HA... ...BORN

...dition

S... ...gy

The...

Collins

For customisable print and digital resources that support this new edition of *Sociology Themes and Perspectives* visit Collins Sociology Web
www.collinseducation.com/sociologyweb

Published by HarperCollins *Publishers* Limited
77–85 Fulham Palace Road
Hammersmith
London W6 8JB

First Edition published in 1980 by University Tutorial Press
Second Edition published in 1985 by University Tutorial Press
Third Edition published in 1990 by Unwin Hyman Ltd
Fourth Edition published in 1995 by Collins Educational
Fifth Edition published in 2000 by Collins Education
Sixth Edition published in 2004 by Collins Education

10 9 8 7 6 5 4 3

British Library Cataloguing in Publication Data
A catalogue record for this publication is available from the British Library.

ISBN 978-0-00-724595-6

Project managed by Sarah Pearsall and Graham Bradbury
Text design and typesetting by Patricia Briggs
Cover design by Angela English
Consultant reader: Pete Langley
Index by Indexing Specialists (UK) Ltd
Printed and bound by L.E.G.O. S.p.A. Italy

Picture credits

pp. vi/1 Rex Features; pp. 18/19 Alamy/Homer Skyes; pp. 90/1 Corbis; pp. 142/3 Alamy/ Marwood Jenkins; pp. 212/13 Corbis; pp. 278/9 Alamy/Janine Weidel; pp. 320/1 Rex Features; pp. 394/5 Alamy/Marco Secchi; pp. 458/9 Alamy/Photofrenetic; pp. 520/1 Rex Features; pp. 598/9 Photos.com; pp. 662/3 Alamy/Bettina Strenske; pp. 710/11 Rex Features; pp. 742/3 Alamy/Adrian Sherratt; pp. 786/7 Alamy/Tetra Images; pp. 834/5 Photos.com.

Acknowledgements

Tables 1.14 and 1.15 from *Social Mobility in Europe* by Richard Breen, published by Oxford University Press, 2004, tables 3.6 and 3.17. Reprinted with permission of Oxford University Press.

Figure 4.6, 'Distributional impact of changes in the tax-benefit system 1997–2004/5 (projected)' from 'Inequality and poverty under New Labour' by T. Sefton and K. Stewart in *A More Equal Society?* edited by J. Hills and K. Stewart, published by Policy Press, Bristol, 2005. Reprinted with permission of Policy Press and the authors.

Figure 6.12, 'Crime and opportunities' from *Environmental Criminology* by P.J. Brantingham and P.L. Brantingham, published by Waveland Press Inc, 1990.

Figure 13.1, 'Age structure of England and Wales in five-year age groups, 1871', from *The British Population, Patterns, Trends and Processes* by D. Coleman and J. Salt, published by Oxford University Press 1992.

Preface to the seventh edition

Sociology Themes and Perspectives was first published in 1980 with the aim of providing a systematic introduction to sociology for UK A level students, undergraduates and the general reader. Since then, in its various editions, it has sold over one million copies worldwide. This edition aims to build on the success of previous editions and has been improved in a number of ways. There is an entirely new chapter on Age and the Life Course as well as extensive updates of existing chapters. The new content ensures very thorough coverage of the new A level specifications and the most exciting developments in the subject.

The division of labour for the writing of the various editions was as follows. Mike Haralambos wrote the first two editions, with Robin Heald as the co-author of the Organizations and Bureaucracy chapter (no longer a separate chapter). With the exception of two chapters, Martin Holborn wrote all the new material for the third, fourth, fifth and sixth editions and Mike Haralambos edited it. Paul Trowler wrote the Communication and the Media chapter for the fifth edition and updated it for the sixth edition. Stephen Moore wrote Chapter 5, Health, Medicine and the Body, for the sixth edition. For the seventh edition Martin Holborn wrote the new chapter on Age and the Life Course and updated the material for all other chapters with the exceptions of Education (updated by Mike Haralambos), Health, Medicine and the Body and Crime and Deviance (both updated by Stephen Moore) and Communications and the Media (updated by Sarah Burch). Many thanks to Stephen and Sarah for their excellent work on these chapters.

Apart from the authors, many people contribute to the publication of a book. The authors would like to thank friends and colleagues whose encouragement and enthusiasm have contributed a great deal to the different editions. Thanks to Jim O'Gorman, Lata Patel, Liz Ronayne, Louisa Turner, Morag Campbell, Joan Blake, Linda Barton, Alison Robinson, Frances Smith, Christine Robinson, Peter Adamson, Dave Beddow, Maurice Gavan, Vincent Farrell, Pauline Cowburn, Jan Pedley, Bob Trafford, Jane Hankinson and Terry Richards. Many thanks also to those who provided skilful editorial support for previous editions: Chris Kingston, Simon Boyd, Josephine Warrior, Pat McNeill, Patricia Briggs, Sarah Pearsall, Kay Wright and Emma Dunlop. For this edition Thomas Allain-Chapman initiated the project and it was commissioned by Abi Woodman and Paul Cherry. Marie Insall saw the project through to completion. Martin would particularly like to thank Abi and Marie for their understanding and support when circumstances made it difficult to keep to schedule. The manuscript for this edition was superbly edited by Sarah Pearsall who also did an outstanding job of managing the later stages of the work. Many thanks to Pete Langley who provided very useful and perceptive editorial comments, Patricia Briggs for excellent design and Graham Bradbury for proofreading. It has been very enjoyable and rewarding working with such a talented and professional team.

Mike Haralambos would like to thank Pauline for her unwavering support and encouragement over the four years that it took to write the original manuscript. She took over many responsibilities and remained cheerful and optimistic when it seemed as though the book would never be completed. He would also like to thank Barbara Grimshaw and Jean Buckley for typing the original manuscript.

Martin Holborn would like to thank his family, Emma, Henry and Ted Holborn, for all their support; particularly Emma for her patience, encouragement, love and practical help during the writing of the last four editions.

Finally, thanks again to everybody who has read the book over the last twenty-eight years since its first publication. We hope it helps you to see the social world a little differently and that it encourages you to think sociologically.

Martin Holborn
Mike Haralambos
November 2007

Contents

INTRODUCTION

Sociological perspectives

According to Mills, sociology should be about examining the biography of individuals in the context of the history of societies. The sociological imagination is not just of use to sociologists; it is important to all members of society if they wish to understand, change and improve their lives.

Introduction

Sociology is one of a number of social sciences (including economics, psychology and human geography) which attempt to explain and understand the behaviour of human beings in society. Unlike some social sciences (such as economics) it does not confine itself to one particular area of social life such as the economy. Indeed, sociologists have studied a vast and diverse range of topics including shopping, popular music, sexuality, the body, ethnic conflict, poverty, sport, science, health, drug use, the law, war, religion, migration, death, colonialism, housework, mobile phones, humour and murder. It is hard to think of any significant area of social life which has never been the subject of a sociological study. Because the subjects it examines are so numerous and so varied, sociology cannot be defined simply in terms of the subjects it studies. It is more useful to define sociology in terms of its approach or approaches to explaining social life rather than its subject matter.

Compared to psychology, sociology is much less concerned with the individual, and much more concerned with humans in groups. The size of the groups studied in sociology can vary considerably, ranging from studies of delinquent gangs or school classes, to studies of institutions (such as the education system or the family), studies of whole societies (for example, British society or the society of the Sioux Indians of South Dakota), and even the study of the globe as a whole (see Chapter 15). However, whatever the scale and scope of a sociological study, to be sociological it must look beyond the individual to understand and explain human behaviour. Rather than explaining human behaviour simply in terms of individual mental states, sociology sees patterns of behaviour as related to the wider social context in which people live. This point can be illustrated through a number of examples, all of which explain apparently individual behaviour (depression, suicide and murder) in sociological ways.

1 In the 1970s and 1980s researchers studied the causes of depression amongst a sample of women in London (Brown and Harris 1978, 1989). The study found that the chances of women becoming depressed could not be explained simply in terms of a tendency towards pyschological problems. Instead, depression was triggered by stressful long- or short-term life events such as losing a job, being evicted from your home or being in poverty. The research also found that the chances of suffering from a stressful life event were directly related to income and class background. The lower your income and social class, the greater your chances of

being made redundant, losing your home and so on. Working-class women also had less supportive social networks to help them cope with the stresses and strains of life than middle-class women. The researchers therefore concluded that a person's mental state was substantially influenced by their economic and class position in society. (See pp. 314–17 for further details of this study and other sociological studies of mental illness.)

2 In 1897, Emile Durkheim published a study of suicide which showed that rates of suicide varied considerably between countries and between social groups. For example, England consistently had a higher suicide rate than France, and married people had lower suicide rates than the unmarried. Durkheim concluded that suicide, an apparently individual act, was actually shaped by social factors. One factor which Durkheim thought was important was the extent to which individuals were involved in or integrated into social groups. For example, married people with children who belonged to a close-knit religious community were much less likely to commit suicide than childless single people who were not involved in a religious community (see pp. 795–803 for a discussion of Durkheim and other sociological theories of suicide).

3 Another act which has often been seen as a highly individual one is murder or homicide. Yet murder too can be seen as an act which is strongly influenced by social factors. Your chances of being murdered or of becoming a murderer vary considerably depending on the social groups to which you belong and the society in which you live. In 1999 the homicide rate (homicides per 100,000 of the population) was 1.45 in England and Wales, 6.26 in the USA, 20.52 in Russia and 56.49 in South Africa. In contrast, Japan had a homicide rate of just 1.04 in the same year (discussed in Holborn, 2005). Such huge differences cannot be explained in terms of individual characteristics or motivations of offenders. Instead they can be seen as resulting from differences between the societies. There are various possible differences which could account for variations in the homicide rate, but one interesting and plausible theory is put forward by James Gilligan (2001). Gilligan believes that differences in homicide rates are related to the amount of inequality in society. According to Gilligan, high levels of inequality lead to shame amongst those who are doing poorly, and shame is a breeding ground for violence and murder.

No reliable figures have been produced on the murder rate in Iraq in the aftermath of the invasion by the USA and Britain in 2003. However, there is no doubt that by 2006 it had become one of the most dangerous places on earth to live. Again, a sociologist would not explain this only in terms of the motivations of individual killers, but would also look at factors such as the causes of ethnic conflict in Iraq and even the global context in which the invasion took place.

Another reason why psychological explanations alone cannot explain homicide is that very few offences can be attributed to the mental illness of the offender. For example, in 2002/3 only 41 of 1,007 homicides in England and Wales involved a suspect who was mentally disturbed (Cotton, 2004). Evidence from Britain suggests that men are much more likely to turn into killers than women; that murderers are overwhelmingly from lower social classes; that some minority ethnic groups are more likely to be victims of homicide than others; and that very few murderers are elderly (Brookman, 2005).

Culture, inequality and society

In sociology, then, it is essential to understand the social context in which human behaviour takes place. At the most basic level, this involves understanding the culture of the society in which social action occurs.

To all intents and purposes a newborn human baby is helpless. Not only is it physically dependent on older members of the species but it also lacks the behaviour patterns necessary for living in human society. It relies primarily on certain biological drives, such as hunger, and on the charity of its elders to satisfy those drives. The infant has a lot to learn. In order to survive, it must learn the skills, knowledge and accepted ways of behaving of the society into which it is born. It must learn a way of life; in sociological terminology, it must learn the **culture** of its society.

Ralph Linton states that 'The culture of a society is the way of life of its members; the collection of ideas and habits which they learn, share and transmit from generation to generation.' In Clyde Kluckhohn's elegant phrase, culture is a 'design for living' held by members of a particular society.

Culture and socialization: norms, subcultures and identity

To a large degree culture determines how members of society think and feel: it directs their actions and defines their outlook on life. Culture defines accepted ways of behaving for members of a particular society. Such definitions vary from society to society. This can lead to considerable misunderstanding between members of different societies, as the following example provided by Otto Klineberg (1971) shows.

Amongst the Sioux Indians of South Dakota, it is regarded as incorrect to answer a question in the presence of others who do not know the answer. Such behaviour would be regarded as boastful and arrogant, and, since it reveals the ignorance of others, it would be interpreted as an attempt to undermine their confidence and shame them. In addition, the Sioux regard it as wrong to answer a question unless they are absolutely sure of the correct answer. Faced with a classroom of Sioux children, a white American teacher, who is unaware of their culture, might easily interpret their behaviour as a reflection of ignorance, stupidity or hostility.

The process by which individuals learn the culture of their society is known as **socialization**. Primary socialization, probably the most important aspect of the socialization process, takes place during infancy, usually within the family (see Chapter 8 for a discussion of the family). By responding to the approval and disapproval of its parents and copying their example, the child learns the language and many of the basic behaviour patterns of its society.

In Western society, other important agencies of socialization include the educational system (see Chapter 10), religion (see Chapter 7), the mass media (discussed in Chapter 12), the occupational group and the peer group (a group whose members share similar circumstances and are often of a similar age). Within its peer group, the young child, by interacting with others and playing childhood games, learns to conform to the accepted ways of a social group and to appreciate the fact that social life is based on rules.

Socialization is not, however, confined to childhood. It is a lifelong process which continues as people change jobs or roles and as society itself changes.

Socialization teaches members of society the **norms**, or informal rules, which govern behaviour. Norms specify the type of behaviour that is considered appropriate in particular situations. For example, norms of dress give guidelines on what to wear on particular occasions. The same clothes would not be considered appropriate at a graduation ceremony, at a party, on a building site or on the beach. Norms vary from society to society. The loincloths worn by the Bushmen of the Kalahari (Thomas, 1969) would not be considered appropriate dress (at least in most contexts) in Britain or other Western European countries.

As well as varying from society to society, culture and norms also change. A change in society such as the introduction of new technology can lead to new ways of behaving. The growth of text messaging, for example, has led to a whole new culture with its own language and its own norms (or informal rules) about appropriate behaviour. Rich Ling (1997) used interviews to study mobile phone use among Norwegian teenagers. He found that they had developed their own norms about the use of phones. For example, the teenagers frowned upon their peers who talked into their mobile phones loudly and ostentatiously in public places as if they were making important business calls. The teenagers regarded such behaviour as 'harry' (tacky) and 'soss' (vulgar). Most of the teenagers conformed to this norm and used their phones discreetly.

Although it is possible for the sake of simplicity to treat each society as having a particular and distinct culture, in reality this is unlikely to be the case. First, apart from a handful of relatively isolated tribal societies (see below), most societies now contain a mix of people from different cultural backgrounds. Migration and other international movements of people (see pp. 152–8) have led to the creation of ethnically and culturally pluralistic societies. Second, all societies have divisions between subcultures. A **subculture** can be defined as a social group within society which has a lifestyle which is distinctive from the culture of the society as a whole. For example, sociologists have studied a variety of youth cultures such as goths, moshers and punks. Members of each group have distinctive ways of dressing and they tend to listen to particular types of music. However, they are not completely different from other members of society, sharing much in common with their peers who do not belong to the subculture. Thus goths might wear distinctive black clothing and make-up, and listen to Bauhaus, The Cure, Marilyn Manson and Slipknot, but in many other ways they live conventional lives.

Individuals can choose whether to belong to particular youth cultures, but they have less choice about some of the social groups to which they belong. Major social divisions such as those between men and women, ethnic groups and social classes exist independently of the choices made by individuals, and these too lead to subcultural differences.

Culture and subcultures are an important source of social identity. **Social identity** has been defined as 'our understanding of who we are, and who other people are' (Jenkins, 1996). People tend to associate themselves or identify with those who are similar to themselves, and to feel more distant from those who are dissimilar.

At a basic level, people tend to associate themselves with those from the same society. So, for example, people from Britain, France, Pakistan or Nigeria may see themselves as British, French, Pakistani or Nigerian, even if they are living outside their country of origin. They may mix with people from that society, support sports teams from their country of origin and so on. So, for example, some British people who have settled in Spain have relatively few social contacts with the local Spanish population, choosing instead to mix mainly with other Britons. They see themselves as British rather than Spanish, read English language newspapers, and make little effort to integrate into the local population or adopt Spanish culture.

Subcultures can also be an important source of social identity. Thus goths see themselves as a distinctive group, and they may tend to associate more with other goths than with peers who are part of different youth cultures.

Inequality and social divisions

As well as specific youth subcultures, there are a number of important social divisions within any society which tend to give rise to subcultural differences in lifestyle. These social divisions are also important as sources of inequality and differences in identity. (Social divisions are seen as particularly important in conflict theories in sociology – see pp. 8–9 for details.)

Issues of inequality concern differences in access to scarce resources. When there are insufficient resources to satisfy everybody, then humans often compete to obtain access to those resources. For example, if there is insufficient food for everybody to have the diet they would like, or insufficient housing to meet everybody's aspirations, then inequality can develop between those who are more successful and those who are less successful in gaining the desired resources. To simplify, there are two main types of inequality in Western capitalist societies:

1 **Inequality of power.** Power concerns the ability of a person or group to get what they wish regardless of the wishes of others (see Chapter 9). For example, the president of the United States has much more power than an ordinary citizen of the country. The president can declare war and direct the most powerful armed forces in the world, giving him/her enormous power. On a more mundane level, one partner in a marriage may get their own way more often than the other partner, giving them greater power than their spouse.
2 **Material inequality** concerns access to wealth and income. Those individuals, institutions or countries with great wealth have an advantage over those that are poor. They control more resources, they have more choices, and they have greater power. Thus, for example, Bill Gates, the founder of Microsoft and one of the wealthiest men in the world, is greatly advantaged compared to an impoverished labourer in a 'third world' country. Chapter 1 (Stratification, class and inequality) is largely concerned with the consequences of material inequality within societies.

Inequality gives rise to social divisions between groups in society. Geoff Payne defines social divisions as 'those substantial differences between people that run throughout our society' (Payne, 2006). Any social division involves at least two groups or categories. As Payne comments, 'one category is better positioned than the other and has a better share of resources because it has greater power over the way our society is organised'. Payne goes on to say, 'Membership of a category is closely associated with a social identity that arises from a sense of being similar to other members and different from other categories' (Payne, 2006, p. 5). It could be added that just as each group develops a distinctive identity, it also tends to develop a distinctive lifestyle and subculture. A large number of social divisions can be distinguished within any society, but there are some social divisions which are seen as particularly important by sociologists. Each of these will now briefly be discussed.

1 **Social class divisions** result from economic or material inequality between social groups. In modern Western societies many sociologists have distinguished between social classes which result from economic inequality. A variety of social class categories have been put forward by sociologists, but many have distinguished between an upper class, a middle class and a working class. At the risk of oversimplification, the upper class owe their position to the ownership of wealth, the middle class to qualifications and the possession of well-rewarded jobs, while the working class do manual work which requires fewer formal qualifications and tends to be low-paid. This social division can produce subcultural differences in many areas of social life, including leisure activities (for example, visiting the opera or playing bingo), accent, clothing and so on. Chapter 1 explores the significance of social class and similar types of social division in detail. Social class differences are seen as particularly important in Marxist theories of society (see pp. 9–11).
2 **Gender divisions** are concerned with the differences and inequalities between men and women in society. Although male and female roles have become less sharply differentiated in some societies than they were in the past, they are still a very important source of inequality and difference. For example, as Chapter 2 shows, in contemporary Britain men still earn more than women, and women are much less likely than men to occupy elite positions in society. Furthermore, there are still considerable differences in the behaviour and roles associated with masculinity and femininity. In Britain, for example, women still do the vast majority of the caring work for children and the elderly, while men still dominate in areas such as politics and business. Gender divisions are central to feminist theories of society (see p. 11).
3 **Ethnic divisions** are directly related to cultural differences between groups which believe they have a common origin (see pp. 158–60 for a detailed definition of ethnicity). Different ethnic groups might have different patterns of marriage and family life, wear distinctive clothes, have their own language, and their own religion, and eat distinctive food. However, ethnicity is not just linked to culture; there is also likely to be inequality between different ethnic groups. In the USA, for example, black Americans have much lower average living standards than the white majority. In Britain, some minority ethnic groups (such as Chinese and Indians) have been much more successful than other groups (such as Bangladeshis) in achieving a high living standard.
4 All societies also have divisions between **age groups**. In traditional, pre-industrial societies such as the North American Pomo Indians (Aginsky, 1940), elders tended to have higher status and more power than younger members of the group. Amongst Pomo Indians the elderly were regarded as wise, and younger members of the tribe looked up to them. In modern industrial societies, both the elderly and children tend to have low status and, particularly in the case of children, little power. Chapter 8 examines age divisions in the context of family life.

Class, gender, ethnicity and age are probably the most important social divisions studied by sociologists. Other significant divisions include religious differences (see Chapter 7), divisions between the disabled and the able-bodied (see pp. 311–12) and differences in sexuality (between heterosexual, homosexual and bisexual). These and other social divisions are a central theme within this book and within sociology as a whole.

Having examined some of the basic concepts and issues within sociology, we will now go on to briefly consider the way in which human societies have developed, before looking at the theories which sociologists have used to explain the social divisions and social changes which are central to sociology theory and research.

The development of human societies

Some sociologists believe that human societies have passed through certain broad phases of development. Many sociologists distinguish between premodern and modern societies. The distinction is a very general one and can neglect differences between the societies of each type. Nevertheless, the distinction is both influential and useful. It is useful because it has allowed sociologists to identify some of the key changes that have taken place in human history. They have then been able to discuss the significance of these changes. Some sociologists, though by no means all, argue that a new type of society, the postmodern society, has recently developed or is developing.

In this section, we will briefly introduce some of the main ideas associated with the distinctions between premodern, modern and postmodern societies. These concepts have a very important role in the development of sociological thinking and will be developed in detail throughout the book.

Premodern societies

Premodern societies took a number of forms. Anthony Giddens distinguishes between three main types: hunting and gathering societies, pastoral and agrarian societies and non-industrial civilizations (Giddens, 1997).

Hunting and gathering societies

The earliest human societies survived by gathering fruit, nuts and vegetables and by hunting or trapping animals for food. They usually consisted of small tribal groups often numbering fewer than fifty people. Such societies tended to have few possessions and little material wealth. What possessions they did have were shared. According to Giddens, they had relatively little inequality, although elder members of the tribe may have had more status and influence than younger ones. Hunting and gathering societies have largely disappeared, but Giddens calculates that some 250,000 people (just 0.0001 per cent of the world's population) still survive largely through hunting

Hunter-gatherers in Namibia

Source: Corbis

and gathering. Hunters and gatherers still exist in regions of Africa, New Guinea and Brazil, but few have remained untouched by the spread of Western culture.

Pastoral and agrarian societies

According to Giddens, these first emerged some 20,000 years ago. **Pastoral societies** may hunt and gather but they also keep and herd animals (for example, cattle, camels or horses). Animal herds provide supplies of milk and meat and the animals may also be used as a means of transport. Unlike hunting and gathering societies, pastoral societies make it possible for individuals to accumulate wealth in the form of their animals. They therefore tend to have more inequality than hunting and gathering bands. They also tend to be nomadic, since they have to move around to find pasture for their animals. Because of this they are likely to come into contact with other groups. The individual societies have tended to be larger than hunting and gathering bands and in all may number as many as 250,000. There are still some pastoral societies in parts of the Middle East, Africa and Asia.

Agrarian societies rely largely upon the cultivation of crops to feed themselves. Like the herding of animals, this provides a more reliable and predictable source of food than hunting and gathering and it can therefore support much larger populations. Such societies are not likely to be nomadic. Food such as grain is often stored and it is possible for individuals to accumulate substantial personal wealth. Agrarian societies can therefore have considerable inequality.

Agriculture remains the main way of earning a living in many parts of the world today. Giddens quotes 1990 figures which showed that over 90 per cent of the population of Nepal and Rwanda, over 80 per cent of the population of Uganda, and nearly 70 per cent of the Bangladeshi population worked in agriculture. However, the culture of contemporary agrarian societies has not remained entirely traditional. Most have been influenced by the culture of modern, industrial societies.

Non-industrial civilizations

These types of society first developed around 6000 BC. According to Giddens, they 'were based on the development of cities, showed very pronounced inequalities of wealth and power, and were associated with the rule of kings and emperors'. Compared to the hunting and gathering and early pastoral and agrarian societies, they were more developed in the areas of art and science and had more institutionalized and centralized systems of government. Non-industrial civilizations also invented writing.

Some of these civilizations expanded across wide areas and developed their own empires. Examples of non-industrial civilizations include the Aztecs, the Maya and the Incas in Central and South America; Ancient Greece and the Roman Empire in Europe; Ancient Egypt in Africa; and Indian and Chinese civilizations in Asia. Most of them had substantial armed forces, and some, such as the Romans, managed major military conquests. None of these civilizations survived indefinitely and none exist today. Despite their importance, none has had as big an impact on the development of human society as modern industrial societies. These first emerged in the eighteenth and nineteenth centuries.

Modern industrial societies

According to Lee and Newby (1983), in the early nineteenth century 'there was widespread agreement among observers and commentators at this time that Northern Europe and North America were passing through the most profound transformation of society in the history of mankind'.

Lee and Newby identify four main transformations that took place:

1. **Industrialism**. The industrial revolution, which started in the late eighteenth century, transformed Britain, and later other societies, from economies based largely on agriculture to economies based largely on manufacturing. New technology led to massive increases in productivity, first in the cotton industry and then in other industries. An increasingly specialized division of labour developed – that is, people had more specialist jobs. Social life was no longer governed by the rhythms of the seasons and night and day; instead people's lives were based on the clock. Instead of working when the requirements of agriculture demanded, people started working long shifts of fixed periods (often twelve hours) in the new factories.
2. **Capitalism**. Closely connected to the development of industrialism was the development of capitalism. Capitalism involves wage labour and businesses run for the purpose of making a profit. Before the advent of capitalism many peasants worked for themselves, living off the produce they could get from their own land. Increasingly, peasants lost their land and had to rely upon earning a wage, either as agricultural labourers or as workers in the developing factories. Capitalist businesses were developed with the aim of making a profit year after year. New classes emerged – principally a class of entrepreneurs who made their living by setting up and running capitalist businesses, and a working class of wage labourers employed in the entrepreneurs' factories.
3. **Urbanism**. The development of industry was accompanied by a massive movement from rural to urban areas. In Britain in 1750, before the industrial revolution, only two cities had populations of over 50,000 (London and Edinburgh). By 1851, twenty-nine British cities had a population of more than 50,000. The population no longer needed to be thinly spread across agricultural land, and was increasingly concentrated in the centres of capitalist industry. Urbanism – the growth of towns and cities – brought with it numerous social problems such as crime, riots, and health problems caused by overcrowding and lack of sanitation. To many commentators the new towns and cities also destroyed the traditional sense of community that they associated with the rural villages. They believe that urbanism undermined the informal mechanisms of social control (such as gossip), which operated in

close-knit communities, but which became ineffective in the anonymity of urban life.

4 **Liberal democracy**. Before the changes of the eighteenth and nineteenth centuries, the right of kings and queens to rule was rarely questioned (an exception being the English Civil War of the seventeenth century). The monarch was accepted as God's representative on earth, and their authority was not therefore open to question. However, in the French Revolution of 1789 the French monarchy was overthrown. Similarly British monarchical rule in America was overthrown by the American War of Independence (1775–83). In both cases there was a new emphasis on the citizenship rights of individuals – individuals were now to have a say in how their countries were ruled rather than accepting what they were told by monarchs. This opened the way for the development of political parties and new perspectives on society. How society was to be run became more a matter for debate than it had ever been before.

Modernity

Taken together, the changes described above are often seen as characterizing modern societies, or as constituting an era of modernity. Modernity involves the following concepts: a belief in the possibility of human progress; rational planning to achieve objectives; a belief in the superiority of rational thought over emotion; faith in the ability of technology and science to solve human problems; a belief in the ability and rights of humans to shape their own lives; and a reliance upon manufacturing industry to improve living standards. Sociology developed alongside modernity and, not surprisingly, it has tended to be based upon similar foundations. Thus early sociological theories tended to believe that societies could and would progress, that scientific principles could be used to understand society, and that rational thought could be employed to ensure that society was organized to meet human needs. For most of its history, sociological thinking has been dominated by such approaches. However, some thinkers, including some sociologists, believe that modernity is being, or has been, replaced by an era of postmodernity.

Postmodernity

Some sociologists believe that in recent years fundamental changes have taken place in Western societies. These changes have led to, or are in the process of leading to, a major break with the old concept of modernity. They suggest that people have begun to lose their faith in science and technology. People have become aware, for example, of the damaging effects of pollution, the dangers of nuclear war and the risks of genetic engineering. They have become more sceptical about the benefits of rational planning. For example, many people doubt that large, rational, bureaucratic organizations (such as big companies or the British National Health Service) can meet human needs. They have lost faith in political beliefs and grand theories that claim to be able to improve society. Furthermore, few people now believe that communism can lead to a perfect society. The modern belief in progress has therefore been undermined and there has been a movement away from science and rationalism. Some people have turned to non-rational beliefs such as New Age philosophies (see pp. 420–3) and religious cults as a reaction against scientific rationalism.

According to some postmodernists, these changes are linked to changes in the economy. Industrial society has been superseded by post-industrial society. Relatively few people in Western societies now work in manufacturing industry. More and more are employed in services and particularly in jobs concerned with communications and information technology. Computer technology has meant that fewer people are needed to work in manufacturing, and communications have become very much faster. Furthermore, in affluent Western countries people are spending a higher proportion of their income on leisure. When they purchase products it is often as much for the image that they represent as the quality and usefulness of the products. Thus people will pay high prices for clothes with designer labels. The media have also become increasingly important in people's lives and in the economy.

Although some of these changes have undoubtedly taken place, some sociologists do not believe that the changes are sufficiently large and significant to justify the claim that there has been a shift from modern to postmodern society. Others believe not just that societies have changed, but also that new theories of society are necessary. Their views will be examined after we have considered some of the longer-established sociological theories.

Theories of society

In this section we will examine some of the most influential theories of society. A **theory** is a set of ideas which claims to explain how something works. A sociological theory is therefore a set of ideas which claims to explain how society or aspects of society work. The theories described in this section represent only a selection from the range of modern sociological theories. They have been simplified and condensed to provide a basic introduction. Since they are applied to various topics throughout the text, an initial awareness is essential. Criticism of the theories has been omitted from this chapter for the sake of simplicity, but it will be dealt with throughout the text and in detail in Chapter 14.

There are many variations on the basic theories examined in this chapter. Again, for simplicity, most of these variations will not be mentioned at this stage, but will be introduced when they become relevant to particular topics.

Functionalism

Functionalism first emerged in nineteenth-century Europe. The French sociologist Emile Durkheim was the most influential of the early functionalists. The theory was developed by American sociologists such as Talcott

Parsons in the twentieth century, and it became the dominant theoretical perspective in sociology during the 1940s and 1950s, particularly in the USA. From the mid-1960s onwards its popularity steadily declined, due partly to damaging criticism, partly to competing perspectives which appeared to provide superior explanations, and partly to changes in fashion.

The key points of the functionalist perspective may be summarized by a comparison drawn from biology. If biologists wanted to know how an organism such as the human body worked, they might begin by examining the various parts such as the brain, lungs, heart and liver. However, if they simply analysed the parts in isolation from each other, they would be unable to explain how life was maintained. To do this, they would have to examine the parts in relation to each other, since they work together to maintain the organism. Therefore they would analyse the relationships between the heart, lungs, brain and so on to understand how they operate and to appreciate their importance. In other words, any part of the organism must be seen in terms of the organism as a whole.

Functionalism adopts a similar perspective. The various parts of society are seen to be interrelated and, taken together, they form a complete system. To understand any part of society, such as the family or religion, the part must be seen in relation to society as a whole. Thus where a biologist will examine a part of the body, such as the heart, in terms of its contribution to the maintenance of the human organism, the functionalist will examine a part of society, such as the family, in terms of its contribution to the maintenance of the social system.

Structure

Functionalism begins with the observation that behaviour in society is structured. This means that relationships between members of society are organized in terms of **rules** which stipulate how people are expected to behave. Rules can be formal (for example, laws) or informal. Informal rules are known as norms. **Norms** are specific guides to action, which tell you, for example, how you are expected to dress and behave at a funeral or at a party. Social relationships are patterned and recurrent because of the existence of rules.

Values provide general guidelines for behaviour. They provide the overall beliefs about what is good or bad, desirable or undesirable in a society. For example, in Western societies values such as honesty, privacy, ambition and individual achievement are important. Values are translated into more specific directives in terms of norms. The value of privacy produces a range of norms, such as those that stipulate that you should knock before entering a room and that you should ask people's permission before photographing them.

Norms are associated with particular **roles** in society. Roles are formal or informal social positions which carry expectations of certain types of behaviour. Examples of roles include lecturer, student, friend, brother, doctor, cleaner and so on. Thus lecturers and students are expected to behave in different ways because there are norms governing the behaviour within these different roles.

The structure of society can be seen as the sum total of normative behaviour – the sum total of social relationships, which are governed by norms. The main parts of society, its institutions – such as the family, the economy, and the educational and political systems – are major aspects of the social structure. Thus an institution can be seen as a structure made up of interconnected roles or interrelated norms. For example, the family is made up of the interconnected roles of husband, father, wife, mother, son and daughter. Social relationships within the family are structured in terms of a set of related norms.

Function

Having established the existence of a social structure, functionalist analysis turns to a consideration of how that structure functions. This involves an examination of the relationship between the different parts of the structure and their relationship to society as a whole. This examination reveals the functions of institutions. At its simplest, function means effect. Thus the function of the family is the effect it has on other parts of the social structure and on society as a whole. In practice, the term function is usually used to indicate the contribution an institution makes to the maintenance and survival of the social system. For example, a major function of the family is the socialization of new members of society. This represents an important contribution to the maintenance of society, since order, stability and cooperation largely depend on learned, shared norms and values.

Functional prerequisites

In determining the functions of various parts of the social structure, functionalists are guided by the following ideas. Societies have certain basic needs or requirements that must be met if they are to survive. These requirements are sometimes known as **functional prerequisites**. For example, a means of producing food and shelter may be seen as a functional prerequisite, since without food and shelter members of society could not survive. A system for socializing new members of society may also be regarded as a functional prerequisite, since, without culture, social life would not be possible. Having assumed a number of basic requirements for the survival of society, the next step is to look at the parts of the social structure to see how they meet such functional prerequisites. Thus a major function of the economic system is the production of food and shelter. An important function of the family is the socialization of new members of society.

Value consensus

From a functionalist perspective, society is regarded as a system. A system is an entity made up of interconnected and interrelated parts. From this viewpoint, it follows that each part will in some way affect every other part and the system as a whole. It also follows that, if the system is to survive, its various parts must have some degree of fit or compatibility. Thus a functional prerequisite of society involves at least a minimal degree of integration between the parts. Many functionalists argue that this integration is based largely on value consensus, that is, on agreement about values by members of society. Thus if the major values of society are expressed in the various parts of the social structure, those parts will be integrated. For example, it can be argued that the value of materialism integrates many parts of the social structure in Western industrial society. The economic system produces a large range of goods, and ever-increasing productivity is regarded as an important goal. The educational system is partly concerned with producing the skills and expertise to expand production and increase its efficiency. The family is an important unit of consumption, with its steadily rising demand for consumer durables such as washing machines, DVD players and microwaves. The political system is partly concerned with improving material living standards and raising productivity. To the extent that these parts of the social structure are based on the same values, they may be said to be integrated.

Social order

One of the main concerns of functionalist theory is to explain how social life is possible. The theory assumes that a certain degree of order and stability is essential for the survival of social systems. Functionalism is therefore concerned with explaining the origin and maintenance of order and stability in society. Many functionalists see shared values as the key to this explanation: value consensus integrates the various parts of society. It forms the basis of social unity or social solidarity, since individuals will tend to identify and feel kinship with those who share the same values as themselves. Value consensus provides the foundation for cooperation, since common values produce common goals. Members of society will tend to cooperate in pursuit of goals that they share.

Having attributed such importance to value consensus, many functionalists then focus on the question of how this consensus is maintained. Indeed the American sociologist Talcott Parsons stated that the main task of sociology is to examine 'the institutionalization of patterns of value orientation in the social system'. Emphasis is therefore placed on the process of socialization whereby values are internalized and transmitted from one generation to the next. In this respect, the family is regarded as a vital part of the social structure. Once learned, values must be maintained. In particular, those who deviate from society's values must be brought back into line. Thus mechanisms of social control are seen as essential to the maintenance of social order.

Conflict perspectives

Although functionalists emphasize the importance of value consensus in society, they do recognize that conflict can occur. However, they see conflict as being the result of temporary disturbances in the social system. These disturbances are usually quickly corrected as society evolves. Functionalists accept that social groups can have differences of interest, but these are of minor importance compared to the interests that all social groups share in common. They believe that all social groups benefit if their society runs smoothly and prospers.

Conflict theories differ from functionalism in that they hold that there are fundamental differences of interest between social groups. These differences result in conflict being a common and persistent feature of society, and not a temporary aberration.

There are a number of different conflict perspectives and their supporters tend to disagree about the precise nature, causes and extent of conflict. For the sake of simplicity, in this introductory chapter we will concentrate upon two conflict theories: Marxism and feminism. Other conflict theories will be introduced later in the book. (For example, the influential conflict theory of Max Weber is dealt with in Chapter 1, pp. 29–30.)

Marxism

Marxist theory offers a radical alternative to functionalism. It became increasingly influential in sociology during the 1970s, partly because of the decline of functionalism, partly because it promised to provide answers that functionalism failed to provide, and partly because it was more in keeping with the tenor and mood of the times. 'Marxism' takes its name from its founder, the German-born philosopher, economist and sociologist, Karl Marx (1818–83). The following account is a simplified version of Marxist theory. It must also be seen as one interpretation of that theory: Marx's extensive writings have been variously interpreted and, since his death, several schools of Marxism have developed. (See Marx and Engels, 1950a, 1950b, for extracts from Marx's most important writings.)

Contradiction and conflict

Marxist theory begins with the simple observation that, in order to survive, humans must produce food and material objects. In doing so they enter into social relationships with other people. From the simple hunting band to the complex industrial state, production is a social enterprise. Production also involves a technical component known as the **forces of production**, which includes the technology, raw materials and scientific knowledge employed in the process of production. Each major stage in the development of the forces of production will correspond with a particular form of the social relationships of production. This means that the forces of production in a hunting economy will correspond with a particular set of social relationships.

Taken together, the forces of production and the social relationships of production form the economic basis or **infrastructure** of society. The other aspects of society, known as the **superstructure**, are largely shaped by the infrastructure. Thus the political, legal and educational institutions and the belief and value systems are primarily determined by economic factors. A major change in the infrastructure will therefore produce a corresponding change in the superstructure.

Marx maintained that, with the possible exception of the societies of prehistory, all historical societies contain basic contradictions, which means that they cannot survive for ever in their existing form. These contradictions involve the exploitation of one social group by another: in feudal society, lords exploit their serfs; in capitalist society, employers exploit their employees. This creates a fundamental conflict of interest between social groups, since one gains at the expense of another. This conflict of interest must ultimately be resolved, since a social system containing such contradictions cannot survive unchanged.

We will now examine the points raised in this brief summary of Marxist theory in greater detail. The major contradictions in society are between the forces and relations of production. The forces of production include land, raw materials, tools and machinery, the technical and scientific knowledge used in production, the technical organization of the production process, and the labour power of the workers. The 'relations of production' are the social relationships which people enter into in order to produce goods. Thus in feudal society they include the relationship between the lord and vassal, and the set of rights, duties and obligations which make up that relationship. In capitalist industrial society they include the relationship between employer and employee and the various rights of the two parties. The relations of production also involve the relationship of social groups to the means and forces of production.

The **means of production** consist of those parts of the forces of production that can be legally owned. They therefore include land, raw materials, machinery, buildings and tools, but not technical knowledge or the organization of the production process. Under capitalism, labour power is not one of the means of production, since the workers are free to sell their labour. In slave societies, though, labour power is one of the means of production, since the workforce is actually owned by the social group in power. In feudal society, land, the major means of production, is owned by the lord, and the serf has the right to use land in return for services or payment to the lord. In Western industrial society, the capitalists own the means of production, whereas the workers own only their labour, which they hire to the employer in return for wages.

Exploitation and oppression

The idea of contradiction between the forces and relations of production may be illustrated in terms of the infrastructure of capitalist industrial society. Marx maintained that only labour produces wealth. Thus wealth in capitalist society is produced by the labour power of the workers. However, much of this wealth is appropriated in the form of profits by the capitalists, the owners of the means of production. The wages of the workers are well below the value of the wealth they produce. There is thus a contradiction between the forces of production, in particular the labour power of the workers which produces wealth, and the relations of production which involve the appropriation of much of that wealth by the capitalists.

A related contradiction involves the technical organization of labour and the nature of ownership. In capitalist society, the forces of production include the collective production of goods by large numbers of workers in factories. Yet the means of production are privately owned, and the profits are appropriated by individuals. The contradiction between the forces and relations of production lies in the social and collective nature of production and the private and individual nature of ownership. Marx believed that these and other contradictions would eventually lead to the downfall of the capitalist system. He maintained that, by its very nature, capitalism involves the exploitation and oppression of the worker. He believed that the conflict of interest between capital and labour, which involves one group gaining at the expense of the other, could not be resolved within the framework of a capitalist economy.

Contradiction and change

Marx saw history as divided into a number of time periods or epochs, each being characterized by a particular mode of production. Major changes in history are the result of new forces of production. Thus the change from feudal to capitalist society stemmed from the emergence, during the feudal epoch, of the forces of production of industrial society. This resulted in a contradiction between the new forces of production and the old feudal relations of production. Capitalist industrial society required relations of production based on wage labour rather than the traditional ties of lord and vassal. When they reach a certain point in their development, the new forces of production will lead to the creation of a new set of relations of production. Then, a new epoch of history will be born which will sweep away the social relationships of the old order.

However, the final epoch of history, the communist or socialist society that Marx believed would eventually supplant capitalism, will not result from a new force of production. Rather it will develop from a resolution of the contradictions contained within the capitalist system. Collective production will remain but the relations of production will be transformed. Ownership of the means of production will be collective rather than individual, and members of society will share the wealth that their labour produces. No longer will one social group exploit and oppress another. This will produce an infrastructure without contradiction and conflict. In Marx's view this would mean the end of history, since communist society would no longer contain the contradictions which generate change.

Ideology and false consciousness

In view of the contradictions that beset historical societies, it appears difficult to explain their survival. Despite its internal contradictions, capitalism has continued in the West for over 200 years. This continuity can be explained in large part by the nature of the superstructure. In all societies the superstructure is largely shaped by the infrastructure. In particular, the relations of production are reflected and reproduced in the various institutions, values and beliefs that make up the superstructure. Thus the relationships of domination and subordination found in the infrastructure will also be found in social institutions. The dominant social group or ruling class – that is, the group which owns and controls the means of production – will largely monopolize political power, and its position will be supported by laws which are framed to protect and further its interests.

In the same way, beliefs and values will reflect and legitimate the relations of production. Members of the ruling class produce the dominant ideas in society. These ideas justify their power and privilege and conceal from all members of society the basis of exploitation and oppression on which their dominance rests. Thus, under feudalism, honour and loyalty were 'dominant concepts' of the age. Vassals owed loyalty to their lords and were bound by an oath of allegiance that encouraged the acceptance of their status. In terms of the dominant concepts of the age, feudalism appeared as the natural order of things. Under capitalism, exploitation is disguised by the ideas of equality and freedom. The relationship between capitalist and wage labourer is defined as an equal exchange. The capitalist buys the labour power that the worker offers for hire. The worker is defined as a free agent, since he or she has the freedom to choose his or her employer. In reality, equality and freedom are illusions: the employer–employee relationship is not equal. It is an exploitative relationship. Workers are not free, since they are forced to work for the capitalist in order to survive. All they can do is exchange one form of 'wage slavery' for another.

Marx refers to the dominant ideas of each epoch as **ruling class ideology**. **Ideology** is a distortion of reality, a false picture of society. It blinds members of society to the contradictions and conflicts of interest that are built into their relationships. As a result they tend to accept their situation as normal and natural, right and proper. In this way a **false consciousness** of reality is produced which helps to maintain the system. However, Marx believed that ruling class ideology could only slow down the disintegration of the system. The contradictions embedded in the structure of society must eventually find expression.

Although highly critical of capitalism, Marx did see it as a stepping stone on the way towards a communist society. Capitalism would help to develop technology that would free people from material need; there would be more than enough to feed and clothe the population. In these circumstances it would be possible to establish successful communist societies in which the needs of all their members were met. Despite its pessimistic tone, Marxism shares with functionalism the modern belief that human societies will improve, and that rational, scientific thinking can be used to ensure progress.

Feminism

There are several different versions of feminism, but most share a number of features in common. Like Marxists, feminists tend to see society as divided into different social groups. Unlike Marxists, they see the major division as being between men and women rather than between different classes. Like Marxists, they tend to see society as characterized by exploitation. Unlike Marxists, they see the exploitation of women by men as the most important source of exploitation, rather than that of the working class by the ruling class. Many feminists characterize contemporary societies as patriarchal; that is, they are dominated by men. For example, feminists have argued that men have most of the power in families, that they tend to be employed in better-paid and higher-status jobs than women, and that they tend to monopolize positions of political power. The ultimate aim of these types of feminism is to end men's domination and to rid society of the exploitation of women. Such feminists advance a range of explanations for, and solutions to, the exploitation of women. However, they all believe that the development of society can be explained and that progress towards an improved future is possible.

Some feminist writers (sometimes called **difference feminists**) disagree that all women are equally oppressed and disadvantaged in contemporary societies. They believe that it is important to recognize the different experiences and problems faced by various groups of women. For example, they do not believe that all husbands oppress their wives, that women are equally disadvantaged in all types of work, or that looking after children is necessarily oppressive to women. They emphasize the differences between women of different ages, class backgrounds and ethnic groups. Like other feminists, they believe that the oppression of women exists, but they do not see it as affecting all women to the same extent and in the same way. For example, a wealthy white woman in a rich capitalist country is in a very different position from a poor black woman living in an impoverished part of Africa. Since their problems are different, they would require very different solutions.

Despite their disagreements, feminists tend to agree that, at least until recently, sociology has neglected women. Certainly until the 1970s, sociology was largely written by men about men. There were relatively few studies of women, and issues of particular concern to women (such as housework and women's health) were rarely studied. A number of feminists criticize what they call **malestream** sociology. By this they mean mainstream, male-dominated sociology. They have attacked not just what male sociologists study, but also how they carry out their studies. For example, they have suggested that feminist sociology should get away from rigid 'scientific' methods and should adopt more sympathetic approaches. These can involve working in partnership with those being studied rather than treating them as simply the passive providers of data (see pp. 809–11).

As feminist scholarship has developed it has started to examine numerous aspects of social life from feminist viewpoints. Many of the resulting studies will be examined in later chapters. (Feminist perspectives are discussed in detail on pp. 100–21.)

Interactionism

Functionalism and Marxism have a number of characteristics in common. First, they offer a general explanation of society as a whole, and as a result are sometimes known as **macro-theories**. Second, they regard society as a system, hence they are sometimes referred to as **system theories**. Third, they tend to see human behaviour as shaped by the system. In terms of Talcott Parsons's version of functionalism, behaviour is largely directed by the norms and values of the social system. From a Marxist viewpoint, behaviour is ultimately determined by the economic infrastructure. Some versions of feminism have similar characteristics in that they explain how society works in terms of the existence of a patriarchal system and explain the behaviour of males and females in terms of that system. (Other feminist theories are very different and share some features in common with interactionism.)

Interactionism differs from functionalism, Marxism and most feminist theories in that it focuses on small-scale interaction rather than society as a whole. It usually rejects the notion of a social system. As a result it does not regard human action as a response or reaction to the system. Interactionists believe that it is possible to analyse society systematically and that it is possible to improve society. However, improvements have to be made on a smaller scale and in a more piecemeal way than implied by macro- or system theories.

Meaning and interpretation

As its name suggests, interactionism is concerned with **interaction**, which means action between individuals. The interactionist perspective seeks to understand this process. It begins from the assumption that action is meaningful to those involved. It therefore follows that an understanding of action requires an interpretation of the meanings that the actors give to their activities. Picture a man and a woman in a room and the man lighting a candle. This action is open to a number of interpretations. The couple may simply require light because a fuse has blown or a power cut has occurred. Or they may be involved in some form of ritual in which the lighted candle has a religious significance. Alternatively, the man or woman may be trying to create a more intimate atmosphere as a prelude to a sexual encounter. Finally, the couple may be celebrating a birthday, a wedding anniversary or some other red-letter day. In each case a different meaning is attached to the act of lighting a candle. To understand the act, it is therefore necessary to discover the meaning held by the actors.

Meanings are not fixed entities. As the above example shows, they depend in part on the context of the interaction. Meanings are also created, developed, modified and changed within the actual process of interaction. A pupil entering a new class may initially define the situation as threatening and even hostile. This definition may be confirmed, modified or changed depending on the pupil's perception of the interaction that takes place in the classroom. The pupil may come to perceive the teacher and fellow pupils as friendly and understanding and so change his or her assessment of the situation. The way in which actors define situations has important consequences. It represents their reality in terms of which they structure their actions. For example, if the pupil maintains a definition of the classroom as threatening and hostile, they may say little and speak only when spoken to. Conversely, if the definition changed, there would probably be a corresponding change in the pupil's actions in that context.

Self-concepts

The actions of the pupil in the above example will depend in part on their interpretation of the way others see them. For this reason many interactionists place particular emphasis on the idea of the self. They suggest that individuals develop a **self-concept**, a picture of themselves, which has an important influence on their actions. A self-concept develops from interaction processes, since it is in large part a reflection of the reactions of others towards the individual: hence the term **looking-glass self** coined by Charles Cooley (1864–1929) (discussed in Coser, 1977). Actors tend to act in terms of their self-concept. Thus if they are consistently defined as disreputable or respectable, servile or arrogant, they will tend to see themselves in this light and act accordingly.

The construction of meaning

Since interactionists are concerned with definitions of situation and self, they are also concerned with the process by which those definitions are constructed. For example, how does an individual come to be defined in a certain way? The answer to this question involves an investigation of the **construction of meaning** in interaction processes. This requires an analysis of the way actors interpret the language, gestures, appearance and manner of others and their interpretation of the context in which the interaction takes place.

The definition of an individual as a delinquent is an example. Research has indicated that the police are more likely to perceive an act as delinquent if it occurs in a low-income inner-city area. The context will influence the action of the police, since they typically define the inner city as a 'bad area'. Once arrested, a male youth is more likely to be defined as a juvenile delinquent if his manner is interpreted as aggressive and uncooperative, if his appearance is seen as unconventional or slovenly, if his speech is defined as ungrammatical or slang, and if his posture gives the impression of disrespect for authority, or arrogance. Thus the black American youth from the inner-city ghetto with his cool, arrogant manner and colourful clothes is more likely to be defined as a delinquent than the white 'all-American girl' from the tree-lined suburbs.

Definitions of individuals as certain kinds of persons are not, however, simply based on preconceptions which actors bring to interaction situations. For example, the police will not automatically define black juveniles involved in a fight as delinquent and white juveniles involved in a similar activity as non-delinquent. A process of negotiation occurs from which the definition emerges. Often negotiations will reinforce preconceptions, but not necessarily. The young blacks may be able to convince the police officer that the fight was a friendly brawl which did not involve intent to injure or steal. In this way they may successfully promote images of themselves as high-spirited teenagers rather than as malicious delinquents. Definitions and meanings are therefore constructed in interaction situations by a process of negotiation.

Negotiation and roles

The idea of negotiation is also applied to the concept of role. Like functionalists, interactionists employ the concept of role but they adopt a somewhat different perspective. Functionalists imply that roles are provided by the social system, and individuals enact their roles as if they were reading off a script that contains explicit directions for their behaviour. Interactionists argue that roles are often unclear, ambiguous and vague. This lack of clarity provides actors with considerable room for negotiation, manoeuvre, improvisation and creative action. At most, roles provide very general guidelines for action. What matters is how they are employed in interaction situations.

For example, two individuals enter marriage with a vague idea about the roles of husband and wife. Their interaction will not be constrained by these roles. Their definition of what constitutes a husband, a wife and a marital relationship will be negotiated and continually renegotiated. It will be fluid rather than fixed, changeable rather than static. Thus, from an interactionist perspective, roles, like meanings and definitions of the situation, are negotiated in interaction processes.

While interactionists admit the existence of roles, they regard them as vague and imprecise and therefore as open to negotiation. From an interactionist perspective, action proceeds from negotiated meanings which are constructed in ongoing interaction situations.

Postmodernism

The challenge to modernism

Since the 1980s, postmodern perspectives have become increasingly influential in sociology. These perspectives take a number of forms, and the more radical of these represent a major challenge to the perspectives examined so far.

Some postmodern theorists content themselves with describing and explaining what they see as the crucial changes in society. They retain elements of conventional approaches in sociology. For example, they still believe that it is possible to explain both human behaviour and the ways in which societies are changing. They no longer assume that the changes are progressive, but they stick to a belief that they can be explained through developing sociological theories. Some postmodernists go much further than this. They argue that conventional, modern approaches in sociology, which grew out of modern society, must be abandoned. While approaches such as Marxism, functionalism, feminism and interactionism might have explained how the social world worked in previous eras, they are no longer useful. New theories are needed for the postmodern age. They support this claim in two main ways.

First, some postmodernists argue that social behaviour is no longer shaped as it used to be by people's background and their socialization. They argue that factors such as class, gender and ethnic group influence people a great deal less than they used to. Instead, people are much freer to choose their own identity and lifestyle. Thus, for example, people can choose whether to be heterosexual or homosexual, they have more choice about where they live and where they travel, what sort of people they mix with and what clothes they wear. The boundaries between social groups are breaking down and you can no longer predict the sorts of lifestyles that people will adopt. If so much choice exists, then many of the aspects of social life studied by modern sociologists are no longer important and their studies are no longer useful.

Second, some postmodernists question the belief that there is any solid foundation for producing knowledge about society. They argue that modern sociologists were quite wrong to believe that sociology could discover the truth by adopting the methods of the physical sciences. From their perspective, all knowledge is based upon the use of language. Language can never describe the external world perfectly. Knowledge is essentially subjective – it expresses personal viewpoints which can never be proved to be correct.

Postmodernists such as Jean Baudrillard argue that it has become increasingly difficult to separate media images from anything even approximating to reality (see pp. 893–4). Society has become so saturated with media images that people now sometimes confuse media characters with real life. For example, they talk about soap opera characters as if they were real people rather than dramatic roles.

Postmodernists such as Jean François Lyotard (see pp. 891–3) are particularly critical of any attempt to produce a general theory of how society works (for example, Marxism or functionalism). Lyotard believes that all attempts to produce such theories are doomed to failure. They cannot truly explain something as complex as the social world. Generally such theories are simply used by groups of people to try to impose their ideas on other people, for example in communist or fascist societies. General theories are therefore dangerous and should always be rejected. In Lyotard's view, modern sociological theories fall into this category and should be rejected.

Difference

Many writers who adopt some of the stronger claims of postmodernism emphasize differences between people rather than similarities between members of social groups. They believe that it is the job of the researcher to uncover and describe these differences rather than to make generalizations about whole social groups. This involves acknowledging that there are many different viewpoints on society and that you should not judge between them. All viewpoints are seen as being equally valid; none is superior to any other. Sociologists should not try to impose their views on others, but should merely enable the voices of different people to be heard. This is very different from the goals of other sociologists (such as Marxists and functionalists) who set out to produce scientific explanations of how society works and how social groups behave.

Postmodern perspectives will be examined and evaluated in more detail later in relation to particular topics. The theory of postmodernism will be discussed in detail in Chapter 14.

Human behaviour and sociological research

The last section looked briefly at five theoretical perspectives in sociology. This section deals with philosophical views of human behaviour. These views have influenced both the type of data sociologists have collected and the methods they have employed to collect the data.

Views of human behaviour can be roughly divided into those that emphasize external factors and those that stress internal factors. The former approach sees behaviour as being influenced by the structure of society, which is objective and exists outside the individual's consciousness. The latter approach places more emphasis upon the subjective states of individuals: their feelings, the meanings they attach to events, and the motives they have for behaving in particular ways. From this point of view, the way that people respond to external factors is shaped by the way that the individual interprets them.

The use of this 'dichotomy' (sharply defined division) is somewhat artificial. In practice most sociologists make use of the insights provided by both approaches when carrying out research and interpreting the results. There are also a number of variations on each approach. For example, as a later section will show (see pp. 15–16), phenomenologists differ in their approach from other sociologists who emphasize the importance of internal influences upon human behaviour.

Positivism

Many of the founders of sociology believed it would be possible to create a science of society based upon the same principles and procedures as the natural sciences, like chemistry and biology, even though the natural sciences often deal with inanimate matter and so are not concerned with feelings, emotions and other subjective states. The most influential attempt to apply natural science methodology to sociology is known as **positivism**.

Auguste Comte (1798–1857), who is credited with inventing the term sociology and regarded as one of the founders of the discipline, maintained that the application of the methods and assumptions of the natural sciences would produce a 'positive science of society'. He believed that this would reveal that the evolution of society followed 'invariable laws'. It would show that the behaviour of humans was governed by principles of cause and effect that were just as invariable as the behaviour of matter, the subject of the natural sciences.

In terms of sociology, the positivist approach makes the following assumptions. The behaviour of humans, like the behaviour of matter, can be objectively measured. Just as the behaviour of matter can be quantified by measures such as weight, temperature and pressure, methods of objective measurement can be devised for human behaviour. Such measurement is essential to explain behaviour.

For example, in order to explain the reaction of a particular chemical to heat, it is necessary to provide exact measurements of temperature, weight and so on. With the aid of such measurements it will be possible to observe accurately the behaviour of matter and produce a statement of cause and effect. This statement might read $A \times B = C$, where A is a quantity of matter, B a degree of heat and C a volume of gas. Once it has been shown that the matter in question always reacts in the same way under fixed conditions, a theory can be devised to explain its behaviour.

From a positivist viewpoint, such methods and assumptions are applicable to human behaviour. Observations of behaviour based on objective measurement will make it possible to produce statements of cause and effect. Theories may then be devised to explain observed behaviour.

The positivist approach in sociology places particular emphasis on behaviour that can be directly observed. It argues that factors that are not directly observable – such as meanings, feelings and purposes – are not particularly important and can be misleading. For example, if the majority of adult members of society enter into marriage and produce children, these facts can be observed and quantified. They therefore form reliable data. However, the range of meanings that members of society give to these activities – their reasons for marriage and procreation – are not directly observable. Even if they could be accurately measured, they might well divert attention from the real cause of behaviour. One person might believe they entered marriage because they were lonely, another because they were in love, a third because it was the 'thing to do', and a fourth because they wished to have children. Reliance on this type of data for explanation assumes that individuals know the reasons for marriage. This can obscure the real cause of their behaviour.

The positivists' emphasis on observable 'facts' is due largely to the belief that human behaviour can be explained in much the same way as the behaviour of matter. Natural scientists do not enquire into the meanings and purposes of matter. Atoms and molecules do not act in terms of meanings, they simply react to external stimuli. Thus if heat, an external stimulus, is applied to matter, that matter will react. The job of the natural scientist is to observe, measure and then explain that reaction.

The positivist approach to human behaviour applies a similar logic. People react to external stimuli and their behaviour can be explained in terms of this reaction. They enter into marriage and produce children in response to the demands of society: society requires such behaviour for its survival and its members simply respond to this requirement. The meanings and purposes they attach to this behaviour are largely inconsequential.

It has often been argued that systems theory in sociology adopts a positivist approach. Once behaviour is seen as a response to some external stimulus (such as economic forces or the requirements of the social system), the methods and assumptions of the natural sciences appear appropriate to the study of humans. Marxism has sometimes been regarded as a positivist approach, since it can be argued that it sees human behaviour as a reaction to the stimulus of the economic infrastructure. Functionalism has been viewed in a similar light. The behaviour of members of society can be seen as a response to the functional prerequisites of the social system. These views of systems theory represent a considerable oversimplification. However, it is probably fair to say that systems theory is closer to a positivist approach than the views that will now be considered.

Social action perspectives

Advocates of social action perspectives argue that the subject matters of the social and natural sciences are fundamentally different. As a result, the methods and assumptions of the natural sciences are inappropriate to the study of humans. The natural sciences deal with matter. To understand and explain the behaviour of matter it is sufficient to observe it from the outside. Atoms and molecules do not have consciousness: they do not have meanings and purposes that direct their behaviour. Matter simply reacts unconsciously to external stimuli; in scientific language, it 'behaves'. As a result, the natural scientist is able to observe, measure and impose an external logic on that behaviour in order to explain it. Scientists have no need to explore the internal logic of the consciousness of matter simply because it does not exist.

Unlike matter, humans have **consciousness** – thoughts, feelings, meanings, intentions and an awareness of being. Because of this, humans' actions are **meaningful**: humans define situations and give meaning to their actions and those of others. As a result, they do not just react to external stimuli, they do not merely behave – they act.

Imagine the response of early humans to fire caused by volcanoes or spontaneous combustion. They did not simply react in a uniform manner to the experience of fire. They attached a range of meanings to it and these meanings directed their actions. They defined fire as a means of warmth and used it to heat their dwellings; they saw it as a means of defence and used it to ward off wild animals; and they saw it as a means of transforming substances and employed it for cooking and hardening the points of wooden spears. Humans do not just react to fire, they act upon it in terms of the meanings they give to it.

If action stems from subjective meanings, it follows that the sociologist must discover those meanings in order to understand action. Sociologists cannot simply observe action from the outside and impose an external logic upon it. They must interpret the internal logic that directs the actions of the actor.

Max Weber (1864–1920) was one of the first sociologists to outline this perspective in detail. He argued that sociological explanations of action should begin with observing and interpreting the subjective 'states of minds' of people. As the previous section indicated, interactionism adopts a similar approach, with particular emphasis on the process of interaction. Where positivists emphasize facts and cause-and-effect relationships, interactionists emphasize insight and understanding. Since it is not possible to get inside the heads of actors, the discovery of meaning must be based on interpretation and intuition. For this reason, objective measurement is not possible and the exactitude of the natural sciences cannot be duplicated. Since meanings are constantly negotiated in ongoing interaction processes, it is not possible to establish simple cause-and-effect relationships. Thus some sociologists argue that sociology is limited to an interpretation of social action.

Nevertheless, both Weber and the interactionists did think it was possible to produce causal explanations of human behaviour, so long as an understanding of meanings formed part of those explanations. Some sociologists, particularly phenomenologists, take the argument further and claim that it is impossible for sociologists to find the causes of human action.

Phenomenology

To phenomenologists, it is impossible to measure objectively any aspect of human behaviour. Humans make sense of the world by categorizing it. Through language they distinguish between different types of objects, events, actions and people. For instance, some actions are defined as criminal and others are not; similarly some people are defined as criminals while others are seen as law-abiding. The process of **categorization** is subjective: it depends upon the opinions of the observer. Statistics are simply the product of the opinions of those who produce them. Thus crime statistics are produced by the police and the courts, and they represent no more than the opinions of the individuals involved. If sociologists produce their own statistics, these too are the result of subjective opinions – in this case the opinions of sociologists.

Phenomenologists believe that it is impossible to produce factual data and that it is therefore impossible to produce and check causal explanations. The most that sociologists can hope to do is to understand the meaning that individuals give to particular phenomena. Phenomenologists do not try to establish what causes crime; instead they try to discover how certain events come to be defined as crimes and how certain people come to be defined as criminal. Phenomenologists therefore examine the way that police officers reach decisions about whether to arrest and charge suspects. In doing so, they hope to establish the meanings attached to the words 'crime' and 'criminal' by the police. The end product of phenomenological research is an understanding of the meanings employed by members of society in their everyday life.

Although there are differences between those who support social action and those who support phenomenological views, they all agree that the positivist approach has produced a distorted picture of social life.

Peter Berger (1966) argues that society has often been viewed as a puppet theatre with its members portrayed as 'little puppets jumping about on the ends of their invisible strings, cheerfully acting out the parts that have been assigned to them'. Society instils values, norms and roles, and humans dutifully respond like Berger's puppets. However, interactionists and phenomenologists believe that humans do not react and respond passively to an external society. They see humans as actively creating their own meanings and their own society in interaction with each other. In this respect they have similarities with some of the postmodern approaches discussed earlier (see p. 13).

Sociology and values

The positivist approach assumes that a science of society is possible. It therefore follows that objective observation and analysis of social life are possible. An objective view is free from the values, moral judgements and ideology of the observer: it provides facts and explanatory frameworks which are uncoloured by the observer's feelings and opinions.

An increasing number of sociologists argue that a **value-free** science of society is not possible. They maintain that the values of sociologists directly influence every aspect of their research. They argue that the various theories of society are based, at least in part, on value judgements and ideological positions. They suggest that sociological perspectives are shaped more by historical circumstances than by objective views of the reality of social life.

Those who argue that an objective science of society is not possible maintain that sociology can never be free from ideology. The term **ideology** refers to a set of ideas which present only a partial view of reality. An ideological viewpoint also includes values. It involves a judgement not only about the way things are, but also about the way things ought to be. Thus ideology is a set of beliefs and values which provides a way of seeing and interpreting the world, which results in a partial view of reality. The term ideology is often used to suggest a distortion, a false picture of reality. However, there is considerable doubt about whether reality and ideology can be separated. As Nigel Harris (1971) suggests, 'Our reality is the next man's ideology and vice versa'.

Ideology can be seen as a set of beliefs and values that express the interests of a particular social group. Marxists use the term in this way when they talk about the ideology of the ruling class. In this sense, ideology is a viewpoint that distorts reality and justifies and legitimates the position of a social group.

Karl Mannheim (1948) uses the term in a similar way. He states that ideology consists of the beliefs and values of a ruling group which 'obscures the real condition of society both to itself and others and thereby stabilizes it'. Mannheim distinguishes this form of ideology from what he calls **utopian ideology**. Rather than supporting the status quo – the way things are – utopian ideologies advocate a complete change in the structure of society. Mannheim argues that such ideologies are usually found in oppressed groups whose members want radical change. As their name suggests, utopian ideologies are based on a vision of an ideal society, a perfect social system. Mannheim refers to them as 'wish-images' for a future social order. Like the ideologies of ruling groups, he argues that utopian ideologies are a way of seeing the world which prevents true insight and obscures reality.

Mannheim's ideas will now be applied to two of the major theoretical perspectives in sociology: Marxism and functionalism. It has often been argued that Marxism is largely based on a utopian ideology, and functionalism on a ruling class ideology. Marxism contains a vision and a promise of a future ideal society – the communist utopia. In this society the means of production are communally owned and, as a result, oppression and exploitation disappear. The communist utopia provides a standard of comparison for present and past societies. Since they inevitably fall far short of this ideal, their social arrangements will be condemned. It has been argued that the communist utopia is not a scientific prediction but merely a projection of the 'wish-images' of those who adopt a Marxist position. Utopian ideology has therefore been seen as the basis of Marxist theory.

By comparison, functionalism has often been interpreted as a form of ruling class ideology. Where Marxism is seen to advocate radical change, functionalism is seen to justify and legitimate the status quo. With its emphasis on order and stability, consensus and integration, functionalism appears to adopt a conservative stance. Rapid social change is not recommended since it will disrupt social order. The major institutions of society are justified by the belief that they are meeting the functional prerequisites of the social system.

Although functionalists have introduced the concept of **dysfunction** to cover the harmful effects of parts of the system on society as a whole, the concept is rarely employed. In practice, functionalists appear preoccupied with discovering the positive functions and the beneficial effects of social institutions. As a result, the term function is associated with the idea of useful and good. This interpretation of society tends to legitimate the way things are. Ruling class ideology has therefore been seen as the basis of functionalist theory.

It is important to note that the above interpretation of the ideological bases of Marxism and functionalism is debatable. However, a case can be made to support the view that both perspectives are ideologically based.

The view that Marxism and functionalism are ideologically based would certainly be supported by **postmodernists**. Postmodernists do not just reject these particular perspectives – they reject any attempt to produce a theory of society as a whole. They see such theories as dangerous. This is because they can lead to one group trying to impose its will on others. From this viewpoint it is neither possible nor desirable to try to remove values from sociology. Instead, a range of different values should be accepted and tolerated. People have a right to be different from one another and to hold different views. It is not the job of the sociologist to arbitrate between these different values and say which is better.

Some sociologists reject this standpoint. Critical social scientists (whose ideas are examined on pp. 804–8) do not deny that values must inevitably enter into sociology. However, they do not believe that sociologists should just accept the range of different values present in society. Rather, it is the duty of social scientists to try to improve society. If, like postmodernists, they were simply to accept the range of different values that exists, they would be shirking their responsibility. By refusing to make any judgement about whose values are better, they would be accepting the way society is. Taken to extremes, this would mean, for example, that the values of the rapist are no worse than those of the rape victim; the values of racists are no worse than those of people who campaign against racism; and the values of capitalists who exploit their workers are no worse than those of people who try to help the poor. Critical social scientists argue that sociologists should take sides and they should try to use their work to fight injustice and improve society. This view is generally supported by the American sociologist C. Wright Mills, whose ideas are examined below.

The sociological imagination

Although sociologists vary in their perspectives, methods and values, they all (with the exception of some postmodernists) share the aim of understanding and explaining the social world. Combining the insights offered by different approaches might be the best way of achieving this goal.

Structural theories of society, such as functionalism and Marxism, emphasize the importance of society in shaping human behaviour. On the other hand, approaches such as interactionism emphasize the importance of human behaviour in shaping society. Many sociologists today believe that good sociology must examine both the structure of society and social interaction. They believe that it is only by combining the study of the major changes in society and individual lives that sociologists can develop their understanding of social life.

This idea is not new. It was supported by the very influential German sociologist Max Weber (1864–1920) (see pp. 874–8), and more recently has been examined in depth by the British sociologist Anthony Giddens (see pp. 888–90). However, perhaps the clearest exposition of this view was put forward by the American sociologist C. Wright Mills.

Mills called the ability to study the structure of society at the same time as individuals' lives the 'sociological imagination' (Mills, 1959). He argued that the sociological imagination allowed people to understand their 'private troubles' in terms of 'public issues'. Unemployment, war and marital breakdown are all experienced by people in terms of the problems they produce in their personal lives. They react to them as individuals, and their reactions have consequences for society as a whole. However, to Mills, these issues can only be fully understood in the context of wider social forces. For example, very specific circumstances might lead to one person becoming unemployed, but when unemployment rates in society as a whole rise, it becomes a public issue that needs to be explained. The sociologist has to consider 'the economic and political institutions of the society, and not merely the personal situation and character of a scatter of individuals'.

According to Mills, then, sociology should be about examining the biography of individuals in the context of the history of societies. The sociological imagination is not just of use to sociologists; it is important to all members of society if they wish to understand, change and improve their lives. Perhaps sociology can be seen as succeeding when it allows people to achieve this imagination, and the theories and studies examined in the rest of the book can be judged in these terms.

CHAPTER 1

Social stratification

There is certainly a powerful business elite in Britain today, just as there always has been. Those with real power – to change the course of events, to influence and alter government policy, to control important institutions – probably constitute maybe less than half the full membership of the 'super-class' – a 'hyper-class', an elite within an elite. Lansley, 2006

Introduction

Inequality

Although people have long dreamed of an **egalitarian** society, a society in which all members are equal, such a society has never existed. All human societies from the simplest to the most complex have some form of social inequality. In particular, power and prestige are unequally distributed between individuals and social groups and in many societies there are also marked differences in the distribution of wealth.

1. **Power** refers to the degree to which individuals or groups can impose their will on others, with or without the consent of those others.
2. **Prestige** relates to the amount of esteem or honour associated with social positions, qualities of individuals and styles of life.
3. **Wealth** refers to material possessions defined as valuable in particular societies. It may include land, livestock, buildings, money and many other forms of property owned by individuals or social groups.

In this chapter we study the unequal distribution of power, prestige and wealth in society.

Social inequality and social stratification

It is important at the outset to make a distinction between social inequality and social stratification. The term **social inequality** simply refers to the existence of socially created inequalities. **Social stratification** is a particular form of social inequality. It refers to the presence of distinct social groups which are ranked one above the other in terms of factors such as prestige and wealth. Those who belong to a particular group or stratum will have some awareness of common interests and a common identity. They will share a similar lifestyle which, to some degree, will distinguish them from members of other social strata. The Indian caste system provides one example of a social stratification system.

In traditional India, Hindu society was divided into five main strata: four *varnas* or castes, and a fifth group, the outcaste, whose members were known as untouchables. Each caste was subdivided into *jatis* or subcastes, which in total numbered many thousands. *Jatis* were occupational groups – there were carpenter *jatis*, goldsmith *jatis*, potter *jatis*, and so on.

Castes were ranked in terms of ritual purity. The Brahmins, or priests, members of the highest caste, personified purity, sanctity and holiness. At the other extreme, untouchables were defined as unclean, base and impure, a status that affected all their social relationships. They had to perform unclean and degrading tasks such as the disposal of dead animals. They were segregated from members of the caste system and lived on the outskirts of villages or in their own communities.

In general, the hierarchy of prestige based on notions of ritual purity was mirrored by the hierarchy of power. The Brahmins were custodians of the law, and the legal system they administered was based largely on their pronouncements. Inequalities of wealth were usually linked to those of prestige and power and the Brahmins tended to be the largest landowners. Although the caste system has been made illegal in modern India, it still exercises an influence, particularly in rural areas.

As shown by the caste system, social stratification involves a **hierarchy of social groups**. Members of a particular stratum have a common identity, similar interests and a similar lifestyle. They enjoy or suffer the unequal distribution of rewards in society as members of different social groups.

Social stratification, however, is only one form of social inequality. It is possible for social inequality to exist without social strata. For example, some sociologists have argued that class systems of stratification have broken down in Western societies so that there are no longer distinct classes whose members have a common lifestyle or a sense of shared identity (see pp. 84–6). However, whether classes still exist or not, there is no disputing that there are still great differences in the wealth, power and status of individuals in Western society, and therefore continuing social inequality.

Stratification systems

Before looking at some of the major issues raised in the study of social stratification, it is necessary to examine certain aspects of stratification systems.

Subcultures

First, in such systems there is a tendency for members of each stratum to develop their own **subculture**, that is, certain norms, attitudes and values which are distinctive to them as a social group. When some members of society experience similar circumstances and problems that are not common to all members, a subculture tends to develop. Studies of class stratification have often focused on the nature of class subcultures and whether they are still as strong as they used to be (see for example pp. 58–63). Recent work inspired by the writings of the French sociologist Pierre Bourdieu (see pp. 67–73) has revitalized an interest in the relationship between class and culture.

Social mobility

Strata subcultures tend to be particularly distinctive when there is little opportunity to move from one stratum to another. This movement is known as **social mobility**. Social mobility can be upward, for example moving from the working to the middle class, or downward.

Stratification systems which provide little opportunity for social mobility may be described as **closed**, and those with a relatively high rate of social mobility as **open**. In closed systems an individual's position is largely **ascribed**: often it is fixed at birth and there is little he or she can do to change status. In open systems status is achieved, and the individual has some chance of changing their position. Caste provides a good example of a closed stratification system: individuals automatically belonged to the caste of their parents and, except in rare instances, spent the rest of their life in that status. In class systems, social mobility is possible and some people will be upwardly mobile and improve their position through talent, hard work or even good luck.

Life chances

A person's position in a stratification system may have important effects on many areas of life. It may enhance or reduce life chances, that is, their chances of obtaining those things defined as desirable and avoiding those things defined as undesirable in their society. Gerth and Mills, referring to Western society, state that life chances include:

> *Everything from the chance to stay alive during the first year after birth to the chance to view fine arts, the chance to remain healthy and grow tall, and if sick to get well again quickly, the chance to avoid becoming a juvenile delinquent and, very crucially, the chance to complete an intermediary or higher educational grade.* Gerth and Mills, 1954, p. 313

Having considered social stratification in general terms, we will now look at this subject from the various sociological perspectives.

Social stratification – a functionalist perspective

Functionalist theories of stratification set their explanations in the framework of larger theories which seek to explain the operation of society as a whole. They assume that society has certain basic needs or **functional prerequisites** that must be met if it is to survive. They therefore look to social stratification to see how far it meets these functional prerequisites.

Functionalists assume that the parts of society form an integrated whole and thus they examine the ways in which the social stratification system is integrated with other parts of society. They maintain that a certain degree of order and stability is essential for the operation of social systems. They therefore consider how stratification systems help to maintain order and stability in society.

Talcott Parsons – stratification and values

Like many functionalists, Talcott Parsons believed that order, stability and cooperation in society are based on **value consensus** – a general agreement by members of society concerning what is good and worthwhile. Parsons argued that stratification systems derive from common values. If values exist, then it follows that individuals will be evaluated and placed in some form of rank order. In other words, those who perform successfully in terms of society's values will be ranked highly and they will be likely to receive a variety of rewards. At a minimum they will be accorded high prestige because they exemplify and personify common values.

For example, if a society places a high value on bravery and generosity, as was the case with the Sioux Indians in North America, those who excel in terms of these qualities will receive a high rank in the stratification system. The Sioux warrior who successfully raided the Crow and Pawnee – the traditional enemies of his tribe – capturing their horses and distributing them to others, would receive a variety of rewards. He might be given a seat on the tribal council, a position of power and prestige. His deeds would be recounted in the warrior societies and the women would sing of his exploits. Other warriors would follow him in raids against neighbouring tribes and the success of these expeditions might lead to his appointment as a war chief. In this way, excellence in terms of Sioux values was rewarded by power and prestige.

Because different societies have different value systems, the ways of attaining a high position will vary from society to society. Parsons argued that American society values individual achievement, and efficiency, and 'puts primary emphasis on productive activity within the economy'. Thus successful business executives who have achieved their position through their own initiative, ability and ambition, and run efficient and productive businesses, will receive high rewards.

Parsons's argument suggests that stratification is an inevitable part of all human societies. If value consensus is an essential component of all societies, then it follows that some form of stratification will result from the ranking of individuals in terms of common values. It also follows from Parsons's argument that there is a general belief that stratification systems are just, right and proper, because they are basically an expression of shared values. Thus American business executives are seen to deserve their rewards because members of society place a high value on their skills and achievements.

This is not to say there is no conflict between the haves and have-nots, the highly rewarded and those with little reward. Parsons recognized that in Western industrial society there will be 'certain tendencies to arrogance on the part of some winners and to resentment and to a "sour grapes" attitude on the part of some losers'. However, he believed that this conflict is kept in check by the common value system which justifies the unequal distribution of rewards.

Organization and planning

Functionalists tend to see the relationship between social groups in society as one of cooperation and interdependence. In complex industrial societies, different groups specialize in particular activities. As no one group is self-sufficient, it alone cannot meet the needs of its members. It must, therefore, exchange goods and services with other groups, and so the relationship between social groups is one of **reciprocity** (mutual give and take).

This relationship extends to the strata in a stratification system. An oversimplified example is the argument that many occupational groups within the middle class in Western society plan, organize and coordinate the activities of the working class. Each class needs and cooperates with the other, since any large-scale task requires both organization and execution. In societies with a highly specialized division of labour, such as industrial societies, some members will specialize in organization and planning while others will follow their directives. Parsons argued that this inevitably leads to inequality in terms of power and prestige:

> *Organization on an ever increasing scale is a fundamental feature of such a system. Such organization naturally involves centralization and differentiation of leadership and authority; so that those who take responsibility for coordinating the actions of many others must have a different status in important respects from those who are essentially in the role of carrying out specifications laid down by others.* Parsons, 1964, p. 327

Thus those with the power to organize and coordinate the activities of others will have a higher social status than those they direct.

Power

As with prestige differentials, Parsons argued that inequalities of power are based on shared values. Power is legitimate authority in that it is generally accepted as just and proper by members of society as a whole. It is accepted as such because those in positions of authority use their power to pursue **collective goals** which derive from society's central values. Thus the power of the American business executive is seen as legitimate authority because it is used to further productivity, a goal shared by all members of society. This use of power therefore serves the interests of society as a whole.

Summary and evaluation

Parsons saw social stratification as both inevitable and functional for society.

1. It is inevitable because it derives from shared values which are a necessary part of all social systems.
2. It is functional because it serves to integrate various groups in society.

Power and prestige differentials are essential for the coordination and integration of a specialized division of labour. Finally, inequalities of power and prestige benefit all members of society since they serve to further collective goals which are based on shared values.

Parsons has been strongly criticized on all these points. Other sociologists have seen stratification as a divisive rather than an integrating force. They have regarded it as an arrangement whereby some gain at the expense of others, and questioned the view that stratification systems derive ultimately from shared values. We will examine these criticisms in detail in later sections.

Kingsley Davis and Wilbert E. Moore – role allocation and performance

The most famous functionalist theory of stratification was first presented in 1945, in an article by the American sociologists Davis and Moore entitled 'Some Principles of Stratification'.

Effective role allocation and performance

Davis and Moore began with the observation that stratification exists in every known human society. They attempted to explain 'in functional terms, the universal necessity which calls forth stratification in any social system'. They argued that all social systems share certain functional prerequisites which must be met if the system is to survive and operate efficiently. One such functional prerequisite is **effective role allocation and performance**. This means that:

1. All roles must be filled.
2. They must be filled by those best able to perform them.
3. The necessary training for them must be undertaken.
4. The roles must be performed conscientiously.

Davis and Moore argued that all societies need some 'mechanism' for ensuring effective role allocation and performance. This mechanism is social stratification, which they saw as a system that attaches unequal rewards and privileges to the different positions in society.

If the people and positions that make up society did not differ in important respects there would be no need for stratification. However, people differ in terms of their innate ability and talent, and positions differ in terms of their importance for the survival and maintenance of society. Certain positions are more **functionally important** than others. These require special skills for their effective performance and the number of individuals with the necessary ability to acquire such skills is limited.

A major function of stratification is to match the most able people with the functionally most important positions. It does this by attaching high rewards to those positions. The desire for such rewards motivates people to compete for them, and in theory the most talented will win through. Such positions usually require long periods of training that involve certain sacrifices, such as loss of income. The promise of high rewards is necessary to provide an incentive to encourage people to undergo this training and to compensate them for the sacrifice involved. It is essential for the well-being of society that those who hold the functionally most important positions perform their roles diligently and conscientiously. The high rewards built into these positions provide the necessary inducement and generate the required motivation for such performance. Davis and Moore therefore concluded that social stratification is a 'device by which societies ensure that the most important positions are conscientiously filled by the most qualified persons'.

Functional importance

Davis and Moore realized that one difficulty with their theory was showing clearly which positions are functionally most important. A position may be highly rewarded without necessarily being functionally important. They suggested that the importance of a position can be measured in two ways:

1. It can be measured by the 'degree to which a position is functionally unique, there being no other positions that can perform the same function satisfactorily'. Thus it could be argued that doctors are functionally more important than nurses since their position carries with it many of the skills necessary to perform a nurse's role but not vice versa.
2. The second measure of importance is the 'degree to which other positions are dependent on the one in question'. Thus it may be argued that managers are more important than routine office staff since the latter are dependent on direction and organization from management.

To summarize, Davis and Moore regarded social stratification as a **functional necessity** for all societies. They saw it as a solution to a problem faced by all social systems, that of 'placing and motivating individuals in the social structure'. They offered no other means of solving this problem and implied that social inequality is an inevitable feature of human society. They concluded that differential rewards are functional for society, because they contribute to the maintenance and well-being of social systems.

Melvin M. Tumin – a critique of Davis and Moore

Davis and Moore's theory provoked a lengthy debate. Melvin Tumin, their most famous opponent, produced a comprehensive criticism of their ideas.

Functional importance

Tumin began by questioning the adequacy of their measurement of the functional importance of positions. Davis and Moore tended to assume that the most highly rewarded positions are indeed the most important. Many occupations, however, which afford little prestige or economic reward, can be seen as vital to society. Tumin therefore argued that 'some labour force of unskilled workmen is as important and as indispensable to the factory as some labour force of engineers'.

In fact, a number of sociologists have argued that there is no objective way of measuring the functional importance of positions. Whether lawyers and doctors are considered as more important than farm labourers and refuse collectors is simply a matter of opinion.

Power and rewards

Tumin argued that Davis and Moore ignored the influence of power on the unequal distribution of rewards. Differences in pay and prestige between occupational groups may be due to differences in their power rather than their functional importance.

The pool of talent

Davis and Moore assumed that only a limited number of individuals have the talent to acquire the skills necessary for the functionally most important positions. Tumin regarded this as a very questionable assumption for two reasons:

1 An effective method of measuring talent and ability has yet to be devised (as the chapter on education in this book indicates).
2 The pool of talent in society may be considerably larger than Davis and Moore assumed (as the chapter on education suggests). As a result, unequal rewards may not be necessary to harness it.

Training

Tumin also questioned the view that the training required for important positions should be regarded as a sacrifice and therefore in need of compensation. He pointed to the rewards of being a student – leisure, freedom and the opportunity for self-development. He noted that any loss of earnings can usually be made up during the first ten years of work and continuing high pay after that may not be justified.

Motivation

The major function of unequal rewards, according to Davis and Moore, is to motivate talented individuals and allocate them to the functionally most important positions. Tumin rejected this view. He argued that social stratification can, and often does, act as a barrier to the motivation and recruitment of talent. The hurdles which people from lower strata need to overcome in order to succeed can be daunting and can discourage rather than motivate people. This is reflected in the tendency for those from lower social classes to leave the education system earlier than those from higher classes. For example, children from middle-class backgrounds are still much more likely to progress to higher education than those from working-class backgrounds (see p. 626).

Tumin also argued that Davis and Moore failed to consider the possibility that those who occupy highly rewarded positions erect barriers to recruitment. Occupational groups often use their power to restrict access to their positions, so creating a high demand for their services and increasing the rewards they receive. For example, Tumin claimed that the American Medical Association deliberately restricted entry into the profession to ensure a shortage of doctors in order to maintain their high wages.

Inequality of opportunity

Tumin concluded that stratification, by its very nature, can never adequately perform the functions which Davis and Moore assigned to it. He argued that those born into the lower strata can never have the same opportunities for realizing their talents as those born into the higher strata. Tumin maintained:

> *It is only when there is a genuinely equal access to recruitment and training for all potentially talented persons that differential rewards can conceivably be justified as functional. And stratification systems are apparently inherently antagonistic to the development of such full equality of opportunity.* Tumin, 1953, in Bendix and Lipset, 1967, p. 55

Social divisions

Finally, Tumin questioned the view that social stratification functions to integrate the social system. He argued that differential rewards can 'encourage hostility, suspicion and distrust among the various segments of a society'. From this viewpoint, stratification is a divisive rather than an integrating force. Tumin concluded that in their enthusiastic search for the positive functions of stratification, functionalists have tended to ignore or play down its many dysfunctions.

The debate between Davis and Moore and Tumin took place in the 1940s and 1950s. Interest in the issues raised by this debate has recently been revived with the development of market liberal (sometimes called neoliberal or 'New Right') perspectives in sociology. In the next section we will analyse the market liberal theories of social stratification.

Social stratification – a market liberal perspective

The ideas of market liberals (also known as neoliberals or the New Right) became influential in the 1980s. In politics, they were closely associated with the British prime minister Margaret Thatcher and the American president Ronald Reagan. They are also associated with the policies of George Bush junior. The American economist Milton Friedman and the Austrian academic Friedrich Hayek contributed much to the development of market liberal thinking (see, for example, Friedman, 1962 and Hayek, 1944). In British sociology, Peter Saunders and David Marsland have been perhaps the most prominent advocates of this perspective.

Marsland's views on poverty will be examined in Chapter 4 (pp. 238–9) and Saunders's theory of stratification is discussed below.

This approach bases its theories on **nineteenth-century liberalism**. This regarded the free market in capitalist economies as the best basis for organizing society. **Market forces** encourage competition, which stimulates innovation and efficiency. Businesses have to make products that are cheaper or better than those of their competitors in order to survive. Free market economies are based upon the choices made by individuals when spending their money, selling their labour or purchasing other people's labour. They therefore promote **individual liberty**.

Like their nineteenth-century liberal counterparts, the market liberal/New Right sociologists believe that excessive state intervention in the economy must be avoided. The state should not act to redistribute resources and interfere with the workings of the free market. If it tries to do so it will undermine economic efficiency. Inefficient concerns propped up by the government needlessly use up resources. State intervention may take away the motivation for people to work hard. There is little incentive to strive for success if individuals know that the state will help them no matter how little effort they make. Government interference may also create injustice, taking from those who have earned their rewards and giving to those who are undeserving. Furthermore, as the state becomes stronger, the freedom of individuals may be suppressed. For all these reasons market liberals are strongly opposed to Marxism and socialism.

Peter Saunders – stratification and freedom

Saunders (1990) is generally sympathetic to Davis and Moore's theory of stratification: he is certainly much less critical than Tumin. He points out that even critics like Tumin accept that all societies have been stratified – there has never been a completely egalitarian society. Furthermore, he suggests that systems which reward different positions unequally can be shown to have beneficial effects, such as motivating people to work hard.

However, Saunders does not argue that unequal rewards are the only way that a society can fill the important positions with capable people. He says that 'it is possible to imagine a society where all positions are rewarded equally in terms of material resources and formal status'. Such a society would have serious problems, however. Some people would not be happy to do the jobs they were allocated and others would not put in the effort needed to do their jobs properly. Saunders believes:

> *In the absence of economic rewards and penalties, the only sanctions available would be those involving the threat or use of physical force. Such people, in other words, would have to be jailed, or forcibly set to work in supervised colonies, or even executed as an example to others.* Saunders, 1990, p. 65

This would be necessary because allowing people to get away with doing less than their fair share of work would undermine the whole system because it would reduce the commitment of others.

Saunders does not therefore accept the functionalist claim that stratification systems based upon economic differences are inevitable. However, he certainly agrees with functionalists that they are desirable. He admits that capitalist societies tend to create more inequality than socialist societies. He also argues that socialist societies are bound to be more repressive than capitalist ones in making people perform their roles. In the absence of adequate economic rewards, force must be used. Saunders even predicts that as countries such as China and the states of the former Soviet Union move towards market-based economies, 'state coercion may be expected to decline'.

Equality and justice

In developing his own theory of stratification, Saunders distinguishes three types of equality:

1. **Formal** or **legal equality** involves all members of society being subject to the same laws or rules. Individuals are judged according to what they do (for example, whether they break the law) and not according to who they are. Saunders sees this type of equality as being an integral part of Western capitalist societies, although he admits that 'in practice it is not always as rigorously applied as it might be'. Legal equality does not imply that everybody ends up in the same position.
2. The second type of equality, **equality of opportunity**, means that people have an equal chance to become unequal. Individuals compete for success and those with greater merit achieve more. Merit might involve the ability to work harder or the possession of attributes or characteristics which are valued in a society. A society based on this type of equality is often called a meritocracy.
3. **Equality of outcome** goes further than the idea of equality of opportunity. Saunders explains:

> *If a meritocracy is like a race where everybody lines up together at the start, a fully-fledged egalitarian society would be like a perfectly handicapped race where everyone passes the finishing tape at the same time no matter how hard and fast they have tried to run.*
> Saunders, 1990, p. 44

Broadly, Saunders accepts the principles behind the first two conceptions of equality but rejects the third. Following the ideas of Hayek, he argues that attempts to create equality of outcome undermine equality of opportunity and legal equality. To obtain equality of outcome you have to treat people differently. For example, 'affirmative action' programmes or 'positive discrimination', designed to equalize the achievements of men and women or blacks and whites, result in discrimination. Whites and males are discriminated against while blacks and females enjoy discrimination in their favour.

Saunders uses an example put forward by another market liberal writer, Robert Nozick (1974), to show how pursuing equality of outcome leads to injustice. A group of students could agree before an exam that they should all be given a mark of 50 per cent. All would pass and none would have to fear failure, but the result would not be just. Some individuals would feel rightly aggrieved if they were stripped of 30 per cent of the marks they would normally have gained and which they had earned through their own efforts.

Saunders and Nozick therefore adopt a conception of equality based on legal equality and the idea of entitlement. Social justice is served when people are allowed to keep those things to which they are entitled. So long as people have earned the resources or money they possess legally through their own work or 'uncoerced exchanges with others', then there should be no question of them being robbed of their possessions. If people pass their wealth on to others, then the recipients become entitled to keep it.

Saunders does, however, admit that there is one flaw in this argument. In a society such as Britain it is not clear that all of the wealthy are actually entitled to what they own. Some of the land in private hands has been passed down to the descendants of Norman warlords who helped William the Conqueror conquer England. Saunders does not want to see the wealth of landowners such as the Duke of Westminster or the Queen taken from them. To do so would undermine 'the whole basis of modern-day property ownership'. He therefore turns to a second justification for inequality which comes from the work of Hayek.

Both Saunders and Hayek believe that inequality is justified because it promotes economic growth. By allowing and encouraging people to pursue their own self-interest, the interests of society as a whole are promoted. Some entrepreneurs who set up businesses fail. When this happens they bear the costs of their own failure. When they succeed, they may, as Saunders says, 'accumulate a fortune, but in doing so they will have added to the productive power and wealth of the society as a whole'.

Competition ensures that goods and services increase in quality and fall in price, making them available to a wider section of the population. Not everyone will be able to afford consumer products initially, or indeed in the end, but living standards will constantly increase. The efforts of entrepreneurs make some of them rich, but at the same time 'the rest of society grows more affluent as it gains by their efforts'. Saunders cites cars, air travel, colour televisions, home computers and central heating as examples of things that have become affordable for ordinary people.

Opportunity and inequality

Saunders clearly believes that competition in capitalist societies benefits the population. He argues that Britain is close to being a meritocracy (Saunders, 1996). Although he does not claim that Britain or similar societies are perfect meritocracies, in which everyone has genuinely equal opportunities to use their talents to achieve success, he does believe that the distribution of economic rewards is closely related to merit.

He argues that much of the apparent inequality of opportunity between classes in capitalist societies may be due to the unequal distribution of ability and effort. In other words, the children of middle-class parents may deserve to be more successful than those from working-class backgrounds because they tend to have greater genetically inherited ability and because they work harder. If this is the case, then it is not surprising if the children of the middle class get better jobs and higher pay than the children of the working class. Nor is this evidence of inequality of opportunity, as the differences of outcome may well be based on merit.

Saunders's claim that Britain is close to being a meritocracy is highly controversial. It will be discussed in detail later in the chapter in the light of studies of social mobility (see pp. 75–81).

Saunders also emphasizes the increasing opportunities for people from all backgrounds as the proportion of well-paid, middle-class jobs in the occupational structure steadily increases. In societies such as Britain and the USA there are fewer people who are unsuccessful than there were in the past. Whatever the **relative** chances of people from different classes getting a higher-class job, the **absolute** chances have increased for everybody. Capitalism creates more well-paid, skilled and white-collar jobs for which people from all backgrounds can compete. Saunders concludes:

> *Capitalism is dynamic because it is unequal, and any attempt to equalize wealth and income will succeed only at the expense of stifling initiative, innovation and social and economic development.* Saunders, 1990, p. 53

A critique of the market liberal perspective

The market liberal perspective on stratification is open to a number of criticisms. Some of Tumin's criticisms of Davis and Moore are also relevant to market liberal theories. For example, market liberals can be accused of playing down the possible harmful effects of stratification in undermining social cohesion and integration. Saunders's view that socialist societies are inevitably more repressive than free market capitalist ones could be seen as an unjustified, sweeping generalization. For example:

1. Early capitalism was partly based upon the use of slave labour.
2. In South Africa, until relatively recently, a capitalist free market economy went hand-in-hand with the apartheid system which separated 'races' and gave black South Africans very few opportunities.
3. In Chile, a democratically elected socialist government under the leadership of President Allende was overthrown in the 1970s in a coup led by General Pinochet. Pinochet followed free market economic policies and his seizure of power was partly engineered by the USA. Yet his regime was far more repressive than that of his predecessor. One of the Pinochet regime's first actions was to round up thousands of potential opponents and take them to the national football stadium where many were executed.

Examples such as these suggest that the free market and freedom do not inevitably go hand-in-hand.

Gordon Marshall and Adam Swift – social class and social justice

Marshall and Swift (1993) make a detailed evaluation of Saunders's views on stratification. They criticize him for trying to argue in favour of both equality of opportunity and formal or legal equality. These two principles may sometimes coincide, but often they do not. For example, Marshall and Swift argue:

> *If a millionaire chooses to bequeath his money to an untalented layabout then justice as entitlement demands that he be permitted to do so, and forbids taxation of the inheritance despite the fact that any normal conception of justice as desert or merit is here clearly violated.* Marshall and Swift, 1993, p. 191

Marshall and Swift then go on to examine the meritocracy thesis. They question the view that market forces necessarily reward merit. Success in business, for example, may depend as much on luck as on the hard work or personal attributes of the entrepreneur.

Furthermore, Marshall and Swift provide evidence which they claim shows that capitalist societies are not genuinely meritocratic. They use data from a study conducted by Gordon Marshall, Howard Newby, David Rose and Carolyn Vogler (1988). This study found that patterns of social mobility were influenced by class, even when educational attainment was taken into account. People from working-class backgrounds had less chance than those from higher-class backgrounds of obtaining a position in one of the top classes even when they had the same level of educational qualifications.

This undermines Saunders's claim that inequalities between classes could be the result of genetic differences. Working-class people with, for example, the ability to get a degree were still disadvantaged because of their class background. As Marshall and Swift say:

> *If people find their place in the occupational order according to meritocratic principles, then the impact of class background should not be apparent in class destinations, except as this is mediated by educational achievements.* Marshall and Swift, 1993, p. 202

The free market does not guarantee that merit is equally rewarded for all social groups. Social justice may therefore be promoted if the state intervenes to try to make job allocation meritocratic. (For more details of the study by Marshall *et al.* see p. 60. For a fuller discussion of whether there is equality of opportunity in Britain, see pp. 75–82.)

Social stratification – a Marxist perspective

Marxist perspectives provide a radical alternative to functionalist views of the nature of social stratification. They regard stratification as a divisive rather than an integrative structure. They see it as a mechanism whereby some exploit others, rather than as a means of furthering collective goals.

Marxists focus on social strata rather than social inequality in general. Functionalists, such as Parsons and Davis and Moore, say little about social stratification in the sense of clearly defined social strata whose members have shared interests. However, this view of social stratification is central to Marxist theory.

Marx's views will first be briefly summarized and then examined in more detail. For details of Marx's theory of stratification, see Marx (1978 [1867], 1974 [1909]), Marx and Engels (1848), and Bottomore and Rubel (1963).

Classes

1. In all stratified societies there are two major social groups: a **ruling class** and a **subject class**.
2. The power of the ruling class comes from its ownership and control of the **means of production** (land, capital, labour power, buildings and machinery).
3. The ruling class exploits and oppresses the subject class.
4. As a result, there is a basic **conflict** between the two classes.
5. The various institutions of society, such as the legal and political systems, are instruments of ruling-class domination and serve to further its interests.
6. Only when the means of production are **communally owned** will classes disappear, thereby bringing an end to the exploitation and oppression of some by others.

From a Marxist perspective, systems of stratification derive from the relationships of social groups to the means of production. Marx used the term 'class' to refer to the main strata in all stratification systems, although most modern sociologists would reserve the term for strata in capitalist society. From a Marxist viewpoint, a class is a social group whose members share the same relationship to the means of production.

For example, in a feudal epoch, there are two main classes distinguished by their relationship to land (the crucial element of the means of production in an agricultural society). They are the **feudal nobility** who own the land, and the **landless serfs** who work the land. Similarly, in a capitalist era, there are two main classes: the **bourgeoisie** or capitalist class, which owns the means of production, and the **proletariat** or working class, whose members own only their labour which they hire to the bourgeoisie in return for wages.

Classes and historical epochs

Marx believed that Western society had developed through four main epochs:

1. Primitive communism
2. Ancient society
3. Feudal society
4. Capitalist society

Primitive communism is represented by the societies of prehistory and provides the only example of a classless society. From then on, all societies are divided into two major classes: masters and slaves in ancient society, lords and serfs in feudal society and capitalists and wage labourers in capitalist society.

During each historical epoch, the labour power required for production was supplied by the subject class, that is, by slaves, serfs and wage labourers respectively. The subject class is made up of the majority of the population, whereas the ruling or dominant class forms a minority. The relationship between the two major classes is discussed below.

Classes did not exist during the era of primitive communism, when societies were based on a socialist mode of production. In a hunting and gathering band, the earliest form of human society, the land and its products were communally owned. The men hunted and the women gathered plant food, and the produce was shared by members of the band. Classes did not exist since all members of society shared the same relationship to the means of production. Every member was both producer and owner; all provided labour power and shared the products of their labour.

Hunting and gathering is a subsistence economy, which means that production only meets basic survival needs. Classes emerge when the productive capacity of society expands beyond the level required for subsistence. This occurs when agriculture becomes the dominant mode of production. In an agricultural economy, only a section of society is needed to produce the food requirements of the whole society. Many individuals are thus freed from food production and are able to specialize in other tasks. The rudimentary division of labour of the hunting and gathering band is replaced by an increasingly more complex and specialized division.

For example, in the early agricultural villages, some individuals became full-time producers of pottery, clothing and agricultural implements. As agriculture developed, **surplus wealth** – that is, goods above the basic subsistence needs of the community – was produced. This led to an exchange of goods, and trading developed rapidly both within and between communities. This was accompanied by the development of a system of private property. Goods were increasingly seen as commodities or articles of trade to which the individual rather than the community had right of ownership.

Private property and the accumulation of surplus wealth form the basis for the development of class societies. In particular, they provide the preconditions for the emergence of a class of producers and a class of non-producers. Some people are able to acquire the means of production, and others are therefore obliged to work for them. The result is a class of non-producers which owns the means of production, and a class of producers which owns only its labour.

Dependency and conflict

From a Marxist perspective, the relationship between the major social classes is one of mutual dependence and conflict. Thus, in capitalist society, the bourgeoisie and proletariat are dependent upon each other. Wage labourers must sell their labour power in order to survive, as they do not own a part of the means of production and lack the means to produce goods independently. They are, therefore, dependent for their livelihood on the capitalists and the wages they offer. The capitalists, as non-producers, are dependent on the labour power of wage labourers, since, without it, there would be no production.

However, the mutual dependency of the two classes is not a relationship of equal or symmetrical reciprocity. Instead, it is a relationship of exploiter and exploited, oppressor and oppressed. In particular, the ruling class gains at the expense of the subject class and there is therefore a conflict of interest between them. This may be illustrated by Marx's view of the nature of ownership and production in capitalist society.

The capitalist economy and exploitation

The basic characteristics of a capitalist economy may be summarized as follows:

1 **Capital** may be defined as money used to finance the production of commodities for private gain.
2 In a capitalist economy, goods, and the labour power, raw materials and machinery used to produce them, are given a monetary value.
3 The capitalists invest their capital in the production of goods.
4 Capital is accumulated by selling those goods at a value greater than their cost of production.

Capitalism therefore involves the investment of capital in the production of commodities with the aim of maximizing profit in order to accumulate more capital. Money is converted into commodities by financing production; those commodities are then sold and converted back into money at such a price that the capitalists end up with more money than they started with.

Capital is privately owned by a minority, the capitalist class. In Marx's view, however, this capital is gained from the exploitation of the mass of the population, the working class. Marx argued that capital, as such, produces nothing. Only labour produces wealth. Yet the wages paid to the workers for their labour are well below the value of the goods they produce.

The difference between the value of wages and commodities is known as surplus value. This surplus value is appropriated in the form of profit by the capitalists. Because they are non-producers, the bourgeoisie are therefore exploiting the proletariat, the real producers of wealth.

Marx maintained that in all class societies the ruling class exploits and oppresses the subject class.

Power and the superstructure

Political power, in Marxist theory, comes from economic power. The power of the ruling class therefore stems from its ownership and control of the means of production. As the **superstructure** of society – the major institutions, values and belief systems – is seen to be largely shaped by the economic infrastructure, the relations of production will be reproduced in the superstructure. Therefore, the dominance of the ruling class in the relations of production will be reflected in the superstructure. In particular, the political and legal systems will reflect ruling-class interests since, in Marx's words, 'the existing relations of production between individuals must necessarily express themselves also as political and legal relations'.

For instance, the various ownership rights of the capitalist class will be enshrined in and protected by the laws of the land. Thus the various parts of the superstructure can be seen as instruments of ruling-class domination and as mechanisms for the oppression of the subject class.

In the same way, the position of the dominant class is supported by beliefs and values which are systematically generated by the infrastructure. As noted on page 000, Marx referred to the dominant concepts of class societies as **ruling-class ideology**, since they justify and legitimate ruling-class domination and project a distorted picture of reality. For example, the emphasis on freedom in capitalist society, illustrated by phrases such as 'the free market', 'free democratic societies' and 'the free world', is an illusion that disguises the wage slavery of the proletariat.

Ruling-class ideology produces **false class consciousness**, a false picture of the nature of the relationship between social classes. Members of both classes tend to accept the status quo as normal and natural and are largely unaware of the true nature of exploitation and oppression. In this way, the conflict of interest between the classes is disguised and a degree of social stability produced, but the basic contradictions and conflicts of class societies remain unresolved.

Class and social change

Class struggle

Marx believed that the **class struggle** was the driving force of social change. He stated that 'the history of all societies up to the present is the history of the class struggle'.

A new historical epoch is created by the development of superior forces of production by a new social group. These developments take place within the framework of the previous era. The merchants and industrialists who spearheaded the rise of capitalism emerged during the feudal era. They accumulated capital, laid the foundations for industrial manufacture, factory production and the system of wage labour, all of which were essential components of capitalism. The superiority of the capitalist mode of production led to a rapid transformation of the structure of society. The capitalist class became dominant, and although the feudal aristocracy maintained aspects of its power well into the nineteenth century, it was fighting a losing battle.

The class struggles of history have been between minorities. Capitalism, for instance, developed from the struggle between the feudal aristocracy and the emerging capitalist class, both groups in numerical terms forming a minority of the population. Major changes in history have involved the replacement of one form of private property by another, and of one type of production technique by another: capitalism involved the replacement of privately owned land and an agricultural economy by privately owned capital and an industrial economy.

Marx believed that the class struggle that would transform capitalist society would involve none of these processes. The protagonists would be the bourgeoisie and the proletariat, a minority versus a majority. Private property would be replaced by communally owned property. Industrial manufacture would remain as the basic technique of production in the new society.

Marx believed that the basic contradictions contained in a capitalist economic system would lead to its eventual destruction. The proletariat would overthrow the bourgeoisie and seize the means of production, the source of power. Property would be communally owned and, since all members of society would now share the same relationship to the means of production, a classless society would result. Since history is the history of the class struggle, history would now end. The communist society which would replace capitalism would contain no contradictions, no conflicts of interest, and would therefore be unchanging. However, certain changes were necessary before the dawning of this utopia.

Class consciousness

Marx distinguished between a 'class in itself' and a 'class for itself'. A **class in itself** is simply a social group whose members share the same relationship to the means of production. Marx argued that a social group only fully becomes a class when it becomes a class for itself. At this stage, its members have class consciousness and class solidarity. **Class consciousness** means that false class consciousness has been replaced by a full awareness of the true situation, by a realization of the nature of exploitation. Members of a class then develop a common identity, recognize their shared interests and unite, so creating **class solidarity**. The final stage of class consciousness and class solidarity is reached when members realize that only by **collective struggle** can they overthrow the ruling class, and take positive steps to do so.

Marx believed that the following aspects of capitalist society would eventually lead to the proletariat developing into a 'class for itself':

1. Capitalist society is by its very nature unstable. It is based on contradictions and antagonisms which can only be resolved by its transformation. In particular, the conflict of interest between the bourgeoisie and the proletariat cannot be resolved within the framework of a capitalist economy. The basic conflict of interest involves the exploitation of workers by the capitalists.
2. Marx believed that this first contradiction would be highlighted by a second: the contradiction between **social production** and **individual ownership**. As capitalism developed, the workforce was increasingly concentrated in large factories where production was a social enterprise. Social production juxtaposed with individual ownership illuminates the exploitation of the proletariat. Social production also makes it easier for workers to organize themselves against the capitalists. It facilitates communication and encourages a recognition of common circumstances and interests.

Polarization of the classes

Apart from the basic contradictions of capitalist society, Marx believed that certain factors in the natural development of a capitalist economy would hasten its downfall. These factors would result in the **polarization** of the two main classes: the gap between the proletariat and the bourgeoisie will become greater and the contrast between the two groups will become more stark. Such factors include:

1. The increasing use of machinery will result in a **homogeneous working class**. Since 'machinery obliterates the differences in labour', members of the proletariat will become increasingly similar. The differences between skilled, semi-skilled and unskilled workers will tend to disappear as machines remove the skill required in the production of commodities.
2. The difference in wealth between the bourgeoisie and the proletariat will increase as the accumulation of capital proceeds. Even though the real wages and living standards of the proletariat may rise, its members will become poorer in relation to the bourgeoisie. This process is known as **pauperization**.
3. The competitive nature of capitalism means that only the largest and most wealthy companies will survive and prosper. Competition will depress the intermediate strata – those groups lying between the two main classes – into the proletariat. Thus the **petty bourgeoisie**, the owners of small businesses, will sink into the proletariat. At the same time the surviving companies will grow larger and capital will be concentrated into fewer hands.

These three processes – the obliteration of the differences in labour, the pauperization of the working class, and the depression of the intermediate strata into the proletariat – will result in the polarization of the two major classes.

Marx believed he could see the process of polarization in nineteenth-century Britain. He wrote that 'society as a whole is more and more splitting into two great hostile camps … bourgeoisie and proletariat'. The battle lines were now clearly drawn: Marx hoped that the proletarian revolution would shortly follow and the communist utopia of his dreams would finally become a reality.

Marx's work on class has been examined in detail because it continues to influence many sociologists and it has influenced many of the debates within the sociology of stratification.

Social stratification – a Weberian perspective

The work of the German sociologist Max Weber (1864–1920) represents one of the most important developments in stratification theory since Marx. Weber believed that social stratification results from a struggle for scarce resources in society. Although he saw this struggle as being primarily concerned with economic resources, it can also involve struggles for prestige and for political power.

Market situation

Like Marx, Weber saw class in economic terms (Weber, 1947). He argued that classes develop in market economies in which individuals compete for economic gain. He defined a class as a group of individuals who share a similar position in a market economy, and by virtue of that fact receive similar economic rewards. Thus, in Weber's terminology, a person's 'class situation' is basically their **market situation**. Those who share a similar class situation also share similar life chances. Their economic position will directly affect their chances of obtaining those things defined as desirable in their society, for example access to higher education and good quality housing.

Like Marx, Weber argued that the major class division is between those who own the forces of production and those who do not. Thus those who have substantial property holdings will receive the highest economic rewards and enjoy superior life chances. However, Weber saw important differences in the market situation of the propertyless groups in society. In particular, the various skills and services offered by different occupations have differing market values. For instance, in capitalist society, managers, administrators and professionals receive relatively high salaries because of the demand for their services. Weber distinguished the following class groupings in capitalist society:

1. The propertied upper class
2. The propertyless white-collar workers
3. The petty bourgeoisie
4. The manual working class

In his analysis of class, Weber disagreed with Marx on a number of important issues:

1. Factors other than the ownership or non-ownership of property are significant in the formation of classes. In particular, the market value of the skills of the propertyless groups varies and the resulting differences in economic return are sufficient to produce different social classes.
2. Weber saw no evidence to support the idea of the polarization of classes. Although he saw some decline in the numbers of the petty bourgeoisie (the small property owners) due to competition from large companies, he argued that they enter white-collar or skilled manual trades rather than being depressed into the ranks of unskilled manual workers. More importantly, Weber argued that the white-collar 'middle class' expands rather than contracts as capitalism develops. He maintained that capitalist enterprises and the modern nation-state require a 'rational' bureaucratic administration which involves large numbers of administrators and clerical staff. Thus Weber saw a diversification of classes and an expansion of the white-collar middle class, rather than a polarization.
3. Weber rejected the view, held by some Marxists, of the inevitability of the proletarian revolution. He saw no reason why those sharing a similar class situation should necessarily develop a common identity, recognize shared interests and take collective action to further those interests. For example, Weber suggested that individual manual workers who are dissatisfied with their class situation may respond in a variety of ways. They may grumble, work to rule, sabotage industrial machinery, take strike action, or attempt to organize other members of their class in an effort to overthrow capitalism. Weber admitted that a common market situation might provide a basis for collective class action, but he saw this only as a possibility.
4. Weber rejected the Marxist view that political power necessarily derives from economic power. He argued that class forms only one possible basis for power and that the distribution of power in society is not necessarily linked to the distribution of class inequalities.

Status situation

While class forms one possible basis for group formation, collective action and the acquisition of political power, Weber argued that there are other bases for these activities. In particular, groups form because their members share a similar **status situation**. Whereas class refers to the unequal distribution of economic rewards, status refers to the unequal distribution of 'social honour'.

Occupations, ethnic and religious groups, and, most importantly, lifestyles, are accorded differing degrees of prestige or esteem by members of society. A **status group** is made up of individuals who are awarded a similar amount of social honour and therefore share the same status situation. Unlike classes, members of status groups are almost always aware of their common status situation. They share a similar lifestyle, identify with and feel they belong to their status group, and often place restrictions on the ways in which outsiders may interact with them.

Weber argued that status groups reach their most developed form in the caste system of traditional Hindu society in India. Castes and sub-castes were formed and distinguished largely in terms of social honour; lifestyles were sharply differentiated and accorded varying degrees of prestige.

Social closure

Castes also provide a good example of the process described by Weber as social closure. **Social closure** involves the exclusion of some people from membership of a status group. In the caste system social closure is achieved through prohibitions which prevent members of a caste from marrying outside their caste. The caste system is an extreme example of social closure since the exclusion of outsiders from the status group is so complete.

Another example of social closure was the apartheid system in South Africa which lasted from the 1940s until 1992. The population was divided into whites, Asians, black Africans, and 'coloured' people descended from more than one 'race'. These different groups were kept apart in public places (for example, they were required to use different public toilets), they had to live in different neighbourhoods and they were prohibited from marrying someone from a different group. Not surprisingly, the better facilities and neighbourhoods were reserved for the dominant white population.

Other status groups erect less formidable barriers to entry. In modern Britain, studies of elite self-recruitment suggest that certain types of job, such as senior positions in the civil service, are usually filled by those who have attended public school. Although individuals who went to state schools have some chance of entering these jobs, public school-educated elites largely reserve such positions for themselves and their children. (For details of elite self-recruitment see Chapter 9.)

Class and status groups

In many societies, class and status situations are closely linked. Weber noted that 'property as such is not always recognized as a status qualification, but in the long run it is, and with extraordinary regularity'. However, those who share the same class situation will not necessarily belong to the same status group. For example, the *nouveaux riches* (the newly rich) are sometimes excluded from the status groups of the privileged because their tastes, manners and dress are defined as vulgar.

Status groups can cut across class divisions. For example, homosexuals from different class backgrounds are involved in gay rights organizations and events such as the annual Gay Pride celebration in Britain.

Weber's observations on status groups are important because they suggest that in certain situations status rather than class provides the basis for the formation of social groups. In addition, the presence of different status groups within a single class, and of status groups which cut across class divisions, can weaken class solidarity and reduce the potential for class consciousness. These points are illustrated by Weber's analysis of 'parties'.

Parties

Weber defined parties as groups which are specifically concerned with influencing policies and making decisions in the interests of their membership. In Weber's words, parties are concerned with 'the acquisition of social "power"'.

Parties include a variety of associations, from the mass political parties of Western democracies to the whole range of pressure or interest groups, which include professional associations, trade unions, and organizations such as the Automobile Association, Greenpeace and the RSPCA. Parties often, but not necessarily, represent the interests of classes or status groups. In Weber's words, 'Parties may represent interests determined through "class situation" or "status situation" ... In most cases they are partly class parties and partly status parties, but sometimes they are neither.'

The combination of class and status interests can be seen in a group such as the Nation of Islam in the USA. As well as being a religious group it is also active in trying to achieve political change. It represents a status group but it also represents class interests – the majority of its members are working-class.

Weber's view of parties suggests that the relationship between political groups and class and status groups is far from clear-cut. Just as status groups can both divide classes and cut across class boundaries, so parties can divide and cut across both classes and status groups. Weber's analysis of classes, status groups and parties suggests that no single theory can pinpoint and explain their relationship. The interplay of class, status and party in the formation of social groups is complex and variable and must be examined in particular societies during particular time periods.

Marx attempted to reduce all forms of inequality to social class and argued that classes formed the only significant social groups in society. Weber argues that the evidence provides a more complex and diversified picture of social stratification.

Modern theories of stratification

Many contemporary studies of stratification are based upon either a Marxist or a Weberian perspective. Some modern sociologists have remained close to the original theories of Marx and Weber. Others have drawn their inspiration from one or other of these classic sociologists, but have made significant alterations to their original theories in an attempt to describe and explain the class structures of capitalist industrial societies. Such sociologists can be referred to as new or neo-Marxists and neo-Weberians.

There has been a long-standing debate between those who draw their inspiration from Marx and those who follow Weber as to which approach is more useful as a way of developing a sociological understanding of class. We will analyse this debate in later sections of this chapter when we deal with the different classes in contemporary capitalism. In the next section, we will consider one attempt to combine the approaches developed by Marx and Weber into a single theory of stratification.

W.G. Runciman – the class structure, roles and power

In an attempt to determine the number of classes in British society, W.G. Runciman has developed a new approach to analysing the stratification system (Runciman, 1990). This approach uses both Marxist concepts, such as 'the means of production', and Weberian ones, such as 'marketability'.

Roles and classes

Runciman starts by arguing that the class structure consists of sets of roles. A role is defined as a position 'embodying consistently recurring patterns of institutional behaviour informed by mutually shared beliefs about their incumbents' capacity directly or indirectly to influence the behaviour of each other'. Occupational roles are the most important, but not everyone has an occupational role. Those without jobs should also be assigned roles according to the 'economic power attaching to whatever different roles they occupy'. A person married to someone with a job should be seen as having the same role as their spouse, assuming they share the economic power of their spouse. Where partners have different jobs, then both should be given the class of the one with the higher ranking role, again assuming that they share their economic power. Whether power is shared cannot be determined theoretically, but needs to be determined from the evidence in each case.

For those with jobs, classes should be determined using the concept of a career. In other words, it is necessary to take account of promotion prospects as well as current position. Some male white-collar workers, for example, might be seen as being in a higher class than some female white-collar workers who have similar jobs but much less chance of moving into management. Where individuals have more than one role (for example, if they have two jobs), the highest ranking role should again be used to determine a person's class.

Classes and power

Runciman then goes on to explain how roles should be allocated to classes. He defines classes as 'sets of roles whose common location in social space is a function of the nature and degree of economic power (or lack of it) attaching to them through their relation to the institutional processes of production, distribution and exchange'.

Economic power can come from three sources:

1 **Ownership**, or 'legal title to some part of the means of production'.
2 **Control**, or 'a contractual right to direct the application to the process of production of some part of the means of production, whether fixed or financial assets or labour'. Managers and supervisors are examples of people who possess control by virtue of their jobs.
3 **Marketability**, or the possession of an 'attribute or capacity' which can be sold to employers. In other words this refers to the skills, qualifications and the ability to carry out physical labour possessed by individual workers.

The class an individual belongs to is determined by examining a combination of these three types of economic power. People can end up in a higher class by having ownership, control or marketability, or indeed any combination of the three.

Runciman illustrates this approach with the example of three engineers. Engineer A is an employee who earns £40,000 per year and has a good pension scheme. Engineer B owns a small engineering business which he has been able to buy through mortgaging his house. After paying interest, he makes £10,000 per year profit. Engineer C is a self-employed freelance engineer who employs his wife as his secretary and earns between £10,000 and £40,000, depending on how successful a year it is.

All three of these people should be placed in the same class, according to Runciman. They have different sorts of power. The first derives most of his power from control, the second from ownership and the third from marketability, but each has about the same amount of power.

Those towards the bottom of the stratification system have little or no control over production, they have very little wealth, and little or nothing in the way of marketable skills or capacities.

The seven classes

Runciman identifies seven classes based upon the possession of different amounts of ownership, control and marketability. These are detailed in Table 1.1 with Runciman's estimate of the percentage of the British population in each class.

The highest class, which he calls the upper class, contains between one-tenth and one-fifth of 1 per cent of

Table 1.1 The Runciman classes

Class	Size in 1990
Upper class	0.1%–0.2%
Upper middle class	<10%
Middle middle class	20%
Lower middle class	20%
Skilled working class	20%
Unskilled working class	30%
Underclass	5%

Source: W.G. Runciman (1990) 'How many classes are there in contemporary British society?' *Sociology*, vol. 24, no. 3, pp. 377–96

the population. It is made up of the owners of the means of production, the most senior managers, and those with absolutely exceptional marketability. Runciman cites examples of each of these three types: the Duke of Northumberland, who qualifies in terms of ownership; the chief executive of Shell, who has control; and 'the senior partners of the biggest firms of City accountants', who have marketability. Runciman specifically excludes very highly paid entertainers because their role is 'irrelevant' to 'the institutional processes of production, distribution and exchange'.

Runciman chooses to divide the middle class into three groups. The higher-grade professionals, senior civil servants and managers are placed in the highest of these three classes, and routine white-collar workers in 'more or less "deskilled"' jobs are placed in the lowest. He argues that there is a sufficient gap in the economic power of these two extremes in the middle class to justify the inclusion of a third group in between. This middle middle class includes lower professions and middle managers. Proprietors who are not in the upper class are allocated to one of the middle classes according to what 'the scale and kind of their property makes appropriate'. Runciman argues that workers such as shop assistants, checkout operators and copy- and audio-typists have insufficient economic power in terms of the marketability of their skills to be placed in the middle class. Instead, they are seen as part of the working class.

The working class itself is divided in two: an upper or skilled working class, and a lower or unskilled working class. Semi-skilled workers are seen as belonging to the lower working class since, according to Runciman, it has become common for workers with minimal skills to be defined as semi-skilled. When he uses the terms skilled, semi-skilled and unskilled, Runciman is not referring to some abstract measure of technical knowledge which is required to carry out jobs. He is thinking instead of the different degrees of marketability, control and ownership that individual workers possess. Thus a worker might be placed in the upper working class on the grounds of ownership if they own their own tools, on the grounds of control if they have control over the operation of machinery, or on the grounds of marketability if their skills are in demand.

Runciman also distinguishes an underclass at the bottom of the stratification system. It consists of those 'whose roles place them more or less permanently at the economic level where benefits are paid by the state to those unable to participate in the labour market at all'. In effect, members of the underclass have no control, ownership or marketability. (We discuss Runciman's views on the underclass in more detail later in the chapter; see p. 66.)

Operationalizing the class scheme

Runciman made no attempt to use his class scheme for research, but he did suggest how that might be done. It would be necessary to determine individuals' jobs, the amount and source of their income, their 'actual and prospective capital resources', and their economic position within the household. These different types of information could then be combined to determine a person's class.

Evaluation of Runciman

There are a number of problems with Runciman's class scheme. It would be extremely difficult to use in research since it means gathering a wide range of data on individuals and the households in which they live. Many respondents to a survey might be unwilling or unable to give precise details of, for example, their wealth.

Runciman also offers no clear dividing lines between the classes: it is unclear how much marketability, power or control a person needs for them to be placed in a particular class. His view that groups such as the self-employed or small proprietors should not be seen as constituting separate classes is somewhat controversial. Runciman himself admits that such groups might be distinctive in terms of 'intergenerational mobility rates' and 'socio-political attitudes', but he is still unwilling to allocate them to a separate class because they do not necessarily have similar amounts of economic power.

In addition, because Runciman uses a gradational approach to class, where the differences between classes are a matter of degree rather than kind, his decision to settle on seven classes seems rather arbitrary. He could just as easily have settled on a six- or an eight-class model.

Rosemary Crompton (1993), however, argues that Runciman's scheme is one of the few approaches to the class structure that has had some success in coming to terms with the social changes that have taken place in Britain since the Second World War. She argues that these changes include:

> *a move away from the conventionally established 'class' boundary between manual and non-manual work following the expansion of the service sector and the routinization and feminization of much lower-level white-collar employment; an emphasis on the diversity of middle-class locations, and the identification of the poorest and most deprived as an 'underclass' – this identification being linked, to varying degrees, with the condition of state dependency. A major element of continuity, however, lies in the persisting concentration of economic, organizational and political power within an 'upper' class which comprises only a small minority of the population.* Crompton, 1993, pp. 191–2

Her description of changes in the class structure provides a succinct summary of some of the main social trends which will be discussed in this chapter. We will now proceed to consider changes in three of the main elements of the stratification system: the occupational structure, the distribution of income, and the distribution of wealth.

Changes in the British stratification system

As we discovered in the previous section, most contemporary theories of stratification have been influenced by the pioneering work of Marx or Weber. Despite the differences between these sociologists, both gave primary importance to material inequalities. Marx saw the most important divisions in any system of stratification as stemming from differences in the ownership of wealth, and specifically ownership of the means of production. Weber also saw ownership of wealth as an important criterion for distinguishing classes. Weber, however, placed more emphasis than Marx on divisions within the propertyless class – the class whose members did not own sufficient property to support themselves without working. Income levels and other life chances for this group depended largely upon the market situation of the occupational group to which the individuals belonged.

No system of class stratification is fixed and static. The distribution of resources within the class system constantly changes, and the size and market situation of occupational groups also alter over time. The next sections will describe some of the broad patterns of change in the occupational structure and the distribution of income and wealth in Britain in the twentieth century. Later sections will examine the changing position of particular classes in more detail.

Changes in the occupational structure

Sociologists from Marx and Weber onwards have debated how best to define social classes. Many, though not all, now base their class categories, at least partly, upon occupational groupings. Official government statistics distinguish between **socio-economic groups**, which, it is claimed, bring together people with jobs of similar social and economic status.

Scales of social class

Although there are disagreements about where the boundary between the middle and working classes should be placed, it is often the case that manual workers are regarded as being working-class, and non-manual workers as middle-class.

Until recently, official statistics on occupations were based upon the Registrar General's scale which distinguished **manual** jobs according to levels of skill, with separate categories being used for the **unskilled**, **semi-skilled** and **skilled** manual worker. Non-manual jobs are also usually divided into three categories: **routine non-manual** jobs, which include clerical and secretarial work; **intermediate non-manual** jobs, which include teachers, nurses, librarians and some managers; and the highest class in this scheme, which includes professionals, such as doctors and accountants, as well as senior managers.

The old scale was replaced in 2001 by the National Statistics Socio-economic Classification (NS-SEC), which provides broadly similar data but using different categories. Because of this it is difficult to make precise statements about recent changes in the occupational structure, but it is certainly possible to identify broad changes.

Although calculated in different ways, Tables 1.2 and 1.3 are both based upon the idea of socio-economic grouping. Table 1.2 shows changes in the occupational structure between 1911 and 1971. Table 1.3 is calculated on a different basis but shows changes between 1975 and 2000. (Table 1.3 includes personal service workers in the same category as semi-skilled manual and so includes a wider range of workers in the lower classes than Table 1.2.)

The shift to non-manual employment

The information contained in Tables 1.2 and 1.3 shows that there was a long-term trend during the twentieth century for the proportion of non-manual jobs to increase, and for manual jobs to decrease. In 2000 just 44 per cent of all workers had manual jobs, whereas in 1911, according to Routh (1980), 79 per cent of jobs were manual. According to the General Household Survey, the proportion of manual and personal service workers

Table 1.2 Occupational class of the working population in Great Britain 1911–71: percentages in different classes

	All					Males					Females				
	1911	1921	1931	1951	1971	1911	1921	1931	1951	1971	1911	1921	1931	1951	1971
1 Professionals															
a) Higher	1.00	1.01	1.14	1.93	3.29	1.34	1.36	1.50	2.56	4.87	0.20	0.18	0.29	0.52	0.55
b) Lower	3.05	3.52	3.46	4.70	7.78	1.61	2.02	2.03	3.16	5.95	6.49	7.07	6.83	8.18	10.95
2 Employers, administrators, managers															
a) Employers and proprietors	6.71	6.82	6.70	4.97	4.22	7.74	7.69	7.65	5.74	5.07	4.28	4.74	4.44	3.22	2.75
b) Managers and administrators	3.43	3.64	3.66	5.53	8.21	3.91	4.28	4.54	6.78	10.91	2.30	2.11	1.60	2.73	3.51
3 Clerical workers	4.84	6.72	6.97	10.68	13.90	5.48	5.40	5.53	6.35	6.38	3.30	9.90	10.34	20.41	27.00
4 Foremen, inspectors, supervisors	1.29	1.44	1.54	2.62	3.87	1.75	1.91	2.00	3.28	5.04	0.18	0.32	0.45	1.14	1.84
5 Skilled manual	30.56	28.83	26.72	24.95	21.56	32.99	32.30	29.96	30.36	29.08	24.78	20.50	19.09	12.75	8.48
6 Semi-skilled manual	39.48	33.85	35.00	32.60	25.23	33.63	28.30	28.85	27.92	20.82	53.42	47.11	49.51	43.12	32.90
7 Unskilled manual	9.63	14.17	14.81	12.03	11.94	11.55	16.72	17.92	13.84	11.89	5.05	8.07	7.45	7.94	12.02

Source: G. Routh (1980) Occupation and Pay in Great Britain 1906–79, Macmillan, London, pp. 6–7

Table 1.3 Socio-economic group by sex, 1975 to 2000

All persons aged 16 and over Great Britain									
Socio-economic group	1975 %	1981 %	1985 %	1991 %	1993 %	1995 %	1996 %	1998 %	2000 %
Men									
Professional	5	4	6	7	7	7	6	8	8
Employers and managers	15	15	19	19	20	21	22	20	21
Intermediate and junior managers	17	17	17	17	17	17	17	19	19
Skilled manual and own account non-professional	41	41	37	38	37	35	35	33	33
Semi-skilled manual and personal service	17	18	16	14	14	15	15	15	14
Unskilled manual	5	5	5	5	4	4	5	5	5
Women									
Professional	1	1	1	1	2	2	2	2	3
Employers and managers	4	5	7	9	10	10	9	11	12
Intermediate and junior managers	46	46	48	48	49	49	50	50	50
Skilled manual and own account non-professional	9	9	9	9	8	8	9	8	7
Semi-skilled manual and personal service	31	29	27	22	22	22	23	22	21
Unskilled manual	9	10	7	11	10	8	8	8	8
Total									
Professional	3	2	3	4	4	4	4	5	5
Employers and managers	9	9	13	14	15	15	15	16	16
Intermediate and junior managers	32	32	33	33	34	34	34	34	35
Skilled manual and own account non-professional	24	24	23	23	22	21	21	20	20
Semi-skilled manual and personal service	24	24	22	18	18	19	19	18	18
Unskilled manual	7	8	6	8	7	6	6	6	6

Source: A. Walker *et al.* (2001), *Living in Britain: results from the 2000 General Household Survey*, The Stationery Office, London p. 22

Table 1.4 Employees in England and Wales by socio-economic classification (NS-SEC), 2001/2006: percentages

All employees	Second quarter 2001	First quarter 2006
1 Higher managerial and professional	13.2	14.6
2 Lower managerial and professional	28.5	31.1
3 Intermediate occupations	14.9	14.1
5 Lower supervisory and technical	12.8	12.2
6 Semi-routine occupations	17.5	16.5
7 Routine occupations	13.1	11.4

Source: Labour Force Survey, Office for National Statistics

declined from 55 per cent to 44 per cent between 1975 and 2000. However, there have been marked increases in professional, managerial, and routine non-manual work.

Table 1.4 contains more recent information based upon the NS-SEC scale. This scale uses seven occupational groupings and the statistics distinguish between employees and the self-employed. In Table 1.4 small employers and own-account workers (group 4) are not included, as they are mainly self-employed, and nor are the long-term unemployed. In the NS-SEC scheme groups 1 and 2 are similar to the highest classifications in the Registrar General's scale and they are sometimes combined to form a 'managerial and professional occupations' category. Although the categories do not correspond exactly to the manual/non-manual divide, groups 5, 6 and 7 are sometimes combined to form a 'routine and manual occupations' category, and groups 3 and 4 are sometimes linked in an 'intermediate class'.

Table 1.4 shows that in England and Wales there was a continuing shift towards managerial and professional employment in the first few years of the twenty-first century and a continuing decline in routine occupations and intermediate occupations. In 2006 45.7 per cent of the economically active population were employed in professional and managerial jobs compared to just 40.1 per cent in lower supervisory, technical or routine occupations. On the basis of these figures, there is no evidence that the expansion of higher classes at the expense of lower classes is coming to a halt.

The shift towards non-manual employment has been caused both by the decline of manufacturing and by the growth of services:

1 Manufacturing industry has declined, while service industries, which employ a lower proportion of manual workers, have expanded. Ken Roberts comments that 'Over half of the manufacturing jobs that existed in the 1970s have gone, and in some industries the workforces have really collapsed' (Roberts, 2001, p. 65). Roberts points out that at one time three-quarters of a million people were employed in coalmining and in 1981 it still employed 218,000 miners. By 1994, however, there were just 8,500 coalminers left.

   Other traditional heavy industries in which employment has declined rapidly include steel manufacture, shipbuilding and dock work. Other manufacturing industries have also declined. This is partly because new technology has increased productivity so that fewer workers are needed to produce the same quantity of goods. Roberts points out that industrial output has stayed about the same in Britain despite a declining workforce. A second reason is that British manufacturing has lost out in competition with businesses in lower-wage economies in Latin America, Eastern Europe and the Far East. Workers in such countries produce an increasing proportion of manufactured goods consumed in Britain.

   There have also been important changes in manual work connected to the decline of manufacturing:

   The old working class was employed in coalmines, shipyards, steel plants and engineering workshops; the new working class is employed in supermarkets, security firms, contract cleaners, fast food and other catering establishments, and suchlike. **Roberts, 2001, p. 68**

2 The service sector has grown considerably. According to Roberts, there was considerable growth in public sector services (such as local government, health and education) from the 1940s to the 1970s, but growth then came to a halt. Financial and business services grew rapidly from the 1960s to the 1980s, but were then hit by the effects of computer technology which reduced the size of the workforce needed. According to Roberts, recent growth in the service sector has largely come from the development of consumer services in leisure industries such as hotels, catering and retailing.

Gender, full-time and part-time work

Women, particularly married women, increasingly started taking paid employment during the twentieth century, but they are not equally distributed throughout the occupational structure. Although women are more likely to have non-manual jobs than men, most female non-manual workers are concentrated in the lowest-paid sectors of non-manual work, and have routine non-manual jobs. As Table 1.5 shows, only 23 per cent of women were managers, senior officials or professionals in 2005, compared to 32 per cent of men. Although the proportion of women who have such jobs has been rising, women

Table 1.5 All in employment: by sex and occupation, 2005

United Kingdom	Percentages Men	Women
Managers and senior officials	18	11
Professional	14	12
Associate professional and technical	13	15
Administrative and secretarial	4	22
Skilled trades	20	2
Personal service	2	14
Sales and customer service	5	12
Process, plant and machine operatives	12	2
Elementary	12	11
All occupations	100	100

Note: Figures include people aged 16 and over

Source: Labour Force Survey, Office for National Statistics

with non-manual jobs are still concentrated in the associate professional and technical, and administrative and secretarial categories. Men were ten times more likely than women to have skilled manual jobs in 2005 (20 per cent as opposed to 2 per cent). In both the middle class and the working class, women tend to be concentrated in the lower-paid and lower-status sectors of each class.

There have also been significant trends in the proportions of men and women in full-time and part-time work. In the UK in 1971 more than 90 per cent of men but less than 60 per cent of women aged 16 to 64 were in employment. By 2005, 79 per cent of men and 70 per cent of women were employed (*Social Trends 2006*, pp. 52–3).

However, it remains the case that women are much more likely to work part-time than men. According to the UK Labour Force Survey, in the first quarter of 2006 there were 1.656 million men employed part-time but 5.694 million women. Although a large majority of part-time work is still done by women, there was a much bigger increase in part-time work amongst men than there was amongst women between 2001 and 2006. Women still seem to have a disadvantaged position in the labour market, and still earn less than men (see pp. 121–4), but there may be some move away from men working full-time and taking on the role of main breadwinner in families.

The changing distribution of income

The importance of income

Some sociologists have argued that inequalities in industrial societies are being progressively reduced; others go further and claim that class divisions are disappearing. Income has an important effect upon life chances: for example, on the chances of owning one's own home, and on life expectancy. If income inequalities were gradually disappearing this would be strong evidence that class divisions were weakening.

Some government policies seem designed to achieve greater income equality by redistributing income from more affluent to poorer groups. However, as we will see in the following sections, income can be measured in various ways and official statistics should be used with caution. In addition, it should not be assumed that long-term trends in income distribution will continue for ever: there is evidence that there have been significant changes in these trends in Britain in recent years. In particular, a long-term trend towards a more equitable distribution of income has been reversed.

The measurement of income distribution

Official statistics measure income in a variety of ways:

1 **Original income** refers to income from sources such as employment, occupational pensions, gifts, alimony payments, and investments. Figures on original income do not include benefits such as state pensions, family credit and income support, which are paid by the state.
2 **Gross income** is a measure of all sources of income. Most individuals are not, however, free to spend all of their gross income, because some of it is deducted to pay income tax and national insurance contributions.
3 **Disposable income** is a measure of gross income less the above deductions.
4 Some taxes (indirect taxes) are not paid directly out of income, but are paid by consumers as part of the purchase price of goods. For example, value added tax (VAT) is payable on most categories of goods in the UK. Duties are also payable on products such as petrol, tobacco and alcohol. **Post-tax income** is a measure of income after the above taxes, and taxes such as the council tax, are deducted.
5 **Final income** adds on to income after taxes the value of benefits provided by the state which are not given in cash, for example medical care and education.

By examining these different measures it is possible to discover the effects of government policy on the distribution of income. Figure 1.1 gives data for 2003–4 based on the Family Expenditure Survey.

The effects of taxation and benefits

Figure 1.1 demonstrates that even after taxation and benefits are taken into account, considerable income inequalities remain. In 2003–4, the poorest 20 per cent of households received just under half the average final income, while the richest 20 per cent received nearly twice the national average. However, it is clear that benefits help to reduce income inequality. In particular, benefits boost the very low original income of the poorest 20 per cent of households. In 2003–4 61 per cent of the income of the poorest households came from benefits compared to 2 per cent for the richest.

Overall taxation and benefits also reduce the final income of richer groups in the population, although less than the higher rates of income tax for high earners would suggest. This is partly because poorer groups in the population tend to pay a higher proportion of their income in indirect taxes (such as VAT and duties) than richer groups.

Figure 1.1 Average household income in the UK, by quintile group, 2003–4

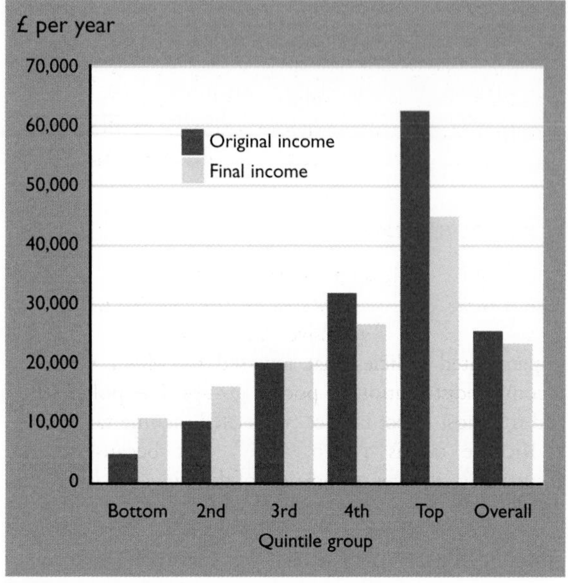

Source: Family Expenditure Survey, National Statistics

The official government figures need to be treated with some caution. Only about 70 per cent of households approached agree to participate in the Family Expenditure Survey. Furthermore, there is no guarantee that the information obtained is entirely reliable. Individuals may not declare all their income, particularly if they have not been truthful to the Inland Revenue or the DSS. The figures may be particularly prone to underestimating the income of the highest earners, who have more opportunities to hide substantial amounts of income than middle- and lower-income groups.

Sources of income

Income comes from a number of sources. According to British government statistics, wages and salaries are the most important source of income in the UK. For those of working age, in 2003–4, 74 per cent of all household income came from wages and salaries, 10 per cent from self-employment, 7 per cent from disability and other benefits, 3 per cent from private pensions, 2 per cent from investments, 1 per cent from tax credits and 3 per cent from other income sources (*Social Trends 2006*, p. 70).

The sources of income vary considerably for households in different socio-economic groups. For example 71 per cent of the income of those who had never worked or were long-term unemployed came from benefits, compared to 1 per cent of the income of those in higher managerial and professional occupations.

Trends in income distribution 1949–79

Despite the limitations of the official figures, they do at least provide some indication of the overall historical trends in the distribution of income. In 1979 the Royal Commission on the Distribution of Income and Wealth published a report examining the changes in the distribution of income and wealth between 1949 and 1978–9.

They found that over this period there was some income redistribution, but mainly towards middle-income groups rather than those on the lowest levels. The top 10 per cent of income earners reduced their share of total income by 3.7 per cent, but the bottom 30 per cent also had their share reduced, in this case by 2.5 per cent. Although there was a slight shift in income distribution – from the top half of income earners to the bottom half – middle-income groups were the beneficiaries.

Changes in taxation

The Royal Commission report was published in 1979, the same year as Margaret Thatcher's Conservative government came to power. Successive Conservative governments implemented policies that reversed the slight trend for income redistribution to poorer groups. The policies that had the most direct impact concerned income tax.

Income tax is a **progressive tax** because higher earners pay a higher proportion of their income in this tax than lower earners. If overall levels of income tax are cut, and if the higher rates in particular are reduced, the redistributive effects of taxation become smaller. Between 1979 and 1997 the basic rate of income tax was reduced from 33 to 23 per cent, while the highest rate fell from 80 to 40 per cent. In 1992 a lower-rate band of 20 per cent was introduced on the first £2,000 of taxable income; this was widened to £4,300 in 1998.

By the early 1990s the government was running into problems financing government spending and was forced to raise extra taxes. Although most of the extra revenue needed was raised through increases in indirect tax, there was an increase in national insurance contributions of 1 per cent in 1994. National insurance contributions are effectively a form of direct tax, and between 1979 and 2001 contributions were raised from 6.5 per cent to 10 per cent.

In 1997 a new Labour government was elected in Britain, the first Labour government for eighteen years. Although traditionally committed to a redistributive tax system, the incoming government pledged not to increase income tax rates and to stick to Conservative spending limits in its early years in government. However, after this period a number of tax changes were introduced, many of which were designed specifically to help the low paid by cutting their tax bills. The main changes were as follows:

1. The introduction of a Working Families Tax Credit, which reduced the income tax bills for families with one or more children and at least one adult in employment. Poorer families received the full tax credit, but the value of the tax credit tapered off to zero for higher earners.
2. A Children's Tax Credit was introduced in 2001 which lowered tax bills for those with children, although this benefit was gradually withdrawn for higher-rate tax payers. In 2003 the Working Families Tax Credit and Children's Tax Credit were combined into the Integrated Child Credit.
3. The reduction of the tax rate on the lower-rate tax band from 20 per cent to 10 per cent.
4. In 2003 an Employment Tax Credit was introduced, reducing tax bills for lower wage earners.
5. The standard rate of income tax was cut to 22 per cent in 2000.

These measures primarily benefited lower- and middle-income earners – particularly those in employment – and some were specifically designed to reduce poverty and boost the income of the low paid. As we shall see, the evidence suggests that these policies certainly had an impact on slowing and nearly stopping the growth in income inequality, but did not significantly reduce income inequality.

Since 1979 there has been a marked shift towards indirect taxation, which tends to take a greater proportion of the income of lower-income groups than it takes from those on higher incomes. In 2003–4 the top fifth of households paid only 11 per cent of their income in indirect taxes, compared to 28 per cent for the bottom fifth.

In 1979 the twin VAT rates of 8 per cent and 12.5 per cent were replaced with a single rate of 15 per cent. This was raised again to 17.5 per cent in 1991. In 1993 it was announced that VAT would be extended to include domestic fuel and would be charged at 8 per cent. In 1997 the new Labour government cut the VAT rate on domestic fuel from 8 per cent to 5 per cent.

Other important types of indirect tax are the duties levied on petrol, alcohol and tobacco. The new Labour government also introduced a range of direct taxes on items such as air travel which had not previously been taxed.

Recent changes in the distribution of income

As outlined above, the Royal Commission on the Distribution of Income and Wealth found that there was some income redistribution from the rich to the poor between 1949 and 1978–9. However, there is clear evidence that changes in taxation introduced by Conservative governments between 1979 and 1997 reversed this trend.

A study of household income inequality by Goodman, Johnson and Webb (1997) showed that any long-term trend towards more equitable income distribution in the UK had been reversed by the late 1990s. The poorest 10 per cent and the poorest 50 per cent of the population both saw a fall in the proportion of national income they received between 1981–3 and 1991–3. This was particularly pronounced in the poorest tenth of the population, whose share fell from 4.1 per cent to 2.9 per cent. On the other hand, the richest tenth of the population saw a rise from 21.3 per cent to 26.2 per cent over the same period.

Goodman *et al.* found a number of reasons for these trends. One was a rise in inequalities in pay for male workers during the 1980s. Unemployment among males rose particularly fast in households where nobody else was working, making those households completely reliant upon benefits. Technological changes and government policies led to a reduction in the demand for unskilled labour and increasing unemployment and falling wages for unskilled workers. More people became reliant upon self-employment as their main source of income. The self-employed are disproportionately found among both the highest-earning and the lowest-earning groups, further widening income inequalities.

Long-term trends in the distribution of disposable income are shown in Figure 1.2, based on research by the Institute for Fiscal Studies (IFS). The figure shows changes in the income of different groups: the median (households in the middle of the income distribution scale), the 90th percentile (those near the top) and the 10th percentile (those near the bottom). According to this research the big increase in income inequality in the 1980s stabilized in the first half of the 1990s, but in the second half of the decade a slow increase in income inequality resumed, though it began to level off in the early years of the twenty-first century (*Social Trends 2006*). Particularly evident from this figure is the very small increase in the disposable income of poorer groups and the rapid growth in income of the most affluent.

New Labour under Tony Blair was elected to power in 1997. Figure 1.2 suggests some slowing in income inequality in the early years of their government, but it does not show what happened in the later years.

Further research by the IFS (Brewer *et al.*, 2006) provides a clear picture of more recent trends. This research shows that in the 1996/7 to 2000/1 period there was a continuing, though slow, increase in income inequality, but from 2000/1 to 2004/5 income inequality fell. This is shown in Figure 1.3 which is based on the Gini coefficient, a statistical measure of inequality. (The Gini coefficient would be 0 if the income of all individuals was identical, and 1 if one person had all the income in a society. The higher the figure, therefore, the greater the level of inequality.)

Overall, during Labour's first eight years in office after 1997, income inequality was little changed, with the increases in the first term in office being roughly matched by the falls in the second term. The IFS comment that this might appear surprising given changes such as the introduction of tax credits and the fall in unemployment, which should have boosted the incomes of low-income families. They suggest that rising inequality within the labour market, and particularly the rapidly increasing incomes of the highest earners, may help to explain the failure of Tony Blair's governments to reduce the overall level of inequality.

The researchers were pessimistic that government policies would do much to further reduce inequality in the future. Writing in 2006, they said that, 'Given the policy and spending commitments that have already been announced, there … seems little room for further commitments that might serve to reduce income inequality substantially' (Brewer *et al.*, 2006, p. 26).

At the very top of the income distribution scale, the best paid continue to thrive and to see their income grow more rapidly than other groups. A survey for the *Observer* (Connor, 2006) found that the highest-paid executive in Britain was Jean-Pierre Garnier, chief executive of GlaxoSmithKline, whose total remuneration package was worth £10.6 million in 2006, a 16 per cent increase on the previous year. Second on the list was Lord Brown, chief executive of BP. In 2006 he had a basic salary of just £1.5 million, but with pension contributions, bonus and incentive plans his total package was worth £10 million, an increase of 19 per cent on 2005. Although three of the ten best-paid British executives had seen their income fall, Sir Tom McKillop of AstroZeneca had enjoyed a pay rise of 47 per cent to £4.6 million. With generous bonuses for many workers in the City of London in recent years, and the rapidly rising incomes of many top sports stars and entertainers, the income growth of the most affluent has restricted any tendency towards greater overall income equality.

Figure 1.2 Distribution of real disposable household income, UK/Great Britain, 1971–2004

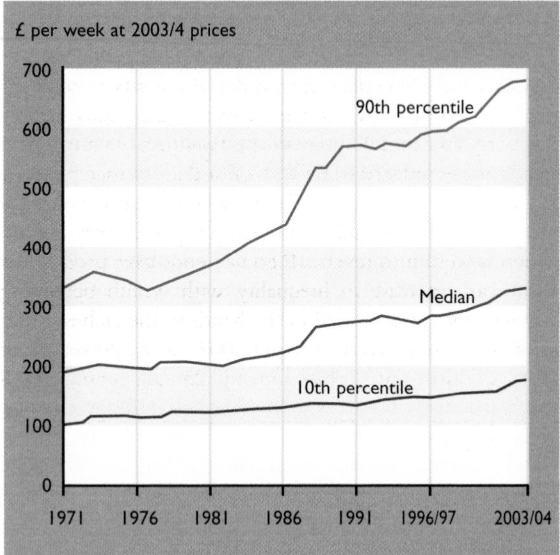

Note: Figures adjusted to 2003/4 prices using the retail price index less local taxes. Equivalized household disposable income before deduction of housing costs. Data from 1993/4 onwards are for financial years; source of data changed in 1994/5, definition of income changed slightly and geographic coverage changed from UK to Great Britain

Source: *Social Trends 2006*, p. 77

Figure 1.3 Income inequality and the Gini coefficient, 1996–2005

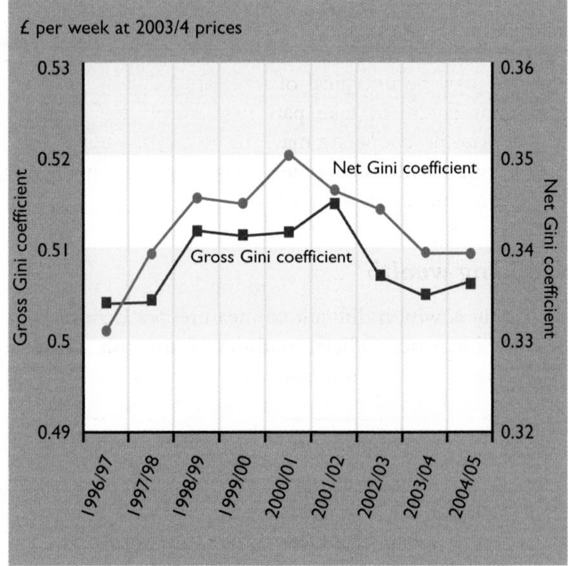

Note: The Gini coefficients have been calculated using incomes before housing costs have been deducted

Source: M. Brewer, A. Goodman, J. Shaw and L. Sibieta (2006) *Poverty and Inequality in Britain 2006*, IFS, London, p. 25

The changing distribution of wealth

The importance of wealth

Inequalities in the distribution of wealth, like inequalities in the distribution of income, are an important indicator of class divisions and class inequality. A particular form of wealth – the means of production – is especially important to Marxist sociologists. Like income, wealth can affect life chances, but to Marxists, ownership of the means of production also gives power. (Today, ownership of the means of production usually takes the form of share ownership.) Wealth is also important in Weberian theories of stratification, although it is given less emphasis than in Marxist theories.

If it could be shown that over the years there had been a major redistribution of wealth from the rich to the poor, this would indicate a reduction in class inequalities. However, wealth is perhaps even more difficult to measure than income, and reliable data prove elusive.

Measuring wealth

The definition and measurement of wealth, like income, are not straightforward. One problem is that the government does not collect information on wealth for tax purposes.

There is no wealth tax on the living, but taxes do have to be paid on the estates of those who have died. Figures on the value of estates left by the deceased are sometimes used to calculate the overall distribution of wealth. However, they may not be a reliable guide to the distribution of wealth among the living; for instance, individuals may transfer some of their wealth to other family members before they die. Moreover, those who die tend to be older than other members of the population, and wealth is not equally distributed between age groups.

Another method of collecting information on wealth distribution is to use survey research, but this too has its drawbacks. Those who refuse to cooperate with the research may be untypical of the population as a whole, and their failure to take part may distort the findings. Those who do cooperate may not be entirely honest, and the richest members of society may be particularly prone to underestimating their wealth.

Defining wealth

Not only is wealth difficult to measure, but defining it is also problematic. Official statistics distinguish between marketable wealth and non-marketable wealth:

1 **Marketable wealth** includes any type of asset that can be sold and its value realized. It therefore includes land, shares, savings in banks, building societies or other accounts, homes (minus any outstanding mortgage debts), and personal possessions such as cars, works of art and household appliances. The figures on marketable wealth exclude the value of occupational pensions, which cannot normally be sold. If such pensions are included in the figures, the statistics show wealth as being more equally distributed than is otherwise the case.
2 **Non-marketable wealth** includes items such as salaries and non-transferable pensions.

From a sociological point of view, the official figures on wealth are not ideal. They fail to distinguish between wealth used to finance production and wealth used to finance consumption. Wealth used for production (for example, shares) is of particular interest to Marxist sociologists because they believe that power largely derives from ownership of the means of production. The distribution of wealth used for consumption is of less interest to Marxists, though it does give some indication of lifestyle. Such figures are also useful for indicating the distribution of various life chances, for instance the chance that different social groups have of owning their own home.

Trends in wealth distribution

Despite the limitations of the available figures, it is possible to discern overall trends in wealth distribution in the UK over the twentieth century. Research by Westergaard and Resler (1976) showed that there was some reduction in inequalities of wealth between 1911 and 1960. In 1911, 69 per cent of personal wealth was owned by the richest 1 one per cent of the population, and 92 per cent by the richest 10 per cent. By 1960 the share of personal wealth owned by the richest 1 per cent had fallen to 42 per cent and the share of the richest 10 per cent had gone down to 83 per cent. These data suggest that there was a considerable reduction in the degree of wealth inequality during the early and middle years of the twentieth century, with much more redistribution of wealth than of income.

Table 1.6 shows that the trend towards greater equality of wealth distribution continued until the early 1990s, when it went into reverse. Recent trends have produced a significant increase in inequality, with wealth becoming particularly concentrated in the hands of the richest 1 per cent of the population. Thus in 2002 the wealthiest 1 per cent of the population owned 23 per cent of all

Table 1.6 Distribution of wealth in the United Kingdom, 1976–2002

	1976	1981	1986	1991	1996	2001	2002
Percentage of marketable wealth owned by:							
Most wealthy 1%	21	18	18	17	20	22	23
Most wealthy 25%	71	73	73	71	74	72	74
Most wealthy 50%	92	92	90	92	93	94	94
Total marketable wealth (£ billions)	*280*	*565*	*955*	*1711*	*2092*	*3477*	*3464*

Note: Figures include people aged 16 and over

Source: *Social Trends 2002* and *2006*

marketable wealth, and the wealthiest 25 per cent owned 74 per cent, leaving the other 75 per cent of the population to share the remaining 26 per cent between them.

A number of factors have contributed to the trends noted above. Westergaard and Resler (1976) suggested that in the earlier years of the twentieth century the most significant redistribution was within the wealthiest groups, rather than between them and the less well-off. A major reason for this was the transfer of assets from wealthy individuals to friends and other family members in order to avoid death duties.

In recent decades a rising proportion of the population have become home owners, and the rapid rise in house prices between 1991 and 2004 helped increase the wealth of many. Housing is the single most important type of personal wealth in the UK, followed by assets held in life assurance policies and pension funds (*Social Trends 2006*). When non-marketable wealth such as investments in pension funds is included in the statistics, wealth is less unequally distributed. Although an increasing proportion of the population have some significant assets, the rise in housing values and in pension and life assurance assets has benefited those in the richer half of the population more than those in the poorer half. Few of the poor have substantial pension rights or own their own homes.

The recent increase in the proportion of total wealth owned by the richest 1 per cent is particularly marked. This has been seen by some commentators as being part of the rise of a new group, the **super-wealthy** (Lansley, 2006). A combination of factors has contributed to this situation, including reductions in the highest rates of income tax, the enormous bonuses that can be earned by finance workers in the City of London, and the profits that can be earned by those companies that are successful in a global economy (see pp. 43–4 for more discussion of the wealthy). In addition, the taxation system, which has limited the top rate of tax to 40 per cent, has failed to close loopholes which allow the very wealthy to minimize the UK taxes they pay or to avoid paying them altogether (see below).

Share ownership

Shares are a particularly important type of wealth, used to finance production. In Britain there has certainly been an increase in recent years in the percentage of the population who own shares. Westergaard and Resler estimated that in 1970 only 7 per cent of adults over the age of 25 owned shares. In 1995–6, according to the Family Resources Survey, around 16 per cent of adults in the UK owned shares.

Much of the increase in share ownership was due to the Conservative government's privatization programme, which encouraged small investors to buy shares in companies such as British Telecom and British Gas. In the 1990s share ownership was increased by the demutualization of building societies such as the Halifax, and the flotation of insurance companies such as Norwich Union. For example, around 9 million people were entitled to shares as a result of the flotation of the Halifax in 1997.

However, many of the new shareholders created by these flotations sold their shares very quickly. Furthermore, most new shareholders have only a very small stake in the companies in which they have invested, and in reality they may have little influence upon the way that the companies are run.

Most privately owned shares remain in the hands of a small minority of the population. Furthermore, the importance of privately held shares has declined. In 1963 individuals owned 54 per cent of the equity in private companies, but by 2004 this was down to just 14.1 per cent (*Share Ownership 2005*). On the other hand, the proportion of share equity held by life assurance and pension funds increased from 16.4 per cent to 32.9 per cent over the same period. While these assets might belong to individuals, they have little control over how their money is invested. An increasing proportion of share equity is owned by non-UK citizens, companies or institutions, rising from just 7 per cent in 1963 to 32.6 per cent in 2004, reflecting the globalization of capitalism (*Share Ownership 2005*).

Taxation and wealth

Successive governments in Britain have made much less attempt to tax wealth than income. Before 1974 the main tax on wealth was estate duty, paid on the estate of someone who had died. It was easy to avoid this tax by transferring assets before death. The rules were tightened up in the 1970s and 1980s so that some tax could be levied on wealth handed over within seven years before death. However, it is still possible to avoid paying the tax by establishing trusts. The current wealth tax, inheritance tax, has a tax-free allowance (in 2008, the first £325,000 of an estate was tax-free), and it is possible to give away some money in the years before one dies without paying tax on it.

As well as taxes directly concerned with wealth, company taxation and the taxation of individual income also have important consequences for the overall distribution of wealth. Drawing on a range of sources, Stewart Lansley (2006) suggests that the rich enjoy much more advantageous tax arrangements than the rest of the British population. He provides a range of evidence and examples to back this up.

A study by C. Larkin (2004) found that since 1985, the richest 20 per cent in Britain have actually paid a lower proportion of their income in taxation than the poorest 20 per cent. The study estimated that in 2002 the richest 20 per cent paid about 35 per cent of their income in taxes while the poorest 20 per cent paid around 38 per cent.

Offshore trusts are used to avoid paying tax. There are now around seventy countries which act as tax havens. The Cayman Islands is one of the most important. The country's population is just 35,000 but there are around 48,000 corporations and trusts registered there. It has been estimated that $11.5 trillion has been put into offshore tax havens where the funds are exempt from tax. Big British companies owned or partly owned by wealthy individuals take advantage of such arrangements. Richard Branson's Virgin Group consists of some 300 companies and most of them are registered offshore to avoid taxes.

Another way of avoiding tax is to live abroad, or for one's spouse to live abroad. Phillip Green, chief executive of Arcadia (which runs BHS amongst other companies), is one of Britain's richest men. In 1998 his wife moved to Monaco, which has no income tax. By making his wife the owner of most of his assets, Green is able to continue working in Britain while paying very little UK tax. In

2005 Green's companies paid his wife a dividend of £1.2 billion. By paying it to his wife he avoided paying corporation tax at 25 per cent, thus depriving the British Inland Revenue of more than £300 million.

Many wealthy foreigners are allowed to live in Britain, or run British companies, while paying little, if any, tax. Lansley says that 'Russian oligarchs, Greek shipping magnates and Swedish entrepreneurs' have all made Britain their home because of the sympathetic treatment they receive from the British tax authorities. Rupert Murdoch's News International has 'paid hardly anything in tax in the UK since the late 1980s', although one study put the profits of the subsidiaries of News Corp's UK holding company at £1.4 billion over eleven years (Lansley, 2006, p. 187).

Lansley argues that however unfair this might seem to the ordinary UK tax payer, it is neither illegal nor surprising. Tony Blair in particular has argued that high taxes on the rich are counter-productive since the rich will tend to take their wealth elsewhere to avoid British taxes. However, Lansley is critical of a situation where:

> *The great majority of individuals pay their dues, while the very rich individuals and also the large corporations increasingly choose and have the power to opt out of their tax obligations.* Lansley, 2006, p. 197

Classes in capitalist societies

We will now examine the changing position of particular classes within the class structure of capitalist societies, using British and American data. Three main classes – the upper class, the middle class and the working class – will be considered in turn, though, as we will show, the location of the boundaries between these classes is disputed.

Most of the views dealt with in the following sections have been influenced by Marxist or Weberian theories of stratification.

The upper class

John Westergaard and Henrietta Resler – a Marxist view of the ruling class

Class divisions

In a study first published in 1975, John Westergaard and Henrietta Resler argued, essentially from a Marxist perspective, that Britain was dominated by a **ruling class**. They claimed that the private ownership of capital provided the key to explaining class divisions.

Westergaard and Resler argued that in detail the class system was complex, but in essence it was simple: the major division was still between capital and labour. Sociologists who focused on the details of class – for example, the differences between manual and routine white-collar workers – merely obscured the overall simplicity of the system. Such differences were insignificant compared to the wide gulf that separated the ruling class from the bulk of the wage- and salary-earning population.

Distribution of wealth

To support their argument, Westergaard and Resler pointed to the concentration of wealth in the hands of a small minority, the richest 5 per cent of the population. Although there has been some change in the distribution of wealth in Britain since 1900, this has largely taken place within the richest 10 per cent. The expansion of home ownership has spread wealth a little more widely, but the ownership of capital in private industry has remained highly concentrated.

Ruling-class power

Westergaard and Resler argued that the maintenance of inequalities of wealth was due to the power of the ruling class. They maintained:

> *The favoured group enjoyed effective power, even when its members took no active steps to exercise power. They do not need to do so – for much of the time at least – simply because things work that way in any case.* Westergaard and Resler, 1976, p. 143

It is generally taken for granted (by members of society and governments alike) that investments should bring profit and that the living standards of the propertyless should be based on the demands of the market for their skills. In general, governments have favoured the interests of capital, assuming that the well-being of the nation is largely dependent upon the prosperity of private industry.

Composition of the ruling class

Westergaard and Resler believed that the ruling class was made up of perhaps 5 per cent, and at most 10 per cent, of the population. It included the major owners of the means of production, company directors, top managers, higher professionals and senior civil servants, many of whom are large shareholders in private industry. The subordinate classes consist of the bulk of the wage- and salary-earning population.

Westergaard and Resler put forward what was essentially a conventional Marxist view of the ruling class. They assumed that the ruling class continued to exist. They claimed that it was a united group which continued to dominate British society, and argued that social changes had not significantly redistributed wealth and power. These views have been challenged by market liberal theorists.

Peter Saunders – a market liberal (New Right) view of higher classes

An influential economic elite

Peter Saunders (1990) does not deny that there is a small group of people in British society who have considerable wealth and more power than other members of society. He accepts that many directors and top managers own shares in their own and other companies, and he also accepts that there is 'an interlocking network at the top of British industry and finance in which the same names and faces keep cropping up with different hats on'. He notes that the hundred largest companies produce more than half of Britain's manufacturing output, and therefore:

> *a few thousand individuals at most are today responsible for taking the bulk of the key financial and administrative decisions which shape the future development of British industry and banking.* Saunders, 1990, p. 88

However, Saunders rejects the Marxist view that such people constitute a capitalist ruling class. He sees them as merely 'an influential economic elite'.

Wealth, ownership and the capitalist class

Saunders identifies some groups who might be seen as a capitalist class. These consist of families who continue to own majority shareholdings in established large companies, entrepreneurs who have built up and still own big businesses, and large landowners.

Such people, however, control only a small fraction of the British economy. Most businesses are run by directors and managers whose income and power derive principally from their jobs and not from their ownership of wealth. Saunders claims that less than 25 per cent of the top 250 British companies are run by managers and directors who own 5 per cent or more of the company's shares. The remaining 75 per cent are part of the 'economic elite', but they do not own substantial parts of the means of production, so they cannot be seen as part of the capitalist class.

Furthermore, Saunders argues that 'it has become much more difficult than it once was to identify a distinctive capitalist class'. Although few people are very rich, many people have a direct stake in owning British enterprises. During the course of the twentieth century the proportion of shares owned by individuals declined. Most shares, and a large proportion of commercial land, are now owned by banks, unit trusts, building societies and pension funds. Millions of ordinary people therefore have investments tied up in the capitalist economy by virtue of their pension schemes, endowment mortgages, life insurance policies and savings in banks and building societies. In addition, the privatization programme has widened direct share ownership. Saunders therefore claims that the capitalist class 'has fragmented into millions of tiny pieces', and says: 'To see these pieces look around you.'

The ruling class

From Saunders's point of view, then, directors and managers lack the wealth to be seen as a capitalist class. He further argues that they lack the power to be a ruling class. Although they make many important investment decisions, they do not monopolize power and they frequently fail to get their own way. There are many areas of society that they do not control. These include the government, the mass media and the education system. Indeed, members of the economic elite are 'sometimes dismayed' when politicians, editors and educationalists fail 'to defer to their wishes and interests'.

Saunders believes that the class divisions of previous centuries have been weakened by the development of capitalism. Inequality is essential if a society is to be just and successful, but the success of capitalism spreads wealth and power more widely. In doing so it ensures that the most wealthy do not rule society.

John Scott – *Who Rules Britain?*

John Scott (1982, 1991, 1997) has provided the most comprehensive description and analysis of the development of the upper classes in Britain. His analysis suggests that there have been important changes within higher classes in British society, but he does not believe the upper class has disappeared. He discusses many of the trends mentioned by Saunders but denies that they show the death or fragmentation of the ruling class.

Scott uses Weberian concepts and borrows some elements of elite theory. (Elite theory is examined in Chapter 9.) In the end, however, he supports the Marxist view that Britain retains a ruling class, although he does believe that the British ruling class is part of an international grouping.

The persistence of the capitalist class

Scott rejects the view that a capitalist class is disappearing. He says unequivocally that 'there is in Britain today a capitalist class whose members owe their advantaged life chances to the occupancy of capitalist economic locations' (Scott, 1991).

During the twentieth century certain types of property became more widely owned. More people now own their own houses and possess consumer goods and cars. Such possessions, however, are **property for use**. They are important for the lifestyle and life chances of individuals and families, but they do not place individuals in a capitalist class. Capitalists own **property for power**. This consists of capital invested in land, shares and commercial enterprises in general. True capitalists own considerable amounts of capital and not just, for example, a few hundred shares in one company.

Scott says that property and the income it can generate are the primary bases for the privileges of the capitalist class, but property may be accumulated through work. He rejects the view that there has been a managerial revolution which has undermined the power of the capitalist class. A considerable number of top managers and directors are able to join the capitalist class themselves. The rest are only likely to retain their jobs if their actions favour the capitalist class.

Scott also attacks the idea that institutional control over many large companies has led to the disappearance of a capitalist class. Even if in theory the assets of pension schemes, banks, insurance companies and similar institutions are owned by a multitude of small investors, in practice they are controlled by a few key members of the capitalist class. The policies of these institutions are largely determined by their directors, who themselves are often members of the capitalist class in their own right. It is these finance capitalists who make the key investment decisions that affect the lives of millions.

Within this group is an inner core who sit on the boards of more than one company. Far from leading to the death of the capitalist class, institutional control improves coordination and cooperation within it.

The composition of the capitalist class

The capitalist class, then, includes many of the directors of the largest companies, especially those with multiple directorships, successful entrepreneurs and those who have inherited substantial amounts of wealth. Scott claims that in Britain this means about 0.1 per cent of the adult population.

Table 1.7 shows the richest forty families/individuals in Britain in 2005, according to research carried out by the *Sunday Times*. All of them had achieved billionaire status.

The ruling class

Having claimed to have established that a capitalist class still exists, Scott goes on to try to show that it remains a ruling class. He says that a ruling class exists when 'there is both political domination and political rule by a capitalist class'. He goes on to argue:

> *This requires that there be a power bloc dominated by a capitalist class, a power elite recruited from this power bloc, in which the capitalist class is disproportionately represented, and there are mechanisms which ensure that the state operates in the interests of the capitalist class and the reproduction of capital.* Scott, 1991, p. 124

By a **power bloc**, Scott means a group of people who can monopolize political power over a country for some time. The **power elite** are those people from the power bloc who occupy key positions in the state. In Britain these positions include those held by the prime minister, members of the cabinet, MPs, senior judges and top civil servants.

Scott quotes figures showing that top civil servants and others in elite positions continue to be predominantly recruited from public school backgrounds. (Figures on elite self-recruitment are discussed in Chapter 9.) Scott concludes that the evidence on self-recruitment shows that a power bloc continues to exist and is dominated by members of the capitalist class.

Whether Conservative or Labour governments have been in power, their policies have become increasingly constrained by the interests of capitalism and capitalists. Governments have to pay close attention to the financial markets if they are going to borrow money, maintain the exchange rate of the currency and attract investment into the country. They cannot afford to ignore the interests of capitalists. In particular, government policy is strongly influenced by an inner core of finance capitalists in the City of London. The 'City point of view', advocated by this group, is 'rooted in short-term commercialism' and 'involves a commitment to free international capital flows, stable sterling exchange rates, and tight monetary controls'.

Changes in the ruling class

Scott certainly believes that there have been changes in the ruling class. At the beginning of the twentieth century it was based around an 'upper circle of status superiors', many of whom had connections to the aristocracy. Aristocratic connections are far less important today and members of the ruling class have an increasingly international role. The growing importance of multinational corporations means there are greater links between the business classes of different societies. British public schools are still important for the recruitment of members of the British ruling class and the maintenance of ruling-class networks, but international business schools are growing in importance. Nevertheless, Scott believes that both in Britain and in other countries a distinctive, nationally based ruling class remains. The character of the ruling class may have changed, but its survival and continued domination of British society have never been in question.

Stewart Lansley – a new 'super-class'

Scott's work is becoming a little dated, but is generally supported by more recent research. Stewart Lansley (2006) argues that a powerful and wealthy minority continues to be dominant in Britain. He admits that the composition of the dominant group may be changing. One change is that a few more successful entrepreneurs from humble backgrounds are joining the ranks of the wealthy (for example, individuals such as Alan Sugar). The traditional establishment and 'old money' have lost some influence and successful entertainers and sportspeople have joined the ranks of the wealthy.

Nevertheless, Lansley agrees with Scott that a wealthy business elite continues to be the most powerful group in Britain. These individuals are still largely drawn from privileged backgrounds, and they have got substantially richer since New Labour come to power in 1997. They have become what Lansley calls a 'super-class' of the very wealthy as the rich have prospered. Within this class there are some who have more wealth and power than the rest. Lansley concludes:

> *There is certainly a powerful business elite in Britain today, just as there always has been. Those with real power – to change the course of events, to influence and alter government policy, to control important institutions – probably constitute maybe less than half the full membership of the 'super-class' – a 'hyper-class', an elite within an elite.* Lansley, 2006, p. 145

Leslie Sklair – the global system and the transnational capitalist class

So far the idea of an upper or ruling class has been examined largely from the viewpoint of individual societies, in particular Great Britain. Advocates of the theory of **globalization** argue, however, that it is misleading to study individual nation-states as independent entities. They believe that national boundaries are becoming less important and power is increasingly

Table 1.7 The billionaire count, Britain, 2005

	Name	Worth (£bn)	Source of wealth
1	Lakshmi Mittal	£14.80	Steel
2	Roman Abramovich	£7.50	Oil, investments
3	The Duke of Westminster	£5.60	Property
4	Hans Rausing and family	£4.95	Food packaging
5	Phillip and Christina Green	£4.85	Retailing
6	Oleg Deripaska	£4.38	Aluminium
7	Sir Richard Branson	£3.00	Transport, mobile phones
8	Kirsten and Jorn Rausing	£2.58	Inheritance, bloodstock, investments
9	David and Simon Reuben	£2.50	Property, metal trading
10	Spiro Latsis and family	£2.40	Banking, shipping
11	Bernie and Slavica Ecclestone	£2.32	Motor racing
12	Charlene and Michael de Carvalho	£2.27	Inheritance, brewing, banking
13	Mahdi al-Tajir	£2.10	Oil, investments, bottled water
	Sri and Gopi Hinduja	£2.10	Industry, finance
15	Joe Lewis	£2.00	Foreign exchange dealing
16	John Fredriksen	£1.89	Shipping
17	Lord Sainsbury and family	£1.71	Supermarkets
18	Earl Cadogan and family	£1.65	Property
19	Sergio Mantegazza and family	£1.54	Travel
20	Roddie Fleming and family	£1.50	Banking
21	Eddie and Malcolm Healey	£1.45	Property, kitchens
22	Nadhmi Auchi	£1.40	Finance
	Mary Czernin and the Howard de Walden family	£1.40	Property
24	Michael Moritz	£1.35	Finance
25	Leonard Blavatnik	£1.30	Industry
	Clive Calder	£1.30	Music
	Richard Desmond	£1.30	Publishing
	Sir Terry Matthews	£1.30	Telecommunications
29	John Caudwell	£1.28	Mobile phones
	Bruno Schroder and family	£1.28	Finance
31	Philippe Foreil-Destezet	£1.27	Recruitment services
32	The Aga Khan	£1.25	Head of the Ismaili people
33	Sir David and Sir Frederick Barclay	£1.20	Media, retail, property
	Viscount Portman and family	£1.20	Property
35	Lady Grantchester and the Moores family	£1.16	Retailing, football pools
36	Paul Fentener van Vlissingen	£1.10	Inheritance
	Michael Lemos	£1.10	Inheritance
	Sir Ken Morrison and family	£1.10	Supermarkets
39	James Dyson	£1.05	Household appliances
40	Roger and Peter De Haan	£1.02	Leisure

Note: Figures include people aged 16 and over

Source: *Sunday Times* Rich List, 3 April 2005

exercised in **transnational relationships**, relationships that cut across state boundaries. Thus, rather than looking for or studying a class that might be dominant in a particular nation, it is necessary to consider the possibility that a single class might exercise power across many nations.

According to Leslie Sklair (1995) the contemporary world is a **global system** in which nation-states are only one set of actors. The global system is made up of a number of **transnational practices**. Sklair identifies a wide range of transnational or global phenomena including travel, tourism, finance, and products which are sold worldwide, but he focuses on three main transnational practices. He defines transnational practices as 'practices that originate with non-state actors and cross state borders' and identifies three spheres in which they operate: the **economic**, the **political** and the **cultural-ideological**. These correspond to the transnational practices of the **transnational corporation (TNC)**, the **transnational capitalist class** and the **culture-ideology of consumerism**.

Sklair sees the capitalist economy as the foundation of the global system and the source of the increasing power of the transnational capitalist class. World production is increasingly dominated by incredibly wealthy corporations. Individual states bend over backwards to attract inward investment from such corporations, while vast numbers of people throughout the world are persuaded to buy the products of these same corporations through advertising.

Thus, for example, corporations such as McDonald's, General Motors, Sony, Ford and Coca-Cola can exercise as much power as many nation-states. Their products, and the ideology which encourages people to consume those products, are increasingly penetrating the 'third world' of poorer nations, the former communist countries and even the more urbanized parts of China.

The transnational capitalist class

The most powerful class in a global system consists of those groups that exercise power across nation-states as well as within them. The transnational capitalist class, the 'driver' of global capitalism, comprises the executives of TNCs and their local affiliates, 'globalizing state bureaucrats', 'capitalist-inspired politicians and professionals' and 'consumerist elites (merchants, media)'.

This class is seen as making system-wide decisions that affect the whole of the global system as it seeks to maintain that system in order to further its interests. It opposes protectionism – through which countries erect tariff barriers to make it difficult for imports to compete with domestic industry. It supports free trade because that offers the best possibilities for corporations to make global profits. The transnational capitalist class also tries to deal with the threat posed by 'anti-capitalist global system movements', particularly the green movement.

Although Sklair does not claim that ruling classes within individual countries have lost all power, he does say that 'as the transnational practices of the global capitalist system become increasingly powerful, only those domestic (i.e. non-transnational) practices that do not threaten the global capitalist project are tolerated'. Politicians, for example, who try to put domestic interests before those of global capitalism will soon find that investment flows out of the country, leaving them little choice but to change tack.

An evaluation of Sklair

Given the enormous influence of world capitalism, Sklair is undoubtedly right to point to the existence of a powerful capitalist class whose activities are not confined to individual nation-states. Theories of upper and ruling classes need to pay more attention to their relationship to non-nationals who exercise power from outside countries.

However, Sklair's analysis of the transnational capitalist class tends to underplay the differences of interest which might exist between different groups of capitalists (between finance capitalists and those involved in manufacturing, for example). Indeed, the whole analysis of capitalism tends to focus on production through the activities of TNCs to the neglect of finance. Sklair has relatively little to say about the power of, for example, bankers in the global system.

Furthermore, nation-states do retain considerable bargaining power in their relations with transnational corporations. As such it can be argued that both domestic and transnational ruling or upper classes have considerable power and neither should be ignored in the analysis of ruling classes. (See Chapter 9 for a discussion of globalization, power and the nation-state.)

Other views

1 **Elite theories** accept that power is concentrated in the hands of a few, but deny that the power comes from wealth. Instead, they see power deriving from the occupation of top jobs in society (see Chapter 9 for further details).
2 **Pluralists** deny that higher social classes monopolize power and believe that in liberal democracies the wishes of the people determine government policy. According to this view, power is dispersed and not concentrated in the hands of the upper classes (see Chapter 9 for details).

Chapter 9 will examine these quite different views about the 'top' of the stratification system.

The middle class

Marx and the middle class

The most usual way of defining the **middle class** is to see it as consisting of those individuals who have **non-manual** occupations, that is, occupations which involve, in some sense, an intellectual element. If the distinction between manual and non-manual labour is used to distinguish the middle class, then, as we indicated earlier (see pp. 33–5), it is a growing sector of capitalist industrial societies such as Britain.

The attempt to analyse the position of the middle class in the class structure has been a major preoccupation of sociologists of stratification. This has been the case particularly for Marxist and neo-Marxist sociologists, since the growth of the middle class has often been cited as evidence against Marx's theory of class.

According to many interpretations of his work, Marx saw capitalist society as divided into only two classes of any importance: the bourgeoisie and the proletariat. This leaves no room for a middle class. In reality, though, Marx recognized the existence of intermediate classes (for example, members of the petty bourgeoisie, such as shopkeepers and small business people). Moreover, the growth of what is usually called the middle class has largely been the result of the increasing amount of white-collar work. In Volume 3 of *Capital* Marx noted this trend when he argued that the increasing size of enterprises made it impossible for them to be run by a single person. In these circumstances there was a need for 'the employment of commercial wage-workers who make up the actual office staff'.

Although he identified the trend towards more non-manual workers, Marx made no detailed attempt to explain how they fitted into his theory of stratification. On the surface, at least, as non-owners of the means of production, they can hardly be considered as part of the bourgeoisie. Nor, it is often argued, can they be seen as part of the proletariat. Many commentators suggest that non-manual workers enjoy considerable advantages in employment over their manual counterparts: they tend to enjoy greater job security, shorter working hours, longer holidays, more fringe benefits and greater promotion prospects.

Life chances

A variety of studies have shown that non-manual workers enjoy advantages over manual workers in terms of their life chances. They are likely to enjoy higher standards of health, and to live longer; they are less likely to be convicted of a criminal offence; they are more likely to own their own house and a variety of consumer goods.

The Office for National Statistics (ONS) has compiled a range of statistical evidence on inequalities between classes in England and Wales (*Focus on Social Inequalities 2004*).

In 2002, 77 per cent of year 11 children with parents in higher professional occupations obtained five or more GCSEs at grade C or above, compared to 32 per cent of those with parents in routine occupations.

Educational qualifications are closely linked to success in the labour market. In 2003 the unemployment rate for those without formal educational qualifications was about twice that for those who had qualifications. Lack of qualifications and low income are associated with a lack of access to facilities such as computers at home. In 2001–2, 86 per cent of households with a weekly disposable income of over £1,000 had a home computer, compared to 15 per cent of households with an income under £200.

Most importantly of all, class differences affect health and life expectancy. In 1997–8 the life expectancy of men with professional jobs was 7.4 years longer than that of men with unskilled manual jobs; and the life expectancy of female professionals was 5.7 years longer than that of female unskilled manual workers.

In 2002 the infant mortality rate was significantly higher for children of unskilled families than it was for children from higher classes. Furthermore, those in higher socio-economic groups were much less likely to report themselves as having poor health than those from lower socio-economic groups. In 2001 rates of long-standing illness were five times higher amongst the long-term unemployed than amongst professional workers.

Conflicting perspectives on the middle class

In Weberian terms, the sort of evidence outlined above can be used to suggest that there is a middle class in Britain, distinguished from the working class by its superior market situation and life chances. From this point of view, the middle class is held to consist of non-manual workers. However, this relatively simple and straightforward view has, for a variety of reasons, been rejected by many sociologists:

1. The distinction between manual and non-manual work is not seen by some as an adequate way of distinguishing between classes. Often Marxist and neo-Marxist sociologists try to distinguish classes according to their role within the economic system, while Weberians are more likely to analyse class in terms of the market situation of particular occupational groups.
2. On the face of it, the middle class contains an extremely diverse group of workers, ranging from secretaries to accountants, shop assistants to managers, shopkeepers to social workers.
3. The position of particular occupational groups – their wages, conditions of employment and responsibilities – changed during the course of the twentieth century, and these changes may in turn have affected the class structure as a whole.

These complications have led to a whole variety of views as to the composition of the middle class and its place in the social structure. Some have argued that there is a distinctive and relatively homogeneous middle class; others that the middle class as such does not exist. Some of those who accept the existence of a middle class believe that it is divided into many different strata; others that it is divided, but only into two main groupings.

The precise location of the boundaries between the middle class and the classes above and below it has also been the subject of dispute. Before we examine the place of the middle class as a whole in the class structure, we will examine the main strata of the middle class in detail.

The upper middle class

For the sake of convenience, different parts of the middle class will be examined in two main sections. In this first section we will consider the position of the more highly rewarded groups, including professionals, senior managers and administrators, and more successful small business people.

In the early twentieth century, small business people (the self-employed and shopkeepers) made up a greater proportion of the working population than they did in 1971. As the size of many businesses grew, the number of employers was reduced. Guy Routh (1980) found that the number of employers in Britain declined from 763,000 in 1911 to 621,000 in 1971. The number of self-employed also fell by 24,000 over the same period.

Obviously, larger employers might be considered part of the upper class, but the others are often seen as part of the 'old' middle class. Marx predicted that this group, which he referred to as the petty (or petite) bourgeoisie, would be progressively squeezed into the proletariat. They would be unable to compete with larger companies which could buy and sell in bulk and take advantage of advanced technology (Marx and Engels, 1848).

Although up to 1971 the trends provided support for Marx's view on the likely fate of the petty bourgeoisie, data since the 1980s indicate a reversal of previous trends. According to official figures, the numbers of self-employed and small proprietors rose from 1,954,000 in 1971, to 3.6 million in 2003 (*Labour Market Trends 1997; Social Trends 2006*). Nevertheless, most of the expansion of the upper middle class is accounted for by the growth of white-collar employment.

Some sociologists distinguish between different strata of the upper middle class, identifying, for example, higher professionals, lower professionals, and managers as separate groups. Others see the upper middle class as being more homogeneous. In the following section we will examine the position of one stratum of the upper middle class – the professions – in the class structure.

The professions in the class structure

The growth of the professions

The professions were one of the fastest growing sectors of the occupational structure during the twentieth century. According to Routh (1980), the number of people employed in the professions rose from 4 per cent of the employed population in 1911 to 11 per cent in 1971. Using a slightly different definition of the professions, the government's Labour Force Survey calculated a rise in the proportion of employees in the UK in professional work between 1991 and 2005 from 10 per cent to 14 per cent among men and from 8 per cent to 12 per cent among women (*Social Trends 1997, 2006*). Similar trends are evident in all Western industrial capitalist societies.

Several reasons have been given for the rapid growth of the professions. The increasing complexity of business demands financial and legal experts such as accountants and lawyers. The development of industry requires more specialized scientific and technical knowledge which results in the development of professions such as science and engineering. The creation of the welfare state and the expansion of local and national government have produced a range of 'welfare professions', and have led to the growth of the medical and teaching professions, as well as the greater employment of professionals in government bureaucracies. From another viewpoint, the growth of the professions may also be associated with the attempts of more and more groups of workers to get their jobs accepted as 'professional'.

Higher and lower professionals

In terms of their market situation, the professionals can be divided into two groups: the higher and lower professionals.

1. The higher professionals include judges, barristers, solicitors, architects, planners, doctors, dentists, university lecturers, accountants, scientists and engineers.
2. The lower professionals include school teachers, nurses, social workers and librarians.

Historical research by Routh suggests there have long been significant differences in earnings between the two groups. Routh found that in 1913–14 higher professional men earned 230 per cent of average male pay and 159 per cent in 1978. The equivalent figures for male lower professionals were 109 and 104 per cent.

Recent figures show continuing high rewards for professionals in general. The *Annual Survey of Hours and Earnings 2005* showed that the mean weekly gross pay was £349.60 per week but for professional occupations it was £594.10. The survey does not distinguish between higher and lower professions as a whole but some of the sub-categories do correspond to the higher and lower professional groups. For example, in 2005, health professionals (which includes the higher professions of doctors, vets, opticians and psychologists) had gross weekly earnings of £920.00 per week, while associate health and welfare professionals (which includes the lower professions of nurses, midwives, physiotherapists and occupational therapists) earned only £412.80 per week. Teaching and research professionals (mainly lower professions) earned £563.30 per week in 2005.

Various sociological theories have been put forward to explain both the advantaged position of the professions in general and the differences between higher and lower professions.

The functionalist perspective on professions

Bernard Barber (1963) offers a functionalist view of the role and rewards of higher professionals. He argues that professionalism involves 'four essential attributes':

1. Professionalism requires a body of systematic and generalized knowledge that can be applied to a variety of problems. For instance, doctors have a body of medical knowledge which they apply to diagnose and treat a range of illnesses.
2. Professionalism involves a concern for the interests of the community rather than self-interest. Thus the primary motivation of professionals is public service rather than personal gain: doctors are concerned primarily with the health of their patients rather than with lining their own pockets.
3. The behaviour of professionals is strictly controlled by a code of ethics, which is established and maintained by professional associations and learned as part of the training required to qualify as a professional. For example, doctors take the Hippocratic Oath, which lays down the obligations and proper conduct of their profession. Should they break this code of conduct, their association can strike them from the register and ban them from practising medicine.

4. The high rewards received by professionals, which include the prestige accorded to professional status as well as earnings, are symbols of their achievements. They denote the high regard in which professionals are held and reflect the value of their contribution to society.

Barber argues that the knowledge and skills of professionals provide them with considerable power, and it is therefore essential for the well-being of society that this power is used for the benefit of all. He claims that professionals make important contributions to the functional well-being of society and, in addition, their services are highly regarded in terms of society's values. Professionals are highly rewarded as a result.

Criticisms of functionalism

Functionalist explanations of the role and rewards of professionals have been strongly criticized on the grounds that they make the following assumptions, all of which are questionable:

1. Professionals make important contributions to the well-being of society as a whole.
2. They serve all members of society rather than particular groups.
3. They are concerned with service to the community rather than with self-interest.

In recent years there has been increasing criticism of the view that professionals provide valuable services to society. Teachers have been attacked for allowing children to underachieve. Lawyers have been accused of mystifying the legal system to the point where the layperson finds it largely unintelligible, and of sometimes helping the guilty to go free while the innocent are convicted.

Individual cases of professional misconduct or incompetence have reduced public trust in the professions. For example, in 2000 the British GP Harold Shipman was found guilty of murdering fifteen of his patients through administering lethal injections – official investigations suggest he may have murdered many more patients. Social workers and other child protection workers were severely criticized in the inquiry into the death of Victoria Climbié in London in 2000 for failing to take effective action to protect her despite extensive evidence that she was being physically abused by her guardians. The reputation of nurses was dented when Beverley Allitt was given thirteen life sentences in 1993 for killing patients in her care in Lincolnshire. In the USA, the accountants of the energy company Enron were found to have misrepresented the company's profits and shredded evidence relating to the company's collapse.

Such examples suggest that the functionalist argument that the higher professions confer positive benefits on society is at least questionable.

The Weberian perspective on professions – market strategy

From a Weberian point of view, the professions can be seen as occupational groups that have succeeded in controlling and manipulating the labour market in such a way that they can maximize their rewards. Thus Noel and José Parry (1976) define professionalism as 'a strategy for controlling an occupation in which colleagues set up a system of self-government'. The occupation is controlled primarily in the interests of its members. From this perspective, professionalism can be said to involve the following factors:

1. There is restricted entry into the occupation, provided by the profession's control of the training and qualifications required for membership and the numbers deemed necessary to provide an adequate service. By controlling supply, professionals can maintain a high demand for their services and so gain high rewards.
2. Professionalism involves an association that controls the conduct of its members 'in respects which are defined as relevant to the collective interests of the profession' (Parry and Parry, 1976). In particular, professional associations are concerned with promoting the view that professional conduct is above reproach and that professionals are committed to public service. This serves to justify high occupational rewards. By claiming the right to discipline their own members, professional associations largely prevent public scrutiny of their affairs and so maintain the image which they project of themselves.
3. Professionalism involves a successful claim that only members are qualified to provide particular services. This claim is often reinforced by law. Thus in Britain, for example, a series of laws have guaranteed solicitors a monopoly on particular services. These monopolies are jealously guarded: the Law Society has prosecuted unqualified individuals for performing services which are defined as a legal monopoly of the law profession.

In these ways, professions can control rival occupational groups which might threaten their dominance of a section of the market. Parry and Parry conclude that, by adopting the strategy of professionalism, certain occupational groups are able to extract high rewards from the market.

Viewing professionalism as a **market strategy** provides an explanation for the differing rewards of various so-called professions. Some of the occupational groups that claim professional status lack many of the attributes of professionalism. In terms of Parry and Parry's definition, they are professions in name only. They have little control over their market situation and, as a result, receive lower rewards than occupational groups that are more fully professionalized.

Parry and Parry illustrate this point by a comparison of doctors and teachers. They claim that doctors receive higher rewards than teachers because they are more fully professionalized. This is largely due to the fact that doctors were able to organize themselves into a professional group before the state intervened in medicine and became a major employer of medical practitioners.

The British Medical Association was founded in 1832, and the Medical Registration Act of 1858 granted doctors a monopoly on the practice of medicine and gave them important powers of self-government. Once established as a professional body, doctors had considerable control over their market situation.

Teachers, by contrast, failed to achieve professionalism before state intervention in education. Because the state was largely responsible for initiating and paying for mass education, it was able to establish greater control over teachers. In particular, the state controlled both the supply of teachers and standards for entry into the occupation. Because they lack the market control which professionalism provides, teachers have turned to trade unionism to improve their market situation. Parry and Parry conclude that the differences in occupational reward between doctors and teachers are attributable to the degree of professionalization of the two groups.

The Weberian perspective on professions – the professional project

The Weberian approach to the professions is reflected in the work of Keith Macdonald (1997) who discusses the **professional project** – the attempt to establish an occupational group as an accepted profession – a complex and continuous process.

Occupational groups do not suddenly achieve professional status at a particular point in their development – they continually struggle to enhance their status as the profession develops. According to Macdonald, the professional project aims to establish a 'monopoly in the market for services based on their expertise, and for status in the social order'. This is particularly important for professions because what they sell is intangible, since it takes the form of 'services which cannot be seen in advance in the shop-window, as it were, but which also require the customer to trust the practitioner with their lives, their health, their money, their property and even their immortal souls'. Achieving the appropriate status is vital to gaining the necessary trust.

Macdonald discusses how professions try to establish their position. First, they need to develop a strategy of **social closure**; that is, they exclude others from practising their profession. Second, they have to establish their own **jurisdiction**, and define the area over which they have expertise to claim a right to practise. Third, they have to **train** the members of their profession. Fourth, they have to try to **monopolize their professional expertise** to make sure that others cannot make claims on their area of jurisdiction. Fifth, they need to attain **respectability**.

Macdonald uses the example of accountancy to illustrate these points. In the mid-nineteenth century clerical workers with fairly basic book-keeping skills carried out accountancy functions. Gradually, accountants have established professional organizations such as the Institute of Chartered Accountants and Certified Public Accountants, gained a legal monopoly of some types of work (such as auditing the accounts of local authorities), confined recruitment almost exclusively to graduates, and succeeded in raising the social status and rewards of accountancy. Accountants are now among the highest paid and most influential professionals in Britain.

Professions as servants of the powerful

The Weberian claim that the professions are able to act primarily in their own interests has been called into question. It has been argued that the higher professionals primarily serve the interests of the wealthy and powerful. Accountants and lawyers are employed in the service of capital, architects build for the wealthy, and doctors and psychiatrists in private practice care for the physical and mental needs of the rich.

Some Marxists have argued that the professions have been weakened so they can no longer pursue their own interests. Harry Braverman (1974) claims that deskilling has taken place in many white-collar jobs. As the skill content of the work has been reduced, so some white-collar workers have lost the advantages they previously enjoyed over manual employees. They have become **proletarianized**.

Although primarily concerned with routine white-collar work, Braverman believes that some professional jobs have also become deskilled. The people who do these jobs lose the power they once had, their work is closely regulated, and they are made aware of their subordination. Examples include draughtsmen, technicians, engineers, accountants, nurses and teachers. Such groups find that their work becomes more and more routine as it is divided into specialist tasks. Their pay levels are threatened as they become unable to control the supply of labour into their profession: there is always a 'reserve army' of suitably qualified workers ready to step into their jobs.

The declining independence of the professions

Braverman's views are rather general, and certainly exaggerate the decline in the autonomy of the professions, but other sociologists have suggested ways in which the position of professional groups in the class structure has deteriorated. Terence Johnson (1972) has pointed to the limits that can be placed on some professions by their clients or employers. For example, in the accountancy profession most practitioners are employed by companies and are not independent advisers. Accountants are expected to be loyal first and foremost to their company, and not to their profession.

It may be true that during the course of the last century some groups of professionals increasingly became employees, rather than being employers or self-employed; and it may also be true that some professional groups have had their independence and autonomy reduced. However, it is an exaggeration to claim that they have been proletarianized. Higher professionals in particular continue to enjoy many advantages over manual workers, and, for that matter, routine non-manual workers. They also have much more power than either group.

Barbara and John Ehrenreich – the professional–managerial class

Although many sociologists see professionals as a distinctive part of the upper middle class, others have argued that they have much in common with managers. Barbara and John Ehrenreich (1979), arguing from a neo-Marxist point of view, claim that there is a distinctive **professional–managerial class**, which consists of 'salaried mental workers who do not own the means of production and whose major function in the social division of labour may be described broadly as the reproduction of capitalist culture and capitalist class relations'. Members of this class include teachers, social workers, psychologists, entertainers, writers of advertising copy, and middle-level administrators, managers and engineers.

Origins and functions

Unlike some other Marxists, the Ehrenreichs believe that there are three main classes in capitalist society, rather than two (the bourgeoisie and the proletariat). They see the third class, the professional–managerial class, as having the following functions which they carry out for the bourgeoisie:

1. The first function of the class is to organize the process of production, for example by developing new technology and new methods of management.
2. The second function is to exercise social control over children and the working class. This is carried out by professionals such as teachers and social workers.
3. A third function is to propagate ruling-class ideology. This is carried out by groups such as entertainers, teachers and advertising copywriters.
4. The final function is helping to develop the consumer goods market, ensuring that the working class consume new products produced by capitalism.

The overall role of the professional–managerial class, then, is to reproduce the relationship of domination and subordination between the ruling and subject classes.

Interests

The Ehrenreichs believe that the professional–managerial class has quite different interests from the working class, even though both groups consist of wage labourers. This is because the professional–managerial class is paid out of the surplus produced by the working class.

The professional–managerial class also has different interests from the ruling class. Both groups have an interest in maintaining the capitalist system, but the professional–managerial class has an interest in maximizing its own independence or autonomy; the ruling class, on the other hand, tries to restrict it as far as possible.

Criticisms of the Ehrenreichs

The Ehrenreichs provide an interesting attempt to analyse the position of one part of the middle class within a neo-Marxist framework. However, they have been criticized by Marxists and non-Marxists alike.

The American neo-Marxist Erik Olin Wright (1978) does not accept that there is a unified professional–managerial class. He argues that capitalist societies remain polarized between two main classes: the ruling class and the working class. He does not deny that there are groups of workers who are intermediate between these two classes, but he argues that they do not constitute a fully developed class. Instead he sees them as occupying a number of strata which are in 'contradictory class locations'. Some of their interests coincide with those of the working class, and some with those of the ruling class, but they do not have a coherent set of interests of their own and cannot therefore constitute a distinctive class.

Weberian theories

Weberian and neo-Weberian sociologists generally reject the approach to defining and distinguishing classes adopted by the Ehrenreichs. They deny that classes can be defined in terms of their functions for capitalism, and instead stress the importance of the market situation of those in particular occupations.

This has led to one Weberian sociologist, Anthony Giddens (1973), identifying a larger middle class than the professional–managerial class discussed by the Ehrenreichs. From Giddens's point of view, the middle class should also include lower-level white-collar workers (for further details see p. 52).

We will consider the implications of these various views for the analysis of the middle class as a whole after we have discussed the lower middle class in the next section.

Mobility between professions and management

The Ehrenreichs' claim that professionals and managers form one class is rather undermined by research which suggests that there is little mobility between the two groups.

Tony Fielding (1995) uses data from an Office of Population Censuses and Surveys longitudinal study of a 1 per cent sample of the population of England and Wales. He found that between 1981 and 1991 just 10 per cent of professionals had moved into management and similarly only 10 per cent of managers had obtained professional jobs. This suggests that managers and professionals could be regarded as two separate classes rather than one.

The lower middle class

Routine white-collar workers include such groups as clerical workers, secretaries and shop assistants. The growth in their numbers during the twentieth century has led to a long-standing debate about their position in the class structure:

1. Some sociologists argue that they have become **proletarianized**; that is, they have effectively become members of the working class.
2. Others claim that routine white-collar workers still belong to the middle class.
3. A third viewpoint suggests that they form an intermediate group between the middle and working classes.

Proletarianization

The theory of proletarianization suggests that routine white-collar workers have become part of the proletariat and so can no longer be considered middle-class. This viewpoint has most usually been associated with Marxist sociologists who have questioned the assumption that the working class is a rapidly declining section of the population in capitalist societies. They see routine non-manual workers as little different from manual workers: they neither own the means of production nor do they perform important social control functions for capitalists.

For example, the British Marxists Westergaard and Resler (1976) estimated that in 1913–14 male clerks earned 122 per cent of the average manual wage, but by 1971 this had fallen to just 96 per cent. They argued that, at least with respect to earnings, 'male clerks and shop workers are now firmly among the broad mass of ordinary labour; and indeed often well down towards the bottom of the pile'.

Harry Braverman – the deskilling of clerical work

The American Marxist Harry Braverman (1974) supports the proletarianization thesis on the grounds that many routine non-manual jobs have become deskilled. According to Braverman, clerical workers in 1870 shared many similarities with manual craft workers: both had wide-ranging responsibilities and plenty of opportunity to use their initiative and develop their skills. As such, they were valued members of the workforce.

As companies grew larger and their clerical workforce expanded, the work was reorganized so that each worker specialized in particular tasks and clerical work became little more than a production line for mental work.

Braverman also claims that most 'service workers' have been deskilled. He says:

> *the demand for the all-round grocery clerk, fruiterer and vegetable dealer, dairyman, butcher, and so forth, has long ago been replaced by a labour configuration in the supermarkets which calls for truck unloaders, shelf stockers, checkout clerks, meat wrappers, and meat cutters; of these only the last retain any semblance of skill, and none require any general knowledge of retail trade.* Braverman, 1974, p. 371

Computerization has further reduced the skill required of checkout assistants, and the control of stock and the keeping of accounts have also become largely automated.

According to Braverman most routine white-collar work requires little more than basic numeracy and literacy. With the advent of mass compulsory education, the vast majority of the population now have the necessary skills to undertake this type of work. As a result the bargaining position of these workers is little better than that of manual workers.

David Lockwood – a Weberian perspective

According to many Marxists, then, the positions in the class structure occupied by most routine non-manual workers have been proletarianized. In an early study of clerks from a neo-Weberian point of view, however, David Lockwood (1958) denied that clerks had been proletarianized. Lockwood did not follow Weber in identifying an upper class based on the ownership of property; he did, though, use a Weberian approach to distinguish between different groups of employees. He suggested that there were three aspects of class situation: market situation, work situation and status situation.

1. By **market situation** he was referring to such factors as wages, job security and promotion prospects.
2. By **work situation** he meant social relationships at work between employers and managers and more junior staff; this involved consideration of how closely work was supervised.
3. By **status situation** he meant the degree of prestige enjoyed by particular groups of workers in society.

In terms of market situation Lockwood admitted that the wages of clerical workers had dropped but he argued that they had considerable advantages over manual workers in other respects. They had greater job security and were less likely to be laid off or made redundant. They also worked shorter hours, had more chance of being promoted to higher-status jobs and were more likely to be given fringe benefits such as membership of a pension scheme.

Lockwood reached similar conclusions with regard to work situation. He accepted that there had been some changes – in particular the offices had grown in size – but he denied that this had led to clerical workers becoming proletarian. Compared to manual workers, clerks still worked in relatively small units, they had closer contact with management, and clerical jobs tended to be more varied and less standardized than manual work.

Finally, in terms of status situation Lockwood was more willing to concede a deterioration in the position of the clerical workforce. He accepted that mass literacy, the recruitment of growing numbers of clerical workers from manual backgrounds, and of women, had reduced the status of clerical work. However, he still believed their status was superior to that of manual workers.

Lockwood's work is now dated and it is debatable how far his claims apply to contemporary clerical work. Nevertheless, it was an important study, since it established many of the issues that were to occupy later sociologists who studied clerical work.

Evaluation

A variety of sociologists have attacked or defended the theory of proletarianization:

1. A. Stewart, K. Prandy and R.M. Blackburn (1980), like Lockwood, argued that proletarianization had not taken place, though for different reasons. They studied a sample of male white-collar workers in medium or large firms and found high rates of social mobility out of clerical work. Only 19 per cent of their sample were still doing clerical work by the time they reached 30, and 51 per cent had been promoted to higher-status jobs. According to this study, clerical work cannot be seen as proletarian because it is often a stepping stone to a career in management.
2. Rosemary Crompton and Richard Jones (1984) criticized the work of Stewart *et al.*, pointing out that it relied upon an all-male sample. Crompton and Jones found in their research that a big majority of clerical workers were female, and very few (just 1 per cent) had reached management positions. Furthermore, they point out that Stewart *et al.* did not examine whether clerical work had become deskilled – a major part of the proletarianization

thesis. Crompton and Jones found that 91 per cent of their sample of clerical workers did not exercise any control over how they worked: they simply followed a set of routines without using their initiative. As a result their work required very little skill, and this deskilling appeared to be closely linked to computerization. Crompton and Jones concluded that clerical workers, particularly female clerical workers, were a white-collar proletariat, with little chance of promotion to genuinely middle-class jobs.

3 Gordon Marshall, Howard Newby, David Rose and Carolyn Vogler (1988; see also Marshall, 1997) rejected Crompton and Jones's view that clerical work has been deskilled. Their conclusions are based on structured interviews carried out with a sample of 1,770 British men and women. Only 4 per cent of the female clerical workers and none of the male clerical workers said the skill requirements of their job had declined. Marshall *et al.* therefore support the views of Goldthorpe and Lockwood that clerical workers are in an intermediate class between the working and service classes. However, they did find that the vast majority of female personal service workers (such as checkout assistants) claimed to have little control over their work or autonomy at work. They therefore conclude that personal service workers are indeed part of the proletariat.

Marshall *et al.*'s rejection of the proletarianization theory for clerical workers must, however, be regarded with some caution. In particular, the significance of the small number who say their work has been deskilled is open to question. The deskilling argument as advanced by Braverman refers to a time-span of a century or more, stretching back far earlier than the experience of those currently employed in such jobs. Indeed, Marshall *et al.* themselves admit that 'a definitive answer to the question of job techniques and job autonomy could be provided only by systematic and direct observation over a prolonged period of time'.

Middle class, or middle classes?

As we have seen, there is no agreement among sociologists about the position of the middle class, or classes, in the stratification system. They are divided about which non-manual workers should be placed in the middle class, and disagree about whether the middle class is a united and homogeneous or divided and heterogeneous group.

Anthony Giddens – the middle class

The simplest position is taken by Anthony Giddens (1973). He argues that there is a single middle class, based on the possession of 'recognized skills – including educational qualifications'. Unlike the members of the working class, who can sell only their manual labour power, members of the middle class can also sell their mental labour power. Giddens distinguishes the middle class from the upper class because the middle class does not own 'property in the means of production' and so has to work for others to earn a living.

John H. Goldthorpe – the service and intermediate classes

Giddens follows Weber's views quite closely, but other neo-Weberians do not agree that there is a single middle class. John Goldthorpe, in his early work (Goldthorpe, 1980; Goldthorpe *et al.*, 1987), defines class in terms of market and work situation, but in his research does not follow Weber in distinguishing the propertied from the propertyless. Goldthorpe does not therefore clearly distinguish an upper class, nor does he claim that there is a united middle class. He sees the highest class as the service class, and this includes large proprietors as well as administrators, managers and professionals. This class itself is internally divided between those in upper and lower positions. However, he sees no significant division between managers and professionals within the service class.

Goldthorpe's class in the middle is not called the middle class, but the **intermediate class**. It includes clerical workers, personal service workers, small proprietors and lower-grade technicians. To Goldthorpe, these workers have poorer market and work situations than the service class. In his scheme this class is also seen as being internally divided, but nevertheless at the most basic level he sees what is normally regarded as the middle class as being split in two.

In his later work, Goldthorpe (1995) changed tack and argued that there was a primary division between different sections of the middle class based on employment status. That is, the employed, employees and the self-employed are in different positions. Beyond that, there are secondary divisions based on different employee relationships and it is these, rather than the nature of the work tasks that they do, that distinguish classes. What makes the service class distinctive is that it not only receives a salary but is also provided with increments, pension rights and career development opportunities.

Goldthorpe's views are controversial. In particular, many sociologists argue, in contradiction to both of Goldthorpe's approaches, that there is a significant division between professionals and managers in Goldthorpe's service class (for example, Savage *et al.*, 1992). A further problem is that Goldthorpe himself admits that, strictly speaking, large employers should be seen as a separate category from the service class employees. However, in his social mobility research (see pp. 75–6), he incorporates **employees** into his category of the service class because the group is so small. He accepts that this 'means introducing some, though in all probability only a quite small, degree of error'.

Mike Savage, James Barlow, Peter Dickens and Tony Fielding – property bureaucracy and culture

Savage, Barlow, Dickens and Fielding (1992) follow Goldthorpe in claiming that the middle class is not a united group. However, they do not argue that this lack of unity is inevitable, nor that the divisions within the middle class always stay the same. For example, they believe that France has tended to have a more united service class (of managers and professionals) than Britain. Furthermore, they believe that the nature of divisions in the British middle class may have been changing in recent times.

Savage *et al.* distinguish groups in the middle class according to the types of assets that they possess, rather than in terms of a hierarchy according to their seniority in the class structure. The importance of these different groups can change over time and is affected by the particular circumstances in which classes are formed. Thus, for example, in one set of circumstances, professionals might form a more cohesive and influential class than managers; at another time in another place the reverse might be true.

Social classes

Savage *et al.* see social classes as 'social collectivities rooted in particular types of exploitative relationships'. These social collectivities are 'groups of people with shared levels of income and remuneration, lifestyles, cultures, political orientations and so forth'. As collectivities they may engage in social action that will affect how societies develop. However, to do this they have to actively form themselves into classes. **Class formation** does not automatically follow from social divisions. Savage *et al.* therefore examine how class formation has developed in the middle classes.

They point out that there are many social collectivities with a shared lifestyle. What makes a class distinctive is that it is based around exploitative relationships in which some people become better off at the expense of others. These may take place through wage labour (as in Marxist theory), but exploitation can also be found outside the workplace. One example is where a person's contribution to an activity is neither recognized nor rewarded. They illustrate this with the case of a male academic who relies on his wife to type his manuscript or do the housework so that he can get on with writing. He gives her no share of the royalties and no acknowledgement as a co-author. Savage *et al.* say, 'her labour has been "deleted"'.

Classes and types of asset

The three types of asset which give the middle classes their advantaged life chances are: **property assets**, **organizational assets** and **cultural assets**. Individuals may have some combination of these three types of asset, but distinctive middle classes can develop based on each type. Different types of asset have different qualities and provide different possibilities for exploitation:

1. The propertied middle class are those who have **property assets**. This group consists of the 'petty bourgeoisie', which includes the self-employed and small employers. Their property assets are not as great as those of the 'dominant class' made up of landowners, financiers and capitalists. Property assets are easily passed down from generation to generation. They can be stored in the form of various types of capital or in other possessions such as property. Property assets are the most 'robust in conveying exploitative potential'. As Marxist theory claims, you can use capital to hire and exploit the labour of others by not giving them the full value of their labour.
2. **Organizational assets** stem from holding positions in large bureaucratic organizations. These assets are held by managers. In the past a considerable number of people gained organizational assets by working their way up a bureaucratic hierarchy in a company without necessarily having high educational qualifications. Organizational assets are the most fragile type of asset. They cannot be stored and it may be very difficult to pass them down to the next generation. Certainly, today, managers are unlikely to be able to ensure that their children also obtain jobs as managers. In some cases, the assets are specific to a single organization and cannot readily be transferred to another company if the employee tries to move job. On the other hand, employment in organizations does provide opportunities for exploiting the labour of others.
3. **Cultural assets** derive partly from educational attainment and credentials. These sorts of cultural asset are particularly important to professional workers. However, they can also take the form of class taste. They can be found in

> *what Bourdieu calls the habitus, or set of internalized dispositions which govern people's behaviour. Cultural assets are stored physically in people's bodies and minds: the body itself materializes class tastes. They can be reproduced through the passing on of cultural tastes to offspring.* Savage et al., 1992

Class taste can be important in gaining educational qualifications (see the discussion of Bourdieu's concept of 'cultural capital' in Chapter 11). Women play a key role here because of their prevalence in the teaching profession and their importance in the provision of childcare. Cultural assets, however, cannot be used to directly exploit the labour of others. For this to happen they have to be used to accumulate property assets or to achieve positions which bring with them organizational assets.

Different sections of the middle class will tend to try to use their assets to gain other assets that will make their position secure and enable them to exploit other workers and pass down their advantages to their children. So, for example, the cultured will try to use their cultural assets to obtain good jobs or start their own businesses. Managers who have worked their way up in a company may try to gain educational qualifications so they have the option of applying for jobs in other companies. Owners of successful small businesses may pay for a private education for their children in the hope that they will acquire cultural assets.

Middle-class formation in Britain

According to Savage *et al.*, the different sections of the middle class in Britain have all enjoyed different degrees of success at different times.

In recent decades, for example, the emphasis on controlling or reducing public expenditure by successive governments, and the increased stress on market forces, have tended to weaken the position of public sector professionals. There have also been important changes in industry. Companies have been moving away from mass production in very large hierarchical firms, and instead produce smaller batches of more specialized products in less hierarchical and more flexible firms. This new system of production is known as **post-Fordism** (see p. 127). In the process, firms have come to rely more upon self-employed consultants of various types.

Savage *et al.* believe that middle-class professionals working in areas such as advertising and marketing are in the ascendancy. They play an important role in 'defining and perpetuating consumer cultures associated with private commodity production'. Their cultural capital is not legitimated so much by qualifications and employment by the state, as by their ability to make money by tapping into consumer tastes. Managers have become even less of a cohesive grouping than they once were. The internal labour markets of companies have become less important for promotion prospects. Managers have tried to cement their position by gaining greater cultural assets such as educational qualifications. These make them less reliant on single companies.

Savage *et al.* claim, on the basis of such arguments, that there is a new division in the British middle classes between:

> *a public sector, professional, increasingly female, middle class on the one hand, opposed to an entrepreneurial, private sector, propertied middle class on the other. This latter group might include the self-employed, some managerial groupings and the private sector professionals.*
>
> *Historically, we have argued, the professional middle class lorded over the rest: today managerial and private sector professionals may be shifting from its sphere of influence and may be joining the previously marginalized petite bourgeoisie in a more amorphous and increasingly influential private sector middle class.* Savage et al., 1992, p. 218

The culture and lifestyles of the middle classes

Using data from 1988 survey research from the British Market Research Bureau, Savage *et al.* claim to have detected cultural differences between these new middle-class groupings. However, they distinguish three lifestyle groups rather than two. The public sector professionals – such as those working in health and education and social workers, who are described as 'people with cultural assets, but not much money' – were found to have 'an ascetic lifestyle founded on health and exercise'. They drank less alcohol than the middle class as a whole and were heavily involved in sports such as hiking, skating and climbing.

On the other hand, the rather better paid 'private sector professionals and specialists' had a **postmodern** lifestyle. This involved an appreciation of both high art and pop culture, and a combination of extravagance and concern for health and fitness. Thus:

> *appreciation of high cultural forms of art such as opera and classical music exists cheek by jowl with an interest in disco dancing or stock car racing … a binge in an expensive restaurant one day might be followed by a diet the next.* Savage et al., 1992

This lifestyle was postmodern because it rejected traditional cultural values in relation to the worthiness of different types of art, and because it drew on consumer culture and its willingness to combine a wide variety of images and lifestyles (see pp. 682–6 for a discussion of postmodernism).

A third group, consisting largely of managers and civil servants, is described as having an undistinctive lifestyle.

If Savage *et al.* are right, then the middle classes remain divided, but the nature of those divisions has changed significantly over recent decades. These changes have been influenced by the policies of the British state, and the middle classes have also exercised greater choice in deciding to adopt different lifestyles.

Evaluation

The work of Savage *et al.* highlights some important divisions within the middle class. It provides a useful analysis of the basis of middle-class life chances. It does not fall into the trap of assuming that class divisions are static, and rightly emphasizes the active role of groups in developing their own class identities. It concentrates, however, on the higher reaches of the middle class – their theory does not explain the position of routine white-collar workers.

Furthermore, it could be argued that their analysis of contemporary divisions in the middle class is not entirely convincing. Senior managers could be seen as forming an increasingly powerful and influential group in Britain, who may have combined the acquisition of qualifications with gaining increased opportunities for movement between companies. For example, those with MBA (Master of Business Administration) qualifications, particularly from the most prestigious business schools, may find it easier to gain and move between powerful and highly paid jobs.

In a later work, Savage and Butler (1995) admit that some senior managerial groups may have benefited from recent changes. They say, 'it seems likely that the most senior managers of large organizations actually have enhanced powers. Such senior managers are also increasingly likely to be significant property owners of their organizations, through devices such as share options.' They speculate that such managers may have professional backgrounds and they are increasingly forming 'a small cadre who can mobilize organization, property and cultural assets simultaneously'.

The characterization of the lifestyle of different groups seems to be based on rather simplified generalizations. For example, there are plenty of teachers and doctors who drink large amounts of alcohol and who are interested in popular culture. There are also plenty of private sector professionals who have a particular interest in health and fitness.

Derek Wynne – leisure, lifestyle and the new middle class

The Heath

Like Savage *et al.* Derek Wynne examined the changing nature of the middle class in late twentieth-century Britain (Wynne, 1998). Wynne also follows Savage *et al.* in paying attention to cultural features of the middle class.

However, Wynne diverges from them in basing his arguments on a detailed case study of the middle class on one housing estate, and in placing greater emphasis on lifestyle choices than on objective class divisions.

Wynne studied a housing estate called the Heath, which is located in the Cheshire countryside. He used a number of methods: a detailed questionnaire which examined aspects of residents' social life, interviews, and participant observation (Wynne lived in a house on the Heath). An unusual feature of the Heath was the existence of a bar and sporting facilities which were paid for, run by and reserved for residents of the estate. The size and price of the houses on the Heath meant that they were largely bought by middle-class families.

Culture and class

In developing his theory Wynne draws upon the work of the French sociologist Pierre Bourdieu (1984). Wynne follows Bourdieu in arguing that classes are not just based upon **economic capital**. Classes are also shaped by the possession of **cultural capital** (such as educational qualifications), **social capital** (such as networks of friends and contacts) and **symbolic capital** (which involves the recognition of particular cultures as legitimate and superior to others). Classes actively struggle to create their own cultures and get them accepted as superior to other class cultures (see pp. 67–9 for a discussion of Bourdieu).

Drawing on Bourdieu, Wynne argues that classes are not fixed entities but are 'in continual flux and change'. As different groups develop their own cultures and struggle to get them accepted as legitimate symbolic capital, classes continually develop and change. Wynne uses his case study to show how what he calls the **new middle class** developed on a single housing estate in Cheshire.

The new middle class

To Wynne, the new middle class consists of just the sort of people who lived on the Heath. These people are employed in professional and managerial jobs. It is a new class because it is associated with the rapid expansion of work in the service sector of the economy. Members have a high income and are often socially and geographically mobile.

Most residents had moved to the Heath from outside the immediate area and a significant number had working-class origins and had been upwardly mobile to join the middle class. Some had achieved upward mobility through the acquisition of educational qualifications, whereas others had achieved it through promotion at work. Generally, those in professional jobs had relied more on qualifications to achieve their position, whereas those in managerial work had relied more on promotion by their employers. The managers tended to possess less educational capital (or qualifications) than the professionals. However, managers were likely to have higher pay.

Wynne found that the differences between well-paid but less well-qualified managers and less well-paid but well-qualified professionals came to be reflected in different lifestyles. For example, managers, particularly those of working-class origin and with low educational qualifications, were more likely to use the bar on the estate (Wynne called this group the drinkers). They tended to dominate the bar area, sitting or standing around the bar on a regular basis, sometimes making it hard for others to get served.

On the other hand, the professionals made much more use of the sporting facilities such as tennis and squash courts (Wynne termed this group the sporters). Many of the regular tennis and squash players took their sport seriously and organized matches against other teams. Getting into the squash or tennis team became an important source of social status. These groups ensured there was a complicated booking system for the courts which made it very difficult for the casual player to gain access to these facilities.

Wynne detected other differences in lifestyle between the two groups. Better qualified men tended to make more contribution to housework than the less well qualified. The drinkers enjoyed summer package holidays to hotels in the Mediterranean or North America. Watching horseracing and football were among their hobbies and they liked to eat out at steakhouse restaurants or to go on trips to musicals. The sporters, on the other hand, were more involved in voluntary organizations. They liked to take camping holidays or gite holidays in France. They were interested in avant-garde theatre rather than popular musicals. While the drinkers furnished their homes with fitted carpets and heavy upholstery, the sporters preferred parquet or tiled flooring and favoured sofa-groupings over three-piece suites.

Wynne argues that the drinkers can be seen as a:

> *petite bourgeoisie created from the ranks of the traditional working class whose advancement has occurred without the development of what Bourdieu terms cultural capital. Their position has developed primarily from the economic field and their leisure pursuits can be understood as an amplified version of those traditionally associated with the urban working class.* Wynne, 1998, p. 133

They are particularly concerned with having enough money to be able to afford an affluent lifestyle. The sporters, on the other hand, are more concerned 'with what is perceived as the "correct" form of consumption than its amount'. Wynne says, 'This group, largely college-educated, could be said to be searching for the cultural requirements of middle classness such as those associated with an appreciation of (high) culture.'

Conclusion

Wynne concludes that the new middle class is divided between two main groups according to differences in lifestyle and particularly the sort of capital (economic or cultural) which is more valued. This division reflects differences in education, class background and occupation, but it is not entirely determined by these factors. He says that 'leisure practices themselves become important locators of social identity'.

Wynne supports aspects of postmodernism (see pp. 84–6 for a discussion of class and postmodernism). He argues that people can choose their lifestyles and therefore to some extent their class position. Traditional class hierarchies based upon occupational status are undermined by the increasing importance of lifestyle and the fragmentation of the middle classes into different lifestyle groupings. Increasingly, it is consumption (such as the furniture people buy, the films they watch or the leisure facilities they use) that produces class distinctions, rather than economic divisions.

Evaluation

Wynne produces an interesting empirical study of differences between groups in the middle class. However, his conclusions could be seen as contradicting his research. He identifies clear differences in lifestyle, but his research suggests these are not simply a matter of choice. Rather, the differences seem to stem from systematic differences in paths to middle-class occupations. In terms of the categories used by Savage *et al.* (see above) the drinkers owe their position largely to **organizational assets** (management jobs), whereas the sporters owe their position more to the possession of **cultural assets** (particularly educational qualifications).

The divisions on the Heath could be seen as stemming more from objective class differences than from lifestyle choices. Wynne's conclusion seems to be based less upon the evidence of his own study and more upon a commitment to the view of postmodernists that people simply choose identities and lifestyles.

The working class

The market situation of manual workers

In most occupational classifications, the working class is usually regarded as consisting of manual workers. As we saw previously (see p. 46), there are important differences in the life chances of manual and non-manual workers. There are also important differences in their market and work situations:

1. Non-manual workers, on average, receive higher wages than their manual counterparts.
2. Manual workers have relatively few opportunities for promotion and their pay structure is unlikely to include incremental increases.
3. Compared to non-manual workers, manual workers have a greater risk of redundancy and unemployment.
4. White-collar workers tend to get more fringe benefits. Such benefits include company pension schemes, paid sick leave, the use of company cars, and so on.

Structure, consciousness and action

The above evidence suggests that manual workers form at least part of the working class in Britain. Marxist-influenced sociologists would also include routine non-manual workers in the working class.

However, many sociologists have argued that social class involves more than a similar market situation and similar life chances. Sharing a particular place in the social structure tends to lead to a shared consciousness or awareness of class, which in turn leads to actions which reflect this consciousness. Ray Pahl (1989, discussed in Devine *et al.*, 2005, p. 5) labelled this as the 'SCA approach' or 'structure-consciousness-action approach'. It follows Marx's belief that, at least in the long term, the working class would develop class consciousness and ultimately take revolutionary action. They would develop awareness of group identity, and some appreciation of and commitment to common interests. They would also develop some similarity of lifestyle and would usually share certain norms, values and attitudes distinct from those of other classes.

Until recently, much of the research on the working class was based upon the SCA approach. It tended to look for evidence of shared identity, the development of class consciousness and collective action by the working class. Where these characteristics were lacking it sought to explain the reasons for their absence. The following sections examine the arguments and research based upon this approach.

David Lockwood – the proletarian traditionalist

One of the most influential ways of looking at the working class using the SCA approach was developed by David Lockwood (1966). He identified and described the type of manual worker who exemplified the idea that the working class would develop a distinctive lifestyle and a strong sense of class consciousness. He called this type of manual worker the **proletarian traditionalist**.

Lockwood did not believe that this group was representative of the whole of the working class, but he did believe that the proletarian traditionalist was typical of close-knit working-class communities such as those based around dock work, coalmining and shipbuilding. When sociologists have discussed the extent to which the working class might have changed, they have sometimes made comparisons with the proletarian traditionalist.

The proletarian traditionalist lived in communities dominated by a single occupational group (such as coalminers, fishermen, steel workers or dockers). These communities are relatively isolated from the wider society. Consequently, they tend to produce a strong sense of belonging and solidarity. The workers are very loyal to their workmates and 'a strong sense of shared occupational experiences makes for feelings of fraternity and comradeship'.

Friendship with workmates extends into leisure activities. Workmates are often neighbours and relatives as well. They spend much of their leisure time together in pubs and working men's clubs. There is little geographical and social mobility, so the sense of belonging to a community is reinforced. The strong social networks 'emphasize mutual aid in everyday life and the obligation to join in the gregarious pattern of leisure'.

The proletarian traditionalist is not an individualist. Lockwood describes 'a public and present-oriented conviviality' which 'eschews individual striving "to be different"'. Unlike the middle class, proletarian traditionalists do not pursue individual achievement by trying to gain promotion at work or success in running their own businesses. Instead they identify strongly with the pursuit of collective goals. This is often expressed through strong loyalty to a trade union. This loyalty comes from an emotional attachment to the organization rather than from a calculation of the benefits that union membership might bring.

The proletarian traditionalist's attitude to life tends to be fatalistic. From this perspective there is little individuals can do to alter their situation, and changes or improvements in their circumstances are largely due to luck or fate. In view of this, life must be accepted as it comes. Since there is little chance of individual effort changing the future, long-term planning is discouraged in favour of **present-time orientation**. There is a tendency to live from day to day, and planning is limited to the near future. As a result, there is an emphasis on **immediate gratification**. There is little pressure to sacrifice pleasures of the moment for future rewards; desires are to be gratified in the present rather than at a later date. This attitude to life may be summarized by the following everyday phrases: 'what will be will be', 'take life as it comes', 'make the best of it', 'live for today because tomorrow may never come'.

By comparison, middle-class subculture is characterized by a **purposive approach** to life; humanity has control over its destiny and, with ability, determination and ambition, can change and improve its situation. Associated with this attitude is an emphasis on **future-time orientation** and **deferred gratification**. Long-term planning and deferring or putting off present pleasures for future rewards are regarded as worthwhile. Thus individuals are encouraged to sacrifice money and/or leisure at certain stages of their lives to improve career prospects.

Images and models of class

In addition to particular values and attitudes, members of society usually have a general image or picture of the social structure and the class system. These pictures are known as images of society or, more particularly, **images of class**.

The proletarian traditionalist tends to perceive the social order as sharply divided into 'us' and 'them'. On one side are the bosses, managers and white-collar workers who have power, and on the other, the relatively powerless manual workers. There is seen to be little opportunity for individual members of the working class to cross the divide separating them from the rest of society.

This view of society is referred to as a **power model**. Research has indicated that traditional workers may hold other images of society and that their perceptions of the social order are not as simple and clear-cut as the above description suggests. However, the power model appears to be the nearest thing to a consistent image of society held by a significant number of traditional workers.

By comparison, the middle-class image of society resembles a ladder. There are various strata or levels differentiated in terms of occupational status and lifestyle. Given ability and ambition, opportunities are available for individuals to rise in the social hierarchy. This view of the social order is known as a status or **prestige model**.

The above account of proletarian traditionalists is largely based on a description of men. Working-class communities have usually been seen as having strongly segregated gender roles. Husbands have been regarded as the main breadwinners, while wives have retained responsibility for childcare and housework. Husbands and wives tend to spend leisure time apart. While the men mix with their work colleagues, women associate more with female relatives. The bond between mother and daughter is particularly strong. (For a detailed description of gender roles in a traditional working-class community see Chapter 8.)

The description is also one which has been applied largely to white men rather than to members of minority ethnic groups.

Social change and the decline of working-class consciousness

The proletarian traditionalists with their distinctive lifestyle, strong sense of group solidarity and loyalty to collective organizations such as unions seem to fit well with the Marxist view that the working class would become increasingly class conscious and radical. However, sociologists have identified a number of social changes which might suggest that the working class is shrinking, becoming increasingly divided and losing its potential for class consciousness.

1. Manual workers constitute a declining proportion of the employed population of advanced capitalist societies. For example, since 1945 jobs in manufacturing have fallen by 54 per cent, while jobs in services have increased by 45 per cent (*Social Trends 2006*, p. 57).
2. Employment in the type of jobs which produced the proletarian traditionalist has declined rapidly. A process of **deindustrialization** has particularly affected industries such as mining, shipbuilding and steel production, all of which have shrunk dramatically.
3. The expansion of non-manual jobs has created considerable opportunities for upward social mobility from the working class to the middle class, which may have weakened class identity. This may have encouraged members of the working class to pursue individual achievement rather than maintaining solidarity with other workers in organizations such as trade unions.
4. The living standards of the population as a whole have risen rapidly in countries such as Britain and many members of the working class enjoy relatively high living standards. Even if they are working in manual jobs, they may aspire to middle-class lifestyles and may have little sense of working-class consciousness.
5. Rather than being a united group, the working class may be increasingly divided between those in different occupations and between those who are more or less successful.

The idea that the working class was failing to develop class consciousness as Marx predicted has a long history. As early as the 1950s some commentators were arguing that rising living standards were creating a new group of affluent members of the working class who had started to act like members of the middle class. **Affluent manual workers** were seen as developing a privatized home-based lifestyle and as becoming more concerned with purchasing consumer goods than with showing solidarity with their workmates.

Another variation on this theme suggests that home ownership, particularly among former council house tenants, has transformed the attitudes and values of some sections of the working class. Such theories have generated considerable discussion and research, which will now be examined.

Embourgeoisement

Writing in the nineteenth century, Marx predicted that the intermediate stratum would be depressed into the proletariat. During the 1950s and early 1960s a number of sociologists suggested that just the opposite was happening. They claimed that a process of **embourgeoisement** was occurring whereby increasing numbers of manual workers were entering the middle stratum and becoming middle-class. From the 1950s onwards it was suggested that a growing group of affluent manual workers were joining the middle class. As a consequence, the stratification system was increasingly dominated by a middle class which was growing rapidly.

Economic determinism

The theory used to explain this presumed development was a version of **economic determinism**. It was argued that the demands of modern technology and an advanced industrial economy determined the shape of the stratification system. For instance, the American sociologist Clark Kerr (Kerr *et al.*, 1962) claimed that advanced industrialism requires an increasingly highly educated, trained and skilled workforce which, in turn, leads to higher-paid and higher-status occupations amongst manual workers.

The supporters of embourgeoisement argued that middle-range incomes led to middle-class lifestyles. The process of embourgeoisement was seen to be accelerated by the demands of modern industry for a mobile labour force. This tended to break up traditional close-knit working-class communities found in the older industrial areas. The geographically mobile, affluent workers moved to newer, suburban areas where they were largely indistinguishable from their white-collar neighbours.

J. Goldthorpe, D. Lockwood, F. Bechhofer and J. Platt – the affluent worker in the class structure

In a famous study entitled **The Affluent Worker in the Class Structure**, conducted in the 1960s, Goldthorpe, Lockwood, Bechhofer and Platt (1968a, 1968b, 1969) presented the results of research designed to test the embourgeoisement hypothesis. They tried to find as favourable a setting as possible for the confirmation of the hypothesis. If embourgeoisement were not taking place in a context that offered every opportunity, then it would probably not be occurring in less favourable contexts.

Goldthorpe *et al.* chose Luton, then a prosperous area in southeast England with expanding industries. A sample of 229 manual workers was selected, plus a comparative group of 54 white-collar workers drawn from various grades of clerical work. The study was conducted from 1963 to 1964 and examined workers from Vauxhall Motors, Skefko Ball Bearing Company and Laporte Chemicals. Nearly half the manual workers in the survey had come from outside the southeast area in search of stable, well-paid jobs. All were married and 57 per cent were home owners or buyers. They were highly paid relative to other manual workers and their wages compared favourably with those of many white-collar workers. However, white-collar workers retained many of their market advantages such as fringe benefits and promotion chances.

If affluent manual workers were becoming middle-class they should be largely indistinguishable from white-collar workers in these areas. However, the research did not find that this was the case.

Instrumental orientation to work

The affluent workers defined their work in **instrumental** terms, as a means to an end rather than an end in itself. Work was simply a means of earning money to raise living standards. Largely because of this instrumental orientation they derived little satisfaction from work. They had few close friends at work and rarely participated in the social clubs provided by their firms. Most affluent workers felt that there was little chance for promotion. They were concerned with making a 'good living' from their firms rather than a 'good career' within their company.

Like the traditional worker, affluent workers saw improvements in terms of wages and working conditions as resulting from collective action in trade unions rather than individual achievement. However, they lacked a strong sense of class solidarity and union loyalty. The affluent workers joined with their workmates as self-interested individuals to improve their wages and working conditions. Thus the **solidaristic collectivism** of the traditional worker had largely been replaced by the **instrumental collectivism** of the affluent worker.

By contrast, white-collar workers did not define work in purely instrumental terms. They expected and experienced a higher level of job satisfaction. They made friends at work, became involved in social clubs and actively sought promotion.

Goldthorpe *et al.* concluded that, in the area of work, there were significant differences between affluent manual workers and white-collar workers.

Friendship, lifestyle and norms

Goldthorpe *et al.* found little support for the view that affluent manual workers were adopting middle-class lifestyles. Affluent workers drew their friends and companions from predominantly working-class kin and neighbours, while the white-collar workers mixed more with friends made at work and with people who were neither kin nor neighbours. Furthermore, the affluent workers showed no desire to seek middle-class status.

However, in one respect there was a convergence between the lifestyles of the affluent worker and the lower middle class. Both tended to lead a **privatized and home-centred existence**. The affluent workers' social relationships were centred on, and largely restricted to, the home. Their time was spent watching television, gardening, doing jobs around the house and socializing with their immediate family. There was no evidence of the communal sociability of the traditional working class.

Images of society

In terms of their general outlook on life, affluent workers differed in important respects from traditional workers. Many had migrated to Luton in order to improve their living standards rather than simply accepting life in their towns of origin. In this respect, they had a purposive rather than a fatalistic attitude. However, as we noted previously, the means they adopted to realize their goals – instrumental collectivism – were not typical of the middle class as a whole. In addition, their goals were distinct from those of the middle class in that they focused simply on material benefits rather than on a concern with advancement in the prestige hierarchy.

This emphasis on materialism was reflected in the affluent workers' images of society. Few saw society in terms of either the **power model**, based on the idea of 'us and them', characteristic of the traditional worker, or the **prestige model**, which was typical of the middle class. The largest group (56 per cent) saw money as the basis of class divisions. In terms of this money model, or **pecuniary model**, they saw a large central class made up of the majority of the working population.

Although differing from traditional workers, the affluent workers' outlook on life and their image of society did not appear to be developing in a middle-class direction.

Political attitudes

Finally, Goldthorpe *et al.* found little support for the view that affluence leads manual workers to vote for the Conservative Party. In the 1959 election, 80 per cent of the affluent worker sample voted Labour, a higher proportion than for the manual working class as a whole. However, support for the Labour Party, like support for trade unions, was often of an instrumental kind. There was little indication of the strong loyalty to Labour that is assumed to be typical of the traditional worker.

The 'new working class'

Goldthorpe *et al.* tested the embourgeoisement hypothesis under conditions favourable to its confirmation, but found it was not confirmed. Instead they found that affluent manual workers differed from both the proletarian traditionalist and the middle class. They therefore suggested that affluent workers were the vanguard of an emerging **new working class**. While the new working class was not being assimilated into the middle class, there were two points of **normative convergence** between the classes: privatization and instrumental collectivism.

These characteristics had developed as traditional working-class norms adapted to a new situation. Lockwood (1966) believed that the privatized instrumentalist revealed by the affluent worker study would gradually replace the proletarian traditionalist as the predominant group in the working class.

Fiona Devine – affluent workers revisited

Fiona Devine (1992) directly tested Lockwood's claim that the privatized instrumentalist would become the typical member of the working class.

Between July 1986 and July 1987 she conducted in-depth interviews with a sample of sixty-two people from Luton. The sample consisted of thirty male manual workers employed on the shop floor at the Vauxhall car plant, their wives, and two further wives of Vauxhall workers whose husbands refused to participate. By returning to Luton, Devine was able to make direct comparisons between her own findings in the 1980s and those of Goldthorpe *et al.* in the 1960s.

Geographical mobility

Like the earlier study, Devine's found high levels of geographical mobility. Some 30 per cent of the sample had grown up away from Luton. However, unlike Goldthorpe *et al.*, she did not find that they had moved to Luton in search of higher living standards. With high levels of unemployment in the 1980s many had gone to Luton in search of greater job security. Some of those who had moved from London had done so in order to find more affordable housing.

Orientation to work

Devine found that those in her sample were interested in using work as a means of improving their living standards. However, they were 'faced with the threat of redundancy and unemployment which hung over their daily lives'. Thus, while they wanted to 'better themselves', they were more concerned with attaining greater security. They expected no more than 'small, cumulative gains' in their living standards. Their consumer aspirations were more limited than those of their 1960s counterparts, though they were still rather greater than those supposed to be possessed by the 'traditional' working class.

The 1980s sample continued to belong to and support trade unions. Furthermore, they saw unions as a 'collective means of securing working-class interests'. Money was not their only concern, and other issues led to feelings of solidarity with fellow workers. Devine says that 'their poor conditions of work, for example, were often shared with fellow workers, and this was recognized to be the case'. They were also concerned about the distribution of power at work, and were interested in securing humane and fair treatment for their colleagues and themselves in their working lives. Many of them were critical of unions, but these criticisms were directed at union tactics and not at the principle of having unions to defend working-class interests.

Overall, Devine follows Goldthorpe *et al.* in describing the workers' orientation to work as instrumental collectivism, but she found more evidence of collectivism in the 1980s than had appeared to be present in the 1960s. The concern with money and living standards did not prevent them from feeling a sense of solidarity with fellow workers.

Friendship, lifestyle and norms

Like Goldthorpe *et al.*, Devine did not find that Vauxhall manual workers were befriending members of the middle class. In some respects they had traditional working-class friendship patterns: men had friends from work and many wives retained close contacts with relatives. Men still enjoyed leisure outside the home with other men, particularly playing sports or going to the pub. Traditional gender roles were also in evidence; although many wives had paid employment they still had primary responsibility for domestic chores. This reduced their freedom to engage in leisure outside the home.

Nevertheless, Devine did find important differences between her sample and the supposed characteristics of traditional workers. She says that they 'were not engaged in extensive sociability in pubs, clubs or whatever', and they did not have a communal existence based on their neighbourhoods. Their lifestyles 'did not totally revolve around the immediate family in the home' but at particular stages in the life cycle the home was very important. Families with young children had restricted opportunities for leisure in the community. Men were often working overtime to help provide materially for the family, and women had most of the responsibility for childcare. In short, their lifestyle was neither as communal as that of the proletarian traditionalist, nor as home-centred and privatized as Goldthorpe *et al.*'s affluent workers.

Images of society

The images of society held by Devine's sample were found to be very similar to those in the earlier study. They had a 'pecuniary model of the class structure'. Most saw themselves as belonging to a 'mass working/middle class' in between the very rich and the very poor. This did not, though, prevent them from sharing certain values with the traditional working class. Many felt resentment at those who had inherited money and a sense of injustice at the existence of extreme class inequalities. One said: 'I disagree with a silver spoon. People should work for their money, not inherit it.' They wanted some redistribution of wealth away from the very rich and, with it, the creation of a somewhat more egalitarian society.

Political attitudes

Devine did find evidence of declining support for the Labour Party. Only 24 of the 62 in the sample had voted Labour in the 1979 or 1983 elections. On the surface this would seem to support the view that affluent workers were increasingly voting for individualistic and instrumental reasons.

However, Devine did not find that disillusioned Labour Party supporters had abandoned their belief in the values traditionally associated with voting Labour. Instead, they had withdrawn their allegiance, perhaps only temporarily, because of the party's political failings. They were highly critical of the 'Winter of Discontent' in 1978–9 when a Labour government had presided over widespread strikes. They were also unhappy about the breakdown in relations between the party and the unions, and critical of the party's performance in running the economy during the 1970s, and of internal divisions during the 1980s.

A number of the disillusioned voters felt fatalistic about politics. While they still felt that theoretically the Labour Party represented working-class interests, they doubted its ability to deliver economic prosperity or low unemployment. Nine of the disillusioned Labour voters said they intended to vote Conservative at the next election. Yet they hardly embraced the Conservative Party with wholehearted enthusiasm: for them, 'the only positive attraction of the Conservatives was their policy of selling council houses which was seen as "giving people the chance to better themselves"'.

Conclusion

Devine's findings were rather different from those of Goldthorpe *et al.* some three decades earlier. She did not find that her sample had become the increasingly instrumental privatized workers predicted. She says:

> *The interviewees were not singularly instrumental in their motives for mobility or in their orientations to work. Nor did they lead exclusively privatized styles of life. Their aspirations and social perspectives were not entirely individualistic. Lastly, the interviewees were critical of the trades unions and the Labour Party, but not for the reasons identified by the Luton team [i.e. Goldthorpe* et al.*].* Devine, 1994, p. 9

Devine rejects the idea of a 'new' working class and denies that the affluent workers have been persuaded to accept capitalist society uncritically. They have aspirations as consumers and their living standards have risen, but they would still like to see a more egalitarian society. They have lost faith in the ability of unions and the Labour Party to deliver this objective, but they have not fundamentally changed their values.

G. Marshall, H. Newby, D. Rose and C. Vogler – continuities in the working class

There is considerable support for Devine's findings in a study of the British stratification system carried out by Gordon Marshall, Howard Newby, David Rose and Carolyn Vogler (1988). Based on a national sample of 1,770 adults, the study found that 'sectionalism, instrumentalism, and privatism among the British working class are not characteristics somehow peculiar to the recent years of economic recession'.

Marshall *et al.* claim that historical studies show that there were artisans who put primary emphasis on their home life, and who had an instrumental attitude to work, well back into the nineteenth century. Furthermore, their data on contemporary workers suggest that these workers retain some commitment to their work and do not follow completely privatized lifestyles. For example, 73 per cent of the sample thought that their work was at least as important as any non-work activity, and over half numbered one or more workmates among their friends. Marshall *et al.* concluded that there was no evidence of a significant shift towards instrumentalism and privatism.

Mike Savage – working-class identities reconsidered

In a recent article, Mike Savage (2005) has re-examined some of the filed data produced in the affluent worker studies of the 1960s. He has done so in order to critically examine the conclusions drawn by Goldthorpe and Lockwood *et al.* and to reinterpret aspects of their data. Savage does not dismiss the conclusions of Goldthorpe and Lockwood *et al.* Indeed he says, 'My argument here largely reiterates the conclusions drawn by researchers of the time, who emphasized the fragmented and contradictory nature of class identities' (Savage, 2005, p. 930). However, Savage believes that the interpretation of the findings in the affluent workers study was shaped by the preconceptions about class and class consciousness which were characteristic of sociology of the time. Savage interprets some of the data from the study rather differently from Goldthorpe and Lockwood *et al.*

- Goldthorpe and Lockwood *et al.* claimed that few of their respondents saw society in terms of a power model, but Savage found considerable evidence that a high proportion of respondents did believe there was a fundamental class divide between the rich and the rest. They may not have explicitly said that the rich had most of the power, but according to Savage the respondents did believe there was a close connection between money, 'the exercise of power, marriage and inheritance' (Savage, 2005, p. 934).
- Savage argues that many respondents had a stronger class identification than was realized by the researchers. Goldthorpe and Lockwood *et al.* saw class largely in terms of the occupation you had and its position in the class structure. Most respondents did not see class in this way but understood it as involving a combination of criteria including money, status and power. Most of the respondents (78 per cent) were willing to identify themselves as being working-class or lower-class, but they also tended just to think of themselves as 'ordinary'. They distanced themselves somewhat from sociological views of class, emphasizing that they were 'normal individuals', but they contrasted this with people from the upper class who were not considered to be 'normal' in the same way. In particular they saw themselves as normal because they had to earn their own living whereas the upper class did not.

On this basis Savage argues that 'Luton affluent workers might not have been so distinct from other groups within the working class which were researched at the same time and where there is evidence that respondents recognized power divisions' (Savage, 2005, p. 943).

A number of recent studies of class, such as those conducted by Charlesworth (2000) and Skeggs (1997) (see pp. 69–70 and 70–2), have claimed that people distance themselves from a working-class identity. They 'dis-identify' from class. Savage believes that such conclusions are misleading. His analysis suggests that there is considerable continuity in working-class identities. Despite all the changes in the working class, the emphasis on being ordinary in contrast to the upper class remains. Savage concludes, in contrast to Goldthorpe and Lockwood *et al.*, that 'working-class identities are not linked to particular work experiences' and the search for subtle differences in the class identities of different sections of the working class may have missed the extent to which the working class shares at least a basic class identity.

Divisions in the working class

Marxism and the homogeneous working class

Marx and Engels (1848) predicted that members of the working class would become increasingly homogeneous, or alike. The American Marxist Harry Braverman (1974) agreed with Marx. He claimed that the pursuit of profit had led to more and more automation in factories. This in turn had reduced the need for skilled workers and had led to an increasingly undifferentiated and unskilled working class.

Whether the working class has become more homogeneous has been debated by sociologists:

1. Ralf Dahrendorf (1959) argued that technology had led to an increasingly divided working class. Ever more complex machinery required more skilled workers to design, build and maintain it. This led to divisions in the working class between skilled, semi-skilled and unskilled manual workers.
2. Roger Penn (1983) agreed with Dahrendorf that the working class was divided, but argued that it was nothing new. From a study of cotton and engineering workers in Rochdale from 1856 to 1964 he found that there had always been divisions between workers with different levels of skill. Even those working in the same industry were often represented by different unions which reflected levels of skill. The unions defended the interests of their members, sometimes at the expense of other groups within the working class.
3. Ivor Crewe (1983) argued on the basis of research on voting behaviour that the working class was becoming divided into a new and an old working class on the basis of sectoral cleavages. Sectoral cleavages were specific factors, to do with residence, work, housing and union membership, which caused divisions in the working class.

   Crewe believed that there was a **new working class** whose members possessed one or more of the following characteristics:
   - They live in the south.
   - They are not union members.
   - They work in private industry.
   - They own their own homes.

   They could be distinguished from the diminishing numbers of old working class who lived in the north, belonged to unions, worked directly or indirectly for the government, and lived in council houses. Crewe found that the old working class were still very likely to vote Labour, but the new working class was increasingly deserting the Labour Party, the traditional party of the working class.
4. Gordon Marshall, Howard Newby, David Rose and Carolyn Vogler (1988) used data from their study of the British stratification system to evaluate the claim that the working class was divided. In general terms, they supported the view that the working class was divided into strata according to the level of skill involved in their work, but denied that the types of sectoral divisions identified by Crewe were significant. Like Penn, they argued that skill divisions were nothing new. Unlike Crewe, they found little

evidence that sectoral cleavages made much difference to voting intentions. Only housing tenure was found to be of any importance. Council house tenants were more likely to vote Labour, but the vast majority of council house tenants were working-class anyway.

5 Warwick and Littlejohn (1992) studied four communities in a mining area of West Yorkshire, surveying a total of 324 households in 1986 and 1987. Although they found some differences in the voting behaviour of council tenants and owner-occupiers, they did not follow Crewe in claiming that housing tenure itself was the cause of increased divisions within the working class. Instead, they argued that housing tenure reflected a polarization between the relatively economically secure who have regular employment, and the rest. For the less well-off members of the working class, insecure employment, low income and poor health, and residence in council housing, tended to go together. Rising unemployment in the economic recessions, combined with the sale of council houses to the better-off, had led to a 'cleavage between citizens who still have clear means of participating in democracy, and those who are being pushed into what some call an "underclass"'.

As we shall see, the idea of an underclass is extremely controversial and has been extensively debated (see pp. 64–6).

Class consciousness

Many Marxist sociologists argue that the contradictions of capitalism will eventually lead to a class-conscious proletariat. Class consciousness involves a full awareness by members of the working class of the reality of their exploitation, a recognition of common interests, the identification of an opposing group with whom their interests are in conflict, and a realization that only by collective class action can that opponent be overthrown. When practical steps are taken in pursuit of this goal, the working class becomes a 'class for itself'. Evidence from a variety of studies suggests that the working class is a long way from becoming a class for itself.

It has often been argued that the image of society held by proletarian traditionalists contains certain elements of class consciousness. The power model, with its emphasis on 'us and them', implies some recognition of common class interests, an indication of class solidarity, and at least a vague awareness of an opponent with whom the workers are in conflict. However, the affluent worker studies of Goldthorpe *et al.* suggested the proletarian traditionalist was already in decline and being replaced by a new working class as early as the 1960s.

Writing in 2001, Ken Roberts argues that most manual workers still see themselves as working-class, but beyond this there is little evidence of class consciousness. According to Roberts, the working class has become **disorganized**, and consequently lacking in class consciousness. He says that the working class has 'lost not only its capacity to act collectively but even to develop shared knowledge of its interests and common aspirations' (Roberts, 2001, p. 109). Roberts believes the working class has become **disempowered** by losing control over its key organizations (such as the Labour Party) and through a reduction in the influence of working-class movements. He gives a number of examples of this disorganization and disempowerment:

1 Trade union membership has declined and in some cases union membership is higher in middle-class groups than in working-class groups.
2 The Labour Party is no longer the party of the working class. In the 1990s the Labour Party tried to disassociate itself from being a party representing working-class interests. It weakened its links with trade unions and tried to build closer links with employers.
3 Not only have the above organizations ceased to be based in the working class, but members of the working class have also distanced themselves from them. Roberts argues that, compared to the 1960s, 'fewer manual workers today are even instrumentally attached to trade unions and the Labour Party' (Roberts, 2001, p. 109).
4 The Co-op, which used to be an organization dedicated to serving the interests of working-class consumers, 'has become just another retailer'.
5 Close-knit working-class communities in which working-class solidarity developed have been broken up by factors such as the decline of heavy industry, urban redevelopment and geographical mobility.
6 The working class has also become disorganized in its leisure. Roberts says: 'Working men's clubs and other community, free-time organizations have been largely replaced by television and commercial leisure.'

As well as the working class becoming disempowered and disorganized, it has also become **devalued**. Roberts believes that members of the working class find it increasingly difficult to take pride in being working-class. He claims that 'identifying with the working class is no longer associating oneself with a powerful group, or a way of life with features that others should envy' (Roberts, 2001, p. 109). To back up this claim, he quotes research by Beverley Skeggs (1997) into a group of working-class women in northwest England (see pp. 70–2 for a discussion of this research). Skeggs found that the women believed it was stigmatizing to be working-class and aspired to being seen as respectable. Roberts admits that men may feel differently from women about being working-class, but nevertheless claims that 'those who remain working-class nowadays are likely to feel that they are being left behind' (Roberts, 2001, p. 110).

The persistence of class consciousness

Not all sociologists believe that the working class is losing its sense of class consciousness. Fiona Devine (1992, 1994) believes that the seeds of class consciousness remain within the working class. Her study of affluent workers in Luton during the 1980s (see pp. 59–60 for further details) found considerable evidence of the persistence of class consciousness. The workers wanted to improve their living standards and those of their families, but that did not prevent them from perceiving society as unjust or from desiring change. They shared with other workers a similar living standard and a desire to improve it and gain increased security.

According to Devine, these shared experiences and desires were a basis for class solidarity. The affluent workers' sense of injustice focused on the very rich. Many resented the fact that, unlike ordinary members of society, the very rich did not have to work for a living. This led the affluent workers to hope for:

> *a more equitable distribution of resources in society as it stood, and, by implication, a more equal, free and democratic society in which people would be more justly and fairly rewarded than at present.* Devine, 1994, p. 8

Trade unions and the Labour Party were still regarded as 'collective means of securing both individual and collective ends'. However, support for them had declined because some of Devine's sample thought they had failed in delivering improvements for the working class.

While there was a strong awareness of a class division between the very rich and ordinary workers, there was less consciousness of a split between the working class and the middle class. Most of the sample thought that class divisions had declined in significance and saw themselves as belonging to a large class of 'ordinary' working people. Nevertheless, those who were employed at the Vauxhall plant still experienced a strong sense of class division at work:

> *Manual workers at the car plant were aware of a sense of superiority and separateness held by the foremen and white-collar workers which placed them in an inferior position. The status aspects of the organization of the workplace and people's attitudes of social superiority were a considerable source of grievance.* Devine, 1994

The affluent workers of the 1980s were more pessimistic about the prospects for changing society, but they had not lost the desire for change, nor their sense of class inequality. To Devine, they retained a considerable amount of class consciousness.

Inconsistencies in class consciousness

There is a tendency in many studies of class consciousness to assume that workers hold a clear, consistent and coherent image of society, and to mould data into neat, tidy categories. However, many individual workers do not hold clear and consistent views on society, as was found in a study of the ideology of 951 unskilled manual workers in Peterborough, conducted in 1970–1 by R.M. Blackburn and Michael Mann (1975). They found that both right- and left-wing views co-existed in the workers' ideology. Blackburn and Mann concluded that the workers did not possess consistent images of society.

In fact, Blackburn and Mann suggest that there is every reason to expect that this should be the case. The workers' experience of subordination and exploitation in the workplace tends to produce a power model of society and radical attitudes that demand a change in the status quo. However, the workers are also exposed to the ideology of the dominant class broadcast by the mass media and transmitted by the educational system and various other institutions. This ideology is conservative: it supports the existing social arrangements and states that the relationship between capital and labour is right, natural and inevitable. As a result, workers 'remain confused by the clash between conservatism and proletarianism, but touched by both'.

Beliefs and actions

On the basis of questionnaire research with a national sample of British adults, David Marshall, Howard Newby, David Rose and Carolyn Vogler (1988) reached somewhat similar conclusions to Blackburn and Mann. They claimed that class consciousness often did not produce a coherent view of the world. Respondents quite frequently gave inconsistent answers. For example, some respondents wanted both to leave the economy to market forces and for the government to intervene more in the economy. Some wanted higher taxes but were unwilling to pay higher taxes themselves.

The continuing relevance of class

Nevertheless, Marshall *et al.* emphasize the continuing relevance and importance of class for the British population. Rose and Marshall summarize some of their findings as follows:

> *Over 90 per cent of our respondents could place themselves in one of the conventionally defined class categories; 73 per cent viewed class as an inevitable feature of British society; and 52 per cent recognized the existence of class conflicts over important social issues in Britain.* Rose and Marshall, 1988 p. 23

Furthermore, half of the sample believed there was a dominant class that possessed economic and political power, and a lower class that had no economic and political power. There was a surprisingly widespread sense of injustice about the distribution of income and wealth in British society, with a majority of all social classes believing that the existing distribution was unfair; and, although lower classes were more likely to believe this, the percentage difference between them and higher classes was not particularly great.

Although people felt that society was unjust, and would have liked to see reforms that would make society fairer, they did not believe that such reforms were likely. Marshall *et al.* do not believe that class consciousness is automatically produced by the existence of class divisions. Despite the potential for class consciousness, the British population has not been mobilized in support of a programme that would tackle the sources of their sense of injustice. In this respect, Rose and Marshall point the finger at the Labour Party for having failed to tap the reservoir of potential support for change.

The lower strata

Although some sociologists see the working class as the lowest stratum in capitalist societies, others argue that there is a group beneath it. The most disadvantaged sections of capitalist society have been described in many ways. Kirk Mann says:

> *Terms such as 'the underclass', 'marginalized groups/stratum', 'excluded groups', 'reserve army of labour', 'housing classes', 'the pauper class', 'the residuum', 'relative stagnant population' and, more obviously, the poor, have all been used to describe a section of society which is seen to exist within and yet at the base of the working class.* Mann, 1992, p. 2

Of these terms, **underclass** is the one that has had the widest currency in recent years. Those sociologists who have identified a group of people at the bottom of the stratification system have seen them as having various distinguishing characteristics. These have included being poor, unemployed or dependent on benefits. In some cases they have been defined as a group whose behaviour contravenes the norms and values of society. Thus some sociologists have emphasized the economic distinctiveness of the lower strata, while others have concentrated on their supposed cultural or behavioural differences from the rest of the population.

In the latter case, the lower strata have been seen as constituting a social problem that poses a threat to society. They can also, however, be seen as a sociological problem for theories of stratification. Some theories of stratification have been based upon occupations, leaving the unemployed as a group who are difficult to categorize. In this chapter we will focus on the implications of the existence of lower strata for theories of stratification. Later chapters will discuss the relationship between the underclass and poverty (see pp. 242–7), and the underclass and ethnicity (see pp. 205–7).

Marx's view of the lower strata

The lumpenproletariat

In recent years, sociologists, journalists and politicians have all paid considerable attention to the 'problem' of the lower strata, but this interest is nothing new. In the nineteenth century Karl Marx was among those who expressed views on these groups. He used a number of different terms to describe those at the bottom of the stratification system of capitalist societies.

He used the word **lumpenproletariat** to describe the lowest group of all. The picture he paints of them is less than flattering. They are variously seen as:

> *This scum of the depraved elements of all classes ... decayed roués, vagabonds, discharged soldiers, discharged jailbirds, escaped galley slaves, swindlers, mountebanks, lazzaroni, pickpockets, tricksters, gamblers, brothel keepers, tinkers, beggars, the dangerous class, the social scum, that passively rotting mass thrown off by the lowest layers of the old society.*
> Marx and Engels, 1950a, p. 267

It is unclear from Marx's writing whether he regarded this group as a class or not. Although, at times, he did refer to these people as a class, at other times he dismissed the idea that they can form a class because he saw them as having little potential for developing class consciousness or taking collective action.

Kirk Mann (1992) argues that Marx uses a wide range of criteria to distinguish the lower strata from the rest of the working class. He says, 'Marx links economic, social and psychological issues to the pathology of individuals and social groups.' Marx does not stick to using the purely economic definition of class which characterizes his work on other classes. Furthermore, many of his views are so critical of the lower strata they seem to represent little more than personal prejudice.

One reason perhaps why Marx was so critical of the lumpenproletariat was that he did not see them as having the potential to develop class consciousness. Mann questions this view, suggesting, for example, that urban riots and the existence of claimants' unions (organizations for those drawing benefits) show that this group is no more conservative than the working class.

Unlike Marx, most contemporary sociologists have used the term **underclass** rather than **lumpenproletariat** to describe the groups at the bottom of the stratification system.

Charles Murray – the underclass in America and Britain

The underclass in America

Although not the first writer in recent times to use the term underclass, the American market liberal sociologist Charles Murray has probably done more than anyone else to popularize its usage.

In *Losing Ground*, published in 1984, Murray argues that the USA has a growing underclass which poses a serious threat to American society. He argues that government policies are encouraging increasing numbers of Americans to become dependent on benefits. During the 1960s, welfare reforms led to an increase in the numbers of never-married black single parents, and to many black youths losing interest in getting a job. Increases in the level of benefits and changes in the rules governing them discouraged self-sufficiency.

Murray argues that the growing size of the underclass is a threat to the social and economic well-being of the country because its members are responsible for a rising crime rate and the benefits paid to them are costly to tax payers.

The underclass in Britain

Murray visited Britain in 1989 and wrote an article for the *Sunday Times*. In it he argued that Britain too has a developing underclass, although unlike America it is neither firmly established nor is it mainly composed of minority ethnic groups. Murray defines the underclass in terms of behaviour. He says 'the "underclass" does not refer to a degree of poverty, but to a type of poverty'. These types of poor people were known to him in his youth and:

> *They were defined by their behaviour. Their homes were littered and unkempt. The men in the family were unable to hold a job for more than a few weeks at a time. Drunkenness was common. The children grew up ill-schooled and ill-behaved and contributed a disproportionate share to the local juvenile delinquents.*
> Murray, 1989, p. 20

Describing himself as 'a visitor from a plague area come to see if the disease is spreading', he found signs that Britain too is being infected. These signs consist of figures showing rising rates of illegitimacy, a rising crime rate and an alleged unwillingness among many of Britain's youth to take jobs. In certain neighbourhoods, traditional values such as beliefs in honesty, family life and hard work have been seriously undermined. As a consequence, increasing numbers of children are being raised in a situation where they are likely to take on the underclass values of their parents.

Evaluation of Murray

Murray's views on the underclass add little to theories of stratification. By insisting on using a cultural definition of the underclass he neglects any economic divisions that contribute to the creation of such a class. In many ways his work is better seen as a theory of poverty than as a theory of stratification. We will therefore evaluate his work in more detail in Chapter 4 on poverty and social exclusion (see pp. 242–7), where we will show that in America much of the evidence suggests that the benefits system does not have the effects he claims.

The evidence Murray uses to make the case for an underclass in Britain is flimsy and sometimes contradictory. He blames the underclass for its predicament, explaining the situation in terms of its own aberrant behaviour. To quote Kirk Mann, he sees the British underclass as 'criminally violent bastards who refuse to work'.

Most sociologists view the so-called underclass rather more sympathetically. Unlike behavioural and cultural accounts of the underclass, structural accounts tend to see the lowest strata in society as the victims of inequality. They therefore tend to make more explicit connections between the underclass and the stratification system of society as a whole.

Anthony Giddens – the underclass and the dual labour market

The middle class, working class and underclass

Unlike Murray, Giddens (1973) does not define an underclass in terms of behaviour. Instead he sees it in terms of its economic situation and he also integrates his theory of the underclass into a theory of stratification.

As mentioned earlier in the chapter (see p. 52), Giddens sees the middle class as those who possess educational or technical qualifications. This gives them an advantage in the labour market over the working class, who have only their manual labour power to sell. Members of the underclass also have to rely upon selling their manual labour power, but, compared to the working class, they are at a disadvantage when trying to do so. As a result, they tend to secure employment in the least desirable and most insecure jobs.

The dual labour market

Giddens argues that contemporary capitalist societies have a **dual labour market**. Jobs in the primary labour market have 'high and stable or progressive levels of economic returns, security of employment and some chance of career mobility'. Jobs in the secondary labour market have 'a low rate of economic return, poor job security, and low chances of career advancement'.

Employers need to plan ahead, and to be able to do so they need a reliable and committed group of workers in key positions. High and secure rewards are necessary to ensure the loyalty of these workers. This inevitably raises labour costs. In order to reduce overall costs, workers who are in less important positions and who are more easily replaced are paid much lower wages and are offered less job security. It is these secondary sector workers who come to make up the underclass.

The nature of the underclass

Giddens argues that women and minority ethnic groups are particularly likely to be found in the underclass. Employers recruit women to underclass jobs partly because of 'social prejudice', but also because they are likely to interrupt their careers as a result of marriage and childbirth. Minority ethnic groups are also the victims of discrimination and prejudice. In the UK, African Caribbeans and Asians are more likely than other groups to be in the underclass. Giddens argues that the underclass is likely to be more radical than the working class because their experience of deprivation makes them more sympathetic to radical social change.

Evaluation of Giddens

Critics have questioned Giddens's theory of the underclass.

Kirk Mann criticizes Giddens's theory of the dual labour market. He argues that there is no clear dividing line between a primary and a secondary labour market. For example, some jobs are well paid but with little job security; others are poorly paid but relatively secure. It is unclear from the dual labour market theory whether such jobs should be seen as primary or secondary jobs. Mann also criticizes the theory for failing to explain why some groups of workers (such as women and minority ethnic groups) tend to end up in the secondary labour market. The theory lacks an explanation of sexism and racism.

Duncan Gallie – a heterogeneous underclass

Duncan Gallie (1988, 1994a) is critical of the views of both Murray and Giddens. He accepts that there is a disadvantaged group at the bottom of the stratification system, but he denies that its members are culturally distinct (as Murray suggests) or that they form a class (as Giddens argues).

Gallie (1994a) used research data from a study of six local labour markets in England and Scotland. He found that both the employed and the unemployed had had an average of six jobs during their working life. On average the unemployed had held on to each of their jobs for almost as long as the employed (74 months as opposed to 76 months). Furthermore, the unemployed were more committed to working than the employed: 77 per cent of the unemployed said they would want to work even if they had enough money to retire in comfort, compared to 66 per cent of the employed and self-employed.

Gallie therefore dismisses Murray's claim that the unemployed have a culture that makes them unwilling to work. However, he also dismisses Giddens's claim that the underclass form a social class, arguing that they are too heterogeneous (or varied) to be considered a class. There are differences between males and females, those who are unemployed and those who are in low-paid work, and between the long-term and short-term unemployed. There are 'huge flows' of people into and out of the ranks of the unemployed every month, making the underclass too unstable to develop any class consciousness.

Gallie argues that most of the so-called underclass can simply be seen as the most disadvantaged section of the working class. They tend to display traditional working-class political beliefs, with more of the unemployed than unskilled manual workers saying they supported Labour.

However, Gallie does tentatively suggest that the long-term unemployed could be seen as an underclass because 'Their deprivations are distinctive from those generated directly by the employment relationship and they have the type of stability over time that is assumed by underclass theory.' He still insists that this group has close connections with the working class, though, and cannot be seen as completely distinct.

Evaluation

While Gallie successfully shows that the supposed underclass, particularly the unemployed, may not form a particularly cohesive group, some writers question whether this invalidates the idea of the underclass altogether.

Ken Roberts (1997) argues that the underclass includes a wide variety of groups with different lifestyles, but it may still be a useful concept. He says, 'hustlers, the homeless, and young single mothers do not share a common way of life. Welfare dependants who need to know their rights develop quite different skill repertoires to drug dealers.' Nevertheless, they all have certain characteristics in common. They are all more deprived than the working class, their deprivation may persist over considerable periods of time, and they may have lifestyles and social networks which are distinct from those in employment.

While Roberts is not sure that an underclass exists yet, in contrast to Gallie, he does believe it is quite likely that one is being formed and that it will become well established in the future. (See pp. 245–7 for ethnographic studies relating to the underclass debate.)

W.G. Runciman – the underclass as claimants

The underclass and the class structure

Runciman (1990) has devised a seven-class model of the British class structure based upon differences in control, ownership and marketability. This model was examined earlier in this chapter (see pp. 31–2). Runciman identifies an underclass at the bottom of his class structure. He explicitly rejects Giddens's view that it should be defined as 'a category of workers systematically disadvantaged in the labour market'.

Runciman mentions Gallie's work in suggesting that a different definition of the underclass is needed. He defines the underclass as 'those members of British society whose roles place them more or less permanently at the economic level where benefits are paid by the state to those unable to participate in the labour market at all'. Many are from minority ethnic backgrounds, and many are women, particularly single mothers, but it is their reliance upon state benefits that places them in the underclass, not their gender or ethnicity.

Criticisms of Runciman

Runciman appears to offer a straightforward and plausible definition of the underclass. However, Hartley Dean and Peter Taylor-Gooby (1992) have attacked his views. They point out that Runciman stresses the importance of 'career' in class analysis: that is, the future prospects and past history of individuals in the class system must be examined before allocating them to a class. Yet Runciman fails to take this into account when considering the underclass. For example, figures suggest that on average lone parents stay as lone parents for a mere thirty-five months. Similarly, most of the long-term unemployed have had jobs in the past. They are unstable members of the working class rather than members of a stable underclass.

To Dean and Taylor-Gooby, the so-called underclass is simply too unstable and impermanent to be seen as a class. They also attack Runciman for basing his definition of the underclass on quite different criteria from those used in his definitions of other classes. Members of the underclass are not defined in terms of their relationship to the market but in 'purely institutional terms'. They exist in a relationship with the state, not the economic system.

Conclusion

Whatever the merits or otherwise of different theories of the underclass, Dean and Taylor-Gooby (1992) suggest that there is a constant danger of the term underclass being misused. They say that 'underclass is a symbolic term with no single meaning, but a great many applications. It represents, not a useful concept, but a potent symbol.' It has become a symbol of 'socially constituted definitions of failure'. In society in general it is used to lay the blame on the disadvantaged for the social problems of which they are the victims.

Dean (1991) suggests that the term underclass should be abandoned. Not only is it misused, but in his view no underclass as such exists. He says that it 'does not usefully define a real or tangible phenomenon'. He believes that the debate about the underclass has touched on important issues though. He therefore concludes:

> *Recent structural and cultural changes have intersected, not to produce an 'underclass', but to shift the boundaries between core workers, peripheral workers and non-workers; between the individual and the family; and between the citizen and the welfare state. Such changes have also exacerbated regional inequalities and inner-city decay and, some would argue, may have contributed to rising levels of crime. We should not go in search of the underclass, but strive for a better understanding of structural and cultural changes and their complex interrelationships and effects.* Dean, 1991

(For a discussion of the underclass and poverty see pp. 242–7. For views on the underclass and ethnicity see pp. 205–7.)

Class identity and culture

The previous sections of this chapter owe a great deal to the influence of Marxist and Weberian perspectives on the study of stratification. As discussed earlier (see pp. 56–7), much of it stems from what David Lockwood has called the **structure–consciousness–action model** (Lockwood, 1988, discussed in Savage *et al.*, 2001). According to this model (the SCA model), 'class structure is seen as leading to class action through giving rise to a particular type of class consciousness' (Savage *et al.*, 2001).

However, Savage *et al.* note that an increasing number of sociologists have argued that you cannot simply read-off or predict class consciousness and class identities from people's position in the class structure. Sociologists who reject the SCA model see class identities as being 'ambivalent and weak' rather than coherent and strong, and they see class identity as actively created through cultural processes. In particular, class identities are created through awareness of **difference** from other groups, rather than simply being based upon a strong sense of belonging to one's own group.

While people may be aware of class, they may be reluctant to see themselves as belonging to a particular class, or they may play down their class identity because they do not wish to be associated with a specific class. One reason for this is that their class may be seen as having little **moral worth**. Andrew Sayer believes that people may:

> *feel class pride or shame and care a great deal about how they are positioned with respect to class and how others treat them. They are likely to be concerned about class in terms of recognition of their worth, and want to be respected or respectable.* Sayer, 2005, p. 948

These points are illustrated by Stephanie Lawler (2005) who discusses how the term 'chav' is used to disparage members of the working class who are deemed to dress and act in a way which shows a lack of 'knowledge and taste'. Because chavs are looked down on, people do not call themselves chavs and are likely to deny or dispute the application of the label to them. People might deny being chavs, and people who use the term might deny it has anything to do with class, but to Lawler the idea of chavs 'invokes class distinctions at every turn'. Furthermore, 'chavs' tend to be blamed for their lack of taste, dismissed as morally inferior and have restricted opportunities in life as a consequence. From this viewpoint, questions of culture and taste interact with the economic inequalities of class.

Many of the studies along these lines emphasize cultural differences, particularly differences in lifestyle, between groups in the stratification system. The biggest influence on these studies is the work of Pierre Bourdieu (1984).

Pierre Bourdieu – class and culture

Unlike Marxist and Weberian sociologists, Pierre Bourdieu attaches as much importance to the cultural aspects of class as he does to the economic aspects. In his most influential work on class, *Distinction*, Bourdieu systematically analyses the differences in culture and lifestyle between classes in France (Bourdieu, 1984, first published in French, 1979). However, Bourdieu does not see culture and lifestyle simply as products of economic differences. Culture and lifestyle can themselves shape chances of upward social mobility and becoming better off. Bourdieu argues that there are four main sources of capital in society.

Types of capital

1. **Economic capital** consists of material goods – wealth in such forms as shares, land or property, and income from employment and other sources. Wealth can be passed on quite easily through gifts or inheritance from parents to children.
2. **Cultural capital** can take a number of forms. First, it includes educational qualifications. Second, it includes a knowledge and understanding of creative and artistic aspects of culture, such as music, drama, art and cinema. In this artistic sense of culture, Bourdieu distinguishes different levels of cultural capital.
   (a) The highest level is what he calls **legitimate culture**. This is the culture of the dominant classes in society. It involves an appreciation of works of art in fields such as music and painting, which are considered to be the height of good taste. For example, Bourdieu puts the paintings of Brueghel and Goya in this category. Legitimate culture tends to be appreciated by those with the highest educational qualifications.
   (b) **Middlebrow culture** includes 'the minor work of the major arts'. They are generally accepted as having artistic merit, but are seen as less serious or worthy than legitimate culture. They are popular in the middle classes. Bourdieu gives the example of Gershwin's *Rhapsody in Blue*.
   (c) **Popular taste** is the lowest form of culture. In music, for example, it includes songs 'totally devoid of artistic ambition or pretension'. He cites Petula Clark as an example and suggests that some classical music, such as the Blue Danube, has become so 'devalued by popularization' that it too has become part of popular taste.

   Bourdieu does not argue that there is anything intrinsically superior about higher levels of culture. He sees this cultural hierarchy as socially constructed. It is used by classes to distinguish themselves from one another and by higher classes to establish and maintain their dominant position.

   A third type of cultural capital relates to **lifestyles** and the **consumption** associated with different lifestyles. Even in areas as mundane as eating and dressing, different classes distinguish themselves from one another through their differences in taste. Higher classes tend to prefer food which is 'light', 'delicate' and 'refined', whereas lower classes favour 'the heavy, the fat and the coarse'. Expensive or rare meat and fresh fruit and vegetables are popular with higher classes. Teachers, who have plenty of cultural capital but less economic capital, favour exotic or original cooking (such as Italian or Chinese food) which can be purchased at low cost.

Following on from differences in consumption, a fourth type of cultural capital is that which is **embodied**. People's bodies can themselves come to reflect and represent differences in taste. Diet affects body shape, and the way in which you present your body can suggest that you are 'vulgar' or 'distinguished', lower-class or higher-class. Such things as your haircut, make-up, and whether you have a beard or moustache can all function as social markers indicating your position in class hierarchies. Even your posture and gestures can be indicative of belonging to a particular class.

Cultural capital cannot be passed on from generation to generation in quite as straightforward a way as economic capital. Nevertheless, through socialization and the acquisition of the class habitus (see below) children from families rich in cultural capital do tend to acquire considerable cultural capital for themselves.

3 The third type of capital is **social capital**. Social capital consists of social connections – who you know and who you are friendly with; who you can call on for help or favours.
4 The fourth type of capital is **symbolic capital**. Symbolic capital is similar to the concept of status and refers to 'a reputation for competence and an image of respectability and honourability'.

Capital, class, lifestyle and the habitus

These different forms of capital relate to one another. For example, it may be difficult to accumulate economic capital without the possession of some cultural, social or symbolic capital. Without educational qualifications, the appropriate taste to enable you to mix in the right circles or to impress at an interview, the 'right' social contacts, or a reputation for competence, it might be difficult or impossible to get a well-paid job.

To a certain extent, one type of capital can be used to accumulate a different type of capital. The wealthy who lack cultural capital can spend extra money on education to help increase their children's cultural capital. Similarly those with cultural capital can use it to make social contacts or acquire educational qualifications which might help them make money.

Classes can be distinguished according to both the type and the amount of capital they possess and their past history. Groups who have been upwardly mobile through education may lack the knowledge of 'good' taste to fit in with those who have been established in higher classes for more than one generation. Groups high in cultural capital but low in economic capital (such as teachers) tend to have rather different lifestyles from those with plenty of economic capital but little cultural capital (such as successful small business people). It is out of such differences that each class, or class faction, develops its own habitus.

The **habitus** is 'a structured and structuring structure' consisting of a 'system of schemes generating classifiable practices and works' and 'a system of schemes of perception and appreciation (taste)' (Bourdieu, 1984, p. 171). In other words, the habitus consists of the subjective ways in which different classes understand and perceive the world, and the sorts of tastes and preferences that they have. A habitus tends to produce specific lifestyles. For example, it will influence the sorts of leisure pursuits that different classes follow, who they mix with, what sort of television programmes they watch, which newspapers (if any) they read, how highly they value education, what food they eat, and so on.

Each habitus develops out of a 'position in the structure of the conditions of existence' – in other words out of economic position. The habitus of the working class, for example, reflects their lack of money and their everyday struggle to make ends meet. Bourdieu claims that the working class are not particularly concerned about the aesthetic merits of household objects. It doesn't matter to them if things around the house look nice so long as they are affordable and do the job they were bought for. On the other hand, the habitus of higher classes reflects their economic security and the greater range of choices open to them. They are far more concerned that what they buy for their home looks good and is in the 'best' possible taste. The habitus therefore has a structure and it structures the everyday life of individuals.

A habitus is not fixed and unchanging. As the economic position of different groups changes, so will their habitus. Groups struggle to get their culture accepted as legitimate, and this too may lead to changes, as some tastes gain in legitimacy while others lose ground. As Richard Jenkins puts it in discussing Bourdieu's work, 'struggles about the meaning of things are an aspect of class struggle' (Jenkins, 1992, p. 147).

Success in the cultural field can bring economic success and so change the habitus. However, Bourdieu does not portray the class system as being very fluid. It is reproduced to a considerable degree. Dominant groups can to a large extent use their control over culture and what is considered good taste to maintain their position, pass it on to their children, and devalue cultures that do not stem from their habitus. As Jenkins puts it, 'the process of social reproduction is largely secured through a process of symbolic violence, a process of cultural reproduction'. Those from culturally disadvantaged classes are, by and large, kept in their place by cultural means.

Criticisms of Bourdieu

Despite being extremely influential, Bourdieu's work has come in for some criticism. Richard Jenkins makes four main criticisms of Bourdieu's work on class:

1 Bourdieu's view is rather deterministic. Although he tries to introduce an element of fluidity and change into his theory, the concept of the habitus implies a high degree of reproduction of class cultures from generation to generation. Those in particular classes seem to have a particular culture imposed on them by their position. The importance of individual choice and creativity is underplayed.
2 Bourdieu neglects the importance of social institutions in shaping class structures. For example, he does not discuss how the development of the welfare state may have influenced class culture, particularly among professionals employed by the state.
3 Bourdieu assumes that his study of France can be generalized to class cultures in other countries. Jenkins suggests that different countries may have rather different class cultures and queries how far Bourdieu's theory is applicable to the USA and Britain.

4 Bourdieu does not provide a convincing discussion of the working class. Jenkins says, 'the superficiality of his treatment of the working class is matched only by its condescension'. He questions the idea that the working class are entirely uninterested in questions of taste when buying things for their homes. He asks: 'Does Bourdieu really believe that it is alien to working-class women to furnish and decorate their homes on the basis of aesthetic choices?' (Jenkins, 1992, p. 148). However, as we shall see, some sociologists disagree with Jenkins's view and see Bourdieu's interpretation of working-class life as perceptive.

Whatever the weaknesses of Bourdieu's work, a number of contemporary sociologists have found it useful for developing their own theories and conducting their own studies of class, culture and identity. Some of these will now be examined.

Simon Charlesworth – a phenomenology of working class experience

If Bourdieu has been accused of neglecting working-class culture by some sociologists, the same is certainly not true of the work of Simon Charlesworth. Charlesworth's (2000) study is based upon interviewing people from Rotherham, a town in Yorkshire suffering from the decline of traditional industries and high levels of unemployment.

Charlesworth draws upon a number of theoretical approaches in his study, including phenomenology, but the biggest influence on his work is probably Bourdieu. He makes particular use of Bourdieu's concept of habitus, which he describes as a 'distinct way of being' and 'the socially constituted principle of perception and appreciation of the social world we acquire in a particular context' (Charlesworth, 2000, p. 29).

Unlike Jenkins, Charlesworth sees Bourdieu's portrayal of working-class life as insightful rather than superficial or condescending. He discussed Bourdieu's work with some of those he interviewed and he found that 'people were fascinated by the ideas and knew precisely what Bourdieu was expressing'. His study attempts to build upon Bourdieu's work by providing a rich description of working-class life in Rotherham.

Life in Rotherham

Rotherham has traditionally relied upon mining and steel production for employment. However, the nearby pits and the steelworks have both closed down, leaving what Charlesworth describes as 'devastation'. At one point Rotherham had 'the largest areas of industrial dereliction in Europe'. It suffered badly during the recessions of the 1980s, losing 8,000 jobs (out of a total of 82,000) in 1981 alone. It has not benefited as much as other areas from economic revival, with rates of unemployment, poverty and long-term illness all being much higher than the national average. Charlesworth paints a bleak picture of the town: 'The place, even according to many who live here, is ugly and depressing.' Areas of greenery tend to be covered in rubbish. Shops frequently close to relocate to the nearby Meadowhall shopping mall. The houses are often in poor condition.

However, it is not just the physical aspects of the town that are depressing. Charlesworth argues that the ugliness of the place 'manifests itself not just in the architectural structures that pattern the space, but in the manner and bearing, the comportment and style of behaviour of the people in the town'. There are many examples of this. Charlesworth says that:

> *the majority seem to smoke, too many are overweight, ill, and often lame too young; and too many are clad in dirty, often cheap, clothes. Young children play, till late, on the streets, and many teenagers seem hell-bent on destroying or damaging anything that is public.* Charlesworth, 2000, p. 55

Nights out

Friday and Saturday nights in Rotherham town centre are a key feature of the social life of many of the residents. However, even this is not exactly uplifting. People go out drinking in the pubs and clubs largely to be seen and to pick up, or to be picked up by, others. There is little in the way of meaningful conversation. Having a good body, looking healthy and dressing well enough to appear to have some money are the criteria by which people are valued. Charlesworth describes:

> *open-plan theme pubs and clubs, where the space is designed and used to be observed in. They are what people colloquially term 'meat' or 'cattle' markets. And, indeed, some of the men are steroid-ridden, swollen in a world where muscles matter. Men and women stand up all night and walk around in large circles, parading themselves, and surveying the value of what else is on this market, whilst also assessing what bodies compete with their own.* Charlesworth, 2000, p. 57

Charlesworth claims that 'what is said is unimportant, for this is an arena in which the truth of our society is clear: it is what you are that matters. Existence is bought with the value of the flesh.'

The working-class habitus

Charlesworth believes that the working class in towns such as Rotherham develop a distinctive habitus because of the conditions under which they live. Most of the residents of Rotherham are working-class. Their lifestyle, habits, attitudes, values and physical appearance all stem from the limitations they experience as members of the working class. Charlesworth says, 'the phenomenon of class, inequality, deprivation and powerlessness must be understood through their effect on the manner in which people come to exist in the world' and through the 'states and sensibilities that are social in the sense that they are prior to a particular individual's feeling and govern the range of feelings available'. The class habitus produces 'powerful affinities and aversions to persons, things and spaces' - and this tends to reproduce classes, encouraging them to stick to things which are familiar and appealing to them.

Members of the working class lack the money to develop the symbolic and cultural capital which would allow them to be accepted in middle-class circles. Life involves a daily struggle to maintain their dignity and make ends meet. Taste is based upon necessity rather than upon the much greater choices open to the middle class and affluent. For example, shell suits are a popular form of dress, although they are mocked by middle-class taste. However, from the point of view of the working class in Rotherham, they are a cheap, comfortable and practical type of clothing. They are especially popular with the unemployed, who spend much of their time at home.

In a culture based on necessity, there is little time for the niceties of middle-class taste and culture. Those who try to adopt aspects of middle-class lifestyle may be mocked. The working-class habitus emphasizes everyday, physical experience and devalues art, literature and other aspects of culture appreciated more by the middle class.

Nevertheless, people are all too aware that others have more possibilities and choices than them. As one interviewee put it, 'The best we can 'ope fo' is a video and a shag, if wi lucky.' But to Charlesworth this attitude does not stem from ignorance. It is a product of the circumstances of working-class life in Rotherham. There is little point in hoping for more than a video and a shag if you are going to be constantly disappointed. Furthermore, Charlesworth argues that a central reason for the disappointment is the education system.

Education and speech

It is largely in the education system that the working class learn to devalue themselves and restrict their ambitions. The most important reason why the working class do not thrive in the education system is because their way of talking and their use of language are devalued by the education system. According to Charlesworth, working-class speech stems from 'the urgencies of a world whose solicitations demand constant readiness which impinges upon consciousness'. Working-class people have to justify themselves to their bosses or to state agencies such as the DSS. The constant struggles of life leave little time or space for contemplation. This lack of space for contemplation leads to an immediacy in working-class speech. People get straight to the point – they avoid euphemism; they know they will not be able to get away with pretension.

> *Speech circles around the practical touchstones of working-class life: work and shifts; so many exchanges that go on between working men begin with 'What shift thy on?', or else 'I'm fucked this week, it's Zombie shift'; or in the absence of work, disgust at the bad treatment by the Department of Social Security.* Charlesworth, 2000, p. 215

In their speech, the working class reflect the fact that what they say 'is not valued, so what they say has no consequence'. They can say almost anything without it having much effect or cost. This is reflected in deliberate coarseness and derogatory comments to one another. The closest friends or partners will greet each other with expressions like 'Nah then shag', 'Nah then shithead', 'Ahr [Our] shit-fo'-brains', 'Nah then ugly', 'Nah then yer slapper'. These forms of familiarity reflect the ways that the working class are devalued by other classes. It establishes a common bond between people who can dispense with any pretence of their own value. Anyone who is aloof or posh (for example, teachers, politicians and officials from the DSS) is deeply distrusted.

Not surprisingly, these ways of speaking are not valued in the education system. According to Charlesworth:

> *the education system enshrines the culture of the dominant class as the national culture; it elevates one form of linguistic habitus to the status of legitimate, as the form of speech befitting those who are appropriate for senior and professional positions.* Charlesworth, 2000, p. 220

Success in the education system requires the use of more measured and euphemistic ways of speaking. Working-class speech is likely to be criticized by teachers and lead to a lack of educational success. Working-class speech patterns become 'hopelessly stigmatized', confirming the working class in their low status and largely confining them to jobs that require few qualifications. Knowing the way in which they are stigmatized by higher classes, the working class react by 'frequenting places that operate as protected enclaves which they can retreat to and avoid, with the help of drink and friends, the direct effects upon the body, of valuelessness'.

Evaluation of Charlesworth

Charlesworth's study provides interesting insights into the origin and nature of the habitus of the working class in Rotherham. Some sociologists have welcomed his work enthusiastically. Tim Ednesor (2000) praises Charlesworth for conducting a detailed empirical study of the culture of the working class, a group which Ednesor believes is increasingly neglected in sociological research. To Ednesor, Charlesworth's work challenges the views of those who believe the working class is disappearing. Furthermore, Ednesor comments that, 'the most impressive part of this marvellous book is that it shows how this culture is deeply enmeshed in, and emerges out of, conditions of struggle and necessity'.

However, there are some weaknesses in Charlesworth's work. He paints a rather bleak picture of working-class culture. It may be that Rotherham has suffered more from economic depression than most towns and cities, so the culture he describes may be untypically depressed and depressing. He fails to find much creativity or resistance in working-class culture and does not acknowledge that some people from the working class are successful in the educational system and experience upward social mobility. Charlesworth tends to portray the whole of Rotherham's working class as equally downtrodden and displays little sensitivity for differences within the working class.

Beverley Skeggs – formations of class and gender

The study

Like Charlesworth, Beverley Skeggs (1997) conducted a study of working-class British people using many of the concepts devised by Bourdieu. However, rather than examining the whole of the working class in a particular town, Skeggs conducted an in-depth study of a group of women. Skeggs focuses on how gender and class interact in creating a habitus. Although Skeggs follows Charlesworth in seeing the working class as being somewhat trapped in their habitus, she paints a less bleak picture of working-class life.

Skeggs used participant observation, interviews and secondary sources to study a group of eighty-three women who were enrolled on caring courses in a further education college in a town in northwest England. Overall, she studied the women for eleven years, following their careers after they had left further education. Skeggs describes her research as ethnography which was 'politically motivated to provide a space for the articulations and experiences of the marginalized'.

Working-class women

Skeggs argues that being a working-class woman in late twentieth-century Britain posed considerable problems. While there were some positive identities for working-class men (for example, those associated with trade unionists campaigning for their rights), it was more difficult for working-class women to establish a positive identity. According to Skeggs, 'the label working-class when applied to women has been used to signify all that is dirty, dangerous and without value'.

Unlike middle-class women, working-class women tend to be portrayed as lacking in respectability and as having a dangerous and unrestrained sexuality. Furthermore, working-class women tend to lack all the types of capital identified by Bourdieu. They are likely to have little wealth and be poorly paid, so they lack **economic capital**. They lack the **cultural capital** to succeed in academic subjects in the education system. They lack **social capital** in the form of relationships with those in positions of power, and they lack **symbolic capital** because the cultural and social capital they do have is not regarded as legitimate by people in higher classes. Lacking in capital, and facing negative perceptions of working-class women, they try to make the best possible use of the capital they do have. They try to challenge their working-class identity.

Working-class disidentification

It is not that the women want to be middle-class. They tend to see the middle class as pretentious and snobbish or 'hoity-toity'. But they do not want to be seen as working-class either. The women see the working class as 'poor, deprived, depriving, dangerous and degraded. They are well aware of the jokes about "Sharons and Kevins", about "takiness", about "white high-heeled shoes"' (Skeggs, 1997, p. 76). The women wish to avoid these connotations and so seek '(dis)identification' with the working class in particular and class in general. For example, one woman says: 'I just don't think class is a very useful term. I think I am probably classless. You know I'm not really one nor the other.' Another woman says:

> *I think it's just daft trying to fit people into pigeonholes. They say because you live on a council estate you must be working class … But loads of people own their own houses and just because they are on council estates it doesn't make any difference.* Skeggs, 1997, p. 77

This desire to **disidentify** with and escape from perceptions of themselves as working-class is particularly evident in two main areas:

1 First, by doing caring courses the women tried to establish that they were **respectable** and **responsible**. They lacked the capital necessary to get into higher education or well-paid jobs, and the academic side of the caring courses had little appeal. However, the practical side of the courses was appealing to them and related to their experiences of caring within families. The responsibility of looking after others (for example, in care homes) 'offered a means to feel good, even morally superior' and this was 'a powerful incentive when set against the prospect of unemployment'.

   The courses themselves emphasized the importance of respectability, for example through teaching good hygiene and discussing the effects of inadequate or irresponsible parenting. The women were able to come to think of themselves as caring and therefore respectable people, although the courses were 'framed by class relations that placed working-class women in a relationship of continually proving themselves as adequate to the standards of others. This means that their production of subjectivity is always open to scrutiny by others.'

2 A second area in which they tried to distance themselves from being seen as working-class was their **sexuality**. Here again they felt scrutinized by others and were concerned about being seen as tarty. Lacking in other forms of capital, they were aware that as young women they had a potential value in the 'marriage market'. However, if they dressed or acted in such a way as to be seen as 'tarts' or 'sluts' then they would be devalued. The women distinguished 'between being looked at in "admiration" and looked at as "sexual object". The former was acceptable, whereas the latter was not. Part of their cultural capital consisted of how to look good without looking tarty. Considerable time, money and effort were expended in getting this right. They developed rules such as '"you can't wear jeans and high heels" and "you can't wear white stiletto shoes and mini-skirts"'.

   Skeggs comments that 'all of the women wanted to be seen as desirable. To be valued was a validation of themselves.' However, they were usually more bothered about knowing that they could get a man rather than actually getting one. Ultimately, they did want to marry and settle down. They saw marriage as offering them respectability. There were fears about being 'left on the shelf' because it would show 'a lack of desirability'. Weddings were of great symbolic importance as 'the validation of legitimation'. Apparently marriage offered the women secure symbolic capital as respectable women who distanced themselves from the connotations of being working-class.

Although these women tried to distance themselves from class associations and refused to see themselves as working-class, Skeggs believes that class was fundamental to them. The place of the women in the class structure shaped the opportunities open to them. It also permeated their lives and particularly the ways in which they tried to make the most of such capital as they had. Skeggs says:

> *Class was completely central to the lives of the women. It was not only structural, in the sense that the division of labour organized what economic opportunities were available for them ... but also operated through a multitude of capital transformations and trading.* Skeggs, 1997, p. 161

Their attempts to distance themselves from a working-class identity ensured that class was important in their lives.

Evaluation

Skeggs's research was an in-depth study using a relatively small sample. This is both its main strength and its main weakness. It is a strength because it enabled Skeggs to develop a thorough understanding of the lives of the women she studied and to see processes of change over the eleven years she followed them. It enabled Skeggs to identify differences between the women and to avoid making sweeping generalizations. For example, Skeggs discusses one woman who goes against the views of the other women by seeing nothing wrong in sleeping around with many different men.

However, because Skeggs uses a small and untypical sample, it is hard to know how far her findings can be generalized to other working-class women. Because all the women were doing a caring course at a particular college, they may have been more concerned about appearing respectable than other working-class women.

The next study to be considered in this section examines class in less depth, but uses a somewhat larger and more diverse sample.

Mike Savage, Gaynor Bagnall and Brian Longhurst: *Class Identities in Northwest England*

The study

Between 1997 and 1999, Mike Savage, Gaynor Bagnall and Brian Longhurst (2001) conducted research based on 178 in-depth interviews on class identities in the Manchester area. The interviews were conducted in four areas:

1. Cheadle: a lower middle-class suburb of Manchester where the interviewees were a mixture of working-class and lower middle-class.
2. Wilmslow: a very affluent suburb where the sample consisted almost exclusively of highly paid managers and professionals.
3. Ramsbottom: an 'old industrial mill village' where a mixture of working-class people and managers and professionals lived, many on new estates.
4. Chorlton: a suburb near the centre of Manchester where most of the residents were young and middle-class, with jobs in the public sector or in the media and arts. A few long-established working-class residents were also interviewed.

Attitudes to class and identity

Savage *et al.* avoided using the term class early in the interviews. Nevertheless, about one-third of respondents referred to class before the term had been used by the interviewer. Often the question 'What type of people live around here?' would elicit a response about the class of residents. As Table 1.8 shows, however, a large majority of people were ambivalent about having a class identity.

Relatively few respondents thought Britain was becoming a classless society. This was demonstrated in a number of things they said. Some talked about 'the haves and have nots', others referred to the existence of an 'establishment', but few were willing to assign themselves, without qualification, to a class. Savage *et al.* comment: 'People have little difficulty in talking about class "out there", but do not like to think about class closer to home with respect to their own identity.' Savage *et al.* suggest that people tend to see class as '"out there", as part of the social fabric, whereas people themselves are "individuals", who by definition cannot be parts of classes'.

People were unwilling to see themselves as simply a product of their class background. They saw themselves as having more control over their lives than the idea of class might imply. Most people were therefore defensive about stating a class identity and, in line with Beverley Skeggs's arguments (see above), tended to 'disidentify' with class.

However, Savage *et al.* did find some people who identified clearly with a class. In Wilmslow, some of the older male professionals with high levels of cultural capital were happy to see themselves as middle-class. Furthermore, there was a minority of people who had 'a degree of inverted class pride in coming from working-class backgrounds'. Savage *et al.*

Table 1.8 Class identities

Respondents (and percentage of them in each place)

Place	Mentioning class spontaneously	Ambivalent about class identity	Thinking UK is becoming classless	Working class identifiers	Middle class identifiers	No class	N
Cheadle	16 (37%)	34 (79%)	3 (7%)	17 (40%)	8 (19%)	18 (42%)	43
Wilmslow	17 (40%)	30 (70%)	8 (19%)	3 (7%)	30 (70%)	10 (23%)	43
Ramsbottom	11 (24%)	31 (67%)	11 (24%)	12 (26%)	15 (33%)	19 (41%)	46
Chorlton	18 (39%)	32 (70%)	7 (15%)	6 (13%)	28 (61%)	12 (26%)	46
TOTAL	62 (35%)	127 (71%)	29 (16%)	38 (21%)	81 (46%)	59 (33%)	178

Source: M. Savage, G. Bagnall, B. Longhurst 'Ordinary, ambivalent and defensive: class identities in the Northwest of England', *Sociology*, Vol. 34, No. 4 Nov. 2001

go on to comment that '"Working classness" is not an entirely stigmatized identity that people tend to distance themselves from. This underestimates the continued moral force of working-class identities, at least for men.'

For the most part, though, it was those from working-class backgrounds who were most likely to feel threatened by the idea of class and deny that they belonged to a class. Those with more cultural capital, such as young university-educated respondents in Chorlton, were more willing to think about how class categories might apply to them. Most still ended up denying that they could be put in clear-cut class categories, but they were willing to think about how class affected their lives. They demonstrated a degree of 'reflexivity' by discussing how their own experiences related to class.

Savage *et al.* therefore argue that three main groups can be distinguished:

1 A 'defensive ambivalent majority'.
2 A small group of upper middle-class and working-class people who have strong class identities.
3 A group of 'reflexive class identifiers'.

Even those who were willing to express some class identity tended to be at pains to stress that they were just ordinary people, like everybody else. Some of those who saw themselves as working-class thought they were ordinary because the vast majority of ordinary people worked for a living. Some of those who identified themselves as middle-class saw themselves as ordinary because they were the class in the middle. Middle-class identifiers often distanced themselves from any idea that they might be 'snobbish'.

Conclusions

Despite the existence of a minority who retain clear class identities, Savage *et al.* generally support Skeggs's claim that it is common to disidentify with class. While using some of Bourdieu's concepts (for example, the concept of cultural capital), they disagree with his view that people are constantly concerned to 'display and construct cultural distinction of one type or another'. Instead, most of the sample tried to show that they were no different from others, that they were ordinary. But that did not mean that they avoided thinking in class terms altogether. Most recognized that classes existed, even if they did not want to see themselves as belonging to one. Furthermore, in seeing themselves as ordinary, they were acknowledging that there were others who were not ordinary, who were in a different class from themselves. Class had by no means disappeared from their understanding of the social world and their own identity. Instead, Savage *et al.* argue, 'We see then in people's accounts of class, a highly charged but complex ambivalence in which classes and individuals are held to be different yet so inherently related.' (For a review of the affluent worker studies by Savage see pp. 60–1.)

Geoff Payne and Clare Grew – Class ambivalence

The research by Savage *et al.* has been criticized by Geoff Payne and Clare Grew (2005). Payne and Grew conducted their own research in two English rural areas which were not in the northwest. Like Savage *et al.*, Payne and Grew used face-to-face in-depth interviews; their sample consisted of thirty-nine people.

Payne and Grew question the findings of Savage *et al.* that a high proportion of the population are ambivalent about class. They argue that the findings of their study were a product of the way the research was conducted and the way the data were interpreted. Savage *et al.* asked respondents, 'Do you think Britain is becoming classless?', immediately before asking them, 'What social class do you think you belong to?' Payne and Grew suggest that respondents were likely to see the second question as an extension of the first. The complexity of the issues involved in the first question may have led to answers which appeared ambivalent.

Furthermore, Savage *et al.* counted any answers which revealed any uncertainty whatsoever as showing ambivalence. For example, those who said, 'I suppose I am middle-class', were classified as ambivalent. Payne and Grew suggest that such replies might reflect 'general ambivalence' about changes in class as much as ambivalence about class position, because respondents were still reflecting on the previous question about classlessness.

In their own research Payne and Grew found only four people who completely rejected both the idea that society still had classes and the idea that they belonged to a class. All the other respondents talked in class terms, but the ways in which they discussed class were complex and varied.

A total of fourteen criteria were used to talk about class, including: 'money, income and financial inequalities', 'housing', 'aristocracy/upper-class people', 'educational qualifications', 'inter-personal attitudes expressing class superiority/inferiority', 'aspirations, getting on and personal achievement' and 'lifestyle'. 'Job types' and 'capitalism/the class system' were mentioned, but very infrequently.

The meaning of class for the interviewees was not only complex, but often it did not conform to sociologists' definitions of class. The apparent ambivalence in their responses reflected this complexity and the differences between their own understandings of class and those of sociologists. Payne and Grew say:

> ***interviewees normally express their views about class in a somewhat confused way, because they are being asked to handle a generally multi-faceted concept at short notice … The rejection of a simple label, therefore, is not necessarily a rejection of class self-identification.***
> Payne and Grew, 2005, p. 903

Conclusion

If Payne and Grew are to be believed, then levels of self-identification with different classes may be higher than Savage *et al.* believe. The methodological complexities of studying class leave considerable room for different interpretations of interview data. Despite the differences between them, the studies of Charlesworth, Skeggs, Savage *et al.* and Payne and Grew all found that class continues to exert a strong influence on people's lives. The first three studies also show that Bourdieu's approach can be used to understand both cultural differences between classes and class inequality.

Beverley Skeggs – the re-branding of class

Popular culture and the denigration of the working class

In more recent work, rather than conducting detailed empirical research into working-class culture, Beverley Skeggs (2005) looks at how working-class culture is presented in **popular culture**. She also broadens the debate about class and culture to consider the changing role of culture in shaping class divisions in general.

Skeggs argues that culture is increasingly important in capitalist societies. Capitalist businesses do not just sell physical commodities (such as cars, washing machines and food); they increasingly sell 'signs' and 'experiences'. For example, it might be the designer label that sells an item of clothing rather than the quality of the material itself; and leisure industries are increasingly based around experiences such as holidays, travel and adventure activities rather than physical products. Thus culture is more and more important for making a profit.

Culture has been *commodified* and this has made 'culture central to exploitation and surplus value production' (Skeggs, 2005, p. 47). Culture is now a vital part of advertising. For example, the fashion group Benetton's advertising has made extensive use of 'racial signifiers to generate a "multi-cultural" appeal' (Skeggs, 2005, p. 47). In this process, the cultures of different classes are valued differently, with working-class culture being seen as particularly lacking in value. Although always devalued, working-class culture is now seen as even more morally worthless than in the past and is identified with 'waste', and seen as 'lacking in taste, as un-modern, backward, as escapist, as dangerous, unruly and without shame' (Skeggs, 2005, p. 49). Even the bodies of the working class are seen negatively as representing such characteristics. Skeggs uses several examples to illustrate this process.

1 Skeggs discusses a survey conducted in the *Daily Mirror* in 1997 in which readers were invited to classify themselves through filling in a questionnaire containing twenty questions. Only three were about economic issues, with the rest about culture. Readers were asked to tick statements they strongly agreed with, including: 'I have sex too much', 'I go to Tuscany for my holidays', 'I never read books' and 'I take bottles, papers and cans to be recycled'. According to Skeggs, the scoring system inferred that working-class practices (such as having too much sex, owning big dogs, not reading, and going on cheap holidays in the sun) were less morally good than middle-class practices (such as recycling, going to Tuscany, exercising sexual restraint and taking physical exercise).
2 Skeggs discusses work by Tasker (1998) which examines film portrayal of working-class women. According to Tasker (and Skeggs), films such as *Pretty Woman*, *Working Girl*, and *Up Close and Personal* are concerned with how morally worthless working-class women can be transformed by changing their appearance and the way they speak to pass as middle-class. In these examples, class differences are **embodied** – they are part of the physical characteristics of the girls concerned.
3 Another example which links working-class tastelessness and moral inferiority is the way ownership of satellite dishes is portrayed. Skeggs quotes research by Brunsdon (1997) which equates the tastelessness of satellite dishes with a working-class identity.
4 Finally, Skeggs refers to research by Haylett (2001) which examined Tony Blair's choice of a run-down council estate in south London in 1997 to make an announcement about social inclusion. Skeggs says that Haylett:

> *shows how this announcement used the white working-class poor as symbols of a generalized 'backwardness' and specifically a culturally burdensome whiteness. The white working class become represented as the blockage not just to social inclusion, but to the development of a modern nation that can play on the global stage.* Skeggs, 2005, p. 56

Working-class culture as a resource

Skeggs does not believe that working-class culture is always denigrated in popular culture. In some cases it is seen as a 'resource' for the middle class who are attracted to its image of being authentic, tough or primitive. These characteristics can sometimes be used to sell commodities.

However, the middle class are sometimes laughed at in popular culture for their naivety about a working class they do not understand, and for their pretentiousness in trying to be working-class. This is reflected in the television comedy *The Royle Family*, which ridicules middle-class pretentiousness, and in the Pulp song 'Common People' in which the person who wants 'to live like common people' is despised and told, 'You'll never watch your life slide out of view, and dance and drink and screw 'cos there's nothing else to do' (quoted in Skeggs, 2005, p. 61).

However, portrayals in popular culture which give some value to working-class culture and ridicule middle classes who have a romantic attachment to working-class culture are very much in the minority and working-class culture is usually devalued. Behaviour which is seen as pathological in the working class (such as too much sex) is glamorized in the middle class. In the television programme *Sex and the City* the sexual desires of the lead characters are treated sympathetically because the characters have 'enough volume of other forms of cultural capital to offset connotations of pathology and denigration' (Skeggs, 2005, p. 63).

Culture and class conflict

Skeggs concludes that just as cultural factors have become increasingly important in differentiating between classes, so culture is also increasingly important in class conflict. She says, 'Class struggle becomes not just about the entitlement to the labour of others but the entitlement to their culture, feelings, affect and dispositions.' As the economy is increasingly dominated by the exchange of cultural signs, classes who lack the 'right' culture will see their economic opportunities restricted. Struggles over the moral worth of different cultures therefore become struggles over economic capital as well.

Conclusion

Skeggs's views reflect the increasing acceptance in the sociology of class stratification that both economic and cultural factors are crucial in understanding class. For example, Rosemary Crompton and John Scott (2005) stress that 'Culture and economy are intertwined' and argue that the study of both aspects of class is crucial to a full understanding of class divisions. They support a 'pluralistic stance in relation to research on class and stratification', in which research inspired by Bourdieu and more conventional types of research on economic inequality or class consciousness are all valued.

The next section examines research which is very different from the studies of culture considered in this section. The study of social mobility is largely quantitative rather than qualitative, and stresses economic opportunity above cultural differences. As Crompton and Scott imply, though, it is just as important for understanding class in contemporary societies as the types of research discussed in this section.

Social mobility

Ascription and achievement

This section examines the nature of social mobility in capitalist society. It is generally agreed that the rate of **social mobility** – the amount of movement from one stratum to another – is significantly higher in industrial societies than in pre-industrial societies. Industrial societies are therefore sometimes described as open. In other words, they have a relatively low degree of closure. In particular, it is argued that status in pre-industrial societies is largely ascribed, whereas in industrial societies it is increasingly achieved. As a result, ascribed characteristics such as class of origin, sex, race and kinship relationships have less influence on an individual's social status. Status is seen to be achieved on the basis of merit: talent, ability, ambition and hard work are steadily replacing ascribed characteristics as the criteria for determining a person's position in the class system.

The importance of social mobility

Sociologists are interested in social mobility for two main reasons:

1. Ken Roberts (2001) believes that social mobility is important because it gives some indication as to 'whether we are an equal opportunity society'. It reveals the extent to which people from different class backgrounds have the same opportunities to achieve higher class or higher status positions in society.
2. Roberts also argues that social mobility should be studied because it can help 'to establish the extent to which occupation-based classes are demographic entities'. Classes which have a relatively stable membership – where most of the children born into the class stay in that class – are more likely than unstable classes to 'develop distinctive class cultures'. Where there are high rates of mobility into and out of the class, the members of that class may have little sense of shared interests and will be unlikely to develop a strong and distinctive class culture.

For both these reasons the study of social mobility plays a vital part in understanding the class structure of any society.

Types of social mobility

Sociologists have identified two main types of social mobility:

1. The first, **intragenerational mobility**, refers to social mobility within a single generation. It is measured by comparing the occupational status of an individual at two or more points in time. Thus if a person begins their working life as an unskilled manual worker and ten years later is employed as an accountant, they are socially mobile in terms of intragenerational mobility.
2. The second type, **intergenerational mobility**, refers to social mobility between generations. It is measured by comparing the occupational status of sons or daughters with that of their fathers (or less frequently with that of their mothers). Thus if the daughter of an unskilled manual worker becomes an accountant, she is socially mobile in terms of intergenerational mobility.

This section will focus mainly on intergenerational mobility, the type of social mobility most frequently studied by sociologists.

The Oxford Mobility Study

The first major study of social mobility in Britain was conducted by David Glass in 1949 (Glass, 1954), but it had significant methodological flaws. The next major study of social mobility in England and Wales was conducted in 1972 and published in 1980, with an updated version published in 1987 (Goldthorpe, 1980; Goldthorpe *et al.*, 1987). Known as the Oxford Mobility Study, it is based on a seven-class scheme devised by John Goldthorpe.

Absolute mobility

The 1972 study revealed relatively high rates of **long-range mobility** (movement across several classes) compared to Glass's 1949 study. For example, 7.1 per cent of sons of class 7 fathers (the lowest class, containing unskilled and semi-skilled manual workers) were in class 1 (the highest class, containing higher professionals and high-grade managers) in 1972. The study found high rates of **absolute mobility** (the total amount of social mobility); in no social class did more than 50 per cent of the sample originate from the same social class.

The Oxford Mobility Study also found there was more **upward** than **downward mobility** because the proportion of non-manual jobs in the occupational structure had increased while the proportion of manual jobs had decreased (see below). It also found that the chances of those from working-class backgrounds reaching a higher social class had improved during the course of the century.

Relative mobility

On the surface, these findings seem to support the claim that British society is becoming more open. However, the study found that relative mobility chances varied greatly between the classes, and the relative chances had changed little during the course of the century.

The concept of **relative mobility** refers not to the total amount of social mobility, but to the comparative chances of those from various class backgrounds reaching particular positions in the social structure. Thus 45.7 per cent of sons with class 1 fathers – but just 7.1 per cent of those with class 7 fathers – ended up in class 1.

By comparing the relative mobility chances of different generations it is possible to determine whether the class structure has become more open. In Figure 1.4 those born in 1908–17 are compared with those born in 1938–47. The seven-class scheme usually used by Goldthorpe is simplified by amalgamating classes to reduce the number of classes to three. (The service class consists of classes 1 and 2, the intermediate class of classes 3, 4 and 5, and the working class of classes 6 and 7.)

Figure 1.4 shows that the chances of members of all social classes attaining service-class jobs increased over the period studied. However, this was largely the result of changes in the **occupational structure**: service-class jobs as a proportion of male employment rose from 13 per cent to 25 per cent, while intermediate jobs declined from 33 per cent to 30 per cent, and working-class jobs from 54 per cent to 45 per cent. The relative chances of the sons of those from different classes taking advantage of the increasing room at the top of the stratification system changed little.

This has been neatly summarized by Kellner and Wilby (1980) as the **1:2:4 rule of relative hope**. This rule suggests that over the period covered, as a rough estimate, whatever the chances of a working-class boy reaching the service class, they were twice as great for intermediate-class boys, and four times as great for service-class boys. In other words, there has been no significant increase in the openness of the British stratification system.

Trends since the Oxford Mobility Study

In a follow-up study Goldthorpe and Payne (1986) brought figures on social mobility more up to date by examining data from the 1983 British Election Survey. They wanted to discover whether economic recession in the period 1972–83 had produced different patterns of mobility from those found in the Oxford study, carried out during a period of economic expansion.

Overall, they found few differences between the results of the two studies. Service-class jobs continued to expand as a proportion of all male jobs; absolute mobility continued to increase, but relative mobility stayed about the same.

However, they did find that unemployment had affected the position of all classes, and the working class in particular. There were still opportunities for upward mobility from the working class, but members of the working class were more likely to become unemployed than members of the higher classes.

Elite self-recruitment

The Oxford Mobility Study and Goldthorpe's later work suggest that there is not a high degree of social closure at the top of the British stratification system, but Goldthorpe can be criticized for ignoring the existence of small elites, or, in Marxist terms, a ruling class. Goldthorpe's class 1 is a relatively large grouping, containing 10–15 per cent of the male working population. Studies that concentrate on small elite groups within class 1 reveal a much higher degree of closure.

The process by which members of wealthy and powerful groups are drawn from the children of those who already belong to such groups is known as **elite self-recruitment**. Thus the Oxford study, while showing a relatively high rate of mobility into class 1, does not indicate the degree of elite self-recruitment. A number of studies (discussed on pp. 533–4) show high levels of elite self-recruitment. Though class 1 as a whole appears fairly open, elite groups within that class are relatively closed.

Figure 1.4 Relative mobility chances of different generations

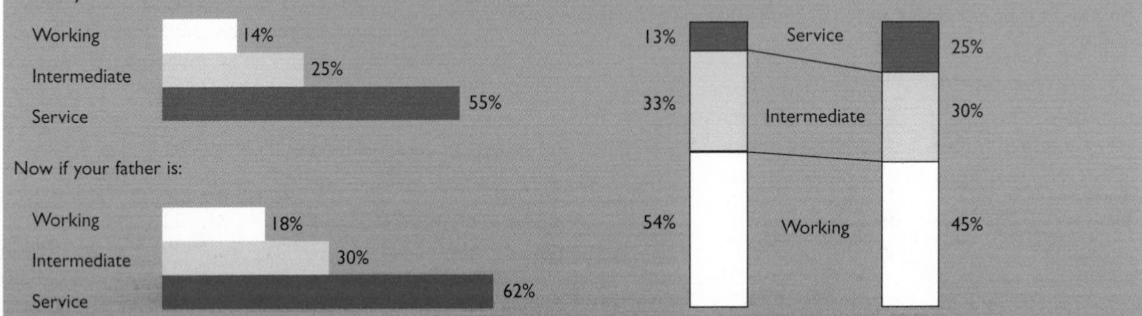

Source: P. Kellner and P. Wilby (1980) *The Sunday Times*, 13 January

Gender and mobility

J.H. Goldthorpe and C. Payne's views on gender and social mobility

A second major problem with the Oxford Mobility Study is the fact that it ignores women. Goldthorpe believes that the unit of stratification in industrial societies is the family. The class position of the family is given according to the occupation of the main breadwinner, which is usually a man. Other sociologists hotly dispute this view. (For details of the debate on gender and stratification see pp. 82–3.)

With specific reference to gender and social mobility, Goldthorpe and Payne (1986) have examined data from the 1983 British Election Survey to determine what difference it makes to the results of studies of social mobility if three different approaches are adopted to including women in the data:

1 In the first approach, women are included but their class is determined by their husband's occupation. Goldthorpe and Payne found this made little difference to either the absolute or relative rates of intergenerational social mobility found in studies using an all-male sample.
2 In the second approach, the occupation of the partner in full-time employment with the highest class position is used to determine the class of both partners. Single women are included on the basis of their own job. This approach also made little difference to relative mobility rates, although Goldthorpe and Payne conceded that it does at least allow information on women who are unattached or who are heads of households to be included.
3 In the third approach, individuals are allocated to classes on the basis of their own jobs. This showed that absolute mobility rates for women and men were very different. This was largely due to the fact that women are distributed differently from men in the occupational structure (see pp. 32–5). However, once again this method of including women in the data made little difference to the intergenerational, relative mobility rates of different classes. In other words, the social mobility chances of women compared to other women from different classes were as unequal as the chances of men compared to men from other classes.

Goldthorpe and Payne therefore concluded that the non-inclusion of women in earlier studies of social mobility was not important, since it made little difference to the overall results, at least in terms of determining the openness of the stratification system.

Alternative views

Michelle Stanworth (1984) is highly critical of Goldthorpe for insisting on categorizing women in social mobility studies according to the class of their husband. She prefers an approach based upon individuals being allocated to a class according to their own job.

Some research seems to support Stanworth's view, in that it shows important differences in the social mobility of men and women. Anthony Heath (1981) has used data from the 1972 and 1975 General Household Surveys to examine the intergenerational mobility of women. He compared women's social class with their father's class (though not their mother's) and reached the following conclusions:

1 Women of class 1 and 2 origins were much more likely to be downwardly mobile than men of the same class origin. This was largely because of the preponderance of females in class 3 (routine non-manual jobs).
2 Women from higher social classes were less likely to follow in their father's footsteps than men from the same classes.
3 On the other hand, women of class 5, 6 or 7 origins were far more likely to be upwardly mobile to class 3 than their male counterparts, although Heath points out that whether this movement can be considered 'upward mobility' is a moot point. As indicated earlier, some sociologists do not believe that routine non-manual workers have any significant advantages over most manual workers (see pp. 50–2).

Heath argues that the disadvantages suffered by the daughters of fathers in the higher classes are greater than the advantages experienced by the daughters of fathers from lower classes. If Heath is to be believed, then the British stratification system is less open than studies based on males would suggest.

Rather similar conclusions have been reached by Pamela Abbott and Geoff Payne (1990). They used data from a study of social mobility in Scotland to compare men and women. This study was carried out by Geoff Payne in 1974–5 and used a sample of 5,000 men born between 1909 and 1955 and 3,500 wives of these men.

The study found that many more women than men were downwardly mobile, fewer women were upwardly mobile, and very few of the women who did manage to be upwardly mobile ended up in the top two classes. Once again this suggests that the omission of women from data can give a misleading impression of absolute mobility rates. (For recent findings on female mobility rates see pp. 79–82.)

Pamela Abbott, Claire Wallace and Melissa Tyler (2005) argue that the openness of the stratification system for men is a result of the lack of openness for women. They say:

> *Women's preparedness to 'have a job' rather than following a career is certainly important in explaining male mobility; few 'dual income' families actually have two partners following careers – more often the man has a career and the woman fits her work into the demands of that career.* Abbott *et al.*, 2005, p. 70

The NCDS study of mobility

A more recent study of social mobility in Britain was carried out by Mike Savage and Muriel Egerton (1997). Savage and Egerton used data from the National Child Development Survey, a study of a national sample of children born in 1958. Savage and Egerton's study (the NCDS study) is based upon the class people had reached in 1991 when aged 33. Unlike the Oxford Mobility Study it included data on the social mobility of women. Women's social mobility was measured in relation to their father's occupation, not that of the chief earner in their household during their childhood.

Ken Roberts (2001) has adapted data from Savage and Egerton's study and the Oxford Mobility Study to make direct comparisons between the cohorts in the two studies in order to indicate changes in social mobility in the twentieth century. The comparisons use a simplified three-class model of service, intermediate and working classes.

Table 1.9 shows the destinations of those in the Oxford Mobility Study, while Table 1.10 shows their origins. Table 1.11 shows the destinations of those in Savage and Egerton's study, and Table 1.12 their origins. Table 1.13 compares the destinations of men and women in the Savage and Egerton study.

The extent of upward mobility

In the period between the two studies the class structure continued to change, with the contraction of the working class and the expansion of higher classes. This provided opportunities for intergenerational upward mobility from the working class. Despite this, it can be seen from Tables 1.9 and 1.11 that the chances of escaping from the working class had not greatly increased. A total of 55 per cent of sons from working-class backgrounds remained working-class in the NCDS study, compared to 57 per cent in the earlier Oxford study. However, the chances of those from working-class origins reaching the service class had significantly increased (from 16 per cent to 26 per cent). Nevertheless, those of service-class origin were still much more likely to end up with service-class jobs. In the NCDS study service-class sons were still more than

Table 1.9 Class outflows of males in the Oxford Mobility Study

Sons	Fathers			
	Service %	Intermediate %	Working %	Total %
Service	59	30	16	27
Intermediate	25	36	27	30
Working	15	34	57	44

Source: K. Roberts (2001) *Class in Modern Britain*, Palgrave Macmillan, p. 197

Table 1.10 Class inflows of males in the Oxford Mobility Study

Fathers	Sons			
	Service %	Intermediate %	Working %	Total %
Service	32	12	5	14
Intermediate	35	37	24	31
Working	33	50	71	55

Source: K. Roberts (2001) *Class in Modern Britain*, Palgrave Macmillan, p. 197

Table 1.11 Class outflows of males in the Savage and Egerton study

Sons	Fathers			
	Service %	Intermediate %	Working %	Total %
Service	61	40	26	36
Intermediate	20	26	19	21
Working	18	34	55	43

Source: K. Roberts (2001) *Class in Modern Britain*, Palgrave Macmillan, p. 197

Table 1.12 Class inflows of males in the Savage and Egerton study

Fathers	Sons			
	Service %	Intermediate %	Working %	Total %
Service	32	18	8	19
Intermediate	28	32	20	26
Working	40	50	72	56

Source: K. Roberts (2001) *Class in Modern Britain*, Palgrave Macmillan, p. 197

Table 1.13 Class inflows of males and females in the Savage and Egerton study

	Fathers							
	Service %		Intermediate %		Working %		Total %	
	Males	Females	Males	Females	Males	Females	Males	Females
Service	61	45	40	35	26	24	36	30
Intermediate	20	40	26	43	19	39	21	40
Working	18	16	34	22	55	37	43	29

Source: K. Roberts (2001) *Class in Modern Britain*, Palgrave Macmillan, p. 197

twice as likely to end up with service-class jobs as working-class sons were (61 per cent as opposed to 26 per cent).

The origins of class members

Tables 1.10 and 1.12 show changes in class inflows, that is, the background from which members of a class come. They give an indication of the extent to which different classes share a common class origin. Table 1.10 shows that in the Oxford study the service class came from diverse origins with fairly equal proportions coming from service-, intermediate- and working-class backgrounds. The working class, however, continued to be recruited very largely from the working class (71 per cent coming from working-class backgrounds). By the time of the NCDS study, 40 per cent of the service class were of working-class origin, but the working class remained largely composed of those of working-class origin (72 per cent).

Female mobility

Table 1.13 provides evidence of recent trends in female mobility compared to male mobility. In line with the studies discussed above, the NCDS study found significant differences in the mobility of men and women. It found that women were much more likely than men to move into the intermediate class from other classes. For example, 19 per cent of males but 39 per cent of females with working-class fathers ended up in the intermediate class. However, females with a service-class origin were less likely than men with this origin to follow fathers into the service class. Only 45 per cent of daughters stayed in the service class, compared to 61 per cent of sons. Savage and Egerton (1997) also found some evidence that daughters from all origins who ended up in the service class were more likely than men to end up in lower professional jobs (such as teaching and nursing) rather than higher professional and managerial jobs.

Conclusion

Discussing these findings, Roberts (2001) argues that 'very wide inequalities of life chances that operate in the middle class's favour' continue to exist. However, there is some evidence of greater openness in the class system. Furthermore, the middle classes have rather diverse origins. As the middle classes grow, however, Roberts believes that they will recruit increasing proportions of their membership from the middle class, which will tend to favour the development of a 'distinctive lifestyle, consciousness and politics'.

Although the working class continues to recruit most of its members from the working class, Roberts believes it may become more disorganized. With more opportunities for upward mobility, those who fail to be upwardly mobile may blame their position on their own inadequacies. Furthermore, the most talented people of working-class origin may tend to be upwardly mobile, with the result that the working class loses potential leaders who could organize and represent the class.

International comparisons of social mobility

Upward and downward occupational mobility

As previous sections have shown, there are many technical difficulties in carrying out studies of social mobility, and these have made it difficult to make international comparisons of social mobility rates. Occupational classification schemes used to distinguish classes have varied from society to society and comparable sets of data have not always been available. However, in recent years international comparisons of social mobility rates have become possible. One reason for this is that a number of countries have adopted similar occupational classification schemes based upon or similar to those of Goldthorpe's class scheme which has influenced the classification scheme adopted for British government statistics (called the NS-SEC – see p. 34).

An international comparison of mobility rates was published in 2004 by R. Breen (discussed in Scott, 2005), which produced figures on the proportions of the population who were upwardly and downwardly mobile. The results are shown in Tables 1.14 and 1.15.

Table 1.14 Mobility of men in eight countries, %

	Germany	France	Italy	Ireland	Great Britain	Sweden	Poland	Hungary
Upward mobility								
1970s	31.7	25.9	-	21.6	32.8	35.1	22.1	26.9
1980s	33.6	29.1	29.0	27.9	33.1	35.3	24.8	34.7
1990s	33.3	29.9	35.9	21.4	21.7	36.6	26.3	35.9
Downward mobility								
1970s	12.4	17.9	-	18.4	17.9	19.0	18.8	26.2
1980s	12.2	16.8	11.8	14.7	17.7	19.4	18.0	21.1
1990s	13.0	16.4	10.4	14.1	19.0	18.6	19.6	17.8

Source: R. Breen (ed.) (2004) *Social Mobility in Europe*, Oxford University Press, p. 48

Table 1.15 Mobility of women in seven countries, %

	Germany	France	Italy	Great Britain	Sweden	Poland	Hungary
Upward mobility							
1970s	25.8	27.8	-	27.5	23.9	19.5	23.2
1980s	29.6	32.9	38.5	29.0	27.5	31.7	38.8
1990s	32.2	33.2	36.7	30.6	33.5	34.1	42.0
Downward mobility							
1970s	22.8	13.9	-	24.6	31.5	14.4	30.8
1980s	19.2	12.8	12.5	23.7	28.9	16.8	19.4
1990s	15.2	12.8	11.3	22.5	24.4	16.2	13.7

Source: R. Breen (ed.) (2004) *Social Mobility in Europe*, Oxford University Press, p. 66

Table 1.14 shows that fairly high proportions of men achieved upward social mobility in all the societies studied, while downward mobility rates were substantially lower. This suggests that all the societies experienced some contraction of working-class jobs and some expansion of middle-class jobs. The highest rates of upward mobility across the three decades were in Germany, Sweden and Britain, and the lowest rates in Ireland, Poland and France. However, the overall **fluidity** – the total amount of male mobility both upwards and downwards – was lowest in France, Ireland and Poland and highest in Britain, Sweden and Hungary.

Amongst women, upward mobility rates had increased quite significantly for women in most countries and in some countries had overtaken men's rates. However, in several countries women had higher rates of downward mobility than men by the 1990s. In Britain in the 1990s women were still doing somewhat less well than men; they had lower rates of upward mobility and higher rates of downward mobility.

This comparative study also examined how far class origin influenced educational success and how far occupation was determined by educational qualifications. In the most meritocratic countries class should have little effect on educational success while occupational status should be strongly influenced by qualifications. Sweden was found to be the most meritocratic of the countries, and Britain was the least meritocratic. Indeed, in Britain there was no evidence of any decline in the influence of class background on educational qualifications achieved.

Income and social mobility

In a novel approach to studying social mobility Jo Blanden, Paul Greg and Stephen Machin (2005) conducted research on intergenerational mobility based upon income differences rather than occupational grouping. Using income rather than occupation as a measure of social mobility allowed simple comparisons to be made between countries and between cohorts (groups of people born at different times). Income levels are a direct measure of inequality, unlike occupation, since earnings can vary considerably within occupations as well as between them, but they are less directly linked with definitions of social class based upon occupations.

Blanden *et al.* divided the population into quartiles: that is, they distinguished between the lowest 25 per cent of income earners, the next 25 per cent earning below median income, the next 25 per cent earning above median income, and the top 25 per cent of earners. British data were based upon the National Child Development Survey (of a cohort born in 1958) and the British Cohort Study (of a cohort born in 1970). Data were also collected on seven other countries: the USA, Canada and five other European countries (see Table 1.18).

Tables 1.16 and 1.17 show the results for the two cohorts based upon earnings when 33 or 30. They show that for sons born in 1958, 31 per cent of sons born into the bottom quartile of income earners were still in the bottom quartile when they were 33, and 17 per cent had reached the top quartile. However, for sons born in 1970 only 16 per cent had reached the top quartile and 38 per cent were still in the bottom quartile. Thus there was less upward mobility for the cohort born more recently, contradicting conventional mobility studies which suggest that upward social mobility has been increasing. Blanden *et al.* therefore argue that 'intergenerational mobility has fallen over time in Britain; equality of opportunity declined for those born in 1970 compared with those born in 1958' (2005, p. 8). Furthermore this change was not found to be characteristic of other countries. They looked at similar data on the USA and found that upward mobility had increased over time.

Comparing mobility rates across all eight countries, Blanden *et al.* found that Britain had one of the lowest levels of social mobility. They examined the strength of the relationship between father's (or in some countries parents') earnings and children's earnings for the most recent cohort for which they had data. Table 1.18 shows the results. The higher the correlation then the closer the relationship between the earnings of fathers (or parents) and sons, and hence the lower the rate of mobility. The table shows that Britain (.271) and the USA (.289) had much higher rates than any other countries. All other countries had very similar rates to one another, with correlations between .139 (Norway) and .171 (West Germany). These results reinforce Breen's findings that Britain has comparatively little social mobility compared with most other countries.

In addition to examining the amount of mobility, Blanden *et al.* also examined the reasons behind the decline in mobility, by looking at educational qualifications. They measured the level of educational qualification by calculating how many years it would take the individual to get to their highest level of qualification after compulsory schooling had ended. They found that educational qualifications were becoming more strongly linked to level of income over time. However, the link between parental income and educational qualifications was also becoming stronger. The sons of affluent parents were taking much more advantage of increased opportunities in education than the sons of poorer parents, cementing their place amongst future high earners and leaving little opportunity for those from poorer backgrounds to get into the top quartile of earners. A rising proportion of children stayed on in education after the age of 16 from the mid-1980s to the late 1990s, but staying-on rates rose faster amongst the more affluent groups than amongst the less affluent.

Blanden *et al.* also examined more recent data from the British Household Panel Survey on a cohort of boys born in the late 1970s, to discover recent trends in the relationship between income and educational attainment. For this group, who reached the age of 16 in the mid-1990s, there was a weakening in the relationship between family income and staying on in education after 16. An increasing proportion of 16-year-olds from all backgrounds were staying on in post-compulsory schooling. However, there was a marked strengthening in the relationship between parental income and whether or not the children got a degree. The research found that:

> *Young people from the poorest income groups have increased their graduation rate by just 3 percentage points between 1981 and the late 1990s, compared with a rise in graduation rates of 26 percentage points for those with the richest 20 percent of parents.* Blanden et al., 2005, p. 11

(See Chapter 10 for more details on this and other studies of changes in educational opportunity and achievement.)

Table 1.16 Transition matrix for sons born in 1958

	Sons' earnings quartile when aged 33 in 1991			
	Bottom	2nd	3rd	Top
Parental income quartile when son aged 16				
Bottom	.31	.28	.23	.17
2nd	.30	.28	.23	.19
3rd	.22	.25	.25	.28
Top	.17	.20	.28	.35

Source: J. Blanden, P. Greg and S. Machin (2005) *Intergenerational Mobility in Europe and North America*, Centre for Economic Performance, London, p. 8 (data drawn from the National Child Development Survey)

Table 1.17 Transition matrix for sons born in 1970

	Sons' earnings quartile when aged 30 in 2000			
	Bottom	2nd	3rd	Top
Parental income quartile when son aged 16				
Bottom	.38	.25	.21	.16
2nd	.29	.28	.26	.17
3rd	.22	.26	.28	.25
Top	.11	.22	.24	.42

Source: J. Blanden, P. Greg and S. Machin (2005) *Intergenerational Mobility in Europe and North America*, Centre for Economic Performance, London, p. 8 (data drawn from the British Cohort Study)

Table 1.18 Internationally comparable estimates of intergenerational mobility

Country	Dataset	Sons born	Sons earnings measure	Measure of parental status	Intergenerational partial correlation
Britain	British Cohort Study	1970	2000 (Age 30)	Parental income 1980 and 1986 (average)	.271
USA	Panel Study of Income Dynamics	1954–1970	Age 30	Parental income when son aged 10 and aged 16	.289
West Germany	Socio-Economic Panel	1960–1973	2000	Parental income 1984 and 1988 (average)	.171
Canada	Intergenerational Income Data (from tax registers)	1967–1970	1998	Parental income when son aged 16	.143
Norway	Register data	1958	1992 and 1999 (average)	Father's earnings 1974	.139
Denmark	Register data	1958–1960	1998 and 2000 (average)	Father's earnings 1980	.143
Sweden	Register data	1962	1996 and 1999 (average)	Father's earnings 1975	.143
Finland	Quinquennial census panel	1958–1960	1995 and 2000 (average)	Father's earnings 1975	.147

Source: J. Blanden, P. Greg and S. Machin (2005) *Intergenerational Mobility in Europe and North America*, Centre for Economic Performance, London, p. 8

Evaluation and conclusion

Blanden *et al.*'s study does have some limitations. It only examined the social mobility and educational achievement of boys and it moved away from using conventional class categories in favour of considering income groups. The international comparisons were made on the basis of data collected in slightly different ways at slightly different times (see Table 1.18). However, the research is based upon sizeable samples, and measures of income inequality may be more reliable than complex occupational schemes used to determine people's class origin.

The study presents convincing evidence that, at least for men in Britain, there is now greater inequality of opportunity than there was a few decades ago. Parental income is having an increasing influence on children's income and chances of obtaining higher educational qualifications. This finding is in marked contrast to the views of those sociologists who believe that class inequality is declining in importance, or may even be disappearing. Such views will be examined below (see pp. 83–9).

Gender and social class

The issue of social mobility illustrates how gender was neglected in many early studies. When men were the main breadwinners in most families and comparatively few married women worked in paid employment, women seemed of little importance in theories of class to the predominantly male sociologists carrying out research. However, as women have increasingly combined paid work with domestic tasks and have become as numerous as men in the labour force, it has become impossible to construct theories of stratification without considering the position of women. The inclusion of women poses a number of theoretical problems for theories of stratification because women are more likely to work part-time than men, some women are housewives, and male and female partners may have jobs in different classes.

On the one hand, women might be seen as a part of the class structure without in any way forming a distinctive group within it. In other words, individual men and women are first and foremost members of a class rather than members of the gender groups 'male' and 'female'. This suggests that a working-class woman has more in common with a working-class man than with a middle-class woman.

Alternatively, gender groupings might be seen to cut across social class, and perhaps even be more important than class. This view implies that a working-class woman would have more in common with a middle-class woman than with a working-class man.

There are numerous variations on these points of view. In the following sections we demonstrate different ways in which sociologists have struggled to resolve the problem of the relationship between class and gender.

The household as the unit of class analysis

The first and simplest way to deal with the relationship between gender and class is to more or less ignore it. In official statistics in Great Britain a person's class is determined by the occupation of the 'head' of their household.

Before the 1981 census males were always considered to be the heads of households in which women also lived. Thus all the women in such a household were deemed to have the same class as the male 'head'. In the 1981 census the possibility of having a female 'head' of the household was first accepted, but in practice the class of the household was still very likely to be determined by the occupation of the husband. Single women and those in all-female households make up the vast majority of women whose class is measured in terms of their own occupation.

Ann and Robin Oakley (1979) point out that many sociological studies have followed this procedure. The family has been taken as the unit of stratification, and the family's class has been derived from the occupation of the family's head.

One supporter of this approach is Frank Parkin (1972). He argues that the social and economic rewards of women are largely determined by their marital and family relationships and, in particular, by the status of the male breadwinner. Parkin states:

> *If the wives and daughters of unskilled labourers have some things in common with the wives and daughters of wealthy landowners, there can be no doubt that the differences in their overall situation are far more striking and significant.* Parkin, 1972, p. 19

In other words, the inequalities of sexual status are insignificant compared to the inequalities of class status. However, Nicky Britten and Anthony Heath (1983) point to an obvious problem with this approach. In some families, which they term cross-class families, it is the woman who has the higher-class occupation on the Registrar General's scale: for example, a male manual worker married to a female non-manual worker. From an analysis of the data from the Child Health and Education Study of 1980, Britten and Heath found significant differences between these families and those in which both husband and wife had a manual job. For example, over 79 per cent of cross-class families had an income of over £99 per week, compared to 67 per cent of families with two manual workers. This might indicate that in cross-class families the wife's occupation is the best indicator of the family's class position.

Nevertheless, some sociologists maintain, with only slight reservations, that a woman's social class should still usually be determined with reference to her husband's occupation. For instance, Westergaard and Resler (1976) assert that the life chances of households are still largely shaped by men's positions in the labour market rather than the position of their female partners. In other words, Westergaard and Resler would claim that they are not being sexist, they are simply taking account of the 'facts': the class position and life chances of a family – indeed the type of employment of the wife – are all largely dependent on the husband's job.

John Goldthorpe – husbands, wives and class positions

John Goldthorpe (1983) further defends this position. He agrees with Parkin, and Westergaard and Resler, that the family is the unit of stratification. Furthermore, he relates class to a family's position in the labour market. He does not believe, though, that a male, where present, should automatically be considered head of a household. The head should be defined as 'the family member who has the greatest commitment to, and continuity in, the labour market'.

In theory this position might pose problems for existing methods of measuring class. If it were found that many wives had a greater involvement in, and commitment to, the labour market than their husbands, then the class position of many families might have been mistakenly defined in the past.

Furthermore, if there were many families in which it was unclear whether the husband or the wife had the greater involvement in the labour market, and their jobs placed them in different classes, it would be difficult to determine in which class to place many families. According to Goldthorpe, these problems do not arise for the following reasons:

1. First, by using data from the Oxford Mobility Study (for further details of this study see pp. 75–6), Goldthorpe claims that the vast majority of working wives withdraw from work once or more during their working life. Thus it is their husbands who have a greater commitment to paid work and therefore it is on the basis of the husband's work that the class of the family should be calculated.
2. Second, Goldthorpe denies that there are a large number of cross-class families in which the wife has a higher social class than the husband. He argues that many families only appear to be cross-class families because the class of the wife has been determined in an inappropriate manner. Most female non-manual workers have routine or unskilled white-collar jobs. Goldthorpe claims that these women have a much less favourable market situation than their male counterparts in lower-level non-manual jobs. The female workers tend to receive lower pay and fewer fringe benefits and enjoy less job security. In these circumstances it makes little sense to place such families in the middle class: the woman's job does not provide the family with middle-class life chances, and the husband's job is still the best measure of the family's class.

Criticisms of Goldthorpe

In a reply to Goldthorpe, Anthony Heath and Nicky Britten insist that 'women's jobs do make a difference', although they accept some of Goldthorpe's criticisms of the concept of cross-class families.

They admit that some non-manual jobs for women offer little significant advantage over male manual jobs. They accept that women working in sales (for example, shop assistants) and in personal services (for example, hairdressing) do not have what could reasonably be called middle-class jobs. However, those in professional, supervisory and managerial occupations clearly have a superior market situation to husbands in manual jobs. Furthermore, female junior office workers also have advantages over male manual workers. Heath and Britten therefore conclude that most families with female non-manual workers must still be regarded as cross-class families.

Stronger criticisms of Goldthorpe are advanced by Michelle Stanworth (1984). She argues quite simply that husbands and wives should be allocated to classes as individuals rather than as part of a family unit. Using data from the General Household Survey of 1979, she found that only 19 per cent of working men were the sole providers of financial support for their wives. Furthermore, she also suggests that the material situations of husband and wife are not necessarily the same. There may be inequalities within the family – for example, if the husband has more money to spend on personal consumption than the wife.

Individuals and families as units of stratification

David Rose and Gordon Marshall (1988) agree to some extent with both Goldthorpe and Stanworth. Their research into social class in Britain conducted in 1984 (see pp. 60 and 63 for further details) found that some class actions taken by women seemed to be affected more by the class of their family than by their own class. For example, the voting intentions of wives were better predicted by the class of their husband than by their own class.

On the other hand, Rose and Marshall found that class fates were affected more by the class of the individual than by the class of their family. Women had less chance of upward social mobility than men, regardless of their husband's occupation. Rose and Marshall concluded:

> *An approach to class analysis which takes the individual as the unit of analysis is as legitimate as one which takes families as the basic unit. Indeed, we believe that both approaches are important because social classes are made up of neither individuals nor families but of individuals in families.* Rose and Marshall, 1988, p. 18

(For details of studies which examine aspects of gender and class identity see pp. 70–2.)

The death of class?

There have long been claims that class is becoming less significant, that class analysis is no longer useful for sociologists, or even that social class is dying. According to David Lee and Bryan Turner (1996), as early as the end of the nineteenth century the German Eduard Benstein argued that improvements in the conditions of the masses were making class-based politics outdated. More recently, postmodern theorists have argued strongly that class is losing its significance or even dying.

Jan Pakulski and Malcolm Waters – postmodernism and the death of class

Class and other social divisions

In their book *The Death of Class* (1996) the Australian sociologists Jan Pakulski and Malcolm Waters claim that, 'like beads and Ché Guevara berets, class is passé, especially among advocates of the postmodernist avant-garde and practitioners of the new gender-, eco- and ethnocentred politics'. In other words, they believe that it is unfashionable to consider class important. While they admit that fashion alone should not dictate how sociologists see the world, they go on to say that 'arguments about the salience of class can no longer be dismissed as symptoms of ideological bias, intellectual weakness or moral corruption'. This is because, they claim, there is growing empirical evidence that class is losing its significance.

According to Pakulski and Waters, classes only exist if there is a 'minimum level of clustering or groupness', and such clusterings or groupness are no longer evident. People no longer feel they belong to class groupings, and members of supposed classes include a wide variety of very different people. Pakulski and Waters do not claim that social inequality is disappearing, but they do argue that there are new 'cleavages that are emerging in post-class society' which overshadow class differences. If people do not act as members of classes and do not see class-based issues as of special significance, then sociologists should not give special importance to class. To Pakulski and Waters, class can be seen as just one, not very important, division in society, along with 'race', ethnicity, gender, age, etc.

Types of society

Pakulski and Waters argue that the stratification systems of capitalist societies have gone through three phases.

In **economic-class society**, which existed in the nineteenth century, society was divided into property owners and workers. The property-owning class controlled the state, and culture was divided into 'dominant and subordinate ideologies and into high and low cultures'.

Organized-class society existed during roughly the first seventy-five years of the twentieth century. The state became the dominant force in society and it was 'typically ruled by a single unified bloc, a political–bureaucratic elite, that exercises power over subordinated masses'. The state elite exercised a strong control over the economy and may have followed policies of redistribution or state ownership of some industries. With this type of government in office the mass of the population tried to influence the state through political parties rather than through conflicts within industry.

In the last quarter of the twentieth century capitalist societies developed into **status-conventional societies**. In this phase stratification became based on cultural rather than economic differences. Pakulski and Waters say, 'the strata are lifestyle- and/or value-based status configurations. They can form around differentiated patterns of value consumption, identity, belief, symbolic meaning, taste, opinion or consumption.' People can choose their lifestyles and values and are therefore not restricted in the groups they can join by their background or job. Because people's tastes and identities can change rapidly, the stratification system 'appears as a shifting mosaic'. There are many different groupings within society based on these cultural differences and status depends on the values of these groupings.

Economic inequalities become much less important in shaping status differences. 'Symbolic values', the value of different images, become the crucial factor shaping stratification, and the conventions which establish these values form the basis of hierarchies in status-conventional societies. For example, the décor of your house becomes more important than the value of your house. Similarly, low-paid but desirable jobs in the media might give you more status than less well-paid but unfashionable jobs in manufacturing industry.

Pakulski and Waters distinguish four key features of the change in the stratification system in status-conventional societies:

1 **Culturalism**. Stratification is based on lifestyles, aesthetics and information flows. 'Material and power phenomena are reducible to these symbolically manifested lifestyle and value phenomena.'
2 **Fragmentation**. In this new type of society people have many different statuses based on their membership of different groups and different patterns of consumption. There is a 'virtually infinite overlap of associations and identifications that are shifting and unstable'.
3 **Autonomization**. Individuals become more autonomous or independent in their values and behaviour. People choose how to act and what to believe and you can no longer predict these things from their class background or other characteristics.
4 **Resignification**. People can change their preferences and identifications, leading to great fluidity and unpredictability in the status system of society. People constantly change what they see as especially significant.

In arguing for this change in the nature of stratification, Pakulski and Waters are highly critical of those theorists who, as they see it, cling to outdated notions about the centrality of class. They say that sociology is still failing:

> *to recognize that oppression, exploitation, and conflict are being socially constructed around transcendent conceptions of individual human rights and global values that identify and empower struggles around such diverse focuses as postcolonial racism, sexual preferences, gender discrimination, environmental degradation, citizen participation, religious commitments and ethnic self-determination. These issues have little to do with class. In the contemporary period of history, the class paradigm is intellectually and morally bankrupt.* Pakulski and Waters, 1996

To Pakulski and Waters, class politics is dead, and issues to do with ethnicity, gender, religion and cultural differences and preferences are far more important. People have become more interested in saving the environment than fighting for class interests, and a much wider variety of issues has become politically important.

Reasons for the death of class

Pakulski and Waters offer a number of explanations for the death of class. Class divisions in earlier years of the twentieth century were first undermined by the growth of increasingly interventionist states. The most interventionist states of all were fascist (for example, Nazi Germany) or communist (for example, the USSR). In other societies the development of welfare states and consensus between governments, business and unions reduced the direct impact of class relationships.

More recently there has been a shift towards 'market–meritocratic' relationships, where the state intervenes less in the economy and society. Alongside this, the division of labour has become more complex, and educational qualifications and professional skills have become more important than class background in shaping job opportunities.

Property has increasingly moved from private hands to being owned by organizations. Fewer large businesses are owned by individuals or families. Property ownership has also become more dispersed, making property 'a decreasing source of power'. Many people own their own homes and have some savings. Pakulski and Waters argue that in capitalist societies wealth became progressively more equally distributed during the twentieth century.

Pakulski and Waters accept that there is some evidence that in recent years class inequalities have started to grow in countries such as the USA, Australia and the UK. However, they argue that the changes are small, the trends inconsistent and any overall effect unimportant. In any case, 'short-term fluctuations are probably influenced more by the changing cash value of assets than by the redistribution of ownership'. For example, changes in house prices and share values affect the overall distribution of wealth as much as houses and shares changing hands.

With wider distribution of wealth, more people are able to consume products well in excess of what they need for physical survival. As a result, there is much more opportunity for individuals to demonstrate taste and to choose products that match their identities. Similarly they can judge others in terms of what they consume. Thus the ecologically aware might judge those who have more money but who consume ecologically damaging products to be inferior. Thus, consumption:

> *is becoming the standard by which individuals judge others and themselves. Consumer goods become signs of association and lifestyle. They are consumed for the images they convey, rather than because of utility or aesthetics, much less out of necessity. Few consumers would seriously believe, for example, that they can make a difference to the environment, much less to a clean domestic environment, by using 'green' household cleaning materials, but they can, by consuming them, indicate a commitment to environmentalist values.* Pakulski and Waters, 1996

Globalization of the world economy has meant that class inequalities within individual countries have become less important (see Chapter 9 for a discussion of globalization). Since exploitation now stretches beyond nations there is much less common ground for class conflict developing within particular societies. Partly as a consequence of this, voting and party allegiance become less based on class and there is a 'decline in the use of class imagery and consciousness in politics'. For example, Pakulski and Waters quote studies of voting in Britain, France, Germany, Sweden and the USA which suggest that there has been a decline in the strength of the relationship between manual workers voting for left-wing parties and non-manual workers voting for right-wing parties. In its place, 'new politics' based on non-class issues has grown in significance. They say:

> *class simply does not fit the wars and conflicts of the Middle East, the rise of Islamic fundamentalism, the Bosnian conflict, or the religious and ethnic conflicts of the Indian subcontinent. National, religious, regional, ethnic, gender, racial and sexual preference identities are much more important.* Pakulski and Waters, 1996

Although these various identities and non-class sources of conflict have always existed, they used to be overshadowed by class issues. Now, they overshadow class issues. Pakulski and Waters thus conclude that 'the intellectual armoury of class theory is about as useful for the contemporary social scene as a cavalry brigade in a tank battle'.

Even apparently new classes, such as the 'underclass', cannot be seen in conventional class terms. According to Pakulski and Waters, 'membership of the underclass is a function not of its members' exploitation but of their incapacity to consume. An earlier generation of social scientists wrote of poverty as a culture. Perhaps it is time to do so once again.'

Criticisms of Pakulski and Waters

Although Pakulski and Waters identify some important changes in capitalist societies, not surprisingly their claim that class is dying has attracted strong criticism:

1. Some writers have criticized Pakulski and Waters for using inconsistent and confused definitions of class. Harriet Bradley (1997) points out that at some points they use primarily economic definitions of class but at others they 'measure the existence of class in terms of its presence or absence in political discourse'. However, whether politicians talk in class terms is not crucial to whether class in economic terms exists. Bradley argues that, 'such definitional sleight of hand serves to write class altogether out of the script, where a more balanced assessment might suggest that class is legitimately seen as one of many aspects of social inequality and political identification'. Indeed, as earlier parts of this chapter have indicated, in Britain at least, people continue to believe that classes exist and see themselves as belonging to particular classes (see p. 63).
2. By claiming that consumption patterns and differences in lifestyle have become more significant than class differences, Pakulski and Waters neglect the obvious point that class differences influence the types of lifestyle that different groups can afford. It seems strange that they appear to think that the

underclass choose a poverty-stricken lifestyle rather than that they adopt such a lifestyle due to lack of money.

The culture of poverty theory, which Pakulski and Waters mention approvingly, has come in for sustained and highly damaging criticism (see pp. 240–2). Of course, people with similar levels of income can make different decisions about their lifestyles and consumption patterns, but those with few resources are inevitably excluded from the many choices that are only available to those with sufficient income or wealth. As John Westergaard (1996) puts it, 'consumer power, after all, is money power: quite simply, the rich and the comfortably off have much more of it than ordinary wage-earners, let alone the poor who are out of wage work'.

3 Pakulski and Waters have been criticized for making unsubstantiated generalizations. For example, Bradley (1997) points out that Pakulski and Waters claim that patriarchy is dying because new technology is freeing women from housework and the demands of childbearing. No real evidence is used to back up this claim, which contradicts a sizeable amount of feminist research. Furthermore, Bradley asks, 'what is one to make of wildly overstated generalizations like this: "the family is more or less entirely losing its function of social and cultural reproduction"?'

Bradley accuses much of *The Death of Class* of being 'a rehashing of the usual postmodern truisms about change, invoking consumerism, fragmentation and destabilization with insufficient empirical backing'. To other critics, this lack of empirical backing – the lack of adequate evidence – is also true of their claims about class.

Gordon Marshall (1997) argues that their work 'misrepresents the evidence in order to substantiate their arguments'. Pakulski and Waters quote work by Peter Saunders which argues that the consumption of housing might lead to a division between home owners and those in rented housing, without acknowledging Saunders's own admission that class remains the key factor shaping voting patterns in Britain.

Pakulski and Waters also claim that height differences between the classes are being reduced and ignore evidence that middle-class people in Britain are still, on average, about five centimetres taller than working-class people. Marshall concludes that, 'these illustrations confirm that the postmodernist critique of class analysis has largely detached itself from empirical reality'.

Ulrich Beck – risk society – 'beyond status and class'

Risk society

It is not only postmodernists who have suggested that classes may be dying out. Ulrich Beck also argues that contemporary societies are undergoing transformation, but not into postmodern societies. Instead, he sees society as changing to a risk society (Beck, 1992). According to Beck, there have been three main stages in the development of societies: **premodernity**, **simple modernity**, and **reflexive** or **late modernity**.

In simple modernity, religion and tradition were replaced by 'technological rationalization' and a sense of certainty which came from a belief in the ability of science and technology to solve problems. However, in the period of reflexive modernity, a **risk society** becomes established. In simple modernity most conflicts concerned the distribution of wealth. A shortage of wealth was a widespread problem: most people suffered from 'genuine material need'. People's chances in life were significantly undermined by a lack of money. The risks associated with poverty, lack of job security and inequality were at the forefront of people's concerns.

The inequalities produced by the class structure in simple modernity were analysed by writers such as Karl Marx and Max Weber. Since there was insufficient wealth to go around, the most important conflicts in society concerned the distribution of wealth. These sorts of issues remain paramount in the 'third world', where poverty and material scarcity are still major problems.

However, in Western Europe and other affluent societies, technological developments have led to a greatly increased productive capacity and a reduction in material need. It has become possible to produce enough to meet people's essential material needs. As Beck puts it, 'the struggle for one's "daily bread" has lost its urgency'.

In countries such as Germany, material scarcity ceased to be the main problem from the early 1970s. However, this did not mean the end of all problems and conflicts. Instead, a new series of problems began to confront such societies. The societies changed from **wealth-distributing societies** to **risk-distributing societies**. The central problem in society changed from creating and distributing wealth to managing the risks that were created by science and technology. In particular, science and technology came to be seen as creating problems rather than simply solving them. There was a growing awareness of the hazardous side effects and destructive potential of science and technology.

The problems of risk society

Beck uses a number of examples to illustrate the problems of risk society:

1 Thanks to developments in agriculture, shortage of food is no longer a problem in the rich countries. However, a plentiful supply of processed food has led to unhealthy diets, obesity and consequent health problems.
2 Atomic energy has helped to produce abundant energy supplies, but nuclear waste and the possibility of nuclear accidents create serious health risks for people.
3 Toxins in the environment, particularly in the air, water and foodstuffs, produce 'systematic and often irreversible harm'. The toxins are often invisible and people are not immediately aware of the risks they create.

Many of these risks are not confined to particular social groups. They may be as likely to afflict the wealthy as the poor, and are beyond the control of individuals. For example, the risks of atomic accidents do not just affect those working at or living near to a nuclear power plant. Radioactivity knows no geographical limits and can spread across national borders.

The rich may make some effort to avoid or minimize risks. For example, they can buy food which has less chance of being affected by pollutants – hence the popularity of organic food. They might choose to buy second homes or go on holiday in areas where environmental risks are low. However, they cannot avoid risks altogether. Like radioactivity, air and water pollution cannot be entirely avoided. Acid rain caused by industrial pollution in one country might affect another country. Some risks, such as the greenhouse effect and global warming and the depletion of the ozone layer, are global in nature. Nobody can avoid them. As Beck puts it, the only way to avoid all risks would be by 'not eating, not drinking and not breathing'.

In the latest phase of modernity the predominant concern becomes how to control the risks. People are no longer exclusively concerned 'with making nature useful, or with releasing mankind from traditional constraints, but also and essentially with problems resulting from techno-economic development itself' (Beck, 1992, p. 19). The biggest concerns of late modernity are problems created by modern science and technology. For these reasons Beck defines the latest period of modernity as **reflexive modernity**. In reflexive modernity people are concerned to reflect upon modernity itself and the problems it creates.

Individualization and the decline of class

In the risk societies of reflexive modernity the social groupings which were so significant in simple modern societies begin to lose their importance. In particular, class and status groups lose social significance.

Beck does not deny that inequalities between rich and poor remain. Furthermore, he accepts that the basic features of capitalism do not change. He says, 'the fundamental conditions of wage labour have remained the same'. However, according to Beck, 'ties to a social class recede mysteriously into the background for the actions of people. Status-based social milieus and lifestyles typical of a class culture lose their lustre' (Beck, 1992, p. 88).

Despite the continuance of inequality, people no longer feel a sense of class identity or base their lifestyle around class membership. The main reason for this is that risks are no longer related to class membership. In simple modernity, the working class were much more insecure than higher classes. In reflexive modernity, risks created by science and technology affect all classes. People cannot protect themselves against them by having a high income.

Even economic insecurity ceases to be based on class differences. Beck argues that in Germany unemployment has affected all classes. Between 1974 and 1983 about a third of Germans, from every class, experienced at least one period of unemployment. In this situation people do not experience risk as a class-based problem: it has the potential to affect everybody. Beck therefore believes that social inequality has been individualized. People experience and worry about risk as individuals rather than as members of a particular class.

A number of factors work together to encourage individualization and to undermine class cultures and identities. Education becomes increasingly important in determining opportunities. There is increased experience of social mobility and competition between people for jobs. Employment becomes less stable. People change jobs more often and fewer have a job for life. In all these respects, individuals have to make their own way through life rather than experiencing life in terms of class membership. They experience it as individuals involved in planning and shaping their own destiny.

Classes are increasingly divided between those with different levels of educational qualifications. As people become geographically mobile, moving from job to job, residential areas are no longer based around particular classes. Beck says, 'People from a great variety of social backgrounds are mixed together and social relations in the neighbourhood are much more loosely organized.' In these circumstances, people can no longer rely on relating to others in terms of class culture. 'The newly formed social relationships and social networks now have to be individually chosen; social ties, too, are becoming reflexive, so that they have to be established, maintained, and constantly renewed by individuals.'

In politics, too, the importance of class declines. Political conflicts increasingly take the form of 'temporary coalitions' between individuals concerned about a particular problem, such as an ecological threat. Risks which affect all classes become an important focus of political concern.

People continue to experience discrimination resulting from 'ascribed characteristics'. Conflicts in terms of such characteristics as 'race, skin colour, gender, ethnicity, age, homosexuality, physical disabilities' rise to prominence as the importance of class declines.

Beck does not argue that class solidarity disappears completely, or immediately. There is a gradual process whereby class loses its social significance. The end result will be a situation where 'Class society will pale into insignificance beside an individualized society of employees.'

Evaluation of Beck's Risk Society

Beck's work on risk society has been widely influential, but it has also been subject to criticism. A key criticism is that Beck greatly exaggerates the shift from a society in which risks stemmed from scarcity to a society in which risks affect all classes however well-off they might be.

Alan Scott (2000) argues that even in pre-industrial times the rich could not isolate themselves from all risks. Problems such as harvest failure could affect the food supply of the rich. Infectious diseases, which were responsible for many deaths, and natural disasters knew no class boundaries. Scott also argues that in contemporary societies money can give far more protection from risks than Beck acknowledges. Scott says, 'Those who can, do move away from areas of high pollution, environmental degradation and danger.' They cannot isolate themselves from total catastrophe (such as nuclear war).

Beck recognizes that inequality continues to exist, but he does not acknowledge the extent to which this still affects life chances. As discussed earlier (see p. 46), class differences continue to affect life expectancy and child mortality.

Beck can also be criticized for simply asserting that class no longer has a significant effect on identity, or influences differences in lifestyle. There is much empirical research that suggests class identities still exist (see, for example, Marshall *et al.*, 1988, pp. 55–6) and that class still influences lifestyle (see, for example, Devine, 1992, pp. 53–4 or Skeggs, 1997, pp. 69–70). Like postmodernists such as Pakulski and Waters, Beck has a tendency to make unsubstantiated generalizations.

John H. Westergaard – the hardening of class inequality

John Westergaard (1995, 1996b) takes a very different approach from that of Pakulski and Waters and Beck. He argues that, far from dying, class differences became stronger in the late twentieth century, particularly in Britain. While the claims of postmodernists, Beck's work and politicians' rhetoric might suggest that class is less important, the objective reality is that class divisions are becoming more important, not less.

Westergaard broadly follows Weberian and Marxist approaches to class, saying that 'class structure is first of all a matter of people's circumstances in life as set by their unequal places in the economic order'. He goes on to state unequivocally, 'in that sense, class structure has recently hardened in Britain'. He tries to substantiate this claim with a range of empirical evidence.

Evidence of the hardening of class structure

Westergaard (1996b) quotes a variety of statistics from British government sources to back up his claim:

1. Between 1980 and 1990 the earnings of the highest-paid 10 per cent of white-collar workers rose by approximately 40 per cent in real terms, while the poorest-paid 10 per cent of blue-collar workers saw virtually no rise in their real incomes.
2. The share of total household income going to the poorest 20 per cent of households fell from 10 per cent in the late 1970s to 7 per cent by the late 1980s, while the share of the richest 20 per cent grew from 37 per cent to 44 per cent.
3. Private ownership of property has become more concentrated. Thus the share of marketable wealth owned by the richest 5 per cent of the British population rose from 36 per cent at the start of the 1980s to 38 per cent at the end of that decade.

Westergaard argues that the power of the highest social classes, and of big business, has also been growing. He says that:

> *the power of private business has grown, of course, as free market policies intended. To take just one instance, business representation in the governance of public education and health has been consistently stepped up; and, more generally, business-style prescriptions for 'cost-efficiency' have spread widely in the conduct of public-sector affairs.* Westergaard, 1996b

The denationalization of public enterprises (such as British Steel and British Airways) has concentrated more power in the hands of private businesses. Changes in the City of London have increased the power of finance capitalists, while the influence of trade unions has declined. According to Westergaard, 'a small network of top people from top corporations and institutions', including 'insurance companies and pension funds', wields enormous power which 'comes from the mass of corporate assets whose strategic deployment they lead'. The top class comprises less than 1 per cent of the total population but, from this viewpoint, its power steadily increased from 1979 to the late 1990s.

Reasons for the hardening of class inequality

The main reasons for these changes, according to Westergaard, are economic and political. Economic growth has become more varied and the North American and Western European economies have faced growing competition from Asia. Transnational corporations have developed faster than nationally based companies.

British government policies changed from 1979 onwards in response to these developments. What Westergaard calls the 'class compromise' of the 1940s involved redistributive taxation and a commitment to the welfare state and state ownership of some industries. Conservative governments strengthened the importance of market relationships in the economy and reduced the progressive elements in taxation. There were increased inequalities in earnings as the market value of unskilled labour declined and the market value of some types of skilled labour increased. The government accepted, even encouraged, the growth of these inequalities as necessary in a competitive market economy.

Class and other divisions

Westergaard accepts the point made by postmodernists such as Pakulski and Waters that there are important divisions other than class. However, he does not accept that these divisions have superseded class. As suggested above, divisions along consumption lines reflect differences in income to a considerable extent.

Westergaard accepts that gender divisions are an important aspect of inequality. However, class and gender divisions 'twine together, to reinforce the effects of class rather than go against them'. For example, most women with white-collar jobs are married to men with white-collar jobs, and working-class women are largely married to working-class men. Many families therefore enjoy the material benefits of two white-collar salaries, whereas few households have the income from one blue-collar wage boosted by a partner's higher professional or managerial salary. Women suffer the same sorts of class disadvantages as men. The main difference is that, typically, they are worse off than men.

Similarly, ethnic divisions are an important source of disadvantage, but again they tend to reinforce rather than contradict class divisions. Westergaard argues that 'racial division – on this score much like gender division – comes to expression in good part as low placement of its victims precisely in the economic order of production and distribution: that is in the structure of class'.

Nor does Westergaard see a sharp division between an underclass and the rest of the class structure. Those who are usually seen as part of the underclass tend to be those from working-class backgrounds who have retired or cannot find work. The unemployed or retired middle class tend to have savings or pensions which mean they are not as disadvantaged as those held to be in the underclass.

Class 'in itself' and class 'for itself'

Westergaard comments, in concluding his argument, that 'we are still left with a puzzle: when class division "in itself" has sharpened, why does class division "for itself" seem to have faded?' If the inequalities between classes are greater, why does there appear to be less class consciousness? He argues that, in Britain at least, the Labour Party may be largely responsible. As the party which traditionally represents the interests of the disadvantaged, it is important in expressing and mobilizing class consciousness in the working class. However, factors such as internal party disputes and the widespread strikes in the late 1970s, under a Labour government, led to disillusionment with the party. In order to regain support it abandoned many of its traditional policies, which were in favour of redistribution to the less well-off. This left no major party to articulate the interests of a class-conscious working class.

Nevertheless, Westergaard maintains that there is the potential for the revival of class consciousness and left-wing policies. Reviewing opinion poll evidence, he says, 'Many people, then, appear to want to see "fairer shares". And although many are sceptical about the means to that end, popular conceptions are nevertheless quite out of line with fashionable social theory and right-wing ideology.' Like Marshall *et al.* (see p. 63) and many other sociologists, he thinks that class is far from dead – indeed in some respects it is not only alive but kicking the disadvantaged in society harder than for many decades.

Summary and conclusions

Westergaard's data are now a little dated, but the evidence of this chapter on more recent trends and research tends to support his views. Inequalities of income and wealth have not declined significantly in recent years (see pp. 39–41) and the data do not suggest Britain has become a meritocratic society. Research on social mobility between different levels of income shows that opportunities for upward mobility have been declining, Britain is less meritocratic than most similar societies, and class increasingly affects access to higher education (see pp. 635–6).

The boundaries between classes may have become increasingly blurred, but that does not prevent people from recognizing the existence of inequality and injustice in society (see pp. 62–3). Undoubtedly there have been important changes in class structure, class culture and class consciousness, but objectively class inequality continues to exercise considerable influence over people's lives. Subjectively, many people may resist seeing themselves as part of a class, but cultural differences between classes are an integral and essential part of everyday experience (see Skeggs, 1997, 2005 – pp. 70–2 and 74–5, Charlesworth, 2000 – pp. 69–70, and Wynne, 1998 – pp. 54–6). Indeed, ethnographic studies of class perhaps bring home more eloquently than statistics on social mobility that claims of the death of class are much exaggerated.

CHAPTER 2

Sex and gender

Look at me! look at my arm! ... I have plowed and planted, and gathered into barns, and no man could head me – and ain't I a woman? I could work as much as any man (when I could get it), and bear de lash as well – and ain't I a woman? Sojourner Truth, quoted by hooks, 1981

Introduction

In the Bible, Original Sin in the Garden of Eden was woman's. She tasted the forbidden fruit, tempted Adam, and has been paying for it ever since. In the Book of Genesis, the Lord said:

> *I will greatly multiply thy sorrow and thy conception; in sorrow thou shalt bring forth children; and thy desire shall be to thy husband, and he shall rule over thee.* Genesis 3:16

Sociologists would regard the above quotation as a mythological justification for the position of women in society. Many women might see it as an accurate description of their status through the ages, that is:

1 Women produce children.
2 Women are mothers and wives.
3 Women do the cooking, cleaning, sewing and washing.
4 They take care of men and are subordinate to male authority.
5 They are largely excluded from high-status occupations and from positions of power.

These generalizations have applied to the vast majority of known human societies. Some sociologists and anthropologists believe that there does not exist, and never has existed, a society in which women do not have an inferior status to that of men. In recent decades, particularly with the development of feminist (and post-feminist) ideas, the explanation for such differences has been hotly debated.

Feminism and 'malestream' sociology

A number of writers now use the term 'malestream sociology' to describe mainstream, male-dominated sociology. Many feminists have argued that early sociology was dominated by men and produced a distorted picture of the social world as a result. Pamela Abbott, Claire Wallace and Melissa Tyler (2005) identify five main criticisms of **malestream** sociology advanced by feminists:

1 Sociology has mainly conducted research about men. For example, until relatively recently most studies of education and work studied all-male samples.
2 Even when all-male samples have been used, then the results have been generalized to apply to all people, and not just to men.
3 Areas of social life of particular concern to women were rarely studied and were not seen as important. For example, there were no sociological studies of housework or childbirth before the 1970s.

4 When 'women are included in research they are often presented in a distorted and sexist way'. For example, early studies of female criminality tended to assume that there had to be something very wrong with women who became criminals, as women were normally passive and law-abiding (see pp. 371–2).

5 Finally, Abbott *et al.* suggest that 'when sex and gender differences are included as variables they are just added on, ignoring the fact that the explanatory theories used are ones which have justified the subordination and exploitation of women'. For example, the functionalist theories of Talcott Parsons have seen the domestic role of women as essential to the functioning of the social system (see pp. 462–3). Conventional sociological theories did not consider the possibility that society might be patriarchal or male-dominated.

Abbott *et al.* sum up by saying that there is:

> *at best no recognition that women's structural position and consequent experiences are not the same as men's and that sexual difference is therefore an important explanatory variable; and at worst women's experiences are deliberately ignored or distorted. Furthermore, the ways in which men subordinate and dominate women are either ignored or seen as natural.* Abbot et *al.*, 2005, p. 10

Despite the strength of these criticisms there is no doubt that since feminism began to influence sociology in the early 1970s the limitations of malestream sociology have been addressed. There is certainly less sex-blind and sexist sociology being produced now than prior to the 1970s.

Abbot *et al.* accept that considerable progress has been made, but in their view it is patchy and varies depending on the topic.

1 Some topics in sociology have been 'revived or reconstructed from feminist perspectives'. These include sexuality, the body, identity and cultural sociology.
2 In other areas reconstruction has not taken place, but feminism has made 'a significant impact'. These include the sociology of the family, health, education, crime, age, popular culture and the mass media.
3 However, there are some areas where feminism has not had a major impact on sociology, particularly class stratification, the sociology of politics and sociological theory.

Abbott *et al.* suggest that all feminists agree that existing sociology is inadequate, but they disagree about what needs to be done to improve it. There are three main approaches to this problem:

1 Some feminists believe that **integration** is the answer. They see the main problem as the way in which sociology ignores certain issues, and believe that if the gaps in malestream sociology are filled in by feminists then sociology will cease to be biased. However, Abbot *et al.* reject this approach, arguing that feminist research will be marginalized if it is simply tacked on to existing sociology. Furthermore, this approach fails to recognize and address the extent to which men 'subordinate and exploit' women even within sociology itself.
2 A second approach is **separatism**, which supports the idea of a 'sociology *for* women *by* women'. Advocates of separatism believe that a truly feminist sociology can only thrive away from malestream influence. While more sympathetic to this way of addressing bias in sociology than they are to integration, Abbott *et al.* still believe that it will not entirely solve the problem. Like integration, it carries the risk that feminist sociology will be marginalized by the men who continue to be dominant in the subject.
3 According to Abbott *et al.*, the best option is **reconceptualization**. This aims for the 'total and radical reformation of sociology so that it is able to incorporate women adequately' (2005, p. 13). From this viewpoint, theories must be rejected unless they are able to explain the experiences of women as well as men. Not only will this eliminate sexism from sociology, but it will improve theorizing so that it applies to all humans and not just males. A 'total rethinking' would embed feminism within the discipline so that it could never be marginalized again. Abbott *et al.* admit that it would be very difficult to achieve full reconceptualization because of the continued dominance of men in sociology, but they believe it is worth aiming for and that it is possible to make progress.

This chapter provides illustrations of how feminist sociology has contributed to the development of the subject, and to the understanding of the social world in general. Other chapters in the book demonstrate its contribution to specific areas such as poverty, the family, education, crime and deviance, religion, health and methodology. While feminist sociology may not have achieved everything that Abbott *et al.* would like it to, there is no doubt that sociology is a lot less 'malestream' than it was thirty years ago.

Sex and gender

Commonsense views on differences between men and women tend to assume that there are distinct, consistent and highly significant biological differences between the sexes. Amy S. Wharton describes this view in the following way: 'The claim that sex marks a distinction between two physically and genetically discrete categories of people is called **sexual diomorphism**. Many view sexual diomorphism in humans as a biological fact' (Warton, 2005, p. 18). The idea of sexual diomorphism has certainly been very influential and continues to be supported by many people. However, as early as the 1960s, writers were beginning to question some of the assumptions on which sexual diomorphism is based and to suggest that the differences between men and women were as much social as biological.

The distinction between sex and gender was the starting point for the development of alternative views. The first person to make this distinction was the American psychoanalyst Robert Stoller (1968). Stoller made the commonsense observation that the vast majority of the population can clearly be categorized as male or female according to their physical characteristics: 'external genitalia, internal genitalia, gonads (the organs which produce sex cells), hormonal states and secondary sex characteristics'. Because of these differences, women are capable of bearing and suckling children, whereas men are not. In addition, differences in physique between men and women usually mean that men are stronger and more muscular.

Biological differences are widely believed to be responsible for the differences in both the behaviour of men and women and the roles that they play in society. Stoller cautioned, though, against such an assumption. He said:

> *Gender is a term that has psychological and cultural connotations; if the proper terms for sex are 'male' and 'female', the corresponding terms for gender are 'masculine' and 'feminine'; these latter might be quite independent of (biological) sex.* Stoller, 1968, p. 9

In other words, it does not necessarily follow that being a woman means being 'feminine', nor that being a man means behaving in a 'masculine' way: girls are not necessarily caring and compassionate; boys do not have to be aggressive and competitive.

Most, though not all, sociologists of gender and feminists support this position. However, it is not immediately obvious how their claims can be justified. The belief that it is 'natural' for men and women to behave differently is widespread, and is supported by many scientists and some psychologists and sociologists. Their views will now be critically examined.

Sex and gender differences

Hormones and the brain

Some scientists believe that variations in the behaviour and social roles of men and women can be explained in terms of hormones and brain differences. Hormones are bodily secretions whose functions include the regulation of the development of male and female bodies so that they become capable of reproduction. The production and release of hormones are controlled by the hypothalamus in the brain. Both sexes produce a full range of sex hormones from a variety of glands (including the ovaries and testes). Normally women produce greater amounts of progesterone and oestrogen, while men produce more testosterone and other androgens. The higher levels of androgens in the male stop the hypothalamus from regulating hormonal production cyclically, which it does in the female menstruation and ovulation cycle. The activity of a wide range of hormones is closely integrated with the activity of the nervous system, and so hormones can influence behaviour, personality and emotional disposition.

Animal research has sometimes been used to link androgens and aggressive behaviour. Research suggests that castrated male rats tend to fight less, while female rats given extra androgens after birth are more aggressive in adult life than other female rats. Goy and Phoenix (1971) claim that female rhesus monkeys given extra androgens display more 'rough and tumble play' than other females. Some studies seem to show a direct link between testosterone levels in human males and aggression, using supposed measures of aggression such as being in jail. In an analysis of studies of testosterone and male aggression, John Archer found some correlation between testosterone levels and criminal records (discussed in Archer and Lloyd, 2002).

Criticisms of hormonal explanations

However, as methods of showing that male and female human behaviour is governed by hormones, all these studies are suspect. Ruth Bleier (1984) points to a number of flaws in using animal behaviour to explain human behavioural differences. In general, she observes that it is dangerous to assume that the same hormonal changes would result in the same changes in behaviour in humans as they do in animals. She does not accept that such experiments are conclusive.

The rhesus monkey experiments have been criticized by Ann Oakley. Oakley (1981) accepts that dominant males in monkey groups have higher testosterone levels than low dominance monkeys. However, she argues that social context affects hormone levels. Experiments show that when low dominance monkeys are caged with females only, their testosterone levels rise. Dominance, or lack of it, might affect testosterone levels, as well as vice versa.

In a review of research, John Archer and Barbara Lloyd (2002) discuss the possible connection between testosterone and aggression and violent crime in men. Although some studies do suggest a connection, findings have varied considerably between studies, with many showing no such connection.

One of the best studies, conducted by Halpern *et al.* (1994) (discussed by Archer and Lloyd), studied testosterone and aggression in 12 to13-year-old boys who were followed for three years. Although levels of testosterone increased rapidly over this period, the boys did not become more aggressive. Furthermore, there was no correlation between levels of testosterone at the start of the study and levels of aggression over the three years.

Archer and Lloyd suggest that aggression has more to do with 'masculine values, in particular those associated with reputation and honour', than it has to do with hormone levels. Males tend to become aggressive when they perceive others to be challenging their reputation and honour. Definitions of reputation and honour are strongly influenced by peer groups. Archer and Lloyd concede that hormones might contribute to the tendency of males to develop peer groups in which honour is defended through aggressive behaviour. However, they argue that there is an 'interaction between biological and social processes'. Social behaviour is not simply determined by hormones, and hormones only influence behaviour in the context of particular 'historical and cultural settings'.

Brain lateralization

There are claims that hormones have indirect effects on male and female brain development, as well as the direct effects discussed above. One area of research has concentrated on the issue of **brain lateralization**. According to John Nicholson (1993) and others, the right and left hemispheres of the brain specialize in different tasks. Nicholson argues that in about 95 per cent of the population the left hemisphere specializes in verbal and language skills, while the right is mainly responsible for visuo-spatial abilities, which relate to the 'ability to locate objects in space'.

J.A. Gray and A.W.H. Buffery (1971) believe that the left hemisphere of the brain is more dominant in girls after the age of 2, and that boys have greater abilities in those functions concentrated in the right hemisphere. According to Gray and Buffery, this difference is due to hormonal influences on the brain, and accounts for the results of some tests which appear to show that girls have greater verbal ability than boys, but that boys perform better in spatial and mathematical tests.

John Nicholson (1993) is willing to accept that there are differences in the development of male and female brains and that testosterone may be linked to visuo-spatial abilities. However, men with very high testosterone levels in childhood actually do less well in visuo-spatial tests than men with very low levels. This suggests that a balance between male and female hormones is necessary to develop high-level visuo-spatial abilities. Nicholson also points out that 'gender differences, where noted, are small, and are almost certainly exacerbated by social factors'.

There is even less evidence to support the view that girls have better linguistic skills than boys. Bob Connell (2002) examined the findings of meta-analysis studies – that is, studies which combine the findings of previous research to reach a conclusion about a particular issue. According to Connell, such studies show that differences in verbal ability between boys and girls have declined over time to the point where they are now 'virtually nonexistent'.

Furthermore, Connell believes there is little evidence to show that brain differences lead to differences in personality between males and females. Once again, meta-analysis shows that personality traits of men and women are converging over time, and the remaining differences are small. Connell argues that, 'Across a wide range of the traits and characteristics measured by psychology, sharp gender differences are rare. Small differences, or no differences, are common' (2002, p. 46). Where differences are found, they tend to be very specific (for example, differences in ability in a specific branch of science), or they are limited to particular samples (such as American university students) or circumstances (such as the amount of aggression produced in response to particular provocation). Connell concludes that, 'We begin to get a picture of psychological sex differences and similarities, not as fixed, age-old constants of the species, but as the varying products of the active responses people make to a complex and changing social world' (2002, p. 46).

Another way in which scientists have tried to demonstrate a difference between male and female brains is by examining the **corpus callosum** – the nerve fibres which link the left and right hemispheres of the brain. A number of scientists have suggested that men and women think in different ways, and that women are more likely to use both hemispheres of the brain simultaneously. This would lead to differences in the corpus callosum between men and women. Women would tend to have more fibres connecting the two sides of the brain and the corpus callosum would appear to be a different shape.

A number of studies have claimed to find significant differences. For example, the psychiatrist and neurologist Edith Caplan has argued that women do indeed have a thicker corpus callosum than men (quoted in Fausto-Sterling, 2000, p. 116). However, Fausto-Sterling argues that such claims are based upon flimsy evidence. After looking closely at the relevant studies, Fausto-Sterling concludes that the nature of this part of the brain has meant that nobody has as yet found a reliable method of measuring or recording its size and shape. She says the 'corpus callosum ... is a structure that is difficult to separate from the rest of the brain, and so complex in its irregular three dimensions as to be unmeasurable'.

Sociobiology – the evolution of human behaviour

There have been a number of attempts to relate sex differences to differences in the behaviour of men and women by using evolutionary ideas. Of these, perhaps the most influential today is **sociobiology**.

Sociobiology was first developed by E.O. Wilson (1975) and has been applied to sex and gender by David Barash (1979). It is based in part on Charles Darwin's **theory of evolution**, but it goes well beyond Darwin's original theory.

Like Darwin, sociobiologists believe that humans and other species develop and change through a process of natural selection. Individuals of a species vary in their physical characteristics, and those which are best adapted to their environment are most likely to survive and reproduce. Since offspring tend to have characteristics similar to those of their parents, due to **genetic inheritance**, the characteristics of a species can change as the fittest survive.

Thus, to use a simple example, giraffes have gradually evolved long necks because members of the species with longer necks had better access to food supplies in the upper levels of trees than their shorter-necked counterparts. As longer-necked giraffes and their offspring tended to survive longer, a long neck became encoded in the genetic make-up of the species.

Sociobiologists go beyond Darwin in two main ways:

1 They argue that it is not just physical characteristics that evolve, but also **behaviour**.
2 They believe that behaviour in animals and humans is governed by a genetic instruction to maximize the chances of passing on their genes to future generations

by **breeding** – that is, they try to ensure that they have offspring which survive. At the heart of sociobiology's attempt to explain differences in the behaviour of female and male humans is the claim that the two sexes employ different strategies to maximize their chances of passing on their genes.

Barash (1979) points out that human males produce millions of sperm during their lifetime, while females usually produce only one egg at a time, and about 400 in total during their lifetime. Furthermore, the female gestates the foetus in her body. The male therefore has an interest in making as many females as possible pregnant, so as to produce the maximum number of offspring who will carry his genes. However, since the female invests so much time and energy in each of her offspring, she must look for quality in her mates, so that each of her offspring has a good chance of ultimate survival. She therefore selects only the most genetically suitable male partners.

Wilson and Barash go on to assert that different reproductive strategies produce different behaviour in males and females and also lead them to occupy **different social roles**. In terms of sexual behaviour, men are likely to be more promiscuous, while women are more circumspect in their pursuit of the best possible genetic partner. Wilson (1975) says that 'it pays males to be aggressive, hasty, fickle and undiscriminating. In theory, it is more profitable for women to be coy, to hold back until they can identify males with the best possible genes.'

Barash talks about there being advantages for men in 'playing fast and loose', and having a 'love 'em and leave 'em' attitude. Wilson claims that rape by males can be explained in this way.

Sociobiologists believe that women can tolerate infidelity by their partners more readily than men. Infidelity by men has little cost for women, but if the woman is unfaithful, the man may devote energy to raising someone else's child.

To Wilson and Barash, these differences have wider implications. Because a woman is always certain whether a child is genetically hers, she will be more willing to devote attention to childcare, and in a modern society may therefore be more willing to become a housewife. In addition, women's search for the best male to father their children leads to them seeking to marry males of a higher social status than themselves. Because women can produce so 'few' children, men must compete for access to the comparatively scarce reproductive capacities of females. The larger and more aggressive males will be more successful. Females do not need to compete for mates in this way, and ultimately this leads to the dominance of males over females.

One way in which men tried to attract females in early societies was through showing that as successful hunters they were the best providers. To sociobiologists, the roots of war and territoriality are to be found in the aggressive male's attempts to secure and retain access to his own females by preventing their access to other males.

Sociobiologists back up these sweeping claims largely with animal studies. They provide examples of ape species in which dominant males are more successful in mating, and cite male lions' domination of female prides. Wilson even claims there are examples of 'gang rape' by mallard ducks.

However, Barash denies that any of the views held by sociobiologists are sexist. He sees males and females as simply biologically different, each pursuing the maintenance of their genes in their own way.

Wilson admits that human males and females are not compelled to behave in the ways described above; they may choose different types of behaviour. But if they do, it goes against their biological predisposition and makes them less efficient at maintaining the species.

Criticisms of sociobiology

Sociobiologists assume a direct link between patterns of genetic inheritance and behaviour in humans. However, there is no scientific evidence that such a link exists.

In contrast to animals, human behaviour is shaped by environment rather than instinct. Steven Rose, Leon Kamin and R.C. Lewontin note that, unlike most animals:

> *the human infant is born with relatively few of its neural pathways already committed. During its long infancy connections between nerve cells are formed not merely on the basis of specific epigenetic programming but in the light of experience.* Rose *et al.*, 1984, p. 145

Bleier (1984) is dismissive of sociobiology. She accuses it of being ethnocentric: of assuming that all human behaviour corresponds to that in the white capitalist world. For example, sociobiologists merely assert that females are 'coy' and males 'aggressive' without examining different societies.

Oakley (1972) points out that there are many societies in which women are far from 'coy'. She claims that 'amongst the Trobrianders, as also among the Lesu, Kurtatchi, Lepcha, Kwoma, and Mataco, women frequently take the initiative in sexual relationships'.

According to the critics, then, sociobiology tries to explain 'universal' human behaviour which is not universal at all. Furthermore, the evidence sociobiologists use from the animal world to support their case is selective. It ignores all the examples of animal species where males are not aggressive and dominant. Bleier notes that in some species of ape and monkey there are no dominance hierarchies at all. In others, such as Japanese macaques, the rank of a male within the troop depends on the rank of his mother. Bleier points out that recent studies have revealed a wide variety of behaviour patterns in apes. There are examples of female apes who 'protect territory, fight for their own or other mothers' young, take food from males, and bond with other females to fight aggressive males'. In short, sociobiologists simply ignore the evidence which contradicts their view.

For this reason, many feminists regard sociobiology as a spurious attempt to provide 'scientific' justification for male power.

John Nicholson (1993) argues that sociobiology is based upon the **naturalistic fallacy**. Gender is seen as being natural and inevitable. The way men and women behave cannot be changed and should therefore be left well alone. Nicholson believes that this is untrue. Gender differences are not natural and can be changed. The naturalistic fallacy gives sociobiology an inherently conservative bias: it opposes changes in the status quo. This is despite the fact that it is possible to argue that gender divisions are far from ideal and may have negative consequences.

For example, it could be argued that it would have been counterproductive for men in hunter-gatherer societies to father large numbers of children, because they would have been unable to provide food and protection for them and their mothers. As a result, many of them would have died. We could therefore make a perfectly reasonable case for saying that it would actually have been the 'stay-at-home man who had the best chance of being survived by children carrying his genes'.

Another problem with sociobiology is that it has great difficulty in explaining behaviour such as homosexuality or voluntary celibacy which preclude the possibility of passing on genes to offspring.

Biology and the sexual division of labour

Biologically based explanations of the differences in behaviour of men and women have not been confined to those who have located these differences in the hormones, brains or genes of the two sexes. Other writers, including anthropologists, have focused on more obvious physical differences between males and females, and related these to the allocation of social roles.

George Peter Murdock – biology and practicality

George Peter Murdock was an anthropologist who argued that biological differences between men and women were the basis of the **sexual division of labour** in society (Murdock, 1949). However, he did not suggest that men and women are directed by genetically based predispositions or characteristics to adopt their particular roles. Instead, he simply suggested that biological differences, such as the greater physical strength of men and the fact that women bear children, lead to gender roles out of sheer practicality. Given the biological differences between men and women, a sexual division of labour is the most efficient way of organizing society.

In a cross-cultural survey of 224 societies, ranging from hunting and gathering bands to modern nation-states, Murdock examined the activities assigned to men and women. He found tasks such as hunting, lumbering and mining to be predominantly male roles, and cooking, water-carrying and making and repairing clothes to be largely female roles. He stated that:

> *Man with his superior physical strength can better undertake the more strenuous tasks, such as lumbering, mining, quarrying, land clearance and housebuilding. Not handicapped, as is woman by the physiological burdens of pregnancy and nursing, he can range farther afield to hunt, to fish, to herd and to trade. Woman is at no disadvantage, however, in lighter tasks which can be performed in or near the home, e.g. the gathering of vegetable products, the fetching of water, the preparation of food, and the manufacture of clothing and utensils.* Murdock, 1949, p. 7

Thus, because of her biological function of childbearing and nursing, woman is tied to the home, and because of her physique she is limited to less strenuous tasks.

Murdock found that the sexual division of labour was present in all of the societies in his sample and concluded that 'the advantages inherent in a division of labour by sex presumably account for its universality'.

Talcott Parsons – biology and the 'expressive' female

Similar arguments are advanced to account for the role of women in industrial society. As we will see in Chapter 8, Talcott Parsons (1955) saw the isolated nuclear family in modern industrial society as specializing in two basic functions:

1. The **socialization** of the young
2. The **stabilization** of adult personalities

For socialization to be effective, a close, warm and supportive group was essential. The family met this requirement and, within the family, the woman was primarily responsible for socializing the young. Parsons turned to biology for an explanation. He stated:

> *In our opinion the fundamental explanation of the allocation of roles between the biological sexes lies in the fact that the bearing and early nursing of children establish a strong presumptive primacy of the relation of mother to the small child.* Parsons, 1955, p. 23

Thus, because mothers bore and nursed children, they had a closer and stronger relationship with them. This was particularly so in modern industrial society, where the isolation of the nuclear family led to a strong relationship between mothers and their children.

Parsons characterized the woman's role in the family as **expressive**, which meant she provided warmth, security and emotional support. This was essential for the effective socialization of the young.

It was only a short step from applying these expressive qualities to her children to applying them also to her husband. This was her major contribution to the second function of the isolated nuclear family: the stabilization of adult personalities. The male breadwinner spent his working day competing in an achievement-oriented society. This **instrumental** role led to stress and anxiety. The expressive female relieved this tension by providing the weary breadwinner with love, consideration and understanding.

Parsons argued that there had to be a clear-cut sexual division of labour for the family to operate efficiently as a social system, and that the instrumental and expressive roles complemented each other and promoted family solidarity.

Although Parsons moved a long way from biology, it formed his starting point for explaining the sexual division of labour.

Ann Oakley – the cultural division of labour

Ann Oakley (1974) explicitly rejects the views of Murdock and Parsons. She does not accept that there is any natural or inevitable division of labour or allocation of social roles on the basis of sex. She says:

> *Not only is the division of labour by sex not universal, but there is no reason why it should be. Human cultures are diverse and endlessly variable. They owe their creation to human inventiveness rather than invincible biological forces.* Oakley, 1974

Oakley first takes Murdock to task, arguing that the sexual division of labour is not universal, nor are certain tasks always performed by men, others by women. She maintains that Murdock's interpretation of his data is biased because he looks at other cultures through both Western and male eyes. In particular, she claims that he prejudges the role of women in terms of the Western housewife–mother role.

Culture and gender roles

Oakley finds plenty of evidence from Murdock's own data to attack the assumption that biology largely determines the sexual division of labour. There are 14 societies in Murdock's sample of 224 in which lumbering is done either exclusively by women or shared by both sexes, 36 societies in which women are solely responsible for land clearance, and 38 in which cooking is a shared activity.

Oakley then examines a number of societies in which biology appears to have little or no influence on women's roles:

1. The Mbuti Pygmies, a hunting and gathering society who live in the Congo rainforests, have no specific rules for the division of labour by sex. Both men and women hunt and share responsibility for the care of children.
2. Among the Australian Aborigines of Tasmania, women were responsible for seal hunting, fishing and catching opossums (tree-dwelling mammals).
3. Turning to present-day societies, Oakley notes that women form an important part of the armed forces of many countries, particularly China, the former USSR, Cuba and Israel. In India, women work on building sites, and in some Asian and Latin American countries they work in mines.

Culture and the housewife–mother role

Oakley also attacks the argument of Parsons that modern industrial societies require women to have an 'expressive' role within the family. Oakley argues that the expressive housewife–mother role is not necessary for the functioning of the family unit – it merely exists for the convenience of men. She claims that Parsons's explanation of gender roles is simply a validating myth for the 'domestic oppression of women'. She points to research evidence which shows that it is not detrimental to the well-being of children if their mothers work.

Oakley concludes that gender roles are culturally rather than biologically determined since comparisons between different cultures show that the behaviour and roles of men and women are highly variable.

Figure 2.1 Caring professions are often perceived as 'feminine'

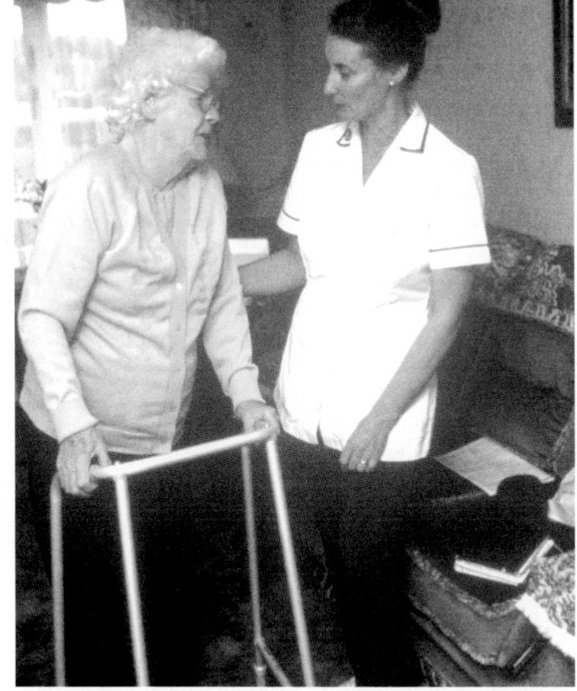

Source: Sally and Richard Greenhill

Figure 2.2 Manual work is often perceived as 'masculine'

Source: Photofusion

The social construction of gender roles

Oakley believes that gender roles are **culturally** rather than **biologically** produced. Whatever the biological differences between males and females, it is the culture of a society that exerts most influence in the creation of masculine and feminine behaviour. If there are biological tendencies for men and women to behave in different ways, these can be overridden by cultural factors.

Socialization and gender roles

Oakley (1974) outlines how socialization in modern industrial societies shapes the behaviour of girls and boys from an early age. Basing her work on the findings of Ruth Hartley, Oakley discusses four main ways in which socialization into gender roles takes place:

1. The child's self-concept is affected by **manipulation**. For example, mothers tend to pay more attention to girls' hair and to dress them in 'feminine' clothes.
2. Differences are achieved through **canalization**, involving the direction of boys and girls towards different objects. This is particularly obvious in the provision of toys which encourage girls to rehearse their expected adult roles as mothers and housewives. Girls are given dolls, soft toys and miniature domestic objects and appliances to play with. Boys, on the other hand, are given toys which encourage more practical, logical and aggressive behaviour, for example bricks and guns.
3. Another aspect of socialization is the use of **verbal appellations**, such as 'You're a naughty boy', or 'That's a good girl'. This leads young children to identify with their gender and to imitate adults of the same gender.
4. Male and female children are exposed to **different activities**. For example, girls are particularly encouraged to become involved with domestic tasks. In addition, numerous studies have documented how stereotypes of masculinity and femininity are further reinforced throughout childhood, and indeed adult life. The media have been particularly strongly attacked by feminists for tending to portray men and women in their traditional social roles.

Criticisms of Oakley

Oakley's work was enormously influential and was important for challenging the idea that differences between males and females were not natural. Nevertheless she has been criticized for the narrowness of her approach, which is based upon the idea that individuals are simply socialized into different sex roles.

1. Nickie Charles (2002) notes that Oakley's approach does not explain why, in most societies, men and not women are socialized into a dominant role. Unlike radical and Marxist feminism, sex-role theory provides no explanation of power differences.
2. Oakley's work implies that within particular societies there is a clear set of gender roles into which males and females are socialized. However, recent studies of masculinity and postmodern feminism suggest that male and female gender roles can vary considerably within individual societies (see pp. 114–16 and 138–41). It is hard to explain these differences in terms of sex-role theory.
3. Bob Connell (2002) criticizes Oakley for portraying socialization as a passive process in which children simply absorb what they learn from parents and other agents of socialization. To Connell, this ignores the active seeking of **pleasure** in acting out gender roles (for example, dressing up in sexy clothes). It neglects **resistance** to socialization, for example by boys who do not like sport and girls who want stereotypically masculine careers. It also fails to discuss the **difficulty** that some people have in living up to masculine or feminine roles. To Connell, the view that people are simply socialized into sex roles cannot explain the enormous changes there have been in the roles of males and females in society. In short, Connell believes that socialization theories are far too simplistic and he advocates a much more complex view of how gender differences are reproduced or changed over time (see pp. 138–41).

Gender attribution

From the viewpoint of writers such as Oakley, gender is socially constructed in the sense that differences in the behaviour of males and females are learned rather than being the inevitable result of biology. Suzanne J. Kessler and Wendy McKenna (1978) go a stage further. As ethnomethodologists (see Chapter 15, pp. 885–7), they are interested in the ways that members of society categorize the world around them. From their perspective, gender attribution – the decision to regard another person as male or female – is socially produced in much the same way as gender roles.

For most people, it seems obvious whether someone is male or female, and it is taken for granted that a decision about the sex of another will coincide with the biological 'facts'. Kessler and McKenna disagree; they deny that there is any clear-cut way of differentiating between men and women.

Two or more sexes?

This startling claim is backed up by a range of arguments and evidence. Kessler and McKenna try to demonstrate that there are exceptions to every rule which is supposed to distinguish the sexes.

The full range of hormones is present in both men and women, thus hormones do not provide a clear dividing line between the sexes. Some women have high androgen levels, while some men have comparatively low levels of this hormone.

Some individuals have male chromosomes (XY), but are insensitive to the effects of androgen and thus appear to be physically female. Despite their male genetic make-up, they are invariably identified as females.

Other individuals have a condition known as **Turner's syndrome**. They have neither XY chromosomes, nor the normal female pairing of XX. Instead, they have a single X chromosome, normally indicated by 'XO'. A small number of people with this condition do have a few XYY chromosomes as well as the predominant XO. They have a female appearance but can fail 'sex tests' for women's athletics competitions.

Kessler and McKenna argue that the main way of determining gender at birth is through an inspection of the genitals. However, even this may produce ambiguous evidence. Some babies and adults have both male and female genitals, a condition known as **hermaphroditism**.

Kessler and McKenna note that, despite these anomalies, both the public and scientists tend to see males and females as opposites, refusing to recognize the possibility of an intermediate state. However, this has not always been the case. Some societies have recognized a third gender role: the *berdache*. A number of North American Indian tribes contained *berdache*. They were usually 'men' who dressed and in some ways acted like women. In some societies they had a high status, in others a low one, but in all cases they were treated as a distinct gender. In Western industrial society, hermaphrodites are almost always categorized as male or female. In tribes such as the Potock of East Africa they would be more likely to be allocated to a third category.

Allocation to sexes

Having questioned the most basic assumption (that there are just two sexes), Kessler and McKenna go on to discuss how individuals are allocated to sexes by others. This process was studied by interviewing **transsexuals** – people who seem biologically normal but who feel themselves to be members of the 'opposite' sex. Some, but not all, transsexuals undergo operations to alter their genitals, usually changing from male to female.

Normally gender and genitals are equated with each other: the connection between them is taken for granted. However, people are not expected to ask others whom they have just met to remove their clothes so that they can determine which sex they are. Various types of evidence are pieced together so that a gender attribution can be made by the observer. Someone with the appearance and behaviour of a female or male will simply be assumed to have the appropriate genitals. The existence of transsexuals means that this assumption is not always accurate. Biological males sometimes live as, and are accepted as, females.

How then do people decide what gender another person is? According to Kessler and McKenna there are four main processes involved:

1. The **content and manner of the speech** of others are taken into account. Some male-to-female transsexuals have trained themselves to appear to be women by putting more inflection in their voice and by having more mobile facial movements when talking. Others introduce themselves as 'Miss' to settle any doubt there might be in an observer's mind.
2. Another important factor in gender attribution is **public physical appearance**. For example, female-to-male transsexuals may disguise their breasts by wearing baggy clothing or by using strapping.
3. The information people provide about their **past life** helps to determine gender attribution. Again, transsexuals have to be careful to avoid suspicion. They may need a cover story. In one case a female-to-male transsexual explained his pierced ears by saying he had once belonged to a tough street gang.
4. The final important factor is the **private body**. Usually there is little problem in keeping the body covered, but transsexuals may need to avoid certain situations (such as visiting beaches or sharing rooms with others) if they have not undergone the appropriate operations to change their sex physically.

Taking on the identity of a sex to which they do not belong biologically is difficult and demanding for the transsexual. For most people, hormones, chromosomes, genitals and the gender attributed to them will all coincide. Nevertheless, the exceptions studied by Kessler and McKenna demonstrate that even the most basic division – that between male and female – can be seen as being at least in part a social construct.

Anne Fausto-Sterling – *Sexing the Body*

Transgendered people

In *Sexing the Body* (2000) Anne Fausto-Sterling follows Kessler and McKenna in challenging conventional views about sex differences. Like them, she examines the significance of hermaphrodites and those with a variety of chromosome abnormalities and with syndromes that affect sensitivity to hormones. She attacks **dualistic** views of sex differences – that you must be either male or female. This type of thinking has led to insistence by many doctors that babies born with ambiguous genitals have to undergo operations to make them one thing or another, girl or boy. Such operations can be psychologically and physically traumatic. People may end up with a body that does not match the sex that they feel they should be. In some cases, babies seen as being essentially girls have been deemed to have a clitoris which is too long, too like a penis, and have had the clitoris removed. This has prevented them achieving orgasm in later life.

Fausto-Sterling is highly critical of such approaches. She argues that the existence of more than two sexes should be accepted and operations to alter the genitals of babies or children should be avoided. She says:

> *We are moving from an era of sexual dimorphism to one of variety beyond the number two. We inhabit a moment in history when we have the theoretical understanding and practical power to ask a question unheard of before in our culture: 'Should there be only two sexes?'* Fausto-Sterling, 2000

Her own answer to this question is a resounding no. When society insists on assigning individuals to one of two sexes it can do great harm. From her viewpoint, **transgendered people**, who have male and female characteristics, need to have their rights to equality, and their right to be different, recognized.

The social determination of sex

Like Kessler and McKenna, Fausto-Sterling believes that the way people are assigned to a particular gender is a social process. For example, the rules for determining whether someone is male or female vary according to context and are not fixed. She uses the example of sporting events where competitors are sometimes tested to see if they are male or female to ensure that 'males' do not cheat by trying to pass as 'females'. For example, in the 1988 Olympics the Spanish hurdler Maria Patio (who had always lived as a woman and appeared to be female) was disqualified from the women's event when it was found that she had the Y chromosome. It turned out that she was affected by androgen insensitivity. Her cells could not detect the testosterone produced by her body, so she developed the physical appearance of a woman. The declaration that she was not a woman caused her many problems. She was stripped of her titles, banned from competition and her boyfriend left her. She fought the ruling that she could not compete as a woman and was reinstated in 1992, having succeeded in persuading the authorities that she was more female than male. Like Kessler and McKenna, then, Fausto-Sterling asserts that the decision that somebody is one sex or another is always a social one.

Science and gender

Fausto-Sterling does not confine her work to re-examining the significance of chromosome abnormalities, transsexuals and hermaphrodites. She also discusses a range of biological theories about the differences between men and women. For example, she examines the idea that the corpus callosum is different in males and females (see above, p. 94) and she discusses theories which examine the influence of hormones on behaviour. She is critical of all these theories and argues that scientists are profoundly influenced by the 'political, social and moral' context in which they work. The interpretation of scientific research, and the sort of research that gets done, reflect the assumptions of scientists and the nature of gender in the society in which they live. For example, the belief that men and women think differently caused scientists to try to measure the corpus callosum and to interpret highly ambiguous results as showing significant differences.

However, Fausto-Sterling does not dismiss biological science altogether. Indeed, she argues that any full understanding of gender must incorporate an understanding of the body. She believes that gender differences become **embodied** – become part of people's bodies. Like Rose *et al.* (1984) (see p. 95), she notes that scientists have demonstrated that the development of the neural connections in the brain is related to the experiences that people have. As people learn gendered behaviour, their brains develop in a way which reflects this. Therefore, 'events outside the body become incorporated into our very flesh'. However, she does not believe that gender differences are simply created by bodily differences. Rather, biological and social factors interact to create a particular **gender system** in which both body and social behaviour tend to reinforce one another in a 'double-sided process that connects the production of gendered knowledge … to the materialization of gender within the body'.

Sex and gender differences – conclusion

Anne Fausto-Sterling is not the only writer to have tried to move beyond the debate on whether sex or gender shapes the behaviour of men and women. It is now quite widely accepted that biology and culture – bodies and the social meaning attributed to them – are interconnected and it is difficult, or even impossible, to separate the two elements out.

In recent years there has been an increased theoretical emphasis upon the differences among women, and the differences among men. It has been recognized that there are a variety of ways to be feminine and a variety of ways to be masculine. There has been less emphasis on the sex/gender differences between men in general and women in general. These new approaches will be discussed later in the chapter (see pp. 115–16 and 117–18).

One particularly influential approach is put forward by Bob Connell (1995, 2002), who sees biology and culture as 'fused' together. Connell's views will be discussed in detail in the section on masculinity (see pp. 138–41).

Gender inequality

So far in this chapter we have examined explanations for differences between men and women. These differences have sometimes been seen as the basis for inequalities between them, and we will now look at those inequalities in more detail. The development of feminism has led to attention being focused on the subordinate position of women in many societies. Feminist sociologists have been mainly responsible for developing theories of gender inequality, yet there is little agreement about the causes of this inequality, or about what actions should be taken to reduce or end it. More recently, the focus has changed from an emphasis on inequality to an emphasis on difference.

Several feminist approaches can be broadly distinguished:

1. Radical feminism
2. Marxist and socialist feminism
3. Liberal feminism
4. Black feminism
5. Postmodern feminism

Some feminists argue that it is no longer useful to distinguish different perspectives, that there is considerable overlap between these approaches, and that each contains a variety of views. Nevertheless, the distinction between these perspectives is important, as it helps to clarify some of the major disputes within feminism. Feminists themselves often assign themselves to one of these categories, and most feminists still employ them.

We will briefly outline each perspective before examining in more detail how they have been applied to particular aspects of gender inequality.

Radical feminism

Radical feminism blames the exploitation of women on men. To a radical feminist, it is primarily men who have benefited from the subordination of women. According to Valerie Bryson (1999), radical feminists see women as 'an oppressed group who had to struggle for their own liberation against their oppressors – that is, against men'. Pamela Abbott, Claire Wallace and Melissa Tyler (2005) argue that radical feminism is 'concerned with women's rights rather than gender equality'. It does not seek to minimize the differences between men and women, but instead believes that there is a 'female or feminine nature that has been concealed and/or distorted throughout history; one that needs to be liberated and revalued' (2005, p. 33). This emphasis on a female perspective and female interests is known as **gynocentrism**.

Radical feminists see society as **patriarchal** – it is dominated and ruled by men. From this point of view, men are the ruling class, and women the subject class. The family is seen by some radical feminists as the key institution oppressing women in modern societies. The family is certainly given more prominence than in Marxist sociology, where, as part of the superstructure, it is given only secondary importance.

Radical feminists tend to believe that women have always been exploited and that only revolutionary change can offer the possibility of their liberation. However, there are disagreements within this group about both the origins of women's oppression and the possible solutions to it. Some radical feminists, such as Shulamith Firestone (1972), believe women's oppression originated in their biology, particularly in the fact that they give birth. In this respect, however, Firestone is unusual. Other radical feminists see men's biology as the problem. Mary Daly (1978), for example, blames female oppression on male aggression. A number of radical feminists believe that rape and male violence towards women are the methods through which men have secured and maintained their power.

Because men are seen as the enemies of women's liberation, many radical feminists reject any assistance from the male sex in their struggle to achieve the rights they seek. **Separatist feminists** argue that women should organize independently of men outside the male-dominated society. A few, like the Leeds Revolutionary Feminist Group (1982), argue that only lesbians can be true feminists, since only they can be fully independent of men.

A particularly radical group, **female supremacists**, argue that women are not just equal but are actually morally superior to men. They wish to see patriarchy replaced by **matriarchy** (male rule replaced by female rule). From such perspectives, men are responsible not only for the exploitation of women, but also for many other problems. These may include conflict, war, destruction of the environment, the abuse of science so that it fails to meet human needs, and so on.

Rosemarie Tong (1998) distinguishes between two groups of radical feminists. The first group, **radical-libertarian feminists**, believe that it is both possible and desirable for gender differences to be eradicated, or at least greatly reduced. They therefore aim for a state of androgyny in which men and women are not significantly different. The ideal state is one in which women and men take on the more desirable characteristics of each sex. They believe that differences between the masculine and feminine are socially constructed. If they are removed, then equality between men and women can follow.

The second group, **radical-cultural feminists**, believe in the superiority of the feminine. As Tong puts it:

> *Far from believing that the liberated woman must exhibit both masculine and feminine traits and behaviour, these radical-cultural feminists expressed the view that it is better to be female/feminine than it is to be male/masculine. Thus women should not try to be like men.* Tong, 1998

According to Tong, they celebrate characteristics associated with femininity, such as 'interdependence, community, connection, sharing, emotion, body, trust, absence of hierarchy, nature, immanence, process, joy, peace and life'. They are hostile to characteristics associated with masculinity, such as 'independence, autonomy, intellect, will, wariness, hierarchy, domination, culture, transcendence, product, asceticism, war and death'.

Tong accepts that such a distinction between radical-libertarian feminists and radical-cultural feminists can be overstated, but believes that it does reflect real and significant differences.

Criticisms of radical feminism

According to Valerie Bryson (1999), other feminists have criticized radical feminism in the following ways:

1. The concept of patriarchy has been criticized for being 'descriptive and ahistorical'. It describes the position of women without providing any explanation for it. It also tends to ignore variations in experience of oppression by women of different class and ethnic backgrounds.
2. Some critics have claimed that radical feminism encourages women to focus only on negative experiences of relationships with men, and to ignore, for example, experiences of happy marriages. Bryson suggests that this may have led to a reputation for feminism as a 'complaining, whining and negative creed, irrelevant to the lives of go-ahead young women'.
3. It has also been argued that radical feminism tends to portray 'women as essentially good and men as essentially bad', which leads to an 'inaccurate and unworkable view of men as "the enemy", which suggests that they cannot be trusted as fathers, friends, sexual partners or political allies'.

Marxist and socialist feminism

Marxist and socialist feminists do not attribute women's exploitation entirely to men. They see **capitalism** rather than patriarchy as being the principal source of women's oppression, and capitalists as the main beneficiaries. Like radical feminists, they see women's unpaid work as housewives and mothers as one of the main ways in which women are exploited. Although men in general benefit, it is primarily capitalists who gain from women's unpaid work, since new generations of workers are reproduced at no cost to the capitalist. (For a discussion of this issue see Chapter 8.)

Thus Marxist and socialist feminists relate women's oppression to the production of wealth, while radical feminists attribute greater importance to childbearing. Marxist feminists also place much greater stress on the exploitation of women in paid employment. The disadvantaged position of women is held to be a consequence of the emergence of private property and subsequently their lack of ownership of the means of production, which in turn deprives them of power.

Although Marxist and socialist feminists agree with radical feminists that women as a group are exploited, particularly since the advent of capitalism, they are more sensitive to the differences between women who belong to the ruling class and proletarian families. Nevertheless, both the working class and women, whatever their class, are oppressed groups in society, so there is considerable potential for cooperation between women and the working class. In this respect, women have interests in common with the working class, and Marxist and socialist feminists see greater scope for cooperation between women and working-class men than do radical feminists.

Marxist feminists share with radical feminists a desire for revolutionary change; however, they seek the establishment of a **communist society**. In such a society (where the means of production will be communally owned) they believe gender inequalities will disappear. This view is not shared by radical feminists, who believe that women's oppression has different origins and causes, and therefore requires a different solution.

There is no clear-cut division between Marxist and socialist feminists; they share much in common. Marxist feminists, though, tend to seek more sweeping changes than socialist feminists. Socialist feminists tend to give more credence to the possibility of capitalist societies gradually moving towards female equality. They see more prospect for change within the democratic system.

Criticisms of Marxist and socialist feminism

Although very influential in the 1970s and 1980s, Marxist and socialist feminism has lost influence in recent decades. While aspects of their arguments have been adopted by other feminists, relatively few feminists now call themselves Marxists or socialists. Marxist and socialist feminism has been criticized on a number of grounds:

1. Some have argued that it is essentially a masculine theory which cannot be adapted to explain the position of women. It emphasizes class inequality and economic factors to the extent that it neglects other sources of gender inequality such as culture, violence and sexuality. Black feminists criticize it for neglecting race and ethnicity.
2. Many feminists have argued that women's experience of communist and socialist regimes has often been far from happy. In China, for example, women's fertility has been greatly restricted by coercive policies to reduce the birth rate, and women have rarely attained the highest positions of power under communist regimes.
3. Abbott *et al.* (2005) argue that the main problem with Marxist feminism is the lack of emphasis on the way men oppress women, with too much emphasis being placed on how the position of women relates to the capitalist system. They argue that 'there is no necessary and inevitable congruence between the interests of patriarchy and the interests of capital', so that much Marxist feminist theory is based on false assumptions.
4. Abbott *et al.* also claim that this type of feminism 'tends to be relatively abstract and far removed from the everyday experiences of women in their relationships with men' (2005, p. 38).

Liberal feminism

Liberal feminism does not have such clearly developed theories of gender inequalities as radical and Marxist and socialist feminism. Nevertheless, liberal feminism probably enjoys greater popular support than the other perspectives. This is largely because its aims are more moderate and its views pose less of a challenge to existing values. Liberal feminists aim for gradual change in the political, economic and social systems of Western societies.

To the liberal feminist, nobody benefits from existing gender inequalities; both men and women are harmed because the potential of females and males alike is suppressed. For example, many women with the potential to be successful and skilled members of the workforce do not get the opportunity to develop their talents to the full, while men are denied some of the pleasures of having a close relationship with their children. The explanation of this situation, according to liberal feminists, lies not so much in the structures and institutions of society, but in its culture and the attitudes of individuals.

Socialization into gender roles has the consequence of producing rigid, inflexible expectations of men and women. Discrimination prevents women from having equal opportunities.

The creation of equal opportunities, particularly in education and work, is the main aim of liberal feminists. They pursue this aim through the introduction of legislation and by attempting to change attitudes. In Britain, they supported such measures as the **Sex Discrimination Act** (1975) and the **Equal Pay Act** (1970) in the hope that these laws would help to end discrimination.

Liberal feminists try to eradicate sexism and stereotypical views of women and men from children's books and the mass media. They do not seek revolutionary changes in society: they want reforms that take place within the existing social structure, and they work through the democratic system. Since they believe that existing gender inequalities benefit nobody (and are particularly harmful to women), liberal feminists are willing to work with any members of society who support their beliefs and aims.

Abbott *et al.* (2005) believe that liberal feminism is a **modernist** theory because of its emphasis on human progress through rational thought, its belief that a just society can be planned and its belief in emancipation. It stresses the rights of individuals and is based upon the assumption that men and women are very similar to one another because of their shared humanity.

Although the least radical of feminist perspectives, it has probably had more impact than any other in improving women's lives. (For an example of the views of a liberal feminist, see the work of Natasha Walter (1998).)

Criticisms of liberal feminism

Valerie Bryson (1999) identifies the following criticisms that have been directed at liberal feminism:

1 Liberal feminism is criticized for being based upon male assumptions and norms. These include a belief in the value of individual achievement and competition, an emphasis on the importance of paid work, and a belief in rationality. All these beliefs are encouraging women to be more like men and therefore deny 'the value of qualities traditionally associated with women such as empathy, nurturing and cooperation'.
2 Liberalism is accused of emphasizing public life (such as politics and work) at the expense of private life. For example, it tends not to see personal relationships in terms of power struggles and politics and it therefore sees them as of little importance in explaining gender inequalities.
3 Liberal feminism is rejected by Marxist and radical feminists for advocating changes that are too limited to free women from oppression, and by Black and postmodern feminists for assuming that all groups of women have shared interests.
4 Abbott *et al.* (2005) criticize liberal feminism for failing to properly explain the exploitation of women, because it takes no account of structural sources of inequality.
5 Abbott *et al.* also criticize liberal feminism for failing to challenge existing perspectives on the social world: it argues that women should be included in samples, but not that theories need reformulation to take account of the experiences of women.

In general, women who do not share the liberal vision of an open competitive society based upon the principle of equality of opportunity do not support liberal feminism. However, many would acknowledge that liberal feminism has resulted in some improvements for women in Western societies.

Black feminism

Black feminism has developed out of dissatisfaction with other types of feminism. Abbott *et al.* (2005) identity four main criticisms that Black feminists level at feminism:

1 It is **ethnocentric**, claiming to address issues concerning women in general but actually concentrating on 'women's experience derived from white perspectives and priorities'.
2 It perpetuates a '**victim ideology**', seeing black women as the helpless victims of racism and sexism and ignoring the extent to which black women have resisted oppression and actively shaped their own lives.
3 They also accuse white feminists of **theoretical racism** for expecting black women to write about their experiences rather than contribute to the development of feminist theory.
4 Another criticism is that white feminists sometimes engage in **cultural appropriation** of black women's culture. bel hooks (1982), for example, argues that the singer Madonna has appropriated overt, aggressive sexuality associated with black women in popular culture. While white feminists celebrate Madonna's stance as liberating, this 'is scarcely of use to Black women who might wish to challenge racist representations of themselves as explicitly and overtly sexual' (hooks, 1982, p. 50).

Black feminists have put forward suggestions about how Black feminism can contribute to an understanding of the social world. bell hooks (1981) argues that other feminists, as well as male anti-racists, have not addressed the particular problems faced by black women. Writing in 1981, hooks claimed that black women in the USA had not joined:

> *together to fight for women's rights because we did not see 'womanhood' as an important aspect of our identity. Racist, sexist socialization had conditioned us to devalue our femaleness and to regard race as the only relevant label of identification.* hooks, 1981

Black women had joined in the fight for civil rights, but the organizations were dominated by men, and women's issues received no consideration.

hooks argues that contemporary black women could learn a lot from some of their nineteenth-century counterparts who had pioneered a distinctive Black feminism. She describes the views of Sojourner Truth, a black American woman who had campaigned for black women to gain the right to vote along with black men. Truth had said that if black women failed in their campaign for voting rights, but black men succeeded, then 'the coloured men will be masters over the women, and it

Figure 2.3 Sojourner Truth, a campaigner for black women's suffrage

Source: Corbis

will be just as bad as it was before' (quoted in hooks, 1981). At a convention of the women's rights movement in Ohio in 1852, white males argued that women should not have equal rights to men because they were physically inferior to men and were unsuited to heavy manual labour. Sojourner Truth countered this argument in a passionate speech saying:

> *Look at me! look at my arm! ... I have plowed and planted, and gathered into barns, and no man could head me – and ain't I a woman? I could work as much as any man (when I could get it), and bear de lash as well – and ain't I a woman?* hooks, 1981, p. 160

Truth's speech highlighted the differences in the experiences of black women and white women. For some Black feminists these differences are the legacy of slavery. Patricia Hill Collins (1990) says that slavery 'shaped all subsequent relationships that black women had within African-American families and communities, with employers, and among each other, and created the political context for women's intellectual work'. To Collins, writing in 1990, most feminist theory has 'suppressed black women's ideas' and has concentrated on the experiences and grievances of white and usually middle-class women. For example, feminist critiques of family life tended to examine the situation of middle-class wives who were in a very different position from most black women. There was a 'masculinist bias in black social and political thought' and a 'racist bias in feminist theory'.

Black feminism could correct that bias by drawing on black women's experiences. Many black women had been employed as domestic servants in white families. From this position they could see 'white power demystified'. They could see whites as they really were, yet they remained economically exploited outsiders. Thus Black feminists could draw upon the 'outsider-within perspective generated by black women's location in the labour market' and could develop a 'distinct view of the contradictions between the dominant groups' actions and ideologies'.

Like hooks, Collins draws inspiration from the insights of Sojourner Truth to show how black women can attack patriarchal ideology. For example, they could attack the belief that women are fragile and weak by drawing on their own experience of physically demanding labour.

Rose M. Brewer (1993) sees the basis of Black feminist theory as an 'understanding of race, class and gender as simultaneous forces'. Black women suffer from disadvantages because they are black, because they are women, and because they are working-class, but their problems are more than the sum of these parts: each inequality reinforces and multiplies the other inequalities. Thus black women's problems can be represented as stemming from 'race class gender' rather than 'race + class + gender'. The distinctive feature of Black feminism to Brewer is that it studies the 'interplay' of race, class and gender in shaping the lives and restricting the life chances of black women.

Heidi Safia Mirza (1997) argues that there is a need for a distinctive Black British feminism. She does not claim that black British women have a unique insight into what is true and what is not, but she does believe that this group can make an important contribution to the development of feminist and other knowledge. They can challenge the distorted assumptions of dominant groups by drawing on their own experiences. They offer 'other ways of knowing' and can 'invoke some measure of critical race/gender reflexivity into mainstream academic thinking'.

In particular, Black British feminists can challenge the predominant image of black British women as passive victims of racism, patriarchy and class inequality. They can undermine the image of 'the dutiful wife and daughter, the hard (but happy and grateful!) worker, the sexually available exotic other, the controlling asexual mother, or simply homogenized as the "third world" woman'. Instead, Black British feminists have been able to show how black British women have been 'brave, proud and strong'. They have struggled against domestic violence; tried to overcome sexism and racism in school; developed alternative family forms in which women have autonomy; and challenged the activities of the police and immigration authorities. They have made their own voice heard rather than relying on others to tell their story.

Black feminist thought has had some influence on postmodern feminism. This will be discussed on pp. 115–18.

Criticisms of Black feminism

1. Black feminism may have introduced the idea that differences between women are as important as similarities and shared interests, but it can be accused of emphasizing one difference ('race'/ethnicity) at the expense of others (such as class or sexuality).
2. Similarly Black feminism can be criticized for failing to address the oppression experienced by white women.

The origins of gender inequalities – feminist views

Although many feminists clearly align themselves with one of the perspectives that we have just outlined, others do not. Thus, in the subsequent sections, not all the explanations for gender inequalities that we will discuss can be neatly attributed to one perspective.

Feminists do not agree about the origins of inequality between men and women. Some believe that women have always had a subordinate position in all societies; others argue that the origins of gender inequalities can be traced back to particular historical events.

The following are some influential examples of radical feminist theories of gender inequality.

Shulamith Firestone – a radical feminist view

In her book *The Dialectics of Sex*, published in 1970, Firestone was one of the first to outline a radical feminist explanation of female inequality. To Firestone, *sexual oppression* was the first and most fundamental form of oppression. Unlike Marxists, Firestone does not attach primary importance to economic differences in the explanation of inequality. Although she acknowledges the importance of the work of Marx and Engels, she criticizes them for confining their studies to economic production. In her view, they ignored an important part of the material world: 'reproduction'.

Firestone believes that what she calls the **sexual class system** was the first form of stratification. It pre-dated the class system and provided the basis from which other forms of stratification evolved. Inequalities and the division of labour between men and women arose directly from biology. Biological differences produced a form of social organization she calls the biological family. Although societies vary in the roles of men and women and the form the family takes, all societies share the **biological family**, which has four key characteristics, described below.

The biological family

1. Women are disadvantaged by their biology. Menstruation, the menopause and childbirth are all physical burdens for women, but pregnancy and breast-feeding have the most serious social consequences. At these times, when women are pregnant or looking after infants, they are 'dependent on males (whether brother, father, husband, lover or clan, government, community-at-large) for physical survival'.
2. Women's dependence on men is increased by the long periods during which human infants are dependent, compared to the infants of other species.
3. The interdependence between mother and child, and in turn their dependence on men, has been found in every society, and it has influenced the psychology of every human being. Dependence on men produced unequal power relationships and **power psychology**.
4. The final characteristic of the biological family is that it provides the foundations for all types of inequality and stratification. Men derived pleasure from their power over women and wished to extend their power to the domination of other men. The sexual class system provided the blueprint and prototype for the **economic class system**. The economic class system provided the means through which some men came to dominate other men. Because the sexual class system is the basis for other class systems, Firestone believes that it must be destroyed before any serious progress can be made towards equality. She says: 'the sexual class system is the model for all other exploitative systems and thus the tapeworm that must be eliminated first by any true revolution'.

Biology and equality

Because sexual class has a biological origin, **biological equality** is the only effective starting point for securing its elimination. Firestone believes that effective birth control techniques have helped to loosen the chains of women's slavery by giving them more control over whether they become pregnant. Even so, the pill and other contraceptives have not freed women from pregnancy altogether; this would only be possible if babies could be conceived and developed outside the womb. Once this occurred, women would no longer be forced into dependence on men for part of their lives.

Yet even this would only be the first step towards a complete revolution. In addition to the biological changes, the economic class system and the cultural superstructure would have to be destroyed. Economic equality would have to follow biological equality, and power psychology would need to be overcome.

The strength of Firestone's argument lies in its ability to explain all forms of stratification, but this radical feminist perspective on inequality has been subject to criticism. Firestone does not explain variations in women's status in different societies at different times. For example, in some societies women do not have primary responsibility for childcare and women's biology does not seem to make them dependent on men for long periods (as we saw in Oakley's discussion on the cultural division of labour, p. 97). If this is the case, then biology alone may not explain gender inequalities.

Sherry B. Ortner – culture and the devaluation of women

Sherry B. Ortner (1974) agrees with Firestone that women are universally oppressed and devalued. However, she claims that it is not biology as such that ascribes women to their status in society, but the way in which every culture defines and evaluates female biology.

Ortner argues that in every society, a higher value is placed on **culture** than on nature. Culture is the means by which humanity controls and regulates nature. By inventing weapons and hunting techniques, humans can capture and kill animals; by inventing religion and rituals, humans can call upon supernatural forces to produce a successful hunt or a bountiful harvest. By the use of culture, humans do not have to submit passively to nature: they can regulate and control it.

Women and nature

This universal evaluation of culture as superior to nature is the basic reason for the devaluation of women. Women are seen as closer to nature than men, and therefore as inferior to men.

Ortner argues that women are universally defined as closer to nature because their bodies experience menstruation, pregnancy, childbirth and lactation. Furthermore they are primarily responsible for the care and socialization of young children, who are seen as less cultured and therefore closer to nature than adults. Women are closely associated with family life, distancing them from activities such as politics, warfare and religion which are seen as the province of men.

Ortner also argues that **woman's psyche**, her psychological make-up, is defined as closer to nature. Because women are concerned with childcare and primary socialization, they develop more personal, intimate and particular relationships with others, especially their children, than men do.

Criticisms of Ortner

Ortner fails to show conclusively that in all societies culture is valued more highly than nature. Although many societies have rituals that attempt to control nature, it is not clear that nature is necessarily devalued in comparison to culture. Indeed it could be argued that the very existence of such rituals points to the superior power of nature.

Stephanie Coontz and Peta Henderson (1986) provide some examples to contradict Ortner. Among the Sherbo of West Africa, children are seen as close to nature, but adults of both sexes are seen as close to culture. Coontz and Henderson also claim that not all societies devalue nature. The Haganers of Papua New Guinea distinguish culture and nature, but do not rank one above the other.

Michelle Zimbalist Rosaldo – the public and the domestic

The anthropologist Michelle Zimbalist Rosaldo (1974) was the first to argue that women's subordination was the consequence of a division between the public and the private (or domestic) world.

She argues that there are two distinctive areas of social life:

1 The domestic, which she defines as 'institutions and modes of activity that are organized immediately around one or more mothers and their children'. As her use of the word 'mother' implies, she believes that it is usually women who are associated with this sphere.
2 The public, which, in contrast, is seen as being primarily the province of men. She defines the public sphere as 'activities, institutions and forms of association that link, rank, organize or subsume particular mother–child groups'.

Thus the domestic sphere includes the family and life in the place of residence of the family, while the public sphere includes the activities and institutions associated with rituals and religion, politics and the economy.

Like Firestone and Ortner, Rosaldo argues that women have been disadvantaged in every known society. Although she accepts that biology is the basis of women's oppression, she argues, like Ortner, that the link between the two is indirect. It is the *interpretation* given to women's biology that leads to their disadvantages, not the biology itself. This interpretation ties them to the rearing of children and the domestic sphere.

Men, on the other hand, are better able to keep their distance from domestic life. As a result, they do not need to show the same personal commitment to other humans as that required from mothers. Men are associated more with abstract authority, and with the political and religious life of society as a whole. Rosaldo argues that as a consequence of men's involvement in religious and political life, they can exercise power over the domestic units which are the focus of women's lives.

Although Rosaldo argues that women have less power than men in all societies, she does believe that inequalities between the sexes are greater in some societies than in others. Thus the Mbuti Pygmies of Africa have a relatively egalitarian society because men and women cooperate in both domestic and economic life. Yet even here men retain some independence from the domestic sphere by having separate and secret flute cults.

Criticisms of Rosaldo

Undoubtedly the distinction between the domestic or private sphere and the public sphere provides a useful way of analysing and explaining the relative powerlessness of women in many societies. If women are largely excluded from the institutions that exercise power in society, then it is hardly surprising that men possess more power than women. Furthermore, this distinction helps to explain how the position of men and women in society has changed (see, for example, the section on 'The origins of gender inequalities and industrialization', pp. 108–9).

However, Linda Imray and Audrey Middleton (1983) argue that women's activities tend to be devalued even when they take place in the public sphere. When women take paid employment outside the home, the jobs they do are often regarded as being of less importance than those of men. From this point of view, the devaluation of women must have deeper roots than their association with domestic life. Certainly, as we will see in later sections, the increasing employment of women outside the private home has not produced equality for women within work.

Firestone, Ortner and Rosaldo all agree that women's subordination to men is universal. They all to some extent agree that the ultimate source of inequality between the sexes is biology, or the interpretation placed on biology. These views are not accepted by all sociologists. Marxist and socialist feminists question the view that women's subordination has always been universal. They claim that it is necessary to examine history to find out how and why inequality between the sexes came about.

We will examine some of these viewpoints in the next section.

The origins of gender inequalities – Marxist and socialist perspectives

Marx's associate, Friedrich Engels, devoted more attention to the sociology of gender than Marx himself. In *The Origin of the Family, Private Property and the State* (1972), Engels outlined his theory of how human societies developed.

Engels – inequality and private property

In the earliest phases of societal development (which Engels called **savagery and barbarism**), gender inequalities favoured women rather than men. There was a division of labour by sex, with men mainly responsible for procuring food and women mainly responsible for the domestic sphere, but women were not subordinate to men. Private property existed in only a rudimentary form and consisted mainly of simple tools, utensils and weapons. What private property there was passed down through the female, not the male, line. This was because monogamous marriage did not exist. Both men and women could have sex with as many partners as they chose. Consequently, men could never be sure that their children were theirs. In contrast, since women give birth, they have no such doubt about their offspring, and so property was passed on to children by the women.

According to Engels, it was during the period of barbarism that women suffered a 'world-historic' defeat. Men gained the upper hand when animals were domesticated and herded and became an important form of private property. Then meat and other animal products became crucial parts of the economy of early societies. Men gained the responsibility for owning and controlling livestock, and were unwilling to allow this important property to be passed down the female line; through owning livestock men overthrew the dominance of women in the household. In Engels's words, 'the man seized the reins in the house also, the woman was degraded, enthralled, the slave of the man's lust, a mere instrument for breeding children'.

In order to ensure that they could identify their own children, men increasingly put restrictions on women's choice of sexual partners. Eventually, during the period Engels calls **civilization**, monogamous marriage was established. By this stage, men had gained control over what was now the patriarchal family.

Criticisms of Engels

Unfortunately, Engels's theory was based upon unreliable anthropological evidence. His history of early societies no longer seems plausible in the light of more recent research into simple societies (which we discuss later in this chapter). Nevertheless, Engels's pioneering Marxist theory of the origins of gender inequalities laid the foundations upon which later Marxist and socialist feminists have built. Engels suggested that particular historical conditions led to the subordination of women, and he directed attention towards the material, economic reasons that could account for this.

Stephanie Coontz and Peta Henderson – women's work, men's property

Stephanie Coontz and Peta Henderson (1986) provide an example of an attempt to explain women's subordination from a Marxist/socialist perspective. They agree with Engels on a number of important points but provide a more complex theory based upon more empirical evidence.

Coontz and Henderson argue that most early societies began not with female dominance, but with equality between the sexes. They accept that, from earliest times, there was a division of labour by sex, but this in itself did not make inequality inevitable. In most (though not all) societies, some women were excluded from hunting and risky tasks, such as trading and warfare, that could involve travel over long distances. However, it was only pregnant women and nursing mothers who had these restrictions placed on them. It was social convenience, rather than biological necessity, that led to an early division of labour. For example, it was difficult for women nursing children to combine this activity with warfare, as young babies could prove a considerable inconvenience in battle. Women did, nevertheless, become successful warriors in some societies (for example, in Dahomey in West Africa).

Despite the existence of a sexual division of labour, Coontz and Henderson believe that the earliest societies were **communal** – the resources produced by men and women alike were shared by everyone. Meat from the hunt and gathered vegetables were given to both the kin and the non-kin of those who produced the food. Even strangers would usually be fed. In these circumstances it was not important to identify the father of a specific child, since the offspring of particular individuals had no special rights to food.

Property and gender inequality

Like Engels, Coontz and Henderson argue that the introduction of herding and agriculture laid the foundations for gender inequalities. These new modes of production made it more likely that a surplus would be produced which could be accumulated or distributed.

However, the most important factor in the transition to a society with gender stratification was the appearance of a form of communal property to which a group of kin had exclusive rights. **Kin corporate property**, as Coontz and Henderson describe it, meant that for the first time non-kin and strangers lost their right to share food and other resources. In these circumstances, parenthood and kinship relationships became important, and senior members of kinship groups gained control over property. Age and seniority began to be associated with greater economic power, as well as higher status.

Patrilocality and gender inequality

Some societies had a system of **patrilocality**; in other words, wives went to live with their husband's kin. Women, as gatherers, continued to act as producers, but they lost control over the products of their labour. What they produced no longer belonged to their own kin corporate group but to that of their husband. Other societies were **matrilocal**: husbands moved to live with their wife's kin group. Coontz and Henderson claim that such societies were more egalitarian; women retained greater power because there was less opportunity for men to concentrate property in their own hands.

However, matrilocal societies tended to be less successful. Patrilocal societies had more chance of expanding through the practice of **polygamy**. Men could marry a number of women and, in doing so, increase the labour force. The extra wives could gather and process more food. Patrilocal societies therefore expanded at the expense of matrilocal ones, which meant that more people were living in societies in which men were dominant.

This theory of the development of gender inequalities is perhaps more sophisticated than that of Engels, and rests upon sounder anthropological evidence. Despite its claims to provide an entirely social explanation, though, it still uses a biological starting point. It assumes that women's capacities to give birth and suckle children tended to result in a division of labour in which women were largely responsible for cooking and gathering, and men for hunting.

The origins of gender inequalities and industrialization – a liberal feminist approach

Ann Oakley has been a prominent figure in the development of feminist sociology. She does not align herself strongly with a particular feminist perspective. Her work includes elements of socialist feminism, arguments that fit well with radical feminism, and studies that fall more within the liberal feminist tradition. The study discussed below fits most closely with the liberal feminist tradition because it suggests that women's oppression is not universal but is historically variable. She emphasizes the importance of opportunities (or lack of opportunities) in paid work in explaining gender inequality.

Oakley (1981) traces the changing status of women in British society from the eve of the industrial revolution, in the eighteenth century, to the 1970s. She claims that 'the most important and enduring consequence of industrialization for women has been the emergence of the modern role of **housewife** as "the dominant mature feminine role"'. In this section, we summarize Oakley's views on the emergence of the housewife role.

The family as the unit of production

In pre-industrial Britain the family was the basic unit of production. Marriage and the family were essential to individuals for economic reasons, since all members of the family were involved in production. Agriculture and textiles were the main industries, and women were indispensable to both. In the production of cloth, the husband did the weaving while his wife spun and dyed the yarn. On the farm, women were in charge of dairy produce. Most of the housework – cooking, cleaning, washing, mending and childcare – was performed by unmarried offspring. The housewife role (which involved the domesticity of women and their economic dependence on men) had yet to arrive. Public life, concerned with economic activity, and the private life of the family were not as distinct as they are today.

The factory as the unit of production

During the early stages of industrialization (which Oakley dates from 1750 to 1841), the factory steadily replaced the family as the unit of production. Women were employed in factories where they often continued their traditional work in textiles.

The first major change that affected their status as wage earners was the Factory Acts, beginning in 1819, which gradually restricted child labour. Children became increasingly dependent upon their parents and required care and supervision, a role that fell to women. Oakley argues that 'the increased differentiation of child and adult roles, with the child's growing dependence, heralded the dependence of women in marriage and their restriction to the home'.

Restrictions on women's employment

From 1841 until the outbreak of the First World War in 1914, a combination of pressure from male workers and philanthropic reformers restricted female employment in industry. Women were seen by many male factory workers as a threat to their employment. As early as 1841, committees of male factory workers called for the 'gradual withdrawal of all female labour from the factory'. In 1842 the Mines Act banned the employment of women as miners. In 1851 one in four married women were employed; by 1911 this figure was reduced to one in ten.

Helen Hacker states that, with the employment of women as wage earners:

> *Men were quick to perceive them as a rival group and make use of economic, legal and ideological weapons to eliminate or reduce their competition. They excluded women from the trade unions, made contracts with employers to prevent their hiring women, passed laws restricting the employment of married women, caricatured the working woman, and carried on ceaseless propaganda to return women to the home and keep them there.*
>
> Hacker, 1972

Victorian ideology, particularly that of the upper and middle classes, stated that a woman's place was in the home. No less a figure than Queen Victoria announced: 'Let woman be what God intended, a helpmate for man, but with totally different duties and vocations' (quoted in Hudson, 1970). The following quotations from articles in the *Saturday Review* illustrate the ideal of womanhood in mid-Victorian times. In 1859:

> *Married life is a woman's profession, and to this life her training – that of dependence – is modelled.*

And in 1865:

> *No woman can or ought to know very much of the mass of meanness and wickedness and misery that is loose in the wide world. She could not learn it without losing the bloom and freshness which it is her mission in life to preserve.* Quoted in Hudson, 1970, pp. 53–4

Oakley claims that during the second half of the nineteenth century these attitudes began to filter down to the working class. Thus a combination of factors, which included ideology, the banning of child labour, and restrictions on the employment of women, locked the majority of married women into the mother–housewife role.

The return to paid employment

Oakley states that from 1914 to 1950 there was a 'tendency towards the growing employment of women coupled with a retention of housewifery as the primary role expected of all women'. During these years, women received many legal and political rights (for example, the vote in 1928), but these had little effect on the central fact of their lives: the mother–housewife role.

Oakley concludes that industrialization has had the following effects on the role of women:

1. The 'separation of men from the daily routines of domestic life'
2. The 'economic dependence of women and children on men'
3. The 'isolation of housework and childcare from other work'

In twentieth-century British society the role of housewife–mother became institutionalized as 'the primary role for all women'.

These generalizations perhaps became less valid as time progressed. Subsequent sections will suggest that women have made significant gains in terms of increasing their economic independence, and there may also have been some increase in male participation in childcare. Even so, the changes produced by the industrial revolution still exert a powerful influence on the organization of Western societies and Western culture. Furthermore, Oakley believes that the extent to which women have shaken off the housewife role has been greatly exaggerated (see pp. 497–8).

Gender in contemporary societies – radical feminist perspectives

For radical feminists, **patriarchy** is the most important concept for explaining gender inequalities. Although literally it means 'rule by the father', radical feminists have used it more broadly to refer to male dominance in society. From this point of view, patriarchy involves the exercise of power by men over women. Kate Millett was one of the first radical feminists to use the term and to provide a detailed explanation of women's exploitation by men.

Kate Millett – radical feminism and sexual politics

In her book *Sexual Politics* (1970), Kate Millett argues that politics is not just an activity confined to political parties and parliaments, but one which exists in any 'power-structured relationships, arrangements whereby one group of persons is controlled by another'. Such relationships of domination and subordination can exist at work, when a man instructs his female secretary to make a cup of tea, or in the family, when a husband's meal is cooked by his wife. Political relationships between men and women exist in all aspects of everyday life.

According to Millett, such relationships are organized on the basis of patriarchy, a system in which 'male shall dominate female'. She believes that patriarchy is 'the most pervasive ideology of our culture, its most fundamental concept of power'. It is 'more rigorous than class stratification, more uniform, certainly more enduring'.

Like other radical feminists, Millett suggests that gender is the primary source of identity for individuals in modern societies. People react to others first and foremost as men and women, rather than in terms of their class membership. It is a rigid system of stratification: sex is ascribed and almost impossible to change.

The basis of patriarchy

Millett identifies eight factors which explain the existence of patriarchy:

1. She claims that biology in the form of superior male strength has played some part in creating gender inequality. However, early socialization is even more important because it encourages males to be aggressive and females to be passive. Males and females are taught to behave and think in ways which reinforce the biological differences that exist.
2. Millett points to **ideological** factors in her search for the roots of patriarchy. Again, she attaches importance to socialization. Men are socialized to have a dominant temperament. This provides men with a higher social status, which in turn leads to them filling social roles in which they can exercise mastery over women.
3. Millett also considers **sociological** factors to be important. She claims that the family is the main institution of patriarchy as it plays an important part in maintaining patriarchy across generations, socializing children into having different temperaments and leading them to expect and accept different roles in later life.
4. Millett discusses the **relationship between class and subordination**. She believes that women have a caste-like status that operates independently of social class. Even women from higher-class backgrounds are subordinate to men. This relationship is maintained by the ideology of romantic love which obscures the

real situation in which women become dependent on men in families.

5 Millett also believes that **educational factors** handicap women and this is reinforced by women's economic dependency. Even in contemporary societies the paid work that women do is usually menial, badly paid and lacking in status. Much of it (housework, for example) is unpaid. Economic inequalities are reinforced by educational ones. Women tend not to study high-status subjects such as the sciences which lead to the best job opportunities.
6 Millett argues that men also retain patriarchal power through **myth and religion**. Religion is used as a way of legitimating masculine dominance. As Millett puts it, 'patriarchy has God on its side'. To illustrate this point she notes that the Christian religion portrays Eve as an afterthought produced from Adam's spare rib, while the origins of human suffering are held to have their source in her actions.
7 An additional source of men's power is **psychology**. Patriarchal ideology is 'interiorized' by women because of all the above factors. Women develop a passive temperament and a sense of inferiority which is reinforced by media images of women.
8 Millett identifies **physical force** as the final source of male domination. Patriarchy is ultimately backed up by force. She points to many examples of the use of violence against women, such as the stoning to death of adulteresses in Muslim countries, 'the crippling deformity of footbinding in China, [and] the lifelong ignominy of the Veil in Islam'. In modern Western societies women are also the victims of violence. Rape and other forms of sexual violence are ever-present threats and ways in which all women are intimidated by all men.

Criticisms of Millett

Millett made an important contribution towards explaining the disadvantaged position of women within society. However, her work has been criticized by socialist and Marxist feminists. They have identified three main weaknesses in her theory of sexual politics:

1 Sheila Rowbotham (1982) argues that patriarchy is too sweeping a category. Because Millett regards all societies as patriarchal, she fails to explain the particular circumstances which have produced male domination in its current forms. To Rowbotham, the term patriarchal implies that male domination has some universal, perhaps biological, cause. This implication 'ignores the multiplicity of ways in which societies have defined gender'.
2 Rowbotham also questions the assumption in Millett's work that all men exploit all women. She says that 'patriarchy cannot explain why genuine feelings of love and friendship are possible between men and women, and boys and girls, or why people have acted together in popular movements'.
3 Another criticism of Millett, and radical feminists in general, is that they ignore the material basis of much of the oppression of women. To Marxist and socialist feminists, it is capitalism rather than patriarchy that explains women's oppression in modern societies.

Gender in contemporary societies – Marxist and socialist perspectives

Marx and Engels and women under capitalism and communism

Apart from explaining the origins of inequality between men and women, Engels (1972) also tried to foresee how women's position in society would change as capitalism developed. Engels believed that economic factors caused women's subservience to men, and only economic changes could lead to their liberation. He stated that 'the predominance of the man in marriage is simply a consequence of his economic predominance and will vanish with it automatically'. Men enjoyed greater power than women because it was men who owned the means of production, or who earned a wage outside the home.

However, Marx and Engels believed that capitalism would eventually lead to some reduction in inequalities between men and women. They argued that the demand for female wage labour would raise the status and power of proletarian women within the family. Female employment would largely free women from economic dependence upon their husbands and so from male dominance within the family.

Although women have entered the labour force in increasing numbers, some Marxist and socialist feminists deny that this has led to the changes anticipated by Marx and Engels. As we will indicate in a later section, women continue to be financially disadvantaged compared to men, even when they take paid employment. They tend to get lower wages and lower-status jobs than men (see pp. 121–4). Furthermore, they still seem to have less power than men within the family (see Chapter 8).

Engels believed that true equality between men and women would arrive with the establishment of communism, when the means of production would be communally owned. Engels predicted that the communal ownership of the means of production would be accompanied by the socialization of housework and childcare. Sexual inequality would end. Gender roles would disappear.

Evidence from former communist countries suggests that Engels was wrong. In a review of studies of the USSR, Nickie Charles (1993) found that women did make some progress under communism. However, in 1991, just before the USSR broke up with the collapse of communism, average wages for women were only about two-thirds of those for men, and women still took responsibility for most of the childcare.

Evidence reviewed by Charles suggested that after the end of communism women's position in the labour market deteriorated in most post-communist countries. Certainly neither communism nor the introduction of capitalist free markets resulted in an end to gender inequality.

Contemporary Marxist feminism

Some Marxist feminists have argued that women's position in society primarily benefits capitalism and capitalists rather than men. Margaret Benston (1972) argues that capitalism benefits from a large reserve labour force of women 'to keep wages down and profits up'. (For a discussion of the reserve army of labour theory see p. 127.) In their role as secondary breadwinners, married women provide a source of cheap and easily exploitable labour. Because women have been socialized to comply and submit, they form a docile labour force which can be readily manipulated and easily fired when not required.

Compared to male workers, women are less likely to join unions or to go on strike or take other forms of militant action against employers. Even when women join unions, they often find themselves in male-dominated organizations. To some degree, sexist ideology splits the working class along sex lines and thereby makes them easier to control.

Some Marxists also believe that women benefit capitalists and the capitalist system in their capacities as mothers and housewives by reproducing labour power at no cost to employers. (We discuss this in more detail in Chapter 8.)

Criticisms of Marxist feminism

There are a number of difficulties with Marxist approaches that explain gender inequalities in terms of how they benefit capitalism. Some Marxist feminists claim that such explanations ignore many of the questions raised by feminists. In terms of the Marxist theory, women appear insignificant: they sit on the sidelines of the grand struggle between capital and labour. Marxism may explain capitalism, but it does not explain patriarchy.

Heidi Hartmann (1981) does not believe that Marxism on its own can explain gender inequalities, because it is 'sex-blind'. In other words, Marxism can explain why capitalists exploit workers, but not why men exploit women. For example, it might be possible to explain in Marxist terms how it benefits capitalism for housework and childcare to be carried out free of charge, but not why women in particular should be responsible for these tasks. Capitalism would benefit as much from househusbands as housewives.

Hartmann accepts that Marxism can play an important part in explaining gender inequalities; however, she believes that feminism must be fully incorporated into any adequate theory. Hartmann provides an example of an attempt to cement a 'marriage' between Marxist and feminist theory.

The 'marriage' of Marxism and feminism

Hartmann (1981) claims that Marxism explains the creation of particular jobs, but it is 'indifferent' to who fills them. Thus it does not explain why women have lower-paid and lower-status employment outside the home, nor why they continue to carry the main burden of domestic responsibilities, even when they are working as well.

Hartmann follows radical feminists in seeing society as patriarchal, but she believes that patriarchy has a material base. Patriarchy is maintained through the way that men control women's labour power. Men deny women access to jobs that pay a living wage, forcing them to be dependent on men. This allows men to control the unpaid labour done by women as housewives and mothers. Because of men's dominance within the family they also control women's bodies and sexuality. Women who are married become almost their husband's property.

Hartmann believes that capitalism and patriarchy are very closely connected, or 'intertwined', but they are not the same and she does not believe that the interests of men as a group and capitalists as a group are identical. For example, ruling-class men may benefit from increasing numbers of women entering the labour force, whereas working-class men may prefer their wives to stay at home to perform personal services for them.

The possible conflict of interests has been resolved as capitalism and patriarchy have learned to coexist in a partnership that fundamentally damages neither partner. For example, in the nineteenth century, male-dominated unions were able to get laws passed limiting women's right to do paid work. Employers had to pay male workers a 'family wage' to support wives who were not working. This cut capitalist profits and restricted the supply of labour, but it placated men, since their power over women was maintained. At the same time capitalists gained because it reduced the likelihood of class-conscious action by male workers.

Hartmann accepts that the increasing participation of women in work today has made them slightly less dependent on men, but the wages tend to be too low to give them true independence.

In Hartmann's analysis Marxism and feminism remain something of an unhappy marriage.

Sylvia Walby – *Theorizing Patriarchy*

Sylvia Walby (1990, 1997) has developed an approach to understanding gender in contemporary societies which does not fit into any of the types of feminism described in earlier sections. Indeed, she starts her 1990 book, **Theorizing Patriarchy**, by pointing out the main criticisms that have been made of other approaches.

Criticisms of existing perspectives

1. Radical feminism has been criticized for 'a false universalism which cannot understand historical change or take sufficient account of divisions between women based on ethnicity and class'.
2. Marxist feminism has been criticized for concentrating on gender inequalities under capitalism and

therefore being unable to explain the exploitation of women in non-capitalist societies.

3 Liberal feminism has been seen as lacking 'an account of the overall social structuring of gender inequality'. Its approach can provide no more than partial explanations. For example, it offers no explanation of how gender inequalities first developed.
4 Walby also criticizes what she calls **dual-systems theory**. By this she means approaches such as that of Hartmann (see above) which explain women's exploitation in terms of two separate systems of capitalism and patriarchy. Walby criticizes Hartmann for underestimating the amount of tension between capitalism and patriarchy and for failing to take account of aspects of patriarchy such as violence and sexuality.

Walby tries to improve on other perspectives by incorporating their strengths into her own theory while avoiding their weaknesses.

Patriarchy

To Walby, the concept of patriarchy must remain central to a feminist understanding of society. She says that '"patriarchy" is indispensable for an analysis of gender inequality' (Walby, 1990). However, her definition of patriarchy is different from that of other feminists. She argues that there are six patriarchal structures which restrict women and help to maintain male domination. These are:

1 Paid work
2 Patriarchal relations within the household
3 Patriarchal culture
4 Sexuality
5 Male violence towards women
6 The state

Each of these structures has some independence from the others, but they can also affect one another, reinforcing or weakening patriarchy in a different structure. Each structure is reproduced or changed by the actions of men and women, but the existence of the structure also restricts the choices that humans, particularly women, can make.

Walby claims that patriarchy is not a fixed and unchanging feature of society and she accepts that changes have taken place in the nature of patriarchy.

Walby does not regard relations between males and females as the only source of inequality. She acknowledges that there are also 'divisions between women based on ethnicity and class' and she discusses the ways that patriarchy, racism and capitalism interact.

We will now examine how Walby describes the role of different aspects of patriarchy in explaining gender inequalities.

The structures of patriarchy

Paid employment

Walby believes that **paid employment** has been and remains a key structure in creating disadvantages for women. In nineteenth-century Britain, regulations excluded women from whole areas of work. In the twentieth century women gained more access to work but were still disadvantaged compared to men. Men continue to dominate in the best-paid jobs, and women are still paid considerably less than men and do most of the part-time work. Many women choose not to work, or work part-time, because of poor job opportunities.

Household production

According to Walby, households sometimes involve distinctive **patriarchal relations of production**. Individual men directly exploit women by gaining benefits from women's unpaid labour, particularly in the home. Women still do most of the housework and childcare and some women suffer violence and abuse in marriage. However, easier divorce means women are not as trapped as they once were by marriage. Furthermore, some Black feminists see family life as less exploitative than life in the labour market where there is considerable racism.

Culture

Walby believes that the **culture** of Western societies has consistently distinguished between men and women and has expected different types of behaviour from them, but the type of behaviour expected has changed.

In the nineteenth century women were thought more feminine if they confined their activities to the domestic sphere and did not take paid work. Walby claims that 'the key sign of femininity today … is sexual attractiveness to men'. Furthermore, 'it is no longer merely the femininity of young single women that is defined in this way, but increasingly that of older women as well'. Sexual attractiveness was also important in Victorian times, but less important than today. It was also 'relatively undercover' compared to contemporary culture.

Escaping from the confinement of domesticity has created greater freedom for women, but the new emphasis on sexuality is not without its costs. Pornography, in particular, increases the freedom of men while threatening the freedom of women. To Walby, 'the male gaze, not that of women, is the viewpoint of pornography', and pornography encourages the degradation of women by men and sometimes promotes sexual violence.

Sexuality

Walby argues that 'heterosexuality constitutes a patriarchal structure', but again the nature of it has changed.

In the nineteenth century women's **sexuality** was subject to strict control within monogamous marriage, where the husband's pleasure was far more important than the wife's. In the twentieth century better contraception and the greater ease of divorce increased women's sexual freedom. Walby quotes research which suggests that more women were being unfaithful to their husbands and that in general women had experienced sexual liberalization. However, Walby believes that 'the sexual double standard is still alive and well'. Young women who are sexually active are condemned by males as 'slags'; those who are not are seen as 'drags'. On the other hand, males with many sexual conquests are admired for their supposed virility.

There is more pressure on women today to be heterosexually active and to 'service' males by marrying or cohabiting with them. Thus heterosexuality remains patriarchal, even though women have made some genuine gains.

Violence

Like other feminists, Walby sees violence as a form of power over women. The use of violence, or the threat of violence, helps to keep women in their place and discourages them from challenging patriarchy.

According to Walby, the lack of reliable evidence from the past makes it impossible to determine whether the amount of violence against women by men has increased or decreased. She does believe, however, that the state, and in particular the police, have become more willing to take action against the worst offenders. Nevertheless, action against violent husbands is still infrequent and some women continue to be subject to male violence, while other women continue to fear it.

The state

State policies relating to gender have changed considerably since the nineteenth century. For example, there has been:

> *the cessation of legal backing to exclusionary practices in employment; the increased ease of divorce and financial provision for non-wage earners; the ending of state backing to exclusionary practices in education and the removal of most forms of censorship of pornography; the decriminalization of contraception and abortion under most circumstances; and minor changes in the law making it marginally easier for a woman to leave a violent man.* Walby, 1990

Most of these changes have brought gains for women but, to Walby, 'the state is still patriarchal as well as capitalist and racist'. State policies are no longer directed at confining women to the private sphere of the home, yet there has been little real attempt to improve women's position in the public sphere and equal opportunities legislation is rarely enforced.

From private to public patriarchy

As well as identifying specific changes in patriarchy, Walby argues that there has been a change in the overall structure of patriarchy. In the nineteenth century, patriarchy was predominantly private; in the twentieth century, it became public. Table 2.1 summarizes how Walby characterizes this change.

Private patriarchy

In private patriarchy an **individual patriarch**, the male head of household, controls women 'individually and directly in the relatively private sphere of the home'. It is 'the man in his position as husband or father who is the direct oppressor and beneficiary, individually and directly, of the subordination of women'. Women remain oppressed because they are prevented from entering the public sphere in areas such as employment and politics.

Household production was the most important structure of private patriarchy, but its importance has now declined.

The shift away from private patriarchy

The shift away from private patriarchy was in part a consequence of **first wave feminism**. Between 1850 and 1930, women in the USA and Britain campaigned for much more than just voting rights. They also sought:

> *the containment of predatory male sexual behaviour (Christabel Pankhurst's slogan was 'Votes for women, chastity for men'), access to employment, training and education, reform of the legal status of married women so they could own property, for divorce and legal separation at the woman's behest as well as that of the husband … for the collective rather than private organization of meal preparation.* Walby, 1990

These campaigns took place 'against the background of an expanding capitalist economy' and capitalists requiring a larger workforce. There was pressure from male trade unionists to continue to exclude women from employment so that they could not compete for men's jobs.

The result was a series of compromises in which women gained greater access to the public sphere, capitalists were able to employ more women in their enterprises, and male workers ensured that women were restricted in the employment opportunities open to them (see pp. 110–11 for further details). These compromises led to the emergence of a new public form of patriarchy.

Table 2.1 Private and public patriarchy

Form of patriarchy	Private	Public
Dominant structure	Household production	Employment/State
Wider patriarchal structures	Employment State Sexuality Violence Culture	Household production Sexuality Violence Culture
Period	Nineteenth century	Twentieth century
Mode of expropriation	Individual	Collective
Patriarchal strategy	Exclusionary	Segregationist

Source: S. Walby (1990) *Theorizing Patriarchy*, Blackwell, Oxford, p. 24

Public patriarchy 'is a form in which women have access to both public and private arenas. They are not barred from the public arenas, but are nonetheless subordinated within them.' In the public sphere, women tend to be segregated into certain jobs which are lower-paid and are given a lower status than men's jobs. The state and employment become the dominant structures of patriarchy, but the other structures remain important. Women are no longer exploited so much by individual patriarchs, but instead are exploited collectively by men in general through their subordination in public arenas. As Walby puts it, 'women are no longer restricted to the domestic hearth, but have the whole society in which to roam and be exploited'.

Variations in patriarchy

Walby believes that there has been some reduction in patriarchal exploitation in certain areas as a result of the changes. There is a generational difference in the way older and younger women have experienced patriarchy, with younger women being somewhat less oppressed. However, the effect is not the same for all groups of women. For example, Walby believes that Muslim women are more restricted by family structures than other women, and are therefore more subject to private patriarchy than other groups. Afro-Caribbean women, on the other hand, are more likely than other ethnic groups to have paid employment and to head their own families, and are therefore more subject to public patriarchy.

Furthermore, there has been a polarization in the position of women from different classes. Middle-class women compete with men in the public sphere on less unequal terms than working-class women. Job opportunities have begun to open up for well-educated women, and some women are playing a greater part in political and social movements; however, patriarchy remains very restrictive for working-class women and those with few qualifications. In a post-Fordist economy (see pp. 127–8 and website) many women are still restricted to part-time, low-paid and insecure employment.

Evaluation of Walby

Walby's theory of patriarchy incorporates the insights of many different feminists. Nevertheless, her work has been criticized. Floya Anthias and Nira Yuval-Davis (1992) criticize her for using what they see as a **three-systems approach**. According to them, Walby treats gender, 'race' and class as separate systems which interact with one another. Anthias and Yuval-Davis believe that patriarchy, capitalism and racism are all part of one system, which advantages some groups and disadvantages others.

Jackie Stacey (1993) praises Walby for 'an all-encompassing account of the systematic oppression of women in society' and for showing an awareness of historical changes in the position of women. However, she criticizes her for her use of the concept of structure. Stacey says that 'some structures are more clearly conceptualized than others (for example, paid employment and culture)'. In the case of some other structures, Walby does not make such a good case for the existence of relatively fixed relationships which contain women. Stacey believes that Walby neglects 'any consideration of identity and lived experience' by focusing on a structuralist analysis which 'fails to explain how people negotiate such a system'.

To Stacey, good feminist sociology pays more attention to the subjective states of women and to how women come to terms with or resist oppression. Similar reservations are expressed by Anna Pollert (1996), who questions the usefulness of the whole concept of patriarchy.

Anna Pollert – *The Poverty of Patriarchy*

Anna Pollert (1996) has criticized the use of the term patriarchy by feminists in general, and by Sylvia Walby in particular. She notes that feminists have attacked the use of male **grand narratives**, such as the Marxist analysis of capitalism and the whole idea of progress, but have stubbornly stuck to using the idea of patriarchy. Pollert, on the other hand, believes that the concept is of little use and tends to hold back feminist analysis rather than helping it to develop.

Pollert's central point is that the idea of patriarchy often involves the use of a **circular argument**. Patriarchy is used both as a description of inequalities between men and women and as an explanation of those inequalities. She uses the example of Heidi Hartmann's work (see p. 111). According to Pollert, Hartmann sees patriarchy as based upon male control over female labour power. In doing so, she fails to explain how men come to control women's labour power in the first place. Hartmann argues that the control comes from the exclusion of women from independent work and control over their work, but this can only be explained in terms of the control over women's labour power which it is supposed to be explaining. Thus Pollert believes that Hartmann is arguing, in effect, that men have control over women because men have control over women. Such circular arguments are typical of most theories that employ the concept of patriarchy.

Other theories, such as that of Walby, can be criticized because they claim, but fail to establish, that patriarchy is a system which forms part of society. Thus Walby sees patriarchy as a system which is sustained by substructures such as violence, sexuality, culture and so on. Pollert does not believe that patriarchy is a system or a structure in the same sense as capitalism. She says that 'there is no intrinsic motor or dynamic within "patriarchy" which can explain its self-perpetuation. Capitalism, on the other hand, does have such an internal dynamic: the self-expansion of capital – profit – which drives the system.' Capitalists are constrained to pursue profit. If they fail to do so, they will go out of business. Gender systems are not constrained in the same way. Men and women can treat each other differently, or even change sex, 'without social production grinding to a halt, or abolishing all gender relations between men and women'.

Pollert believes that theories such as those of Walby lose sight of 'agency'. That is, they neglect the choices made by individual actors as they reproduce or resist existing sets of social relationships. She describes Walby's division of patriarchy into six structures as 'an arbitrary exercise' which 'leads to the static perspective of arbitrating parts in which agency is even more absent than before'.

Pollert believes that Walby has not succeeded in

breaking free from dual-systems theory, seeing capitalism and patriarchy as two separate if linked systems. Pollert argues that they are not separate at all. She says 'class relations are infused with gender, race and other modes of social differentiation from the start'. Because class and gender are intertwined it is inappropriate to use structural analysis to understand how they relate to one another. Instead, it is necessary to carry out detailed empirical studies of how they and other social differences relate to each other in particular contexts.

Pollert is in favour of using a materialist analysis which stresses economic inequalities and favours detailed qualitative research. She herself has conducted research of this type with women working in a hosiery factory (Pollert, 1981).

However, as Pollert acknowledges, this is not the only way in which sociologists have reacted to criticisms of structural concepts such as patriarchy. Postmodernists, too, have tended to reject any overarching theory of gender in favour of describing the viewpoints of different women. Pollert rejects postmodernism because it uses obscure language which is hard for ordinary people to understand. It is also **relativistic**, that is, it records the viewpoints of different women but is unwilling to say that any viewpoint is stronger than any other. It therefore loses any sense of trying to change and improve the lives of women.

Notwithstanding Pollert's criticisms, postmodernism has become a major influence on the theories of gender which we will now consider.

Postmodernism, sex and gender

Destabilizing theory

Pollert (1996) notes that some sociologists who have rejected structural concepts such as patriarchy have turned to **postmodernism** as an alternative to detailed empirical studies. As we have just seen, Pollert herself rejects postmodernism, but in recent years it has become an increasingly influential approach to the study of sex and gender.

Michèlle Barrett and Anne Phillips (1992) argue that new feminisms have developed because of a dissatisfaction with the general theories characteristic of traditional male-dominated social science. Feminism has always been suspicious of theories developed by men, but in the past liberal and socialist feminists have embraced aspects of male theories. Recently, however, there has been 'a sweeping attack on the falsely universalizing, overgeneralizing and over-ambitious models of liberalism, humanism, and Marxism. Many feminists have joined sympathies with poststructuralist and postmodernist critical projects'. Barrett and Phillips describe this attack as a process of **destabilizing theory**. The apparent certainties offered by the liberal, Marxist/socialist and radical feminisms developed in earlier decades are no longer uncritically accepted. Despite the differences between these types of feminism, they were united in seeking to find the causes of women's oppression in inequalities in society. That consensus has now broken down.

Barrett and Phillips argue that this change was stimulated by three main factors:

1 The development of Black feminism. Dual-systems theories (see p. 112) could not readily accommodate a third system.
2 Increased suspicion of the distinction between sex and gender. Both psychoanalysis and the belief that some aspects of femininity (such as mothering) were positively superior to masculinity led some feminists to question the idea that men and women could be both equal and alike. Female difference came to be seen in a more positive light.
3 Postmodern ideas were having an increasingly influential role in social science generally.

Tensions and affinities between postmodernism and feminism

Susan Hekman (1990) argues that there are both affinities and tensions between postmodernism and feminism. She says that:

> *despite the similarities between the two movements, however, there is at best an uneasy relationship between postmodernists and feminists. Few feminists are willing to label themselves postmodernists and, similarly, many postmodernists are profoundly sceptical of the feminist movement.* Hekman, 1990

This tension exists because feminism could, in certain respects, be seen as a modern social theory. It is modern in the sense that it offers a general theory of how society works and it seeks to find ways to ensure progress towards a better society. Postmodernists reject the possibility both of a general theory and of a recipe for improving society.

However, there are important affinities between postmodernism and feminism. Hekman points out that both question conventional scientific models of knowledge. Feminists, for example, argue that knowledge can come from women's experiences rather than from positivist data produced by methods such as questionnaires (see Chapter 13). Both feminists and postmodernists question Enlightenment thinking (see Chapter 14), in the sense that neither believe that male rationality is adequate for understanding the social world. Furthermore, both question what Hekman calls the 'fundamental dichotomies of Enlightenment thought, dichotomies such as rational/irrational and subject/object' (see pp. 890–1).

Hekman believes that the affinities between feminism and postmodernism are sufficiently great for them to be able to combine into a **postmodern feminism**. Certainly, such an approach has become increasingly popular and has posed an important challenge to more conventional feminisms.

The main features of postmodern feminism

Postmodern feminism has some similarities with aspects of Black feminism. Postmodern feminism tends to reject the claim that there is a single theory that can explain the position of women in society. It encourages the acceptance of many different points of view as equally valid. In particular, it tends to deny that there is any single, unitary essence to the concept 'woman'. Groups of women (for example, black women, lesbian women, white middle-class women) and individual women are different. Furthermore, groups of women and individual women change constantly and are therefore impossible to pin down to some essence or core.

Pamela Abbott, Claire Wallace and Melissa Tyler (2005) argue that 'central to postmodern theory is the recognition that identity is multiple and provisional – race, sex, age, sexuality, and so on are constantly revised and renegotiated'. They go on to say that, 'By rejecting the idea of a central core constituting the person, postmodernism shifts attention away from the subject as a manifestation of her "essence" to "the subject in process" – never unitary and never complete.' Incomplete subjects – subjects who are always developing – also tend to be different from one another.

Postmodernism tends therefore to celebrate differences and to attack the idea that some characteristics are to be preferred to others. For this reason, postmodern feminists sometimes reject the idea that women can progress by taking on the characteristics and gaining the social positions traditionally reserved for men. Many postmodern theories reject the idea of progress altogether. Postmodern feminists see the whole idea of progress as a product of a dominant, male rationality. Some see ideas such as 'justice' and 'equality' as concepts associated with male reason, which seeks to manipulate and control the world. They reject these sorts of aims, which they see as the product of masculine styles of thinking.

Nevertheless, postmodern feminists have suggested ways in which the interests of women in general can be pursued. Unlike more conventional feminisms, though, these have more to do with the **use of language** than with such things as improving job opportunities, freeing women from biological constraints or getting men to do more housework. Such approaches see their principal aim as **deconstructing male language** and a masculine view of the world.

According to postmodern feminists, males see the world in terms of pairs of opposites (for example, male/female, good/evil, true/false, beautiful/ugly). They take the **male as normal** and the **female as a deviation** from the norm. For example, Sigmund Freud saw women as men who lacked a penis and who envied males for possessing one (penis envy). **Deconstruction** involves attacking linguistic concepts typically regarded in a positive way and reinterpreting their opposites in a positive light. Deconstructionists thus turn conventional thinking on its head. For example, they might regard femininity, evil, falsehood and ugliness as desirable characteristics.

In fact, postmodern feminists go further than this, questioning the whole idea of truth by claiming that language cannot represent some external reality. Not only should the binary opposition projected by male thought be rejected, but also language itself fails to represent a feminine understanding of the world. Language is the ally of male rationality. It is used to impose an artificial order on the world, and to express the masculine desire to manipulate and control, to plan and achieve objectives. Languages that have been developed primarily by men are inadequate for understanding the ways in which women understand and experience the world.

To postmodernists, woman is the **other**, that which is not man. However, as Tong (1998) puts it, 'otherness, for all its associations with oppression and inferiority, is much more than an oppressed, inferior condition. It is also a way of being, thinking, and speaking allowing for openness, plurality, diversity and difference.' By making the voices of different women heard and taken seriously, it becomes possible to escape from the straitjacket of male thought and male, modern language. Such ideas have their origins in the work of French social theorists such as Jacques Lacan and Jacques Derrida. Derrida has been particularly influential and his ideas will now be examined.

Influences on postmodern feminism

Jacques Derrida

Jacques Derrida is a French writer who has had a great influence on postmodern feminism (see Kamuf, 1991, for extracts from Derrida). Derrida is often described as a **poststructuralist**. **Poststructuralism** is a general term to describe diverse theorists who reject the view that there are rigid social structures, and who emphasize the importance of language (see Chapter 11, pp. 681–2). Other poststructuralists include Jacques Lacan and Michel Foucault (see pp. 559–62).

Derrida's ideas derive from **linguistics**, the analysis of language. By questioning the nature of language, Derrida opens up a whole range of implications for the study of society in general, and sex and gender in particular.

The Swiss linguistic theorist Ferdinand de Saussure first distinguished between the **signifier**, a word, and the **signified**, the thing to which it refers. Thus the word 'dog' is a signifier that refers to the signified, the actual animal. Saussure argued that signifiers were arbitrary. For example, there was no necessary connection between the word 'dog' and the animal to which it referred. Any other word would serve just as well as the signifier. However, Derrida went much further in questioning the nature of language and in doing so opened up questions of sex and gender.

Derrida argued that language was a self-contained system of signifiers. Signifiers referred not to some independent reality but to other signifiers. Thus the word 'dog' can only be understood with reference to other words or signifiers such as 'animal', 'bark' and so on. There is an unbridgeable gap between objects and the way we describe them. The objects are physically separate from those people who describe them and separated in time. We use the term 'dog' as an alternative to producing an actual dog to illustrate what we are talking about. Using the sign or signifier 'dog' is therefore based on the absence of a dog itself. Derrida uses the French word *différence* to indicate how the signifier is unlike the signified. *Différence* has two meanings in French: being unlike or dissimilar, and being delayed. *Différence* indicates, therefore, that words are fundamentally different from the things to which they refer and are postponed or delayed representations of things which are not present.

This abstract analysis of language leads Derrida to be highly suspicious of any claims to have established the truth. Since language cannot truly represent an objective reality, claims to absolute truth cannot be accepted. Attempts have been made to find a sign on which all other concepts can be based. Examples include God, and matter, but none have removed the distance between the subject and object, the human being and what they are describing.

Derrida argues that existing belief systems are based upon the use of **binary oppositions**. That is, they are based upon a belief in pairs of opposites. Sarup (1988) notes that some key oppositions according to Derrida are 'signifier/signified, sensible/intelligible, speech/writing ... space/time, passivity/activity'. Usually, however, one of the pair is suppressed, while the other is brought to the fore and regarded as superior. Thus good is seen as superior to evil, activity as superior to passivity, and so on. Such binary oppositions are closely connected to ideologies which make strong distinctions between what is desirable and what is not. It is possible to undermine these binary oppositions, and therefore the ideologies on which they are based, by the process of **deconstruction**.

Deconstruction involves showing how the favoured term only has a meaning in contrast with its opposite. Thus good has no meaning unless its opposite, evil, exists. Furthermore, Derrida tries to show that there is really no reason for privileging one term at the expense of its opposite. Good is no better than evil, and evil no worse than good. By turning pairs of opposites against one another, he tries to undermine the whole idea that binary opposition should form the basis for thinking about the world.

Derrida's work tends to support **relativism**, that is, denying that any one truth can be found. Any particular text can be taken apart and shown to have contradictions within it. (By text Derrida means any written or visual document that can be interpreted. Examples include books, articles, films, paintings and so on.) By revealing these contradictions it is possible to show that a text can have different meanings, with no one interpretation able to stand as superior to the others. The meaning of texts is also relative because of **intertextuality**. By this Derrida implies that texts are given their meaning by referring to meanings in other texts. However, these texts in turn only derive their meaning from further texts, so the meaning of any single text can never stand alone or be finally determined.

At times, Derrida's work touches directly on issues to do with gender. He regards male/female and nature/culture as unacceptable dualisms in Western thought. He is also critical of phallocentric (or penis-centred) language which, according to Tong (1998), 'connotes a unitary drive towards a single supposedly reachable goal'. Just as male sexuality involves the aim of orgasm and ejaculation, so male language is based upon achieving an identified objective. It puts little emphasis on the enjoyment of experience rather than the achievement of goals.

We will now examine the views of some postmodern feminists who have been influenced by Derrida.

Postmodern feminists

Hélène Cixous

Hélène Cixous is a French novelist and feminist writer who sees language as a key part of gender difference. She says:

> *Everything is word, everything is only word ... we must grab culture by the word, as it seizes us in its word, in its language ... Indeed, as soon as we are, we are born into language and language speaks to us, language dictates its law.* Cixous, quoted in Haste, 1993

Cixous believes that language is male-dominated or, as she terms it, **phallocentric**. Its form is masculine. Both *how* things are said and *what* is said (and written) reflect masculinity and particularly male sexuality. Like Derrida, Cixous believes that male thought and language can be seen as phallic. She complains of 'the woman who still allows herself to be threatened by the big dick, who's still impressed by the commotion of the phallic stance' (Cixous, 1981a).

Male sexuality, the sexuality of the phallus, has a single focus, the penis, and is directed towards particular goals such as penetration and orgasm. Men have tended to define women in terms of a lack of a penis. Most men are afraid of women because they fear castration, and women, lacking a penis, are seen as being like castrated men. However, Cixous believes that, in reality, female sexuality, which she calls *jouissance*, is much more subtle and varied than male sexuality. Women can find pleasure in different parts of their bodies and can achieve greater pleasure than that offered by the phallus. Women's sexuality, and indeed the whole feminine perspective on the world, has been repressed and needs to escape from this repression and express itself openly.

In 'Castration or decapitation' Cixous (1981b) illustrates her ideas by using a Chinese story. In the story, the king tells his general, Sun Tse, to train his 180 wives to be warriors. The general agrees and proceeds to try to teach the king's wives to march in time. However, the wives ignore the instructions and instead talk and laugh among themselves. Sun Tse regards this as mutiny and persuades the king that his wives should be executed for their actions. The king agrees and starts by beheading two of them. The rest of the wives now start following instructions and duly march to order as required. To Cixous, this is an example of the 'masculine economy' which:

> *is governed by a rule that keeps time with two beats, three beats, four beats, with pipe and drum, exactly as it should be. An education that tries to make a soldier of the feminine by force, the force history keeps reserved for woman ... Women can keep their heads only on condition that they accept complete silence, turned into automatons.* Cixous, 1981b

Cixous then explains how women can begin to counter male force. She says that women and femininity should:

> *start speaking, stop saying that she has nothing to say! Stop learning in school that women are created to listen, to believe, to make no discoveries. Dare to speak her piece about giving ... Speak of her pleasure and, God knows, she has something to say about that, so that she gets to unblock a sexuality that's just as much feminine as masculine, 'de-phallocentralize' the body, relieve man of his phallus, return him to an erogenous field and a libido that isn't stupidly organized round that monument, but appears shifting, diffused, taking on all the others of oneself.* Cixous, 1981b

Such a change would not be easy. Current male-dominated language is incapable of expressing feminine sexual pleasure.

Cixous goes into further detail about the aspects of male language that need to be countered. Following Derrida, she claims that phallocentric language is based around dualisms, or pairs of opposites. These are all related to 'the couple man/woman' (Cixous, 1981a).

Examples include:

- Activity/Passivity
- Sun/Moon
- Culture/Nature
- Day/Night
- Father/Mother
- Head/Heart
- Intelligible/Sensitive
- Logos/Pathos
- Man/Woman

The oppositions are hierarchical, with the masculine ranked higher than the feminine.

Despite the strength of phallocentrism in culture and language, Cixous does believe that change is possible. Furthermore, men could benefit from the change as well as women. Cixous does not think that there is an absolute difference between men and women. Femininity and masculinity can be present in both sexes. If women can develop ways of expressing the joy of femininity and succeed in speaking out, more men as well as women will benefit from the revelation of the feminine.

Helen Haste – The Sexual Metaphor

Like Cixous, Helen Haste (1993) also attaches great importance to the role of language and to the existence of dualisms. However, Haste puts particular emphasis on the role of **metaphors** in language. Metaphors are not merely comparisons between one thing and another, they also shape the way that people see the world and how they act. Gender differences go deeper than patriarchy or capitalism; they are enshrined in language. Different metaphors are used to understand the lives of men and those of women. Haste says, 'the lives of modern industrial men can be metaphorically constructed in terms of finite, achievable tasks'.

Women, however, experience their lives differently, in terms of cycles, rather than in terms of tasks which are completed and followed by another task. Haste says that 'women's lives are experienced, in so many areas, as cycles – physical and biological cycles, diurnal cycles of nurturance and preparation of food, cycles of caring, cleansing, and the annual cycles of family life'. Only men working in agriculture have such close involvement with cycles.

Like Cixous, Haste believes that it is difficult to express and understand female experiences through a language dominated by men, and particularly by male metaphors. One such metaphor is the idea of 'Man the Hunter'. This has been used to reinforce dualisms such as public and private: men should go out into the public sphere and do the literal or metaphorical hunting, while women should be confined to the private sphere. Haste says:

> *Man the Hunter illustrates some key points of my argument. The image implies a scenario or script for certain aspects of male behaviour. It contains a set of rules for behaviour, motives, skills and – most importantly – relations with others. The scenario is understood by all members of the culture. It gives meaning and symbolism beyond the literal context – the commercial entrepreneur is perceived as a metaphoric hunter, and his actions are construed in terms of a hunter's performance, skillfully pursuing prey, seeking spoils and returning to the female for approval.* Haste, 1993, p. 29

Such metaphors maintain dualistic thinking. Since the Enlightenment, the contrast between masculine rationality and female emotion has been a central dualism. Haste is critical of feminists who accept the male conception of rationality and simply assert that females can be as rational as men. Haste argues that there are distinctive and equally valid feminine ways of looking at the world. Male conceptions of truth see it as something to be arrived at through the detached, impersonal use of logic. Female conceptions of truth see it as linked more to experience and negotiation with others. Thus she argues that:

> *one cannot know, either simply through detachment and objectification; one must gain knowledge through participation. Language and communication are vitally important, because our concepts depend on the language available to us. Persuasion – the recognition of the other person's point of view and the accommodation of one's arguments to that point of view – is essential for comprehension and the development of ideas.* Haste, 1993, p. 33

For women, who in contemporary cultures are defined as the 'Other' – that which is not male – the search for truth is the search for authenticity. They need to find out who they really are and move beyond being defined and defining themselves as simply the non-masculine.

Haste acknowledges that there have been significant changes in recent decades. For example, she points out that the most significant 'is the growing recognition that women are sexually autonomous beings who have their own sexual needs and their own sexual desires'. This change has also benefited men because it has led to their 'liberation from the need to pursue and to perform Olympically, and freedom to seek mutual sexual enjoyment and a more fulfilling and satisfying sexual egalitarianism'. But while Haste wants greater equality between the sexes, she does not want the sexes to become alike. The masculine view of the world should no longer be accepted as the only view. Women should no longer be seen as the Other to the male. What is needed is an acceptance of different viewpoints. She concludes that:

> *the metaphor of the two-way mirror in which both perspectives are possible is, in my view, the only one which can resolve this – just as recognizing pluralism is the only way to resolve the debates that pit monolithic rationality against the chaos of relativism.* Haste, 1993

Postmodern feminism – an evaluation

Rosemarie Tong (1998) is among those who are generally supportive of postmodern feminism. She argues that it encourages an awareness and an acceptance of differences: differences between men and women, the masculine and the feminine, and different types of masculinity and femininity. It supports an acceptance of the validity of the points of view of the 'excluded, ostracized, and alienated so-called abnormal, deviant, and marginal people'.

However, some critics accuse postmodern feminism of doing almost the opposite, of losing sight of inequality and oppression and mistakenly reducing them to differences in the use of language. Thus Sylvia Walby (1992) argues that the emphasis on difference rather than inequality leads postmodernists to 'conceptualize power as highly dispersed rather than concentrated in identifiable places or groups. In the face of the complexity of the social world the postmodernists' response is to deny the possibility of causality and macro-social concepts.' Walby is very much opposed to such tendencies. She admits that there are significant differences between groups of women, yet still thinks that concepts such as 'patriarchy' are valid. This becomes particularly obvious, according to Walby, when you examine the work of writers such as Mies (1986). Mies claims to show that women are disadvantaged throughout the world in rich and poor countries alike. If the exploitation is worldwide, the concept of patriarchy is valid and what unites women is as important as what makes them different from one another.

While Walby criticizes postmodernists for arguing that women are fragmented into many different groups, others have accused postmodern feminism of the opposite, of treating women as all alike. Writers such as Cixous can be seen as arguing that there is an essential difference between men and women. The way they see and experience the world is fundamentally different. Rosemarie Tong (1998) says that 'difference feminists, especially postmodern feminists, celebrated women's bodies, reproductive rhythms, and sexual organs ... critics of postmodern feminism claim that if the truth be told, difference feminists use the term difference in an "essentialist" way'. That is, they have reacted against the view of some conventional feminists who claim that there is no real difference between men and women, by going to the opposite extreme. They have returned to what might be seen as discredited arguments that men and women are fundamentally different.

Tong rejects this criticism. She believes that writers such as Cixous distinguish between femininity and masculinity as ways of understanding the world, but do not make absolute distinctions between men and women. Men can have feminine perspectives and women masculine ones. However, this line of criticism does show that there are significant differences between postmodern feminists. Some seem to celebrate the diversity of femininity, while others concentrate more on the distinctiveness of femininity.

Like most other broad perspectives within the social sciences, there are significant differences within each school of thought, which can make generalizations about their strengths and weaknesses dangerous. Nevertheless, postmodern feminists do seem to be united in their emphasis on the importance of language. Language may well have been neglected by other social theories, but the emphasis on language leads to a neglect of other sources of inequality and difference. For example, postmodern feminists say little about the use of physical force by males, or about inequalities of wealth and income, which might play an important role in maintaining gender inequalities in general. They also say little about the way in which gender differences might have a negative effect on the world as a whole. The same cannot be said of the next approach, which examines the global impact of gender differences in many areas of social life.

Ann Oakley – *Gender on Planet Earth*

Postmodernism as a delusional system

In an important contribution to feminist thinking, Ann Oakley (2002) develops a global perspective on the impact of gender inequalities. Oakley draws upon a number of strands of feminist thinking including liberal, socialist and radical feminism (see below). However, she goes beyond all of them by introducing a global perspective and by discussing the impact of patriarchy on the social world as a whole, not just on gender inequality. Although Oakley draws ideas from most types of feminism, she is dismissive of postmodernism, calling it a 'delusional system'. She has three main criticisms:

1. Oakley criticizes postmodernism for 'obscurity'. She says the language used by postmodernists is 'dense, imprecise, long-winded, grammatically complex, hugely inaccessible', and it therefore completely fails in one of its central aims, 'demystifying and opening up knowledge to multiple perspectives' (2002, p. 190).
2. Oakley says that postmodernism 'wraps intellectuals in sterile debates and isolates them from important social movements'. It seems little concerned with real issues, with global injustices, with social problems, and Oakley scathingly argues that 'A main function of postmodernism is to support the careers of postmodernists' (190–1).
3. Oakley also criticizes postmodernism for its blanket attack on science. She agrees that there are many distortions in science but she believes that a systematic approach to gathering evidence and evaluating ideas is important. According to Oakley, Jean François Lyotard's (see pp. 891–3) attack on science was based on very little knowledge of science. Indeed Lyotard later admitted that he 'made up stories' about science (quoted in Oakley, 2002, p. 191).

For these reasons Oakley does not accept the postmodernist view that other forms of theory are invalid, and instead she tries to develop feminism to push towards greater understanding of a changing world.

Feminism and patriarchy

Feminism

Oakley does not align herself with any particular feminist theory in *Gender on Planet Earth*, but the influence of different types of feminism is apparent.

1. From **liberal feminism** Oakley takes the idea that equality is the overall objective. She does not want one gender to be dominant but instead wants the

overall system of patriarchy to change. She does not generalize about all men – for example, she says that many men are opposed to violence. However, she does criticize the 'dominant form of masculinity in Western culture' which 'is both aggressive and misogynist'. She differs from some radical feminists because she does not believe that men are biologically programmed to be violent.

2 From **socialist feminism** Oakley takes the view that capitalism and patriarchy are jointly responsible for the world's problems. For example, discussing male violence she claims that 'The values of capitalism – competitiveness, profit and self-seeking materialism – interact with those of (white middle-class) men as the dominant group' (2002, p. 38).
3 From **radical feminism** she takes the idea that masculinity is a threat to the world and that feminine values are in some ways superior and better for the world. To Oakley, masculine values lack 'caring, empathy, compassion, altruism and forgiveness' (2002, p. 38). Like many radical feminists, she emphasizes the damage done by male violence.

Putting together these different strands of feminism, Oakley argues that feminism 'was/is about the claiming of rights and opportunities on a non-gendered, non-discriminatory basis'. It 'sees particular institutional structures … as linked to a more deep-seated and long-lived system of masculine power and privilege, which is itself closely tied to the economic and moral structures of capitalism' (2002, p. 116).

Oakley takes a structural view of society, arguing that you need to understand 'the ways in which the behaviour of men, women and children, including inside families, is influenced by these wider processes of power and economics' (2002, p. 116). It is the overall structure of patriarchy and capitalism that causes the problems, not men as individuals. Indeed, she argues that both men and women 'collude' in maintaining the sex/gender system. However, the positions of men and women in this system are not equal – men do have more power than women.

To Oakley, feminism is not just about the problems of women, the behaviour of men, or inequality between men and women. She admits that important strides forward have been made in terms of women's rights and that some forms of gender inequality have been reduced. We no longer live in a society where there is any restriction on women's property ownership, education or choice of marital partners Men are rarely completely dominant and discrimination is less obvious and more subtle than it used to be. However, Oakley believes that patriarchy is the 'default mode: what's always there and will always happen unless it's actively contended' (2002, p. 27).

The extent of change can also be exaggerated. Oakley quotes figures for Britain showing that 87 per cent of the care of young children is still done by women, that far more women than men are low-paid, that only 18 per cent of MPs are women, and so on. Furthermore, patriarchy as a system leads to a wide range of social practices and institutions which are damaging and destructive for the planet as a whole. To Oakley, unless this is challenged, the future will be bleak.

The effects of the patriarchal system

Oakley identifies a wide variety of ways in which she believes that patriarchy and capitalism are damaging or destroying the planet and its inhabitants.

1 **Transport**. Oakley is a keen cyclist and she extols the virtues of cycling in terms of the lack of damage to the environment. She quotes figures which show that cycling greatly reduces mortality rates. However, the dominant patriarchal system promotes car use above cycling. Cars, of course, contribute greatly to global warming, and enormous numbers of people die on the roads each year. Some of them are cyclists because roads are rarely designed to be safe and user-friendly for cyclists, and motorists are often inconsiderate of the safety of cyclists. The dominance of the car, just like the dominance of men in public life, is simply taken for granted.
2 **Violence**. It is not only men who are violent, but evidence suggests that men commit about 90 per cent of all violence. Oakley claims that there is a 'global picture of violence against women', including 'genital mutilation … violence associated with prostitution and pornography; dowry-related murder; selective malnourishment of female children; sexual abuse of girls; and corporate crimes affecting women in their roles as childbearers and houseworkers' (2002, p. 32). She discusses the violence of men during war and the violence that results from the crimes of corporations which are dominated by men. Most homicides are committed by men, but many more people die as a result of poor health and safety at work.

   Individualized explanations cannot explain the general pattern of male violence, and Oakley does not claim that men are inevitably violent. Instead she sees violence as stemming from what men learn about being masculine, and from attempts to maintain patriarchy as a system. For example, men are most likely to become violent as individuals when their sense of masculinity or their authority is questioned by others, especially if it is questioned by women. Thus, men may kill their female partners if they are unfaithful, or refuse to do their bidding.
3 **Nature and the environment**. In a chapter entitled 'The Rape of Mother Earth', Oakley argues that:

> *We live in a toxic world which poses a major threat to public and personal wealth. It's a world which is intrinsically and perpetually exploitative of human and natural resources, including entire ecosytems … Most environmental damage happens because of the earth's domination by the Western lifestyle, which depends on constantly rising levels of consumption, an addiction to technology, and meat as the basis of the human diet. Its most toxic aspect is the form of material and social relations which produces the logic that the earth's resources are there to be bought and sold … The most culpable are men and male-dominated transnational corporations. The major victims are the poor, women and children and the populations of Third World countries.* Oakley, 2002, p. 127

In Western societies the 'good life' involves driving cars, eating meat, and using large quantities of energy. All these damage the earth, contributing to problems such as global warming. Women are far more likely to be vegetarians than men and less likely to be 'corpse-eaters'. Chemical fertilizers used for animal feed contribute to global warming and pollution, cattle produce methane gas which is a greenhouse gas, and land which goes to feed animals could be used to produce crops for human consumption. Most environmental campaigners are women, and most of those who oppose the violence of slaughtering animals for food are also female. Transnational corporations are male-dominated and they contribute tremendously to climate change by promoting an 'energy-intensive export-oriented model of development' (2002, p. 142)

4 **Reproduction.** Another area in which patriarchy is highly damaging is the control of female reproduction by largely male/capitalist medicine and technology. A wide variety of measures 'involve the invasion of the female body'. These include IVF, sterilization, contraception, caesarian sections and other surgical/medical techniques used in childbirth. Oakley accepts that caesarian sections are sometimes necessary, but the numbers are now much greater than the number required for medical reasons. Doctors in private practice seek extra income through doing unnecessary caesarian sections, and doctors often use the technique to control the time of birth to suit their work schedules. Another way in which women can be 'butchered' by obstetricians is through the unnecessary use of episiotomies (cuts in the vagina to make the passage of the baby easier or quicker).

5 **Delusional systems.** Oakley believes that patriarchy is maintained by belief systems (which she calls delusional systems). These include postmodernism (see above), psychoanalysis and economics. All of them, in different ways, justify and help to sustain patriarchy and/or capitalism. Psychoanalysis (first developed by Sigmund Freud) is described as a 'secular religion', with absurd sexist ideas such as the belief that women suffer from 'penis envy'. To Oakley, there is no convincing evidence to back up its theories, and plenty of evidence that it has little or no therapeutic effect.

She is just as critical of economics, arguing that its convoluted mathematical formulae bear little relationship to the real world, and that economic forecasts are usually very wide of the mark. She maintains that many of the theories of economics simply do not work in real economies. Furthermore, economic calculations of gross domestic product ignore the contribution of women's unpaid work to the economy as a whole.

Oakley is also highly critical of sociobiology (see pp. 94–5 for a discussion and critique of sociobiology). All of these delusional systems contribute to a passive acceptance of patriarchal and capitalist society. Psychoanalysis turns the individual in on themselves and so discourages any questioning of the social order; while laws of economics portray self-seeking individualism as both inevitable and desirable.

Conclusion and evaluation

Conclusion

Oakley admits that in Western societies many 'old forms of patriarchy have disappeared: husbands and fathers can't, by and large, any longer tell women what to do ... The wages paid to employed women can't just be set according to the whims of (benevolently?) sexist bosses' (2002, p. 216). However, she argues that feminism is just as vital as ever, if we are to understand

> *not only (most obviously) the enduring problem of gender inequality, but the domination of our planet by individual and corporate masculine violence towards women, children, animals, nature and other men, and the fashion for forms of transport and food that damage human beings and entire systems.* 2002, p. 216

The gender system can turn men into 'alienated beasts, and women, if we are honest, into scared outsiders'. To Oakley, unless the gender system is changed, humans will miss the opportunity to 'make our next few billion years' inhabitation of planet earth a better time both for the planet and for us'.

Evaluation

Oakley succeeds in linking gender into very important issues, particularly environmental issues, which are neglected by most other feminists. However, in doing so she perhaps stretches the boundaries of feminism a little and is not always convincing in showing that patriarchy is the cause of the problems. Indeed, in many cases it could be argued that capitalism is a more important factor than patriarchy.

Following Walby's criticisms of Hartmann (see p. 112), Oakley could also be accused of using a dual-systems approach in which the tensions between patriarchy and capitalism are not fully explored. Following Pollert's criticism of the use of the term 'patriarchy' (see pp. 114–15), Oakley could be accused of failing to show that patriarchy is a system or a structure. Although Oakley refers to patriarchy as a system, most of her descriptions seem to depict cultural practices which are not as clearly interlinked and interdependent as the parts of a system. With a book as wide-ranging and ambitious as Oakley's some limitations may be inevitable, but she can be praised for helping to extend the scope of feminist analysis.

Gender and paid employment

Gender inequalities at work

While Oakley broadens the issues addressed by feminists to include global environmental and peace issues, many feminists concentrate on gender inequality, particularly inequality in paid employment. Postmodernists place little emphasis on paid work, but both Marxist feminists and liberal feminists see employment opportunities as crucial to understanding gender inequalities. Liberal feminists have argued that a combination of legislation and changed attitudes can open up economic opportunities for women.

Equal opportunity legislation

In 1970 the Equal Pay Act was passed in Britain. This specified that women were entitled to the same pay as men if they were doing the same or broadly similar work, or if their work was shown through a job evaluation scheme to be of the same value as that carried out by men. A five-year period was allowed for the implementation of the Act.

In 1982, however, the European Court decided that the Equal Pay Act was not consistent with EC legislation and it was strengthened. A 1984 amendment allowed women to claim equal pay for work of equal value if they could show that their job made demands as great as the work carried out by male employees in the same organization in terms of factors such as skill, effort and decision making.

The 1975 Sex Discrimination Act barred discrimination on the grounds of sex in employment, education, and the provision of goods, services and premises. In employment, women were to be given equal access to jobs, and equal chances for promotion. Some types of job (for example, an attendant in a female public toilet) were excluded from the provisions of the Act, if there was considered to be 'a genuine occupational qualification by sex'.

Legislation was further strengthened by the 2006 Equality Act, which, from 2007, required all public bodies to take an active role in removing illegal discrimination against women.

Gender and the labour force

There have been considerable increases in recent years in the proportion of women who work. Figure 2.4 shows that, between 1971 and 2005, employment rates for men declined while those for women increased. In 1971, 92 per cent of men of working age were employed, compared to 56 per cent of working-age women. By spring 2005 only 80 per cent of men were working while the proportion of women had risen to 70 per cent (*Social Trends 2006*, p. 52).

However, a much higher proportion of women than men work part-time. According to the Labour Force Survey (spring 2005), 42 per cent of women in employment worked part-time, but just 10 per cent of men. Most of the rise in female employment has been due to the growing numbers of married mothers who work. In 2004, 67 per cent of mothers with dependent children were in employment, almost as many as the 70 per cent of women without dependent children in employment (*Social Trends 2006,* p. 54). Lone mothers are less likely to be in work than other women – only 53 per cent had jobs in 2004.

Gender and earnings

In 1970, women working as full-time employees earned about 63 per cent of the average male full-time employees' wage. In 1975 the figure was substantially higher at 71 per cent. There was then little further rise until the 1980s. In 2005 the figure stood at 82 per cent (EOC, 1997, 2002a; *New Earnings Survey 2005*).

The gap is rather less when calculated in terms of the median rather than the mean hourly pay. (The median pay is the pay of the person in the middle of the range from the lowest paid to the highest paid. The mean pay is the average pay. The median pay for men is lower than the mean pay because a few men who are very high earners inflate the mean pay of men.) In 2005 the median hourly earnings of women employed full-time were 13 per cent lower than those of equivalent men. There is evidence that there was a gradual narrowing of the gender pay gap between 2001 and 2005 after a period of stability in relative earnings. However, there is a much bigger gap between the hourly pay of men employed full-time and that of women who work part-time. The median pay gap for part-time female workers stood at 41 per cent in 2005 and the mean pay gap at 38 per cent (Women and Work Commission, 2006).

Significant differences in the pay of men and women remain even when they are carrying out similar types of work. Amongst professionals there are substantial pay gaps in the hourly earnings of men and women: in 2005 women in the medical profession earned 23 per cent less, in the legal profession 21 per cent less, in accountancy 15 per cent less, and science and technology professionals earned 14 per cent less (Women and Work Commission, 2006, p. 11). Despite the legislation of the 1970s, women are still paid less than men in a wide variety of occupations.

Although women make up an increasing proportion of the labour force, they are not equally represented throughout the occupational structure. There is both **horizontal** and **vertical segregation** in men's and women's jobs. Horizontal segregation refers to the extent to which men and women do different jobs. Vertical segregation refers to the extent to which men have higher-status and higher-paid jobs than women.

Figure 2.4 Employment rates in the UK, by sex (men aged 16–64, women aged 16–59)

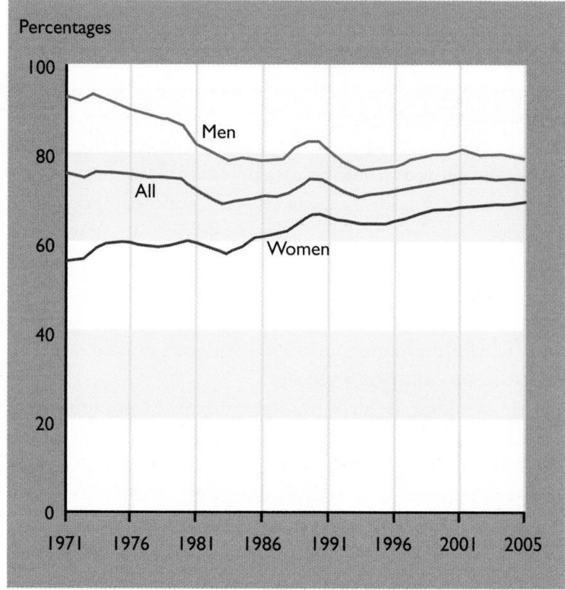

Source: *Social Trends 2006*, p. 52 (figures based on Labour Force Survey, 2005).

In terms of horizontal segregation, the Women and Work Commission noted that:

> *Nearly two-thirds of women are employed in 12 occupational groups: the five 'c's – caring, cashiering, catering, cleaning and clerical occupations – plus teaching, health associate professionals (including nurses), and 'functional' managers, such as financial managers, marketing and sales managers and personnel managers.* 2006, p. 10

Men are employed in a wider range of occupations. Table 2.2 shows that women predominate in sectors such as health and social work, education and hotels and restaurants, while men predominate in construction, transport, storage and communication, and manufacturing.

Another way of examining horizontal segregation is to look at employment figures by occupation type. This also gives some indication of vertical segregation because some types of occupation tend to be higher-status and better-paid than others. Table 2.3 shows that men predominate in manual occupations, particularly in skilled trades, whereas women predominate in personal service, administrative and secretarial, and sales and customer service. Men still comprise nearly two-thirds of managers, but by 2005 there were almost as many female as male professionals. The proportion of female managers and professionals has been increasing in recent years. The Women and Work Commission noted that in 2005 three-quarters of pharmacists, nearly 40 per cent of accountants, about a third of doctors and almost 50 per cent of lawyers were women.

Table 2.2 Employment in Great Britain, by sector, 2005 (employees and self-employed aged 16 and over)

	Women		Men	
Industry sectors	thousands	%	thousands	%
Health & social work	2638	79	703	21
Education	1810	73	666	27
Hotels & restaurants	652	56	519	44
Banking, insurance & pension provision	592	51	567	49
Public administration & defence	963	51	933	49
Wholesale, retail & motor trade	2088	50	2067	50
Real estate, renting & business activities	1330	42	1824	58
Manufacturing	921	25	2693	75
Transport, storage & communication	453	24	1439	76
Construction	215	10	1895	90
All sectors[1]	12668	47	14558	53

[1] Including those not shown separately.

Source: *EOC Facts about Women and Men in Great Britain 2006*, Equal Opportunities Commission, Manchester, p. 21 (figures based on Labour Force Survey, 2005).

Table 2.3 Employment in Great Britain, by occupation, 2005 (employees and self-employed aged 16 and over)

	Women		Men	
Occupational groups	thousands	%	thousands	%
Personal service	1767	84	339	16
Administrative & secretarial	2750	81	653	19
Sales & customer service	1479	69	677	31
Associate prof. & technical	1898	50	1911	50
Elementary	1405	45	1724	55
Professional	1451	42	1988	58
Managers & senior officials	1393	34	2679	66
Process, plant & machine ops	269	13	1776	87
Skilled trades	247	8	2798	92
All occupations[1]	12668	47	14558	53

[1] Including those not classified by occupation.

Source: *EOC Facts about Women and Men in Great Britain 2006*, Equal Opportunities Commission, Manchester, p. 23 (figures based on Labour Force Survey, 2005).

Vertical segregation is even more marked when specific jobs are considered. Table 2.4 shows some of the high-paid and low-paid jobs in 2005 in the UK, the average hourly pay, and the proportions of males and females doing the jobs. It shows that 83 per cent of directors and chief executives (average earnings £56.33 per hour) were men; and 74 per cent of waiters and waitresses (average earnings £5.50 per hour) were women. Men predominate in all the higher-paid jobs except personnel, training and industrial relations managers; while women predominate in all the lower-paid jobs except sports and leisure assistants, where the numbers of men and women are equal.

Generally, the more senior the position, the lower the proportion of women. According to the Equal Opportunities Commission report *Sex and Power: Who Runs Britain?* (EOC, 2006), women were under-represented in elite positions. In 2004 only 9 per cent of senior judges, 10 per cent of senior police officers and 13 per cent of national newspaper editors were women. Women held only 10.5 per cent of the directorships of the FTSE 100 companies (the 100 largest companies on the London Stock Exchange), and 19.7 per cent of MPs and 27.3 per cent of cabinet members were female. Although most teachers are women, in 2004 only 31.8 per cent of head teachers were female. In 2005, less than 1 per cent (0.8 per cent) of senior ranks in the armed forces and only 10.2 per cent of senior police officers were female. The report notes some improvements in the representation of women but calculates that at current rates of change it would take forty years before 50 per cent of top directors were female, and 200 years before there were as many female as male MPs.

Explanations for gender inequalities in employment

As we have seen in previous sections, women face a number of disadvantages in paid work:

1. They tend to be paid less than men.
2. They are more likely to be in part-time work.
3. They tend to be concentrated in the lower reaches of the occupations in which they work.
4. They tend to do particular types of jobs, usually those with a low status.

Table 2.4 Occupational segregation in the United Kingdom, 2005 (employees on adult rates)

		Employees		
	Average pay, £[1]	% women	% men	Thousands
High-paid jobs				
Directors & chief executives of major organizations	56.33	17	83	87
Medical practitioners	33.01	37	63	176
Financial managers & chartered secretaries	29.92	32	68	176
Solicitors & lawyers, judges & coroners	25.89	47	53	94
Management consultants, actuaries, economists & statisticians	24.10	30	70	84
ICT managers	23.94	21	79	163
Marketing & sales managers	22.68	29	71	513
Personnel, training & industrial relations managers	22.37	58	42	95
HE teaching professionals	21.83	41	59	132
Financial institution managers	21.02	43	57	149
Low-paid jobs				
Sports & leisure assistants	7.09	50	50	84
Receptionists	7.07	95	5	219
Packers, bottlers, canners & fillers	6.78	52	48	115
School midday assistants	6.24	96	4	114
Sales & retail assistants	6.16	72	28	1170
Cleaners & domestics	6.04	76	24	590
Retail cashiers & checkout operators	5.85	67	33	221
Kitchen & catering assistants	5.74	73	27	376
Waiters & waitresses	5.50	74	26	133
Bar staff	5.43	60	40	176

[1]Mean hourly pay (£) excluding overtime of all employees, full-time and part-time.

Source: *EOC Facts about Women and Men in Great Britain 2006*, Equal Opportunities Commission, Manchester, p. 24 (figures based on Annual Survey of Hours and Earnings, 2005).

Some explanations for these inequalities argue that gender inequalities in earnings are justified by the characteristics, behaviour or choices of women; while others see the structure of the labour market or the patriarchal nature of society as responsible. Amongst the theories that see society as responsible for women's low pay there are a variety of influences from different strands of feminism. For example, some are influenced by liberal feminism and emphasize differences in socialization and lack of equal opportunity, while others are influenced by radical feminism and emphasize male intimidation and sexism.

The first theory to be examined, however, is influenced by functionalist sociology and economic theory rather than feminism, and contends that there are good reasons for women receiving lower wages.

Functionalism and human capital theory

As we discussed earlier in the chapter (see pp. 96–7), the functionalist Talcott Parsons argued that women are naturally suited to the 'expressive' role of childcare, whereas men are more suited to the 'instrumental' role of competing in the labour market. This implies that women with children will give up or interrupt their careers in order to care for their children.

Human capital theory, which is advocated by some economists, argues that women's lack of commitment to paid employment is the cause of the disadvantages they suffer in the labour market. Women often choose to take career breaks or to work part-time because they wish to combine work with raising a family. Because they are likely to abandon or interrupt their careers at an early age, women have less incentive to invest their time in undertaking lengthy programmes of training or education. They are therefore of less value to employers than their more highly trained and more skilled male counterparts.

Similarly, on average, women will have less experience in their jobs than men because they are less likely than men to be in continuous employment. This makes it difficult for women to be promoted to higher-status and better-paid jobs. Once again, women are paid less than men because they are worth less to the employer. Their lack of training, qualifications and experience, which all result from the demands of childcare, create disadvantages for them in the labour market.

From the point of view of the household it is rational for women to take more responsibility for childcare than men. Only women become pregnant and give birth, making some break from the labour market inevitable for women who have children. As this will tend to lead to women having lower wages than men, households benefit from men concentrating on their careers to maximize the family income.

Anne Witz (1993) is among the many critics of functionalist and human capital approaches. She argues that even when women do work continuously without taking career breaks they still tend to end up in the lower-paid and lower-status jobs.

Teresa Rees (1992) points out that American research designed to test human capital theory has found that only about half the pay differentials between men and women can be explained in terms of the theory.

Peter Sloane (1994) investigated human capital theory using data collected for the Social Change and Economic Life Initiative, which studied the labour markets of Rochdale, Swindon, Aberdeen, Coventry, Kirkcaldy and Northampton between 1985 and 1988. Sloane found that professional qualifications had a big impact on pay, raising pay by 30 per cent compared to non-qualified groups. However, he also found that gender was an important variable, even when controlling for factors such as education, experience and training, which are seen as important by human capital theory. Males still enjoyed a 29 per cent earnings advantage over females, which could not be explained in human capital terms. Human capital theory also ignores causes of inequality between male and female employees located within the structure of the labour market. These will be examined later in this section.

Catherine Hakim – preference theory

Catherine Hakim (2004) does not dismiss human capital theory out of hand, as she believes it does offer useful insights into gender inequality. However, the theory implies that the same factors cause gender inequality in all societies and that inequality stems from rational choices made to maximize family income. Hakim disagrees with both of these points. She argues that the position of women has changed, opening up more choices. She claims that inequality simply stems from personal preferences rather than rational choices designed to maximize family income.

Hakim believes that, until relatively recently, women did not have genuinely equal opportunities. Before the 1960s a number of barriers made it very difficult for all but a small minority of women to be able to pursue a career on anything like equal terms with men. However, five changes have transformed the situation so that there are now much better labour market opportunities for women. These changes are:

1. The **contraceptive revolution** (from about 1965) – the introduction of the pill made it possible for women to control their own fertility.
2. The **equal opportunities revolution**, which Hakim believes 'ensured that for the first time in history women obtained equal rights to access all positions, occupations and careers in the labour market' (2004, p. 14). Hakim does not deny that there may still be some instances of discrimination against women, but broadly she believes that women can get into any area of paid employment.
3. The **expansion of white-collar occupations**, which has created a large reservoir of jobs which women find attractive.
4. There has also been an expansion of **jobs for secondary earners** – for example, jobs with flexible hours, job-shares and part-time jobs.
5. Increased affluence has led to a situation in which **personal preferences** about work have become more important than financial necessity in determining work patterns. Many women can afford to work part-time, or even not at all, because they have partners who are paid enough to meet basic household costs.

Now that these changes have taken place, at least in countries such as Britain and the USA, groups of women have begun to choose different lifestyles. Three different groups emerge:

1 **Adaptive women** combine paid work and family work without prioritizing one or the other. They are likely to vary the balance between the two depending on circumstances such as the age of their children. They want the best of both worlds and are often attracted to flexible or part-time jobs. According to Hakim, this is the biggest group of women, accounting for up to two-thirds of women, depending on the country.
2 **Work-centred women** decide to focus on career development and they fit family life around their work. They are a minority group amongst women (usually less than 20 per cent), and for this reason Hakim believes that men will tend to remain dominant in the workplace.
3 **Home-centred women** represent about 20 per cent of women and they prefer not to do paid work unless required to by a shortage of money. Home-centred women may be well qualified; they may be attracted to higher education because of the opportunities it offers in the marriage market (they can find a good husband) as well as in the labour market.

Hakim backs up her research with data from her own surveys in Spain and Britain, which show, for example, that the employment decisions of adaptive and home-centred women are affected by whether good childcare is available, but work-centred women are not influenced by this.

Hakim's research has proved controversial and has come in for strong criticism from some sociologists.

1 Crompton and Le Feuvre (1996, discussed in Abbott *et al.*, 2005) found, from a study of women working in pharmacy and banking in Britain and France, that there were no clear-cut categories of women. For example, part-time workers were just as committed to their work and careers as those who worked full-time.
2 Research by Houston and Marks (2003, discussed in Women and Work Commission, 2006) found that there were many factors other than personal preference which affected women's attitude towards paid employment. Their study of 400 women who had given birth to their first child found that 14 per cent who had wanted to work were not doing so, and 10 per cent of those who wanted to work full-time were working part-time. The women gave a variety of reasons for not following the working pattern they preferred, including stress or exhaustion and employers who would not allow them to work part-time or flexibly.
3 Pamela Abbott, Claire Wallace and Melissa Tyler (2005) point out that Hakim's theory ignores the way that structural constraints limit and shape choices. They say:

it is essential to remember that when women 'choose' to combine their commitments to unremunerated work with paid employment, the choices they make and their orientations to both are the outcome of a relatively narrow range of choices and the socially constructed expectations of women's roles and responsibilities. They are also shaped by material factors such as social class inequalities, and racial and ethnic power relations, as well as issues such as disability. Abbott *et al.*, 2005, p. 249

The theories which we will now go on to examine focus on how social structures, particularly the structure of the labour market, affect opportunities for women, the kinds of jobs they do and the level of pay they receive.

The dual labour market theory

R.D. Barron and G.M. Norris (1976) were among the first British sociologists to apply **dual labour market theory** to gender inequalities. From this point of view, there are two, not one, labour markets. The **primary labour market** is characterized by high pay, job security, good working conditions and favourable promotion prospects. The **secondary labour market** consists of lower-paid jobs with less job security, inferior working conditions and few opportunities for promotion.

Primary and secondary labour markets often exist side by side within a company, but transfer from the secondary to the primary is difficult, perhaps impossible. Primary sector workers in a firm include professional and managerial staff and highly skilled manual workers. Secondary sector workers include those doing unskilled or semi-skilled manual or non-manual jobs.

According to Barron and Norris, dual labour markets result from the tactics used by employers to obtain the types of labour they require. Employers are prepared to offer relatively high rewards to retain primary sector workers with the necessary skills and experience, but they regard secondary sector workers as more dispensable. Secondary sector workers can be easily replaced, and there is therefore little incentive to offer them high wages, job security or promotion prospects.

Both men and women can be found in the secondary sector, but Barron and Norris believe that women are more likely to have jobs in this sector. Employers tend to ascribe characteristics to women which make them particularly suited to these types of job: they are seen as easy to replace, as having less interest in gaining additional skills, and as less concerned than men with the size of their wage packets (since men are expected to be the main breadwinners within families). The relatively low status of women in society and their tendency not to belong to unions weaken their position further and make it especially difficult for them to get a foothold in primary sector employment. Once recruited to the secondary sector, women are likely to remain captives within it for the rest of their working lives.

Veronica Beechey (1986) identifies a number of limitations to the dual labour market theory:

1 Some women in skilled manual jobs (for example, in the textile industry) still receive low pay although their work is very similar to primary sector men's jobs.
2 Many women do have jobs in the primary sector, but not in industry: for example, nurses, teachers and social workers. The dual labour market theory is not particularly good at explaining the position of women outside manufacturing industry.
3 The dual labour market theory cannot explain why women gain promotion less often than men, even when they are doing the same jobs.

A study by Brendan Burchell and Gill Rubery (1994) also contradicted dual labour market theory. Their study was based upon an analysis of data on work attitudes and work histories in Northampton in the mid-1980s, collected for the Social Change and Economic Life Initiative (Scott, 1994). This research found no simple division between a primary and secondary labour market but instead found five clusters of groups in the labour market. These were:

1. The **primary segment** in the most secure and advantaged jobs
2. **Stickers**, who were relatively satisfied with their work and did not wish to change to gain promotion
3. **Female descenders** (96 per cent of this group were women), who had lost ground in the labour market after giving up full-time work to look after children
4. The **young and mobile**
5. **Labour market descenders**, who had lost position due to unemployment

Although men were over-represented in the most advantaged groups (78 per cent of the primary group were men), and women were over-represented in the most disadvantaged groups, there was no perfect fit between male advantage and female disadvantage. For example, 20 per cent of the young and mobile were women, as were 22 per cent of the primary segment. Most of the labour market descenders who had suffered unemployment were male.

Women as a reserve army of labour

Marxists and Marxist feminists tend to dismiss the sorts of approaches that have been discussed so far, on the grounds that they fail to relate the position of women to the workings of the capitalist economy as a whole. Veronica Beechey (1986) developed a Marxist approach which explains the position of women in the labour market in terms of how capitalism operates.

Marx argued that capitalism required a **reserve army of labour**, that is, a spare pool of potential recruits to the labour force. According to Marx, because of their inbuilt contradictions, capitalist economies went through cycles of slump and boom, and it was essential to be able to hire workers during the booms, and fire them during the slumps. One of the main functions of the reserve army is to reduce the wages of all members of the labour force. A group of unemployed people looking for work creates competition in the workforce. This gives employers an advantage and allows them to reduce wages and increase the rate of exploitation. According to Beechey, women may be particularly suited to form part of the reserve army of labour in Britain because they are less likely to be unionized than men, less likely to be entitled to redundancy payments, and, because of domestic responsibilities, more likely to accept part-time work.

The reserve army of labour theory certainly seems to explain some of the changes that took place in the proportions of women working in Britain during the twentieth century. For example, it would appear to account for the increased employment of women during the two world wars. However, like the other theories examined in this section, it has serious drawbacks. For example, Beechey herself admits that it cannot explain horizontal segregation in the labour market (why women are largely confined to certain types of job). Furthermore, in recent times female part-time and full-time employment has continued to grow, suggesting that it is increasingly difficult to see women's participation in the labour market as a temporary phenomenon. High levels of female employment have continued through both booms and slumps, while unemployment has risen most among men. Thus, while women continue to have more flexible patterns of work than men, they cannot be seen as a reserve army of labour as such.

Linda McDowell – gender and post-Fordism

Linda McDowell (1992) argues that fundamental changes have taken place in the labour market since the late 1960s and these have had important effects on gender and employment. McDowell uses the theory of **post-Fordism** to understand changes in the labour market (for a detailed discussion of post-Fordism, see website). This theory argues that businesses have moved away from mass production towards the flexible production of small batches of specialized products. In doing so, they employ a core of highly skilled workers who are capable of using their skills to produce a wide variety of products. Other work is carried out by part-time workers, or workers on short-term contracts, or is contracted out to other firms. McDowell argues that these changes are reflected in the increased use of part-time female labour and the reduction in the employment of males in full-time permanent jobs.

Women have been used to fill the increasing proportion of jobs in parts of the growing service sector. These types of jobs have traditionally been done by women. Part-time workers are cheaper to employ because they do not have the same rights to unemployment benefit or Jobseeker's Allowance and sick pay as full-time workers; their wages tend to be lower than those of full-time workers; and they are easier to dismiss because they do not have the same legal protections under employment legislation. In most areas of business, employers have been determined to cut costs and to have a more flexible labour force to cope with recessions and increased competition.

Some women have benefited from these changes. A few have found secure and well-paid employment as core workers and have 'captured the labour market opportunities and rewards traditionally reserved for male workers'. Most, however, have not fared so well. The majority of new jobs have been part-time, not because workers wanted part-time work but because it was most convenient for employers. Furthermore, according to the New Earnings Survey, pay per hour for female part-time workers fell from 81 per cent of that for female full-time workers in 1980 to 75 per cent in 1989. With the decline in the availability of well-paid and secure work for working-class men, this has left many working-class women considerably worse off.

John Lovering (1994) conducted an investigation into how restructuring or reorganization within businesses had affected gender divisions in employment. He examined nine different employers in Swindon, including an engineering company, a food manufacturing company, a small hospital, a motorway service station, a shop and a high-technology research company. He found significant differences between employers, but many had very traditional patterns of male and female employment. The longest-established manufacturing and public service industries tended to retain the strongest and most conventional division of labour, with more men in the high-status and full-time jobs.

Lovering did detect some evidence of change within the companies that came closest to being post-Fordist. Restructuring manufacturing companies and newly developing service employers tended to have more flexible ways of operating. He says that 'some new jobs were being created, and this was associated with attempts to reduce or modify the sex-typing of employment'. New opportunities were opening up for internal promotion, with meritocratic considerations gaining in importance over gender stereotyping. Both the service station and the retailer offered some internal promotion opportunities that women were able to take advantage of. Nevertheless, even in such businesses, there was still little likelihood of women getting right to the top.

Lovering's research suggests that a move towards post-Fordism is characteristic of only some employers. Where it has happened, there may be some increase in opportunities for women. He further points out that women will only be able to take advantage of these limited increases in opportunities if they can gain the qualifications and experience which will allow them to apply for the new jobs.

Men, trade unions and women in the labour market

Marxist feminist approaches to women and employment (such as the theory of the reserve army of labour) stress the relationship between the economic system and women's work. However, such approaches tend to ignore the role of men – and particularly male workers – in restricting women's employment opportunities. Sylvia Walby (1986) argues that unions have been an important factor in producing female disadvantage in employment. From a study of engineering, clerical work and textiles in Britain, she claims that two main strategies have been used by males in these industries: the exclusion of women altogether, or the confinement of women to the lower grades of work.

In many parts of the engineering industry, exclusion was the main tactic (at least until 1943), while in clerical and textile work male unionists used grading. In the weaving industry, for example, men were successful in allowing only a few women to be promoted to overlookers. In recent years, male unionists have resorted to tactics mainly involving grading, as legislation has made it difficult to exclude women from whole areas of employment.

Although Walby follows Marxists in describing modern societies as capitalist, she puts particular stress on the concept of patriarchy in trying to explain gender inequalities in employment. She sees unions as patriarchal institutions. Her own research suggests that they are usually dominated by men, and they tend to act in the interests of male employees, even when women form a majority of the union's membership. Nevertheless, she accepts that women have made some gains in the union movement in recent years, and they have had some success in persuading unions to take gender equality more seriously.

Walby believes that work is a major factor shaping domestic relationships. Women suffer such disadvantages in the labour market that they become only too willing to accept the main responsibility for domestic tasks. As she puts it, 'housework is as good as anything else a woman is likely to get'.

Rosemary Crompton (1997) accepts that trade unions may have played an important part in disadvantaging working women in the past. However, she argues that now that an increasing proportion of union members are women, unions have had to take women's interests more seriously. She comments that 'the situation is now transformed as trade unions give both the recruitment of female members and the promotion of equal opportunities policies a high priority'.

Radical feminism and female employment

Radical feminists believe that women's disadvantages in the labour market stem from the exploitation of women by men and have little to do with the operations of capitalism. They concentrate in particular on how men exercise power over women at work and protect their own interests by intimidating women and excluding women from senior positions. Radical feminists claim that one way that men do this is through the use of **sexual harassment**.

Elizabeth A. Stanko (1988) defines sexual harassment as:

> *unwanted sexual attention. Its behavioural forms are many and include visual (leering); verbal (sexual teasing, jokes, comments or questions); unwanted pressures for sexual favours or dates; unwanted touching or pinching; unwanted pressures for sexual favours with implied threats of job-related consequences for non-cooperation; physical assault; sexual assault; rape.* Stanko, 1988, p. 91

Men back up these types of harassment with their power within organizations. They are usually in a position to hire or fire women and may take action against them if they complain. According to Stanko, sexual harassment is a common occurrence at work. She refers to a number of British studies which found that over half of the women questioned had experienced sexual harassment.

Stanko believes that men use sexual harassment to intimidate women who seek to enter areas of traditionally male employment. In such jobs, 'men's working environments become part of men's territories'. The men talk about sport and about women. They may have pin-ups of nude females in the workplace and they resent any challenge to the assumption that they can maintain a working environment which is male-dominated. Stanko says:

> *Sexual jokes, comments, teasing or touching of women are part of the building and sustaining of male solidarity ... Women, it is commonly assumed, by entering into men's territory, must expect and accept these displays of male heterosexuality.* Stanko, 1988, p. 97

In jobs predominantly done by women, the situation is somewhat different. Here, 'sexualizing women who work in traditional occupations serves to eroticize women's subordination'. Waitresses and barmaids, for example, are expected to be sexually attractive and to accept that during their work they may be the recipients of unwanted attention from males. Secretaries 'to some extent become office wives'. Some leave their jobs if their male boss seeks to start an affair.

Another radical feminist, Rosemary Pringle (1992), argues that the work of female secretaries is largely governed by patriarchal images of the job. It is difficult for secretaries to be taken seriously or to have their work valued, because of those images. Secretaries rarely have a clear job description and instead their work is viewed largely in terms of ideas about femininity. Pringle claims that if 'secretaries are represented as women, they are represented almost exclusively in familial or sexual terms: as wives, mothers, spinster aunts, mistresses and femmes fatales'. At every place of work where she conducted her study, at least one person assumed that because Pringle was studying secretaries she must be investigating sexual scandals. Pringle argues that 'the emphasis on the sexual has made it easy to treat the work as trivial or invisible'. Secretaries are sometimes seen as doing little but sitting around and gossiping, 'filing their nails or doing their knitting'. A secretary is often viewed as 'the extension of her boss, loyal, trustworthy and devoted'. The dominant images of secretaries make it very difficult for them to be regarded as skilled workers or considered as possible candidates for promotion into management.

Lisa Adkins – the sexualization of women's work

Lisa Adkins (1995) goes even further in seeing the gendering, and particularly the sexualization, of work as an essential feature of the labour market. Although generally supportive of the kinds of view advocated by Stanko and Pringle, Adkins believes that they still 'assume that capital produces jobs (the places in a hierarchy of waged-workers within the labour market), while (on top of this) the patriarchal control of women's labour limits women's access to those jobs'. To Adkins, though, the places in the labour market often have a gendered character – there are jobs for men or jobs for women, and not jobs that can be filled by either sex. Furthermore, what she calls sexual work is integral to many of the women's jobs. Sexuality does not just permeate the workplace for women, it is also linked to the 'production of men's economic and other advantages in the labour market'.

Adkins bases her arguments largely on research she conducted into women's work in hotels and pubs and at a leisure park. Adkins found that many pub and hotel chains had a deliberate policy of employing married couples. Typically, they employ the husband as the manager but specify in the contract that the wife must contribute to the running of the hotel or pub. Couples in this sort of contract are usually paid about 25 per cent more than a single man. The wife, however, is not paid a salary in her own right – the husband simply receives a higher salary.

Breweries and hotel chains prefer married couples for a number of reasons. First, they get cheap labour, effectively paying only about a quarter of the salary they would need to pay to employ a second manager. Second, they believe that married couples will be more reliable and harder working than single men. Third, 'companies regard wives as "sexual attractions" who will boost sales. Wives being present encourages men to use the establishments.'

The wives studied by Pringle were usually subject to direct control by their husbands. The husbands chose which jobs were done by which partner, often handpicking the most interesting or easiest work for themselves. Women's jobs usually included a combination of serving customers and doing the accounts.

Adkins thinks these arrangements are important because they show that family-based systems of production are alive and well in contemporary capitalist and patriarchal societies. In such systems women's labour amounts to the provision of sexualized services for men, a theme which Adkins develops in her detailed research into a large hotel (which she calls 'Global Hotel') and an amusement park ('Fun Land').

There was strong horizontal segregation at both Global Hotel and Fun Land. At Fun Land operatives of high-speed rides were exclusively young and male, while most catering assistants were female. Operatives of children's rides were a mixture of women and men. Adkins found that the criteria for selecting female catering assistants (whose jobs included serving food and working in bars) included looking attractive. No such criteria were applied to men. Two young women who looked 'too butch' to be catering assistants were given jobs as operatives of the children's rides. These operatives had little contact with male customers.

Adkins found that the female employees were subject to continual sexual harassment from customers and from male operatives. While some senior staff frowned on the behaviour of the male operatives, they did nothing to prevent it. As far as customers were concerned, it was made clear to the young women that they were expected to cope with the attentions of male customers and they were prohibited from responding to them aggressively. Making the male customers feel good by smiling and making light of their sexual innuendoes and other sexualized behaviour was seen as part of their job.

This type of sexual servicing was essentially part of the product being offered by Fun Land. Women who were unable or unwilling to provide it, by not being young or attractive enough or by complaining about harassment, were not employed, or were employed on children's rides, or in some cases were dismissed. For example, the one woman who had the nerve to complain about sexual harassment was sacked for being 'too domineering'.

At Global Hotel similar patterns emerged. The chefs, cooks and bar staff were predominantly male while the waiters/waitresses were predominantly female. The company had personnel specifications to help managers appoint appropriate people to particular jobs. One criterion which was common to all the predominantly female jobs was 'being attractive'. No necessity to 'be attractive' was specified for the male-dominated jobs. Furthermore, Global Hotel's manuals specified that women were required to 'look attractive, clean and fresh' while working, whereas men were not. Like their counterparts at Fun Land, female workers at Global Hotel were expected to make the male customers who harassed them feel good rather than complain about their behaviour.

Adkins concludes that, in many service sector jobs, being sexually attractive and engaging in sexual servicing are integral parts of women's work. Their job is as much about sexuality as it is about serving food or drinks or otherwise dealing with customers' practical needs. A consequence of this is that the 'compulsion on women to carry out sexual work locates men as a more powerful group of workers' and therefore helps to produce patriarchal relationships.

Evaluation

Approaches such as those developed by Stanko and Pringle illustrate how men may use intimidation and ideological power to maintain their domination at work.

Adkins's work suggests how sexuality may be integral to much service sector work undertaken by women. These studies add extra dimensions to an understanding of gender inequalities and gender differences at work but, like all the approaches examined so far, they are somewhat limited in scope. They emphasize the importance of some sources of gender inequality at work while neglecting others. For example, Stanko pays little attention to the operation of the labour market as a whole.

Most of the studies examined so far have tended to emphasize the importance of one main source of female disadvantage in the labour market. It is likely that in reality a number of factors work together to disadvantage women in this sphere. In the final part of this section we will examine a study which incorporates a wider range of factors into its explanation.

The Women and Work Commission – *Shaping a Fairer Future*

In 2006 a Commission set up by the British government reported its findings on how to tackle the pay gap between men and women (Women and Work Commission, 2006). The report, entitled *Shaping a Fairer Future*, broadly follows a liberal feminist approach, arguing that reform, legislation and tackling sexist socialization can largely solve the problem of unequal pay between men and women. Although mainly concerned with identifying practical steps to address inequality, it does also discuss possible causes of gender inequality in employment.

The Commission noted that there had been significant progress in the position of women in the labour market in the thirty years since the introduction of the Equal Pay Act, but that women continued to be seriously disadvantaged. It found that gender inequality led to women's skills being underutilized, resulting in lost productivity and output. This was costing the UK economy a potential £2–9 billion per year. Research showed that there were over one million women who were not working who would like to do so, and that nearly 15 per cent of female part-time workers would like to increase their hours. The report outlined the following causes of, and possible solutions to, gender inequality in the labour market:

1 **Culture**. The Commission found that the pay gap between men and women was small when they first started work. Young women, being better qualified than young men, started in the labour market in a strong position, but as their careers developed women tended to lose out. The Commission quoted research by Manning and Swaffield (2005) which found that after ten years in the labour market women's pay was on average 12 per cent lower than that of men. About half of this difference was due to the sorts of jobs that men and women did; the other half was due to other factors. The concentration of women in lower-paid occupations was therefore the single most important factor holding back women's pay, and the Commission largely attributed this to cultural factors. It found that gender stereotyping was still strong among young people, with most 14 to 16-year-olds readily distinguishing between what they saw as 'men's' and 'women's' jobs. This was reinforced by careers advice which did not question gender stereotypes. Careers advisers rarely pointed out to girls that many of the careers they were interested in were low-paid, and the report quoted evidence showing that most girls were unaware of pay differentials.

Since 2004 all school pupils have been required to get some work experience, but pupils are usually offered placements which are gender-stereotypical. The report discusses an Equal Opportunities Commission study which found that high proportions of males and females said they would like to try jobs traditionally associated with the other sex, but few got the chance to do so. It recommended that there should be 'taster' days to give pupils an opportunity to experience non-traditional work.

The report found that stereotypes developed when the children were young, and these needed to be challenged in schools. Gender stereotyping was further reinforced by the introduction of specialist status for schools. All-girls schools tended to specialize in arts subjects, while all-boys schools tended to specialize in science and technology. The report recommended that schools consider adopting non-gender-stereotypical specialisms. It also suggested that the media could play an important part in breaking down stereotypes by providing role models. For example, about two-thirds of forensic science students were female, a fact which was attributed to the BBC series Silent Witness in which Amanda Burton played a female forensic pathologist.

2 A second key factor in causing gender inequality is the problems faced by women in **combining work and family life**. The report quotes research in the UK Time Use Survey which found that mothers still did three-quarters of the childcare during the week and two-thirds at weekends. Furthermore, a big majority of care work for elderly relatives is still done by women.

Domestic responsibilities often led to women taking career breaks, and this greatly disadvantaged women. As a result of career breaks women lost experience, compared to males who did not take them, and this could lead to lower wages. This cost some women as much as £250,000 in lost earnings during their working life.

The Commission quoted research by Francesconi and Gosling (2005) which found that a single year working part-time before returning to full-time work typically led to a 10–15 per cent reduction in pay. Part-time jobs tend to be concentrated in low-paid sectors, and many skilled women, such as trained teachers, could not get part-time work which used their professional qualifications. The researchers conclude that 'There is a lack of quality part-time work and flexible working at senior levels, arising from the long-hours culture and "prestenteeism" – the need to be seen at work' (Women and Work Commission, 2006, p. 35). The report therefore recommended that firms should be encouraged to offer more quality part-time jobs.

Employers should use increased flexibility in employment practices to make use of underutilized skills amongst female workers and address skills shortages. It was necessary to make 'flexibility part of the corporate working culture'. Help was also needed for women returning to work, perhaps by extending the New Deal (which helps the unemployed find employment or training) to this group. However, most important of all was the extension of good-quality, affordable childcare to all working mothers. The government already had a strategy in place, but the Commission thought it should be extended to help those who did not work standard nine-to-five hours.

3 The third area that needed addressing was developing lifelong opportunities for women in **training**. This would not only help individual women, but could also address skills shortages. There were shortages in many traditionally male areas of employment, such as engineering, construction and information technology. Retraining women in these areas would reduce these shortages. Women's wages could also be raised by encouraging employers to provide more training for low-skilled female workers, for example in order to 'professionalize' occupations such as care work.

4 The fourth main area examined was **workplace practice**. In this context the Commission noted a number of ways in which employers might inadvertently disadvantage women, resulting in low pay. Addressing the pay gap meant challenging biased evaluations of the worth of different jobs. For example, predominantly female sales assistants were paid an average of £5.44 per hour, compared to £7.03 per hour in the largely male occupation of elementary goods storage. Both jobs required similar levels of skill yet one was paid much more than the other.

The report also suggested that the pay structures used by employers could sometimes lead to lower pay for women. Job evaluation schemes sometimes discriminated if they did not fully recognize the skills needed in female-dominated jobs. Starting pay for women returners was often too low, and pay scales related to length of service could be unfair. For many jobs, productivity does not increase significantly after the first few years' service, yet pay continues to rise. Women who took maternity leave sometimes missed out on bonuses and incentives.

The Commission therefore welcomed the use of equal pay reviews where the whole pay structure of an employer was examined to see whether it conformed to equal pay principles. In some organizations, pay reviews had led to significant improvements for women. For example, in the NHS, the Agenda for Change had introduced a non-discriminatory job evaluation scheme. However, Commission members were split on whether such reviews should be compulsory. They agreed that the Equal Pay Act was somewhat ineffective. Few cases were brought under this legislation because of the time, complexity and cost of a successful claim. They noted and welcomed the fact that the 2006 Equality Act (which would come into effect in 2007) required all public bodies to act to remove unlawful discrimination against women, and some members of the Commission thought that this should be extended to the private sector. Other members believed that compulsory pay reviews would be too much of a burden on employers and believed a voluntary policy was preferable.

The Commission concluded that change was desirable and achievable. It emphasized the role of government in making change happen and recommended that there should be a new cabinet subcommittee to oversee the implementation of their proposals.

Evaluation

The Commission certainly identified some important causes of the pay gap, and outlined a number of practical proposals to address it. However, it perhaps overestimated the degree to which piecemeal government intervention could deal with this problem. The reduction in the pay gap has been disappointing, given over thirty years of government intervention. Furthermore, the Commission did not take into consideration the sorts of structural and cultural factors identified by Marxists and radical feminists. These groups would be sceptical that the modest measures proposed by the Commission could make a fundamental difference.

Feminism and the future

In the 1970s and 1980s feminism became an increasingly influential force in sociology and in Western societies. It was partly responsible for increased opportunities for women in many areas of social life. However, by the 1990s the status of feminism in society and in social thought began to be challenged. Feminist and anti-feminist ideas have developed in a variety of directions. There has been something of a backlash against feminism from those who believe either that the movement has gone too far, or that it has already substantially achieved its objectives. Within feminism there has been a degree of fragmentation, with specific groups (such as Black feminists, lesbian feminists, and eco-feminists – who combine feminist and ecological beliefs) representing different strands of feminist thought.

To some extent, this reflects a view that it might be impossible or undesirable to develop a single, all-embracing feminist project for transforming society. There is now increased emphasis on the differences between groups of women, rather than on inequality between women and men. However, not all feminists agree that the emphasis on difference is a good thing and some have argued that feminism is as necessary now as it was in the 1970s. This section examines claims about whether feminism is still needed, and, if so, how feminist thought should develop in the future.

Susan Faludi – *Backlash*

In her 1992 book, *Backlash: The Undeclared War Against Women*, Susan Faludi argues that the women's liberation movement has run into increased opposition. Women have been told by politicians, business leaders and advertisers, among others, that they have won the war for women's rights, and now enjoy equality with men. However, they are warned at the same time that the rights they have won have been at considerable cost. Faludi says:

> *Behind this celebration of women's victory, behind the news cheerfully and endlessly repeated, that the struggle for women's rights is won, another message flashes. You may be free and equal now, it says to women, but you have never been more miserable.* Faludi, 1992, p. 1

In America, for example, magazines and newspapers have claimed that professional career women are prone to infertility and health problems such as alcoholism and hair loss, while women without children and women who do not get married are prone to depression or hysteria. Feminism is portrayed as the root cause of these problems.

Faludi denies that women have attained equality. For example, despite some narrowing in pay differentials between men and women, significant differences remain in both the USA and Britain (see pp. 122–3 for recent figures).

Faludi is also critical of many of the claims about the supposedly harmful effects of women's liberation. She quotes numerous studies which have found that single women and women with careers tend to have more healthy and fulfilling lives than married housewives. Faludi found that:

> *The psychological indicators are numerous and they all point in the same direction. Married women in these studies report about 20 per cent more depression than single women and three times the rate of severe neurosis. Married women have more nervous breakdowns, nervousness, heart palpitations and inertia. Still other afflictions disproportionately plague married women: insomnia, trembling hands, dizzy spells, nightmares, hypochondria, passivity, agoraphobia and other phobias, unhappiness with their physical appearance and overwhelming feelings of guilt and shame.* Faludi, 1992

To Faludi, then, the backlash is not a genuine attempt to improve the lives of women, but rather represents an attempt by men to reassert their dominance. Even so, Faludi is generally optimistic that this attempt will not succeed. She claims, in 1992, that there is 'no good reason why the 1990s cannot be women's decade', and she concludes:

> *whatever new obstacles are mounted against the future march towards equality, whatever new myths invented, penalties levied, opportunities rescinded or degradations imposed, no one can ever take from women the justness of their cause.* Faludi, 1992

Postfeminism

The backlash described by Faludi has been termed **postfeminism** in some circles. However, this term has also been applied to more theoretical developments that have had consequences for the women's movement. Under the influence of postmodernism (see pp. 115–18), some women have begun to question the idea that there can ever be a single project to liberate women. This view argues that women are a highly diverse group and no one group of feminists can claim to speak for all women.

Furthermore, any set of solutions to the general problems of gender inequality is unlikely to be suitable for all groups of women. Like postmodernists, postfeminists reject the idea of a single **metanarrative**, or big story, which claims to offer a single design for improving the world. This change has entailed a focus on the differences between women rather than the inequalities between men and women. Thus Ann Brooks (1997) says:

> *postfeminism as understood from this perspective is about the conceptual shift within feminism from debates around equality to a focus on debates around difference. It is fundamentally about, not a depoliticization of feminism, but a political shift in feminism's conceptual and theoretical agenda.* Brooks, 1997

As part of this shift, the usefulness of terms such as 'patriarchy' and 'women' has been questioned. Postfeminists argue that such terms are over-generalized and falsely assume that oppression is the same for all women and that all women are fundamentally the same.

Brooks attributes this shift to the 'political impact of women of colour's critique of the racist and ethnocentric assumptions of a largely white, middle-class feminism', and to an increasing interest in sexual differences between women (for example, heterosexual women and lesbians).

Writers such as Brooks and others see this change as progressive, and agree that diverse feminisms have played an important part in the women's movement. Thus, for example, Imelda Whelehan (1995) says, 'an important function of black feminism has been to keep alive the vitality of the social and political environment from which it emerged'.

As socialist and Marxist feminism lost popularity and influence in Britain, the **new feminisms** kept women's issues in the public eye. Yet Whelehan warns against abandoning the ideas and language of the earlier era. She says that it 'is important not to lose sight of the early aims of second wave feminism. No matter how simplistic some of their constructions seem today, early critiques made those important steps towards forging a language specific to the experiences of women.' Terms such as patriarchy may indeed be over-generalized, but they have helped to unite women in trying to understand their common experiences and therefore have created a basis for political action to improve the position of all women.

As we will see later, Whelehan (2000) has argued that feminists need to guard against a revival of sexism and patriarchal attitudes. Rather like Faludi, she claims that there has been something of a 'backlash' against feminism, which threatens to reverse some of the gains made by women over the last few decades (see pp. 134–5).

Natasha Walter – *The New Feminism*

Natasha Walter (1998) offers a very different view of contemporary feminism and the future of feminism from that of postfeminists. She rejects the view that there are no longer common causes for which women need to unite. Although she acknowledges that there has been considerable progress for women in Britain, she believes there is still a long way to go before women achieve equality. Furthermore, she is critical of both postmodern and radical feminism. Postmodern feminism has placed too much emphasis on language and the idea of **political correctness**, which has alienated many women. Radical feminism has placed too much emphasis on the idea of transforming **personal life**. While this is of some importance, Walter believes that it leads people to miss the bigger picture in which women remain unequal.

In Walter's view, the new feminism needs to return to looking for political rather than personal solutions to the continued inequality faced by women. Essentially, she advocates a return to the agenda of liberal feminism, which seeks to achieve equality between men and women through gradual reform of politics and aspects of society. Through such reform, women gain more power, so they are in a position to improve opportunities for themselves and for other women. However, Walter is also influenced by aspects of socialist feminism in her emphasis on material factors as the key to explaining and eradicating inequality.

Progress and the problems of feminism

Walter starts off by documenting a wide range of improvements in the position of women in Britain. She says, 'everywhere you look there are women who are freer and more powerful than they have ever been before'. More women are working; they are doing better than males in the education system; they have reached positions of great power and status (such as prime minister, head of MI5, speaker of the House of Commons); they have more control over when and whether to have children; similar numbers of men and women are entering the legal and medical professions; and women feel able to act in traditionally 'masculine' ways. Above all, women seem to have the independence and confidence to choose the lifestyle they wish, free of most of the constraints which limited their options in the past.

In these circumstances, many women feel that feminism is irrelevant to their lives. According to Walter, many British women associate feminism with a rather restrictive and intolerant creed. They see feminism as telling them that men are the enemy. They regard it as an inflexible set of beliefs which intrudes into their personal lives and tells them they must not wear make-up, accept pornography or use politically incorrect phrases. It tells them how they should make love so that women's sexual pleasure is always paramount.

All these aspects of feminism (which tend to be associated with radical or postmodern feminism) are off-putting to women. Walter's own research suggests that many women do not want to call themselves feminists because of these associations. They reject the view that every aspect of personal life is political and dislike the excessive emphasis on language and political correctness – they dislike being told what they are and are not allowed to say.

Continuing problems and inequality

Despite her assertion that women in Britain have much more freedom than in the past, Walter believes that women share common problems and that feminism needs to bring all women together to solve them. Although most women do not want to call themselves feminists, they do agree that women face difficulties. Ordinary women often start discussions about women in Britain with the phrase 'I'm not a feminist but …'. They then go on to identify problems which women face.

Walter believes that most of the grievances that women share are to do with a lack of **equal opportunities**. New feminism needs to address these issues rather than abandoning them. Walter identifies five main areas in which women continue to be disadvantaged – areas which need to be tackled by the new feminism. These are:

1. Inequality at work
2. A lack of high-quality affordable childcare
3. Women's continued responsibility for most childcare and domestic work
4. Higher rates of poverty amongst females than amongst males
5. Higher rates of domestic and sexual violence suffered by women than by men

Solutions

To Walter, such problems need to be tackled through feminism becoming part of the **mainstream** of British society, not through women isolating themselves from men and 'patriarchal' institutions. Women getting power is the key to achieving their aims. However, Walter is also happy to accept men as feminists. There is no reason why men who agree with promoting greater equality cannot become feminists and use their power to promote feminist causes.

To Walter, the continuing inequality in British society can ultimately only be tackled through politics. If women merely change their personal lives, it will not change the systems and structures which give rise to inequality. Women need to campaign for better childcare, improvements in the criminal justice system to deal with male violence, and so on. She concludes:

> *Today, women and men are building a new feminism that is working for ordinary, everyday equality. It isn't a movement that seeks to mould people's desires, but a movement that wants everyone to have the freedom to follow their ambitions and dreams without being stifled by the dead weight of inequality that has moulded our society for too long.* Walter, 1998, p. 257

Evaluation

Walter clearly identifies areas in which women have failed to achieve equality with men. She attempts to make feminism relevant to women in contemporary Britain and suggests ways of countering the negative image which feminism sometimes suffers, and she suggests ways of addressing inequality which seem realistically achievable.

However, Whelehan (2000) criticizes Walter for providing a misleading characterization of feminism and an acceptance of popular myths about it. To Whelehan, the idea of political correctness, attempts to tackle stereotypes of femininity and the insistence that the personal is political have all made an important contribution to increasing the choices open to women. While Whelehan welcomes Walter's attempt to make feminism relevant to a new generation, she is concerned that Walter may be abandoning too many of the concerns of other feminist approaches.

Imelda Whelehan – *Overloaded*

As indicated above, Imelda Whelehan (2000) disagrees with Walter that women have achieved freedom in their personal life and that a concern with culture is no longer relevant to women in Britain. Instead, Whelehan argues that patriarchy and **sexism** are making a comeback in the guise of **lad culture**. Attempts to attack the idea of political correctness disguise the revived sexism which has become more complex and sophisticated than sexism in the past, but is just as damaging and just as offensive.

Feminism and girl power

Whelehan's study examines the portrayal of gender in the media and popular culture generally. She argues that we are entering 'an era of "retrosexism" – nostalgia for a lost, uncomplicated past peopled by "real" women and humorous cheeky chappies'. This is clearly evident in increasing hostility to feminism in popular culture. Feminism has become the unacceptable 'f word'. In the media, independent women tend to be portrayed as 'psychotic or neurotic'. Examples include Glenn Close as a deranged businesswoman in the 1987 film *Fatal Attraction*, and Demi Moore in the 1994 film *Disclosure* as the boss who uses an accusation of sexual harassment to get back at a colleague who spurns her sexual advances.

Feminism is attacked as being boring, in favour of censorship, and against having fun. Women are portrayed as having already achieved equality through the celebration of **girl power**, a phrase popularized by the Spice Girls. The Spice Girls and women such as Madonna are portrayed as having achieved independence and control over their own lives. Madonna 'flouted the rules of conventional female behaviour with her overtly sexual style', while the Spice Girls along with other girl bands 'offer a ground-breaking model of intervention into a male-dominated arena'. Whelehan, however, suggests a number of reasons to question the idea that girl power, with its emphasis on individual choice and empowerment, offers a real alternative to conventional feminism:

1. Girl power ignores the continuing existence of structural inequality which holds women back. Listening to the Spice Girls proclaiming girl power will not prepare women for 'the gritty realities of the job market'. Whatever the rhetoric, women continue to suffer discrimination, disadvantage and lower wages.
2. Women such as Madonna and the Spice Girls are highly untypical. Few women have had the same degree of success or have been able to achieve the same measure of control over their lives. They are used as examples to show that women have achieved equality, but they are the exception rather than the rule.
3. Whelehan argues that 'Much of girl power seems to involve meeting aggression, particularly sexual aggression, with similar aggression – like the archetypal "ladette" who adopts traditionally "male behaviour" in an attempt to subvert or deflect male lechery.' There is often little difference between the new ladette and the old-fashioned 'dolly bird'. While the ladette might be more sexually aggressive she is still a sex object for the titillation of men. Whelehan argues that the presenter Denise van Outen, a 'ladette *par excellence*', has a similar look to Barbara Windsor, who was the 'dolly bird' in many of the highly sexist *Carry On* films.

The singleton

Another increasingly common way of portraying women in the media is in terms of the 'Bridget Jones effect'. The 1996 book and 2001 film *Bridget Jones' Diary* portray a woman who is aware of feminism, but is also desperate to find a decent man before she gets too old. It portrays the single woman, or the **singleton**, who is

> *the elder sister of the ladette. Once 'snogging and shagging' of the early years are over and she has reached a certain level in her career, the biological imperative to 'nest' takes over. It is only then that the singleton realizes that her success in other fields has been at the expense of the only thing that 'really' matters – finding a man.*
> Whelehan, 2000, p. 136

This theme is also the basis for the television series *Sex and the City* and *Ally McBeal*. The message of all these media portrayals is that, however independent and resourceful a woman is, in the end she has to make herself attractive to men. They play upon women's fears of being left single, of leaving it too late to find a partner with whom to have children, and their fear that they might be sacrificing true fulfilment in their search for independence and material success. They therefore offer a kind of postfeminist message that taking feminist ideas too far will undermine women's happiness.

Lads

If the portrayal of women is damaging to feminism, the portrayal of men is even worse. In particular, **retrosexism** (a nostalgia for and return to traditional sexism) is particularly evident in the popularity of **laddism**. Laddism involves a celebration of the worst and often extremely sexist behaviour of young men. It is most clearly evident in relatively new and very popular men's magazines such as *Loaded*, *Maxim* and *FHM*. Commenting on *Loaded*, Whelehan says, 'the lads' frame of reference is very clearly demarcated – sport, pop, alcohol, soft drugs, heterosex and soft porn. Further, this is the domain of the male, and the male alone, where women function only as objects.'

An important feature of the magazines is the use of scantily clad or naked women. Whelehan describes an article on the accomplished actress Helen Mirren which is accompanied by six pictures of her nude or semi-nude. She is described as 'a lot more than just a bit of middle aged crumpet' (quoted in Whelehan, 2000, p. 59), but her sexuality is the focus of the whole article. In the same magazine there are even 'descriptions of sex as the act of silencing shrill women'. For example, the May 1997 edition included the following letter: 'Whatever happened to that annoying bird Sarah from Clevedon – who kept writing in to beg for a shag? A good work fella! Blue Peter badge to whoever managed to shut her up by giving her a proper seeing to!' (quoted in Whelehan, 2000, p. 59).

Conclusion

Whelehan argues that the media have 'constantly reinvented ways to make women's oppression seem sexy'. Retrosexism is based on a myth that women today are in control of their lives and that feminism is no longer necessary. In reality, women continue to suffer poverty, discrimination and a 'new/old patriarchy' which treats women as little more than 'sexual beings'. Although Whelehan accepts that women have made progress in some areas, she considers that 'feminism's success has been announced rather prematurely'. Furthermore, it is not just material inequality that needs addressing. The popularity of retrosexism means that much still needs to be done by feminists in challenging patriarchal culture.

Germaine Greer – *The Whole Woman*

In *The Whole Woman* (2000) Germaine Greer launches an even stronger attack on new feminism, postmodernism and all those who think that feminism has achieved many or all of its objectives. She goes much further than Whelehan in denying that women have made substantial progress, and even attacks the emphasis on equality evident in the work of Natasha Walter.

In 1970 Greer published *The Female Eunuch*, which was an influential text for feminists of that era. Some thirty years later she argues that, although women have made some advances, there are still very many areas in which they are far from liberated. Greer advocates a version of radical feminism. She sees patriarchy as deeply entrenched in culture and society and very difficult to eradicate. She identifies the continued existence of patriarchy in a number of areas. The following are just some examples.

1 In sexuality it is men who have gained sexual freedom rather than women. There is still an overwhelming emphasis in heterosexuality on penetration of the vagina by the penis, and an increasing expectation that women will service male sexual fantasies. The more subtle and varied ways in which women gain sexual pleasure are neglected.
2 Women are still expected to be obsessively concerned with their bodies and physical appearance. Far from being free to dress and appear as they choose, women are subject to rigid restrictions. For example, it is considered unacceptable for women to leave their armpits and legs unshaven, or for them to allow pubic hair to protrude from their bikini. Vast amounts of money are spent on fruitless attempts to get rid of cellulite (perfectly natural fat) and on cosmetic surgery. Increasing numbers of women take botulin, a toxin, to freeze their faces to reduce wrinkling. Even beauty contests are making a comeback. Women are simply not allowed to be themselves.
3 Women are still afraid of men. The interests of 'the dominant male' are maintained by those who teach women to be afraid of violent males, of rapists and of flashers. Greer says: 'The father who, if his teenage daughter is out at night, insists on collecting her and bringing her home in his car, is unconsciously instilling fear into her at the same time that he consciously exercises control over her.'
4 In 1970 Greer wrote: 'Women have very little idea of how much men hate them.' She argues that male hatred of women is still the norm. She gives some horrific individual examples. Jacqueline Newton was attacked by her husband, who poured hydrochloric acid and paint-stripper over her. Susan McDonald was viciously beaten, raped and attacked with a rusty pick by her male partner. Although these may be extreme examples, Greer argues that 'all men hate some women some of the time' and 'some men hate all women all of the time'. She quotes British Medical Association figures which show that more than a quarter of women have experienced domestic violence from male partners. However, in a male-dominated legal system few of the men who perpetrate such violence are punished. She quotes figures which show that, out of 512 reported incidents of domestic violence in London in 1997, only thirteen resulted in the man being convicted. Men sometimes get off lightly when they are convicted by claiming they have been provoked by 'nagging' from the women they have attacked. Men are also very likely to get away with rape.

Liberation

Greer is dismissive of the claims of some postmodernists and new feminists who celebrate increased lifestyle choices for women. She says: 'A "new feminism" that celebrates the right (i.e. duty) to be pretty in an array of floaty dresses and little suits put together for starvation wages by adolescent girls in Asian sweatshops is no feminism at all.' The reference to the poverty of women in parts of the developing world shows that Greer is concerned with material inequality. However, it is not equality that Greer seeks for women, but **liberation**. For Greer, true liberation will only come when women do not have to be like men to succeed and do not have to dress and act in ways that men want them to. She does not want women to adopt the competitiveness and aggression of men and she wants them to stop pandering to male sexual fantasies.

Women continue to be oppressed through 'intimate relationships'. Unlike Walter, Greer believes that the 'personal is still political' and liberation will only come from women being able to express their femininity in a social world in which patriarchy no longer holds sway.

Evaluation and conclusion

Greer's work offers a powerful critique of the idea that women have now been liberated and feminism is no longer necessary. However, Whelehan (2000) argues that Greer's work does contain some 'huge sprawling generalizations' which may be hard to justify. She also argues that Greer offers little incentive for men to get involved in working with women for female liberation. Nevertheless, Whelehan praises Greer, saying that 'her impassioned though sometimes unsupported assertions carry a clout, a clout that few feminists can rival'.

Greer's work, along with that of the other writers examined in this section, shows that feminists continue to offer a lively and insightful analysis of contemporary society. As this section has demonstrated, there is a variety of contemporary feminist views. Where they all agree is in arguing that patriarchy, in one form or another, still exists and that feminism is still needed.

Masculinity

In the earlier parts of this chapter we saw how feminists have succeeded in putting the sociology of gender – and of women in particular – on the sociological map. Before 1970, few sociological studies were conducted about women and women's lives. Yet, paradoxically, some male sociologists have argued that men have also in some senses been 'invisible' in much sociology. While most studies have been conducted by men and the subjects of the research have been men, few have been about masculinity. Men are simply taken for granted in studies; they are assumed to be the norm and their behaviour is not explained in terms of gender or compared to that of women.

In this section we examine some of the attempts that have been made to put right this 'neglect' of masculinity and to explore how masculinity shapes the lives of men and the social world in general.

David D. Gilmore – *Cultural Concepts of Masculinity*

Masculinity, sex and gender

In his 1990 book, *Manhood in the Making: Cultural Concepts of Masculinity*, the anthropologist David D. Gilmore discusses the way masculinity is defined in a wide range of societies. Gilmore describes masculinity as 'the approved way of being an adult male in any given society', and his study is an attempt to discover the extent to which this varies from place to place. He uses both his own field data from ethnographic research and the findings of other anthropological studies.

Gilmore does not see masculinity as a set of characteristics entirely determined by biology. He says that feminists 'have convincingly demonstrated that the conventional bipolar model based on biology is invalid and that sex (biological inheritance) and gender (cultural norms) are distinct categories'. He also says that 'the answer to the manhood puzzle must lie in culture'. Nevertheless he does not believe that biology is unimportant. He claims that 'culture uses or exaggerates biological potential in specific ways'. Nearly always this involves making a very clear distinction between masculinity and femininity.

In the vast majority of societies masculinity is defined in fairly similar ways, suggesting that biological differences do play some part in influencing the cultural definitions which are adopted.

The typical features of masculinity

Gilmore suggests that there are three typical features of masculinity found in most societies:

1. **Man the impregnator**. Men are expected to impregnate women. To do this they are normally required to take the initiative in courtship and sexual encounters. They are expected to compete with other men for access to women. For example, in Sicily, 'masculine honour is always bound up with aggression and potency. A real man in Sicily is "a man with big testicles".'
2. **Man the provider**. Having impregnated women, in most societies men are then expected to provide for them and their offspring. According to Gilmore, in the Mediterranean, 'the emphasis on male honour as a domestic duty is widespread'. In the traditional Greek peasant village, the honour of fathers rests upon their ability to provide their daughters with large dowries. Men of the Sambia in New Guinea have their manhood measured partly through their competence in hunting. Women are not allowed to hunt. Men who fail in hunting are subject to ridicule and may have difficulty in finding a wife.
3. **Man the protector**. The third way in which most cultures define masculinity is in terms of men's role as protectors. Men must protect their women from other men and any threats which might arise.

   For example, in the East African Samburu tribe, males have to demonstrate their bravery during *moranhood*. This starts at around the age of 14 or 15 and lasts about twelve years. The first test is a circumcision ritual which is performed without anaesthetic. The boy must not flinch, despite the pain as his foreskin is cut off, or 'he is forever shamed as a coward'. Later in *moranhood*, the male proves himself by rustling cattle from other tribes. He runs the risk of being caught and beaten or even killed by the victims of the rustling. However, success confirms that the male has become manly; it makes him attractive to females and shows that he will be able to take care of a family.

Masculinity and society

Gilmore argues that the roles of impregnator, provider and protector have some features in common. They are all dangerous or competitive and failure in any of the roles carries high costs.

Gilmore suggests that this feature of masculinity may have benefits for society. Men are persuaded to do things which are necessary for society's survival which they would not otherwise do because of their desire for self-preservation. He says, 'we may regard "real manhood" as an inducement for high performance in the social struggle for scarce resources, a code of conduct that advances collective interests by overcoming inner inhibitions'.

However, Gilmore does not see the type of masculinity described above as an inevitable feature of all societies. Rather, it is one of a number of strategies of adaptation which can reconcile 'individual and social needs' through rewards and punishments. In a few societies, masculinity has a very different meaning. Societies can work with a wide variety of definitions of masculinity.

Men in Tahiti and Semai

Tahiti, one of the Society Islands in Polynesia, has a much less marked differentiation between masculinity and femininity than most societies. Furthermore, the Tahitian concept of masculinity does not require men to act as providers and protectors. There is little need for men to take physical risks since there is no warfare, and there are few dangerous occupations. The lagoon offers a plentiful supply of fish, so risky deep-sea fishing is not necessary. Families cooperate in economic activities and there is no social pressure to be economically successful. Indeed, traditional Tahitian culture encourages a 'laconic attitude towards work'. It also encourages men to be timid and passive. They are expected to ignore insults and they very rarely fight one another.

Tahitian men are neither protective of their women nor possessive towards them. When an English ship, the *Dolphin*, arrived at Tahiti in 1767, the ship's captain reported that the Tahitian women 'came down and stripped themselves naked and made all the alluring gestures they could to entice them onshore' (quoted in Gilmore, 1990). The Tahitian men actually encouraged the women to do this, and a later French explorer found that Tahitian men were extremely hospitable and even offered him their daughters.

The Semai people live in central Malaysia. Both men and women are strongly opposed to violence and aggression. Aggression is denoted by the word *punan*, which also means taboo. The Semai try to avoid doing anything that frustrates another person or goes against their wishes. As a consequence, both men and women are usually expected to agree to a request for sex, even if they are married and the person requesting sex is not their spouse. However, it is also considered *punan* if a person repeatedly pesters another person for sex. There is very little jealousy and Semai men and women tolerate the extra-marital affairs of their spouses as being no more than a loan.

The Semai do not engage in competitive sport and are not materialistic. Men do not have to compete with each other because farming is cooperative; if one man has too little land to get by, he simply asks another man for some of his. It is *punan* to refuse. Although the Semai do hunt, and hunting is reserved exclusively for males, the hunting is not dangerous or difficult. They hunt nothing larger or more dangerous than small pigs, they stop hunting before noon when it gets too hot, and 'if they encounter danger, they run away and hide without any shame or hesitation'.

There are some differences between men and women in both Tahitian and Semai society (although among the Semai they are not particularly pronounced), but neither society has a cultural image of the 'real man'. Gilmore suggests that the unusual characteristics of masculinity in these societies may result from the material circumstances in which the societies exist.

Animals confronted with danger produce adrenalin, which makes them more able to flee or to stay and fight the source of the danger. In humans, the choice between fight or flight is shaped by cultural conditioning. Most cultures seem to have put more emphasis on men fighting than fleeing, but the Tahitians and Semai are exceptions. This may be due to the plentiful supply of food and other resources in both societies and the lack of 'serious hazards' in their environments, such as dangerous animals or aggressive neighbours.

Gilmore admits that it is impossible to show conclusively that the ideology of passivity is caused by the material context. It could be that the culture creates a situation where the people have little material ambition and are content with what they have. Therefore they have no need to be competitive. He suggests that there might be a 'feedback relationship in which the ideology, once formed, assists in and intensifies a matching adaptation to the environment'. Whatever the factors giving rise to these cultures, it is clear that the ideology of 'Man the Impregnator–Provider–Protector' is not universal.

Evaluation

Many feminists could criticize Gilmore for his apparent claim that men usually protect and provide for women. As we have seen in earlier sections of this chapter, far from protecting their wives, some men abuse and attack them; and it is often the case that women work harder than men. However, Gilmore's work does succeed in showing that culture has a strong influence on ideologies of masculinity and that masculinity can therefore assume very different forms.

Victor J. Seidler – rationality and masculinity

Although Gilmore does use some examples from technologically advanced industrial or post-industrial societies, he relies mainly on examples from more traditional agricultural societies. Victor J. Seidler (1989, 1994) concentrates instead on men in Western societies.

The Enlightenment

According to Seidler, ideas of masculinity in Western societies are closely connected with the thinking and beliefs associated with the **Enlightenment**. The Enlightenment is the name given to a range of interconnected philosophical, scientific and social beliefs which developed in Western Europe in the seventeenth and eighteenth centuries.

Enlightenment thinking rejected emotion, superstition and belief in the supernatural as ways of understanding the world. It argued that the natural world could only be understood through objective, detached, unemotional science. Knowledge could only come from reason and rationality. Reason was contrasted with nature. As Seidler puts it, 'Nature is real but is bereft of consciousness and of value. It exists as separate and independent of the consciousness that is attempting to grasp it.' To understand the physical world, humans had to detach themselves from it.

To Seidler and many other writers, Enlightenment thinking is the foundation of **modernity**. Modernity is a phase in human history in which it is believed that humans can use scientific knowledge to ensure progress. Science allows nature to be conquered and controlled for the benefit of people. (We discuss these ideas in more detail in Chapter 14.)

Masculinity, femininity and modernity

In modernity, science came to be associated with masculinity. For example, the late sixteenth- and early seventeenth-century British philosopher Francis Bacon talked 'quite unashamedly about the new sciences as a masculinist philosophy'. In *The Protestant Ethic and the Spirit of Capitalism*, Max Weber described how the rational pursuit of profit encouraged by certain forms of Protestantism helped to produce the rationalization of the modern world (see pp. 406–9 and 874–8 for a discussion of Weber). It was only men, though, who were seen as capable of understanding and controlling nature through reason. Women were seen as being closer to nature than men. As such they were regarded as being more emotional, less able to be detached, impersonal and rational.

Emotions were valued less than reason. Men fear the consequences of being emotional. Emotions have no place, particularly in public arenas such as work, and so men suppress them. Seidler says that 'it is as if we do not have emotional needs of our own as men, for needs are a sign of weakness'. Seidler sees the association of men with reason and rationality, and women with nature and emotion, as harmful and destructive. It damages personal relationships, making it difficult for men to build strong relationships with women.

The association of men with reason contributes to the creation and maintenance of male, patriarchal power at every level. Men are liable to tell their female partners in arguments that they are being irrational and emotional and refuse to discuss matters further until the woman 'calms down'. Men are 'constantly talking for others, while presenting themselves as the neutral voice of reason'.

Evaluation

Seidler's argument provides some interesting insights into the nature of masculinity in Western societies. However, it is somewhat abstract and is not based upon detailed empirical evidence. He admits that it may not be possible to generalize his claims about masculinity, saying: 'I am talking from a particular experience of white, middle-class Jewish masculinity.' He also admits that it is not possible to identify one dominant form of masculinity in Western society. Feminism and an increasing distrust of science have both contributed to the creation of a wider variety of masculinities in contemporary Western societies. We will examine some of these in the next section.

R.W. Connell – *Masculinities*

Bob Connell (1995, 2002) developed the study of masculinity by examining how masculinity is changing in contemporary societies and by looking at the variety of meanings that masculinity can have. He uses detailed empirical evidence to back up his arguments. Connell's work makes a significant contribution to the development of theories of gender in general, as well as of masculinity in particular.

The nature of gender

Connell's arguments are based upon a rejection of conventional approaches to the analysis of gender. He identifies three conventional approaches to this issue:

1. Those which see **biological differences** between male and female bodies as the cause of differences between women and men.
2. Those which believe that **culture** determines gender differences so that 'the body is a more or less neutral surface or landscape on which a social symbolism is imprinted'.
3. Those which see gender as a product of a **combination** of biological and cultural factors.

An earlier section of this chapter examined these three approaches (see pp. 93–100). Connell, however, sees all three as inadequate. He believes there is plenty of evidence that behaviour is not determined by biology. For example, there are cultures in which it is normal for men to engage in homosexuality at some points in the life cycle, and there have been cultures where rape did not exist, or was extremely rare. Connell also rejects **cultural determinism**, the idea that behaviour is entirely shaped by culture. This is because bodies cannot be conceived as blank canvases on which culture can create any type of behaviour. He says that 'bodies, in their own right as bodies, do matter. They age, get sick, enjoy, engender, give birth. There is an irreducible bodily dimension in experience and practice; the sweat cannot be excluded.'

However, Connell does not conclude that biological and cultural factors can be seen as separate but interacting aspects of gender. Rather, the two need to be fused by seeing the body as an active agent in social processes. The body acts within social institutions and social relationships – for example, the institutions surrounding professional, masculine sport. But sport is also a bodily activity. Thus, 'running, throwing, jumping or hitting' are 'symbolic and kinetic, social and bodily, at one and the same time, and these aspects depend on each other'. Bodily performance is part of being masculine or feminine. It can enable people to act in gendered ways, prevent people from acting in gendered ways, or persuade people to reinterpret their own gender.

The following example from Connell's own field research illustrates these points. One interviewee, Don Merideth, describes how physical experiences led him to change his conception of his own sexuality. Don Merideth described how he got pleasure from the stimulation of his anus while having sex with a woman. This physical sensation led him to believe that he should have homosexual relationships. The body led him towards a different set of social and physical practices.

Connell therefore sees bodies as 'both objects and agents of practice', and the practices of bodies as involved in 'forming the structures within which bodies are appropriated and defined'. Bodies, whether male or female, are an active and integral part of social action and the construction of gender, and are not separable from the societies in which they live.

Types of masculinity

Having established a foundation for the study of masculinities, Connell then discusses the different forms masculinity can take. Masculinities constantly change, new forms can emerge and old forms decline, but in any particular era a broad distinction can be made between hegemonic and other types of masculinity.

Hegemonic masculinity is the form of masculinity that claims and tries to maintain a dominant influence over social life in a particular society at a particular time. Hegemonic masculinity never enjoys complete dominance, it is always contestable. It can be challenged by women and also by other masculinities. Thus white, heterosexual and middle-class masculinity might be dominant in contemporary Western societies, but black, homosexual and working-class masculinities also exist and sometimes challenge hegemonic masculinity.

Hegemonic masculinity may try to maintain its dominance through control over institutional structures. It can also be maintained through a 'rich vocabulary of abuse'. For example, the masculinity of heterosexual males can be put down through words such as 'wimp, milksop, nerd, turkey, sissy, lily liver, jellyfish, yellowbelly, candy ass, ladyfinger, pushover, cookie pusher, cream puff, motherfucker, pantywaist, mother's boy, four-eyes, ear-'ole, dweeb, geek, Milquetoast, Cedric, and so on. Here too the symbolic blurring with femininity is obvious.'

With some masculinities, hegemonic masculinity tries to maintain a situation of **dominance** and **subordination**. Thus heterosexual masculinity generally tries to keep homosexual masculinity subordinate. Many men are not subordinate to hegemonic masculinity but engage in relationships of complicity with it. That is, they go along with aspects of hegemonic masculinity and try to gain by sharing in hegemonic masculinity's power over women and subordinate masculinities. However, they may be unable or unwilling to live up to the ideals of masculinity held by the hegemonic type. Connell says, 'marriage, fatherhood and community life often involve extensive compromises with women rather than naked domination or an uncontested display of authority'.

Within sets of gender relations, particular masculinities (or femininities) may be marginalized. Without necessarily being rejected outright, they are not acknowledged and accepted as legitimate. Thus, in contemporary European societies the achievements of black sportsmen might be celebrated, but black masculinity in general is far from being fully accepted.

Each society, at a particular stage in its development, possesses a set of gender practices, or different ways of being male and female. It also possesses sets of relationships between masculinities and femininities, relationships of domination, subordination, complicity and marginalization. Together these practices and relationships create a **gender order** characteristic of the society. However, the gender order can always change.

The changing gender order

According to Connell, the period 1450–1650 saw the establishment of a hegemonic masculinity which he calls **gentry masculinity**. This was partly a product of empire building by white European men who conquered countries which were colonized. This sort of masculinity was 'emphatic and violent' and sometimes underwent periods of crisis.

The gender order of gentry masculinity has gradually been replaced over the last 200 years by 'new hegemonic forms and the emergence of an array of subordinated and marginalized masculinities'. These changes were caused by a combination of factors, including challenges from women to hegemonic masculinity, changes in industrial capitalism, and the end of empire with decolonization. A key change was a move from the outright use of violence to achieve domination to a greater emphasis on the use of bureaucratic rationality in organizations. The importance of the gentry declined and hegemonic masculinity became split between managers, who dominated through holding positions of authority, and professionals, whose dominance came from the possession of technical expertise.

The use of violence increasingly shifted to the colonies and away from the colonial powers. However, traces of the masculine ideology of the empire builders remained important. Thus Connell argues that 'wilderness, hunting and bushcraft were welded into a distinct ideology of manhood by figures such as Robert Baden-Powell, the founder of the scouting movement'.

In the late nineteenth century, hegemonic masculinity succeeded in defining homosexuality as a deviant and subordinate form of masculinity. Homosexual conduct was criminalized and began to be seen as males engaging in feminized or bestial behaviour. The expulsion of women from work in heavy industry created the ideology of separate spheres, with the women's sphere confined to the private arena of domestic life. Among some of the working class there was the development of 'rough, disorderly masculinities among the marginalized "dangerous classes"'.

As the twentieth century progressed, the split between professional and managerial masculinity became more significant. The challenge to hegemonic masculinity from women increased. Some men began to take notice of feminist critiques of masculinity and tried to develop alternatives. Homosexual masculinity established itself as an alternative to hegemonic masculinity. Migration from former colonies to rich capitalist nations led to the establishment of new minority ethnic communities. These communities added to the diversity of the masculinities present in the rich countries. The hegemonic masculinities of such countries (Connell refers to them as metropolitan countries) have seen their influence spread throughout most of the world. Globalization (see pp. 548–57 for a discussion of globalization) has allowed the mass media to spread the ideology of this type of masculinity worldwide. The image of masculinity produced by commercial sport has become influential, as has the association of masculinity with 'fast cars and powerful trucks'.

Despite the enormous wealth, power and influence of hegemonic masculinity in the metropolitan countries, it faces unprecedented challenges from the increasing variety of femininities and masculinities in the metropolitan countries themselves. Thus, 'the meaning of masculinity, the variety of masculinities, the difficulty of reproducing masculinity, the nature of gender and the extent of gender inequality all come into question and are furiously debated'.

Research into masculinities

As part of his study, Connell conducted detailed research into four distinctive groups of Australian men. He traced the life history of each of these men through the use of in-depth tape-recorded interviews. On the basis of these interviews he claimed to have found evidence of 'crisis tendencies' in the contemporary gender order. According to Connell, hegemonic masculinity is increasingly challenged, making it difficult for people to agree about what it means to be masculine. In his research, Connell picked out four particular groups of men in which 'the construction or integration of masculinity was under pressure':

- He described the first group as those who wish to **live fast die young**. This group of interviewees consisted of five working-class men aged between 17 and 29. All of them had experienced long periods of unemployment, had little in the way of educational qualifications, and one was illiterate. They had all grown up in working-class households, some of which were very poor.

  In many ways these young men engaged in a form of exaggerated masculinity in which violence played an important part. Although they were divided about whether they should use violence towards women, they were all willing to use violence against other men if the occasion demanded it. All were subject to 'compulsory heterosexuality' (a phrase Connell borrows from Adrienne Rich). They felt obliged both to be heterosexual and to make that heterosexuality clear to others. At least part of the time the men demonstrated a 'thin, contemptuous misogyny, in which women are treated basically as disposable receptacles for semen'. Some of them rode motorbikes and engaged in showy displays of their masculine toughness.

Connell believes that this group of men were demonstrating a form of 'protest masculinity', a 'marginalized masculinity, which picks up themes of hegemonic masculinity in the society at large but reworks them in the context of poverty'. Lacking the material success of other men, they try to make up for this through aggressive public displays of how tough and masculine they are. They try to maintain a strong 'front'. However, Connell does not believe that 'protest masculinity' is a straightforward exaggeration of conventional masculinity. The men had less rigid views about social roles than they did about violence and the body – particularly sexuality. Some even claimed to believe in 'equal rights' for women.

2 The second group consisted of six men involved in the **environmental movement**. All were heterosexual and all had been looked after primarily by their mother in childhood. Each of these six men had largely embraced hegemonic masculinity in their early life, but had distanced themselves from it as they got older. They had followed very different paths towards the environmental movement, but for all of them this movement challenged hegemonic masculinity. There were several main themes in the movement which had this effect. These included 'a practice and ideology of equality ... emphasis on collectivity and solidarity', 'a practice and ideology of personal growth' and 'an ideology of organic wholeness'.

The environmental movement questions the hierarchical dominance characteristic of hegemonic masculinity. It encourages group cooperation rather than individual competitiveness. It emphasizes developing as a person rather than achieving material success and encourages a connection with nature rather than an acceptance of the alienation of rationalization.

All of the men had become familiar with feminist thinking, five of them as a direct consequence of involvement in environmentalism. Connell suggests that there was a certain degree of tension in the personalities of these men between identifying with their father (and brothers) and identifying with their mother, who had mainly been responsible for looking after them. From childhood they had experienced the strength and resourcefulness of women and as a consequence they were open to taking feminist ideas seriously. Many of them experienced considerable guilt about the way men can treat women and had made a conscious decision to be different from the sort of men who accept hegemonic masculinity.

3 The third group Connell studied were what he calls **very straight gays**. This group of eight men, aged in their twenties, thirties and forties, were all homosexual (though most had also had heterosexual relationships) and all lived in Sydney. All had grown up in fairly conventional families with employed fathers and mothers doing most of the parenting. They all maintained a fairly conventional masculine outward appearance. Some were critical of gay men who were effeminate and of those who were 'hyper-masculine', dressing in leather. In these ways they had fairly conventional definitions of masculinity despite rejecting the 'compulsory heterosexuality' usually associated with it.

Connell says, 'the choice of a man as sexual object is not just the choice of a body-with-penis, it is the choice of embodied-masculinity. The cultural meanings of masculinity are, generally, part of the package.' Connell argues that 'young people's sexuality is a field of possibilities, not a deterministic system'. He does not believe that some men are predestined to be homosexual and others heterosexual. Both types of sexuality are 'produced by specific practices'. They come from the bodily experience of sex, which develops into a 'sexual closure' in which one type of sexuality is chosen above the other. These choices, though, are not just personal and physical, because they take place within the 'large-scale structure of gender'. They are also social in that there is now a well-established gay community in cities such as Sydney, with its own infrastructure of shops, bars, organizations and so on. Therefore 'coming out' can 'also mean coming in to an already constituted gay milieu'.

All the men in this group had first been brought up with the values and practices of hegemonic masculinity, but had defined their own sexuality in homosexual terms and had then become involved with the gay community. In some respects they remained conventional and were influenced by hegemonic ideas on what masculinity was. However, in their personal relationships with other men, they tended to have a more egalitarian outlook than is typical of hegemonic male/female relationships. Furthermore, simply by having an established alternative to hegemonic masculinity they show that different types of masculinity are possible.

4 The final group, **men of reason**, were part of hegemonic masculinity. These nine men, aged from the mid-twenties to the mid-forties, were all working in professional jobs and were all heterosexual. They all had post-school education. Their conception of masculinity was largely based upon the idea that men, unlike women, were rational. Unlike some working-class men, they did not associate masculinity so strongly with violence. Many were hostile to unconventional masculinities such as that of gay men.

Despite the apparently conventional and coherent nature of these men's masculinity, Connell did find some evidence of tensions within it. Although their masculinity encouraged them to embrace rationality, this was 'incompatible with men's categorical authority over women'. In principle, they accepted the logic of equal rights for men and women at work, but in practice they could find it hard to accept a female boss. Thus one man, Greg, had an emotional crisis, because he worked for his sister's company, and she was unwilling to give him much say in how the company was run.

Connell argues that the 'instrumental rationality of the marketplace has a power to disrupt gender' and this creates a certain tension. One of the interviewees, Hugh, was beginning to have doubts about conventional or hegemonic masculinity and was starting to question his competitive ethos and his sense of superiority to women.

Conclusions

Connell's study shows that there are many different masculinities, even among individuals from similar backgrounds, and that these masculinities can constantly change. Most masculinities are somewhat contradictory and there are elements within them that contradict or question the conventional gender order.

Most men continue to benefit from hegemonic masculinity. According to Connell, men still remain dominant in social life, but male dominance is no longer automatically accepted. Connell is not particularly optimistic about the future, but he does believe that divisions between masculinities make change possible. He thinks there are areas in which positive steps can be taken. These include 'the politics of the curriculum, work around AIDS/HIV and anti-racist politics'.

Connell believes that men are most likely to produce positive changes by working with other groups (such as the women's movement, the gay liberation movement and the green movement) rather than through concentrating on introspective 'men's groups' alone. While he is strongly in favour of overthrowing hegemonic masculinity, he does not deny that there are some aspects of it which are worth preserving. He says that:

> *abolishing hegemonic masculinity risks abolishing, along with violence and hatred, the positive culture produced around hegemonic masculinity. This includes hero stories from the Ramayana to the Twilight of the Gods; participatory pleasures such as neighbourhood baseball; abstract beauty in fields such as pure mathematics; ethics of sacrifice on behalf of others. That is a heritage worth having, for girls and women as well as boys and men (as the rich heritage of feminine culture is worth having, for boys and men as well as girls and women).* Connell, 1995

Summary and conclusions

Much of the early sociology of gender was concerned to show that gender issues, and women in particular, were neglected in malestream research. Feminists attacked what they saw as sexist assumptions in male-dominated sociology and tried to establish that an understanding of society could not be achieved without taking account of feminist thought.

One of the first targets of feminists was the idea that men and women were predetermined to act in different ways because of their biology. Feminists such as Oakley saw gender roles as socially constructed and believed that there was nothing inevitable about masculine and feminine ways of behaving. More recently, writers such as Connell and Fausto-Sterling have suggested that the body cannot simply be ignored, and that bodily (or biological) and social aspects of gender are interconnected or even fused together.

As the influence of feminism in sociology developed, it became clear that there were several different strands within feminist thinking. Most of these concentrated on the inequality between men and women, but gave different explanations of that inequality. Postmodern feminism, on the other hand, paid more attention to differences between women (or men). Some postfeminists questioned whether the old concern with inequality was really necessary, given improvements in the position of women in society. However, many feminists, including Germaine Greer, Ann Oakley, Imelda Whelehan and Sylvia Walby, reject the idea that feminism is no longer necessary, arguing that patriarchy is still a dominant force in society. Certainly research on specific areas of social life, such as paid employment, suggests that gender equality is very far from being achieved.

Feminist sociology has not just contributed to the understanding of the position of women in society. It has also made an important contribution to sociological theory in general, and to an understanding of men. With the development of studies of masculinity, sociologists now have a better understanding of how society shapes gender relations and gender experiences for both men and women.

Despite some important improvements in the position of women in society (partly stimulated by the work of feminists and sociologists of gender) the evidence suggests that there are still many areas of social life where gender differences and inequalities remain. If Ann Oakley is to be believed, studying gender remains important not just to improve the lot of women, but also to understand and ultimately tackle problems such as war and environmental damage.

CHAPTER 3
'Race', ethnicity and nationality

[Institutional racism is] the collective failure of an organization to provide an appropriate and professional service to people because of their colour, culture or ethnic origin. MacPherson, 1999

Introduction

Racism and conflict between ethnic and national groups have long been a feature of human societies. We can illustrate this with a number of examples.

In 1601 Queen Elizabeth I issued a proclamation saying that 'Negroes and blackamoors' should be deported from England because they were 'infidels' and they were contributing to economic and social problems such as poverty and famine.

According to the historian Philip D. Curtin (1965), in the eighteenth century some 9.5 million Africans were transported across the Atlantic to become slaves in North and South America and the Caribbean. John Taylor, a writer and traveller, described the black slaves in Jamaica as 'these ignorant pore souls' who differed 'from bruite beast, only by their shape and speech'. In 1884, long after the abolition of slavery, the *Encyclopaedia Britannica* continued to express similar views. It claimed that the African Negro occupied the lowest position in the evolutionary scale and this was supposedly demonstrated by their abnormally long arms and lightweight brains.

Another group who were widely seen as inferior in nineteenth-century Britain were the Irish. Frederick Engels, Karl Marx's friend and collaborator, described the Irish in *The Condition of the Working Class in England*. Writing in 1844–5, he said:

> ***The southern facile character of the Irishman, his crudity, which places him but little above the savage, his contempt for all human enjoyments, in which his very crudeness makes him incapable of sharing, his filth and poverty, all favour drunkenness.*** Engels 1973, first published 1844

Over half a century later, in 1901, the London writer Joseph Bannister was no less critical of a different group of people in his book *England Under the Jews*. He described Jews as 'Yiddish money pigs' who were unwilling to take baths and so were particularly prone to skin and blood diseases. Bannister believed that Britain was becoming dominated by Jews, and in a private letter to a Jew he said: 'It is a pity that some kind of vermin exterminator could not be invented by which your vile breed could be eliminated.'

Anti-Semitic feeling (hostile feelings towards the Jewish people) went beyond mere words in Hitler's Nazi Germany. In *Mein Kampf* (completed in 1927) Hitler outlined his view that the true Germans were a racial group called the Aryans. The Aryan race had been corrupted by contact with inferior races such as the Slavs and Jews, but Hitler aimed to put this right by creating an Aryan 'master race'. In 1935 the Nuremberg Laws withdrew the civil rights of Jews and forbade mixed marriages between Jews and Aryans. The 'Final Solution' to the Jewish 'problem' involved gassing millions of Jews (along with gypsies, homosexuals and others) in concentration camps such as Auschwitz, Belsen and Dachau.

In the 1990s, after the end of communist rule in Yugoslavia, civil war broke out between the Muslims, the Croatians and the Serbs. The conflicts largely concerned the boundaries and ethnic composition of new states as Yugoslavia broke up. In parts of Bosnia whole ethnic groups were driven out of an area so that it might be claimed by another group. This process became known as **ethnic cleansing**. Many thousands died as the Bosnian Serbs tried to seize territory from the Muslims and besieged towns and cities such as Gorazde, Srebrenica and Sarajevo.

In the late 1990s Serbia engaged in ethnic cleansing on a massive scale in Kosovo, another region of the former Yugoslavia. Hundreds of thousands of ethnic Albanians were driven from their homes and became refugees in neighbouring states. In response, the military alliance of NATO (including the United States, the United Kingdom, France and Germany) went to war with Serbia.

Examples of conflict and inequality between racial, ethnic or national groups are by no means confined to history. In Northern Ireland there is conflict between Catholics and Protestants, in Sri Lanka between Tamils and the Sinhalese. In Spain some Basques seek an independent state, and in East Timor guerrilla leaders have striven to regain independence from their Indonesian invaders. In Burundi and Rwanda, two ethnic groups – the Hutus and the Tutsis – have been in conflict for decades, resulting in the deaths of many thousands of people. In 1994–6 there was renewed violence, and large numbers of Tutsis were massacred by the Hutus.

Following the US and British invasion of Iraq in 2003 and the overthrow of Saddam Hussein's regime, sectarian violence broke out principally between Iraqi Sunni Muslims (split between Arabs and Kurds) and Iraqi Shiite Muslims (mainly Arab with a small Kurd minority). There were numerous incidents and many thousands were killed. In one incident, in September 2005, 114 people were killed by a car bomb in the Shi'a district of Kadhimiya, Baghdad. Armed Shi'a militias were reported to have carried out many vigilante attacks on Sunnis. In addition there was ongoing violence between the occupying troops and different factions in the Iraqi population.

In Britain, racially motivated attacks against British Asians and African Caribbeans continue to take place. In 2001 riots broke out involving clashes between British Asians and whites in the northern English towns of Oldham, Bradford and Burnley. There have also been attacks on asylum seekers. In August 2001, Firsat Yildiz, a Turkish asylum seeker living in Glasgow, was murdered in what was thought to be an unprovoked racist attack.

In the wake of the terrorist attacks on the USA on 11 September 2001, Arabs, Muslims and others who were mistaken for Arabs or Muslims were attacked. In Arizona a Sikh man was killed in a drive-by shooting; in New York a man attempted to run over a Pakistani woman in a car park; in London a Muslim minicab driver was viciously attacked and left paralysed from the neck down.

In Britain, France and other European countries, extreme right-wing parties such as the British National Party, the National Front and Le Pen's Front National, which oppose immigration and blame social problems on minority ethnic groups, continue to attract support. In the USA evidence suggests that many years after the enactment of civil rights legislation American blacks and Hispanics are still seriously disadvantaged in areas such as employment and education.

In this chapter we will examine some of the reasons why conflict and inequality between racial, ethnic and national groups continue to occur. Broadly, these explanations prioritize one or more of the following factors:

1. Some see biological differences between 'races' as the crucial factor.
2. Some emphasize the process of migration as crucial since this brings contact and potentially conflict and inequality between those from different ethnic, racial or national backgrounds.
3. Those who emphasize ethnicity stress cultural rather than biological differences between groups of people.
4. Those who emphasize racism stress power differences and discrimination between different groups.
5. National identity can lead to people differentiating themselves from others and can be the basis for conflict and inequality.

There is considerable overlap between these issues, and most sociologists would accept that ethnicity, migration, nationality and racism are closely connected and interrelated. Different sections of the chapter will focus on different issues while also discussing connections between the issues. 'Race' or biological difference is discussed first, because some sociologists dismiss the idea that biological differences, in themselves, can account for patterns of social life.

'Race'

Biological theories of 'race' attempt to establish a relationship between **phenotype**, or physical characteristics, such as hair and skin colour, and **genotype**, or the underlying genetic differences between groups of humans. (The word 'race' is placed in inverted commas because, as we shall see, there is debate over whether there is any scientific basis for distinguishing so-called 'races'.) As science has developed, the dominant thinking about this relationship has changed.

Michael Banton – theories of 'race'

Michael Banton (1987) has described the various attempts that have been made to divide human beings into different biological or racial groups. He distinguishes three main types of theory: those which see 'race' as lineage; those which see it as type; and those which see it as subspecies.

Race as lineage

According to Banton, the word 'race' was not used in English until 1508, when it appeared in a poem by the Scotsman William Dunbar. At that time 'the Bible was accepted as the authority on human affairs' and ideas on racial difference were therefore based on biblical teaching.

This meant that it was generally accepted that all humans were ultimately descended from Adam and Eve. The idea of 'race' as lineage adopted a **monogenesist view**: humans belonged to a single species and had a common origin.

However, it was believed that as humans became dispersed around the globe, distinctive **lineages** or lines of descent developed. These corresponded to differences in physical appearance and geographical origin between human groups. People had become different as the result of migration to different environments, but ultimately because 'God had guided the course of events'.

In some respects the idea of 'race' as lineage implied that all humans were basically equal. However, some claimed that God had made people different in order to make them suited to particular areas of the earth. For example, many thought that only Africans could work effectively in the extreme heat of the tropics. Banton argues: 'The message was that each people was adapted to its own environment and therefore should stay where they were.'

In the seventeenth and eighteenth centuries, British and American writers rarely used the word 'race', but by the nineteenth century a new approach to classifying groups of humans was gaining popularity.

'Race' as type

The idea of 'race' as **type** is based upon a belief that all humans do not share a common origin and that humanity is divided into distinctive groups. It is therefore a **polygenetic theory**, that is, a theory that humanity has several origins rather than one. This new approach to 'race' developed in different countries at around the same time, but some of the most influential views originated in America.

The Philadelphian doctor Samuel James Morton based his arguments on the measurement of skulls. In 1839 Morton distinguished five 'races':

1. **Caucasian** (from Europe, India and parts of North Africa and the Middle East)
2. **Mongolian** (Chinese and Eskimos)
3. **Malay** (from Malaysia and the Polynesian Islands)
4. **American** (native Americans from North and South America)
5. **Ethiopian** (from sub-Saharan Africa)

From his measurements Morton claimed that 'Caucasians' had the largest cranial capacity and 'Ethiopians' the smallest. Morton equated cranial capacity with the size of the brain, and the size of the brain with intellectual development. He believed therefore that Europeans were more advanced than sub-Saharan Africans.

Morton's ideas were developed further by J.C. Nott and G.R. Gliddon in their book *Types of Mankind*, published in Philadelphia in 1854. Nott and Gliddon believed there were distinctive groups of humans of a relatively permanent kind. These separate types gave rise to differences in behaviour between groups of humans. Furthermore, different types of human were naturally antagonistic to one another.

Nott and Gliddon clearly believed in the superiority of white races. They claimed that Caucasians (who are supposed to originate from the Caucasus mountains) 'have in all ages been the rulers' and had shown themselves to be the only humans capable of developing democracy. On the other hand, dark-skinned 'races' were 'only fit for military governments'.

Nott and Gliddon's work was typical of that of many other writers in asserting that there were distinct biologically different 'races'. These 'races' behaved in different ways: some had remained 'pure' and untainted by interbreeding; and some of them were superior to others.

Banton comments that Nott and Gliddon's notions of racial purity and of racial inferiority and superiority were close to the racial views of the Nazis. An even bigger influence on Nazi thinking was the French writer Arthur de Gobineau. Writing in the 1850s, he claimed that there was a distinctive Aryan 'race' which had migrated from a homeland in the East and which was superior to all other 'races'. According to Gobineau, the Aryans had then spread out and were responsible for establishing most of the world's major civilizations. These included the civilizations of Egypt, Rome, China, Greece, Assyria and even Mexico and Peru.

'Race' as subspecies

The idea of 'race' as **subspecies** combines elements of the idea of 'race' as lineage and that of 'race' as type. The origins of this conception of 'race' are to be found in the work of the British biologist Charles Darwin and his **theory of evolution**.

According to Banton, Darwin saw a species as 'a class which was distinctive because its members inherited common characters but inherited them in different combinations which were subject to continual modification'. Members of the same species can breed with one another and produce fertile offspring. However, because species are constantly changing and evolving it is possible for different branches, subgroups or subspecies to develop. Where groups within a species become geographically separated and breed only within that group, they develop their own distinctive characteristics.

Darwin saw **evolution** as a slow process resulting from **natural selection**. Those members of a species that were best adapted to their environment were most likely to breed and therefore to pass on their genetic characteristics to future generations. There was also an element of **sexual selection** involved. Females would tend to select the most attractive males of their species with which to breed. Gradually the characteristics that made members of a species or subspecies more likely to breed and produce offspring became increasingly typical of the group as a whole.

Different human 'races' could develop in the same way as different subspecies of animal. Natural selection, sexual selection and chance variations in genes could result in distinct human groups with different physical appearances. Thus, although all humans had a common origin, they could evolve to form different races.

Banton does not accept that the term 'race' is a useful one. He says: 'Race as a folk-concept differentiating present-day groups on the basis of their appearance has no theoretical value' (Banton, 1997). Some reasons why it may have no theoretical value will be explored below.

Herbert Spencer – human subspecies and social evolution

The idea of 'race' as subspecies became increasingly popular in the latter part of the nineteenth century. The English functionalist sociologist Herbert Spencer developed his ideas about **social evolution** at the same time as Darwin was developing his ideas about biological evolution (Spencer, in Andreski, 1971). In applying evolutionary ideas to the study of society Spencer developed influential ideas about the relationship between 'race' and human social development.

The mixture of races

Spencer believed that societies could sometimes benefit from the mixing of races. For example, he claimed that the Romans gained strength from amalgamating with 'other Aryan tribes, Sabini, Sabelli and Samnites'. England too had benefited from the interbreeding of closely related groups, including 'different divisions of the Aryan race' and 'varieties of Scandinavians'.

However, the outcome was rather different when societies were composed of mixed races that were less closely related. Spencer believed that this could result in infertility after several generations, and unstable societies. Spain had an incongruous mixture of 'Basques, Celtic, Gothic, Moorish [and] Jewish' groups. Such societies required strong central government to keep the diverse 'racial groups from engaging in conflict with one another' and Spencer believed that too much government regulation hindered social evolution.

The evolutionary scale

According to Spencer, then, societies could consist of one race, but often consisted of a mixture of several. The precise mixture helped determine whether or not a society became more evolved and civilized. Spencer developed a complex scheme for categorizing societies based on whether they had a complex or simple structure, and whether they were stable or unstable:

1. A **simple society** was 'a single working whole' which was not divided into different sections, groups or tribes.
2. A **compound society** was one where 'the simple groups have their respective chiefs under a supreme chief'.
3. **Doubly compound societies** were more complex still, with a number of compound societies united under a single government.

Spencer left the reader in no doubt that simple societies were less developed and therefore inferior to more complex ones. He described them as 'uncivilized' and referred to some as 'savage tribes'. More complex societies had evolved further, and were more civilized and better adapted to their environment.

To Spencer, social life and the evolutionary process involved the 'survival of the fittest'. Those individuals, groups and species that were not well adapted to their environment would die out. If the native populations of conquered colonies died out, then this was simply because they were not well adapted.

The limitations of nineteenth-century ideas on 'race'

Although more sophisticated than theories of 'race' as type, the idea of 'race' as subspecies has also been used to suggest that certain 'races' are superior to others. All the approaches to 'race' examined so far have based their analysis on phenotypical differences in physical appearance between groups of humans. However, nineteenth-century scientists did not possess the scientific knowledge necessary to relate phenotypical differences to underlying genotype or genetic differences. Advances in genetics after the Second World War made this possible.

Steve Jones – genetics and evolution

Genetic differences

The geneticist Steve Jones (1991, 1994) examined theories of 'race' in the light of increasing understanding of human genetics. There are 50,000 genes in each human being and these genes determine the differences between humans. Genetic research has found some differences between groups of humans. For example, changes in fewer than ten genes determine skin colour. According to Jones, climatic variations have led to the evolution of differences in these genes among people from different climatic areas. Ultraviolet light from the sun allows humans to produce vitamin D in the skin. Vitamin D is essential to avoid the disease rickets. Dark-skinned people do not manufacture vitamin D as easily as light-skinned people do. In less sunny climates those with dark skins are less likely to survive into adulthood and are therefore unable to pass on their genes by having children.

There are genetic differences too between Europeans and the Japanese. Europeans are more tolerant of alcohol because their livers are more capable of breaking it down. In Japan a genetic variant of the liver enzyme is less effective at coping with alcohol. The Japanese drink less alcohol than the Europeans because when they do drink they tend to feel nauseous and their faces go red.

Genetic research also suggests that Africans 'are on a branch of the human family that split off from the others early on, and most of the rest of us are more closely related to each other than we are to the populations so far tested in Africa' (Jones, 1991).

In the Pacific there seem to be two main genetic groups. One consists of the Australian Aborigines and the people of New Guinea. Genetics suggests they have been settled in that area for a very long time. The peoples of other Pacific islands, on the other hand, are more closely related to East Asians and may have moved to the area more recently.

The absence of 'races'

Despite describing the existence of genetic differences between human groups, Jones does not believe that there is any genetic justification for distinguishing 'races'. He gives a number of reasons for this:

1. He suggests that, to be able to show that there are different 'races', 'the different peoples should be quite distinct from one another in a *large* sample of their

genes, not just those for skin colour'. However, this is not the case. Geneticists have not found that the genes governing skin colour are related to other genetic patterns. Jones says: 'The patterns of variation in each system are independent of each other. Our colour does not say much about what lies under the skin.'

2 Genetic diversity has relatively little to do with 'race'. About 85 per cent of the variations in human genes result from differences between individuals from the same country. A further 5 to 10 per cent of genetic diversity comes from differences between countries in the same continent and populated by the same supposed 'race' (for instance, differences between the English and the Spanish, or between Nigerians and Kenyans). Jones concludes: 'The overall genetic differences between "races" – Africans and Europeans, say – are no greater than that between different countries within Europe or within Africa. Individuals – not nations and not races – are the main repository of human variation' (Jones, 1991).

3 Overall, humans are much more homogeneous than other species. For example, one of Jones's areas of expertise is the genetic variations between snails. His research shows that variations between the snail populations in different Pyrenean valleys are greater than the variations between Australian Aborigines and English people. He says: 'If you were a snail it would make good biological sense to be a racist: but you have to accept that humans are tediously uniform animals.'

Social definitions of 'race'

Steve Jones believes that many attitudes towards 'race' have no scientific basis. He argues:

> *Humanity can be divided into groups in many ways: by culture, by language and by race – which usually means by skin colour. Each division depends to some extent on prejudice and, because they do not overlap, can lead to confusion.* Jones, 1991

Societies use different definitions of 'race'. Under apartheid in South Africa anyone who had just a single white ancestor was regarded as non-white or coloured, no matter what their actual skin colour was. In Haiti, on the other hand, the former ruler Papa Doc claimed that he lived in a white nation. Although most of the inhabitants had a dark skin colour nearly everyone could claim one or more white ancestors.

Some supposed 'races' are figments of the imagination. Genetic research suggests, for example, that there is no such thing as an 'Aryan race' and there is no evidence of a distinct Caucasian 'race' with its origins in the Caucasus mountains.

Attitudes to 'race'

Jones notes that thinking about 'race' has usually gone beyond classifying human groups. He says: 'It is a tiny step from classifying people to judging them.' According to him, the idea of 'distinct pure races which differed in quality had a disastrous impact'. Hitler's attempt to eradicate Jews was based upon 'scientific' claims that they were an inferior 'race'. In 1923 the US president Calvin Coolidge passed immigration laws establishing quotas ensuring that most immigrants were from Western and Northern Europe. This policy was based on the claim that there would be racial deterioration if 'Nordic' people interbred with those from other 'races'. Jones concludes that 'Much of the story of the genetics of race – a field promoted by some eminent scientists – turns out to have been prejudice dressed up as science.'

To Jones, issues such as racism are moral issues rather than scientific ones, as modern science has shown that there can be no biological argument for racism. There are variations in human genotypes which affect physical characteristics (phenotypes). However, they are not sufficiently significant to allow different 'races' to be identified and they are not related to the culture, behaviour or morality of different groups of humans.

John Richardson and John Lambert – sociology and 'race'

Like Steve Jones, John Richardson and John Lambert (1985) criticize biological approaches to 'race'. They describe the idea of pure 'races' as 'misleading in the extreme' and deny that clear-cut, biologically different 'races' can be distinguished. However, they do not say that 'race' should not be studied by sociologists. Whatever the scientific limitations of the concept, it is widely believed that 'races' exist and this belief influences the behaviour of many members of particular societies. Richardson and Lambert refer to W.I. Thomas's dictum that 'if people define a situation as real, it is real in its social consequences'. Since people define 'race' as real, it has social consequences. The study of these consequences forms an important part of the sociology of 'race'.

The doctrine of racial superiority

As well as attacking biological definitions of 'race', Richardson and Lambert criticize the idea that some 'races' can be seen as superior to others. They outline three main problems with the doctrine of **racial superiority**:

1 There is no clear connection between biological differences and differences in behaviour and culture in groups of humans. Richardson and Lambert do not deny that biology has some bearing on social and cultural behaviour, but they claim that any links are 'remote and indirect'.

2 Social explanations of behavioural and cultural differences between human groups are far more convincing than biological ones. Biology is much less important in shaping human behaviour than it is in shaping animal behaviour. Richardson and Lambert say: 'Unlike animals, human beings are not so rigidly bound to inbuilt instincts or innate biological triggers; on the contrary, human survival and progress is enhanced if cultural flexibility prevails.' The same 'race' can produce very different cultures in different parts of the world. (An example might be Afrikaners in South Africa who developed a different culture under the apartheid system compared to the more

liberal culture of the Netherlands, which is where their ancestors originated.)

3 It is impossible to find any objective criteria by which to measure the 'superiority' or 'inferiority' of human groups. The Victorian Britons who argued for the superiority of white Europeans assumed that their urban, industrial societies were superior to other 'primitive' ones. However, as Richardson and Lambert comment:

> *Claims of 'progress' appear less convincing when we consider the subsequent problems of industrial pollution, personal alienation, and the possibility of nuclear warfare. The African pygmy or Mongolian herdsman is arguably in a more 'harmonious' relationship with his physical environment than is the urban inhabitant of London or New York.* Richardson and Lambert, 1985

In any case, if cultural achievements and technological developments are a measure of superiority and inferiority, history shows that different 'races' have been the most advanced at particular points in time. There were highly developed African civilizations such as the Ashanti and Zimbabwe when Europe was still in the 'Dark Ages'. Richardson and Lambert quote J.H. Goldthorpe, who claims that in 1600 China was perhaps the most developed nation, followed by India and Arabia. The evidence does not therefore support the belief that Europeans are innately superior to people from other parts of the world.

The social construction of 'race'

To Richardson and Lambert, and to most other sociologists, 'race' is a **social construction**: it has no biological basis. It has more to do with 'what people make of physical differences' and the 'everyday or commonsense notions which influence them'. How people define 'races' and their attitudes to different 'races' are influenced by the dominant belief systems of the society in which they live. For example, stereotypes about particular groups vary from place to place and time to time. Furthermore, 'In some societies, at certain times, people are found to attach little weight to racial differences, while in other contexts we might find intense hostility and pronounced patterns of racial "exclusion" and "inclusion"' (Richardson and Lambert, 1985).

In Richardson and Lambert's view, though, people do not just passively accept definitions of 'race' in a particular society. Through their actions and interactions with others they may reinforce or challenge existing beliefs about 'race', or they may help to create new beliefs. At the same time their beliefs and actions 'take place within particular historical and cultural contexts which tend to limit human choices and make certain types of cultural response and behaviour more likely than others'.

In later sections of this chapter we will analyse in more detail how 'race' is socially constructed. In particular, the sections on racism examine the way in which stereotypical beliefs about 'races' are created and sustained (see pp. 168–88).

Ethnicity is usually seen as defining groups in terms of their cultural characteristics rather than their supposed biological differences. In a later section we will discuss the concept of ethnicity, which many see as a more valid way of classifying human groups than 'race' (see pp. 158–68).

Migration and 'race' relations

Human groups which regard themselves as biologically or culturally different often live in close proximity to one another. Some sociologists have seen the process of **migration** and the social relationships and social changes that result from it as the key to understanding 'race' relations. Before discussing these theories, we will look briefly at patterns of migration to Britain. (Social policy issues in relation to migration are discussed later in this chapter – see pp. 149–52.)

Migration to Britain

Immigration until 1945

Britain has long had an ethnically diverse population. John Richardson points out:

> *The early Roman invaders encountered a mixed population of Britons, Picts and Celts, and when the Romans finally withdrew from these shores in 410 AD the succeeding centuries witnessed a series of forays and scattered settlements by varied groups of Angles, Saxons, Jutes, Danes and Vikings. This diversity was significantly enhanced by the arrival of the Normans.* Richardson, 1990

Since Roman times there have been successive waves of migration to Britain. Some of the most significant periods of migration are described below.

1 In the sixteenth, seventeenth and eighteenth centuries England accepted large numbers of Protestant refugees fleeing from religious persecution in Europe.

2 There have been Jewish immigrants to Britain for several centuries, but the main period of Jewish immigration to Britain took place between 1870 and 1914. In that period, 120,000 Jews fled persecution in Eastern Europe to settle in Britain.

3 Between 1820 and 1910 there was a massive emigration from Ireland. Nearly half the population left to escape starvation and poverty in their native country. Although many went to the USA, others settled in British cities such as Liverpool, London, Glasgow and Manchester.

4 Immigration laws were tightened in the twentieth century, but during the Second World War it proved impossible to control the entry of refugees. Along with British troops, large numbers of Poles, Belgians and French were evacuated to Britain from Dunkirk. Refugees also came to Britain from Czechoslovakia, Norway, Greece and Denmark. The Polish made up the largest group of all: by the end of 1945 there were nearly 250,000 Poles in Britain.

5 The biggest groups of immigrants to Britain since the Second World War have come from the Asian

subcontinent and the Caribbean. The Nationality Acts of 1914 and 1948, which severely restricted immigration from most parts of the world to Britain, imposed no restrictions on immigration to Britain from Commonwealth and Empire countries. Subjects of the British Empire had the right to enter Britain, vote, work and join the armed forces.

In the aftermath of the Second World War, Britain was experiencing a serious labour shortage. The government set up a working party to explore the possibility of employing more people from the Commonwealth in Britain. It suggested that female workers could be recruited for the health service.

In 1948 the first ships carrying groups of immigrants from Commonwealth countries arrived in Britain. The very first was the *Empire Windrush*, which carried 492 Jamaicans to Britain to seek work. London Transport recruited thousands of workers from Barbados, Trinidad and Jamaica. In some cases it paid the new workers' fares. Many, though by no means all, New Commonwealth immigrants were recruited to do relatively low-paid and unskilled jobs which employers could not fill with white British workers.

Although most of the earliest migrants in this period were from the West Indies, by 1962 they were outnumbered by immigrants from Pakistan and India. Most of the first immigrants from southeast Asia were men, with their families being more likely to follow later. Early migration from the West Indies included a higher proportion of women than that from India and Pakistan, and a second generation, born in Britain, developed more quickly. There were also long-established African Caribbean communities in cities such as Cardiff, Liverpool and London.

Politics and immigration control

Since at least the thirteenth century (when Edward I expelled Jews from Britain in 1290), immigration to Britain has been a politically contentious issue. This was certainly the case with the New Commonwealth immigration from 1945 to 1961.

There were tensions between the migrants and the white British population. In 1958 there were clashes between local whites and the African Caribbean population in Notting Hill in London. There was discrimination against minority ethnic groups with the **colour bar** – notices or adverts banned black people from renting property, joining clubs or obtaining other goods or services.

In 1968 the Conservative politician Enoch Powell made a famous speech in which he predicted that a multicultural Britain would prove to be disastrous. Powell claimed that Britain must be 'literally mad' to be allowing dependants of migrants to be entering the country. He argued that it would eventually lead to racial conflict and serious violence. He said: 'As I look ahead, I am filled with foreboding. Like the Roman, I seem to see "the River Tiber foaming with much blood"' (quoted in Layton-Henry, 1992).

Although Powell was sacked from his position in the shadow cabinet, politicians of both main parties were persuaded to introduce tight restrictions on immigration in response to such views. A succession of Acts was passed restricting the rights of Commonwealth citizens to settle in Britain.

The 1962 Commonwealth Immigrants Act had denied the right of entry to Britain unless strict criteria were met. In 1967, large numbers of East African Asians had entered Britain, particularly from Kenya. The Kenyan government had introduced an 'Africanization' policy and many Asians fled to Britain. East African Asians had not been covered by the 1962 Act, so the government rushed in new legislation. The 1968 Commonwealth Immigration Act imposed immigration controls on all Commonwealth citizens who did not have one parent or grandparent who was a UK citizen or born in the UK. Andrew Pilkington comments:

> *The act proved to be racially discriminatory in nature. For its effects were to allow Kenyan whites to enter Britain but to prevent Kenyan Asians from doing so until they were lucky enough to be granted one of the limited number of vouchers issued each year.* Pilkington, 1984

The Acts of the 1960s were followed by more legislation designed to curb immigration, particularly from non-white citizens of Commonwealth countries. This included the 1971 Immigration Act, the 1981 British Nationality Act, and the 1988 Immigration Act. This legislation largely succeeded in minimizing immigration from the Caribbean and the Asian subcontinent, but by the 1990s the government's attention had turned to other categories.

In 1993 the Asylum and Immigration Appeals Act was introduced. This was designed to try to reduce the number of people seeking **asylum**. Asylum seekers apply to enter a country in order to escape persecution in the country they are fleeing from. The British government which introduced the Act claimed that the system was being abused by 'economic migrants' – people who were not fleeing persecution but simply seeking a higher standard of living in Britain.

The Act removed the right of appeal for visitors to Britain who were refused entry. Asylum seekers retained the right of appeal, but they had to appeal within forty-eight hours of a decision by an immigration officer not to admit them. This might be difficult for asylum seekers who were unlikely to have either access to legal advice or a detailed knowledge of the regulations.

Asylum seekers lost their rights to public housing while they were awaiting a decision. They were also required to be fingerprinted, and regulations specified that their application would be refused if they failed to disclose all relevant information. In February 1996 new restrictions were introduced on the eligibility of asylum seekers for social security payments.

Attempts to limit the number of asylum seekers were also made through extending the need for visas to visitors from an increasing number of countries. Between 1985 and 1989, visa requirements were introduced for people from Sri Lanka, India, Bangladesh, Pakistan and Turkey. By the mid-1990s visas were required for people visiting Britain from over 100 countries. As Robin Cohen points out, it might be difficult for someone who was being persecuted by a regime to apply for a visa to leave the country. He says:

Now refugees were required to carry a passport from the very authorities who might be persecuting them. As to a visa, a visit to an accessible British embassy might well be interpreted as an act of dissent in itself. Cohen, 1994

The introduction of new legislation led to some politically embarrassing incidents which revealed the inhumanity of the legislation and the way it was being applied. For example, in 1993 over half of the 323 passengers on a pre-Christmas flight from Jamaica to London were detained by the British immigration authorities on the grounds that they might be 'Yardies' – members of Jamaican organized crime groups.

Recent immigration and asylum legislation

In 1999 a new Immigration and Asylum Act was introduced. This Act aimed to speed up the process of deciding cases so that most cases would be decided within six months. While most people welcomed this, other measures were more controversial. One such measure was the decision to replace an entitlement to welfare benefits with vouchers, worth £35 per week, which asylum seekers could use to obtain goods necessary for subsistence.

The Act also introduced a new system whereby asylum seekers were dispersed around the UK to avoid concentrations of asylum seekers in places such as Dover and London. This was partly a response to hostility from local residents in some areas where there was a high concentration of asylum seekers.

The Parekh Report (Parekh *et al.*, 2000; see pp. 209–11 for further details) strongly criticized these measures, specifically the 'indignity of subsisting on vouchers and being bussed around the country to communities that are often ill-prepared and hostile, and the lack of proper financial, educational and community support'. The report suggested that asylum seekers felt isolated by being dispersed and there were inadequate skills in local areas to help them put forward claims for asylum and develop their skills in speaking English. In Glasgow, one asylum seeker was murdered. Lydia Morris (2002) notes that the dispersal system 'has generated considerable concern about the potential for racial harassment'.

The 1999 Act made further attempts to restrict the inflow of asylum seekers. It imposed prohibitively expensive fines (£2,000 per illegal passenger) on lorry drivers found entering Britain with illegal immigrants on board. It also increased the number of airline liaison officers abroad in an attempt to curb the number of people travelling to Britain on illegal papers. Airlines also suffered penalties if they transported such people to Britain.

The Parekh Report points out that such measures make it virtually impossible for people fleeing persecution to enter Britain legally. The countries persecuting them would be unlikely to issue visas for them to leave and seek asylum. People are therefore forced into remaining in a country where they are in danger, or paying for fake documentation, or paying to be smuggled into Britain. The dangers of such a situation were demonstrated in 2000 when fifty-eight Chinese people attempting to enter Britain in the back of a lorry suffocated to death.

Some of the measures introduced in 1999 were so ineffective, or were so heavily criticized, that they were rapidly reconsidered. In 2002 a new Nationality, Immigration and Asylum Bill was introduced to change aspects of the 1999 Act. The voucher system was repealed and the policy of dispersing asylum seekers was replaced by a system of accommodation centres. However, aspects of these policies were also controversial, with some commentators questioning the wisdom of confining asylum seekers in large, isolated accommodation centres. Lydia Morris comments that there were several potential problems:

The quality and location of the centres will be important in determining the character and overall success of the new provisions, and difficulties are likely to stem from under-resourcing and problems securing planning permission. Unless the centres offer acceptable standards and are located in non-threatening areas, then drop-out from the system is likely to continue. Morris, 2002

Also controversial was a proposal to educate the children of asylum seekers away from mainstream schools, making integration with the local community difficult.

The Asylum and Immigration Act of 2004 introduced a wide range of measures with the stated purpose of 'strengthening the UK's borders to deter illegal immigration'. These included: creating a new offence of being without a valid immigration document without reasonable excuse; increased fines for those who employ illegal immigrants; and withdrawing support for the families of failed asylum seekers who were not cooperating with returning home. The Act also allowed the secretary of state to designate certain countries as safe, therefore invalidating any claims for asylum from people of those countries.

Yet another bill was introduced in 2005 (the Immigration, Asylum and Nationality Bill), which proposed stronger border controls, such as fingerprinting all visa applicants, and that the granting of indefinite leave to remain for refugees should be stopped. The Refugee Council has criticized many of these measures. For example, it says the offence of failing to provide a valid immigration document without reasonable excuse 'effectively allows the Home Office to decide on an asylum case based upon information about how the applicant came to the UK rather than about the merits of individual cases' (Refugee Council, 2005).

Immigration and the European Union

Britain's laws on refugees and migration have been affected by membership of the European Union. The EU (formerly the European Community) has always allowed the free movement of people between member states, and since 1993 citizens of each member state have become citizens of the EU as well. However, the EU has adopted what has become known as a 'fortress Europe' policy, which has tried to largely exclude non-EU citizens from entry to the community.

In 1990 five of the original members of the EU signed the Schengen Agreement, which tried to create common policies over issues relating to migration and asylum. Britain did not sign, preferring to retain its own restrictive rules. However, it did sign the Dublin Convention in

1990. This prevented asylum seekers from applying for asylum in more than one EU country. According to Cohen (1994), it was an attempt to make sure that asylum seekers did not take advantage of any weak link in Europe's borders by making multiple applications to different states. Thus, while membership of the EU has made movement within the community easier, it has done little for the plight of asylum seekers from elsewhere.

The politics of asylum seekers

From the mid-1990s onwards, asylum seekers became a highly charged political issue. The Parekh Report described 'a series of increasingly vitriolic press campaigns. Targeted groups have included Tamils, Turkish Kurds and Somalis.' The report argues that before the mid-1980s, asylum seekers 'were seen as brave people fleeing persecution, in contrast to the workers and families against whom immigration control was directed'. However, attitudes began to change when a number of Tamils from Sri Lanka began to arrive seeking asylum from persecution. This was because 'Single young men from South Asia were precisely the people against whom UK immigration control had been targeted for 30 years.' They were often therefore portrayed as bogus – they were using claims to be persecuted as an excuse to gain entry to a country where they could have a better lifestyle. In short, they were regarded as economic migrants posing as asylum seekers.

The Parekh Report quoted a Dover newspaper which lumped asylum seekers together with other undesirables. The paper said: 'Illegal immigrants, asylum seekers, bootleggers and scum-of-the-earth drug-smugglers … have targeted our beloved coastline. We are left with the backdraft of a nation's human sewage' (quoted in Parekh *et al.*, 2000). Similar media images of groups such as the Kurds and Somalis were also common. Such a 'culture of disbelief' was not confined to the media. Immigration officials were increasingly 'geared much more towards preventing "abuse" and discouraging arrivals, than to providing protection'.

The Parekh Report argues that both media and official responses to asylum seekers are highly damaging. Such responses are very similar to the 'immigration scares' from earlier decades and they tend to feed the sort of racism that can lead to violence against minority groups. The report argues that asylum seekers are the most socially excluded group in Britain. However, some government policies have increased their exclusion rather than reduced it. The report suggests that delays in processing asylum applications, attempts to prevent people from seeking asylum, and severe limitations on the right of asylum seekers to work, all mean that the community is unable to benefit from their talents and skills. Rather than being seen as a burden, they should be seen in terms of their potential to be a useful asset. The Parekh Report claims that the hostility to asylum seekers from politicians suggests that the latter 'are not genuinely committed to addressing all forms of racism' and it 'undermines Britain's development as a cohesive but diverse society'.

Further criticisms of policies on asylum seekers in Britain and elsewhere are put forward by Mathew J. Gibney (2004). He points out that rules governing the treatment of refugees were introduced in the 1951 United Nations Geneva Convention as the result of the shameful lack of support provided for Jews fleeing Nazi persecution in some countries. Asylum seekers are simply those who are seeking refugee status, yet the vilification of asylum seekers has made it very difficult for refugees to flee persecution.

According to Gibney, a number of changes in the world have led to the increased hostility towards refugees. These include easier and cheaper travel, increasing numbers of refugees from non-European countries, and the decline in demand in Western countries for unskilled and semi-skilled labour.

In response to increased applications for asylum in the 1990s, many countries, including Britain, found new ways to exclude asylum seekers, by preventing the arrival of refugees. If refugees cannot enter Britain or other countries where they might seek asylum, then they are unable to have their claims for asylum considered. For the genuine refugees any chance to escape persecution is denied.

Various techniques have been used to prevent refugees entering countries of refuge. Britain has introduced new visa requirements for nationals from many countries, it has introduced sanctions against carriers if they bring people without proper papers to Britain, and it has sent British immigration officers to overseas airports to stop potential asylum seekers boarding planes.

Gibney does not deny that some asylum seekers may be economic migrants rather than those fleeing persecution, but he thinks the numbers of economic migrants are small. Most asylum seekers are genuine refugees from violent countries, such as Iraq, Afghanistan, the former Yugoslavia, Sri Lanka and Turkey, where there is a real risk of individuals being persecuted. Gibney says that, 'Few states have made any real attempts to disentangle refugees … from the web of restrictions.' Few refugees are able to enter Britain legally, so, in Gibney's view, Britain is failing (like many other countries) in its responsibility to help refugees, as set out in the 1951 Geneva Convention.

Whatever the merits of these arguments, the media coverage seems to have given a misleading impression of the scale of applications for asylum in the UK. In 2004 the inflow of asylum seekers was only slightly above the average for EU countries. In that year there were 0.7 asylum seekers per 1,000 of the UK population (*Social Trends 2006*). This was above the EU average (0.6 per 1,000 people), but much lower than in some other countries. For example, rates were 11.0 per 1,000 in Cyprus, 3.0 in Austria, 2.6 in Sweden and 2.1 in Slovakia.

British migration since 1961

As a consequence of some of the changes discussed above, immigration from the New Commonwealth (including Pakistan) declined from 136,000 in 1961 to 68,000 in 1972 and 22,800 in 1988. It rose to an average of 36,100 per year in the 1996–2000 period. The majority were allowed to come to Britain as the dependants of British citizens rather than as immigrants in their own right. By 2000 there were more immigrants from the European Union and the Old Commonwealth (such as Canada, Australia and New Zealand) than there were from the New Commonwealth (such as Pakistan, India and the West Indies).

In recent years, patterns of immigration have become complex, with immigrants originating in a wide variety of countries. In 2004 the largest number of immigrants who were granted settlement were from Asia, and the second largest number were from Africa, with immigration from non-EEA (European Economic Area) European countries coming third (*Social Trends 2006*). People from the EEA are allowed to live in Britain if they are employed or able to support themselves without receiving benefits. *Social Trends* points out that from 1991 to 1994 the most rapid rises in immigration were from Africa (which tripled) and from non-EEA European countries (which almost quadrupled).

At the same time, Britain has become a net importer of people. In 1991 the numbers of immigrants to and emigrants from the UK were about the same, but in 2004 there was estimated to be a net inflow of 222,600 immigrants. There have also been inflows of people to the UK from Eastern European states which have joined the European Union, such as Poland. (Poland became an EU member in 2004.)

Despite the increased immigration from Europe, there is little doubt that many of the immigration rules have been specifically designed to limit the numbers of Asian and African-Caribbean migrants to Britain. This is despite the fact that there are many migrants from other parts of the world. Writing in 1992, Richard Skellington and Paulette Morris noted: 'The word "immigrant" is often wrongly used to refer only to black people. The majority of immigrants are white – from Eire or the Old Commonwealth (Australia, New Zealand and Canada) or from other European countries.' They point out that the 1981 census found that, of 3.4 million people in Britain who were born elsewhere, 1.9 million were white.

However, Robin Cohen (1994) argues that Britain's policies towards migration have not just been based on excluding black and Asian immigrants. At various times a range of groups, some of them white, have been seen as unsuitable for immigration to Britain. The reasons are tied up with nationalistic conceptions of British identity, which will be explored later in the chapter (see pp. 192–4).

Britain's minority ethnic population

It is only comparatively recently that the British government has started collecting data specifically on minority ethnic groups. The 1991 census included a question asking people to assign themselves to an ethnic group from a list of options. There were a number of problems with this data:

1. The options were by no means exhaustive: for example, no 'Irish' category was included and a considerable number of respondents described themselves as belonging to the ethnic group category 'other'.
2. The figures were based upon self-assigned ethnic groups, and were therefore shaped by the subjective views of the respondents.
3. The question mixed up nationality (e.g. Bangladeshi) and skin colour (e.g. 'Black other').
4. The figures did not distinguish between people from distinctive cultural groups but with the same national origin (e.g. Indian Sikhs and Hindus).

Nevertheless, because the census is more comprehensive than any other survey, it provides perhaps the most reliable estimate of the size of the minority ethnic population in Britain.

Furthermore, the 2001 census addressed some of these problems. For the first time people were able to describe their ethnic origin as 'White Irish', and a new category of 'mixed race' was included. Table 3.1 shows that in 2001, 4,635,000 people described themselves as belonging to a non-white minority ethnic group, some 7.9 per cent of the British population. This was a big increase from the 3,015,000 who stated they were from a minority ethnic group in 1991. Part of this increase may have been due to the inclusion of the category 'mixed race', which was chosen by 677,000 people. Some of these individuals may have described themselves as white in the previous census in the absence of a mixed race option.

The largest minority ethnic group was Indian Asian or Asian British, which made up 1.8 per cent of the population, followed by Pakistani Asian or Asian British (1.3 per cent), Black Caribbean (1 per cent), Black African (0.8 per cent), Bangladeshi (0.5 per cent), Chinese (0.4 per cent), 'Other' (0.4 per cent), 'Other Asian' (0.4 per cent) and 'Black other' (0.2 per cent). 'Mixed race' was chosen by 1.2 per cent. In addition, 1.2 per cent of the population described themselves as 'White Irish'.

Although Britain's minority ethnic population is growing, there is evidence that an increasing proportion of members of minority ethnic groups were born in Britain. In 1994 the *Fourth National Survey of Ethnic Minorities* was carried out by the Policy Studies Institute (Modood *et al.*, 1997). It collected data from a representative sample of 5,196 people of Caribbean and Asian origin and a comparative group of 2,868 white people. The survey revealed, not surprisingly, that a growing proportion of members of minority ethnic groups had been born in Britain: 62 per cent of the population of Caribbean origin had been born in Britain compared to 54 per cent in 1982. The figures were lower for other groups, reflecting the timing of migration. In 1994, 47 per cent of those of Indian origin were born in Britain. The equivalent figures were 41 per cent for African Asians, 52 per cent for Pakistanis and 44 per cent for Bangladeshis. In all groups the vast majority of children were born in Britain.

More recently, the 2001 census found that 90.7 per cent of people in England were born in the UK. Although the major minority ethnic groups in the UK are well established and many of their members were born in the UK, some sociological approaches to 'race' and ethnicity have seen the process of migration as important in understanding the position of minority ethnic groups in societies. These approaches will now be examined.

Migration and assimilation

One influential approach to studying relationships between ethnic groups, or **race relations**, focuses on the process of migration by minority ethnic groups to a new society. It has sometimes been called the **immigrant–host model** because it tends to conceive of relationships between ethnic groups as between a dominant 'host' society and a smaller immigrant group.

Table 3.1 The UK population by ethnic group, 2001

	Total population 2001 Count	Total population 2001 %	Minority ethnic population 2001 %
White	54,153,898	92.1	n/a
Mixed	677,117	1.2	14.6
Asian or Asian British			
Indian	1,053,411	1.8	22.7
Pakistani	747,285	1.3	16.1
Bangladeshi	283,063	0.5	6.1
Other Asian	247,664	0.4	5.3
Black or Black British			
Black Caribbean	565,876	1.0	12.2
Black African	485,277	0.8	10.5
Black other	97,585	0.2	2.1
Chinese	247,403	0.4	5.3
Other	230,615	0.4	5.0
All minority ethnic population	4,635,296	7.9	100
All population	58,789,194	100	n/a

Source: Office for National Statistics, 2003: (http://www.statistics.gov.uk/cci/nugget)

The immigrant–host approach has usually adopted an optimistic view of 'race' relations. Sociologists using this perspective have usually believed that eventually the immigrant group will adapt to the way of life of the host society and will be **assimilated** into it. Conflict based on 'race' and ethnicity will tend to decline or even disappear with the passage of time.

The immigrant–host model has sometimes been seen as similar to a functionalist view of society. Some sociologists who have used it see the host society as characterized by a basic consensus and a shared culture. The immigrant group is seen as temporarily disrupting the consensus and shared culture, before the society gradually adapts to the newcomers and the immigrants adapt to the society. The emphasis is usually on the second of these processes: the immigrants are expected to fit in with their new society more than the society is expected to adapt to them. Thus, like functionalism, the immigrant–host model emphasizes stability, shared moral values and slow evolutionary change involving a process of adaptation. Furthermore, one of the pioneers of this general approach, Robert E. Park, followed functionalists in using biological analogies in his work.

Robert E. Park – 'race' relations and migration

The nature of 'race' relations

Robert E. Park was a leading member of the Chicago School of Sociology, based at Chicago University, which developed influential theories of social life during the 1920s and 1930s. At the time, Chicago was a rapidly growing city and large numbers of people from diverse groups were migrating to Chicago, both from within the USA and from other countries. The Chicago sociologists engaged in detailed empirical research in their city, and it was in this context that Park developed his theory of 'race' relations.

Park describes 'race' relations as

the relations existing between peoples distinguished by marks of racial descent, particularly when these racial differences enter into the consciousness of the individuals and groups so distinguished, and by doing so determine in each case the individual's conception of himself as well as his status in the community. Park, 1950

'Race' relations only existed where people had a sense of belonging to different groups and there was some conflict between them. Thus, according to Park, there were no 'race' relations in Brazil. Although Europeans and Africans lived together in Brazil, there was almost no **race consciousness** and therefore little potential for conflict.

Park believed that different 'races' originated with the dispersal of a once-concentrated population. The **great dispersion** was partly stimulated by the search for a more abundant food supply, and it was, 'like the migration of plants and animals, centrifugal'. Each dispersed human group then 'developed, by natural selection and inbreeding, those special physical and cultural traits that characterize the different racial stocks'.

Eventually the **centrifugal dispersion** of humans was replaced by a **centripetal force** that brought people from the different 'racial stocks' together. European migration and conquest created 'race' relations in many parts of the world, and the mixing of different groups in cities had the same effect. Thus, Park says, 'It is obvious that race relations and all that they imply are generally, and on the whole, the products of migration and conquest.'

Interracial adjustments

Park claimed that a complex process of **interracial adjustment** followed migration or conquests that brought different 'races' into contact. This process involved 'racial competition, conflict, accommodation and assimilation'.

Competition was a universal, biological phenomenon: the 'struggle for existence'. Just as plants might struggle for sunlight, humans struggled for scarce and prized goods and, in particular, land. Failure in this struggle could lead to extinction both in plant or animal species and in human 'races'. For example, the native population of Tasmania 'seem to have been hunted like wild animals by the European immigrants, as were, at one time, the Indians in the USA'. Competition does not always take such an extreme form as this, but it continues so long as there are different 'races' which have 'racial consciousness'.

Competition is a struggle by groups and individuals in the ecological order; **conflict** is a struggle between individuals in the social order. Park gives the example of conflict between 'negroes' and whites in the southern states of the USA over 'jobs and places of relative security in the occupational organization of the community in which they live'.

If competition and conflict divide 'races', then accommodation and assimilation bring them together. Conflict ceases, at least temporarily, when the status and power of different 'races' have become fixed and are generally accepted.

Accommodation allows people 'to live and work on friendly terms' but it does not ensure that relations will remain harmonious. The groups with less power and status may eventually decide that their position is unsatisfactory and they may seek to improve it through engaging in competition.

On the other hand, **assimilation** provides a permanent solution to the problems created by 'race' relations. Assimilation can involve two processes:

1. 'A process that goes on in society by which individuals spontaneously acquire one another's language, characteristic attitudes, habits and modes of behaviour'
2. 'A process by which individuals and groups of individuals are taken over and incorporated into larger groups'

Park claimed that Italians, French and Germans had resulted from the assimilation of a variety of racial groups, and that the USA had been able to assimilate a variety of groups with 'ease and rapidity'. He was unclear about whether assimilation was inevitable or not. In one article he said, 'the race relations cycle which takes the form, to state it abstractly, of contacts, competition, accommodation and eventual assimilation, is apparently progressive and irreversible'.

However, Park recognized that, at the time he was writing, Japanese and 'negro' Americans had not assimilated into American society. He suggested that this was because both groups had 'a distinctive racial hallmark' in the form of physical differences from white Americans. The Irish, for example, could become 'indistinguishable in the cosmopolitan mass', but for other groups the situation was different. Park argues:

> *Where races are distinguished by certain external marks these furnish a permanent physical substratum upon which and around which the irritations and animosities, incidental to all human intercourse, tend to accumulate and so to gain strength.* Park, 1950

An evaluation of Park

The work of Park has undoubtedly been influential. For example, Sheila Patterson (1965) used the immigrant–host model in a study of African-Caribbean immigrants in Brixton in the 1950s. She painted an optimistic picture of gradual assimilation between the immigrants and the 'hosts'. Park too was generally optimistic about race relations in the long run, although he seemed to believe that conflict would not necessarily disappear between all racial groups. Unlike some sociologists who have used the immigrant–host perspective, he did not believe that the migrants would necessarily adapt to the lifestyle of the hosts. For example, he was well aware that in some societies immigrants from Europe had become dominant, and in some cases had wiped out the indigenous population completely. Nevertheless in several ways Park's work is open to criticisms that have been made of immigrant–host theories.

John Richardson and John Lambert – a critique of the immigrant–host model

Strengths and weaknesses of the immigrant–host model

Richardson and Lambert (1985) are generally critical of the immigrant–host model, but they do believe that it has some strengths. They believe that the process of migration can influence relationships between ethnic groups and that it is therefore well worth studying. They argue:

> *The model effectively drew attention to the dislocation caused by migration, it bravely addressed the complexities of assimilation, and it demonstrated the dynamic processes of change, rather than settling for a misleadingly static view of black–white conflict.* Richardson and Lambert, 1985

It raised important issues and, although it 'failed to supply satisfactory answers to all the issues, at least it stimulated further development of the debates'.

Richardson and Lambert identify four main flaws or limitations in the immigrant–host model:

1. They argue that it tends to be unclear about the status of the different stages that are usually outlined. Sometimes it is seen as inevitable that a society will move through these stages, with a gradual movement towards assimilation; at other times the process seems less than inevitable. Park recognized that there could be long delays before a society moved on to the next stage and that sometimes reversals were possible. However, at times Park also suggested that the 'race relations cycle' was an inevitable process. Thus some of the theories contradict themselves. Richardson and Lambert argue that concepts like accommoda-

tion and assimilation 'are not really spelled out, and in practice it remains difficult to identify the exact stage of "adjustment" which has been reached'.

2. Richardson and Lambert question the assumption built into these theories that assimilation is desirable. The theories tend to assume that migrant groups will, or should, want to give up their distinctive cultures to become fully integrated into the host society. They tend to neglect the possibility that both the immigrants and the hosts might value the cultural diversity of a multicultural society. The model also places most of the emphasis on the migrants changing and does not see the need for major changes in the host society. It can therefore be seen as ideologically biased in supporting the cultural domination of the majority ethnic group in a society.
3. The immigrant–host model attaches little importance to the existence of racism as a cause of ethnic conflict and inequality. Many writers argue that, in Britain and elsewhere, ethnic conflict results from the deeply and widely held racist views of the host society. The hosts are far more than suspicious or cautious about the newcomers: they have been brought up to have stereotypical views and hostile attitudes. (Racism is discussed in detail on pp. 168–88.)
4. The immigrant–host model has been criticized by conflict theorists for assuming that there is a consensus in the host society. It hides divisions between males and females and different classes as well as between ethnic groups. It tends to ignore the cultural diversity and the wide variations in values that may already exist in the host society. For example, some groups may be very strongly opposed to immigration and hold entrenched racist views, while other groups might welcome cultural diversity and be in favour of relaxing or removing immigration controls.

Conclusion

While processes of migration remain important, it can be argued that they are becoming less important in Britain. As discussed above, increasing proportions of the main minority ethnic groupings have been born in Britain and are not migrants. They can be seen as belonging to one of an increasingly diverse range of British cultures. It is no longer possible (if it ever was) to see Britain as possessing one dominant culture from which other cultures diverge. As will be discussed later, some sociologists see Britain as possessing a range of increasingly well-established new ethnicities (see pp. 194–8). These may be hybrids of different cultural traditions. They are too far removed from the process of migration to be seen in terms of an immigrant–host model (see pp. 152–5).

Stephen Castles and Godula Kosack – a Marxist view of migration

In a 1973 study of migration to France, Germany, Britain and Switzerland, Castles and Kosack advanced a very different theory of migration from the immigrant–host model. Rather than seeing relations between immigrants and hosts in terms of cultural differences, they argued that migration had to be examined in the context of the international capitalist system.

They found that immigrants in the four countries studied had a number of similarities. These were: a 'subordinate position on the labour market, concentration in run-down areas and poor housing, lack of educational opportunities, widespread prejudice, and discrimination from the host populations and authorities'. Castles and Kosack argued that these similarities showed that the diverse immigrant groups 'had the same function and position in society, irrespective of their original backgrounds'.

Migration and the international economic system

Castles and Kosack regard migration as resulting from the development of the international economic system. According to them, the richer European nations have exploited the poorer nations of the world, causing their underdevelopment. From colonial times onwards the 'third world' has been used as a source of cheap, easily exploited labour and cheap raw materials. The colonies were not allowed to develop, or in some cases even maintain, industries that competed with those of their European masters. The poor in the 'third world' were then used as a reserve army of labour by successful capitalist nations during periods of economic prosperity and high employment. Development has also been uneven in Europe, leaving potential migrants in some of the more impoverished rural areas of southern Europe.

Migration tends to increase the inequalities between richer and poorer nations. Those who migrate are a valuable resource: they are usually young and vigorous. The society into which they were born has had to pay to maintain them during their childhood when they were not able to contribute to the wealth of their nation. Castles and Kosack therefore see 'migration as a form of development aid for the migration countries' – these countries are able to take advantage of labour which has cost them little or nothing to produce. Furthermore, migrants may be willing to work for relatively low wages, undercutting other workers and reducing the labour costs of capitalists.

'Race prejudice' and the working class

As well as directly serving the interests of the ruling class by reducing its wage bills, immigration can also help to cement its power in capitalist societies. According to Castles and Kosack, prejudice against immigrants has three main functions:

1. It serves to 'conceal and legitimate the exploitation' of immigrant workers 'by alleging that they are congenitally inferior'. Injustice and discrimination that would otherwise be unacceptable are tolerated if they are directed at a supposedly inferior group.
2. Immigrant workers are often used as scapegoats for the problems created by the capitalist system. They provide a convenient explanation for problems such as unemployment and housing shortages. In reality,

though, such problems result from 'the deficiencies of capitalist society, which is unable to provide adequate living conditions and to guarantee security to the whole of the working population'.

3 **Race prejudice** serves to divide the working class. Workers are persuaded to accept discriminatory measures against immigrant workers and this means that there is little prospect of the working class uniting to oppose capitalist power.

Castles and Kosack conclude that immigration benefits the ruling class by reducing its labour costs and by preventing the working class from seeking to change the status quo, which works to the advantage of the richest and most powerful members of society. (We discuss Marxist views on 'race' and ethnicity further on pp. 177–8.)

Stephen Castles and Mark J. Miller – *The Age of Migration*

The increase in migration

In a later study, published in 1993, Castles, writing with Mark Miller, described the internationalization of migration since 1973. He was more optimistic in this study about the effects of migration than he was in 1973.

Castles and Miller argue that migration has increased as 'third world' countries have become more and more involved in the world capitalist system. In countries that are developing, there is considerable migration from rural to urban areas, and as this happens more people acquire 'the financial and cultural resources necessary for international migration'.

Rich capitalist countries have tried to restrict migration, but are unable to do so completely. There are considerable numbers of illegal immigrants to some richer countries, for example to the USA from Mexico. In any case most countries now have established minority ethnic populations, so that, 'even if migration were to stop tomorrow', cultural pluralism would affect the countries 'for generations'.

There are enormous pressures encouraging migration and, as a result, 'most highly developed countries and many less-developed ones have become far more culturally diverse than they were even a generation ago'.

The consequences of cultural pluralism

Castles and Miller argue that many countries now have no choice but to come to terms with the existence of a variety of ethnic groups within their national boundaries. 'Marginalization and isolation' of minority ethnic groups have served only to strengthen their ethnic identity and, for some minorities, their culture has become 'a mechanism of resistance'. Consequently, 'even if serious attempts were made to end all forms of discrimination and racism, cultural and linguistic differences will persist for generations'.

Although discrimination against and exclusion of minority ethnic groups are undesirable in themselves, the cultural pluralism they engender opens up new possibilities. A new **global culture** develops, encouraged by the mass media, international travel and migration. People become more familiar with the cultures of different societies and ethnic groups. Therefore 'difference need no longer be a marker for strangeness and separation, but rather an opportunity for informed choice among a myriad of possibilities'. International migration might even, Castles and Miller suggest, 'give hope of increased unity in dealing with the pressing problems which beset our small planet'.

To Castles and Miller, then, it is no longer possible for most countries to adopt the 'monocultural and assimilationist models' that were advocated by supporters of the immigrant–host theories.

However, some countries have been relatively isolated from international migration for many years. With the break-up of the USSR and the Soviet bloc in Eastern Europe, a number of countries were suddenly exposed to enormous social changes. In such a situation, 'narrow traditional cultures seem to offer a measure of defence' for those subject to these pressures. Hence **exclusionary nationalism** led to civil war in areas such as the former Yugoslavia.

Citizenship and migration

In 'Citizenship and the other in the age of migration', Stephen Castles explores the consequences of migration further (Castles, 2000, first published 1999). He argues that the increase in global migration creates a possible clash between ideas of **nationality** and **citizenship**. He defines a nation as 'a cultural community of people who believe that they have a common heritage and a common destiny'. On the other hand, citizenship involves the possession of certain rights as a result of being recognized as a member of a particular state. In well-integrated nation-states, the national (who identifies with the community) and the citizen (who possesses social and political rights in the territory) may be combined. Increasingly, however, migration creates a situation where they are not. Castles asks: 'what of migrants who settle in one country without abandoning their cultural belonging in another? The migrant has always been the "Other" of the nation. National identity is often asserted through a process of exclusion.'

If migrants are excluded from wider society, they will tend to 'focus their activities within the ethnic community … This in turn increases the suspicion of the majority population that "alien enclaves" are developing.' Racism directed at immigrant groups makes it impossible for them to integrate with the majority population, producing a self-fulfilling prophecy – the idea that they are unwilling to integrate creates a lack of integration.

Castles reiterates his view, expressed in *The Age of Migration*, that it is becoming difficult for countries with many immigrants to sustain the view that 'the problem of cultural diversity would solve itself over time through the assimilation of minorities'. It is not just racism and exclusion which prevent this: globalization makes it much easier for migrants to maintain a distinctive ethnic identity. Cheap and quick travel and rapid communications allow them to keep in close touch with their country of origin. This can cause problems when a group adopts 'extreme separatism – such as Islamic fundamentalist groups in France, Germany, and Britain'. However, Castles thinks such responses to migration are rare, and 'in most cases, ethnic mobilization, especially by members of the second generation, is concerned with combating discrimination and achieving equal treatment within mainstream society'.

Castles concludes that to accommodate the diverse populations created by migration, countries need to accept that those who are citizens of the country will not always adopt a national identity to the exclusion of their ethnic identity. He says: 'The continuing attempt to base citizenship on membership of an imagined cultural community leads to political and social exclusion and the racialization of difference.' This leads to increased social divisions and conflicts between those who see themselves as belonging to the nation and the immigrant or minority ethnic 'other'. Castles offers an alternative way of dealing with citizenship and nationality in the age of migration, based upon three principles:

1. All people who are permanent residents within a country need to have the same citizenship rights whatever their legal position – for example, whatever passport they hold.
2. Social and economic policies need to be followed that prevent forms of social exclusion such as high levels of unemployment for immigrant or minority ethnic groups.
3. Political, social and economic institutions need to be reformed so that they no longer exclude or discriminate against people because they are not seen as belonging to the national culture of the country.

Evaluation

Castles's work raises important issues. For example, in 2002 the British Home Secretary initiated a scheme whereby people applying for British citizenship would be required to learn about aspects of British culture. This would seem to go against Castles's view that it is necessary for countries with high levels of immigration to have greater acceptance of cultural diversity and to move away from equating citizenship and nationality. If Castles's analysis is correct, then such an approach would be likely to do more harm than good, by trying to maintain the myth that Britain has a single, dominant, shared culture to which immigrants must assimilate.

Robin Cohen – *Migration and its Enemies*

Cosmopolitanism

Robin Cohen (2006) is another writer who has examined both the causes and consequences of global patterns of migration. Like Castles he believes that the increase in migration has enormous implications for societies throughout the world. He also shares a degree of optimism with Castles. For example, he too believes that increased contact between people of different ethnic backgrounds can reduce conflict and distrust between ethnic groups.

Increased contact has led to the creation of more **cosmopolitanism**. Cosmopolitan individuals tend to be those who have migrated or travelled extensively. As a consequence they have become used to being at ease with different cultures, languages and countries. Rather than showing overwhelming allegiance to a particular nation-state or ethnic group, they have 'complex repertoires of allegiance, identity and interest'. They are unlikely therefore to be intolerant of others or racist.

Privileged and exploited migrants

However, cosmopolitanism is only one side of the coin – the increase in global migration also has another, much less attractive side. Cohen starts his book by discussing the case of the Chinese cockle-pickers, who on 5 February 2004 were drowned by the incoming tide in Morecambe Bay. Nineteen died, all of them illegal immigrants to Britain. They had paid large amounts of money to Chinese people-smuggling gangs for the privilege of living in squalid housing and working on the dangerous sands of the bay for only £7 per hour.

Cohen argues that this case illustrates the continuing exploitation of cheap migrant labour. Although patterns of migration have undoubtedly changed, there is also continuity with the past in that some migrants are still being used as a **reserve army of cheap labour**. Cohen's theory, though, is much more complicated than that of Castles and Kosack (see above, pp. 155–6). There are now large numbers of privileged as well as exploited migrant groups in the world.

Cohen divides migrants into three groups: **citizens**, **denizens** and **helots**.

1. **Citizens** are those who have full nationality in a country by virtue of birth or naturalization, established immigrants who have acquired citizenship rights, or refugees who have been accepted as legitimate under the rules of the 1951 Geneva Convention which defined refugees. Refugees may not have full citizenship rights, such as the ability to vote in elections, but they can work and tend to enjoy benefits and protections under the law similar to those of other citizens.

   From the end of the Second World War until the oil price rises of the early 1970s, many affluent countries encouraged migration and allowed migrants to become citizens. However, this took place during a period of labour shortages, and as unemployment began to rise most countries became reluctant to grant such rights to large numbers of people. Countries such as Canada and Australia, which still actively seek migrants who will become citizens, tend to cherry-pick migrants with the qualifications and skills that are in short supply. Former colonial powers, such as Britain and France, have largely withdrawn the right of citizens of their former colonies to emigrate to them.
2. **Denizens** are those who have some rights in the country they move to, or who are accepted or even welcomed without being given full citizenship. They include those who have dual nationality, recognized asylum seekers, and special entrants who are allowed to stay in the country for particular reasons. Many of the more privileged denizens are well-paid and highly qualified citizens of other countries, often employed by transnational corporations. While they may not have the right to vote, they often have highly advantageous contracts which offer such benefits as travel allowances, health insurance and private education for their children.

There are large numbers of denizens working in the oil-rich Middle-East (e.g. Saudi Arabia). However, some of the labour recruited for such countries does not enjoy such good conditions and is recruited from poorer countries to do low-paid work, such as domestic service.

3 **Helots** are the most exploited group of migrants. They include illegal migrants, people who overstay their visas, asylum seekers whose claims have not been accepted, and unskilled workers tied to particular projects. The lack of citizenship rights and economic security makes helots particularly vulnerable and likely to be exploited.

Helots are often denigrated in the societies to which they have moved. An example is the hostility to asylum seekers in Britain (see above, p. 151). Cohen says there is often a 'powerful attempt to try to exclude, detain or deport foreigners who are regarded as disposable units of labour power to whom the advantages of citizenship, the franchise and social welfare are denied'.

Some helots are **unfree labour**, whose situation is only a little better than that of slaves. These include women who are forced to work in the sex industry, often as prostitutes, to pay back those who financed their travel to another country. In Japan there are large numbers of Thai women working as unfree labour in the sex industry; there are Eastern European women working in Western Europe, and so on.

States expend vast amounts of money and effort trying to exclude helots. For example, Britain has made considerable efforts to reduce the number of asylum seekers, and the USA has tried to prevent illegal immigrants from Mexico from crossing the border. However, in a globalized world such attempts are less than successful.

Despite the hostility to helots and their weak position, they are not always entirely powerless. In the USA illegal migrants are crucial to the economy of some states, as they are needed to provide labour, especially in service industries. Consequently, they have been able to organize and demand greater rights. Many politicians are ambivalent towards these groups: exploiting popular antagonism towards them for political reasons, while recognizing the important role they play in the economy.

The future of migration

Cohen does not accept that migration can be understood simply in terms of the needs of the capitalist system, as claimed by Marxist theories such as those of Castles and Kosack. Migration should also be understood in terms of 'the view from below' – that is, the perspective of the migrants. Even exploited illegal immigrants may well earn considerably more than they would have back home, if they come from low-wage economies. Some can save enough to return home in a better financial position, and some find ways to acquire rights in the country to which they have migrated.

Given the great inequality between richer and poorer nations, the movement of migrants from one to the other is likely to continue, whatever the efforts to restrict the movement by the rich countries. Controls on people leaving countries have largely been abandoned since the collapse of the Soviet Union (under the old regime, citizens were prevented from leaving to go to the West).

In a post 9/11 world, migration is sometimes seen as a terrorist threat as well as an economic one, adding to the fears that can be used to whip up hostility towards migrants. There is also an increasing attack on diversity which is perceived in some countries to be a threat to national culture. In the USA, for example, some social scientists have argued that the country must remain a 'melting pot' in which different cultures become blended together. The multiculturalism which immigration threatens to bring is not acceptable. From the point of view of such commentators, immigration can be seen as a 'threat to public order, economic prosperity, social well-being or cultural cohesion'.

However, Cohen believes that migration is bound to continue, and there is a strong case for allowing more migration. The global capitalist economy now largely permits free movement of capital. Furthermore, the labour-intensive service sector is increasingly important in richer countries. Many service sector jobs (for example, care of the elderly) cannot be exported to other countries as easily as manufacturing jobs, so richer countries will have to allow significant numbers of workers in from low-wage economies.

If large-scale migration is bound to continue, will it inevitably lead to increased hostility towards minorities, ethnic conflict, and an ever greater fear of immigrants? Cohen is not entirely pessimistic. First, the trend towards cosmopolitanism which comes from globalization will tend to counteract hostility towards immigrants. Second, in an insecure world, citizenship can be a matter of life or death. Migrants will fight for rights in their new countries and will sometimes succeed in gaining ground. Finally, governments are increasingly accepting the existence of diverse ethnic groups within society. They have largely given up the belief that groups will assimilate and have accepted that society will be diverse, pluralistic or multicultural, providing some basis on which real or potential conflicts can be resolved. (For more details of Cohen's work see pp. 192–3.)

Ethnicity

Thomas Hylland Eriksen – the nature of ethnicity

Like the immigrant–host model, sociological approaches based on the idea of ethnicity place great emphasis on culture. They distinguish human groups primarily according to the distinctiveness of their lifestyles. They tend to attach little importance to 'race' as a biological difference between humans, although they do recognize that it is important when groups of humans *believe* they belong to a particular 'race'. However, unlike the immigrant–host model, approaches based around the idea of ethnicity do not assume that in the long term immigrant groups will assimilate by adopting the culture of the host society.

Eriksen supports the use of the concept of ethnicity and rejects the idea that there are distinct 'races'. He argues that 'there has been so much interbreeding between human populations that it would be meaningless to talk of fixed boundaries between races' (Eriksen, 2002). Like other writers, such as Steve Jones (1991, 1994; see pp. 146–7), Eriksen points out that there is sometimes greater genetic variation within so-called 'races' than there is between supposed 'races'. Furthermore, he notes that 'no serious scholar today believes that hereditary characteristics explain cultural variations'. Although the concept of 'race' exists as a cultural construct, and can therefore influence human actions, Eriksen believes it has no objective existence.

The definition of ethnicity

To Eriksen, the term ethnicity as used by contemporary anthropologists and sociologists has far more value than the concept of 'race'. Eriksen sees ethnicity as relating to 'aspects of relationships between groups which consider themselves, and are regarded by others, as being culturally distinctive'. Nevertheless, he admits that the boundaries between the concepts of 'race' and ethnicity are somewhat blurred, for the following reasons.

1. Ethnic groups often have a belief that they have a common origin and they therefore share common ancestors and potentially common racial characteristics.
2. Some supposed 'racial' groups such as African Americans have become *ethnified*; that is, they have tended to adopt cultural characteristics which might distinguish them as an ethnic group.
3. Some ethnic groups have been racialized in the perceptions of others; that is, others have come to see such groups as having a common genetic origin and shared traits. For example, in Mauritius, an ethnically diverse island in the Indian Ocean, Creoles (who are largely of African or Malagasy descent) are usually seen as 'lazy, merry and careless' by others, while Hindus are seen as 'stingy, dishonest, hardworking' and Muslims as 'religious fanatics, non-minglers'.

Nevertheless, Eriksen believes that the cultural emphasis in the term ethnicity makes it a much more useful concept than 'race' and distinguishes it from other related concepts such as nationalism (see pp. 188–94). To Eriksen, ethnic groups can never exist in isolation. The idea of ethnicity implies that the culture of one group is different from that of another group. Very often there is a hierarchy of ethnic groups within a society, with some groups enjoying more status and greater material rewards than other groups. Thus Eriksen says: 'The term ethnicity refers to relationships between groups whose members consider themselves distinctive, and these groups may be ranked hierarchically within a society.' For ethnic groups to develop, there must be some contact between groups of people who 'entertain ideas of each other as being culturally different from themselves'. It is the belief that they are different rather than any underlying reality that is important. Thus Eriksen claims that there was relatively little difference between Serb and Croat culture in the former Yugoslavia, yet this did not prevent bloody ethnic conflict between the groups in the 1990s.

Ethnic groups can believe they are different from one another in a variety of ways, but they tend to have myths of common origin and they nearly always have ideologies encouraging endogamy (they encourage or require marriage partners to be chosen from within the same ethnic group).

Shared cultural characteristics are not always sufficient for ethnic identities to develop. For example, 'social classes', 'the inhabitants of Somerset' or 'the members of a science-fiction association' are not ethnic groups. While Eriksen does not see any one criterion as central for distinguishing ethnic groups, all the above groups of people lack a sufficiently strong sense of common bond to form ethnic groups. They do not have any notion of shared ancestry, they do not see themselves as sharing common 'blood', they do not have the same religion and they do not discourage marriage outside of the cultural group.

Types of ethnicity

Having defined ethnicity, Eriksen goes on to distinguish between different types of ethnic group.

1. **Urban ethnic minorities** consist of groups of immigrants and their descendants concentrated in towns and cities. Such concentrations include a variety of minority ethnic groups of non-European origin in Europe (such as South Asians in Britain), Hispanics in the USA, Chinese in Indonesia and Koreans in Japan. Such groups may suffer from discrimination but they are unlikely to organize to demand their own separate states.
2. **Indigenous people** are 'aboriginal inhabitants of a territory, who are politically relatively powerless and who are only partly integrated into the dominant nation-state'. Examples of this category include Maoris in New Zealand, Aborigines in Australia, the Sami of northern Scandinavia and tribal groups in the Amazon basin. They may retain elements of a 'non-industrial mode of production' and Eriksen does not therefore regard indigenous groups such as the Welsh or the Basques as belonging in this category.
3. **Proto-nations** or **ethnonationalist movements** are minority ethnic groups who are actively seeking an independent state. Eriksen gives a number of examples, including Tamils in Sri Lanka, Kurds and Palestinians. They have a good deal in common with nations but do not have control over their own territory. Proto-nations in Europe with aspirations to political independence include the Basques in France and Spain and Bretons in France.
4. **Ethnic groups in plural societies** are groups seen as culturally distinctive within 'colonially created states'. During colonialism such societies became more ethnically diverse as a result of migration organized or encouraged by the colonial power. Examples of such societies include Kenya, Indonesia, Jamaica and Mauritius. In Mauritius, for example, the population consists of five ethnic groups: Creoles (of African or Malagasy descent), Hindus (of Indian descent), Muslims (of Indian descent),

Sino-Mauritians (of Chinese descent) and Franco-Mauritians (of French or British descent) plus Coloureds (of 'mixed' descent). Such ethnic groups are unlikely to seek independent nationhood but are likely to compete for resources with one another and may well hold stereotypical views of each other.

5 **Post-slavery minorities** are minority ethnic groups who are the descendants of slaves, particularly those of African origin in the Americas. Sometimes members of such groups develop a culture based upon 'a rediscovered Africanness' – for example, Rastafarians in Jamaica. Sometimes they celebrate having a hybrid identity – for example, African Americans. Eriksen comments: 'Their identity politics tend to be based on their shared history of uprooting and suffering.' Very often they retain at least some elements of their original culture, although they may modify it in a new setting.

Despite the undoubted superiority of the concept of ethnicity over the concept of 'race', it is not without its problems. Some of these problems are explored by John Richardson.

John Richardson – ethnicity and other classification systems

Richardson (1990) identifies three main classification systems:

1 'Race'
2 Black/white
3 Ethnicity

He argues that there are some advantages in using ethnicity rather than 'race' or black/white. Like most sociologists he disputes the existence of clear-cut biological groups in the population. He therefore rejects the use of the concept of 'race'. He also raises a number of problems with using the term black. It can be a confusing term, since sometimes it is used to refer only to those of African Caribbean origin, and sometimes, in countries like Britain, it is used more broadly to refer to disadvantaged minorities. However, when it is used in the latter sense, it is still not usually seen as appropriate to apply it to groups such as the Chinese, Cypriots and people from the Middle East, even though they are sometimes as disadvantaged in Western industrialized societies as groups who are commonly referred to as black. Another problem is that many Asians do not regard themselves as 'black'.

In some ways, then, Richardson sees ethnic groups as a more acceptable term than the available alternatives. He sees ethnicity as based upon cultural differences between groups and says: 'This classificatory approach is attractive in so far as it highlights socio-cultural criteria (unlike the conventional "race" systems) and it accommodates a potentially wide range of groups (unlike the two-category black/white model).'

Nevertheless, Richardson believes that there are also serious problems with the idea of ethnicity. In particular it can be very difficult to distinguish clearly between ethnic groups. Many groups are themselves subdivided and they may overlap with other groups. Ethnic groups can be distinguished in different ways, leading to different classifications. Thus, for example, **territorial origin** could lead to distinctions between Bangladeshis, Pakistanis and Indians, whereas **religious affiliation** would lead to a distinction between Hindus, Sikhs and Muslims. **Linguistic criteria** could produce a third system of classification.

Steve Fenton – the strength of ethnicity

The work of Eriksen demonstrates that ethnicity can take a number of forms. Richardson shows that ethnic identity can be based upon different criteria and that ethnic boundaries can be somewhat blurred. Steve Fenton (1999) emphasizes that ethnic identification can have different degrees of intensity. Ethnicity may provoke strong passions and lead to violence. It may dominate people's lives. On the other hand, it may be a relatively minor source of identity and have only limited relevance in everyday life.

According to Fenton, ethnicity is never the only identity that people have and therefore 'no one is a full-time ethnic, at least not in the same way in all settings'. For example, 'The young student of South Asian ancestry in Britain is not a full-time South Asian, the Malay businessman in Kuala Lumpur is not a full-time Malay.' The importance of ethnicity varies between societies, but for an individual it also varies according to the context and circumstances in which they find themselves. Its intensity is highly variable.

Fenton distinguishes broadly between what he terms **hot** and **cold** ethnicity.

1 **Hot ethnicity** involves appeals to 'blood and passion'. Ethnic identities may be mobilized in this way in support of nationalist movements or where there is intense conflict between ethnic groups. The importance of strong group loyalty is emphasized in hot ethnicity.
2 **Cold ethnicity** is much less impassioned and involves 'calculation and instrumentality'. Here the appeal is less emotional. Instead, supporting and identifying with an ethnic group is contingent upon deriving benefits from group membership. For example, cold ethnicity might involve a business person using ethnic ties to develop business contacts, or a politician using their ethnicity to improve their chances of re-election.

Fenton also distinguishes three different ways in which ethnicity can be 'a dimension of social life and structure'. These also involve ethnicity assuming different degrees of importance.

1 Ethnicity as a **command principle** involves ethnicity requiring different sorts of behaviour. In this situation society structures social action strongly in different ethnic groups. For example, in Mississippi in the 1930s blacks and whites were very restricted in the ways they could relate to one another. Fenton says, 'black–white relationships of equality, or of marriage, or where black was superordinate to white, were practically excluded'.
2 Ethnicity as a **flexible principle** involves greater freedom of choice. Where divisions between ethnic

groups are not so clear-cut, or do not require particular behaviours to the same extent as they did in Mississippi, then the degree to which ethnicity shapes behaviour is more variable. Thus in Malaysia, for example, membership of different ethnic groups has some importance but is not the overriding identity which shapes the relationship between individuals.

3 Ethnicity as **nil principle** involves situations where ethnicity has no importance. Either the law or 'broad customary consensus' may require that ethnicity plays no part in social action. For example, ethnicity as nil principle should operate in the awarding of grades in exams in societies such as Britain.

Although the categories used by Fenton are not clear-cut, and the intensity of ethnicity may be a matter of interpretation, his arguments do highlight how ethnicity can assume varying degrees of importance in different situations.

Conclusion

There are problems with all approaches to defining ethnicity and classifying different types of ethnicity. Nevertheless it can be argued that the idea of ethnic groups is the least unsatisfactory way of dealing with the problem of classification. Despite its limitations, it is more flexible and adaptable than other approaches, and can accommodate changes in people's perceptions about the groups to which they belong. Groups such as the Irish in England can be accommodated within the ethnicity framework, whereas they cannot under the other alternatives, such as 'race'.

The ethnicity approach is not limited to describing immigrant groups and different facets of ethnicity (such as language, religion and territorial origin). It can be used as the basis of classification as appropriate to the sociological issue or issues under consideration. Above all, it recognizes that social divisions between such groups are created, maintained, altered and challenged by humans and that they are not the inevitable product of supposed biological differences. The idea of 'race', though, remains a useful term when ethnic groups are thought by themselves or by others to be distinguished by phenotype (physical appearance).

Studies of ethnicity

Studies of ethnicity often take the form of **ethnographic studies**: studies of the lifestyles of groups of people. Such studies do not always focus on migrants and their descendants, but in Britain the main focus has been on people of Caribbean and South Asian origin.

Migrants from the Caribbean and from South Asia were the subject of a number of early studies. These studies usually compared the lifestyles of African Caribbeans or South Asians in Britain with their lifestyles in their native land in order to evaluate the extent to which the British context had affected their cultures.

Later studies, which have taken place since a second generation (and then later generations) of British-born African Caribbeans and South Asians has become established, have tended to examine the extent to which traditional cultures have changed across the generations. Recent studies often make particular use of the concept of **identity**, though they generally also use the concept of **culture** extensively. The studies we will look at are only a small sample of the numerous studies that have been undertaken, but they are fairly typical of this type of research.

Roger Ballard – Sikhs and Mirpuri Muslims

Early work

Roger Ballard conducted research into South Asian communities in Britain between the 1970s and the 1990s. In his first major study, conducted with Catherine Ballard between 1971 and 1974 (Ballard and Ballard, 1977), he examined the lifestyles of Sikhs in Leeds. The Ballards compared these lifestyles with those of Sikhs from the Jullundur Doab region of the Punjab, the area from which most of the Sikhs in Leeds had originated.

Most of the earliest migrants were men who arrived to work with the intention of returning to South Asia. Many of the earliest male migrants made little attempt to preserve traditional Sikh culture and values. Few took part in religious rituals and many did not bother wearing turbans or growing long hair and beards. Seeing their stay as temporary, and without having to worry about their family being corrupted by Western culture, they felt little need to try to protect themselves from Western influences.

However, once they were joined by their families, Sikhs in Leeds became more concerned to ensure that their traditional family life and religion were preserved. Far from encouraging assimilation, the establishment of a more permanent Sikh community led to a more distinctive ethnic identity.

As a second generation born in Leeds grew up, they adopted some elements of Western materialism and children sometimes clashed with their parents over issues such as whether they could wear British-style clothes. However, these behaviours represented little more than a temporary period of teenage rebellion. In general, even the second generation were concerned to maintain key aspects of Sikh culture.

Furthermore, the common experience of racism meant that they developed close links and a shared sense of identity with other South Asian groups in Britain. However, the Ballards do not believe that this was simply a result of the external constraints of racism. The internal preferences, the desire to maintain their cultures, were also vital factors in ensuring that the Sikhs and other Asian groups actively chose to maintain important aspects of their lifestyles.

Divisions in the Asian community

In an article published in 1990, Roger Ballard updated his earlier work and described changes in Asian communities in the late 1970s and 1980s. In the earlier study, he and Catherine Ballard had suggested that South Asians in Britain were being drawn closer together. In his later article, Ballard stresses that there are strong divisions between South Asian groups in Britain. He argues:

> *As it becomes increasingly obvious that settlers of different backgrounds are following varied, and often sharply contrasting, social trajectories, so it is becoming steadily more difficult, and increasingly inappropriate, to make generalizations which are valid for all 'Asians' in Britain.*
> Ballard, 1990

He notes that there are divisions according to class, caste, region of origin, religion and different experiences of migration. In order to try to explain these divisions he compares the Sikhs who originated in Jullundur Doab in India (who are discussed above) with Muslims from the Mirpur District in Kashmir, Pakistan.

Differences between the Sikhs and Muslims

Both the Jullunduris and Mirpuris migrated to Britain from predominantly rural areas, and in both groups the main aim of the early migrants was to earn money to send back to Asia. However, after arrival in Britain they followed different paths.

The Sikhs were reunited with their families earlier than the Muslims and enjoyed more economic success. Many Sikhs set up their own businesses, and others aspired to – and succeeded in gaining – middle-class jobs and statuses. By 1990 most had moved away from the inner cities and their children were enjoying educational success comparable with that of middle-class white children.

Most of the Mirpuri Muslims became 'international commuters' during their early years as migrants. They would work for a time in Britain before returning home to spend some time with their families. They would then return to Britain to earn more money. A few set up their own businesses, although they were not as numerous nor as successful as those of the Sikhs. Most, however, relied upon unskilled or semi-skilled work in industries such as textiles and engineering. Their wages were comparatively low, and from the 1970s onwards they were more likely to be hit by unemployment. Even after being joined by their families most were unable to afford to buy homes away from the inner cities. Their children enjoyed less academic success than their Sikh counterparts.

Economic reasons for the differences

Having described the differences, Ballard then sets out to explain them. One important reason for the greater success of the Sikhs was the greater prosperity of their region of origin. Jullundur Doab is a relatively affluent agricultural area with fertile land and a good infrastructure. Mirpur also has fertile land but it has a higher population density so landholdings tend to be small, it is difficult to irrigate and the infrastructure is poor. As a consequence of these differences, migrants from Jullundur Doab tended to have more craft and business skills and higher educational qualifications than the Mirpuris. They also tended to be more literate. Relying on unskilled and semi-skilled work in traditional manufacturing industries made the Mirpuris much more likely to lose their jobs once recession hit Britain.

However, Ballard does not believe that such differences in economic situation can, on their own, account for the contrasting fortunes of the two groups. He argues that cultural differences may also be part of the explanation.

Cultural reasons for the differences

Ballard is very cautious about attributing too much importance to cultural factors. He expresses concern about the possibility of resorting to 'sweeping and inevitably stereotypical assertions about the allegedly "conservative" or "liberal" characteristics of the two religious traditions'. Nevertheless, he does believe that differences in religion and in community and family life could partly explain differences in the fortunes of South Asian groups. Ballard identifies three important cultural differences:

1. Muslims are allowed to marry close kin and often do so, whereas it is not permitted for Sikhs and Hindus. This means that kinship networks for Muslims tend to be more close-knit and geographically limited in scope.
2. The tradition of purdah is stronger in Islam than in Sikhism and it places greater restrictions on women in public places. As a result, Muslim women in Pakistan are less likely than Sikh women in India to travel long distances or to take up paid employment outside the home.
3. Sikhs and Hindus cremate their dead, whereas Muslims bury them. Consequently Muslims tend to develop stronger ties to a particular village or region where their ancestors are buried.

Together, these factors make Muslim families less geographically mobile and more close-knit and inward looking. As a result, the male Mirpuri immigrants were rather more cautious about bringing their wives and children to Britain than the Sikh men. As international commuters, sometimes for up to fifteen years, the Muslim men used up a lot of their money on travel. Furthermore, a higher proportion of their income was sent back to Asia to be spent or invested there. By the time the men decided that their families should settle in Britain the administrative obstacles had become greater, slowing down the process of family reunion even more.

Muslim families had therefore had less time to become established in Britain and improve their living standards than some other groups of Asians. Once in Britain, Muslim wives were less likely to take paid employment, thus limiting the earning power of the family. Thus, although the differences in the economic success of the two groups have been influenced by economic factors and the structural features of society, cultural factors such as religion and kinship patterns have had a part to play as well.

Conclusion

Ballard stresses at the end of his article that his account is oversimplified. He points out that 'Sikhs' and 'Mirpuris' are not homogeneous groups. For example, members of different Sikh castes such as the Jat (peasant farmers) and the Ramgarhia (craft workers) have followed rather different paths. Furthermore, not all Jullunduris are Sikh and many British Pakistanis come from regions other than Mirpur.

Nevertheless, Ballard's work does show that it may only become possible to explain inequalities between ethnic groups if sociologists can develop a sophisticated understanding of cultural differences, as well as examining wider structural forces.

Tehmina N. Basit – *Eastern Values; Western Milieu*

Although Ballard is very cautious in his conclusions, he does emphasize that British Muslims are more inward looking towards their own communities than other ethnic groups in Britain. Tehmina N. Basit (1997) takes a rather different view.

Basit conducted in-depth interviews with twenty-four British Muslim girls and twenty-four of their parents. The girls were drawn from two schools in two towns in the east of England and she also interviewed eighteen of the girls' teachers in these schools. As well as comparing the girls and their parents, Basit compared the teachers' perceptions of the girls with the girls' perceptions of themselves. The aim of the study was 'to discover what was shaping the identities and ambitions of a group of teenagers and how they were coping with the differences in culture and religion to make sense of their lives'.

Identities

Basit found that both the girls and their parents had a strong sense of their identity as Asians and Muslims, but she did not see them as inward looking. The girls did tend to think of themselves essentially as Asian. However, they usually linked this identity with their religion and culture. For example, one girl described herself as 'Asian, because I wear Asian clothes; eat Asian food; I go according to the rules of my religion: that makes me Asian'. However, the girls did not just see themselves as Asian. They also saw themselves as British. Because they were born in Britain, and had lived in Britain all their lives, they saw themselves as both Asian and British. One girl said: 'At school, I look different because of my colour and my dress, so I am Asian. But I was born here, so I am also British.'

Most of the girls had visited their country of origin and they, and their parents, kept in close contact with relatives in South Asia. Their parents wanted them to be familiar with the 'religion, history, culture and language' of their country of origin. However, they acknowledged that their daughters would not feel at home if they ever returned to Pakistan or Bangladesh to live.

The parents tended to have more of an Asian than a British identity. Some parents felt that they faced hostility and discrimination in Britain, making it difficult for them to feel British. Nevertheless, they saw things as different for their children. One said: 'Though they are our children, and we are Pakistani, they cannot adjust to that environment (rural Pakistan) because this country and this culture have also had an impact on them.'

The identities of the girls reflected this. The girls wanted to hang on to Asian elements of their identity, while finding ways to adapt and negotiate this identity in the context of British society. Basit says, 'the girls, themselves, are also constantly negotiating their own identities and subsequently creating distinct identities in different contexts without compromising their ethnicity, language and religion'. The girls were critical of both Asian and British culture and they adopted elements of both, but also adapted them to create unique identities of their own. Basit describes their identities as dynamic rather than static. The girls look in two different directions at once – Asian culture and British culture – and their sense of identity changes as they grow up and as they encounter different situations.

British Muslim girls – myths and reality

By comparing the views of the non-Asian teachers she interviewed with those of the girls themselves, Basit tries to evaluate some common views about British Muslim girls.

1 In terms of religion, Basit found that most teachers correctly recognized that Islam was important to the girls. However, many saw it as 'an oppressive religion into which these girls were being indoctrinated by their dictatorial parents'. Religion was certainly important to the girls, but they did not experience it as oppressive. While all the girls espoused the Islamic faith, there were wide variations in the extent to which they and their families practised the religion. Most of the girls fell somewhere in between staunch adherence to Islam and a superficial belief in the religion. They practised some elements of it but not others.

2 A number of teachers believed that family life, like religion, was oppressive for the girls. They believed that Asian women were dominated in patriarchal families where they were taught to be submissive to parental authority and men in general. The teachers saw it as particularly oppressive that some families would not let the girls go out unaccompanied in the evenings, and they were often hostile to the idea of arranged marriage, seeing it as an infringement of individual liberty.

The girls' own perceptions of family life were quite different. They had little or no sense of oppression. They accepted that they should respect their parents rather than simply obey them unthinkingly. This respect was part of a general respect for older people, including women. This was misinterpreted by some teachers as the girls being submissive.

All the parents in the study valued their daughters just as much as their sons and some of the men saw women as having an elevated status within Islam. Both the girls and their parents saw some of the restrictions on their behaviour as protective rather than oppressive. They were part of the obligation to maintain family honour and respect other family members.

Generally the girls had no wish to find their own boyfriends and saw arranged marriage in a positive light. They believed that their parents with their greater experience would have a good chance of finding a suitable marriage partner. All the girls felt that they would have a choice about whether to marry the potential husbands found by their parents.

Generally the girls and their parents saw Asian family life in a very positive light. They had no wish to adopt Western approaches, which they saw as having clear disadvantages, such as high divorce rates. A number of the parents accepted that there were some Muslim families in which women were not treated as the equals of men, in accordance with Islamic teaching. However, none of the girls in the study felt that they were treated unfairly by their parents, and there was little evidence of generational conflict.

3 Basit found that in terms of education, a number of teachers felt that some Muslim girls were not motivated to have high aspirations at school. Sometimes they felt that parents were uninterested in their daughters' education because they expected them to get married rather than pursue a career. According to Basit, this did not match the reality. She says: 'though many parents whom I interviewed had little or no education themselves … they wanted their daughters to receive a good education'.

The girls themselves were usually positive about going to school, partly to meet friends, but also because they too wanted educational success. Furthermore, despite the fact that most of the girls came from a working-class background, all of them wanted to continue into further education, and despite the beliefs of their teachers, many of them wanted to study for a degree. Far from seeing their future in terms of being housewives, the vast majority wanted to work even after they got married. Most aspired either to well-paid and high-status jobs such as being a lawyer or an accountant, or to working in professions such as nursing or teaching. However, the girls were concerned not to pursue careers which might compromise their religious and cultural values by requiring them to do things that were un-Islamic.

Conclusions

Reflecting on the difference between the teachers' perceptions and the reality of the girls' lives, Basit argues that 'Muslims are perhaps the most misunderstood religious group in Britain'. Far from sticking rigidly to the culture of their parents, the girls were developing a dynamic culture in which they adopted 'aspects of the indigenous culture which do not clash with their religio-cultural ethos'. For the girls, the desire to combine careers with marriage was a particularly important part of the indigenous culture they were adopting. But this did not indicate any desire to abandon the religion or family values of previous generations. Their culture and their identities were continuously undergoing changes or metamorphoses embracing these diverse influences.

Basit offers a highly sympathetic insider's view of British Muslim culture and identities. As such, her study is important for challenging some of the stereotypes about Islam which are a feature of Islamophobia (see pp. 181–3). However, the sample she uses is small and geographically limited. Furthermore, she confines her study to adolescent girls. A somewhat different view of British Asian culture and identities is provided by the work of Claire Alexander (see pp. 185–6).

Evaluation

All the studies examined in this section tend to see minority ethnic groups in Britain as having distinct cultures. More recent studies of ethnicity in Britain have tended to adopt a rather different approach. A number have argued that it is no longer possible to see sharp distinctions between the culture of minority ethnic groups and that of the white majority in Britain. They stress that members of minority ethnic groups are very diverse and there is increasing overlap between different cultures. Many such studies are linked to new theoretical approaches in the study of 'race' and ethnicity. Most have drawn upon the insights provided by studies of racism. These newer approaches to British ethnicity will be examined later in the chapter, once some of the theoretical developments on which they are based have been considered (see pp. 194–8 and pp. 201–2).

James McKay – primordial and mobilizationist explanations of ethnicity

So far in this section we have examined how ethnicity can be defined and we have considered some ethnographic studies of ethnicity. However, we have not yet dealt with explanations of how ethnic groups come to be formed in the first place. James McKay (1982) and others have identified two main types of explanation of how ethnic groups form: primordial and mobilizationist.

Primordial approaches

McKay notes that the **primordial** approach was first proposed by the American sociologist Shils in 1957. Shils claimed that people often had a primordial attachment to the territory in which they lived, or from which they originated, to their religion and to their kin. This attachment involved strong feelings of loyalty and, Shils said, 'a state of intense and comprehensive solidarity' (quoted in McKay, 1982).

Some writers see primordial attachments as a basic feature of social life and a natural and inevitable phenomenon in human groups. From this point of view humans always divide the world into groups of insiders and outsiders, 'us' and 'them', and have an emotional and intuitive bond with those who belong to their group. This comes either from socialization or from some basic psychocultural need for belonging. Primordial ethnic attachments may persist for centuries or millennia, and can be the basis for intense conflict between ethnic groups over long periods.

McKay suggests that a strength of the primordial approach is that it can account for 'the emotional strength of ethnic bonds', but he is also critical of the approach. He claims that it tends to be 'deterministic and static':

1 It assumes that members of ethnic groups have little choice about their sense of attachment, whereas in reality ethnic attachments vary in strength from individual to individual.
2 It tends to assume that all individuals will have an ethnic identity and thus offers no explanation for the existence of 'rootless cosmopolitans'.
3 The approach cannot easily deal with changes in ethnic identity among groups.
4 The primordial approach attaches so much importance to basic human emotions that it tends to 'talk as if ethnic and group identities existed in a political and economic vacuum'.

Mobilizationist approaches

The **mobilizationist** approach suggests there is nothing inevitable or natural about ethnicity. Ethnic identities are actively created, maintained and reinforced by individuals and groups 'in order to obtain access to social, political and material resources'. People use the symbols of ethnic identity to further their own ends, and ethnic groups tend to be formed when people believe they can gain some advantage by forming them. For example, South Asians or African Caribbeans in Britain might develop an ethnic identity because they believe that membership of an ethnic group offers practical and emotional support in a hostile, racist society. By forming ethnic groups it might be possible to achieve changes in the law or other political changes which strengthen their position.

McKay is slightly more sympathetic to this approach than he is to the primordial model, but he still believes that it has its limitations. It tends to underestimate the emotional power of ethnic bonds and assumes that ethnicity is always related to common interests being pursued by the group. McKay argues that this is not always the case. He says, 'the fact that some ethnic groups pursue political and economic interests does not mean that all ethnic groups have identical goals'.

Furthermore, this approach sometimes confuses class and ethnic stratification, seeing the two as being little different. Ethnicity, though, involves more than class interests and can cut across class boundaries. In places such as Northern Ireland, South Africa and the Lebanon, ethnic conflicts have been stronger than conflict between classes, and people have tended to identify with their ethnic group regardless of their social class.

Combining the approaches

McKay believes the **affective, emotional ties** emphasized in the primordial model and the **instrumental ties** stressed in the mobilizationist model tend to be interrelated and both are 'manifestations' of ethnicity. Rather than being irreconcilable opposites, the two theories can be combined. Ethnicity may be based primarily on mobilizationist, or primordial, interests in different sets of circumstances, which can change over time and so change the basis of attachment in a particular ethnic group. Ethnicity is not fixed; it changes, and a single approach cannot account for all the variations within and between ethnic groups.

Thomas Hylland Eriksen – the ascription and achievement of ethnicity

Eriksen (2002) offers some support for McKay's view that ethnicity cannot be explained simply in terms of the political mobilization of ethnic identities or in terms of primordial attachments. However, Eriksen uses slightly different concepts from those of primordial and mobilizationist approaches and instead discusses the issues in terms of ascription and achievement.

Eriksen does not believe that ethnicity is just a matter of primordial attachments. Ethnicity is never a fixed characteristic of groups with a distinctive culture which derives from their origins. For example, in both Mauritius and Trinidad there are significant ethnic groups of Indian origin. In Mauritius, Indians are in a majority and tend to be dominant in government. There, Indians are seen as good politicians, but they do not have a major role in business on the island. In contrast, in Trinidad, Indians are in a minority and a considerable number of them are successful business people. These differences cannot be explained in terms of a common Indian culture.

To Eriksen, there are always cultural differences both within and between groups of human beings. Those who are believed to belong to an ethnic group are not all the same, and they may share things in common with those who are held to belong to other ethnic groups. An ethnic group only comes to exist through its relationship with other groups – that is, when differences between groups come to be seen as socially significant (see pp. 158–9). For example, Protestants and Catholics in Northern Ireland only constitute ethnic groups because they see themselves – and are seen by others – as being different. The two ethnic groups do not exist because they have clearly distinct cultures. There are many areas of overlap and similarity between them, though the central difference in religious affiliation remains. However, the antagonistic relationship between them marks them as distinct ethnic groups.

Eriksen gives examples of how ethnic identities can be achieved through mobilization. He refers to an ethnographic study of a village in Bosnia where Catholic Croatians and Muslims, who had lived side-by-side in harmony for centuries, entered into violent conflict with one another as Serbs, Croats and Muslims fought over the control of territory in Bosnia (Bringa, 1996; quoted in Eriksen, 2002).

Eriksen generally sees ethnicity as a characteristic which develops to serve a purpose rather than something which develops out of primordial instincts. Black slaves in the USA developed a common identity as black people despite coming from different parts of Africa, where there were different cultures and languages. Because of 'their identical treatment, they also had shared political interests in promoting their rights and, later, contesting the hegemonic world views promoted by the colonial or white … groups'.

Eriksen therefore places great emphasis on the active creation of ethnicity and its development and mobilization on the basis of shared interests. However, to Eriksen, ethnicity is not simply achieved in this way – it is not just a matter of choice or political manipulation. Ethnicity is also strongly shaped by the processes through which people learn a culture and their attachment to particular groups. He emphasizes the importance of

> *socialization, the transmission of knowledge and skills from one generation to the next, the power of norms, the unconscious importance of religion and language for identity and a sense of community. For how are societies integrated, if not through culture, which cannot be seen merely as a socially constructed heritage but rather as a shared system of communication?* Eriksen, 2002

There are real differences between ethnic groups which cannot simply be created or abandoned at will. Furthermore, people cannot usually choose which group they belong to – to some extent we are born into ethnic groups, although the boundaries between groups are not absolutely fixed. Eriksen therefore argues that 'ethnic identities are neither ascribed nor achieved: they are both'. Ethnicity is not based upon absolute cultural divisions between groups. The differences have to be made relevant in a social situation. However, our identification with a particular ethnic group is not always within our control and there are real differences in the cultures of different groups.

Conclusion

The work of both Eriksen and McKay suggests that there are a number factors leading to the development of ethnic identities and distinctions between ethnic groups. Neither believes that a single explanation can account for ethnicity. Both see it as a complex phenomenon, which is not static but changing, and can take a variety of forms.

Michael E. Brown – the causes of ethnic conflict

Ethnic conflict and the 'New World Order'

Although McKay and Eriksen's work has implications for understanding ethnic conflict, it does not directly address this issue. Michael E. Brown (1997) has drawn upon the work of a number of other writers in trying to explain the existence of ethnic conflict in the contemporary world.

Brown starts by noting that in the early 1990s there was considerable optimism in many quarters about the prospects for ethnic relationships. With the collapse of communism in the Soviet Union and Eastern Europe, it was hoped that different states in the international community could work together to prevent or resolve conflict. For example, some people claimed that the international cooperation during the Gulf War – in which the USA and other countries (including Britain) repelled the Iraqi invasion of Kuwait – heralded the arrival of a **New World Order**.

In the New World Order, states and ethnic groups would be reluctant to act in repressive or violent ways towards other states or ethnic groups because they would fear the consequences of the reaction from the international community. However, far from ushering in a new and more harmonious era, the end of the Cold War seems to have been followed by widespread and intense ethnic conflict. Brown points out:

> *The war in Bosnia-Herzegovina has received the most attention in the West because of the intense coverage it has received from the Western media, but equally if not more horrific conflicts are under way in Afghanistan, Angola, Armenia, Azerbaijan, Burma, Georgia, India, Indonesia, Liberia, Sri Lanka, Sudan and Tajikstan. Other trouble spots abound – Bangladesh, Belgium, Bhutan, Burundi, Estonia, Ethiopia, Guatemala, Iraq, Latvia, Lebanon, Mali, South Africa, Spain and Turkey, for example – and the prospects for ethnic conflict in Russia and China cannot be dismissed.* Brown, 1997

Defining ethnicity

Brown tries to explain why such conflict has become prevalent, but first he tries to define ethnicity. He believes that six criteria must be met for a group of people to qualify as an ethnic group:

1. They must have a name that identifies them as a group.
2. They must 'believe in common ancestry'. It is not essential that this common ancestry is real or that genetic ties exist – it is the belief that matters.
3. They need to have shared beliefs about their collective past. These beliefs often take the form of myths.
4. They must have some degree of shared culture which is 'generally passed on through a combination of language, religion, laws, customs, institutions, dress, music, crafts, architecture, even food'.
5. The group has to have a sense of attachment to a specific territory.
6. Members of the group must believe that they constitute an ethnic group.

Conflict between such groups can take a wide variety of forms. It may take place through political processes with no violence involved. An example is the campaign by some French Canadians to win autonomy for Quebec. On the other hand, the conflict may be very violent, as in the civil war in Bosnia. However, not all civil wars qualify as ethnic conflict. For example, the war between the Khmer Rouge and other groups in Cambodia is a war between political groups rather than ethnic ones. Nevertheless ethnic conflict is widespread.

The causes of ethnic conflict

Brown distinguishes between three main types of explanation for ethnic conflict: the **systemic**, the **domestic** and the **perceptual**.

Systemic explanations suggest that ethnic conflict results from 'the nature of the security systems in which ethnic groups operate'. An obvious systemic requirement before conflict is likely to occur is that the groups live close to one another. Brown suggests that fewer than 20 of the 180 or so states in the world are ethnically homogeneous. This creates the potential for an enormous amount of conflict, but, fortunately, not all ethnic neighbours end up in conflict.

Using the ideas of the political scientist Posen, Brown suggests that conflict will not break out when national, regional or international authorities are strong enough to prevent it by controlling the potentially opposing groups. Without this control, conflict can occur when a particular group believes it is in their interests to resort to violence. This can happen if they believe they will be more secure by launching a preemptive strike rather than waiting to be attacked.

Conflict can also result when it is difficult to distinguish between the offensive and defensive forces of a potential adversary. When empires such as the Soviet Union break up, ethnic groups may have to provide for their own defence for the first time. Lacking sophisticated military equipment, they usually have to rely largely on infantry. Although infantry may be intended for defensive purposes, they can easily be seen as a potentially offensive force and encourage a preemptive strike.

Furthermore, the break-up of empires often produces a situation in which ethnic groups are surrounded by other groups who are potentially hostile. Some groups develop state structures faster than others, and the faster-organizing group may seek to take advantage of the situation by seizing land. Many of these conditions existed in Bosnia, with Serbs trying to seize land from the Croats and from the Muslims, who were in the weakest position of all.

Where a newly independent ethnic state has nuclear weapons it is less vulnerable to external attack, and ethnic conflict between new nation-states is unlikely. Larger, newly independent, former Soviet states with nuclear weapons have tended to face less external threat than those without such weapons.

Domestic explanations of ethnic conflict relate to factors such as 'the effectiveness of states in addressing the concerns of their constituents, the impact of nationalism on inter-ethnic relations, and the impact of democratization on inter-ethnic relations'.

Using the ideas of Jack Snyder, Brown suggests that nationalistic sentiments are aroused in situations where people feel vulnerable because they feel they lack a strong state to protect them. In parts of Eastern Europe and the former USSR some groups have felt vulnerable because the state has been weak, or because they have found themselves in a state dominated by another, possibly hostile, ethnic group. Some minority ethnic groups have been blamed for economic failures by the majority population and have responded by trying to establish their own states. Ethnic nationalism involves trying to establish a nation-state based around a particular ethnic group. Such a state may not respect the rights of minorities, and ethnic conflict is likely to result.

Drawing on a range of theories, Brown goes on to suggest that processes of democratization can produce problems in multi-ethnic societies. When an old regime has collapsed, and new arrangements are being discussed, there can be major problems if there are ethnic groups who feel they were mistreated under the previous regime. They may seek retribution for past wrongs or they may feel unable to work with members of other ethnic groups in a democratic system. Problems will be particularly acute where a powerful majority ethnic group rides roughshod over the wishes and interests of less powerful smaller groups. Politicians may seek to exploit ethnic differences to increase their support, and in doing so they will heighten people's consciousness of those differences and increase the significance they attach to them.

Perceptual explanations are concerned with the way in which ethnic groups perceive one another. Hostility can be increased through myths and false histories which distort and demonize members of another group. Brown uses the example of Serbs and Croats. He says:

> *Serbs, for example, see themselves as heroic defenders of Europe and they see Croats as belligerent thugs; Croats see themselves as valiant victims of oppression and Serbs as congenital oppressors. Under such circumstances, the slightest provocation from either side simply confirms deeply held systems of belief and provides the justification for a retaliatory response.* Brown, 1997

Myths about other ethnic groups are particularly likely to develop where an authoritarian regime has suppressed the histories of minority ethnic groups for a long time. Such regimes tend to suppress the critical examination of past history, leaving little opportunity for myths to be challenged. It is not surprising, therefore, that Eastern Europe and the former USSR have seen high levels of conflict.

Conclusion

Brown concludes that ethnic conflict is most likely where ethnic groups are living in close proximity in an area where there is no strong central authority, particularly if the groups have hostile perceptions of one another based upon beliefs that they have been mistreated in the past. The end of the Cold War created such a situation in a number of regions, and no New World Order capable of limiting ethnic conflict has yet emerged.

Brown is not completely pessimistic. Conflict may lead to ethnic reconciliation. For example, in Spain there has been a degree of reconciliation between the Spanish state and the Basques, Catalans and Galicians, who have all achieved some degree of autonomy. Peaceful separation sometimes takes place, an example being the separation of Czechoslovakia into Slovakia and the Czech Republic. However, there are also many situations in which different groups cannot agree on a constitutional settlement and ethnic war ensues. This may involve the slaughter of civilians and the creation of large numbers of refugees.

Ethnic wars can also have chain-reaction effects. As new states are formed, a new problem can be created as another ethnic group finds itself in a minority in a new state. For example, when Georgia became independent from Russia, the Ossetian minority began to seek their own state with other Ossetians in Russia.

Brown succeeds in identifying a number of reasons for the increase in ethnic conflict in areas of the world which have become politically unstable. His arguments are perhaps less convincing in explaining the revival of ethnic conflict and nationalism in some parts of the world (such as Western Europe) which have not experienced high levels of instability. Some commentators have linked such phenomena to a general process of **globalization** (see, for example, pp. 548–57). Other explanations for ethnic conflict can be found in later sections on racism and nationalism (see pp. 177–88 and 188–94).

Ethnicity – an evaluation

The ethnicity approach certainly has some advantages over biological theories of 'race' and the immigrant–host model. Unlike the former, it does not base its arguments upon physical distinctions, which modern genetics has found to be of little significance. Unlike the immigrant–host model, it does not assume that minority groups will assimilate by adopting the culture of the majority.

The ethnicity approach tends to be sympathetic to cultural diversity and to support **multiculturalism** – the belief that ethnic or cultural groups can peacefully coexist in a society and show respect for one another's cultures. At least in theory, ethnographic studies allow the development of an insider's view of different cultures, and therefore facilitate a greater understanding of those cultures than is likely from other sociological approaches. Such studies also have the strength of recognizing the role that minority ethnic groups have in shaping their own lives: they are not presented as the helpless captives of biology or the passive victims of racism. Ethnographic studies can reveal subtle variations and divisions within ethnic groups which are often lost in other approaches.

However, the ethnicity approach is far from perfect. Critics tend to argue that it places too much emphasis on the culture of minority ethnic groups. While emphasizing how minority ethnic groups shape their own lives, it sometimes neglects the wider forces which constrain members of minority ethnic groups. Racism and structural features of society – both of which may cause inequality – tend to be neglected.

Marxists and other conflict theorists believe that the analysis of racism and inequalities stemming from the structure of society should be the starting point for an understanding of ethnic difference and inequality, and not a subsidiary theme. The ethnicity approach is sometimes criticized for offering unconvincing explanations of why people form ethnic groups in the first place. The racism approach and conflict theories claim to offer superior explanations. We will examine racism and conflict approaches in the next section.

The ethnicity approach has theoretical links to symbolic interactionism. Both tend to use participant observation as a research method and both emphasize the importance of seeing the social world from the actor's point of view. It is not surprising, then, that the ethnicity approach shares many of the limitations of symbolic interactionism. Not only does it tend to neglect social structure, but it also relies upon research methods that can be seen as subjective. The findings of participant observation studies depend very much upon the observer's interpretations and they are liable to be questioned.

The ethnicity approach is often associated with multiculturalism. However, multiculturalism is not accepted as politically desirable by all sociologists. We will discuss the values underpinning multiculturalism in the final part of this chapter (see pp. 208–9).

A further problem is that ethnicity approaches tend to see sharp distinctions between different ethnic groups. Andrew Pilkington (2003) comments that, 'When we study ethnic groups, there is the very real danger that the boundaries between them will be overdrawn and the cultural distinctiveness of each exaggerated.' Some recent approaches to ethnicity see ethnic groups as in a constant state of flux, with the boundaries between them shifting and the cultures intermingling. Theories of globalization suggest that the differences between cultures will become less marked as time progresses. Nevertheless, the widespread conflict between ethnic groups suggests that many people do believe they belong to an ethnic group. For this reason it still seems worthwhile to study the cultural similarities and differences between groups of humans who feel they share a common ethnicity.

Racism

Introduction

Many of the ethnicity approaches discussed in the last section recognize the existence of racism and accept that racism influences the behaviour of minority ethnic groups. However, they place more emphasis on the choices made by members of minority ethnic groups than on the constraints that can result from the hostility and discrimination of the ethnic majority. Sociological approaches that attach particular importance to racism emphasize the limitations imposed on minority ethnic groups by such hostility and discrimination. The focus of attention is not the group itself, but the wider society in which it is a minority group. There is more concern with the inequalities between ethnic groups than with cultural differences, and racism is therefore a particularly important concept in conflict approaches to 'race' and ethnicity.

In this section we will start by considering definitions of racism and related terms, before discussing the extent of racism. We will then examine explanations for the existence of racism.

Definitions

Prejudice and discrimination

The terms prejudice and discrimination are general ones that can be applied to many issues other than those to do with 'race' and ethnicity. For example, people may be prejudiced against people who are very short, or may discriminate against other people because they are women.

In the *Dictionary of Race and Ethnic Relations* (1996), E.E. Cashmore defines **prejudice** as 'learned beliefs and values that lead an individual or group of individuals to be biased for or against members of particular groups'. Prejudice is therefore about what people think and is not necessarily translated into actions.

Discrimination, on the other hand, is about actions. Cashmore defines it as 'the unfavourable treatment of all persons socially assigned to a particular category'. Both prejudice and discrimination are often based on stereotypes about particular groups of people.

Stereotypes are oversimplified or untrue generalizations about social groups. For example, short people might be stereotyped as being unusually aggressive, and women as being weak and passive. When stereotypes imply negative or positive evaluations of social groups, they become a form of prejudice, and when they are acted on they become discrimination.

Early sociologists of 'race' and ethnicity often use the terms **racial prejudice** and **racial discrimination** to describe prejudice or discrimination directed at groups because of their membership of a supposed racial or ethnic group. However, the use of these terms has become less common and racism has largely replaced them as the most widely used term.

Racism

Racism is a controversial term with no single, generally accepted definition. Robert Miles (1989, 1993) discussed the origins of the term and identified a number of different ways in which it has been used. According to Miles, **racism** is a relatively new word. There was no entry for it in the *Oxford English Dictionary* of 1910. Its first use in English seems to date from the 1930s. At that time it was used as a description of the nineteenth-century theories which claimed that there were distinct, biologically differentiated 'races'. As scientists began to reject this view, some termed their nineteenth-century counterparts who advocated it racists. Racism also came into use in the 1930s as a description of the beliefs of Hitler and the Nazi party in Germany.

This definition was an extremely narrow one. It meant that racism only existed if it was based upon a belief that there were biologically distinct races. The view that racism was a mistaken view about biological divisions between human groups was reflected in a definition used by UNESCO. During the 1950s and 1960s this organization arranged four conferences at which experts from different countries came together to produce agreed statements about 'race' that could be issued by the UN. The fourth statement defined racism for the first time, saying: 'Racism falsely claims that there is a scientific basis for arranging groups hierarchically in terms of psychological and cultural characteristics that are immutable and innate' (quoted in Miles, 1989). While broadening the definition to include beliefs about psychological and cultural differences, this still retained the idea that racism had to be based upon supposedly scientific theories.

This view was rejected by the British Weberian sociologist John Rex. Rex specifically stated that racist theories did not have to be based upon a scientific justification. He defined racism as 'deterministic belief systems about the differences between the various ethnic groups, segments or strata'. Racist theories attributed characteristics to human groups which were determined by factors beyond their control, and which could not be changed. Rex said:

> *It doesn't really matter whether this is because of men's genes, because of the history to which their ancestors have been exposed, because of the nature of their culture or because of divine decree. Whichever is the case it might be argued that this man is an X and that, being an X, he is bound to have particular undesirable qualities.* Rex, 1986

Rex's description of racism retains the idea that the word refers to theories about the differences between groups and the desirability or undesirability of these differences. Many contemporary definitions of racism do not limit the meaning of the term so that it refers only to theories and beliefs. Some also use racism to refer to behaviour which is based upon such theories and beliefs.

John Solomos (1993), for example, defines it as 'those ideologies and social processes which discriminate against others on the basis of their putatively different racial membership'. It need not be based upon any specific theory about biological or cultural superiority because, to Solomos, 'racism is not a static phenomenon'. People may hold stereotypical views about those from different supposed racial groups and may discriminate against them without necessarily believing the group to be inferior. Some sociologists have described a **new racism** which does not involve clearly articulated beliefs about the superiority or inferiority of particular groups (see pp. 178–9 for details).

A broad definition such as Solomos's perhaps comes closest to the meaning attached to racism in everyday language. People may be described as **racist** when they discriminate against members of other 'races' or express derogatory or stereotypical beliefs about them, regardless of what sort of theory, if any, underlies their actions or beliefs.

Precise definitions of racism continue to vary between contemporary sociologists. We will examine these differences in the rest of this section.

Cultural racism

Richardson (1990) defines **cultural racism** as 'a whole cluster of cultural ideas, beliefs and arguments which transmit mistaken notions about the attributes and capabilities of "racial groups"'. This definition is in line with many definitions of racism – for example, it has much in common with Rex's definition. However, cultural racism always refers to the attributes of a society's culture rather than the beliefs held by individuals. An individual might hold racist beliefs, but it would only be an example of cultural racism if those beliefs were widely shared.

The idea of cultural racism is similar to some definitions of institutional racism which we will discuss later.

Racialism

To add to the confusion, some sociologists distinguish between racism and racialism. Rex, for example, describes **racialism** as 'unequal treatment of various racial groups', as opposed to racism, which involves beliefs about racial groups. In other words, racialism involves actions, whereas racism does not; it is only concerned with what people think. Racialism is therefore a form of discrimination. This distinction is not usually made in everyday language and has not been adopted by all sociologists.

Institutional racism

The term institutional racism is perhaps even more controversial than racism. Not only is it used in widely varying ways, but some have questioned whether institutional racism actually exists.

According to Miles, the idea of **institutional racism** originated in the work of American Black Power activists in the 1960s. In 1968 Carmichael and Hamilton defined racism as 'the predication of decisions and policies on considerations of race for the purpose of subordinating a racial group and maintaining control over that group'. Racism could be individual and overt, where people consciously and openly discriminated against blacks. However, it could also take the form of institutional racism. This was often covert or hidden. It did not require conscious discrimination since it took place as a result of 'the active and pervasive operation of anti-black attitudes' (quoted in Miles, 1989).

The idea of institutional racism was further developed by American sociologists such as Robert Blauner. Like Carmichael and Hamilton, Blauner argued that racism need not be conscious or based on individual prejudice. Blauner argued that racism was built into the way that major American institutions worked. Racism was 'located in the actual existence of domination and hierarchy', and it ensured the continued domination of particular races by others. Like Carmichael and Hamilton, some sociologists have defined institutional racism in terms of the domination of blacks by whites and have not used it to apply to any other racial groups.

Wellman (1993) argues that racism is concerned with protecting an advantaged position in society. Since, in American society at least, whites tend to be advantaged and blacks disadvantaged, only whites can be racist. Another American sociologist, Katz, argues that all white Americans are inevitably racist regardless of their individual beliefs because racism is 'perpetuated by Whites through their conscious and/or unconscious support of a culture and institutions that are founded on racist policies and practices' (quoted in Miles, 1989).

In Britain, the term institutional racism has also been used in a variety of ways. David Mason (1982) identifies five of them:

1 The **conspiracy version** occurs when those in positions of power in public institutions deliberately set out to discriminate against racial groups. Mason cites the Scarman Report, which investigated the Brixton riots of 1981. Scarman denied that Britain was an institutionally racist society: 'If by that what is meant is that it is a society which knowingly, as a matter of public policy, discriminates against black people.'
2 The **structural Marxist** view of institutional racism does not depend upon the existence of conscious prejudice and discrimination. This argues that racism results from the consequences of state policy regardless of the intentions behind it. In other words, if government policy results in inequality between racial groups, then this demonstrates that the state is racist whether or not individuals who hold positions in the state are racist as individuals. The state acts to serve the interests of capitalists by trying to ensure profitability for their enterprises. In doing so it is bound to follow racist policies. For example, it might encourage the immigration of cheap easily exploited labour when it is needed, and then use that labour force as a scapegoat for the failings of capitalism when unemployment rises and there is a shortage of adequate housing.
3 The **unintended consequences** approach to institutional racism has been particularly influential. This argues that the actions of institutions in society can lead to racial disadvantage and inequality as a consequence of those institutions following policies that were not designed to be racist. For example, in a 1960s study of housing in Birmingham, Rex and Moore (1967) found that minority ethnic groups tended to end up in poor housing and had little success in obtaining council housing. This was partly because the council gave preference to those who had lived in the area longest. As fairly recent immigrants, most members of minority ethnic groups were well down the list.

   Similarly, Lord Scarman found that policing policies in Brixton in London, designed to reduce the number of 'street crimes' by stopping and searching suspects on the streets, resulted in discrimination against African Caribbeans. Since they were most likely to be present on the streets when the police were looking for suspects, they were more likely to be stopped and arrested.

   In neither case was the policy motivated by racial prejudice but in both it had the effect of discriminating against minority ethnic groups. Sometimes it may be a question of what an organization does not do rather than the active policies it follows. For example, if job vacancies are not advertised in newspapers read by minority ethnic groups, then this can restrict their job opportunities even if the selection procedure adopted by an institution tries to provide equal opportunities.

   A definition of institutional racism which incorporated at least an element of the unintended consequences approach was adopted by the Stephen Lawrence Inquiry (MacPherson, 1999). This was an inquiry into the racially motivated murder of Stephen Lawrence, a young black man, who was stabbed to death by a group of white youths in London on 22 April 1993. The inquiry also investigated the failure of the Metropolitan police to convict anybody of the crime despite the availability of good evidence. The inquiry defined institutional racism as:

   > *The collective failure of an organization to provide an appropriate and professional service to people because of their colour, culture, or ethnic origin. It can be seen or detected in processes, attitudes and behaviour which amount to discrimination through unwitting prejudice, ignorance, thoughtlessness and racist stereotyping which disadvantage minority ethnic people.* MacPherson, 1999

4 The **colonialism version** of institutional racism suggests that the role in which minority racial or ethnic groups enter a society can result in institutional racism. Mason notes that John Rex argues that New Commonwealth immigrants to Britain were forced to take menial roles in keeping with their status as migrants from former colonies. Robert Blauner developed a similar argument in relation to black Americans with the status of former slaves. In both cases the initial disadvantages created long-term inequalities because the minority ethnic groups tended to be located at the bottom of their respective society's stratification system and upward social mobility was very difficult.
5 The final type of institutional racism identified by Mason is **political opportunism**. This claims that institutional racism results not so much from prejudice but from the workings of the democratic process. Political groups will try to gain votes by taking advantage of 'race', like any other issue, to increase their popularity, since the primary aim of all politicians is to win elections. Thus all major political parties in Britain have sought to win over voters by supporting immigration controls, and parties like the British National Party and National Front have sought electoral success by advocating openly racist views and policies.

Criticisms of the concept of institutional racism

In view of the wide variations in the way the term institutional racism has been used, it is not surprising that it has become a controversial concept. Even those who use it themselves tend to criticize sociologists who use the term in different ways.

Robert Miles (1989), for instance, sees institutional racism as 'exclusionary practices' which disadvantage racial groups but are no longer justified in terms of racist beliefs. Using this fairly narrow definition he criticizes wider definitions. He argues that broad definitions of institutional racism which see it as stemming from the structure of society are 'inseparable from a theory of stratification that is simplistic and erroneous'. They assume that all members of minority ethnic groups are equally disadvantaged by the structural factors. Consequently these approaches to the concept are not able to account for the differences in success between minority ethnic groups.

Miles is particularly critical of approaches which suggest that institutional racism is simply 'what "white" people do'. These rely too much on attributing racism to individual behaviour and ignore the possibility that there are some structural constraints limiting opportunities for the victims of institutional racism. Furthermore, they limit the application of the concept to one historical situation – the institutional racism of 'whites' against 'blacks' – when racism can and has appeared in other contexts.

This last point is also raised by John Richardson. He suggests that some views on racism 'run the risk of transforming race relations in Britain into a simple morality play in which white "villains" persecute black "victims" (although in the wings there are black "heroes" and "heroines" waiting to rescue the victims)' (Richardson, 1990). As Richardson points out, this denies the possibility of racism between minority ethnic groups or even that directed against whites.

Institutional racism – conclusion

Some sociologists interpret the existence of inequalities between ethnic groups as evidence of institutional racism. If, for example, African Caribbeans do less well in the British education system than other groups, this could be viewed as a clear indication that the education system suffers from institutional racism.

However, this is not necessarily the case. Other factors, such as social class or family background, *could* account for the differences and it cannot be automatically assumed that the education system is responsible. Structural accounts of institutional racism, though, tend to rely upon such evidence. If racism has nothing to do with the beliefs or actions of individuals and is simply the outcome of policies, whatever those policies were intended to achieve, then the only evidence that can be used to show that institutional racism exists is evidence of inequality.

This account of institutional racism tends to obscure the causes of inequalities between ethnic groups by attributing them to something that cannot be measured and is just assumed to be all-pervasive. For this reason, perhaps the term is most useful when it is used to refer to actual policies and practices in institutions which can be shown to have the effect of disadvantaging some groups.

This view is supported by John Richardson, who says that 'institutional racism implies that racism is found in the chief policies of our dominant institutions'. While some sociologists do not use the term unless it can be shown that there was a deliberate intention to discriminate, Richardson believes that this usage is too restrictive. He argues: 'regardless of the original intentions of the personnel involved, there is little doubt that their policies – or sometimes lack of policies – nevertheless have damaging social consequences for the less powerful ethnic and racial minorities' (Richardson, 1990).

Racism and the law

In the 1960s and 1970s the British government passed laws making some forms of racial discrimination illegal. In the late 1990s the adequacy of these laws was questioned in the wake of the murder in London of Stephen Lawrence and the subsequent failure of the Metropolitan police to secure a conviction for this racially motivated crime. Partly as a result of this and the subsequent MacPherson Report (see p. 170), new legislation was passed. In this section we will outline that legislation and briefly consider how effective it has been.

The 1965 Race Relations Act

The 1965 Race Relations Act banned discrimination on the grounds of 'race, colour, or ethnic or national origin' in 'places of public resort' such as restaurants and on public transport. It also made it illegal to incite racial hatred in speech or writing.

The Act was widely criticized for being too limited. It did not cover discrimination in housing or employment – both of crucial importance to people's life chances. Furthermore the **Race Relations Board** which enforced the legislation had little power. Zig Layton-Henry (1992) says, 'it quickly found that most of the complaints it received were outside its jurisdiction, and even those it could deal with it had little power to enforce'.

The 1968 Race Relations Act

The 1968 Race Relations Act extended the scope of the earlier Act to include employment, housing and the provision of commercial and other services. Discriminatory advertising and notices were banned. The Race Relations Board was given the power to investigate complaints of racial discrimination, institute conciliation procedures, and, if those did not work, take legal proceedings.

The 1968 Act certainly strengthened race relations legislation but it still had important limitations. The Race Relations Board had to wait for complaints to be made and could not investigate discrimination where the victims might not be aware that they had been unfairly treated. The Act still excluded some important areas of 'social' life, particularly the police: complaints against them on the grounds of racial discrimination continued to be investigated by the police themselves.

Layton-Henry suggests that the small number of cases that were dealt with effectively by the Board indicates that it still lacked teeth. From April 1969 to April 1970, 982 complaints were investigated. In 734 cases it was decided that there was no discrimination, and 143 of the cases where it did find discrimination were related to advertising. Layton-Henry suggests that this was because the legislation was effective in dealing with discrimination in that area.

However, the Board was less effective in dealing with discrimination in employment and housing. It is much harder to prove that discrimination has taken place in these areas, and consequently few cases were brought to court. In fact, of the 2,967 complaints investigated by the end of March 1972, only seven resulted in court cases. The penalties for those who were convicted usually involved the payment of very small sums in damages.

The 1976 Race Relations Act

In 1976 a new Race Relations Act came into force. This introduced the idea of indirect discrimination: for example, using unjustifiable requirements or conditions which had the effect of discriminating against a minority ethnic group, even if the criteria of exclusion were not directly ethnic or racial ones. For instance, if an employer stipulated that potential employees had to have been born in the UK or that they could not live in an inner-city area, then these policies could be seen as indirectly discriminatory, since members of minority ethnic groups were more likely to fall into these categories.

The Act also established the **Commission for Racial Equality**, which had the task of promoting racial harmony and could give legal assistance to those who believed they had been the victims of discrimination. Layton-Henry says that the Commission for Racial Equality was 'a much more powerful body than its predecessors, with much greater scope and powers for strategic initiatives in enforcing the law'.

However, like most other commentators, Layton-Henry believes that the Commission for Racial Equality did not achieve as much as might have been possible with stronger powers and more resources. It continued to be difficult to bring prosecutions and, with limited resources, the Commission often had to make difficult decisions about which cases and investigations to pursue and which to drop. Furthermore, Layton-Henry comments: 'The return of the Conservatives in 1979 created a less favourable environment for the Commission's work as the new government was generally hostile to what it called the "race relations industry" and reluctant to allocate resources to it' (Layton-Henry, 1982).

The Race Relations Amendment Act 2000

In 1997 a Labour government was elected which was more sympathetic to anti-racist measures. In 1999 the MacPherson Report on the murder of Stephen Lawrence was published. The report was highly critical of the Metropolitan police for their handling of the case and particularly for their failure to treat the murder as a racially motivated crime. The report also found evidence of widespread institutional racism in the criminal justice system (see p. 170). Partly as a result of this, new government legislation was introduced which became the Race Relations Amendment Act 2000. This greatly strengthened the previous legislation in a number of ways:

1. It extended the 1976 Act to include all the functions of nearly all public authorities, including the police, educational institutions, the NHS and any private or voluntary agencies providing public sector services. There were some exceptions in the new Act, such as the security services, and immigration authorities were still able to discriminate on the basis of national or ethnic origin, but not on grounds of race or colour. The previous legislation only covered certain areas – education, housing and the provision of goods or services. The new legislation covered all areas of public service. Unlike the previous legislation, it applied to the regulatory and enforcement powers of the police, the prison service, licensing bodies and local authorities. For example, it made it illegal for the police to discriminate on racial grounds when carrying out duties such as controlling demonstrations, deciding whether to arrest somebody, or conducting stops and searches.
2. Most importantly, and for the first time, the new Act introduced a positive duty on public bodies to actively eliminate unlawful discrimination and promote equality of opportunity. It required all such bodies to consider the implications for racial equality in everything they did. Furthermore, the Commission for Racial Equality can issue a compliance notice on bodies it believes are not carrying out their duties. This positive duty came into operation in 2001.

Although there are some limitations on the scope of this legislation, there is no doubt that the Race Relations Amendment Act enormously increases the power of the Commission for Racial Equality and the potential for using the law to tackle racism. However, it remains to be seen whether the most recent legislation has more impact than the previous laws. Shifts in a society's culture, although slower to produce change, may have a greater effect in the longer term.

In the next section, we will examine whether there is any evidence that legislation and/or cultural changes have led to a reduction in racism in Britain.

The extent of individual racism

British Social Attitudes Surveys

Useful data, which give some indication of changes in the amount of individual racism, have been produced by the British Social Attitudes Surveys. Since 1983 these annual surveys of a representative sample of the British population have included questions on racism. In general, the results of the surveys offer some grounds for optimism. The surveys found that the percentage who described themselves as 'Very or a little prejudiced against people of other races' declined from 35 per cent in 1983, to 31 per cent in 1991 and 28 per cent in 2000. Although this is a small decrease, it does suggest some reduction in racism over that period.

In the 2000 survey, a number of questions were included which related racism to national identity (Jowell *et al.*, 2000). The survey asked a sample of 2,718 people in England whether they saw themselves as ambiguously or unambiguously English or British, or some combination of the two. The survey found that those from minority ethnic groups were unlikely to define themselves as English. Only 6 per cent of those who described themselves as black and 7 per cent of those who defined themselves as Asian defined themselves as English rather than British. Furthermore, in the sample as a whole, those who defined themselves as English were more likely to express racist views.

Table 3.2 shows that 70 per cent of those who saw themselves as 'unambiguously English' agreed or strongly agreed that 'immigrants take jobs away from people who were born in Britain', compared to 37 per cent of those who saw themselves as unambiguously British. Overall only 16 per cent thought that minority ethnic groups had been getting ahead and this was a bad thing, but 34 per cent agreed that 'attempts to give equal opportunities to blacks and Asians in Britain had gone too far or much too far'. This suggests that there is still a long way to go before racist views die out, especially among those with an English identity.

More recent data are provided by an ICM opinion poll conducted for the *Observer* in September 2001. In the poll only 9 per cent agreed that 'To be truly British it is necessary to be white.' However, a further 30 per cent believed that 'people from ethnic minorities need to demonstrate a real commitment to this country before they can be considered British'. Another question which might indicate the extent of racism asked people to agree or disagree with the statement 'It would not bother me if a member of my family married someone from a different ethnic background': 18 per cent disagreed. However, a larger percentage thought that the rise of multicultural society in Britain was causing problems: 35 per cent thought it increased social tension, 32 per cent thought it led to a shortage of adequate housing, 31 per cent thought it led to rising crime rates, and 25 per cent thought it eroded the traditional British way of life. These findings suggest that between one-quarter and one-third of the population hold at least some beliefs which could be defined as racist. (For details of a further poll conducted in the aftermath of the attacks on the USA on 11 September 2001, see pp. 449–51.)

Conclusion – studies of individual racism

These studies give some indication of how willing people are to say they are racist or prejudiced and they give an indication of changes over time. However, they do not measure how many people act in a racist or racialist way.

Furthermore, the studies have methodological limitations. They rely upon measuring the strength of the racist beliefs held by individuals, beliefs which respondents in questionnaire or interview research may be unwilling to admit. They are based upon the idea that racism is a characteristic of individuals, and perhaps a minority of individuals, rather than a feature of a society's culture or structure. They therefore add little to an understanding of cultural racism or institutional racism. At the very least, they need supplementing with studies of other types of racism.

Racial harassment

One way of examining the actual incidence of racism is to study racial harassment. As part of the Policy Studies Institute's Fourth National Survey of Ethnic Minorities, questionnaire data on the incidence of racial harassment was collected from interviews with 5,196 members of minority ethnic groups.

Satnam Virdee (1997) noted that racial harassment had come to public attention partly because of some particularly vicious attacks. He gives the example of Rohit Duggal, a schoolboy in southeast London who was

Table 3.2 Attitudes towards immigration and minority ethnic groups by national identity

	% who think:				
	Immigrants take jobs	Bad that ethnic minorities got ahead	Equal opportunities gone too far	Racially prejudiced	*Base*
National identity					
Unambiguously English	70	26	46	37	253
Ambiguously English	51	21	38	38	238
More English than British	48	18	39	33	389
Equally English and British	44	14	33	26	999
More British than English	36	13	32	28	298
Ambiguously British	48	14	31	26	119
Unambiguously British	37	14	26	17	235
All	**44**	**16**	**34**	**28**	2,718

Notes:
Immigrants take jobs: per cent who strongly agree that 'immigrants take jobs away from people who were born in Britain'
Bad that ethnic minorities got ahead: per cent who think that ethnic minority groups in England have been getting ahead in the last few years and that this is a bad thing
Equal opportunities gone too far: per cent who think that 'attempts to give equal opportunities to blacks and Asians in Britain have gone too far'
Racially prejudiced: per cent who say they are 'very or a little prejudiced against people of other races'

Source: Jowell *et al.* (2000), p. 168

stabbed to death in a racially motivated attack. In all, according to Virdee, fifteen people were killed in such attacks in Britain in the period 1992–4. However, Virdee argues that more everyday forms of harassment, such as racially motivated attacks on property and racist verbal abuse, can also have serious effects.

The findings of the PSI study are summarized in Table 3.3. Virdee found that, although racially motivated physical attacks affected only about 1 per cent of the minority ethnic population, this was about 20,000 attacks per year. He estimated that around 40,000 people had their property damaged for racially motivated reasons, and some 230,000 were racially abused or insulted. This compares with about 10,000 racially motivated incidents reported to the police in the same year.

Most of the racial attacks – 67 per cent – were committed by complete strangers, and 62 per cent of the racial insults came from strangers. However, most of the racial attacks on property were committed by neighbours (52 per cent), with 36 per cent committed by complete strangers. Some incidents took place at work: 8 per cent of racial attacks and 11 per cent of racial insults were committed by workmates.

Although racial insults may be less serious than racial attacks, they can still have important consequences. The researchers asked members of minority ethnic groups about the effects of racial incidents. About one in seven said they had taken some measures in the previous two years to avoid racial harassment. Of this group, 58 per cent had 'started to avoid going out at night', 54 per cent had 'made home more secure', 35 per cent had 'started to visit shops at certain times only', 23 per cent had 'stopped children playing outside', 23 per cent had 'stopped going out without partner', and 20 per cent had 'started to avoid areas where only white people live'. Virdee concludes that for these people racial harassment 'has a significant impact on the quality of life they are able to lead'.

The British Crime Survey provides a useful source of data about racially motivated assaults. On the basis of the 2003/4 survey it was estimated that around 206,000 racially motivated incidents had taken place in the previous year. The 2002/3 survey results revealed that less than 1 per cent of whites, 2 per cent of blacks, 3 per cent of Asians and 4 per cent of people of mixed race believed they had been victims of a racially motivated crime in the previous twelve months. Minority ethnic groups were found to be more worried about crime than whites.

Inequalities between ethnic groups in Britain

In this section we examine the statistical evidence for the extent of material inequality between ethnic groups in Britain. The inequalities may be caused by individual racism, cultural racism or institutional racism, but may also be the result of other factors such as cultural differences or class inequality. (Details of inequalities between ethnic groups are discussed elsewhere in the book. See pp. 649–61 for data on ethnic groups and educational achievement, pp. 235–7 on ethnicity and poverty, pp. 305–6 on 'race' and health, and pp. 359–67 on 'race', ethnicity and crime.)

Employment, unemployment and earnings

Figure 3.1 shows that in 2000 the average net weekly pay of white men was higher than that of men in all ethnic groups apart from Indian men. Bangladeshi men had the lowest net weekly pay, while Indian men had seen the biggest proportional increases in pay between 1994 and 2000. These findings come from a Cabinet Office report on minority ethnic groups in the labour market. The report examined whether the inequalities between ethnic groups could be explained in terms of factors such as educational achievement, or whether simply belonging to an ethnic group was itself a disadvantage. The report found that, 'After taking into account the key variables that can be quantified all ethnic minorities remain disadvantaged in terms of employment and occupational status.' It suggested that the differences could be explained, at least partially, in terms of the continued existence of racism.

The differences in earnings between ethnic groups are reflected in variations in the risk of living in a low income household. In 2002/3 16 per cent of whites lived in low

Table 3.3 People who were subjected to some form of racial harassment in the last 12 months

	Cell percentages						
	Caribbean	Indian	African Asian	Pakistani	Bangladeshi	Chinese	All ethnic minorities
Racially attacked	1	1	1	1	1	0	1
Racially motivated property damage	2	2	3	3	1	1	2
Racially insulted	14	9	12	11	8	16	12
Any form of racial harassment	15	10	14	13	9	16	13
Weighted count	1,567	1,292	799	862	285	391	5,196
Unweighted count	1,205	1,273	728	1,185	591	214	5,196

Source: T. Modood *et al.* (1997) *Ethnic Minorities in Britain*, PSI, London, p. 266

Figure 3.1 Average net weekly pay of men in main job, in Britain, 1994–2000

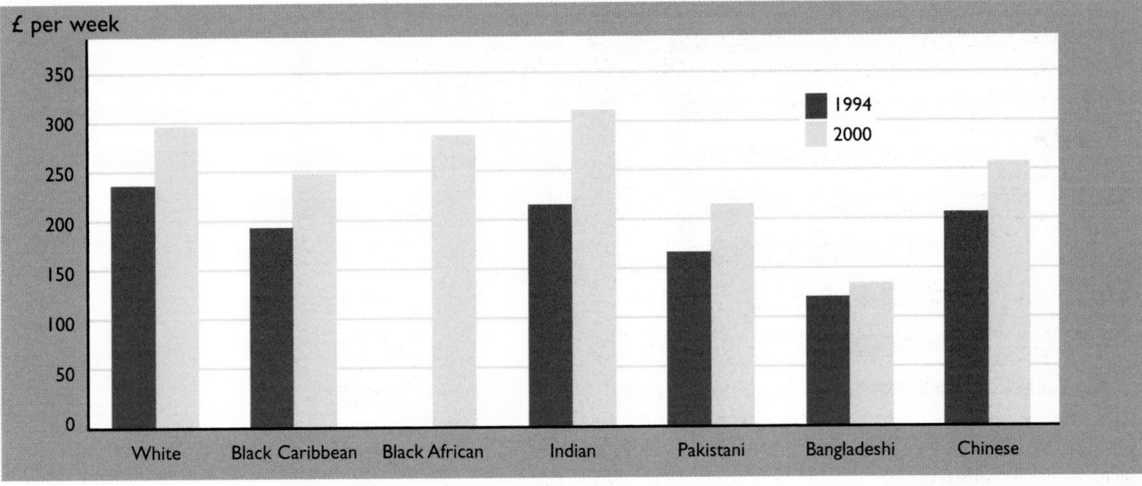

Note: Sample sizes for Black African (1994) net weekly pay are too small to be accurate and are excluded.

Source: *Labour Force Survey, 1994–2000*, National Statistics, London.

Figure 3.2 Average net weekly pay of women in main job, in Britain, 1994–2000

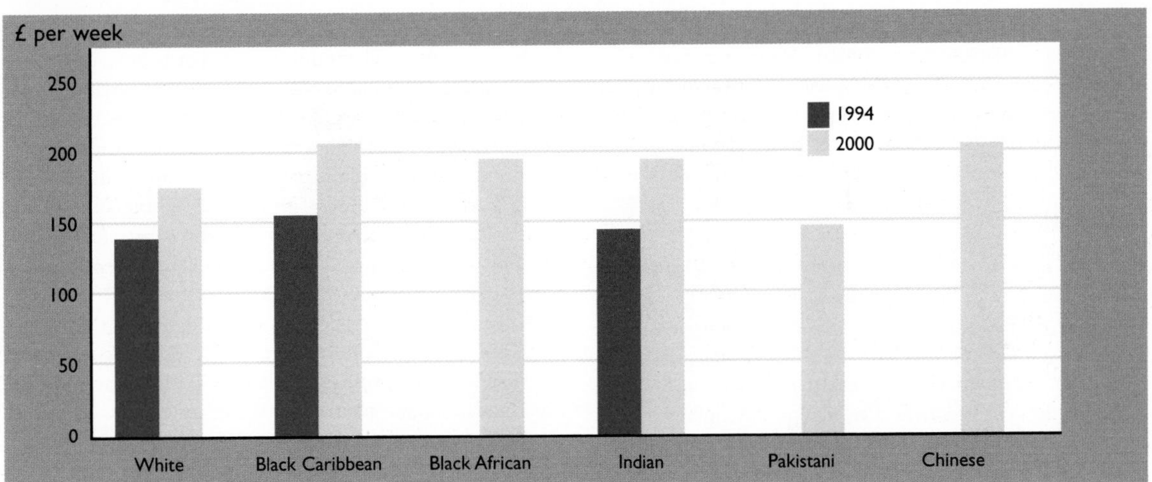

Note: Sample sizes for Black African, Pakistani and Chinese (1994) net weekly pay are too small to be accurate and are excluded.

Source: *Labour Force Survey, 1994–2000*, National Statistics, London.

income households, compared to 20 per cent of Indians, 23 per cent of Chinese, 27 per cent of blacks, and no less than 59 per cent of Pakistanis/Bangladeshis (Home Office, 2005).

Figure 3.2 shows that the position was rather different for women, with women from all ethnic groups apart from Pakistani earning more than white women.

Minority ethnic groups tend to be disadvantaged in terms of their position in the class structure. According to data from the 1998–2000 Labour Force Survey, 41 per cent of whites were in the top two classes of professional, managerial and technical workers. The proportion of Indian men (47 per cent) and Chinese men (44 per cent) in the top classes exceeded the proportion of whites. However, only 33 per cent of black men, 31 per cent of Pakistani men and 23 per cent of Bangladeshi men were in the highest groups.

Among white women, 34 per cent were in the two highest classes. Among minority ethnic women, Chinese women were doing better than their white counterparts (41 per cent were in the highest two classes), black women were doing as well as white women (34 per cent in the highest classes), but only 33 per cent of Indian women and 29 per cent of Bangladeshi/Pakistani women had higher-class jobs. Overall the inequalities were greater among men than among women, with Pakistanis and Bangladeshis doing least well in both cases.

Figure 3.3 shows that unemployment rates vary considerably by ethnic group. In 2004 White British men had an unemployment rate of 5 per cent, much lower than that for most ethnic groups. Black Caribbean men had a rate of 14 per cent, Black African, mixed and Bangladeshi groups all had a rate of around 13 per cent, with rates of 11 per cent for Pakistani men, 10 per cent for Chinese men, and 7 per cent for Indian men.

Data on women in different ethnic groups show very considerable differences in labour market participation. *Social Trends 2006* suggests that cultural and religious reasons

Figure 3.3 Unemployment rates of men: by ethnic group, 2004

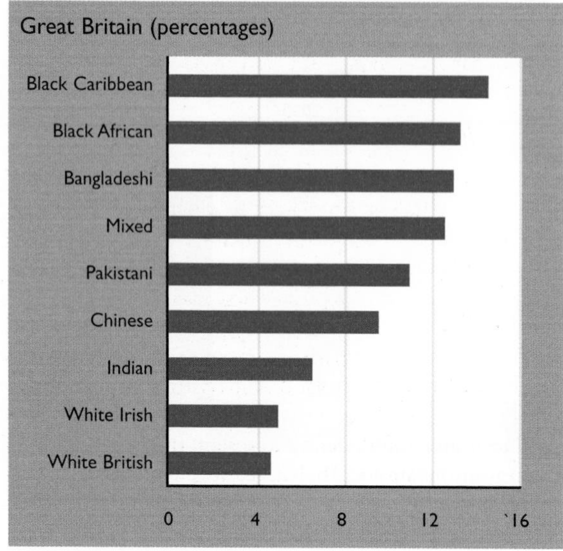

Source: *Social Trends 2006*, National Statistics, London, p. 6.

Figure 3.4 Economic inactivity rates of women: by ethnic group, 2004

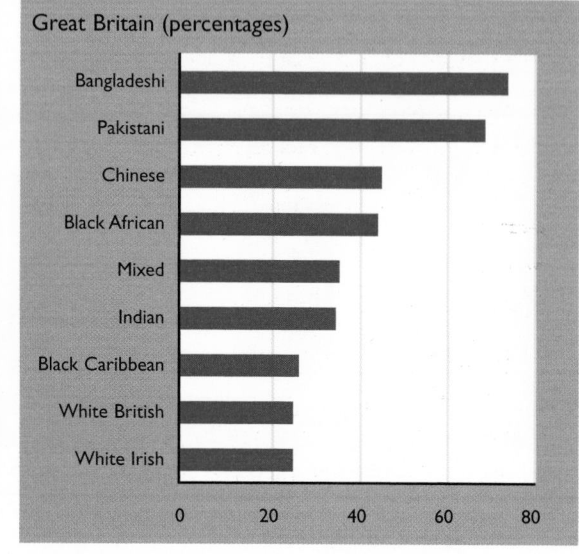

Source: *Social Trends 2006*, National Statistics, London, p. 5.

partly explain the very high rates of inactivity amongst Pakistani and Bangladeshi women shown in Figure 3.4. Fully three-quarters of working-age Bangladeshi women were not taking part in the labour market in 2004, compared to one-quarter of White British women.

Housing

Another area in which minority ethnic groups are disadvantaged is in terms of their living conditions and housing. Andrew Pilkington (2005) comments that 'Minority ethnic communities are much more likely than Whites to live in cities and other urban centres, and within these within deprived areas.' Partly as a consequence of this they are more likely to live in substandard housing. The Home Office (2005), quoting the English House Condition Survey of 2001, noted that 40 per cent of minority ethnic households but only 32 per cent of white households lived in what was defined as 'non-decent homes'. The Home Office report also noted that 30 per cent of Bangladeshis, 21 per cent of Pakistanis, 7 per cent of Black Caribbeans and 7 per cent of Indians lived in overcrowded homes, compared with 2 per cent of whites (quoted in Pilkington, 2005, p. 82).

Inequality and disadvantage

The inequalities discussed above may or may not be the result of some form of racism. Although some definitions of institutional racism see these types of inequality as good evidence of racism, it could be that they have nothing to do with racism but are caused by other factors which affect the opportunities for different groups.

One study which tries to untangle the influence of different factors was conducted by the Home Office (2005). Using data from the Labour Force Survey the Home Office measured whether the higher rates of unemployment for minority ethnic groups could be explained by lack of educational qualifications and living in deprived areas. The study found that even when these factors were taken into account, most minority ethnic groups were still doing less well than other groups in finding employment. They calculated an **ethnic penalty** – the strength of the disadvantage that stemmed simply from being part of a particular group. The ethnic penalty for whites and Chinese was 0 per cent, for Black Caribbeans/Africans and Indians it was 5 per cent, and for Pakistanis/Bangladeshis it was 11 per cent.

Commenting on these findings, Andrew Pilkington says: 'The existence of ethnic penalties indicates that racial discrimination continues to play a role in accounting for the disadvantaged position of minority ethnic groups in the labour market' (Pilkington, 2005, p. 82).

Conclusion

Data from this section and elsewhere in the book suggest that there has been some reduction in most types of inequality between whites and minority ethnic groups in Britain. Patterns of inequality vary by ethnic group, with African Asians and Indians generally faring better than African Caribbeans and Bangladeshis.

In all types of inequality there are important gender differences. For example, women from some minority ethnic groups who are in employment have enjoyed considerable success in achieving high-status jobs, while their male counterparts have been less successful. Furthermore, some of the inequalities may be a product of class differences rather than a direct consequence of ethnicity. It is therefore important not to generalize about minority ethnic groups as a whole.

Overall, though, it is clear that minority ethnic groups continue to have poorer life chances than the white population in Britain (with the possible exception of the Irish). Many sociologists attribute much of the inequality to racism, theories of which we will now examine.

Theories of racism

Some influential theories of racism have assumed that racism is a characteristic of an abnormal minority of the population and that the abnormality which causes racism is psychological. However, most sociological explanations relate racism to wider factors in the structure of society.

Oliver C. Cox – a Marxist theory of racism

Ethnicity, 'race' and racism

Oliver C. Cox (1970) developed an early theory of racism based on Marxist ideas. In 1948 he published his book *Caste, Class and Race* in which he rejected approaches that saw racism as something that had always existed and was a product of natural human sentiments.

To Cox, the idea of 'race' was itself a human creation. In his view, **ethnic groups** were any socially distinct groups which 'lived competitively in a relationship of superordination or subordination with respect to some other people or peoples within one state, country or economic area'. Ethnic groups could be divided into those that were distinguished by culture, and those that were distinguished by 'race'.

'Races' were identified according to physical characteristics but these characteristics did not have to reflect any real biological differences between groups. Cox said, 'a race may be thought of as simply any group of people that is generally believed to be, and accepted as, a race in any given area of ethnic competition'. It was the belief in difference that was important, not any real differences that might exist.

To Cox, racism was a comparatively recent phenomenon. It could not therefore have its origins in universal human sentiments which automatically made ethnic groups hostile to one another. He argued that 'one should miss the point entirely if one were to think of racial antagonism as having its genesis in some "social instinct" of antipathy between peoples'. According to Cox, there was no racism in ancient civilizations:

1 In Ancient Greece, people were divided into Greeks and barbarians. The difference was not a racial one but was based on whether people were familiar with Greek language and culture. Those who were not familiar were barbarians.
2 In Ancient Rome, citizenship was the key distinction. Freeborn people who possessed Roman citizenship could come from any part of the empire and were not restricted by ethnic or racial group.
3 The early Roman Catholic Church distinguished between Christians and heathens and heretics on the basis of religious belief, and people from any racial group could convert to the religion and be accepted as equals. Even the early Portuguese explorers who were ruthless in their dealings with Africans did not see the latter as racially inferior; the Portuguese held to the Christian belief that all people were equal in the eyes of God.

However, towards the end of the fifteenth century things changed and racism began to develop.

Capitalism and racism

In 1493, as a result of Spanish pressure, Pope Alexander VI issued a papal bull putting 'all the heathen peoples and their resources – that is to say, especially the coloured peoples of the world – at the disposal of Spain and Portugal'. At that point, according to Cox, racism was born.

To Cox, racism is not 'an abstract, natural, immemorial feeling of mutual antipathy between groups, but rather a practical exploitative relationship with its socio-attitudinal facilitation'. In other words, racism is a set of beliefs used to justify and therefore to sustain the exploitation of one group by another. It had its origins in the development of capitalism with its need to systematically exploit labour power.

The 'capitalist exploiter, being opportunistic and practical, will utilize any convenience to keep his labour and other resources freely exploitable'. It was hard to justify the use of slave labour in terms of religious beliefs, which saw all humans as equal. It was therefore necessary to 'argue that the workers are innately degraded and degenerate, consequently they naturally merit their condition'.

Early capitalism went hand-in-hand with colonialism. As European nations conquered other areas of the world, they were able to exploit the workforce in the colonies and to justify their actions through racism. To Cox, racism is always something developed by the exploiters against the exploited. He argues: 'race prejudice must be actually backed up by a show of racial excellence, secured finally by military might' and 'the superior race controls the pattern of all dependent race prejudices'.

If racism is something developed to justify exploitation, it cannot be developed by those who are exploited. It is not only whites who are capable of racism, but by chance it was whites who developed capitalism, and therefore it was they who first developed racism. According to Cox, if capitalism had not developed, then 'the world might never have experienced race prejudice'.

Criticisms of Cox

Many writers since Cox have agreed with him that racism is related to capitalism and colonialism. However, many have also denied that racism can only exist within capitalism and that colonialism and capitalism are the only causes of racism. Social psychologists tend to disagree with Cox's view that only white people can be racist, arguing that individuals from any ethnic group can be racist.

Cox's work has influenced some Marxists, but most now reject his views as too simplistic. John Solomos says: 'The model of Marxism with which Cox was familiar was based on the conceptual baggage of "base" and "superstructure" and an instrumental view of the state as the agent of the capitalist class' (Solomos *et al.*, 1982).

Cox saw racism as determined by the economic system. It existed because capitalism needed it to exist. The state acted in a racist way because the state was the instrument of the ruling class.

Many contemporary Marxists argue that such views are far too simplistic. The capitalist class is not all-powerful and the needs of the capitalist system do not in themselves determine everything that happens. An alternative approach has been developed at the Birmingham Centre for Contemporary Cultural Studies.

The Birmingham Centre for Contemporary Cultural Studies – a neo-Marxist theory of racism

A theoretical approach to racism

In a collection of articles entitled *The Empire Strikes Back*, published in 1982, a group of sociologists at the Birmingham Centre for Contemporary Cultural Studies developed a neo-Marxist approach to racism. In an introductory article, John Solomos, Bob Findlay, Simon Jones and Paul Gilroy outlined the main features of this approach.

They agreed with Cox that racism was influenced by colonialism, but argued that racism pre-dated colonialism and was shaped by many other factors. According to them, the nature of racism in Britain was not fixed, but changed as history progressed. They agreed with other Marxist writers that racism was connected to the exploitation of migrant labour in capitalist societies, but again argued that this was not the only important factor. To them, 'The construction of race as a "problem" has not come about by evolutionary means. It has emerged from a whole series of events: struggles, breaks, and discontinuities.' It was necessary to examine these complex events in order to understand racism.

Solomos *et al.* believed that it was necessary to examine the part played by minority ethnic groups themselves in resisting and challenging racism, and to consider how the working class came to accept racist beliefs. Racism was not something that was just imposed on exploited groups in society by an all-powerful ruling class. Although some exploited groups rejected racism, others accepted it, and racist ideas were incorporated into their commonsense understanding of the world.

Like most Marxists, Solomos *et al.* accept that economic factors are important in shaping social life. In Britain in the 1970s and early 1980s, issues to do with 'race' developed against a backdrop of economic crisis and rising unemployment. However, Solomos *et al.* said, 'there is no one-to-one correspondence between the "crisis of race" and the economic crisis', pointing out that 'economic decline preceded popular acknowledgement of crisis, and the expulsion of blacks as a solution to national problems has a long history in British political thought'.

A variety of historical and political factors shaped the situation, along with the development of the economy. The cultures of the working class and of minority ethnic groups, and the policies followed by the British state, all interacted to produce a particular form of racism in the 1970s and early 1980s.

According to Solomos *et al.*, this period saw the emergence of a **new racism** which stressed the cultural differences between ethnic groups rather than biological superiority and inferiority of particular 'races'. It drew upon long-established beliefs about British nationalism which went back centuries, and which appealed to some sections of the white working class. In a later chapter in *The Empire Strikes Back*, Errol Lawrence tried to describe and explain the emergence of this new racism.

Errol Lawrence – the origins of racism in Britain

According to Lawrence, racist ideas have a very long history. Even before colonialism, 'white' was associated with goodness and purity, whereas 'black' was associated with evil. Hence, for example, the distinction between black and white magic. The Christian religion had always characterized non-Christians as pagans. In early contacts between Europeans and other peoples, non-Europeans were usually portrayed as uncivilized.

With the advent of colonialism, racist ideas were developed further. Members of the British working class fought in the wars in which colonies were captured, and in the twentieth century they fought again in independence struggles in countries such as Kenya. Lawrence claims that by the time colonies were gaining independence colonial people had come to be seen as 'children needing protection or as the equally immature "brutal savage"'. Either way the newly independent states were seen as needing strong guidance from their former British 'masters'. Their success or failure was likely to be determined by the extent to which they adopted European culture and institutions.

According to Lawrence, in the 1970s the ruling class in Britain succeeded in 'reorganizing the commonsense racist ideologies of the white working class, around the themes of "the British nation", "the British people" and "British culture"'. The racist ideas that developed were not 'mere "relics" of a distant imperial past', but they did contain strong elements of ideologies developed during colonial times. These stressed the distinctive nature of British culture and the great traditions of British militarism which allowed Britain (and its working-class soldiers) to conquer large parts of the world.

Although the racist images 'are cross-cut by other contradictory images about the essential equality of all people ... they nevertheless tend to pull popular opinion towards racist opinions and interpretations'. This meant that 'black cultures are still likely to be viewed as "primitive" in comparison to British "civilization"'.

The new racism

In the economic and political instability of the 1970s, 'immigrants' came to be seen as a cause of the problems. The emphasis was no longer on outright inferiority but more on difference. British strength came from its way of life, and the presence of 'aliens' with different cultures was sapping this strength and causing national decline. The British way of life was being undermined by 'foreigners', and it was unnatural for people with very different lifestyles to live together.

The new racism attacked the family life of African Caribbeans and Asians. African Caribbeans were seen as incapable of maintaining stable families consisting of parents and children. Such families were viewed as the bedrock of British society. Asians, on the other hand, had unnaturally large extended families which led to overcrowding and the isolation of Asians from the beneficial effects of British culture.

From this point of view, individuals could not be truly British simply by having a British passport or even by being born in Britain. Rather, they had to think of themselves as British and have a British lifestyle and values. Neither African Caribbeans nor Asians were seen as measuring up to these criteria. They had different 'identities', 'loyalties' and 'anti-British attitudes'. Their presence was therefore bound to cause conflict between the 'immigrants' and the real 'British'. According to the logic of the new racism, the only solution to the problem was for the 'immigrants' to leave Britain and return to the countries where their culture was more acceptable.

To Lawrence, the new racism was a response to the crisis in British society. Unemployment, rising crime and the apparent breakdown of family life were all causes of concern, and minority ethnic groups were convenient scapegoats for these problems. However, the new racism was not an automatic and inevitable consequence of economic change. It had to be created using elements of old racist ideas; it had to be accepted by, and make sense to, the white working class; and it had to overcome opposition from anti-racists.

Paul Gilroy – *There Ain't No Black in the Union Jack*

Paul Gilroy was one of the contributors to *The Empire Strikes Back* (see above). In 1987 his own book, *There Ain't No Black in the Union Jack*, was published. This extended the earlier analysis. Like Lawrence, Gilroy examined the new racism, but he also discussed minority ethnic cultures. In doing so, Gilroy was attempting to produce a more complete understanding of 'race' and ethnicity than studies that concentrated on racism or ethnicity alone. His study discusses a wide range of issues which overlap with the issues we consider in a number of sections in this chapter.

Race formation

Gilroy rejects both biological definitions of 'race' and studies of ethnicity which regard ethnic groups as having very strong and distinctive cultures which are slow to change. In his view, **'race' formation** involves an ongoing process in which groups 'define themselves and organize around notions of "race"'. It is a 'continuous and contingent process' which varies from place to place and time to time. It is affected by racism but also by the conscious choices made by those who see themselves as belonging to racial groups.

Resistance to racism and political organization by 'races' play important roles in the process of 'race' formation. Gilroy says, 'it is struggle that determines which definition of "race" will prevail and the conditions under which they will endure or wither away'. For example, in Britain the term 'black' had begun to be used to refer both to African Caribbeans and to Asians. This implies the possibility of Afro-Asian unity in a struggle against racism. More recently, however, 'black' has become more commonly used to refer to African Caribbeans alone. To Gilroy, 'this development has its origins in an understanding of "race" which stresses the obstacles to political accommodation erected between culture and ethnicity'. It has resulted from struggles over the meaning of 'race', and Gilroy believes it reflects the increasing influence of the new racism, which puts great emphasis on cultural differences.

Although influenced by Marxism, Gilroy moves further from Marxist orthodoxy than the Birmingham Centre for Contemporary Cultural Studies had done in *The Empire Strikes Back*. He accepts that struggles over 'race' have been influenced by the development of capitalism – for example in its use of slave and migrant labour – but he denies that the exploitation of 'races' is a form of class exploitation.

Nor does Gilroy believe that conflict between 'races' is simply a form of class conflict. He says: 'The processes of "race" and class formation are not identical. The former is not reducible to the latter even where they become mutually entangled.' Racial divisions are separate and distinct from class divisions and Gilroy talks of 'the evident autonomy of racism from production relations'. Indeed, to Gilroy, class conflict is becoming less important in modern capitalist societies. Instead, conflict has become much more based around new social movements which are concerned with non-economic issues. Examples include the 'women's movements, youth movements, anti-nuclear and peace movements, ecological movements, and various urban and citizen movements'.

Racism

Gilroy agrees with Lawrence that there is a new form of racism in Britain and that it is based around cultural rather than biological distinctions. Gilroy sees this racism as intimately linked to 'discourses of patriotism, nationalism, xenophobia, Englishness, Britishness, militarism and gender difference'. The new racism involves specifying who may be regarded as a legitimate member of 'the Island Race' and who is considered an outsider. So-called 'immigrants', many of whom were actually born in Britain, are usually regarded as outsiders. They are portrayed as culturally different and therefore as threatening the British way of life. Their difference undermines a homogeneous British culture which is seen as having given Britain its strength.

This image of strength is stressed in celebrations of past military victories and was invoked during the 1982 war against Argentina over the Falklands. According to Gilroy, during that war the white residents of the Falklands were seen as coming from the same cultural community as white British people. They were portrayed as being genuinely British even though they lived 8,000 miles from Britain itself.

Similar attitudes prevailed in relation to the athlete Zola Budd. In 1984, Budd, a talented white South African distance runner, was given British citizenship because her grandfather had been British. Her application for citizenship was processed rapidly and accepted enthusiastically by the government. This contrasted with the much greater difficulties experienced by Asians and West Indians who tried to secure British citizenship in order to emigrate to Britain.

Indeed many Asians and African Caribbeans who do have British citizenship and may have been born in Britain are sometimes treated as more alien than whites from New Commonwealth countries such as the Falklands and South Africa. When black protesters demonstrated against Zola Budd because she refused to denounce apartheid in South Africa, the *Sun* newspaper said that they should be 'returned to their original homelands' because 'there is no place for them in Britain'.

Gilroy believes that 'the link between crime and blackness has become absolutely integral' to the new racism. Through much of the 1950s and 1960s African Caribbeans were not portrayed as being particularly prone to criminality. Their presence in Britain was portrayed as creating housing problems and they were certainly subject to much racial discrimination.

However, the turning point was a speech by the Conservative politician Enoch Powell. In 1968 he described the plight of an old white woman who had lived in a particular street all her life. Gradually, more and more blacks moved into her street. According to Powell, after she had refused a black neighbour's request to use her phone one night, she began to suffer verbal abuse from blacks in her area. Gilroy comments that in Powell's speech: 'The anarchy represented by black settlement is counterpoised to an image of England in which Britannia is portrayed as an old white woman, trapped and alone in the inner city' (Gilroy, 1987). She was surrounded by hostile aliens in her home – a corner of Britain had been taken over by outsiders.

In Powell's view the aliens were liable to be criminals. In 1976 he argued that 'mugging' was a racial crime because it was predominantly carried out by blacks. This view of blacks as criminals was reinforced by media reporting of so-called 'muggings' and various inner-city disturbances in the 1970s and 1980s. (For details of a study of the 'panic' over mugging see pp. 361–3.)

Ethnic absolutism

As we saw earlier in the chapter (see p. 149), in his 1968 speech, Powell had said: 'As I look ahead, I am filled with foreboding. Like the Roman, I seem to see "the River Tiber foaming with much blood".' The blood would be the inevitable consequence of immigration, which led to people from different cultures living side-by-side.

Gilroy calls the view that there are completely different cultures **ethnic absolutism**. He criticizes people like Powell for believing that cultures are fixed and unchanging. For Gilroy, there are many overlaps between black and white cultures in Britain, and indeed British culture, particularly youth culture, has become increasingly influenced by black culture.

Gilroy believes that cultures are constantly changing and he attacks all those who analyse ethnic cultures as separate entities. This includes not only right-wing politicians who support the 'repatriation' of British blacks, but also some left-wing thinkers and sociologists who study ethnicity. They too can be ethnic absolutists when they portray groups of Asians or African Caribbeans as having quite distinct cultures from other British people.

Thus Gilroy is hostile to the sort of studies that we discussed in the 'Ethnicity' section of this chapter.

Black culture

In discussing black culture Gilroy concentrates on the music and youth culture of African Caribbeans. He sees black culture as being formed partly as a response to racism and exploitation. For example, from slave songs to reggae, rap and hip-hop, black music and lyrics have expressed radical sentiments. However, black culture is much more than simply a reaction to racism; it is actively created in different contexts from diverse influences. Some of those influences are African and pre-date the large-scale exploitation of blacks by whites.

Black culture is an international culture which has been influenced by the **diaspora**, or dispersal, of African peoples throughout the world. In Britain there are strong Caribbean and African American influences. Reggae music and the sound systems over which it is traditionally played have influenced black youth in Britain, as have North American traditions of soul and rap. Most styles of black music are based around African rhythms which were preserved in slave music and passed down to succeeding generations.

Black music and culture not only have international origins, they are also influential throughout the world. Gilroy claims, for example, that 'Rastafari culture has been carried to locations as diverse as Poland and Polynesia, and hip-hop from Stockholm to Southall.'

Black culture has also influenced white youth. Gilroy attacks ethnic absolutists by pointing out how elements of black music have been adopted by whites. The Beatles' early records contained cover versions of rhythm and blues and rock and roll songs originally recorded by black American artists. Later, reggae rhythms started to be incorporated into mainstream pop music.

In Britain, Gilroy finds some evidence that racial divisions may be being weakened by music. In West London some Asians had become involved in hip-hop. White and black musicians worked together in the 1970s in groups like the Specials, who played ska music (a variation on reggae) and attacked racism in their lyrics. Gilroy quotes at length from David Emmanuel's 1984 hit 'Cockney Translation'. In this song cockney and black slang are translated:

Cockney say scarper we scatter
Cockney say rabbit we chatter
We say bleach Cockney knackered
Cockney say triffic we say wackard
Cockney say blokes we say guys
Cockney say alright we say ites!
We say pants Cockney say strides
Sweet as a nut … just level vibes. Seen.

To Gilroy, this suggested the increasing possibility of the black and white working classes working together to resist racism and class exploitation. Despite the differences between blacks and whites, their cultures were not completely separate and they influenced one another. Gilroy concludes on an optimistic note, suggesting that black and white cooperation offers an image of a better future. Eventually the different cultures may become so similar that people will no longer even think of each other as belonging to different 'races'.

Evaluation

Gilroy's work has been criticized by more conventional Marxists. They have criticized him for failing to define 'race' clearly and for continually referring to groups as 'races'. To Miles (1989) there is no biological basis for 'races'. 'Races' therefore do not exist and the term 'race' should not be used. Miles also criticizes Gilroy for arguing that class conflict has been replaced by 'race' conflict and other non-economic forms of conflict. To Miles and other Marxists, class conflict is far from dead, and economic exploitation continues to be an important factor in the exploitation of minority ethnic groups and the production of racism.

Whatever its limitations, Gilroy's work represents an important advance over most earlier approaches to 'race' and ethnicity. It combines the study of minority ethnic cultures with an examination of racism and in doing so avoids the narrow focus of many of the other studies we have examined in this chapter. Gilroy also discusses the relationship between 'race', racism, ethnicity and nationality in suggesting that in Britain racism has become increasingly closely connected with a form of British nationalism.

In some respects Gilroy's work anticipated a number of theoretical developments. These include the idea that new ethnicities are developing, that ethnic identities are not static but change continually, that identities are becoming fragmented, and that there is a complex relationship between 'race', ethnicity and nationality. These sorts of theoretical developments will be discussed later in the chapter (see pp. 194–204). First, however, we will consider how some of the new approaches to racism and ethnicity have been applied to British Asians.

Islamophobia, British Asians and racism

Islam and racism

Some of the new approaches to understanding racism and ethnic groups have been applied to an understanding of attitudes to Islam in general and to British Asians in particular. It can be argued that in the 1990s Muslims in Britain and elsewhere began to experience new forms of racism. First, it has been suggested that young Asian men increasingly came to be seen as a threat to law and order in British towns and cities. In this respect there was something of a shift from racism directed at British African Caribbean youth (see, for example, the panic over 'mugging', pp. 361–3) to racism directed at Asian youth. This included a concern about the development of Asian gangs (see below).

Second, it has been argued that Muslims have increasingly been seen as a problem by the media and in political debate in Western societies. The Parekh Report commented: 'Recently, Muslims have emerged as the principal focus of racist antagonisms ("Islamophobia") based on cultural difference' (Parekh *et al.*, 2000). Such concern was exemplified by the response to riots in towns in the north of England in 2001, the reaction to the attacks in the USA on 11 September 2001, and the reaction to the suicide bombers on the London underground in 2005 (often referred to as 7/7).

An opinion poll was conducted by ICM for the *Observer* in Britain shortly before and shortly after the September 2001 attacks (in August–September 2001 and November 2001). Following the attacks, 60 per cent of the sample agreed that British Muslims should 'make a special effort to state their allegiance to Britain', and 58 per cent thought that those who expressed support for Bin Laden should be deported. In a number of areas there was evidence of a change in attitudes as a result of the attacks. Before the attacks, 21 per cent of the population thought race relations were getting worse, but afterwards this rose to 36 per cent. Before the attacks, 59 per cent agreed that 'immigrants should embrace the British way of life rather than embrace their own lifestyle'; afterwards 71 per cent agreed with this statement.

After the 7/7 bombings the British media expressed particular concern that the suicide bombers were apparently 'home-grown' terrorists – they were British citizens brought up in Britain. Tahir Abbas says, 'Certainly, the 7/7 attacks on London have added to direct and indirect forms of Islamophobia. There is considerable evidence of violence towards individuals, communities and mosques, impacting on the experience of Muslims living in Britain' (Abbas, 2005, p. xv).

The term Islamophobia is used to refer to a particular form of discrimination or prejudice. Rather than being directed against a 'race' or a particular minority ethnic group, Islamophobia can be seen as a form of racism directed at people because of their religious beliefs. We will now examine a number of attempts to understand this phenomenon. In this section, we will first examine Islamophobia in general before looking at the effects on British Muslims in more detail.

The Runnymede Trust – the nature of Islamophobia

In 1997 the Runnymede Trust argued that there had been a rapid growth in anti-Muslim prejudice. Just as anti-Jewish feeling in earlier European history had led to the development of a new term to describe it (anti-Semitism), so the growing hostility to Muslims required a new word, **Islamophobia**. The Runnymede Trust defined Islamophobia as 'unfounded hostility towards Islam' which could lead to 'unfair discrimination against Muslim individuals and communities, and to the exclusion of Muslims from mainstream political and social affairs' (Runnymede Trust, 1997). It accepted that to be critical of aspects of Islam was not in itself an example of Islamophobia. For example, followers of other religions could disagree with Islamic theology; secular humanists of no religious faith might be critical of religion; and Islamic regimes which did not respect human rights or contravened international law could legitimately be criticized. However, the Runnymede Trust distinguished between

Table 3.4 Closed and open views of Islam

Distinctions	Closed views of Islam	Open views of Islam
1 Monolithic/diverse	Islam is seen as a single monolithic bloc, static and unresponsive to new realities	Islam is seen as diverse and progressive, with internal differences, debates and development
2 Separate/interacting	Islam is seen as separate and other – (a) not having any aims or values in common with other cultures; (b) not affected by them; (c) not influencing them	Islam is seen as interdependent with other cultures – (a) having certain shared values and aims; (b) affected by them; (c) enriching them
3 Inferior/different	Islam is seen as inferior to the West – barbaric, irrational, primitive, sexist	Islam is seen as distinctively different, but not deficient or inferior, and as equally worthy of respect
4 Enemy/partner	Islam is seen as violent, aggressive, threatening, supportive of terrorism, engaged in 'a clash of civilizations'	Islam is seen as an actual or potential partner in joint cooperative enterprises and in the solution of shared problems
5 Manipulative/sincere	Islam is seen as a political ideology used for political or military advantage	Islam is seen as a genuine religious faith, practised sincerely by its adherents
6 Criticisms by West	Criticisms of Islam made by 'the West' are rejected out of hand	Criticisms by 'the West' and other cultures are considered and debated
7 Discrimination	Hostility towards Islam is used to justify discriminatory practices towards Muslims and exclusion of Muslims from mainstream society	Debates and disagreements with Islam do not diminish efforts to combat discrimination and exclusion
8 Islamophobia seen as natural/problematic	Anti-Muslim hostility is accepted as natural and 'normal'	Critical views of Islam themselves are subjected to critique, lest they be inaccurate and unfair

Source: Runnymede Trust (1997) *Islamophobia*, Runnymede Trust, London, p. 4.

closed and open views of Islam. These two competing approaches are summarized in Table 3.4.

The report identified eight differences between closed and open views of Islam:

1 Closed views of Islam see it as a single, unchanging and inflexible religion. The open view acknowledges that there are divisions in Islam and it is dynamic and constantly changing. The report points out that there are numerous differences within Islam: for example, between generations, between Muslims in different regions, between different interpretations of the Qur'an and between those who are critical of human rights abuses in some Islamic countries and those who are not.
2 Closed views see Islam as a completely separate and independent religion. The open view accepts that there are many similarities between Islam and other monotheistic religions such as Christianity and Judaism.
3 Closed ways of thinking about Islam see it as inferior, uncivilized, irrational, violent and repressive. Open views accept that there are differences between Muslims and others, but do not see Muslims as inferior. They acknowledge, for example, that sexism, intolerance and literal interpretation of scriptures are found in all religions and are not confined to, nor pervasive within, Islam.
4 A fourth characteristic of closed views of Islam is that it is seen as a 'violent and aggressive' enemy. Open views recognize that most Muslims are opposed to the actions of terrorists who claim to be Islamic, and opposed to regimes in Islamic countries which are aggressive. The Runnymede Trust quotes a number of newspaper columnists (e.g. Bernard Levin), political scientists (e.g. Samuel Huntingdon) and military leaders (such as the Secretary General of NATO) who have described Islam or Muslim fundamentalism as the enemy of, and a threat to, Western civilization. The Runnymede Trust is more supportive of a speech given by Prince Charles in 1996 which called for bridge-building between the West and Islam, although there were critical reports of the speech in the British press.
5 Closed views of Islam see the religion as being manipulated by political leaders to further their own ends and to give political or military advantage to their states. Open views accept that adherents of the religion are sincere in their beliefs, like any other religious people.
6 Closed views of Islam believe that Muslims reject out of hand all criticism made by Westerners, whereas open views show an awareness of the fact that criticisms are debated by Muslims.
7 Closed views include the belief that discrimination against Muslims can be justified because in some respects they deserve it. This view often goes hand-in-hand with attacks on 'political correctness' and the promotion of anti-immigrant and anti-Asian feeling. For example, the Runnymede Trust (1997, p. 18)

quotes a British newspaper columnist who complains: 'With the wishy-washy excuse that "it's their culture", we are supposed to tolerate idiots slaughtering goats on the streets in Kensington, groups of idiots burning books on the streets in Bradford and wealthy bigger groups building mosques on streets everywhere.' Open views allow reasoned criticism of Islam, but are committed to the eradication of all discrimination and racism.

8 Finally, closed views see it as natural and normal that Westerners should be hostile to Islam as an alien religion which goes against Western values. Open views, however, can be critical of Islam, but they acknowledge that the critics of Islam may themselves be wrong and they accept that their own arguments should be open to scrutiny.

Conclusion

The Runnymede Trust concludes that Islamophobia, just like anti-Semitism, has the potential to cause major problems for Western societies. It argues that Islamophobia 'inhibits the development of a just society characterized by social inclusion and cultural diversity. For it is a constant source of threat and distress to British Muslims and implies that they do not have the same rights as other British citizens.' It can lead to young Muslims joining extremist groups, it increases the chance of social disorder, it makes it harder for moderate or mainstream Muslims to have their views heard, it obstructs cooperation and interchange between Muslims and non-Muslims, and it can harm international relations.

While the Runnymede Trust provides an interesting description and definition of Islamophobia, it does not really explain where Islamophobia comes from. The search for an explanation is more prominent in the work of Edward Said.

Edward Said – Orientalism and Islam

The nature of Orientalism

In *Orientalism* (1995) Edward W. Said argues that the idea of the **Orient** is a European invention. Europeans have for hundreds of years divided the world into two contrasting halves, the West or **Occident**, and the East or **Orient**. Said argues that the image of the Orient is an integral part of the way in which Westerners, particularly Europeans and North Americans, understand themselves. Groups construct identities in contrast with others. Said says: 'the development and maintenance of every culture requires the existence of another different and competing alter ego'. The image of the 'Other' or 'Others' is constantly recreated and can change over time, although images of the Orient have remained fairly consistent. Said claims:

> *Debates today about 'Frenchness' and 'Englishness' in France and England respectively, or about Islam in countries such as Egypt and Pakistan, are part of the same interpretive process which involves the identities of different 'others', whether they be outsiders and refugees, or apostates and infidels.* Said, 1995

Thus, for example, the image of the Orient as somewhere that is different is an important part of the way Europeans see themselves.

Said defines **Orientalism** as 'a way of coming to terms with the Orient that is based on the Orient's special place in European, Western experience'. Orientalism is found in the writings of academics and novelists and in the speeches of politicians. Initially it was France and Britain which developed Orientalism, because they dominated the Orient as colonial powers. However, other European countries such as Germany have played some part in developing Orientalism, and since the Second World War the USA has become the dominant force.

Said sees Orientalism as a **discourse**, a way of thinking and talking about something that involves the exercise of power (see pp. 559–62 for a discussion of the concept of discourse developed by Michel Foucault). It has helped the West to maintain **hegemony**, or political domination, over the Orient, although the hegemony has been resisted (see pp. 539–40 for a discussion of Gramsci's concept of hegemony).

One principle of Orientalism is that it claims that Westerners understand the Orient better than those from the Orient. For example, the French writer Flaubert used his encounter with an Egyptian courtesan as a basis for claiming that he could accurately describe the characteristics of Oriental women. The discourse of Orientalism has had a long and widespread currency and this has given it durability and strength, so that images of the Orient still enjoy much credibility today.

Images of the Orient

What sorts of images of the Orient has Orientalism promoted? Said draws upon a speech by the British politician Balfour given in the House of Commons in 1910. Balfour claimed that British occupation of Egypt was justified because Egyptians, as Orientals, were incapable of governing themselves. Left to their own devices, they would install a government which was a despotic tyranny and which would do nothing to further the country's interests. Britain understood Egypt and how to help it progress better than the Egyptians themselves. From Balfour's point of view, 'Subject races did not have it in them to know what was good for them' (Said, 1995).

Said also refers to the ideas of Cromer, an administrator of the British Empire in India and Egypt. Cromer believed that

> *Orientals or Arabs are … gullible, 'devoid of energy and initiative', much given to 'fulsome flattery', intrigue, cunning and unkindness to animals … Orientals are inveterate liars, they are 'lethargic and suspicious', and in everything oppose the clarity, directness, and nobility of the Anglo-Saxon race.* Said, 1995

A key feature of Orientalism, according to Said, is the view of Orientals as lacking the ability to think logically, thus requiring superior, logical, Occidental minds to think for them. To Said, Orientalism is an **essentialist** viewpoint, one that claims there are fundamental or essential differences between Orientals and Occidentals. Said is dismissive of such essentialism, arguing that 'words such as "Orient" and "Occident" correspond to no stable reality that exists as a natural fact'. In reality, there is no common personality or culture in Eastern countries, but great variety. Eastern countries are 'heterogeneous, dynamic and complex'. Orientalism disguises the interests of the Occident by promoting myths about the Oriental 'Other' which are used to justify interventions in other countries and which help to sustain stereotypical views.

Said argues that the discourse of Orientalism is now applied to Islam and fundamentalism, and the same basic characterization of Orientals continues. It is also evident in the portrayal of the Arab–Israeli conflict. This tends to be portrayed in terms of a 'simple-minded dichotomy of freedom-loving, democratic Israel and evil, totalitarian, and terroristic Arabs'.

Covering Islam

In 1997 the second edition of Edward W. Said's book *Covering Islam* was published. In this, he extended and updated some of the arguments developed in *Orientalism*. He argued that there had been 'an intense focus on Muslims and Islam in the American and Western media, most of it characterized by a ... highly exaggerated stereotyping and belligerent hostility'. Furthermore, he claimed that it had become acceptable to denigrate Islam in a way that was no longer acceptable for other religious or ethnic groups. He says:

> *Malicious generalizations about Islam have become the last acceptable form of denigration of foreign culture in the West; what is said about the Muslim mind, or character, or religion, or culture as a whole cannot now be said in mainstream discussion about Africans, Jews, other Orientals, or Asians.* Said, 1997

These generalizations tend to portray Islam in terms of 'its violence, primitiveness, atavism, threatening qualities'.

Said gives numerous examples of what could be seen as racist comments in the Western media. He quotes Peter Rodman, a former member of the United States National Security Council, who wrote that the West was being 'challenged from the outside by a militant, atavistic force driven by hatred of all Western political thought' (quoted in Said, 1997). He also quotes Bernard Lewis, a British professor living and writing in the USA, who tends to portray 'the whole of Islam as basically *outside* the known, familiar, acceptable world that "we" inhabit, and in addition that contemporary Islam has inherited European anti-Semitism for use in an alleged war against modernity'. Said also notes that popular films, such as *True Lies*, now portray the enemies of the USA not as dangerous communists, but as evil Arab terrorists with an irrational desire to kill Americans.

Said argues that such views must be seen in the context of world politics and the interests of the USA in particular. He accepts that Muslims have been involved in terrorism and attacks on US forces – for example, attacks in Somalia and Lebanon, hostage taking in the Middle East, and the terrorist destruction of Pan Am flight 103 over Lockerbie. However, such aggression is largely the result of the perception of the USA as hostile to Islam. Said points out that the USA or its close ally Israel have

> *bombed and invaded several Islamic countries (Egypt, Jordan, Syria, Libya, Somalia, Iraq), they have (in Israel's case) occupied Arab-Islamic territory in four countries, and in the United States' case are seen in the United Nations as openly supporting the military occupation of these territories.* Said, 1997

Said points out that Israel has ignored many United Nations resolutions requiring it to leave the territories it has occupied in Palestine, and he argues that most Arabs and Muslims see Israel as 'an arrogant regional nuclear power, contemptuous of its neighbours, heedless in the frequency of its bombings, killings (which far exceed the number of Israelis killed by Muslims), dispossessions, and dislocations, especially so far as the Palestinians are concerned'. Said argues that US policy in the Middle East places the interests of 4 million Israelis above those of 200 million Arab Muslims.

While the USA proclaims its democratic credentials and insists that it is a tolerant liberal democracy, it is quite willing to prop up undemocratic regimes which are sympathetic to the USA. In countries such as Saudi Arabia, Indonesia, Morocco and Jordan the USA has backed 'often isolated minority governments, alienated from most of their people'. The support for Israel, the use of military force, and the support for unpopular regimes have made the USA unpopular with many Muslims, despite America's connections with political elites in some Islamic countries.

According to Said, the stereotypical portrayal of Islam is related to the hostility directed towards the USA by many Muslims. The USA, since the collapse of communism in the 1990s, has become the world's only superpower and now expects to exercise its power and influence throughout the world. Said comments: 'The tendency to consider the whole world as one country's imperium is very much in the ascendancy in today's United States.' The Islamic world is the one grouping which is holding out against the dominance of the USA. Said says: 'whereas the other great cultural groupings appear to have accepted the United States' role, it is only from within Islam that signs of determined resistance are still strong'.

Said therefore sees stereotyping of Islam as a response to the defiance of the Islamic world in resisting the dominance of the USA and the West. This stereotype is promoted and reinforced by the Western media and there have been 'deliberate attempts to stir up feelings of anger and fear about Islam in Americans and Europeans'. Such attempts are all the more successful because they draw upon the long-established principles of Orientalism.

Evaluation

Said succeeds in setting the rise of Islamophobia in a wider context than most writers. He places particular emphasis upon the role of the media, but perhaps fails to take sufficient account of the range of messages in the Western media, some of which are sympathetic to Islam and to Palestinians in particular. By concentrating on the broad picture, Said says little about how hostility towards Muslims develops in particular local contexts and at specific times. The next study we will consider looks in detail at how hostility towards British Asians in general developed in relation to the claim that Asian youths were forming 'gangs'.

Claire E. Alexander – *The Asian Gang*

The moral panic over Asian youth

Claire E. Alexander (2000) argues that the late 1990s witnessed a moral panic about the 'problem' of Asian youth. In previous decades there had been moral panics about British black youth, focusing on such issues as 'Rastafarian drug dealers, black rioters, muggers and yardies'. Generally, British Asian communities were portrayed as much less of a problem. Alexander says: 'Britain Asian communities were held to be ... holistic and coherent, alien and incomprehensible perhaps, but peaceable, law-abiding, successful and – the odd scare about immigration aside – largely unproblematic.' However, a series of factors came together to produce growing concern in the media and elsewhere about British Asians in general and Asian youth in particular.

1 In 1989, the Muslim leaders in Iran issued a fatwa (or death sentence) against the British Asian writer Salman Rushdie for his comments on the Islamic religion in his novel *The Satanic Verses*.
2 The Gulf War of 1990 increased hostility to those of Middle Eastern origin.
3 A number of media reports gave the impression of Asian youth as a problem. For example, in 1993 a *Panorama* documentary entitled *Purdah in the Underclass* expressed concern that there was 'an emergent Muslim ghetto culture'. In 1996 the *London Evening Standard* ran a story about 'Asian Teenage Gangs Terrorising London' (quoted in Alexander, 2000), and other papers, including the *Daily Mail* and the *Independent*, also ran stories about Asian gangs.
4 In 1995 there were riots in Bradford in which Asian youths seemed to be expressing unhappiness at the way their community was being policed. Alexander says that coverage of this gave 'the image of a backward, tradition-bound culture struggling in the face of progressive Western values'.
5 This image of British Asians built upon a long-standing negative portrayal of Asian women as victims of 'patriarchal absolutism', in which they were subservient to men and forced into arranged marriages against their will.

Alexander also notes that the negative coverage began to differentiate between sections of the Asian community. Increasingly, Bangladeshi and Pakistani Muslims were coming to be seen as particularly problematic and particularly backward looking. Alexander argues: 'In Britain concerns over Islamophobia, or alternatively, religious fundamentalism, have concurred in the position of Islam at the centre of political and academic discourse as Public Enemy Number One – Britain's most unwanted, as it were.'

The myth of the Asian gang

As well as examining media portrayal of British Asian youth, Alexander also conducted an ethnographic study of young Asian men while she was working on a youth project in south London in the mid-1990s. While working on the project there were a number of violent incidents involving clashes between the young Asian men and local black youths. These incidents received considerable coverage in the local press implying that they represented the development of a new and worrying phenomenon, the Asian gang, which was in conflict with local black gangs. However, Alexander argues that the Asian 'gang' was essentially a myth.

1 There were only a 'relatively few encounters' and they were 'transformed by a dual discourse, closely intertwined, of "gangs" and of "race", which served to obscure the more mundane – perhaps even banal – explanations'. The main protagonist was an African boy from Nigeria called Hansel. The trouble started when Hansel and one of his friends tripped up two of the Asian boys, Malik and Hanif. Hanif was later attacked by Hansel and some friends and was on the receiving end of a black eye and head injuries. In another incident a group of black boys had a fight with some Asians at their school and a number of 'minor scuffles' followed.
2 It was true that these clashes were largely between black youths and a group of Asians, all but one of whom was of Bengali (Bangladeshi) origin. However, the Asian group was loose-knit and they did not see themselves as constituting a gang. Rather, they were simply a group of friends, a peer group which evoked some sense of loyalty and shared identity. They were not intent upon developing a reputation for violence or toughness. However, they would come to the defence of other members of the peer group if they felt they were being attacked.
3 The clashes were not based on straightforward conflict between 'races'. They were specific to the particular people who were directly involved. For example, on one occasion a group of Asians went looking for Hansel shortly after he had attacked one of their number. They surrounded a young black man known to be a friend of Hansel's, but rather than attacking him they simply questioned him about Hansel's whereabouts and apologized to him once they realized he had not been involved in the previous violence. Although peer groups did tend to follow ethnic lines, this was not always the case and notions of community sometimes meant that the youths identified with other local youths who were from different ethnic groups.

Alexander found that there was, in reality, no Asian gang. The conflict was not specifically based on 'race'; it was based around local and personal relationships. She comments:

> *The spectre of 'race' must then be viewed and understood through a more local and personal lens, which fragments any more universal perception of difference reified and naturalized in notions of 'the Gang'. Central to the conflict was a more specific, time-bound and localized notion of personal and collective positionality.* Alexander, 2000

Conclusion

Alexander's study embraces both the study of racism and the study of ethnicity. From the study of racism she develops the idea that the boys were the victims of misrepresentation in the media, which portrayed them as belonging to a gang. This in turn was part of a wider discourse which held that Asian youths were abandoning the relative passivity of their parents and posing a new threat to law and order.

From the study of ethnicity Alexander develops an understanding of the peer groups and wider communities to which the boys belonged. However, she does not follow other studies of ethnicity in seeing the Bangladeshi community in the area she studied as forming a completely distinct ethnic subculture. She emphasizes the overlap between the Asian boys she studied and other ethnic groups, and the fragmentation and diversity within the group. She describes her own views as being close to the views of those who have developed theories of new ethnicity and hybridity (see pp. 194–8), but she is not entirely happy with their approach either.

The boys had a sense of identity in which they saw themselves as Muslim or Bengali rather than as British Asians. Alexander therefore argues that the boys were not so much mixing elements from different ethnic subcultures as creatively developing their own peer groups and subcultures within a society in which they were disadvantaged, marginalized and subject to a new form of racism: a type of Islamophobia which portrayed them as a violent, criminal threat. The development of these peer groups was strongly linked with family and local attachments.

Alexander warns against drawing any wider conclusions about Asians in Britain from a local study. (For a discussion of the issue of multiculturalism and Asians in Britain see pp. 208–9. For a discussion of studies of ethnicity and British Asians see pp. 161–4.)

Islam and Islamophobia in Britain since 9/11

Since the Runnymede Trust's report, further developments in Britain and internationally have led to more discussion about the nature of Islam and the extent of Islamophobia. These include the 9/11 attacks, the 7/7 attacks (on the London underground), the invasions of Afghanistan and Iraq (as part of the 'War on Terror'), and the alleged Islamic terrorist plot to blow up airliners travelling from Britain to the USA in 2006.

In *Muslim Britain: Communities Under Pressure* (Abbas, 2005) a number of writers explored the impact of some of these events on the nature and extent of Islamophobia, on Muslim communities, and on the relationship between Muslims and non-Muslims in Britain. To some extent they support the findings of the Runnymede Trust report, and, if anything, they suggest that there has been an intensification of the conflicts surrounding these issues.

Ceri Peach – the British Muslim community

Ceri Peach (2005) sets the scene for the discussion by providing details of the British Muslim community. Using data from the 2001 census Peach found that there were 1,591,000 Muslims in Britain (up from about 1 million in 1981). Of these 68 per cent were of South Asian origin, with 42 per cent of Pakistani origin. There were also 96,000 black African Muslims (most of them from Nigeria and Somalia), 93,000 Muslims from the Middle East, 36,000 North African Muslims, and 60,000 from Eastern Europe (mainly Bosnia and Kosovo).

Peach observes that compared to other religious groups in Britain the Muslim population is 'largely young and rural in origin. It is poor, badly housed and poorly educated, suffers high levels of male unemployment and has a very low female participation rate in the labour market' (2005, p. 23). The low number of women in paid employment means that there are few dual-income households, resulting in large numbers of households with a low income. Compared to other groups, the Muslim population is 'a very religious population and holds strong family values'. It is largely concentrated in Greater London, the West Midlands, Greater Manchester and West Yorkshire.

Tahir Abbas and Chris Allen – the intensification of Islamophobia

Tahir Abbas (2005) examines the impact of 9/11 and its aftermath on British Muslims, particularly those from South Asia. Abbas believes that these events have led to an intensification of Islamophobia, which he defines as, 'the fear or dread of Islam or Muslim'. Partly this is due to the media which give extensive coverage to 'extremist groups' and 'Islamic terrorism'. However, Abbas also detects evidence of increasing Islamophobia in British politics.

The idea of 'community cohesion' was prominent in the Cantle Report into the riots in northern towns and cities in 2001. To Abbas, this is a thinly disguised attack on Muslims for preserving strong religious beliefs and ethnic identity. Abbas criticizes the then Home Secretary David Blunkett for a speech in which he demanded allegiance tests and attacked 'the excess of cultural diversity and moral relativism'. This represented an attack on previous multicultural policies which had encouraged acceptance of the idea of Muslims retaining a separate identity.

Some public policies have continued to adopt a multicultural approach (for example, wider availability of halal food), but Abbas thinks state policies towards Islam 'have been at best inconsistent, at worst patchy'. He points out that South Asians continue to suffer more problems of poor housing, unemployment and poor health than other groups in the population. Furthermore, following 9/11 there has been an increase in violent attacks on Muslims and increased support for far right groups who are hostile to Muslims.

Abbas argues that there is a danger of an upward spiral of hostility between Western societies and their Muslim minorities. Incidents such as the Madrid train bombings in 2004 and the holding of British Muslims without trial by the USA in Guantanamo Bay can lead to 'further unrest, political turmoil, and violent action and reaction'.

Although Abbas is concerned about future developments, he does think that the problems are resolvable. He believes that multiculturalism which fully respects ethnic and religious diversity can work, especially if combined with attempts to reduce poverty and inequality.

Chris Allen (2005) agrees with Abbas that the problem of Islamophobia has increased since 9/11. He argues that Muslims are increasingly seen as 'monstrous others' who are either 'terrorist warriors against the West or apologists defending Islam as a peaceful religion'. Muslims tend to be seen as the 'enemy within', and since the report by the Runnymede Trust in 1997 the negative perceptions of Muslims have become more widely and more firmly established.

Allen suggests that not enough was done as a result of the Runnymede Trust report to challenge Islamophobia. The Anti-Terrorism, Crime and Security Bill (2001) did outlaw religiously motivated harassment, violence and criminal damage, but failed to protect Muslims from other types of discrimination. The shift in discrimination from 'race' to religion has caught out politicians, and groups such as the BNP (British National Party) have taken advantage of the situation. For example, a BNP leaflet entitled *The Truth about Islam* suggested that the word ISLAM stood for 'Intolerance, Slaughter, Looting, Arson and Molestation'.

Attacks on Islam are not just confined to groups like the BNP but can also be found in the media. Even in the *Guardian*, traditionally a very anti-racist paper, Polly Toynbee declared herself to be 'an Islamophobe and proud' (quoted in Allen, 2005, p. 61). She justified this statement by quoting carefully selected passages from the Qur'an which appeared to condone violence.

Like Abbas, Allen notes that politicians have also joined in attacking Muslims. Allen is rather less optimistic about the future than Abbas. He thinks that existing Islamophobia has been exacerbated by 9/11 and other events. He concludes that 'The situation, therefore, is complex. A dangerous cocktail has been mixed on the basis of a pre-existing phenomenon now shaken with the hyperbolic exaggerations emerging from the fog of 9/11.'

Humayan Ansari – British Muslim attitudes to jihad, martyrdom and terrorism

Allen and Abbas examined the development of Islamophobia in response to 9/11 and the 'War on Terror'. Humayan Ansari (2005), another contributor to *Muslim Britain: Communities Under Pressure*, examined how British Muslim attitudes corresponded to Islamophobic stereotypes.

Ansari conducted questionnaire research with a sample of Muslim South Asians. The sample was evenly split between males and females; 80 per cent were aged 16–44; and most were religiously devout – 80 per cent fasted during Ramadan and 69 per cent said religion was 'very important' to them. Ansari asked the respondents about their attitudes to *jihad*, martyrdom and terrorism.

Islamophobic portrayals of Muslims tend to suggest that all British Muslims support or at last sympathize with the idea of *jihad* as a holy war against the West, and they see martyrdom and terrorism as legitimate ways of attacking the West. Ansari found that, in reality, there was a wide range of views in the Muslim community. For example, there was not even any consensus about how the word *jihad* should be understood.

Ansari points out that there have been many different interpretations of *jihad* over the centuries but it is generally seen as meaning something like 'the use of one's utmost power, efforts, endeavours, or ability in contending with an object of disapprobation' or 'striving towards a worthy goal'. It thus has a much wider meaning than the idea of holy war against non-Muslims which is often attributed to it by people who are not Islamic.

Within Islam, some scholars emphasize a peaceful meaning for *jihad*, which comes from the term *al-jihad al-akbar* which means 'higher *jihad* or the struggle against one's own desires and temptations' (Ansari, 2005, p. 147). Other scholars, however, emphasize another meaning for *jihad*, *al-jihad al-asghar*, which means 'lesser *jihad* or armed fighting in the path of Islam' (p. 147). The latter meaning tends to be used by militant Islamists, and Abbas found that most of his respondents saw *jihad* as a war against those who threaten Islam. Others, however, saw it as a general struggle against oppression, and a minority saw it more as an inner struggle for peace, truth and faith. A significant number of respondents therefore saw *jihad* quite differently from the way it is portrayed by Islamophobes.

Martyrdom and suicide in Islamic belief are also much more complex than they are portrayed to be in most non-Islamic sources. According to Ansari, Islam does allow an individual to fight against the foes of Islam knowing it will result in their death, but it does not permit suicide. Suicide bombers may therefore be condemned on the grounds that they are committing suicide, or condoned on the grounds that they are sacrificing themselves for their religion.

In the sample studied, 47 per cent said violence could never be justified against non-Muslims, and just 26 per cent said that it could be justified. Individual responses varied considerably and there was no consensus. Abbas comments that 'these findings reveal that views regarding suicide and martyrdom are complex and variable, and very much depend on factors such as the context and the target of attack'. Thus, some thought that violence was justified in the case of Palestinians who they felt were oppressed by Israel, but not in other cases where Muslims were not suffering obvious oppression. However, most respondents were strongly opposed to terrorism, which they associated with the killing of innocent people. Furthermore, the 'overwhelming view … was that the events of September 11 were terrorist acts and wrong'. Some of the Muslims questioned did think that 9/11 could be explained in terms of American foreign policy, but that it could not be justified.

Ansari's research suggests that most British Muslims do not hold the sorts of views attributed to them in Islamophobic accounts. Their views were complex, and although there was sympathy with the suffering of Muslims elsewhere in the world, and some sympathy with the views of radical Muslims, there was less sympathy for their actions. Most of the Muslims questioned held moderate views, but they did feel there had been increased hostility towards them since 9/11.

Ron Geaves – British citizenship and Muslim identity

Tahir Abbas and Chris Allen emphasize the increasingly strong divisions between Muslims and non-Muslims in Britain. Humayan Ansari found that Islamophobic views which help to create the divisions exaggerate and oversimplify the beliefs of Muslims in Britain. Ron Geaves (2005), however, argues that in some ways parts of the Muslim and the non-Muslim communities have moved closer together. He therefore paints a much more positive picture of the situation for Muslims in Britain than the writers discussed above.

First-generation Muslims who came to Britain as migrants from South Asia tended to look inwards to the local Muslim community, and did little to develop wider contacts. Consequently, British Muslims had little sense of being British citizens. However, time and events have begun to change the situation so that British Muslims have a broader outlook. One of the first events to contribute to this was the Salman Rushdie affair.

There were protests from Muslims around the world about Rushdie's portrayal of the prophet Mohammed in *The Satanic Verses*. This linked global Islam with local politics as Islamic groups demonstrated to have *The Satanic Verses* removed from bookshops and libraries. It involved British Muslims in campaigns to widen the blasphemy laws. In the process they began to engage with national politics. Young Muslims, in particular, became more involved in political processes. Partly because of this, new organizations developed, such as the Muslim Association of Britain (MAB) and the Muslim Society of Britain (MSB). These organizations have moved beyond traditional Muslim political concerns and developed an interest in campaigns for social justice and equal rights. Since 9/11 groups such as this have faced new challenges. Geaves comments:

> *a new language of integration and cohesion was voiced by national politicians demanding controls on imported imams, intercontinental marriages and far more rigid controls on political and economic migrants. While their elders continued with the management of the mosques and the maintenance of traditional religious and cultural domains, young British Muslims were once again confronted with the question of what it means to be Muslim and British.* Geaves, 2005, p. 71

This question was given further importance by the second Gulf War when Britain and the USA invaded Iraq. Most British Muslims were opposed to the invasion, but they were not alone since there was also widespread opposition from white British people. Muslim opposition was mainly organized by the Muslim Association of Britain which joined the wider Stop the War group. For the first time in British political history, a strong Muslim-based protest movement joined forces with protestors from non-Muslim backgrounds. To Geaves, this is important because such alliances 'challenge essentialist thinking regarding ethnicity by exemplifying the creation of hybrid or flexible identities' (2005, p. 74) (see pp. 194–8 for a discussion of hybrid identities).

Geaves believes that such hybrid identities are increasingly in evidence among young British Muslims who are developing new ways to combine their religious beliefs with a sense of British citizenship. This belief was supported by an interview which Geaves conducted with a group of female Muslim university students. The young women felt that British citizenship was important because of the acceptance of religious diversity and because it gave them the democratic right to oppose government policies. They saw no contradiction between being able to express their ethnic and religious identity and taking a full part in democratic political life in Britain.

These Muslims have 'come out' of the closet of narrowly Islamic community politics and found a place on the wider political stage. Geaves is therefore very optimistic that there has been a 'qualitative transformation in identity politics and the formation of a moderate Muslim identity which creatively interacts with British citizenship as a result of the aftermath of 9/11 and the conflicts generated by British and US foreign policy' (2005, p. 76). This identity is 'more fruitful than the anti-West rhetoric of the "Islamists"', and it shows that British Muslims are not anti-democratic as many Islamophobic views suggest.

Evaluation

The complex problem of the relationship between Islam and the non-Islamic world is a crucial issue in many parts of the world and is much wider than the issue of relations between Muslims and non-Muslims in Britain. However, the British examples suggest both that there are increased levels of conflict and that there is increasing engagement between the two groups. Thus, the various events in Britain and abroad that have brought this relationship to the fore have provided opportunities for new identities and alliances to develop, as well as creating conditions where more conflict is created. (For more discussion of Islamic identity and the relationship between Islam and the West see pp. 449–50.)

Nationalism and identity

Nationalism

The importance of nationalism

Stuart Hall (1992) pointed out that both of 'the great discourses of modernity', liberalism and Marxism, led people 'to expect not the revival but the gradual disappearance of the nationalist passion'. In Marxist theory, classes, not nations, would become the great historical actors, while liberalism saw national differences being eroded by a global market in which trade linked all parts of the world.

A number of contemporary sociologists also claim that a process of **globalization** has been taking place. In this process national boundaries become less significant in social life. Communication systems such as satellite TV transcend such boundaries. The world's financial markets are linked by technology so that movements in share prices in one country can instantaneously affect prices on the other side of the world. International organizations such as the UN and the EU also reduce the importance of nations, while travel gives individuals a less localized view of the world (see pp. 548–57).

However, many people have argued that there has been a great resurgence of **nationalism** in recent decades. Individuals usually seem to identify more with their nation than with any other grouping. Nationalism could be seen as being present in the 'new racism' described by Gilroy in the preceding section (see pp. 179–81), and in demands for independence by the Scottish and Welsh in Britain, the Basques in Spain and the Bretons in France. Nationalism was important in the collapse of the USSR, with demands for independence for Lithuania, Estonia, Ukraine and elsewhere contributing to the break-up of the country. In the former Yugoslavia, violent civil war raged as Croatians, Serbs and Muslims fought for territory in future independent states.

Benedict Anderson (1983) claims that 'since World War II every successful revolution has defined itself in nationalist terms': 'The "end of the era of nationalism" so long prophesied is not remotely in sight. Indeed, nation-ness is the most universally legitimate value in the political life of our time.' Whether or not Anderson is right to attach so much importance to nationalism, it has certainly been neglected in much social theory and it is clearly an important feature of social life and one which shows little sign of becoming less important.

The definition of nationalism

Anderson argues that a **nation** is 'an imagined political community – and imagined as both inherently limited and sovereign':

1. It is **imagined** because most members of even a small nation never meet one another or hear one another, yet they feel they all belong to one community. Whatever inequalities divide members of a nation it is 'always conceived as a deep, horizontal comradeship'.
2. It is **limited** in the sense that nations include some people who are regarded as belonging, while excluding others as outsiders. No nation claims to include the whole of humanity.
3. It is **sovereign** because nationalism seeks or celebrates independence and self-government for a group of people.

Anderson claims that racism and nationalism are quite different concepts:

1. **Racism** is based on 'dreams of eternal contamination'. It sees groups of people as having fixed, biological characteristics. For example, Jews, 'the seed of Abraham', are 'forever Jews no matter what passport they carry or what languages they speak and read'.
2. **Nationalism**, on the other hand, does not see individuals as inevitably belonging to a particular group of people. It is possible to become a member of a nation, while it is not possible to become part of a 'race' to which the individual did not originally belong.

Anderson's view that racism and nationalism are quite different has not been accepted by most sociologists. Robert Miles (1989) argues that 'ideologies of racism and nationalism have a common historical origin'. Racism was originally used to justify the exploitation of non-Europeans in various parts of the world. With the end of colonialism, the kind of racism which saw distinct biological groupings in humanity was to some extent replaced by nationalism, in which individuals see their nation as superior to other nations. To Miles, racism and nationalism are similar because 'both claim the existence of a natural division of the world's population into discrete groups which exist independently of class relations'. Both are used by people to justify beliefs that particular groups are superior to other groups.

However, Miles does acknowledge one important difference between nationalism and racism. He says: 'the ideology of nationalism, unlike that of racism, specifies a particular political objective (national self-determination) and therefore a blueprint for political organization on a world scale'. Thus, although Miles disagrees with Anderson about the relationship between nationalism and racism, he agrees that nationalism is based upon a belief that a group of people should have a sovereign state.

Thomas Hylland Eriksen (2002) examines the relationship between ethnicity and nationalism. To Eriksen, 'Nationalism and ethnicity are kindred concepts.' Both are based upon the belief that a group of people is distinctive and has a shared culture. However, nationalism and ethnicity are different and the difference he identifies has a similar basis to the definitions of nationalism put forward by Anderson and Miles.

Eriksen argues that a nationalist ideology 'is an ethnic ideology which demands a state on behalf of the ethnic group'. Eriksen admits that this simple definition poses certain problems when considering some examples of nationalism and ethnicity. Nationalism is sometimes used to try to unite diverse ethnic groups and it therefore 'stresses shared civil rights rather than shared cultural roots'. In Mauritius, for example, Mauritian nationalism is used to try to overcome the divisions between Hindus, Muslims, Chinese, French and Africans.

Another problem is that there are some marginal cases which could be seen as examples of nationalism *or* ethnicity. These may occur when some members of a group want full independence, while others want greater independence within an existing state. Scottish and Basque nationalism are both examples. Although there is general agreement that nationalism is related to sovereignty, precise definitions vary and there is no agreement about the exact relationship between nationalism, 'race' and ethnicity.

David McCrone – *The Sociology of Nationalism*

In *The Sociology of Nationalism* (1998) David McCrone conducts a comprehensive review of sociological theories of nationalism. He finds that no one theory can account for the diverse forms that nationalism takes, but that a number of theories can contribute to an understanding of this phenomenon.

Civic and ethnic nationalism, state and nation

McCrone starts his analysis by distinguishing between **civic nationalism** and **ethnic nationalism**. In civic nationalism, nationalist sentiments are tied to belonging to a particular state. Thus in the USA many different ethnic groups share, to some degree, a sense of loyalty to the nation. It is their common citizenship that unites them rather than a common ethnic background. In other situations nationalism focuses more on ethnicity than on citizenship. For example, for Serbs and Croats in the former Yugoslavia, what unites these groups of people is a belief in a common ethnic origin.

However, McCrone admits that such a distinction can be criticized. Even in countries in which a civic concept of nationalism is dominant, ethnic groups sharing a common civic nationality may be hostile to one another. McCrone asks: 'How is one to make sense of endemic racism against the "Other" in Western societies which profess overwhelmingly civic definitions of citizens?' An example would be racism directed against British African Caribbeans and Asians by white British people. Ethnic pluralism can sometimes be at odds with civic nationalism.

McCrone also distinguishes between the nation and the state. Often they are seen as one and the same thing, as in the term nation-state, but this is not always the case. The state is essentially a political and administrative unit, but people may feel a sense of national identity which does not coincide with political boundaries. There are examples in Western societies of what McCrone calls 'stateless nations', where groups in particular regions seek greater autonomy or independent states. These include Scotland in the United Kingdom, Catalunya in Spain, and Quebec in Canada. Stateless nations need not necessarily have a strong ethnic identity. McCrone says, 'Scottishness is based upon living in a common territory' and not upon a shared culture.

To McCrone, the relationships between state and nation, territory and ethnicity, are complex; consequently, there can be no single theory of nationalism. In order to make sense of this complexity McCrone broadly distinguishes four types of nationalism. Each of these will now be discussed.

Nationalism and the development of the modern nation-state

This type of nationalism is related to the development of the nation-state in Western society. Examples of such states include the United Kingdom, France and the USA. This type of nation-state is generally seen as a product of modernity. The nation-state began to emerge with the decline of dominant religious thinking and a greater acceptance of secular authority. It is therefore often linked with the Enlightenment (see pp. 890–1).

The emergence of the nation-state was also connected with the break-up of empires, particularly the Austrian, Ottoman and Russian empires. The territorial boundaries of nations came to demarcate the most important political units and, with these political divisions, nationalist sentiments became more important.

However, different writers have provided a variety of explanations for the development of the Western nation-state. Some have seen its development as related to the growth of industrialism, others to the growth of capitalism. Some have argued that political leaders were important in promoting nationalist sentiment and creating the idea of a nation out of very little. On the other hand, some sociologists believe that existing ethnic divisions were important in providing a starting point for the development of nation-states.

McCrone argues that all these factors played some role. He accepts that economic changes played an important part, but is critical of those approaches that deny there were any ethnic or cultural factors involved. He believes that, where they existed, cultural and ethnic differences had to be highlighted by those who were trying to create nation-states. Ethnicity on its own was never enough to create a modern nation-state, but it could help. What was crucial was that ethnic nationalism, where it was important, was converted into a more civic form. McCrone says of nationalism: 'The more implicit and embedded it is, the more powerful it can be. That is why what is called "civic" nationalism is a much more powerful mobilizer in the long term than its "ethnic" variant' (McCrone, 1998).

Colonialism and nationalism

The second type of nationalism discussed by McCrone developed in **colonies** and **postcolonial** societies. Very often those opposed to colonial rule would appeal to a national identity in trying to mobilize opposition to colonial powers such as Britain and France. Anti-colonial movements often advocated and achieved secular states. However, with the economic failure of some of these states, nationalism in some postcolonial societies has become more associated with ethnicity and religion.

People in many postcolonial societies have ambiguous identities, with nationality, religion and ethnicity all making claims on their loyalty. For example, in postcolonial Egypt people could think of themselves as Arab, Islamic or Egyptian. Different identities were in competition for people's allegiance. In countries like India and Algeria the nationalist movements which achieved independence made little appeal to religion or ethnicity. However, when they failed to deliver the 'economic, social and cultural liberation' that they promised, then secular liberation was 'outflanked by counter-risings which mobilized culture and religion'. A clear example is the overthrow of the secular Shah of Iran by the Islamic regime of Ayatollah Khomeini in 1979.

McCrone believes that a key component of postcolonial nationalism is what he calls 'the dialectic with the other'. Nationalists define their nation in terms of difference from somebody else, in this case the colonial power. The dialectical relationship between colonialism and postcolonialism can help explain the changing nature of nationalism. Although nationalism emerged in opposition to colonialism, it often took the form of a kind of mirror image. While opposing colonialism and asserting the difference between the colony and the colonial power, it often took on the type of state structure and the ideology of the nation-state that had been introduced by the colonizer. Postcolonial states such as India adopted the 'secularism, science and democracy' that were associated with colonialism. But other non-secular and non-scientific kinds of nationalism did not die out altogether. These have revived as the secular state – founded as a mirror image of colonialism – has failed to fulfil its promise.

Neo-nationalism

McCrone uses the term **neo-nationalism** to refer to nationalist independence movements in Western stateless societies such as the Basque country, Scotland and Quebec. He argues that this type of nationalism is hard to explain in terms of conventional theories. Most theories of Western nation-states assumed that the nineteenth century saw the successful establishment of distinct nations and that regional differences within nation-states would tend to disappear as time progressed.

Using the examples of Quebec, Catalunya and Scotland, McCrone argues that neo-nationalism develops when a set of circumstances coincide. It usually develops in areas with a strong **civil society**. (Civil society can be defined as the public life of a society as compared to the activities of the state and private life within households.) The key features of civil society are the economy and the family/domestic sphere. Neo-nationalism tends to develop in regions with strong economies rather than weak ones. It was noticeable that Scottish nationalism was given a boost by the discovery of North Sea oil. Neo-nationalism also tends to develop in areas where people have multiple national identities. Scots sometimes identify themselves as British, Catalans as Spanish, and so on. McCrone comments: 'This plurality is a political resource which can be played in appropriate circumstances rather than a fixed characteristic.'

Neo-nationalism is normally based on relatively new political parties. There is usually no exact correspondence between support for such parties (for example, the Scottish National Party (SNP)) and independence. Some people who vote for such parties may not actually seek independence, but may see the party as a way of gaining greater autonomy short of independence. This illustrates the ambiguity that is often present in such movements.

Finally, neo-nationalism tends to occur in nation-states which are part of larger supranational organizations, such as the European Union or the North American Free Trade Association (NAFTA) (of which Canada is a member). Such organizations suggest that it is difficult to have a truly independent economy. If the British economy is closely integrated with the European economy, there seems less for Scotland to lose by becoming independent from the rest of Britain. An independent Scotland within the EU appears to be a less risky proposition than a Scotland which simply goes it alone. Thus the closer links between societies involved in globalization actually create the space in which regional identities and independence movements can develop.

McCrone believes that neo-nationalism is largely civic rather than ethnic in nature. He denies that you can see neo-nationalism 'as a throwback to atavistic or ethnic forms of nationalism', or reduced 'to mere forms of pressure group politics'. Instead, neo-nationalism must be seen as a 'multifaceted and adaptable ideology' which links issues of identity to issues of economic and cultural power.

Post-communist nationalism

The collapse of communism in the USSR and Eastern Europe led to major changes. Some states disappeared (for example, Yugoslavia and Czechoslovakia). Czechoslovakia was divided into the Czech Republic and Slovakia; East and West Germany were fused together; countries such as Poland, Latvia, Lithuania and Estonia regained their independence; and new states such as Ukraine, Georgia and various central Asian republics emerged out of what had been the Soviet Union.

McCrone argues that there was a great deal of dissatisfaction with the communist regimes and nationalism became the focus of opposition to communism. A number of explanations have been suggested for why nationalism should be the focus. One of the most common is what McCrone calls the **deep freeze theory**. This suggests that deep-seated, historic ethnic divisions were held in check by totalitarian communist regimes. When communism thawed out and opposition became possible, traditional rivalries between ethnic groups reappeared. An alternative theory suggests that politicians simply encouraged nationalist sentiment in order to secure popular support for their own leadership. For example, Slobodan Milosevic used the appeal of Serbian nationalism to increase his personal support.

McCrone does not deny that both these theories have some merit, but he believes that both are too simplistic. Instead, he turns to the work of Roger Brubaker (1996) and argues that it provides the most satisfactory way of understanding post-communist nationalism. Brubaker distinguishes three types of post-communist nationalism:

1. The **nationalizing state** is the form of nationalism in which a state, often a new one, tries to persuade its citizens to share a common identity. In Western Europe nationalizing states have been fairly successful in achieving a common identity based on citizenship, but not in Eastern Europe.
2. **National minorities** are groups who have a primary allegiance to another, often neighbouring, state. For example, there are significant groups of ethnic Hungarians in Romania and vice versa. National minorities are not so significant in Western Europe.
3. **National homelands** are the territories with which people who claim particular nationalistic ethnicities identify. Thus Romania is the national homeland for ethnic Romanians in Hungary.

Since there is rarely a perfect fit between nationalizing states, national minorities and national homelands in the former communist countries, there is a lot of potential for nationalistic conflict and for politicians to emphasize or exploit national identities. This is particularly true of territories that used to be part of the Soviet Union. The Soviet Union officially classified people as belonging to different national minorities and so heightened a sense of national identity.

Having discussed Brubaker's analysis of nationalism, McCrone goes on to apply elements of it to a discussion of Yugoslavia. McCrone suggests that Yugoslavia failed to become established as a nationalizing state because too few people saw themselves as Yugoslavian. Members of the Communist Party, some of the young people, and those from mixed parentage saw themselves as Yugoslavian, but most people did not. Furthermore, different areas of Yugoslavia corresponded reasonably closely with the national ethnic groups, Serbs and Croats. There was therefore a strong basis for establishing ethnic homelands with independent states.

The problem with Bosnia was that it had no dominant national ethnic group. The biggest group in the population (about 44 per cent) were Muslims, descendants of people who had converted to Islam when the area was part of the Ottoman Empire. Only a minority of ethnic Muslims actually practised Islam, but they had no ethnic allegiance to a Serbian or Croatian homeland.

Bosnia-Herzegovina was a largely secular and pluralistic region with no ethnic basis for a nationalizing state. There was no strong sense of Bosnian citizenship. As McCrone says, this put the people of Bosnia-Herzegovina at a 'severe disadvantage when faced with enemies who aligned ethnicity, religion and citizenship in a much more potent and threatening way'. The consequence was a bloody civil war in which the people of Bosnia, especially the Muslims, were caught between the territorial ambitions of Serb and Croat nationalisms.

The future of nationalism

McCrone concludes that many early theorists of nationalism were quite wrong to believe that it would decline in importance. The ideology of nationalism – that people should have a nation-state to which they belong – has never been stronger. Other ideologies, such as socialism, have lost popularity while nationalism has become more popular. Nationalistic conflict remains possible in many parts of the world since only a minority of states are ethnically and culturally homogeneous. There are both stateless nations (where an ethnic group has no state of its own) and nationless states (where a territory is culturally heterogeneous).

In some ways the power and importance of states have been undermined by globalization (see pp. 548–57) and by supranational bodies such as the European Union. However, nationalism has survived and prospered because it is a flexible, adaptable ideology. As societies undergo rapid change and there is more confusion and fluidity over identity (see below for a discussion of identity), nationalism can be an effective ideology for uniting groups of people. McCrone concludes:

> *Nationalist movements can, then, encapsulate cultural defence, the pursuit of political resources from the centre, as well as being vehicles for social identity in rapidly changing societies. It will not be possible to reduce any nationalism automatically to any one of these, but the rapidly increasing rate of social change makes it more rather than less likely as a potent vehicle of social protest.*
> McCrone, 1998

Robin Cohen – British nationality and identity

Compared to countries in Eastern Europe and some other parts of the world, Britain is a long-established state. Nevertheless Robin Cohen (1994) believes that what it means to be British is not clear-cut. He argues that there are a number of ways in which a British identity is ambiguous or unclear. His arguments illustrate how even in Western Europe the relationship between nationality and identity is far from straightforward.

Cohen discusses what he calls the **fuzzy boundaries** of being British. The idea of fuzzy boundaries originates from the idea of fuzzy logic in mathematics. This is a method in which you proceed by trying to eliminate the uncertain edges of a problem to focus better on the problem itself. Similarly, Cohen believes, you can get to the core of what it means to be British by looking at the frontiers that divide Britons from others. These frontiers can be internal, such as the frontier between being British and being English, or external, such as the frontier between Britons and 'aliens'. Cohen identifies six frontiers:

1. **The Celtic fringe.** This includes the Irish, Welsh and Scots. Despite the Act of Union between England and Scotland in 1707, Cohen believes 'the Scots have always been regarded with an element of fear and not a little incomprehension by the English'. He believes that oil revenues have provided an important impetus towards independence in Scotland. The Welsh have a rather less strong sense of independent identity than the Scots. They would find it more difficult to prosper with economic independence and have less history as an independent nation. Nevertheless the Welsh language and events such as the National Eisteddfod provide some basis for a separate Welsh identity. Irish national consciousness is both much stronger and more problematic for England. Despite the strong Irish identity there are overlaps between being Irish and being English. Northern Ireland Unionists identify much more closely with England than with Eire. Eire citizens can travel freely to the United Kingdom and vote in British elections. For the English the Celtic fringe is 'a familiar but inexplicit internal boundary'.
2. **The dominions.** A number of aspects of English and British identity are linked to the history of colonization. Large numbers of white British people settled in dominions such as Canada, New Zealand, Australia, South Africa and Rhodesia. All of these countries have achieved independence and, at least at some point in their history, have been ruled by the white settlers from Britain. Cohen believes that in all these countries a British identity became dominant. Many citizens of the countries managed to retain British passports, and their legal and education systems have usually retained close links with the corresponding British systems. White citizens of these countries are sometimes regarded as the 'kith and kin' of white British citizens. However, as Cohen points out, the association of British with white has become increasingly problematic. Although British immigration law and citizenship rules were influenced by a racist desire to maintain a white British identity (see pp. 149–50), they have not succeeded in maintaining what Cohen calls 'the myth of a racially exclusive British identity'. Even for racists, it is increasingly difficult to portray British identity in exclusively white terms. Despite independence, and the demise of an exclusively white British identity, some white communities in former colonies try to cling on to a British, and often a specifically English, identity.
3. **Empire and Commonwealth.** Cohen believes that the British Empire was about more than military conquest and political domination of other countries. It was also concerned with an attempt 'to establish a cultural and national superiority of worldwide proportions: an empire where, truly, the sun never set'. Despite independence, many former colonies have a legacy of colonization. Some of their institutions still follow the model established by the colonial power.

The Indian civil service is one example. Furthermore, the Commonwealth maintains institutional links between former colonies and the 'motherland'. Such connections have led to some former colonies, for example in the West Indies, retaining an element of British identity. Cohen argues, though, that British political leaders, particularly Margaret Thatcher, have attached little importance to the Commonwealth. On the other hand, it continues to remain an important institution in relation to the monarchy.

4 **The Atlantic connection.** If Margaret Thatcher was unenthusiastic about the Commonwealth, she put much more emphasis on the so-called 'special relationship' between Britain and the USA. There are, of course, historical connections between Britain and the USA. Not only was America a British colony, but there are also large numbers of Americans descended from British emigrants. Although the USA is very culturally diverse, WASP (White Anglo-Saxon Protestant) culture remains the most influential of its cultures. Furthermore, English remains the dominant language in the USA. Cohen therefore concludes that 'a cousinhood between the British and many Americans remains: a fuzzy frontier somewhere between a self-hood and an other-hood'.

5 **Britain and Europe.** Britain does not have the same linguistic links with Europe as it has with the USA. However, through the European Union, Britain's political ties with Europe are closer than those with the USA. While older British people tend to be resistant to the idea of closer European integration, this is not the case with the young. Cohen claims:

> *The slow drip-feed of European integration is influencing the younger generation – who increasingly study, work, travel and holiday on the Continent and who forget their kith and kin abroad, deride the British Empire and neglect the idealistic notion of a multiracial Commonwealth.* Cohen, 1994

There is therefore a movement towards a more European identity for some young Britons.

6 **Aliens.** The frontier between the British and 'aliens' is less fuzzy than other frontiers. The maintenance of a British identity essentially rests upon defining some groups as 'others', people who do not belong, who have no claims to be British. Defining the alien involves 'a distinction between the self (the acceptable, the insider), and who the other (the stranger, the outsider, the alien) is'. As the fuzzy boundaries show, though, this distinction is not clear-cut and can change over time.

Evaluation

Cohen's work illustrates the ambiguity, complexity and changing nature of one national identity – British identity. Colonialism and decolonization, migration, travel and political change have affected nearly all parts of the globe. It seems likely that the boundaries of national identity are fuzzy in many other countries apart from Britain. Nationalism is sometimes used as an ideology to try to remove some of the fuzziness. Issues of identity have become increasingly important in contemporary sociology and in the study of 'race', ethnicity and nationality in particular. The next section considers the development of British identities in an era of globalization.

Andrew Pilkington – nationalism and identity in a global age

British national identity

Andrew Pilkington argues that national identities are socially created. Although many nations claim to have a 'long ancestry', most are in reality quite new creations. Pilkington believes there is nothing **primordial** (see pp. 164–5) in national identities because 'the idea of a nation as community which demands people's loyalty and aspires to exercise control over a particular territory is distinctly modern' (Pilkington, 2002). For most of human history, people have lived in small communities and have generally identified with those communities, kinship groups or perhaps wider religious groupings.

National identities only became important in the eighteenth and nineteenth centuries. It was only then that political and economic changes encouraged the development of a strong national identity and communications were sufficiently developed to convey national identities to large communities. However, according to Pilkington, national identities have become pervasive. Like other writers, he acknowledges that while nations often aim for the creation of a state for a people, states and nations are not the same thing. He points out: 'Some states (including the United Kingdom) are multinational and some people who share a common national identity (for example the Kurds) are scattered in a number of states.'

Turning his attention to Britain, Pilkington argues that there was no British national identity before the Act of Union of England and Scotland in 1707. This development 'necessitated the construction of a British national identity'. This involved the construction of 'Others' who were not British and whose difference helped to define the distinctive features of the British. Particularly important Others were Catholics (British identity was portrayed as a Protestant identity) and the French.

Although British identity was initially confined to the elite, the spread of mass literacy and the development of mass forms of communication resulted in the diffusion of British identity to other sectors of society. To encourage the deployment of British identity, 'a variety of stories, symbols, images and rituals' was developed to provide a sense of shared identity. These included, for example, the pageantry of the British monarchy (even though the monarchs were predominantly of German descent) and stories about British heroes who fought the French and other foreigners and created the British Empire. However, British national identity never overwhelmed other identities – other national identities, particularly Scottish, Welsh and English identities, remained, as did distinctive ethnic identities. Nevertheless British identities were to some extent racialized, with Britain being portrayed as white in the popular media.

Because Pilkington sees national identities as socially constructed, he believes there is always the possibility of them changing. For example, the racialized aspects of British national identity have been challenged in parts of the media. Pilkington quotes a 1997 study (Law, 1997) which found that around three-quarters of media coverage of 'race' issues had an anti-racist message. However, one of the most significant factors affecting British national identity in recent times has been **globalization**.

Globalization and identity

Like many other sociologists (see pp. 548–57), Pilkington believes that globalization is taking place. He sees it as involving the increasing 'interconnectedness of societies' partly as a result of the development of communications and information technology. Globalization produces contradictory results which affect nationalism.

1. It can lead to 'cultural homogenization'. For example, people in most countries in the world now drink Coca-Cola and watch films made in Hollywood.
2. On the other hand, there is an increasing 'fascination with difference' so that 'ethnically distinctive products are also now available around the world'.

Another contradiction is between: **centralization** in political units, such as the European Union, and in business in transnational corporations; and **decentralization**, for example the break-up of the USSR and the demands of some ethnic and national groups for greater political autonomy, or their own states.

These developments have had important effects on British national identity. Some British people feel that British national identity has come under a **dual threat**. The forces of centralization have threatened national identity from *above*, particularly through the growing power of the European Union. On the other hand, forces of decentralization are seen by some as threatening Britain from *below*, through what is seen as a strengthening of the identities of ethnic and national minorities in Britain. One response is a retreat into a very restrictive and defensive 'definition of "Englishness"'.

The people who put forward this response are sometimes called **Little Englanders**. One example was the Conservative MP John Townsend, who was strongly anti-European and who claimed in 1989 that the majority of English people would have preferred, if asked, that Britain should stay 'an English-speaking white country' (quoted in Pilkington, 2002). Pilkington sees Townsend as a 'cultural racist' who regards English 'white' culture as superior to other cultures.

However, the Little Englander reaction to globalization is not the only response. There are also examples of a diametrically opposed approach which, instead of retreating to a narrow and restrictive sense of identity, tries to embrace **multiple identities**. Pilkington quotes the example of Gordon Brown, then Chancellor of the Exchequer, who claimed in an interview that he could see himself as being Scottish, British and European simultaneously. In the interview he also said: 'I see Britain as being the first country in the world that can be a multicultural, multi-ethnic, and multinational state … We have a chance to forge a unique pluralist democracy where diversity becomes a source of strength' (quoted in Pilkington, 2002). Thus Pilkington argues that just as there are contradictory trends within globalization, there are contradictory responses regarding its implications for national identity in Britain.

The differences in response are also evident in minority ethnic groups. A defensive response is found, according to Pilkington, among some groups of British Asians. He says: 'Aware that they are often not accepted as British, some Asians respond by "strengthening local identities" and asserting their essential difference from other ethnic groups.' This was evident in the reaction of some Muslims to the publication of Salman Rushdie's *The Satanic Verses*, which was perceived as attacking Islam.

On the other hand, Pilkington believes that there is considerable evidence of 'new hybrid identities' which mix aspects of different cultures. This is found both in British Caribbean and in British Asian youth. One example is bhangra music, which emerged in the 1980s and 'fused traditional Bengali and Punjabi music with hip-hop and house'.

Pilkington concludes that there are important shifts in the nature of British national identity. In the past, cultural racism, which excluded minority groups from a British identity, was dominant, but this is increasingly being challenged. While some have responded to globalization by reasserting cultural racism or through religious fundamentalism, there are 'regimes of representation' – ways of portraying ethnic groups – 'which challenge the old stereotypes'. There are a number of examples of the challenge to defensive responses to globalization, including 'representing the nation in an ethnically inclusive way and the creation of hyphenated identities such as Black-British and British-Asian'. We now turn our attention to studies which follow Pilkington in arguing that new ethnicities and identities are being formed.

New ethnicities and identities

Pilkington's work on the effects of globalization on British identities has much in common with recent empirical studies examining ethnic identities. Unlike traditional studies of ethnicities, this new approach emphasizes the changing nature of ethnic identities, and with these changes the creation of new ethnicities. The idea of new ethnicities has a good deal in common with some of Paul Gilroy's work (see pp. 179–81), but it tends to put less emphasis on racism and more on issues to do with identity. In this respect it is close to some postmodern theories which will be examined shortly (see pp. 198–204).

Stuart Hall – new ethnicities

Stuart Hall first used the term **new ethnicities** in an article originally published in 1989 (Hall, 1996). He relates the concept to developments in black cultural politics, particularly in Britain. In an earlier phase of black cultural politics, the term 'black' was used to refer to all people of Asian, African Caribbean and African origin. It was used as a 'way of referencing the common experience of racism and marginalization in Britain and came to provide the organizing category of a new politics of resistance'. The experiences and interests shared by these black groups were seen as more significant than the cultural and other differences that divided them. The cultural politics resulting from this process involved challenging the negative representations of black people common in white British culture. Stereotypes of black people could be challenged in the printed media, TV, art, music and so on. To facilitate this challenge black people struggled to gain access to these media, which were dominated by whites.

The new cultural politics

By 1989 Hall believed that a new era in black cultural politics was emerging. Although the old struggles had been far from won and were continuing, new trends were developing alongside the old cultural politics. This change involved the 'end of the innocent notion of the essential black subject'. Hall explains that this involved 'the recognition of the extraordinary diversity of subjective positions, social experiences and cultural identities which compose the category "black"'. In other words, there was an increased awareness of differences between groups. These differences could be religious, class-based, ethnic, age-related, to do with gender and sexuality, and so on.

Hall puts particular emphasis on *class,* **sexuality**, **gender** and **ethnicity**. He argues that the representation of black people is increasingly focused on black people from a particular ethnic group, with a particular sexual preference, from a specific class background and for whom their masculinity or sexuality is significant. The new cultural politics tends to celebrate difference rather than ignore it. Hall uses the example of the film *My Beautiful Laundrette*, in which gender differences, class differences, ethnic differences and differences between gay and heterosexual people in an Asian community are featured strongly.

Films such as *My Beautiful Laundrette* challenge the idea that the major cultural division in society is between true Britons, who are white, and others. By showing the diversity of English people it challenges 'the exclusive and aggressive form of English identity [which] is one of the core characteristics of British racism today'. The new cultural politics of ethnicity shows that everybody speaks from a particular position in terms of their ethnicity and other characteristics. However, they are not confined to *only* speaking from that position. Asian filmmakers, for example, need not just make Asian films for Asian audiences. Their films can explore issues other than those which are confined to ethnicity, and which are of interest to others beyond their own ethnic group.

The idea of new ethnicities therefore suggests that differences within ethnic groups provide the basis for a plurality of ethnic identities. In doing so they weaken the importance of the divisions between black and white, and show that all ethnic groups are internally differentiated. These differences (for example, differences in sexuality) cross-cut ethnicity and make people from different ethnic groups more aware of what they might have in common. At the same time they show the diversity of British people and challenge predominant conceptions of what it means to be British.

Hall also briefly acknowledges that new ethnicities might involve novel forms of 'hybridization' and 'cut and mix'. Elements from different ethnic cultures might be combined to develop novel ethnic identities. This idea of **hybridization** is explored in greater detail in a later article, which also tries to place the emergence of new ethnicities in a global context.

Stuart Hall – 'Our mongrel selves'

Capitalism and nationalism

In his article 'Our mongrel selves' (1992), Hall examines the relationship between capitalism, nationalism, ethnicity and identity. He argues that capitalism has had contradictory effects: it created the nation-state and with it nationalism, but in recent times capitalism has also promoted forces which have undermined national cultures. On the one hand, the global nature of the world has produced **transnational imperatives**. On the other hand, 'globalization seems to have led to a strengthening of "local" allegiances and identities'.

In Western Europe a number of countries have seen the development of movements calling for greater degrees of regional autonomy or complete independence; in Eastern Europe and the former USSR there has been 'a revival of ethnic nationalisms among peoples submerged for decades within the supranationalism of the Soviet sphere of influence'. Political changes such as the collapse of Soviet communism and the process of globalization have weakened nation-states and their attempts to impose a single all-embracing culture on diverse ethnic groups within their boundaries. The ethnic groups have taken advantage of the situation to reassert their distinctive identities.

To Hall, attempts to promote nationalism in the modern world can be very dangerous. Most modern nation-states 'are inextricably multicultural – mixed ethnically, religiously, culturally and linguistically'. When groups within the boundaries of a state assert their rights and celebrate their differences, it can lead to violent conflict. In the former Yugoslavia it led to 'ethnic cleansing' – attempts to make whole areas 'ethnically pure' by killing or driving out members of other ethnic groups. In some states attempts to impose a single national culture on diverse groups have led to the development 'of an openly racist far right'. In France the Front National calls for the 'repatriation' of so-called 'immigrants', as do organizations such as the British National Party. In Germany, Turkish workers have been attacked and killed by right-wing nationalists.

However, Hall does not see nationalism as bad in itself. It has also been used by groups seeking independence from colonial powers which have oppressed them. Nationalism 'isn't necessarily either a reactionary or progressive force'; it can be either.

Identity

According to Hall, the forces outlined above are causing people to have a confused sense of identity: a mixed-up view of who they are. The ethnic and cultural diversity of most countries, different nationalisms and the process of globalization, all contribute to the confusion. Many people have a number of identities simultaneously and may act and think in terms of belonging to a whole variety of groups. Hall says:

Modern people of all sorts and conditions, it seems to me, have had, as a condition of survival, to be members, simultaneously, of several overlapping 'imagined communities'; and the negotiations across and between these complex borderlines are characteristic of modernity itself. Hall, 1992

The novelist Salman Rushdie provides a good example of identity confusion. Born in Asia and brought up a Muslim, he is a British citizen who was condemned to death by Ayatollah Khomeini in Iran for the allegedly anti-Islamic nature of his novel *The Satanic Verses*. Hall quotes Rushdie as arguing that '*The Satanic Verses* celebrates hybridity, impurity, intermingling', and describing how mass migration has led to the creation of 'our mongrel selves'. Rushdie sees himself as representing a diverse mix of national, racial, religious, cultural and political identities.

Hall gives a graphic example of people's multiple identities, illustrating how issues of gender, politics and class can add to the confusion created by racial, ethnic and national differences. In 1991 the American president, George Bush, nominated a black conservative judge, Clarence Thomas, for the Supreme Court. A former colleague of Thomas, Anita Hill, then accused him of sexually harassing and propositioning her. People took different sides in the ensuing arguments according to their sense of identity. Hall says:

Some blacks supported Thomas on racial grounds; others opposed him on sexual grounds. Black women were divided, depending on whether their 'identities' as blacks or as women prevailed. Black men were also divided depending on whether their sexism overrode their liberalism. White men were divided, depending not only on their politics, but also on how they identified themselves with respect to racism and sexism. White conservative women supported Thomas, not only on political grounds, but also because of their opposition to feminism. White feminists, often liberal on race, opposed Thomas on sexual grounds. And because judge Thomas is a member of the judicial elite and Anita Hall, at the time of the alleged incident, was a junior employee, there were issues of social class position at work in these arguments too. Quoted in Pilkington, 1993

Hall concludes that nationalism and ethnic absolutism are major threats to the modern world. With such pluralism in most parts of the world, tolerance of human diversity is essential if humans are to live together in anything approaching harmony. He says: 'The capacity to live with difference is, in my view, the coming question of the twenty-first century.'

In general terms new ethnicities facilitate living with difference by making ethnic absolutism and aggressive nationalism seem redundant. If there is no essential difference between different nationalities and ethnicities, if differences within ethnicities and nationalities are as important as differences between them, if many people have hybrid identities, then hatred and violence between groups become less likely.

Evaluation of Hall

Hall's influential work identifies important cultural changes in contemporary societies. However, aspects of it have been questioned. Solomos and Back (1996) argue that views such as those of Hall do not fully analyse 'the creation of new essentialisms on the basis of religion, ethnicity or race'. Hall fails to explain new ways in which people make absolute distinctions between different groups. These cannot all be attributed to a revival of nationalism brought about by global change. They might actually emerge out of the sorts of processes which create new ethnicities. Far from liberating people from their prejudices, they may encourage people to reassert them.

Bhatt (1994, quoted in Solomos and Back, 1996) believes that intolerant and fundamentalist beliefs sometimes develop in minorities because they feel threatened by the sorts of processes outlined by Hall. They fear that their cultural distinctiveness will disappear as elements of other cultures become incorporated into their own. They may act to defend their own culture in ways that seem threatening and intolerant to people from other cultural traditions.

A further criticism of Hall is that he tends to support his arguments with evidence from the work of particular black filmmakers, artists, etc. Solomos and Back comment that Hall fails to show that 'new ethnicities' are important outside this context. The same, however, cannot be said of those who have conducted the sorts of empirical studies we will now examine.

Tariq Modood – new ethnicities and identities

Interview research

Tariq Modood and colleagues have conducted detailed empirical studies of ethnicity and identity in Britain (Modood *et al.*, 1994; Modood, 1997). In *Changing Ethnic Identities* Modood, Beishon and Virdee report on research involving semi-structured and group interviews with seventy-four British people of Caribbean or South Asian origin. The interviews were conducted in 1993 and examined issues such as family life, religious belief and identity. Modood *et al.* argued that previous research in this area had tended to explain identity either in terms of a cultural affiliation to a particular ethnic group, or in terms of a political reaction to racism. Modood *et al.* believe that both ethnic origin and reactions to racism are important in forming identities, but neither on its own is sufficient to explain the development of identities.

In their study Modood *et al.* found a wide variety of identities among the British. There were considerable differences between such aspects of identity as the importance attached to religion, to ethnic origin, and to being British. Among some, hybrid identities such as black British and Asian British were developing. Thus Modood *et al.* broadly accept the arguments of writers such as Stuart Hall that new ethnicities are beginning to emerge.

Modood *et al.* found that, among Caribbeans, most thought of themselves as black. First-generation British Caribbeans (that is, those born in the Caribbean) were most likely to describe themselves as West Indian, although a large minority used the term black. A black identity was most common among the second generation (who were born in Britain) but significant minorities preferred terms such as black British. They tended to prefer to describe themselves as African Caribbean rather than as West Indian, and very few of the second generation thought the Caribbean island from which their parents had emigrated particularly significant.

Many British Caribbeans felt there was considerable similarity between British and Caribbean culture. They tended to think Caribbean culture had less in common with South Asian culture than it had with British culture. Nevertheless, some second-generation Caribbeans felt commonality with South Asians, based upon a common experience of racism. In this case they tended to see black as a term covering both Caribbeans and South Asians. Some also thought that there were new fusions being created between Caribbean, Asian and/or white youth culture.

A number of Caribbeans pointed out that the way they thought of themselves varied from situation to situation. For example, for the first generation, island labels (for example, Jamaican or Antiguan) could be significant when mixing with others of Caribbean origin. One female respondent said she used to think of herself as Antiguan until she visited Antigua and people called her 'English girl'.

Some of those interviewed commented that they felt British, but that this could be undermined by the experience of racism. One said: 'We try to live British, but are not accepted as British'; another said: 'If you are black they do not accept you as British even if we are here for another 100 years. White people don't see me as being British, I am always made conscious of that.' For one girl it was difficult to feel British because she felt excluded from many of the symbols and signs representing Britishness. She said: 'Rule Britannia, Britannia rules the waves. Britons never, never, never will be slaves. Bull-shit, we were the slaves.' Nevertheless, many of those who were born in Britain did feel British even though they felt they were not fully accepted as such by some or all white people. Others rejected British identity in favour of an alternative.

Among South Asians, 'the first generation identified with their specific ethnic or religious identity rather than with a pan-Asian ethnicity or British nationality'. However, there were variations between groups. Most Punjabi Sikhs thought of themselves as Indian rather than as Sikh. Among other groups there was a wide range of identifications based on religion (Hindu or Muslim), region (for example, Gujarati or Punjabi) or nationality (Indian, Pakistani or Bangladeshi). A few first-generation Pakistanis used hybrid terms such as Pakistani British, but such terms were much more common in the second generation. Some of the second generation, though, simply saw themselves as Asian and a small number as black. This last group tended to have Caribbean friends with whom many shared a common interest in music. Some other young Asians thought there were wide cultural differences between themselves and Caribbeans.

Overall, Modood *et al.* found a major difference between the first and second generations of South Asians. Most of the first generation 'had a strong sense of belonging to the society in which they were brought up and saw themselves as law-abiding, hard-working citizens at peace with British society but culturally distinct from it'. Only a few of the first generation took an active interest in developing a more British identity. In the second generation, some

> *saw themselves in terms of a bi-culturalism but the majority felt they were culturally more British than anything else. Few, however, felt they could call themselves British in an unproblematic way. By thinking of Britishness in terms of 'whiteness', backed up by violence, racial discrimination, harassment, abusive jokes and cultural intolerance, some white people made it very difficult for non-whites to identify with Britain in a positive way.*
>
> Modood *et al.*, 1994

Despite this, those who had adopted a bi-cultural identity, such as British Asian, managed to be positive about the British element of their identity while wishing to retain religious or ethnic elements of their identity as well.

Survey research

In later research, Modood (1997) analysed data from the 1994 PSI survey on minority ethnic groups in Britain (see pp. 173–4 for further details of this study). This provided statistical data on a large representative sample of minority ethnic groups. Some of the main findings are summarized in Table 3.5. In the table the figures refer to rounded multiples of 10 per cent (thus 2 means approximately 20 per cent, 8 means approximately 80 per cent and so on).

The table shows that a large majority of all the groups thought of themselves as belonging to a minority ethnic group. However, only a minority in all the groups, apart from the Chinese, did not think of themselves as British. Modood comments that ethnic identity, as revealed in this table, is more to do with 'whom one belongs with' than it is to do with people's actual behaviour. The highest scores tend to refer to membership (for example, membership of a religion) rather than routine participation in activities like wearing ethnic clothes.

Distinctive cultural practices were found to be more common among Caribbeans than among South Asians. Among South Asians, Pakistanis and Bangladeshis were more likely to have distinctive, ethnically based cultural practices than Indians and African Asians. For example, they were more likely to wear Asian clothes and to prefer schools of their own religion.

Modood *et al.* also examined changes between generations. Among South Asians generally, there was a progressive decline in cultural distinctiveness in the younger generation. Among Caribbeans it was more complex. For example, nearly 50 per cent of Caribbeans aged 35–49 did not think of themselves as British, yet a substantial minority (about one in six) of Caribbeans born in Britain did not even identify themselves as belonging to an African Caribbean ethnic group. Among Asians diversity of identity was most evident between generations; among Caribbeans there was great diversity within generations as well as between them.

Conclusions

Modood and colleagues concluded that ethnic identity,

> *far from being some primordial stamp upon an individual, is a plastic and changing badge of membership. Ethnic identity is a product of a number of forces: social exclusion and stigma and political resistance to them, distinctive cultural and religious heritages as well as new forms of culture, communal and familial loyalties, marriage practices and coalitions of interests and so on.*
>
> Modood et *al.*, 1994

Table 3.5 Ethnicity as 'difference': an overview

	Caribbean	Indian	African Asian	Pakistani	Bangladeshi	Chinese
Thinks of self as member of ethnic group	8	9	9	9	9	9
Has a religion other than one of the historic Christian churches	1	9	10	10	10	3
Women sometimes wear 'ethnic' clothes/ adornments (figures in parentheses refer to those who usually do)	3 (1)	9 (5)	9 (3)	10 (8)	10 (9)	-
Men sometimes wear 'ethnic' clothes/ adornments (figures in parentheses refer to those who usually do)	1 (-)	6 (1)	5 (-)	9 (1)	8 (1)	-
Uses a language other than English	2	9	9	10	10	8
Has visited country of origin of family in last 5 years	4	5	4	6	4	6
Parents chose one's spouse (16–34-year-olds only)	-	2	2	6	5	-
Would like quarter or more of pupils at child's school to be from own ethnic group	5	3	3	5	4	1
Would mind if a close relative were to marry a white person	1	4	3	5	4	1
Does not think of oneself as British	4	4	3	4	4	6

Source: T. Modood (1997) 'Culture and identity', in Modood *et al.*, *Ethnic Minorities in Britain*, PSI, London.

They found an 'emerging and evolving plurality' of ethnicities, old and new. Modood (1997) does not believe that the changes are simply a watering-down of ethnic cultures and identities in a British context. While certain cultural practices (for example, religious observances or wearing ethnic clothes) might be less important for the second generation than the first, ethnic identities had become politicized rather than being taken for granted. Such identities are no longer based primarily around the private sphere of family life, but are more in the public sphere. The second generation is generally more willing than the first to campaign for political change and to assert its ethnic identity in public with pride. At the same time more of the younger generation than the old identify themselves as being at least partly British. New ethnicities have a little less to do with culture than traditional ethnicities and more to do with identity and politics. They are less distinctive and more likely to take on hybrid forms.

New ethnicities – conclusion

The main strength of studies of new ethnicities such as those of Modood is that they try to combine insights from the study of identity, racism and ethnicity. They acknowledge that identities are shaped by the experience of racism, the cultural heritage of ethnic groups, and experience in local communities. The emphasis on diverse identity in much of the work on new ethnicities does run the risk of implying that people are free to choose whatever identity they wish. However, Modood acknowledges that such choices are limited and shaped by racism.

The study of new ethnicities succeeds in demonstrating some of the complexities of identity in contemporary societies. However, it does perhaps exaggerate the extent to which hybrid ethnic identities are new. For example, Jewish, Irish and other ethnic groups have long-established British communities which might be seen as involving hybrid ethnicities and identities. As Modood's study lacks a historical perspective, it cannot show that hybrid ethnicities are a genuinely novel phenomenon. However, some sociologists certainly believe that fundamental changes have taken place in the nature of ethnicity and identity. Many who support such beliefs have been strongly influenced by postmodernism.

Modernity, postmodernity, racism, ethnicity and identity

A number of sociologists have attacked modernity for causing racism. Far from seeing the Enlightenment belief in rationality as likely to undermine racist beliefs, they have argued that modernity has actually encouraged racism. Postmodern and poststructural theorists have also argued that racism arises out of a modern tendency to see the world in terms of **binary oppositions**, or pairs of opposites. Western modernity has contrasted itself with 'others' who are taken to be very different. Out of this process racism develops.

A number of advocates of poststructural and postmodern theories argue that traditional, modern sociology has tended to work with categories (such as 'race', ethnicity and nation) which are too rigid and inflexible to deal with a complicated contemporary world. They argue that postmodern analysis can break down these simplistic ways of thinking about issues and substitute new perspectives. It is claimed that these perspectives are more suited to understanding a world in which people have complicated, multiple and ambiguous identities. These approaches would agree that 'new ethnicities' are developing, but they go further than writers like Modood, arguing that such changes should lead to whole new ways of thinking about racism and ethnicity.

Zygmunt Bauman – *Modernity and the Holocaust*

How modernity caused the Holocaust

In *Modernity and the Holocaust* (1989) Zygmunt Bauman argued that the Holocaust was a product of modernity. The mass extermination of Jews (and others) in Nazi Germany was not simply the result of anti-Semitism, an illogical racism directed against Jews. Rather, the Holocaust was a product of the central features of modernity. Bauman says:

> *The truth is that every 'ingredient' of the Holocaust – all those many things that rendered it possible – was normal ... in the sense of being fully in keeping with everything we know about our civilization, its guiding spirit, its priorities ... of the proper ways to pursue human happiness together with a perfect society.* Bauman, 1989

The links between modernity and the Holocaust take a number of forms:

1 The Holocaust was a product of modern, bureaucratic rationality (see pp. 874–8 for a discussion of bureaucracy). The German bureaucracy (particularly the SS) was charged with the task of removing Jews from Germany. In keeping with the principles of modern bureaucracy, the people involved did not question the aims given to them by their political masters. They simply sought the most technically efficient means to achieve the objective. Moving Jews to Poland caused administrative problems for those Germans who had to govern the annexed territory. Another proposal was to send Jews to Madagascar, a colony of defeated France. However, this proved impractical as well. The distances involved and British naval capabilities meant that millions of Jews could not easily be sent there. Mass extermination was adopted simply because it was the most technically efficient means of getting rid of the Jewish presence in Germany. Bauman says: 'The "Final Solution" did not clash at any stage with the rational pursuit of efficient, optimal goal-implementation. On the contrary, *it arose out of a genuinely rational concern, and it was generated by bureaucracy true to its form and purpose.*' Bureaucratic organization can be used to serve any end, and the modern ethos that bureaucrats should not question the purpose of their organization precludes them from taking steps to prevent events such as the Holocaust.

2 Evidence from Holocaust survivors suggests that most members of the SS responsible for carrying out the Holocaust did not appear to be psychologically disturbed sadists. They appeared to be relatively normal individuals. However, they were able to participate in such inhuman acts because they were authorized to do so by their superiors and because the killing was routinized. They subjected themselves to the discipline of the organizations to which they belonged. Accepting organizational discipline is another feature of rational organization in modernity. The honour of civil servants depends upon their ability to follow the orders of their political masters, even if they disagree with those orders. Furthermore, modern, rational organization tends to make the consequences of individual actions less obvious. The part played by each member of a bureaucratic system may seem distant from the final consequences. Thus an official who designated people as 'non-Aryan' in Nazi Germany would be unlikely to think of themselves as responsible for mass murder. Even the actual killing was sanitized by the use of gas chambers. Earlier methods had included machine-gunning victims. However, this was both inefficient and made the inhumanity of what was going on more obvious to the perpetrators. Gas chambers minimized such difficulties.

3 Modernity is based upon the existence of nation-states with clear-cut boundaries. Jews were regarded as 'foreigners within' in European states. Bauman claims that 'in premodern Europe the peculiar flavour of Jewish otherness did not on the whole prevent their accommodation into the prevailing social order'. Premodern societies were divided by estates or castes, and Jews were just one more different group. Modern nation-states emphasize the homogeneity of the nation in order to foster nationalist sentiment. Their desire to maintain boundaries involves excluding alien others. This produces the conditions in which racism can thrive.

4 From the Enlightenment onwards, modern thinking has maintained that human societies can progress through the application of rational, scientific knowledge in planning society. The anti-Semitism that was expressed in an extreme form in the Holocaust was backed up by German scientists who could supposedly prove the inferiority of Jews. The mass extermination of Jews was justified on the grounds that it would improve German society. Such projects to transform society are typically modern and would not be considered in premodern societies, which lacked such a sense of progress.

Conclusion

Bauman concludes that the possibility of the Holocaust was created by modernity. He does not deny that modernity has had its benefits, but he believes that it created the conditions in which racism can thrive. This is particularly because modernity detaches morality from rationality and technical efficiency.

In later work Bauman goes on to discuss postmodernity (Bauman, 1992). He argues that in postmodernity authority becomes dispersed among different groups of experts and is not centralized in the hands of the state. This returns more moral responsibility to the individual, who can now at least choose which authority to take notice of. Bauman therefore believes that postmodernity reduces the chances of events such as the Holocaust occurring. It opens up more opportunity for challenges to racism and more likelihood of the tolerance of diversity. Like postmodern theorists such as Lyotard (see pp. 891–3), Bauman associates postmodernism with the acceptance of pluralism and the rejection of harmful attempts to direct the development of society.

Davis Goldberg – *Racist Culture*

In his book *Racist Culture* (1993), Davis Goldberg follows Bauman in relating racism to modernity. However, Goldberg does not focus on the Holocaust but looks more broadly at the development of racisms.

Premodern and modern societies

Goldberg argues that racism did not exist in premodern societies. For example, in Ancient Greece, slaves and barbarians were the victims of exclusion and discrimination. However, they were not differentiated from other people in terms of race, but were simply seen as politically different. Similarly, he believes that people were not seen in racial terms in medieval Europe. According to Goldberg, the term 'race' only began to be used in the fifteenth century and only became important with the development of modernity. Goldberg defines modernity as developing in the West from the sixteenth century onwards. He sees the 'modern project' as 'a broad sweep of socio-intellectual traditions', including:

> *the commodification and capital accumulation of a market-based society, the legal formation of private property and systems of contract, the moral and political conception of rational self-interested subjects, and the increasing replacement of God and religious doctrine by reason and nature as the final arbiters of justificatory appeal.* Goldberg, 1993

These changes involved fundamental shifts in what Goldberg calls the **conceptual order**. The conceptual order was concerned with the way people thought about things, and in particular how they thought about their own identity in relation to others. Individuals no longer thought of themselves as the subjects of God, but, instead, as rational, independent individuals subject only to reason. Individuals developed a strong sense of themselves as possessing a cohesive identity. This sense of identity developed out of **liberalism**. This was because liberalism

> *is committed to* individualism *for it takes as basic the moral, political and legal claims of the individual over and against those of the collective. It seeks* foundations *in* universal principles *applicable to all human beings or rational agents in virtue of their humanity or rationality.* Goldberg, 1993

These principles would seem to be ill-suited to encouraging racism. If all people are united by reason, then there is little justification for treating them differently because of their 'race'. Furthermore, liberalism is committed to the idea of progress through planned improvements in society, and it also 'takes itself to be committed to equality'. Goldberg adds: 'From the liberal point of view, particular differences between individuals have no bearing on their moral value, and by extension should make no difference concerning the legal or political status of individuals.'

Despite all this, Goldberg finds that many prominent liberal thinkers have been racist. The examples he cites include the philosophers David Hume and John Stuart Mill and the nineteenth-century British politician Benjamin Disraeli. Paradoxically, modernity and liberalism give rise to racism when, on the surface, it appears that they should do just the opposite. How does Goldberg explain this?

Liberals and racism

Goldberg argues that the emphasis on the rationality of humanity implied a comparison with the non-rational. The non-rational could be found both in premodern thought and in non-Western societies. Along with the development of colonialism, Western, rational liberals began to categorize other groups of humans as less rational or non-rational.

Goldberg comments that the 'concept of race has served, and silently continues to serve, as a boundary constraint upon the applicability of moral principles'. Modern liberal beliefs in the morality of equality and liberty did not extend to those who were conquered, and in some cases enslaved, by the colonial powers such as Spain, France, Portugal and Britain. Goldberg says: 'The rational, hence autonomous and equal subjects of the Enlightenment project turn out, perhaps unsurprisingly, to be exclusively white, European and bourgeois.'

Along with modernity's belief in rationality went scientific investigations based upon **empiricism**. Empiricism claims that it is possible to classify the world by carrying out detailed observations, and as such it has much in common with positivism (see pp. 788–90 for a discussion of positivism). Empirical observations of humans formed the basis for classifying them into different races. Specialized disciplines emerged which lent scientific respectability to racism. Biology and anthropology were combined to make claims that biological differences between groups of humans formed the basis for differences in culture. The supposedly primitive and non-rational cultures of some societies were taken as evidence of biological inferiority.

The dominant liberal ideas of modernity did see humans as having rights. For example, in the eighteenth century the French and American revolutions asserted the rights of American and French citizens. However, the belief in rights failed to protect non-whites from racism because those rights were seen as being limited to certain groups. Goldberg says:

> *The rights others as a matter of course enjoy are yet denied people of color because black, brown, red and yellow subjectivities continue to be disvalued; and the devaluation of these subjectivities delimits at least the*

applicability of rights or restricts their scope of application that people of color might otherwise properly claim.
Goldberg, 1993

The West and its 'others'

Goldberg draws on the work of Edward Said (1995, first published 1978) in discussing how the devaluation of non-whites came about (see pp. 183–4). In his book *Orientalism* Said explains how the West established a discourse (see pp. 559–62 for a discussion of discourse) in which the Orient was portrayed in a stereotypical and largely negative way. The East was seen as mysterious and exotic, but also less rational than, and therefore inferior to, the West. The West defined the East as 'the other', that which it was not, and in doing so cemented its own sense of superiority.

Following Said, Goldberg believes that, through the process of naming others as Orientals, the West was able to exercise power over them. By claiming to have knowledge about them, it denied those in Arab and other Eastern countries the opportunity to define who they were themselves. In doing so it effectively denied them the ability to act for themselves. Goldberg says:

> *Naming the racial Other, for all intents and purposes is the Other. There is, as Said makes clear in the case of the Oriental, no Other behind or beyond the invention of knowledge ... These practices of knowledge and naming construction deny all autonomy to those so named and imagined, extending power, control, authority and domination over them. To extend Said's analysis of the 'Oriental' to the case of race in general ... racialized social science knows ... what is best for the Other – existentially, politically, economically, culturally.* Goldberg, 1993

Because Western social scientists and politicians claimed to understand the Orient better than Orientals themselves, they could claim to be in a better position to govern them – and make decisions that were in their interests – than they could themselves. Hence they could justify colonialism.

Racisms

Even though, in Goldberg's view, modernity caused racism, he does not believe that racism will simply disappear with the end of modernity. In fact he does not think that there is one racism, but rather many different **racisms**. He acknowledges that, as modern societies have developed, the nature of these racisms has changed. They have become less based upon biology, and more based upon cultural and other differences between racial groups. People justify excluding others in a variety of ways. Different tactics are needed to counter different racisms.

Nevertheless, Goldberg does express some optimism that changes in society might be making it easier to challenge racisms. In general, he believes that there has been a trend towards postmodernism in Western societies. To Goldberg, postmodernism involved losing a single, unified sense of identity. People have more mixed, varied and insecure identities. This makes it more difficult to sustain the view that other people have unified identities based around their supposed 'race'. In these circumstances some people even start to contemplate taking on something of the identity of 'the Other' – that is, of those who are supposed to define who you are by being different. Goldberg concludes:

> *We must accordingly be prompted to think the once unthinkable: that whites ... be intellectually and culturally influenced by the thought of black people; that whites and blacks think through the conditions for being black, indeed, for whites to be black.* Goldberg, 1993

Ali Rattansi – a 'postmodern' frame

In their discussions of 'race', racism, ethnicity and identity, Goldberg and Bauman are most concerned with criticizing modernity and its role in creating racisms. Ali Rattansi is more concerned with developing a postmodern approach to these issues. However, he is rather tentative in advocating postmodernism, and puts 'postmodern' in quotation marks to show that he has reservations about the term. Nevertheless he tries to outline a postmodern frame, or framework, for understanding Western 'racisms, ethnicities and identities'.

Decentring and de-essentialization

In Rattansi's view, a key element of any postmodern frame must involve a 'decentring and de-essentializing of the subject and the social' (Rattansi, 1994). To Rattansi, **decentring the subject** means rejecting the view that people have a strong and unambiguous sense of identity. People do not know who they are in an unproblematic way, but tend to have confused, ambiguous and sometimes contradictory identities. The concept also involves rejecting the view that people can and do make sense of the world through the exercise of reason. Like other critics of Enlightenment thinking, Rattansi believes that subjective and emotional elements of humans are an integral part of the way humans understand and relate to the external world.

De-essentialization involves rejecting the belief that there are any fundamental or unchanging features of societies or humans. Thus Rattansi rejects the view that there is such a thing as human nature, and denies that there are features that are characteristic of all societies. Thus, for example, de-essentialization would reject the Marxist view that all societies can be understood in terms of their mode of production, and Parsons's view that all societies have the same functional prerequisites (see pp. 859–61 and 867–70). Identities and societies are fluid; they change constantly and are therefore hard to pin down.

Nevertheless Rattansi does discuss factors that have helped to form Western identities. Like Goldberg, he argues that Western identities have at least partly been formed by making comparisons with 'Others', particularly the non-white peoples who were colonized by Western imperial powers. In this context he argues that 'modernity cannot be understood without grasping racism as its other, "darker" side'.

Modern thinking not only produced racism out of a sense of superiority to its 'others', but it also insisted upon strong classification systems. The belief in the power and authority of rationality leads modernists to divide people into groups. However, Rattansi argues that a postmodern frame is bound to undermine classifications of people into 'races', ethnic groups or nations. By 'decentring and de-essentializing' it undermines the basis of racism or destructive nationalism. He says: 'There are no unambiguous, water-tight definitions to be had of ethnicity, racism and the myriad terms in-between. Indeed, all these terms are permanently "in-between", caught in the impossibility of fixity and essentialization.'

Rattansi rejects the view that there are biological differences between 'races' and that there are clear-cut cultural differences between ethnic groups or nationalities. He does not believe that such views are always destructive or harmful – sometimes they can be used to mobilize support for progressive changes. For example, he regards the use of the idea of an 'African race' by some black American activists as a useful resource in the struggle against white racism. Nevertheless he argues that the idea of a distinctive African race could still be seen as racist.

Ethnicity and representation

Within a postmodern framework, the idea of **ethnicity** is not seen in absolute terms but as part of 'a cultural politics of representation'. **Representation** involves 'the construction and constant recreation of ethnic identities through the production of images and narratives in visual texts of "popular" and "high" culture'. In other words, ethnic identities and ethnic groups are only created through people's active efforts to portray such groups as existing. They are more imagined than real. Nevertheless, they have real consequences. People use the representation of ethnic groups to try to gain advantages over other groups. They use the idea of ethnicity to claim superiority to, or authority over, other groups, and to mobilize support for their political projects. Although it is becoming less common, people sometimes try to represent group differences in terms of biological 'race' rather than cultural ethnicity. Rattansi calls this process **racialization**.

Because of the fluid nature of concepts such as ethnic groups and nations, a postmodern approach to these concepts should be based upon trying to **deconstruct** existing ideas on ethnicity and nationality. This involves taking the concepts apart and trying to show that they do not describe real groups at all. For example, conventional sociology might compare the examination performance and school exclusion rates of British Asians, African Caribbeans and whites. It might conclude that teachers stereotype non-white pupils, place them in lower streams and so on (see pp. 652–3 for examples of studies of this type). Rattansi attacks such studies for failing to deconstruct or take apart the categories involved. Not all teachers stereotype pupils. Not all pupils react in the same way when they are stereotyped. There are important differences and divisions within minority ethnic and white groups. To give just one example, female African Caribbean pupils might be more prepared to make compromises at school than many male African Caribbean pupils, who are more likely to rebel against racism.

A postmodern frame also criticizes the idea of **institutional racism** (see pp. 169–70). The idea of institutional racism, like concepts such as ethnicity, tends to overgeneralize and ignore ambiguities and inconsistencies. Institutions such as the state, schools and hospitals tend to be 'fragmented and internally divided'. In some contexts they might operate in racist ways, in other contexts they do not. They are influenced by diverse professional ideologies (for example, those of psychiatry, medicine, education, and social work) which train their practitioners in different ways.

Furthermore, in some places there is more effective resistance to racism than in others. Contradictions may arise in ideologies. For example, 'among teachers there is the popular liberal notion of treating individual students in supposedly "colour-blind" terms, which has the effect of ignoring the effects of racism and racialized economic disadvantage'. Ethnicity, 'race' and racism must be studied in specific local contexts, since generalizations about these concepts are impossible.

Rattansi is generally supportive of ideas such as those of Stuart Hall that 'new ethnicities' are developing (see pp. 195–6). He agrees that ethnic identities are being combined in novel ways that undermine the old idea that there are clear-cut distinctions between groups. Rattansi attributes this to the process of **globalization**. He also believes that there is a shift away from the use of the term 'black' to refer to all non-white people. The use of this term by disadvantaged minorities was part of a struggle to challenge racial or ethnic stereotypes, to substitute positive images and to try to gain access to the media to promulgate such views. Rattansi calls these processes 'a struggle over relations of representation'. This has largely been replaced by a new phase: 'a politics of representation'. This tries to move away from the idea of the 'essential black subject': that is, the idea that all black people share a good deal in common.

In the politics of representation, the '"positive" images are now regarded as suffocating the possibilities for exploring the huge variety of ethnic, subcultural and sexual identities pulsating in the minority communities'. Some of these developing cultures are themselves influenced by postmodern and poststructural thinking. An example is the 'postmodern rap' of the British South Asian rapper, Apache Indian.

Rattansi admits that this postmodern framing approach raises some questions that have yet to be answered. For example, he accepts that there may be questions about the ability of this approach to challenge racism. Nevertheless, he believes that the celebration of ethnic diversity and of new ethnicities is a positive and progressive development that allows the sociology of 'race' and ethnicity to move beyond the rather tired debates of the past.

Kenan Malik – a critique of postmodern theories

Kenan Malik is highly critical of postmodern approaches to 'race' and rejects the view that modernity can be seen as responsible for racism. He does not deny that racism has been a powerful and corrosive force in modern societies, but he does not see racism as a product of modernity itself. Furthermore, he does not believe that the celebration of difference, which he sees as a key feature of postmodern thinking, is the way to undermine racism. Instead, he argues that racism can best be tackled by reviving some of the principles on which modernity is based. In particular he believes that the application of universal principles is preferable to acknowledging and celebrating variety in human groups. Before examining Malik's own viewpoint, though, we will discuss his comments on the sorts of postmodern theories we have looked at in this section.

Criticisms of other theories

First, Malik (1996) criticizes Bauman's claim that the Holocaust was a product of modernity. For Malik, the Holocaust arose in specific historical circumstances rather than being a product of modernity in general. If blame for the Holocaust can be attributed to anything, it should be to capitalism rather than reason.

Modernity involves a belief in reason and the application of science, while capitalism involves economic relationships based upon the pursuit of profit. The two are not the same; indeed, capitalism may make it difficult to achieve the equality that was the objective of many modern thinkers. The inequalities produced by capitalism may encourage people to think of other 'races' as inferior, but this is not the same as saying that racism is produced by science and reason. As Malik says, 'By conflating the social relations of capitalism with the intellectual and technical progress of "modernity", the product of the former can be laid at the door of the latter.'

Malik is also critical of the claim that the Holocaust can be blamed on modernity simply because modernity provided the technological means to accomplish mass extermination. Modern technology has also been used to alleviate problems such as famine and material poverty. The existence of advanced technology in itself cannot be held responsible for the political decision to use technology to exterminate people by gassing. Malik says:

> *I find it odious that scholars can in all seriousness equate mass extermination with the production of McDonald's hamburgers or of Ford Escorts, or make a comparison between technology aimed at improving the material abundance of society and political decisions which annihilate whole peoples and destroy entire societies.* Malik, 1996

Second, Malik criticizes the work of Goldberg. He agrees with Goldberg that racism was not present in premodern societies, but does not believe that it developed as an inevitable consequence of modern rationalism. There was no necessary connection between the scientific method and belief in rationality and the categorization of people by 'race'. Malik says:

> *Belief in reason, espousal of the scientific method and a universalistic conviction do not of themselves imply a racial viewpoint. That in the nineteenth century science, reason and universalism came to be harnessed to a discourse of race is a development that has to be explained through historical analysis; it is not logically given by the nature of scientific or rational thought.* Malik, 1996

In reality, Malik claims, Enlightenment philosophy introduced the idea that humans could be equal and, in theory at least, its aims were 'to set all human beings free'. To Malik, what needs to be explained is why such philosophies changed to accept the idea of different races. Malik's explanation for this will be examined shortly.

Third, Malik criticizes the claims of writers such as Goldberg and Said that racism can be understood in terms of the concept of the 'Other'. Malik does not believe that modernity causes people automatically to compare themselves to other people, and that as a result racism develops. Malik suggests that such claims are so sweeping as to be seriously misleading. In his view, it cannot be assumed that, over many centuries, Westerners have seen all non-Westerners as the 'Other' in the same way. Western views of other people have been related to specific contexts and circumstances. For example, different meanings have been given to the possession of a black skin at different times and in different places in modern history. At one time most Westerners thought that it was acceptable to enslave people with black skins. That is no longer the case. The meaning of 'otherness' is often disputed and contentious, and not all modern, post-Enlightenment thinkers have been persuaded of the truth of racist beliefs.

The origins of racism

Malik himself explains racism in terms of a clash between Enlightenment ideas and the social relations produced by capitalism. In the eighteenth century the universalistic Enlightenment idea that all humans were equal was widely held. For example, the French philosopher Rousseau, writing in 1770, distinguished between physical inequality (such as strength) and moral or political inequality. While the first type of inequality came from nature, the second type was created by humans and reflected both privilege and prejudice. In Rousseau's thinking – which was very much in line with the Enlightenment thinking from which modernity developed – there was no room for racism. There was prejudice against 'racial' groups in the eighteenth century, but liberals influenced by Enlightenment ideas were opposed to slavery.

Furthermore, a supposedly 'scientific' theory of racism only developed in the nineteenth century. Malik argues that this resulted from inequality within Western, capitalist society. While the Enlightenment had taught that people were equal, people's experiences of society had shown them the development of a disadvantaged working class. These disadvantages seemed to be passed down from generation to generation, and this encouraged advantaged groups to believe that members of the working class were biologically inferior to themselves. This tendency was further encouraged by concern among the elite about the pace of social change, the apparent breakdown of traditional moral values and the danger of working-class unrest. In these circumstances it was the working-class rather than non-Western others who were first seen as part of an inferior 'race'. Malik comments:

> *For the Victorians race was a description of social distinctions, not of colour differences. Indeed, as I have already argued, the view of non-Europeans as an inferior race was but an extension of the already existing view of the working class at home.* Malik, 1996

A good example is the widespread view among the Victorian elite that the working-class Irish in the country were a biologically inferior group.

It was the inability of capitalism to deliver the equality that modernity had promised that led to 'scientific' thinking becoming racist. It was only after the working class had begun to be thought of in racist terms that racial thinking began to be applied to non-European groups.

If Malik is right, then postmodernists have, at the very least, been too critical of modernity. There is no reason why rational modern thought cannot be turned against racism. It may be possible to combat racism in a more positive way than simply encouraging an acceptance of human diversity. For Malik, postmodernists have abandoned the struggle to produce greater equality in favour of unequal diversity. Malik regards this as an undesirable and unnecessary admission of defeat.

Minority ethnic groups in the labour market and stratification system

There is considerable evidence that minority ethnic groups are disadvantaged in the British labour market. As we have seen, minority ethnic groups are more likely to suffer from unemployment (see pp. 175–6). Furthermore, earlier in this chapter we saw that those from minority ethnic groups tend to get paid lower wages and have lower-status jobs (see pp. 174–5). Although there are differences between ethnic groups, most groups continue to suffer from disadvantages even when factors such as fluency in English and educational qualifications are taken into account.

Discrimination in the labour market

The most straightforward explanation of disadvantage suffered by minority ethnic groups in employment is that it results from the racism and prejudice of employers. In other words, employers discriminate against minority ethnic groups by refusing to employ them, employing them only in low-status and low-paid jobs, or refusing to promote them.

Evidence to support this point of view is provided from a study by Colin Brown and Pat Gay (1985) carried out in 1984–5. They conducted research in London, Birmingham and Manchester, in which bogus applications were made for a variety of jobs by letter and by telephone. The supposed applicants were identified as being from minority ethnic groups by the use of Hindu names for 'Asian' applicants and a Jamaican educational background for 'West Indian' applicants. In telephone applications ethnic accents were used to differentiate minority ethnic applicants from 'white' applicants.

Brown and Gay found that positive responses were significantly less common to applications from those who were identified as being from minority ethnic groups. Some 90 per cent of white applicants, but only 63 per cent of Asian and 63 per cent of West Indian applicants, received positive responses.

Brown and Gay compared their results with those of similar studies carried out in 1973–4 and 1977–9. They found that the level of discrimination had remained about the same in all three studies. They concluded that 'there is no evidence here to suggest that racial discrimination in job recruitment has fallen over the period covered by these studies'.

A study using similar methods was conducted in 1993 by Kim Hoque and Mike Noon (1993). In this case applications were made by letter to the UK's top 100 companies. The speculative applications were from two equally well-qualified candidates called 'Evans' and 'Patel', and the study found that, overall, companies were less responsive and helpful to 'Patel'.

Similar studies were repeated during the 1990s in local areas. Reporting on the findings of such studies, Modood (1997) comments: 'Objective tests suggest that the proportion of white people who are likely to carry out the most basic acts of discrimination has been stable at about a third for several decades.'

The PSI's *Fourth National Survey of Ethnic Minorities*, conducted in 1994, asked a number of questions about discrimination in employment. The survey found that 28 per cent of Caribbean people, 19 per cent of African Asians, 15 per cent of Indians, 7 per cent of Chinese, and 5 per cent of Pakistani/Bangladeshi people believed they had been refused a job for religious or racial reasons (Modood, 1997). Comparing these results with those of the previous survey, Modood found a slight increase in reported discrimination of this type among Caribbeans, but a slight decrease among South Asians.

These figures must be used with some caution. They rely upon the subjective beliefs of the respondents to the survey, who might not be in a position to assess accurately whether they had been the victims of racial discrimination. Discrimination could be more common or less so than the figures indicate. However, the figures do suggest that at least some of the disadvantages experienced by minority ethnic groups in the labour market could be the result of racism. Furthermore, a 2001 report which discussed the findings of employment tribunals found that racial discrimination and harassment continued in the labour market (Cabinet Office, 2003, p. 38).

Minority ethnic groups as an underclass

Some sociologists have tried to develop a more theoretical approach to explaining the position of minority ethnic groups in the labour market and in society as a whole. Some British and American sociologists have suggested that minority ethnic groups form an **underclass**. While some have defined the underclass in cultural terms, others have seen the underclass as a structural feature of society. The idea of an underclass has already been discussed in detail (see pp. 64–6 for a discussion of the underclass in relation to stratification, and see also pp. 242–7 for a discussion of the underclass and poverty). In this section we will concentrate on the relationship between the concepts of underclass and ethnicity.

Charles Murray – Losing Ground

In his 1984 book *Losing Ground*, the American neoliberal sociologist Charles Murray argued that the USA had developed a black underclass. This underclass was distinguished by its behaviour. Murray claimed that increasing numbers of young blacks were withdrawing from the labour market: they were unwilling to work. At the same time there were increasing numbers of black single parents who had never been married.

Murray denied that such changes were the result of poverty and lack of opportunity. He argued that in the 1950s participation by blacks in the labour market was higher than in the 1960s, yet there was greater economic prosperity and lower unemployment in the 1960s than in the 1950s.

To Murray, the real reason for the changes in behaviour lay in welfare benefits. In his view the policy of Aid to Families with Dependent Children removed many of the incentives for men to work to support their families, and it enabled mothers to bring up their children on their own. The stigma of relying upon benefits had been reduced as more and more benefits were introduced for people with low incomes.

American critics of Murray have pointed out that Aid to Families with Dependent Children was introduced some twenty years before the number of single-parent black families began to rise rapidly. Lydia Morris criticizes Murray for failing to explain the withdrawal of black youth from the labour market. The young unemployed have no automatic entitlement to benefit in the USA, so their behaviour cannot be explained in terms of the welfare system.

Some American sociologists have agreed with Murray that the USA has developed a black or minority ethnic underclass, but they have not agreed about the causes. They have attributed its development to structural forces rather than the operation of the welfare system and the behaviour of welfare claimants. The most influential alternative view of the American underclass was advanced by W.J. Wilson.

W.J. Wilson – The Truly Disadvantaged

In his book *The Truly Disadvantaged* (1987), Wilson argues that blacks and Hispanics living in inner-city areas have come to form an underclass because of forces beyond their control. The disadvantages faced by urban blacks and Hispanics have historical roots and have created problems that continue to make it difficult to escape from the ghetto.

When poor blacks migrated from the rural south of the USA to the cities of the north, they faced the obstacle of racism when they tried to find work. The migrants had few skills and little prospect of career advancement. Their low levels of economic success encouraged whites to develop crude racial stereotypes which produced further problems for the ghetto poor. What work the blacks could find was largely unskilled and in manufacturing industry.

In the 1970s manufacturing industry began to decline, and the industry which survived the recession moved away from city centres. Service sector work increased but much of it required qualifications which minority ethnic groups in the inner cities did not possess. Some blacks and Hispanics had enjoyed success, gained qualifications and secured well-paid jobs. However, these individuals moved out of the city centres to the suburbs, leaving behind the most disadvantaged. The poor had become trapped in areas where there were few opportunities to improve their lot. Wilson says: 'The underclass exists mainly because of large-scale and harmful changes in the labor market and its resulting spatial concentration as well as the isolation of such areas from the most affluent parts of the black community.'

In 1990, in an address to the American Sociological Association, Wilson abandoned the use of the term underclass (Wilson, 1991). Although he stuck by his analysis of the problems faced by minority ethnic groups in the inner cities of the USA, he argued that the term underclass had become a liability. It had been adopted by right-wing commentators who had used it to indicate that the problems of the poor were of their own making. To Wilson, the problems resulted more from impersonal economic forces, and the connotations the term had taken on were unfortunate. He therefore suggested that the groups he was describing should be called the ghetto rather than the underclass.

Some American critics have argued that Wilson underestimates the effects produced by racism. Their view is that the black middle class is small and that even those blacks with good jobs do less well than their white counterparts with similar qualifications. Problems for American blacks in the labour market are not confined to the poor.

The underclass in Britain

Some sociologists have argued that there is a British underclass composed mainly or exclusively of minority ethnic groups. They have followed Wilson in arguing that the underclass has been created by structural forces, and have tended to be critical of sociologists such as Murray who see the underclass in cultural terms. One of the most influential views of this type was advanced by Anthony Giddens (1973).

Giddens argued that the underclass was composed of those with a disadvantaged position in the labour market. As well as lacking skills and qualifications, they may also have to face prejudice and discrimination. Women and minority ethnic groups are most likely to suffer from these problems and are therefore most likely to be found in the underclass. As we saw in Chapter 1 (see pp. 64–5), Giddens believed that migrants were very likely to end up in the underclass.

To Giddens, when minority ethnic groups such as Asians and West Indians in Britain and Algerians in France are heavily concentrated in the lowest-paid jobs or are unemployed, then an underclass exists. When members of the underclass do have jobs they are mainly in the secondary labour market which consists of relatively unskilled jobs with few promotion prospects.

This view was supported by a study conducted in Birmingham by John Rex and Sally Tomlinson (1979). The study found that minority ethnic groups tended to be concentrated in **secondary labour market** jobs such as metal goods manufacture. Relatively few members of minority ethnic groups obtained **primary labour market** jobs (skilled jobs with promotion prospects). (See pp. 126–7 for a discussion of primary and secondary labour markets.)

Marxist approaches

Marxist sociologists agree with writers such as Giddens that minority ethnic groups are disadvantaged in capitalist societies. However, they do not agree that they form an underclass in Britain. They reject the importance attached to status in underclass theories and place more emphasis on the workings of the economy and the role of minority ethnic groups in the economic system.

Stephen Castles and Godula Kosack – a reserve army of labour

In a study of immigrant workers in France, Germany, Switzerland and Britain, Stephen Castles and Godula Kosack (1973) found that immigrants faced similar problems in the labour market to those identified in Birmingham by Rex and Tomlinson (see above). In these four European countries immigrants were found to be concentrated in low-paid jobs or in jobs with poor working conditions. Most were manual workers in unskilled or semi-skilled work and they suffered high rates of unemployment. Castles and Kosack claim that in Britain this situation is mainly due to discrimination. In France, Germany and Switzerland the migrant workers are foreigners in the country in which they are working and restrictive laws and regulations prevent them from gaining employment in the more desirable jobs.

Discrimination and restrictive regulations are, however, only the immediate causes of the plight of immigrants. The poor treatment of immigrants ultimately derives from the need in capitalist societies for a **reserve army of labour**: it is necessary to have a surplus of labour in order to keep wage costs down, since the greater the overall supply of labour, the weaker the bargaining position of workers.

Furthermore, as Marxists, Castles and Kosack believe that capitalist economies are inherently unstable. They go through periods of boom and slump, and a reserve army of labour needs to be available to be hired and fired as the fluctuating fortunes of the economy dictate. After the Second World War, capitalist societies exhausted their indigenous reserve army of labour; women, for example, were increasingly taking paid employment. Capitalist countries in Europe therefore turned to migrant labour and immigration to provide a reserve pool of cheap labour which could be profitably exploited.

Castles and Kosack do not believe that such workers form an underclass outside and below the main class structure. They regard them as being part of the working class. Like other workers, they do not own the means of production and so share with them an interest in changing society. However, Castles and Kosack believe that immigrant and migrant workers are the most disadvantaged groups within the working class and as such they form a distinctive stratum. Thus Castles and Kosack believe that the working class is divided into two, with minority ethnic groups constituting one working-class grouping and the indigenous white population the other.

This situation is beneficial to the ruling class in capitalist societies. Minority ethnic groups are blamed for problems such as unemployment and housing shortages. Attention is diverted from the failings of the capitalist system. The working class is divided and cannot unite, develop class consciousness or challenge ruling-class dominance. (For further details of Castles and Kosack's work see pp. 155–6.)

Andrew Pilkington – the underclass reconsidered

Despite the differences between the theories on ethnicity and employment examined so far, they share a good deal in common. Andrew Pilkington suggests:

> *There is considerable agreement that ethnic minorities still constitute a replacement population – employed (if at all) in predominantly non-skilled manual work; with few chances of promotion; subject to poverty; and substantially segregated from the white working class.* Pilkington, 1999

However, Pilkington believes that the underclass and Marxist theories are not supported by empirical evidence. He analyses figures from the census, the Labour Force Survey and the PSI study conducted by Modood et al. (see pp. 173–4). None of these sources of data show that minority ethnic groups are overwhelmingly concentrated at lower levels of the occupational structure.

Furthermore, there is evidence that all minority ethnic groups are making progress in the occupational structure. Research from the PSI study, for example, shows that between 1982 and 1994 all ethnic groups made progress both in absolute terms and relative to whites. Pilkington produces a chart based upon the PSI figures which uses a scale to allocate numerical values to position in the occupational structure – the higher the score the higher the position. Figure 3.5 shows the results of this calculation for men. It shows that Indian men had overtaken white men in terms of job status, while all other groups had made significant progress. The available data on women from the survey suggested that 'Caribbean women made the most progress, followed by Whites and African Asians, with Indians lagging a little behind' (Pilkington, 1999).

Pilkington argues that it is dangerous to make generalizations about ethnic groups in Britain, as different ethnic groups have enjoyed varying degrees of success in the British labour market. The least successful have been Bangladeshis and Pakistanis, who 'are the only groups where the majority of members experience any of the forms of disadvantage thought to be characteristic of an underclass'. Even for these groups, though, there has been significant progress over time and 'the majority of men … do not experience persistent unemployment and the majority of households are not concentrated in inferior housing'.

Like other ethnic groups, Bangladeshis and Pakistanis tend to be polarized between the successful and the unsuccessful, and there is therefore no basis for seeing either group as constituting an underclass. Pilkington accepts that all minority ethnic groups have certain factors in common. They all 'continue to face racial discrimination and experience some racial disadvantage'. However, he concludes: 'Our analysis in short points to too much ethnic diversity and relative progress to warrant talk of a racially defined underclass.'

Figure 3.5 Relative progress in job levels of male employees

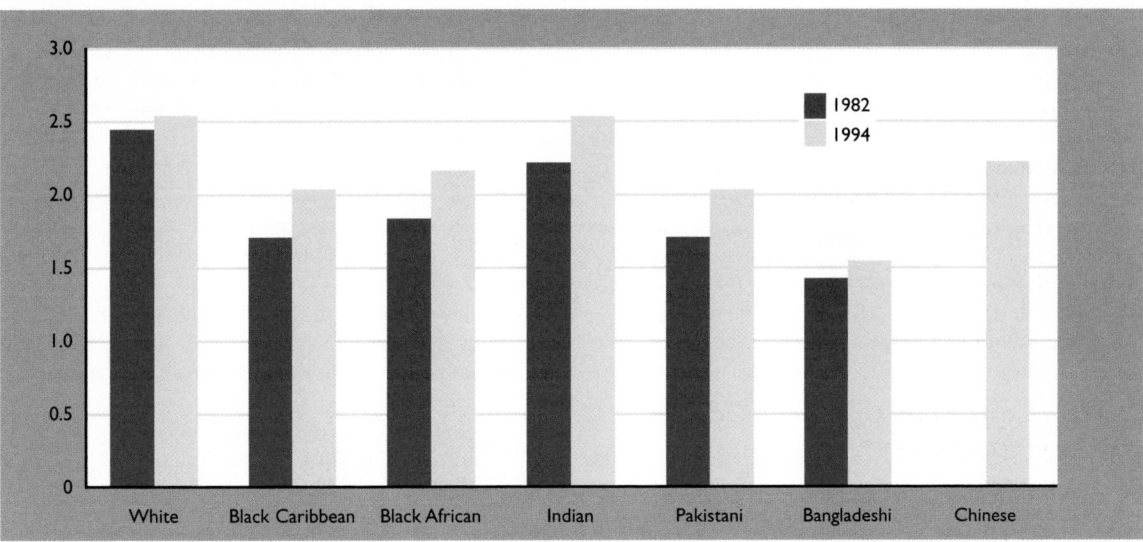

Note: Based on average job-level score derived from the following scale:
4 = professional, managerial, employer 3 = other non-manual 2 = skilled manual and foremen
1 = semi-skilled manual 0 = unskilled manual

Source: A. Pilkington (1999) 'Racial disadvantage and ethnic diversity', in M. Haralambos (ed.) *Developments in Sociology*, vol. 15, Causeway Press, Ormskirk.

Conclusion

Writers such as Heidi Mirza (1992) support aspects of Pilkington's argument. Mirza warns of the dangers of labelling minority ethnic groups as failures in the labour market and other areas of social life. She points out that women of Caribbean origin have enjoyed considerable success in British society (see pp. 653–4). That does not mean that the relatively successful groups are immune from discrimination – they might have been even more successful if discrimination had not occurred. However, any full explanation of inequalities in the labour market would need to take account of a range of factors other than discrimination. These would include gender, class, age and cultural differences.

'Race', ethnicity, social policy and social theory

Social policies and social theories relating to 'race', ethnicity, migration and nationality have always been influenced by the dominant views on the nature of 'race' and ethnicity and on the nature of any problems associated with migration and national identity. This was certainly true in the nineteenth century. Sociologists generally accepted the view of scientists and others that humanity was divided into distinct biological 'races', some of which were superior to others. Not surprisingly, they tended to see themselves and their own 'race' as being at the top of the hierarchy.

Thus, to sociologists like Herbert Spencer (1971), white Europeans generally belonged to the most evolved 'races'. Spencer's beliefs did not stem from individual arrogance or ignorance. Colonialism undoubtedly contributed to persuading most people in Victorian Britain that their 'race' was superior to the other 'races' that they and other European powers had conquered and ruled.

Today, most scientists and social scientists dismiss the idea that there are distinct 'races', never mind the belief that some 'races' are superior to others (see pp. 146–8).

'Race' and immigration

As described earlier (see p. 147), the doctrine of racial superiority was gradually replaced by the view that there were important cultural differences between ethnic groups, which could, potentially at least, cause serious problems. These grew in importance, as large-scale migration between and within countries became more common, and people from different ethnic groups increasingly lived close together.

Sociologists supporting the immigrant–host model were unlikely to claim that certain 'races' were superior to others. To them, the problems of race relations were created by the difficulties encountered when immigrants or strangers settled in an established host society.

However, these views were still strongly influenced by the values of the sociologists who expressed them: it was always the 'immigrants' who were the problem, disrupting the harmony of the host society. The hosts were seen as largely tolerant and some were even welcoming. Any fault lay with those who would not adapt to their new surroundings. From this point of view the hosts were generally willing to accept the strangers; they were not filled with racism or hatred.

The views associated with the immigrant–host model seem to remain common among British whites today. For example, an ICM opinion poll in 2001 found that over 70 per cent of the sample thought that 'immigrants should embrace the British way of life' (see p. 173 for more details of this poll).

Integration and assimilation

Although it is increasingly seen as inappropriate to regard minority ethnic cultures as inferior, there is still an influential school of thought which argues that integration is the key to harmony between ethnic groups. This approach has been coming back into fashion in recent years in response to such events as the 9/11 and 7/7 terrorists attacks (see p. 181), the growing debate over the relationship between Islam and Western societies, adverse media coverage of immigration, and the disturbances in Oldham, Bradford and Burnley in 2001.

The disturbances in Oldham, Bradford and Burnley were investigated in the Cantle Report (Cantle, 2001), which initiated a debate about whether assimilation was preferable to multiculturalism. The report argued that the rioting, which involved clashes between Asians, the police and others, was to a large extent the result of the segregation of the different communities. It argued that what these towns lacked was a 'sense of community cohesion'; and it claimed that there was an extreme **polarization** between the different communities:

> *Separate educational arrangements, community and voluntary bodies, employment, places of worship, language, social and cultural networks, means that many communities operate on the basis of a series of parallel lives. These lives often do not seem to touch at any point, let alone overlap and promote any meaningful exchanges.* Cantle, 2001

The report argued that what was needed was 'greater knowledge of, contact between, and respect for, the various cultures that now make up Great Britain'.

While such sentiments sound laudable enough, and are far less stark than ideas that 'immigrants' should assimilate to 'our' way of life, Roger Ballard (2002) argues that they involve the same underlying message. He sees the Cantle Report as 'strongly assimilationist (because vigorously anti-segregationist)' in its call for community cohesion. He also believes that attempts to integrate communities will be unlikely to succeed. There are four main reasons for this:

1. It is a 'routine feature of all plural societies' that there will be segregation between ethnic groups. It should not be seen as exceptional or necessarily undesirable.
2. Coercive attempts to reduce the gap between communities tend to have undesirable consequences and make the divisions wider. One or more of the communities involved tends to resent the attempt to get them to change. Trying to impose majority culture on minority cultures is only likely to strengthen the determination of the minority to protect their own culture.
3. Attempts to develop a degree of homogeneity are doomed to failure. It is far better to find ways in which the communities can find a *modus vivendi*, a way of living together, without interference or resentment. This is the 'least-worst option' and the only workable one in diverse societies.
4. To Ballard, a *modus vivendi* can only be achieved when there is recognition of minority ethnic cultures 'in all spheres of public activity'. All schools, hospitals and political institutions, for example, should recognize that special provisions might be needed to accommodate the needs and preferences of those from minority cultures. Only then will 'members of every component in our plural society begin to feel that they have a valued and meaningful stake in the established social order'. However, Ballard is not confident that this can be achieved. He describes it as 'radically at odds with Home Office thinking', which still emphasizes the need for minority assimilation and for minorities to change those values which are at odds with the core values of British citizenship.

Multiculturalism

Ballard's rejection of assimilation is more in tune with developments within sociology than the Cantle Report. Sociologists have increasingly challenged the idea that 'immigrants' need to change their cultures. From the 1960s onwards, the mood, at least among some groups in Western societies, has moved in favour of greater tolerance of diverse cultures. In the USA, the civil rights and Black Power movements encouraged minority ethnic groups to take pride in their distinctiveness. In Britain, legislation has outlawed discrimination and made open racism less respectable and acceptable.

Rather than just expecting 'immigrants' to integrate, new approaches to issues of 'race' and ethnicity seemed necessary. One approach was to emphasize the desirability of ethnic pluralism. This suggested that the cultures of minority ethnic groups should not necessarily change to allow integration, but rather should remain distinctive and separate. Studies of ethnicity were carried out to develop a greater understanding of the diverse ways of life of different ethnic groups.

This approach produced policies of **multiculturalism**. From this viewpoint, schools, for example, should accommodate all ethnic groups: the diet, religious practices, clothing, beliefs and values of different ethnic groups should all be catered for in the education system.

Radical critics of this approach tended to dismiss it. James Donald and Ali Rattansi (1992) call it the 'saris, samosas and steel-bands syndrome'. In their view, it focused on the 'superficial manifestations of culture' and did not really address the underlying problems faced by minority ethnic groups. Donald and Rattansi argue that multiculturalism ignores the 'continuing hierarchies of power and legitimacy'. If minority ethnic groups are allowed or encouraged to wear saris, eat samosas and play in steel bands, that does not necessarily mean that their cultures have the same power and legitimacy as white culture.

Donald and Rattansi argue that the 'limits to this approach were cruelly exposed by intellectual as well as political responses to *The Satanic Verses* affair in the late

1980s'. Politicians and writers alike tended to side with Salman Rushdie against the British Muslim community who called for the book to be banned for blasphemy.

According to some sociologists, the emphasis on culture in multiculturalism has its own dangers. The new racism identified by Solomos *et al.* (1982) (see pp. 178–9) and the ethnic absolutism described by Gilroy (1987) (see p. 180) are based on the idea that ethnic groups are incompatible because their cultures are incompatible. Repatriation, which used to be justified on the grounds of biological difference, was supported by politicians such as Enoch Powell on cultural grounds. Rivers of blood would flow simply because very different cultures could not mix. Although contemporary politicians tend to express their views less bluntly, recent debates have returned to the issue of multiculturalism and it has come in for renewed criticism (see below).

Anti-racism

Sociologists who stress the importance of racism suggest that the problems of 'race' and ethnicity cannot be solved by encouraging tolerance of different cultures. To some, racism is deeply ingrained in the minds, culture and institutions of whites. Whites possess most of the power in countries such as the USA and Britain, and racism ensures that they keep their power. From this point of view minority ethnic groups have to fight to gain power rather than rely on the tolerance of well-meaning liberals. The policies associated with this approach are often called **anti-racist**. They involve seeking out, exposing and destroying the open or hidden racism present in society and its institutions.

Burnage High School in south Manchester became a notorious example of this approach in 1986 when Ahmed Iqbal Ullah was murdered by a white boy in the school playground, despite the school's vigorous anti-racist policy. Children in the school were taught about the evils of racism but that did not prevent the murder. The school banned white children from attending the funeral.

While nearly all sociologists today condemn racism, some disagree with some of the policies of anti-racism. Paul Gilroy argues that anti-racism has sometimes practised **moralistic excesses**. It has 'drifted towards a belief in the absolute nature of ethnic categories' and has therefore fallen into the trap of emphasizing 'race' to the exclusion of everything else. It sees the world in terms of black and white. Whites are the oppressors, blacks are the oppressed. All whites are racist, as are their institutions. Gilroy says:

> *The anti-racism I am criticizing trivializes the struggle against racism and isolates it from other political antagonisms – from the contradiction between capital and labour, from the battle between men and women. It suggests that racism can be eliminated on its own because it is readily extricable from everything else.* Gilroy, 1987

To Gilroy, the views of some anti-racists are no longer plausible. Not only are issues of 'race' and ethnicity bound up with other issues, but also racial and ethnic identities and cultures themselves cannot be separated into distinct and neat categories. Like Stuart Hall (1992), Gilroy believes that in the modern world there has been so much intermingling of different cultures that it is no longer appropriate to treat different 'races' as discrete groups.

Postmodernism

Postmodernists tend to share Gilroy's view that new types of ethnic identity are developing as the cultures of different ethnic groups are mixed. However, postmodernists tend to support a type of radical multiculturalism rather than hope for the virtual disappearance of 'racial' differences. For example, Goldberg (1993) advocates a 'shift from the fundamental public commitment to ignore difference and particularity in the name of universality to a public celebration of diversity and an openly acknowledged and constantly recreated politics of difference'.

Rather than treat everybody the same and pretend that there are no differences, we should acknowledge the differences. We should create space for different voices to be heard. For example, black lesbian females should have as much chance to express their views as white heterosexual males. Different religions, age groups, classes, ethnic groups and people with different sexualities must all have a voice in contemporary society. They all need to record their own history, to express how they experience society and to celebrate their own identities. Their differences should not be suppressed under an Enlightenment philosophy that all people are fundamentally the same.

Kenan Malik (1996) strongly opposes this approach. He says: 'The philosophy of difference is the politics of defeat, born out of defeat. It is the product of disillusionment with the possibilities of social change and the fragmented world.' He accuses postmodern thinkers of accepting and even encouraging the oppression of minority ethnic groups. From Malik's point of view, postmodernists sometimes seem to want such groups to remain oppressed. This is so that they can articulate their experiences and maintain their distinctive identities, which are partly based on their oppression.

Malik believes that a 'social revolution' is necessary. What is needed is a revolution in which people refuse to accept defeat and start to believe again that it is possible to intervene to make society better. Racism can be defeated by an active struggle against it.

Most postmodernists would not accept that their views are based upon accepting racism. They see the acceptance of diversity as liberating.

The Parekh Report

Despite the disagreements between Malik and postmodernists it may be possible to reconcile their conflicting viewpoints. According to the Parekh Report (Parekh *et al.*, 2000), there is no conflict between recognizing and celebrating diversity *and* tackling racism. Both are essential if 'multi-ethnic Britain is to have a successful or harmonious future'. The report argues that there are six key elements to what it calls 'building and sustaining a community of citizens and communities':

1. Britain will need to 'rethink the national story and national identity'. The report argues that it is very misleading to think that Britain is, or ever has been, a homogeneous society. Britain was only formed in 1707 after the Act of Union united England, Scotland and Wales. It is only 'imagined' to be a single society

and has long consisted of several nations, different religious communities (e.g. Catholics and Protestants), regions and so on. Even England cannot be seen as a homogeneous entity. 'Depending on whether you're black, white, old, young, privileged, disadvantaged, healthy, sick, living in the provinces or the cities, England means a million different things to a million different people.' Devolution, globalization, membership of the European Community and 'the breakdown in older class hierarchies' have all complicated the picture further. In these circumstances, Britain has no majority culture to which minorities could assimilate.

2 The identities of British people are 'in transition'. 'All communities are changing and all are complex, with internal diversity and disagreements, linked to differences of gender, generation, religion and language.' Furthermore, these communities are changing, overlapping with one another and influencing one another, and as this happens hybrid cultures develop. It is no longer possible to identify clear dividing lines between communities.

In 1990 the Conservative politician Norman Tebbit devised the 'cricket test' to tell if people were truly British. He argued that true Britons would support England at cricket rather than, for example, India, Pakistan or the West Indies. The Parekh Report argues that this test is out of date. It claims that

> ***people today are always juggling different, not always wholly compatible, identities. South Asians and African Caribbeans support India, Pakistan and the West Indies against England, but England against Australia, especially where the English team includes Asian and black players. This is just one aspect of the complex, multifaceted, post-national world in which national allegiance is played out.*** Parekh et al., 2000

3 The Parekh Report states that there is a need for 'cohesion, equality and difference'. These aims might be seen as contradictory; for example, it might be difficult to achieve cohesion and equality while also accepting difference.

There are different models of how these aims can be achieved. The **nationalistic model** is based upon the idea that 'the state promotes a single national culture and expects all to assimilate to it'. However, the report rejects this model because, it argues, there is no single, dominant, national culture, and, even if there was, those who do not subscribe to it should not be treated as second-class citizens. Instead, it argues for a combination of liberal and plural models.

In a **liberal model** 'there is a single political culture in the public sphere but substantial diversity in the private lives of individuals and communities'. There needs to be some core of shared values relating to the public sphere: for example, in relation to how disputes are settled. However, a problem with this model is that a monocultural public realm may undermine a multicultural private realm. For example, if public holidays are based upon Christian tradition, this undermines and devalues other religious traditions.

The report therefore argues that elements of a **plural model** should be accepted. In this model, there should be public recognition of diversity. Public services in particular should try to meet the needs of different communities and not just be orientated towards the needs of the majority. The Stephen Lawrence case is cited as an example of how one public service, the police, failed to meet the needs of minority communities subjected to racially motivated attacks.

4 So far, the Parekh Report advocates a form of multiculturalism. However, the fourth key element takes into account the arguments of anti-racists. The report argues that there are many different forms of racism, which can be based on religion, language and culture as well as skin colour. All of these forms undermine attempts to produce a community of citizens and all need to be vigorously tackled.

5 The Parekh Report also follows more **radical** and **structural** views on 'race' and ethnicity by arguing that inequality and social exclusion must be tackled if progress is to be made. Specific efforts should be made to help disadvantaged minorities, which involve, for example, helping members of minorities find employment, developing welfare systems to reduce ethnic disadvantage, and financing and encouraging local initiatives which tackle specific community problems.

Inequality and social exclusion need to be tackled for all groups, but this cannot be done in a culture-blind way. For example, reducing inequality in housing by improving council housing would not help Pakistani people much, as they mainly rent privately or are owner-occupiers. Institutional racism requires special measures to eradicate it, and anti-poverty measures need to take account of cultural differences (for example, in household size and patterns of family life) if they are going to meet the needs of all communities.

6 The report argues that a sense of citizenship can be encouraged through developing a **pluralistic human rights culture**. Here some progress has been made with the incorporation into British law of the European Convention on Human Rights, which provides for a range of rights for individuals.

The Parekh Report accepts that there will always be the potential for conflict over contested issues, such as the attempt to 'balance the right to free speech and the right to freedom from incitement to racial hatred', and there can be incompatibility between the logic of multiculturalism and the logic of human rights. Nevertheless the report believes that the adoption of human rights is necessary to 'lay down the moral minimum'.

This, on its own, though, is not enough to produce a more harmonious society. Whatever the state stipulates, only the development of mutual respect in everyday life between individuals from different communities can secure a satisfactory future for multi-ethnic Britain. As the Parekh Report admits, combining values such as equality and diversity, liberty and solidarity, is not an easy task. There are theoretical problems in reconciling apparently conflicting standpoints and there are practical problems in implementing them.

Multiculturalism and contemporary politics

The Parekh Report received a lot of hostile coverage from the British press (Pilkington, 2005). For example, the *Daily Telegraph* claimed that the report stated that the word 'British' had racist connotations. Pilkington argues that this, and much of the reporting, was inaccurate and misleading. Quotes were taken out of context and key arguments misrepresented. Pilkington suggests that this seems to indicate that there is little chance of the report's recommendations being implemented and its aims being achieved.

Pilkington also suggests that there has been something of a 'retreat from multiculturalism'. Multiculturalism has not just been questioned by the press but also by academics and even by the Chair of the Commission for Racial Equality. David Goodhart (2004, discussed in Pilkington, 2005) criticizes multiculturalism on the grounds that it undermines solidarity. If ethnic groups are encouraged to maintain very different cultures, then different social groups will feel little sense of common identity. According to Goodhart, this discourages support for the welfare state. People are unwilling to contribute taxes to help pay for the welfare of ethnic groups whom they see as having little in common with themselves. Goodhart believes that this is why ethnically diverse societies (such as the USA) tend to have much less generous welfare states than ethnically homogeneous societies such as Sweden.

Trevor Phillips, then Chair of the Commission for Racial Equality, attacked multiculturalism in 2004, arguing that the separation of communities prevented integration. Furthermore, as Pilkington points out, some critics of the New Labour government have argued that, after 2001, it lost its way in dealing with ethnic disadvantage. A number of sociologists and other commentators have claimed that New Labour began to emphasize assimilation rather than multiculturalism and became more concerned with issues such as terrorism rather than issues such as racism.

However, Pilkington believes that this view oversimplifies the situation and ignores some government initiatives. For example, in 2005 the then Home Secretary Charles Clarke announced measures designed to tackle racial inequality. Furthermore, despite the hostile reception the Parekh Report received, the Runnymede Trust (which commissioned the report in the first place) claimed that by 2003 more than two-thirds of the report's recommendations had already been acted upon.

Thus, despite the hostility to many of the policies designed to tackle ethnic inequality and conflict, a wide variety of measures have continued to be taken to tackle the problems. Pilkington concludes: 'What we need to do is adopt an attitude of cautious optimism and seek through our actions to reinforce those tendencies that promote racial equality' (Pilkington, 2005, p. 94).

Summary and conclusions

This chapter has examined a number of criteria – 'race', ethnicity and nationality – which can produce divisive differences in the identities of groups of humans. The nature of these identities has shifted over time.

In the nineteenth century, 'racial' differences were seen as the most important. By the late twentieth century, there was more emphasis on ethnicity, with cultural rather than biological differences assuming more importance in creating social divisions. With the rise of Islamophobia around the start of the twenty-first century, religious identity became increasingly mixed with ethnicity as divisions and conflict between groups with different identities showed no sign of disappearing.

Strong nationalist sentiment can also lead to conflict – for example, it can encourage hostility to new groups of immigrants who are deemed to be different from the 'host' population. The nature of these divisions and conflicts changes over time and varies between societies, but, despite this, such divisions seem remarkably persistent.

Sociologists are divided over the causes, but conflicts of interest, cultural differences, the exploitation of some groups by others, racism based on learnt stereotypes, and the encouragement of nationalism by political leaders all play a part. In a globalizing world where the movement of peoples leads to more ethnically mixed societies, the potential for increased ethnic, 'racial' and national divisions and conflict continues to grow.

However, as the Parekh Report concludes, there are some reasons for optimism. Societies such as Britain may still suffer from ethnic inequality, but there is evidence that there is less inequality than in the past. In Britain and elsewhere, there is growing awareness of racism, and racism is increasingly considered unacceptable. For example, in the British reality TV programme *Big Brother*, participants have been severely criticized for racist remarks.

Yet even as overt racism becomes taboo in some places, in other parts of the world racially or ethnically motivated wars and even genocide are still taking place. While it is possible to address some of the problems which cause ethnic conflict and racial hatred, there are still many underlying factors which seem likely to continue to cause such problems in the future.

CHAPTER 4

Poverty, social exclusion and the welfare state

Individuals, families and groups in the population can be said to be in poverty when they lack the resources to obtain the types of diet, participate in the activities and have the living conditions and amenities which are customary, or at least widely encouraged or approved, in the societies to which they belong. Their resources are so seriously below those commanded by the average individual or family that they are, in effect, excluded from the ordinary living patterns, customs and activities. Townsend, 1979

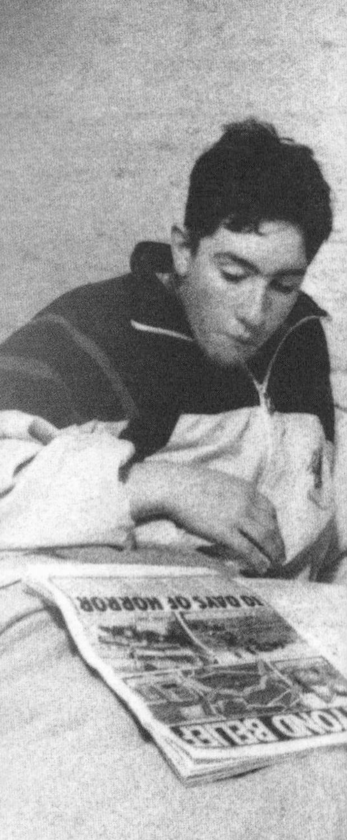

Introduction

The terms **poverty** and **social exclusion** imply undesirable states. They suggest that individuals or groups suffering from poverty or social exclusion need to be helped so that their situation can be changed. In other words, poverty and social exclusion are usually seen as social problems. Most societies have developed institutions designed to deal with social problems such as poverty, and these institutions are often referred to as the **welfare state**. This chapter examines the problems in defining and measuring poverty, the causes of poverty and social exclusion, and the ways in which these social problems can be reduced or eradicated.

The welfare state has sometimes been seen as the most effective way of dealing with poverty, social exclusion and other social problems. However, some sociologists have argued that the welfare state does little to alleviate poverty and social exclusion, and others have even suggested that it is a cause of poverty. There are competing perspectives on how the welfare state works and how it should work, ranging from those who see it as essential to solving numerous social problems, to those who see it as counterproductive and as creating more problems than it solves.

The terms 'poverty', 'social exclusion' and the 'welfare state' are all controversial and the definitions of poverty and social exclusion will be discussed below. The welfare state will be discussed in detail later in the chapter but it is useful at this point to have a preliminary definition. The historian Asa Briggs defines the welfare state as 'a state in which organized power is deliberately used (through politics and administration) in an effort to modify the play of market forces' (Briggs, 2000, p. 18, first published 1969). To Briggs, the welfare state exists where governments decide that private enterprise is failing to meet what the government sees as the social needs of its citizens. The welfare state might intervene to meet such needs by providing services or by redistributing resources to those in need through a benefits system. Before discussing the controversies surrounding the welfare state we will examine two of the problems which it is supposed to tackle, poverty and social exclusion.

The definition and measurement of poverty

Before it is possible to explain the existence of poverty, or to decide what to do about it, it is first necessary to decide what poverty is. The definition of poverty matters because how it is defined determines how much poverty there is believed to be. The definition can also influence the explanations of poverty and the possible solutions that are put forward. As Ruth Lister puts it, 'how we define poverty is critical to political, policy and academic debates about the concept. It is bound up with explanations and has implications for solutions' (Lister, 2004, p. 12).

Some definitions minimize the amount of poverty believed to exist in countries such as Britain and suggest that it is a minor problem which can be dealt with through minor reforms. Other definitions suggest that poverty is still widespread and imply that much greater changes are needed to tackle the problem. It is therefore important to examine competing definitions before proceeding further.

Since the nineteenth century, when rigorous studies of poverty first began, researchers have tried to establish a fixed standard against which to measure poverty. There have been three main areas of controversy over the basic principles on which such a standard can be based.

Absolute and relative poverty

First, researchers have disputed whether poverty should be measured in **absolute** or **relative** terms. Some writers have argued that there is a common minimum standard that can be applied to all societies below which individuals can be said to be 'in poverty'.

Measures of **absolute poverty** are usually based upon the idea of **subsistence**. In other words, people are in poverty if they do not have the resources to maintain human life.

Supporters of the concept of **relative poverty**, however, tend to dismiss this view. They argue that a definition must relate to the standards of a particular society at a particular time. According to this view, the point at which the dividing line that separates the poor from other members of society is drawn will vary according to how affluent that society is.

Material and multiple deprivation and social exclusion

The second area of controversy concerns whether poverty can be defined purely in **material terms**, or whether the definition should be wider. Some sociologists assume that poverty consists of a lack of material resources – in British society, for instance, a shortage of the money required to buy those commodities judged to be necessary to maintain an acceptable standard of living.

Other commentators, though, believe that poverty involves more than **material deprivation**. They see poverty as a form of **multiple deprivation** which can have many facets. For example, some have argued that inadequate educational opportunities, unpleasant working conditions, or powerlessness can all be regarded as aspects of poverty. None of these conditions is necessarily directly related to the income of the individual. Each implies that broader changes than simply increasing the income of the worst-off members of society are necessary if poverty is to be eliminated.

Many commentators now favour the use of the term **social exclusion** to refer to a situation in which multiple deprivation prevents individuals from participating in important areas of society's activities. Thus the socially excluded might be unable to find work, take part in leisure activities or actively participate in a society's politics beyond voting at elections.

Inequality and poverty

The third area of controversy concerns the relationship between **inequality** and poverty. From one point of view, any society in which there is inequality is bound to have poverty. In other words, if all those individuals with below average incomes were defined as poor, then the only way that poverty could be eradicated would be to abolish all inequality in income. This is because if some people have higher than average incomes, inevitably others must fall below the average.

Most sociologists who adopt a relative definition of poverty accept that some reduction in inequality is necessary if poverty is to be reduced, but they do not believe it is necessary to abolish inequality altogether. They argue that it is possible to establish a minimum standard, a **poverty line**, which might be below the average income. The poor within a society can then be defined as those whose income or resources fall so far short of the average that they do not have an acceptable standard of living. Thus it would be possible to have a society with some inequality where poverty no longer exists.

We will now look at these competing definitions and methods of measuring poverty, paying particular attention to the way that these definitions have been used, and the statistics they produce.

Absolute poverty

The concept of absolute poverty usually involves a judgement of basic human needs and is measured in terms of the resources required to maintain health and physical efficiency. Most measures of absolute poverty are concerned with establishing the quality and amount of food, clothing and shelter deemed necessary for a healthy life.

Absolute poverty is often known as **subsistence poverty** since it is based on assessments of minimum subsistence requirements. This means that those who use absolute measurements usually limit poverty to material deprivation. Absolute poverty is generally measured by pricing the basic necessities of life, drawing a poverty line in terms of this price, and defining as poor those whose income falls below the line.

There have been many attempts to define and **operationalize** (put into a form which can be measured) the concept of absolute poverty. An example of an absolute definition of poverty was provided by the 1995 Copenhagen World Summit on Development. The summit agreed that there should be a two-tier definition of poverty. One tier was an **absolute definition** and the other was an **overall definition**. Absolute poverty was defined as:

> *a condition characterized by severe deprivation of basic human needs, including food, safe drinking water, sanitation facilities, health, shelter, education and information. It depends not only on income but also on access to services.* United Nations, 1995

Overall poverty was seen as a broader concept incorporating absolute poverty but also including such features as 'lack of participation in decision-making and in civil, social and cultural life'. This is close to definitions of relative poverty and social exclusion, which will be discussed later. First, however, the problems of absolute definitions will be considered.

Criticisms of the concept of absolute poverty

The concept of absolute poverty has been widely criticized. It is based on the assumption that there are minimum basic needs for all people, in all societies. This is a difficult argument to defend, even in regard to subsistence poverty measured in terms of food, clothing, drinking water and shelter. Such needs vary both between and within societies.

Thus Peter Townsend (1970) argues, 'it would be difficult to define nutritional needs without taking account of the kinds and demands of occupations and of leisure time pursuits in a society'. For instance, the nutritional needs of the nomadic hunters and gatherers of the Kalahari Desert in Africa may well be very different from those of office workers in London. Within the same society, nutritional needs may vary widely, between, for example, the bank clerk sitting at a desk all day and the labourer working on a building site.

A similar criticism can be made of attempts to define absolute standards of shelter. Jack and Janet Roach give the following illustration:

> *City living, for example, requires that 'adequate' shelter not only protects one from the elements, but that it does not present a fire hazard to others and that attention be paid to water supplies, sewage, and garbage disposal. These problems are simply met in rural situations.* Roach and Roach, 1972

Thus, for instance, flush toilets, which may well be considered a necessary part of adequate shelter in the city, might not be considered essential fixtures in the dwellings of traditional hunting and gathering societies.

The concept of absolute poverty is even more difficult to defend when it is broadened to include the idea of basic cultural needs, such as the need for education and information. Such 'needs' vary from time to time and from place to place, so that any attempt to establish absolute, fixed standards can be problematic. For example, the minimum education considered adequate for a person in a remote agricultural community in a poor country might be very different from that considered adequate for an individual in an urban environment in an affluent society. Similarly, it is very hard to define an adequate level of access to information. Clearly, the expectations regarding access to information will be very different in a society where few have access to information technology and one where access to the internet is widespread and considered essential.

Any absolute standard of cultural needs is based in part on the values of the researchers, which, in turn, reflect their particular cultures. Peter Townsend (1970) notes that when societies are compared in terms of recreational facilities, 'cinema attendance and ownership of radios take precedence over measures of direct participation in cultural events', such as religious rituals and other ceremonies. This is a clear illustration of Western bias.

Budget standards and poverty

One common approach to measuring poverty is to use what has been called the **budget standards** approach. This involves calculating the cost of those purchases which are considered necessary to raise an individual or a family out of poverty. It has been used in some classic and contemporary studies of poverty in Britain. The British government used it in calculating the level at which to set the means-tested benefit National Assistance (now called Income Support) when it was introduced in 1948. It has also been used by the US government in setting benefit levels.

Some of the earliest and most famous studies of poverty were conducted by Seebohm Rowntree in York (Rowntree, 1901, 1941; Rowntree and Lavers, 1951). In his early work, the budget standards approach was originally based upon something very close to an absolute definition of poverty. (In Rowntree's later work, and in contemporary sociology, budget standards have been based upon more relative definitions of poverty.)

Seebohm Rowntree – trends in poverty

Rowntree's original method of defining or measuring poverty comes closest to the use of an absolute and material or subsistence definition in Britain.

Rowntree conducted a study of poor families in York in 1899 and drew a poverty line in terms of a minimum weekly sum of money 'necessary to enable families ... to secure the necessaries of a healthy life' (quoted in Coates and Silburn, 1970). The money needed for this subsistence level of existence covered fuel and light, rent, food, clothing, and household and personal items, and was adjusted according to family size. According to this measure, 33 per cent of the survey population lived in poverty.

Rowntree conducted two further studies of poverty in York, in 1936 and 1950, based largely on a similar methodology. However, in the later studies he included allowances for some items which were not strictly necessary for survival. These included newspapers, books, radios, beer, tobacco, holidays and presents. Despite the inclusion of the extra items, he found that the percentage of his sample population in poverty had dropped to 18 per cent in 1936 and 1.5 per cent in 1950. He also found that the causes of poverty had changed considerably over half a century. For example, inadequate wages – a major factor in 1899 and 1936 – were relatively insignificant by 1950. Table 4.1 summarizes the results of Rowntree's surveys.

By the 1950s it appeared that poverty was a minor problem. 'Pockets' remained (for example, among the elderly), but it was believed that increased welfare benefits would soon eradicate this lingering poverty. The conquest of poverty was put down to an expanding economy (the 1950s were the years of the 'affluent society'), to government policies of full employment and to the success of the welfare state. It was widely believed that the operation of the welfare state had redistributed wealth from rich to poor and significantly raised working-class living standards.

Throughout the 1950s and 1960s, researchers became increasingly dubious about the 'conquest of poverty'. Rowntree's concept of subsistence poverty and the indicators he used to measure poverty were strongly criticized. His measurement of adequate nutrition is a

Table 4.1 Rowntree's studies of York

Percentage of those in poverty			
Causes of poverty	1899	1936	1950
Unemployment	2.31	28.6	–
Inadequate wages	51.96	42.3	1.0
Old age		14.7	68.1
Sickness	5.11	4.1	21.3
Death of chief wage earner	15.63	7.8	6.4
Miscellaneous (incl. large family)	24.99	2.5	3.2
Totals	100	100	100
Percentage of survey population in poverty	33	18	1.5

Source: Adapted from K. Coates and R. Silburn (1970) *Poverty: The Forgotten Englishmen*, Penguin, Harmondsworth, p. 46.

case in point. With the help of experts, Rowntree drew up a diet sheet that would provide the minimum adequate nutritional intake, and, using this, he decided upon the minimum monies required for food. It was very unlikely, however, that this minimum budget would meet the needs of the poor. As Martin Rein argues, it was based on:

> *an unrealistic assumption of a no-waste budget, and extensive knowledge in marketing and cooking. An economical budget must be based on knowledge and skill which is least likely to be present in the low-income groups we are concerned with.* Rein, 1970

Rowntree's selection of the 'necessaries of a healthy life' was based on his own opinions and those of the experts he consulted. In his original 1899 study, these necessities were very limited and genuinely included only the basic items necessary for living in an industrial society. However, as we saw earlier, in his later research he extended the range of what he considered necessities quite considerably. In the 1936 survey, he expanded the idea of 'human needs' to include personal items such as a radio, a holiday, books and travelling. These items were estimated to cost 5 shillings (25 pence). Thus, in his later work, Rowntree used a measure of poverty significantly above subsistence level. Furthermore, the inclusion of such items as holidays anticipated the views of some of the supporters of relative poverty.

Some recent commentators, such as Ruth Lister (2004), have suggested that Rowntree did not himself believe that only those in subsistence poverty should be seen as poor, and that his work paved the way for later, relative, definitions of poverty.

Despite Rowntree's broadening of the definition of poverty in later work, his studies revealed a dramatic decline in the amount of poverty. Rising living standards and improvements in the state benefits available to those on low incomes seemed to have reduced the poor to a very small fraction of the British population. In the 1960s, though, poverty was 'rediscovered', as researchers developed and applied the concept of relative poverty.

Jonathan Bradshaw, Deborah Mitchell and Jane Morgan – the usefulness of budget standards

Since Rowntree's pioneering work there have been a number of attempts to develop the budget standards approach. One example is the work of the Family Budget Unit (Bradshaw *et al.*, 1987; Bradshaw, 2001).

Bradshaw *et al.* (1987) admit that the budget standards approach, which prices the necessities needed to avoid poverty, has its limitations. For example, they accept that it 'inevitably involves judgements – judgements about what items should be included, about the quantity of items that are required and about the price that should be fixed to the items'.

Nevertheless, they think that the budget standards approach is useful because it focuses attention on the amount paid in benefits to the recipients of welfare. It offers sociologists the chance to assess whether benefit levels can provide adequately for people's needs.

Bradshaw *et al.* accept the criticisms of Rowntree's work which point out that it is unrealistic to expect people to have a no-waste budget. To overcome this problem, they base their research on how people actually spend their money, rather than on how experts think they ought to spend it. Bradshaw *et al.* used data from a government survey of family expenditure, the Family Finances Survey, to study how families spent their money.

On the basis of information provided by experts and consumer groups, they worked out the cost of a 'low cost but acceptable' (LCA) standard of living and a 'modest but adequate' (MDA) standard. The LCA standard includes housing costs, heating costs for the lower floor of a house only, bus fares, the cost of second-hand bikes, the cost of one coach journey to a holiday destination about forty miles away each year, and so on. Thus, while there is some provision for leisure, the standards are fairly basic. The MDA standard is higher and allows full participation in society, including running a car and taking an annual holiday.

Howard *et al.* (2001) compared the cost of these budgets with income support levels. They estimated that in 1998 income support levels left a couple with two children under 11 years of age £32.29 a week short of the LCA standard. Income support levels were just 79 per cent of the LCA standard. By 2001 increases in income support for children had reduced the shortfall, but the family would still be £11.17 a week short and were still only receiving 93 per cent of what they needed to meet basic necessities. Furthermore, Howard *et al.* describe the LCA budget as 'a very basic standard of living in the twenty-first century'. Income support levels were well short of the more generous MDA standard.

Evaluation

Pete Alcock (1997) argues that the budget standards approach either relies upon accepting the opinion of experts about what constitutes an adequate budget, or assumes that 'anyone seeing the evidence of the inadequacy of the weekly budget will recognize the existence of poverty'. Such an assumption is unlikely to be justified. Some will see the budget levels chosen as too generous, others as too mean. The definition is therefore either 'tautological … or one based only on the judgement of experts'.

Paul Spicker (1993) also argues that the approach of Bradshaw *et al.* has its limitations. He points out that people's quality of life is not entirely determined by how they spend money. For example, living standards can be improved by the unpaid labour of family members. However, Spicker does support the collection of data on what people actually spend rather than what experts say they should spend. He concludes: 'if there is a way to identify patterns of deprivation as a matter of fact with levels of income, this seems to be it'.

A further problem with the budget standards approach is that it is difficult to take account of regional variations in the cost of living. Lucinda Platt (2006) points out that many costs vary from place to place and budget standards studies tend to generalize about the income needed to attain certain living standards across wide geographical areas.

Relative poverty and deprivation

In view of the problems associated with absolute and subsistence standards of poverty, many researchers have abandoned them. Instead, they have defined and measured poverty in terms of the standards specific to a particular place at a particular time. In this section we will consider those definitions.

In a rapidly changing world, definitions of poverty based on relative standards will be constantly changing. In Western society, products and services such as hot and cold running water, refrigerators and washing machines, medical and dental care, full-time education and cars are moving or have moved from being luxuries, to comforts, to necessities. Thus, in Peter Townsend's words, any definition of poverty must be 'related to the needs and demands of a changing society'.

Moreover, some sociologists have argued that it is necessary to discuss poverty in terms of lifestyles. It is not sufficient to see poverty simply as lack of material possessions and of the facilities necessary for material well-being. These sociologists believe that poverty also exists where members of society are excluded from the lifestyle of the community to which they belong.

Peter Townsend – poverty as relative deprivation

Peter Townsend carried out a number of studies of poverty, including one of the most detailed ever undertaken in Britain (Townsend, 1979). During the 1960s and 1970s he played a major part in highlighting the continuing existence of poverty, and in forcing the issue back onto the political agenda. He was also the leading supporter of defining poverty in terms of relative deprivation: he stressed that poverty should be defined in relation to the standards of a particular society at a particular time. Furthermore, he believed that poverty extended beyond a simple lack of material resources.

Relative deprivation

Townsend asserts, 'poverty can be defined objectively and applied consistently only in terms of the concept of relative deprivation'. He justifies this claim on the grounds that society determines people's needs: for example, it determines and conditions even the need for food. It affects the amount of energy that 'different sections of the population habitually expend not only at work but in community and family pursuits'. Their individual obligations as parents, wives or husbands, friends or neighbours, as well as the work they have to do, influence how many calories they have to consume each day.

Society also determines what types of foodstuff are available and influences patterns of food consumption through its culture. For instance, tea is closely tied up with British culture and lifestyles: members of British society are expected to be able to offer visitors to their homes a cup of tea, and many workers would be outraged if management threatened to remove their right to a mid-morning tea break. Tea, Townsend reminds us, is 'nutritionally worthless' but 'psychologically and socially essential' in Britain.

Townsend argues that the concept of relative deprivation should be thought of in terms of the resources available to individuals and households, and the styles of living that govern how those resources are used. He believes that concentrating exclusively on income to assess a household's material situation ignores other types of resources that might be available. It neglects capital assets (those who own their home may be better off than those who rent), and ignores occupational fringe benefits, gifts, and the value of public social services such as education and health care.

Townsend also believes it is necessary to move beyond consumption (the purchase of goods) to an examination of how resources affect participation in the lifestyle of the community. He argues that poverty involves an inability to participate in approved social activities that are considered normal, such as visiting friends or relatives, having birthday parties for children, and going on holiday. The cost of such activities can vary greatly – a month on a Mediterranean cruise is considerably more expensive than a weekend camping close to home – but, to Townsend, individuals suffer deprivation if they cannot afford even the cheapest form of such activities.

On the basis of these arguments, Townsend defines poverty as follows:

> *Individuals, families and groups in the population can be said to be in poverty when they lack the resources to obtain the types of diet, participate in the activities and have the living conditions and amenities which are customary, or at least widely encouraged or approved, in the societies to which they belong. Their resources are so seriously below those commanded by the average individual or family that they are, in effect, excluded from the ordinary living patterns, customs and activities.* Townsend, 1979

In *Poverty in the United Kingdom* (1979), Townsend used the above definition to measure the extent of poverty in the UK. His research was based upon a social survey using questionnaires. In 1968–9 his researchers collected information on 2,052 households, containing 6,098 individuals, in 51 parliamentary constituencies in Britain.

The deprivation index

In order to put his definition of poverty into operation, Townsend devised a **deprivation index**. This index covered a total of sixty specific types of deprivation relating to households, diets, fuel and lighting, clothing, household facilities, housing conditions and amenities, working conditions, health, education, the environment, family life, recreation and social activities. From this original list, he selected twelve items he believed would be relevant to the whole of the population (and not just to certain sections of it), and calculated the percentage of the population deprived of them. The results of his findings are shown in Table 4.2.

Each household was given a score on a deprivation index. The more a household was found to suffer deprivation, the higher its score. Townsend then calculated the average score for households with different levels of income, expressed as a percentage of basic supplementary benefit levels. He claimed to find a threshold for levels of income below which the amount of deprivation suddenly increased rapidly. This threshold was found to be at about 150 per cent of basic supplementary benefit levels. He therefore decided to classify all households that did not have this level of resources as 'suffering from poverty'.

Townsend adjusted the income deemed necessary for each family according to the numbers in it, whether adults were working, the age of any children, and whether any members were disabled. Because of the procedures he had followed, he felt able to claim that his figures and definition were 'scientific' and 'objective'.

On the basis of these calculations, Townsend found that 22.9 per cent of the population (or 12.46 million people) were living in poverty in 1968–9. This compared with 6.1 per cent in poverty according to the state standard, or 9.2 per cent according to the relative income standard. Townsend found that poverty was much more widespread than other research had suggested.

Table 4.2 The deprivation index

Characteristics	% of population
1 Has not had a week's holiday away from home in last 12 months	53.6
2 Adults only. Has not had a relative or friend to the home for a meal or snack in the last four weeks	33.4
3 Adults only. Has not been out in the last four weeks to a relative or friend for a meal or snack	45.1
4 Children only (under 15). Has not had a friend to play or to tea in the last four weeks	36.3
5 Children only. Did not have party on last birthday	56.6
6 Has not had an afternoon or evening out for entertainment in the last two weeks	47.0
7 Does not have fresh meat (including meals out) as many as four days a week	19.3
8 Has gone through one or more days in the past fortnight without a cooked meal	7.0
9 Has not had a cooked breakfast most days of the week	67.3
10 Household does not have a refrigerator	45.1
11 Household does not usually have a Sunday joint (three in four times)	25.9
12 Household does not have sole use of four amenities indoors (flush WC; sink or washbasin and cold-water tap; fixed bath or shower; and gas/electric cooker)	21.4

Source: P. Townsend (1979) *Poverty in the United Kingdom*, Penguin, Harmondsworth, p. 250.

Criticisms of Townsend's early research

Despite the enormous impact Townsend's early work had on British poverty research, some writers criticized it. David Piachaud (1981, 1987) argued that the index on which Townsend's statistics were based was inadequate. Commenting on the items included in the index, Piachaud writes: 'it is not clear what they have to do with poverty, nor how they were selected'. In particular, he questioned the view that going without a Sunday joint and not eating fresh meat or cooked meals are necessarily associated with deprivation: it might reflect social and cultural differences. He claims: 'it is no indicator of deprivation if someone chooses to stay at home, eating salads and uncooked breakfasts'.

A problem that all researchers into poverty face is that of finding a point at which it is possible to draw a poverty line. Townsend claimed to have found such a point, below which deprivation starts to increase rapidly. Piachaud believes that the selection of this point (at 150 per cent of basic supplementary benefit levels) is as arbitrary as any other. He examined Townsend's data closely and disputed the view that deprivation starts to increase rapidly below this level of income. Other researchers, such as M. Desai (1986), have reanalysed Townsend's data, and have supported his claim that there is a poverty threshold.

Perhaps the most damaging criticism of Townsend advanced by Piachaud concerns the implications of his definition of poverty for measures designed to eradicate it. Using Townsend's deprivation index as a measure of poverty, all inequality of wealth and income could be removed from society, but poverty might still remain if people chose to become vegetarian or not to go on holiday. As Piachaud puts it, 'taken to its logical conclusion, only when everyone behaved identically would no one be defined as deprived'. To tackle what Townsend calls poverty would involve creating uniformity in people's behaviour, because Townsend did not attempt to discover whether it was choice or shortage of money which led to people in his survey scoring points on the deprivation index.

Amartya Sen (1981, 1985) argues that there is 'much to be said' for Townsend's concept of relative deprivation. However, Sen believes that relative deprivation, even including all its variants, cannot really be the only basis for the concept of poverty. He suggests that there is an

> *irreducible core of absolute deprivation in our idea of poverty, which translates reports of starvation, malnutrition and visible hardship into a diagnosis of poverty without having to ascertain first the relative position.* Sen, 1985

Thus, if famine were very widespread in a society, it would make little sense to argue that there was no poverty on the grounds that there was little inequality since everybody was short of food.

Sen accepts that the resources needed to avoid absolute deprivation vary from society to society. The diet and shelter required in different circumstances will vary, but to him that does not prevent poverty researchers from determining when people have too little for their most basic needs. For Sen, 'the approach of relative deprivation supplements rather than supplants the analysis of poverty in terms of absolute dispossession'.

Townsend (1995) has continued to argue that an international poverty line can be based on a concept of relative deprivation. He claims that when absolute measures of poverty are used to compare nations, they tend to suggest there is little poverty in richer countries. Since Townsend believes that poverty remains a substantial problem in countries such as the USA and Britain, he does not accept that absolute international poverty lines are adequate. Instead, he argues that international comparisons can be made by identifying a poverty threshold for each society, below which people start to suffer from relative deprivation. However, the problem remains that this still involves making comparisons on the basis of poverty lines that are unique to each country.

Despite Townsend's defence, Sen may have a point in arguing that different types of poverty should be distinguished. Most of Sen's research has been conducted in developing countries where absolute deprivation, however defined, remains a real problem. At least in terms of international comparisons, the idea of absolute deprivation as poverty may still be useful.

In more recent research, Townsend, along with others, has further developed the way he has measured relative deprivation and poverty (Gordon *et al.*, 2000). This research will be examined shortly.

Joanna Mack and Stewart Lansley – *Poor Britain*

In the 1980s, London Weekend Television financed a study of poverty built on Townsend's methods (Mack and Lansley, 1985). It was conducted by Joanna Mack and Stewart Lansley, and took account of many of the methodological criticisms of Townsend made by sociologists such as Piachaud.

Mack and Lansley followed Townsend in defining poverty in relative terms, and in attempting to measure directly the extent of deprivation. Unlike Townsend, however, they tried to distinguish between styles of living which people could not afford, and those which they chose not to follow.

Furthermore, Mack and Lansley devised a new way of determining what were the 'necessities' of life in modern Britain. They accepted the point made by Piachaud that taste might influence whether some people went without items on a deprivation index. In order to overcome this problem, they decided to include in their research a question relating to each item that respondents said they lacked, asking them whether it was by choice, or through necessity because of financial shortage. Those who said it was a matter of choice were not defined as being deprived of that item.

In addition, Mack and Lansley excluded some items from the index which groups with high income were as likely, or nearly as likely, to say they lacked by choice as groups on low incomes. They suggested that where these particular items were concerned, the cost of them depended to a significant extent on where people lived. (For example, the cost of a garden would be much greater in an area with very high housing costs.) Lack of a television set was also ignored because nearly everyone had one. After the exclusion of such items, Mack and Lansley argued that their figures would accurately reflect the extent of involuntary deprivation.

Public perception of necessities

The second area in which this study tried to improve on Townsend's work was in the selection of items for inclusion in the index. Mack and Lansley wanted to avoid the accusation that their choice of items was purely arbitrary. They asked respondents in their research what they considered to be necessities in contemporary Britain. Although the answers represented no more than the subjective opinions of members of society, they did at least give some indication of what the population considered to be customary, socially approved and of vital importance to social life.

Furthermore, Mack and Lansley claimed to have discovered a large degree of consensus about what items were seen as necessities. They decided to assume that an item became a necessity when 50 per cent of the respondents in their study classified it as one. Lack of a television, lack of self-contained accommodation, lack of a garden and lack of money for public transport were excluded for reasons that have already been explained. This left them with a deprivation index of twenty-two items. Mack and Lansley went on to measure the extent of poverty, which they defined as 'an enforced lack of socially perceived necessities', on the basis of this index. Only those people who lacked three or more items were considered to be poor.

Mack and Lansley produced the following results, using a sample of 1,174 people who were questioned in February 1983. According to their calculations, there were 7.5 million people in poverty in Britain – 5 million adults and 2.5 million children – equivalent to 13.8 per cent of the population. Although this figure is substantially less than that reached by Townsend in 1968–9, it still showed that poverty remained a significant problem in contemporary Britain. Furthermore, the figures are not comparable because they are calculated in a different way. Mack and Lansley themselves suspected that poverty was increasing, not decreasing, due to such factors as the reduction in benefit levels and rising unemployment in the early 1980s.

The follow-up study

Mack and Lansley carried out a follow-up study in 1990, using a sample of 1,800 people. Once again, they conducted a survey to determine public perceptions of necessities. They found that these had changed. For example, a weekly outing for children, having children's friends round once a fortnight, a telephone and a best outfit for special occasions were all now seen as necessities by more than half the population. These were therefore added to the index. Televisions were also included and new items were added such as 'a decent standard of decoration in the home' and 'fresh fruit and vegetables every day'. This produced an index of thirty-two items.

Table 4.3 The public's perception of necessities (percentage classing items as necessary)

	Omnibus survey: items considered		Main stage survey: items that respondents…	
	Necessary	Not necessary	Don't have, don't want	Don't have, can't afford
Beds and bedding for everyone	95	4	0.2	1
Heating to warm living areas of the home	94	5	0.4	1
Damp-free home	93	6	3	6
Visiting friends or family in hospital	92	7	8	3
Two meals a day	91	9	3	1
Medicines prescribed by the doctor	90	9	5	1
Refrigerator	89	11	1	0.1
Fresh fruit and vegetables daily	86	13	7	4
Warm, waterproof coat	85	14	2	4
Replace or repair broken electrical goods	85	14	6	12
Visits to friends of family	84	15	3	2
Celebrations on special occasions such as Christmas	83	16	2	2
Money to keep home in a decent state of decoration	82	17	2	14
Visits to school, e.g. sports day	81	17	33	2
Attending weddings/funerals	80	19	3	3
Meat, fish or vegetarian equivalent every other day	79	19	4	3
Insurance of contents of dwelling	78	20	5	8
Hobby or leisure activity	76	20	12	7
Washing machine	75	22	3	1
Collect children from school	75	23	36	2
Telephone	71	28	1	1
Appropriate clothes for job interviews	69	28	13	4
Deep freeze/fridge freezer	68	30	3	2
Carpets in living rooms and bedrooms	67	31	2	3
Regular savings (of £10 per month) for rainy days or retirement	66	32	7	25
Two pairs of all-weather shoes	64	34	4	5
Friends or family round for a meal	64	34	10	6

continued…

Changes between 1983 and 1990

The 1990 study found that there had been a big increase in poverty. The number of people lacking three or more of the necessities, and therefore in poverty according to Mack and Lansley's definition, had risen from 7.5 million in 1983 to 11 million in 1990. The number in severe poverty, defined as lacking seven or more items, had gone up from 2.5 million in 1983 to 3.5 million in 1990.

Two-thirds of the poor in 1990 were found to be dependent on state benefits. Mack and Lansley argued that much of the increase in the numbers of poor resulted from specific changes in the benefits system, such as a slow increase in the level of the basic state pension and the level of income support (previously supplementary benefit). Both rose at a considerably slower rate than average earnings.

David Gordon *et al.* – Poverty and Social Exclusion in Britain (the PSE study)

After the 1990 research there was a nine-year gap before this type of poverty research was done again. In 1999, research was carried out for the Joseph Rowntree Foundation by David Gordon *et al.* (2000; see also Pantazis *et al.*, 2006). Although the research team included both Jonathan Bradshaw and Peter Townsend, the methods adopted largely followed those developed by Mack and Lansley. The research was based upon a survey of public views on necessities conducted by the Office for National Statistics Omnibus Survey, using a sample of 1,855 people, and a further detailed survey using interviews of a sample of 1,534 people drawn from those who had taken part in

...continued

	Omnibus survey: items considered		Main stage survey: items that respondents...	
	Necessary	Not necessary	Don't have, don't want	Don't have, can't afford
A small amount of money to spend on self weekly not on family	59	39	3	13
Television	56	43	1	1
Roast joint/vegetarian equivalent once a week	56	41	11	3
Presents for friends/family once a year	56	42	1	3
Holiday away from home once a year not with relatives	55	43	14	18
Replace worn out furniture	54	43	6	12
Dictionary	53	44	6	5
An outfit for social occasions	51	46	4	4
New, not second-hand, clothes	48	49	4	5
Attending place of worship	42	55	65	1
Car	38	59	12	10
Coach/train fares to visit friends/family quarterly	38	58	49	16
An evening out once a fortnight	37	56	22	15
Dressing gown	34	63	12	6
Having a daily newspaper	30	66	37	4
A meal in a restaurant/pub monthly	26	71	20	18
Microwave oven	23	73	16	3
Tumble dryer	20	75	33	7
Going to the pub once a fortnight	20	76	42	10
Video cassette recorder	19	78	7	2
Holidays abroad once a year	19	77	25	27
CD player	12	84	19	7
Home computer	11	85	42	15
Dishwasher	7	88	57	11
Mobile phone	7	88	48	7
Access to the internet	6	89	54	16
Satellite television	5	90	56	7

Note: percentage of people answering 'Don't know' not shown in table

Source: D. Gordon *et al.* (2000) *Poverty and Social Exclusion in Britain*, Joseph Rowntree Foundation, York, p. 14.

the government's General Household Survey. The second sample was stratified to take account of household income as revealed in their responses to the General Household Survey, with a booster sample of those in low income households.

Defining and measuring poverty

This research attempted to operationalize the United Nations concept of 'overall poverty' (see pp. 214–15). It therefore considered whether people lacked a broad range of items due to low income, and also the extent to which people were excluded from taking part in essential social activities. While largely following the work of Mack and Lansley, some modifications were made. As well as considering poverty, the broader issue of social exclusion was addressed. (The findings on social exclusion are discussed separately: see pp. 229–32.)

As in Mack and Lansley's survey, necessities were defined as items that more than 50 per cent of the sample believed were essential in modern Britain. A number of items were added to the list of possible necessities, including some items concerning children and some related to social obligations. Using data from the Omnibus Survey, twenty-eight items were deemed necessities by more than 50 per cent of respondents. Six of these items (a television, a fridge, beds and bedding for everyone, a washing machine, prescribed medicines, and a deep freeze/fridge freezer) were excluded from the analysis because they 'did not add to the reliability or validity of the definition of necessities in terms of distinguishing between rich and poor' (Gordon *et al.*, 2000, p. 18).

Table 4.3 shows the percentage of people who deemed different items a necessity, and the percentage of people who lacked these items, either because they didn't want them or could not afford them.

The researchers then questioned the respondents in the sample taken from the General Household Survey about which items defined as necessities they lacked due to lack of money. Using these data, a poverty threshold was established. Statistical techniques were used to calculate a threshold which 'maximizes the difference between "poor" and "not poor"', and 'minimizes the differences within these groups'. It was found that the optimum definition for the poor on this basis comprised those who lacked two or more necessities of the twenty-two in the final list. (As noted above, in the 1983 survey, only those lacking three or more necessities were defined as poor.) The researchers argue that these procedures meant that 'the level of deprivation that constitutes poverty is based on a scientific calculation, not an arbitrary decision'.

Findings

Table 4.4 shows the overall findings of the survey. The population was divided into four groups.

1 The poor were defined as those who lacked two or more necessities and did not have relatively high incomes: 25.6 per cent were defined as poor.
2 Those who did not lack two or more necessities but had relatively low incomes were defined as 'vulnerable to poverty': 10.3 per cent fell into this group. Some members of this group had recently lost their job and might struggle to keep themselves out of poverty in the future.
3 1.8 per cent of the sample were unable to afford two or more necessities despite having a relatively high income. This group were defined as having risen out of poverty. They were likely to have experienced a recent rise in income, but had not yet been able to afford all the necessities.
4 The remaining group, which constituted 62.2 per cent of the sample, were defined as not poor.

The study found that about 9 million people could not afford adequate housing, over 10 million people could not afford one or more essential household goods, and one-third of British children lacked at least one necessity (Pantazis *et al.*, 2006).

Changes over time

In order to compare the 1999 findings with those from Mack and Lansley's study of 1983, Gordon *et al.* also calculated the percentage of the population who lacked *three* or more necessities (the definition used by Mack and Lansley). They found that on this basis the percentage of households experiencing poverty had increased from 14 per cent in 1983 to 24 per cent in 1999. Between 1983 and 1999 an extra half a million people joined the ranks of the poor each year. This was despite a big increase in average living standards over the same period. Even after taking inflation into account, average income rose 51 per cent between 1983 and 1998/9. So why had poverty increased despite this rise in living standards? Gordon *et al.* provide two main explanations.

1 Despite the rise in average income, after allowing for increases in housing costs and inflation the income of the poorest households actually decreased over the period. The incomes of the richest grew rapidly, creating growing income inequality and a rise in relative poverty.
2 To some extent the public's perceptions of necessities had changed. In 1999 possession of a telephone and 'friends or family round for a meal' were both considered necessities by more than 50 per cent of the sample for the first time, and some new items were added to the list of necessities. Fewer people thought that carpets, new clothes and presents for friends and family were necessities than in previous surveys, but they remained as indicators of poverty since they were still seen as necessities by more than 50 per cent of the population.

Table 4.4 Poverty and social exclusion survey, poverty classifications

	Number	%
Poor	393	25.6
Vulnerable to poverty	158	10.3
Risen out of poverty	28	1.8
Not poor	955	62.2
Total	1534	100.0

Source: D. Gordon *et al.* (2000) *Poverty and Social Exclusion in Britain*, Joseph Rowntree Foundation, York, p. 18.

Criticisms of Mack and Lansley and Gordon et al.

Use of a public opinion poll to determine what are considered necessities is an advance over Townsend's approach, which relied largely on the judgements of the researcher. However, even Mack and Lansley's and Gordon *et al.*'s methods are heavily influenced by the choices made by the researchers. They have to choose what items to question the public about before they can determine what is considered deprivation. Many other items apart from those chosen could have been included.

The researchers also shaped the findings by defining poverty as lacking three or more items in Mack and Lansley's research, and two or more items in the case of Gordon *et al.* If they had settled on four items as the dividing line they would have produced different estimates of the total number in poverty. As David Piachaud (1987) pointed out, Mack and Lansley's approach 'still requires expert involvement in defining questions and determining answers'.

A further problem is that such studies may exaggerate the number of items identified as necessities. Stephen Sinclair (2003) says, 'these surveys may arrive at an over-generous estimation of poverty because they ask questions almost exclusively about the condition and rights of the poor, and might prompt more favourable answers'. Furthermore, Lucinda Platt (2006) suggests that it is arbitrary to define an item as a necessity when a bare majority of people (anything over 50 per cent) regard it as one. The definition of poverty in these studies is supposed to be based upon a 'consensus', but in reality the opinion polls found large variations in what different groups of the population saw as necessities.

Piachaud also pointed out that there was a problem in Mack and Lansley's research with individuals who spent their money on items that are not considered necessities. For example, some people could not afford to pay for an adequate diet or adequate housing because they spent large amounts of money on cigarettes or leisure pursuits. To Piachaud, there needs to be 'some judgement about what margin, if any, needs to be allowed for non-necessities'. Again, this involves the use of the opinion of 'experts' and further undermines the claim that the results of such studies are based upon definitions of poverty supported by the general public.

Robert Walker (1987) provides an alternative to the use of experts or opinion polls in trying to determine what constitute necessities. He argues that Mack and Lansley's approach fails to do justice to the complexity of the problem. The survey data they use gave respondents no chance to determine what quality of goods and services people need. For example, is a threadbare carpet adequate, or should it be in a better condition? Moreover, Mack and Lansley gave the respondents no opportunity to include items they were not asked about, and no chance to discuss the issues involved and reflect in depth on the necessities of contemporary living.

Walker therefore proposes that basic needs should be determined not by groups of experts or by survey methods, but by panels of ordinary people who are given the opportunity to have in-depth discussions. These members of the public could then produce costed descriptions of the minimum acceptable basket of goods and services needed by different family types. In this way, a definition of poverty could be based upon a genuine consensus among a sample of the population, rather than being based upon the majority voting system used in Mack and Lansley's survey research.

An obvious problem with Walker's approach is the assumption that a consensus would be reached. It is quite likely that the members of the public on the panel would disagree about a minimum acceptable living standard. Furthermore, there would be no guarantee that the same living standard would be agreed by a different panel. Once again, an objective or 'democratic' definition of poverty would prove elusive.

If all methods of determining what constitutes a necessity are flawed, it is also very difficult to make comparisons over time of rates of relative poverty. The inclusion of entirely new items in the 1990 and 1999 indexes, and changes in public perceptions of necessities, raise questions about the comparability of the data from the three studies. Obviously, the more items that are included as necessities, the greater the number of people who will be found to be lacking necessities.

All figures on poverty are a product of the methods used to operationalize definitions of poverty. However, comparability over time is somewhat easier using definitions of poverty based upon official statistics. These will now be examined.

Official statistics on poverty

Some countries use an official poverty line and produce regular statistics on poverty. The USA is an example. Other countries, such as Britain, do not have an official poverty line but do produce some statistics on low incomes.

Statistics on official poverty, or low incomes, are not necessarily based upon sophisticated sociological definitions of poverty. What is more, statistics from different countries are calculated in a variety of ways and therefore cannot always be compared. Nevertheless, official statistics do provide valuable information about the extent of poverty, or at least low incomes. They also give some indication of how poverty is distributed between different social groups.

British statistics

Types of official statistics

The British government has not always had an official poverty line, but it has for many years published a variety of statistics relevant to poverty. From 1972 to 1985 the government published statistics on **low income families**, and from 1985 to 1995 the Institute for Fiscal Studies and the House of Commons Social Security Committee continued the statistical series (Howard *et al.*, 2001). These statistics measured the number of people living at or just above the level of the main means-tested state benefit, supplementary benefit/income support. Figures were produced for those receiving 100 per cent and 140 per cent of the benefit.

Until 1995 these figures were used by most bodies as the nearest thing to a governmental definition of poverty. However, these figures have now been discontinued. As Flaherty *et al.* (2004) point out, they depended upon political decisions taken by the government of the day on the level of benefits they chose to provide. Indeed, if the government put up benefits then more people would be defined as poor since the threshold for escaping officially defined poverty would be raised.

Nevertheless, figures on the proportion of people claiming the main state means-tested benefit still give some indication of trends in welfare dependency and low income. Only 8 per cent received such benefits in 1979. This rose to a peak of 15 per cent in 1993, falling slightly to 13.9 per cent in 2003 (Flaherty *et al.*, 2004).

Because of some of the problems discussed above, low income family statistics were replaced by figures based on average (or, more accurately, median) income. **Households below average income** statistics were introduced in 1988 (though figures going back as far as 1979 have been produced), and by 1995 they were being used as the nearest thing to an official measure of poverty. After the Labour government was elected in 1997 they became the basis for an official poverty line which was used when setting targets for the reduction of child poverty.

These figures measure the number of households receiving 60 per cent of the median income before and after housing costs. (Calculating the median income involves ranking all families in terms of income and using the family that is ranked exactly half-way up this ranking.) All figures are adjusted to take account of the size of households and the number of children and adults they contain, and are based on government surveys, currently the Family Resources Survey. This method allows figures to be produced which show the number of households falling below different levels in relation to average income. For example, the number of households receiving 50 per cent or less of the average household income is sometimes taken as a measure of the numbers in poverty.

Government figures are based on those receiving 60 per cent of median income. In 2004/5 a couple with two children required £268 per week to avoid being in poverty by this definition, while a lone parent with two children required £186 per week, a single person required £100, and a childless couple £183 (CPAG, 2006a; Brewer *et al.*, 2006).

Households below average income (HBAI) statistics provide a useful measure of income inequality and can be used as one way of measuring relative poverty. Giles and Webb (1993) argue that the figures are useful because they are not tied to benefit levels, which are affected by political decisions. Figures such as the proportion of households receiving less than half the average income allow clear comparisons over time and between countries.

However, Giles and Webb note that the figures were never intended to be a measure of poverty and what they actually measure is simply income distribution. Furthermore the percentage of median income that is taken to represent the poverty line is somewhat arbitrary. There is no agreement about whether figures should be based on statistics before or after housing costs. The Child Poverty Action Group (Howard *et al.*, 2001) argue that figures after housing costs are more useful because there are big regional differences in housing costs and families on low income may have little chance of cutting these costs because they are already likely to be living in some of the cheapest available accommodation. However, others see figures before housing costs as more useful because they are based on total income. A further problem is that the figures do not include people in residential institutions, students, homeless people or those living in bed and breakfast accommodation, since these are not covered in the Family Resources Survey.

Despite these problems, HBAI statistics are the best available comprehensive official figures relating to poverty. Their findings will now be examined.

Trends in households below average income (HBAI)

According to the Child Poverty Action Group (CPAG, 2006b), there has been a significant overall increase in poverty in terms of HBAI figures since 1979, although in recent years levels have fallen from a peak in 1999/2000. Using 60 per cent of median income after housing costs as the cut-off point, they found that the number of people in poverty had increased from 7.1 million (13 per cent of the population) in 1979, to 11.4 million or 20 per cent in 2005/6. However this had fallen from 1999/2000 when 13.3 million or around 23 per cent of the population were in poverty by this definition (Howard *et al.*, 2001). The government also uses 60 per cent of median income as the

Figure 4.1 Relative poverty in Britain: percentage of individuals in households with income below various fractions of median AHC (after housing costs) income

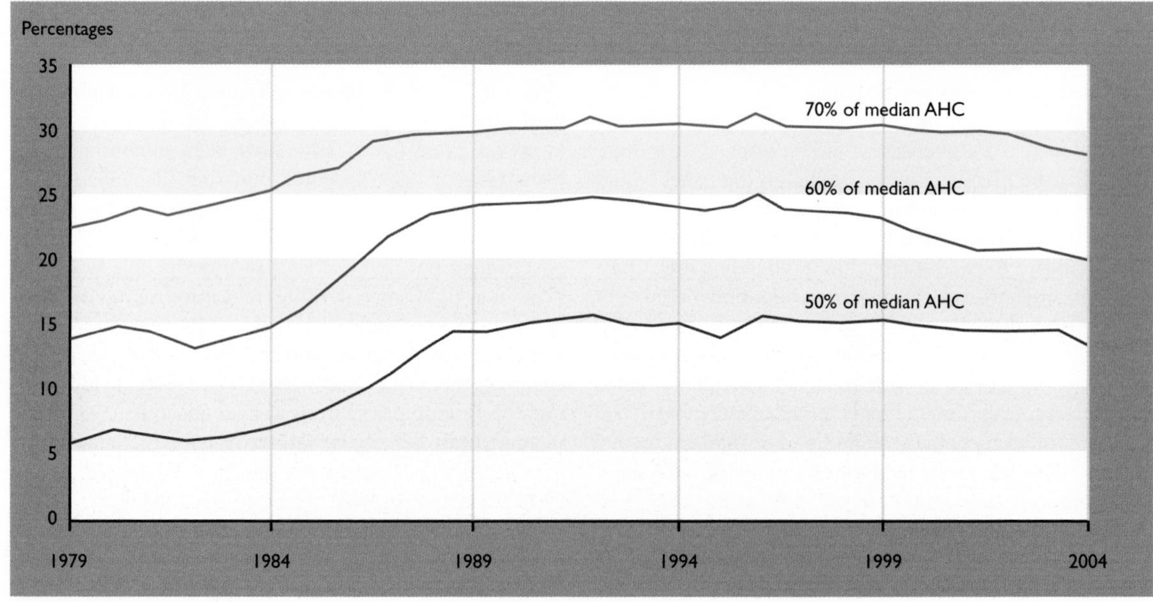

Source: M. Brewer, A. Goodman, J. Shaw and L. Sibieta (2006) *Poverty and Inequality in Britain*, IFS, London, p. 29.

cut-off point for poverty. According to this measure the increase in poverty has been substantial.

The election of a Labour government under Tony Blair in 1997 introduced a new policy of trying to tackle poverty. One of the Labour government's stated aims was to reduce and eventually eradicate child poverty (see p. 259). In 1999 Tony Blair made a speech saying that his government's aim was to end child poverty within twenty years. He set an interim target of reducing child poverty by at least 25 per cent by 2004.

There is evidence that the Labour government was making progress in reducing poverty in general in its first few years in office. Figure 4.1 shows trends in poverty, where poverty is defined as 50 per cent, 60 per cent (the government figure) and 70 per cent of median income after housing costs. The graph shows poverty rates peaking around the time Blair's government was elected to power, before starting to decline slowly.

Research by Brewer *et al.* found that in 1996/7 24.8 per cent of the population in Britain had an income of less than 60 per cent of the median after housing costs, and by 2004/5 this had fallen to 19.9 per cent. The equivalent figures before housing costs were 18.4 per cent in 1996/7 and 16.1 per cent in 2004/5. Indeed, whether poverty is defined as 50 per cent, 60 per cent or 70 per cent of median income, before or after housing costs, there was a significant fall over this period.

In terms of child poverty there was also some progress. According to government figures, the percentage of children living below poverty thresholds declined from 24.9 per cent to 19.5 per cent between 1996/7 and 2004/5 before housing costs, and from 33.3 per cent to 27.2 per cent after housing costs (quoted in Brewer *et al.*, 2006). Despite this, Brewer *et al.* calculated that the government had still failed to meet its target of reducing child poverty by 25 per cent by 2004. Furthermore, by 2004/5 the government was falling well behind on its target to cut child poverty by 50 per cent by 2010 and to eradicate it by 2020.

Although the reductions in child poverty fall short of government targets, they do at least represent progress and reverse a long-term trend in relative poverty.

The overall figures showing the changing proportions of people in poverty mask important differences in the composition of the poor. Figure 4.2 shows the risk of being in poverty according to household characteristics. It shows that the unemployed, those in lone-parent households, Pakistanis/Bangladeshis and black non-Caribbeans all have very high risks of poverty. Having children and having only a part-time worker in a household also lead to a significant increase in the chances of being in poverty.

The chances of different groups being in poverty have changed over time. Figures quoted by Flaherty *et al.* (2004) show that between 1979 and 2000/1 the proportion of the poor who were pensioners or couples with children declined, while the proportions who were single, couples without children or lone parents increased. We will explore more reasons for some of these differences in risk later in the chapter (see pp. 232–7).

Figure 4.2 Risk of income poverty by household characteristics, 2004/5

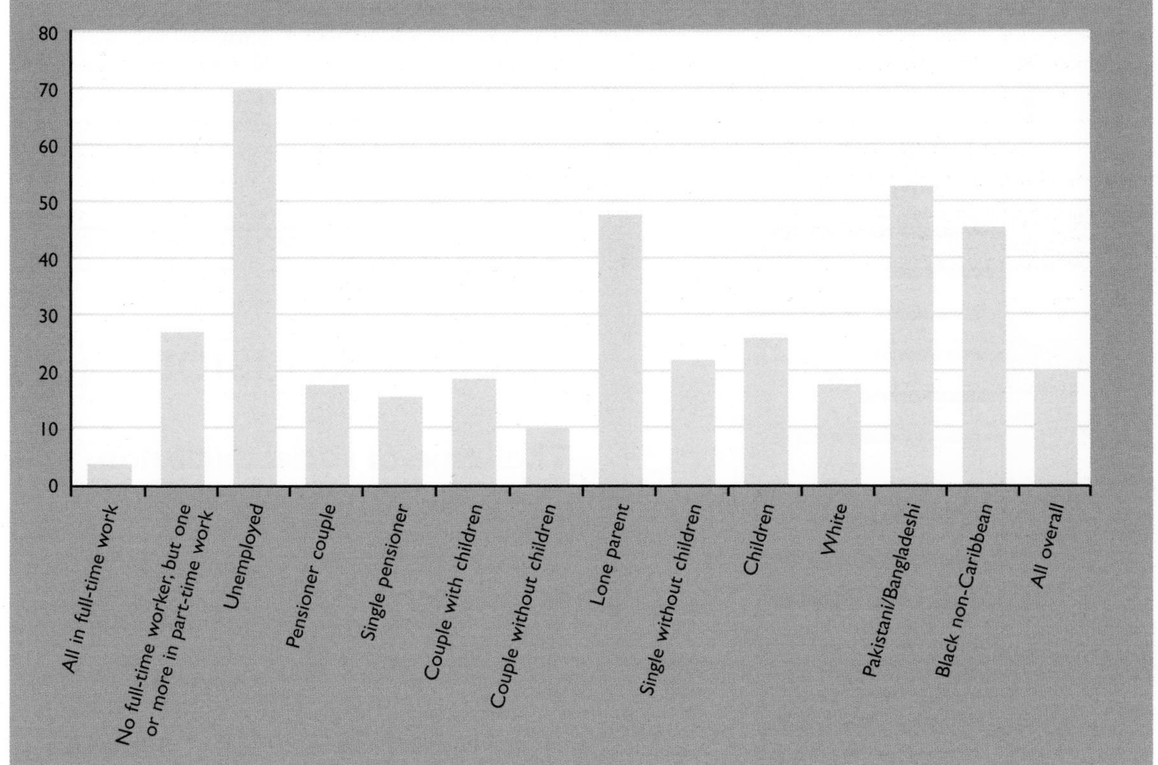

Note: Income poverty defined as the household having an income below 60 per cent of median after housing costs.

Source: CPAG (2006) *Poverty: The Facts: Update 2006*, CPAG, London, p. 2.

Figure 4.3 Poverty rates in the EU: percentage of individuals in each country with an income below the risk-of-poverty threshold, set at 60 per cent of median income

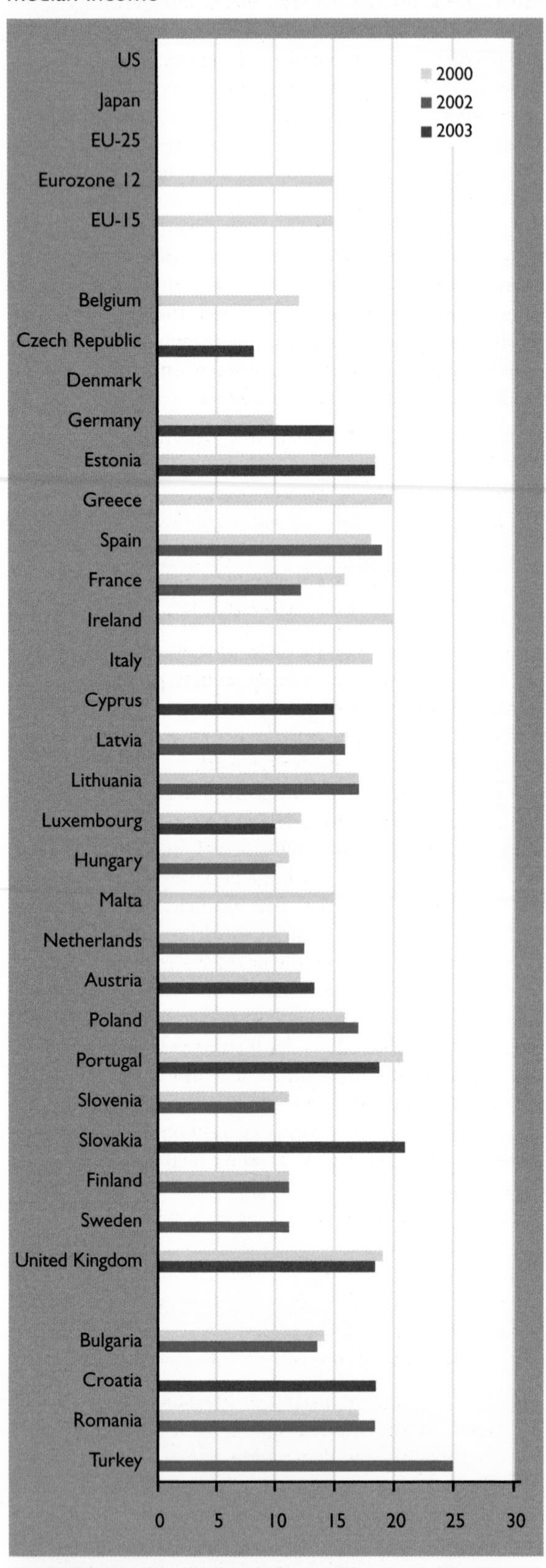

Source: EU Structural Indicators: Update to the Statistical Annex to the 2005 Report from the Commission to the Spring European Council (http://europa.eu.int/com).

International comparisons

Poverty in the European Union

Although the European Union prefers the term 'social exclusion' to poverty, it has not yet devised any way of comparing rates of social exclusion in different countries. However, a number of different definitions of poverty have been used to compare rates across Europe. Figure 4.3 provides statistics based on households below 60 per cent of median income in 2000, 2002 and 2003, though figures for all countries were not available in all these years. It includes EU members along with some countries which were then being considered for future membership. Since it uses the same 60 per cent cut-off point the figures can be compared with the statistics used by the British government to measure its progress on reducing child poverty.

In 2000 the UK's poverty rate, at around 18 per cent, was above the EU average of 15 per cent. Of existing EU countries, only Slovakia, Portugal, Ireland and Greece recorded higher rates than the 2000 rate in the UK. Of applicants for membership only Turkey had a higher rate than the UK. There was some reduction in the UK rate by 2003 but it still had one of the highest poverty rates in Europe.

Poverty worldwide

While there are no up-to-date figures on poverty worldwide calculated in a similar way to the European and British figures, the United Nations does produce useful statistics, using a different measure of poverty. The UN produces figures based upon a combination of income poverty, unemployment, mortality and literacy (UN, 2005). The 2005 report found that there were fourteen countries with lower rates of human and income poverty than the UK, with Sweden, Norway, the Netherlands, Denmark and Germany having the lowest rates of all. Thus, although the UK has lower rates of poverty than most countries in the world, a substantial number of developed countries have less poverty than the UK.

Social exclusion

The issue of social exclusion

In recent years, some commentators have tried to broaden the issues involved in thinking about the most deprived groups in society by using the term **social exclusion** rather than poverty. In some ways, this represents an extension of Townsend's idea of relative deprivation, as it goes beyond confining the question of deprivation to commodities that can be directly purchased.

Tania Burchardt, Julian Le Grand and David Piachaud (2002) note that the term 'social exclusion' originated in continental Europe but has rapidly become influential in British politics and in debates about social policy. Pete Alcock (1997) notes that the EU's European Social

Charter mentions the term and the promotion of social inclusion is now a strategic goal of the EU. Burchardt *et al.* (2002) also note that shortly after coming to power in Britain in 1997, the Labour government set up an inter-departmental **Social Exclusion Unit**.

Despite the increasing political importance of the term, there is no agreed definition or way of measuring social exclusion. Burchardt *et al.* describe it as a 'contested term'. A number of ways of defining the concept will now be considered.

Social exclusion, the underclass and poverty

Before considering what social exclusion is, it is important to distinguish it from some things which it is not. Most commentators agree that the concept of social exclusion should be distinguished from concepts of the **underclass** and **poverty**.

According to David Byrne (1999), the term 'social exclusion' 'has replaced that pejorative US import, "the underclass"'. For people such as Charles Murray, the underclass socially exclude themselves by not trying to participate fully in society (see pp. 242–4). Byrne rejects this interpretation, arguing that social exclusion draws attention to the relationship between those who are excluded and those who do the excluding. Byrne argues, 'exclusion is something that is done by some people to other people', therefore the socially excluded cannot be seen as an underclass.

Similarly, social exclusion should be distinguished from poverty. Poverty refers to a lack of material resources, whereas all definitions of social exclusion include a broader range of ways in which people may be disadvantaged in society. Many of these types of deprivation concern the inability to participate fully in society in ways that are only partly shaped by material resources. For example, the socially excluded might include the unemployed, who lack a role in the formal economic system; those who do not register to vote, who lack a role in the political system; and isolated elderly individuals, who live alone and lack a role in the social system. While there is no agreement on what exactly should be included in the definition of social exclusion, there is agreement that it includes more issues than those covered by poverty. It is also often seen as a more dynamic concept than poverty. For example, Alcock argues:

> *What the EU commentators were doing in their discussion of the problem of social exclusion was attempting to broaden the debate and research on poverty and deprivation beyond the confines and experiences of the poor to encompass the reaction to poverty by other social agencies and individuals throughout society. In this sense, they argue that, rather than being a state of affairs – as poverty has often been conceived – social exclusion is really a process involving us all.* Alcock, 1997

Brian Nolan and Christopher T. Whelan (1996) also stress that social exclusion is a dynamic concept:

> *Talking of social exclusion rather than poverty highlights the gap between those who are active members of society and those who are forced to the fringe, the increasing risks of social disintegration, and the fact that, for the persons concerned and for society, this is a process of change and not a fixed or static situation.* Nolan and Whelan, 1996

Progressive and regressive views of social exclusion

The shift from the discussion of poverty to the discussion of social exclusion has been seen as both a **progressive** and a **regressive** step. Some have argued that the shift is regressive because it involves deflecting attention away from dealing with poverty and therefore means that governments can avoid doing much to help the most disadvantaged. Nolan and Whelan claim that one reason for its introduction to European debates was that the British Conservative government was unwilling to accept the existence of poverty, but it was willing to discuss the rather vaguer term 'social exclusion'. Some critics of the idea of social exclusion therefore see it as a way of avoiding the issue of poverty and therefore avoiding tackling income inequality. For example, Nolan and Whelan suggest that the EU is keen on using the term 'social exclusion' because it might be:

> *more palatable, and perhaps more effective in terms of EU decision-making, to talk in terms of the need to accompany the integration of economies with measures to promote social integration and combat social exclusion rather than to highlight the possibility that economic integration could result in poverty for some vulnerable people and areas.* Nolan and Whelan, 1996

They even suggest that the idea of social exclusion could be used to justify cutting welfare payments on the grounds that it would encourage those who were excluded (the unemployed) to try to escape from social exclusion by looking harder for work.

Others argue that the change from discussing poverty to discussing social exclusion is a progressive step. From this point of view, dealing with social exclusion involves tackling income inequality but it also means tackling many other forms of injustice. For example, Roger Lawson (1995) describes social exclusion in Britain and the USA as becoming 'detached from the broader social and economic experiences of mainstream society'. He believes that social exclusion has been increasing because of the 'risks of family breakdown, reinforced gender inequalities … more hostile and fearful relationships in local communities [and] the most disturbing of recent trends … hardened racial cleavages and … new forms of xenophobia and racism among the less privileged'. Tackling such problems would involve measures to deal with racism, to encourage a stronger sense of community, and to combat sex discrimination and other causes of gender inequality.

Ruth Lister (2004) on the whole sees social exclusion as a useful concept although she believes it should be used as well as poverty and not instead of it. She identifies several advantages of the concept of social exclusion.

1. It encourages a 'broad and dynamic' analysis which looks at the relationship between a wide range of factors linked to deprivation.
2. The concept involves the notion of a relationship between the excluded and the rest and it therefore focuses attention on how the advantaged maintain their position. This leads to a better understanding of disadvantage than approaches which concentrate solely on the situation of the disadvantaged themselves.

3 Because of this, social exclusion can be seen as drawing attention to the existence of injustice.
4 The idea of social exclusion also highlights the 'denial' of a wide range of 'social rights' (for example, educational and housing rights) which are not covered by the concept of poverty.
5 The emphasis on relationships, injustice and the denial of rights allows issues relating to discrimination based on social divisions such as gender, ethnicity and sexuality to be included in the analysis of social exclusion.

Lister suggests that it is possible to see social exclusion as a more 'multi-dimensional' and 'multi-level' concept than poverty. She concludes that:

> *Provided social exclusion is not treated as an alternative to poverty, it can serve a useful conceptual function as a lens, which both sharpens the focus on a number of important aspects of poverty and also advances ... [a] broad framework of analysis of poverty.* Lister, 2004, p. 98

Weak and strong definitions of social exclusion

Although David Byrne agrees with Lister that social exclusion can be a useful concept, he argues that whether social exclusion is seen as progressive or regressive compared to poverty depends upon what sort of definition is used. Drawing upon the work of John Veit-Wilson (1998; discussed in Byrne, 1999), Byrne argues that **weak** and **strong** definitions of social exclusion can be distinguished.

Byrne uses the definition of Carol and Alan Walker as an example of a weak definition. The Walkers distinguish between poverty and social exclusion in the following way:

> *We have retained the distinction regarding poverty as a lack of the material resources, especially income, necessary to participate in British society and social exclusion as a more comprehensive formulation which refers to the dynamic process of being shut out, fully or partially, from any of the social, economic, political or cultural systems which determine the social integration of a person in society. Social exclusion may therefore be seen as the denial (or non-realization) of the civil, political and social rights of citizenship.* Walker and Walker, 1997; quoted in Byrne, 1999

Byrne sees this as a weak definition of social exclusion because it does not require any great increase in equality to tackle it. It is based upon the idea of individual rights and ignores the 'democratic socialist project of collective transformation' in which the working class escapes from exploitation. Furthermore, Byrne argues that this definition of social exclusion pays little attention to power. It is concerned primarily with integrating people in society rather than making them more equal.

Byrne is much more supportive of strong definitions of social exclusion. Here he quotes Madanipour *et al.* (1998):

> *Social exclusion is defined as a multi-dimensional process in which various forms of exclusion are combined: participation in decision-making and political processes, access to employment and material resources and integration into common cultural processes.* Byrne, 1999

To Byrne, this is a strong definition because it emphasizes the importance of both material inequality and inequalities of power. Tackling social exclusion in this sense would require redistribution of income, but it would also require radical changes in the structure of society.

The different definitions of social exclusion tend to reflect the theoretical and political preferences of those who produce the definitions. However, the concept of social exclusion plays a valuable role in broadening the debate about what constitutes a good quality of life to include more than purely material considerations. It also encourages policy makers to coordinate a wide range of policies that try to improve the position of the disadvantaged.

However, because of its breadth and because it is multi-dimensional, social exclusion is difficult to define precisely and measure reliably. As with relative poverty, there are even greater problems in using this concept to compare different societies which have different norms and patterns of social interaction. Tackling some aspects of social exclusion (for example, a decline in a sense of community) may be beyond the power of governments. These problems have not prevented attempts to measure social exclusion and to evaluate the effectiveness of government policies designed to reduce it. We will now examine a governmental and a non-governmental attempt to measure social exclusion.

Official statistics on social exclusion

Opportunities for all

Since 1999 the British government's Department of Work and Pensions (DWP) has published an annual report to monitor progress on what it calls its 'evidence-based strategy for tackling poverty and social exclusion'. The reports are based on evaluating the success or otherwise of government strategy in tackling a variety of causes of symptoms of poverty and social exclusion. The fourth report identified the following dimensions of poverty and social exclusion.

1 **Lack of resources.** The report suggests an adequate income is necessary 'to provide people with the resources to live active fulfilling lives'. It argues that short-term low income may not be a major problem, but if low income is long-term it can lead to serious social exclusion. Poverty needs to be tackled because it can lead to 'cycles of deprivation' in which deprivation can be passed on from one generation to the next. It also believes that poverty can exacerbate other aspects of social exclusion by 'making it difficult for the deprived to afford to participate in many socially important activities'.
2 **Lack of opportunities to work.** 'For most people of working age and their families work is the key to ensuring a decent and prosperous life.' Not only does work help protect against low income; it also helps

people avoid the negative impact of unemployment on health and provides people with the social networks necessary to avoid other types of exclusion.

3 **Lack of opportunities to learn.** According to the DWP report, 'A lack of education and training is arguably the most important driver behind poverty and social exclusion.' It argues that skills are increasingly important in the contemporary labour market and without them there is a high risk of unemployment.
4 **Suffering health inequalities.** The report argues that poor health may prevent people from taking advantage of opportunities 'to work, to learn and to participate in society'. It notes that class (or socio-economic group), ethnicity and gender have an influence on health inequalities.
5 **Lack of decent housing.** Poor housing or homelessness can lead to health problems, including mental health problems. Inadequate heating is one aspect of poor housing.
6 **Disruption of family life.** Here lone parenthood and the break-up of relationships are cited as problems because they can be associated with a fall into low income and tend to place a considerable strain on the parent primarily responsible for children.
7 **Living in a disadvantaged neighbourhood.** Some areas experience problems such as high crime, poor services and poor health, which can make individuals' problems worse. The report notes that living in a neighbourhood with a poor reputation can adversely affect one's chances of finding employment.

The report goes on to argue that where people experience several aspects of poverty and social exclusion the different factors work together to reinforce social exclusion. Particular areas might suffer particular problems as those with skills move away to live in more desirable neighbourhoods. The report also stresses how poverty and social exclusion can be transmitted 'throughout a person's life, through generations and through communities'.

By the eighth report, published in 2006, the indicators of social exclusion were grouped into those concerning children and young people, people of working age, people in later life and communities. The data collected in the report do not try to measure poverty and social exclusion as experienced by individuals. Rather, the data examine whether government policies and other social changes are leading to a reduction or an increase in poverty and social exclusion. The report provides data on changes in levels of social exclusion based upon a range of indicators. By the fourth report, forty-one main indicators were being used, some of which were subdivided to give a total of fifty-nine indicators overall. The findings are summarized in Table 4.5.

The table provides a summary of the direction of movement of the data underlying the indicators. It assesses overall progress by looking at the trend since the baseline. It also shows the direction of movement of the most recent data. It is important to note that, because many of the indicators draw on data from sample surveys, small changes in data could be attributed to sampling variability. The most recent data reported range from 1996 to 2002 depending on the data source.

Compared with the baseline year of 1996, the 2006 report found a worsening trend in seven of the indicators while there were improvements in forty. In nine areas there was little change and in three areas the necessary data were not available to make a valid comparison. In terms of more recent trends between 2002 and 2006, there were just two areas in which things were deteriorating: the proportion of teenage parents in education, employment or training was declining; and the gap between the educational attainment and participation of children looked after by local authorities and that of their peers was widening.

Problems with the DWP reports

There are a number of problems with the attempt to measure poverty and social exclusion in the DWP reports.

1 Stephen Sinclair (2003) points out that the reliability of some of the findings could be questioned. He says, 'some of the changes indicated ... may only be small and could be due to the method of data collection (e.g. where evidence is drawn from a sample survey)'.
2 Unlike studies of relative poverty (see, for example, Gordon *et al.*, 2000), the report produces no overall figure for the number of individuals experiencing poverty and social exclusion. It does not specify how many forms of poverty/social exclusion an individual needs to experience before they are poor/socially excluded. There is also no weighting given to indicate the relative importance of the different measures, some of which might be seen as far more important than others.
3 The selection of criteria for measuring social exclusion is somewhat arbitrary. The criteria included have been altered between reports. There is therefore no clear and coherent justification for some items to be included while others are not. Furthermore, there may be a tendency for reports to include only those criteria which are easily measured, which fit in with the government's political priorities, and which show signs of improvement. As we shall shortly see, alternative ways of measuring social exclusion tend to produce a less rosy picture.

Despite these problems, the reports show that Labour governments since 1997 have accepted that problems of poverty and social exclusion exist, and they have collected appropriate data and initiated policies to try to tackle them. How effective those policies have been will be discussed later (see pp. 257–9).

The Joseph Rowntree Foundation – monitoring poverty and social exclusion

An alternative source of information on the extent of, and trends in, poverty and social exclusion is provided in an annual report produced for the Joseph Rowntree Foundation (Palmer *et al.*, 2005). This has some similarities with the DWP reports:

Table 4.5 Direction of movement of indicators of poverty and social exclusion from baseline of 1996 and between 2002 and 2006 (direction of latest trends)

Indicator		Covers	Trend since baseline	Direction of latest data
Children and young people				
1	Children in workless households	GB	✓	≈
2	Low income:			
	a) Relative	GB	✓	✓
	b) Absolute	GB	✓	✓
	c) Persistent	GB	✓	✓
3	Teenage pregnancy:			
	a) Teenage conceptions	England	✓	≈
	b) Teenage parents in education, employment or training	England	✓	✗
4	An increase in the proportion of children in disadvantaged areas with a 'good' level of development	England	▲	▲
5	Key Stage 2 (11-year-olds) attainment	England	✓	≈
6	Attainment:			
	a) 16-year-olds achievement	England	✓	✓
	b) Schools below floor target	England	✓	✓
7	19-year-olds with at least a Level 2 qualification	England	▲	✓
8	School attendance	England	≈	≈
9	Improvement in the outcomes for looked-after children:			
	a) Education gap	England	✗	✗
	b) Not in education, employment or training	England	≈	≈
	c) Stability in the lives of looked-after children	England	✓	≈
10	16 to 18-year-olds in learning	England	≈	≈
11	Infant mortality	England and Wales	✗	≈
12	Serious unintentional injury	England	✓	≈
13	Smoking prevalence for			
	a) Pregnant women	England	✓	✓
	b) Children aged 11 to 15	England	✓	≈
14	Obesity for children aged 2 to 10	England	✗	≈
15	Re-registrations on Child Protection Register	England	✓	≈
16	Housing that falls below the set standard of decency	England	✓	✓
17	Families in temporary accommodation	England	✗	≈
People of working age				
18	Employment rate	GB	✓	≈
19	Employment of disadvantaged groups:			
	Disabled people	GB	✓	✓
	Lone parents	GB	✓	≈
	Ethnic minority people	GB	✓	✓
	People aged 50 and over	GB	✓	≈
	Lowest qualified	GB	✗	≈

continued...

Indicator	Covers	Trend since baseline	Direction of latest data
20 Working-age people in workless households	GB	✓	✓
21 Working-age people without a Level 2 NVQ qualification or higher	England	✓	✓
22 Long periods on income-related benefits	GB	✓	≈
23 Low income:			
a) Relative	GB	≈	≈
b) Absolute	GB	✓	≈
c) Persistent	GB	≈	≈
24 Smoking rates:			
a) All adults	England	✓	≈
b) Manual socio-economic groups	England	✓	≈
25 Death rates from suicide and undetermined injury	England	✓	≈
26 Rough sleepers	England	✓	≈
27 Drug use (16 to 24-year-olds):			
a) Use of Class A drugs	England and Wales	≈	≈
b) Frequent use of any illicit drug	England and Wales	≈	✓
People in later life			
28 Low income:			
a) Relative	GB	✓	✓
b) Absolute	GB	✓	✓
c) Persistent	GB	✓	✓
29 People contributing to a non-state pension	GB	✗	≈
30 People making continuous contributions to a non-state pension	GB	≈	≈
31 Healthy life expectancy at age 65	England	≈	≈
32 Being helped to live independently:			
a) Receiving intensive home care	England	✓	✓
b) Receiving any community-based service	England	▲	▲
33 Housing that falls below the set standard of decency	England	✓	✓
34 Fear of crime	England and Wales	✓	≈
Communities			
35 Employment rates in deprived areas	GB	✓	✓
36 Crime rates in high-crime areas	England and Wales	✓	≈
37 Housing that falls below the set standard of decency	England	✓	✓
38 Households in fuel poverty	England	✓	≈
39 Life expectancy at birth	England	✗	≈
40 Attainment gap at Key Stage 2 (11-year-olds)	England	✓	✓
41 Road accident casualties in deprived areas	England	✓	✓

✓ data moving in right direction
✗ data moving in wrong direction
≈ data showing broadly constant trend or no significant movement
▲ only baseline data available or insufficient data available to determine a trend

Source: Department of Work and Pensions (DWP) (2006) *Opportunity for All: Eighth Annual Report on Poverty and Social Exclusion*, DWP, London, pp. 5–8.

1 It uses approximately the same number of indicators to measure poverty and social exclusion (fifty instead of fifty-nine).
2 It uses much of the same government data and some of the indicators are the same (for example, both use 60 per cent of median income as a measure of income poverty/relative income).
3 It is published annually and tries to measure changes in poverty and social exclusion, both over the previous year and over the medium term.

However, it is different in a number of ways:

1 It uses a somewhat broader range of indicators than the DWP reports. This is because the indicators chosen do not depend upon the policy targets of the government.
2 The Rowntree Foundation reports are often rather less optimistic and rather more critical of government policy than those of the DWP. Palmer *et al.* (2005) comment that this is because they examine areas where the government may not have specific targets to improve the situation. For example, in considering housing, the Rowntree Foundation looks at the numbers of homeless people (who may or may not be sleeping rough), whereas the DWP reports collect data on rough sleepers. The Rowntree Foundation reports also include more data relating to crime, financial exclusion (such as numbers without bank accounts) and low pay. However, unlike many earlier reports, the 2005 report was broadly in line with the DWP report in terms of the trends shown by the indicators of social exclusion.
3 Compared to the DWP reports, there are more data concerning which groups are suffering from different types of social exclusion.

Findings

In the 2005 report, data were included for medium-term changes over the previous five years and for shorter-term changes over the previous year. As Table 4.6 shows, over the medium term six indicators had worsened, eighteen had improved, and the rest were mixed or steady. Over the previous year only two indicators had worsened (school exclusions and the numbers requiring help to live at home), while twenty had improved.

The Rowntree Foundation report found that 12 million people were below the income poverty threshold of 60 per cent of median income. This represented a fall of almost 2 million on the peak figure in the 1990s, but it was still nearly twice the number in poverty at the end of the 1970s. The report suggested that useful progress had been made towards the government's targets for cutting child poverty (see p. 258), but questioned whether current policies were sufficiently effective to reach the targets. Two of the main initiatives designed to achieve the targets, the minimum wage and the Working Families Tax Credit, had already been introduced and had taken effect. The report stressed that low wages continued to be a major cause of both poverty and social exclusion, with the minimum wage being inadequate to ensure that people escaped poverty. Nevertheless the report found that, overall, the increase in the number of people employed was the main reason for the reduction in poverty rather than changes in benefits.

The 2005 report was particularly critical of the lack of progress in improving the position of the disabled. It found that no less than 30 per cent of the working-age disabled were below the poverty line (see p. 237 for further discussion of poverty and the disabled).

In terms of education, the Rowntree Foundation report found evidence of significant reductions in social exclusion. Educational outcomes were improving, although the rate of improvement had slowed since 1999. Levels of attainment had improved amongst deprived groups, but 40 per cent of those receiving free school meals still failed to get five or more GCSEs at grade C or above.

The report found that health inequalities were 'deep and persistent'. For example, infant deaths were still 50 per cent higher amongst families with manual workers than amongst those with non-manual workers. There had been more progress in terms of crime, with rates of violence and burglary dropping by as much as 50 per cent over the previous decade. But it was still the poor and socially excluded who were bearing the brunt of crime. Households which had no contents insurance were three times more likely to be burgled than those which had insurance.

There was a mixed picture in terms of housing. The proportion of low-income households which had central heating had risen, but then so had the number of homeless people. Over five years there had been a 20 per cent rise in people accepted as homeless by local authorities.

Evaluation

It could be argued that the Rowntree Foundation reports provide a more impartial discussion than the DWP reports because of their independence from government. They are therefore not tied to using indicators that are restricted to areas in which the government has targets and policy initiatives. Furthermore, careful justifications are given for selecting particular indicators.

Despite this it can still be argued that other indicators could be used. For example, it is unclear why the number of burglaries should be an indicator of social exclusion while the number of violent offences is not. While the reports use a wider variety of indicators than the DWP reports, they are still restricted to using indicators for which statistical data exist. Most of these data are produced by the government and therefore government policy might still have some influence on the indicators chosen.

Such problems are inherent in trying to measure a complex and multi-faceted concept such as social exclusion. Whatever its limitations, the Rowntree Foundation may still provide the best available overview of changes in levels of social exclusion.

The social distribution of poverty and social exclusion

The chances of being in poverty or being socially excluded in Britain (and indeed elsewhere) are not equally distributed. Some groups are much more prone to ending up in poverty or being socially excluded than others, while the chances relating to particular groups change over time.

In this section we will briefly outline some of the variations in poverty rates.

Table 4.6 Summary of the 2005 report monitoring poverty and social exclusion indicators

Indicator	Trends over time: Over the medium term	Trends over time: Over the latest year of available data
Low income		
1 Numbers in low income	Improved	Improved
2 Low income by age group	Mixed	Mixed
3 Low income by family type	Improved	Mixed
4 Out-of-work benefit levels	Mixed	Mixed
5 Long-term recipients of out-of-work benefits	Steady	Steady
6 In receipt of tax credits	n/a	n/a
Children		
7 In low income households	Improved	Improved
8 In workless households	Improved	Improved
9 Concentrations of poor children	Steady	Steady
10 Low birthweight babies	Worsened	Steady
11 Child health and well-being	Steady	Steady
12 Underage pregnancies	Steady	Steady
13 Low attainment at school (11-year-olds)	Improved	Improved
14 Low attainment at school (16-year-olds)	Steady	Steady
15 School exclusions	Worsened	Worsened
Young adults		
16 Without a basic qualification	Steady	Steady
17 School leavers	Steady	Steady
18 With a criminal record	Improved	Improved
19 In low income households	Steady	Steady
20 Unemployment	Steady	Steady
21 Low pay	Steady	Steady
Working-age adults aged 25+		
22 Low income and work	Worsened	Mixed
23 Low income and disability	Steady	Steady
24 Wanting paid work	Improved	Steady
Working-age adults aged 25+ (continued)		
25 Work and disability	Improved	Improved
26 Workless households	Steady	Steady
27 Low pay by gender	Steady	Improved
28 Low pay by industry	n/a	n/a
29 Low pay and disability	n/a	n/a
30 Insecure at work	Steady	Steady
31 Support at work	Improved	Steady
32 Premature death	Improved	Improved
33 Limiting longstanding illness	Steady	Improved
34 Mental health	Steady	Improved
Pensioners		
35 In low income households	Improved	Improved
36 No private income	Improved	Steady
37 Non-take-up of benefits	Worsened	Steady
38 Excess winter deaths	Steady	Steady
39 Limiting longstanding illness	Steady	Improved
40 Help to live at home	Worsened	Worsened
41 Anxiety	Steady	Improved
Communities		
42 Polarisation of low income	Improved	Improved
43 Concentrations of low income	n/a	n/a
44 Victims of crime	Improved	Improved
45 Transport	Steady	Steady
46 Without a bank account	Improved	Improved
47 Without home contents insurance	Improved	Improved
48 Without central heating	Improved	Improved
49 Homelessness	Worsened	Improved
50 In mortgage arrears	Improved	Improved

Source: G. Palmer *et al.* (2005) Monitoring Poverty and Social Exclusion in Britain 2005, Joseph Rowntree Foundation, York, pp. 17–18.

Economic and family status and lone parenthood

Figures 4.4 and 4.5 show the risk of poverty according to economic and family status in Britain in 2001/2. They are based on the numbers of individuals in households receiving below 60 per cent of median household income after housing costs have been deducted. Figure 4.4 shows that participation in the labour market greatly reduces the risk of poverty. Retirement and unemployment are both strongly associated with poverty.

Figure 4.5 shows that lone parenthood leads to a high risk of poverty: 53 per cent of lone parents are poor. Couples without children are much less likely to be poor than those living in other household types.

Jan Flaherty, John Veit-Wilson and Paul Dornan (2004) explored some of the reasons why there are such high rates of poverty amongst lone parents. They found that the main reason for poverty amongst this group is lack of participation in the labour market. Single lone parents who have never married are the group with the highest rates of unemployment. They often lack work experience and

Figure 4.4 The risk of income poverty by economic status in 2001/2

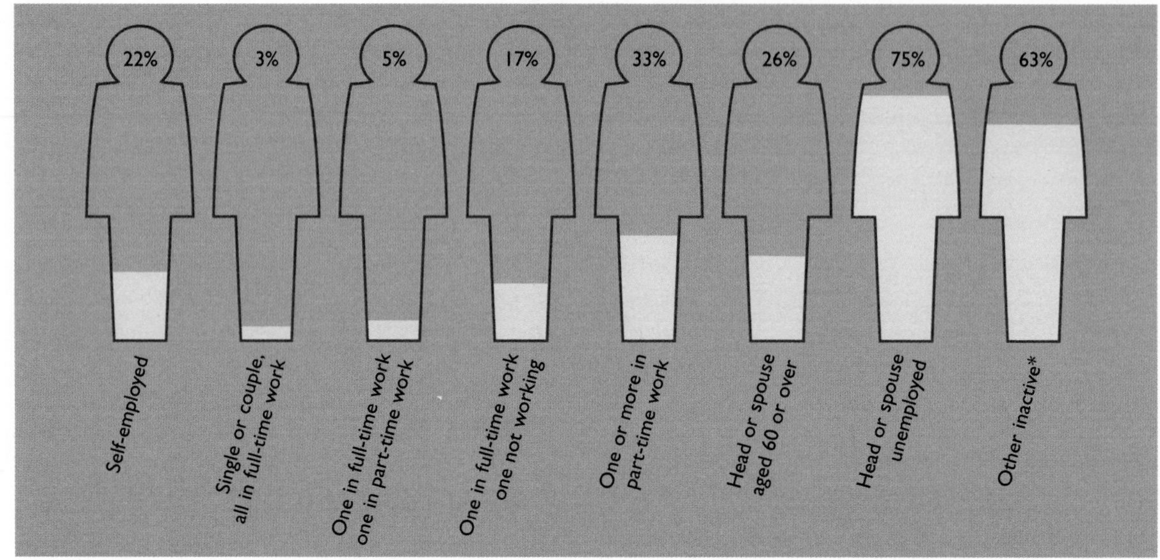

* Other inactive = all those not included in previous groups (this group includes the long-term sick, disabled people and non-working lone parents)

Source: J. Flaherty, J. Veit-Wilson and P. Dornan (2004) *Poverty: The Facts*, CPAG, London, p. 39.

Figure 4.5 The risk of income poverty by family status in 2001/2

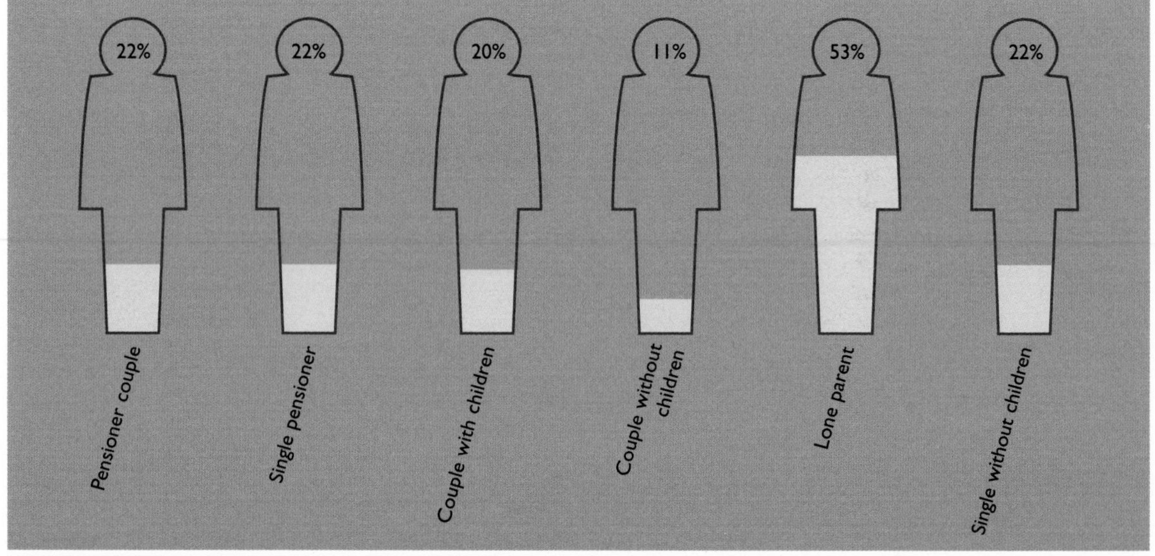

Source: J. Flaherty, J. Veit-Wilson and P. Dornan (2004) *Poverty: The Facts*, CPAG, London, p. 40.

qualifications, making it difficult for them to find work. The responsibilities of childcare make gaining experience or improving qualifications difficult, sometimes leading to long-term poverty. Where they do find work, it is often part-time, temporary or low-paid and produces insufficient income to raise them out of poverty.

The problems of never-married lone parents can be exacerbated by the effects of deprivation. For example, low income can lead to ill-health which makes it even more difficult to raise one's living standards. Flaherty *et al.* quote a survey which found that more than half of lone parents went without meals to save money. Divorced, separated or widowed lone parents can face similar problems. However, those who have accumulated more resources, experience or qualifications than young, never-married lone parents face less acute problems. Nevertheless, according to Flaherty *et al.*, 50 per cent of women who separate from their partners to become lone parents experience a fall in income.

The low income of lone parents has been seen as a problem by successive governments, concerned about the cost of providing welfare benefits as well as about the impact of poverty. The main policy of the Blair Labour government to tackle lone parent poverty was the New Deal for Lone Parents (NDLP). This aimed to raise the proportion of lone parents in paid employment from 44 per cent in 1999 to 70 per cent in 2010. It therefore saw increased employment rather than increased benefits as the principal way to tackle poverty in this type of family.

Ruth Levitas, Emma Head and Naomi Finch (2006) used data from the Poverty and Social Exclusion Survey (Gordon *et al.* 2000; see pp. 220–2) to analyse the position of lone parents. This survey found that many types of deprivation made the situation of lone mothers worse than that of mothers with partners, and made poverty difficult to escape from. These included an increased likelihood of damp homes, cramped accommodation, inadequate heating and long-standing illness. As well as material deprivation, lone mothers were also likely to suffer from many forms of social exclusion. They socialized less with friends and family than parents with a partner, and they went on holiday less frequently. Lone mothers had less help when ill and less help with informal care than partnered mothers.

Levitas *et al.* conclude that the problems of lone mothers 'are primarily practical and material. The poverty of lone mothers impinges on their social participation' (2006, p. 408). This lack of social participation means they do not have the social contacts required to enable them to cope with their situation and to escape poverty. Levitas *et al.* believe that these problems should be seen in a wider context. They say, 'The combination of widening general inequality with persistent gender inequality in the distribution of paid and unpaid work places lone parents in a particularly vulnerable position' (2006, p. 422). In this vulnerable position lone mothers sometimes fail to escape poverty even when they do find work, since the work they get may well be low-paid. (For more discussion of lone parenthood see pp. 485–8.)

Gender and poverty

Research suggests that in most countries in the world women are more likely to experience poverty than men (Lister, 2004). In European countries, with the exception of Sweden, poverty rates are higher for women than for men. In Britain, government figures on households below average income provide information on the proportions of men and women in poverty (defined as those in households receiving less than 60 per cent of median income). In 2001/2, 18 per cent of men and 21 per cent of women were in poverty.

Gender differences in the risk of poverty are confirmed by other studies. The PSE study (see pp. 220–2) found that women had a 14 per cent greater risk of poverty than men (quoted in Flaherty *et al.*, 2004). Furthermore, simple figures on poverty do not reveal the 'hidden poverty' which might be suffered by women (see below); and women might be more likely to experience intense poverty than men.

The over-representation of women in poverty statistics has been called the 'feminization of poverty' (Lister, 2004). This term was first used by Dina Pearce to point out that female poverty was becoming increasingly visible. According to Pearce (discussed in Lister, 2004), women had always been more prone to poverty than men, but their poverty was disguised because there were fewer female-headed households where women were the only adults to be included in poverty statistics.

Nevertheless, according to Lister, the deprivation suffered by women continues to be underestimated because of the existence of **hidden poverty**. Hidden poverty occurs when a family has sufficient resources overall to raise it above the poverty line, but those resources are not distributed equally between family members. Studies of money management and consumption patterns suggest that in a considerable number of households men have more control over the household income than women, and women spend less on their own needs than men. Women may sacrifice an adequate diet or neglect their own clothing needs so that the needs of their children or male partner can be met.

Flaherty *et al.* (2004) have identified a number of reasons why women in the UK are more likely to experience poverty than men.

1. Women are still slightly less likely than men to be in paid employment.
2. There is a gender pay gap, which means that women earn less per hour than men (see pp. 121–4).
3. Women are more likely than men to have low-paid work. For example, women are more likely to be homeworkers, who tend to be particularly low paid. It has been estimated that more than two-thirds of those earning less than the minimum wage are women (see Flaherty *et al.*, 2004, p. 267).
4. Most part-time workers are women. Part-time work tends to be lower paid than full-time work, and offers fewer opportunities for career advancement.
5. Women continue to be primarily responsible for childcare, and for care of the elderly, the sick and other vulnerable groups. These responsibilities can have a number of consequences which increase the risk of poverty. Career breaks to fulfil such obligations can reduce the prospects of career advancement and lead to low wages. They may also restrict national insurance contributions (on which the state pension is based) and payments into private pension schemes. This increases the risk of poverty for women in old age.
6. Many carers are unable to work because of their responsibilities, and benefits for carers are very low.
7. On average, women live longer than men, and the majority of elderly pensioners are women. Elderly pensioners are particularly likely to become poor.
8. Most lone parents are female and, as discussed above, being a lone parent is strongly associated with poverty.

Ruth Lister argues that the high rates of both official and hidden poverty for women reflect, 'on the one hand, structural factors associated with women's economic dependence and male power and, on the other, the agency of women who sacrifice their own needs on behalf of other family members, especially children' (2004, p. 57). Lister (1995) also argues that women are not just more likely to suffer poverty; they also have more responsibility for dealing with its effects. She says, 'It tends to be women who manage poverty and debt as part of their general responsibility for money management in low-income families.' This may lead to extra stress and ill-health. Lister also suggests that women may suffer from 'time poverty' because of their continued responsibility for most domestic labour.

Ethnicity and poverty

Official statistics on ethnicity and poverty have only recently become available. An ethnic breakdown is now included in households below average income figures (see Table 4.7). Using 60 per cent of median income after housing costs as the cut-off point, in 2004/5 all minority ethnic minority groups had a greater risk of poverty than whites. The risks were particularly great for Pakistanis/Bangladeshis who were almost three times as likely as whites to be below the poverty line. Most members of minority ethnic groups do not live in poverty, and some have very high incomes, but there are a number of factors which give minority ethnic groups an above-average risk of poverty.

Flaherty *et al.* (2004) suggest the following reasons for high rates of poverty amongst minority ethnic groups.

1. Members of minority ethnic households are less likely to be employed and more likely to be unemployed than whites. For example, in 2002 only 10 per cent of Pakistani/Bangladeshi households had all adults in paid employment, compared to 57 per cent of white households. Black African graduates in 2002 were seven times more likely than white graduates to be unemployed.
2. Although members of minority ethnic groups have a wide variety of jobs, they do tend to be concentrated in certain types of jobs, creating a degree of labour market segregation. Minority ethnic groups are more likely to have unskilled or semi-skilled jobs than whites and historically have tended to be concentrated in sectors of manufacturing industry which have been in decline. With the exception of Chinese and Indian men, minority ethnic men are less likely than others to have professional or managerial jobs. A variety of reasons have been suggested for these patterns, including discrimination by employers (see pp. 204–7).
3. Partly as a result of labour market segregation, minority ethnic workers are more likely to be low paid. This is particularly true of Bangladeshi and Pakistani workers. Flaherty *et al.* note that in 2002 average weekly net earnings of Pakistanis and Bangladeshis were around half those of white workers, although average pay of Indian men was around 3 per cent higher than that of white men. (For more details of ethnicity and earnings see pp. 174–6.)
4. Educational disadvantage is a factor which helps to explain the low average pay of some minority ethnic groups. Flaherty *et al.* suggest that poverty may be a contributory factor in relation to people achieving low qualifications, which in turn increases the chances of remaining poor. They point out that more than 30 per cent of Pakistani and black pupils and more than 50 per cent of Bangladeshi pupils are poor enough to receive free school meals, and those who are eligible for free school meals are amongst the least likely to be successful in GCSEs. (For more discussion see pp. 649–61.)
5. It may be difficult for minority ethnic groups to escape from poverty because they tend to live in deprived areas where job opportunities are limited and public services, such as schools, may not be of the highest quality. In 2000, 70 per cent of people from minority ethnic groups were living in the eighty-eight most deprived local authority areas.
6. Minority ethnic groups are also disproportionately likely to live in poor-quality housing where overcrowding and problems such as damp can affect people's health. According to Flaherty *et al.*, Bangladeshi and Pakistani people are more than three times as likely as the general population to report poor health. Overall, members of minority ethnic groups have above-average rates of mental illness, and there is some evidence that they are less well served by the NHS than other groups. Flaherty *et al.* say that 'Experiencing racism, unemployment, benefit-level incomes and overcrowding were identified as impacting upon the physical and mental health of many people from ethnic minorities' (2004, p. 199).
7. Flaherty *et al.* also argue that minority ethnic groups can end up in poverty as a result of difficulties with the benefits system. First-generation immigrants are unlikely to have the continuous contributions record to build up entitlement to full benefits. The complexity of claiming some benefits leads to low take-up rates from minority ethnic groups, and further problems arise from 'direct and indirect discrimination through conditions placed on "people from abroad"

Table 4.7 Percentage of minority ethnic groups in poverty (60% of median income) in Britain, 2004/5

		Percentage below 60% of median before housing costs	Percentage below 60% of median after housing costs
White		15	18
Mixed		19	33
Asian/Asian British		33	39
of which	Indian	28	30
	Pakistani/Bangladeshi	44	52
Black/Black British		24	34
of which	Black Caribbean	21	25
	Black Non-Caribbean	27	45
Chinese or other		26	36
All		16	20

Source: DWP (2006) *Households Below Average Income 2004/05*, DWP, London.

such as sponsorship and tests of residence' and 'failure to provide interpretation and translation facilities' (Flaherty *et al.*, 2004, p. 199). If members of minority ethnic groups are recent immigrants they may be denied benefits if they cannot show 'habitual residence' in Britain. Furthermore, 'awareness of differential treatment based on racist assumptions may lead to the non take-up of benefit entitlements'.

8 The biggest problems of all are faced by asylum seekers and refugees who are very likely to be from minority ethnic backgrounds. Asylum seekers can neither work nor claim social security benefits until their applicaion for asylum has been considered. They are given some financial support by the National Asylum Support Service but at a considerably lower level than Income Support and it is insufficient to raise them above the poverty line. Flaherty *et al.* quote a study which found that 85 per cent of the organizations which support asylum seekers said their clients experienced hunger, and 80 per cent said they had too little income to maintain good health. If asylum seekers are granted refugee status, their position improves, but they can face long delays in processing claims for benefits. They have worse employment prospects than any minority ethnic group and they are particularly likely to find only temporary and low-paid work.

Pete Alcock (1997) argues that social exclusion is often as much a problem for minority ethnic groups as material deprivation. It can involve lack of access to good-quality housing, unequal access to health care and social services, and substandard education facilities. He says, 'deprivation in housing, health and education adds significantly to the financial inequality of Black people in Britain, and they have remained important despite the introduction in the 1960s of race relations legislation'. Racial harassment may produce a sense of isolation and fear and thus exacerbate the social exclusion produced by other inequalities.

Poverty and disability

Another often-neglected factor related to poverty is disability. According to British government figures on households below average income, 22 per cent of households with one or more disabled adults were in poverty in 2004/5, compared to 14 per cent of households with no disabled adults (DWP, 2006, p. 30); and 28 per cent of households in which there was both a disabled adult and a disabled child were in poverty.

Oppenheim and Harker (1996) suggest that high rates of poverty among the disabled are partly due to 'labour market exclusion and marginalization'. Most households containing a sick or disabled person receive no income from employment, and such households, not surprisingly, are much more likely than other households to depend on benefits. Oppenheim and Harker argue that such households 'face the risks of poverty because of inadequate benefits'. Disabled people also tend to have higher spending costs on such items as special diets, transport and heating than other people do.

Alcock (1997) points out that disabled people may also suffer from social exclusion as well as material poverty. He notes that Townsend's pioneering research (see pp. 217–18) found that disabled people were likely to have poorer housing and fewer holidays. Alcock also argues that, 'participation in social activities and leisure pursuits may be restricted by reduced mobility or sensory deprivation, leading to an overall reduction in the quality of life of people with disabilities compared with most able-bodied people'. However, Alcock does not see such exclusion and poverty as being an inevitable consequence of the disability itself. Rather, they are caused by a society which discriminates against those with disabilities. This may be through active discrimination, or by failing to provide the resources and facilities necessary to minimize the impact of disability. He says:

> *In the case of disability it is very much a case of non-reaction leading to problems for persons with disabilities. Modern industrial societies, and even modern welfare states, have largely been constructed on the basis that the people who inhabit them, who produce and reproduce them and benefit from them, are able-bodied. This is true of workplaces, public and private buildings, transport systems, information and telecommunications networks, retail outlets – indeed almost all venues for social interaction.*
>
> *The places where serious attempts have been made to overcome these problems are few and far between and the welfare state generally fails to provide the extra resources disabled people need to overcome the social exclusion that can result. Furthermore, the carers of those with disabilities often find that they become excluded from areas of social life, such as employment. They too are restricted in their movements and social interactions by the societal assumption that people are able-bodied.* Alcock, 1997

Since Alcock wrote this, the Disability Discrimination Act of 2005 has come into force, strengthening the laws against discrimination on the grounds of disability and requiring larger businesses and organizations to take reasonable steps to accommodate the needs of disabled people. However, it may be some time before the physical environment becomes completely user-friendly for disabled people. Furthermore, as the experience of legislation outlawing racial and sex discrimination has shown, discrimination can be difficult to detect and laws banning it difficult to enforce.

Individualistic and cultural theories of poverty and social exclusion

In the previous sections we considered the definition, measurement and extent of poverty and social exclusion. In this section we consider explanations for poverty. Some of the earlier theories to be considered concentrate particularly upon poverty, but many of the more recent ones examine both poverty and social exclusion.

Individualistic theories

The earliest theories of poverty were also perhaps the simplest. They placed the blame for poverty on the poor themselves. Those who suffered from very low incomes did so because they were unable or unwilling to provide adequately for their own well-being. From this point of view, neither society nor the social groups to which individuals belonged were accountable, and society should not therefore be responsible for providing for the needs of the poor. Such individualistic theories of poverty were particularly popular in the nineteenth century.

Herbert Spencer – 'dissolute living'

The nineteenth-century English sociologist Herbert Spencer was a severe critic of the poor. He dismissed the views of those who showed sympathy with the 'poor fellow' who was living in poverty. Why, he asked, did they not realize that he was usually a 'bad fellow', one of the 'good-for-nothings ... vagrants and sots, criminals ... men who share the gains of prostitutes; and less visible and less numerous there is a corresponding class of women' (Spencer, 1971).

According to Spencer, it was unnatural to help those engaged in 'dissolute living' to avoid the consequences of their actions. Those who were too lazy to work should not be allowed to eat. The key to explaining why particular individuals became poor lay in an examination of their moral character.

Spencer thought that the state should interfere as little as possible in the lives of individuals. If the Poor Law or welfare system gave the poor more than an absolutely minimum amount, laziness and moral decline would spread through the population. Individuals would be attracted to the easy life on offer to those not prepared to work for their own living. As a result, society would suffer. Its economy would not be successful.

Spencer believed strongly in the ideas of evolution that were so popular in late Victorian Britain. It was Spencer – not, as is often thought, the biologist Charles Darwin – who coined the phrase 'survival of the fittest'. For society to evolve and become more successful, the most able and the hardest working would have to be allowed to keep the rewards of their efforts. The weak, the incompetent and the lazy should be condemned to a life of poverty, because it was no more than they deserved. Poverty was a necessity for society, for without it the incentive to work would be missing.

Evaluation

Few sociologists today accept individualistic explanations of poverty. At the very least, sociologists see poverty as a characteristic of a social group, such as a family or a community, and not as a characteristic of individuals. Some sociologists would go further and argue that it is not the generosity but the inadequacy of the welfare state, or the structure of society itself, which is responsible for the existence of poverty in the midst of affluence. For some, individualistic explanations of poverty are no more than an 'ideological smokescreen' to hide the injustices suffered by the poor. To the American writer William Ryan (1971), it is an example of 'blaming the victims' for what they suffer at the hands of others.

Market liberal (New Right) perspectives – the culture of dependency

The politics of the Conservative governments (1979–97) of Margaret Thatcher and John Major were associated with the ideas of **market liberals** (sometimes referred to as **neoliberals** or the **New Right**). A central plank of their policies was the claim that the welfare state was leading to a **culture of dependency**.

Hartley Dean and Peter Taylor-Gooby (1992), critics of the concept of a culture of dependency, have identified its key characteristics:

1. It assumes that people often act in ways that are motivated by rational calculations about the effort needed to secure rewards. If, for example, too much effort is required to secure a small rise in income, people will not bother to work.
2. To some extent contradicting the first point, people are strongly influenced by others around them, particularly those in the same neighbourhood. If few people go out to work in an area, then others living there may not bother to work themselves.
3. The theory has a moral dimension. It extols the virtues of self-reliance and hard work, and denigrates dependence on others and laziness. For example, in 1987 John Moore, then Secretary of State for Health and Social Security, said, 'dependence in the long run decreases human happiness and reduces human freedom ... the well-being of individuals is best protected and promoted when they are helped to be independent'.

A few contemporary sociologists, such as David Marsland, have adopted the philosophy of the New Right and have used some of the thinking behind the concept of dependency culture to explain poverty.

David Marsland – poverty and the generosity of the welfare state

Marsland (1996) is rather dismissive of most of the approaches to poverty discussed in this chapter. He argues that a 'poverty lobby' has distorted the picture of deprivation in Britain and greatly exaggerated its extent. He claims that groups such as the Joseph Rowntree Foundation 'deliberately confuse poverty with inequality' and 'exaggerate the extent of poverty absurdly'. He accuses those who argue for the existence of widespread poverty of acting out of self-interest, and says the 'legend of poverty is elaborated by mischief-makers and professional sentimentalists as an antidote to their own failed neurotic dreams'. He also claims that these people completely fail to examine the evidence impartially, and that 'the persistence of poverty guarantees a meaning for the lives of all those for whom the humdrum satisfactions of successful domesticity and useful practical work are either unavailable or never enough'.

Arguing for an absolute rather than relative definition of poverty, Marsland suggests that steadily improving living standards resulting from capitalism have largely eradicated poverty. He sees inequality as a desirable feature of society because it rewards unequal effort and ability, and in doing so creates incentives for people to work harder. Furthermore, he believes the incomes of the least well-off groups in Britain have, in any case, been rising.

Marsland (1989) argues that, for most people, low income results from the generosity of the welfare state rather than from personal inadequacy as such. He is particularly critical of **universal welfare provision**: the provision of welfare for all members of society regardless of whether they are on low or high incomes. Examples of universal provision in Britain include education, health care and child benefits.

Marsland believes such benefits have created a culture of dependency. He says, 'the expectation that society, the state, the government, "they", will look after our problems tricks us into abdicating from self-reliance and social responsibility' (Marsland, 1989). He argues that welfare 'hand-outs' create incentives for staying unemployed; they discourage competition and self-improvement through education. Furthermore, by increasing public expenditure, they take money away from investment in industry and thus hinder the production of wealth.

Marsland does not believe that all benefits should be withdrawn, but he believes they should be restricted to those in genuine need who are unable to help themselves. Benefits should be targeted at groups such as the sick and disabled, and should not be given to those who are capable of supporting themselves. Such groups make up only 5–8 per cent of the population, far fewer than the enormous proportion of the population who receive benefits. According to Marsland, reliance upon the huge, centralized bureaucracy of the welfare state 'weakens the vitality of the family, the local community, and voluntary associations, which are the natural arenas of genuine mutual help'. He concludes:

> *Critics of universal welfare provision are not blaming the poor, as welfarist ideologues allege. On the contrary, these are the foremost victims of erroneous ideas and destructive policies imposed on them by paternalists, socialists, and privileged members of the professional New Class.* Marsland, 1989

We will examine government policies that have been influenced by market liberal thinking and market liberal theories of welfare in later sections (see pp. 272–3).

Criticisms of Marsland

Bill Jordan (1989) argues that Marsland is wrong to attribute the culture of dependency to universal welfare provision. If such a culture exists, it is created by 'targeted', means-tested benefits received by only the very poor. He says, 'selective systems trap people in poverty and passivity, and exclude them from the opportunities and incentives enjoyed by their fellow-citizens'. If, for example, those in work have to pay for education and health care, and the unemployed do not, then 'many unskilled and partially disabled people will not be able to afford to work'.

Jordan claims that societies that rely upon means-tested benefits, such as the USA, tend to develop a large underclass, which has little chance of escaping from poverty. If members of the underclass take low-paid jobs, they lose benefits and the right to free services, and they may end up worse off. In such societies the only way to persuade some people to work is to impose heavy penalties on them if they do not.

To Jordan, poverty does not result from an over-generous welfare system, but instead it is caused by a system which is too mean. He claims that the only way to tackle poverty is to have 'universal provision, which brings everyone up to an acceptable level. Far from creating dependence it frees people from dependence.'

Hartley Dean and Peter Taylor-Gooby – The Explosion of a Myth

Dean and Taylor-Gooby (1992) attempted to explode the 'myth' of dependency culture. They argue that it is 'based upon socially constituted definitions of failure' and does not really identify a difference between the independent and the dependent. Nobody is truly independent in contemporary Britain, or in similar societies: 'When we speak of individual autonomy, or the sovereignty of the worker, the consumer or the citizen, we must remember that the human individual remains dependent upon other human individuals and social structures' (Dean and Taylor-Gooby, 1992). For example, workers are dependent on employers, consumers are dependent on those who supply the goods, and the citizen is dependent on the state for 'physical security and the regulation of other human individuals and social structures'. The benefit claimant is not in a qualitatively different position from other members of society who are also dependent in various ways.

Dean and Taylor-Gooby's objections to dependency theory are not solely philosophical. In 1990 they carried out eighty-five in-depth interviews with social security claimants of working age in south London and Kent. This research found that many benefit claimants had not lost interest in working. Only fourteen of those interviewed showed little interest in working; and of this group, four nevertheless hoped to come off benefits eventually, eight had health problems or caring responsibilities which prevented them from working, one had taken early retirement, and only one had rejected the idea of working. He was a man in his fifties who described himself as an anarchist, who had rejected the work ethic after a career working as a technician in the oil industry.

Dean and Taylor-Gooby did find evidence that the benefits system discouraged some people from taking low-paid work. Over half of those interviewed made some reference to the problems associated with losing means-tested benefits if they went out to work. This seems to support Jordan's claim that it is means-tested benefits (such as income support and family credit), rather than universal benefits, which can create disincentives to work. But there was no evidence that the disincentives had led to a dependency culture. For example, only twenty-one people said their circle of friends and relatives contained many claimants. As Dean and Taylor-Gooby observe, 'clearly most respondents could not be said to be enmeshed in a claiming culture'.

According to this study, the ambitions, attitudes and social networks of most benefits claimants are little different from those of other members of society. They want to earn their own living and would prefer not to have to turn to the state for a basic income. For them, the state is a last resort, and one they would rather avoid. Dean and Taylor-Gooby conclude: 'the social security system does not foster a dependency culture, but it constructs, isolates and supervises a heterogeneous population of reluctant dependants'.

Dean and Taylor-Gooby's findings have been criticized for using a sample concentrated in the south of England, where unemployment has generally been low. Critics argue that they might have obtained different results if they had studied the effects of social security in areas with higher rates of unemployment, such as northeast England, Wales or Scotland.

The culture of poverty

Many researchers have noted that the lifestyle of the poor differs in certain respects from that of other members of society. They have also noted that poverty lifestyles in different societies share common characteristics. The circumstances of poverty are similar, in many respects, in different societies. Similar circumstances and problems tend to produce similar responses, and these responses can develop into a culture – that is, the learned, shared and socially transmitted behaviour of a social group.

This line of reasoning has led to the concept of a **culture of poverty** (or, more correctly, a subculture of poverty), a relatively distinct subculture of the poor with its own norms and values. The idea of a culture of poverty was first introduced in the late 1950s by an American anthropologist, Oscar Lewis (1959, 1961, 1966). He developed the concept from his fieldwork among the urban poor in Mexico and Puerto Rico. Lewis argued that the culture of poverty is a **design for living** transmitted from one generation to the next.

A design for living

As a design for living which directs behaviour, the culture of poverty has the following elements:

1. On the individual level, according to Lewis, the major characteristics are a strong feeling of marginality, helplessness, dependence and inferiority, a strong present-time orientation with relatively little ability to defer gratification, and a sense of resignation and fatalism.
2. On the family level, life is characterized by free union or consensual marriage, a relatively high incidence of abandonment of mothers and children, a trend towards mother-centred families and a much greater involvement of maternal relatives. There are high rates of divorce and desertion by the male family head, resulting in matrifocal families headed by women.
3. On the community level, 'the lack of effective participation and integration in the major institutions of the larger society is one of the crucial characteristics of the culture of poverty' (Lewis, 1961). The urban poor in Lewis's research do not usually belong to trade unions or other associations, they are not members of political parties, and 'generally do not participate in the national welfare agencies, and make very little use of banks, hospitals, department stores, museums or art galleries'. For most, the family is the only institution in which they directly participate.

Perpetuating poverty

The culture of poverty, then, is seen as a response by the poor to their place in society. According to Lewis, it is a 'reaction of the poor to their marginal position in a class-stratified and highly individualistic society' (Lewis, 1961).

The culture of poverty goes beyond a mere reaction to a situation. It takes on the force of culture because its characteristics are guides to action that are internalized by the poor and passed on from one generation to the next. As such, the culture of poverty tends to perpetuate poverty, since its characteristics can be seen as mechanisms that maintain poverty: attitudes of fatalism and resignation lead to acceptance of the situation, while the failure to join trade unions and other organizations weakens the potential power of the poor.

Lewis argued that, once established, the culture of poverty tends to perpetuate itself from generation to generation because of its effect on children. By the time 'slum' children are aged 6 or 7, they have usually absorbed the basic values and attitudes of their subculture and are not psychologically geared to take full advantage of changing conditions or increased opportunities which may occur in their lifetime.

Lewis argued that the culture of poverty best described and explained the situation of the poor in colonial societies or those societies in the early stages of capitalism, as in many developing countries. Although the culture of poverty was common in such societies, not everyone adopted it. In advanced capitalist societies and (the then) socialist societies, the culture of poverty was non-existent, weakly developed or affected a fairly small minority. In the USA, for example, Lewis estimated that only 20 per cent of the poor adopted the lifestyle of the culture of poverty.

Other sociologists, however, have argued that the idea of a culture of poverty can be applied to most of the poor in advanced industrial societies. For example, in *The Other America*, Michael Harrington writes of the American poor:

> *There is, in short, a language of the poor, a psychology of the poor, a world view of the poor. To be impoverished is to be an internal alien, to grow up in a culture that is radically different from the one that dominates the society.*
> Harrington, 1963

Criticisms of the culture of poverty theory

Since its introduction, the culture of poverty theory has received sustained criticism. The actual existence of a culture of poverty has itself been questioned. Research in low-income areas in Latin American and African countries, which should have provided evidence of a thriving culture of poverty, has cast some doubt on Lewis's claims.

For example, William Mangin's (1968) research in the *barriadas* of Peru, shanty towns surrounding major cities, reveals a high level of community action and political involvement. Members of the *barriadas* often organize their own schools, clinics and bus cooperatives, have a high level of participation in community politics and show little of the family break-up described by Lewis.

Audrey J. Schwartz's (1975) research in the slum areas, or *barrios*, of Caracas in Venezuela revealed little evidence of apathy and resignation, present-time orientation or broken families, and she concluded that the subculture of the *barrios* did not perpetuate and maintain poverty.

Evidence from advanced industrial societies has cast further doubt on the culture of poverty thesis, and, in particular, its application to Western society. From their research in Blackston (a pseudonym for a low-income Black American community), Charles and Betty Lou Valentine (1970) state, 'it is proving difficult to find community patterns that correspond to many of the subcultural traits often associated with poverty in learned writings about the poor'. They found a great deal of participation in local government, constant use of welfare institutions and 'a veritable plethora of organizations', from block associations to an area-wide community council.

More recent qualitative research in Britain, conducted for the Joseph Rowntree Foundation and summarized in a book by Elaine Kempson (1996), provides substantial support for the argument that no more than a small proportion of those on low income have a culture of poverty.

The research discussed by Kempson consisted of thirty-one qualitative studies funded by the Joseph Rowntree Foundation. It found that there was:

> *no lack of commitment to working, even among those who had been unemployed for some time. Getting a job was seen as the best chance people on low incomes had of improving their standard of living or repaying the money owed to creditors.* Kempson, 1996

Indeed, some people went to extremes in their pursuit of work. One man, for example, visited the Job Centre four times a week, checked the local paper, visited local factories asking for work and had written over 100 letters. Some men visited factories in groups asking for work. However, such tactics were rarely successful, and many people on low income experienced considerable barriers to even looking for work. Age, lack of skills, poor health and disability and even having too little money to get on a bus to go and ask employers for work were all problems. This suggested that **situational constraints** were more important than culture in keeping people on low income. This view will now be examined.

Situational constraints – an alternative to a culture of poverty

The second and major criticism of the culture of poverty has centred on the notion of culture. Despite the research referred to above, there is evidence from both advanced and developing industrial societies to support Lewis's characterization of the behaviour of the poor.

The use of the term 'culture' implies that the behaviour of the poor is internalized via the socialization process and once internalized is to some degree resistant to change. It also implies that aspects of the behaviour of the poor derive from values. Again, there is the suggestion of resistance to change.

Thus Lewis, with his notion of culture, suggests that, despite the fact that it was initially caused by circumstances such as unemployment, low income and lack of opportunity, once established, the subculture of low-income groups has a life of its own. This implies that if the circumstances which produced poverty were to disappear, the culture of poverty might well continue. This is made even more likely by Lewis's view that the culture of poverty is largely self-contained and insulated from the norms and values of the mainstream culture of society. The poor, to a large degree, therefore live in a world of their own.

Culture versus situational constraints

These arguments have been strongly contested. Rather than seeing the behaviour of the poor as a response to established and internalized cultural patterns, many researchers view it as a reaction to situational constraints. In other words, the poor are constrained by the facts of their situation – by low income, unemployment and so on – to act the way they do, rather than being directed by a culture of poverty.

The situational constraints argument suggests that the poor would readily change their behaviour in response to a new set of circumstances once the constraints of poverty were removed.

The situational constraints thesis also attacks the view that the poor are largely insulated from mainstream norms and values. It argues that the poor share the values of society as a whole, the only difference being that they are unable to translate many of those values into reality. Again, the situational constraints argument suggests that once the constraints of poverty are removed, the poor will have no difficulty adopting mainstream behaviour patterns and seizing available opportunities.

Mainstream values

In his classic study, *Tally's Corner*, Elliot Liebow (1967) strongly supported the situational constraints thesis. The study is based on participant observation of black 'streetcorner men' in a low-income area of Washington, DC.

The men are unemployed, underemployed (working part-time) or employed in low-paid, unskilled, dead-end jobs as manual labourers, elevator operators, janitors, bus boys and dishwashers. Their view of work is directed by mainstream values. The men want jobs with higher pay and status but they lack the necessary skills, qualifications and work experience. They regard their occupations from the same viewpoint as any other member of society. In Liebow's words, 'both employee and employer are contemptuous of the job'.

When streetcorner men blow a week's wages on a 'weekend drunk', or pack in a job on an apparent whim, the middle-class observer tends to interpret this behaviour as evidence of present-time orientation and inability to defer gratification. Liebow, however, argues that it is not the time orientation that differentiates the streetcorner man from members of the middle class, but his future. Whereas middle-class individuals have a reasonable future to look forward to, the streetcorner man has none. His behaviour is directed by the fact that 'he is aware of the future and the hopelessness of it all'.

In the same way, Liebow argues that it is not inability to defer gratification that differentiates the streetcorner man from members of the middle class, but simply the fact that he has no resources to defer. Middle-class individuals are able to invest in the future, to save, to commit time and effort to their jobs and families, both because they have the resources to invest and because of the likelihood that their investment will pay off in the form of promotion at work and home ownership and home improvement. The streetcorner man lacks the resources or the promise of a pay-off if he invests what little he has. With a dead-end job or no job at all, and insufficient income to support his wife and family, he is 'obliged to expend all his resources on maintaining himself from moment to moment'.

Liebow argues that what appears to be a cultural pattern of immediate gratification and present-time orientation is merely a situational response, a direct and indeed a rational reaction to situational constraints. Rather than being directed by a distinctive subculture, the behaviour of the streetcorner man is more readily understandable as a result of his inability to translate the values of mainstream culture – values which he shares – into reality.

Family life and situational constraints

Liebow applies similar reasoning to the streetcorner man's relationship with his wife and family. The men share the values of mainstream culture. They regard a conventional family life as the ideal and strive to play the mainstream roles of father and breadwinner. However, their income is insufficient to support a wife and family. Faced daily with a situation of failure, men often desert their families. Liebow writes, 'to stay married is to live with your failure, to be confronted with it day in and day out. It is to live in a world whose standards of manliness are forever beyond one's reach.'

Increasingly, the men turn to the companionship of those in similar circumstances, to life on the streetcorner. Their conversation often revolves around the subject of marriage and its failure, which is explained in terms of what Liebow calls the theory of manly flaws. The failure of marriage is attributed to manliness, which is characterized by a need for sexual variety and adventure, gambling, drinking, swearing and aggressive behaviour. Men often boast about their 'manly flaws', illustrating their prowess with a variety of anecdotes, many of which have little relation to the truth. The theory of manly flaws cushions failure and, in a sense, translates it into success, for, at least on the streetcorner, manly flaws can bring prestige and respect. In Liebow's words, 'weaknesses are somehow turned upside down and almost magically transformed into strengths'.

On closer examination, however, Liebow found little support for the streetcorner man's rationale for marital failure. Marriages failed largely because the men had insufficient income to maintain them. The matrifocal families that resulted were not due to a culture of poverty, but simply to low income. The emphasis on manliness was not a valued aspect of lower-class culture, but simply a device to veil failure. Liebow concludes:

> *The streetcorner man does not appear as a carrier of an independent cultural tradition. His behaviour appears not so much as a way of realizing the distinctive goals and values of his own subculture, or of conforming to its models, but rather as his way of trying to achieve many of the goals and values of the larger society, of failing to do this, and of concealing his failure from others and himself as best he can.* Liebow, 1967

Liebow therefore rejects the idea of a culture of poverty or lower-class subculture, and sees the behaviour of the poor as a product of situational constraints, not of distinctive cultural patterns. The idea that situational constraints may shape the behaviour of the disadvantaged more than culture has been reiterated by some critics of the theory of the underclass (see the work of Steve Craine, discussed on pp. 245–7).

Situational constraints and culture

A compromise between the extremes of Liebow on the one hand and Lewis on the other is provided by Ulf Hannerz (1969). He sees some virtue in both the situational constraints and the culture arguments.

Hannerz, a Swedish anthropologist, conducted research in a black low-income area of Washington, DC. In his book, *Soulside*, he argues that if a solution to a problem such as the theory of manly flaws becomes accepted by a social group, it is learned, shared and socially transmitted, and is therefore cultural. To some degree it is based on values, since the theory of manly flaws provides a male role model to which to aspire. This model is therefore not simply a cushion for failure, a thinly veiled excuse. To some degree, it provides an alternative to the mainstream male role model.

Like Liebow, Hannerz sees the theory of manly flaws as a response to situational constraints, but unlike Liebow he argues that if these constraints were removed, this 'model of masculinity could constitute a barrier to change'. However, Hannerz concludes that situational constraints are more powerful in directing the behaviour of the poor than cultural patterns. He argues that the cultural patterns that distinguish the poor exist alongside and are subsidiary to a widespread commitment to mainstream values. He does not see 'the ghetto variety of the culture of poverty as a lasting obstacle to change' (Liebow, 1967). Since the behaviour of the poor contains a cultural component, it may hinder change once the situational constraints are removed. There may be a cultural lag, a hangover from the previous situation, but Hannerz believes this would only be temporary.

The underclass and poverty

In recent years the concept of an underclass has become widely used and increasingly controversial. In Chapter 1 we discussed the underclass debate in terms of its relevance to theories of stratification. However, some theories based on the concept are also highly relevant to poverty. For example, similar ideas to those employed in individualistic and cultural theories of poverty have been used to explain the existence of an underclass.

Charles Murray – the underclass in Britain

As outlined in Chapter 1 (pp. 64–5), Charles Murray is an American sociologist who first developed ideas on the underclass in his home country. In 1989 he visited Britain and claimed that Britain too was developing an underclass. This section examines the debate surrounding his original article (Murray, 1989). The next section examines the debate relating to a subsequent article published in 1993.

Murray believes that members of the underclass are not simply the poorest members of society, but they are also those whose lifestyles involve a 'type of poverty'. According to Murray, this involves particular forms of behaviour. He says:

> *When I use the term 'underclass' I am indeed focusing on a certain type of poor person defined not by his condition, e.g. long-term unemployed, but by his deplorable behaviour in response to that condition, e.g. unwilling to take the jobs that are available to him.* Murray, 1989

Other types of 'deplorable behaviour' typical of the underclass are committing crimes and having illegitimate children. Murray does not claim that all poor people, nor all those who are unemployed or reliant upon benefit, engage in deplorable behaviour. It is only a minority who act in this way, but ultimately their behaviour will influence others. He claims:

> *Britain has a growing population of working-aged, healthy people who live in a different world from other Britons, who are raising their children to live in it, and whose values are contaminating the life of entire neighbourhoods ... for neighbours who don't share those values cannot isolate themselves.* Murray, 1989

Murray puts forward evidence in three areas to support his claims.

Illegitimacy

First, he looks at **illegitimacy**. He points out that in 1979 Britain had an illegitimacy rate of 10.6 per cent of births, which was low compared to most Western industrial societies. By 1988, though, it had risen to 25.6 per cent, higher than many comparable countries and not far behind the USA.

Murray cites figures to show that most illegitimate children are born to women from lower social classes and not to middle-class career women, and he suggests that in some areas the absence of a father has become the norm. For example, he relates a story about a girl in Birkenhead who was embarrassed when her father went to watch her in a school play because he was the only father there.

Murray notes that the majority of births are jointly registered to a mother and father (69 per cent in 1987), and of these 70 per cent give the same address, suggesting they live together. Even so, Murray does not believe this undermines his argument. He questions whether relationships between cohabiting parents are as stable as those between married ones, although he admits he has no evidence to show that the former are less stable. To Murray, the rising illegitimacy rate is important because illegitimate children will tend to 'run wild', and the lack of fathers results in 'a level of physical unruliness which makes life difficult'.

Crime

Second, Murray associates the development of an underclass with **rising crime**. Writing in 1989, he claimed that the rate of property crime in Britain at the time was at least as high and probably higher than that in the USA. In 1988, for example, England had a burglary rate of 1,623 per 100,000 of the population, compared to a US rate of 1,309 per 100,000. Violent crime was lower in Britain, but Murray pointed out that it was rising rapidly, even though the proportion of young males in the population was falling.

Murray argues that crime is particularly damaging because communities become fragmented if rates of victimization are high. People become defensive and suspicious of one another and retreat into their homes. As crime becomes more common and more widely accepted, young boys start to imitate the older males and take up criminal activities themselves. As the crime rate rises further, the community becomes ever more fragmented and informal social controls which encourage conformity are weakened.

Unemployment

Third, Murray does not see **unemployment** itself as a problem; instead, it is the unwillingness of young men to take jobs that creates difficulties. He says there is an 'unknown but probably considerable number of people who manage to qualify for benefit even if in reality very few job opportunities would tempt them to work'. Like illegitimacy and crime rates, unemployment is much higher in the lowest social class of unskilled manual workers, some of whom are becoming members of the underclass.

According to Murray, attitudes to work were changing in Britain at the end of the 1980s. Those in their thirties and forties who found themselves unemployed were generally much more committed to work than younger groups. The older generations of working-class males saw it as humiliating to rely on benefits, while the younger generations were happy to live off the state. Murray says that 'talking to the boys in their late teens and early twenties about jobs, I heard nothing about the importance of work as a source of self-respect and no talk of just wanting enough income to be free of the benefit system'.

In Murray's view, such attitudes are disastrous. He claims: 'when large numbers of young men don't work, the communities around them break down'. Young men without jobs are unable to support a family, so they are unlikely to get married when they father children and thus the illegitimacy rate rises. Supporting a family is one way for young men to prove their manhood. In the absence of family responsibilities they find other, more damaging ways to prove themselves, for example through violent crime.

Causes and solutions

Murray sees the increase in illegitimacy as a consequence of changes in the benefits system. He calculates that, at 1987 prices, an unemployed single mother with a young child received just £22 a week in benefits in 1955. Furthermore, she had no special privileges on housing lists. The stigma of illegitimacy was also much greater. However, the value of benefits grew, the Homeless Person's Act of 1977 made pregnant women and mothers

history, but not as they pleased, nor under circumstances of their own choosing'.

Craine distinguishes between three types of transition for these school leavers (using concepts developed by Ken Roberts):

1 Three participants had a **traditional** post-school transition. That is, they went straight into employment. All three were married with children and were no longer living with parents by their mid-twenties. They came from homes where parents had stable jobs, and their parents' workplace contacts had been useful in finding jobs.
2 The second group had a **protracted** transition. For four to seven years they moved between employment, unemployment and government schemes before finally finding more permanent employment. This group lost none of their commitment to the labour market and continued to struggle to find work despite frequent set-backs. They tended to come from families which were not regarded as the most 'rough' or the most 'respectable' in the area, but somewhere in the middle. For each of them, at least one person in their family was working.
3 The third and largest group experienced a **cyclical** transition. This 'entailed early careers in which participants became trapped on a (not so) merry-go-round of unemployment, government schemes and special programmes, youth jobs, work in the informal economy, more unemployment, more schemes, and so on'. Those trapped in this cycle called it the **Black Magic Roundabout**.

Life on schemes

People who found themselves on the Black Magic Roundabout were usually placed on schemes which offered no real training or prospect of employment. The schemes involved work such as clearing graveyards, cleaning up canals, decorating the homes of elderly people, and so on. Girls tended to be given 'feminized' work such as office, cleaning and care work, while boys were given the heavier manual tasks. Those on the schemes were derisive about them and they believed that others saw them as having the lowest possible status. Craine says, 'trainees complained of inadequate facilities, lack of "proper" training, pointless "boring" and repetitive tasks and of being "treated like shit", like "some sort of moron", "like dirt"'.

All of those studied were derisive about the social and life skills training on the schemes, and many felt their dignity was undermined by their movement into and out of dead-end schemes. One said, 'it was like a bloody circus except we were the clowns'. Craine found that the schemes were ineffective in finding people work. In total, the thirty-nine young people had been on nearly ninety schemes, for a total time of nearly sixty years. Only one person had gained access to a job through a scheme.

The hopelessness of the situation was expressed by people in various ways. One local graffiti artist had painted a 'piece' on a wall near the local careers office. Craine says, 'it displayed the familiar characters from the children's television series, *The Magic Roundabout*, but the faces of the various characters, Dylan, Dougal, Zebedee, etc., were grotesquely distorted with sinister, demonic eyes and embittered scowls, their faces drawn in pain or anguish.' Craine discovered that this image was related to a local cult among the unemployed of watching daytime repeats of *The Magic Roundabout* on television. However, the idea of going round in a circle on the roundabout was also 'a pictorial metaphor for futility and alienation ... which concisely articulated the revolving door of cyclical post-school transitions'.

Underclass behaviour

In the context of the Black Magic Roundabout, some of the young people studied did engage in behaviour which some writers have associated with the underclass. Among the females, the choice was between domestic drudgery within male-dominated marriages, lone parenthood or alternative ways of earning an income. Nine of the girls had become lone parents by 1990, four were earning a living illegally (one through prostitution, one through fraud and drug dealing, and two through 'working on the side'), and the remainder were married or cohabiting with men. From their point of view, almost anything was better than the Black Magic Roundabout. Becoming a mother or wife provided a more socially accepted role than being unemployed or on dead-end schemes, while illegal activities offered the only realistic prospect of earning a good living.

For the males, failure to find long-term work usually led to 'retreat into the norms, values and alternative status systems of their peer group subcultures. Participants built on a collective sense of identity constructed out of an exaggerated version of working-class machismo.' Most of them had fathered one or more children, but their macho emphasis on emotional detachment and their insecurity and lack of reliable income meant that only three of those undergoing cyclical transitions had established long-term relationships. Eight of the group had become involved in crime and the lives of some were made even more unstable by spending time in prison.

Among the long-term unemployed males, Craine found no lack of energy and imagination. That energy and imagination, however, was largely directed towards 'alternative careers'. These might start out as minor benefit fiddles, but later their illegal careers would progress further. Some were given work by two local 'hard' families, the Hattons and the Donoghues. This might involve acting as ticket touts, unlicensed street trading, or selling unofficial programmes at the GMex or other venues. For example, they sold poor-quality unofficial programmes at performances by the ice skaters Torville and Dean. By wearing white coats, they appeared to be official programme vendors. Craine argues that such alternative careers provided 'income, autonomy and status from living off their wits'. These were not available from the opportunities provided by conventional work (because they could not obtain any), or on government schemes.

The alternative careers often progressed beyond the initial stage. The next, 'intermediate stage' involved 'totting and hustling'. Totting was systematic benefit fraud; hustling activities included selling stolen goods, shoplifting and casual drug dealing. The final stage involved more serious criminal activities: 'dealing' or systematic drug dealing; 'hoisting' or organized shoplifting; 'grafting' or organized burglary and other types of theft; and 'blagging' or robbery, armed or otherwise.

Conclusion

On the surface, Craine's study appears to provide ammunition for those who argue that there is an underclass problem caused by the cultural characteristics of its members. However, Craine argues that the culture he found is not passed down from generation to generation as Murray suggests. Rather, it is a creative solution to an intolerable situation.

Nor did Craine find that the welfare state encourages passivity. Rather, because benefits are too low for people to live on, it encourages people to earn their living in imaginative and entrepreneurial ways outside the law. Craine therefore found that 'benefit dependence, paradoxically, promotes a distorted "parody" of dominant values and encourages "the penny capitalism of the poor"'. The development of alternative careers is not due to benefit dependence or pathological culture, but to lack of legitimate opportunities. He explains it in terms of:

> *an interconnected and cumulative ecology of disadvantage, which included: stigmatized residential location; (for some) absentee fathers; enduring poverty; transgenerational unemployment; negative policy interventions in housing benefits and training; plus the cynicism and alienation engendered by post-school labour market experiences.* Craine, 1997

Not all of those on the Black Magic Roundabout turned to crime or lone parenthood. Some were provided with 'forms of social support and policy intervention which helped to promote and sustain positive outcomes for disadvantaged young people'. In some cases, family members, housing professionals or probation officers helped individuals gain access to legitimate opportunities. However, it is likely to be a minority of the disadvantaged young who go down such paths if:

> *we follow the New Right apologists of the underclass thesis and rest by our analyses and future policy agenda on empirically deficient notions of social pathology and individual moral defectiveness. In the meantime, socially excluded youth will continue to construct their own solutions and make their own history – no doubt fuelling further reactionary myths and stereotypes as they do.* Craine, 1997

Conflict theories of poverty and social exclusion

From a conflict perspective it is the failure of society to allocate resources and provide opportunities fairly that explains the problems of poverty and social exclusion. Poverty and social exclusion are not held to be the responsibility of those who suffer from them. Instead, such people are seen as the victims.

To some extent conflict theorists disagree about the reasons why society has failed to eradicate poverty and social exclusion.

1 Some see the failings of the welfare state as mainly responsible.
2 Others place more emphasis on the lack of power and weak bargaining position of the poor and socially excluded, which places them at a disadvantage in the labour market. The poor are either unable to sell their labour or are prevented from receiving sufficient rewards from it to lift themselves out of poverty.
3 Many conflict theorists relate the existence of poverty and social exclusion to wider structural forces in society, in particular the existence of a stratification system.
4 Marxists tend to believe that poverty and social exclusion are inherent and inevitable consequences of capitalism. They cannot envisage the defeat of poverty and the eradication of social exclusion without the total transformation of society.

Thus, although there are broad similarities between the sociologists we will look at in the following sections, there are also some areas of disagreement.

Poverty and the welfare state

Recent studies of poverty have found that those who rely upon state benefits for their income are among the largest groups of the poor. If poverty is defined in relative terms, and the definition that is advanced means that benefit levels do not raise the recipient above the poverty line, then a great deal of poverty can simply be attributed to inadequate benefits.

Nevertheless, it might be argued that the welfare state still makes a major contribution to reducing poverty, or at least to improving the relative position of those who are poor. It is widely assumed that one effect of the welfare state is to redistribute resources from the rich to the poor, since, at first sight, it appears that both taxation and welfare payments do this.

Taxation

This view has been challenged by some conflict sociologists. Some taxes are certainly **progressive** – that is, they lead to the better-off paying a greater proportion of their income to the government than the lower income groups pay. **Direct taxes**, such as income tax, are levied at different levels according to income, and those on very low pay may not even reach the threshold at which tax must be paid.

However, **indirect taxation** (taxes levied on the purchase of goods) tends to be **regressive**. Taxes such as VAT (Value Added Tax) and duties on alcohol and tobacco tend to take up a greater proportion of the income of poorer sections of the community than that of richer ones.

Between 1978–9 and 1997 the tax burden on the low paid increased, while the burden on the high paid was reduced. Direct taxation became less progressive, indirect taxation increased, and the relative position of those on low incomes worsened. For example, Christopher Giles and Paul Johnson (1994) examined the effects of tax changes between 1985 and 1995 in a study for the Institute for Fiscal Studies. They found that as a result of tax changes the poorest decile (that is, the poorest 10 per cent of the population) lost an average of £3 per week, or 2.9 per cent of their income, over that period, while the richest decile gained £31.30, or 5.5 per cent of their income.

However, it cannot be argued that all governments have pursued taxation policies which advantage the rich and disadvantage the poor and socially excluded. From 1997 the Labour government introduced a number of taxation policies which benefited those on lower incomes, particularly those with children. These included the introduction of tax credits for those on lower incomes, such as the Working Families Tax Credit. From 2003 the Working Tax Credit was introduced to benefit lower-income families without children.

Although the Labour government retained a policy of not increasing income tax rates, in 2003 it did raise national insurance contributions, which are in effect a form of direct taxation. Despite all the changes designed to help the poor, research suggests that there were only modest changes in income inequality under Tony Blair's government (see below). This may partly be because taxation policies should not be seen in isolation. They can have indirect effects which might offset their intended consequences. Abigail McKnight (2002) points out that tax credits are in effect a subsidy to low-paid workers. If governments provide such subsidies then there is a temptation for employers to cut wages to their low-paid workers, thereby reducing any positive effects tax credits might have. (See pp. 249–51 for a discussion of low pay.)

Welfare, poverty and social exclusion

The provision of welfare is one of the principal means that governments have of tackling poverty and social exclusion. Not only can money be redistributed to groups such as the elderly, the sick, the disabled and the unemployed, through benefits, but also welfare services such as social services, health and education can be used to reduce many forms of social exclusion. However, although welfare appears to benefit the poor and socially excluded, some conflict theorists have questioned whether this is the case in some parts of the welfare state.

Undoubtedly, some welfare benefits primarily benefit those on the lowest incomes: income support, unemployment benefit and family credit are all directed at the poorest members of society. However, writing in 1982, Julian Le Grand suggested that the **strategy of equality** through the provision of social services had failed. From an examination of education, health care, housing and transport subsidies, he argued that the better-off members of British society had benefited considerably more than the poor.

In education, the children of top income groups were more likely to stay on in education after the age of 16, and were more likely to go to university. Le Grand calculated that the families in the top 20 per cent of income groups received nearly three times as much expenditure on their children's education as those in the bottom 20 per cent.

In the field of health care, Le Grand claimed that those on higher incomes, again, benefit more from the services provided. The actual amounts spent on different income groups did not vary a great deal; however, lower socio-economic groups were more likely to suffer from illness, and therefore needed more medical care than the higher groups. It was this extra care that they did not receive. Le Grand found that 'the evidence suggests that the top socio-economic group receives 40 per cent more NHS expenditure per person reporting illness than the bottom one'.

Le Grand found a similar picture in relation to housing expenditure. Poorer households received substantially greater benefits than richer ones from various forms of direct expenditure on housing. General subsidies on the supervision and maintenance of council housing and rent rebates and allowances (now replaced by housing benefits) favoured lower-income groups. However, higher-income groups benefited considerably more from indirect expenditure, such as tax relief on mortgage interest payments (later abolished) and the lack of capital gains tax on homes.

Le Grand concluded that the welfare state failed to promote greater equality, and in some areas there would be less inequality if the welfare state did not exist.

More recent changes in welfare

Le Grand's analysis is now very dated and there have been many changes in welfare since 1982. Nevertheless there are many areas in which his conclusions can still be supported.

1. Although some means-tested benefits might involve redistribution of money to the poorest, they may still fail to raise people above the poverty line. Piachaud and Sutherland (2001) calculated that basic income support levels do not allow recipients to escape poverty (defined as 60 per cent of median household income before housing costs). A lone parent with one child received 83.9 per cent of the income necessary to escape poverty, and a couple with one child just 67.7 per cent of the necessary income.
2. There are a number of ways in which it is possible for higher earners and the rich to avoid paying income tax. These include using overseas tax havens and taking advantage of tax-free savings accounts such as Individual Savings Accounts (introduced in 1999).
3. The better-off may also gain more from education than poorer groups. Despite the expansion of higher education, there are still big class differences in participation in higher education (see pp. 235–6). Labour governments have continued with policies of encouraging competition between schools by introducing **quasi-markets** in which schools are funded according to their success in attracting pupils (see pp. 617–18). Many critics argue that these policies are divisive and lead to those from richer backgrounds securing places at the most successful schools while the poor tend to receive a less satisfactory education at the more unpopular state schools (see pp. 618–20 for a full discussion).

Nevertheless, Labour governments since 1997 have made efforts to tackle inequality and social exclusion in the education system. For example, they have extended free pre-school education and have introduced fees so that university students (who still predominantly come from middle- and upper-class backgrounds) contribute towards the cost of their education.

Abigail McKnight, Howard Glennerster and Ruth Lupton (2005) point out that Labour governments have provided additional grants to disadvantaged schools, and introduced Education Action Zones (which were superseded by the Excellence in Cities initiative) to improve education in the poorest areas. Despite these efforts, McKnight *et al.* conclude that 'there is still a long way to go before school funding is sufficiently differentiated to meet the additional needs of the most disadvantaged pupils' (2005, p. 51).

4 Norman Ginsburg (1997) noted that housing policy was designed to encourage home ownership. The consequence was that spending on new council housing was severely restricted, and by 1996 some 1.7 million council or housing association homes had been sold to their tenants. The Conservative governments between 1979 and 1997 also pushed for increases in council rents towards market levels. Rents rose 36 per cent in real terms between 1988–9 and 1993–4. This was designed to encourage private landlords to rent out properties as well as to increase public revenues. However, the result has been increasing expenditure on housing benefit, as the government has had to help the poorest meet these increased costs. This is despite cuts in the level and scope of housing benefit. Ginsburg noted, 'the government has capped housing benefit for private tenants, thereby pushing some households below the poverty line and even making some households homeless.

5 Michaela Benzeval (1997) found a growing health gap between the rich and poor in Britain. She says, 'throughout the 1980s and 1990s a considerable body of evidence accumulated that showed the poor health experience in terms of premature mortality and excess morbidity of people living in disadvantaged circumstances'. She quotes a variety of studies showing these inequalities. She argues that Conservative government policies towards health focused on introducing 'market mechanisms' into the NHS and showed very little concern for health inequalities. (See pp. 298–303 for a discussion of health inequalities.)

In 2005, Franco Sassi noted that Labour governments after 1997 did have some targets for reducing health inequalities between classes in certain areas. These included infant mortality, life expectancy, and death rates from heart disease, cancer and strokes. Part of the plan to achieve this involved developing Health Action Zones in some deprived areas. Furthermore, attempts to tackle child poverty were likely to have some effect in reducing inequalities. However, Sassi argues that such policies do 'not constitute a sufficiently aggressive redistributive policy to produce radical changes in many aspects of health inequalities' (Sassi, 2005, p. 91).

Overall, there is little reason to believe that government policies up until 1997 did any more to redistribute resources to the poor or to tackle social exclusion than they did when Le Grand first discussed the failure of the strategy of equality. Indeed, Pete Alcock (1997) suggests that the Conservative governments of 1979–97 actively pursued a **strategy of inequality**. They encouraged greater inequality between rich and poor. In doing so, they increased poverty and social exclusion.

Since 1997, the Labour government has had targets to reduce child poverty and social exclusion generally, and there is evidence that they have had some success in a number of areas (see pp. 273–5). A number of conflict sociologists previously critical of the welfare state, such as Hills *et al.* (2002), accept that the welfare state has done more to tackle inequality, poverty and exclusion than under previous administrations. However, there is evidence that it has had only a limited impact in reducing inequality. Indeed, comparing the highest and lowest earners, inequality continued to grow.

Tom Sefton and Holly Sutherland (2005) found that between 1996/7 and 2002/3 the share of total income of the poorest 10 per cent in Britain before housing costs actually went down from 3.1 per cent to 2.8 per cent. The next poorest 30 per cent saw no change in the proportion of total income they received, but the richest 10 per cent saw their share increase from 26.1 per cent to 27.7 per cent. This is despite evidence that changes in the tax–benefit system under the Blair government were heavily weighted towards benefiting lower-income groups. Figure 4.6 shows the impact of such changes between 1997 and 2004/5.

Writing in 2005, John Hills and Kitty Stewart concluded that, in some respects, Britain did become a more equal society between 1997 and 2005, but 'there is still a very long way to go before we reach an unambiguous picture of success, and sustained effort will be needed to make further progress' (Hills and Stewart, 2005, p. 346).

Poverty, social exclusion, the labour market and power

Not all of those who experience poverty or social exclusion in countries such as Britain rely on state benefits for their income. Nor can their poverty be primarily attributed to the failure of the social services to redistribute resources. A considerable proportion of the poor are employed, but receive wages that are so low that they are insufficient to meet their needs.

Abigail McKnight (2002) argues that 'poverty and low pay are entwined over the life course and across generations'. According to her research, childhood poverty is likely to lead to low pay in adult life, persistent low pay during working life causes poverty, and those who are low paid as workers are much more likely to experience poverty in old age. The low paid are also more likely than other groups to experience periods of unemployment; and all these links increase the likelihood of the low paid experiencing various forms of social exclusion. For example, McKnight quotes research which shows that children from low-income families do less well in standard literacy and numeracy tests and leave education with lower qualifications than those from higher-income backgrounds. This in turn increases their chances of being low paid and socially excluded themselves.

McKnight notes that a number of recent policies have helped the low paid. These include the introduction of a minimum wage in 1999 (originally set at £3.60 per hour)

Figure 4.6 Distributional impact of changes in the tax–benefit system, 1997 to 2004/5 (projected)

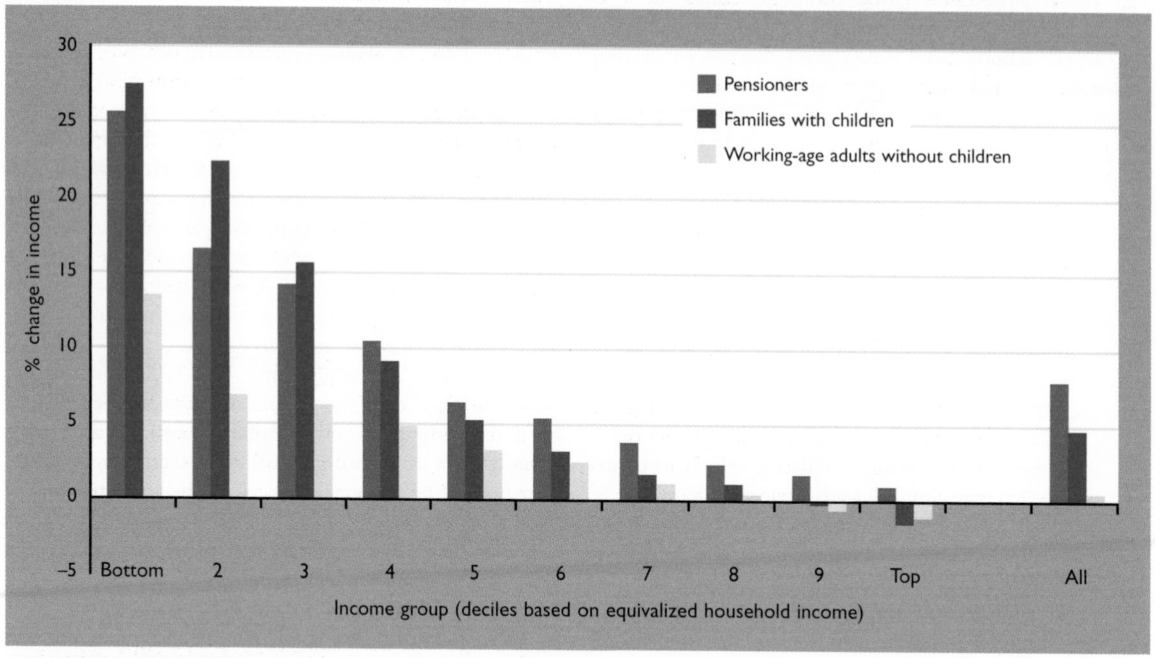

Source: T. Sefton and H. Sutherland (2005) 'Inequality and poverty under New Labour', in J. Hills and K. Stewart (eds) *A More Equal Society?* Policy Press, Bristol, p. 245.

and the introduction of various tax credits to boost the income of the low paid (see p. 274). However, she argues that, despite this, the overall rise in living standards means that 'work is now less likely to raise a household out of poverty than in the past'. While British Labour governments since 1997 have introduced a number of measures to get the unemployed back into work, they have not made much progress in tackling the root causes of low pay, nor have they introduced effective policies to help the low paid into better-paid jobs.

A number of underlying causes of low pay have been suggested.

Market situation and poverty

Weberian theories can be used to suggest some of the underlying reasons for low pay. Weber (1947) argued that a person's class position is dependent upon his or her **market situation**. It depends upon the ability of individuals and groups to influence the labour market in their own favour so as to maximize the rewards they receive.

The following explanations have been put forward to account for the market situation of the low paid:

1 In advanced industrial societies, with increasing demand for specialized skills and training, the unemployed and underemployed tend to be unskilled with low educational qualifications. Liebow's streetcorner men, for example, with few skills or qualifications, can command little reward in the labour market.
2 With increasing mechanization and automation, the demand for unskilled labour is steadily contracting.
3 Competition from manufacturers in low-wage 'third world' economies tends to force wages in Britain down.
4 Many, though by no means all, low-paid workers are employed either in declining and contracting industries or in labour-intensive industries such as catering. It has been argued that the narrow profit margins of many such industries maintain low wage levels.

Post-Fordism, globalization and poverty

Writing about poverty in advanced industrial countries, Enzo Mingione (1996) argues that increases in poverty are linked to changes in the world economic system. He believes there has been a shift from **Fordist** to **post-Fordist** production in the world economy. This involves a decline in heavy industry and mass production, and a shift to the service sector and those companies making smaller production runs of more specialized products. This results in a reduction in the number of full-time staff with secure employment and an increase in casual, insecure and temporary employment. (See p. 127 for more details on post-Fordism.)

Globalization involves a reduction in the importance of national boundaries, a willingness of companies to shift investment overseas in search of cheap labour and freer trade, and consequently greater international competition. At the same time, there has been an increase in the number of women working or seeking employment. Together, such changes have made growing numbers of people vulnerable to poverty. Fewer people can rely upon keeping their jobs over many years. With more women working, the idea of the family wage – a man earning enough to support a whole family – has decreased in importance. More families today rely upon having two earners. Unskilled female workers generally find it easier than men to secure jobs in the growing service sector.

Mingione (1996) comments that, 'the balance between the loss of stable manufacturing jobs and the growth in services is having a serious negative impact, particularly in de-industrializing cities'.

Secure jobs have also become harder to find as a result of the privatization of many welfare services. Subcontractors are less likely than local authority employers to provide workers with permanent jobs, partly because they have no guarantee of keeping contracts indefinitely. The problems of those who are poor are worsened by welfare systems that were designed when the advanced economies provided more permanent jobs. Such systems tend to be ineffective at ensuring that people avoid poverty and social exclusion when their circumstances change quickly.

Mingione also argues that the fragility of marriage in many countries, and the 'weakening of kinship networks', have reduced the 'community solidarity' which in earlier times helped people through such periods of hardship.

David Byrne – the new reserve army of labour

Byrne (1999) agrees with Mingione that changes in the world economic system have led to an increase in poverty and social exclusion. He argues that there has been a move towards 'post-industrial flexibility' involving a shift towards post-Fordism. However, to Byrne, this has not just resulted from changes in the global economy. Rather, in many countries there has been a deliberate policy of 'destroying the organizational capacities of workers at the point of production'. In Britain, for example, legislation was enacted in the 1980s and 1990s which made it much more difficult for trade unions to organize effective strikes to campaign for higher wages. To Mingione, this process has been a vital part of creating the 'labour market flexibility' necessary to sustain the new economic system. Flexibility is achieved through 'obligation to engage in poor work'. Benefits systems increasingly require people to take employment – any employment, no matter how low paid – or risk losing their benefits. With weak trade unions and the obligation to work, employers can hire and fire low-paid workers with ease.

According to Byrne, this group of workers constitutes a **new reserve army of labour**. The idea of a reserve army of labour has been advanced by a number of Marxist sociologists. It suggests that capitalism requires a substantial group of the unemployed who are desperate for work. They will therefore be willing to work for lower wages than those currently employed. This will tend to keep wage levels low and enable capitalists to make profits.

From Byrne's point of view, the development of welfare programmes and the greater bargaining power of unions had gone some way towards reducing the importance of the reserve army of labour. However, for the new form of post-Fordist capitalism to work, a new reserve army of labour is needed. This group is willing or is forced to move from one low-paid job to another as the labour requirements of employers change in a rapidly changing economy. Contemporary capitalism does not require large numbers of people who are permanently unemployed, but it does require the low-paid flexible workers created by the changes discussed above.

According to Byrne, the new reserve army of labour forms a group of people who tend to be socially excluded. Their social exclusion is exacerbated by the **spatial structure** of urban areas. The poor and socially excluded tend to be concentrated in certain areas of towns and cities – areas where there are few job opportunities and the schools are unlikely to produce great educational success. At the other extreme, the most successful members of society, the least excluded, can access private services or ensure they live in the areas with the best state services. Byrne comments: 'For many people, where they live determines what sort of schooling their children get and that determines much of their future life course.'

Poverty and stratification

Most conflict theorists move beyond explaining why particular individuals and groups are poor in an attempt to relate poverty to the organization of society as a whole. They claim that poverty is rooted in the very structure of society. The key concept used in this explanation is that of **class**, but some conflict theorists see class and poverty as less closely connected than others.

Peter Townsend – poverty, class and status

In the conclusion to *Poverty in the United Kingdom* (1979), Peter Townsend states, 'the theoretical approach developed in this book is one rooted in class relations'. In particular, he sees class as a major factor determining 'the production, distribution and redistribution of resources', or, in other words, who gets what. However, according to his definition, poverty is also related to the cultural patterns of a society, the lifestyles which govern 'the expectations attaching to membership of society'. The relationship between different classes is not a sufficient explanation of poverty because it does not entirely explain how lifestyles develop and certain types of social behaviour become expected.

Townsend's use of the word 'class' is closer to that of Weber than that of Marx. He argues that the distribution of resources is not always directly related to the interests of capital and capitalists. Some agencies of the state, he claims, act in their own interests, or act as checks on the operations of capitalists, and not simply as committees for handling the affairs of the bourgeoisie. For example, the civil service might be more concerned with preserving its own status and power than with maximizing profits for capitalists. Agencies such as the Health and Safety Executive, which is concerned with implementing the legislation governing health and safety at work and elsewhere, may limit the behaviour that is allowed in the pursuit of profit. The labour market, Townsend points out, is not just influenced by individuals and groups competing for higher pay, but also by institutions such as the Equal Opportunities Commission. Such institutions therefore also have an effect on the extent of poverty.

Townsend uses the Weberian concept of status to explain the poverty of those reliant on state benefits. The poor are a group who, in addition to lacking wealth, lack prestige. In Townsend's view, the low-status groups include retired elderly people, the disabled, the chronically sick, one-parent families and the long-term unemployed. As a consequence of their low status, their opportunities for access to paid employment are severely restricted.

The internationalization of poverty

In his later writing, Townsend (1993) stressed the international dimension of poverty. International agencies such as the World Bank and the International Monetary Fund (IMF) influence the distribution of resources in the world. The IMF can impose conditions on governments which borrow money from it, which in turn affect the poor. For example, it can ask governments to cut public expenditure by reducing the welfare programmes on which the poor rely.

Although these institutions mainly affect the poor in the 'third world', others, such as the European Community (EC), have an important impact on the poor in the 'first world'. For example, European employment legislation affects the rights of low-paid and part-time workers in member countries.

Furthermore, the internationalization of industry affects poverty in the 'first' and 'third' worlds alike. Cheap labour in 'third world' countries may be paid poverty wages. This can also create poverty in the 'first world', as jobs are transferred from the high-wage economies of Europe, North America and Japan to low-wage economies, and, as a result, unemployment rises in the 'first world'. Alternatively, 'first world' workers may be forced to take pay cuts as a consequence of competition from low-wage economies in Africa, Asia and South America. These pay cuts may push them into poverty.

Townsend argues, therefore, that poverty can no longer be explained or understood by examining any one country in isolation.

Marxism, class and poverty

Marxist theories of poverty place less emphasis than most other theories on differentiating the poor from other members of the working class. Rather than seeing them as a separate group, Ralph Miliband (1974) believes they are simply the most disadvantaged section of the working class. Westergaard and Resler (1976) go further, claiming that concentrating on the special disadvantages of the poor 'diverts attention from the larger structure of inequality in which poverty is embedded'. Marxists would see Townsend as failing to emphasize these wider structures sufficiently. Miliband concludes:

> *The basic fact is that the poor are an integral part of the working class – its poorest and most disadvantaged stratum. They need to be seen as such, as part of a continuum, the more so as many workers who are not 'deprived' in the official sense live in permanent danger of entering the ranks of the deprived; and that they share in any case many of the disadvantages which afflict the deprived. Poverty is a class thing, closely linked to a general situation of class inequality.* Miliband, 1974

Poverty and the capitalist system

To many Marxists, poverty can be explained in terms of how it benefits the ruling class. Poverty exists because it serves the interests of those who own the means of production. It allows them to maintain the capitalist system and to maximize their profits.

Poverty and the labour market

Members of the subject class own only their labour, which they must sell in return for wages on the open market. Capitalism requires a highly motivated workforce. Since the motivation to work is based primarily on monetary return, those whose services are not required by the economy, such as the aged and the unemployed, must receive a lower income than wage earners. If this were not the case, there would be little incentive to work.

The motivation of the workforce is also maintained by unequal rewards for work. Workers compete with each other, as individuals and groups, for income, in a highly competitive society. In this respect, the low-wage sector forms the base of a competitive wage structure. Low wages help to reduce the wage demands of the workforce as a whole, since workers tend to assess their incomes in terms of the baseline provided by the low paid. J.C. Kincaid (1973) argues that 'standards of pay and conditions of work at the bottom of the heap influence the pattern of wages farther up the scale'. He maintains that low wages are essential to a capitalist economy, since this helps to keep all wages low.

For a recent variation on these Marxist views, see Byrne's discussion of the new reserve army of labour (p. 251).

Evaluation

Although the Marxist views of poverty discussed above were first advanced decades ago, they still provide one credible explanation for why poverty exists in capitalist societies. Indeed, with the increased emphasis on market forces in societies such as Britain, Westergaard (1996) asserted that Marxist theories were becoming more relevant than ever. However, they are less successful than other conflict approaches in explaining why particular groups and individuals become poor or socially excluded. They are not particularly sensitive to variations in income within the working class, and fail to differentiate clearly the poor and socially excluded from other members of the working class, or to provide an explanation for their poverty. By concentrating on the wider structural origins of poverty and social exclusion, they neglect the particular reasons why certain individuals and groups are more likely to become poor or socially excluded than others.

Some sociologists have tried to develop a framework for understanding poverty and social exclusion which takes account of the different levels of explanation, from the individual to the structural, which can be used to explain these phenomena.

Burchardt, Le Grand and Piachaud – an integrated framework for explaining social exclusion and poverty

Burchardt, Le Grand and Piachaud (2002) put forward 'a framework for understanding social exclusion'. They argue that some social scientists have emphasized economic factors in causing social exclusion, others have stressed the importance of behaviour, while others have examined the impact of particular government policies. Some have concentrated on the economic aspects of poverty, while others have focused primarily on social processes that lead to exclusion. Burchardt *et al.* believe that all these elements need to be combined to provide a full explanation of poverty and social exclusion.

To suggest how this might be achieved, Burchardt *et al.* provide a visual representation of how a full theory might appear. As Figure 4.7 shows, they argue that individual, family, community, local, national and global factors can all have an influence. For example, an individual's disability, their family responsibilities, the social services available locally, the local labour market, the availability of transport for disabled people, governmental policies on welfare and the global economic climate could all affect an individual's chances of being in poverty or suffering social exclusion.

Furthermore, Burchardt *et al.* believe that an integrated approach needs to examine both **past** and **present** influences on the opportunities available to people and the outcomes that result from the interaction of the various factors involved. This is illustrated in Figure 4.8. From their point of view, the events of the past lead to people acquiring different amounts of **capital**, and these in turn shape the opportunities open to people.

However, following the ideas of Pierre Bourdieu (see pp. 67–9), Burchardt *et al.* argue that capital can take a number of forms:

- **Human capital**: this depends on genetic inheritance, childhood circumstances (family, health, housing, poverty, social environment, etc.), education and training.
- **Physical capital**: ownership of housing, land, equipment, etc.
- **Financial capital**: ownership of financial assets or liabilities.

Figure 4.7 An integrated approach

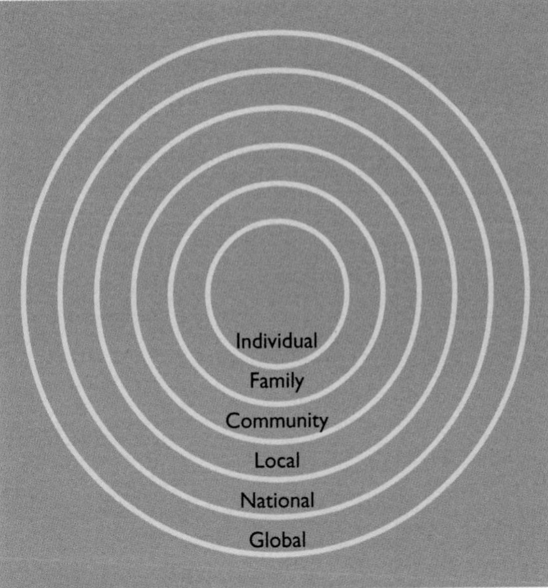

Individual: e.g. age, gender, race, disability; preferences, beliefs and values
Family: e.g. partnership, children, caring responsibilities
Community: e.g. social and physical environment, schools, health and social services
Local: e.g. labour market, transport
National: e.g. cultural influences, social security, legislative framework
Global: e.g. international trade, migration, climate change

Source: T. Burchardt, J. Le Grand and D. Piachaud (2002) *Understanding Social Exclusion*, Oxford University Press, Oxford, p. 7.

Figure 4.8 Framework for analysing social exclusion

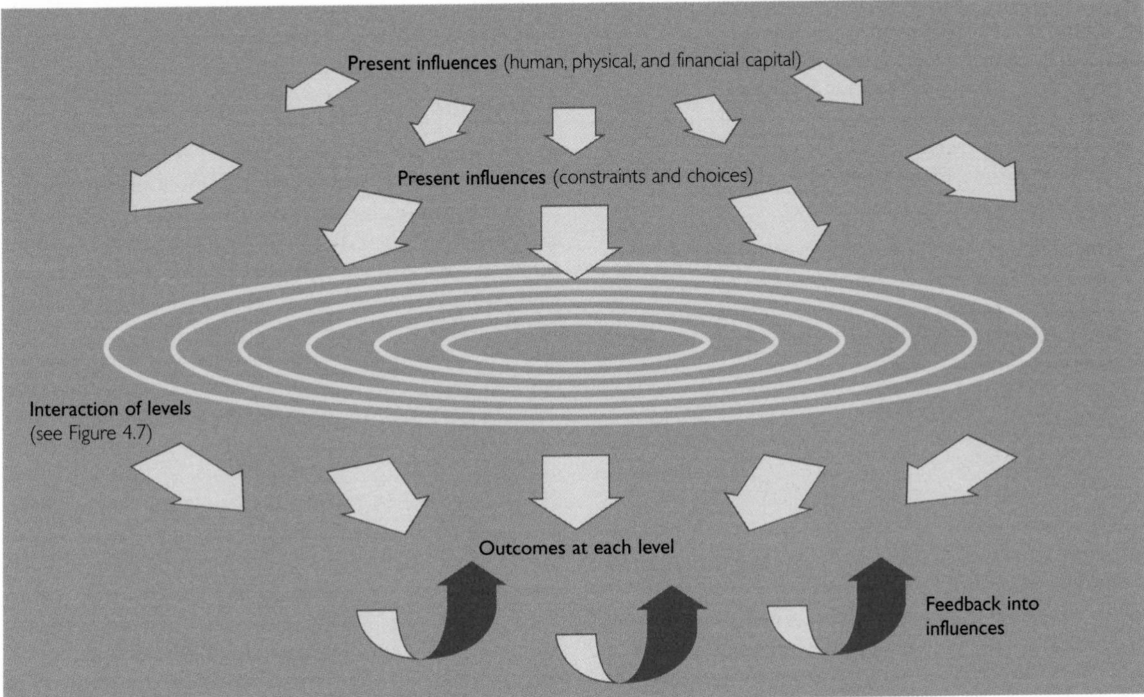

Source: T. Burchardt, J. Le Grand and D. Piachaud (2002) *Understanding Social Exclusion*, Oxford University Press, Oxford, p. 9.

These types of capital may be interrelated. For example, ownership of financial capital can obviously be used to acquire physical capital. Ownership of human capital in the form of educational qualifications can help people to acquire financial capital, but financial capital can also help them to acquire human capital by paying for education.

Present influences on whether individuals or groups experience poverty and social exclusion are divided by Burchardt *et al.* into external influences, which are 'constraints facing an individual or community' (e.g. the availability of job vacancies), and internal influences, which involve 'choices individuals or communities make'.

Burchardt *et al.* therefore accept that **cultural factors** can play a part in influencing choices such as whether people pursue a particular career or stay on in post-compulsory education. However, these choices are not made in a vacuum, but in the context of levels of capital that people already possess and in the context of their individual and family circumstances, the community in which they live, and national and global circumstances. For those who are poor to start with, who have low levels of human, physical and financial capital, who have problematic personal and family circumstances, or who live in a deprived community, constraints may make it very difficult or even impossible to escape poverty or social exclusion.

Brian Barry – social exclusion, poverty and social justice

Barry (2002) developed aspects of the approach outlined by Burchardt *et al.* He also explored the relationship between inequality and poverty, and poverty and social exclusion. As such, his work provides a useful example of how contemporary conflict theorists explain poverty and social exclusion.

Barry defines social exclusion in this way: 'individuals or groups are socially excluded if they are denied the opportunity of participation, whether they actually desire to participate or not'. Money, or financial capital, is very important in determining the extent to which people can participate in a range of socially important activities. However, wider factors, such as the provision of public services, are also crucial. For example:

> *inexpensive and reliable public transport that runs long hours will enable poor people to travel for economic, social and political purposes. In its absence, the participation of those who cannot afford to run a car or hire a taxi will be severely limited.* Barry, 2002

It is not just individual choices and individual circumstances which shape the chances of social exclusion, but also national policies and local services. Barry also stresses that choices themselves are influenced by the circumstances in which they are made. For example, 'lack of job opportunities among the adults in an area tends to depress scholastic motivation and thus contributes to poor educational outcomes that condemn the next generation to extremely limited opportunities in their turn'. Like Burchardt *et al.*, therefore, he stresses that past influences can have important effects in shaping present influences and choices.

Although Barry focuses on social exclusion he does argue that inequality and poverty are crucial to understanding and explaining social exclusion. Many aspects of social exclusion are directly related to material factors. For example, 'the opportunity to get a fair trial is closed to those who cannot afford high-quality legal representation in the absence of a well-funded system of legal aid'. On the other hand, the wealthy tend to have the power to avoid social exclusion.

> *It is scarcely necessary to point out the many ways in which opportunities for disproportionate political influence flow directly from the ability to make large financial contributions and from possession of other resources such as ownership of media of mass communication.* Barry, 2002

Barry concludes that inequality tends to produce 'stratified social exclusion'. Although the choices of individuals can influence the degree to which they are excluded, the existence of inequality tends to produce systematic patterns of social exclusion. In Britain, the 'great bulk of goods and services are allocated through the market'. Those who cannot afford them, those who are poor, will tend to become socially excluded. For them, their exclusion is not voluntary.

However, there is another group of people, the very rich, who may be excluded through choice. Many of the rich choose to send their children to private schools, and some live on private estates protected by gates or even security guards. These, the most privileged group, do not just benefit from the possession of physical and financial capital; they also have more useful **social contacts** than other members of society. They can gain extra opportunities through their contacts with other rich and influential people.

Barry therefore concludes that social exclusion cannot be tackled just by trying to deal with individual manifestations of the problem (such as truancy or lack of good public transport). From his point of view, some **redistribution of income** is also necessary.

Evaluation

Barry's arguments are somewhat vague and generalized. However, they do suggest how a number of explanations of poverty might work together. Barry sees social exclusion as influenced by individual choices, but these are shaped by constraints and wider social factors. Past events have an important role in shaping present circumstances and choices.

To Barry, social exclusion is different from poverty, but it is strongly influenced by the existence of poverty in particular and social inequality in general. Barry relates social exclusion and poverty to the existence of a stratification system in which power, like wealth, is distributed very unequally. Whatever the merits of his particular arguments, his work does suggest how some of the theories described in this section might be complementary.

We have now outlined various responses to the problems of defining and measuring poverty, and explanations of the causes of poverty and social exclusion. In the next section we will turn our attention to possible solutions to these problems.

Policies on poverty and social exclusion

Governments do not always have specific policies targeted at reducing poverty. However, there have been a number of periods in Britain, the USA and elsewhere when governments have developed programmes aimed specifically at poverty reduction. Whether they have such programmes or not, government policies always have an influence on the extent of poverty and many have themselves been influenced by some of the theories of poverty examined in this chapter. This section briefly examines some of the programmes and policies which have impacted upon poverty and social exclusion. Later sections examine the welfare state in detail.

The culture of poverty and policies in the USA

The war on poverty

An early attempt to tackle poverty occurred in the USA in the 1960s. The 'war on poverty' was based on the assumption that poverty was caused by some problem with the poor themselves. The war on poverty commenced in 1964 when the US President, Lyndon B. Johnson, launched the Economic Opportunity Act and formed the Office of Economic Opportunity to coordinate measures to fight poverty. The comments of an American anthropologist, Thomas Gladwin, represent the verdict of many social scientists on this campaign:

> *The whole conception of the war on poverty rests upon a definition of poverty as a way of life. The intellectual climate in which it was nurtured was created by studies of the culture of poverty, notably those of Oscar Lewis ... [which] provide the basis for programs at the national level designed very explicitly to correct the social, occupational and psychological deficits of people born and raised to a life of poverty.* Gladwin, 1967

The Office of Economic Opportunity created a series of programmes designed to resocialize the poor and remove their presumed deficiencies. For example, the Job Corps set up residential camps in wilderness areas for unemployed, inner-city youth with the aim of 'building character' and fostering initiative and determination. There were also 'work experience' programmes designed to instil 'work habits'. The aim of many of these schemes was to undo the presumed effect of the culture of poverty by fostering ambition, motivation and initiative.

In comparison with the above programmes, direct aid in the form of cash payments to the poor received a low priority. Edward James, in *America Against Poverty* (1970), a study of the 1960s war on poverty, stated that direct aid was the 'least popular anti-poverty strategy in America'.

Why the war on poverty was lost

The war on poverty was not designed to eradicate poverty by providing the poor with sufficient income to raise them above the poverty line. By changing the poor it was hoped to provide them with the opportunity to become upwardly mobile.

By the late 1960s, many social scientists felt that the war on poverty had failed. The poor remained stubbornly poor despite the energy and resolve of the Office of Economic Opportunity. Sociologists increasingly suggested that solutions to poverty must be developed from stratification theory rather than the culture of poverty theory. Thus Miller and Roby (1970) argued that poverty was an aspect of inequality, and not merely a problem of the poor. It could only be solved through restructuring society as a whole.

However, such a view had little influence on subsequent governments in the USA or British governments between 1979 and 1997. In both cases the main influence on policies towards the poor was the New Right. Policies influenced by the New Right are discussed below.

Poverty and the expansion of welfare in Britain

In Britain, governments have not declared war on poverty. Between 1945 and 1979 successive governments were less averse than their American counterparts to providing cash payments to the poor, and to providing universal services (such as education and health care) to everyone regardless of ability to pay. Governments added to the provisions of the welfare state, partly with the aim of alleviating poverty.

Critics argue that these developments were inadequate. According to Kincaid (1973), benefits to the poor were 'pitifully low' and 'left millions in poverty'. The harsher edges of poverty may have been blunted by the welfare state, but poverty, at least in relative terms, remained. Welfare professionals may have cushioned some of the misery produced by poverty, but they had not solved the problem.

Market liberal solutions

After 1979, the Conservative governments of Margaret Thatcher and John Major followed a rather different course. Inspired by the ideas of market liberals, they decided to try to reduce welfare expenditure, move away from universal benefits and services, and target resources towards the poor.

The intention was to free economic resources to create a more dynamic economy. As the economy grew, and living standards rose, economic success would 'trickle down' to those on low incomes, so that their living standards would rise along with everyone else's. Reducing or replacing universal benefits would destroy the dependency culture which made people rely too heavily on state hand-outs. Means-tested benefits, such as income support, would go only to those who were not in a position to help themselves and who were in genuine need.

The welfare system was changed in line with these policies in April 1987. Supplementary benefit was replaced by income support. Before 1987 the single-payments system allowed those on a low income to claim money for necessities such as household equipment, furniture, clothing and bedding, which they could not otherwise afford. This system was replaced by the social fund, under which loans rather than grants for such necessities became the norm. These loans had to be paid back out of benefits received. Only those who could afford to pay back the loans were offered them: some individuals were too poor to be given loans. The government argued that this system would make claimants more responsible and encourage them to plan ahead in managing household budgets.

The government also cut the amount spent on housing benefit. Much of the money saved by this measure was spent on replacing family income supplement with family credit. Both were means-tested benefits designed to boost the incomes of those with low incomes, but family credit was more generous.

In September 1988 the Conservative government raised the age at which people became entitled to income support from 16 to 18. The intention was to prevent the young from becoming victims of the dependency culture. In theory, all 16- to 17-year olds were guaranteed a place on a Youth Training Scheme (YTS) which would provide them with an income.

In 1990 full-time students lost their right to unemployment benefit and other means-tested benefits during their holidays.

Between 1992 and 1997 a whole range of further measures and changes was introduced. Marilyn Howard (1997) has outlined the main ones.

- The Child Support Agency, introduced in 1993, tried to shift the burden for supporting lone mothers from the state to absent fathers, who were now required to pay child maintenance.
- In 1994 a habitual residence test was introduced which made it more difficult for people who have recently moved to Britain to receive benefit.
- In 1995 invalidity benefit was replaced by incapacity benefit, designed to make it more difficult for people to claim that they are unfit for work and therefore eligible for the benefit. The government has also shifted much of the burden of responsibility for sickness benefits to employers.
- In 1996 the Jobseeker's Allowance was introduced for the unemployed. Under this scheme, an unemployed person receives benefit only if they sign a Jobseeker's Agreement detailing how they intend to search for work. Those who do not comply can be instructed to undertake training schemes. The Jobseeker's Allowance lasts for only six months, whereas unemployment benefit could be claimed for a year. Earnings-related elements, where benefits depend on previous earnings, have virtually disappeared from the benefits system.

Criticisms of market liberal policies

Critics argue that, far from reducing poverty, these measures increased it. Many of those reliant on welfare had their income cut. With the replacement of single payments by the social fund, some people were unable to buy necessities. The Child Poverty Action Group claimed that there were insufficient YTS places for all 16- to 17-year-olds. Those who were not supported by their families and who could not find employment or a place on a training scheme could end up destitute and homeless.

The Conservative government, however, claimed that its policies benefited those on low incomes. According to government figures, the average income of the poorest 20 per cent of the population rose by 5.5 per cent in real terms between 1979 and 1985. This, the government claimed, supported its view that the benefits of economic growth would trickle down to those on low incomes.

However, the economist John Hills (1995) pointed out that the government's figures did not take account of changes in indirect taxes such as VAT and duties on petrol, alcohol and tobacco. Hills claims that when these are taken into account the real income of the poorest 20 per cent of households actually fell by 6 per cent between 1979 and 1986. Over the same period the richest 20 per cent of households saw their real income rise by 26 per cent. If Hills's figures are correct, they seem to undermine the market liberal claim that prosperity will automatically solve the problem of poverty.

Most of the evidence contained in earlier sections of this chapter suggests that poverty increased from the late 1980s until 1997, again indicating that market liberal policies may have added to the problem rather than solving it. Carey Oppenheim (1997) found no evidence of a 'trickle down' effect. In the introduction to the Child Poverty Action Group's 1997 book, *Britain Divided*, Alan Walker summarizes the effect of Conservative policies in the following way:

> *The fact is that many thousands of poor families can trace the start of their misfortune back to the recession of the early 1980s, a recession that was deepened and prolonged by government policies, and subsequent changes of administration have not improved their position but, rather, have been responsible for worsening it. As this book shows, poverty and social exclusion have increased remorselessly over the last 18 years and not one of the four Conservative Governments have had an explicit policy to combat them.* Walker and Walker, 1997

(For further discussion of Conservative and market liberal perspectives on the welfare state, see pp. 268–73. The policies of the Labour government elected in 1997 are examined on pp. 257–9.)

Welfare and redistribution as solutions to poverty and social exclusion

A number of sociologists believe that the way to solve problems of poverty and social exclusion is to reform the provision of welfare to encourage the redistribution of wealth.

Peter Townsend (1997) sees the solution to poverty as resting on a wider range of measures. He argues the need for a national plan to eradicate poverty. This would be in line with an agreement signed by the Conservative government at the United Nations Copenhagen Summit on Social Development in 1995. This agreement called for the signatories to eliminate absolute poverty, greatly reduce relative poverty and tackle the structural causes behind poverty.

Townsend believes such a plan might ultimately require the development of a kind of international welfare state. With the progress of globalization, it is increasingly difficult for individual countries to increase taxes and risk discouraging inward investment. Under such a framework, national governments would then be able to:

1 Introduce limits on wealth and earnings and ensure that there were adequate benefits for the unemployed.
2 Ensure there was a link between benefit levels and average earnings to make sure that the relatively poor shared in increased prosperity.
3 Make sure that taxation was progressive, thus redistributing wealth from the rich to the poor.
4 Implement policies of job creation through the use of grants and by taking on more government employees so that unemployment was greatly reduced.

Despite the radical nature of the changes he proposes, Townsend stops short of suggesting revolutionary change. He says, 'it would be wrong to suggest that any of this is easy or even likely. The citadels of wealth and privilege are deeply entrenched and have shown a tenacious capacity to withstand assaults.'

Pete Alcock (1997) stresses that tackling poverty and social exclusion cannot be separated from a government's overall economic and social policies. He maintains that the purpose of the welfare state is not just to provide a safety net, or even to redistribute wealth. Rather, it is an integral part of maintaining the whole social and economic system:

> *The introduction of state welfare is the product of the process of economic adjustment within capitalist society in which state intervention in the reproduction and maintenance of major services, such as health and education, has become a necessary means of ensuring the continuation of existing economic forces, just as much as a means of redistributing resources to the poor.*
> Alcock, 1997

According to Alcock, capitalist societies such as Britain cannot do without welfare states, and the rich as well as the less fortunate benefit from the way the welfare state produces and reproduces workers. Those who see welfare simply as a way of redistributing wealth have missed the point that state policies can have a big impact by influencing the initial distribution of wealth. Thus policies on wealth, income, investment and employment can help to avoid the need for redistribution by preventing individuals from falling into poverty or suffering from social exclusion.

Marxist solutions

Given the sort of difficulties that Townsend mentions (see above), some Marxist sociologists do not accept that such changes are possible within a capitalist system. While capitalism remains, significant changes in the provisions of the welfare state are impossible. The 'walls of the citadels of wealth and privilege' will not be breached without a full-scale assault which seeks not merely to breach them, but to destroy them altogether.

Because Marxists see poverty as simply one aspect of inequality, the solution to poverty does not involve reforms to the social security system, or the provision of additional payments or services to those defined as poor. Instead, it requires a radical change in the structure of society. Westergaard and Resler (1976) maintain that no substantial redistribution of wealth can occur until capitalism is replaced by a socialist society in which the forces of production are communally owned. They argue that as long as the free market system of capitalism determines the allocation of reward, inequality will remain largely unchanged.

Clearly, Marxist views are ideologically based. Sociologists who adopt these views are committed to the principles of socialism and equality. They regard capitalism as an exploitative system and condemn the inequality it generates. However, there seems little immediate prospect that the changes they propose will take place in Britain, the USA or other capitalist countries. A communist revolution does not seem imminent and neither the former nor the few remaining communist countries have eradicated poverty altogether. However, reforming governments have made less dramatic attempts to tackle poverty through government policies.

'New Labour' – 'A hand up, not a hand-out'

New Labour philosophy

The New Labour government which took office in Britain in 1997 claimed it had policies that would combat the problems of poverty and social exclusion. Prime minister Tony Blair argued that what the poor needed was a 'hand up, not a hand-out'. In other words, they needed to be given the support they required to help themselves, rather than simply depending on state benefits.

Robert M. Page (2002) discussed some of the key features of New Labour's approach as outlined by the then Home Secretary, David Blunkett, in his book *Politics and Progress* (Blunkett, 2001). Page notes that Blunkett argues that welfare should involve **reciprocity**. People should not expect something for nothing. Welfare **rights** also entail **responsibilities**. For example, those receiving benefit because they are unemployed should have an obligation to actively seek work and to accept any suitable work they are offered. From Blunkett's point of view, welfare should 'empower individuals to … seize control of their future'. To Blunkett, welfare involves moral expectations that people should take responsibility for their own behaviour, but this should be in a context in which general fairness and social justice are promoted. Furthermore, Blunkett accepts that everyone is entitled to a reasonable minimum living standard regardless of their ability to work.

Another important aspect of New Labour's approach was to combine a concern with poverty with wider issues of social exclusion. This implies a broader strategy than the more traditional left-wing approach in which redistribution of wealth and income was the main aim. Hills (2002) says: 'Simply giving cash, for instance, does not by itself make someone part of mainstream society.'

Although by no means all policies could be seen as reflecting this changed philosophy of welfare, there are a number of policy areas which do reflect the values underpinning New Labour's approach. The Labour government's policies appear to be based on the view that, on the one hand, the poor and excluded need opportunities and that they will be willing to take advantage of these once they have the training, education, work experiences or childcare facilities they need. On the other hand, at least some claimants need to be compelled to take advantage of the opportunities by the threat of lost benefit. While the former policies are associated with more left-wing sociologists, such as Peter Townsend, the latter are more typical of market liberal writers, such as Charles Murray.

A number of New Labour policies designed to tackle poverty will now be briefly outlined. New Labour philosophy and policies regarding welfare in general will be examined in more detail later in the chapter (see pp. 273–5).

New Labour policies

Among the policies introduced were the following:

1 The launch of a Social Exclusion Unit designed to help the socially excluded reintegrate into society. According to Patrick Wintour and Nick Cohen (1997), the unit would try to tackle truancy, discourage drug dependency by withdrawing benefits for those who refused drug rehabilitation courses, and allow tenants more control over big estates.
2 A strategy was introduced to reduce and eventually eradicate child poverty. In 1999, targets were set to abolish child poverty by 2020, halve it by 2010 and reduce it by a quarter by 2004. Child poverty was defined as living in a household with less than 60 per cent of the median income for that type of household.
3 The main strategy for achieving a reduction in child poverty was to change the tax and benefit system to raise the incomes of low-income households. In particular, measures were introduced to raise the incomes of those in low-paid work. A minimum wage was introduced in 1999, and new tax credits were introduced, first to boost the incomes of working parents, and then those of other groups (see p. 274). Child benefits were also raised.
4 A number of measures were introduced to encourage people back into work and cut unemployment. Early on, the money from a 'windfall tax' on the profits of privatized utilities, such as gas and electricity companies, was spent on providing more training and job opportunities for the young unemployed. This 'Welfare to Work' scheme gave people under the age of 25 who had been unemployed for more than six months one of four options. These were: (1) subsidized employment with businesses (the companies getting £60 a week and £750 for training); (2) for those without qualifications, up to 12 months' full-time study; (3) six months' employment with a voluntary sector employer; (4) six months' work with the environmental taskforce. Those unwilling to take part risked losing their entitlement to benefit. Another scheme was introduced to give lone parents advice and guidance on how to get back to work. From 2001, single parents were required to attend an interview each year to explore their opportunities for employment.
5 A number of government policies were designed to tackle particular types of social exclusion. A wide range of measures was designed to raise the educational standards for children from disadvantaged backgrounds (see pp. 621–2). These included literacy and numeracy hours for primary schools, Education Action Zones in the areas with poor educational outcomes, attempts to raise the numbers staying on in education after 16, and after-school homework clubs designed for children who found it difficult to study at home. A number of measures attempted to tackle social exclusion in particular neighbourhoods through the New Deal for Communities and the Single Regeneration Budget, which provided extra resources in the most disadvantaged areas.

Criticisms of New Labour policies

The policies of New Labour have received both support and criticism. While some have argued that they have involved a shift away from a genuine concern with eradicating poverty and inequality, others have argued that the policies have begun to make a significant difference. Some of the more critical views will be examined first.

In its early years in office Tony Blair's government showed little willingness to increase benefits to raise the living standards of the poor. Its most controversial early measure was to reduce the benefits available to single parents, in line with a policy the Conservative government had intended to implement before it was voted out of office. New Labour was elected promising that it would not exceed the previous government's spending plans and was therefore reluctant to commit itself to extra spending on the large welfare budget. It was also elected promising there would be no increase in income tax rates, making it difficult to embark on a costly programme designed to alleviate poverty or tackle social exclusion.

A number of commentators believed the Labour Party was moving away from its traditional concern with redistribution of wealth and income. Stephen Sinclair (2003) argues, 'some benefits have been increased in real terms above the level of inflation, but usually these have been targeted at particular groups – such as disabled people or children – who are unable to work'. Much less had been done for the unemployed who were capable of working. Sinclair goes on to say:

> *The reluctance to increase benefits which government Ministers themselves acknowledge are very low reflects New Labour's reluctance to provide 'something for nothing' and reduce the gap between the richest and the poorest in society. In an interview just before the 2001 election, the Prime Minister acknowledged that he was not very troubled by the large and growing inequalities of income and wealth in Britain, and did not believe that improving the situation of those on low incomes necessarily meant reducing the gap between them and those who are better off. This is quite a shift from traditional Labour thinking, which held that poverty and inequality were closely connected and, in fact, poverty was caused by a concentration of income and wealth.* Sinclair, 2003

Sinclair quotes research conducted in 2002 which suggests that some £5.5 billion would need to be redistributed from rich to poor to substantially raise the income of the poorest 4 million households.

New Labour policies and changing values

Writing in 1998, Ruth Levitas also detected a change in the dominant values of the Labour Party. She argued that New Labour's shift away from a concern with poverty towards a concern with social exclusion represented an important ideological change. She distinguished three discourses, or ways of thinking and talking, about social exclusion.

1 RED, or the 'redistributionist discourse ... in which social exclusion is intertwined with poverty'. This approach emphasizes that poverty and social exclusion can only be tackled by taking some money away from the rich to give to the poor.
2 MUD, or the 'moral underclass discourse', which explains poverty and social exclusion in terms of cultural influences on the behaviour of the poor. This discourse may use the language of the underclass advocated by Charles Murray (see pp. 242–4), but is also reflected in some uses of the term 'social exclusion' and in arguments about the 'responsibilities' of benefit claimants and other groups of the poor. From this point of view, the problems can be tackled by changing the behaviour of those who have defective attitudes.
3 SID, defined by Levitas as a 'social integrationist discourse', which 'sees inclusion primarily in terms of labour market attachment'. This discourse argues that both the financial and non-financial aspects of the problems of poverty and social exclusion are caused by the lack of social integration among those who do not have paid employment. From this point of view, creating greater social solidarity is the key to tackling problems, and the best way to do this is to ensure that everybody who can, does paid work.

An increasingly important part of political debate in Britain involves 'the contested meaning of social exclusion'. While everybody agrees that social exclusion is a bad thing, there is no agreement about what lies behind it or what to do about it. Levitas believes New Labour has not emphasized the traditional Labour Party concern with RED (the redistributionist discourse) and instead has emphasized a mixture of SID (social integrationist discourse) and MUD (moral underclass discourse). Above all, tackling social exclusion has been seen as involving greater social integration and social solidarity.

Levitas argues that this discourse owes much to the ideas of Emile Durkheim and his concern with the importance of a collective conscience in creating greater social solidarity (see pp. 396–7 and 858–9). Levitas believes that this emphasis will not lead to the changes necessary to get rid of poverty and social exclusion. To Levitas, 'a more radical egalitarian approach to inclusion', which involves 'a critique of capitalism', is needed. From this point of view, without greater equality the social exclusion of the most disadvantaged is unlikely to disappear.

New Labour achievements

However, not all commentators agree that Labour governments since 1997 deserve such criticism. For example, Robert M. Page (2005) argues that government policies have made significant differences. First, the government accepted a relative definition of poverty (60 per cent of median income) and set out with targets to reduce poverty for children. It also had less explicit targets to reduce pensioner poverty.

Page points out that both official and other sources show that child poverty fell significantly under the Labour government (see p. 225 for the figures). The introduction of the Minimum Income Guarantee and Pensioner Credit schemes improved the financial position of pensioners; and winter fuel payments for those aged 60 and over, and free TV licences for all pensioners of 75 or over, also helped to reduce pensioner poverty.

Although there were no explicit policies designed to reduce poverty for working-age adults, the introduction of the minimum wage, working and child tax credits and 'Welfare to Work' programmes helped adults on low incomes. Page comments that it is difficult to assess how effective Labour policies designed to get people into work have been, but the overall strength of the economy has produced a buoyant labour market.

Furthermore, Page points out that the government had policies designed to tackle social exclusion as well as poverty. The 2004 report of the Department of Work and Pensions found improvements in thirty-five of the fifty-eight indicators of social exclusion, with a deterioration in just three indicators. Page concludes that, overall, New Labour has made 'steady progress' in dealing with problems such as poverty and social exclusion. He admits that for more progressive or radical commentators this might seem inadequate, while others would see the achievements as impressive.

(This chapter has dealt largely with poverty and social exclusion in the UK. For analysis of problems of poverty in 'third world' countries see Chapter 15.)

The welfare state

Introduction: types of welfare

The issue of welfare concerns the well-being of populations within particular societies or states. Welfare is concerned which such issues as meeting basic needs including those for clean water, food and shelter; preventing or dealing with absolute or relative poverty; and providing health, education and other services.

Pete Alcock (2003) identifies four main sectors which meet or help to meet such needs in contemporary societies.

1 The **informal sector** involves family, neighbours or friends assisting people in times of need. It includes parents educating, feeding and housing their children, a neighbour helping out an elderly pensioner, or a person allowing a homeless friend to stay with them. As Alcock says, 'Informal care is not organised or regulated and in practice is based upon

individual dedication and goodwill or reciprocal agreements' (Alcock, 2003, p. 178). Informal care is extremely important in the provision of welfare, and, Alcock points out, it allows other sectors to operate as they do. Private, voluntary and state provision tend to supplement informal provision.

However, because it is informal and its providers are unpaid, it is hard to measure the total worth of informal provision. Some providers of informal care do receive support from the state – for example, some of those who care for the elderly receive Attendance Allowance. However, much of the cost is borne by individuals.

Feminists point out that most informal care is provided by women (see pp. 275–6), and suggest that this reinforces gender inequalities. Social democrats also criticize over-reliance upon informal care, arguing that the lack of regulation and organization means there is no guarantee that this sector can provide comprehensive, fair or high-quality care (see pp. 265–7). On the other hand, the New Right (see pp. 268–73) tend to see the family as the cornerstone of society and are generally in favour of the expansion of informal care at the expense of state provision.

2 The **voluntary sector** consists of organizations, which are usually registered charities, which are set up to deal with social problems such as old age, homelessness or child abuse. Examples of such organizations include Help the Aged, Shelter and the NSPCC (National Society for the Prevention of Cruelty to Children). Although less important than the state or informal sectors, Alcock estimates that in Britain in 2002 the voluntary sector spent some £15.6 billion on the provision of welfare.

The voluntary sector is very diverse and some organizations receive help with funding from the state, though most rely to some extent on charitable donations. Many voluntary organizations work with the state in providing services (e.g. the NSPCC). However, many also have a campaigning role (e.g. the Child Poverty Action Group) and as such may actively try to change government policy.

Advocates of all perspectives on the welfare state recognize that the voluntary sector can make an important contribution to welfare provision. Market liberals are particularly keen on the way it can encourage individuals to take on responsibility for others through volunteering to help. However, social democrats generally oppose an over-reliance upon the voluntary sector, arguing that only the state has the resources to guarantee the provision of the welfare services that are needed. Although most voluntary organizations can afford to employ some people, they often rely a great deal on unpaid volunteers. Volunteers may not have the same level of expertise or training as employees. As the income of voluntary organizations is not guaranteed they may not be able to offer the same level of service from year to year.

3 The **private sector** consists of welfare services provided by private companies which charge for their services and which usually aim to make a profit. Examples include private hospitals, schools and nursing homes. Alcock points out that private provision was particularly encouraged by the market liberal Conservative government of Margaret Thatcher (1979–90), although most state provision was retained. From this perspective it is more efficient if welfare is delivered by private companies rather than the state, because competition between companies raises standards and cuts costs (see pp. 265–7).

Private provision sometimes exists alongside state provision (for example, in health and education), providing an alternative for those who can afford to pay privately. Social democrats and Marxists, however, are highly critical of private provision, arguing that it contributes to inequality and prevents social justice (see pp. 267–8 and 275–6).

4 The **state sector** (or welfare state) involves the state or government providing welfare services. This sector is the main focus of this part of the chapter, and competing perspectives on the welfare state (and its relationship with other sectors) will now be examined.

Defining the welfare state

As discussed earlier (see p. 213), Asa Briggs defined the welfare state as 'a state in which organized power is deliberately used (through politics and administration) in an effort to modify the play of market forces' (Briggs, 2000, p. 18, first published 1969). From this point of view, the welfare state exists in societies where there is a market for goods, services and labour, typically capitalist societies. The welfare state develops where the government decides that the population's essential needs and well-being will not be adequately provided for without government intervention. Thus Anthony Giddens explains that:

> *Most industrialized and industrializing countries in the world today are welfare states. By this it is meant that the state plays a central role in the provision of welfare, which it does through a system which offers services and benefits that meet people's basic needs for things such as healthcare, education, housing and income. An important role of the welfare state is managing the risks faced by people over the course of their lives: sickness, disability, job loss and old age.* Giddens, 2006, p. 365

However, Giddens goes on to point out that both the level of spending and the range of services offered by welfare states vary considerably from country to country. He comments that:

> *Some countries have highly developed welfare systems and devote a high proportion of the national budget to them. In Sweden, for example, tax revenues represent about 53 per cent of the gross domestic product (GDP). By comparison, other western nations take far less in tax. In the UK, tax revenues represent around 38 per cent of GDP and in the USA just under 30 per cent.* Giddens, 2006, p. 366

This is partly because policy makers and academics have advanced conflicting views on what they think the role of welfare should be. This has led to the development of distinctive perspectives on welfare which tend to reflect different political views.

At different periods in the development of the welfare state in Britain and elsewhere, different perspectives have been dominant and have had a major influence on government policy. Some perspectives emphasize the need to keep the welfare state as small as possible, while others believe that most areas of welfare should be provided by the government. These competing perspectives also have varying views on the provision of welfare by other sectors. For example, some believe that the private, voluntary and informal sectors should have a major role in the provision of welfare, while others believe that the role of one or more of these sectors should be minimized.

Before considering the competing perspectives we will first briefly examine the history of the British welfare state until the Beveridge Report of 1942, which laid the foundations for the modern welfare state.

The origins of the welfare state in Britain

Michael Hill – the history of social policy

The Poor Law and the origins of state welfare

Michael Hill (2003) provides a useful summary of the history of social policy in Britain, including a description of the origins of the modern welfare state.

Hill argues that government welfare policy goes as far back as the sixteenth and seventeenth centuries. Before 1601, help for the poor was largely provided informally by family and friends, with some involvement from churches. In 1601 the Poor Law Act was introduced in England and this is often seen as the first direct state involvement in welfare. Under this law the Acts of Settlement stipulated that parishes were responsible for providing help to the poor from their parish, paid for by local property taxes or rates. As agriculture developed and towns began to grow, there were increased population movements. To deal with these it was stipulated that the poor had to return to their parish of birth to receive help.

Although this basic system remained in place for over two centuries, it became increasingly unworkable. Hill comments that:

> *As the UK became industrialized and urbanized, this strictly local system of administration came under strain. Population movements gradually rendered the Acts of Settlement obsolete. The tasks of the Poor Law became more costly and more complex as parishes had to cope with, for example, trade recessions and outbreaks of infectious diseases, each affecting large numbers of people in the new towns and cities.* Hill, 2003, pp. 14–15

The growth of state intervention in the nineteenth century

As a result of these problems, the Poor Law was completely overhauled with the Poor Law Amendment Act of 1834. Under this Act a new Poor Law Commission was established to oversee the administration of help to the poor. Parishes were grouped together in Poor Law unions to provide assistance to the poor. These unions were required to set up poor houses where the poor were forced to live if they wished to receive assistance – a type of assistance known as **indoor relief**.

Poor houses were deliberately designed to be unattractive so that the poor would only use them as a last resort. The intention was to cut down the growing costs of **outdoor relief**, which had been given to those outside poor houses, and to encourage people into work. As Hill comments, 'The system was intended to ensure that those who received help were worse off ("less eligible") than the poorest people in work' (2003, p.15). However, in practice, as time passed, the Poor Law unions increasingly gave outdoor relief to the sick and elderly.

Nineteenth-century social policy was not confined to dealing with the problem of poverty. A number of new measures were also introduced to deal directly with social problems caused by the industrial revolution and rapid urbanization as the population grew and people moved from rural areas to the developing towns and cities.

1. Measures were introduced to limit the working hours of children and women and to improve health and safety in factories and other places of work. A centralized factory inspectorate was set up.
2. As awareness grew of the link between poor sanitation and infectious diseases, steps were taken to improve sewage disposal and provide a supply of clean water. The Municipal Corporations Act of 1835 provided the local government structure to enable these problems to be tackled at a local level. From 1871 local authorities were required to employ medical officers to deal with public health issues.
3. State support for education also began in the nineteenth century, starting in 1833 with grants to support the work of church schools which provided some education for the poor. In 1870 the state started providing primary education, and in 1880 schooling became compulsory for the first time between the ages of 5 and 10.
4. State-funded health provision developed slowly in the nineteenth century, but Poor Law hospitals were available to some of the most needy. Local authorities were also allowed to provide hospitals to control infectious diseases and care for the mentally ill.

Despite all these changes, 'The dominant view amongst the governing classes in the last part of the nineteenth century was that state involvement in dealing with social issues and problems should be kept to a minimum' (Hill, 2003, p. 17). While some members of the middle class were concerned about the effects of social problems such as crime and disease, they tended to support voluntary, charitable provision rather than state intervention.

Nevertheless, around the turn of the century there was growing awareness of social problems such as poverty. This was highlighted in research by Charles Booth in London

(1902–3) and Seebohm Rowntree (1901) (see pp. 215–16). Furthermore, local government reform in 1888 and 1894 strengthened the ability of local authorities to provide welfare services. With the election of a Liberal government in 1906 there was a new impetus to the development of a rudimentary welfare state.

The foundations of the welfare state 1906–39

Even before the Liberals took power from the Conservatives in 1906, there was a growing belief that the existing system of helping the poor was inadequate. In 1908 the Liberals introduced the Old Age Pensions Act to help the elderly. In 1911 the National Insurance Act was introduced to assist some people suffering from sickness or unemployment.

The old age pension provided a basic, means-tested benefit for the elderly poor. Means-tested benefits only go to those who are deemed to have too low an income or insufficient savings to support themselves.

The National Insurance Act provided a contributory scheme, whereby only those who had paid sufficient contributions into the scheme were entitled to financial support in sickness or unemployment. This introduced state payments to doctors who treated patients under the scheme, and today GPs continue to be paid by the NHS in a similar way.

Hill comments that, under the Liberal government, 'Key foundations of the UK system of social policy were laid at this time. What was established was essentially an embryonic welfare state for male breadwinners, with a strong influence on what was to come' (2003, p. 21).

Between the end of the First World War in 1918 and the start of the Second World War in 1939 there was a gradual extension of the role of the state in the provision of welfare. The state began to subsidize the building of local authority housing (council houses), provision for the unemployed was extended (though it remained meagre for most), a contributory pension scheme for working men was introduced in 1925, and education beyond the primary stage grew. Despite these developments, state welfare provision remained patchy because it had developed in a piecemeal way. Though the principle of state provision was well established, there was no overall plan on which state provision was based. However this was to change in the 1940s with the publication of the Beveridge Report and the introduction of the Butler Education Act.

The Beveridge Report and the birth of the modern welfare state

Background to the Beveridge Report

During the Second World War the British government took control of more aspects of social policy than had ever been the case during peacetime. Centralized government planning did not just involve organizing the military effort. It also involved aspects of social policy such as rationing of food, the control of rents, price control and the organization of the evacuation of children to the countryside from cities that were at risk of bombing. There was enormous government expenditure which created full employment, with more people employed by the state than ever before. Hill comments that 'The wartime state had many of the characteristics of the "welfare state", which is popularly regarded as having been created after the war' (2003, p. 25).

The conduct of the war and the organization of social and economic policy by the state suggested that the state could effectively take on a wider role than it had hitherto enjoyed. During the war a coalition government was formed which included the main political parties, and 'planning of the peace was widely accepted as a legitimate political task during the war' (Hill, 2003, p. 24). Some commentators also claim that all social classes experienced hardship during the war, creating the political conditions in which a comprehensive review of welfare could be welcomed. Cliff Alcock, Sarah Payne and Michael Sullivan comment:

> *It might be claimed that … the shared danger of war time created a greater sense of social solidarity than had hitherto been the case. Conscripts were drawn from different walks of life and social classes were thrown together and formed close bonds of comradeship.* Alcock *et al.*, 2004

Together, the new-found confidence in state planning and increased social solidarity helped to create the impetus which led to the commissioning of the Beveridge Report.

The Beveridge Report

The Social Insurance and Allied Services Report (better known as the Beveridge Report; Beveridge, 1942) was commissioned by the government to find out how the existing welfare benefits and services could be improved. Sir William Beveridge, who wrote the report, had trained as a lawyer but had served as a civil servant, amongst other things setting up and directing labour exchanges.

The report attracted great public interest and sold some 635,000 copies (Fraser, 1984). Although it focused on the provision of social insurance it argued that 'social insurance should be treated as one part only of a comprehensive policy of social insurance' (extracts from Beveridge, 1942, p. 1). It therefore proposed a comprehensive overhaul of state welfare provision, covering all the major welfare issues in which the state was involved. To this end Beveridge identified 'five giants on the road of reconstruction', which were 'Want … Disease, Ignorance, Squalor and Idleness' (Beveridge, 1942, p. 1).

1 **Want** was concerned with lack of 'income security' which could lead to people having an inadequate income to live on. This tended to affect people who were unemployed, sick, old or widowed. From Beveridge's point of view, therefore, it mainly affected households without somebody in paid employment.

   To tackle this problem Beveridge suggested that social insurance schemes should be extended to cover more circumstances and made more generous. He further suggested the introduction of child allowances to cover the extra costs of looking after children.

   Beveridge proposed a combination of means-tested benefits (which depended on income or savings), benefits which depended upon previous contributions, and benefits received by everybody regardless of income or contributions (universal benefits). A basic means-tested benefit was to be provided as a safety-net for all those who had no other source of income. Beveridge believed that this benefit should be based upon calculations made by

Rowntree which estimated the amount of money required to meet basic needs (Thane, 1982). These measures were to be funded by a flat-rate national insurance scheme to which employers and employees would contribute. Although national insurance was the main focus of the report, mention was also made of the other 'giants' which needed to be tackled.

2 The second giant was **disease**. Beveridge believed that this could be tackled through the provision of a health service available to all citizens.
3 The third giant, **ignorance**, had to be tackled through the provision of state education, particularly through the provision of a state-funded, universal, secondary education system.
4 The issue of **squalor** was mainly concerned with housing. To tackle this, Beveridge proposed an extensive programme of building affordable council houses to rent.
5 **Idleness** was to be avoided through ensuring that the mass unemployment of the 1930s was never repeated. The theories of the British economist John Maynard Keynes (1936) suggested that unemployment could be avoided if the government spent enough money to stimulate the economy and thereby create the demand for workers. As Hill comments, 'There was a commitment to the maintenance of full employment, with the Keynesian doctrine that budgetary management could achieve this now a matter of economic orthodoxy' (2003, p. 27).

The principles of the Beveridge Report

In many ways the Beveridge Report was the basis for radical changes in British society. Derek Fraser comments that the overall package of measures was designed to be comprehensive. He says:

> *the Beveridge plan for social insurance envisaged in return for a single weekly contribution a cradle-to-grave provision of sickness, medical, unemployment, widows', orphans', old-age, maternity, industrial injury and funeral benefits. It was universal in coverage of both risks and persons and would provide subsistence benefits for all.* Fraser, 1984, p. 214

However, Beveridge himself had moderate, reforming and liberal political views. He did not see the welfare state as aiming to create a more egalitarian society, nor did he want or expect the state to take on more and more responsibilities. His aims were more narrowly focused on solving particular social problems. The state was to provide a safety-net and help for citizens 'from the cradle to the grave', but Beveridge did not expect them to become dependent upon welfare provision.

One of the principles of the Beveridge Report was that

> *The state should offer security for service and contribution. The state in organising security should not stifle incentive, opportunity, responsibility; in stabilising a national minimum, it should leave room and encouragement for voluntary action by each individual to provide more than the minimum for himself and his family.* Beveridge, 1942, p. 1

Beveridge did not believe that the welfare state would become more and more expensive, but quite the contrary. He expected that as social problems were progressively reduced, welfare expenditure in most areas would fall. With a well-educated, fully employed workforce, fewer people would need to claim benefits. Better health care would reduce illness and so cut the financial burden on the state.

Vic George and Paul Wilding (1994) characterize Beveridge as a **reluctant collectivist** – he saw the welfare state as 'a mechanism for making good the failure of the market to control avoidable ills rather than an instrument for social and economic change or for promoting the good life' (George and Wilding, 1994, pp. 62–3). Collective action was needed by the state to help individuals when necessary – when basic needs were not met by the market in a capitalist economy – but the welfare state should not try to achieve more than this. Because of this, Beveridge has been attacked both by left-wing sociologists and commentators, who see him as too moderate in his aims, and by right-wing sociologists and commentators, who believe that Beveridge's approach to welfare involves far too much state intervention.

Implementation of the Beveridge proposals

Broadly speaking, most of Beveridge's proposals were introduced. The report received widespread backbench support in parliament, and Pat Thane claims it 'caught the public imagination and came to symbolise the hope for a different, more just world' (1982, p. 252). Some measures were introduced by the wartime coalition government, but many were implemented by the Labour government of Clement Attlee which won power in 1945. The following were some of the main welfare changes.

1 The Education Act of 1944 (often known as the Butler Act) introduced universal, free state secondary education and raised the school leaving age to 15 with effect from 1947.
2 According to Hill, 'Beveridge's insurance scheme was broadly put into legislation' (2003, p. 25). Family allowances were introduced immediately, with most of the other measures introduced by the Labour government. However, contrary to Beveridge, the insurance principle – that one had to pay contributions to get the benefits – was somewhat undermined by making the length of time one had to contribute to get an old age pension very short.
3 In 1948 the National Health Service (NHS) was set up, providing GPs and hospital services free for everyone.
4 The post-war Labour government was influenced by the views of Beveridge and the theories of Keynes (see pp. 541–2) and tried to maintain high levels of employment. Pat Thane says, 'The Labour government talked the language of planning whilst practising a modified version of Keynesian management, approved by the treasury' (1982, p. 257). In one respect the government intervened directly in the economy, nationalizing (taking into state ownership) the unprofitable power and transport industries.
5 In terms of housing, the Labour government introduced a policy of publicly financing the building of new towns and embarked upon a major house-building programme which resulted in one million new houses built by 1951.

Criticisms of the Beveridge and Keynesian approaches to welfare

Beveridge and Keynes have been criticized from both the right and the left of the political spectrum.

1 Market liberals (who in some contexts are known as neoliberals or the New Right) have been critical of both Beveridge and Keynes for advocating so much state intervention in welfare and the economy. They see this as having a negative effect, discouraging self-reliance, initiative and entrepreneurship, and undermining economic efficiency and growth.

David Marsland, a leading advocate of a market liberal approach to welfare, argues that the Beveridge Report 'had the effect, whatever the author's intentions, of discouraging individualism, self-reliance, voluntary organisations, and private initiatives. It tipped the balance in the development of social policy decisively against competition and in favour of planning' (1992, p. 146). In Marsland's view, state involvement in welfare should be minimal, with most welfare provided by the voluntary, private and informal sectors.

According to George and Wilding (1994), Keynes has been criticized by market liberals for ignoring the negative effects of government spending to boost the economy. From the right-wing point of view this leads to the creation of an inefficient state welfare system and inefficient nationalized industries. The workers in those sectors know that the government will support them even if they are inefficient and unprofitable, giving them little incentive to be efficient, hard-working or entrepreneurial.

2 Although Beveridge himself saw his proposals as radical, some left-wing critics of Beveridge have seen his proposals and the policies which followed as far from radical. Christopher Pierson notes that a number of critics of Beveridge have suggested that the changes 'represented not a radical charter for a new social order, but a tidying up and codification of pre-war legislation' (2006, p. 139).

Social democratic and Marxist theorists have variously criticized the type of welfare state that resulted from Beveridge for failing to redistribute income and wealth to create a fairer society, for failing to eradicate poverty, and/or for being a tool used by the ruling class to maintain social order (see pp. 265–7 and 267–8 for an examination of Marxist and social democratic perspectives). Although there are a variety of left-wing positions, all agree that the welfare state as established in Britain in the 1940s was inadequate to produce social justice.

3 According to George and Wilding (1994), some feminists were critical of Beveridge for basing his approach on the assumption that the mother role was a primary one for women. Anthony Giddens supports this viewpoint, arguing that 'the vision for the welfare state was predicated on a patriarchal conception of families – the male breadwinner was to support his family while his wife tended to the home' (2006, p. 370). However, there were some feminists who welcomed the introduction of Family Allowance which gave women who were not in paid work some income independent of a male partner's wage.

4 The Beveridge model also came in for criticism and ultimately modification by the Labour governments of Tony Blair from 1997 to 2007. Blair – who characterized his government as being 'New Labour' – supported the idea of a **Third Way**, which is neither left-wing nor right-wing, but which combines ideas which have traditionally been associated with both ends of the political spectrum.

As Robert M. Page (2005) points out, New Labour has claimed that the welfare state needs to be modernized to provide adequate services in a changing world. In particular, New Labour has introduced the idea of consumer choice, which has traditionally been associated with the private provision of welfare and right-wing thinking rather than Labour governments. From this point of view, Beveridge's approach has become less appropriate as living standards have risen and the users of welfare services have expected and demanded a better service, in line with the improved service that consumers expect in other areas of social life.

Furthermore, from a New Labour point of view, the Beveridge model did too little to encourage people to be self-reliant. This view argues that welfare should provide people with a 'hand up not a hand-out' – that is, people should be assisted, when they need it, to help themselves, but should not be encouraged to become reliant on hand-outs without doing anything in return. New Labour thinking has therefore been broadly sympathetic to the aims of Beveridge, but has argued that the welfare state has failed to achieve its aims, and needs bringing up to date if it is to become more effective.

The influence of Beveridge and Keynes

Despite the range and the strength of criticisms of Beveridge, there is no doubt that his vision of welfare has been extremely influential. In the post-war period, the broad thrust of the approach to social welfare and the economy advocated by Beveridge and Keynes remained dominant for many years.

Alcock argues that despite the Conservatives replacing Labour in 1951, 'the same state-welfare services were maintained in almost exactly the same form' (2003, p. 7). During this period there was what was frequently referred to as the **post-war consensus**, in which both the major parties, Labour and Conservative, followed policies based upon the principles laid down by Keynes and Beveridge. These policies are sometimes referred to as **Butskellism**.

The term Butskellism was first used in *The Economist* magazine in 1954 (Alcock, 2003). It combines the surnames of Hugh Gaitskell (the Labour Chancellor in the 1945 Labour government) and Rab Butler (the Conservative Chancellor in the 1951 Conservative government). The consensus represented by this term involved the Labour leadership rejecting the most left-wing thinking in its party, and the Conservative leadership abandoning the more right-wing thinking in its party. Alcock describes it in this way: 'This consensus seemed to represent an accommodation in Conservative thinking to the role of state intervention … and a recognition in Labour thinking of the abandonment of the need for a future socialist revolution' (2003, p. 7).

Aspects of the post-war consensus survive in the British welfare state up to the present day. For example, the principle that health care should be provided universally to all citizens, free at the point of use, has largely survived (despite some charges such as those for prescriptions). The idea of universalism – that some services should be free to all – 'was seen as promoting national solidarity. It would integrate the nation by involving the entire population in a common set of services' (Giddens, 2006, p. 370). It has proved politically difficult to change this principle despite opposition from market liberals (see pp. 268–73).

However, the post-war consensus came under some pressure from social democratic thinking from the 1960s onwards, and this had some influence on reforms to the welfare state under Labour governments of the 1960s and 1970s (see below). Nevertheless, arguably it was not until the election of a radical Conservative government under Margaret Thatcher in 1979 that the post-war consensus began to fall apart. Before examining this period, and market liberal thinking on welfare, social democratic views will first be considered.

Social democratic views on welfare

Butskellism, or the post-war consensus, was never completely dominant in the years after 1945, and as time went by it was increasingly challenged by the political left. Both inside and outside the Labour Party, there were always some who had more radical ambitions for the welfare state than those put forward by Beveridge.

According to Pierson (2006), social democratic perspectives have the following essential features.

1. Like Marxists, social democrats believe that capitalist industrial societies have been based upon the exploitation of the working class (see pp. 26–9), but, unlike Marxists, they believe it is possible to get rid of injustice within a capitalist system and without having a revolution. Through democratic processes, including trade union activity and involvement in parliamentary democracy, workers can ensure that their position gradually improves.
2. Social democrats believe that the class structure has become less polarized between capitalists and workers, and not more polarized as Marx predicted (see pp. 26–9). The middle class has grown with the development of public sector employment, leading to a more complex class structure.
3. Social democrats believe that in the above situation capitalism can grow without economic crises, and living standards can improve at the same time as income and wealth become more equally distributed.

From this point of view, then, state intervention can correct the problems created by industrial capitalist societies. Through democratic politics a socialist society, in which people are much more equal than they were in early capitalism, can be created without the need for revolution.

Social democratic thinking is gradualist and reformist – change is a gradual process and involves reform of society without revolution. As Pierson comments, though, the socialist aims of social democracy are rather vague. Social democrats often tend to disagree about how much inequality should remain after reform has taken place. Furthermore they are sometimes unclear about what they see as the proper balance between state intervention and the free market. The following sections look at some of the influential social democratic thinkers.

T.H. Marshall and citizenship

A major influence on social democratic thinking was the work of T.H. Marshall (1950). Marshall argued that the development of the welfare state involved the progressive development of citizenship rights. According to Marshall, as industrial societies evolved, citizens gained different types of rights. As each was gained, this allowed further progress to be made.

The first types of rights to be gained were **civil rights**, which are the 'rights necessary for individual freedom – liberty of the person, freedom of speech, thought and faith, the right to own property and to conclude valid contracts, and the right to justice'. Once these rights had been established, it allowed people to campaign for **political rights**, which are 'the right to participate in the exercise of political power, as a member of a body invested with political authority or as the elector of the member of such a body' (Marshall, 2000, first published 1950, p. 32).

These democratic rights gave ordinary citizens the ability to shape government policy and ultimately resulted in the granting of **social rights**. Social rights are the type of rights associated with the development of a welfare state and include:

> *the whole range, from the right to a modicum of economic welfare and security to the right to share to the full in the social heritage and to live as a civilized being according to the standards prevailing in the society. The institutions most closely connected with it are the educational system and the social services.* Marshall, 2000, first published 1950, p. 32

Social rights also include the right to employment.

At first sight the emphasis on rights sounds little different from the Beveridge approach to welfare, but for Marshall the insistence on everyone being entitled to rights was based on egalitarian principles. Rights assumed a degree of equality between all citizens since everybody had the same rights. Marshall admitted that this could be at odds with a capitalist society in which individuals and businesses competed for material success, and some did better than others. This inevitably gave rise to class inequality, but Marshall saw the welfare state as a way of greatly reducing this inequality. As the state intervened more and more in the economy and society, providing extra income to the poor and taking extra taxes from the rich, inequality would be reduced and classes would weaken. Marshall did not believe that complete equality between individuals was possible, or even desirable. However, he did think that the welfare state could and should gradually create a more egalitarian society where the rights of citizens shaped society more than free market economics.

Richard Titmuss

Another important contributor to the development of social democratic views on welfare was Richard Titmuss (Titmuss, 2000, first published 1968). Like Marshall, Titmuss was concerned about the creation of greater social justice and greater equality, but he also saw the welfare state as being able to achieve additional aims. According to Vic George and Paul Wilding (1994), Titmuss believed that the welfare state could 'promote altruism and social integration in society' (George and Wilding, 1994, p. 82). From this point of view, the welfare state could bring people together and give them a shared sense of citizenship. Furthermore, it could encourage particular values whereby people felt a shared responsibility for the well-being of fellow citizens. The main way in which these aims could be achieved was through the provision of universal social services – that is, social services available to all which are not based on means-tests.

Titmuss identified universal social services as Family Allowance, the NHS, free state education, and pensions provided through national insurance. None of these were means-tested – they did not depend on the income of the recipients but were provided by right. Because they were universal, all members of society could potentially share in the benefits, and similarly everybody contributed towards paying for them when they were able to do so.

Titmuss believed that the existence of universal benefits and services got rid of the stigma associated with claiming means-tested benefits. The recipients of means-tested benefits are sometimes looked down on as scroungers, but if everybody can claim a benefit or use a service as of right, there is no basis for looking down on the recipients. The funding, provision and use of universal aspects of the welfare state bind all citizens together in the knowledge that they depend upon each other.

To Titmuss, universal benefits get rid of the complexity and administrative costs of means-testing and they avoid the humiliation of having to ask for assistance and reveal one's income. They therefore have a high take-up rate, and nobody is left without help because they are too proud to ask or because claiming is too difficult. Thus, for example, there is no stigma attached to drawing an old-age pension, sending children to a state school or using the NHS, because they are all regarded as citizens' rights. In contrast, means-tests are designed to exclude people from the right to a benefit and they therefore treat people not as citizens or consumers, but as applicants.

Titmuss also felt that means-tested services tend to degenerate into poor quality services because they are not used by richer and more powerful members of society who can pressurize politicians into improving them. Means-tested benefits can also produce a poverty trap. People are discouraged from working to get out of poverty because, as their income rises, they lose benefits and are hardly any better off (or even worse off) as a result of working.

Titmuss was aware, however, that universalism did not necessarily produce greater equality. He quoted work by Peter Townsend which showed that relative deprivation still existed in Britain in the 1960s and that the gap between the rich and the poor remained very substantial (see pp. 217–18 for Townsend's work on relative poverty). Titmuss therefore thought that universalism was not, on its own, enough to achieve social democratic aims, and so he also advocated 'positive, selective discrimination' to give extra help to the most disadvantaged. **Positive discrimination** might be offered in terms of 'income maintenance, in education, in housing, in medical care, in mental health, in child welfare and in the tolerant integration of immigrants and citizens from overseas' (Titmuss, 2000, first published 1968, p. 48).

Titmuss therefore concluded that the welfare state needed to be based on universal social services, but it also needed to be able to provide extra help and resources for the most needy in ways that were socially acceptable and which were not socially divisive or stigmatizing to the recipients. (For views that are critical of universal provision, see pp. 268–9 and 238–9.)

Social democratic perspectives and government policy

Social democratic thinking had some influence on the Labour governments of 1964–70 and 1974–9. For example, it influenced the introduction of comprehensive schools which in some areas replaced the tripartite system. The tripartite system was introduced in 1944 and provided grammar schools for the more academically able, and secondary modern and technical schools for the less academic. The system was selective, with the selection based upon performance in an intelligence test known as the eleven-plus (see Chapter 10, pp. 626–7).

Social democrats saw this system as divisive because grammar schools were dominated by middle- and higher-class children, while secondary moderns had a predominantly working-class intake. It therefore reinforced existing class divisions. Furthermore, grammar schools were often seen as providing a better education which gave pupils more opportunities for access to higher education. Secondary modern schools were viewed as providing fewer opportunities for upward mobility.

It was hoped that the introduction of comprehensive schools would break down social barriers, create more equal opportunities and give more working-class children access to higher education and middle-class jobs. The comprehensive system was first introduced by the Labour minister Anthony Crosland in 1965 and Crosland was a prominent advocate of social democratic policies (Alcock, 2003).

Social democratic thinking also influenced the raising of taxes for those with high incomes and, following the ideas of Richard Titmuss, there were some attempts to provide positive discrimination for the particularly disadvantaged. In some of the poorest areas, for example, Education Action Zones were introduced to boost the educational opportunities of some of the most deprived children. However, social democratic influence on government policies only went so far. Michael Hill argues that the period from 1964 to 1979 did not see radical changes in the welfare state but instead was a period of 'consolidation and modification' (2003, p. 28).

Evaluation of the social democratic perspective

Christopher Pierson (2006) argues that the social democratic perspective on welfare has some advantages over previous perspectives. In its analysis of how the welfare state changes, it acknowledges both the importance of political factors and that of social changes such as industrialization, technological change and the development of capitalism. Thus it explains the development of the welfare state as resulting both from the development of working-class movements and political parties, and from the way in which the welfare state helps to meet the needs of capitalism for a trained and healthy workforce. Furthermore, Pierson agrees with social democrats such as T.H. Marshall that expanding citizenship rights are a crucial element of the welfare state and help to create greater integration in society.

However, Pierson argues that social democrats are naively optimistic in seeing the development of welfare as unproblematic progress leading to some sort of socialist utopia. Societies which have the social democratic model have not solved all their problems. Pierson points out that Sweden, which has perhaps the most advanced welfare state in the world, has had serious problems. He says that Sweden's 'status as the exemplar of social democratic state success has been very seriously compromised (with an unemployment rate which by the late 1990s was almost double that of the US' (Pierson, 2006, p. 40).

In the late 1970s the British welfare state was also experiencing considerable problems. Derek Fraser argues that the 'intellectual consensus began to disintegrate' (1984, p. 251). There was no longer universal acceptance that the welfare state should continue to expand along the lines supported by social democrats or even by Beveridge. Britain was suffering an economic crisis, with rising unemployment, very high inflation, considerable industrial unrest leading to strikes, and the government forced to borrow large amounts of money to fund its activities. In these circumstances, spending on the welfare state came under pressure and the New Right (later termed market liberals or neoliberals) questioned every aspect of social democratic policies. This culminated in 1979 in the election of a Conservative government under Margaret Thatcher which had a very different philosophy and policies. (See below for market liberal criticisms of social democrats.)

Social democratic views on the welfare state have also been attacked by those supporting other perspectives.

1. Marxists believe that anything approaching equality cannot be achieved in a capitalist society and they believe that social democratic policies on welfare fail to redistribute wealth and income from the rich to the poor (see pp. 247–8). Marxists therefore believe that social democrats do not go far enough in wanting only to reform capitalism.
2. Some feminists believe that the social democratic emphasis on the rights of workers leads to a neglect of the rights of women, particularly in their roles as mothers and domestic labourers (see pp. 275–6).

New Labour's Third Way approach to welfare accepts some aspects of social democratic thinking while combining it with elements of market liberalism (see pp. 273–4).

Despite all these criticisms there is some evidence that social democratic policies have had some success in achieving their aims. For example, there is evidence that for much of the twentieth century inequalities of wealth and income were reduced (see pp. 35–41). Furthermore, some aspects of universal welfare provision supported by social democrats still enjoy widespread political support. In particular, no major political party in Britain has seriously questioned the principle of a National Health Service which is free at the point of use.

Marxist perspectives on the welfare state

The welfare state, capitalism and the control of workers

Marxist sociologists of the welfare state take a more radical left-wing view than social democrats. They believe that ultimately the welfare state exists to benefit capitalists and capitalism. So long as capitalism exists, welfare states will not fundamentally improve the position of the proletariat. Marxists believe that ultimately a communist or socialist society will have to replace capitalism before the proletariat can genuinely have their interests promoted.

Marxists' views on the welfare state reflect their views on the state generally. As discussed elsewhere (see pp. 535–9), some Marxists see the state as being directly controlled by the bourgeoisie. They point to the statement by Marx and Engels that, 'The executive of the state is but a committee for managing the common affairs of the whole bourgeoisie' (Marx and Engels, 1950a, first published 1848). However, other Marxists, such as Poulantzas (1969, 1976), believe that the welfare state has some independence (or relative autonomy) from direct rule by capitalists. From this viewpoint, the welfare state acts in the long-term interests of the capitalist class as a whole rather than the short-term interests of individual capitalists. For example, the state might put the long-term stability of the capitalist system before short-term profits. A number of Marxists see the welfare state in this light. On the surface, it appears to be benefiting the working class (for example, by providing them with social security or health care), but in the long term it helps to maintain capitalism. An example of this viewpoint is provided by Norman Ginsburg (1979).

Ginsburg believes that the welfare state has the following functions.

1. It contains the 'inevitable resistance and revolutionary potential of the working class' (1979, p. 2). It does this by appearing to provide genuine help for the working class, making society more fair and redistributing income from the rich to the poor. In reality this is a myth since the welfare state is largely paid for out of the taxes of the working class (see pp. 41–2).
2. The welfare state helps to maintain a reserve army of labour. It provides basic support for the unemployed who may be needed by capitalists in times of economic boom. Both the unemployed reserve army, and members of the working class in jobs, are willing to work for low wages because of fear of unemployment. This helps to maintain the profitability of capitalist companies.
3. The social security system helps to maintain the patriarchal family by promoting the idea of the male breadwinner and the female housewife-mother. The

responsibility of the male breadwinner for his family helps to discipline male workers. It discourages them from striking or leaving their jobs.

4 The welfare state is there to manage and regulate capitalism, to smooth out the problems created by slumps and booms, and not to benefit workers. Any benefits to workers are an unintended by-product of this central purpose. Ginsburg says, 'Only secondarily and contingently does it act as a means of mitigating poverty or providing income maintenance' (1979, p. 2).

Other strands in Marxist thinking suggest that a very important function of the welfare state is to control the working class. Christopher Pierson (not himself a Marxist) outlines a number of points made by Marxists along these lines.

1 Welfare reforms have often been introduced by ruling elites to discipline or control the workforce rather than to redistribute wealth or create a fairer society.
2 The welfare state has enabled monitoring of and control over the lives of the proletariat through the activities of groups such as social workers, health visitors and teachers.
3 The working class themselves have little control over welfare provision. The welfare roles of working-class institutions such as friendly societies and trade unions have largely been taken over by the state. This has reduced the ability of the working class to organize in opposition to capitalism, or even to provide services genuinely focused on their needs. State welfare typically gives the working class little or no power; it is usually bureaucratic and anti-democratic.
4 The minimum welfare provision that exists 'has demobilized working-class agitation for more radical economic and political change' (Pierson, 2006, p. 53). In effect, the working class have been bought-off relatively cheaply.

Arguments for Marxist views

Pierson argues that there is some evidence to support these views.

First, early welfare, such as the Poor Law, was clearly intended as a measure to control the working class by making poor relief so unattractive it encouraged people to work at any price (see pp. 261–2).

Second, the receipt of state benefits has become increasingly dependent on 'a record of regular employment, "willingness to work clauses", a qualifying period and cut-off points for payment of benefits' (Pierson, 2006, p. 53). All of these measures are intended to ensure that those on benefits are not supported unless they make the maximum possible contribution to the capitalist economy.

Third, the working class were often opposed to aspects of the welfare state because they would undermine working-class self-help.

Fourth, Pierson claims that there is a lot of historical evidence that many of the reformers who introduced new welfare services explicitly introduced them to create a more healthy, well-trained or docile workforce.

Arguments against Marxist views

Pierson argues that despite some evidence to support Marxist views there is also much evidence to contradict these views. Some governments, particularly those influenced by social democratic thinking, have gone much further than capitalists wanted in providing benefits and services for the working class. The cost of financing these has ultimately come out of the profits generated by capitalism.

Many changes in welfare have led to significant improvements for the working class. For example, even early national insurance and pensions schemes were a great improvement on the previous Poor Laws. Pierson also believes that even the modest levels of benefit available for the unemployed, the sick or the disabled have discouraged some claimants from taking paid employment.

Pierson agrees that much of the welfare state is paid for out of the taxes of workers, but believes that overall the welfare state is 'mildly redistributive' since the better-off do pay higher rates of tax (see pp. 35–8).

From Pierson's point of view, Marxist perspectives exaggerate the degree to which the welfare state benefits capitalism, but it does benefit capitalism to some degree. At the same time, though, it also improves the position of workers. Pierson says, 'The capitalist class could not have a healthier, better educated, reliable (and thus more profitable) source of surplus value without improving the health, education and housing of the working class' (Pierson, 2006, p. 56).

(For a discussion of changes in the welfare state from a neo-Marxist point of view, see the section on the work of Bob Jessop in Chapter 9, pp. 540–2. For details of Marxist views on poverty and welfare see pp. 247–9.)

Whatever the merits or otherwise of Marxist views of the welfare state, they are completely contradicted by the views of market liberals who criticize the welfare state for harming the interests of capitalists rather than benefiting them. Their views will now be examined.

Market liberal perspectives on the welfare state

The main features of market liberal perspectives

This perspective has been described by Christopher Pierson as 'perhaps the most prominent (and successful) opponent of the post-war orthodoxy' (2006, p. 41). Pierson argues that there are two strands to this perspective:

1 First, the market liberal strand which 'argues the case for a freer, more open and competitive economy' (2006, p. 42). This perspective argues that the state should do as little as possible, while capitalist enterprise and the free market should do as much as possible.
2 The second strand comes from conservative thinking which is more concerned with 'restoring social and political authority throughout society' (2006, p. 42). This strand of thinking is particularly critical of the welfare state for encouraging dependency on welfare and undermining (as they see it) traditional institutions such as the family. It is reflected, for example, in the views of Charles Murray (see pp. 64–5).

Supporters of these views in the Conservative governments of 1979 to 1997 (particularly under Margaret Thatcher) were referred to as the New Right, although the terms market liberal and neoliberal are often used interchangeably. Pete Alcock (2003) has described the main features of this approach.

According to Alcock, much of this perspective is based upon the writings of Hayek. Hayek argued that the free market was the best way to allocate resources. Through the decisions of individuals to buy or not to buy products and services, the providers were given information about what people wanted. Through pricing, the providers of goods and services could discover how much people were prepared to pay for goods and services. In contrast, if the state provided goods and services, there was no system of pricing to show whether the products were of a good enough quality for people to buy, and no direct way of knowing whether demand was being met.

Market mechanisms encourage competition and innovation which allow consumers' needs to be met and new goods and services to be constantly introduced. Through competition and increased efficiency the price of products and services tends to be forced down, providing better value for consumers. Furthermore, according to Hayek, a capitalist free market tends to be associated with individual freedom. Welfare states lead to the government accumulating power which can lead to restrictions on individual liberty. As Alcock says, Hayek

> *argued that state intervention involved an unwarranted interference with the freedom of individuals to organise their own affairs and, therefore, that intervention was only justified if its aim was to protect individual freedom (for example the use of the criminal law to protect private property).* Alcock, 2003, p. 198

Alcock argues that neoliberals (the term Alcock uses for market liberals) have three main grounds for objecting to the welfare state and wanting to keep state expenditure on welfare to a minimum.

1 On economic grounds, the welfare state leads to an excessive tax burden on private industry. The profits of private industry go to pay for welfare which prevents reinvestment in private enterprise. This undermines incentives for enterprises to take risks, because much of the profit will go to the government in taxation. Lacking competition, services provided by the state tend to become more and more expensive. Because of the drain on private enterprise, government expenditure can lead to recession, which causes high unemployment and increases the financial demands on the welfare state.

2 Market liberals object to the welfare state because they believe it creates **perverse incentives** and can create a dependency culture. For example, people are given perverse incentives to have children in order to claim benefits (see Murray's views on the underclass, pp. 64–5). Charles Murray (1989, 1994) also believes that welfare claimants become dependent on welfare and they lose the ability to support themselves. The welfare state may also create a poverty trap where the poor are better off claiming benefits than they are taking low-paid work, further reducing their chances of becoming self-supporting.

3 Market liberals also object to what they believe are the political consequences of the welfare state. Neoliberals have devised a theory of political behaviour called **public choice theory**, which assumes that politicians will act in their own self-interest. Since their interests are best served by being re-elected, they tend to make excessive promises about how much they can do for voters, and these promises tend to involve the expansion of the welfare state. Alcock describes this view in the following way: 'no one in the political process has any interest in controlling the expansionary tendencies of state welfare, with the result that it acquires the momentum of a runaway train (with, it is argued, ultimately much the same disastrous consequences for those on board)' (2003, p. 200).

In addition to the above criticisms of the welfare state, neoliberals argue that employees also act in their own self-interest. They too have a shared interest in the continued expansion of the welfare state because it pays their salaries. Welfare state employees tend to view more and more problems as requiring state intervention, and without any competition there is no way of controlling expenditure or ensuring that work is done efficiently. Thus Vic George and Paul Wilding (1994) say:

> *New Right thinkers are also fiercely critical of the basic instruments of welfare state policies, that is bureaucracies and professionals. For the New Right they are not disinterested eunuchs of policy implementation, but are strongly interested and extremely powerful parties. They have a very clear interest in expansion, and some see them indeed, as the main beneficiaries of welfare state programmes.* George and Wilding, 1994, p. 28

Market liberals tend to argue for a **minimalist welfare state** – one that does the bare minimum necessary to prevent extreme poverty and major social problems. They accept the need for a very basic means-tested benefit to act as a safety net, but they are reluctant to support expensive, universal, state-provided services. However, some market liberals go even further than this and see almost the whole of the welfare state as unnecessary or damaging.

James Bartholomew – The Welfare State We're In

James Bartholomew (2006) is a radical market liberal critic of the British welfare state. He argues that Britain would actually have been better off if the welfare state had never been developed. A journalist and former banker, Bartholomew argues that the welfare state has not just failed to achieve its objectives, but has actually been counter-productive, making many of the problems it was supposed to solve worse.

In a detailed critique Bartholomew examines and finds fault with all aspects of the welfare state.

Benefits and pensions

According to Bartholomew, the state first got involved with providing a basic income to the poor after Henry VIII dissolved the monasteries in the 1530s. He did so to fund extravagant state expenditure but in the process he removed an effective voluntary system of assistance to the poor. Ever since then, from the Elizabethan Poor Law to income support today, the state has experimented with more or less generous benefits, but none of the schemes have worked.

Bartholomew believes that unemployment is linked to benefit levels. The higher the benefits paid by the state, the less incentive people have to work, and the higher the unemployment rate. The rise in unemployment from the 1960s to the early 1980s was produced by gradually rising benefit levels, and after they were cut in the 1980s, unemployment fell.

By 2002 recorded unemployment had fallen below 1990s levels, but Bartholomew suggests that the benefit system had just created hidden unemployment. By 2002 over 2.4 million people were claiming incapacity benefit, which is more generous than income support and lasts indefinitely. Bartholomew argues that many of the claimants are simply feigning back-ache or psychological problems in order to claim incapacity benefit.

Bartholomew believes that the welfare system creates incentives for fraud and he estimates that fraudulent claims cost the government £15 billion per year. Worse than that, it creates a state of mind in which lying is considered acceptable because 'everybody does it'. He sees means-testing as responsible for many problems and says, 'Those on means-tested benefits ... get the message "Don't tell the truth" because they can get benefits if they lie about their assets or their income' (Bartholomew, 2006, p. 79). This in turn tends to create a more dishonest society and contributes to rising crime.

Bartholomew particularly criticizes Labour Chancellor Gordon Brown's policy of extending means-testing. The introduction of tax credits (see pp. 273–4) has meant that more and more people can gain means-tested income from the government. This has created a massive and expensive bureaucracy to administer the benefits. It has also created disincentives to save for old age because pensioners on low incomes receive pension credits. Bartholomew concludes that:

> *It would have been better if modern social security ... had never been started. Britain today would have been a better place with better people. There would be fewer who were seriously poor in monetary terms and in their spirit.*
> Bartholomew, 2006, p. 85

He also thinks that without welfare benefits family life would be more stable. Like Charles Murray he argues that state provision for lone parents has made divorce and single parenthood an option.

Another consequence of state benefits is inadequate provision for retirement. People who retire and have to live on a basic state pension get their income topped up by the state. This means that those on low pay have little or no incentive to save for their retirement. Even those with modest savings lose their entitlement to extra benefits. According to Bartholomew, the situation was better for the elderly when they made their own provision through non-profit-making Friendly Societies. Furthermore, state pensions discourage people from working after the age of 65 and 'this reduces the contact that older people have with the rest of society. It makes them poorer – socially as well as financially – than they would otherwise be' (Bartholomew, 2006, p. 302).

Health

Bartholomew believes that, compared to health services in other advanced countries, the NHS is woefully inadequate. Despite more and more resources being poured into the NHS there is a shortage of doctors in general and consultants in particular, the number of hospital beds has been cut, there is a shortage of equipment, and waiting lists are very long. Calculations suggest that over 15,000 people a year die unnecessarily because the NHS is so much worse than the health systems of other advanced countries. This is equivalent to the death toll from a major train crash every day.

There are a number of reasons for this. Hygiene is poor, with the result that the 'super bug' MRSA is widespread. Survival rates for major diseases are lower than in comparable countries. Bartholomew believes that the NHS fails to make good use of its resources because a state-run bureaucracy lacks the financial incentives to perform well. To keep within budget, there are incentives in the NHS to do less, carry out fewer operations, see fewer patients, keep fewer people in hospital beds and so on. In contrast, when a new system was introduced in Stockholm under which hospitals were paid on the basis of how many operations they performed, productivity shot up 19 per cent.

In Britain there is an enormous bureaucracy administering the system which drains resources from patient care. Left unchecked, bureaucracies tend to grow over the years, as those employed in administration and management try to protect their jobs, increase their wages and expand the empires that they manage. Bartholomew therefore sees the NHS as 'remarkably inefficient and riddled with waste', and he concludes that 'the structure which predated the NHS was better' (2006, p. 150). As a result, people are increasingly deserting the state system.

Education

Bartholomew is no less critical of state education. He believes that the overall educational standards of the British population have fallen over recent decades, and compare unfavourably with the educational standards of other countries. For example, he quotes research by Robert Coe of Durham University which used the International Test of Developed Abilities (ITDA test) to look at the knowledge and ability of British children in different subjects. This research found that from 1988 to 1998 results in these tests fell for sixth-form biology from 63.7 to 53.4, and they also fell in all other subjects tested. Over the same period, the number of students achieving the highest grades at A level increased considerably, suggesting that A levels were getting easier and the rise in pass rates and grades hid a deterioration in standards.

Bartholomew quotes figures which suggest that private schools achieve considerably better results than state schools even when factors such as social class and income are taken into account. Furthermore, state education has not achieved other objectives such as reducing inequality and improving economic performance. It has not significantly reduced the education gap between higher and lower social classes, with the children of professionals still being more than ten times as likely as the children of the unskilled to study for degrees. According to Bartholomew, there is no correlation between education spending and economic success. Japan, for example, spends considerably less than Britain but is significantly more prosperous.

As in the case of the NHS, Bartholomew sees one of the reasons for this as being the waste of resources. A lot of the money spent on the education system is not spent directly on teaching but on administration and bodies such as OFSTED (which carries out inspections) and QCA (which oversees examinations and the National Curriculum).

Another problem is that union power has prevented pay being linked to teacher performance, which has meant that schools cannot reward their best staff to motivate and retain them. Bartholomew concludes by saying that, 'To ask the state not to waste money or be less bureaucratic is like asking a zebra to give up its stripes' (2006, p. 219).

Housing

Bartholomew also discusses the role of the welfare state in the provision of housing. Drawing on the work of Young and Willmott (see pp. 476–8), he argues that, although well-intentioned, the development of council housing had disastrous consequences.

As Wilmot and Young observed, the building of new council estates in east London disrupted traditional working-class communities and undermined the support networks which were a crucial part of family life. According to Bartholomew, many of the so-called slums that were cleared in the 1960s and 1970s were sound houses which simply needed refurbishment. Some were replaced by tower blocks which were badly designed, often poorly built and did not meet the needs of most of their residents. They became breeding grounds for crime and very unpopular with those who lived in them.

Bartholomew believes that council housing was unsuccessful because there were no market forces to ensure that people got the sort of housing that they needed. If privately built houses are unpopular, developers cannot sell them at a profit. Council tenants do not have the same choices as private buyers or people who rent in the private sector, so central planners do not have to make sure that tenants or purchasers will be content with the accommodation. In addition, council tenants have no stake in the housing and therefore they are not likely to take care of it. Bartholomew therefore applauds the scheme introduced by Margaret Thatcher's Conservative government in the 1980s whereby council tenants were given the right to buy the houses in which they lived. He also welcomes the increased availability of privately rented housing which gives consumers much more choice than those who are allocated housing from a council waiting list.

Taxation

Finally Bartholomew examines the way welfare provision is financed – that is, through taxation. He believes that higher taxes stifle entrepreneurship and consequently reduce economic growth. They discourage investment by companies and mean that incentives for the unemployed to take work are reduced.

Bartholomew supports these claims by comparing the UK with Hong Kong. Until it was handed back to China, Hong Kong was administered as a British colony, but one which followed very different policies. The Financial Secretary in Hong Kong from 1961 was John Cowperthwaite, and he kept taxes very low (no more than 15 per cent) and limited state spending on welfare. In contrast, the UK had much higher taxes and the government spent a much greater proportion of the total wealth of the country (gross national product or GNP). By 1970 over 40 per cent of GNP was spent by the government in the UK, and it has stayed at nearly 40 per cent or more ever since. Bartholomew notes that since the 1960s Hong Kong has had more rapid economic growth than the UK and he attributes this to the low taxes and low government spending.

Bartholomew even argues directly against the social democratic view that a developed welfare state and high taxation can lead to greater equality and can help the poor. In his view, high taxation does not just harm the rich, it also hits the poor. Bartholomew calculates that even those in relative poverty (which he defines as 60 per cent of average earnings) have to pay tax. In his view, economic growth helps the poor much more than high taxation, as high levels of employment provide opportunities for the less well off to earn more. Economic growth from 1911 to 1960 led to a reduction in the gap in earnings between rich and poor. Bartholomew says, 'there are counter-arguments and conflicting data, but there is some reason to think that capitalism over time does spread wealth to the less well off disproportionately' (2006, p. 323).

Conclusion

Bartholomew concludes that Britain would have been better off without the welfare state. Services such as housing, health and education are provided much more effectively by the private sector than the state. Without the welfare state, families would have been much stronger and the informal sector would therefore have been better able to provide for people's needs.

Bartholomew believes that voluntary welfare and organizations such as Friendly Societies can be just as effective as the state in meeting the needs of the most vulnerable, and, without the welfare state, people are much more responsible in making provision for themselves and other family members. Without the need to fund an expensive welfare system, taxes are much lower, economic growth is greater, and as society becomes more prosperous the living standards of the poor improve and inequality may actually be reduced. Although he stops short of saying that all state welfare should immediately be stopped, Bartholomew applauds countries such as New Zealand, Switzerland and the USA where welfare is less well developed than in the UK and where cut-backs have been made.

Evaluation of Bartholomew

Bartholomew's work offers a radical challenge to the views of Beveridge, social democrats and others who support the welfare state. He undoubtedly identifies some ways in which the welfare state has been inefficient or has failed to provide a good service. However, although his views are backed up by plenty of evidence, there are many details of his work which can be criticized. The following are a few examples.

1 There has been extensive criticism of the view that social security leads to a culture of dependency and encourages lone parenthood (see pp. 244–7).
2 Government statistics clearly show that taxation and welfare spending do boost the final incomes of the poorest members of society (see pp. 18–19).
3 Evidence suggests that inequality in Britain, in terms of both income and wealth, did fall for most of the twentieth century, but began to rise again after 1979, and the growth of income inequality levelled off after 1997 (see pp. 17–23). Inequality therefore tended to fall in the periods when the welfare state was being developed and started rising again under the market liberal government of Margaret Thatcher, which cut back on state welfare spending (see pp. 35–8). When welfare spending increased again under New Labour, the growth of inequality was curtailed. The evidence could therefore be seen to directly contradict Bartholomew's assertion that rising state spending increases inequality.
4 The idea that lower taxation and lower government spending lead to higher economic growth is simplistic and it is often contradicted by evidence. A whole variety of factors affect growth and economic development. Some economists follow Keynes in arguing that government spending tends to stimulate economic growth. For example, from a study of eighteen countries between 1960 and 1985, Francis G.. Castles and Steve Dowrick (1990) found that increasing government expenditure did not reduce economic growth and could in some circumstances increase it.
5 It is also highly questionable whether higher government expenditure leads to higher unemployment. For example, figures quoted by Michael Hill (2003, pp. 246–7) show that in 2001 Spain had the second lowest rate of spending (as a proportion of GDP) on social security in the European Union, but the highest rate of unemployment. The UK had lower than average spending on social security, but above average levels of unemployment. There was no correlation between rate of spending and rate of unemployment.
6 Like other market liberal thinkers, Bartholomew does not adequately explain how non-state welfare could provide comprehensive, affordable and accessible welfare. Informal and voluntary welfare depend upon individual generosity in terms of both time and money, and there is no guarantee that these sectors will treat individuals equitably. For example, popular causes, such as the welfare of children, are likely to attract more voluntary support than unpopular causes such as the treatment of drug addicts.

Pete Alcock argues that the voluntary sector 'is varied, flexible, innovative, non-bureaucratic, accessible and, perhaps most significantly, cheap; but it is also unpredictable, unstable, incomplete and sometimes oppressive and exclusionary' (2003, p. 176). Informal care is also unpredictable and incomplete and, as feminists argue (see pp. 275–6), tends to rely disproportionately on women. Alcock argues that private provision has advantages, but in a capitalist economy private enterprise has to make money and it will not provide services which are not profitable. Nor will it provide services for those who cannot afford them. Thus 'poor people faced with charges are therefore unable to pay for services that they desperately need' (Alcock, 2003, p. 157).

Further criticisms of market liberal theory are provided elsewhere in the book (see pp. 239–40).

Market liberal theory and social policy

For the reasons examined above no government in Britain or in other advanced capitalist countries has abolished state welfare. However, some countries, such as the USA, have spent less on welfare than other capitalist countries, and some, such as New Zealand, have substantially reduced spending on state welfare.

In Britain, the period of Conservative government from 1979 to 1997 was strongly influenced by market liberal thinking, particularly during Margaret Thatcher's time as prime minister (1979–90). During this time there were cuts in and changes to welfare benefits, taxes were lowered, attempts were made to cut government spending, and state services such as education and health care were reformed.

Part of this reform involved the introduction of market forces into state services. For example, schools were encouraged to compete against one another for pupils, and were provided with funding partly on the basis of how many pupils they attracted (see pp. 622–4). Schools, GP practices and hospitals were given greater financial independence and more control over resources, in the hope they would be run in a more business-like and efficient manner.

Areas where market forces of supply and demand have been introduced into the state sector have been termed **quasi-markets**. These have come in for heavy criticism. Pete Alcock (2003) points out that they can be very expensive to administer. Other critics point out that the consumer choice they are supposed to provide is often illusory. For example, many parents do not get to send their children to their preferred school because the most successful schools tend to be over-subscribed. Wealthier parents may be better able to manipulate such markets than poorer parents, for example by buying expensive houses in the catchment area for a successful school (see pp. 618–20). This can lead to the perpetuation of class inequalities.

In some ways the Conservative governments failed to achieve their own aims. As Christopher Pierson (2006) points out, health expenditure rose over the period from 6 per cent to 7.6 per cent of GDP, while education expenditure stayed about the same at around 5 per cent. Welfare professionals were increasingly monitored (for example, teachers were monitored by OFSTED). Although this contributed to achieving one market liberal aim of encouraging a better service for welfare users, it also increased costs and bureaucracy. Thus, the Conservatives were not as radical in their reforms of the welfare state as some market liberals would have liked. At the same time they were criticized by those on the left for introducing quasi-markets, cutting some services and increasing inequality.

Although the Conservative government was replaced by a Labour government in 1997, the new government did not abandon all the previous policies. The Conservatives had not fully implemented market liberal policies, and likewise the incoming Labour government did not advocate only social democratic policies. Instead, it sought to be a 'New Labour' Party which was to follow a 'Third Way' which, they claimed, was neither left-wing nor right-wing.

New Labour and the Third Way

Anthony Giddens and the Third Way

The 'Third Way' is a term which has been used in a number of countries to describe a political philosophy which aims to move, as in the title of a book by Anthony Giddens, *'Beyond Left and Right'* (Giddens, 1994). In Britain it has been used to describe the approach of Tony Blair's New Labour government from 1997 to 2007 – an approach which was advocated by the leading British sociologist, Anthony Giddens. Giddens was an adviser to Tony Blair during his early years in office.

According to Giddens (2000), the Third Way as supported by Tony Blair involved a rejection of aspects of the social democratic view of the welfare state. Giddens argues that Tony Blair was critical of the social democratic approach because it put too much emphasis on **equality of outcome** – that is, members of society ending up more equal. Pursuing equality of outcome emphasizes people's **rights**, but it pays little attention to their **responsibility** or **effort**. It leaves little room for rewarding people who make extra effort or who live up to their responsibilities (such as saving for retirement, caring for their children, paying their taxes, or obeying the law).

The Third Way approach places more emphasis on **equality of opportunity** rather than equality of outcome. From this point of view, it is acceptable for people to end up unequal so long as they all have the opportunity to be successful. Rewards should be based upon merit rather than seen as a universal entitlement. Third Way thinking suggests that it is perfectly compatible with social justice if some people become much more successful and richer than others, so long as their rewards reflect ability rather than simply the effects of a privileged background.

To Giddens, another problem with the social democratic view on welfare is that it encouraged 'ever higher levels of public spending almost regardless of what was actually achieved, or the impact on competitiveness or job creation' (2000, p. 6). Like market liberals, supporters of the Third Way think that state spending should be constrained and that it is undesirable to have ever rising taxes. However, unlike market liberals, Third Way supporters do see state intervention in the economy and society as being very important, though they accept that the welfare state has failed to meet its objectives and is in need of major reform.

Giddens believes that the social democratic approach is based upon **passive welfare** provision, while an improved, Third Way approach needs to be based upon **active welfare**. Rather than people becoming passively dependent upon financial support from the state, they need to be enabled to actively help themselves out of welfare dependency.

The Third Way places much more emphasis on social exclusion than on poverty (see pp. 257–9), because tackling social exclusion avoids dependency by opening up opportunities. For example, if social exclusion in education is tackled by cutting truancy and school exclusions, fewer children will grow up poorly educated and unable to hold down jobs. If single parents are helped to find work and given access to high-quality, affordable childcare, then there will be less welfare dependency and more opportunity.

Giddens argues that the welfare state must take account of changes in the world such as increased rates of lone parenthood, an ageing population, and globalization. If Britain and other countries are to remain competitive, then the state must provide the opportunities and the help so that people can actively support and take responsibility for themselves and their families. The Labour Party in Britain has described this policy as offering a 'hand up' not a 'hand-out'. For example, unemployed claimants of benefits are seen as having a responsibility to actively look for work, and to undergo retraining if necessary. They are not seen as having an unlimited right to state support if they fail to live up to their responsibilities.

This approach sees the state as very important, but it does not see it as the solution to all problems. It believes the state can work with voluntary organizations and the informal and the private sectors to increase opportunities and tackle exclusion.

Giddens believes that the Third Way offers a genuine alternative to both market liberal (which he calls neoliberal) approaches, and social democracy. He argues that neoliberalism 'is a deeply flawed approach to politics because it supposes that no responsibility needs to be taken for the social consequences of market-based decisions' (Giddens, 2000, p. 33). A welfare state is necessary to ensure that those from disadvantaged backgrounds have opportunities to succeed, to reduce social exclusion and to provide 'social goods' (such as education and health) 'that a decent society must involve'.

However, Giddens believes that the social democratic approach is equally unacceptable. It fails to recognize that 'All welfare states create problems of dependency, moral hazard, bureaucracy, interest-group formation and fraud' (2000, p. 33). Furthermore, welfare states do not eradicate inequality and they can undermine individual initiative and economic competitiveness. From this point of view, the only solution is to have an active welfare state which counteracts the injustices created by a free-market economy, while rewarding effort, encouraging responsibility and providing opportunity in such a way that it avoids the pitfalls that come from the social democratic model of welfare.

New Labour and the welfare state

New Labour's implementation of Third Way thinking has been reviewed by Robert M. Page (2005). Page notes that Blair and his government claimed that the welfare state needed modernizing for four reasons.

- First, it needed to create an active welfare state which developed the skills and **social capital** (see pp. 863–7) of individuals. This would limit welfare expenditure, and increase Britain's competitiveness by maximizing the contribution of individuals to the economy. Everybody who could find work, or who could be retrained, would be encouraged to do so.

This view resulted in 'Welfare to Work' programmes which required claimants to actively seek employment, and to undergo training or do voluntary work if they were to receive benefits long-term. Particular schemes were aimed at encouraging and facilitating lone parents, the young, those over 50 and the disabled to find work. To make work worthwhile the minimum wage was introduced, and tax credits were also introduced to make sure that it paid to come off benefits (see below). Higher education was also expanded to improve the skills of the workforce, though tuition fees were introduced to help pay for this (see pp. 621–2).

2 A modernized welfare state would 'focus on the needs of service users rather than the interests of providers' (Page, 2005, p. 6). Through monitoring, welfare professionals would be forced to focus on government targets. Thus league tables for schools and hospitals and organizations such as OFSTED (which carries out school inspections) and NICE (the National Institute for Clinical Excellence) would ensure that welfare state institutions were doing a good job and were providing value for money. Quasi-markets in education and health (in which money followed the choices made by service users) would make welfare providers responsive to parents, patients and other welfare users. Like its Conservative predecessor, the Labour government advocated increased choice for service users.

3 To enable greater choice, the Labour Party tried to develop a wider range of service providers. For example, in schooling, they introduced city academies and specialist schools, and encouraged faith schools. In doing so they encouraged cooperation between the public sector and other welfare providers. For example, private companies helped to fund city academies, and religious groups (from the voluntary sector) helped to run faith schools. New Labour tried to break down barriers between public and private provision, encouraging cooperation between the two. For example, the Private Finance Initiative used private capital to build public facilities (such as hospitals). State organizations were also encouraged to become more independent so that they would become less bureaucratic and more entrepreneurial, like the private sector. Schools were given more autonomy, and most NHS services were reorganized into Primary Care Trusts (PCTs) which were responsible for most health services in their area apart from hospitals. From 2003 all hospitals and PCTs could apply for Foundation Status which allowed them considerable autonomy over their own finances (they could, for example, borrow money privately), their priorities and even pay scales for staff.

4 New Labour put more emphasis on means-testing than social democrats (who tend to favour universalism), and less emphasis on means-testing than market liberals (who tend to favour it). It sought to combine the two approaches in what was called a **progressive universalist** strategy. This strategy involves providing assistance to a wider range of people than those targeted by means-tested benefits, but not to everybody as is the case with universal benefits and services. The main policy used to implement this approach was tax credits.

New Labour introduced tax credits for those with children (the child tax credit) and for pensioners (the pension tax credit). The child tax credit was paid to most families with children, but was based on a sliding scale so that higher earners received less and those on very high incomes received nothing. According to Page, the aim was partly to reduce the stigma of means-tested state benefits and increase the take-up. There was less stigma attached because it was not just the poor who were entitled to this state support and because the payments were received through pay packets or pensions rather than as a direct state benefit. It was hoped that this would increase social solidarity and support for welfare, as most people were getting help, but avoid wasting money by giving help to the wealthy.

Evaluation of New Labour policies

Although most of New Labour's policies are not in line with social democratic thinking, there have been some policies which are. These include aims to reduce child poverty (see p. 225), some positive discrimination (such as the introduction of Sure Start to help children in disadvantaged areas (see p. 621)), and the introduction of a minimum wage (see p. 258). Nevertheless, some of the strongest criticisms have come from a social democratic perspective. These have been summarized by Page (2005).

1 New Labour has been criticized for failing to tackle income inequalities. Page, writing in 2005, noted that according to the Gini coefficient (see p. 38), income inequality rose under New Labour, largely as a result of the increase in the incomes of the very rich. However, Hills and Stewart (2005) noted that there was a small reduction in relative poverty and some improvement in the position of low-income groups. Page concludes that:

> *Although New Labour's policies have helped to slow the increase in income inequality, a reduction in overall inequality is unlikely unless they are prepared to cap the rise in earnings of the highest paid and increase benefit levels for all groups of claimants.* Page, 2005, p. 14

2 New Labour have also been criticized by left-wing commentators for using the Private Finance Initiative, by which private sector money is used to finance government capital costs such as those for building schools and hospitals. The costs of repaying the borrowed money can be costly in the long term. For example, Page quotes one study which showed that the government would have to pay back a total of £400 million for a hospital in Cumberland which initially cost just £87 million.

3 Left-wing critics also argue that the introduction of markets into public services can lead to increased inequality. For example, if some Foundation Trusts in the NHS are more successful than non-Foundation Trusts, they may provide a better service, leading to inequality of provision in different areas. Similarly, parents in affluent catchment areas with more

popular and successful schools will tend to get a better education for their children than those in deprived catchment areas with under-subscribed schools (see pp. 634–5). Page suggests that such policies can end up being 'socially divisive'.

4 Another policy which can be socially divisive is the encouragement of faith schools. Page says that, 'While such a move might meet the interests of parents, religious segregation of this kind is unlikely to foster greater social integration and inclusiveness' (2005, p. 15).

5 The expansion of higher education has generally been supported by social democrats, but they have been critical of the use of tuition fees to fund it. Although there are schemes to help students from poorer backgrounds, students are still likely to incur substantial debts while studying for a degree. There is some evidence that this discourages participation by students from less affluent backgrounds. Most social democrats supported higher income tax on high earners or an additional income tax on graduates as more egalitarian ways of funding higher education expansion.

6 Some feminists have criticized the New Labour emphasis on getting as many people as possible, including lone parents, into paid employment. Page says that 'this emphasis has inevitably resulted in the devaluing of unpaid activities such as caring and voluntary work' (2005, p. 15).

7 Social democrats and other left-wingers have attacked the movement in policy away from the rights of **citizens** towards treating users of the welfare state as **consumers**. From this point of view, using collective services can encourage a sense of social solidarity, while a consumerist approach encourages individualism. The choices of individuals can also undermine the interests of the wider community. For example, while some parents will be able to get their children into popular schools, others will be left with their children being educated in unpopular and therefore under-funded schools. Without spare places in hospitals, schools and other welfare services, only some people will get the choices that they want and these will tend to be the better-informed middle and higher classes.

Page summarizes these criticisms as follows:

> *These criticisms highlight crucial differences between 'old' and 'new' Labour. Traditionalists remain sceptical about New Labour's assertion that a more modest egalitarian strategy and welfare reform are pre-requisites for electoral success in the modern era. Traditionalists still hold to the belief that a key role for any Labour government is to offer a transformative egalitarian vision for the future. Accordingly they reject the accommodation that New Labour has made with business interests, their loss of confidence in public services and the too ready willingness to promote individualism and consumerism rather than the collective good and citizenship.* Page, 2005, p. 17

From a very different viewpoint, New Labour policies have been criticized by market liberals such as James Bartholomew (2006). Bartholomew criticizes the Labour government under Tony Blair for continuing to increase state spending on welfare, for failing to reduce taxes, for failing to make significant moves away from state welfare provision towards private welfare provision, and for expanding the costly and inefficient bureaucracies which run the welfare state.

Bartholomew is particularly critical of the policies of Gordon Brown when Chancellor of the Exchequer under Tony Blair. Bartholomew believes that means-tested benefits are damaging to incentives for hard work and entrepreneurship, yet Gordon Brown extended the scope of means-testing through tax credits. Writing in 2006, Bartholomew said:

> *It is now estimated that 28 per cent of households are on one means-tested benefit or another. Nine out of ten families are able to claim the child tax credit – which involves filling in a fifty-six question form accompanied by forty-seven pages of advisory notes.* Bartholomew, 2006, p. 80

(For a full account of Bartholomew's view on the welfare state see pp. 269–71.)

Conclusion

Given New Labour's attempts to follow a 'middle way', it is not surprising that it has come under attack from left and right. Nevertheless, most critics have found some merit in New Labour policies. For example, James Bartholomew (2006) does recognize that changes to taxes and benefits have ensured that people are at least slightly better off if they move from benefits into work. Social democratic commentators tend to believe that New Labour policies are better than market liberal policies. For example, John Hills and Kitty Stewart (2005) believe that New Labour policies have been significantly different from those of the preceding Conservative governments. They argue that these policies have 'turned the tide' and prevented inequality from growing any greater. Furthermore, under New Labour, Britain has become a more equal society in some respects, but there is 'still a very long way to go' before the policies could be considered an unambiguous success.

Whether New Labour policies have succeeded in providing better-quality welfare services or good value for money remains open to debate, but the comparatively modest 'Third Way' reforms clearly fail to satisfy more radical right-wing or left-wing views on welfare. (For a radical left-wing view on welfare, see the discussion of Marxist perspectives (pp. 267–8).)

Feminist perspectives on welfare

All the perspectives on the welfare state examined so far have been subject to criticism from feminists. Drawing on a range of feminist writing, Christopher Pierson (2006) has summarized the arguments put forward by feminists. He argues that there is considerable variation between feminist theorists of social policy and welfare, but they all agree on three key issues.

1 They agree that gender issues are neglected by other perspectives and need to be studied.

2 They agree that other perspectives concentrate too much on production and the formal economy of

work, taxation, etc., and pay too little attention to reproduction and the informal economy of unpaid caring and domestic labour.

3 Feminists argue that the welfare state is primarily used or consumed by women and largely produced by women, as most welfare employees are female.

According to Pierson, feminists have 'characteristically represented the welfare state as organized in the interests of men, and of capital, at the expense of women' (2006, p. 67). However, he notes that some feminists have begun to recognize that there have been some reforms which have benefited women in recent years.

Feminist criticisms of the welfare state

Pierson identifies the following criticisms put forward by feminists.

1 In the 1970s and 1980s Marxist feminists criticized the welfare state for being based upon the assumption that women would do unpaid work to reproduce the labour force for the benefit of capitalism. The tax and benefits systems assumed that men would be the main breadwinners, giving married women less entitlement to unemployment and other benefits because it was assumed that they were supported by their husband's wage. From this viewpoint, women were a **reserve army of labour** who were easy to recruit as an extra workforce in times of boom and dismiss in times of recession (see p. 127).
2 Later feminists began to see this analysis as an oversimplification. As women's employment grew, some argued that the welfare state was increasingly exploiting women as underpaid workers within the welfare state (for example, as cleaners, secretaries, nurses, low-grade administrators and so on). While women were given careers in the welfare state, most senior positions were held by men, reinforcing patriarchal dominance.
3 Other feminists criticized the welfare state for failing to provide adequate services for women. For example, it did not provide high-quality, affordable universal childcare for women who wished to pursue a career.

Some more recent feminists have argued that the welfare state does not universally oppress women as earlier feminists had assumed. Pierson points out that some of these writers have identified countries (for example, Sweden) where women are well provided for by welfare state services such as childcare and there are good career opportunities for women in welfare state jobs. More recent feminist writing has therefore tended to criticize the welfare state in more subtle ways.

Pierson argues that 'The newer literature has … developed a more nuanced reading of the salience of key welfare terms such as "dependence" and above all "care" (2006, p. 69). For example, Daly and Lewis (2000) (discussed in Pierson, 2006) see care as involving the psychological as well as the physical well-being of the young and the old. Care is primarily women's work whether it is done in the state, private, informal or voluntary sector.

The concept of care shows how the experience of welfare in all sectors tends to differ for men and women. When men are cared for, it is primarily by women, and the welfare state maintains and reinforces this relationship. Daly and Lewis believe that the welfare state is experiencing a crisis around care because of the increasing proportion of the population who are elderly, and the increasing numbers of women in paid employment who are unavailable to do unpaid care in the informal sector. Even when care work is paid in the private or state sectors, wages are usually low, making it difficult to recruit people to do the work.

Another key theme in recent feminist writing on welfare is a reconsideration of the idea of citizenship. Pateman (1988) and Lister (2001) (discussed in Pierson, 2006) both argue that the idea of citizenship represented in the Beveridge Report and supported by T.H. Marshall is gendered. Qualification for full citizenship rights largely depends upon having paid employment and making full national insurance contributions – criteria which do not fit well with women's role as the primary carers. In their view, the nature of social citizenship needs to be changed so that it is available much more widely and just as accessible to women as to men.

Summarizing the contribution of feminist theories of welfare, Pierson concludes that it has established two key points:

1 First, most welfare is provided in the informal, domestic sector, and this has been neglected by male theorists of welfare.
2 Second, formal state welfare cannot be understood or effectively reformed unless its relationship to welfare provided in the family is taken into account.

Evaluation of the feminist view

Pierson argues that feminist arguments are generally supported by the fact that women are more vulnerable to poverty than men (see p. 235). This implies that the welfare state is less effective in meeting women's needs than men's. Pierson says, 'In the most basic area of income maintenance, the welfare state has probably failed women more comprehensively than any other group' (2006, p. 73).

However, Pierson believes that some feminists tend to make rather generalized claims about welfare states. In some countries, such as Sweden, the poverty rate is very low and there is little gender difference in the risk of poverty. Furthermore, the position of women has been improving in many countries. He says, 'In fact, *formal* inequality of welfare rights for men and women has tended to recede (but certainly not disappear) over the past ten to fifteen years, especially within the European Union' (2006, p. 73).

Nevertheless, the feminist analysis remains valid because of those areas where differences in welfare rights continue. In Britain these include women's greater rights to parental leave than men, and the fact that Child Allowance is usually paid to women, both of which assume that women have primary responsibility for childcare. Because of their caring roles women still continue to lose out on benefits largely based on contributions from paid work, including pensions.

Summary and conclusions

Poverty, social exclusion and the welfare state are all politically and ideologically divisive issues. Poverty and social exclusion tend to be seen as social problems, and the welfare state is sometimes viewed as the main solution to such problems.

Those on the political left tend to define poverty in relative terms, see it as a major and widespread problem, and believe that state intervention is the best way to deal with it. For example, Peter Townsend's views on poverty (see pp. 217–18) have much in common with the social democratic view that progressive taxation and a large and generous welfare state are the solutions to poverty (see pp. 265–7).

On the other hand, those on the political right tend to define poverty in absolute terms; they often believe that rising living standards in capitalist societies have greatly reduced poverty; and they see the welfare state as the cause of, rather than the solution to, many social problems. Thus Charles Murray's views on the underclass and the reasons why lone parents end up poor (see pp. 242–4) have much in common with James Bartholomew's view on the damaging effects of the welfare state (see pp. 269–71).

Although Bartholomew claims that Britain would have been better off without the welfare state, few sociologists or politicians would go that far. Most accept that some state intervention in capitalist societies is necessary to promote social order, stability and, at the very least, equality of opportunity. The 'Third Way' of New Labour has tried to square the circle by combining elements of right-wing and left-wing thinking on poverty and welfare, but in doing so has not fully satisfied advocates of any of the other approaches and perspectives.

Writers from all perspectives agree that society must find some way to look after the welfare of its members and to avoid excessive poverty, but they disagree about the balance between state, informal, private and voluntary provision. However, there is no doubt that, compared to the nineteenth century, Britain and similar societies now have much less absolute poverty and the mass of the population enjoy much greater income security and better education and health care than they once did.

CHAPTER 5

Health, medicine and the body

by Stephen Moore

Health is not merely the absence of disease, but a state of complete physical, mental, spiritual and social well-being. World Health Organization, 1974

Introduction

Being ill can be an unpleasant and possibly life-threatening experience. Once the illness starts, there may be little that we can do about it except retire to bed, take our medicine and wait to get better. One thing is clear: illness is something physical over which we may have little – if any – control. Given these circumstances, it seems that the role of sociology in understanding health and illness is very limited indeed.

Despite this, sociologists have explored the nature of health, illness and medicine, and have found that things are not as clear-cut as would first appear. There is a social dimension to health and illness. In fact, much of what we know as health and illness can only be understood in a social context. Both health and illness vary across times and cultures. It is arguable whether there is such a thing as the 'normal' body, as ideas about what is normal also change. The practice of medicine and the role of the medical professions are also critically explored by sociology. Sociologists suggest that the practice of medicine as we understand it today is not necessarily as effective as it claims, but the medical professions rely upon our belief in its effectiveness in order to gain prestige and financial reward.

In this chapter we are going to explore this **social** aspect of health and illness. The chapter begins with an exploration of the contesting definitions of health and illness. These definitions polarize between those used by the medical profession, which are essentially physiological in nature, and the socially based definitions used by ordinary people. Within these socially based or subjective definitions there are variations that appear to be closely related to the degree of interference in everyday life that a physical symptom generates. Health and illness for most people therefore relate to the extent to which people can get on with their 'ordinary' lives, irrespective of physical (or even mental) abnormality.

Having explored these differing definitions of health and illness, there is a detailed presentation of the various theoretical perspectives that sociologists have brought to the study of health, illness and medicine. These provide very different sociological insights, but also reveal different views on the efficiency and the benefits of medicine for society.

The presentation of these theoretical debates also provides an introduction to a number of the issues examined in greater depth in the chapter. The first of these is the significance of the **biomedical model of health**. This is the dominant approach to understanding the body as used by the medical profession. Specifically, it sees the body as similar to a machine, which goes wrong if not correctly maintained. The role of medicine is to encourage decent maintenance and to intervene if anything goes wrong. The importance of this model of medicine cannot be overestimated, as most health care systems in the world are based upon it, including the National Health Service (NHS) in Britain. However, sociologists have very significant criticisms of the model, which are examined in some detail. Not the least of these is that levels of illness and death actually began to decline *before* the introduction of modern medical techniques. Sociologists therefore tend to point to living conditions as more important than medicine in combating disease.

Nevertheless, the dominant model of medicine is the biomedical model, which underpins the power and status of doctors. This has contributed to a process known as **medicalization**, which refers to the way in which increasing areas of social life are seen as falling under the remit of doctors. Having identified this process, sociologists have also critically examined the phenomenon. An exploration of medicalization would not be complete without a discussion of the linked debate about the basis of power of the medical professions and their role in society.

If health and illness were simply the results of physiological factors, we would expect illness to be spread randomly across the various social groupings in society. However, the statistics on health suggest that there is a close relationship between patterns of ill-health and social class, and to a lesser extent gender and 'race'. This suggests that social factors play an important role in health and illness.

The 'site' of illness is, of course, the body. The chapter therefore goes on to examine what sociology has contributed to our understanding of the body. This discussion takes a rather surprising turn, for sociologists suggest that medicine has had a profound influence upon the way we look upon our bodies, and that how we view our bodies has changed over time. This seems to suggest that bodies are not just 'natural' things, but also social objects.

An example of debates over the idea of the body – and in particular what is regarded as normal and abnormal – is the issue of **disability**. Under this heading, we look at the way in which people with impairments – that is, people with some physical handicap – are transformed into socially marginalized, disabled people. One way of describing the attitude towards disabled people is that there is a **social stigma** attached to being disabled. They share this status with other groups, such as those who are HIV-positive and those suffering from forms of cancer. It seems that people attach moral attributes to illness and disability, with some people being viewed as brave or innocent, while others are seen as being punished for their immoral or unhealthy lifestyles.

Another stigmatized group is the mentally ill, and the chapter moves on to explore the issue of mental illness in society, including the controversial argument, supported by a number of sociologists, that there may well be no such thing as mental illness at all.

The end of the chapter, perhaps appropriately, discusses death and dying. Sociologists have long been interested in the process of death. Indeed, one of the classics of sociology, Durkheim's *Suicide*, tackles this very issue. Death, sociologists argue, is not the completely individual act that most people believe it to be, but takes place, and can only be understood, within a social framework.

Defining health and illness

Health and illness are terms that most people use in everyday life without giving them much thought. However, when people are asked to define exactly what health and illness mean, a considerable divergence in views and understandings emerges and this is reflected in the academic debates about the nature of health and illness. Definitions of health and illness polarize between those that rely upon 'objective', 'scientific' criteria at one extreme, and those that are based on people's subjective awareness, at the other.

The traditional medical view is that there is such a thing as a normal functioning body, which has a limited degree of variation. When operating within the normal boundaries of these variations, a person can be defined as healthy, and when they are outside these normal boundaries, they are ill or their organs are diseased. Health can be defined, within this framework, as the **absence of disease**. The definition of disease is based upon medical concepts developed over the last few hundred years, presented as the truth about how the body functions correctly. It assumes a state of health unless symptoms emerge that demonstrate a deviance from normality. (We discuss the idea of a 'normal' body on p. 307, and the role of medicine in defining the normal body on pp. 309–11.)

At the other extreme, there is the definition of health employed by the World Health Organization – part of the United Nations. This suggests that health is

> *not merely an absence of disease, but a state of complete physical, mental, spiritual and social well-being.* WHO, 1974

This **positive** approach acknowledges the concept of disease, but brings a much broader social element into the definition, suggesting that health is not just a physical state, but also a wider sense of well-being, closely linked to our social surroundings. At this end of our definitional spectrum, the actual physical state is less important than the overall sense of well-being.

This debate over the meaning of health has led sociologists to research just how ordinary people themselves define health – known as the **lay model of health** perspective. The research indicates that alongside the negative and positive definitions discussed above, people also use **functional definitions**, which refer to health as the ability to perform normal daily activities.

Mildred Blaxter (1983, 1990) undertook two studies on how people defined their own health: one of a large cross-section of the population involving 9,000 people, and a second solely of socially disadvantaged families. In both cases she found that a negative definition of illness was used, with people defining health as the absence of disease.

However, there were clear differences between the various age groups, and between the sexes. Younger males tended to emphasize issues linked to strength and fitness, while older males stressed mental well-being. Younger women concentrated on vitality and the ability to cope in various circumstances, while older women talked about contentment, but also included wider issues such as social relationships.

In her earlier research, Blaxter found that poorer families seemed more likely to place greater stress on health and illness in terms of the disruption to their lives and an ability to 'accommodate' minor illnesses, while still 'getting on' with their lives. 'Healthy children were those who were never kept off school, or for brief periods only, or at least managed to be active' (Blaxter, 1983).

Howlett *et al.* (1992) used Blaxter's data in a more detailed examination of ethnic differences in definitions of health. Their results suggested that there were differences between the various ethnic groups, with people of Asian origin defining health in a functional way, while those of African Caribbean origin were more likely to include elements of energy and physical strength in their definitions of health. Interestingly, they were also more likely to see illness as the result of bad luck.

Conrad (1994) has included a further element when it comes to defining health and illness, arguing that ordinary people may also add a moral dimension to their definitions of health and illness – so that some illnesses are seen as being worse than others because of the perceived moral implications. For example, sexually transmitted diseases are viewed more negatively than most other forms of illness, and even various kinds of cancer can carry a stigma.

Although the research outcomes on definitions of health are not particularly clear, what does emerge is that health is not a simple concept; rather, it is multi-faceted, with different groups defining it in different ways.

Disease and illness

Health, like poverty, is a relative concept according to sociologists, and we have seen that concepts of health vary according to social group, so that poorer people are less likely to define themselves as ill, as are older people. Younger and more affluent people tend to have higher standards of what they consider to be good health.

However, it would be absurd to deny that there are certain conditions which exist objectively – these may vary from lung cancer and heart disease at one extreme, to skin inflammations at the other. This has led some sociologists to distinguish between disease and illness. A classic statement is Eisenberg's claim:

> *Illnesses are experiences of disvalued changes in states of being and social function: diseases are abnormalities in the structure and function of body organs and systems.*
> Eisenberg, 1977

Eisenberg suggests that **illness** is something that people experience as having an unpleasant impact upon their lives and activities, while **disease** refers to abnormal and harmful physical changes in the body. It is possible to have a disease and not be ill, and to be ill and not have a disease.

Having a disease and not being ill

In 1947 Erwin Ackernecht, a medical historian, studied the incidence of spirochetosis – a skin disease – among a number of indigenous peoples in South America. The disease was so widespread that it was regarded as normal and men who did not have the disease were actually discriminated against, including a ban on them marrying.

Blaxter (1990) found that British people diagnosed with such serious conditions as diabetes would still define themselves as 'healthy', unless the symptoms were particularly acute.

Having an illness and not having a disease

L'Esperance (1977) explored the way in which the disease of 'hysteria' was linked to the oppression of women in the nineteenth century. Hysterical women exhibited a range of symptoms, including crying and sometimes laughing for 'no reason'. There was no incidence of men having 'hysteria'. The medical opinion of the time was that it was caused by women trying to do activities beyond their natural abilities. This might be because women sought employment or to involve themselves in politics or other non-domestic activities. The resulting bodily stress was too much and 'hysteria' resulted. 'Effective cures' were rest and a return to the domestic environment.

There was in fact no such disease as hysteria, but by labelling a range of medical conditions as hysteria, and suggesting that its cause lay in a changing social role, women who challenged their subordinate position could be labelled as ill. Therefore the women could be said to have had an 'illness' but not a 'disease'.

A much more topical current debate on the link between illness and disease is that on ME (myalgic encephalomyelitis, also known as chronic fatigue syndrome) and 'Gulf War Syndrome' – in both these cases sufferers exhibit genuine debilitating symptoms, yet a significant proportion of medical opinion denies that any objective 'disease' exists.

Definitions of health and their significance for policy

This debate over the meaning of health and illness holds great significance for sociology, but also has very important implications for health policy.

At the time of the introduction of the NHS in 1948, most reforming politicians believed that, because of a previous lack of decent health care, a huge backlog of 'ill people' had built up. People were desperately in need of a wide range of operations to cure diagnosed illnesses. The belief was that in the first few years of the NHS there would be a huge amount of illness to clear up, and then, once this had been achieved, demand for services from the NHS would decline. The funding projections for the NHS were based on this belief.

By the early 1950s, the government realized that the demand for health services was actually growing, and in 1952 the first NHS funding crisis occurred. It was only then that health service staff realized that health and illness were not fixed, objective states, but varied over time. What were considered acceptable standards of health in 1948 were unacceptable in 1958, when a health service was available to provide care. This problem of increased spending and increasing demands on the NHS as a result of changes in the definition of illness has continued right up to the present, with continuing crises over the ability of the NHS to match increasing demands for health care.

Sen (2002) conducted a comparative study of lay views on health in India and the USA. He concluded that the higher the levels of education in a population, the higher the levels of reported illness and hence demand for health care, with the USA having a significantly higher reportage of ill-health than India. This is despite the fact that on 'objective' measures, standards of health were significantly higher in the USA.

Theoretical approaches to illness

The functionalist perspective

The functionalist approach to the sociology of health and illness derives from the work of Talcott Parsons.

At the time Parsons began writing on health and illness in the early 1950s, very few sociologists had paid any attention to the idea of illness. However, Parsons, in his determination to demonstrate that functionalism provided a complete theory of society, wanted to show that even the apparently biological aspects of social life could be understood through the lens of sociology.

The starting point for Parsons is that all social actions can be understood in terms of how they help society to **function** effectively or not. When a person is sick, they are unable to perform their social roles normally. Parsons argued that the best way to understand illness sociologically is therefore to view it as a form of **deviance**, which disturbs society's functioning, in just the same way that crime does. Therefore, like crime and any other form of deviance, illness needed to be controlled in some way, and the deviant helped or forced into performing their social role once again. This led Parsons to explore the relationship between illness and social control.

Talcott Parsons: the sick role

In *The Social System* (1951), Talcott Parsons put forward one of the most famous concepts in the sociology of health and illness: the **sick role**.

Instead of accepting the idea of sickness as a biological concept, Parsons suggested that it was a social concept, so being ill meant acting in different, deviant ways compared to the norm. Being sick was therefore a form of social role, with people acting in particular ways according to the culture of society. In modern Western societies, this involves four elements, two of which are **rights** and two of which are **obligations**.

The rights of the sick role

1. The sick person has the right to be exempted from normal social obligations, such as attending employment, or fully engaging in family activities. However, the extent to which the person can take on the sick role and so avoid normal duties depends upon the seriousness of the illness and other people's acceptance that they are genuinely ill. For example, employers might reject an employee's claim to be sick and unable to work. They may argue that the person is merely feigning illness. In cases like this, a medical expert is called upon to decide on the validity of the claim to be sick.
2. The sick role is something that the person can do nothing about and for which they should not be blamed – they therefore have the right to be 'looked after' by others. The sick role effectively absolves the person from any blame for their social deviance.

Obligations of the sick role

As well as these two rights, there are two related obligations:

1. The sick person must accept that the situation they are in is undesirable and that they should seek to get well as soon as possible.
2. The sick person must seek professional help and cooperate with the medical profession to get better.

According to Parsons, the rights of the sick role are completely dependent on the sick person undertaking these obligations – if not, their illness is not regarded as legitimate and they are seen as unfairly appropriating the sick role.

By suggesting that illness is just one of a number of forms of deviance that could be harmful to society, Parsons expands the idea of illness to include a social dimension. Being ill becomes not just a physical abnormality, but also a social abnormality. Illness is deviant and dangerous to society, and must be controlled. The sick role provides a way in which society can swiftly deal with the deviance and bring people back to their normal pattern of functioning, which benefits society.

Criticisms of the sick role

The concept of the sick role has been strongly criticized by a number of sociologists.

The first criticism is that it only applies to acute illness; it is not a useful concept when looking at chronic illness, where people are unwell for a long time with no apparent prospect of improvement and the obligation to get better as soon as possible simply cannot apply. Parsons (1975) responded to this criticism by saying that although complete recovery is not possible, people can 'manage' their illness, carrying on as normal a life as possible.

A second criticism is that Parsons assumes that the sick role occurs only when the doctor legitimates the illness. However, according to Eliot Friedson (1970), before consulting the doctor, there is a complex set of **lay-referrals**, by which he means that the ill person will consult others close to them as to whether they might be ill and the significance of the symptoms. Only after this process will the person go to the doctor.

Friedson argues that other people besides the medical professional are important in deciding whether a person can occupy the sick role or not, and that the likelihood that the person will be granted the sick role can best be understood in terms of a process of **legitimacy**.

Friedson suggests three possible variations of legitimacy. In the first situation, the person is considered to have an illness from which they can recover and they are granted conditional access to the sick role. This was the model as put forward by Parsons.

In the second situation, where the person simply cannot get well and suffers from obvious long-term symptoms or even faces death, access to the sick role is unconditionally legitimate, once granted – so there are no obligations to get better.

The third case is where the illness is stigmatized by others. For example, sexually transmitted diseases may be seen as the fault of the ill person and therefore the sick role may be regarded as illegitimate and it is unlikely that the rights of the sick role will be granted.

Parsons further assumes that all people who are ill attend the doctor's surgery. However, most research indicates that there is a large amount of illness that is simply ignored or not defined as such. In one study, Scambler *et al.* (1981) asked a sample of women to keep diaries of their health status for six weeks. On average there were eleven 'consultations' with other people around them for every consultation with the doctor. The women were most likely to consult their husbands, followed by female friends, then their mothers, and finally other female relatives.

The decision to attend a doctor's surgery also reflects patterns of social class, gender and ethnicity, with working-class people, women and minority ethnic groups having considerably lower rates of attendance than other groups.

Finally, Parsons's image of the doctor–patient relationship has been heavily criticized. Bryan Turner (1995), in particular, argues that Parsons portrays doctors as universally beneficent, competent and altruistic, and patients as compliant, passive and grateful. Neither of these images necessarily fits the reality. Instead, doctors pursue their own careers and incomes as well as provide medical expertise. Patients, too, have their own needs and wishes when they attend the surgery, and these may not fit the role of unquestioning compliance, which Parsons seems to suggest. Turner suggests that the doctor–patient relationship can better be understood as a site of conflict between the differing needs and desires of doctors and patients.

Howard Waitzkin (1971) later applied a modified version of the sick role to six specific organizational settings: the family, the mental hospital, the totalitarian state, prisons, the armed forces and conscription (when people of a certain age are required by law to undertake a period of military service). In each of these settings, he argued, the sick role provided a way for the system to allow a limited amount of deviance, thereby avoiding more serious damage to society.

One example of this was the way that the sick role prevented serious conflict in the United States during the period of the Vietnam War. This war was unpopular among many sections of the American public and there was considerable opposition to it from young people. However, the US government was also conscripting young men – sometimes against their will – to fight in the war. The sick role enabled significant numbers of young males to escape conscription on the grounds of physical or mental unsuitability. However, the sick role was not used equally across American society. Much larger numbers of educated, articulate young males were certified as sick than poorer uneducated males. It was exactly these educated young males who would have put up the greatest opposition to taking part in the war. As a result of the sick role, social discord was more limited than it would have been.

Waitzkin's version of Parsons's sick role was intended to show that the basic idea of the sick role was a useful analytical tool, but that Parsons failed to explore the significance of differences in power and how the sick role could be used to benefit the more powerful in society. This stress on inequality of power leads us to the materialist or political economy perspective on health and illness, which is discussed after the next section.

Safilios-Roschild: the rehabilitation role

Parsons's idea of the sick role (see pp. 282–3), where people who are ill are allowed to default on their normal social roles as long as they try to get better by following medical advice, has been criticized because it cannot be applied to disabled people, nor to those with chronic illness. In response to this criticism, Safilios-Roschild (1970) developed the notion of the **rehabilitation role**. This provides a social role for disabled and chronically ill people, which involves a person accepting and learning to accommodate to their condition. This can only be achieved through maximizing whatever abilities they have and by cooperating with medical professionals in a process of rehabilitation. This rehabilitation process involves seeking to return the individual to normality and also the individual adjusting psychologically to their new identity.

The political economy perspective

This perspective derives primarily from Marxism. In a similar argument to that of the functionalists, political economy writers argue that medicine is closely related to the concept of social control. It is used to define normality, punish deviance and maintain social order. However, the crucial difference is that, unlike functionalism, it sees medicine as operating on behalf of the controlling groups in society.

According to Vicente Navarro (1986), capitalism benefits from medicine in three main ways:

1. Medicine ensures that the population remains healthy enough to contribute to the economic system, by working in offices and factories to produce profit for the ruling class. Definitions of health and illness are crucially linked to the ability to produce goods – a healthy person is one who is productive and therefore profit-making for capitalism; an unhealthy person is one who produces no wealth. Doctors ensure that people are fit enough to work.
2. Medicine has an ideological function by masking the differences in health by social class, gender and ethnicity, which are caused by differences in wealth, income, and living and working conditions. The medical profession does this by providing an explanation of ill-health as the result of bad luck, or of the individual engaging in activities that put

health at risk. The wider social factors are therefore ignored and any blame for ill-health is placed upon the individual.

Lesley Doyal and Imogen Pennell (1979) have suggested that these wider factors causing ill-health are a direct result of capitalism. For example, the role of capitalism in generating pollution which causes a wide range of respiratory diseases and cancers is largely ignored; and only limited controls are placed upon products such as alcohol and tobacco which are known to cause serious ill-health, but which make enormous profits.

They also point to more specific conditions of employment under capitalism, which lead both directly and indirectly to ill-health through, for example, industrial accidents, high stress levels and alienation.

> *So deep is the frustration engendered by work that the incidence of heart attacks among manual workers is higher than that in any other stratum of society. People 'die from work' not only because it is noxious or dangerous – 8 per cent of all working hours are lost through accidents – but because it is intrinsically 'killing'.* Navarro, 1986

Navarro also points out a neglected feature of medicine: its ineffectiveness. He claims that levels of ill-health for the working class have increased under capitalism and that medicine can do little about it. Navarro argues that, despite its ineffectiveness, medicine has grown because it is a key way of **depoliticizing** an essentially political situation – which is that the causes of ill-health lie in capitalism. Yet the more that capitalism harms working-class people, the greater is the provision of health care to mask this. So the very ineffectiveness of medicine actually ensures its expansion in capitalism. 'Such medicine is but a device to convince those who are sick and tired of society that it is they who are ill, impotent, and in need of technical repair' (Illich, 1976).

3 This stress on the biomedical explanations for illness leads to treatments being based upon the use of drugs and advanced technology. In turn, the production of these goods is highly profitable to capitalism. Therefore, not only does capitalism create the conditions for poor health, but it also profits from the attempts to cure that same poor health.

Ellen Annandale (1998) uses the example of the breast implants provided by a US company, Dow Corning, to show how capitalism benefits from illness. This company began manufacturing breast implants (which increase the size of the bust), made from a type of silicone gel, in 1963. The gel implant was used in over a million transplants. In the 1970s, surgeons began to complain that the gel was 'leaking' from the implants in many cases and causing serious medical problems. However, after discussions with the company and representatives of the plastic surgeons using the gel, the controlling authority, the US Federal Drugs Agency, refused to intervene and ban the use of silicone. By the late 1990s there were so many cases of problems that were directly traceable to the silicone implants that, in a US court case, the jury found that the company had continued to provide the implants even when it knew that there were medical dangers associated with their use. In separate court cases in the 1990s, Dow Corning agreed to pay over $4 billion in compensation to women suffering from related medical problems.

This example, according to those supporting the political economy perspective, illustrates the way in which profit dominates approaches to health in capitalism.

Criticisms of the political economy perspective

The political economy perspective has been very influential, but it has also received numerous criticisms.

Nicky Hart (1985) has argued that it fails to recognize that capitalism has provided real health care gains as well as increased life expectation for the majority of the population. Bryan Turner (1995) has added the point that capitalist societies have been much more effective in advancing the health of the majority of the population than have socialist societies.

Furthermore, Hart points out that much of the Marxist critique of 'capitalism' is in fact a critique of US health care, where the system is largely privatized and exploitative of the poor. It is far less accurate in its description of British and Northern European health care systems, which are freely available to all without payment, and where there is a large body of law which seeks to limit damage to health by work practices and pollution.

> *The general impression left by Marxist writers is that capitalism is disastrous for human health. The argument is advanced from the position of a socialist utopia undefined beyond the identification of certain negative features of capitalism ... From this hazy perspective, capitalism is treated as a blanket category with no account taken of the substantial differences between contemporary market societies in standards of health and welfare provision.* Hart, 1985

In response to this, Vicente Navarro replied that it was possible to make short-term gains within capitalism, and that the health care gains have been as a result of working-class pressure for higher wages, better working conditions and higher standards of health care. However, capitalism itself does not provide these advances without the pressure. Furthermore, Navarro argues that although it is true that absolute standards of health have improved – all social groups have improved their health standards under capitalism – the relative gap between rich and poor has either remained static or actually grown wider at the extremes.

Postmodern approaches to health

Advances in medicine and the overall increase in levels of health have created the belief that most people will live long, healthy lives. As a result, there is an increasing emphasis on 'life planning' and 'self-identity ... as the constraints of life-threatening disease, early death and insecurity have given way to a more predictable life course', according to Michael Bury (1997). The experience of chronic illness therefore threatens much of what has come to be accepted as normal in contemporary society.

Bury (1982) interviewed patients with rheumatoid arthritis who had only recently been diagnosed with the disease. As a result of these interviews, Bury argued that chronic illness constitutes a major disruptive force in people's lives, undermining the taken-for-granted assumptions they had about the world and their place in it and forcing them to review their lives, their own bodies and their own identities. He called this process **biographical disruption**. As a result, people begin to appreciate the tenuous nature of their own lives, and this involves a recognition of the worlds of pain and suffering, possibly even death, which are normally only seen as distant possibilities or the plight of others.

This, in turn, leads people to rethink their own lives, in terms of what it has been about and who they really are – there are profound disruptions in explanatory systems normally used by people, such that a fundamental rethinking of the person's biography and self-concept is involved.

Not only does the onset of disease change a person's perception of their life and their body; it also leads to a disruption of relationships, physical activities and economic issues. Arthritis can lead to a physical dependence on others, and this might disturb the balance we all have in terms of giving and receiving help, with the arthritic person unable to give, but only able to receive.

Bury emphasizes that responses to illness are strongly influenced by the physical, economic and relationship resources that people have. The more of these they are able to muster, then the more likely they are to maintain a positive body image and be able to live a more 'normal' life.

Gareth Williams (1984) interviewed people who had been suffering from rheumatoid arthritis for a considerable time – Williams calls them 'seasoned professionals'. The aim was to see what the longer-term effects of suffering from a chronic illness are. Williams confirms Bury's argument that the diagnosis of serious illness has a 'biographically disruptive' effect on the individual, but he found that over time a process of **narrative reconstruction** is used by people to create a sense of coherence and order.

This narrative reconstruction provides an explanation or narrative of how and why they got the disease – as opposed to anyone else or as opposed to any other disease. The individuals construct a narrative that makes sense of the illness and places it in the context of their lives. In doing so, they may well ignore or downgrade the 'correct' medical version of causes – instead, they seek some form of meaning for the illness in their lives. The respondents in the study tended to highlight what they saw as significant social events in their lives, such as a family death, or a particularly bad employment experience, which they saw as connected to the illness. According to Williams, narrative reconstruction is used to 'reconstitute and repair ruptures between body, self, and world by linking and interpreting different aspects of biography in order to realign present and past and self and society'.

Criticism of biographical disruption: the importance of wider factors

There may not necessarily be disruption as suggested by Bury and Williams. Indeed a disease could confirm an already existing view of oneself. An example of this is provided by Danièle Carricaburu and Jenine Pierret (1995), who conducted two-hour interviews with forty-four HIV-positive men, twenty of whom were gay, and twenty of whom were heterosexual haemophiliacs, all living around Paris. Carricaburu and Pierret compared the views of those who were infected through gay sex and haemophiliacs who were infected through blood transfusions. They found that the gay men went through the process of disruption as suggested by Bury, but the haemophiliacs actually engaged in a form of 'biographical reinforcement', as they had already organized their lives and their awareness of themselves as being ill. When they discovered they were HIV-positive, this simply reinforced their view of themselves as haemophiliacs who were far more likely to die and who had to live their lives with an expectation of uncertainty.

Carricaburu and Pierret argue that their study indicates that how people respond to disease is not individual, but a reflection of membership of a particular group – in this study, gay men and haemophiliacs – and that this membership has a strong influence on the process of biographical disruption.

Support for the importance of the wider social context in understanding the illness narrative, and, in particular, issues of ethnicity, gender, class and age, has come from a number of researchers.

Pound *et al.* (1998) explored the experiences of strokes among older, working-class people in the East End of London and found that these people saw their illness as just another crisis to be faced in their 'hard-earned' lives. They had lived in poverty and had seen ill-health and deprivation all around them throughout their lives – so a stroke was not a 'biographically disruptive' event. Age and class were therefore crucial factors in their understanding of illness and in how they coped with it.

Interactionist perspectives on health and illness

Symbolic interactionism has probably been the most influential theoretical approach in the sociology of health and illness, with studies focusing on the processes involved in people arriving at the decision to seek professional help, the interaction between the ill person and the medical professional in arriving at a definition of the illness, and the impact on the person of being labelled as ill.

Symbolic interactionists reject the notion that illness is a direct result of some form of disease; instead, they perceive it as a form of social deviance. What constitutes illness is a result of social definitions. People may well have a serious disease, but this does not automatically result in the people defining themselves as ill. This definition is the outcome of a long process, which may result in the label 'ill' being applied to some groups and not others. This approach is exactly the same as that taken by symbolic interactionists to explain other forms of social deviance, such as crime or sexual aberration. As Rosenberg (1989) puts it: 'Disease does not exist as a social phenomenon until it is somehow perceived as existing.'

One example of the social construction of a disease is Repetitive Strain Injury (RSI). The causes and seriousness of RSI have been debated, with a variety of explanations being put forward which tend to reflect the different interests of the groups involved, according to Tesh (1988). Employers have suggested that RSI is not serious and is actually the outcome of poor posture by employees using their computers. Psychiatrists argue that it is not a physical condition but related to dislike of the particular employment, which manifests itself in a psychosomatic condition. Unions claim that RSI is a serious and common problem resulting from the stress and pace of work faced by employees engaged in routine keyboard operations for eight hours each day. Whether RSI is therefore a disease, claims Tesh, will depend upon political and power issues, and not on any physical condition.

A second area of interest is **illness behaviour**, the term used by sociologists to explore the patterns of behaviour that people engage in when they decide whether or not they are actually unwell and what they should do as a result of their decision.

Mechanic defines illness behaviour thus:

> ***The way in which symptoms are perceived, evaluated and acted upon by a person who recognizes some pain, discomfort and other signs of organic malfunction.*** Mechanic, 1968

The first point noted by sociologists about illness behaviour is that the vast majority of people who feel 'unwell' do not visit a doctor. For example, in a study by Scambler *et al.* (1981) in which seventy-nine women aged 16–44 years were asked to keep a diary of how they felt over a period of six weeks, only one in eighteen women who reported symptoms actually visited a doctor. Freund and McGuire (1991) have called this the **illness iceberg**, referring to the fact that there is so much illness compared to the relatively small amount that is presented to doctors.

Yet doctors often complain that patients too often attend GP practices with trivial complaints. For example, one national study of GPs by Cartwright and Anderson (1981) found that over 25 per cent of doctors believed that more than half of their consultations were for complaints that were too trivial to warrant seeing a doctor.

Becker *et al.* (1977) explored what influenced people in visiting the doctor and developed the **health belief model**, which consists of three stages:

Stage 1 Factors that lead the person 'to undertake recommended compliance behaviour'.

Stage 2 'Modifying and enabling factors', which affect the first stage.

Stage 3 'Compliant behaviour', which refers to the likelihood that the person will follow the recommendations of the health professional, as a result of the influence of stages one and two.

Within the first stage the factors include:

- An individual's *motivations* to define themselves as ill or not; for example, some people are uninterested in their own health.
- The *value of illness threat reduction* – according to Becker *et al.*, this refers to a person's subjective estimate of the extent of harm to their body from the illness and the extent of interference with their social roles.
- The *extent to which they will benefit* from defining themselves as ill and receiving treatment.

The second stage of 'modifying and enabling factors' includes such things as the age of the person, the possible costs of the treatment (financial, social and physical), the attitudes of the medical professionals towards them, and finally the social importance of the people telling them to consult a medical professional and to follow their advice.

The third and final stage refers to factors that influence whether the person will follow the recommendations of the professional. Thus people may follow none, some or all of the medical recommendations, depending upon the continuing outcome of the interaction of factors in stages one and two.

This may seem complex, but in essence Becker *et al.* are saying that being ill, seeking medical advice and following medical advice are as much a result of social factors as medical ones. Furthermore, being ill, seeking help and following advice are the result of a complex interaction between the individual, their perceptions of health, illness and the medical profession, and the views of the social network that surrounds them.

Criticism of interactionist perspectives

Day and Day (1977) criticized social interactionist accounts of health and illness for concentrating on the negotiations between medical professionals and patients while ignoring wider social factors such as social inequality, pollution and stress, which provide the actual causes of the ill-health.

Feminist approaches to health

As discussed elsewhere in this book (see p. 11), it is inaccurate to see feminism as one agreed perspective within sociology. Instead, there are a number of differing feminist positions. These can include liberal feminism, socialist feminism and radical feminism. Divisions are apparent in the theoretical debates on feminism within the sociology of health and illness.

Liberal feminism

The liberal feminist approach has focused in particular on inequalities of health between males and females and has sought explanations for these differences within the different roles and economic positions of men and women. From this perspective, if women can obtain the same economic and social status as men, then improvements in standards of health must follow.

Similarly, this approach has sought equality of numbers of men and women in the higher-status medical professions, and research has been undertaken to demonstrate the smaller number of women who occupy senior medical positions, and also the way in which nursing is regarded as a lower-status, 'female' profession.

Liberal feminism also points to the lack of power that women have in their relations with the medical profession, and demands a greater say in women's health – particularly in childbirth and contraception.

Ellen Annandale (1998) comments that other forms of feminism criticize liberal feminism because of its willingness to work within the patriarchal system: as patriarchy is the root of the oppression of women, it is therefore impossible to work within it. She also notes that radical feminists accuse liberal feminism of primarily operating for the benefit of white, middle-class women, as it advocates opening up the professions and positions of power on an equal basis to women. Only those challenging for top professional positions could therefore ever benefit.

Finally, Annandale claims that radical feminists suggest that liberal feminists view the female body and emotionality as 'handicaps', which must be overcome by women to achieve equality. As we will see later, radical feminists see the body and emotionality as central to the very nature of being a woman.

Socialist feminism

This approach links Marxist and feminist arguments, and there are considerable tensions within it between those who argue that essentially Marxism underpins the approach, and those who argue that it is based upon feminism with Marxist ideas added to it.

In terms of health and illness, the approach mirrors the stress of the liberal feminist model on inequalities of health and illness. However, socialist feminists emphasize that it is not possible to change the roles of males and females within a capitalist patriarchal society, as liberal feminists seek to do. Instead, it is necessary to amend fundamentally the nature of the economic system and replace capitalism with a socialist society in which males and females have equal roles and statuses.

According to Lesley Doyal (1995), for example, medicine supports capitalism by defining illness as that which stops workers from being productive. As regards women, medicine supports patriarchy by defining women's health in terms of the ability to reproduce physically the next generation of workers, the ability to undertake the domestic tasks needed to run a household, and the ability to act as a 'reserve army of labour' when additional workers are needed.

Women's health is also functional to capitalism in that there is significant profit to be made from taking 'normal' female bodily activity and turning it into a concern of medicine. New technologies and drugs are developed and sold for pregnancy, childbirth, hormonal cycles and to avert signs of ageing.

Doyal (1995) provides a detailed breakdown of the differences in health between the genders. The basic cause of women's ill-health is the fact that they are expected to work outside the home and then also to take major responsibility for domestic work – what she calls the 'double day'. According to Doyal, 'it is the cumulative effects of … working in production and reproduction … that are the major determinants of women's state of health'.

Doyal then draws evidence together to argue that women work more in the home than men, and are expected to do more caring than men. Heterosexual sex is dangerous for women, both because of the sexual diseases passed on to them, including cervical cancer, and the physical and emotional damage caused by sexual abuse. Women are not in control of their own fertility – it is more likely that men are – and so the resulting 'inability to influence one of the most fundamental aspects of biological functioning can have profound effects on both physical and mental health'. Also, the hazards, low pay and stress of their occupations damage women. Finally, many women are prescribed drugs which help them cope with the stress of their lives – as does cigarette smoking – but which are harmful in the long term.

Health care, according to Doyal, is a set of social relationships that function to reproduce class, gender and ethnic hierarchies.

Radical feminism

Radical feminists see the basis of contemporary society as the exploitation and oppression of women by men. This simple fact underpins all of society. Gaining equal rights or overthrowing capitalism would in themselves produce no real gain for women. They argue that no matter what the divisions between women in terms of ethnicity or social class, there is still an underlying common exploitation shared by all women.

Ehrenreich (1978) provides an insight into the way patriarchal medicine acts as an agent of social control. She argues that medicine depoliticizes the social causes of ill-health for women, as it provides individualistic explanations of ill-health rather than pointing to the common problems faced by all women. Furthermore, the apparently neutral and scientific discipline of medicine actually contains a strong measure of social control: 'The "scientific" knowledge of doctors is sometimes not knowledge at all, but rather social messages (e.g. about the proper behaviour of women) wrapped up in technical language.'

Ehrenreich and English (1978) have provided a specific example of how medicine has been used historically to control women. Their study explored the way that women were treated during the latter part of the nineteenth century, and in particular they examined the dominant medical theories of female health prevalent at the time. One particularly important belief was that the organs in the body vied with each other for the body's energy. This was especially significant for women, as the predominant belief was that the primary role of women was to reproduce. If women engaged in other activities, then this might prevent energy going to the female organs linked to reproduction. Ehrenreich and English's research also showed that doctors traced most women's medical problems – including headaches and even sore throats – to 'disorders' of the uterus and the ovaries.

Women were also viewed as 'naturally' frailer than men, and thus it was regarded as better that they should not exhaust themselves with a range of activities such as higher education or sport. The result was that medicine effectively helped justify the repression of women, as 'medical arguments seemed to take the malice out of sexual oppression'.

Radical feminists argue that this control of women through medicine continues today.

Graham and Oakley (1986) used data from interviews with women in London and York who had recently given birth to claim that men and women have fundamentally different ways of viewing the entire process of pregnancy and childbirth – what Graham and Oakley refer to as different **frames of reference**.

Whereas male doctors stress the 'medical' aspects only, women are more likely to see the experience in the context of their work, home and family. Male doctors viewed childbirth as a potentially problematic event, whereas the mothers viewed it as a normal part of life. Furthermore, when doctors obtain information from women – ostensibly on medical grounds – they then use this to exert control and direct the activities of women, and in so doing take away some of the intense emotions involved in childbirth.

This process of obtaining information, in itself, reflects the dominant male doctor/female 'patient' relationship. Graham and Oakley give the example of how, when the pregnant women were being given a medical examination, they were already lying down when the doctor entered the cubicle, thereby placing the woman in a position of powerlessness. When the examination was over, the nurse (rather than the doctor) would then ask the woman if she wanted to ask the doctor any questions – once again, according to Graham and Oakley, this reaffirms the dominant position of the doctor and the lesser status of both nurse and woman.

Although the majority of women felt intimidated into not asking questions, for the minority who did so, the replies from the doctors were less about giving information and more about reassuring the pregnant woman that everything would be all right, or making a joke of the situation. For the very few women who continued to press for information, the doctors would then use medical terminology to reaffirm the relative status positions of doctor/patient: he is the expert and she is the patient who has to place trust in him.

This sort of research led to the development of feminist organizations which sought to take back control over reproduction from (male) doctors. The Association of Radical Midwives, for example, sought to give power back to women.

Criticisms of radical feminism

Radical feminists take what is known as an **essentialist** position regarding males and females, implying that all women are, by nature, the same. Women are therefore biologically and socially connected, no matter what their social circumstances. If the patriarchal interventions of males could be resisted, then women would be able to coexist in some natural female way.

Annandale (1998) has pointed out that feminist critics of the radical feminist position dispute this claim that all women share some *natural* connection. Women, like men, are different from one another, and the way to understand these differences is through exploring culture, not nature.

Models of health

Sociologists take the view that health and illness are social constructs just as much as they are medical constructs. This is not, however, the dominant way in which health and illness are perceived and defined in contemporary Western societies. Instead, a biological model of health and illness is seen as 'real' and this medical/biological model largely determines the way that health services are provided.

On the other hand, sociological approaches suggest that the only way to understand health and illness is to place them within social, political and historical circumstances.

Until the nineteenth century, when the biomedical model began to take over, traditional health models (which we now know as complementary or alternative medicine) dominated health care. These traditional models of health care rapidly diminished in significance under the onslaught of the new scientific ways of approaching health.

In this section, we look at the way in which modern Western medicine has come to be dominated by a particular **biomedical model of disease** and the implications of this for health provision. This is followed by a discussion of how complementary and alternative approaches have recently made a come-back.

The biomedical model

The biomedical model, on which contemporary medical practice is based, has four core elements:

1 Mind–body dualism
2 Specific aetiology
3 Mechanical metaphor
4 Objective science

Mind–body dualism is the belief that the mind and our ways of thinking can be completely separated from the body. The concept developed as a result of the way that scientific thought itself emerged in the seventeenth century under the influence of the philosopher René Descartes. Descartes' argument was that the mind was the controlling force of the body, which acted at the will of the mind. The mind was therefore distinct from the body. This was in opposition to the teachings of the time. The Catholic Church saw the body and mind (and soul) as inseparable. The gradual acceptance of Descartes' ideas and the decline in the influence of the Catholic Church led to the belief that it was morally correct to dissect bodies for anatomical research. As a result of this research, explanations were developed about how the body 'worked'. A longer-term result was that disease was seen as the outcome of some malfunctioning part of the body, while the mind and wider social factors came to be seen as irrelevant.

Specific aetiology refers to the way in which modern medical models assume a specific cause for a disease (such as a virus or bacteria): by targeting this cause, the disease can be cured. This idea of narrowing down the cause to a specific causal agent was strongly influenced by the work of researchers such as Pasteur and Koch, both of whom worked in the nineteenth century.

Until the work of Pasteur on bacteria and Koch on the tubercle bacillus (which causes TB, a disease which was a major killer in Britain until the early twentieth century), it was generally believed that disease was caused by 'miasma' or 'polluted air'. Miasma could be detected by unpleasant smells and was the result of dirt and decay.

Pasteur and Koch showed, instead, that specific micro-organisms were transmitted in a variety of ways, including coughs, sneezes and in water. Through these means humans passed on infections to each other. As a result of this, medicine came to view all diseases as having a specific cause ('aetiology' refers to searching for 'the cause'). Finding and addressing this specific cause would lead to a cure.

Doctors regard the human body as similar to a very complex and advanced machine. They look at the functions that each part of the body performs and seek to 'repair', heal or replace the non-functioning parts. This **mechanical metaphor** also derived from the division between the mind and body and the emergence of the belief in specific aetiology. According to Dixon (1978), with the establishment of specific disease categories, the main task of diagnosis became that of examining and measuring the individual's body to determine what exactly the 'symptoms' were and then to compare these to the known symptoms produced by a particular disease. The patient's disease could then be classified and treated. Diseases came to be regarded as universal and independent of culture or background.

Freund and McGuire (1991) comment that the acceptance of the mechanical metaphor has led to medicine 'developing specializations along the lines of the machine parts, emphasizing individual systems or organs to the exclusion of the totality of the body'.

The **objective science** of medicine is the belief, widely accepted in most scientific and even social scientific disciplines, that there is such a thing as the scientific method, which provides the 'truth' about the object under study. By rigorously following the correct methods, the results will reveal an objective reality.

The development of scientific thinking took place from the Enlightenment onward, and was based upon the belief in an objective world, existing out there, beyond human beings. The role of science was to gain an understanding of this world in order to change it for the use of humans (see pp. 890–1 for more detailed discussion of the development of scientific thought).

Medicine fully subscribes to this belief and seeks the origins of ill-health through rigorous research techniques. The usefulness of alternative methods of explaining and curing disease can only be uncovered by an assessment using these research techniques. This explains the rejection of 'alternative medicines', such as homeopathy, as they do not fit the criteria of science (see pp. 295–8).

One of the results of adopting the scientific approach to disease has been the increasing use of, and reliance upon, technology to research and cure diseases.

The biomedical model now dominates health provision, although it is being challenged increasingly by a reinvigorated traditional model, now known as complementary or alternative medicine. Sociologists have therefore sought to explain why the biomedical model gained such dominance at the expense of other approaches to health.

History as progress

A traditional explanation for the dominance of the biomedical model has been that it is the outcome of **progress**.

> *Surrounded by a sea of ignorance and irrationality, some scholars, working over centuries, have brought together more and more precise knowledge of how the human body is structured and how it functions under normal conditions or under conditions of illness.* Unschuld, 1986

The 'history as progress' model emphasizes the influence of Descartes and the work of Pasteur and Koch on micro-organisms as examples of a steady forward progression in science, which has led inexorably to the current biomedical model. Textbooks for medical students routinely provide this explanation of the development of the biomedical model.

Changing relationships

Jewson (1976) suggested that modern medicine developed through three stages to its present biomedical model, and that these stages reflect changing relationships between patients, doctors and forms of knowledge.

The first of Jewson's three stages is that of **bedside medicine**, which lasted from the Middle Ages to the eighteenth century. Doctors were dependent on the patronage of wealthy individuals for employment. It was the role of the doctor to ask the patient what was wrong with them, and, on the basis of what the patient said, the doctor would seek to cure them. The important point is that the doctor responded to the view of illness provided by the patient.

The second stage was the growth of **hospital medicine** in the nineteenth century. The patient now entered hospital and was dependent upon the knowledge of the professionally trained doctor. The doctor now led the enquiry into the disease, by asking where the pain was and eliciting other symptoms from the patient. The doctor was only interested in the symptoms, not in the views of the patient. The treatment was then based upon what doctors had been trained to associate with specific symptoms.

The third and contemporary stage, Jewson claims, is that of **laboratory medicine**. Here, both the doctor and the patient are displaced by the scientific tests conducted in the laboratory. The doctor's role is to carry out tests and then hand them over for scientific analysis by machines and technicians. Healing now depends upon the results of the tests more than the guess of the doctor, based upon asking for information on the symptoms. Statistical tests will tell the patient whether they have a disease or not, as the tests will say whether their body functioning is normal or abnormal. The view of the patient and to some extent that of the doctor are irrelevant.

Criticisms of the biomedical model

Despite its dominance, the biomedical model has been subjected to considerable criticism by sociologists. Perhaps the best-known attack on the model has come from Thomas McKeown in *The Role of Medicine* (1979).

McKeown argues that 'the improvement of health during the past three centuries was due essentially to provision of food, protection from hazards, and limitation of numbers'. He does not dispute the role of medicine overall, but argues that 'it is sometimes extremely effective; but often it is ineffective, or merely tides the patient over a short illness, leaving the underlying disease condition and prognosis essentially unchanged'.

The Role of Medicine is a detailed study of mortality rates in England and Wales from the early eighteenth century onwards. McKeown concludes that the single most important factor in lowering death rates was improvement in nutrition from the early eighteenth century onwards. He also estimates that improvements in hygiene accounted for about one-fifth of the entire decline in the death rate from the mid-nineteenth century onwards.

When it comes to the introduction of immunization, McKeown suggests that this was highly effective in combating the remaining cases of diseases such as polio and TB. However, the most significant decline in these diseases actually occurred *before* the introduction of immunization. Therefore, immunization was useful only for the small minority of people who were still prone to these diseases after the major decline had already taken place (see Figure 5.1).

McKeown is not arguing that modern biomedical models are of no use, simply that they are much less effective than other, apparently non-medical, factors in explaining the great decline in the mortality rate over the last two hundred years.

McKeown also admits that modern medical techniques may be useful in helping people get well after an illness, but they have only had a marginal impact on levels of mortality.

McKeown says that if only one factor had to be chosen to explain why individuals were more or less prone to disease, he would suggest that it is the genetic makeup they have inherited from their parents. McKeown would therefore strongly support the potential effectiveness of research into genetics – an area of research which does take a highly scientific approach.

Earlier, we noted that the biomedical model was only one way of understanding health and illness, but that it has come to be seen by medical professionals and policy makers as the only scientifically correct model. However, there is considerable evidence to show that for 'ordinary people' alternative models for understanding health and illness are still very important, and that there has not been complete acceptance of the biomedical model.

Chrisman (1977) reviewed a range of previous studies which had focused on what people saw as the causes of illness, and suggested that these could be categorized into four types of explanations:

1 **Invasion** – where something has come from outside and entered the person's body, such as a 'germ'.
2 **Degeneration** – when a person is 'run-down'.
3 **Mechanical** – when some part of the body, such as a heart or kidney, misfunctions.
4 **Balance** – where an individual's body, life or even relationship with others is disturbed in some way.

Blaxter (1983) illustrates the significance of these 'causes' in people's understanding of illness. In her research she studied forty-six working-class women, asking them their views on health and illness. Of 587 examples of illness mentioned in the transcripts from her in-depth interviews with the women, in only about 150 cases was there any discussion of the causes.

Blaxter argued that although the explanations given for disease were not 'scientifically' correct – in the sense of what a doctor might point to as the specific cause of illness – they did show an accurate and sophisticated awareness of the conditions that produced disease, such as stress, poverty, environmentally poor surroundings and so on, all of which could lead to a person being 'run-down' (degeneration).

The single most common explanation provided for disease in her study concerned stress or strain – which falls clearly within Chrisman's category of balance. Cancer, which was seen as a frightening, mysterious disease that could happen to anybody, without apparent reason, is an example of invasion, and heart attacks were viewed as mechanical breakdowns.

Michael Calnan (1987) found evidence of social class differences in explanations of illness, with middle-class women more likely to explain cancer as due to a mixture of smoking and hereditary factors than working-class women. Other studies have also found some differences in explanations of illness by social class. Blaxter and Peterson (1992) found that the greater the economic and social deprivation, the more fatalistic women were about their health chances, viewing illness as something they could do little about. Similarly, Pill and Stott (1986) found that when they compared home owners (used as an indicator of higher income) with people living in social housing, those living in social housing were more likely to exhibit fatalistic attitudes towards ill-health.

Causes of illness would appear to vary according to a range of factors, but clearly the degree of deprivation is important in the form of definition used. It seems that fatalistic attitudes to health are adopted which possibly

Figure 5.1 Respiratory tuberculosis: death rates per million, England and Wales, 1838–1970

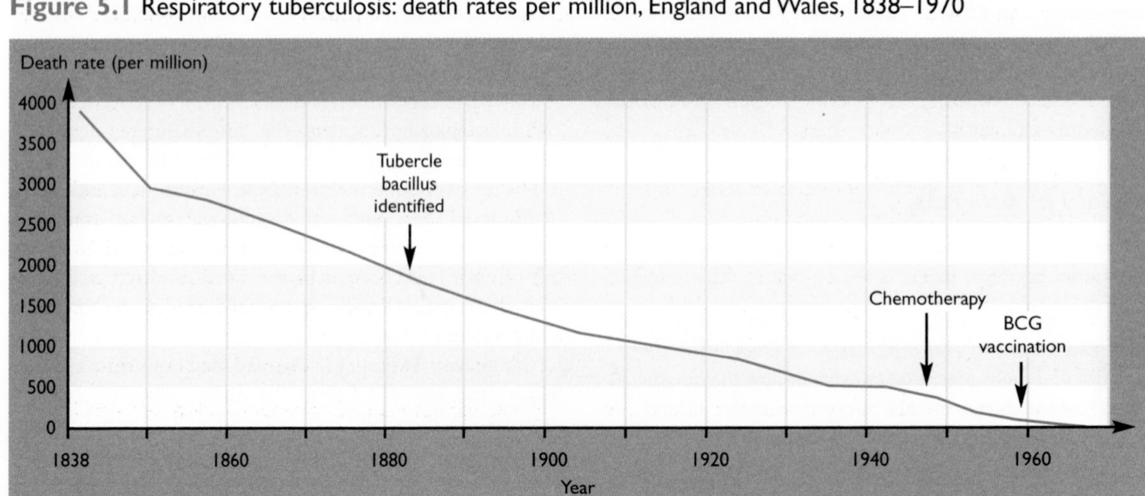

Source: T. McKeown (1976) *The Modern Rise of Population*, Edward Arnold, London.

reflect the powerlessness that poorer people feel. More affluent people would appear to have a more positive view about their ability to prevent illness.

All of these studies demonstrate that the biomedical model of illness does not coincide with how ordinary people understand and explain illness. In addition, people seem to have a clear awareness of the impact of life experiences on health, which is largely absent from the biomedical model.

Medicalization

The dominance of the biomedical model in medicine, discussed earlier, has led to a number of concerns regarding the increased power of the medical profession and the way it has extended its control into other spheres of life. The first person to draw attention to this was Eliot Friedson (1970), who suggested that the high status accorded to medicine and the medical profession had led to other issues, more properly defined as social problems, such as gambling, drug use and crime, being inappropriately redefined as illness, to be dealt with by doctors.

The idea was taken up by Irving Zola (1981), who suggested that 'medicine is becoming a major institution of social control, nudging aside, if not incorporating, the more traditional institutions of religion and the law'.

Ivan Illich: *Limits to Medicine*

Ivan Illich (1976) explored the concept of **medicalization**, arguing that activities and conditions that might otherwise have been ignored, or seen as a social problem or a normal part of life, have all come to be defined as medical issues, which fall under the expertise of the medical profession. This is despite convincing evidence that medicine has had very limited success in treating a wide range of conditions. Furthermore, Illich links this to the idea of **iatrogenesis**, by which he means the increased levels of illness and social problems caused by medical intervention.

Illich claims that **industrialization** is the main force which helped create both the professionalization and bureaucratization of wide swathes of modern society – in particular, education and medicine. According to Illich, the medical profession has created the belief that it has indispensable knowledge and skills, which cannot be provided by anyone else. In fact, the power of the medical profession is so great that it can even persuade people to believe that they know less about their own bodies and the most effective way to care for them than doctors do.

The outcome of this, Illich argues, is that the medical profession actually *harms* public health: 'the medical establishment has become a major threat to health'.

Illich describes the process of iatrogenesis as having three elements:

1. **Clinical iatrogenesis** refers to the fact that many technological and pharmaceutical 'advances' have such serious side-effects that they may actually be worse than the original condition. As Illich puts it: 'The pain, dysfunction, disability and even anguish which result from technical medical intervention now rival the morbidity due to traffic, work and even war-related activities' (Illich, 1976).
2. **Social iatrogenesis** is created by the activities of a medical profession that wishes to expand its role into the wider society. The result is a passive and docile population who have become increasingly reliant upon drugs and the medical interpretation of social and physical events.
3. **Structural iatrogenesis** describes the most powerful aspect of Illich's critique of the medical profession and refers to the fact that the medical profession has gradually reduced the ability of people to cope with normal processes of body change and life. People are unable to cope with sickness, pain and death – they are seen as abnormal and something to be avoided. Yet, as Illich points out, these are integral parts of the human condition and need to be seen as such. 'The so-called health professions have an even deeper structurally health-denying effect insofar as they destroy the potential of people to deal with their human weakness, vulnerability and uniqueness in a personal and autonomous way.'

Illich argues that iatrogenesis has had a profound effect on society. He suggests that the role of the medical profession needs to be restricted, and ordinary people need to take back control over their own bodies. They must also learn to cope with pain, illness and death as earlier generations did.

Marxist approaches to medicalization

Whereas Illich links the harm done by medicine to industrialization, Marxist approaches to health and illness seek to locate these issues within the broader framework of **capitalism**. The health care system is part of a wider process of oppression: 'With scientific medicine, health care has grown into an industry which helps maintain the legitimacy of the social order and which in part creates new sectors of production' (Renaud, 1975).

According to Marxists such as Vicente Navarro (1980), the biomedical model of health is shaped by the ideology of capitalism, as it stresses the individual nature of illness and ignores the social patterns of disease which are closely related to social class. In doing so, it directs attention away from the exploitative nature of capitalism and the 'real' underlying causes of disease. Medicine, Navarro argues, 'makes palatable those diswelfares generated by the economic system'.

These causes, which include environmental and occupational factors, as well as poverty, can only be addressed by changing the economic and social bases of society, upon which capitalism rests. The activities of the medical profession ensure that people instead see health as an individual problem, with illness striking people by bad luck. A famous quote by McKinlay illustrates this:

> *To use the upstream–downstream analogy, one could argue that people are blamed (and in a sense even punished) for not being able to swim after they, perhaps against their own volition, have been pushed in to the river by manufacturers of illness.* McKinlay, 1974

Ehrenreich and English: feminism and medicalization

Medicalization and the resulting control of women's health by (male) doctors has been one of the central debates within the radical feminist approach to medicine (see p. 287).

According to Ehrenreich and English (1978), by the nineteenth and early twentieth centuries menstruation and pregnancy were treated as abnormal and as forms of sickness. Doctors attributed a range of disorders, including headaches, sore throats and even indigestion, to the uterus and ovaries. Surgical removal of ovaries, hysterectomy and clitoridectomy were all procedures used to treat unrelated illnesses and mental conditions, including what was regarded as excessive sexual desire. The result of all this was that women's activities and behaviour were restricted under the guise of medical concern.

Ehrenreich and English examined the illness known as 'hysteria' in Victorian England among middle-class and upper-class women (see p. 281). Hysteria had numerous symptoms, including screaming, crying and laughing. According to Ehrenreich and English, these were probably a response to the highly restricted, sexually controlled lives of the women. However, 'hysteria' was defined in medical terms as a disease, and the cure usually consisted of up to two months lying in bed, during which time the patient would be encouraged to cope with her emotional 'problems'. Ehrenreich and English suggest that by defining the situation in terms of a medical condition, this allowed male doctors to avoid discussion of women's rights and their oppression.

Walsh (1980) examines the relationship of the medical profession to contraception and argues that the discourse surrounding the use of contraception and the regulation of women's reproduction is still 'contested'. Women see it as their right to choose any form of contraception, while the medical profession regard it as an issue of medical judgement. This difference in viewpoint is taken even further in the debate over abortion.

Conrad and Schneider: *Deviance and Medicalization*

Conrad and Schneider (1980) examined how gambling changed from being viewed as an immoral act in the nineteenth century to being viewed as an illness during the twentieth century. According to Conrad and Schneider, gambling acquired its immoral image because it clashed with the dominant nineteenth-century American value, derived from Protestantism, of success as the reward for hard work. Gambling rewarded those who were lucky, not the hard-worker. Therefore, gambling was a deviant act, which was open to explanation through all the normal approaches to deviance.

Conrad and Schneider describe a process of 'prospecting', by which various groups seek to provide a socially dominant explanation for the deviant action. During the twentieth century there were various attempts to stake a claim to the area, and in 1943 Edmund Bergler published a paper in a medical journal claiming that 'neurotic gamblers' were ill. This was followed in 1957 by a book devoted to the subject.

However, other groups were also competing to provide an explanation for gambling, and in 1957 Gamblers Anonymous was formed, which laid claim to explain and combat addiction to gambling, but from a non-medical perspective. According to Conrad and Schneider, at this point there was no guarantee that the medical explanation for gambling would become the dominant one. However, in 1978 funding was provided for a hospital-based therapy programme in Maryland, USA, and this was crucial in giving legitimacy to the notion of gambling as a medical issue. The dominance of the medical definition was finally assured when the American Association of Psychiatrists formally included a new entry of *pathological gambling* in the handbook of recognized diseases, *The Diagnostic and Statistical Manual*.

Thus, a medical condition of pathological gambling now exists, which provides both an explanation and a course of therapy to combat the disease. Alternative definitions have been marginalized in the USA.

Lay demand for medicalization

The argument that it has been solely the medical professions who have pushed the boundaries of medicalization into progressively broader areas of social life has been criticized by Moynihan and Smith (2002). They argue that, increasingly, it is the wider population who are demanding to have the illnesses which they believe they suffer from formally recognized. In particular, campaigns have been mounted to ensure that Attention Deficit Hyperactivity Disorder (ADHD), ME/Chronic Fatigue Syndrome and Gulf War Syndrome should all come to have full recognition as diseases. Moynihan and Smith point out that, in these cases, it is the medical professions who are objecting to the designation of disease status and who are seeking to draw boundaries between what they perceive as 'objective' disease and conditions such as these.

However, as we shall see later, although more and more areas of social life are becoming medicalized, there is a parallel movement in which people are increasingly challenging both the medical professions and the biomedical model of health care. So, despite this increase in medicalization, there is also a shift to using more traditional forms of medicine, including complementary and alternative approaches.

Professions and power in medicine

The medicalization thesis suggests that significant areas of social life, which have nothing to do with medicine, have been taken over by health professionals. Related to this is the debate over just how doctors have achieved such a high status in society, which allows them to have such power.

Initial discussions of the medical professions, by functionalist writers, tended to stress that these were very specific, highly skilled jobs dominated by educated people motivated more by an ethos of well-being for the community than personal gain (Carr-Saunders and Wilson, 1933). However, writers supporting this claim still struggled to make a clear distinction between professions and non-professions. Eventually, a series of traits was identified that distinguished professions from other occupations.

Millerson: the traits of a profession

One such list applied to the medical profession can be found in the work of Millerson (1964).

1 Millerson suggests that a profession is based on *theoretical knowledge*, as opposed to practice developed from what works and what does not. There is therefore a body of academic knowledge underpinning the role.
2 Millerson also suggests that a profession has a clearly developed programme of *specialized education*, such as found in 'medical schools'. These specialize in providing the specific, high-level education required.
3 Professionals must undergo a series of *formal examinations*, which they must pass in order to practise.
4 Professionals must have an *independent body* to represent their interests, but also to regulate the quality of care. Those who do not maintain the levels of care cannot continue to practise.
5 There is a compulsory *professional code of behaviour* and anyone breaking this is prevented from working in medicine.
6 The aim of the profession is the *public good*, as opposed to personal financial interests.

This trait approach has been criticized for simply providing an idealized list of the characteristics of members of the medical profession. It provides no evidence to prove that these traits are true.

Talcott Parsons: the functions of the profession

A similar approach has been taken by functionalists, but writers such as Parsons (1951) have located these traits within the broader perspective of functionalist theory.

According to the theory, the medical profession is an important occupation in society, and as such must attract some of the most intelligent people. To do this, it needs to be highly rewarded in both financial and status terms, but it must also have a series of safeguards (the traits) to ensure that the highest standards are achieved.

The medical profession is further characterized by its provision of a vocation based upon two of the **pattern variables** of functionalist theory: universalism and affective neutrality. (Pattern variables are the culturally approved ways in which people are encouraged to behave in order that society should run smoothly.)

Universalism is the value that ensures that all people are treated similarly, and there is no favouritism based on family/friendship connection, or payment. This is crucial, as doctors must seek to provide the highest standards of health care to all members of society, without favour. Furthermore, as people put their lives in the hands of doctors and do not have the specific knowledge required to question the doctor's authority, it is crucial that they can completely trust the doctor.

Affective neutrality means that the professional will not let personal views or interests affect the way they carry out their professional duties. This is important, as doctors often deal with issues they may find morally distasteful and they must do so without letting these feelings show.

The medical profession's high status and financial reward, allied to strict adherence to the pattern variables, ensure that there is a specialization of skill and knowledge by the most able, which benefits the smooth and effective functioning of the social system.

Criticism of functionalist approaches

Turner (1995) has criticized these sorts of trait and functionalist analyses of the professions because, first, they largely reproduce the image which the professions themselves want the public to believe, and second, they ignore the power of the professional bodies, which allows them to manipulate their clients and obtain high levels of reward. Turner points out that these analyses provide an image of the historical development of professions which suggests that they have always striven to attain those particular positive traits. Turner suggests instead that any examination of the history of the professions would show that this is not the case.

Friedson: a 'Weberian' view of the professions

A third approach to understanding the professions in medicine has been provided by Eliot Friedson (1970), who argues that professions operate in order to gain **social closure** through professional dominance.

Friedson is strongly influenced by Weber, who introduced the concept of social closure into sociology. According to Weber, social groups are constantly vying for position in the status hierarchy of any society. One method of maintaining a high position, once it is obtained, is to restrict membership to a limited number of people, usually from similar backgrounds. By doing this, the closed group is able to maintain its privileges. Friedson suggests the best way to understand the position of doctors is to see their dominance as a profession as a form of social closure, whereby they have forced other, competing providers of health care into subordinate positions.

The various traits which Millerson describes can therefore be looked on as techniques of closure: doctors define a particular form of knowledge and set examinations so that only specially chosen people may enter the profession – usually from the same social class background and with a high percentage of men. Those who would not 'fit in' are filtered out in the process of selection by the medical schools. Once in the profession, the only people who can judge the work of the doctor are colleagues, who will prefer to maintain the fiction that all doctors are equally competent than to let the public know that some doctors are incompetent.

Finally, the myth that doctors are interested in the general good rather than in financial gain perversely allows doctors to make high financial demands for their services, *precisely because* they are working for the good of the public rather than themselves.

Friedson points out that doctors have been so successful that they have not only gained a monopoly over medical practice, but they have also been able to define the roles and tasks of other health care providers. Friedson uses the term **paramedical professions** for the whole range of other providers, including nurses and midwives.

Bryan S. Turner: *Medical Power and Social Knowledge*

Turner (1995) develops this Weberian approach by arguing that professionalization by doctors is no more than 'an occupational strategy to maintain certain monopolistic privileges and rewards'. Turner points to the work of Jamous and Peloille (1970), who provide a useful explanation of how this professional dominance occurred.

According to Jamous and Peloille, the basis for the social prestige of a profession is the degree of **social distance** between the client and the professional. Social distance refers to the degree of access to knowledge or other social resources. Social distance – and therefore prestige – is at its greatest when the professional has access to knowledge which the client is unable to control or check. If the body of knowledge can be codified and simply broken down into clear guidelines for action, then social distance is closed, prestige is lost and skills become routinized.

Jamous and Peloille refer to this as the **indeterminacy/technicality ratio**, where indeterminacy refers to the ability of the professional to keep the patient mystified as to the exact process by which the doctor has reached a decision. Doctors, particularly surgeons, have been especially successful in maintaining a high degree of indeterminacy, which provides them with high levels of status.

Bryan Turner has also examined the relationship between the different health care professions, trying to find out how doctors have managed to emerge as the highest-status health care professionals. Turner argues that doctors do not intrinsically perform better or more functionally useful tasks than other health care occupations. What they have successfully achieved is autonomy (they control themselves) and dominance over other health care practitioners who were historically in competition with them.

They have done this, Turner argues, partly through the high status achieved via a high degree of indeterminacy, as described above, and partly through a process of **occupational domination**, which can be achieved in three different ways:

1 **Subordination** refers to the process of forcing other health care occupations to undertake tasks as delegated to them by doctors. Examples of this are nurses and midwives, who are formally required to submit to the occupational knowledge of doctors.
2 **Occupational limitation** refers to the situation where the dominant medical profession forces other groups to limit their activities to a particular part of the body, such as dentistry, or to a specific form of medical practice, such as chiropractic.
3 **Exclusion** occurs where the dominant medical profession can prevent competing occupations from performing health care practice, through challenging their knowledge base or by preventing access to paid occupations. For example, doctors have successfully excluded homeopathy from formal recognition as a type of medicine within the NHS.

Occupational strategies and gender: a feminist approach

As Anne Witz (1992) has pointed out, it is noticeable that many of the health care providers who were either squeezed to the margins – such as homeopaths – or placed in subordinate paramedical professions – such as nurses and midwives – were women. Witz suggests this is not just coincidence – the processes of occupational closure discussed earlier are based partly on gender inequalities. She argues that only by adding a gender dimension to discussions of professionalization in medicine can a full understanding of the process be gained.

Witz's starting point is that in the battle to gain professional status and inclusion, men have greater economic, political and prestige resources to draw upon. Witz argues that two processes in particular have been used to limit women's entry into professions. The first of these is a **gendered exclusionary strategy** by which women are blocked from entering the profession through a variety of means, such as preventing them obtaining the necessary educational qualifications.

A second, related, tactic is **gendered demarcatory strategies**, where women are restricted to a particular sphere of medical activity, under the control of male professionals. Examples of this are nursing and midwifery.

On the other hand, Witz argues that women have pursued various **inclusionary** strategies to become full members of professions, or to have their sphere of medical activity recognized as a profession.

Witz (1992) provides an analysis of how male doctors subordinated the female role of midwifery. Before the emergence of modern medicine, women dominated midwifery and it was extremely unusual for males to attend births. Few of the skills used by midwives were written down; instead, they were handed down from one generation to another, through practice. There was also no system of licensing: women were free to practise and pregnant women could choose whom they wanted to attend them. Sporadic attempts from the seventeenth century onwards by males to enter and later to dominate the profession largely failed.

However, after 1858, when the Medical Registration Act was passed in Britain, doctors were given a monopoly over medical provision, and the Act quickly began to regulate other areas of health activities. Midwifery was seen as an important area to be brought under the control of doctors and so a campaign began to subordinate midwifery to medicine.

General practitioners (GPs) were very keen to take over the role of midwifery and relegate midwives to the role of nurses – a tactic of deskilling. However, the new specialism of (male) obstetricians was prepared to support the registration of midwives as long as it was able clearly to demarcate their tasks and limit them to 'normal' births.

Midwives, faced with a choice of deskilling and exclusion by GPs, or limitation of their spheres of competence and subordination by obstetricians, chose the latter. As a result, midwives were licensed by the General Medical Council and could be struck off this register if they were deemed to have stepped outside their new, restricted competencies. All this was introduced in the 1902 Midwives Act.

Witz's analysis describes the activities of doctors who sought to take over midwifery, and also the tactics used by midwives in their struggle for medical control. The initial tactic of midwives was similar to that of the doctors, in that they attempted to introduce a formal system of education and licensing to allow them to attend the complete range of labours, from normal to abnormal. Witz describes this as **revolutionary dual closure**, which refers to the attempt to close off this area of practice by excluding doctors and by developing a specialist area of knowledge. However, doctors foiled this plan, and midwives were forced into a tactic of **accommodative dual closure**. Here, they accepted a subordinate role to obstetricians, but retained control over 'normal' births, and a licensing system was introduced which gave them a monopoly over 'normal' childbirth. By means of an alliance with obstetricians they closed this area of health care practice to GPs.

Challenges to the dominance of doctors

In the last twenty-five years there has been an increasing challenge to the occupational dominance of doctors. Sociologists have suggested three differing processes which might help to explain this.

Haug (1973) argued that a form of **de-professionalization** has taken place in medicine, as doctors have lost their monopoly over medical knowledge within a better-educated society. This fits in with the development in late modernity of a stress on individual choice, which is as evident in medicine as elsewhere. Thus, there has been an enormous growth in alternative models of health care, such as homeopathy and the use of herbal medicines.

McKinlay and Arches (1985) argued instead that a process of **proletarianization** is taking place. The increase in management control of the health care system and the growth in numbers of doctors employed by the NHS, with carefully regulated working conditions, have combined to limit the traditional autonomy of doctors. The increase in the use of technology for diagnosing and testing patients has further emphasized this deskilling process.

Carpenter (1993) pointed to increasing challenges from other health care professionals, who seek to achieve professionalization themselves and thereby break free from the occupational dominance of doctors. Carpenter gives the example of how nurses have attempted to improve their occupational position by engaging in professionalization. According to Carpenter, nursing has passed through three stages in its professional project:

1. The first stage was from the mid-nineteenth century to the early part of the twentieth century. Under the influence of Florence Nightingale, nurses accepted that they were subservient to doctors, although a non-threatening, semi-autonomous role was constructed by nurses.
2. The second stage overlapped with the first, and covered much of the twentieth century up to the 1970s. During this time, nurses sought occupational control through exclusionary closure, by having a state-supported registration scheme and a disciplinary council (run by nurses) to oversee nursing.
3. The third stage of the 'new professionalism' was the move to obtain full professional status. This involved redefining nursing as 'clinical nursing', with most of the traditional basic care work being reclassified as appropriate for less-qualified health care assistants, who were to be supervised by nurses. A new knowledge base and occupational speciality were also proposed for the clinical nurses, and new specialisms were introduced, such as nurse practitioners and primary nursing. These developments specifically addressed the necessary traits of professionalism, while challenging the dominance of doctors – for instance, nurses were given power by parliament to prescribe a limited range of drugs.

A Marxist view of the professions in medicine

All the approaches we have looked at so far are derived from Weberian analyses and regard professional groups as competing for prestige, using whatever elements of power they are able to muster. However, Marxist analyses have also been used to explain the position of professional groups. For example, Vicente Navarro (1978) argued that the professions play a key role in social control in capitalist societies by hiding the real causes of ill-health.

Navarro rejects the Weberian argument that prestige comes from occupational closure. Instead, he argues that prestige follows from the fact that the professions already exist and have a clear location within the capitalist stratification structure. High prestige merely serves to reinforce the professionals' class position – it is not the basis of it.

Complementary or alternative medicine

Complementary medicine and **alternative medicine** are the two most commonly used terms to describe a whole range of approaches to health which reject many of the assumptions of the biomedical model discussed earlier (pp. 288–91). These approaches include a vast range of 'remedies' or 'therapies', of which the best known are probably homeopathy, osteopathy, acupuncture and herbalism. Although there has been an upsurge of interest in alternative medicines recently, in fact most of these approaches actually predate the biomedical model, but were superseded during the period of modernity (see pp. 890–1), when approaches which did not conform to the notion of 'scientific rigour' were discounted (Saks, 1998).

Complementary/alternative medicines cover such a wide range of approaches that it is difficult to provide a precise definition, apart from the negative statement that they generally share a belief that the biomedical model's perception of the person as a form of biological machine which can be repaired through surgical or pharmaceutical intervention is mistaken. Complementary/alternative medicines instead see each person as unique and argue that both the mind and the body of the person must be taken into account in seeking to cure them.

As Cant and Sharma (1999) state:

> *Alternative medicine is at best a fluctuating and heterogeneous category, incapable of being sharply and universally demarcated from other forms of healing, or at least not in a way that is immediately applicable to the range of national situations. It is also a negative and formal category (that which is not biomedicine) rather than a substantive one.* Cant and Sharma, 1999, p. 8

According to Cant and Sharma, the use of a range of terms for complementary/alternative medicines – which include 'unofficial', 'unorthodox', 'holistic' and 'non-conventional' – reflects both the range of models of health which underlie these differing medicines, and the ability of the more powerful biomedical professions to have them defined as somehow subservient to (complementary) or less proven (alternative) than biomedicine. Cant and Sharma suggest that, for simplicity, the term 'complementary medicines' should be used when discussing the range of non-biomedical approaches which are used in Britain, but that the term 'alternative medicines' should be used when discussing them in an international context. The NHS uses both terms interchangeably – for example, it publishes an 'NHS Directory of Complementary and Alternative Medicines' – whilst the BMA tends to use the term 'alternative medicine'. In this discussion we will therefore use the term 'complementary/alternative medicines'.

Complementary/alternative medicines are widely used in the UK. Ernst and White (2000) conducted a national survey to find out the extent of usage of complementary therapies in the UK. They concluded that over 20 per cent of the population used some form of complementary therapy, most commonly herbalism, aromatherapy, homoeopathy, acupuncture/acupressure, massage and reflexology. They also calculated that over £1.6 billion is spent each year on complementary/alternative medicines as a whole.

However, it is not that people are necessarily rejecting conventional biomedical approaches and substituting complementary/alternative medicines for them; rather it would appear that people are more likely to use both approaches. Eisenberg *et al.* (2001) conducted a national study in the USA on the perceptions and use of conventional medicine and complementary therapies. They concluded that over 80 per cent saw a combination of approaches as being the most effective.

According to Sharma's (1992) research in Britain, people use complementary/alternative medicines for chronic health conditions that have not responded to orthodox medicine, and because there is a perception that there are fewer side-effects. In addition, users of complementary/alternative practitioners feel they are treated better by the practitioner, compared to a doctor, and that they are given 'more plausible' explanations of their conditions. Although there is evidence of disillusionment with biomedical medicine, people continue to use this alongside complementary/alternative approaches. Interestingly, only a minority tell their GP that they are using non-orthodox treatment.

Explaining the resurgence of complementary/alternative medicine

Two differing explanations have been offered for the re-emergence of complementary/alternative medicine, according to Saks: a postmodern and late modern explanation; and a neo-Weberian explanation.

Complementary/alternative medicines, modernity and late modernity

Saks (1998) points out that the rise of the biomedical model to a dominant position reflects, and is a partial cause of, **modernity** – a period in history characterized by rational thinking and organization and large-scale industrial production.

Socially, modernity was linked to the development of social classes and, within that, the growth of the professions. Before the dominance of the health care professions, based on biomedical models, there was a range of approaches to health care, including astrology, herbalism and spiritual healing. However, newer ways of predominantly rational thinking, which sought coherent, all-encompassing explanations for the physical and social worlds, emerged from the seventeenth century onwards. One result of this newer way of thinking and acting was the gradual marginalization of the broader range of health care options, other than biomedical ones, as these were viewed as being irrational or superstitious. By the mid-nineteenth century, as we saw earlier, medical doctors, with their scientifically based explanations for disease and bodily functioning, had gained a monopoly of medical practice.

This period from the mid-nineteenth to the mid-twentieth century saw the high tide of modernity, and with it enormous prestige being granted to experts and professionals, especially doctors.

However, modernity and modernist ways of thinking have gradually become challenged by those who argue that rational, scientific thinking and all-encompassing theories seeking to explain the natural and social worlds have over-reached themselves. Sociologists have argued that we have moved into a period of **late, or post-, modernity** in which society is characterized much more by the acceptance of a plurality of different styles of living and thinking.

Linked to this has been a general decline in the uncritical acceptance of the power of professionals in all spheres, including medicine. A further development has been the increase in the emphasis on the individual and their right to choose lifestyles, and this has been expressed through consumerism. According to Bakx (1991), the decline in the cultural dominance of biomedicine and the medical profession has resulted in the re-emergence of the plurality of complementary/alternative approaches to health. Individuals, according to Bakx, now feel empowered to make choices about their health and also their healing. This empowerment has been given a strong impetus by the increasingly obvious failure of biomedicine to combat chronic (long-term) illnesses, as opposed to acute medical problems. In the more affluent countries the increase in life expectancy has led to chronic illnesses becoming more important to a growing number of people, and there is therefore a greater interest in methods of alleviating these forms of illness.

Bakx suggests that, in a postmodern world, people wish to be actively involved in choosing solutions to problems; the medical professions, on the other hand, expect people or 'patients' to be passive and accepting of the medical decisions made by doctors:

> *From the viewpoint of advocates of the postmodern, therefore, the rise of complementary therapies could be seen to challenge orthodox medicine's epistemological authority, in the wake of the growing plurality of knowledge claims – as biomedicine becomes elativized into yet another discourse in a web of indeterminacy.* Saks, 1998, p. 208

For postmodern writers, therefore, the emergence of complementary/alternative medicines reflects a broader shift in society from modern to late or postmodern, and the future for biomedical approaches will be that they will increasingly be seen as just one option for consumers to choose from amongst a plurality of health choices.

Neo-Weberian approaches

The neo-Weberian explanation for the re-emergence of complementary/alternative medicine draws on Friedson's arguments (1994), which we examined earlier, in which he suggests that the dominance of the medical profession was the result of a successful occupational strategy to marginalize competing approaches. Saks (1998) argues that the relationship between the medical profession and complementary/alternative medicines is actually motivated by 'interest-based politics', with the biomedical profession seeking to protect their interests.

Specifically, the British Medical Association has been successful, until recently, in ensuring that only those forms of medicine which conform to the requirements of positivistic models of scientific endeavour can truly be regarded as 'medicine'. Indeed, by setting the benchmark of what is considered to be sufficient standards of evidence for measuring the effectiveness of medical intervention, the biomedical tradition has largely been successful in maintaining its superior position, unchallenged.

However, challenges by complementary/alternative medical organizations, which have become increasingly well organized and aggressive, have led to a declining confidence in the superiority of biomedical approaches. This decline in confidence was reflected by the falling numbers of children being vaccinated against mumps, measles and rubella (MMR). In 1998 a medical researcher, Wakefield, published an academic journal article which argued that there might be a link between autism and the MMR vaccination. The medical profession as a whole sought to discredit the argument, but the fall in MMR vaccinations of almost 10 per cent over a period of ten years (instead of an expected increase) perhaps demonstrates an emerging lack of trust (see Table 5.1 and Figure 5.2). Indeed, possibly as a result of the fall in take-up of the vaccination, the number of cases of mumps in the UK showed a sharp increase between 2001 and 2004.

The British Medical Association has begun to recognize this situation and has shifted its tactics from seeking to exclude complementary/alternative medicines to attempting to *subordinate* them.

Cant and Sharma (1999) use a historical and global perspective to explain the relationship between complementary/alternative and biomedical approaches. They suggest that most of the sociologists writing about medicalization have failed to take a historical or global perspective on health and have instead focused on the British and US health care systems, both unusually

Table 5.1 Immunization of children by their second birthday,[1] UK, percentages

	1981[3]	1991/92	1994/95	1999/2000	2004/05
Tetanus	83	94	96	95	94
Diphtheria	83	94	95	95	94
Poliomyelitis	82	94	95	94	94
Whooping cough	45	88	95	94	94
Measles, mumps rubella[2]	54	90	91	88	82

[1] Children reaching and immunized by their second birthday.
[2] Data exclude Scotland
[3] Includes measles-only vaccine for 1981. Combined vaccine was not available prior to 1988.

Source: Office for National Statistics (2006) *Social Trends 36*, Palgrave Macmillan, Basingstoke.

Figure 5.2 Notification of measles, mumps and rubella, 1991–2004

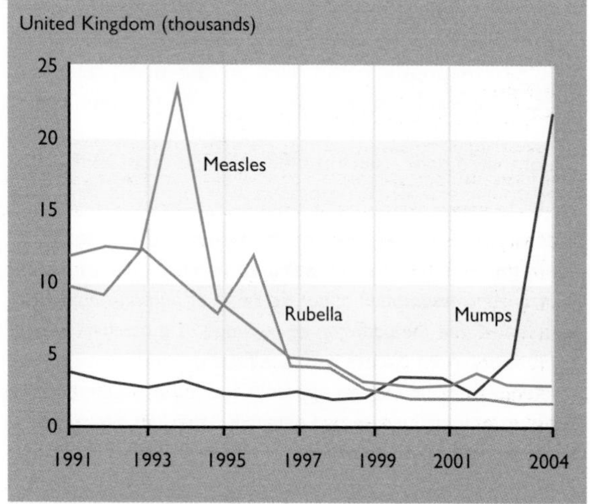

Source: Health Protection Agency, Centre for Infections; National Health Service in Scotland; Communicable Disease Surveillance Centre (Northern Ireland).

dominated by the biomedical approach. They point out that complementary/alternative medical approaches pre-dated biomedical ones and have continued to exist in various forms across all societies. According to Cant and Sharma, it is clear that biomedicine has remained just one health option available to people across the world, and the apparent dominance of the biomedical model has not been as clear-cut as commonly supposed.

This argument is supported by Bakx (1991), who suggests that we can distinguish between popular, folk and biomedical approaches. By popular, Bakx means informal caring, mainly carried out by women in the home, while 'folk' medicine refers to the complete range of alternative therapies, including physical manipulation, herbal remedies and those focusing on the mind.

Bakx argues that most health care has always taken place through popular and folk approaches; it is only state or insurance systems that have been based on biomedicine.

Conclusion

The dominance of the health 'market-place' by biomedical approaches still remains, but increasingly complementary/alternative medicine has re-emerged, reflecting a more consumerist approach to health and a decreasing level of trust in professionals. Cant and Sharma describe this current health care system as one of 'medical pluralism', by which they mean that there are different health providers and people will not simply choose between them, but use more than one at the same time.

Inequalities of health

Illness and death are generally regarded as resulting from genetic inheritance and from chance. All that an individual can do is to seek to lead as healthy a lifestyle as possible in order to maintain a healthy body and live as long as possible. As far as individuals are concerned, this may well be a reasonable way to look at one's health.

The biomedical model of health is based on the belief that the body can be viewed as a machine, which can go wrong or is poorly constructed in the first place. This chapter has explored the significance of the biomedical model of health for how medicine understands and seeks to combat disease (see pp. 288–91). Thomas McKeown sums up the sociological position:

> *Medical science and services are misdirected, and society's investment in health is not well used, because they rest on the erroneous assumption about the basis of human health. It is assumed that the body can be regarded as a machine whose protection from disease and its effects depends primarily on internal intervention. The approach has led to indifference to the external influences and personal behaviour which are the predominant determinants of health.* McKeown, 1979

One of the strongest 'cards' that sociologists have to play in their argument that it is social factors which 'cause' disease is the very clear relationship between health, disease and social divisions.

The clear outcome of sociological research is that standards of health and length of life are clearly distributed along the divisions of class, ethnicity, geography and gender. 'Chance' plays a small part in our health – far more important are social factors, which create the context in which people live their lives.

Measuring health

Before discussing the extent and causes of health inequalities, we need to understand the various definitions used in the debates.

Mortality rates refer to the number of people dying within any particular period, per 100,000 of the population. Mortality data are collected from the official registration of deaths, and the reason for death is usually based upon that stated on the death certificate. As we shall see later, how death certificates are completed can significantly influence the statistics upon which sociological explanations for health inequalities are based.

An alternative measure, often used, is that of the Standardized Mortality Ratio (or SMR). This assumes that the figure 100 stands for the average chance of death of all 16- to 65-year-olds in the population. If any particular social group has a figure above 100 then it suggests that they have a higher chance of death during that age period; if the figure is below 100 then conversely it means they have a lower chance of death than the average.

The term **morbidity** is sometimes used instead of illness or disease. Statistics used in this chapter are taken from a range of different sources. Some studies use self-reported measures of health, where individuals are asked about their own perception of their health. Other studies rely upon visits to doctors and hospital attendance. Others use medical statistics, derived from treatment patterns.

Studies of health inequality

Modern studies of the differences in mortality and morbidity can be traced back to the Black Report (1980; Townsend and Davidson, 1982).

The Black Report gathered evidence of differences in the SMRs of different social classes in Britain, using the official registry of deaths and then categorizing the SMRs by the Registrar General's classification. This involves the division of occupations into five groups or classes and is the official classification of social class used by the government. The study also drew on a wide range of morbidity statistics, largely from official sources.

The conclusions of the study were unambiguous:

> *In the case of adults between the ages of 15 and 64, for virtually all causes of death there is a consistent inverse relationship between social class and mortality. That is, the higher the social class group, the lower its SMR, and conversely the lower the social class group, the higher its SMR.* Black Report, 1980

The Black Report goes on to argue:

> *Over time ... the relative position of social class groups has remained remarkably stable ... So while mortality has been improving for the population as a whole, the gap between social class groupings has remained wide.*

The Black Report suggests that possible explanations for the differences in social class could be categorized under four headings:

1 **Artefact**: the differences are a reflection of the methodologies used to measure mortality and social class.
2 **Social selection**: the differences in social class reflect the fact that healthier people are more able to work their way up the social class structure.
3 **Cultural differences**: working-class people are more likely to engage in unhealthy lifestyles.
4 **Material differences**: the economic differences in Britain lead directly and indirectly to poorer health for the less well off and an increased chance of early death.

The Black Report has been extremely influential and these categories of explanation are still those used today. (These explanations are explored in detail on pp. 300–3.)

A more recent attempt to provide statistics on health inequalities was the Acheson Report (1998). This provided evidence of continuing inequalities and suggested that the relative differences between the social classes were actually *increasing* at the extremes of the social class divide.

In the 1970s the mortality rate among men in social class V was twice as high as for those in social class I, but by the 1990s it had increased to three times as high (see Figure 5.3). The increased differential occurred because death rates declined for all social classes, but declined more slowly for the lower social classes. Specifically, it fell by 40 per cent for social classes I and II and 30 per cent for classes IIN, IIM and IV, but only by 10 per cent for social class V. Acheson acknowledges that there has been a decline in the numbers of people in social class V, so to give a clearer measure the report combined classes IV and V, and compared this with II and I. This showed that people in social classes IV and V combined had a 68 per cent higher chance of death before the age of 65 than those in social classes I and II, compared to 53 per cent in the 1970s.

Looking at life expectancy, those in the two highest social classes increased their life expectancy by 2.0 years in the thirty years between 1970 and 2000, while those in the lower social classes experienced a smaller increase of 1.4 years.

In 1997–9, the infant mortality rate among the 'routine and manual' occupational group was 13 per cent higher than for the total population. In 2001–3, it was 19 per cent higher.

Infant mortality rates, too, are lower for those babies born into the middle classes.

Morbidity

The research shows that although mortality rates had fallen overall, the gap between the classes had grown between the times of the two reports (Black and Acheson). The situation seems even worse in terms of morbidity.

According to the Acheson Report there has been a slight increase in long-standing illness overall, and the gap has increased significantly. For example, among those aged 45–64, 17 per cent of professional men reported a limited long-standing illness, compared with 48 per cent of unskilled men. Among women, 25 per cent of professional women compared to 45 per cent of unskilled women reported limited long-standing illness in this age group.

Figure 5.3 The widening mortality gap between social classes, men of working age, England and Wales, 1930–93

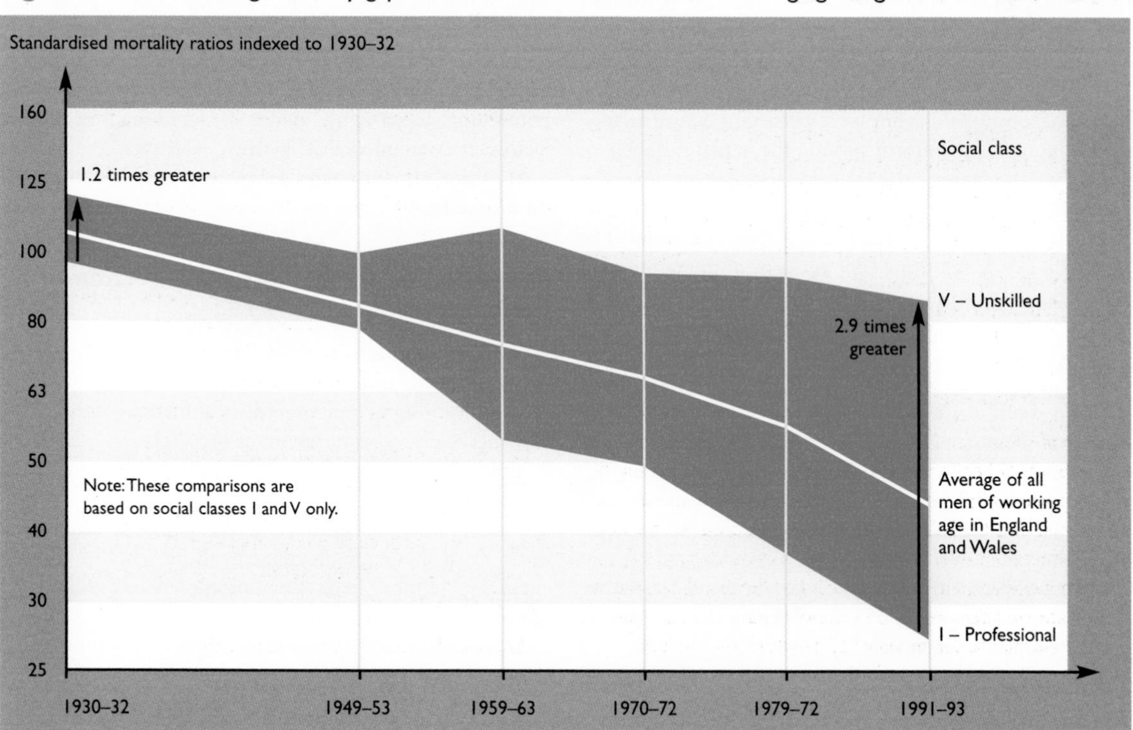

Source: Department of Health (1999) *Saving Lives: Our Healthier Nation*, The Stationery Office, London.

Class and gender differences are not limited to physical health; there were significant variations in mental health too. Fifteen per cent of women in social classes I and II were likely to suffer from mental illness, compared to 24 per cent in social classes IV and V.

Social class explanations for health inequalities

As discussed earlier, the Black Report was the first study that clearly and unambiguously demonstrated a link between social class and poor health. It suggested that there were four differing explanations:

1 Statistical artefact
2 Self-selection
3 Cultural differences
4 Material differences

Although the Black Report was published as long ago as 1980, the fourfold division into competing explanations is still the one most commonly used in academic discussion – though a considerable range of additional studies has been added. The following section follows this framework.

Statistics, health and social class: the artefact explanation

The Black Report and numerous other studies since have demonstrated a clear statistical link between mortality, ill-health and social class. However, the significance of the link has been disputed by a number of sociologists.

Illsley (1986, 1987), in particular, criticized the statistics in the Black Report for concentrating on the relative inequality between the highest and lowest classes, while neglecting absolute improvements in the health of most people.

Illsley explained this apparent contradiction by saying that although the mortality and morbidity rates of the lowest occupational groups were becoming worse relative to the higher occupational groups, the actual numbers of people in the lowest groups were in steep decline. For example, according to Illsley, during the period for the collection of statistics for the Black Report, the number of people in class V fell from 12.9 per cent of the population to 8.4 per cent, while class I increased from 1.8 per cent to 5 per cent.

This problem was specifically addressed by the Acheson Report which, as we saw earlier (p. 299), combined different social classes in order to readjust the figure. The Acheson Report compared social classes I and II (combined) with IV and V (combined). Even when the classes were combined, the report concluded there was a widening of the gap in mortality and morbidity between the higher and lower social classes.

Another problem with the mortality and morbidity statistics in relation to social class concerns the categorization of people's occupations.

Carr-Hill (1987) pointed out that when he examined death certificates, he found that the 'profession' recorded was often incorrectly categorized and this meant that statistics based on death certificates might well be inaccurate. An example of how important this could be is illustrated by the work of Le Grand and Pamuk on health inequalities.

Le Grand's (1985) evidence was collected by examining individual death certificates, while Pamuk (1985) collated existing information which distinguished social class groups. The outcome was that Le Grand found smaller differences between groups than Pamuk.

From a more radical Marxist perspective, Scambler (2002) criticized the measurement of social class used in the Black and Acheson reports, as well as that used by the government in its White Paper, *Saving Lives: Our Healthier Nation* (Department of Health, 1999).

Scambler raised the issue of just how accurate the Registrar General's measure of social class and the other classificatory schemes used in the various studies has been in *sociological* terms. Scambler argues that by using socio-economic divisions, such as the Registrar General's classification, attention is taken away from the ruling class. This has produced a framework in which the debate over health inequalities ignores the massive differences in wealth and power between the ruling class and the majority of the population – a majority which includes professionals in social classes I and II.

Some sociologists, such as Saunders (1993), are doubtful about the usefulness of social class in understanding contemporary society. They suggest that conventional uses of the term 'social class' ignore differences in consumption and other specific lifestyle activities, which have become increasingly important in recent decades. (See pp. 24–5 for Saunders's views on social class.)

Saunders suggests that by focusing on consumption rather than occupation, more specific factors can be isolated which influence health. Support for this comes from Smith and Jacobson's (1988) study, which showed that women aged 15–59 at death and who had no access to a car had an SMR of 135, compared to an SMR of only 83 for women with access to a car. The equivalent figures for men were 121 and 85. The large-scale British Regional Heart Study studied 8,000 middle-aged men in Britain, controlling for a wide range of social and economic factors. It concluded that for men who were neither car owners nor home owners, social class had little influence on mortality.

Ill-health and social class: the direction of the relationship

A second approach to understanding the relationship between health and social class has been to explain social class position as an outcome of health status, rather than viewing health as an outcome of social class.

Illsley (1987) argued that it is perfectly reasonable to assume that fitter, healthier people are more likely to take the higher social positions at the expense of those who suffer from illness or disability, as those who are fit and energetic are more likely to be promoted and to have the opportunity to work hard.

In support of this argument, Wadsworth (1986) used information from a national sample of males and found a close relationship between illness in childhood and adult social status. For example, 36 per cent of those from non-manual backgrounds who experienced ill-health in childhood suffered downward social mobility, compared to 23 per cent of those who had good health.

This sort of argument has been rejected by Shaw *et al.* (1999), who argue that any examination of the evidence will show that those from poorer backgrounds are faced with a range of economic, social and employment factors which combine to create ill-health. From this point of view, class position shapes health and not the other way round.

Cultural factors

The third type of explanation suggested in the Black Report emphasized cultural factors.

This sort of approach suggests that people from lower social classes may be more likely to engage in risky or unhealthy lifestyles, which have an effect upon long-term health, and can lead to early death (see Figure 5.4). The obvious examples are that smoking cigarettes leads to heart disease and various forms of cancer, and eating fatty foods leads to obesity and heart disease.

An extensive range of research studies over the last twenty years (summarized in Department of Health, 1999) have shown that working-class people are more likely to smoke, eat less fruit and vegetables, consume higher amounts of sugar and have diets with higher levels of fat. All of these things can lead to higher levels of morbidity and increased death rates. Consumption of alcohol, too, is higher among working-class males.

Research has also shown that there is a relationship between levels of exercise and social class. There is also a higher rate of domestic accidents among poorer families.

The key point underlying this approach is that the 'blame' for the high-risk lifestyle can be located either with the individual or with the social milieu in which they live. Those who support this approach argue that the only way to eradicate differences in health between social classes is to provide educational campaigns which persuade people to engage in 'healthier' lifestyles, including changes in diet, exercise regimes and smoking levels.

Critics of this approach argue that working-class people are more likely to engage in risky behaviour as a rational response to their circumstances.

A good example of this is Graham's (1993) research on smoking behaviour among low-income mothers. Graham argues that smoking is a way for poorer women to cope with the situation in which they live. It may also be a way of saving money, as smoking cigarettes can be used as a substitute for eating. In later research, Graham and Blackburn (1998) demonstrate that mothers on income support have much lower levels of 'psycho-social health' than the majority of the population and, for them, smoking provides a means of relief.

Keith Paterson (1981) argues that the cultural approach fails to consider the underlying structure of society, which he believes actually creates these risks. As a result, risks themselves are depoliticized. For example, it is the inequalities and poverty of capitalism which ensure that certain groups in the population are unable to afford 'healthier' foods. Furthermore, capitalism may benefit from the continuation of these differences in lifestyle. Capitalists make profits from selling unhealthy foods, so they continue to advertise and promote unhealthy lifestyles.

Figure 5.4 Smoking, lung cancer and social class

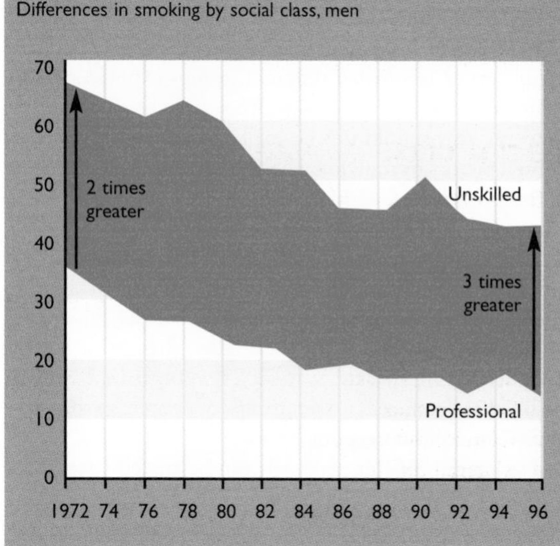

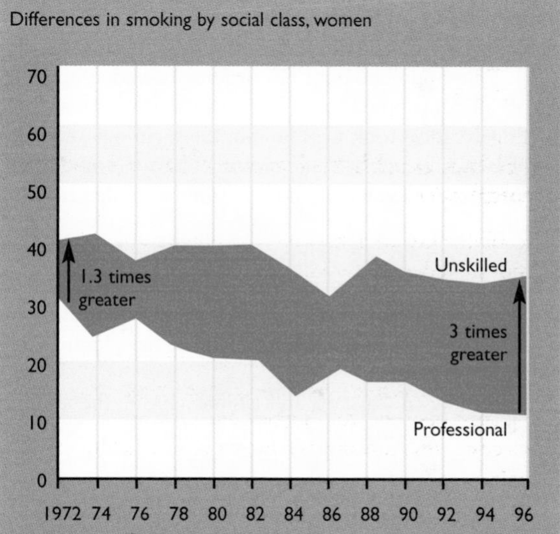

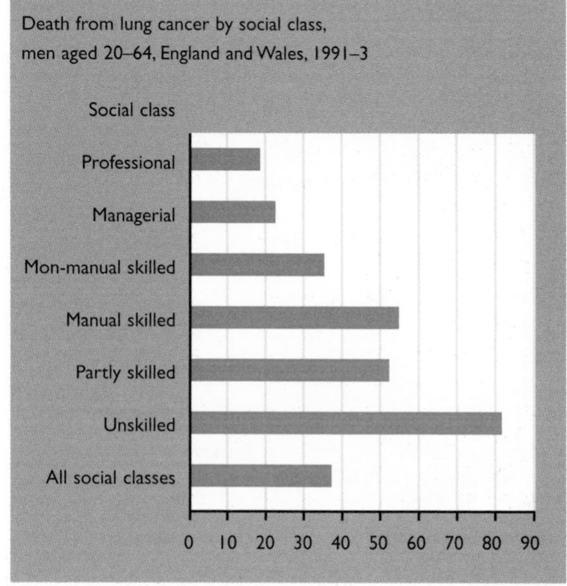

Source: Department of Health (1999) *Saving Lives: Our Healthier Nation*, The Stationery Office, London.

The materialist or structural approach to health argues that the main influences on a person's health chances can be traced back to the structure of society and the resulting conditions of life which different groups experience. The poorer a person, the less chance they have of good health. However, this should not be explained solely in terms of cultural factors or individual behaviour, but should be seen in the context of wider, political, economic and social structures.

This approach does not deny the differences in behaviour which lead to ill-health and high mortality rates among less affluent groups, but argues that the differences are not the real reasons for the higher rates of ill-health. Instead, it claims that the way society is organized systematically disadvantages certain groups of people, so that they inevitably experience poor health.

The origins of this approach can be traced back as far as Engels, Marx's collaborator, who undertook an extensive study of Manchester factory workers in the latter part of the nineteenth century (Engels, 1974, first published 1845). He concluded that ill-health was a direct outcome of capitalists' pursuit of profit. The dangerous work, long hours and poor pay (leading to under-nourishment) all contributed to the early death of workers.

Engels's ideas took firm hold in the sociology of health and illness, and a great range of studies have pointed to the importance of wider economic factors in determining health.

Accident rates are highest among those in the more dangerous manual occupations, such as factory and building work. Martin *et al.* (1987) argue that those who live in poorer housing conditions tend to have higher rates of respiratory disease.

According to Carstairs and Morris (1989), the association between eating habits and ill-health (see p. 301) can be understood less as cultural choice and more as a response to lack of income to buy better quality foodstuffs. This is illustrated by Lobstein's (1995) study of the cost of healthy and unhealthy food in London. In 1988 and 1995, Lobstein compared prices and foodstuffs available in a more affluent part and a poorer part of London. It emerged that healthy food actually cost less in the more affluent areas of London than in the poorer areas, while unhealthy foodstuffs were slightly cheaper in the poorer areas than in the more affluent areas. Poorer people were more likely to have to pay more for healthy food.

Furthermore, the structure and ownership of food outlets have an impact upon the food choices of poorer people. A survey by the Department of Health (1996) found that the total number of food retailers had declined by 35 per cent in the previous twelve-year period as a result of the growth in out-of-town supermarkets and a decline in smaller, local shops. Wrigley (1998) argues that these supermarkets are less available to poorer people without access to cars; and even if they do have transport, the costs of travel will leave them with less money for food.

The significance of diet for determining health standards is underlined by Blane *et al.* (1997), who calculated that 15 per cent of all early deaths are caused by poor diets.

One of the clearest studies demonstrating the link between material circumstances and ill-health comes from the American Multiple Risk Factor Intervention Trial, in which over 300,000 men were screened for a period of sixteen years for a range of health and socio-economic factors (Davey-Smith *et al.*, 1996). A clear pattern emerged: the age-adjusted relative death rate of the poorest group of subjects was twice that of the richest group. If the relative rates were further adjusted for differences between income groups in cigarette smoking, blood pressure, cholesterol levels, heart disease and diabetes, then the mortality rates of the poorest groups remained proportionately much higher than the more affluent groups, despite taking these factors into account. This suggested that socio-economic factors had a strong influence on the mortality rates independently of standards of health.

Doyal and Pennell (1979) argue that material factors which cause ill-health are not an unfortunate by-product of differences in society, but an inevitable outcome of capitalist society. For example, they point out the dangers to the health of workers employed in factories where chemicals and asbestos are used. Evidence to support the link between employment and ill-health was provided by Richard Clapp *et al.* (2005) who suggest that about 12 per cent of deaths from cancer are workplace-related, and work by Meldrumm *et al.* (2005) which indicates that between 15 and 20 per cent of deaths from lung disease are caused by work conditions.

Doyal and Pennell also argue that the sheer pace and pressure of work in capitalist societies causes illness and stress – particularly for those employed in manual work:

> *Industrial health strategies have been developed within the limits set by a capitalist economy and the overall thrust has been towards the adjustment of workers to the pace and the physical conditions of the production process, rather than the reverse.* Doyal and Pennell, 1979

Beyond the workplace, they argue that higher levels of cigarette smoking result from the advertising industry's portrayal of smoking as both desirable and a form of stress relief for the poor.

Doyal and Pennell also claim that differences in dietary intake by the poorest people are partly a result of differences in income. The poor cannot afford to buy better food; more importantly, the food industry, in its search for profit, produces poor-quality and harmful food, high in chemicals, salts and sugars. Such food causes obesity and ill-health:

> *Most people in the developed capitalist world now have enough to eat, but the balance and the quality of their diet have produced a new kind of malnutrition – obesity. Too much food (often of the wrong kind) ... now constitutes a major health problem.* Doyal and Pennell, 1979

Doyal and Pennell directly link health differences, caused by working conditions and cigarette smoking and food consumption, to the nature of capitalism and its search for ever greater profits. The state, rather than protecting the interests of workers by controlling standards of food and enforcing health and safety at work, instead collaborates with the interests of the owners of commerce and industry to allow practices which lead to poor health:

> *Thus government policies with regard to food or any other potentially dangerous commodity are constrained by a range of economic and social interests which are often in direct conflict with wider health needs.* Doyal and Pennell, 1979

Materialist explanations and the life course model

Shaw *et al.* (1999) reviewed most of the main studies conducted in Britain over the previous twenty years, as well as conducting their own research into geographical inequalities. Overall, Shaw and her colleagues were convinced that the main reason for inequalities in health could be traced back to material factors. However, they found that this general approach ignores too many individual and group variations in health. They suggest that, within the overall material approach, sociologists should also be aware of the way the poorest people accumulate a range of disadvantages in health over their lifetime. There is no one cause or set of causes, but a slow process of disadvantage caused ultimately by the social factors that create inequality.

Shaw *et al.* identify a number of critical periods in the life course (such as nutrition, growth and health in childhood, and job loss and insecurity) when health is affected by events. Events build up through a 'multiplier effect' to damage health over time.

Beyond class: inequality and social capital

Recently, sociologists have become increasingly interested in the concept of **social capital**, and refer to the social advantages which certain groups have over others. The best-known example of the use of social capital in an analysis of health differences is a study by Wilkinson.

Wilkinson: Unhealthy Societies

Wilkinson (1996) argues that there is a clear, quantifiable relationship between income inequality and poor health. He bases his conclusions on detailed statistical surveys of mortality levels, income distribution and levels of wealth drawn from a number of countries, primarily the UK, the USA and Japan.

Wilkinson suggests that an **epidemiological transition** occurs once a country achieves a certain standard of living (which he estimated as a Gross Domestic Product (GDP) of $5,000 per head of population). At this level of national wealth, death rates decline quite markedly; the diseases which kill so many people in poorer countries decline; and death is more likely to come from diseases such as cancer, which occur later in life.

Wilkinson says:

> *The term [epidemiological transition] is used to demarcate the change from predominantly infectious causes of death, still common in poorer countries, to the degenerative diseases which have become the predominant cause of death in richer countries.* Wilkinson, 1996

Poorer countries which have not reached the epidemiological transition will have significantly different – and worse – standards of health compared to richer countries.

However, beyond this threshold level, Wilkinson argues, any further increases in total societal wealth will have very limited impact on overall mortality rates. Therefore:

> *Apparently regardless of the fact that health differences within societies remain so closely related to socio-economic status, once a country has passed through the epidemiological transition, its whole population can be more than twice as rich as any other country without being healthier.* Wilkinson, 1996

The only factor which can improve the health of the less well off in a society which has passed through the epidemiological transition is an increase in income equality. To support this claim, Wilkinson draws upon statistics on mortality and income distribution for the more affluent nations belonging to the OECD (Organization for Economic Cooperation and Development), and provides more detailed information drawn from studies in the United States, England and Wales, and Japan.

According to Wilkinson, it is not the absolute standard of living which is important, but the *distribution* of income in society. He goes on to calculate that a shift of 7 per cent in the share of income going to the bottom 50 per cent of the population would result in a two-year increase in their life expectancy.

Wilkinson's explanation for the link between levels of inequality and health derives from the earlier work of Putnam and his concept of social capital (see Chapter 15, pp. 863–6). Wilkinson argues that where there is a high degree of income inequality in a rich country, social divisions become exacerbated, levels of trust and strength of community life tend be lower, and rates of social anxiety and chronic stress tend to be higher.

The result is a **culture of inequality** characterized by a 'more hostile and less hospitable social environment' which leads directly to poor health and the 'experience of low social status or subordination' felt by the poorest in an unequal society.

Wilkinson's work is particularly interesting because it links the various levels of analysis that other writers have explored. It incorporates materialist or structural arguments as the background for cultural differences, which in turn place greater stress on individuals.

Criticisms of Wilkinson

Scambler (2002) points out that Wilkinson has been criticized for his certainty that the epidemiological transition takes place at $5,000 GDP per head of population, and that there are errors in the calculations which led to this figure. Furthermore, Wilkinson is vague on exactly how the concept of social trust can be measured. He also fails to spell out the mechanism by which a lack of social trust can lead to ill-health.

Wilkinson relies upon secondary sources from a range of different organizations in a number of countries for his statistics on wealth, inequality and mortality. These statistics are based upon different definitions of inequality and wealth, and different methodologies are used to collect the data. If these statistics are unreliable, then his theory may also be questionable.

Gender and health inequalities

Gender differences

Self-report studies, which are studies based on asking people to rate their own levels of health, are regularly

Figure 5.5 Life expectancy at birth, by deprivation group and sex, 1994–9

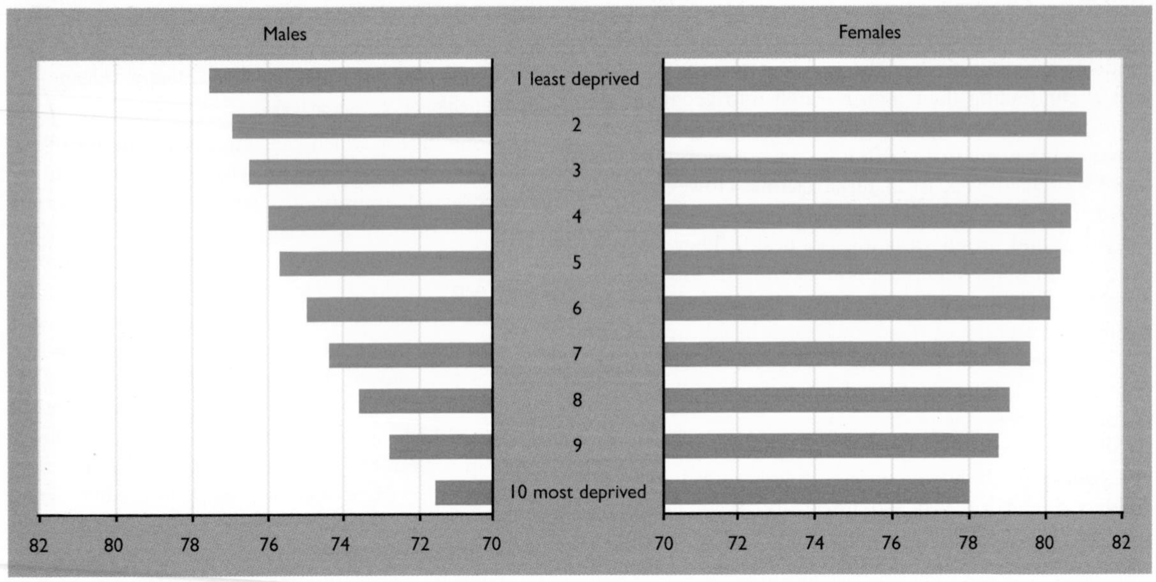

Source: Office for National Statistics (2006) *Social Trends 36*, Palgrave Macmillan, Basingstoke, p. 100, figure 7.2.

conducted by the British government. These consistently show that women have higher rates of illness and 'restricted activity' than men. They also have significantly higher levels of depression. However, women are more likely to live longer than men – though the additional years of life are often dogged by poor health.

Explanations for gender differences in health and mortality

Three kinds of explanations have been suggested for differences in morbidity and mortality between males and females.

1. **Artefact**: explanations of differences between men and women are often based on self-reports, which involve individuals assessing their own levels of illness. This has led some commentators to suggest that the higher levels of ill-health reported by women reflect their subjective beliefs rather than objective reality. However, a study by MacIntyre (1993) found that men were significantly more likely than women to over-rate their symptoms in comparison to a clinical observer. As a result, MacIntyre suggests that the real rates of illness for women are significantly higher than the official figures indicate.
2. **Genetic**: although most sociologists would argue that the major part of the explanation for differences in health can be traced to social factors, there is an acceptance that some of the explanation is based upon genetic factors. Waldron (1983), for example, argues that women have greater resistance to heart disease because of genetic differences.
3. **Social causation**: the main explanations for gender inequalities centre on three social factors: risk, social deprivation and female roles.

Risk

One of the most notable differences between male and female patterns of mortality is the higher death rate of young males aged 17–24 (see Figure 5.6). This is closely linked to the younger male's propensity to take risks and the associated higher death rate from motor vehicle accidents. Furthermore, males have higher rates of cigarette smoking and alcohol consumption. Lyng (1990) suggests that one way to understand the higher-risk activities of males is to see them in terms of the male role in society, which encourages young males to engage in what he terms 'edgework' – that is, deliberately risky behaviour.

Social deprivation

All the evidence available links poverty to ill-health. This leads Miller and Glendinning (1989) to argue that women are much more economically disadvantaged than men, on average receiving about 80 per cent of male wages, forming the overwhelming majority of single parents, and being more likely to be reliant upon state benefits. The result is considerably poorer health among women in general.

Female roles

Graham (1984) argues that within households, as a result of having day-to-day responsibility for household budgets, women are more likely to reduce spending upon themselves when income is limited, and to spend it upon the male partner and children instead.

Popay and Bartley (1989) suggest that not enough attention has been paid to the health consequences of domestic labour, and that the 'labour conditions' of the home can be compared with factory conditions. Thus, such things as noise, damp, cold and stress caused by repetitive work all have an impact on the morbidity of women at home.

Popay and Bartley studied the domestic labour patterns of 1,700 households in London, and found that women with children spent 64 hours each week on domestic tasks if they had a full-time job, 75 hours if they had a part-time job, and 87 hours if they had no employment. Popay and Bartley argue that the number of hours of work and the poor conditions contribute to women's poor health compared to men.

Figure 5.6 Prevalence of major accidents, by gender and age, England, 1996

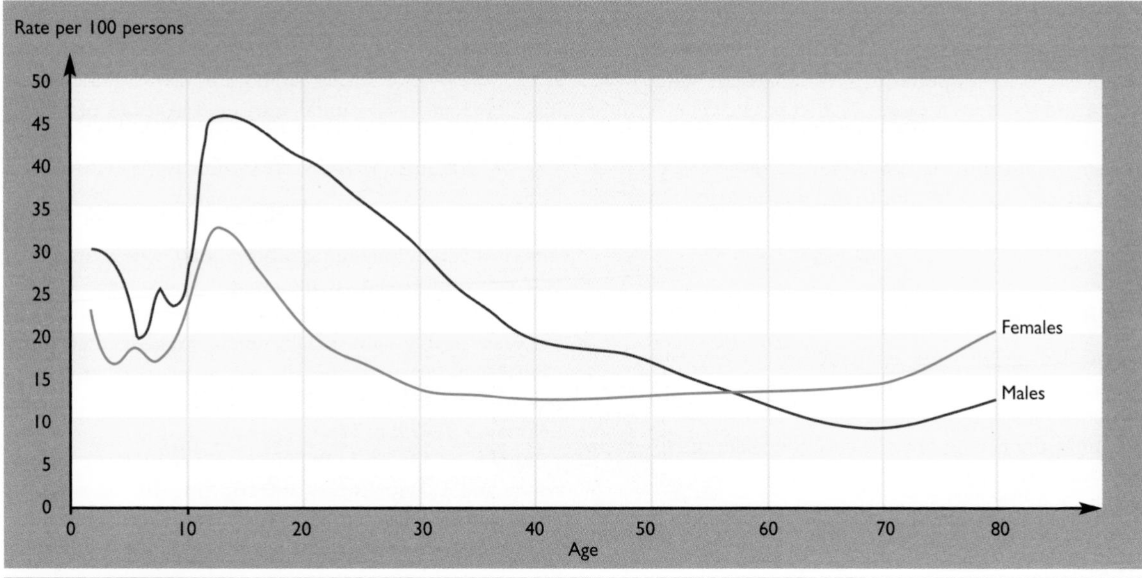

Source: Department of Health (1999) *Saving Lives: Our Healthier Nation*, The Stationery Office, London.

Table 5.2 Standardized mortality ratios, by country of birth, selected causes, men and women aged 20–69, England and Wales, 1989–99

	All causes		Coronary heart disease		Stroke		Lung cancer		Breast cancer
	Men	Women	Men	Women	Men	Women	Men	Women	Women
All countries	100	100	100	100	100	100	100	100	100
Scotland	132	136	120	130	125	125	149	169	114
Ireland	139	120	124	120	138	123	151	147	92
East Africa	110	103	131	105	114	122	42	17	84
West Africa	113	126	56	62	271	181	62	51	125
Caribbean	77	91	46	71	168	157	49	31	75
South Asia	106	100	146	151	155	141	45	33	59

Source: Department of Health (1999) *Saving Lives: Our Healthier Nation*, The Stationery Office, London.

'Race' and health

Pearson (1991) argues that collecting data on 'race' and health is problematic, as definitions of 'race' and ethnicity vary between studies. For example, the term 'Asian' can include a range of different groups of people varying in nationality, place of birth, religion and language.

Some patterns emerge, however, with people from the Indian subcontinent having the highest levels of heart disease and those from Caribbean backgrounds suffering particularly high levels of strokes (see Table 5.2).

The explanations for such health variations focus on genetic, cultural and socio-economic factors. According to Nettleton (1995), however, 'although genetic differences may have some influence … they are unable to account for the wider "racial" patterning of health status'.

Cultural accounts of different health and lifestyle behaviour have been particularly common and influential on government policy. Cultural differences have included the higher levels of rickets among 'Asian' children because of a dietary deficiency in vitamin D.

The problem with the cultural explanation is that when it is imposed upon social class differences in health, it tends to place the blame upon individuals and regard improvements in health as lying in the choices of the persons themselves. Positive cultural health practices may be ignored: for example, the low rates of smoking and alcohol consumption among many Asian groups.

> *In this perspective, racialized inequalities in both health and access to health care are explained as resulting from cultural differences and deficits … Institutional racism and racial discrimination have no part in this equation.* Ahmad, 1993

If we turn to wider socio-cultural factors, particularly associated with 'race', rather different reasons emerge for health variations between ethnic groups.

The first piece of evidence is (as for women) the higher rate of poverty and deprivation among minority ethnic groups in Britain. This includes poorer housing conditions, a concentration in some of the most deprived neighbourhoods, employment in more hazardous areas of work and in shift-work, higher unemployment and lower wages.

Linked to all this, minority ethnic groups suffer from racism and the stress it causes. Nettleton (1995), in a study of Asian women in northern England, concluded that the women regarded 'social isolation, fear and frequency of racist attacks, and cold and damp housing to be the main causes of their poor physical and mental health'.

Health and place

Social class, gender and ethnicity are all key factors in understanding health inequalities, but another element has also been recognized by sociologists – that of place. Using data from the census, Shaw *et al.* (1999) identified which parliamentary constituencies had the highest number of people dying before retirement age (the mortality rate) and which had the lowest numbers dying. They then constructed two lists: one containing all the constituencies with the 1 million people with the highest mortality rate; the other with the constituencies with the 1 million people with the lowest rate.

They then controlled, for the million people dying early in each list, for gender and social class. What emerged was that irrespective of class and gender there were still enormous differences in the chances of living beyond retirement age. Shaw *et al.* point out: 'Had the mortality ratios of the "worst health" million been the same as the "best health" million then 62 per cent of the deaths under 65 would not have occurred in the period 1991–5.'

Shaw *et al.* argue that these differences in chances of death are linked by a mixture of 'spatial', social and economic factors, which combine over a person's lifetime to affect the age of death.

Joshi *et al.* (2000) argue that there is a distinction to be made between social composition and social context in understanding health inequalities. **Social composition** refers to particular groups which share certain characteristics – for example, social classes, ethnic groups and gender divisions. **Social context** refers to the social dynamics of individuals with their physical environment and with each other. Therefore Joshi *et al.* suggest that we need to look beyond the traditional categories of social class, gender and 'race'.

Beyond class, gender and ethnicity: the emergence of social capital

It is precisely this movement beyond class, 'race' and gender that is taken up by proponents of the concept of social capital. The concept has been most closely linked to the work of Putnam (1995). There is also a clear link to Durkheim's much earlier writings on social integration and anomie.

Putnam says:

> *By social capital I mean features of social life – networks, norms, and trust – that enable participants to act together more effectively to pursue shared objectives ... To the extent that the norms, networks and trust link substantial sectors of the community and span underlying social cleavages ... [then] those who have wider and more closely integrated social networks ... feel a sense of well-being.* Putnam, 1995

Social capital has become increasingly used by sociologists to provide an explanation of health and mortality differences between groups in society, as an alternative to class, gender or ethnicity-based analyses. Work by Cooper *et al.* (1999) gave strong support to the argument that high levels of social capital, measured in terms of a sense of belonging to the local community and active membership in local organizations, were directly related to good health.

Putnam himself claimed that, 'As a rough rule of thumb, if you belong to no groups but decide to join one, you cut your risk of dying over the next year in half' (2000, p. 331); and Halpern, in a review of the links between health and social capital, suggests that social capital 'may act to buffer the effects of social stress and that its presence might generate a sense of wellbeing and belonging' (1999, p. 22).

However, David J. Pevalin and David Rose (2004) conducted a major survey, interviewing 10,000 adults in 5,000 separate households over a period of nine years. They used a range of sophisticated techniques to measure the extent of social capital that each individual had; this involved a range of questions on friendships, group membership, degree of social support and sense of trust in the community. The outcome of their research was not particularly supportive of the arguments for social capital.

Pevalin and Rose concluded that social capital did have an impact on health, but was less important than social deprivation. They concluded that 'programmes or policies that encourage ... social capital through involvement in the community may produce benefits for health but they will do little to negate the more fundamental inequalities in health'.

This seems to suggest that social capital interacts with other material factors, particularly social deprivation, to influence levels of health. A good example of this interaction is provided by Wilkinson's international study of the relationship between social capital, inequality and health (see p. 303 for a discussion of this study).

Conclusion

Poor health and high death rates are not the result of random factors, but are patterned along lines of ethnicity, gender and social class. Without doubt there are very considerable methodological problems concerning the definitions and measurement of health and mortality and their relationship to different social categories. However, despite the inaccuracies, enough evidence has been uncovered to prove that social factors play a powerful role in deciding the health chances and the length of life of individuals. Exactly which social factors have the greatest impact in bringing about specific diseases is only slowly becoming understood, but they appear to be those linked to wider social processes rather than those which appear to have an immediate impact on health.

> *It is clear that with the continued existence of poverty and inequality, those living in less advantaged social circumstances receive the worst end of the deal whatever the actual diseases and the set of exposures which mediate between social disadvantage and disease are.*
> Shaw *et al.*, 1999

The body

The focus of all medicine is the human body, yet curiously, until relatively recently, the body was not seen as something which was relevant to sociological research; rather the body was seen as something natural which was outside the domain of sociology.

This **naturalistic** perspective is closely linked with the biomedical model we discussed earlier (see pp. 288–91). This approach sees the body as a natural, biological entity in which a normal functioning body can be distinguished from an abnormal body. This model stresses how knowledge and understanding of the workings of the body have been developed over time by doctors and medical researchers. It is the view of the 'body' taught in medical schools and demonstrated in anatomy textbooks.

Thomas Laqueur (1990), for example, studied the way in which males and females were understood in medical discourse up to the nineteenth century. According to Laqueur, the accepted understanding of the body until the 1800s was that males and females had identical sexual organs; it was merely that the male ones were on the outside and the female's on the inside, with the ovaries referred to (and perceived) as the female testicles and so on. According to Laqueur, the normal body was that of the male, reflecting ideological views on the superiority of the male over the female.

A similar conclusion was arrived at by Lawrence and Bendixen (1992) who studied medical textbooks published from the latter part of the nineteenth century up to 1989; once again the diagrams and text referred to the male body as the norm, with the female body either not appearing in the textbooks at all, or referred to as a variant of the male body.

Sociologists are not saying that the contemporary anatomical understanding of the body is incorrect, merely that the way it is looked at and comprehended – the clinical gaze, as Foucault terms it (pp. 309–10) – does have a social element which needs exploring,

The impact of society on the body

The first and perhaps simplest approach to the sociology of the body stresses the way in which social factors interact with the biological to influence the shape and health of the body. For example, Connell (1987) argues that males are not

Figure 5.7 Plastinated runner, by Gunther von Hagens

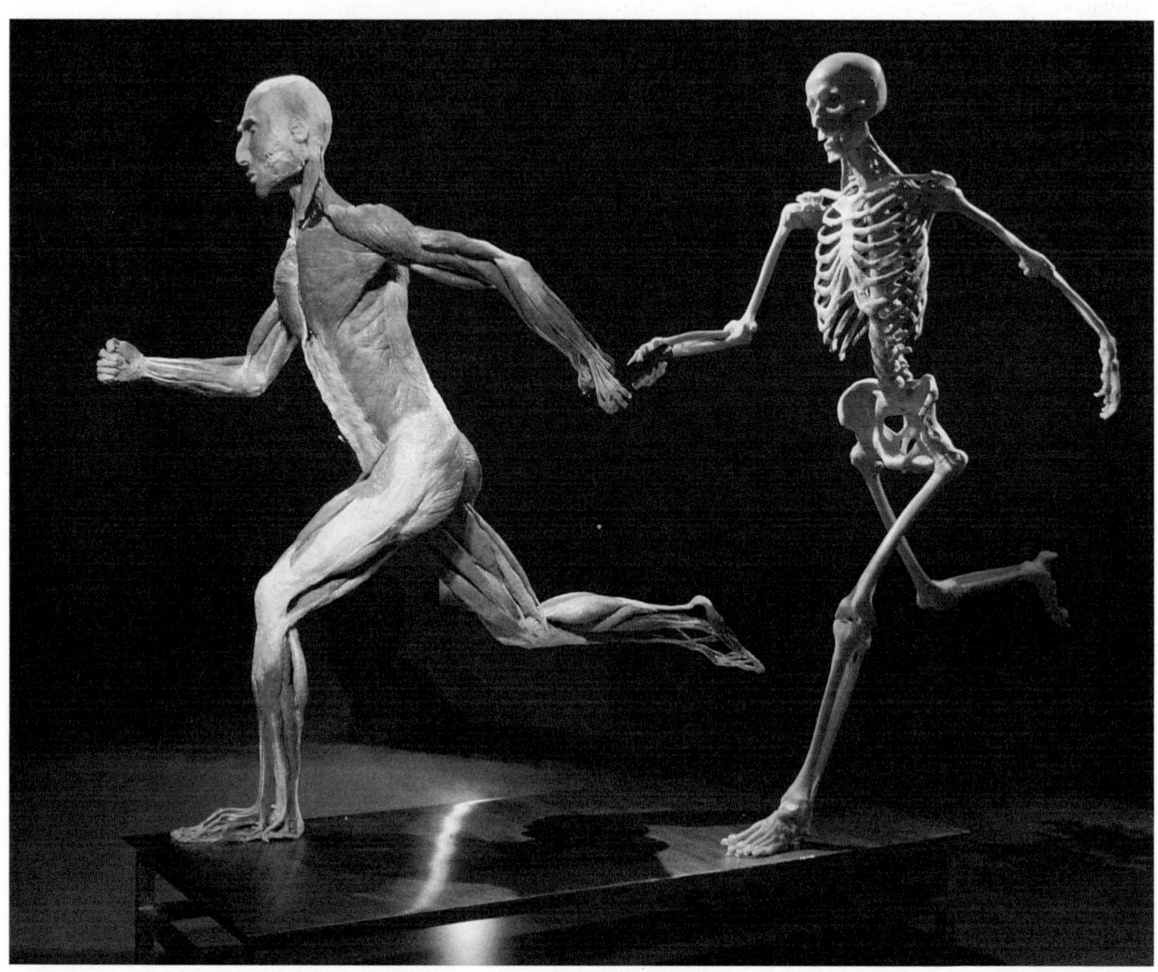

Source: Getty Images

necessarily naturally stronger, taller and more muscular than females. Indeed, variations within the sexes are possibly as great as between the sexes. However, males are encouraged to engage in sport from an early age and the consequence of the stress on male strength and sporting prowess is that men tend to be more likely to develop a muscular physique.

This is not necessarily biologically determined and Connell points to other societies, such as the Berber women in the Atlas Mountains of Morocco, where it is the women who are expected to undertake the more strenuous tasks and who therefore develop more muscular physiques. So, the actual physiques of males and females are partly developed from the expectations we have of 'correct' male and female bodies.

Dickens (2001), writing from a Marxist perspective, argues that capitalism has a major impact on the form of bodies, in that different types of employment and life experiences can alter the body, such that capitalism comes to 'modify human biology in its own image'.

Evidence to support this comes from Bury and Wadsworth's longitudinal study of individuals over forty-three years (cited in Bury, 1991). They concluded that obesity and raised blood pressure levels were directly linked to deprivation over an individual's lifetime.

In Britain a government survey published in 2006 found that 30 per cent of women in manual occupations were obese, compared with 16 per cent in professional occupations (NHS Information Centre, 2006).

Finally, Freund *et al.* (2003) examined the impact of repetitive manual labour on the bodies of men engaged in this form of work. They suggest that a process of both **overload** and **underload** takes place in manual labour, with excessive pace of work overloading the physical body, and dull, repetitive tasks leading to an underload when it comes to mental stimulation. They argue that this has a direct impact upon the body and upon health, with increased signs of ageing and higher levels of heart attacks.

Giddens, the body and late modernity

Anthony Giddens (1991) linked changes in the way the body is perceived with the move from modernity to late modernity (see pp. 895–9). He argues that in late modernity identity and appearance are crucial concepts, and that the key to understanding these concepts is through an examination of how people see their bodies.

In particular, Giddens argues that in late modernity people see their bodies as things which can be altered and shaped according to fashion or individual whim. In much the same way that people have traditionally chosen to express an image through their clothes, in late (or, as Giddens calls it, 'high') modernity, they can also express themselves through altering their bodies. This may involve cosmetic surgery and tattooing and piercing, as well as dieting and using beauty treatments. Giddens calls this sense of being able to look 'from the outside' at one's own body, **reflective mobilization**.

Late modernity has therefore altered notions of health and illness, giving people choice over what they want their body to be. However, this choice also causes problems, as it creates anxieties in people over just what choices they *ought* to make – Giddens calls this the **manufactured uncertainty of everyday life**. People are more open to suggestion as to what choice to make, and the suggestions are usually generated by the media, which provide images of what the perfect body is like. Giddens claims this has significant implications for health, as people use drugs or diet in order to achieve socially valued body shapes.

Giddens argues that this idea of self-transformation also has implications for sexual identification, which was once seen as fixed, with one type of sexuality regarded as normal and others regarded as perversions. Today, Giddens suggests, 'normal sexuality is simply one type of lifestyle choice amongst others'.

According to Featherstone (1991), the body has been the focus of this consumption, and he describes the body as the 'visible carrier of the self'.

Lash and Urry (1994) argue that this new period of consumption has led to a new form of capitalism, which they call **disorganized capitalism**. This form of capitalism is even more effective than the old one at getting people to pay for goods and services. A wide range of new services have sprung up to exploit concerns about health, identity and the body. Whereas these things had always been seen as 'natural', in late modernity they are consumer items which can be bought.

This has led to the growth in private health care, health farms, expensive diets and the purchase of over-the-counter health products. For example, in the USA, Weight Watchers, a commercial slimming organization, claims 8 million members. In Britain, a study showed that only 10 per cent of women claimed that they had never dieted (Ogden, 1992).

The body as a project

According to Chris Shilling (2003), human bodies are best seen as unfinished social and physical constructions which are transformed through social influences. Shilling refers to the 'body as a project' and argues that individuals now see the body as an entity which 'should be worked at and accomplished as part of an individual's self-identity' (2003, p. 5). Shilling argues that this is the case because technology now allows people to alter their bodies, and also because in late modernity there is increasing awareness that the body is unfinished and can be shaped in line with lifestyle choices.

In a society dominated by issues of risk and uncertainty, the body has become a secure site, over which people feel able to exercise some control. 'If one feels unable to exert control over an increasingly complex society, at least one can have some effect on the size, shape and appearance of one's body' (Shilling, 2003, p. 6).

Shilling is partly influenced by Giddens, but also by Norbert Elias, who was probably the first sociologist to explore the sociology of the body in *The Civilizing Process* (1978).

Elias argues that Western society has engaged in a civilizing process since medieval court society. Up until early medieval times social interaction was characterized by unpredictability and emotions – rationality and polite behaviour, in our understanding of the terms, simply did not exist. Physical actions too were not socially restricted as today – so bodily functions and sexual activity were relatively uncontrolled.

However, during the medieval period a slow process began whereby 'manners' and appropriate behaviour concerning defecation, sex and general behaviour began to develop. Slowly, according to Elias, self-control began to be internalized, with increasing levels of social control linked with a sense of shame. According to Shilling, this increasing level of bodily control was linked to three processes.

1 **Socialization** is the process by which people are discouraged from carrying out bodily functions in public. Indeed, natural bodily functions such as defecation came to be seen as something which should not be discussed or performed in view or sound of others.
2 **Rationalization** occurs when people are expected to exercise self-control and to restrain their feelings (or concern over pain).
3 **Individualization** is the belief that we are separate and distinct from others and that we should maintain our body at some socially acceptable distance from the bodies of others.

All three processes have significant implications for health and health care which we will explore later.

One other influence on Shilling was the writings of Pierre Bourdieu, best known in sociology for his work on cultural capital (see pp. 632–4). Bourdieu later developed the notion of 'capital' and suggested that, apart from cultural capital, people had different access to three other types of capital. The first of these is **economic capital**, referring to income and wealth, but the remaining two are closely connected to the body – **symbolic capital**, which refers to the presentation of self in everyday life, and **physical capital**, referring to body shape, manner of walking and mode of speech.

According to Shilling (1991), different social groups are able to convert symbolic and physical capital into other forms of capital – for example, working-class males with high levels of physical capital may seek to use this to obtain economic capital through professional sport.

Jocalyn Lawler: handling the body

So far, we have discussed the idea of the body in a somewhat theoretical manner which may appear rather distant from health concerns. However, in *Behind the Screens: Nursing, Somology and the Problem of the Body* (1991), Jocalyn Lawler explores how nurses deal with a part of their work in which they are required to engage in forms of bodily contact which are normally proscribed, at least between strangers, in contemporary society. Lawler suggests that they are able to do so by adopting four basic **rules** and by seeking to create a set of **specific contextors** within which the social interaction with their patients takes place.

The four rules are: that patients are expected to comply with the instructions of the nurse; that the patient should accept that they are dependent on the nurse (and therefore do what they are told); the modesty rule that patients should behave appropriately when private and potentially embarrassing body-care actions are being carried out; and finally the privacy rule, which suggests that nurses should seek to ensure appropriate privacy for the patient.

These rules, however, take place within a framework of 'contextors' which seek to define the social situation in such a way that the rules will function most easily. The first of the five specific contextors is that the nurse wears a uniform, which makes a symbolic statement about the relationship between professional and patient. The second contextor is that the nurse acts in an appropriate (professional) manner, which depersonalizes the situation. Third, the nurse seeks to minimize the sense of personal shame when the patient is touched intimately or has defecated or vomited. The nurse will do this by understating the situation. The term Lawler uses for this is 'minfism'. Fourth, the nurse will ask family and friends to leave before carrying out care, so as not to expose the patient to shame. Finally, in the 'discourse of privatization', discussions about body functions and embarrassing aspects of patient care are conducted in private.

Lawler suggests that nurses (the majority of whom are female) seek to apply the rules and contextors wherever possible; however, these are at their most fragile in nursing situations involving areas of sexuality and the male organs. According to Lawler the most likely cause of problems is when the nurse defines the situation along the professional relationship of nurse and patient, but the patient defines the situation as a sexual one. Here the nurse must seek to move the definition of the situation towards a clearly professional one, imposing this upon the patient.

Lawler's research points to the way in which certain actions of the body have become seen as shameful and disgusting, and illustrates the social constructions that are necessary to deal with these elements of shame.

The individual body and the social body

Two writers, however, have gone somewhat beyond other sociologists in their discussions of the body – Foucault and Turner. Whereas the writers we have looked at so far seek to understand the place and meaning of the body in society, Turner and Foucault have been particularly interested in developing a sociology which seeks to draw close links between the control of individual bodies and developments in control of the 'social body'.

Michel Foucault: The Birth of the Clinic

Without doubt the most important figure in understanding the development of health and medicine is the French social scientist, Michel Foucault.

Foucault's starting point is that there is no objective reality 'out there' waiting to be explored. Instead, social reality is created in various ways through the activities of people. The resulting social reality provides a **discourse**, which is a way of conceptualizing an issue and provides a framework for discussion and action.

According to Foucault, discourses create 'effects of truth' – that is, we believe the resulting perception of the world as being true. In particular, Foucault (1973) argues that the changing medical approach and views of disease resulted in particular ways of viewing the body, through what he calls the **clinical gaze** (*le regard*).

According to Foucault, towards the end of the eighteenth century a change took place in the mainstream approach to disease. Because of extensive medical malpractice a new form of clinic was set up in France to provide medical training. This was characterized by a new approach which emphasized clinical observation, bedside teaching and physical examinations. The technological invention which helped this new form of investigation was the stethoscope, which allowed doctors to pinpoint exactly where the problem was located.

The clinic provided doctors with a perfect place for close observation of large numbers of patients, and because it provided health care for poor people who had no other place to go, there were few objections to the intimate examination of the body. Over time the 'clinical gaze' created a completely new way of looking at the body, which 'directs attention to certain structures, certain similarities, certain symptoms and not others [and] in so doing forms a set of rules for reading the body and for making it intelligible' (Armstrong, 1983). The role of the doctor is to be a neutral observer who identifies, classifies and charts the route of the disease in the body. The patient has come to be viewed as simply a body, not a whole person.

This new way of looking at the body did not appear because of a revolutionary advance in understanding the body. Instead, the new way of looking actually reflected wider political and social changes in French society.

These wider changes were a growth in new forms of surveillance and control, as well as the new science of classifying people, which were appearing in a range of settings at this time. There were examinations in schools, inspections in military barracks, and new forms of punishment of criminals – in particular, being sent to prison to be reformed.

This links to a much wider theme of the relationship between power and knowledge which runs through Foucault's work. For Foucault, all knowledge has implications for power relationships, and the history of modern human society is that of increasing control over the mass of the population.

States originally could only control people through violence or threats of violence and therefore the punishment for deviance was usually brutal. Gradually, new forms of knowledge developed which enabled states to control people in more effective ways – and medicine plays a key role in this. It helped to develop the idea of surveillance (the doctor surveys the body) and it also generated concepts of normal and deviant (by distinguishing between the normal and diseased body).

Gradually, the state could withdraw from having to punish and coerce the mass of the population, as they learned to do this for themselves, by internalizing notions of normal and deviant/pathological. A parallel to be drawn today is the way that people monitor their own health, taking exercise, eating 'correctly' and thereby accepting that there is a 'correct' form of body and standard of health, from which it is a mistake to deviate.

Other sociologists have drawn on the work of Foucault. Armstrong (1983) developed Foucault's thesis, agreeing that the twentieth century saw the development of the clinical gaze, but Armstrong suggests that this involved the extension of the gaze far beyond the confines of the body (and medicine), out into the social sphere.

Armstrong studied the growth of 'dispensaries' (clinics) in the early part of the twentieth century. Originally, these were developed as the location for new arrangements to contact and screen tuberculosis patients (TB was a major cause of death at the time). The dispensaries coordinated home visits, checked on patients, and ensured, via follow-ups, that the patients were treated. As a result of this, a geographical and social awareness of disease began to be developed. No longer was disease seen as an individual problem, but instead the social origins and social distribution of the disease were gradually established.

According to Armstrong, the activities of the dispensaries raised consciousness within the communities of the social location of diseases, and this justified the extension of the dispensaries' activities. Whereas Foucault and other writers stressed the significance of the physical sciences, Armstrong suggests that the new social science techniques – such as surveys – served to map ever more accurately the social bases of disease to create new categories of ill people, and new specialities, such as geriatrics and paediatrics.

In later work (1993) Armstrong suggests that this process has advanced so far that almost everyone can be categorized as ill or potentially ill, and the boundaries between the sick and the healthy are no longer clear.

> *The dream of the new medicine has reformed the relationship between health and illness. No longer are they polar opposites ... they have become inextricably linked ... On the one hand health is contained within illness; the disabled, the chronically sick, the dying and diseased can promote their health by appropriate health behaviour ... Equally the germ of illness is now contained in health. Health has become a temporal trajectory containing the seeds of illness, which nevertheless, can be countered by preventive action ... healthy living.* Armstrong, 1993, p. 65

Bryan Turner: Regulating Bodies

Like Foucault, Bryan Turner is interested in the body mainly because he sees it as providing an insight into broader social changes. In *Regulating Bodies* (1992) Turner explores the way in which bodies are controlled in society. He suggests that there are three key institutions dealing with the individual's body: the law, religion and medicine.

Turner suggests that over time the influence of each of the institutions has shifted, with religion originally being dominant and gradually being nudged aside by the law and, more importantly, medicine. Not only has medicine now come to dominate how the body is treated, but also medicine now serves a moral purpose. However, according to Turner, these moral elements of medicine are 'typically disguised and they are ultimately legitimized by an appeal to scientific rather than religious authority ... medicine occupies the space left by the erosion of religion' (Turner, 1992, p. 23).

Turner suggests that there is a clear parallel in (late) modern society between the regulation of individual bodies and the regulation of the social body. In particular, he identifies four tasks which he claims are central to social order.

1. **Reproduction**, which refers to social institutions which control sexuality and other physical needs.
2. The **regulation** of bodies, which occurs through medical surveillance and through the systems of crime control.

3 The need for **restraint**, which is where self-control is applied to ensure that a person does not simply follow their emotions.
4 **Representation**, which refers to the way in which we physically present our bodies to others.

Turner's work is, like Foucault's, rather challenging, but what he is seeking to do in his writing is to demonstrate how the control of the 'social body' or society of people can be seen as closely linked to control of the individual body, and it is a mistake to separate them.

Turner, like Giddens, sees a major change in the role of bodies in late modernity. According to Turner, late modernity has seen a decline in the traditional value placed on hard work and has emphasized consumption, hedonism and play, so that the work ethic has been replaced by the play ethic. Identity comes more from consumption (dress, image and style) than it does from production (a person's job).

> *Through consumption we are urged to shape our lives by the use of our purchasing power. We are obliged to make our lives meaningful by selecting our personal lifestyle from those offered to us in advertising, soap operas, and films, to make sense of our existence by exercising our freedom to choose in a market in which one simultaneously purchases products and services, and assembles, manages and markets oneself.* Rose, 1989

Conclusion

The sociology of health and illness has taken an important step in challenging the notion that the body is a biological entity which exists independently of society. Sociologists have shown that the body can be understood and responded to through a social framework as well as a biological one. One important consequence of this has been a flowering of studies in the sociology of disability.

Disability

On the issue of disability and the related area of chronic (long-term) illness, sociology has provided a very strong alternative to the biomedical model. Traditionally, disability has been viewed as a physical deviation from the normal body, and as a consequence disabled people are unable to perform what are regarded as normal tasks. However, an alternative model of disability (and of chronic illness) has been suggested by a number of sociologists working in this area.

Oliver: disability and the myth of the personal tragedy

Perhaps the best known of these sociologists is Oliver (1990), who argues that the biomedical model of disability leads to what he calls an ideology of **personal tragedy** which stresses the need for the individual disabled person to come to terms with 'their' problem, by struggling to cope as best they can.

Oliver calls this the personal tragedy model because it tends to describe disability as some terrible personal problem, which has ruined that person's life. He suggests that this model has now become taken for granted, achieving 'ideological hegemony' in the way that disabled people are viewed.

In place of the individualistic or personal tragedy model, Oliver argues that disability should be seen as a social problem and that it can only be understood within a wider social and economic framework, that is, within a social model.

Oliver argues that a clear distinction can be made between impairment and disability. A person may have a physical impairment of some kind, but it only becomes a disability when the society organizes social and economic features in such a way as to translate the impairment into a disability. For example, if the only means to enter a cinema is by using steps, then a person who has an impairment which leads them to use a wheelchair becomes disabled. However, if a ramp is provided and the ticket booth is at a lower height, and adequate spaces are provided for wheelchair users, then the person is no longer disabled. So, disability derives from organizing society in such a way as to change impairment into disability.

Vic Finkelstein: capitalism and disability

Finkelstein (1980) argues that disability is the product of capitalist society and the linked processes of urbanization and industrialization. Before these processes took place, disabled people were not segregated from the population and were not regarded as a specific group. They were simply individuals who formed part of a huge marginal, often destitute, group on the edge of society who eked out a living by begging and by agricultural work. The idea of disabled people as a specific group with a distinguishable 'place' in society simply did not exist. People were, of course, aware of 'cripples', and they were discriminated against – but not as a specific, identifiable category (see pp. 309–10 on Foucault's concept of the gaze).

However, with the development of industrialization and the shift to machine-based work within factories, there was no need for the labour of disabled people. Without access to work, disabled people became an economic burden for society and came to be defined as a social problem. They became an identifiable group who were now excluded and segregated from the mass of the (able-bodied) productive population.

According to Finkelstein, people with impairments were now seen as abnormal and came to be compared to the 'normal', able-bodied population. Their physical or mental abnormalities led them to be categorized as a medical problem and placed under the control of the medical professions. In Victorian Britain, the form of medical care for such groups was to segregate them into large institutions, along with the mentally ill, the old and the poor. This kind of segregation lasted for over a hundred years, with disabled people being 'cared for' in such places.

However, a gradual shift by the medical profession took place in the middle of the twentieth century, with doctors seeking to 'cure' disabled people by making them fit enough to return to society and to take employment. Finkelstein therefore suggests that disability shifted from being an abnormality to being a sickness which could be partially cured, so that people could enter the world of work and thus re-enter society.

Criticism of Finkelstein

Tom Shakespeare (1994) disagrees with Finkelstein's argument that the origins of prejudice against disabled people derive from capitalist society. He suggests instead that prejudice against disabled people is implicit in 'cultural representation, in language and in socialization'. According to Shakespeare, all societies have reacted negatively to impairment and this is often reflected in the ways that disabled people are portrayed in the culture. Shakespeare therefore suggests that the oppression of disabled people pre-dates industrial capitalism, and thus the origins of prejudice lie less in the place of disabled people in the labour market and more in wider cultural representations.

Bourdieu and physical capital

Pierre Bourdieu is probably best known in sociology for his work on cultural capital (see pp. 632–4) in which he points out that the educational success of children in school is influenced by the amount of educational support, knowledge and resources (all of which he brackets together as cultural capital) that there is in the home.

Bourdieu later developed the notion of 'capital' and suggested that, apart from cultural capital, people had different access to three other types of capital: **economic capital**, **symbolic capital** and **physical capital** (see pp. 67–9).

Disabled people will have lower levels of symbolic and physical capital, according to Bourdieu's argument, and thus are less able to impose their definitions of normality on the wider 'able-bodied' society. The lower level of physical capital derives from the fact that they do have some form of physical impairment; and the lower level of symbolic capital derives from the process of stigmatization of disabled people.

Bourdieu (1984) later went on to extend and explain the issues surrounding symbolic and physical capital. In his book, *Distinction: A Social Critique of the Judgement of Taste*, he introduced the notion of **habitus**, which refers to the internalized or embodied sense of being and place in society. Habitus is constructed by certain powerful institutions, and in the case of disability the most important institution is that of medicine, which has influenced social views on disabled people by helping to create the notion of inferiority and dependence.

Bourdieu goes even further and suggests that this denial of symbolic capital to disabled people is a form of 'symbolic violence', which undermines their sense of value.

A good example of symbolic violence is provided in the early writing of Kathy Charmaz (1983). Charmaz's study was concerned with the way in which people who had become 'disabled', through an accident or chronic ill-health, became concerned about the loss of their previous self-image – indeed what they had seen before as their very 'selves'. These people faced a number of dilemmas in their attempts to hold on to a sense of self as the impact of disability chipped away at their identities:

1. Charmaz notes that they seek approval from others and look for any sign of change in their attitudes to them.
2. They also tend to use the tactic of expressing their dependence on others as a means of securing the other person's loyalty to them, despite the fact that increased dependence actually places considerable strain on relationships.
3. They are more likely to express their true feelings of loss and hurt in a way which is not usually acceptable in society, and in doing so they may further discourage the intimate association of others.
4. Finally, they constantly battle with the culturally accepted measure of a person's worth by what they can achieve, and this in particular constantly undermines their self-belief.

In a later book, Charmaz (1993) explores the different ways in which chronically ill and disabled people can approach their situation. She suggests that there is a range of responses, from those who merely see their disability as an *interruption* in their lives, downplaying the impact on them and their idea of self, and those who see it as an *intrusion*, to those who actually *'immerse'* themselves in their identity as disabled.

Conclusion

The notion of disability is usually linked to the idea of an imperfect or abnormal body, which in turn is seen as both a personal problem (how will the individual cope?) and a medical problem (how can medicine provide cures to make these people normal?). However, the sociology of disability suggests these are the wrong questions. Instead, sociologists distinguish between the original state of 'people with impairments' (that is, some physical difference which might mean that certain actions are difficult or impossible) and 'disabled people' (that is, people who are seen as inadequate and abnormal and who need help to become like able-bodied people). Having impairments, they argue, is being different, while being disabled is the result of prejudice which sees people with impairments as inferior and abnormal. Furthermore, the impact on disabled people is not just in terms of their disadvantaged position in society, but also in their perceptions of themselves and their worth.

Illness, blame and stigma

Illness, although a physical problem, is also viewed in moral terms. Despite the dominance of the biomedical model over traditional medicine in the understanding of health and disease (see pp. 288–91), traditional views on links between ill-health and moral failings still seem to exist. This is reinforced by the fact that many scientific theories of health lay the 'blame' for illness on personal behaviour – for example, smoking, eating too much or not taking exercise. This turns illness into a **moral issue**, where the individual is in the wrong for being ill.

Helman (1986) provides a famous example from his time as a GP in a middle-class suburb of London. He found that patients distinguished between colds and 'chills' on the one hand, and fever and 'flu' on the other. Colds and chills were explained as resulting from penetration of the body by cold or damp 'outside'. Although the cold and damp were natural conditions beyond the control of the patients, they still blamed themselves for not having taken appropriate precautions – dressing suitably and keeping out of the cold. However, when it came to 'flu' or fever, these were explained by 'bugs' which they could not avoid 'catching'. Thus, they were not to blame.

This kind of thinking results in people with certain types of illness being seen as guilty (for example, people with lung cancer caused by smoking), while others are viewed as innocent victims (for example, children with leukaemia).

Illnesses with a negative moral label attached include lung cancer and obesity. The person who suffers from such a disease is regarded as blameworthy because aspects of their chosen lifestyle are believed to have caused the disease. For instance, AIDS is linked to sexual activity, lung cancer to smoking, and obesity to over-eating and lack of exercise.

In contemporary society, the reason why people are ill is understood within a **narrative of risk**. We live in a risk-filled world in which our health is constantly under threat, and it is everyone's duty to avoid becoming ill. Thus, 'irresponsible' sexual activity or excessive alcohol or cigarette consumption are seen as the moral failings of the individual concerned. Therefore the cause of their illness is their own 'wrong' lifestyle.

Clarke (1992) compared the presentation of cancer, heart disease and AIDS in articles in popular Canadian and US magazines over a period of more than twenty years. She found there were clear moral differences in the way the diseases were understood and how those suffering from them were viewed. Cancer was seen as a mysterious evil creature which attacked the body, and which was associated with loss of hope, fear and almost certain death. Heart disease was seen as morally neutral: the machinery of the heart was malfunctioning; if caught in time, the disease was manageable and did not result in any stigma to the person concerned. Being HIV-positive or having AIDS was viewed in terms of a punishment for an immoral lifestyle.

These images of illness can have a powerful effect upon how people with disease see themselves – they may feel guilty for actually having the disease. Susan Sontag, who wrote a book about her own experience of cancer, comments that modern diseases such as cancer and AIDS are: 'a powerful means of placing the blame on the ill. Patients who are instructed that they have, unwittingly, caused their disease are also made to feel that they have deserved it' (Sontag, 1988).

The resulting shame and the sense of being different and inferior have been examined by Erving Goffman.

Erving Goffman: *Stigma*

Goffman (1968) suggests that certain people who have undesired 'differentness' are stigmatized, in that others regard them as 'tainted and discounted'. One of the major types of stigma relevant to the sociology of health and illness is 'physical deformity'.

Goffman is less interested in the origins of stigma than in the impact it has on the social interaction of the stigmatized person and how they perceive themselves. According to Goffman, whenever there is a significant difference between a person's virtual identity (what the normal person is like) and their actual identity, then negative consequences are likely to follow.

Goffman distinguishes between a **discrediting stigma**, such as a clearly visible disfigurement or disability, and a **discreditable stigma**, where the negative 'undesired differentness' is not obvious, and the person has the possibility of hiding it.

People who have discrediting attributes, according to Goffman, deal with their potentially difficult day-to-day interaction with others through **impression management**. This lowers the chances of humiliation or other problems. One particular technique is **covering**, by which the person will engage in most normal activities, but will seek to minimize the impact of their stigma by conforming as much as possible to standard norms of behaviour.

People with discreditable attributes can seek to hide their attributes and avoid stigma, or undertake **information management** by controlling what they tell others. Goffman says that a person trying to give the impression they are 'normal' may face considerable problems in managing information, as they will always live in fear of being exposed. The two main strategies for the person with discreditable attributes are **passing** and **withdrawal**. Passing is seeking to hide the discreditable attribute, and withdrawal is when the person withdraws from social contacts wherever possible.

Scambler and Hopkins (1986) used Goffman's concept of stigma to study people with epilepsy. However, they made a further distinction in the concept of stigma, by distinguishing between **enacted stigma** and **felt stigma**.

> *Enacted stigma refers to instances of discrimination against people with epilepsy on the grounds of their perceived unacceptability or inferiority … Felt stigma refers principally to the fear of enacted stigma, but also encompasses a feeling of shame associated with 'being epileptic'.* Scambler and Hopkins, 1986

People respond negatively to those with epilepsy (enacted stigma) and so individuals with the disease have to find ways of managing it (felt stigma). Scambler and Hopkins suggest people will respond in at least four ways to felt stigma.

1 **Selective concealment**, where people do not tell the majority of those with whom they interact in the workplace or in leisure activities. Disclosure is only made to a few close, trusted friends and family. Usually, people follow a plan of disclosure: they plan under what circumstances they can hide their illness and in what situations they should let others know. For example, the issue of a person's epilepsy was raised and explained in carefully thought out

situations and staged circumstances during trips away or in long periods spent with friends.

2 **Covering up** the discreditable condition and keeping it secret. This runs the risk of being 'uncovered', as Goffman also pointed out.
3 **Medicalizing their behaviour** to evoke sympathy.
4 **Condemning the condemners**, where people challenge the enacted stigma, often through political action.

Although Scambler and Hopkins applied their analysis specifically to epilepsy, these responses could equally be applied to a wide range of stigmatized illnesses.

For example, disabled people are one of the largest groups who deal with stigma. A significant proportion have chosen to condemn the condemners and have developed a powerful lobby to resist the stigma attached to disability. As far back as 1981, the British Council of Organizations of Disabled People was formed from a range of smaller groups to represent the interests of disabled people, and the academic journal *Disability and Society* was first published in 1986. The aim was to clash head on with political, medical and social science interpretations of disability.

Stigma and mental illness

Hall *et al.* (1993) asked adults how they thought they would react if they came into contact with mentally ill people. Although the majority agreed they would talk to mentally ill people, a significant proportion preferred to have the most limited social interaction possible. For example, over 25 per cent did not want their children to attend a party where a mentally ill person lived, and 35 per cent would not want to live next door to a person suffering from paranoid schizophrenia.

Philo *et al.* (1996) conducted a content analysis of Scottish (fictional and non-fictional) media coverage of mental illness over a period of one month. They found that over 66 per cent of all images presented showed mentally ill people as violent towards others, and a further 18 per cent as violent towards themselves. Only 4 per cent of coverage was critical of the accepted images of mental illness portrayed in the rest of the media.

In the second part of their study, Philo and colleagues examined how a sample of people responded to these media images. Their conclusions supported the work of Hall *et al.* in finding that the majority of people derived their images of mental illness from the media; indeed, people sometimes still associated violence with mental illness, despite personal acquaintance with mentally ill individuals who exhibited no violent tendencies at all.

Criticism of the concept of stigma

James Charlton (1998) criticized these approaches to understanding stigma, at least when they are applied to disability. Although the theoretical notion of stigma can be successfully applied to disability, Charlton questions its usefulness in the real world. He suggests that the reality for disabled people across the world is that they are poor as a result of being excluded from decent employment, as well as because of stigmatizing attitudes. For Charlton, emphasis on issues of felt stigma draws attention away from the central point of their exclusion from a reasonable quality of life. Sociological concepts such as stigma actually help to maintain the oppression of disabled people by masking this fundamental reality. According to Charlton, the only way to understand chronic illness and disability is through a structural perspective which focuses on the reasons for their poverty.

Mental illness

Although the majority of sociological research has focused on physical illness, there is also a long tradition of writing about mental illness. The majority of this sociological writing has taken to task the more traditional, non-sociological approaches to mental illness, particularly their two basic assumptions: first, that there is such a thing as mental illness; and second, that explanations for the illness are located in the individual experience or physical well-being of the mentally ill person.

Within sociology itself, however, there are different perspectives, which take rather different views on the nature and significance of mental illness.

One school of thought, broadly based on interactionist writings, disputes the very notion of mental illness, and explores the reasons why certain forms of behaviour are viewed as mental illness and why certain people come to be labelled as mentally ill. In a similar vein, Foucault also argues that mental illness is constructed, though he does not agree with specific interactionist arguments.

A second approach, which we can term structuralist, broadly accepts the notion of mental illness, but examines the way in which it is unequally distributed across the various social groups in society.

Mental illness as a social construction

Thomas Scheff: Being Mentally Ill

Scheff (1966) argues that there is no such thing as mental illness. Instead, it is better understood as a category for all bizarre behaviour which cannot be explained through other means (such as alcohol or drug use). Scheff argues that people who behave bizarrely are not mentally ill; rather, their behaviour does not make sense to others.

Scheff claims that most people pass through periods in their lives when they might behave oddly, but in the majority of cases this behaviour is not labelled as deviant and therefore has no consequences. It is only a small minority whose behaviour comes to be regarded as evidence of mental illness.

Scheff says, a 'stereotyped image of mental illness is learned in early childhood and continually reaffirmed, inadvertently, in ordinary social interaction'. The way we view and respond to mental illness is the result of the wider socialization process in childhood – 'going mad', 'acting like a lunatic' – and then this is strengthened by

psychiatric profession too, according to writers such as Chesler (1972), who argues that cultural views on appropriate behaviour for women permeate psychiatry.

According to Williams and Watson (1996), over 50 per cent of all women who use psychiatric services have experienced sexual or physical abuse at some point in their lives – evidence which supports the argument that mental illness is directly related to women's lack of power in society.

Mental illness and minority ethnic groups

In a national survey of British people and mental illness, Nazroo (1997) concluded:

1 British people of African Caribbean origin are more likely to suffer depression than the majority of the population. The rates for most other forms of mental illness are broadly similar to those of the majority population.
2 People of South Asian origin have lower rates of depression than the majority population.

However, these rates are not necessarily reflected in the levels of treatment provided by the NHS. Koffman *et al.* (1997), for example, found that people from African Caribbean backgrounds were significantly over-represented in treatment for psychotic disorders, with one and a half times the rate of admission for treatment compared to the majority population.

Pilgrim and Rogers (1999) note that people of African Caribbean origin are much more likely than white people to make contact with psychiatry through the police, courts or prisons. Rates of contact via the police are more than two and a half times higher than for white people, and through the courts or prisons the figure increases to twenty-nine times higher.

According to Fernando (2002), higher rates of treatment for people of African Caribbean origin reflect cultural bias in Western psychiatry, rather than any actual higher levels of illness. Browne (1990) suggests the practices of the police and courts effectively discriminate against young African Caribbean males so that they are much more likely to be compulsorily treated for mental illness.

The most commonly accepted explanation for higher levels of mental illness among certain minority ethnic groups is that they suffer higher levels of material deprivation; this, combined with their experiences of discrimination, leads to high levels of stress. However, Pilgrim and Rogers (1999) argue that this alone cannot be the full explanation, because people of Asian origin and African Caribbean origin both suffer from material deprivation and racism, but there are significantly higher levels of mental illness among those of African Caribbean origin.

Conclusion

Sociologists have disputed the accounts of mental health provided by psychiatrists, arguing instead that it is a socially created concept, though explanations for its creation vary. Those who come to be defined as mentally ill are more likely to be the poorest and the least powerful.

Death and dying

Inevitably, everyone dies: it is simple and inescapable. The relevance of sociology appears to be limited and only biology seems important.

However, sociologists have for a long time been fascinated with the social aspects of death. Sociology's original and most famous study of death remains Durkheim's *Suicide*, in which he argues that death can best be understood in a social context. Later writings by Douglas and Atkinson followed up Durkheim's insights by pointing out that even death has different meanings to different people.

The study of suicide has generally been incorporated into the sociology of deviance, rather than the sociology of health and illness. Nevertheless, the sociology of health and illness has expressed considerable interest in the nature of death and dying.

Philippe Ariès (1981) explores the ambiguity of death in Western societies and how it has changed over time. He distinguishes five forms of death:

1 **Tame death** dates from 'the earliest times', when death was an ever-present reality and could be expected at any time. Death was less about the person than about the community. It was 'tame' in the sense that it was spoken about and recognized.
2 **Death of the self** is a form of death that developed in the late medieval period and was the beginning of an awareness that death was individual.
3 **Remote** or **imminent death** refers to death in the seventeenth and eighteenth centuries, when religion was in decline and scientific, rational thought on the increase. Ariès refers to this period as 'the turning of the tide' in attitudes to death. Death now was lonely and associated with separation.
4 **Death of the other**: in the nineteenth century a new, romantic version of death emerged in novels, and the idea of people being reunited in an afterlife became fashionable.
5 **Invisible death** is the contemporary form of death in Western society. It is isolated, taking place in a hospital where it is hidden and invisible.

Norbert Elias (1985) also provided an overview of changes in dying. According to Elias, our attitudes to death fit into an overall change in Western society, which he terms the 'civilizing process'. This process (which we discussed earlier on pp. 308–9) includes the development of restraint over all forms of extreme behaviour and feelings. Death, which is likely to promote strong emotions, is 'screened off' as a way of limiting the potential emotionally laden behaviours. As death is now much less likely for the young, instead becoming a remote occurrence, the dying are also 'pushed further behind the screens, are isolated'.

Ariès and Elias agree on the move to an isolated and invisible death. However, Elias rejects the idea that dying was 'better' in earlier times, as Ariès seems to suggest. Elias makes the point that modern death gives people the chance to die 'serenely and calmly', whereas historically the majority of people died in 'torment and pain'.

Death and dying in contemporary society

Ariès and Elias provide historical overviews of death. Other sociologists have explored the actual process of dying in contemporary society.

Allan Kellehear (1990) argues that there is a model of the **good death**, which people aspire to in contemporary Western societies. This provides the framework within which family and professionals, as well as the dying person, seek to arrange the death:

1. The doctor makes it clear to the patient that they are going to die, and this is accepted by the patient.
2. The person is able to sort out financial and personal issues with those around them.
3. The person is able to continue working until late on. This is important, as it maintains a sense of social worth.

Kellehear shows how these components of a good death reflect contemporary social values, including a belief in modern medicine and science, the need to care for one's family and the moral value of working. Thus, correct patterns of death are closely related to the values of society and are as much social as biological. People do not simply die; they die in socially regulated ways.

Glaser and Strauss: negotiating death

In their study of patients dying in Californian hospitals in the 1960s, Glaser and Strauss (1965) noted that a process of **negotiation** often took place between patients, medical staff and family, as each of them sought to manage death in what they considered the best way. Glaser and Strauss observed that there were four different forms of awareness.

Closed awareness is when patients are not aware they are dying, but others are. This occurs when the medical staff believe that the patient does not want to know that they are dying and it would be better for the patient – and the hospital staff – if they are not told.

Glaser and Strauss then suggest that at some point there is a move to **suspected awareness**, when the dying person thinks they are dying and attempts to elicit the information from others. This places the medical staff in a dilemma, until eventually the patient comes to realize they are going to die.

At this point there is a shift to **mutual pretence**, when both sides know that the person is going to die but no one admits or discusses it. This generally gives way to **open awareness**, when finally the dying person accepts their death.

However, not all of these stages may be gone through and the process can stop at any time.

Sudnow and the management of death

Even when death is negotiated there is still a stigma attached to it in Western societies. It is often necessary to 'manage death' to avoid impact on others.

For example, other patients in a hospital may not wish to know about the deaths of those around them. David Sudnow (1967), in an ethnographic study of a US hospital, described how patients and visitors were shielded from the reality of death by the staff, who were careful about when they moved bodies from the ward, and sought whenever possible to hide them from the other patients.

Sudnow pointed out that it is also difficult for hospital staff to cope with constant deaths, so they develop mechanisms to make death routine. This **routinization of death** – when it becomes 'just another part of the job' – enables staff to avoid any psychological impact on themselves.

Lawton and the unbounded body

Julia Lawton (2000, 2002) explored the decisions to allow some people to die in a hospice and others to be sent home to die. Developing the ideas of Elias (see pp. 317–18), she concluded that the key to the decision lay in the extent to which the body was 'unbounded'. By unbounded, Lawton means those who were not in control of their bodily functions so that they were incontinent, vomiting, weeping pus or suffering other bodily losses. According to Elias, the civilizing process means that these unpleasant and unsightly bodily losses should be carried out in privacy as it offends our sense of dignity. The hospice therefore provided a shelter in which the unbounded body could be hidden from others, thus limiting the shame of the dying person.

This sense of unboundedness also has an impact on the behaviour of the dying person, such that those who exhibit these bodily losses are far more likely to withdraw into themselves, cutting off interaction with the wider world. Indeed Lawton suggests that they lose a sense of self, as they also become distant from themselves, feeling ashamed and disgusted by their own bodies.

Conclusion

How people die has changed over time, moving from a public to a more private and isolated activity. However, the process of death still needs to be managed so that people can achieve what is considered a socially 'good' death, and so that those professionals who deal with the dying are 'protected' from the emotional toll of death.

Summary and conclusions

The sociology of health and illness has moved from being a minor area of sociology, relatively marginal to the major debates in the subject, to a much more central position.

By questioning the taken-for-granted notions of what is meant by health and illness, and the nature of the disabled versus the normal body, sociology has presented a significant challenge to simplistic physiological explanations. What was previously seen as biologically fixed is recognized as having a social element.

This extension of the social into the physiological has also reached into explanations of why some people (or groups of people) are more likely to suffer from illness and shorter life spans than others. However, although there is general acceptance of the importance of social explanations in helping to understand health and illness, within sociology there is little consensus as to the exact mechanisms which link social class, gender, ethnicity and geography to different levels of health – with the explanations ranging from those which stress the wider economic structure of society, to those which stress individual lifestyle choices.

The sociology of health and illness has also provided a clear insight into the role and position in society of the medical profession. Doctors have held a position of great prestige in society for over 150 years, and during that time their explanations and methods of dealing with disease have, until recently, rarely been challenged. However, sociological research suggests that their power emerged as much from an ability to marginalize rivals, such as nurses, midwives and complementary/alternative therapists, as from straightforward efficacy in dealing with diseases. Doctors, sociology argues, are one health interest group amongst a range of such groups, and have achieved their dominance through political activity.

Health, illness and the role of the medical profession are also linked to politics in a broader sense, with writers such as Foucault and Turner pointing to the way in which the development of medicine has been linked to the emergence of new, subtle and powerful forms of social control in society which extend even to what is considered the appropriate form of normal human body.

Earlier, we mentioned how sociology has managed to demonstrate that illness (and how it is treated) cannot be seen solely in physiological terms, but also has a social dimension. This is most vividly illustrated by the sociological exploration of death. Sociologists have demonstrated that dying too has this social dimension, with culturally appropriate ways of dying and responses to death existing in each society and changing over time.

The sociology of health and illness can claim to be an area of sociology which has challenged the idea that there are areas of knowledge which are 'natural' and can only be understood through a physiological framework. It has shown that sociology has a relevance in a much wider range of areas than traditionally accepted.

CHAPTER 6
Crime and deviance

The heart of the capitalist economic system is the protection of private property ... It is not surprising, then, to find that criminal laws reflect this basic concern. Chambliss, 1976

Introduction

In everyday language to **deviate** means to stray from an accepted path, and many sociological definitions of deviance simply elaborate upon this idea. In other words, we often find that deviance consists of those acts which do not follow the norms and expectations of a particular social group. Deviance may be **positively sanctioned** (rewarded), **negatively sanctioned** (punished) or simply accepted without reward or punishment.

In terms of the above definition of deviance, soldiers on the battlefield who risk their lives above and beyond the normal call of duty may be termed deviant, as may physicists who break the rules of their discipline and develop a new theory. Their deviance may be positively sanctioned: a soldier may be rewarded with a medal, and a physicist with a Nobel Prize. In one sense, though, neither is deviant, since both conform to the values of society: the soldier to the value of courage, and the physicist to the value of academic progress.

By comparison, murderers deviate not only from society's norms and expectations, but also from its values, in particular the value placed on human life. Their deviance generally results in widespread disapproval and punishment.

A third form of deviance consists of acts that depart from the norms and expectations of a particular society but are generally tolerated and accepted. The person with a house full of cats or someone with an obsession for collecting clocks would fall into this category. Usually their eccentricities are neither rewarded nor punished by others. Such people are simply defined as a 'bit odd' but harmless, and are therefore tolerated.

The sociological study of deviance

In practice, the field of study covered by the sociology of deviance is usually limited to deviance that results in negative sanctions. The American sociologist Marshall B. Clinard (1974) suggested that the term 'deviance' should be reserved for behaviour which is so much disapproved of that the community finds it impossible to tolerate. Although not all sociologists would accept this definition, it does describe the area usually covered by studies of deviance.

In terms of Clinard's definition, **crime** and **delinquency** are the most obvious forms of deviance. Crime, or offending, refers to those activities that break the law of the land and are subject to official punishment; **youth offending**, or delinquency, refers to criminal acts which are committed by young people. A new term, anti-social behaviour, refers to a wide variety of acts, often committed by young people, which disturb other members of society, without necessarily involving theft or turning to crime, which promises greater rewards than legitimate means.

Merton stressed that membership of the lower strata is not, in itself, sufficient to produce deviance. Only in societies such as the USA, where all members share the same success goals, does the pressure to innovate operate forcefully on the lower classes. Merton argues that those who innovate have been 'imperfectly socialized so that they abandon institutional means while retaining success-aspirations'.

3 The third possible response is **ritualism**. Those who select this alternative are deviant because they have largely abandoned the commonly held success goals. The pressure to adopt this alternative is greatest for members of the lower middle class whose occupations provide less opportunity for success than those of other members of the middle class. (We analyse the market situation of the lower middle class in Chapter 1, pp. 50–2.) However, compared with members of the working class, they have been strongly socialized to conform to social norms. This prevents them from turning to crime. Unable to innovate, and with jobs that offer little opportunity for advancement, their only solution is to scale down or abandon their success goals.

   Merton paints the following picture of typical lower middle-class 'ritualists'. They are low-grade bureaucrats, ultra-respectable but stuck in a rut. They are sticklers for the rules, follow the book to the letter, cling to red tape, conform to all the outward standards of middle-class respectability, but have given up striving for success. Ritualists are deviant because they have rejected the success goals held by most members of society.

4 Merton terms the fourth, and least common, response, **retreatism**. It applies to 'psychotics, autists, pariahs, outcasts, vagrants, vagabonds, tramps, chronic drunkards and drug addicts'. They have strongly internalized both the cultural goals and the institutionalized means, yet are unable to achieve success. They resolve the conflict of their situation by abandoning both the goals and the means of reaching them. They are unable to cope, and 'drop out' of society, defeated and resigned to their failure. They are deviant in two ways: they have rejected both the cultural goals and the institutionalized means. Merton does not relate retreatism to social class position.

5 **Rebellion** forms the fifth and final response. It is a rejection of both the success goals and the institutionalized means, and it replaces them with different goals and means. Those who adopt this alternative wish to create a new society. Merton argues that 'it is typically members of a rising class rather than the most depressed strata who organize the resentful and rebellious into a revolutionary group'.

To summarize, Merton claimed his analysis showed how the culture and structure of society generate deviance. The overemphasis upon the cultural goals of financial success and high status in American society, at the expense of institutionalized means, creates a tendency towards anomie. This tendency exerts pressure for deviance, a pressure which varies depending on a person's position in the class structure.

Evaluation of Merton

Critics have attacked Merton's work for neglecting the power relationships in society as a whole, within which deviance and conformity occur. Laurie Taylor (1971) criticized Merton for not carrying his analysis far enough: for failing to consider who makes the laws and who benefits from the laws. To continue Taylor's analogy, the whole game may have been rigged by the powerful with rules that guarantee their success. These rules may be the laws of society.

Merton has also been criticized for assuming that there is a value consensus in American society and that people only deviate as a result of structural strain. His theory has been attacked as being too deterministic because it fails to explain why some people who experience the effects of anomie do not become criminals or deviants.

Some critics believe that Merton's theory over-predicts and exaggerates working-class crime, and under-predicts and underestimates middle-class or white-collar crime. Taylor, Walton and Young (1973) believe that Merton's theory cannot account for politically motivated criminals (such as freedom fighters) who break the law because of commitment to their cause rather than the effects of anomie.

However, some sociologists have defended Merton's theory. Robert Reiner (1984) points out that Merton himself acknowledged that not all Americans accept the success goals of the American Dream. Nevertheless, such goals are sufficiently widespread in the lower strata to account for their deviance.

Reiner also notes that 'Merton was well aware both of the extensiveness of white-collar crime in the suites, and of the way that official statistics disproportionately record crimes in the streets'. Merton explained white-collar crime by suggesting that American society placed no upper limit on success. However wealthy people were, they might still want more.

Nevertheless, Reiner maintains that Merton's view that there was more working-class crime remains quite plausible, since those failing to become wealthy in legal ways will be under more pressure to find alternative routes to success. Reiner also believes that Merton's theory can be developed to accommodate most of the criticisms. Thus Taylor *et al.*'s political criminals could be included in Merton's rebellion adaptation.

Subculture theorists, whose work will be examined shortly, have also criticized Merton. However, as Reiner points out, their work represents an attempt to refine and develop Merton's theory rather than rejecting it altogether.

Some empirical support for Merton is provided by Hannon and Defronzo (1998, quoted in Jones, 2001). In a study of 406 metropolitan counties in the USA they found that those with higher levels of welfare provision had lower levels of crime. They argued that the welfare provision opened up opportunities for people to achieve the goal of material success through legitimate means and therefore reduced anomie and the crime which could result from it.

Despite the criticisms, Merton's theory remains one of the more plausible attempts to explain crime rates in whole societies. Joachim J. Savelsberg (1995) argues that Merton's strain theory can help to explain the rapid rises in the crime rate in post-communist Poland, Czechoslovakia, East Germany and Russia. Poland is an example of how dramatic these rises sometimes were. Poland had its first free elections in 1989. Between 1989 and 1990 the official crime rate in Poland increased by no less than 69 per cent.

Merton's work, however, can hardly explain all crime. Since his original work, other sociologists have modified and built on his theory in order to try to develop more complete explanations for crime and delinquency.

Structural and subcultural theories of deviance

Structural theories of deviance are similar to Merton's theory. They explain the origins of deviance in terms of the position of individuals or groups in the social structure.

Subcultural theories explain deviance in terms of the subculture of a social group. They argue that certain groups develop norms and values which are to some extent different from those held by other members of society. For example, some groups of criminals or delinquents might develop norms that encourage and reward criminal activity. Other members of society may regard such activities as immoral, and strongly disapprove of them.

Subcultural theories claim that deviance is the result of individuals conforming to the values and norms of the social group to which they belong. Members of subcultures are not completely different from other members of society: they may speak the same language, wear similar clothes, and attach the same value to family life. However, their subculture is sufficiently different from the culture of society as a whole to lead to them committing acts that are generally regarded as deviant.

Albert Cohen's analysis of youth offending provides a synthesis of both approaches. The development of subcultures is explained in terms of the position of groups or individuals in the social structure.

Albert K. Cohen – the delinquent subculture

Cohen's work (1955) was a modification and development of Merton's position. From his studies of delinquency, Cohen made two major criticisms of Merton's views on working-class deviance:

1. First, he argued that delinquency is a collective rather than an individual response. Whereas Merton saw individuals responding to their position in the class structure, Cohen saw individuals joining together in a collective response.
2. Second, Cohen argued that Merton failed to account for **non-utilitarian crime** – such as vandalism and joyriding – which does not produce monetary reward. Cohen questioned whether such forms of offending were directly motivated by the success goals of the mainstream culture. He agreed, however, that Merton's theory was 'highly plausible as an explanation for adult professional crime and for the property delinquency of some older and semi-professional thieves'.

Cohen began his argument in a similar way to Merton. Lower working-class boys hold the success goals of the mainstream culture, but, due largely to educational failure and the dead-end jobs that result from this, they have little opportunity to attain those goals. This failure can be explained by their position in the social structure. Cohen supported the view that **cultural deprivation** accounts for the lack of educational success of members of the lower working class. (The theory of cultural deprivation is outlined in Chapter 10, pp. 629–30.)

Stuck at the bottom of the stratification system, with avenues to success blocked, many lower working-class boys suffer from **status frustration** – that is, they are frustrated and dissatisfied with their low status in society. They resolve their frustration, not by turning to criminal paths to success, as Merton suggested, but by rejecting the success goals of the mainstream culture. They replace them with an alternative set of norms and values, in terms of which they can achieve success and gain prestige. The result is a **delinquent subculture**. It can be seen as a collective solution to the common problems of lower working-class adolescents.

The delinquent subculture not only rejects the mainstream culture, it also reverses it. In Cohen's words, 'the delinquent subculture takes its norms from the larger culture but turns them upside down'. Thus, a high value is placed on activities such as stealing, vandalism and truancy, which are condemned in the wider society. Cohen described the delinquent subculture in the following way: 'Throughout there is a kind of malice apparent, an enjoyment of the discomfiture of others, a delight in the defiance of taboos.' He illustrates this theme with the example of a boy defecating on the teacher's desk.

But the delinquent subculture also offers positive rewards. Those who perform successfully in terms of the values of the subculture gain recognition and prestige in the eyes of their peers. Thus stealing becomes, according to Cohen, not so much a means of achieving success in terms of mainstream goals, but 'a valued activity to which attaches glory, prowess and profound satisfaction'.

Cohen argued that, in this way, lower working-class boys solve the problem of status frustration. They reject mainstream values, which offer them little chance of success, and substitute deviant values, in terms of which they can be successful. Cohen thus provides an explanation for delinquent acts which do not appear to be motivated by monetary reward.

Evaluation of Cohen

Steven Box (1981) believed Cohen's theory was only plausible for a small minority of offenders. He questioned Cohen's view that most young people who offend originally accepted the mainstream standards of success. Rather than experiencing shame and guilt at their own failure, Box argued, they feel resentment at being regarded as failures by teachers and middle-class youths whose values they do not share and cannot accept. They turn against those who look down on them; they will not tolerate the way they are insulted.

Cohen has also been criticized for his selective use of the idea of lower-class subculture. David Bordua (1962) argued that he used it to explain the educational failure of lower working-class youngsters, with the notion of cultural deprivation, but he did not use it to explain youth offending. Thus, whereas cultural deprivation is passed on from one generation to the next, this does not seem to happen with the delinquent subculture. It appears to be created anew by each generation reacting to its position in the social structure.

David Matza (1964) questioned the view that most delinquents are strongly opposed to mainstream values and strongly committed to delinquent gangs. Matza's research in the USA suggested that the majority of youths who were seen as delinquent accepted most of the mainstream values of society and only occasionally and in special circumstances committed offences. Few were strongly involved in a delinquent subculture; they simply drifted into delinquency from time to time without any commitment to delinquent values or a delinquent way of life.

Despite such criticisms, Cohen's ideas continue to offer insights into delinquency. Many would agree with Cohen that the search for status is an important aspect of delinquent behaviour.

Richard A. Cloward and Lloyd E. Ohlin – *Delinquency and Opportunity*

In *Delinquency and Opportunity* the American sociologists Richard A. Cloward and Lloyd E. Ohlin (1961) combined and developed many of the insights of Merton and Cohen. While largely accepting Merton's view of working-class criminal deviance, they argued he had failed to explain the different forms that deviance takes. For example, why do some offenders concentrate on theft while others appear preoccupied with vandalism and violence?

Cloward and Ohlin argued that Merton had only dealt with half the picture. He had explained deviance in terms of the **legitimate opportunity structure** but he failed to consider the **illegitimate opportunity structure**. In other words, just as the opportunity to be successful by legitimate means varies, so does the opportunity for success by illegitimate means.

By examining access to, and opportunity for entry into, illegitimate opportunity structures, Cloward and Ohlin provided an explanation for different forms of deviance.

They began their explanation of working-class delinquency from the same point as Merton: that is, there is greater pressure on members of the working class to deviate because they have less opportunity to succeed by legitimate means. Cloward and Ohlin then distinguished three possible responses to this situation: the 'criminal subculture', the 'conflict subculture' and the 'retreatist subculture'. The development of one or other of these responses by young people depends upon their access to, and performance in terms of, the illegitimate opportunity structure.

Structure and subculture

1. **Criminal subcultures** tend to emerge in areas where there is an established pattern of organized adult crime. In such areas a 'learning environment' is provided for the young: they are exposed to criminal skills and deviant values, and presented with criminal role models. Those who perform successfully in terms of these deviant values have the opportunity to rise in the professional criminal hierarchy. They have access to the illegitimate opportunity structure. Criminal subcultures are mainly concerned with **utilitarian crime** – crime which produces financial reward.
2. **Conflict subcultures** tend to develop in areas where young people have little opportunity for access to illegitimate opportunity structures. There is little organized adult crime to provide an 'apprenticeship' for the young offenders and opportunities for them to climb the illegitimate ladder to success. Such areas usually have a high turnover of population and lack unity and cohesiveness. This situation tends to prevent a stable criminal subculture from developing. Thus access to both legitimate and illegitimate opportunity structures is blocked. The response to this situation is often gang violence. This serves as a release for anger and frustration, and a means of obtaining prestige in terms of the values of the subculture.
3. Finally, Cloward and Ohlin analysed Merton's retreatist response in terms of legitimate and illegitimate opportunity structures. They suggested that some lower-class adolescents form **retreatist subcultures**, organized mainly around illegal drug use, because they have failed to succeed in both the legitimate and illegitimate structures. As failed criminals or failed gang members, they retreat, tails between their legs, into retreatist subcultures.

Evaluation of Cloward and Ohlin

Cloward and Ohlin produced a more sophisticated version of structural and subcultural theory. By combining the work of Merton and Cohen, and adding the notion of the illegitimate opportunity structure, they attempted to explain the variety of forms that deviance might take. Nevertheless, the theory has not been without its critics.

Roger Hopkins Burke (2001) identifies three main criticisms of Cloward and Ohlin:

1. The idea of the criminal subculture is based on gangs in Chicago in the 1920s and 1930s and it is highly debatable how far the analysis would be applicable today.
2. Hopkins Burke argues that their theory is based upon a false assumption that the working class is a homogeneous group.
3. He believes that Cloward and Ohlin offer 'a grossly simplistic explanation of drug misuse, which is, in reality, fairly common among successful middle-class professional people'.

Taylor *et al.* (1973) argued that Merton, Cohen, and Cloward and Ohlin share one major fault in common: they all assume that everybody in America starts off by being committed to the success goal of achieving wealth. Taylor *et al.* believe that individuals pursue a much greater variety of goals. An individual, for example, may refuse to take a new job or accept a promotion which offers higher pay, because it would disrupt their family life, reduce the amount of leisure time they enjoy, or result in greater stress.

Nevertheless, it is clear that some people in the USA, Britain and elsewhere place considerable emphasis on material success. The **marketization** of capitalist societies (see pp. 355–9 for a discussion of crime and marketization) may have made these theories increasingly relevant. For example, Cloward and Ohlin's analysis of illegitimate opportunity structures could be applied to the organization of the supply of illegal drugs in towns and cities.

Nigel South (1997) believes the British drug trade is largely based around disorganized crime (which can be compared to Cloward and Ohlin's conflict subcultures), although some of the trade is based around professional criminal organization (more akin to criminal subcultures). Some drug users themselves could be seen as part of a retreatist subculture. Thus, once again, it is possible to use classic theories to understand contemporary patterns of criminality. (See also Simon Winlow's study of crime in Sunderland, pp. 383–6.)

The underclass and crime

Charles Murray – welfare, culture and criminality

Some contemporary sociologists have developed a cultural explanation for crime which uses the concept of underclass rather than that of subculture. Some accounts of the underclass, such as that of Charles Murray (1989), do not accept that the underclass share the same values as other members of society. They see the underclass as responsible for a high proportion of crime, and explain their criminality in terms of their rejection of mainstream values and norms.

Murray largely attributes the development of such values to the generosity of welfare states. The payments provided by welfare states have made it possible for young women to become single parents and for young men to reject the idea that it is important to hold down a job (see pp. 64–5 and 242–4 for further discussion of Murray's views).

Inequality, the underclass and crime

Although not a supporter of Murray's theory, Stephen Jones (1998) argues that there is 'a growing underclass who inhabit the run-down areas found in most American cities'. He believes this gives rise to rather different criminal activities compared to those found in the lower class in America in the 1950s. He says: 'Gangs are now divided far more on racial grounds and their major activities centre on drugs. Disputes over territory are based on seemingly rational economic grounds rather than expressions of male machismo' (Jones, 1998).

Ian Taylor (1997) also believes that an underclass exists in American and British cities. However, he does not explain either the existence of the underclass or any involvement in criminality in the same way as Murray. He argues that the marketization of American and British society, the declining demand for unskilled labour, and rising inequality are all responsible for the development of an underclass. Young, unskilled, working-class males have been particularly affected by the long-term effects of increasing inequality and declining job opportunities. Taylor describes the situation in Britain in the following way:

> *Many of the older industrial areas of England, Scotland, and Wales ... began to be plagued by quite unknown levels of theft and burglary, car stealing, interpersonal violence, and also by a crippling sense of fear and insecurity, which cuts thousands of their residents off from the pleasures of the broader consumer society and the compensations of friendship and neighbourhood.* Taylor, 1997

To Taylor, then, underclass criminality is a consequence of material deprivation rather than an unacceptable culture.

Evaluation of underclass theories of crime

Underclass theories have been extensively criticized. In both Britain and America, some people have questioned the view that there is a distinctive underclass culture, and some that there is an underclass at all. Some sociologists have seen the idea of an underclass as far more applicable in the USA than in Britain. Others have accepted that an underclass may exist, but deny that it has an ethnic component (see pp. 64–6 and 204–7).

Perhaps the strongest arguments against underclass theories of criminality have been against the sort of theory espoused by Murray. For example, Henrik Tham (1998) compared welfare policies and official crime rates in Britain and Sweden in the 1980s and 1990s. In Sweden, compared to Britain, there was less increase in inequality and less use of imprisonment; and Sweden's generous welfare payments were maintained at a much higher level than in Britain. However, crime rates increased more rapidly in Britain than they did in Sweden. Tham argues that this evidence undermines Murray's claim that the generosity of welfare payments can be held responsible for underclass crime. Rather, Tham argues, crime is more closely related to increases in inequality.

Tham himself recognizes that the use of official crime rates is open to criticism, but his work does offer more support for theories such as those of Ian Taylor, than for cultural interpretations of the underclass.

Further criticisms of Murray are to be found in the work of Jane Mooney (1998). Mooney reviewed research in Britain in order to evaluate Murray's claim that single parenthood is associated with criminality. She found that 'there is not a single substantial scrap of evidence' that such a link exists. She quotes a leaked Cabinet paper which found no direct association between single parenthood and criminality, and points out: 'The five million crimes reported to the police every year, with another ten million or more unreported, cannot conceivably be blamed on that fraction of single mothers who are on income support and have adolescent sons.'

Mooney accepts that poverty may be linked to criminality, and that many single parents are poor, but denies that single parenthood as such is important. She believes such views are blaming the victims of social inequality for society's ills. According to her own research into single parenthood in London, single mothers tend to be victims of crime, not perpetrators. Thus, about one in five single mothers in her research had been violently attacked in the previous year – twice the average rate for all women in her study.

Crime and official statistics

Many theories of crime are based in part on official statistics provided by the police, the courts, and other government agencies involved in law enforcement. In countries such as Britain and the USA, these statistics consistently show that some groups are more involved in crime than others. The working class, the young, males, and members of some minority ethnic groups are all more likely to commit crimes than the middle class, the elderly, females and whites – according to official data.

Some sociologists have taken these figures at face value and have then proceeded to explain why such groups should be so criminal. Merton, Cohen, and Cloward and Ohlin (see pp. 323–6) all assume that working-class men are the main offenders, although they differ in their explanations as to why this should be so. If it could be shown that the reliability of the figures is open to question, it would raise serious doubts about their theories.

In Britain, official statistics on crime are published annually. They provide criminologists, the police, the courts, the media, and anyone else who is interested, with two main types of data.

First, the official statistics provide information on the total number of crimes 'known to the police'. This information is often taken as an accurate measure of the total amount of crime. The data allow comparisons to be made between crimes, and with previous years. Often the figures receive widespread publicity through the media, particularly if they show increases in crime over previous years. This can lead to concern that the country is being engulfed in a crime wave.

Figure 6.1 shows long-term trends in crimes recorded by the police in Britain from 1876 to 2000. It shows that rates remained very low until the 1950s, but increased rapidly for most of the period after that. However, there were some falls in crime during the 1990s.

Figure 6.2 shows trends from1981 to 2006–7 in more detail. It shows crime in England and Wales reaching a peak in 1992 before falling back. There is a break in the figures because in 1998–9 the counting rules for recording indictable (or more serious) offences were

Figure 6.1 British crime trends, 1976–2000

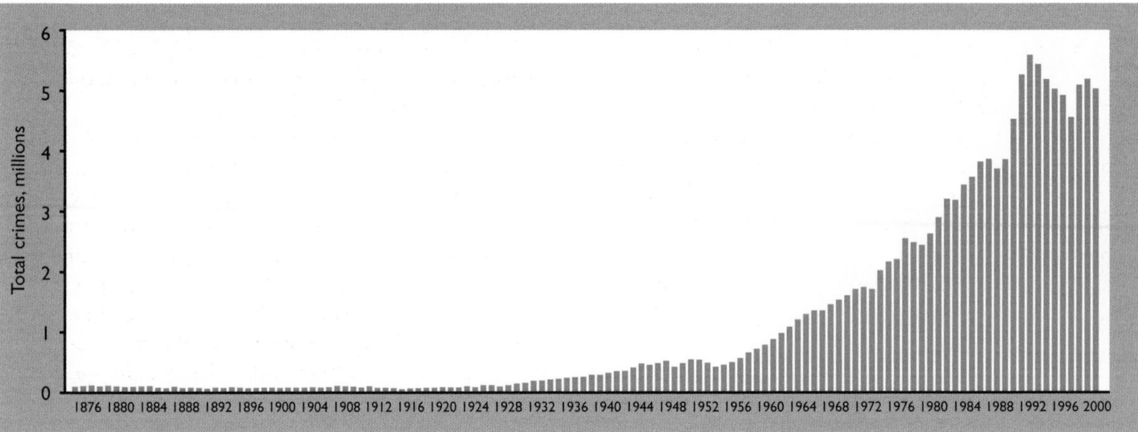

Source: M. Maguire (1997) 'Crime statistics, patterns and trends', in M. Maguire, R. Morgan and R. Reiner (eds) *The Oxford Handbook of Criminology*, Oxford University Press, Oxford, p. 158.

Figure 6.2 Trends in recorded crime in England and Wales 1981–2006/7

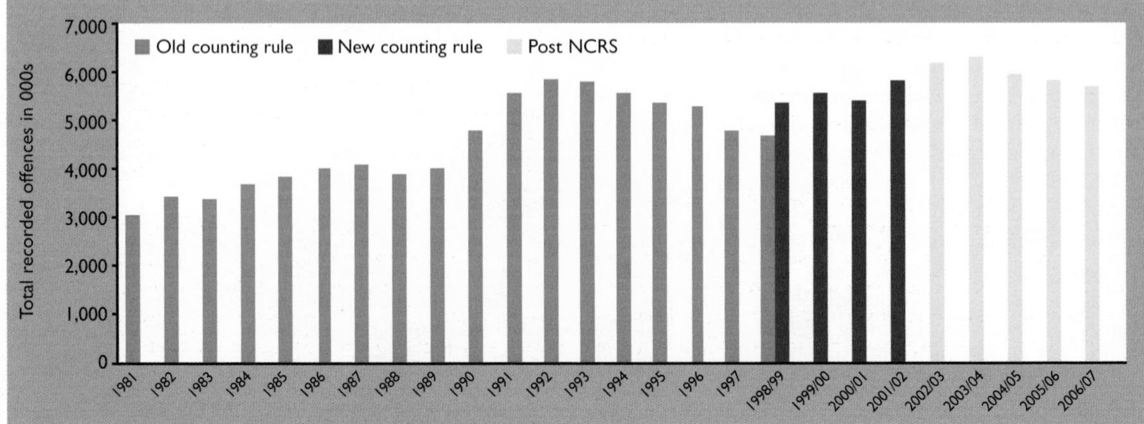

Source: S. Nicholas, C. Kershaw and A. Walker (2007) *Crime in England and Wales 2006/7*, Home Office Statistical Bulletin, London, p. 18.

changed. As Mike Maguire (2002) notes, these changes increased the amount of recorded indictable crime considerably. After 1997, offences of criminal damage to the value of £20 or less were recoded as indictable for the first time. This increased the total amount of recorded crime by about 7 per cent. In 1998 common assault and assault on a police officer began to be recorded as indictable crime, increasing the number of violent offences recorded considerably.

The counting system was changed again in 2002 and it appeared that the amount of crime had increased, but this apparent increase merely reflected the fact that the figures are now more accurate.

In 2006/7, drug offences accounted for 4 per cent of recorded crime, violent crime 19 per cent, burglary 11 per cent, theft of or from vehicles 14 per cent, other thefts 23 per cent, and criminal damage 22 per cent. More serious crimes are very rare; all sexual crimes, for example, comprise just 1 per cent of recorded crime.

It should be noted that the figures discussed above do not include all crimes. Many crimes dealt with by agencies other than the police are not recorded in the police figures because they are dealt with administratively rather than through prosecutions. Maguire (2002) points out that this can include tax evasion and benefits fraud. He also points out that offences recorded by police forces which are not the responsibility of the Home Office are not included in the main statistics. These include the Ministry of Defence Police, the British Transport Police and the UK Atomic Energy Police, who between them deal with about 80,000 notifiable offences per year.

The second type of data the official statistics provide is information on the social characteristics of those who have been convicted of offences, such as their age and gender. It is on these figures that a number of theories of crime have been based.

Each of these sets of figures will now be examined in detail.

Unrecorded crime

It is quite obvious that not all crimes that take place are recorded by the police. There is much evidence of a substantial 'dark figure' of unrecorded crimes.

Before a crime is recorded, at least three things must happen:

1. It must come to someone's attention that a crime has taken place.
2. It must be reported to the relevant agency.
3. That agency must be willing to accept that the law has been broken.

Not all crimes, though, have a specific victim who is aware that they have been wronged. If you return home to find a broken window and valuable items missing from your house, it will not take you long to work out that you have been burgled. Crimes such as tax evasion, however, do not have a single victim to report the offence. In this case the victim is the community as a whole, which has been deprived of tax revenue. The extent of this type of crime is difficult to measure, since it can only be uncovered by investigation. However, it is possible to estimate the amount of crime of which victims are aware, but which is not reported to the police, or not recorded as crime by them.

Victimization studies

In 1983 the Home Office Research and Planning Unit published the first British Crime Surveys. These studies contain data on crime in Britain. The first study was conducted in 1981 and published the following year. By 1998 seven surveys had been completed and from 2000 it became an annual publication.

The studies complement the annual police statistics. Instead of relying on police records, the Home Office carries out **victimization studies**. These involve asking individuals if they have been the victim of crime in the previous year. People are also asked whether they reported the crimes, and whether the police recorded them. The 2006/7 British Crime Survey used a sample of 47,000 adults, aged 16 or over, in England and Wales. The overall response rate is typically over 75 per cent.

The Home Office now regards these studies as providing a source of information which is more reliable for certain crimes than the police statistics. The British Crime Survey does not cover thefts from businesses and shops, and frauds; it also excludes 'victimless crimes' (e.g. possession of drugs) and, because it is a victim-based survey, murders are not included. One very important omission is that the British Crime Survey does not cover crimes committed against those under the age of 16.

Information was collected on a range of offences committed during 2006/7 (Nicholas *et al.*, 2007). The survey found that only 41 per cent of these crimes were reported to the police. Figure 6.3 shows that the rate of reporting varied considerably by type of crime, so that 93 per cent of vehicle thefts and 81 per cent of burglaries were reported, but reporting rates were relatively low for crimes such as assault without injury, at 36 per cent, and 'theft from the person', at 35 per cent. Only 32 per cent of acts of vandalism were reported to the police.

There are a number of reasons for the non-reporting of crime – the most frequent was that victims perceived the crimes to be too trivial, or they believed that the police would or could not do much about them (71 per cent of unreported incidents). For violent crime, however, a large proportion of the incidents were not reported because victims considered the issue to be a private matter and dealt with it themselves (34 per cent). People were more likely to report a crime when they would benefit from reporting it, as in the case of car theft and burglary where crime incident numbers are required in order to make an insurance claim.

Once an incident had been reported, the police did not always accept that an offence had taken place. Indeed, until the late 1990s, it was estimated that up to 40 per cent of incidents reported to the police were not recorded by them as crimes in the categories of crime used in the British Crime Survey. However, partly as a result of the findings of the British Crime Survey, police methods of recording crime changed in 1997, and then again in 2002,

Figure 6.3 Percentage of reported British Crime Survey crimes estimated to have been reported to the police 2006/7

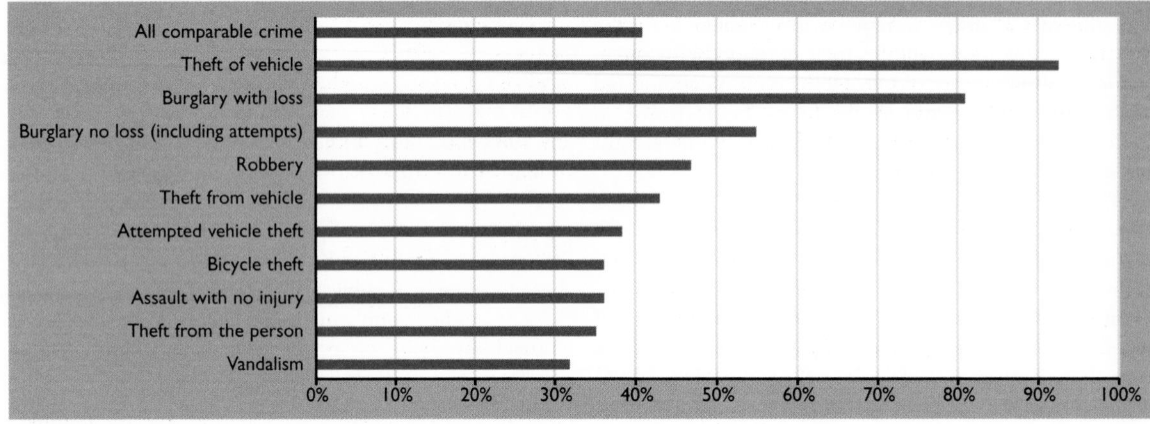

Source: S. Nicholas, C. Kershaw and A. Walker (2007) *Crime in England and Wales 2006/7*, Home Office Statistical Bulletin, London, p. 25.

Figure 6.4 Indexed trends in crime since 1981 (1981 = 1.00)

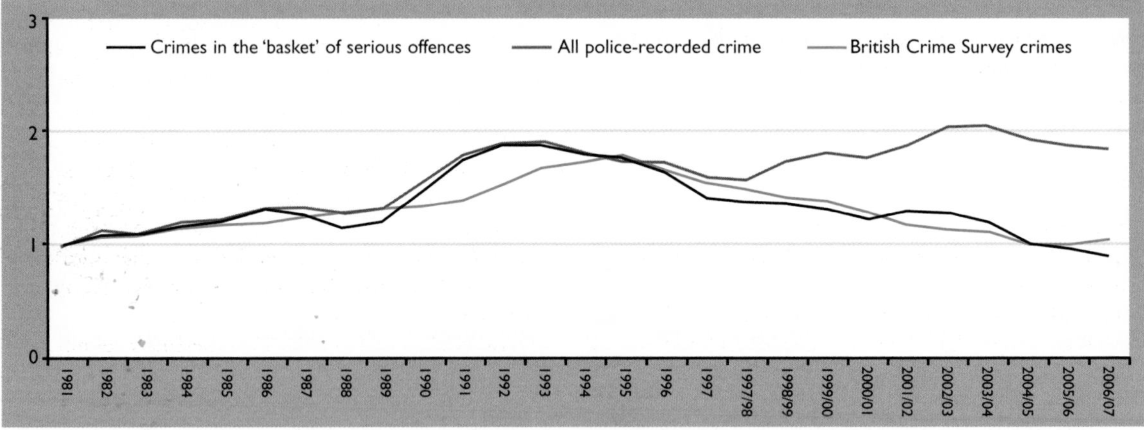

Source: S. Nicholas, C. Kershaw and A. Walker (2007) *Crime in England and Wales 2006/7*, Home Office Statistical Bulletin, London.

with the result that police-recorded crime rose very significantly, as shown in Figure 6.4.

Although victimization studies provide an indication of trends in crime and an estimate of how many crimes remain unrecorded, the data from them are not entirely reliable. Hazel Croall (1998) points out a number of problems with the British Crime Surveys:

1 Like other victim surveys the British Crime Surveys can only record crimes which victims are aware of and they therefore exclude many crimes.
2 The results 'reflect respondents' definitions of events which may not be the same as legal classifications. They are also limited by respondents' memory.'
3 Because the survey is restricted to households it does not record crimes committed against businesses or crime committed in or against institutions.
4 The early Crime Surveys only interviewed people over the age of 16 and therefore omitted most crimes committed against younger age groups.

Given these problems, the trends revealed in victimization studies should be treated with caution. However, they are probably more reliable than those shown in the police-recorded statistics because they include so many crimes which are not reported.

The characteristics of offenders – self-report studies

Only a small proportion of offenders are successfully prosecuted and find their way into the official statistics. In 2006/7 only 26 per cent of indictable offences in England and Wales were cleared up (Nicholas *et al.*, 2007). Overall, it has been estimated that only about 3 per cent of crime in England and Wales ends with a conviction (Maguire, 2002). It is possible, at least in theory, that the people who are caught, tried and convicted are a representative cross-section of all those who commit offences. On the other hand, it could be that some sections of society are much more likely to be convicted than others, irrespective of whether they have committed more crimes.

A number of sociologists have devised an alternative to official statistics for discovering the characteristics of criminals. **Self-report studies** use questionnaires or interviews to collect information about individuals, and ask them to admit to the number of crimes they have committed. The data collected can then be compared with official conviction rates to discover which offenders are most likely to be convicted.

Steven Box (1981) reviewed forty such studies on delinquency, conducted in a number of different countries. On the basis of this evidence, Box rejects the view presented in the official statistics that working-class youths are much more likely to engage in delinquency than middle-class youths. He says, 'we should be very sceptical of those who continue to argue that delinquency is located at the bottom of the stratification system'.

In a later study, conducted by Graham and Bowling (1995), it was found that social class had no influence on whether young British males and females would admit to having committed offences. However, it was found that those from lower classes were more likely to admit to more serious offences.

Of course, it is possible that those replying to questionnaires or interviews might not be truthful about the amount of crime they commit. Various tests have been carried out to check on the results of these studies. These tests range from the use of lie detectors, to questioning adolescents' friends about crimes they claim to have taken part in. Generally, it has been found that about 80 per cent of those who reply tell the truth.

Self-report studies are not, therefore, entirely reliable. However, they do locate many more offenders than those who are convicted and appear in official statistics. As such they are probably considerably more reliable than the latter.

Victims of crime

While the chance of being a victim of a minor offence is relatively high, there are very few (relatively speaking) victims of serious crime.

The risk of being a victim of crime is not equal for all; it varies by geographical area, age, gender and patterns of social activity. So, for example, young males who live in poorer areas and who go out three or more times a week are at most risk of becoming the victim of a violent offence.

Stranger violence is relatively rare. Most violent offences are committed by someone who is known or recognizable to the victim, and in the case of women, this is most likely to be a partner or ex-partner. Women are most likely to be raped by men they know, with over 50 per cent of rapes committed by someone known 'extremely well' by the victim, and a further 29 per cent by someone known to the victim. Over half of all offences involve repeat rapes by the same perpetrator over a period of time.

The risk of becoming a victim of burglary or vehicle theft is much higher in run-down areas, particularly in inner-city areas where there are high levels of rented accommodation. Poorer households containing a single parent are also at greater risk.

People from minority ethnic groups are also more at risk of personal crimes – particularly street robbery – possibly because members of minority ethnic groups tend to live in inner city areas and have higher levels of poverty and single parenthood.

As we have just seen, the probability of being a victim of crime is not spread randomly across the population. However, even more noticeable is that a relatively small proportion of the population is subjected to a high proportion of all offences. This is because some victims of crime are repeatedly offended against. In 2006/7, for example, 32 per cent of those who had been the victims of vandalism once were victimized at least once again, and 28 per cent of people who were the victims of violence were attacked on at least one other occasion. This is known as **repeat victimization**.

Repeat victimization refers to a person being the victim of the same offence at least twice. However, sociologists have also suggested another category, known as **multiple victimization**, where the person has been the victim of any crime more than once in a year. In 2006/7, 34 per cent of victims accounted for 62 per cent of all crime.

White-collar crime

So far it has been suggested that official statistics do not give an accurate picture of the extent of offending among middle- and working-class adolescents. Unfortunately, few self-report studies have been conducted on adults, so it is not possible to compare official statistics and the findings of self-report studies on adult crime. Even so, there is evidence that offences committed by adults of high social status are less likely to lead to arrests and convictions than those committed by adults of low social status.

Edwin Sutherland was the first sociologist to study what has come to be known as 'white-collar crime'. Sutherland (1960) defines **white-collar crime** as 'crimes committed by persons of high social status and respectability in the course of their occupations'. Such crimes include bribery and corruption in business and politics, misconduct by professionals such as doctors and lawyers, the breaking of trade regulations, food and drug laws, and safety regulations in industry, the misuse of patents and trademarks, and misrepresentation in advertising.

David Nelken (2002) believes Sutherland's definition is open to criticism. For example, crimes may be committed by people of high social status outside of their occupations. Some crime may be the responsibility of organizations or corporations (often called **corporate crime**) rather than committed by individuals. Furthermore, the phrase 'persons of high social status' is ambiguous, since Sutherland gives no clear definition of 'high social status'.

Gary Slapper and Steve Tombs (1999) argue that some of the definitional problems can be overcome by distinguishing between white-collar and corporate crime. In their view, the term 'white-collar crime' should only be applied to 'crimes by the individually rich or powerful which are committed in the furtherance of their own interests, often against corporations or organizations within which they are working'. Corporate crimes, on the other hand, are crimes committed by or for corporations which act to further their interests rather than those of the individual employer.

Whatever the problems with Sutherland's definition, he did succeed in identifying a category of offence which subsequent research and events have suggested is widespread. For example, in the business world in the UK, Ian Taylor argues that there has been:

> *an enormous explosion of fraud and corruption that has accompanied the construction of a free market economy since 1979, and which has escalated since the Big Bang of 27 October 1986, when the London Stock Exchange was significantly opened up to a largely unregulated system for the marketing of financial securities.* Taylor, 1992

One common type of fraud is **insider dealing**, in which shares in a company are bought by individuals who know that the company is about to be the subject of a takeover bid. These individuals illegally use their knowledge to make a killing on the stock market.

Some of the most significant crimes of this type took place in the USA in the 1980s. A number of employees of the investment bank Drexel Burnham Lambert were involved in the issuing of junk bonds. These are bonds issued with high yields in order to finance takeover bids, but often with little financial backing behind them to give security to investors. Using illegal insider trading, Drexel Burnham Lambert was able to make $800 million in 1986 alone (Punch, 1996). The leading participant, Michael Milken, served several years in prison and paid fines totalling $650 million. However, he is still believed to be extremely wealthy, having made no less than an estimated $1 billion over a five-year period.

In an even more spectacular example of the losses that can result from irresponsible financial deals, in 1998 it was found that an investment fund, or hedge fund, Long-Term Capital Management (LTCM), had made losses running into billions of US dollars. The fund had borrowed some $900 billion, more than 250 times its capital, to gamble on such things as future interest rates in Europe. Such was the scale of the collapse that it threatened the whole Western banking system. In November 1998, major Western governments decided to put together a $3.5 billion rescue package.

Larry Elliot (1998) puts such sums of money in context by comparing the amounts spent on propping up LTCM with those pledged for disaster relief in November 1998 when disastrous floods hit Central America. Thousands were killed and the economies of countries such as Honduras were devastated, yet Western governments initially pledged help of just $100 million in emergency aid – less than a thirtieth of that being spent bailing out LTCM.

Slapper and Tombs (1999) identified another area of corporate crime in which losses have been enormous: the mis-selling of pensions in the UK. Many leading pension providers have been found to have provided illegal and misleading advice to people investing in personal pensions, leading them to make costly decisions to invest in inappropriate personal pensions. Slapper and Tombs admit it is hard to estimate the total amount involved with any degree of certainty, but the Financial Services Authority put the figure at £11 billion in 1998. Slapper and Tombs comment:

> *this figure of £11 billion – even if ultimately an overestimate, and even though not an annual but a 'once-and-for-all' cost – dwarfs the costs of almost all estimates of all forms of street crime put together.*
> Slapper and Tombs, 1999

Pension funds have also sometimes been the subject of fraud. Perhaps the most famous businessman accused of fraud was Robert Maxwell. He was the owner of Mirror Group Newspapers and numerous other businesses before his mysterious drowning near the Canary Islands in 1991. Maxwell had used money from the pension fund of Mirror Group employees to stave-off the collapse of his business empire. When it finally collapsed, it left debts of some £2 billion.

The inadequacy of the City regulation of business and banking was also illustrated by the bankruptcy of BCCI (the Bank of Credit and Commerce International) in 1991. The bank lost more than $10 billion in trading that was not recorded in its accounts, and by making fictitious loans.

More recently, major scandals have emerged concerning US companies which had produced accounts which misled investors about their financial position. In 2001 it was revealed that the US company Enron had concealed huge debts. The company was forced into bankruptcy and had to sell assets to try to meet some of the claims of creditors owed around $50 billion. The following year another giant American company, WorldCom, admitted accounting 'errors' totalling $7.65 billion. The company was forced into bankruptcy and had to announce plans to make 17,000 workers redundant.

Corruption on a massive scale took place during the 1970s when enormous amounts of money were lent, perfectly legally, by banks to governments in less developed countries such as the Philippines (where President Marcos invested vast sums in bank accounts abroad) and Mexico (where it has been estimated $40 billion went missing). The end result of such loans and the corruption that they encouraged was a worldwide debt crisis in which many poorer nations ended up heavily indebted to richer countries (George, 1988).

Offences committed by businesses do not just involve loss of money; some also result in injury, disability or loss of life. In 1984 an escape of poisonous gas from a chemical plant at Bhopal in India killed more than 3,000 people and caused permanent injury to a further 20,000. The escape of gas was caused by inadequate safety procedures at the plant, which was owned by a subsidiary of the US multinational corporation Union Carbide. No criminal charges were brought against the company when it agreed to pay $470 million in compensation to victims and their families.

Personal harm

Another tragic example of the consequences of negligence was the *Herald of Free Enterprise* disaster in 1987: 188 people died when the P&O car ferry sank after setting sail from Zeebrugge harbour with its bow doors open.

Inadequate safety precautions can lead to death tolls which dwarf that from street crimes. For example, in 2001–2 there were 886 homicides in Britain, according to police statistics (Simmons *et al.*, 2002). However, according to Michael Streeter (1997), in the late 1990s the effects of asbestos (which can cause the fatal lung disease mesothelioma) alone killed about 3,500 people per year in Britain. According to Streeter, the number of deaths resulting from exposure to asbestos were rising and were spreading beyond the traditional victims – building-site workers – to groups such as clerical workers and teachers, who had been exposed during construction work at their places of employment. The actions which resulted in these deaths may not have been illegal, but their consequences in terms of loss of life were very serious.

Serious injuries can also result from inadequate safety precautions, which may or may not contravene regulations. According to Barrie Clement (1997), figures from the British Health and Safety Executive show that in 1996

100 people were blinded at work, and 1,158 had an amputation as a result of an accident. However, the Health and Safety Executive only actually investigated six of the blindings. There were 302 fatal accidents at work in 1996.

The most dramatic example of the possible effects of crimes like these is the thalidomide affair. The drug thalidomide was manufactured by Chemie Grunethal of Germany; it was used as a sleeping pill or tranquillizer. However, the use of the drug by pregnant women led to over 8,000 seriously deformed babies being born throughout the world. Despite numerous examples of adverse reactions from clinical tests, the drug was marketed with little delay, the advertising proclaiming that it was 'completely safe'. The company was slow to withdraw the product even when the drug's disastrous effects were known.

Politicians and officials

White-collar crimes involving politicians and state officials come to light from time to time. The Watergate affair is one of the best-known examples. The US President Richard Nixon was forced to leave office in 1974 as a result of his involvement in the break-in and attempted bugging of the offices of political opponents, and his involvement in using illegal sources of money to fund political campaigns.

In another US political scandal, Irangate, government officials were found to have been involved in the exchange of arms for hostages with the government of Iran, which went against stated US policy.

In Britain, accusations were made that members of the Thatcher government knowingly allowed companies to export products for military use, including parts for a 'supergun', to the government of Iraq. This contravened the British government's own ban on such exports during the Iran–Iraq war.

Another member of the Conservative government, Jonathan Aitken, was found to have accepted hospitality at the Paris Ritz Hotel from Mohamed Al Fayed in return for asking questions in parliament. Aitken was later imprisoned for conspiracy to pervert the course of justice, as a result of trying to cover up what had happened.

Michael Woodiwiss (1993) claims that the US government has a history of promoting drug trafficking. During the Vietnam War, 'opponents charged that the CIA was knowingly financing its operations from opium money'. This was confirmed in a book written by Orrin DeForest, a senior investigations officer with the CIA. To raise more money, army officers allowed heroin to be smuggled back to America in the corpses of American soldiers. The bodies were cut open and had up to 25 kg of heroin concealed inside.

Gregg Barak (1994) accuses the US government of backing, at various times, repressive dictators in the Philippines, Brazil, South Korea, Cuba, Iran and Argentina; of helping to overthrow or undermine democratically elected governments in countries including Chile, Jamaica, Guatemala and Nicaragua; and of the use of illegal means to deal with domestic protest movements, such as the Black Panthers, the American Indian Movement, and anti-war movements during the 1960s.

In 1998, President Clinton ordered the bombing of a chemical factory in Sudan on the grounds that it was manufacturing chemical weapons. However, according to Ed Vulliamy and colleagues (1998), America's own tests could find no evidence that chemical weapons were being made there. The result was to destroy some of Sudan's capacity to produce desperately needed medicines.

The underestimation of white-collar and corporate crime

A number of factors combine to reduce the apparent extent and seriousness of white-collar crime.

1. It is difficult to detect: many white-collar crimes are 'crimes without victims'.
2. In cases of bribery and corruption, both parties involved may see themselves as gaining from the arrangement, both are liable to prosecution, and therefore neither is likely to report the offence.
3. In cases where the victim is the public at large (such as misrepresentation in advertising), few members of the public have the expertise to realize that they are being misled, or a knowledge of the legal procedure to redress the wrong. In such cases, detection and prosecution are often left to a government agency which rarely has the personnel or finances to bring more than a few cases to court in the hope of deterring the practice.

White-collar crimes, if detected, are rarely prosecuted. In the thalidomide affair no individual was ever found guilty of a criminal offence. Only one court case, in Canada, for compensation for one deformed baby, was ever completed. With their massive resources and skilled lawyers, the companies involved used delaying tactics to such an effect that every other case was settled out of court.

Often, white-collar crimes are dealt with administratively by the various boards, and commissions and inspectorates are appointed to deal with them. 'Official warnings' rather than prosecutions are frequently the rule. In the case of professionals, their own associations usually deal with misconduct and, again, prosecution is rare. In extreme cases, doctors and lawyers may lose their licence to practise, but more often than not their professional associations simply hand down a reprimand.

The sociological study of white-collar crime provides some support for the view that there is one law for the rich and another for the poor. Sutherland (1960) argues that there is a consistent bias 'involved in the administration of criminal justice under laws which apply to business and the professions and which therefore involve only the upper socio-economic group'. The matter is neatly summarized by Willy Sutton, a professional bank robber:

> *Others accused of defrauding the government of hundreds of thousands of dollars merely get a letter from a committee in Washington asking them to come in and talk it over. Maybe it's justice but it's puzzling to a guy like me.*
> Quoted in Clinard, 1974

Official statistics probably underestimate the extent of white-collar and corporate crime to a far greater degree than they underestimate the extent of crime in general. As a result, official statistics portray crime as predominantly working-class behaviour.

In this context, deviant norms and values develop. Having been defined and treated as outsiders, the hippies tend to express and accentuate this difference. Hair is grown longer, clothes become more and more unconventional. Drug use becomes transformed from a peripheral to a central activity, especially as police react more strongly against the deviance they have helped to create.

Young argued that, because of increased police activity, 'drug taking in itself becomes of greater value to the group as a symbol of their difference, and of their defiance of perceived social injustices'. In this situation a deviant subculture evolves and deviant self-concepts are reinforced, all of which makes it increasingly difficult for the hippies to re-enter conventional society.

Howard Becker – the origins of 'deviant' activity

Howard Becker's approach stressed the importance of the public identification of a deviant. It suggested that a **deviant label** can lead to further deviance, and can even change individuals' self-concepts so that they come to regard themselves as deviant for the first time.

However, Becker argued that this process is by no means inevitable. Ex-convicts do get jobs and go 'straight'; drug addicts do sometimes give up their habit and re-enter conventional society.

Furthermore, Becker tried to explain how individuals get involved in deviant activities in the first place. He conducted his own study of marijuana smoking in order to explain how the habit could start, and noted that various conditions had to be met if the first experimentation with the drug was to lead to regular use.

As an interactionist, Becker emphasized the importance of the **subjective meanings** given to experiences. Thus the physical experiences that result from taking drugs are interpreted by the individual as he or she interacts with others. With regard to marijuana, Becker says, 'The user feels dizzy, thirsty; his scalp tingles, he misjudges time and distance.' These effects will not necessarily be defined as pleasurable: other experienced smokers will need to reassure the new user that the effects are indeed desirable, and should be sought again.

Unlike the other theories of crime and deviance that we have looked at in this chapter, Becker examined becoming deviant as a process. Whereas Merton (1968) identified a single cause of deviance (anomie) to explain deviance throughout a person's life, Becker stressed that the reasons for deviance might change as time passes and circumstances alter. Thus the reason why someone tries marijuana for the first time could be quite different from the reasons for continuing after being caught and labelled.

Becker used what he called a 'sequential' approach to the explanation of deviance; and at any stage in the sequence it is possible that the deviant will return to conformity.

Edwin M. Lemert – societal reaction as the 'cause' of deviance

Like Becker, Edwin M. Lemert (1972) emphasized the importance of **societal reaction** – the reaction of others to the deviant – in the explanation of deviance. Lemert distinguished between 'primary' and 'secondary' deviation.

Primary deviation

Primary deviation consists of deviant acts before they are publicly labelled. There are probably any number of causes of primary deviation and it is largely a fruitless exercise to enquire into them, for the following reasons:

1. Samples of deviants are based upon those who have been labelled and are therefore unrepresentative. For example, it makes little sense to delve into the backgrounds of convicted criminals to find the cause of their deviance, without examining criminals who have not been caught.
2. Many so-called deviant acts may be so widespread as to be normal in statistical terms. Thus, most males may at some time commit a homosexual act, engage in delinquent activities, and so on.

In fact, Lemert suggested that the only thing that 'known' deviants probably have in common is the fact that they have been publicly labelled as such.

Not only is the search for the causes of primary deviation largely fruitless, but also primary deviation itself is relatively unimportant. Lemert argued that it 'has only marginal implications for the status and the psychic structure of the person concerned'. Thus Lemert suggested that the odd deviant act has little effect on individuals' self-concepts and status in the community, and does not prevent them from continuing a normal and conventional life.

Secondary deviation

The important factor in 'producing' deviance is societal reaction – the public identification of the deviant, and the consequences of this for the individual concerned. **Secondary deviation** is the response of the individual or the group to societal reaction.

Lemert argued that studies of deviance should focus on secondary deviation, which has major consequences for the individual's self-concept, status in the community and future actions. In comparison, primary deviation has little significance: 'In effect the original "causes" of the deviation recede and give way to the central importance of the disapproving, degradational, and isolating reactions of society.'

Thus, Lemert claimed that societal reaction can be seen as the major 'cause' of deviance. This view, he argued, 'gives a proper place to social control as a dynamic factor or "cause" of deviance'. In this way, Lemert neatly reverses traditional views of deviance: the blame for deviance lies with the agents of social control rather than with the deviant.

Stuttering and societal reaction

Lemert was particularly convincing in his paper entitled 'Stuttering among the North Pacific Coastal Indians', which examines the relationship between societal reaction and deviance.

Previous research had indicated a virtual absence of stuttering among North American Indians: indeed, most tribes did not even have a word for this speech irregularity. However, Lemert's investigation of deviance among various tribes living in the North Pacific coastal area of British Columbia revealed evidence of stuttering both before and after contact with whites. In addition, the languages of these tribes contained clearly defined concepts of stutterers and stuttering. It is particularly significant that their inland neighbours, the Bannock and Shoshone, had no words for stuttering, and research, using a large-scale sample of members of these tribes, found no evidence of actual stuttering.

The North Pacific coastal Indians had a rich ceremonial life, involving singing, dancing and speech-making. Their legends and stories were filled with references to famous orators and outstanding speeches. From an early age, children were initiated into ceremonial life, and parents stressed the importance of a faultless performance. There were rigorous and exacting standards to be met; rituals had to be performed exactly as they should be. If they did not meet these standards, children shamed their parents and suffered the ridicule of their peers. In particular, there was a highly developed sensitivity to any speech defect. Children and parents alike were anxious about any speech irregularity and responded to it with guilt and shame.

Lemert concluded that stuttering was actually produced by societal reaction. The concern about, and the reaction to, speech irregularities actually created them. He argued that the culture, both past and present:

> *seems favourable to the development of stuttering, that stutterers were and still are socially penalized, that parents tended to be specifically concerned or anxious about the speech development of their children, that children were anxious about ritual performances involving solo verbal behaviour.* Lemert, 1962

In other American Indian societies, where such concerns were largely absent, stuttering was unknown. Thus, Lemert argued, societal reaction, prompted by a concern about particular forms of deviance, can actually produce those forms of deviance.

Labelling theory and social policies

Stephen Jones (2001) reviewed the policy implications of interactionist and labelling theories. He argues that these theories have two main implications. First, they suggest that as many types of behaviour as possible should be decriminalized. Second, they imply that, when the law has to intervene, it should try to avoid giving people a self-concept in which they view themselves as criminals. This might involve trying to keep people out of prison or warning people rather than prosecuting them.

Both of these approaches have had some influence. For example, in Britain, the *Independent* newspaper started a campaign in 1997 to legalize cannabis. In countries such as the Netherlands some 'soft' drugs have been effectively legalized.

However, in Britain, the main impact of such thinking has probably been on juvenile justice. Jones suggests there have been rather inconsistent policies in this area, but there have been some attempts to avoid stigmatizing young offenders. These have included using cautions rather than prosecutions, introducing separate juvenile courts (under the Children and Young Person's Act, 1993), and granting anonymity to young offenders.

For adults, the only measure of this nature was contained in the Rehabilitation of Offenders Act, 1974. This allowed offenders to withhold from employers information about most offences, once a period of time (which depended on the offence) had elapsed.

However, as Jones points out, such policies became less popular during the 1990s. In some quarters there has been a renewed emphasis on the public shaming of offenders in order to deter others. Examples of this include writing to men accused of kerb crawling, so that their wives find out about their offence, and the naming of paedophiles in newspapers.

In 2000, after the murder of a young girl, Sarah Payne, the *News of the World* newspaper started a (so far unsuccessful) campaign for the public to be informed of the identity of sex offenders. As Jones points out, this had the ironic effect not of reducing crime as was intended, but of increasing it, when vigilante attacks took place on suspected paedophiles. One unfortunate victim of such attacks in South Wales was actually a paediatrician rather than a paedophile.

This evidence suggests that, whatever the strengths and weaknesses of labelling theory, its influence declined in the 1990s. However, it also suggests that labelling can actually increase offending by those determined to punish suspected offenders.

Criticisms of the interactionist perspective

In terms of sociological theory, in the 1960s the interactionist view of deviance enjoyed wide popularity. For many sociologists, the work of writers such as Becker, Lemert and Goffman became the accepted, orthodox perspective on deviance. Nevertheless, in the 1970s it began to provoke strong criticism. Interactionists rallied to the defence of their work and attempted to show that the criticisms were unjustified.

The definition of deviance

The first line of criticism attacked the interactionist definition of deviance. Becker and Lemert argued that deviance was created by the social groups who defined acts as deviant. Taylor, Walton and Young (1973), however, claimed that this view was mistaken. To them, most deviance can be defined in terms of the actions of those who break social rules, rather than in terms of the reaction of a social audience.

For example, it is true that in some circumstances deliberately killing another person may be regarded as justified: you may be acting in self-defence, or carrying out your duties as a soldier. However, no matter who makes up the social audience, a 'premeditated killing for personal gain' will always be regarded as deviant in our society. As Taylor *et al.* put it, 'we do not live in a world of free social meanings': in many circumstances there will be little or no freedom of choice in determining whether an act is regarded as deviant or not.

They promise cooperation with the juvenile officers, assuring them that their son or daughter is suitably remorseful.

As a result, the middle-class juvenile is often defined as ill rather than criminal, as accidentally straying from the path of righteousness rather than committed to wrongdoing, as cooperative rather than recalcitrant, as having a real chance of reforming rather than being a 'born loser'. He or she is typically 'counselled, warned and released'. Thus, in Cicourel's words, 'what ends up being called justice is negotiable'.

Cicourel based his research on two Californian cities, each with a population of around 100,000. The socio-economic characteristics of the two populations were similar. In terms of structural theories, the numbers of delinquents produced by the pressures of the social structure should be similar in each city. However, Cicourel found a significant difference in the numbers of delinquents arrested and charged. He argues that this difference can only be accounted for by the size, organization, policies and practices of the juvenile and police bureaux.

For example, the city with the highest rate of delinquency employed more juvenile officers and kept more detailed records on offenders. In the second city, the delinquency rate fluctuated sharply. Cicourel argues that in this city the response of the police to delinquency 'tends to be quite variable depending on publicity given to the case by the local paper, or the pressure generated by the mayor or chief or Captain of Detectives'. Thus, societal reaction can be seen directly to affect the rate of delinquency.

Cicourel argues that delinquents are produced by the agencies of social control. Certain individuals are selected, processed and labelled as deviant. Justice is the result of negotiation in the interaction process. The production of delinquents is also dependent on the ways in which police and juvenile bureaux are organized, their policies, and the pressures that are brought to bear on them from local media and politicians.

In view of these observations, Cicourel questions structural and subcultural theories of deviance which see deviance as a product of pressure from the social structure. He concludes: 'The study challenges the conventional view which assumes "delinquents" are "natural" social types distributed in some ordered fashion and produced by a set of abstract "pressures" from the "social structures".'

Criticisms of Cicourel

Cicourel's study provides some useful insights into juvenile justice in the USA. He attempts to show how the meanings held by the various officials lead to some individuals being defined as delinquent. As Stephen Jones points out, his study exemplifies:

> *some of the gains that such an approach has provided. In the early 1960s, criminological orthodoxy did not question official statistics or formal processes: by the beginning of the twenty-first century no study of the subject could conceivably be undertaken without their unreliability being emphasized at an early stage.* Jones, 2001

However, Jones also argues that phenomenology has been criticized for its 'subjectivist and relativist nature'. Some critics, such as Taylor, Walton and Young (1973), certainly argue that Cicourel fails to explain how subjective meanings originate. He fails to show why, for instance, the police see the 'typical delinquent' as coming from a low income family. In common with other phenomenologists and ethnomethodologists, he does not explain who has power in society, and how the possession of power might influence the definition of crime and deviance.

The same cannot be said of Marxists, whose theories on deviance we will now examine.

Traditional Marxist perspectives on deviance

Sociologists such as William Chambliss (1976, 1978), Milton Mankoff (1976), Frank Pearce (1976; Pearce and Tombs, 1993; Pearce and Woodiwiss, 1993) and Laureen Snider (1993) have used Marxist concepts to provide a framework for understanding deviance in capitalist societies.

Such sociologists see power as largely being held by those who own and control the means of production. The superstructure reflects the relationship between the powerful and the relatively powerless: the ruling and subject classes. As part of the superstructure, the state, the agencies of social control, the law, and definitions of deviance in general, reflect and serve ruling-class interests.

As an instrument of the ruling class, the state passes laws which support ruling-class interests, maintain its power and coerce and control the subject class. (Marxist views on the role of the state are examined in Chapter 9, pp. 535–9.) Laws are not an expression of value consensus but a reflection of ruling-class ideology. Thus a general commitment to laws on the part of members of society as a whole is an aspect of false class consciousness, since, in practice, laws benefit only the ruling minority.

In the next few sections we will consider these views and their implications in detail. Neo-Marxist and other conflict perspectives on deviance will be examined later in this chapter.

Who makes the law? Who benefits?

From a Marxist perspective, laws are made by the
which represents the interests of the ruling class of laws

Many sociologists have noted the large n or example,
dealing with property in capitalist soci the history of
Hermann Mannheim (1960) wro ny other countries,
criminal legislation in England an was given by the law to
shows that excessive prominen y'. According to William
the protection of prope laws were largely unnecessary in
Chambliss (1976), such
feudal society, where land – unmovable property – was the

main source of wealth, and landowners were 'the undisputed masters of the economic resources of the country'.

However, the increasing importance of trade and commerce (which involve movable property) and the eventual replacement of feudalism by capitalism resulted in a vast number of laws protecting the property interests of the emerging capitalist class. Chambliss argues:

> *The heart of a capitalist economic system is the protection of private property, which is, by definition, the cornerstone upon which capitalist economies function. It is not surprising, then, to find that criminal laws reflect this basic concern.* Chambliss, 1976

Laureen Snider (1993) notes that the capitalist state is often reluctant to pass laws which regulate large capitalist concerns and which might threaten their profitability. She points out that capitalist states often spend vast sums of money trying to attract investment from corporations. They offer new investors tax concessions, cheap loans and grants, and build expensive infrastructures to help companies operate successfully. Having tried so hard to attract inward investment, the state is unwilling to risk alienating large corporations. Snider says: 'The state is reluctant to pass – or enforce – stringent laws against pollution, worker health and safety, or monopolies. Such measures frighten off the much sought-after investment and engender the equally dreaded loss of confidence.'

Non-decision making

Just as important as laws that are passed are laws that are not passed. **Non-decision making** is as important as decision making. In Chapter 9 it is argued that the ruling class have the power to ensure that only 'safe decisions' are taken, and to prevent many issues from ever reaching the point of decision. Chambliss (1976) applies this argument to the law.

Chambliss suggests that much of what takes place in the creation of rules is 'non-decision making'. He gives examples of situations which might well be legally defined as criminal if the ruling class did not control beliefs about what should and should not be defined as such. Thus, a movie magnate hires a nightclub and spends $20,000 on a lavish birthday party for his daughter, while people are starving a few blocks away. The wife of the US Attorney General has 200 pairs of shoes, while, in the Appalachian Mountains, parents cannot afford to buy their children a single pair. Such behaviour is justified by ruling-class ideology with statements such as: 'They've earned their money; they have a right to spend it as they see fit.'

Few break through the barriers of false class consciousness. Angela Davis, a former leader of the Black Panthers, a militant Black American organization, is the exception rather than the rule when she claims: 'The real criminals in this society are not all the people who populate the prisons across the state, but those people who have stolen the wealth of the world from the people' (quoted in Taylor *et al.*, 1973). In her eyes, the real criminals are members of the capitalist class. Ruling-class control of the superstructure prevents such views from becoming widespread, from developing into major issues, and from being translated into law.

Who breaks the law? Who gets caught?

Corporate crime

Sociologists who have been strongly influenced by Marxism tend to argue that crime is widespread in all social strata.

Laureen Snider (1993) argues: 'Many of the most serious anti-social and predatory acts committed in modern industrial countries are corporate crimes.' Snider claims that corporate crime does more harm than the 'street crimes', such as burglary, robbery and murder, which are usually seen as the most serious types of crime. Writing in 1993, she pointed out that figures suggest that corporate crime costs more, in terms of both money and lives, than street crime.

For example, in a typical year in the USA about 20,000 people are murdered, and in Britain about 600. This compares in the USA with an annual death toll of 14,000 from industrial accidents (many resulting from breaking safety regulations), 30,000 from 'unsafe and usually illegal' consumer products, 100,000 from occupationally induced diseases, and 'hundreds of thousands of cancer deaths are caused by legal and illegal environmental pollution'. In Britain, workplace accidents account for 600 deaths and 12,000 injuries annually.

According to Snider, street crime involves losses of around $4 billion each year in the USA. However, losses from corporate crime are more than twenty times greater. In recent years, 312 US savings and loan companies have been unable to pay their debts, due to fraudulent activities such as insider dealing, failing to disclose accurate information in accounts, and racketeering. The General Accounting Agency has estimated the total cost of bailing out these companies as a minimum of $325 billion and, more probably, around $500 billion. This means it is likely to cost every household in the USA $5,000.

Despite the enormous costs of corporate crime, both the penalties and the chances of prosecution for those involved in it are usually small. Snider argues that enforcement agencies are expected to balance the costs of enforcing regulations (for example, in lost profits or jobs) with the benefits. Prosecutions are normally used as a last resort, and it is more likely to be small businesses which are taken to court rather than the big corporations which do most harm.

Quoting from a variety of studies, Snider notes that under US anti-trust legislation there were 1,551 prosecutions from 1890 to 1969, but only 4.9 per cent of offenders received a prison sentence. In fact, for the first seventy-one years of the legislation no business leaders were imprisoned – the only people sent to jail were labour leaders. Some 80 per cent of the fines imposed were under $5,000.

Why break the law? Why enforce the law?

Capitalism and crime

Many Marxists see crime as a natural 'outgrowth' of capitalist society. They argue that a capitalist economic system generates crime for the following reasons:

1 The economic infrastructure is the major influence upon social relationships, beliefs and values. The capitalist mode of production emphasizes the maximization of profits and the accumulation of wealth.
2 Economic self-interest rather than public duty motivates behaviour.
3 Capitalism is based on the private ownership of property. Personal gain rather than collective well-being is encouraged.
4 Capitalism is a competitive system. Mutual aid and cooperation for the betterment of all are discouraged in favour of individual achievement at the expense of others. Competition breeds aggression, hostility and – particularly for the losers – frustration.

Chambliss (1976) argues that the greed, self-interest and hostility generated by the capitalist system motivate many crimes at all levels within society. Members of each stratum use whatever means and opportunities their class position provides to commit crime. Thus, in low income areas, the mugger, the petty thief, the pusher, the pimp and the prostitute use what they have got to get what they can. In higher income brackets, business people, lawyers and politicians have more effective means at their disposal to grab a larger share of the cake.

Given the nature of capitalist society, and particularly American society, David Gordon (1976) argues that crime is rational, it makes sense. In a 'dog-eat-dog' society, where competition is the order of the day, individuals must fend for themselves in order to survive. This is particularly true for the American poor, since the USA has minimal welfare services compared to other advanced industrial societies. Gordon concludes: 'Most crimes in this country share a single important similarity – they represent rational responses to the competitiveness and inequality of life in capitalist societies.'

Selective law enforcement

From a Marxist viewpoint, the selective enforcement of the law has a number of important consequences. As noted above, the occasional prosecution of ruling-class crime perpetuates the fiction that the law operates for the benefit of society as a whole, that the state represents the public interest, and that the extent of ruling-class crime is small. Conversely, frequent prosecution of members of the subject class has equally important consequences.

David Gordon argues that the practice of law enforcement in the USA supports the capitalist system in three ways:

1 By selecting members of the subject class and punishing them as individuals, it protects the system which is primarily responsible for their criminal deviance. Individuals are defined as 'social failures' and as such they are responsible for their criminal activities. In this way, blame and condemnation are directed at the individual rather than the institutions of capitalism.
2 The imprisonment of selected members of the subject class 'legitimately' neutralizes opposition to the system. American blacks are heavily over-represented among those arrested for 'street crimes' such as robbery and aggravated assault.
3 Gordon argues that defining criminals as 'animals and misfits, as enemies of the state', provides a justification for incarcerating them in prisons. This keeps them hidden from view. In this way the most embarrassing extremes produced by the capitalist system are neatly swept under the carpet. If something were really done to help those who broke the law, if their problems were made public, the whole system might be questioned.

Gordon therefore concludes that the selective enforcement of the law serves to maintain ruling-class power and to reinforce ruling-class ideology.

Evaluation of conventional Marxism

Marxist theories have come in for heavy criticism from a number of quarters:

1 Feminist sociologists have argued that Marxist theories put undue emphasis upon class inequality. From their point of view, Marxist theories ignore the role of patriarchy in influencing the way the criminal justice system operates. Marxists have also been accused of neglecting the importance of racism in the enforcement of laws.
2 Marxists have been criticized for assuming that a communist system could eradicate crime. Before the end of communism in the Soviet Union and Eastern European countries, crime had not been eradicated.
3 Stephen Jones (2001) points out that capitalism does not always produce high crime rates. For example, in Switzerland, which has long embraced a capitalist system, crime rates are very low.
4 Some Marxists have a rather simplistic view of the distribution of power in capitalist societies. While the group which Marxists define as a ruling class might have a disproportionate amount of power, it may be misleading to see this group as monopolizing power. A range of non-Marxist theories suggest that the distribution of power is more complex than Marxists tend to believe (see pp. 525–35 and 542–8). Stephen Jones points out that the activities of capitalists are sometimes criminalized. He gives the example of insider trading. If it were not illegal, capitalists would be free to make substantial profits out of their knowledge about proposed mergers and takeovers. The illegality of such activity suggests that capitalists cannot always get the laws they want.
5 'Left realists' tend to see Marxist theories as putting undue emphasis on corporate crime, at the expense of other types of crime. Left realists argue that crimes such as burglary, robbery and other violent crimes cause greater harm than Marxist theories seem to imply. The victims of such crimes are usually working-class, and the consequences can be devastating for them. To left realists, Marxism offers a rather one-sided view of crime and, in doing so, offers no way of dealing with the types of crimes which are of most concern to most members of the population. (These views are discussed in more detail on pp. 345–50.)

6 Postmodern criminology rejects Marxist criminology as a 'metanarrative' which is neither believable nor defensible. These views will be examined later in the chapter (see pp. 386–90).

Although it has fallen somewhat out of fashion in recent years, Marxist criminology continues to influence some sociologists who do not call themselves Marxists. In a study of corporate crime, Gary Slapper and Steve Tombs (1999) describe their approach as 'critical social science'. They stop far short of advocating communism, but still believe that key features of Marxist analysis are essential to explain corporate crime:

> *For us, a society with a strong competitive ethos ... an increasing commodification of all human relationships and practices ... and a capitalist economy constantly pushing people with targets to hit, promotions to seek and demotions to avoid, recessions to try to survive, and so on, can thus be seen as a society likely to engender corporate crime.* Slapper and Tombs, 1999

Echoing writers such as Chambliss and Snider, they go on to say:

> *Where certain sorts of crime, like corporate crime, are scarcely policed, rarely prosecuted and hardly ever punished with severe sanctions, the structure of the criminal justice system also contributes to the facilitation of corporate crime as an option for achieving business goals.* Slapper and Tombs, 1999

Furthermore, Marxism has influenced a range of other approaches to the sociology of crime and deviance. Some of these will be examined in the next section.

Deviance – neo-Marxist and radical perspectives

There are a number of critical perspectives that have developed since the heyday of conventional Marxism. Some of these have drawn their inspiration in large measure from Marxism, despite using elements from other theories. These can be referred to as neo-Marxist approaches. Others owe rather less to Marxism and are perhaps better defined as radical theories of crime and deviance. Some feminist approaches (examined on pp. 372–4) can also be seen as radical theories.

Neo-Marxism

Neo-Marxist sociologists of crime and deviance accept that society is characterized by competing groups with conflicting interests. Furthermore, they are all critical of existing capitalist societies, and they share a concern about the unequal distribution of power and wealth within such societies. However, none of them believe that there is a simple and straightforward relationship between the infrastructure of society and deviance. Although most of these sociologists have been strongly influenced by Marxism, their work differs in important respects from that of the Marxists we have examined so far. It can therefore be termed a **neo-Marxist** approach to deviance.

Ian Taylor, Paul Walton and Jock Young – *The New Criminology*

In 1973, Ian Taylor, Paul Walton and Jock Young published *The New Criminology*. It was intended to provide a radical alternative to existing theories of crime and deviance. In some respects, Taylor *et al.*'s views are similar to those of the Marxist writers who have just been examined:

1 They accept that the key to understanding crime lies in the 'material basis of society'. Like Marx, they see the economy as the most important part of any society.
2 They believe that capitalist societies are characterized by inequalities in wealth and power between individuals and that these inequalities lie at the root of crime.
3 They support a radical transformation of society: indeed, they suggest that sociological theories of crime are of little use unless they contribute in a practical way to the 'liberation of individuals from living under capitalism'.

However, in important respects they differ from more conventional Marxist approaches. As such, we can see *The New Criminology* as a neo-Marxist perspective on crime.

Crime, freedom and political action

Much of Taylor *et al.*'s work is concerned with criticizing existing theories of crime. Marx himself is judged by them to have produced inadequate explanations of crime. He is criticized for coming close to providing an economically deterministic theory.

Taylor *et al.* insist that criminals choose to break the law. They reject all theories that see human behaviour as directed by external forces. They see the individual turning to crime 'as the meaningful attempt by the actor to construct and develop his own self-conception'.

The New Criminology denies that crime is caused by biology, by anomie, by being a member of a subculture, by living in areas of social disorganization, by labelling, or by poverty. It stresses that crimes are often deliberate and conscious acts with political motives. Many crimes against property involve the redistribution of wealth: if a poor resident of an inner-city area steals from a rich person, the former is helping to change society. Deviants are not just the passive victims of capitalism: they are actively struggling to alter capitalism.

Like conventional Marxists, Taylor *et al.* wish to see the overthrow of capitalism and its replacement with a different type of society. Unlike conventional Marxists, they refer to the type of society they wish to see as 'socialist' rather than 'communist'. They place greater emphasis than many Marxists on freedom in any future society. They wish to see a society in which groups which are now seen as deviant are tolerated. They believe that hippies, minority ethnic groups, homosexuals, and perhaps even drug users, should simply be accepted in an ideal society, and not turned into criminals by persecution.

A 'fully social theory of deviance'

In the final chapter of *The New Criminology*, Taylor *et al.* attempt to outline what they believe would be a **fully social theory of deviance**. They identify seven aspects of crime and deviance which they believe should be studied:

1. The criminologist first needs to understand the way in which wealth and power are distributed in society.
2. He or she must consider the particular circumstances surrounding the decision of an individual to commit an act of deviance.
3. It is necessary to consider the deviant act itself, in order to discover its meaning for the person concerned. Was the individual, for example, showing contempt for the material values of capitalism by taking drugs? Was he or she 'kicking back' at society through an act of vandalism?
4. Taylor *et al.* propose that the criminologist should consider in what ways, and for what reasons, other members of society react to the deviance. How do the police or members of the deviant's family respond to the discovery of the deviance?
5. The reaction then needs to be explained in terms of the social structure. This means that the researcher should attempt to discover who has the power in society to make the rules, and to explain why some deviant acts are treated much more severely than others.
6. Taylor *et al.* then turn to labelling theory. They accept that it is necessary to study the effects of deviant labels. However, they emphasize that labelling may have a variety of effects. The amplification of deviance is only one possible outcome. Deviants may not even accept that the labels are justified: they might see their actions as morally correct and ignore the label as far as possible.
7. Finally, Taylor *et al.* say that the relationship between these different aspects of deviance should be studied, so that they fuse together into a complete theory.

Evaluation of The New Criminology

The New Criminology has attracted criticism from a number of quarters:

1. Roger Hopkins Burke believes *The New Criminology* is both too general to be of much use in explaining crime and too idealistic to be of any use in tackling crime. He says:

   The New Criminology *provided a very generalized prescription for a crime-free, socialist 'good society'. From the standpoint of the twenty-first century, it can be seen as utopian, reflecting the optimistic nature of the times in which it was written; while the generality of the work itself meant it could offer very little to substantive theory at all.* Hopkins Burke, 2001

2. Feminist sociologists have criticized *The New Criminology* for concentrating on male crimes and ignoring gender as a factor in criminality.
3. Some 'left realist' criminologists have accused *The New Criminology* of neglecting the impact of crime on the victims, of romanticizing working-class criminals (who in reality largely prey on poor people rather than stealing from the rich), and of failing to take street crimes seriously (see pp. 345–50 for a discussion of left realism).

In 1998, twenty-five years after *The New Criminology* was published, Paul Walton and Jock Young evaluated the impact of their earlier work.

Paul Walton (1998) argued that the central aim of *The New Criminology* was an attempt to undermine 'correctionalism' – that is, the belief that the sociology of crime and deviance should be used to try to get rid of deviant or criminal behaviour.

To Walton, many traditional theories of crime 'acted as little more than an academic justification for existing discriminatory practices in the penal and criminal justice system'. *The New Criminology* advocated greater tolerance of a wider variety of behaviour.

Although Walton believes traditional forms of correctionalist criminology have survived, *The New Criminology* did succeed in opening up a new, radical approach to criminology. He accepts that some of the newer approaches in criminology – such as feminism, left realism and postmodernism – have been somewhat critical of *The New Criminology* (see pp. 345–50 and 386–90). Furthermore, he accepts some of their criticisms, such as the feminist view that *The New Criminology* neglected gender. However, he argues that even these more recent approaches were all built on foundations laid by *The New Criminology*. Walton says, 'realist criminology, feminist criminology and postmodern criminology are all committed to creating a more just and equitable society'. In that respect they are a continuation of the traditions of *The New Criminology*.

Jock Young is now a leading proponent of left realist criminology, which has been critical of *The New Criminology*. However, like Walton, he defends its role in attacking conventional theories of crime and deviance. He stresses that *The New Criminology* emphasized the importance of explaining both the actions of offenders and the workings of the criminal justice system. It did not, as some critics seem to believe, put sole emphasis on the way in which the state defines some people's behaviour as criminal and ignores the crimes of others. In this respect Young sees *The New Criminology* as a precursor to his later approach, left realism (see pp. 345–50).

There have been few attempts to put a 'fully social theory of deviance' into practice. Two possible examples of such attempts include the work of Stuart Hall and colleagues on the moral panic over mugging (see pp. 360–2), and the later work of Ian Taylor in trying to develop a socialist criminology (see pp. 355–8).

Left realism

Since the early 1980s a number of sociologists have developed a perspective on crime and deviance usually referred to as **left realism**. Among the most prominent supporters of this perspective are Jock Young, John Lea, Roger Matthews and Richard Kinsey. Left realism originated in Britain, but has begun to influence criminologists in other parts of the world, including Canada and Australia. Left realist criminologists are critical of perspectives which see longer sentences and more prisons as the solution to crime, but they also oppose the views of what they term 'left idealists'. In their view, this includes a variety of Marxists, neo-Marxists and radical feminists.

Politically, left realists tend to see their approach as being close to the position of the British Labour Party. Lea and Young (1984) describe themselves as socialists and support the reform of society rather than the revolutionary change advocated by some Marxists. They argue that right-wing politicians in industrial capitalist societies have been particularly successful in presenting themselves as the parties representing the forces of law and order. Left idealists have not provided alternative policies on law and order, since they have suggested that social justice cannot be achieved without a radical transformation of society. Left realists have tried to counter the popularity of right-wing law-and-order policies by presenting what they see as realistic proposals for change, within the framework of existing societies, which address the concerns of ordinary people.

In Young's (1997) view, you have to be 'tough on crime', but this does not just mean being tough on criminals. It also means being tough in trying to change the social factors which have a long-term impact on crime rates, and being tough in trying to ensure that the criminal justice system really does promote social justice.

Furthermore, you have to be tough on theories of crime. To Young, simplistic theories should be regarded with suspicion. The social world is complicated and constantly changing. What works now may not work in the future. What works for one type of crime, may not work for another. Left realists therefore set out to produce an overall theory which is sufficiently flexible to be able to deal with different aspects of crime and justice at different times and places.

The problem of crime

One of the basic tenets of left realism is that crimes other than white-collar crimes are a serious problem and they need to be explained and tackled. Left realists counter a number of arguments which criminologists have advanced to suggest that such crimes are not serious:

1. Jock Young (1993) argues that there has been a real and significant increase in street crime since the Second World War. According to this view, criminology has undergone an **aetiological crisis** (or crisis of explanation), resulting from the rapid increase in officially recorded street crimes in most democratic industrial societies. In Britain, the USA and most Western European countries, crime rates recorded by the police have risen alarmingly. Some sociologists have tried to deny that the apparent increase is real by pointing to the unreliable nature of criminal statistics. From this point of view, increased reporting of crime and changes in police recording of crime might account for the figures. However, Young believes the rises have been so great that changes in reporting and recording cannot account for all of the increase. He points to evidence from the British Crime Survey (see pp. 329–30 for details) which shows that over the last hundred years there has been an increase in crime overall. There is more reporting of crimes, but there are also more victims.
2. Some sociologists have advanced the view that the chances of being the victim of street crime are minimal. Lea and Young (1984) point out that, while the average chances of being a victim are small, particular groups face high risks. It is not the rich who are the usual targets of muggers or thieves, but the poor, the deprived, minority ethnic groups and inner-city residents. For example, Lea and Young calculate that unskilled workers are twice as likely to be burgled as other workers. In some of the poorer areas of London, the chances of being mugged are four times the average for the city as a whole. In the USA, figures indicate that black men and women are more likely to be murdered than to die in a road accident. Young (1997) has calculated that in the mid-1990s black Americans were 8.6 times as likely to be murdered as white Americans. It is the deprived groups in society who are most likely to be harmed by these crimes; it is also these groups who suffer most if they are the victims of some of these offences. Those with low incomes suffer more if they are robbed or burgled: crime adds to and compounds the other problems that they face.
3. Crime is widely perceived as a serious problem in urban areas and this perception has important consequences. Left realists have carried out a considerable number of victimization studies, examining such issues as the extent of crime and attitudes towards crime. These studies have been conducted in, among other places, Merseyside, Islington, Hammersmith and Fulham. In the Second Islington Crime Survey no less than 80.5 per cent of those surveyed saw crime as a problem affecting their lives. Fear of crime was widespread. Some 35 per cent sometimes felt unsafe in their own homes. Many people altered their behaviour to avoid becoming victims of crime. This was particularly true of women. The authors said, 'women are not only less likely to go out after dark, but also stay in more than men because of fear of crime'.
4. Lea and Young (1984) attack the idea that offenders can sometimes be seen as promoting justice. For example, they attack the image of the criminal presented in parts of *The New Criminology* as a type of modern-day Robin Hood. They deny that muggers can be seen as stealing from the rich and redistributing income to the poor. As we saw earlier,

state devote too much of their time and energy to dealing with certain types of crime, and not enough to others. In the former category are minor drug offences and juvenile 'status' crimes, such as under-age drinking; in the latter there is a wide range of offences where he believes tighter control by the state is necessary. These include racially motivated attacks, corporate crime, pollution, and domestic crimes of physical and sexual abuse.

Tackling the social causes of crime

Young (1992, 1997) does not believe that crime can be dealt with simply by improving the efficiency of the police. As we saw in earlier sections, he and other left realists see the problem of crime as rooted in social inequalities. Only if those inequalities are significantly reduced will the problem of crime be reduced.

Young and Matthews (1992) argue that 'objectives within the criminal justice system are linked to wider social and political objectives of greater equality, opportunity and freedom of choice'. Young (1992) suggests that improving leisure facilities for the young, reducing income inequalities, raising the living standards of poorer families, reducing unemployment and creating jobs with prospects, improving housing estates, and providing 'community facilities which enhance a sense of cohesion and belonging', all help to cut crime.

Young does not believe that the criminal justice system is the main source of crime control. He says, 'It is not the "thin Blue Line", but the social bricks and mortar of civil society which are the major bulwark against crime' (Young, 1997). Young insists that 'social causation is given the highest priority'. Order will only arise in a just society, and all solutions must therefore address the question of whether they enhance social justice. Long-term problems, therefore, need to be addressed, but more immediate measures can be taken, so long as they enhance the overall aim of increasing social justice.

The multi-agency approach

Left realists have not tended to say a great deal about how the wider social causes of crime, such as excessive income inequality, can be tackled. They have concentrated on suggesting shorter-term and more readily achievable ways of reforming institutions. However, such proposals are not limited to the police.

Young (1992) advocates a 'multi-agency' approach. For example, councils can improve leisure facilities and housing estates, while the family, the mass media and religion have a role in improving the 'moral context' which permits so much crime. Social services, victim support schemes and improved security can help alleviate the problems of actual or potential victims. In Young's view, the public also has a vital role to play in dealing with crime.

The square of crime

As we have seen in the above discussion, left realists have examined many facets of crime. These include the causes of crime, the nature of crime statistics, policing, public attitudes towards crime and the police, the chances of being a victim of crime, and so on. In recent years these elements have been brought together into one theoretical approach to the understanding of crime. This has been called the **square of crime**.

Figure 6.6 The square of crime

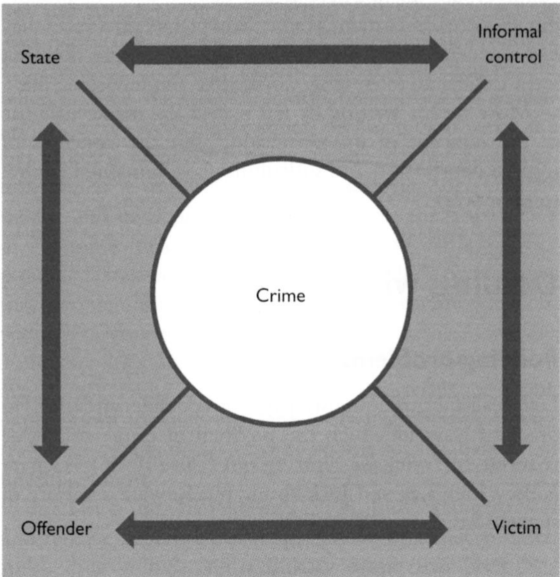

Source: *Sociology Review*, February 1993, p. 28.

As Figure 6.6 shows, the square of crime involves four elements:

1 The state and its agencies
2 The offender and their actions
3 Informal methods of social control (sometimes called 'society' or 'the public')
4 The victim

Left realists believe that crime can only be understood in terms of the interrelationships between these four elements. Roger Matthews states:

> *Crime is, in an important sense, a socially constructed phenomenon. Its meaning is profoundly influenced by considerations of time and space. Its construction is based upon the interaction of four key elements – victims, offenders, the state and the public.* Matthews, 1993

The idea that crime is socially constructed, that social factors determine who and what are considered criminal, is nothing new. Labelling theorists, phenomenologists and Marxists all agree this is the case. The idea that crime needs to be examined from different angles is not new either. For example, *The New Criminology* (Taylor *et al.*, 1973) proposed just such an approach, and Young (1997) acknowledges that in this respect it served as a precursor to left realism.

However, left realism claims to go beyond these approaches in a number of ways. Left realists pay far more attention to victims and public opinion than the approaches mentioned above. *The New Criminology* pays little or no attention to victims, in examining crime. Matthews and Young (1992) claim many other theories concentrate on just one part of the square of crime: labelling theory on the state, control theory on the public, positivism on the offender, and victimology on the victim.

Left realists do not accept that one element of the square of crime is always of prime importance. The importance of different elements varies from crime to crime. Matthews and Young say:

> *Each particular form of crime will have a different set of determinants within this framework and will involve a different combination of the key elements within the square. Thus corporate crime and street crime involve different types of victim–offender relation and are regulated by a different combination of formal and informal controls.* Matthews and Young, 1992

Multiple aetiology

Whatever the type of crime, though, left realists believe that each of these four elements is crucial, and together they determine what crime is, as well as what causes it and how it might be dealt with. Young calls this the principle of **multiple aetiology** – that is, it is caused by several different factors. Crime by its very nature is a product of formal and informal rules, of actions by offenders, and of reactions by victims and the state and its agencies. It is therefore important to try to understand why people offend, what makes the victims vulnerable, the factors that affect public attitudes and responses to crime, and the social forces that influence the police.

For example, when examining changes in violent behaviour in a country, both alterations in the amount of violence and alterations in public and police attitudes about what constitutes serious violence have to be examined. Young says:

> *Deviance and control cannot be studied independently of each other. You cannot study changes in policing without changes in patterns of crime ... Systems of social control profoundly affect deviance and changes in deviance patterns of control.* Young, 1992

The idea of the square of crime can be illustrated by considering the different elements that go to make up crime. For crime to exist there must be laws prohibiting behaviour. The existence or otherwise of those laws is influenced by the public. For an infraction to take place there must be an offender (or someone perceived as an offender) and, usually, a victim.

A variety of social factors influence the behaviour of the victim. For many offences it is the victim who decides whether the offence is reported. Victims will be influenced by prevailing social values in deciding whether they think an offence is immoral, illegal and worth reporting. The relationship between victim and offender might affect both the victim's willingness to report the crime and the impact that the crime has on him or her. For example, wives might be unwilling to report the domestic violence of their husbands, or they might see the behaviour as 'normal'. The crimes of a spouse will have a different impact compared to those of a stranger.

The response of the police or other authorities then determines whether the offender is defined as criminal or not. Public opinion can have an impact on the behaviour of authorities. As labelling theorists point out, the decisions and actions of the criminal justice system can influence the future behaviour of those convicted of crime. Changes in any of these areas can affect the crime rate and the problems which criminality poses for society.

Evaluations of left realism

Since left realism is highly critical of many existing theories of crime and deviance, it is not surprising that it has itself been the subject of criticism.

Failure to explain the causes of crime

Gordon Hughes (1991) attacks left realism on a number of counts, but argues that its major failing is in its attempts to explain the causes of street crime. On one level, left realists have simply failed to carry out the necessary research. Hughes says, 'The empirical investigation of offenders' motives remains the yawning gap in the NLR research on crime.'

The concentration on victimization studies has prevented left realists from gathering their own data on the motives of offenders. The data they have collected are largely quantitative and statistical and cannot reveal the subjective states of offenders. Thus, according to Hughes, 'NLR offers no empirical account of the subjective worlds of the street criminal but, instead, appears to rely for the most part on speculation'.

The reliance upon subculture theory

Hughes also criticizes left realism for its reliance upon subculture theory. He says, 'NLR uses subcultural analysis without any fundamental or radical revision'. By doing so, it falls into the trap of repeating some of the errors of the original subculture theories. For example, it assumes there are shared values throughout society and that it is only when these break down that crime becomes likely. It is equally possible to argue that crime stems from the existence of many different sets of values, some of which tolerate certain types of crime.

To Hughes, left realism tends to concentrate on the criminal subculture in terms of Cloward and Ohlin's categories (see pp. 326–7), or the adaptation of innovation in terms of Merton's approach (see pp. 323–4). In doing so, it neglects other responses to relative deprivation, such as retreatism or ritualism. Hughes also claims that concentrating upon the criminal subculture in relation to minority ethnic groups might lead to 'a further fanning of the stereotype, "black = criminal"'.

Hughes concludes that the work of left realists tends to oversimplify the causes of crime; it 'reduces law-breaking to the effects of deprivation and selfishness', while giving less sophisticated explanations of the various responses to deprivation than those offered by Albert Cohen, Merton or Cloward and Ohlin.

Relative deprivation

Stephen Jones (1998) argues that left realism fails to explain why some people who experience relative deprivation turn to crime, while others do not. According to Jones, the theory of relative deprivation tends to over-predict the amount of crime. There is less crime, particularly property crime, than might be expected if the theory were correct. In fact, Jones also believes that the theory serves better as a theory of property crime than of violent crime. It is easy to understand why those who suffer from relative deprivation might turn to theft or burglary to solve their material problems; it is less easy to see what they might gain from violence.

Furthermore, Jones does not believe that the left realist solution to crime, of reducing inequality, would get rid of relative deprivation. Many people might still feel deprived even if the gap between them and the better-off was narrowed.

The focus on victims

While left realists are certainly right to point out that other approaches have tended to neglect victims, some commentators think that there are flaws in their emphasis on victims. Jones (1998) argues that left realists only listen to victims on certain issues. Thus, while they take victims' accounts of their fear of crime at face value, they do not ask victims about the causes of crime. Instead, they impose their own explanations, which might have little credibility to victims. Jones says, 'victims are only empowered at the level of providing information'.

Furthermore, to Jones, left realists only really take account of the views of certain types of victims. Their studies have been concentrated on urban areas where crime rates are high. This might give a misleading impression of how harmful crime is, since it neglects suburban and rural areas where crime has much less impact on people's lives.

Corporate and organized crime

Left realists are certainly aware of corporate crime and see it as a major problem. However, Vincenzo Ruggiero (1992) argues that they have neglected its investigation, and that this type of crime cannot be readily understood within the framework of their theory. He says they do not consider how crime can be integrated into work carried out for corporations. Nor do they examine the ways in which offenders can themselves be the victims of criminal organizations (for example, the drug-taker being exploited by the pusher, or the prostitute by the pimp). Victims tend to be seen as the victims of aberrant individuals within the square of crime, not as the victims of corporations or 'central and local authorities'. Lip-service is paid to issues such as corporate crime, but they are not integrated into the theory.

The strengths of left realism

Most of the critics acknowledge that left realist criminology has made some contribution to the development of sociological theories of crime and deviance. Gordon Hughes (1991) sees it as having the following strengths:

1. It has revived some useful sociological concepts, such as relative deprivation.
2. It has promoted debate and theoretical development within the subject.
3. It has highlighted the problems that street crime can cause for weak members of society.
4. It has explored the position of victims much more than most previous theories, and it 'avoids the worst excesses of both "the right" and "the left" in neither glorifying nor pathologizing the police and other state agencies'. Overall, though, Hughes concludes: 'In its efforts to expunge itself of its own past sins of romanticism, NLR has jettisoned many of the valuable gains made by radical theory over the past two decades.'

Left realism and social policy

Whatever its merits (or lack of them) left realism has probably had more influence on policies concerning crime than most sociological theories. A number of its proposals have been adopted. For example, the police in Britain increasingly employ civilians to do routine tasks, thus giving them more time to investigate crime. The police now put much greater emphasis on crimes of domestic violence and racially motivated crimes.

One of the biggest changes in policing which can partly be traced back to left realism has been the introduction of neighbourhood policing. **Neighbourhood policing** involves dedicated groups of police officers who are directly responsible to local communities through public meetings in which the public engage in discussion with the police officers and agree policing priorities. Every police force in Britain has been required to introduce neighbourhood policing.

A second area of policing which left realism has influenced is the growth of **police community support officers**. These are police employees who work in collaboration with police officers to provide low-level, community policing. They have fewer powers than police officers and are expected to have a closer relationship with the public, who are encouraged to see them as the eyes and ears of the police rather than as 'enforcers' of the law.

However, Jones (2001) argues that local accountability might not be particularly desirable. Local politics tends to be dominated by a minority of activists who may not represent the interests or wishes of the wider population.

More generally, there are similarities between the policies of the 'New' Labour Party in Britain and the theories of left realism. Labour's slogan 'Tough on Crime, Tough on the Causes of Crime' echoes the ideas of left realists, although British Labour Party policies have not focused on reducing inequality as much as left realists would like.

A wide range of initiatives have been introduced by New Labour which reflect, at least partially, the arguments put forward by left realism. For example, New Labour has invested heavily in deprived neighbourhoods through the 'Communities that Care' initiative, which focuses on physical and social reconstruction of the most deprived areas in England and Wales. These projects set clear targets which include lowering crime rates and the fear of crime.

The influence of left realism has also been counterbalanced by right realist theories (see below), which stress a far tougher and more aggressive policy to combat crime. Nevertheless, left realists have influenced some policy initiatives which may have had some impact on crime and how it is dealt with. This is more than can be said for many theories of crime and deviance.

Jock Young – *The Exclusive Society*

In his more recent writing, Jock Young (1999, 2002) has built upon left realist criminology but broadened the issues addressed and changed aspects of his approach. While this work uses a number of ideas from left realism (for example, the idea of relative deprivation), it also has significant differences from Young's earlier work:

1. It suggests somewhat more radical solutions to the problems of crime in contemporary society than left realism. This work is not so concerned with practical and limited proposals to reduce the problem of crime.
2. It relates crime to major structural changes in society and is less concerned with the details of how particular crimes might be explained.
3. Young relates the problem of crime to the nature of modernity and the issue of social exclusion. In doing so he looks at both the causes of crime and different social reactions to crime.

Inclusive to exclusive society

Young argues that in the last third of the twentieth century a shift took place in advanced industrial societies from **inclusive** to **exclusive** societies. Following Giddens (see pp. 895–9), Young sees this as a move from the era of **modernity** to the era of **high modernity** (Young also uses the term 'late modernity' interchangeably with the term 'high modernity').

According to Young, the 1950s and 1960s can be seen as the 'Golden Age' of modern, capitalist societies (Young takes the idea of the Golden Age from the work of the British historian Eric Hobsbawm). In the Golden Age most members of the working class could find secure employment. The state was committed to trying to maintain full employment, or something near to it, through intervention in the economy using the ideas of the economist J.M. Keynes (see p. 541).

The economy was based upon Fordist mass production, which provided considerable stability. The welfare state provided important citizenship rights for all members of society. Women were increasingly included in the formal economy as large numbers of married women found paid employment. Compared to today, family life was relatively stable, with much lower rates of divorce and fewer lone-parent families. Young comments that in the Golden Age:

> *The world of work is paralleled by the sphere of leisure and the family; underwritten by the division of labour between the sexes, the family becomes the site of consumption, the celebration of an affluent lifestyle, the essential demand side of Keynsianism, and is presented with an ever-expanding array of consumer goods to measure individual success.* Young, 1999

Core values shared by most of the population centred around work and family life. A sense of community was stronger than today. All of these characteristics together produced an 'interwoven and buttressed structure'. Most people were included within this structure.

Of course, not everything in the garden was rosy. There were criminals, but they were a minority. There was a broad consensus about who the minority were and which behaviours could be tolerated and which could not. Values about right and wrong were absolute and not open to negotiation, but society was generally tolerant of minor misdemeanours.

By the 1970s, however, this structure was beginning to unravel. According to Young, this was brought about by a shift from Fordist to post-Fordist production. **Post-Fordism** moved away from the mass production of standardized products towards more specialist production of a wider range of products. It brought with it greater economic insecurity as unemployment became more common. It led to more people being employed in insecure work in the secondary labour market (see pp. 126–7). There were more short-term contracts and fewer 'safe' careers where you could expect a job for life. The number of male manual jobs available declined as manufacturing shifted to the 'third world', where wages are much lower. All of this increased the amount of **economic exclusion**.

Young uses the ideas of the British writer Will Hutton to suggest that Britain had developed into a '40:30:30 society'. In such a society, '40 per cent of the population is in tenured secure employment, 30 per cent in insecure employment, and 30 per cent marginalized, idle or working for poverty wages' (Young, 2002).

As increasing numbers became economically excluded, exclusion began to spread to other areas of social life. Young (2002) describes the 'rise of structural unemployment, the decay of community, the breakdown of family, the fears of crime, and the intrusions of disorder'. In this situation, those who are successful and in secure employment begin to fear and exclude the unsuccessful. They perceive them as the cause of society's problems and use them as scapegoats to explain increasing crime and disorder. This only leads to further exclusion, as the successful try to isolate themselves from the less successful – for example, by living in private estates surrounded by high walls and protected by security guards.

Relative deprivation in the exclusive society

According to Young, a major reason for rising crime rates in the exclusive society of high modernity is the problem of **relative deprivation**. Both absolute and relative deprivation were present in the Golden Age of modernity, but they were less intense. There are a number of reasons for this.

1. While living standards generally have risen, inequality between the richest and poorest has increased. In a globally competitive capitalist economy, the rewards for the most successful are astronomical. On the other hand, the increasing numbers of the excluded have to make do with poverty wages or benefits which decline relative to wages.
2. **Marketization** (see pp. 355–7 for a discussion of marketization) places greater emphasis on individual material success and intensifies the feeling of deprivation experienced by the less successful. Young says: 'market values encourage an ethos of every person for themselves'. This undermines communities and means that people no longer compare their success (or lack of it) just with that of their neighbours. Everybody aspires to the material success enjoyed by those in secure and well-paid employment.
3. Young develops this idea by arguing that high modernity produces high levels of **cultural inclusion** for all members of society, but combines

this with **social and economic exclusion.** Young quotes studies of American ghettos where there is 'full immersion in the American Dream: a culture hooked on Gucci, BMW, Nikes, watching television eleven hours a day, sharing the mainstream culture's obsession with violence' (Young, 2002). The ideas of meritocracy and opportunity are very influential, yet some people are 'systematically excluded' from achieving success. As Young says, Merton's idea of anomie (see pp. 323–4) is very similar to the idea of relative deprivation in the exclusive society of high modernity.

4 While relative deprivation is greatest at the bottom of the social structure, it is not confined there. Many of those who have achieved some success feel deprived. In part this is because the ideology of meritocracy, which suggests everybody gets what they deserve, contrasts with the reality of 'chaos in the market of rewards'. Some people appear to get much more than they deserve – for example, some footballers and the highly paid bosses of unsuccessful companies. Many people do not experience promotions or wage structures at work as being particularly meritocratic. They feel they deserve more.

5 The middle classes also experience what Young calls 'relative deprivation downwards'. In some respects they feel deprived compared to those who are less well-off than themselves. They can feel discontented when groups who were previously excluded gain greater social recognition. 'Discontent rises when migrants are assimilated or when lower classes are granted citizenship, or when ethnic minorities, once separate, become part of the mainstream' (Young, 2002). As the gap in social recognition between some successful and some marginal groups narrows, the successful can feel their relative position is declining.

Furthermore, the middle classes can feel deprived relative to those who they feel 'are getting an easy ride' on the back of their taxes. To achieve material success the middle classes need to be disciplined, they need to work hard; often, both partners in a household will work full-time, leaving them short of time for leisure or to care for children. Working hours have increased and employees need to show extra commitment to get on. Young says, 'children are often not seen for long after the weary commute home; people talk of "quality time" as a euphemism for "little"; the weekends seem short and enjoyment has to be snatched, often with the liberal aid of alcohol'. Having made sacrifices, they resent those who get away without the same sacrifices. Young argues:

> *It cannot be an accident that the stereotype of the underclass – with its idleness, dependency, hedonism, and institutionalized irresponsibility; with its drug use, teenage pregnancies, and fecklessness – represents all the traits which the respectable citizen has to suppress to maintain his or her lifestyle.* Young, 2002

While they do not want to join the underclass, they resent the way the underclass are under less pressure to act responsibly.

6 The sense of relative deprivation on all sides is exacerbated by the proximity of different social groups to one another. It is not just a matter of general cultural inclusion: the excluded also come into physical contact with the included. They carry out much of the routine and menial service work for the included – serving them food, cleaning their houses and workplaces, serving them in shops. However, this is experienced as exclusion rather than inclusion, for it simply heightens the sense of relative deprivation they experience.

Crime in the exclusive society

According to Young, the combination of relative deprivation and the individualism of capitalism proves a 'potent cause of crime'. As a result, the nature of crime changes considerably. These changes are summarized in Table 6.1.

Crime becomes more widespread and is no longer confined to a deviant minority. Furthermore, crime becomes nastier. In the 1950s most burglaries were directed at commercial property in Britain, but by the 1990s most crime was directed at domestic property. There is also a considerable increase in hate crime directed at people because of their age, sexuality, gender, ethnicity or simply because they are poor. Much of this is encouraged by a sense of relative deprivation downwards. According to Young (2002), in high modernity, 'crime occurs throughout the structure of society and ... its origins lie not in a separate aetiology but in the structure of society and its values'.

What those core values are becomes more contested. The definition of crime and the criminal becomes more problematic. People become less tolerant of those who are deemed to have acted in criminally deviant ways, and want harsher punishments. They feel threatened by a rising tide of crime and what they perceive as a deterioration in public behaviour.

At the same time the boundary between acceptable and unacceptable behaviour becomes blurred. For example, the idea of 'political correctness' is intolerant of many behaviours which were previously considered acceptable. However, the idea of political correctness is itself very controversial and is disputed by many. Crimes such as domestic violence have become less tolerated, but the boundaries of acceptable violence are disputed (for example, whether it is acceptable to smack children).

In the absence of close-knit communities and with a greater plurality of identities – for example, as a result of ethnic diversity – a consensus about what constitutes crime breaks down.

Table 6.1 The deviant other in late modernity

	Modernity	Late modernity
Society	Inclusive	Exclusive
Size	Minority	Majority
Values	Absolutism	Relativism
Adherence	Consensus	Pluralism
Distinctiveness	Distinct	Blurred/continuum/overlap/crossover
Threshold	Tolerant	Intolerant

Source: J. Young, *The Exclusive Society*, Sage, London, 1999, p. 16.

Crime and social policy

What then can be done about crime in high modernity? One approach is that adopted by the New Labour government in Britain. According to Young, this has been based upon 'new inclusionism', whereby the government has tried to reintegrate some of the excluded back into society. A range of policies have been adopted, both forceful (such as the requirement that everyone on long-term state benefits must have an employment interview) and supportive (such as the various 'credits' which people on low pay or in part-time work can claim to 'top-up' their salaries).

The Labour government has also introduced extensive legislation concerning 'anti-social behaviour'. Two Acts in 1998 and 2003 targeted a whole new range of behaviour, some of which was previously illegal and some not. Interestingly, the definition of an anti-social (and therefore illegal) act was one which was deemed to have caused 'harassment or distress to someone not of the same household'. As such, a huge range of behaviours are included, over 150 in all – for example, noisy neighbours, teenagers hanging around on the streets, graffiti, etc.

Young believes such anti-social behaviour policies are unlikely to succeed. He sees them as essentially nostalgic. They try to recreate the Golden Age of close-knit communities, stable families and secure employment. Government wage 'credits' and employment schemes do not create secure long-term employment, but merely encourage employers to provide low-paid insecure employment where people are still socially excluded. Dealing with noisy neighbours or getting teenagers off the streets cannot magically recreate communities or reconstitute stable families.

To Young, the causes of increased crime are deep-seated and stem from the structure of society. As such, radical solutions are needed. Any solution must tackle the unfairness in the way rewards are allocated. A sense of relative deprivation can only be reduced if rewards are seen to be distributed more on the basis of merit. Tackling this would involve dealing with the problem of inherited wealth, reducing race, sex and other forms of unfair discrimination, and reducing gross disparities in wages which have little relationship to the value of people's work.

Young accepts that society is unlikely to go back to generally agreed definitions of what is right and wrong, of what should be considered criminal and what should not. However, the way to deal with the diversity of values in modern societies is not to stigmatize some groups as outsiders whose values are inferior.

Young is opposed to the idea of multiculturalism, which sees modern societies as divided into distinct groups with separate cultures. He argues that there is a great deal of overlap between different cultures and no absolute distinctions between ethnic groups, age groups, the 'underclass', and so on. Rather, modern societies have great cultural diversity, 'which is not a catalogue of fixed features but … a plethora of cultures, ever changing, ever developing, transforming themselves and each other' (Young, 1999). In such circumstances, respect for and tolerance of diversity are needed and the impetus towards seeing whole groups as criminal should be resisted. There should be an 'intense democratic debate' about how those from different cultures can work together and how crime can be defined. To sum up, Young says:

> *The solution is to be found not in the resurrection of past stabilities based on nostalgia and a world that will never return, but on a new citizenship, a reflexive modernity which will tackle the problem of justice and community, of reward and individualism, which dwell at the heart of liberal democracy.* Young, 1999

Evaluation

Young provides an interesting analysis of crime, societal reactions to crime, and wider changes in society. His recent work broadens left realism and answers some of its critics, for example by placing greater emphasis on inequality and including more discussion of social structure.

However, Young's work is rather abstract compared to earlier left realism. Rather than offering practical and specific policies to deal with crime, it offers vague and idealistic solutions. For example, Young makes no specific suggestions about how the distribution of rewards can be made more just in modern societies. Furthermore, many of his ideas are based upon a rather simplistic contrast between a Golden Age of modernity and the chaos and uncertainty of high modernity. He perhaps overestimates the degree of stability and the strength of community in Britain in the 1950s and 1960s.

Many of the themes in Young's recent work, such as marketization, globalization and modernity, will be discussed later in this chapter (see pp. 355–9 and 386–90).

Right realist criminology

Attempts to find 'realistic' solutions to the problems of crime have not been confined to left-wing sociologists. Right-wing sociologists have also tried to develop new theoretical approaches to explain and suggest solutions to crime. Right realist theories are particularly associated with American sociologists such as James Q. Wilson and Richard Herrnstein. Although not popular among British social scientists, right realist views have influenced British governments and certainly have similarities to some populist views about what should be done about crime in Britain.

Right realist views are theoretically very different from left realist views and, as we will see, have been strongly attacked. However, in practice, New Labour has combined elements of both right realism and left realism in their policies since 1997.

James Q. Wilson – *Thinking about Crime*

Poverty, rationality, community and crime

In *Thinking about Crime* (1975), James Q. Wilson attacked many of what he took to be conventional views about crime among social scientists. He denies that trying to eradicate poverty will lead to major reductions in crime. He argues that, in the 1960s in the USA, major anti-poverty programmes were accompanied by enormous increases in the amount of crime. He therefore believes that crime can neither be explained nor tackled by welfare programmes or policies designed to redistribute wealth and income. He points out that many poor people (for example, those who are elderly or sick) do not commit crimes, and so poverty itself cannot be considered a cause of crime.

Wilson concentrates particularly on what he calls 'predatory street crime', such as burglary, robbery, theft and murder. He argues that the general public are far more concerned about such crimes than they are about victimless crime or white-collar crime. Furthermore, street crimes are particularly important because they undermine communities, and successful communities are the best protection against rising crime.

Wilson sees crime as being the result of rational calculations. People will commit crime if the likely benefits exceed the likely costs. This might suggest that harsher sentences and more police are the answer to crime. If punishments were greater and there was more chance of being caught, then people would commit fewer crimes. However, Wilson believes that such an approach can have only a limited impact. In reality, the chances of getting caught for a particular crime are quite small. If offenders do not believe they are going to get caught, or if punishments only take place long after offences, then even severe penalties will not deter people. Certain and swift penalties are likely to be effective, but, until they can be assured by the criminal justice system, other types of measure are also needed.

There are other ways of changing the balance between the gains and losses of committing crimes. One example is the prescription of methadone to heroin addicts. This offers addicts an alternative and less destructive substitute drug, which helps to limit the side-effects of giving up heroin. Combined with a clampdown on the supply of heroin, leading to an increase in price, the heroin problem can be contained. The costs of taking the drug are increased, while the costs of giving up are reduced. At the same time, former addicts have more chance to enjoy the benefits of a conventional lifestyle.

Another effective way of dealing with crime is to try to prevent the disintegration of communities. This is more effective than trying to rely upon deterrent sentencing. Where strong communities exist, they can deter crime, because people who are disgraced by being found to be involved in crime will lose their standing in the community. Where a community is strong, this loss will be important to people and they will try to avoid it. The problem is that crime itself undermines communities. Wilson says:

> *Predatory street crime does not merely victimize individuals, it impedes and, in the extreme case, even prevents the formation and maintenance of community. By disrupting the delicate nexus of ties, formal and informal, by which we are all linked with our neighbours, crime atomizes society and makes its members mere individual calculators estimating their own advantage.* Wilson, 1975

This tends to lead to even higher crime rates. In the absence of a community, people no longer gain by conforming to the community's values.

'Broken windows'

In a later article, Wilson and George Kelling (1982) spell out how to avoid the collapse of community as a consequence of criminality. They believe that it is crucial to try to maintain the character of neighbourhoods and prevent them from deteriorating. If a single window, broken by vandals, goes unmended; if incivilities such as rudeness and rowdiness on the streets go unchallenged; then problems will quickly grow. More windows will be vandalized, unruly youths will start hanging around on the streets, and law-abiding citizens will become afraid to go out. Freed from close observation by respectable members of the community, those inclined to criminality will commit more and more street crimes.

On the other hand, if residents believe attempts are being made to maintain law and order, they will be more likely to report crime and discourage incivilities and anti-social behaviour in public places. Informal social controls will be maintained, and street crime will not get out of hand.

The crucial role of the police, then, is to stop an area from deteriorating by clamping down on the first signs of undesirable behaviour. They should try to keep drunks, prostitutes, drug addicts and vandals off the streets. They should try to make law-abiding citizens feel safe. Their role is to maintain public law and order in areas where it has yet to break down.

Controversially, Wilson and Kelling believe it is a waste of valuable resources to put much effort into the worst inner-city areas. Once law and order have broken down, the police are unlikely to be able to restore it by arresting people. Their time is better spent concentrating on those areas where there is still hope.

James Q. Wilson and Richard Hernstein – *Crime and Human Nature*

In a later book written with Richard Hernstein (Wilson and Hernstein, 1985), Wilson's work took a slightly different tack. Wilson and Hernstein claim there is a substantial biological element in causing crime. They argue that some people are born with a predisposition towards crime. Their potential for criminality is more likely to be realized if they are not properly socialized. If parents fail to teach them right from wrong, and particularly if they fail to punish them immediately for misbehaving, those who are prone to crime become much more likely to commit criminal acts in later life.

In close-knit nuclear families, children can be conditioned to have a conscience, which will keep them out of trouble with the law. Where such families are absent (for example, single-parent families), effective socialization is unlikely. Furthermore, Wilson and Hernstein believe that the quality of socialization has declined with the development of a more permissive society in which anything goes.

Despite the role they see for biology and socialization, Wilson and Hernstein still believe that people possess free will. Ultimately, people choose whether to commit crimes, by weighing up the costs and benefits. Unfortunately, an over-generous welfare system discourages people from putting in the hard work necessary to hold down a job. It is too easy to live off benefits. At the same time, in an increasingly affluent society, the potential gains from crime are constantly increasing. For many people, the benefits of crime come to outweigh the costs, and the crime rate rises.

In dealing with such problems the authorities should be pragmatic. Just as they should concentrate on neighbourhoods which have a chance of being saved, so they should concentrate on individuals who can be turned away from crime. Habitual and professional criminals may be beyond redemption, and for them lengthy sentences may be the only answer. For others, early intervention can be effective in deterring them from taking up crime on a more permanent basis.

Evaluation of right realism

Some aspects of right realist thinking have been influential. In parts of both the USA and Britain, 'Zero Tolerance' policing has been influenced by the idea that it is effective to clamp down at the first sign that an area is deteriorating. The idea of Zero Tolerance is that, by proceeding against minor offences, the police will discourage the people in a locality from moving on to more serious crime.

However, in a review of research on the ideas of Wilson and Kelling, Roger Matthews (1992) found little evidence that tolerating broken windows and public incivilities led to an increase in crime. Matthews argued that the level of incivility was determined by the level of crime, and not the other way round.

Stephen Jones (2001) believes factors such as lack of investment are far more important in determining whether a neighbourhood declines. He argues that the approach advocated by Wilson and Kelling would lead to an unfair criminal justice system. The police would concentrate their attention on minor offenders, and sometimes on people who have not broken the law at all but are merely rude or unruly. More serious offenders would be given less police attention and would therefore be more likely to get away with their offences. Furthermore, even if particular neighbourhoods could be made more orderly, there is a danger that the uncivil, disorderly and criminal members would simply move their activities to a neighbouring area with a less strong sense of community.

Despite these criticisms, it could well be argued that the anti-social behaviour initiatives introduced by New Labour are partly a result of right realist thinking. The argument put forward by Wilson that clamping down on disorder will lead to stronger neighbourhoods is exactly the policy followed by New Labour, with the introduction of anti-social behaviour orders (ASBOs) which require those convicted of anti-social behaviour to desist from undertaking certain activities and from going to certain places. The belief is that as people become more confident that the local authority will back them when they challenge 'troublemakers', the more likely they will be to do so. As a result, community cohesion will improve.

Jones is also critical of the work of Wilson and Hernstein. He dismisses the biological elements of their theory as based upon outdated and already discredited theories. He argues that they ignore issues of class, ethnicity and gender, fail to consider the role of inequality and unemployment in causing crime, and neglect white-collar and corporate crimes (many of which can be very harmful).

Jones points out that, in the USA, elements of a right realist approach have been adopted. For example, repeat offenders have become subject to the 'three strikes and you're out' rule in some states. This stipulates that after three serious offences an offender should automatically get a life sentence. However, despite such measures and a rapid increase in levels of imprisonment, the crime rate has risen inexorably in the USA. This comes as no surprise to the next group of theorists we will consider, for they concentrate on the very issues that Jones accuses right realists of neglecting.

Marketization, globalization, inequality and crime

Some left realists, such as Jock Young, have considered how changes in Western societies in the 1980s and 1990s might have encouraged rises in crime rates. These issues have been developed further by sociologists considering the impact of marketization, globalization and rising inequality on society.

These themes have generally been developed by left-of-centre sociologists sympathetic to the view that the New Right policies of political leaders such as Margaret Thatcher in the 1980s in Britain, and more recently George Bush in the USA, have done immense harm. Politically, their views tend to stand somewhere between those of Marxists and left realists: they want more radical changes than those prescribed by left realists, but they stop well short of advocating a total transformation of society. They tend to refer to themselves as social democratic or socialist criminologists, or sociologists of crime and deviance. They are particularly critical of the increasing importance of market forces in Western capitalist societies, and have analysed the impact this has had on society in general and crime in particular.

Ian Taylor – 'The political economy of crime'

> *In Britain, as in the United States, an understanding of the pattern of crime is inextricably connected to an understanding of the political economy, not just of unemployment, but more broadly of the new inequality characteristic of free market societies.* Taylor, 1997

Ian Taylor does not believe such changes are confined to Britain and the USA. They are also typical of Europe:

> *As we approach the end of the century, the advance of 'economic liberalism' – or of a free market, untrammelled (and, indeed, encouraged) by governments – is observable right across Europe – from Ireland to Russia, from Spain to 'social-democratic' Scandinavia.* Taylor, 1998a

Taylor is interested in how changes in the global economy and the ways in which politicians have responded to these changes have affected crime.

Social changes

Taylor identifies a number of important changes in the world economy, in the responses of governments, and in culture:

1. Multinational corporations have shifted their activities from country to country in the search for profitability. Taylor generally agrees with the theory of post-Fordism, which suggests that mass production of standardized products is no longer a viable way to ensure long-term profit. These changes have reduced the job security of full-time workers and increased the amount of part-time, temporary and insecure employment.
2. The deregulation of stock exchanges and opening-up of world markets to increased competition have made it more difficult for governments to exercise control over the economies of the countries they govern. Increased economic instability has resulted.
3. The state has reduced its role in social and economic planning, and its involvement in 'the provision of public goods in areas like health and welfare, transport, housing and urban planning' (Taylor, 1997). Some of these areas have been increasingly opened up to market forces and competition, and there have been cut-backs in the provision of welfare.
4. The European Community has increasingly become an exclusively economic community, which puts primary emphasis on economic growth and, in particular, on trying to gain an increasing share of world markets. Ruggiero, South and Taylor (1998) comment that, in Europe, 'the emphasis on the market is leaving little space for the development of public and state institutions, and for their consequent production of social cohesion and social justice'. Instead, it has become 'dominated by corporations, monopolies and oligarchies'.
5. These changes have resulted in a change in society's cultures towards **marketization**. Increasingly, ordinary members of society are encouraged to see social life in market terms – to calculate the economic costs and benefits of making particular decisions. This includes criminals. People are also encouraged to see themselves as consumers who are entitled to be able to buy what they want. In the media, in particular, there is:

   > *a discourse which identifies the viewer or the listener as a consumer of 'goods', and which glorifies the idea of choice across a range of different market places (unlimited tourist experiences, multiple channel television, a range of private health and personal insurance schemes, etc.).* Taylor, 1998a

   Taylor does not believe that marketization and the idea of the consumer completely pervade European societies, but he does believe they are increasingly influential.

These changes have had a profound impact on crime.

The impact on crime

Marketization and opportunities for criminality

The development of capitalism has produced new opportunities for criminal activity. The deregulation of financial markets has provided increased opportunities for crimes such as insider trading, where financiers use privileged knowledge of proposed takeovers to make a financial killing. Taylor (1997) lists numerous examples, including the case of the Wall Street stockbrokers Drexel, Burnham and Lambert (see p. 332). They were accused of manipulating the US stock market and committing various frauds and, in 1990, agreed to pay $650 million to the Securities and Exchange Commission as punishment for their activities. In Britain, the collapse of Barings Bank in 1996, after their futures trader Nick Leeson had lost some £860 million, is perhaps the best-known example of financial crime.

Deregulation has also encouraged the development of tax havens, such as the Cayman Islands, which are not just used for avoiding tax, but also for laundering and hiding money gained through criminal activities.

According to Taylor, marketization has also increased the opportunities for various types of crime based directly upon the growth of consumer societies. Examples include insurance fraud by claimants and salespeople, and VAT, customs and pension scheme fraud.

The development of the European Community has provided enormous scope for defrauding the European Commission of money by making false claims for various subsidies and other payments. Taylor quotes an estimate that the European Commission loses some $7 billion per year due to fraud.

Changes in employment and unemployment

Other crimes are related to the changing nature of employment and unemployment. Taylor (1998b) believes there has been a fundamental shift in employment patterns in capitalist societies. Both mass manufacturing and the public sector have experienced substantial job losses, even in the most successful capitalist countries such as Germany.

Furthermore, there is little prospect of anything like a return to full employment. Taylor notes that the latest economic thinking suggests that Britain could enjoy economic growth of 3 per cent a year without any increase in employment opportunities. Jobless growth can take place because high technology businesses can meet rising demand through the use of new technology, without taking on more workers. Many of the jobs that are created are flexible, temporary or part-time.

These changes have two main effects:

1. In the areas most affected by unemployment, Taylor describes 'the massively destructive effects that this joblessness clearly has had on the self-respect of individuals and communities'. This effect has been so strong because unemployment has become a more or less permanent feature of some areas. There is little hope of a major improvement, and the longer that high levels of unemployment last, the greater the cumulative effects. Lack of opportunity and hope leads some to turn to crime. Taylor points out that officially recorded burglary increased by 122 per cent between 1979 and 1991, theft/handling stolen goods by 95 per cent, and robberies by 262 per cent.

2 Changing patterns of work have created more opportunities and incentives for criminal activity based on work. Ruggiero *et al.* (1998) believe that subcontracting encourages the employment of people who are working illegally, such as illegal immigrants, those who are fraudulently claiming benefit, or those who are employed in conditions or at wage levels which fail to conform to national laws. Such practices are particularly common in the clothing, food and building industries. Subcontractors often feel they have to break the rules so as to cut costs, in order to get and retain contracts in very competitive industries.

Materialism and inequality

While the precise nature of employment opportunities is related to particular types of crime, the overall increase in criminality is underpinned by growing materialism and widening inequality. On the one hand, success is increasingly portrayed in terms of achieving a lifestyle associated with the consumption of expensive consumer goods. Taylor says:

> *Television programmes and magazines (for example* Hello! *magazine, the quintessential product of our times) seem obsessed by the lifestyles of individuals who have been successful in business or the media; great interest is shown in the material goods that have been acquired by the successful (from items of clothing to cars) and in the various pleasures of personal consumption in which they indulge.* Taylor, 1998b

On the other hand, inequalities have widened rapidly. For example, Taylor quotes British government figures showing that, in 1988–9, the most affluent 20 per cent of the population received 41 per cent of national income, compared to 35 per cent ten years earlier. Meanwhile, the share of the bottom 10 per cent fell from around 10 per cent to 6.9 per cent.

Taylor sees the prevalence of crimes such as car theft as related to these changes. Stealing a car allows someone to possess one of the most highly prized of consumer goods, even if only on a temporary basis.

Drugs and globalization

Perhaps the area of crime where globalization and marketization have had the biggest impact is the drugs trade. Drawing on Mike Davis's book *City of Quartz* (1990), Taylor (1997) argues that cities such as Los Angeles have been badly affected by deindustrialization and lack of opportunities for young working-class men. At the same time, the culture of entrepreneurship has encouraged many young blacks, who confront the additional problem of racism, to pursue illegitimate opportunities in the drugs business.

In the 1980s new opportunities opened up in Los Angeles because of a shift in the 'cocaine trail' from Florida to California. As crack cocaine became increasingly popular, there were opportunities to set up crack houses in which crack was distilled and cut. Towards the end of the 1980s it was estimated there were more than 10,000 members of drugs gangs in Los Angeles, and about one gang-related killing per day.

But it was not just poverty and inequality in inner cities and the culture of entrepreneurship which encouraged the drugs trade – factors connected to globalization were also important.

In a globalized economy, countries such as Peru, Colombia, Sri Lanka and Burma have been left behind. Some 'third world' countries, such as Brazil, Mexico, South Korea and Taiwan, have developed substantial industries, but other countries have not. The less successful countries have turned to the production of drugs, because crops from which drugs are derived require little technology or investment, and can command high prices when used to produce drugs. Meanwhile, the massive profits of the global drugs trade can be hidden in the growing offshore tax havens such as the Cayman Islands.

Dealing with crime

Taylor accepts that left realists have provided some useful suggestions as to how to deal with the crime problem. These include greater police accountability and a multi-agency approach to dealing with problems (see p. 348). However, he thinks that more emphasis needs to be placed on:

> *'the big issues' – the realities of market society with all its social and cultural effects (joblessness; the homelessness, poverty and deprivation) at the heart of civil society; the massive subversion of institutions, especially local authorities but also the whole apparatus of welfare state provision with respect to health, income support, and so on that until the late 1970s were working, however imperfectly, in the public interest.* Taylor, 1998b

However, Taylor does not believe there can simply be a return to the past. Too much has changed to make that possible. Nevertheless, he believes there is a need to try to 'reinvent the lost sense of community, public civility and/or sense of shared citizenship that characterized English life before the free market experiment'.

New Labour politicians might argue that they have undertaken many of the changes that Taylor claimed were needed. Great emphasis has been placed on reconstructing communities and investing in run-down areas. Although the Labour government has not adopted the four-day week suggested by Taylor, they have introduced a wide range of policies to encourage people into work, usually through the use of tax credits. They have also introduced a minimum wage and increased holiday entitlement. Furthermore, there has been considerable investment in trying to reconstruct community cohesion through community neighbourhood projects.

Taylor also cites approvingly the 1980s programme on the Paris metro which involved the frequent removal of litter and graffiti as well as the introduction of more security officers to create an increased feeling of security. Much of New Labour policy on anti-social behaviour has involved similar innovations on the streets of the UK.

However, the core ideas surrounding marketization and globalization have not been influential, despite support for them from other research, as we shall see later.

Evaluation of Taylor

Taylor's work has the great merit of trying to explain crime in the context of important changes in capitalist societies. Unlike many previous theorists, Taylor does not try to develop a general theory of crime, which could be applicable to any place or time, but he discusses it in the context of recent trends towards globalization and marketization. Furthermore, many of his arguments seem very plausible. However, he does tend to produce rather generalized arguments which lack a detailed examination of criminal motivation. It is therefore difficult to evaluate how directly any increase in criminality can be linked to the changes he discusses.

However, some support for the idea that crime can be linked to marketization can also be found in British studies. One such study will now be examined.

Dick Hobbs and Colin Dunningham – entrepreneurship and 'glocal' organized crime

Entrepreneurial criminals and crime networks

In an ethnographic study of organized crime in Britain conducted during the 1990s, Dick Hobbs and Colin Dunningham (1998) examine how criminal careers are related to wider economic changes. They argue that organized crime increasingly involves individuals together in loose-knit networks, who treat their criminal career rather like they would a business career. They are constantly on the look-out for new business opportunities, and often mix legitimate and illegitimate enterprises.

Just as Fordist mass production has given way to post-Fordist flexible production in the formal economy, similar changes have taken place in organized crime. The large criminal organizations of the 1960s (such as those of the Krays and the Richardson brothers in London) have largely disappeared.

As part of their study, Hobbs and Dunningham carried out research in a depressed post-industrial town, which they called Downtown. They found no evidence that there was any large criminal organization in the area. Instead, individuals with extensive criminal contacts acted as 'hubs', connecting the diverse activities of different loose groupings of criminals.

Nevertheless, Hobbs and Dunningham see criminal activities as being firmly rooted in local contexts. Criminal entrepreneurs develop their careers, at least initially, in local areas. They rely very much on networks of contacts to find opportunities to make money. Eventually, some become involved in wider networks – for example, those involving drug smuggling. They may even emigrate, but generally they retain strong local links.

Thus, Hobbs and Dunningham do not believe that organized crime is increasingly dominated by large multinational or even global criminal organizations (such as the Mafia). Instead, it works as a **glocal** system. That is, there are some global connections involved, but it remains locally based.

Hobbs and Dunningham particularly studied criminals with contacts in Downtown, the run-down area in which their study was based. They illustrate their claims with a number of case studies.

Case studies

- Bill and Ben started their careers separately as burglars. They ended up in prison together, and on their release started working together, stealing from building sites. They quickly progressed to stealing plant machinery from sites and developed a close relationship with building workers and contractors in the local area, to whom they sold most of the stuff they had stolen. This proved profitable and, after about five years, Ben diversified into property development, arranging fraudulent mortgage deals, and the importation of cannabis. However, disputes with business partners led to the collapse of the cannabis business and, faced with financial problems, Ben had to go back to being a small-time crook.

  Bill was more successful. He bought a share in a pub which proved very profitable. He made a lot of money stealing from lorry compounds. He would drive a lorry equipped with false number-plates into a secure compound and pay for the night's stay. He would then leave, but a number of associates would hide in the lorry. When the security guards had gone, they would proceed to break into other lorries and move goods from them into their own lorry. Bill would return at opening time and drive away with the now lucratively laden vehicle.

  Bill built up contacts with local businesses and criminals through his pub and started supplying imported amphetamines. He also got involved in selling stolen designer clothes and CDs.
- Dave Peters was one of the most successful criminals studied by Hobbs and Dunningham. He started his career by collaborating with various criminal organizations which imported cannabis. He soon progressed to running a team of burglars and became involved in managing a chain of pubs. He made so much money that he moved to the Costa del Sol from where he ran a shipping business. Among other activities, the shipping business supplied Dave Peters's growing chain of clubs, which he bought throughout Europe. Despite these international connections, he also kept a warehouse near Downtown, which acted as a centre for the disposal of stolen goods.
- Ned was another successful criminal. To those who did not know him better, he was a successful local businessman who drove a Mercedes, lived in an expensive house, and spent much of his time at a local leisure club. However, Ned had made much of his money by fixing greyhound races, dealing in cannabis through a local network, and disposing of stolen goods. He was given a nine-month prison sentence when the police found him in possession of stolen whisky. After that, he changed to a career as a plumber and was able to secure large contracts by using bribes.

  Ned became involved with a gang who carried out armed robberies, but he feared another prison term and took to acting as a police informer as insurance against further convictions. His legitimate business interests flourished, but he continued to have occasional involvement in activities such as drug importation, disposing of stolen goods, and selling counterfeit currency.

Conclusion

Hobbs and Dunningham believe their study shows how legal and illegal businesses become intermeshed in local entrepreneurial networks. While they tie into broader networks, local contacts and knowledge remain crucial to these criminals.

The criminals described in the case studies are in many ways exemplary entrepreneurs. They are very flexible and are constantly looking for profitable openings in various markets. They are products of a 1980s and 1990s enterprise culture which has opened up illegitimate opportunities in some of the areas where legal paths to success have become severely restricted. (See also Simon Winlow's study *Badfellas*, discussed on pp. 383–6, which reaches similar conclusions.)

Evaluation

All of the studies examined in this section have drawn upon older theories of crime and deviance. The Marxist critique of capitalism, Merton's discussion of anomie, and Cloward and Ohlin's discussion of illegitimate opportunities have all influenced the writers discussed above. However, Taylor and Hobbs and Dunningham try to place their theories and studies in the context of changes in contemporary economies, and they believe that social changes have strengthened the link between crime and capitalism.

While their theories are not particularly original, they do seem to highlight important changes in the nature of crime. They would be more convincing if they used detailed comparisons with the 1970s and earlier to show that the criminality they try to explain is quantitatively or qualitatively different from what has gone before. If they could do this, they would be able to demonstrate more convincingly that marketization is responsible for much of the contemporary crime 'problem'.

'Race', ethnicity and crime

The issue of 'race' and crime

Hazel Croall (1998) argues that an interest in 'race', ethnicity and crime dates back to the nineteenth century, when 'the Irish were portrayed as part of the "dangerous classes"' and were therefore sometimes seen as likely to be involved in crime.

Coretta Phillips and Ben Bowling (2002) argue that the issue of 'race' and crime returned to public attention in the 1970s because of interest in the 'consistent pattern of over-representation of African/Caribbean people in prison in Britain'. This raised important questions about whether the over-representation was caused by British African Caribbeans being more criminal than other ethnic groups, or was the result of discriminatory treatment by the criminal justice system.

In the 1990s the relationship between racism, ethnicity and victimization became a new focus of attention. This was partly in response to the murder of the African Caribbean teenager Stephen Lawrence in 1993. He was killed by a gang of white youths who stabbed him to death, having first shouted racist abuse at him. So far, despite the existence of substantial evidence against alleged offenders, nobody has been convicted of the crime. An inquiry was set up into the incident – the Macpherson Inquiry (Macpherson, 1999) – which found serious failings in the police and accused the Metropolitan police of 'institutional racism' (see pp. 169–70). The report raised issues about the way the police dealt with racially motivated attacks and the extent to which criminality by different ethnic groups might be racially motivated.

The next section will examine the relationship between 'race', ethnicity and offending, and following that we will return to the issue of 'race', ethnicity and victimization.

Images of minority ethnic offending

According to Phillips and Bowling (2002), 'in the 1970s, a quarter of a century after the onset of mass migration from the West Indies and Indian subcontinent, there was an official consensus that the settler communities offended at lower rates than the majority population'. A House of Commons Select Committee Report in 1972 found that African Caribbean crime rates were no higher than those of whites, while Asian crime rates were substantially lower. However:

> *This position dramatically altered in the mid-1970s in the face of increased conflict between the police and the African Caribbean communities, and the accumulation of police statistics which documented higher arrest rates – particularly for robbery and theft from the person – among African Caribbean youth in London.* Phillips and Bowling, 2002

As a result, 'black criminality' began to be seen as a problem. In contrast, in the late 1970s, Asians were still considered to have low crime rates. The general image of Asian communities was that they were close-knit and well regulated by family ties, so that Asian youth tended to avoid involvement in crime.

However, Phillips and Bowling argue that, by the 1990s, Asians too were beginning to be seen as a problem because of their apparent involvement in some types of crime. In 1994 a group of young Bangladeshi men murdered a man in King's Cross; in 1995 there was urban disorder in Bradford involving Asians; and there were 'riots' involving Asians in Oldham, Burnley and Bradford in 2001 (see p. 208).

Parts of the media began to develop an image of the 'Asian gang' (see pp. 185–6 for a discussion of the 'Asian gang'). This emphasis on growing Asian crime rates has more recently been overshadowed by discussions of terrorism.

From the 1980s onwards, though, some social scientists began to challenge the idea that members of minority ethnic groups were any more prone to criminality than their white counterparts.

The 'myth of black criminality'

In an early contribution to the debate about 'race' and crime, Paul Gilroy (1983) argued that black criminality was a myth. He rejected the view that black criminals belong to an 'alien culture' or that minority ethnic groups are poorly socialized and therefore become criminals. Instead, he sees minority ethnic groups as defending themselves against a society which treats them unjustly.

Both British Asians and African Caribbeans originate from former colonies of Britain and the original migrants to Britain carried with them 'the scars of imperialist violence'. The anti-colonial struggles against British imperialism allowed these ethnic groups to learn how to resist exploitation. Once they arrived in Britain these ethnic groups used the same techniques they had first developed in Asia and the Caribbean: marches, demonstrations and riots. In areas such as Southall, Toxteth, Brixton, Handsworth and St Paul's Bristol (all scenes of inner-city rioting in the late 1970s and early 1980s) they hit back against police harassment, racially motivated attacks and discrimination.

Although Gilroy sees minority ethnic crime as part of a political struggle, he denies that minority ethnic groups are any more prone to crime than other groups. He claims the myth of black criminality has been created as a result of the police having negative stereotypes of African Caribbeans and Asians. African Caribbeans are seen as 'wild and lawless' and more specifically as potential 'muggers'. Asians are also regarded with suspicion and are often seen as possibly being illegal immigrants.

Gilroy (1983) provides some evidence to support such views. He refers to a police officer in Brixton saying to a reporter: 'We are here to give our coloured brethren all the help we can – all they need to go somewhere else.' Gilroy also points out that the Police Federation magazine claimed that Jamaica had deliberately shipped convicts to Britain during the early period of migration in order to export its crime problems.

For these reasons, Gilroy argued that statistics which showed a disproportionate involvement of African Caribbeans in street crime could not be trusted. They reflected the prejudice of the police rather than any real tendency for this group to be more criminal than white British people.

Policing the Crisis – mugging, the state, and law and order

The views of Gilroy were supported to some extent in a study conducted by the Birmingham Centre for Contemporary Cultural Studies. Stuart Hall, Chas Critcher, Tony Jefferson, John Clarke and Brian Roberts (1979) attempted to provide a detailed explanation of the crime of mugging in Britain. Although their argument was somewhat contradictory (at times they seemed to suggest that African Caribbeans were more criminal than whites), its main thrust was that African Caribbeans were much more likely to be labelled as criminals than whites. They argued that at least certain sections of the police were racist and that concern about street crime, particularly mugging, was an unjustified moral panic.

'Mugging', the media and moral panic

In the thirteen months between August 1972 and August 1973, sixty events were reported as muggings in the national daily papers. Dramatic individual cases of such crimes were highlighted in the media. On 15 August 1972, Arthur Hills was stabbed to death near Waterloo Station in London. For the first time, a specific crime in Britain was labelled a mugging in the press. On 5 November 1972, Robert Keenan was attacked by three youths in Birmingham. He was knocked to the ground, and had some keys, five cigarettes and 30p stolen. Two hours later, the youths returned to where he still lay, and they viciously kicked him and hit him with a brick.

It was stories such as these which highlighted an apparently new and frightening type of crime in Britain. Judges, politicians and the police lined up with the media in stressing the threat that this crime posed to society. Many commentators believed the streets of Britain would soon become as dangerous as those of New York or Chicago. The Home Secretary in the House of Commons quoted an alarming figure of a 129 per cent increase in muggings in London in the previous four years.

Hall *et al.* (1979) see these reactions as a moral panic. (A **moral panic** is an exaggerated outburst of public concern over the morality and behaviour of a group in society.) They try to explain why there should be such a strong reaction to, and widespread fear of, mugging.

They reject the view that the panic was an inevitable and understandable reaction to a new and rapidly increasing form of violence. As far back as the nineteenth century, footpads and garrotters (who half-strangled their victims before robbing them) had committed violent street crimes similar to those of the modern mugger. Violent robberies were not, therefore, a new crime at all – indeed, as recently as 1968, an MP had been kicked and robbed in the street without the crime being labelled a mugging.

Hall and his colleagues note that there is no legally defined crime called mugging. Since in law there is no such crime, it was not possible for the Home Secretary accurately to measure its extent. Hall *et al.* could find no basis in the criminal statistics for his figure of a 129 per cent rise over four years. From their own examination of the statistics there was no evidence that violent street crime was rising particularly fast in the period leading up to the panic. Using the nearest legal category to mugging – robbery, or assault with intent to rob – the official statistics showed an annual rise of an average of 33.4 per cent between 1955 and 1965, but only a 14 per cent average annual increase from 1965 to 1972. This type of crime was growing more slowly at the time the panic took place than it had done in the previous decade.

For these reasons, Hall and his colleagues could not accept that the supposed novelty or rate of increase of the crime explained the moral panic. They argued that both mugging and the moral panic could only be explained in the context of the problems faced by British capitalism at the start of the 1970s.

Capitalism, crisis and crime

Economic problems produced part of the 'crisis'. Hall *et al.* (1979) accept the Marxist view that capitalist economies tend to go through periods of crisis when it is difficult for firms to sell their goods at a profit. During the 1970s, they argue, the British economy was characterized by just such a crisis. There was a declining rate of profit, rising unemployment and falling wages. This crisis coincided with the mugging panic.

The crisis of British society, however, went beyond economic problems. It was also a crisis of 'hegemony', a term first used by Antonio Gramsci. **Hegemony** is the political leadership and ideological domination of society. (Gramsci and hegemony are discussed in more detail on pp. 539–40.) According to Gramsci, the state tends to be dominated by parts of the ruling class. They attempt to win support for their policies and ideas from other groups in society. They try to persuade the working class that the authority of the state is being exercised fairly and justly in the interests of all. A crisis in hegemony takes place when the authority of the state and the ruling class is challenged.

In 1970–2 the British state faced both an economic crisis and a crisis of hegemony. From 1945 until about 1968 there had been what Hall *et al.* (1979) call an **inter-class truce**: there was little conflict between the ruling and subject class. Full employment, rising living standards and the expansion of the welfare state secured support for the state and acceptance of its authority by the working class. As unemployment rose and living standards ceased to rise rapidly, the basis of the inter-class truce was undermined. It became more difficult for the ruling class to govern by consent.

Hall *et al.* provide a number of examples of the challenge to the authority – to the hegemony – of the state:

1 Northern Ireland degenerated into open warfare.
2 There was a growth in student militancy and increased activity from the Black Power movement.
3 The unions posed perhaps the biggest single threat: in 1972 there were more workdays lost because of strikes than in any year since 1919. The miners were able to win a large pay-rise by using flying pickets, which prevented coal reaching key industries and power stations.

Since the government was no longer able to govern by consent, it turned to the use of force to control the crisis. It was in this context that street crime became an issue. Mugging was presented as a key element in a breakdown of law and order. Violence was portrayed as a threat to the stability of society, and it was the black mugger who was to symbolize the threat of violence.

In this way the public could be persuaded that society's problems were caused by 'immigrants' rather than the faults of the capitalist system. The working class was effectively divided on racial grounds, since the white working class was encouraged to direct its frustrations towards the black working class.

Crisis and the control of crime

The government was also able to resort to the use of the law and direct force to suppress the groups that were challenging them. Force could be justified because of the general threat of violence. Special sections of the police began to take action against the 'mugger'. The British Transport Police was particularly concerned with this crime and it set up a special squad to deal with violent crime on the London Underground. Hall *et al.* claim the police in general, and this special squad in particular, created much of the mugging that was later to appear in the official statistics.

Hall *et al.* give examples of police pouncing unannounced on African Caribbean youths of whom they were suspicious. Often this would provoke a violent reaction in self-defence by the youths, who would then be arrested and tried for crimes of violence. Many of the 'muggers' who were convicted following incidents like these had only police evidence used against them at trial. 'Victims' of their crimes were not produced because, Hall *et al.* imply, there were no victims in some cases. Labelling helped to produce the figures that appeared to show rising levels of black crime, which in turn justified stronger police measures.

Hall *et al.* do not claim that the reactions to crime, 'mugging', and other 'violence' were the result of a conspiracy by the ruling class. The police, the government, the courts and the media did not consciously plan to create a moral panic about street crime; the panic developed as they reacted to changing circumstances.

Neither were the media directly manipulated by the ruling class or the government: different newspapers included different stories, and reported mugging in different ways. Nevertheless, there was a limited range of approaches to the issue in the press. Most stories were based on police statements or court cases, or were concerned with the general problem of the 'war' against crime. Statements by the police, judges and politicians were therefore important sources of material for the press. Consequently, the newspapers tended to define the problem of mugging in similar ways to their sources: criminal violence was seen as senseless and meaningless by most of the press. It was linked to other threats to society, such as strikes, and was seen as a crime which needed to be stamped out as quickly as possible.

Black crime

Although *Policing the Crisis* concentrates on the moral panic about crime, Hall *et al.* also make some attempt to explain African Caribbean criminality. Many immigrants to Britain from the Commonwealth arrived in the 1950s and early 1960s. They were actively encouraged to come to the country during a period of full employment and labour shortage. London Transport, for example, recruited large numbers of West Indians to fill low-paid jobs which might otherwise have remained vacant.

The recession in the early 1970s hit immigrant groups hard. They became a 'surplus labour force', many of whom were not required for employment. Those who remained in employment often had to do menial and low-paid jobs, which some referred to as 'white man's shit work'. Some opted out of the employment market altogether. They turned to 'hustling' for money, using petty street crime, casual drug dealing, and prostitution to earn a living. Street crime was a survival strategy employed by an unwanted reserve army of labour.

Policing the Crisis – *an evaluation*

Policing the Crisis provides a sophisticated analysis of the crime of 'mugging' from a neo-Marxist perspective. It suggested that the rise in African Caribbean criminality was largely the result of police labelling, but that some individuals were forced into crime in order to survive.

David Downes and Paul Rock (1988) criticized the book for contradicting itself. It appeared to claim simultaneously that African Caribbean street crime was not rising quickly, that it was being amplified by police labelling, and that it was bound to rise as a result of unemployment. According to this criticism, Hall *et al.* were trying to have their cake and eat it. They changed their view on whether these crimes were rising or not, according to how it fitted their argument.

Despite the contradictions in *Policing the Crisis*, the general approach adopted by Gilroy and Hall *et al.* tends to see any over-representation of minority ethnic groups in crime as largely a product of labelling. It tends to deny that African Caribbeans are any more prone to criminality than anybody else. This approach has been heavily criticized by left realist criminologists such as John Lea and Jock Young, whose views will now be examined.

John Lea and Jock Young – minority ethnic criminality

John Lea and Jock Young (1984) argue that it is not entirely a myth that certain types of crime are more common among minority ethnic groups than among whites. They believe the official statistics on the ethnic background of offenders are not entirely fabricated. They are particularly critical of Paul Gilroy, but by implication they also reject the main thrust of the argument put forward by Stuart Hall and his colleagues.

Lea and Young attack Paul Gilroy for suggesting that the disproportionate number of black males convicted of crimes in Britain was caused by police racism. Lea and Young quote figures showing that 92 per cent of crimes known to the police are brought to their attention by the public, and only 8 per cent are uncovered by the police themselves. In such circumstances, they argue, it is difficult to believe that the preponderance of blacks in the official figures is entirely a consequence of discrimination by the police.

Lea and Young also make use of statistics on 'race' and crime produced by the Home Office researchers, Stevens and Willis. Lea and Young calculate that the differences in offending between ethnic groups found by Stevens and Willis could only be explained entirely in terms of police racism if the police had arrested a substantial majority of African Caribbean offenders but a small minority of white offenders. Thus, 66 per cent of all African Caribbean offenders and just 21 per cent of all white offenders would have to have been arrested for the figures to be explicable entirely in terms of racism. Lea and Young believe discrimination on such a scale was unlikely. They see it as more plausible to believe that there were real differences between offending rates, with African Caribbeans having a higher offending rate than whites for some crimes.

They also point to a number of aspects of criminal statistics which cannot be explained by police racism alone. The recorded rate for crimes committed by whites is consistently slightly higher than that recorded for Asians. Lea and Young maintain that 'police racism would have to manifest itself very strangely indeed to be entirely responsible for such rates'.

Furthermore, in the 1960s the recorded rates for crimes committed by first-generation African Caribbean immigrants were lower than the national average. Even today, the official statistics for offences such as burglary show the rate for African Caribbeans to be lower than that for whites. If these statistics were produced by police racism, then the police must have exercised positive discrimination in favour of some minority ethnic groups at times.

Lea and Young accept that policing policies and police racism exaggerate the minority ethnic crime rate. Nevertheless, they believe there has been a real increase in the number of certain crimes (particularly robbery) committed by African Caribbeans. They find it hard to understand why writers such as Gilroy (see p. 360) cannot bring themselves to believe that unemployment and racial discrimination might result in minority ethnic groups committing more street crime than others.

Lea and Young are even more critical of Gilroy's claim that such African Caribbean crime as there is results from a continuation of the 'anti-colonial struggle' conducted in the former colonies. They point out that most young West Indians are second-generation immigrants who have lived in Britain since birth. Most of their parents appear, from the statistics in the 1950s and 1960s, to have been highly law-abiding. It is hard to see how they could have passed down the tradition of the 'anti-colonial struggle' to their children.

In any case, most of the victims of crimes committed by African Caribbeans are also African Caribbeans. How, Lea and Young enquire, can crimes committed against members of their own community be seen as a political attack on the white racist state? To them, it is far more plausible that street crime is a reaction to the oppression that African Caribbeans have experienced in Britain. They see their criminality as a response to relative deprivation (they have less experience of material success than their white peers), a sense of marginalization (produced partly by unemployment) and the formation of subcultures which are supportive of some types of criminal activity in some areas. (For a discussion of the use of these concepts by left realists, see pp. 345–7.)

Evaluation

Unlike Lea and Young, Phillips and Bowling (2002) believe the differences in the criminality of African Caribbean and Asian people could be accounted for by police racism. They suggest this is:

> *consistent with cultural stereotyping and the 'heightened suspicion' of African/Caribbeans that has emerged in empirical studies in the last two decades. This contrasts sharply with the stereotyping of Asians as passive, traditional, and self-regulating with strong family ties.* Phillips and Bowling, 2002

From this point of view, the differences between ethnic groups may well be explained, at least in part, by racial stereotypes and discrimination within the criminal justice system.

Whatever the merits of this argument, it is certainly true that the dispute between writers such as Gilroy, Hall *et al.* and Lea and Young over the real incidence of criminality among minority ethnic groups was based upon very limited evidence. It was only in 2000, in response to the Macpherson Inquiry (concerning the handling of police investigations into the death of Stephen

Lawrence), that the government first started publishing detailed statistics on ethnicity and crime.

These statistics and recent empirical studies provide more detailed evidence than was available in the 1970s and 1980s about the extent of both minority ethnic criminality and racism in the criminal justice system. This evidence will be examined shortly.

Gilroy and Hall *et al.* concentrated exclusively on African Caribbean crime. Lea and Young also concentrated on crime committed by this ethnic group, although they did comment on the lower crime rate among British Asians. Before examining recent data on ethnicity, racism and crime, we will now briefly examine studies of criminality among British Asians.

Studies of British Asian crime

Ben Bowling and Coretta Phillips (2002) note that by the late 1990s ethnographic studies had begun to examine crime among British Asians. They review a number of studies, including those by Desai (1999) and Mawby and Batta (1980).

Bowling and Phillips note that earlier ethnographic studies had generally portrayed Asian communities as '"inward-looking", "tightly-knit", self-regulating, passive and ordered by tradition with strong family ties'. These characteristics were assumed to explain low rates of criminality among British Asians.

For example, a study by Mawby and Batta (1980) examined criminality among British Asians in Bradford. Mawby and Batta pointed out that most British Asians in Bradford were relatively poor, of working-class backgrounds and living in inner-city areas. All these factors suggested they should be heavily involved in crime. However, the study found that they committed few crimes and those that they did commit tended to be of a minor nature. Mawby and Batta explained that the emphasis on *izzat*, or family honour, encouraged conformism among British Asians in Bradford. They were afraid of dishonouring the family name and they were therefore reluctant to commit crime.

More recent studies, such as that by Desai, have found 'groups of Asian males who were willing to take the risks of moving around town and were rebelling against their parent culture' (Bowling and Phillips, 2002). Desai found that some young Asian men were taking a more aggressive stance in combating racist attacks against them and were more willing to use violence to defend their communities against perceived threats from outside. According to Desai, some Bangladeshi boys were making a self-conscious attempt to counter the image of themselves as weak and passive. Some cultivated a 'Bengali Bad Boy Image' (Bowling and Phillips, 2002).

Not all ethnographers of Asian communities have reached similar conclusions. A study by Claire Alexander (2000) argued that the media image of a growing problem of Asian gangs was something of a myth (see pp. 185–6). Although there was some violence in the area of south London she studied, it was greatly exaggerated by the media. There were no clearly defined Asian gangs, and friendships and conflicts in the area could cut across divisions between ethnic groups.

Conclusion

As in the case of African Caribbean crime, there is no agreement about the extent of criminality among British Asians. Nor is there any agreement about the extent to which differences between ethnic groups can be held to explain patterns of criminality. While it seems plausible that cultural factors might explain differences between African Caribbean and British Asian criminality, the research that has been carried out has been small-scale and therefore inconclusive. Recent researchers have come to somewhat contradictory conclusions about the extent to which British Asian culture has been changing and could account for patterns of crime.

Patterns of criminality

If the evidence about the causes of minority ethnic crime is somewhat limited, there has been no shortage of recent research on the extent of such crime or the extent of racism in the criminal justice system.

Table 6.2 provides data on the representation of ethnic groups at different stages of the criminal justice process in

Table 6.2 Representation of ethnic groups at different stages of the criminal justice process, 2004/5

	Ethnicity					
	White	Black	Asian	Other	Unknown/ Not recorded	Total
General population (aged 10 and over) at 2001 census	91.3	2.8	4.7	1.2	0.0	100
Stops and searches	74.7	14.1	7.1	1.5	2.6	100
Arrests	84.3	8.8	4.9	1.4	0.6	100
Cautions	83.8	6.4	4.4	1.2	4.2	100
Youth offences	84.7	6.0	3.0	0.6	3.3	100
Crown Court	75.7	13.0	7.4	3.9	–	100
Prison population	76.8	13.5	5.4	0.9	0.7	100
Prison receptions	80.8	10.2	5.4	0.8	0.5	100

Source: Home Office (2002) *Race and the Criminal Justice System*, Home Office, London, p. 14.

2004/5. The table shows that black ethnic groups are particularly over-represented. In 2004/5, 'black' people made up 2.8 per cent of the population but accounted for 14.1 per cent of stops and searches, 8.8 per cent of arrests, 10.2 per cent of prison receptions and 13.5 per cent of the prison population. Asian ethnic groups made up 4.7 per cent of the population and accounted for 4.9 per cent of arrests and 5.4 per cent of the prison population. White ethnic groups were less likely to be arrested or cautioned than other ethnic groups and were also less likely than other groups to be sent to prison.

In 2004/5 there were 839,977 stops and searches of persons recorded by the police. Of these, 118,165 (14 per cent) were of black people, who form 2.8 per cent of the population, 59,954 (7 per cent) of Asian people, who form 4.7 per cent of the population, and 12,733 (1.5 per cent) of people of 'Other' origin who comprise 1.2 per cent of the population. At first sight, this seems to support the argument of those who claim that 'black' groups in the population are disproportionately selected by the police for stop and search. However, the majority of people stopped and searched are young males, and the number of stops and searches of young black males roughly reflects their proportion in the population, as the 'black' population is younger overall than the white population. A similar demographic profile is demonstrated by the Asian population.

Figures such as these do not reveal whether the over-representation of minority ethnic groups results from discrimination within the criminal justice system, or whether these groups actually have higher crime rates. We will now examine the research relating to this issue.

Evidence of racism in the criminal justice system

This section examines whether the differences in recorded crime between minority ethnic groups and the rest of the population can be explained in terms of differences in offending rates or in terms of racism within the criminal justice system. This is largely based upon reviews of the evidence by Coretta Phillips and Ben Bowling (2002; Bowling and Phillips, 2002), but it also includes data from elsewhere.

Policing and stops and searches

Phillips and Bowling (2002) argue that discrimination against minority ethnic groups starts with decisions about policing. The criminalization of minority ethnic groups starts with 'the over-policing of neighbourhoods where ethnic minorities, particularly African/Caribbeans, are heavily concentrated'. In the 1970s and 1980s there was ample evidence of this, with 'oppressive policing techniques, such as mass stop and search operations, the use of riot squads using semi-military equipment, excessive surveillance, unnecessary armed raids, and police use of racially abusive language'.

Despite the Stephen Lawrence case and the subsequent concern about racism in policing techniques, by 1999/2000 black people were still five times more likely than whites to be stopped and searched. However, these figures should be treated with some caution. It may be that there are simply more members of minority ethnic groups available to be stopped and searched in the urban areas where such stops are likely to take place.

Phillips and Bowling quote Home Office research which used CCTV cameras in five urban areas and compared the number of black, white and Asian people on the streets with the numbers stopped and searched. It found that Asians were less likely to be stopped than other groups. For African Caribbeans, the results were mixed, with more stops and searches in some areas than others. Furthermore, research based on the British Crime Survey of 2000 found that the incidence of stops and searches of African Caribbean people could be explained in terms of factors other than race, such as age, income and area of residence.

Nevertheless, Phillips and Bowling (2002) argue that the preponderance of African Caribbean suspects among those stopped and searched suggests that this makes 'a modest but significant contribution to the over-representation of black people in the arrest population'.

The most recent figures, published since Phillips and Bowling's study, show a significant increase in stops and searches of minority ethnic groups. In 2000–1, 12 per cent of people stopped were black and 6 per cent were Asian.

A number of studies have found evidence of racism within the police which might account for a greater tendency for the police to suspect members of minority ethnic groups, stop them or arrest them. A study by Ben Bowling (1999; discussed in Bowling and Phillips, 2002) 'found that police officers saw racism as a "natural" and inevitable resentment of ethnic minorities in what had been at one time "white areas" … ethnic minorities were seen to be "taking over"'. Many police officers in the study felt that African Caribbeans and Asians antagonized white people by failing to adapt to 'British culture'.

The Macpherson Inquiry into the Stephen Lawrence case examined a range of evidence and supported the view that there was institutional racism in the police (see pp. 169–70 for a definition of institutional racism). John Mewing, the Chief Constable of Derbyshire, admitted:

> *In the police service there is a distinct tendency for officers to stereotype people. That creates problems in a number of areas, but particularly in the way officers deal with black people. Discrimination and unfairness are the result. I know because as a young police officer I was guilty of such behaviour.* Macpherson, 1999

Further evidence of racism in the police was put forward in a study by Her Majesty's Inspectorate of Constabulary (1997; discussed in Bowling and Phillips, 2002). Bowling and Phillips found that there were so many complaints from the public about racism by the police that even if some complaints were not genuine, there were 'pockets of wholly unacceptable racist policing'.

Certainly, there is evidence that people from minority ethnic groups have limited faith in the police. The Youth Lifestyles Survey of 1998–9 questioned 4,848 people aged 12–30 (Flood-Page *et al.*, 2000). It found that 58 per cent of blacks felt the police treated African Caribbeans less fairly than white people. It also found that 41 per cent of Indians and 45 per cent of Pakistanis and Bangladeshis felt that Asians were treated less fairly than whites by the police.

Arrests

Looking at data for 1999–2000, Phillips and Bowling note that about four times as many African Caribbean people were arrested as would be expected in terms of their proportion of the general population (see Figure 6.7). The difference between African Caribbeans and whites was even greater in terms of imprisonment, with African Caribbeans having about eight times the imprisonment rates of whites (Figures 6.8 and 6.9). Therefore, African Caribbean people who were arrested were considerably more likely to be imprisoned than their white counterparts.

African Caribbean people made up a disproportionate number of those arrested for robbery (28 per cent), and Asian people a disproportionate number of those arrested for fraud and forgery. There is evidence that, once arrested, minority ethnic groups are more likely to deny the offence, use their right to silence and choose to have legal advice. Phillips and Bowling suggest that all these responses to arrest may reflect 'ethnic minorities' opinions of police'.

The suspicion with which minority ethnic groups tend to view the police is well documented in a number of surveys. If defendants do not admit an offence they cannot escape with a caution. Because of this, whites who are arrested are more likely to be cautioned and they avoid the possibility of a conviction.

Figure 6.7 Arrests by ethnic group, 2000–1

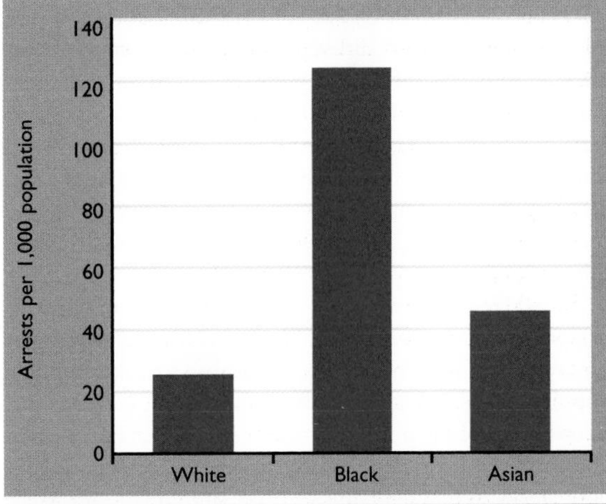

Figure 6.8 Female prisoners by ethnic group

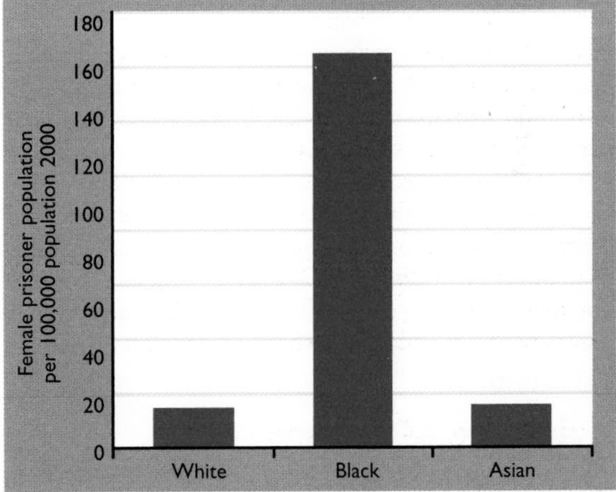

Figure 6.9 Male prisoners by ethnic group

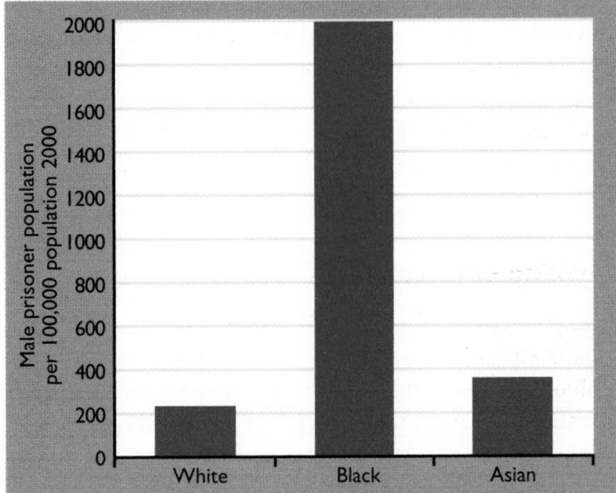

Source: Home Office (2002) *Race and the Criminal Justice System*, Home Office, London, pp. 4, 6.

Prosecuting and sentencing

The Crown Prosecution Service (CPS) decides whether to proceed with prosecutions. It does so if it considers that there is a 'realistic prospect of conviction' and the prosecution would be in the public interest. Phillips and Bowling quote two studies which have examined differences between ethnic groups over decisions to prosecute: studies by Phillips and Brown (1998) and Mhlanga (1999). Both studies found that the CPS were more likely to terminate cases involving minority ethnic groups. On the surface this might suggest discrimination in favour of minority ethnic groups. However, Phillips and Bowling suggest two other possible causes.

1. It may be that the police tend to forward cases involving minority ethnic groups to the CPS where the evidence is weak because the police tend to have negative stereotypes of minority ethnic groups.
2. The decisions of the CPS may reflect the ethnic mix of the organization. Minority ethnic groups are seriously under-represented in the police. In 2001 less than 4 per cent of the police service but more than 10 per cent of the CPS were from minority ethnic backgrounds.

Once it has been decided to bring a prosecution, minority ethnic groups are more likely than whites to be tried in a Crown Court rather than a Magistrates Court. In part, this might result from a tendency for minority ethnic groups to elect for jury trial, even though this exposes them to risking the heavier sentences which tend to be given by Crown Courts.

A detailed Home Office (2006) study of sixteen police force areas in 2005 found that a greater proportion of white defendants (75 per cent) were found guilty in the Crown Court in 2004 than black (68 per cent) or Asian defendants (66 per cent). Of those sentenced in these sixteen areas, custodial sentences were given to a greater proportion of black offenders (68 per cent) and those in the 'Other' category (68 per cent) than white (61 per cent) or Asian offenders (60 per cent).

For drug offences, 80 per cent of black offenders sentenced received a custodial sentence, compared with 74 per cent of Asian offenders and 62 per cent of white offenders. For fraud and forgery, 61 per cent of black offenders received a custodial sentence, compared to 54 per cent of Asian offenders and 49 per cent of white offenders. A slightly different pattern is apparent for robbery offences, where 87 per cent of Asian offenders and 83 per cent of black offenders received a custodial sentence. This compares to 85 per cent of white offenders.

However, the Home Office study points to the difficulty in comparing the seriousness and circumstances of each offence and suggests that the sentences largely reflect these factors.

Earlier research conducted by Roger Hood (1992) took into account a range of legally relevant factors such as previous convictions and the seriousness of the offence. The study found that when these factors were taken into account, black men were 5 per cent more likely than white men to be given a custodial sentence. Furthermore, black males who were sent to prison were given sentences which were on average three months longer than those of whites who had committed equivalent offences. The disparity was even greater among Asian men, who received sentences which were on average nine months longer than those of white men.

Among female defendants there was less evidence of discrimination, but black women did have a greater chance of being given a custodial sentence than white women, taking into account relevant factors. Phillips and Bowling argue: 'Hood's findings represent a clear example of direct discrimination against people of African/Caribbean origin, which has a clear contributory effect to the higher proportion of African/Caribbean people in prison in England and Wales.'

Self-reported crime

Self-report studies have been used to try to discover whether the rate of offending among minority ethnic groups really is higher than that among whites. There are, however, methodological problems which raise questions about the reliability and validity of the figures. Phillips and Bowling point out:

> *The self-report technique is obviously limited by the necessity to rely on the honesty of interviewees. Further methodological weaknesses include the under-measuring of serious offences, and the under-sampling of groups of people such as the homeless and those in institutions who may be more involved in offending.* Phillips and Bowling, 2002

Nevertheless, self-report studies give some indication of the chances of crimes committed by different groups leading to arrests. They are free from any bias that might result from police discrimination.

Phillips and Bowling refer to a Home Office study conducted by Graham and Bowling in 1995. This used a general sample of 1,700, plus a booster sample of 800 people from minority ethnic groups. All those in the sample were aged between 14 and 25. Overall, the study found that 44 per cent of whites, 43 per cent of 'blacks', 30 per cent of Indians, 28 per cent of Pakistanis and 13 per cent of Bangladeshis admitted having committed one or more crime. Furthermore, it found that drug use was most common among white youths. Among males, 46 per cent of whites had used one or more illegal drugs, compared to 29 per cent of Indians, 24 per cent of 'blacks', 12 per cent of Pakistanis and 10 per cent of Bangladeshis. Among females, 27 per cent of whites had used illegal drugs, compared to 25 per cent of 'blacks', 16 per cent of Pakistanis, 7 per cent of Indians and 2 per cent of Bangladeshis.

Phillips and Bowling note that very similar results have been found in subsequent studies. Bowling and Phillips (2002) admit that self-report studies do not reveal the 'real' rates of offending in ethnic groups because of the methodological problems of such studies. Nevertheless, they conclude: 'The consistent findings from self-report drug use and offending surveys add weight to the argument that official crime data exaggerate the extent of offending among ethnic minority communities.'

Conclusion

Phillips and Bowling (2002) conclude that it is impossible to calculate the extent to which the over-representation of some minority ethnic groups among those convicted of crime is due to racism. It is impossible because some studies are contradictory and none of the evidence is perfect, and because of the complex nature of criminal justice itself.

Nevertheless, their work does highlight numerous studies which suggest that individual and institutional racism plays some part in creating the high arrest and imprisonment rates of British African Caribbean men in particular.

Race and victimization

Table 6.3 shows the risk of victimization by ethnic group according to data from the British Crime Survey of 2000. It shows that members of minority ethnic groups are more likely to be victims of crime than other groups. However, the assumption that this is directly related to race issues has been criticized by a number of studies.

Table 6.3 Differential risk of victimization by ethnicity according to data from the British Crime Survey 2000

	White	Black	Indian	Pakistani/ Bangladeshi
Burglary	4	6	6	5
Vehicle theft	13	17	14	16
All household offences	25	25	27	29
Assault	3	3	2	2
Threats	3	3	3	3
Robbery/theft from person	2	4	4	2
All personal offences	8	10	7	7

Source: A. Clancy, M. Hough, R. Aust and C. Kershaw (2001) *Crime Policing and Justice: The Experience of Ethnic Minorities: Findings from the 2000 British Crime Survey*, Home Office Research Study 223, Home Office, London, p. 12.

The 2004/05 BCS indicated that ethnicity was not independently associated with risk of victimisation for either personal or all violent incidents. Instead other factors; age and sex, frequency of visiting pubs or bars, living in an area with high levels of perceived anti-social behaviour and marital status were the strongest predictors of risk of victimisation. Home Office, 2006, p. 8

According to Clancy *et al.* (2001), much of the difference in victimization can be explained in terms of social factors, such as the areas in which minority ethnic groups live, the higher rates of unemployment among minority ethnic groups, and the younger age structure of minority ethnic groups compared to whites. Indeed, their statistical analysis suggests that such factors are more important than ethnicity.

Nevertheless, ethnicity explains some of the difference in victimization rates. Furthermore, Phillips and Bowling point out that some of the 'social factors such as inner-city residence and unemployment may themselves be partly explained by discrimination in housing and employment'.

Data from the British Crime Survey and other sources suggest that the increased risk of victimization – particularly in violent crime – is reflected in increased fear of crime among minority ethnic groups. Phillips and Bowling (2002) comment: 'On the street, and especially at home alone at night, ethnic minorities feel less safe than white people and that feeling affects their individual freedom of movement.'

Given that minority ethnic groups have less faith in the police than whites (see p. 364), the problems of increased risk of victimization are compounded by a lack of faith in the ability of the criminal justice system to deal with the racially motivated and other crimes to which they fall victim. The Macpherson Inquiry into the Stephen Lawrence case highlighted the complacency and inefficiency of the police in dealing with a racially motivated incident. While considerable efforts have been made to tackle this problem, it remains to be seen how successful these efforts will be.

'Race', ethnicity and crime – conclusion

Bowling and Phillips (2002) conclude that minority ethnic groups' involvement in crime and criminal justice is closely related to **social exclusion**. Social exclusion relates both to minority ethnic groups as victims of crime and as suspects or perpetrators.

Criminological research shows that victimization clusters in conditions of social exclusion, such as high unemployment, high housing density and poor schools. On the basis of the social and economic position of ethnic minority communities, structural theories of crime – including those based on such concepts as anomie, strain, social disorganization, absolute and relative deprivation – would all posit that people from ethnic minority communities are disproportionately likely to be found in criminogenic contexts. Bowling and Phillips, 2002

To Bowling and Phillips, the evidence on whether minority ethnic groups commit more crime than whites is inconclusive. However, they believe it is clear that black people are more likely to be **criminalized** – that is, they are more likely to be turned into a criminal by being arrested and imprisoned. This in turn leads to greater social exclusion and therefore to a greater chance of criminalization. Social exclusion can therefore lead to a vicious circle which creates increased chances of minority ethnic involvement in crime, as victims and as people who are criminalized.

David J. Smith (1997) reviewed evidence about ethnicity and crime and reached broadly similar conclusions. However, he places slightly more emphasis than Bowling and Phillips on discrimination, and rather less on social exclusion. He argues:

It seems likely ... that ... discrimination against black minorities interacts with high rates of offending amongst those same groups ... The interaction between racial stereotypes, discrimination, antagonism to authority, and actual rates of offending amongst young black people produces a cycle of deviance amplification. Smith, 1997

Gender and crime

Gender and patterns of crime

Writing in 1979, Carol Smart stated:

Our knowledge is still in its infancy. In comparison with the massive documentation on all aspects of male delinquency and criminality, the amount of work carried out on the area of women and crime is extremely limited. Smart, 1979

Smart put forward a number of reasons for this neglect:

1. Women tend to commit fewer crimes than men, so female offenders are seen as less of a problem for society.
2. Most crimes committed by women seem to be of a comparatively trivial nature and may therefore be considered unworthy of research.
3. Sociology and criminology have both tended to be dominated by males. In the main, they have been studied by men and the studies have been about men.
4. Traditional criminology is motivated by a desire to control behaviour that is regarded as problematic. Since women's criminality has been seen as much less problematic than men's, it has received correspondingly less attention.

Although the years since Smart's study have seen much more interest in the study of female crime and deviance, some general theories in this area of sociology continue to neglect gender as a factor influencing criminality. This is despite the fact that official figures suggest that gender is perhaps the most significant single factor in whether an individual is convicted of crime. Sociological theories which fail to explain this relationship could therefore be seen as inadequate.

Official statistics, criminality and gender

According to official statistics, in 2005, 1.8 million offenders were found guilty of, or cautioned for, offences in England and Wales, and of these 79 per cent were male. The ratio of male offenders to female offenders is four to one.

Theft and handling stolen goods was the most common offence category for both males and females, but males committed over 70 per cent of the offences. Just over half of all offences committed by women were offences of theft, whereas for men the proportion was one-third. In all other categories of offences, the proportion of women offenders was between 10 and 20 per cent, except in the case of sexual offences and burglary where the figures were much lower, at 2 and 5 per cent respectively.

Such figures are neither unusual nor surprising. In Britain, there has been a long-standing tendency for men to commit many more crimes than women, and a similar pattern is repeated in many other countries. Frances Heidensohn (1997) quotes American research which shows that, in 1993, females accounted for only 24 per cent of arrests of those aged under 18, and 19 per cent of those in older age groups.

Heidensohn's own research, conducted in the mid-1980s, found that females made up 20 per cent or less of offenders in a variety of European countries. Heidensohn also refers to more recent research which shows low rates of offending for women in countries as diverse as Brazil and India.

Heidensohn (1997) quotes a number of historical studies of offenders in Britain, which show women accounting for small proportions of the total number of law-breakers. Thus, one study of the Home Counties in 1782–7 found that women made up just 12 per cent of those convicted; another found that women accounted for a steady 17 per cent of convictions from 1860 to 1890. However, one study, which examined cases at the Old Bailey from 1687 to 1912, found that 45 per cent of defendants were women (Feeley and Little, 1991; quoted in Heidensohn, 1997). This study may be unrepresentative because it concentrated on one court.

Official figures such as these have raised three main questions about gender and crime:

1 Do women really commit fewer crimes than men, or are the figures misleading? Some sociologists have suggested that women's offences are consistently under-recorded by the authorities.
2 Although women continue to commit comparatively few crimes, some people have suggested that the proportion of crimes committed by women has been increasing. If women are becoming more criminal how can this be explained?
3 Why do those women who do break the law commit crimes?

In the following sections we examine the answers that sociologists have given to these questions.

Figure 6.10 Offenders found guilty of, or cautioned for, indictable offences: by gender and type of offence, 2005

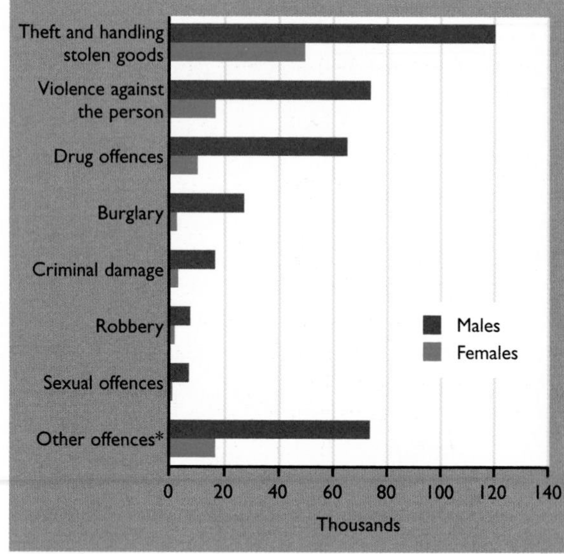

* Includes fraud and forgery and indictable motoring offences

Source: *Social Trends 2007*, HMSO, London, p. 142.

Pollak – the 'masked' female offender

Writing in 1950, Otto Pollak argued that official statistics on gender and crime were highly misleading. He claimed the statistics seriously underestimated the extent of female criminality. From an examination of official figures in a number of different countries, Pollak claimed to have identified certain crimes that are usually committed by women but which are particularly likely to go unreported:

1 He assumed that nearly all offences of shoplifting and all criminal abortions were carried out by women, and then asserted that such crimes were unlikely to come to the attention of the authorities.
2 He also argued that many unreported crimes were committed by female domestic servants.
3 Pollak accepted official definitions of crime when he pointed out all the offences of prostitution that were not reported. Male clients of prostitutes were assumed to have engaged in no illegal activities.
4 He even went so far as to suggest that women's domestic roles gave them the opportunity to hide crimes such as poisoning relatives and sexually abusing their children.

Pollak then went on to give reasons as to why there should be an under-recording of female crime:

1 He argued that the police, magistrates and other law enforcement officials tend to be men. Brought up to be chivalrous, they are usually lenient with female offenders, so fewer women appear in the statistics. However, he regarded this as only a minor factor.
2 A more important factor, according to Pollak, is that women are particularly adept at hiding their crimes. He attributed this to female biology. Women have become accustomed to deceiving men because traditional taboos prevent women from revealing pain and discomfort resulting from menstruation. Furthermore, women also learn to mislead men during sex. Men cannot disguise sexual arousal when they get an erection, whereas women can take part in sexual intercourse while faking interest and pleasure.

Criticisms of Pollak

Not surprisingly, Pollak's totally inadequate analysis has been subject to fierce criticism.

Stephen Jones (2001) points out that Pollak gave no real evidence that female domestic servants commit many crimes against their employers or that women are better at concealing crimes than men. Jones says: 'Pollak's methodology nowadays appears hardly satisfactory: for example, he failed to take account of changes in the law against abortion in several of the countries he studied.'

Heidensohn (1985) also criticizes Pollak, noting that later research indicates that much shoplifting is committed by men. She also comments that 'concealment of menstruation is by no means universal and changed sexual mores have long since made nonsense of his view of passive, receptive females brooding vengeance'. Heidensohn regards Pollak's work as being based upon an unsubstantiated stereotypical image of women, and notes his unwillingness to attribute male crime to a biological predisposition to aggression and violence.

Although Pollak's work has no credibility today, he was important for being the first to suggest that statistics greatly underestimate female criminal activity. Some sociologists have supported the idea that female criminals are seriously under-represented in official statistics.

Criminality, sex and the law

In theory at least, the vast majority of laws are sex-blind: the possibility of being charged, or the type of offence for which you are charged, does not depend upon your sex. However, there are a few laws that only apply to members of one sex. For example, in Britain, only men can be convicted of rape or offences of homosexuality. On the other hand, only women can be convicted of infanticide or soliciting as prostitutes. In reality, only a very small proportion of crimes come into one of these categories, and legal definitions therefore make little difference to the overall statistics for male and female crime.

Leniency towards female offenders

Nevertheless, a number of writers have put forward evidence to support the **chivalry thesis**, which claims that women are let off relatively lightly by the predominantly male police, judges, magistrates, etc. in the criminal justice system.

One type of study that has been used to support such claims is the **self-report study**, in which individuals are asked about what crimes they have committed. (For further comments on this type of study, see pp. 329–30.) Although such studies have their methodological limitations, they do give some indication of the extent of unreported crime and the chances that different groups have of escaping the discovery and prosecution of their offences.

Some self-report studies have implied that female offenders are more likely to escape conviction than males. In 1992, John Graham and Benjamin Bowling (1995) conducted research into self-reported offending among 1,721 14- to 25-year-olds in England and Wales. Although they found that males were more likely to commit offences than females, the differences were not as great as those shown in official statistics. The study found that 55 per cent of males and 31 per cent of females admitted having committed an offence; 28 per cent of males and 12 per cent of females admitted an offence in the previous twelve months. In official statistics around four times as many men as women are convicted in a typical twelve-month period.

Similar results were produced by the Youth Lifestyles Survey (Flood-Page *et al.*, 2000). This was conducted in 1998–9 and used a sample of 4,848 12- to 30-year-olds in England and Wales. The study only included reasonably serious offences and did not include drug use. It found that 11 per cent of females compared to 26 per cent of males admitted offending in the previous year. These general figures suggest some difference in the likelihood of male and female offenders being convicted. Furthermore, the study found that 1 per cent of the women said they had been cautioned or taken to court in the last twelve months (1 in 11 self-reported offenders) compared to 4 per cent of men (more than 1 in 7 self-reported offenders). However, such figures should be used with caution.

Another area in which there is apparent evidence for chivalry – that is, treating females more leniently than males – is in the cautioning of offenders. Writing in 1981, Anne Campbell pointed out that female suspects were more likely than male suspects to be cautioned rather than prosecuted. Official statistics show that this remains true. In 1999, of males recorded as offending, 30.1 per cent were cautioned and 69.9 per cent were convicted. In the case of women, 47 per cent were cautioned and 53 per cent were convicted (Home Office, 2000b).

A study by Hilary Allen (1989), based upon an examination of 1987 criminal statistics, showed apparent leniency towards female offenders. For example, 73 per cent of women, but only 54 per cent of men, found guilty of indictable motoring offences, were given fines. This difference very largely resulted from more men being given prison sentences.

Allen (1987) also found evidence that women sometimes escape prison in very serious cases (including manslaughter), where a male defendant might have been expected to receive a prison term. In 1976, Campbell (1981) compared a self-report study on her own sample of 66 urban schoolgirls, aged 16, with similar data on a sample of 397 16-year-old males, collected by West and Farrington. These sources of data showed that 1.33 offences were committed by males for every 1.0 committed by females. This contrasted with 1976 official figures on convictions, which showed 8.95 male convictions for every female conviction.

Evidence against the chivalry thesis

In contrast, most other researchers have not found support for the chivalry thesis. Steven Box (1981) reviewed the data from self-report studies in Britain and the USA. Although a few of these studies indicate some leniency towards females, the majority do not. He is able to conclude:

> ***The weight of evidence on women committing serious offences does not give clear support to the view that they receive differential and more favourable treatment from members of the public, police or judges.*** Box, 1981

He goes on to say: 'it would not be unreasonable to conclude that the relative contribution females make to serious crime is fairly accurately reflected in official statistics'.

A closer examination of the self-report studies discussed above could support Box's argument. Both the study by Graham and Bowling and the Youth Lifestyles Survey found that females were less likely than men to be involved in the more serious offences. The seriousness of the offence could explain the lower proportions of females among the convicted and cautioned than among self-reported offenders, rather than leniency in the criminal justice system. Furthermore, neither study considers older offenders, among whom males may be particularly predominant.

All self-report studies rely upon the respondent's ability and willingness to tell the truth. Some researchers have tried to measure crime more directly, using observation. Abigail Buckle and David P. Farrington (1984) carried out a small-scale observational study of shoplifting in a British department store in southeast England in 1981. Shoplifting is one crime where numbers of female offenders nearly match numbers of male offenders in the official statistics. This study found that 2.8 per cent of the 142 males observed shoplifted, but only 1.4 per cent of the 361 females did so. Obviously this study uses far too small a sample to draw firm conclusions, but, as one of the few attempts to measure crime directly, it does provide some evidence against the chivalry thesis.

Sentencing policy

Another approach to evaluating the chivalry thesis is to examine sentencing policy. In 1983, David P. Farrington and Alison Morris conducted a study of sentencing in Magistrates Courts. They started out by noting that some official figures did imply more leniency towards women. For example, in 1979, 6.6 per cent of men but only 2 per cent of women found guilty of indictable crimes were imprisoned. Farrington and Morris examined data on sentencing for 408 offences of theft in Cambridge in the same year. Some 110 of these offences were committed by women.

Although men received more severe sentences than women, the research found that the differences disappeared when the severity of offences was taken into account. Farrington and Morris (1983) concluded: 'There was no independent effect of sex on sentence severity.'

However, these findings were not replicated in a study carried out by Roger Hood in the West Midlands in 1989, which used a sample of 2,884 male and 433 female defendants in Crown Courts. Hood (1992) compared the sentencing of men and women, controlling for variables which he had found affected the sentencing of men. He found that white women were given custodial sentences 34 per cent less often than men in similar cases, and black women 37 per cent less often.

However, as we will discover in later sections, this does not necessarily mean that women are always treated sympathetically by the legal system.

Criminal justice as biased against women

A rather different point of view is put forward by those who argue that women are treated more harshly by the criminal justice system than men. This view can be supported by evidence which suggests that male offenders are sometimes treated more sympathetically than their female victims. This is particularly the case with rape trials. Carol Smart (1989) argues that such trials 'celebrate notions of male sexual need and female sexual capriciousness'. She quotes trial judges in rape cases in support of this claim:

> *It is well known that women in particular and small boys are likely to be untruthful and invent stories.* Judge Sutcliffe, 1976

> *Women who say no do not always mean no. It is not just a question of how she says it, how she shows and makes it clear. If she doesn't want it she only has to keep her legs shut.* Judge Wild, 1982

> *It is the height of imprudence for any girl to hitch-hike at night. That is plain, it isn't really worth stating. She is in the true sense asking for it.* Judge Bertrand Richards, 1982

Sandra Walklate (1998) believes that, in effect, it is the female victim rather than the male suspect who ends up on trial. Women have to establish their respectability if their evidence is to be believed.

Walklate quotes a study by Adler (1987) which found that women who were single mothers, had a criminal record, were punks, had children in care, lived in a commune or supported the Greenham Common peace camp (an all-female protest camp against nuclear weapons) were all regarded by courts as lacking in respectability and therefore credibility.

Walklate agrees with Carol Smart that rape trials continue to see things from the male point of view, which accepts that men become unable to restrain their sexual desires once women give them any indication they might be available for sex.

Many researchers have claimed that men are treated leniently in cases of domestic violence. In a pioneering study of domestic violence by Dobash and Dobash (1979), it was found that police officers were 'very unlikely to make an arrest when the offender has used violence against his wife'. Walklate (1998) points out that, since this study, the police, encouraged by feminist campaigners, have made attempts to take domestic violence more seriously. The Metropolitan police and other police forces have set up Domestic Violence Units to monitor the way the police deal with such cases, and in British police forces generally there is an increased emphasis upon prosecuting offenders. Nevertheless, Walklate believes there 'are obviously still difficulties in ensuring that women are responded to appropriately by all officers called to the scene'.

Double standards in criminal justice

A number of empirical studies and commentaries on gender and crime have reached the conclusion that males and females are treated differently and inequitably by the justice system, but not always to the detriment of women. Basing her arguments on a review of available evidence, Heidensohn (1985) suggests that women are treated more harshly when they deviate from societal norms of female sexuality. Sexually promiscuous girls are more likely to be taken into care than similar boys. On the other hand, courts may be reluctant to imprison mothers with young children.

To Heidensohn, the justice system is influenced by attitudes to gender in society as a whole. These are based upon 'dual' and 'confused' assumptions about women, which see women as 'virgin and whore, witch and wife, Madonna and Magdalene'.

As we noted earlier, Hilary Allen's (1987, 1989) studies of sentencing found that women were treated quite leniently in the case of motoring offences. Allen found that women were more likely to escape with low-tariff punishments across a range of offences and were certainly less likely to be sent to prison. However, she also found that women were more likely than men to be put on probation for some offences.

Like Heidensohn, Allen argues that these policies are tied up with conventional definitions of femininity and masculinity. Men's offences are often put down to aggression or greed. Men are more likely to be fined and imprisoned partly because they are seen as being less central to family life than women. The loss of money from a fine or the loss of a parent through imprisonment is regarded as less problematic for a family if the offender is a man than if it is a woman.

Women are seen as being less inherently deviant than men, and courts find it harder to understand their criminal activity. Consequently courts are more likely to order reports on female offenders in the search for 'underlying psychological meanings'. Probation may be used instead of a fine, with the intention of helping the female offender. In this case, though, what could be seen as 'chivalry' by the courts could also be seen as disadvantaging women and reinforcing sexist ideologies about masculinity and femininity.

Similar conclusions are reached by Pat Carlen (1997). She argues:

> *The majority of British born women who go to prison in England, Wales and Scotland are less likely to be sentenced for the seriousness of their crimes and more according to the court's assessment of them as wives, mothers and daughters. If they are young and their parents or state guardians believe them to be beyond control, if they are single, divorced or separated from their husbands, or if their children are in residential care, they are more likely to go to prison than those who, though their crimes may be more serious, are living more conventional lives.* Carlen, 1997

Carlen quotes from her own earlier research into Scottish sheriffs (judges). In interviews, the sheriffs stated they were unlikely to imprison women who were good mothers, but were much more inclined to punish childless women, or women whose children were in care, with a custodial sentence.

Although women who conform to the ideals of femininity held by male judges sometimes get off relatively lightly, others are less lucky. Some alternatives to prison, such as community service, are unsuitable for women who cannot afford childcare, so they tend to get prison sentences as the only practicable option. Carlen claims that some pregnant women who are very poor or homeless are sent to prison so that their children are born in what the courts see as more desirable surroundings.

If writers such as Heidensohn, Allen and Carlen are correct, then the British criminal justice system is highly **gendered**. That is, its decisions (whether they benefit men or women) are at least partly based on the sex and gender characteristics (as well as the class and ethnicity) of those it deals with. As such, the idea of equality before the law is an illusion.

The causes of female crime and deviance

Physiological causes

Some of the earliest attempts to explain female criminality were based upon physiological or biological theories. One of the pioneers of biological theories of male crime, Caesare Lombroso, also attempted to explain female crime. Writing with William Ferrero in *The Female Offender*, Lombroso devoted considerable attention to comparing anatomical features of female criminals and non-criminals (Lombroso and Ferrero, 1958; first published in English 1895). For example, he reported data comparing brains and skulls, the width of cheekbones, size of jaws and even the size of the thighs of prostitutes and 'normal' women! Nevertheless, his overall argument is that, rather than being the cause of female criminality, biology tends to prevent women from becoming criminal.

Writing about male crime, Lombroso had suggested that criminals could be identified through the presence of 'stigmata' or physical abnormalities, such as having an extra toe or nipple. Lombroso and Ferrero found few examples of such abnormalities among female criminals. To them, this suggested that most female offenders were not true, biological, criminals – they broke the law only occasionally and their crimes were not serious. Lombroso and Ferrero claimed that women had a deficient moral sense, and were inclined to be vengeful and jealous, but 'in ordinary cases these defects were neutralized by piety, maternity, want of passion, sexual coldness, by weakness and an underdeveloped intelligence'.

Nevertheless, Lombroso and Ferrero did believe that a few women were born criminals. These women were so exceptional and started life with such 'enormous wickedness' that each was 'consequently a monster'. They tended to be more masculine than other women.

Lombroso's work has long been discredited. For example, Heidensohn comments:

> *His work was fanciful rather than scientific. His detailed measurements were not subject to any tests of significance and his 'analysis' of photographs of 'fallen women' is as objective as an adjudication in a beauty contest.*
> Heidensohn, 1985

Such criticisms have not prevented some later sociologists from seeking biological explanations both for women's conformity, and, when it occurs, for their deviance. For example, Anne Moir and David Jessel (1997) explain some violent female crime as resulting from hormonal changes associated with Premenstrual Syndrome (PMS). Most sociologists, however, have rightly focused on possible social causes of female crime.

Female crime and women's liberation

Freda Adler (1975) first put forward the suggestion that women's liberation was resulting in increasing levels of female criminality and creating new and more serious types of female criminal. She rejects the idea that female crime can be explained in biological terms. For example, she points out that there are 'many passive men with normal androgen levels who are less aggressive than women'. She argues that differences in the behaviour of men and women are socially determined, and that changes in society have led to changes in behaviour.

Adler quotes a number of studies in the USA which show increasing levels of female involvement in traditionally male-dominated crimes such as robbery and embezzlement. She claimed there were similar trends in Western Europe, New Zealand and India. Adler believed the main reason for this was that just as women were taking on what had been male social roles in the world of work, they were also taking on male roles in the criminal world.

On the surface, there appears to be some evidence to support Adler's argument in the rising crime rates for women. Frances Heidensohn (2002) accepts there has been some increase in the proportion of crimes committed by women in Britain. She observes that in the 1950s women committed about one-seventh of recorded crime, but by 1999 this had increased to around one-sixth. She also notes an increase in the USA, with the proportion of people arrested who were female rising from 13 per cent in 1975 to 19 per cent in 1995. However, Heidensohn does not support the theory that female liberation has been the cause of the increase in female criminality. She comments:

> *Criminal women are amongst those least likely to be affected by feminism (and those most affected by it, middle-class white women, are the least likely to be criminal). Moreover, criminal women tend to score highly on 'femininity' scores, whereas 'masculine' scoring women tend to be less delinquent.* Heidensohn, 2002

In a study of female offenders in the USA, Chesney-Lind (1997) reaches a similar conclusion. She found no evidence of any link between women's liberation and female criminality in the 1970s, arguing that poor, marginalized women were more involved in crime than liberated women. She did find some evidence of female involvement in drug-related crime, including violent crime, in the 1990s. However, she again argues that this has nothing to do with women's liberation. Rather, such activities by women are usually connected to prostitution; thus, women's involvement in criminality continues to be shaped by conventional gender roles.

Pat Carlen – women, crime and poverty

In 1985, Pat Carlen (1988) conducted a study of thirty-nine women aged 15–46 who had been convicted of one or more crimes. She carried out lengthy and in-depth unstructured taped interviews with each of the women. Most were from the London area and twenty were in a prison or youth custody centre at the time of interviewing. Most of the women were working-class (as are most women with criminal convictions) and they had committed a range of offences. Twenty-six had convictions for theft or handling stolen goods, sixteen for fraud or similar offences, fifteen for burglary, fourteen for violence, eight for arson, six for drugs offences, and four for prostitution-related crime.

Carlen does not believe that liberation has resulted in an increase in crimes by women. Most of her sample had been touched little by any gains that women had experienced in, for example, access to a wider range of jobs. Instead, most had experienced their opportunities becoming increasingly restricted.

Carlen argues that the working-class background of most of her sample is fairly typical of female offenders convicted of more serious crimes, although she is aware that 'white-collar' female criminals might be escaping conviction for their offences. She says: 'when women do break the law those from lower socio-economic groups are more liable to criminalization than are their middle-class sisters'.

By reconstructing the lives of such women from in-depth interviewing, Carlen hoped to identify the sets of circumstances that led to their involvement in crime.

Control theory

Carlen adopts **control theory** as her theoretical approach. Control theory has influenced a considerable number of criminologists and was first explicitly outlined by an American sociologist, T. Hirschi, in 1969. It starts with the assumption that humans are neither naturally wicked and prone to crime, nor are they naturally virtuous and prone to conformity. Instead, humans are essentially rational and they will turn to crime when the advantages seem to outweigh the disadvantages and are more appealing than the likely rewards of conformity.

According to Carlen, working-class women have been controlled through the promise of rewards stemming from the workplace and the family. Such women are encouraged to make what she calls the 'class deal' and the 'gender deal'. The **class deal** offers material rewards such as consumer goods for those respectable working-class women who work dutifully for a wage. The **gender deal** offers 'psychological and material rewards ... emanating from either the labours or the "love" of a male breadwinner'. When these rewards are not available, or women have not been persuaded that these rewards are real or worth sacrifices, the deals break down and criminality becomes a possibility.

Factors encouraging deviance

Carlen found that the women she studied attributed their criminality to four main factors. These were drug addiction (including alcohol), the quest for excitement, being brought up in care, and poverty. She places particular emphasis on the last two factors: very often the abuse of drugs and the desire for excitement were the consequence of being brought up in care or of being poor.

In all, thirty-two of the women had always been poor, four of the remaining seven were unemployed at the time of being interviewed, and only two had good jobs. A majority of the women (twenty-two) had spent at least part of their lives in care.

Rejection of the class deal

Poverty and being brought up in care led to the women rejecting the class and gender deals. Few of the women had experience of the possible benefits of the class deal. They had never had access to the consumer goods and leisure facilities which society portrays as representing the 'good life'.

Attempts to find a legitimate way of earning a decent living had been frustrated. For example, six of the women had been through the Youth Training Scheme, but they had returned to being unemployed at the end of their training. A number had gained qualifications in prison but had found them to be of no use in finding a job. Many had experience of day-to-day 'humiliations, delays and frustrations' in trying to claim benefits. They had 'a strong sense of injustice, oppression and powerlessness'. Crime was a way of resisting the injustices and trying to solve the problems of poverty. The women had little to lose by turning to crime, and potentially a good deal to gain.

Rejection of the gender deal

According to Carlen, women generally are deterred from committing crime because they are brought up to see themselves as the 'guardians of domestic morality'. They also have less opportunity to commit crimes because they are more closely supervised than males, first by parents and later by husbands. Patriarchal ideology promises women happiness and fulfilment from family life. For most of the women in the study, though, the gender deal had not been made, or had been rejected. They had been freed from family life, or so closely supervised that they felt oppressed by the family. Carlen says:

> *When young girls have been brought up in situations where absolutely no rewards (and many severe disabilities) have been seen to emanate from families, when, too, the technologies of gender discipline have been unusually harsh or oppressive, women's adult consciousness has been constituted within an immediate experience of the fundamental oppression inherent in the gender deal … they have resisted it.* Carlen, 1988

Some of the women had been sexually or physically abused by their fathers. Eight of them had been physically attacked by male partners. For the twenty-two women who had been in care, there had been little opportunity to 'acquire the psychological commitment to male-related domesticity'. Spending time in care broke attachments to friends and family and reduced some of the potential social costs of isolation which could result from crime. Running away from care, usually with no money, or leaving care, sometimes homeless and unemployed, could easily lead on to crime. Carlen describes the situation of women leaving care:

> *Ill-equipped (both materially and by their previous experiences) for living on their own, many of the women had soon begun to think that crime was the only route to a decent standard of living. They had nothing to lose and everything to gain.* Carlen, 1988

Convictions and prison sentences merely served to restrict the women's legal opportunities even further and make the attractions of crime greater.

Conclusion

Carlen's study was based upon a small sample of mainly working-class women involved in fairly serious crimes. It is therefore dangerous to generalize from her findings. Nevertheless, her study does provide strong support for the view that criminal behaviour becomes more likely when society's mechanisms of social control break down. Other sociologists have examined social control mechanisms to explain why women seem so much more likely to conform than men.

Frances Heidensohn – women and social control

As earlier sections have indicated, however inaccurate official statistics may be, it seems clear that women do commit fewer serious crimes than men. Frances Heidensohn (1985) has tried to explain why this should be so. Like Pat Carlen, she uses control theory as the basis of her explanation. Building on the work of other sociologists, she argues that male-dominated patriarchal societies control women more effectively than they do men, making it more difficult for women to break the law. Control operates at home, in public and at work.

Control of women at home

Being a housewife directly restricts women by limiting their opportunities for criminality. Heidensohn describes domesticity as 'a form of detention'. The endless hours spent on housework and the constant monitoring of young children leave little time for illegal activities. A 'very pervasive value system' persuades women that they must carry out their domestic responsibilities dutifully or they will have failed as mothers and wives. Women who challenge the traditional roles of women within the family run the risk of having them imposed by force. Heidensohn says, 'many observers confirm that wife-battering is in fact an assertion of patriarchal authority'.

If they are the main or only wage earner, men may also use their financial power to control women's behaviour.

Daughters as well as wives are more closely controlled by the family. They are usually given less freedom than boys to come and go as they please or stay out late at night, and are expected to spend more time doing housework.

Control of women in public

In public, women are controlled by the male use of force and violence, by the idea of holding on to a 'good' reputation, and by the 'ideology of separate spheres'.

Women often choose not to go out into public places because of the fear of being attacked or raped. Heidensohn quotes the 1986 Islington Crime Survey, which found that 54 per cent of women, but only 14 per cent of men, often or always avoided going out after dark because of fear of crime. She quotes Susan Brownmiller's claim that rape and fear of rape 'is nothing more or less than a conscious process of intimidation by which all men keep all women in a state of fear'. Heidensohn stops short of endorsing this view, but she does argue that the sensational reporting of rapes and the unsympathetic attitude of some police officers and judges to rape victims act as forces controlling women.

Women also tend to limit their behaviour in public places because of the risk of being labelled unrespectable, of being seen as a 'slag, slut or bitch'. The wrong sort of 'dress, demeanour, make-up and even speech' can damage a woman's reputation in the eyes of men (Heidensohn, 1985).

The **ideology of separate spheres**, which sees a woman's place as being in the home, 'has become part of the system that subtly and sometimes brutally confines women'. Women are not expected to raise their concerns in public and place them on the political agenda. If they try, they may be ridiculed and told to return to where they belong – in the home. Such a fate befell the Greenham Common women who, during the 1980s, protested about the siting of American nuclear weapons in Britain.

Control of women at work

At work, women are usually controlled by male superiors in the hierarchy, and workers' own organizations – trade unions – are also dominated by men. Women may also be intimidated by various forms of sexual harassment that discourage female employees from asserting themselves or from feeling at home at work. Sexual harassment 'ranges from whistles and catcalls and the fixing of pinups and soft porn pictures, to physical approaches and attacks which could be defined as possibly indecent and criminal'. Heidensohn quotes surveys which find that up to 60 per cent of women have suffered some form of sexual harassment at work.

Conclusion

Heidensohn's argument about the causes of conformity by women fits in well with Carlen's views on the causes of deviance. Both are based on control theory and both agree that crime and deviance by women take place when controls break down and women lose the real or imagined incentives to conform. Heidensohn suggests that some female criminals may be those who have 'perceived the bias of the system and decided to push against it'.

For other women, it is the restrictions themselves that force them into reliance upon crime. Heidensohn says: 'women are particularly vulnerable because they are so economically exploited'. If they lose the 'protection' of a man they may turn to crimes such as prostitution as the only way to earn a reasonable living.

Evaluation

Many of Heidensohn's arguments are based upon generalizations, some of which do not apply to all women. She does not always support her claims with strong empirical evidence. Furthermore, she admits that many of the empirical tests of control theory have been carried out on juvenile offenders rather than adults, and that control theory does sometimes portray women as being passive victims (Heidensohn, 1997).

However, Heidensohn does present a plausible explanation of why such a gap remains between men's and women's crime rates. In doing so she highlights some of the inequalities that remain between men and women.

Socio-spatial criminology

All criminal activity is conducted within a place, and all those who engage in criminal behaviour inhabit and live out their lives in physical places. There has therefore been a long history of studying where offenders come from and where they commit their offences in order to better understand their behaviour. In recent years this study of place has also extended to very specific attempts to prevent offending.

We will start with a brief exploration of the historical approaches which related places to offending, and then explore in more depth current approaches.

C.R. Shaw and H.D. McKay – *Juvenile Delinquency and Urban Areas*

C.R. Shaw and H.D. McKay were two researchers at the University of Chicago in the early part of the twentieth century, at a time of enormous inward migration to the city. They discovered a geographical pattern to offending behaviour based on a meticulous record of the addresses of offenders.

In their famous study, *Juvenile Delinquency and Urban Areas* (1942), Shaw and McKay used a system previously devised by E.W. Burgess, another Chicago sociologist who had divided the city into five main concentric zones. Each of these had a different economic and social profile. There was a central business district, and then further out from this a mixed area of poor housing and industrial units, and then, moving outwards from this, three more zones of increasing affluence. The poorer district surrounding the central business zone was described as the 'zone of transition', as it was assumed that as people became more affluent, they would move outward to the more affluent zones.

When their statistical analysis of offending was applied to this model, Shaw and McKay discovered that offending was highest in the 'zone of transition' which surrounded the central business district, and declined the further out the zone. What was even more interesting was that they found similar patterns in other US cities and that even when the population of the 'zone of transition' changed, the levels of offending still remained highest here. Therefore, there were strong grounds to link offending with a geographical area, and not with specific offenders who lived there.

Shaw and McKay suggested that the high levels of population turnover, linked to significant levels of poverty and poor housing, all combined to create a state of social disorganization. The influx of new immigrants prevented the development of strong and, most importantly, shared values to prevent them engaging in offending.

Shaw and McKay later amended the concept of 'social disorganization' to mean a distinct set of values which provides an alternative, non-conformist set of values to those of the mainstream society – known as **cultural transmission theory**. This approach is one of the bases for the development of subculture theory (see pp. 325–7 for a discussion of subculture theory).

Evaluation of Shaw and McKay

Critics such as Anthony Bottoms (2007) have suggested that Shaw and McKay confused where people lived with where they committed the offences. Bottoms points out that these are two very different issues, which Shaw and McKay failed to distinguish. We will see the importance of this later in relation to policies to combat crime.

Second, Bottoms points out that the concentric zone model does not fit most European cities and certainly is inappropriate for cities where any town planning and provision of social housing by the state are implemented. Indeed, British research failed to reproduce the clear pattern of concentric circles, finding instead that, although crime rates varied by area, the patterns were far more complex.

Finally, Shaw and McKay's model of cultural transmission is simply very difficult to prove or disprove, because the proof lay in the higher levels of offending, but the higher levels of offending were also what was being explained in the first place. So the problem is also the explanation.

A tradition of mapping offending did develop, but later studies tended to focus more on where offences took place rather than on where the offenders lived.

One particularly important study by Wilkstrom (1991) examined crime patterns in Stockholm using police data on various offences and where they were committed. What Wilkstrom found was that city centres did have higher levels of offending, as did poorer districts and affluent areas adjacent to poorer districts. Crimes of violence were more likely in the poorer districts, while burglary was more likely in the affluent adjacent areas. It was possible to make even more detailed analyses – for example, levels of domestic violence were higher in some poorer areas than in others.

Opportunity theory and cognitive maps

The essential point of **socio-spatial criminology** is to move away from an analysis which focuses on the individual and towards one which sees neighbourhood or spatial characteristics as more useful. Given that there are clear, but complex patterns which emerge when studying both the residences of offenders and the places where offences are most likely to be committed, the next step is to explain why certain places have higher levels of offences than others.

The first two explanations – opportunity theory and cognitive maps – are distinct but have often been combined, particularly by Home Office researchers, and have been very influential in policing circles.

Felson and Clark have suggested that the best way to explain why and where offending occurs is to use **opportunity theory**. They suggest that the likelihood of an offence occurring depends upon two factors: target attractiveness and accessibility.

1. **Target attractiveness** refers to how attractive the object to be stolen is to the offender – for example, most thieves would prefer something portable and highly valuable (a laptop computer) over an immobile, low-value object (a settee).
2. **Accessibility** refers to how easy the object is to steal in terms of access to it, ease of escape and likelihood of the offence being witnessed.

Marcus Felson: routine activities theory

Routine activities theory developed out of this approach and is most closely linked to the writings of Marcus Felson (2002). Opportunity theory states that:

> ***the probability that a violation will occur at any specific time and place might be taken as a function of the convergence of likely offenders and suitable target in the absence of capable guardians.*** Cohen and Felson, 1979, p. 590

Felson argues that crimes are most likely to be committed when the day-to-day activities of potential offenders come in contact with opportunities to commit crime.

In a study of professional burglars in Texas City, Cromwell *et al.* (1991) found that offenders weighed up the possibility of being caught against the attractiveness of the objects to be stolen as the key elements in their decision to break into a property (which supports opportunity theory), but they were far more likely to break into properties in areas which they knew well, as this increased their confidence in being able to escape afterwards (which supports routine activities theory).

Cohen and Felson's approach, however, extends the socio-spatial approach further than just explaining the activities of professional burglars – in two ways. First, it suggests that crimes are likely to occur where there is no 'capable guardian' to keep watch, such as a police officer, neighbours or informal social control engendered by a sense of community.

Second, they point out that it is not just place which is important, but also time. The same place can be safe during the day, but can become an area of crime in the evening and night (it could also be that different crimes are committed at different times). The best example of this is the high street of any town. During the day there will be relatively few crimes, but those which occur are likely to be offences such as theft. In the evening, when large numbers of young people are out drinking, the crime level may well increase, including the number of violent crimes.

Thus Cohen and Felson's approach helps explain why most violent offences occur in the evenings and weekends in city centres, and why burglaries are most likely to occur in poorer areas and in areas adjacent to them. Furthermore, it throws light on the fact that those who are most likely to be victims of violence tend to be young males, who go out three or more times a week, who drink alcohol and who are themselves most likely to commit offences – as they are the ones whose routine activities place them in the most likely situation to be victims/offenders.

Patricia and Paul Brantingham: cognitive maps

Patricia and Paul Brantingham (1991) argue that although people believe they share a common knowledge of a particular city or area where they live, actually they have quite different perceptions of these areas, depending upon where they live, and their routes from home to work, and places of entertainment. The Brantinghams suggested that each person carries, in their mind, a rather different image or map of their city, and they coined the term **cognitive maps** to describe these images (see Figure 6.11).

According to the Brantinghams, offenders are most likely to commit crimes when they encounter opportunities in areas which are cognitively familiar to them, and they are far less likely to offend in areas outside their cognitive maps. This provides an explanation for the patterns of crime we noted earlier – for burglary, for example.

Research by Carter and Hill (1979) in Oklahoma City extends the relevance of cognitive maps. Carter and Hill studied burglars to find out why they chose certain places rather than others. The research indicated that the burglars made strategic decisions (where to burgle) through their cognitive maps, and tactical decisions (which houses, when and how) after this.

A study in Sheffield by Wiles and Costello (2000) found that offenders travelled only two miles on average to commit their offences and invariably the area chosen was within their routine activities and cognitive maps.

Figure 6.11 Crime and opportunities

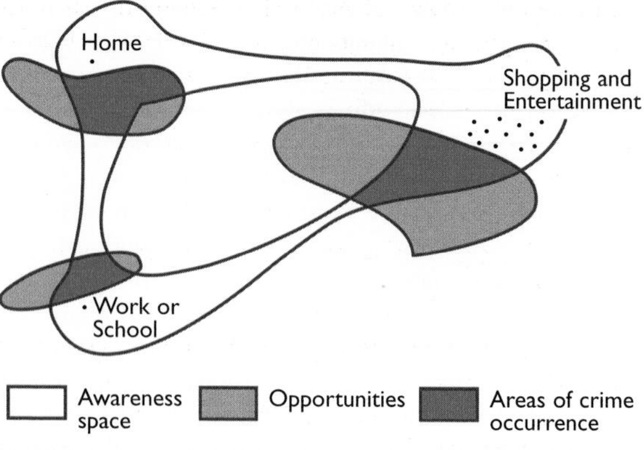

Source: P.J. Brantingham and P.L. Brantingham (1984) *Environmental Criminology*, Waveland Press, Prospect Heights, IL, p. 362.

An evaluation of administrative criminology

These three approaches – opportunity theory, routine activities theory and cognitive maps – have been placed together by sociologists such as Jock Young and described as '**administrative criminology**'. The term is used because the approaches have been strongly influential in government and policing policies (the administration).

The insights provided by administrative criminology have enabled the police and local authorities to make it more difficult for burglars to break into houses (by providing more lighting, blocking access to the rear of properties, etc.), and to make objects less attractive to them (by indelible ink marking). Administrative criminology has also been influential in policing city centres and in the decision to have flexible licensing hours so that large groups of young people are not turned out of pubs in city centres at exactly the same time.

However, the term administrative criminology is a pejorative one. These approaches do not explain the reasons why people commit offences, merely the circumstances in which they are more likely to commit them. According to Young, this means that they fail to explore the true underlying issues which generate crime, and it is this which makes the approaches particularly attractive to policy makers.

A second line of criticism focuses on the 'rationality' of the decision making of offenders. All three approaches, but opportunity theory in particular, assume that offenders make calculated decisions regarding their offending. Other studies, however, suggest that decisions regarding offending are not rational. Researchers such as Jack Katz (1988) argue that offending is often motivated by thrills and the search for excitement. We explore this critique in our discussion of cultural criminology in the next section.

Cultural criminology

One of the defining elements of the so-called 'administrative criminology' is that it is largely based on rational thinking – offenders make choices from a range of opportunities provided by their everyday lives. This led to a wide range of anti-crime initiatives which sought to make the potential offender think twice about committing a crime by putting obstacles in their way.

However, even while this approach held great sway in sociological and policy thinking, another tradition existed which cast great doubt upon the idea that rationality was involved in the vast bulk of offences, particularly offences committed by young males.

These alternative approaches stress irrationality, emotion and self-image as being the key elements of offending. Furthermore, these approaches stress that rather than using positivistic methods to help distinguish between offenders and non-offenders, it is much better to use ethnographic and biographical methods.

These various approaches have most recently been grouped together under the heading of **cultural criminology**, which seeks to bring a wide variety of influences into the study of crime – in particular, influences drawn from cultural studies, philosophy, urban studies and anthropology. As Keith Hayward and Jock Young (2004) put it, cultural criminology's main remit is to keep 'turning the kaleidoscope on the way we think about crime and the legal and societal responses to rule breaking'.

The sociologist who is most closely associated with this approach is Jeff Ferrell, who first coined the term 'cultural criminology'. However, it is important to remember, as Ferrell points out, that cultural criminology is 'less a definitive paradigm than an emergent array of perspectives' (2004, p. 396). What follows, then, is a short overview of a very broad range of approaches which only share the common approach of rejecting the rational explanations and suggesting that emotions and self-image are far more important in understanding crime.

The origins of cultural criminology can be traced back to the influences of David Matza.

David Matza – delinquency and drift

The American sociologist David Matza (1964) was the first sociologist to suggest that many sociological theories of delinquency are misleading; in particular, those that present an over-deterministic view of the origins of deviance. (**Determinism** is the doctrine that states that people have little or no freedom to direct their own actions since they are controlled by external forces.) 'Trapped by circumstances', the individual is automatically propelled down the path of deviance. Matza believes that this view ignores the choices and alternatives which are always available for human action.

In contrast to subculture theories (see pp. 325–7), Matza argues that male delinquents are not in opposition to society's norms and values. In fact, to a considerable extent they are committed to the same norms and values as other members of society. Far from being committed to crime, delinquents are only occasional, part-time law-breakers; they are 'casually, intermittently, and transiently immersed in a pattern of illegal activity'.

Techniques of neutralization

If delinquents, then, are generally committed to conventional norms and values, how is it possible for them to contemplate illegal acts? Matza claims that in certain circumstances they are able to 'neutralize' the moral bind of society: they are able to convince themselves that the law does not apply to them on this particular occasion. Deviance becomes possible when they use **techniques of neutralization** which temporarily release them from the hold that society has over them.

Techniques of neutralization include:

1. Denial of responsibility for a deviant act – the delinquents may remove responsibility from themselves by blaming their parents or the area in which they live.
2. Denial of injury resulting from the act – the delinquents may argue that joyriding does not harm anyone, it is just a bit of mischief, and that they were borrowing rather than stealing the car.
3. Denial that the act was basically wrong – an assault on a homosexual or a robbery from an extortionate store owner can be presented as a form of 'rough justice'.
4. Condemnation of those who enforce the rules – the police may be seen as corrupt, teachers as unjust and hypocritical.
5. Appeal to higher loyalties – the delinquents may argue that they broke the law not out of self-interest but to help their family or friends.

Matza argues that the use of techniques of neutralization throws serious doubts on the idea of deviant subcultures.

1. Techniques of neutralization are evidence of guilt and shame, which indicates at least a partial acceptance of mainstream norms and values. If there really were a delinquent subculture, there would be no need to resort to techniques of neutralization, since there would be no guilt to neutralize.
2. Techniques of neutralization often employ one set of mainstream norms to justify breaking others. Thus assaulting homosexuals is justified because it supports mainstream norms of sexual behaviour. Again, this shows some degree of commitment to mainstream culture.

Subterranean values

Once potential delinquents have freed themselves from the normal constraints society exercises over them, delinquency becomes a possibility. They are in a state of **drift** and may or may not break the law. Whilst the state of drift explains why people can break the law, it does not explain why they should wish to.

Matza explains the attraction to deviance in terms of **subterranean values**. This set of values encourages enjoying oneself, acting on the spur of the moment, self-expression, aggression and seeking excitement. These values, according to Matza, exist throughout society alongside **formal values** which encourage hard work and planning for the future. The 'respectable' member of society will only act in accordance with subterranean values during leisure activities, such as drinking in a bar, visiting the bowling alley, or playing football.

Delinquents do not hold different values from other members of society; they simply express subterranean values at the wrong place and time. For example, they may seek excitement at school, or they could be aggressive while at work. Again, Matza stresses that delinquents share more in common with other members of society than earlier theories would suggest.

The mood of fatalism and the mood of humanism

So far Matza has explained why delinquency is possible, and why it is attractive to some adolescents. This is not sufficient, however, to explain why they embark on delinquency. Before this is likely, some 'preparation' may be necessary: they may have to learn some of the skills they will require (such as those needed to break into a car) from more experienced delinquents. They also need a strong push to step over the dividing line between deviance and conformity for the first time. As they drift they may be pushed towards or away from deviance according to the circumstances.

The final decision to step over the line comes when adolescents experience the **mood of fatalism.** They feel powerless: other people are pushing them around, telling them what to do. To overcome this feeling they need to take some action which will make things happen, and 'restore their **mood of humanism**'. They wish to stop feeling like a victim of circumstances, and to prove to themselves that they too are human beings who can influence events around them.

Committing a delinquent act assures them of at least some response, even if it is a negative one. At the very least they can expect their action to be noticed, and to lead to a police investigation. Once they have taken this step, it becomes easier to contemplate other delinquent acts, but Matza emphasizes that delinquency never becomes more than an occasional activity. He stresses the choices that are available to all human beings, including delinquents.

Jack Katz – *Seductions of Crime*

The second major influence on cultural criminology is the work of Jack Katz (1988), who argues that what is missing from an understanding of offending is the part played by emotion, and particularly humiliation and rage.

Katz explores a number of crimes, including murder, and argues that:

> *Running across these experiences of criminality is a process juxtaposed in one manner or another of humiliation which turns into rage ...the badass with searing purposiveness tries to scare humiliation off ... young vandals and shoplifters innovate games with risks of humiliation, running along the edge of shame for its exciting reverberations [sic]. Fashioned as street elites, young men square off against the increasingly humiliating social restrictions of childhood by mythologizing differences with other groups of men.* Katz, 1988, pp. 312–13

Katz suggests that it is best to approach crime by looking at the particular act as a means of resolving an 'intolerable' position. The seduction of committing an act of murder occurs when the killer is faced with a situation where he can only maintain 'his' self-respect by going through with the act, where the actual act of murder is a release of tension, humiliation and shame. This moment of killing is described by Katz as 'righteous slaughter'.

By committing murder the killer experiences a heightened sense of release from the humiliation, but also a sense of control over the forces of humiliation and shame. The emotions at the time of murder are impossible to understand outside that moment of rage, and therefore seeking to apply rational explanations simply will not work. As Katz describes it, the moment of murder provides a 'blindness to the temporal boundaries of existence, they take us out of time and thus provide an escape ... rage is mercifully blind to the future ... blotting out all other experience and is indifferent to reasoned argument'.

The most extreme crime explored by Katz is murder, but there are many less serious crimes which he argues can also be understood by the emotion being used to evade or resist an intolerable situation. Katz suggests that people engage in 'sneaky thrills' in a range of minor crimes such as shoplifting, which have the 'emotional power of thrill' which in turn is linked to the possibility of detection and its consequences.

Katz's rejection of rationality and placing of emotion centre-stage, whether in committing murder or in seeking thrills through shoplifting, has been very influential and fits closely with the work of Lyng on 'edgework'.

S. Lyng – 'Edgework'

Writing at approximately the same time as Katz, Lyng also places emotions at the centre of his analysis of offending (and of a range of other activities too). Lyng (1990) argues that in a world of mundane rationality, certain individuals and groups seek a contrived loss of control. That is, people (usually young males) put themselves in potentially risky circumstances in order to enjoy the thrills of being on the edge of danger. Examples of this outside offending include free-fall parachuting, fast motorcycling, hang-gliding and white-water rafting. Lyng coins the term 'edgework' for these sorts of activities.

Lyng describes **edgework** as involving:

> *a clearly observable threat to one's physical or mental well-being or one's sense of an ordered existence. The archetypal edgework experience is one in which the individual's failure to meet the challenge will result in death or at the very least debilitating injury ... involving the ability to maintain control over a situation that verges on complete chaos, a situation most people would regard as entirely uncontrollable.* Lyng, 1990, pp. 858–9

Lyng agrees with Katz that at the time of committing the offence, the person involved in the edgework experience finds themselves in a 'hyper-reality' which seems much more real than their day-to-day existence. However, Lyng disagrees with Katz as to the basis of the emotional state. For Katz, the rage is a way of coping with intolerable circumstances; for Lyng, edgework involves a chance to exercise their skill at maintaining themselves at the very boundary of danger without actually coming to harm.

Lyng's approach has often been used to explain joyriding, where a car is stolen and then driven dangerously, sometimes in front of an admiring crowd, before being abandoned and wrecked (or set on fire, see below).

The writings of Matza, Katz and Lyng all stress the importance of emotion and reject rational/deterministic approaches. However, in the UK particularly, a newer generation of writers, such as Jack Hayward and Mike Presdee, have sought to locate the idea of emotions within a context, and in doing so have looked back to the Centre for Contemporary Cultural Studies (CCCS) for their inspiration.

The CCCS at Birmingham University (see pp. 771–4) produced a series of very influential publications in the 1970s which, from a Marxist perspective, sought to understand youth culture and offending in terms of 'resistance' to capitalist society.

The newer, late modernist approach, which Hayward, Presdee and others have developed, stresses that emotions are key to understanding the activities of offenders (particularly youth offenders), but that the emotions and the reasons for expressing them did not occur in a social vacuum.

Using a mixture of ideas from different sources, their central argument is that societies have always given people 'cultural spaces' to engage in deviant activity at certain agreed times of year – in particular the notion of 'carnival', which still lingers on in formal festivities in Venice and Rio de Janeiro for example.

Presdee (2004) in particular argues that the traditional 'carnivals' allowed the expression of emotion and resentment against the power of the higher orders in pre-capitalist society, and for a few days the normal order was turned upside down. At carnivals, church ceremonies were made fun of, and the priesthood and royalty were mocked. At the end of carnival, life and the social order returned to normal.

It is through these official carnivals that 'misrule', 'resentment' and 'resistance' are lived out, as the 'logic of late capitalism' asserts itself within the weave of everyday life. It is at this moment that the search for the carnivalesque becomes an essential element within the culture of everyday lived life, as we seek to find solace in transgression in order to free ourselves from the rules, regulations and regimentation of rational contemporary life. In some way the carnivalesque promises freedom.

Presdee suggests that there is no modern equivalent of this form of carnival, and thus expression of emotions and rejection of the current social order have no formalized outlet. For Presdee, the apparent anti-social behaviour of youth is an expression of this rejection, or a form of carnival.

For Hayward, the emotional expression which can be found in offending is one where people engage in a search for true emotions, which are denied in a capitalist economy where the only means of self-expression is through ownership of goods. As Hayward puts it, cultural criminology attempts 'to reflect the peculiarities and particularities of the late-modern socio-cultural milieu' (2004, pp. 155–63).

For both writers, then, emotions, and thrills in particular, are the key to understanding why people engage in offending, but these emotions are engendered within particular social contexts, wherein certain groups are denied expression of their identities.

As Presdee states:

> *Cultural criminology highlights the currents of carnivalesque excitement, pleasure, and risk-taking that animate everyday life, but equally so the many capillaries of daily control designed to contain and commodify these experiential currents.* Presdee, 2004

Mike Presdee: 'Burning issues: young people and the fascination for fire'

Presdee (2004) points out that in any one week in England and Wales there are on average 2,100 fires recorded which are started deliberately and which result in at least two deaths and costs of £40 million. The majority of these fires involve the burning of cars, with approximately 200 burnt out every day

For Presdee the way to approach the problem of arson is to explore it outside the boundaries set by seeking rational motives (for example, to hide the evidence after a car has been used for joyriding, or to make a false insurance claim), and to see it in terms of fun, pleasure and irrationality.

As Presdee puts it:

> *cultural criminology reflects ... the history of the discourses of 'limit' and 'transgression'; 'boundary making' and 'boundary breaking'; 'control' and 'hedonism'; 'rationality' and 'irrationality', alongside the examination of the 'inner' experience of individuals free from moral reasoning and safe from the 'outside' world. The individual 'inner' experience becomes the seat of wrongdoing and immorality par excellence. It is when this inner experience becomes exteriorized into the rebelliousness and resistance of carnival (or fête) that disorder becomes defined as law breaking rather than harmless fun – much the same way in which there is an instance when the fascination with fire becomes arson.* Presdee, 2004, p. 278

In order to understand the meaning of fire to young people, Presdee asked sixth formers at a 'high school' in the southeast of England to write about 'their experiences as well as their feelings for fire and what it meant to them'. In addition, he observed November 5th celebrations by young people.

Cultural criminologists routinely delve outside traditional sociological sources for their explanations and Presdee explores philosophical, psychological and anthropological discussions of fire. He concludes that:

> *Fire has slowly permeated our emotional makeup, entering our cultural consciousness in a deep and layered way. Fear yet fascination; destruction yet creation; death yet life. These dualities of fire lie buried within us, erupting from time to time, whenever and wherever the passage or survival of social life and social identity becomes a burning issue.* Presdee, 2004

Presdee suggests that deep within the culture there are powerful yet ambivalent feelings about fire, which most of the time lie dormant and controlled; but on certain carnivalesque occasions the thrill of fire is utilized. He quotes one of the sixth formers commenting that:

> *Last year on the last day at school before the summer holidays all the year 12s was burning their blazers!! There were fires all down the road! You couldn't wear those again!! (Jackie, 17)* Presdee, 2004

Presdee suggests that young people were using the power of fire to mark their passage from one social status to another – a form of rite of passage. He also argues that it symbolically destroys the power of adults over them as they leave school for perceived freedom from adult (teacher) restraint. Fire was chosen because of deep-seated cultural ambivalence about fire, but also as a clear signal of rebellion against the dominant culture.

When observing the November 5th celebrations, Presdee watched as the young people who were having an 'unofficial' bonfire engaged in what could best be described as edgework – running across the fire and placing burning pallets on top of the bonfire in order to have mock fights. The possibility of harming themselves was played with, and the aim of the action was to go as far as possible to put themselves in danger without actually getting burned.

Presdee regards this behaviour as reflecting the need for people in late modernity to 'transgress', and in so doing find space within the dominant rational processes that make up the organization of our society. He suggests that if there were greater opportunities for 'carnival' the need for transgression would be less: 'For late-modernity, carnival is dead but the need to transgress and resist is not ... carnival life, transgressive life, still happens in the creases of everyday-life creating instability, disorder and disturbance' (Presdee, 2004).

Cultural criminology: an evaluation

Cultural criminology has breathed life into a number of areas of sociology and has also made useful links to cultural studies. Cultural criminology cannot be seen as a coherent approach to understanding crime, but as a general movement of sociologists who wish to link criminological concerns more tightly with emotions, self-image and the idea that social action is increasingly influenced by the media and the perceptions of reality which can be found there.

Cultural criminology also argues for a move away from the scientific, 'positivistic' methods practised by criminologists, with their emphasis on finding the differences between those who commit crime and those who do not through the use of statistics and computer analysis of interviews. In their place, cultural criminology argues for an increase in ethnographic (observational) research, with sociologists getting back out on to the streets to look at everyday life in a different way.

Cultural criminology also explores new areas. For example, one of the writers most closely associated with cultural criminology, Jeff Ferrell (2004), has conducted work on the meaning of the shrines people construct on roadsides to mark the place where someone has died in a car accident. Ferrell's research involved visiting and photographing the sites. Ferrell has also studied people who live off the proceeds of rooting through 'trash' left out by householders in California and selling anything of value they can find. Both of these are areas which have never been explored before by sociologists.

However, cultural criminology does have weaknesses. The research produced is almost always observational and draws upon a wide variety of sociological and non-sociological influences. Whilst refreshing and challenging, the arguments produced remain highly theoretical as cultural criminologists are not particularly interested in proving their arguments by statistical methods or other means. Cultural criminology also tends to focus on interesting but perhaps marginal issues, such as those studied by Ferrell. It has not produced a coherent set of arguments explaining deviance and offending.

However, there are writers in this tradition who have sought to explore more substantial issues, in particular Elijah Anderson (1999), who explored the idea of 'respect' amongst inner-city black youths in the United States. Anderson argues that the desire for respect and the search for self-esteem is a powerful emotional need for everyone, and it finds expression amongst the young males in his study in ideas of toughness and masculinity (these issues are discussed in more detail on pp. 380–2). 'Shows of deference by others can be highly soothing, contributing to a sense of security, self-confidence and self-respect' (Anderson, 1994, p. 89).

Masculinities and crime

Early feminist approaches in criminology highlighted the neglect of women in criminological theory. At the same time they paved the way for a consideration of how masculinity could help in explaining crime. While traditional criminological studies have been written by men, about men and (arguably) for men, few have explicitly examined the links between masculinity and crime. They have tended to concentrate on crimes committed by males and ignore crimes committed by females, but have not considered what it might be about masculinity which leads to an apparently higher crime rate.

The few studies that have made links between masculinity and crime have tended to use very simple models. Thus, Tim Newburn and Elizabeth A. Stanko (1994) argue that 'the dominant theoretical models have rarely gone beyond the simple association of masculinity with, say, machismo'.

Theorists such as Walter Miller (1962) did relate crime to a working-class, male-dominated culture of toughness, but Miller's analysis remained unsophisticated. Others, such as Lombroso and Ferrero (1958), who first published their work in the nineteenth century, related gender differences in crime to biological differences. However, quite apart from their other faults (see p. 371 for a discussion), such theories completely ignore how social factors shape what it means to be thought of as a 'real man' or a 'real woman'.

Of the increasing number of attempts to discuss the relationship between criminality and masculinities, James W. Messerschmidt's is perhaps the most influential.

James W. Messerschmidt – *Masculinities and Crime*

Messerschmidt (1993) notes that most crimes are committed by males and therefore any study of crime must include a detailed study of masculine values. He begins his analysis by criticizing what he sees as the failure of previous criminology to deal with the relationship between masculinity and crime. Previous attempts to address this issue have been based either on biology or on what Messerschmidt calls **sex-role theory**, in which it is argued that male and female roles are taught in childhood and define the person's behaviour for the rest of their life.

Messerschmidt rejects both these approaches – biological accounts on the grounds that cross-cultural comparisons do not reveal any universal masculine characteristics, and sex-role theory on the grounds that it portrays men and women as being far too passive. He says, 'men and women are active agents in their social relations'. They do not simply act out the roles they have been taught, but make active decisions about how to behave as circumstances change.

Thus Messerschmidt believes that a theory explaining why men commit crimes should take account of different **masculinities** – the different ways in which people have perceived being masculine. Different conceptions of masculinity tend to lead to different social actions, in general, and different types of criminality, in particular.

Messerschmidt's approach

Messerschmidt adopts a version of Anthony Giddens's **structuration** theory (see pp. 888–90) as a theoretical approach for understanding gender and crime. Like Giddens, he believes social structures exist, but they only exist through structured social action. In other words, people's actions are needed to reproduce social structures. If they change the way they behave, the structures change. For example, patriarchal structures will change if men and women start behaving differently in families and sharing housework equally.

On the other hand, pre-existing structures do shape social action. For example, the relatively low wages available to most women in a gendered labour market encourage those women who are involved in partnerships with men to concentrate on domestic tasks, because their partner can earn more through paid employment.

Accomplishing masculinity

Gender is something people do, something they **accomplish**. In everyday life they try to present themselves in their interactions as adequate or successful men or women. They constantly monitor and adjust their social actions in the light of the circumstances.

> *Masculinity is accomplished, it is not something done to men or settled beforehand. And masculinity is never static, never a finished product. Rather, men construct masculinities in specific social situations (although not in circumstances of their own choosing); in doing so men reproduce (and sometimes change) social structures.* Messerschmidt, 1993

From this viewpoint, a man chatting with his mates at a bar, a man having sex with his girlfriend, or a man playing football, are all trying to accomplish masculinity.

However, men do not all construct the same type of masculinity. An individual's situation may or may not provide easy access to dominant forms of masculinity. Some men are not in a position to accomplish certain highly valued types of masculinity and must try to find alternative ways to be real men. Messerschmidt says, 'Although masculinity is always individual and personal, specific forms of masculinity are available, encouraged, permitted, depending on one's class, race, and sexual preference.'

Hegemonic and subordinated masculinities

Following the work of Connell (see pp. 138–41), Messerschmidt divides masculinity into two main types: hegemonic and subordinated masculinities. **Hegemonic masculinities** are the dominant and most highly valued types of masculinities. **Subordinated masculinities** are less powerful and carry lower status – examples include homosexual masculinity and the masculinity of African Americans.

The nature of hegemonic masculinity varies from place to place and time to time, but it is generally based upon the subordination of women. Hegemonic men benefit from their power over women. Men with less dominant forms of masculinity may also try to get benefits from power over women, but it is less easy for them to do so.

The importance of this for crime is that criminal behaviour can be used as a resource for asserting masculinity. Indeed, Messerschmidt goes so far as to argue:

> *Crime by men is a form of social practice invoked as a resource, when other resources are unavailable, for accomplishing masculinity. By analysing masculinities, then, we can begin to understand the socially constructed differences among men and thus explain why men engage in different forms of crime.* Messerschmidt, 1993

Using a wide variety of research findings, largely from other sociologists' studies, Messerschmidt explores why different groups of males turn to different types of crime in attempts to be masculine in different ways.

Masculinities and crime in youth groups

White middle-class boys tend to enjoy educational success and frequently also display some sporting prowess. In these ways they are able to demonstrate the possession of some characteristics of hegemonic masculinity. However, this is achieved at a price. Characteristics such as independence, dominance and control largely have to be given up in school. In order to achieve success, white middle-class boys are, to an extent, **emasculated** – their masculinity is undermined. They have to act in relatively subservient ways to school teachers.

However, outside school white middle-class boys try to demonstrate some of the characteristics that are repressed within school. This involves engaging in pranks, acts of vandalism, excessive drinking and minor thefts. Because of their background, these boys are usually able to evade becoming labelled as criminals by the authorities.

Such young men adopt an **accommodating masculinity** within school. This is a 'controlled, cooperative, rational gender strategy of action for institutional success'. Outside, they adopt more of an **oppositional masculinity**, which goes against certain middle-class norms but asserts some aspects of hegemonic masculinity they are denied in school.

White working-class boys also experience school as emasculating. However, they have less chance of academic success and so cannot easily access the type of masculinity based on academic success available to middle-class youth. They therefore tend to construct masculinity around the importance of physical aggression. It is important to be tough or hard and to oppose the imposition of authority by teachers and others. Theirs is an oppositional masculinity both inside and outside school. Messerschmidt quotes the 'lads' in Paul Willis's study of anti-school peer groups as an example (see pp. 605–8 for details of this study).

A third group, lower working-class boys from minority ethnic groups, have great problems finding reasonably paid, secure employment. They do not expect to be able to express their masculinity as breadwinners by holding down a steady job and supporting a family. Their parents may be too poor to buy them consumer goods with designer labels which confer status. With little chance of asserting their masculinity through success within school or work, the focus of these young men's lives is the street. They are unable to access the advantages of hegemonic masculinity through legitimate means and instead turn to violence and crime. They use violence inside and outside school to express their masculinity. They become more involved in serious property crime than white working-class youths. This at least offers some possibility of the material success associated with hegemonic masculinity.

Messerschmidt quotes a number of American studies showing how robbery is used to make the offenders feel more masculine than their victims, how gang and turf warfare is part of an attempt to assert masculine control, and how rape is sometimes used to express control over women.

Messerschmidt describes the particularly horrific case of the 'Central Park Jogger Rape', which took place in New York in 1989. Four adolescent African Americans beat and repeatedly raped a young, white, female jogger, before dragging her unconscious to a ravine and leaving her for dead. Messerschmidt says, 'Such group rape helps to maintain and reinforce an alliance among the boys by humiliating and devaluing women, thereby strengthening the fiction of masculine power.'

Of course, men in such groups do not necessarily resort to rape. They may be able to establish their masculinity through consenting sexual conquests instead. Like their white middle-class and working-class counterparts, lower working-class, minority ethnic males 'do' masculinity within the limits of the social structures that constrain them. Their recourse to a more violent and aggressive form of masculinity reflects the 'social conditions of poverty, racism, negated future' which limit their options.

Examples of links between different types of masculinity and crime

Messerschmidt also discusses how different types of masculinity can be expressed by different adult males in a variety of contexts leading to crime.

Pimping

On the street, pimping is one way to express masculinity. Pimps usually exercise strong control over the prostitutes they 'run'. By getting the women to turn most of their earnings over to them, they can also enjoy a degree of material success. They have more chance of expressing their masculinity in this way than by struggling to find and keep low-paid work. Furthermore, they can assert their masculinity by adopting 'the cool pose of the badass', which involves 'use of "poses" and "postures" that connote control, toughness and detachment'.

Pimps are loud and flamboyant and display their success through using luxury consumer goods. For black pimps, this is a way 'to transcend class and race domination', because they can assert their ability to earn money through work, and their power to exercise authority and control. However, their lifestyle and flashy displays are despised by more successful, white middle-class men, and, in effect, they only end up confirming their status as inferior men.

White-collar crime

To achieve success in large-scale corporations managers must do whatever is necessary to make their company profitable. In this sort of masculine culture it is not surprising that corporate and white-collar crimes are accepted, even encouraged, when they are the only way to guarantee profits. Messerschmidt quotes an engineer at Ford explaining why nobody questioned the continued production of the Pinto model in the USA. This car was prone to bursting into flames if it was in a rear-end collision, and a number of people died as a result, but it continued in production. The engineer explained that safety 'didn't sell', and that anyone questioning the production of the Pinto would, quite simply, have been sacked.

Domestic violence

The family is another area where men express different types of masculinity and dominance over women. Messerschmidt argues that relatively powerless men use wife-beating, violent rape and even murder to reassert masculine control when their masculinity is threatened by women. Thus, much violence occurs when the man believes that his wife (or children) has not carried out her duties, obeyed his orders, or shown him adequate respect.

Evaluation of Messerschmidt

Messerschmidt's work provides some valuable insights into the relationship between masculinity and crime. It uses a sophisticated theoretical approach which allows for the existence of different types of masculinity and for the way that these masculinities can change. It makes plausible attempts to link different types of crime to different types of masculinity and it appears to provide a basis for explaining why men are more criminal than women. Tony Jefferson (1997) describes Messerschmidt's work as 'a brave attempt'.

However, Jefferson criticizes Messerschmidt's work on a number of grounds. He argues that Messerschmidt fails to explain why particular individuals commit crimes rather than others. For example, only a small minority of African American men carry out rapes.

Other criticisms can also be made. Messerschmidt seems to advance rather stereotypical and negative views of men in general, and of working-class and non-white men in particular. There is no room in his book for men who might commit politically motivated crimes in a fight against an oppressive government, and little for men who reject the idea that being a real man involves asserting control over women.

Other writers, such as Bob Connell (1995) (see pp. 138–41), do not always portray men in such a negative light. Furthermore, perhaps Messerschmidt exaggerates the importance of masculinity in the explanation of crime. If Messerschmidt is to be believed, then nearly all crimes committed by men are an expression of their masculinity. While Messerschmidt may be right that it is difficult to understand male crime without reference to masculinities, he may be wrong to assume that it can be explained by this alone.

Masculinity and postmodernity

Messerschmidt's discussion of masculinity and crime falls, broadly speaking, within the range of theories which see society through the lens of late or high modernity. Many of these theories, including that of Messerschmidt, take Giddens's work as their starting point.

However, postmodern theorists also explore gender identity and crime. One of the better known examples of this approach is the work of Richard Collier.

Richard Collier – *Masculinities, Crime and Criminology*

Although Collier (1998) generally sees the work of Messerschmidt as an advance upon previous work in this area, he is still critical of aspects of Messerschmidt's approach.

1. Collier argues that the idea of hegemonic masculinity is of limited usefulness. To Collier, it is simply a list of traits which are not exclusive to men. Women can possess the same traits. Furthermore, the characteristics of hegemonic masculinity are used to explain a vast range of crimes, from burglary, rape and sexual abuse to traffic offences and corporate crime. Collier says: 'To account for such a diversity is, clearly, asking a great deal of the concept of masculinity.'

2 The use of the concept of hegemonic masculinity by Messerschmidt can be seen as tautological. Crime is regarded as the way in which criminals are expressing their masculinity, and masculinity is regarded as the cause of their crime.
3 Collier believes the description of hegemonic masculinity is simply based upon 'a range of popular ideologies on what constitutes ideal or actual characteristics of "being a man"'. As such, popular stereotypes are simply being reproduced in academic work.

Collier argues that a postmodernist approach is needed to understand the relationship between masculinity and crime – one which can 'address the complexity of the multi-layered nature of the social subject'. Stereotypes and images of masculinity are important, because they do affect people's understanding of what it means to be masculine. However, they are always interpreted in particular contexts. To Collier, men do not simply try to 'accomplish masculinity', because masculinity is multi-faceted and whether crimes are perceived as related to masculinity only emerges in the 'discourse' that surrounds crime.

There is considerable uncertainty over what it means to be masculine because of 'the changing configurations of childhood, family and fatherhood, of heterosexual social practices and the sexed subject'. Collier believes it is preferable to examine the subjective expression of masculinity by individuals or groups of men through crime than it is to generalize about hegemonic and other forms of masculinity. Generalizations are dangerous because 'male "identities" are precariously achieved and never fixed'.

Collier's approach can be illustrated by his case study of Thomas Hamilton.

Masculinity, crime and Thomas Hamilton

On 13 March 1996 Thomas Hamilton shot and killed sixteen primary school children and their teacher at their school in Dunblane in Scotland. He then committed suicide by shooting himself.

Hamilton was a local man who was 43 and single. He lived alone, but kept in frequent contact with his mother, who lived locally. He had been a scoutmaster but was forced to leave because of 'inappropriate behaviour'. He had failed, despite a number of attempts, to be reinstated.

Collier argues that the media tended to portray Hamilton as a 'monster' whose actions were 'grotesque'. It was implied that he might be a 'repressed homosexual' because he had an interest in children through the scout movement and because he was too close to his mother, he was single and had never been married. Hamilton was seen essentially as a failure as a man, who became violent because of his inability to express his masculinity. The media saw him as an 'inadequate nobody, a man considered unable to succeed in society – financially, socially, sexually, academically, in sport or in work'.

However, to Collier, this is an inadequate explanation of Hamilton's behaviour. It is based upon a static and generalized account of masculinity which does little to explain why Hamilton should choose to express his masculinity in such a violent way. Collier therefore tries to explain his behaviour in a more subtle way, which takes account of the multi-faceted nature of his masculinity and of the 'interface between the contexts in which Hamilton lived at the level of social structure and the specificities of his own life history'.

Based upon details of Hamilton's life, Collier argues that there was no evidence that Hamilton was a predatory paedophile. It was more likely that he felt a need to control and direct young boys in order to influence their development.

However, most care of young children is carried out by women, and men who become involved with young children can be regarded as potential paedophiles. In this context, Hamilton had 'forcefully resisted the label "pervert"; he had "fought back", protesting his "normality" to everybody from the Queen to the Ombudsman'. Hamilton had written many letters claiming that he should be allowed to run boys clubs or be a scoutmaster.

Thwarted in his attempts to express his masculinity by acting as an authority figure to boys, he found other ways to express it – in particular, through an interest in guns which allowed him to draw upon 'images of hyper-masculine toughness'. By attacking the school, he was asserting male authority and turning it upon the feminized world of the primary school. His murderous assault was not, therefore, a case of Hamilton losing control – it was 'a means of taking control'.

Evaluation

Collier provides interesting and perceptive interpretations of the relationship between masculinity and crime in the case of Thomas Hamilton (and in other case studies discussed in his book). He develops useful arguments about the dangers of generalizing about masculinities and shows how the analysis of individuals' identities can be revealing.

However, Collier himself sometimes makes generalized statements about masculinity, which are little different from those put forward by writers such as Messerschmidt, whom Collier criticizes. For example, Collier sees 'learnt tendencies of aggressive heterosexual manliness' as widely shared.

Simon Winlow – *Badfellas*

Simon Winlow's study, *Badfellas* (2001), examines the changing masculinities among working-class men in northeast England. Like Collier, Winlow is interested in the relationship between masculinity and violence. However, unlike Collier, Winlow is not particularly concerned with variations in the masculinity of individuals. Rather, he is concerned with how a whole local culture has changed, along with the nature of criminal masculinity.

Winlow's study draws upon a wide variety of theoretical approaches in sociology and criminology, including the sociology of masculinity, subcultural theory, theories of modernity and postmodernity, and theories of globalization. His study is also a richly detailed ethnographic account of crime in a particular location.

In the late 1990s Winlow conducted an ethnographic study of bouncers and associated criminal activity in the Sunderland area. Winlow was born and brought up in Sunderland. He came from the same background as many of the doormen; he knew a number of them personally, and because of this was able to obtain work as a doorman himself. He conducted a participant observation study and supplemented this with some informal interviewing and the use of secondary sources such as previous studies of the working class in Sunderland.

Social change in Sunderland and the northeast

Winlow argues that changes in Sunderland must be set in the context of social and economic change. These changes have taken on a number of key characteristics.

1 Sunderland has experienced rapid and profound deindustrialization. By the late 1980s, the mainstays of the local economy such as shipbuilding and mining were no longer employing large numbers of people. Associated trades such as welding and boiler making had also largely gone. Winlow describes Sunderland as 'a perfect example of a locality firmly rooted in the industrial modern age', but, he says, it 'is currently transforming economically, socially and culturally to cope with the advent of post-industrial and postmodern society'.
2 With the decline of heavy manual industries dominated by male full-time employment, part-time female employment has assumed more significance. There has been a shift to a post-industrial economy in which service sector and leisure-related employment has become increasingly important. This is particularly evident in the night-time economy, where legal and illegal activities coexist. Clubs, bars, taxi services, drug dealing, prostitution, strip clubs and cheap hotels all offer services to the mainly young people determined to enjoy themselves on their nights out. They also offer both legal and illegal opportunities for employment. Winlow sees the night-time economy as reflecting key features of a move towards a postmodern society.

   Drawing on the work of the postmodernist Jean Baudrillard (see pp. 893–4), Winlow argues that this is a context where images and signs become all-important in the creation of changing self-identities:

   > ***young people bond with mates and seek mates, get drunk, take drugs and seek out fun in a "hyper-real" world where almost any hedonistic desire seems within reach, and the baggage of one's normative identity can be left at the door …***
   >
   > ***… this environment is seemingly the very epitome of the postmodern. Use and sign value appear to merge in the consumption of designer beers and designer drugs, even as high fashion is donned by the majority rather than the lucky few and simulation is apparent at every turn.*** Winlow, 2001

3 A third major change is the impact of globalization. Although Sunderland retains a distinctive locality, influenced by its own tradition and culture, it is increasingly shaped by and in contact with wider cultures. The media have a significant influence. Winlow explains how he 'witnessed young males who strive to be Robert De Niro in *Goodfellas*'. He describes how one of the men discussed in his study, Sartie, has a particular interest in rap and hip-hop music even though he has never been to the USA and has no direct contact with the black American inner-city culture out of which the music grew.

   As we shall see, Winlow also found that local criminals were increasingly becoming involved in much wider criminal networks extending to other countries. In this process Winlow claimed to detect 'the merging of the global and the local to produce the contemporary cultural environment in the northeast'.
4 The fourth major change was the increasing importance of entrepreneurship in the local economy. With the decline of full-time employment opportunities, especially for men, people were looking to find new ways to earn a living. High levels of unemployment encouraged more of the local men to try their luck at entrepreneurial business activities. Some took advantage of the new international or even global networks connecting the northeast to other parts of the world.

Putting all these changes together, Winlow describes and explains a major shift in masculine identities in the northeast of England.

Crime in modern industrial societies

Winlow argues that, in the modern era, prior to the decline of heavy industry in Sunderland, it was important to men to 'prove their masculinity through physical labour'. Work not only allowed men to show their physical prowess, it also meant they were 'able to keep a wife and family'. However, the prime concern was not to demonstrate their masculinity to women, but to other men. Shop-floor masculinity involved 'strength, skill, autonomy, camaraderie', and, outside work, being able to 'hold your drink' was also important.

While a full-time job and family responsibilities offered a route into working-class respectability, the culture of working-class men in Sunderland also 'incorporated violence and an "immediate aggressive style of behaviour"'. This emphasis on being able to use violence was also found in the criminal aspects of working-class culture. Here, Winlow draws upon the work of Cloward and Ohlin (see pp. 326–7). He argues that in the modern industrial era there were few opportunities to make a living out of crime. There was little in the way of organized crime and therefore no significant illegitimate opportunities. In these circumstances a conflict subculture developed, characterized by petty crime and the use of violence to gain status. Winlow says, 'Violence was … a crucial signifier of self-image, a reflection upon a culture that favourably judged those who maintained a credible use of force.'

Winlow illustrates these arguments with a case study about Tommy, a 58-year-old former 'hard man', now too old to be a physical threat to younger hard men, but in his day a respected and feared man in Sunderland. Tommy worked in the local shipyards, but in his spare time he worked as a doorman at local dancehalls such as the Palladium. He also sometimes acted as a minder for local pubs. However, he never earned much money for these services. He was more likely to be rewarded with free beer than significant payment. Furthermore, his career as a doorman was cut short by his tendency to drink excessively and to start fights rather than prevent them. Nevertheless, his role gained him a local reputation, the admiration of some young women and status in the subculture.

Figure 6.12 Masculinity can be expressed through job role – how does masculinity manifest when there is no work?

Source: Rex Features

Figure 6.13 Legitimate protection?

Source: Rex Features

Masculinity in post-industrial society

By the late 1990s the nature of masculinity in Sunderland was changing, as was the nature of local crime. For many unskilled working-class men, there was little prospect of finding reasonably secure full-time employment. With an increase in the number of women working, the traditional role of men as the main breadwinner in a family had been undermined. Because of such changes, 'males become undesirable marriage partners' and the number of female-headed households increases. In this situation, traditional masculinities adapt to new circumstances. Winlow says:

> *As a shop-floor masculinity is now out of reach, its component parts are sifted, sorted and evaluated and those that can be moulded to fit in with the new post-industrial and postmodern cultural habitat are translated and made to work in this new environment.* Winlow, 2001

One aspect of traditional masculinity that is retained is the emphasis on violence. Being a hard man continues to be a way of gaining status. However, in the changed circumstances it assumes a new significance and becomes a way of earning a living, an entrepreneurial activity, as well. Working as a doorman, Winlow found that the other doormen increasingly saw their work as more of a career than a hobby. They were paid for their efforts in maintaining order and used it as a springboard for getting involved in potentially rewarding criminal activities. For example, some doormen started selling drugs, or importing and selling cheap duty-free beer and spirits to licensees and publicans.

Another criminal activity involved protection rackets. Some bouncers were involved with criminals who were paid by pub owners for ensuring there was no trouble on their premises. On one occasion, Winslow witnessed a violent attack by those involved in a protection racket on a man who had started a fight in one of the pubs they were minding. There was a degree of rivalry between different groups who minded pubs in different parts of the city. This could sometimes give rise to violent confrontations as one group tried to muscle in on pubs in another group's area.

To sum up, Sunderland had now developed a thriving criminal subculture in which crime was not just important for status, but also as a way of earning a living. There was a considerable degree of organization in this subculture, with various legal businesses and illegal activities being interlinked. For example, legitimate security firms were connected to protection rackets and apparently legal businesses were used to launder money from illegal activities.

The criminal subculture was developing international and global connections, particularly those related to importing cheap alcohol and drugs. For those involved in these activities, it was vital that they maintained their reputation as hard men. Any sign of weakness could encourage rivals to challenge them. With little in the way of legitimate job prospects the men involved used their **bodily capital** to earn a living. Many of the doormen and other hard men would actively try to develop their physique through body building.

However, success in the criminal subculture involved more than just being big and muscular. Winlow says, 'Just as important as the physical ability to carry out one's job is the sign value of one's body, speech and body language, facial expression and demeanour.' You had to look intimidating to discourage people from challenging you, as well as maintain your reputation and actually win fights. Ideally, you would also try to advertise your apparent success by wearing 'Ralph Lauren shirts and fake Rolex watches'. Thus, to Winlow, even the violent world of Sunderland's criminal subculture is a postmodern world where signs are an important commodity.

Conclusion and evaluation

Winlow concludes that the nature of masculinity and criminality in the Sunderland area has changed along with the nature of opportunities in the area. Without access to a stable masculine identity derived from long-term employment in heavy industry, crime becomes an appealing career option, along with the chance to enjoy 'the immediacy of one's own lived existence and the chance to live "life as a party"'.

Winlow accepts that not all crime in Sunderland is professional. However, even non-professional crime can act as preparation for a criminal career. He says, 'Petty crime and non-profit-making crime will not disperse with the arrival of a criminal entrepreneurial ethic. Car crime, burglary, shoplifting, vandalism, violence and other assorted crime are, in themselves, all potential testing grounds for formative and potentially fragile masculinities.' Some of those involved will go on to professional crime.

Winlow provides a detailed account of the changing nature of crime in one British city. It is particularly credible because of his closeness to the culture he is describing and because he could use his local knowledge to witness criminal violence. It draws upon a wide range of concepts from sociology and appears to make sense of changing conceptions of masculinity.

However, it is difficult to know how typical the northeast is of other areas of the country. His emphasis on violent and professional crime means that he says relatively little about petty and casual street crime and delinquency, and about crime which lacks a financial motive. Sometimes his attempts to link criminality to postmodernity appear a little tenuous. A street culture involving excessive drinking, drugs and the enjoyment of other hedonistic pleasures is certainly nothing new and has existed for many decades.

Postmodernism and criminology

Apart from the work of Winlow, a number of other attempts have been made to apply theories of postmodernism to the understanding or explanation of crime and deviance. One of the most influential postmodern approaches to criminology attempted to combine postmodernism with feminism to produce a new way of thinking about crime.

Carol Smart – postmodern feminism and female criminality

Traditional criminology

In an article entitled 'Feminist approaches to criminology, or postmodern woman meets atavistic man' (Smart, 1995; first published 1990), Carol Smart examines the relationship between postmodernism, feminism and criminology. She starts by attacking both traditional approaches in criminology (such as biological, psychological and subcultural theories) and newer approaches, such as left realism (see pp. 345–50). To Smart, they all share certain central characteristics and they all adopt a version of positivism:

1. They all try to find the causes of criminality.
2. The aim of all of them is to try to eradicate crime.
3. They all assume that scientific methods are the best way of finding the truth about crime.
4. They all believe it is possible to develop a **metanarrative** – a master theory – which will explain crime.

Smart does not reject some of the aims of approaches such as left realism. She thinks left realists have their hearts in the right places when they want to 'reduce the misery to which crime is often wedded' and they seek 'policies which are less punitive and oppressive'. The trouble is:

> *Science is held to have the answer if only it is scientific enough. Here is revealed the faith in the totalizing theory, the master narrative which will eventually – when the scales have fallen from our eyes or sufficient connections have been made – allow us to see things for what they really are.* Smart, 1995

Conventional criminology is based on a modernist paradigm. Such a paradigm assumes there will be progress, that sciences such as criminology can deliver knowledge that is superior to all other knowledge. It arrogantly believes 'it is only a matter of time before science can explain all, from the broad sweep of societal change to the motivations of the child molester'.

Deconstructing positivism and modernism

Smart rejects the modernist paradigm and, more specifically, traditional, positivist approaches. She argues that the modernist approach is 'male or phallagocentric', with a typical masculine obsession with control and domination over others (in this case, criminals). It is politically suspect because it denies a voice to anyone other than the scientific criminologist. The voices of 'lesbians and gays, black women and men, Asian women and men, feminists and so on' are drowned out by the strident assertions of the scientists, who are usually white, Western men.

Traditional criminology panders to the requirements of often-oppressive states which will not provide money for research that does not correspond to their agenda. To Smart, no general theory of crime is ever possible, no matter how much research is done and how sophisticated scientific methods become. Modernism is an 'exhausted mode' of thinking. It has failed to deliver the goods, and failed to reduce crime rates for governments.

A central reason for this is that it has been quite wrong to see crime as a single type of phenomenon. Different crimes involve very different types of behaviour. Often, some of the most important characteristics of behaviours which are lumped together in the category 'crime' have nothing to do with them being against the law. Postmodern approaches are better able to deconstruct such behaviours, to show that they are not what they seem. Thus:

> *The thing that criminology cannot do is deconstruct 'crime'. It cannot locate rape and child sexual abuse in the domain of sexuality, nor theft in the domain of economic activity, nor drug use in the domain of health. To do so would be to abandon criminology to sociology, but more importantly it would involve abandoning the idea of a unified problem which requires a unified response – at least at the theoretical level.* Smart, 1995

If criminology admitted there was no single type of activity that constituted crime, there would be no need for criminology, and criminologists would be out of jobs. Smart does not therefore regard it as surprising that criminologists try to stick to the myth that a theory of crime is possible. However, she believes that feminist theory offers potentially superior approaches to studying the various types of behaviour that are categorized as crimes.

Feminist approaches to criminology

Smart draws on the work of Sandra Harding (1986, 1987) in distinguishing three types of feminism: feminist empiricism, standpoint feminism, and feminist postmodernism.

1 **Feminist empiricism** argues that previous work has been largely written about men by men. It argues that the balance of research is sexist, with women largely being left out. It therefore believes more empirical research needs to be carried out about women. Smart notes that there has been a big increase in criminological studies of women (some of them have been discussed in this chapter). However, she believes such an approach makes little difference to criminology as a whole. Conventional criminology can carry on using the same methods and theories and simply acknowledge that it is writing about men and not humanity as a whole. Feminist criminologists can fill in the gaps in knowledge about women, but without allowing the discipline to progress in any other way.

2 **Standpoint feminism** offers a more radical challenge. This approach believes that true knowledge can be created by listening to the oppressed and disadvantaged. Women who are actively engaged in the struggle against patriarchal society can understand how society works. Standpoint feminist criminologists have listened, for example, to female victims of rape, sexual harassment and domestic violence. The accounts of female victims are intended to replace the dominant accounts of such crimes, which have previously come largely from male police officers and male criminologists.

While Smart welcomes the attempt to see the world from the viewpoint of the subjugated, she does not believe that it goes far enough. For example, it is unable to explain the involvement of men in crime and it cannot understand masculinity. This is because it cannot examine the viewpoint of dominant groups in society.

3 Smart is convinced that the best feminist approach is feminist postmodernism. **Feminist postmodernism** rejects the view that there is one scientific, criminological theory which can explain crime. It rejects the view that all men, or all women, are essentially the same. There is no essence of humanity, masculinity or femininity which can explain crime. Indeed, crime itself has no core of essential characteristics through which it can be understood. People have fractured identities. Individuals have many different aspects to their identity, involving their ethnicity, class, gender, age, experiences, etc. Everyone is different. Similarly, crimes are very different acts committed by very different people for very different reasons. Criminology needs to be de-essentialized: it must stop looking for essential characteristics which do not exist. Smart says, 'The core element of feminist postmodernism is the rejection of the one reality which arises from "the falsely universalizing perspective of the master" (Harding, 1987).'

Standpoint feminism seeks to substitute the truth of the oppressed for the truth of the oppressors. Feminist postmodernism:

> *does not seek to impose a different unitary reality. Rather, it refers to subjugated knowledges, which tell different stories and have different specificities. So the aim of feminism ceases to be the establishment of the feminist truth and becomes the aim of deconstructing Truth and analysing the power effects that claims to truth entail.* Smart, 1995

What Smart argues, then, is that postmodern feminist criminologists should take apart the claims made by other theorists and practitioners about crime. They should show how male criminologists, police, judges, and so on, make false claims about crime and how it should be dealt with. Their claims are designed to, and often do, give them power over others.

Smart follows Foucault's ideas on power (see pp. 559–62) in arguing that power exists in all social relationships and derives from discourses, and from claims to the possession of knowledge. Power is not concentrated in any one place, it is not monopolized by any one group. Power, including the power of men, can only be challenged by resistance in each place, each time it is used. Knowledge which claims to be the truth has to be challenged.

Smart uses the example of rape to illustrate her ideas. She says postmodern feminists can challenge the way rape is portrayed in court cases. They can attack the way the vagina is portrayed as a passive and vulnerable receptacle and the penis as a weapon. They can attack the view of judges that women dressed in short skirts are 'asking for it', and undermine the idea that men cannot control their sexual urges once they have gone so far. They can examine the way in which male and female sexualities are portrayed in courts, the media and elsewhere. They can reveal the inconsistencies and contradictions involved in these portrayals, and by doing so challenge and undermine the prevailing discourses through which power is exercised over women.

Conclusion

Smart concludes by arguing that criminology has little to offer feminism. Its modes of analysis are outdated and of little use. Criminology has been revived by feminism, particularly postmodern feminism, and not the other way round. She therefore believes 'it might be that criminology needs feminism more than the reverse' and 'it is very difficult to see what criminology has to offer to feminism'.

Pat Carlen – a critique of postmodern feminist criminology

Pat Carlen (1992) is sympathetic to some of the arguments advanced by Smart. She accepts it is unlikely that one theory could explain all crime, and agrees there is no fundamental essence which distinguishes criminal behaviour from all other behaviour. She agrees with Smart that standpoint feminism is wrong to assume that the truth can be discovered simply by letting oppressed women speak for themselves. However, she does not believe that all attempts to explain or even to control crime can be seen as part of a failed, male, modernist project. Attempts to produce theories of crime can illuminate the causes of specific crimes committed by particular groups of women. Furthermore, they can be used in support of progressive policies which can tackle injustice.

Nor does Carlen believe, as some postmodernists do, that you should simply respect and celebrate the lifestyles of different groups of oppressed women. For example, her own research (see pp. 373–4 for details) revealed connections between female criminality, homelessness and drug addiction. Using this knowledge to try to reduce homelessness and drug addiction, and therefore crime, is seen by Carlen as progressive rather than regressive. It is not the imposition of a phallocentric, modernist view of the world on reluctant women, but a genuine attempt to understand people's problems and help them to overcome them. Carlen comments:

> *Women with drink or drug addictions often choke to death on their own vomit. Others have Aids as a result of either sharing needles or engaging in prostitution to fund their habits. Sleeping rough, nursing bleeding sores and suffering withdrawal symptoms are not particularly life-enhancing processes either. Not one woman of the many I have known with addictions has celebrated her addictive state; many have themselves referred to 'destructive lifestyles', 'abusing my body' and 'killing myself'.* Carlen, 1992

Just because such views might be shared by the criminal justice system and conventional criminologists does not mean that they are wrong. Deconstructing such views will not do anything to alleviate the deprivations faced by such women.

To Carlen, trying to explain crime does not mean that you inevitably fall into an essentialist trap. You do not inevitably end up with the same biases as the more sexist male criminologists or the more oppressive parts of the criminal justice system. You can recognize that crime and criminals are very different, that no one theory will do, without abandoning the attempt to explain crime.

Carlen has no objection to the sort of critical deconstruction of bias in the criminal justice system advocated by Carol Smart. However, she does not believe that criminology should confine itself to only conducting that sort of study. To do so would risk losing sight of what she sees as the fundamental aim of feminist criminology, which is:

> *To ensure that the penal regulation of female lawbreakers does not increase their oppression as unconventional women, as black people and as poverty-stricken defendants still further; and to ensure that the penal regulation of lawbreaking men is not such that it brutalizes them and makes them behave even more violently or oppressively towards women in the future.* Carlen, 1992

Evaluation

Both Smart and Carlen claim that feminist criminology can be used to promote social justice. However, they believe that different theoretical and methodological approaches can best achieve this. While Smart advocates a methodology based on deconstruction and a theory based on postmodernism, Carlen supports more conventional methodologies and more traditional theories which claim to be able to explain crime.

Perhaps both approaches can help illuminate the relationship between gender and crime. For example, they could be used to understand both why some men commit rapes, and how the actions of rapists and victims are dealt with by the courts. Of the two theorists, Carlen seems the more willing to accept the use of a variety of approaches in studying crime and criminal justice.

John Lea – 'Criminology and postmodernity'

Although not himself a postmodernist, John Lea (1998) reviewed the ways in which postmodernism has been, or could be, applied to criminology. Lea believes criminology is an obvious target of attack for postmodernists:

> *Criminology and penology were central pillars of the postwar 'grand narratives' of social engineering and welfare reformism, the blueprints for the good society that are now so discredited. The crisis of modernity is a part of the crisis of criminology.* Lea, 1998

Scientific theories held the promise of solving the problem of crime. Instead, the crime rate rose almost inexorably. If the scientific study of crime did nothing to help control it, postmodernists may argue that the time has come to abandon the objective of the scientific explanation and control of crime. To Lea, postmodernism has the potential to contribute to understanding three aspects of crime: the nature of crime, explaining the causes of crime and controlling crime.

The nature of crime

Lea suggests *deconstruction* is the main method that postmodernists advocate for understanding the nature of crime. Postmodernists such as Carol Smart (discussed above) see traditional criminology as obscuring the nature of crime by regarding all crime as the same sort of phenomenon. Lea says, 'taking the example of rape, deconstruction exposes how the definition of an activity such as rape involves its repression of its other characteristics – as a form of sexuality'.

However, such an approach raises its own problems. The idea that rape is essentially a form of sexuality could itself be deconstructed to show that this definition repressed other aspects of rape (for example, that it was to do with power, or to do with crime after all). This raises the problem of **infinite regress**. Every deconstruction could itself be deconstructed in a process that would be never-ending and would lead nowhere. In practice, what has to happen is that deconstruction stops at some point. Smart stops at the point of saying that rape is to do with sex, but such a decision seems arbitrary and simply reflects Smart's own preconceptions about rape.

An alternative approach to deconstruction is similar to that of standpoint feminism (see p. 387), where a particular social group is held to be the key to understanding a phenomenon. Thus, lesbians, gays, members of minority ethnic groups, working-class women, disabled men, or whoever, might be seen as having a privileged viewpoint from which to deconstruct particular crimes.

However, this seems to be reverting to a form of **foundationalism** (the belief that there is a firm foundation for some absolute truth), which postmodernists reject. Furthermore, the views of oppressed groups might have been distorted or contaminated by the ideologies of more powerful groups. Thus, for example, gays and lesbians might have been persuaded by heterosexuals that heterosexuality is more normal than homosexuality.

A third type of deconstruction suggests that the search for truth be abandoned in favour of knowledge that works – that is, knowledge which is effective in achieving some objective. Thus, if a particular theory of crime can be applied to reduce crime, it should be accepted, whether or not the theory stands up to close examination.

However, as Lea points out, what works is very much influenced by the distribution of power in society. So, for example, a theory that much sex between married men and women was in fact rape by the man would be resisted and rejected by men, who have more power than women. Thus, you would end up accepting only those theories that reflected the desires and interests of the powerful. Lea says, 'what began as a radical critique of dominant discourses of power ends up prostrating itself before them. What "works" in any situation is precisely a product of the dominant relationship of power!'

Lea believes that criminology has long included a type of deconstruction in the form of labelling theory. Criminologists have already critically examined the nature of crime, and postmodern advocates of deconstruction have not produced a coherent and superior alternative. Furthermore, criminology already has its own ways of analysing the influence of power on the definition of crime.

Deconstruction can show that power is always involved in defining crime, but this has long been acknowledged by Marxist, feminist and various other critical types of criminology. Such approaches can relate the definition of crime to the distribution of power in particular societies at particular times. Postmodern deconstruction is less satisfactory because all it can do is show how some sort of power relationship is always involved in definitions of crime.

The causes of crime

Lea, quoting the ideas of Lyotard (see pp. 891–2), argues that postmodern approaches to the causes of crime reject the idea that some grand theory or grand narrative can explain crime. Carol Smart, for example (see pp. 386–7), rejects what she calls 'positivist' approaches in criminology. Instead, postmodern theories can only look for 'local truths', explanations of particular, individual examples of crime.

Postmodernists tend to reject the idea that different crimes can be linked together and common factors which cause them can be found. Each criminal act is, in effect, to be regarded as a unique event. Postmodernists also tend to see crime, like everything else, as part of a process of 'the experimental creation of lifestyles' and a 'process of free self-creation'. Individuals may choose an identity as a bank robber or a heroin addict. From this postmodern viewpoint, crime is simply a product of 'the general condition of freedom itself'.

Lea finds such an approach to explaining criminality unsatisfactory. While it avoids being deterministic, it goes to the opposite extreme and abandons any claim to be able to explain crime in general. It is unable to explain, for example, why certain groups are likely to resort to certain types of crime rather than others. While crime might be widespread, certain types of crime are more associated with particular groups: corporate crime with corporate executives, street crimes with the marginal and oppressed. Postmodern criminology cannot explore such links.

The control of crime

In this area, Lea sees postmodernism as making a more useful contribution. According to Lea, postmodernism argues that there has been a move away from formal methods of social control based on a centrally planned criminal justice system. Under modernity, the control of crime was based on the idea that all citizens share certain rights, and that these should be administered impartially by the police, courts, welfare agencies and so on. However, it was also recognized that informal social control, which worked through social pressure, was also important. The state intervened to buttress informal social control outside the criminal justice system through 'a variety of social rights to welfare and education, parental and children's rights and so on'. Various types of treatment and 'care' were used where informal social control was not working, in addition to punishment through the criminal justice system.

Lea believes that things have changed with the move towards a postmodern society. He says:

> *If postmodernization has any meaning then it lies in the hypothesis that decentralized informal mechanisms come to dominate and partially replace formal centralized institutions and their accompanying discourses or grand narratives, and at the same time that formal criminal justice institutions operate in an increasingly informal way.* Lea, 1998

Increasingly, for example, private security firms, such as those responsible for watching over shopping malls, replace the police in providing private security. Control is achieved less through punishing offenders than by denying some people access to places where they might offend. In some American estates and in blocks of flats in Britain, for example, security firms exclude undesirables from entering.

There has been a decline in the idea of public space in which anyone can move freely without being watched, monitored or vetted. Closed-circuit television (CCTV) is not just confined to private spaces, but is increasingly used to monitor the streets of towns and cities as well.

In some ways, such changes can be seen in a postmodern light as celebrating diversity. Different groups are confined to certain areas of towns or cities. Lea says, 'the blacks in the ghetto and the whites in the protected central city and the segregated and secured suburbs are all, equally, manifestations of difference'.

In each area people are treated differently. There is a move away from seeing people as citizens with rights, and a move towards seeing them as consumers or customers. Policing policies tend to become more localized in focus. Ghettos and suburbs are seen as having different policing needs and are treated differently. Thus, the criminal justice system starts to take account of people's diverse lifestyles and needs.

Lea sees some of these changes as welcome. In postmodern societies there seems more likelihood that policing can become sensitive to the needs of minorities. However, such a change also carries dangers. There is a danger that the ghettos will either be left alone to fend for themselves, or that they will be repressed through military-style policing. If people are treated as consumers, then those with no spending power are less likely to have their needs met. No one can afford private security in the areas where people are most likely to be the victims of crime.

In the end, the acceptance and celebration of difference are unlikely to solve the problems of the most disadvantaged. These members of society are left at the mercy of the forces of global capitalism. Although there are some advantages in abandoning the idea of citizenship rights in favour of valuing difference, it is ultimately self-defeating. Rather than liberating people, it condemns the weak to be neglected.

Although different social groups, such as minority ethnic groups, gays, women, inner-city dwellers and so on, demand slightly different things from the criminal justice system, they are all seeking some form of justice. Thus, to Lea, controlling crime must rely upon retaining some notion of justice, and some idea of the basic rights of citizens. Without this it is likely to be the voices of the powerful which drown out the demands of others.

Evaluation

Lea accepts that postmodernism can offer something to criminology in describing changes in society. It has identified some novel developments in the way crime is controlled. However, he does not believe it offers a viable method for studying crime, or an acceptable approach to dealing with it. He agrees with Pat Carlen (1992) that postmodern criminology has failed to demonstrate that it should supersede other approaches.

Transgressive criminology

In the late 1960s, David Matza (1969) argued that positivistic criminology had been extremely successful in redefining the nature of the sociology of crime and deviance, by separating the study of crime from the study of the state. Matza said, 'criminological positivists succeeded in what would seem impossible. They separated the study of crime from the working and theory of the state.'

What Matza was suggesting was that criminologists had accepted that their job was to explore why some people broke the law and others did not. This was to be achieved by comparing the attributes, behaviour and beliefs of the law-breakers with those of the people who conformed to the laws. But the key question was: who makes those laws and why are they made?

This challenge was later taken up by radical or Marxist criminologists who, from their particular standpoint, asked exactly these questions, but then sought the answer within the Marxist perspective. Their approach was to analyse the way in which the state made laws and enforced them for the benefit of the ruling class (see pp. 340–2).

However, during the 1990s a broader definition of the sociology of crime and deviance emerged, which looked beyond traditional constraints. The argument here was that criminology had been too tightly bound by both positivists and radical criminologists, and that the notion of 'harm' was open to debate. It was in this atmosphere that a number of new areas emerged.

This new **transgressive criminology** (so-called because it goes beyond the boundaries of normal criminology) includes a huge range of issues, from the harm caused to women and children by the power of men, to the harm caused by the existence of poverty and inequality, both nationally and internationally. This broad range of interests is both the strength and weakness of transgressive criminology: a strength because it breaks away from the link with breaking the law and low-level deviance, but a weakness in that it loses any focus.

Two examples are explored here, green criminology and crimes of the state, to give a flavour of the debates.

Green criminology

Half of the world's wetlands were lost during the twentieth century; logging and conversion have shrunk the world's forests by as much as 50 per cent; some 9 per cent of the world's tree species are at risk of extinction; and fishing fleets are 40 per cent larger than the ocean can sustain, and nearly 70 per cent of the world's major marine fish stocks are overfished or being fished to their biological limits. Since 1980, the global economy has tripled in size and the world's population has grown by 30 per cent to 6 billion people (Halsey, 2004, p. 834).

Green criminology can be seen as an extension of the globalization of criminological concerns. It involves moving the focus of criminological study away from law-breaking and deviant activity to a much broader discussion of environmental activities on a global basis, which harm societies – even societies other than where the activities may actually be taking place.

Green criminology is radical in nature in two main ways:

1. Rather than focusing on law-breaking, its interests lie in the causes and consequences of the harm done to the environment – even when that harm is legal.
2. Unlike most criminology, it is just as much concerned about harm to animals and plants as it is about harm to humans.

Lynch and Stretsky argue:

> *In general, criminologists have often left the study of environmental harm, environmental laws and environmental regulations to researchers in other disciplines. This has allowed little room for critical examination of individuals or entities who/which kill, injure and assault other life forms (human, animal, plant) by poisoning the earth.* 2003, p. 231

The idea of 'harm' has led to considerable debate, as there is no agreed definition of 'harm to the environment'.

Indeed, environmental standards and laws vary from country to country, so what is wrong to one group or government may be acceptable to others. As Halsey and White (1998) point out, the notion of harm is 'inherently ideological' and is constructed through the political process, with competing interest groups seeking to have their definition of harm accepted. Therefore a coherent approach to green criminology can only be constructed when there are global standards regarding the environment.

Three approaches to understanding environmental harm and the role of green criminology have emerged.

The first approach accepts as its starting point the laws regarding the environment and concentrates on violations of them. So, Situ and Emmons (2000) state that 'an environmental crime is an unauthorised act or omission that violates the law'. This approach accepts as given that there are national and international laws and regulations which lay down the limits of harm which can be done to the environment. Criminological studies in this tradition document and explore the reasons for breaches of the laws in much the same way that 'traditional' criminology approaches law-breaking.

This approach has been criticized by Braithwaite and Drahos (2000) for ignoring the ability of powerful groups to frame the law in such a way as to reflect their interests. This criticism provides the link to the second approach to green criminology, which argues that 'harm' ought to include those activities which may be labelled as legal but nevertheless have a 'negative environmental impact'. So, criminologists in this tradition accept that 'harming the environment' must provide the basis of any analysis, rather than simply law- or regulation-breaking

In many ways, this approach, which is taken by Chunn *et al.* (2003) for example, is similar to that of Marxist writers in that the law is seen as reflecting the interests of powerful groups in (world) society, with their ability to label certain activities as harmful or otherwise. Like Marxists, green criminologists suggest that large, global corporations are closely involved in influencing what is regarded as legal.

White (2007) argues that a result of the power of large corporations has been the emergence of a definition of environmental harm which is strongly influenced by the ideology of 'sustainable development', as developed by the World Bank. The concept of **sustainable development** argues that ecological concerns should be seen within the wider framework of economic growth and the expanding consumption of the earth's resources, which, it is argued, are necessary for the maintenance of a decent standard of living for the richer countries and the development of the poorer nations.

However, Halsey and White (1998) argue that this is based on the proposition that continuing economic expansion will not harm the earth in any fundamental way. White suggests that this ideology reflects the 'hegemonic dominance of anthropocentric, and specifically capitalist, conceptions of the relationship between human beings and nature' (2007, p. 280).

The difference between these first two approaches can be illustrated using a real-life environmental disaster. In 1984, the Union Carbide plant in Bhopal in India was involved in one of the most serious environmental disasters ever. The plant routinely used a mixture of highly toxic gases in its production process. As a result of poor maintenance and negligence, there was a large explosion which resulted in more than 3,000 deaths and 20,000 serious, permanent injuries and disabilities (with high levels of birth defects in the children born soon after).

The explanation for the environmental 'crime' committed here is offered in the Situ and Emmons approach in terms of the failure of the (US) company to ensure that correct maintenance checks were carried out. Greed and inefficiency are focused on, and the explanation falls within the broad approach used by those explaining white-collar crime.

However, following the approach advocated by Chunn *et al.*, the focus of the explanation lies first in decisions by large multinational companies to locate dangerous and polluting chemical plants in countries where labour is cheap and where there is relatively lax enforcement of laws regarding worker safety or environmental damage. This approach also focuses on the fact that the plant was located near an area where poor people lived, where cheap labour could be obtained and where there was limited likelihood of opposition to the siting of the plant.

A third approach has been put forward by Beck, with his concept of the 'risk society'. Beck (1992) argues that during the period of modernity societies were faced with issues of scarcity, and social conflict was based on gaining access to these scarce resources. Beck suggests that out of this conflict social class and many modern political structures developed.

However, technologically advanced and socially complex 'late modern' societies have resolved this issue of scarcity. There are adequate resources for all and thus class conflict declines. One outcome of the production of goods and services, though, has been massive damage to the environment, which has, in turn, generated new forms of dangers or 'risks' which humanity has never had to face before.

Beck points out that although nuclear energy has produced adequate power output, we are faced with the threat that a malfunctioning nuclear power station can represent – for example, as demonstrated by the nuclear accidents at Chernobyl in Ukraine in 1986 and Three Mile Island in the USA in 1979. Beck also points to pollution through toxins in the environment and the health dangers of processed foodstuffs. Beck argues that these risks are different from those faced by humanity throughout history in that past global risks were not manufactured by humans themselves but were the outcome of natural processes.

Beck suggests that despite the clear evidence that catastrophe may well occur as a result of technological pollution and environmental degradation, there still remains a failure to grasp the true causes, and that there is a 'loss of sociological thinking' about the environment. He argues that the definition of harm and the causes of this harm are generally regarded as 'matters of nature and technology or of economics and medicine' (Beck, 1992).

Beck suggests, then, that most thinking about environmental risk is characterized by 'lack of social thinking', but it is not necessarily the outcome of the influence of large corporations. The point that Beck makes is vividly illustrated by the paucity of green criminological studies. Green criminology, like the other subjects mentioned in this 'transgressive criminology' section, is still in its infancy.

In order to clarify just how sociologists should go about the process of studying environmental crimes, and to get over the problem of whether it is the role of sociologists to study only those who break the law, Nigel South (1998) suggested a twofold framework for understanding green crimes. The first part of the framework is what he calls 'primary crimes'. The second part is crime which develops out of 'the flouting of rules that seek to regulate environmental disasters' (Carrabine *et al.*, 2004).

Primary crimes consist of harm done to the environment and people by activities such as:

- **Air pollution**. The burning of fossil fuels releases about 6 billion tons of carbon into the air each year, which, by the time it settles, increases the existing levels by 3 billion tons. This increase is caused by industrial output, vehicles and planes. According to South (in Carrabine *et al.*, 2004), potential criminals here are governments, big business and consumers.
- **Deforestation**. Between 1960 and 1990 approximately 20 per cent of the world's tropical forest was lost. This is important, not just because of the role of forests in converting carbon dioxide to oxygen, but because between 75 and 95 per cent of all living species live in these forests. According to South, the world is losing about 10 million hectares of forest each year, which is an area approximately the size of South Korea. He suggests that 'new crimes and criminals would include those who deal in the destruction of rainforests and valuable lands'.
- **Species decline**. South notes that we lose fifty species a day, with 46 per cent of mammal and 11 per cent of bird species said to be at risk. By 2020 10 million species are likely to become extinct. South also points to how overfishing has depopulated the oceans of the world.
- **Water pollution**. 25 million people die each year as a result of contaminated water and 500 million people lack access to fresh, clean drinking water. The seas of the world are also polluted, with one-third of all fish at risk. Since 1990, over 1.1 million tons of oil have been leaked or spilled into the world's oceans.

All the activities described above are currently legal under international law and South is suggesting that the amount of harm they cause should allow these issues to be debated under the umbrella of criminology rather than as solely 'environmental' concerns.

The second part of South's framework is crime which develops out of 'the flouting of rules that seek to regulate environmental disasters'. According to South these include hazardous waste and organized crime, and state violence against oppositional groups.

Hazardous waste and organized crime

The disposal of hazardous waste is an extremely lucrative business, given its complexity and the care that must be taken. Because of lax international controls, this area has attracted organized crime. In Italy, there are currently investigations involving the Mafia's control of waste contracts, and earlier reports cited by South suggest that significant parts of the Gulf of Naples are polluted by illegal dumping. The situation is so bad that it has been estimated that authorized dumping accounts for only 10 per cent of all disposal outflows into the gulf.

Illegal dumping is a huge international trade, with illegal transports of waste travelling from richer countries to poorer ones, where the material is simply dumped with no regard for human or animal lives. Ruggiero (1996) points out that as the people in richer nations become more aware of the problems of pollution caused by hazardous waste, and the requirements imposed upon legal disposal firms by governments grow, the greater the potential profits of the illegal dumpers.

State violence against oppositional groups

South points out that although governments condemn 'terrorism', some are prepared to use illegal and violent methods when they need to. One famous example was the blowing up of the Greenpeace ship *Rainbow Warrior* by French secret services operatives in 1985, in which one of the crew was murdered. South cites Day (1991) who argues that the *Rainbow Warrior* case was unusual in that it became public. According to Day there have been numerous other examples of government interference which have never been uncovered.

However, South's division of green crimes into two main types fits uneasily with the evidence, which seems to suggest an overlap between the two categories, with many states actively involved in illegal environmental practices.

Evaluation

Green criminology has not progressed very far since the early 1990s when it first emerged as a concern. The problem is that it extends the scope of criminology to cover such a wide area that it is difficult to place boundaries around the subject matter, as it shades into environmental issues. Furthermore, as noted above, the decision as to what is or is not harm is as much a moral, political and ideological argument as it is a criminological one.

Crimes of the state

This idea that governments themselves may be capable of committing crimes was, until recently, overlooked in criminology. However, after the collapse of the Marxist-Stalinist regimes of Eastern Europe, Stan Cohen (2001) argued that future debates in criminology will be less concerned about causes of crime and more about human rights and crimes by states against their citizens.

With the rise of fundamentalist Islamic terrorism and the US-driven 'war on terror', the issue of human rights has become even more important. Once the issue was raised, it became obvious that throughout the world, in countries such as China, Chechnya, Iran, Syria and Burma – to pick just a few – human rights are routinely abused. But crucially for the study of criminology, the abuse and torture which take place are practised by agents of the state, on behalf of the government, almost always in contravention of the law of those countries.

The starting point, therefore, for any analysis of crimes of the state is cases such as the above where agents of the government ignore their own laws. However, as in the case of green criminology there are also concerns about the treatment of populations under the control of a government even if that government states that what it is doing is legal.

This argument was raised most forcefully by Herman and Julia Schwendinger (1975) who argued that sociologists have a duty to look at the forms of social control imposed by states and to decide whether they are reasonable or not. Sociologists should not simply accept the laws as passed by national and international governments, but go beyond this to explore the harm perpetrated by governments in the name of having to maintain social control.

This argument was taken forward by William J. Chambliss (1989) who suggested that the role of criminology was to explore 'the crimes of the state'. Chambliss undertook this task from a Marxist perspective and examined how states were involved in a range of illegal activities including money-laundering, arms smuggling and state-organized assassinations.

Chambliss's approach was limited by a Marxist-based analysis and it was not until Eugene McLaughlin's study in 2001 that sociologists began to explore the state from a Weberian perspective. Weber had defined the state as 'claiming the monopoly of the legitimate use of physical force within a given territory'. McLaughlin argues that in democracies, state agencies can use force wherever it is seen as being in the interests of the public. Yet, the public interest is a highly contested area, for what is seen as being in the public interest by one group may not be seen in the same way by another.

This is reflected in the debate over what constitutes a terrorist act and who are terrorists. The US and British governments routinely use the term 'war on terror' and refer to fundamentalist Islamic acts of violence as 'terrorist' acts perpetrated by terrorists. Yet the same governments used completely different language in their own activities against fundamentalists in Iraq and Afghanistan, which resulted in many more deaths. (Even having this debate in a textbook is difficult, as the term 'fundamentalist' is also one carrying certain connotations.)

Therefore, from a sociological perspective, it is perfectly possible to ask questions about the activities of democratic governments and how definitions are arrived at of what constitutes 'crimes' and abuse of human rights. Nigel South (in Carrabine *et al.*, 2004) has suggested that this discussion over what is a crime of the state can be extended to the use of torture and capital punishment.

Evaluation

The criminology of crimes of the state suffers a similar fate to that of green criminology. Once sociologists move away from the law or low-level deviance as their subject matter, they encounter great difficulties in avoiding ideological debates about what constitutes harm or abuse. However, in response, sociologists such as Stan Cohen would argue that merely by raising the issue of harm and human rights as a matter of debate, the sociology of crime and deviancy has continued its pathbreaking role of exploring new areas ignored by other branches of sociology.

Summary and conclusions

This chapter has examined one of the broadest and most complex areas of sociology. Sociological approaches to crime and deviance have, for almost one hundred years, pushed the boundaries of sociology in new directions. Traditionally criminology has drawn heavily from the perspectives of functionalism, Marxism, feminism and social interactionism (labelling theories) to provide the grounds upon which most of the debates have taken place. However, arguably criminology has been rather more 'applied' in its focus than other areas of sociology in seeking to provide more specific answers to the 'problem' of crime. This has encouraged other developments beyond the traditional theoretical foundations we have just mentioned, which have introduced some quite novel ideas to sociology.

Feminism, though important by itself, has also given birth to the study of 'masculinity' and its relationship to crime. Criminological theorists from the socio-spatial school have explored the impact of 'place' on crime and linked this to patterns of leisure activities in society. This exploration of place has extended to the impact of global changes on local crime – or 'glocalism' as it has been called. Other 'left realist' writers have suggested that the way that policing interacts with communities is important in explaining crime levels.

More contemporary work, particularly by Jock Young, suggests that late modernist consumerism is crucial in explaining crime and that those who are excluded from the ability to consume are still left with the desire to possess the products and lifestyles promoted as signs of success. Desire is, of course, an emotion and one of the two most recent innovations in criminology has been to rediscover and explore the impact of emotions (love, hate, excitement) on criminality. The other contemporary innovation has been the emergence of a 'green' criminology which has 'transgressed' beyond the normal boundaries of the subject matter and focused attention upon the deliberate and systematic despoiling of the planet by industrial societies.

This chapter has therefore sought to lay out and chart a course through these and numerous other debates within the sociology of crime.

CHAPTER 7
Religion

By sacred things one must not understand simply those personal things which are called gods or spirits; a rock, a tree, a spring, a pebble, a piece of wood, a house, in a word anything can be sacred. Durkheim, 1912

Introduction – definitions of religion

1 'In the beginning was the Word, and the Word was with God, and the Word was God.' The God of Christianity is a supreme being, his word is the ultimate truth, his power is omnipotent. His followers worship him and praise him and live by his commandments.
2 The Dugum Dani live in the Highlands of New Guinea. They have no god, but their world is inhabited by a host of supernatural beings known as mogat. The mogat are the ghosts of the dead. They cause illness and death and control the wind and the rain. The Dugum Dani are not pious – they do not pray. Their rituals are not to honour or worship the mogat but to placate and appease them.
3 Scientology originated in the writings of a US science fiction writer, L. Ron Hubbard. It started as a type of therapy named Dianetics in which a therapist (or auditor) questions a subject (known as a preclear) wired to a machine similar to a lie detector (called an e-meter). The aim is to clear the mind of the preclear of negative blockages, known as engrams. But Scientology also contains spiritual beliefs. Alan Aldridge describes these beliefs in the following way: 'Scientology built a complex cosmological and metaphysical system on the basis of Dianetics. Human beings are in essence spiritual entities, thetans. Immortal, omniscient and omnipotent, thetans created the universe … but foolishly became trapped in their own creation … eventually forgetting their own origins and status as thetans' (Aldridge, 2000, p. 14). In this belief system, humans are in effect Gods, but Gods who have lost their way.

Religious beliefs of one sort or another are present in every known society, but their variety seems to be endless. Any definition of religion must encompass this variety. However, it is difficult to produce a definition broad enough to do so without incorporating phenomena that are not normally thought of as religions. Two main approaches have been adopted in tackling this issue: those that rely upon **functional** definitions and those that use **substantive** definitions.

1 One way of defining religion is to see it in terms of the **functions** it performs for society or individuals. An example of this approach is provided by Yinger, who defined religion as 'a system of beliefs and practices by means of which a group of people struggles with the ultimate problems of human life' (quoted in Hamilton, 1995). However, Hamilton notes two main problems with such a definition.

First, it allows the inclusion of a wide variety of belief systems in the category 'religion'. For example, by this definition communism could be regarded as a religion even though it explicitly rejects religious beliefs. Second, it is based upon assumptions about the roles and purposes of religion. However, these roles and purposes might vary between societies and it should be the job of sociology to uncover them by empirical investigation, not to assume what they are from the outset. Third, phrases such as 'the ultimate problems of human life' are open to varied interpretations. Hamilton points out that for some people the ultimate problems of life might be 'simply how to enjoy it as much as possible, how to avoid pain and ensure pleasure'. It is clear that many other aspects of social life, apart from religion, address such issues – for example, medicine and leisure.

2 Other approaches are based upon **substantive** definitions; that is, they are concerned with the content of religion rather than its function or purpose. Substantive definitions can take a number of forms.

Durkheim (1961, first published 1912) defined religion in terms of a distinction between the sacred and the profane. Sacred objects – for example, the cross in Christianity – produce a sense of awe, veneration and respect, whereas profane objects do not. However, as critics have pointed out, in some cases explicitly religious objects are not always treated with respect.

A common approach to a substantive definition of religion is to define it in terms of supernatural beliefs. Thus Roland Robertson (1970) states that religion 'refers to the existence of supernatural beings that have a governing effect on life'. A supernatural element is combined with institutional aspects of religion in Melford Spiro's (1965) definition of religion as 'an institution consisting of culturally patterned interaction with culturally postulated superhuman beings'. However, as Hamilton points out, such definitions run into problems because certain belief systems which are commonly regarded as religions, such as Buddhism, do not contain a belief in supernatural beings.

All definitions emphasize certain aspects of religion and exclude others. Functional definitions tend to be too inclusive – it is too easy to qualify as a religion; while substantive ones tend to be too exclusive – it is too difficult to qualify as a religion. We will look at a variety of definitions throughout the chapter. It should be borne in mind that these definitions tend to reflect the theoretical assumptions and the specific arguments being advanced by individual sociologists. This is particularly evident in the debate on **secularization** (the question of whether religion has declined). Varying definitions allow the advocates and critics of the theory to include evidence that supports their case and exclude evidence that contradicts it.

The problems of definition should not, however, be exaggerated. The disputes tend to occur over phenomena that can be considered to be on the fringes of religion (such as New Age movements), and there is general agreement that such belief systems as Hinduism, Islam, Christianity, Buddhism and Judaism *are* religions.

Religion – a functionalist perspective

The functionalist perspective examines religion in terms of society's needs. Functionalist analysis is primarily concerned with the contribution religion makes to meeting those needs. From this perspective, society requires a certain degree of social solidarity, value consensus, and harmony and integration between its parts. The function of religion is the contribution it makes to meeting such functional prerequisites – for example, its contribution to social solidarity.

Emile Durkheim

The sacred and the profane

In *The Elementary Forms of the Religious Life*, first published in 1912, Emile Durkheim presented what is probably the most influential interpretation of religion from a functionalist perspective. Durkheim argued that all societies divide the world into two categories: the **sacred** and the **profane** (the non-sacred). Religion is based upon this division. It is 'a unified system of beliefs and practices related to sacred things, that is to say things set apart and forbidden'.

It is important to realize that:

> *By sacred things one must not understand simply those personal things which are called gods or spirits; a rock, a tree, a spring, a pebble, a piece of wood, a house, in a word anything, can be sacred.* Durkheim, 1961, first published 1912

There is nothing about the particular qualities of a pebble or a tree that makes them sacred. Therefore, sacred things must be symbols, they must represent something. To understand the role of religion in society, the relationship between sacred symbols and what they represent must be established.

Totemism

Durkheim used the religion of various groups of Australian Aborigines to develop his argument. He saw their religion, which he called **totemism**, as the simplest and most basic form of religion.

Aborigine society is divided into several clans. A clan is like a large extended family, with its members sharing certain duties and obligations. For example, clans have a rule of **exogamy** – that is, members are not allowed to marry within the clan. Clan members have a duty to aid and assist each other: they join together to mourn the death of one of their number and to revenge a member who has been wronged by someone from another clan.

Each clan has a totem, usually an animal or a plant. This totem is then represented by drawings made on wood or stone. These drawings are called *churingas*. Usually churingas are at least as sacred as the species which they represent and sometimes more so. The totem is a symbol. It is the emblem of the clan. 'It is its flag; it is the sign by which each clan distinguishes itself from all others.' However, the totem is more than the churinga which represents it – it is the most sacred object in Aborigine ritual. The totem is 'the outward and visible form of the totemic principle or god'.

Durkheim argued that if the totem 'is at once the symbol of god and of the society, is that not because the god and the society are only one?' Thus, he suggested, in worshipping god, people are in fact worshipping society. Society is the real object of religious veneration.

How does humanity come to worship society? Sacred things are 'considered superior in dignity and power to profane things and particularly to man'. In relation to the sacred, humans are inferior and dependent. This relationship between humanity and sacred things is exactly the relationship between humanity and society. Society is more important and powerful than the individual. Durkheim argued: 'Primitive man comes to view society as something sacred because he is utterly dependent on it.'

But why does humanity not simply worship society itself? Why does it invent a sacred symbol like a totem? Because, Durkheim argued, it is easier for a person to 'visualize and direct his feelings of awe toward a symbol than towards so complex a thing as a clan'.

Religion and the 'collective conscience'

Durkheim believed that social life was impossible without the shared values and moral beliefs that form the **collective conscience**. In their absence, there would be no social order, social control, social solidarity or cooperation. In short, there would be no society. Religion reinforces the collective conscience. The worship of society strengthens the values and moral beliefs that form the basis of social life. By defining them as sacred, religion provides them with greater power to direct human action.

This attitude of respect towards the sacred is the same attitude applied to social duties and obligations. In worshipping society, people are, in effect, recognizing the importance of the social group and their dependence upon it. In this way, religion strengthens the unity of the group: it promotes social solidarity.

Durkheim emphasized the importance of **collective worship**. The social group comes together in religious rituals full of drama and reverence. Together, its members express their faith in common values and beliefs. In this highly charged atmosphere of collective worship, the integration of society is strengthened. Members of society express, communicate and understand the moral bonds which unite them.

According to Durkheim, the belief in gods or spirits, which usually provide the focus for religious ceremonies, originated from belief in the ancestral spirits of dead relatives. The worship of gods is really the worship of ancestors' souls. Since Durkheim also believed that souls represent the presence of social values, the collective conscience is present in individuals. It is through individual souls that the collective conscience is realized. Since religious worship involves the worship of souls, Durkheim again concludes that religious worship is really the worship of the social group or society.

Criticisms of Durkheim

Durkheim's ideas are still influential today, although they have been criticized:

1. Critics have argued that Durkheim studied only a small number of Aboriginal groups, which were somewhat untypical of other Aboriginal tribes. It may therefore be misleading to generalize about Aboriginal beliefs from this sample, never mind generalizing about religion as a whole.
2. Most sociologists believe that Durkheim overstated his case. While agreeing that religion is important for promoting social solidarity and reinforcing social values, they would not support his view that religion is the worship of society. Durkheim's views on religion are more relevant to small, non-literate societies, where there is a close integration of culture and social institutions, where work, leisure, education and family life tend to merge, and where members share a common belief and value system. His views are less relevant to modern societies, which have many subcultures, social and ethnic groups, specialized organizations, and a range of religious beliefs, practices and institutions. As Malcolm Hamilton (1995) puts it, 'The emergence of religious pluralism and diversity within a society is, of course, something that Durkheim's theory has great difficulty dealing with.'
3. Durkheim may also overstate the degree to which the collective conscience permeates and shapes the behaviour of individuals. Indeed, sometimes religious beliefs can be at odds with and override societal values. Hamilton makes this point strongly:

> *The fact that our moral sense might make us go against the majority, the society, or authority, shows that we are not quite so dependent upon or creatures of society as Durkheim claims. Society, powerful as it is, does not have the primacy that Durkheim believes it has. Ironically, it often seems to be the case that religious beliefs can have a much greater influence upon and hold over the individual than society does, since it is often out of religious convictions that individuals will fly in the face of society or attempt to withdraw from it, as in the case of many sectarian movements.* Hamilton, 1995

Bronislaw Malinowski

Like Durkheim, Malinowski (1954) uses data from small-scale non-literate societies to develop his thesis on religion. Many of his examples are drawn from his fieldwork in the Trobriand Islands off the coast of New Guinea. Like Durkheim, Malinowski sees religion as reinforcing social norms and values and promoting social solidarity. Unlike Durkheim, however, he does not see religion as reflecting society as a whole, nor does he see religious ritual as the worship of society itself. Malinowski identifies specific areas of social life with which religion is concerned, and to which it is addressed. These are situations of emotional stress that threaten social solidarity.

Religion and life crises

Anxiety and tension tend to disrupt social life. Situations that produce these emotions include **crises of life** such as birth, puberty, marriage and death. Malinowski notes that in all societies these life crises are surrounded with religious ritual. He sees death as the most disruptive of these events and argues:

> *The existence of strong personal attachments and the fact of death, which of all human events is the most upsetting and disorganizing to man's calculations, are perhaps the main sources of religious beliefs.* Malinowski, 1954

Religion deals with the problem of death in the following manner. A funeral ceremony expresses the belief in immortality, which denies the fact of death, and so comforts the bereaved. Other mourners support the bereaved by their presence at the ceremony. This comfort and support check the emotions that death produces, and control the stress and anxiety that might disrupt society. Death is **socially destructive**, since it removes a member from society. At a funeral ceremony the social group unites to support the bereaved. This expression of social solidarity reintegrates society.

Religion, prediction and control

A second category of events – undertakings that cannot be fully controlled or predicted by practical means – also produces tension and anxiety. From his observations in the Trobriand Islands, Malinowski noted that such events were surrounded by **ritual**.

Fishing is an important subsistence practice in the Trobriands. Malinowski observed that in the calm waters of the lagoon, 'fishing is done in an easy and absolutely reliable manner by the method of poisoning, yielding abundant results without danger and uncertainty'. However, beyond the barrier reef in the open sea there is danger and uncertainty: a storm may result in loss of life and the catch is dependent on the presence of a shoal of fish, which cannot be predicted. In the lagoon, 'where man can rely completely on his knowledge and skill', there are no rituals associated with fishing, whereas fishing in the open sea is preceded by rituals to ensure a good catch and protect the fishermen. Although Malinowski refers to these rituals as magic, others argue that it is reasonable to regard them as religious practices.

Again, we see ritual used for specific situations that produce anxiety. Rituals reduce anxiety by providing confidence and a feeling of control. As with funeral ceremonies, fishing rituals are social events. The group unites to deal with situations of stress, and so the unity of the group is strengthened.

Therefore, we can summarize by saying that Malinowski's distinctive contribution to the sociology of religion is his argument that religion promotes social solidarity by dealing with situations of emotional stress that threaten the stability of society.

Criticisms of Malinowski

Malinowski has been criticized for exaggerating the importance of religious rituals in helping people to cope with situations of stress and uncertainty. Tambiah (1990; discussed in Hamilton, 1995) points out, for example, that magic and elaborate rituals are associated with the cultivation of taro and yams on the Trobriand Islands. This is related to the fact that taro and yams are important because men must use them to make payments to their sisters' husbands. Men who fail to do so show that they are unable to fulfil significant social obligations. These rituals are therefore simply related to the maintenance of prestige in that society and have little to do with cementing solidarity or dealing with uncertainty and danger. A particular function or effect that religion sometimes has, has been mistaken for a feature of religion in general.

Talcott Parsons

Religion and value consensus

Talcott Parsons (1937, 1964, 1965a) argued that human action is directed and controlled by norms provided by the social system. The cultural system provides more general guidelines for action in the form of beliefs, values and systems of meaning. The norms which direct action are not merely isolated standards for behaviour: they are integrated and patterned by the values and beliefs provided by the cultural system. For example, many norms in Western society are expressions of the value of materialism. Religion is part of the cultural system. As such, religious beliefs provide guidelines for human action and standards against which people's conduct can be evaluated.

In a Christian society the Ten Commandments operate in this way. They demonstrate how many of the norms of the social system can be integrated by religious beliefs. For example, the commandment 'Thou shalt not kill' integrates such diverse norms as the way to drive a car, how to settle an argument and how to deal with the suffering of the aged. The norms that direct these areas of behaviour prohibit manslaughter, murder and euthanasia, but they are all based on the same religious commandment.

In this way, religion provides general guidelines for conduct which are expressed in a variety of norms. By establishing general principles and moral beliefs, religion helps to provide the consensus which Parsons believes is necessary for order and stability in society.

Religion and social order

Parsons, like Malinowski, sees religion as being addressed to particular problems that occur in all societies. He argues that in everyday life, people 'go about their business without particular strain'. If life were always like this, 'religion would certainly not have the significance that it does'. However, life does not always follow this smooth pattern. The problems that disrupt it fall into two categories.

The first 'consists in the fact that individuals are "hit" by events which they cannot foresee and prepare for, or control, or both'. One such event is death, particularly premature death. Like Malinowski, and for similar reasons, Parsons sees religion as a mechanism for adjustment to such events and as a means of restoring the normal pattern of life.

The second problem area is that of 'uncertainty'. This refers to endeavours in which a great deal of effort and skill have been invested, but where unknown or uncontrollable factors can threaten a successful outcome. One example is humanity's inability to predict or control the effect of weather upon agriculture. Again, following Malinowski, Parsons argues that religion provides a means of adjusting and coming to terms with such situations through rituals which act as 'a tonic to self-confidence'.

In this way, religion maintains social stability by relieving the tension and frustration that could disrupt social order.

Religion and meaning

As a part of the cultural system, religious beliefs give meaning to life; they answer, in Parsons's rather sexist words, 'man's questions about himself and the world he lives in'. This function of religion is particularly important in relation to the frustrations we discussed in the last section, which threaten to shatter beliefs about the meaning of life and so make human existence meaningless. Why should a premature death occur? It is not something people expect to happen or feel ought to happen. Social life is full of contradictions that threaten the meanings people place on life. Parsons argues that one of the major functions of religion is to 'make sense' of all experiences, no matter how meaningless or contradictory they appear.

A good example of this is the question of suffering: 'Why must men endure deprivation and pain and so unequally and haphazardly, if indeed at all?' Religion provides a range of answers: suffering is imposed by God to test a person's faith; it is a punishment for sins; and suffering with fortitude will bring its reward in heaven. Suffering thus becomes meaningful.

Similarly, the problem of evil is common to all societies. It is particularly disconcerting when people profit through evil actions. Religion solves this contradiction by stating that evil will receive its just deserts in the afterlife.

Parsons (1965a) therefore sees a major function of religion as the provision of meaning to events that people do not expect, or feel ought not to happen – events that are frustrating and contradictory. Religion 'makes sense' of these events in terms of an integrated and consistent pattern of meaning. This allows intellectual and emotional adjustment. On a more general level, this adjustment promotes order and stability in society.

Criticisms of the functionalist approach

The functionalist perspective emphasizes the positive contributions of religion to society and tends to ignore its dysfunctional aspects. With its preoccupation with harmony, integration and solidarity, functionalism neglects the many instances where religion can be seen as a divisive and disruptive force. It bypasses the frequent examples of internal divisions within a community over questions of religious dogma and worship – divisions that can lead to open conflict. It gives little consideration to hostility between different religious groups within the same society, such as Catholics and Protestants in Northern Ireland, Shia and Sunni Muslims in Iraq, or Hindus and Muslims in India. In such cases religion can be seen as a direct threat to social order. As Charles Glock and Rodney Stark state in their criticism of functionalist views on religion:

> *We find it difficult to reconcile the general theory with considerable evidence of religious conflict. On every side it would seem that religion threatens social integration as readily as it contributes to it. The history of Christianity, with its many schisms, manifests the great power of religion not merely to bind but to divide.* Glock and Stark, 1965

The Marxist perspective on religion, which we are going to consider next, provides an interesting contrast to functionalist views.

Religion – a Marxist perspective

In Marx's vision of the ideal society, exploitation and alienation are things of the past. The means of production are communally owned, which results in the disappearance of social classes. Members of society are fulfilled as human beings: they control their own destinies and work together for the common good. Religion does not exist in this communist utopia because the social conditions that produce it have disappeared.

To Marx, religion is an illusion which eases the pain produced by exploitation and oppression. It is a series of myths that justify and legitimate the subordination of the subject class and the domination and privilege of the ruling class. It is a distortion of reality which provides many of the deceptions that form the basis of ruling-class ideology and false class consciousness.

Religion as 'the opium of the people'

In Marx's words, 'Religion is the sigh of the oppressed creature, the sentiment of a heartless world and the soul of soulless conditions. It is the opium of the people' (Marx, in Bottomore and Rubel, 1963). Religion acts as an opiate to dull the pain produced by oppression. It is both 'an expression of real suffering and a protest against suffering', but it does little to solve the problem because it helps to make life more bearable and therefore dilutes demands for change. As such, religion merely stupefies its adherents rather than bringing them true happiness and fulfilment.

Similarly, Lenin argued that 'religion is a kind of spiritual gin in which the slaves of capital drown their human shape and their claims to any decent life' (cited in Lane, 1970).

From a Marxist perspective, religion can dull the pain of oppression in the following ways:

1. It promises a paradise of eternal bliss in life after death. Engels argued that the appeal of Christianity to oppressed classes lies in its promise of 'salvation from bondage and misery' in the afterlife. The Christian vision of heaven can make life on earth

more bearable by giving people something to look forward to.

2 Some religions make a virtue of the suffering produced by oppression. In particular, those who bear the deprivations of poverty with dignity and humility will be rewarded for their virtue. This view is contained in the well-known biblical quotation, 'It is easier for a camel to pass through the eye of a needle, than for a rich man to enter the Kingdom of Heaven.' Religion thus makes poverty more tolerable by offering a reward for suffering and promising compensation for injustice in the afterlife.

3 Religion can offer the hope of supernatural intervention to solve problems on earth. Members of religious groups such as the Jehovah's Witnesses live in anticipation of the day when the supernatural powers will descend from on high and create heaven on earth. Anticipation of this future can make the present more acceptable.

4 Religion often justifies the social order and a person's position within it. God can be seen as creating and ordaining the social structure, as in the following verse from the Victorian hymn 'All things bright and beautiful':

> *The rich man in his castle,*
> *The poor man at his gate,*
> *God made them high and lowly,*
> *And ordered their estate.*

In this way, social arrangements appear inevitable. This can help those at the bottom of the stratification system to accept and come to terms with their situation. In the same way, poverty and misfortune in general have often been seen as divinely ordained as a punishment for sin. Again, the situation is defined as immutable and unchangeable. This can make life more bearable by encouraging people to accept their situation philosophically.

Religion and social control

From a Marxist viewpoint, religion does not simply cushion the effects of oppression, it is also an instrument of that oppression. It acts as a **mechanism of social control**, maintaining the existing system of exploitation and reinforcing class relationships. Put simply, it keeps people in their place. By making unsatisfactory lives bearable, religion tends to discourage people from attempting to change their situation. By offering an illusion of hope in a hopeless situation, it prevents thoughts of overthrowing the system.

By providing explanations and justifications for social situations, religion distorts reality. It helps to produce a **false class consciousness** which blinds members of the subject class to their true situation and their real interests. In this way it diverts people's attention from the real source of their oppression and so helps to maintain ruling-class power.

Religion is not, however, solely the province of oppressed groups. From a Marxist perspective, ruling classes adopt religious beliefs to justify their position both to themselves and to others. The lines 'God made them high and lowly / And ordered their estate' show clearly how religion can be used to justify social inequality, not simply to the poor, but also to the rich.

Religion is often directly supported by the ruling classes to further their interests. In the words of Marx and Engels, 'the parson has ever gone hand in hand with the landlord'. In feudal England the lord of the manor's power was frequently legitimated by pronouncements from the pulpit. In return for this support, landlords would often richly endow the established church.

Because religion was an instrument of oppression, it followed that if oppression came to an end then religion would no longer be necessary. Marx stated: 'Religion is only the illusory sun which revolves around man as long as he does not revolve around himself' (Marx and Engels, 1957). In a truly socialist society, individuals revolve around themselves, and religion – along with all other illusions and distortions of reality – disappears.

Evidence to support Marxism

There is considerable evidence to support the Marxist view of the role of religion in society.

The caste system of traditional India was justified by Hindu religious beliefs. In medieval Europe, kings and queens ruled by divine right. The Egyptian Pharaohs went one step further by combining both god and king in the same person. Slave-owners in the southern states of America often approved of the conversion of slaves to Christianity, believing it to be a controlling and gentling influence. It has been argued that in the early days of the industrial revolution in England, employers used religion as a means of controlling the masses and encouraging them to remain sober and to work hard.

A more recent example which can be used to support Marxism is discussed by Steve Bruce (1988). He points out that, in the USA, conservative Protestants – the 'New Christian Right' – consistently support right-wing political candidates in the Republican Party, and attack more liberal candidates in the Democratic Party. The New Christian Right supported Ronald Reagan in his successful campaign for the presidency in 1984. In the 1988 presidential campaign, however, Reagan was unsuccessfully challenged for the Republican nomination for president by a member of the New Christian Right, Pat Robertson. Robertson was one of a number of television evangelists who tried to gain new converts to their brand of Christianity and who spread their political and moral messages through preaching on television.

Another president who drew support from the New Christian Right was George W. Bush. When he was re-elected in 2004, an exit poll found that two-thirds of voters who attended church more than once a week voted for him (Schifferes, 2004). George Bush consistently supported right-wing and morally conservative views during his presidency.

According to Bruce, the New Christian Right support 'a more aggressive anti-communist foreign policy, more military spending, less central government interference, less welfare spending, and fewer restraints on free enterprise'. Although Bruce emphasizes that they have had a limited influence on American politics, it is clear that they have tended to defend the interests of the rich and powerful at the expense of other groups in the population.

The limitations of Marxism

Conflicting evidence suggests that religion does not always legitimate power; it is not simply a justification of alienation or a justification of privilege, and it can sometimes provide an impetus for change. Although this is not reflected in Marx's own writing, nor in much of Engels's earlier work, it is reflected in Engels's later work and in the perspectives on religion advanced by more recent neo-Marxists. We will examine these views in the next section.

Furthermore, the fact that religion sometimes acts as an ideological force in the way suggested by Marx does not explain the existence of religion. As Malcolm Hamilton points out:

> *To say, however, that religion can be turned into an instrument of manipulation is no more to explain it than saying that because art or drama can be utilized for ideological purposes this explains art or drama.*
> Hamilton, 1995

It does not explain the existence of religion where it does not appear to contribute to the oppression of a particular class. Nor does it explain why religion might continue to exist when, in theory at least, oppression has come to an end.

In the USSR under communism after the 1917 revolution the state actively discouraged religion and many places of worship were closed. The communist state placed limits on religious activity, and the religious instruction of children was banned. Nevertheless, religion did not die out under communism as Marx predicted. For example, in 1988, Geoffrey Hoskins argued: 'The Soviet Union is already a much more "religious" country than Britain or most of Western Europe.'

When the USSR began to divide and Communist Party rule was abandoned, religious convictions became even more evident. Quoting data from the International Social Survey Program, Andrew Greeley (1994) notes that, in 1991, 47 per cent of the Russian population claimed to believe in God. The strength of the religious revival is revealed by the fact that 22 per cent of the population were former non-believers who had converted to a belief in God.

This evidence suggests that Marx was wrong to believe that religion would disappear under communism, and that there must be other reasons for the existence of religion apart from those put forward by Marx.

Engels and neo-Marxists – religion as a radical force

Engels – Christianity and social change

Roger O'Toole (1984), commenting on the Marxist sociology of religion, argues: 'Beginning with the work of Engels, Marxists have undoubtedly recognized the active role that may be played by religion in effecting revolutionary social change.' Thus, in *On the History of Early Christianity*, Engels compared some of the early Christian sects that opposed Roman rule to communist and socialist political movements (Marx and Engels, 1957). He said, 'Christianity got hold of the masses exactly as modern socialism does, under the shape of a variety of sects.' While Christianity originated as a way of coping with exploitation among oppressed groups, it could become a source of resistance to the oppressors and thus a force for change.

Otto Maduro – the relative autonomy of religion

Maduro is a neo-Marxist. While accepting many aspects of Marx's analysis of religion, he places greater emphasis on the idea that religion has some independence, or 'relative autonomy', from the economic system of the bourgeoisie (Maduro, 1982). He denies that religion is always a conservative force and, indeed, claims that it can be revolutionary. He says, 'Religion is not necessarily a functional, reproductive or conservative factor in society; it often is one of the main (and sometimes the only) available channel to bring about a social revolution.'

Maduro claims that, up until recently, Catholicism in Latin America tended to support the bourgeoisie and the right-wing military dictatorships which represented its interests. The Catholic Church has tended to deny the existence of social conflicts between oppressive and oppressed classes. It has recognized some injustices, such as poverty and illiteracy, but has suggested that the solution lies with those who already have power. The Catholic Church has also supported members of the clergy who have assisted private enterprise and government projects; it has celebrated military victories but has failed to support unions, strikes and opposition political parties.

On the other hand, Catholic priests have increasingly demonstrated their autonomy from the bourgeoisie by criticizing them and acting against their interests. Maduro believes members of the clergy can develop revolutionary potential where oppressed members of the population have no outlet for their grievances. They pressurize priests to take up their cause, and theological disagreements within a church can provide interpretations of a religion that are critical of the rich and powerful.

All of these conditions have been met in Latin America and have led to the development of **liberation theology** (for further details of liberation theology, see p. 409).

Having discussed Marxist and neo-Marxist views on religion, we will now turn to a consideration of the relationship between gender and religion. Some feminist theories of religion have similarities with Marxist theories.

Gender, feminism and religion

Feminist theories of religion follow Marxist theories in arguing that religion can be an instrument of domination and oppression. However, unlike Marxism, they tend to see religion as a product of **patriarchy** (see p. 112 for a discussion of patriarchy) rather than as a product of capitalism. They see religion as serving the interests of men rather than those of a capitalist class. Indeed, such a view of religion is not confined to female and feminist sociologists. For example, Anthony Giddens argues:

> *The Christian religion is a resolutely male affair in its symbolism as well as its hierarchy. While Mary, the mother of Jesus, may sometimes be treated as if she had divine qualities, God is the father, a male figure, and Jesus took the human shape of a man. Woman is portrayed as created from a rib taken from a man.* Giddens, 1997

The secondary and often subordinate role of women in Christian doctrine is also typical of most other religions. Karen Armstrong (1993) argues: 'None of the major religions has been particularly good to women. They have usually become male affairs and women have been relegated to a marginal position.' Although women may have made significant advances in many areas of life, their gains in most religions have been very limited.

Women continue to be excluded from key roles in many religions (although the Church of England finally allowed the ordination of women priests in 1992). This is despite the fact that women often participate more in organized religion (when they are allowed to) than men. (For a discussion of gender and religious participation and belief, see pp. 423–5.)

Feminist writers are interested in how women came to be subservient within most religions and how religion has been used to cement patriarchal power. More recently, some sociologists have examined how women have begun to try to reduce the imbalance between males and females within religion.

Gender inequality in religion

The origins of gender inequality

A number of writers have noted that, historically, women have not always been subordinate within most religions. Karen Armstrong (1993), for example, argues that in early history 'women were considered central to the spiritual quest'. In the Middle East, Asia and Europe, archaeologists have uncovered numerous symbols of the Great Mother Goddess. She was pictured as a naked pregnant woman and seems to represent the mysteries of fertility and life. As Armstrong puts it:

> *The Earth produced plants and nourished them in rather the same way as a woman gave birth to a child and fed it from her own body. The magical power of the earth seemed vitally interconnected with the mysterious creativity of the female sex.* Armstrong, 1993

There were very few early effigies of gods as men. As societies developed religious beliefs in which there were held to be many different gods and goddesses, the Mother Goddess still played a crucial role. Armstrong says the Mother Goddess was:

> *absorbed into the pantheons of deities and remained a powerful figure. She was called Inanna in Sumner, in ancient Mesopotamia, Ishtar in Babylon, Anat or Asherah in Canaan, Isis in Egypt and Aphrodite in Greece. In all these cultures people told remarkably similar stories about her to express her role in their spiritual lives. She was still revered as the source of fertility.* Armstrong, 1993

Not surprisingly, since they had goddesses, these societies also had female priests. However, the position of women in religion began to decline as a result of invasions:

> *In Mesopotamia, Egypt and India, Semitic and Aryan invaders from the north brought with them a male-orientated mythology which replaced the Goddess with more powerful masculine deities. These invasions had begun as early as the fourth millennium but became more and more devastating.* Armstrong, 1993

Armstrong argues that an Amorite myth dating from about 1750 BC marked the start of the eventual decline of the goddess. In it the goddess Tiamat, the goddess of the sea, is replaced by the male god of Babylon, Marduk. Male gods such as the Hebrew Yahweh became increasingly important and they introduced a 'more martial and aggressive spirituality'.

The final death knell of goddesses came with the acceptance of monotheism – belief in a single god rather than many. This originated with Yahweh, the god of Abraham. Furthermore, this 'God of Israel would later become the God of the Christians and the Muslims, who all regard themselves as the spiritual offspring of Abraham, the father of all believers'.

Jean Holm – inequality in major religions

Jean Holm (1994) reviewed some of the ways in which women are subordinated or exploited in contemporary religions and devalued by different religious beliefs. She argues that, while the classical teachings of many religions have stressed equality between men and women, in practice women have usually been far from equal. She says, 'Women do, of course, have a part to play in many religions, but it is almost always subordinate to the role of men, and it is likely to be in the private rather than the public sphere.' She gives a number of examples.

In Japanese folk religions women are responsible for organizing public rituals, but only men can take part in the public performances. In Chinese popular religion women are associated with Yin and men with Yang. However, Yang spirits are more important and powerful. In Buddhism, both men and women can have a religious role, as monks and nuns, respectively. However, all monks are seen as senior to all nuns. Orthodox Judaism only allows males to take a full part in ceremonies. In Islam, in some regions, women are not allowed to enter mosques for worship, and men have made all the legal rulings.

Christianity has also been male-dominated. Holm says:

> *Many of the most influential ideas were worked out by (celibate) men in the first five centuries of the Church's history, and the significant developments of the medieval Church and the Reformation were also shaped by men.* Holm, 1994

In Hinduism only men can become Brahmanic priests. Sikhism is perhaps the most egalitarian of the major religions, since all offices are equally open to men and women. However, even in Sikhism only a small minority of women have significant positions within the religion.

Women's second-class status is often related to female sexuality. Holm comments: 'Menstruation and childbirth are almost universally regarded as polluting. In many traditions women are forbidden to enter sacred places or touch sacred objects during the menstrual period.' For example, Hindu women are prohibited from approaching family shrines when pregnant or menstruating. Muslim women are not allowed to touch the Qur'an, go into a mosque or pray during menstruation.

Despite documenting these inequalities, Holm is not entirely pessimistic. As we will see later, she does detect evidence of changes in which the inequality between men and women in religion is being slowly reduced (see below, p. 404).

Feminist perspectives on religion

Simone de Beauvoir – religion and The Second Sex

Jean Holm describes some of the inequalities between males and females within different religions. However, she goes into little detail about why such inequalities exist. The French feminist Simone de Beauvoir provides such an explanation in her pioneering feminist book *The Second Sex* (1953, first published 1949). To de Beauvoir, religion acts for women in very similar ways to those in which Marx suggested religion could act for oppressed classes. De Beauvoir says, 'There must be a religion for women as there must be one for the common people, and for exactly the same reasons.' Religion can be used by the oppressors (men) to control the oppressed group (women) and it also serves as a way of compensating women for their second-class status.

De Beauvoir notes that men have generally exercised control over religious beliefs. She says, 'Man enjoys the great advantage of having a God endorse the code he writes.' That code uses divine authority to support male dominance. As de Beauvoir says, 'For the Jews, Mohammedans, and Christians, among others, man is master by divine right; the fear of God will therefore repress any impulse towards revolt in the downtrodden female.'

However, in modern societies, 'religion seems much less an instrument of constraint than an instrument of deception'. Women are deceived by religion into thinking of themselves as equal to men, despite their evident inequality. In some ways women are portrayed by religion as being closer to God than men, even if they are unlikely to hold positions of power within religions. As mothers, women have a key religious role: 'a mother not only engenders the flesh, she produces a soul for God'. Women are taught to be relatively passive, but in some ways this makes them appear more godly than the men whose 'agitation for this and that is more than absurd, it is blameworthy: why remodel this world which God himself created?'.

Like Marx's proletariat, religion gives women the false belief that they will be compensated for their sufferings on earth by equality in heaven. In this way the subjugation of women through religion helps to maintain a status quo in which women are unequal. Women are also vital to religion because it is they who do much of the work for religious organizations and introduce children to religious beliefs. Thus, de Beauvoir concludes:

> *Religion sanctions woman's self-love; it gives her the guide, father, lover, divine guardian she longs for nostalgically; it feeds her day-dreams; it fills her empty hours. But, above all, it confirms the social order, it justifies her resignation, by giving hope of a better future in a sexless heaven. This is why women today are still a powerful trump in the hand of the Church; it is why the Church is notably hostile to all measures likely to help in women's emancipation. There must be religion for women; and there must be women, 'true women', to perpetuate religion.* de Beauvoir, 1953

Nawal El Saadawi – *The Hidden Face of Eve*

Patriarchy, Islam and the limited role of religion

Simone de Beauvoir writes from the perspective of a Western, Christian woman. Nawal El Saadawi is an Egyptian feminist writer and a leading advocate of women's rights in the Arab world. She was sacked from her post as Egypt's Director of Public Health by the then-ruler, Sadat, and has been imprisoned for her political activities. In *The Hidden Face of Eve* (1980) she discusses female oppression in the Arab world and elsewhere and considers the importance of religion in creating and perpetuating oppression.

El Saadawi recounts some of her personal experience of oppression. For example, she describes in chilling terms her terror as a young girl when her parents forced her, without warning or explanation, to undergo 'female circumcision', where part of her clitoris was amputated. She argues that Arab girls are often victims of sexual aggression by men (often their fathers, brothers or other relations). She also discusses prostitution, slavery and abortion and argues that all of these areas provide evidence of patriarchal dominance of Arab men over Arab women.

El Saadawi notes that oppressive practices such as female circumcision have often been attributed to the influence of Islam. However, she denies that the oppression of women is directly caused by religion in general, or Islam in particular. Female circumcision has been practised in a considerable number of countries, not all of them Islamic. Authentic religious beliefs tend to be opposed to any such practices because, 'if religion comes from God, how can it order man to cut off an organ created by Him as long as that organ is not diseased or deformed?' Authentic religion aims at 'truth, equality, justice, love and a healthy wholesome life for all people, whether men or women'.

Furthermore, other religions are often more oppressive than Islam. El Saadawi says, 'If we study Christianity, it is easy to see that this religion is much more rigid and orthodox where women are concerned than Islam.' To El Saadawi, the oppression of women is caused by 'the patriarchal system which came into being when society had reached a certain stage of development'. Nevertheless, she does see religion as playing a role in women's oppression. Men distort religion to serve their own interests, to help justify or legitimate the oppression of women.

The origins of oppressive religion

El Saadawi argues that religion started to become patriarchal through the misinterpretation of religious beliefs by men. She cites the Greek mythological story of Isis and Osiris. The male Osiris is overpowered by the evil Touphoun. His body is cut into small pieces and dispersed in the sea, and his sexual organ is eaten by fish. Despite this, Isis (who is female) is able to reassemble Osiris's body. To El Saadawi, this story clearly implies female superiority, but it has been interpreted quite differently by men. They have emphasized the superiority of Osiris because he was created from the head of the god Zeus, who was greater than Osiris, according to Homer and other writers, because he was more knowledgeable. In reality, El Saadawi says, all the male gods were created by, or given the ability to move by, the greatest deity of them all, the goddess Isis.

Similar distortions have entered the story of Adam and Eve, which is accepted by both Christians and Muslims as part of the story of creation. Eve is usually portrayed by males as a temptress who created sin in the world, but was created from Adam's spare rib. However:

> *if we read the original story as described in the Old Testament, it is easy for us to see clearly that Eve was gifted with knowledge, intelligence and superior mental capacities, whereas Adam was only one of her instruments, utilized by her to increase her knowledge and give shape to her creativity.* El Saadawi, 1980

Like other writers, El Saadawi argues that forms of religion oppressive to women developed as monotheistic religions (believing in a single god) became predominant. Such religions 'drew inspiration and guidance from the values of the patriarchal and class societies prevalent at the time'. For example, the Jewish religion drew upon the patriarchal power of Abraham to produce a situation in which 'a Hebrew household was embodied in the patriarchal family, under the uncontested and undivided authority of the father'.

Islamic society also developed in a patriarchal way through the dominance of a male minority who owned herds of horses, camels and sheep. As a consequence, 'Authority in Islam belonged to the man as head of the family, to the supreme ruler, or the Khalifa (political ruler), or Imam (religious leader).' Although the Qur'an stipulated that both men and women could be stoned to death for adultery, this fate was very unlikely to befall men. This was because men were permitted several wives (but women were not permitted several husbands) and because men could divorce their wives instantaneously. There was therefore little need for men to commit adultery. Even today, in countries such as Egypt, women are still subject to extremely restrictive marriage laws.

El Saadawi describes Christ as a revolutionary leader who opposed oppression. Early Christianity had stricter moral codes than other religions, and codes which treated the sexes fairly equally. Nevertheless, at a later stage:

> *the religious hierarchies that grew and fattened on the teachings of Christ allowed the system of concubinage to creep in once more. Despite the limitations placed by Christianity on man's sexual freedom, woman was maintained in her inferior underprivileged status as compared with him. The patriarchal system still reigned supreme and grew even more ferocious with the gradual shift to a feudal system.* El Saadawi, 1980

In the fourteenth century, for example, the Catholic Church declared that women who treated illnesses, without special training, could be executed as witches.

Conclusion

El Saadawi concludes that female oppression is not essentially due to religion but due to the patriarchal system that has long been dominant. Religion, though, has played its part:

> *The great religions of the world uphold similar principles in so far as the submission of women to men is concerned. They also agree in the attribution of masculine characteristics to their God. Islam and Christianity have both constituted important stages in the evolution of humanity. Nevertheless, where the cause of women was concerned, they added a new load to their already heavy chains.* El Saadawi, 1980

The only way for women to improve their lot is to struggle for their own liberation. Arab women have been doing this for longer than their Western counterparts. As early as fourteen centuries ago, Arab women successfully campaigned against the universal use of the male gender when referring to people in general in the Qur'an. El Saadawi believes any recent gains in the position of Arab women have been due to a combination of social, economic and political changes and their own struggles. She argues that women have benefited from socialist revolutions wherever they have taken place. Revolutions will further the cause of women even more if the positive aspects of the Qur'an can be emphasized and the patriarchal misinterpretations abandoned. Thus El Saadawi is not hostile to religion itself, but only to the domination of religion by patriarchal ideology.

Women and resistance to religious oppression

Signs of hope

Apart from El Saadawi, the theorists examined above have tended to portray women as the passive victims of religious oppression, and religions themselves as universally oppressive. Increasingly, however, sociologists have come to acknowledge that women can no longer be seen as being so passive. Jean Holm (1994), acting as editor of a book dealing with women and different religious traditions, sees 'signs of hope' in the religious situation of women. Rita Gross (1994) detects signs of a 'post-patriarchal' Buddhism that might be developing in Western countries.

Leila Badawi (1994) notes aspects of Islam that are positive for women. Unlike Christian women, Islamic women keep their own family name when they get married. Muslims also have considerable choice over which interpretation of Islam, or school of law, they give their allegiance to. Some schools of law have much more positive attitudes to women than others.

Alexandra Wright (1994) notes that Reform Judaism has allowed women to become rabbis since 1972. Holm notes that even in 1994 there were already three female Anglican bishops. Some Christian religions, particularly Quakerism, have never been oppressive to women. Kanwaljit Kaur-Singh (1994) points out that 'Sikh Gurus pleaded the cause of the emancipation of Indian womanhood and did their best to ameliorate the sordid condition of women'.

Thus it should not be assumed that all religions are, and always have been, equally oppressive to women. Furthermore, even apparently oppressive practices may be open to varied interpretations.

Helen Watson (1994) argues that the veiling of Islamic women can be interpreted as beneficial to Muslim women. She examines three personal responses by Islamic women to veiling and finds that wearing veils can be used in a positive way by Islamic women in a globalized world.

As Western culture tries to influence Islamic countries, and more Muslims live in the Western world, the veil can take on new meanings for women. For example, Nadia, a second-generation British-Asian woman studying medicine at university, actively chose to start wearing a veil when she was 16. She was proud of her religion and wanted others to know that she was Muslim. She felt that 'It is liberating to have the freedom of movement, to be able to communicate with people without being on show. It's what you say that's important, not what you look like.' She found that, far from making her invisible, wearing a veil made her stand out, yet it also helped her to avoid 'lecherous stares or worse' from men.

Watson concludes that veiling is often a reaction against an increasingly pervasive Western culture. Some Muslim men, too, have begun to reject Western-style clothes – for example, by refusing to wear ties. All this can be seen as 'a sign of the times' which entails the assertion of independence, separate identity and a rejection of Western cultural imperialism. Rather than seeing the veil as a sign of male oppression, it has become 'a reaction against the secular feminism of the West, and as part of the search for an indigenous Islamic form of protest against male power and dominance in public society'.

Watson's work serves as a caution to sociologists who interpret in simplistic terms the practices of religions which are not their own. It shows that the meaning of religion needs to be carefully interpreted. In studies of religion, account needs to be taken of the meaning of religion to its believers; it is not just based upon reading holy texts and observing religious practices. Watson's work suggests that practices that may appear oppressive can take on a variety of meanings.

Nevertheless, Watson's conclusions should be treated with some caution. Her observations are based upon studying only three women. She appears to have made no attempt to find Muslim women who felt they were forced into wearing the veil against their will by men or patriarchal society. Attempts by women to subvert patriarchy by changing the meaning of traditional practices may not always succeed in liberating women from domination through religion. There is always a danger that they might have the opposite effect.

Religion and social change

There are a number of possible relationships between religion and social change. Religion may be a factor that impedes social change, or it may help to produce it. Another possibility is that religion itself has no influence on changes in society, but that there is nevertheless a causal relationship between the two. From this point of view, it is social change in society as a whole that leads to changes in religion.

Religion as a conservative force

Functionalists, Marxists and feminists have generally dismissed the possibility that religion can cause changes in society. They believe religion acts as a conservative force and that it is changes in society that shape religion, not vice versa.

Religion can be seen as a 'conservative force' in two senses, depending on the meaning attached to the word 'conservative'. The phrase **conservative force** is usually used to refer to religion as preventing change and maintaining the status quo. Functionalists have claimed that it acts in this way because it promotes integration and social solidarity. As we discovered in previous sections, from a functionalist perspective, religion provides shared beliefs, norms and values, and helps individuals to cope with stresses that might disrupt social life. In these ways it facilitates the continued existence of society in its present form. Marx had similar views, although he saw religion as maintaining the status quo in the interests of the ruling class rather than those of society as a whole.

'Conservative' may, however, be used in another way: it can refer to traditional beliefs and customs. Usually, if religion helps to maintain the status quo, it will also maintain traditional customs and beliefs. For example, the stance of successive popes against the use of contraception has restricted the growth of artificial methods of birth control in Roman Catholic countries. But in some circumstances religion can support social change while at the same time promoting traditional values. This often occurs when there is a revival in 'fundamentalist' religious beliefs. Such beliefs involve a return to what a group claims are the 'fundamentals' or basic, original beliefs of a religion. For example, in Iran in 1979 an Islamic revolution took place which both changed society and involved a return to traditional values.

Fundamentalism involves the reassertion of traditional moral and religious values against changes that have taken place and those who support the changes. If fundamentalists are successful, they succeed in defending traditional values, but at the same time they change society by reversing innovations that have taken place.

Perhaps the most dramatic example of fundamentalism causing social change through the imposition of a return to traditional values has been in Iran. Under the last Shah,

Iranian society underwent a process of change. One aspect of this change was the liberalization of traditional Islamic attitudes to women. In 1979 the Shah was deposed during a revolution which was partly inspired by Islamic fundamentalism. The liberalization that took place under the Shah was reversed. In this case, it can be argued, religious beliefs contributed to producing revolutionary change. Religion did not therefore act as a conservative force in one sense of the word. Nevertheless, in terms of supporting traditional values, it did act as a conservative force. The two meanings of the word 'conservative' should therefore be distinguished. (For a discussion of fundamentalism, see pp. 445–8).

Changes in society and religion

Most sociologists agree that changes in society lead to changes in religion:

1 Talcott Parsons (1937, 1964, 1965a), for example, believed that, as society developed, religion lost some of its functions (for further details, see pp. 398–9).
2 Marx believed that a change in the infrastructure of society would lead to changes in the superstructure, including religion. Thus, Marx anticipated that, when a classless society was established, religion would disappear (Marx and Engels, 1957).
3 As later sections of this chapter will show, supporters of the secularization theory think industrialization has led to profound changes that have progressively reduced the importance of religion in society (see pp. 429–36).
4 A number of sociologists have claimed that changes involved in the advent of postmodernism and globalization have produced changes in religion (see pp. 451–6).

So far, then, it appears to be generally agreed that (1) religion helps to maintain the status quo, and (2) changes in religion result from changes in the wider society. Some sociologists, however, have argued that religion can cause social change.

Max Weber – *The Protestant Ethic and the Spirit of Capitalism*

Functionalists and Marxists emphasize the role of religion in promoting social integration and impeding social change. In contrast, Weber (1958, first published 1904) argued that in some circumstances religion can lead to social change: although shared religious beliefs might integrate a social group, those same beliefs may have repercussions which in the long term can produce changes in society.

Marx is generally regarded as a **materialist**. He believed that the material world (and particularly people's involvement with nature as they worked to secure their own survival) shaped people's beliefs. Thus, to Marx, the economic system largely determined the beliefs that were held by individuals. In Marxist terms, the mode of production determined the type of religion that would be dominant in any society.

Unlike Marx, Weber rejected the view that religion is always shaped by economic factors. He did not deny that, at certain times and in certain places, religion may be largely shaped by economic forces, but he denied that this is always the case. Under certain conditions the reverse can occur, that is, religious beliefs can be a major influence on economic behaviour.

Weber's **social action theory** argues that human action is directed by meanings and motives. (See Chapter 15, pp. 874–8, for a discussion of Weber's general theory.) From this perspective, action can only be understood by appreciating the **worldview** – the image or picture of the world – held by members of society. From their worldview, individuals obtain meanings, purposes and motives that direct their actions. Religion is often an important component of a worldview. In certain places and times, religious meaning and purposes can direct action in a wide range of contexts. In particular, religious beliefs can direct economic action.

Capitalism and ascetic Protestantism

In his most famous book, *The Protestant Ethic and the Spirit of Capitalism*, Weber examines the relationship between the rise of certain forms of Protestantism and the development of Western industrial capitalism. In the first part of his argument Weber tries to demonstrate that a particular form of Protestantism, ascetic Calvinist Protestantism (see pp. 406–8), preceded the development of capitalism. He also tries to show that capitalism developed initially in areas where this religion was influential. Other areas of the world possessed many of the prerequisites, yet they were not among the first areas to develop capitalism. For example, India and China had technological knowledge, labour to be hired, and individuals engaged in making money. What they lacked, according to Weber, was a religion that encouraged and facilitated the development of capitalism.

The first capitalist nations emerged among the countries of Western Europe and North America that had Calvinist religious groups. Furthermore, most of the earliest capitalist entrepreneurs in these areas came from the ranks of Calvinists.

Having established a relationship – a correlation between Calvinism and capitalism – by comparing religion and economic development in different parts of the world, Weber goes on to explain how and why this type of religion was linked to capitalism.

Calvinist Protestantism originated in the beliefs of John Calvin in the seventeenth century. Calvin thought there was a distinct group of the **elect** – those chosen to go to heaven – and that they had been chosen by God even before they were born. Those who were not among the elect could never gain a place in heaven, however well they behaved on earth.

Other versions of Christianity derived from the beliefs of Martin Luther. Luther believed that individual Christians could affect their chances of reaching heaven by the way that they behaved on earth. It was very important for Christians to develop faith in God, and to act out God's will on earth. In order to do this they had to be dedicated to their calling in life. Whatever position in society God had given them, they must conscientiously carry out the appropriate duties.

At first sight, Lutheranism seems the doctrine more likely to produce capitalism. However, it encouraged people to produce or earn no more than was necessary for their material needs. It attached more importance to piety and faith than to the accumulation of great wealth.

The doctrine of predestination advocated by Calvin seems less likely to produce capitalism. If certain individuals were destined for heaven regardless of their earthly behaviour – and the rest were equally unable to overcome their damnation – there would be little point in hard work on earth.

Weber points out, though, that Calvinists had a psychological problem: they did not know whether they were among the elect. They suffered from a kind of inner loneliness or uncertainty about their status, and their behaviour was not an attempt to earn a place in heaven, but rather to convince themselves that they had been chosen to go there. They reasoned that only the chosen people of God would be able to live a good life on earth. If their behaviour was exemplary they could feel confident that they would go to heaven after death.

Therefore, the interpretation that the Calvinists put on the doctrine of predestination contributed to them becoming the first capitalists.

The Protestant ethic

The **Protestant ethic** which Weber describes (and which enabled Calvinists to convince themselves that they were among the elect) developed first in seventeenth-century Western Europe. The ethic was **ascetic**, encouraging abstinence from life's pleasures, an austere lifestyle and rigorous self-discipline. It produced individuals who worked hard in their careers or **callings**, in a single-minded manner. Making money was a concrete indication of success in one's calling, and success in one's calling meant that the individual had not lost grace in God's sight.

John Wesley, a leader of the great Methodist revival that preceded the expansion of English industry at the close of the eighteenth century, wrote:

> *For religion must necessarily produce industry and frugality, and these cannot but produce riches. We must exhort all Christians to gain what they can and to save all they can; that is, in effect to grow rich.* Quoted in Weber, 1958, first published 1904

These riches could not be spent on luxuries, fine clothes, lavish houses and frivolous entertainment, but in the glory of God. In effect, this meant being even more successful in terms of one's calling, which in practice meant reinvesting profits in the business.

The Protestants attacked time-wasting, laziness, idle gossip and more sleep than was necessary – six to eight hours a day at the most. They frowned on sexual pleasures; sexual intercourse should remain within marriage and then only for the procreation of children (a vegetable diet and cold baths were sometimes recommended to remove temptation). Sport and recreation were accepted only for improving fitness and health, and condemned if pursued for entertainment. The impulsive fun and enjoyment of the pub, dance hall, theatre and gaming house were prohibited to ascetic Protestants. In fact, anything that might divert or distract people from their calling was condemned. Living life in terms of these guidelines was an indication that the individual had not lost grace and favour in the sight of God.

The spirit of capitalism

Weber claimed that the origins of the spirit of capitalism were to be found in the ethic of ascetic Protestantism. Throughout history there had been no shortage of those who sought money and profit: pirates, prostitutes and money lenders in every corner of the world had always pursued wealth. However, according to Weber, both the manner and purpose of their pursuit of money were at odds with the spirit of capitalism.

Traditionally, money seekers engaged in speculative projects: they gambled in order to gain rewards. If successful they tended to spend money frivolously on personal consumption. Furthermore, they were not dedicated to making money for its own sake. Weber argued that labourers who had earned enough for their family to live comfortably, and merchants who had secured the luxuries they desired, would feel no need to push themselves harder to make more money. Instead, they sought free time for leisure.

The ascetic Protestant had a quite different attitude to wealth, and Weber believed this attitude was characteristic of capitalism. He argued that the essence of capitalism is 'the pursuit of profit and forever renewed profit'.

Capitalist enterprises are organized on rational bureaucratic lines. Business transactions are conducted in a systematic and rational manner, with costs and projected profits being carefully assessed. (We examine Weber's views on rational action in this chapter and in detail in Chapter 15, pp. 874–8.)

Underlying the practice of capitalism is the **spirit of capitalism** – a set of ideas, ethics and values. Weber illustrates the spirit of capitalism with quotes from two books by Benjamin Franklin, *Necessary Hints to Those that Would be Rich* (1736) and *Advice to a Young Tradesman* (1748). Franklin writes: 'Remember that time is money.' Time-wasting, idleness and diversion lose money. 'Remember that credit is money.' A reputation for 'prudence and honesty' will bring credit, as will paying debts on time. Business people should behave with 'industry and frugality' and 'punctuality and justice' in all their dealings.

Weber argued that this spirit of capitalism is not simply a way of making money, but a way of life which has ethics, duties and obligations. He claimed that ascetic Protestantism was a vital influence in the creation and development of the spirit and practice of capitalism: a methodical and single-minded pursuit of a calling encourages rational capitalism. Weber wrote: 'restless, continuous, systematic work in a worldly calling must have been the most powerful conceivable lever for the expansion of the spirit of capitalism'. Making money became both a religious and a business ethic. The Protestant 'interpretation of profit-making justified the activities of the businessman'.

Weber claimed that two major features of capitalist industry – the standardization of production and the specialized division of labour – were encouraged by Protestantism. The Protestant 'uniformity of life immensely aids the capitalist in the standardization of production'. The emphasis on the 'importance of a fixed calling provided an ethical justification for this modern specialized division of labour'.

Finally, Weber noted the importance of the creation of wealth and the restrictions on spending it, which encouraged saving and reinvestment:

> *When the limitation of consumption is combined with this release of acquisitive activity, the inevitable result is obvious: accumulation of capital through an ascetic compulsion to save. The restraints that were imposed on the consumption of wealth naturally served to increase it, by making possible the productive investment of capital.* Weber, 1958, first published 1904

The ascetic Protestant way of life led to the accumulation of capital, investment and reinvestment. It produced the early businesses that expanded to create capitalist society.

Materialism and Weber's theory

Weber, then, believed he had discovered and demonstrated that religious beliefs could cause economic change. He claimed he had found a weakness in Marx's materialism which implied that the economic system always shaped ideas.

However, it should be stressed that Weber did not discount the importance of the economy and material factors. He said, 'It is, of course, not my aim to substitute for a one-sided materialistic an equally one-sided spiritualistic causal interpretation of culture and of history.' Capitalism was made possible not just by Calvinist Protestantism, but also by the technology and economic system of the countries in which it developed. Material factors were as important as ideas in its development; neither could be ignored in any explanation.

Religion, modernity and rationality

As well as proposing an explanation for the origins of capitalism, Weber also had a good deal to say about the likely consequences of the changes produced by the development of Protestantism. His theories have had a tremendous influence on general ideas about changes in Western societies, and in particular on the concepts of modernity and secularization. **Modernity** refers to both a historical period and a type of society which is often seen as developing along with industrialization, science and capitalism (see pp. 890–1). **Secularization** refers to the decline of religion (see below, pp. 429–45). Robert Holton and Brian Turner (1989), for example, argue that the central themes of all of Weber's sociology were 'the problems of modernization and modernity, and that we should regard rationalization as the process which produced modernism'.

As we have seen above, in *The Protestant Ethic and the Spirit of Capitalism* Weber argued that ascetic Protestantism helped to produce modern capitalism. With that went an emphasis on rational calculation, since pursuing the maximum possible profit required an appraisal of the profits that would be produced by following different lines of action. The capitalist would then follow whatever path would produce the greatest profit.

Weber (1947) distinguished between formal rationality and substantive rationality. **Formal rationality** involved calculating the best means to achieve a given end, and the calculations had to be in a numerical form. **Substantive rationality** involved action designed to meet some ultimate goal, such as justice, equality or human happiness. Capitalist behaviour put primary emphasis upon the formal rationality of accounting in the pursuit of profit maximization. Substantive rationality, including the morality provided by religious beliefs, tended to fade into the background in capitalist societies.

To Weber, rationality would not be confined to capitalist enterprise in the modern world. As Holton and Turner point out, it would also involve 'a rational legal system, the separation of the home and the workplace, rational financial management, and the emergence of a rational system of administration'. Weber's ideas on bureaucracy are a good example of his belief that modern societies would be increasingly characterized by rationality (see pp. 874–8). However, to Weber, and to many later sociologists, rationality can be at odds with the faith that is required by religion.

Religions do not expect their followers to try to test their beliefs scientifically, nor do they expect religious beliefs to be based upon weighing up the costs and benefits of joining a religious group. Followers should simply believe in the truth of their religion. In the rationalized modern world, though, Weber thought it would be increasingly difficult for followers of religion to maintain their faith. Discussing Protestant sects in the USA, Weber said, 'closer scrutiny revealed the steady progress of the characteristic process of "secularization" to which all phenomena that originated in religious conceptions succumb' (Weber, in Gerth and Mills, 1948). In short, ascetic Protestantism would contribute to the development of capitalism, which required a rational approach to social life, which would in turn undermine religion. Protestant religions therefore contained the seeds of their own destruction. As Malcolm Hamilton puts it:

> *Once on its way, the modern economic system was able to support itself without the need of the religious ethic of ascetic Protestantism, which in many ways could not help but sow the seeds of secularization in modern society by its own promotion of worldly activity and consequent expansion of wealth and material well-being. Calvinistic Protestantism was its own gravedigger.* Hamilton, 1995

Weber – an evaluation

The ideas of Weber and other sociologists on modernity, rationality and secularization will be discussed later in the chapter (see pp. 429–45). The following discussion therefore concentrates on his specific ideas relating to *The Protestant Ethic and the Spirit of Capitalism*.

Since its publication, Weber's book has received both criticism and support from researchers:

1. Sombart (1907), an early critic, argued that Weber was mistaken about the beliefs held by Calvinists. According to Sombart, Calvinism was against greed and the pursuit of money for its own sake.

   Weber himself countered this argument. He pointed out that it was not the beliefs of Calvinists that were important in themselves. The doctrine of predestination was not intended to produce the rational pursuit of profit, but nevertheless that was one of its unintentional consequences, and the evidence lay in the way that ascetic Protestants actually behaved.
2. A second criticism points to parts of the world where Calvinism was strong, but capitalism did not develop until much later. For example, Switzerland, Scotland, Hungary and parts of the Netherlands all

contained large Calvinist populations, but were not among the first capitalist countries.

Gordon Marshall (1982) dismisses this criticism. He argues that the critics demonstrate a lack of understanding of Weber's theory. Weber did not claim that Calvinism was the only factor necessary for the development of capitalism. His theory cannot therefore be disproved simply by finding Calvinist countries that failed to become capitalist comparatively early. In his own study of Scotland, Marshall found that the Scots had a capitalist mentality but were held back by a lack of skilled labour and capital for investment, and by government policies that did not stimulate the development of industry.

3 A potentially more damaging criticism of Weber's theory originates from Marxist critics such as Kautsky (1953). Kautsky argues that early capitalism preceded and largely determined Protestantism. He sees Calvinism as developing in cities where commerce and early forms of industrialization were already established. In his view, Protestantism became the ideology capitalists used to legitimate their position.

This is a chicken and egg question – which came first: Calvinism or capitalism? The answer depends upon how capitalism is defined. To Weber, pre-capitalist money-making ventures were not organized rationally to ensure continued profit. Marshall (1982) disputes this. He suggests that the medieval merchant classes behaved quite rationally considering the conditions of the time. It was not their psychological attitude that encouraged them to make what Weber saw as risky investments, but the situation they faced. In England the risks involved in trading were balanced by investments in land. Buying landed estates was not an example of conspicuous consumption, but of the prudent spreading of investments. In the Netherlands, too, the business classes spread their risks, but more money went into merchant trading because of the price of land. Even so, defenders of Weber insist that a distinctive rational capitalist entrepreneur did not emerge until after Calvinism.

4 A fourth criticism of Weber does not deny that Calvinism was an important factor that helped lead to capitalism, but questions whether it was the religious beliefs of Calvinists that led to them becoming business people. According to this view, non-conformist Calvinists devoted themselves to business because they were excluded from holding public office and joining certain professions by law. Like the Jews in Eastern and Central Europe, they tried to become economically successful in order to overcome their political persecution.

In reply to this criticism, supporters of the Protestant ethic thesis argue that only Calvinist minorities developed the distinctive patterns of capitalist behaviour which involved rational planning for slow but sure capital growth; only they could develop capitalist businesses before capitalism was established.

Despite the considerable effort devoted to discussing Weber's theory by historians and sociologists alike, no agreement has been reached about its accuracy. Nevertheless, whatever the merits of this particular study, Weber does successfully highlight the theoretical point that ideas – in this case, religious ideas – can conceivably lead to economic change.

Religion and social change – conclusion

Many sociologists do now accept that religion can be a force for change. Despite the examples that can be used to support the functionalist and Marxist view that religion promotes stability, other examples contradict their claims.

G.K. Nelson (1986) points to a number of cases where religion has undermined stability or promoted change:

1 In Northern Ireland, Roman Catholicism has long been associated with Irish Republicanism.
2 In the USA in the 1960s the Reverend Martin Luther King and the Southern Christian Leadership Council played a leading role in establishing civil rights and securing legislation intended to reduce racial discrimination.
3 Also in the 1960s, a number of radical and revolutionary groups emerged within the Roman Catholic Church in Latin America. They preached liberation theology, arguing that it was the duty of church members to fight against unjust and oppressive right-wing dictatorships. Thus, in 1979, Catholic revolutionaries supported the Sandinistas when they seized control in Nicaragua.
4 In Iran, Islamic fundamentalism played a part in the 1979 revolution, led by the Ayatollah Khomeini.
5 Poland provides another example of religion stimulating change. The Roman Catholic Church opposed the communist state in Poland, and it supported the attempts of the free trade union Solidarity to achieve changes in Polish society. In 1989 the communist monopoly on power was broken when Solidarity was allowed to contest and win many seats in the Polish parliament.
6 In South Africa, Archbishop Tutu was a prominent opponent of apartheid.

Examples such as these lead Nelson to conclude that, 'far from encouraging people to accept their place, religion can spearhead resistance and revolution'. In many cases when religion has been a force for change in society, the society that results may be strongly influenced by that religion.

Engels (Marx and Engels, 1957), unlike Marx, did realize that in some circumstances religion could be a force for change. He argued that groups which turned to religion as a way of coping with oppression could develop into political movements which sought change on earth rather than salvation in heaven. Some contemporary neo-Marxists have followed Engels and developed this view (see p. 401 for further details).

Conservative or radical religion?

Like Nelson, Merideth B. McGuire (1981) acknowledges that religion can be a force for change. However, she develops the analysis further than Nelson by examining the factors that determine whether religion acts as a radical force or not. She identifies four main factors:

1 The **beliefs** of the particular religion. Religions that emphasize adherence to strong moral codes are more likely to produce members who are critical of society and who seek to change it. If a religion stresses concern with this world, it is more likely to result in actions by its members which produce change than a religion which confines itself to a concern with sacred and spiritual matters. Thus Protestantism can have more impact on social change than Buddhism.
2 The **culture** of the society in which a religion exists. In societies where religious beliefs are central to the culture (such as in Latin America), anyone wishing to produce change tends to use a religious legitimation for their actions. In Britain, however, religion plays a less central role in societal culture, so it tends to play a less important role in justifying changes in society.
3 What McGuire describes as the **social location** of religion is the third important factor. This concerns the part that religion plays in the social structure. Again, the greater the importance of religion, the greater its potential to play a part in producing change. Where an established church or other religious organization plays a major role in political and economic life, there is considerable scope for religion having an impact on processes of change.
4 The **internal organization** of religious institutions. According to McGuire, religions with a strong, centralized source of authority have more chance of affecting events. On the other hand, the central authority might try to restrain the actions of parts of the organization. For example, in 1978 at the Puebla Conference in Mexico, the Pope clashed with Latin American Roman Catholic bishops who were advocating liberation theology.

McGuire provides only a sketchy outline of the factors determining whether religion acts as a conservative force maintaining the status quo or as a force for change. Nevertheless she does provide a starting point for analysing the relationship between religion and social change. (For a discussion of the related issue of whether religion causes conflict, see pp. 448–51.)

In the next section we will examine different types of religious organization and the wide variety of ideologies that have been supported by different organizations. We will also discover that conservative and radical ideologies tend to be associated with different types of religious organization.

Religious organizations

Individuals may have their own religious beliefs without belonging to any particular organization: they may form their own personal and unique relationship with a god or some source of spiritual power. However, many members of society express their religious beliefs through organizations, and the organizations tend to shape those beliefs. Social factors influence the types of organization that are created, who joins them and how they develop. At the same time, religious organizations may themselves influence society.

Before we examine these issues, it is necessary for us to distinguish between the different types of religious organization. There have been a number of attempts to categorize them, but no system fits perfectly the enormous variety of organizations that have existed throughout the world. Nevertheless, it is possible broadly to distinguish some main types of religious organization.

The church

Ernst Troeltsch in 1931 was one of the first writers to try to distinguish different types of religious organization. Troeltsch used the term **church** to refer to a large religious organization. Individuals do not have to demonstrate their faith to become members of a church – indeed, often they are born into it. In some churches the practice of baptism ensures that all the children of members are automatically recruited before they are old enough to understand the faith.

In principle a church might try to be **universal** – to embrace all members of society – but in practice there might be substantial minorities who do not belong. Because of its size, members of a church are drawn from all classes in society, but the upper classes are particularly likely to join. This is because, in Troeltsch's words, a church usually 'stabilizes and determines the political order' (Troeltsch, 1981).

Churches are sometimes closely related to the state. For example, the Roman Catholic Church in the Middle Ages had important political, educational and social functions. Even in contemporary Britain the queen is both head of the Church of England and head of state.

Churches are likely to be ideologically conservative and support the status quo. This type of organization accepts and affirms life in this world: members can play a full part in social life and are not expected to withdraw from society.

In many circumstances a church will jealously guard its monopoly on religious truth, and will not tolerate challenges to its religious authority. For example, the Roman Catholic Church at one time used the Inquisition to stamp out heresy – opinions that differed from the established beliefs of the church. Churches are formal organizations with a hierarchy of professional, paid officials.

The above definition of a church is reflected in a typology of religious organizations developed by Roy Wallis (1976). Wallis distinguished organizations in terms of whether they were **respectable** because they supported the norms and values of the wider society, or **deviant** because they did not. They were also distinguished according to whether they were **uniquely legitimate** (they claimed a monopoly on religious truth), or **pluralistically legitimate** (they accepted that other organizations could have legitimate religious beliefs as well). As Figure 7.1 shows, Wallis regarded churches as respectable and uniquely legitimate institutions.

Figure 7.1 A typology of religious organizations

	Respectable	Deviant
Uniquely legitimate	CHURCH	SECT
Pluralistically legitimate	DENOMINATION	CULT

Source: Source: R. Wallis, *The Road to Total Freedom: A Sociological Analysis of Scientology*, Heinemann, London, 1976, p. 13.

However, Steve Bruce (1996) argues that this sort of definition of a church is primarily useful in describing premodern Christian societies. He says, 'The notion of the church derives its force from the growth of Christianity and the historic forms of Catholic, Orthodox, and Coptic churches. These bodies sought to be coextensive with their societies.' However, in 1517, Martin Luther, a German priest, began to question some of the teachings and practices of the medieval church. This led to the Reformation, in which competing religious views developed, including the Protestant Church of England established by Henry VIII. A plurality of sects with competing doctrines also developed.

To Bruce, the development of religious pluralism in societies undermines the maintenance of the church type of religious organization. He says, 'when a population becomes divided between a number of organizations, that fragmentation undermines the conditions for the church form' (Bruce, 1995). This is because it becomes more difficult for the state to lend exclusive support to one religion, and because a single set of religious beliefs is no longer taken for granted and reinforced by all groups in society. Thus, for Bruce, churches, in the sense meant by Troeltsch, are essentially historical phenomena which cannot continue to exist in modern societies. Indeed, Bruce sees the Church of England as a denomination rather than a church.

A number of examples can illustrate Bruce's point. A variety of organizations, which call themselves churches or which could be seen as churches, do not conform to the characteristics outlined by Troeltsch:

1. The percentage of the population who are active members of a church can vary widely. For example, according to the 2005 English Church Census (Brierley, 2006a), in England in 2005 only 870,000 people attended Anglican churches (most were in the Church of England) and 893,100 attended Roman Catholic churches.
2. Many churches today do not claim a monopoly on religious truth – other religions are tolerated. In England there is a growing diversity of religious groupings which are tolerated by the Church of England.
3. Churches are not always ideologically conservative and they do not always support the dominant groups in a society. Davie (1989) claims there is a growing gap within the Church of England between lay members, who tend to be conservative, and senior officials such as bishops, who tend to be more radical.
4. In some circumstances churches are not connected to the state, and may even act as a focus of opposition to it. Before the overthrow of communism in Poland the Roman Catholic Church opposed the communist government, and in many parts of Latin America liberation theology has also led to conflict between the Catholic Church and the state.

In some contemporary societies churches continue to retain some of their traditional characteristics. Churches in industrial societies tend to be larger and more conservative than other religious groups. Some industrialized societies have retained fairly strong churches which continue to conform to most of the characteristics outlined by Troeltsch.

Describing the Roman Catholic Church, Roy Wallis and Steve Bruce (1986) claim: 'In those places where it is dominant, e.g. Spain, Portugal and the Republic of Ireland, it acts as a universal church, claiming authority over the society as a whole.' However, even in these countries, the power and influence of the Catholic Church may be declining. For example, in 2005 same-sex marriages became legal in Spain, a measure strongly opposed by the Catholic Church.

In many other countries the Roman Catholic Church is even less dominant and has to coexist peacefully with a plurality of other religions, making no special claims on the state. Similarly, in Iran there is close identification between Islam and the state, but this is not the case in Muslim countries such as Turkey and Egypt.

Denominations

Troeltsch's original categorization of religious organizations included only churches and sects. It did not include 'denominations'. As Troeltsch based his work on an analysis of religion in sixteenth-century Europe, his classification was not capable of describing the variety of religions in the USA, or for that matter in modern Britain.

According to Stark and Bainbridge (1985), the term **denomination** is usually used to refer to an organization that shares several but not all of the supposed features of a church. It is often seen as a kind of watered-down church which has some similarities to a sect (we will discuss sects in the next section). In 2005, there were 227 different Christian denominations in England (Brierley, 2006a).

In a study of religion in the USA, H.R. Niebuhr (1929) was the first sociologist to differentiate clearly between denominations and churches. A denomination has been seen as having the following features:

1. Unlike a church, a denomination does not have a universal appeal in society. For example, the 2005 English Church Census found 289,400 attending Methodist churches, 287,600 attending Pentecostal churches and 254,800 attending Baptist churches (Brierley, 2006a).
2. Like churches, denominations draw members from all strata in society, but unlike churches they are not usually so closely identified with the upper classes. Often a considerable number of denominations exist within a particular society. In the USA there is no established church, but a large range of denominations.

3 Unlike a church, a denomination does not identify with the state and approves the separation of church and state.
4 Denominations do not claim a monopoly on religious truth. They are prepared to tolerate and cooperate with other religious organizations. This is reflected in Roy Wallis's definition of a denomination as a religious organization which is respectable but also pluralistically legitimate (see Table 7.1 and discussion on pp. 411–12).
5 Denominations are usually conservative: members generally accept the norms and values of society, although they may have marginally different values from those of the wider society. Some denominations place minor restrictions on their members. For instance, Methodists are discouraged from drinking and gambling, but drinking in moderation is tolerated, and drinkers are not excluded from the denomination.
6 In other respects, denominations have the same characteristics as churches: new members are freely admitted and they have a hierarchy of paid officials.

Steve Bruce sees the lack of a claim to a monopoly on religious truth as the defining feature of denominations. Furthermore, he sees them as increasingly important:

> *The last two hundred years has seen gradual evolution of churches and sects into denominations. The church form has been made untenable by the gradual increase in cultural pluralism and by the unwillingness of the state to continue to force reluctant people into the state church.*
> Bruce, 1995

However, the blurring of boundaries between religious organizations as they change has made the concept of the denomination no less problematic than the concept of the church. It covers a wide range of organizations, from Jehovah's Witnesses to Methodists, from Pentecostalists to Baptists. Some organizations are classified as sects by some sociologists but as denominations by others.

Alan Aldridge (2000) argues that in some contexts a religious organization might be seen as a respectable denomination, while in other contexts it is seen as less acceptable and therefore more like a sect. For example, the Church of the Latter Day Saints (or Mormons) is seen as respectable and more like a denomination in the USA, but in Britain it is sometimes seen as deviant and therefore more like a sect.

Sects

According to Troeltsch (1981), **sects** have characteristics that are almost diametrically opposed to those of churches:

1 They are both smaller and more strongly integrated than other religious organizations.
2 Rather than drawing members from all sections of society and being closely connected to the state, Troeltsch claimed that sects are 'connected with the lower classes, or at least with those elements in Society which are opposed to the State and Society'.
3 Far from being conservative and accepting the norms and values of society, sects are 'in opposition to the world'. They reject the values of the world that surrounds them, and their detachment may be 'expressed in the refusal to use the law, to swear in a court of justice, to own property, to exercise dominion over others, or to take part in war'.
4 Sect members may be expected to withdraw from life outside the sect, but at the same time they may wish ultimately to see changes take place in the wider society.
5 Members of a sect are expected to be deeply committed to its beliefs. They may be excluded from the sect if they fail to demonstrate such a commitment.
6 Young children cannot usually enter the sect by being baptized if they are not old enough to understand the significance of the ceremony. They must join voluntarily as adults, and willingly adopt the lifestyle and beliefs of the sect. In particular, they must sacrifice 'worldly pleasures' in order to devote themselves to their religious life. In this sense, sects exercise a stronger control over individuals' lives than, for example, the modern Church of England. Sects share this characteristic with religions such as Islam in countries where religious beliefs still have a strong hold over social life.
7 Like the Roman Catholic Church in Europe in the Middle Ages, sects tend to believe they possess a monopoly on religious truth.
8 Unlike churches, sects are not organized through a hierarchy of paid officials. If central authority exists within a sect, it usually rests with a single **charismatic leader**, whose personality and perceived special qualities persuade the followers to adhere to his or her teachings.

More simply, Roy Wallis (1976) defined sects as **deviant groups** which see themselves as **uniquely legitimate**. They deviate from society's norms or values in a significant way and, like churches, do not accept the right of other religions to claim any authority for their beliefs (see Table 7.1, p. 411).

Sects were originally groups which broke away from the dominant religion in a society because of a disagreement over the interpretation of the religion. Steve Bruce describes the process of sect formation in the following way:

> *From time to time the church would face dissent or revolt. People would protest against ecclesiastical pomp and wealth or would seek to live out a more radical form of the faith. Those who could not be contained within the church – for example, as a religious order – broke away to form 'sects'. As they often challenged the state as much as the church, they were met with repression. For this, if for no other reason, sects were normally small.* Bruce, 1995

To Bruce (1996), the original sects were a product of the 'upheavals of the reformation' but, as noted above, some of them developed to become denominations which were tolerated as religious diversity became more accepted. However, Bruce also acknowledges that sects can prosper in modern societies, where people have more opportunity to form their own subcultures. Even with the greater toleration of contemporary societies, though, some sects may come into serious conflict with the wider society and its values.

One example was the People's Temple, an American sect of the 1970s. When this sect came to an end it had just 900 members. It was founded in California by the Reverend Jim Jones and, although it recruited a considerable number of relatively affluent whites, it had a particular appeal to black ghetto dwellers of northern California.

The sect had a radical ideology: it claimed to be based upon a Marxist philosophy and it strongly opposed prejudice and discrimination. Sect members gradually withdrew from the outside world and they were strictly controlled by their charismatic leader.

Jim Jones moved the sect to the rainforests of Guyana and set up a commune at 'Jonestown'. In 1978 the entire membership died after taking cyanide. Some committed suicide on the orders of their leader; others were murdered by being tricked into taking the poison.

In the 1990s there were a number of religious movements in which deaths of some of the followers occurred in violent circumstances. Perhaps the best-known example was the Branch Davidians. Founded by their charismatic leader, David Koresh, they established a commune at Waco in Texas. Koresh demanded absolute loyalty from members. In February 1993 the Bureau of Alcohol, Tobacco and Firearms attempted to search their premises, only to be met by gunfire. Four ATF agents were killed and sixteen were wounded. After a lengthy siege the FBI attempted to arrest those inside using armoured vehicles. A fire started, resulting in the deaths of more than eighty Branch Davidians, including twenty-two children. A subsequent investigation found that sect members had started the fire themselves, although survivors insist this was not the case.

Although the People's Temple and the Branch Davidians are extreme examples of sects, many other religious organizations display similar characteristics. However, there are also numerous exceptions. It is possible to find sects of vastly different sizes, with a wide variety of ideologies, contrasting attitudes to the outside world, varying degrees of control over their membership, and with or without a professional clergy and a charismatic leader.

Bryan Wilson (1982) accepts that Troeltsch's description of sects may have been accurate in relation to European countries, until quite recently. However, it does not account for or adequately describe the proliferation of sectarian groups in Europe and the USA in recent decades. Some of the **new religious movements**, which come close to Troeltsch's description of sects, will be examined shortly.

Cults

According to Bruce (1995), Troeltsch mentioned 'mysticism' as another tradition within Christianity in addition to the church and sect. Bruce describes it in this way: 'Unlike the other forms, this was a highly individualistic expression, varying with personal experiences and interpretations.' To Bruce, this corresponds to the idea of a **cult**, which he sees as a 'loosely knit group organized around some common themes and interests but lacking any sharply defined and exclusive belief system'.

A cult tends to be more individualistic than other organized forms of religion because it lacks a fixed doctrine. Cults tolerate other beliefs and indeed their own beliefs are often so vague that they have no conception of heresy. Cults often have customers rather than members and these customers may have relatively little involvement with any organization once they have learnt the rudiments of the beliefs around which the cult is based.

This rather general description corresponds fairly closely to one type of new religious movement identified by Wallis (1984): the World-Affirming Movement (see p. 415). Wallis himself defined cults as deviant religious organizations which do not claim to have a monopoly on the truth (they are pluralistically legitimate – see Table 7.1, p. 411).

A competing definition of cults is offered by Stark and Bainbridge (1985) who define them in terms of their novelty in a particular society (see p. 416). Furthermore, there is overlap between the New Age movement and cults since some aspects of the New Age movement are based around cults (see below, pp. 420–3).

There is therefore no single definition of cults which is accepted by all sociologists. Nevertheless there have been a number of useful attempts to classify smaller religious groupings. Some of these will now be examined and in the process competing definitions of cults will be discussed further.

New religious movements, sects and cults

Roy Wallis – The Elementary Forms of the New Religious Life

The development of a range of new religions and the revival of some old ones, in the 1970s, led Roy Wallis to categorize these **new religious movements** (Wallis, 1984). He was not aiming to provide a classification which would apply to all places at all times, but just to understand developments in Britain in the mid- to late twentieth century. Nevertheless his typology has proved influential and has been applied in other contexts. His views are illustrated in Figure 7.2.

Wallis divides new religious movements into three main groups. Like Troeltsch, the principal criterion he uses to categorize religious organizations is their relationship to the outside world. He therefore distinguishes between them according to whether the movement and its members **reject**, **accommodate** or **affirm** the world. He represents his typology with a triangle, and notes the existence of some groups (those in the central box) which do not fit neatly into any single category.

World-rejecting new religious movements

The **world-rejecting new religious movements** have most of the characteristics of a sect described by Troeltsch:

1. They are usually clearly religious organizations with a definite conception of God. For example, members of the Unification Church, better known as the 'Moonies' – after their leader, the Reverend Sun Myung Moon – pray in a conventional way to a 'Heavenly Father'.
2. In other respects, though, such groups are far from conventional. Their ideology is invariably highly

Figure 7.2 Types of new religious movement

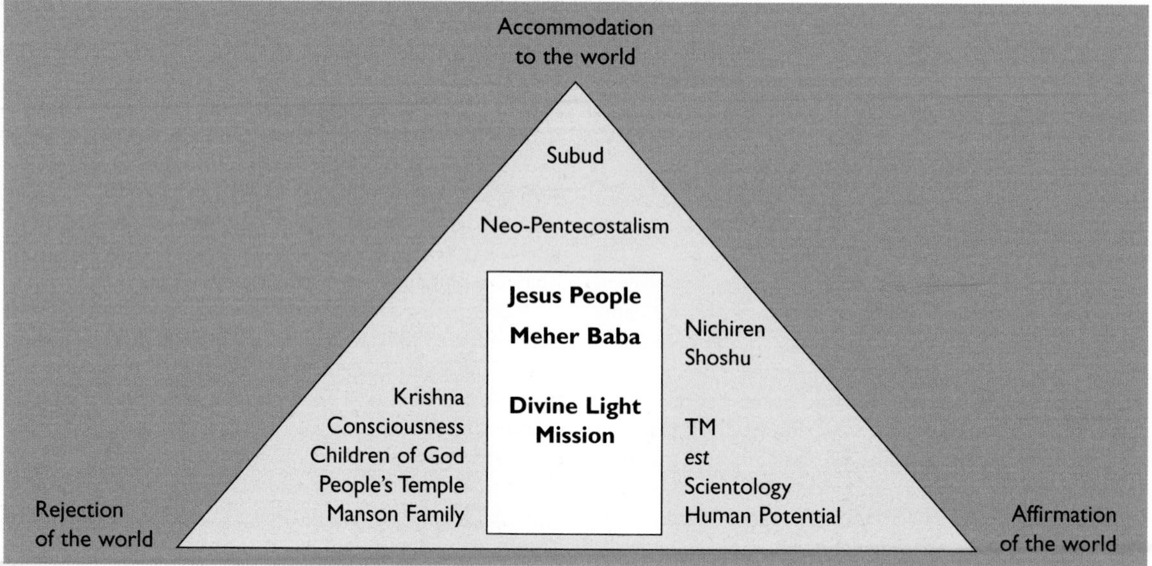

Source: R. Wallis, *The Elementary Forms of the New Religious Life*, Routledge & Kegan Paul, London, 1984.

critical of the outside world, and the movement expects or actively seeks change.

3 In order to achieve salvation, members are expected to make a sharp break from their conventional life when they join the movement. Organizations of this type act as **total institutions**, controlling every aspect of their members' lives (a concept developed by Erving Goffman). As a result, they often develop a reputation for 'brainwashing' their members, since families and friends find it hard to understand the change that has taken place in a member.
4 Limited contact with the outside world may be allowed, to facilitate fundraising. Moonies in San Francisco help to support the group by selling flowers.
5 The leadership of the group may be quite prepared to have contact with the outside world in an attempt to try to change society without waiting for divine intervention. For example, Jim Jones, leader of the ill-fated People's Temple, had close contacts with Californian politicians.
6 Although they are usually radical, there can be conservative elements in the beliefs and actions of such organizations. The Unification Church is strongly anti-communist, and has supported South Korean military dictatorships. Many of the movements are morally puritanical, forbidding sex outside marriage, for example. The Moonies are particularly strict about restricting sex to monogamous marriage.
7 World-rejecting new religious movements vary enormously in size: the Moonies have an international following – in 1995 they claimed 926,000 members (Brierley, 2001) – while other groups are small and locally based.
8 Most of these movements tend to be based around some form of communal lifestyle, and as such develop unconventional ways of living. The commune of the Branch Davidians in Waco, Texas is a case in point.

Thus, despite the variations within these groups, none of them are content with the world as it is.

Wallis sees most world-rejecting new religious movements as sects. He defines sects as groups that claim to be uniquely legitimate and which advocate religious doctrines that are widely regarded as deviant. They have 'an authoritative locus for the attribution of heresy' and are hostile to the state and non-members.

World-accommodating new religious movements

The **world-accommodating new religious movements** are usually offshoots of an existing major church or denomination. For example, neo-Pentecostalist groups are variants of Protestant or Roman Catholic religions, while Subud is a world-accommodating Muslim group.

Typically, these groups neither accept nor reject the world as it is; they simply live within it. They are primarily concerned with religious rather than worldly questions. As Wallis puts it:

> *The world-accommodating new religion draws a distinction between the spiritual and the worldly in a way quite uncharacteristic of the other two types. Religion is not constructed as a primarily social matter; rather, it provides solace or stimulation to personal interior life.* Wallis, 1984

The religious beliefs of followers might help them to cope with their non-religious social roles, but the aim of the religion is not to create a new society, nor to improve the believers' chances of success in their lives. Instead, world-accommodating groups seek to restore the spiritual purity to a religion, which they believe has been lost in more conventional churches and denominations. Pentecostalists hold that the belief in the Holy Spirit has been lost in other Christian religions. The Holy Spirit speaks through Pentecostalists, giving them the gift of 'speaking in tongues'. Most of the members of world-accommodating groups live conventional and conforming lives outside their religious activities.

World-affirming new religious movements

The **world-affirming new religious movements** are very different from all other religious groups, and may indeed lack some of the features normally thought to be central to a religion. Wallis (1984) says such a group 'may have no "church", no collective ritual of worship, it may lack any developed theology or ethics'. However, these groups do claim to be able to provide access to spiritual or supernatural powers, and in that sense can be regarded as religions.

Rather than rejecting existing society or existing religions, world-affirming groups accept the world as it is and they are not particularly critical of other religions. What they offer the follower is the potential to be successful in terms of the dominant values of society by unlocking spiritual powers present in the individual. Salvation is seen as a personal achievement and as a solution to personal problems such as unhappiness, suffering or disability. Individuals usually overcome such problems by adopting some technique that heightens their awareness or abilities.

World-affirming movements are not exclusive groups: they seek as wide a membership as possible. Rather than trying to convert people as such, they try to sell them a service commercially. Followers carry on their normal lives except when undergoing training; often, courses are held at weekends or at other convenient times so as not to cause disruption. There is little social control over the members, or customers, and they are not normally excluded from the group if they fail to act in accordance with its beliefs.

An example of a world-affirming new religious movement is provided by Transcendental Meditation (TM). TM is based upon the Hindu religion, but during at least some periods of its development the religious elements have been played down. First introduced to the West in the late 1950s, it achieved prominence in 1968 when the Beatles met its leading proponent, the Maharishi Mahesh Yogi.

TM involves a meditational technique whereby a follower is given a personal mantra on which to concentrate for twenty minutes in the morning and evening. It is claimed that this technique can provide 'unbounded awareness', which can have beneficial effects for individuals and for society. Initiation is a simple matter and can take place in just a couple of hours, with further follow-up sessions lasting just a few hours more. However, some followers go on to take an advanced course in the powers of TM, the Siddi programme, which claims to provide occult powers, such as the ability to levitate. Some go on to form an inner core of more dedicated followers whose dedication can come to resemble that of members of world-rejecting movements.

To Wallis, most world-affirming new religious movements are cults. Cults are like sects in that they have religious beliefs that are widely regarded as deviant, but, unlike sects, cults tolerate the existence of other religions. Cults are 'loosely structured, tolerant, and non-exclusive'. They have a rapid turnover in membership and are relatively undemanding on their followers.

The 'middle ground'

Wallis realized that no religious group will conform exactly to the categories he outlines. He says, 'all actual new religious movements are likely to combine elements of each type to some extent' (Wallis, 1984). Indeed, he points to a number of groups that occupy an intermediate position, such as the Healthy Happy Holy Organization (3HO) and the Divine Light Mission. Comparing them to the three main groups, he says: 'They combine in various degrees all three types, and more particularly elements of the conventional society and the counter-culture.'

3HO, for example, is similar to world-accommodating new religious movements in that it is an offshoot of an established religion, in this case Sikhism. Like world-affirming movements, it employs techniques that it is claimed will bring personal benefits, such as happiness and good health. In common with TM, 3HO hopes its teachings will have spin-offs for the outside world: in fact, nothing less than world unity. 3HO is not exclusive. Classes are provided for those who are not full members, so that they can receive benefits from the teachings. Even fully committed members are expected to have conventional marriages and to hold down conventional jobs.

On the other hand, 3HO does have some characteristics in common with world-rejecting movements. The organization has a clear concept of God. Members dress unconventionally in white clothing and turbans. They live in communes or ashrams, but the ashrams do not involve total sharing: individuals pay for their own room and board. Some restrictions are placed on behaviour: members of 3HO are vegetarians and abstain from alcohol, tobacco and mind-altering drugs.

Occupying as it does the **middle ground**, 3HO allows its followers to combine elements of an alternative lifestyle with conventional marriage and employment.

Roy Wallis – an evaluation

James A. Beckford (1985) commends Wallis's scheme for recognizing that new religious movements do not always fit neatly into one category or another, and for outlining the differences in the types of individuals recruited by different types of movement (we outline Wallis's views on recruitment on p. 418). However, Beckford also offers some criticisms of Wallis:

1. He argues that Wallis's categories are difficult to apply. It is not made clear whether the teachings of the movement or the beliefs and outlooks of the individual members distinguish the different orientations to the world.
2. Beckford thinks that Wallis pays insufficient attention to the diversity of views that often exists within a sect or cult.

Nevertheless, Beckford does not deny that a **typology**, or list of types, of new religious movements is useful. In contrast, Stark and Bainbridge, whose views we examine next, reject the idea of using a typology to distinguish new religions.

Rodney Stark and William Sims Bainbridge – un-ideal types

The problems of typologies

According to Stark and Bainbridge (1985), none of the typologies of new religious movements, sects, churches and denominations developed by other sociologists are a sound basis for categorization. All of them consist of lists of characteristics that each type is likely to have. However, these characteristics are not found in every religious organization placed in each category. Not all churches try to convert all members of society and not all sects are exclusive.

Such characteristics used to distinguish organizations are **correlates**: sets of characteristics that tend to be found together in the same organizations. They are not, however, **attributes**: characteristics that an organization must have if it is to be defined as a church, denomination, sect or cult. Defining types of organization in terms of correlates tends to lead to confusion, since most organizations are in some way exceptions to the rule.

Stark and Bainbridge therefore argue that typologies of religious organization should be abandoned altogether. They claim that religious groups can be compared in terms of a single criterion: the degree of conflict that exists between them and the wider society. The use of such a definition allows clear comparisons. For example, the Catholic Church in the USA is nearer to the sect end of the continuum than the Catholic Church in the Republic of Ireland. Such a definition also allows changes over time to be clearly described: organizations might change and become more, or less, in tension with the social environment.

Sects and cults

Stark and Bainbridge then go on to argue that there are different kinds (they are careful to avoid using the word 'types') of religious movement in a high degree of tension with their social environment:

1. **Sects** are groups that are formed as an offshoot of an existing religion as a result of division or schism within that religion.
2. **Cults**, on the other hand, are new religions, or at least they are new in a particular society. Some result from cultural importation, where a religion from other societies is introduced into a society in which it had not previously been practised. Thus, Eastern religions introduced into the USA are examples of imported cults. Some cults, though, are entirely new. These result from cultural innovation; they are unconnected to existing religions.

Stark and Bainbridge go on to suggest that cults exhibit different degrees of organization and can be divided into three types:

1. **Audience cults** are the least organized and involve little face-to-face interaction. Contacts are often maintained through the mass media and the occasional conference. Many of the members of the audience for such cults may not know each other. Astrology is an example of an audience cult, as is the belief in UFOs.
2. **Client cults** are more organized and usually offer services to their followers. In the past they tended to offer 'medical miracles, forecasts of the future, or contact with the dead', though more recently they have 'specialized in personal adjustment'. Scientology, for example, offers its clients the opportunity to clear 'engrams' (repressed memories of painful experiences) from the brain, while the Reich Foundation offers the promise of the 'monumental orgasm'.
3. **Cult movements** involve followers much more. They try to satisfy all the religious needs of their members and, unlike client and audience cults, membership of other faiths is not permitted. They do, however, vary considerably in their power. Some require little more than occasional attendance at meetings and acceptance of the cult's beliefs, but others shape the whole of a person's life. The Reverend Sun Myung Moon's Unification Church is an example of a cult movement. Many client cults become cult movements for their most dedicated followers – for example, practitioners of TM who take the Siddi programme (see p. 415 for a short description of TM).

A well-publicized example that would probably fit Stark and Bainbridge's definition of a cult movement was the Heaven's Gate cult. This was a doomsday cult with an interest in computer technology and science fiction. It started in the mid-1970s and required members to refrain from sex, drugs and alcohol. The leader, Marshall Applewhite, who liked to be addressed as 'Do' or 'The Representative', even had himself castrated so that he did not become distracted by physical pleasures. The group believed the earth was about to be recycled to become a garden for some future generation. The leader told his followers they needed to leave their earthly bodies so as to get closer to heaven. When the comet Hale-Bopp passed close to earth in 1997, the cult members committed suicide, believing that their spirits would ascend to a spacecraft which was following close behind the comet.

Conclusion

Stark and Bainbridge offer a different – and they would claim, superior – method of distinguishing religious organizations from that of Wallis. They make some useful distinctions between different types of cult; however, in doing so, they contradict themselves. They develop their own typology and fail to notice that some groups will not conform to all the characteristics they attribute to audience cults, client cults or cult movements.

Reasons for the growth of sects, cults and new religious movements

Religious sects and cults are not a new phenomenon: they have existed for centuries. Bruce (1995) traces the emergence of the first sects to the Reformation of the church in the sixteenth century and the upheavals that accompanied it. Despite this, most existing sects and cults originated in the twentieth century, and the 1960s in particular saw the appearance of many new organizations.

Membership has grown steadily in both Britain and the USA. According to *Religious Trends 3* and *5* (Brierley, 2001, 2005), there were 14,350 members of new religious movements in Britain in 1995. By 2000 this had grown to 29,503 and by 2005 to 37,412. In 2005 there were 829 individual groups that were members of new religious movements (an increase from 775 groups in 2000). However, these figures did not include a number of important non-trinitarian groups (those not believing in the trinity of 'Father, Son and Holy Spirit'), which are often seen as new religious movements by sociologists. When these groups are added in there were 547,178 members of new religious movements and non-trinitarian religions in 2005, up from 539,968 in 2000 (Brierley, 2005).

Between 1995 and 2005 the number of Scientologists grew from 121,800 to 165,000; and the number of Moonies from 390 to 1,200; though the number of Spiritualists fell from 40,000 to 30,000. It should be borne in mind that these figures are produced in different ways and many are estimates. For example, Scientology 'membership' is an estimate of those who have completed a Scientology course.

The growth of sects and cults can be explained either in terms of why particular individuals choose to join, or in terms of wider social changes. In reality these reasons are closely linked, since social changes affect the number of people available as potential recruits.

Marginality

Max Weber (1963, first published 1922) provided one of the earliest explanations for the growth of sects. He argued they were likely to arise within groups that were **marginal** in society: members of groups outside the mainstream of social life often feel they are not receiving the prestige and/or economic rewards they deserve. One solution to this problem is a sect based on what Weber called 'a theodicy of disprivilege' (a **theodicy** is a religious explanation and justification). Such sects contain an explanation for the disprivilege of their members and promise them a 'sense of honour', either in the afterlife or in a future 'new world' on earth.

Bryan Wilson (1970) pointed out that a variety of situations could lead to the marginalization of groups in society, which in turn could provide fertile ground for the development of sects. These situations include defeat in war, natural disaster or economic collapse. Radical and undesirable changes such as these are not the only circumstances that can encourage sect development.

In part, the growth of sects in the USA in the 1960s was accomplished through the recruitment of marginal and disadvantaged groups. The Black Muslims, for example, aimed to recruit 'the negro in the mud', and the sect seemed to offer hope for some of the most desperate blacks.

However, for the most part, in the 1960s and 1970s the membership of the world-rejecting new religious movements was drawn from among the ranks of young, white, middle-class Americans and Europeans. Wallis (1984) does not believe that this contradicts the theory that marginal members of society join world-rejecting sects. He argues that many of the recruits had already become marginal to society. Despite their middle-class backgrounds, they were usually 'hippies, drop-outs, surfers, LSD and marijuana users'. Their marginality may have been further increased by arrests for drug use or activities involved with radical politics. They were attracted to the communal lifestyle which the sect offered.

Relative deprivation

However, this does not explain why quite affluent middle-class youth should become marginal members of society in the first place. The concept of 'relative deprivation' can be used to explain their actions. **Relative deprivation** refers to subjectively perceived deprivation: that which people actually feel. In objective terms the poor are more deprived than the middle class, but in subjective terms certain members of the middle class may feel more deprived than the poor. They do not lack material wealth, but feel spiritually deprived in a world they see as too materialistic, lonely and impersonal. According to Wallis (1984), they therefore seek salvation in the sense of community offered by the sect.

Stark and Bainbridge (1985) also employ the concept of relative deprivation in explaining the origin of sects. They define sects as organizations which break away from an established church, and they believe it is the relatively deprived who are likely to break away. Splits take place when churches begin to compromise their beliefs. When the more successful members of a religion try to reduce the amount of tension between that religion and the outside world, the less successful resent it and break away.

Social change

A number of sociologists, such as Bryan Wilson (1970), argue that sects arise during periods of rapid social change when traditional norms are disrupted, social relationships come to lack consistent and coherent meaning, and the traditional universe of meaning is undermined.

Wilson uses the example of the early Methodist movement, which had the characteristics of a sect. He sees the rise of Methodism as the response of the urban working class to the 'chaos and uncertainty of life in the newly settled industrial areas'. He claims they had to evolve 'new patterns of religious belief to accommodate themselves to their new situation'. In a situation of change and uncertainty, the sect offers the support of a close-knit community organization, well-defined and strongly sanctioned norms and values, and a promise of salvation. It provides a new and stable universe of meaning, which is legitimated by its religious beliefs.

More generally, Bruce (1995, 1996) attributes the development of a range of religious institutions, including sects and cults, to a general process of **modernization** and **secularization**. He believes that the weakness of more conventional institutionalized religions has encouraged some people to consider less traditional alternatives. In the Middle Ages the church form of organization was dominant. With the Reformation, splits within the church led to the creation of the new sects.

As modern societies developed and faith in traditional sources of authority (such as churches) declined, religious pluralism and diversity were increasingly tolerated. The denomination became the characteristic form of religion – a watered-down version of the intolerant beliefs of churches and sects which believed that only they knew the truth.

More recently, in what Bruce believes is a more secular world in which people are less likely to hold strong commitments, cults have become more popular. These require fewer sacrifices and less commitment than churches and sects and are therefore more tolerable to a modern clientele. However, a small number of people are willing to join the stricter sects. Bruce's views on specific types of new religious movement will be examined below.

The growth of new religious movements

Wallis (1984) pointed to a number of social changes which he believed accounted for the growth of new religious movements in the 1960s. Some of these had important effects on youth in particular:

1. The growth of higher education and the gradual lengthening of time spent in education created an extended period of transition between childhood and adulthood. Youth culture developed because there was an increasing number of young people who had considerable freedom but little in the way of family or work responsibilities.
2. At the same time there was a belief that developing technology would herald the end of poverty and economic scarcity.
3. Radical political movements were also growing in the 1960s, providing an alternative to dominant social norms and values.

Wallis claimed that in these circumstances world-rejecting new religious movements were attractive because of the potential they seemed to offer for 'a more idealistic, spiritual and caring way of life, in the context of more personal and loving social relationships'.

Bruce (1995) sees world-rejecting movements as having a particular appeal to the young. Many had become disillusioned by the failure of the counter-culture in the 1960s to radically change the world. The hippie culture and the commune movement had disintegrated largely because of drugs and exploitation of the movement. The disillusioned young people sought another path to salvation through religion rather than peace and love.

Wallis (1984) provided only a very sketchy explanation of recruitment to world-accommodating religious movements. He claimed that those with a substantial stake in society, but who nevertheless have reasons for being dissatisfied with existing religions, tend to join them. Research suggests that groups such as Erhard's Seminar Training have members with above-average incomes and education who are somewhat older than members of world-rejecting groups. To Wallis, what they offer is a 'means of coping with a sense of inadequacy among social groups which are, by the more obvious indicators, among the world's more successful and highly rewarded individuals'. It is primarily the emphasis placed upon individual success in terms of status, income and social mobility that stimulates these 'religions' to develop.

Actually achieving success may in another sense motivate individuals to join these groups. Individuals may feel that in the successful performance of their social roles (such as their jobs) they lose sight of their real selves. A world-affirming religious movement might allow the rediscovery of this real 'self'.

Bruce (1995, 1996) believes that world-affirming new religious movements are predominantly a response to the **rationalization** (see pp. 875–7) of the modern world. Because of rationalization, 'modern life is so fragmented that many people find it increasingly difficult to draw on their public roles for a satisfying and fulfilling sense of identity' (Bruce, 1995). Jobs, for example, are simply a means to an end, to earn a living, and offer little sense of satisfaction or fulfilment. People no longer have a sense of calling in their work and may not identify strongly with their workmates. People have, however, been encouraged to value achievement, yet many lack the opportunities to be as successful as they would like. World-affirming movements can offer a solution. They provide a technique which claims to be able to bring people both success and a spiritual element to their lives.

The explanations provided above offer some general reasons why world-affirming movements should be popular in advanced industrial societies, but they do not explain why particular individuals should join, nor why they are popular at particular periods of time. More specific theories have been devised to account for what Wallis calls 'movements of the middle ground'.

Several sociologists studying these movements have claimed that they help to reintegrate people into society, while allowing them to retain some elements of an alternative lifestyle. These movements appeal to those members of the counter-culture or world-rejecting religious movements who have become disillusioned, or feel they need to earn a living in a conventional way. They offer a stepping-stone back towards respectability. Thus, Mauss and Peterson describe the members of one such group, the Jesus Freaks, as 'penitent young prodigals' (quoted in Wallis, 1984).

These middle-ground groups were particularly successful from the mid-1970s onwards, when economic recession and the decline in the numbers of people willing to adopt alternative lifestyles provided a large pool from which members might be recruited.

The development of sects

Sects as short-lived organizations

In 1929, H.R. Niebuhr made a number of observations about the way in which religious sects changed over time. He argued that sects could not survive as sects beyond a single generation. Either they would change their characteristics, compromise and become denominations, or they would disappear altogether. He advanced the following arguments to support this view:

1. Sect membership was based upon voluntary adult commitment: members chose to dedicate themselves to the organization and its religion. Once the first generation started to have children, though, the children would be admitted as new members when they were too young to understand the teachings of the religion. These new members would not be able to sustain the fervour of the first generation. Consequently, the sect might become a denomination.

2 Sects that relied upon a charismatic leader would tend to disappear if the leader died. Alternatively, the nature of the leadership would change: no longer would the charisma of an individual hold the sect together. This would allow the bureaucratic structure of a denomination to emerge, with its hierarchy of paid officials.
3 Niebuhr argued that the ideology of many sects contained the seeds of their own destruction. Sects with an ascetic creed would encourage their members to work hard and save their money. As a result the membership would be upwardly socially mobile, and would no longer wish to belong to a religious group which catered for marginal members of society. Once again the sect would have to change or die: either becoming a denomination or losing its membership.

According to Niebuhr, then, there was no possibility of a sect surviving for a long period of time without losing its extreme teachings and rejection of society. One example that illustrates this well is that of the Methodists before they became a denomination: as the Methodist membership rose in status in the nineteenth century, the strict disciplines of the sect and its rejection of society were dropped, and it gradually came to be recognized as a denomination.

A number of sects have also disappeared because of the mass suicide (or murder) of their members. The examples of the People's Temple, the Branch Davidians and the Heaven's Gate group have been discussed above (see pp. 413 and 416).

The life cycle of sects

However, Bryan Wilson (1966) rejected Niebuhr's view that sects are inevitably short-lived. He pointed out that some sects do survive for a long time without becoming denominations. To Wilson, the crucial factor is the way the sect answers the question: 'What shall we do to be saved?' Sects can be classified in terms of how they answer this question. Only one type, the **conversionist sect**, is likely to develop into a denomination. Examples include the **evangelical sects**, typical of the USA, which aim to convert as many people as possible by means of revivalist preaching. Becoming a denomination does not necessarily compromise such a sect's position. It can still save souls.

The other types of sect cannot maintain their basic position in a denominational form. **Adventist sects**, such as the Seventh Day Adventists and Jehovah's Witnesses, provide an example of the reason why. Adventist sects await the Second Coming of Christ, who will judge humanity and establish a new world order. Only sect membership will guarantee a place in the new order. The rich and powerful and those who follow conventional religions will be excluded from Christ's kingdom on earth. Adventist sects are founded on the principle of separation from the world in the expectation of the Second Coming. To become a denomination they would have to change this basic premise. Separation from the world and denominationalism are not compatible.

Thus, Wilson concludes that a sect's prescription for salvation is a major factor in determining whether or not it becomes a denomination.

In more recent writing, Wilson (2003) again notes that many sects with a long history have survived (for example, the Amish, the Quakers, Jehovah's Witnesses, Mormons, Seventh Day Adventists and Pentecostalists). Wilson contradicts Niebuhr, arguing that many of these groups have successfully followed a policy of recruiting the children of sect members into the organization. The more successful have managed to keep the children somewhat isolated from secular influences in the outside world. Wilson believes that such sects will not disappear in the near future. Most have established efficient bureaucracies which provide continuity and the organizational basis for continued survival.

However, Wilson does believe that sects will face difficulties. Ever-improving educational standards and opportunities may lead to children questioning the fundamentalist beliefs held by some sects. Also, globalization makes it increasingly difficult for sects to isolate themselves from the outside world. However, globalization also offers new opportunities for sects to organize and recruit new members in disadvantaged, 'third world' countries. In poorer countries there is a greater pool of relatively or absolutely deprived potential recruits than there is in richer 'first world' countries. Most Seventh Day Adventists and Pentecostalists now come from 'third world' countries. This in itself poses problems for sects, which tend to develop splits (or schisms) between branches from richer and poorer countries. Thus Wilson predicts that sects will survive, but the branches in Western, 'first world' countries may decline as those in the 'third world' gain in strength.

Internal ideology and the wider society

Roy Wallis (1984) takes a more complex view of the paths followed by sects: he thinks the chances of sects surviving, changing or disappearing are affected both by the internal ideology of the sect and by external social circumstances.

World-rejecting sects often change their stance as time passes. Like Niebuhr, Wallis sees the possibility that such groups may soften their opposition to society and become more world-accommodating. This seems to have been particularly common in the 1970s, when economic recession discouraged some members from dropping-out and rejecting society altogether. The Children of God, for example, weakened their opposition to other religions and no longer thought of non-members as servants of Satan.

Wallis accepts that charismatic leaders have difficulty in retaining personal control over a religious movement indefinitely, and that this may also result in changes. If the organization grows, a process which Weber described as the **routinization of charisma** can take place. A more bureaucratic organization develops so that some of the leader's personal authority becomes vested in his (or untypically her) officials or representatives. Nevertheless, the changes may stop well short of denominationalization.

Wallis also recognizes that sects can disappear. World-rejecting sects may actually be destroyed by the charismatic leader, as in the case of Jim Jones's People's Temple. Social changes may lead to the members becoming less marginal in society, so threatening the basis on which the sect was founded. However, as new groups in society become marginal, new sects will arise.

According to Wallis, then, world-rejecting sects tend to be unstable, but new ones emerge, and those that survive may become more world-accommodating while continuing to exist as sects.

World-affirming movements often sell their services as a commodity, so they are vulnerable to a loss of support from their consumers. To the extent that they sell themselves in the market-place, they are subject to the same problems as a retailer. If the public no longer needs, or gains benefits from, their services, they will lose customers. To Wallis, though, world-affirming movements are more likely to change to attract a new clientele than to cease to exist. For example, in the 1970s, Transcendental Meditation (TM) tried to broaden its appeal by emphasizing the practical benefits – the worldly success – that the meditation claimed to offer.

Wallis believes that world-affirming movements are flexible and can change relatively easily as they seek to survive and prosper. In some circumstances they can also become more religious and spiritual (like world-rejecting movements) for at least an inner core of followers.

The position of the movements of the middle ground is by its very nature more precarious. Since they are in an intermediate position they are likely to shift between being world-rejecting and world-affirming, depending upon circumstances and the needs and wishes of the membership. This can lead to splits within the movement or the establishment of rival organizations. One British movement of this type, the Process, was founded in 1963 and split into two separate groups in 1973.

Wallis says little about how world-accommodating movements develop, but these seem the most stable of the new religious movements. Indeed, some are not particularly new: Pentecostalism has survived little-changed since the early years of the twentieth century. As Wallis points out, this type of 'new' religious movement has most in common with denominations.

Thus, although Wallis does not agree with Niebuhr that sects inevitably disappear or become denominations, his work does suggest there may be tendencies in these directions, particularly for world-rejecting movements.

The New Age

Examples of the New Age

The **New Age** is a term that has been applied to a range of ideas which started to become prominent in the 1980s. Although some of these beliefs were organized as new religious movements (particularly as world-affirming new religious movements) and as cults of various types (particularly client cults and audience cults), in many cases they were not closely attached to particular organizations (Heelas, 1996; Bruce 1995, 2001). Rather, New Age ideas were spread through aspects of the culture of particular societies in films, shops, seminars, meetings, music, television programmes, public lectures and so on.

In recent writing Paul Heelas *et al.* (2005) have termed this environment the **holistic milieu**. The holistic milieu contrasts with the **congregational domain** in which people attend places of collective worship on a regular basis, typically once a week. The holistic milieu is less visible than the congregational domain, but involves one-to-one encounters (for example, between a healer and a client) and small group activities (for example, yoga groups).

Examples of New Age beliefs include interest in clairvoyance, contacting aliens, belief in 'spirit guides' and 'spirit masters', various types of meditation and psychotherapy, belief in paganism, magic, tarot cards, ouija, astrology and witchcraft, an interest in self-healing and natural or traditional remedies for ill-health (for example, yoga, aromatherapy, reflexology), spiritually inclined ecology such as a belief in Gaia (the Greek goddess who has been used to represent the sacred and interconnected nature of all life), and so on.

Manifestations of the New Age can be found in gatherings such as the annual Mind, Body and Spirit Convention, which has been held in London since 1977; in publications on topics such as Feng Shui, mysticism and Shamanism; in shops that sell tapes of sounds from nature, which can be used for relaxation or meditation; in communes such as the Findhorn community in Scotland (which grew vegetables with the help of plant spirits rather than fertilizers); and in more conventionally organized groups such as the Scientologists and some Buddhist groups.

The themes of the New Age

What have such a diverse range of activities and beliefs got in common? Paul Heelas (1996) believes that the central feature of the New Age is a belief in **self-spirituality**. People with such beliefs have turned away from traditional religious organizations in their search for the spiritual and instead have begun to look inside themselves. The New Age 'explains why life – as conventionally experienced – is not what it should be; it provides an account of what it is to find perfection; and it provides the means for obtaining salvation'. However, that salvation does not come from being accepted by an external god; it comes from discovering and perfecting oneself. Often, this means going beyond one's conscious self to discover hidden spiritual depths. Heelas says:

> *Perfection can be found only by moving beyond the socialized self – widely known as the 'ego' but also as the 'lower self', 'intellect' or the 'mind' – thereby encountering a new realm of being. It is what we are by nature.* Heelas, 1996

In this process we find our spiritual core. New Agers tell people, 'You are Gods and Goddesses in exile', who only need to cast off the cloaks that hide this to uncover their true potential. There are many different ways (in the words of a Doors song) to 'break on through to the other side'. These include 'psychotherapies, physical labour, dance, shamanic practices, magic, or for that matter, fire-walking, sex, tennis, taking drugs or using virtual-reality equipment' (Heelas, 1996).

According to Heelas, the New Age values personal experience above 'truths' provided by scientists or conventional religious leaders. In this respect **detraditionalization** is a key feature of the New Age: it rejects the authority that comes from traditional sources and sees individuals and their sense of who they are as the only genuine source of truth or understanding. A good example of this attitude was a notice above the door of

Bhagwan Shree Rajneesh's ashram (commune) at Puna, which said: 'Leave your minds and shoes here'.

The New Age stresses that you can become responsible for your own actions, you do not need to be governed by preconceived ideas. It also emphasizes freedom to discover your own truth and discover your own way to the truth. Although many aspects of the New Age draw on traditional mystical and religious teachings, these are seen as ways of getting in touch with your own spirituality rather than as doctrines that must be rigidly followed. They allow the discovery of truth as an abstract concept, as an inner and spiritual phenomenon, rather than revealing a particular and specific version of the truth. According to Heelas, the movement believes 'the same wisdom can be found at the heart of all religious traditions'.

Variations within the New Age

Although Heelas detects many common themes in the New Age, as outlined above, he also discerns some variations in New Age beliefs. Following Roy Wallis's typology of new religious movements (see pp. 413–15), Heelas distinguishes between aspects of the New Age which tend towards the world-affirming and those which are more world-rejecting.

World-affirming aspects of the New Age stress how to experience the best of the **outer world**. For example, New Age teachings might help people to be successful in business. HarperCollins (the publishers of this book) in the 1990s ran company-wide courses following the New Age 'Values and Vision' training of Tishi. Transcendental Meditation now has its own University of Management in the Netherlands. There are numerous other examples and all claim to be able to help companies to become more profitable and individuals more successful.

World-rejecting aspects of New Age stress how to experience the best of the **inner world**: how to achieve inner spirituality and turn away from any concern with worldly success.

Most New Age beliefs, though, offer the **best of both worlds**, claiming that people can become both successful and spiritually fulfilled. Not surprisingly, then, the radicalism of different New Age beliefs differs considerably. While some almost celebrate capitalism, others are strongly opposed to aspects of it. This is particularly true of ecologically inclined parts of the movement. Nevertheless, Steve Bruce believes that even these types are less radical than some of the new religious movements of earlier decades. Bruce says of environmentalism:

> *It is critical of aspects of the modern world, especially those such as pollution that can be seen as side-effects of greed and over-consumption, and in that sense the New Age is 'alternative', but there is little of the blanket condemnation of the present world found in out-and-out world-rejecting new religions.* Bruce, 1995

The appeal of the New Age

Some writers have argued that the appeal of the New Age comes from the failure of the modern world to deliver personal satisfaction. John Drane believes the New Age is a:

> *response to the acknowledged failure of the scientific and materialist worldview to deliver the goods. The great Enlightenment vision of a better world for everyone has simply not materialized. Not only has the fundamental human predicament not improved, but as the twentieth century progressed, things actually got worse.* Drane, 1999

Drane follows the views of postmodernists in arguing that Western societies are turning against institutions and belief systems associated with the Enlightenment (see p. 891). Modern rationality, which followed from the Enlightenment, produced such disasters as the First World War, the Holocaust, numerous other bloody conflicts, the depletion of the ozone layer and global warming. People have lost faith in institutions such as the medical profession, which is now seen as more interested in 'covering their overheads than in the health and welfare of those they treat'.

Although the churches had 'an uneasy relationship with Enlightenment values', they adapted to and largely adopted those values. The churches are therefore viewed with suspicion and distrust. According to Drane, many people believe that, 'because of the dominance of rationalism and reasonableness, the current establishment options ... are pale remnants of the spiritual fire that started them'.

Disillusioned with the inability of the churches to satisfy their craving for spirituality, New Agers seek to develop their own spirituality. Drane sees this change as part of a move towards postmodernity (see pp. 453–5 for a discussion of postmodernism and religion).

However, both Steve Bruce (1995) and Paul Heelas (1996) argue that the New Age can best be explained as a product of modernity, rather than postmodernity (Bruce, in particular, is critical of the idea of postmodernity). Rather than being the product of a break from modernity, the New Age results from the latest stage in the development of modernity in Western societies. (See pp. 890–1 for a discussion of modernity.)

Bruce claims that the New Age appeals most to affluent members of society, particularly the 'university-educated middle classes working in the "expressive professions": social workers, counsellors, actors, writers, artists, and others whose education and work causes them to have an articulate interest in human potential'. They may have experienced personal development themselves and therefore find it plausible to believe that there is the potential for further development for themselves or others. These are also the sorts of people who have been most exposed to a belief in individualism, which is characteristic of modern societies. Modern societies are relatively egalitarian and democratic, so the views and beliefs of individuals are given more credence than was once the case, whereas the views of experts and traditional authorities are regarded with more scepticism. Bruce says:

> *This is the importance of the New Age. It illustrates the zenith of individualism. Individualism used to mean the right to act as one wished provided it did not harm others and the right to hold views radically at odds with the consensus. It has now shifted up in abstraction from a behavioural and ethical principle to an epistemological claim [a claim about how you know what is true and what is not]. It is now asserted as the right to decide what is and what is not true.* Bruce, 1995

Bruce comments on the way in which many aspects of the New Age draw heavily upon Eastern religions, such as Hinduism and Buddhism. For example, Transcendental Meditation is based upon Hinduism, and Soka Gakkai is a popular Western form of Buddhism. However, to make them attractive in a Western context, the religions tend to be stripped of the need for self-discipline. Traditional forms of Hinduism and Buddhism require 'a very long struggle against the temptations of the flesh'. As part of the New Age they require much more modest sacrifices. For example, TM requires only twenty minutes' meditation twice a day. Buddhism and Hinduism in the East also stress the smallness and passing, insignificant nature of the individual in comparison with the permanent and vast nature of the universe. Bruce comments that in Western, materialist societies few would be willing to make heavy sacrifices in the pursuit of spirituality. Nor are individuals prepared to accept their own insignificance. The New Age interpretation of Eastern religions appeals because it:

> *flatters the arrogance of the Westerner. Or to put it another way, though it talks of empowerment, it requires as an entry price a certain degree of self-confidence, a belief that one is already rather splendid. At the very least you have to believe that you have a self that people should want to hear you talk about endlessly.* Bruce, 2001

The New Age is a symptom of the extreme **relativism** of knowledge; that is, what you believe comes to depend simply on your subjective point of view and is not based upon general acceptance of definite claims by scientists and experts. It is also, in Bruce's eyes, a symptom of the decline of traditional religion. If people have little faith in the claims of scientists, they have even less in those of traditional religious leaders.

Paul Heelas (1996) reaches broadly similar conclusions. He sees the main appeal of the New Age as stemming from aspects of mainstream culture. However, it provides a more critical, **radicalized** and more religious, **sacrilized** version of mainstream culture. On the surface it appears to reject mainstream culture, but in fact it is based on an extreme emphasis on the individualism that is typical of modernity. This individualism leads to people becoming 'disembedded, desituated or detraditionalized selves'. People have no roots in the locality where they were born or brought up. They no longer have unquestioning faith in political, moral or religious codes, or in the leaders who promote them. People are thrown back on their own resources to make sense of the world and to create their own identity.

The individualism of modernity takes two forms:

1. **Utilitarian individualism** encourages people to seek to maximize their own happiness and material success. This is linked both to the desire for consumer goods and to those aspects of the New Age which aim to provide people with techniques to make them more successful in business or in their careers.
2. **Expressive individualism** emphasizes the importance of being yourself, of discovering your authentic or true self. This links to those aspects of the New Age which are more inner-directed.

Heelas examines four more specific ways in which modernity might link to the appeal of the New Age:

1. Modernity gives people a 'multiplicity of roles'. For example, they have work roles, family roles, roles as consumers, as members of various organizations, as friends and so on. In the modern world there may be little overlap between these roles; people are unlikely to live close to, and socialize primarily with, their workmates, or to live in the same community all their lives, or to work with members of their family. Because of this, people may end up with a fragmented identity – they have no central, core concept of who they are. The New Age offers ways of finding an identity.
2. Consumer culture encourages people to try to become the perfect person by, for example, wearing the right clothes, using the best make-up, having the healthiest diet, etc. This creates a 'climate of discontent' as people fail to achieve the perfection portrayed by the advertisers. This encourages people to try new ways of gaining perfection, including those offered by the New Age.
3. Following Bryan Wilson (see p. 417), Heelas suggests that periods of rapid social change, in which traditional norms and values are disrupted, might lead people to seek certainty and security in religious or spiritual beliefs.
4. The decline of conventional religion, particularly Christianity, leaves people without strong spiritual alternatives to the New Age when they are seeking solutions to the problems created by modernity.

Heelas sees the last of these explanations as the least important. However, he believes that all may have some role to play in explaining the appeal of the New Age. All are linked to modernity, but people experience modernity in very different ways. Some people experience modernity as (in a phrase used by Weber) an 'iron cage'. They feel trapped by the power of bureaucracies, the routines of work and the demands of success in capitalist societies. Yet, for all its demands, modernity does not offer most people a satisfying sense of identity – of who they are and why they exist. The New Age offers a solution.

Others experience modernity as a 'crumbling cage' in which they have too much freedom and too few guidelines about how to behave. Again, the New Age offers possible solutions for people prepared to look within themselves for the answers.

Of course, there are other ways of dealing with the dilemmas of modernity. As Heelas acknowledges, some people – for example, Christian fundamentalists in the USA – turn to traditional religion. Others might throw themselves into their work or become entranced by consumer culture. Nevertheless, the popularity of the New Age is only made possible by the nature of modernity.

In later work Paul Heelas *et al.* (2005) argue that the growth of New Age and related beliefs is part of a **spiritual revolution** which is taking place in modern societies. They claim that there has been a **subjective turn** in modern societies. People no longer put such emphasis on carrying out particular social 'roles, duties and obligations' (2005, p. 2). This involves living 'life-as a member of a community or tradition, whether it takes the form of a kinship system, a feudal system, a nation-state, a class system or a particular religion' (2005, p. 3). Instead there is an increased emphasis on **subjective life**. This 'has to do with states of consciousness, states of mind, memories, emotions, passions, sensations, bodily experiences, dreams, feelings, inner conscience and sentiments – including moral sentiments like compassion' (2005, p. 3).

In the congregational domain (see p. 444) of traditional churches and denominations, religious life is 'life-as' – as a believer and a follower who defers to the authority of religious organizations and their leaders. In the holistic milieu there are few prescriptions and you discover your own spirituality.

The subjective turn is not confined to the religious and spiritual spheres, but is found in every part of modern life. For example, it is found in child-centred education, consumer culture and patient-centred health. In work it is reflected in an emphasis on the personal development of employees rather than the responsibilities the employee has to the employer.

The New Age – conclusion

On the surface the New Age seems to contradict the view of sociologists such as Weber that the modern world would become increasingly rational. There seems to be little rationality in the claim by the New Ager Shirley MacLaine that she is responsible for the birth of her parents (quoted in Heelas, 1996), or that spirit guides, astrology or messages from 'an energy personality essence no longer focused in physical reality' (quoted in Bruce, 1995) can help us to live our lives better. But if Bruce and Heelas are correct, then the rationality of modernity also brought with it an individualism in which apparently non-rational beliefs could flourish.

Some writers disagree with Bruce and Heelas, seeing the existence of such beliefs as evidence that we have moved beyond modernity into an era of postmodernity (see pp. 453–5 on postmodernity and religion). There is no agreement either on whether the New Age is evidence of the resurgence of spiritual belief or a manifestation of secularization (see pp. 439–40). But Heelas and Woodhead (see pp. 444–5) seem to be on strong ground in arguing that the New Age is related to a decline in traditional beliefs and that it is closely linked with other social and cultural developments in modern societies.

Social groups and religiosity

Whatever the type of religious organization or movement, there is a tendency to attract more members, participants or believers from some social groups than from others. This section examines these variations and discusses possible reasons for the differences.

The main social divisions which affect religious belief or participation are gender, ethnicity, age and social class.

Social class and religiosity

Social class will not be examined in detail here because it has been discussed in other sections of the chapter. Thus Marxist theory (see pp. 399–401) suggests a relationship between class and religion as it sees religion as a response to class exploitation. Radical religions are often a response to deprivation (see, for example, the discussion of liberation theology (p. 409) and Islamic fundamentalism (pp. 445–8)). The previous section on different types of religious organization (pp. 410–20) examines the class composition of each type, as does the discussion of the New Age (pp. 420–3).

Social class differences interact with other types of social division. For example, working-class and middle-class women tend to have different patterns of religious belief and observance (see p. 424). The way social divisions interact in shaping religiosity will be discussed as the section progresses.

Gender and religious participation

An earlier section suggested that women were disadvantaged in many religions (see pp. 402–5). However, research suggests that in many groups women are more religiously active than men. According to the 2005 Church Census (Brierley, 2006a), 57 per cent of those attending one of the main churches or denominations in 2005 were women. This represented an increase from 55 per cent in 1979 but was down from a peak of 58 per cent in 1989. Women also attend churches more often than men, being more likely to attend at least once a week.

Although recent opinion poll evidence on gender and religious belief is not available, older evidence suggests that here too women tend to be more religious than men. An opinion poll conducted in 1990 and discussed in *Religious Trends 5* (Brierley, 2005) found that 84 per cent of women believed in God, compared to 64 per cent of men, and 57 per cent of women but only 39 per cent of men believed in life after death.

Evidence concerning New Age beliefs suggests that they are overwhelmingly followed or practised by women (see p. 425). Among minority ethnic groups who are not Christians the pattern is more complex. The Policy Studies Institute's *Fourth National Survey of Ethnic Minorities* (Modood *et al.*, 1997) found that Muslim women were more likely to say religion was 'very important' to them than were Muslim men. Men, however, were more likely to attend mosques. For example, only 5 per cent of Muslim men aged 16 to 24 said they never attended mosques, compared to 32 per cent of women in the same age group. Modood *et al.* point out though that many mosques do not welcome women, so differences in attendance do not necessarily indicate that Muslim women are less religious than Muslim men.

Various explanations have been put forward to account for the apparent greater participation in and commitment to religion amongst women in most religions.

Alan S. Miller and John P. Hoffman – 'Risk and religion'

Alan S. Miller and John P. Hoffman (1995) examine a number of explanations for women's greater religiosity.

They argue that two main types of explanation have been put forward by other sociologists.

1 Many sociologists examine **differential socialization**. According to this view 'females are taught to be more submissive, passive and obedient and nurturing than are males and these attributes are associated with higher levels of religiosity' (Miller and Hoffman, 1995, p. 63). These characteristics are more often found in traditional religious beliefs. For example, religions such as Christianity emphasize obedience to God and also characteristics such as being loving which are associated with female gender roles. Male roles place less emphasis on these characteristics. This theory is backed up by research evidence from the USA which shows that men who are submissive, passive, obedient and nurturing tend to be more religious than men who are not.
2 The second explanation argues that the differences result from the **structural locations** of men and women in society. Women are less involved in the labour force than men and more involved in bringing up children. Not only do women have more time for church-related activities but their lack of paid work also gives them a greater need for the sense of personal identity which religion can provide. Some US research suggests that religion is seen as a household activity. Socializing children through taking them to church can be regarded as an extension of female childcare roles.

These two explanations are not mutually exclusive. Indeed the socialization of males and females tends to lead to them occupying different social locations which in turn reinforce gender differences. Plausible though these explanations are, Miller and Hoffman argue that they cannot entirely explain the difference between male and female religiosity. They quote research which suggests that even when socialization and location in the social structure are controlled for, women are still more religious than men. They argue, therefore, that a third factor, attitude to **risk**, is also important.

Not being religious can be seen as risk-taking behaviour. There is nothing to lose by being religious, but not being religious risks being condemned to hell after death. Miller and Hoffman also point out that sociologists such as Malinowski see an important function of religion as dealing with risk (see pp. 397–8). Using survey research from the USA (*A Continuing Study of the Lifestyles and Attitudes of Youth*) Miller and Hoffman show that men tend to be less averse to risk than women, and that both men and women who are more averse to taking risks have higher levels of religiosity. They conclude that women's greater concern about risk is an important additional factor alongside socialization and structural location explaining women's greater religiosity.

Steve Bruce – religion and secularization

Unlike Miller and Hoffman, Steve Bruce (1996) does not see attitudes to risk as being significant in explaining gender differences in religiosity. He does follow Miller and Hoffman in seeing differences in male and female roles as being important, but he goes beyond their ideas by linking gender differences to secularization and by discussing gender and New Age beliefs.

Bruce starts by suggesting that religion tends to have an affinity with aspects of femininity which make women 'less confrontational, less aggressive, less goal oriented, less domineering more cooperative and more caring'. This affinity does not just apply to traditional religion and indeed is particularly strong with spiritual beliefs such as those of the New Age. Women are very attracted to the 'healing, channelling and spirituality' side of New Age beliefs because they are more in keeping with female gender roles. The minority of men involved in the New Age tend to be more interested in parapsychology than the more feminine aspects of the movement.

Bruce also believes that women are more interested in traditional religions because 'the churches have always been interested in the control of sexuality and the instruction of the next generation, both matters which are concentrated on the domestic hearth in which women have a major role to play'. According to Bruce there is a sharp division in the modern world between the **public sphere** (of paid work, politics, etc.) and the **private sphere** (of the domestic world of the family and personal life). Bruce believes that as a result of secularization (see pp. 429–55) religion has become less and less important in the public sphere and increasingly confined to the private sphere. Since women are more involved with the private sphere than men, and religion has become a largely private matter, women have tended to become more religious than men. As religion has declined generally, men with their predominantly public-sphere social roles have lost their religiosity more quickly than women

To Bruce, then, within an overall pattern of decline, religion has declined less amongst women than amongst men. However, the type of religion which has retained an appeal for some women varies by social class. Working-class women tend to retain a belief in forms of religion and spirituality in which they are more passive. They believe in a powerful God, or in 'obscure forces beyond their control', such as fortune-telling, superstition and charms. Middle-class women, on the other hand, have more experience of controlling and improving their own lives. Consequently, they tend to follow religions which allow more individual autonomy, and forms of spirituality which facilitate personal development. They are attracted to New Age beliefs which promote the growth and development of the self (see pp. 420–3 for a discussion of the New Age).

Linda Woodhead – female religiosity and gendering secularization

Like Bruce, Linda Woodhead connects gender differences in religiosity to changes in society, including secularization, and she discusses both traditional religion and New Age and similar spiritual beliefs. However, she develops a more sophisticated explanation of the relationship than Bruce. Furthermore, Woodhead does not follow Bruce in arguing that religion and spirituality are simply declining. In work with Paul Heelas (Heelas *et al.*, 2005), Woodhead argues that there is a **spiritual revolution** taking place involving a shift away from the traditional religions of the congregational domain towards the spiritualities of the holistic milieu (see pp. 444–5). Furthermore, she believes that to some extent religions of the congregational domain are changing as well.

Woodhead (2005) believes that processes of secularization have had an influence on Western societies, but they can only be understood if they are related to gender. From the nineteenth century, modernization led to a process of rationalization, described by Weber (see pp. 874–8). The world of work and public institutions became increasingly organized around the rational principles of bureaucracies (see pp. 876–8). This had a 'corrosive effect' on religion as it left little room for the non-rational faith required by religion. However, this process largely affected men. The housewife role became increasingly important for middle-class women and this isolated them to some extent from rationalization. Women were not 'absorbed into rationalized values' and so were not as likely to become disillusioned with the church's teachings as men.

Male church-going declined, but female church-going did not, leading to women becoming the majority of those involved in churches. Churches became 'increasingly feminized or domesticized'. They placed more emphasis on 'love, care and relationships' and less on God as an all-powerful and punitive ruler, though they continued to buttress male power through paternalistic images of God as a 'loving father'. As churches became feminized, they lost prestige and became even less appealing to most men.

By the 1970s the process of married women returning to the labour force was well under way. By now the dominance of women as church-goers was well established, reinforced by the 'feminine' nature of the religious beliefs espoused by most churches. However, large numbers of women were increasingly exposed to the rationalized culture of paid work. This led to a rapid decline in church-going by women.

Woodhead believes that it is largely the changes in women's lives that account for the decline of Christian churches and denominations in Western countries since the 1970s. However, this does not mean that women are now no more religious than men. Women are still more interested than men in religion and spirituality, for a number of reasons:

1 Women are still less involved in the public world of work than men. More women than men work part-time and women are still much more likely than men to have the main responsibility for childcare.
2 Woodhead argues that, contrary to much theory, there are three rather than two spheres in contemporary societies. These are:
   - **Primary institutions** (such as those associated with work and politics)
   - **Secondary institutions** (which are associated with caring for others; these include the family and religion)
   - An **individual sphere** (in which people are concerned with their own autonomous and individual selves)

   Religion, since it has been feminized, retains some plausibility for those whose lives are based in secondary institutions, and, since this is mainly women, they are still more likely than men to be involved in churches and denominations. Elsewhere, Woodhead (2001) argues that the emphasis on relationships in feminized churches remains more attractive to women than to men. Both church religion and women's lives emphasize 'relationships of love, trust and care'.
3 New Age beliefs or the holistic milieu (Heelas *et al.*, 2005; see pp. 444–5) also tend to be dominated by females. Woodhead argues that this is the case because it helps to resolve 'an unresolved clash between "traditional" female roles based around domestic labour and the new more masculinised roles, which become available to women as they enter the paid workforce in increasing numbers' (Woodhead, 2007). In paid work one's sense of self largely derives from one's position or job, whereas in family roles one's sense of self is more concerned with relationships with others (as wife, parent and so on). The holistic milieu allows this tension to be bypassed because it creates a new 'type of selfhood in which identity is not dictated by social position and experience, but discovered from within'. If work and family life give a person different views of who they are there is a danger that their overall sense of self will be confused or even contradictory. The spirituality of the holistic milieu offers the promise of discovering a true self which is not contradictory but reflects the whole person.

Conclusion

Woodhead's work is more developed than that of other writers on this topic and adds significantly to the understanding of secularization as well as of gender differences in religiosity. However, as Woodhead herself admits, gender and religiosity is a somewhat neglected area of research and further investigation is required to make these theories more convincing. Research into gender and religiosity amongst minority ethnic groups is even less developed, but there have been useful attempts to understand the relationship between ethnicity and religiosity in general.

Religion, ethnicity and age

This section looks at both ethnicity and age, as these two factors can interact closely in influencing religious belief and religious practice.

Ethnic groups and religion in Britain

There are two main sources of information on religion and ethnicity in Britain: the Policy Studies Institute's *Fourth National Survey of Ethnic Minorities* (Modood *et al.*, 1997) and the 2001 census. The PSI survey is older and is based upon a sample, but provides a range of information. The census is, of course, a national survey, but it only provides information on religious identity and gives no indication of the strength of that identity.

The findings of the 2001 census are shown in Table 7.1. Not surprisingly, it shows that there are significant variations in the religious identities of different ethnic groups and in the chances of being religious or not. Fully 52.6 per cent of Chinese had no religion, as did 23.25 per cent of those with mixed ethnic backgrounds and 15.45 per cent of White British. Very few Asians said they had no

Table 7.1 Ethnic groups in England and Wales by religion, 2001

	Christian	Buddhist	Hindu	Jewish	Muslim	Sikh	Any other religion	No religion	Religion not stated	All people	*Base*
White	75.89	0.12	0.02	0.83	0.38	0.01	0.25	15.34	7.67	100	*47520666*
British	75.94	0.11	0.01	0.48	0.14	0.01	0.24	18.48	7.62	100	*45533741*
Irish	85.42	0.19	0.02	0.16	0.14	0.02	0.26	6.38	7.42	100	*641804*
Other White	62.67	0.33	0.09	2.39	8.61	0.04	0.67	18.91	9.38	100	*1345321*
Mixed	52.46	0.70	0.87	0.47	9.72	0.42	0.58	23.28	11.64	100	*981034*
White and Black Caribbean	60.70	0.22	0.06	0.16	0.58	0.03	0.38	28.40	12.47	100	*237420*
White and Black African	56.44	0.59	0.21	0.23	13.34	0.04	0.35	17.92	10.88	100	*78911*
White and Asian	43.95	0.97	1.86	0.44	16.08	1.12	0.68	24.06	10.84	100	*189015*
Other Mixed	48.19	1.17	1.22	1.09	14.10	0.35	0.88	21.69	11.29	100	*155686*
Asian or Asian British	4.06	0.61	23.46	0.08	60.10	13.93	0.91	1.36	6.49	100	*2273737*
Indian	4.89	0.18	45.00	0.06	12.70	29.06	1.75	1.7	4.63	100	*1036807*
Pakistani	1.09	0.03	0.08	0.05	92.01	0.05	0.04	0.60	6.16	100	*714826*
Bangladeshi	0.50	0.06	0.60	0.05	92.48	0.0	0.01	0.43	5.83	100	*280830*
Other Asian	13.42	4.85	26.76	0.30	37.31	6.22	0.93	3.44	6.79	100	*241274*
Black or Black British	71.10	0.13	0.26	0.08	9.33	0.05	0.43	7.66	11.05	100	*1139577*
Black Caribbean	73.76	0.17	0.29	0.10	0.79	0.02	0.59	11.23	13.04	100	*563843*
Black African	68.87	0.07	0.21	0.05	20.04	0.09	0.21	2.31	8.14	100	*479665*
Other Black	66.61	0.20	0.36	0.13	5.97	0.07	0.66	12.09	13.93	100	*96069*
Chinese or Other Ethnic Group	27.18	15.30	0.69	0.54	12.80	0.52	0.69	33.68	8.63	100	*446702*
Chinese	21.56	15.12	0.07	0.05	0.33	0.03	0.49	52.60	9.75	100	*226948*
Other Ethnic Group	32.98	15.49	1.32	1.06	25.68	1.02	0.90	14.08	7.48	100	*219754*
All people	71.75	0.28	1.06	0.50	2.97	0.63	0.29	14.81	7.71	100	*52041916*
Base	*37338486*	*144453*	*552421*	*259927*	*1546626*	*329358*	*150720*	*7709267*	*4010658*	*52041916*	

Source: Census, April 2001, Office for National Statistics, London.

religion, including just 0.43 per cent of Bangladeshis; 11.23 per cent of Black Caribbeans had no religion, but fewer Black Africans – just 2.31 per cent. White Irish people were much less likely to have no religious beliefs than other Whites.

The predominant religions of ethnic groups reflected the religions of their place of origin: over 90 per cent of Pakistanis and Bangladeshis said they were Muslim. Hindus, Sikhs and Muslims were the biggest groups amongst Indians, while over three-quarters of Whites regarded themselves as Christian. Most Black or Black British people saw themselves as Christian, though a significant minority of Black Africans were Muslim. Most of the Chinese who stated they were religious identified themselves as Christian or Buddhist.

The PSI survey (Modood *et al.*, 1997) broke down religious affiliation in more detail. One of its findings was that Black Caribbeans had high rates of participation in New Protestant groups (twentieth-century sects such as Seventh Day Adventists and the New Testament Church of God): 25 per cent of people of Caribbean origin belonged to such groups, compared to just 1 per cent of whites. The survey also found big ethnic differences in the importance attached to religion. Only 11 per cent of white members of the Church of England saw religion as very important in their lives, compared to 32 per cent of white Roman Catholics, 43 per cent of Hindus, 71 per cent of Caribbean members of New Protestant churches and 74 per cent of Muslims. These differences were also reflected in the likelihood of attending religious services or prayer meetings: 62 per cent of Muslims, 57 per cent of Caribbean followers of New Protestant religions, 39 per cent of Sikhs, 29 per cent of white Roman Catholics, 27 per cent of Hindus, but just 9 per cent of white Church of England followers attended weekly.

Figure 7.3 Imam leads prayers

Source: Alamy/Ian Miles – Flashpoint Pictures

Figure 7.4 Young people perform religious rituals in a Hindu temple

Source: Alamy/Stan Kujawa

Figure 7.5 Rabbi reading Torah

Source: Corbis

These figures indicate that, with the exception of the Chinese, all minority ethnic groups (including the Irish) are more religious than the white majority in Britain. Pakistani and Bangladeshi Muslims tend to be the most religious but they are rivalled by black followers of Christian New Protestant denominations.

John Bird – explanations for high levels of religiosity

John Bird (1999) identifies five important reasons why you would expect higher levels of religiosity amongst minority ethnic groups.

1 Many ethnic groups 'originate in societies with high levels of religiosity' (Bird, 1999, p. 116). For example, Bangladesh, Pakistan and, to a slightly lesser extent, India all have high levels of religious observance and belief.
2 In an environment where people belong to a minority group, religion can 'act as a basis for community solidarity' (p. 116). Solidarity based on religious affiliation can perform important social functions for new migrants, giving them 'a point of contact in a new country, a source of marriage partners, social welfare and so on' (p. 118).
3 Following on from this point, Bird argues that 'Maintaining a religious commitment is also a way to maintain other aspects of cultural identity such as language, art, patterns of marriage, cooking and so on' (p. 116).
4 The importance of religion can be maintained through processes of socialization and 'there is often strong family pressure to maintain religious commitment'.
5 Bird also examines the possibility that minority ethnic groups might have strong religious beliefs because it helps them cope with oppression. Disadvantaged minority ethnic groups tend to be working-class, and their religious beliefs can express their position in the social structure. Drawing on research by Ken Pryce (1979) in Bristol, and Hinnels (1997), Bird suggests that Pentecostalism may perform a dual function for British African Caribbeans. First, it can be 'a way to adjust to a society in which Afro-Caribbeans face discrimination and social injustice' (p. 124). Bird claims that Pentecostalism can act in the way Marx suggested as the 'opiate of the masses' (see pp. 399–400). However it can also help people to combat disadvantage by improving their social and economic position. Pryce (1979) pointed out that it encouraged hard work and thrift which could lead to Pentecostalists gaining greater economic security.

In Pryce's study some African Caribbeans adopted another religion of the oppressed, Rastafarianism. Rastafarianism offers the promise of salvation through a return to Africa and is sometimes associated with radical political views. Bird describes Rastafarianism as 'a typical religious sect based upon material underprivileged' (1999, p. 125).

The decline of minority ethnic religion?

Steve Bruce accepts that minority ethnic groups are more likely to engage in religious activity than the ethnic majority, but he argues that this is largely for social reasons.

Bruce argues that the vitality of religion is largely a response to the social situation of minority ethnic groups rather than an expression of deep religious commitment. He sees the strength of minority ethnic religions as caused by either:

1. **cultural defence** (where an ethnic group is protecting its sense of identity and maintaining ethnic pride through religion); or
2. **cultural transition** (where an ethnic group uses religion to cope with the upheaval of migration).

Bruce believes, however, that, over time, ethnic groups in Britain become more integrated and are increasingly influenced by the wider secular society. As a consequence, their religious beliefs will decline.

A more complex view is taken by George Chryssides (1994) who argues that in Britain the religions of immigrant groups and their descendants have had three main paths open to them. The first option is **apostasy**, where a particular set of religious beliefs is abandoned in a hostile environment. The second is **accommodation**, where religious practices are adapted to take account of the changed situation. The third option is **renewed vigour**, where the religion is reasserted more strongly as a response to the actual or perceived hostility towards it. Examples of all three responses can be found.

Chryssides cites the case of Morris Cerello, a Sikh who converted to Christianity, as an example of apostasy. An example of accommodation might be a Sikh who removed his turban because he believed it would improve his chances at a job interview. Those who insist on strong religious orthodoxy from their children might be practising their religion with renewed vigour.

Chryssides acknowledges that minority ethnic religions have faced difficulties in Britain. They have had to establish places of prayer and deal with situations where religious observation might be difficult. However, the general pattern has been characterized by accommodation and renewed vigour rather than apostasy. Buildings have been bought and converted into mosques and temples, and religious beliefs and practices have been retained or adapted rather than abandoned. For example, many Islamic women have found ways to dress modestly while incorporating Western elements into their clothing. Religious marriage ceremonies have been adapted to meet the requirements for a legal marriage under British law.

The vigour of minority ethnic religions in Britain is demonstrated by the existence of some first-generation converts to these religions. Chryssides notes that Buddhism has been particularly successful in attracting new followers who have been brought up within the Christian tradition.

Some writers argue that there has been a revival of religion, which directly contradicts the claims of the advocates of the secularization thesis. For example, Gilles Kepel, in a book called *The Revenge of God* (1994), argues that there has been a resurgence of Judaism, Christianity and Islam in the modern world. According to Kepel, this has affected these religions, whether they are the religion of a minority or a majority in a particular society. Thus, for example, British Muslims have retained or strengthened their faith, not as a way of coping with cultural transition, but because they have been influenced by a worldwide Islamic revival. (For a discussion of Islamic and other faiths in the context of fundamentalism, see pp. 448–51.)

Evidence to help evaluate the competing claims is provided by the PSI survey (Modood et al., 1997) and by the 2005 English Church Census (Brierley, 2006a).

The English Church Census only measures attendance at Christian churches, and cannot therefore give any indication about the religions of non-Christians. However, it did find that church attendance had gone up among all minority ethnic groups between 1998 and 2005, and among black British people it had increased by 23 per cent. Brierley accepts that part, but not all, of this increase is due to immigration, but he also thinks that black churches have been successful because of their 'intense community involvement' (2006a, p. 92).

The PSI survey (Modood *et al.*, 1997; see pp. 425–7 for further details) produced more mixed findings. Table 7.2 shows the proportions of different age groups who said religion was very important to the way they lived their life. The table shows that young Chinese, White and Caribbean people were less likely than older people from their ethnic group to see religion as very important. Amongst Indians,

Table 7.2 'Religion is very important to how I live my life', by age, cell percentages

	White	Caribbean	Indian	African Asian	Pakistani	Bangla-deshi	Chinese	All ethnic minorities
All	13	34	47	43	73	76	11	46
16–34	5	18	35	37	67	67	7	35
35–49	13	43	56	40	81	92	8	52
50+	20	57	59	64	83	81	31	62
Weighted count	*2857*	*779*	*637*	*400*	*437*	*145*	*194*	*2592*
Unweighted count	*2857*	*587*	*627*	*373*	*595*	*298*	*109*	*2589*

Source: T. Modood, 'Culture and identity', in T. Modood *et al.*, *Ethnic Minorities in Britain*, PSI, London, 1997, p. 308.

African Asians, Pakistanis and Bangladeshis the age differences in religious belief were not as marked, but 16–34-year-olds were still less religious than those who were aged 50 and over. The general decline provides some support for Bruce's belief that secularization would affect minority ethnic groups, but there are a number of reasons for being cautious about any such conclusion.

1 Modood still found very high levels of religious belief among minority ethnic groups (see above, pp. 426–7). Only 4 per cent of Muslims, for example, said that religion was not important to them. Furthermore, as discussed above, black Christian churches have been growing in recent times.
2 Modood's research is rather dated. It is possible that since the time he was writing some minority ethnic religions, particularly Islam, may have experienced renewed vigour amongst the young.
3 Studies of age and religion suggest that if the young are less religious than the old, this does not necessarily mean that secularization is taking place. The issue of age and religion will now be discussed in more detail.

Age, generation and religiosity

Research evidence shows that in Britain the young tend to be less religious than the old. It is not just among minority ethnic groups (see above) that this age difference exists; the English Church Census (Brierley, 2006a) found similar results. The census found a rapid decline in young people attending church in the 1990s, that the average age of the church-goer had increased from 37 in 1979 to 45 in 2005, and that in 2005 59 per cent of churches had nobody attending between the ages of 15 and 19. This lack of interest in the religious or spiritual is also found in New Age beliefs, with Heelas *et al.* (2005) observing that most of those involved in the holistic milieu are middle-aged or older (see pp. 444–5).

David Voas and Alisdair Crockettt (2005) note that there are three possible explanations for lack of religiosity amongst the young.

1 The differences could be the result of **age**. Many commentators have suggested that people tend to get more religious as they get older and therefore see themselves as coming closer to death. Religious belief might also be affected by life events such as having children. People may return to active involvement in religion because they think it is important for the socialization of their children. From this perspective, substantial numbers of the young or middle-aged will return to religion as they get older.
2 The differences could be explained by a **period effect**. Those born in a particular period (a cohort) might be particularly unlikely or likely to be religious because of specific events or social changes in the era when they were growing up. An example of such a theory is put forward by Brierley, commenting on the rapid decline in church-going among the young in the 1990s. Brierley says, 'Those in "Generation Y", defined by some as those born in the 1980s, have been found to have little spiritual interest, being rather focused on "happiness"' (2006a, p. 118).
3 The differences could be due to the progressive decline of religion, so that each generation is less religious than the previous one. Supporters of this view generally favour the theory of secularization of religious decline (see pp. 429–45).

Voas and Crockettt examined data from the British Social Attitudes Survey to consider which of these theories was most plausible. The data allowed them to see whether a cohort was more or less religious than other cohorts and whether their attitude to religion changed as they aged.

Voas and Crockett found little evidence that people became markedly more religious over time, or that it was specific cohorts that were becoming less religious. They say, 'Although many individual adults become more, or less religiously committed our investigation suggests that in the aggregate such age and period effects have little impact' (Voas and Crockettt, 2005, p. 24). Instead they concluded that in Britain 'change has occurred because each generation has entered adulthood less religious than its predecessors'. In part, they claimed, this was because each generation was less likely to socialize their children into religious beliefs than the previous generation.

The conclusions reached by Voas and Crockett may not apply to all types of religious and spiritual belief. Different conclusions are reached by Heelas *et al.* (2005) with respect to spiritual beliefs of the holistic milieu. They claim that this type of belief is growing rapidly despite few young people being involved, because people do not usually start to engage with such spiritualities until middle age.

The conclusions of Voas and Crockett appear to provide support for the theory that religion is declining – the theory of secularization. However, secularization theory is hotly contested and will now be examined in detail.

Secularization

Support for the secularization thesis

Although sociologists have disputed whether religion encourages or inhibits social change, most agree that changes in society will lead to changes in religion. Furthermore, many have claimed that social change would lead to the weakening or even disappearance of religion.

In the nineteenth century it was widely believed that industrialization and the growth of scientific knowledge would lead to **secularization**, which very broadly can be defined as the process of religious decline. Auguste Comte (1986, first published 1830–42), the French functionalist sociologist, believed that human history passed through three stages. Each stage was characterized by a different set of intellectual beliefs:

1 In the first, **theological stage**, religious and superstitious beliefs would be dominant.
2 These would be weakened as society passed into the second, **metaphysical stage**, during which philosophy would become more important.

3 Religious belief would disappear altogether in the final, **positive stage**, in which science alone would dominate human thinking and direct human behaviour.

Durkheim did not agree that religion was doomed to total obsolescence. He once commented that there was 'something eternal in religion' (Durkheim, 1961, first published 1912). Nevertheless, he did anticipate that religion would be of declining social significance. In an industrial society in which there was a highly specialized division of labour, religion would lose some of its importance as a force for integrating society. Social solidarity would increasingly be provided by the education system rather than the sort of religious rituals associated with the more simple societies.

Weber, too, anticipated a progressive reduction in the importance of religion. He thought that in general people would act less in terms of emotions and in line with tradition, and more in terms of the rational pursuit of goals. **Rationalization** would gradually erode religious influence (Weber, 1958, 1963, first published 1904, 1922; Gerth and Mills, 1954) (for further details see p. 408).

Marx did not believe that industrial capitalism as such would herald the decline of religion, but he did believe it would set in motion a chain of events that would eventually lead to its disappearance (Marx and Engels, 1950a). Religion, according to Marx, was needed to legitimate inequality in class societies (see pp. 399–400), but capitalism would eventually be replaced by classless communism, and religion would cease to have any social purpose.

Many contemporary sociologists have followed in the footsteps of these founders of the subject. They have argued that science and rationality, the decline of traditional values, and the increasingly specialized division of labour, would tend to undermine religion in particular and faith and non-rational beliefs in general. These views are largely based upon an analysis of the nature of **modernity**.

Modern societies are seen to be incompatible with the retention of a central role for religion. That is not to say that supporters of the secularization thesis necessarily believe that religion will disappear completely. Instead, they argue that in some sense religion will decline in significance. For example, Bryan Wilson – a leading advocate of secularization – defined secularization as 'the process whereby religious thinking, practice and institutions lose social significance' (Wilson, 1966).

However, a major problem with the concept of secularization is that it is given different meanings by different sociologists. Problems arise in evaluating the theory of secularization because of the absence of a generally agreed definition. Glock and Stark (1969) argue: 'Perhaps the most important attribute of those who perceive secularization to be going on is their commitment to a particular view of what religion means.'

Jose Casanova (2003) identifies a particularly significant division between two uses of the term secularization. One way of using the term sees secularization broadly as 'the secularization of societal structures or the diminution of the significance of religion' (Casanova, 2003, p. 19). In this definition the main emphasis is on the separation of the religious sphere from other areas of social life, so that religious institutions and religious beliefs play an ever-decreasing role in influencing public life. Religion becomes an essentially private matter and it has little influence on public policies, political debate and the way that society as a whole is run.

The other main way of using the term is narrower and refers to 'the decline of religious beliefs and practices among individuals' (Casanova, 2003, p. 19). In this case the emphasis is on such issues as how many people believe in God and how many attend churches or other places of worship.

Steve Bruce (2002) sees the debate on secularization as even more complex and fragmented. He says, 'there is no one secularization theory. Rather, there are clusters of descriptions and explanations that cohere reasonably well.' The following sections examine the main clusters of description and explanation that have been discussed in the debate about whether or not religion is declining.

Institutional religion – participation

Statistical evidence

Some researchers have seen religious institutions and the activity associated with them as the key element in religious behaviour. From this viewpoint they have measured the importance of religion in society in terms of factors such as church attendance, church membership, and participation in ceremonies such as marriages, which are performed in church.

In these respects, a good deal of the statistical evidence does seem to point towards secularization, at least in the UK. However, the evidence needs to be examined carefully: some of it does not appear to support the secularization thesis; the evidence varies between countries; and the reliability and validity of many of the statistics are open to question. (For an explanation of the terms validity and reliability, see pp. 816–17.)

We will now examine the statistics relating to different types of participation in institutional religion.

Church attendance in Britain

Some of the strongest evidence for the secularization thesis as applied to Britain seems to come from church attendance statistics. The earliest available survey statistics on church attendance originate from the 1851 'Census of Religion'. This found just under 40 per cent of the adult population attending church. In England and Wales the numbers had dropped to 35 per cent by the turn of the century and 20 per cent by 1950.

The most recent data come from Church Censuses carried out in 1979, 1989, 1998 and 2005. The figures are based on an attempt to collect information from every Christian church and denomination, including the House Church movement, in which small groups of Christians meet in people's homes. These surveys found that 12 per cent of the population of England attended church in 1979, declining to 10 per cent in 1989, 7.5 per cent in 1998 and 6.3 per cent in 2005 (Brierley, 2006a). Using these surveys, estimates have been produced for adult attendance at institutional and free churches between 1979 and 2005 in England, with projections for 2015 based on previous trends. The results are given in Tables 7.3 and 7.4. The tables also show percentage changes between the various censuses.

Table 7.3 Institutional church attendance in England, 1979–2005

	1979	Change	1989	Change	1998	Change	2005	Change	2015E
Roman Catholic	1,991,000	−14%	1,715,900	−28%	1,230,100	−28%	893,100	−32%	608,000
Anglican	1,671,000	−24%	1,266,300	−23%	980.600	−11%	870,600	−24%	660,000
United Reformed	190,000	−21%	149,300	−18%	121,700	−43%	69,900	−53%	33,100
Orthodox	10,000	+23%	12,300	+105%	25,200	+2%	25,600	+2%	26,100
Total	3,862,000	−19%	3,143,800	−25%	2,357,600	−21%	1,859,200	−29%	1,327,200

Source: P. Brierley, *Pulling Out of the Nose Dive*, Christian Research, London, 2006, p. 26.

Table 7.4 Free church attendance in England, 1979–2005

	1979	Change	1989	Change	1998	Change	2005	Change	2015E
Methodists	621,000	−18%	512,300	−26%	379,700	−24%	289,400	−31%	200,000
Pentecostals	228,000	+4%	236,700	−9%	214,600	+34%	287,600	+3%	298,000
Baptists	290,000	−7%	270,900	+2%	277,600	−8%	254,800	−11%	226,000
Independent Churches	235,000	−27%	298,500	−36%	191,600	−1%	190,500	−11%	170,000
New Churches	64,000	+161%	167,000	+20%	200,500	−8%	183,600	−10%	166,000
Smaller denominations	141,000	−19%	113,600	−18%	93,100	+9%	101,100	−14%	87,000
Total	1,579,000	+1%	1,599,000	−15%	1,357,100	−4%	1,307,000	−12%	1,147,000

Source: P. Brierley, *Pulling Out of the Nose Dive*, Christian Research, London, 2006, p. 31.

The tables show a continuing overall pattern of decline for both institutional and free churches. The decline has been rapid in the Anglican churches (of which the Church of England is by far the most important) and in the Roman Catholic Church. The United Reformed Church and Methodism have also declined rapidly. Though some types of church have grown, these tend to be religious organizations with fewer worshippers.

Peter Brierley (2006a) notes that the rate of decline did slow down between 1998 and 2005 compared with the period between 1989 and 1998. This led him to be moderately optimistic about the future of English churches and he entitled a recent book *Pulling Out of the Nose Dive*. He also noted that over 1,100 new churches opened between 1998 and 2005. However, 1,300 churches closed and the growth of some churches was more than offset by the decline of others.

Other types of participation in organized religion have also declined. Attendance at special Christian ceremonies such as baptisms and marriages has declined. In the 1920s and 1930s, over 90 per cent of babies were baptized, but by 1970 baptisms were down to 64 per cent and in 1990 down to 51 per cent, and down to 45 per cent in 2001 (Brierley, 2005).

There has also been a noticeable drop in the number of marriages conducted in church. According to Bruce, nearly 70 per cent of English couples were married in the Church of England at the start of the twentieth century. By 1990 the number had fallen to 53 per cent. According to *Religious Trends 3*, 37.8 per cent of marriages in England and Wales in 1995 took place in a church. In 2005 fewer than 70,000 out of a total of more than 238,000 marriages took place in a church (Brierley, 2005). However, Brierley

Figure 7.6 United Methodist Church service

Source: Topfoto

Table 7.5 Total UK church statistics

Year	Membership		Churches	Ministers	Sunday attendance	
	Total in UK	% of pop			Total in GB	% of pop
1990	6,634,335	11.5	49,321	35,558	5,369,770	9.6
1995	6,303,726	10.8	48,999	35,074	4,794,850	8.5
2000	5,913,572	10.0	48,250	34,537	4,379,880	7.6
2001	5,862,651	9.9	48,420	34,546	4,315,040	7.3
2002	5,766,614	9.7	48,165	34,144	4,224,220	7.1
2003	5,700,628	9.6	47,973	34,576	4,133,400	6.9
2005	5,634,324	9.4	47,635	34,449	3,976,060	6.8
2010E	5,190,471	8.6	46,735	33,457	3,528,710	6.0
2020E	4,550,551	7.2	43,890	31,639	2,683,950	4.4

Source: P. Brierley, *Religious Trends 5*, 2005/2006, Christian Research, London, 2005, p. 2.23.

points out that this was partly due to the expansion of 'approved premises' where weddings could take place outside churches or register offices.

Table 7.5 shows the number of church members, the number of separate congregations or churches, and the number of ministers in the UK from 1990 to 2005, with projections for 2010 and 2020. The data reveal steady falls in the membership of churches, the number of churches and the number of ministers. By 2005, only 9.4 per cent of the UK adult population were members of any church, compared to 11.5 per cent in 1990.

However, changes in membership vary from church to church. Between 2000 and 2005, membership of Anglican, Roman Catholic, Presbyterian, Baptist, Independent and Methodist churches fell, while membership of new churches, Pentecostal churches and Orthodox churches rose (*Religious Trends 5*).

Membership of some non-Christian churches and other religious organizations has been increasing. Non-trinitarian religions increased their membership from over 511,000 in 1995 to over 547,000 in 2005 (Brierley, 2001, 2005). Non-trinitarian churches include Jehovah's Witnesses, Mormons and Christedelphians.

Furthermore, many non-Christian religions have been growing. Estimates compiled by Brierley (2005) suggest that the number of active Muslims increased from 768,000 in 2000 to 893,000 in 2005. Over the same period active Hindus increased from 273,000 to 305,000, Sikhs from 164,000 to 184,000, and Buddhists from 49,000 to 54,000. The number of active Jews declined from 88,000 to 86,000.

New religious movements, which take the form of sects or cults, involve much smaller numbers than the major non-Christian religions. *Religious Trends 5* lists thirty-four such movements and estimates that their membership, along with that of other new religious movements, has increased from 29,503 in 2000 to 37,412 in 2005. Other groups which are defined as sects or cults are listed in *Religious Trends 5* as non-trinitarian churches. According to the *Religious Trends* figures, between 1995 and 2000 membership of the Unification Church (Moonies) rose from 1,000 to 1,200, and the number of Scientologists increased from 144,400 to 165,400.

All of the above figures should be viewed with caution. Many are estimates, and, as we will see below, interpreting religious statistics is difficult and controversial. Nevertheless, they do give some indication of membership trends.

A further indication of overall religious trends in Britain is provided in Figure 7.7, which was originally produced by Peter Brierley for *Religious Trends 5* and is based upon various sources including Church Censuses, the national census, and membership figures. Some figures are estimates. Members of the Christian community are defined as 'those who would positively identify as belonging to a church even if they may only attend irregularly, or were just baptised as a child' (Brierley, 2005, p. 2.2). It would include those who would choose Christian as their religion in the national census.

Figure 7.7 shows a steady fall in the percentage of Christians, but the fall in the Christian community is not as rapid as the fall in regular church-going. The proportion of the population who are Christians remains high at 72 per cent, down from 76 per cent in 1980. The figure suggests a doubling of the proportion belonging to non-Christian religions (up from 3 per cent to 6 per cent) but only a small increase in the non-religious from 21 per cent to 22 per cent. (For a discussion of the 2001 census on which these statistics are partly based, see pp. 435–6.)

Religious participation in the rest of the world

A very different impression of the state of religion is given once the discussion is broadened beyond the UK. For example, rates of religious participation are much higher in some parts of the world than they are in Britain. According to Grace Davie (2002), around 40 per cent of people in the USA state that they attend church weekly, and an even higher proportion attend monthly. Writing in 1993, C. Kirk Hadaway, Penny Marler and Mark Chaves also noted that rates of self-reported church attendance in the USA were around 40 per cent, with Protestant attendance the same as it had been in the 1940s. Rates of attendance for Catholics in the USA did decline in the 1960s and early 1970s, but had not fallen any further.

Grace Davie (2002) suggests that Europe may be the 'exceptional case' – the only part of the world in which there is real evidence of secularization. Even in terms of Christian belief, there is little evidence of religious decline in the USA, sub-Saharan Africa or Latin America. Indeed, according to Davie, in many parts of the world Christianity is thriving.

In Latin America and Africa there has been a big growth in Pentecostalist churches, and even in Far East countries such as South Korea and the Philippines Christianity has boomed. Furthermore, very high attendance is still recorded even in two European countries, the Republic of Ireland and Poland.

The World Christian Encyclopaedia, compiled by David Barrett (discussed in Brierley, 2001), took statistics from around the world to estimate global changes in religious affiliation. Barrett estimated that 34.5 per cent of the world's population were Christian in 1900 and this had declined only marginally to 33 per cent in 2000. While Christianity had declined in Europe, it had increased significantly in Africa, Latin America and Asia.

In 2001 Peter Brierley quoted figures which suggested that between 1970 and 2000 there had been a small decrease in the proportion of the world's population who were Christian, but a big increase in the proportion who were Muslim, and overall a decline in the proportion who were not religious.

The most recent figures for world religious affiliation are shown in Figure 7.8. The figures are based on a wide range of sources and include those who have only a weak religious identity. On this basis less than one-sixth of the world's population were non-religious in 2005. These figures provide a picture which contrasts with the apparent religious decline in Britain.

Interpreting the evidence on participation and membership

Most of the long-term evidence on membership and attendance in Britain seems to support the secularization theory. Although recent years have seen a growth in smaller religious organizations, compared to the

Figure 7.7 Religious structure of the population of Great Britain, 1980 to 2000

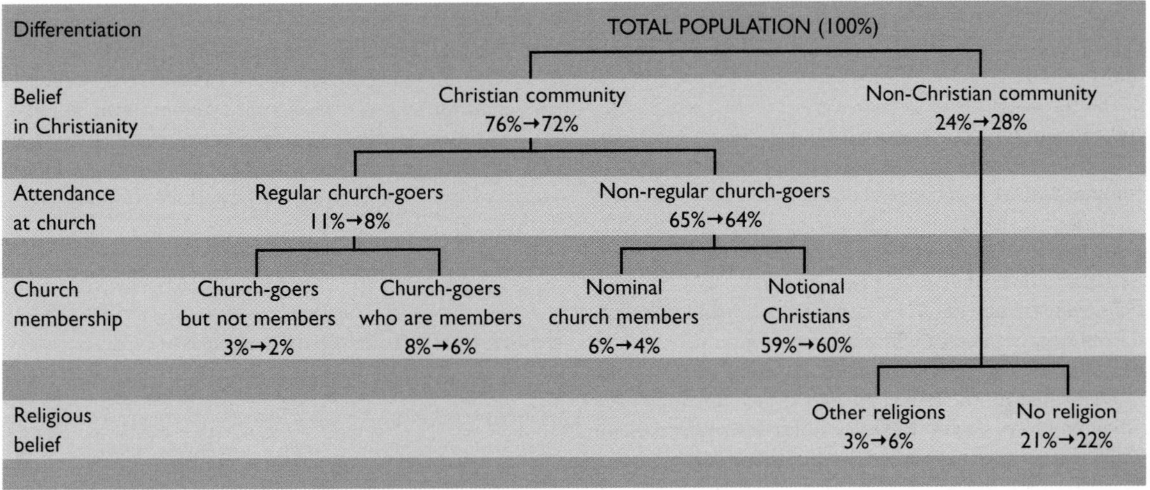

Source: P. Brierley, *Religious Trends 5*, 2005/2006, Christian Research, London, 2005, p. 2.2.

Figure 7.8 Major religions of the world ranked by number of adherents

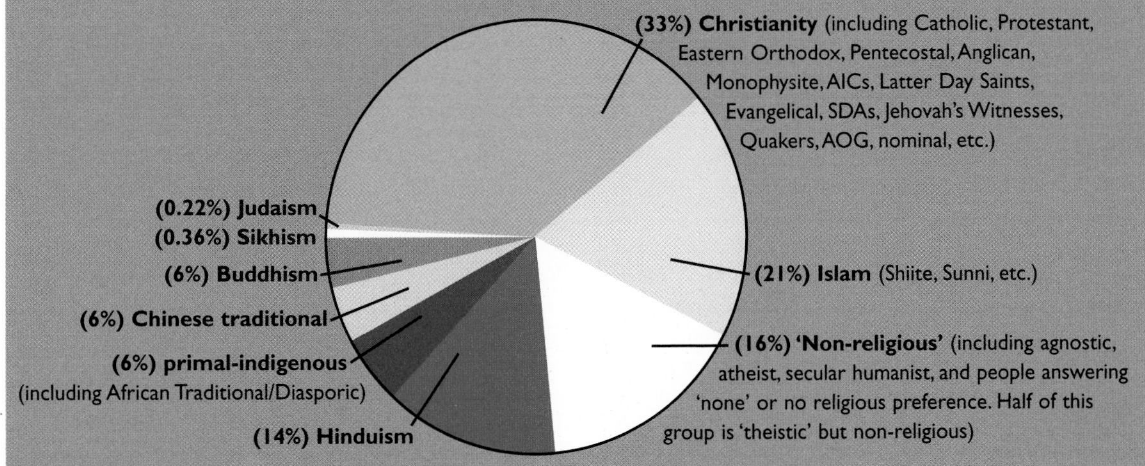

Source: http://www.adherents.com/Religions-By-Adherents.html

nineteenth century and early decades of the twentieth century there is little doubt that fewer people attend a place of worship or belong to a religious organization.

In the USA and the world as a whole, though, the evidence seems to support the views of those who question the secularization thesis. However, the evidence is far from conclusive and needs to be used with care. As Grace Davie (1989) says, 'Religious statistics are notoriously hard to handle.'

Both the reliability and the validity of the statistics are open to question. Nineteenth-century church attendance figures for Britain pose special problems because the methods of data collection used do not meet today's standards of reliability. More recent British figures may be hard to trust as well. Some commentators argue that attendance and membership figures may be distorted by the ulterior motives of those who produce them. Some churches – for example, the Roman Catholic Church – may underestimate the numbers in their congregation in order to reduce the capitation fees they have to pay to central church authorities. Others, particularly Anglican churches, may overestimate the figures to produce impressive totals, particularly where there may be a risk of a church with a small congregation being closed down.

Membership figures can be calculated in different ways, and various churches, denominations and other religious groups use different criteria:

1. Members of the Roman Catholic Church in Britain and the Church of England are normally taken to be those who have been both baptized and confirmed. The numbers may therefore include people who, although officially members, have taken no part in church life since their confirmation.
2. The Church of Wales, on the other hand, bases its figures on those attending Easter Communion.
3. Figures giving the numbers who are held to be members of the Jewish religion simply document the number of Jewish heads of household, regardless of how often or whether they attend a synagogue.

Because of these variations, statistics on church membership are highly unreliable, and the trends indicated by the figures may be misleading.

In the USA the attendance statistics are based on survey evidence. Hadaway *et al.* (1993) questioned the reliability of the evidence. They conducted a detailed study of church attendance in a part of Ohio. In most of the churches they were able to get attendance counts from the clergy; in others they estimated attendance by counting cars in church car parks. They compared these results with findings from their own telephone poll. Their conclusion was that, overall, actual church attendance was about half that claimed in polls. Twice as many people claimed to attend church or a synagogue as actually did so. People exaggerated their church attendance, probably because church attendance was seen as socially desirable behaviour, and people were unwilling to admit their lack of attendance.

The problems of providing accurate figures on membership of or participation in religion are multiplied when attempts are made to produce statistics about religions throughout the world. The definitions of religiosity and the procedures for producing statistics vary considerably from country to country. Since they lack a consistent methodology, and the problems of data collection in some parts of the world may be considerable, it is difficult to know whether much credence can be given to estimates of the proportion of the world's population who are religious.

The decline in church attendance in Britain can be interpreted in a number of ways:

1. David Martin (1969) claimed that in Victorian Britain church attendance was a sign of middle-class respectability to a greater extent than it is today. Many Victorians may have attended church to be seen, rather than to express deep religious convictions.
2. Some sociologists argue that a decline in institutional religion cannot be taken as indicating a decline in religious belief and commitment. Religion today may be expressed in different ways. Religion may have become increasingly privatized; people develop their own beliefs and relationship with God and see religious institutions as being less important. (For some evidence to support this claim see the discussion of census data below, pp. 435–6.)
3. It is also possible that many individuals who hold religious beliefs, and whose behaviour is also partly directed by such beliefs, are not formally registered as church members. Statistics on participation in religious institutions provide only one type of indicator of the religious commitment of individuals and may be only tenuously linked to the strength of religious beliefs.

We will now examine some evidence relating to religious belief and activity outside the context of religious organizations.

Belief, church-going and atheism

Opinion poll evidence is perhaps the simplest type of data relating to religious beliefs. However, there are a variety of questions that can and have been asked about religious beliefs, and the questions asked determine the impression given by the data.

Opinion poll data generally find that many more people retain religious beliefs than are members of religious organizations or regular attendees at places of worship. Table 7.6 is compiled from a variety of Gallup polls and the Opinion Research Business survey 'The Soul of Britain, 2000' (taken from Bruce, 2001).

More recently a *Financial Times*/Harris poll used slightly different questions. The poll was conducted in several countries and the results are shown in Table 7.7.

The figures show that in 2000, 70 per cent of people in Britain retained some sort of belief, while only 15 per cent rejected the idea of a God, spirit or life force altogether. The *Financial Times*/Harris poll found that in 2006, 35 per cent of people in Britain believed in some form of God or supreme being, and 35 per cent were agnostic, with 17 per cent being atheist. The rise in the number of atheists and the small percentage of clear believers suggest a further decline in religious belief since 2000, but the figures are not strictly comparable with earlier studies because of the different options used. Furthermore, the findings of all opinion polls of this type

Table 7.6 Belief in God, Britain, 1947–2000

Year	2000 (%)	1990 (%)	1981 (%)	1947 (%)
There is a personal God	26	32	41	45
There is some sort of spirit or life force	21	41	37	39
There is something there	23	na	na	na
I don't really know what to think	12	15	16	16
I don't really think there is any sort of God, spirit or life force	15	10	6	na
None of these	3	1	na	na

na = not asked

Source: S. Bruce (2001) 'Religion, the global and the post-modern', in M. Haralambos (ed.) *Developments in Sociology*, Vol. 17, Causeway Press, Ormskirk, 2001, p.12.

Table 7.7 Belief in God or supreme being: 'Thinking now about religion, would you say that you are a ...?'

	Great Britain	France	Italy	Spain	Germany	United States
Believer in any form of God or any type of supreme being	35	27	62	48	41	73
Agnostic (one who is sceptical about the existence of God but not an atheist)	35	32	20	30	25	14
Atheist (one who denies the existence of God)	17	32	7	11	20	4
Would prefer not to say	6	6	8	8	10	6
Not sure	7	4	3	3	4	3

Note: Percentages may not add up exactly to 100% due to rounding

Source: 'Religious views and beliefs vary greatly by country, according to the latest *Financial Times*/Harris poll' (http://www.prnewswire.com.cgi-bin.pl?ACCT=104&STORY=/www/story/12... (11/01/2007))

are open to different interpretations. They could be seen as providing strong evidence for or against secularization, depending on whether a narrow or broad definition of religion is employed.

As with all opinion poll data, there are question marks over the strength of the relationship between what people say and what they do. As Malcolm Hamilton says, saying you believe in God:

> *does not mean that it has any consequences for behaviour, is held with any conviction, or has any real meaning. What the surveys show is not that people are religious but that they have a propensity to say yes to this sort of survey question.* Hamilton, 1998

Steve Bruce (2001) argues that the opinion poll data show a strong weakening of religious beliefs. Belief in a personal God has declined markedly, as has belief in 'some sort of spirit or life force'. A belief that 'there is something there' is a very weak and insignificant belief compared to a belief in an organized religion such as Christianity. Bruce argues that this represents a big increase in scepticism towards religious beliefs. He says, 'people are moving away from what they cannot believe without wishing to go so far as to say they do not believe'. Such vague beliefs have little cultural influence and hardly affect people's day-to-day behaviour.

Nevertheless, looking beyond Great Britain, there are clearly some countries where religious beliefs are much more widespread. For example, the *Financial Times*/Harris poll discussed above found that in the USA 73 per cent and in Italy 62 per cent said they believed in some form of God, and only 4 per cent in the USA and 7 per cent in Italy said they were atheists.

However, data from the 2001 census in Britain suggest that religious beliefs of a fairly traditional kind remain common. In the 2001 census, respondents were, for the first time, invited to state their religious affiliation. The question was not compulsory, but over 92 per cent chose to answer it. Furthermore, a surprisingly high percentage – 71.6 per cent – stated they were Christian; 2.7 per cent described themselves as Muslim, 1 per cent Hindu, 0.6 per cent Sikh, 0.5 per cent Jewish, 0.3 per cent Buddhist, and 0.3 per cent 'other religion', with 15.5 per cent saying they had no religion and 7.3 per cent not answering.

Bruce could argue that many of those saying they were Christian would have very weak beliefs, which would have little influence on their lives. Nevertheless, a Christian identity remained surprisingly common.

There are, however, some question marks over the validity of the figures. Following a campaign on the internet to encourage people to give annoying answers or to show their love of the *Star Wars* films, over 390,000 people (about 0.7 per cent) gave their religion as 'Jedi' or 'Jedi Knight'. This group was included along with agnostics, atheists and heathens in the 15.5 per cent described as having 'no religion', but it does suggest that not everybody took the question entirely seriously. Furthermore, research just a year later in 2003, conducted as part of the British Social Attitudes Survey, found that no less than 41 per cent said they had no religion (discussed in Brierley, 2005). This raises serious questions about the validity of the data produced by the census.

Religious belief and participation may be the most obvious areas in which to look for evidence in favour of or against secularization. However, some theorists deny that these are crucial to the secularization thesis. For example, José Casanova (1994) argues that these aspects of religion are essentially irrelevant to secularization. For him, it is the role of religion that is important, in particular the process of differentiation (see pp. 436–7). We will now examine aspects of theories of secularization which focus more on the role of religion in society.

Institutional religion – disengagement, differentiation and societalization

Disengagement

Some researchers, as we have just noted, have seen the truly religious society in terms of full churches. They have therefore seen empty churches as evidence of secularization. Others have seen the truly religious society as one in which the church as an institution is directly involved in every important area of social life. In terms of this emphasis, a **disengagement** or withdrawing of the church from the wider society is seen as secularization.

David Martin (1969) saw this view as concerned with decline in the power, wealth, influence and prestige of the church. Compared to its role in medieval Europe, the church in contemporary Western society has undergone a process of disengagement. In the Middle Ages, there was a union of church and state. Today, apart from the right of bishops to sit in the British House of Lords, the church is hardly represented in government.

Steve Bruce (1995) argues that the state churches have lost their power as they have become more distant from the British state. This distancing has given them the freedom to be more critical of governments. For example, during the period of Conservative government from 1979 to 1997, the Church of England criticized nuclear weapons policy, and lack of help for the poor in the inner cities. However, the government took little or no notice of the views expressed by church leaders.

José Casanova (1994, 2003) accepts that secularization in this sense may have taken place in some European countries, but he sees Europe as an exception to the rule since in most countries religion is becoming more prominent in public life. According to Casanova (1994), from the 1980s onwards, increasing attention was paid to religion by politicians, social scientists and the general public, and religious leaders were increasingly willing to enter public and political debate. Casanova says: 'During the entire decade of the 1980s it was hard to find any serious political conflict anywhere in the world that did not show behind it the not-so-hidden hand of religion.' Examples include the conflicts between Jews and Muslim Arabs in the Middle East, and between Muslims, Serbs and Croats in Bosnia.

Religion played an important part in the revolts that led to the collapse of communism in Eastern Europe and the former USSR. The 'Moral Majority' of fundamentalist Christians became influential in the USA. Even in Britain some issues have forced religion onto the public agenda: for example, the conflict between Protestants and Catholics in Northern Ireland; and in 1989 the Salman Rushdie affair highlighted a clash between religious and secular values in Britain (the Iranian leader Ayatollah Khomeini declared Rushdie's book *The Satanic Verses* blasphemous to Islam and issued a fatwa, or religious death sentence, against Rushdie).

Casanova therefore believes there has been a **deprivatization** of religion. Before the 1980s, religion was becoming confined to the private sphere. It was considered a matter of personal conscience, and religious organizations were withdrawing from trying to influence public policies. From the 1980s, this was reversed, with religions again trying to exert an influence on public life.

Casanova therefore sees the privatization of religion as a 'historical option', which has been followed in some societies at some times, but it is not an inevitable or irreversible aspect of modernity, and since the 1980s it has become an increasingly unpopular option.

In more recent writing, Casanova (2003) argues that the public role of religion is not just confined to particular societies. Some religious movements and organizations have taken on a **transnational** character. For example, Islamic fundamentalism and the Pentecostal movement transcend national boundaries and are a political force in the world in their own right.

Structural and social differentiation

An alternative to the view that disengagement equals secularization is provided by Talcott Parsons (1951, 1960, 1965a). Parsons agreed that the church as an institution had lost many of its former functions. He argued that the evolution of society involves a process of **structural differentiation**: various parts of the social system become more specialized and so perform fewer functions. (This idea forms part of Parsons's theory of social evolution, outlined in Chapter 15, pp. 859–61.)

However, the differentiation of the units of the social system does not necessarily lessen their importance. As we saw in a previous section, Parsons argued that religious beliefs still give meaning and significance to life. Churches are still the fount of religious ethics and values.

As religious institutions become increasingly specialized, Parsons maintained that their ethics and values become increasingly **generalized**. In American society, for instance, they have become the basis for more general social values.

Steve Bruce (1995) discusses essentially the same process as Parsons, although in Bruce's case he terms it **social differentiation**. Unlike Parsons, he sees it as a feature of secularization that stems from the rationalization of the modern world. In the fourteenth century the medieval church tried to assert control over activities like money lending, defining them as sinful. Social differentiation means that the church now has much less opportunity to involve itself in non-religious spheres. Indeed, to Bruce, social life becomes dominated by the logic of capitalist production, with its emphasis on calculability, efficiency and profit. Religious faith and morality become less and less significant in the culture and institutions of modern societies:

> *Modernization sees the freeing of economic activity from religiously sanctioned controls and the development of the world of work as an autonomous sphere driven only by its own values. Gradually, other aspects of life go the same way. Education, social welfare, health care, and social control have mostly passed out of church control, and where churches still run such activities they do so in ways that differ little from secular provision.* Bruce, 1995

Unlike Parsons, Bruce sees differentiation as affecting individuals as well as institutions. Modern societies have become increasingly egalitarian. People no longer have fixed roles which are ascribed at birth. There are no longer rigid hierarchies in which everybody knows their place. There is much greater occupational and geographical mobility. People frequently mix with strangers without knowing their status. As a result, it is increasingly difficult for people to see themselves as subject to the power of an omnipotent God. Bruce says, 'The idea of a single moral universe in which all manner and conditions of people have a place in some single grand design became less and less plausible.' Institutional religion therefore exercises a less significant hold over individuals.

Societalization

Bruce (1995, 2002) uses the term **societalization** (first used by Bryan Wilson) to refer to a process in which social life becomes fragmented and ceases to be locally based. Like social differentiation, he sees this as a consequence of a general process of modernization. Modern societies do not have close-knit communities. People's lives are increasingly dominated by large impersonal bureaucracies, and in suburbs people rarely know and mix with their immediate neighbours. People interact with one another at the level of society as a whole rather than within local communities.

According to Bruce, the decline of community undermines religion in three ways. First, without a strong sense of community, churches can no longer serve as the focal point for communities. For example, large proportions of the community will not turn out for a local wedding or funeral at the parish church because most people will not know the people getting married or the deceased. Bruce says: 'When the total, all-embracing community of like-situated people working and playing together gives way to the dormitory town or suburb, there is little held in common left to celebrate.'

Second, people's greater involvement with the broader society in which they live leads them to look far more widely for services. They are less likely to turn to the local priest or vicar for practical or emotional support.

Third, the cultural diversity of the society in which people live leads them to hold beliefs with less certainty. Bruce (1995) says, 'Beliefs are strongest when they are unexamined and naively accepted as the way things are.' In a society where we no longer get constant reinforcement of a particular religious view:

> *Religious belief is now obviously a matter of choice. We may still choose to believe, but we cannot easily hide from ourselves the knowledge that we choose God rather than God choosing us. God may still be respected and loved but that he no longer need be feared means that one major source of motivation for getting religion right has been removed.* Bruce, 1995

According to Bruce, then, fundamental changes in social life in modern societies lead to institutional religion losing its social base, many of its social roles and its main source of legitimation. However, Bruce may exaggerate the extent of change and the consequences for religion. For example, there has been a long-standing debate about whether, and to what extent, there has been a decline of community, with many commentators questioning the view that there has been a straightforward movement from strong to weak communities (see, for example, Slattery, 1985).

Bruce asserts the decline of community without examining the evidence in detail. Similarly, some writers have questioned the dominance of religious worldviews in the past (see below, p. 438). However, Bruce is certainly correct to point out that there has been a growth of religious diversity in many modern societies. The significance of this will now be considered.

Institutional religion – religious pluralism

Some researchers imply that the truly religious society has one faith and one church. This picture is influenced by the situation in some small-scale, non-literate societies, such as the Australian Aborigines, where the community is a religious community. Members share a common faith and at certain times of the year the entire community gathers to express this faith in religious rituals.

In terms of Durkheim's (1961, first published 1912) view of religion, the community is the church. Medieval European societies provided a similar picture: there the established church ministered to the whole society.

A number of sociologists essentially follow this line of thinking. Steve Bruce (1992) argues that religious pluralism results from a variety of sources, all of which have 'undermined the communal base to religious orthodoxy'. England expanded to incorporate Scotland and Ireland, which had different religious traditions, while migration has led to a plurality of religious groups in both North America and Europe. Industrialization reduced the contact between social classes and helped to create new, predominantly working-class versions of Christianity, such as Methodism.

Modernization and industrialization bring with them the **social fragmentation** of society into a plurality of cultural and religious groups. As we have seen above, Bruce believes that as a consequence the state can no longer support a single religion without causing conflict. The **plurality of religions** reminds individuals that their beliefs are a personal preference, a matter of choice, and no longer part and parcel of their membership of society. Indeed, Bruce sees these processes as absolutely central to secularization.

Strong religion (Bruce, 2002), which dominates people's lives and shapes how they live in profound ways, cannot be widespread in a fragmented society. It may survive in isolated pockets (such as in Amish communities in the USA or in some sects), but to continue such communities must try to isolate themselves from the secular climate of the wider society.

Weak religion, which is more a matter of personal choice and does not claim to be the only legitimate religion, is more suited to fragmented societies. It accepts there may be more than one way to spiritual truth and does not seek to dominate individual lives to the same extent as strong religion. In this form, religion can be more widespread in modern secular societies, but because it is voluntary, a matter of choice, and does not govern how people live their lives, it has little social impact. Weak religion is typified by liberal Protestant churches, the New Age and some cults.

However, contrary to Bruce's view, it could be argued that a truly religious society is simply one in which religious beliefs and institutions thrive. It is not necessary for everyone to share the same religious beliefs for religion to be important. Northern Ireland is a case in point. There the divisions between Catholics and Protestants are associated with higher rates of church membership and attendance than in other parts of the UK.

In some modern societies (such as the USA) it could be the case that religious pluralism exercises a strong influence on society in general, encouraging a toleration of diversity in which a plurality of beliefs can thrive. However religious pluralism is perceived in modern societies, it largely stems from two sources: from the existence of different ethnic groups with their own religious traditions, and from the growth of new sects and cults. These will now be examined.

Ethnicity and religious diversity

Steve Bruce (1996) acknowledges that certain ethnic groups often retain strong religious beliefs. However, he does not see this as an argument against the secularization thesis. This is because Bruce believes religion remains strong because of its social importance rather than because the members of the group have deep religious convictions as individuals.

Bruce claims that religion tends to serve one of two main purposes for ethnic groups: **cultural defence** or **cultural transition**:

1 Religions take on the role of **cultural defence** where:

> *there are two (or more) communities in conflict and they are of different religions (for example, Protestants and Catholics in Ulster, or Serbs (Orthodox), Croats (Roman Catholic) and Bosnian Muslims in what used to be Yugoslavia), then the religious identity of each can call forth a new loyalty as religious identity becomes a way of asserting ethnic pride.* Bruce, 1996

From Bruce's point of view, it is their ethnic identity that is important, rather than religiosity. In Northern Ireland he cites the example of Ian Paisley's Democratic Unionist Party. It represents Northern Ireland Protestants who strongly support the union of Northern Ireland within the UK. (They opposed the original peace proposals in 1998–9.) Most of the activists in this party are members of the evangelical Protestant Free Presbyterian Church. Only a tiny percentage of the Northern Irish population, about 1 per cent, are Free Presbyterians, but Ian Paisley's party gets much more support than that. This is because, according to Bruce, ethnic Protestants identify themselves with the party's opposition to a united Ireland, not because they are attracted to the religious convictions of the party's activists.

2 **Cultural transition**

> *involves religion acquiring an enhanced importance because of the assistance it can give in helping people cope with the shift from one world to another. It might be that the people in question have migrated; it might be that they remain in the same place while that place changes under their feet.* Bruce, 1996

Religion is used as a resource for dealing with situations where people have to change their identity to some extent. For example, Asian and African Caribbean migrants to Britain and their descendants can use mosques, temples and churches as centres for their communities, and their religion as a way of coping with the ambiguities of being Asian or black and British.

However, Bruce believes that religion loses this role where a group becomes increasingly integrated into the host community. For example, Irish Catholics who migrated to England and Scotland were originally subject to considerable hostility and discrimination from the host population. Catholicism was very important to this group for several generations. However, as Irish Catholics have married outside their own ethnic group and have enjoyed increasing success, prosperity and acceptance by other members of the population, the importance of their religion as a focus for community identity has declined.

Bruce concludes: 'Cultural defence and cultural transition may keep religion relevant but they will not create a religious society out of a secular one.'

However, this interpretation is not shared by everybody. The historian Callum G. Brown (1992) questions Bruce's claim that it can be seen as evidence of secularization when religion has a role in cultural defence or cultural transformation for particular ethnic groups. Brown sees 'ethnic defence' as a key function of religion in the modern world. He denies there was ever a 'Golden Age' in which religion provided a single, unifying worldview for all members of a society. There has always been some diversity in religious outlooks and there have always been some who were sceptical or hostile towards religion. The role of religion has changed, but that is not the same thing as decline. Brown says: 'Religion adapts to different social and economic contexts. It is not static, unchanging and unyielding to different situations. Such changes that churches undergo do not necessarily mean secularization.' In particular, he argues that contemporary religion might draw its strength from individual communities (including ethnic communities) rather than from society as a whole. A religiously plural society can also be a non-secular society; both the USA and Britain are examples.

Certainly, there is plenty of evidence that religion can and often does remain strong among ethnic groups. (See pp. 425–9 for further details.)

Sects, cults and secularization

The continuing proliferation of sects has been interpreted by some researchers in much the same way as the spread of denominations and religious pluralism in general. It has been seen as a further fragmentation of institutional religion and therefore as evidence of the weakening hold of religion over society.

Accurate measurements of the numbers of sects and the size of their memberships are not available, but estimates have been made. Although Roy Wallis (1984) believed there was a decline in new religious movements in the late 1970s and early 1980s, more recent figures suggest they have been growing (see p. 432). There are certainly more sects today than there were before the Second World War.

The apparent vitality of sects seems to provide evidence against the secularization theory. World-rejecting sects are perhaps the most religious type of organization, since they demand greater commitment to the religion than other organizations. If they are stronger than in the past, it suggests religion retains a considerable appeal for the populations of advanced industrial societies. Andrew Greeley (1972) believes that the growth of new religious movements represents a process of **resacrilization**: interest in, and belief in, the sacred is being revived. Societies such as Britain and the USA are, if anything, becoming less secular.

Rodney Stark and William S. Bainbridge (1985) also deny that secularization has taken place. Some established churches may have lost part of their emphasis on the supernatural, but Stark and Bainbridge believe that secularization never advances far because new religious groups with more emphasis on the supernatural constantly emerge. They put forward statistical evidence to support this claim. According to their figures on religious activity in different states of the USA, cults thrive where conventional religions are weak. For example, in California relatively few people are church-goers but many believe in supernatural phenomena.

Nevertheless other sociologists see the growth of sects as evidence of secularization. Peter Berger (1970) argues that belief in the supernatural can only survive in a sectarian form in a secular society. In order to maintain a strong religious belief and commitment, individuals must cut themselves off from the secularizing influences of the wider society, and seek out the support of others of like mind. The sect, with its close-knit community organization, provides a context in which this is possible. From this viewpoint, the sect is the last refuge of the supernatural in a secular society. Sects are therefore evidence of secularization.

Bryan Wilson (1982) takes a similar view, maintaining that sects are 'a feature of societies experiencing secularization, and they may be seen as a response to a situation in which religious values have lost social pre-eminence'. In other words, sects are the last outpost of religion in societies where religious beliefs and values have little consequence.

Bryan Wilson is particularly scathing in his dismissal of the religious movements of the young in the West, such as Krishna Consciousness, which emerged during the 1960s in the USA. He regards them as 'almost irrelevant' to society as a whole, claiming: 'They add nothing to any prospective reintegration of society, and contribute nothing towards the culture by which a society might live.'

By comparison, Methodism, in its early days as a sect, provided standards and values for the new urban working class, which helped to integrate its members within the wider society. In addition, its beliefs 'steadily diffused through a much wider body of the population'.

Wilson thinks that the new religious movements show no such promise. Their members live in their own enclosed, encapsulated little worlds. There they emphasize 'hedonism, the validity of present pleasure, the abandonment of restraint and the ethic of "do your own thing"'. Wilson is scornful of their 'exotic novelty', which he believes offers little more than self-indulgence, titillation and short-lived thrills. He believes that movements which seek the truth in Asian religions and emphasize the exploration of the inner self – such as Krishna Consciousness – can give little to Western society. They simply 'offer another way of life for the self-selected few rather than an alternative culture for mankind'. Rather than contributing to a new moral reintegration of society, they just provide a religious setting for 'dropouts'. They do not halt the continuing process of secularization and are 'likely to be no more than transient and volatile gestures of defiance' in the face of a secular society.

Similar conclusions are reached by Steve Bruce (1995, 1996, 2002). He argues that new religious movements only recruit very small numbers compared to the massive decline in mainstream Christian religions. World-rejecting new religions have affected the smallest number. World-accommodating new religions have influenced a greater number, yet even in this case numbers are small. Bruce (2002) estimates that the active membership of Eastern-based spiritual groups such as Hare Krishna and TM 'is not likely to be much above 10,000 – fewer than the number lost to the Christian churches in a month'.

Furthermore, these religious movements have the least impact on people's lives. To Bruce (1996), 'people who chant in Soka Gakki or meditate in TM or attend EST seminars (Erhard's Seminar Training) or Insight weekends' carry on their lives very much as normal and there 'are no consequences for the operation of the social system'.

Secularization and the New Age

Bruce has also commented on the significance, or in his view the lack of significance, of the New Age. Like new religious movements, he sees the New Age as posing little or no threat to the validity of the theory of secularization. Although it affects more people than sects, 'it cannot aspire to promote radical and specific change because it does not have the cohesion and discipline of the sect' (Bruce, 1996).

The beliefs advocated by the New Age are **diffuse** (Bruce, 2002). Diffuse religion promotes individualism and tolerance – people can believe whatever they choose and need not follow a single set of teachings. According to the New Age, what works for you is your truth, while others can have different truths. This solves the problem of living in pluralistic societies such as Britain. It allows many different beliefs to exist side by side.

However, diffuse religion produces only 'slight commitment and little agreement about detail'. People will not make sacrifices or change their lives in profound ways for diffuse religion. Without a community to constantly reiterate and reinforce a set of beliefs, and without agreement that access to a single truth requires devotion to a religious organization, New Age beliefs are very weak and it is difficult to sustain serious commitment to them. In fact, Bruce (1996) believes that the New Age is simply an extreme form of the individualism that is characteristic of modern societies. As such it has a role as 'symptom and as a cause in the erosion of faith in orthodoxies and the authority of professional knowledge'.

However, Bruce believes that toned-down aspects of New Age beliefs may become accepted as parts of the 'cultural mainstream'. For example, New Age has had some impact on people's concern for the environment and willingness to give credence to alternative medicines.

It could be argued that Bruce underestimates the significance of the effects he identifies. If substantial numbers of people are willing to question scientific orthodoxy and place some trust in beliefs which require a degree of faith, this in itself could be taken as evidence against the secularization theory.

Paul Heelas (1996) certainly regards the New Age as rather more significant than does Bruce. He quotes a 1993 Gallup opinion poll which found that in Britain 26 per cent of people believed in reincarnation, 40 per cent in some sort of spirit, 17 per cent in flying saucers and 21 per cent in horoscopes; while a 1989 Gallup poll found that no less than 72 per cent had 'an awareness of a sacred presence in nature'.

Some indication of the vitality of the New Age is provided by a study conducted by Paul Heelas, Linda Woodhead and colleagues in the town of Kendal in Cumbria, in northern England (Kendal Project, 2001a, 2001b; Heelas *et al.*, 2005). The study attempted to find every religious group in Kendal, and groups with a spiritual dimension in Kendal and within a five-mile radius.

The researchers identified twenty-six different churches, and on 26 November 2000 a total of 2,315 people attended these churches. They also found a total of sixty-two groups with a spiritual dimension, including:

> *23 yoga groups; 7 Tai Chi groups; 7 dancing, singing drumming or arts and crafts groups; 5 healing groups; 4 groups with an earth-based spirituality; 4 syncretic or interfaith groups; 4 therapy or self-discovery groups; 4 women's groups; 3 Buddhist groups; and several other specialized groups such as Bahai and Sai Babba.* Kendal Project, 2001a

All of these groups used a language of spiritual growth. They also found ninety people who practised alternative therapies, of whom sixty-three said their practice had a spiritual dimension.

From their research they were able to estimate that about 450 people attended groups and about 280 saw a spiritual practitioner. Therefore, a total of around 730 people were involved in spiritually inclined but non-Christian activities in a single week. This compared to 674 who worshipped in Anglican churches in a typical week. This high level of active participation showed New Age beliefs to be quite significant in the lives of many people in Kendal (see pp. 444–5).

Using a broad definition of the New Age, then, there appears to be widespread belief in some of its claims among a high proportion of the population, and active participation among a significant minority.

Some New Age magazines are quite successful (with circulation figures in the tens of thousands), and in the USA there are several thousand New Age bookshops. Heelas argues that aspects of New Age beliefs are deeply embedded in contemporary Western culture. They are a 'radicalized' version of 'humanistic expressivism'. The New Age might not be much like a traditional religion; but to Heelas it provides a strong argument against the view that modern societies have become secular and rational. It is just that individuals have turned within themselves in the search for spirituality, rather than looking to the external authority of church religions. Heelas *et al.* (2005) see this as part of a spiritual revolution involving a shift from the congregational domain of conventional religion towards the self-spirituality of the holistic milieu (see pp. 444–5).

Institutional religion – the secularization of religious institutions in the USA

According to Will Herberg (1960), the main evidence for secularization in the USA is not to be found in a decline in participation in religion, but in a decline in the religiosity of churches and denominations themselves. The major denominations have increasingly emphasized this world as opposed to the other world; they have moved away from traditional doctrine and concern with the supernatural; they have compromised their religious beliefs to fit in with the wider society. Because of this, they have become more like the secular society in which they are set.

Herberg's general views have been supported by Heelas and Seel (2003). Reviewing evidence from the USA, they claim that the more subjective religions, which allow considerable freedom to believers, have been the most successful in the USA in recent years. There has been a move away from traditional religions which involve being disciplined to act in accordance with religious beliefs. This view is linked to more general claims about the **subjectivization of religion** (in which individuals develop their own personal religious views) which emerged in the Kendal Project (see pp. 444–5 for further details).

However, other writers have strongly challenged Herberg's views. Roof and McKinney (1987) accept that Herberg's analysis had much merit when it was written in the 1950s, but they argue, 'it failed to ring true in the America of the 1980s'. In particular, not all religious groupings seem to have turned their back on what Herberg would see as authentic religion. Like other commentators, Roof and McKinney note the growth of conservative Protestant religions (sometimes called the New Christian Right), which seem to combine a serious commitment to religious teachings, a strong element of theological doctrine and a refusal to compromise religious beliefs. As such, they seem to directly contradict Herberg's claims about secularization within religious institutions.

Institutional religion – the New Christian Right

Roof and McKinney categorize the following religious groups in America as conservative Christians: Southern Baptists, Churches of Christ, Evangelicals/ Fundamentalists, Nazarenes, Pentecostalists/Holiness, Assemblies of God,

Churches of God and Adventists. Using survey data, they estimated that conservative Protestants made up 15.8 per cent of the American population in 1984. Their evidence suggests these groups have been growing since the 1920s. They quote a 1976 Gallup poll which found that 34 per cent of the population said they had been 'born again'.

Roof and McKinney's data also show that conservative Protestants are more likely than any other religious group in the USA to attend church and believe in God. They have rejected any move towards liberal values and instead strongly support traditional morality. Conservative Protestants have been strong opponents of abortion, extra-marital or pre-marital sex, homosexuality and the relaxation of divorce laws. They have supported literal interpretations of the Bible, campaigning against the teaching of evolutionary biology on the grounds that it contradicts the biblical account of God's creation of the earth.

More recent data suggest that conservative Christian groups have continued to grow at the expense of more moderate, mainline Protestant denominations. Almond *et al.* note that membership of the Southern Baptists increased from around 10 million in 1960 to 17 million in 2000, and membership of Pentecostalist denominations increased from less than 2 million to nearly 12 million over the same period (Almond *et al.*, 2003). In contrast, membership of mainline denominations fell. The United Methodists lost more than 2 million members, falling from over 10 million in 1960 to under 8 million in 2000, and Episcopalians also declined from 3.5 million to 2 million.

The limited impact of the New Christian Right

Although the New Christian Right has set up its own radio and TV stations and publishing houses and has campaigned in numerous elections, Steve Bruce (1988, 1996) argues that they have had very little impact. Very few of its members who have stood for national office have won their elections. Only five senators have supported the New Christian Right and they have failed to get any new Federal legislation passed. Opinion polls have shown no shift towards their views on moral issues. In Bruce's (1996) view they have achieved no more than to 'remind cosmopolitan Americans that fundamentalists were not extinct and still had some rights'.

Bruce acknowledges that the USA is less secular than Britain, but he believes the New Christian Right may have merely slowed down the process of secularization within its own religious institutions, and has failed to do any more than that. Indeed, he believes the only reason the New Christian Right gets so much attention is that its members are unusual for holding strong religious convictions in a largely secular world.

Internal secularization in Britain

Less attention has been devoted to the possibility that British churches and denominations have undergone secularization. However, Steve Bruce (1988) believes that British mainstream churches have abandoned, or at least watered down, a number of their religious convictions. These include beliefs in the virgin birth, Christ's bodily resurrection (the former Bishop of Durham, David Jenkins, called it a 'conjuring trick with a bag of bones'), heaven and hell, and the expectation that Christ would return to earth. Bruce also points out that most British Christian churches have ceased to claim a monopoly on religious truth.

In the previous sections we examined approaches to secularization largely in terms of institutional religion. Our focus now changes to a more general view of the role of religion in Western society and is concerned with the influence of religious beliefs and values on social norms and values, social action and consciousness. As in previous sections, assessments of the importance of religion depend largely on the observer's interpretation of what constitutes a 'religious society' and religiously motivated action.

Religion and society – desacrilization

A number of sociologists have argued that the sacred has little or no place in contemporary Western society, that society has undergone a process of **desacrilization**. This means that supernatural forces are no longer seen as controlling the world, action is no longer directed by religious belief, and human consciousness has become secularized.

Disenchantment

Weber's interpretation of modern society provides one of the earliest statements of the desacrilization thesis. He claimed that modern society is 'characterized by rationalization and intellectualization and, above all, by the "disenchantment of the world"' (Weber, quoted in Gerth and Mills, 1948). The world is no longer charged with mystery and magic; the supernatural has been banished from society. The meanings and motives that direct action are now rational.

Weber's concept of rational action and his view that modern society is undergoing a process of rationalization are examined in detail in Chapter 15 (pp. 874–8). Briefly, rational action involves a deliberate and precise calculation of the importance of alternative goals and the effectiveness of the various means of attaining chosen goals.

For example, if an individual's goal is to make money, he or she will coldly and carefully calculate the necessary initial investment and the costs involved in producing and marketing a commodity in the most economical way possible. His or her measurements will be objective: they will be based on factors that can be quantified and accurately measured. He or she will reject means to reach that goal which cannot be proven to be effective.

Rational action rejects the guidelines provided by emotion, by tradition or by religion. It is based on the cold, deliberate reason of the intellect, which demands that the rationale for action can only be based on the proven results.

Science and reason

A number of sociologists have accepted Weber's interpretation of the basis for action in industrial society. In

Religion in a Secular Society (1966), Bryan Wilson stated: 'Religious thinking is perhaps the area which evidences most conspicuous change. Men act less and less in response to religious motivation: they assess the world in empirical and rational terms.'

Wilson argued that the following factors encouraged the development of rational thinking and a rational worldview:

1. Ascetic Protestantism, which 'created an ethic which was pragmatic, rational, controlled and anti-emotional' (see pp. 406–9).
2. The rational organization of society, which results in people's 'sustained involvement in rational organizations – firms, public service, educational institutions, government, the state – which impose rational behaviour upon them'.
3. A greater knowledge of the social and physical world, which results from the development of the physical, biological and social sciences. Wilson maintained that this knowledge was based on reason rather than faith. He claimed: 'Science not only explained many facets of life and the material environment in a way more satisfactory [than religion], but it also provided confirmation of its explanation in practical results' (Wilson, 1966).
4. The development of rational ideologies and organizations to solve social problems. Ideologies such as communism and organizations such as trade unions offer practical solutions to problems. By comparison, religious solutions, such as the promise of justice and reward in the afterlife, do not produce practical and observable results.

Wilson argues that a rational worldview is the enemy of religion. It is based on the testing of arguments and beliefs by rational procedures, on assessing truth by means of factors that can be quantified and objectively measured. Religion is based on faith and as such is non-rational. Its claim to truth cannot be tested by rational procedures.

Peter Berger (1970) developed some of Weber's and Wilson's ideas within the framework of the sociology of knowledge. He maintained that people in Western society increasingly 'look upon the world and their own lives without the benefit of religious interpretations'. As a result there is a secularization of consciousness. Berger argued that the 'decisive variable for secularization' is 'the process of rationalization that is the prerequisite for any industrial society of the modern type'. A rational worldview rejects faith which is the basis of religion. It removes the 'mystery, magic and authority' of religion.

Steve Bruce (2002) stresses the importance of **rationalization**, rather than science itself. He argues that science and religion can coexist quite easily. Religious faith, where it is backed up and supported by a strong religious community, is not susceptible to being disproved by science. This is because 'some people are quite capable of sustaining beliefs long after the point where the impartial observer might suppose those beliefs refuted by the evidence (creationism, for example)'. However, technological advances have given individuals a greater sense of control over the natural world and less need to resort to supernatural explanations or remedies. Bruce says:

> *We may still go to church to celebrate the successful conclusion of the harvest but we use chemical fertilizers and weed-killers rather than prayer to ensure a good crop. When all the conventional medical solutions have been exhausted, we may pray for the health of a loved one, but only a very few small sects reject conventional medicine and trust instead to the Lord.* Bruce, 1988

However, the general spread of rationalization is much more important than any direct influence of science and technology, particularly in the planning of social life in bureaucracies. Bruce says:

> *A world of rationality is less conducive to religion than a traditional society. Everything is seen as potentially improvable. Everything can be made more efficient. We find it very easy to talk about means and procedures but very difficult to discuss transcendental means.* Bruce, 1996

Bruce acknowledges that such events as the death of a loved one or an injustice suffered may lead people to turn to God. There are some things in the modern world that science and rationality cannot deal with. However, when people do turn to God, they do so as individuals. Furthermore, they tend to do so as a last resort after the rational, scientific alternatives have all been fully exhausted. Thus:

> *When we have tried every cure for cancer, we pray. When we have revised for our examinations, we pray. We do not pray instead of studying, and even committed believers suppose that a research programme is more likely than a mass prayer meeting to produce a cure for Aids.* Bruce, 1996

Although the argument that science and/or rationalism have triumphed over religion and superstition appears strong, not everybody finds it convincing. For example, the development of New Age beliefs seems to suggest that the non-rational has a place in contemporary societies (see pp. 420–3 and 439–40). Furthermore, there is plenty of evidence which appears to point to a religious revival on a global scale (see pp. 432–3).

Also, the theory of **postmodernism** suggests that societies have begun to move beyond the scientific rationality of modernity, partly because they have started to mistrust science. People are increasingly aware of the failures of science (including the failure to find a cure for AIDS) and, more importantly, the negative side-effects that can be produced by science and technology. Examples might include global warming, air pollution, increasing cancer rates, the depletion of the ozone layer, and so on. In these circumstances people may turn to religion, of one sort or another, as an alternative to science, which some see as creating as many problems as it solves. The relationship between religion and postmodern society will be examined shortly (see pp. 453–5).

In this section we have considered the desacrilization thesis; that is, the view that religion and the sacred have largely been removed from the meanings that guide action and interpret the world, and from the consciousness of humanity. This view is difficult to evaluate since it is largely based on the impressions of particular researchers rather than 'hard' data. In addition, it compares industrial society with often unspecified pre-industrial societies in which, presumably, religion provided a guide to action and a basis for meaning. We will deal with the problems involved in this approach in the next section.

Religion in pre-industrial societies

As we saw in the previous sections, the term 'secularization' has been used in many different ways. Whichever way it has been used, though, the supporters of the theory of secularization have tended to take it for granted that pre-industrial societies were highly religious. Some researchers have challenged this view.

The anthropologist Mary Douglas (1973) argues that the use of supposedly 'religious', small-scale non-literate societies as a basis for comparison with modern 'secular' societies is unjustified:

> *The contrast of secular with religious has nothing whatever to do with the contrast of modern with traditional or primitive ... The truth is that all varieties of scepticism, materialism and spiritual fervour are to be found in the range of tribal societies.* Douglas, 1973

It is simply an illusion concocted by Westerners that 'all primitives are pious, credulous and subject to the teaching of priests or magicians'.

In the same way, the search for the 'Golden Age' of religion in the European past may provide an equally shaky standard for comparison. From his study of religion in sixteenth- and seventeenth-century England, K.V. Thomas states: 'We do not know enough about the religious beliefs and practices of our remote ancestors to be certain of the extent to which religious faith and practice have actually declined' (quoted in Glasner, 1977).

Secularization – international comparisons

International variations

Some sociologists studying secularization have concentrated on making observations about, and researching into, particular modern industrial societies. They have, nevertheless, often assumed that secularization is a universal and perhaps inevitable process. Bryan Wilson (1966) claimed, for example, 'Secularization, then, is a long-term process occurring in human society.' However, by concentrating on Britain and the USA, sociologists have taken a rather narrow view of social change and religion. For instance, they have not accounted for the revival over recent years of Islamic fundamentalism in Iran and other countries.

David Martin (1978) takes a wider view than most sociologists by looking at the changing role of religion in a range of societies. Martin's research shows very different patterns of religious practice in various advanced industrial countries. In predominantly Roman Catholic countries, such as Italy and Spain, there tends to be more religious participation than in predominantly Protestant countries such as Britain. Attendance tends to be particularly low in countries where the church is closely tied to the state. For example, Sweden has attendance rates of only some 5 per cent.

Religion is strongest in those modern industrial societies where a plurality of religious and ethnic groups express their cultural differences through membership of and participation in religion. Thus religion remains comparatively strong in the USA because its population is largely made up of ethnic and national groups who were originally migrants to the USA.

Martin (1991a, 1991b) has also drawn attention to the contrasting fates of religions in different 'third world' countries. In some Latin American countries the Roman Catholic Church remains a key institution in society, and Protestantism has made few converts. In others, such as Brazil, there have been many converts to Protestantism.

In Islamic societies religious change also varies from country to country. In Tunisia and Egypt the state has become more secular: Islamic beliefs do not have a great influence on political decisions. In Iran the Islamic revolution of 1979 took the country in the opposite direction, with religious leaders gaining most of the political power. In other countries there is a continuing conflict between the religious and the secular. In Sudan, for example, there are strong advocates of religious pluralism and tolerance, but there are others who wish to see an Islamic state established. In Turkey attitudes towards religion are ambivalent. Some see religion as a cause of 'backwardness'. Others see it as the vital foundation on which the moral values of the society rest.

Grace Davie (2002, 2006) also argues that the strength and nature of religion vary enormously around the world. Within Europe there are some countries, such as Poland and the Republic of Ireland, where religious participation remains very high. In most parts of Europe, however, participation has fallen; but this makes Europe the 'exceptional case' not the norm for the rest of the world (Davie, 2002).

Even in Europe, the decline of religion may be exaggerated. Although most people might not wish to be actively involved in religion, they are still broadly supportive of churches as institutions, they have no wish to see them disappear, and indeed welcome them as a resource they can draw on in times of need. Many people are happy in the knowledge that in times of personal or national crisis they can turn back to religion and religious leaders for guidance. Davie calls this vicariousness – people enjoy the benefits of religion without themselves taking an active role.

Davie (2002) describes the vitality of religion in the USA, Africa, Latin America and the Far East (for example, in South Korea). She particularly draws attention to the success of Pentecostalist churches in Latin America and elsewhere. She comments:

> *There are now about a quarter of a billion Pentecostalists in the modern world, making this the fastest growing form of Christianity in the modern world. And in Latin America, Pentecostalist initiatives eclipse their secular equivalents, a point on which all commentators agree.* Davie, 2006, p. 138

Some sociologists who have discussed religion on a global scale argue that, far from secularization taking place, religion is undergoing a major revival. Gilles Kepel (1994) claims that any trend towards secularization was reversed around 1975. Furthermore, the various religious revivals were very ambitious – they were aimed at 'recovering a sacred foundation for the organization of society – by changing society if necessary'.

Kepel uses the examples of Christians in the USA and Europe, Jews in Israel, and Muslims throughout the world to support his case. All of these revivals represent attempts to counter secularism. They are a reaction to the apparent failure of attempts to base the policies of nation-states upon secular principles. He says, 'They regard the vainglorious emancipation of reason from faith as the prime cause of the ills of the twentieth century, the beginnings of a process leading straight to Nazi and Stalinist totalitarianism.' As such, they are very much a reaction against modernity.

Some people who support the theory of secularization accept that it is not a universal process. Steve Bruce (2002) for example, is quite specific in arguing that secularization applies to pluralistic, democratic Western societies such as those of Europe and North America. Such societies are socially fragmented and lack the strong communities necessary to sustain religion as an important force in society. This more limited use of the concept of secularization is more defensible than the claim that secularization is an inevitable and global phenomenon.

Secularization – conclusion

Problems with proving or disproving secularization

As the views of sociologists such as Martin and Kepel illustrate, the secularization thesis has not been definitively proved or disproved. This is partly because sociologists, from Weber to Wilson and from Comte to Casanova, have used the term 'secularization' in many different ways. This has led to considerable confusion, since writers discussing the process of secularization are often arguing about different things.

Glock and Stark (1969) argue that researchers have been unable to measure the significance of religion because they have not given adequate attention to defining religion and religiosity. Until they have clearly thought out and stated exactly what they mean by these terms, the secularization thesis cannot be adequately tested.

There is some evidence that contemporary theorists of secularization do pay more attention to differentiating between different issues that have been considered under the heading 'secularization'. For example, Bruce (1995, 1996, 2002), a strong advocate of the theory of secularization, accepts that religion can remain an important part of individual beliefs, but he believes that religion has lost its social and political significance.

Casanova and types of secularization

José Casanova (1994) distinguishes three aspects of secularization:

1 Secularization as **differentiation**. In these terms secularization takes place when non-religious spheres of life (such as the state and the economy) become separate from and independent of religion.
2 Secularization as a **decline of religious beliefs** and practices. In this case secularization takes place when fewer individuals take part in religious activities or hold religious beliefs.
3 Secularization as **privatization**. With this type of secularization, religion stops playing any part in public life and does not even try to influence how politicians make decisions or individuals in society choose to live their lives.

Casanova believes recent history shows that religious beliefs and practices are certainly not dying out, and that 'public religions' have increasingly re-entered the public sphere. Thus, to him, it is only in the first sense that secularization has taken place. Religion no longer has a central position in the structure of modern societies, but neither has it faded away.

The Kendal Project and subjectivization

One attempt to provide a single theory to explain and understand religious change has been provided by the Kendal Project (Heelas *et al.*, 2003, 2005). In this study, which took place between 2000 and 2001, a 'body count' of attendees at religious ceremonies was carried out, along with a number of interviews, a street survey and ethnography. The study was based on Kendal, a town in northern England. Heelas *et al.* found that while attendance at churches was declining, more people were becoming involved in spiritually inclined groups and alternative therapies connected to the New Age (see pp. 420–3 for details).

Heelas *et al.* divided more conventional congregations into three groups:

1 Those that emphasize 'individuals in the living of their unique lives'.
2 Those that emphasize that individuals live unique lives 'but offer normative prescriptions about the forms these lives should take'.
3 Those that 'pay little or no attention to unique lives, and require unique subjectivities to be sacrificed on the altar of a higher good'.

The first type came closest to the spiritual beliefs of the New Age. The last type was more typical of strict, traditional religions, where the teachings of the religion are expected to be obeyed with little or no question. Heelas *et al.* found that congregations with the first type of beliefs were likely to be growing fastest, while those with the third type of beliefs were likely to be contracting. Long-established religions which 'have traditionally located authority in individual experience', such as Unitarianism and Quakerism, were thriving.

Along with the growth in interest in the New Age, this led Heelas *et al.* to suggest that both secularization and sacrilization were occurring at the same time. These changes were part of a spiritual revolution in which the nature of spirituality was changing.

Secularization was defined as a decline in traditional theistic religions (based on a strong belief in God). The decline was evident in the falling numbers involved in the **congregational domain**, where members of congregations meet together to pray in places of worship.

On the other hand, **sacrilization**, and increased emphasis on the sacred, was taking place in the holistic milieu. The **holistic milieu** involves support for 'body–mind spirituality' and is evident in New Age beliefs and the beliefs of some religions.

According to the Kendal Project, then, secularization is only taking place in the narrow sense of a decline in traditional religion. From a broader perspective, beliefs are shifting away from traditional religion towards more individualist, spiritually inclined beliefs. Heelas *et al.* attribute this change to the **subjectivization** of social life.

The idea of subjectivization originated in the work of the American sociologist Charles Taylor. He argued that people increasingly see themselves as unique individuals with hidden depths. In part, this can be linked to the development of consumer culture. As consumers, individuals have considerable choice and they tend to feel they can help to shape their own lives through these choices. Through their consumer choices (such as choosing clothes, interior décor and cars) they can express their own individuality. Religions which deny this unique individuality are unpopular because they are not consistent with widespread values and beliefs. Other religious and spiritual beliefs are much more compatible with the mood of the times.

The various conclusions reached by different sociologists reflect the different ways in which secularization is defined and the different areas of the world that are studied. Without an agreed definition of secularization, there is unlikely to be agreement about whether or not it is taking place. However, there is some agreement that religion is changing and that, at least in parts of Europe, traditional church-based religion is in decline. While most sociologists agree that there is increasing interest in New Age beliefs, some (such as Bruce) see this as insignificant, whereas others (such as Heelas *et al.*) see it as evidence of important cultural change.

Most theorists who either support or attack the theory of secularization are now willing to admit that the theory cannot be unproblematically applied to all groups in all modern societies. It can therefore be argued that the national, regional, ethnic and social-class differences in the role of religion make it necessary to relate theories to specific countries and social groups.

Fundamentalism and religious divisions in the modern world

The nature and definition of fundamentalism

The theory of secularization suggests a progressive decline in religion, but, as the previous section indicates, there are many parts of the world where religion appears to be thriving or reviving. In a number of contexts the term **fundamentalism** has been used to describe the nature of religion, particularly where it is undergoing an enthusiastic revival in strongly held beliefs.

In a major comparative study of *Strong Religion* (or fundamentalism), Gabriel Almond, R. Scott Appleby and Emmanuel Sivan (2003) identify fundamentalist movements amongst Jews in Israel, Muslims in Pakistan, Palestine, Egypt, and the Russian regions of Dagestan and Chechnya, Sikhs and Hindus in India, Christians in the USA and Ireland, and even Buddhists in Sri Lanka.

Almond *et al.* note that in five countries fundamentalist groups have taken control of the state. In 1979 the pro-Western Shah of Iran was toppled in an Islamic revolution. In the Sudan in 1993, and in Turkey and Afghanistan in 1996, Islamic regimes also gained control. In India in 1998 and 1999 a Hindu fundamentalist party won the national elections. Since Almond *et al.* were writing, Hamas, a Palestinian fundamentalist group, have also come to power (in 2006).

Elsewhere – for example, in Pakistan and the USA – fundamentalist groups may not have gained outright power, but there have been political leaders (such as George Bush) who have had some sympathy with fundamentalist views.

Islamic fundamentalism has perhaps been subject to more attention than other forms, particularly after the Islamic fundamentalist group Al Qaeda's 9/11 attacks in the USA, the train bombings in Madrid in 2004, and the suicide bombings in London in July 2005. However, fundamentalism is by no means confined to Islam. Furthermore, most Islamic people (like most Christians, Hindus and the followers of other religions) are not usually regarded as fundamentalists.

Fundamentalism is sometimes linked to violence, particularly terrorism, though this is not always the case.

According to Steve Bruce (2000), the term fundamentalism was first used in the 1920s when conservative evangelical Protestants published a series of pamphlets in which they called for a return to 'The Fundamentals of the Faith'. Bruce says they 'reasserted what they saw as the core of Protestant truth against the liberal and progressive spirit of the age' (2000, p. 10). These Protestants were therefore 'anti-modernist' in that they objected to the way in which, as they saw it, their religion was becoming diluted in the modern world.

Bruce notes that all religions will have some elements within them that are conservative and traditional, but he sees fundamentalism as involving more than this. In his view, fundamentalism describes 'movements that respond to problems created by modernization by advocating society-wide obedience to some authentic and inerrant text or tradition and by seeking the political power to impose the revitalized tradition' (Bruce, 2000, p. 94).

Almond *et al.* (2003) reached a definition of fundamentalism after an extensive comparative research project. They defined it as 'a discernible pattern of religious militance by which self-styled "true believers" attempt to arrest the erosion of religious identity, fortify the borders of the religious community, and create viable alternatives to secular institutions and behaviors' (Almond *et al.*, 2003, p. 17).

These two definitions are similar in that both see fundamentalism as a response to a perceived threat to a religion. However, Bruce's definition is perhaps a little narrower. He only defines a movement as fundamentalist if it claims authority for a sacred text and if it seeks society-wide obedience.

Although fundamentalists claim to be reasserting the true meaning of a religion, it should be borne in mind that religions are usually open to many different interpretations. Those claiming to be returning to the original teachings of a religion may well disagree with one another. Thus, Fred Halliday (1994), commenting on Islamic fundamentalism, says, 'no such essential Islam exists: as one Iranian thinker puts it, Islam is a sea in which it is possible to catch almost any fish one wants'. In other words, each particular fundamentalist interpretation of a religion is only one among many.

There is often much room for dispute over what the fundamentals of a religion actually are, although the adherents to a particular version of fundamentalism tend to believe that theirs is the one, true version of the faith.

Steve Bruce – fundamentalism and secularization

Secularization and modernization

The British sociologist Steve Bruce (2000) is a strong advocate of the theory of **secularization** or religious decline (see pp. 429–45). The theory of secularization strongly influences his explanation of fundamentalism. Bruce sees fundamentalism as a reaction to **modernization**.

Modernization involves **societalization** (in which social life becomes increasingly fragmented) and **differentiation** (in which religious life is separated from other aspects of social life such as the economy) (see pp. 436–7 for further discussion). Modernization also involves **rationalization**, in which social life is planned to achieve certain goals, not based upon faith or prayer (see p. 442).

A further feature of modernity is a tendency towards **egalitarianism**, in which all members of society share certain rights. For example, it involves increasingly egalitarian gender roles as women gain full citizenship rights.

According to Bruce, all of these processes challenge the authority of religion, and in some circumstances groups with strongly held religious beliefs will try to defend their religion against the perceived threat to it.

In 'first world' countries, such as the USA, modernization has provided a local and immediate challenge to religious belief as such countries have modernized. Elsewhere – for example, in Islamic countries such as Iran and Turkey – a process of modernization has been imposed upon society from outside by regimes friendly to the West. Examples include the regimes of the Shah of Iran and Kemal Ataturk in Turkey.

In either set of circumstances, Bruce believes that 'the main cause of religious fundamentalism is the belief of religious traditionalists that the world around them has changed so as to threaten their ability to reproduce themselves and their tradition' (2000, p. 95).

The causes of fundamentalism

However, Bruce believes that the existence of a group who feel threatened by secularization and modernization is not sufficient in itself to create a fundamentalist reaction. A number of other factors are also important.

1 Some religions have more potential for developing fundamentalist groups than others. Religions which do not have a single sacred text (such as the Bible or Qur'an) struggle to develop fundamentalist movements. For example, unlike Islam or Christianity, Hinduism is a diverse religion with many Gods and no central sacred text. This makes it more difficult to create a movement claiming to express the 'true' nature of the religion. What Bruce calls **ideological cohesion** makes it much easier to mobilize people and claim their allegiance. Thus, although there has been some Hindu fundamentalism, it has not been as prominent as Islamic fundamentalism. Indeed, Bruce sees both Hindu fundamentalism in India and Sinhalese Buddhist fundamentalism in Sri Lanka as being more an expression of nationalism than of religious orthodoxy.

2 Fundamentalist beliefs tend to be stronger where a group believes it has a common external enemy. Ideological cohesion is not just a property of religious belief; it can develop where a group is united through hostility to a common enemy. Thus Hinduism started to develop some degree of unity when Hindus began to unite in hostility to rule by the British Raj. Similarly, many Islamic fundamentalist groups are united in hostility to the USA and its allies.

3 A third factor is the way in which belief systems are controlled within a religion. Roman Catholicism has not given rise to fundamentalism. According to Bruce this is because religious authority is centralized with the Pope and the Vatican. Such is their authority that dissenters are unlikely to be able to claim that their version of the religion is more true. On the other hand, both Protestantism and Islam are less centralized, and 'authoritative knowledge is democratically available. Any right-spirited person can determine God's will by reading the scriptures or studying the Qur'an' (Bruce, 2000, p. 98).

4 Religious fundamentalism does not just require religious beliefs and organization; it also needs a supply of potential recruits. To Bruce this means that it needs 'members of particular social strata that feel especially threatened, dispossessed or relatively deprived by modernization' (2000, p. 99). In the USA, some Christians, particularly from the South, who felt threatened by the liberal secularism of Washington politicians fell into this category. In Palestine, Hamas has found a supportive constituency amongst young, often unemployed or poor Muslims, who feel anger at their treatment by Israel.

5 The path that fundamentalism takes is also affected by its relation to politics. In the USA, New Right Christian fundamentalists have had ample opportunity to promote their cause through conventional democratic politics. Where this avenue is not open, fundamentalism is more likely to take a violent turn. American Christian fundamentalists have on occasion used violence – for example, against abortion clinics – but violent action is much more common amongst Islamic fundamentalists.

Furthermore, Christianity started out as a deviant religion which was persecuted under Roman rule. Christians were forced to accept a distinction between church and state so that they would 'Render unto Caesar the things that were Caesar's and unto God the things that are God's' (Matthew 22:21, quoted in Bruce, 2000, p. 106).

In contrast, Islam quickly came to dominate states that were led by Islamic leaders. The Prophet himself was a political leader. According to Bruce this has led to followers of Islam seeking political control and, unlike followers of Christianity, not being satisfied with maintaining religious belief without political power.

Christianity emphasizes being religious through holding the correct beliefs (**orthodoxy**), whereas Islam places more emphasis on being religious through one's actions (**ortho-praxis**). Bruce believes that the emphasis on action and on gaining political power, combined with the lack of opportunity for democratic progress in some Muslim countries, makes it more likely that Islamic fundamentalists will turn to violence than Christian fundamentalists.

Bruce's analysis emphasizes that many of the causes of fundamentalism (such as modernization and the existence of groups who are relatively deprived) lie outside religions themselves. However, he does think that religion is important in its own right and is more than a justification for political movements which would have existed anyway. He says,

> *It would be bizarre if something which took up so much of people's wealth and time, and that so dominated so many cultures, did not matter: that it merely served as a cafeteria of convenient legitimations for any sort of behaviour.* Bruce, 2000, p. 103

To Bruce, therefore, it is necessary to look at both wider sociological causes of fundamentalism, and factors which lie within the religions themselves. He sees fundamentalism as a 'rational response of traditionally religious peoples to social, political and economic changes that downgrade and constrain the role of religion in the public world' (Bruce, 2000, p. 117). The response is rational, because Bruce believes that the threat to traditional religion from secularization is real and very strong. He believes that the social changes which threaten religion are so strong that 'Fundamentalism in the West has no chance of winning' (Bruce, 2000, p. 121).

Outside the West its prospects are better, and Islamic fundamentalism, in particular, has centuries-old roots which mean that it is unlikely to disappear any time soon. However, Bruce still believes it faces an uphill struggle. He quotes a study of Jordanians (Antoun, 1994, discussed in Bruce, 2000) who had worked or studied in the West before returning to their village. Although the Jordanians valued Islam and valued many of the traditional aspects of village life, they accepted the need to become more Western by accepting science, technology and rational bureaucracy. Ultimately, Bruce believes, these kinds of secular Western influence will undermine traditional religions throughout the world.

Evaluation

Bruce provides many useful insights into the nature and causes of fundamentalism. However, his views are strongly influenced by his support for the theory of secularization. His view that Islamic fundamentalism is more likely to become violent than other forms is controversial. Linked to this, he places more emphasis on the nature of religious beliefs in explaining fundamentalism than some other sociologists. Karen Armstrong (2001) (see below) places much more emphasis than Bruce on the specific political and economic circumstances that might have encouraged the development of militant Islam, and less emphasis on the nature of the religion itself.

Gabriel Almond, R. Scott Appleby and Emmanuel Sivan – *Strong Religion*

Levels of explanation

In *Strong Religion*, Gabriel Almond, R. Scott Appleby and Emmanuel Sivan (2003) discuss the findings of a major comparative study of fundamentalist religions throughout the world. A total of seventy-five case studies were carried out by researchers over a twenty-year period, and interviews were conducted in the Middle East, North Africa and the United States.

Like Bruce, Almond *et al.* regard some Hindu, Sikh and Buddhist movements as fundamentalist, alongside Muslim and Christian ones. They also follow Bruce in seeing fundamentalism as a reaction to the social changes associated with modernization and secularization (see their definition of fundamentalism on p. 445). However, they take a somewhat broader range of factors into account than Bruce does in explaining the rise of fundamentalism.

Almond *et al.* argue that fundamentalism can be understood at three levels.

1. The **structural** level is concerned with long-term contextual conditions such as structural unemployment, the existence of persecuted ethnic groups or dislocated people, social changes such as secularization, the theology of a religion or economic situation.
2. However, **contingency** and **chance** are also important. Structural factors might create the general situation in which fundamentalism is likely to develop, but specific historical events help to determine whether this is translated into actual movements.
3. The third set of factors concern **human choice** and **leadership** (Almond *et al.*, 2003, p. 116). Even when other factors create the right conditions for fundamentalism, it will not develop without religious leaders who can mobilize large numbers in support of their beliefs. Each of these types of factor will now be examined.

Structural causes of fundamentalism

The first and central structural cause of fundamentalism is **secularization**. Without secularization there would be no need for a fundamentalist movement. Like Bruce, though, Almond *et al.* think that the nature of religious organizations is also important. They argue that religions where individual congregations have some independence are more likely to develop breakaway groups, including fundamentalist ones. If the beliefs of the religion are 'explicit and coherent, codified in texts' (Almond *et al.*, 2003, p. 123), then it is easier to claim to have discovered the true interpretation of the religion.

So far, Almond *et al.* identify very similar factors to Bruce, but they also think that **education** and **communication** are important. For example, the growth of higher education in the USA tended to undermine traditional religious beliefs and increased the influence of **rationalism**. This in turn encouraged some Christians to feel beleaguered and to turn to fundamentalism.

The development of communications has led to globalization, and with it the influence of Western secular rationalism has spread to non-Western countries. However, it has also provided opportunities for fundamentalists to organize and spread their message. Thus the New Christian Right in the USA have made extensive use of the media, including starting their own TV stations. The internet has been important in spreading Islamic fundamentalism worldwide. It also allows the 'demonstration effect' or copy-cat behaviours such as some suicide bombings.

A strong **civil society** – for example, with trade unions or political parties – can help to diffuse the anger and resentment which can feed fundamentalism. However, inequality and deprivation tend to encourage strong religious beliefs. Almond *et al.* quote a study in the USA by Nancy Ammerman (1990, discussed in Almond *et al.*, 2003) which found that Christian fundamentalism amongst Southern Baptists thrived amongst those from working-class backgrounds.

Major **migration** movements also encourage the development of fundamentalism. Where large numbers of people are displaced – for example, Palestinians after the creation of the Israeli state in 1948 – this can breed the resentment on which fundamentalism feeds. Recent migrants who form a minority in a country can also become fundamentalist if they feel their religion and traditions are under threat.

Economic problems can be a major stimulus to fundamentalism. Almond *et al.* say that 'recessions, depressions, inflation, strikes, unemployment and famine may produce grievances among groups in the population inclining them favourably to fundamentalist arguments' (2003, p. 130). However, economic problems can make fundamentalist movements unpopular where they have gained political power, as has occurred at various times in Sudan, Turkey and Iran.

The final structural cause mentioned by Almond *et al.* is **Western imperialism**. Fundamentalism is often tied up with nationalist movements against Western control and influence in colonies, former colonies and countries with pro-Western regimes. A prime example is the 1979 Iranian revolution against the Shah, who was supported by the USA and other Western powers. Another example is the growth of fundamentalism amongst Palestinians after Israel seized land from them during the 1967 Arab–Israeli war.

Contingency and chance

All of the above structural factors make the development of fundamentalism more likely, but it also usually takes a specific shock or trigger to mobilize populations into active participation in fundamentalist movements. Some chance events, such as a particularly poor harvest in a country which is already struggling to feed its population, are made more likely by structural conditions. Others, however, are completely unpredictable. For example, part of the reason for the success of the Iranian revolution in 1979 was the illness of the Shah, who was suffering from terminal cancer, which made it very difficult for him to respond effectively to the threat from fundamentalism.

Human choice and leadership

Even with the right structural conditions and chance factors encouraging fundamentalism, leaders are still needed to persuade people to follow a fundamentalist path. Leaders may be of different types. **Ideological catalysers** are often charismatic individuals able to gain a loyal following due to the force of their personality. They can also have an impact by articulating an ideology which expresses the grievances of a particular group of people and gives them direction. Ayatollah Khomeini, who became leader of Iran in 1979, is an example. In contrast, **organizers** and **coalition makers** rely more on their bureaucratic and political skills to lead a movement. Almond *et al.* use Bob Jones, a fundamentalist Baptist in the USA, as an example of this type of leader.

Conclusion and evaluation

Almond *et al.* conclude that fundamentalism will only thrive when the right combination of structural factors, chance factors and leadership comes together at a specific place and time. If the structural conditions have created a 'mobilizable mass of potential followers' and a 'cataclysmic, transformative event occurs', then the 'trigger creates a new set of circumstances that provides an opening for a fundamentalist movement to expand and assert itself under the guidance of a charismatic and authoritarian leader' (Almond *et al.*, 2003, p. 135).

Almond *et al.* provide a sophisticated and thoroughly researched analysis of the factors leading to the growth of fundamentalism. They examine a wider range of factors and place less emphasis than Steve Bruce does on the characteristics of particular religions. Nevertheless their explanations have much in common since both see fundamentalism as a response to Western secularization amongst poor or relatively deprived groups, or groups who feel particularly threatened by social change. (For further views on fundamentalism see the views of Armstrong, pp. 449–51, and Giddens, pp. 452–3.)

Religion and conflict in the contemporary world

The issue of fundamentalism illustrates the fact that religion appears to be associated with conflict in many parts of the world. These conflicts might include terrorism, civil war, or riots. This section examines some of the competing views of this relationship.

The section starts by considering the view that it is inevitable that different religions, or at least the 'civilizations' associated with them, will tend to clash. However, Karen Armstrong argues that conflict between Islam and the West is far from inevitable, but is the product of particular conditions. Finally, Steve Bruce largely supports this view, arguing that the role of religion in conflict can be exaggerated, and apparently religious conflict can have other roots as well.

Samuel P. Huntington – 'The clash of civilizations'

Samuel P. Huntington sees religion as developing a very important role in the modern world. In Huntington's theory, the groups involved are civilizations rather than nation-states or religions as such. However, there are often close relationships between religions and civilizations.

The relationships between different civilizations are increasingly important because 'the world is becoming a smaller place. The interactions between peoples of different civilizations are increasing; these increasing interactions intensify civilization consciousness' (Huntington, 1993). According to Huntington, the increasing contacts between different groups can sometimes have the effect of intensifying the emphasis upon differences rather than bringing groups closer together, and in doing so can cause conflict.

Civilizations

To Huntington, a 'civilization is a cultural entity'. He says, 'Civilizations are differentiated from each other by history, language, culture tradition, and, most important, religion.' The civilizations he distinguishes are 'Western, Confucian, Japanese, Islamic, Hindu, Slavic-Orthodox, Latin American and possibly African civilization'.

In the contemporary world, sources of identity that are not religious or based on civilization have declined in significance. The end of the Cold War and the collapse of communism have meant that people are less divided by political differences. Economic change, improved communications, travel and migration have weakened the nation-state. On the other hand, regional economic cooperation (for example, in the EU and the North American Free Trade Area) strengthens civilization consciousness. Huntington says, 'In much of the world religion has moved in to fill this gap, often in the form of movements that are labelled "fundamentalist". Such movements are found in Western Christianity, Judaism, Buddhism and Hinduism, as well as Islam.' Because of this, Huntington believes that, far from the world becoming secularized, there is evidence of **unsecularization**.

Clashes between civilizations

Huntington believes there will increasingly be clashes between civilizations. He argues: 'As people define their identity in ethnic and religious terms, they are likely to see an "us" versus "them" relation existing between themselves and people of different ethnicity or religion.'

Geographical closeness increases the likelihood of clashes. Thus, there tend to be high rates of conflict along the borders (or fault lines) between civilizations. Hence, there were clashes in the former Yugoslavia, where Orthodox, Christian and Muslim civilizations met. In the Middle East there are clashes between Islam, Judaism and Western Christianity. Huntington sees the Gulf War of 1990 as partly a clash between Arabs and the West (although there were Arab nations on both sides). In Asia there is the clash between Muslims and Hindus in the Indian subcontinent. China has repressed Buddhists in Tibet and Muslim minorities in China itself.

Increasingly, political leaders use an appeal to civilization consciousness to try to mobilize support. Thus, Saddam Hussein argued that Islamic countries should unite against American imperialism, and the Orthodox Serbs appealed for support from Orthodox Russia in the Bosnian conflict.

According to Huntington, then, most of the conflict in the world can now be related to religious divisions rather than political ones. For example, 'In the 1930s the Spanish Civil War provoked intervention from countries that politically were fascist, communist and democratic. In the 1990s the Yugoslav conflict is provoking intervention from countries that are Muslim, Orthodox and Western Christian.'

Implications for the future

Huntington does not argue that sources of conflict and identity other than civilizations and their religions will disappear or become insignificant. However, he believes that civilizations will become more important than ideology and other sources of conflict. The implication is that religion will become more rather than less important in global terms.

Although at the moment Western Christian civilization is dominant, in the future it will increasingly be challenged. China, for example, has developed nuclear weapons, and Islamic countries such as Pakistan, India and Iran have been trying to develop them (India carried out underground nuclear tests in 1998). There is the possibility of an arms race between Eastern civilizations based on Islamic and Confucian religions.

However, as there is no likelihood of a world or global civilization developing, the different civilizations will have to learn to live with one another. Unfortunately, Huntington's theory gives little reason for optimism that they will do so.

Karen Armstrong – 11 September 2001, Islam and the West

Cultural difference and conflict

Huntington sees increasing contact between cultures and religion as an important consequence of global changes. His work stresses the likelihood of conflict between differing civilizations and religions. If clashes between civilizations are indeed becoming more important, then the clash between Islam and Western society appears to be the most prominent example.

Since the Iranian revolution of 1979 there has been hostility between some Islamic fundamentalists and some Western nations. The attacks on the United States on 11 September 2001 by Islamic militants highlighted the clash and led to further conflict, with President Bush's 'war on terror', which was largely directed at Islamic countries such as Afghanistan and Iraq.

According to Huntington's views, such clashes are more or less inevitable because of the importance of cultural differences and the emphasis placed upon them in a world where different cultures come into closer contact.

This view is challenged by Karen Armstrong, who argues that there is nothing inherently incompatible about the West and the Muslim world. Rather, political and economic factors are behind these increased tensions.

Islam and the failure of modernization

Armstrong argues:

> *About a hundred years ago, almost every leading Muslim intellectual was in love with the West … Politicians and journalists wanted their countries to be just like Britain or France; philosophers, poets even some of the ulama (religious scholars) tried to find ways of reforming Islam according to the democratic, liberal model of the West.* Armstrong, 2001

Some claimed that Western societies were becoming in one respect more Islamic than Islamic countries. Islam advocates the sharing of resources, and at that time a trend towards greater equality was evident in some Western European countries.

The main appeal of Western societies a hundred years ago stemmed from **modernization**. According to Armstrong, modernization has a number of key features.

1. Modern societies are based upon developing new technology and continually reinvesting profit, rather than upon producing an agricultural surplus.
2. This development greatly increases productivity, and the development of industry frees humans from some of the constraints imposed by reliance upon nature.
3. Higher levels of education are needed if people are to become effective workers in the changing economy and this leads to demands for greater democratic rights.
4. The needs of the economy tend to mean that previously excluded groups, such as religious minorities and women, are allowed to take a fuller part in economic activity.
5. These changes lead to the development of the 'modern spirit', which involves greater 'political, intellectual and scientific' independence for people and an emphasis on 'innovation'.

In Western societies modernization took some three hundred years and was a painful and turbulent process. In the twentieth century many Muslim countries attempted the same process in a much shorter time. Armstrong says:

> *The Muslim world has had an especially problematic experience of modernity. These countries have had to modernize far too rapidly. They have had to attempt the process in a mere 50 years instead of 300 years. In addition, in the Muslim world modernity did not bring freedom and independence, it came in the context of political subjugation.* Armstrong, 2001

Western imperialism and human rights

Most Muslim countries, including Egypt, Sudan, Libya and Algeria, were occupied by Western countries. In many countries there were attempts at introducing democracy, but in the end autocratic leaders were imposed by the West. In Iran, for example, the British and then the Americans backed the Pahlavi shahs as dictatorial leaders. The shahs were sympathetic to the West, on which they depended, and this gave the West access to the considerable Iranian oil supplies.

The Shah Muhammad Reza Pahlavi was installed in power in 1953 in a coup supported by the CIA and British intelligence services. He proved to be a particularly ruthless dictator who ordered a massacre in Tudeh Square in 1978 in which nearly 900 people died. He was overthrown the following year in an Islamic revolution.

In Iraq, in 1979, the USA and Britain supported the installation of Saddam Hussein as a dictator because he was hostile to Iran. They supplied him with arms for several years before turning against him.

The West has been keen to support Islamic regimes where it has suited their purposes. Thus Osama Bin Laden was supplied with weapons by the West when he was fighting the occupation of Afghanistan by the Soviet Union. In the Middle East, the USA has provided unwavering support for Israel, its main ally in the area, despite Israel's illegal occupation of Palestinian lands for more than three decades.

Apart from denying Islamic people human rights and democratic government, the influence of the West tended to divide Islamic societies into a Western-educated elite and the mass of the population. Any material benefits provided by modernization, or by the exploitation of oil, tended to go to the elite, while the mass of the population received little. In some Muslim countries (such as Indonesia) Muslims are employed by Western companies as very cheap labour to make 'our nice shirts and jeans'.

The causes of fundamentalism

With both their political and economic ambitions frustrated,

> *many have turned to Islam. The secularist and nationalist ideologies, which they had imported from the West, seemed to have failed them, and by the late 1960s, Muslims throughout the Islamic world had begun to develop what we call fundamentalist movements.* Armstrong, 2001

According to Armstrong, fundamentalism is 'a part of the modern scene'. All fundamentalist movements (including Christian and Jewish ones) believe that Western, secular values aim to wipe out their religions completely. Armstrong says, 'Fundamentalists believe that they are fighting for survival, and when people feel that their backs are to the wall, they can often lash out violently.'

In Palestine, in the attacks on the USA on 11 September 2001, and elsewhere, this is precisely what has happened.

Future prospects

According to Armstrong, there is no fundamental reason why Western and Islamic civilizations should clash. She points out: 'The vast majority of fundamentalists … do not take part in acts of violence.' Although Bin Laden began what he described as a 'holy war' against the USA in 1998,

> *This is … entirely contrary to the central tenets of Islam, which essentially preaches peace. Far from declaring war, as bin Laden has done, on 'Jewish-Christian crusaders', the Koran insists that Muslims treat the 'People of the Book' with courtesy and respect.* Armstrong, 2001

Furthermore, there are very few circumstances in which the Qur'an permits the declaration of war.

Like other religions, Islam is open to a number of interpretations. Fundamentalist interpretations have become popular because of the failure of modernization and the constant interference of Western countries in the Islamic world in ways which damage Muslims but support Western interests. Thus, Armstrong argues that political and economic factors are behind the clash between some Muslims and the West, and not fundamental religious differences or the cultural incompatibility of civilizations.

Armstrong is not, therefore, as pessimistic as Huntington. She believes it could be possible to reduce hostility between the West and Islam. However, it will not be achieved through a 'war on terror'. Instead, what is needed is that people in Western societies campaign through the democratic system to persuade their governments to adopt foreign policies which are fairer to Islamic countries. In the long term, what is needed is a '"one-world" mentality, which could do as much, if not more than our fighter planes, to create a safer and more just world'.

Steve Bruce – conflict, religion and other causes

Huntington's work suggests that religions (or at least cultural differences between civilizations) cause much of the conflict in the modern world. On the other hand, Armstrong places much more emphasis on social, political and economic factors causing the clash between Islam and the West. Steve Bruce (2000) argues that the role of religion in conflict varies. Sometimes religion is no more than a justification for war or violence which has little to do with religion. At other times religion is important in its own right. But often religious and non-religious factors are intertwined and cannot be separated. There are therefore three types of relationship between religion and conflict:

1 Bruce argues that

Religion is commonly invoked to justify what are essentially secular national or ethnic conflicts, even when the combatants are the same religion. In the First World War, Christian leaders blessed their troops and claimed divine support, but very few people involved thought that they were involved in a specifically religious crusade. 2000, p. 8

According to Bruce, a more recent example of this sort of situation was the civil war in the former Yugoslavia in the 1990s. Croats, Serbs and Bosnian Muslims fought one another and religion must have played some role since each group follows a different faith (Croats are Roman Catholic and Serbs are Orthodox). However, the war was largely based on ethnic divisions and concerned control of territories rather than the truth of different faiths.

2 Bruce believes that at the opposite extreme some conflicts are essentially to do with religion. Some participants in conflict see themselves as engaged in a **crusade** (a Christian mission to spread their religion) or ***jihad*** (the Islamic equivalent). Thus Bruce believes that Osama Bin Laden has largely religious motives for his leadership of Al Qaeda, and that Iranian attempts to export its Islamic revolution have also been religiously motivated.

3 In most cases, however, religious and secular motives are 'inseparably intertwined' (Bruce, 2000, p. 9). There is often an overlap between religious groups, national boundaries and ethnic divisions, so a war might be fought for religion, country and ethnicity simultaneously. In these circumstances,

religion is not just a convenient sign of difference (like the contrasting colour shirts of opposing football teams), it is often also deeply embedded in the ethnic or national identity. It provides each side with a justification for seeing itself as superior (we obey God) and the enemy as inferior (they are the Infidel). Bruce, 2000, p. 9

Bruce goes on to argue that even within a single conflict a variety of religious, secular and mixed motives can be present. For example, amongst those who fought the Russians in Chechnya and Dagestan in 1999 were

secular nationalists who wished to push the Russians out of the southern Caucasus ... Muslim fundamentalists keen to regain for the true faith land that had once been Islamic, and ... people who saw the creation of a new state as the best way of promoting the true faith. Bruce, 2000, p. 9

Conclusion

Bruce's analysis suggests that the role of religion in producing conflict can be both exaggerated and underestimated. It may be uncommon for differences in religious belief in themselves to create conflict, though this can happen. More commonly, religion is used to mobilize or strengthen existing divisions and reinforce existing sources of conflict. If Bruce and Armstrong are correct, then Huntington is wrong to see conflict between civilizations or religions as unavoidable, since political, economic and social changes can make clashes between those of different faiths much less likely.

High modernity, postmodernity and religion

Karen Armstrong sets her arguments about Islamic fundamentalism in the context of ideas of modernization. This suggests that in some countries the failure of modernization has led to religious revivals. On the other hand, advocates of secularization, such as Steve Bruce, argue that the development of modernity led to secularization, and fundamentalism is a largely futile attempt to reverse it. According to these arguments, the role of religion becomes marginalized in modernity because science and rationality supplant faith in religious beliefs, and because the differentiation of institutions largely relegates religion to a private sphere. This would suggest that theories which argue that modernity has changed, or that it has been replaced by postmodernity, might imply there is the potential for a religious revival.

Thus, theories of high modernity, along with theories of postmodernity, might be able partly to explain the apparent revival of religion discussed in the sections above. David Lyon (1996), for example, notes: 'Religion, then, is reappearing in sociological accounts of post- or late-modern societies.'

Two theories in which religion has reappeared will now be examined, followed by a discussion of whether the New Age can be seen as a postmodern phenomenon.

Anthony Giddens – high modernity and religious revival

The main features of high modernity

In *The Consequences of Modernity* (1990) and *Modernity and Self-Identity* (1991) Anthony Giddens argues that modern societies have moved into a new phase of **high modernity**. He sees this as a development of modernity and a radicalization of certain features of modernity. However, although high-modern societies develop out of modern ones, they are significantly different.

Like Steve Bruce, Giddens sees modernity as involving rationalization and differentiation. However, high modernity takes these a step further.

First, there is increased **reflexivity**. This involves the constant monitoring of social life in order to improve it. People become increasingly willing to change their beliefs, practices and institutions in the light of new knowledge and experience. The Enlightenment (see pp. 890–1) seemed to offer the promise of certainty through scientific knowledge. However, high modernity leads to an unsettling uncertainty because of this constant willingness to change. It also produces a tendency to undermine the traditional. Giddens (1991) says, 'Modern institutions differ from all preceding forms of social order in respect of their dynamism, the degree to which they undercut traditional habits and customs.' Sociology itself is part of the reflexivity. It involves critically analysing social arrangements rather than taking them as given and retaining them simply because they are traditional.

Second, there are fundamental changes in the organization of time and space. The **separation of time and space** involves a process whereby 'the advent of modernity increasingly tears space away from place by fostering relations between "absent" others, locationally distant from any given situation of face-to-face interaction' (Giddens, 1990). In other words, new communications technology (such as the internet and satellite communications) and the globalization of social life (see pp. 548–57 for a discussion of globalization) mean that social relationships increasingly take place between people who live and work in different parts of the globe.

Third, and closely related to the separation of time and space, **disembedding** occurs. By this Giddens (1990) means 'the "lifting out" of social relations from local contexts of interaction and their restructuring across indefinite spans of time-space'. What happens in a particular locality may be shaped by events far away. For example, hill sheep farmers may be affected by the fall-out from a nuclear accident thousands of miles away (as in the case of Chernobyl), or a factory may have to close because of economic changes in other continents.

People can no longer place their trust in others whom they know from their immediate locality. Instead, they must trust that expert systems will prove reliable and effective in meeting their needs. For example, people trust that the systems are in place to ensure that the aeroplane in which they travel has been properly serviced and the pilot properly trained. They do not need to know the mechanics and the pilot personally to have sufficient confidence to place their lives in their hands.

Religion and high modernity

At first sight, Giddens's description of high modernity does not appear to be a place where religion will flourish. Traditional beliefs (such as religions) are questioned. Technical systems and science are highly developed and very important. As local communities become less significant, religious beliefs are less likely to be reinforced by the communities in which people live. Indeed, in *The Consequences of Modernity* Giddens suggests that religion faces an uphill task. He admits that secularization does not involve the disappearance of religion. However:

> *Most of the situations of modern social life are manifestly incompatible with religion as a pervasive influence upon day-to-day life. Religious cosmology is supplanted by reflexively organized knowledge, governed by empirical observation and logical thought, and focused upon material technology and socially applied codes. Religion and tradition were always closely linked, and the latter is even more thoroughly undermined than the former by the reflexivity of modern social life, which stands in direct opposition to it.* Giddens, 1990

In essence, Giddens does little more than restate conventional versions of the secularization thesis using his own terminology. However, in his 1991 book, *Modernity and Self-Identity*, he adopts a rather different position. Here he argues that high modernity provides the conditions for a resurgence of religion. He says, 'Religious symbols and practices are not only residues from the past; a revival of religious or, more broadly, spiritual concerns seems fairly widespread in modern societies.' But why should this be?

The answer largely lies in the consequences of modernity for the individual sense of self. As tradition loses its grip on social life, individual selves become increasingly reflexive. That is, people make more conscious choices about who they are and what they wish to become. They do not simply accept their position in society and their sense of self that comes from socialization. However, individuals face problems in developing their sense of self.

First, rational knowledge has replaced the certainty that comes from tradition with the certainties of science. Nevertheless, in every field, there are competing experts making divergent claims about what is true and what is not. Individuals have to choose between the claims of these experts in many areas of their life. Examples might include conflicting advice on the most fashionable clothes, the most healthy diet or the best moral values.

High modernity is therefore characterized by increasing doubt in people's minds about all sorts of aspects of their lives. As Giddens (1991) puts it, 'Modernity institutionalizes the principle of radical doubt and insists that all knowledge takes the form of hypotheses: claims which may very well be true, but which are in principle always open to revision.'

Second, what Giddens calls 'existential questions' – questions about why people exist – tend to be separated from everyday life in high modernity. People whose condition or behaviour makes you think about the purpose of existence tend to be kept apart from others in institutions or some physically separate place. Giddens says, 'The mad, the criminal and the seriously ill are physically sequestered from the normal population, while "eroticism" is replaced by "sexuality" – which then moves behind the scenes to become hidden away.' As a result, 'The sequestration of experience means that, for many people, direct contact with events and situations which link the individual lifespan to broad issues of morality and finitude are rare and fleeting.' People are isolated from thinking about death, what happens to you after you die, why you should act in a 'sane' way, why you should conform, and from sex itself, and they are therefore in somewhat of a moral vacuum.

As people try to make sense of their lives and themselves in a reflexive way but within a moral vacuum, 'Personal meaninglessness – the feeling that life has nothing worthwhile to offer – becomes a fundamental psychic problem in circumstances of late modernity.' Religion and spirituality can step in to fill the vacuum that has been left, although it can also be filled by various forms of 'life politics – concerned with human self-actualization'. Thus people might feel a sense of personal fulfilment through joining an ecological movement and trying to live in harmony with the earth, rather than through joining a religious movement.

Religious movements are another way of overcoming this sense of meaninglessness. Unlike the past, though, and typical of other aspects of high modernity, there is now a great choice of religious beliefs and movements to consider. Reflexive individuals have to decide for themselves which cult, sect, denomination or church, or which New Age beliefs to follow (if any). Religions offer 'a return of the repressed, since they directly address issues of the moral meaning of existence which modern institutions so thoroughly tend to dissolve'.

Fundamentalism

There is one type of religious revival which Giddens sees as particularly worrying: fundamentalism. He sees religious fundamentalism of various types as a response to the way in which high modernity undermines certainty and detraditionalizes society. It is a relatively new phenomenon – the term 'fundamentalism' has only come to be widely used in the past thirty years or so – and it represents a rejection of key aspects of high modernity. Giddens (1994) describes it as 'tradition defended in the traditional way – but where that mode of defence has become widely called into question'.

Fundamentalists – for example, some Protestant fundamentalists in the USA – simply assert they are right through an appeal to traditional beliefs. They react against a globalized world – in which differences and disputes are usually resolved by discussion and dialogue – by refusing to compromise or even consider that they might be wrong. They assert their religious beliefs and will allow no contradictions.

To Giddens, such an approach to religion is dangerous in the contemporary world because of the dispersal of different people across the globe and the rapid communications and increased levels of migration and travel. In a globalized world the different ethnic and religious groups who live in close proximity have to be more tolerant of one another if serious conflict is to be avoided.

Evaluation of Giddens

James A. Beckford (1996) identifies strengths and weaknesses in Giddens's views on religion and high modernity. To Beckford, it is a strong theory because it appears to account for both the traditional types of religion (for example, traditional fundamentalism) and novel types (such as cults). It also appears convincing because 'Giddens regards the survival of religion as a central consequence of high modernity rather than as an awkward or incidental freak show on the side'.

Nevertheless, it does seem contradictory that religion should revive in a society characterized by the use of rational thought to monitor every aspect of life. To Beckford, Giddens can only explain this by reverting to untestable claims about the needs of individuals. Basically, religion comes down to the need for some moral certainty and some sort of answer to existential questions such as why we are here. Beckford says, 'he seems to posit the existence of a "real" self, which is resistant to the pressures of high modernity'. This argument has a 'distinctly functionalist ring about it', since it is based on the idea that people have basic needs which must be met. Beckford goes on to say:

> *The repressed morality asserts itself. This 'volcanic' or emergent vision of moral agency is inadequate insofar as it runs the risk of implying that the real moral agent is pre- or even non-social. It is difficult to avoid the suspicion that the 'return of the repressed' is a rabbit pulled out of a theoretical hat when all other tricks have failed to make sense of the persistence of religion at a time when, according to the theory of high modernity, religion's chances of survival are extremely slim.* Beckford, 1996

Certainly, this interpretation would seem to fit with the apparent change in Giddens's views on the fate of religion, noted earlier in this section.

Zygmunt Bauman – religion and postmodernity

Although Bauman (1992) is a theorist of postmodernity, his analysis of religion has some similarity to that of Giddens. Like Giddens, Bauman sees contemporary societies as developing out of key features of modernity. He also agrees with Giddens that there is increased reflexivity in the contemporary world and that this poses problems for individuals. Furthermore, he follows Giddens in arguing that religious revival results from the problems faced by individuals. Nevertheless, Bauman's characterization of changes in society and his explanations for any religious revival are rather different from those of Giddens.

To Bauman, modernity was characterized by a search for universal truths. Postmodernity tears down or deconstructs any claims to universal truth. Bauman sees postmodernity as a 'state of mind' in which there is a 'universal dismantling of power-supported structures'. People no longer accept that others have authority over them and that they must live their lives according to rules imposed by any form of external authority. To Bauman, postmodernity:

> *means licence to do whatever one may fancy and advice not to take anything you or the others do too seriously ... It means a shopping mall overflowing with goods whose major use is the joy of purchasing them; and existence that feels like a life-long confinement to the shopping mall. It means the exhilarating freedom to pursue anything and the mind-boggling uncertainty as to what is worth pursuing and in the name of what one should pursue it.* Bauman, 1992

This uncertainty raises problems with morality and ethics. Modernity tried to put ethical problems on one side. They were reduced to or replaced by rules or laws. People were encouraged to behave in particular ways because the rules (for example, of bureaucracies) or laws of society said they should. The rules and laws were justified on rational grounds as providing the best means for achieving given ends. Thus, Bauman says, 'Modernity was, among other things, a gigantic exercise in abolishing individual responsibility other than that measured by the criteria of instrumental rationality and practical achievement.'

However, once postmodernity has torn away the belief that there can be a rational basis for perfecting society, it leaves individuals with no external rules to govern their lives. This leads to a renewed emphasis on the ethical and the moral, but now it is personal ethics and morality that are important. Bauman says:

> *The ethical paradox of the postmodern condition is that it restores to agents the fullness of moral choice and responsibility whilst simultaneously depriving them of the comfort of universal guidance that modern self-confidence once promised ... In a cacophony of moral voices, none of which is likely to silence the others, the individuals are thrown back on their own subjectivity as the only ultimate ethical authority.* Bauman, 1992

Morality becomes privatized, a matter of personal choice. Yet morality cannot be abandoned altogether. Individuals still seek to evaluate themselves and their own worth. They still want to make their lives meaningful.

In modernity individuals tended to have what Bauman calls 'life-projects', things they wished to achieve, ambitions they wanted to fulfil. In postmodernity people seek a process of 'self-constitution'. Rather than achieving things, they want to be somebody. They want to be 'visible' to others. They want to get noticed and to be admired or respected. Uncertain about their own worth, people want the reassurance of people noticing and admiring them. They need to think of the lifestyle they adopt, the things they consume and the moral beliefs they adopt as superior to those of other people.

In the absence of any one set of rules about how to behave, what is good taste or which moral beliefs are true, people have only two possible sources of reassurance. First, they can seek justification for their choices from 'experts' in a particular field. There may be many competing experts, but to have some outside support is better than to have none. Second, they can rely upon a 'mass following' supporting their choices. They can try to be a trend-setter, or at least to follow the crowd so that they are not too out of step with others, too unfashionable.

With all these choices available, and with individuals responsible for their own morality, people turn to experts in morality – religious leaders – for guidance. Bauman concludes there is a 'typically postmodern heightened interest in ethical debate and increased attractiveness of the agencies claiming expertise in moral values (e.g. the revival of religious and quasi-religious movements)'.

Evaluation of Bauman

James A. Beckford (1996) is even more critical of Bauman than he is of Giddens. He sees Bauman's analysis as rather contradictory. Some types of religion or quasi-religion might seem to fit aspects of his theory. Thus the 'playfulness of some New Age beliefs' seems to fit in with the supposed lack of seriousness in postmodern consumer culture. However, to Beckford, it is simply contradictory for Bauman to say that postmodernity undermines faith in external authorities and that it makes people seek the authority of religious experts for their beliefs. Beckford says, 'This sounds suspiciously like an argument about the appeal of authority and moral principles at a time – postmodernity – when such things were not supposed to be important.'

According to Beckford, Giddens, Bauman and other theorists who believe there has been a fundamental change in contemporary societies in recent times are faced with a problem. They need to explain the 'continuous importance of religion throughout history' in the context of claims about major changes in social life. Beckford does not believe there has been a massive religious revival, because he does not believe there was any preceding massive decline in religion. If he is right, then perhaps the theorists of postmodernity and high modernity have exaggerated the extent of change in social life. It is a view that would probably attract some sympathy from Paul Heelas, who has examined the significance of the New Age for theories of postmodernity (see pp. 455–6).

David Lyon – *Jesus in Disneyland*

David Lyon (2000) uses aspects of the work of both Giddens and Bauman in developing his theory of religion and **postmodernity**. Unlike Bauman, Lyon does 'not assume that postmodernity has by any means supplanted modernity'. Unlike Giddens, he believes that societies have moved beyond high modernity and that postmodernity is an increasingly important feature of many societies. Lyon characterizes the move towards postmodernity in terms of two key social changes:

1 The spread of **computer and information technology** (CIT) allows ideas to be disseminated throughout the world as part of globalization. On the internet, for example, it is possible to gain information about almost any type of religious or spiritual belief. CIT, along with aspects of globalization such as increased geographical mobility and travel, reduces the extent to which people's identities are based upon local communities. It opens up a wider range of possible beliefs for people. Global flows of information and ideas make it harder for people to maintain fixed and unchanging sets of beliefs.
2 Following Bauman, Lyon argues that growing **consumerism** is a feature of postmodernity. Consumer culture means that 'people are free to choose on their own what to do with their time, their homes, their bodies, and their gods'. Just as people are used to being able to choose what fashions they wear and what cars they drive, so people feel they should be able to choose what they believe in.

To Lyon, these changes do not mean that religion is declining. Instead, religion is just relocating to a different sphere: the **sphere of consumption**. In a world which emphasizes choice, people are less willing to accept the authority of a church, but still seek meaning in their lives. Lyon argues that work has become less important in providing people with a central identity. Changes in the economy have meant that people are less likely to keep a job for life, and more likely to change jobs and careers frequently. People's identities are more fluid and more open to personal choice.

Religion, too, can be chosen in the postmodern world, but, in the absence of any other central identity, can become an important source of identity for individuals. People still seek a **narrative** or story to put their lives in context, but they are less willing to accept an externally imposed narrative of an established church. Lyon says:

> *The grand narratives of modernity or of the so-called Christian West may in some respects be fading. But does this really mean that no narratives, no stories, are available any longer, or that what remains has no sacred aspects? I think not. Rather, the available stories are much more fluid, malleable, and personalized.* Lyon, 2000

Lyon gives the example of religious belief in Canada. He quotes a survey which found that 75 per cent of Canadians do not attend religious services regularly. However, 80 per cent of non-attendees still 'draw selectively on religious beliefs and practices, still identify with a religious tradition and turn to religion for rites of passage'. Religion has far from disappeared. People have simply become selective consumers. There has been a general shift from religion as a **social institution** of great importance, to religion as a **cultural resource** which remains important to individuals in their lives.

To illustrate his arguments, Lyon uses the image of 'Jesus in Disneyland'. He refers to an occasion when there was a Harvest Day Crusade at Disneyland in Anaheim, California. There were several stages on which a variety of Christian singers and other artists performed and the evangelist Greg Laurie preached the Christian gospel. According to Lyon, this was an example of religion interacting with the most postmodern of settings, Disneyland.

Disneyland is often considered postmodern because it is a fantasy world where the images (such as the image of Mickey Mouse), or signs, have no connection with reality, but are treated as if they are real. For example, some people take the trouble to get the 'autographs' of Mickey Mouse and other characters (or rather, people in costumes) (see pp. 893–4 for Baudrillard's comments on Disneyland).

According to Lyon, the Harvest Day Crusade is an example of how religion is adapting to postmodernity and becoming part of it. Religion is no longer confined to traditional institutions such as churches, but can be found in many different settings.

Lyon believes that an important feature of postmodernity is **dedifferentiation**. This involves a process whereby the distinction between different features of social life becomes less clear-cut; boundaries become increasingly blurred. One example is the way in which the distinction between high culture (for instance, classical music) and low culture (pop music) blurs (see pp. 684–6 for a discussion of postmodernism and popular culture). In the case of Jesus in Disneyland the distinction between religion and popular culture is blurred. Religion can be found anywhere: in 'a detraditionalized world of deregulated religion', people 'seek credible ways of expressing faith in contemporary modes, but outside the walls of conventional churches. They work out ways of coming to terms with the circulating signs, and in this case strike a deal with Disney.'

Evaluation of Lyon

Lyon seems to be on strong ground in arguing that religion has spread outside the confines of traditional churches and found new ways to try to appeal to a wide audience. However, sociologists such as Bruce (2002) see this as evidence of **secularization** rather than an indication of the continuing vitality of religion. It produces only **weak religion** (see pp. 439–40), which has little impact on the way people live their lives. It is also very debatable whether such developments can be seen as indicative of a move to postmodernity. As we shall see, Paul Heelas also discusses religion outside the established church and he sees detraditionalization and dedifferentiation as characteristic of postmodernity. However, he concludes that a particular area of non-traditional religion, the New Age, is a modern rather than a postmodern phenomenon.

Paul Heelas – postmodernity and the New Age

Why the New Age appears postmodern

Paul Heelas (1996) argues that in a number of ways the New Age appears to have characteristics that are associated with postmodernism:

1 First, it seems to involve **dedifferentiation** and **detraditionalization**. Scott Lash (1990) has argued that postmodernism involves dedifferentiation – that is, a breakdown in traditional categories such as those between high culture and popular culture. The New Age appears to involve a breakdown in the distinction between traditional religious beliefs and popular culture. Furthermore, Heelas says, 'dedifferentiation is a major theme of the movement. In most versions of New Age thought, inner spirituality does not acknowledge difference. All people are held to share the same inner spirituality, together with the spirituality of the natural order as a whole.' The New Age is detraditionalized simply because it rejects the established traditions of conventional religions such as Christianity.
2 Like postmodernism, the New Age appears to accept **relativism**. It does not accept one set of ideas as revealing the whole truth, and it is prepared to accept that there is merit in the viewpoints of different groups. The same characteristics are thought to be typical of postmodernism, which rejects metanarratives that claim to provide definitive guides to the truth and how social life should be organized (see pp. 891–3 for details of the idea of metanarratives).
3 The New Age seems to have strong links with the **consumer culture** that writers such as Bauman see as central to postmodernity. New Agers can 'consume' different practices from week to week. For example, people might 'participate in "shamanic" weekends, followed by some "Zen", or "yoga", and then a visit to some "Christian"-inspired centre'.
4 Like postmodernism, the New Age emphasizes the importance of **experience** over the achievement of particular ends. Heelas suggests that both consumers – for example, when they are shopping – and New Agers might experience 'euphoric intensities' which lead to the 'disintegration of the subject'. They become so involved in their activities that they forget who they are and simply enjoy the experience.
5 Heelas points out that some writers have made the simple link that both the New Age and the idea of postmodernity are about the advent of a new era.

Why the New Age is not postmodern

Despite the apparent similarities and connections between postmodernism and the New Age, Heelas rejects the idea that the New Age is postmodern. He argues that the New Age has a very strong, central **metanarrative** at its heart. Although it rejects what he calls cultural metanarratives (for example, about how society should be developed), it replaces them with an 'experiential metanarrative'. This metanarrative claims to be able to reveal absolute truths and to provide people with the basis for planning their lives.

Although there might be different paths towards the type of inner wisdom that New Agers seek, a core set of beliefs exists which allows people to make judgements about themselves and others. Heelas says the New Age 'shows a considerable degree of unity in its basic discourse of self-spirituality'. Furthermore, committed New Agers do not think of these beliefs as trivial, playful or no more important than the consumer goods they choose to buy. They treat their beliefs as serious ones, just as others might treat more conventional religions. They differentiate between their spirituality and less important parts of their lives.

Heelas also points out that many aspects of New Age beliefs are not particularly new. There is a long tradition of similar thinking going back to the theosophy movement (founded in India towards the end of the nineteenth century), which was an early form of self-religion. In any case, many New Age beliefs derive from ancient sources.

Heelas concludes that the New Age can be seen as emphasizing an individualism which 'involves the ascription of value and truth to the self'. Individualism is a key feature of Western culture and of modern societies. Because of this there is no justification for regarding the New Age as postmodern. Heelas says, 'the New Age is quite clearly an aspect of modernity'.

Indeed, Heelas argues that there is no clear-cut division between a modern and a postmodern era. You can find examples from social life in the past which seem postmodern, and examples from the present which do not appear to be postmodern at all. Heelas says it is 'much more profitable to think in terms of a dynamic interplay between detraditionalization and retraditionalization, tradition-maintenance and tradition-construction, than it is to think in terms of nineteenth-century-like periodizations'. History, including the history of religion, is more complicated than the idea that we have moved from modernity to postmodernity would suggest.

Compared with theories of secularization, theories of postmodernity leave more room for religion to be seen as an important feature of contemporary society. On the surface such theories seem to be buttressed by the evidence of religious revival on a global scale. However, this evidence needs to be approached with caution. Sociologists, like other people, tend to interpret the evidence to fit their preconceptions, and some theorists of postmodernity and globalization may have exaggerated the importance of religion. Similarly, however, advocates of secularization may have underestimated the continuing significance of religion. As Beckford (1996) says, 'from time to time sociology is swept by enthusiasm for novel concepts or theories'.

It is important that the most recent fashions are regarded with as much scepticism as the older ones. Without this scepticism sociology would become stuck with the favoured concepts of a particular generation of sociologists, whether they remained appropriate to changing societies or not.

Summary and conclusions

Although sociological theories of religion differ in many ways, they all address fundamental questions about the reasons why religion, in some form or another, is found in all societies. They put aside questions of whether religion is true, and all agree that social explanations can be found for the existence of religion. To simplify, functionalists explain the existence of religion in terms of its contribution to social order. Both Marxists and feminists see religion as maintaining the power of minority groups in society: the ruling class and men, respectively.

Theories of religion also address the effects of religion on society, and an examination of historical and contemporary examples shows that religion can contribute to instability, social change and conflict, as well as stability, maintenance of the status quo and harmony.

Until fairly recently, most Western sociologists of religion expected the importance of religion to gradually decline as modernity advanced, but the theory of secularization has become increasingly disputed. The existence of fundamentalist religion, widespread conflict associated (at least in part) with religion, and the growth of non-rational beliefs such as the New Age have all stimulated sociological interest in religion.

There is no doubt that religion continues to have an important social role for many individuals and most societies, and the study of religion is very important for understanding the nature and direction of social changes in the world today.

CHAPTER 8
Families and households

It is no longer possible to pronounce in some binding way what family, marriage, parenthood, sexuality or love mean, what they should or could be; rather these vary in substance, norms and morality from individual to individual and from relationship to relationship. Beck and Beck-Gernsheim, 1995

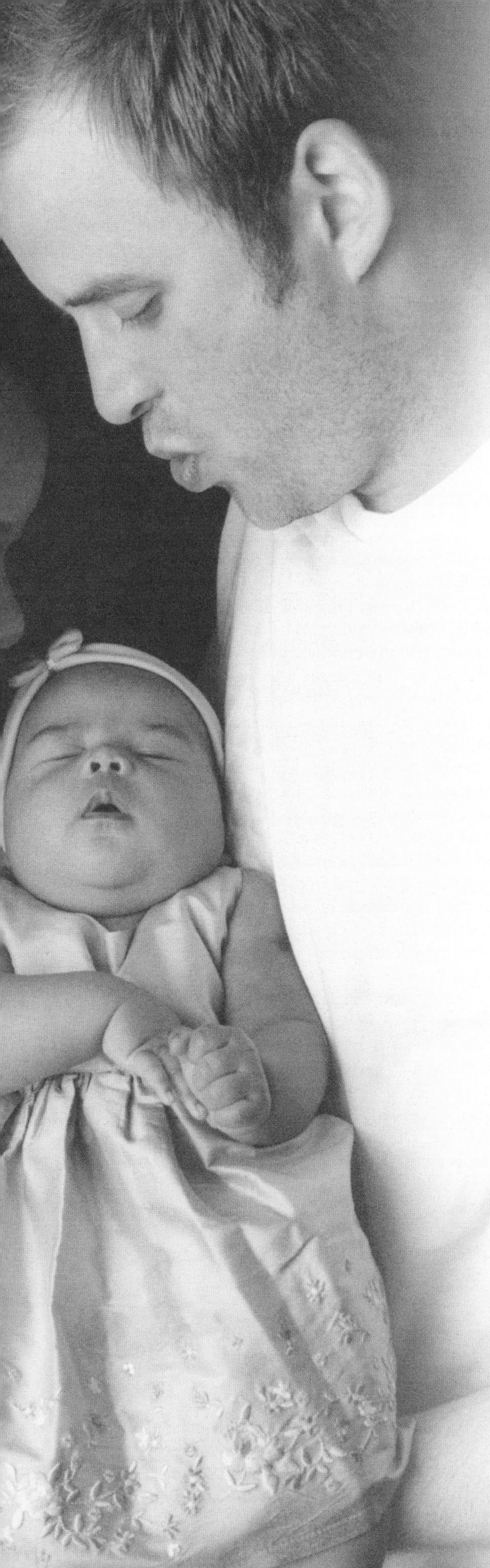

Introduction

The family has often been regarded as the cornerstone of society. In premodern and modern societies alike it has been seen as the most basic unit of social organization and one which carries out vital tasks, such as socializing children.

Until the 1960s few sociologists questioned the importance or the benefits of family life. Most sociologists assumed that family life was evolving as modernity progressed, and that the changes involved made the family better suited to meeting the needs of society and of family members. A particular type of family, the **nuclear family** (based around a two-generation household of parents and their children), was seen as well adapted to the demands of modern societies.

From the 1960s, an increasing number of critical thinkers began to question the assumption that the family was necessarily a beneficial institution. Feminists, Marxists and critical psychologists began to highlight what they saw as some of the negative effects and the 'dark side' of family life.

In the following decades the family was not just under attack from academic writers. Social changes also seemed to be undermining traditional families. Rising divorce rates, cohabitation before marriage, increasing numbers of single-parent families and single-person households, and other trends all suggested that individuals were basing their lives less and less around conventional families.

Some have seen these changes as a symptom of greater individualism within modern societies. They have welcomed what appears to be an increasing range of choice for individuals. People no longer have to base their lives around what may be outmoded and, for many, unsuitable conventional family structures. Others, however, have lamented the changes and worried about their effect on society. Such changes are seen as both a symptom and a cause of instability and insecurity in people's lives and in society as a whole. This view has been held by traditionalists who want a return to the ideal of the nuclear family. For them, many of society's problems are a result of increased family instability.

Some postmodernists argue that there has been a fundamental break between the modern family and the postmodern family. They deny that any one type of family can be held up as the norm against which other family types can be compared. While modern societies might have had one central, dominant family type, this is no longer the case. As a result, it is no longer possible to produce a theory of 'the family'. Different explanations are needed for different types of family.

Alongside these developments in society and sociology, family life has become a topic of political debate. What was once largely seen as a private sphere, in which politicians should not interfere, is now seen as a legitimate area for public debate and political action. As concern has grown in some quarters about the alleged decline of the family, politicians have become somewhat more willing to comment on families. Sometimes they have devised policies to try to deal with perceived problems surrounding the family.

In short, the family has come to be seen as more problematic than it was in the past. The controversies that have come to surround families and households are the subject of this chapter. We begin by examining the assumption of the 'universality' of the family.

Is the family universal?

George Peter Murdock: the family – a universal social institution

In a study entitled *Social Structure* (1949), George Peter Murdock examined the institution of the family in a wide range of societies. Murdock took a sample of 250 societies, ranging from small hunting and gathering bands to large-scale industrial societies. He claimed that some form of family existed in every society, and concluded, on the evidence of his sample, that the family is universal.

Murdock defined the family as follows:

> *The family is a social group characterized by common residence, economic cooperation and reproduction. It includes adults of both sexes, at least two of whom maintain a socially approved sexual relationship, and one or more children, own or adopted, of the sexually cohabiting adults.* Murdock, 1949

Thus the family lives together, pools its resources and works together, and produces offspring. At least two of the adult members conduct a sexual relationship according to the norms of their particular society.

Such norms vary from society to society. For example, among the Banaro of New Guinea, the husband does not have sexual relations with his wife until she has borne a child by a friend of his father. The parent–child relationship, therefore, is not necessarily a biological one. Its importance is primarily social, children being recognized as members of a particular family whether or not the adult spouses have biologically produced them.

Variations in family structure

The structure of the family varies from society to society. The smallest family unit is known as the **nuclear family** and consists of a husband and wife and their immature offspring. Units larger than the nuclear family are usually known as **extended families**. Such families can be seen as extensions of the basic nuclear unit, either **vertical extensions** – for example, the addition of members of a third generation such as the spouses' parents – and/or **horizontal extensions** – for example, the addition of members of the same generation as the spouses, such as the husband's brother or an additional wife. Thus the functionalist sociologists Bell and Vogel define the extended family as 'any grouping broader than the nuclear family which is related by descent, marriage or adoption'.

Either on its own or as the basic unit within an extended family, Murdock found that the nuclear family was present in every society in his sample. This led him to conclude:

> *The nuclear family is a universal human social grouping. Either as the sole prevailing form of the family or as the basic unit from which more complex forms are compounded, it exists as a distinct and strongly functional group in every known society.* Murdock, 1949

However, as we will discover in the following sections, Murdock's conclusions might not be well founded.

Kathleen Gough – the Nayar

Some societies have sets of relationships between kin which are quite different from those which are common in Britain. One such society was that of the Nayar of Kerala in southern India, prior to British rule being established in 1792. Sociologists disagree about whether this society had a family system or not, and thus whether or not it disproves Murdock's claim that the family is universal.

Kathleen Gough (1959) provided a detailed description of Nayar society. Before puberty all Nayar girls were ritually married to a suitable Nayar man in the *tali* rite. After the ritual marriage had taken place, however, the *tali* husband did not live with his wife, and was under no obligation to have any contact with her whatsoever. The wife owed only one duty to her *tali* husband: she had to attend his funeral to mourn his death.

Once a Nayar girl reached or neared puberty she began to take a number of visiting husbands, or *sandbanham* husbands. The Nayar men were usually professional warriors who spent long periods of time away from their villages acting as mercenaries. During their time in the villages they were allowed to visit any number of Nayar women who had undergone the tali rite and who were members of the same caste as themselves, or a lower caste. With the agreement of the woman involved, the *sandbanham* husband arrived at the home of one of his wives after supper, had sexual intercourse with her, and left before breakfast the next morning. During his stay he placed his weapons outside the building to show the other *sandbanham* husbands that he was there. If they arrived too late, then they were free to sleep on the veranda, but could not stay the night with their wife. Men could have unlimited numbers of *sandbanham* wives, although women seem to have been limited to no more than twelve visiting husbands.

An exception to the family?

Sandbanham relationships were unlike marriages in most societies in a number of ways:

1. They were not a lifelong union: either party could terminate the relationship at any time.
2. *Sandbanham* husbands had no duty towards the offspring of their wives. When a woman became

pregnant, it was essential according to Nayar custom that a man of appropriate caste declared himself to be the father of the child by paying a fee of cloth and vegetables to the midwife who attended the birth. However, it mattered little whether or not he was the biological parent, so long as someone claimed to be the father, because he did not help to maintain or socialize the child.

3 Husbands and wives did not form an economic unit. Although husbands might give wives token gifts, they were not expected to maintain them – indeed, it was frowned upon if they attempted to. Instead, the economic unit consisted of a number of brothers and sisters, sisters' children, and their daughters' children. The eldest male was the leader of each group of kin.

Nayar society, then, was a **matrilineal** society. Kinship groupings were based on female biological relatives and marriage played no significant part in the formation of households, in the socializing of children, or in the way that the economic needs of the members of society were met.

In terms of Murdock's definition, no family existed in Nayar society, since those who maintained 'a sexually approved adult relationship' did not live together and cooperate economically. Only the women lived with the children. Therefore, either Murdock's definition of the family is too narrow, or the family is not universal.

Gough claimed that marriage, and by implication the family, existed in Nayar society. In order to make this claim, though, she had to broaden her definition of marriage beyond that implied in Murdock's definition of the family. She defined marriage as a relationship between a woman and one or more persons in which a child born to the woman 'is given full birth-status rights' common to normal members of the society.

Matrifocal families – an exception to the rule?

Murdock's definition of the family includes at least one adult of each sex. However, both today and in the past, some children have been raised in households that do not contain adults of both sexes. Usually these households have been headed by women.

A significant proportion of black families in the islands of the West Indies, parts of Central America such as Guyana, and the USA do not include adult males. The 'family unit' often consists of a woman and her dependent children, sometimes with the addition of her mother. This may indicate that the family is not universal as Murdock suggests, or that it is necessary to redefine the family and state that the minimal family unit consists of a woman and her dependent children, own or adopted, and that all other family types are additions to this unit.

Female-headed families are sometimes known as **matriarchal** families and sometimes as **matrifocal** families, although both of these terms have been used in a number of senses. We will use the term 'matrifocal family' here to refer to female-headed families.

Can we then see the matrifocal family as an exception to Murdock's claim that the family is universal, or, if it is accepted as a family, as an exception to his claim that the nuclear family is a universal social group?

Support for Murdock

Supporters of Murdock could argue that the matrifocal family usually makes up a minority of families and is not regarded as the norm in any of the societies mentioned above. Furthermore, matrifocal families could be seen as the result of nuclear families breaking down rather than being an alternative family form which is valued and which people aspire to.

However, even if matrifocal families are in the minority, this does not necessarily mean that they cannot be recognized as an alternative family structure. In many societies which practise polygyny, polygynous marriages are in the minority, yet sociologists accept them as a form of extended family.

Members of matrifocal families regard the unit as a family and, from her West Indian data, González (1970) argues that the female-headed family is a well-organized social group which represents a positive adaptation to the circumstances of poverty. By not tying herself to a husband, the mother is able to maintain casual relationships with a number of men who can provide her with financial support. She retains strong links with her relatives, who give her both economic and emotional support.

The above arguments suggest that the matrifocal family can be regarded as a form of family structure in its own right. If these arguments are accepted, it is possible to see the matrifocal family as the basic, minimum family unit and all other family structures as additions to this unit.

The female-carer core

This view is supported by Yanina Sheeran. She argues that the female-carer core is the most basic family unit:

> *The female-carer unit is the foundation of the single-mother family, the two-parent family, and the extended family in its many forms. Thus it is certainly the basis of family household life in Britain today, and is a ubiquitous phenomenon, since even in South Pacific longhouses, pre-industrial farmsteads, communes and Kibbutzim, we know that female carers predominate.* Sheeran, 1993

In Britain, for example, Sheeran maintains that children usually have one woman who is primarily responsible for their care. These primary carers are often but not always the biological mother; they may 'occasionally be a grandmother, elder sister, aunt, adoptive mother or other female'.

Sheeran seems to be on strong ground in arguing that a female-carer core is a more basic family unit than that identified by Murdock, since in some societies families without an adult male are quite common. However, she herself admits that in Britain a small minority of lone-parent households are headed by a man. Thus it is possible to argue that the female-carer core is not the basis of every individual family, even if it is the basis of most families in all societies.

Matrifocal families, and one-parent families in general, are becoming more common in Britain. We will consider the significance of this development later in this chapter (see pp. 485–8).

Gay families

Another type of household that may contradict Murdock's claims about the universality of the family, as defined by him, is the gay or lesbian household. By definition, such households will not contain 'adults of both sexes, at least two of whom maintain a socially approved sexual relationship' (Murdock, 1949). Such households may, however, include children who are cared for by two adult females or two adult males. The children may have been adopted, or be the result of a previous heterosexual relationship, or they may have been produced using new reproductive technologies involving sperm donation or surrogate motherhood. A lesbian may have sex with a man in order to conceive a child to be raised by her and her female partner.

Most children of gay couples result from a previous heterosexual relationship. Lesbian mothers are more common than gay fathers, due to the difficulties gay men are likely to encounter in being granted custody or adopting children. Official statistics are not produced on the number of gay couples raising children, but there is little doubt that the numbers are increasing. This raises the question of whether such households should be regarded as families.

Rather like lone-parent families, households with gay parents are seen by some as not being 'proper' families. In most Western societies the gay couple will not be able to marry and any children will have a genetic connection with only one of the partners. However, Sidney Callahan (1997) argued that such households should still be seen as families. He claimed that, if marriage were available, many gay and lesbian couples would marry. Furthermore, he believed that the relationships involved are no different in any fundamental way from those in heterosexual households. Callahan therefore claimed that gay and lesbian households with children should be regarded as a type of family, at least where the gay or lesbian relationship is intended to be permanent. He concluded:

> *I would argue that gay or lesbian households that consist of intimate communities of mutual support and that display permanent shared commitments to intergenerational nurturing share the kinship bonding we observe and name as family.* Callahan, 1997

Although gay couples still cannot marry in Britain, since December 2005 they have been able to register a civil partnership. Civil partnerships give gay couples many of the same legal rights as married couples. Figures released by National Statistics show that a total of 15,672 civil partnerships were registered in the UK between December 2005 and the end of December 2006. An unknown number of these civil partners were looking after children, but the fact that these couples have registered civil partnerships does seem to strengthen Callahan's claim that they should be seen as families.

The universality of the family – conclusion

Whether the family is regarded as universal ultimately depends on how the family is defined. Clearly, though, a wide variety of domestic arrangements have been devised by human beings which are quite distinctive from the 'conventional' families of modern industrial societies. As Diana Gittins (1993) puts it, 'Relationships are universal, so is some form of co-residence, of intimacy, sexuality and emotional bonds. But the forms these can take are infinitely variable and can be changed and challenged as well as embraced.'

It may be a somewhat pointless exercise to try to find a single definition which embraces all the types of household and relationship that can reasonably be called families.

Having examined whether the family is universal, we will now examine various perspectives on the role of families in society.

The family – a functionalist perspective

George Peter Murdock – the universal functions of the family

Functions for society

From his analysis of 250 societies, Murdock (1949) argued that the family performs four basic functions in all societies, which he termed the **sexual**, **reproductive**, **economic** and **educational**. They are essential for social life since without the sexual and reproductive functions there would be no members of society, without the economic function (for example, the provision and preparation of food) life would cease, and without education (a term Murdock uses for socialization) there would be no culture. Human society without culture could not function.

Clearly, the family does not perform these functions exclusively. However, it makes important contributions to them all and no other institution has yet been devised to match its efficiency in this respect. Once this is realized, Murdock claimed, 'The immense utility of the nuclear family and the basic reason for its universality thus begin to emerge in strong relief.'

Functions for individuals and society

The family's functions for society are inseparable from its functions for its individual members. It serves both at one and the same time and in much the same way. The sexual function provides a good example of this. Husband and wife have the right of sexual access to each other, and in most societies there are rules forbidding or limiting sexual activity outside marriage. This provides sexual gratification for the spouses. It also strengthens the family, since the powerful and often binding emotions which accompany sexual activities unite husband and wife.

The sexual function also helps to stabilize society. The rules which largely contain sexual activity within the family prevent the probable disruptive effects on the social order that would result if the sex drive were allowed 'free play'. The family thus provides both 'control and expression' of sexual drives, and in doing so performs important functions, not only for its individual members, but also for the family as an institution and for society as a whole.

Murdock applied a similar logic to the economic function. He argued that, like sex, it is 'most readily and satisfactorily achieved by persons living together'. He referred in glowing terms to the division of labour within the family, whereby the husband specializes in certain activities, the wife in others. For example, in hunting societies men kill game animals which provide meat for their wives to cook and skins for them to make into clothing. This economic cooperation within the family not only fulfils the economic function for society as a whole, but also provides 'rewarding experiences' for the spouses working together, which 'cement their union'.

Murdock argued that his analysis provided a 'conception of the family's many-sided utility and thus of its inevitability'. He concluded: 'No society has succeeded in finding an adequate substitute for the nuclear family, to which it might transfer these functions. It is highly doubtful whether any society will ever succeed in such an attempt.'

Criticisms of Murdock

Murdock's picture of the family is rather like the multi-faceted, indispensable boy-scout knife. The family is seen as a multi-functional institution which is indispensable to society. Its 'many-sided utility' accounts for its universality and its inevitability.

In his enthusiasm for the family, however, Murdock did not seriously consider whether its functions could be performed by other social institutions and he does not examine alternatives to the family. As D.H.J. Morgan (1975) notes in his criticism, Murdock does not state 'to what extent these basic functions are inevitably linked with the institution of the nuclear family'.

In addition, Murdock's description of the family is almost too good to be true. As Morgan states, 'Murdock's nuclear family is a remarkably harmonious institution. Husband and wife have an integrated division of labour and have a good time in bed.' As we will see in later sections, some other researchers do not share Murdock's emphasis on harmony and integration.

Talcott Parsons – the 'basic and irreducible' functions of the family

Parsons (1959, 1965b) concentrated his analysis on the family in modern American society. Despite this, his ideas have a more general application, since he argued that the American family retains two 'basic and irreducible functions' which are common to the family in all societies. These are the 'primary socialization of children' and the 'stabilization of the adult personalities of the population of the society'.

Primary socialization

Primary socialization refers to socialization during the early years of childhood, which takes place mainly within the family. **Secondary socialization** occurs during the later years when the family is less involved and other agencies (such as the peer group and the school) exert increasing influence.

There are two basic processes involved in primary socialization: the **internalization of society's culture** and the **structuring of the personality**.

If culture were not internalized – that is, absorbed and accepted – society would cease to exist, since without shared norms and values social life would not be possible. However, culture is not simply learned, it is 'internalized as part of the personality structure'. The child's personality is moulded in terms of the central values of the culture to the point where they become a part of him or her. In the case of American society, personality is shaped in terms of independence and achievement motivation, which are two of the central values of American culture.

Parsons argued that families 'are "factories" which produce human personalities'. He believed they are essential for this purpose, since primary socialization requires a context which provides warmth, security and mutual support. He could conceive of no institution other than the family that could provide this context.

Stabilization of adult personalities

Once produced, the personality must be kept stable. This is the second basic function of the family: the **stabilization of adult personalities**. The emphasis here is on the marriage relationship and the emotional security the couple provide for each other. This acts as a counterweight to the stresses and strains of everyday life, which tend to make the personality unstable.

This function is particularly important in Western industrial society, since the nuclear family is largely isolated from kin. It does not have the security once provided by the close-knit extended family. Thus the married couple increasingly look to each other for emotional support.

Adult personalities are also stabilized by the parents' role in the socialization process. This allows them to act out 'childish' elements of their own personalities which they have retained from childhood but which cannot be indulged in adult society. For example, father is 'kept on the rails' by playing with his son's train set.

According to Parsons, therefore, the family provides a context in which husband and wife can express their childish whims, give and receive emotional support, recharge their batteries, and so stabilize their personalities.

Criticisms of Parsons

This brief summary of Parsons's views on the family is far from complete. Other aspects will be discussed later in this chapter (pp. 474–5; see also Chapter 2, p. 96), but here we will consider some of the arguments which criticize his perspective:

1. As with Murdock, Parsons has been accused of idealizing the family with his picture of well-

adjusted children and sympathetic spouses caring for each other's every need. It is a typically optimistic, modernist theory which may have little relationship to reality.

2 His picture is based largely on the American middle-class family, which he treats as representative of American families in general. As Morgan (1975) states, 'there are no classes, no regions, no religious, ethnic or status groups, no communities' in Parsons's analysis of the family. For example, Parsons fails to explore possible differences between middle-class and working-class families, or different family structures in minority ethnic communities.
3 Like Murdock, Parsons largely fails to explore functional alternatives to the family. He does recognize that some functions are not necessarily tied to the family. For instance, he notes that the family's economic function has largely been taken over by other agencies in modern industrial society. However, his belief that its remaining functions are 'basic and irreducible' prevents him from examining alternatives to the family.
4 Parsons's view of the socialization process can be criticized. He sees it as a one-way process, with the children being pumped full of culture and their personalities being moulded by powerful parents. He tends to ignore the two-way interaction process between parents and children. There is no place in his scheme for the children who twist their parents around their little finger.
5 Parsons sees the family as a distinct institution which is clearly separated from other aspects of social life. Some contemporary perspectives on the family deny that such clear-cut boundaries can be established (see pp. 516–17). The family as such cannot therefore be seen as performing any particular functions on its own in isolation from other institutions.

The very positive view of the family advanced by functionalists has not been supported by sociologists who advocate more radical and conflict perspectives. These include Marxists, feminists and some postmodernists. Their views will now be examined.

Marxist perspectives on the family

Friedrich Engels – the origin of the family

The earliest view of the family developed from a Marxist perspective is contained in Friedrich Engels's *The Origin of the Family, Private Property and the State* (Engels, 1972, first published 1884).

Like many nineteenth-century scholars, Engels took an evolutionary view of the family, attempting to trace its origin and evolution through time. He combined an evolutionary approach with Marxist theory, arguing that, as the mode of production changed, so did the family.

During the early stages of human evolution, Engels believed the means of production were communally owned and the family as such did not exist. This era of **primitive communism** was characterized by promiscuity. There were no rules limiting sexual relationships and society was, in effect, the family.

Although Engels has been criticized for this type of speculation, the anthropologist Kathleen Gough argues that his picture may not be that far from the truth. She notes that the nearest relatives to human beings, chimpanzees, live in 'promiscuous hordes', and this may have been the pattern for early humans.

The evolution of the family

Engels argued that, throughout human history, more and more restrictions were placed on sexual relationships and the production of children. He speculated that, from the promiscuous horde, marriage and the family evolved through a series of stages, which included polygyny, to its present stage, the monogamous nuclear family. Each successive stage placed greater restrictions on the number of mates available to the individual.

The monogamous nuclear family developed with the emergence of private property, in particular the private ownership of the means of production, and the advent of the state. The state instituted laws to protect the system of private property and to enforce the rules of monogamous marriage. This form of marriage and the family developed to solve the problem of the inheritance of private property. Property was owned by males and, in order for them to be able to pass it on to their heirs, they had to be certain of the legitimacy of those heirs. They therefore needed greater control over women so that there would be no doubt about the paternity of the offspring. The monogamous family provided the most efficient device for this purpose. In Engels's words:

> *It is based on the supremacy of the man, the express purpose being to produce children of undisputed paternity; such paternity is demanded because these children are later to come into their father's property as his natural heirs.* Engels, 1972, first published 1884

Evidence for Engels's views

Engels's scheme of the evolution of the family is much more elaborate than the brief outline described above. It was largely based on *Ancient Society*, an interpretation of the evolution of the family by the nineteenth-century American anthropologist Lewis Henry Morgan.

Modern research has suggested that many of the details of Engels's scheme are incorrect. For example, monogamous marriage and the nuclear family are often found in hunting and gathering bands. Since humanity has lived in hunting and gathering bands for the vast majority of its existence, the various forms of group marriage postulated by Engels (such as the promiscuous horde) may well be figments of his imagination.

However, Gough (1972) argues that 'the general trend of Engels' argument still appears sound'. Although nuclear families and monogamous marriage exist in small-scale societies, they form a part of a larger kinship group. When individuals marry they take on a series of duties and obligations to their spouse's kin. Communities are united by kinship ties and the result is similar to a large extended family. Gough argues:

> *It is true that although it is not a group marriage in Engels' sense, marriage has a group character in many hunting bands and in most of the more complex tribal societies that have developed with the domestication of plants and animals. With the development of privately owned, heritable property, and especially with the rise of the state, this group character gradually disappears.*
> Gough, 1972

Further aspects of Engels's views on the family are examined in Chapter 2, pp. 106–7.

Eli Zaretsky – personal life and capitalism

Eli Zaretsky (1976) analysed developments in the family in industrial societies from a Marxist perspective. He argues that the family in modern capitalist society creates the illusion that the 'private life' of the family is quite separate from the economy. Before the early nineteenth century the family was the basic unit of production. For example, in the early capitalist textile industry, production of cloth took place in the home and involved all family members. Only with the development of factory-based production were work and family life separated.

In a society in which work was alienating, Zaretsky claims the family was put on a pedestal because it apparently 'stood in opposition to the terrible anonymous world of commerce and industry'. The private life of the family provided opportunities for satisfactions that were unavailable outside the walls of the home.

Zaretsky welcomes the increased possibilities for a personal life for the proletariat offered by the reduction in working hours since the nineteenth century. However, he believes the family is unable to provide for the psychological and personal needs of individuals. He says, 'it simply cannot meet the pressures of being the only refuge in a brutal society'. The family artificially separates and isolates personal life from other aspects of life. It might cushion the effects of capitalism but it perpetuates the system and cannot compensate for the general alienation produced by such a society.

Furthermore, Zaretsky sees the family as a major prop to the capitalist economy. The capitalist system is based upon the domestic labour of housewives who reproduce future generations of workers. He also believes the family has become a vital unit of consumption. The family consumes the products of capitalism and this allows the bourgeoisie to continue producing surplus value. To Zaretsky, only socialism will end the artificial separation of family private life and public life, and produce the possibility of personal fulfilment.

Criticisms

Jennifer Somerville (2000) argues that Zaretsky, even after the qualifications he makes, exaggerates the importance of the family as a refuge from life in capitalist society. She suggests that Zaretsky underestimates 'the extent of cruelty, violence, incest and neglect' within families. He also exaggerates the extent to which family life is separated from work. According to Somerville, during the early stages of capitalism most working-class women had to take paid work in order for the family to survive financially, and relatively few stayed at home as full-time housewives. Somerville herself advocates a feminist approach (see p. 470), and we will now start to examine competing feminist views on the family.

Feminist perspectives on the family

The influence of feminism

In recent decades feminism has probably had more influence on the study of the family than any other approach to understanding society. Like Marxists, feminists have been highly critical of the family. However, unlike other critics, they have tended to emphasize the harmful effects of family life upon women. In doing so, they have developed new perspectives and highlighted new issues.

Feminists have, for example, introduced the study of areas of family life such as housework and domestic violence into sociology. They have challenged some widely held views about the inevitability of male dominance in families and have questioned the view that family life is becoming more egalitarian. Feminists have also highlighted the economic contribution to society made by women's domestic labour within the family.

Above all, feminist theory has encouraged sociologists to see the family as an institution involving power relationships. It has challenged the image of family life as being based upon cooperation, shared interests and love, and has tried to show that some family members, in particular men, obtain greater benefits from families than others.

Recently, some feminists have questioned the tendency of other feminists to make blanket condemnations of family life. Some have argued that feminists should recognize the considerable improvements in family life for women over the last few decades. Others have emphasized the different experiences of women in families. Some feminists have rejected the idea that there is such a thing as 'the family' rather than simply different domestic arrangements. All feminists, however, continue to argue that family life still disadvantages women in some ways.

In later sections of this chapter we will consider the impact of feminism on the study of conjugal roles, domestic labour, social policy and marriage. In the next section, however, we will examine some of the feminist theoretical approaches to understanding the family.

Marxist feminist perspectives on the family

Marxists such as Engels and Zaretsky acknowledge that women are exploited in marriage and family life but they emphasize the relationship between capitalism and the family, rather than the family's effects on women. Marxist feminists use Marxist concepts but see the exploitation of women as a key feature of family life. The next few sections will examine how these theories have been applied to the family. (More details of the Marxist feminist approach can be found in Chapter 2, pp. 101–2.)

The production of labour power

Margaret Benston stated:

> *The amount of unpaid labour performed by women is very large and very profitable to those who own the means of production. To pay women for their work, even at minimum wage scales, would involve a massive redistribution of wealth. At present, the support of the family is a hidden tax on the wage earner – his wage buys the labour power of two people.* Benston, 1972

The fact that the husband must pay for the production and upkeep of future labour acts as a strong discipline on his behaviour at work. He cannot easily withdraw his labour with a wife and children to support. These responsibilities weaken his bargaining power and commit him to wage labour. Benston argues:

> *As an economic unit, the nuclear family is a valuable stabilizing force in capitalist society. Since the husband–father's earnings pay for the production which is done in the home, his ability to withhold labour from the market is much reduced.* Benston, 1972

Not only does the family produce and rear cheap labour, it also maintains it at no cost to the employer. In her role as housewife, the woman attends to her husband's needs, thus keeping him in good running order to perform his role as a wage labourer.

Fran Ansley (1972) translates Parsons's view that the family functions to stabilize adult personalities into a Marxist framework. She sees the emotional support provided by the wife as a safety valve for the frustration produced in the husband by working in a capitalist system. Rather than being turned against the system which produced it, this frustration is absorbed by the comforting wife. In this way the system is not threatened. In Ansley's words:

> *When wives play their traditional role as takers of shit, they often absorb their husbands' legitimate anger and frustration at their own powerlessness and oppression. With every worker provided with a sponge to soak up his possibly revolutionary ire, the bosses rest more secure.*
> *Quoted in Bernard, 1976*

Ideological conditioning

The social reproduction of labour power does not simply involve producing children and maintaining them in good health. It also involves the reproduction of the attitudes essential for an efficient workforce under capitalism. Thus, David Cooper (1972) argues that the family is 'an ideological conditioning device in an exploitive society'. Within the family, children learn to conform and to submit to authority. The foundation is therefore laid for the obedient and submissive workforce required by capitalism.

A similar point is made by Diane Feeley (1972), who argues that the structure of family relationships socializes the young to accept their place in a class-stratified society. She sees the family as an authoritarian unit dominated by the husband in particular and adults in general. Feeley claims that the family with its 'authoritarian ideology is designed to teach passivity, not rebellion'. Thus children learn to submit to parental authority and emerge from the family preconditioned to accept their place in the hierarchy of power and control in capitalist society.

Criticisms

Some of the criticisms of previous views of the family also apply to Marxist approaches. There is a tendency to talk about 'the family' in capitalist society without regard to possible variations in family life between social classes, ethnic groups, heterosexual and gay and lesbian families, lone-parent families, and over time. As Morgan (1975) notes in his criticism of both functionalist and Marxist approaches, both 'presuppose a traditional model of the nuclear family where there is a married couple with children, where the husband is the breadwinner and where the wife stays at home to deal with the housework'. This pattern is becoming less common and the critique of this type of family may therefore be becoming less important.

Marxist feminists may therefore exaggerate the harm caused to women by families and may neglect the effects of non-family relationships (apart from class) on exploitation within marriage. Thus, for example, they say little about how the experience of racism might influence families. They also tend to portray female family members as the passive victims of capitalist and patriarchal exploitation. They ignore the possibility that women may have fought back against such exploitation and had some success in changing the nature of family relationships. Furthermore, they are not usually prepared to concede that there may be positive elements to family life. As we shall see, some liberal feminists and difference feminists are more prepared to accept that there may be some positive advantages for women in some families.

Radical feminist perspectives on the family

There are many varieties of radical feminism. However, Valerie Bryson (1992) argues that they share at least one characteristic in common. According to her, all radical feminism 'sees the oppression of women as the most fundamental and universal form of domination'. Society is seen as **patriarchal**, or male-dominated, rather than capitalist, and women are held to have different interests from those of men.

Radical feminists do not agree on the source of male domination, but most do see the family as important in maintaining male power. We will now analyse a range of major radical feminist theories of the family.

Christine Delphy and Diana Leonard – *Familiar Exploitation*

Types of feminism

Christine Delphy and Diana Leonard (1992) are unlike most radical feminists in that they attach considerable importance to material factors in causing women's oppression. In this respect their views have some similarity with Marxist feminist theories. In particular, Delphy and Leonard attach special importance to work and say that their approach 'uses Marxist methodology'. Nevertheless, they see themselves as radical feminists since they believe that it is men, rather than capitalists or capitalism, who are the primary beneficiaries of the exploitation of women's labour. To them, the family has a central role in maintaining patriarchy:

> *We see the familial basis of domestic groups as an important element in continuing the patriarchal nature of our society: that is, in the continuance of men's dominance over women and children.* Delphy and Leonard, 1992

The family as an economic system

Delphy and Leonard see the family as an **economic system**. It involves a particular set of 'labour relations in which men benefit from, and exploit, the work of women – and sometimes that of their children and other male relatives'. The key to this exploitation is that family members work not for themselves but for the head of the household. Women in particular are oppressed, not because they are socialized into being passive, but because their work is appropriated within the family.

Delphy and Leonard identify the following features as the main characteristics of the family as an economic system:

1. Every family-based household has a social structure that involves two types of role. These are head of household and their dependants or helpers. Female heads of household are uncommon – the vast majority are men.
2. The male head of household is different from other members because he 'decides what needs doing in a given situation' and assigns tasks to other members or delegates to them. Other family members may change his mind about decisions, but it is his mind to change. He makes the final decision.
3. The head of household provides maintenance for other family members, and they receive a share of family property on his death. However, they have to work for him unpaid.
4. The type and amount of work family members have to do are related to sex and marital status. Female relatives have to do unpaid domestic work; wives in addition have to carry out 'sexual and reproductive work'. Although the precise allocation of tasks varies from household to household, domestic work remains a female responsibility.
5. Money and resources for maintenance, and money inherited by dependants, are not related to the amount of work done. A man must provide for his dependants' basic needs, and may be very generous, but, unlike an employer, he does not purchase labour power by the hour, week or amount produced. The amounts inherited by family members are related more to position – with, for example, sons inheriting more than daughters – than to work.
6. The relations of production within the family often, therefore, involve payment in kind (such as a new coat or a holiday) rather than payment in money.
7. The economic relationships rarely involve formal contracts or bargaining. This means family members must use informal methods of negotiation. For example, 'Wives and children have to study their husbands and fathers closely and handle them carefully so as to keep them sweet.'
8. 'The head of the family may have a near monopoly over, and he always has greater access to and control of, the family's property and external relations.'
9. When dependants, particularly wives, have paid employment outside the home, they still have to carry out household tasks, or pay others out of their wages to do housework or care for children for them.

Who gets what from the family

Having outlined how the family works as an economic system, Delphy and Leonard go on to examine in more detail who contributes to and who benefits from family life. They admit that most men do some housework, but point out that such tasks are usually done by women. They claim that time-budget studies show that women do about twice as much domestic work each day as men. Furthermore, women are still expected to care for children and the sick, except in special circumstances (for example, if the wife is disabled).

As well as carrying out housework and caring for children, the sick and older people, women also contribute a great deal to their husbands' work and leisure by providing 'for their emotional and sexual well-being'.

Drawing on the work of a British sociologist, Janet Finch, Delphy and Leonard describe some of the types of help provided by wives. Sometimes they provide direct help – for example, doing office work for a self-employed husband, or doing constituency work if he is an MP. They may stay at home to answer the phone or arrange dinner parties for colleagues of their husband.

Wives also give moral support, 'observing and moderating his emotions, arranging entertainment and relaxation, and supplying personal needs'. Wives are there to listen when their husbands unburden themselves of their work problems. They provide 'trouble-free sex', which is important since 'men frequently unwind best post-coitally'. Wives also make the house into a home so that it is 'comfortable, warm and undemanding'. Women even control their own emotions so that they can provide emotional care for husbands. They 'flatter, excuse, boost, sympathize and pay attention to men', all to give them a sense of well-being.

In contrast, men make little contribution to their wives' work and the husband's career remains the central one.

Delphy and Leonard believe, then, that wives contribute much more work to family life than their husbands. Despite this, they get fewer of the material benefits of family life than men. Men retain ultimate responsibility for family finances, and women consume less than male family members. The (usually) male head of household has the 'decision-making power' to determine what goods are produced or bought for the family and who uses them. For instance, 'the food bought is the sort he likes, and he gets more of it and the best bits'.

Husbands get more leisure time, more access to the family car, or to the best car if there is more than one; and sons get more spent on their education than daughters. In every area of family consumption it is the status of different family members which shapes who gets what.

Empirical evidence

Delphy and Leonard use four main sources to try to back up their claims. Three of these are studies of British factory workers and their families. They use Goldthorpe and Lockwood's 1962 study of affluent workers in Luton (see pp. 58–9 for further details), a 1970s study of 500 workers and their wives in a Bristol company which made cardboard packing cases, and a 1980s study of redundant steel workers in Port Talbot, Wales. They also use data from Christine Delphy's own studies of French farming families. In these studies they found some evidence to support their theories. In all these contexts they found that men were dominant and women did a disproportionate share of the work.

Conclusion and summary

Delphy and Leonard believe the family is a patriarchal and hierarchical institution through which men dominate and exploit women. Men are usually the head of household, and it is the head who benefits from the work that gets done. Women provide '57 varieties of unpaid service' for men, including providing them with a 'pliant sexual partner and children if he wants them'. Wives do sometimes resist their husbands' dominance – they are not always passive victims – but 'economic and social constraints' make it difficult for women to escape from the patriarchal family.

Evaluation

Delphy and Leonard provide a comprehensive analysis of the family from a radical feminist perspective. They highlight many ways in which the family can produce or reinforce inequalities between women and men. However, their work can be criticized both theoretically and empirically:

1. Theoretically, Delphy and Leonard do not succeed in demonstrating that inequality is built into the structure of the family. Their argument is based upon the assumption that all families have a head, usually a man, and it is the head who ultimately benefits from family life. However, they do not show theoretically or empirically that all families have a head who has more power than other family members, or that power is never shared equally between men and women.
2. Empirically, their work is based upon unrepresentative data. The three British studies used are all of manual workers, and all of them are dated. Most researchers have found less gender inequality in middle-class families than in working-class families.
3. Delphy's study of French farming families was specifically directed at testing their theories, but farming families are hardly typical of other families. Family members tend to work in the family business – the farm – and few wives have an independent source of income which could reduce marital inequality.

Delphy and Leonard tend to make rather sweeping statements about inequality which may not apply equally to all families. In doing so they perhaps overstate their case by denying the possibility of exceptions.

Germaine Greer – *The Whole Woman* and the family

Germaine Greer is another radical feminist who argues that family life continues to disadvantage and oppress women (Greer, 2000). Greer believes that there are many non-economic aspects to the exploitation of women in families and she therefore takes a wider view than Delphy and Leonard. Greer's general views are examined in Chapter 2 (see p. 135); this section will focus on her specific comments on the family.

Women as wives

Greer argues there is a strong ideology suggesting that being a wife (or as she puts it a 'female consort') is the most important female role. The wives of presidents and prime ministers get considerable publicity, but the likes of Hillary Clinton and Cherie Blair have to be very much subservient to their husbands. Such a role demands that the woman

> *must not only be seen to be at her husband's side on all formal occasions, she must also be seen to adore him, and never to appear less than dazzled by everything he may say or do. Her eyes should be fixed on him but he should do his best never to be caught looking at her. The relationship must be clearly seen to be unequal.* Greer, 2000

This inequality extends to all other, less celebrated relationships, but this does little to undermine the enthusiasm of women for getting married. Greer complains that the 'ghastly figure of the bride still walks abroad', and notes that the average wedding costs over £10,000. However, the honeymoon period will not last for ever, and inequalities will soon appear:

> *Having been so lucky as to acquire a wife, [the husband] begins to take the liberties that husbands have traditionally taken, comes and goes as he pleases, spends more time outside the connubial home, spends more money on himself, leaves off the share of the housework that he may have formerly done. She sees her job as making him happy; he feels that in marrying her he has done all that is necessary in making her happy.* Greer, 2000

Yet all this is a 'con' because it is men who need marriage more. Married men score much higher on all measures of psychological well-being than unmarried men, whereas single women tend to be more content than married women. Wives are seen as having a duty to keep their husbands interested in sex with them, even though they may no longer 'fancy' their husband. However, they have no realistic chance of maintaining his sexual interest because 'Wives are not sexy. Male sexuality demands the added stimulus of novelty.'

Greer points out that families are now much less stable than they were, with very high divorce rates in Britain. According to Greer, this is largely due to the unhappiness of wives, who are no longer content to accept oppression by their husbands. Three-quarters of divorces are initiated by women.

However, far from being concerned about family instability, Greer sees it as a positive development, because it shows that women are becoming less willing to accept unsatisfactory relationships. She comments:

> *The truth behind the so-called decline in family values is that the illusion of stable family life was built on the silence of suffering women, who lived on whatever their husbands thought fit to give them, did menial work for a pittance, to buy the necessities that their husbands would not pay for, put up with their husband's drinking and their bit on the side, blamed themselves for their husband's violence towards them, and endured abuse silently because of their children.* Greer, 2000

Women as mothers

If women get little fulfilment from being wives, perhaps motherhood offers women better prospects? Greer does not deny that motherhood can be intrinsically satisfying, but she claims that it is not valued by society. She says: 'Mothers bear children in pain, feed them from their bodies, cherish and nourish and prepare to lose them.' Children are expected to leave their mother's home when quite young and to owe their mother little or nothing. Many of the elderly who die of hypothermia are mothers, yet their children accept no responsibility for helping or supporting them. Society attaches no value to motherhood. Greer says:

> *'Mother' is not a career option; the woman who gave her all to mothering has to get in shape, find a job, and keep young and beautiful if she wants to be loved. 'Motherly' is a word for people who are frumpish and suffocating, people who wear cotton hose and shoes with a small heel.* Greer, 2000

This is reflected in 'the accepted ideal of feminine beauty', according to which women are 'boyishly slim and hipless' and the 'broad hips and full bosom of maternity' are seen as 'monstrous'. Women are expected to 'regain their figure' as quickly as they can after childbirth.

In childbirth, medical attention focuses on the well-being of the baby, while the mother's health takes a back seat. After birth, women find that 'mothers and babies are not welcome in adult society, in cinemas, theatres, restaurants, shops or buses'. Women are often expected to return to work 'to service the family debt', and end up exhausted.

Nevertheless, women who are mothers have a final function to perform: 'to take the blame'. Both children and society at large blame mothers for what goes wrong in the children's lives. Single mothers are particularly targeted by commentators and politicians as scapegoats for social problems such as crime and unemployment.

Women as daughters

According to Greer, then, family life does little to benefit women in their adult roles as mothers and wives. However, it is also unrewarding for them as daughters.

Greer suggests recent evidence shows that daughters are quite likely to experience sexual abuse from fathers, stepfathers and other adult male relatives. Greer sees this as a particularly horrendous extension of patriarchal relations within families. Men expect to exercise control over women within families and believe women should service their needs. As adults, women become less willing to accept such subservience, but female children become a relatively easy target of exploitation.

Such abuse is 'very much commoner than we like to believe' and is not confined to 'a special group of inadequate individuals'. Instead, it is an extension of male heterosexuality. Greer says: 'It is understood that heterosexual men fancy young things, that youth itself is a turn-on, but no one is sure how young is too young. Why after all are sexy young women called "babes"?'

Conclusion and evaluation

Given the dismal prospects for women within patriarchal families, Greer argues that the best bet for women is segregation. Women do not need to dissociate themselves from men completely, but they would benefit from living in **matrilocal** households where all the adults are female. Greer says: 'Such segregated communities may hold great advantages for women and children, especially if they can find a way of incorporating older women who are now the majority of the elderly living alone on benefit.' The only alternative is for women to continue to accept their 'humiliation' by men in conventional families.

Germaine Greer's work is very provocative and makes some important points about the position of women in contemporary society. However, it does make sweeping generalizations, many of which are not backed up by research evidence.

Jennifer Somerville (2000) is very critical of Greer. Somerville argues that Greer underestimates the progress made by women over recent decades. She also argues that Greer offers little in the way of practical policy proposals that might make a real difference to women's lives and she fails to discuss the effectiveness of policies that have been introduced.

Jennifer Somerville – a liberal feminist perspective on the family

Compared to Greer, Jennifer Somerville (2000) herself offers a more measured critique of the family from a feminist perspective, with more concern for realistic policies which might improve the position of women. Her proposals involve relatively modest reform rather than revolutionary change within society. For these reasons Somerville can be seen as a liberal feminist, although she does not use this term herself.

Somerville argues that many young women do not feel entirely sympathetic to feminism, yet still feel some sense of grievance. To Somerville, many feminists have failed to acknowledge the progress that has been made for women. In particular, women now have much greater freedom to take paid work even if they are married and have young children. They also have much more choice about when or whether they marry or cohabit, become single mothers, enter lesbian relationships, or live on their own.

The increased choice for women, and the tendency for working-class and middle-class families alike to have both partners in employment, have helped to create greater equality within marriage. Somerville argues: 'Some modern men are voluntarily committed to sharing in those routine necessities of family survival, or they can be persuaded, cajoled, guilt-tripped or bullied.' Despite this, however, 'Women are angry, resentful, but above all disappointed in men.' Many men do not take on their full share of responsibilities and often these men can be 'shown the door'.

Somerville raises the possibility that women might do without male partners, especially as so many prove inadequate, and instead get their sense of fulfilment from their children. Unlike Germaine Greer, though, Somerville does not believe that living in households without adult males is the answer. She says, 'the high figures for remarriage suggest that children are not adequate substitutes for adult relationships of intimacy and companionship for most women'. Such a solution fails to 'mention desire – that physical and energizing interest in the Other – which defies being tailored to the logic of equality and common sense'.

From Somerville's viewpoint, heterosexual attraction and the need for adult companionship will mean that heterosexual families will not disappear. However, nor will 'the conflicts endemic to current inequalities in heterosexual unions'. These will lead to more women cohabiting, living in non-family households or on their own; but most will return to 'further renewed attempts at a permanent commitment to partnership, involving ever more complex familial networks of relationships, responsibilities and residences'.

What is therefore needed is a principled pragmatism in which feminists devise policies to encourage greater equality within relationships and to help women cope with the practicalities of family life. One area that Somerville thinks is particularly important is the introduction of new policies to help working parents. The working hours and the culture of many jobs are incompatible with family life. Many jobs, whether done by men or women, are based on the idea of the male breadwinner who relies upon a non-working wife to take full responsibility for children. This makes equality within marriage difficult to attain and contributes to the tensions which do much harm to many families.

Somerville therefore believes: 'There is a crisis in family life and it does stem from the contradiction between the partial achievement of feminist ideals for women's greater equality and the institutional framework of their lives which assumes their inequality.' If that institutional framework can be changed, for example by increased flexibility in paid employment, then the liberal feminist dream of egalitarian relationships between men and women will move closer to being a reality.

Evaluation

Somerville's arguments are largely based upon a review of other feminist approaches to the family and consequently her study is not backed up by detailed empirical evidence or by specific suggestions for changes in social policies. However, her work does recognize that significant changes have taken place in family life, it suggests ways of making feminism more appealing to the majority of women, and it offers the realistic possibility of gradual progress towards greater equality within the family.

To radical feminists such as Delphy and Leonard and Greer such an approach will fail to deal with the persistence of patriarchal structures and a patriarchal culture in contemporary family life.

Difference feminism

Marxist and radical feminist approaches to the family are not particularly sensitive to variations between families. Both approaches tend to assume that families in general disadvantage women and benefit men (and, in the case of Marxist approaches, benefit capitalism). Both can be criticized for failing to acknowledge the variety of domestic arrangements produced by different groups, and the range of effects that family life can have.

Jennifer Somerville (2000) does take some account of the existence of increased pluralism in the forms of family life. However, some feminists have taken this line of reasoning considerably further and have seen variations in the family situations of women as the defining issue in their theories. Thus, they have argued that women in single-parent families are in a different situation compared to women in two-parent families; women in lesbian families are in a different position to women in heterosexual families; black women are often in a different family position to white women; poor women are in a different position compared to middle-class women, and so on. Feminists who analyse the family in these terms have sometimes been referred to as 'difference feminists'.

Difference feminists have been influenced by a range of feminist theories, including liberal feminism, Marxist feminism and radical feminism (see pp. 101–3). Their work often has affinities with postmodern theories of the family (see pp. 517–18) and with ideas relating to family diversity (see pp. 482–95). However, they share a sufficiently distinctive approach to be considered a separate feminist perspective on the family.

Michèlle Barrett and Mary McIntosh – *The Anti-social Family*

One of the earliest examples of a theory of the family put forward by difference feminists is provided by the work of Michèlle Barrett and Mary McIntosh (1982). Their work was influenced by Marxist feminism but moves beyond the kinds of Marxist feminist views discussed earlier (see p. 466).

Barrett and McIntosh believe that the idea of 'the family' is misleading, given the wide variations that exist in life within families and the varieties of household types in which people live. (Family and household diversity is discussed on p. 466.) If there is no one normal or typical family type, then it may be impossible to claim that the family always performs particular functions either for men or for capitalism.

The 'anti-social' family

Barrett and McIntosh believe there is a very strong ideology supporting family life. To them, 'the family' is 'anti-social' not just because it exploits women, and benefits capitalists, but also because the ideology of the family destroys life outside the family. They say, 'the family ideal makes everything else seem pale and unsatisfactory'. People outside families suffer as a consequence. Family members are so wrapped up in family life that they neglect social contact with others. 'Couples mix with other couples, finding it difficult to fit single people in.'

Life in other institutions (such as children's homes, old people's homes and students' residences) comes to be seen as shallow and lacking in meaning. Barrett and McIntosh argue that homes for those with disabilities could be far more stimulating if life in institutions were not devalued by the ideology of the family.

Like other feminists, Barrett and McIntosh point out that the image of the family as involving love and mutual care tends to ignore the amount of violent and sexual crime that takes place within a family context. They note that 25 per cent of reported violent crimes consist of assaults by husbands on their wives, and many rapes take place within marriage.

They do not deny that there can be caring relationships within families, but equally they do not think that families are the only places in which such relationships can develop. In their view, the ideology that idealizes family life:

> *has made the outside world cold and friendless, and made it harder to maintain relationships of security and trust except with kin. Caring, sharing and loving would all be more widespread if the family did not claim them for its own.* Barrett and McIntosh, 1982

Linda Nicholson – 'The myth of the traditional family'

Like Barrett and McIntosh, Linda Nicholson (1997) believes there is a powerful ideology which gives support to a positive image of family life. She argues that this ideology only supports certain types of family while devaluing other types. Nicholson contrasts what she calls the 'traditional' family with 'alternative' families. She is an American feminist and her comments largely refer to the USA, but they may be applicable more generally to Western societies.

The 'traditional' family

Nicholson defines the traditional family as 'the unit of parents with children who live together'. The bond between husband and wife is seen as particularly important, and the family feels itself to be separate from other kin. This family group is often referred to as the nuclear family (see p. 474). When conservative social commentators express concern about the decline of the family, it is this sort of family they are concerned about. They tend to be less worried about any decline of wider kinship links involving grandparents, aunts, uncles and so on.

Nicholson claims that the nuclear family which is idealized by many commentators is a comparatively recent phenomenon and only became the norm for working-class families in the 1950s, and even then it was uncommon among African Americans. Furthermore, alternative family forms were already developing even before the traditional family reached its zenith. Nicholson says:

> *Even as a certain ideal of family was coming to define 'the American way of life', such trends as a rising divorce rate, increased participation of married women in the labour force, and the growth of female-headed households were making this way of life increasingly atypical. In all cases such trends preceded the 1950s.* Nicholson, 1997

Some of these changes actually altered what was perceived as a 'traditional' family. For example, it came to be seen as 'normal' for married women to work, even if they had small children. Other changes, though, were seen as producing alternative families. Alternatives to traditional families included, 'Not only gays and lesbians but heterosexuals living alone; married couples with husbands at home caring for children', as well as stepfamilies, single parents, heterosexual couples living together outside marriage, and gay or lesbian couples with or without children.

The merits of different family types

Alternative families, or alternatives to traditional families, tend to be devalued. They are seen as less worthy than traditional families. However, Nicholson rejects this view. Alternative families are often better than traditional ones for the women who live in them. For example, poor black women in the USA derive some benefits when they live in mother-centred families, often without men. They develop strong support networks with other friends and kin, who act as a kind of social insurance system. They help out the families who are most in need at a particular time if they are in a position to do so.

Such families do have disadvantages. If they have some good fortune and come into money, each family is expected to share resources. This makes it difficult for individual families to escape poverty. Furthermore, the lack of stable heterosexual partnerships means 'children frequently do not have the type of long-term relationships with father figures which is normative within middle-class households'.

Traditional families also have disadvantages:

- Because both partners now tend to work, they have tremendous time pressures, making it difficult to carry out satisfactory and rewarding childcare.
- Children who are the victims of abuse by parents have relatively little opportunity to turn to other relatives for help.
- Traditional families place a heavy burden of expectation on the partners, and, with work and childcare commitments, it may be difficult for them to provide the love and companionship each partner expects.
- The traditional family also precludes and excludes gay and lesbian relationships.

However, traditional families do have some advantages:

- Their small size tends to encourage intimacy between family members, and, when the relationships work, they can be rewarding and long-lasting.
- Traditional families can be economically successful because they are not usually expected to share their resources with others.

Conclusion

The fact that they have some advantages does not mean that traditional families are better than alternative types. From Nicholson's point of view, different types of family suit different women in different circumstances. She believes the distinction between traditional and alternative families should be abandoned. The distinction implies that traditional families are better, when this is often not true. In any case, the idea of the traditional family misleadingly implies that such families have long been the norm, when in fact they have only become popular in recent times, and have never been totally dominant.

By the late 1990s so many people lived in alternatives to traditional families that the idea of the traditional family had become totally outdated. Nicholson therefore concludes that all types of family and household should be acknowledged and accepted because they could suit women in different circumstances. She advocates the celebration of greater choice for people in deciding on their own living arrangements.

Cheshire Calhoun – lesbians as 'family outlaws'

Like Linda Nicholson, Cheshire Calhoun (1997) develops a type of difference feminism influenced by postmodernism. Unlike Nicholson, she focuses on lesbian families rather than looking at the merits of a variety of family forms for women. Calhoun is a postmodern, difference feminist from the United States.

Lesbians and families

Calhoun argues that traditional feminists are right to argue that women are exploited within families, but wrong to argue that the exploitation of women is an inevitable feature of family life. Rather, exploitation results from the heterosexual family.

In lesbian families, there is no possibility that women can become dependent on men and exploited by them. Some lesbian feminists argue that women should avoid forming families, but Calhoun disagrees. According to her, it is not family life itself that leads to the exploitation of women; rather, it is family life within patriarchal, heterosexual marriages that is the problem. Lesbian marriage and mothering can avoid the exploitative relationships typical of heterosexual marriage. Indeed, lesbian partners may be able to develop forms of marriage and family life which can point the way to creating more egalitarian domestic relationships.

This view is in stark contrast to a more conventional view that lesbians and gays cannot develop proper marriages or construct genuine families. According to Calhoun, gays and lesbians have historically been portrayed as 'family outlaws'. Their sexuality has been seen as threatening to the family. They have been portrayed as 'outsiders to the family and as displaying the most virulent forms of family-disrupting behaviour'.

However, Calhoun believes the anxiety among heterosexuals about gays and lesbians has in fact been caused by anxiety about the state of the heterosexual nuclear family. Rather than recognizing and acknowledging the problems with such families, heterosexuals have tried to attribute the problems to corrupting outsiders or outlaws: that is, gays and lesbians.

According to Calhoun, modern family life is essentially characterized by choice. Lesbians and gays introduced the idea of chosen families. You can choose whom to include in your family without the restrictions of blood ties or the expectation of settling down with and marrying an opposite-sex partner. Now, however, heterosexuals also construct 'chosen families' as they divorce, remarry, separate, choose new partners, adopt children, gain stepchildren and so on.

Rather than seeing the above changes in a positive light, many commentators have seen them as a threat to families and the institution of marriage. This time there have been two main types of family outlaw who have been scapegoated and blamed for the changes. These are 'the unwed welfare mother and ... the lesbian or gay whose mere public visibility threatens to undermine family values and destroy the family'.

Conclusion

Calhoun concludes that such scapegoating of lesbians and gays is used to disguise the increasingly frequent departures from the norms of family life by heterosexuals. She says:

> *Claiming that gay and lesbian families are (or should be) distinctively queer and distinctively deviant helps conceal the deviancy in heterosexual families, and thereby helps to sustain the illusion that heterosexuals are specially entitled to access to a protected private sphere because they, unlike their gay and lesbian counterparts, are supporters of the family.* Calhoun, 1997

Thus the ideology of the heterosexual family has played an important part in encouraging discrimination and prejudice against gays and lesbians.

To Calhoun, gay and lesbian relationships, with or without children, are just as much family relationships as those of heterosexual couples. She does not believe that arguing for them to be accepted as such in any way legitimates the heterosexual, patriarchal family that has been so criticized by radical and Marxist feminists.

In the contemporary world, heterosexual families engage in 'multiple deviations from norms governing the family'. A wide variety of behaviours and family forms have become common and widely accepted. Accepting gays and lesbians as forming families involves the acceptance of just one more variation from traditional conventional families. It has the potential benefit of reducing the anti-gay and anti-lesbian prejudice that has been promoted in the name of preserving the family.

Difference feminism – conclusion

The feminists discussed in this section all avoid the mistake of making sweeping generalizations about the effects of family life on women. They tend to be sensitive to the different experiences of family life experienced by women of different sexual orientations, ethnic groups, classes and so on (although each writer does not necessarily discuss all the sources of difference that affect how families influence women's lives). In these respects they can be seen as representing theoretical advances upon some of the Marxist and radical theories discussed earlier.

However, some difference feminists do sometimes lose sight of the inequalities between men and women in families by stressing the range of choices open to people when they are forming families. By stressing the different experiences of women they tend to neglect the common experiences shared by most women in families. Nevertheless, this general approach may be right to suggest that it is possible (if not common) for both men and women to develop rewarding and fulfilling family relationships.

The last few sections have examined the family from a variety of perspectives. The focus now changes to various themes that are significant to our understanding of the family as a unit of social organization. The first theme is the effect of industrialization and modernization on the family.

The family, industrialization and modernization

The pre-industrial family

A major theme in sociological studies of the family is the relationship between the structure of the family and the related processes of industrialization and modernization. **Industrialization** refers to the mass production of goods in a factory system which involves some degree of mechanized production technology. **Modernization** refers to the development of social, cultural, economic and political practices and institutions which are thought to be typical of modern societies. Such developments include the replacement of religious belief systems with scientific and rational ones, the growth of bureaucratic institutions, and the replacement of monarchies with representative democracies (see pp. 890–1 for an introduction to the concept of modernity).

Some sociologists regard industrialization as the central process involved in changes in Western societies since the eighteenth century; others attach more importance to broader processes of modernization. However, there are a number of problems that arise from relating the family to industrialization or modernization:

1 The processes of industrialization and modernization do not follow the same course in every society.
2 Industrialization and modernization are not fixed states but developing processes. Thus the industrial system in nineteenth-century Britain was different in important respects from that of today. Similarly, British culture, society and politics are very different now from how they were two hundred years ago.
3 Some writers dispute that we still live in modern industrial societies and believe that we have moved into a phase of postmodernity. The issue of the family and postmodernity will be examined later in the chapter (see pp. 517–19).

Further difficulties arise from the fact that there is not one form of pre-industrial, or premodern, family, but many.

Much of the research on the family, industrialization and modernization has led to considerable confusion because it is not always clear what the family in modern industrial society is being compared to. In addition, within modern industrial society there are variations in family structure. As a starting point, therefore, it is necessary for us to examine the family in premodern, pre-industrial societies in order to establish a standard for comparison.

The family in non-literate societies

In many small-scale, non-literate societies the family and kinship relationships in general are the basic organizing principles of social life. Societies are often divided into a number of kinship groups, such as **lineages**, which are groups descended from a common ancestor. The family is embedded in a web of kinship relationships. Kinship groups are responsible for the production of important goods and services. For example, a lineage may own agricultural land which is worked, and its produce shared, by members of the lineage.

Members of kinship groups are united by a network of mutual rights and obligations. In some cases, if individuals are insulted or injured by someone from outside the group, they have the right to call on the support of members of the group in seeking reparation or revenge.

Many areas of an individual's behaviour are shaped by his or her status as kin. An uncle, for example, may have binding obligations to be involved with aspects of his nephew's socialization and may be responsible for the welfare of his nieces and nephews should their father die.

Something of the importance of family and kinship relationships in many small-scale societies is illustrated by the following statement by a Pomo Indian of northern California:

> *What is a man? A man is nothing. Without his family he is of less importance than that bug crossing the trail. In the white ways of doing things the family is not so important. The police and soldiers take care of protecting you, the courts give you justice, the post office carries messages for you, the school teaches you. Everything is taken care of, even your children, if you die; but with us the family must do all of that.* Quoted in Aginsky, 1968

In this brief description of the family in small-scale, pre-industrial society we have glossed over the wide variations in family and kinship patterns which are found in such societies. Even so, it does serve to highlight some of the more important differences between the family in kinship-based society and the family in industrial society.

The 'classic' extended family

A second form of pre-industrial, premodern family, sometimes known as the classic extended family, is found in some traditional peasant societies. This family type has been made famous by C.M. Arensberg and S.T. Kimball's study of Irish farmers, entitled *Family and Community in Ireland* (1968).

As in kinship-based societies, kinship ties dominate life, but in this case the basic unit is the extended family rather than the wider kinship grouping. The traditional Irish farming family is a **patriarchal extended family**, so-called because of the considerable authority of the male head. It is also **patrilineal** because property is passed down through the male line. Within the family, social and economic roles are welded together, status being ascribed by family membership.

On the farm, the father–son relationship is also that of owner–employee. The father–owner makes the important decisions (such as whether to sell cattle) and directs the activities of all the other members of the extended family. He is head of the family and 'director of the firm'.

Typically, the classic extended family consists of the male head, his wife and children, his ageing parents who have passed on the farm to him, and any unmarried brothers and sisters. Together, they work as a 'production unit', producing the goods necessary for the family's survival.

Some people have argued that, as industrialization and modernization proceed, kinship-based society and the classic extended family tend to break up, and the nuclear family – or some form of modified extended family – emerges as the predominant family form.

Talcott Parsons – the 'isolated nuclear family'

Structural isolation

Talcott Parsons argued that the **isolated nuclear family** is the typical family form in modern industrial society (Parsons, 1959, 1965b; Parsons and Bales, 1955). It is 'structurally isolated' because it does not form an integral part of a wider system of kinship relationships. Obviously there are social relationships between members of nuclear families and their kin, but these relationships are more a matter of choice than binding obligations.

Parsons saw the emergence of the isolated nuclear family in terms of his theory of social evolution. (This theory is outlined in Chapter 15, pp. 860–1.) The evolution of society involves a process of **structural differentiation**. This simply means that institutions evolve which specialize in fewer functions. As a result, the family and kinship groups no longer perform a wide range of functions. Instead, specialist institutions such as business firms, schools, hospitals, police forces and churches take over many of their functions.

This process of differentiation and specialization involves the 'transfer of a variety of functions from the nuclear family to other structures of the society'. Thus, in modern industrial society, with the transfer of the production of goods to factories, specialized economic institutions became differentiated from the family. The family ceased to be an economic unit of production.

The family and the economy

Functionalist analysis emphasizes the importance of integration and harmony between the various parts of society. An efficient social system requires the parts to fit smoothly rather than abrade. The parts of society are **functionally related** when they contribute to the integration and harmony of the social system.

Parsons argued that there is a functional relationship between the isolated nuclear family and the economic system in industrial society. In particular, the isolated nuclear family is shaped to meet the requirements of the economic system.

A modern industrial system with a specialized division of labour demands considerable geographical mobility from its labour force. Individuals with specialized skills are required to move to places where those skills are in demand. The isolated nuclear family is suited to this need for geographical mobility. It is not tied down by binding obligations to a wide range of kin and, compared to the pre-industrial families described above, it is a small, streamlined unit.

Status in the family

Status in industrial society is **achieved** rather than **ascribed**. An individual's occupational status is not automatically fixed by their ascribed status in the family or kinship group. Parsons argued that the isolated nuclear family is the best form of family structure for a society based on achieved status.

In industrial society, individuals are judged in terms of the status they achieve. Such judgements are based on what Parsons termed **universalistic values** – that is, values that are universally applied to all members of society. However, within the family, status is ascribed and, as such, based on **particularistic values** – that is, values that are applied only to particular individuals. Thus a son's relationship with his father is conducted primarily in terms of their ascribed statuses of father and son. The father's achieved status as a bricklayer, school teacher or lawyer has relatively little influence on their relationship, since his son does not judge him primarily in terms of universalistic values.

Parsons argued that, in a society based on achieved status, conflict would tend to arise in a family unit larger than the isolated nuclear family. In a three-generation extended family, in which the children remained as part of the family unit, the following situation could produce conflict. If the son became a doctor and the father was a labourer, the particularistic values of family life would give the father a higher status than his son. Yet the universalistic values of society as a whole would award his son higher social status. Conflict could result from this situation, which might undermine the authority of the father and threaten the solidarity of the family.

The same conflict of values could occur if the nuclear family were extended horizontally. Relationships between a woman and her sister might be problematic if they held jobs of widely differing prestige.

The isolated nuclear family largely prevents these problems from arising. There is one main breadwinner, the husband–father. His wife is mainly responsible for raising the children and the latter have yet to achieve their status in the world of work. No member of the family is in a position to threaten the ascribed authority structure by achieving a status outside the family which is higher than the achieved status of the family head.

These problems do not occur in premodern, pre-industrial societies because occupational status is largely ascribed, since an individual's position in the family and kinship group usually determines his or her job.

Parsons concluded that, given the universalistic, achievement-oriented values of industrial society, the isolated nuclear family is the most suitable family structure. Any extension of this basic unit might well create conflict which would threaten the solidarity of the family.

As a consequence of the structural isolation of the nuclear family, the **conjugal bond** – the relationship between husband and wife – is strengthened. Without the support of kin beyond the nuclear family, spouses are increasingly dependent on each other, particularly for emotional support. As we outlined previously, Parsons argued that the stabilization of adult personalities is a major function of the family in modern industrial society. This is largely accomplished in terms of the husband–wife relationship.

Criticism of Parsons

So far, the arguments examined in this section suggest that modernization and industrialization led to a shift from predominantly extended to predominantly nuclear family types. The nuclear family is portrayed by Parsons as being well adapted to the requirements of modern industrial societies. Furthermore, the nuclear family is generally portrayed in a positive light. David Cheal (1991) sees this view as being closely related to the modernist view of progress.

Cheal describes **modernism** as 'a self-conscious commitment to and advocacy of the world-changing potential of modernity'. Writers such as Parsons put forward a modernist interpretation of the family. Cheal strongly attacks Parsons's views.

Parsons saw the change towards a nuclear family as part of the increased specialization of institutions. The family was seen as an increasingly well-adapted specialist institution which interacted with other specialist institutions such as those of the welfare state. Cheal is very sceptical of the modernist view of the family advocated by Parsons. He claims that the faith in progress expressed by writers such as Parsons and Goode ignored contradictions within modernity. Changes in different parts of society did not always go hand-in-hand. For example, increased employment of women in paid jobs did not lead to men sharing domestic tasks equally. From Cheal's point of view, there is nothing inevitable about modern institutions developing in such a way that they function well together. Furthermore, Cheal argues:

> *Parsons' generalizations about family life were often seriously parochial, reflecting narrow experiences of gender, class, race and nationality. Inevitably, that resulted in Parsons drawing some conclusions that have not stood up well to empirical investigation, or to the passage of time.* Cheal, 1991

Peter Laslett – the family in pre-industrial societies

The family in kinship-based society and the classic extended family represent only two possible forms of family structure in pre-industrial society. Historical research in Britain and America suggests neither was typical of those countries in the pre-industrial era.

Peter Laslett, a historian, studied family size and composition in pre-industrial England (Laslett, 1972, 1977). For the period between 1564 and 1821 he found that only about 10 per cent of households contained kin beyond the nuclear family. This percentage is the same as for England in 1966. Evidence from America presents a similar picture.

This surprisingly low figure may be due in part to the fact that people in pre-industrial England and America married relatively late in life and life expectancy was short. On average, there were only a few years between the marriage of a couple and the death of their parents. However, Laslett found no evidence to support the formerly accepted view that the classic extended family was widespread in pre-industrial England. He states: 'There is no sign of the large, extended co-residential family group of the traditional peasant world giving way to the small, nuclear conjugal household of modern industrial society.'

The 'Western family'

Following on from his research in England, Laslett (1983, 1984) began to draw together the results of research into pre-industrial family size in other countries. He reached the conclusion that the nuclear family was not just typical of Britain. He uncovered evidence that there was a distinctive **Western family** found also in northern France, the Netherlands, Belgium, Scandinavia and parts of Italy and Germany. This type of family was typically nuclear in structure: children were born relatively late, there was little age gap between spouses, and a large number of families contained servants. This contrasted with Eastern Europe and other parts of the world (such as Russia and Japan), where the extended family was more common.

According to Laslett, it was at least possible that the predominance of the nuclear family was a factor that helped Western Europe to be the first area of the world to industrialize. He reversed the more common argument that industrialization led to the nuclear family, claiming that the nuclear family had social, political and economic consequences which in part led to industrialization.

Criticisms of Laslett

Although Laslett successfully exploded the myth that the extended family was typical of pre-industrial Britain, his conclusions should be viewed with some caution.

Michael Anderson (1980) points out some contradictory evidence in Laslett's own research. Laslett's research might have shown average household size to be under five people, but it also revealed that a majority of the population in pre-industrial Britain (53 per cent) lived in households consisting of six or more people.

Anderson also refers to other research which suggests a much greater variety of household types than Laslett's theory of the Western family implies. For instance, research has shown that in Sweden extended families were very common. Furthermore, there is evidence of considerable variation within Britain: the gentry and yeoman farmers, for example, tended to have much larger households than the average.

For these reasons, Anderson is critical of the idea of the 'Western family'. He believes pre-industrial Europe was characterized by family diversity without any one type of family being predominant.

Michael Anderson – household structure and the industrial revolution

Michael Anderson's own research into the effects of industrialization on families does not, however, support the view that during industrialization extended families began to disappear (Anderson, 1971, 1977).

Using data from the 1851 census of Preston, Anderson found that some 23 per cent of households contained kin other than the nuclear family – a large increase over Laslett's figures and those of today. The bulk of this 'co-residence' occurred among the poor. Anderson argues that co-residence occurs when the parties involved receive net gains from the arrangement:

> *If we are to understand variations and changes in patterns of kinship relationships, the only worthwhile approach is consciously and explicitly to investigate the manifold advantages and disadvantages that any actor can obtain from maintaining one relational pattern rather than another.* Anderson, 1971

Extended families and mutual aid

Preston in 1851 was largely dependent on the cotton industry. Life for many working-class families was characterized by severe hardship, resulting from low wages, periods of high unemployment, large families, a high death rate and overcrowded housing. In these circumstances the maintenance of a large kinship network could be advantageous to all concerned.

In the absence of a welfare state, individuals were largely dependent on kin in times of hardship and need. Ageing parents often lived with their married children, a situation that benefited both parties. It provided support for the aged and allowed both the parents to work in the factory, since the grandparents could care for the dependent children. Networks of mutual support were useful in the event of sickness or unemployment or if children were orphaned. Co-residence also allowed the sharing of the cost of rent and other household expenses.

Anderson's study of Preston indicates that, in the mid-nineteenth century, the working-class family functioned as a mutual aid organization. It provided an insurance policy against hardship and crisis. This function encouraged the extension of kinship bonds beyond the nuclear family. Such links would be retained as long as they provided net gains to those involved. Anderson concludes that the early stages of industrialization increased rather than decreased the extension of the working-class family.

Michael Young and Peter Willmott – four stages of family life

Michael Young and Peter Willmott conducted studies of family life in London from the 1950s to the 1970s. In their book *The Symmetrical Family* (1973) they attempt to trace the development of the family from pre-industrial England to the 1970s. Using a combination of historical research and social surveys, they suggest that the family has gone through four main stages. In this section we will concentrate on their analysis of the working-class family.

Stage 1 – the pre-industrial family

Stage 1 is represented by the pre-industrial family. The family is a unit of production: the husband, wife and unmarried children work as a team, typically in agriculture or textiles. This type of family was gradually supplanted as a result of the industrial revolution. However, it continued well into the nineteenth century and is still represented in a small minority of families today, the best examples being some farming families.

Stage 2 – the early industrial family

The Stage 2 family began with the industrial revolution, developed throughout the nineteenth century and reached its peak in the early years of the twentieth century. The family ceased to be a unit of production, since individual members were employed as wage earners.

Throughout the nineteenth century, working-class poverty was widespread, wages were low and unemployment high. Like Anderson, Young and Willmott argue that the family responded to this situation by extending its network to include relatives beyond the nuclear family. This provided an insurance policy against the insecurity and hardship of poverty.

The extension of the nuclear family was largely conducted by women who 'eventually built up an organization in their own defence and in defence of their children'. The basic tie was between a mother and her married daughter, and, in comparison, the conjugal bond (the husband–wife relationship) was weak. Women created an 'informal trade union' which largely excluded men. Young and Willmott claim: 'Husbands were often squeezed out of the warmth of the female circle and took to the pub as their defence.'

Compared to later stages, the Stage 2 family was more often headed by a female. However, unlike the situation of New World black families (see p. 861), this resulted more from the high male death rate than from desertion by the husband.

The Stage 2 family began to decline in the early years of the twentieth century, but it is still found in many low income, long-established working-class areas. Its survival is documented in Young and Willmott's famous study entitled *Family and Kinship in East London*. The study was conducted in the mid-1950s in Bethnal Green, a low income borough in London's East End. Bethnal Green is a long-settled, traditional working-class area. Children usually remain in the same locality after marriage. At the time of the research, two out of three married people had parents living within two to three miles.

The study found that there was a close tie between female relatives. Over 50 per cent of the married women in the sample had seen their mother during the previous day, over 80 per cent within the previous week. There was a constant exchange of services such as washing, shopping and babysitting between female relatives. Young and Willmott argued that in many families the households of mother and married daughter were 'to some extent merged'. As such they can be termed extended families, which Young and Willmott define as 'a combination of families who to some degree form one domestic unit'.

Although many aspects of the Stage 2 family were present in Bethnal Green, there were also indications of a transition to Stage 3. For example, fathers were increasingly involved in the rearing of their children. (For details of a later study which examined how Bethnal Green had changed by the 1990s, see pp. 492–4.)

Stage 3 – the symmetrical family

In the early 1970s Young and Willmott conducted a large-scale social survey in which 1,928 people were interviewed in Greater London and the outer metropolitan area. The results formed the basis of their book, *The Symmetrical Family*.

Young and Willmott argue that the Stage 2 family has largely disappeared. For all social classes, but particularly the working class, the Stage 3 family predominates. This family is characterized by 'the separation of the immediate, or nuclear family from the extended family'. The 'trade union' of women is disbanded and the husband returns to the family circle.

Life for the Stage 3 nuclear family is largely home-centred, particularly when the children are young. Free time is spent doing chores and odd jobs around the house, and leisure is mainly 'home-based', for example, watching television. The conjugal bond is strong and relationships between husband and wife are increasingly 'companionate'. In the home, 'They shared their work; they shared their time.' The nuclear family has become a largely self-contained, self-reliant unit.

Young and Willmott use the term **symmetrical family** to describe the nuclear family of Stage 3. 'Symmetry' refers to an arrangement in which the opposite parts are similar in shape and size. With respect to the symmetrical family, conjugal roles, although not the same – wives still have the main responsibility for raising the children, although husbands help – are similar in terms of the contribution made by each spouse to the running of the household. They share many of the chores, they share decisions, they work together, yet there is still men's work and women's work. Conjugal roles are not interchangeable but they are symmetrical in important respects.

Reasons for the rise of the symmetrical family

Young and Willmott give the following reasons for the transition from Stage 2 to Stage 3 families:

1. A number of factors have reduced the need for kinship-based mutual aid groups. They include an increase in the real wages of the male breadwinner, a decrease in unemployment and the male mortality rate, increased employment opportunities for women and the provision of a wider range of services and benefits by the welfare state.
2. Increasing geographical mobility has tended to sever kinship ties. In their study of Bethnal Green, Young and Willmott showed how the extended kinship network largely ceased to operate when young couples with children moved some twenty miles away to a new council housing estate.
3. The reduction in the number of children, from an average of five or six per family in the nineteenth century to just over two in 1970, provided greater opportunities for wives to work. This in turn led to greater symmetry within the family, since both spouses are more likely to be wage earners and to share financial responsibility for the household.
4. As living standards rose, the husband was drawn more closely into the family circle, since the home was a more attractive place with better amenities and a greater range of home entertainments.

Class and family life

Young and Willmott found that the home-centred symmetrical family was more typical of the working class than the middle class. They argue that members of the working class are 'more fully home-centred because they are less fully work-centred'. Partly as compensation for boring and uninvolving work, and partly because relatively little interest and energy are expended at work, manual workers tend to focus their attention on family life. Young and Willmott therefore see the nature of work as a major influence on family life.

The 'Principle of Stratified Diffusion'

In *The Symmetrical Family* Young and Willmott devise a general theory which they term the **Principle of Stratified Diffusion**. They claim this theory explains much of the change in family life in industrial society. Put simply, the theory states that what the top of the stratification system does today, the bottom will do tomorrow. Lifestyles, patterns of consumption, attitudes and expectations will diffuse from the top of the stratification system downwards.

Young and Willmott argue that industrialization is the 'source of momentum': it provides the opportunities for higher living standards and so on. However, industrialization alone cannot account for the changes in family life: it cannot fully explain, for example, why the mass of the population have chosen to adopt the lifestyle of Stage 3 families. To complete the explanation, Young and Willmott maintain that the Principle of Stratified Diffusion is required.

Industrialization provides the opportunity for a certain degree of choice for the mass of the population. This choice will be largely determined by the behaviour of those at the top of the stratification system. Values, attitudes and expectations permeate down the class system; those at the bottom copy those at the top.

A Stage 4 family?

Applying the Principle of Stratified Diffusion to the future (writing in 1973), Young and Willmott postulated the possible development of a Stage 4 family. They examined in detail the family life of managing directors, which, in terms of their theory, should diffuse downwards in years to come.

Managing directors were work-centred rather than home-centred – 'my business is my life' was a typical quote from those in the sample. Their leisure activities were less home-centred and less likely to involve their wives than those of Stage 3 families. Sport was an important area of recreation, particularly swimming and golf. The wife's role was to look after the children and the home. As such, the managing director's family was more asymmetrical than the Stage 3 family.

Young and Willmott suggest that changes in production technology may provide the opportunity for the Stage 4 family to diffuse throughout the stratification system. As technology reduces routine work, a larger number of people may have more interesting and involving jobs and become increasingly work-centred.

Young and Willmott admit: 'We cannot claim that our 190 managing directors were representative of managing directors generally.' However, given the evidence available, they predict that the asymmetrical Stage 4 family represents the next major development.

Evaluation

A number of features of Young and Willmott's work are open to criticism. Many feminists have attacked the concept of the symmetrical family, arguing that there has been little progress towards equality between husband and wife (see p. 497 for details). There is also little evidence that the Principle of Stratified Diffusion has led to the Stage 4 family becoming typical of all strata. Married women have continued to take paid employment and few working-class families can afford to adopt the lifestyle and family arrangements of managing directors.

Later research by Peter Willmott has not used or supported the concept of the Stage 4 family, as we will see below.

The middle-class family

Quantity and quality of contacts

A major problem in studies of the family is the difficulty of measuring the importance of kin beyond the nuclear family. In a study of middle-class family life carried out in Swansea, Colin Bell (1968) questioned whether the frequency of actual face-to-face contacts between kin provides an accurate assessment. Bell points to the importance of contact by telephone and mail. He also distinguishes between the quantity and quality of contacts. For example, bumping into mum on a street corner in Swansea may have far less significance than a formal visit to her mother by a middle-class daughter.

In his study, Bell found a low level of direct face-to-face contact with kin beyond the nuclear family. Despite this relatively low level of contact, he argues that, compared to the working class, 'Middle-class kin networks may have fewer day-to-day demands but I think that there is little evidence to suggest that they necessarily show any different affective quality.' Thus direct contact may be less frequent but the emotional bonds are the same.

Similar conclusions were reached by Graham Allan (1985) in research conducted in a commuter village in East Anglia. Although he found some evidence that the relationship between working-class wives and their mothers was particularly close, in general there was little difference between the middle-class and working-class kinship networks. In both cases relationships were characterized by a 'positive concern' for the welfare of the kin regardless of the frequency of face-to-face contacts.

Contemporary family networks

Peter Willmott – networks in London

In research conducted during the 1980s in a north London suburb, Peter Willmott (1988) found that contacts with kin remained important in both the middle and working class. In the area he studied, about a third of the couples had moved to the district in the previous five years. Only a third of all the couples had parents or parents-in-law living within ten minutes' travelling distance. However, despite the distance between their homes, two-thirds of the couples saw relatives at least weekly. Working-class couples saw relatives more frequently than middle-class couples, but the differences were not great.

Maintaining contact was relatively easy for most families because so many had access to cars. Most also had homes that were sufficiently spacious for relatives to come and stay. Some 90 per cent had telephones which enabled them to keep in touch with relatives even if they did not meet face-to-face.

Willmott also found that 'relatives continue to be the main source of informal support and care, and that again the class differences are not marked'. For example, nearly 75 per cent had relatives who sometimes helped with babysitting and 80 per cent looked to relatives to help them when they needed to borrow money.

Margaret O'Brien and Deborah Jones – families and kinship in east London

Margaret O'Brien and Deborah Jones (1996) conducted research in Barking and Dagenham, in east London, in the early 1990s. They collected survey data on 600 young people and their parents in this predominantly working-class area. They compared their findings with a 1950s study of the same area conducted by Peter Willmott (1963).

O'Brien and Jones found that, compared with the 1950s, this area had developed a greater variety of types of family and household. Of the young people surveyed, 14 per cent lived with a step-parent and 14 per cent lived in lone-parent families. According to census statistics, over one-third of births in the area took place outside marriage. There were many dual-earner families, with 62 per cent of women in their sample working in paid employment, and 79 per cent of men. In Willmott's 1950s study, family life was much more homogeneous. Then, 78 per cent of people were married and just 1 per cent were divorced. Most single people were young and lived with their parents.

Despite the move towards a greater plurality of family and household types, O'Brien and Jones did not find that there had been any major erosion in the importance attached to kinship. In both Willmott's and O'Brien and Jones's research, over 40 per cent of the sample had grandparents living locally. In the 1990s, 72 per cent of those studied had been visited by a relative in the previous week, and over half the sample saw their maternal grandparent at least weekly. Twenty per cent had a large network of local kin numbering over ten relatives.

O'Brien and Jones conclude that there has been a **pluralization of lifestyles**, an increase in marital breakdowns and a big rise in dual-earner households. However, they also found that 'kin contact and association do not appear to have changed significantly since Willmott's study of the borough in the 1950s'. This suggests a greater continuity in kin relationships, at least among the working class in London, than that implied by some other studies.

Families and kinship in the 1980s and 1990s

All of the above studies are based upon specific geographical areas at a particular point in time. The British Social Attitudes Surveys of 1986 and 1995 contained a number of questions on families and kinship (reported in Jowell *et al.*, 1989, and McGlone *et al.*, 1996). The surveys used large representative samples of the British population. The results of these two surveys were analysed by Francis McGlone, Alison Park and Kate Smith (1998).

Changes in family contacts

McGlone *et al.* (1996) start by noting that a number of important changes that might affect family life took place between 1986 and 1995. These included: a rising proportion of elderly people in the population; increasing levels of divorce, cohabitation, lone parenthood, and births outside marriage; a decline in male unskilled jobs and an increase in female employment; and some young people staying reliant on their families for longer. Despite these changes, McGlone *et al.* actually found considerable continuity between 1986 and 1995.

The British Social Attitudes Surveys revealed that even in 1995 contacts with relatives remained quite frequent. For example, in 1995, 47 per cent of people without dependent children and 50 per cent of those with dependent children saw their mother at least once a week. Furthermore, 35 per cent of those without children and 45 per cent of those with children saw their father at least once a week. (All figures refer to the proportions of those with living relatives of the type specified.)

The proportions were even higher for those who lived within one hour's drive of their relatives. Among this group, for example, 75 per cent of those without children under 16 saw their mother and 63 per cent saw their father at least once a week. Among those with children, 70 per cent saw their mother and 69 per cent saw their father at least once a week. Telephone contact was also common. Among women with a dependent child, 78 per cent talked to their mother at least once a week, 54 per cent to their father, 45 per cent to an adult sibling, and 39 per cent to another relative.

In line with other studies, it was found that there were significant social class differences. For example, 65 per cent of manual workers but only 39 per cent of non-manual workers with a dependent child saw their mother at least once a week.

Although contacts with relatives remained frequent in 1995, a comparison with 1986 did find that they had declined somewhat. In 1986, 59 per cent of those with dependent children saw their mother at least once a week, declining to 50 per cent in 1995. Contacts with all other relatives had fallen as well. However, the falls were partly accounted for by people living further apart. The fall in contact with mothers was less for those who lived within an hour's driving distance than for the group as a whole. Contacts with fathers remained unchanged and those with adult siblings had increased.

What fall there had been was largely accounted for by non-manual workers, particularly middle-class families where the woman was in full-time paid employment. It appeared that in many dual-earner families there was too little time to maintain regular weekly contact with parents and other relatives. There was no significant change in maternal and paternal contacts among manual workers.

Table 8.1 Proportion with a dependent child who see specified relative living within one hour's journey time at least once a week (1986 and 1995)

	1986		1995	
	%	Base	%	Base
Mother	76	269	70	328
Father	69	196	69	253
Adult sibling	55	300	56	336
Other relative	70	313	64	383

Note: The base for each percentage comprises all those with the specified relative living within one hour's journey time (non-resident) and with dependent children.

Source: F. McGlone, A. Park and K. Smith (1998) *Families and Kinship*, Family Policy Studies Centre, London, p. 17.

Families and help

As earlier studies suggested, even where there was a lack of contact between family members, that did not necessarily mean that kinship networks had become unimportant.

The British Social Attitudes Surveys of 1986 and 1995 asked people who they would go to for help with things such as doing household and garden jobs, support during illness, and borrowing money. For household jobs and help while ill, most said they would turn first of all to a spouse or partner, while turning to other relatives was the second most popular choice. For borrowing money, the most popular options were borrowing from other relatives or from a bank.

Among those who had received help in the previous five years, a high proportion had got that help from relatives. For example, 59 per cent of those without a child under 16 and 71 per cent of those with a child, who had received a loan or gift of money, had got it from a parent or in-law, and over a third of those who had received help when ill had got it from one of these sources.

McGlone *et al.* conclude that family members remain the most important source of practical help. While people tend to turn first to a spouse or partner, after that they turn to other relatives, with friends or neighbours being less important.

Attitudes to families

Here, McGlone *et al.* found that 'the majority of the adult population are very family centred'. Table 8.2 summarizes the results of the study in this area. It shows that less than 10 per cent thought that friends were more important to them than family members. The vast majority thought that parents should continue to help children after they had left home, and around 70 per cent thought that people should keep in touch with close family members. A majority thought that you should try to keep in touch with relatives such as aunts, uncles and cousins, even if you did not have much in common with them.

Conclusions

McGlone *et al.* found that families remain very important to people in contemporary Britain. They argue that their study confirms the results of earlier research showing that families remain an important source of help and support, and that family contacts are still maintained even though family members tend to live further apart. Their research suggests that the 'core' of the family does not just include parents and children – in most households grandparents are part of the core as well.

McGlone *et al.* also found that differences between social classes remained significant, with the working class still more likely to have frequent contacts than the middle class. Despite all the social changes affecting families between 1986 and 1995, kinship networks beyond the nuclear family remain important to people.

Survey research on family contacts

More recent research has been carried out for the British Social Attitudes Survey (Park *et al.*, 2001). This research investigated the likelihood of adults seeing family members. The results are summarized in Table 8.3. They show that only 10 per cent of those who had a mother who was still living saw her less than 'several times a year', while 20 per cent saw their father less often than this. Seventy-one per cent saw their brother or sister at least 'several times a year'; and only 4 per cent of those with adult children saw them less frequently.

Government research for the Omnibus Survey (a government survey) found that 61 per cent of grandpar-

Table 8.2 Attitudes towards the family, by whether there is a dependent child

	No child under 16		All with child under 16		Age of child Under 5		Age of child 5 to 15	
% agreeing	%	Base	%	Base	%	Base	%	Base
People should keep in touch with close family members even if they don't have much in common	74	1,407	68	595	66	265	69	330
People should keep in touch with relatives like aunts, uncles and cousins even if they don't have much in common	59	1,414	49	594	42	264	54	330
People should always turn to their family before asking the state for help	54	1,394	42	594	36	264	46	329
I try to stay in touch with all my relatives, not just my close family	50	1,381	43	583	42	259	43	324
I'd rather spend time with my friends than with my family	15	1,370	11	584	9	263	13	321
Once children have left home, they should no longer expect help from their parents	15	1,413	6	596	8	264	4	332
On the whole, my friends are more important to me than members of my family	8	1,393	7	588	8	264	6	324

Source: F. McGlone, A. Park and K. Smith (1998) *Families and Kinship*, Family Policy Studies Centre, London.

Table 8.3 Frequency[1] of adults seeing relatives and friends, 2001 (Great Britain, percentages)

	Mother	Father	Sibling	Adult child	Best friend[2]
Daily	8	4	2	12	9
At least several times a week	19	14	10	17	21
At least once a week	24	24	18	22	28
At least once a month	17	16	16	14	18
Several times a year	19	19	25	10	16
Less often	7	11	15	2	4
Never	3	9	7	2	–
All[3]	100	100	100	100	100

[1] By people aged 18 and over. Those without the relative and those who live with the relative are excluded.
[2] Best friend is the respondent's own definition.
[3] Includes respondents who did not answer.

Source: *Social Trends 2003*, Office for National Statistics, London, 2003, p. 44.

ents saw their grandchildren at least once a week and a further 17 per cent at least every month. Grandparents also made use of technology to contact their grandchildren: 60 per cent used letter, telephone, fax or e-mail to keep in touch at least once a week, and 12 per cent used one of these methods at least once a month. This research shows that both face-to-face and other contacts between family members remain quite frequent.

The isolated nuclear family?

The evidence we have presented so far under the heading of 'The family, industrialization and modernization' provides a somewhat confusing picture. On the one hand there is Talcott Parsons's isolated nuclear family, and on the other a large body of evidence suggesting that kin beyond the nuclear family play an important part in family life and that the importance of that role may not have been greatly diminishing.

In America, a number of researchers have rejected Parsons's concept of the isolated nuclear family. Sussman and Burchinal (1971), for example, argue that the weight of evidence from a large body of research indicates that the modern American family is far from isolated. They maintain that the family can only be properly understood 'by rejection of the isolated nuclear family concept'.

Parsons replied to his earlier critics in an article entitled 'The normal American family' (1965b). He argued that close relationships with kin outside the nuclear family are in no way inconsistent with the concept of the isolated nuclear family. Parsons stated: 'the very psychological importance for the individual of the nuclear family in which he was born and brought up would make any such conception impossible'.

However, he maintained that the nuclear family is structurally isolated. It is isolated from other parts of the social structure, such as the economic system. For example, it does not form an integral part of the economic system as in the case of the peasant farming family in traditional Ireland.

In addition, the so-called 'extended families' of modern industrial society 'do not form firmly structured units of the social system'. Relationships with kin beyond the nuclear family are not obligatory – they are a matter of individual choice. In this sense, 'extended kin constitute a resource which may be selectively taken advantage of within considerable limits'. Thus, extended families do not form 'firmly structured units' as in the case of the classic extended family or the family in kinship-based societies.

Many recent studies of family life would support Parsons's view that relationships with extended kin, though often maintained, are a matter of choice. However, as we will see later in the chapter, it may be that nuclear families themselves no longer (if they ever did) make up a vital structural unit in contemporary societies. There is evidence that the decision to form a nuclear family is increasingly also a matter of choice (see pp. 514–15).

The dispersed extended family and the beanpole family

A number of attempts have been made to characterize contemporary families in the light of the research which has found that people often continue to maintain contact with extended family members even if they live some distance away.

On the basis of research carried out in London in the 1980s, Peter Willmott (1988) claimed that the **dispersed extended family** is becoming dominant in Britain. It consists of two or more related families who cooperate with each other even though they live some distance apart. Contacts are fairly frequent, taking place on average perhaps once a week, but less frequent than they were among extended families who lived close together. Cars, public transport and telephones make it possible for dispersed extended families to keep in touch. Members of dispersed extended families do not rely on each other on a day-to-day basis.

Willmott sees each nuclear family unit as only partially dependent upon extended kin. Much of the time the nuclear family is fairly self-sufficient, but in times of emergency the existence of extended kin might prove invaluable. Thus Willmott argues that, in modern Britain, 'although kinship is largely chosen, it not only survives but most of the time flourishes'.

The research discussed by McGlone *et al.* (1998) reaches broadly similar conclusions. Kinship networks outside the nuclear family are still important. Indeed, they argue that the core of families with dependent children includes not just the nuclear family but also grandparents. Despite all the social changes that could have weakened kinship, people still value kinship ties and for the most part try to retain them even when they live some distance from their relatives.

Support for this view is provided by Julia Brannen (2003). Drawing on research in which she was involved (Brannen *et al.*, 2000), Brannen argues that there are strong

intergenerational links (links between generations) in contemporary British families. This is partly because people are living longer and therefore there are more families with three or even four generations alive than there were in the past.

Brannen *et al.* (2000) found that grandparents are increasingly providing informal childcare for their grandchildren. In addition, grandparents often give financial help to their children and grandchildren. According to Brannen *et al.*'s research, adults still provide practical or emotional support for elderly parents in many families, and sometimes help them out financially as well.

Although these family links are generally regarded as optional, they are commonplace and play a crucial role in maintaining family cohesion. Brannen (2003) claims that these intergenerational links tend to survive changes in families such as those resulting from divorce. For example, lone parents may rely more on help with childcare from grandparents than parents living with a partner do.

In contrast to the intergenerational links, Brannen *et al.* found that **intragenerational links** (links between those from the same generation, for example siblings and cousins) were somewhat weaker. Brannen therefore characterizes contemporary family structures as being long and thin – she compares them to a beanpole. She concludes:

> *Many multigenerational families are now long and thin – typically described as beanpole families; they have fewer intragenerational ties because of high divorce rates, falling fertility and smaller family size, but more vertical intergenerational ties because of increased longevity.*
> Brannen, 2003

Although there are some differences in the way that Willmott, McGlone *et al.* and Brannen *et al.* characterize contemporary British families, they all agree that extended kinship networks remain important.

In this section we have focused on how social changes have affected household composition and kinship networks in Britain. Some of the research has been based upon the assumption that a single family type has been dominant in Britain in different eras. We will now examine whether there is (or ever has been) such a thing as the 'typical family' in Britain.

Family diversity

Introduction

Although some historians such as Michael Anderson (1980) have pointed to a variety of household types in pre-industrial times and during industrialization, it has generally been assumed that a single type of family is dominant in any particular era. Whether the modern family is regarded as nuclear, modified extended, modified elementary or dispersed extended, the assumption has been that this type of family is central to people's experiences in modern industrial societies. However, recent research has suggested that such societies are characterized by a plurality or diversity of household and family types, and that the idea of a typical family is misleading.

The 'cereal packet image' of the family

Ann Oakley (1982) described the image of the typical or 'conventional' family. She says 'conventional families are nuclear families composed of legally married couples, voluntarily choosing the parenthood of one or more (but not too many) children'.

Leach (1967) called this the 'cereal packet image of the family'. The image of the happily married couple with two children is prominent in advertising, and the 'family-sized' packets of cereals and other types of product are aimed at just this type of grouping. It tends also to be taken for granted that this type of family has its material needs met by the male breadwinner, while the wife has a predominantly domestic role.

The monolithic image of the family

The American feminist Barrie Thorne (1992) attacked the image of the 'monolithic family'. She argues: 'Feminists have challenged the ideology of "the monolithic family", which has elevated the nuclear family with a breadwinner husband and a full-time wife and mother as the only legitimate family form.' She believes the focus on the family unit neglects structures of society that lead to variations in families: 'Structures of gender, generation, race and class result in widely varying experiences of family life, which are obscured by the glorification of the nuclear family, motherhood, and the family as a loving refuge.' The idea of 'The Family' involves 'falsifying the actual variety of household forms'. In fact, according to Thorne, 'Households have always varied in composition, even in the 1950s and early 1960s when the ideology of The Family was at its peak.' By the 1990s such an ideology was more obviously inappropriate, since changes in society had resulted in ever more diverse family forms.

Family and household diversity in Britain

The view that such images equate with reality was attacked by Robert and Rhona Rapoport (1982). They drew attention to the fact that in 1978, for example, just 20 per cent of families consisted of married couples with children in which there was a single breadwinner.

In 1989, Rhona Rapoport argued that family diversity was a global trend: a view supported by a study of family life in Europe. At the end of the 1980s the European Co-ordination Centre for Research and Documentation in Social Sciences organized a cross-cultural study of family life in fourteen European nations (Boh, 1989). All European countries had experienced rising divorce rates and many had made it easier to get divorced. Cohabitation appeared to have become more common in most countries, and the birth rate had declined everywhere. Katja Boh argued that, overall, there was a consistent pattern of convergence in diversity. While family life retained considerable variations from country to country, throughout Europe a greater range of family types was being accepted as legitimate and normal.

As Table 8.4 shows, since the Rapoports first advanced the idea of family diversity, there has been a steady decline in the proportion of households in Great Britain consisting of married couples with dependent children, from 35 per cent in 1971 to just 22 per cent in 2005. There has been a corresponding increase in single-person households in the same period, with the proportion of households of this type rising from 18 per cent in 1971 to 29 per cent in 2005. Furthermore, the proportion of households that were lone-parent households with dependent children more than doubled, from 3 per cent in 1971 to 7 per cent in 2005. The proportion of all lone-parent households rose from 7 per cent to 10 per cent over the same period. (Lone-parent families are discussed in more detail on pp. 485–8.)

Types of diversity

The fact that the 'conventional family' no longer makes up a majority of households or families is only one aspect of diversity identified by the Rapoports. They identify five distinct elements of family diversity in Britain:

1 There is what they term **organizational diversity**. By this they mean there are variations in family structure, household type, and patterns of kinship network, and differences in the division of labour within the home. For example, there are the differences between conventional families, one-parent families, and **dual-worker families**, in which husband and wife both work.

   There are also increasing numbers of reconstituted families. These families are formed after divorce and remarriage. This situation can lead to a variety of family forms. The children from the previous marriages of the new spouses may live together in the newly reconstituted family, or they may live with the original spouses of the new couple. Although it might be seen to reflect a failure to create a happy family life, some adults in a reconstituted family may find positive aspects of reconstitution.

   On the basis of a study conducted in Sheffield, Jacqueline Burgoyne and David Clark (1982) claim some individuals in this situation see themselves as 'pioneers of an alternative lifestyle'. They may choose to remain unmarried to their new partner, and may find advantages in having more than two parental figures in their children's lives. Sometimes they believe stepsiblings gain from living together. Some couples in the Sheffield study felt a considerable sense of achievement from the successful reconstitution of a family. (For further details on divorce, see pp. 504–7.)
2 The second type of diversity is **cultural diversity**. There are differences in the lifestyles of families of different ethnic origins and different religious beliefs. There are differences between families of Asian, West Indian and Cypriot origin, not to mention other minority ethnic groups. (We discuss ethnic family diversity in more detail on pp. 488–92.) Differences in lifestyle between Catholic and Protestant families may also be an important element of diversity.
3 There are differences between middle-class and working-class families in terms of relationships between adults and the way in which children are socialized (see p. 477).
4 There are differences that result from the stage in the life cycle of the family. Newly married couples without children may have a different family life from those with dependent children or those whose children have achieved adult status.

Table 8.4 Households: by type of household and family (Great Britain, percentages)

	1971	1981	1991	2001	2005
One person					
Under state pension age	6	8	11	14	15
Over state pension age	12	14	16	15	14
One-family households					
Couple					
No children	27	26	28	29	29
1–2 dependent children	36	35	30	19	18
3 or more dependent children	9	6	5	4	4
Non-dependent children only	8	8	8	6	6
Lone parent					
Dependent children	3	5	6	7	7
Non-dependent children only	4	4	4	3	3
Two or more unrelated adults	4	5	3	3	3
Multi-family households	1	1	1	1	1
All households (=100%) (millions)	18.6	20.2	22.4	23.8	24.2

Source: *Social Trends 2006* (2006) Office for National Statistics, London, p. 22.

5 The fifth factor identified by the Rapoports as producing family diversity is **cohort**. This refers to the period during which the family passed through different stages of the family life cycle. Cohort affects the life experiences of the family. For example, those families whose children were due to enter the labour market in the 1980s may be different from other families: the high rates of unemployment during that period may have increased the length of time that those children were dependent on their parents.

Continuing diversification

More recently, Graham Allan and Graham Crow (2001) commented on a continuing trend towards the diversification of family types. They argue that there is now 'far greater diversity in people's domestic arrangements', so that there is no longer a clear 'family cycle' through which most people pass. That is, most people no longer pass through a routine series of stages in family life whereby they leave home, get married, move in with their spouse, and have children who in turn leave home themselves. Instead, each individual follows a more unpredictable family course, complicated by cohabitation, divorce, remarriage, periods living alone and so on.

This diversity is based upon increased choice. Allan and Crow say: 'Individuals and families are now more able to exercise choice and personal volition over domestic and familial arrangements than previously, their options no longer being constrained by social convention and/or economic need.' In part, this is due to 'the increasing separation of sex, marriage and parenthood'. Most people feel they do not have to get married before having sex, and being a parent outside of marriage is increasingly accepted as a legitimate option.

According to Allan and Crow, such is the diversity that

> *in an important sense there is no such thing as 'the family'. There are many different families; many different family relationships; and consequently many different family forms. Each family develops and changes over time as its personnel develop and change.* Allan and Crow, 2001

However, while there is increased choice, Allan and Crow emphasize that families are not egalitarian institutions – some members have more power over changes than others.

Allan and Crow identify the following demographic changes as contributing to increased family diversity:

1 The divorce rate has risen. This has affected most countries in the Western world, not just Britain.
2 Lone-parent households have increased in number. This is partly due to increased divorce, but also because pregnancy is no longer automatically seen as requiring legitimation through marriage.
3 Cohabitation outside marriage is increasingly common. In the early 1960s only one in twenty women lived with their future husband before marriage, but by the late 1980s one in two did so.
4 Marriage rates have declined. This is partly because people are, on average, marrying later, but also 'lifetime marriage rates also appear to be falling … even by middle age, significantly fewer of the generation born in the 1960s and 1970s will have married compared to the cohorts of the 1940s and 1950s'.
5 A big increase in the number of stepfamilies also contributes to increased diversity.

Allan and Crow, writing some two decades after the Rapoports originally identified family diversity, believe the trend towards family diversity has continued and strengthened in the intervening period.

We will now examine a number of different aspects of the increasing diversity of family and other intimate relationships.

Gay and lesbian families and the decline of the heteronorm

Differences in sexuality have contributed to increasing diversity according to many sociologists. Gay and lesbian households have become more commonplace – certainly there are more openly gay and lesbian households than there were several decades ago. As Jeffrey Weeks, Catherine Donovan and Brian Heaphey (1999) argue, 'During the past generation the possibilities of living an openly lesbian and gay life have been transformed.' As discussed earlier (see p. 462), many sociologists believe that such households, where they incorporate long-term gay or lesbian relationships, should be seen as constituting families.

According to Weeks *et al.*, homosexuals and lesbians often look upon their households, and even their friendship networks, as being **chosen families**. Some see their relationships as involving a greater degree of choice than those in more conventional heterosexual families. They choose whom to include in their family and negotiate what are often fairly egalitarian relationships.

Some see their families as an alternative type of family which they are consciously developing. Weeks *et al.* argue that this may be part of wider social changes in which 'we culturally prioritize individual choice and the acceptance of diversity. Commitment becomes increasingly a matter of negotiation rather than ascription.' (Their views are similar to those of Anthony Giddens – see pp. 512–14 for details.)

Sasha Roseneil (2005) develops the idea of chosen families further. She uses the term **heteronorm** to refer to the belief that intimate relationships between heterosexual couples are the normal form that intimate relationships take.

Roseneil believes that the heteronorm is increasingly breaking down. She points to television series such as *Friends*, *Seinfeld*, *Ellen* and *Will and Grace* as examples where it is the 'sociability of a group of friends rather than a conventional family, which provides the love, care and support essential to everyday life in the city' (Roseneil, 2005, p. 242).

Roseneil goes on to argue that there is an increasing blurring of the boundaries between intimate sexual relationship and friendship. This is particularly true of lesbian and gay intimacies where 'Friends become lovers, lovers become friends and many have multiple sexual partners of varying degrees of commitment (and none).' Indeed, an individual's 'significant other may not be someone with whom she or he has a sexual relationship' (Roseneil, 2005, p. 244).

The increasing flexibility and diversity of sexual relationships and friendship might be most marked amongst homosexuals, but it is also developing among heterosexuals. Roseneil therefore argues that there is a 'decentring of heterorelations' so that the heterosexual couple is less central to the social life of individuals, the culture of society and public policies. She says that 'individuals are increasingly being released from hetero-sexual scripts and the patterns of heterorelationality that accompany them' (Roseneil, 2005, p. 247).

This shift has resulted from social changes such as the rise in divorce, the increase in births outside marriage and heterosexual relationships, the increase in single-person households and the growth of lone parenthood. Roseneil points to the passing of the UK's Civil Partnerships Act of 2004 (which allows civil partnerships between gay and lesbian couples) as a symptom of this change. She concludes that: 'The heterosexual couple, and particularly the married, co-resident heterosexual couple with children, no longer occupies the centre-ground of western societies and cannot be taken for granted as the basic unit of society' (Roseneil, 2005, p. 247).

New reproductive technologies

Unlike gay and lesbian relationships, new reproductive technologies add an entirely new dimension to family diversity. In 1978 the first 'test-tube baby', Louise Brown, was born. The process is called *in vitro* fertilization and involves fertilizing an egg with a sperm in a test-tube, before then implanting it in a woman's womb. The woman may or may not be the woman who produced the egg.

Surrogate motherhood involves one woman carrying a foetus produced by the egg of another woman. This raises questions about who the parents of a child are, and about what constitutes a family. As noted earlier (see pp. 472–3), Calhoun sees this as undermining the centrality of the reproductive couple as the core of the family, and it introduces a greater range of choices into families than was previously available.

John Macionis and Ken Plummer (1997) show how new reproductive technologies can create previously impossible sets of family relationships. They quote the case of Arlette Schweitzer, who in 1991 gave birth in South Dakota in the USA to her own grandchildren. Her daughter was unable to carry a baby and Arlette Schweitzer acted as a surrogate mother. She gave birth to twins, a boy and a girl. Macionis and Plummer ask, 'is Arlette Schweitzer the mother of the twins she bore? Grandmother? Both?' Such examples, they say, 'force us to consider the adequacy of conventional kinship terms'.

They note that such technologies have largely been made available to heterosexual couples of normal child-rearing age, but they have also been used by lesbians, homosexuals, and single and older women. The implication of new reproductive technologies is that biology will no longer restrict the possibilities for forming or enlarging families by having children. They therefore add considerably to the range of potential family types and thus contribute to growing diversity.

Single parenthood

The increase in single parenthood

As mentioned earlier, single-parent families have become increasingly common in Britain. According to government statistics, in 1961, 2 per cent of the population lived in households consisting of a lone parent with dependent children, but by 2005 this had increased sixfold to 12 per cent (HMSO, 2002a; *Social Trends 2006*). Between 1972 and 2002 the percentage of children living in single-parent families increased from 7 per cent to 23 per cent (*Social Trends 1998, 2006*).

According to European Union figures (Lehemann and Wirtz, 2004), in 2003, lone-parent households with dependent children made up 3 per cent of households in Europe, but 5 per cent of households in Britain. Britain had the second highest proportion of such households in Europe, exceeded only by Sweden with 7 per cent. In Italy, Luxemburg and Spain only 1 per cent of households contained single parents with dependent children.

Although useful, these figures need to be interpreted with caution. They provide only a snapshot picture of the situation at one point in time and do not represent the changing family life of many individuals. Many more children than the above figures seem to suggest spend part of their childhood in a single-parent family, but many fewer spend all of their childhood in one. Children may start their life living in a single-parent family. However, the single parent may well find a new partner and marry or cohabit with them. The child will then end up living with two parents.

The British Household Panel Survey revealed that about 15 per cent of lone mothers stopped being lone parents each year. This was usually because they had established a new relationship (quoted in *Social Trends 1998*).

It should also be noted that many children who live in a single-parent household do see and spend time with their other parent. Furthermore, even in two-parent families, one parent (usually the mother) might be responsible for the vast majority of the childcare. In terms of children's experience, then, the distinction between single-parent and two-parent households is not clear-cut.

The causes of single parenthood – demographic trends

Single parenthood can come about through a number of different routes. People who are married can become single parents through:

1. Divorce
2. Separation
3. Death of a spouse

Lone parents who have never been married:

- may have been living with the parent of the child when the child was born, but they subsequently stopped living together.
- may not have been living with the parent of the child when the child was born.

Official statistics give some indication of the frequency of the different paths to lone parenthood, but do not provide a complete picture.

Figures for Britain based on the General Household Survey of 2005 show that 27 per cent of families with dependent children were lone-parent families. Of these, 24 per cent were headed by lone mothers and just 3 per cent by lone fathers. In 1971 only 1 per cent of households were headed by a never-married lone mother, but by 2005 this had risen to 11 per cent. The proportion of families headed by a divorced, separated or widowed lone mother rose from 6 per cent to 13 per cent over the same period.

Allan and Crow (2001) note that the increase in lone parenthood is clearly due to two factors: an increase in marital breakdown (particularly divorce), and a rise in births to unmarried mothers. They claim that both these trends 'reflect an acceptance of diversity and individual choice which was far less pronounced in previous eras'. However, as we shall see shortly, there may be limits to the extent to which attitudes have changed.

David Morgan (1994) suggests the rise in lone parenthood could partly be due to changing relationships between men and women. He says important factors causing the rise could include 'the expectations that women and men have of marriage and the growing opportunities for women to develop a life for themselves outside marriage or long-term cohabitations'.

The causes of single parenthood – changing attitudes

The increase in single mothers may partly result from a reduction in the number of 'shotgun weddings' – that is, getting married to legitimate a pregnancy. Mark Brown (1995) suggests that in previous eras it was more common for parents to get married, rather than simply cohabit, if they discovered that the woman was pregnant. Marriages that resulted from pregnancy were often unstable and could end up producing lone motherhood through an eventual divorce or separation. Now, the partners may choose to cohabit rather than marry and, if their relationship breaks up, they end up appearing in the statistics as a single, never-married, parent.

Evidence from the British Social Attitudes Survey gives some indication of changing attitudes towards having children outside marriage and towards lone parenthood in particular. Alison Park *et al.* (2001) analysed data from the British Social Attitudes Survey and found that younger age groups are much more accepting of parenthood outside marriage. For example, in 2000, of those born between 1915 and 1924, 90 per cent agreed that 'people who want children ought to get married'. This compared to just 33 per cent of those born between 1976 and 1982.

The British Social Attitudes Surveys also show a gradual increase in the acceptance of parenthood outside marriage over time. In 1989, 70 per cent agreed that 'people who want children ought to get married', but by 2000 this was down to 54 per cent. By 2000, only 27 per cent agreed that 'Married couples make better parents than unmarried couples'.

However, these figures do not reveal how acceptable people found single parenthood as such, rather than births outside marriage. There is evidence that people continue to disapprove of teenage pregnancy, which is often seen as closely linked to single parenthood. Figures from the British Social Attitudes Survey show that 82 per cent disagree or strongly disagree with the statement 'Teenage pregnancy isn't really that much of a problem in Britain today'. In part, this was because people felt that women on their own would struggle to bring up children. Forty-two per cent agreed or strongly agreed that 'Bringing up a child is simply too hard for a woman of any age to do alone'; 33 per cent disagreed or strongly disagreed. However, respondents were particularly concerned about the ability of teenage single mothers to cope: 83 per cent agreed or strongly agreed that 'Bringing up a child is simply too hard for most teenagers to do alone'. Only 6 per cent disagreed or strongly disagreed.

Thus, while the public have become more accepting of children being born outside marital relationships, many remain concerned about lone parenthood, particularly where the parent is a teenager.

Some time before Allan and Crow (2001), the Rapoports (1982) claimed that the lone-parent family was increasingly becoming accepted as one aspect of growing family diversity. They believed it was an important 'emerging form' of the family which was becoming accepted as a legitimate alternative to other family structures.

Other writers, too, have claimed that the stigma attached to lone parenthood has been decreasing. According to David Morgan (1994), the reduction in stigma is reflected in the decreasing use of terms such as 'illegitimate children' and 'unmarried mothers', which seem to imply some deviation from the norms of family life, and their replacement by concepts such as 'single-parent families' and 'lone-parent families', which do not carry such negative connotations. The reduction in the stigma of single parenthood could relate to 'the weakening of religious or community controls over women'.

However, there is little evidence that a large number of single parents see their situation as ideal and actively choose it as an alternative to dual parenthood. Burghes and Brown (1995) conducted research on thirty-one lone mothers and found that only a minority of the pregnancies were planned. None of the mothers had actively set out to become lone mothers and all of them attributed the break-up of their relationship to 'violence in the relationship or the father's unwillingness to settle down'. In this small sample, all aspired to forming a two-parent household, but had failed to achieve it despite their preference.

Lone parents, benefits and the underclass

According to some sociologists the increase in lone parenthood is largely a result of the generosity of welfare payments. Charles Murray's theory of the underclass (discussed on pp. 64–5 and 242–4) is the most influential version of this viewpoint.

A number of politicians have supported this view. According to Mary McIntosh (1996), the former US President Bill Clinton suggested that Murray's explanation for the development of the underclass was basically correct. New Labour politicians in Britain have been less willing to suggest openly that lone motherhood is caused by welfare payments. However, they have developed a 'New Deal' for lone parents which encourages them to find employment rather than relying upon benefits (see pp. 511–12 for a discussion of New Labour policies on families).

However, there are a number of reasons for supposing that the welfare state is not responsible for the increases:

- Some commentators do not believe that lone parenthood gives advantages to those seeking local authority housing. In 1993 John Perry, policy director of the Institute of Housing, said:

I've not been able to find a single housing authority which discriminates in favour of single parents over couples with children. The homeless get priority, but there is no suggestion that a homeless single parent gets priority over a homeless couple. Quoted in the *Independent on Sunday*, 11 July 1993

2 As the next section indicates, lone parents who are reliant upon benefits tend to live in poor housing conditions and have low standards of living. There is little material incentive to become a lone parent.

3 There is evidence that a large majority of lone parents do not wish to be reliant on state benefits. They would prefer to work for a living but find it impractical to do so. The 1998 British government Green Paper, *Supporting Families*, quoted figures showing that 44 per cent of lone mothers had paid employment, and 85 per cent of the remainder would like to be employed.

Research for the Department for Work and Pensions (DWP, 2006) has shown that the New Deal for Lone Parents has raised the proportion of lone parents who are not reliant upon state benefits to about 20 per cent. DWP figures from 2004 (DWP, 2004) showed a rise in the proportion of lone parents in employment from 27 per cent in 1991 to 56 per cent ten years later.

As well as the New Deal for Lone Parents other New Labour policies have contributed to this change. The implementation of a National Childcare Strategy has made childcare more widely available for lone parents who wish to work, and tax credits have made work more financially worthwhile for many (McKnight, 2005).

Allan and Crow (2001) say, 'it is a mistake to assert that lone-parent families, including single-mother ones, are promulgating radically different values to those held by more prosperous families ... in the main lone-parent families do not reject or denigrate a two-parent model'. Indeed, lone parenthood is often a temporary and relatively short-lived family situation. Lone parents may cohabit with a new partner, get married, or be reconciled with their previous partner to form a new two-parent household. Drawing on a number of studies, Allan and Crow estimate that the average length of time spent as a lone-parent family is around five years.

This view is backed up by government research. A longitudinal study carried out for the Department for Work and Pensions (DWP, 2004) found that, of those who were lone parents in 1991, a third were living with a new partner in 2001, while a further 17 per cent had had a new partner since 1991 but were lone parents again in 2001.

The consequences of single parenthood

Single parenthood has increasingly become a contentious issue, with some arguing it has become a serious problem for society. For example, in a letter to *The Times* in 1985, Lady Scott said:

A vast majority of the population would still agree, I think, that the normal family is an influence for good in society and that one-parent families are bad news. Since not many single parents can both earn a living and give children the love and care they need, society has to support them; the children suffer through lacking one parent. Quoted in Fletcher, 1988

Similar sentiments have been expressed by British Conservative politicians and, when they were in government, such views began to influence social policies (see pp. 509–10). New Labour politicians have been less inclined to condemn single parenthood outright, but the Labour government's 1998 Green Paper, *Supporting Families*, did say, 'marriage is still the surest foundation for raising children'.

Sociologists such as Charles Murray have even gone so far as to claim that single parenthood has contributed to creating a whole new stratum of society, the underclass – a claim discussed in detail in Chapter 1 (pp. 64–6).

Mary McIntosh (1996) says: 'Over recent years, the media in the United Kingdom have been reflecting a concern about lone mothers that amounts to a moral panic.' She claims that, as a group, lone mothers have been stigmatized and blamed for problems such as youth crime, high taxation to pay for welfare benefits, encouraging a culture of dependency on the state, and producing children who grow up to be unemployable. She says, 'Perhaps the most serious charge is that they are ineffective in bringing up their children.'

However, while most commentators agree that single parenthood can create problems for individual parents, many sociologists do not see it as a social problem, and some believe it is a sign of social progress. As Sarah McLanahan and Karen Booth have said:

Some view the mother-only family as an indicator of social disorganization, signalling the 'demise of the family'. Others regard it as an alternative family form consistent with the emerging economic independence of women. McLanahan and Booth, 1991

Single parenthood and living standards

However single parenthood is viewed, there is little doubt that it tends to be associated with low living standards. The General Household Survey of 2005 found that lone-parent families were disadvantaged in comparison to other British families. In 2005, 41 per cent of lone-parent families had a gross household income of £200 per week or less, compared to 8 per cent of married couples with dependent children and 11 per cent of cohabiting couples with dependent children.

Many of these differences stem from the likelihood of lone-parent families relying upon benefit. According to the Department for Work and Pensions Green Paper on welfare reform (2006), of 1.8 million lone parents, 787,000 were receiving income support.

Lone parents may also receive maintenance payments from the non-resident parent or parents of their children. The Child Support Agency (CSA) was set up in 1993 to pursue non-resident parents for maintenance payments. (In 2006 it was announced that it would be replaced in 2008 with a Child Maintenance and Support Commission.)

However, Allan and Crow (2001) argue that the CSA provides little help to lone parents. By the late 1990s only around 30 per cent of non-resident parents were making any contribution towards their child's maintenance. (CSA Quarterly Summary Statistics from 2003 show that by then around 75 per cent of non-resident parents who were required to pay maintenance were making at least some payment.) Furthermore, the non-resident parents have little incentive to pay if the lone parent is receiving income support, since the receipt of maintenance payments leads to income support being cut.

Maintenance payments assist lone parents who are employed and earning more than income support levels, but this affects only a minority of lone parents. Lone parents who are employed tend to be on low wages. Most work part-time, and the vast majority are women and as such suffer from 'gendered inequality in the labour market' (Allan and Crow, 2001).

Not all lone-parent families are poor. A few are very affluent, but the majority do suffer from poverty. According to Flaherty *et al.* (2004), in 2001/2 government figures on households below 60 per cent of median earnings showed that 53 per cent of lone-parent families were in poverty, a much higher figure than for any other household type (see Figure 4.5, p. 234).

Other effects

More controversial than the low average living standards of lone parents is the question of the psychological and social effects on children raised in such families. McLanahan and Booth (1991) listed the findings of a number of American studies which seem to indicate that children are harmed by single parenthood. These studies claimed that such children have lower earnings and experience more poverty as adults; that children of mother-only families are more likely to become lone parents themselves; and that they are more likely to become delinquent and engage in drug abuse.

The findings of such studies must be treated with caution. As McLanahan and Booth themselves point out, the differences outlined above stem partly from the low income of lone-parent families and not directly from the absence of the second parent from the household.

In a review of research on lone parenthood, Louie Burghes (1996) notes that some research into the relationship between educational attainment and divorce suggests that children in families where the parents divorce start to do more poorly in education before the divorce takes place. Burghes argues that this implies 'it is the quality of the family relationships, of which the divorce is only a part, that are influential'.

The more sophisticated research into the effects of lone parenthood tries to take account of factors such as social class and low income. These studies find that 'the gap in outcomes between children who have and have not experienced family change narrows. In some cases they disappear; in others, statistically significant differences may remain. Some of these differences are small' (Burghes, 1996).

Some support for this view is provided by research by Sara Arber (2000). Arber found that the children of lone parents did overall suffer more ill-health than other children. However, this difference disappeared for the children of lone parents in employment, who suffered no more ill-health than other groups.

E.E. Cashmore (1985) questioned the assumption that children brought up by one parent are worse off than those brought up by two. Cashmore argues that it is often preferable for a child to live with one caring parent than with one caring and one uncaring parent, particularly if the parents are constantly quarrelling and the marriage has all but broken down.

Cashmore also suggests single parenthood can have attractions for the parent, particularly for mothers, since conventional family life may benefit men more than women. He says:

> *Given the 'darker side of family life' and the unseen ways in which the nuclear unit serves 'male power' rather than the interests of women, the idea of parents breaking free of marriage and raising children single-handed has its appeals.* Cashmore, 1985

It can give women greater independence than they have in other family situations. However, Cashmore does acknowledge that many lone mothers who are freed from dependence on a male partner end up becoming dependent on the state and facing financial hardship. He concludes: 'Lone parents do not need a partner so much as a partner's income.'

David Morgan (1994) believes the evidence does suggest that the children of single parents fare less well than those from two-parent households. He qualifies this by saying, 'we still do not know enough about what causes these differences'. As with the effects of financial hardships, the children could be affected by the stigma attached to coming from a single-parent family. Morgan argues: 'It is possible, for example, that school teachers may be more likely to label a child as difficult if they have the knowledge that a particular child comes from a single-parent household.'

For Morgan, it is very difficult to disentangle the direct and indirect effects on children of being brought up in a single-parent household, and therefore dangerous to make generalizations about such effects.

Ethnicity and family diversity

Ethnicity can be seen as one of the most important sources of family diversity in Britain. Ethnic groups with different cultural backgrounds may introduce family forms that differ significantly from those of the ethnic majority.

British sociologists have paid increasing attention to the family patterns of minority ethnic groups. They have been particularly concerned to establish the extent to which the family relationships typical of the societies of origin of the minority ethnic groups have been modified within the British context. Thus, sociologists have compared minority ethnic families in Britain both with families in the country of their origin and with other British families.

Although some changes in the traditional family life of these groups might be expected, the degree to which they change could provide important evidence in relation to the theory of increasing family diversity. If it is true that cultural diversity is becoming increasingly accepted in Britain, then these families could be expected to change little. If, however, the families of minority ethnic groups are becoming more similar to other British families, then family diversity resulting from ethnic differences might be only temporary.

Statistical evidence

Statistical evidence does suggest there are some differences in the prevalence of different household types in different ethnic groups.

The size of households varies significantly by ethnic group. According to figures from the General Household Survey (2006), amongst the main ethnic groups the smallest household size is found among Black Caribbeans (2.22), followed by whites (2.27), Indians (2.93) and Pakistanis (4.04), with Bangladeshis (4.38) having the largest households. These differences can partly be explained by differences in household and family types.

The Labour Force Survey in autumn 2002 found significant differences in the proportions of different household types in different ethnic groups. Table 8.5 shows that just 9 per cent of Pakistani/Bangladeshi households and 5 per cent of Indian households consisted of lone parents with dependent children, compared to 25 per cent of Black Caribbean and 26 per cent of Black African families. Perhaps surprisingly, there was a lower proportion of lone parents among white households (8 per cent) than among Pakistani/Bangladeshi households.

Among all Asian groups a high proportion of households consisted of couples with dependent children – for example, 57 per cent of Pakistani/Bangladeshi households and 43 per cent of Indian households – compared to 29 per cent of white households and just 22 per cent of Black Caribbean households.

The sample sizes of some minority ethnic groups in the Labour Force Survey are quite small, but other research confirms that there are significant differences between the household and family types of different ethnic groups.

The Policy Studies Institute's *Fourth National Survey of Ethnic Minorities*, conducted in England and Wales in 1994, also found important differences between the families and households of different ethnic groups (Modood *et al.* 1997; see p. 152 for further details of the survey). Table 8.6 shows the marital status of adults under 60 in different ethnic groups. It shows that whites and Caribbeans had higher rates of divorce and cohabitation than other groups, and that Indians, African Asians, Pakistanis and Bangladeshis were the ethnic groups who were most likely to be married.

Using data from previous surveys, Tariq Modood *et al.* were able to calculate the proportions of families with children in different ethnic groups which were headed by lone parents at different points in time. Table 8.7 shows that there had been a substantial increase in lone parenthood in all three ethnic groups, but that the increase had been most noticeable in minority ethnic groups. The rate among South Asian families had risen most quickly, but from a very low base, so that by 1994 they were still by far the least likely group to have formed lone-parent families.

Rates among Caribbean families had also risen rapidly and were probably the highest rates at the time of all three surveys (there were no figures for whites in the 1974 survey). It is significant that very high rates of single parenthood were not present among families of Caribbean origin in 1974. This would suggest that diversity of family types among minority ethnic groups has developed over time. The family types of minority ethnic groups have not remained static and Modood *et al.* conclude that minority ethnic families in Britain changed rapidly between the 1970s and the 1990s. However, as both statistics and qualitative studies suggest, the patterns of ethnic groups do remain somewhat different. There has not been a convergence to a single, typical, British family type, characteristic of all ethnic groups.

We will now examine the significance of variations in family life by ethnic group.

Table 8.5 Proportions of working-age households by household type and ethnic origin of the household reference person,[1] UK, autumn 2002, percentages

Ethnic origin of household reference person	One person	Couple, no children	Couple with dependent children	Lone parent with dependent children	Other	All household types
White[2]	20	25	29	8	17	100
Mixed[3]	27	15	21	24	13	100
Indian	12	14	43	5	26	100
Pakistani/Bangladeshi	6	8	57	9	19	100
Other Asian	18	*	40	*	27	100
Black Caribbean	31	8	22	25	15	100
Black African	23	7	30	26	14	100
Other Black	30	14	16	30	*	100
Chinese	22	18	23	*	32	100
Other	23	13	36	12	16	100
All ethnic groups	20	24	29	9	18	100

[1] Excludes cases where ethnic origin of head of household is not known.
[2] Includes British and other white. [3] Includes all mixed origin.
* Sample size too small for estimate.

Source: 'Labour Market Spotlight' (2003) *Labour Market Trends*, April, p. 167.

Table 8.6 Marital status, adults under 60

	Percentages						
	White	Caribbean	Indian	African Asian	Pakistani	Bangladeshi	Chinese
Single	23	41	21	21	19	22	34
Married	60	39	72	72	74	73	62
Living as married	9	10	3	2	3	1	1
Separated/divorced	7	9	3	3	3	1	3
Widowed	1	2	2	1	2	3	–
Weighted count	4,194	1,834	1,539	960	1,053	344	467
Unweighted count	4,187	1,298	1,560	951	1,709	815	271

Note: Analysis based on all individuals in survey households who were neither dependent children nor aged 60 or more.

Source: T. Modood *et al.* (1997) *Ethnic Minorities in Britain*, PSI, London, p. 24.

Table 8.7 Proportion of families with children which were lone-parent families, 1974–94

	White	Caribbean	South Asian
1974 (household definition)	n.a.	13	1
1982 (household definition)	10	31	5
1994 (household definition)	16	36	5

Source: T. Modood *et al.* (1997) *Ethnic Minorities in Britain*, PSI, London, p. 40.

South Asian families

Roger Ballard (1982, 1990) examined South Asian families in Britain and compared them to families in South Asia itself. Migration from this area began in the 1950s and was mainly from the Punjab, Gujarat and Bengal. Although there are important differences in family life within these groups, which stem from area of origin, religion and caste, Ballard identifies some features generally held in common.

Families in South Asia are based traditionally around a man, his sons and grandsons, and their respective wives and unmarried daughters. These family groups ideally live and work together in large multi-generational households, sharing both domestic and production tasks. In practice, in the past, many households were not as large as might be expected. A high death rate limited the number of generations living together, and sons might establish different households after their father's death when the family land was divided up.

Changes in South Asian families

Ballard found that some changes had taken place in Asian families in Britain. Women were increasingly working outside the home, and production was less frequently family-based because wage labour provided the most common source of income. Ballard claims married couples in Britain expected more independence from their kin. In some families extended kinship networks were less important than they traditionally are because some of the kin remained in South Asia or lived in distant parts of Britain. Families were also split into smaller domestic units, partly because British housing was rarely suited to the needs of large groupings.

The strengthening of South Asian families

Despite these changes, Ballard says:

> *It should not be assumed that such upheavals have either undermined or stood in contradiction to family unity. On the contrary, migration has taken place within the context of familial obligations and has if anything strengthened rather than weakened them.* Ballard, 1982

Many migrants found that British culture seemed to attach little value to family honour and placed relatively little emphasis on maintaining kinship ties. As a result, many first-generation immigrants became conservative and cautious in their attitudes to family life. They were vigilant in ensuring that standards of behaviour in the family did not slip and kept a close check on their children.

Ballard found that many children had the experience of two cultures. They behaved in ways that conformed to the culture of the wider society for part of the time, but at home conformed to their ethnic subculture. Although children increasingly expected to have some say in their choice of marriage partners, they generally did not reject the principle of arranged marriages.

The majority of families relied on wage labour, but some of the more successful began to establish family businesses (such as buying a shop), which provided a new focus for the family's economic activities.

Ballard found that, despite the distances involved, most families retained links with their village of origin in South Asia. Extended kinship links could stretch over thousands of miles. He found that money was sometimes sent to help support family members who remained in South Asia.

In Britain, despite the housing problems, close family ties remained. By living close together, or buying adjoining houses and knocking through a connecting door, people were able to retain strong family links.

Ballard concluded that South Asians had suffered comparatively little disruption to family life as a result of settling in Great Britain.

Ghazala Bhatti – Asian children at home

In a more recent ethnographic study, Ghazala Bhatti (1999) carried out research into fifty British Asian families living in a town in southern England. The research was largely based upon in-depth interviews: forty-four of the families were Muslim with Pakistani or Bangladeshi backgrounds, and six were of Indian origin: four were Hindu and two Sikh.

Like Ballard, Bhatti found there was a continuing emphasis on loyalty to the family and on trying to maintain traditional practices related to marriage. For example, most families were keen to maintain links with relatives in India or Pakistan. If they could afford it, they would return 'back home' to the Asian subcontinent to see relatives, on a family trip lasting several weeks. Many families felt some obligation to help out their kin in India or Pakistan financially. Bhatti says that the tradition of *bhai chaara* (literally, brother's help) is taken very seriously.

As in other studies of Asian family life, Bhatti found that *izzat* or family honour was also taken very seriously, with particular emphasis being placed on the behaviour of daughters. Bhatti found that mothers saw their family roles as being of paramount importance. She says: 'Motherhood bestowed status upon these women and they saw child rearing as their most important role and duty in life.' Paid work was seen as much less important than caring for children and others. Fathers, on the other hand, saw their family responsibilities more in terms of a traditional breadwinner role. Bhatti says: 'Asian fathers felt they had to provide for their families. They saw themselves as heads of their households.'

So far, the evidence from Bhatti's research suggests Asian families retained their distinctive emphasis upon traditional family life and family obligations well into the 1990s. But was there any evidence that the younger generation was moving away from this towards patterns prevalent among the white population of Britain?

Bhatti did find some evidence of conflict between different generations. In four of the families studied, 'open clashes had developed between parents and children'. In all these cases, the elder brother had 'decided to marry an English girl instead of somebody of his own kin'. The parents of these children all felt that they had failed as parents and worried about whether their younger children would follow a similar path.

However, Bhatti stresses that these families are 'not the norm'. There were some tensions between the generations in many of the other families, but for the most part these were minor and generally the children seemed happy to adhere to traditional patterns of family life. Bhatti therefore found that the distinctiveness of Asian families was largely continuing and therefore contributing to the family diversity of Britain.

Asian families in the PSI national survey

Data on families collected in the Policy Studies Institute's *Fourth National Survey of Ethnic Minorities* were analysed by Richard Berthoud and Sharon Beishon (1997). They found that British South Asians 'were more likely to marry and marry earlier than their white equivalents. Few of them lived as married and separation and divorce were relatively rare.' Nearly all South Asian mothers were married and 'a relatively high proportion of South Asian couples, including many with children, lived in the same house as the young man's father'. Nevertheless, there was some evidence that family patterns were changing.

There were some divorces and some single parents in South Asian communities, and another sign of change was a fall in the number of children born to each married couple. The study also found some evidence of changing attitudes to family life, with, for example, young people expecting more say in the choice of marriage partner than their parents had expected.

Families in the West Indies

Research into the family life of West Indians in Britain and in the Caribbean has found greater diversity in their cultural patterns. Jocelyn Barrow (1982) argues that there are three main West Indian family types in the Caribbean:

1. The **conventional nuclear family**, or 'Christian marriage', which is often little different from nuclear families in Britain. Families of this type tend to be typical of the more religious or economically successful groups in the population.
2. The **common-law family**, which is more frequently found among the less economically successful. An unmarried couple live together and look after children who may or may not be their biological offspring.
3. The **mother household**, in which the mother or grandmother of the children is head of the household and, for most of the time at least, the household contains no adult males. This type of household often relies a good deal on the help and support of female kin living nearby to enable the head of the household to fulfil her family responsibilities.

West Indian families in Britain

To a large extent, research has shown that a similar mixture of family types exists among West Indian groups in Britain. Geoffrey Driver (1982), however, found that in some cases what appears to be a nuclear family is rather different beneath the surface. He uses the example of a family called the Campbells. In this family the wife took on primary responsibility both for running the household and for being the breadwinner after her husband lost his job. In reality, then, this was a mother-centred family, even though it contained an adult male.

Barrow (1982) found that mother-centred families in Britain, whether or not they contained an adult male, could rely less on the support of female kin than they could in the West Indies. They were much less likely to live close to the relevant kin, and in some cases appropriate kin were still in the West Indies, and could not therefore be called upon to provide assistance.

However, Barrow discovered that equivalent networks tended to build up in areas with high concentrations of West Indians. Informal help with childcare and other domestic tasks is common among neighbours, and self-help projects such as pre-school playgroups are frequent features of West Indian communities.

Mary Chamberlain (1999) studied the importance of brothers, sisters, uncles and aunts to Caribbean families in the UK and the Caribbean. She found that siblings often played a significant part in the upbringing of their younger brothers and sisters or of their nephews and nieces. Like Barrow, Chamberlain found that distance from kin made it difficult or even impossible for relatives to play such a significant role in childcare as they played in many families in the Caribbean. Nevertheless, some British African Caribbeans were able to choose to live close to their relatives, and brothers, sisters, aunts and uncles played a greater role in the upbringing of children than is typical in white British families.

Berthoud and Beishon (1997), who analysed the data from the PSI survey, found some distinctive features of black family life in Britain, but also a great deal of variety between families. They say that 'the most striking characteristic is a low emphasis on long-term partnerships, and especially on formal marriage'. British African Caribbean families had high rates of divorce and separation and were more likely than other groups to have children outside of marriage. Among this group there were also high proportions of lone mothers, but African Caribbean lone mothers were much more likely than those from other groups to have paid employment. Nevertheless, over half of Caribbean families with children were married or cohabiting in long-term relationships.

Tracey Reynolds (2002) argues that the concentration on female-headed households among Black Caribbean families in Britain is rather misleading. She emphasizes the diversity and fluidity of Black Caribbean families. In part this reflects cultural diversity within the Black Caribbean community. Family patterns vary between Caribbean islands and these variations are reflected in Britain. For example, in Jamaica, female-headed households are dominant, but in Barbados and Antigua nuclear households are more common.

In Britain (and in the Caribbean) Black Caribbean family diversity is increased by the existence of **visiting relationships**. Even where there is no adult male in the household, the female head of household may still have a male partner, who does not live with her but visits frequently. The visiting man may play a full and active role as a parent.

Sometimes visiting relationships are maintained because they have advantages in terms of claiming social security benefits. However, Reynolds's own research suggests they are often seen as a stepping-stone towards a stable, cohabiting relationship, which might ultimately lead to marriage. Other women, though, valued the independence that a visiting relationship brought and had no desire to cohabit with and marry their partner.

Reynolds concludes that the

> *tendency in policy research to present Black, female-headed households as the unitary Black family model disguises the fluid and adaptive nature of Black family relationships and living arrangements and also the fact that, similar to families in other racial and ethnic groups, the Black family has diverse family and household patterns.* Reynolds, 2002, p. 69

Ethnicity and family diversity – conclusion

The general picture provided by these studies suggests that immigrants and their descendants have adapted their family life to fit British circumstances, but they are still influenced by family patterns in their country of origin. This would suggest that the presence of a variety of ethnic groups has indeed contributed to the diversity of family types to be found in Britain. These minority ethnic groups have succeeded in retaining many of the culturally distinctive features of their family life.

Nevertheless, there is also evidence of changes taking place in the families of minority ethnic groups, and British culture may have more effect on future generations. Each ethnic group contains a variety of different family types, which are influenced by factors such as class and stage in the life cycle, which relate to diversity in white families. David Morgan warns:

> *While seeking to recognize ethnic diversity in a multicultural society, ethnic boundaries may be too readily or too easily constructed by, say, white Western analysts. There may be oversimplified references to 'the Chinese family', 'the Muslim family' and so on just as, in the past, there have been oversimplified references to 'the Jewish family'.* Morgan, 1996

Minority ethnic families have not just contributed to family diversity through each group having its own distinctive family pattern. They have also contributed to it through developing diverse family patterns within each ethnic group.

Geoff Dench, Kate Gavron and Michael Young – Bethnal Green revisited

The study

Ethnic and other forms of diversity are reflected in a 1990s study carried out by Geoff Dench, Kate Gavron and Michael Young (2006) in the East End of London. They returned to Bethnal Green to see how family life had changed in the area since Young and Willmott had carried out pioneering family research some decades earlier (see pp. 476–7). As part of the study they surveyed 799 residents from all ethnic groups, and a separate sample of 1,021 Bangladeshis, as well as carrying out in-depth interviews. Dench *et al.* comment that:

> *In the old East End, it was families, and especially mothers and motherhood, which constituted the heart of local community life. Family ties gave people the support and security which made life tolerable, and provided a model for organizing relationships with close neighbours. Being a member of a family gave you kin and quasi-kin locally and made the world a safe place.* Dench et al., 2006, p. 103

Some of the older respondents recalled family life in Bethnal Green in the 1950s with fondness. However, Dench *et al.* found that the earlier family patterns had largely disappeared.

The new individualism

Amongst the white population, only a few families remained which had strong kinship networks in the local area. These families tended to be based around family businesses where different family members worked together and local contacts were important for maintaining business. The businesses were usually handed down the male line, but women were important in maintaining family ties and ties with the local community.

These families apart, family life in Bethnal Green in the 1990s was characterized by much greater fluidity and variety than had been the case in the 1950s. For example, the survey found that 21 per cent of the sample were living in single-person households. Of these, 52 per cent were single, 30 per cent widowed, 14 per cent divorced or separated and 4 per cent married. A further 9 per cent lived in households which consisted of unrelated adults.

Dench *et al.* argue that a new individualism had developed. In part this had been an unintended consequence of developments in the welfare state. In the early post-war years, state welfare reform based upon the Beveridge Report (see pp. 262–3) had tried to supplement the welfare provided by families and communities. By the 1960s, however, state welfare placed an increased emphasis on the citizenship rights of individuals. This resulted in the welfare state taking over many of the support roles for individuals which had previously been provided by families. There was a 'bureaucratisation of caring' (Dench *et al.*, 2006, p. 105). This change allowed individuals to be more independent of families, which in turn led to women having more freedom to take paid work.

The new individualism is reflected in changes in families and households.

> *Many people are now living in very casual, fluid households, or in more than one place, or in unconventional relationships. On top of this, the rise of ... single parenthood ... means that many are engaged in undisclosed cohabitation which they simply do not discuss ... for fear of losing benefits.* Dench et *al.*, 2006, p. 109

Family life is much more varied than in the 1950s. Cohabitation, divorce, separation and single parenthood are all more common. Individual families take a wide variety of forms. For example, in one family where the parents were separated, they still spent time together and the woman spent a lot of time with her estranged husband's relatives.

Although some of the changes had benefited women, they were still usually the ones left caring for children. At the same time, male detachment from family concerns was becoming more common. More men were living apart from their children and although some played a full and active part in their children's lives, others did not.

The slide back towards conventionality

Despite all these changes, Dench *et al.* did not find widespread rejection of marriage among the white population. Some single mothers had escaped from unsatisfactory relationships and were not keen to find another partner immediately, but most young women still saw marriage as the ideal. Most cohabitants saw cohabitation as a step on the road to marriage. There was little evidence that single mothers who were reliant upon state benefits were happy with their situation – most were hoping to get off benefits as soon as possible.

Despite all the changes, then, Dench *et al.* detected a 'slide back towards conventionality' (2006, p. 115). Not only did people still value conventional marriage, but most disapproved of gay couples and there was a widespread feeling that family patterns had moved too far from traditional patterns. Many people believed that casual and fluid relationships were acceptable before children were born, but once you became a parent more stable households were preferable. The middle-class residents who had moved into the area seeking affordable housing were particularly likely to believe that the additional responsibilities of parenthood were best addressed in stable relationships.

For the white residents of Bethnal Green, then,

> *life for most people still seems to follow broadly the same path as it always has, that is from childhood, through a period of independence, on to parenthood and the interdependence between adults characteristic of married life. What has changed is ... that many (middle-class) now wait longer before becoming parents.* Dench et *al.*, 2006, p.116

Once women became parents they felt more constrained and they lost some of their sense of having the freedom to choose whatever life they wished, especially as women still had primary responsibility for childcare.

Bangladeshi families

According to Dench *et al.*, the new individualism that had affected white family life had had little discernible impact on Bangladeshi family life. Out of the sample of over 1,000 Bangladeshis, only four lived in single-person households. These consisted of one single woman, one single man, a man with a wife in Bangladesh and one divorced man.

The reason why so few Bangladeshis live alone, according to Dench *et al.*, is that divorce and separation rates are very low in the Bangladeshi community, widows tend to live with their children, and the elderly are still usually cared for by their children.

Furthermore, couple households were very uncommon: only two of the Bangladeshi households consisted of a married couple with no children. On the other hand, extended families were common: 61 per cent of the sample consisted of a married couple with their children, and 25.7 per cent were extended family households. In most cases extended families developed because young couples decided to live with the husband's parents.

The Bangladeshi households were large, with an average size of nearly six. Dench *et al.* found that Bangladeshis' families were close-knit and supportive. Many of the Bangladeshis interviewed were critical of white families for failing to support vulnerable family members such as elderly parents. Dench *et al.* say that most Bangladeshis 'still believe in the moral solidarity of the family and the importance of putting family interests before those of the individual' (2006, pp. 84–5).

Bangladeshi men have a religious obligation to marry and be involved in family life. Men also feel a strong obligation towards their mother, and, by marrying, a son can get domestic help for his mother from his wife. It is also considered part of a son's duty towards his mother to have children to continue the family line. Some Bangladeshi women, however, are not happy with having to take on responsibility for their mother-in-law, and some therefore prefer to marry a man from Bangladesh in the hope that his mother will not come and settle with them.

Dench *et al.* challenge the view that Bangladeshi families are male-dominated or patriarchal. A man's role is to serve his family through paid work, not to dominate it. In the Bangladeshi community the family is seen as the centre of power and is more important than the public world of work. Bangladeshi wives are less likely to work than their white counterparts, but that does not mean that they lack power. Dench *et al.* comment: 'Far from conforming to the notion of the compliant "little women", in our study Bangladeshi mothers – certainly those in the senior generation – emerge in the domestic context as decidedly matriarchal, in firm control of their families' (2006, p. 86).

Conclusion

The study by Dench *et al.* clearly shows that in the four decades since Young and Willmott's previous study, there had been enormous changes in the family life of Bethnal Green. Little remained of the extended family networks typical amongst the white population of the 1950s. The strongest family networks were amongst the Bangladeshi community, but they had distinct family patterns of their own which added to the overall diversity. In the white population, the new individualism undermined traditional patterns of family life. However, marriage and family were still valued, particularly by those who had children, and Dench *et al.* detected a move back towards valuing conventional family life amongst some residents.

Robert Chester – the British neo-conventional family

The conclusions of Dench *et al.* suggest that it might be too simple to argue that British family life is characterized by diversity and that conventional family life is no longer valued. In an early attack upon the idea that fundamental changes are taking place in British family life, Robert Chester (1985) argued that the changes had been only minor. He claimed the evidence advanced by advocates of the theory of family diversity was misleading, and the basic features of family life had remained largely unchanged for the vast majority of the British population since the Second World War. He argued:

> *Most adults still marry and have children. Most children are reared by their natural parents. Most people live in a household headed by a married couple. Most marriages continue until parted by death. No great change seems currently in prospect.* Chester, 1985

Percentage of people versus percentage of households

Chester believed that a snapshot of household types at a particular time does not provide a valid picture of the British family.

The first point that Chester made is that a very different picture is produced if the percentage of people in various types of household is calculated, instead of the percentage of households of various types. Households with parents and children contain a greater percentage of the population than the percentage of households they make up. This is because family households tend to have more members than other types of household.

Chester's arguments were based upon figures from 1981. As Table 8.8 shows, the way the figures are calculated does make a difference. In 1981, 40 per cent of households were made up of two parents and children, but over 59 per cent of people lived in such households. In 2005, 27 per cent of households consisted of two parents plus children, but 44 per cent of people lived in this type of household. Despite the changes, just under half the population were still living in nuclear, two-generation households, with a further 26 per cent living in couple households.

The nuclear family and the life cycle

The second point made by Chester was that life cycles make it inevitable that at any one time some people will not be a member of a nuclear family household. Many of those who lived in other types of household would either have experienced living in a nuclear family in the past, or would do so in the future. He said: 'The 8 per cent living alone are mostly the elderly widowed, or else younger people who are likely to marry.' He described the parents-and-children household as 'one which is normal and is still experienced by the vast majority'.

The 'neo-conventional family'

According to Chester, there was little evidence that people were choosing to live on a long-term basis in alternatives to the nuclear family. However, he did accept that some changes were taking place in family life. In particular, many families were no longer 'conventional' in the sense that the

Table 8.8 Households and people in households in Great Britain, 1981 and 2005

Type of household	1981 Households (%)	1981 People (%)	2005 Households (%)	2005 People (%)
One person	22	8	31	14
Married or cohabiting couple	26	20	29	26
Married or cohabiting couple with dependent children	32	49	21	36
Married or cohabiting couple with non-dependent children	8	10	6	8
Lone parent with dependent children	4	5	7	8
Other	9	8	6	8

Source: Social Trends (1982) HMSO, London, and General Household Survey, 2005 (2006) Office for National Statistics, London.

husband was the sole breadwinner. He accepted that women were increasingly making a contribution to household finances by taking paid employment outside the home.

However, Chester argued that, although, according to his figures, 58 per cent of wives worked, often they only did so for part of their married lives, and frequently on a part-time basis. Many gave up work for the period when their children were young; a minority of married mothers (49 per cent) were employed; and only 14 per cent of working married mothers had full-time jobs. Chester argued: 'The pattern is of married women withdrawing from the labour force to become mothers, and some of them taking (mostly part-time) work as their children mature.'

Although Chester recognized this was an important change in family life compared to the past, he did not see it as a fundamental alteration in the family. He called this new family form – in which wives have some involvement in the labour market – the **neo-conventional family**. It was little different from the conventional family apart from the increasing numbers of wives working for at least part of their married lives.

Family diversity – conclusion

While Chester makes an important point in stressing that nuclear families remained very common and featured in most people's lives, he perhaps overstated his case. As Table 8.8 shows, there has been a continuing reduction in the proportion of people living in parents-and-children households, from 59 per cent in 1981 to 44 per cent in 2005. The percentages of people living alone or in lone-parent households have increased. Thus, since Chester was writing, there has been a slow but steady drift away from living in nuclear families in Britain.

In 1999 Elizabeth Silva and Carol Smart summed up the situation by arguing that fairly traditional family forms remain important. They note:

> *In 1996, 73 per cent of households were composed of heterosexual couples (with just under 90 per cent of these being married), 50 per cent of these households had children, and 40 per cent had dependent children ... only 9 per cent of households with dependent children were headed by lone parents.* Silva and Smart, 1999

Nevertheless, they argue, 'personal choices appear as increasingly autonomous and fluid'.

Jennifer Somerville (2000) believes the decline of the traditional family can be exaggerated. She notes that the argument that traditional families have declined is often based on a comparison with figures from 1971. However, this is misleading because the 1960s were an untypical decade in which women 'had a greater propensity to marry than in previous generations and married at the earliest age ever recorded since civil registration began in 1837'. In succeeding decades, women went back to a pattern of marrying and having children later in life.

Furthermore, echoing the arguments of Chester, she points out that most of the figures are based upon snapshots of how many are married with children at a particular time, rather than a life-cycle approach which looks at how many marry and have children at any point in their lives. Somerville claims that only about 5 per cent of people never marry at some stage in their lives.

However, she recognizes there are 'considerable discontinuities with the past'. These include the 'separation of sex from reproduction', so that pre-marital sex is now the norm and cohabitation outside or before marriage is increasingly common. Childlessness is becoming more common, and there are many more working mothers and much more divorce than several decades ago. Lone parenthood is also more common, though it is often transitory, with most lone parents finding a new partner (or their children reaching adulthood) within a few years of becoming lone parents.

Somerville also accepts that minority ethnic groups add to the diversity of British family life. She therefore identifies a broader range of changes that increase diversity in family life than Chester. Nevertheless, she reaches the conclusion that 'changes should be seen in the context of continuing commitment by the vast majority of the population to a framework of belief in the value of family life and to behaviour which seeks to approximate to that ideal'.

This analysis is rather more balanced than that advanced by the Rapoports, who in 1982 first put forward the idea that there was a new era of choice and diversity in British family life. They argued that it was increasingly acceptable to form alternative households and families to conventional nuclear ones. They said:

> *Families in Britain today are in a transition from coping in a society in which there was a single overriding norm of what family life should be like to a society in which a plurality of norms are recognized as legitimate, indeed, desirable.* Rapoport and Rapoport, 1982

The statistical evidence indicates increasing diversity and several sociologists have tried to link ideas of choice and diversity with their particular views on modernity and postmodernity. (These views will be examined on pp. 512–19.) However, sociologists such as Chester and Somerville believe most people continue to aspire to a conventional family life.

Having surveyed the ways in which the structure of the family may have changed over the years, we will now investigate whether the functions of the family have also changed.

The changing functions of the family

The loss of functions

Some sociologists argue that the family has lost a number of its functions in modern industrial society. Institutions such as businesses, political parties, schools and welfare organizations now specialize in functions formerly performed by the family. Talcott Parsons argued that the family has become:

on the 'macroscopic' levels, almost completely functionless. It does not itself, except here and there, engage in much economic production; it is not a significant unit in the political power system; it is not a major direct agency of integration of the larger society. Its individual members participate in all these functions, but they do so as individuals, not in their roles as family members. Parsons, 1955

However, this does not mean that the family is declining in importance – it has simply become more specialized. Parsons maintained that its role is still vital. By structuring the personalities of the young and stabilizing the personalities of adults, the family provides its members with the psychological training and support necessary to meet the requirements of the social system. Parsons concluded: 'the family is more specialized than before, but not in any general sense less important, because society is dependent more exclusively on it for the performance of certain of its vital functions'. Thus the loss of certain functions by the family has made its remaining functions more important.

The maintenance and improvement of functions

Not all sociologists would agree, however, that the family has lost many of its functions in modern industrial society. Ronald Fletcher, a British sociologist and a staunch supporter of the family, maintained that just the opposite has happened. In *The Family and Marriage in Britain* (1966) Fletcher argued that not only has the family retained its functions but also those functions have 'increased in detail and importance'. Specialized institutions such as schools and hospitals have added to and improved the family's functions, rather than superseded them.

1. Fletcher maintained that the family's responsibility for socializing the young is as important as it ever was. State education has added to, rather than removed, this responsibility, since 'Parents are expected to do their best to guide, encourage and support their children in their educational and occupational choices and careers.'
2. In the same way, the state has not removed the family's responsibility for the physical welfare of its members. Fletcher argued: 'The family is still centrally concerned with maintaining the health of its members, but it is now aided by wider provisions which have been added to the family's situation since pre-industrial times.'

   Rather than removing this function from the family, the state provision of health services has served to expand and improve it. Compared to the past, parents are preoccupied with their children's health. State health and welfare provision has provided additional support for the family and made its members more aware of the importance of health and hygiene in the home.
3. Even though Fletcher admitted that the family has largely lost its function as a unit of production, he argued it still maintains a vital economic function as a unit of consumption. Particularly in the case of the modern home-centred family, money is spent on, and in the name of, the family rather than the individual. Thus the modern family demands fitted carpets, three-piece suites, washing machines, television sets and 'family' cars.

Young and Willmott (1973) make a similar point with respect to their symmetrical Stage 3 family (see p. 477). They argue: 'In its capacity as a consumer the family has also made a crucial alliance with technology.' Industry needs both a market for its goods and a motivated workforce. The symmetrical family provides both. Workers are motivated to work by their desire for consumer durables. This desire stems from the high value they place on the family and a privatized lifestyle in the family home. This provides a ready market for the products of industry.

In this way the family performs an important economic function and is functionally related to the economic system. In Young and Willmott's words, 'The family and technology have achieved a mutual adaptation.'

Feminism and economic functions

Feminist writers have tended to disagree with the view shared by many sociologists of the family that the family has lost its economic role as a unit of production and has become simply a unit of consumption. They tend to argue that much of the work that takes place in the family is productive but it is not recognized as such because it is unpaid and it is usually done by women. The contribution to economic life made by women is frequently underestimated.

The radical feminists Christine Delphy and Diana Leonard (1992) accept that industrialization created new units of production such as factories, but deny that it removed the productive function from the family. Some productive functions have been lost, but others are performed to a much higher standard than in the past. They cite as examples 'warm and tidy rooms with attention to décor, and more complex meals with a variety of forms of cooking'.

The family has taken on some new productive functions, such as giving pre-school reading tuition to children, and functions such as washing clothes and freezing food have been reintroduced to the household with the advent of new consumer products.

Delphy and Leonard also point out that there are still a fair number of families which continue to act as an economic unit producing goods for the market. French farming families, which have been studied by Christine Delphy, are a case in point. (Delphy and Leonard's work is discussed in more detail on pp. 467–8; and housework is discussed on pp. 497–9.)

Summary and conclusions

Most sociologists who adopt a functionalist perspective argue that the family has lost several of its functions in modern industrial society, but they maintain that the importance of the family has not declined. Rather, the family has adapted and is adapting to a developing industrial society. It remains a vital and basic institution in society.

Others dispute the claim that some of these functions have been lost, or argue that new functions have replaced the old ones. From all these viewpoints the family remains a key institution.

All the writers examined here have a tendency to think in terms of 'the family' without differentiating between different types of family. They may not, therefore, appreciate the range of effects family life can have or the range of functions it may perform.

Graham Allan and Graham Crow (2001) argue that attempts to identify the functions of the family can be criticized because of the 'excessively abstract and over-general nature of functionalist frameworks of analysis which, by treating family forms as things shaped by external forces, allowed little scope for individual agency or variations from the norm'. Postmodernists and difference feminists certainly reject the view that there is any single type of family which always performs certain functions. (See pp. 517–19 for a discussion of postmodernism and pp. 470–2 for a discussion of difference feminism.)

The writers discussed above also tend to assume that families reproduce the existing social structure, whether this is seen as a functioning mechanism, an exploitative capitalist system, or a patriarchal society. Yet families are not necessarily supportive of, or instrumental in reproducing, existing societies. With increasing family diversity, some individual families and even some types of family may be radical forces in society. For example, gay and lesbian families sometimes see themselves as challenging the inegalitarian relationships in heterosexual families (see p. 462 for a discussion of gay and lesbian families).

In this section we have discussed the various functional roles that the family performs; in the next section we focus on roles within the family.

Conjugal roles

A major characteristic of the **symmetrical family** – which Young and Willmott (1973) claimed was developing when they were writing in the 1970s – was the degree to which spouses shared domestic, work and leisure activities. Relationships of this type are known as **joint conjugal** roles, as opposed to **segregated conjugal** roles.

In Young and Willmott's Stage 2 family, conjugal roles – the marital roles of husband and wife – were largely segregated. There was a clear-cut division of labour between the spouses in the household, and the husband was relatively uninvolved with domestic chores and raising the children. This segregation of conjugal roles extended to leisure. The wife associated mainly with her female kin and neighbours; the husband with his male workmates, kin and neighbours. This pattern was typical of the traditional working-class community of Bethnal Green.

In the Stage 3 symmetrical family, conjugal roles become more joint. Although the wife still has primary responsibility for housework and child rearing, husbands become more involved, often washing clothes, ironing and sharing other domestic duties. Husband and wife increasingly share responsibility for decisions that affect the family. They discuss matters such as household finances and their children's education to a greater degree than the Stage 2 family.

Young and Willmott argue that the change from segregated to joint conjugal roles results mainly from the withdrawal of the wife from her relationships with female kin, and the drawing of the husband into the family circle. We looked at the reasons they gave for this in a previous section (see pp. 477–8). The extent to which conjugal roles have been changing and what this indicates about inequalities between men and women have been the subject of some controversy. These controversies will now be discussed.

Inequality within marriage

Although much of the recent research on conjugal roles has been concerned with determining the degree of inequality between husband and wife within marriage, there has been no generally accepted way of determining the extent of inequality. Different researchers have measured different aspects of inequality. Some have concentrated on the division of labour in the home: they have examined the allocation of responsibility for domestic work between husband and wife and the amount of time spent by spouses on particular tasks. Others have tried to measure the distribution of power within marriage.

Young and Willmott are among those who have argued that conjugal roles are increasingly becoming joint. However, many sociologists who have carried out research in this area have found little evidence that inequality within marriage has been significantly reduced.

Conjugal roles, housework and childcare

The symmetrical family

Young and Willmott's views on the symmetrical family (see above) have been heavily criticized. Ann Oakley (1974) argues that their claim of increasing symmetry within marriage is based on inadequate methodology. Although their figure of 72 per cent (for men doing housework) sounds impressive, she points out that it is based on only one question in Young and Willmott's interview schedule: 'Do you/does your husband help at least once a week with any household jobs like washing up, making beds (helping with the children), ironing, cooking or cleaning?' Oakley notes that men who make only a very small contribution to housework would be included in the 72 per cent. She says: 'A man who helps with the children once a week would be included in this percentage, so would (presumably) a man who ironed his own trousers on a Saturday afternoon.'

Housework and childcare

A rather different picture of conjugal roles emerged in Oakley's own research (1974). She collected information on forty married women who had one child or more under the age of 5, who were British or Irish born, and aged between 20 and 30. Half of her sample were working-class, half were middle-class, and all lived in the London area.

She found greater equality in terms of the allocation of domestic tasks between spouses in the middle class than in the working class. However, in both classes few men had high levels of participation in housework and childcare: few marriages could be defined as egalitarian. In only 15 per cent of marriages did men have high levels of participation in housework; for childcare the figure was 30 per cent.

Since these pioneering pieces of research, more sophisticated methods have been developed for examining the domestic division of labour.

Survey research

Survey research has used large samples to produce more reliable data. The British Social Attitudes Survey conducted research on household tasks in 1984, 1991 and 1997. It detected a trend towards men undertaking an increasing proportion of domestic tasks, but the change has been slow and women still do most of the domestic work.

The 1997 British Social Attitudes Survey also included comparative data from Europe, but only included data on a restricted range of household tasks (Jowell *et al.*, 1998) (see Table 8.9). It showed a small reduction in the gendered nature of washing and ironing in Britain (it was a mainly female task in 84 per cent of households in 1991, while the equivalent figure for 1997 was 79 per cent). There was also a small reduction in the tendency for men to be responsible for making repairs around the house (although the precise wording of the relevant question changed between surveys). Washing and ironing were less female-dominated in Britain than in other countries, but in Sweden looking after sick family members was considerably less likely than it was in Britain to be a mainly female activity.

Childcare

Mary Boulton (1983) argues that studies which focus upon the allocation of tasks in the home exaggerate the extent of men's involvement in childcare, and she denies that questions about who does what give a true picture of conjugal roles. To her, childcare:

> *is essentially about exercising responsibility for another person who is not fully responsible for herself and it entails seeing to all aspects of the child's security and well-being, her growth and development at any and all times.* Boulton, 1983

Boulton claims that, although men might help with particular tasks, it is their wives who retain primary responsibility for children. It is the wives who relegate non-domestic aspects of their lives to a low priority.

Some empirical support for Boulton is provided by a study conducted by Elsa Ferri and Kate Smith (1996). They produced data based upon the National Child Development Survey. This survey followed, as far as possible, the lives of everybody born in Great Britain in a specific week in 1958. The data came from the 1991 survey when those involved were 33 years old. By that time, the sample included 2,800 fathers and 3,192 mothers.

The survey found it was still very unusual for fathers to take primary responsibility for childcare. For example, according to the male respondents, in dual-earner families where both worked full-time the father was the main carer in only 2 per cent of families, the wife was the main carer in 24 per cent of families, and childcare was shared equally in 72 per cent of families. When mothers were asked the same question they said that they were the main carer in 32 per cent of families and men in just 1 per cent.

Even when the woman had paid employment outside the home and the man did not, it was still more common for the woman than the man to take main responsibility for routine childcare or childcare in the event of illness. This suggests that the increasing employment of married women outside the home had made comparatively little impact on the contribution of the male partner to childcare.

The study also found little evidence for the development of egalitarian gender roles in relation to other types of housework. Ferri and Smith say, 'Thus, for example, two-thirds of full-time working mothers said they were responsible for cooking and cleaning, and four out of five for laundry.'

Time

Another way to study gender roles is to examine time spent on different tasks. This gives some indication of whether, in total, men or women spend more time on paid and unpaid work.

Jonathan Gershuny (1992, 1999) examined how social changes have affected the burden of work for British husbands and wives. Perhaps the most important change affecting this area of social life has been the rise in the proportion of wives taking paid employment outside the home. Sociologists such as Oakley have argued that women have increasingly been taking on a dual burden: they have retained primary responsibility

Table 8.9 Household division of labour, 1997

% saying always or usually the woman:	Western Germany	Britain	Irish Republic	Netherlands	Sweden*
Washing and ironing	88	79	85	87	80
Looking after sick family member	50	48	50	47	38
% saying always or usually the man:					
Makes small repairs around the house	80	75	69	78	82
Base (households with partners only)	*1,604*	*601*	*607*	*1,255*	*883*

* For Sweden the base varies for the different tasks and this is the smallest unweighted base.

Source: R. Jowell *et al.* (1998) *British and European Social Attitudes*, Fifteenth Report, Ashgate, Aldershot, p. 32.

for household tasks while also being expected to have paid employment.

Gershuny examined 1974 and 1975 data from the BBC Audience Research Department, and 1997 data from an Economic and Social Research Council project, to discover how the share of work had changed (Gershuny, 1999, discussed in Laurie and Gershuny, 2000). In 1997 women continued to do in excess of 60 per cent of the domestic work even when both partners were working full-time. However, Gershuny did find a gradual shift towards husbands doing a higher proportion of domestic work. Overall, he found little difference in the amount of time men and women in employment spent on paid and unpaid work.

However, Graham Allan (1985) suggests the work that women carry out in the home may be tedious and less satisfying than the more creative tasks that are frequently done by men. He says: 'much female domestic work is monotonous and mundane, providing few intrinsic satisfactions'.

Recent survey research suggests that, overall, there is little difference between men and women in the time spent on paid and unpaid work. In 2000–1 and 2005 (ONS, 2001; Lader *et al.*, 2006) the British government conducted detailed time-use surveys which involved collecting data using questionnaires and self-completed time diaries in a sample of over 5,000 homes.

In the 2000 survey, men spent a total of 6 hours 20 minutes per day on employment and study, housework and childcare, compared to 6 hours 26 minutes per day spent by women. In 2005, men spent 5 hours 41 minutes on these activities, compared to 5 hours 58 minutes spent by women (see Table 8.10). Therefore, the gap between men and women had widened from six minutes to seventeen minutes.

Furthermore, in 2005 men had a total of 5 hours 25 minutes' leisure a day, compared to women's 4 hours 53 minutes. However, these figures include all men and women, not just those who cohabit with a partner of the opposite sex. Lader *et al.* found that 'Men and women in partnerships have similar totals of work and leisure time, with men overall having a little more work time than women' (2006, p. 23). Much of the overall difference could be explained by the fact that women who were not in a partnership were much more likely than single men to be lone parents, and single women also tended to spend longer working than single men.

Table 8.10 Time spent on main activities by sex, in Great Britain, 2005 (people aged 16 and over)

	Hours and minutes per day	
	Males	Females
Sleep	8.04	8.18
Resting	0.43	0.48
Personal care	0.40	0.48
Eating and drinking	1.25	1.19
Leisure		
Watching TV/DVD and listening to radio/music	2.50	2.25
Social life and entertainment/ culture	1.22	1.32
Hobbies and games	0.37	0.23
Sport	0.13	0.07
Reading	0.23	0.26
All leisure	*5.25*	*4.53*
Employment and study	3.45	2.26
Housework	1.41	3.00
Childcare	0.15	0.32
Voluntary work and meetings	0.15	0.20
Travel	1.32	1.22
Other	0.13	0.15

Source: *Time Use Survey 2005*, http://statistics.gov.uk?CCI?nugget.asp?ID=7&Pos=1&ColRank=2&Rank=352

Conjugal roles and power

Another approach to studying conjugal roles is to examine power within marriage. This has usually been attempted through an examination of who makes the decisions.

A study by Irene Hardill, Anne Green, Anna Dudlestone and David Owen (1997) examined power in dual-earner households in Nottingham using semi-structured interviews. The households were classified into those where the husband's career took precedence in making major household decisions (such as what part of the country to live in), those where the wife's career took precedence, and those where neither career clearly took precedence over the other. In nineteen households the man's career came first, in five the woman's career took precedence, and in six neither career was clearly prioritized. It was most likely to be the man who decided where the couple were to live, and men tended to make decisions about cars. However, husband and wife usually made a joint decision about buying or renting a house.

Although men dominated in most households, this was not the case in a significant minority of households where there appeared to be more egalitarian relationships.

Power can also be examined in terms of the control of money. Jan Pahl (1989, 1993) was the first British sociologist to conduct detailed studies of how couples manage their money. Her study was based upon interviews with 102 couples with at least one child under 16. The sample, although small, was fairly representative of the population as a whole in terms of employment, class, housing and ownership of consumer goods. However, the very rich were under-represented.

The study found four main patterns of money management:

1 **Husband-controlled pooling** was the most common pattern (thirty-nine couples). In this system, money was shared but the husband had the dominant role in deciding how it was spent. This system was often found in high-income households, especially if the wife did not work. It was also common if the woman worked part-time or if she had a lower-status job than her husband. This system tended to give men most power.

2 **Wife-controlled pooling** was the second most common category, involving twenty-seven couples. In this system, money was shared but the wife had the dominant role in deciding how it was spent. This group tended to be middle-income couples, especially where the wife was working and had a better-paid job than her husband or was better educated. This tended to be the most egalitarian system of financial control.
3 **Husband control** was found in twenty-two couples. Among these couples the husband was usually the one with the main or only wage, and often he gave his wife housekeeping money. Some of these families were too poor to have a bank account; in others only the husband had an account. Sometimes the women worked, but their earnings largely went on housekeeping. In some systems of husband control, the husband gave his wife a housekeeping allowance out of which she had to pay for all or most of the routine costs of running the household. This system tended to lead to male dominance.
4 **Wife control** was the least frequent pattern, found in just fourteen couples. This was most common in working-class and low income households. In a number of these households neither partner worked and both received their income from benefits. In most of these households neither partner had a bank account and they used cash to pay any bills. Although this system appeared to give women more power than men, it was most common in poorer households where the responsibility for managing the money was more of a burden than a privilege.

Inequality and money management

According to Pahl, the most egalitarian type of control is wife-controlled pooling. In households with this system the male and female partners tend to have similar amounts of power in terms of decision making, and they are equally likely (or unlikely) to experience financial deprivation. They also tend to have similar amounts of money to spend on themselves.

Wife-controlled systems appear to give women an advantage over men. However, they tend to be found in households where money is tight and there is little, if anything, left over after paying for necessities. Often women will go short themselves (for example, by eating less, delaying buying new clothes and spending little on their leisure) rather than see their husband or children go short.

Husband-controlled systems tend to give husbands more power than their wives. In these households men usually spend more on personal consumption than wives.

Where husband-controlled pooling occurs, men tend to have more power than women, but the inequality is not as great as in systems of husband control. In the highest-income households there is usually sufficient money to meet the personal expenditure of both partners.

Overall, then, Pahl found that just over a quarter of the couples had a system (wife-controlled pooling) associated with a fair degree of equality between the partners. This would suggest that in domestic relationships, as in a number of other areas, women have not yet come close to reaching a position of equality.

More recent research by Laurie and Gershuny (2000) analysed data from the British Household Panel Survey from 1991 and 1995. This showed movement away from the housekeeping allowance system (in which the man gives the woman an allowance to pay for household expenses), which was being used by just 10 per cent of households by 1995.

The use of shared management systems had increased marginally to 51 per cent in 1995. However, there was more evidence of change towards greater equality in terms of major financial decisions. In 1991, 25 per cent of couples said the male partner had the final say on big financial decisions, but by 1995 this had declined to 20 per cent. The proportion saying the male and female partners had an equal say had risen from 65 per cent to 70 per cent over the same period. Greater equality was particularly in evidence where the women were well qualified and had high earnings, especially if they were employed in professional or managerial jobs.

Overall, Laurie and Gershuny concluded that while there was some evidence of a movement towards greater equality, 'we are still far from a position in which the balance between the sexes in the workplace, corresponds to the balance of work, and economic power, in the home'.

Conjugal roles and emotion work

Jean Duncombe and Dennis Marsden – emotion work

Drawing on the work of various sociologists, Jean Duncombe and Dennis Marsden (1995) argue that some forms of domestic work cannot be measured in conventional surveys. In particular, alongside such tasks as housework and childcare members of households also carry out **emotion work**.

The term 'emotion work' was first used by Arlie Hochschild (1983) to describe the sort of work done by female airline cabin crew in trying to keep passengers happy. Duncombe and Marsden also try to develop the work of N. James (1989), who discussed how 'from a very early age girls and then women become subconsciously trained to be more emotionally skilled in recognizing and empathizing with the moods of others'.

Hochschild and James were mainly interested in emotion work in paid employment. Duncombe and Marsden examine the implications of their ideas for relationships between heterosexual partners.

Their research was based on interviews with forty white couples who had been married for fifteen years. They asked the couples, separately and together, how their marriage had survived for so long in an age of high divorce rates. They found that many women expressed dissatisfaction with their partner's emotional input into the relationship and the family. Many of the women felt emotionally lonely. A number of the men concentrated on their paid employment, were unwilling to express feelings of love for their partner, and were reluctant to discuss their feelings. Most of the men did not believe there was a problem. They did not acknowledge that emotion work needed to be done to make the relationship work.

Duncombe and Marsden found that many of the women in the study were holding the relationship together by doing the crucial emotion work. In the early stages of the relationship, the partners, but particularly the women, **deep act** away any doubts about their emotional closeness or suitability as partners. At this stage any doubts are suppressed because they feel in love and are convinced of the worth of the relationship.

Later, however, 'with growing suspicions, they "shallow act"' to maintain the 'picture for their partner and the outside world'. **Shallow acting** involves pretending to their partners and others that the relationship is satisfactory and they are happy with it. They 'live the family myth' or 'play the couple game' to maintain the illusion of a happy family. This places a considerable emotional strain on the woman, but it is the price to pay for keeping the family together. However, eventually some women begin to 'leak' their unhappiness to outsiders. In the end this may result in the break-up of the relationship and separation or divorce.

In the meantime, women's greater participation in emotion work can be 'a major dimension of gender inequality in couple relationships'. With married women increasingly having paid employment, they can end up performing a **triple shift**. Having completed their paid employment they not only have to come home and do most of the housework, they also have to do most of the emotion work as well.

As women have gained paid employment this type of inequality has not reduced. Progress in this area would require even more fundamental changes. Duncombe and Marsden say:

> *In fact if we consider what would be a desirable future, the most important change would be for boys and men to become meaningfully involved in the emotional aspects of family life and childcare from an early age. And this would require not only a massive reorganization of work and childcare but also a deep transformation in the nature of heterosexual masculinity.* Duncombe and Marsden, 1995

Gillian Dunne – the division of labour in lesbian households

In an interesting departure from studies of conjugal roles in heterosexual households, Gillian Dunne (1999) conducted a study of the division of labour in lesbian households. She examined thirty-seven cohabiting lesbian couples who took part in in-depth, semi-structured interviews.

Dunne found that 'A high level of flexibility and even-handedness characterized the allocation of employment responsibilities in partnerships.' A number of the couples were responsible for the care of at least one child, making it difficult for both to work full-time. However, unlike most heterosexual couples, one of the partners did not usually take primary responsibility for childcare. The birth mother of the child was not necessarily the main carer, and the partners often took turns to reduce their paid employment to spend more time with the children.

The women were also asked to keep time-budget diaries. These revealed that in most households there was a fairly equitable division of time spent on household tasks. In 81 per cent of households neither partner did more than 60 per cent of the housework. Where the division of tasks was more skewed towards one partner than the other, it was usually the case that the one who did less housework spent much longer in paid employment.

Many of the women felt that their sameness as women and the lack of different gender roles made it easier to share tasks equitably. One of the women said, 'I suppose because our relationship doesn't fit into a social norm, there are no pre-set indications about how our relationship should work. We have to work it out for ourselves.'

Dunne concludes that the boundaries between masculinity and femininity and the hierarchical nature of gender relationships, with men being dominant, help to produce conventional domestic divisions of labour in heterosexual households. The best way to change this is to give greater value to 'feminine' tasks such as childcare and housework.

Many middle-class women have avoided the consequences of men's lack of involvement in housework by employing other women to help with domestic tasks. Their career opportunities have been gained at the expense of low-paid, exploited, working-class cleaners, nannies, childminders, etc. To Dunne, this is not an acceptable solution, since it helps to perpetuate the exploitation of women in what she sees as a patriarchal society. Dunne says:

> *We have a common interest in dissolving gender as a category of both content and consequence. This involves acting upon our recognition that gender has a social origin, is possessed by men as well as women and can thus be transcended by both. In practical terms, this means recognizing and celebrating the value of women's traditional areas of work rather than accepting a masculine and capitalist hierarchy of value which can lead to women passing on their responsibilities to less powerful women.* Dunne, 1999

Inequality within marriage – conclusion

Dunne's study of lesbian households suggests equitable domestic divisions of labour can be achieved. However, it is not easy to achieve them in the context of a culture that still differentiates quite clearly between masculinity and femininity.

Most of the evidence suggests women are still a long way from achieving equality within marriage in contemporary Britain. They are still primarily responsible for domestic tasks and they have less power than their husbands within marriage. In terms of the amount of hours spent 'working', though, the general picture of inequality seems to be less clear-cut. Husbands of wives with full-time jobs do seem to be taking over some of the burden of housework, although the change is slow and some inequality remains.

Marriage, marital breakdown and family decline

Many social and political commentators in Western societies have expressed concern about what they see as the decline of marriage and of family life. Many see this as a threat to the family, which in turn they see as the bedrock of a stable and civilized society.

For example, Brenda Almond (2006) believes that the family is fragmenting. She argues that there has been a shift away from concern with the family as a biological institution based upon the rearing of children, towards the family as an institution which emphasizes 'two people's emotional need or desire for one another' (Almond, 2006, p. 107).

There is an increased emphasis on the needs of individuals and less emphasis on society's need for the rearing of children in stable relationships. There is increasing social and legal acceptance of marital breakdown, cohabitation, gay and lesbian relationships and so on, all of which lead to the decline and fragmentation of families. Almond believes that the decline of the family is damaging to society, and steps should be taken to reverse the trend.

Another writer who believes that the family and marriage are in decline is Patricia Morgan (2003). She argues that factors such as increased cohabitation, declining fertility, the decline in the proportion of married people, the increase in single parenthood and childbirth outside marriage, and the rise in the numbers living alone are all indicative of this decline. Like Almond, she sees this as harmful for society, for individuals and for children. For example, cohabiting couples are much more likely to split up than married couples, causing, according to Morgan, problems for children and for a society which may have to provide financial support for the resulting lone-parent family.

In addition, cohabitation, divorce and the delaying of marriage until later in life all contribute to the low fertility rate. This leads to an ageing of the population, which places a massive burden on those of working age who need to support the growing proportion of elderly in the population.

The threats to marriage and family life fall into two main categories: threats resulting from alternatives to marriage and conventional families; and threats resulting from the breakdown of marriages.

On the surface, the evidence for a crisis in the institution of marriage and in family life seems compelling. However, as we will see, the evidence needs to be interpreted carefully and the crisis may not be as acute as it first seems.

'Threats' from alternatives to marriage

First, it is argued that marriage is becoming less popular – decreasing numbers of people are getting married. More people are developing alternatives to conventional married life. These alternatives can take a number of forms.

Marriage rates

Writing in the 1980s, Robert Chester (1985) was among those who noted that marriage rates among young adults had declined in many Western countries. First, Sweden and Denmark experienced falling marriage rates among the under-thirties. The trend continued in Britain, the USA and West Germany in the early 1970s, and later spread to France.

In England and Wales the first-marriage rate (number of marriages per 1,000 single people) was 74.9 in 1961, rising to 82.3 in 1971, but by 2004 it was just 24.7 (*Population Trends*, 2006). Amongst women the rate was 83 in 1961, 97 in 1971 and 30.8 in 2004. As Figure 8.1 shows, the number of first marriages fell from a peak of nearly 400,000 per year in the mid-1960s to well under 200,000 per year by 2003.

However, Chester did not see these sorts of figures as conclusive evidence for a decline in the popularity of marriage. He said, 'Mainly we seem to be witnessing a delay in the timing of marriage, rather than a fall-off in getting married at all.' He thought future generations might marry less frequently, but he believed there would be only a small (if any) reduction in marriage rates.

Chester was certainly right about the delay in marriage since much of the decline in first marriages does seem to be due to people delaying marriages. According to British government statistics, in 1961 the average age at first marriage in the UK was 25.6 years for men, and 23.1 years for women. In 2004 the average age at first marriage was considerably older: 31.4 years for men and 29.1 years for women (*Population Trends*, 2005). Some commentators are keen to point out that most people do get married at some stage in their lives. According to Jon Bernardes:

> *It is important to realize that around 90 per cent of all women marry in the UK today compared to 70 per cent in the Victorian era. Britain has one of the highest rates of marriage in the European Union. By the age of 40 years, 95 per cent of women and 91 per cent of men have married.* Bernardes, 1997

Recent figures suggest continued reductions in the proportion who have never married. The Government Actuary's Department (2005) calculated that in 2003 89 per cent of 45- to 64-year-old men and 93 per cent of

Figure 8.1 Marriages and divorces in the UK, 1950–2003

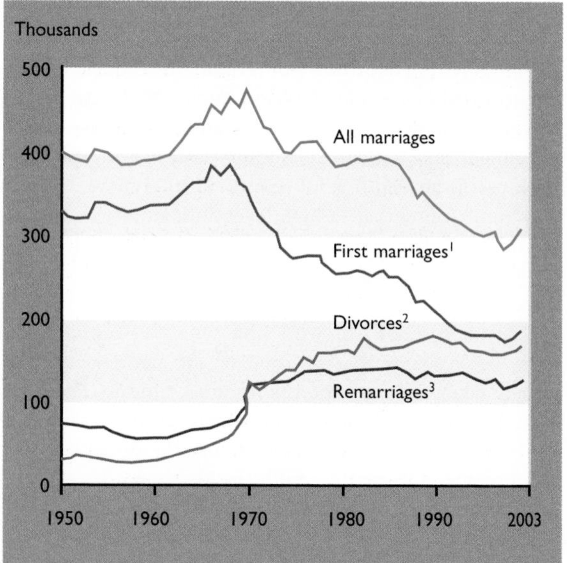

[1] For both partners
[2] Includes annulments. Data for 1950 to 1970 for Great Britain only
[3] For one or both partners

Source: *Social Trends 2006*, Office for National Statistics, London, p. 26.

women had married at least once. However, they predicted that the lower rates of marriages in younger age groups would lead to an increase in the never-married. They projected that by 2031 amongst the 45–64 age group only 66 per cent of men and 71 per cent of women would have been married at least once.

Whether these projections prove accurate remains to be seen, but if the proportion of the never-married amongst older age groups does rise this much, it would suggest more than a simple delay in the timing of marriage.

Cohabitation

One alternative to marriage is cohabitation by couples not legally married. According to *Social Trends 2006*, between 1986 and 2004/5 the proportion of non-married adults aged under 60 who were cohabiting rose from 11 per cent to 24 per cent amongst men, and from 13 per cent to 25 per cent amongst women. Amongst cohabiting men, 23 per cent were single, 12 per cent were widowed, 36 per cent were divorced and 23 per cent were separated. Amongst women the proportions were 27 per cent single, 6 per cent widowed, 29 per cent divorced and 23 per cent separated.

Whilst there is no doubt that cohabitation has become increasingly common, there is no agreement about the significance of this trend.

Patricia Morgan (2003) sees it as part of a worrying trend in which marriage is going out of fashion and the family is in serious decline. Morgan believes that cohabitation used to be seen primarily as a prelude to marriage but increasingly it is part of a pattern which simply reflects an 'increase in sexual partners and partner change' (2003, p. 127). She quotes statistics from the British Household Panel Survey showing that less than 4 per cent of cohabiting couples stay together for more than ten years as cohabitants, although around 60 per cent get married.

A different view is taken by Joan Chandler (1993). She sees the increase in cohabitation as rather more significant: 'The time couples spend cohabiting is lengthening and increasingly they appear to be choosing cohabitation as a long-term alternative to marriage.' Chandler suggests this is reflected in the increasing proportion of children born out of marriage – partners no longer feel as much pressure to marry to legitimize a pregnancy. She argues:

> *Many of today's parents have detached childbearing and rearing from traditional marriage and 28 per cent of children are now born to unmarried mothers. However, many fewer are born to residentially lone parents, as 70 per cent of these children are jointly registered by parents who usually share the same address.* Chandler, 1993

Although Chandler sees cohabitation as increasingly popular, she does point out that it is nothing new. Unofficial self-marriage (where people simply declare themselves to be married – sometimes called 'living over the brush') was very common in past centuries. She quotes research which estimates that as many as a quarter to a third of couples lived in consensual unions in Britain in the eighteenth century.

Changing public attitudes to cohabitation were discussed by Anne Barlow, Simon Duncan, Grace James and Alison Park (2001). Using data from a number of British Social Attitude Surveys, Barlow *et al.* found clear evidence of changing public attitudes. More people were beginning to see it as acceptable to have children without getting married. In 1994, 70 per cent agreed that 'People who want children ought to get married', but by 2000 this was down to 54 per cent.

They found increasingly liberal attitudes to pre-marital sex, with the proportion thinking that it was 'not wrong at all' increasing from 42 per cent in 1984 to 62 per cent in 2000. By 2000 more than two-thirds of respondents (67 per cent) agreed it was 'all right for a couple to live together without intending to get married', and 56 per cent thought it was 'a good idea for a couple who intend to get married to live together first'.

Barlow *et al.* also found clear evidence that younger age groups were more likely to find cohabitation acceptable than older age groups, but all age groups had moved some way towards greater acceptance of pre-marital sex and cohabitation. Barlow *et al.* argue: 'Over time … there is a strong likelihood that society will become more liberal still on these matters, although particular groups, such as the religious, are likely to remain more traditional than the rest.'

However, they do not suggest that this indicates the breakdown of marriage as a respected institution. In the 2000 survey, 59 per cent agreed that 'marriage is still the best kind of relationship'. A mere 9 per cent agreed that 'there is no point getting married – it is only a piece of paper', while 73 per cent disagreed.

Despite the increasing acceptance of cohabitation, Barlow *et al.* therefore argue that, 'overall, marriage is still widely valued as an ideal, but that it is regarded with much more ambivalence when it comes to everyday partnering and (especially) parenting'.

Many people showed considerable commitment to their relationships even if they were not married. On average, current cohabitants had been together for six and a half years. For some, extended cohabitation was a prelude to marriage. Barlow *et al.* therefore argue that many people still value long-term, stable heterosexual relationships. While many see marriage as preferable to cohabitation, cohabitation is increasingly accepted as a valid alternative.

Barlow *et al.* suggest Britain will 'probably move towards a Scandinavian pattern, therefore, where long-term cohabitation is widely seen as quite normal, and where marriage is more of a lifestyle choice than an expected part of life'.

Declining fertility and birth rates

Patricia Morgan (2003) points out that total fertility rates (the number of children born per woman of childbearing age) have fallen. In the 1870s, around five children were born per woman, but this declined to below two in the 1930s. Many people delayed getting married or having children during the Second World War, but after the war there was a baby boom. This led to the total fertility rate peaking at 2.94 in 1964. By 1995 it had fallen to 1.77. According to Social Trends 2006, it fell further to 1.63 in 2001 before returning to 1.77 in 2004.

In part, the decline in fertility is a consequence of women having children later in life. According to *Social*

Trends 2006, in 1971 the average age of mothers at first birth was 23.7 but by 2004 it had risen considerably to 27.1. The average age for all births also rose, from 26.6 in 1971 to 28.9 in 2004. The later women leave it before they have their first child, the fewer fertile years they have remaining, making it likely that they will have fewer children.

Morgan (2003) sees the decline in fertility as part of the general decline in family life. She links it to the rise in cohabitation, noting that women who are cohabiting rather than married are more likely to have only one child. She points out that the birth rate would be even lower and the average age at birth even higher were it not for a rise in the number of pregnancies amongst unmarried teenage girls.

However, from another point of view there is nothing surprising about a decline in the birth rate and it does not necessarily indicate a decline in family life. According to a number of geographers (see Waugh, 2000), the decline can be seen as a part of a demographic transition which takes place in all developed societies. According to this model, the birth and fertility rates fall for the following reasons:

1. Access to contraception, sterilization and abortion make family planning easier.
2. An increased desire for material goods coupled with an increasing cost of raising children creates incentives for smaller families.
3. The emancipation of women, and their consequent greater participation in paid work, leads to women combining careers with motherhood. This encourages women to have fewer children and to delay childbirth until their careers are established.
4. A decline in the death rate for young children, as a result of improvements in hygiene and medical care, means that there is less pressure to have many children in case one or more of them dies before reaching adulthood.

Eventually these changes can lead to a situation where, without immigration, the population declines since there are more deaths than births. If the decline in births and fertility is seen as an inevitable consequence of social change, it does not necessarily indicate a declining commitment to family life. Indeed, some theorists have argued that as fewer children are born, the family simply becomes more child-centred. More time and energy are devoted to the smaller number of children in each family.

Single-person households

An alternative to marriage is to live on one's own. Many single-person households may be formed as a result of divorce, separation, the break-up of a partnership involving cohabitation, or the death of a partner. However, others may result from a deliberate choice to live alone.

There is statistical evidence that single-person households are becoming more common. According to government statistics, in 1971 6 per cent of people lived alone in Great Britain, but by 2005 this had doubled to 12 per cent. Over the same period the proportion of one-person households rose from 18 per cent to 29 per cent. In part this increase is due to the ageing of the population, but it is also a result of an increase in the proportion of the young living alone.

According to *Social Trends 2006*, there was a doubling in the proportion of young people aged 25 to 44, and men aged 45 to 64, living alone between 1986/7 and 2005/6. Richard Berthoud (2000) used data from the General Household Survey to show that the proportion of people in their twenties who lived alone increased from 3 per cent in 1973 to 9 per cent in 1996.

Jon Bernardes (1997) believes there are strong social pressures discouraging people from remaining single because society portrays marriage as the ideal state. He says, 'Predominant ideologies emphasize the "normality" of forming intimate partnerships and the "abnormality" of remaining single for too long.' However, despite Bernardes's claims, the increasing frequency of single-person households among those below retirement age does suggest there is greater acceptance of a single status as an alternative to marriage or cohabitation.

Jennifer Somerville (2000) certainly sees the rise in single-person households as a significant trend. She argues there has been a particularly large rise in the percentage of young men who live alone, both because of later marriage and increased divorce.

John Macionis and Ken Plummer (1997) claim that among women aged 20 to 24 in the USA the proportion who were single (although not necessarily living alone) increased from 28 per cent in 1960 to 67 per cent in 1994. They comment: 'Underlying this trend is women's greater participation in the labour force: women who are economically secure view a husband as a matter of choice rather than a financial necessity.'

Fran Wasoff, Lynn Jamieson and Adam Smith (2005), however, analysed data from the British Household Panel Survey between 1991 and 2002 to discover how the situation of people living alone changes over time. They found that only 7 per cent remained living alone throughout the whole period. They therefore argue: 'This suggests that transition between solo living and living with others is commonplace and that the boundaries between solo living and family living are frequently crossed' (Wasoff *et al.*, 2005, p. 213).

Furthermore, Wasoff *et al.* used data from the Scottish Household Survey to show that most people living on their own retain frequent contacts with other family members. For example, 59 per cent had been to visit relatives in the last fortnight (compared to 68 per cent of those who did not live alone). For most young people, solo living is a temporary phase which often ends with cohabitation or marriage, and during solo living most people retain family contacts.

Marital breakdown

The second type of threat to contemporary marriage and family life is the apparent rise in marital breakdowns. The usual way of estimating the number of such breakdowns is through an examination of the divorce statistics, but these statistics do not, on their own, provide a valid measure of marital breakdown.

Marital breakdown can be divided into three main categories:

1 **Divorce**, which refers to the legal termination of a marriage.
2 **Separation**, which refers to the physical separation of the spouses: they no longer share the same dwelling.
3 So-called **empty-shell marriages**, where the spouses live together, remain legally married, but their marriage exists in name only.

These three categories must be considered in any assessment of the rate of marital breakdown.

Divorce statistics

Despite minor fluctuations, there was a steady rise in divorce rates in modern industrial societies throughout the twentieth century.

In 1911, 859 petitions for divorce were filed in England and Wales, of which some three-quarters were granted. The number of divorces gradually increased in the first half of the twentieth century, but was still relatively low during the 1950s at less than 40,000 a year. However, the numbers doubled between 1961 and 1969 and doubled again by 1992. The number of divorces peaked in 1993 at 180,000 before dropping a little to 155,000 in 2000. There was an increase to 167,100 in 2004 (*Social Trends 2006*), though the number declined to 153,399 the following year (National Statistics News Release, September 2006).

Figure 8.1 (see p. 502) shows trends in divorce between 1950 and 2003 and illustrates the closing gap between the number of first marriages and the number of divorces.

The proportion of marriages that are remarriages has also been rising. For example, government statistics show that 15 per cent of all marriages in the UK in 1961 were remarriages for one or both partners; by 2005 this figure had risen to approximately 40 per cent.

Whichever way the figures are presented, the increase in divorce is dramatic. This rise is not confined to Britain. The USA has an even higher rate than Britain, and nearly all industrial societies have experienced an increase in the divorce rate over the past few decades.

Separation statistics

Reliable figures for separation are unobtainable. In Britain some indication is provided by data from the 2001 census, which suggest that around 2 per cent of people are separated and living alone. The number of judicial separations increased in the 1960s by about 65 per cent according to Chester (1985), but this did not necessarily mean an increase in separations, since the number of unrecorded separations is unknown. Today few separations are officially recorded so there are no official statistics which give a reliable indication of long-term trends in separation.

Empty-shell marriages

Estimates of the extent of empty-shell marriages can only be based on guesswork. Even where data exist, the concept is difficult to **operationalize** (that is, put into a measurable form). For example, if a couple express a high level of dissatisfaction with their relationship, should this be termed an empty-shell marriage?

Historical evidence gives the impression that empty-shell marriages are more likely to end in separation and divorce today than in the past. William J. Goode argues that in nineteenth-century America:

> *People took for granted that spouses who no longer loved one another and who found life together distasteful should at least live together in public amity for the sake of their children and of their standing in the community.*
> Goode, 1971

Even though an increasing number of empty-shell marriages may end in separation and divorce today, this does not necessarily mean that the proportion of such marriages, in relation to the total number of marriages, is decreasing.

In view of the problems involved in measuring marital breakdown it is impossible to be completely confident about overall rates of breakdown. However, levels of divorce are now so high that it is probably true that more marriages break down today than they did several decades ago.

Explanations for marital breakdowns

In *When Marriage Ends* (1976), Nicky Hart argued that any explanation of marital breakdown must consider the following factors:

1 Those which affect the value attached to marriage
2 Those which affect the degree of conflict between the spouses
3 Those which affect the opportunities for individuals to escape from marriage

We will first consider these factors from a functionalist perspective. From this viewpoint, behaviour is largely a response to shared norms and values. It therefore follows that a change in the rate of marital breakdown is to some degree a reflection of changing norms and values in general, and, in particular, those associated with marriage and divorce.

The value of marriage

Functionalists such as Talcott Parsons and Ronald Fletcher argue that the rise in marital breakdown stems largely from the fact that marriage is increasingly valued. People expect and demand more from marriage and consequently are more likely to end a relationship which may have been acceptable in the past. Thus Fletcher (1966) argues, 'a relatively high divorce rate may be indicative not of lower but of higher standards of marriage in society'.

The high rate of remarriage apparently lends support to Parsons's and Fletcher's arguments. Thus, paradoxically, the higher value placed on marriage may result in increased marital breakdown.

Research suggests that people do still attach a high value to marriage. From their analysis of the British Social Attitudes Survey, Barlow *et al.* (2001) found that most people do regard marriage as more than 'just a piece of paper'. However, they also regard cohabitation as an acceptable alternative (see p. 503 for further details). Thus, Barlow *et al.* found no evidence that people attach a higher value to marriage than they used to. Other explanations therefore seem more plausible.

Hart (1976) argues that the second set of factors that must be considered in an explanation of marital breakdown are those which affect the degree of conflict between the spouses.

From a functionalist perspective it can be argued that the adaptation of the family to the requirements of the economic system has placed a strain on the marital relationship. It has led to the relative isolation of the nuclear family from the wider kinship network. William J. Goode (1971) argues that, as a result, the family 'carries a heavier emotional burden when it exists independently than when it is a small unit within a larger kin fabric. As a consequence, this unit is relatively fragile.'

Edmund Leach (1967) makes a similar point. He suggests the nuclear family suffers from an emotional overload, which increases the level of conflict between its members.

In industrial society the family specializes in fewer functions. It can be argued that, as a result, there are fewer bonds to unite its members. The economic bond, for example, is considerably weakened when the family ceases to be a unit of production.

N. Dennis (1975) suggests that the specialization of function which characterizes the modern family will lead to increased marital breakdown. Dennis argues that this can place a strain on the strength of the bond between husband and wife. Put simply, when love goes, there is nothing much left to hold the couple together.

Similar points have been made by sociologists who would not regard themselves as functionalists. Graham Allan and Graham Crow (2001) believe 'marriage is less embedded within the economic system' than it used to be. There are fewer family-owned businesses and, most importantly, husbands and wives now usually have independent sources of income from paid employment. Since fewer people now rely as much as they used to on membership of the family to maintain their income, they are less willing to accept conflict with their spouse and more willing to contemplate divorce. Allan and Crow (2001) say, 'incompatibilities which were tolerated are now seen as intolerable; and the absence of love, once seen as unfortunate but bearable, is now taken as indicative of the irretrievable breakdown of marriage'.

These changes particularly affect the willingness of married women to contemplate divorce. It is increasingly likely that married women will have an independent source of income. Official statistics seem to support the view that it is largely wives' dissatisfaction with marriage that accounts for the rising divorce rate. In 2005, 69 per cent of divorces were granted to wives, and in over half of these cases the husband's behaviour was the reason for the divorce (National Statistics News Release, September 2006). This was a dramatic change in comparison with 1946, when wives accounted for 37 per cent of petitions for divorce and husbands for 63 per cent.

Modernity, freedom and choice

Colin Gibson (1994) combines elements of the previous two arguments in claiming that the development of modernity has increased the likelihood of conflict between spouses. The way modernity has developed puts increasing emphasis upon the desirability of individual achievement. Gibson argues that people now live in an 'enterprise and free-market culture of individualism in which the licence of choice dominates'. He adds: 'A higher divorce rate may be indicative of modern couples generally anticipating a superior standard of personal marital satisfaction than was expected by their grandparents.'

People increasingly expect to get most of their personal satisfaction from their home life, and 'television programmes reinforce the feeling that togetherness is the consummate life style'. However, the emphasis on togetherness is somewhat undermined by 'the Thatcherite manifesto of unfettered self-seeking interest', so that conflict between spouses becomes more likely if self-fulfilment is not delivered by the marriage.

Individualistic modernity and the ideology of the market emphasize consumer choice, and, if fulfilment is not forthcoming through your first choice of marriage partner, then you are more likely to leave and try an alternative in the hope of greater satisfaction. In the past it was difficult for women in particular to escape from unsatisfactory marriages, but with greater independence – resulting from paid employment and other sources – this is no longer the case. Gibson says, 'Greater freedom to judge, choose and change their mind has encouraged women to become more confident and assertive about what they expect from a marriage.' They increasingly exercise that freedom by leaving marriages that fail to live up to what they expect.

A similar view was supported by Graham Allan and Graham Crow (2001). They argue that marriage is increasingly viewed as a 'relationship rather than a contract'. By getting married, people do not see themselves as entering a binding, lifelong contract; rather, they are hoping to establish a personally satisfying relationship: 'Love, personal commitment and intrinsic satisfaction are now seen as the cornerstones of marriage. The absence of these emotions and feelings is itself justification for ending the relationship.'

Furthermore, as the divorce rate rises, divorce is 'normalized' and 'the emergent definition of marriage as centrally concerned with personal satisfaction and fulfilment is bolstered further'.

(For a general discussion of the relationship between modernity and changes in the family, see pp. 512–14.)

The ease of divorce

So far we have considered the factors which affect the value attached to marriage and those which affect the degree of conflict between spouses. The third set of factors that Hart considers essential to an explanation of marital breakdown are those which affect the opportunities for individuals to escape from marriage. This view is backed up by the British and European Social Attitudes Survey carried out in 1997 (Jowell *et al.*, 1998). It found that 82 per cent of their sample disagreed with the view that 'Even if there are no children a married couple should stay together even if they don't get along'.

If, as the functionalists argue, behaviour is directed by norms and values, a change in the norms and values associated with divorce would be expected. It is generally agreed that the stigma attached to divorce has been considerably reduced. This, in itself, will make divorce easier.

Colin Gibson (1994) believes secularization has weakened the degree to which religious beliefs can bind a couple together and make divorce less likely (see pp. 429–45 for a discussion of secularization). He says, 'Secularization has also witnessed the fading of the evangelical bond of rigid morality which intertwined the cultural fabric of conformist social mores and habits and the declared public conscience.'

Along with a decline in religious beliefs, there has also been a decline in any set of shared values that might operate to stabilize marriage. He describes the change in the following way:

> *Within our pluralistic society it has become increasingly difficult to sustain an identifiable common culture containing generally held values, aspirations and symbols. George Formby and his ukulele had a cultural identity embracing men and women, rich and poor, young and old; the vocal form of Madonna does not offer the same symbolic universality.* Gibson, 1994

In the absence of any central, shared beliefs in society, anything goes, and there is little or no stigma attached to divorce.

Divorce legislation

The changing attitudes towards divorce have been institutionalized by various changes in the law which have made it much easier to obtain a divorce. In Britain before 1857 a private Act of Parliament was required to obtain a divorce. This was an expensive procedure beyond the means of all but the most wealthy.

Since 1857 the costs of obtaining a divorce have been reduced and the grounds for divorce have been widened. Divorce legislation was influenced by the idea of **matrimonial offence**, the notion that one or both spouses had wronged the other. This was the idea behind the Matrimonial Causes Act of 1857, which largely limited grounds for divorce to adultery. Although divorce legislation in 1950 widened the grounds to include cruelty and desertion, it was still based on the same principle.

The Divorce Reform Act, which came into force in 1971, no longer emphasized the idea of matrimonial offence and so avoided the need for 'guilty parties'. It defined the grounds for divorce as 'the irretrievable breakdown of the marriage'. This made divorce considerably easier and accounts in part for the dramatic rise in the number of divorces in 1971 (see Figure 8.1, p. 502).

New legislation relating to divorce was introduced at the end of 1984. This reduced the period a couple needed to be married before they could petition for divorce from three years to one year. It also altered the basis on which financial settlements were determined by the courts. From 1984 the conduct of the partners became something the courts could take into account. If the misbehaviour of one partner was responsible for the divorce, they could be awarded less than would otherwise have been expected. The intention behind this seemed to be to counteract what some saw as the anti-male bias in maintenance payments from men to their ex-wives.

The Family Law Act of 1996 introduced a number of new measures. No longer did it have to be demonstrated that one or both partners were at fault in order to prove that the marriage had broken down. Instead, the partners simply had to assert the marriage had broken down and undergo a 'period of reflection' to consider whether a reconciliation was possible. Normally this period was one year, but for those with children under 16, or where one spouse asked for more time, the period was eighteen months.

The Act also encouraged greater use of mediation, rather than relying on solicitors, to resolve issues such as the division of money and arrangements for children. However, after trials, most of these measures were delayed indefinitely and have not been implemented. One part of the Act that was introduced (in 1997) allowed a spouse who had been the victim of violence from their husband or wife to obtain a non-molestation order.

Despite a reduction in costs, divorce was still an expensive process during the first half of the twentieth century. It was beyond the means of many of the less wealthy. This was partly changed by the Legal Aid and Advice Act of 1949, which provided free legal advice and paid solicitors' fees for those who could not afford them.

The economics of divorce were further eased by the extension of welfare provisions, particularly for single parents with dependent children. The Child Support, Pensions and Social Security Act of 2000 (which was implemented in 2002) provided for absent parents to contribute a fixed proportion of their take-home pay towards maintenance costs. This varied from 15 per cent for one child to 25 per cent for three children. Although many consider these provisions far from generous, they do provide single-parent families with the means to exist. (For a discussion of changes relating to parental responsibilities for children after divorce, see pp. 516–17.)

Conclusion

A decline in the rate of marriage, increasing cohabitation outside marriage, the rising number of single-parent families and single-person homes, and the apparent increase in marital breakdown all seem to suggest the decline of marriage as an institution in modern Britain. Yet all of these changes are open to different interpretations, and none – at least on its own – seems likely to make marriage obsolete in the near future.

It is easy to exaggerate the extent to which there has been a retreat from marriage. Robert Chester (1985) says, 'On the evidence, most people will continue not only to spend most of their lives in a family environment, but also to place a high value on it.'

The socialist feminist sociologists Pamela Abbott and Claire Wallace (1992) are also rather sceptical of the belief that the family and marriage are in danger of falling apart. They suggest this view has been encouraged by the New Right (right-wing politicians and thinkers whose views and policies are discussed on pp. 509–10). To Abbott and Wallace, such people have succeeded in setting the agenda of public debate about the family by trying to portray it as under serious threat from moral decay in society as a whole, and they have carefully interpreted the evidence to support their case. Abbot and Wallace say:

> *We are told how many marriages end in divorce, how many children live in single-parent families and so on. Yet we can also look at these statistics another way – to show the stability of the family. Six out of ten couples who get*

married in the 1990s, according to present trends, will stay together until one of them dies. Seven out of eight children are born to parents living together, three-quarters of whom are legally married. Only one in five children will experience parental divorce by the time he or she is 16; that is, four out of five children born to a married couple will be brought up by them in an intact family. In 1985, 78 per cent of British children under 16 were living with both natural parents who were legally married. Abbott and Wallace, 1992

Abbott and Wallace recognize the increasing diversity of family forms, but see the alleged decline of the family and marriage as having been exaggerated for political ends.

Jennifer Somerville (2000) argues that there have been major changes in marriage and family life, but she too thinks they can be exaggerated. Lone parenthood, single-person households, increased cohabitation and the normalization of pre-marital sex are all aspects of contemporary society. However, the vast majority of people in Britain still get married, most marriages still continue until one spouse dies, most people still live in households headed by a married couple, and extended kinship networks remain strong in most people's lives. Somerville therefore argues:

diversification of family forms and relationships ... must be seen in the context of a commitment by the vast majority of the population to a framework of belief in the value of family life and behaviour which seeks to approximate to that ideal. Somerville, 2000

The family, politics and social policy

Despite the traditional British belief that politicians should not interfere in the family, state policies have always had an impact on family life. Taxation, welfare, housing and education policies all influence the way in which people organize their domestic life. The policies adopted can encourage people to live in certain types of household and discourage them from living in other types. Furthermore, in recent decades the family has come to be seen as a legitimate and important subject of public debate.

Bias towards conventional families

Feminists and other radical critics of government policies have sometimes seen them as biased. They have argued that they tend to favour the traditional nuclear family in which there are two parents: a male breadwinner and a wife who stays at home when there are young children. Allan (1985) argues: 'Much state provision ... is based upon an implicit ideology of the "normal" family which through its incorporation into standard practice discourages alternative forms of domestic organization from developing.'

To Allan, these policies encourage 'the standard form of gender and generational relations within families'. In other words, they assume that one family member will put primary emphasis during their life on childcare rather than work; that families will usually take care of their elderly and sick; and that wives are economically dependent on their husbands.

Daphne Johnson (1982) argues that schools are organized in such a way that it is difficult for single-parent families and dual-worker families to combine work with domestic responsibilities. School hours and holidays mean that families with children find it difficult for the adult members to combine the requirements of employers with their domestic responsibilities.

Roy Parker (1982) claims that state assistance (of a practical rather than financial nature) tends not to be given to the elderly and sick if they live with relatives. It is assumed that the family will care for them. In both the care of the elderly and infirm and the care of children, this generally means wives will be expected to take up these domestic responsibilities, or at least to work only part-time.

It can be argued that, in recent years, Parker's argument has become increasingly valid, at least in terms of its application to elderly people. The state has encouraged families to take responsibility for their elderly members, either in practical or financial terms. Furthermore, the elderly are increasingly required to use their savings to pay for their care in old age rather than receiving free care from the state.

The situation in relation to childcare is less clear-cut. The government now guarantees two and a half hours of approved childcare per weekday for all 3- and 4-year-olds. However, it is not possible to offset the costs of childcare against earnings to reduce the size of tax bills. This reduces the incentive for mothers (or the primary carer) to seek paid employment, since any childcare costs have to be paid out of income from employment which is liable to taxation.

The **Working Tax Credit** and **Child Tax Credit** (introduced in April 2003) do, however, allow help with childcare, but the Working Tax Credit only applies to low income families where both partners are in paid employment. This discourages women in these families from staying at home to look after their children.

In public housing policy the formal emphasis is usually upon making children's needs a priority. However, Lorraine Fox Harding (1996) believes that in practice married couples with children tend to be favoured over single parents with children. Single parents are usually provided with the least desirable housing. Furthermore, 'Most dwellings are constructed for the nuclear family and are planned and designed by men. Units are privatized and self-contained. The centrality of family housing reinforces dominant notions of family and non-family households.' Few council or other public houses have been built to accommodate groups larger than conventional nuclear families.

Fox Harding believes regulations relating to maternity leave and pay reinforce traditional gender roles. In Britain, unlike some other European countries, fathers have very limited rights to leave from work on the birth of a child, compared with women. Furthermore, 'Benefits for pregnancy and the period after childbirth are inadequate, reflecting the assumption that women have the support of a male partner.'

In 1993 the **Child Support Agency** was established. It oversees the payment of maintenance by 'absent' parents to the parents responsible for looking after the children. Its work therefore covers divorced, separated and never-married couples who live apart.

The agency was set up to make sure that fathers in particular would find it more difficult to escape financial responsibility for their children. In this respect it can be seen as supporting the traditional family by imposing financial costs on those who do not live in one. (In 2006 it was announced that the Child Support Agency would be replaced in 2008 by a Child Maintenance and Support Commission which would have similar functions.)

The Child Support Agency has been highly controversial and highly criticized. For example, many argue that its main aim is not to help children but rather to save the Treasury money, since maintenance payments usually reduce the benefits paid to single mothers. Indeed, in its first year the agency was set a target of saving £530 million of taxpayers' money. However, it was clear that Conservative ministers supported the agency not just to save money, but also because they saw it as helping to uphold moral values relating to parental responsibility. As we will see, the Labour government elected in 1997 in some ways continued to support such policies on similar grounds.

As Fox Harding notes, cuts in welfare provision in the 1980s and 1990s had the effect of extending family responsibilities beyond the immediate, nuclear family. This was in contrast to earlier decades of the twentieth century, when there was a tendency for the state to take over responsibilities that had previously been left to families. Fox Harding gives the example of care of the elderly and care of offspring aged 18–25. In both cases cuts in benefits have put the onus on families to help, even though they have not been made legally responsible for doing so. Fox Harding also sees the increased emphasis on absent parents supporting their offspring as an example of the state's attempt to extend familial responsibilities.

Policies which do not support conventional families

Not all government policies can be seen as supporting conventional families or traditional gender roles within them. For example, there have been some measures which might be seen as undermining traditional male dominance within families. Fox Harding points out that in 1991 the House of Lords ruled that men were no longer exempt from being charged with raping their wives. Traditional patriarchal authority relations within families have been further undermined by increasing intolerance of men using violence to discipline their wives or children.

The gradual liberalization of divorce laws shows a willingness to accept that marriage does not guarantee the long-term stability of a family. Some legal concessions have been made to recognize the rights of cohabitants who are not married. Fox Harding says, 'there are some rights which have been extended to cohabitees, such as succession to tenancies and inheritance in certain circumstances, and the right to have orders made to restrain violence'. Cohabiting gay or lesbian couples have few legal rights relating specifically to such relationships (although from 2005 they were able to register civil partnerships).

Brenda Almond (2006) believes that recent policies undermine traditional family structures. She claims that tax legislation discriminates against families where there is one breadwinner. They cannot use their partner's tax allowances and two-earner families tend, therefore, to pay less tax than one-earner families.

Almond believes that the liberalization of divorce laws undermines the idea of marriage as a lifelong commitment, and that the recognition of civil partnerships for gay and lesbian couples sends signals to people that conventional families are no longer seen as preferable to other living arrangements.

Pamela Abbott and Claire Wallace – the family and the New Right

Pamela Abbott and Claire Wallace (1992) examined the view of the family and social policy put forward by the New Right (sometimes called market liberals or neoliberals) in Britain and the USA in the 1980s. Instead of arguing that government policy was biased in favour of the conventional family, the New Right argued that government policy was undermining it and policies had to be changed.

In Britain, New Right thinking was promoted by individual journalists and academics – for example, Paul Johnson and Roger Scruton – and by 'think-tanks' such as the Centre for Policy Studies and the Adam Smith Institute.

In the USA a variety of pressure groups campaigned to reassert traditional morality and family relationships. Abbott and Wallace describe them as a 'Pro-Family' movement and say it 'developed out of an alliance of political, religious, anti-feminist and pro-life anti-abortion groups'.

In Britain, the 'Pro-Family' movement was not as strong, but the anti-abortion movement and individuals like Victoria Gillick (who campaigned to stop doctors prescribing contraceptives to girls under 16 without parental consent) and organizations like Families Need Fathers (which is opposed to divorce) supported similar causes to their American counterparts.

Abbott and Wallace argue that the New Right advocated 'liberal economic policies with support for conservative social moral values'. Members of the New Right saw the family as being under threat from permissiveness, social change and government policies, and this in turn threatened the stability of society. To them, the family operates properly when it remains stable and the wife is responsible for socializing children so that they conform to society's norms and values. The husband, as principal breadwinner, is disciplined by the need to provide for his family.

The New Right saw many signs of the family becoming unable to carry out its proper role. These included 'working mothers (who by taking paid work fail to put the needs of their children first), increased divorce rates, higher numbers of single-parent families and open homosexuality'. Members of the New Right argued that such changes played a major role in causing social problems such as crime, delinquency and drug abuse.

The New Right and politics

In trying to influence political debate and the actions of governments, the New Right tried to change what it saw as harmful social policies.

Abbot and Wallace argue that the New Right attacked welfare systems for encouraging deviant lifestyles and family forms. For example, welfare payments allowed mothers to bring up their children in single-parent families, taxation policies discriminated against married couples, divorce laws made it easier to end marriage, and abortion laws and the relaxation of laws against homosexuality undermined traditional morality.

Indeed, from this point of view, government policy further undermined the family by taking from conventional families and giving to deviant households. Welfare payments to single mothers drove up taxation to the point where wives with young children were forced to take paid employment to make ends meet. As a result, even those who wished to live in conventional nuclear families, with the mother at home, were unable to do so, and more children were socialized in unsatisfactory ways.

The New Right was in a position to influence social policy because of the election of political leaders sympathetic to its views. These included Ronald Reagan, president of the USA from 1980 to 1988, and Margaret Thatcher, who was prime minister of Britain throughout the 1980s.

In a speech in May 1988, Thatcher said:

> *The family is the building block of society. It's a nursery, a school, a hospital, a leisure place, a place of refuge and a place of rest. It encompasses the whole of society. It fashions beliefs. It's the preparation for the rest of our life and women run it.* Quoted in Abbott and Wallace, 1992

The New Right and policies

On the surface, it would appear that the New Right had a major impact on government policy on both sides of the Atlantic. Abbott and Wallace do identify some policies that were influenced by its ideas. For example, the 1988 budget changed taxation so that cohabiting couples could no longer claim more in tax allowances than a married couple. It also prevented cohabiting couples from claiming two lots of income tax relief on a shared mortgage when a married couple could only claim one.

However, in many other ways the New Right failed to achieve the changes it wanted. In terms of moral policies, divorce was actually made easier in 1984, and further legislation gave 'illegitimate' children the same rights as those born within marriage.

Conservative governments did not introduce any tax or benefits policies to encourage mothers to stay at home with young children and, to Abbot and Wallace, many Thatcherite policies actually undermined family life. Such policies included: the freezing of child benefit, economic policies which forced up unemployment, the emphasis on home ownership and opposition to the provision of council housing, and cuts in education spending and the real levels of student grants. All of these policies hit the finances of families, with the result that, far from encouraging self-reliance, 'Many families and individuals have had their ability to care for themselves reduced, not increased.'

To Abbott and Wallace, the main purpose of government policies under Thatcher was to reduce public spending; maintaining the traditional family was very much a secondary consideration. They conclude:

> *The welfare and economic policies advocated by the New Right – in so far as they have been implemented by the Thatcher and Reagan administrations – have been more concerned with reasserting the rights of middle-class men and maintaining capitalism than they have been with a genuine concern for men, women and children and the quality of their lives.* Abbott and Wallace, 1992

The family under John Major's government

Margaret Thatcher left office in 1990 and was replaced as prime minister by John Major. Major remained in office until the Labour Party displaced the Conservatives in government in the election of 1997.

Ruth Lister (1996) reviewed the approach to the family adopted by John Major. She notes that Major did take an interest in the family as an issue. He gave specific responsibility for family matters to a cabinet member (Virginia Bottomley). He also ended the erosion in the value of child benefit in an apparent attempt to give extra support to families with children. The Child Support Agency, which tried to get absent fathers to pay maintenance costs for their children, was also launched during Major's period in office.

A White Paper concerned with adoption came down strongly in favour of giving priority to married couples, and against allowing adoption for gay and lesbian couples. Many of Major's cabinet ministers made strong attacks upon single parents, particularly at the 1993 Conservative Party conference. Lister describes this as an 'orgy of lone-parent bashing'. John Major himself launched a 'Back to Basics' campaign at the same conference, which included an emphasis on the virtues of conventional family life.

However, the Back to Basics campaign floundered after a number of embarrassing revelations about the personal lives of several Conservative MPs and ministers. According to Lister, from 1994 John Major encouraged his cabinet colleagues to tone down their rhetoric criticizing single parents.

In general, Major's period in office saw a considerable concern about families, but little change in government policies. Lister therefore concludes that the Major government:

> *is more likely to be remembered for the 'moral panic' about the breakdown of the 'family' and for the backlash against lone-parent families that it helped to unleash, together with the legacy it inherited in the form of the Child Support Act, than for any distinctive policies of its own directed towards families and women.* Lister, 1996

Carol Smart and Bren Neale – childcare and divorce

Carol Smart and Bren Neale (1999) examined one particular area of family policy – laws relating to childcare after divorce – during the era of Margaret Thatcher and John Major's administrations. They detected a significant shift in the emphasis in policies during this period.

In the 1960s and 1970s, most legislation involved **liberalizing** the law in response to public demand for more freedom to choose how they organized their family life. People were becoming increasingly unwilling to accept that their own happiness should be restricted by laws which reinforced conventional morality and made it difficult for them to divorce.

However, by the 1980s, governments were changing the emphasis towards trying to combat some of the negative effects they believed stemmed from the liberal legislation. In particular, they were concerned about the effects of divorce on children and felt it was important to ensure that parents honoured their responsibilities to children after divorce. Smart and Neale say:

> *There has been a notable shift from a 'permissive' approach of the late 1960s, which basically led to governments responding to popular pressure concerning the private sphere and personal morality, towards social engineering designed to mitigate the perceived harms generated by the previous permissiveness.* Smart and Neale, 1999

This change of emphasis was evident in a number of Acts of Parliament: the Children's Act (1989), the Child Support Act (1991) and the Family Law Act (1996). Earlier divorce legislation had encouraged the idea of the 'clean break' between ex-spouses on divorce, so that they could start a new life and put the problems of their dissolved marriage behind them. This new legislation emphasized the priority that should be given to the needs of children and was based upon the principle that both biological parents should share responsibility for their offspring.

Divorce was regarded as a social problem in this legislation because it could disadvantage the children. The Children's Act (1989) stopped the practice of awarding custody of children to one or other parent and introduced 'an automatic presumption that mothers and fathers simply retained all the parental responsibility they enjoyed during marriage beyond legal divorce'. While the courts could decide on where children lived and how much access the non-resident parent could have, joint responsibility was assumed and parents were encouraged to make their own arrangements where possible.

Smart and Neale argue that this legislation was intended to reinforce parental aspects of traditional family responsibilities, while acknowledging it would be impossible to force spouses to stay together against their will. The implicit aims were to:

- *prioritize first families;*
- *discourage clean breaks on divorce;*
- *prioritize parenthood over spousal obligations;*
- *prioritize biological parentage and descent;*
- *challenge the popular understanding of divorce as a solution to private problems;*
- *identify divorce as a social problem.*

In all these ways the policy was intended to emphasize moral values associated with traditional families without actively trying to prevent the formation of the types of family diversity which are the result of divorce.

In terms of this analysis, then, aspects of the conventional family were supported by legislation in this period, albeit in a form which recognized the existence of diversity. Smart and Neale do not examine how far these principles continued to be important after the Labour government took office in 1997. This issue will be examined next.

The family and New Labour

Family values

Although support for 'family values' has traditionally been associated with more right-wing thinkers and political parties, it has begun to exercise some influence over the British Labour Party.

Elizabeth Silva and Carol Smart (1999) claim the 'political mantra on the family is not peculiar to Conservative governments but has also become a theme of New Labour in Britain'. They quote Tony Blair's 1997 conference speech in which he said: 'We cannot say we want a strong and secure society when we ignore its very foundations: family life. This is not about preaching to individuals about their private lives. It is addressing a huge social problem.' He went on to cite teenage pregnancies, families unable to care for their elderly members, poor parental role models, truancy, educational underachievement and even unhappiness as among the social problems which could stem from the failure to achieve successful family life. Blair pledged that the government would examine every area of government policy to see how it could strengthen family life.

Silva and Smart suggest that Blair was really talking about a specific type of family life. They say, 'Strong families are, of course, seen as conjugal, heterosexual parents with an employed male breadwinner. Lone mothers and gay couples do not, by definition, constitute strong families in this rhetoric.' However, they believe that Blair and the Labour government recognized that social change had occurred and that it was not possible to follow policies that pretended that most people continued to live in conventional families.

Supporting Families

This concern with families led to the Labour government setting up a committee, chaired by the home secretary Jack Straw, to produce a consultation paper, or Green Paper. This was published in 1998 under the title *Supporting Families*. The Green Paper suggested a whole range of measures to provide 'better services and support for parents', such as a National Family and Parenting Institute to coordinate and publicize services available to families. It suggested a greater role for health visitors in helping out families. It also made proposals which would help people to balance the requirements of work and their home life. These included longer maternity leave, a right to three months' unpaid leave for both parents, and a right to time off (from employment) for family reasons.

The paper included measures designed to strengthen marriage and to reduce the number of marriage breakdowns. These included giving registrars a greater role in advising married couples, and improvements to the information couples received before marriage. It also suggested making pre-nuptial agreements (for example, about who gets what in the event of divorce) legally binding.

The paper suggested it was necessary to take measures to cut teenage pregnancies because these were associated with wider social problems. With regard to single parents, the Green Paper heralded the introduction of a **New Deal**. This involved ensuring that single parents received personal help and advice to assist them in returning to paid employment if they wished to do so. For low income families a **Working Families Tax Credit** was to be introduced which allowed them to claim some tax relief against a proportion of the childcare costs they incurred by going to work.

Conclusion

In general the measures proposed and introduced by the New Labour government were based around strengthening conventional families. However, they certainly moved away from the idea that families should have a single earner and that women should stay at home to look after children. As described above, a number of measures were taken to help parents combine paid work with domestic responsibilities. The Green Paper said:

> *We also need to acknowledge just how much families have changed. Family structures have become more complicated, with many more children living with stepparents or in single-parent households. They may face extra difficulties and we have designed practical support with these parents in mind.* Supporting Families, 1998

The paper accepted that single parents and unmarried couples could sometimes raise children successfully, but none the less said that 'marriage is still the surest foundation for raising children and remains the choice of the people in Britain'. No mention was made of providing support for single people.

Alan Barlow, Simon Duncan and Grace James argue that New Labour 'proclaims moral tolerance. Nevertheless, it still firmly states that marriage is the ideal state and that living with two biological and preferably married parents is the best for children' (Barlow *et al.*, 2002, p. 116). They note, though, that there is a strong emphasis on paid work 'as a moral duty and not the unpaid caring that most lone mothers place first' (p. 114).

Although not condemning lone mothers, New Labour sees two parents as preferable because this makes it easier for one or both adults to do paid work and therefore avoid reliance upon benefits. Barlow *et al.* see New Labour as having done little to introduce policies to support alternatives to conventional family life. For example, they have not introduced new rights for people who cohabit.

Despite a toning down of the rhetoric criticizing unconventional families and non-family groups, the policies of New Labour continued to idealize stable, long-lasting marriage and nuclear families. Jennifer Somerville (2000) says that Tony Blair's government idealized the family as 'a working example of mutual interdependence, care and responsibility'. It also 'increased the expectations of parental responsibility with regard to financial support for children, children's conduct and educational achievement'. Aspects of New Labour thinking still reflect the family agenda originally pushed to the forefront of politics in Britain by the New Right.

However, at least in one area, the Labour government took steps to introduce legal protection for an alternative to conventional marriage. Not only did it introduce civil partnerships for gay and lesbian couples, but it also banned discrimination on the basis of sexuality, including in applications for adoption, meaning that gay and lesbian families gained an unprecedented degree of legal recognition.

Families, modernity and postmodernity

Much of this chapter has suggested that significant changes have taken place in family life in Europe and North America (as well as elsewhere) over the last few decades. Although some sociologists have stressed that it is important not to exaggerate the extent of the changes, all acknowledge that at least some changes have taken place.

A number of sociologists have related the changes to the concepts of modernity or postmodernity. They have seen them as part and parcel of changes in society as a whole. Although the sociologists examined in this section disagree about whether social changes should be seen as part of the development of modernity or as part of a postmodern stage in the development of society, there are some similarities in the sorts of changes they relate to the development of the family.

Anthony Giddens – *The Transformation of Intimacy*

In an influential book, the British sociologist Anthony Giddens argues that major changes have taken place in intimate relationships between people (particularly relationships between sexual partners). He relates these changes to the development of what he calls high modernity (his concept of high modernity is discussed on pp. 895–9).

Romantic love

Giddens (1992) argues that premodern relationships in Europe were largely based around 'economic circumstance'. People got married to particular people largely to provide an economic context in which to produce a family. For the peasantry, life was so hard it 'was unlikely to be conducive to sexual passion'. Married couples, according to research quoted by Giddens, rarely kissed or caressed. The aristocracy also married for reasons to do with reproduction and forming economic connections between families.

However, in the eighteenth century the idea of **romantic love** began to develop, first among the aristocracy. Romantic love involved idealizing the object of one's love and, for women in particular, telling stories to oneself about how one's life could become fulfilled through the relationship.

The idea of romantic love was closely connected to the emergence of the novel as a literary form – romantic novels played an important part in spreading the idea of romantic love. It was also related to the limitation of family size. This allowed sex, for women, to gradually become separated from an endless round of (at the time very dangerous) pregnancy and childbirth. Romantic love contains the idea that people will be attracted to one another and this attraction will lead to the partners being bound together.

In theory, romantic love should be egalitarian. The bond is based upon mutual attraction. In practice, however, it has tended to lead to the dominance of men. Giddens says, 'For women dreams of romantic love have all too often led to grim domestic subjection.' Sex is important in romantic love, but a successful sexual relationship is seen as stemming from the romantic attraction, and not the other way round. In the ideal of romantic love, a woman saves herself, preserves her virginity, until the perfect man comes along.

Plastic sexuality

Giddens argues that in the most recent phase of modernity the nature of intimate relationships has undergone profound changes. Virginity for women is no longer prized, and few women are virgins on their marriage day. **Plastic sexuality** has developed. With plastic sexuality, sex can be freed from its association with childbirth altogether. People have much greater choice over when, how often and with whom they engage in sex.

The development of plastic sexuality was obviously connected to the development of improved methods of contraception. To Giddens, however, it began to emerge before these technological developments and has more social than technical origins. In particular, as we will see, it was tied up with the development of a sense of the self that could be actively chosen.

Confluent love and the pure relationship

The emergence of plastic sexuality changes the nature of love. Romantic love is increasingly replaced by **confluent love**. Confluent love is 'active contingent love' which 'jars with the "forever", "one-and-only" qualities of the romantic love complex'.

In earlier eras divorce was difficult or impossible to obtain and it was difficult to engage openly in pre-marital relationships. Once people had married through romantic love they were usually stuck with one another however their relationship developed. Now people have much more choice. They are not compelled to stay together if the relationship is not working.

The ideal which people increasingly base relationships on is the **pure relationship**, rather than a marriage based on romantic passion. Pure relationships continue because people choose to stay in them. Giddens says: 'What holds the pure relationship together is the acceptance on the part of each partner, "until further notice", that each gains sufficient benefit from the relationship to make its continuance worthwhile.'

Love is based upon emotional intimacy and only develops 'to the degree to which each partner is prepared to reveal concerns and needs to the other and to be vulnerable to that other'. These concerns are constantly monitored by people to see if they are deriving sufficient satisfaction from the relationship to continue it. Marriage is increasingly an expression of such relationships once they are already established, rather than a way of achieving them.

However, pure relationships are not confined to marriage or indeed to heterosexual couples. In some cases and in some ways gay and lesbian relationships may come closer to pure relationships than heterosexual ones. Furthermore, pure relationships do not have to be based upon exclusivity if both partners agree that they will not limit their sexual relationships to one another.

In general, Giddens sees pure relationships as having the potential for creating more equal relationships between men and women. They have an openness and a mutual concern and respect which make it difficult for one partner to be dominant. However, that does not mean that Giddens has an entirely positive view of contemporary marriage and other intimate relationships – far from it. He documents a whole range of emotional, psychological and physical abuses that can occur within contemporary relationships. The pure relationship is more of an ideal than a relationship that has actually been achieved by most intimate couples. But Giddens does think there is a trend towards such relationships, because their development is intimately bound up with the development of modernity.

Modernity and self-identity

Giddens sees **institutional reflexivity** as a key, perhaps the key, characteristic of modernity. In premodern times institutions were largely governed by tradition. They carried on in certain ways because they had operated that way in the past. Modernity involves the increasing application of reason. Reason is used to work out how institutions can work better. Reflexivity describes the way in which people reflect upon the institutions that are part of the social world and try to change them for the better.

Increasingly, such reflexivity reaches into all areas of social life, including very personal areas. For example, publications such as the Kinsey Report (a survey of sexual behaviour among Americans) opened up sex to critical reflection. An increasing number of self-help books, magazine columns and so on are written to help people reflect upon and try to improve their sex lives. Giddens says, 'the rise of such researches signals, and contributes to, an accelerating reflexivity on the level of the ordinary, everyday sexual practices'.

Reflexivity extends into the creation of self-identity. People can increasingly choose who they want to be. They are no longer stuck with the roles into which they are born and confined by the dictates of tradition. Within the limits of the opportunities available to them, people can increasingly shape who they are and who they think themselves to be.

Giddens argues there is a 'reflexive project of the self' which 'is oriented only to control. It has no morality other than authenticity, a modern day version of the old maxim "to thine own self be true".' People want to discover who they really are, and trying different relationships can be an important part of this process. Seeking a pure relationship may, for example, allow an individual to try to decide whether they are truly homosexual, heterosexual or bisexual.

People have far more choice of lifestyle than in the past, and trying different ones may be part of creating a self-identity. Giddens says, 'Today, however, given the lapse of tradition, the question "Who shall I be?" is inextricably bound up with "How shall I live?"'

Conclusion

If Giddens's analysis is correct, then it certainly seems to explain the increasing rates of divorce and other relationship breakdowns and the greater pluralism of family forms. The continuing popularity of marriage could be seen as part of the quest for the pure relationship. Certainly, Giddens seems to be on strong ground in arguing that there is more sense of choice in personal relationships than in the past.

However, Giddens may underestimate the degree to which factors such as class and ethnicity continue to influence the form that relationships take. Furthermore, other sociologists, while agreeing that there is now more choice, see this as resulting from somewhat different processes from those discussed by Giddens. Some see the changes in a much more negative light than Giddens does.

Ulrich Beck and Elisabeth Beck-Gernsheim – *The Normal Chaos of Love*

Another influential interpretation of changes in relationships and family life was put forward by the German sociologists Ulrich Beck and Elisabeth Beck-Gernsheim (1995, first published in German in 1990). Beck and Beck-Gernsheim follow a similar line of argument to Giddens in claiming that changes in family life and relationships are being shaped by the development of modernity. They also follow Giddens in arguing that modernity is characterized by increasing individual choice, in contrast to an emphasis upon following tradition in premodern societies. However, they characterize this process as involving **individualization** rather than reflexivity, and see it as having rather different consequences from those outlined by Giddens.

Individualization

Individualization involves an extension of the areas of life in which individuals are expected to make their own decisions. Beck and Beck-Gernsheim say: 'The proportion of possibilities in life that do not involve decision making is diminishing and the proportion of biography open to decision making and individual initiative is increasing.' Like Giddens, they contrast this increasing choice with a premodern era in which choice was much more limited and tradition much more important in shaping social life.

Beck and Beck-Gernsheim trace the origins of the process of individualization back to a range of factors, including the influence of the Protestant ethic (see pp. 407–9), urbanization and secularization. Most important of all, though, was an increase in personal mobility, both social and geographical. As modern societies opened up, moving place and moving jobs became easier, and this presented individuals with more choices about how to run their lives.

In the second half of the twentieth century this process went on to a new stage in which there was a rapid increase in available choices. The reasons for this included the opening up of educational opportunities, the improvement in the living standards of the lower classes, which freed them from the daily grind of trying to survive in poverty, and improved labour market opportunities for women. This last change has led to new uncertainties in gender roles and has particularly affected intimate relationships.

Choice in families and relationships

If premodern societies gave people little choice about their roles in families and marriages, they did at least provide some stability and certainty. Beck and Beck-Gernsheim say that for individuals the 'severing of traditional ties means being freed of previous constraints and obligations. At the same time, however, the support and security offered by traditional society begin to disappear.' In the absence of such supports and security, individuals have to try to create personal relationships that will provide for their needs.

Beck and Beck-Gernsheim say the nuclear family seems to offer 'a sort of refuge in the chilly environment of our affluent, impersonal, uncertain society, stripped of its traditions and scarred by all kinds of risk. Love will become more important than ever and equally impossible.' Love is important because people believe they can express and fulfil their individuality through a loving relationship. Love offers the promise of an 'emotional base' and a 'security system', which are absent in the world outside. However, contemporary societies prevent the formation of such relationships.

Love in the context of successful family relationships has come to depend on individuals finding a successful formula. It can no longer be based upon norms and traditions, since these no longer exist in a form that is generally or even widely accepted. People try out a number of arrangements, such as cohabitation, marriage and divorce, in their search for love. In each relationship they have to work out solutions for how to order their relationships anew. Beck and Beck-Gernsheim describe the situation in the following way:

> *It is no longer possible to pronounce in some binding way what family, marriage, parenthood, sexuality or love mean, what they should or could be; rather these vary in substance, norms and morality from individual to individual and from relationship to relationship. The answers to the questions above must be worked out, negotiated, arranged and justified in all the details of how, what, why or why not, even if this might unleash the conflicts and devils that lie slumbering among the details and were assumed to be tamed ... Love is becoming a blank that lovers must fill in themselves.* Beck and Beck-Gernsheim, 1995

The causes of conflict

The amount of choice in itself causes the potential for conflict, but there are other factors that make it even more likely. Earlier periods of industrial modern societies were based upon relatively clear-cut gender roles involving a male breadwinner and a female carer and homemaker. Industrial work by men was founded upon the assumption of a wife who was carrying out housework and childcare tasks. With increased opportunities for women in education and employment, this has changed. Now, both men and women might seek fulfilling careers.

Furthermore, the demands of the capitalist workplace contrast markedly with those of domestic life. Beck and Beck-Gernsheim comment: 'Individual competitiveness and mobility, encouraged by the job market, run up against the opposite expectations at home where one is expected to sacrifice one's own interests for others and invest in a collective project called family.'

The family is the arena in which these contradictions and conflicts are played out. Men and women argue over who should do the housework, who should look after the kids and whose job should take priority. The results of the arguments are unlikely to satisfy both parties. In the end one person's career or personal development has to take a back seat. In a world where individualization has proceeded so far this is bound to cause resentment.

Conclusion

Beck and Beck-Gernsheim believe these contradictions lead to 'the normal chaos of love'. Love is increasingly craved to provide security in an insecure world, but it is increasingly difficult to find and sustain. The quest for individual fulfilment by both partners in a relationship makes it difficult for them to find common ground. Beck and Beck-Gernsheim conclude pessimistically that 'perhaps the two parallel lines will eventually meet, in the far distant future. Perhaps not. We shall never know.'

Giddens's conclusions seem a little over-optimistic, those of Beck and Beck-Gernsheim seem rather too pessimistic. Some couples do manage to work out their differences and produce mutually satisfactory relationships. However, Beck and Beck-Gernsheim may be right to suggest that the apparent greater choice over relationships can create problems in making them work.

David H.J. Morgan – past-modern sociology and family practices

Past-modern sociology

David Morgan (1996, 1999) has attempted to develop an approach to studying the family which takes account of recent changes in family life without fully embracing postmodernism. He borrows the term **past-modern** from R. Stones (1996) to characterize his approach. Morgan claims this approach draws upon a wide variety of influences, including feminism, postmodernism and interactionism. It tries to avoid the sort of modern approach to studying 'the family' which assumes families have a fixed structure and clear boundaries between themselves and the outside world. He would reject, therefore, the kinds of approaches used by Parsons (see p. 463 and pp. 474–5) and Young and Willmott (pp. 476–8), which tend to see a single dominant type of family evolving alongside the development of modern societies.

On the other hand, Morgan is also opposed to an extreme version of postmodernism 'that would threaten to empty sociological enquiry (of any kind) of any content' (Morgan, 1999). Morgan believes we should acknowledge the changes taking place in family lives, but we should not reject the use of all empirical evidence. He says: 'the assemblage of carefully collected "facts" about family living is not to be despised but neither is it to be seen as the culmination of family analysis'.

Changes in family living

Morgan believes modern approaches to studying family living have become outdated because of changes in families and societies. Both are increasingly characterized by 'flux, fluidity and change'. 'The family' is not a static entity which can be frozen at a moment in time so that its form can be clearly analysed. Rather, it is constituted by ongoing processes of change, and overlaps considerably (and in changing ways) with the society that surrounds it. In the conventional sociological way of thinking about families:

> *Family living is not about hospital waiting lists, size of classrooms or the availability of public transport. Yet such matters, in the experiences of individual members, may be at least as much to do with routine family living as the matters subsumed under the statistical tables [such as those about household size, divorce rates and so on].*
> Morgan, 1999

Morgan's alternative approach attempts to take account of the blurred boundaries between families and the outside world, and the constantly changing nature of family life.

Family practices

Morgan believes the study of the family should focus on **family practices** rather than, for example, family structure. Family practices are concerned with what family members actually do, and with the accounts they give of what they do.

Unlike some postmodernists, Morgan does not believe that what families do should be reduced to the descriptions of what they do. He believes there is a social reality that really exists and can be described and analysed by sociologists. That reality is independent of sociologists' descriptions of it. However, that should not stop sociologists from also discussing the way in which people talk about and describe their own family lives.

Morgan goes on to outline the central themes brought out by the idea of family practices:

1. 'A sense of interplay between the perspectives of the social actor, the individual whose actions are being described and accounted for, and the perspectives of the observer.' For example, researchers should examine how far individuals see themselves as members of families, and they should consider where people draw the boundary between their family and non-family members.
2. 'A sense of the active rather than the passive.' People do not just occupy particular roles, they actively construct their lives. Gender, class and family relationships are all worked out by people in the course of their actions; they are not predetermined. Even something as apparently passive as sleeping involves actively working out what are seen as appropriate sleeping arrangements for different family members.
3. 'A focus on the everyday.' Routine family practices, such as how breakfast is organized and consumed, can tell you as much, if not more, about family life as examining less mundane events, such as weddings.
4. 'A stress on regularities.' Although family life may change frequently, there are often regular patterns that reoccur, particularly in daily routines. Sociologists

should not lose sight of these regularities, which may well be part of the taken-for-granted life of families.

5 Despite the importance of regularities, Morgan also believes there should be 'a sense of fluidity'. Family practices will flow into practices from other spheres of social life. He says:

> *Thus a family outing might consist of a variety of different family practices while also blending with gendered practices, leisure practices and so on. Further, the family outing may well be linked in the perceptions of the participants to other such outings, to anticipated future outings and the planning involved in each case.*
> Morgan, 1999

6 'An interplay between history and biography.' The focus should not be entirely upon the experience of family life on an everyday basis, but should also be linked to a consideration of the historical development of society as a whole. Family outings, for example, are linked to 'a wider historical framework to do with the development of leisure, transportation and shifting constructions of parenthood and childhood'.

Although a little vague, Morgan's past-modern approach does offer the possibility of analysing family life in a way which is sensitive to contemporary changes but which also rests upon detailed evidence. It suggests that some of the older debates about family structure and the 'typical' or 'conventional' family may be becoming less useful for understanding family life today. It also offers the possibility of examining areas of family life (such as outings and use of health services) which have not usually been the focus of study for sociologists of 'the family'.

Carol Smart and Bren Neale – *Family Fragments?*

A positive sense of self

In a study of divorce and parenthood based upon interviews with sixty parents in West Yorkshire, Smart and Neale (1999) make use of aspects of the work of both Giddens and Morgan. Following Giddens, Smart and Neale found that the process of divorce often involves an attempt to re-establish a positive sense of self by moving beyond a relationship that has failed to provide satisfaction.

As discussed earlier (see pp. 510–11), Smart and Neale believe divorce law in the 1960s and 1970s embraced the idea that individuals should have the opportunity to re-establish a sense of self after divorce by accepting the idea of a 'clean break'. Freed from any need to continue to associate with their former spouse, each divorcee could go about constructing a new sense of identity and perhaps seeking a new 'pure' relationship.

However, in the 1980s and 1990s new laws undermined the possibility of a clean break, at least where there were children from the marriage. Divorcing couples were forced to continue a relationship with their former spouse through the need to negotiate over childcare responsibilities.

Furthermore, Smart and Neale argue that a problem with Giddens's ideas is that he fails to distinguish between the situations of men and women. Influenced by feminist thinking, Smart and Neale maintain that men and women can be in different situations when they try to develop a new identity after divorce. In their research, they found that, 'In order to reconstitute the self on divorce therefore, it was necessary for many women to disconnect themselves and to cease to be bound up with their former partners.'

Some women were intimidated by their former husbands, and some had been victims of violence. Many remained in what had been the marital home and their former partners would show little respect for the idea that it was now the woman's space. For example, one of the women studied, Meg Johnson, initially tried allowing her husband to look after their children in the marital home at weekends while she stayed at her mother's. However, she soon tired of this arrangement because she felt she didn't have her own independence or space. Indeed, Smart and Neale comment: 'issues of space and independence were a common theme for very many of the mothers'. They go on to say: 'Women's sense of powerlessness seemed to be embedded in their inability to become their "own" person once again.'

The situation was rather different for men. None of them expressed concern about lack of independence or space or felt this was hindering them from establishing a new identity. Nevertheless, they did experience a sense of powerlessness and frustration. 'Many of the fathers in our sample experienced having to negotiate with their ex-wives as demeaning and as a tangible sign of their powerlessness.' What troubled them was not their loss of an independent identity, but their loss of power over others. They were no longer able to exercise the same degree of control over their ex-wives as they had done when they were married to them.

Power

Smart and Neale use these arguments to distinguish between **debilitative powerlessness** and **situational powerlessness**. They define debilitative powerlessness as 'an effacement of the self' – the loss of a sense of control over one's own identity and destiny. This was the sort of powerlessness most usually experienced by women. They defined situational powerlessness as something 'which is experienced as an inability to control others and a denial of rights'.

Although both types of powerlessness could be experienced by men or women, the latter type was most commonly experienced by men because the children usually lived with the mother, at least for most of the week. Furthermore, Smart and Neale argue that debilitative powerlessness is ignored in public debates, whereas men have succeeded in putting situational powerlessness on the agenda of public debate and political discussion. 'Men's rights' (or their lack of them) in relation to children after divorce have been highlighted in the media and elsewhere, while the difficulties women face in feeling free of their former partner are not usually recognized.

Family practices

In this aspect of their work, then, Smart and Neale accept much of Giddens's arguments about identity and the changing nature of relationships, but they criticize him for assuming that men and women face the same problems. To Smart and Neale, the experience of divorce is gendered; it is different for men and women.

In other aspects of their work, Smart and Neale express approval for Morgan's ideas and illustrate some of his points. Like Morgan, they argue that family life should be seen in terms of 'family practices'. Research into families should focus on what goes on in families and recognize that they change, although certain patterns of activity may be common and may be repeated frequently.

To Smart and Neale, it is fruitless to try to analyse 'the family' as a static entity. Relationships and patterns of family life are flexible and change. Nowhere is this more evident than in family relationships after divorce, especially since legislation has made it unlikely that there will be a clean break between divorcing parents.

The biological father continues to play a part in family life, even when he lives apart from his former spouse and children. Social fathers (the new partners of divorced mothers) have little formal role or responsibility for their new partner's children, but obviously have an important role within the household and an important relationship with the mother.

Grandparents may also have a role. Sometimes the grandparents from the father's side will have more contact with the children than the father himself. A father in one household may have important attachments to children in another. All this means that 'the family' is no longer a single entity based on common residence in one household. Instead, there are 'fragments of families spread across a number of households'.

Smart and Neale go on to argue that 'Divorce will inevitably come to mean something different – less an end to marriage and more the start of a set of relationships based on parenthood.' In addition, they note that the increasing frequency of gay and lesbian parenting and new reproductive technologies (such as surrogate motherhood) will lead to further complexity in family and household relationships. They conclude that these changes

> *will produce a very different spatial dimension in family connections and brings us directly back to David Morgan's concept of family practices. As Morgan has argued, we need increasingly to think in terms of 'doing' family life rather than in terms of 'being' in a family or part of an institution called a family.* Smart and Neale, 1999

Judith Stacey – the postmodern family

The shift to the postmodern family

Unlike Giddens, Beck and Beck-Gernsheim, and Morgan, the American sociologist Judith Stacey (1996) believes contemporary societies such as the USA have developed the **postmodern family**. Like the other writers examined in this section, she associates changes in the family with a movement away from a single dominant family type and with greater variety in family relationships. She says, 'I use the term postmodern family … to signal the contested, ambivalent, and undecided character of our contemporary family cultures.' She goes on: 'Like postmodern culture, contemporary Western family arrangements are diverse, fluid, and unresolved. Like postmodern cultural forms, our families today admix unlikely elements in an improvisational pastiche of old and new.'

Stacey does not see the emergence of the postmodern family as another stage in the development of family life; instead, it has destroyed the idea that the family progresses through a series of logical stages. It no longer makes sense to discuss what type of family is dominant in contemporary societies because family forms have become so diverse. Furthermore, there can be no assumption that any particular form will become accepted as the main, best or normal type of family.

Stacey believes this situation is here to stay. It will be impossible for societies to go back to having a single standard (such as the heterosexual nuclear family) against which all families are compared and judged. Societies will have to come to terms with such changes and adapt to cope with the greater variety and uncertainty in family life.

Although some commentators deplore the decline of the conventional, heterosexual nuclear family, diversity is here to stay. Social attitudes and social policies will have to adjust to this diversity if postmodern families are to have a good chance of facilitating fulfilling lives for their members.

Postmodern families in Silicon Valley

Stacey's claim that the postmodern family is characteristic of the USA is based upon her own research into family life in Silicon Valley, conducted during the mid-1980s. Silicon Valley in California is the 'global headquarters of the electronics industry and the world's vanguard post-industrial region' (Stacey, 1996). Usually, trends in family life in the USA take on an exaggerated form in Silicon Valley. For example, divorce rates in this area have risen faster than in other areas of the country. Trends there are generally indicative of future trends elsewhere.

Most sociologists have tended to argue that higher-class and middle-class families lead the way in new family trends and that working-class families then follow later (see, for example, Willmott and Young's idea of the symmetrical family, p. 477). Stacey's research suggests the reverse might be true with the rise of the postmodern family. Her research focused on two working-class extended-kin networks in Silicon Valley, and uncovered the way in which these families had become adaptable and innovative in response to social changes.

According to Stacey, the modern family was largely based around the idea of the male as the primary breadwinner, earning a 'family wage'. In other words, the man earned enough to keep the whole of the family. However, this sort of family life only became available to working-class families relatively late in the twentieth century. It was not until the 1960s that some working-class men started earning enough to keep a whole family. Furthermore, the situation was to be short-lived. By the late 1970s, economic changes began to threaten the viability of families dependent on a working-class male wage earner.

The two central people in the two kinship networks studied by Stacey's research were Pam and Dotty: working-class women who had to adapt their family life to changing personal circumstances and the changing society that surrounded them.

Pam and Dotty

Both Pam and Dotty got married to manual workers around the end of the 1950s and the start of the 1960s. Both their husbands were of working-class origin, but both worked hard and worked their way up in the electronics industry until they had middle-class jobs. Despite this, neither husband was earning enough to maintain their family in the sort of middle-class lifestyle they desired. Pam took on some cleaning and childcare work, but she kept it a secret from her husband to avoid injuring his male pride in being the sole breadwinner. Dotty took on a range of temporary and low-paid jobs.

In the early 1970s Pam and Dotty both started courses at their local college – courses designed to give them a chance of getting better work. At the college they were exposed to feminist ideas for the first time and this encouraged them to take steps to change their marriages and family life. Both were unhappy with aspects of their marriage. Both husbands took little part in family life and were unwilling to help with housework. Dotty's husband, Lou, physically abused her. For these reasons both women left their husbands.

Pam got divorced, studied for a degree, and pursued a career working for social services. Some time later Pam became a born-again Christian and remarried. Her second marriage was a more egalitarian one and her family network was far from conventional. In particular, she formed a close relationship with her first husband's live-in lover and they helped each other out in a range of practical ways.

Dotty eventually took her husband back, but only after he had had a serious heart attack which left him unable to abuse her physically. Furthermore, the reconciliation was largely on Dotty's terms and her husband had to carry out most of the housework. Dotty meanwhile got involved in political campaigns in the community, particularly those concerned with helping battered wives. Later, she withdrew from political campaigning and took part-time work in an insurance office. Her husband and two of her adult children died. One of her deceased daughters left four children behind and Dotty successfully obtained custody of the children, against the wishes of her son-in-law, who had abused members of his family. Dotty then formed a household with one of her surviving daughters, who was a single mother.

These complex changes in the families of Pam and Dotty showed how two working-class women developed their family life to take account of changes in their circumstances in a rapidly changing environment. Stacey comments that by the end of the study, 'Dotty and Pamela both had moved partway back from feminist fervour, at the same time both had moved further away from the (no longer) modern family'. Furthermore, none of Pam's or Dotty's daughters lived in a conventional, modern nuclear family.

The working class and the postmodern family

Stacey found that the image of working-class families clinging on to conventional family arrangements longer than the middle class was quite erroneous. She says: 'I found postmodern family arrangements among blue collar workers at least as diverse and innovative as those found within the middle-class.'

The women she studied had drawn upon the tradition of working-class and African American women being supported by their female kin (such as mothers, daughters, sisters and aunts) to find new ways of dealing with the changes to their family circumstances. In post-industrial conditions, when jobs were less secure and workers were expected to work 'flexibly', women drew on such traditions to find ways of coping with uncertainty and change. Stacey says the working-class women she studied were:

> *Struggling creatively, often heroically, to sustain oppressed families and, to escape the most oppressive ones, they drew on 'traditional' premodern kinship resources and crafted untraditional ones. In the process they created postmodern family strategies.*
>
> *Rising divorce and cohabitation rates, working mothers, two-earner households, single and unwed parenthood, along with inter-generational female-linked extended kin support networks appeared earlier and more extensively among poor and working-class people.* Stacey, 1996

Gay and lesbian families

Stacey argues that gay and lesbian families have also played a pioneering role in developing the postmodern family. In the early 1970s gay and lesbian organizations were often strongly anti-family, but by the late 1980s this attitude had been reversed. There was a major 'gay-by boom' – that is, a boom in babies and children being looked after by gay and lesbian couples.

Stacey quotes research which suggests that by the late 1980s, 6–14 million children were being brought up in gay and lesbian families. Gay and lesbian families are themselves extremely diverse, but because of the prejudice they sometimes face they form a 'new embattled, visible and necessarily self-conscious, genre of postmodern kinship' (Stacey, 1996).

Furthermore, 'self-consciously "queer" couples and families, by necessity, have had to reflect much more seriously on the meaning and purpose of their intimate relationships'. This forced reflection makes them more creative and imaginative in developing family forms to suit their circumstances, and it makes them more likely to include people from outside conventional nuclear family relationships in their family circle. Stacey believes:

> *Gays and lesbians improvisationally assemble a patchwork of blood and intentional relations – gay, straight, and other – into creative, extended kin bonds. Gay communities more adeptly integrate single individuals into their social worlds than does the mainstream heterosexual society, a social skill quite valuable in a world in which divorce, widowhood and singlehood are increasingly normative.* Stacey, 1996

Within this creativity and flexibility, gay and lesbian couples have increasingly asserted a right to claim, if they wish, aspects of more conventional family relationships for themselves. This has involved, for example, claiming custody of children, lesbian women intentionally becoming pregnant so that they can raise a child with their partner, and trying to have same-sex marriages legally recognized. Slowly, they have made gains on all these fronts, although at the time Stacey was writing same-sex marriage had not become legal in the USA. (A court case over the legality of same-sex marriage was pending in Hawaii.)

Stacey argues that research indicates that gay and lesbian relationships are at least as suitable for raising children as heterosexual marriages. Generally, research finds there is virtually no difference in the psychological well-being and social development of children with gay or lesbian carers and those with heterosexual carers. Stacey says: 'The rare small differences reported tend to favour gay parents, portraying them as somewhat more nurturant and tolerant, and their children in turn, more tolerant and empathetic, and less aggressive than those raised by non-gay parents.'

Stacey believes children raised in gay and lesbian families are less likely to be hostile to homosexual relationships and more likely to try them for themselves. However, she regards this as an advantage rather than a problem. This is because it discourages intolerance of families who are different, and in a world of increasing family diversity this is essential. It also allows people more freedom to explore and develop their sexuality, free from what Adrienne Rich has called 'compulsory heterosexuality' (quoted in Stacey, 1996).

Conclusion

Stacey does not believe the development of the postmodern family has no disadvantages. She acknowledges that it creates a certain degree of unsettling instability. Nevertheless, she generally welcomes it as an opportunity to develop more egalitarian and more democratic family relationships.

As we have seen earlier in the chapter (see pp. 494–5, for example), it is questionable how far the undoubted diversification of families has supplanted more conventional families. It is possible that Stacey exaggerates the extent of change. Neither gay and lesbian families nor families in Silicon Valley are likely to be typical American families or typical of families in Britain and elsewhere.

Summary and conclusions

Many of the earliest sociological attempts to understand families and households were from a functionalist perspective. They tended to assume that the family was a basic, universal institution of society. They accepted that family life changed as society evolved, but believed that in any one era a single family type, which met the needs of society and individuals, would be dominant.

Arguably, functionalism had an idealized and romanticized view of the family. Certainly, sociological research and theorizing have challenged the assumptions on which functionalism was based. Marxists and feminists, amongst others, have questioned whether the family can be seen as functional for individuals and for society. They have highlighted what they see as exploitative and abusive aspects of family life such as the unpaid work of women and domestic violence.

Increasingly, theoretical approaches to the family, such as difference feminism and postmodernism, have emphasized the variety of family types and living arrangements that exist in contemporary society. By and large, they have welcomed these changes as offering increased freedom and choice for individuals.

Research certainly confirms that nuclear family households are becoming less common in Britain and similar societies, and that households and families are becoming more diverse. Not everybody welcomes these trends, as some see them as threatening the stability of society by undermining an essential institution, the family.

Political and sociological debate about the family reflects the division of opinion about family change, with issues such as lone-parent families, gay 'marriage' and the use of new reproductive technologies attracting controversy. Whether the changes are regarded as desirable or not, most sociologists accept that important changes are taking place which reflect broader changes in society as a whole. Changes in family and household structure may well reflect changes in the nature of relationships within families and changes in the expectations that people bring to marriage, family life and cohabitation.

CHAPTER 9

Power, politics and the state

... by their very existence they have proved to be the destroyers of the democratic aspirations and the effective debate which should lie at the heart of an open society.

Hywel Williams on Britain's power elites, 2006, p. 26

Introduction

In this chapter we are mainly concerned with the nature and distribution of power in modern industrial societies.

Many sociologists argue that political sociology is the study of power in its broadest sense. Thus Dowse and Hughes state that 'politics is about "power", politics occurs when there are differentials in power' (Dowse and Hughes, 1972). In terms of this definition, any social relationship that involves **power differentials** is political. Political relationships would extend from parents assigning domestic chores to their children to teachers enforcing discipline in the classroom; from a manager organizing a workforce to a general ordering troops into battle. Feminist sociologists have played an important role in developing the idea that power relationships are present in everyday life as well as in the activities of states (see pp. 109–11 for an example).

However, the traditional study of politics has concentrated on the state and the various institutions of government such as Parliament and the judiciary. Sociologists have been particularly concerned with the state, but they have examined it in relation to society as a whole, rather than in isolation.

Sociologists often distinguish between two forms of power – authority and coercion:

1. **Authority** is that form of power which is accepted as legitimate – that is, right and just – and therefore obeyed on that basis. Thus, if members of British society accept that Parliament has the right to make certain decisions and they regard those decisions as lawful, parliamentary power may be defined as legitimate authority. Similarly, pupils or students might accept that their teachers have the right to make decisions about the marks that should be awarded to their work and when their work should be handed in.
2. **Coercion** is that form of power which is not regarded as legitimate by those subject to it. Thus, from the point of view of some Basque nationalists, the activities of the Spanish police and army in the Basque region may be regarded as coercion. After the invasion of Iraq by American and British troops, some Iraqis rejected the legitimacy of the occupation and carried out violent attacks on the occupying troops.

However, the distinction between authority and coercion is not as clear-cut as the above definitions suggest. It has often been argued that both forms of power are based ultimately on physical force, and that those who enforce the law are able to resort to physical force whether their power is regarded as legitimate or not. Furthermore, some sociologists have suggested that power can have several faces or dimensions.

Nevertheless, one of the most influential sociological views of power, that of Max Weber, is largely based on distinguishing different types of authority. Weber's work provides a useful starting point for a consideration of how sociological ideas about power have developed.

Defining power

Max Weber – power and types of authority

Max Weber defined **power** as:

> *the chance of a man or a number of men to realize their own will in a communal action even against the resistance of others who are participating in the action.* Weber, in Gerth and Mills, 1948

In other words, power consists of the ability to get your own way even when others are opposed to your wishes.

Weber was particularly concerned to distinguish different types of **authority**. He suggested there were three sources: charismatic, traditional, and rational–legal.

Charismatic authority

Charismatic authority derives from the devotion felt by subordinates for a leader who is believed to have exceptional qualities. These qualities are seen as supernatural, super-human, or at least exceptional compared to lesser mortals.

Charismatic leaders are able to sway and control their followers by direct emotional appeals which excite devotion and strong loyalties. Historical examples which come close to charismatic authority might include Alexander the Great, Napoleon and Fidel Castro. More ordinary people, such as teachers or managers, may also use charisma to exercise power.

Traditional authority

Weber called the second type of authority **traditional authority**. In this case authority rests upon a belief in the 'rightness' of established customs and traditions. Those in authority command obedience on the basis of their traditional status, which is usually inherited. Their subordinates are controlled by feelings of loyalty and obligation to long-established positions of power.

The feudal system of medieval Europe is an example of traditional authority: monarchs and nobles owed their positions to inherited status and the personal loyalty of their subjects.

Rational–legal authority

The final type of authority distinguished by Weber was **rational–legal authority**. In this case, unlike charismatic and traditional authority, legitimacy and control stem neither from the perceived personal qualities of the leader and the devotion they excite, nor from a commitment to traditional wisdom. Rational–legal authority is based on the acceptance of a set of impersonal rules.

Those who possess authority are able to issue commands and have them obeyed because others accept the legal framework that supports their authority. Thus a judge, a tax inspector or a military commander are obeyed because others accept the legal framework that gives them their power. The rules on which their authority is based are rational in the sense that they are consciously constructed for the attainment of a particular goal and they specify the means by which that goal is to be attained. For example, laws governing the legal system are designed to achieve the goal of 'justice'.

Ideal types

Weber stressed that, in reality, authority would never conform perfectly to any of his three types. His three categories are **ideal types**, each of which defines a 'pure' form of authority. In any particular example, authority may stem from two or more sources. It is therefore possible to find examples of authority which approximate to one of these types, but it is unlikely that a perfect example of any could be found.

Weber's attempts to define power and authority have been highly influential. The pluralist view of power and the state has adopted Weber's definition as a basis for measuring who has power in modern industrial societies.

Pluralists concentrate on the **will** (or desires) of individuals or groups to achieve particular ends. The wishes that people have are then compared to actual decisions taken by a government. The group whose wishes appear to be carried out are held to possess greater power than those who oppose them. Therefore, power is measured by comparing the stated wishes of individuals or groups who seek to influence government policy, with the actions taken by their government. (Pluralist views on power and the state are discussed fully below; see pp. 525–30.)

Steven Lukes – a radical view of power

Despite the acceptance of Weber's definition of power by many sociologists, some writers believe it is too narrow. Steven Lukes (1974, 2006) has put forward a **radical view** of power as an alternative. He argues that power has three **dimensions** or **faces**, rather than just one.

Decision making

Like pluralists, Lukes sees the first face of power in terms of **decision making**, where different individuals or groups express different policy preferences and influence the making of decisions over various issues. Lukes would accept that if a government followed the policies advocated by the trade unions, this would represent evidence that the unions had power. However, he believes it is misleading to concentrate entirely on decisions taken, for power can be exercised in less obvious ways.

Non-decision making

The second face of power does not concern decision making, but rather focuses on **non-decision making**.

Power may be used to prevent certain issues from being discussed, or decisions about them from being taken.

From this point of view, individuals or groups exercising power do so by preventing those who take a decision from considering all the possible alternative sources of action, or by limiting the range of decisions they are allowed to take.

For example, a teacher might offer students the opportunity to decide whether to do a piece of homework that week or the following week. The class appears to have power, for they have been given the opportunity to reach a decision. In reality, however, most power still rests with the teacher, who has limited the options open to the students. The students are not free to decide whether or not they do this particular piece of work, nor can they choose to reject doing homework altogether.

Shaping desires

The third face of power strays even further from an emphasis on decision making and the preferences expressed by members of society. Lukes claims that power can be exercised by **shaping desires** – manipulating the wishes and desires of social groups. A social group may be persuaded to accept, or even to desire, a situation that is harmful to them.

Some feminists would argue that men exercise power over women in contemporary Britain by persuading them that being a mother and a housewife are the most desirable roles for women. In reality, feminists claim, women who occupy these roles are exploited by, and for the benefit of, men.

Lukes's definition of power

Having examined the nature of power, Lukes is able to conclude that power can be defined thus: 'A exercises power over B when A affects B in a manner contrary to B's interests' (2006, p. 30). In other words, Lukes argues that power is exercised over those who are harmed by its use, whether they are aware they are being harmed or not.

Lukes has been responsible for refining the concept of power, and showing that it has more than one dimension. As he himself admits, though, what is in a person's interests, or what is good for them, is ultimately a matter of opinion. A mother and housewife might deny that her role in society is any less desirable than that of her husband. She might also deny that she is being exploited.

Despite this problem, the radical definition of power has become increasingly influential. Marxist sociologists in particular have used this definition to attack the evidence used by sociologists advocating other perspectives.

We will develop this issue of defining and measuring power as the various theories are examined in detail. Next, however, we will analyse the role of the state in relation to power.

The state

Definitions and development of the state

The definition of the state is probably less controversial than the definition of power. Weber provided a definition with which most sociologists are in broad agreement. He defined the state as 'a human community that (successfully) claims the monopoly of the legitimate use of physical force within a given territory' (Weber, in Gerth and Mills, 1948).

In modern Britain, the state rules over a clearly defined geographical area, which includes England, Northern Ireland, Wales and Scotland (although there is now devolution of power to Scotland, Wales and Northern Ireland).

Only the central authority is believed by most members of society to have the right to use force to achieve its ends. Other groups and individuals may resort to violence, but the actions of terrorists, football 'hooligans' and murderers are not seen as legitimate. The state alone can wage war or use the legal system to imprison people against their will.

On the basis of Weber's definition, the state can be said to consist of the government or legislature which passes laws, the bureaucracy or civil service which implements governmental decisions, the police who are responsible for law enforcement, and the armed forces whose job it is to protect the state from external threats.

Many sociologists see the state as consisting of a wider set of institutions and, in Britain, would include welfare services, and the education and health services. Some go even further and see nationalized industries as part of the state. However, in developing their theories of the state most sociologists have concentrated upon the more central institutions, such as the government and the civil service.

The twentieth-century world came to be dominated by nation-states which laid claim to territory in every corner of the world (see pp. 188–94 for a discussion of nationalism). However, although states which conform to Weber's definition have existed for thousands of years, and include ancient Greece, Rome and Egypt, and the Aztecs of Central America, the state is a comparatively new feature of many societies.

Anthropologists have discovered a number of stateless 'simple' societies. These are sometimes called **acephalous** or headless societies. For example, in the 1930s, E.E. Evans-Pritchard (1951) carried out a study of the Nuer society in Africa. The society consisted of some forty separate tribes, none of which had a head or chief. Important decisions appear to have been reached informally through discussions between members of each tribe. In this society there was no government or other institution which claimed a monopoly of the legitimate use of force, and the society was not based upon a clearly defined territory. As such, Nuer society can be seen as stateless.

A number of commentators believe the modern centralized state is also a relatively new feature of many parts of Europe. They suggest it did not develop until after the feudal period.

Under feudalism the legitimate use of force was not concentrated in the hands of a centralized authority. While, in theory, the monarch ruled at the centre, in practice, military power and the control of particular territories were in the hands of feudal lords in each region. Gianfranco Poggi (1978) has described how, for example, in the Maconnâis in feudal France, the King was a 'dimly perceived, politically ineffective figure'. Only in the seventeenth century did the French monarchy successfully establish its authority over the aristocracy in the regions. Furthermore, it was only in the nineteenth century that transport and communications had developed sufficiently for it to become possible for the centralized state to exercise close control over the far-flung corners of its territory.

The modern state

The centralized state developed comparatively recently in many areas of the world. However, its importance in modern, industrialized societies increased dramatically in the nineteenth and twentieth centuries. In Britain, for instance, in this period the state greatly extended its involvement in, and control over, economic affairs, and the provision of welfare, health care and education.

The increasing importance of the state in industrial societies has prompted sociologists to devote considerable attention to this institution. In particular they have debated which groups in society control the state and in whose interests the state is run. We will now examine the competing sociological perspectives on power and the state, beginning with a functionalist perspective.

Power – a functionalist perspective

Most sociological theories of power follow Weber's definition in two important respects:

1. Weber's definition implies that those who hold power do so at the expense of others. It suggests there is a fixed amount of power, and, therefore, if some hold power, others do not. This view is sometimes known as a **constant-sum** concept of power. Since the amount of power is constant, power is held by an individual or group to the extent that it is not held by others.
2. The second important implication of Weber's definition is that power-holders will tend to use power to further their own interests. Power is used to further the sectional interests of particular groups in society. This view is sometimes known as a **variable-sum** concept of power, since power in society is not seen as fixed or constant. Instead, it is variable in the sense that it can increase or decrease.

Talcott Parsons – the variable-sum concept of power

Power and collective goals

Talcott Parsons's view of power was developed from his general theory of the nature of society. He began from the assumption that value consensus is essential for the survival of social systems. From shared values derive collective goals, that is, goals shared by members of society. For example, if materialism is a major value of Western industrial society, collective goals such as economic expansion and higher living standards can be seen to stem from this value. The more Western societies are able to realize these goals, the greater the power that resides in the social system. Steadily rising living standards and economic growth are therefore indications of an increase of power in society.

Parsons's view of power differentials within society also derived from his general theory. Since goals are shared by all members of society, power will generally be used in the furtherance of collective goals. As a result, both sides of the power relationship will benefit and everybody will gain by the arrangement. For instance, politicians in Western societies will promote policies for economic expansion which, if successful, will raise the living standards of the population as a whole.

Thus, from this viewpoint, the exercise of power usually means that everybody wins. This forms a basis for the cooperation and reciprocity that Parsons considered essential for the maintenance and well-being of society.

Authority and collective goals

As we saw in Chapter 1, Parsons regarded power differentials as necessary for the effective pursuit of collective goals. If members of society pool their efforts and resources, they are more likely to realize their shared goals than if they operate as individuals. Cooperation on a large scale requires organization and direction, which necessitate positions of command. Some are therefore granted the power to direct others.

This power takes the form of authority. It is generally regarded as legitimate, since it is seen to further collective goals. This means that some are granted authority for the benefit of all.

Power in Western democracies

Parsons's analysis of the basis of political power in Western democracies provides a typical illustration of his views on the nature of power. He argued:

> *Political support should be conceived of as a generalized grant of power which, if it leads to electional success, puts elected leadership in a position analogous to a banker. The 'deposits' of power made by constituents are revocable, if not at will, at the next election.* Parsons, 1967

Just as money is deposited in a bank, members of society deposit power in political leaders. Just as depositors can withdraw their money from the bank, so the electorate can withdraw its grant of power from political leaders at the next election. In this sense, power resides ultimately with members of society as a whole. Finally, just as money generates interest for the depositor, so grants of power generate benefits for the electorate, since they are used primarily to further collective goals. In this way, power in society can increase.

Criticisms

Many sociologists have argued that Parsons's views of the nature and application of power in society are naive. They suggest he has done little more than translate into sociological jargon the rationalizations promoted by the power-holders to justify their use of power. In particular, they argue that Parsons has failed to appreciate that power is frequently used to further sectional interests rather than to benefit society as a whole. We will analyse these criticisms in detail in the following sections.

Power and the state – a pluralist perspective

Pluralism is a theory which claims to explain the nature and distribution of power in Western democratic societies. **Classical pluralism** was the original form that this perspective took, but it has been heavily criticized. Some supporters of this perspective have modified their position and have adopted an **elite pluralist** view which takes account of some of those criticisms.

We will first describe and evaluate classical pluralism, before considering elite pluralism at the end of this section.

Classical pluralism

This version of pluralism has important similarities with the Parsonian functionalist theory. Pluralists agree with Parsons that power ultimately derives from the population as a whole:

1. They accept that the government and state in a Western democracy act in the interests of that society and according to the wishes of its members.
2. They see the political systems of countries such as the USA, Britain and France as the most advanced systems of government yet devised, and regard them as the most effective way for a population to exercise power and govern a country.
3. They regard the exercise of power through the state to be legitimate rather than coercive, since it is held to be based upon the acceptance and cooperation of the population.

Pluralists, however, part company from Parsons in three important respects.

The nature of power

First, pluralists follow Weber in accepting a constant-sum concept of power. There is seen to be a fixed amount of power which is distributed among the population of a society. They do not accept Parsons's variable-sum concept of power, which sees it as a resource held by society as a whole.

Sectional interests

Second, they deny that democratic societies have an all-embracing value consensus. They would agree with Parsons that members of such societies share some interests and wishes in common. For example, most citizens of the USA share a commitment to the constitution of the country and the political institutions such as the presidency, the Congress and the electoral system.

However, pluralists do not accept that members of society share common interests or values in relation to every issue. They believe industrial society is increasingly differentiated into a variety of social groups and sectional interests, and, with the increasingly specialized division of labour, the number and diversity of occupational groups steadily grow. Groups such as doctors, teachers, business people and unskilled manual workers may have different interests. Each group may be represented by its own union or professional association, and these groups may put forward conflicting requests to the government.

Pluralists do not deny the existence of class, or divisions based on age, gender, religion or ethnicity. However, they do deny that any single division dominates any individual's wishes or actions. According to their view, each individual has a large number of different interests. A male manual worker might not just be a member of the working class, he might also be a car owner, a mortgage payer, an avid reader of library books and a father of two children in higher education. Therefore, while he has certain interests as a manual worker, other interests stem from other aspects of his position in society. As a car owner he has an interest in road tax and petrol prices being kept low, as a mortgage payer in interest rates being reduced, as a library user in more government expenditure on this service, and as a father in the reinstatement of student grants. Another range of interests could be outlined for a female professional.

To the founder of the pluralist perspective, the nineteenth-century French writer de Tocqueville (1945, first published 1835), a democratic political system requires that individuals have a large number of specific interests. He believed democracy would become unworkable if one division in society came to dominate all others. Such a situation could lead to a tyranny of the majority: one group in society would be in a permanent majority and the interests and wishes of the minority could be totally disregarded. Countries which have a major split between two main ethnic or religious groups can have such problems.

The state

The third difference compared to the functionalist view follows from the pluralists' denial that a complete value consensus exists. Since individuals have different interests, political leaders and the state cannot reflect the interests of all members of society in taking any single decision.

To pluralists, the state is seen as an **honest broker** which takes account of all the conflicting demands made on it by different sections of society. The state mediates between different groups, ensuring that all of them have some influence on government policy, but that none gets its own way all the time. On one particular occasion the government might take a decision which favours car owners, such as deciding to build a new motorway. On another it might decide against such a project in order to take account of the protests of environmentalists. On a third, the government might reach a compromise, concluding that the road is necessary but changing the route in order to protect an area of particular environmental importance.

Pluralists argue that every group over a period of time has its interests reflected in governmental decisions, but because of the divisions within society, it is not possible for the state to satisfy everyone all of the time. In Raymond Aron's (1968) words, 'government becomes a business of compromise'.

Classical pluralism – political parties and interest groups

Political parties

From a pluralist perspective, competition between two or more political parties is an essential feature of representative government. **Political parties** are organizations which attempt to get representatives elected to positions in parliaments or their local equivalents. Pluralists claim that competition for office between political parties provides the electorate with an opportunity to select its leaders and a means of influencing government policy.

This view forms the basis of Seymour M. Lipset's definition of **democracy**. According to Lipset:

> *Democracy in a complete society may be defined as a political system which supplies regular constitutional opportunities for changing the governing officials, and a social mechanism which permits the largest possible part of the population to influence major decisions by choosing among contenders for political office.* Lipset, 1981, first published 1959

For efficient government, Lipset argued that competition between contenders for office must result in the granting of 'effective authority to one group' and the presence of an 'effective opposition' in the legislature as a check on the power of the governing party.

Pluralists claim that political parties in democratic societies are representative for the following reasons:

1. The public directly influences party policy, since, in order to be elected to govern, parties must reflect the wishes and interests of the electorate in their programmes.
2. If existing parties do not sufficiently represent sections of society, a new party will usually emerge, such as the Labour Party at the beginning of the twentieth century in Britain, or Respect, a left-wing party led by George Galloway which was opposed to British troops remaining in Iraq. In the 2005 general election Galloway won the Bethnal Green and Bow seat from the Labour Party.
3. Parties are accountable to the electorate, since they will not regain power if they disregard the opinions and interests of the public.
4. Parties cannot simply represent a sectional interest since, to be elected to power, they require the support of various interests in society.

However, as Robert McKenzie (1969) stated, political parties must not be seen 'as the sole "transmission belts" on which political ideas and programmes are conveyed from the citizens to the legislature and the executive'. During their time in office and in opposition, parties 'mould and adapt their principles under innumerable pressures brought to bear by organized groups of citizens which operate for the most part outside the political system'. Such groups are known as **interest** or **pressure groups**.

Interest groups

Unlike political parties, interest groups do not aim to take power in the sense of forming a government. Rather, they seek to influence political parties and the various departments of state. Nor do interest groups usually claim to represent a wide range of interests. Instead, their specified objective is to represent a particular interest in society.

Interest groups are often classified in terms of their aims as either protective or promotional groups:

1. **Protective groups** defend the interests of a particular section of society. Trade unions such as the National Union of Teachers (NUT), professional associations such as the British Medical Association, and employers' organizations such as the Confederation of British Industry are classified as protective groups. Membership of protective groups is usually limited to individuals of a particular status: for example, only teachers can join the NUT.
2. **Promotional groups** support a particular cause rather than guard the interests of a particular social group. Organizations such as the RSPCA and Friends of the Earth are classified as promotional groups. Membership of promotional groups is potentially larger and usually more varied than that of protective groups, since they require only a commitment to their cause as a qualification for joining.

In practice, the distinction between protective and promotional groups is not clear-cut, since the defence of an interest also involves its promotion.

Interest groups can bring pressure to bear in a number of ways:

1. By making contributions to the funds of political parties, such as trade union contributions to the Labour Party.
2. By appealing to public opinion. An effective campaign by an interest group can mobilize extensive public support, especially if it attracts widespread coverage by the mass media, and its arguments are seen to be valid. Certain conservation groups have successfully adopted this strategy. In the mid-1990s, protesters campaigning for rights for the disabled chained themselves to buses at the entrance to Downing Street. Another example is the campaign launched by rock musicians at the 1999 Brit Awards for the cancellation of a large part of the 'third world's' debt, which was followed up by the Live 8 concerts in 2005.
3. By the provision of expertise. It has often been argued that, in modern industrial society, governments cannot operate without the specialized knowledge of interest groups. By providing this expertise, interest groups have an opportunity to directly influence government policy. In Britain, representatives of interest groups now have permanent places on many government advisory committees.

4 By various forms of civil disobedience or direct action. This approach has been used by a wide variety of interest groups. Examples include Fathers4Justice (who campaign for the rights of divorced fathers), whose members threw flour at the prime minister, Tony Blair, in the House of Commons in 2004, and the Animal Liberation Front which has used a variety of methods including freeing animals bred for laboratory experiments. Hunt saboteurs tried to prevent fox hunting by disrupting hunts, while in 2004 pro-hunt protestors managed to gain entry to the House of Commons to protest. Campaigners for lower fuel duties blocked roads and disrupted the distribution of petrol in 2000.

5 By illegal payments to elected representatives and state officials – in other words, bribery. In 1994 it was revealed that at least one MP in Britain had received payments from Mohamed Al Fayed in return for asking questions on his behalf in the House of Commons. Although not illegal, this example does suggest that money has sometimes been used to buy access to MPs and government ministers.

Interest groups and democracy

Pluralists see interest groups as necessary elements in a democratic system for a number of reasons.

Voting in elections involves only minimal participation in politics for members of a democracy. Classical pluralists believe that as many people as possible should participate as actively as possible in politics. They do not believe that in Britain, for instance, voting once every five years is an adequate level of participation.

Interest groups provide the opportunity for many individuals – who are not members of political parties – to participate in politics. For example, many members of groups such as Amnesty International (which campaigns for human rights) or environmental organizations such as Friends of the Earth and Greenpeace are not members of political parties. Some commentators have noted that membership of political parties in Britain has been falling while many pressure groups have seen membership rising (see Garnett, 2005). (For more discussion of political participation, see pp. 590–5.)

Interest groups are also necessary because even those who have voted for a government may not agree with all its policies. In a party-political system it is necessary to choose between the overall packages offered by the opposing parties. Interest groups make it possible to alter some parts of a governing party's policies while retaining those with which a majority of the population agree.

Clearly, it is also vital that those who voted for a losing party have some opportunity to allow their voice to be heard. To the classical pluralist, the large number and diversity of pressure groups allow all sections of society to have a say in politics.

Before an election, a party seeking office outlines its proposed policies in a **manifesto**. The electorate can choose whom to vote for on the basis of the alternative manifestos put forward. However, manifestos cannot be completely comprehensive: new issues may arise. In the 2001 election in Britain no reference was made to Iraq in the manifestos of the major parties, since a possible invasion of Iraq had not been openly suggested at that time.

Interest groups provide the means through which the public can make their views known to a governing party as circumstances change and new issues arise. Furthermore, interest groups can mobilize public concern over issues that have been neglected or overlooked by the government.

The Refugee Council is a British interest group which draws the attention of the public and government alike to the plight of refugees who are generally seen in an unsympathetic light by the media and many politicians. A variety of environmental pressure groups did much to push the issue of global warming on to the political agenda before it was accepted as a crucial issue by most political parties.

According to classical pluralists, then, all sections of society and all shades of political opinion are represented and reflected in a wide variety of groups in Western democracies. Anyone who feels that they are being neglected by the government can form a new pressure group in order to rectify the temporary flaw in the operation of the democratic system.

Measuring power

Pluralists have provided empirical evidence to support their claim that Western societies are governed in accordance with democratic principles. The evidence they advance is based upon an attempt to show that a government's policies reflect a compromise between the wishes of the various sectional interests in society. They therefore concentrate upon the first face of power: decision making.

Pluralists compare the decisions taken by a government with the wishes of its general public, and the wishes expressed by different groups in the population. By examining evidence from opinion polls and the stated policy preferences of interest groups, pluralists reach the conclusion that countries such as Britain and the USA are genuinely democratic.

Empirical studies by pluralists

One of the most famous studies supporting the pluralist view is *Who Governs?* by Robert A. Dahl (1961). Dahl investigated local politics in New Haven, Connecticut, in the USA. He examined a series of decisions and found that different interest groups had influence over different issues.

For example, business interests, trade unions and the local university were involved in the issue of urban renewal. The mayor and his assistants made the major decisions in consultation with the various interest groups and produced a programme that was acceptable to all parties concerned.

Similarly, Christopher J. Hewitt (1974) examined twenty-four policy issues which arose in the British Parliament between 1944 and 1964. He found that business interests did not dominate the decisions. The government took account of a wide range of different views, often reaching a compromise position between different standpoints. Opinion poll data were available on eleven of the issues and in every case but one – the abolition of capital punishment in 1957 – government policies followed public opinion.

In another study, Wyn Grant and David Marsh (1977) found that the CBI (Confederation of British Industry) had no more influence over government policy in important areas than trade unions and a variety of pressure groups. Even a pressure group as small as the Warwickshire Conservation Society was able to persuade the government to modify its policies on the disposal of poisonous wastes in the Disposal of Poisonous Wastes Act of 1972.

Pluralism and contemporary British politics

Although there have been no detailed studies of recent policies from a pluralist perspective, it is possible to argue that there is plenty of evidence of governments taking note of a variety of interest groups. It also appears that the government often follows policies supported by public opinion.

Although balancing a range of interests may not have been particularly typical of Margaret Thatcher's period as prime minister (1979–91), it was more characteristic of John Major's period in office (1991–7) and that of Tony Blair (1997–2007). For example, John Major tried to balance the views of pro- and anti-Europeans by his policy of 'wait and see' over whether Britain should enter a single European currency. The New Labour Party under Tony Blair openly tried to respond to the views of a wide range of pressure groups and to take account of a range of sectional interests. His government, for example, took account of the views of trade unions by introducing minimum wage legislation and by giving unions a right to recognition by the employer where certain conditions are met.

On the other hand, the Blair government did not reinstate all the trade union laws repealed under the Conservatives – measures which would have been strongly opposed by the CBI and other groups. Furthermore, the Labour government has actively tried to include business leaders in the government and to take account of business interests and wishes.

Pluralism – a critique

A large body of evidence from studies such as those of Dahl in the US, and Hewitt and Grant and Marsh in Britain, appears to support the classical pluralist position. However, there are a number of serious criticisms of pluralism. These criticisms are concerned both with the methods pluralists use to measure power, and with empirical evidence which seems to contradict their claim that power is dispersed in Western democracies.

Non-decisions and safe decisions

Marxists and other conflict theorists have suggested that pluralists ignore some aspects of power. In particular, it is argued that they concentrate exclusively on the first face of power, decision making.

John Urry (in Urry and Wakeford, 1973), for example, believes that pluralists ignore the possibility that some have the power to prevent certain issues from reaching the point of decision. As a result of this **non-decision making**, only safe decisions may be taken – decisions which do not fundamentally alter the basic structures of capitalist societies.

From this point of view, it is in the interests of the powerful to allow a variety of interest groups to influence safe decisions. This fosters the illusion of real participation and helps to create the myth that a society is democratic. It disguises the real basis of power and so protects the powerful.

Pluralists can also be criticized for ignoring what Steven Lukes (1974, 2006) has identified as the third face of power. They do not take account of the possibility that the preferences expressed in opinion polls or by pressure groups might themselves have been manipulated by those with real power – for example, those who control institutions such as the media and the education system, which can play a part in shaping individuals' attitudes and opinions.

The consequences of decisions

Other writers have identified further ways in which power can be measured. Westergaard and Resler (1976) argue: 'Power is visible only through its consequences'. Government legislation may fail to have its intended effect. Despite an abundance of legislation aimed at improving the lot of the poor, Westergaard and Resler believe there has 'been little redistribution of wealth'. Although studies of actual decisions might give the impression that the interests of the poor are represented in government decisions, in fact studies of the results of those decisions might provide a very different picture.

In more recent writing, Westergaard (1995, 1996) argues that class inequalities have 'hardened' and the power of private business has grown (see pp. 88–9).

In any case, many sociologists deny that governments in Western democracies monopolize power. A government might, for example, seek to reduce the level of unemployment in order to secure victory at the next election. However, it is not within the government's power to control all the actions of large corporations, who can decide whether to close existing factories, making some of their workforce redundant, or to invest their profits overseas. This may be increasingly true if some theorists of globalization are to be believed (see pp. 548–57).

Contradictory evidence

The above points pose fundamental questions about the pluralists' method of measuring power, but pluralism can also be criticized on its own terms. Some of the evidence suggests that some interest groups have more influence over government decisions than others. Decision making by governments does not always appear to support the view that power is equally distributed among all groups in society, or that the state acts impartially as an 'honest broker'.

Many interest groups which have attracted tremendous support or have represented large groups in the population have had little influence. For example, it can be argued that the wishes of trade unions were consistently ignored by the governments of Margaret Thatcher and John Major from 1979 to 1997. For some eighteen years these pressure groups representing many millions of workers had very little influence on government decisions affecting them.

Wyn Grant (2003) argues that economic policy in contemporary Britain is largely shaped by political and financial elites, particularly the treasury, the prime minister and the Bank of England.

Unions had little impact on New Labour policies after 1997 except in the case of the introduction of the minimum wage. In the early years of the New Labour government the CBI was consulted closely, but the relationship became strained as the government introduced regulatory restrictions which were opposed by some business leaders.

According to Grant, current economic policy is influenced more by international organizations such as the World Bank, the International Monetary Fund and the OECD (Organization for Economic Cooperation and Development) than it is by pressure groups.

If anything, promotional groups seem to possess much less influence than protective groups. For example, the Campaign for Nuclear Disarmament (CND) has not succeeded in getting rid of British nuclear weapons. The pressure group Stop the War Coalition was formed in 2001 to oppose the 'War on Terror' but gained most support in opposing the British and US invasion of Iraq. On 15 February 2003 it organized a demonstration in London opposing the imminent invasion. According to the BBC, police estimates, which were the lowest estimates, put the number of demonstrators at 750,000, making it the biggest demonstration in British history. Despite this, the organization failed to influence government policy and the invasion of Iraq went ahead on 20 March 2003.

Some small pressure groups have managed to change government policy in recent years. ASH (Action on Smoking and Health) succeeded in getting a ban on smoking in enclosed public places introduced in England in 2007. Anti-fox hunting groups succeeded in getting a ban introduced in 2005; and in 1997 a handgun ban was introduced following a successful campaign in the wake of shootings in Dunblane, Scotland. However, the government has ignored the wishes of many larger groups with wider public support.

Unrepresented interests

Classical pluralists assume not only that interest groups have equal power, but also that all major interests in society are represented by one group or another. This latter assumption is also questionable.

The fairly recent emergence in Britain of consumer associations and citizens' advice bureaux can be seen as representing the interests of consumers against big business, and of citizens against government bureaucracies. It cannot be assumed that such interests were absent, unthreatened or adequately represented before the existence of such organizations. For instance, the unemployed are a group who, unlike employers and employees, still lack a protective pressure group to represent them.

Another group who have little power or political influence are refugees and asylum seekers. In Britain, some asylum seekers who have their applications turned down are not deported but are banned both from working and from claiming benefits, leaving them no opportunity to earn a living legally. While there are some promotional pressure groups which try to defend their interests (such as Amnesty International and the Refugee Council), these organizations have had little influence on government policy. For example, in 2002, 10,410 asylum seekers were forcibly removed, and the government has introduced a range of measures designed to make it more difficult for asylum seekers to get to Britain and successfully claim asylum. These measures include:

> *a clampdown on entitlement to benefits, the closure of the Sangatte transit camp near Calais, tighter security around the Channel Tunnel and the extension of the number of 'white list' countries, whose asylum seekers are rapidly returned with no right of appeal.* Morris, 2003

Reappraisals of classical pluralism

It is not surprising that, given the strength and number of criticisms advanced against classical pluralism, some of its supporters have modified their positions to take account of some of the weaknesses of classical pluralism.

David Marsh (1983) described a number of attempts to explain the distribution of power and the operation of the state as **elite pluralist theories**. These theories share important similarities with classical pluralism:

1. They see Western societies as basically democratic.
2. They regard government as a process of compromise.
3. They agree that power is widely dispersed.

On the other hand:

1. They do not accept that all members of society have exactly the same amount of power.
2. They do not concentrate exclusively on the first face of power.
3. They see elites, the leaders of groups, as the main participants in decision making.

Wyn Grant – pressure groups and elite pluralism

In more recent work, Wyn Grant (1999) has supported what is essentially an elite pluralist position. Focusing on the role of pressure groups, he notes a number of important changes in British politics:

1. The power of the pressure groups – which were most influential in the 1970s – has declined. Thus the TUC and the CBI have lost their central role in discussions with the government, although they still retain some influence.
2. The number of pressure groups has greatly expanded, so that very few interests can now claim to be unrepresented.
3. Pressure groups no longer focus so exclusively on Westminster and on changing government policy. There are now 'multiple arenas' in which they try to exert influence. These include the European Union and the courts, and in the future will include the devolved parliaments in Wales, Scotland and Northern Ireland. Some pressure groups try to influence people's activities directly rather than trying to get the government to act. For example, the oil company Shell was persuaded not to dump its disused oil rig Brent Spar in the North Sea partly by boycotts of products encouraged by environmental pressure groups.

4 Linked to the above point is an increased use of various forms of direct action. Examples include the firebombing of milk tankers in Cheshire by radical, vegan, animal rights campaigners; the release of mink from mink farms by the Animal Liberation Front; the attempts by anti-roads campaigners to prevent road building; and the attempts of farmers to blockade ports to prevent the importation of Irish beef. Such methods have mixed results, but some, at least, are effective. Direct action not only gains publicity; it can also sometimes increase the costs of activities – for example, building roads or farming mink – so that economic disincentives are created.

5 Despite the increase in direct action, there has also been an increase in the number of pressure groups consulted by governments. Some groups previously regarded as outsider groups (such as Greenpeace) have become accepted by governments as suitable groups to consult over matters that concern them. Nevertheless, Grant still believes that a distinction between insider and outsider groups remains valid. Like other elite pluralists, he believes insider groups tend to have more influence than outsider groups, although the latter group can sometimes achieve their objectives through direct action.

Grant concludes: 'For all the talk of a "new" Britain and a "new" politics, there is much that looks like "business as usual" in the world of pressure group politics.' Pressure groups still help to ensure that Britain is essentially democratic, but it remains true that some groups have more influence than others.

Evaluation of pluralism

Clearly, elite pluralism does answer some of the criticisms advanced against classical pluralism. It allows for the possibility that, at least temporarily, some interests may not be represented and some groups may have more power than others. It acknowledges that all individuals may not play an active part in politics, and it does not rely exclusively on measuring the first face of power, decision making. However, the analysis of elite pluralists may not be satisfactory in at least three ways:

1 In showing that democracies do not work perfectly, their own evidence raises doubts about the basic pluralist view that power is widely dispersed in Western industrial societies.

2 While they note the existence of elite leaders, they fail to discuss the possibility that these elites monopolize power and use it in their own interests.

3 Elite pluralists take account of two faces of power, but ignore the third. They do not discuss the power of some members of society to influence the wishes of others.

Pluralism and elite pluralism both see a healthy democracy as one in which large numbers of people are involved in politics, either through participation in political parties or pressure groups, or through voting. However, there has been a significant decline in at least some forms of participation in recent years. Turnout at general elections has fallen, as has membership of political parties. There is also evidence of more disillusionment with politics. This raises questions about the pluralist view that Western democracies are truly democratic (see pp. 546–8).

Elite theory

Elite theory differs from both pluralism and functionalism in that it sees power in society as being monopolized by a small minority (or elite). Elite theory sees society as divided into two main groups: a **ruling minority** who exercise power through the state, and the **ruled**.

There are, however, a number of ways in which elite theorists differ. They do not agree as to whether elite rule is desirable or beneficial for society; they differ in their conclusions about the inevitability of elite rule; and they do not agree about exactly who constitutes the elite or elites.

Classical elite theory

Elite theory was first developed by two Italian sociologists: Vilfredo Pareto (1848–1923) and Gaetano Mosca (1858–1911). Both saw elite rule as inevitable and dismissed the possibility of a proletarian revolution leading to the establishment of a communist society. As such they were arguing against Marx's view of power and the state.

Because of the inevitability of elite rule neither saw it as desirable that any attempt should be made to end it. Pareto and Mosca agreed that the basis of elite rule was the superior personal qualities of those who made up the elites. Pareto believed that elites possessed more cunning or intelligence, while Mosca saw them as having more organizational ability. Since people were unequal, some would always have more ability than others, and would therefore occupy the elite positions in society.

According to both theorists, apart from the personal qualities of its members, an elite owes its power to its internal organization. It forms a united and cohesive minority in the face of an unorganized and fragmented mass. In Mosca's words: 'The power of the minority is irresistible as against each single individual in the majority.'

Major decisions that affect society are taken by the elite. Even in so-called democratic societies these decisions will usually reflect the concerns of the elite rather than the wishes of the people. Elite theorists picture the majority as apathetic and unconcerned with the major issues of the day. The mass of the population is largely controlled and manipulated by the elite, passively accepting the propaganda which justifies elite rule.

Although there are broad similarities in the work of these two classical elite theorists, there are also some differences.

Pareto (1963, first published 1915–19) believed that history consisted of one type of elite replacing another, a process he called the **circulation of elites**. He identified two types of elite: cunning foxes, and strong and decisive lions. Each type had their weaknesses, meaning they would eventually be superseded by the other type.

Like Pareto, Gaetano Mosca (1939) believed that rule by a minority was an inevitable feature of social life. Mosca argued that different qualities would create elites in different sorts of society, but even democracies would be dominated by elites. He accepted that democracies were more open than other sorts of society, but believed that representative democracy still allowed a small group to take control of the reins of power and rule over the disorganized mass of the population.

Pareto's view of elites has been heavily criticized for being based on little or no systematic evidence and for placing undue emphasis on psychological characteristics. Furthermore, most sociologists today would not accept that elites should necessarily be seen as superior to other groups in society.

However, the general idea of elite theory – that small groups can become dominant through organization and through holding positions of power – remains influential. A number of sociologists have developed the principles of classical elite theory in more modern contexts.

Elite theory and the USA – C. Wright Mills

Whereas Pareto and Mosca attempted to provide a general theory to explain the nature and distribution of power in all societies, the American sociologist C. Wright Mills (1956) presented a less ambitious and less wide-ranging version of elite theory. He limited his analysis to American society in the 1950s.

Unlike the early elite theorists, Mills did not believe that elite rule was inevitable; in fact he saw it as a fairly recent development in the USA. Unlike Pareto, who accepted the domination of the masses by elites, Mills roundly condemned elite rule. Since he saw elite rule as based upon the exploitation of the masses, he adopted a conflict version of elite theory. Because the elites and the masses had different interests, this created the potential for conflict between the two groups.

The power elite

Writing in the 1950s, Mills explained elite rule in institutional rather than psychological terms. He argued that the structure of institutions was such that those at the top of the institutional hierarchy largely monopolized power. Certain institutions occupied key pivotal positions in society and the elite comprised those who held **command posts** in those institutions.

Mills identified three key institutions:

1. The major corporations
2. The military
3. The federal government

Those who occupied the command posts in these institutions formed three elites. In practice, however, the interests and activities of the elites were sufficiently similar and interconnected to form a single ruling majority, which Mills termed the **power elite**. Thus the power elite involved the 'coincidence of economic, military and political power'. For example, Mills claimed: 'American capitalism is now in considerable part military capitalism.' As tanks, guns and missiles poured from the factories, the interests of both the economic and military elites were served. In the same way, Mills argued that business and government 'cannot now be seen as two distinct worlds'. He referred to political leaders as 'lieutenants' of the economic elite, and claimed their decisions systematically favoured the interests of the giant corporations.

The net result of the coincidence of economic, military and political power was a power elite which dominated American society and took all decisions of major national and international importance.

Elite unity

However, things had not always been so. The power elite owed its dominance to a change in the 'institutional landscape'.

In the nineteenth century, economic power was fragmented among a multitude of small businesses. By the 1950s it was concentrated in the hands of a few hundred giant corporations 'which together hold the keys to economic decision'.

Political power was similarly fragmented and localized and, in particular, state legislatures had considerable independence in the face of a weak central government. The federal government eroded the autonomy of the states, and political power became increasingly centralized.

The growing threat of international conflict led to a vast increase in the size and power of the military. The local, state-controlled militia were replaced by a centrally directed military organization.

These developments led to a centralization of decision-making power. As a result, power was increasingly concentrated in the hands of those in the command posts of the key institutions.

According to Mills, the cohesiveness and unity of the power elite were strengthened by the similarity of the social backgrounds of its members and the interchange and overlapping of personnel between the three elites. Members were drawn largely from the upper stratum of society; they were mainly Protestant, native-born Americans, from urban areas in the eastern USA. They shared similar educational backgrounds and mixed socially in the same high-prestige clubs. As a result, they tended to share similar values and sympathies, which provided a basis for mutual trust and cooperation.

Within the power elite there was frequent interchange of personnel between the three elites: a corporation director might become a politician and vice versa. At any one time, individuals might have footholds in more than one elite.

Elite dominance

Mills argued that American society was dominated by a power elite of 'unprecedented power and unaccountability'. He claimed that momentous decisions such as the American entry into the Second World War and the dropping of the atomic bomb on Hiroshima were made by the power elite with little or no reference to the people.

Despite the fact that such decisions affected all members of society, the power elite was not accountable for its actions, either directly to the public or to any body which represented the public interest. Mills saw no real differences between the two major political parties – the Democrats and the Republicans – and therefore the public was not provided with a choice of alternative policies.

In Mills's analysis, the bulk of the population was pictured as a passive and quiescent mass controlled by the power elite which subjected it to 'instruments of psychic management and manipulation'. Excluded from the command posts of power, the 'man in the mass' was told what to think, what to feel, what to do and what to hope for by a mass media directed by the elite. Unconcerned with the major issues of the day, 'he' was preoccupied with 'his' personal world of work, leisure, family and neighbourhood. Free from popular control, the power elite pursued its own concerns – power and self-aggrandizement.

Hywel Williams – *Britain's Power Elites*

The rise of elite power in Britain

Although Mills was writing more than fifty years ago in the USA, some contemporary writers believe that his ideas are applicable to Britain in the twenty-first century. Hywel Williams (2006) explicitly pays tribute to the pioneering work of Mills in his book *Britain's Power Elites: The Rebirth of a Ruling Class.*

Like Mills, Williams sees the development of dominant power elites as a historically specific event, in this case happening in Britain since the early 1990s. Williams also follows Mills in identifying three elites, in this case the political elites, the professional elites, and the financial/business elites. These elites have gradually managed to gain power and have used it to consolidate and then further their own interests.

Williams sees elite power as stemming partly from the occupation of key positions, but he also sees control over money and the manipulation of language as important. Williams puts particular stress on the power of the financial/business elite, especially those working in the City of London. According to Williams, political and professional elites usually have to defer to the financial muscle of the City which has become vital to Britain's economy.

Elites also use language to persuade the population that there is no alternative to their rule. Williams says:

> *Occupying positions at the very apex of our society, they use the language of national interest, valour and endeavour in order to keep themselves in power. But by their very existence they have proved to be the destroyers of the democratic aspirations and the effective debate which should lie at the heart of an open society.* 2006, p. 26

Having outlined his general views on elite power in Britain, Williams goes on to examine the position of each group of elites in turn.

The political elites

Williams sees 'The upper echelons of the party machines' – particularly MPs and active members of the House of Lords – as Britain's **political elites**. Ministers have much more power than MPs and they work closely with senior civil servants. Ministers and civil servants share a 'fundamental mental similarity as management types' (Williams, 2006, p. 27).

Like Mills, Williams sees democratic choices as largely illusory; in reality there is now little difference between the main parties, and leaders such as Tony Blair and David Cameron are more or less interchangeable, with very similar policies. Williams says:

> *Political and journalistic ingenuity in Britain is directed towards the conversion of molehills into mountains as interchangeable managers seek to seduce a few thousand floating voters with the cut of their jib, the sweetness of their smile and the persuasively soft drape of a tailored suit.* 2006, p. 28

Not only has government been reduced to a managerial role as ideological differences between parties have disappeared, but the scope of that role has also been curtailed. Privatization and a decline in the belief that the government can control the economy have restricted what politicians are expected to do. Much more has been left to the 'free market'.

However, Williams believes that politicians remain 'hugely influential' as the 'conduits of power'. They link business, professional and political elites together through 'their capacity of knowing who to talk to, along with an expertise in knowing how and when that talking has to be done' (2006, p. 39).

Furthermore, the political elite manages to retain some of its power through the use of patronage. They make appointments to numerous agencies such as regulators of public services. They also have the ability to employ private sector consultants and managers who are brought in to advise or run institutions such as city academies. There are very strong links, therefore, between political and professional elites who work for the private and public organizations employed by the state.

Political elites also have strong links with financial/business elites. In 2001, the House of Commons Register of Members' Interests showed that 58 of the 646 MPs had significant business interests, such as executive or non-executive directorships. Furthermore, ministers who leave office and MPs who step down are often offered roles in business upon their departure.

Williams also provides evidence that elites tend to be self-perpetuating; elite positions are often passed on to relatives of existing members of the elite. He points out that even in the Labour Party many senior figures have a family history of holding senior positions. Examples include Charles Clarke, Hilary Benn and David and Ed Miliband, all cabinet ministers in recent Labour governments.

With their links to other elites and tendency to recruit new members from elite families, Williams believes there is little chance of political elites introducing radical change that undermines elite power. He observes that Labour politicians might start out as radicals, but by the time they become cabinet ministers the radical edge has gone and they act dutifully to defend elite privilege. Politicians such as Jack Straw, Peter Hain and Charles Clarke all abandoned the radical activism of youth as they climbed to cabinet rank.

The professional elites

The professional and management elite is far more numerous than the political elite, but, according to Williams, it has thrived only since the end of the 1970s. Williams believes, however, that the gains have been at the expense of some autonomy for professionals. Their professional expertise is not regarded with the same deference as it once was. Groups such as doctors, solicitors and teachers have lost some independence and have increasingly become the servants of business or the state. They are controlled through targets and their work is increasingly monitored and evaluated.

The old professions (such as the scientific, legal and medical professions) have done well in terms of wages, but much power has shifted to what Williams calls the **new professions**. The new professionals set targets to try to ensure 'delivery' in the public and private sector. Rather than possessing distinct expertise in a specific area of knowledge, they use management jargon to assert their right to monitor and control others. Williams describes them as 'professional elites who, for an hourly computed fee, stand ever-ready to regulate, assess and measure the quality of the work done by those in the public sector who work for a fraction of their own salaries' (2006, p. 100).

The archetypal example of a new professional is the management consultant who is paid to go into a public or private sector organization to advise on how it should be run. Williams notes that in 2004–5 management consultants earned no less than £1 billion advising the government.

There has also been a rapid expansion of public sector workers since New Labour came to power in 1997, many of whom are involved in regulating, administering, managing and monitoring the work of other public sector workers rather than using their expertise to provide services. Lacking any real, useful expertise, these groups maintain power through the ability to 'dominate argument by jargon, evasion and enclosed systems of thought' (Williams, 2006, p. 160). For all professionals, success now depends less upon developing professional expertise and has more to do with acquiescing to the demands of their paymasters, private business or the state.

The financial and business elite

While political and professional elites are both powerful, Williams believes that the financial and business elite is more powerful than either. He claims that financial and business elites have more power than at any time in British history. Other elites have to defer to them. Many professionals are employed in the private sector and political decisions are only taken if they do not damage financial and business interests.

The City of London is now much more important than manufacturing industry. The vast wealth created by financiers in the City underpins the British economy and the government cannot risk alienating City opinion. Decisions such as whether to adopt the euro or opt for closer European integration are 'largely governed by what suits the City and its needs as a centre for foreign exchange dealing' (Williams, 2006, p. 165).

As manufacturing and the wealth of landowners have declined, the financial institutions of the City have gained pre-eminence. This has partly been fuelled by mergers and takeovers which create vast fees and bonuses for City workers. The wages and bonuses of City elites dwarf those of political and professional elites. For example, in 2006 the chief executive of Standard Chartered Bank earned some £2 million, and some traders in financial instruments can receive bonuses of £5 to £10 million.

With such sums available it is not surprising that members of other elites are drawn towards the City. Former senior civil servants, cabinet ministers and government advisers are increasingly employed in City jobs or company directorships. Political parties, including the Labour Party, increasingly rely upon donations from business people to keep their party afloat; and corporations benefit greatly from the government as a customer. Pharmaceutical companies sell drugs to the NHS, often at inflated prices. Arms manufacturers such as BAE (formerly British Aerospace) rely on government military contracts for the bulk of their sales.

The links between the public and private sectors have become much closer. The PFI (Private Finance Initiative) allows government spending (for example on building new hospitals) through the use of private money. This makes the government reliant upon business for its programme, and makes healthy profits for financial and business elites who have to be repaid with interest.

Conclusion

Williams concludes that financial and business elites now sit at the apex of a pyramid of power in Britain. They, along with less prominent elites, have taken power in a quiet and unobtrusive 'very British coup' (2006, p. 219). They have been able to do so because other centres of power, such as the trade unions and the church, have declined.

The Labour Party, which used to represent the interests of workers rather than capital, has become entangled with the interests of the financial and business elites. It has not been easy for these elites to become dominant, and they have had to work hard to maintain their grip on power. But their position has become more entrenched over time as they have become more organized. Like Mills, therefore, Williams sees elite power as stemming from a lack of well-organized opposition to these elites.

Elite self-recruitment in Britain

Williams's account of elite power in Britain is supported by numerous examples, but a lack of systematic evidence. One way of establishing whether a relatively closed elite exists is to examine where its members come from. If they are largely recruited from the ranks of the children of the elite, this process is known as **elite self-recruitment**. A number of researchers have found that the majority of those who occupy elite positions in Britain are recruited from the minority of the population with highly privileged backgrounds. This appears to apply to a wide range of British elites, including politicians, judges, higher civil servants, senior military officers, and the directors of large companies and major banks.

There is also evidence that there may be some degree of cohesion within and between the various elites. Individuals may occupy positions within more than one elite: cabinet ministers and other MPs may hold directorships in large companies. Individuals may move between elites: the former businessman Geoffrey Robinson became a minister in Tony Blair's first cabinet in 1997. Directors may also sit on the boards of a number of different companies.

Elites are also likely to have a common educational background: many members of elites attended public schools and went to Oxford or Cambridge University. John Rex argues that this type of education serves to socialize future top decision makers into a belief in the legitimacy of the status quo. It creates the possibility that the elites will be able to act together to protect their own interests. Rex suggests:

> *The whole system of 'Establishment' education has been used to ensure a common mind on the legitimacy of the existing order of things among those who have to occupy positions of power and decision.* Rex, 1974

The following studies provide evidence for the existence of such elites in Britain.

The educational background of British elites

Studies of the background of British elites were more common in the 1970s than they have been in recent decades. However, sporadic research has provided some contemporary evidence on elites in Britain.

Research by the Sutton Trust (2005a) examined the background of those at the top of the legal profession. Around 7 per cent of the UK population attend private schools, but in 2004 75 per cent of Law Lords and Judges of Appeal, and 69 per cent of barristers at the leading chambers, had been educated privately; 81 per cent of these judges and 82 per cent of the barristers had been to Oxford or Cambridge University. Furthermore, the evidence suggested that there had been little change over time. For example, the percentage of the most senior judges who had been to private school had declined by just 1 per cent between 1989 and 2004.

The Sutton Trust (2006) also conducted research into the background of the 100 leading news journalists in the UK. It found that the proportion of these journalists who had been to private schools actually increased between 1986 and 2005, from 49 per cent to 54 per cent. In 2005, 45 per cent had been educated at Oxford or Cambridge University.

There is no information available on the school education of chief executives of major companies; however, information is available on their university education. A report by the London Chamber of Commerce (2006) found that 25 per cent of the chief executives of Britain's 100 largest companies had been to Oxford or Cambridge University, and 33 per cent had been to one of the top thirteen universities in the country. This economic elite therefore had a less privileged educational background than the elites discussed above, but they were still much more likely to have attended a prestigious university than the population as a whole.

Detailed data have been collected on political elites. Researchers found a decline in the proportion of MPs attending private schools. For example, Borthwick *et al.* (1991) found that the proportion of Conservative MPs who had been privately educated declined between 1979 and 1987.

However, recent research shows that the privately educated are still substantially over-represented in British politics. According to Byron Criddle (2005), 18 per cent of Labour MPs elected in 2005 had been to private schools, as had 60 per cent of Conservative MPs and 39 per cent of Liberal Democrats. The Sutton Trust (2005b) found that 25 per cent of members of the Labour government had been educated privately. Furthermore, in the House of Lords 62 per cent of members had been educated outside the state sector.

Criddle (2005) also examined the occupations of MPs elected in 2005. Most came from professional or business backgrounds; just 10 per cent of Labour, 1 per cent of Conservative and 2 per cent of Liberal Democrat MPs had previously had a manual, working-class occupation.

If anything, those at the top of government are even more likely to come from elite backgrounds than backbench MPs. David Cracknell, Isabel Oakeshott and Alan Schofield (2007) examined the makeup of Tony Blair's last cabinet and Gordon Brown's first cabinet in 2007. There were twenty-three ministers in the last Blair cabinet, of whom seven had been to private schools and eight to Oxford or Cambridge. Brown's first cabinet had twenty-two members, of whom nine had been privately educated and over half (thirteen) had attended Cambridge or Oxford University.

Elite theory in the USA and Britain – an evaluation

The evidence provided by C. Wright Mills and researchers in Britain shows that those occupying elite positions often come from privileged backgrounds, and that there are connections between different elites. Williams's work suggests that power is increasingly concentrated in the hands of financial and business elites. However, the significance of these findings and the accuracy of these claims are open to dispute.

Some Marxists claim that the evidence points to the existence of a ruling class based upon economic power, rather than a ruling elite based upon the occupation of 'command posts'.

Furthermore, it has been argued that elite theory fails to measure power adequately: it does not show that elites actually have power, nor that they exercise power in their own interests against the interests of the majority of the population. Elite theory largely assumes that the elite have power and use it for their own ends.

For example, Robert A. Dahl (1973) criticized Mills from a pluralist perspective. He claimed that Mills had simply shown that the power elite had the 'potential for control'. Mills conducted no research to show that they used this potential to further their own interests.

Dahl's criticism of Mills applies with equal force to British studies of elite self-recruitment. Furthermore, the British studies make no attempt to measure the second and third faces of power (they make no reference to non-decision making, nor do they discuss how the wishes of the population may be manipulated by elites). As such, studies of elite self-recruitment may reveal something about patterns of social mobility but they provide little direct evidence about who actually has power.

Williams looks beyond patterns of elite self-recruitment but he fails to show that elites always act in their own interests at the expense of the interests of the bulk of the population. Some would claim that professional, political and financial/business elites have raised prosperity and the quality of public services in Britain and have not merely feathered their own nest.

From a very different point of view, Marxists and some other conflict theorists would claim that all elite theory fails to identify the underlying basis for power. In particular, Marxists argue that power derives from wealth in the form of owning the means of production, rather than from the occupation of senior positions in society. We will examine Marxist views on power and the state in the next section.

Power and the state – Marxist perspectives

Marxist perspectives, like elite theory, see power as concentrated in the hands of a minority in society. Marxist theorists also agree with those elite theorists who see power being used to further the interests of the powerful.

Marxist theories stress that the powerful and the powerless have different interests and that these differences may lead to conflict in society. Unlike elite theory, though, Marxist approaches do not assume that power rests with those who occupy key positions in the state. They see the source of power as lying elsewhere in society. In particular, Marxists put primary emphasis upon economic resources as a source of power.

A wide variety of Marxist theories of power have been developed. We start this section by examining the work of Marx himself, and his friend and collaborator Engels, before going on to consider the views of those who have developed less orthodox Marxist views.

Marx and Engels on power and the state

According to Marx, power is concentrated in the hands of those who have economic control within a society (Marx, 1974, 1978, first published 1909 and 1867; Marx and Engels, 1950b). From this perspective, the source of power lies in the economic infrastructure:

1. In all class-divided societies the means of production are owned and controlled by the ruling class. This relationship to the means of production provides the basis of its dominance. It therefore follows that the only way to return power to the people involves communal ownership of the means of production.
2. In a communist society, power would be more equally distributed among the whole of the population, since the means of production would be communally owned rather than owned by individuals.

As we have seen in previous chapters, in capitalist society ruling-class power is used to exploit and oppress the subject class, and much of the wealth produced by the proletariat's labour power is appropriated in the form of profit or surplus value by the bourgeoisie. From a Marxist perspective, the use of power to exploit others is defined as **coercion**. It is seen as an illegitimate use of power since it forces the subject class to submit to a situation which is against its interests. If ruling-class power is accepted as legitimate by the subject class, this is an indication of **false class consciousness**.

Ruling-class power extends beyond specifically economic relationships. In terms of Marxist theory, the relationships of domination and subordination in the infrastructure will largely be reproduced in the superstructure (see pp. 26–9 for a definition of these terms). The state (as part of the superstructure) reflects the distribution of power in society. The decisions and activities of the state will favour the interests of the ruling class rather than those of the population as a whole.

Despite the general thrust of the arguments of Marx and Engels, there are, as we will see, some inconsistencies in their statements about the state.

The origins and evolution of the state

Engels claimed that in primitive communist societies the state did not exist. Kinship (or family relationships) formed the basis of social groupings (Engels 1884, in Marx and Engels, 1950b). These societies were essentially agricultural, and no surplus was produced beyond what was necessary for subsistence. It was therefore impossible for large amounts of wealth to be accumulated and concentrated in the hands of a few. There was little division of labour, and the means of production were communally owned.

Only when societies began to produce a surplus did it become possible for a ruling class to emerge. Once one group in society became economically dominant, a state developed.

Engels believed the state was necessary to 'hold class antagonisms in check'. In primitive communist societies all individuals shared the same interests; in class societies, a minority benefited from the existing social system at the expense of the majority. According to Engels, the exploited majority had to be held down to prevent them from asserting their interests and threatening the position of the ruling class. Thus, in ancient Athens, the 90,000 Athenian citizens used the state as a method of repressing the 365,000 slaves.

The simplest way the state could control the subject class was through the use of force or coercion. Engels pointed to the police, the prisons and the army as state-run institutions used to repress the exploited members of society.

Engels believed coercion was the main type of power used to control the population in early states. In ancient Athens and Rome, and the feudal states of the Middle Ages, ruling-class control of the state was clearly apparent. For example, the feudal state consisted exclusively of landowners; serfs possessed neither private property nor political rights.

However, Engels believed that more advanced forms of the state were less obviously a coercive tool of the ruling class. Indeed, Engels described democracies as the 'highest form of state', for with such a state all members of society appear to have equal political power. Each individual in societies with universal suffrage can vote, and in theory therefore has as much influence over government policy as every other individual. According to Engels, this would tend to mean that the existing social order would be perceived as fair, just and legitimate, since the state would be seen to reflect the wishes of the population. As such, the state would not need to rely so heavily on the use of force: in most cases the authority of the state would be accepted by the population.

In reality, however, Engels believed democracy was an illusion. Real power continued to rest with the owners of the means of production, and not with the population as a whole.

One way in which the ruling class could ensure that the state continued to act in its interest was through corruption. Troublesome officials who threatened to follow policies harmful to the bourgeoisie could be bribed. A second way to determine government policies was through the use of the financial power of capitalists. The state often relied upon borrowing money from the bourgeoisie in order to meet its debts. Loans could be withheld if the state refused to follow policies beneficial to the bourgeoisie.

The end of the state

Marx and Engels did not believe that the state would be a permanent feature of society. Since they believed its purpose was to protect the position of the ruling class and to control the subject class, they argued it would become redundant once classes disappeared. In the immediate aftermath of the proletarian revolution, the proletariat would seize control of the state. They would use it to consolidate their position, establish communal ownership of the means of production, and destroy the power of the bourgeoisie. Once these objectives had been achieved, class division would no longer exist, and the state would 'wither away'.

The views of Marx and Engels on the state are neatly summed up in the Communist Manifesto, where they say: 'The executive of the modern state is but a committee for managing the common affairs of the whole bourgeoisie' (Marx and Engels, 1950a, first published 1848).

However, Engels did accept that in certain circumstances the state could play an independent role in society, where its actions would not be completely controlled by a single class. Engels argued that, at particular points in history, two classes could have roughly equal power. He claimed that in some monarchies of seventeenth- and eighteenth-century Europe the landowning aristocracy and the rising bourgeoisie were in opposition to each other and both were equally powerful. In this situation the state could take an independent line, since the warring classes effectively cancelled each other out.

Furthermore, in his more empirical studies, Marx recognized that there might be divisions within states in capitalist countries. For example, in *The Class Struggles in France 1848–1850* (Marx, in Marx and Engels, 1950a), Marx acknowledged a difference in interests between finance capitalists on the one hand and the industrial bourgeoisie on the other. Finance capitalists (many of whom were large landowners) had an interest in the government of France retaining the huge debt it had at the time, since financiers could benefit from lending money to the French state. On the other hand, the industrial bourgeoisie were being harmed by the taxes needed to service the debt.

Marx and Engels inspired many later Marxists to devote a great deal of attention to the study of power and the state, but their original work is sometimes vague, and it is sometimes inconsistent. It has been interpreted in different ways.

Furthermore, the work of the founders of Marxism has not been entirely free from criticism from more recent Marxists. Consequently, a number of contrasting Marxist theories of the state have been developed. These differ over the precise way in which they see the bourgeoisie controlling the state, the extent to which they believe the state enjoys independence from ruling-class control, and the importance they attach to this institution for maintaining the predominance of the bourgeoisie in capitalist societies.

Ralph Miliband – the capitalist state

The British sociologist Ralph Miliband (1969) followed Marx and Engels in seeing power as being derived from wealth. Miliband believed the state could sometimes act as the direct tool or instrument of those who possess economic power, the ruling class. They used it to preserve their economic dominance, maintain their political power and stabilize capitalist society by preventing threats to their position. However, Miliband did accept that in some circumstances direct intervention by the wealthy was not necessary in order for the state to act in their interests.

Elites and the ruling class

To Miliband, the state was run by a number of elites who ran the central institutions. These elites included cabinet ministers, MPs, senior police and military officers, and top judges. Together, they acted largely to defend the ruling class or bourgeoisie: Miliband believed that all the elites shared a basic interest in the preservation of capitalism and the defence of private property. Miliband attempted to justify his claims by presenting a wide range of empirical evidence:

1. He tried to show that many of those who occupy elite positions are themselves members of the bourgeoisie. For example, he pointed out that in Britain people from business backgrounds made up about 33 per cent of British cabinets between 1886 and 1950.
2. He claimed that the non-business person in the state elite will, in any case, act in the interests of the bourgeoisie. He argued that groups such as politicians, senior civil servants and judges tend to come from a similar background to the bourgeoisie; they have often been to the same schools and may have family ties with them. Consequently, they will tend to share a similar outlook and follow policies which support bourgeois interests. Even those from

working-class backgrounds who make it into the elite will have to have adopted bourgeois values to get there.

3 Miliband claimed that the actions of the state elites have, in practice, tended to benefit the ruling class. He pointed out that judges saw one of their primary duties as the protection of private property. He suggested Labour governments had done little to challenge the dominance of the ruling class and redistribute wealth.

Legitimation

Miliband also advanced an explanation as to why the majority of the population should accept a state which acts against their interests. He examined various ways in which the subject class was persuaded to accept the status quo. In effect, he considered the third face of power, claiming that the economic power of the ruling class enabled them partly to shape the beliefs and wishes of the remainder of the population.

He believed this took place through the process of **legitimation**, which indoctrinated the public into the acceptance of capitalism. In particular, advertising is used to promote the view that the major concern of big business is public service and the welfare of the community, while persuading people that the way to happiness and fulfilment involves the accumulation of material possessions – in particular, the acquisition of the products of capitalism.

To sum up, Miliband argued that there is direct interference by members of ruling elites in the state. Their dominance is further cemented through the socialization of state personnel from non-elite backgrounds into the values of the elite, and the manipulation of the beliefs of the mass of the population so that they will lend support to pro-capitalist policies.

Nicos Poulantzas – a structuralist view of the state

Nicos Poulantzas (1969, 1976) criticized Miliband's view of the state and provided an alternative Marxist interpretation which places less stress on the actions of individuals and more on the role of social structure. A **structuralist** approach emphasizes the importance of social structure, and minimizes the importance of the actions of individuals in society. As such, Poulantzas saw much of the evidence advanced by Miliband as irrelevant to a Marxist view of the state.

The state and the capitalist system

Poulantzas described the state as 'the factor of cohesion of a social formation': in other words, the state was vital for maintaining the stability of the capitalist system. As part of the superstructure, it would automatically tend to serve the interests of the ruling class. It was not necessary for members of the ruling class to occupy elite positions within the state: the existence of a capitalist system was itself sufficient to ensure that the state functioned to benefit the ruling class.

Similarly, the background of members of the state elite was of little importance: it was not their class origin but their class position which determined their behaviour. Since they occupied positions in a state, which inevitably functions to benefit the bourgeoisie, their job would ensure that they acted in the interests of the bourgeoisie, regardless of their background. They would not take actions harmful to capitalist interests.

Relative autonomy

Poulantzas took this argument a stage further. He claimed:

> *The capitalist state best serves the interests of the capitalist class only when members of this class do not participate directly in the state apparatus, that is to say when the ruling class is not the politically governing class.*
> Poulantzas, 1969

Poulantzas argued that the ruling class did not directly govern, but rather its interests were served through the medium of the state. As such, the state was relatively autonomous. To some degree it was free from the ruling class's direct influence, independent from its direct control. However, since the state was shaped by the infrastructure, it was forced to represent the interests of capital.

Poulantzas argued that the relative autonomy of the state was essential if it was to represent capital effectively. The state required a certain amount of freedom and independence in order to serve ruling-class interests. If it were staffed by members of the bourgeoisie, it might lose this freedom of action.

The following reasons have been given for the relative autonomy of the capitalist state:

1 As a group, the bourgeoisie is not free from internal divisions and conflicts of interest. To represent its common interests the state must have the freedom to act on behalf of the class as a whole.

2 If the bourgeoisie ruled directly, its power might be weakened by internal wrangling and disagreement, and it might fail to present a united front in conflicts with the proletariat. The relative autonomy of the state allows it to rise above sectional interests within the bourgeoisie and to represent that class as a whole.

3 The state must have the freedom to make concessions to the subject class, which might be opposed by the bourgeoisie. Such concessions serve to defuse radical working-class protest and to contain the demands within the framework of a capitalist economy.

4 Finally, the relative autonomy of the state enables it to promote the myth that it represents society as a whole. The state presents itself as a representative of 'the people', of 'public interest' and 'national unity'. Thus, it has an ideological role; the state disguises the fact that essentially it represents ruling-class interests.

Repressive and ideological state apparatus

Poulantzas did not disagree with Miliband about the importance of legitimation. However, he went much further in seeing this process as being directly related to the state. He used a broader definition of the state than Miliband. He divided it into the **repressive apparatus** – the army, government, police, tribunals and administration – which exercises coercive power, and the **ideological apparatus** – the church, political parties, the unions, schools, the mass media and the family – which is concerned with the manipulation of values and beliefs, rather than the use of force.

Most writers do not see institutions such as the family as constituting part of the state. Poulantzas argued that they should be categorized in this way because they were necessary for the survival of capitalism as they fostered false class consciousness.

Criticisms of Poulantzas

Miliband (1972) tried to defend himself against the criticisms made by Poulantzas, and he put forward his own criticisms of the latter's work. In particular he accused Poulantzas of **structural super-determinism**. In other words, Miliband did not believe that ultimately all aspects of the behaviour of the state were determined by the infrastructure. Such a theory, he claimed, could not account for the differences between fascist and 'democratic' states within capitalist systems.

Furthermore, Miliband argued that Poulantzas's theory was not backed up by empirical evidence. It was not sufficient to simply assert that the state must act in the interests of capitalism.

Miliband also questioned the definition of the state proposed by Poulantzas. He expressed great scepticism about the claim that institutions such as the family could be seen as part of the state. He accepted that they might have an ideological role, but in his view they possess so much independence or autonomy that it is ridiculous to see them as part of the state.

It can also be argued that the theory of relative autonomy is impossible to prove or disprove. If the theory is accepted, any action the state takes can be interpreted one way or another as benefiting the bourgeoisie. If it does not appear to benefit them directly, it can be dismissed as a mere concession to the proletariat. Some neo-Marxists argue that concessions can be more than token gestures. To writers such as Gramsci, the working class do have some power and can influence the actions of the state. (We will analyse neo-Marxist views later in this chapter – see pp. 539–41.)

Evidence to support Marxism

Marxist writers have adopted more sophisticated methods of measuring power than either pluralists or elite theorists. They have examined all three faces of power identified by Steven Lukes (1974), and have also extended the concept to include the effects of decisions.

The effects of decisions

As we saw earlier, the decision-making approach to measuring power used by pluralists has been heavily criticized. Marxists such as Westergaard and Resler (1976) argued that power can only be measured by its results: if scarce and valued resources are concentrated in the hands of a minority, that group largely monopolizes power in society. Put simply, the proof of the pudding is in the eating: whoever reaps the largest rewards holds the largest share of power.

Westergaard and Resler believed that the welfare state does little to redistribute income, for it is largely financed out of the taxes paid by the working class. More recent research conducted by Westergaard (1995) suggests that, if anything, the 1980s and early 1990s saw increased inequality in Britain (see pp. 88–9). (This is also backed up by recent research on widening inequality – see pp. 35–41.)

Concessions to the working class

In Britain, as in other advanced capitalist societies, the state has implemented a wide range of reforms which appear to benefit directly either the subject class in particular or society as a whole. These include legislation to improve health and safety in the workplace, social security benefits such as old-age pensions and unemployment and sickness benefit, a national health service, and free education for all.

However, these reforms have left the basic structure of inequality unchanged. They have been largely financed from the wages of those they were intended to benefit and have resulted in little redistribution of wealth. They can be seen as concessions, which serve to defuse working-class protest and prevent it from developing in more radical directions which might threaten the basis of ruling-class dominance.

Non-decision making

Marxists have also been concerned to examine the second face of power: non-decision making. John Urry, in criticizing Dahl, argued that he:

> *ignores the process by which certain issues come to be defined as decisions and others do not. The study of decisions is the failure to study who has the power to determine what are decisions.* Urry, in Urry and Wakeford, 1973

Many Marxists believe the range of issues and alternatives considered by governments in capitalist societies is strictly limited. Only safe decisions are allowed – those which do not in any fundamental way challenge the dominant position of the bourgeoisie. The sanctity of private property is never questioned; the right of workers to keep the profits produced by their labour is never seriously proposed; and communism is never contemplated as a realistic alternative to capitalism.

Ideology

According to Marxists, the ability of the ruling class to suppress such questions is related to the third face of power. Numerous studies claim that the bourgeoisie are able to produce false class consciousness among the working class.

Westergaard and Resler (1976) argued that ruling-class ideology (see p. 41) promotes the view that private property, profit, the mechanisms of a market economy and the inequalities which result are reasonable, legitimate, normal and natural. If this view is accepted, then the dominance of capital is ensured, since 'no control could be firmer and more extensive than one which embraced the minds and wills of its subjects so successfully that opposition never reared its head'.

If anything, the plausibility of such arguments has been increasing in recent decades. Countries such as Britain and the United States have embraced capitalist free markets wholeheartedly. A number of sociologists have commented on the increased influence of the market economy in different areas of social life, including education, crime and the welfare state (see pp. 618–20, 355–8 and 268–73).

The regimes of leaders such as Ronald Reagan and Margaret Thatcher tried to reduce government spending on welfare and state intervention. Margaret Thatcher's Conservative governments in Britain (1979–91) privatized numerous state-owned industries and tried to introduce competitive, capitalist-like relationships into parts of the welfare state such as the National Health Service (NHS).

When the Labour Party was elected to power in Britain in 1997 it promised not to increase income tax or raise higher-rate tax for the highest earners. The Labour government under Tony Blair and Gordon Brown has worked closely with business people, for example by using private capital on state projects through the Private Finance Initiative.

Nevertheless, Marxist views have been widely criticized.

Criticisms of Marxism

Marxists provide a considerable amount of evidence to support their views. However, the Marxist theory of the state cannot explain why the state became stronger rather than 'withering away' in communist countries. Furthermore, Marxists fail to take account of the possibility that there are sources of power other than wealth. Some conflict theorists deny that wealth is the only source of power, despite seeing economic power as important. If they are correct, then Marxists certainly exaggerate the degree to which those with economic power dominate state decisions and determine the effects of those decisions.

Even if the interests of capitalists are very influential, that does not necessarily support the Marxist view that the state acts in the interests of a minority. Anthony H. Birch suggests that all Marxist evidence shows is that 'the perceived need to maintain economic growth places serious constraints on government policy' (2001, p. 211). Opinion poll evidence suggests that most voters see economic growth as important, and it is plausible to claim that most of the population benefit from rising living standards. Therefore the pro-capitalist nature of much government policy could as easily be seen as a product of democratic choice as a product of ruling-class domination.

We will now consider the state from a neo-Marxist viewpoint.

Neo-Marxist approaches to power and the state

A number of writers have put forward theories of the state and the distribution of power in society which are heavily influenced by Marxism, but which differ in some significant way from the original writings of Marx and Engels. This section examines the work of such writers.

Antonio Gramsci – hegemony and the state

Antonio Gramsci (1891–1937) is among the most influential twentieth-century theorists who were themselves influenced by Marx. Gramsci was an Italian sociologist and political activist. A leader of the Italian Communist Party, he is partly remembered for the part he played in the Turin Factory Council Movement, in which industrial workers in Turin unsuccessfully attempted to seize control of their workplaces. From 1926 until his death, Gramsci was imprisoned by Mussolini's fascist government, and his main contributions to sociological theory are contained in his *Prison Notebooks* written during that time (Gramsci, 1971).

Gramsci parted company with conventional Marxists in arguing against **economic determinism**: he did not believe that the economic infrastructure determined to any great degree what occurred in the superstructure of society. He talked of a 'reciprocity between structure and superstructure': although the infrastructure could affect what took place in the superstructure, the reverse was also possible.

Gramsci did not deny that the economic infrastructure of society was important: it provided the general background against which events took place. An economic crisis might increase political awareness among the proletariat, for instance. However, he believed the actions of groups trying to maintain or change society were at least as important.

Political and civil society

Unlike traditional Marxists, Gramsci divided the superstructure of society into two parts: political society and civil society. Political society consisted of what is normally thought of as the state. This was primarily concerned with the use of force by the army, police and legal system to repress troublesome elements within the population. Civil society consisted of those institutions normally thought of as private, particularly the church, trade unions, the mass media and political parties.

In a novel way Gramsci claimed 'the state = political society + civil society'. He used a very broad definition of the state, for he did not think of it in terms of particular institutions but rather in terms of the activities of a dominant class in society.

Hegemony

At one point in his work Gramsci described the state as:

> *the entire complex of practical and theoretical activities with which the ruling class not only justifies and maintains its dominance, but manages to maintain the active consent of those over whom it rules.* Gramsci, 1971

If the ruling class managed to maintain its control by gaining the approval and consent of members of society, then it had achieved what Gramsci called **hegemony**. Hegemony was largely achieved, not through the use of force, but by persuading the population to accept the political and moral values of the ruling class. Here Gramsci stressed the importance of ideas in society: effective ruling-class control was only maintained to the extent that the ruling class could retain command of the beliefs of the population through civil society.

Gramsci's view on how hegemony could be maintained comes close to Marx's view of false class consciousness. However, unlike the views Marx sometimes expressed, Gramsci did not see the ruling class as ever being able to impose entirely false beliefs and values on the population, nor did he see the state as ever being able to act as a simple instrument or tool of ruling-class dominance. The state could only remain hegemonic if it was prepared to compromise and take account of the demands of exploited classes, and, for the following three important reasons, ruling-class hegemony could never be complete.

Historic blocs

In the first place, Gramsci saw both the ruling and subject classes as being divided. The ruling class was divided into groups such as financiers, small and large industrialists and landowners, while industrial workers and agricultural peasants represented a major division within the subject class. No one group on its own could maintain dominance of society. Hegemony was only possible if there was some sort of alliance between two or more groups.

Gramsci called a successful alliance – which achieved a high level of hegemony – a **historic bloc**; but because of the different elements it contained it would always be something of a compromise between the groups involved.

Concessions

The second reason why the hegemony of one group would never be complete was that the state always had to make some concessions to the subject class. Gramsci said, 'hegemony undoubtedly presupposes that the interests and tendencies of the groups over which hegemony is to be exercised are taken into account'. From this point of view, the ruling class had to make concessions in order to be able to rule by consent instead of relying on the use of force. It had to adopt some policies that benefited the subject class.

Dual consciousness

If the ruling class were able to indoctrinate the population completely, then clearly it would not be necessary for them to make concessions. However, Gramsci maintained that this was never possible. He believed that individuals possessed **dual consciousness**. Some of their ideas derived from the ruling class's control over civil society and its ability to use institutions such as the church and schools to persuade people to accept that capitalism was natural and desirable. However, in part, individuals' beliefs were also the product of their activities and experiences. To a limited extent they would be able to see through the capitalist system, and realize that their interests lay in changing it. For example, their day-to-day experience of poor working conditions and low wages would encourage them to believe that, at the very least, some reforms of the system were necessary.

The overthrow of capitalism

According to Gramsci, then, power derived only in part from economic control; it could also originate from control over people's ideas and beliefs. Since the ruling class was unable to control the ideas of the population completely, it could never completely monopolize power. Similarly, the subject class would always have some influence over the activities of the state. The activities of political society would benefit them to the extent that they were able to realize where their interests lay and wrest concessions from the ruling class.

Like Marx, Gramsci looked forward to a proletarian revolution, but he saw such a revolution arising in a rather different way. He did not accept that the contradictions of the capitalist economic system made a revolution a foregone conclusion.

The revolutionary seizure of power in tsarist Russia by the Bolsheviks was only possible because of a complete absence of ruling-class hegemony in that country. The rulers lacked the consent of the subject classes and so those classes were able to overthrow them with a direct frontal attack. Gramsci termed such a violent revolutionary seizure of power a 'war of manoeuvre', in which direct action was taken to secure victory.

In most advanced capitalist countries, though, he saw the ruling class as having much more hegemony than they had possessed in Russia. Consequently, countries such as Italy and Britain needed a good deal more preparation before they would have the potential for a proletarian revolution. Gramsci called such preparation a 'war of position' – a kind of political trench warfare in which revolutionary elements in society attempted to win over the hearts and minds of the subject classes.

It was only when individuals had been made to realize the extent to which they were being exploited, and had seen through the ideas and beliefs of the ruling class, that a revolution was possible. For this to happen, 'intellectuals' had to emerge within the subject classes to mould their ideas and form a new historic bloc of the exploited, capable of overcoming ruling-class hegemony.

Bob Jessop – *The Future of the Capitalist State*

Bob Jessop (2002) is a British sociologist who draws upon a range of Marxist, neo-Marxist and other approaches in analysing the contemporary state. His work is influenced by Marx himself, as well as by Poulantzas, Gramsci, Niklas Luhman (a non-Marxist theorist) and the theory of post-Fordism. His work is primarily concerned with how the state is changing in response to economic change involving a shift from Fordist mass production to the more specialized production of post-Fordism. Jessop sees this change as involving a movement to 'a globalizing, knowledge-driven economy'.

Like Marxists, Jessop believes that a capitalist economic system exercises a strong influence on the state in Western Europe and North America. However, unlike writers such as Miliband, he does not believe that the state is directly run by capitalists, and unlike Poulantzas he does not even believe that the state necessarily always serves the interests of capitalism.

Operational autonomy

Capitalism never exists in a pure form and is never based upon perfect competition. For example, monopolies can artificially put up prices and may be able to prevent competitors entering the market who might lower prices. Furthermore, labour power cannot be reproduced simply through market relationships. Bringing up children to the point at which they can provide labour power is largely done outside the market relationship. For example, parents are not paid to look after their children, and the education of most children is provided by the government.

Jessop therefore argues, 'it is precisely because capitalism cannot secure through market forces alone all the conditions needed for its own reproduction that it cannot exercise any sort of economic determination in the last instance over the rest of the social formation'. If the economic system cannot reproduce and regulate itself without some assistance from non-capitalist institutions, other parts of society are bound to have some autonomy from the economy.

So the state operates in the context of a capitalist system and it has a vital role in making the system work. However, it will not always succeed. States in capitalist societies do not always make decisions that will allow private companies to flourish and make profits. The state is institutionally separate from the capitalist economy and it will not automatically operate as a 'simple instrument' of capitalism (as Miliband suggested), or as a 'functioning mechanism for reproducing capitalist relations of production', as Poulantzas claimed. Jessop therefore says:

> *There is no guarantee that political outcomes will serve the needs of capital – even assuming that these could be objectively identified in advance in sufficient detail to provide the basis for a capitalistically rational plan of state action and inaction. The operational autonomy of the state is a further massively complicating factor in this regard. Indeed, to the extent that it enables the state to pursue the interests of capital in general at the expense of particular capitals, it also enables it to damage the interests of capital in general.* Jessop, 2002

Jessop therefore goes further than Poulantzas, arguing that the state has more than relative autonomy: it has **operational autonomy**, meaning that it can be harmful to capitalism. In this respect, Jessop's ideas are close to those of Gramsci. The state can reflect different alliances between different classes, and politicians may direct the state towards different 'hegemonic projects'. For example, after Margaret Thatcher came to power in Britain in 1979, Thatcherism changed the direction in which the British state was heading (see below).

Ecological dominance

Nevertheless, globalization (see pp. 548–57) and the increasing penetration of market forces into many parts of life (see pp. 613–15 for the example of education) have led to an increasingly strong influence of capitalism over non-economic parts of society. But, rather than controlling the state, capitalism merely exercises **ecological dominance**. This means that the influence of the capitalist system over other parts of society is greater than the influence of the non-capitalist parts of society over capitalism.

The capitalist system does this in a number of ways:

1. Capitalists can threaten to remove their capital from states which do not follow policies which favour their interests. Since states cannot risk big rises in unemployment and a reduction in their own income, they are unlikely to follow policies which are hostile to capitalism.
2. Capitalism has extended its influence into more and more areas of social life, including politics, education, health and science. For example, the roles of private health care, private education and scientific research funded by corporations have all increased.
3. Capitalism can try to impose a 'profit-seeking logic' on other systems even where there is no direct buying and selling of goods or services by consumers involved. For example, market forces have been introduced into aspects of state-funded health and education (see pp. 272–3).

The capitalist state has used its operational autonomy to change the way in which it regulates capitalism. Jessop therefore calls his approach to the state a **regulationist** approach: it analyses the way the state regulates the capitalist economy, whether it succeeds in benefiting the capitalist system or actually harms it. His particular focus is on an overall shift in the system of regulation which has taken place over the last few decades.

The Keynesian welfare state

In particular, Jessop argues that there has been a general shift in state policies away from what he calls the **Keynesian welfare state** towards the **Schumpeterian workfare postnational regime**.

J.M. Keynes was a British economist who wrote influential books from the 1930s onwards (e.g. Keynes, 1936) and whose ideas influenced a number of Western governments after the Second World War. The Keynesian welfare state (KWS) pursued a policy of full employment through government intervention in the economy. This was done to try to avoid the problems of unemployment experienced in the 1930s. Where the free market failed to prevent instability and high unemployment the state would intervene by employing more people itself (in nationalized industries, government and welfare services) and by increasing government spending to stimulate the economy.

It was assumed that the government could largely shape the performance of a national economy through controls over issues such as trade and the movement of capital. Regulation of the economy involved bargaining with workers, and the extension of welfare rights was used to persuade trade unionists to agree to make deals with the government and employers.

A 'mixed economy' was accepted, in which private industry was important, but when the free market failed to produce the outcomes desired by the government, the government would intervene to compensate for 'market failures'.

The KWS was based upon Fordist production and consumption. Goods were mass produced and consumers bought and used these goods *en masse*. There were variations on the KWS in different countries.

1. The USA had a more liberal welfare regime with greater emphasis on the free market and less on state intervention.

2 Some of the smaller countries, such as Sweden, had more social democratic welfare regimes with higher government spending on welfare and an emphasis on the export of high-value goods.
3 Some of the larger European countries such as Germany had more conservative corporativist welfare regimes, where there was a considerable amount of government intervention and 'close coordination between industry and finance'.
4 Southern European countries had a welfare model which took more account of the large numbers employed in agriculture.

Whatever their differences, they shared much in common in the way that they actively managed what they assumed to be relatively closed national economies. Globalization had not developed to any extent and the KWS therefore believed it could effectively control its own economy.

The Schumpeterian workfare postnational regime

According to Jessop, from the mid-1970s onwards Western economies began to shift towards post-Fordism. **Post-Fordism** involves a movement away from mass production and mass consumption to the production of more specialized products. To Jessop, it also involves a move towards a **knowledge-based economy**, in which products become less important than knowledge, with the development of new information and communications technologies.

Another important development was the growing significance of globalization (see pp. 548–57). In an increasingly globalized economy, success comes from competing with businesses throughout the world by means of constant innovation. This idea is associated with the work of Joseph Schumpeter, a twentieth-century Austrian political economist. Jessop describes Schumpeter's ideas in the following way:

> *Competitiveness depends on developing the individual and collective capacities to engage in permanent innovation – whether in sourcing, technologies, products, organization or marketing ... Thus Schumpeterian competitiveness depends on dynamic efficiency in allocating resources to promote innovations that will alter the pace and direction of economic growth and enable the economy to compete more effectively.* Jessop, 2002

Given the emphasis on innovation and the development of globalization, it becomes much harder for economies to be controlled centrally. The role of the state shifts away from direct intervention in the economy to creating the conditions where innovative businesses can thrive. This leads to a greater emphasis on public–private sector partnerships rather than nationalized industries, and the prime aim of social policy becomes economic success rather than social justice or the provision of welfare. For example, education becomes focused upon producing highly educated, well-trained and flexible workers rather than producing greater equality (see pp. 612–24 for a discussion).

In what Jessop calls the **workfare state**, benefits cease to be an automatic entitlement for those out of work. The unemployed are deemed to have a responsibility to seek work and if necessary retrain to make themselves employable in a competitive economy.

The regime is termed **postnational** because it is focused on international competition rather than regulating the national economy.

Jessop accepts that just as there are variations on the Keynesian welfare state, so there are different varieties of the Schumpeterian workfare postnational regime. Some regimes are keener on privatization (for example, Margaret Thatcher's governments), while others place more emphasis on public–private partnerships (for example, Tony Blair's governments). The movement towards this type of regime is not automatically determined by economic needs, and there is considerable room for different policies within this general framework.

Nevertheless, all Western economies have moved towards being Schumpeterian workfare postnational regimes, since governments have perceived this to be necessary to achieve economic success.

Conclusion and evaluation

How has this affected the power of the state? To Jessop, there has been some 'hollowing out' of the state – it has lost some of its functions. Economies are less directly regulated by states and depend more on networks of economic relationships which cross national boundaries.

Nevertheless, the state still has a vital role and retains considerable power. The state moves from direct government of the economy towards more indirect governance, in which it provides the framework for economic activity but relies increasingly on 'networking and other forms of self-organization' by corporations and other organizations involved in the economy.

Jessop's analysis does not suggest that economic influences on states have declined. The Schumpeterian state is at least as concerned with the reproduction of capital and the interests of capitalism as the Keynesian welfare state. Neither is directly controlled by capitalism, but both are attempts to ensure that capitalism continues to function effectively.

Jessop's analysis provides a sophisticated contemporary development of a neo-Marxist view. It avoids being over-deterministic in suggesting that the state is directly controlled by capitalists, while taking account of changes in the nature and policies of states. However, Jessop makes only limited and rather general attempts to explain exactly how capitalism or capitalists exercise control or influence over states. Furthermore, to some writers he still underestimates the power of states. This view will now be examined.

State-centred theories of power

The approaches we have considered so far have been society-centred: they see the state and its actions as shaped by external forces in society as a whole. We will now look at an alternative perspective which has a completely different viewpoint.

Eric A. Nordlinger – the autonomy of democratic states

Society-centred and state-centred approaches

According to Eric A. Nordlinger (1981), theories of power and the state are either society-centred or state-centred. To Nordlinger, all the perspectives on the state and power examined so far are society-centred, and society-centred approaches have 'a pervasive grip upon citizens, journalists and scholars alike'. Pluralism sees the state's actions as determined by the democratic will of the people; elite theory sees its actions as shaped by the wishes of a small group of powerful people; Marxism sees the state as shaped by the interests of a ruling class. Although some Marxist and neo-Marxist theories concede that the state may have some autonomy, they do not go far enough, because, in the final analysis, the state is portrayed as being unable to go against ruling-class interests.

Nordlinger criticizes all these approaches, saying:

> *The possibility that the state's preferences have at least as much impact on public policy as do society's is ignored; the state's having certain distinctive interests and divergent preferences is not considered; the state's many autonomous actions are not calculated; the state's numerous autonomy-enhancing capacities and opportunities are not examined.* Nordlinger, 1981

Nordlinger argues that society-centred approaches have been so dominant that a very distorted and one-sided view of the state and power has been produced. Although society can and does influence the state, the reverse sometimes happens. This is what Nordlinger describes as the **state-centred approach** to the theory of power. The state acts independently or autonomously to change society.

This is true of democracies, as well as other types of state, even though they are supposed to be under the control of the electorate.

The autonomy of the democratic state takes three forms.

Type 1 state autonomy

Type 1 state autonomy occurs when the state has different wishes from those of major groups in society, and implements its preferred policies despite pressure for it not to do so. For example, state policy in Sweden is often formulated by royal commissions. About 80 per cent of those who serve on the commissions are civil servants, and the recommendations are usually followed even when they are unpopular with the electorate or are opposed by elites outside the state.

In Norway, public–private committees which formulate public policy are often chaired by civil servants and, again, their recommendations are normally accepted whatever the opposition to them.

To Nordlinger, there are many ways in which the state can enhance its autonomy from society. These include:

1. Using secretive systems of decision making
2. Using honours, appointments or government contracts to persuade opponents to accept proposals
3. Using the state's resources to counter resources used by opponents (for example, using the funds in the state bank to prop up a currency that is being undermined by speculators)
4. Threatening to change a range of policies in such a way as to harm the interests of opponents of the state's policies
5. Taking actions or issuing statements which cause mistrust among different groups of opponents.

Because the state has considerable power of its own, it is sometimes able to utilize it to prevent effective opposition.

Type 2 state autonomy

Type 2 state autonomy occurs when the state is able to persuade opponents of its policies to change their minds and support the government. Nordlinger argues that this is quite common and examples of it can be found in classical pluralist studies such as Dahl's *Who Governs?* (see p. 527).

Although Dahl claimed that the authorities in New Haven were responsive to public opinion and the policies they adopted were shaped by interest groups, Nordlinger believes the authorities played an active role in manipulating public opinion. For example, Dahl himself pointed out there had been little or no interest in a programme of urban renewal until the mayor put the issue on the agenda and persuaded various interest groups to support him. None of the interest groups agreed with his proposals when they were first put forward.

From this viewpoint, then, Dahl's own evidence showed that the state could act autonomously in shaping public opinion, rather than having its policies shaped by public opinion.

Type 3 state autonomy

Type 3 state autonomy occurs when the state follows policies which are supported, or at least not opposed, by the public or powerful interest groups in society. Very often, significant groups in society may be unsure of what policies to support and leave it up to the state to decide. For example, between 1948 and 1971 the USA's grain farmers, industrial workers and exporters made little attempt to influence America's international monetary policy. Although the policy affected them a great deal, they were unable to predict the effects of the state's policies and so were content to accept whatever policies the state adopted.

On many issues concerned with the state itself there is considerable apathy on the part of the public, and the state has considerable freedom of manoeuvre, even though the issues may be of great importance. Nordlinger suggests such issues tend to include 'possible changes in the state unit's formal powers relative to one another, policy implementation responsibilities, budgetary allotments, staffing, organization, and standard operating procedures'.

Nordlinger's views suggest that the state has considerable autonomy over many issues, whether there is opposition from society or not. While he recognizes that the autonomy is only partial, he perhaps goes further in attributing independence to the state than other state-centred approaches. His theory is backed up by a limited number of empirical examples.

Other sociologists have conducted more detailed research in their attempts to show that the state acts as an independent source of power.

Theda Skocpol – *Bringing the State Back In*

The autonomy of states from society

Theda Skocpol (1985) is perhaps the most influential of the state-centred theorists. She has written extensively about the state as a source of power and is a strong supporter of what she calls *Bringing the State Back In*. She argues that pluralists, functionalists, Marxists and neo-Marxists have all tended to see the state as shaped by external pressures and have neglected the possibility that the state can shape society. Like Nordlinger, she is critical of such approaches. For example, she says:

> *Virtually all neo-Marxist writers on the state have retained deeply embedded society-centred assumptions, not allowing themselves to doubt that, at base, states are inherently shaped by classes or class struggles and function to preserve and expand models of production. Many possible forms of autonomous state action are thus ruled out by definitional fiat.* Skocpol, 1985

To Skocpol, states can have considerable autonomy and, as actors, have the potential capacity to achieve their policy goals. These goals 'are not simply reflective of the demands or interests of social groups, classes or society', for states can have their own goals and pursue their own interests.

Skocpol believes one of the main aims of states and parts of states is to increase their own power. She suggests: 'We can hypothesize that one (hidden or overt) feature of all autonomous state actions will be the reinforcement of the prerogatives of collectivities of state officials.' 'Policies different from those demanded by societal actors will be produced' as states 'attempt to reinforce the authority, political longevity, and social control of the state organizations'.

Skocpol gives a number of examples of states acting in pursuit of their own interests.

- In 1968 in Peru there was a coup organized by career military officers who used state power to plan economic growth, weaken opposition groups in society, and try to impose order.
- In Britain and Sweden, according to Skocpol, the civil services often oppose the policies of elected politicians and have some success in ensuring that their policies are not implemented in such a way as to undermine the power of the state.
- In the USA, both the White House and the State Department are fairly insulated from public opinion and democratic control, and they often act autonomously. Skocpol's own research found that in the USA, after the First World War, the Department of Agriculture was a powerful part of the state which acted independently in the pursuit of its own interests.

State capacities

Although all states have the potential to achieve their own goals, their capacity to do so will be affected by a number of factors:

1. Skocpol says, 'sheer sovereign integrity and the stable administrative control of a given territory are preconditions for any state's ability to implement policies'. Unless a state can largely command the territory for which it is responsible, it will have no power base from which to achieve its aims.
2. States that have a reliable and substantial source of income are more powerful than those that do not. For example, if a state relies heavily upon the export of a single commodity or product (as some 'third world' states do), then it is vulnerable to a decline in demand for the product or a reduction in its value. On the other hand, economies that export a wide variety of products have a more reliable income.
3. States that govern rich societies obviously have more potential for raising domestic taxes than those that govern poor societies. This can strengthen their power base.
4. States that are forced to borrow large amounts of money can end up in a weaker position than those that have sufficient revenue to finance their activities.
5. States also tend to increase their power if they can recruit many of the most able and highly educated members of society into their ranks. Not only does this tend to improve the organization of the state, it also deprives non-state organizations and groups of the personnel who would be most likely to challenge and undermine the state's power.

Skocpol believes that whether a state becomes powerful or not partly depends upon how well organized groups in society are. She criticizes Marxists for claiming that states always reflect the interests of a dominant class, saying:

> *the political expression of class interests and conflicts is never automatic or economically determined. It depends on the capacities classes have for achieving consciousness, organization, and representation. Directly or indirectly, the structures and activities of states profoundly condition such class capacities.* Skocpol, 1985

To Skocpol, Marxist political sociology 'must be turned, if not on its head, then certainly on its side'. The state shapes the activity of classes as much as classes shape the activity of the state.

States' capacities are profoundly affected by their relationships with other states. Large and powerful armed forces increase the capacity of a state to defend its own territory or seize the territory of other states. Control over territory is the basis of the state's ability to raise revenue and finance its activities. States can be weakened by wars, especially if they incur crippling costs or they suffer military defeats. External threats can result in internal weakness and sometimes contribute to the state losing its autonomy from society.

States and social revolutions

In her most substantial empirical study, Skocpol (1979) compared revolutions in France (1788), China (1911) and

Russia (1917). She argued that in all these cases the activities of the states and the weak position that the states found themselves in played a vital role in causing revolutions.

The French, Chinese and Russian states acted in ways which undermined their own power and produced a situation where the state was overthrown by particular classes. Although class conflict was important in all of the revolutions, none of them could be understood without considering the role of the state as an autonomous actor. Skocpol argues that, in all three cases, 'The revolutionary crises developed when old-regime states became unable to meet the challenges of evolving international situations.'

According to Skocpol, in France, China and Russia, it was the weakness of the state which ultimately caused the revolution. She comments: 'In all three cases ... the ultimate effect of impediments to state-sponsored reforms was the downfall of monarchical autocracy and the disintegration of the centralized administrative and military organizations of the state.'

In each case the state could have acted differently by introducing more effective reforms earlier to prevent the development of a revolutionary situation. Each regime was brought down by a combination of external pressures from other states and the way 'agrarian relations of production and landed dominant classes impinged upon state organizations'.

For example, in France, the state failed to find a way to raise sufficient taxes from the landed classes to pay for wars waged by the state. While class relationships were important, none of the revolutions could be understood without reference to the actions taken by the states involved.

In all three countries the revolution led to the collapse of the old regime, but it was replaced sooner or later by a regime with even more centralized power and more autonomy than the old state: the Napoleonic regime in France, and communist regimes in China and Russia. According to Skocpol, these were all clear examples of states which could exercise power and which could sometimes act to pursue their own interests rather than the interests of groups within society.

Evaluation of state-centred theories

One of the problems with state-centred theories is that they are often unclear about their precise theoretical position. Thus Bob Jessop argues:

> *In their eagerness to criticize society-centred analysis, they have failed to distinguish three different sorts of claim about the state. It is not clear whether they are: (a) rejecting the so-called society-centred approach in its entirety and arguing that the state should be the independent variable; (b) bending the stick in the other direction for polemical purposes, one-sidedly emphasizing the importance of the state as a crucial causal factor; or (c) suggesting that a combination of society and state-centred perspectives will somehow provide a complete account of state–society relations.* Jessop, 1990

Most critics are prepared to accept that the actions of the state should be taken into account in studies of power. However, many believe that Skocpol and similar writers exaggerate the importance of the state in an attempt to support their approach. Furthermore, Jessop argues that it is artificial and misleading to see the 'state' and 'society' as being quite separate institutions. He sees state and society as so intimately connected that it is not possible to separate them completely in accounts of power.

Both Jessop and Gregor McLennan argue that state-centred approaches offer misleading analyses of the so-called society-centred approaches which they are attacking. Jessop claims they rest on a '"straw-man" account of the society-centred bias in other studies'. In reality, Jessop suggests, other theories do take account of the power of the state. McLennan (1989) argues in similar fashion that many Marxists, such as Poulantzas, recognize that the state has 'relative autonomy' and that its actions are not entirely determined by society. McLennan concludes: 'Pragmatically it is always degrees of autonomy we are dealing with.'

This is true both of Skocpol's work and of many Marxist theories of power, and the theoretical difference between these approaches has been greatly exaggerated by many of the advocates of a state-centred approach.

Noam Chomsky, capitalism and the power of the US state

As the above evaluation suggests, theories of power do not necessarily have to be exclusively state-centred or society-centred. Some approaches recognize both – that the state can be shaped by external forces (such as social classes, elites, the capitalist system or the electorate) and that the state exercises power independently. An example of this is the work of the radical American social scientist Noam Chomsky.

In numerous books Chomsky (1996, 1999, 2000, 2002, 2003, 2006) has criticized the use of power by the American state and suggested that state policies are shaped by powerful elites. These elites have a strong stake in promoting the interests of capitalism in general, and their own economic interests in particular. Their actions, and the actions of the USA and many other states, are in turn shaped by the operation of capitalism.

Chomsky's more theoretical work is largely concerned with linguistics, so he does not discuss theoretical sociological issues such as the nature of power or the differences between Marxism and elite theory in any detail. Nevertheless, his work provides a useful example of how different approaches can be combined with a detailed analysis of the use of power by the world's only 'superpower', the USA.

Democracy and corporations

In books such as *Powers and Prospects* (1996) and *Profit over People* (1999) Chomsky argues that the USA is neither truly democratic, nor does it support genuine democracy in other parts of the world. While people have the right to vote, the choices they are offered are very limited.

Both the main parties in the USA (the Democrats and the Republicans) have very similar policies. Furthermore, those policies are shaped by the interests of big business, particularly large corporations. Chomsky (1999) says, 'the governing institutions are not independent agents but reflect the distribution of power in the larger society'. In the wider society, large corporations have the dominant power. Chomsky describes these corporations as 'unaccountable private tyrannies'. The directors of corporations are accountable only to their shareholders; the general public have no say whatsoever over their actions.

Neoliberalism and democracy

According to Chomsky, over several decades the US government has pursued a consistent policy of expanding the power of these corporations. Among the powerful elites in Washington, a consensus has developed over the desirability of neoliberal economic and social policies. (Neoliberals are sometimes known as market liberals or the New Right – see pp. 23–6 and 268–73 for discussions of the New Right.)

Neoliberals claim that 'democracy and freedom' as well as prosperity are promoted by encouraging free-market economics. According to this view, businesses should be left alone, free of government interference to buy and sell their products throughout the world. Governments should cut taxes for the rich and where possible reduce government expenditure on welfare. In theory, neoliberalism advocates free trade without duties, tariffs or other obstacles to the free movement of commodities around the world.

According to Chomsky, however, in practice neoliberalism promotes neither freedom nor democracy, nor for most people in the world does it promote prosperity. In the USA, neoliberalism has reduced the power of ordinary US citizens to influence government policy by increasing the wealth and power of unelected and unaccountable directors and executives of corporations. Even if governments truly wished to shape society according to the wishes and interests of the majority, their ability to do so has been gradually eroded. As the role of the state is minimized in favour of private enterprise, the state loses some of its capacity to shape the economy or improve the lot of ordinary people with welfare programmes.

The supporters of neoliberalism have used their power over US foreign policy to influence the government to use violence, terrorism and economic power to undermine or destroy regimes which are deemed to be damaging to US interests. Some of the regimes which have been changed by these methods were democratic (for example, in the 1970s, the elected regime of Allende in Chile was overthrown in a CIA-sponsored coup by the dictator General Pinochet). On other occasions, the US government and corporations use their power to support tyrannical regimes with no semblance of democracy (for example, Saddam Hussein's Iraq before 1991). More examples of US foreign policy are discussed below.

Neoliberalism and economic power

Just as the USA's claim to support democracy is a distortion of the truth, so is its claim to support free markets. According to Chomsky, the USA only supports free markets and free trade to the extent that this promotes the economic interests of US corporations. Chomsky says:

> *Free market doctrine comes in two varieties. The first is the official doctrine imposed on the defenceless. The second is what we might call 'really existing free market doctrine': market discipline is good for you, but not for me.*
> Chomsky, 1999

For example, the government of the USA provides large subsidies to many industries, particularly the aircraft, computer and advanced technology industries. This gives them an unfair advantage over foreign competitors which do not enjoy such subsidies.

US agriculture is also supported while foreign competitors are undermined. For example, the US Food for Peace aid plan was used to dump subsidized wheat in Colombia, undermining Colombia's own wheat-growing industry, which was unable to compete. President Clinton's policies of quotas for limiting the import of textiles led to the collapse of the Kenyan textile industry.

In contrast, poor countries are required to abandon subsidies and remove quotas and tariffs if they are to receive help from the USA or international institutions such as the World Bank or International Monetary Fund. These organizations are dominated by the USA, which contributes most money to them. They are likely to insist on 'structural adjustment' policies before providing aid or loans to poor countries in need of financial help. These open up the countries to US exports while the USA continues to protect its own industries from competition. As a consequence, there has been an increase in poverty in many poorer nations, particularly in Africa and Latin America.

The USA and its corporations have other ways of using their economic power to shape the policies and economies of other countries to favour US interests. Between the end of the Second World War and 2000, there were 116 examples of sanctions being imposed on countries (Chomsky, 2000). Of these, 80 per cent were initiated by the USA. For example, the USA has imposed sanctions on Cuba since 1961 because of its disapproval of the communist regime.

The threat of sanctions, which can have a devastating effect on the weak economies of small nations, can be enough to ensure compliance with US wishes. The USA has used such a threat to persuade Asian countries such as Taiwan and South Korea to open their markets to US exports in negotiations over the international trade treaty, GATT (General Agreement on Tariffs and Trade).

Many poorer countries suffer from enormous debts to Western governments, banks and institutions such as the IMF and World Bank. Chomsky (1999) argues that the USA uses the debt crisis to ensure it retains effective control over the policies of governments in indebted countries.

Military power

The USA does not simply use its economic dominance to shape the world in its own interests. Where necessary, it can use its overwhelming military power. During the Cold War, in which the USA and the communist USSR competed for global influence, the USA used the threat of Soviet communism as a justification for military action (Chomsky, 2000). For example, it justified the war in Vietnam in terms of the dangers of the spread of communism.

Since the end of the Cold War, with the collapse of the Soviet Union in the early 1990s, the USA has become the dominant military power in the world. It has continued to use its military power to promote US interests in general and the interests of US corporations in particular. In recent years this has often been justified on the grounds that the US is acting against rogue states (Chomsky, 2000) or against international terrorism (Chomsky, 2003). However, in reality, Chomsky believes the USA is the biggest 'rogue state' of all.

The USA has supported numerous regimes which have carried out extreme violations of human rights – for example, General Suharto's regime in Indonesia. It ignored, for many years, the Indonesian invasion of East Timor (1975) in which opposition was brutally repressed. It supported Saddam Hussein in Iraq, despite his use of 'weapons of mass destruction' against the Kurds, at least until the regime invaded Kuwait in 1991.

The USA has consistently supported Israel despite its illegal occupation of Palestinian territory in the West Bank and Gaza. The USA has also been quite willing to ignore atrocities perpetrated by Russia in Chechnya, and by Turkey against the Kurds, and repression by the Chinese authorities in Western China and Tibet.

Such abuses of human rights have been overlooked because these countries supported the US 'War on Terror', including the invasion of Afghanistan, in the aftermath of the terrorist attacks on the USA in September 2001 (Chomsky, 2003).

When Bill Clinton was president, Turkey was one of the biggest recipients of weapons from the USA, despite the Turkish government's actions against the Kurds in which 'millions of them were driven out of their homes, thousands of villages destroyed, maybe tens of thousands killed, every imaginable kind of barbaric torture'.

In Nicaragua in the 1980s, the USA 'had to basically attack it' to overthrow a regime unfriendly to the USA. The result was 'tens of thousands of people killed, and the country virtually destroyed. It is now the second poorest country in the hemisphere. It may never recover.'

In 1985 a bomb was planted outside a mosque in Beirut, killing eighty people and wounding 250. According to Chomsky, 'The bomb was aimed at a Muslim sheik, who escaped. It was traced back to the CIA and British intelligence, and that's not particularly contested' (Chomsky, 2003).

In the 1960s the US war in Vietnam led to the deaths of an unknown but very large number of Vietnamese (Chomsky estimates three to four million), and the Americans made widespread use of chemical weapons.

Chomsky therefore argues that the USA is at least as much a 'rogue state' as other states which it has targeted in its 'War on Terror'. Indeed, according to Chomsky, the USA is itself responsible for arming and sponsoring other terrorists, and on one occasion (the car bomb in Beirut in 1985) initiating terrorism itself.

The USA has also invaded Panama, bombed Libya and the Sudan (1998) and, in the 'War on Terror', invaded both Afghanistan (2002) and Iraq (2003).

Chomsky (2006) is very critical of the invasion and occupation of Iraq. He argues that the USA has stretched the justification for war. It has portrayed the Iraq invasion as justified as a preventive war – waged to prevent a possible war in the future. Such a justification is not valid under international law but the USA is able to impose it simply because of its military, economic and political predominance.

The war is also a way of enhancing US power since it serves as a warning to other states, telling them 'you had better watch out, you could be next' if you fail to do America's bidding.

Chomsky argues that no 'sane person' would deny that a desire for control over Iraq's oil reserves was a major reason for the invasion of Iraq. Having invaded, the USA has made sure that its economic interests are served by the new regime. He says, 'the occupying forces have imposed an economic regime that no sovereign state would accept for a moment, which completely opens up Iraq to takeover by foreign corporations' (Chomsky, 2006, p. 81). Military power can therefore serve to enhance the economic power of the USA and its corporations.

Chomsky reiterates the point that the USA frequently uses violence when reflecting upon the significance of the September 2001 attacks in the USA. He argues that these attacks were unprecedented, not because of their scale, but because the victim was the United States. Usually, the victims of terrorist or military attacks are victims of the USA or its allies.

The media

If the United States commits serious offences and abuses its power, then why does the population not use its voting rights to remove the government?

Chomsky argues that the media are used by the powerful to persuade the population to acquiesce or even enthusiastically support the actions of the government. In *Media Control: The Spectacular Achievement of Propaganda* (2002), Chomsky claims that the information provided to the public is 'narrowly and rigidly controlled'. This usually involves whipping up public fear about a supposed external threat to the USA.

For much of the period after the Second World War, the communist threat from the USSR and its allies was emphasized. More recently, the media have promoted the idea of another serious threat: 'international terrorists and narco-traffickers and crazed Arabs and Hussein, the new Hitler, was going to conquer the world'.

All these threats are greatly exaggerated, or even complete myths, but it is difficult for the public to become aware of this because dissenting voices are rarely given media exposure. For example, there was almost no coverage in the American media of the democratic opposition to Saddam Hussein's regime in Iraq when he was an ally of presidents Reagan and George Bush (Senior).

Individuals might feel uneasy with American policy or media portrayals, but they feel too isolated from mainstream opinion to mount an effective challenge to these ideas.

The public are kept in ignorance of offers made to resolve conflicts peacefully. For example, according to Chomsky, after the invasion of Kuwait, Iraq offered to withdraw completely from Kuwait in return for the UN Security Council considering the Arab–Israeli conflict and the existence of weapons of mass destruction.

Because the mass of the population are kept in ignorance of alternatives to government policy, they become a 'bewildered herd', struggling to make sense of situations in which the information available to them is little more than propaganda.

Conclusion and evaluation

Chomsky offers a powerful critique of the foreign policy of the USA and links this to a theory of power which examines economic and military power and the power of the media. His views are supported with numerous examples. He stresses the power of the USA as the world's only superpower, but he does allow that 'the US is powerful, but not all-powerful'. For example, he recognizes that Western Europe and Japan and other prosperous Asian countries also have considerable economic power.

Nevertheless, Chomsky could be accused of exaggerating the power of capitalist corporations and the US government and neglecting other sources of power, such as the populations of democratic countries. Pluralists (see pp. 525–8) would reject his claim that the public are no more than a 'bewildered herd', and a number of sociologists of the media argue that radical and dissenting views are not uncommon in the mass media (see pp. 720–1).

Chomsky's work lacks theoretical clarity. For example, he does not discuss whether the powerful should be seen as a ruling elite or a ruling class, and he has no clear definition of power or way of measuring it. However, Chomsky's work also has a number of strengths. He makes extensive use of concrete examples of the use of power, rather than simply discussing power in the abstract. While he might exaggerate the power of the USA compared to other states, there is no doubt that the USA is very powerful, and few sociological theories of power address the issue of US power explicitly.

The next theories to be examined question the idea that nation-states retain the power they once enjoyed.

Globalization and the power of the nation-state

Many sociologists and others have begun to argue that the analysis of power cannot be confined to examining the distribution of power within particular nation-states. Approaches which claim that **globalization** has taken place tend to see the power that exists outside nation-states as restricting their activities and limiting their power. From this point of view, power relationships increasingly cut across national boundaries, and states lose some of their capacity to act independently and shape social life within their boundaries.

John Baylis and Steve Smith – *The Globalization of World Politics*

In *The Globalization of World Politics* John Baylis and Steve Smith (2005) outline the main features of the theory of globalization. They start by using the terrorist attacks on the United States on 11 September 2001 (generally known as 9/11) to illustrate the idea of globalization.

The attacks of 9/11 took place in a single country – the USA – but the events were seen around the world almost instantaneously on TV screens. The attacks were carried out by Al Qaeda, a loosely organized non-state organization with followers in around fifty countries. They were arranged using globalized technology such as international bank accounts and the internet. Those involved used international air travel – a feature of globalization – both to stage the attacks and to travel.

There were intense reactions to the events around the world, ranging from jubilation to shock. The attacks hit buildings – the Pentagon and the World Trade Centre – which had global connections, and the victims came from some ninety different countries. The causes of the attacks have been related to what has happened elsewhere in the world including the stationing of US troops in Saudi Arabia and events in Palestine. To Baylis and Smith, then, 9/11 symbolizes globalization extremely well.

Baylis and Smith define **globalization** as 'the process of increasing interconnectedness between societies such that events in one part of the world more and more have effects on peoples and societies far away' (2005, p. 8). Globalization has social, economic and political consequences. In each of these areas the world seems to be 'shrinking' so that geographical distance plays less of a role in limiting social life. Baylis and Smith accept that globalization is not new, but claim that recent developments have led to qualitative changes in the social world. One of these changes may be that a 'new world political system has emerged as a result of globalization' (Baylis and Smith, 2005, p. 9).

Baylis and Smith identify a number of arguments which can be used to claim that globalization has led to a new era in politics.

1. 'The pace of **economic transformation** is so great that it has created a new world politics. States are no longer closed units and they cannot control their economies' (2005, p. 11). This leads to some loss of state power since other actors now have considerable influence over national economies.
2. **Electronic communications** (such as the internet) change the nature of the social groups within which the individual can interact, making geographical location much less important. This opens up the possibility of new political relations that cross state boundaries.

3 There is a move towards a **global culture**, strongly influenced by American culture, which reduces the importance of national culture in governing nation-states.
4 'The world is becoming more **homogeneous**' as differences between people are declining.
5 **'Time and space are collapsing'** as a result of modern communications and media shrinking the world.
6 A **global polity** may be emerging with the development of transnational political movements (for example, pressure groups such as Amnesty International, and new social movements (see pp. 568–73), as well as transnational and international bodies such as the United Nations, the European Union and the World Bank).
7 A **cosmopolitan culture** is developing where people from different parts of the world live in the same locality and diverse cultures mix together.
8 'A **risk culture** is emerging with people realizing both that the main risks that face them are global (pollution and AIDS) and that states are unable to deal with them' (2005, p. 11). (See pp. 86–8 for a discussion of the idea of risk society.)

Baylis and Smith argue that the above points are often highlighted by those who see globalization as a progressive force leading to desirable changes in world politics. However, Baylis and Smith acknowledge that there are also powerful criticisms both of the view that globalization is taking place, and, if it is, that it is desirable.

1 First, some question the view that globalization really is a new phenomenon which significantly reduces the power of nation-states. Hirst and Thompson (1996) (see below) are amongst those who are sceptical about the claims of globalization theorists.
2 Globalization may have affected rich Western societies much more than poorer societies where modern communications are not widely available. For example, only a minority of the population of the world are connected to the internet.
3 The supporters of globalization tend to ignore the effects on those who lose out as a result of globalization in an economically divided world. Radical theorists of globalization (for example, Sklair – see pp. 551–2) see it as facilitating more explicit exploitation of the poor.
4 Globalization has negative effects in allowing the development of problems such as global terrorism, the international drugs trade and people smuggling.
5 The idea of global governance may be an illusion and to the extent that it exists it may not be subject to democratic control in the same way as the government of nation-states (see the work of Held and McGrew for a discussion of global governance – pp. 555–6).

Baylis and Smith do not side with either the views of those who emphasize the benefits and extent of globalization, or the views of those who are more sceptical. The following sections exemplify the competing views on globalization and discuss these controversies further. We start with a very strong advocate of globalization, Kenichi Ohmae.

Kenichi Ohmae – *The Borderless World*

As a management consultant and 'business guru', Kenichi Ohmae (1994) is primarily concerned with the significance of globalization for large corporations. However, his analysis also encompasses changes in the distribution of power and the role of nation-states. He is one of the most uncompromising and wholeheartedly enthusiastic advocates of globalization and so his views form a convenient starting point.

The interlinked economy

According to Ohmae, political borders have become increasingly insignificant in a globalized world, especially in the most developed economic regions. In particular, Ohmae sees the United States, Japan and Europe as forming one, giant, **interlinked economy** (ILE), which is being joined by rapidly developing countries such as Taiwan, Singapore and Hong Kong. He claims the ILE 'is becoming so powerful that it has swallowed most consumers and corporations, made traditional national borders almost disappear, and pushed bureaucrats, politicians, and the military towards the status of declining industries'.

Ohmae sees such developments as stemming from an opening up of the world economy so that trade between people in different nation-states becomes very easy. This in turn is a consequence of rapid improvements in communications. Through such developments as cable and satellite TV, cheaper, easier and more frequent international travel, and (since Ohmae was writing) the rapid development of the internet, individuals are increasingly able to see what people consume in other countries. It has also become much easier for individuals to buy what they want from other countries. Ohmae says:

> *Today, of course, people everywhere are more and more able to get the information they want directly from all corners of the world. They can see for themselves what the tastes and preferences are in other countries, the styles of clothing now in fashion, the sports, the lifestyles.*
> Ohmae, 1994

In the past, governments could exercise considerable control over the flow of information to their citizens. Now this is no longer possible. If people see that what they are getting is substandard they will look abroad for something better or insist upon improvements. For example, in Japan the population grew dissatisfied with the standard of their housing. According to Ohmae, ten million Japanese travel abroad each year. Seeing how others live led them to insist that the government take steps to improve the standard of the housing available to them.

The lack of control governments now have over information is paralleled by the lack of control they can have over the economy. It is becoming increasingly difficult for governments to protect their domestic industries from foreign competition. It is difficult to enforce attempts to impose tariff barriers designed to prevent imports, and, in any case, it is counter-productive. Tariffs are only effective in some low-income economies. India, for example, protects its domestic car industry from external competition. The end result is over-priced and outdated cars which consumers do not like. In higher-income countries, people demand access to the best goods produced anywhere in the world. According to Ohmae, this is not only good for the consumer, it is good for the country's economy as well.

According to Ohmae, most wealth is no longer produced by manufacturing, and most jobs are created when economies are open to investment from any companies, be they domestic, foreign or multinational. He says, 'such functions as distribution, warehousing, financing, retail marketing, systems integration and services are all legitimate parts of the business system and can create as many, and often more, jobs than simply manufacturing operations'.

Global citizens and regional links

Individuals have become **global citizens**. They 'want to buy the best and the cheapest products, no matter where in the world they are produced'. Regional economic links have become more important than national economies, and distant parts of the world are connected through business and other ties.

Californian businesses often have stronger links with Asian businesses than with businesses in other areas of the USA. Hong Kong has strong links with parts of Canada, since many business people from Hong Kong moved to Canada because they feared the consequences of Hong Kong reverting to Chinese control. There are clusters of investment by Japanese companies in Alsace-Lorraine and South Wales.

If national governments try to limit or stifle these links, they undermine economic growth and incur the displeasure of their citizens. Nor can governments use economic policies to control their economies in the way they used to. Financiers can move money around the globe in vast quantities almost instantaneously. Governments cannot set tax rates or interest rates, or try to fix the value of their currency, without taking account of these facts.

National policies can soon be rendered ineffective if financiers and corporations move their currency or their businesses elsewhere. Indeed, Ohmae argues that corporations should no longer see themselves as being based in a particular country. To be successful they have to produce the best products in the world. The development costs of being the best are often enormous and only global success will repay the initial investment. To achieve such success they need to have footholds throughout the interlinked economy and adapt their businesses and products to meet local conditions. This cannot be achieved unless businesses lose their sense of being based primarily in a single country.

Governments and consumers

According to Ohmae, then, governments have largely lost their power to regulate and control both their national economies and information within their boundaries.

Another important governmental function, providing military security, is also becoming redundant. In the interlinked economy it makes little sense for nations to fight over territory. Invading your neighbour would involve destroying property owned by your own citizens, and disrupting economic activity which contributes to your own country's wealth. States such as Singapore have little in the way of armed forces, yet they do not live in fear of external military threats.

In Ohmae's view of the world, power has shifted decisively from governments to individual consumers. Both governments and companies alike have to accommodate the demands of consumers, if they are to get re-elected, or win and keep customers. It is a world in which there is a plurality of cultures, in which 'people vary in how they want to live'. Regimes that try to maintain or impose a single, national culture (such as communist regimes) are doomed to failure.

If states have lost much of their economic role and power, and their role in controlling information, and if they are losing their military role, and no longer have a national culture to protect, are they still necessary? Do they still have any power?

Ohmae thinks they are necessary and that they retain some limited powers. They are necessary, essentially, to produce the conditions in which consumers, workers and corporations can thrive in the global economy. They are still necessary to provide the infrastructure (such as roads and a legal system) which makes it possible for businesses to operate. Above all, though, they need to ensure the best possible education for their citizens. Ultimately, Ohmae believes that economic success results from having a highly educated, entrepreneurial and well-informed population. To achieve these limited objectives, governments still need to raise taxes. However, if their taxes are too high, the effect will be counter-productive, since businesses will simply relocate elsewhere.

Evaluation

Ohmae's view of a world in which political borders are largely irrelevant and power is transferred to consumers is open to many criticisms. He ignores the continuing role of nation-states in controlling access to their territories as markets for businesses. Although there has been movement towards freer trade in the world economy, completely free trade has not yet come close to fruition. The three biggest capitalist blocs of Japan, North America and the European Union continue to restrict the trade allowed with each other and with nations outside these blocs.

Ohmae surely exaggerates the decline in the importance of the military capability of states. Neither consumers nor corporations have the ability to use military force to impose their will on others. As Nigel Harris (1992) says, 'States have a monopoly within their territory of the use of physical power while companies rarely have more than security guards.' Individual consumers have even less ability to impose their will on others through the use of force.

Even if Ohmae is correct in believing that the power of the nation-state has declined, it is surprising that he attributes so much power to consumers. Many other theorists of globalization argue that power has shifted to corporations rather than to consumers (see below). Some theorists, such as Hirst and Thompson (see pp. 553–4), raise serious questions about the existence of globalization, while others, such as Giddens, accept that globalization has happened, but make far less extreme claims about the decline of state power. Some of these alternative views will now be considered.

Globalization and transnational corporations

As long ago as 1971, Raymond Vernon published a book claiming that the power of nation-states was being eclipsed by the power of multinational (now often called transnational) corporations. Vernon said, 'Suddenly, it seems, the sovereign states are feeling naked. Concepts such as national sovereignty and national economic strength appear curiously drained of meaning.'

Vernon believed the power of nation-states was declining, but he saw it as shifting to corporations rather than consumers. **Multinational** and **transnational corporations** are defined in different ways by different writers, but, as a minimum definition, they are business organizations which operate in more than one country.

Most of the larger transnational corporations operate in numerous countries and their activities involve vast sums of money. For example, the 1995 United Nations Conference on Trade and Development found that global sales by the foreign affiliates of transnational corporations amounted to $5.2 trillion, which was more than the total value of all goods and services traded in the world (which amounted to $4.8 trillion) (World Investment Report, 1995).

In view of the increased popularity of theories of globalization, it is not surprising that some sociologists have argued that power has shifted to such corporations in a globalized world. One such sociologist is Leslie Sklair.

Leslie Sklair – *Sociology of the Global System*

Leslie Sklair (1993, 1995, 2003) believes that states retain some power, but that any understanding of the global system must focus primarily upon transnational corporations (TNCs).

Transnational practices

Using data from a variety of sources, Sklair (2003) points out: 'The largest TNCs have assets and annual sales far in excess of the Gross National Products of most of the countries in the world.' In 2001 there were 240 TNCs with a turnover in excess of $20 billion per year. In the same year, more than half (71) of the 132 countries of the world with a population over 2 million had a gross national income of less than $20 billion. Comparing corporate revenues and state revenues (what governments receive in income from taxes), thirty-five of the biggest economic actors in the world were corporations and just fifteen were governments in 2002.

Sklair claims:

> *Such well-known companies as Ford, General Motors, Shell, Toyota, Volkswagen, Nestle, Sony, Pepsico, Coca-Cola, Kodak, Xerox (and many others most of us have never heard of) have more economic power at their disposal than the majority of the countries of the world.* Sklair, 1993

Sklair argues that TNCs have grown rapidly in recent years and have increased their 'global reach'. They increasingly earn their income outside their home country. IBM, BP, McDonald's, Coca-Cola and British American Tobacco all earn more than half their income from abroad.

Sklair's model is based upon the idea of **transnational practices**. He defines these as 'practices that originate with non-state actors and cross state borders'. These are distinguished from international relations which involve the relations between nation-states. According to Sklair, transnational practices are increasingly important, compared to international relations.

Transnational practices take place in three main spheres:

1 The economic
2 The political
3 The cultural–ideological

These correspond to the practices of:

1 The transnational corporation
2 The transnational capitalist class
3 The culture–ideology of consumerism

Sklair sees the transnational corporation as the **vehicle** of the global system. He points to the enormous wealth of such corporations and the crucial role they have in most national economies.

The transnational capitalist class is the **driver** of the global system. This class consists of executives of TNCs, 'globalizing state bureaucrats', 'capitalist-inspired politicians and professionals' and 'consumerist elites (merchants, media)'. It is seen as making system-wide decisions which affect the whole of the global system, and it attempts to make decisions which further its own interests within the system. Although it includes some politicians based in particular nation-states, the class opposes protectionism, which puts national interests above those of the class as a whole.

The culture–ideology of consumerism involves the worldwide spread of the ideology, which stresses the benefits of consumerism. It has become so important because of the near-universal spread of the mass media. Sklair (1995) says cheap televisions, cassettes and radios 'now totally penetrate the First World, almost totally penetrate the urban Second and Third Worlds, and are beginning to penetrate deeply into the countryside in every country'.

TNC power

Like Ohmae, then, Sklair largely sees the decline of the power of the state as a consequence of the development of capitalism. Unlike Ohmae, he believes that power largely rests with TNCs rather than consumers. Sklair claims:

> *Effective TNC control of global capital and resources is almost complete. There are few important national resources that are entirely exempt from economic transnational practices. Transnational capitalist classes rule directly, through national capitalist political parties or social democratic political parties that cannot fundamentally threaten the global capitalist system, or they exert authority indirectly to a greater or lesser extent as the price levied on the non-capitalist states as a sort of entrance fee into the global capitalist system.* Sklair, 1995

To Sklair, consumers are effectively indoctrinated by the ideology of the corporations. Far from ensuring that a globalized world acts in their interests, they, for the most part, tamely consume the products that capitalist ideology pushes. He says: 'The control of ideas in the interests of consumerism is almost total.'

Despite his more extreme claims, Sklair does recognize both that there is some opposition to the capitalist global system and that nation-states retain some power. There are some anti-global social movements which challenge the ideology of consumerism, including environmental movements. However, Sklair does not believe they have the power to mount a serious challenge to global capitalism.

States are more powerful than anti-globalization movements. Sklair admits, for example, that the USA remains enormously powerful, certainly compared to some 'third world' states and even the larger TNCs. He says:

> *All the Fortune 500 corporations [the biggest corporations in the world] do not have the same economic impact on the United States, for example, as a few copper TNCs have had on Chile, or fruit companies on Central America, or mining corporations on Southern Africa.* Sklair, 1995

In a few parts of the world, such as China, TNCs have had little success in gaining power at the expense of the state.

The consequences of globalization

Although Sklair accepts that globalization is more entrenched in some parts of the world than in others, he believes it has had a tremendous impact in the world as a whole.

Sklair (2003) sees the effects of globalization as being largely negative. He believes globalization has created two crises for the world: the crisis of class polarization and the crisis of ecological unsustainability.

1 The crisis of class **polarization** involves growing inequality, both within and between nations. In a globally competitive economy, the winners get very rich as they exploit a global market, while the losers get very poor.

   Sklair refers to lots of evidence to support his claim that there is growing global inequality. The United Nations Development Report (2000) found that the gap between the income of the richest and poorest countries had grown from about 3 to 1 in 1820, to 43 to 1 in 1973, and 72 to 1 in 1992. The UN Research Institute for Social Development estimated that the number of people living on less than $1 a day increased from 1,196,500,000 in 1987 to 1,214,200,000 in 1998.

   Furthermore, inequality within many countries has grown. For example, according to a United Nations Development Programme Report (2000), in Brazil the poorest 20 per cent of the population received just 2.5 per cent of national income. In 1998 even the World Trade Organization, an institution dedicated to the expansion of global trade, had to admit that the expansion and liberalization of trade had led to 'non-trivial adjustment costs' for some people (quoted in Sklair, 2003). Sklair gives an example of such costs. In Mexico between 1981 and 2000 the purchasing power of the minimum wage in terms of staple food (tortillas) declined by nearly three-quarters.

2 Sklair sees the crisis of **ecological unsustainability** as at least as serious as the crisis of class polarization. He gives some examples:

> *Agricultural lands, rainforests and other wooded areas, grasslands, and sources of fresh water are all at risk. Many rivers and other aquatic ecosystems are suffering severe ecological distress ... Ocean fishing is ... a very important source of food and income for poor people living near coastlines, and over-fishing by large commercial fleets has increased the pressure on the livelihood of these poor communities.* Sklair, 2003

   Sklair describes transnational corporations as 'deeply implicated' in many ecological problems: their activities either create the problems or make them much worse. He accepts there has been some progress in certain areas, for example reducing the release of CFC gasses, and that there is increased public awareness of some problems. However, both TNCs and many individuals are reluctant to change. TNCs are unwilling to take environmental measures at the expense of their profits. Individuals in rich countries are reluctant to take necessary measures at the expense of their lifestyle (for example, using public transport instead of cars). To Sklair, this is because many have become 'addicted to a greater or lesser extent to the culture–ideology of consumerism'.

Sklair concludes by arguing that the two crises are linked. The consumption of the rich countries driven by the culture–ideology of consumerism, and the exploitation of natural resources by TNCs which produce the culture–ideology of consumerism, together produce both class polarization and an ecological crisis.

As the resources of the world are exploited by corporations to make short-term profits, the poor who rely upon natural resources to make a living become still poorer. In short, the world is largely run by and for the benefit of the transnational capitalist class and those who share in the wealth created by TNCs. Sklair therefore argues: 'Those who own and control the institutions that drive globalization presently wield most of the power in the global system.'

Evaluation

Sklair's analysis is more subtle and better supported by evidence than that of Ohmae. It also recognizes that the global system may have serious disadvantages. It seems more plausible to argue that power has shifted to TNCs than to say, as Ohmae does, that consumers are virtually all-powerful.

Nevertheless, Sklair may well exaggerate the power of TNCs. His emphasis is on companies involved in production and he says little about the significance of global financiers, bankers and speculators. Yet finance capitalism involves bigger and more rapid flows of resources than does investment abroad by TNCs.

Other theorists such as Jeffrey Frieden (1991) attribute much more importance to finance capitalism. Furthermore, Sklair concentrates almost exclusively on economic aspects of globalization.

Paul Hirst and Grahame Thompson – questioning globalization

'International' economies and globalized economies

Paul Hirst and Grahame Thompson's *Globalization in Question* (1996) makes an attempt to test the theory of globalization empirically. Like Sklair, Hirst and Thompson put the role of transnational corporations (TNCs) or multinational corporations (MNCs) at the forefront of their argument. They start their analysis by distinguishing between a globalized economy and an international economy.

They argue that a **globalized economy** consists of a system in which 'distinct national economies are subsumed and rearticulated into the system by international processes and transactions. The international economic system becomes autonomized and socially disembedded, as markets and production become truly global.' In other words, nation-states become almost irrelevant to patterns of economic activity, and the existence of national boundaries makes little or no difference to patterns of trade.

In an **international economy**, though, 'processes that are determined at the level of the national economy still dominate and international phenomena are outcomes that emerge from the distinct and differential performance of the national economies'. In other words, the world is made up of interacting national economies.

TNCs and MNCs

Hirst and Thompson regard corporations as a key test of whether the world economy is global or international. They distinguish between MNCs (multinational corporations) and TNCs (transnational corporations). In MNCs the national base is important and they are effectively regulated by their home government. In contrast, TNCs are globally based and 'footloose'. They have an international management team and are potentially willing to base their operations, including if necessary their headquarters, anywhere in the world.

Hirst and Thompson use their own data (based on an analysis of the sales, assets and profits of 500 corporations in 1987, and the sales and assets of more than 5,000 corporations in 1992–3) to test whether corporations are still MNCs or have become TNCs.

According to their analysis, both sets of data show that home-based activities dominate in terms of such measures as the number of subsidiaries and affiliates, the location of assets, and the place where profits are produced. For example, in 1992–3, 75 per cent of both German and Japanese manufacturing corporations' sales were in the home region/country. The corresponding figure for the UK was 65 per cent, and for the USA 67 per cent. They conclude that MNCs are dominant in a largely international economy.

Nation-states and power

Hirst and Thompson adopt a more balanced position when discussing economic governance and nation-states. They accept that 'the combined effects of changing economic conditions and past public policies of dismantling exchange controls have made ambitious and internationally divergent strategies of national economic governance far more difficult'. States have to adopt increasingly similar policies if they are to succeed in the contemporary world.

Furthermore, Hirst and Thompson admit that states have a reduced capacity 'to act autonomously on their societies'. They give the example of the socialist government of France in the 1980s. It tried to combat unemployment and recession by pumping money into the economy, but the negative reaction of foreign investors and financiers forced it to abandon the policy.

Along with the loss of economic power, Hirst and Thompson believe there has also been a loss of military power. This is because it has become inconceivable for most developed nations to pursue policies through military force in a post-Cold War but nuclear era. It is simply too risky to embark on military campaigns with the possibility of a nuclear response.

States may even have lost some ideological power. With increasingly heterogeneous populations, states are less able to call on nationalist loyalty. The diversity of populations makes it difficult to produce loyalty to any one set of values.

Although Hirst and Thompson believe the state's capacities have been reduced and in some ways changed, they do not believe they have been eliminated altogether. The state retains a role as a 'facilitator and orchestrator of private economic actors':

> *It still retains one central role that ensures a large measure of territorial control – the regulation of populations. People are less mobile than money, goods or ideas: in a sense they remain 'nationalized', dependent on passports, visas, and residence and labour qualifications.*
> Hirst and Thompson, 1996

It is this quality which gives the state democratic legitimacy. It can claim to speak for a body of people and thus can play a crucial role in negotiating international agreements. Hirst and Thompson see such agreements as crucial in the contemporary international economy. They conclude: 'Politics is becoming more polycentric, with states as merely one level in a complex system of overlapping and often competing agencies of government.'

Evaluation

Hirst and Thompson can be criticized on a number of grounds.

First, their analysis ofTNCs and MNCs leaves room for alternative interpretations. They themselves point out: 'The fact that only 30 per cent or so of company activity is conducted abroad does not tell us anything about the strategic importance of that 30 per cent to the overall business activity of firms.'

Leslie Sklair (2003) makes the point that the strategies of many corporations are based around a desire to expand their activities outside their countries of origin. This, Sklair argues, is apparent from their annual shareholders' reports. Sklair also points out that data on foreign investment does not show whether corporations act in the interests of their home country. Sklair argues that they do not, but act in accordance with the interests of their shareholders and the global capitalist class that largely runs them.

A further problem with this aspect of Hirst and Thompson's argument is that the definition of the 'home region' on which their figures are based (see above) is extremely broad. Thus the German 'home region' is taken to include the rest of Europe and the Middle East and Africa, the US home region includes Canada, and the Japanese home region covers the whole of southeast Asia.

Hirst and Thompson perhaps use an over-restrictive definition of TNCs in order to allow them to arrive at the conclusion that there are few genuine TNCs. Furthermore, as Anthony Woodiwiss (1996) points out, Hirst and Thompson are arguing against a rather extreme view of the 'borderless world' (derived from the writings of Ohmae), which is not representative of the more qualified accounts of globalization.

Second, aspects of their argument seem to point in the opposite direction to the conclusions they reach. Their emphasis on international regulation just adds plausibility to the theory of globalization, since increased international regulation is only necessary because of globalization.

Third, Woodiwiss argues that they are so keen to find evidence to support their ideas that they tend to ignore potentially contradictory evidence. In particular, they neglect the transnational influences on economies other than those involving corporations (for example, tourism and changes in exchange rates).

Hirst and Thompson are also criticized by Kate Nash (2000) who believes that they misrepresent most theories of globalization. According to Nash, Hirst and Thompson criticize theories of globalization for seeing the nation-state as virtually redundant. However, Nash believes that most theories merely portray the state as in a more difficult position as a result of globalization, and in this respect are not very different from the views of Hirst and Thompson themselves.

Nash also believes that there is plenty of evidence of corporations taking a more global outlook, and she criticizes Hirst and Thompson for neglecting developing aspects of globalization such as global environmental problems – for example, global warming.

Despite these problems, Hirst and Thompson do succeed in raising serious doubts about the more extreme versions of globalization. They show that home markets remain important to corporations and that most corporations retain strong attachments to their country of origin. They also show that the continued control over territory and ability to represent populations mean that states continue to have sources of power which are not available to other institutions.

Anthony Giddens – globalization and high modernity

Unlike Hirst and Thompson, Anthony Giddens generally supports the theory of globalization. Indeed, as we will see, he explicitly criticizes Hirst and Thompson. However, Giddens is also critical of the extreme version of the theory advanced by Ohmae, as he steers a path between those who deny that globalization has taken place and those who think it has completely transformed the world.

Globalization and time–space distanciation

Anthony Giddens (1990) defines globalization as 'the intensification of worldwide social relationships which link distant localities in such a way that local happenings are shaped by events occurring many miles away and vice versa'. This often includes events which take place in other nation-states and which may be outside the control of any state.

Giddens sees this process as involving **time–space distanciation**, in which interaction is stretched across space so that people no longer have to be physically present to interact with one another. Technological innovations such as the internet and satellite communications make this possible and reduce the time it takes to communicate with people in other parts of the world. National boundaries become less significant and states are less able to control what happens in the world.

Competition and the global economy

Part of this process involves increasing competition between businesses in different societies. Businesses have to compete globally if they are to be successful. They cannot rely upon monopolizing their own domestic market. This is because the opening up of world trade prevents national governments from protecting businesses from foreign competition.

Giddens puts forward some evidence to support his claim that globalization is taking place. He attacks Hirst and Thompson's views by arguing that world trade is more important and more open than ever before. According to Giddens (1999), only 7 per cent of the gross domestic products of the richest nations consisted of exports in 1950. By 1970 it was 12 per cent, and by 1997 it had risen further to 17 per cent.

Furthermore, Giddens also points out that a much-expanded role has developed for world financial markets. According to Giddens, 'Over a trillion dollars a day is turned over in currency exchange transactions.' Furthermore, institutional investors who can shift money around the world extremely rapidly have become incredibly powerful. According to Giddens's figures, in the USA in 1996 they held assets of $11.1 trillion. Even if Hirst and Thompson are right to point out that much trade is regional, Giddens is convinced 'there is a "fully global economy" on the level of financial markets'.

Nation-states and power

Where do these economic changes leave the governments of nation-states? Giddens believes that the changes do restrict their power. Nation-states have to compete to attract inward investment from major transnational corporations and they have to keep institutional investors happy. They cannot therefore afford to levy very high taxes in order to pay for expensive welfare programmes. If they tried to tax too highly, businesses would go elsewhere and deprive the government of the business revenue they need to fund their welfare programmes. Giddens says:

The new period of globalization attacks not only the economic basis of the welfare state but the commitment of its citizenry to the equation of wealth with national wealth. The state is less able to provide effective central control of economic life. Giddens, 1994

However, this does not lead Giddens to agree with writers such as Ohmae that the nation-state has lost its power and become insignificant. Giddens (1999) asks, 'Is the nation-state becoming a fiction as Ohmae suggests, and government obsolete? They are not, but their shape is being altered.' It is true that governments lose some economic power, but other powers are retained, even enhanced.

Giddens believes governments can sometimes use nationalist sentiments to increase the support they gain from their populations. Furthermore, he believes that 'Nations retain, and will for the foreseeable future, considerable governmental, economic and cultural power, over their citizens and in the external arena.'

However, he believes that to exercise such powers they increasingly need to collaborate with other states, with transnational actors, and with regions and localities within their own states. Each of these has become more important, and national governments, without being stripped of power, do increasingly share it with other groups and organizations.

Evaluation

Giddens provides perhaps the most balanced analysis of globalization. Although parts of his argument are not particularly well backed up with evidence, he does show an awareness of the continuing power of states and of some of the limitations that have been put on that power.

David Held and Anthony McGrew – democracy and the cosmopolitan order

David Held and Anthony McGrew are British sociologists who have given detailed consideration to the implications of globalization for the state. In *Globalization/Anti-Globalization* (2002) Held and McGrew critically examine existing theories and outline their own approach.

Globalists and sceptics

Held and McGrew argue that it is possible to distinguish between two types of theorist of globalization: the **globalists** and the **sceptics**. The globalists believe that globalization has taken place, while the sceptics argue that it has not. Ohmae, Sklair and Giddens are all examples of globalists, whereas Hirst and Thompson are examples of sceptics.

Held and McGrew argue that both positions have some merit, but both are open to criticism. Both are able to support their case because they tend to use different types of evidence. Held and McGrew say:

Sceptics put primary emphasis on the organization of production and trade … while globalists tend to focus on financial deregulation and the explosive growth of global financial markets over the last twenty-five years. Held and McGrew, 2002

Furthermore:

Sceptics stress the continuing primacy of the national interest and the cultural traditions of national communities, while globalists point to the growing significance of transnational political problems – such as worldwide pollution, global warming and financial crises – which create a growing sense of the common fate of humankind. Held and McGrew, 2002

Neither of these viewpoints is 'mere rhetoric or ideology' and both have strengths and weaknesses.

Held and McGrew believe the sceptics are on strong ground in arguing that there is nothing new about high levels of international trade and direct investment. Furthermore, the sceptics' case is supported by historical evidence about migration. In the late nineteenth century, migration was on a similar scale to that seen today. As a consequence, ethnically mixed societies have long been common.

Held and McGrew support the sceptics' case in arguing that members of nation-states retain strong national identities, and local cultures have not become homogenized by global culture. They say, 'the role of national (and local) culture remains central to public life in nearly all political communities; and … imported foreign products are constantly read and reinterpreted in novel ways by national audiences'. Thus, for example, audiences all over the world might watch the same films, but their interpretation will vary from society to society. Rather than undermining cultural differences, these variations in interpretation might actually strengthen them.

Nevertheless, Held and McGrew believe the globalists are right about many things. They agree with them that there have been institutional changes in the economy which have encouraged globalization. These include 'the establishment of a global trading system, the integration of financial markets, and the spread of transnational production systems'.

They agree that politics has become increasingly globalized, with international and global political institutions such as the EU and UN becoming more important.

They also believe that environmental problems are often global in scale. Furthermore, there are more global social movements, including global environmental groups (such as Greenpeace) and a global anti-capitalist movement. (For a discussion of global social movements, see pp. 567–8.)

The transformationalist stance

Held and McGrew argue that it is possible to find a good deal of common ground between the globalists and the sceptics. Both agree that 'economic interconnectedness' has grown over recent decades and both agree that transnational problems such as money laundering and global terrorism have become more significant.

There is no question that international and global institutions such as the World Trade Organization have become more important. Neither side disputes that significant changes have taken place which 'require new modes of thinking about politics, economics and cultural change'.

To Held and McGrew, all these examples suggest that globalization is real and having a significant impact on social life. However, they do not go as far as the extreme globalists who see globalization as having had a fundamental effect on all areas of social life. Rather, they see globalization as a process which has had a big impact on some areas of social life, but not all.

They therefore adopt what they call a **transformationalist** stance, which 'accepts a modified version of the globalization argument, emphasizing that while contemporary patterns of global, political, economic and communications flows are historically unprecedented, the direction of these remains uncertain, since globalization is a contingent process replete with conflicts and tensions'. There is nothing inevitable about globalization, and the existence of forces opposed to globalization means that in the future the process might change direction or even be reversed.

However, Held and McGrew believe that, so far, globalization has had the most influence on politics and on states, and it is in this area that they develop ideas about the best way to respond to globalization.

States and politics

Held and McGrew claim that the roles and functions of states have changed considerably as a result of globalization. States no longer exercise the same degree of control over their territory and have to take increasing account of external influences. States operate at 'the intersection of regionalizing and globalizing networks and trends'. The state is a very significant actor, for example, in international and multilateral organizations such as the UN, EU and NATO, and in influencing investment decisions of transnational corporations through domestic economic policy.

However, there are fewer occasions on which states can exercise power without reference to other actors, other states, or international and transnational bodies. As a result of globalizing tendencies, even the most powerful states (such as the USA) are rarely able to act without any reference to the power of external groups or institutions. The sovereignty of the nation-state has not been lost altogether, but 'sovereignty has been transformed'.

Held and McGrew say that the sovereignty of states 'has been displaced as an illimitable, indivisible and exclusive form of public power, embodied in an individual state, and embedded in a system of often multiple, often pooled, power centres and spheres of political authority'. The increasing importance of international law and IGOs (intergovernmental organizations) such as the World Trade Organization (WTO) limit state freedom to act entirely independently. The result is an 'unbundling of the relationship between sovereignty, territoriality and political power'.

According to Held and McGrew, politics is becoming more complex and multi-layered. Power is exercised by institutions other than the state. New social movements (see pp. 566–75) (which try to influence how others exercise power) often operate across different states. They may also try to influence the behaviour of people or institutions other than those of nation-states. For example, environmental groups try to influence individual consumers, intergovernmental organizations, and multinational institutions such as the EU.

These changes create problems for democracy. Democracy is based upon the assumption that a group of people can exercise control over their own affairs. As it becomes more difficult to confine issues within national boundaries, it becomes harder to operate democracy along these lines. As well as bringing people together, globalism can create 'fragmentation' and 'disintegrative trends'. Closer global ties bring diverse cultures together and can increase the chances of conflict and war between people of different cultures and national identities.

Cosmopolitan social democracy

However, these problems are not impossible to deal with. Held and McGrew argue that the difficulties can be tackled through **cosmopolitan social democracy**. This involves making globalizing institutions and organizations accountable, just as democratically elected governments are accountable to their electorate. Cosmopolitan social democracy could be achieved with:

> *the opening up of IGOs to key stakeholders and participants; greater equity in the distribution of the world's resources; the protection of human rights and fundamental freedoms; sustainable development across generations; and peaceful dispute-settling in leading geopolitical conflicts.* Held and McGrew, 2002

Held and McGrew admit this will not be easy. However, they believe that foundations are in place which can be built on. Institutions such as the UN and the International Criminal Court are a useful starting point. Admittedly, many proposals at the UN have been vetoed by permanent members of the security council (the USA, Russia, China, the United Kingdom and France). However, the UN does at least provide a vision of a world in which there are agreed procedures to settle disputes and global standards for human rights are enforced. Indeed, Held and McGrew believe there has already been substantial progress towards the 'entrenchment of cosmopolitan values concerning the equal dignity and worth of all human beings'.

They do not believe, though, that cosmopolitan social democracy can be achieved by a single institution. They envisage 'multi-layered governance' in which a variety of institutions work to deal with problems at the local, national, regional or global level.

They believe that non-governmental organizations like Amnesty International and Oxfam can play an important role, and new social movements can help to push for a more just and better-governed globalized world. However, they admit that 'aspirations for global democracy and social justice' will have to 'overcome fierce opposition from well-entrenched geopolitical and geoeconomic interests'.

Conclusion and evaluation

The views of Held and McGrew are perhaps somewhat idealistic. While many states are affected by global issues, that does not necessarily mean they have the same interests in relation to those issues. For example, poor 'third world' countries have an interest in changing some aspects of the global economy which benefit the rich 'first world', and which the latter therefore wants to retain. The disagreements among member states of the EU and the inability of the UN to take effective action in places such as Bosnia, Kosovo, Chechnya and Palestine suggest that Held and McGrew's vision of international democracy and cooperation will not easily become reality.

There were fundamental disagreements between states about the invasion and occupation of Iraq by the USA and the UK in 2003, and there were disputes over the legitimacy of the action under international law. Writers such as Noam Chomsky are unlikely to believe that either the USA or transnational corporations will relinquish power to make the world more democratic (see pp. 545–8).

Kate Nash summarizes these types of objections to the notion of cosmopolitan democracy. She says that Held:

> *does not give enough attention to the continuing power of nation-states. It is argued that they simply cannot be made subject to international law in the way Held proposes since, without a global state, there is no global peacekeeping force beyond that which they provide. As long as political institutions are international rather than supranational, they depend on nation-states.* 2000, p. 254

Nevertheless, Held and McGrew may well be right to point out that democracy must tackle the problem of globalization if power is not to become more distant from the citizens of nation-states. Identifying the problem is easier than finding the solution, but it can at least be seen as a step in the right direction.

Michael Mann – the sources of social power

Michael Mann (1986, 1993) developed his own distinctive theory of power and tied it to an account of the development of societies from 10,000 BC to the present day. In doing so, he returned to the all-embracing questions about societal development which so concerned the 'classical' sociologists, Marx, Weber and Durkheim. Furthermore, Mann has a considerable advantage over these eminent sociologists, since he has access to up-to-date historical and archaeological evidence which was unavailable to them.

Mann's work incorporates elements from the theories of power discussed in the two preceding sections of this chapter:

1. He agrees with writers such as Skocpol that the state can be an independent source of power, arguing that 'political power' is as important as ideological, military and economic power.
2. He follows theories of globalization in claiming that theories of power cannot be confined to examining how power is distributed within national boundaries. Like Held and McGrew and others, Mann believes that networks of power can stretch across countries and across the globe. He does not, however, see this as a particularly new phenomenon, claiming that networks of power have long extended across sizeable geographical areas.

In some ways Mann's work represents a more fundamental challenge to theories of power than state-centred approaches and the theory of globalization, for he starts his analysis by attacking perhaps the most basic concept of sociology, that of 'society'.

The non-existence of 'society'

Mann says: 'if I could, I would abolish the concept of "society" altogether'. Although he continues to use the word 'society' for the sake of convenience, he is anxious to point out that 'societies are not unitary. They are not social systems (closed or open); they are not totalities.'

Mann claims it logically follows from this standpoint that non-existent societies cannot be divided into parts or subsystems, as they are by Parsons, nor can they be analysed in terms of 'levels', as in the Marxist division between the infrastructure and the superstructure. Furthermore, Mann rejects the idea of societal evolution because of his belief that societies are not unitary.

How, then, is Mann able to justify his rejection of so many central concepts in sociological theory? His main argument is very simple: human behaviour is not, and has never been, exclusively related to, or caused by, a particular territory in which an individual lives. In the modern world, for example, the development of the mass media has led to many aspects of culture extending across national boundaries. Nor is the spread of cultural influences particularly new: for centuries, major religions such as Islam and Christianity have had an influence which transcends national boundaries.

Like theorists of globalization, Mann claims that a society such as Britain is not a political unit which can be analysed independently. Britain is a member of the military alliance NATO, and of the economic grouping of nations, the EU. Many companies in Britain are owned by multinational corporations which are based abroad. Through trade, the British economy is affected by other countries, and cultural products from all parts of the world are imported.

In order to understand the culture, politics, military activity and economics of Britain, therefore, it is necessary to consider what happens in other parts of the world. Throughout history, according to Mann, trade, war and conquest have ensured that there has never been an isolated society.

Power networks and types of power

On the basis of such observations, Mann reaches the view that 'societies are constituted of multiple overlapping and intersecting sociospatial networks of power'. In order to understand social life, sociologists need to study the way that humans enter into social relationships which involve the exercise of power.

Since power is so central to his theory, Mann spends some time explaining what he means by the word and distinguishing different forms of power. He sees **power** as the ability to pursue and attain goals through mastery of the environment. Power, in this sense, can take two separate forms:

1. **Distributional power** is power over others. It is the ability of individuals to get others to help them pursue their own goals. Distributional power is held by individuals.
2. In contrast, **collective power** is exercised by social groups. Collective power may be exercised by one social group over another: for example, when one nation is colonized by another. It may also be exercised through mastery over things: for example, the ability to control part of nature through an irrigation scheme.

Having distinguished between different types of power, Mann goes on to explain the two main ways in which it can be exercised:

1. **Extensive power** is 'the ability to organize large numbers of people over far-flung territories in order to engage in minimally stable cooperation'. An example of extensive power would therefore be the influence over believers exercised by a major religion.
2. **Intensive power**, on the other hand, is the ability 'to organize tightly and command a high level of mobilization or commitment from the participants'. Thus a religious sect might be seen as having intensive power in comparison to the more extensive power of a church.

In the final part of Mann's analysis of different types of power, he identifies a difference between authoritative and diffused power:

1. **Authoritative power** is exercised when conscious, deliberate commands are issued, and those to whom they are issued make a conscious decision to follow them. A football player following a referee's instruction to leave the field would be an example of authoritative power.
2. **Diffused power** spreads in a more spontaneous way. It involves power relationships, but ones which operate without commands being issued. Mann uses the example of market mechanisms: a company can go out of business not because someone commands that it does, but because it is unable to compete with other companies producing the same types of product. Often this type of power produces behaviour that appears as 'natural' or 'moral', or as resulting from 'self-evident common interests'.

By combining the distinctions between intensive and extensive, and authoritative and diffused power, Mann is able to distinguish four principal types of power. Examples of these four types of power are given in Table 9.1.

The sources of power

So far, this account of Mann's theory has explained the types of power that he believes exist, but not where that power comes from. Central to his approach is the simple idea that power can have four sources: these can be economic, ideological, political and military.

Table 9.1 Michael Mann – examples of social power

	Automotive	Diffused
Intensive	Army command structure	A general strike
Extensive	Militaristic empire	Market exchange

Source: M. Mann (1986) *The Sources of Social Power*, vol. 1. Cambridge University Press, Cambridge, p.9.

Mann follows Marx in thinking that economic power is important, but he does not attribute the primary role to it that Marx does, because of the importance of the three other sources.

Ideological power involves power over ideas and beliefs; **political power** concerns the activities of states; and **military power** the use of physical coercion. In Marxist theory these sources of power are often seen as being united. From a Marxist point of view, the group that has **economic power** – those who own the means of production – will also have ideological power through their ability to promote false class consciousness. Furthermore, the economically ruling class will exercise control over the state and will therefore have political power; and, through the state, it will also monopolize military power.

However, Mann disagrees with the Marxist view, claiming that each source of power can be independent of the others. Ideological power can be wielded by churches or other religious organizations, which may have little or no economic power. The political power of a state does not ensure that it will have ideological power. In communist Poland, for example, much of the population appeared to attach more importance to the ideas of the Roman Catholic Church and the free trade union Solidarity than to those of the communist state.

Even political and military power are not necessarily tied together. In feudal Europe, military power rested mainly in the hands of individual lords and not with the state. In modern societies, in a *coup d'état* the army actually takes power from the political rulers. Thus, in Chile, General Pinochet led a military coup in which power was seized from President Allende's elected government.

Of course, Mann accepts that in a particular society at a particular time, two or more of the four sources of power might be monopolized by a social group. However, all power never rests in one set of hands. Since no society is completely independent, networks of power will stretch across national boundaries, thus preventing a single group within a society from having all the power.

An example of Mann's approach

In his explanation of social changes Mann explains how these various sources of power are related to each other. For example, he demonstrates how, shortly after AD 1300, an innovation in military strategy led to a number of important social changes in Europe, and in particular to a weakening in the influence of feudalism.

At the battle of Courtrai, Flemish infantrymen were faced by an attack from French mounted knights. At the time, semi-independent groups of armoured mounted knights were militarily dominant and the normal tactic for infantry who were attacked by them was to flee. On this occasion, though, the Flemings were penned against a river and had no alternative but to fight. By adopting a close-knit formation, the pike phalanx of the Flemings was able to unseat many of the knights and secure victory.

As a result, feudal mounted armies lost their dominance, and societies such as the Duchy of Burgundy, which did not adapt to the changed circumstances, declined. Furthermore, the change led to a centralization of state power and a reduction in the autonomy of feudal lords. It became recognized that mixed armies of cavalry, infantry and artillery were the answer to the pike phalanx, and states could more easily provide the resources to maintain this type of army than could individual lords. Thus, changes in the nature of military power led to an extension of the political power of the state.

On the surface, it might appear that this significant episode in history is an example of military technology determining the course of social change, but Mann believes ideological and economic factors were also important. He suggests that pike phalanxes could not have succeeded if the individuals in them had not been convinced that those on either side of them would stand firm. In societies such as Flanders and Switzerland, such trust was likely to develop because of the way of life of the burghers and free peasants there. Furthermore, the different types of army produced by the Flemings and the Swiss on one side, and feudal societies on the other, were related to their respective abilities to produce an economic surplus to finance their armies.

Thus, the four sources of social power were all linked: an extension of military power was related to the nature and distribution of ideological and economic power and led to an increase in the political power of the state. In this example, military power was particularly important, but, according to Mann, in other episodes in history, any of the sources of power can assume a central role.

Conclusion

Other theories of power and the state tend to emphasize a particular source of power. Marxism stresses the importance of economic power, pluralism stresses ideological power in democracies, and elite and state-centred theories emphasize political power. Mann's approach argues that any complete theory must embrace all of these, as well as including military power.

Michel Foucault – power/knowledge

The nature of power

The work of Michel Foucault (1926–84) provides an influential and novel view of power. Like Mann, he saw power as something that is not concentrated in one place or in the hands of particular individuals. However, he goes much further from conventional views of power than Mann does. Foucault's complex (and sometimes obscure and contradictory) writings suggest that power is found in all social relationships and is not just exercised by the state. Nevertheless, much of his work is concerned with the way in which the state develops its ability to classify and exercise power over populations.

To Foucault, power is intimately linked with knowledge: **power/knowledge** produce one another. The extension of the power of the state therefore involves the development of new types of knowledge, which enable it to collect more information about and exercise more control over its populations. This involves the development of **discourses**: ways of talking about things which have consequences for power.

However, Foucault does not just think of power in coercive terms: as well as restricting people, power can enable them to do things. Furthermore, and paradoxically, Foucault only sees power as operating when people have some freedom. Power never allows total control and, indeed, constantly produces resistances and evasions as people try – and often succeed – in slipping from its grasp.

Foucault's ideas will now be examined in more detail.

Madness and Civilization

Much of Foucault's early work was taken up with an account of how the state increasingly tried to regulate and control populations. Before the eighteenth century, governments made little attempt to control, regulate or even monitor the behaviour of the mass of the population. Few statistics were produced and few records were kept.

In *Madness and Civilization* (1967) Foucault describes how such phenomena as unemployment, poverty and madness started to be seen as social problems by states in the eighteenth century. Before that, the mad were largely free from state interference. Although they were sometimes cast out of towns, they were permitted to wander as they wished in rural areas. Alternatively they were put to sea together in 'ships of fools'. However, this system of dealing with the mad was replaced by places of confinement (such as madhouses) in which the mad, the poor and the sick were separated and isolated from the rest of the population.

Foucault argues that this was due to a new concern in European culture with a sense of responsibility for such social problems and a new work ethic. It was felt that something should be done with the mad; and others were punished for the new sin of laziness.

By the start of the nineteenth century, however, the policy of confining these diverse groups together came to be seen as a mistake. For example, although the unemployed were forced to work in the madhouses, this just led to them doing some of the work needed in the local area, thus increasing unemployment and making the problem worse. Consequently, new methods were used to separate the different groups of undesirables.

New scientific disciplines, such as psychiatry, were developed to categorize people (as sane or mad, and as suffering from different illnesses). In this process the discourses of the social sciences came to be involved in power relationships. According to Madan Sarup (1988), by 'discourse' Foucault meant 'practices that systematically form the objects of which they speak'.

From this viewpoint, the practices of psychiatry (and, connected to them, the knowledge contained in theories) created the mentally ill. Psychiatry was a discourse and a tactic used to control particular groups in the population. The technique of classifying people as mentally ill was an important part of the state's gradual development of systems of administration. Administration allowed the monitoring of people and hence offered the potential for controlling their behaviour.

However, classifying and monitoring people did not just involve a straightforward coercive use of power by the state. Rather, it created the possibility of localized power/knowledge relationships that took place at an individual level. For example, power/knowledge related to the discourse of psychiatry created the possibility of power being exercised in individual interactions between psychiatrists and their patients. In Foucault's view, though, the power is part of the discourse of psychiatry, and not something which is held by individual psychiatrists.

Discipline and Punish

Many of the themes first explored in *Madness and Civilization* were explored further in a later book, *Discipline and Punish* (1991, first published 1975). In this book, Foucault traced the changes in the nature and purposes of punishment in the eighteenth century.

The book starts with a graphic account of the execution of the French murderer Damiens in Paris in 1757. Damiens was first placed on a scaffold where pieces of flesh were torn from him using red-hot pincers. Lead, oil, resin wax and sulphur were melted together and then poured on to the flesh wound. Each of his four limbs was then attached to a separate horse so that they could pull him apart. However, initially this failed, and a knife had to be used on Damiens to make it easier for the horses to pull his body apart. Still alive, his head and the trunk of his body were tied to a stake and set on fire.

By the late eighteenth century such public punishments were starting to die out. Punishment was increasingly hidden. People were executed behind closed doors using swifter methods (such as the guillotine or hanging), and many people were locked away in prisons. Here, they were subjected to a regimented regime involving a strict timetable of work, sleep, education and so on.

Changes in punishment

Foucault argues that these changes involved a fundamental shift in the nature of punishment. In the early eighteenth century, punishment focused on the body; it involved the direct infliction of pain as a way of making the offender suffer for his crimes, and as a way of discouraging others. By the late eighteenth and early nineteenth centuries, this had changed. It was no longer the body that was the main focus of punishment, but the soul. The punishment consisted of a loss of rights – particularly the right to liberty – rather than the suffering of pain. The certainty of being caught was intended to deter people, rather than the public humiliation of execution or being placed in the stocks.

Furthermore, the intention was to reform the offender rather than simply to make him suffer. Foucault admits there was no clear-cut break between these two systems of punishment (executions continued to be used, for example), but he argues that, nevertheless, there was a definite shift from one approach to another.

What was being judged also subtly changed. In the earlier period people were judged for what they had done. By the later period they were judged for what sort of a person they were. The motivation behind the crime began to be taken into account because of what it revealed about the offender. The punishment used varied according to the motivation. Foucault says:

> *The question is no longer simply: 'Has the act been established and is it punishable?' But also: 'What is this act, what is this act of violence or this murder? To what level or to what field of reality does it belong? Is it a phantasy, a psychotic reaction, a delusional episode, a perverse action?' It is no longer simply: 'Who committed it?' But: 'How can we assign the causal process that produced it? Where did it originate in the author himself? Instinct, unconscious, environment, heredity?'* Foucault, 1991

A whole range of experts were involved in answering these questions: experts such as psychologists and psychiatrists, educationalists, and members of the prison service. Control over punishment became fragmented and wrapped up in specialist knowledge. Foucault says, 'A corpus of knowledge, techniques, "scientific" discourses is formed and becomes entangled with the practice of the power to punish.'

Foucault tries to show that, even as the state developed techniques for controlling populations, it also ceded power to the experts who had the knowledge deemed necessary to exercise power in ways suitable for reforming people.

The exercise of power/knowledge

However, Foucault does not argue that such knowledge/power relationships are entirely '"negative" mechanisms that make it possible to repress, to exclude, to prevent, to eliminate'. Instead, he believes there are also 'positive' aspects to them. They can be positive in the sense that they make it possible for certain things to be achieved. Foucault gives the example of how punishments can be used to motivate workers to step up their efforts and provide more of the labour power that society might need.

Foucault is also insistent that power is not something simply possessed by individuals. He says, 'power is exercised rather than possessed'. An individual does not simply hold power; they can use power if they can muster the right 'dispositions, manoeuvres, tactics, techniques' to achieve what they want.

Furthermore, power is only exercised by getting people to do something when they have a choice not to. It is not simply physical coercion, where there are no options open to those over whom power is exercised. In fact (in a later work) Foucault makes it clear that he thinks there are very few circumstances in which people have no choice. In most circumstances somebody would have a choice of resisting by the possibility 'of committing suicide, of jumping out through the window, of killing the other' (Foucault, 1988, quoted in Hindess, 1996).

From Foucault's point of view, then, it is always possible to resist the exercise of power, to refuse to go along with what others are trying to get you to do. When attempts are made to exercise power, the result always has an element of uncertainty. Indeed, Foucault believes that power can sometimes be reversed. At one point in his work he argues that the fact 'that I am older and that at first you were intimidated can, in the course of the conversation, turn about and it is I who can become intimidated before someone, precisely because he is younger' (Foucault, 1988, quoted in Hindess, 1996).

In *Discipline and Punish* Foucault reiterates his belief that power/knowledge are virtually inseparable. He says:

> *We should admit that power produces knowledge ... that power and knowledge directly imply one another; that there is no power relation without the correlative constitution of a field of knowledge, nor any knowledge that does not presuppose and constitute at the same time power relations.* Foucault, 1991

Partly because power is so wrapped up with knowledge, there is almost always some chance to resist the exercise of power by challenging the knowledge on which it is based. For example, a psychiatric patient could question the accuracy of a psychiatrist's diagnosis.

Because power/knowledge imply one another, power relationships are present in all aspects of society. They 'go right down into the depths of society ... they are not localized in the relations between the state and its citizens or on the frontier between classes'.

Thus, Foucault would see most of the views of power discussed in this chapter as inadequate because they are too limited in scope. Marxism is too limited because it only focuses on class relationships of power. Pluralism and elite theory are inadequate because they concentrate on power exercised by the state. None of them look at power in the everyday activities of people and the commonly used discourses involved in interaction.

Government and discipline

Although Foucault does not believe that power/knowledge is only exercised through the state, that does not mean that he thinks that power/knowledge is absent from the state. Attempts are made by states and other authorities to govern, manipulate and control behaviour. Although never entirely successful, sophisticated techniques can be devised to do this.

In *Discipline and Punish*, for example, Foucault goes into considerable detail about the way in which activities overseen by the state involve power/knowledge. For example, he discusses the **panopticon**, a prison design proposed by the English philosopher Jeremy Bentham. Although never fully implemented, aspects of it were incorporated into the design of some prisons, as illustrated in Figure 9.1.

The key feature of the panopticon was a central tower which allowed prison warders to see into every cell and therefore to observe the activities of all the inmates. The use of backlighting would mean that the warders would be able to see into cells without the inmates knowing whether they were being observed at any particular time. Inmates would therefore have to restrain their activities and act in a disciplined manner all the time, just in case they were being watched.

Foucault saw discipline as an important feature of modern societies. Techniques of **surveillance** are used to check on people's behaviour in places such as schools, hospitals and elsewhere. However, the possibility of being watched also encourages **self-discipline**: people become accustomed to regulating and controlling their own actions, whether or not somebody is checking up on them.

Discipline gives people the ability to regulate and control their own behaviour. According to Foucault, it is based upon the idea that humans have a soul that can be manipulated. This is far more effective than trying to punish individual bodies by inflicting extreme pain, in the way described earlier in the execution of Damiens. Instead of punishing bodies, you try to produce docile bodies – bodies which pose no threat to order because they are self-disciplined.

Discipline is an important part of governing, but it is not confined to the activities of the government. It is also present in the activities of organizations (from nineteenth-century factories to contemporary corporations). Furthermore, it is never entirely successful. As Barry Hindess (1996) describes it, 'The suggestion is, then, that we live in a world of disciplinary projects, all of which suffer from more or less successful attempts at resistance and evasion. The result is a disciplinary, but hardly disciplined society.'

Figure 9.1 Bentham's panopticon prison design

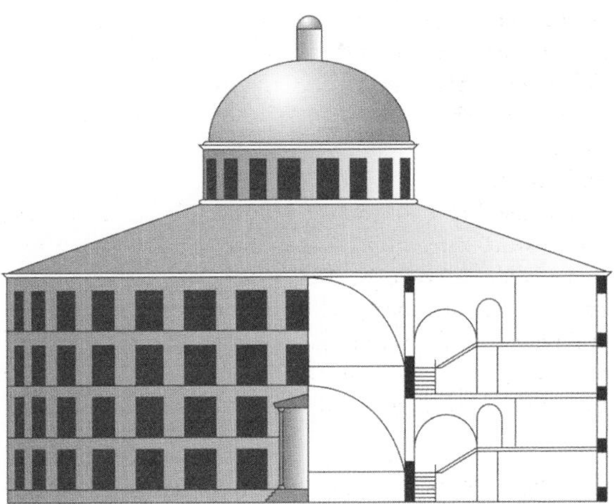

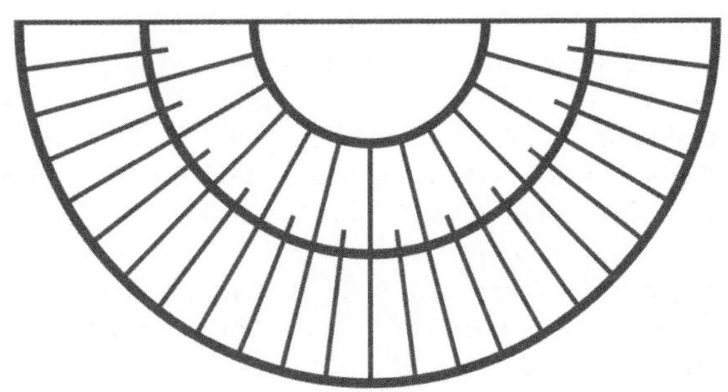

In Foucault's view, government extends far beyond the activities of the state and, particularly, the passing and enforcement of laws. Attempts at government through discipline are almost ubiquitous features of modern societies, but such attempts are never completed and never entirely successful. The unruly pupil, the worker who sabotages machinery, and the psychiatric patient who denies their diagnosis are as much a feature of modern society as the disciplined citizen with a docile body.

Evaluation

Foucault's work provides a number of important insights into the nature of power. For example, he succeeded in showing that knowledge is closely connected to power, he demonstrates that power can be found in many social relationships other than those involving the state, and he makes the important observation that power is unlikely to be absolute. He is aware that people often resist or evade attempts to exercise power.

In many ways, then, his work is subtler than that of other writers, such as some Marxists (who tend to see power as concentrated in the hands of an economic ruling class), elite theorists (who see it as concentrated in the hands of those in key positions), and pluralists (who focus on the decisions of the state to the exclusion of other ways of exercising power).

However, it can be argued that Foucault underestimates the importance of the sources of power discussed in some of these theories. For example, he neglects the power that can be exercised through the control of economic resources, such as the power to shut down a plant by shifting production elsewhere. He neglects the power that can be exercised through the use of military force.

On a smaller scale, Foucault might exaggerate the power of a mental patient to resist or evade their diagnosis; and, of course, the power of prisoners is usually strictly limited and does not include the power to change their sentence. Foucault tends to focus too much on the power associated with knowledge rather than other types and sources of power.

Foucault's work on power is in some ways contradictory. On the one hand, it documents the increased ability of governments and others to watch, record, manipulate or even control the activities of populations. On the other hand, it insists that power is only exercised when people have some freedom, and it claims that resistance is always possible. Thus his work seems to point in opposite directions.

Foucault's work also involves a strange definition of power which directly contradicts more conventional definitions. In most views of power (such as Weber's, discussed on p. 522), power is exercised precisely when people do not have freedom to act as they choose rather than when they do.

Despite these problems, Foucault certainly succeeded in developing ideas that have proved to be provocative and have stimulated both research and theorizing. He also provided an interesting analysis of how modern societies develop techniques of social control.

Postmodernism, politics and new social movements

There is a variety of postmodern approaches to politics. Most, like Foucault, see politics as involving a wider range of activities than those confined to the state and political parties. They all tend to identify a difference between modern politics and postmodern politics. They vary in the sort of changes they associate with postmodern politics and the significance they attach to those changes.

We will start by examining some of the more extravagant claims made by postmodernists, and then discuss postmodern theories that make more modest claims about changes in the nature of power and politics. The most extreme view of all is perhaps that of Jean Baudrillard. He goes way beyond Foucault's claim that power is dispersed, arguing that power has disappeared and politics is no longer real.

Jean Baudrillard – the end of politics

Perhaps the most extreme postmodern view of power and politics is advanced by Jean Baudrillard (1983). Baudrillard's basic position is that signs (such as words and visual images) no longer reflect or represent reality. Instead, signs have become totally detached from reality and indeed disguise the fact that reality no longer exists (see pp. 893–4 for a detailed discussion). In this process, politics becomes simply about the manipulation and exchange of signs to produce the appearance of a non-existent reality. We have entered an era of **simulacra**: signs which mask the fact that reality no longer exists.

Examples of the end of politics

Baudrillard gives a number of examples of this process:

1. Party politics in Western democracies give the impression of offering a real choice between different parties with differing policies. In reality, this is an illusion. The differences between parties (such as the Republicans and Democrats in the USA) are minuscule, and the same homogeneous political elite occupy state positions whoever wins the election. Having elections maintains the impression that political conflict continues to exist.
2. To Baudrillard, wars have also lost their reality: they have become simulacra. That is not to say that they do not have real effects. Baudrillard concedes that 'the flesh suffers just the same, and the dead ex-combatants count as much there as in other wars'. However, wars do not exist in the sense that they involve 'the adversity of adversaries, the reality of antagonistic causes, the ideological seriousness of war

– also the reality of defeat or victory'. Baudrillard gives the example of the bombing of Hanoi by the USA during the Vietnam War. He thinks that this bombing had no military purpose, since America had already decided to withdraw its forces, but it did allow the Vietnamese to pretend to be reaching a compromise and the Americans to feel less bad about leaving. The bombing was a simulacrum because it hid the reality that nothing was at stake – the bombing could make no difference to the outcome.

3 Baudrillard seems to believe that contemporary politicians have no real power. He describes Presidents Johnson, Nixon, Ford and Reagan as puppet presidents who lacked the power to change the world. Their main purpose was to maintain the illusion that politics continued as normal. To Baudrillard, they were simply the 'mannequins of power'.

4 Baudrillard believes that even the most potentially devastating political conflict, the Cold War, hid the absence of power. In the Cold War the possession of vast arsenals of nuclear weapons by the main (supposed) protagonists (the USA and the USSR) was irrelevant. The destructiveness of the weapons cancelled each other out and made any actual war impossible. The situation therefore 'excludes the real atomic clash – excludes it beforehand like the eventuality of the real in the system of signs'.

Baudrillard therefore believes that real power and actual politics have disappeared into a system of signs which is based around simulacra – signs which have no relationship to an actual reality. He talks of 'the impossibility of a determinant position of power', and describes 'power itself eventually breaking apart … and becoming a simulation of power'.

Evaluation

Baudrillard's claims are so extravagant that they are hard to justify. He provides no definition of power, so it is difficult to evaluate his claim that it has disappeared.

Baudrillard admits that people are killed in real wars, and he does not justify his claim that there are no real victors and vanquished in wars. For example, the USA did lose the Vietnam War, and a regime to which it was hostile did take control of the government. By any reasonable definition of power and politics, this was a political defeat for the USA and a victory for their Vietnamese enemies, since the Vietnamese regime gained power against the wishes of the US government. There are many similar examples which seem to contradict Baudrillard's arguments.

Baudrillard may have more of a point in arguing that it often makes little difference which political party wins elections in countries such as the USA. However, he still fails to show that there are no significant differences between the policies of different parties.

Baudrillard tends to make sweeping generalizations backed up by examples whose significance is debatable. He does not systematically examine the evidence which might support or refute his case. For this reason, his claims, while interesting, are open to serious doubt.

Other postmodernists do not go as far as arguing that power has disappeared and that politics is just an illusion. They do, however, claim to have identified some important changes in power and politics in a postmodern era. (For further evaluation of Baudrillard, see pp. 893–4.)

Jean-François Lyotard – the decline of metanarratives

Politics and language-games

As discussed elsewhere (see pp. 891–3 for a detailed account), Jean-François Lyotard associates postmodernism with a decline of **metanarratives**. By this he means that people no longer place their faith in big, all-embracing theories about how the world works or about society. In politics they lose their belief in political ideologies such as Marxism and fascism.

However, it is not just particular sets of political beliefs that lose people's support; rather, people become sceptical that any set of beliefs can provide an effective understanding and resolution of the problems of humanity. People no longer think that a perfect society is attainable.

The implication of this view is that politics will become less about arguments over major ideologies and will become more localized and limited in scope.

Lyotard sees knowledge in general as the main source of power in postmodern societies. As people lose their faith that any one metanarrative can provide comprehensive knowledge, knowledge breaks down into a series of different, specialist language-games. Politics therefore becomes increasingly linked to specialist language-games and less concentrated in the hands of states.

Furthermore, knowledge itself becomes evaluated according to whether it is useful, rather than whether it is true. That is, if knowledge can be used to achieve certain specific aims, then it is accepted, whether or not it can be shown to be true in terms of scientific theories. Lyotard (1984) says knowledge 'will continue to be, a major, perhaps the major – stake in the competition for power'.

Useful knowledge is not confined to states, and is increasingly possessed by multinational corporations and by other organizations and individuals that are part of civil society. Lyotard is aware that power can be exercised through coercion (which could be exercised, for example, by state-controlled military forces), but he sees such power as becoming much less important than that exercised by those who possess the most useful knowledge.

Evaluation

Lyotard's work opens up a number of ideas on power and politics, which have been developed and reiterated by later postmodernists. These include: the equation of power with knowledge; the possibility that the state loses much of its power; the idea that politics becomes fragmented; and the idea that people become concerned with single issues rather than grand ideologies.

While there may be some truth in all of these ideas, they are also open to criticism. For example, this sort of approach tends to ignore military power; it may underestimate the power of nation-states (see pp. 553–5); and it ignores the continuing importance of some 'metanarratives'. For instance, nationalist metanarratives remain a powerful force in areas such as Serbia; and religious metanarratives remain powerful in Islamic Iran.

Some critics have argued that most Western societies are dominated by the idea of free-market capitalism, which is no less of a metanarrative than the ideology of communism.

Such examples suggest that centralized state power and big issues remain important in contemporary politics. (For further evaluation of Lyotard, see pp. 891–3.)

Nancy Fraser – postmodern politics and the public sphere

The public sphere

Nancy Fraser argues that there has been a shift from predominantly modern to predominantly postmodern politics in contemporary societies. Such a shift involves a change in the public sphere. She defines the **public sphere** as those aspects of social life other than the economy and the activities of the state. She describes it as 'the space in which citizens deliberate about their common affairs' and as 'a site where social meanings are generated, circulated, contested and reconstructed' (Fraser, 1995). Fraser believes the public sphere has undergone important changes which involve a transition in the nature of politics.

The public sphere in modern societies

According to Fraser, in modern societies three main assumptions were made about the public sphere:

1. It was assumed that democratic debate was possible between people even if they had different statuses. Thus a poor person with a low-status job had as much chance to participate in debate in the public sphere as someone who was rich, successful and in a high-status job.
2. It was thought preferable to try to integrate everyone into one arena in which the concerns, the preferences and the beliefs of the public were discussed. It was thought undesirable for groups to discuss issues separately from one another. It was believed that 'a single, comprehensive public sphere is always preferable to a nexus of multiple publics'.
3. In the modern conception of the public sphere it was believed that people should discuss what was in the public interest, what was good for everyone, rather than arguing for their own private interests and what was good for them.

Fraser questions all of these modern assumptions about the public sphere:

1. In practice, inequalities between members of the public restricted the chances disadvantaged groups had to make their voices heard and their opinions count. What Fraser calls 'protocols of style and decorum' – ways of talking and acting – served to mark out higher-status individuals from lower-status ones. Lacking the appropriate protocols, women and those from minority ethnic groups and lower classes found it difficult to get their views listened to and respected.
2. In a situation where substantial inequalities exist, Fraser denies it is desirable to have public debate confined to a single, overarching public sphere. She believes it is far better to have multiple public spheres in which members of different social groups or those with specialist interests discuss issues with one another. In these groups people can develop alternative competing views to those of the political mainstream, and then compete to get their views on to the political agenda. Fraser says:

   > *Members of subordinated social groups – women, workers, people of colour, and gays and lesbians – have repeatedly found it advantageous to constitute alternative publics. I have called these 'subaltern counterpublics' in order to signal that they are parallel discursive arenas where members of subordinated groups invent and circulate counter discourses.* Fraser, 1995

   Eventually, groups such as feminists may succeed in getting their ideas taken seriously and effecting some changes in society.
3. Fraser also rejects the idea that people should not push their private interests in the public sphere. She argues that what starts out as being a private interest can come to be accepted as an issue of public concern. For example, when feminists started raising the issue of sexual harassment their ideas were not taken seriously. Most people considered the behaviour they complained of to be no more than 'innocent flirting'; others saw it as a purely personal matter.

   Fraser argues that the personal and the private can be political, and you cannot presume in advance that certain things should be off limits for public debate. Furthermore, labelling issues such as sexual harassment as private simply serves to perpetuate and reinforce the power of privileged groups – in this case, men.

   The divide between the public and the private is an artificial division of modern societies and it should not be allowed to shape public, political debate. People themselves should be the only arbitrators of what should be discussed in the public sphere and it should not be limited by any conception of what is in the public interest.

Postmodernism and the public sphere

Fraser therefore believes that modern assumptions about the public sphere need to be replaced by postmodern ones. These should involve:

1. Elimination of the inequalities between social groups which prevent people from having equal power in public, political debate.
2. Acceptance and encouragement of different groups having their own debates.
3. Rejection of the idea that supposedly 'private' issues should be off limits for public debate.

Fraser therefore advocates a pluralistic politics in which the widest possible participation takes place. She sees politics as operating outside the formal mechanisms of party politics and parliamentary government, and involving a wide variety of groups talking, discussing and arguing. She sees issues such as gender, ethnicity and sexuality as very important in postmodern politics. Class also remains important, but it is no longer the dominant issue it once was.

To Fraser, inequalities stemming from class, race, gender and sexuality cut across each other and influence debates in the public sphere. The interplay of different types of inequality is characteristic of postmodern politics. She illustrates these points with reference to the discussion of the issue of Clarence Thomas in US politics (this case is also referred to in Chapter 3, p. 196).

Clarence Thomas and postmodern politics

Clarence Thomas is a US judge who was nominated in 1991 to be appointed to the Supreme Court of the USA. Clarence Thomas is black and has generally conservative views. His nomination was generally supported by right-wing politicians. However, after being nominated, a black woman, Anita Hill, accused him of sexually harassing her some years earlier when she was working with him in a junior position.

The argument over whether Thomas should be confirmed in his appointment was played out in the public sphere, even though it involved behaviour – sexual harassment – which some saw as a private issue. It involved issues of race, gender and class differences. The struggle over the appointment involved trying to present the case as a particular sort of issue (a class, gender or race issue). It showed the importance of language in postmodern politics because the argument rested upon the words used to define the issue.

The Senate Judiciary Committee, which reviewed the proposed appointment, initially decided not to publicize the accusations made by Hill. However, pressure from feminist groups, who accused the committee of sexism, brought the issues into the open for public debate. The feminists succeeded, therefore, in getting the question of sexual harassment accepted as being of legitimate public concern.

However, the White House, who proposed Thomas in the first place, managed to argue that other aspects of Judge Thomas's private life (including a claim that he had admitted watching pornographic movies when he was a law student) were not relevant to public debate.

Anita Hill was not so successful in ruling her private life out of bounds for public scrutiny. Fraser says, 'Soon the country was awash in speculation concerning the character, motives, and psychology of Anita Hill.' She was accused by different people of being 'a lesbian, a heterosexual erotomaniac, a delusional schizophrenic, a fantasist, a vengeful spurned woman, a perjurer, and a malleable tool of liberal interest groups'.

Anita Hill had some success in presenting herself as a woman who was the victim of discrimination and inappropriate behaviour by a man. Although they were both black, Judge Thomas had more success in using the issue of race to defend himself. Fraser describes how he claimed that the hearings were 'a "high-tech lynching" designed to stop "an uppity Black who deigned to think for himself". He spoke about his vulnerability to charges that played into racial stereotypes of black men as having large penises and unusual sexual prowess.' In doing so, he tried (largely successfully) to make Anita Hill appear to be behaving like a white racist. Fraser says, 'the result was it became difficult to see Anita Hill as a black woman'. The position of black women became marginalized.

Thomas succeeded in claiming some of the protections of privacy that had historically been given to white men. Hill was not able to get the same protections. This was not, perhaps, too surprising given that, historically, 'black women have been highly vulnerable to sexual harassment at the hands of masters, overseers, bosses and supervisors'.

Class issues were also involved in the case. As Hill's superior when he was alleged to have harassed her, it could be argued that Thomas was trying to exploit his superior class position to obtain sexual favours. However, supporters of Thomas in the media portrayed the issue quite differently. They depicted Anita Hill as a professional, intellectual yuppie, while Judge Thomas was depicted as an ordinary bloke with down-to-earth and commonsense views. This depiction ignored the fact that Hill was born into rural poverty.

In the end, Thomas was confirmed as a Supreme Court judge.

Conclusion

Fraser claims this whole episode neatly illustrates the nature of postmodern politics. It shows how arguments over how issues are defined are crucial. It shows how arguments over what should be allowed into the public sphere and what should be kept private are of key importance. It demonstrates how inequalities between a range of social groups continue to shape postmodern politics in debates in the public sphere. It shows how debates in the public sphere influence the activities of the state. Finally, it shows how, in the public sphere, a wide variety of different voices can be heard.

The Thomas/Hill case led to:

> *the fracturing of the myth of homogeneous 'communities'. The 'black community', for example, is now fractured into black feminists versus black conservatives versus black liberals versus various other strands of opinion that are less easy to fix with ideological labels. The same thing holds true for the 'women's community'. This struggle showed that women don't necessarily side with women just because they are women.* Fraser, 1995

Postmodern politics is more complicated than modern politics ever was.

Evaluation

Fraser makes some useful observations about contemporary politics. Certainly, she seems on strong ground in arguing that issues relating to what should be private and what can be public are important, and in claiming that gender, ethnicity and sexuality are important political issues as well as class. However, she may exaggerate the difference between modern and postmodern politics.

Although they might have been less prominent in the past, issues such as gender and ethnicity have not been absent from politics in previous eras. (Examples include arguments over the introduction of voting rights for women and campaigns to abolish slavery.) Furthermore, there has always been a plurality of groups (such as pressure groups) trying to get their particular issues to the top of the political agenda. If there has been a move towards the sort of postmodern politics described by Fraser, then it may be a matter of degree rather than a clear-cut break with a very different system of modern politics.

New social movements and the new politics

Postmodern theories of power and politics, such as that of Fraser, stress the fragmentation and widening of political debate, and relate it to a decline in the importance of conventional party politics. These themes can all be linked to the emergence and development of what have come to be known as **new social movements**, which are seen by some sociologists as a key aspect of changes in the nature of politics in contemporary capitalist societies. The main characteristics of new social movements will be outlined first, before discussing a range of views on the significance of these movements.

Simon Hallsworth – 'Understanding new social movements'

Simon Hallsworth provides a useful introduction to the main characteristics of new social movements.

Defining new social movements

According to Hallsworth (1994), the term 'new social movements' is generally applied to 'movements such as feminism, environmentalism, the anti-racist, anti-nuclear and civil rights movements which emerged in liberal democratic societies in the 1960s and 1970s'. They are movements which are 'held to pose new challenges to the established, cultural, economic and political orders of advanced ... capitalist societies'.

The term is not usually applied to movements supporting traditional values (such as the anti-abortion movement), to long-established social movements (such as trade unions), or to conventional political parties. It is sometimes used broadly to incorporate religious movements like the Moonies, the Human Potential Movement and some ostensibly non-political groups such as New Age travellers.

New social movements and issues

New social movements tend to have an **issue basis**. They are focused on particular social issues. These broadly divide into two types:

1. The first type are concerned with issues to do with 'the defence of a natural and social environment perceived to be under threat'. In this category are animal rights groups (such as the Animal Liberation Front), anti-nuclear groups (such as the Campaign for Nuclear Disarmament) and environmental groups (such as Greenpeace and Friends of the Earth). They tend to be opposed to 'a perceived tendency inherent in the logic of the modern industrial order to plunder and annihilate the natural world'. The more radical ones believe their campaigns can show the way towards a quite different sort of society, in which people live in more harmonious ways with animals, the natural environment and each other. Others have more modest aims, such as encouraging recycling to limit damage to the environment.
2. The second type have a 'commitment to furthering the provision of rights to historically marginalized constituencies in societies such as women, ethnic minority groups and gay people'. Feminist, anti-racist and gay rights groups come into this category, as do groups campaigning for the rights of the disabled.

The novel features of new social movements

New social movements represent a departure from conventional party and pressure-group politics in a number of ways:

1. Such groups have tried to extend the definition of what is considered political to include areas such as individual prejudice, housework and domestic violence.
2. They have generally rejected the development of bureaucratic organizations in favour of more informal structures. Hallsworth says, 'they are usually characterized by low levels of bureaucracy, decision-making premised upon the idea of full participation, the appointment of few (if any) full-time officials, and a blurring of the social distance between officials and other members'. They are not content to delegate to, or be represented by, elites. Instead, they seek a participatory democracy.
3. New social movements tend to be diverse and fragmented, with many organizations and informal groups concerned with the same issues. There is no central leadership to coordinate the activities of the different groups. Feminism provides a good example of this (see pp. 100–4 for a discussion of different types of feminism).
4. Unlike political parties, they do not seek power for themselves. Unlike traditional pressure groups (such as unions and employers' organizations), they do not use threats to withdraw resources (such as labour power or capital) to achieve their objectives. Instead, they use a wide range of tactics, from illegal direct action (sometimes including bombs) to civil disobedience. They also use a variety of means, such as publishing books and appearing on television, to win people over to their causes.
5. New social movements tend to pursue very different values compared to conventional politicians. Generally, economic issues related to improving people's material living standards are not given much prominence. They are mainly concerned with what Hallsworth and others call 'post-materialist values'. These are more to do with quality of life than with material comfort. They are the product of societies in which it is assumed that people's basic material needs (such as food and shelter) can be easily met.
6. According to Hallsworth, members of new social movements tend to have certain social characteristics

which distinguish them from members of more conventional political organizations. Most members tend to be young (particularly between 16 and 30). They also tend to be from neither traditional working-class nor upper-class backgrounds. Instead, they are mainly from a new middle class, 'who tend either to work principally in the public/service sector of the economy (such as teachers, social workers, nurses etc.) or who are born to parents who work in the public sector'. Those who are outside conventional employment, particularly students and the unemployed, are also over-represented in these movements.

Conclusion

Hallsworth concludes that new social movements:

> *may be conceived as the heralds of distinctly new forms of politics in Western liberal democratic societies. Considered in this way their uniqueness is apparent in the novelty of the issues they have sought to contest; in the post-material values they have sought to advocate; in their distinctive organizational form and structure; in the form of political activity with which they are associated; as well as by the distinctive profile of their membership.* Hallsworth, 1994

Robin Cohen and Shirin M. Rai – global social movements

'Old' and 'new' social movements

Robin Cohen and Shirin M. Rai (2000) adopt a rather different standpoint from that of Hallsworth. While Hallsworth claims to be able to distinguish distinctive features of new social movements, Cohen and Rai question the usefulness of any distinction between old and new movements. They suggest two main reasons why the distinction is not clear-cut.

1. There is no clear difference between old movements concerned with class issues and new social movements concerned with life politics or identity politics. They point to the existence of movements such as 'Utopian communes, cargo cults … and the Women's Christian Temperance Union, all of which were concerned with non-class issues and existed long before the 1960s'.
2. Human rights movements have also existed for many decades, and they defy easy categorization into 'new' or 'old' social movements. Cohen and Rai see these movements as including 'the anti-racist, indigenous peoples, pro-refugee, anti-apartheid, anti-torture movements and campaigns against corporate social irresponsibility'. They believe such movements show concern both for issues of power and inequality (or 'emancipatory politics'), and for issues to do with identity (or 'life-politics').

Changes in social movements

Nevertheless, Cohen and Rai do not deny that recent decades have seen some changes in the nature of social movements. These changes include the following:

1. Social movements have introduced 'tactical and organizational innovations', which have made use of the media and technological developments. For example, groups such as Greenpeace may stage dramatic protests which are likely to attract media attention. Generally, social movements have become more aware of the need to get their message heard throughout the media and have found a variety of ways of doing so. They have also made more use of technologies such as the internet, e-mail and mobile phones to drum up support and organize protests.
2. The new technology has enabled many social movements to become global rather than confined to local or national arenas. They have responded to globalization by organizing on a global scale themselves. Thus, the environmental movement links campaigns in different countries and emphasizes how many problems (such as air and sea pollution or global warming) cut across national boundaries. Some movements make universal demands, such as demands for fundamental human rights.

Transnational and global social movements

Cohen and Rai therefore argue that it is useful to distinguish between **global social movements** (most of which are new and are concerned with issues in several countries or issues affecting the world as a whole) and social movements concerned with issues within individual countries. Examples of global social movements include the Worldwide Fund for Nature (with some 4.7 million members in 2000), Greenpeace (around 3 million members in 158 countries) and Friends of the Earth (around a million members in 56 countries). They are able to organize activities in many countries. For example, the Worldwide Fund for Nature had projects in 56 countries in 2000; Greenpeace managed to get 5 million signatures from around the world in a campaign opposing nuclear testing; and Friends of the Earth has persuaded retailers in different countries to boycott timber from the rainforests.

Cohen and Rai prefer the term 'global social movements' to the term 'transnational social movements', although they admit that not all these movements cover every part of the globe. This is because Cohen and Rai believe that the most successful movements, particularly the women's movement, religious movements, the human rights movement, the peace movement and the environmental movement, all have a genuinely global organization and outlook.

Cohen and Rai suggest five reasons for the development of these global social movements.

1. Social movements have responded to the proliferation of international organizations. The number of IGOs (international governmental organizations such as NATO and the Universal Postal Union) and INGOs (international non-governmental organizations) has grown rapidly. Since many of them make important policy decisions, global social movements have developed to try to influence them.
2. Cheap communications and travel have made global organization feasible for social movements with limited resources.
3. Political activities have adapted to the increased power of transnational corporations. For example,

parts of the labour movement such as unions have developed increasingly strong transnational networks to react to the movement of jobs between nations by transnational corporations.

4 The environmental movement has been forced to organize globally because of the obvious global or at least transnational consequences of many environmental problems.

5 Some social movements have aims which 'have an implied universal logic'. The workers' movement implores 'workers of the world' to 'unite', the women's movement is concerned with the rights of all women, and the human rights movement asserts universal human rights.

6 Some values are becoming increasingly widespread across different countries. For example, the idea of democratization is becoming increasingly influential even in countries which are, as yet, far from being democratic.

Evaluation

Cohen and Rai make useful points about the dangers of seeing 'new' social movements as entirely new. They also suggest important connections between globalization and the development of social movements.

However, they rather neglect novel features of some social movements based within particular nation-states. For example, local ecological campaigns such as those against new road building in parts of Britain have developed new methods of direct action and new ways of attracting publicity. An example is the tactics used by 'Swampy' and others, who dug and stayed in tunnels to try to prevent roads being built.

Cohen and Rai may also overstate the extent to which some social movements (such as the labour movement) have become global.

Malcolm J. Todd and Gary Taylor – new social movements and democracy

Malcolm J. Todd and Gary Taylor (2004) place much more emphasis than Cohen and Rai on the decline of other forms of politics as an explanation for the rise of new social movements. They see this as one of three central reasons for the growth of these movements.

1 The decline of party politics

Todd and Taylor say, 'it is often argued that voter apathy, declining membership of political parties and increased cynicism towards political leaders have pushed the modern democratic system towards a crisis of legitimacy' (2004, p. 4). People have become further disillusioned by the use of **'spin doctors'** by political parties – people who manipulate political stories to ensure a party's policies are portrayed in the best possible light by the media.

The electorate have become sceptical about the information they are provided with by politicians, regarding it as, at best, half-truths. They also see political parties as offering little real choice. There are no longer major ideological divisions between the parties and they simply disagree over 'the best ways to manage market capitalism' (Todd and Taylor, 2004, p. 6). The policies of the different parties all become similar because everybody is trying to attract the votes of the undecided 'floating voters' who determine the outcome of elections.

Todd and Taylor go on, 'The working class, in particular, have become more contemptuous of the political system, and this has manifested itself, in part, in declining turnout at elections' (2004, p. 5). Left-of-centre parties no longer focus their attention on the needs of poorer groups, so these groups take less part in formal politics since it fails to offer them adequate representation.

Todd and Taylor believe that substantial numbers choose to abstain because of their hostility to conventional parties – they are not simply apathetic. Large numbers of non-voters are 'active citizens' who take part in community affairs and political protests. Lacking faith in or enthusiasm for party politics, they may become involved in new social movements. (For more discussion of the decline of conventional politics, see pp. 595–6.)

2 The decline of class and ideology in politics

Todd and Taylor argue that, 'Whereas so-called "old" social movements attempted to gain access to the state through parliamentary politics and focused on economic redistribution, "new" social movements focus increasingly (though not exclusively) on issues like social identity, culture, lifestyle and human rights' (2004, p. 19). They are less associated with an ideology (such as socialism, liberalism or conservatism) which reflects class interests.

Class identities are less important than they were and the mainstream parties do not base their appeal on class differences any more. Movements such as feminism, nationalism and ecology have raised issues and sources of identity which are distinct from class, and this has influenced the development of new social movements.

3 The fragmentation of democracy

Another reason for the growth of new social movements is the **fragmentation of democracy**. Whereas in the past the government of the day made most of the important decisions, this is no longer the case. In a 'post-industrial democracy' power is more diffused, with corporations and international and transnational organizations (such as the EU, UN and World Bank) having considerable power as well.

In these circumstances, active citizens set up organizations to exert influence or protest and often adopt novel methods to convey their message or achieve their aims. Sometimes these involve direct action rather than traditional methods of campaigning.

Todd and Taylor believe that, in part, the fragmentation of democracy reflects a fragmentation of identity as well as the fragmentation of power. As class identities influence people less, other identities (such as gender, ethnicity, sexuality and attitude to the environment) draw political activists to a range of causes and issues and consequently a range of new social movements.

Todd and Taylor therefore explain the growth of new social movements in terms of both changes in society and changes in politics. They mention a shift towards postmodernity as a possible way of interpreting the changes in society, but they do not wholeheartedly embrace postmodernism. For example, they still see class as being important. Furthermore, they do not believe that new social movements can replace party politics which they believe is still needed to make decisions which represent broad public interests.

Much stronger support for the theory of postmodernity is provided by the next sociologists to be considered.

Stephen Crook, Jan Pakulski and Malcolm Waters – social movements and postmodernization

Stephen Crook, Jan Pakulski and Malcolm Waters (1992) associate the development of social movements with a process they define as **postmodernization**. This involves a clear shift from the politics of modern societies to a new politics of postmodernizing societies. Although postmodernization is an ongoing process and may not yet be complete, they believe 'new politics marks both a substantive and permanent change in the political complexion of advanced societies'.

Old politics in modern societies

According to Crook *et al.*, politics in modern societies had a number of key features:

1. It was dominated by political parties drawing their support from particular classes.
2. It was largely concerned with the sectional interests of these classes.
3. It was dominated by the activities of elites who were supposed to represent the interests of particular socio-economic groups.
4. The state was the key focus of political activity and the exercise of power. In Europe the bureaucratic–corporatist state was developed. **Corporatism** involved allowing the representatives of the two sides of industry (capital and labour, or employers and workers) access to state decision making through their organizations. In Britain, for example, these were principally the CBI (Confederation of British Industry) and the TUC (Trades Union Congress). Negotiations between these groups were used to reach compromise solutions and blunt the impact of class conflict.
5. In the old politics, political activity was seen as belonging to a separate, specialized sphere of social life, which was not the concern of ordinary people in their everyday activities.

New politics in postmodernizing societies

However, according to Crook *et al.*, old politics of this sort has largely given way to a new politics which is very different.

New politics has the following characteristics:

1. The class basis of support for political parties declines. Left-wing parties can no longer rely upon working-class support, and right-wing parties can no longer rely on members of the middle and upper classes voting for them. The electorate becomes more volatile and identifies less with a particular class.
2. Politics becomes less concerned with sectional interests and more concerned with moral issues that affect everyone. For example, a concern with animal rights, world peace or ecology is not confined to particular classes but is based upon a universal appeal to moral principles. Furthermore, people's political views become associated with their choice of lifestyle rather than with class membership. Thus ecological movements will be supported by those who choose to live green lifestyles (for example, by recycling their waste, or cycling rather than travelling by car) rather than by people from any particular class.
3. The new politics moves away from people relying upon elites to represent them. In the new politics, social movements encourage everyone to become involved in campaigns over certain issues. The members of new social movements are often suspicious of leaders and want to retain democratic control over their own organizations.
4. The new politics is not focused on the activities of the state, nor is it based upon the incorporation of sectional interest groups into state decision making. Unions and employers' organizations lose some of their influence on government, and the focus of politics moves from the state to civil society.
5. This change is so great that the new politics 'spills over and fuses with the socio-cultural arena … protests combine with leisure activities and merge into a total counter-cultural *Gestalt*'. Political views do not just reflect lifestyle; choosing to live in a particular way is a political statement and a form of political activity.

Postmodernization and the shift to new politics

What then has caused the shift to the new politics?

Perhaps the most important factor is what Crook *et al.* call **class decomposition**. Members of social classes become less similar to one another. There is progressive social **differentiation**: that is, even people from the same backgrounds become increasingly dissimilar to one another.

Members of the bourgeoisie become divided between owners and managers. The working class becomes divided according to the region they live in, their level of skill, and 'a growing diversity of lifestyles and consumption patterns'. The middle class also becomes increasingly heterogeneous, with divisions between professional, administrative and technical workers and between state employees and those working in private industry.

New social movements do tend to attract particular groups in the population, such as the young, the geographically mobile, the well educated and those in creative and welfare professions. However, according to Crook *et al.*, this represents 'socio-cultural rather than socio-economic' divisions. It is related to lifestyle and consumption patterns rather than class divisions. (For more details of Pakulski's views on class, see pp. 84–6.)

Another important cause of the shift to the new politics is the increasing importance of the mass media in postmodernizing societies. As the media come to penetrate all areas of social life, politics becomes increasingly about the manipulation of words and symbols in the mass media. In this situation, political issues are:

> *always contextualized, and linked with the global issues and general values, often in the form of such doom scenarios as nuclear holocaust and greenhouse disaster. This dramatizes them, adds a sense of urgency, and generates mass anxiety which proves to be an exceptionally potent propellant for action.* Crook et al., 1992

The media therefore contribute to people taking a more global outlook, which makes it less likely that they will confine their political concerns to narrow sectional interests.

Conclusion

Crook *et al.* conclude that postmodernization has led to a permanent shift in politics, resulting in 'the increased diversity of political processes – more open organizational structures, more diverse elites, more fluid and fragmented alliances and loyalties, and more complex networks of communication'. They go on to argue: 'Even if the inevitable normalization strips the new politics of some of its formal idiosyncrasies, the diversity that constitutes a major departure from the class-structured partisan politics of the past will persist.'

Evaluation

Crook *et al.* identify some significant trends in contemporary politics, but they may exaggerate them. Some writers argue that there has been little if any decomposition of classes (see pp. 88–9). Others have questioned the view that the class basis of voting has significantly declined (see pp. 579–81). Trade unions and employers may still have an important role in contemporary politics and, from a Marxist point of view, writers such as Crook *et al.* ignore the continuing powerful influence of the capitalist economy on politics (see pp. 535–9).

Perhaps a more balanced view of new social movements and new politics is taken by the next writer to be considered, Anthony Giddens.

Anthony Giddens – social movements and high modernity

Like Crook *et al.*, Anthony Giddens (1990) believes that important changes have been taking place in politics in contemporary societies. Unlike Crook *et al.*, Giddens believes these changes are part of developments in modernity rather than part of a transition to postmodernity. As modernity has developed, and moved into a phase which he calls **high modernity** or **radicalized modernity**, changes have taken place; these have been changes in emphasis rather than complete transformations.

Giddens characterizes modernity as having four institutional dimensions, illustrated in Figure 9.2.

1. **Capitalism** is 'a system of commodity production centred upon the relation between private ownership of capital and propertyless wage labour'. The analysis of capitalism has been the focus of much of the sociology developed by Marxists.
2. **Industrialism** is 'the use of inanimate sources of material power in the production of material goods, coupled to the central role of machinery in the production process'.
3. **Surveillance** 'refers to the supervision of the activities of subject populations in the political sphere'. Following Foucault (see pp. 559–62), this may take place in workplaces, prisons, schools and similar institutions. It is largely the concern of nation-states and, with the advent of modern societies, the ability of states to monitor their populations greatly increases.
4. **Military power** concerns 'control of the means of violence'. This again is largely the prerogative of the nation-state, and the development of military technology leads to the industrialization of war and increases the ability of the nation-state to use violence.

According to Giddens, social movements develop which correspond to these four institutional dimensions. These are illustrated in Figure 9.3.

Social movements concerned with each of the four dimensions have existed throughout the modern period. However, in high, or radicalized, modernity the emphasis

Figure 9.2 The institutional dimensions of modernity

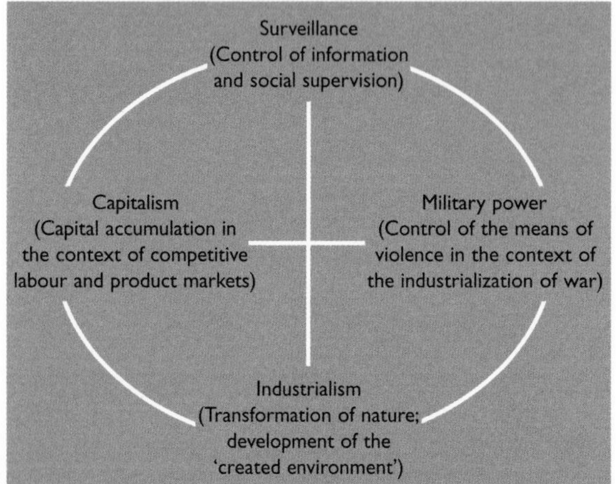

Source: A. Giddens (1990) *The Consequences of Modernity*, Polity Press, Cambridge, p. 59.

Figure 9.3 Types of social movements

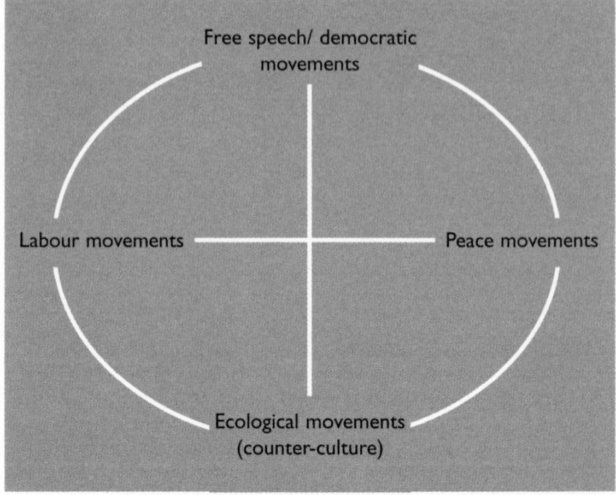

Source: A. Giddens (1990) *The Consequences of Modernity*, Polity Press, Cambridge, p. 159.

in political activity shifts away from labour movements, which were most prominent in the early period of modernity.

1 **Labour movements** correspond to the institution of capitalism. They are specifically concerned with 'attempts to achieve defensive control of the workplace through unionism and to influence or seize state power through socialist political organization'.
2 **Free speech/democratic movements** correspond to the institutional dimension of surveillance. Like labour movements, they have a long history within modernity. In earlier periods they were often closely linked to labour movements. At the same time as trying to gain economic improvements for their members, they often also tried to win them greater rights to democratic participation. In recent times, free speech/democratic movements have tended to become separated from labour movements and have campaigned in their own right. A British example is Charter 88, which campaigns for, among other things, the introduction of a Bill of Rights for British citizens.

The other two types of movement – ecological and peace movements – Giddens describes as 'newer in the sense that they have come to increasing prominence in relatively recent years'. However, he does not believe they are completely new; both have a history dating back to much earlier in the modern period.

1 **Peace movements** are concerned with the means of violence. Pacifist movements go back to earlier wars, such as the First World War, when the industrialization of war meant that war was becoming increasingly destructive. However, peace movements have become more prominent because of the 'growth in high-consequence risks associated with the outbreak of war, with nuclear weaponry forming the core component in contemporary times'.
2 **Ecological movements** correspond to the institutional realm of industrialism. The 'created environment' is therefore their area of concern. Like peace movements, they are not completely new. In the nineteenth century, ecological movements were linked with romanticism and were mainly intended to 'counter the impact of modern industry on traditional modes of production and upon the landscape'. In the late twentieth century they assumed greater prominence, partly because of the increased risks associated with possible global ecological catastrophes (such as global warming and the depletion of the ozone layer).

Conclusion

Giddens therefore sees globalization (see pp. 554–5) and increases in risk as major factors leading to the growing prominence of social movements concerned with peace and ecology. However, he stresses that such movements are not entirely new, and nor have they replaced other actors as a source of power or the location of political activity.

To Giddens, party politics, the nation-state, and the economic power of business remain crucially important in high-modern societies. Discussing how power can be exercised to improve modern societies, he says:

> *Peace movements, for example, might be important in consciousness raising and in achieving tactical goals in respect of military threats. Other influences, however, including the force of public opinion, the policies of business corporations and national governments, and the activities of international organizations, are fundamental to the achieving of basic reforms.* Giddens, 1990

Social movements might be increasingly important, but they have not eclipsed or replaced other political arenas.

Evaluation

Giddens's views are based upon a rather abstract model of modernity and its institutional dimensions, which is not really supported by detailed empirical evidence. Because his discussion is pitched at a high level of generality, he goes into little detail about such issues as the background and objectives of those who join social movements, and the way they are organized.

Nevertheless, his work is useful because it shows an awareness of continuities in the development of politics and social movements, which are neglected by some other writers – writers who may exaggerate the degree to which such movements are genuinely novel.

The anti-capitalist and anti-globalization movement

Perhaps the most recent and novel manifestation of a new social movement is the **anti-capitalist** or **anti-globalization** movement. This movement does not fit neatly into previous categories of social movement, its aims are not particularly well defined, and it involves a wide range of groups, each of which has slightly different concerns.

Nevertheless, it is possible to see it as a single movement because of an overarching hostility to capitalism and the effects of globalization. It involves elements of peace movements, ecological movements and labour movements, but is characterized more by informal alliances rather than by any hierarchical organization. Unlike conventional labour movements, it does not represent particular groups of workers, but is concerned with issues that affect workers throughout the world.

The most obvious manifestations of this movement have been demonstrations that have taken place at meetings of leading politicians from Western capitalist countries or influential capitalist organizations. For example, there were major protests at the G8 summit (a meeting of the leaders of the eight leading industrial/capitalist countries) at Genoa on 20–21 July 2001. During these protests there was serious violence in which a local youth was shot dead (Callinicos, 2003). In Seattle in 1999 there was a big demonstration involving some 40,000 demonstrators focused on a meeting of the World Trade Organization.

The movement uses a wide range of methods of protest, some quite novel (e.g. culture jamming – see below).

We will now examine the work of two writers who both support the anti-capitalist or anti-globalization movement and who have analysed the reasons for its increasing prominence.

Alex Callinicos – *An Anti-Capitalist Manifesto*

The anti-capitalist movement

Alex Callinicos (2003) argues that in the late 1990s a distinctive new movement began to take shape. Callinicos describes it as an **anti-capitalist movement**. Although sometimes called anti-globalization, he sees this as an inappropriate title. Many of those involved welcome some aspects of globalization, such as increased global sharing of culture, resources, and even styles of cooking. To Callinicos, it is specifically the influence of global capitalism that the movement's supporters are opposed to.

The movement brings together those campaigning about a variety of issues. What these issues share in common is that the problems involved can all be seen as produced by global capitalism in general and the power of global corporations in particular. Callinicos says the movement:

> *does not simply campaign over specific grievances or issues – say to do with free trade or the environment or Third World debt – but is motivated by a sense of the interconnection between an immense variety of different injustices and dangers.* Callinicos, 2003

For example, the movement is concerned with the way that rich countries prevent the import of agricultural goods from poor countries (e.g. through the European Union Common Agricultural Policy), which contributes to poor countries falling into debt, causing increased poverty. It is concerned with the way that large corporations systematically exploit workers in the 'third world', damage the environment and support repressive regimes which allow the easy exploitation of workers.

Callinicos admits that the movement embraces a wide variety of political positions, from those who support relatively moderate reforms to revolutionaries. Some want better controls of global capitalism to reduce the harm it does, while others advocate the complete overthrow of capitalism. Those who support revolution disagree over what to replace capitalism with. Some are socialists, others anarchists, while others are mostly influenced by the environmental movement.

Nevertheless, Callinicos believes they can work together because of the loose-knit nature of the movement. As there are no overall leaders, no single statement of the movement's aims and no formal organization, it is often possible for participants to cooperate on the basis of the aims they share rather than be divided by differences.

The emergence of anti-capitalism

Callinicos sees the emergence of the anti-capitalist movement as being a significant new development in thinking about society. The 1990s witnessed the increasing dominance of neoliberalism (neoliberalism, or market liberalism, is very similar to the thinking of the New Right; see pp. 23–5 and 268–72). Communism in the Soviet Union and Eastern Europe had collapsed, and many Western politicians and social scientists argued that there was no longer any alternative to free-market capitalism.

In the USA the **Washington Consensus** emerged, which believed that US-style capitalism should spread around the world, supported if necessary by the use of military power (see pp. 545–8). Politicians such as President Clinton in the USA and Tony Blair in the UK, and sociologists such as Anthony Giddens, claimed to offer a **Third Way** (between capitalism and socialism), but to Callinicos this was not significantly different from neoliberalism. Callinicos argues that the Third Way involves an acceptance of economic globalization, free markets and a belief that nothing can be done about inequality. As such it is little different from neoliberalism.

In the USA, one social scientist, Francis Fukuyama (1992), declared 'the end of history'. He believed that major ideological disputes were a thing of the past – everybody now accepted there was no alternative to capitalism.

In sociology and other social sciences, postmodernism became increasingly popular. Postmodernists such as Baudrillard argued that politics had become meaningless because the social world was increasingly constituted by images rather than reality (see pp. 893–4).

However, the Seattle protests of 1999 were a turning point and marked the revival of radical politics and radical social science, which stress issues such as inequality and injustice.

Reasons for the growth of the anti-capitalist movement

Callinicos believes that this shift back towards radical social science theories such as Marxism was largely stimulated by the development of protest movements, particularly the anti-capitalist movement. But why did this movement appear with apparent suddenness at the end of the 1990s? Callinicos attributes this development to a number of factors.

1. In part, the movement is a response to globalization. The increased prominence of global or transnational institutions such as the United Nations, European Union and G8 has prompted more of a global outlook from protest movements. In addition, campaigning non-governmental organizations (NGOs) such as Amnesty International and Greenpeace have developed and linked together local campaigns. They have gained prominence through involvement in conferences such as the 1992 Rio Summit on global warming.
2. The network of activists throughout the world has developed as a result of specific campaigns, such as Jubilee 2000, a campaign to alleviate 'third world' poverty by cancelling 'third world' debt to the richer nations.
3. In 1997–8 East Asia experienced an acute financial crisis which raised questions about the sustainability of prosperity through global capitalism. Even capitalist financiers such as George Soros began to question the viability of global capitalism in its current form. For many future protestors, the crisis in East Asia 'demonstrated the dangers of a deregulated world economy where huge flows of speculative capital could make or break countries overnight'.
4. In 1993 the NAFTA (North American Free Trade Agreement) was concluded. This established new,

more liberal, trade between various American countries including the USA, Canada and Mexico. There was considerable opposition to the agreement. After it was implemented in 1994, southeastern Mexico experienced a peasants' uprising. The peasants were protesting about their loss of access to common land as a result of the agreement. This highlighted the effect of neoliberal policies on indigenous people, and the opposition to the agreement was a precursor of later protest movements.

5 Neoliberal economic policies also met resistance in some richer countries. For example, in France there were public sector strikes in late 1995 which contributed to the development of a new left group in that country which was opposed to aspects of globalization.

Together, these various events stimulated the development of an anti-capitalist movement which was beginning to develop loose networks across the globe. It was further encouraged through the writings of leading radicals such as Chomsky in the USA (see pp. 545–8) and Bourdieu in France (see pp. 87–9). According to Callinicos, another important influence was the work of Naomi Klein, and in particular her bestselling book *No Logo*.

The work of Naomi Klein will now be examined.

Naomi Klein – *No Logo*

In *No Logo* (2000) Naomi Klein offers a radical critique of global or transnational corporations. The main focus of her study is the development of marketing and branding by corporations such as Coca-Cola and Nike. She also examines what she sees as the negative impact of such corporations and the development of anti-capitalist social movements opposed to their activities. Because of its popularity, her work has encouraged the further development of the movement.

Brands not products

Klein argues that:

> *astronomical growth in the wealth and cultural influence of multinational corporations over the last fifteen years can arguably be traced back to a single, seemingly innocuous idea developed by management theorists in the mid-1980s: that successful corporations must primarily produce brands as opposed to products.* Klein, 2000

Since the second half of the nineteenth century, companies have mass marketed products. However, it was only in the 1940s that marketing experts began to realize the importance of **branding**. From that time on, it was not so much the product as the brand that was marketed. Most jeans, cola drinks and cigarettes are very similar products, but companies need to persuade consumers that their brand is the best. Consequently, corporations put a tremendous amount of resources into promoting brands such as Levi Strauss, Coca-Cola and Marlboro. Each tried to develop a distinctive brand image which would appeal to consumers throughout the world.

By the 1980s, however, corporations were discovering that rather than promoting the product as a brand, it was possible to promote the company, or the logo of the company, as a brand in its own right. Once the company itself and its logo were sufficiently well established in the minds of the public, the company could diversify and sell a wider variety of products through their association with the logo.

In Britain, for example, Richard Branson's Virgin company has used its logo not just to promote its original products (records and music shops) but also to sell cola, mobile phones, airline and rail services, financial services, etc. Particular symbols such as the swoosh symbol of Nike, the golden arches of McDonald's and the Coca-Cola logo have become globally recognizable and powerful marketing tools for promoting the respective businesses.

For consumers, it is increasingly the logo that it is important for them to buy rather than the product it relates to. Often, logos are associated with particular lifestyles. For example, Nike has tried to associate the swoosh symbol with the ideal of sport. Nike has branched far beyond its original business (selling trainers and sports footwear) to encompass all aspects of sport. Not only does Nike now sell a whole range of sports goods, it actually bought the Ben Hogan golf tour in 1992 (renaming it the Nike tour), and it has its own agency for managing sports stars.

Nike has particularly benefited from promoting its association with the world's greatest basketball player, Michael Jordan, to establish itself as a 'superbrand'. Klein says Nike is 'a shoe company that is determined to unseat pro sports, the Olympics and even star athletes, to become the very definition of sport itself'.

Promoting the superbrand

As companies try to establish themselves as superbrands, they start to compete with other superbrands. Ideally, they want their logo to be the most recognizable logo on earth. The competitors of Nike are no longer just other sportswear companies such as Adidas and Reebok; they are also competing with Coca-Cola, McDonald's and many others for global recognition of their brand.

To maintain and enhance the position of their brand, global corporations are prepared to go to almost any lengths. For example:

1 They are willing to spend vast amounts of money on advertising and marketing. In 1997 Nike alone spent some $500 million on advertising, compared to less than $50 million in 1987. Between 1979 and 1998, overall advertising expenditure in the USA rose from $50 billion to just under $200 billion. From 1985 to 1998 there was a 700 per cent increase in US corporate sponsorship spending.

2 Corporations are willing to extend advertising and marketing into virtually every area of social life. They sponsor television programmes, sporting events, rock music tours, and are increasingly involved in sponsoring education and advertising in schools and universities. Klein suggests the activities of corporations are beginning to limit freedom of enquiry within education. For example, corporations have threatened to withdraw funds from universities whose academics publish anything critical of the corporation or its products.

3 Corporations also try to make use of every trend in youth culture to make their products seem more 'cool'. Nike is so focused on 'borrowing style, attitude and imagery from black urban youth that the company has its own word for the practice: bro-ing'. The corporations try to incorporate anything that could be seen as anti-capitalist or against their interests into their marketing. Lou Reed of the Velvet Underground has done adverts for Honda. The Beatles song 'Revolution' and John Lennon's 'Instant Karma' have both been used in Nike adverts. The image of the Cuban revolutionary Che Guevara has been used to sell soft drinks; and Red or Dead have used the communist leaders Mao and Lenin to sell handbags. In these circumstances, even radical messages tend to be drowned out by the pervasive manipulation of images by corporations.
4 Companies who wish to establish their brand as predominant often try to put the opposition out of business. According to Klein, the coffee-shop chain Starbucks sometimes tries to buy up the independent cafés in an area or outbid independent café owners for the leases on their properties.
5 Takeovers and mergers are frequently used to ensure the promotion and predominance of a particular brand. Klein gives some examples:

> *Disney buys ABC, which then broadcasts its movies and cartoons. Time Warner purchases Turner Broadcasting, which then cross-promotes its magazines and films on CNN. George Lucas buys block stocks in Hasbro and Galoob before he sells the toy companies the licensing rights for the new Star Wars films, at which point Hasbro promptly buys Galoob to consolidate its hold on the toy market.* Klein, 2000

6 Corporations use various forms of censorship to block messages critical of their activities or which pose even the slightest threat to the exclusivity of their brand. McDonald's took two environmental protestors (the 'McLibel two') to court in Britain for criticizing McDonald's environmental record and claiming their food was unhealthy. McDonald's also 'continues busily to harass small shopkeepers and restaurateurs of Scottish descent for that nationality's uncompetitive predisposition towards the Mc prefix in its surnames'. For example, it sued both a sandwich shop called McMunchies in Buckinghamshire and a Ronald McDonald who owned a restaurant in Illinois.

No space – no choice – no jobs

So far, Klein's work suggests a world in which branding by multinational corporations has become the dominant cultural force across the globe. In Klein's words there appears to be **no space** for alternative or oppositional messages and **no choice** but to buy the products and services sold by the corporations.

Furthermore, Klein argues that the activities of corporations have a damaging effect on employment, leading to **no jobs**. The corporations spend so much of their money on promoting their brand, they have little left to pay the workers who make their products. Jobs are exported from the richer 'first world' countries to sweatshops in the 'third world', where workers are exploited with very low wages. Many of the jobs that remain in the richer countries are temporary, part-time or insecure.

Nevertheless, Klein does not believe that corporations are totally dominant. As well as exploring the rise of branding and the power of corporations she also examines the rise of social movements opposing corporations.

Culture jamming

The first reaction against corporate branding discussed by Klein is **culture jamming**. The term was coined by a group in San Francisco in 1984 and referred to their practice of visually changing an advertisement in order to reveal what they saw as the real meaning. For example, Joe Camel (advertising Camel cigarettes) became Joe Chemo.

In the late 1990s, culture jamming revived and became increasingly prominent. Klein suggests a number of reasons for this.

1 The pervasiveness of adverts and logos and the lack of non-commercialized space for alternative messages made adverts an obvious target for radicals. Graffiti artists such as the New Yorker Rodriguez de Gerada began openly to change billboards in public spaces. Such artists believe the concentration of media ownership in the hands of a few has undermined freedom of speech. The reaction against this has 'created a climate of semiotic robin hoodism'.
2 Technological developments, particularly the development of the internet, have made it much easier to make parodies of adverts widely known. It has also facilitated the development of a global network of '"hacktivists" who carry out their own raids on the Internet, mostly by breaking into corporate websites and leaving their own messages behind'. New technology also makes it easier to manipulate images to subvert their meaning.
3 Culture jamming has also become popular because commercialism has been 'able to overpower the traditional authority of religion, politics and schools'. While these might have been targets of anti-establishment campaigners in the past, the dominance of corporations makes corporations the most attractive target now.
4 Many culture jammers were influenced by earlier feminist, anti-racist and anti-homophobia campaigns which drew attention to the use of stereotypical images by the media. This made radicals more aware of the importance of media image and more focused on changing or undermining media images they found exploitative.
5 In American universities and schools, advertisers began placing adverts in bathrooms and toilets. These arenas have traditionally been the preserve of graffiti artists and it was not long before students began subverting these intrusive advertising signs. Students began to be concerned not just about the content of adverts but also about their pervasiveness, and some became culture jammers.
6 By creating a society obsessed with logos, the large corporations set themselves up as targets. Klein says: 'We are a celebrity-obsessed culture, and such a

culture is never in finer form than when one of its most loved icons is mired in scandal.' Any association with prominent logos is glamorous and attractive, even for those who are undermining the logos through culture jamming. Attacking logos is also appealing for culture jammers because it is so effective. Modern corporations may not rely upon particular workers or factories to make their products (they can easily move production somewhere else), but they do rely on the positive appeal of their logo.

Campaigns

Companies such as Shell, McDonald's and Nike have been the subject of quite effective campaigns which have provided their logos with less appealing associations than those promoted by the companies.

For example, the Nike swoosh has been dubbed the 'Swooshstika' and associated with very poor pay and conditions in the 'third world' factories where its products are largely made.

Shell has been linked by its critics to the execution by the Nigerian government in 1995 of the Nigerian campaigner Ken Saro Wiwa. He had campaigned against Shell operations which had damaged the land of the Ogoni people of the Niger delta. Some culture jammers hung dummies from Shell logos at petrol stations with the slogan 'Shell Kills Ogoni'.

In June 1997 there were pickets at 500 McDonald's outlets and leaflets critical of many aspects of McDonald's business were distributed. At one outlet there was 'a street performance featuring an axe-wielding Ronald McDonald, a cow and lots of ketchup'. McDonald's attempt to silence its critics by suing two protestors for libel backfired when the 'McLibel' case simply drew attention to the accusations made by the protestors.

Activists feel they can do little to challenge the dominance of corporations through conventional political campaigns and so they are attracted to what they feel is the far more effective method of culture jamming.

The limits to culture jamming

Despite her obvious enthusiasm for culture jamming, Klein is aware it has its limitations. It might inconvenience particular multinational companies, but 'the conduct of the individual multinationals is simply a by-product of a broader global economic system that has steadily been removing almost all barriers and conditions to trade, investment and outsourcing'.

When one company loses business because of bad publicity, another company, which may be little better, is usually the beneficiary. For example, Adidas has benefited from campaigns against Nike, although Klein argues it has followed similar, exploitative employment practices.

Furthermore, anti-branding campaigns can do little to embarrass companies that do not rely upon brands – for example, mining companies and steel companies which have poor safety records but no brand image.

The broader movement

Nevertheless, Klein believes the anti-branding culture jamming movement has laid the foundation for wider global social movements. It has drawn attention to links between politically repressive regimes, the exploitation of workers, the activities of corporations, and brands. As such, it has stimulated the development of broad coalitions between different campaigners. This has been evident in the protests at meetings of world leaders. Klein says: 'world leaders can't have lunch these days without somebody organizing counter-summit gatherings that bring together everyone from sweatshop workers trying to unionize to teachers fighting the corporate takeover of education'.

In 1998 the movement achieved some success by persuading the OECD (Organization for Economic Cooperation and Development) to drop the Multilateral Agreement on Investment. The opponents condemned the agreement as 'a secret conspiracy to ensure global domination by multinational companies'.

Thus Klein is optimistic that it may be possible to build an opposition to the dominance of corporate capitalism 'that is as global, and as capable of coordinated action, as the multinational corporations it seeks to subvert'.

Conclusion and evaluation

Both Callinicos and Klein are committed supporters of the global movements against corporations and capitalism. Their views are undoubtedly influenced by their political involvement. Both may exaggerate the impact that the movement has had thus far. Since both are themselves actively involved in promoting the movement they may also exaggerate the importance of particular events and the activities of particular groups of activists.

However, they do also identify underlying changes in society (such as globalization and new technologies) which might help account for the development of the movement. Furthermore, their work certainly contributes to the understanding of what appears to be a new and significant political phenomenon – a transnational alliance of campaigners against aspects of the global capitalist system.

Voting behaviour

Despite the increasing importance of new social movements and other forms of political participation outside party politics, voting remains the most obvious way in which citizens can influence politics in parliamentary democracies.

In parliamentary democracies, governments are formed through competition between political parties in elections. This process is the subject of this section, which focuses on patterns of voting in Britain. A later section (see pp. 595–6) examines reasons why this type of participation may have declined.

A number of theories have been put forward to explain patterns of voting in Britain. We will examine these theories in turn, starting with those that were popular in the 1960s, and then examining those which have been more influential in recent years.

David Butler and Donald Stokes – the theory of partisan alignment

Until the 1970s, patterns of voting in post-war Britain were predictable. Most **psephologists** (those who study voting behaviour) agreed on the basic characteristics of British voting and on the explanation of these characteristics. David Butler and Donald Stokes (1974) were perhaps the most influential psephologists during the 1960s and early 1970s and their views became widely accepted.

There were two main features of the British political system at this time: partisan alignment and a two-party system. These were closely related to each other and, together, seemed to make it relatively easy to explain British voting.

Class and partisan alignment

The theory of **partisan alignment** (strong adherence to a particular party) explained voting in the following way:

1. It suggested that class, as measured by a person's occupation, was the most important influence on voting.
2. It claimed that most voters had a strongly partisan self-image: they thought of themselves as 'Labour' or 'Conservative'.
3. This sense of identity led to voters consistently casting their votes for the party with which they identified. Few people changed their votes from election to election, there was little electoral volatility, and there were few **floating voters** who were prepared to consider changing their allegiance.

Using the evidence from Butler and Stokes's research into the 1964 election, Ivor Crewe found that 62 per cent of non-manual workers voted Conservative, and 64 per cent of manual workers voted Labour (Sarlvick and Crewe, 1983).

Butler and Stokes themselves produced a range of figures which appeared to confirm that most voters had a strongly partisan self-image, and that this self-image was closely related to voting. In 1964, for example, only 5 per cent of those they questioned did not claim to identify with a party. Of those who did identify with a party, only 12 per cent said they identified 'not very strongly', while 41 per cent identified 'fairly strongly' and 47 per cent 'very strongly'. In the local elections in May 1963, 85 per cent of those with a Conservative partisan self-image voted Conservative, and 95 per cent of those who identified with the Labour Party voted Labour.

The strength of these political ties was reflected in the low **swings** (percentage changes in votes) between Conservative and Labour in successive elections. In the general elections of the 1950s the average swing was just 1.6 per cent. Few people changed the party they voted for because of the strength of their attachment to one or other of the major parties. As late as 1974 Butler and Stokes felt justified in saying 'class has supplied the dominant basis of party allegiance in the recent past'.

The two-party system

The second main feature of British voting patterns, the **two-party system**, was perhaps even more striking: together, the Labour and Conservative parties dominated the political scene. In no election between 1945 and 1966 did their combined vote fall below 87.5 per cent of those cast, and the third most popular party, the Liberals, gained in excess of 10 per cent of the vote only once (in 1964).

The results did not surprise psephologists. If class determined voting, and there were two classes, then inevitably there would be two dominant parties to represent those classes. The Conservatives gained so many votes because middle-class non-manual voters identified with that party, while the Labour Party enjoyed similar levels of support among working-class manual voters. There was little room left for a third party.

The Liberals were not believed to represent any particular class, and therefore could not rely on strongly partisan support from any particular section of the electorate. This was reflected in the very low vote they received in some elections: in 1951 the Liberals gained only 2.5 per cent of the votes cast.

Political socialization

So far we have examined the evidence for partisan alignment and the existence of a two-party system. However, this does not explain why there should be such a strong relationship between class and voting.

The explanation provided by Butler and Stokes was essentially very simple. To them, **political socialization** held the key to explaining voting. As children learned the culture of their society, they also learned the political views of parents and others with whom they came into contact. Butler and Stokes stated quite emphatically: 'A child is very likely indeed to share the parents' party preference.'

They saw the family as the most important agent of socialization, but, by the time an individual was old enough to vote, other socializing institutions would have had an effect as well. Butler and Stokes argued that schooling, residential area, occupation and whether they belonged to a union would all influence the way people voted.

The Conservative Party could expect to get most support from those who:

- attended grammar or public schools
- lived in middle-class areas where many people were homeowners
- were not members of unions.

Labour support would be most likely to come from those who:

- attended secondary modern schools
- lived in working-class areas (and particularly on council estates)
- were union members.

The most important factor, though, was whether voters had a manual or non-manual occupation.

All of these factors were important because they influenced the extent to which voters came into contact with members of different classes and therefore whether they mixed with partisan Labour or Conservative supporters. Generally speaking, all of these factors reinforced the effects of the voter's class background. For instance, children with parents who voted Labour were more likely to go to secondary modern schools and become trade union members.

In emphasizing the effects of socialization, Butler and Stokes were denying that the **policy preferences** of an individual were important. Voters were not thought to pay much attention to the detailed policies outlined in party manifestos. They did not choose who to vote for on the basis of a rational assessment of which package of policies on offer would benefit them most. They voted emotionally, as an expression of their commitment to a particular party. To the extent that they had preferences for policies, these were largely shaped by the parties themselves: voters would trust their party to implement the best policies.

The 'problem' of deviant voters

The partisan alignment theory of voting was so widely accepted that in 1967 Peter Pulzer claimed: 'Class is the basis of British party politics; all else is embellishment and detail.' However, the partisan alignment theory could not explain the existence of **deviant voters**: those who did not conform to the general pattern.

Throughout the post-war period a significant number of the British electorate were deviant voters. Deviant voters are normally defined as manual workers who do not vote Labour, and non-manual workers who do not vote Conservative. In other words, deviant voters are those who do not vote for the party which is generally seen as representing their class.

The precise number of deviant voters fluctuated between elections, but generally there were considerably more manual workers who did not vote Labour than non-manual workers who did not vote Conservative.

A number of explanations were put forward to explain their behaviour.

1. McKenzie and Silver (1972) argued that some working-class Conservative voters were **deferential**. They voted Conservative because they believed that their candidates, who tended to come from higher-class backgrounds, were better equipped to be rulers of the country than candidates from middle- or working-class backgrounds.
2. McKenzie and Silver believed some working-class Conservatives voters were **secular** voters. They lacked strong party attachments and voted for the party they believed would do most to raise their living standards. In the case of these voters they believed the Conservatives would benefit them more than Labour.
3. Butler and Rose (1960) suggested that **contradictory socializing influences** on individuals would reduce their sense of loyalty to the party of their class. If, for example, one parent voted Labour and the other Conservative, there would be a considerable chance of their children becoming deviant voters in later life. Social mobility could also lead to deviant voting if individuals ended up in a different class from that of their parents. For example, individuals from a working-class background who experienced upward social mobility and gained middle-class jobs might vote according to their background rather than according to their current class position.
4. Butler and Rose also suggested that one section of the manual workforce was increasingly adopting middle-class attitudes and lifestyles. As a result of this process of **embourgeoisement** they were increasingly likely to vote Conservative. However, the theory of embourgeoisement has been heavily criticized (see pp. 58–60); and research by Goldthorpe *et al.* (1968a) found that 80 per cent of affluent manual workers in Luton still voted Labour.
5. Goldthorpe *et al.* themselves found that deviant voting was more likely to result from **cross-class attachments**, for example where a man with a manual job was married to a woman with a non-manual job or vice versa.
6. While most research focused on working-class voters who supported the Conservatives, Frank Parkin (1968) was one of the few writers who also analysed the reasons for deviant voting by middle-class Labour supporters. He found that these middle-class radicals were likely to have occupations 'in which there is a primary emphasis upon either the notion of service to the community, human betterment or welfare and the like or upon self-expression and creativity'. Such occupations include teaching and social work. Since Labour is seen as the party most concerned with social welfare, voting Labour is a means of furthering the ideals which led people to select these occupations.

Theories of dealignment

Bo Sarlvick and Ivor Crewe – partisan dealignment

Ivor Crewe was among the first commentators to criticize the approach of Butler and Stokes and to identify changing trends in British voting. In this section we will first discuss his work with Bo Sarlvick, published in 1983.

Sarlvick and Crewe argued that Butler and Stokes could not explain the reduction of class-based voting since 1974. Evidence suggested that embourgeoisement could not account for the decline in partisanship. Nor could Sarlvick and Crewe find any evidence that there had been a sudden and dramatic increase in voters whose parents had different party loyalties. They accepted that there had been more social mobility, but it was nothing like enough to account for the rise in deviant voting.

The decline in partisan voting

Table 9.2 summarizes some of the main findings of the British Election Studies, of 1964 and 2001, which were conducted by a number of different researchers using survey techniques to collect standardized information about a large sample of voters. The findings appear to

Table 9.2 Class voting, 1964 and 2001 (percentages)

Vote	1964 Social class Non-manual	1964 Social class Manual	2001 Social class Non-manual	2001 Social class Manual
Conservative	62	28	34	20
Labour	22	64	38	61
Other	16	8	28	19

Source: H.D. Clarke, D. Sanders, M.C. Stewart and P. Whiteley (2004) *Political Choice in Britain*, Oxford University Press, Oxford, p. 42.

confirm Sarlvick and Crewe's theory that partisan dealignment has taken place in Britain.

Table 9.2 shows an increase in the proportion of voters not supporting the party that traditionally represents their class, and, as part of that trend, increasing support for parties other than Labour and the Conservatives.

Sarlvick and Crewe originally defined **partisan dealignment** as a situation where 'none of the major occupational groups now provides the same degree of solid and consistent support for one of the two major parties as was the case in the earlier postwar period' (Sarlvick and Crewe, 1983).

In later writings, however, Crewe distinguished between partisan dealignment and class dealignment. Partisan dealignment referred to a decline in the percentage of the electorate who had a strong sense of loyalty to a particular party; **class dealignment** referred to a decline in the relationship between the working class and Labour voting and the middle class and Conservative voting.

Table 9.3 shows different measures of the strength of the relationship between class and voting, including a measure of the amount of absolute class voting. This is the percentage of voters who were middle-class and voted Conservative or who were working-class and voted Labour. In other words, it measures the percentage of non-deviant voters. In 1983 manual Labour voters together with non-manual Conservative voters were in the minority at 47 per cent.

The Alford Index is another measure of the degree to which class influences voting, on a scale of 1 to 100. For Labour, if the score were 100, then all manual workers who voted would vote Labour. If the score were 0, Labour would gain the same proportion of votes in the middle class as in the working class. For the Conservatives, if the score were 100, then all non-manual workers who voted would vote Conservative. If the score were 0, the Conservatives would gain the same proportion of votes in the working class as in the middle class.

By this measure, the decline in partisan voting in the working class has been dramatic. It fell substantially between 1964 and 1983, dropping from 42 to 25. (In a later study of the 2001 election, Harold Clarke *et al.* found the Alford Index figure was 23 (Clarke *et al.*, 2004).)

From such evidence, Sarlvick and Crewe concluded that most voters were no longer strongly loyal to a party on the basis of their class, and that there was much greater volatility in the electorate. In the four elections of the 1970s, for example, less than half of the electorate (47 per cent) voted Labour or voted Conservative four times in a row.

Table 9.3 Measures of class voting, 1964–92

	Absolute class voting	Alford index (Labour)	Alford index (Conservative)
1964	63	42	34
1966	66	43	35
1970	60	33	31
Feb 1974	55	35	29
Oct 1974	54	32	27
1979	55	27	25
1983	47	25	20
1987	49	25	19
1992	54	27	20

Source: D. Denver (1994) *Elections and Voting Behaviour in Britain*, 2nd edition, Harvester Wheatsheaf, London, p. 62

The causes of partisan dealignment

First, Sarlvick and Crewe argued, factors other than class seemed to be increasingly related to voting. Such factors included whether voters rented or owned their housing, and whether they were members of trade unions. In 1979 the Conservatives were 51 per cent ahead of Labour among non-manual workers who were not in trade unions, but only 7 per cent ahead of those who were members. Labour was 33 per cent ahead of the Conservatives among manual trade union members, but actually 1 per cent behind among non-union manual workers.

Sarlvick and Crewe believed that class boundaries were being blurred by factors such as these. There were fewer 'pure' members of the working class who had manual jobs, lived in council houses and belonged to trade unions; and fewer 'pure' members of the middle class who had non-manual jobs and were non-unionized. The increasing numbers of unionists in the middle class and the increasing numbers of home owners in the working class had reduced the level of partisan alignment with the traditional party of their class, and had resulted in class dealignment as well.

The second explanation of partisan dealignment put forward by Sarlvick and Crewe provided a more fundamental challenge to the theories of Butler and Stokes. They argued that it was misleading simply to see the voters as captives of their socialization, unable to make rational choices about which party to vote for. Instead, Sarlvick and Crewe claimed that voters' active decisions about which party's policies best suited them had to be included in any explanation of voting.

From their analysis of the 1979 general election, Sarlvick and Crewe argued that 'voters' opinions on policies and on the parties' performances in office "explain" almost twice as much as all the social and economic characteristics taken together'.

According to Sarlvick and Crewe, the main reason why the Conservatives won in 1979 was simply that the electorate was unimpressed with the performance of the previous Labour government and supported most Conservative policies. Some issues were particularly important. Sarlvick and Crewe found that Conservative proposals designed to limit the power of trade unions and plans to privatize some state-funded industries were the most important policies which persuaded Labour voters to switch to the Conservatives.

Despite the significance Sarlvick and Crewe attached to the policy preferences and active choices of the electorate, they did not claim that class was of no importance. They stated: 'The relationships between individuals' social status and their choice of party have by no means vanished. But as determinants of voting they carry less weight than before.'

Traditional theories could not be completely rejected: Sarlvick and Crewe still saw class as the most important aspect of a person's social status, but parties which wished to win elections could not just rely on the loyalty of their supporters – their policies had to appeal to voters as well.

Anthony Heath, Roger Jowell and John Curtice – the continuing importance of class

The views of Sarlvick and Crewe relating to the 1983 general election were questioned in another study conducted by Anthony Heath *et al.* (1985). This study used different and arguably more sophisticated research methods (Heath *et al.*, 1985).

Redefining class

The first, and perhaps most important, methodological change involved the definition and measurement of class. Heath *et al.* argue that defining the middle class as non-manual workers and the working class as manual workers is theoretically inadequate. They claim that classes can be more adequately defined in terms of **economic interests**, that is, according to their situation in the labour market. They therefore use a version of John Goldthorpe's neo-Weberian class scheme to distinguish five classes.

The five classes are:

1. The **salariat**, which consists of managers, administrators, professionals and semi-professionals who have either considerable authority within the workplace or considerable autonomy within work.
2. **Routine non-manual workers**, who lack authority in the workplace and often have low wages.
3. The **petty bourgeoisie**, which consists of farmers, the owners of small businesses, and self-employed manual workers. Their situation depends upon the market forces that relate to the goods and services they supply. They are not wage labourers and they are not affected in the same way as other workers by employment and promotion prospects. This group cuts across the usual division between manual and non-manual workers.
4. **'Foremen' and technicians**, who either supervise other workers or who have more autonomy within work than the fifth class.
5. **Manual workers** – Heath *et al.* do not separate manual workers in terms of the degree of skill their job requires, since they do not believe skill levels have a significant impact on voting.

Apart from using new class categories, another important feature of Heath *et al.*'s work is the way they deal with the voting of women. Nearly all of the previous studies classified women voters according to the occupation of their husband if they were married. Heath *et al.* argue that women's own experience of the workplace will have a greater impact on their voting than that of their husband.

Table 9.4 summarizes Heath *et al.*'s findings on class voting in the 1983 election.

The continuing importance of class

The results suggest a stronger relationship between class and voting (in 1983) than the results of studies using conventional definitions of class:

1. The working class remained a stronghold of Labour support.
2. 'Foremen' and technicians (who would normally be categorized as part of the skilled working class) were strongly Conservative.
3. The petty bourgeoisie (some of whom would normally be defined as manual workers) were the strongest Conservative supporters.
4. The salariat and routine non-manual workers gave most of their support to the Conservatives, but it was also in these classes (as well as in the working class) that the Alliance gained its greatest share of the vote. The Alliance was formed when some Labour Party members broke away to form the SDP (Social Democratic Party) and made an electoral pact with the Liberals – they later united to form the Liberal Democrats.

Examining the results of one election does not reveal whether or not class-based voting has declined. Heath *et al.* therefore attempted to measure the strength of the relationship between class and voting since 1964. It is more difficult to measure this relationship using a fivefold division of the population into classes, so they decided to measure the strength of the relationship between class and voting by measuring the likelihood of the salariat voting Conservative and the working class voting Labour.

From their figures they calculated an **odds ratio** which determines the relative likelihood of a class voting

Table 9.4 Class voting in the 1983 election

Class	Conservative	Labour	Alliance	Others
Petty bourgeoisie	71%	12%	17%	0%
Salariat	54%	14%	31%	1%
Foremen/ Technicians	48%	26%	25%	1%
Routine non-manual	46%	25%	27%	2%
Working class	30%	49%	20%	1%

Source: A. Heath, R. Jowell and J. Curtice (1985) *How Britain Votes*, Pergamon, Oxford, p. 20.

for the party it could be expected to. The figures in Table 9.5 show how many times more likely it is for the working class to vote Labour and the salariat to vote Conservative than vice versa.

Table 9.5 produced some unexpected findings. There appear to have been wide variations in the relationship between class and voting, but no long-term dealignment. According to this measurement, 1983 was an average election and not a year in which the influence of class was at its lowest since the Second World War.

Table 9.5 Odds ratio for working class voting Labour and salariat voting Conservative in general elections, 1964–83

Election	1964	1966	1970	1974 (Feb)	1974 (Oct)	1979	1983
Odds ratio	9.3	7.3	3.9	6.1	5.5	4.9	6.3

Source: Adapted from A. Heath, R. Jowell and J. Curtice (1985) *How Britain Votes*, Pergamon, Oxford, p. 20.

Changes in the class structure

Heath *et al.* claim that much of the change in levels of support for the different parties is the result of changes in the distribution of the population between classes. For example, the working class has shrunk as a proportion of the electorate, while the salariat and routine non-manual groups have grown.

However, changes in the class structure alone cannot explain all the changes in levels of support for the parties in elections. Heath *et al.* calculated what percentage of the vote each party would have gained in 1983 if they had kept the same levels of support in each class as they had in 1964. These figures showed that the Labour Party did even worse than expected, the Conservative Party failed to take advantage of changes in the social structure, while the increase in Liberal/Alliance support was far greater than would be anticipated. Consequently, Heath *et al.* conclude that factors other than changes in the social structure must have affected patterns of voting.

Rejection of policy preference theories

Heath *et al.* reject the view that detailed policy preferences account for these changes. They measured people's views on various policies and asked them where they thought the major parties stood on these issues. They also asked voters which issues they thought were most important:

1. Unemployment and inflation came top of the list, and on both Labour had the most popular policies.
2. The Alliance proved most popular on the third most important issue (whether there should be more spending on welfare or tax cuts), while Labour and the Conservatives tied a little way behind.
3. Conservative and Alliance policies proved most popular on the fourth most important issue, defence.

On the basis of this evidence, Labour should have won a handsome victory. If the six most important issues were taken into account, Labour and the Conservatives would have received the same share of the vote. Heath *et al.* therefore reject the policy preference or **consumer theory** of voting; their evidence suggests that it cannot explain the Conservative victory in 1983.

Party images

Despite rejecting the consumer theory, Heath *et al.* do not deny that the actions taken by a political party affect the vote it obtains, but they believe that it is not the party's detailed policies that matter, but its overall political stance in the eyes of the electorate. They say, 'It is not the small print of the manifesto but the overall perception of the party's character that counts.'

If voters believe that a party has the same basic ideology as they have, they will be likely to vote for it. From this point of view, Labour lost so badly in 1983 because many voters believed it had moved too far to the left, despite the extent to which they agreed with its policies.

Class, ideology and voting behaviour

Heath *et al.* use a more complex model of ideology than the simple left/right distinction that is usually employed. They argue that there are two main dimensions to ideological differences on issues:

1. **Class issues** are mainly economic: they concern such questions as whether industries should be nationalized or privatized, and whether income and wealth should be redistributed. The ideology which supports nationalization and redistribution can be called left-wing, and the opposite right-wing.
2. **Liberal issues** concern non-economic questions such as whether there should be a death penalty, whether Britain should retain or abandon nuclear weapons, and whether or not there should be a strong law-and-order policy. For the sake of convenience, the ideology which supports the death penalty, the retention of nuclear weapons and strong law-and-order policies will be called 'tough', while its opposite will be called 'tender'.

In terms of these differences, the Labour Party supports left-wing and tender policies, the Conservative Party supports right-wing and tough policies, and (according to Heath *et al.*) the Alliance was perhaps slightly to the right of centre on class issues and more tender than tough on liberal issues. Liberal supporters have a distinctive ideological position and, according to Heath *et al.*, it is one that is becoming increasingly popular with the electorate.

From their analysis of changes in voters' ideology, Heath *et al.* found that there had been distinct shifts. On average, voters increasingly supported right-wing economic policies, but more tender social policies. These changes seemed to have benefited the Alliance more than the other major parties, both of whom had experienced a significant move away from their ideology on one of the two dimensions. The study found that the main reason for the high level of Alliance support in 1983 was the increasing proportion of voters whose ideological position roughly coincided with that of the Alliance.

Summary

The complex and highly sophisticated theory of voting devised by Heath *et al.* differs from both the partisan alignment and policy theories. Class remains very important but it does not directly determine the party voted for. It is not specific policies that matter, but the class of the voters and how they perceive the ideological position of the parties. From this point of view, the prospects for the parties in the future will be partly determined by changes in the class structure, but they can also affect their chances of success by the way they present themselves to the electorate.

Competing theories of voting

The work of Sarlvick and Crewe and Heath *et al.* on the 1983 and earlier elections established a number of issues relating to voting which have been the subject of controversy ever since. In the next section we will examine each of the following issues in turn in the light of the 1997, 2001 and 2005 elections. (In each of these elections Labour won a comfortable majority, in contrast to the 1983 election when the Conservatives won a very large majority.)

1. How far has dealignment taken place in British politics? Are individuals now less likely to identify with particular parties than they were in the past?
2. To what extent does class continue to influence patterns of voting in Britain today? Is there evidence of continued class dealignment?
3. How far do the policy preferences of voters determine the outcome of elections? Can the results of elections be explained simply in terms of which party has the most popular policies?
4. Does the ideological image of political parties compared to the ideology of the electorate determine how well parties do in elections? Is the party with the best ideological image most likely to win an election?
5. How far can patterns of voting be explained in terms of non-class factors which cut across class cleavages, such as gender, ethnicity and region?

Having examined these issues we will then consider other theories of voting which have gained popularity since the controversies between Sarlvick and Crewe on the one hand and Heath *et al.* on the other.

Dealignment and voting

Ivor Crewe and Katrina Thompson – dealignment or realignment in 1997?

Ivor Crewe and Katrina Thompson (1999) used the British Election Study (a study which conducts an exit poll after each general election) relating to the 1997 election to examine whether the dealignment Sarlvick and Crewe had claimed to detect in earlier elections (see pp. 577–9) had continued in 1997.

Realignment might have taken place if significant numbers of voters had started to identify with particular parties, when they had not done so in the past. There would be evidence of realignment if the big increase in the Labour vote represented a corresponding increase in its number of loyal supporters. On the other hand, 1997 might not indicate realignment if the Conservatives had been 'defeated by a temporary protest of dissatisfied voters'.

On the surface, the 1997 election did provide evidence of a dramatic realignment. According to Crewe and Thompson, it saw the biggest change in party identification since 1964. Conservative identifiers went down from 45 per cent to 39 per cent between 1992 and 1997, while Labour identifiers rose from 33 per cent to 46 per cent. The percentage of Conservative identifiers was the lowest it had been since 1964. All of this seemed to indicate that Labour had replaced the Conservatives as the natural majority party, only able to be defeated in exceptional circumstances. If that was the case, then 1997 would certainly have been a critical realigning election.

However, Crewe and Thompson interpreted the data differently. They argue that questions about party identification measure little more than current voting preferences. Party identification changes in line with voting and says little about long-term commitments. According to Crewe and Thompson, a better indication of partisanship is found in those who *strongly* identify with a particular party.

On this measure of what Crewe calls partisan dealignment, there had been a dramatic decline. In 1964, 44 per cent of voters very strongly identified with a political party; by 1997 it was just 16 per cent. Furthermore, in 1997 it was the youngest voters – those in the 18–24 age group – whose partisanship was the weakest. While Labour benefited from a large swing in votes, it could not claim to have gained a large block of loyal and partisan followers.

Crewe and Thompson note that the Labour Party continued to enjoy very high levels of popularity in the period after the election. With so many new supporters, the aftermath of the election provided the potential for substantial realignment towards the Labour Party. Crewe and Thompson describe an 'opportunity to harden the overwhelming but soft partisanship of young voters into a New Labour generation; but these same voters are open to conversion to another party if the government is perceived to fail'.

Labour's success was caused by 'ideological convergence' with other parties, as it shifted towards the ideological middle ground. It was not based on attracting loyal support from particular social groups, nor was it based on specific policy issues. The electoral success and post-election popularity of Labour were largely based upon short-term political factors, such as a divided Conservative Party and a 'buoyant economy', rather than more long-term or fundamental factors.

For Crewe and Thompson, then, the 1997 election did not show a return to partisan alignment with more voters being committed to one party or another. Rather, it confirmed that most of the electorate no longer had strong party loyalties.

Partisanship and voting in recent elections

Given that Ivor Crewe originally proposed the theory of partisan dealignment after the 1983 election, it is perhaps unsurprising that he found evidence to support this theory in the result of the 1997 election. Does the evidence suggest there has been any direct increase in partisanship in recent elections?

Figure 9.4 suggests that partisan alignment has continued to decline. David Sanders, Harold Clarke, Marianne Stewart and Paul Whiteley (2005) found that the percentage strongly identifying with a party was down to just 9 per cent in 2005, one-fifth of the level (45 per cent) in 1964. A further 40 per cent identified fairly strongly with a political party. The total percentage of very or fairly strong identifiers declined from 84 per cent in 1964, to 54 per cent in 2001, and further to 49 per cent in 2005. Sanders *et al.* describe these figures as showing 'an era of dramatically weakened partisanship' (2005, p. 6).

Another possible indication of dealignment is the very low turnout in recent elections. As Whiteley *et al.* (2005) point out, in 2001 only 59 per cent of the electorate bothered to vote, the lowest figure in any election since women got the same voting rights as men in the 1920s. Some 41 per cent of the electorate were not sufficiently partisan to vote at all. In the 2005 general election, as Sanders *et al.* point out, there was only a very modest recovery of voter turnout to 61 per cent.

Evidence such as this suggests that there has been a long-term decline in partisan identification with particular parties. Whether that decline can be related to a declining influence of social class on voting will now be considered.

Class and voting

Geoffrey Evans, Anthony Heath and Clive Payne – class and voting in 1997

Part of Crewe and Sarlvick's original argument that dealignment was taking place suggested class dealignment was occurring (see pp. 577–9). This view was questioned by Heath *et al.* in their study of the 1983 election (see pp. 579–81). This issue was discussed by Geoffrey Evans, Anthony Heath and Clive Payne (1999) in relation to the 1997 election.

Evans *et al.* used a seven-class model devised by John Goldthorpe and Anthony Heath, rather than the simple division between manual and non-manual workers. They found that in 1997 unprecedented proportions of the service classes and other non-manual classes voted Labour. Labour did even better among working-class voters but, compared to elections in the 1960s, the gap, in terms of the support Labour got, between middle-class and working-class voters was much narrower. Evans *et al.* note that Labour did no better among the working class in 1997 than they had in the 1960s, but between 1964 and 1997 their middle-class support more than doubled.

Evans *et al.* measured the overall relationship between class and voting, using a composite measure of 'changes in the odds ratios between classes and parties across elections' (see pp. 579–81 for a description of odds ratios). They found 'a generally declining trend from the highest point in 1964 to the lowest in 1997 with some fluctuations in-between'. In 1997, for example, the class–voting relationship was only about 60 per cent as strong as it had been in 1964.

Up until this point Anthony Heath had tended to argue that class influences on voting remained strong (for example, in Heath *et al.* 1994). However, after the 1997 election, Heath and his colleagues (Evans *et al.*, 1999) were prepared to admit that class was exercising a decreasing influence on voting patterns. Evans *et al.* argued that this change was largely the result of changes in the Labour Party and its relationship with working-class voters.

Statistically, much of the variation in the relationship between class and voting was caused by changes in the relationship between class and Labour voting. Evans *et al.* suggested, therefore, that it might be the changing character of the Labour Party that was largely responsible for the weakening relationship between class and voting. In particular, it might be caused by changes in the

Figure 9.4 Levels of party identification in Britain, 1964–2005

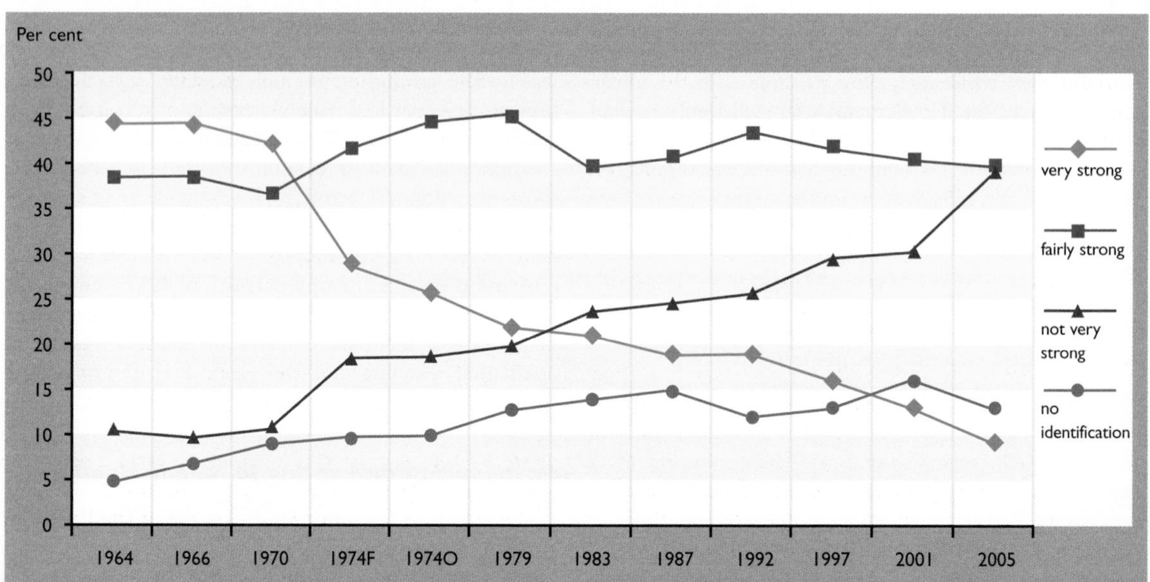

Source: D. Sanders, H. Clarke, M. Stewart and P. Whiteley (2005) *The 2005 General Election in Great Britain: Report for the Electoral Commission*, University of Essex, p. 6.

ideology and policies of Labour, so that it became a party appealing to all classes (a 'catch-all party') rather than one which aimed its appeal specifically at the working class.

Evans *et al.* noted that a study by Ian Budge (1999) of election manifestos had found that the Labour Party had moved well away from a left-wing ideology by 1997 in an attempt to appeal to middle-class voters. Evans *et al.* looked at data from the British Election Studies which measured whether voters thought there was a 'good deal', 'some', or 'not much' difference between the parties. In 1997 only 33 per cent of voters thought there was a good deal of difference between the parties. This compares to 46 per cent giving this reply in 1964 and as many as 82 per cent in 1983 and 84 per cent in 1987.

In general, then, it appeared that the voters accurately perceived that the ideological gap between the parties had narrowed by 1997. Evans *et al.* attribute the decline in class-based voting to this reduction in the perceived ideological gap between the parties. In particular, the Labour Party attracted so many middle-class votes in 1997 because it had largely abandoned left-wing policies which would appeal to working classes but alienate middle classes.

The big fluctuations in the class and voting relationship between elections did not suggest the changes were part of an inevitable and long-term trend in society. Rather, they were a product of short-term political changes within parties. If this was the case, then the relationship between class and voting might strengthen in the future if a more clear-cut ideological division between the Conservative and Labour parties returned.

Evans *et al.* therefore conclude that the dip in class voting in 1997 does not show that it was a critical election, since it did not necessarily signal a permanent change. They say, 'The future strength of class voting therefore depends more upon party strategy and electoral appeals than upon secular trends in society.'

Class and voting in 2001 and 2005

Pippa Norris (2001) used opinion poll evidence from the 2001 election and reached somewhat different conclusions from those of Evans *et al.* From this evidence she found that Labour lost most support among the unskilled working class, while increasing its support in the lower-middle class. The Conservatives, on the other hand, actually gained support in both the skilled and unskilled working class, while losing further support among the middle classes who have traditionally supported the Conservatives. In 2001 Labour actually won more votes than the Conservatives in the lower-middle class.

Norris agrees with Evans *et al.* (1999) that the apparent continuing reduction of class-based voting may be largely due to the success of Labour in establishing itself as a party which appeals to all classes. She suggests that Tony Blair used a 'careful ideological balancing act' which involved a 'strategy of straddling the centre-ground, promising improved public services but no rise in income tax, a safe pair of hands handling the economy but better health and education'. Nevertheless, Norris still argues that 'class voting is withering away in British politics'.

Similar conclusions were reached by those conducting the British Election Study of the 2001 election. Clarke *et al.* (2004) found that class had only a weak relationship with voting, however that relationship was measured. As well as using the Alford Index of class voting (see p. 578) they also used a measure of relative class voting using odds ratios, first suggested by Heath *et al.* (see pp. 579–81). Even using the relative measure, which Heath *et al.* had used to show that class was still important, the influence of class more than halved between 1964 and 2001 (falling from a figure of 6.4 to 2.7).

Clarke *et al.* go further, arguing that class influence may have been exaggerated for many years. In election studies in 1964 and 1966 more than half of respondents said they did not think of themselves as belonging to a particular class. Clarke *et al.* therefore suggest that:

> *the 'class tribes' always have been considerably smaller than commonly supposed. If upwards of one half of the British electorate lack class self-identifications, a model of their voting behaviour in which (absent) class identities drive party support cannot be correct.*
> Clarke *et al.*, 2004, p. 44

David Kavanagh and David Butler analysed opinion poll evidence for the 2005 election and found that 'the social class divide is perhaps weaker than ever when it comes to voting' (2005, p. 197). According to MORI polls the Conservative lead over Labour amongst the professional and managerial classes fell considerably between 2001 and 2005 to just 10 per cent (38 per cent of these voters supported the Conservatives and 28 per cent Labour). Kavanagh and Butler say, 'There is perhaps no more striking measure of how New Labour, even when its vote share fell, has managed to capture a large part of what had been Conservative core vote' (2005, p. 197).

Amongst unskilled and semi-skilled manual workers the Labour vote fell back 7 per cent to less than half (48 per cent), while the Conservative share increased by 1 per cent to 25 per cent.

However, not all commentators are quite so dismissive of the influence of class on voting in recent elections. Pippa Norris and Christopher Wlezien (2005) found from opinion poll evidence that during the course of the 2005 campaign class differences in voting became more marked in response to the messages put forward by the parties. They found that it was 'fairly clear that the campaign did in some way activate class interests, with implications for the distributions of Labour and Conservative voters' (Norris and Wlezien, 2005, p. 228).

Class and voting – conclusion

A wealth of evidence suggests that class is a less important variable in shaping voting behaviour than it was in the past. However, that does not mean that class has become insignificant. There are still important differences in the voting behaviour of different classes. As Evans *et al.* (1999) suggest, it is quite possible that class-based voting will increase again if the Labour and Conservative parties try to strengthen their appeal to their traditional supporters in the working class and middle class, respectively.

Furthermore, class differences may be related to other social differences (such as region and ethnicity) which have some influence on voting. We will now examine how far non-class-based theories of voting can explain recent patterns of voting behaviour.

Non-class divisions and voting

As we saw earlier (see pp. 577–9), Sarlvick and Crewe argued that a range of characteristics other than class were increasingly influencing voting behaviour after 1974. They claimed that the working class was increasingly divided in terms of whether individuals were trade union members or not, or whether they rented accommodation or owned their own homes, with trade union members who were council tenants most likely to vote Labour.

In later work, Crewe (1992) suggested there was an increasing north/south cleavage in the working class, with manual workers in northern England, Wales and Scotland more likely to vote Labour than those in the south. In research into the 1987 elections Crewe (1987a, 1987b) argued that there was a new division opening up in the middle class. The middle class who worked in the public sector and who were university educated were more likely to vote Labour than those who worked in the private sector and who had not attended university.

According to Crewe and Sarlvick, the divisions in the working class tended to work against the Labour Party. As trade union membership fell and fewer people lived in council houses, and the proportion of the working class living in the south grew, Labour was likely to lose support from its traditional working-class voters. On the other hand, Labour was likely to gain some support in the middle class because more people were going to university, but also lose some because the number of public sector workers was falling. However, the overall effect would be to further reduce the closeness of the association between class and voting as these non-class cleavages became increasingly important.

Issues such as trade union membership, housing tenure, public versus private sector workers and educational qualifications have received relatively little attention in recent elections, although some analysis has been conducted.

In a study of the 2001 election, David Butler and Dennis Kavanagh (2002) examined figures from a MORI opinion poll. They found that some of these cleavages continued to be significant. For example, 43 per cent of home owners voted Conservative and 32 per cent Labour, whereas 60 per cent of council tenants voted Labour and only 18 per cent Conservative. They also found that 50 per cent of trade unionists voted Labour and just 21 per cent Conservative.

On the surface, this seems to lend credence to the view that non-class cleavages remain an important influence on voting. However, these figures did not break down the voters by class, so the differences may have been largely due to differences in the class backgrounds of these groups rather than their housing tenure and membership or otherwise of unions. Furthermore, according to the figures used by Butler and Kavanagh, Labour lost support among trade unionists and council tenants between 1997 and 2001, suggesting that these cleavages were becoming less important as influences on voting.

Harold Clarke, David Sanders, Marianne Stewart and Paul Whiteley (2004) carried out more sophisticated research on the effects of home ownership on voting in the 2001 election. They attempted to control for other relevant variables in order to find out whether it had an independent effect on voting. They found that home ownership had some effect on voting, making people less likely to vote Labour, and the strength of this effect had not changed much between 1992 and 2001.

Region and voting

John Curtice and Alison Park (1999), using data from the British Election Study of the 1997 election, found that the swing from Conservative to Labour was bigger in the southern parts of England than in the northern parts.

There was also a good deal of tactical voting. In particular, in constituencies where either a Liberal Democrat or a Labour candidate seemed well placed to unseat a Conservative MP, anti-Conservative voters seemed to switch to the party which had the best chance of defeating the Conservatives.

One consequence of these shifts was that the Conservatives lost more seats than they would have done if the fall in their vote had been evenly spread. Curtice and Park believe that the trends in the 1997 election represented **dealignment** rather than **realignment**.

Between the mid-1950s and the mid-1980s regional factors exercised an increasing influence on voting. Even when factors such as class were taken into account, Labour gained more support in the north, while the Conservatives increased their support in the south. The 1997 election reversed these trends and therefore reduced the influence of region in shaping people's voting preferences. Curtice and Park calculate that, between 1987 and 1997, a quarter of the regional gap in voting preferences disappeared, although southerners were still more likely to vote Conservative than northerners.

Curtice and Park argued that this change largely resulted from the Labour Party deliberately targeting southern voters. As part of their modernization strategy, the Labour Party set out to shed policies that were unpopular with southern voters. In particular, Labour abandoned its commitment to nationalization (which had been Clause 4 of its constitution), distanced itself from trade unions, and promised not to increase income tax.

Data from the British Election Study of 1997 found that, throughout the country, Labour was perceived as being more right-wing than it had been in previous elections. People had noticed the changes in policy and this had affected people's image of the party.

Furthermore, by 1997, those in the south saw the Labour Party as more right-wing than those in the north. This could explain why Labour gained more ground in the south of the country, where much of the electorate was hostile to the more left-wing positions Labour had adopted in previous elections. Curtice and Park comment: 'overall, Labour's modernization project was particularly successful in overcoming negative perceptions and associations that the southern voter had of the party in the 1980s'.

Curtice and Park conclude that most of the evidence points to the influence of region declining in the 1997 election. The north–south divide became less significant, and the closing of the ideological and policy gap between Labour and the Liberal Democrats weakened some people's attachment to either of these parties. The main reason for these changes was that people's perceptions of the parties had changed. The electorate's reasons for choosing to vote for a particular party had not altered radically, but people thought that the Labour Party had changed, making it more attractive to southern voters in particular. This would suggest that the ideological image of parties is an important factor shaping voting behaviour.

Clarke *et al.* (2004) examined data on region and voting in elections between 1992 and 2001. Controlling for other variables they found that Labour gained more support from northern England, Scotland and Wales than the Conservatives or the Liberal Democrats. However, from the 1997 election onwards the situation changed, with Labour actually getting disproportionate support in southern England. They suggest that this 'reflects the success of Tony Blair's attempts to attract "middle England" voters to New Labour' (Clarke *et al.*, 2004, p. 70).

Ron Johnstone, Charles Pattie and David Rossiter (2005) found that regional differences held fairly steady for the Labour and Conservative parties in the four elections between 1992 and 2005. For example, Labour lost about 6 per cent of its support nationally between 2001 and 2005 and it declined by about the same amount in every region except Wales and southwest England – regions where it performed poorly.

However, there was some regional shift in Liberal Democrat voting in 2005. The party did well in regions outside its traditional stronghold in the southwest, thereby broadening the regional basis of its support.

Overall, Johnstone *et al.* do not see regional factors in themselves as having a very strong influence on voting. They argue that the type of constituency found in each region affects voting patterns much more than the characteristics of the region as a whole. Labour still does well in regions with manufacturing industry, in deprived inner cities and in constituencies with high proportions of low-status voters, while the Conservatives still do well in constituencies which are rural, white-collar and have disproportionately high-status populations. What has changed, though, is that in the 1997, 2001 and 2005 elections Labour won more 'middle Britain' constituencies, whereas in 1992 the Conservatives took a big majority of these seats.

Ethnicity

Shamit Saggar and Anthony Heath (1999) looked at the relationship between ethnicity and voting. Using data that went back to 1974, they found no evidence of a major shift in the voting of minority ethnic groups. Labour attracted between 72 per cent and 83 per cent of minority ethnic votes in the six elections between October 1974 and 1997; the Conservatives between 7 per cent and 18 per cent.

In 1997 an overwhelming 84.8 per cent of blacks and Asians voted Labour, 11.3 per cent voted Conservative and 3.2 per cent voted for the Liberal Democrats. Saggar and Heath conclude that the 1997 election reinforced existing patterns of minority ethnic voting and that there was no evidence of a major shift in support.

There has been a lack of similar research on the last two elections. However, Andrew Russell (2002) argues that the indirect evidence shows that in 2001 minority ethnic groups continued to give overwhelming support to the Labour Party. He notes that only two of the seventy-five seats with the highest proportion of minority ethnic voters did not return a Labour candidate. Conservative attempts to increase support from minority ethnic voters were somewhat undermined by a speech by a Conservative backbencher, John Townsend, which attacked both immigration and asylum seekers.

The 2005 election saw a significant move away from the Labour Party amongst the British Muslim population. Edward Fieldhouse and David Cutts (2005) found that in the thirty-nine constituencies with the biggest Muslim populations the vote share of the Liberal Democrats increased by nearly 9 per cent, largely at the expense of the Labour Party. In the constituencies with the lowest Muslim populations the Liberal Democrat vote increased by just over 3 per cent, and in those with intermediate levels of Muslim voters the increase was just under 6 per cent.

This apparent move away from Labour and towards the Liberal Democrats amongst Muslims has been widely attributed to the invasion of Iraq in 2003 and the subsequent war. The Liberal Democrats were the only party to oppose the war, and opinion poll evidence suggests that Muslims also tended to be opposed. Pippa Norris and Christopher Wlezien (2005) note data from the British Election Study which showed that 83.1 per cent of Muslims disapproved of the Iraq war, compared to 67.1 per cent of all voters.

Further evidence of Muslim anti-war and anti-Labour sentiment was provided in the constituency of Bethnal Green. This seat was won by George Galloway. Galloway was expelled from the Labour Party in 2003 and he stood as a candidate for the newly formed Respect Party with a left-wing and strongly anti-war manifesto. He succeeded in ousting the sitting Labour MP Oona King (who had supported the war). Bethnal Green has 45,000 Muslim voters and Galloway's victory depended on substantial Muslim support.

Thus, although Labour may continue to enjoy strong support from most minority ethnic groups, the 2005 election shows that it is possible for Labour to alienate minority ethnic support and lose some of their votes.

Gender

In studying the 1997 election, Pippa Norris (1999b) found evidence of a change in the relationship between gender and voting. In the 1960s and 1970s, women in Britain were proportionally more likely to vote Conservative and less likely to vote Labour than men.

In most countries, women have traditionally given more support to right-wing parties than men. Recent studies in a number of countries have suggested that the gender gap in voting is reducing. In some countries, such as the USA, the traditional gender pattern has been reversed. Women have moved from being more right-wing than men to being more left-wing.

Norris's views are based on a calculation of the difference between male and female voting. This involves calculating 'the difference in the Conservative–Labour lead among women minus the Conservative–Labour lead among men' (Norris, 1999b). For example, if the Conservatives had an 8 per cent lead over Labour among women but a 3 per cent lead among men, the gender gap would be 5 per cent.

The figures show that the gender gap has fluctuated considerably, from about 17 per cent in 1951 and 1955, to around 2 per cent in 1987 and about 4 per cent in 1997. However, overall there does seem to have been a gradual reduction in the gender gap.

Norris finds that the relationship between gender and voting is influenced by age. Older women are more likely to vote Conservative than older men, whereas younger women are more likely to vote Labour than younger men. Norris argues:

> *The most plausible reason for this we can suggest is that the younger generation of women spent their formative years during the height of the second wave women's movement, the social revolution in sex roles which occurred in the 1960s, and the change in cultural values associated with feminism.* Norris, 1999b

As older generations of women die and younger generations reach voting age we might therefore expect the gender gap in voting to be reversed, so that women become more inclined to vote Labour than men.

Norris concludes that the 1997 election did not involve a radical change in patterns of gender and voting. Women were still more likely to vote Conservative overall than men were. However, she does anticipate a gradual change in patterns of gender and voting in line with the leftward drift she has detected among women.

Rosie Campbell and Joni Lovenduski (2005) found evidence to support Norris's prediction of a gradual shift in the relationship between gender and voting. Using data from British Election Studies from 1992 to 2001 and from MORI opinion polls for 2005, they found that by 2005 the gender gap had indeed reversed so that women were more likely to vote Labour than men (see Table 9.6). This was true of all age groups under the age of 54, and young female voters were particularly likely to vote Labour.

Campbell and Lovenduski suggest that this change might have as much to do with party policies as to do with social changes. They point to deliberate attempts by the Labour Party to attract women voters. They say, 'since 1997 the Labour Party has campaigned on issues that are known to be higher priorities for women voters than for men. Women are more likely than men to say that health and education are the most important election issues' (Campbell and Lovenduski, 2005, p. 194).

Table 9.6 The Conservative–Labour gender gap 1992–2001

Year	Size of the gender gap
1992	–5.8
1997	–4.5
2001	–1.1
2005	+6.0

Source: British Election Studies, 1992–2001, and MORI opinion polls, 2005 (www.mori.com).

Social factors and voting – conclusion

This section has shown that a variety of social factors other than social class can influence voting behaviour. Of the factors discussed, membership of a minority ethnic group has perhaps the biggest influence and is strongly associated with voting Labour. However, the minority ethnic populations make up only a small proportion of the British population (see p. 152) and therefore have only a limited impact on overall patterns of voting in Britain. Overall differences between men and women are small, and many of the other factors discussed (such as home ownership and union membership) are closely related to social class differences.

The evidence therefore suggests that while the influence of social class has declined, it remains important. Social class has not been eclipsed by other social factors in shaping voting patterns. Instead, social class seems to operate alongside a range of other factors. Furthermore, the changing ideological and policy stances of the parties seem to have an important effect on the extent to which particular social factors become influential in specific elections.

Policy, ideology and economics

Policy preference

If social factors on their own cannot explain the patterns of voting in the 1997 and 2001 elections, can they be explained in terms of the policies of parties and the policy preferences of the electorate?

As discussed earlier (see pp. 577–9), Sarlvick and Crewe (1983) certainly thought that these factors would exercise an increasing influence on election outcomes and voting. On the other hand, Heath *et al.* (1985) argued that party image and its relationship to the ideology of the electorate were more important in determining voting.

Of course, the policies of a party and its ideological image tend to go hand in hand. As a party seeks to change its image (for example, by becoming more 'middle of the road' and less 'extreme') it will tend to change its policies to show that its ideology has changed. It can therefore be difficult to disentangle these two theories. Indeed, psephologists have advanced arguments to suggest that both policy preference and ideological image can account for Labour's victories in 1997, 2001 and 2005.

David Denver (2002) argues that in the 2001 election there was a strong link between the policy preferences of the electorate and the outcome of the election. He believes voters' views were much closer to those of Labour than those of the Conservatives in 2001 on the issues they thought were most important.

The Labour Party advocated increased spending on public services in its campaign, while the Conservatives promised to cut tax. In an ICM poll only 4 per cent favoured lower taxes at the expense of spending on public services, while 57 per cent were prepared to accept increased taxation to finance better public services.

Conservative policies were more popular in some areas, such as opposition to joining the euro, but these were well down the list of priorities as stated by the public in opinion polls.

However, Denver admits that the image of parties may be more important than their detailed policies. Many voters are unfamiliar with the details of the policies in election manifestos, but they are likely to have a general idea of the party's overall ideology. Denver says:

> *Even if many voters cannot easily distinguish the precise policies put forward by a party or have no clear ideas about how the parties have been performing, they often form vague general impressions that may be influential in determining their vote.* Denver, 2002

Policies and the 2005 election

Paul Whiteley, Marianne Stewart, David Sanders and Harold Clarke (2005) argue that policy preferences were very important in the 2005 election. They argue that voters can no longer be placed on an ideological spectrum between left and right (see below) because the ideological difference between the parties has declined. So, for example, disagreements over issues such as taxation and public services are more to do with the technicalities of making policies work effectively than to do with fundamental differences of principle. Furthermore some issues which were relevant in 2005, such as the war in Iraq and how to deal with terrorism, had little to do with divisions between left and right.

Whiteley *et al.* argue that not all issues are equally important. They believe that **valence issues** are particularly important. These are issues where there is no disagreement about the ends of government policy, but there are disagreements about the means. People tend to vote for the party best able to deliver what most of the electorate want, such as a strong economy, better health care and education, low crime, and security. Refining this model further, Whiteley *et al.* argue that **issue salience** has a big impact on individual voters – that is, they are influenced by the issues that are most important to them.

To examine the impact of different factors on voting in 2005, Whiteley *et al.* used a variety of measures based on data from the British Election Study Campaign Panel Survey of Voters.

1. First, they measured the ideological position of voters on EU membership, lower taxation versus increased public spending, and tackling crime versus preserving civil liberties. They compared the individual's ideological position with their perception of the position of different parties.
2. They examined valence issues by looking at voters' views on the performance of the economy, their emotional reaction to the economic situation, and their evaluations of Labour and Conservative positions on a range of other policy areas. These included the NHS, education, asylum and crime.
3. Finally, they measured the salience of various issues by asking voters which were the most important issues to them and which parties had the best policies on these issues. The results are shown in Table 9.7.

From these data, Whiteley *et al.* found that ideological differences could not explain much of the variation in voting patterns. On the other hand, valence issues, such as the economy and delivery of public services, had a major impact on voting and tended to benefit Labour.

The Labour vote fell compared to the 2001 election partly because the salience of other issues, including asylum seekers/immigration and crime, had increased for the electorate. These were policies on which the Conservatives were seen as having stronger policies than Labour by many voters, and this helped to increase their vote.

The Iraq war had a similar effect for the Liberal Democrats. Only a few people cited it as a key issue but for those voters it did seem to increase the likelihood of them supporting the Liberal Democrats, the only party to oppose the war.

Whiteley *et al.* see voter preferences on the issues they see as most salient as the most important factor shaping voting, but they acknowledge that other factors are important too. Some voters remained partisan supporters of one of the main parties and were not persuaded to change their vote even if they were not happy with some of their party's policies.

Also important was leader image. Whiteley *et al.*'s research suggested that Tony Blair had lost public credibility over his claims that Iraq had weapons of mass destruction. However, Michael Howard, the Conservative leader, was not popular either so the Conservatives did not capitalize fully on the unpopularity of the prime minister. Whiteley *et al.* therefore conclude that, 'Taken together, a triumvirate of valence issues, leader images and partisanship gave Mr. Blair just enough of what he needed to stay in No. 10' (2005, p. 163).

However, the importance of policy in the 2005 election is questioned by John Bartle and Samantha Laycock (2006). Using data from the British Election Study, they pointed out that the only major issue which a majority (55 per cent) thought Labour had handled very or fairly well was the economy: 45 per cent said they had handled terrorism very or fairly well, but only 38 per cent said the same about education, 34 per cent about the NHS, 27 per cent about taxation and crime, 21 per cent about Iraq, and just 9 per cent about asylum.

Given these figures, it was surprising that Labour still managed to win, albeit with only about 36 per cent of the vote. Bartle and Laycock argue that the main reason for Labour's success was not so much the popularity of Labour, but the poor image of the Conservatives. The Conservatives were widely seen as 'being stuck in the past' and were thought to favour the privileged over ordinary citizens and the poor.

Furthermore, there is evidence from previous elections that, on their own, party policies compared to the policy preferences of the electorate cannot predict the way people will vote. For example, discussing the 1987 election, even Ivor Crewe (who first developed the policy preference model) found that it could not explain the outcome. The Conservatives won in 1987 even though Labour had the most popular policies on unemployment, defence and education – according to opinion polls, three of the four most important policy areas for the electorate. Crewe (1987a) said: 'Had electors voted purely on the main issues Labour would have won.'

Ideology and voting

Despite the claim of Whiteley *et al.* that policy preferences are key to understanding voting, a number of political scientists still see the ideology of parties and party image

Table 9.7 Most important issue facing country, and party best able to handle it, 2005

Most important issue	Labour	Conservatives	Liberal Democrats	Other	Don't know/ None	*Total citing issue*
Asylum seekers/Immigration	10	42	3	19	27	*23*
Crime	20	35	6	2	37	*14*
National Health Service	36	15	10	2	37	*14*
Economy general/Unemployment	54	18	5	3	21	*9*
Education	31	11	25	1	32	*4*
Taxation	9	39	18	4	30	*4*
Terrorism	43	15	2	3	38	*4*
Political pathologies	2	27	20	10	41	*3*
Europe/Euro	13	34	8	33	13	*2*
Environment	9	0	9	62	18	*2*
Housing prices/Cost of living	22	6	12	3	57	*2*
Iraq war	10	13	35	7	35	*2*
Social pathologies	27	14	17	7	35	*2*
Public services	35	22	12	4	27	*2*
Tony Blair's leadership	8	45	19	5	24	*2*
Civil liberties	3	20	53	5	20	*1*
Values/Morality	6	16	13	9	56	*1*
Miscellaneous other issues	27	15	12	7	40	*8*
Not sure/Don't know	9	4	3	2	82	*2*
Party preference/All most important issues	23	26	9	9	33	

Source: P. Whiteley, M. Stewart, D. Sanders and H. Clarke (2005) 'The issue agenda and voting in 2005', in P. Norris and C. Wlezien (eds) *Britain Votes 2005*, Oxford University Press, Oxford, p.154.

as very important. Before considering this, though, we will examine changing party ideologies in recent elections.

Ian Budge – changes in party policy and ideology

After the 1997 election, Ian Budge (1999) examined the major policy positions of the Labour Party, the Conservative Party and the Liberal Democrats (previously the Liberals and the Liberal/Social Democrat Alliance) in every election since 1945. Each sentence in the manifestos was analysed in terms of whether it adopted a left-wing or a right-wing stance. Budge then calculated whether, overall, the manifesto had a preponderance of left-wing or right-wing policies.

Table 9.8 gives some indication of the sorts of policies that were judged to be left-wing or right-wing. Figure 9.5 charts the findings of the study.

Figure 9.5 shows some significant movements in party ideology. Between 1992 and 1997 the Labour Party manifesto moved sharply to the right, so that for the first time in post-war history there were more right-wing than left-wing policies. Furthermore, Labour had leapfrogged over the Liberal Democrats, so that Labour's manifesto was the more right-wing.

However, Budge did not conclude that these changes were necessarily indicative of a permanent transformation. The Liberal Democrats held their position on the centre-left, and the 'Conservatives kept, broadly speaking, their Thatcherite right-wing posture'. The Labour Party certainly changed its stance, but it deviated 'only from their leftward shift of position in 1992'. Having temporarily shifted to more left-wing policies in the previous election, Labour continued its general move to the right, which had begun in 1983.

Budge does not believe this change will necessarily be permanent. Having established a stronger electoral position, the Labour Party might well move back towards more left-wing policies, perhaps with a renewed emphasis on welfare spending. Budge nevertheless argued that Labour's ideological shifts could help explain its electoral popularity. Labour's ideological position was more in tune with the electorate than that of the Conservatives.

Judith Bara and Ian Budge (2001) conducted a similar study of the 2001 election. Based on their analysis of election manifestos, they found that Labour moved very slightly back towards left-wing policies, but still had an overall preponderance of right-wing over left-wing policies. The Liberal Democrat manifesto shifted a little towards the centre and had fewer left-wing policies than in the previous manifesto. The Conservatives remained right-wing overall, but shifted towards the centre to some degree.

Table 9.8 Budge's left–right coding scale

Codings of manifesto sentences Right emphases (sum of %s for) minus	Left emphases (sum of %s for)
Pro-military	Decolonization
Freedom, human rights	Anti-military
Constitutionalism	Peace
Effective authority	Internationalism
Free enterprise	Democracy
Economic incentives	Regulate capitalism
Anti-protectionism	Economic planning
Economic orthodoxy	Pro-protectionism
Social services limitation	Controlled economy
National way of life	Nationalization
Traditional morality	Social services expansion
Law and order	Education expansion
Social harmony	Pro-labour

Source: I. Budge (1999), 'Party policy and ideology: reversing the 1950s?' in G. Evans and P. Norris (eds) *Critical Elections: British Parties and Voters in Long-Term Perspective*, Sage, London, p. 5.

Figure 9.5 British parties' ideological movement on a left–right scale, 1945–97

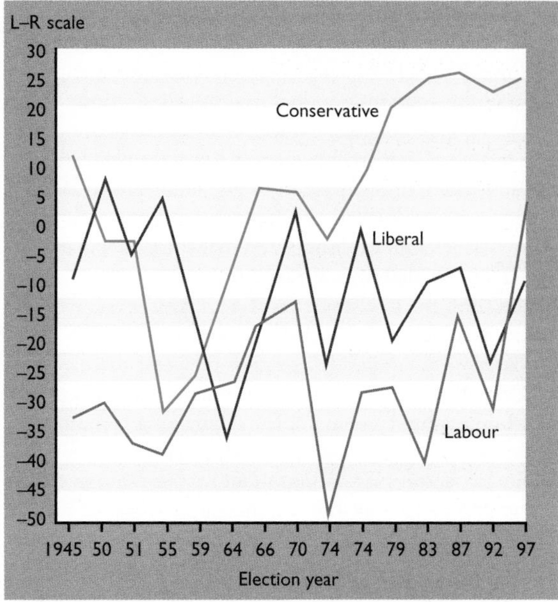

Source: H.-D. Klingemann *et al.* (1994) *Parties, Policies and Democracy*, Westview Press, Boulder, quoted in I. Budge, 'Party policy and ideology: reversing the 1950s?' in G. Evans and P. Norris (eds) (1999) *Critical Elections: British Parties and Voters in Long-Term Perspective*, Sage, London, p. 5.

Bara and Budge concluded that the manifestos were closer together ideologically than at any time since 1945, but the Conservative position still remained well to the right of most of the electorate. It was not surprising therefore that they failed to win in 2001. Bara and Budge argued: 'if they wish to expand their popular base they have nowhere to go in policy terms but centre-left – seeking to propagate "Caring Conservatism" on a more sustained and extended basis'.

Although there is no comparable study of policies in the 2005 election, there was little evidence of major ideological shifts.

Labour continued to be led by Tony Blair who remained committed to policies that captured the centre ground, and rejected any return to 'old Labour' policies to appeal to the left wing. The Conservatives under Michael Howard emphasized the traditional right-wing policy of restricting immigration. The Liberal Democrats remained in some ways to the left of the Labour Party – for example, supporting a higher 50 per cent rate of tax on those earning over £100,000 per year (Kavanagh and Butler, 2005). Indeed, Whiteley *et al.* (2005) argue that there was little change in the ideological stance of the main parties between 2001 and 2005.

In 2005 David Cameron took over as leader of the Conservative Party, and, arguably, began a process of trying to move the Conservatives on to the centre-ground of ideology. Commenting on Cameron's leadership in 2006, Phillip Lynch said: 'There is some unease amongst Thatcherites and social Conservatives about the new leader's reluctance to promise lower taxes, his retreat from pro-market policies on health and education, and his social liberal attitudes on drugs' (2006, p. 5). Cameron also emphasized green issues, not a traditional concern of right-wing parties.

In 2007 Gordon Brown took over as prime minister and leader of the Labour Party. At the time of writing it is too early to say whether his ideological stance will be similar to that of Tony Blair or slightly more left-wing. However, if anything, the parties may be coming even closer together ideologically, making it difficult for voters to identify with a particular party due to the lack of a distinctive ideological image.

The economy and voting

A final theory which has been put forward to explain voting suggests that the key factor in elections is the economy. According to this theory, the electorate will tend to vote for the party that they believe will manage the economy best. The governing party will tend to do badly in elections if the economy has been performing poorly, while the opposition will tend to do well. Conversely, if the economy is doing well, the government tends to be rewarded with strong electoral support.

A variation on this theory argues that **'pocket-book' voting** takes place. According to this theory, voters will tend to favour the party they believe is likely to do most to raise their standard of living. For example, voters tend to support parties they think will enable them to earn more, pay less tax or receive more benefits.

Commenting on the 1987 election, Ivor Crewe (1987a) argued that voters put primary emphasis on their own prosperity. Despite the unpopularity of many of their policies, the Conservatives won the 1987 election because most people thought they would be better off under the Conservatives than under Labour. A Gallup poll in 1987 found that 55 per cent thought the Conservatives were more likely to produce prosperity than other parties, whereas only 27 per cent thought they were less likely to do so.

David Sanders *et al.* (2001) suggest that economic factors could easily be seen as explaining Labour's victory in the 2001 election. Compared to European averages at the time of the election, inflation and unemployment were low, and the economic growth rate was high. Both wages and retail spending were rising, and although mortgage rates were higher than elsewhere in Europe, they were very low and falling in comparison to previous years in Britain.

However, looking at previous elections, Sanders *et al.* argue that it cannot be suggested that the performance of the economy determines election results in any simple way. In 1997 the Conservatives were in power and by most measures the economy was doing well and people's living standards were rising. Nevertheless they lost the election. In 1992 the Conservative government retained power despite the country being in the depths of a recession.

Sanders *et al.* do not, however, reject the view that economic factors play an important role in election results and voting behaviour. Instead, they argue that the crucial factor is not the objective performance of the economy and the prosperity or otherwise of voters, but the subjective view of voters about the economic competence of different parties.

In the 1992 election, despite the recession, the Conservatives still enjoyed the confidence of most voters as the party most competent to manage the economy. Labour still retained something of a reputation, dating back to its last period in office in the 1970s, as a party which spent too much money and could not manage the economy well.

However, in 1992, shortly after John Major had been re-elected as Conservative prime minister, Britain was forced to withdraw from membership of the ERM (Exchange Rate Mechanism) – a system which was supposed to limit variations in the exchange rates of different European currencies. The position of sterling was undermined by currency speculation. The government was seen to have lost control over economic policies. Sanders *et al.* argue that this episode destroyed the Conservative reputation for competent economic management.

In 1997 Labour was able to persuade sufficient voters that it could manage the economy competently, to enable it to win the election. By the time of the 2001 election Labour had been able to demonstrate that it could run the economy without causing serious problems, and it retained enough support to return with a large majority.

Sanders *et al.* back up these claims with evidence from a number of opinion polls, which show that voters' perceptions of the economic policies and competencies of the parties changed significantly between 1992 and 2001. They conclude:

> *The objective economy appeared to have almost no effect on Labour's victory in 2001. But the subjective economy – the calculations about economic competence and about the economic future that voters make inside their heads – continued to exert a very powerful influence on voters' electoral preferences.* Sanders et *al.*, 2001

Certainly, it appears difficult for a party to win enough votes to gain power if few members of the electorate believe it can manage the economy competently.

In the 2005 election, Sanders *et al.* (2005) found that slightly more people (50 per cent) felt negatively about the economic situation than positively (48 per cent). Nevertheless, Labour enjoyed a substantial lead over the Conservatives in terms of who the electorate thought would handle the economy better: 51 per cent expected the Labour Party to handle the economy very well or fairly well, compared to 30 per cent who said they thought the Conservatives would do so.

Martin J. Smith (2005) believes that the economy featured much less in the 2005 election than in most previous elections. Opposition parties steered clear of the issue because they saw it as a strong policy for Labour. As a consequence Labour was never seriously challenged over economic issues and 'a myth of Labour's invulnerability on the economy developed' (Smith, 2005, p. 238). The absence of any effective attack on Labour's economic record may well help to explain their third successive victory despite the decline in their support.

Voting behaviour – conclusion

None of the theories of voting behaviour discussed above seems able, on its own, to explain the results of elections. Yet all put forward plausible theories of how British people vote. A variety of social factors, including social class, appear to influence voting. However, they do not determine how people vote. Voters make their own judgements about the policies, ideological stance and economic competence of different parties.

Furthermore, as voters' preferences change, parties may change their policies and ideological stance to try to attract more votes. On the other hand, parties themselves may persuade the electorate to change their views on issues. Voting behaviour is therefore a complex and dynamic process. It is not surprising that no single theory can provide an entirely satisfactory explanation for it.

The decline of politics?

A number of earlier sections in this chapter have examined the possibility that the nature of politics has changed.

1. The idea of globalization implies that nation-states have become less powerful as they have lost control over their own territories.
2. The postmodernist Jean Baudrillard proclaimed the end of politics, while Jean-François Lyotard argued that individuals no longer believe in the 'metanarratives' that justify the ideology of political parties and political movements.
3. The rise of new social movements suggests that conventional parliamentary politics is becoming less and less important.
4. Some political scientists argue that the ideological differences between political parties in Britain have

declined, and thus the electorate have little meaningful choice when they cast their votes in a general election. From this point of view, the differences between the policies of the different parties are minimal and voters are likely to be uninspired by political debate.

Some social scientists have begun to argue that these and other factors have led to most of the population becoming disillusioned either with party politics, or all forms of politics. This section discusses whether disillusionment with politics is growing and is reflected in declining involvement in politics and belief in politicians.

The Power Inquiry

Disillusionment with parties and elections

The 2001 general election saw turnout fall to an unprecedentedly low level of less than 60 per cent. This led to concern about the state of Britain's democracy and resulted in the Joseph Rowntree Foundation setting up a commission of inquiry into disengagement from politics. The commission was chaired by Baroness Kennedy QC and included members from different political parties.

In 2006 the commission reported its findings (Power Inquiry, 2006). The commission found that:

1. Turnout in the 2001 general election was just 59.4 per cent, its lowest level in the post-Second World war era (see Figure 9.6). In the 2005 election it rose just 1 per cent. In addition, local election turnouts had been low for several decades. In the 1990s only around 25 per cent of voters bothered to cast their vote in elections for metropolitan councils in England, and turnout in European parliament elections has never exceeded 40 per cent.
2. Party membership has declined even more dramatically (see Figure 9.7). Conservative membership has declined most rapidly, from over 2 million in 1964 to less than 400,000 in 2001. Labour membership has also seen a sharp fall. Overall, in 2001 membership of the three biggest parties was less than one-quarter of its 1964 levels. In 2001 less than 2 per cent of the population were members of a political party.
3. Even these low figures exaggerate active participation in party politics. The commission found that most party members play little active role in party affairs. Over three-quarters of Conservatives and 65 per cent of Labour members said they had no active involvement in party activities in the average month. A study in 1990 found substantially more likelihood of party members playing an active role in their party, indicating that activism had declined.
4. Another indication of declining concern with politics is the fall in party allegiance (see also pp. 577–9). In 1997, 14.7 per cent of the British electorate claimed to have a 'very strong' allegiance to a political party, compared to 43.8 per cent in 1964.
5. More qualitative evidence supported the impression given by the statistical data. The inquiry invited submissions from individuals and organizations about their views on elections and party politics. Of the 1,500 submissions received, 'the very great majority had nothing positive to say about parties and elections' (Power Inquiry, 2006, p. 48). A series of focus groups run by the inquiry also revealed similarly negative opinions on these issues.

Figure 9.6 General election turnout, 1945–2005

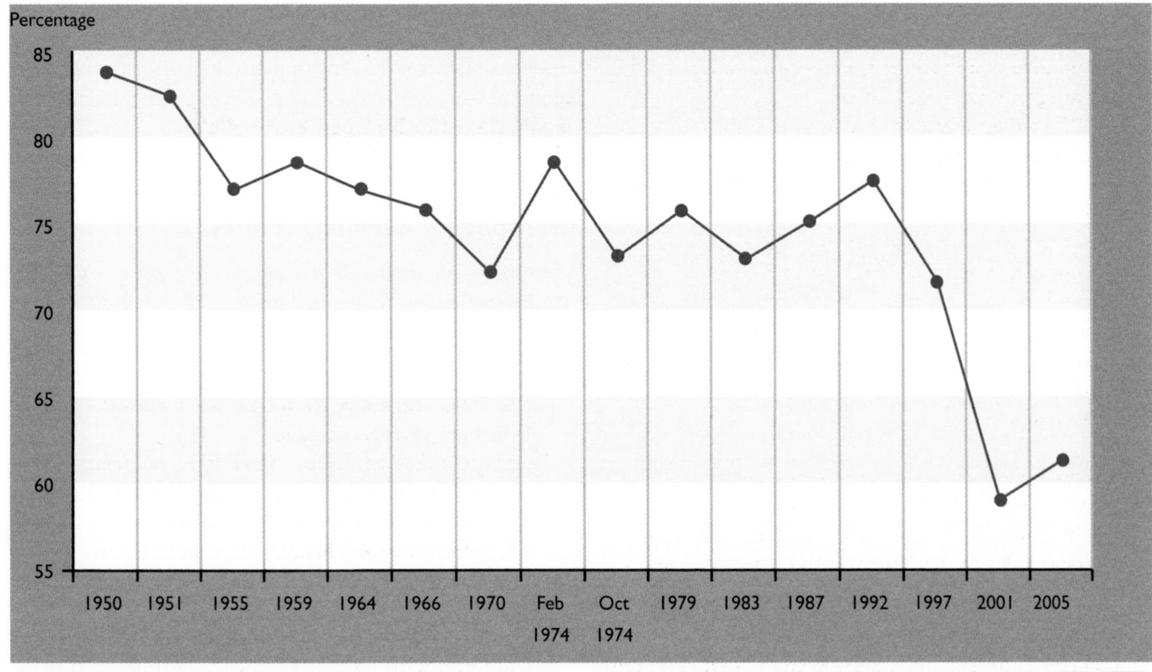

Source: The Power Inquiry (2006) *Power to the People: The Report of Power: An Independent Inquiry into Britain's Democracy*, Joseph Rowntree Foundation, York, p. 46.

Figure 9.7 Membership of the three main parties, 1964–2001

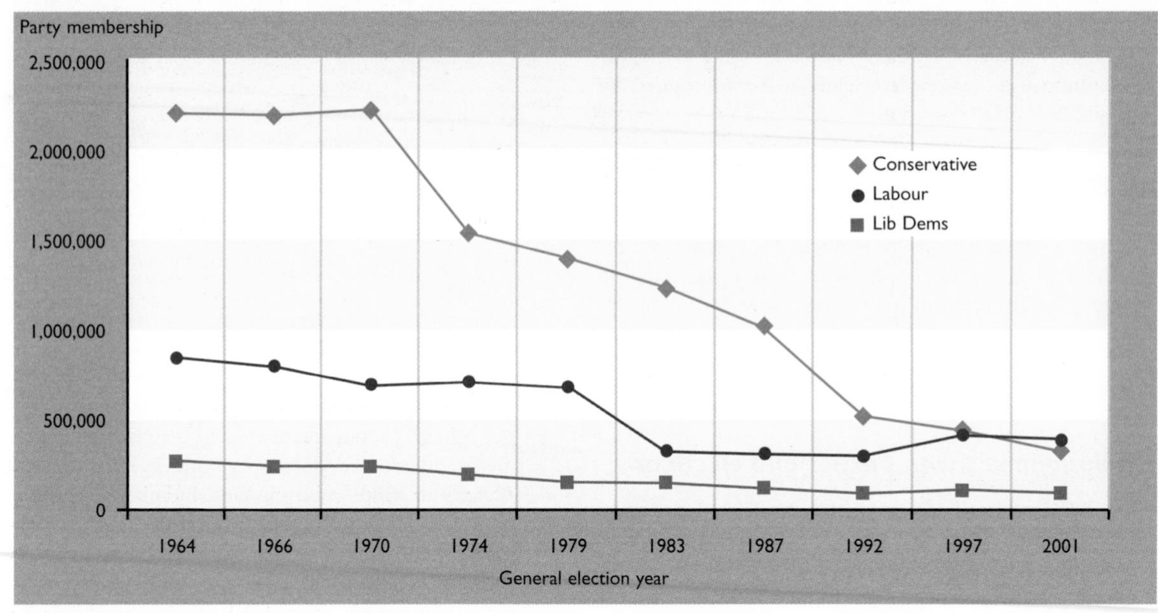

Source: The Power Inquiry (2006) *Power to the People: The Report of Power: An Independent Inquiry into Britain's Democracy*, Joseph Rowntree Foundation, York, p. 47.

The myth of apathy

How then could this negativity be explained? The inquiry examined the view that it was part of general political apathy. However, it argued that this was a 'myth' and that interest in politics was alive and well outside narrow party politics and elections. Furthermore, it found plenty of evidence that British citizens were willing to get involved in other aspects of community affairs such as voluntary work or charitable fundraising. The inquiry therefore criticized the theory of declining social capital put forward by Putnam in the United States (see pp. 863–6).

For example, it quotes Home Office research which showed that the percentage of British adults who volunteered for community activity increased from 47 per cent in 2001 to 50 per cent in 2005. Even amongst those at risk of social exclusion, volunteering stood at 43 per cent in 2005.

The inquiry also refers to research for the Citizen Audit of Britain which found that 62 per cent of the population donated to a campaigning organization or political party, and 30 per cent were involved in raising money, 42 per cent had signed a petition, 25 per cent had contacted a public official, and 13 per cent had tried to change a law through contacting a politician.

The inquiry's own research found a good deal of commitment amongst those involved with campaigning organizations. Many organizations had been growing. For example, membership of Greenpeace rose from 30,000 in 1981 to 221,000 in 2002; a Countryside Alliance demonstration in 2002 drew a crowd estimated at 400,000; some estimates for those attending a demonstration against the Iraq war in 2003 put the number as high as 1,500,000; and 150,000 attended the Live 8 concert in 2005 with hundreds of thousands taking part in demonstrations and events elsewhere.

Another area of increasing activity is consumer boycotts. The Citizen Audit in 2000 found that 31 per cent of the population had boycotted products or producers for political or ethical reasons in the previous twelve months. Support for Fairtrade goods and ethical investments has increased dramatically over recent years.

Another area of growth has been the development of blogs and discussion forums which deal with politics or current affairs.

The inquiry accepted that some groups are more likely to participate in these types of activity than others, with the poorly educated and low income groups least likely to take part. However, the inquiry argues that this sort of evidence shows there is a healthy interest in current affairs and political issues generally and a willingness to participate in public activities. This, however, is in stark contrast to the declining interest and participation in formal politics.

Reasons for declining interest

The inquiry identified a number of reasons why the decline in interest had taken place:

1. Citizens did not feel they had any genuine influence over political decisions. Even party members felt that ordinary members had little say over the policies pursued by their party.
2. Many were unhappy with the political parties themselves. They felt that the parties acted to gain power at the expense of sticking to principles. Furthermore, the main parties were felt to be too similar, giving voters little real choice when it came to elections.
3. There was widespread criticism of the electoral system. With single-member constituencies many people who voted did not vote for a winning candidate, and their votes were effectively wasted. In

many constituencies one party is dominant and there is little chance of control changing from one party to another. Only in marginal constituencies did people feel that their vote really mattered.

4 Individuals were often willing to join or support single-cause organizations or campaigns, but less willing to join or support a political party. Because parties commit to a full range of policies, each party usually has some policies which an individual does not support.
5 A large number of people felt they were ill-informed about politics and, lacking this expertise, they did not feel qualified to get involved.
6 It was also widely felt that the actual process of voting was difficult and inconvenient. For example, elections were held on Thursdays when many people were at work.

The Power Inquiry noted that most of these problems were not new. They further noted that declining participation in party politics was common to many advanced countries. They therefore argued that an underlying cause of these problems was a shift from an industrial to a post-industrial society.

In a post-industrial society there is a large population of well-educated people which 'feels no deference towards those in positions of authority, and is not as bound by the traditional bonds of place, class, and institutions that developed during the industrial era' (Power Inquiry, 2006, p. 18). Lacking deference or a sense of identity linking them to a political party, they tend to identify less closely than previous generations with one party.

A second group is 'permanently marginalized' because they have lost out in the move to post-industrialism. They suffer poverty, poor education and other forms of deprivation. They are not generally affiliated to organizations such as trade unions which used to link the working class to the Labour Party.

The party system in Britain still reflects a divide between the middle and working class, but classes have changed and class identity has declined in significance, making party identification problematic for most voters. As a result, the political system 'cannot respond to the diverse and complex values and interests of the individuals which make up our post-industrial society' (Power Inquiry, 2006, p. 19).

The parties have concentrated on attracting undecided, floating voters in marginal constituencies, with little concern for engaging most of the population in political life. They have simply tried to win elections, at the expense of invigorating political life.

Solutions

The Power Inquiry puts forward a long list of changes which might improve this situation. These include: lowering the voting age to 16; having a mostly elected House of Lords; improving citizenship education in schools; a new voting system; making voting easier; and setting up local resource centres where people can access political information. The inquiry also proposes greater power for the House of Commons (rather than the government) and more decentralization of power, making local politics and local elections more important.

Conclusion

The findings of the Power Inquiry have certainly been influential. For example, shortly after becoming prime minister in 2007, Gordon Brown proposed a package of possible constitutional changes, some of which reflected the recommendations of the inquiry. These included giving more power to local government, restricting some power exercised by the government (e.g. the power to engage in military action without a parliamentary vote), and lowering the voting age to 16.

However, both the causes and extent of political disengagement put forward by the Power Inquiry have been questioned by other social scientists.

Gerry Stoker – *Making Democracy Work*

Like the Power Inquiry, Gerry Stoker (2006) argues that there is growing disenchantment with party politics in Britain and elsewhere. He too looks at evidence of declining participation in elections, falling membership of political parties and declining party loyalty. He also notes that large numbers of people are willing to get involved in other forms of politics, such as demonstrations, single issue campaigns and donating money to broadly political causes.

However, Stoker places more emphasis than the Power Inquiry on disengagement from politics outside party politics and elections. He argues that activities such as donating money require little personal involvement, and that most people's involvement in politics is ad hoc rather than sustained. For example, the Iraq war protests drew very large crowds but most of the participants did not continue to campaign throughout the war and occupation. Stoker says, 'Politics is an ad hoc activity from which people tune in or tune out according to the circumstances confronting them. What they lack is any sense of sustained engagement with political institutions and the political system' (2006, p. 35). Most citizens only get involved if they feel they have to, and then without great enthusiasm or commitment.

Causes

Gerry Stoker places more emphasis than the Power Inquiry on the international scope of disenchantment from politics and on underlying causes of disenchantment rather than specific features of the British political system. He discusses a number of possible causes of disenchantment suggested by a variety of commentators.

1 The first possible explanation is that politics is failing because politicians are becoming more corrupt or incompetent. Stoker finds no evidence to support this claim. He quotes studies of corruption which find that countries such as the UK have not experienced any rise in corruption. Nor are politicians regarded as increasingly incompetent. For example, with a recent sustained period of economic growth most people believe that economic management by government is highly competent.
2 Although politicians might not be seen as more corrupt or incompetent there is still a lack of trust in them. This could be because a better educated and

better informed electorate is more likely to be critical of politicians and less likely to defer to their wisdom. Stoker is not convinced by this argument, pointing out that you might expect an educated and well-informed electorate to get more involved in politics not less.

3 A third possible explanation is a general decline in social capital as people become less involved in community activities (see pp. 863–6 for a discussion of social capital). Stoker finds some support for this argument – for example, trade union membership and membership of community and civic groups have declined to some degree in Britain. However, some types of community involvement have grown, such as membership of sports/hobby clubs, so it is unlikely that this could account for most of the disenchantment with politics.

4 A common explanation for the decline of politics is that many issues are moving beyond the control of politicians as a result of globalization. As Stoker says, 'Some writers suggest that the forces of globalization are so powerful that they are sweeping away nation states and making the democracy embedded within them irrelevant' (2006, p. 59). According to extreme versions of globalization theory, governments no longer have the power to control their own economies, and the global market and transnational companies have more power than nation-states (see pp. 548–57).

Stoker does not accept such extreme views, arguing that governments still have considerable power to regulate and control capitalist economies, both within their own territory and through transnational and global institutions such as the EU and World Trade Organization. He accepts that globalization 'does provide a very tough challenge for politics' but believes that it 'has not rendered democratic politics redundant'. Globalization, along with the pace of technological change, has raised questions about the ability of politicians to shape events and has made politics seem more remote, but most people still see politicians as necessary and important.

5 Finally, Stoker considers the possibility that the 'end of history' (and with it the end of ideology) may be the cause of disenchantment. The **end of history** thesis (first put forward by Francis Fukuyama – see p. 572) suggests that, with the collapse of communism at the end of the 1980s, there were no longer any major competing political belief systems to create political controversy and interest in politics. The triumph of liberal democracy signalled the end of intense political debate and engagement over the type of society we should live in.

This idea relates closely to the ideas of the postmodernist Lyotard who believed that postmodernity had led to the end of belief in big stories or metanarratives, such as political ideologies like communism.

Stoker is not impressed by these arguments. He claims that political controversies and ideologies are still very important. What has changed is simply that they have diversified rather than being about a single clash of systems such as that between communism and capitalism. New ideologies have developed, concerned with issues such as environmentalism, nationalism and religious belief. As with globalization, this makes politics more challenging, but it does not, in itself, explain its decline.

Stoker therefore argues that other factors must be the main explanation for disenchantment with politics.

The first factor that he thinks is important is the process of **consumerism** and **individualism**. Consumerism and individualism lead to members of society being able to achieve many of their personal goals through individual choices in the market. Everybody can buy at least some of the goods and services that they want.

Politics is very different from consumerism. It involves compromise between divergent views and wishes, so that disappointment for many is built in to the process. Politicians can never keep everybody happy. Stoker says: 'the discourse and practice of collective decision-making sits very uncomfortably alongside the discourse and practice of individual choice, self-expression and market-based fulfilment of needs and wants' (2006, p. 69). Individuals can only influence political decisions through expressing their views or using voice (using voice means making your views known to politicians in an attempt to influence their policies). But this is an indirect, slow and often ineffective way of getting what you want.

As a result of changes in society with the growth of individualism and consumerism some types of political activism have grown while others have declined. Individualistic and consumeristic involvement has grown. People are willing to contribute money, or boycott goods, as individuals, but they are less likely to join a party or take an active part in a campaigning political group.

Campaigning to influence the government has become increasingly professionalized. Rather than individual citizens taking part in pressure groups, businesses and representatives of particular interest groups pay professionals to lobby the government. Politicians are seen as distant and regarded with suspicion. Members of the public see them as being influenced more by professional campaigners than by voters, further alienating them from party politics.

Conclusions

Like the Power Inquiry, Stoker argues that change is needed if party politics is to be revived. Like the inquiry, Stoker proposes changes to the voting system, increased emphasis upon local politics, and innovations (such as using new technologies) to make participation easier. Other solutions suggested by Stoker are more transparency and monitoring of ethical standards in politics, and making politicians more representative of the electorate, for example by encouraging greater representation for minority ethnic groups.

Although Stoker believes that there are deep-seated changes in society which have led to disenchantment with politics, he still thinks that reform of the political system can create a revival. He admits that some political scientists will reject his views because they believe that a move to postmodernity makes party politics increasingly irrelevant. He acknowledges that others believe that 'structural inequalities, and the power of business interests "hinder an accessible politics"' (Stoker, 2006, p. 201). But he does not believe that this is an insurmountable problem. What he calls 'politics for amateurs' can be revived and the influence of big business and professional lobbyists curtailed.

Colin Crouch – post-democracy

The rise of post-democracy

A less optimistic view of the future of party politics is provided by Colin Crouch (2005). He believes that the barriers to any revival of party politics are very substantial and cannot be removed by tinkering with the political system. Indeed he argues that we have entered an era of **post-democracy** in which the effectiveness and power of democratic institutions and processes have been seriously compromised.

Crouch argues that in some ways democratic government has never been more widespread, with some research suggesting that in 2002 191 countries had something approximating to a democratic system, compared to 147 in 1988. On a strict definition of democracy, only 88 countries were democratic in 2002, but the number had still risen from 65 in 1988.

However, in established democracies such as those in Western Europe, the USA and Japan, democracy is in a far from healthy state. According to Crouch, there is a **crisis of legitimacy** as many citizens begin to question whether the government truly represents their interests. This is because most mature democracies have moved towards a model of **liberal democracy** which:

> *stresses electoral participation, extensive freedom for lobbying activities, which mainly means business lobbies, and a form of polity that avoids interfering in a capitalist economy. It is a model that has little interest in widespread citizen involvement or the role of organizations outside the business sector.* Crouch, 2005, p. 3

Crouch believes that this situation is far from truly democratic and represents such a decline in democracy that it can be described as post-democracy. He sees the high point of democracy as being the Keynesian governments of Britain, Scandinavia and the Netherlands in the 1950s (see pp. 541–2 for a discussion of Keynes).

Keynesian governments intervened in the economy to meet the needs of their citizens. They had developed welfare states. Political parties were well supported and there were high levels of participation in politics by the working class through institutions such as the Labour Party and trade unions.

Since then, and particularly since the 1970s, mass participation has declined and the power of business and financial interests has grown. The dominant concerns of governments have shifted away from the maintenance of full employment and the provision of welfare, to ensuring the success of business and finance in the pursuit of overall economic growth. This shift has occurred because of the global deregulation of financial markets which has increased the power of finance capital and the emphasis on short-term profits for shareholders. Governments are forced to cut corporation tax if they are to persuade firms to locate their businesses in that country.

The underlying cause of the shift to post-democracy is globalization, to which Crouch attaches far more significance than Stoker. According to Crouch the global firm is the most important institution in the post-democratic world. Many global firms do not manufacture their own products and they are not tied to particular companies to do their manufacturing for them. Indeed some concentrate almost entirely on brand image rather than production, contracting out manufacturing to the lowest bidder (see the work of Klein, pp. 573–5).

This institutional model increasingly influences politics so that parties rely more on image than on following policies which reflect the interests of a particular class. In government, too, many activities are subcontracted or privatized, giving the state less direct control over the implementation of policies. For example, the private sector has become increasingly involved in providing health care and education in Britain, either directly (as in private health care) or indirectly (through providing consultants and setting up city academies in the educational sector).

Public administration has increasingly been commercialized. The state has been left to provide residual public services for the most disadvantaged who are amongst the least likely to be actively involved in politics. This makes politics less important than it was, further shifting society towards post-democracy.

The corporate elite

Like Stoker, Crouch believes that professional lobbying by companies has largely replaced mass participation in political parties. In this process power has shifted away from democratic control to a **corporate elite**. This elite:

> *become even more powerful as government concedes to them the organisation of its own activities and bows to the superiority of its expertise. In addition to dominating the economy itself, they become the class that also dominates the running of government.* Crouch, 2005, p. 44

Furthermore, Crouch says:

> *Today ... through the growing dependence of government on the expertise of corporate executives and leading entrepreneurs, and the dependence of parties on their funds, we are steadily moving towards the establishment of a new, dominant, combined political and economic class.* Crouch, 2005, p. 52

Unlike in previous eras, no other class can challenge its political dominance. The working class has declined as a result of deindustrialization. The middle classes are relatively 'incoherent'. They lack a single voice because they are divided between public and private sector workers and between upper and lower middle-class strata.

Crouch concedes that political parties are concerned with gaining support from the middle class, especially the lower middle class, who they see as crucial floating voters who can determine election results. However, both New Labour and the Conservatives portray the interests of the middle classes as being no different from those of business elites. They are viewed as wanting better public services, but the solution put forward is more privatization, in line with the policy that business supports.

Education is portrayed as crucial because it provides opportunities for upward mobility. The middle class believe that their aspirations for their children can be met through the education system. Those aspirations sometimes include achieving a place in the business elite. But Crouch thinks this cannot satisfy most people: since 'social mobility can only be enjoyed by a minority and in competition with everyone else, it is a very odd policy to offer as a general solution to life's discontents' (2005, p. 60).

The Third Way

Like Marxists, Crouch believes that a capitalist class holds much of the power in contemporary Britain. Like elite theorists, he believes that power is concentrated in the hands of a small elite. However, unlike these theorists he does not believe that this has always been the case. He argues that it is only in recent times that the Labour Party in particular has become dominated by business interests.

Crouch sees New Labour as a post-democratic party, which has lost touch with its traditional working-class, activist and trade union support and allied itself to business interests. For example, it has come to rely increasingly on financial support from wealthy donors rather than funding from trade unions.

New Labour under Tony Blair advocated a **Third Way** approach, based upon the ideas of the sociologist Anthony Giddens (see pp. 273–4). The Third Way is supposed to provide an alternative to either capitalism or socialism. For example, public services are still funded by the state, but are made more efficient through being opened up to competition and through being provided by private sector firms.

As well as making politics less important (see above), this obscures lines of responsibility for public services. For example, in rail crashes it has been unclear who is responsible for the safety of a particular section of track because complex systems of subcontracting have been used. When a single public sector body, for example British Rail, is responsible, as it used to be, lines of responsibility are clear. The body is responsible to the government and ultimately the citizen. In post-democratic societies the capacities of the citizen are reduced. Private companies are responsible for policy implementation, and the government is responsible to the electorate only for very broad policy direction.

The future of democracy

Although Crouch borrows much from Marxism and elite theory he is not as pessimistic as them about the future of democracy in advanced capitalist societies. The shift to post-democracy can be reversed if the dominance of corporate elites is addressed. Doing this requires new rules 'to prevent, or at least very closely to regulate, flows of money and personnel between parties, circles of advisors and corporate lobbies' (Crouch, 2005, p. 109). There also needs to be a renewed emphasis upon the idea of public service as an alternative to the profit motive as a basis on which services are provided for citizens.

Like Stoker and the Power Inquiry, Crouch proposes increased power for local democracy. However, Crouch does not believe that changing the mechanisms of politics will be enough. He argues that new identities need to be mobilized so that there are organized interests that can be represented through political parties.

Crouch believes that politics has retained some vitality in social movements such as the ecological movement, feminism, the campaigns for gay rights and the anti-globalization movement. He describes these as 'new global' movements which can only achieve so much as protest movements. The identities adopted by their supporters need to be used to link them to political parties who can represent their interests and restore the link between citizens and party politics.

Crouch describes himself as a 'democratic egalitarian' (2005, p. 122) and concludes by arguing that the only way to create the greater equality he seeks is to harness the vitality of social and protest movements to the party political system through which governments are formed.

Conclusion

Whatever their differences, the Power Inquiry, Stoker and Crouch all agree that party politics is in decline and something needs to be done to change the situation. Crouch places more emphasis on underlying social and structural causes of the change than other writers, but still believes it is possible to reverse the situation.

Given the deep-seated nature of the causes Crouch identifies (such as globalization and the decline of class identities) his suggested solutions may be too superficial to arrest the decline. If the power of corporate elites has become so embedded in the political system, it may be very difficult to significantly restrict their influence on political parties. Nevertheless, like other commentators in this section, Crouch at least makes constructive suggestions about how to make democracy in Britain and elsewhere correspond more closely to the ideal to which it aspires.

Summary and conclusions

This chapter has shown that power can be defined in different ways and that the study of power need not be confined to the study of the state. Foucault, for example, sees power as involved in all social relationships, not just those involved in formal politics.

It has also been demonstrated that power can have many sources, including control of the state, economic resources, the ability to persuade others through ideology, the use of language and the use of military might. As a topic, therefore, the study of power is a very broad one which is integral to all aspects of sociology.

Traditionally, however, the study of power has concentrated on politics and the state. There has been a long-standing debate about whether the state in democratic societies really does reflect the wishes of the citizens, as pluralists claim. Marxists and elite theorists have both rejected this view. Whether their theories are accepted as valid or not, there is a convincing case that power is not equally shared. Clearly some individuals have more opportunity to exercise power both inside and outside the state than others.

The theory of globalization questions the assumption that nation-states monopolize political power. It suggests that transnational or global organizations or processes increasingly exercise power alongside, or even over, the state.

There is no doubt that transnational/global corporations and organizations (such as the World Bank, International Monetary Fund and European Union) do have some power. However, the extent to which power has shifted from the nation-state remains open to debate. States certainly retain the power to make laws, control territory and use military force on a scale which is rarely available to non-state actors (which range from terrorist organizations to institutions such as the United Nations). As Chomsky suggests, there is no doubt that the USA retains enormous power (though even the USA is not always able to control events, as the occupation of Iraq has shown).

Even though power is exercised in many ways, and the power of the nation-state has been challenged, politics remains important in determining such issues as who gets what resources. However, as many sociologists have suggested, the nature of politics might be changing. This could be happening in many ways, including: the decline of class influences on voting and politics in general; disillusionment with party politics; a decline in participation in elections and party politics; increasing citizen involvement in new social movements and global and other protest movements; and the increasing importance of identity politics.

Postmodernists see these types of change as part of wider social processes involving the transformation of Western societies from modern to postmodern. Others are more sceptical that such fundamental changes are taking place, and certainly all the trends listed above can be exaggerated. For example, there are lots of arguments and considerable evidence to suggest that class is still of some significance in politics. Only a minority take part in new social movements; old social movements continue to have an influence; and most people do still vote in general elections. 'New' social movements are not necessarily that new – in Britain at least, political activists have not always worked through parliamentary democracy to pursue their aims.

Nevertheless, it is clearly not true that nothing has changed. Sociologists of power, politics and the state have identified a number of important trends as well as showing how power, in one form or another, is integral to social life.

CHAPTER 10
Education

... we are likely to end up with a more socially differentiated and divisive system of education. In any market there are winners and losers. In this market we may all end up losing out!' Ball et *al.*, 1994

Introduction

In its broadest sense, education is simply one aspect of socialization: it involves the acquisition of knowledge and the learning of skills. Whether intentionally or unintentionally, education often also helps to shape beliefs and moral values.

In small-scale non-literate societies, such as hunting and gathering bands, education was hard to distinguish from other aspects of life. Young people learned their 'lessons' largely by joining in the social group. Knowledge and skills were usually learned informally by imitating examples provided by adults. Although adults sometimes instructed their young, they did so as part of their daily routine. Thus boys accompanied their fathers on hunting trips, while girls assisted their mothers with cooking and gathering vegetables.

In more complex pre-industrial societies, such as those of medieval Europe, specialized educational institutions slowly developed, along with the specialized role of the teacher. However, such developments provided formal education for only a small minority of the population, such as future members of the clergy and the sons of the wealthy. Formal education for the masses was not provided until industrialization was well under way.

The expansion of British education

In Britain, free compulsory education conducted in formal institutions staffed by full-time professionals began in 1870. Although the state had contributed to the provision of education as early as 1833, only with Forster's Education Act of 1870 did it assume full responsibility. In 1880 school attendance was made compulsory up to the age of 10. With the Fisher Education Act of 1918 the state became responsible for secondary education, and attendance was made compulsory up to the age of 14. The school-leaving age was raised to 15 in 1947, and to 16 in 1972.

The raising of the school-leaving age was obviously accompanied by an expansion of schooling. For most of the twentieth century, though, education also expanded as a result of people continuing in education after the compulsory period of attendance, or returning to education later in life. In 1900 only 1.2 per cent of 18-year-olds entered full-time further or higher education; by 1938 the figure had reached 5.8 per cent.

However, the first explosion of post-compulsory education came in the 1950s, 1960s and early 1970s. The Robbins Report of 1963 established the principle that all those capable of benefiting from higher education should be entitled to it. New universities were built, polytechnics were established, and the Open University gave adults fresh educational opportunities. Young people of school-leaving age were encouraged to stay on in school sixth forms, or to attend college. By 2005, 76 per cent of 16- to 18-year-olds in England were participating in some form of education and training (dfes.gov.uk, 2007).

The growth in higher education slowed down in the late 1970s and early 1980s, but rapid growth resumed in the late 1980s and early 1990s. Most existing universities expanded, as did the polytechnics, which were given university status in 1992. The number of higher education students in the UK increased by nearly two-thirds between 1991/2 and 2003/4 (dfes.gov.uk, 2007).

In 1993/4, UK government expenditure on education was £33 billion, 12.6 per cent of total expenditure. By 2002/3, this had risen to £53 billion, 13.5 per cent of total government spending (Annual Abstract of Statistics, 2005).

We will now examine major sociological perspectives on education.

Education – functionalist perspectives

Two related questions have guided functionalist research into education:

1 'What are the functions of education for society as a whole?' Given the functionalist view of the needs of the social system, this question leads, for example, to an assessment of the contribution made by education to the maintenance of value consensus and social solidarity.
2 'What are the functional relationships between education and other parts of the social system?' This leads to an examination of the relationship between education and the economic system, and a consideration of how this relationship helps to integrate society as a whole.

As with functionalist analysis in general, the functionalist view of education tends to focus on the positive contributions education makes to the maintenance of the social system.

Emile Durkheim – education and social solidarity

Writing at the turn of the last century, the French sociologist Emile Durkheim saw the major function of education as the transmission of society's norms and values. He maintained:

> *Society can survive only if there exists among its members a sufficient degree of homogeneity; education perpetuates and reinforces this homogeneity by fixing in the child from the beginning the essential similarities which collective life demands.* Durkheim, 1961, first published 1925

Without these 'essential similarities', cooperation, social solidarity, and therefore social life itself would be impossible. A vital task for all societies is the welding of a mass of individuals into a united whole – in other words, the creation of **social solidarity**. This involves a commitment to society, a sense of belonging, and a feeling that the social unit is more important than the individual. Durkheim argued: 'To become attached to society, the child must feel in it something that is real, alive and powerful, which dominates the person and to which he also owes the best part of himself.'

Education, and in particular the teaching of history, provides this link between the individual and society. If the history of their society is brought alive to children, they will come to see that they are part of something larger than themselves: they will develop a sense of commitment to the social group.

Education and social rules

Durkheim argued that, in complex industrial societies, the school serves a function which cannot be provided either by the family or by the peer group. Membership of the family is based on kinship relationships; membership of the peer group on personal choice. Membership of society as a whole is based on neither of these principles.

Individuals must learn to cooperate with those who are neither their kin nor their friends. The school provides a context where these skills can be learned. As such, it is society in miniature, a model of the social system. In school, the child must interact with other members of the school community in terms of a fixed set of rules. This experience prepares him or her for interacting with members of society as a whole in terms of society's rules.

Durkheim believed school rules should be strictly enforced. Punishments should reflect the seriousness of the damage done to the social group by the offence, and it should be made clear to transgressors why they were being punished. In this way, pupils would come to learn that it was wrong to act against the interests of the social group as a whole. They would learn to exercise self-discipline, not just because they wanted to avoid punishment, but also because they would come to see that misbehaviour damaged society as a whole. Science, and particularly social sciences like sociology, would help the child to understand the rational basis on which society was organized. Durkheim stated:

> *It is by respecting the school rules that the child learns to respect rules in general, that he develops the habit of self-control and restraint simply because he should control and restrain himself. It is a first initiation into the austerity of duty. Serious life has now begun.* Durkheim, 1961, first published 1925

Education and the division of labour

Finally, Durkheim argued that education teaches individuals specific skills necessary for their future occupations. This function is particularly important in industrial society with its increasingly complex and specialized division of labour.

The relatively unspecialized division of labour in pre-industrial society meant that occupational skills could usually be passed on from parents to children without the need for formal education. In industrial society, social solidarity is based largely on the interdependence of specialized skills – for example, the manufacture of a single product requires the combination of a variety of specialists. This necessity for combination produces cooperation and social solidarity.

Thus schools transmit both general values, which provide the 'necessary homogeneity for social survival', and specific skills, which provide the 'necessary diversity for social cooperation'. Industrial society is thus united by value consensus and a specialized division of labour whereby specialists combine to produce goods and services.

Criticisms of Durkheim

Durkheim's views on education are open to a number of criticisms.

1. Durkheim assumes societies have a shared culture which can be transmitted through the education system. Countries such as Britain are now multicultural and it is therefore debatable whether there is a single culture on which schools could base their curriculum.
2. Marxists argue that educational institutions tend to transmit a dominant culture which serves the interests of the ruling class rather than those of society as a whole (see pp. 602–8).
3. In recent decades both New Right and New Labour perspectives on education have tended to emphasize the economic importance of education and have downplayed the significance of transmitting a shared culture (see pp. 613–16 and 621–4).
4. Some researchers question whether in practice schools do act in the way that Durkheim describes. On the basis of a study of comprehensive schools, David Hargreaves (1982) argues that education in modern Britain often fails to transmit shared values, promote self-discipline, or cement social solidarity. Hargreaves believes that in reality British education emphasizes individual competition through the exam system, rather than encouraging social solidarity.

Although Durkheim and Hargreaves both criticize education based upon individual competition in an exam system, other functionalists see competition as a vital aspect of modern education (a view also supported by New Right perspectives; see pp. 602–8). We will now examine their views.

Talcott Parsons – education and universalistic values

The American sociologist Talcott Parsons (1961) outlined what has become the accepted functionalist view of education. Writing in the late 1950s, Parsons argued that, after primary socialization within the family, the school takes over as the **focal socializing agency**: school acts as a bridge between the family and society as a whole, preparing children for their adult role.

Within the family, the child is judged and treated largely in terms of **particularistic** standards. Parents treat the child as their particular child rather than judging her or him in terms of standards or yardsticks that can be applied to every individual. However, in the wider society the individual is treated and judged in terms of **universalistic** standards, which are applied to all members, regardless of their kinship ties.

Within the family, the child's status is **ascribed**: it is fixed by birth. However, in advanced industrial society, status in adult life is largely **achieved**: for example, individuals achieve their occupational status. Thus the child must move from the particularistic standards and ascribed status of the family to the universalistic standards and achieved status of adult society.

The school prepares young people for this transition. It establishes universalistic standards, in terms of which all pupils achieve their status. Their conduct is assessed against the yardstick of the school rules; their achievement is measured by performance in examinations. The same standards are applied to all students regardless of ascribed characteristics such as sex, race, family background or class of origin. Schools operate on **meritocratic** principles: status is achieved on the basis of merit (or worth).

Like Durkheim, Parsons argued that the school represents society in miniature. Modern industrial society is increasingly based on achievement rather than ascription, on universalistic rather than particularistic standards, on meritocratic principles which apply to all its members. By reflecting the operation of society as a whole, the school prepares young people for their adult roles.

Education and value consensus

As part of this process, schools socialize young people into the basic values of society. Parsons, like many functionalists, maintained that value consensus is essential for society to operate effectively. In American society, schools instil two major values:

1. The value of achievement
2. The value of equality of opportunity

By encouraging students to strive for high levels of academic attainment, and by rewarding those who succeed, schools foster the value of achievement itself. By placing individuals in the same situation in the classroom and so allowing them to compete on equal terms in examinations, schools foster the value of equality of opportunity.

These values have important functions in society as a whole. Advanced industrial society requires a highly motivated, achievement-oriented workforce. This necessitates **differential reward for differential achievement**, a principle which has been established in schools. Both the winners (the high achievers) and the losers (the low achievers) will see the system as just and fair, since status is achieved in a situation where all have an equal chance. Again, the principles that operate in the wider society are mirrored by those of the school.

Education and selection

Finally, Parsons saw the educational system as an important mechanism for the selection of individuals for their future role in society. In his words, it 'functions to allocate these human resources within the role-structure of adult society'. Thus schools, by testing and evaluating students, match their talents, skills and capacities to the jobs for which they are best suited. The school is therefore seen as the major mechanism for **role allocation**.

Criticisms of Parsons

Like Durkheim, Parsons fails to give adequate consideration to the possibility that the values transmitted by the educational system may be those of a ruling minority rather than of society as a whole. His view that schools operate on meritocratic principles is open to question – a point which we will examine in detail in later sections.

Kingsley Davis and Wilbert E. Moore – education and role allocation

Like Parsons, Davis and Moore (1967, first published 1945) saw education as a means of role allocation, but they linked the educational system more directly with the system of social stratification. As outlined in Chapter 1, Davis and Moore see **social stratification** as a mechanism for ensuring that the most talented and able members of society are allocated to those positions that are functionally most important for society. High rewards, which act as incentives, are attached to those positions. This means, in theory, that all will compete for them and the most talented will win through.

The education system is an important part of this process. In Davis's words, it is the 'proving ground for ability and hence the selective agency for placing people in different statuses according to their capacities'. Thus the education system sifts, sorts and grades individuals in terms of their talents and abilities. It rewards the most talented with high qualifications, which in turn provide entry to those occupations that are functionally most important to society.

Criticisms of Davis and Moore

General criticisms of Davis and Moore's theory have been examined in Chapter 1 (see pp. 22–3). With respect to the relationship between education and social stratification, there are a number of more specific criticisms:

1. The relationship between academic credentials and occupational reward is not particularly close. In particular, income is only weakly linked to educational attainment.
2. There is considerable doubt about the proposition that the educational system grades people in terms of ability. In particular, it has been argued that intelligence has little effect upon educational attainment.
3. There is considerable evidence to suggest that the influence of social stratification largely prevents the educational system from efficiently grading individuals in terms of ability.

We will consider these points in detail later.

Education, globalization and functionalism

Functionalism has focused on the role of education in the nation-state. From this perspective, education promotes a national identity and strengthens social solidarity within national boundaries. But is this view out of date in an increasingly global society?

Beyond functionalism

Some researchers argue that the traditional functions of education are becoming increasingly inappropriate and/or impractical as globalization progresses. They claim that the transmission of a common national culture is no longer possible in the multicultural societies of a globalized world. The cultures of today's societies are too fragmented and diverse to weld into a national identity based on shared norms and values (Donald, 1992).

In defence of functionalism

Other researchers argue that education continues to play a vital role in national societies. First, increasing cultural diversity means that education remains important for maintaining some degree of social integration – for example, by transmitting a common language and common national goals. Second, the economic functions of education become even more important as competition between nation-states intensifies in the global marketplace. Governments see education and training as the key to national economic progress (Green, 1997; Lauder *et al.*, 2006).

Education – conflict perspectives

Functionalism assumes that education makes positive contributions to society as a whole. An effective education system is seen to benefit all members of society. By contrast, conflict perspectives are based on the view that there is a conflict of interest between groups in society. In particular, the powerful are seen to gain at the expense of the less powerful. From a conflict perspective, education largely serves the interests of the powerful. It maintains their power, justifies their privilege and legitimizes their wealth.

Samuel Bowles and Herbert Gintis – *Schooling in Capitalist America*

The American Marxist economists and sociologists Bowles and Gintis (1976) argue that the major role of education in capitalist societies is the reproduction of labour power. In particular, they maintain that there is 'close "correspondence" between the social relationships which govern personal interaction in the work place and the social relationships of the education system'. According to Bowles and Gintis, this **correspondence principle** provides the key to understanding the workings of the education system. Work casts a 'long shadow' over the education system: education is subservient to the needs of those who control the workforce – the owners of the means of production.

The hidden curriculum

The first major way in which education functions is to provide capitalists with a workforce which has the personality, attitudes and values that are most useful to them. Like Marx, Bowles and Gintis regard work in capitalist societies as both exploitative and alienating; yet, if capitalism is to succeed, it requires a hard-working, docile, obedient and highly motivated workforce, which is too divided and fragmented to challenge the authority of management.

The education system helps to achieve these objectives largely through the **hidden curriculum**. It is not the content of lessons and the examinations that pupils take which are important, but the form that teaching and learning take and the way that schools are organized. The hidden curriculum consists of those things that pupils learn through the experience of attending school, rather than the stated educational objectives of such institutions. According to Bowles and Gintis, the hidden curriculum shapes the future workforce in the following ways:

1. It helps to produce a subservient workforce of uncritical, passive and docile workers. In a study based upon 237 members of the senior year in a New York high school, Bowles and Gintis found that the grades awarded related more to personality traits than academic abilities. They found that low grades were related to creativity, aggressiveness and independence, while higher grades were related to perseverance, consistency, dependability and punctuality.

   Far from living up to the ideal of encouraging self-development, the American education system was creating an unimaginative and unquestioning workforce which could be easily manipulated by employers.
2. Bowles and Gintis claim that the hidden curriculum encourages an acceptance of hierarchy. Schools are organized on a hierarchical principle of authority and control. Teachers give orders, pupils obey. Students have little control over the subjects they study or how they study them. This prepares them for relationships within the workplace where, if workers are to stay out of trouble, they will need to defer to the authority of supervisors and managers.
3. At school, pupils learn to be motivated by external rewards, just as the workforce in a capitalist society is motivated by external rewards. Because students have so little control over, and little feeling of involvement in, their school work, they get little satisfaction from studying. Learning is based upon the 'jug and mug' principle. The teachers possess knowledge which they pour into the 'empty mugs', the pupils. It is not therefore surprising that many pupils do not enjoy the process of schooling. Instead, they are encouraged to take satisfaction from the external reward of a qualification at the end of their studies. The qualification offers the promise of employment, or better-paid employment than would otherwise have been the case.

   The subsequent creation of a workforce motivated by external rewards is necessary, according to Bowles and Gintis, because work in capitalist societies is intrinsically unsatisfying. It is not organized according to the human need for fulfilling work, but according to the capitalist's desire to make the maximum possible profit. As a result, the workers must be motivated by the external reward of the wage packet, just as the pupil is motivated by the external reward of the qualification.
4. Bowles and Gintis claim that another important aspect of the hidden curriculum is the **fragmentation** of school subjects. The student, during the course of the school day, moves from one subject to another: from mathematics to history, to French, to English. Little connection is made between the lessons: knowledge is fragmented and compartmentalized into academic subjects.

   This aspect of education corresponds to the fragmentation of the workforce. Bowles and Gintis believe most jobs in factories and offices have been broken down into very specific tasks carried out by separate individuals. In this way, workers are denied knowledge of the overall productive process, which makes it difficult for them to set up in competition with their employers. Furthermore, a fragmented and divided workforce is easier to control, and this control can be maintained because of the principle of 'divide and conquer'. It becomes difficult for the workforce to unite in opposition to those in authority over them.

The benefits of the education system for capitalism

Bowles and Gintis believe the formal parts of the curriculum correspond to the needs of capitalist employers by providing a surplus of skilled labour. This maintains a high rate of unemployment and ensures that workers of all levels of skill have to compete with each other for jobs. Employers can pay low wages through being able to threaten dismissal and replacement by the reserve army of skilled workers. Since the mental requirements of most jobs are quite low, and most skills can be learned on the job, education tends to over-educate the workforce.

Apart from the direct benefits provided by the education system, just outlined, Bowles and Gintis argue that education also has indirect benefits for capitalism through the **legitimation of inequality**. By making society appear fair and just, class consciousness does not develop and the stability of society is not threatened.

The illusion of equality of opportunity

Unlike functionalists, Bowles and Gintis reject the view that capitalist societies are meritocratic. They believe that class background is the most important factor influencing levels of attainment.

The idea that we all compete on equal terms is an illusion. Although education is free and open to all, and despite the fact that individuals can apply for jobs at will, Bowles and Gintis claim that some have much greater opportunities than others. The children of the wealthy and powerful tend to obtain high qualifications and highly rewarded jobs irrespective of their abilities. The education system disguises this, with its **myth of meritocracy**. Those who are denied success blame themselves, and not the system which has condemned them to failure.

Intelligence, educational attainment and meritocracy

Bowles and Gintis base their argument on an analysis of the relationships between intelligence (measured in terms of an individual's **intelligence quotient** or **IQ**), educational attainment and occupational reward. They argue that IQ accounts for only a small part of educational attainment.

Bowles and Gintis examined a sample of individuals with average IQs. Within this sample they found a wide range of variation in educational attainment, which led them to conclude that there is hardly any relationship between IQ and academic qualifications.

They found a direct relationship between educational attainment and family background. The causal factor is not IQ, but the class position of the individual's parents. In general, the higher a person's class of origin, the longer he or she remains in the educational system and the higher his or her qualifications.

But why do students with high qualifications tend to have higher-than-average intelligence? Bowles and Gintis argue that this relationship is largely 'a spin-off, a by-product' of continued education. The longer an individual stays in the educational system, the more his or her IQ develops. Thus IQ is a consequence of length of stay, not the cause of it.

The above evidence led Bowles and Gintis to conclude that, at least in terms of IQ, the educational system does not function as a meritocracy.

They apply a similar argument to the statistical relationship between IQ and occupational reward. In general, individuals in highly paid occupations have above-average IQs. However, Bowles and Gintis reject the view that IQ is directly related to occupational success. Within their sample of people with average IQs, they found a wide range of income variation. If IQ were directly related to occupational reward, the incomes of those with the same IQ should be similar. Again Bowles and Gintis found that family background was the major factor accounting for differences in income.

They found that the main factors accounting for occupational reward were the individual's class of origin, ethnicity and gender. There is considerable evidence to show that educational qualifications are far more valuable on the job market to the white male than to the white female, to the white male than to the black male, and to the middle-class male than to the working-class male.

Thus Bowles and Gintis argue:

> *The intellectual abilities developed or certified in school make little causal contribution to getting ahead economically. Only a minor portion of the substantial statistical association between schooling and economic success can be accounted for by the school's role in producing or screening cognitive skills.* Bowles and Gintis, 1976

They conclude: 'Education reproduces inequality by justifying privilege and attributing poverty to personal failure.' It efficiently disguises the fact that economic success runs in the family, that privilege breeds privilege. Bowles and Gintis therefore reject the functionalist view of the relationship between education and stratification put forward by Talcott Parsons and Davis and Moore.

Criticisms and evaluation of Bowles and Gintis

The work of Bowles and Gintis has been highly controversial. It has been criticized by Marxists and non-Marxists alike. The critics tend to agree that Bowles and Gintis have exaggerated the correspondence between work and education, and have failed to provide adequate evidence to support their case:

1. M.S.H. Hickox (1982) questions the view that there is a close correspondence between education and economic development. He points out that in Britain compulsory education was introduced long after the onset of industrialization. Despite the fact that for a long time capitalists did not employ a workforce which had had its attitudes and values shaped by education, the development of capitalism did not appear to be affected.
2. Phillip Brown, A.H. Halsey, Hugh Lauder and Amy Wells (1997) argue that, even if education used to produce the sorts of behaviour and personality required by capitalist employers, this may no longer be the case. They suggest that changes in the nature of work organizations have reduced the importance of bureaucratic control and increased the importance of teamworking. However, the exam system, in which people are judged and compete with one another as individuals, discourages the development of teamworking skills.
3. Bowles and Gintis can be criticized for their claims about the way that schools shape personality. They did not carry out detailed research into life within schools. They tended to assume that the hidden curriculum was actually influencing pupils. There are, however, numerous studies which show that many pupils have scant regard for the rules of the school, and little respect for the authority of the teacher. Paul Willis (1977) (see pp. 605–7) showed that working-class 'lads' learned to behave at school in ways quite at odds with capitalism's supposed need for a docile workforce.
4. Bowles and Gintis have been criticized for ignoring the influence of the formal curriculum. David Reynolds (1984) claims that much of the curriculum in British schools does not promote the development of an ideal employee under capitalism. The curriculum does not seem designed to teach either the skills needed by employers or uncritical passive behaviour which makes workers easy to exploit. He says:

> *The survival in schools of a liberal, humanities-based curriculum, the emphasis upon the acquisition of knowledge for the purposes of intellectual self-betterment rather than ... material gain, the limited swing to science within higher education, the continuing*

high status of 'pure disciplines' as against work-related applied knowledge, the decline in commercially important foreign languages at sixth form level ... all suggests a lack of correspondence. Reynolds, 1984

It might be added that the popularity of sociology as an A level subject in Britain could hardly be seen as promoting unthinking workers! Even if the hidden curriculum could be shown to encourage docility, the presence of Bowles and Gintis themselves within the formal curriculum would undermine their claims about education.

5 A further area of criticism concerns the extent to which education legitimates inequality by creating the appearance that success and failure are based upon merit. Hickox (1982) refers to a study by Richard Scase in which only 2.5 per cent of a sample of English workers expressed the view that educational qualifications were an important factor in determining social class. Most of those interviewed placed a far greater emphasis on family background and economic factors. This would suggest that education has not succeeded in legitimating inequality in Britain.
6 Bowles and Gintis have been attacked for failing to explain adequately how the economy shapes the education system. David Reynolds (1984) suggests it is simply not possible for British capitalists or the 'capitalist state' to exercise detailed control over British schools. Local authorities have a considerable amount of freedom in the way they organize schools, and, once they 'shut the classroom door', teachers are not subject to close supervision. Reynolds claims 'a large number of radicals have been attracted into teaching', and because of their independence they have not moulded education to suit the needs of capitalism.

Bowles and Gintis developed their theory of education in the 1970s, and their views became less influential in later decades. However, it can be argued that, since critics first responded to their theory, the British education system has developed in such a way that their analysis may have become more relevant. For example, local authorities have lost some of their power over education because they no longer run colleges, and schools now have greater autonomy. The freedom of teachers has been restricted by the introduction of a national curriculum, and education has become more explicitly designed to meet the needs of employers. These changes will be discussed later in the chapter (see pp. 617–21).

Whatever the merits of Bowles and Gintis's work, many sociologists sympathetic to Marxism have felt the need to modify their approach. Some have denied that parts of the superstructure, such as education, are exclusively shaped by the infrastructure; others have stressed that pupils and students are not simply the passive recipients of education.

Marxism, struggle, and the relative autonomy of education

In response to the criticisms of Bowles and Gintis, Marxists such as Henry Giroux (1984) have advocated a modified approach to the analysis of education within a broadly Marxist framework. Giroux makes the following general points:

1 Working-class pupils are actively involved in shaping their own education. They do not accept everything they are taught, nor is their behaviour entirely determined by capitalism. Pupils draw upon their own cultures in finding ways to respond to schooling, and often these responses involve resistance to the school.
2 Schools can be seen as 'sites' of ideological struggle in which there can be clashes between cultures. Different classes, ethnic and religious groups all try to influence both the content and process of schooling. From this point of view the nature of education is not simply determined by the needs of capitalism, but is also influenced by a continuing struggle between the groups involved.
3 The education system possesses **relative autonomy** from the economic infrastructure. Unlike Bowles and Gintis, Giroux argues that education has partial independence from the needs or requirements of capitalist industry. For example, he points out that in the USA in the early 1980s the education system produced more graduates than the labour market required. Many became unemployed or had to take low-paid jobs that required little training. In this way the myth that education provided equal opportunity and the chance for upward mobility was undermined. Giroux stresses, however, that the independence of education is only partial: in the final analysis, education cannot go against the fundamental interests of capitalism.

Criticisms of relative autonomy

Although in some respects Giroux's work is more subtle than that of Bowles and Gintis, Andy Hargreaves (1982) believes it fails to solve the problems associated with Marxist theories of education. To Hargreaves, there is a massive contradiction built into the theory of resistance and relative autonomy: it claims that education is free to develop in its own way and is influenced by numerous social groups, yet it is still ultimately determined by the economy.

Hargreaves criticizes Giroux for failing to spell out in what circumstances education can develop independently, and how and when economic factors become paramount. He describes Giroux's theory as one in which 'anything goes'. Pupils might be indoctrinated with bourgeois ideology at school, or fight against the authority of the teachers. Both fit the theory of relative autonomy. It therefore becomes impossible to prove the theory wrong: any facts can be made to fit it. As Hargreaves says of such theories, 'they appear to want to have it both ways, to assert both the dependence and independence of schooling; to have their cake and eat it'.

Paul Willis – *Learning to Labour*

In an important and much discussed study, Paul Willis (1977) developed a distinctive, neo-Marxist approach to education. Like Giroux, Willis recognizes the existence of conflict within the education system, and he rejects the view that there is any simple, direct relationship between the economy and the way the education system operates. Like Bowles and Gintis, Willis focuses on the way that education prepares the workforce, but he denies that education is a particularly successful agency of socialization. Indeed, Willis argues that education can have unintended consequences for pupils – consequences which may not be completely beneficial to capitalism.

As well as drawing upon Marxist sociology, Willis adopted some of the research techniques associated with symbolic interactionism. He used a wide variety of research methods in his study of a Midlands school in England in the 1970s. He used 'observation and participant observation in class, around the school and during leisure activities, regular recorded group discussions, informal interviews and diaries'.

In the course of his research Willis did not just rely upon abstract analysis of the relationship between education and the economy, but tried to understand the experience of schooling from the perspective of the pupils. He soon found that schools were not as successful as Bowles and Gintis supposed in producing docile and conformist future workers.

The counter-school culture

The school Willis studied was situated on a working-class housing estate in a predominantly industrial small town. The main focus of his study was a group of twelve working-class boys whom he followed over their last eighteen months at school, and their first few months at work. The twelve pupils formed a friendship grouping with a distinctive attitude to school. The 'lads', as Willis refers to them, had their own **counter-school culture**, which was opposed to the values espoused by the school.

This counter-school culture had the following features. The lads felt superior both to teachers and to conformist pupils, whom they referred to as 'ear 'oles'. The lads attached little or no value to the academic work of the school and had no interest in gaining qualifications. During their time at school their main objective was to avoid going to lessons, or, when attendance was unavoidable, to do as little work as possible. They would boast about the weeks and months they could go without putting pen to paper. They resented the school trying to take control over their time – they constantly tried to win 'symbolic and physical space from the institution and its rules'.

While avoiding working, the lads kept themselves entertained with 'irreverent marauding misbehaviour'. 'Having a laff' was a particularly high priority. Willis described some of the behaviour that resulted:

> *During films in the hall they tie the projector leads into impossible knots, make animal figures or obscene shapes on the screen with their fingers, and gratuitously dig and jab the backs of the 'ear 'oles' in front of them.* Willis, 1977

Throughout school, the lads had an 'aimless air of insubordination ready with spurious justification and impossible to nail down'.

To the lads, the school equalled boredom, while the outside world, particularly the adult world, offered more possibilities for excitement. Smoking cigarettes, consuming alcohol and avoiding wearing school uniform were all ways in which they tried to identify with the adult world. Going out at night was seen as far more important than school. Many of them also had part-time jobs, which were more than just ways of earning cash: they were a means of gaining a sense of involvement in the male, adult world.

The lads' counter-culture was strongly sexist, emphasizing and valuing masculinity and downgrading femininity. It is significant that the lads regarded the ear 'oles as cissies, lacking true masculine attributes. In addition, the counter-culture was racist, seeing members of minority ethnic groups as inferior.

According to Willis, the lads were anxious to leave school at the earliest possible moment, and they looked forward eagerly to their first full-time jobs. While the ear 'oles took notice of career lessons and were concerned about the types of job they would eventually get, the lads were content to go on to any job, so long as it was a male manual job. Such jobs were considered 'real work', in contrast to the 'pen pushers' jobs which the ear 'oles were destined for. Manual labour was seen by the lads as more worthy than mental labour.

Having described the counter-school culture, Willis observes that the education system seems to be failing to manipulate the personalities of pupils to produce ideal workers. They neither deferred to authority nor were they obedient and docile. Furthermore, they did not believe it was worth striving to maximize individual achievement. Yet Willis believes, paradoxically, that the lads were well prepared for the work that they would do. It was their very rejection of school which made them suitable for male, unskilled or semi-skilled manual work.

Shop-floor culture and counter-school culture

When Willis followed the lads into their first jobs, he found important similarities between shop-floor culture and the counter-school culture. There was the same racism and sexism, the same lack of respect for authority, and the same emphasis on the worth of manual labour. Having a 'laff' was equally important in both cultures, and on the shop floor, as in the school, the maximum possible freedom was sought. The lads and their new workmates tried to control the pace at which they worked, and to win some time and space in which they were free from the tedium of work.

According to Willis, both the counter-school culture and the shop-floor culture are ways of coping with tedium and oppression. Life is made more tolerable by having a 'laff' and winning a little space from the supervisor, the manager or the teacher. In both settings, though, the challenges to authority never go too far. The lads and workers hope to gain a little freedom, but they do not challenge the institution head-on. They know that they must do a certain amount of work in the factory or risk dismissal, and they realize that the state can enforce school attendance if it is determined to do so.

Having described and compared the counter-school culture and the shop-floor culture, Willis analyses the significance of his findings for an understanding of the role of education in society.

Willis does not see the education system as simply being a successful agency of socialization which produces false class consciousness. He does believe that education reproduces the sort of labour force required by capitalism, but not directly or intentionally. The lads are not persuaded to act as they do by the school, nor are they forced to seek manual labour; rather, they actively create their own subculture, and voluntarily choose to look for manual jobs. They learn about the culture of the shop floor from fathers, elder brothers and others in the local community. They are attracted to this masculine, adult world, and respond to schooling in their own way because of its lack of relevance to their chosen future work.

Capitalism and the counter-school culture

In the final part of his book Willis discusses the significance of the counter-school culture for capitalist society. Once again he does not simply argue that the lads' culture is entirely beneficial to capitalism, nor does he think it is entirely harmful. Willis claims that in some ways the lads see through the capitalist system, but in other ways they contribute to their own exploitation and subordination.

Willis identifies a number of insights into the workings of capitalism that the lads have, which he calls **penetrations**. The lads see through at least part of the ideological smokescreen that tends to obscure the true nature of capitalism:

1 He says they recognize that capitalist society is not meritocratic. They understand that they are unlikely to be upwardly socially mobile to any great extent.
2 The lads show an appreciation of the limitations of a strategy of pursuing individual achievement for improving their own lives. Willis claims that only collective action can dramatically change the position of the working class, and in their loyalty to their mates at school or on the shop floor the lads recognize this. Collective action might create a classless society or eradicate unemployment, whereas striving for individual achievement will not.
3 The lads can see through careers advice. They know that most of the jobs likely to be available in their area require little skill, and that their studies at school will not prepare them for their work. Even if they worked hard at school, the qualifications they would get would be quite limited. They might be able to move into clerical work, or gain an apprenticeship, but the sacrifices would hardly be worth the small amount of extra pay.
4 They have come to understand the unique importance of manual labour power. In a sense they have followed in the footsteps of Karl Marx and found for themselves that it is labour power that creates wealth.

On the other hand, Willis does not believe that the lads have seen through all of the ideological justifications for capitalism. They have no overall picture of how capitalism works to exploit them, and they tend to be sexist and racist. Their attitudes to women and minority ethnic groups merely serve to divide the working class, making it easier for it to be controlled. Furthermore, the lads' willing entry into the world of manual work ultimately traps them in an exploitative situation. At school they prepare themselves to cope with manual labour, but in doing so they condemn themselves to 'a precise insertion into a system of exploitation and oppression for working-class people'.

In his wide-ranging research, then, Willis tries to show that it is the rejection of school which prepares one section of the workforce (semi-skilled and unskilled manual labourers) for its future role. This is done through the actively created and chosen counter-school culture of some working-class pupils. The reproduction of labour power through education works in an indirect and unintentional way. The lads are not simply suffering from false class consciousness – in part they understand their own alienation and exploitation – yet in the end their own choices help to trap them in some of the most exploitative jobs that capitalism has to offer. As Willis says, 'Social agents are not passive bearers of ideology, but active appropriators who reproduce existing structures only through struggle, contestation and a partial penetration of those structures.'

Paul Willis – criticism and evaluation

Undoubtedly, Willis's study has been influential. Liz Gordon (1984), for example, claims it 'has provided the model on which most subsequent cultural studies investigation within education has been based'. Furthermore, she believes it has encouraged Marxists to pay more attention to the details of what actually happens within education, and it has helped to overcome a tendency to provide oversimplified accounts of the role of education in society. Nevertheless, Willis has his critics.

David Blackledge and Barry Hunt (1985) advance three main criticisms:

1 They suggest Willis's sample is inadequate as a basis for generalizing about working-class education. Willis chose to concentrate on a mere twelve pupils, all of them male, who were by no means typical of the pupils at the school he studied, never mind of school children in the population as a whole.
2 In a related criticism Blackledge and Hunt accuse Willis of largely ignoring the existence of a whole variety of subcultures within the school. They point out that many pupils came somewhere in between the extremes of being totally conformist and being totally committed to the counter-school culture. As we will see in a later section, some interactionist studies have uncovered a wide variety of pupil subcultures and ways of reacting to school (see pp. 641–2).
3 Blackledge and Hunt suggest Willis misinterpreted some evidence. For example, by examining Willis's own evidence they argue there is little basis for claiming that the lads develop the same attitudes to work as previous generations of workers. They point to some differences between one of the lads, Joey, and his father. Joey's father took much more pride in his work than Joey, and showed much less contempt for people outside his circle of friends than Joey did.

It is also questionable how far Willis's findings would apply in contemporary Britain, where there are far fewer unskilled manual jobs available and less chance of finding employment without educational qualifications. Nevertheless, in trying to combine an ethnographic study of the school with an analysis of the role of education, Willis demonstrated how it is possible to move beyond the limited focus of most studies of education.

Glenn Rikowski – education, capitalism and globalization

Glenn Rikowski (2002, 2005) argues that the development of educational systems can be best understood within a Marxist framework. Marx claimed that the higher the development of capitalism, the more institutions of social reproduction – for example, education, health and other social services – become capitalized. This means they are transformed into commodities with the aim of producing surplus value – that is, profit. In this way, education becomes like any other commodity – a product to be bought and sold on the market. Rikowski (2005) argues that 'educational services are increasingly operating in markets' and 'being transformed into commodities'.

Marx claimed that a constant expansion of the market is necessary for the development of capitalism. As a result, there is a built-in tendency for capital to create a world market. Rikowski (2002) argues that today's globalization is 'essentially capitalist globalization'. He sees education as part of this process. Education is becoming a global commodity. As such, the driving force behind educational institutions is the generation of profit.

These developments reflect the logic of capitalism. But, although there are considerable pressures within the system to move capitalism in this direction, the process is not inevitable.

The business takeover of schools

Although there is a long way to go, Rikowski claims that the beginnings of 'the business takeover of schools' are well established. The process works as follows:

1. The state raises the finance for schools.
2. More and more of the school's functions are subcontracted to private industry.
3. Profit is made by running these functions for less than the contract price.
4. As a result, educational activities are steadily being transformed into commodities.

Rikowski points to various aspects of the Labour government's education policy to support his claims. These include:

- Increasing links betweens schools and business, particularly business sponsorship of academies.
- The marketization of schools, with schools competing in the market-place for customers.
- Schools operating increasingly as commercial enterprises – 'selling' their product and becoming successful or failing as a result of consumer demand for their services.

Rikowski argues that if this process continues unchecked, education will be privatized and will be run 'primarily for the benefit of shareholders'.

Globalization and education

Global spending on education is estimated to be around $2,000 billion (Hill, 2006a). A world market in educational services could be extremely profitable. According to Rikowski (2002), the World Trade Organization is steadily opening up educational services across the world to corporate capital, and this is being welcomed by many governments who see education as the key to success in an increasingly competitive global economy.

The UK company Nord Anglia is a forerunner in the trend that Rikowski anticipates. According to its website, the International Schools Division of Nord Anglia Education PLC 'operates schools in Eastern Europe, the Middle East and Far East and is focused on the delivery of high quality British-style education to children and young people between 2–18 years of age' (Nord Anglia, 2007).

In addition, universities are increasingly operating in a similar way to business institutions. For example, university schools of education in the UK generate large amounts of income by acting as consultants for developing school systems in countries such as Chile, Poland and Romania. Rikowski (2002) sees a global trend in which 'educational services will be progressively commercialised, privatised and capitalised'.

Opposition to global capitalism

Despite the above arguments, Rikowski is optimistic about the possibility of opposing the influence of global capitalism in education. He says: 'Education and training are implicated in the social production of the one commodity underpinning the maintenance of capitalist society: labour power. This is capitalism's "weakest link".'

Capitalism is vulnerable to educators who might 'subvert the smooth flow of labour power production by inserting principles antagonistic to the smooth flow of labour power production. Such principles include social justice, equality and solidarity for progressive social change.' Teachers are in a uniquely strong position to challenge capitalism through radical teaching.

Evaluation of Rikowski

Over the last twenty-five years, Marxist sociology has become unfashionable. Rikowski has given a new lease of life to Marxist perspectives on education. As he admits, he is looking at the beginnings of a possible trend. Is the capitalization and globalization of education the agenda for the future?

Rikowski's critics accept that schools are increasingly run on business lines, that they are exposed to market forces, that some educational services are subcontracted to the private sector, and that there is a growing market for the export of educational services. However, this is a long way from saying that education is becoming a global commodity, controlled by global capitalism for the primary purpose of generating ever-increasing profit.

Critics argue that governments control education and will do so for the foreseeable future. Schools for profit are unlikely to appear as part of present or future educational policy in the UK (Hatcher, 2005).

Education – postmodern perspectives

Robin Usher and Richard Edwards – *Postmodernism and Education*

Education and modernity

In their book *Postmodernism and Education* (1994) Robin Usher and Richard Edwards discuss the implications of postmodernism for education. They start by arguing that 'Education is very much the dutiful child of the Enlightenment and, as such, tends to uncritically accept a set of assumptions deriving from the Enlightenment.'

They refer to the work of Lyotard, the leading proponent of postmodernism (see pp. 891–2), who believed that, from the modern perspective, education promised to liberate the whole of humanity from ignorance and backwardness. According to the promises of modernity, education would help to spread the rational and scientific beliefs that would free people from the grip of tradition and superstition. Individuals had always had the potential to think for themselves and to make rational decisions, but they were prevented from doing this in premodern societies by the influence of superstition and tradition.

According to Usher and Edwards, the task of education under modernity was 'one of "bringing out", of helping to realize this potential, so that subjects became fully autonomous and capable of exercising their individual and intentional agency'. Within modernity, education is the key to developing individuals and, in doing so, making social progress possible.

Usher and Edwards follow writers such as Lyotard in arguing that modernity is characterized by a belief in **metanarratives** of human progress (see pp. 891–2 for a discussion of metanarratives). It is education which expresses and disseminates the big stories about progress and helps to give people their belief in progress itself and their faith in science and reason as the ways of achieving it.

Postmodernism/postmodernity and education

If Usher and Edwards are fairly clear about the close relationship between education and modernity, they are less clear about its relationship with postmodernity. Indeed, they are rather unclear about what postmodernity is. They say:

> *To talk about postmodernity, postmodernism or the postmodern is not therefore to designate some fixed and systematic 'thing'. Rather, it is to use a loose umbrella term under whose broad cover can be encompassed at one and the same time a condition, a set of practices, a cultural discourse, an attitude and a mode of analysis.* Usher and Edwards, 1994

If it is unclear what postmodernism, postmodernity and the postmodern are, it is clearer what they are against. They are opposed to any belief that there is a firm foundation to knowledge; they are critical of any attempt to impose one version of the truth on people; and they are against believing that science and rationality can solve all human problems. Thus, Usher and Edwards say, 'postmodernism teaches us to be sceptical of foundationalism in all its forms, of totalizing and definitive explanations and theories and thus of the dominant taken-for-granted paradigms in education, whether these be liberal, conservative or progressive'.

Postmodernism would therefore be suspicious of grand claims such as the following:

- Human potential can be achieved through education.
- Education can produce shared values and social solidarity.
- Education can produce equality of opportunity and a just society.

To Usher and Edwards, postmodernism also denies that there is any single best curriculum that should be followed in schools. If there is no one set of truths that can be accepted, then there is no basis for saying that one thing should be taught in all schools whereas other things should be excluded. Instead, Usher and Edwards argue that education should teach many different things and should accept that there can be different truths. Rather than providing any definitive blueprint for education, postmodernism simply suggests there should be no attempt to impose one set of ideas on all education.

The future of education

How then might the education system develop? Usher and Edwards outline four possibilities:

1. Modern education systems could continue. The view that education can help individuals fulfil their potential could be retained and the current education system could continue largely unchanged.
2. The education system could be reshaped so that it tried to stress traditional values and to impose one set of values on everybody. This could occur as a reaction to the uncertainty and differences between people, which are part of postmodernity.
3. Education could be shaped to reflect the capitalist system. The content of education could be modified so that the primary emphasis is upon knowledge that is useful and helps to make a profit, rather than the main emphasis being on seeking truth. This has some affinity with postmodernism in that it defines knowledge in terms of usefulness rather than truth (see Lyotard's views on the changing nature of knowledge, pp. 891–2), but it still imposes one version of how education should be developed, rather than accepting that education can encompass variety.
4. The final possibility is that education could reflect aspects of postmodernism by taking account of **cultural pluralism** – the cultures and needs of different groups. It could acknowledge the importance to individuals of shaping their own education to meet their personal needs and wishes. Usher and Edwards

say, 'Examples here might be the emphasis on lifelong learning, the recognition and exploration of cultural difference, of educational provision for and by marginalized and oppressed groups.'

This would not entirely remove modern elements from the education system. For example, teaching people to be tolerant and accepting of people from different cultures could be seen as part of the modern, humanist, liberal tradition, which tries to use education to turn individuals into better people.

Nevertheless, it would go some way towards undermining what Usher and Edwards see as the elitism of modern education. According to them, modern education was largely run by and for dominant groups such as white, wealthy males. If pluralism were accepted and minority interests catered for, this would no longer be the case.

The fourth possibility generally finds favour with Usher and Edwards, but they are careful not to put it forward as a definitive statement of how postmodern education should develop. They are conscious of trying to avoid the 'danger of simply replacing one totalizing, oppressive discourse with another ... Therefore any reconfiguration is provisional and open to question.'

Nevertheless, they do concede that different educations are necessary for different people, including groups who are relatively powerless and currently have little influence on the education system.

Robin Usher, Ian Bryant and Rennie Johnston – postmodernism and adult education

In *Adult Education and the Postmodern Challenge* (1997), Robin Usher, writing on this occasion with Ian Bryant and Rennie Johnston, focuses upon postmodernism and adult education. This book reiterates many of the points made in the earlier work by Usher and Edwards. It contrasts the nature of modernity and postmodernity, discusses how postmodernity undermines claims to a single truth, and suggests this will lead to greater diversity within education. However, it goes further in suggesting how elements of postmodernism have already become evident in adult education, and it extends the analysis to discuss how adult education is linked to postmodern consumption.

According to Usher *et al.*, adult education has been particularly responsive to the postmodern trend towards greater choice and diversity. Compared to schooling, there is much more use of flexible and distance learning. This allows greater tailoring of the content and pace of education to meet individual needs.

Postmodernity is characterized by the **decentring of knowledge**: a move away from seeing any particular knowledge as central to all knowledge and superior to other forms of knowledge. This is reflected in the vast range of courses provided for adults by educational institutions. It is also reflected in increased uncertainty about what adult education is for. Liberal adult education, designed to develop people's potential as human beings or to encourage certain humanistic values, competes with a more vocational model which sees adult education as preparation for work. However, both models are beginning to be challenged by education becoming simply another form of consumption.

Education, consumption and identity

According to Usher *et al.*, postmodernism involves a **decentring of the self**. People no longer have a single, overarching sense of identity, of who they are. People's class, religion, place of birth, nationality and so on no longer define, on their own, who people are and how they see themselves. People are increasingly free to create their own identities and to change them almost at will. They do this partly by consuming different products, from the vast array of consumer products available, and by choosing particular lifestyles.

Increasingly, adult education has become simply another consumer product involved in lifestyle choices. Thus, for example, a woman may choose to study Italian to give herself a more cosmopolitan and sophisticated identity; or alternative therapies such as acupuncture because she wants to identify herself with New Age lifestyles. (See pp. 695–9 for a discussion of postmodern identities, and pp. 455–6 for a discussion of the New Age.) In these circumstances, adult education becomes more of a playful, leisure activity, rather than the purposive, goal-oriented activity it was under modernity. Usher *et al.* say:

> *As education in the postmodern becomes detached from legitimizing grand narratives, it becomes increasingly implicated with specific cultural contexts, on localized and particularistic knowledges, on the needs of consumption and the cultivation of desire and on the valuing of a multiplicity of experience as an integral part of defining a lifestyle ... In postmodernity knowledge is valued for its 'interest' and its role in supporting the play of difference.*
> Usher *et al.*, 1997

However, Usher *et al.* also acknowledge that another trend within postmodernism is for knowledge to become a commodity that can be bought and sold. Knowledge is also valued if it is useful and can therefore be exchanged for money in the labour market. Knowledge is no longer valued because it provides 'the truth', though, or because it helps to make people more rational. Essentially, enjoying yourself and making money become most important to people.

Modern educators and intellectuals might scoff at these concerns as being unimportant, trivial and lacking in seriousness. Usher *et al.* do not agree. Indeed, they believe postmodern education can play an important role in helping oppressed groups. Because of its openness, it gives a chance for education to feature the concerns of the oppressed.

Furthermore, being able to consume is important to many groups trying to escape from disadvantage and oppression. Usher *et al.* say, 'There are many examples of oppressed groups who see empowerment in terms of the increased consumption of desired goods and images; as adult educators we ought to recognize this and at the very least not deny it.'

According to Usher *et al.*, adult education is no longer a well-defined field with clear goals. It increasingly overlaps with other areas of life, including leisure and work, and has a multiplicity of meanings and purposes for those involved.

Michael W. Apple – postmodernism, education, power and economics

The problems with postmodernism

Michael W. Apple (1997, first published 1993) welcomes some aspects of the postmodern perspective. He agrees, for example, that it may be misleading to believe that a single grand theory or metanarrative can explain everything about education, and he agrees that issues such as consumption and identity are increasingly important in contemporary societies. However, he also believes that postmodernists concentrate too much on local struggles over education and in doing so lose sight of the bigger picture. He claims that, while postmodernists focus on 'clever rhetorical and cultural battles … over what counts as "appropriate" knowledge and what counts as "appropriate" forms of teaching and knowing', the education system as a whole is being shaped by wider political and economic forces. Postmodernists tend to ignore these forces and therefore neglect the sorts of insights into education offered by Marxists.

While Apple himself would not like to see Marxist perspectives emphasized to the exclusion of postmodern ones, he does not believe that the postmodern approach can afford to ignore what he calls the 'political economy' of education. While postmodernists and cultural theorists are busy arguing among themselves, the education system is being shaped by powerful political and economic forces.

At times Apple is somewhat scathing about aspects of postmodernism and the cultural theory that it uses, saying: 'It moves from theory to theory rapidly, often seemingly assuming that the harder something is to understand or the more it rests on European cultural theory (preferably French) the better it is.' In the process, it 'has often lost any but the most rhetorical connections with the multiple struggles against domination and subordination'.

Power relationships

Apple gives an example of the sort of power relationships ignored by postmodernists. He claims that those types of knowledge that are valued by postmodernists, particularly cultural theory, are not particularly highly valued or important in the exercise of power. Instead, he believes 'technical/administrative knowledge' has been given the highest value, and the possession of such knowledge is used by people to gain positions of power and influence.

This type of knowledge is the type deployed in running large corporations in a competitive global economy. Apple says:

> *An advanced corporate economy requires the production of high levels of technical/administrative knowledge because of national and international economic competition, and to become more sophisticated in the maximization of opportunities for economic expansion, for communicative and cultural control and nationalization, and so forth.* Apple, 1997

Students learn this sort of knowledge when being educated in rapidly developing subjects such as market research and human relations. In the USA there have been cuts in humanities and arts subjects while business-related subjects have been expanding.

However, perhaps the most significant US example of this sort of trend is the TV programme *Channel One*. *Channel One* provides 'news' and commercials. It supplies free videos and TVs to each classroom and a satellite dish for schools which agree that over a three- to five-year period at least 90 per cent of pupils will watch at least 90 per cent of the broadcasts. The schools are monitored to ensure that they comply with the agreement. The offer is hard for cash-strapped schools to refuse and *Channel One* has been very successful. However, *Channel One* broadcasts essentially pro-capitalist, pro-business propaganda and in doing so is shaping the way school children see the world.

Apple concludes that social scientists should not allow postmodernism to make them forget the extent to which capitalism and economic power shape the world. He argues that the way contemporary societies are run 'is still capitalism and that makes a difference to our daily lives', and he says: 'The world may be a text, but some groups seem to be able to write their lines on our lives more easily than others.'

Postmodernism and education – evaluation and conclusion

Because postmodernists are anxious to attack all grand theories (or metanarratives), they try to avoid claiming that their approach is a coherent theory at all. It is largely based upon criticizing other approaches. Nevertheless, postmodernists are unable to avoid putting forward some of their own views, but it is often unclear what exactly they are trying to say.

For example, there is often ambiguity over whether they are describing changes in the education system or advocating change in a particular direction, or both.

It can be argued that, whichever is being claimed, there are serious problems with their analysis. For example, if their ideas are seen as descriptions of actual changes in education, then they may be inaccurate. Developments in the British education system have in some respects (such as the National Curriculum) involved the centralization of power in the hands of the government rather than increased diversity and choice. Some social scientists question whether policies purportedly designed to achieve greater consumer choice have actually had such an effect (see pp. 618–21).

Postmodernists advance little empirical evidence to support the claim that adult education has become about choice of lifestyle rather than gaining qualifications for work. For sociologists such as Apple, commercialization and commodification of education are more important trends than consumer choice.

If their theories are more about how they would like to see the education system change, then they ignore powerful economic and political forces which may work to prevent the sort of changes they would like to see. If education is increasingly dominated by business, then it is unlikely that the curriculum will be increasingly influenced by the interests of local, oppressed groups. Feminists, gay rights activists, anti-racists, campaigners for disabled rights and so on may influence some university courses, but they are unlikely to be able to shape mainstream schooling. Furthermore, as Apple implies, qualifications relating to these sorts of subjects are unlikely to produce knowledge that has the same status and power as qualifications related to business.

Education – social democratic perspectives

The social democratic perspective is a political ideology which has had a major influence on the development of Western democracies. It has also influenced sociological thinking. This can be seen in the sociology of education.

From a social democratic perspective, the state should represent the interests of the population as a whole. This requires a democratic system in which adult members of society elect those who govern them. Democracy is seen as the best way to ensure equal rights – for example, every citizen is equal under the law – and to ensure equal opportunity – every member of society has an equal chance of becoming successful.

In some respects, social democratic views are similar to functionalism. Both see education as a means towards equality of opportunity, and both see education as essential for economic growth. However, many social democrats argue that inequalities in society can (1) prevent equality of educational opportunity, and (2) reduce the effectiveness of education in promoting economic growth.

Social democratic views have had an important influence on the sociology of education, particularly during the 1960s. And they continue to have a major influence on government educational policy in the UK.

Equality of opportunity

Social democrats such as the British sociologist A.H. Halsey argued that the inequalities produced by a free market economy prevented equality of opportunity. It was clear that those who succeeded in the educational system tended to be the sons and daughters of the middle classes, and those who failed were disproportionately from working-class backgrounds. The class system appeared to stand in the way of equal opportunity.

Social democrats believe in a **meritocracy** – a society in which a person's status is achieved on the basis of merit, on their talent and motivation. For a meritocracy to operate effectively, equality of opportunity is essential. Could equality of educational opportunity be provided by reforming the educational system?

In the 1960s, around two-thirds of pupils from middle-class backgrounds attended grammar schools at age 11, compared with only a quarter of pupils from working-class backgrounds. A grammar school education was the route to further and higher education and to high-status, well-paid jobs. Most young people went to secondary modern schools. They were mainly working-class and they were usually seen as educational failures. Clearly, selection at age 11 favoured the middle-class child and did not provide equality of educational opportunity. (The tripartite system of secondary education is examined in detail later in the chapter, see p. 616.)

From a social democratic perspective, this was both unfair and inefficient. It was unfair because it discriminated against working-class pupils. It was inefficient because it did not develop their talents. This 'wastage of talent' failed to produce the highly educated workforce required by a modern industrial economy.

During the 1960s and 1970s, many social democrats argued that a change in the system of secondary education would promote equality of opportunity. Some saw the comprehensive system as the answer – one type of schooling for all. Selection at age 11 would stop and young people from all social classes would receive the same type of education in the same type of schools (except for those in private schools).

Economic growth

According to social democrats, education has a major role to play in economic growth. Halsey *et al.* (1961) stated that:

> *Education is a crucial type of investment for the exploitation of modern technology. In advanced industrial societies it is inevitable that the education system should come into a closer relationship with the economy ... as the proportion of the labour force engaged in manual work declines and the demand for white-collar, professional and managerial workers rises.* Halsey et *al.*, 1961, pp. 1–2

Equality of educational opportunity would make society more meritocratic. It would provide everyone with the opportunity to develop their potential and so maximize their contribution to the economy. In doing so, they would make greater contributions to economic growth which would bring prosperity to all.

Evaluation of social democratic theory

Equality of opportunity

According to social democratic theory, social class is the main barrier to equality of opportunity. The class system prevents education from providing equal opportunity for all young people. There are two main solutions to this problem: first, changing the education system in order to provide all students with an equal chance to succeed; second, changing the class system by reducing the social inequalities which divide society.

Despite attempts by governments to address both of these problems, there has been little change in class differences in educational attainment from the 1940s to the present day. As Britain becomes richer and standards of living for all steadily increase, the gap between the rich and the poor remains basically unchanged. And so does the class gap in educational attainment.

Changes in the educational system have provided greater opportunities – for example, the proportion of young people going on to higher education has increased rapidly. Despite this, the class gap in achieving a place in higher education has grown even wider. It is the sons and daughters of the middle classes who have gained most from the expansion of university places (see p. 626).

Social democratic theory has been criticized for placing too much importance on changing the education system as a means of reducing inequality of educational opportunity. Over the past sixty years, changes in primary, secondary, further and higher education do not appear to have reduced class differences in educational attainment. It appears, in the words of the British sociologist Basil Bernstein (1971), that 'education cannot compensate for society'. In other words, education cannot make up for inequalities in the wider society.

Many social democrats now argue that only a reduction in social inequality in society as a whole can reduce inequality in educational opportunity. Attempts by governments to create a more equal society have largely failed. Although living standards have risen for all members of society, the gap between top and bottom remains largely unchanged.

Economic growth

Does education promote economic growth as social democratic theory claims? Critics make the following points.

First, the school curriculum often fails to meet the requirements of employers. It is not designed to provide the skills needed for economic growth.

Second, more education does not necessarily lead to more growth in the economy. Alison Woolf (2002) analysed educational expenditure and economic growth in a number of countries. She found that, 'among the most successful economies, there is in fact no clear link between growth and spending on education'. In Switzerland, for example, expenditure on education is relatively low, but in terms of per capita income it is one of the richest countries in the world. Among less developed countries, Egypt massively expanded its education spending between 1980 and 1995, but failed to improve its economic position relative to other countries.

Woolf does not believe that all educational expenditure is wasted. As well as acknowledging the importance of high-quality primary and secondary education, she believes it is important to provide 'first-rate facilities' for 'first-rate students'. She believes that trying to educate a larger proportion of the population to degree level limits spending on the most able, who could contribute most to economic growth through, for example, pioneering research.

Despite such criticism, many sociologists and all governments see more education for more people as vital for economic growth in an increasingly competitive global economy. As competition intensifies, growth is seen to be increasingly dependent on the development of scientific knowledge, technological innovation, and a more highly skilled workforce. And education is seen as crucial for these developments (Lauder *et al.*, 2006).

Education – neoliberal/New Right perspectives

Education and the market

The terms neoliberal (or market liberal) and New Right refer to political ideologies rather than sociological theories. They are often used interchangeably.

Neoliberal/New Right perspectives are partly based on theories derived from economics, particularly those that advocate market systems as a way of distributing resources. Market systems are driven by individuals making decisions about what to buy or consume. Because consumers have a choice, the providers or producers of the goods or services have to respond to the preferences of consumers. If they fail to do so, consumers will go elsewhere and the providers/producers will go out of business.

Publicly funded education, however, has not generally been provided by commercial enterprises, but instead has been run by bureaucracies which are accountable to elected politicians.

Some theorists, known as **public choice theorists** – such as J. Buchanan and G. Tullock (1962) – argue that bureaucracy and democracy are likely to produce inefficient and ineffective services in which *producers* rather than *consumers* tend to dominate decision making.

Public services often act as a monopoly: consumers cannot freely choose an alternative provider of free education, health services or refuse collection. Furthermore, because they are publicly funded, the providers cannot go out of business. They therefore have little incentive to respond to the needs of consumers. Instead, it is the needs of the producers which tend to dominate decision making: **producer capture** takes place. For example, education comes to reflect the interests of teachers and the bureaucrats who run the system, rather than the consumers – the pupils and parents – whom the system is intended to benefit.

According to public choice theory, everyone acts according to their own interests. Politicians want votes, teachers and bureaucrats want secure jobs, and it is their interests which become dominant in conventional state education systems. As a result, state expenditure on education increases, which results in rising taxes. This in turn damages the economy. Businesses end up being over-taxed and unable to compete with businesses in other countries. At the same time pupils and parents have little control over education. They have to accept the state education that is on offer and they have little chance to change or shape it. However, neoliberal/New Right thinkers believe that if competition and market systems are introduced into education all of these problems can be remedied.

Among the most influential advocates of the introduction of market forces into education are the US political scientists Chubb and Moe, whose work will now be discussed.

John E. Chubb and Terry M. Moe – 'Politics, markets and the organization of schools'

In their article 'Politics, markets and the organization of schools' (1997, first published 1988), Chubb and Moe put forward their case for the introduction of market forces into education. They argue that problems such as 'declining test scores, loose academic standards and lax discipline' can only be solved through a move towards a market system within education.

Public and private schools

In order to support their arguments, Chubb and Moe compare how public schools (in the USA, state-run schools are called public schools) and private schools are run.

Public schools 'are controlled by democratic authority and administration'. Although individual schools have their own elected school boards, state and federal government play a crucial role in the overall direction of schooling. In any public school, therefore, a wide range of people can be seen as the 'constituents' – that is, the people who have a legitimate say in how the school should be run. These include local and national politicians and administrators, students, parents, and citizens in general, who vote in elections or pay taxes.

Public education is not supposed to be responsive simply to the needs of those who use the services of the school; it is intended to serve wider public purposes as determined by politicians. Usually, the only way of influencing school policy is through expressing your opinion and hoping that your views are taken into account by those in authority. In theory it is possible for the parents of public-sector children to take their children out of the school. However, there are usually only two ways of doing this. One is to pay for private schooling, but many parents are not willing to do this or cannot afford it. The other is to move house to an area with a school that the parents prefer. Moving house, though, involves considerable cost, and many factors other than the quality of the local school influence where people choose to live.

Schools themselves tend to have little freedom and autonomy under a public system of this type because they are accountable to a large group of constituents. These constituents all have their own self-interests and sometimes these will conflict with the interests and wishes of parents and pupils. Politicians need to attract support in order to win elections. To do this they must try to take actions which take account of the wishes of a variety of interest groups. The better organized the interest groups, the more likely they are to influence the government. Chubb and Moe argue that these interest groups:

> *include teachers' unions and associations of administrators, but also a vast array of groups representing more specialized interests – those of minorities, the handicapped, bilingual education, drivers' education, schools of education, book publishers, and accrediting and testing organizations among them.* Chubb and Moe, 1997

Generally, these groups have a vested interest in maintaining existing educational systems, since change costs them money and might undermine their position in the education system. They all want as big a share as possible of the public money that funds education.

The government bureaucrats who run the education system also have 'incentives to expand their budgets, programmes, and administrative controls'. These vested interests tend to undermine the autonomy of schools, restricting their ability to respond to the needs and wishes of parents. At the same time they encourage ever-increasing expenditure on a school system which is unlikely to be providing what parents want.

Private schools have a great deal more room for manoeuvre than public ones. Instead of being shaped by a diverse group of constituents, they are responsible to a smaller and more clearly defined group of consumers: the parents who are paying the fees for children to attend the school. These consumers have two ways of influencing school policies. The most direct way is to remove their children from the school or to choose a different school for their children to attend in the first place. Because schools rely upon the fees paid by parents, this creates a strong incentive for the schools to change if they are failing to attract sufficient pupils.

Because they need to please their clientele in order to survive, private schools have good reason to consult parents and listen to what they have to say. Because they need the fees, they are much more likely to create a match between what they provide and what parents are looking for. Furthermore, private schools are not constrained by governmental and bureaucratic interference. They have much more freedom to change and adapt to what their customers want. Also, they have incentives to keep costs down. The cheaper the fees, the more customers they will attract, so long as they can keep providing the sort of high-quality education that parents want. The fact that parents are willing to pay for private education when they could get free public education demonstrates that private schools must be successful in meeting parents' needs.

Evidence

Chubb and Moe support their claims with research evidence. They collected data from 60,000 students in more than 1,000 schools, and in about 500 of these schools they also collected data from thirty teachers, the principal and some other staff members. They found that private schools were less likely than public ones to be responsible to outside administrators; they were more likely to be closely controlled by school boards; and they had more freedom to hire and fire staff. They also found that parents tended to be more supportive of the private schools and their aims than parents of children in public schools; that staff were more satisfied with the leadership of the principal in the private sector; and that private schools had clearer goals.

Conclusion

Chubb and Moe conclude that public schools must become subject to the same sorts of incentives for improvement and responsiveness as schools in the private sector. Power needs to be decentralized 'to the producers and immediate consumers of educational services', so that schools can get on with providing the sort of education their customers want.

Chubb and Moe suggest this could be achieved through a **voucher system**. All parents could be given a voucher entitling them to purchase for their children education of a value determined by the government. This would encourage public and private sector schools to compete in an open market for children to attend their schools. Successful schools could grow, while the unsuccessful would need to improve to survive. All schools would become more flexible and responsive, although Chubb and Moe concede that 'broad democratic guidance' would be needed to oversee the system.

Education and globalization

Neoliberal/New Right thinkers argue that their views are particularly relevant to success in the global market. These views are summarized by Brown and Lauder (1997) and Lauder *et al.* (2006).

A global economy

The market for goods and services is increasingly global and increasingly competitive. New technology and new knowledge are essential for economic success. A nation's competitiveness in the global arena depends on the skills and knowledge of its workers. The primary purpose of education is to develop these skills and instil this knowledge.

Competition and choice

Raising standards in education is the key to economic success. The way to achieve this is **marketization** – educational institutions must be subject to market forces. This involves competition and choice. Schools must compete for customers in a free and open market. This means that a choice of schools must be available to parents. This will improve standards, as parents will send their children to the most successful schools, and schools will now have an incentive to improve their standards in response to consumer demand. In a marketized education system, public money follows parents' choices, giving successful schools the funds to expand and failing schools an incentive to improve or face closure.

For an educational market to work efficiently, data on the standards achieved by schools must be widely available. Without this, parents, students and politicians cannot make informed decisions. Testing regimes must be put in place to provide information on which to base choice. Students must be regularly assessed and the results published. Schools can then be directly compared and ranked in 'league tables'. Measuring school performance is essential for informed choice and for raising standards.

Criticisms of neoliberal/New Right perspectives on education

Educational markets are unfair

Even with a voucher system it would be misleading to believe that parents would be genuinely equal in the educational market. Some parents have more knowledge and understanding of the education system and more money. They are in a better position to manipulate education markets to get the most out of them.

For example, middle-class parents will be more likely to get their children into the schools with the best reputations, or they will be able to afford to pay for them to attend successful private schools.

Raising standards

Will competition and choice raise standards? A detailed study of evidence from the USA indicates the following. Based on the findings of twenty-five separate studies, the evidence suggests that competition and choice do produce small improvements in student achievement (Levin and Belfield, 2006). However, these 'modest' improvements are well below the levels expected by supporters of market approaches.

Will this modest improvement be spread evenly across the student population, or will some gain more than others? Evidence from the USA suggests that market approaches will lead to greater social inequalities – in particular, the children of higher income parents will gain most, leading to a wider attainment gap between rich and poor (Levin and Belfield, 2006).

Neoliberal/New Right ideas have been widely applied in New Zealand. In some, largely working-class, low-achieving schools, student numbers did decline. But this was mainly because middle-class students moved to schools with higher reputations, leaving their working-class counterparts behind in inferior schools (Lauder *et al.*, 1999).

Selection by schools

In an open market, consumer choice may sometimes result in provider choice. In terms of education, this may lead to schools (the providers) choosing pupils, rather than parents (the consumers) choosing schools. For example, the most successful schools may not have enough places for all the pupils who wish to attend. This means that schools must select (Ranson, 1996).

Given their desire to remain at the top of the league table, there is a pressure on these schools to select those they see as the most able pupils. Such pupils are usually seen as those from middle-class backgrounds. This process is sometimes known as **cream-skimming** or **creaming** (Bartlett and Le Grand, 1993).

Education as a means to an end

Some critics believe that the marketization of education leads to a narrow view of education as a means to an end. For example, Stewart Ranson (1996) argues that markets are based upon the assumption that each individual will pursue an 'instrumental rationality' in which their sole concern will be to maximize their own self-interest. Ranson believes that when individuals act in this way it is because the market encourages them to do so. It undermines values that stress the importance of selflessness and cooperation with others.

Increasingly, a school's success in the market is judged on its test results – its results in Key Stage tests, GCSEs and A levels. There is pressure on both schools and pupils to see examination success as the focus of education. This is a very narrow view of education. It largely ignores major issues and debates, the idea of knowledge for its own sake, and the view that education is about understanding the world and about developing the potential of each pupil.

Neoliberal/New Right perspectives see the major role of education as the development of the skills and knowledge required to compete in the market. This encourages students to see knowledge as information which can be converted into memory, and examination success as a means of obtaining a well-paid job (Lauder *et al.*, 2006).

Educational policy in the UK, 1945–97

This section looks at education policy in the UK from 1945 to 1997. It pays particular attention to the influence of two major perspectives – social democracy and neoliberalism/the New Right – on government policy.

Educational policy, 1945–79

Social democracy provided the framework for educational policy from 1945 to 1979. The social democratic perspective was outlined earlier (see pp. 612–13). The main points are summarized below.

- Society should be based on justice and fairness.
- This means that everyone should have an equal chance to succeed. In other words, society should be meritocratic – there should be equality of opportunity for all.
- Education has an important part to play in a meritocracy. It should provide all young people with an equal chance to develop their talents.
- This will lead to a better educated and more highly skilled workforce. This, in turn, will lead to greater productivity and economic growth.
- As a result, living standards will rise.

The tripartite system

The 1944 Education Act was strongly influenced by social democratic principles. It aimed to provide equality of opportunity for all young people. The school leaving age was raised to 15 and the tripartite system of secondary education was introduced. This system consisted of three types of school: grammar schools for academic pupils, technical schools for those with an aptitude for technical subjects, and secondary modern schools for pupils seen to be best suited to practical tasks and manual jobs.

The tripartite system was introduced to provide separate but equal schools for pupils of different abilities and aptitudes. Each type of school was to have **'parity of esteem'** – equal status – with similar funding, and buildings, equipment and staffing of similar quality. Pupils took an exam – the eleven-plus – to discover which type of school they were suited for.

Criticisms of the tripartite system

1. Grammar schools, attended by around 20 per cent of young people, were seen as the most prestigious type of secondary school. They specialized in academic subjects which led to high-status, well-paid jobs. Secondary modern schools, attended by most young people (around 75 per cent), were seen as low-status institutions. Parity of esteem did not exist.
2. The system wasted talent. Many secondary modern students were not allowed to take O levels, which meant their education finished at the age of 15. They were denied the opportunity to progress further. This prevented many from realizing their potential and from making a full contribution to the economy.
3. One of the main aims of the 1944 Education Act was to increase the opportunities of working-class pupils. Yet the social class divide remained. For example, two-thirds of boys from middle-class backgrounds went to grammar schools but only a quarter of working-class boys (Halsey *et al.*, 1980).

The comprehensive system

By the 1960s, it was clear to many that the tripartite system was wasting talent. The education and skills needed for economic growth were not being provided. Nor was the equality of educational opportunity which the 1944 Act looked forward to. The comprehensive system offered a possible solution. It would provide a single form of state secondary education for all. There would be one type of school – the comprehensive school – for pupils of all backgrounds and all abilities who would be offered the same opportunities to obtain qualifications and training.

Supporters of comprehensive education believed that it would reduce social class differences in educational attainment. But, despite an improvement in the educational qualifications of all school leavers, class differences remained largely unchanged.

A more equal society

It appeared that social class prevented equality of educational opportunity. In other words, class inequality led to inequality in educational opportunity. Some social democrats argued that the only way to move towards equal opportunity was to reduce social inequality in society as a whole. One way to do this was to target resources on the most disadvantaged.

This was the thinking behind **Educational Priority Areas** in the late 1960s. Additional resources were provided for low income areas in England, in the hope of raising standards. The emphasis was on pre-school and primary education. Although it was difficult to evaluate the results, the available evidence suggests that Educational Priority Areas produced little change (Midwinter, 1975). However, governments have continued with this type of policy to the present day.

Conservative educational policy, 1979–97

Neoliberal/New Right policies became increasingly influential during the Conservative governments of 1979 to 1997. These policies were outlined earlier (see pp. 613–16), but they are briefly summarized below with reference to educational policy.

- Education should be mainly concerned with promoting economic growth through improving the skills of the workforce.
- The best way to achieve this is to encourage competition in the educational market-place. The introduction of market forces will make schools more efficient and raise standards.
- Competition will only work if parents have a real choice between schools. They will select the most successful schools for their children. The greater the competition, the greater the incentive for schools to improve. Unsuccessful schools will either have to raise their standards or face the possibility of closure.
- Parents must have a means of assessing the quality of schools. This is provided by government inspections and a rigorous system of testing pupils. The results of these inspections and tests must be made available to parents so that they can make an informed choice.

Schooling

The Education Reform Act of 1988 was the most far-reaching legislation since the 1944 Education Act. It introduced the following measures:

1. **Grant maintained schools**. State schools were allowed to opt out of local authority control if sufficient parents voted to support this move. Known as grant maintained schools, they were funded directly by central government. The idea was to free schools to specialize in particular subjects or particular types of pupils. This, it was hoped, would offer diversity and real choice for parents, and encourage schools to compete in the educational market-place.
2. **City technology colleges**. Diversity, choice and competition were to be extended by the introduction of city technology colleges. Financed by central government and private industry, they would focus on maths, science and technology. They were to be built mainly in inner-city areas, for 11- to 18-year-old students, and they were to compete with existing schools. In the 1990s, the Conservatives introduced two further types of schools: schools specializing in either languages or technology. They were called colleges to indicate their prestige and importance. By 1996, there were 1,100 grant maintained schools, accounting for one in five of all secondary students. There were 15 city technology colleges, 30 language colleges and 151 new technology colleges (Chitty, 2002).
3. **Open enrolment**. Parents were given the right to send their children to the school of their choice. This would encourage schools to compete and improve their results.
4. **Formula funding**. Under this new system of funding, the financing of schools was largely based on the number of enrolments. This was intended to reward successful schools which attracted large numbers of pupils, while giving less successful schools an incentive to improve.
5. **National Curriculum**. For the first time, the government told teachers in England and Wales what to teach, and provided tests – Key Stage tests for pupils at age 7, 11 and 14 – in order to assess parts of the National Curriculum. These tests were also used to assess teachers and schools. The results were to form part of the published material designed to provide parents with information on which to base their choice of school.
6. **Testing and assessment**. The testing and assessment process introduced by the 1988 Education Act was developed during the 1990s. In 1992, state secondary schools in England and Wales were required to publish their Key Stage, GCSE and A level results. In 1997, primary schools were required to publish their Key Stage results. Local and national league tables of schools were based on these results. They were intended to provide parents with information so that they could make an informed choice of school, and to intensify competition between schools by encouraging them to improve their position in the league.

   In 1993, the Office for Standards in Education (Ofsted) was set up to inspect schools in England and Wales. All schools were to be inspected every four years and a report published on the quality of teaching and the standard achieved. Ofsted reports provided further information for the assessment of schools.

Vocational education and training

Conservative governments from 1979 to 1997 aimed to develop a vocational education and training system to meet the needs of industry. Until the 1970s, **vocational training** – training for work – was seen as the responsibility of employers. This view began to change in the 1970s with the rapid rise in youth unemployment. Many argued that this rise was largely due to schools failing to teach appropriate work skills to young people. As a result, industry faced a skills shortage. A number of measures were designed to solve this problem. They included the following:

1. **National Vocational Qualifications (NVQs)**. In 1986, the National Council for Vocational Qualifications was set up to introduce standardized vocational qualifications for particular occupations. By 1990, around 170 NVQs had been established.
2. **General National Vocational Qualifications (GNVQs)**. More general vocational qualifications covering wider areas – for example, leisure and tourism, and health and social care – were available from 1995. They were intended to provide a vocational alternative to traditional academic qualifications such as GCSEs and A levels.
3. **Modern apprenticeships**. From 1995, these programmes combined training at work with part-time attendance at college, with the aim of achieving an NVQ qualification at Level 3 (equivalent to A level).

4 **The new vocationalism**. This term was used to describe new vocational training initiatives introduced in the 1970s and aimed initially at unemployed young people. Started by the Labour government in the early 1970s, they were developed by the Conservatives. For example, the Youth Training Scheme (YTS) was a one-year training scheme for school leavers, combining work experience with education. In 1986, YTS was extended to a two-year scheme. YTS was replaced in 1990 with Youth Training. The only requirement in this scheme was for employers to ensure that trainees followed some sort of training programme which led towards a Level 2 NVQ.

Evaluating educational policy, 1979–97

This section examines sociological studies which have attempted to evaluate the effects of changes in educational policy from 1979 to 1997. These studies were all conducted when the Conservatives were in power. However, in some respects, they are also relevant to evaluating Labour policies after 1997, since Labour retained many of the competitive, market-based reforms introduced by the Conservatives.

Stephen J. Ball, Richard Bowe and Sharon Gewirtz – competitive advantage and parental choice

Between 1991 and 1994, Stephen Ball, Richard Bowe and Sharon Gewirtz conducted a study of fifteen schools in three neighbouring local educational authorities (LEAs) (Ball *et al.*, 1994; Gewirtz *et al.*, 1995). The study included a mixture of LEA-controlled schools, grant maintained schools, two church schools and a city technology college (CTC). The institutions served a variety of areas, some with mainly middle-class populations and some with a higher concentration of working-class residents. Some areas had substantial minority ethnic populations and others did not.

Ball *et al.* visited the schools, attended meetings, examined documents and interviewed a sample of teachers. They also interviewed about 150 parents who had children in primary schools and were at the point of making the choice about the secondary schools their children should attend. In addition, they interviewed some primary head teachers and examined LEA documents about changing patterns of choice. Ball *et al.*'s study attempted to discover the effects that parental choice and the encouragement of competition between schools were having on the education system, and particularly on opportunities for different social groups.

The effects on schools

The study found that the changes were having significant effects on secondary schools. This was particularly true of those schools that were under-subscribed: they had to try to do something to arrest their decline. More successful schools could afford to be fairly complacent, but they too were starting to change some of their practices.

Most schools were 'paying a lot more attention to what parents want for their children's education. Or more precisely what schools think that parents want.' However, it was not the case that schools were equally keen to attract all students. The publication of league tables meant that schools were much more keen to attract academically able pupils who would boost the school's league table performance and thus improve its reputation. According to Ball *et al.*, 'There is a shift of emphasis from student needs to student performance: from what the school can do for the students to what the student can do for the school.'

This emphasis has encouraged some schools to reintroduce streaming and setting and to direct more resources to children who are likely to be successful in examinations and tests. In some cases, it has led to pupils being seen as commodities by the school.

As schools have concentrated on the more able pupils, they have paid less attention to those with Special Educational Needs (SENs). Indeed, Ball *et al.* argue, 'some of the money and energy previously devoted to educational endeavours like SEN work are now focused on marketing activities'. In an effort to attract pupils, some schools are publishing glossy brochures and some have brought in public relations firms. Staff are expected to devote more time and energy to marketing activities such as open evenings.

Ball *et al.* believe these changes have led to 'a significant shift in the value framework of education'. Gewirtz *et al.* see this as involving an overall shift from comprehensive to market values, although individual schools have been affected to different degrees. This shift involves a number of characteristics, which are summarized in Figure 10.1.

Neighbouring schools have ceased to cooperate with each other and instead there is 'suspicion and hostility' between them as they compete for pupils. As competitive

Figure 10.1 The shift from comprehensive to market values

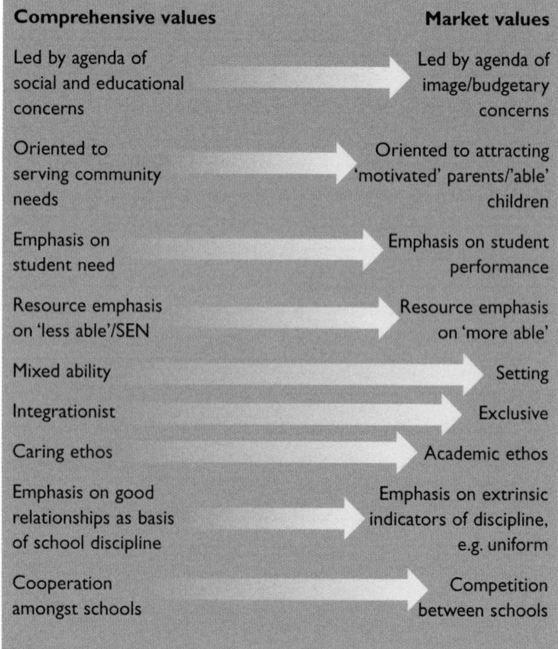

Source: S. Gewirtz, S.J. Ball and R. Bowe (1995) *Markets, Choices and Equity in Education*, Open University Press, Buckingham, p. 150.

market systems are introduced, 'commercial rather than educational principles are increasingly dominant in making curriculum and organization and resource allocation decisions'. Budgetary concerns, such as cutting costs, are seen as more important than educational and social issues (Gewirtz *et al.*, 1995). More attention is devoted to the image of the school, particularly to making it seem to have a traditional and academic focus.

The educational market and degrees of choice

Gewirtz *et al.* found that the amount of choice involved in selecting a school was limited both by the availability of schools and by the ability of parents to discriminate between them. And in this respect, parents were not equal.

Gewirtz *et al.* argue that three broad groups can be distinguished in terms of their ability to discriminate between schools:

1. **Privileged/skilled choosers** are strongly motivated to choose a school for their children and they have the necessary skills to do so. They have the ability to understand the nature of different schools and to evaluate the claims made by schools in their publicity. They are likely to devote considerable time and energy to finding out about different schools and their admission criteria. Privileged/skilled choosers often have the money to make a range of choices that will assist their children's education. These choices may include moving house or paying for private education.

   Privileged/skilled choosers are usually middle-class and some – for example, teachers – benefit from inside knowledge of the education system. This group tends to seek out the most successful 'cosmopolitan schools', which are often over-subscribed and draw their intake from a wide area.

2. **Semi-skilled choosers** 'have strong inclination but limited capacity to engage with the market' (Gewirtz *et al.*, 1995). They are just as concerned to get the best possible education for their children but they do not have the same level of skill as their privileged/skilled counterparts. They tend to lack the 'experiences or inside knowledge of the school system and the social contacts and cultural skills to pursue their inclination to choose "effectively". They are less "at ease" in the medium of school choice than the privileged/skilled choosers.'

   For example, they are less likely to appeal if they do not get their children into their first-choice school. They are more likely to accept rumours about schools and their local reputation at face value than to probe deeper, and they can have difficulties interpreting league table results. Members of this group are less likely to be middle-class than privileged/skilled choosers, and are more likely to choose a local school than a successful cosmopolitan one.

3. **Disconnected choosers** are not inclined to get very involved with the educational market. They are concerned about their children's welfare and education but 'they do not see their children's enjoyment of school or their educational success as being facilitated in any way by a consumerist approach to school choice'.

   They tend to consider a small number of options, and frequently just the two closest schools to where they live. They may not own a car or have easy access to affordable public transport, making the local schools seem the only realistic options. They tend to believe there is little difference between schools, and put more emphasis on the happiness of their child than on the academic reputation of the school.

   The result is that disconnected choosers are more likely to send their children to the local school where their friends are going, rather than have them travel further afield to a supposedly better school. Disconnected choosers are likely to be working-class and are more likely than other choosers to send their children to an under-subscribed school.

These differences result in certain groups being more likely to benefit from the educational market than others. Generally, the higher a person's social class, the more likely they are to benefit from the best state schooling (or to be able to choose private schooling). The market leads to a hierarchy of schools and, even without selection by academic ability, can lead to a growing division between predominantly middle-class and working-class schools.

Conclusion

Ball *et al.* (1994) conclude that the encouragement of parental choice, the publication of exam results in league tables, open enrolment, formula funding, and other policies designed to make education more market-oriented, have all served to make education less egalitarian. Those whose children are already advantaged in the system seem to be gaining even more benefits, while those who are already disadvantaged are losing further ground.

At the same time the ideology of educational institutions is changing in such a way that schools are becoming more concerned with attracting the gifted and the advantaged than with helping the disadvantaged. According to Ball *et al.*'s research: 'we are likely to end up with a more socially differentiated and divisive system of education. In any market there are winners and losers. In this market we may all end up losing out!' (For more discussion of this research, see pp. 634–5.)

Ron Glatter, Phillip Woods and Carl Bagley – 'Diversity, differentiation and hierarchy'

Another study of the marketization of schooling, and particularly the effects of introducing greater choice of school, was conducted by Ron Glatter, Phillip Woods and Carl Bagley (1997). They conducted research in three areas, each of which formed what they call a **local competitive** arena.

Glatter *et al.* believe educational markets are essentially local, with real competition only taking place between schools within travelling distance of one another. For this reason the amount of choice and the nature of the choice open to parents depend upon the choices available locally. Their study therefore aimed to discover whether the changes in the education system had increased, reduced or made no difference to the amount of choice in particular localities. They also examined whether schools had become more hierarchical – that is, whether clearer differences in the status of different schools had emerged. They looked at how schools had responded to the changes and they collected questionnaire data on parental attitudes about diversity.

Competition in different areas

The first area, which they call Marshampton, was a town with a population of about 120,000, with a relatively high proportion of middle-class and professional people. The area contained one long-established private school and, before the changes, six LEA state schools, one of which was a selective grammar school. In response to the educational changes, all the LEA schools had opted for grant maintained status. Thus the marketization of education had produced a change in the types of school available, but no greater diversity.

In fact, Glatter *et al.* detected a move towards uniformity. The schools without sixth forms were all hoping to open their own sixth forms to give their schools greater status and academic credibility. Market pressures were pushing all the schools in a similar direction. A clear hierarchy of schools had emerged in the area, with less successful schools under-subscribed. However, Glatter *et al.* found it was extremely difficult for the less successful schools to improve their position in the hierarchy, because of problems such as a poor reputation and cuts in their budgets. Thus competition was not doing much to improve standards, particularly for those attending the less popular schools.

The second area was Northern Heights, a predominantly working-class area with a substantial Bangladeshi population. It was located in a larger LEA area, Northborough. Northborough had a wide range of secondary schools consisting of two boys' and one girls' grant maintained schools, one boys' and one girls' LEA school, three Roman Catholic schools, three special schools and one independent school.

There were three co-educational comprehensive schools run by the LEA in Northern Heights itself. One of these was an over-subscribed, academically oriented school, while the other two concentrated more on pastoral matters and were under-subscribed. All three of these schools were seeking to offer more of a vocational curriculum to their pupils. About two-thirds of parents in Northern Heights sent their children to one of these schools, while about a third of the residents chose to send their child to a school outside the immediate area.

This area, then, did offer plenty of diversity and choice, and this had been increased since some schools had chosen to opt out of LEA control. However, some parents could not get their first choice. And the element of choice was by no means new. Northborough had adopted a policy of open enrolment, allowing children to choose their school, as early as 1977.

The third area, East Greenvale, was a semi-rural area with numerous villages and three small towns. Each of these towns had an LEA-controlled 13–18 co-educational comprehensive school. The vast majority of children chose to go to the nearest school. Because of the geographical distance between the schools, each operated as almost a local monopoly. Each school was fairly content with the number of pupils they could attract and informally agreed not to 'poach' students from other areas. There was little differentiation between the schools and little opportunity for exercising choice.

Conclusions

The research of Glatter *et al.* demonstrates the extent to which local factors largely determine how the educational market operates. The geography of different areas, the number and nature of existing schools, and the tactics adopted by schools combine to determine how much and what sort of competition there is in particular areas. The introduction of markets into education has unpredictable and varied effects, but in two of the areas of the study it made no marked difference to the choices available to parents.

Glatter *et al.* conclude that the 'secondary school system is not dramatically moving in the direction of greater diversity or reduced hierarchy'. Furthermore, in their study of parents' attitudes, Glatter *et al.* found no real evidence that parents sought diversity. All parents sought 'a caring, child-centred focus', although some parents did want their child's school to stress a more academic focus.

Youth training schemes

Dan Finn – the hidden agenda of YTS

The new vocationalism involved in the various youth training schemes introduced in the 1970s and 1980s has been strongly attacked by some critics. Dan Finn (1987) refused to accept it was really designed to achieve its stated objectives. Finn claimed that in 1983 confidential government papers leaked to the London magazine *Time Out* showed that the real purpose of the Youth Training Scheme (YTS) was to restrict the number of workers joining trade unions, so reducing the bargaining power of the workforce. YTS would also directly reduce the wage levels of young workers.

The government paid employers for 'training' people on YTS, but in fact the trainees could be used as a source of cheap labour. Furthermore, the small allowances paid to people on YTS would depress wage levels generally for young workers. The scheme would also reduce embarrassing unemployment statistics, since those participating were not classified as unemployed. In addition, the government hoped it would help to reduce crime and social unrest (for example, riots) by taking up the free time of young people.

Finn denied there was any truth in the claim that school leavers were unemployable. He believed their unemployment was simply the result of a lack of jobs. He pointed out that many school pupils have experience of the world of work and proved themselves capable of holding down part-time jobs even before they leave school. In a survey of fifth-form (year 11) pupils in Rugby and Coventry, he found that 75 per cent had had some experience of working: they could hardly be totally ignorant of the world of work.

Finn regarded the various youth training schemes as a way of coping with the surplus of labour in the 1970s and 1980s. Rather than being left to their own devices, swelling the unemployment statistics, school leavers would be taught the values and attitudes that would make them an easily exploited workforce. The schemes would help to lower the employment expectations of the working class so that they would 'know their place'.

John Clarke and Paul Willis – the transition from school to work

John Clarke and Paul Willis (1984) reached similar conclusions. They argued that the new vocationalism was a way of producing people who want to work, but are kept in 'suspended animation' until work becomes available. They saw the schemes as resulting from a 'crisis of profitability' in British industry. Trainees could be used as a substitute for full-time employees who would have to be paid more and would be eligible for redundancy payments.

Labour educational policy, 1997–2007

Coming to power in 1997, Tony Blair, leader of the Labour Party, announced that his priorities were 'Education, Education, Education'. This section looks at how Labour translated these priorities into policy and practice.

Labour's educational policy was influenced by both social democratic and neoliberal/New Right perspectives. This section begins by outlining legislation reflecting social democratic concerns with equality of educational opportunity.

The influence of social democratic perspectives

Education Action Zones (EAZs)

Education Action Zones were set up in 1998 to raise the motivation and attainment levels of underachieving pupils in 'deprived', low income, inner-city areas. By 2003, there were seventy-three EAZs in England. They were funded by central government with additional funding from business. Each zone was run by an Action Forum made up of parents, and representatives from local schools and businesses and from local and national government.

An Ofsted report on EAZs praised some initiatives, such as homework and breakfast clubs. The report found some improvement in standards at Key Stage 1 but no change at Key Stage 3 or GCSE (McKnight *et al.*, 2005).

Excellence in Cities (EiC)

The **Excellence in Cities** programme steadily replaced EAZs. It targeted local education authorities in disadvantaged inner-city areas. Like EAZs, it aimed to improve attainment levels of pupils from low income backgrounds. The main initiatives of EiC were special programmes for gifted pupils, city learning centres with IT facilities, learning mentors and low-cost leasing for home computers (Tomlinson, 2005).

An Ofsted evaluation of EiC found that it was more effective than EAZs. Overall, there was a small improvement in Key Stage 3 test results and in attendance levels (McKnight *et al.*, 2005). (For further evaluation of EAZs and EiC, see p. 632.)

Sure Start

This programme targets the under-fours and their families living in the most deprived areas of England. It aims to improve their health, education and employment prospects. **Sure Start** is based on the idea that early intervention – for example, home visits and play centres run by professionals – will have long-term positive results. Started in 1999, by 2003 there were over 500 Sure Start programmes involving some 300,000 children.

Sure Start is difficult to evaluate because (1) each programme is different, and (2) only short-term results are available. The National Evaluation of Sure Start found that its impact on children and their parents after three years was disappointing. However, it is too early to assess its impact on children's formal education (Anning, 2006).

Academies

Academies are designed to replace 'failing' comprehensive schools in low income, inner-city areas. They aim to drive up educational standards. Academies are sponsored by individuals, businesses, faiths, charities, and increasingly by city education authorities. Sponsors contribute up to £2 million and appoint the majority of governors who run the school. Central government contributes around £25 million for each academy. The first three academies were opened in 2002, and there were forty-six by 2006, with a total of at least 200 planned for 2010.

An evaluation of the academies programme by the accountants Price Waterhouse published in 2006 reported mixed results. Although there were some behaviour problems, there were improvements at Key Stages 3 and 4. GCSE results for 2006 showed a rise of 1.8 per cent for students nationally, and 6.1 per cent for students from academies. A report from the National Audit Office concluded that academies are heading in the right direction but more must be done to improve GCSE results in English and maths (*Guardian*, 30.11.2006, 23.02.07).

Despite these generally positive reports, there are strong critics of academies. Some claim that the improvement in results is largely due to academies taking fewer students with special needs or behavioural problems. And others are concerned about the influence of sponsors. For example, the evangelical Christian Sir Peter Vardy sponsors an academy in Gateshead which teaches creationism alongside evolutionary theory in science lessons (Tomlinson, 2005).

Further and higher education (FE and HE)

Labour aimed to widen access to further and higher education – in particular, to increase the number and proportion of working-class students in FE and HE.

The numbers continuing their education after 16 grew steadily throughout the 1990s and 2000s. In the UK, there were 2.23 million students in further education in 1990/1 compared with 5.05 million in 2004/5 (*Social Trends 2007*). However, participation varied by social class. For example, in England and Wales in 2004, 85 per cent of 16-year-olds from the higher professional class were in full-time education, compared to 57 per cent from the routine class (or lower social class) (Youth Cohort Study, 2004).

The **Education Maintenance Allowance (EMA)** was introduced in 2004 in an attempt to reduce the class gap in

FE. EMA is a weekly cash allowance payable to 16- to 19-year-olds from low income families who remain in education. Pilot studies found that staying-on rates increased by around 6 per cent with EMA (McKnight *et al.*, 2005).

There has been a rapid increase in student numbers in higher education in the UK – from 748,000 full-time students in 1990/1, to 1,456,000 in 2004/5 (*Social Trends 2007*). Labour's policy is to continue this increase, with a target of 50 per cent of 18- to 30-year-olds in HE by 2010.

Despite increasing numbers of students from all social classes, the class gap in HE participants has been steadily widening. For example, in Britain in 2001, 79 per cent of young people from professional backgrounds were in HE, compared with 55 per cent in 1991 – a gain of 24 percentage points. At the other end of the scale, 15 per cent of young people from unskilled manual backgrounds were in HE in 2001, compared with 6 per cent in 1991, a gain of only 9 percentage points. This indicates that those at the top of the class system have gained far more from the expansion of places in higher education (Galindo-Rueda *et al.*, 2004).

Labour's policy was aimed to close the class gap in participation in higher education. In fact, just the opposite happened. There is some evidence that Labour's introduction of tuition fees and scrapping of maintenance grants in 1998 reduced participation of those from low income backgrounds (see p. 626). However, the widening gap may simply be a continuation of a long-term trend – a trend which was well under way before Labour's election in 1997 (Galindo-Rueda *et al.*, 2004).

The influence of neoliberal/ New Right perspectives

Specialist schools

Labour continued the Conservative policy of **specialist schools**. They rejected the idea of the 'bog-standard', 'one-size-fits-all' comprehensive. Rather than a single type of school for everyone, schools should specialize in particular subject areas. This would provide diversity and choice within the educational market-place, it would increase competition and it would raise standards. According to former Secretary of State for Education, Estelle Morris, 'Specialist schools and Colleges will have a key contribution to make in raising standards and delivering excellence in schools' (quoted in Chitty, 2002).

State secondary schools can apply to become a specialist school in one or two of ten specialisms – arts, business & enterprise, engineering, humanities, languages, mathematics & computing, music, science, sports and technology. In order for their application to succeed they must raise £50,000 from private sector sponsors, which will be matched by additional government funding. They must also meet performance targets set by central government. Specialist schools are allowed to select 10 per cent of their pupils who show an aptitude in their specialism.

In 1997, Labour inherited 196 specialist schools from the Conservatives. Ten years later, there were over 2,500 specialist schools – over 75 per cent of all secondary schools in England (Tomlinson, 2005; www.standards.dfes.gov.uk/specialistschools).

Evaluation of specialist schools

In 2005, the House of Commons Select Committee on Education and Skills published a report on a two-year investigation into secondary education. Here is a summary of its main findings (Select Committee on Education and Skills, 2005).

- **Specialist schools and standards.** The government claimed that the specialist school policy would raise standards. Although standards have risen in many specialist schools, it is not clear why they have risen. Is it the specialism? An Ofsted report found that schools often achieve better results in subjects outside their specialist area. Improvement might be due to additional government funding during a specialist school's first four years.
- **Social class and specialist schools.** Specialist schools tend to have a higher middle-class intake than non-specialist schools. This may account for their better results. Schools in low income areas have difficulty in raising the funds necessary to become a specialist school.
- **Admissions policy and selection.** Evidence indicates 'a troubling slide away from parents choosing schools for their children and towards schools choosing the pupils they wish to admit'. This is due to a shortage of places in schools which parents choose. Research suggests that some schools will select those they see as the most able pupils in order to boost their results – and these tend to be middle-class pupils.

Responding to this criticism, the government published new rules for admissions in 2006, in order to make the process fairer – for example, by banning interviews with parents and/or pupils (Taylor, 2006).

Various methods have been suggested for dealing with over-subscribed schools. One suggestion is a lottery system whereby pupils are randomly selected. Another suggestion is that, to ensure a range of ability, children take an admission test, they are then placed in ability bands on the basis of the test results, and a number of children are selected from each band (Shepherd, 2007).

Assessment and targets

Labour largely welcomed the testing and assessment regime developed by the Conservatives. Pupils, teachers and schools were rigorously assessed with Key Stage tests, GCSE and A level examinations, Ofsted inspections, and a range of other measures such as truancy rates. These assessments were published and schools ranked in league tables. In addition, performance targets were set for Key Stage tests. The thinking behind assessment and performance targets included the following:

- Measurements of performance are essential if parents are to make an informed choice of school.
- They will encourage schools to compete – for example, to improve their position in school league tables and to increase pupil numbers.
- This will raise standards by providing incentives to improve test and exam results.
- Performance targets will also improve standards by providing clear targets to aim for and by rewarding success.

School league tables

Since 1992, secondary schools have been required to publish their GCSE and A level results. Until recently, league tables were based on examination results. They showed, for example, the percentage of pupils obtaining at least five A*–Cs at GCSE. Now there are additional measures – for example, 'value added' and 'most improved'. The **value added** score measures the difference schools have made between the ages of 11 and 16 – for example, how much a school has improved a pupil's attainment over the five years of secondary education. **'Most improved'** looks at the improvements in GCSE results in particular schools over time.

Evaluation of league tables

League tables have been strongly criticized. Critics argue that they fail to provide an accurate measure of school performance. GCSE results may say more about the social background of pupils than the performance of the school. In general, the higher the proportion of middle-class pupils, the better the school's GCSE results. The value added measure goes some way to meet this criticism but it does not take the social background of pupils into account.

In 2006, social factors were included for the first time. This measure indicates what pupils might be expected to achieve, given their social background. Schools whose pupils exceed this expectation will do well in this league table. Results using this measure show that many schools in low income, 'deprived' areas are doing far better than either the exam results or the value added measures indicate (Crace, 2006).

Despite the introduction of alternative league tables, the original measure – exam results – remains the basis for many parents' judgement of schools. As a result, this will encourage schools to recruit 'able' middle-class pupils and avoid those with special needs and excluded children. Also, the priority given to exam results will encourage teachers to 'teach to the test' – to teach pupils how to pass exams rather than improving understanding and learning (Thrupp and Hursh, 2006).

Vocational education and training

In 2005, Labour leader Tony Blair stated: 'We have to secure Britain's future in a world driven by globalization. We have to change and modernize ... to equip everyone for this changing world.' And the way to do this was to raise standards in education.

In many ways Labour's education policy was driven by neoliberal/New Right ideas which see the main role of education as providing the skills and knowledge required by the workforce in an increasingly competitive global society. According to Sally Tomlinson (2005), 'education was subordinated to the economy'. In this sense, all education was vocational education. From Labour's point of view, the education system must 'respond to a competitive global economy by improving the skills and qualifications of young people' (Tomlinson, 2005, p. 90).

This section looks at Labour's approach to what has traditionally been seen as vocational education and training. However, as the above paragraph argues, Labour policy tended to see all education as vocational.

New Deal for Young People

In 1998, Labour introduced the **New Deal for Young People** (NDYP) with the aim of significantly reducing youth unemployment. The programme was designed for 18- to 24-year-olds who had been unemployed and claiming Jobseeker's Allowance for six months. They were provided with Personal Advisers who guided them through the various options: (1) full-time education or training for up to twelve months; (2) work for six months in either the Environmental Task Force or the voluntary sector; (3) a subsidized job with at least one day a week of training; (4) loss of benefits if they refused to take part in the programme. Between April 1998 and the end of May 2005, 567,900 (46 per cent) of those leaving the programme entered employment (*Social Trends 2006*).

Labour claimed that NDYP was a great success. However, critics point out that youth unemployment was falling significantly when NDYP was introduced and much of the later reduction was due to improvements in the economy rather than to the programme itself. In addition, they argue that 40 per cent of participants in the programme failed to find lasting jobs and that NDYP failed to help the most disadvantaged (Tomlinson, 2005).

Despite these criticisms, researchers see NDYP as moderately successful, resulting in a drop in youth unemployment of around 17,000 a year (Van Reenen, 2004).

Vocational qualifications

National Vocational Qualifications (NVQs) and **Scottish Vocational Qualifications (SVQs)** were introduced in 1987. There has been a steady increase in the take-up of these qualifications: in 1991/2, 153,000 NVQs and SVQs were awarded; this rose to 574,000 in 2004/5 (*Social Trends 2007*). Most were awarded at Level 2 (59 per cent in 2004/5). Labour extended the range of NVQs/SVQs to Level 5, which is equivalent to a degree. In addition, the number of vocational areas covered was increased.

The aim of NVQs/SVQs is to raise skill levels in a wide range of occupations. However, a number of surveys indicate that around two-thirds of employers see little value in these qualifications. And in 2005, the British Social Attitudes Survey found that 54 per cent of respondents believed that employers showed insufficient respect for vocational qualifications (*Social Trends 2007*). In addition, various governments may have overestimated the demand for highly skilled workers. For example, in the 1990s, the fastest growing job was the job of care assistant in hospitals and nursing homes (Strathdee, 2003).

GNVQs (General National Vocational Qualifications) were introduced in 1995 as vocational alternatives to GCSE and A level. They covered broad vocational areas such as health and social care, business and finance, and leisure and tourism.

In 2001, Labour rebranded GNVQs as **vocational GCSEs** and **vocational A levels** in an attempt to raise their status so that they would be seen as equivalent to academic qualifications. Critics have seen this as a cosmetic exercise, seeing most vocational qualifications as primarily a route into lower-paid, lower-status jobs. Traditionally, it has been students from working-class backgrounds who have been channelled into vocational courses (Tomlinson, 2005). It remains to be seen whether the rebranding of GNVQs will change their status and the class profile of the students who take them.

Evaluation of Labour's policies

As previous sections have shown, Labour's educational policies have been influenced by both social democratic and neoliberal/New Right perspectives. From Labour's point of view, policies based on these two perspectives are complementary rather than contradictory. For example, raising standards through competition and choice will also increase the opportunities of those from disadvantaged backgrounds, thereby reducing inequality of opportunity. In the process, the skills of the workforce will be raised, so improving the UK's ability to compete in a competitive global economy.

However, many critics have questioned both the effectiveness and compatibility of Labour's policies.

Sally Tomlinson: Education in a Post-welfare Society

Sally Tomlinson is one of the UK's leading researchers on social policy. Here is a brief outline of some of her views on Labour's educational policy.

Tomlinson believes that Labour has narrowed education to an economic function. It has become preoccupied with raising standards in order for the UK to compete effectively in an increasingly global market. In Tomlinson's words:

> *In an effort to keep the UK economy competitive, education and training are elevated to key positions; 'raising standards', 'learning to compete' and getting education 'right' become major policy objectives.* Tomlinson, 2005, p. 216

Labour saw the application of market principles to schools as the main way to raise standards. Competition and choice would drive up standards in an educational market. However, this almost compulsive preoccupation with 'standards' had a down side. First, it favoured the middle classes. In Tomlinson's words:

> *The application of market principles to education proved extraordinarily effective in reintroducing a complex system of selection, passing as 'diversity' in which, as intended, the greatest beneficiaries were the middle classes.* Tomlinson, 2005, pp. 218–19

The success of some schools in the educational market meant they were over-subscribed. As a result, they were able to select their own customers. The pressure to remain market leaders and maintain their position in the league table led them to select those they saw as most able. In practice, this meant mainly middle-class students.

In a market system schools are judged largely on results. With league tables based on Key Stage tests, GCSEs and A level results, there is considerable pressure on teachers to teach to the tests. The priority has increasingly become 'examination techniques, rote learning and revision'. This, combined with the view of education as being primarily about 'jobs, business, enterprise and competition', may be a threat to the well-being of society.

Tomlinson concludes:

> *Critiques of the narrowing of education to economic ends want to reclaim education as a humanizing, liberalizing, democratizing force, directed, as the UN (1948) Universal Declaration of Human Rights put it, to 'the full development of the human personality and a strengthening of respect for human rights and fundamental freedoms'. Education must also help people make sense of the impact of global changes, combat resurgent xenophobic nationalism, recreate the idea of the common good and move beyond a tawdry subservience to market forces.* Tomlinson, 2005, p. 223

Abigail McKnight, Howard Glennerster and Ruth Lupton: tackling education inequalities

In an article subtitled 'An assessment of Labour's successes in tackling education inequalities', Abigail McKnight, Howard Glennerster and Ruth Lupton (2005) pass judgement on Labour's attempts to reduce inequalities of educational opportunity.

Overall, standards appear to have risen. There have been steady improvements in Key Stage tests, and in GCSE and A level results. Although there were significant class differences in attainment, the percentage point gap between the top and bottom social class groups in terms of GCSE and A level results fell between 1998 and 2003. Despite this, the gap remained wide and was the same in 2003 as it was in 1989.

Participation in further and higher education increased significantly under Labour. However, as noted earlier, there is a significant class gap in continuing full-time education after age 16. Statistics from 1997 to 2001 show that the class gap for participation in higher education has steadily widened.

Labour has directed increased resources towards disadvantaged, low income, inner-city areas. There is some evidence that this may have resulted in moderate improvements. However, it will be some time before the full effects of initiatives such as Sure Start will be felt (McKnight *et al.*, 2005).

Paul Trowler: social and educational inequalities

In *Educational Policy*, Paul Trowler (2003) welcomes improvements in achievement such as GCSE results. He also sees initiatives such as Excellence in Cities, directed at low income, inner-city areas, as a positive move. However, he warns about seeing such initiatives as the answer to significantly reducing inequality of educational opportunity.

Like many sociologists, Trowler argues that changes in the educational system cannot compensate for social inequality in the wider society. As long as social inequality exists, it will be reflected in educational attainment. It follows that a significant reduction in inequality of educational opportunity requires a significant reduction in social inequality in society as a whole. Trowler concludes:

> *Although Labour has learned a lot about educational policy, it continues to have unrealistic expectations of what education can do and has a similarly unrealistic expectation of how far deep-rooted social inequalities can be successfully ameliorated through the educative process.* Trowler, 2003

Class and educational attainment

Differential education attainment refers to the fact that different groups – for example, different class, ethnic and gender groups – have different levels of educational attainment. This section looks at evidence and explanations for class differences in educational attainment.

Research shows that the higher a person's social class, the higher their educational attainment is likely to be. The children of parents in higher social classes are more likely to attain high grades in Key Stage tests and at GCSE; they are more likely to stay on in post-compulsory education and to take and pass A level examinations; and they are more likely to gain university entrance.

These class differences were a feature of British education throughout the twentieth century and they have continued to the present day. Whether there has been any reduction in class differences in educational attainment is debatable. There is some evidence which may indicate a reduction in recent years. However, the gap in educational attainment between the top and bottom classes remains significant.

Measuring class attainment

Measuring class differences in educational attainment is difficult. Researchers use different classifications of social class. This means that their findings cannot be directly compared. Comparison is made more difficult when different measures of attainment are used. For example, when attempting to identify trends, different types of examinations might be involved – for example, O levels and GCSEs.

Despite these problems, one thing is clear – whatever the classification of class and the measure of attainment, class differences in educational attainment are wide, long-standing and show no sign of disappearing.

The statistics used in this section are mainly drawn from the **Youth Cohort Study** – a series of longitudinal surveys based on large samples (14,000 in 2004) of young people in England and Wales. They were contacted at age 16, after completion of compulsory education, and again one and/or two years later.

Two different classifications of social class are used – the SEG (socio-economic group) and the NS-SEC (National Statistics Socio-economic Classification), which replaced SEG in official surveys. These two classifications are not directly comparable.

Class attainment at GCSE

Table 10.1 shows the percentage of 16-year-olds from each social class who attained five or more GCSE grades A*–C from 1989 to 1998. The SEG classification of class is used for these years. Table 10.2 updates

Table 10.1 Attainment of five or more GCSE grades A*–C, by social class, 1989–98 (percentages)

Parental occupation (SEG)	1989	1991	1992	1994	1996	1998	Gain 1989–98
Managerial/professional	52	58	60	66	68	69	+17
Other non-manual	42	49	51	58	58	60	+18
Skilled manual	21	27	29	36	36	40	+19
Semi-skilled manual	16	20	23	26	29	32	+16
Unskilled manual	12	15	16	16	24	20	+8

Source: Adapted from DfES (2005) *Youth Cohort Study: The Activities and Experiences of 16 Year Olds: England and Wales, 2004*, DfES, London.

Table 10.2 Attainment of five or more GCSE grades A*–C, by social class, 2000–4 (percentages)

Parental occupation (NS-SEC)	2000	2002	2004	Gain 2000–4
Higher professional	74	77	77	+3
Lower professional	62	64	65	+3
Intermediate	49	51	53	+4
Lower supervisory	35	34	40	+5
Routine	26	31	33	+7

Source: Adapted from DfES (2005) *Youth Cohort Study: The Activities and Experiences of 16 Year Olds: England and Wales, 2004*, DfES, London.

Table 10.3 Attainment of A/AS levels, by social class, 2002–6 (percentages)

Parental occupation (NS-SEC)	2002	2004	2006	Gain 2002–6
Higher professional	57	63	57	0
Lower professional	42	46	45	+3
Intermediate	24	32	33	+9
Lower supervisory	18	16	23	+5
Routine	11	16	16	+5

Source: Adapted from DfES (2002, 2004, 2006) *Youth Cohort Study: The Activities and Experiences of 18 Year Olds: England and Wales, 2002, 2004, 2006*, DfES, London.

these statistics to 2004, using the NS-SEC classification of class.

Both tables show that the higher the class position, the greater the percentage of students attaining five or more GCSE grades A*–C. For example, in 2004, 77 per cent of students from higher professional backgrounds attained these grades, compared to only 33 per cent from routine backgrounds.

The figures in the final column of each table (headed 'Gain') show the increase in percentage points for each class from the beginning to the end date of the period covered. For example, in 2004, 77 per cent of students from higher professional backgrounds attained five or more GCSE grades A*–C, compared with 74 per cent in 2000. This is a gain of 3 percentage points.

The percentage gain figures for 2000 to 2004 suggest that the class gap is narrowing. The greatest gains are now at the bottom of the class system. The routine class gained 7 percentage points, compared with a gain of 3 by the higher professional class. However, the gap between top and bottom remains wide – a difference of 44 percentage points in 2004.

Class attainment at A level

Table 10.3 shows the percentage of 18-year-olds from each social class in England and Wales who attained A/AS level qualifications from 2002 to 2006. The percentage gain figures indicate a narrowing of class differences, with the greatest gains being made in the middle and lower levels of the class system. However, the gap between top and bottom remains large at 41 percentage points in 2006.

Participation in higher education

Table 10.4 shows the percentage of people in Britain under 21 from each SEG social class who entered undergraduate courses from 1991 to 2001. The figures on the right in the 'Gain' column show that the greatest gainers were those from the professional class, with a gain of 24 percentage points, followed by the intermediate class with a gain of 14 points. In 1991 there was a gap of 49 percentage points between the top and bottom classes. By 2001, this had grown to 64. Clearly it was those at the top who gained most from the expansion of higher education places. (The Age Participation Index from which these figures are drawn was discontinued in 2001.)

Table 10.5 shows the percentage of 19-year-olds in England and Wales from each NS-SEC class who entered undergraduate courses in 2003 and 2005. With the exception of the lower supervisory class, it indicates gains for all social classes, with an increase in the gap between top and bottom classes of 2 percentage points. However, two years is too short a period to indicate a trend.

The following sections examine possible reasons for class differences in educational attainment.

Intelligence, class and educational attainment

An obvious explanation for differences in educational attainment is the intelligence of the individual. In Britain, the 1944 Education Act established the **tripartite system** of education. Children were allocated to one of three types of school – grammar, technical or secondary modern – largely on the basis of their performance in an intelligence test, the eleven-plus.

Educational psychologists, such as Sir Cyril Burt, were influential in the establishment of this system. Burt's research appeared to show that intelligence was largely inherited and could be measured by the use of a test. It therefore made sense to send children to the type of school best suited to their abilities. Grammar schools provided an academic education for those with a high measured intelligence, while secondary modern schools catered for those with a lower measured intelligence.

In the eleven-plus exam there was a strong correlation between results and social class, with middle-class children getting higher average scores. Consequently, more middle-class children gained places at grammar schools.

Burt's research into intelligence was later discredited – many of his results had simply been invented – and the tripartite system was gradually replaced by comprehensive schools which all children attended regardless of intelligence. In most areas the eleven-plus was phased out. Nevertheless, many studies continue to show a correlation between measured intelligence and achievement in education. Working-class children continue to score less well in intelligence tests than middle-class children. This might lead to the conclusion that intelligence continues to explain class differences in achievement.

However, there are many reasons for not jumping to such a simplistic conclusion. As Bowles and Gintis (1976)

Table 10.4 Participation rates in higher education, by social class, 1991–2001 (percentages)

Parental occupation (SEG)	1991	1992	1993	1994	1995	1996	1997	1998	1999	2000	2001	Gain 1991–2001
Professional	55	71	73	78	79	82	79	82	73	76	79	+24
Intermediate	36	39	42	45	45	47	48	45	45	48	50	+14
Skilled non-manual	22	27	29	31	31	32	31	29	30	33	33	+11
Skilled manual	11	15	17	18	18	18	19	18	18	19	21	+10
Partly skilled	12	14	16	17	17	17	18	17	17	19	18	+6
Unskilled	6	9	11	11	12	13	14	13	13	14	15	+9

Source: Adapted from Age Participation Index, 2003, DfES, London.

Table 10.5 Nineteen-year-olds in higher education, by social class, 2003–5 (percentages)

Parental occupation (NS-SEC)	2003	2005	Gain 2003–5
Higher professional	52	59	+7
Lower professional	40	45	+5
Intermediate	26	32	+6
Lower supervisory	17	16	-1
Routine	14	19	+5

Source: Adapted from DfES (2003, 2005) *Youth Cohort Study: The Activities and Experiences of 19 Year Olds: England and Wales, 2003, 2005*, DfES, London.

argued, the fact that above-average intelligence is associated with high academic qualifications does not necessarily mean that one causes the other. Before reaching any conclusions, it is necessary to examine questions such as 'What is intelligence?', 'How is it measured?', 'Where does it come from?'

What is intelligence?

The American psychologist Arthur Jensen (1973) defines **intelligence** as 'abstract reasoning ability' and argues it is 'a selection of just one portion of the total spectrum of human mental abilities'. It is the ability to discover the rules, patterns and logical principles underlying objects and events, and the ability to apply these discoveries to solve problems.

Intelligence is measured by intelligence tests which give an individual's **intelligence quotient** or **IQ**. Such tests are designed to measure abstract reasoning ability, and so exclude questions such as 'Which is the highest mountain in the world?' which test knowledge and memory rather than the ability to reason. Thus a simple IQ test may ask for the next number in the following sequence: 2, 4, 6, 8. This question requires individuals to discover the pattern underlying the sequence of numbers and to apply their discovery to solve the problem.

Despite their widespread use, there is a large body of evidence to suggest that IQ tests are not a valid measure of intelligence, particularly when they are used to compare the intelligence of members of different social groups.

Culture and intelligence

Many researchers argue that IQ tests are biased in favour of the middle class, since they are largely constructed by and standardized upon members of this group. If it is accepted that social classes and other social groups have distinctive subcultures and that this affects their performance in IQ tests, then comparisons between such groups in terms of measured intelligence are invalid.

This argument is best illustrated by the testing of non-Western populations with Western IQ tests. The Canadian psychologist Otto Klineberg (1971) gave a test to Yakima Native American children living in Washington State, USA. The test consisted of placing variously shaped wooden blocks into the appropriate holes in a wooden frame 'as quickly as possible'. The children had no problem with the test but produced low scores because they failed to finish within the required time. Klineberg argues that this does not indicate low intelligence but simply reflects the children's cultural background. Unlike Western culture, the Yakima do not place a high priority on speed.

Such examples suggest that Western IQ tests are inappropriate for non-Western people. The same argument has been applied to the use of IQ tests within Western societies which contain different subcultural groups, including social class subcultures. Thus, the British psychologist Philip Vernon (1969) stated: 'There is no such thing as a culture-fair test, and never can be.' This suggests that conclusions based on comparisons of the average measured IQ of different social groups must be regarded at best with reservation.

Genes and intelligence

There is general agreement that intelligence is due to both **genetic** and **environmental factors**: it stems partly from the genes individuals inherit from their parents, and partly from the environment in which they grow up and live. Environmental influences include everything from diet to social class, from quality of housing to family size. Some social scientists, such as Arthur Jensen (1973) and Richard Hernstein and Charles Murray (1994) in America, and Hans Eysenck (1971) in Britain, argue that IQ is largely inherited. They variously estimate that between 60 and 80 per cent of intelligence is genetically based. And they argue that class differences in intelligence largely account for class differences in educational attainment.

Eysenck (1971) claims: 'What children take out of schools is proportional to what they bring into the schools in terms of IQ.' Jensen (1973) is more cautious when he suggests 'genetic factors may play a part in this picture'. However, he does argue that there is better evidence for the influence of genes on educational attainment than there is for the influence of environmental factors.

Environment and intelligence

Those who argue that differences in IQ between social groups are due largely to environmental factors make the following points. It is not possible to estimate the degree to which IQ is determined by genetic and environmental factors. Research has indicated that a wide range of environmental factors can affect performance in IQ tests. Otto Klineberg summarizes some of these factors:

> *The successful solution of the problems presented by the tests depends on many factors – the previous experience and education of the person tested, his degree of familiarity with the subject matter of the test, his motivation or desire to obtain a good score, his emotional state, his rapport with the experimenter, his knowledge of the language in which the test is administered and also his physical health and well-being, as well as on the native capacity of the person tested.* Klineberg, 1971

In the following sections we will examine evidence which indicates that the relatively low test scores of certain social groups are due, at least in part, to the factors outlined by Klineberg.

David Gillborn and Deborah Youdell – 'The new IQism'

Intelligence and ability

David Gillborn and Deborah Youdell (2001) argue that while the term 'intelligence' is now rarely used in British education, it has largely been replaced by the use of the term 'ability'. Gillborn and Youdell describe this as 'the new IQism' in which '"ability" has come to be understood (by policy-makers and practitioners alike) as a proxy for common sense notions of "intelligence"'. Furthermore, '"ability" is constituted in ways that provide for the systematic disadvantage of particular socially defined groups, especially children of working-class and Black/African-Caribbean heritage'.

The A-to-C economy

Gillborn and Youdell conducted qualitative research in two London secondary schools, which they called Taylor Comprehensive and Clough Grant Maintained, between 1995 and 1997. They carried out interviews and observations with teachers, and pupils between the ages of 13 and 16.

Gillborn and Youdell found that both schools were strongly influenced by the 'A-to-C economy'. This involved getting as many pupils as possible to achieve five or more grade Cs or above in their GCSEs, because league tables of school achievement are largely based on these figures. Because of this emphasis,

> *both schools are increasingly rationing the time and effort they expend on different groups of pupils. The similarity reflects the crucial importance that both schools accord to the level of examination success that is recorded in the officially published performance tables.* Gillborn and Youdell, 2001

The nature of ability

In both schools, teachers tended to assess the chances of individual pupils achieving five or more GCSEs in relation to notions of their 'ability'. They saw ability as something that was fixed and which determined the potential of different pupils. In Taylor Comprehensive, for example, the head teacher argued: 'You can't give someone ability can you? ... You can't achieve more than you're capable of can you?'

Furthermore, teachers tended to believe that ability could be objectively measured. In Clough Grant Maintained, pupils were given tests of 'cognitive ability' when they started at the school. These were taken as good predictors of their eventual performance in GCSEs. Gillborn and Youdell say: 'Ability is seen, therefore, as both fixed and measurable' and it is 'frequently seen in terms of generalized academic potential'.

In all these respects, common ideas about ability are exactly the same as the beliefs about intelligence which shaped the tripartite system in an earlier era.

The beliefs about ability are not confined to teachers. Such beliefs have also informed Labour's policies on education. Gillborn and Youdell note that Labour governments since 1997 have supported the use of 'setting' to distinguish pupils of different 'abilities' and to give them teaching 'appropriate' to those abilities.

Ability, class, and 'race'

Gillborn and Youdell found that in both the schools they studied the pupils complained that 'certain peers are favoured over others'. Many pupils felt that 'clever' middle-class children were punished less, and got away with more; while a number of African Caribbean pupils felt that teachers expected less of them than their white peers. The unwitting discrimination against black and working-class children had a number of consequences:

1. Black and working-class children were less likely than white and middle-class children to be entered for higher levels of GCSE exams and thus had no chance of achieving the highest grades (which could only be obtained in higher tier exams).
2. These children were more likely to be placed in lower sets than other children who had been doing work of the same standard.

These factors were reflected in big differences in levels of achievement by class and ethnic group. For example, in Clough Grant Maintained only 9 per cent of children who got free school meals (and whose families therefore had a low income) gained five or more GCSEs at C or above, compared to 39 per cent of other pupils. (For more discussion of ethnicity in relation to this study, see pp. 649–61.)

Conclusion

Gillborn and Youdell conclude that 'inherited intelligence' has returned in the form of 'fixed ability'. Differences in educational attainment are seen to result from differences in ability. In general, working-class pupils are seen to have less ability than middle-class pupils and blacks less ability than whites. As a result, the education system discriminates against working-class and black pupils, and this lowers their attainment levels. 'Ability' has become the new 'IQism'.

Class subcultures and educational attainment

Various studies have shown that, even when IQ is held constant, there are significant differences in educational attainment between members of different social groups. Thus working-class students with the same measured IQ as their middle-class counterparts are less successful in the educational system. It has therefore been suggested that class stratification is directly related to educational attainment. In particular, it has been argued that the subcultures, the distinctive norms and values, of social classes influence performance in the educational system.

Values, class and educational attainment

This position was first spelled out in detail by the American sociologist Herbert H. Hyman (1967) in an article entitled 'The value systems of different classes'. He argued that the value system of the lower classes creates 'a self-imposed barrier to an improved position'.

Using a wide range of data from opinion polls and surveys conducted by sociologists, Hyman outlined the following differences between working-class and middle-class value systems:

1 Members of the working class place a lower value on education.
2 They place a lower value on achieving high occupational status.
3 Compared to their middle-class counterparts, members of the working class believe there is less opportunity for personal advancement.

The values Hyman outlined did not characterize all members of the working class – a sizeable minority did not share them. In general, however, he concluded that motivation to achieve, whether in school or outside it, is generally lower for members of the working class.

Attitudes and orientations

The British sociologist Barry Sugarman (1970) argued that middle- and working-class subcultures contain different attitudes and orientations which may account for class differences in educational attainment. In particular, he claims that working-class subculture emphasizes fatalism, immediate gratification, present-time orientation and collectivism.

1 **Fatalism** involves an acceptance of the situation rather than efforts to improve it; as such it will not encourage high achievement in the classroom.
2 **Immediate gratification** emphasizes the enjoyment of pleasures of the moment rather than sacrifice for future reward, and will tend to discourage sustained effort with its promise of examination success. It will also tend to encourage early school-leaving for the more immediate rewards of a wage packet, adult status and freedom from the disciplines of school.
3 **Present-time orientation** may further reduce the motivation for academic achievement, whereas an emphasis on long-term goals and future planning can encourage pupils to remain longer in full-time education by providing a purpose for their stay.
4 Finally, **collectivism** involves loyalty to the group rather than the emphasis on individual achievement which the school system demands.

Sugarman therefore concluded that the subculture of pupils from working-class backgrounds places them at a disadvantage in the educational system.

Class subcultures – problems of methodology

Before continuing, it is important to make a number of criticisms of the concept of social class subculture and the methodology used to establish its existence:

1 So-called working-class subculture may simply be a response in terms of mainstream culture to the circumstances of working-class life. Thus, members of the working class may be realistic rather than fatalistic; they might defer gratification if they had the resources to defer, and they might be future-oriented if the opportunities for successful future planning were available.
2 From this point of view, members of the working class share the same norms and values as any other members of society. Their behaviour is not directed by a distinctive subculture. It is simply their situation which prevents them from expressing society's norms and values in the same way as members of the middle class. (This view is examined in detail on pp. 241–2.)
3 The content of working-class subculture is sometimes derived from interviews and questionnaires. Hyman's and Sugarman's data were largely obtained from these sources. However, what people say in response to interviews or questionnaires may not provide an accurate indication of how they behave in other situations. As Robert Colquhoun (1976) notes in his criticism of Sugarman, it cannot simply be assumed that 'a response elicited in a questionnaire situation holds in the context of everyday life situations'. Thus, social class differences in response to interviews and questionnaires may not indicate subcultural differences which direct behaviour in a wide range of contexts.
4 Finally, in a criticism of American studies, R.H. Turner (discussed in Colquhoun, 1976) notes that social class differences reported from interviews and questionnaire data are often slight. Sociologists tend to ignore similarities between classes and emphasize the differences.

J.W.B. Douglas – *The Home and the School*

An influential early longitudinal study (that is, a study of the same group over time) was conducted by J.W.B. Douglas and his associates (1964, 1970). This followed the educational careers of 5,362 British children born in the first week of March 1946, through primary and secondary school up to the age of 16 in 1962.

Douglas divided the students into groups in terms of their ability, which was measured by a battery of tests, including IQ tests. He also divided the students into four social class groupings, and found significant variations in educational attainment between students of similar ability but from different social classes. He also found that length of stay in the educational system was related to social class. Within the 'high ability' group, 50 per cent of the students from the lower working class left secondary school in their fifth year, compared with 33 per cent from the upper working class, 22 per cent from the lower middle class and 10 per cent from the upper middle class.

Parental interest in education

Douglas related educational attainment to a variety of factors, including the student's health, the size of the family, and the quality of the school. The single most important factor appeared to be the degree of parents' interest in their children's education. In general, middle-class parents expressed a greater interest, as indicated by more frequent visits to the school to discuss their children's progress. They were more likely to want their children to stay at school beyond the minimum leaving age and to encourage them to do so. Douglas found that parental interest and encouragement became increasingly important as a spur to high attainment as the children grew older.

Douglas also attached importance to the child's early years, since, in many cases, performance during the first years of schooling is reflected throughout the secondary school. He suggested that, during primary socialization, middle-class children receive greater attention and stimulus from their parents. Middle-class parents were likely to encourage their children to do their best in a wide variety of activities. This forms a basis for high achievement in the educational system.

Leon Feinstein – parental support and education

Leon Feinstein (2003) discussed more recent research which he conducted with others into the factors affecting success in education. Feinstein used data from the National Child Development Study (which followed the development of all children born in one week in March 1958) and the British Cohort Study (which conducted similar research on a group of children born in 1970).

Like Douglas, Feinstein claimed that the main factor influencing educational attainment was the degree of parental interest and support. Class differences in parental support account for class differences in educational attainment.

Parental support was measured by teachers' assessments of how much interest parents showed in their children's education. Feinstein gives the following example to indicate the importance of parental support:

> *in tests of maths attainment the improvement between 11 and 16 of children whose parents exhibited high interest in education was 15 percentage points greater than those of children whose parents exhibited no interest ... By comparison, the average advantage of having two parents who both stayed on at school beyond the minimum leaving age and a father in a professional occupation was only 2 per cent for maths.* Feinstein, 2003

He suggests that the positive effects of parental interest operate through 'motivation, discipline and support'.

Evaluation

The studies discussed above appear to give strong support to the view that class subcultures influence educational attainment, particularly through differences in parental encouragement of children at school. However, they should be viewed with some caution.

A number of arguments have been advanced to suggest that working-class parents are not necessarily less interested in their children's education just because they go to their children's schools less frequently than their middle-class counterparts. Tessa Blackstone and Jo Mortimore (1994) make the following points:

1. Working-class parents may have less time to attend school because of the demands of their jobs. Manual jobs typically involve longer and less regular hours than non-manual jobs.
2. Working-class parents may be very interested in their children's education but they are put off going to school because of the way teachers interact with them. Blackstone and Mortimore argue that it is possible that:

   > *working-class parents feel ill at ease or the subject of criticism when they visit school. Teachers represent authority and parents who have had unhappy experiences at school or with authority figures may be reluctant to meet them.* Blackstone and Mortimore, 1994

3. The data used by both Douglas and Feinstein may not actually measure parental interest in education, but teachers' perceptions of their interest. It is possible that teachers perceive middle-class parents as more interested than working-class parents because of the way they interact with teachers when they do attend school.
4. Feinstein himself introduces an element of caution into his conclusions. He admits, 'parental attitudes are influenced by their economic and social position' and 'moreover, deprivation does have a direct effect on attainment'.

Basil Bernstein – speech patterns

The English sociologist Basil Bernstein suggested that class differences in speech patterns are related to educational attainment.

Since speech is an important medium of communication and learning, attainment levels in schools may be related to differences in speech patterns. Much of the early work in this area was conducted by Bernstein (1961, 1970, 1972). He distinguished two forms of speech pattern which he termed the elaborated code and the restricted code. In general, he argued that members of the working class are limited to the use of restricted codes, whereas members of the middle class use both codes.

Restricted codes are a kind of shorthand speech. Those conversing in terms of the code have so much in common that there is no need to make meanings explicit in speech. Married couples often use restricted codes, since their shared experience and understandings make it unnecessary to spell out their meanings and intentions in detail.

Bernstein stated that restricted codes are characterized by 'short, grammatically simple, often unfinished sentences'. There is limited use of adjectives and adjectival clauses, or adverbs and adverbial clauses. Meaning and intention are conveyed more by gesture, voice intonations and the context in which the communication takes place.

Restricted codes tend to operate in terms of **particularistic meanings**, and as such are tied to specific contexts. Since so much is taken for granted and relatively little is made explicit, restricted codes are largely limited to dealing with objects, events and relationships that are familiar to those communicating. Thus the meanings conveyed by the code are limited to a particular social group: they are bound to a particular social context and are not readily available to outsiders.

In contrast, an **elaborated code** explicitly verbalizes many of the meanings that are taken for granted in a restricted code. It fills in the detail, spells out the relationships and provides the explanations omitted by restricted codes. As such, its meanings tend to be **universalistic**: they are not tied to a particular context. In Bernstein's words, the meanings 'are in principle available to all because the principles and operations have been made explicit and so public'. The listener need not be plugged in to the experience and understanding of the speaker, since the meanings are spelled out verbally.

To illustrate his points, Bernstein gave the example of stories told by two 5-year-olds, one with a working-class, the other with a middle-class, background. The children were given four pictures on which to base their story. In the first, several boys are playing football. In the second, the ball breaks a window. The third shows a woman looking out of the window and a man making a threatening gesture in the boys' direction. The fourth picture shows the boys retreating from the scene.

Using an elaborated code to spell out the detail in the pictures, the middle-class child describes and analyses the relationships between the objects, events and participants, and his or her story can be understood by the listener without the aid of the pictures.

The working-class child, using a restricted code, leaves many of his or her meanings unspoken, and the listener would require the pictures to make sense of the story. This story is therefore tied to a particular context, whereas the first story is free from context and can be understood with no knowledge of the situation in which it was created.

Speech patterns and educational attainment

Bernstein used class differences in speech codes to account in part for differences in educational attainment:

1. Formal education is conducted in terms of an elaborated code. Bernstein stated: 'the school is necessarily concerned with the transmission and development of universalistic orders of meaning'. This places working-class children at a disadvantage because they tend to be limited to the restricted code.
2. The restricted code, by its very nature, reduces the chances of working-class pupils successfully acquiring some of the skills demanded by the educational system.

Bernstein did not dismiss working-class speech patterns as inadequate or substandard: he described them as having 'warmth and vitality', 'simplicity and directness'. However, particularly in his earlier writings, he did imply that, in certain respects, they are inferior to an elaborated code. He suggested that an elaborated code is superior for explicitly differentiating and distinguishing objects and events, for analysing relationships between them, for logically and rationally developing an argument, for making generalizations and for handling higher-level concepts. Since such skills and operations form an important part of formal education, the limitation of working-class pupils to a restricted code may provide a partial explanation for their relatively low attainment.

Class and classification systems

In later work, Bernstein (1996) developed these ideas and tried to make links between classification systems and social class. He attempted to show that working-class children are more likely to classify things in terms of personal meanings and experiences, whereas middle-class children are more likely to classify things in terms of abstract principles.

He reported a study of twenty-nine middle-class and twenty-nine working-class children who were shown pictures of different types of food. He found that the working-class children were likely to classify foods on grounds such as 'I cook this for my mum' or 'I have this for breakfast'. On the other hand, the middle-class children were likely to use criteria such as whether the foods were vegetables, fruits or meats. When asked to reclassify the foods in a different way, the working-class children continued to use criteria related to personal experience, while the middle-class children changed to using personal criteria as well.

Bernstein concludes that middle-class children can easily adopt two different ways of classifying things, whereas working-class children tend to concentrate upon one classification system. This gives middle-class children an advantage, since they feel more comfortable with abstract systems of classification which are frequently used in education.

Criticisms

Bernstein's ideas have provoked strong criticism. In a detailed critique, Harold Rosen (1974) attacks his arguments step by step. He argues that Bernstein's view of social class is vague: at times he talks about the working class in general as having a restricted code; at others he specifies the lower working class. Bernstein lumps together all non-manual workers into a middle class whose members from top to bottom appear equally proficient in handling an elaborated code. He thus ignores possible variety within these classes.

Rosen also notes a lack of hard evidence for elaborated and restricted codes: Bernstein provides few examples to actually prove their existence.

Finally, Rosen accuses Bernstein of creating the myth that the supposed middle-class elaborated code is superior in important respects to working-class speech patterns. Rosen concludes: 'It cannot be repeated too often that, for all Bernstein's work, we know little about working-class language.'

Chris Gaine and Rosalyn George (1999) also criticize Bernstein for a lack of evidence and for using simplified distinctions between the working class and middle class. They suggest that, even if there was a homogeneous working class in the 1960s, when Bernstein's work began, this is not the case now. They say, 'Given the changes in the British class structure … it would be unwise to describe it as anything other than multi-layered and blurred.' They therefore believe it is far too simplistic to assume that the working class have one, dominant speech pattern.

In this section we have examined possible subcultural differences between social classes which may account, in part, for the different attainment levels of members of these groups in the educational system. We will examine the implications and policies that stem from this view in the next section.

Cultural deprivation and compensatory education

The picture of working-class subculture is not an attractive one. It is portrayed as a substandard version of mainstream middle-class culture. Its standard deteriorates towards the lower levels of the working class, and at rock bottom it becomes the culture of poverty, which we outlined in Chapter 4.

Conclusion

The evidence in this section indicates that material aspects of social class have an important effect on educational attainment. In particular, it suggests that Labour's aim to increase working-class access to higher education is not helped by the use of student loans to fund this process.

Education – interactionist perspectives

Explanations of class differences in attainment examined in previous sections have been largely based on factors outside the school. They look at the wider society and argue that an individual's position in the social structure has an important effect on their educational attainment. Structural explanations, in this case explanations based on the class structure, see behaviour as shaped by external factors over which the individual has little control. Their behaviour is seen as largely determined by the directives of class subcultures and the pressures of the class system.

This section looks at education from an interactionist perspective. The focus is narrowed from the wider society to the classroom. Attention is directed to small-scale interaction situations and the meanings which develop and guide action within those situations.

Interactionists argue that a person's **self-concept**, their view of themselves, develops from interaction with others. Interaction in the classroom, with teachers and pupils, helps to shape a person's self-concept; and their self-concept can have a significant effect on their educational attainment.

Typing, labelling and the self-fulfilling prophecy

One of the most important aspects of the interactionist theory of education concerns the ways in which teachers make sense of and respond to the behaviour of their pupils.

In their book *Deviance in Classrooms* (1975), David H. Hargreaves, Stephen K. Hester and Frank J. Mellor analyse the ways in which pupils come to be **typed** or classified. Their study is based on interviews with teachers, and classroom observation in two secondary schools. They examined the way in which teachers 'got to know' new pupils entering their first year at the school.

Teachers have limited knowledge about their new pupils as individuals. They may know about the types of catchment area from which pupils originate, and have a general image of first-year pupils, but apart from this they can only start to build up a picture as the school year progresses. Hargreaves *et al.* distinguish three stages of typing or classification.

The first stage consists of **speculation**. The teachers make guesses about the types of pupils they are dealing with. The researchers noted seven main criteria on which initial typing was based. Teachers distinguished pupils according to:

1 Their appearance
2 How far they conformed to discipline
3 Their ability and enthusiasm for work
4 How likeable they were
5 Their relationships with other children
6 Their personality
7 Whether they were deviant

Hargreaves *et al.* stress that in the speculation phase teachers are only tentative in their evaluations, and they are willing to amend their views if initial impressions prove to be misleading. Nevertheless, they do form a **working hypothesis** – a theory about what sort of child each pupil is.

Each hypothesis is then tested in the second phase, which Hargreaves *et al.* call **elaboration**. Gradually the hypotheses are either confirmed or contradicted, but either way the teachers become more confident in their judgements as their typing is refined.

When the third stage is reached, **stabilization** takes place. By this time the teacher feels 'He "knows" the pupil; he understands him; he finds little difficulty in making sense of his acts and is not puzzled or surprised by what he does or says.' By this time, all the pupil's actions will be evaluated in terms of the type of pupil he or she is thought to be. Some pupils will be regarded as deviant, and for them it will be difficult for their behaviour to be seen in a positive light.

Typing and social class

Although Hargreaves *et al.* emphasize that typing is a gradual process, other sociologists have suggested it can be much more abrupt.

In a study of an American kindergarten, R.C. Rist (1970) found that as early as the eighth day of school the children were permanently seated at three separate tables. Table 1 was reserved for 'fast learners', tables 2 and 3 for the less able. According to Rist, though, it was not, in reality, ability which determined where each child sat, but the degree to which they conformed to the teacher's own middle-class standards. For example, the teacher seemed to take account of whether the children had neat and clean appearances, and whether they were known to come from an educated family in employment. In other words, the kindergarten teacher was evaluating and labelling pupils on the basis of their social class, not on their abilities in the classroom.

The effects of typing

The typing or **labelling** of pupils can have important effects on their progress.

For example, Aaron V. Cicourel and John I. Kitsuse (1963) conducted a study of the decisions of counsellors in an American high school. The counsellors played a significant part in the students' educational careers since they largely decided which students should be placed on courses designed for preparation for college entry. Although the counsellors claimed to use grades and the results of IQ tests as the basis for classifying students in terms of achievement, Cicourel and Kitsuse found significant discrepancies between these measures and the ways in which students were classified.

Cicourel and Kitsuse found that the student's social class was an important influence on the way they were evaluated. Even when students from different social backgrounds had similar academic records, counsellors were more likely to perceive those from middle- and upper-middle-class origins as natural 'college prospects', and place them on higher-level courses.

Cicourel and Kitsuse argued that the counsellors' classifications of students' ability and potential were influenced by a whole range of non-academic factors, such as the students' appearance, manner and demeanour, assessments of their parents, and reports from teachers on their conduct and adjustment. Cicourel and Kitsuse suggest that a counsellor's evaluation of an individual as a 'serious, personable, well-rounded student with leadership potential' may often have more effect than his or her grades upon his or her educational career. They conclude that such procedures do not uphold the 'ideal of equal access to educational opportunities for those of equal ability'.

In an article based on the same research, Cicourel and Kitsuse (1971) examined the meanings employed by counsellors in the definition of students as 'conduct problems'. Again, they found a range of factors which subtly combined to create the counsellors' picture of a conduct problem. These included 'the adolescent's posture, walk, cut of hair, clothes, use of slang, manner of speech'. Again, social class was an important basis for classification, since the characteristics used to type a conduct problem tended to be found in students from low income backgrounds.

Labelling and the self-fulfilling prophecy

Labelling theory argues that once a label is attached to a person there is a tendency for them to see themselves in terms of the label and act accordingly. And there is a tendency for others to see them in terms of the label and act towards them on this basis. This may result in a self-fulfilling prophecy.

The **self-fulfilling prophecy** theory argues that predictions made by teachers about the future success or failure of pupils will tend to come true because the prediction has been made. The teacher defines the pupil in a particular way, such as 'bright' or 'dim'. Based on this definition, the teacher makes predictions or prophecies about the behaviour of the pupil: for example, that they will get high or low grades.

The teacher's interaction with pupils will be influenced by their definition of the pupils. They may, for example, expect higher-quality work from, and give greater encouragement to, those whom they have defined as 'bright' pupils. The pupils' self-concepts will tend to be shaped by the teacher's definition. Pupils will tend to see themselves as 'bright' or 'dim', and act accordingly. Their actions will, in part, be a reflection of what the teacher expects from them. In this way the prophecy is fulfilled: the predictions made by the teacher have come to pass. Thus the pupil's attainment level is to some degree a result of interaction between the pupil and the teacher.

There have been a number of attempts to test the validity of the self-fulfilling prophecy theory. The most famous one was conducted by Robert Rosenthal and Leonora Jacobson (1968) in an elementary school in California. They selected a random sample of 20 per cent of the student population and informed the teachers that these children could be expected to show rapid intellectual growth. They tested all pupils for IQ at the beginning of the experiment. After one year the children were re-tested and, in general, the sample population showed greater gains in IQ. In addition, report cards indicated that teachers believed that this group had made greater advances in reading skills.

Although Rosenthal and Jacobson did not observe interaction in the classroom, they claimed that 'teachers' expectations can significantly affect their pupils' performance'. They suggested that teachers had communicated their belief that the chosen 20 per cent had greater potential to the children, who responded by improving their performance. Rosenthal and Jacobson speculated that the teachers' manner, facial expressions, posture, degree of friendliness and encouragement conveyed this impression, which produced a self-fulfilling prophecy.

Evaluation of self-fulfilling prophecy and labelling theory

Despite the plausibility of the self-fulfilling prophecy theory, it has been criticized. One area of criticism concerns the evidence. Rosenthal and Jacobson have been strongly attacked for the methodology they used in their study. In particular, it has been suggested that the IQ tests they used were of dubious quality and were improperly administered.

In a review of research in this area, C. Rogers summarizes the findings. He says:

> *Some show effects only with younger children, some only with older ones. Some show effects with urban children, but not suburban. Some show quantitative but not qualitative effects on pupil–teacher interactions, while others show the exact opposite.* Rogers, 1982

Notwithstanding these contradictions, Rogers claims that the evidence, on balance, suggests the self-fulfilling prophecy is real – it can occur. However, it does not appear to be an inevitable result of labelling.

There is evidence that not all pupils will live up to their labels. In a study of a group of black girls in a London comprehensive school, Margaret Fuller (1984) found that the girls resented the negative stereotypes associated with being both female and black. They felt that many people expected them to fail, but, far from living up to these expectations, they tried to prove them wrong. The girls devoted themselves to school work in order to try to ensure their success.

This suggests that negative labels can have a variety of effects. However, this observation weakens the forcefulness of the labelling theory. It seems that labels can have an effect, but the type of effect is not always predictable.

Ability grouping

If labelling can affect the attainment of individual pupils, can it affect groups of pupils? In many schools, pupils are organized into **ability groups** – groups based on their perceived ability. There are several types of ability grouping. These include:

- **Streaming**. Pupils are placed in a class on the basis of their general ability. They remain in that class for most subjects.
- **Banding**. This is a less rigid form of streaming. Each band contains two or more classes which may be regrouped for different subjects.
- **Setting**. Pupils are placed in classes on the basis of their attainment in particular subjects. For example, they may be in set 1 for English and set 3 for maths.
- **Mixed ability**. Pupils are randomly or intentionally mixed in terms of their perceived ability (Ireson and Hallam, 2001).

Stephen J. Ball – banding at Beachside Comprehensive

In his book *Beachside Comprehensive* (1981), Stephen J. Ball examines the internal organization of a comprehensive school. At Beachside a system of **banding** was introduced for first-year pupils. Pupils were placed in one of three bands on the basis of information supplied by their primary schools. The first band was supposed to contain the most able pupils, and the third band the least able. However, Ball found that factors other than academic criteria were influential in determining the bands in which the children were placed. In particular, for pupils of similar measured ability, those whose fathers were non-manual workers had the greatest chance of being placed in the top band.

Ball observed that most pupils were conformist and eager when they first entered the school, but gradually the behaviour of the children began to diverge. He attributed this process to teachers' stereotypical views of the different bands. Band one was seen as likely to be hard-working, dedicated and well-behaved. Band three was not expected to be particularly troublesome, but the pupils were expected to have learning problems. Band two was expected to be the most difficult to teach and the least cooperative.

According to Ball, the effect of these views was a progressive deterioration in the behaviour of most band two pupils, which was reflected in higher levels of absence, more non-conformist behaviour and a lack of effort being put into homework.

As a result of teacher expectations, different bands tended to be taught in different ways and encouraged to follow different educational routes. Band one pupils were 'warmed-up': they were encouraged to have high aspirations and to follow O level courses in subjects with a high academic status. In contrast, band two children were 'cooled-out' and directed towards more practical subjects and towards the lower-level CSE exams. The end result was that band two pupils were much less likely than their band one counterparts to take O levels, to stay on at school after the age of 16, or to take A levels.

Ball admits that not all band two children failed. Some were able to overcome the difficulties that placement in this band produced. Nevertheless, there was a strong relationship between banding and performance. Given that there was also a strong relationship between social class and banding, Ball claims 'working-class pupils tend to percolate downwards in the processes of academic and behavioural differentiation'.

Nell Keddie – streaming and classroom knowledge

While Ball examined the workings of a banding system, a study by Nell Keddie (1973) looked at the operation of **streaming** in a large London comprehensive school. As well as looking at the classification and evaluation of students, Keddie studied the ways in which knowledge was evaluated and classified.

Keddie discovered that knowledge defined by teachers as appropriate to the particular course was considered worthwhile; knowledge from the student's experience which did not fit this definition was considered of little consequence. Knowledge presented in an abstract and general form was considered superior to particular pieces of concrete information. The knowledge made available to students depended on the teacher's assessment of their ability to handle it. Thus those students who were defined as bright were given greater access to highly valued knowledge.

Like other researchers, Keddie found a relationship between perceived ability and social class. Pupils were streamed into three groups in terms of ability. There was a tendency for pupils from higher-status white-collar backgrounds to be placed in the 'A' stream, and for those from semi-skilled and unskilled manual backgrounds to be relegated to the 'C' stream.

Keddie observed the introduction of a new humanities course designed for all ability levels. Despite the fact that all streams were supposed to be taught the same material in the same way, Keddie found that teachers modified their methods and the information they transmitted, depending on which stream they were teaching. There was a tendency to withhold 'higher-grade' knowledge from 'C' stream pupils. Some teachers allowed the 'C' stream pupils to make more noise and do less work than those in the 'A' stream.

Keddie argued that teachers classified students in terms of a standard of the 'ideal pupil'. The middle-class pupils in the 'A' stream were closest to this ideal and were therefore given greater access to highly valued knowledge. This resulted in 'the differentiation of an undifferentiated curriculum'.

Keddie then examined the students' definition of the situation, and she accounted for the 'success' of 'A' stream students in the following way. 'A' stream students were more willing to accept on trust the validity of the teacher's knowledge and to work within the framework imposed by the teacher. By comparison, 'C' stream pupils would not suspend their disbelief if the teacher made statements that did not match their own experience. For example, one pupil objected to a teacher's portrayal of the 'British family' because it did not fit his own experience.

From the teachers' viewpoint, such objections slowed down the transmission of the 'body of knowledge' they were concerned with getting across. Many of the questions asked by 'C' stream pupils were defined by teachers as irrelevant and inappropriate, as were their attempts to relate their personal experience to the course. In general, 'C' stream pupils were less willing to work within the guidelines provided by teachers. Keddie ironically commented, 'It would seem to be the failure of high-ability pupils to question what they are taught in schools that contributes in large measure to their educational achievement.'

Keddie concluded that classifications and evaluations of both pupils and knowledge are socially constructed in interaction situations. Appropriate knowledge is matched to appropriate pupils. This results in knowledge defined as high-grade being made available to students perceived as having high ability. It results in pupils perceived as having low ability (in practice, mainly working-class pupils) actually being denied knowledge which is essential for educational success.

Pupil subcultures and identities

Pupils experience school in different ways. They are treated differently by their teachers, given different labels, and often placed in different ability groups. Pupils attach different meanings to their education and find a variety of ways to relate to their experiences.

Schools lay down a set of standards and indicate to pupils how they are expected to behave. However, not all pupils are able and/or willing to conform to these standards. If they fail to do so, pupils may well form their own subcultures which reject some of the values of the school.

David Hargreaves – streaming and pupil subcultures

In an early study of a secondary modern school, David Hargreaves (1967) related the emergence of subcultures to labelling and streaming. Pupils labelled as 'troublemakers' were placed in lower streams; those whose behaviour was more acceptable were placed in higher streams. Those with negative labels attached to them had been defined as failures: first, by being placed in a secondary modern which was seen as a second-rate institution; and second, through the streaming system. Many teachers regarded them as no more than 'worthless louts'.

Faced with the problem of being unable to achieve high status within the school, such pupils attempted to protect their sense of worth and retain a positive self-concept. Students labelled as troublemakers tended to seek out each other's company, and within their group awarded high status to those who broke the school rules. Thus, disrupting lessons, giving cheek to teachers, failing to hand in homework, cheating and playing truant all brought prestige. According to Hargreaves, two distinctive subcultures emerged within the school: the **conformists** and the **non-conformist delinquents**.

Máirtín Mac an Ghaill – masculine identities

Máirtín Mac an Ghaill (1994) studied year 11 students in Parnell School (not its real name), a largely working-class comprehensive in the West Midlands. He identified three working-class male peer groups, each with its own definition of masculine identity and its own subculture. These groups developed in response to:

- the way students were organized into sets
- the curriculum they followed
- the teacher–student relations which resulted from the above
- the students' position within the working class
- the changes in the labour market, for example the rapid decline in unskilled and semi-skilled manual jobs

The three groups Mac an Ghaill identified were:

1. **Macho Lads** – the 'academic failures' placed in the bottom sets for all their subjects. They saw the school as representing 'hostile authority' and making 'meaningless work demands' on them. They developed an anti-school subculture based on acting tough, having a laugh and looking after your mates. They saw academic work as effeminate and often misbehaved in lessons. Teachers saw a major part of their job as policing the Macho Lads.
2. **Academic Achievers** – the 'academic successes' in the top sets. They were highly regarded by teachers and expected to do well. They looked forward to upward social mobility and a professional career. Since academic qualifications were seen as the route to high occupational status, they were positive about the school curriculum. Academic Achievers tended to have skilled working-class backgrounds.
3. **New Enterprisers.** They too saw the curriculum in a positive light, but in their case it was a vocational curriculum with subjects like business studies and technology. They saw their future in the high-skilled sector of the labour market.

Setting and attainment

Streaming and banding were the main types of ability groupings in primary and secondary schools in the 1950s and 1960s. **Setting**, particularly for GCSE examinations, became increasingly common in the late twentieth century. It was seen as a means of improving exam results and league table positions in a competitive educational market-place. It was also a response to Labour's drive to raise standards in order to compete in the global economy. Labour's 1997 election manifesto stated:

> *Children are not all of the same ability, nor do they learn at the same speed. That means 'setting' children in classes to maximise progress, for the benefit of high fliers and slower learners alike.*

Judith Ireson, Susan Hallam and Clare Hurley – setting and GCSE

In a paper entitled 'Ability grouping in the secondary school: effects at Key Stage 4', Judith Ireson, Susan Hallam and Clare Hurley (2001) attempted to measure the possible effects of setting on GCSE results. Their sample consisted of forty-five mixed comprehensives in England, representing three types of ability grouping:

- Mixed ability schools – mostly mixed ability classes in all subjects, with setting in no more than two subjects in year 9.
- Partially set schools – setting in no more than two subjects in year 7, increasing to a maximum of four subjects in year 9.
- Set schools – streaming, banding, or setting in at least four subjects from year 7.

Their main findings were that 'For mathematics, science and English, the amount of setting a pupil experiences from Year 7 to Year 11 does not have an effect on GCSE attainment.'

This conclusion is based on a comparison of schools with different amounts of setting. A different picture is provided by looking at the effects of setting within single schools. This is shown by the following research.

David Gillborn and Deborah Youdell – sets and tiers

GCSE exams are often tiered into foundation and higher tiers. Pupils entered for the foundation tier cannot attain grades A* to B – the highest grade available is grade C. Pupils are often placed in lower and higher tier sets for entry into foundation and higher GCSE tiers.

Research by David Gillborn and Deborah Youdell (2001) in two London secondary schools showed that set placement was based on teachers' assessment of pupils' ability. Working-class and black pupils were more likely to be placed in foundation tier sets even when they had been doing the same work and attaining the same results as middle-class and white pupils in the higher tier sets. This placement was based on teachers' beliefs that pupils from working-class backgrounds and black pupils were less likely to have the ability to attain higher grades at GCSE. As a result, placement in the lower sets denied pupils the knowledge required to obtain the top grades at GCSE.

Interactionist perspectives – an evaluation

The interactionist perspective has the advantage of focusing directly on small-scale interaction situations in schools and colleges. In doing so, it provides detailed evidence of what actually happens within educational institutions. However, this focus can lead researchers to ignore the wider society. It is difficult to support the views of some interactionists who argue that the meanings that guide actions are simply constructed in the classroom. Schools are situated in the wider society. Teachers and pupils are part of that wider society – for example, they bring their social class backgrounds into the school and express them in classroom interaction.

Interactionist studies are usually dated – interactionism is not fashionable today. The more recent studies included in this section are not based on a specifically interactionist perspective. However, they have been included here because they are school-based and deal with similar issues to those of earlier interactionist research.

Gender and educational attainment

In the UK today, girls and young women are outperforming their male counterparts at every level of the educational system – from primary school to university. This is a dramatic and worldwide change that has happened during the last twenty-five years. Across cultures and continents, from the USA to Japan, from Mexico to New Zealand, from Portugal to Korea, girls have reversed the picture that would have been expected twenty-five years ago.

In the 1970s the focus of research was on girls' 'underachievement'. Since the 1990s it has been 'underachieving boys' who have been the focus of gender research in education.

It is important to place the 'gender effect' in perspective. Class has over five times the effect on educational attainment that gender has. And ethnicity has twice the effect (Gillborn and Mirza, 2000). But, as the following section shows, the effect of gender on educational attainment is still significant.

Gender and attainment – the evidence

Key Stage tests

Research over the past sixty years shows that girls have always outperformed boys in primary school tests. The same applied to the eleven-plus (see p. 626). However, girls' scores in the eleven-plus were 'adjusted' in order to

Table 10.6 Percentage of pupils attaining Level 5 or above in Key Stage 3 tests (England)

	English	Maths	Science
Boys in 2005	64	74	70
Boys in 2004	64	73	65
Boys in 2003	61	70	68
Boys in 2002	58	66	65
Boys in 2001	56	64	66
Girls in 2005	78	77	73
Girls in 2004	77	74	67
Girls in 2003	74	72	69
Girls in 2002	75	68	66
Girls in 2001	74	68	66

Source: Adapted from *Social Trends 2006*; and *Gender and Achievement*, standards.dfes.gov.uk.

ensure that equal numbers of girls and boys obtained grammar school places (Tomlinson, 2005). This shameful procedure was kept quiet.

Table 10.6 shows the percentage of girls and boys in England attaining Level 5 or above in Key Stage 3 tests from 2001 to 2005. With the exception of science in 2001, girls' attainment has been consistently higher than that of boys, with the largest difference in English. This generally reflects gender differences at Key Stages 1 and 2. The gender gap grows from Key Stage 1 to 3, particularly in English. For example, in 2004 girls were ahead by 8 percentage points at Key Stage 1 in English and by 13 points at Key Stage 3.

GCSE

Before the introduction of the GCSE examination, the gender gap at age 16 was either slightly in favour of girls or non-existent (Machin and McNally, 2006). From 1988, when GCSEs replaced O levels, the gender gap steadily widened.

Table 10.7 shows the percentage of boys and girls attaining five or more GCSE grades A* to C from 1990 to 2006. Girls' attainment was consistently higher, with the gender gap widening from 7.6 percentage points in 1990 to 10.6 in 2002, followed by a slight narrowing to 9.6 in 2006. Despite the gender gap, it is important to note that the attainment levels of both boys and girls have risen steadily. This also applies to A level results.

A level

In 1975/6 the proportion of young men in the UK attaining two or more A levels or equivalent qualifications was 14.5 per cent, compared with 12.1 per cent for young women – an attainment gap of 2.4 percentage points in favour of men. The gap slowly narrowed until 1987/8 when the percentage for both men and women was the same at 15.1 per cent (*Social Trends 2000*). From then on the attainment gap steadily widened in favour of women. Figure 10.2 illustrates this.

Between 1990/1 and 2004/5 the proportion of young women gaining two or more A levels or equivalent rose from 20 per cent to 45 per cent, and the proportion of young men rose from 18 per cent to 35 per cent. The gender gap increased from 2 percentage points in 1990/1 to 10 in 2004/5. In addition, young women outperform young men in grades in practically all GCE A levels (standards.dfes.gov.uk: Gender and Achievement).

Table 10.7 Percentage of pupils attaining five or more GCSE grades A*–C (England)

Year	All pupils %	Boys %	Girls %	Gender difference %
2006	57.3	52.6	62.2	9.6
2005	55.7	50.8	60.8	10.0
2004	53.7	48.4	58.4	10.0
2003	52.9	47.9	58.2	10.3
2002	51.6	46.4	57.0	10.6
2000	49.2	44.0	54.6	10.6
1998	46.3	41.3	51.5	10.2
1996	44.5	39.9	49.4	9.5
1994	43.3	39.1	47.8	8.7
1992	38.3	34.1	42.7	8.6
1990	34.5	30.8	38.4	7.6

Source: Department for Education and Employment (1999–2000); Department for Education and Skills (2001–5).

Higher education

Figures for higher education (HE) reflect the gender trends for A level. As Table 10.8 shows, student numbers in higher education have grown steadily, with those of women growing faster than those of men. In 1970/1, there were just 621,000 full-time and part-time HE students in the UK, 33 per cent of whom were women. In 1995, women outnumbered men for the first time. By 2004/5, there were 2,494,000 HE students, 57 per cent of whom were women (*Social Trends 2007*).

Figure 10.2 Attainment of two or more GCE A levels or equivalent qualifications, by gender, UK

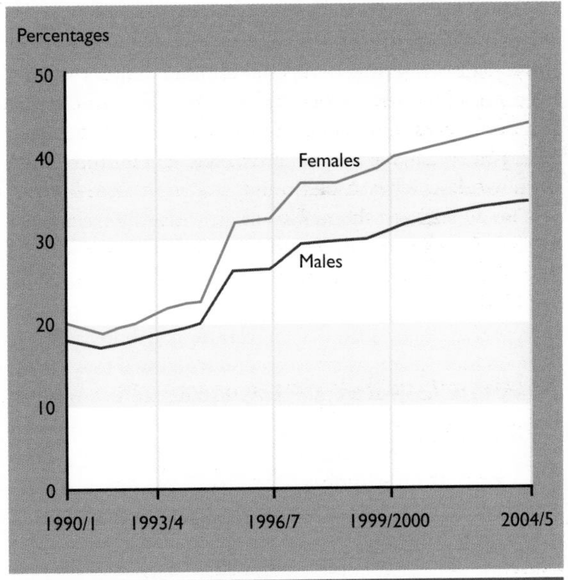

Source: National Statistics Online

Table 10.8 Students in higher education, UK, thousands

	Women	Men
1970/1	205	416
1980/1	301	526
1990/1	491	588
2004/5	1,426	1,068

Source: *Social Trends 2007*.

Table 10.9 shows the proportion of male and female students who achieved first class and upper second class degrees (the top two classes of degrees). In general, women achieve better degrees than men – for example, in 2005/6, 63 per cent of female compared to 56 per cent of male undergraduates were awarded first class or upper second class degrees. The gender gap has remained consistent at around 7 percentage points (Higher Education Statistics Agency, 2007).

Table 10.9 Gender and first and upper second class degrees, UK (percentages)

	Women	Men	Gender gap
1994/5	51	44	7
2004/5	62	55	7
2005/6	63	56	7

Source: Higher Education Statistics Agency, January 2007.

Explaining girls' 'underachievement' – the 1970s and 1980s

In the 1970s and 1980s, the main focus of gender research in education was girls' underachievement. Although the gender gap at 16 was either non-existent or slightly in favour of girls, at A level and degree level boys were outperforming girls. This section looks briefly at explanations for this gender difference after age 16. In one respect, these explanations are now redundant, with girls outperforming boys at every level of the educational system. However, some of the explanations may still be relevant – they may point to factors which, even today, are preventing girls from reaching their full potential.

Early socialization

As Fiona Norman and her colleagues (1988) point out, before children start school, conditioning and sex stereotyping have already begun. From the types of play that girls and boys are encouraged to engage in and the types of toys they are given, different sets of aptitudes and attitudes may be developed.

The educational aspirations of girls may be influenced through playing with dolls and other toys which reinforce the stereotype of women as 'carers'. Boys tend to be encouraged to be more active than girls, and this may be reflected in their attitudes in classrooms. Furthermore, boys are more likely to be given constructional toys which can help develop scientific and mathematical concepts. Stereotypes of men and women can be further reinforced by the media, through magazines, books, computer games, television and advertising.

One possible consequence of early gender stereotyping is that girls may come to attach less value to education than boys. Research conducted by Sue Sharpe (1976) into a group of mainly working-class girls in London schools in the early 1970s found that the girls had a set of priorities which were unlikely to encourage them to attach great importance to education. She found that their concerns were 'love, marriage, husbands, children, jobs, and careers, more or less in that order'. Sharpe argued that, if girls tended to see their future largely in terms of marriage rather than work, then they might have little incentive to try to achieve high educational standards.

In the 1990s, Sharpe repeated her research and found that girls' priorities had changed. Now jobs/careers were their chief concern for the future (Sharpe, 1994). This change may help to explain why the educational attainment of girls at school is now greater than that of boys (see pp. 642–3 for more details).

Socialization in school

Many sociologists have claimed there is bias against girls in the educational system.

Research by Glenys Lobban (1974) found evidence of gender bias in some educational reading schemes. From a study of 179 stories in six reading schemes, Lobban found that only 35 stories had heroines, compared to 71 which had heroes. Girls and women were almost exclusively portrayed in traditional domestic roles and it was nearly always men and boys who took the lead in non-domestic tasks. In at least three of the schemes females took the lead in only three activities in which both sexes were involved: hopping, shopping with parents, and skipping. Males took the lead in seven joint activities: exploring, climbing trees, building things, looking after pets, sailing boats, flying kites and washing cars. Summarizing the findings and the likely effects of the reading schemes, Lobban says:

> *The girls who read them have already been schooled to believe, as our society does, that males are superior to females and better at everything other than domestic work, and the stories in the schemes cannot but reinforce the damage that our society does to girls' self-esteem.*
> Lobban, 1974

Lobban's research was conducted in the 1970s, but more recent research has also found evidence of gender stereotyping. In 1992 Lesley Best and her students examined a sample of 132 books for pre-school-age children in an attempt to discover whether gender bias in children's books had decreased.

They found that in these 132 books, 792 male and 356 female characters were portrayed. There were 94 male heroes but just 44 heroines. Some 75 per cent of the female characters featured in the book were portrayed in family situations, compared to just 15 per cent of the male characters; and men were shown in 69 different occupations, but women in only 18. Some characters were shown in non-traditional roles – there were two female sailors, a female jockey, and a male babysitter, for example – but they were the exception rather than the rule.

Best concluded that, despite the existence of a few non-sexist books, little had changed since Lobban's research. She says:

> *It would seem that there is little attempt made in pre-school books to widen the horizons for either sex by presenting more women in a broad range of jobs or more men taking on a caring role.* Best, 1993

Research which only examines the content of reading schemes or textbooks is rather limited in scope. It does not reveal what effects such books have on children. Recent research has tended to emphasize that children are not simply the passive recipients of socialization processes. Instead, they are actively involved in shaping their own conceptions of what it means to be masculine or feminine.

Behaviour in the classroom – self-confidence and criticism

The active and dominant males in the reading schemes may be reflected in the behaviour of boys and girls in the classroom. From their own classroom observations and from the analysis of other studies, Barbara G. Licht and Carol S. Dweck (1987) reached the following conclusions about gender differences in young children's self-confidence.

Licht and Dweck found that girls lacked confidence in their ability to carry out intellectual tasks successfully. Despite the superior performance of young girls compared to boys in primary schools, it was the girls who generally expected to encounter most difficulty when learning new things.

According to Licht and Dweck, boys are able to shrug off failures by attributing them to a lack of effort on their part, or unfair assessment by teachers. Girls, on the other hand, constantly underestimate their ability, fail to attach significance to their successes, and lose confidence when they fail.

This is because girls blame failure on their own intellectual inadequacies, yet explain success in terms of luck. In doing this, girls fail to convince themselves that they are capable of succeeding, and they come to avoid challenging new situations in which they fear they will fail.

Licht and Dweck do not think that this situation is the result of conscious discrimination by teachers. Indeed, they found that, in line with their own experiences of how girls performed, most primary school teachers expected greater success from their girl pupils. However, by examining fourth- and fifth-grade American classes, Licht and Dweck found differences in the ways that boys and girls were evaluated.

There was very little difference in the amount of praise and criticism that girls and boys received for their academic achievements and failures. Boys, however, were criticized much more frequently for lacking neatness in their work, for failing to make sufficient effort and for misbehaviour in the classroom. Licht and Dweck concluded that girls begin to lose confidence because they get less criticism from teachers. The boys in their study were given ways of explaining away their failures in terms of behaviour that could be modified; the girls had no such excuses to make for themselves.

Although this research is now rather dated, more recent research also suggests that boys continue to get more criticism than girls, but girls still lack self-confidence.

Michelle Stanworth – gender differences in further education

Michelle Stanworth (1983) examined the later stages of the education system in a study of A level classes in a further education college. She interviewed teachers and students from seven different classes in the humanities department. Her findings suggested that a number of the attitudes displayed by teachers would impede the educational progress of girls. These attitudes were not confined to male teachers – they were also typical of their female colleagues.

Teachers found it much more difficult to remember the girls in their classes. Without exception, all the pupils whom teachers said it was difficult to name and recall were girls. Quiet boys were remembered, but quiet girls seemed to blend into the background and made little impression on their teachers.

Stanworth found that teachers held stereotypical views of what their female pupils would be doing in the future. Only one girl was seen as having the potential to enter a professional occupation. Interestingly, she was the most assertive of the girls in the classroom but her academic performance was not particularly good. The most academically successful girl was described by one teacher as being likely to become a 'personal assistant for someone rather important'. Even for this girl, marriage was suggested as one of the most significant aspects of her future life; and male teachers mentioned nothing other than marriage as the future for two-thirds of the female pupils.

When asked which students were given the most attention by teachers, the pupils themselves named boys two and a half times as often as girls, although girls outnumbered boys by nearly two to one in the classes studied. The pupils reported that boys were four times more likely to join in classroom discussions, twice as likely to seek help from the teacher, and twice as likely to be asked questions.

Furthermore, girls were consistently likely to underestimate their ability, while boys overestimated theirs. Pupils were asked to rank themselves in terms of ability in each class. In nineteen of the twenty-four cases in which teachers and pupils disagreed about the ranking, all of the girls placed themselves lower than the teachers' estimates, and all but one boy placed themselves higher.

Stanworth claimed that classroom interaction disadvantaged girls. Teachers had an important role in this, but pupils themselves also 'played an active part in the regeneration of a sexual hierarchy, in which boys are the indisputably dominant partners'.

Stanworth's work was based upon interviews and not direct classroom observation. It therefore gives some indication of what teachers and pupils perceive to be happening in classrooms, but does not actually establish, for example, that teachers give more attention to boys (Randall, 1987). However, later research supports the claim that boys tend to dominate classrooms.

Becky Francis – girls and achievement

In *Boys, Girls and Achievement*, Becky Francis (2000) reviews more recent work on gender in the classroom, and describes her own research in this area. She says:

> *Almost two decades on, research shows that girls' educational achievement has improved despite the continuing male dominance of the classroom, curriculum content (for example, history's focus on the lives of men) and greater demands on teacher time.* Francis, 2000

Francis conducted her own research in three London secondary schools in 1998–9. The schools had different levels of overall achievement and were located in different areas, but all had a majority of working-class pupils. She observed four different classes of 14- to 16-year-olds in each school, visiting each class three times. Half the classes were in English and half in maths. In addition to classroom observations, she interviewed a sample of pupils.

Like earlier researchers, Francis found evidence that classrooms were gendered and tended to be dominated by boys. She found that 'boys tend to monopolize space in the classroom and playground, and … girls tend to draw less attention to themselves than do boys'. In eight of the twelve classes boys were considerably noisier than girls. A number of the teachers, though not all, treated male and female pupils differently. One teacher told pupils that girls tended to be better at languages while boys were better at maths.

There were a number of incidents where boys were disciplined more harshly or more frequently than girls. Francis admits that sometimes this might have reflected the greater noisiness of boys. Girls who were not paying attention tended to talk quietly rather than disrupt the classroom with more obvious, noisy behaviour. One teacher was particularly likely to treat boys and girls differently. He used:

> *a very challenging style with more confident boys in his maths class, frequently putting them on the spot and using sarcasm. In turn, Mr L was far more sympathetic and kind to the girls, and he was more tolerant of any lack of understanding. This may have been because he did not want to intimidate them, but it had the effect of allowing girls to refrain from participation. A number of girls in this class sat at the back of the classroom and were observed regularly chatting together about other subjects while the pupils (mainly boys) at the front of the class were completely engrossed in maths problems.* Francis, 2000

In some classes, other teachers also took 'a more "robust" disciplinarian approach with boys than with girls'.

Unlike researchers such as Stanworth, Francis does not just assume that these differences would only create problems for girls. She acknowledges that sometimes boys could feel picked on and this might discourage them at school. Nevertheless, she still feels that girls were getting less attention and were less likely than boys to be challenged to improve their performance.

Girls could also be disadvantaged outside the classroom. Francis observed some incidents outside the classroom where boys used the threat of violence to prevent girls from challenging their authority.

Francis found evidence that girls were still getting less attention than boys and that schools remained largely male-dominated. However, in some classes there was little evidence that boys and girls were treated significantly differently. Furthermore, Francis did find that some things had changed. For example, she found that pupils no longer took for granted the belief that girls were less academically able than boys. And she also found that boys faced some disadvantages (see pp. 648–9).

Explaining girls' achievement

Over the past twenty-five years, the improvement in the educational attainment of girls and young women has been dramatic and unprecedented. Yet relatively little has been written to explain it. Instead the focus has been on the so-called 'underachievement' of boys. According to Becky Francis and Christine Skelton (2005), 'this reveals the marginalisation of girls, how their school performance is seen as peripheral to that of boys, how they do not count'.

This section looks at some of the explanations for the rise in girls' educational attainment.

Changing attitudes and expectations

Sue Sharpe's (1976) study of working-class school girls in the early 1970s showed that their main priorities for the future were 'love, marriage, husbands and children'. When she repeated this study in the 1990s, she found significant changes. Now, the girls' main concerns were 'job, career and being able to support themselves' (Sharpe, 1994). They were more confident, assertive and ambitious. They saw education as the main route to a good job and financial independence.

In the 1970s, over 80 per cent of girls wanted to get married; by the 1990s this had dropped to 45 per cent. The girls were increasingly wary of marriage. With the rapidly rising divorce rate throughout the 1980s and 1990s, they had seen adult relationships breaking up around them. They had also seen women standing on their own two feet rather than depending on financial support from a man. Paid employment and financial independence were now major concerns.

Although many of the girls in the 1990s expected to work in 'women's jobs' such as primary school teaching, nursing, beautician work and clerical work, they were more likely than girls in the 1970s to consider 'men's jobs' such as car mechanics and firefighters, and to look forward to professional careers such as being a doctor or a lawyer. Given their hopes and concerns, educational success was more important to the 1990s girls than their 1970s counterparts.

The changing attitudes and expectations of girls are reflected both by their parents and by their schools. A number of studies, particularly those of girls from middle-class families, indicate that parents increasingly expect exam success, and in some cases make their daughters feel that they could 'never be good enough' (Francis and Skelton, 2005).

A study entitled *Education and the Middle Class* (Power *et al.*, 2003) showed that girls were often 'driven by the ambitions of the school' to maintain or improve its position in the league tables. This was particularly apparent in all-girls private schools where it was assumed that every student would aim to continue to A level and university. As one girl put it, 'It was just one track and that was that.'

The women's movement and feminism

Many of the rights that feminists and the women's movement fought for in the 1960s and 1970s have now been translated into law. And the ideals on which those rights are based have been increasingly taken for granted. Although today's young women may not see themselves as feminists, they expect equal opportunity in education and in the labour market. According to Mitsos and Browne (1998), the women's movement has provided both incentives and direction for young women in education. In their view, the 'women's movement and feminism have achieved considerable success in improving the rights and raising the expectations and self-esteem of women'.

Changes in the labour market

The decline in heavy industry, the growth in service sector work, and the increasing employment of 'flexible' part-time workers and workers on fixed-term contracts have all expanded employment opportunities for women. The employment rate for working-age women in the UK rose from 56 per cent in 1971 to 70 per cent in 2005; the same period saw a drop in the male rate from 92 per cent to 79 per cent. Jobs in the service industries – where women are typically employed – increased by 45 per cent between 1978 and 2005, while jobs in manufacturing – where men have traditionally been employed – fell by 54 per cent over the same period (*Social Trends 2006*).

The growth in employment opportunities, along with the rise in young women's occupational ambitions, has increased their incentives to gain educational qualifications. Studies of both primary and secondary school pupils show that many girls are now looking forward to jobs that require degree level qualifications (Francis and Skelton, 2005).

Individualization and the risk society

Ulrich Beck (1992) argues that we are moving into 'the second modernity'. Other sociologists see society moving into the late modern period, and still others see a movement into postmodernity. Beck's views have been used to help explain the dramatic worldwide change in women's educational achievements (Francis and Skelton, 2005).

According to Beck, today's society is characterized by **risk** and **uncertainty** and by a process of **individualization**. For example, with the rising divorce rate, marriage is increasingly associated with risk and uncertainty. Employment is becoming increasingly unstable. There are fewer 'jobs for life'; people are changing jobs more often, retraining, improving and/or learning new skills. As a result, the job market and career paths become less predictable.

Risk and uncertainty are accompanied by a process of individualization. People are increasingly thrown back on themselves as individuals – they are more and more responsible for their own fate, their own security, their own future. People are becoming more self-sufficient and self-reliant. Beck (1992) sees women at the forefront of the individualized self; they are 'setting the pace for change'.

In this increasingly insecure, individualized society, individuals must equip themselves for self-reliance and self-sufficiency. Financial independence is one of the main ways of doing this; and education is one of the main routes to well-paid jobs which can provide financial independence.

However, education is not simply a means to financial security. Sociologists who picture a second modernity, a late modernity, or a postmodernity generally agree that there is an increasing emphasis on individuality, on the construction of self and on the creation of identity. Studies of girls in primary and secondary schools illustrate this emphasis. According to Francis and Skelton (2005), 'The majority appear to see their chosen career as reflecting their identity, as a vehicle for future fulfilment, rather than as simply a stopgap before marriage.'

Explaining boys' 'underachievement'

A moral panic

'We are talking about boys. They cannot read, write their own names or speak properly. They are physically and socially clumsy. Increasingly they cannot even do boys' stuff like maths and science.' This quote comes from the editorial of a respected newspaper, the *Observer* (5.1.1998). It reflects the growing concern about so-called 'underachieving', 'underperforming' or 'failing' boys. That same year, Labour produced 'a coordinated plan of action to tackle the underachievement of boys'. Eight years later, Labour Chancellor Gordon Brown was warning of the prospect of 'a wasted generation of boys' (*Guardian*, 13.10.2006). Some commentators suggest that this concern has reached the level of a 'moral panic' among British newspapers and politicians (Francis and Skelton, 2005).

Are boys underachieving?

In the 1970s and 1980s, concern about the 'gender effect' was focused on girls' 'underachievement'. By the 1990s this concern was reversed. Now it was boys 'underachieving'. But were they?

In general, the educational attainment of boys and young men has steadily improved over the past sixty years. This does not indicate underachievement. However, there is evidence that certain boys are underachieving – a higher proportion of working-class boys are doing badly compared with other social groups. But the same can be said for working-class girls.

What has changed is the overall rate of improvement for boys and girls. As the statistics outlined earlier show clearly, girls' educational performance over the last twenty years has improved at a faster rate than boys', resulting in a significant widening of the gender gap. And this applies to boys and girls from all social classes. Whether this should be seen as 'boy's underachievement' is a matter of opinion.

There have been many attempts to explain this widening of the gender gap. Some of these will now be examined. They are based on the assumption that boys are underachieving and that something should be done to raise their educational attainment.

Constructions of masculinity

The school is a major setting for the construction of masculinity. Recent research argues that the form of masculinity constructed in the classroom contributes to the underachievement of male students. Earlier research had made a similar argument with reference to the anti-school subculture developed by some working-class boys, particularly those placed in lower streams, bands and sets. However, studies now indicate that 'laddish' behaviours have spread to most boys – both working-class and middle-class – and to some extent to girls (Jackson, 2006).

In a study entitled *Lads and Ladettes in School* (2006), Carolyn Jackson examined 'laddish behaviour' among 13- to 14-year-old (year 9) boys and girls. Her research was based on interviews with 203 pupils in eight schools and questionnaire data from 800 pupils in six schools.

Laddish behaviour is based on the idea that it is 'uncool' to work and that appearing 'cool' is necessary to be popular. This aspect of laddishness was accepted by the vast majority of boys and girls, whatever their social class background.

Boys' laddish behaviour was constructed within a framework of **hegemonic masculinity** – the dominant and pervasive view of masculinity. It was based on heterosexuality, toughness, power and competitiveness. It was expressed in acting 'hard', being one of the lads, disrupting lessons, having a laugh and being demanding and assertive. Academic work was defined as feminine and uncool.

Students are faced with a dilemma. They want to do well academically, yet they also want to appear cool and to be popular. But if they are seen to work hard, they are a 'geek', a 'nerd' or a 'swot' – terms of derision. The solution is to appear to reject school work, do the requisite amount of messing around, but work secretly, usually at home. This favours middle-class boys who have the resources at home to do their homework quickly and efficiently – the space, privacy, a desk and a computer. They are better able 'to balance the demands of being popular and academically successful' (Jackson, 2006).

If laddish behaviour is holding boys back, then its development should parallel the widening of the gender gap in attainment. Some researchers argue that this is the case. The following are some suggested explanations for the development of laddish behaviours. They point to changes in the wider society which have occurred at the same time as the widening gender gap.

Pressure to succeed and fear of failure

A number of sociologists have seen competitive individualism and individual responsibility as major themes of late modern society. This promotes fears of academic failure and directs responsibility for failure to the individual. Laddish behaviour can be seen as a response to this. The argument that it is uncool to work can be used as an excuse for poor academic performance.

The marketization of schools has placed further pressure on students. Schools compete in the educational market, striving to raise standards and climb league tables. The importance of examination success is increasingly emphasized and students are under growing pressure to achieve high grades. Laddish behaviour can be seen as a defensive strategy to reduce the fear of poor academic performance or to excuse the reality of failure (Jackson, 2006).

Changes in the labour market

Over the past twenty years there has been a rapid decline in unskilled and semi-skilled manual jobs. These 'macho' manual jobs reflected traditional male working-class identities. Their disappearance has left these identities uncertain and threatened. The new jobs in the service sector, such as care work, call centre and office work, require what have traditionally been seen as feminine skills and sensitivities. Working-class boys may have responded to these threats to their traditional identities by turning to laddish behaviour to restore their sense of masculinity (Jackson, 2006).

Reaction to political correctness

Becky Francis (1999) suggests that the rise of 'laddish' behaviour in the 1990s can be seen as a backlash against 'political correctness'. She argues that:

> *This led to a defiant resurgence of traditional 'laddish' values in the media, typified by the men's magazine Loaded and the popular sit-com 'Men Behaving Badly'. Thus, the values of 'lads' were appropriated by and popularised for middle-class (and often middle-aged) men, and the term has gained new prominence in popular and media culture.* Francis, 1999, p. 357

Discourses of male underachievement

A **discourse** is a set of ideas which tell us how to make sense of the world, what kind of questions to ask, what counts as a problem, and how to solve problems. Researchers claim that a number of discourses on male underachievement can be identified from government policy, and the views put forward by educational experts and the media. Two of the discourses outlined in *Failing Boys?* (Epstein *et al.*, 1998) remain relevant today:

1. **The poor boys discourse.** This discourse sees boys as victims. The way schools are run, the organization of teaching and learning, and the examination system all discriminate against boys. Feminism has gone too far in empowering girls and feminizing the curriculum and assessment procedures. Teachers fail to meet boys' learning needs and fail to appreciate and understand their masculinity. Female teachers dominate primary schools, where they control and suppress 'boyness'. This discourse suggests that schools should be made more 'masculine' and that attention and resources should be redirected from girls to boys (Francis, 2006).
2. **The boys will be boys discourse.** In terms of this discourse, boys have a natural inclination to be boys. They are 'naturally clever' but tend to be lazy and difficult to motivate, slapdash, noisy, competitive and demanding. Their boyishness needs to be constructively channelled, with discipline and authority, clear targets to aim for and competitive sports. They must be recognized and treated as boys and their masculinity respected.

Becky Francis and Christine Skelton have identified two further discourses which they see as emerging in recent years – 'problem boys' and 'at-risk boys' (Francis and Skelton, 2005; Francis, 2006).

3. **The problem boys discourse.** This discourse sees boys as a problem. They develop anti-learning behaviour and contribute to their own underachievement. Firm action is needed. In the words of former education minister David Miliband, 'We have to crack the lad culture that stops too many boys from doing well at school' (quoted in Jackson, 2006). Problem behaviour at school is seen as part of a range of antisocial behaviour in the wider society – vandalism, drugs and alcohol misuse, assault and various other crimes. Blame is directed at the boys themselves –

they are irresponsible, they are to blame. This discourse risks demonizing boys and young men.

4 **The 'at-risk' boys discourse.** At-risk boys are not bad, they are vulnerable. They are socially excluded and disconnected from the wider society. Confused, insecure, and with low self-esteem, they take refuge in hegemonic masculinity and resort to bravado to boost their self-esteem. The at-risk boy has a fragile inner self protected by a macho outer shell. He deserves our sympathy and attention. Measures must be taken to build up his self-esteem and re-connect him to society.

Conclusion

As these discourses suggest, boys' 'underachievement' has become a major concern. Large amounts of time and money have been spent on a range of government initiatives aimed at raising boys' educational attainment. Some critics have argued that the whole question of equality of educational opportunity has been reduced to gender and focused on boys. As noted earlier, class has over five times the effect on educational attainment that gender has, and ethnicity has twice the effect (Gillborn and Mirza, 2000). According to some researchers, the focus on gender has diverted attention from class and ethnicity; and the focus on boys has diverted attention from girls (Francis and Skelton, 2005).

Ethnicity and educational attainment

This section looks at the attainment of different ethnic groups. Comparisons over time are difficult because different classifications of minority ethnic groups are used and some groups are omitted from particular sets of statistics.

In England in 2006, 21 per cent of the pupils in primary schools and 17 per cent of those in state schools belonged to a minority ethnic group.

Minority ethnic pupils are more likely to come from low income families. For example, over 60 per cent of Pakistani and Bangladeshi households are defined as in poverty compared to 20 per cent of white households (Modood, 2006).

Key Stages 1–3

Chinese and Indian pupils have consistently scored above the national average in Key Stage tests, with Black African, Black Caribbean, Bangladeshi and Pakistani pupils consistently below the national average. For example, 92 per cent of Chinese pupils in England attained the expected level in Key Stage 2 mathematics in 2006, compared with a national average of 75 per cent. In Key Stage 3 science, 54 per cent of Pakistani pupils attained the expected level, compared with 72 per cent of pupils nationally. In recent years, there has been an overall improvement in Key Stage test results, with Bangladeshi pupils in particular making significant progress (National Curriculum Assessments, SFR 04/2007, dfes).

For all Key Stages, pupils with English as their first language performed better than pupils with English as an additional language.

GCSE

Table 10.10 shows the percentage of pupils in various ethnic groups attaining five or more GCSE grades A*–C in year 11 in England. It shows that all groups improved their results between 1992 and 2006. During this period, the White group was usually just above average. Of the groups listed, Indian pupils had the highest results in 2006, at 72 per cent. However, as shown in Figure 10.3, Chinese pupils had the best GCSE results in 2006.

In recent years, the lower attaining groups have made the greatest gains. Between 2000 and 2006, Bangladeshi pupils gained 28 percentage points, which brought them up to the national average; followed by Pakistani pupils with a gain of 22 percentage points. The attainment level of the Black group has remained consistently low,

Table 10.10 Attainment of five or more GCSE grades A*–C, by ethnicity, England (percentages)

	1992	1994	1996	1998	2000	2002	2004	2006	Gain 1992–2006
All	37	42	44	46	49	51	54	57	+20
White	37	43	45	47	50	52	55	58	+21
Black	23	21	23	29	39	36	34	48	+25
Asian	33	36	38	45	48	52	55	61	+28
– Indian	38	45	48	54	60	60	72	72	+34
– Pakistani	26	24	23	29	29	40	37	51	+25
– Bangladeshi	14	20	25	33	29	41	45	57	+43
– Other Asian	46	50	61	61	72	64	65	65	+19

Source: Adapted from various Youth Cohort Studies.

Figure 10.3 Attainment of five or more GCSE grades A*–C, by ethnicity and gender, England (percentages), 2006

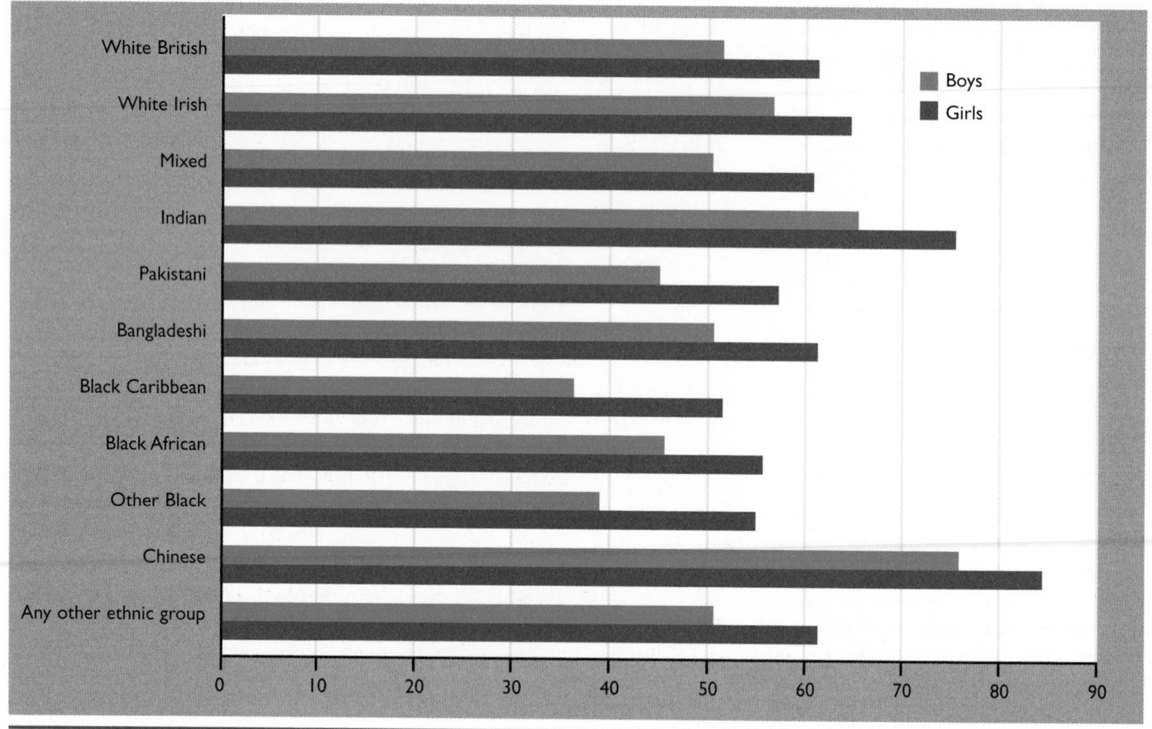

Source: Adapted from *Focus on Ethnicity and Identity*, Office for National Statistics, London; and *National Curriculum Assessments*, SFR 04/2007, DfES, London.

particularly that of African Caribbean boys, as shown in Figure 10.3. However, in recent years, their GCSE results have improved at a faster rate than the national average.

As Figure 10.3 shows, the gender gap applies to every group, though boys in higher attaining groups often get better results than girls in lower attaining groups.

A level

Table 10.11 shows the percentage of 18-year-olds from various ethnic groups with one or more A/AS levels or equivalent Level 3+ qualifications – for example, AVCEs (vocational A levels) or NVQ Level 3 or above. The time period covered is too short to identify a clear trend and in some cases the minority ethnic group samples are too small to reach firm conclusions. The figures generally mirror those for GCSE, with Indians having the best results (60 per cent in 2006), Whites around the national average, and Blacks and Pakistanis/Bangladeshis having the lowest attainment.

In 2006, 47 per cent of 18-year-olds were in full-time education. Young people from minority ethnic groups are also more likely to continue their education after age 16 than the white majority. For example, 84 per cent of Indian and 77 per cent of Black 18-year-olds were in full-time education in 2006, compared to 44 per cent of Whites (Youth Cohort Study, SFR 47/2006). Minority ethnic students are more likely to gain or upgrade their qualifications at an older age.

Table 10.11 Eighteen-year-olds with one or more A/AS level or equivalent Level 3+ qualifications, by ethnicity, England and Wales (percentages)

	2002	2004	2006
All	41	43	46
White	42	43	46
Black	42	30	40
Asian	41	51	48
– Indian	56	58	60
– Pakistani/Bangladeshi	26	39	37

Source: Adapted from various Youth Cohort Studies.

Higher education

In 2006, the government planned to get 50 per cent of young people, aged 30 and below, into higher education. Table 10.12 shows that by 2001/2, minority ethnic groups as a whole had exceeded this target, with 56 per cent starting higher education courses.

Table 10.12 shows entry into higher education on a full-time and part-time basis. Whites had the lowest participation rates at 38 per cent, below Bangladeshis at 39 per cent and Black Caribbeans at 45 per cent. At the top are Black Africans at 73 per cent, followed by Indians at 71 per cent (Connor *et al.*, 2004). Members of minority ethnic groups now make up 16 per cent of home undergraduates in England, nearly double their share of the population (Modood, 2006).

There are some qualifications to this success story. Minority ethnic students are less likely to enter the more prestigious universities, they are more likely to drop out,

Table 10.12 Higher education initial participation rates, England, 2001/2 (percentages)

Ethnic group	Male	Female	All
White	34	41	38
All minority ethnic groups	55	58	56
Black Caribbean	36	52	45
Black African	71	75	73
Black other	56	72	64
Indian	70	72	71
Pakistani	54	44	49
Bangladeshi	43	33	39
Chinese	47	50	49

Source: Adapted from H. Connor, C. Tyers, T. Modood and J. Hillage (2004) *Why the Difference? A Closer Look at Higher Education Minority Ethnic Students and Graduates*, DfES research report RR552, www.dfes.gov.uk/research/data/uploadfiles/RB552.pdf

and they are less likely to attain a high-grade degree. However, this is less applicable to Indian and Chinese students (Modood, 2006).

Social class, ethnicity and attainment

As noted earlier, class appears to be the most important social factor affecting educational attainment. It has a significant effect on the attainment of minority ethnic groups. As with the white majority, the higher the class position of members of the minority ethnic groups, the higher their attainment is likely to be.

Despite this, there are important differences in the influence of class on particular ethnic groups. Compared to whites, some minority ethnic groups achieve higher-level qualifications than their class profile would suggest. In particular, working-class members of some minority ethnic groups tend to do better than their white working-class counterparts.

GCSE and higher education

One measure of income inequality is a comparison of pupils eligible for free school meals (FSM) with those not eligible for free school meals (non-FSM). This measure is used in Figure 10.4 to compare ethnic groups attaining five or more GCSE grades A*–C.

In 2003, 56 per cent of non-FSM and 20 per cent of FSM White British pupils attained these grades – a difference of 36 percentage points between non-FSM and FSM. By comparison, 50 per cent of non-FSM and 43 per cent of FSM Bangladeshi pupils attained these grades – a difference of 7 percentage points. For Chinese pupils, the figures are 76 per cent non-FSM and 69 per cent FSM. In this case, the proportion of low income Chinese FSM students (69 per cent) achieving five or more grades A*–C is significantly larger than the proportion of the higher income non-FSM White group (56 per cent) achieving these grades. It appears that class has a greater effect on white attainment than it has on minority ethnic attainment.

Compared to whites, minority ethnic groups have a larger proportion of members with working-class backgrounds in higher education. This is particularly true for Pakistanis and Bangladeshis – nearly two-thirds of the entrants to higher education from these groups came from households headed by manual workers or the unemployed (Modood, 2004).

Explaining class, ethnicity and attainment

In recent years, Bourdieu's concept of cultural capital has been widely used to explain class differences in educational attainment. To some extent, it may help to explain differences in minority ethnic attainment.

For example, Chinese and Indians have the largest proportion of middle-class members and the highest attainment. Their high attainment may result from having the largest amount of cultural capital. But what about Bangladeshis and Pakistanis who are doing much better than their class profile suggests? In view of their relatively high proportion of low income members, these groups should not, in theory, have the cultural capital to produce their level of attainment. The same applies to the FSM

Figure 10.4 Proportion of pupils achieving five or more GCSE grades A*–C, by ethnic group and FSM status, 2003

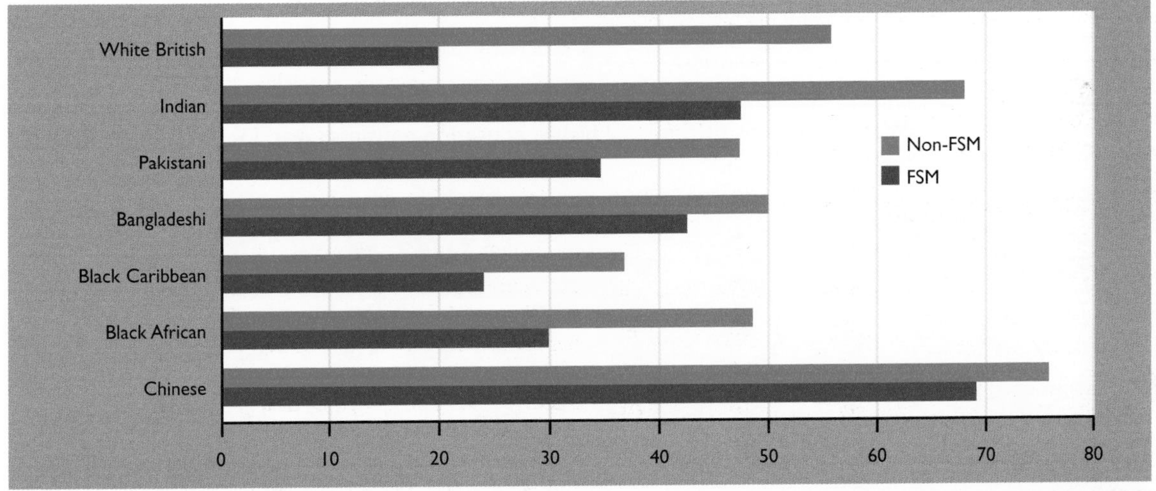

Source: Adapted from DfES (2005) *Ethnicity and Education*, DfES, London.

Chinese pupils, who should not, in theory, have the cultural capital to reach their high attainment at GCSE. Tariq Modood (2004) gives the following possible explanations for this.

Many members of minority ethnic groups may have more cultural capital than would be expected from their present class position. This is because their jobs in the UK were depressed on migration, when they experienced downward mobility compared to their previous occupational status. This may particularly reflect the experience of many Indians and East African Asians. In addition, the occupational status of some migrants may have been depressed by discrimination in the labour market.

A number of things may result from this:

1 A reservoir of cultural capital which derives from earlier occupations.
2 A powerful desire on the part of migrants to improve their position and the prospects for their children.
3 A high value placed on education as a means for doing this.
4 This value is passed on to their children.

As Table 10.13 indicates, minority ethnic parents may place a higher value on education, give their children greater encouragement and expect more from them than many white parents. The scores in the table range from 1 to 5, where 1 represents 'Does not apply/no effect', and 5 'Applies strongly/big effect'.

Racism and education

Much of the research on minority ethnic differences in educational attainment has attempted to explain why certain groups are underachieving. The main focus has been African Caribbean boys and young men.

African Caribbean boys start primary school on a par with their white counterparts. By age 11 they are falling behind, and by age 16 they are the lowest performing ethnic/gender group (judging from GCSE results). To some extent, they 'catch up' and improve their attainment levels in further and higher education.

Some researchers argue that minority ethnic underachievement is due primarily to racism in schools. This racism is usually unconscious and unintentional – the majority of teachers are well-intentioned and not consciously racist (Blair, 2001).

Bernard Coard – racism and underachievement

The year 1971 saw the publication of Bernard Coard's *How the West Indian Child is Made Educationally Sub-normal in the British School System: The Scandal of the Black Child in Schools in Britain*. Coard makes the following points:

1 A disproportionate number of African Caribbean children are placed in ESN special schools – schools for the 'educationally subnormal'.
2 Many have been wrongly placed there, according to the judgement of the head teachers.
3 Once placed in ESN schools, less than 10 per cent ever return to mainstream schools.
4 It is assumed that the ESN child has low capabilities – they cannot cope with the academic requirements of a normal school.

African Caribbean pupils in mainstream schools underachieve. This is due to a number of factors:

1 The racism of many teachers.
2 The low expectations teachers have of black pupils' ability.
3 Low expectations reduce the amount of effort teachers expend.
4 These low expectations also reduce the motivation of pupils, lower their self-esteem, and result in a self-fulfilling prophecy. Placed in lower streams and bands and expected to fail, there is a tendency for this prophecy to come to pass.
5 The black child's 'true identity is denied daily in the classroom … He is made to feel inferior in every way.'

Coard's views have been both strongly supported and strongly criticized.

His analysis was partly based on impressionistic evidence and personal experience, but, despite this, his work remains extremely influential. It was re-published in 2005 as part of a larger volume entitled, *Tell It Like It Is: How Our Schools Fail Black Children* (Richardson, 2005). The contributors to this volume believe that Coard's views remain relevant.

Coard argued that schools systematically fail black pupils, barring them from an education which is rightfully theirs. Some researchers argue that this is the case today. For example, they point to the fact that African Caribbean boys are between four and fifteen times more likely to be excluded than white boys (Richardson, 2005).

Table 10.13 Factors affecting decisions by potential higher education entrants (year 13) to go on to higher education, by ethnic group (mean scores)

Issues affecting decision	Black African	Black Caribbean/ Other	Pakistani/ Bangladeshi	Indian	Chinese/ Asian other	All minority groups	White
Encouragement from family	4.0	4.0	4.0	4.0	3.8	4.0	3.4
Always assumed would go on to higher education	4.0	3.2	4.0	4.1	3.9	3.9	3.1

Source: Adapted from H. Connor, C. Tyers, T. Modood and J. Hillage (2004) *Why the Difference? A Closer Look at Higher Education Minority Ethnic Students and Graduates*, DfES research report RR552, www.dfes.gov.uk/research/data/uploadfiles/RB552.pdf

Cecile Wright – racism in multi-ethnic primary schools

In 1988–9 Cecile Wright (1992) conducted an ethnographic study of four multi-ethnic inner-city primary schools. The study involved: classroom observation of a total of 970 pupils and 57 staff; observation outside the classroom; informal interviews with all the observed teachers, some support staff and the four head teachers; interviews with the parent or parents of 38 children; and an examination of test results in three of the schools.

Wright found that 'the vast majority of the staff … seemed genuinely committed to ideals of equality of educational opportunity'. However, despite these ideals, there was considerable discrimination in the classroom.

Asians in primary schools

In nursery units Asian children were largely excluded from group discussions because teachers assumed they would have a poor command of English. When they did involve the Asian pupils, the teachers tended to speak to them in simplistic, childish language.

In general, in all classes, 'Asian girls seemed invisible to the teachers'. They received less attention than other pupils, and teachers sometimes expressed 'open disapproval of their customs and traditions'. For example, they disapproved when Asian girls tried to maintain some privacy when they had to get changed for PE. Another example of insensitivity was when one teacher was handing out letters for pupils to take to their parents so that they could give permission for their children to go on a school trip. The teacher said to the Asian girls, 'I suppose we'll have problems with you girls. Is it worth me giving you a letter, because your parents don't allow you to be away from home overnight?'

Wright concluded that such comments from teachers made Asian pupils increasingly isolated from other pupils, who picked up on teachers' comments and became hostile to the Asians. It led to the Asian pupils themselves being ambivalent towards the school. For example, when Asian culture and celebrations were introduced into the school curriculum, Asian pupils 'expressed some pride' in having their culture acknowledged but they were also 'concerned that this often exacerbated the teasing, ridicule and harassment which they felt they received daily, particularly from the white children'.

African Caribbeans in primary schools

Despite the hostility of teachers towards Asian cultural traditions, and their assumptions that Asians would have poor language skills, teachers did expect them to have some academic success. The same was not true for African Caribbean children. For these children there were 'expectations of bad behaviour, along with disapproval, punishment and teacher insensitivity to the experience of racism'. In one class, for example, an African Caribbean pupil called Marcus was frequently criticized for shouting out answers to questions, whereas white pupils engaging in the same behaviour were not.

Generally, 'African-Caribbean boys received a disproportionate amount of teachers' negative attentions.' Compared to white boys whose behaviour was the same, they were more likely to be sent out of class, to be sent to see the head teacher or to have privileges withdrawn. African Caribbean Rastafarian children 'were seen by some teachers as a particular threat to classroom management' and were treated even more harshly.

Conclusion

All of the schools made attempts to take account of the multicultural nature of their intake in what they taught. However, they often failed to achieve their objectives in doing so. Teachers would mispronounce words or names relating to minority ethnic groups, causing white children to laugh and black children to be embarrassed. Wright comments: 'This situation unintentionally served to make topics or areas of knowledge associated with minority ethnic values and culture appear exotic, novel, unimportant, esoteric or difficult.'

The difficulties of the minority ethnic children in the primary schools were further exacerbated by racism from other children. White children often refused to play with Asian children 'and frequently subjected them to threatening behaviour, name calling and hitting'. Both Asian and African Caribbean children sometimes had to suffer 'intimidation, rejection and the occasional physical assault'.

Wright concludes that 'some black children are relatively disadvantaged' in primary schools. She argues that the earliest years of education provide 'the foundations of emotional, intellectual and social development', and that these early disadvantages might well hold back the children in later stages of their education.

A problem with Wright's study is that it tends to portray minority ethnic groups as the passive victims of racism. Some sociologists argue that pupils from minority ethnic groups do not necessarily accept negative portrayal or negative treatment by teachers. They therefore emphasize the positive and active part that pupils themselves play in determining how they react to the educational system.

The two studies we will examine next focus on the variety of ways in which minority ethnic groups respond to racism in the education system.

Heidi Safia Mirza – *Young, Female and Black*

In *Young, Female and Black*, Heidi Mirza (1992) describes the results of a study of 198 young women and men, including sixty-two black women aged 15–19 who were the main focus of the study. They all attended two comprehensive schools in south London. Mirza conducted observation in the school, used questionnaires to obtain basic data on the sample, and conducted informal interviews both with members of the sample and with parents. She also used secondary sources such as school records and exam results. She carried out detailed case studies of three black women.

The myth of underachievement

Mirza argues that there is a 'myth of underachievement' for black women. The girls in her sample did better in

Figure 10.5 The majority of primary school staff are committed to ideals of equality and educational opportunity

Source: Sally & Richard Greenhill

exams than black boys and white pupils in the school, and Mirza believes that in general the educational achievements of black women are underestimated.

Mirza also challenges the labelling theory of educational underachievement. Although there was evidence of racism from some teachers, she denies this had the effect of undermining the self-esteem of the black girls. When asked whom they most admired, 48 per cent of the black girls named themselves and over half named somebody who was black.

Some of the girls felt that some teachers put them down and did not give them a chance to prove themselves. However, 'Although the girls were resentful of these attitudes, there was little evidence that they were psychologically undermined by this different treatment.'

Types of teacher

A few teachers Mirza describes as 'overt racists'. One, for example, used the term 'wog' to one of the girls. The girls tried to avoid these teachers if possible and were certainly not prepared to accept their negative definitions of black people.

Another group, whom Mirza describes as 'the Christians', tried to be 'colour blind', recognizing no differences between ethnic groups. Although the behaviour of this group was less damaging than that of the overt racists, it did have its problems. For example, a number of the teachers who fell into this category opposed the setting up of a multi-racial working party because they believed there was no problem of racism to address.

Teachers in this group sometimes failed to push black pupils hard enough for them to achieve success. Sometimes they gave black girls reports that were more glowing than their achievements justified, preventing them from identifying and addressing their own weaknesses before exams came around.

A few of the teachers were active anti-racists, described by Mirza as 'the crusaders'. However, Mirza describes their campaigns as 'often misguided and over-zealous'. They put more effort into promoting these campaigns in the staffroom than they did into preparing for the classroom. Attempts to make classes relevant to black pupils sometimes resulted in no more than bemusement. For example, one teacher introduced a role-play into a class, which involved a girl who had been playing truant meeting her social worker. Although designed to reflect the experiences of black people, none of the black girls in the class had played truant or ever had a social worker.

Another group were described as 'the liberal chauvinists'. Like the crusaders, they were well-intentioned. They wanted to help black pupils, but their 'help' was patronizing and often counter-productive. They felt they understood their problems and knew what was best for them. For example, one teacher stopped a girl entering for all her exams because it was felt she could not cope with the workload. The teacher believed the girl's mother overworked her at home, helping out with household chores. In reality the pupil was desperate to enter for all her exams because she needed them to get on to a social work course. This ambition was thwarted by the teacher's insistence that she did fewer subjects.

Summarizing the actions of the liberal chauvinists, Mirza says:

> *There were numerous examples of teachers' negative assessments, most of which were based on what they believed to be 'informed judgements'. These negative assessments often led to the curtailment of opportunities that should have been available to the black girls in the study in view of their ability and attainment.* Mirza, 1992

The final group identified by Mirza was a group of four black teachers. Mirza found that members of this group were effective teachers who were liked and respected by their pupils from all ethnic groups. Although they showed no favouritism to black pupils, they could be 'of immense value when it came to advising and understanding the girls' needs'.

Conclusion

Overall, Mirza found that the black girls in her study had positive self-esteem, were concerned with academic success and were prepared to work hard. They did sometimes encounter open racism, but most of the teachers were genuinely trying to meet the girls' needs. However, most were failing to do so, and in the process were making it difficult for the girls to fulfil their potential. The girls had to look for

> *alternative strategies with which to 'get by'. These strategies, such as not taking up a particular subject or not asking for help, were employed by the girls as their only means of challenging their teachers' expectations of them, and as such were ultimately detrimental to the education of the pupils concerned.* Mirza, 1992

Mirza therefore believes it was not the effects of labelling as such that held the girls back, nor was it the culture of the girls. Instead, they were simply held back by the well-meaning but misguided behaviour of most of the teachers, and in particular by the power that teachers could exercise over pupils. In the end, however much they rejected the beliefs of their teachers, the girls 'were in no position in the "power hierarchy" to challenge any negative outcomes' that came from the way the teachers interpreted the girls' behaviour.

Máirtín Mac an Ghaill – minority ethnic groups in the sixth form

Máirtín Mac an Ghaill (1992) conducted an ethnographic study of twenty-five African Caribbean and Asian students studying A levels in a sixth-form college in a Midlands city from 1986 to 1988. He used observation and carried out interviews with the students, their parents, their teachers, and representatives of the black community in the area.

To different degrees, all the students 'spoke of the pervasiveness of white racism in relation to, inter alia, British immigration laws, the housing and labour markets, welfare institutions, policing and media presentation'. However, they disagreed over the extent of racism within education, with some arguing that 'they experienced little personal racial antagonism', and others believing 'their schools, as part of the wider society, were seen as significant institutions in reproducing racial exclusiveness'.

Their beliefs about the extent of racism, though, did not directly determine their attitudes to education and their levels of academic success. Those who believed they were labelled as likely failures, and who felt that they were the victims of most racism, were not necessarily those who had the most negative attitudes to education and nor were they those who put least effort into their academic work. The way that students 'perceived and responded to schooling' varied considerably and was influenced by the ethnic group to which they belonged, their gender, and the class composition of their former secondary schools.

Schooling and class

Some of the students had been to predominantly working-class inner-city schools, some to more suburban schools, and one to a private school. Eight females and four males went to single-sex schools. These varying experiences of schooling had affected the attitudes of individual students to the education system. The girl who went to a private school hated it and saw the other girls there as racist snobs. However, she reacted against this situation. She said, 'The place could have made me fail but I was determined to prove them wrong about black people.'

Many of those who went to the inner-city schools identified an anti-academic culture at the schools and linked this with high rates of unemployment in the area. One Asian male, for example, said that teachers treated them as a problem, but without realizing that 'they are one of the main causes of our problems'. Teachers did not expect them to do well, but this student believed 'it's just as bad for the white kids in many ways'.

Some of the girls thought they benefited from going to single-sex suburban schools. Although there was some racism, the environment was more academic and girls had greater chances of success in science subjects since there were no boys to dominate lessons.

Most pupils saw their parents as a major reason for their success in education. Mac an Ghaill says, 'The students explicitly identified with their parents, seeing them as their main support and source of inspiration.' This contradicts the claims of some sociologists that parental culture holds back some members of minority ethnic groups in the education system. However, a few of the girls did believe that their gender was a handicap at home. They were expected to do much more domestic work than their brothers, leaving them less time for their studies.

Gender and ethnicity

Gender also affected their experiences at school. Some of the students felt that African Caribbean boys were treated particularly badly. Teachers saw them as a threat and disciplined them more than other groups. One African Caribbean boy said:

> *The teachers treated black boys much worse than Asians and whites. Like, if we were standing together, they would break us up, saying gangs were bad. But they didn't seem to feel threatened in the same way with Asian and white boys.* Ghaill, 1992

Some students felt that teachers saw Asian girls as having more academic potential than African Caribbean girls. An African Caribbean student called 'Deborah' claimed, 'There's no way that a black girl would be encouraged to do the good subjects. It was music and sport for us.'

Survival strategies

All of the minority ethnic students experienced problems in the education system, but they experienced them differently depending on their gender and their ethnic group. Nevertheless, all of these students had enjoyed some success. They had done so through adopting a variety of survival strategies.

Some of the girls had banded together in their schools and used 'resistance within accommodation'. They would help each other out with academic work and would try to do work that would get them good marks. However, they were less willing to conform to school rules relating to dress, appearance and behaviour in class.

Some of the other minority ethnic pupils were less hostile to their schools and tried to become friendly with specific teachers. They tried to avoid other teachers who were racist, to prevent conflict. As one Asian student said, 'You keep your head down. What choice have you? My mates knew who the racist teachers were and kept out of their way.'

Although only a small-scale study, Mac an Ghaill's research shows the importance of seeing how class, gender and ethnicity interact within the school system. He argues: 'we need to move beyond mono-causal explanations and direct our research to the multifaceted dimensions of a class-based school system that is racially and gender structured'.

This research also shows that negative labelling does not necessarily lead to academic failure among minority ethnic students. Although such labelling creates extra barriers, some students are able to overcome these barriers: 'In so doing, they are rejecting the model of white society presented by teachers and are resisting incorporation into white cultural identities.'

David Gillborn and Deborah Youdell – *Rationing Education*

Ethnicity and achievement in two schools

Research by David Gillborn and Deborah Youdell (2000, 2001) argues that racism contributes to disadvantage minority ethnic groups, particularly African Caribbeans.

Gillborn and Youdell studied two London comprehensive schools (Taylor and Clough schools) over a two-year period, using lesson observation, analysis of documents, and interviews with pupils and teachers. The study was based on pupils in Key Stage 4 (14–16) with a particular focus on GCSEs.

In Clough school, 16 per cent of black pupils but 35 per cent of white pupils achieved five or more higher-grade passes at GCSE. In Taylor school, 47 per cent of white pupils and 24 per cent of black pupils achieved this standard. Thus, in both schools, approximately twice as many white as black pupils were succeeding in terms of this measure. Gillborn and Youdell point out that it is often seen as particularly important that pupils get a C or above in maths, English and a science subject. In Taylor school, no black pupils managed to achieve this, whereas 37 per cent of white pupils did. In Clough school, only 4 per cent of black pupils managed it, compared to 18 per cent of white pupils.

Gillborn and Youdell believe the move back towards selection in education, the emphasis on pupils achieving five or more higher-grade GCSEs, and the introduction of different tiers in GCSE have all contributed to the disadvantages of black (and working-class) pupils. They argue that these changes have produced a system of **educational triage** in which education is rationed. 'Triage' refers to a medical practice, used for example in the event of a disaster, whereby patients are prioritized. Hopeless cases, where the doctors feel there is no hope of survival, are left to die. Doctors prioritize the serious cases where they believe they have a chance of saving the patient. Those with more minor problems, whose lives are not under threat, are given a lower priority and dealt with later.

In the education system, the emphasis is on helping students who have a chance of getting five or more GCSEs at C or above, while those who are certain to succeed are less of a priority. Those who are seen as having no chance of success in these terms are the lowest priority. In itself, this does not inevitably disadvantage minority ethnic pupils, but in practice it does lead to black pupils being held back. Gillborn and Youdell say: 'Selection by "ability" unfairly disadvantages ethnic minority pupils. The colour-blind nature of specific policy proposals belies the racialized reality of contemporary life in Britain and, therefore, threatens racist consequences.'

Racialized expectations

How do Gillborn and Youdell explain these disparities? Most teachers were not openly racist nor did they want to disadvantage black pupils. In fact, 'many teachers are passionately committed to challenging the very inequalities that they participate in reinforcing'.

Like a number of researchers before them, Gillborn and Youdell found that throughout their school careers the expectations held of black pupils were comparatively low and they were systematically denied access to the sets, groups and exams which would give them the best chance of success. Gillborn and Youdell believe that underlying these processes are **racialized expectations** of different ethnic groups.

Without intending to be racist, schools and their teachers tend to interpret the behaviour of pupils from different ethnic groups in different ways. In particular, the actions of black pupils tend to be interpreted as challenging the authority of the teacher or the school, whereas the actions of white pupils are not. In one of the schools a faculty head was concerned about a number of black pupils questioning their low predicted grades. This teacher treated this as evidence of 'a "challenge" and "threat" rather than evidence of high aspirations and motivation to succeed'.

Black pupils certainly felt they were treated more harshly than white pupils. They believed they were picked on even when they were engaging in similar types of behaviour to white pupils. Pupils gave numerous examples of these practices, of which the following are only a small selection.

- In Taylor school, Marcella, a black girl, was temporarily excluded from school for watching a fight, when white girls who did the same were not.
- Also at Taylor school, Awad, a black pupil, was excluded even though he claimed he was the victim rather than the perpetrator of violence, and that he had been beaten up.
- In both schools a number of black pupils believed their placement in low sets or entry for lower tiers of exams was unwarranted, given their academic performance.

Although Gillborn and Youdell found that 'openly racist teachers and consciously discriminatory practices are rare', they did find that 'widespread inequalities of opportunity are endured by black children'. Teachers had an expectation that 'black pupils will generally present disciplinary problems, and they therefore tended to feel that "control and punishment" had to be given higher priority than "academic concerns"'. They also expected black pupils, on average, to do less well than their white peers.

In their turn, most black pupils felt they were disadvantaged. By and large, the black pupils expected to be blamed for disciplinary problems and they expected that teachers would underestimate their future achievements. In these circumstances it was hardly surprising that they ended up doing, on average, less well than the white pupils attending the same schools.

Marketization and the changing priorities

Since the 1990s there has been a growing emphasis on examination success. Schools have been increasingly concerned with their position in league tables. Comprehensive schools for 11–16s are largely judged by the proportion of pupils attaining five or more A*–C grades at GCSE. Head teachers and teachers see this as the dominant measure of their success.

In line with this concern, teachers are increasingly prioritizing their time and effort in order to produce the best GCSE results. As a result, 'some pupils are sacrificed to the more important goal of raising attainment in the league table statistics'. The pupils 'sacrificed' are primarily working-class and African Caribbean.

GCSE exams are tiered. In two-tiered exams, C is the highest grade a pupil entered for the foundation tier can achieve. In maths, which until recently had three tiers, D was the highest grade a pupil entered for the foundation tier could achieve.

Both schools studied by Gillborn and Youdell followed the national pattern of placing pupils into exam sets on the basis of their perceived ability. Pupils seen as 'able' were placed in higher sets and entered for higher-level GCSE exams, while those seen as 'less able' were placed in lower-level sets and entered for foundation level exams. In practice, a disproportionate number of African Caribbean and working-class pupils were placed in lower sets.

Pupils in higher sets had the most experienced teachers and were given more teacher time, support and effort. Pupils in lower sets were 'systematically neglected'. For example, at Clough school, 29 per cent of the white pupils but 38 per cent of the black pupils were seen as 'without hope' of success at GCSE and, in Gillborn and Youdell's words, 'condemned to the group of lost causes'.

Teachers decided which pupils should be assigned to which sets. Discussions were based on their view of what counts as ability and who has it. They assumed that ability is largely fixed, it can be measured and it can predict educational performance. In practice, African Caribbean students were seen as less able and less likely to achieve grade C and above at GCSE. As a result, they were more likely to be placed in lower sets and entered for lower tiers. For example, in Taylor school, 71 per cent of black pupils were entered for foundation level maths. As a result, it was impossible for them to even get a grade C.

Gillborn and Youdell condemn the concept and use of 'ability'. In their words, '"ability" is a loaded, fallacious and highly dangerous concept ... "Ability" offers a supposedly fair means for condemning some children to second-class education.' When teachers see 'ability' as unequally distributed between social groups, its use can disadvantage particular groups. In the case of African Caribbeans, the use of the concept of 'ability', with all its consequences, is racist.

Tony Sewell – *Black Masculinities and Schooling*

So far, explanations for African Caribbean underachievement have focused on racism in schools. This section looks at the African Caribbean writer Tony Sewell's (1997) study of the relationship between family life, identity, street culture and schooling. Sewell's research is based on a study of black students in a boys-only 11–16 comprehensive school. It provides a possible explanation for the decline in the attainment of many African Caribbean boys during secondary education.

Street culture and black masculinity

A high proportion of African Caribbean boys are raised in lone-parent families, usually headed by women. In 2001, 57 per cent of African Caribbean families with dependent children were headed by lone parents, compared with 25 per cent of white families (*Social Trends 2006*). As a result, many boys lack the male role model and the discipline provided by a father figure. According to Sewell, this makes them more vulnerable to peer group pressure.

Some young men are drawn into gangs which emphasize an aggressive, macho form of masculinity. Members demand respect, reject authority figures such as teachers and police, and focus on up-to-the-minute street fashion and music. This form of black masculinity is reflected and reinforced by the media, with gangsta rap and hip-hop fashions and news reports emphasizing black street crime and gun culture.

According to Sewell, this subculture of black masculinity provides a 'comfort zone' for many African Caribbean young men. Acceptance and support from the peer group compensate for their sense of rejection by their fathers and by a society and education system which they often experience as racist.

In schools, this version of black masculinity can lead to opposition to the authority of teachers, a rejection of academic achievement, and a definition of hard work as effeminate. However, Sewell's research indicates that only a minority of African Caribbean boys adopt this approach.

Black masculinities in school

Sewell identified four main groups of black students in the comprehensive he studied:

1. **Conformists.** This was the largest group, making up 41 per cent of the sample. They saw education as the route to success and conformed to the norms and values of the school. They saw this approach as incompatible with the aggressive masculinity of black street culture.
2. **Innovators.** This group (35 per cent) also saw education as important but they rejected the process of schooling and the demands they saw it making on their identity and behaviour. Although anti-school, they attempted to keep out of trouble. They kept their distance from the Conformists and the teachers.
3. **Retreatists.** Students in this category (6 per cent) were loners and kept themselves to themselves. Many had special educational needs.
4. **Rebels.** This group (18 per cent) rejected both the norms and values of the school and the importance of education. Many saw educational qualifications as worthless since racism would disqualify their worth in leading to high-status, well-paid jobs. The rebels reacted aggressively to what they saw as racism in school. They were confrontational and challenging, adopting a macho masculinity and demanding respect. Some modelled themselves on the Jamaican 'Yardman', noted for his supposed physical and sexual prowess.

   The Rebels brought black street culture into school. Teachers sometimes interpreted this as a challenge to their authority when none was intended. For example, many of the Rebels came to school with patterns in their hair. This was banned, despite the fact that white students were allowed to wear ponytails. The Rebels saw this as a lack of respect and responded aggressively. Examples such as this illustrate how an anti-social confrontational subculture can develop.

Evaluation

Tony Sewell's study is controversial. He has been attacked for what his critics see as blaming African Caribbeans for their underachievement. He has been accused of blaming black fathers for deserting their families, blaming black youth for generating a subculture which leads to their own failure, and blaming the black community for failing to support its young people. Critics argue that, in the process, Sewell has diverted attention from what they see as the real cause of black underachievement – a racist society, an institutionally racist education system and economic deprivation.

Supporters of Sewell reject this criticism. They argue that he is attempting to describe and explain rather than allocate blame. Sewell provides a possible explanation for the decline in the attainment of many African Caribbean boys during secondary education. In addition, his research rejects the stereotype of the young aggressive black male personified by the Rebels by showing that they formed only a relatively small minority (18 per cent) of the African Caribbean boys in the school he studied.

Paul Connolly – *Racism, Gender Identities and Young Children*

More recent studies of education have moved away from an exclusive emphasis on differential attainment. Instead, they have examined the way in which the identities of different groups are constructed within the education system. These studies have implications for the understanding of attainment, but that is not their primary focus.

One such study is Paul Connolly's (1998) investigation of three classes of 5- and 6-year-olds in a multi-ethnic inner-city primary school. This study provides interesting insights into the relationship between gender and ethnicity. The study was carried out in 1992–3, using observation, interviews with parents, staff and governors, and group interviews with the children. Connolly also used secondary sources such as files produced by the school.

Although his research was based in the school, Connolly paid particular attention to the wider context in which the schooling took place. He did not see the social relationships within the school as just a product of the education system. Young though the children were, they brought with them to school ways of thinking about masculinity, femininity and ethnicity which played an important role in developing the internal school relationships. Of course, teachers' attitudes and behaviour also played a role. There was evidence of some sexism from teachers, but Connolly stresses the complexities of the factors shaping what went on in the school.

Black boys

Teachers in the school were well aware that it was located in a deprived area. They were concerned about the maintenance of discipline and they brought with them to their work assumptions about different groups. For example, Connolly found that teachers were more likely to criticize the behaviour of black boys than that of other groups. He says:

> *There were many examples gained from observations throughout the school year, where black boys would be sent to stand outside the classroom, told to stand up or move in assemblies, and be singled out and instructed to stand by the wall or outside the staffroom during playtime. While black boys were not the only ones to be disciplined in this way, they were significantly over-represented in these processes.* Connolly, 1998

According to Connolly, teachers were influenced in their perceptions of black boys 'by the broader discourses on "race", crime and the inner city'. Some teachers thought that some of the black male children they were teaching were in danger of growing up to be violent criminals and they saw them as a threat to school discipline. By picking on them they were trying to nip their behaviour in the bud.

However, they also took more positive steps to encourage them to participate enthusiastically and actively in school activities. There was a particular pride taken in the school football teams, in which some of the black boys who were perceived to be badly behaved were players. The emphasis on football, though, created a 'specifically masculine ethos within the school'.

However, it was not just a question of the boys being labelled by teachers and then living up to their labels. The black boys also brought with them to school their own values and attitudes – for example, those relating to masculinity. This contributed to their sense of identity as much as the behaviour of teachers.

One particular group of black boys, whom Connolly dubs the 'Bad Boys', drew upon common perceptions of black male children to base their behaviour upon ideas of 'hyper-masculinity'. They were successful in establishing themselves as some of the toughest in the school, as among the best footballers, and as some of the most attractive to girls in games of 'kiss-and-chase'. This earned them considerable respect from their male peers in the school. It also encouraged them to concentrate on non-academic ways of earning status and so limited their educational progress.

Black girls

Some negative stereotypes were not just confined to boys. Like black boys, black girls were perceived by teachers as potentially disruptive but likely to be good at sports. They were more likely to be singled out for punishment than other girls. However, teachers did tend to believe that black girls were good at some subjects, such as music and dancing. One girl, for example, was often chosen to come to the front of the class to sing her favourite songs.

Despite the predominant perception within the school that girls were more passive than boys, some of the black girls were willing to challenge this. Although boys used various techniques of intimidation to try to maintain their dominance within the school, some of the black girls got together from time to time to turn the tables on the boys. For example, on one occasion eight of the black girls 'captured' a white boy whom they found particularly troublesome. They paraded him around the playground.

The teachers at this school tended to 'underplay the black girls' educational achievements and focus on their social behaviour'. Like their black male counterparts, they were quite likely to be disciplined and punished even though their behaviour did not always seem to justify it. However, this was not the case with all the girls. One of the black girls, Whitney, came from a higher-class background than the others and she was seen as approaching the ideal of a model pupil. Consequently, her work was valued, she received more encouragement than other black girls and she was less likely to be disciplined for bad behaviour.

South Asian boys

South Asian boys developed rather different identities compared to black boys. On the local estates, white residents tended to see Asians as an 'alien wedge' who were more distinctive and different than black people. Asians were seen as having different family lifestyles, which were more close-knit than those of the rest of the community. They were also seen as different by virtue of being able to speak languages other than English, and because of religion. Aspects of these views were reproduced among the teachers in the school.

Some teachers contrasted what they saw as the close and supportive Asian families with the high rates of single parenthood among other groups in the area. However, some teachers also believed that Asian parents might lack the parenting skills necessary to help their children develop social skills. South Asian boys tended to be seen as immature rather than as seriously deviant. Misbehaviour was often seen as 'silly' rather than as a threat to order. Much of their bad behaviour went unnoticed by teachers and was not punished to the same extent as that of black boys.

Partly because they were not seen as challenging the school, the identity of South Asian boys was 'feminized'. They were seen as relatively passive and conformist. Some were even described as 'little' by teachers, and some teachers thought that particular South Asian boys needed 'looking after' because they were vulnerable. Because of this there was a tendency for other boys who wanted to assert their masculinity to pick on South Asian boys and attack them. This reaffirmed their feminized identity and made it very difficult for them to assert their masculinity. They were largely excluded from football – one of the key arenas for asserting masculine identity. Those who did join in football games were sometimes subject to racial abuse.

The South Asian boys had difficulty in gaining status as males. This made it difficult for them to enjoy school and feel confident. However, teachers did have high expectations of their academic work. They expected them to be reliable and keen. They were often praised, and encouraged to try hard and take their work seriously.

South Asian girls

South Asian girls were seen as likely to be even more obedient and hard-working than South Asian boys, and, furthermore, than black and white girls. Teachers more or less took it for granted that South Asian girls would produce a reasonable standard of work and that they would be conscientious. However, Connolly's own observations showed that 'the behaviour of South Asian girls pointed towards a similar mix of work and avoidance of work and obedience and disruption, making their behaviour largely indistinguishable from that of their female peers'.

All of this suggested that South Asian girls would have advantages over other girls. Teachers' expectations were high and this would encourage the girls to live up to them. On the other hand, teachers felt there was little need to give these girls special help. They expected them to cope without it. Teachers got no extra status from helping South Asian girls to achieve academic success. It was expected of them. Some teachers spent more time trying to get pupils from other groups to do well. This was because the teachers would get more of a sense of achievement if these pupils' work improved 'against the odds'.

Like South Asian boys, South Asian girls had high status in terms of their perceived academic ability, but they had a relatively low status among their peers. In some ways they were viewed as extremely feminine because they were regarded as 'quiet, passive, obedient and helpful'. However, they were also regarded as 'the Sexual Other in relation to discourses on boyfriends and the related discursive themes of intimacy, love and marriage'. They were not expected to get involved in games of 'kiss-and-chase', nor were they seen as potential girlfriends by black boys and white boys. Their culture was seen as too alien and inferior by other pupils for them to be seen as possible girlfriends.

Conclusion

Connolly's study shows how gender and ethnicity interact in creating identities among young children, and it highlights some of the ways in which this might influence educational attainment. It shows how teachers define gender and ethnic identities in terms of discourses drawn from the wider society. It also shows how these discourses can be modified and challenged by the pupils themselves as they strive to create their own identities. And finally, it shows the danger of trying to explain the differences in educational achievement between boys in general and girls in general in terms of overall theories which fail to take account of other social divisions, such as ethnicity and class.

Louise Archer – Muslim boys and education

In *Race, Masculinity and Schooling: Muslim Boys and Education* (2003), Louise Archer examined how Muslim boys saw themselves, their schooling and their future. Her sample consisted of thirty-one Muslim boys aged 14–15 in year 10, in four schools in a town in northwest England which she called Mill Town. The data were derived from discussion groups led by three interviewers/discussion leaders – two British women of Pakistani heritage and Archer herself, a white British middle-class woman. The boys were mainly of Pakistani or Bangladeshi heritage. Archer's main aim was to see how the boys 'constructed and negotiated their masculine identities'.

Muslim and black identities

In the discussion groups, all the boys identified themselves first and foremost as Muslim. They saw this as a positive masculine identity. They were proud of belonging to a local and global Muslim brotherhood. They saw this as a strong masculine identity as opposed to the traditional stereotype of a 'weak', 'passive' Asian masculinity.

Although most of the boys were born in England, they did not feel they belonged in England, nor in the countries of origin of their parents or grandparents – mainly Pakistan and Bangladesh. Although they saw themselves as Muslim, many of the boys were not particularly religious in terms of their behaviour – for example, most did not attend the mosque on Friday.

When constructing their identities, the boys drew partly on African Caribbean and African American styles of masculinity. They sometimes referred to themselves as 'black' in comparison to the 'white' majority. Black was seen as 'cool' and 'strong'. The boys sometimes drew on African American 'gangsta' masculinity when constructing their identities. Most claimed to be members of gangs – where they 'talked tough', 'walked the walk' and wore the latest fashions. However, the boundary between a 'friendship group' and a 'gang' was blurred.

The boys' black identity was ambiguous – black 'gangsta' forms of masculinity were drawn on rather than forming the basis for their identities.

Gendered identities

The boys' gender identity as male was constructed in relation to girls. They were aware of boys' supposed 'underachievement' and girls' superior exam performance and they complained that teachers unfairly favoured girls. They responded to this with laddish remarks, seeing 'messing around' and 'having a laugh' as typical of a desirable macho masculinity. This response probably reflected their class position as well as their gender – most of the boys came from working-class families.

The boys saw part of their gender identity as deriving from their Asian Muslim culture. Men are the breadwinners – they have freedom and autonomy, power and control. Women are primarily concerned with domestic matters as housewives and mothers – they are subservient. It is a man's duty to make sure that women's behaviour is appropriate – for example, that their appearance and clothing are respectable. The boys admitted that in certain respects gender roles were unfair but believed that this was part of their religious/cultural tradition and therefore they should abide by it.

However, the boys recognized that the gender relations outlined above were not reflected in their everyday experiences. Muslim girls often refused to do as they were expected – from the boys' point of view, they were often 'out of control'.

Education and the breadwinner identity

The boys saw themselves as future breadwinners and saw education as a means towards successfully performing this role. They held a strong belief in the value of education for 'getting ahead' and obtaining a well-paid job. Most of the boys expressed an interest in continuing their education beyond GCSE and were encouraged by their parents to do so.

Despite this view of education, some of the boys felt that the value of qualifications was reduced by racism. They believed that this made it more difficult for them to translate qualifications into appropriate occupations. Because of this, some saw falling back on family businesses – for example, restaurants – which did not require qualifications, as an alternative route.

The boys described their family lives in 'overwhelmingly positive terms' – home was a source of warmth, love and security. They saw adult Muslim masculinity as involving a breadwinner providing for his family, caring for his parents in their old age, and supporting relatives locally and 'back home' in Bangladesh or Pakistan. Successfully performing this role was a 'source of pride and a symbol of masculinity'; and education was seen as a means to this end.

Evaluation

This is an important study because it illustrates that identities are fluid and complex, they derive from different sources, they change according to the social context and they are always in the process of construction and reconstruction. For example, the boys 'shifted across and between' Muslim, Black, Asian, Bangladeshi/Pakistani, English and British identities, selecting one or more depending on the situation, context or topic of conversation. And the boys' identities were influenced by their ethnicity, their religion, their class, their gender and their experience of family life. Their attitudes towards and experience of education must be seen in terms of this fluid and complex social context.

Archer's insistence on the importance of social context may indicate a weakness in her research method. The data came from small discussion groups led by two British Pakistani women and one white British woman. Each boy had an audience, consisting of other boys in the group and one of these women. Each boy's projection of particular identities will reflect his perception of the audience. Archer recognizes this. However, it may place limitations on her data – for example, what would the boys say in the presence of their father, mother, sister, brother, male friends, female friends and so on? Wider sources of data drawn from different contexts would provide a fuller picture.

Summary and conclusions

Although a very recent development in human history, mass education is here to stay. It is a growth industry with nation-states seeing it as a vital component for success in an increasingly competitive global market-place. Critics of this view see education being reduced to a means of economic development. Sally Tomlinson (2005) voices this concern when she argues that education should be a 'humanizing, liberalizing and democratizing force' rather than narrowed to economic ends. Where in today's National Curriculum is a concern for the welfare and well-being of humanity, for peace and justice, for a better society and global environment, for equal opportunity and tolerance, for exploring ideas and developing critical thought?

Sociologists are members of society. As such, they will be influenced by the issues of the day, the values of society and political ideologies. For example, the social democratic perspective has helped to shape the sociology of education with its emphasis on equality of opportunity. This has led to research which highlights how class, gender and ethnic inequalities have resulted in inequality of educational opportunities. This research shows that class is the main social factor affecting differential educational attainment; and it shows that, despite the efforts of various governments over the past sixty years, class differences in educational attainment have remained largely unchanged.

It is important to know this and even more important to do something about it.

CHAPTER 11

Culture, socialization and identity

Without social identity, there is, in fact, no society. Jenkins, 1996

Introduction

The definition of culture

In the introductory chapter (see p. 2) culture was defined as being the whole way of life found in a particular society. It was suggested that culture was learned and shared by members of a society. However, the concept of culture is a complicated one. In his book *Keywords* (1976), Raymond Williams, a leading theorist of culture, claims: 'Culture is one of the two or three most complicated words in the English language.'

The word 'culture' has in fact been used in a number of different ways, both by sociologists and in everyday conversation. All the ways in which it has been used implicitly or explicitly contrast culture with nature. The things that humans produce or do are cultural, whereas the things that exist or occur without human intervention are part of the natural world. Christopher Jencks (1993) describes culture in this sense as 'all which is symbolic: the learned ... aspects of human society'. However, the various definitions differ as to what aspects of human life and its products should be seen as part of culture.

Jencks distinguishes four main senses in which the word 'culture' is now used:

1. Culture is sometimes seen as a state of mind. Someone becomes cultured if they move towards 'the idea of perfection, a goal or an aspiration of individual human achievement or emancipation'. From this perspective, culture is seen as a quality possessed by individuals who are able to gain the learning and achieve the qualities that are seen as desirable in a cultured human being.
2. The first definition is rather an elitist one, in that it sees some aspects of what is human as superior to other aspects. The second definition is also elitist, but rather than seeing some individuals as superior to others it sees certain societies as superior to others. In this sense, culture is closely related to the idea of civilization. Some societies are more cultured or more civilized than others. This view of culture is closely linked to evolutionary ideas, such as those of Herbert Spencer (see p. 146), who saw Western societies as more evolved than other societies.
3. The third definition sees culture as 'the collective body of arts and intellectual work within any one society'. As Jencks points out, this is a fairly commonsense definition and is widely used. From this point of view, culture is to be found in theatres, concert halls, art galleries and libraries, rather than in all aspects of human social life. Culture in this sense is sometimes called **high culture**.

4 The final definition sees culture as 'the whole way of life of a people'. This definition of culture is adopted by Ralph Linton (1945), who says: 'The culture of a society is the way of life of its members; the collection of ideas and habits which they learn, share and transmit from generation to generation.'

The fourth definition is the one most usually adopted by contemporary sociologists. Culture in this sense incorporates virtually the whole of the subject matter of sociology. Thus it is hard to see the sociology of culture as being very distinct from other areas of sociology. When the third definition is adopted it is easier to identify a distinctive area of sociology which is the sociology of culture. It includes, for example, the sociology of art, the sociology of music and the sociology of literature.

Types of culture

These definitions of culture (particularly the third and fourth) can be developed further through a brief examination of the different types of culture that have been identified by sociologists.

High culture

The term **high culture**, as mentioned above, is usually used to refer to cultural creations that have a particularly high status. They are regarded by arbiters of cultural taste as the epitome of the highest levels of human creativity. The products of long-established art forms are usually seen as examples of high culture. They include opera, the work of highly regarded classical composers such as Beethoven and Mozart, the paintings of artists such as Leonardo da Vinci, and critically acclaimed literature such as the work of Shakespeare and Milton. For many who use the term, high culture is seen as aesthetically superior to lesser forms of culture, such as the next three types we will consider.

Folk culture

Folk culture refers to the culture of ordinary people, particularly those living in pre-industrial societies. Dominic Strinati (1995) says folk culture is often taken to arise 'from the grass roots, is self-created and autonomous and directly reflects the lives and experiences of the people'. Examples of folk culture include traditional folk songs and traditional stories which have been handed down from generation to generation. Folk culture has been seen by some theorists as being less worthwhile than high culture, but nevertheless as worthy of some respect. Strinati describes this view in the following way: 'folk culture can never aspire to be art, but its distinctiveness is accepted and respected'. It is at least an authentic culture and not one that is artificially created.

Mass culture

For its critics, **mass culture** is seen as less worthy than folk culture. If folk culture is seen as characteristic of premodern, pre-industrial societies, mass culture is a product of industrial societies. Mass culture is essentially a product of the mass media, and examples include popular feature films, television soap operas and recorded pop music. As we shall see, some critics of mass culture see it as debasing for the individual and destructive of the fabric of society. While folk culture was created by ordinary people, mass culture is only consumed by them. From this viewpoint, the audience become passive members of a mass society, unable to think for themselves.

Popular culture

The term **popular culture** is often used in a similar way to the term mass culture. Popular culture includes any cultural products appreciated by large numbers of ordinary people with no great pretensions to cultural expertise: for example, TV programmes, pop music, mass-market films such as the *Star Wars* and *Harry Potter* series, and popular fiction such as detective stories. However, while mass culture is usually used as a pejorative term – a term of abuse – this is by no means always the case with the term popular culture. While some do see popular culture as shallow or even harmful, others, including some postmodern theorists, argue that it is just as valid and just as worthwhile as high culture.

Subculture

Subculture is a term widely used in sociology to refer to 'groups of people that have something in common with each other (i.e. they share a problem, an interest, a practice) which distinguishes them in a significant way from other social groups' (Thornton, 1997). The term has been applied to a wide range of groups, including communities who live close together and have a shared lifestyle, youth groups who share common musical tastes and enjoy the same leisure activities (for example, ravers), ethnic groups, people who share the same religious beliefs, members of the same gang, and so on. Some theorists, particularly functionalists, have tended to emphasize the degree to which culture, in the sense of lifestyle, is shared by members of a society. Many other theorists emphasize one or more aspects of cultural pluralism or subcultural variety in society.

Global culture

In terms of scale, the concept of global culture is at the opposite extreme to the idea of subculture. The idea of global culture implies that we are all becoming part of one, all-embracing culture that affects all parts of the world. Mike Featherstone argues that in terms of such a definition, no global culture exists. He says, 'Is there a global culture? If by a global culture we mean something akin to the culture of a nation-state writ large, then the answer is patently a negative one' (1990, p. 1).

Featherstone believes it is clear that people throughout the world do not share a similar lifestyle. However, he does believe that it is reasonable to talk of the *globalization of culture*, as a process in which some aspects of culture cross state boundaries and become widely dispersed across most areas of the world.

Socialization

Anthony Giddens defines socialization as 'the process whereby the helpless infant gradually becomes a self aware,

knowledgeable person, skilled in the ways of the culture in which he or she was born' (Giddens, 2006, p. 163). He goes on to comment that, 'Socialization among the young allows for the more general phenomenon of social reproduction – the process whereby societies have structural continuity over time' (p. 163). Giddens, like many other sociologists, therefore sees socialization as a fundamental process in societies, and one of the main means by which societies are able to endure, as their culture is passed down from generation to generation.

The earliest stages of socialization, in which young children start to acquire the ability to act socially, are referred to as **primary socialization**. Most primary socialization takes place within the family. Primary socialization is often seen as crucially important in helping to shape human beings, but socialization continues throughout life.

Secondary socialization takes place later, with education, religion and the mass media being amongst the most important agents of secondary socialization. Also important are peer groups. **Peer groups** are groups of people with a similar status – for example, groups of friends, school children in the same year, or colleagues in the same job. Socialization within peer groups is less hierarchical than the socialization of children by adults. In peer groups the culture and norms of behaviour develop in the course of interaction rather than being imposed from above. As adults enter new situations – for example, as a result of moving house, changing jobs or taking up a new pastime – socialization takes place as they learn the norms, values and social roles of the social group. Furthermore, the culture of society changes, so the process of socialization is never complete.

This brief description of socialization suggests that it is a highly predictable, conservative process, which maintains the status quo by passing down a shared and relatively stable culture from generation to generation. Some sociological accounts of socialization, such as functionalism, see the process very much in this way. However, as we shall see, this interpretation has been increasingly questioned (see pp. 687–92).

Many social psychologists and sociologists emphasize that children (and for that matter adults) are not just the passive recipients of socialization, but instead are actively involved in the process. Sometimes socialization does not work smoothly and predictably. People are often subject to contradictory socializing influences which encourage different behaviours. Furthermore people may also resist socialization by actively rejecting what they are being taught. Some writers suggest that even young children have their own cultures and therefore do not simply learn cultures passed down to them by adults (see p. 689). Amongst older age groups this active resistance may manifest itself in the formation of **deviant subcultures** (see pp. 325–7 and 771–82).

Socialization is a very important part of child development, but growing up also involves other processes. Gerald Handel (2006) argues that one of these processes is **individuation** – 'the process of becoming an individual person'. Children learn to see themselves as unique individuals with characteristics that separate them from other members of society. People are not carbon copies of their parents, nor are all members of society identical to one another. Individuation gives rise to another crucial sociological concept, that of **identity**. (See pp. 686–92 for a more detailed discussion of socialization.)

Identity

The definition of identity

The concept of **identity** has been defined as 'A sense of self that develops as the child differentiates from parents and family and takes a place in society' (Jary and Jary, 1991). It refers to the sense that someone has of who they are, of what is most important about them. Important sources of identity are likely to include nationality, ethnicity, sexuality (homosexual, heterosexual, bisexual), gender and class. Although it is individuals who have identities, identity is related to the social groups to which the individual belongs and with which they identify. However, there is not always a perfect match between how a person thinks of themselves and how others see them. **Personal identity** may be different from **social identity**. For example, a person perceived by others to be male may see themselves as a woman trapped in a man's body.

The importance of identity

The concept of identity has become increasingly important in sociology. Early sociologists rarely used the concept, although their work often implied a theory of identity. For example, most early studies of social class in Britain tended to see class identity as central to people's sense of who they were. Studies of class consciousness (see, for example, pp. 56–8) often assumed that class identity was normally strong. They downplayed the importance of other identities such as gender, sexuality and ethnicity. Some sociologists believe that studies such as these operated with a modern conception of identity. People's identities were seen as fairly stable, as widely shared within social groups, and as based upon one or two key variables, such as class and nationality.

More recently, poststructuralist and postmodern theories of identity have adopted very different views (see pp. 697–9). They tend to suggest that people's identities have many different facets, that they frequently change and can contain considerable contradictions. For example, people may act in more 'masculine' ways in some situations and more 'feminine' ways in other situations. Furthermore, the meaning of 'feminine' and 'masculine' identities has become less clear-cut. There may now be many different ways to be manly or womanly, rather than just one (see, for example, pp. 690–2).

According to these sorts of perspectives, people actively create their own identities. Identities are no longer reducible simply to the social groups to which people belong. People have a great deal of choice about what social groups to join and, through shopping and other forms of consumption, people can shape and sometimes change their identities. To some writers, most individuals in contemporary societies no longer have a stable sense of identity at all – their identities are fragmented (see pp. 700–4).

Identity and culture

The concept of identity is closely related to the idea of culture. Identities can be formed through the cultures and subcultures to which people belong or in which people participate. However, different theories of identity see the relationship between culture and identity in rather different

ways. Those influenced by modern theories of culture and identity are more likely to see identity as originating in a fairly straightforward way from involvement in particular cultures and subcultures. For example, people living in Britain would be expected to have a strong sense of British identity. Theories influenced by postmodernism tend to stress the complexity of being British and the diversity of ways in which, for example, British people from different ethnic or national origins interpret British identity.

Stephen Frosh describes the view that identity draws from culture but is not simply formed by it:

> *Recent sociological and psychological theory has stressed that a person's 'identity' is in fact something multiple and potentially fluid, constructed through experience and linguistically coded. In developing their identities people draw upon culturally available resources in their immediate social networks and in society as a whole. The process of identity construction is therefore one upon which the contradictions and dispositions of the surrounding socio-cultural environment have a profound impact.* Frosh, 1999

The issue of identity will be explored in much greater depth towards the end of the chapter. First, we will examine a number of perspectives on culture.

Culture – functionalist perspectives

Functionalist sociologists have generally had little to say about culture in the sense of the arts, but have been interested in culture in the sense of norms, values and lifestyles. Functionalists have generally approached the issue of societal culture from an evolutionary perspective. Their emphasis has been on the changing nature of culture as society evolved. Durkheim and Mauss developed an influential functionalist theory which goes back to the origins of human culture.

Emile Durkheim and Marcel Mauss – *Primitive Classification*

The need for classification

In *Primitive Classification* (1963, first published 1903), Emile Durkheim and Marcel Mauss considered some of the most basic questions about how human culture arises. To Durkheim and Mauss, culture only becomes possible once humans are able to distinguish between things and classify them. At birth, humans cannot classify things, and experience simply 'a continuous flow of representations'. This makes it difficult to separate one thing from another. In order to develop a culture, humans have to develop a system for classifying things. Without such a system, they cannot make sense of the world around them.

The origin of classification systems

Where does the model on which classification is based come from? Durkheim and Mauss claimed that the model comes from the structure of society. Because social structures are based upon divisions between social groups, people begin to classify the rest of the world in terms of such divisions.

Durkheim and Mauss believed that Australian aboriginals had the simplest and most primitive societies. They considered that such societies provided important evidence about how human systems of classification might have developed. By examining the work of other anthropologists, Durkheim and Mauss found that the Port Mackay aboriginals had perhaps the simplest classification system of all. The Port Mackay aboriginals were divided into two social groups or **moieties**. These were called the Youngaroo and the Wootaroo. Because their society was divided into two groups, they divided everything else into two groups, corresponding to their moieties. For example, alligators and the sun were classified as Youngaroo, whereas kangaroos and the moon were Wootaroo.

Other aboriginal groups had more complicated systems. For example, the Wakelbura of Queensland classified everything into four groupings. This was because their society was divided into four groups: two moieties – the Mallera and Wutaru – each of which was subdivided into two marriage clans – the Kurgila and Banbey in the Mallera moiety, and the Wongu and Obu in the Wutaru moiety. The Wakelbura classification system reflected these divisions, with two primary classes of things, each of which was further subdivided into two. Furthermore, this affected even what people were allowed to eat. The Banbey, for example, were only allowed to eat food that was classified as Banbey (including kangaroos, dogs, small bees and honey).

Complex classification systems

As the complexity of societies increases, so does the complexity of classification. For example, the Zuni Sioux of North America have an eightfold classification system based upon eight points of the compass. For example, 'the pelican, crane, grouse, sagecock, the evergreen oak, etc. are things of the north; the bear, coyote, and spring grass are things of the west'.

Although such classification systems might appear primitive, they are the basis for all classification and indeed all culture. Like much more advanced and even scientific classification systems, they describe hierarchies, establish relationships between groups of things, and organize the world to make it comprehensible. Thus all understanding is based upon social relationships. Durkheim and Mauss say:

> *Far from being the case ... that the social relations of men are based upon logical relations between things, in reality it is the former which have provided the prototype for the latter ... The first logical categories were social categories; the first classes of things were classes of men.*
> Durkheim and Mauss, 1963, first published 1903

Religion and classification

In other work, Durkheim is equally insistent on arguing that culture has a social origin. In *The Elementary Forms of*

the Religious Life (1961, first published 1912) he extended the arguments of *Primitive Classification* to incorporate religion. He argued that religion is based upon a basic division of the world into the sacred and the profane. He again used the example of Australian aboriginals and advanced the argument that the totem system is concerned with the worship of society (see pp. 396–7 for a full discussion).

In simple societies, Durkheim believed religion was the basis for the **collective conscience** – the shared moral beliefs and values of a society. Although Durkheim does not use the term 'culture' to refer to the collective conscience, what he describes is very similar to the way the term culture is used by some other writers. Durkheim (1947) says: 'The totality of beliefs and sentiments common to average citizens of the same society forms a determinate system which has its own life; one may call it the collective or common conscience.'

As discussed in Chapter 7 (see pp. 396–7), Durkheim believed that the collective conscience exerts a very strong influence on people in pre-industrial societies. These societies are characterized by **mechanical solidarity**. People feel a sense of solidarity because they are similar to one another. There is little division of labour.

As society evolves, the division of labour becomes more specialized. People are no longer so similar to one another. However, they do depend upon one another. For example, teachers need farmers to grow food, and farmers need teachers to educate their children. Durkheim describes this situation of interdependence as **organic solidarity**. In a society of organic solidarity a collective conscience – a shared culture – is still necessary. However, the collective conscience tends to be less strong than it was under mechanical solidarity. Individuals have to be different to carry out their specialized roles. (For example, a boxer needs to be more aggressive than a nurse.)

A specialized division of labour can encourage excessive individualism (which Durkheim calls **egoism**) or even a situation of normlessness (which he calls **anomie**). Anomie can result from changes in society which disrupt existing relationships and bring existing values into question. This can lead to social problems such as a high suicide rate (see pp. 795–8). Nevertheless, it is still possible for society to maintain a collective conscience. Durkheim suggests the education system (see pp. 600–1) and professional associations can help to cement social solidarity among people in industrial societies.

Conclusion

To Durkheim, then, a shared culture, or collective conscience, is necessary if a society is to run smoothly. This shared culture exists over and above the wishes and choices of individuals, and it constrains their behaviour. It is passed down from generation to generation. Durkheim says the collective conscience 'does not change from generation to generation, but, on the contrary, it connects successive generations with one another. It is thus entirely different from particular consciences, although it can be realized only through them.'

People must conform to the culture of their society if they are to avoid the risk of punishment. Although society needs a shared culture, the specialized division of labour and rapid pace of industrial societies can place it under threat and positive steps may have to be taken to support it.

Criticisms and evaluation of Durkheim

Durkheim's work has been extensively criticized. Rodney Needham (1963) questions Durkheim and Mauss's work on primitive classification on the grounds that 'there is a simple lack of correspondence between form of society and form of classification'. For example, Port Mackay moieties are actually divided into marriage clans. You would therefore expect them to adopt a fourfold classification system rather than a binary one. Durkheim and Mauss ignore this evidence because it fails to support their case.

There have also been criticisms of Durkheim's work on religion (see p. 397) and on suicide (see pp. 798–803). In general, Durkheim's work has been criticized for exaggerating the extent to which human culture is determined by social structure. His work leaves little room for human creativity and does little to address subcultural differences between groups. However, Durkheim did pave the way for developing a social theory of culture, and he encouraged many later writers to examine the ways in which social factors might shape culture.

Marxist theories of culture and identity

Karl Marx on culture

Like Durkheim, Marx made little explicit use of the concept of culture. However, contained within his extensive writings there are a number of ideas that could be seen as forming a theory of culture (in the sense of the lifestyle of a society). Furthermore, Marx also developed some ideas on art and literature.

The origins of culture

Like functionalists, Marx argued that human culture has a social origin and cannot be seen as deriving directly from nature or from innate instincts in human beings. Culture comes from humanity's creation of the first societies. Unlike Durkheim, Marx did not see culture developing in terms of primitive classification systems that derive from social structure. Instead, he believed that culture had a material origin in human labour.

As a materialist, Marx believed that material circumstances and economic activity shaped human consciousness. In the **Economical and Philosophical Manuscripts** (first published 1844), Marx argued: 'The animal is immediately identical with its life-activity. It is its life-activity. Man makes his life-activity itself the object of his will and of his consciousness. He has conscious life-activity' (quoted in Baxandall and Morawski, 1974).

In this passage, Marx is arguing that animals do not possess a consciousness separate from activities such as hunting or building nests. While animals produce things, they do so only to meet their immediate needs. However, humans do more than this.

Once humans get together and form social groups they engage in productive activity even when they have no need to. Marx said: 'man produces even when he is free from physical need and only truly produces in freedom therefrom ... Man, therefore, also forms things in accordance with the laws of beauty.' Because humans, once they form social groups, produce more than they need to do for simple physical survival, they begin to produce things for their aesthetic appeal. They produce things because they give pleasure rather than because they meet needs such as hunger or thirst.

To Marx, culture originates in human productive activity. As humans extend the work they do beyond their survival needs, they start to develop self-consciousness. This allows them actively to create their own culture. In *Capital* (first published 1867), Marx elaborated further on this theme. He suggested that the imagination and creativity of the human worker are qualitatively different from the mechanical behaviour of bees or other animals. He said:

> *The poorest architect is categorically distinguished from the best of bees by the fact that before he builds a dell in wax, he builds it in his head. The result achieved at the end of a labour process was already present at its commencement, in the imagination of the worker in its ideal form. More than merely working an alteration in the form of nature, he also knowingly works his own purposes into nature.* Quoted in Baxandall and Morawski, 1974

Alienation and culture

According to Marx, when humans live in freedom, they fulfil themselves through the creative activity of producing things using their imagination. However, problems arise when human freedom is restricted by the existence of private property. Some humans start to accumulate large amounts of private property at the expense of others, and the propertyless begin to lose their freedom. They lack the **means of production**, such as the tools or the land necessary to produce enough for their own physical survival. Instead, they have to work for others who do own the means of production. They lose freedom to organize their productive activity or work. They are compelled to work for the owners of the means of production in order to survive. In short, they become alienated.

Alienation involves a sense of estrangement from the work that people do (the act of production), from other workers, from what they are producing (the end product) – because they no longer own it – and even from their own essential humanity. Alienated workers are unable freely to express their own humanity by using their creativity in their work.

Culture as ruling-class ideology

Marx developed these ideas further by claiming that in class-stratified societies culture can be seen as little more than **ruling-class ideology**. From this point of view culture is simply an expression of the distorted view of the world advanced by the dominant class. It is part of the superstructure of society. The superstructure is shaped by the economic base or infrastructure. The ruling class – the owners of the means of production – use their economic power to shape society's culture. In a famous passage in *The German Ideology* (first published 1846), Marx and Engels argued:

> *The ideas of the ruling class are, in every age, the ruling ideas: i.e. the class which is the dominant material force in society is at the same time its dominant intellectual force. The class which has the means of material production at its disposal, has control at the same time over the means of mental production, so that in consequence the ideas of those that lack the means of mental production are, in general, subject to it. The dominant ideas are nothing more than the ideal expression of the dominant material relationships grasped as ideas.* Quoted in Bottomore and Rubel, 1963

Contemporary Marxists have used such statements as the basis for developing Marxist theories of institutions such as the mass media (see pp. 713–18).

However, the writings of Marx and Engels are open to a range of interpretations and they do not always state that the cultural superstructure of society is entirely shaped by the infrastructure. At other times Marx, or Marx and Engels, argued that the infrastructure influences, or perhaps sets limits on, what happens in the cultural superstructure, but does not totally determine it. Elements within the infrastructure can influence one another as well (see pp. 867–72 for an elaboration of these views).

One interpretation of Marx, then, sees all culture in capitalist societies as a product of ruling-class ideology. The working class are seen as suffering from false class consciousness and their beliefs and culture will therefore be shaped by the ruling class. This theory has been called 'the dominant ideology thesis' (Abercrombie *et al.*, 1980). Other interpretations see the working class and other cultures as possessing some independence or relative autonomy from ruling-class domination and from the economic base.

Culture as the reflection of class differences

A further interpretation of Marx emphasizes class differences between cultures. From this point of view, different classes will always tend to have different cultures because their conditions of material existence are different. The different experiences of living as members of the ruling class or the working class will produce a different view of the world and hence a different culture. Stefan Morawski (1974) describes this interpretation of Marx and Engels's views in the following way: 'Ideology will here be considered as the statement or symptomatic expression of a pattern of social class attitudes, interests, or habits of thought.' Thus, working-class literature will be different from literature produced by the ruling class.

However, Engels accepted the possibility that aspects of culture such as literature could, in the work of some writers, rise above the class origins of the writer and

demonstrate revealing insights into society. An example is Engels's discussion of the German writer Goethe.

According to Engels, at times Goethe's work is restricted by his class background. His comfortable and respectable background as the 'Frankfurt alderman's cautious child, the privy councillor of Weimar' sometimes leads Goethe to celebrate German life. However, at other times, Goethe is 'the poet of genius, who is disgusted by the wretchedness of his surroundings' (quoted in Baxandall and Morawski, 1974).

Here, Engels raises the possibility that people can see through false class consciousness and produce cultural works that show an appreciation of the oppression and exploitation found in class societies. Thus, literature and other forms of art and aspects of culture tend to reflect the experiences of different class groups, but they can sometimes rise above this to uncover something approaching the truth about society.

Marx and Engels believed that eventually the culture of society as a whole would change. Class consciousness would develop in the working class and they would begin to see through the distorted ideology of the ruling class. Capitalism would be replaced by communism and, in the absence of exploitation and ruling-class domination, humans would be able to return to creating things that expressed their true humanity.

(The strengths and weaknesses of the work of Marx and Engels will become clear as we discuss the way their ideas have been used by later Marxists. Criticism and evaluation of Marx and Engels relevant to their theories of culture can also be found on pp. 771–82 and 401.)

Marxist theories of the arts

Marxist and neo-Marxist theories of the general cultures of societies are examined elsewhere in the book (see, for example, pp. 867–70 and 26–9). This section will therefore concentrate on Marxist theories of the arts, and particularly literature.

John Berger – oil paintings and private property

Ruling-class art

One of the most straightforward Marxist theories of art is advanced by John Berger (1972). In *Ways of Seeing* he argues that oil painting – the dominant medium for painters between 1500 and 1900 – came to reflect the worldview of the ruling classes. Berger says: 'The art of any period tends to serve the ideological interests of the ruling class.' He claims that in the period 1500–1900, 'a way of seeing the world, which was ultimately determined by new attitudes to property and exchange, found its visual expression in the oil painting'.

Oil paintings had special characteristics that made them particularly suitable for portraying ruling-class ideology. According to Berger, oil painting has a 'special ability to render the tangibility, the texture, the lustre, the solidity of what it depicts. It defines the real as that which you can put your hands on.' This was important because oil painting came to be primarily concerned with the depiction of wealth or property.

Because of the sense of tangibility that oil painting can produce, it gave substance to the sense of ownership that the ruling class wanted to portray in their paintings. Although paintings had always portrayed things of value, in earlier periods they were usually related directly to the glory of God. As capitalist society developed, painting focused more directly on the wealth and power of the ruling class, elevating money above religious considerations. Berger says:

> *Works of art in earlier traditions celebrated wealth. But wealth was then a symbol of a fixed social or divine order. Oil painting celebrated a new kind of wealth – which was dynamic and which found its only sanction in the supreme buying power of money.* Berger, 1972

The ruling class were able to impose their own view of the world, simply because it was very largely they who commissioned paintings. Large numbers of paintings were commissioned by the wealthy – most of mediocre quality. It was more important to the buyers of the paintings that they portrayed them and their wealth in the way they wanted, than that the painting was of a high quality. Berger says, 'Hack work is not the result of either clumsiness or provincialism; it is the result of the market making more insistent demands than the art.'

Examples of ruling-class art

Berger gives a number of examples to illustrate his claims.

In earlier periods, paintings of Mary Magdalene tended to emphasize the importance of her story – that 'she so loved Christ that she repented of her past and came to accept the mortality of the flesh and the immortality of the soul'. However, by the time of the dominance of oil paintings, the typical portrait of her had changed. She was now portrayed as a woman to be owned by men – simply another possession. Berger says, 'She is painted as being, before she is anything else, a takeable and desirable woman.'

Still-life paintings were more obviously about possessions. These tended to portray such things as tables laden with luxurious foods, as testament to the high living of those who had commissioned them.

Paintings of animals were also popular. However, they were not usually animals in the wild, but 'livestock whose pedigree is emphasized as proof of their value'.

Landscapes were used to celebrate the property of the rich. Berger uses the example of *Mr and Mrs Andrews*, painted by Gainsborough (see Figure 11.1). The Andrews insisted on being included in the landscape which featured land owned by them. According to Berger, 'They are landowners and their proprietary attitude towards what surrounds them is visible in their stance and their expressions.'

Figure 11.1 *Mr and Mrs Andrews*, by Gainsborough, *c.*1748–9, National Gallery, London

Source: The Bridgeman Art Library

Low-life paintings

Of course, not all oil paintings portrayed the property of the rich. However, even some that portray the poor reflect ruling-class ideology. Pictures of 'low life', such as debauched groups in taverns, were popular with the growing bourgeoisie in the sixteenth to nineteenth centuries. The point of such pictures, though, was to tell a moral tale about how the rich deserved their success while the poor had only themselves to blame for their misfortune. Berger says such paintings 'lent plausibility to a sentimental lie: namely that it was the honest and hard-working who prospered, and that the good-for-nothings deservedly had nothing'.

Rembrandt

Despite the emphasis that Berger puts upon ruling-class ideology in influencing oil painting, he does accept that some paintings were able to transcend the narrow concerns of the bourgeoisie. However, such works are exceptional and can only be painted by those who undergo a struggle to free themselves from dominant ways of thinking about the world. According to Berger, one painter who succeeded in this respect was Rembrandt.

In his early work Rembrandt succumbed to the dominant artistic style propagated by the bourgeoisie. In an early self-portrait (see Figure 11.2) Rembrandt portrays himself with his first wife. He is essentially showing off his wife and, to Berger, 'The painting as a whole remains an advertisement for the sitter's good fortune, prestige and wealth.'

In a self-portrait painted thirty years later, when he was an old man (see Figure 11.3), Rembrandt portrays himself in a more sombre and reflective mood and includes none of the trappings of material success. Berger says, 'All has gone except a sense of the question of existence, of existence as a question.' Rembrandt has succeeded in shaking off ruling-class ideology and painting something of more universal and lasting significance.

Evaluation of Berger

Janet Wolff (1981) argues that Berger provides a rather crude and oversimplified explanation of oil paintings. She considers that his study lacks 'an adequate and systematic analysis'. However, Wolff does acknowledge that 'the intervention into the discipline of art history has proved to be extremely critical and influential, and it has stimulated a good deal of more detailed analysis'. Many other Marxist theories of art and literature have adopted a broadly similar approach, but have tried to refine the sorts of arguments put forward by Berger. One example is the work of Lucien Goldmann.

Lucien Goldmann – class and literature

The expression of class worldviews

In his best-known work, *The Hidden God* (1964), Goldmann develops a sociological account of the French writers Pascal and Racine. Unlike Berger, Goldmann does not believe that artistic products tend to reflect ruling-class ideology in a simple way. Instead, he argues that works of art (in this case, great works of literature) reflect the worldview of particular social classes. He says: 'the most important group to which any individual may belong,

Figure 11.2 *Self-portrait with Saskia*, by Rembrandt, *c.* 1635, Gemäldegalerie, Dresden

Source: The Bridgeman Art Library

Figure 11.3 *Self-portrait as an Old Man*, by Rembrandt, *c.* 1664, Galleria degli Uffizi, Florence

Source: The Bridgeman Art Library

from the point of view of intellectual and artistic activity and creation, is that of the social class, or classes of which he is a member'. He justifies this claim by saying that humans in subject classes have to devote most of their effort to physical survival, while those in more dominant classes have to devote their time to maintaining their dominance. Class therefore tends to be prominent in people's thinking about the world.

To Goldmann, most people have only an incoherent and partial class consciousness. However, a few individuals are more perceptive than this. They are:

> ***exceptional individuals who either actually achieve or who come very near to achieving a completely integrated and coherent view of the social class to which they belong. The men who express this vision on an imaginative or conceptual plane are writers and philosophers.*** Goldmann, 1964

Pascal and Racine

Goldmann sees Pascal and Racine as examples of just such exceptional individuals. He argues that they shared a particular **tragic vision** of the world, which reflected the position of a specific class grouping in French society in the seventeenth century. Goldmann refers to this class as the *noblesse de robe*.

The *noblesse de robe* consisted of members of legal and administrative professions who were not directly employed by the monarchy but were tied to the state, which was partially under the control of the monarchy. The worldview of the *noblesse de robe* was therefore likely partially to reflect the worldview of the monarchy.

However, the sort of functions they performed – for example, in the legal profession – inclined them towards a rather different worldview, which was more rationalistic and less inclined to accept the traditional authority of the monarchy. Their worldview therefore contained contradictory elements characteristic of both the monarchy and the rising bourgeoisie, who had a more rationalistic outlook. According to Goldmann, it was this contradictory ideology that was reflected in the tragedies written by Pascal and Racine.

The central feature of the tragedies was 'that everything which God demands is impossible in the eyes of the world, and that everything that is possible when we follow the rules of this world ceases to exist when the eye of God lights upon it'. In short, it was impossible to succeed in the world and to please God. This reflected the impossibility of acting as members of the bourgeoisie and pleasing the king. Thus, the literature of Pascal and Racine directly reflected and expressed the contradictions of the class position of the *noblesse de robe*.

Evaluation of Goldmann

Janet Wolff argues that Goldmann provides a relatively sophisticated and subtle Marxist interpretation of literature. She says:

> ***He relates literature and ideology to class structure without using a simple reductionist equation, but instead insists that social life is a totality. The relationship between literary production is not defined as causal or crudely deterministic, but is presented as mediated through social groups and their consciousness.*** Wolff, 1981

Wolff notes that Goldmann uses the idea of the exceptional individual, who can articulate a class consciousness which others can only partially grasp. To Wolff, this is a considerable advance on the much more deterministic approach of Berger.

However, Goldmann's work is not above criticism and, from a number of viewpoints, may be seen as inadequate.

1 It rather assumes, without strong justification, the primacy of class in shaping experience. To feminists, for example, gender is more important than class in influencing art. Other social groupings, such as ethnic groups and age groups, may also exert an influence on the production of literature and other art forms.
2 Goldmann's work assumes that a class can possess an ideology, that individuals can develop a coherent and consistent view of the world, and that the meaning of a text can be clear to those who interpret it. All of these claims are challenged by a variety of poststructuralists and postmodernists who are deeply critical of such neat assumptions.
3 Despite the autonomy that Goldmann attributes to individual authors, he still advances a rather monocausal account of literature. It is doubtful whether one single factor, such as the expression of the worldview of a particular class, can explain the content of art forms such as literature.

As this chapter develops, a range of other influences upon culture will be discussed.

Neo-Marxist theories of culture

A number of writers have developed what can be described as new or neo-Marxist theories of culture. All of these approaches have been significantly influenced by Marxism, but all tend to argue that culture possesses considerable autonomy or independence from economic influences, and that there is no straightforward correspondence between class and culture.

Raymond Williams – *Culture and Society*

One of the most influential figures in the development of cultural studies in Britain has been Raymond Williams. In a series of important books, Williams (1961, 1965, 1978) examined the relationships between society, culture and art, using some aspects of Marxist theories in the development of his ideas.

Class consciousness and culture

In *Culture and Society* (1961) Williams questions two main aspects of Marxist theories of culture.

First, he argues that the use of the ideas of infrastructure and superstructure is misleading. He says, 'Structure and superstructure, as terms of an analogy, express at once an absolute and fixed relationship. But the reality which Marx and Engels recognize is both less absolute and less clear.' Williams does not deny that economic factors influence culture, but he does deny that they determine culture in a straightforward way. He says:

> *A Marxist theory of culture will recognize diversity and complexity, will take account of continuity within change, will allow for chance and certain limited autonomies, but, with these reservations, will take the facts of the economic structure and the consequent social relations as the guiding string on which a culture is woven.* Williams, 1961

In Williams's work there is much more room for historical detail and individual and group creativity than in some Marxist theories.

Second, Williams argues that Marxist theories of culture have been too concerned with art and literature. As such they have had too narrow a focus. For Williams, Marxist theory emphasizes the interdependence of all aspects of social reality, and such a narrow field as art and literature should not be taken as synonymous with culture. He therefore argues: 'Marxists should logically use "culture" in the sense of a whole way of life, a general social process.'

Working-class culture and bourgeois culture

Williams's own studies include an analysis of working-class culture.

During the industrial revolution and the nineteenth century there was relatively little art and literature produced by the working class, but they did develop their own distinctive lifestyles and institutions. To Williams, the basis of working-class culture was the commitment to acting collectively. Individual members of the working class were too weak to defend themselves individually and too restricted in their life chances to achieve success through individual effort. Therefore, working-class culture has taken shape through 'the collective democratic institution, whether in the trade unions, the cooperative movement, or a political party'.

While Williams draws this general contrast between collective working-class and individualistic bourgeois culture, he does not believe there is an absolute and clear-cut distinction between them. There is some overlap between bourgeois and working-class culture. He says, 'there is both a constant interaction between these ways of life and an area which can properly be described as belonging to or underlying both'. Furthermore, cultures are not the automatically determined products of class structures. Rather, they are actively created by people who are responding to their economic circumstances.

Residual and emergent, alternative and oppositional culture

In a later work, Williams (1978) tries to develop his ideas on the relationship between class and culture. As in his earlier work, he denies there is ever a monolithic, totally dominant ruling-class ideology in society. While there may be a dominant ideology, it is always likely to be challenged

by alternative ideologies. There may be **residual ideologies** (the ideology of a class which is declining but still important) or **emergent ideologies** (the ideologies of new groups that are outside the ruling class). Residual and emergent ideologies may be either **oppositional** (opposed to the dominant ideology) or **alternative** (they coexist with the dominant ideology without challenging it).

Thus, to Williams, there is nothing inevitable about groups outside the ruling class either accepting or rejecting the dominant ideology. Both responses are possible, and of course people may accept some aspects of the dominant ideology while rejecting others.

Evaluation of Williams

Williams's ideas encouraged other writers to take working-class cultures seriously and therefore to study them. Such writers tried to move away from deterministic versions of Marxism and to take account of specific historical circumstances and human creativity. Nevertheless, they did not really resolve the question of the precise relationship between the economy and culture.

Furthermore, many contemporary theorists (for example, most postmodernists) argue that it is difficult to distinguish such a thing as working-class culture, and they would certainly deny that the working class retains a collective culture such as that described by Williams (see, for example, pp. 84–5). For such theorists, even if working-class culture was important in modern societies, it is no longer so in postmodern societies. Although this might not invalidate Williams's historical studies of working-class culture, it does raise questions about whether his theories are useful for understanding contemporary society. Other research suggests that working-class lifestyles remain culturally distinctive (see pp. 62–3).

(For an example of a neo-Marxist theory of youth culture see pp. 771–4.)

Mass culture

In the 1950s there was considerable concern about the impact of what was called **mass culture**. It was argued that the development of the mass media was debasing the culture of ordinary people, creating problems and dangers in Western societies. This view was particularly influential in the USA and was expressed by Bernard Rosenberg in 1957. The critique of mass culture was most fully developed in the work of Dwight Macdonald, whose views will now be examined.

Dwight Macdonald – 'A theory of mass culture'

Types of culture

Macdonald distinguished between **folk art**, **high culture** and **mass culture**.

He saw **folk art** as the 'culture of the common people' in pre-industrial societies. It 'grew from below. It was a spontaneous, autochthonous expression of the people, shaped by themselves, pretty much without the benefit of high culture, to suit their own needs' (Macdonald, 1957). Folk culture did not produce great art, but in its own limited way it had some merit, and it was at least authentic. It emerged out of genuine communities in which people interacted with one another.

High culture was not so explicitly defined. Macdonald took its meaning as almost self-evident. However, he did not just see the classic works of great artists, musicians and writers (for example, Leonardo da Vinci, Beethoven and Shakespeare) as being examples of high culture. He also included the work of twentieth-century avant-gardists (the term **avant-garde** refers to artists who develop challenging and original work in a given field). Macdonald includes in the avant-garde the painter Picasso, the poet Rimbaud, the composer Stravinsky, and the writer James Joyce. High culture is seen as the product of great individuals who are able to produce work that appeals to a minority who can appreciate work of this calibre.

Mass culture is very different from either folk art or high culture. It has little, if any, merit. It is designed to appeal to the lowest common denominator. It is unchallenging and has nothing of significance to say. It does not express a genuine culture in the way that folk art does, nor does it achieve the intrinsic artistic value of high culture. It is simply standardized, commercial kitsch imposed by businesses on the masses to make a profit. (**Kitsch** is a German word for popular culture. It tends to be used as a term of abuse, implying that what it refers to is mindless and worthless.) According to Macdonald:

> *Mass culture is imposed from above. It is fabricated by technicians, hired by businessmen; its audiences are passive consumers, their participation limited to the choice between buying and not buying. The Lords of kitsch, in short, exploit the cultural needs of the masses to make a profit and/or to maintain their class rule.* Macdonald, 1957

Macdonald saw mass culture as a threat to high culture. Like Rosenberg, he saw mass culture as creating a risk of totalitarianism. Macdonald thought that mass society and mass culture had made communist rule in the Soviet Union possible, and had facilitated Hitler's rise to power. It was not just culture that was at stake, but political control as well. Indeed, Macdonald follows something similar to a Marxist line of argument in seeing mass culture as a possible tool of the ruling classes.

The problem of mass culture

Why was mass culture such a problem? Macdonald made a number of claims:

1. He believed that bad culture would drive out good. People found mass culture easier to understand. It took less mental effort. It therefore tended to undermine high culture. Macdonald said:

> *It threatens high culture by its sheer pervasiveness, its brutal, overwhelming, quantity. The upper classes, who begin by using it to make money from the crude tastes of the masses and to dominate them politically, end by finding their own culture attacked and even threatened with destruction by the instrument they have thoughtlessly employed.* Macdonald, 1957

2 As a result, mass culture would end up creating a single, homogenized culture. High culture would be vulgarized and incorporated in a simplified form into mass culture. For example, the high culture of the theatre was undermined by the mass culture of the cinema. Macdonald observed that plays were increasingly put on simply to try to sell movie rights. If the plays were too sophisticated to have the potential to be made into films, they would not be staged. Mass cultural forms, such as detective stories, were adopting a bogus intellectual style to make them seem more artistically important than they really were. Macdonald cites the work of Dorothy L. Sayers as an example. To Macdonald, the distinction between high culture and mass culture was breaking down, so that it was getting harder to distinguish between the two.

3 Macdonald believed that the triumph of mass culture would lead to increased alienation among those who created cultural products. There was a greater division of labour in media such as the cinema, when compared with the theatre, so that individuals were reduced to carrying out mechanical tasks relating to one small aspect of a film.

4 Macdonald claimed that mass culture was leading to 'adultized children and infantile adults'. He quoted research which suggested that American adults were increasingly reading comics and comic strips in newspapers. Adults were also watching children's television programmes, like *The Lone Ranger*, in large numbers, while children were gaining easy access to adult-oriented films and television. The result, according to Macdonald, was the creation of infantile adults – unable to cope with adult life without turning to escapist mass culture for leisure – and over-stimulated children, who grew up too fast.

5 Even more seriously, Macdonald believed that mass culture was undermining the fabric of society. It was creating a **mass society**, in which individuals were **atomized**. They were losing their involvement in small social groups and losing opportunities to interact with one another in a meaningful way. Instead, people were becoming isolated individuals relating only to centralized systems and organizations such as the mass media, political parties and companies. Macdonald said, 'The mass man is a solitary atom, uniform with and undifferentiated from thousands and millions of other atoms who go to make up "the lonely crowd" as David Riesman well calls American society.'

Conclusion

Macdonald's conclusions are those of a gloomy pessimist. He sees little sign that high culture can survive, arguing that even the efforts of the avant-garde are under threat from mass culture. Most people had become trapped in a self-perpetuating mass society and mass culture, their sensibilities and will to resist dulled by several generations' output of mindless mass culture. Only 'heroes' could resist such pressure, and they were few and far between.

Nevertheless, Macdonald did not see the situation as completely hopeless. It was still possible that, despite their dwindling number and influence, a small cultural elite could keep the torch of high culture alight.

Evaluation of mass culture theory

The idea that mass culture is harming society remains influential today. However, it has come under increasing attack and has generally fallen out of favour among sociologists of culture.

In the 1970s Edward Shils (1978) argued that advocates of mass culture theory were wrong to say that there had been a decline in working-class and lower-middle-class culture. He did not deny that most mass culture was not particularly enlightening, but he thought it less damaging for lower classes than the 'dismal and harsh existence of earlier centuries' (quoted in Storey, 1997).

Increasingly, though, sociologists have not just argued that mass culture is not as bad as its critics make out; they have begun to attack the idea that it is appropriate to evaluate cultures as superior or inferior to one another. Furthermore, they have criticized the idea that it is possible to distinguish between just two cultures, high culture and mass culture.

Herbert J. Gans – the plurality of taste cultures

Herbert J. Gans attacked the idea that cultural experts had any right to try to impose their judgements about culture on others. He said, 'all people have a right to the culture they prefer' (Gans, 1974). Gans was an early advocate of the view that America had a large number of different **taste cultures**, all of which were equally worthwhile. Rather than simply distinguishing between worthwhile high culture and worthless mass or popular culture, he identified a range of different cultures, each of which had its own intrinsic worth. Gans identifies five main taste cultures.

High culture

High culture consisted of art, music and 'serious' literature (in fiction, for example, the seriousness was demonstrated by an emphasis 'on character development over plot, and the exploration of basic philosophical, psychological and social issues'). To Gans, high culture was intended for small audiences and he emphasized the importance of the creativity of the creators of the culture (writers, artists, film directors and so on).

High culture paid more attention to 'abstract social, political, and philosophical questions and fundamental societal assumptions more often, more systematically, and more intensively than do other cultures'. However, more popular cultures also addressed moral issues and paid attention to areas such as the problems of earning a living, which were neglected by high culture.

Upper-middle culture

Upper-middle culture was the culture of upper-middle-class, well-educated professionals and managers who had no special knowledge of or involvement in high-culture arts and literature. These people were less concerned with innovative music, literature and art than those involved in high culture. They wanted more plot in the fiction they read. They wanted the heroes in their books to achieve their goals in competition with other people. They enjoyed

some of the work of authors such as Norman Mailer and Arthur Miller, and read publications like *Harper*, *New Yorker* and *Vogue*. Broadway theatre and foreign films were also favoured by those with upper-middle-class culture.

Many women involved in this culture were interested in women's liberation and the cultural products of its advocates. According to Gans, on the one hand upper-middle-class culture rejected anything that was too experimental or too abstract, and on the other hand it rejected anything considered too 'vulgar' or populist. Gans believed this was the fastest-growing culture in America (at the time he was writing) because of the expansion of college education.

Lower-middle culture

Lower-middle culture was the 'dominant taste culture' in the USA. It attracted those in lower professions, such as teaching, and those in administrative jobs. This taste culture was less interested in art, serious film, literature and so on than the other taste cultures examined so far. However, its followers were prepared to watch television series derived from upper-middle culture films (for example, *M.A.S.H.*), and to read magazines like *Cosmopolitan*, or the novels of Harold Robbins.

This taste culture wanted substance that was easy to understand and enjoyable. People involved in this culture would accept elements of high culture if they met these criteria. Thus, for example, they might own reproductions of the more popular paintings of artists such as Van Gogh and Degas (famous for his paintings of ballet dancers).

Gans argued that lower-middle culture was increasingly breaking up into different groups. There were traditional and progressive factions. Traditionalists objected to open discussion of sexuality in lower-middle-class culture, whereas progressives were in favour of it.

Low culture

Low culture was 'the culture of the older lower-middle class, but mainly of the skilled and semi-skilled factory and service workers, and of the semi-skilled white collar workers'. They rejected anything with the pretensions of high culture and stressed substance above all else. They liked stories with morals about individual and family problems, and films with plenty of action. The male hero in low-culture films:

> *is sure of his own masculinity, is shy with 'good' women and sexually aggressive with 'bad' ones. He works either alone or with 'buddies' of the same sex, depends partly on luck and fate for success, and is distrustful of government and all institutionalized authority.* Gans, 1974

Gans cites Clark Gable and John Wayne as examples.

The mass media are important for transmitting low culture. Members of this taste culture enjoy television programmes such as the *Beverly Hillbillies*, rock and country music, and tabloid newspapers with sensational headlines.

Quasi-folk, low culture

Quasi-folk, low culture is described as 'a blend of folk culture and of the commercial low culture of the pre-World War II era'. It represents the tastes of many blue-collar workers and the rural poor. It is described as 'a simpler version of low culture, with the same emphasis on melodrama, action comedies and morality plays'. Comics, old Westerns and soap operas are among the cultural forms that are popular.

Age and ethnicity

As well as these five main, well-established and class-based cultures, Gans also discusses cultures based on age groups or ethnic groups.

According to Gans, youth cultures had existed for some time, but in the 1960s they became more diverse and influential. Some youth cultures were **total cultures**, while others were **partial cultures**. By total cultures Gans meant a whole lifestyle outside of mainstream society, whereas partial cultures involved tastes of groups who remained within mainstream society.

Total cultures

There were five main types of total culture: a drug and music culture; a communal culture, which involved living in communes; a political culture, which was divided into many groups but these groups had in common the desire to overthrow American capitalism; a religious culture, based on religious sects or cults such as the Jesus freaks; and a neo-dadaist culture, concerned with experimenting with a mixture of new artistic, social and political ideas. Although these total youth cultures did not have many followers, they were highly visible and attracted a lot of concern from those in mainstream culture.

Partial cultures

Gans saw the partial cultures as part-time versions of the total cultures. They were more likely to have become commercially exploited, and were closer to mainstream tastes. However, they shared with total cultures a critical perspective on conventional lifestyles and a preference for radical music and other art forms.

According to Gans, **black culture** rose to greater prominence in the 1960s, although black Americans had, of course, always had their own culture. In the 1960s the civil rights movement prompted black Americans to be more proud of their culture and to produce more of their own music, television programmes, films and so on.

Finally, Gans discussed **ethnic cultures**. Each group of immigrants brought their own cultures with them, but they tended to be less important to children born in America than they were to the original immigrants. However, Gans detected a revival of ethnic cultures among such groups as Italians and Poles.

The hierarchy of tastes

Gans was aware that there was no straightforward distinction between these cultures. Individuals might choose to consume cultural products from different taste cultures, and certain types of cultural product might be popular in different taste cultures. Nevertheless, he did believe that an overall taste structure existed.

There was a hierarchy of tastes, with high culture at the top and other cultures ranged below it. But Gans did not see this hierarchy as based on merit. It was largely the product of differences in the class, status and power of those who belonged to the different taste cultures. Thus, high culture and upper-middle culture were seen as better because they were the cultures of the highest class and most powerful groups in American society. These groups were more able to fund and protect their cultures than other groups. For example, Gans notes that sexually explicit material is produced in both high culture (for example, James Joyce's novel *Ulysses*) and low culture (for example, hardcore pornography films and magazines).

In 1973 the US Supreme Court ruled that pornographic material could be acceptable if it had 'some redeeming social value'. This allowed sexually explicit high culture to continue untroubled by agencies of law enforcement, while low-culture pornography was criminalized.

Conclusion

Gans concluded by attacking critics of mass culture for trying to impose their own values on others. He argues that all of the different cultures examined by him fulfil the needs of their audiences for information and entertainment. In a pluralistic and democratic society they are all worthy of respect.

However, Gans did not entirely avoid his own value judgements. He suggested there were ways in which high culture could be seen as superior to other cultures. For example, high culture could deal with more aspects of life because its public was better educated than the public for other cultures. Thus, high culture could consider philosophical issues whereas low culture could not. High culture might also be better able to provide adequate information to help people solve both personal and social problems.

Evaluation

Gans not only provides a strong critique of mass culture theory, he also develops his own conflict theory of culture and taste. His work represents a major advance on theories of mass culture because it recognizes that different cultures can be useful for different audiences, and because it recognizes that there is a plurality of cultures rather than just two.

Gans acknowledges the importance of class, ethnicity and gender in contributing to cultural diversity. His work is in some ways a precursor to postmodern theories of culture which emphasize plurality and diversity (see pp. 682–6). However, for some, his work retains an element of elitism. By arguing that high culture does have some advantages over other cultures, Gans fails to rid himself entirely of judgements about which cultures are more valid.

At an empirical level Gans's work provides an interesting description of American cultures in the 1970s. Clearly, this description may not be applicable to different societies at different times, and his work may perhaps lack detailed arguments about why different groups have different tastes.

Dominic Strinati – a critique of mass culture theory

While Gans criticized mass culture theory by developing his own alternative approach to culture, Dominic Strinati (1995) is simply concerned with evaluating the theory of mass culture. Strinati is even more critical than Gans and attacks mass culture theory on a number of different grounds:

1. Strinati believes mass culture theory is very elitist. He says it 'fails to recognize that mass culture can be understood, interpreted and appreciated by other groups in distinct and "non-elitist" social and aesthetic positions within society'. It makes the false assumption that the masses are 'cultural dopes' willing to consume any old rubbish put before them by the mass media. In fact, the consumers of mass culture are often critical and reject many products (such as films and television programmes) which they find insufficiently interesting or entertaining. Consumers of mass culture are not a passive and undifferentiated mass. They are discriminating in what they choose to consume, and active in deciding how they are going to react (see pp. 862–4 for research which supports such claims).
2. According to Strinati, mass culture theory sees all popular culture as homogeneous – it is all the same. Strinati argues that this is far from being the case, and in reality there is a very wide variety of styles and genres. To take just one example, popular music can hardly be seen as homogeneous when it includes 'rap, soul, jazz, sampling, novelty songs and "serious ballads"'.
3. Strinati does not agree with mass culture theorists like Macdonald that it is possible to distinguish an authentic and superior 'folk culture' from an inauthentic and inferior mass culture. For example, folk blues and country music are not part of 'pure' cultures untainted by outside influences. All have been affected by a range of musical traditions. Furthermore, authenticity does not determine how much an audience enjoys its music. Pop music may be just as enjoyable and seen by its audience as just as good as any of the types of supposedly 'authentic' popular music.
4. The theory of mass culture rests upon the assumption that there is a reasonably clear-cut boundary between high culture and mass culture, but this is not the case. Strinati says:

> *The boundaries drawn between popular culture and art, or between mass, high and folk culture, are constantly being blurred, challenged and redrawn. These boundaries are not given, nor are they consistently objective and historically constant. Rather, they are contested, discontinuous and historically variable.* Strinati, 1995

What was once considered mass culture might increase in status and come to be taken seriously as art. Strinati gives the examples of jazz music, the films of Alfred Hitchcock, and rock-and-roll records which have attained the status of classics.

Cultural politics

To Strinati, the theory of mass culture is a product of cultural politics rather than an objective assessment of the merits of different cultures. It represents a backlash by intellectuals who feel threatened by the growth of popular culture.

Mass culture threatens the hierarchy of taste by giving everybody the chance to choose what they think are the best books, films, music, paintings or images and so on. This undermines 'the symbolic power of intellectuals over the standards of taste which are applied to the consumption of cultural goods'. It is hardly surprising that they choose to fight a rearguard action to defend their cultural power. To Strinati, though, their arguments are unconvincing and unlikely to preserve the authority of their elitist judgements.

Global culture

Like the theory of mass culture, the idea of global culture suggests that the same culture is being shared by many people. Like mass culture, global culture is usually seen as being spread through mass communications. However, the idea of global culture implies less of a moral judgement about the worth of the culture – global culture is not necessarily seen as an inferior culture in the same way as mass culture. This section examines the work of John Storey (2003) who has discussed the concept of global culture in detail.

John Storey – global culture and popular culture

Globalization and global culture

Storey defines **globalization** as 'the name given to the complex relations which characterize the world in the twenty-first century. It refers to the relentless global flows of capital, commodities, and communications across increasingly porous territorial borders' (2003, p. 107).

In the past, the cultures of different areas of the world tended to remain relatively separate from one another. They were separated by **time** and **space**. It was costly and time-consuming to travel from one part of the world to another and in the absence of mass communications the contact between different cultures was limited.

Now, time and space have become much less important in restricting cultural contacts. Cheap travel, extensive migration and tourism, the expansion of world trade, and the development of technology such as satellite communications and the internet have shrunk the world, making contact between those from different cultures easier and more frequent. For example, English Premiership football teams now feature players from around the world, and the local high street has products from all over the globe. Furthermore, 'We encounter the global in the clothes we wear, the music we listen to, the television programmes and films we watch' (Storey, 2003, p. 108).

Homogenization and heterogenization

Storey comments that, 'One dominant view of globalization is to see it as a process of **homogenization**, that is the reduction of the world to an American "global village"' (p. 109). According to this view, American culture – for example, Coca-Cola, Microsoft software, McDonald's, Levi jeans, rock music and Budweiser beer – has become dominant everywhere. American capitalism has been so successful that it has led to 'the successful global imposition of Americanization ... underpinned by the ideological work that its commodities supposedly do in effectively destroying indigenous cultures and imposing an American way of life on "local" populations' (p. 109).

Although Storey accepts that American capitalism has been very successful, he denies that this has resulted in a US-dominated global culture. He puts forward several reasons for this. Culture is not the same as the commodities which people buy. Culture is much more than a series of commodities because it also involves the way in which the commodities are used and relate to people's lifestyles. Consumers are not simply passive, and commodities do not, for example, impose values and norms on people. Their meaning is affected by how they are used in a local context. Even cultural artefacts such as songs are given local meaning. For example, hip-hop originated in the USA but in countries such as South Africa, France and Britain the style has been appropriated and adapted to fit in with local culture.

Storey therefore believes that globalization does not destroy local culture – in some ways it adds to cultural diversity in the world. He says, 'The process is much more contradictory and complex, involving the ebb and flow of both homogenizing and heterogenizing forces and the meeting and mingling of the "local" and the "global"' (p. 112). Like the theory of mass culture, a simplistic theory of global culture assumes that mass communications impose an ideology on a mass audience, and it ignores the way in which the audience can manipulate or oppose the culture.

Hybridization

One important result of the mixing of the local and the global is **hybridization**. The increasing contact between different cultures and between American capitalism and local culture provides many opportunities for cultures to come together in numerous hybrid forms. New forms of culture constantly develop, which fuse together elements from different sources. For example, chicken tikka masala is unknown as a dish in India and represents a hybrid of British and Asian cooking. Many forms of popular music mix influences and often combine local folk music with commercial music from the USA or Europe.

Storey, however, does not believe that there is a simple contrast between local folk culture and global culture. No cultures have truly developed in isolation; what passes for folk culture in particular areas has already been influenced by cultures from other places. However, according to Storey, this process accelerates with globalization, making any idea of an authentic, local, folk culture less and less tenable.

According to Storey, 'Globalization offers the possibility of cultural mixing on a scale never before known' (p. 117). It does undermine local culture, but it

does not lead to a single global culture. While some commodities, particularly American ones, are found worldwide, they are used in different ways in different places. Instead of the world being dominated by an American culture, it is characterized by an ever greater plurality of hybrid cultures which mix influences from different parts of the globe.

Although Storey generally welcomes this development, he is concerned that not all cultures are valued equally. Some cultures – for example, American culture – are more powerful than other cultures. Storey does not believe that certain cultures should be seen as superior to others, but he accepts that some do still enjoy greater prestige than others, with consequences for who has most power in the world. This helps to buttress the power of the most culturally influential states.

Evaluation

Not everybody agrees with Storey's analysis. For example, Leslie Sklair (1993, 1995, 2003) believes that an ideology of consumerism promoted by transnational capitalist corporations has become very influential (see pp. 551–2). Nevertheless Storey's work is useful for countering the exaggerated claims of those who believe that a single culture dominates every corner of the world. (See pp. 548–57 for a broad discussion of globalization.)

Structuralism

Structuralism is an influential approach to the study of culture, which originated in theories of linguistics. Structuralist approaches to culture see language as the key to understanding the social world. They see the social world as a linguistic phenomenon. Most social life is conducted through language, and, from a structuralist point of view, shaped by it. Structuralist thought began with the work of the Swiss linguist, Ferdinand de Saussure.

Ferdinand de Saussure – semiology

Signs

Saussure (1857–1913) is usually seen as the founder of semiology (sometimes called semiotics), or the science of signs. Saussure defines **semiology** as 'A science that studies the life of signs within society' (Saussure, 1966, first published in English in 1959). Saussure defines a **sign** as 'the combination of a concept and a sound image'. Signs, then, consist of two parts. For example, the sign 'tree' consists of:

1. The **concept** of tree – the sort of object that is referred to as a tree.
2. The **sound-image** of tree. This is not the physical sound made when somebody says the word 'tree', but the 'psychological imprint of the sound'. You can recite the word 'tree' to yourself in your imagination without actually saying it, and the ability to do this means that the sound-image is a psychological phenomenon rather than the physical sound when the word is spoken.

Saussure then goes on to use the word **signified** to denote a concept, and the word **signifier** to denote the sound-image. Signified and signifier together form a sign.

The relationship between signifier and signified

Saussure argued that there is an arbitrary relationship between signifier and signified. There is no necessary reason why particular signifiers should be used to denote particular concepts. This is demonstrated by the fact that different languages use different words to signify the concept of tree. He says, 'nothing would prevent the association of any idea with any sequence of sounds'.

Although the signifier has no necessary connection with the signified, people cannot choose what words to use to signify particular concepts. Thus an individual cannot decide to start calling trees 'dogs' and continue to be understood by others. Signs are handed down from one generation to the next. Saussure comments: 'No society, in fact, knows or has ever known language other than as a product inherited from preceding generations.' He therefore sees language as a **social phenomenon** shared by members of a social group and passed down to children. Therefore, it is largely **immutable** – it tends to be fixed and unchanging. Saussure accepts that some changes in language are possible over long periods of time. However, even then, there tend to be only small shifts in the meaning of particular signifiers.

Langue and parole

Saussure does not see language as simply a collection of unrelated signifiers. Signifiers are defined in terms of other signifiers. For example, the signifier 'animal' helps to define the signifier 'dog'. Furthermore, language can only be used if there are some rules governing how different signifiers are strung together to communicate ideas. Each language therefore has a structure consisting of the grammatical rules, words, the meanings that link words together, and so on. Saussure calls this overall structure the **langue**. He distinguishes it from **parole**, which refers to the actual use of language.

The sentences in this book, the words spoken by sociology students in classrooms, the discussions people have in pubs and in their homes are all examples of parole. All require the existence of a langue to make the parole possible. Saussure compares this to the game of chess. In chess the langue consists of the rules governing initial placement of pieces, the movement of pieces, taking opponents' pieces, winning the game, and so on. The parole consists of the actual moves chosen by particular players.

Linguistics

To Saussure, linguistics involves examining parole – examples of the use of language – to understand the underlying structure or langue. A language should be studied as an integrated system with its own logic and

structure. It should not be seen in terms of its links with an external reality. Thus the sign 'dog' should be seen in terms of its relationship with other signs, such as 'animal' and 'bark', rather than in terms of its relationship with the actual creature it describes.

Saussure therefore emphasizes that people experience the world in terms of signs which have particular meanings, rather than experiencing it in a direct material way. John Storey has described the implications of this aspect of Saussure's work. He says:

> *The function of language is to organize and construct our access to reality. It therefore also follows from this that different languages in effect produce a different mapping of the real. When a European gazes at a snowscape, he or she sees snow. An Eskimo looking at the same snowscape would see so much more, the reason being that Eskimos have over fifty words to describe snow. Therefore an Eskimo and a European standing together surveying the snowscape would in fact be seeing two quite different conceptual schemes.* Storey, 1997

Evaluation

Saussure effectively founded the disciplines of semiology and linguistics. However, his work has attracted some criticism. Norman Fairclough (1989, discussed in Strinati, 1995) argues that Saussure exaggerates the extent to which language is shared by members of a society. Fairclough also argues that Saussure neglects the importance of power. More powerful members of society may try to define their own language as superior to other forms, creating the possibility of conflict over what forms of language are afforded the highest status.

However, there is no doubt that Saussure influenced the work of other writers. His ideas laid the foundations for the whole discipline of semiology, which now extends to the analysis of signs other than words (for example, clothing and food). In this sort of study there is an attempt to uncover the meaning system of a set of signs in a way that is similar to the way in which Saussure examined the langue of a language.

Saussure's ideas also influenced the work of structuralists such as Lévi-Strauss, by suggesting to them that human thinking and social relationships could be shaped by underlying structures similar to those that are integral to a langue. (For an example of the application of semiotics, see Hebdige's discussion of youth culture, pp. 772–4.)

Claude Lévi-Strauss – structuralism, myths and kinship

Structures

Saussure's attempts to uncover the basic structure of signs and language influenced the development of structuralism. **Structuralism** analyses the basic structures underlying human thinking and human social groups. The anthropologist Claude Lévi-Strauss (1963, 1986, first published 1963) was the first to develop structuralism, using it to understand such things as kinship systems and myths.

Lévi-Strauss believes there are certain structures which underlie all human thinking and social arrangements. While these structures cannot be directly observed, they can be revealed in human culture, which is shaped by these structures. Since the structures are common to all humans, evidence of them can be found universally. Thus the myths of the Ancient Greeks and North American Indians (or Native Americans) reflect the same structures. Similarly, all kinship systems are based upon the same basic structures. The details of different myths or kinship systems may be very different, but the fundamental structure is the same.

Kinship

Lévi-Strauss (1963) argues that 'kinship phenomena are of the same type as linguistic phenomena'. By this he means that kinship systems are based upon certain laws which apply to all cultures. Just as Saussure believed that all languages had the same relationship between signifiers and the signified, Lévi-Strauss believed that all kinship systems had the same basic relationships.

According to Lévi-Strauss, all kinship systems have sets of relationships, and, like a language, each part of the system only has meaning when related to other elements. Thus, for example, the position of wife can only exist if related to the position of husband, and the position of mother can only exist in relation to the position of son or daughter. Furthermore, the same basic elements of kinship systems are found everywhere. Lévi-Strauss says:

> *The recurrence of kinship patterns, marriage rules, similar prescribed attitudes between certain types of relatives, and so forth, in scattered regions of the globe and in fundamentally different societies, leads us to believe that, in the case of kinship ... the observable phenomena result from the action of laws which are general but implicit.*
> Lévi-Strauss, 1963

So what then is the basic structure of kinship? Lévi-Strauss believes it involves three types of family relationship: 'a relationship between siblings, between spouses, and a relation between parent and child'. In addition there is an **avuncular** relationship between uncle or aunt and nephew or niece. This derives automatically from the existence of relationships between parents and children and between siblings.

This basic structure is 'a direct result of the universal presence of an incest taboo'. The incest taboo prohibits sexual relationships between close relatives such as siblings and parents and children. The existence of this taboo means that 'a man must obtain a woman from another man who gives him a daughter or a sister'. The basic kinship structure needs to exist to establish which members of society are not the kin of an individual – and therefore with whom that individual can have a legitimate sexual relationship.

Within different kinship structures the strength of one relationship will tend to determine the strength of others. In the Trobriand Islands, for example, sibling relationships are fairly weak, so children have closer relationships with their fathers than they do with uncles. In Tonga, on the other hand, sibling relationships are seen as more important than spouse relationships. Consequently, boys have close relationships with uncles – sometimes closer than the relationship with their own father.

Binary oppositions

To Lévi-Strauss, kinship systems are not the only aspects of culture which are universal. He also claimed to find certain **binary oppositions**, or pairs of opposites, which structure all human thinking.

These binary oppositions stem from the way humans tend to divide up the world into 'segments so that we are predisposed to think of the environment as consisting of a vast number of separate things belonging to named classes' (Leach, 1970). Examples of such binary oppositions are nature/culture, man/woman, good/bad. The categories in each binary opposition are mutually exclusive; something cannot be part of nature and culture at the same time. However, the existence of binary oppositions sometimes causes contradictions. Myths are used to try to resolve these contradictions.

Myths

Many myths incorporate elements related to food. Eating food is an essential part of human culture and, according to Lévi-Strauss (1986, first published 1963), humans consume food in ways related to the opposition between nature/culture. **Raw food** is seen as part of nature. Animals, which are part of nature, eat food in raw form. **Cooking**, on the other hand, transforms food into a part of culture because it is something that humans do to food. Left to their own devices, meat or vegetables will rot as part of a natural process. Like raw food, rotted food is seen as part of nature.

Lévi-Strauss argues that food in different states is found in many myths. The discovery of fire and the cooking of food feature prominently in some of them. It is used to make sense of the transition of humans from being animals – which eat raw food, and are therefore part of nature – to being humans who are cultured and have the means to cook food.

Another fundamental problem dealt with in myths is the origin of human beings. In many, if not all, cultures it is believed that humanity had an **autochthonous** origin; that is, that the first humans were created autonomously without being born to a mother and father. In some cultures humans are seen as coming from the earth, in others as being created by God. This belief contradicts human experience, which shows that humans come into being as the result of a union between a man and a woman.

This problem is dealt with in the Oedipus myth, 'which relates the original problem – born from one or born from two? – to the derivative problem; born from different or born from same?' (Lévi-Strauss, 1963). In the Greek Oedipus myth, Oedipus marries his mother Jocasta, kills his father Laios, and slays the Sphinx, a monster who does not want men to live.

Lévi-Strauss notes that the meaning of 'Oedipus' is 'swollen-foot' and that in mythology people who are born from the earth are either unable to walk or are clumsy walkers. He therefore believes Oedipus represents autochthonous birth even though he was born with a mother and a father. The myth is unable to resolve the contradiction between autochthonous and bisexual reproduction, but it does express the contradiction in mythical form. Furthermore, although the contradiction is not resolved, humanity does survive, as the creatures which threaten it (such as the Sphinx) are killed.

As with other myths, Lévi-Strauss does not see the Oedipus myth as the product of a particular culture. He argues that the basic structures of this myth are to be found in very different and widely separated societies. The details of the story may vary, but the structure remains the same. It is therefore a product of the basic structures of human thought, particularly the existence of certain binary oppositions.

Lévi-Strauss concludes that myths serve as an 'intermediary entity' between parole (particular stories or myths) and langue (the basic structures of thought and the human brain). Myths express the structure in the form of particular stories and make it possible to deal with, and sometimes resolve, the contradictions in binary oppositions.

Evaluation

Dominic Strinati (1995) argues that Lévi-Strauss tends to use highly selective evidence in support of his theories. While he uses plenty of examples to back up what he says, he tends to ignore any evidence that contradicts it. For example, Strinati says, 'his analysis of Oedipal myths is only successful because he selects those features of the stories which suit his case, and ignores others which contradict the notion that they are expressions of a universal mental structure.' If they truly expressed a universal mental structure, then all examples would support his theories and there would be no need to be selective.

Because Lévi-Strauss is seeking evidence of universal mental structures, his arguments are **reductionist**: that is, they try to reduce all culture to being the product of fixed mental structures. Lévi-Strauss therefore neglects the importance of history in shaping cultures and makes little attempt to explain the variety of human cultures. Strinati says:

> *Downplaying the importance of history means that the problems posed for any analysis of popular culture by historical variations in cultures and societies are simply not addressed. Indeed, it could be argued that it is impossible to understand the formal structures of language or myth outside of their social and historical contexts.* Strinati, 1995

Strinati also accuses Lévi-Strauss's structuralism of being **deterministic**. It allows no room for human creativity and simply assumes that all culture is automatically shaped by unconscious mental structures, whatever the wishes of individuals. Furthermore, the meaning of culture is always open to interpretation, and this very fact 'suggests that the importance of the human subject cannot be so easily dismissed'.

Finally, Strinati attacks Lévi-Strauss's claim that humans always think in terms of binary oppositions – for example, that between nature and culture. Strinati admits that all societies have to respond to the existence of nature, but they do not necessarily see it as the opposite of culture. Different societies understand nature in different ways; it does not have the same meaning for everybody and it is not always seen in terms of a binary opposition with culture. This point could be extended to all of Lévi-Strauss's examples of binary oppositions. There are plenty of occasions when humans think in more subtle terms than distinguishing between pairs of opposites.

Poststructuralism

Derrida, Lacan and Foucault

Poststructuralism is a rather general term used to refer to the work of writers such as Jacques Lacan, Jacques Derrida (see pp. 116–17) and Michel Foucault (see pp. 559–62).

At first sight these writers have little in common, since they wrote about different issues, using a variety of theoretical approaches. Lacan is influenced by psychoanalysis and is concerned with gender differences in early human development. Derrida's work is based more upon linguistics and focuses on the meaning of language. Foucault's work is wide-ranging and considers issues as diverse as the development of prisons, sexuality, madness and, more generally, the relationship between power and knowledge.

However, they are grouped together as poststructuralists because their work includes some broad philosophical similarities. They are seen as poststructuralists because their work has developed out of a rejection of the idea of structures. Nevertheless, it owes a lot to the emphasis on language found in the work of semiologists and structuralists such as Saussure and Lévi-Strauss.

Poststructuralism and Lévi-Strauss

Poststructuralists reject Lévi-Strauss's belief that it is possible to find certain fixed structures in society which reflect the human mind. They also reject the Marxist view that society has certain structures (such as a class structure) which shape social relationships. Foucault, for example, saw power/knowledge as the key to understanding how society is shaped (see p. 559). Power/knowledge has no fixed form but constantly changes in the course of interaction. Power is not to be found in social structures, but is intimately linked to the way people talk about things and create particular discourses (see p. 559 for a discussion of discourse).

Language, meaning and subjectivity

Chris Weedon (1994, first published 1987) argues that poststructuralists 'share certain fundamental assumptions about language, meaning and subjectivity'. The emphasis on language is to be found in Derrida's discussion of *différence* (see p. 116), Foucault's discussion of discourse, and Lacan's idea of the symbolic order. (Rosemary Tonge (1998) describes the symbolic order as 'a series of interrelated signs, roles and rituals' in which language plays a key role.) Derrida, Foucault and Lacan all agree that the way people understand society and the way society works are shaped by language. As Weedon puts it, 'Language is the place where actual and possible forms of social organization and their likely social and political consequences are defined and contested.'

However, poststructuralists insist that language does not reflect or describe some underlying reality or structure. They argue that it is language that creates reality rather than reflecting it. Madan Sarup (1988) says: 'In poststructuralism, broadly speaking, the signified is demoted and the signifier made dominant.' Sarup points out that Derrida 'believes in a system of floating signifiers pure and simple, with no determinable relation to any extra-linguistic referents at all'. While, for example, Lévi-Strauss looked for the meaning behind myths, poststructuralists deny that any fixed meaning is present.

Derrida argues that the meaning of a text (anything that contains meaningful signs) depends upon how a particular reader interprets it. Thus, if two people interpret a film or book as having different meanings, each interpretation is equally valid. As Sarup (1988) says, 'While structuralism sees the truth as "behind" or "within" a text, poststructuralism stresses the interaction of reader and text.'

Meaning is always related to the particular context in which it is being discussed. Outside that context the meaning might be quite different.

Poststructuralist feminism

Although poststructuralists do not believe it is possible to see behind signs and language to find the truth, many believe that the particular meanings that gain acceptance are of crucial importance. Chris Weedon, a poststructuralist feminist, gives some examples.

Weedon argues that the outcome of rape trials in the United Kingdom is largely determined by the meaning given to the idea of 'natural justice' and the meaning attributed to the word 'rape'. The dominance of masculine definitions of natural justice leads to a situation where men are unlikely to be convicted of rape. This is because it is seen as 'natural' for a man to continue with sex even when a woman says no. From this point of view, it is unjust for courts to find men guilty where women may have appeared to encourage sex. Weedon says:

> ***courts often endorse the view of rape as an active endorsement of male sexuality in the face of female 'provocation'. In the view of some judges, this may take the form of going out alone at night, wearing a mini-skirt or being a prostitute.*** Weedon, 1994, first published 1987

From Weedon's point of view, it is important to challenge this view of natural justice so that courts are more likely to find rapists guilty and punish them.

As a poststructuralist, Weedon sees arguments over language as having a key social and political role. Changing the accepted interpretation of a word or sign in particular contexts can have a crucial role in promoting greater social justice. This process can make use of Derrida's idea of **deconstruction** (see p. 117), in which the meaning of signs is taken apart and found to be contradictory.

Poststructuralism and identity

As well as attacking the idea that signs have any fixed meaning, poststructuralists also reject the idea that

individuals have a fixed sense of who they are – that is, of identity. Poststructuralists use the idea of the subject.

According to Weedon, in conventional views of the subject, '"Subjectivity" is used to refer to the conscious and unconscious thoughts and emotions of the individual which are unique, fixed and coherent and make her what she is.'

Weedon and other poststructuralists reject this view. They argue that individuals do not have a unique, fixed or coherent idea of who they are, or sense of identity. Instead, their identity is shaped through involvement in particular discourses. From this point of view, experience shapes one's subjectivity, but experience itself is only understood in terms of the discourses that surround it. For example, a person does not simply experience 'family life' in a direct way. Instead, they make sense of it through the **discourses** – the ways of thinking and talking about the family – that they come into contact with.

Somebody influenced by feminist discourse will experience being a 'mother' or a 'wife' very differently from somebody influenced by more traditional discourses of the family. Since there is a wide range of discourses available, and each of these may be challenged and changed over time, individuals do not have a settled sense of who they are. Weedon suggests that even the identity of being a woman has no fixed meaning. What people understand by womanhood, and how women see themselves as women, changes as they come into contact with continually changing and contested discourses of femininity (see pp. 692–704 for a fuller discussion of identity).

Poststructuralism attacks the foundations on which most types of social science have been based, and instead focuses on the fluid and indeterminate meaning of language. By undermining conventional approaches in social science, poststructuralism paved the way for postmodern theories of society and culture. These will be examined shortly.

Evaluation of poststructuralism

Poststructuralism focused attention on the importance of language, which was certainly neglected by many other sociologists (including functionalists and Marxists). But the focus on language is the greatest weakness of poststructuralism as well as its greatest strength.

The emphasis on language leads poststructuralists to neglect material reality. For example, Marxists would argue that material wealth has just as much influence on society as discourse, or ways of talking about things. In the end, capitalists have the power to determine which television programmes or films are made and promoted. To socialist and Marxist feminists it is the wealth of men rather than the way language is used that keeps women oppressed.

Like other sociological approaches which deny the existence of absolute truth (such as postmodernism (see pp. 891–4) and ethnomethodology (see pp. 885–7)), poststructuralism advocates **relativism**. It argues that the 'truth' depends simply on who you listen to, which discourse is accepted. Because signifiers are defined in terms of other signifiers, they cannot represent reality.

This creates a problem shared with other relativist approaches: there is no reason to accept poststructuralism above other sociological perspectives. From a poststructuralist viewpoint, each perspective is simply a different discourse and there is no way of testing which are true and which are false.

Poststructuralists clearly believe that their own discourse is superior to other discourses. Some see certain perspectives (for example, feminism) as being more valid than others (for example, functionalism). However, the philosophy underlying their own perspective prevents them from being able to show why their views should be accepted above the views of others. (For an evaluation of Foucault, see p. 562; for an evaluation of poststructuralist and postmodern feminism, see pp. 118–19.)

Modernity, postmodernity, globalization and culture

Stephen Crook, Jan Pakulski and Malcolm Waters – *Postmodernization*

Stephen Crook, Jan Pakulski and Malcolm Waters (1992) argue that contemporary societies are undergoing a process of **postmodernization**. They are in the process of changing from modern to postmodern societies. Crook *et al.* trace the changes involved in this process by comparing modern and postmodern culture.

Modern culture

According to Crook *et al.*, there are three main characteristics of modern culture: differentiation, rationalization and commodification.

Differentiation

Differentiation involves the separating out of different parts of society. Economic, political, social and cultural spheres become increasingly distinct from one another. Drawing on the ideas of Max Weber, Crook *et al.* argue that different aspects of society come to be judged in terms of different criteria. Science is judged in terms of truth; morality and law in terms of goodness and justice; and art in terms of beauty. Each sphere develops its own specialist institutions and occupations.

Initially, the patronage of the rich enabled people to become professional musicians, composers, sculptors and artists. Later, specialist institutions such as art schools developed to train future generations of cultural specialists. Other institutions, such as theatres, art galleries and concert halls, were established to make cultural products more widely available.

Culture was therefore separated or differentiated from other aspects of life. It was produced by specialists, trained in particular institutions, and it was consumed in specific places. This formed the basis for distinguishing between **folk culture** (which could be found among ordinary people) and **high culture**, which was the product of these specialist individuals and institutions.

However, as modernity progressed, new types of popular culture developed, such as the music hall, the charabanc (coach) trip or the seaside holiday resort. In these, too, culture was differentiated from other areas of life, but it had no pretensions to being high culture.

There have been some attempts to break down the division between high culture and everyday life. Avant-garde artists have tried to shock people out of their cultural complacency by portraying everyday objects as art. For example, in 1917 Marcel Duchamp displayed a urinal as a work of art with the title 'Fountain'. He attributed the work to the sanitary engineer who designed the urinal. However, such protests against the splitting of art and life had little impact in modern societies.

Rationalization

According to Crook *et al.*, **rationalization** also shaped modern culture, but not as completely as differentiation. Music was increasingly influenced by harmonic rationalization, in which mathematics was used to help compose harmonic music. There was also considerable rationalization of the reproduction of music and other art forms.

Technology was used to make it possible to recreate or copy culture. For example, the piano allowed the reproduction of a version of complex music on a single instrument. Radios and record players allowed broadcasts and copies of original music to be consumed more widely. Printing technology allowed the reproduction of works of art to become rationalized – people no longer relied upon the efforts of individual artists in order to be able to see pictures.

While some have seen these developments as undermining the distinction between high culture and everyday life, Crook *et al.* disagree. People may be able to sit in their living room listening to Beethoven on their hi-fi while gazing at a print of the Mona Lisa, but this simply serves to reinforce the status of high culture. It gives legitimacy to the idea that certain individuals were the greatest artists or composers.

Nevertheless, in modernity the rationalization of culture can only proceed so far, since the individual creativity of the great artist is still valued.

Commodification

The **commodification** of culture involves turning cultural products into commodities that can be readily bought and sold. From the viewpoint of mass culture theories (see pp. 673–4), this undermines aesthetic values and threatens the purity of high art. It brings to the masses an inferior and debased culture which then threatens the unique qualities of high art.

Crook *et al.* do not agree with this view. To them, the development of **taste** is a key feature of modern culture. Taste only develops when people have enough resources to make choices about what they consume. In early modernity only the highest classes could do this, but as modernity progressed the possibility of choosing what to consume spread to all classes. This does not undermine hierarchies of taste. The taste of higher social classes is still valued above that of lower classes. In modernity classical music is still seen as superior to the latest pop music.

Postmodernization

In modern societies, culture is differentiated from other areas of social life and high culture is differentiated from popular culture. However, **postmodernization** reverses these trends. According to Crook *et al.*, an intensification of some of the processes at work in modernity leads to postmodernization. Differentiation, rationalization and commodification are superseded by hyperdifferentiation, hypercommodification and hyper-rationalization. Although each of these develops from, and intensifies the processes of, modernity, they have the effect of reversing some of the trends evident in modernity. This leads to a new type of culture. Crook *et al.* call this new culture **postculture**.

Hypercommodification

Hypercommodification involves all areas of social life becoming commodified. In modern societies certain areas of social life such as family life, class background and community ties were not commercialized and were major sources of identity. They influenced what you consumed because they influenced taste. Thus, for example, different families from different classes and different localities would tend to eat different types of food, wear different types of clothes and buy different types of furniture. Hypercommodification undermines these differences.

First, all areas of social life are invaded by commodities. Family activities such as eating are invaded by the marketing of products. Consumption increasingly takes place within the home and members of the same family become more inclined to consume different things. Often children have their own television sets, and they sit in different rooms from their parents, watching different programmes and adverts, and even eating different foods. Instead of a uniform family culture, each family member chooses their own lifestyle.

Similarly, members of the same class no longer tend to share the same tastes. They can increasingly choose from a range of **lifestyle options**. Different lifestyles themselves become freed from their association with specific groups. For example, people from many different backgrounds choose to live 'green' lifestyles which express their concern for the environment, or choose to follow particular sports or even particular teams.

According to Crook *et al.*, **style**, unlike taste, is not constrained or shaped by external social factors such as class. Styles are systems of signs: the style you choose says something to others about what sort of a person you are. Styles are shaped only by personal preference – essentially, everybody can become whoever they choose.

Hyper-rationalization

Hyper-rationalization involves the use of rationalized technology to spread cultural consumption more widely and to privatize it. Technology such as the Walkman and satellite TV allows greater individual choice about what to

listen to or watch. Video and cassette recorders extend choice over when and where cultural products are consumed. Again, this allows individuals to choose their own lifestyle. Public cultural events such as theatres and music halls, where people gather to consume cultural products simultaneously, become less important.

Following the ideas of Baudrillard (see pp. 893–4), Crook *et al.* argue that this erodes the distinction between **authentic** and **inauthentic culture**. Media images come to dominate society. Media copies and reproductions begin to replace the authentic, real thing they represent. Eventually images and signs lose their connection with reality and become what Baudrillard calls **simulacra** (see p. 893 for a definition of simulacra).

Hyperdifferentiation

Crook *et al.* argue: 'In postmodernization a thousand flowers bloom.' A fantastic variety of cultural forms develop, with no particular type being dominant. For example, popular music has fragmented into a wide variety of styles, each with its own audience choosing its own preferred style, to go with its chosen lifestyle. As variety becomes the order of the day, it becomes difficult for any particular style to claim to be superior to all others.

Furthermore, hypercommodification leads to the incorporation of high culture into cultural forms that have not traditionally enjoyed much prestige. For example, classical music is used as background music in advertising, films and television programmes.

The increased fragmentation of culture – **hyperdifferentiation** – leads ultimately to **dedifferentiation**, in which distinctions between different types of culture break down. In particular, the distinction between high culture and popular culture is undermined in postmodernizing societies. Not only does high culture get incorporated into popular culture, but also popular culture increasingly claims to be serious art. Each cultural style has its own devotees who see their own preferred styles and art forms as better than others. High culture no longer has an exclusive claim to legitimacy.

Conclusion

Crook *et al.* claim that postculture is characterized above all by fragmentation. Variety and choice are the main features of postculture, where lifestyle preferences replace a hierarchy of tastes based on class and other social differences.

Crook *et al.* did not believe that postculture had become completely dominant at the time they were writing (1992). They saw postmodernization as an ongoing process, but did not deny that elements of modern culture remained important. Nevertheless, they clearly believed that postmodernization was gaining momentum, and envisaged a time when it would have largely undermined modern culture.

Dominic Strinati – postmodernism and popular culture

Crook *et al.* are enthusiastic advocates of the claim that contemporary societies are moving towards postmodernity. Dominic Strinati (1995) is much more sceptical. However, he does provide a commendably clear explanation and discussion of how theories of postmodernism analyse popular culture. He argues that there are five main features of postmodern analysis of popular culture, and he illustrates these arguments with reference to a variety of cultural products. He also examines factors that might have produced postmodern popular culture.

The main features of postmodernism

Strinati identifies the main features of postmodernism as the following:

1. The first is 'the breakdown of the distinction between culture and society'. This involves the development of a 'media-saturated society'. In such a society the mass media are extremely powerful. Rather than reflecting reality the media become so all-consuming that they create our sense of reality. Computer technology helps to create virtual realities which 'potentially replace their real life counterparts'. Increasingly, economic activity is concerned with buying and selling media images rather than physical products.
2. The second main feature of postmodernism is 'an emphasis on style at the expense of substance'. Thus, particular products become popular because they have designer labels which evoke an attractive lifestyle, rather than because they are useful. Society develops a 'designer ideology'. Surface qualities assume more importance than anything deeper. For example, Strinati says that in popular culture:

   surface and style, what things look like, playfulness and jokes, are said to predominate at the expense of content, substance and meaning. As a result, qualities like artistic merit, integrity, seriousness, authenticity, realism, intellectual depth and strong narratives tend to be undermined. Strinati, 1995

   For example, a film will tend to be successful if it is visually appealing, whether or not the plot is any good.
3. There is a 'breakdown of the distinction between art and popular culture'. In postmodern culture, 'anything can be turned into a joke, reference or quotation'. Thus, elements of what used to be thought of as 'high culture' become incorporated into popular culture. The pop artist Andy Warhol, for example, produced a famous print consisting of thirty representations of Leonardo da Vinci's **Mona Lisa**. The work is called 'Thirty are better than One', and it undermines the special aura and uniqueness of the original by emphasizing how easy it is to produce endless copies of the print.

   Strinati says: 'postmodern popular culture refuses to respect the pretensions and distinctiveness of art'. Art has become incorporated into everyday life in societies dominated by signs. Consequently, there is no longer anything special about art.

   The critics of mass culture in the earlier decades of the century were deeply worried about just such a development (see pp. 673–4). If postmodernists are right, the worst fears of these critics have come true. However, postmodernists see no reason to be unhappy about this; they welcome the fun,

spontaneity and variety of the new postmodern culture in which art is part of life.

4 A fourth feature of postmodern culture is the development of 'confusions over time and space'. Following the ideas of David Harvey (1990), Strinati believes that rapid travel, almost instantaneous communications, and the speed with which capital, information and cultures flow from society to society, all lead to confusions over time and space. The media make it possible to witness events on the other side of the globe almost as if you were there. As a result, people's sense of space becomes confused.

Postmodern culture also confuses people's sense of time. For example, architecture is often nostalgic and incorporates styles from previous eras. Theme parks recreate the past and try to create the future. Postmodern films often avoid following a story from beginning to end (linear time), but jump around between past, present and future in a confusing way. The title and content of the film *Back to the Future* show how conventional ideas of linear time can be undermined in postmodern culture.

5 Finally, postmodern culture involves 'the decline of metanarratives'. Drawing on the ideas of Lyotard (see pp. 891–3), Strinati sees postmodernism as involving a decline in people's faith in any big stories, or big ideas, about the world. Postmodernism is 'sceptical of any absolute, universal and all-embracing claim to knowledge', such as 'religion, science, art, modernism and Marxism'. It denies there is any sense of progress in history. In popular culture this manifests itself in the use of collage, where elements from very different sources are brought together in particular cultural artefacts. Postmodern films often mix different genres, and postmodern buildings mix different styles. The implicit message is that no style or genre is better than any other. Everything is equally valid and the search for a single truth is both pointless and dangerous.

Reasons for the emergence of postmodernism

Strinati identifies three main reasons for the emergence of postmodernism:

1 Capitalist societies have placed an increasing emphasis on consumerism. In the earlier stages of capitalism there was more emphasis on production, on developing the productive capacity of machinery, and on meeting people's basic needs. Advanced capitalist societies have, on average, much higher living standards, and there is much more emphasis on getting people to consume products that can be produced in very high numbers. A more affluent population with more leisure time needs to be entertained and persuaded to spend money if companies are to continue to make profits. The media are central to these processes, and consequently media images increasingly dominate society.

2 'New middle-class occupations' have developed which have an interest in promoting postmodern culture. These occupations include design, marketing, advertising and creative jobs in the various media. These jobs involve persuading people about the importance of taste. Once people are persuaded of this, then they will need the expertise of those who claim to be experts in their fields, and they will usually access this expertise through the media.

Strinati also sees groups such as teachers, social workers, lecturers and therapists as important because of their involvement with 'notions of psychological and personal fulfilment and growth'. Such ideas also encourage people to take lifestyle seriously. They therefore encourage them to consume the goods and services required for the lifestyle that they decide is best for them.

Strinati concludes that, for the new occupations in the middle class, 'Their quest for cultural power leads them towards postmodernism and away from the cultures of other classes, such as the high culture of the traditional middle-class intelligentsia.'

3 According to Strinati, postmodernism also comes about because of the 'erosion of collective and personal identities'. There has been a gradual disappearance of identities based upon such things as class, local communities, religion and the nation-state. Yet these have not been replaced by alternative sources of identity. People's identities become more personal and individual, and 'popular culture and the mass media come to serve as the only frames of reference available for the construction of collective and personal identities'. (See pp. 692–704 for a detailed discussion of identity.)

An evaluation of postmodern theories of culture

As well as describing postmodern theories of culture, Dominic Strinati also evaluates them. In doing so he raises a considerable number of problems – with postmodern theories of popular culture in particular, and culture in general.

1 Strinati argues that postmodernists greatly exaggerate their case in suggesting that the mass media 'take over "reality"'. He says, 'The mass media are important, but not that important.' He sees exaggerated claims about the importance of the media as a product of the ideology of those who make a living from the media. They are based on little empirical evidence; there is no reason to suppose that most people cannot distinguish between image and reality. For example, few people believe that the characters in soap operas are real. Postmodernism also fails to explain exactly why the media are so important, and it ignores other areas of social life, such as work and families, which are also important.

2 Postmodern theory also exaggerates the importance of the media in shaping what people consume. People do not just buy products because of their image or the designer label attached to them; they also buy them because they are useful. Furthermore, less affluent members of society simply cannot afford to buy expensive products for the kudos attached to a brand name. What is more, not all sections of society have a culture which attaches importance to the image of products.

3 Strinati questions the logic of postmodernism's claim that metanarratives are in decline. This is because he argues that postmodernism is itself a metanarrative. Strinati says postmodernism:

> *presents a definite view of knowledge and its acquisition, together with a general account of the significant changes it sees occurring in modern societies. It presumes to tell us something true about the world, and knows why it is able to do this.* Strinati, 1995

These are just the characteristics that postmodernists use to describe other metanarratives, of which they are so critical. The popularity of postmodernism therefore undermines the postmodernists' claim that metanarratives are in decline.

4 Strinati has more time for the postmodernists' claim that concepts of time and space have been affected by developments such as faster travel and communications. However, he argues that some people have less opportunity to experience these changes than others. The poorer people of the world do not have access to computer technology, satellite communications or jet travel. In any case, some changes date back to the early decades of the twentieth century (for example, aeroplanes and the cinema), well before postmodernity is supposed to have developed.

As in other areas, postmodernists do not provide detailed evidence that people's consciousness has changed. There are no studies which actually show that people have confused ideas about space and time.

5 Strinati believes that 'postmodernist claims about the breakdown of the distinction between art and popular culture do have a certain plausibility'. However, he argues that these claims can only be applied to the culture of the new middle-class occupations, which he sees as largely responsible for the emergence of postmodernism.

Generally, people still find it possible to distinguish between what they consider art and what they see as popular culture. Furthermore, postmodernists themselves distinguish between 'modern' and 'postmodern' cultural products. If they can do this, then 'the potential for cultural discrimination must remain under postmodernism'. If postmodernists prefer postmodern films, buildings, television programmes and so on to modern ones, it remains open for other groups of people to retain their own preferences, which may be quite different from those of postmodernists.

Strinati believes: 'Rather than dismantling the hierarchy of aesthetic and cultural taste, postmodernism erects a new one, placing itself at the top.' Postmodern cultural products often contain 'clever' references to a variety of styles and genres from previous eras. Only clever, well-informed people (particularly postmodernists), who are familiar with all these different styles and genres, can fully appreciate the subtleties of postmodern art and popular culture.

6 Finally, Strinati evaluates postmodern claims about actual changes in popular culture. He argues that postmodern elements are most common in advertising and architecture, but that in other areas they have had a more limited impact. He looks particularly at the cinema.

Strinati notes that many films, which can be seen as postmodern in some respects, can be seen as modern in other respects. For example, the *Back to the Future* films may involve confusions over space and time, but they also have strong narratives (story lines) – a feature supposed to be characteristic of modern films.

Even *Blade Runner*, the archetypal postmodern film, is partly based upon themes that predate the emergence of postmodernism by many decades. *Blade Runner* follows the theme of Mary Shelley's novel *Frankenstein*, which explored the tragic consequences of trying to replicate human life (the characters in *Blade Runner* are 'replicants' – near-perfect reproductions of human beings).

Strinati believes that many of the supposedly postmodern aspects of the contemporary cinema are nothing new. For example, even early silent films parodied other genres, taking some ideas from music hall. Films which involve nostalgia for the past have also long been made. Westerns and gangster films are two examples.

Strinati concludes that there are many examples of a postmodern influence on aspects of popular culture, but they are only examples. They are not important or numerous enough to justify the rather grand and generalized claims made by many postmodernists. Strinati says: 'While it cannot be dismissed completely, postmodernism seems subject to severe theoretical and empirical limitations. It is certainly inadequate as a basis for developing a sociology of popular culture.'

This is partly because Strinati believes that any adequate theory must take account of two main factors: the tastes of audiences, and the need for the culture industry to make a profit. He says, 'it is doubtful whether power and control over production by themselves are sufficient to determine patterns of cultural consumption'. However, they do have an important role in determining what is produced: a role that is wholly neglected by postmodernists.

Socialization

Perspectives on socialization

As discussed above (pp. 664–5), **socialization** is the process by which individuals become self-aware and learn the culture of their society. Sociologists influenced by all perspectives see socialization as an important process, although they differ in the ways that they conceive that process. This section briefly introduces these different perspectives before examining the process of socialization in more detail.

The functionalist view of socialization

Talcott Parsons (1937, 1951, 1955, 1959) is perhaps the most important functionalist theorist of socialization. Parsons saw socialization as vital to the process by which a **value consensus** is produced in society. Through socialization the individual **internalizes** society's values – they become part of his or her personality. Through this process individuals take on aspects of society's culture, making their behaviour largely predictable, and contributing to the maintenance of social order.

As discussed elsewhere (see pp. 8–9), the creation and maintenance of a value consensus allows society to meet basic needs (or **functional prerequisites**) such as the need for common culture (or **pattern maintenance**, see pp. 859–61). Socialization provides people with common goals; teaches them the appropriate behaviour associated with particular roles (e.g. the roles of mother, teacher, student and friend); and allows them to learn the **norms** (or informal rules) of social life (see p. 3).

Parsons argued that the family is the most important agency of primary socialization (see pp. 463–4). He saw socialization as taking place primarily through **identification** with adults. Children identify with adults of the same sex (particularly mothers and fathers) and tend to imitate them. As discussed elsewhere (see p. 96), Parsons (1955) believed that it is beneficial to society if women take primary responsibility for childcare, while men are the main breadwinners. Therefore, part of socialization involves learning different gender roles in which women are more expressive (or emotional) and men more instrumental (they plan rationally to achieve certain goals).

Parsons saw schools as an important agency of secondary socialization (see pp. 601–2). Parsons (1961) described school as a **focal socializing agency** because it acts as a bridge between the home and society at large. In schools, members of society learn to treat others according to general rules, or **universalistic values**. This contrasts with the family, where children are treated as individuals according to what are believed to be their individual needs. They are treated as a particular person – in terms of **particularistic values** (see pp. 860–1 for details of different types of values linked to pattern variables). At school, therefore, children become accustomed to conforming to abstract, formal rules.

Evaluation

Functionalist views of socialization, such as those put forward by Parsons, have been extensively criticized.

Alvin Gouldner (1970) believes that Parsons underestimates the amount of conflict that can take place in the process of socialization. He says, 'You would never guess from reading functionalist texts on socialization that training children can be a continual, room-to-room battle, invariably exhausting to the parents and repellent to the children' (Gouldner, 1970, p. 429).

In a much quoted criticism of Parsons, Dennis Wrong (1961) argued that sociology in general, and functionalism and Parsons in particular, had an 'oversocialized view of man'. Sociology was far too likely to portray people as conforming to social rules, ignoring the extent to which people deviated from the norms and values which socialization tried to instil in them.

Another critic, Gary Allan Fine (2006, first published 1981), believes that Parsons's approach to socialization is **adultist**. It sees children as the passive recipients of socialization from adults and assumes that children will identify with and imitate adults, particularly same-sex parents. Fine believes that children do not necessarily identify so closely with parents – they can also be strongly influenced by peer groups.

Increasingly sociologists identify the active part played by children in their own development, rather than seeing them as empty vessels which are simply filled with values and norms passed down to them (see pp. 764–5).

Marxism and socialization

Functionalist perspectives tend to see socialization as an entirely positive process. Through socialization the individual becomes a competent and conforming member of society, and this benefits society as a whole. Marxist perspectives on socialization tend to agree that socialization can be an effective way of producing conformity, but they disagree that this benefits society as a whole.

Ideological conditioning

An example of the Marxist view of socialization is provided by the work of David Cooper (1972). Cooper sees the family as 'an ideological conditioning device' which conditions children to accept their own exploitation. The family lays down behaviour patterns in which people submit to those in authority. Children learn to obey their parents, just as they will obey employers in later life. Every child has the potential to be an artist, a visionary, or a revolutionary, and to see through ruling-class ideology, but this is stifled by the submission of the self to the demands of the family.

Social controls implanted by the family are particularly effective because of taboos which saturate family life. For example, after a certain age boys are not expected to kiss their fathers, and breaking this taboo can create feelings of guilt. The association of guilt with breaking family taboos provides the basis for conformity and submission to the laws and requirements of the powerful.

Cooper argues that 'the family specializes in the formation of roles for its members rather than laying down conditions for the free assumption of identity'. Thus children are taught to play the roles of son and daughter, male and female. Such roles are constricting. They confine behaviour within narrow limits and restrict the development of self. They lay the groundwork for 'indoctrination' at school and in society in general.

A similar approach was adopted by Bowles and Gintis (1976) in their study of schooling in the USA. They argue that the **hidden curriculum** socializes children to be subservient and obedient, to be motivated by external rewards (such as exam results and pay packets) and to see inequality in society as legitimate (see pp. 602–4 for a detailed description and discussion).

Evaluation of Marxist approaches

Marxist approaches such as those of Cooper and Bowles and Gintis are vulnerable to many of the same criticisms levelled at Parsons and functionalist approaches. They may exaggerate the success of socialization, suffer from an 'oversocialized' view of people, and underestimate conflict in the process of socialization. This last point is developed by neo-Marxists who emphasize that socialization is not necessarily effective and it can be riven with conflict.

Neo-Marxism and socialization

Paul Willis, Antonio Gramsci and Pierre Bourdieu

Paul Willis's study (1977) of working-class 'lads' in the British education system shows how a **counter-school culture** can develop in which the authority of teachers is constantly questioned. The 'lads' develop a culture in which they are far from being obedient and passive recipients of socialization. However, Willis argues, the 'lads' unintentionally prepare themselves for work through their resistance. They develop a culture which prepares them for the tedium of manual labour in a capitalist society. Ultimately the 'lads' are socialized effectively, but socialization involves the creative responses of a peer group rather than the passive acceptance of rules and norms imposed on them by adults (see pp. 605–7 for a full description and evaluation).

Neo-Marxism tends to suggest that socialization is not as effective as some Marxists assume. The neo-Marxist Antonio Gramsci (1971) (see pp. 539–40) argues that in capitalist societies people possess **dual consciousness**. In part, people are indoctrinated through socialization by institutions such as the state, the education system and religion into accepting capitalist society as legitimate. However, their day-to-day experience of oppression and exploitation – for example, in the workplace – contradicts the **false class consciousness** fostered by the bourgeoisie. Consequently people are unlikely to accept capitalist ideology fully. In part, they see through the capitalist system and realize that it does not always act in their interests.

Another influential neo-Marxist view of socialization is advanced by Pierre Bourdieu (1984). He sees socialization as involving the transmission of **cultural capital** – cultural resources that can be used to acquire other sorts of capital, such as money. Higher-class parents pass down to their children the cultural knowledge necessary for them to succeed in capitalist societies. Because of this process, class inequalities are passed down from generation to generation. Bourdieu emphasizes class differences in socialization and sees socialization as important in maintaining class inequality (see pp. 67–9).

Evaluation

Neo-Marxist theories are more credible than some Marxist theories because they acknowledge that socialization is not as straightforward and free of conflict as some Marxists claim. However, like Marxist theory in general, they tend to assume that class is the basis of socialization and that other sources of inequality and difference are unimportant.

Postmodernists tend to reject the view that class differences are as rigid as they used to be. They argue that people are not restricted by their background and are free to construct their own identities (see pp. 697–9). Postmodernists therefore emphasize individual choice much more than neo-Marxists.

Feminists also believe that neo-Marxists exaggerate the importance of class. However, some feminists do not disagree with Marxists that socialization can be ideological in that it indoctrinates individuals into the acceptance of inequality. However, from their point of view, it largely serves to indoctrinate people with **patriarchal ideology** and the acceptance of gender inequality, rather than indoctrinating people with capitalist, ruling-class ideology (see Chapter 2 for a discussion of patriarchal ideology).

Symbolic interactionism and socialization

Of all the major sociological perspectives, symbolic interactionism has probably developed the most detailed theory of socialization. Drawing heavily on the work of George Herbert Mead (the founder of symbolic interactionism – see Chapter 15, pp. 881–2), Gerald Handel outlines the process of socialization from a symbolic interactionist point of view.

Gerald Handel – the process of socialization

Biology and social interaction

Handel (2006, first published 1978) observes that, at birth, the newborn infant is not able to take part in society by cooperating with others. There are two reasons for this: first, the infant is physically immature, and second, the infant is unsocialized. As the child gets older, he or she goes through **biological maturation** as he or she moves towards adulthood. The child's body grows and develops new capacities. At the same time the child undergoes a process of socialization which enables him or her to function as a member of society.

In order to survive, a newborn baby must receive care from one or more adults. This requires **social interaction** between the baby and carers. This provides the child with their first experiences of the social world. As the child develops, he or she achieves greater maturity through the interaction between physical maturation and socialization. For example, a child cannot learn to read or write until the neuromuscular system has developed sufficiently to make this possible. At the same time, socialization contributes to the mental and physical development of the child. Mental capacities are developed as a child learns societal culture, just as children develop muscles as they exercise.

Handel emphasizes that while biological factors interact with socialization, humans possess considerable **plasticity** – they can be moulded in many different ways through socialization. For example, in some societies children as young as 5 years old are expected to work, whereas in others children are not thought to be capable of working until considerably older.

Empathy, communications and the self

According to Handel, in the process of socialization children develop three key capacities:

1 They develop the capacity for **empathy**. Empathy requires a person to put themselves imaginatively in the position of another person and understand, to some extent, how they might feel. For example, empathy is needed by carers who look after babies – they have to interpret the baby's crying and decide how to help them.
2 Developing the ability to **communicate** is another crucial role of socialization. To take part in society, a child must learn to use symbols such as words which have the same meaning for different people. Socialization facilitates the acquisition of language, both vocabulary and grammar.
3 The third capacity that children must develop through socialization is a **sense of self**. Drawing on the work of the symbolic interactionist Charles Horton Cooley, Handel defines this sense of self as 'the ability to take oneself as an object, *to be conscious that one is an object distinct from other objects*' (p. 14). By distinguishing their self from others the child can begin to regulate their own conduct, evaluate their behaviour and, in time, imagine how their behaviour is viewed by others. Cooley argued that people come to possess a 'looking-glass self' – their sense of who they are becomes a reflection of how others see them.

The development of a self is crucial in socialization because it enables a child to start to align their behaviour with that of others. Instead of simply pursuing their own desires, children start to take account of the opinion of others and to act in ways they believe will reflect well in the looking-glass that others hold up to them.

Handel notes that George Herbert Mead developed these ideas further. Mead explains how children progressively develop a sense of self through play and games. As this occurs, the individual takes more account of reactions of others and therefore becomes socialized into societal culture (see pp. 881–2 for full details).

Socialization agents and peer groups

Unlike most functionalists and Marxists, however, symbolic interactionists such as Handel do not see socialization as a passive process in which children simply learn what they are taught and adults simply teach children to follow agreed norms and values. Nor does socialization involve learning a single, universally shared culture of a society. Handel develops these points by viewing socialization from two perspectives.

First, there is the perspective of the **socialization agents**, such as parents and teachers. They have responsibilities for preparing children for membership of society. Limits are placed on their actions by society. For example, parents can be prosecuted if they fail to care adequately for their children – for example, if they leave young children unattended or if they punish them too severely; and teachers have specific legal responsibilities.

The actions of socialization agents reflect their position in society, but socialization agents also have considerable latitude in how they choose to socialize children. Socialization agents from different backgrounds will tend to bring up children differently, meaning that all children are not raised with identical norms and values. Handel says:

No child is simply born into society but rather into particular locations in society – a social class, an ethnic group, a type of neighbourhood. The socialization agents in different social segments present different expectations to children, who will, accordingly, have different socialization experiences. Handel, 2006, first published 1978, p. 17

For example, Handel claims that studies show that in both the USA and Italy the working class socialize their children to be more obedient than the middle class, who expect their children to show more initiative.

Second, there is the perspective of the child who is being socialized. From the child's perspective, agents of socialization are only one influence; they are also strongly influenced by **peer groups** (groups of children of a similar age to themselves).

Children actively take part in social interaction with other children of a similar age and status, and in peer groups children actively socialize each other. The peer group is a very important **reference group** – a group whose opinion is important to the child and with which the child compares themselves. Handel comments that in the peer group, 'a child learns to function more independently, to acquire and test skills and beliefs that earn him a place among people of the same generation, to develop new outlooks that reflect youthful interests rather than adult ones' (p. 16).

In peer groups socialization operates differently compared to socialization by adults.

1 In peer groups the children take part in making the rules rather than simply following rules passed down to them.
2 Peer groups tend to seek more immediate gratification than agents of socialization, who are concerned with long-term adjustment to society.
3 Peer groups 'provide an alternative to adult standards' (p. 17) and may have values which are different from those of adults. This can lead to **socialization conflict**, when the demands of the peer group contradict rules that derive from parental authority. For example, the peer group might encourage a child to cross a road which parents have forbidden them to cross.

Peer groups are not just important to children. They are also important in the socialization of adults. Although Handel concentrates on the socialization of children, he acknowledges that it is a process that continues throughout life. For example, embarking on a new profession or changing religion involves significant new socialization.

Conflict

Unlike functionalists such as Parsons, Handel sees socialization as a process involving considerable conflict. He says, 'Not only do parents and peers often have different expectations, but there are also many other conflicts – between parents and teachers, parents and other interested commentators such as aunts and uncles, two parents themselves' (p. 18).

However, Handel does tentatively suggest that there may be a **societal demand** – by which he means that 'each society has some conception of the kind of adult it would like its children to become' (p. 18). Thus, despite the considerable variation in how children are socialized, and

the conflict between different agents of socialization, and between the agents and recipients of socialization, in most societies there may be at least some widely shared values and norms which most children internalize through socialization.

Evaluation

The interactionist approach outlined by Handel provides a more complex theory of socialization than that advanced by most functionalists and Marxists. It recognizes that socialization is an active process in which children and adults both play a part, that it can involve conflict, that it continues throughout life, and that it varies between social groups.

However, Handel provides only a very general outline of how socialization takes place, and his views are not backed up by empirical research. Furthermore, like other interactionists he concentrates on day-to-day interaction and makes only passing reference to the role of wider social structures in socialization. Thus, for example, he mentions class differences, but unlike Marxists he has no developed model of the class system or explanation of why classes vary in socialization practices.

Feminist perspectives on socialization

Gender and sex role socialization

There is a variety of feminist views on socialization, with different feminists attaching different degrees of importance to socialization in the development of gender inequalities. Liberal feminists generally place most stress on socialization, but writers from other feminist perspectives also highlight the way in which socialization can contribute to the creation of inequalities between men and women (see pp. 100–4 for a discussion of feminist perspectives).

Perhaps the best-known feminist view on socialization is provided by Ann Oakley. Oakley (1974) argues that there are distinct gender roles for men and women which derive from culture rather than from biology. Gender roles vary from society to society but in all societies they tend to maintain male dominance and female subservience. These roles are learnt through socialization during childhood and shape the behaviour of adults. As discussed elsewhere (see p. 98), Oakley claims that processes such as the manipulation of children's self-image by parents, and the canalization of boys and girls towards different objects and activities, contribute to the reproduction of differences in behaviour between males and females.

Some sociologists, such as Glenys Lobban (1974) and Lesley Best (1992), claim that sex-role socialization continues in school through the stereotypical portrayal of girls and boys in reading schemes (see p. 664). Other feminists have pointed to the influence of the media in perpetuating gender inequalities through stereotypical portrayals of males and females (see pp. 728–9). These types of view have exercised a strong influence in sociology and beyond, and have led to changes in the practices of parents, schools and the mass media, where stereotypes have been challenged.

Evaluation

These feminist approaches to gender and sex-role socialization mirror Marxist concerns about the ideological bias of class socialization. Like Marxists, feminists have tended to see socialization in a negative light, arguing that it is used by the powerful (in this case men) to maintain their power and privilege. Socialization is portrayed as a process supporting and maintaining patriarchy (or male dominance). However, this rather simplistic view of gender and socialization has increasingly been challenged.

1. Some sociologists point out that socialization does not always support patriarchal values and stereotypical gender roles. For example, Barbara Risman and Kristen Myers (2006, first published 1997) point out that some children are now socialized in feminist households where they are encouraged to be hostile to patriarchal or sexist culture. From a study of seventy-five such families, Risman and Myers found that children socialized in this way developed egalitarian views, believing that men and women should be equal. Although they still had some stereotypical views about gender differences (perhaps picked up from agencies of socialization outside the family) they had developed values at odds with those predicted by conventional feminist ideas on socialization.
2. It should not be assumed that males and females simply accept socialization passively. For example, studies of the media have shown that interpretations of the messages put forward by the media vary, and the audience sometimes reject stereotypical portrayals of males and females (see pp. 734–5).
3. Some feminists now see gender socialization as a complex and often contradictory process in which children play an active role, rather than being the passive recipients of a culture which is passed down to them.

We will now examine a study which moves a long way from conventional feminist views on socialization while still examining the process through which gender roles are acquired.

Barrie Thorne – gender in school

The study

In an influential study, Barrie Thorne (1993) examines the process through which gender roles develop in schools in the USA. She observed classrooms and playgrounds and other public spaces in two elementary schools with children aged between 5 and 11. Thorne sees herself as a feminist, and developed an interest in gender and childhood as a result of her own experience when she and her husband tried to bring up their children in a non-sexist way. They found that their efforts were only partially successful, and Thorne decided to explore the role of schools in the production of gender differences.

The complexity of gender socialization

Thorne argues that conventional feminist portrayals of socialization are inadequate for understanding the way

that gender develops. She says that 'the social construction of gender is an active and ongoing process' (p. 4). Children are not simply the passive recipients of socialization, but rather they interact with each other and adults as gender differences develop.

Furthermore, Thorne does not believe that there is a single set of gender roles which can be learnt by boys and girls. She argues that gender differences are complex and variable. Males and females do not behave in the same ways in different situations, and the nature of gender changes with time and context. She says, 'Gender is not something one passively "is" or "has"'; rather, we 'do gender' in our everyday activities.

Thorne talks of 'the sheer complexity of gender relations – the multiple and contradictory meanings, the crosscutting lines of difference and inequality, the fluctuating significance of gender' (p. 5). She follows R.W. Connell (1995) (see pp. 138–41) in arguing that there are many different ways of being feminine or masculine, rather than simply one, leading to greater variation in male and female behaviour than conventional theories of gender socialization assume.

Thorne's approach has a certain amount in common with interactionist perspectives on socialization, because she emphasizes that it is an active rather than passive process, which is fluid and variable and more complex than simply learning a culture. However, she goes beyond interactionism in setting her discussion in the context of wider power relations – in particular the power of men.

Thorne says little about feminist theory but she does say that it is possible to 'recognize the influence of postmodern and deconstructive ideas in the approach I develop' (p. 5). By emphasizing that groups of women can have different interests from one another, and stressing that there is no single fixed, patriarchal structure, Thorne follows the theory of postmodern and difference feminism (see pp. 115–18).

Gender relations and school organization

Thorne starts by examining the way in which school structures gender relations. She notes that rules relating to the mixing or separating of boys and girls vary from school to school. In one class she observed – Mrs Smith's Kindergarten class (5- to 6-year-olds) at 'Ashton School' – boys and girls were organized into mixed tables. However, in Mrs Bailey's class of 10- to 11-year-olds at 'Oceanside School', pupils were allowed to sit where they chose. In fact, boys chose one side of the classroom and girls the other. In this context, gender segregation was chosen by the children rather than imposed on them.

However, in both classrooms there were instances where teachers reinforced gender differences by, for example, organizing contests between boys and girls, referring to 'the boys' and 'the girls' in the classroom, or getting the children to separate into boys' and girls' lines when going for lunch. All these situations could lead to antagonism or rivalry between males and females, and reinforced a sense that the sexes were different. At other times, though, children would be organized into mixed-sex work groups where, by and large, boys and girls worked cooperatively and gender issues were not to the fore.

Friendship and play

Outside formal lessons, children had more choice about who they associated with, and to a large extent seating and activities became sex-segregated. In both schools, at lunchtime boys usually chose to sit with boys, and girls chose to sit with girls. Friendship groups were usually all-male or all-female and much of the time girls and boys played separate games in the playground.

Boys tended to monopolize most of the space in playgrounds, playing football, softball and basketball. Girls tended to stay in spaces closer to the school and were more likely to play with skipping ropes, hopscotch squares and bars on which they could swing. Most of the time children would choose these separate activities and would exclude members of the other sex who wanted to join in – for example, boys might tell a girl who wanted to play football that they already had enough players.

Reasons for gender segregation

Thorne argues that there is no one key reason why gender segregation comes about. She accepts that boys and girls develop an awareness of being different from one another through socialization, but believes that this is not in itself sufficient to explain the segregation. There are many contexts in which boys and girls do mix without obvious conflict, hostility or embarrassment, but in some circumstances the segregation is quite marked.

Thorne goes on to try to explain how this gender separation comes about.

1. She argues that the segregation is much more pronounced in school playgrounds than in the community. This is because gender segregation is more likely in a crowded setting. In neighbourhoods there are fewer children to play with and it is therefore more likely that a child will choose somebody of the other sex as a playmate. Furthermore, there is less likelihood of teasing, either for 'liking' (or fancying) a member of the other sex, or for gender-inappropriate behaviour. In playgrounds boys are often accused of being 'sissies' if they play with girls. Their masculinity and sexuality can be questioned if they are seen as being at all effeminate.
2. Public choosing accentuates gender divisions because choosing is often based on gender as one criterion. In games where teams are chosen, such as football, boys will invariably choose all the boys before choosing girls for their team. However, in handball, teams are not chosen. A person joins a line and waits for their turn. Consequently handball tends to be less gender-segregated.
3. A lack of adult presence tends to increase the separation of the sexes. Adults sometimes intervene to allow mixed-sex games or play on the grounds of fairness, and 'Adult presence legitimates the possibility of entering a turf controlled by the other gender' (p. 56).
4. The segregation is sometimes reinforced by what Thorne calls **borderwork**. This involves marking the boundaries between male and female social groups. One type of borderwork is cross-gender chasing,

with girls chasing boys or vice versa. By definition, boys and girls are in separate teams during cross-gender chasing, but it can also involve a 'ritualized form of provocation' (p. 71). Girls sometimes play 'chase-and-kiss', with the boys trying to avoid the embarrassment of being kissed by a girl. The girls may wear lipstick to smear the boys for extra effect. The boys, on the other hand, may complain that being kissed by the girls gives you 'cooties' – a type of invisible germ. Terms such as 'cootie queens' or 'cootie girls' are sometimes applied to the lowest-status girls, who are the 'female pariahs, the ultimate school untouchables' (p. 74).

Another type of borderwork is the invasion, where one gender group (usually boys) cross into the territory of the other gender group and disrupt their activities. In the playground, boys would sometimes deliberately intervene in and disrupt the girls' rope-jumping games. Such borderwork highlights and dramatizes the differences in human nature attributed to boys and girls. It emphasizes that male and female should be seen as opposites, and it exaggerates gender differences, hiding the extent to which male and female behaviour overlap.

The types of processes discussed above do not just reinforce gender differences, they often also reinforce male power. Boys tend to use physical strength to dominate or disrupt the activities of girls, though girls will sometimes chase off boys intent on causing disruption. In the playground, the children themselves act in various ways to reinforce gender differences, but adults play a part too. In one school the adults sometimes told boys to go away from the areas where girls were playing, because they assumed that the boys were out to cause trouble. However, this prevented any mixing of the sexes.

Overlap between genders

Despite finding many ways in which interaction in schools reinforces or creates gender differences, Thorne is at pains to emphasize that gender differences and stereotypes can be challenged in school, and that these processes do not lead to a dualistic division of children into a feminine and a masculine culture.

Boys and girls do not have wholly distinct cultures – there is much overlap, and some crossing of the gender divide. Even in the playground, there are some boys who join in with 'girls' games' such as jump-rope, and some girls who join in with 'boys' games' such as football. Some games, such as handball, are mixed-gender activities.

Boys who play with girls risk being teased as sissies, but popular boys can get away with playing with girls with less risk of name-calling. It is probably easier for girls to engage in 'tomboy' behaviour than for boys to get involved in what are traditionally girls' activities, especially for stronger and more athletic girls. Furthermore, as noted earlier, in the classroom and in neighbourhoods there are many activities where gender differences are not to the fore and have relatively little significance.

Overall, life in schools does reinforce gender division, but this cannot be seen as a simple process of socialization. Thorne expresses approval for approaches which,

> *Rather than casting children as 'objects of socialization' … grants them agency, tracing various responses to and interpretations of gender prescriptions. By positing a complex and plural approach to gender, these ethnographies also challenge simplistic dualism like girls' culture versus boys' culture.* Thorne, 1993, p. 107

Evaluation

Thorne's study shows how gender roles develop through the interaction between children, and between adults and children, with children playing an active part in their own development. Thorne says, 'I have argued that kids as well as adults take an active hand in constructing gender, and that collective practices – forming lines, choosing seats, teasing, gossiping, seeking access to or avoiding particular activities – animate the process' (p. 157).

However, Thorne's study also suggests that this process still to some extent reproduces existing social roles (such as those of man and woman) and inequalities between social groups. She goes on: 'I have been able to give full attention to children as social actors living in the abundant present, although influenced by larger social forces' (p. 157).

Thorne's study can be seen as developing a more nuanced or sophisticated theory of socialization than that advanced by many sociologists, or even as suggesting that the concept of 'socialization' is inadequate for understanding the way that people develop as social actors. Thorne herself claims that her study moves beyond being 'limited by notions of "socialization" and "development"' (p. 157).

Identity

Introduction – the nature of social identity

Richard Jenkins (1996) argues that **social identity** is 'our understanding of who we are and of who other people are, and, reciprocally, other people's understanding of themselves and of others'. Identity is something that is negotiable and which is created in the process of human interaction. It involves making comparisons between people and therefore establishing similarities and differences between them. Those who are believed by themselves and others to be similar share an identity, which is distinguishable from the identity of people who are believed to be different and who do not, therefore, share the same identity.

To Jenkins, 'social identity is about meanings', and these meanings are socially constructed rather than about essential differences between people. For example, Jenkins discusses the transition to being an old-age pensioner or senior citizen. The change in identity and the social role that accompanies it are based upon an arbitrary distinction between those who are 64 and those who are 65, but it has a tremendous impact on a person's identity. Jenkins says:

Imagine, for example, the morning of your sixty-fifth birthday. With it, as well as birthday cards, will come retirement, a pension, a concessionary public transport pass, special rates every Tuesday at the hairdresser … Although it will be the same face you will see in the bathroom mirror, you will no longer be quite the person that you were yesterday. Nor can you ever be again.
Jenkins, 1996

According to Jenkins, identity is an integral part of social life. It is only by distinguishing the identities of different groups that people are able to relate to other people. An awareness of different identities provides some indication of what sort of person you might be dealing with, and therefore how you can relate to them.

The understanding people have of different identities might be limited, or wrong altogether, but it is a vital part of social life and it makes interaction possible. Jenkins comments:

More often than not, men and women going about their everyday lives are concerned with specific social identities. We talk, for example, about whether people are born gay or become gay as a result of the way they have been brought up. About what it means to be 'grown up'. About what the difference is between Canadians and Americans. We observe the family who have just moved in around the corner and shake our heads: what can you expect, they come from the wrong part of town. We watch the television news and jump to all sorts of conclusions about current events on the basis of identifications such as 'Muslim', 'fundamentalist Christian', or whatever.
Jenkins, 1996

Jenkins concludes: 'Without social identity, there is, in fact, no society.'

Kath Woodward – the formation of identities

Kath Woodward (2000) discusses three central questions about the formation of identities:

1. To what extent can we shape our own identities?
2. How are identities formed?
3. Are there particular uncertainties about identity at this moment in the UK?

Her answers to these questions will be considered in turn.

Agency, structure and interpellation

Woodward argues that identity is to do with the way an individual answers the question 'Who am I?' However, this is not purely a psychological question, it is also a social question because it concerns the groups with which we identify. This involves an element of choice, a degree of individual agency where the person decides they identify with the group. For example, a person might decide to identify with a football team, say Sheffield Wednesday, by attending their matches and wearing clothes signifying that they are a supporter.

To Woodward, identity is 'marked by similarity': you identify with others because of the similarities between you, and the differences between the group you identify with and other groups. For example, Sheffield Wednesday supporters distinguish themselves from supporters of Sheffield United, as well as from teams from other parts of Britain.

Identity also 'combines how I see myself and how others see me'. It is partly internal and subjective, but also partly external and dependent on the judgement of others. While you may choose to support a football team, it is more difficult to make a personal decision about, or to change, your gender identity. You may regard yourself as a man, but if everybody else sees you as a woman, you may be unable to establish the identity you want. Similarly, you may wish to regard yourself as British, but you may not be entitled to British citizenship, and this prevents you from establishing a British identity, at least in official terms.

Thus, to Woodward, identity is always formed through a combination of individual agency and structural constraint. There are limits on the identities you can choose for yourself. Among the important structures which place constraints on individual choices are structures of gender, nationality and class.

How is the individual linked to these structures? In answering this question, Woodward draws on the work of the French Marxist Louis Althusser (1971). Althusser argued: 'when people are recruited into identity positions they are **interpellated** or hailed' (Woodward, 2000). It is as if we are walking down the street and somebody calls out our name – we stop and realize that we are being hailed. Particular symbols and images are used to call out to certain people so that they recognize themselves in them and identify with the group being portrayed. For example, women in 1950s Britain were interpellated by adverts of women happily engaged in domestic activities. This was part of an attempt to encourage women to identify with the identity of housewife and persuade them to return to this role after the ending of the Second World War.

Through interpellation,

we come to feel that an identity is the one that fits us – as a New Labour voter, as a lad, as a mother, as a 'new man', as a European. The process is one of recognition, of looking at yourself and thinking 'that's me'. Woodward, 2000

Developing identities

How is it that people come to recognize themselves in certain images and not others? In explaining how people develop identities in the first place, Woodward draws on a range of different theories from social science.

First, Woodward draws on the work of the interactionist sociologist George Herbert Mead (see pp. 881–2 and 688–90). Mead argued that a crucial part of human development involves being able to imagine how others might see us. For example, if attending a job interview, we are careful to select clothes which will encourage the interviewer to see us as we wish to be seen. Clothes are an example of symbols which signify particular things to others. A suit worn at an interview might be used to signify that the wearer is a serious candidate for a job. Through imagining the way others see us, our personal or subjective sense of identity is linked to the external identity that others have of us.

Woodward comments: 'The ability to visualize and to represent ourselves gives some degree of agency, although

the repertoire of images on which we can draw is always limited by the particular culture which we inhabit.' The meanings of different sorts of clothing, the sorts of identity they project, for example, cannot simply be chosen by us, but are also influenced by our culture.

Second, Woodward draws on the work of the sociologist Erving Goffman. Goffman saw the social world as being rather like a drama, or a performance in a play. His work is therefore sometimes described as a **dramaturgical** approach. Individuals put on a performance for others to convince them about who they are. Like an actor, they have to believe in the role in order to be convincing. In the process, they may become the person they are trying to project an image of. Goffman describes this process as *The Presentation of Self in Everyday Life* (1959) – through presenting him- or herself in particular roles the individual develops identities. Goffman admits that the roles available for us to adopt are not unlimited and that individuals are therefore constrained by the range of social roles available in a particular society at a particular time.

Third, Woodward uses the ideas of the Austrian founder of psychoanalysis, Sigmund Freud. Freud argued that people possess an unconscious mind which contains repressed feeling and desires which they are not aware of. Many of these are concerned with pleasure-seeking and sexuality. To develop into a psychologically well-balanced adult, the child needs to learn to control these desires, and to identify with the same-sex parent. For Freud, childhood experiences were vital for the development of identities in adulthood.

Woodward believes that Freud's work is important in understanding how identities develop. She says: 'we bring childhood experiences, even those about which we are not conscious, to the decisions we make as adults'. She argues: 'identity positions which we take up may be the result of unconscious feelings'. Like Freud, she stresses that 'Both gender and sexuality are important to our understanding of identity. Our sense of who we are is most significantly linked to our awareness of our identities as women and men.'

Uncertainty and identity in the UK

Woodward sees the above processes, which lead to the development of identity, as universal, but she believes that the actual content of identities can change. In particular, she believes there is some evidence of increased uncertainty over identities in the UK. She suggests a number of reasons why this is so.

1. Changes in the social structure have reduced certainties about social class. Heavy manufacturing industry, the basis of the traditional working class, has declined and service sector employment has grown. Thus, in mining communities, traditional masculine identities, based upon being the family breadwinner with a job for life, have disappeared with the closure of pits. Structural economic change has left men struggling to find a new identity in the face of high unemployment and labour market change which gives them no obvious alternatives to their previous identity.
2. Another structural economic change – the increased employment of married women in paid work – has undermined previous certainties about gender identities when the housewife role was dominant. Class and gender identities are interlinked and both have altered in ways which have required the construction of new identities.
3. Family roles are an important source of identity, and family life has also undergone radical changes. Some of the major changes include a decline in the rate of marriage and increases in divorce and single parenthood. Furthermore, even apparently unchanging and biological aspects of identity have been undermined. In 1998 Liz Buttle, a 60-year-old grandmother, was able to give birth with the help of IVF treatment. This undermined the link between age and fertility. As Woodward comments: 'New technologies appear to challenge certainty and the constraints of biology, opening up questions about "who we are" in situations where we might have thought there were no questions.'
4. New social movements have developed, such as the women's movement, movements for gay and lesbian rights, the peace movement, environmental movements, movements for the rights of the disabled, and black civil rights. All of these have encouraged positive identification with new groups or with groups whose identities previously had predominantly negative connotations. In terms of political identities, such movements offer people more choice than political parties, which have tended to be identified with particular classes.
5. Certainty about national identity has also been reduced. Britain is increasingly multicultural and there is increasing emphasis upon Irish, Scottish, Welsh, English and regional identities within Britain.
6. Woodward also recognizes that the growth of consumer culture increases people's choices about identity. What people buy is becoming an increasingly important source of identity, with people distinguishing themselves from others through their preferences for particular products. This is reflected in an increasing emphasis on consumption relating to the body as a source of identity. People can express identity not just through the way they clothe their body, the jewellery they wear (if any) and their hairstyles, but also through cosmetic surgery, working out at the gym, or getting tattoos. Woodard says: 'In contemporary society the body has become a project. People attempt to alter or improve the appearance, size and shape of their bodies in line with … their own designs.'

Conclusion

Despite believing that there is increasing choice and fluidity in the construction of identity, Woodward also recognizes that structural constraints continue to prevent some people from adopting the identities they would like to have. She says:

> *Economic circumstances, changes in employment, poverty, racism and lack of recognition of our ethnic or national identities all deny us access to identities which we might want to take up … Our own bodies put limits on what it is possible to achieve.* Woodward, 2000

Nevertheless, even the relatively disadvantaged and powerless can shape their identities to some extent through taking collective action. Woodward concludes:

> *People reconstruct their own identities, even within the constraints of poverty. Through the collective action of social movements, of class-based action, and through asserting ethnic identities and separate national identities within a multicultural UK, people reshape the social structures that restrict them.* Woodward, 2000

Woodward's work addresses many of the central issues in the sociology of identity. It tries to maintain a balance between arguing that there are increased choices in the construction of identity, and recognizing that there are continuing restrictions or constraints which limit people's choices. As we shall see in the following sections, the issue of freedom versus constraint has been a central controversy in this area of sociology. It is taken up in the work of the next writer to be considered, Stuart Hall, who adopts a sophisticated historical approach to understanding changes in the nature of identity.

Stuart Hall – three concepts of identity

In 'The question of cultural identity' (1992), Stuart Hall argues that ideas on identity have passed through three main stages in which particular conceptions of identity were dominant in thinking about society. These are:

1 The Enlightenment subject
2 The sociological subject
3 The postmodern subject

Premodern identities

Hall (1992) argues that the early stages of modernity 'gave rise to a new and decisive form of individualism, at the centre of which stood a new conception of the individual subject and its identity'.

In premodern societies identities were largely based around traditional structures, particularly related to religion. A person's position in society and their identity came from the position they were born into, which was seen as reflecting the will of God. People were not regarded as being unique individuals with their own identity, but simply part of the 'great chain of being'. This concept saw every living thing as having a place in the scheme of things. There was a hierarchy stretching from God at the pinnacle, through kings and less significant human beings, to animals, plants and inanimate objects at the bottom. A person's identity came from their place in the scheme of things, rather than from any individual or personal attributes.

The Enlightenment subject

However, with the advent of modernity, this changed. Between the sixteenth and eighteenth centuries a new conception of identity became dominant. This new conception of identity had two key features:

1 The individual subject was seen as 'indivisible'. Each person had an identity in their own right, and this identity was unified and could not be broken down into smaller, constituent parts.
2 The identity of each individual was unique.

The individual was not part of something bigger – the great chain of being – but was seen as having a distinct identity of their own.

According to Hall, this conception of identity stemmed from the ideas of the French philosopher, Descartes (1596–1650). Descartes believed there was a basic distinction between the mind and matter. He had a **dualistic conception** of humans: they were divided into two separate parts, the mind and the body. Each individual's mind was separate from every other individual's mind; consequently, each individual was unique. The distinctiveness of the individual mind was expressed in Descartes' famous saying, 'Cogito ergo sum' – 'I think, therefore I am.'

The individual, in this conception of identity, was a unified, whole person with the ability to think for themselves. The individual saw themselves as distinct and separate from other people, complete in their own right. The individual was rational, able to work out things for themselves on the basic of logic, and not limited by their position in society or traditional beliefs. Hall says:

> *The Enlightenment subject was based on a conception of the human person as a fully centred, unified individual, endowed with the capacities of reason, consciousness and action, whose 'centre' consisted of an inner core which first emerged when the subject was born, and unfolded with it, while remaining essentially the same – continuous or 'identical' with itself – throughout the individual's existence. The essential centre of the self was a person's identity.*
> Hall, 1992

The sociological subject

By the nineteenth century a more sociological conception of the subject and individual identity began to develop. Hall sees this as resulting from changes in society.

As industrialization and urbanization began to take hold, society became more complicated. It became increasingly based upon organizations and structures which shaped the lives of individuals. By the early twentieth century, for example, companies run by individual entrepreneurs were giving way to corporations owned by shareholders and run by complex administrations. Furthermore, 'The individual citizen became enmeshed in the bureaucratic and administrative machineries of the modern state.'

Each individual was no longer seen as being unique and separate from other individuals. Rather, the relationship between the individual and society was mediated through 'group processes and … collective norms'. For example, an individual's identity was seen as being tied up with their membership of a particular social class, a specific occupational grouping, their origins in a particular region, their nationality, and so on.

Symbolic interactionism and identity

Hall sees the theory of **symbolic interactionism** as a good example of this conception of individual identity. From the viewpoint of symbolic interactionism, individual

identity is only formed in interaction with others. A person's view of themselves, or **self-concept**, is partly a product of how others see that person.

The symbolic interactionist George Herbert Mead called the self-concept the 'I' (see pp. 881–2). Another interactionist, Charles Horton Cooley (discussed in Hall, 1992), saw humans as having a 'looking-glass self'; their sense of who they were reflected the reactions of other people to them.

From the interactionist viewpoint, people still possessed their own individuality, but it was not an individuality wholly distinct from society. Identity acts as a bridge between the social and the purely individual. By possessing a particular identity, individuals internalize certain norms and values that accompany that identity. It allows their behaviour to be predictable to others and in turn makes behaviour in society more patterned and regular.

This sort of view can be illustrated with the example of social class. A particular class identity would encourage people to behave in particular ways. Traditional working-class and middle-class identities differed, and they were associated with different subcultures (see pp. 56–7). The existence of these subcultures gave substance to and reinforced the class structure of society. Hall comments: 'Identity thus stitches (or, to use a current medical metaphor, "sutures") the subject into the structure. It stabilizes both subjects and the cultural worlds they inhabit, making both reciprocally more unified and predictable.'

This general approach to identity was not confined to interactionists. For example, functionalists such as Parsons saw identity in terms of the existence of social roles which fitted individual personalities into the social system (see pp. 859–61).

Change in late modernity – the postmodern subject

According to Hall, the symbolic interactionist theory of identity and the idea of the sociological subject might have been appropriate analyses in modernity, but they have become increasingly inappropriate in late modernity or the postmodern era (Hall is somewhat unclear as to whether the contemporary era is late-modern or postmodern).

According to Hall, contemporary societies are increasingly characterized by the existence of **fragmented identities**. People no longer possess a single, unified conception of who they are, but instead possess 'several, sometimes contradictory or unresolved, identities'. This fragmentation of identity has a number of sources.

Modernity and change

Modern societies have always been characterized by rapid change. In late-modern societies the pace of change increases, which makes it difficult for people to retain a single, unified sense of who they are.

New social movements

In the past, social class provided something of a 'master identity', which overarched other identities and formed the basis for political conflict. However, in the 1960s and 1970s people began to organize around issues other than class. New social movements developed (see pp. 566–73), concerned with a variety of issues and identities. Hall lists 'feminism, black struggles, national liberation, anti-nuclear and ecological movements' as examples. Instead of people feeling part of a single class, their identity became fragmented in terms of their gender, ethnicity, religion, age, nationality, views on ecology, and so on.

Identity politics

With the rise of new social movements, identity itself became a political issue. **Identity politics**, as it became known, is concerned with the differences between groups of people, and with allowing individuals to express those differences. It emphasizes the importance of hearing different voices, particularly those of oppressed groups such as gays and lesbians, black women, the disabled, and so on.

Feminism

Feminism had a particularly important role. It paved the way in opening up what were previously thought of as private issues (such as housework and domestic violence) to public debate. Feminism therefore 'exposed, as a political and social question, the issue of how we are formed and produced as gendered subjects. That is to say, it politicized subjectivity, identity and the process of identification (as men/women, mothers/fathers, sons/daughters).'

In its early phases feminism replaced the idea of all humans having the same identity, 'mankind', with the idea that men and women were different. It encouraged women to unite as 'sisters' and tried to substitute gender as the 'master identity' instead of class. However, more recently, **difference feminism** has emphasized the differences between women (for example, women from different ethnic origins). This has led to a further fragmentation of identity (see p. 471 for a discussion of difference feminism).

Disciplinary power and surveillance

Another important factor in fragmenting identities is highlighted in the work of Foucault (see pp. 558–62). According to Foucault, societies were becoming increasingly characterized by 'disciplinary power' and 'surveillance'. The behaviour of individuals was increasingly watched, monitored and, where necessary, punished. Such techniques originated in prisons and hospitals, but have since spread to encompass many aspects of society. Since people are monitored and treated as individuals rather than as members of social groups, they become increasingly isolated. This makes it more difficult for them to form coherent identities based upon social interaction.

Globalization

A final, very important, factor in creating fragmented identities is the process of globalization. Hall suggests a number of ways in which globalization might affect identity.

The ease and frequency with which people move around the world, and improvements in communications and the 'global marketing of styles, places and images', can lead to a 'cultural supermarket effect'. People are no longer confined to developing identities based upon the place in which they live, but can choose from a very wide range of different identities. They can adopt the clothes, ways of speaking, values and lifestyles of any group they choose.

On the other hand, global consumerism can also lead to increasing homogeneity, or similarity, between people. Products are marketed worldwide, and the most successful (for example, Coca-Cola) can be found more or less anywhere.

There are therefore contradictory trends within globalization, but both can undermine previously existing identities. The homogenization of the global consumer undermines identities rooted in membership of particular social groups. The ability to make greater choices about identity means that people living in close proximity and even belonging to the same social groups can have quite different identities. Globalization thus opens up a number of possibilities.

Globalization and different sources of identity

Hall then goes on to review the actual effects of globalization on identity. He argues that in modern societies nationality was an important source of identity. Most nation-states emphasized the importance of the nation and tried to use national identity to create solidarity among citizens of different classes, ethnic origins and so on. With globalization, this has not proved so easy or effective. There have been three main responses to globalization in relation to nationality:

1. In some places people have tried to reaffirm national identity as a defensive mechanism. They have perceived a threat to their national identity, from, for example, immigration. Thus, in Britain, such a reaction has created 'a revamped Englishness, an aggressive little Englandism, and a retreat to ethnic absolutism in an attempt to shore up the nation'.
2. The first reaction to globalization is found among majority ethnic groups, but minority ethnic groups sometimes react in defensive ways as well. In response to racism and exclusion, minority ethnic groups have sometimes placed a renewed emphasis upon their ethnic identities and culture. In Britain this has involved 're-identification with cultures of origin (in the Caribbean, India, Bangladesh, Pakistan); the construction of strong counter-ethnicities – as in the symbolic identification of second generation youth, through the symbols and motifs of Rastafarianism, with their African origin'.
3. A third reaction to globalization is the construction of **new identities**. A British example is the construction of a 'black' identity, embracing British African Caribbeans and Asians. The black British identity represents an alternative to the re-identification with cultural origins, as a response to racism and exclusion. In this case identity becomes **hybrid**, mixing more than one existing identity into a new identity (see pp. 193–4).

The first two responses to globalization have had the effect of reviving ethnicity as a source of identity, often in opposition to existing nationalism. In several parts of the world ethnic groups have demanded their own nation-states, as bigger nation-states (such as the USSR and Yugoslavia) broke up. (This led to considerable violence and even civil war in places such as Bosnia and Kosovo.)

Hall sees this strident nationalism, based upon real or imagined ethnic differences, as a worrying trend. He argues that the idea of **ethnic purity** is largely a myth. Nearly all populations come from a variety of ethnic backgrounds. This has become increasingly true in the twentieth century, with the large-scale migration of great numbers of people. Most cultures are hybrid ones and attempts to create 'pure' ethnic identities are very dangerous in such circumstances. (See pp. 195–6 for more discussion of Hall's ideas on ethnicity and nationality, and pp. 188–97 for a general discussion of ethnicity, nationality and identity.)

Conclusion

Hall concludes that, in line with postmodern theory, identity has become **decentred**. Individuals can no longer find a core or centre to their identity, based on class or existing nation-states. Globalization in particular has had 'a pluralizing impact on identities, producing a variety of possibilities and new positions of identification, and making identities more positional, more political, more plural and diverse; less fixed, unified or trans-historical'. It is this uncertainty and diversity which has led some groups to try to create a more stable or unified identity through a renewed emphasis upon their ethnicity.

Zygmunt Bauman – 'From pilgrim to tourist – or a short history of identity'

Zygmunt Bauman (1996) goes much further than Hall in advocating a postmodern view of identity. According to Bauman, identity has not just become fragmented, it has ceased to have any stable base whatsoever. Identity has become simply a matter of choices, and not even choices that are necessarily consistent or regular. Individuals can change their identity as and when they choose.

Modern identity as pilgrimage

According to Bauman, under modernity, identity could be seen as similar to a pilgrimage. In a pilgrimage a person maps out their future life. They have a goal – to reach the place of pilgrimage. All of their actions are geared towards achieving that goal. They must not be distracted along the way by enjoying hospitality or engaging in leisure activities. They need a singleness of purpose. They must treat the world around them as if it were a desert, free from distractions. Furthermore, in the desert sand they can see their footprints stretching back into the distance, reassuring them about how far they have come.

To Bauman, the formation of identity in modern societies was very much like a pilgrimage. People's life strategies were based upon having a clear sense of who they wanted to become. Their lives were geared towards achieving their desired identity. This identity was usually related to their occupation. They worked in this job and tried to have a successful career. They mapped out their future, looking ahead to achieving their career goals, and looking backwards to see how far they had come since embarking on their career.

Postmodernity – 'the world inhospitable to pilgrims'

Pilgrims require a degree of certainty in the world. They have to know that the place of pilgrimage will be there when they arrive, otherwise the pilgrimage will be pointless. Postmodernity undermines pilgrimage as a life strategy by creating uncertainty.

In postmodern societies change is so rapid that there can be no certainty that particular positions, or even particular professions, will still exist in ten, twenty or thirty years' time. Bauman says:

> *Not only have jobs-for-life disappeared, but trades and professions which have acquired the confusing habit of appearing from nowhere and vanishing without notice can hardly be lived as Weberian 'vocations' – and to rub salt into the wound, the demand for the skills needed to practise such professions seldom lasts as long as the time needed to acquire them.* Bauman, 1996

In this situation there is no point in embarking on a pilgrimage. The destination – the job that a successful career will lead to – will have disappeared long before getting there. Because jobs change so rapidly, a person's career achievements so far may well be irrelevant to future jobs and will quickly be forgotten. Similarly, for the pilgrim in a desert, a storm may well come along and blow the sand around to cover up the tracks. The pilgrim can no longer see how far they have progressed.

Postmodern life strategies

In this situation new life strategies are required. These strategies abandon the idea of creating any single, central or permanent identity. Instead, people change their identity at will, putting little commitment into achieving an identity which may at any time become obsolete. Bauman identifies four postmodern life strategies:

1. The **stroller** (or *flaneur*) is somebody who strolls around cities observing and being entertained by the spectacle of city life. He or she has no particular objective in mind but strolls simply as a leisure pursuit. The stroller is a postmodern 'playful consumer' who has replaced the 'heroic producer' (or worker) of modernity.

   Shopping malls have been created as the haunt of the postmodern stroller. Shopping malls are there so that you can 'stroll while you shop and … shop while you stroll'. You can sample an endless range of products and consume whatever you wish, construct whatever identity you choose, and change it the following day if you want. With developments such as multi-channel television and the internet the stroller does not even have to leave the comfort of their armchair to enjoy their pastime.
2. The second life strategy is that of the **vagabond**. In past times, the vagabond wandered from place to place refusing to be tied down to any one location. The authorities disliked the vagabonds because they were unpredictable. They had no particular goals in their wandering, so you could never predict where they would turn up. This was quite different from the utterly predictable movements of the pilgrim.

   The vagabond is always a stranger wherever they wander, and has no settled place in the world. In a postmodern world it makes sense to wander from identity to identity without settling on any one. Indeed, postmodern society makes it more or less impossible to settle. Bauman says:

   > *Now there are few 'settled' places left. The 'forever settled' residents woke up to find the places (places in the land, places in society and places in life), to which they 'belong', no longer existing or no longer accommodating, neat streets turn mean, factories vanish together with jobs, skills no longer find buyers, knowledge turns into ignorance, professional experience becomes liability, secure networks of relations fall apart and foul the place with putrid waste.* Bauman, 1996

   It is little wonder that becoming a wandering vagabond, changing identity at will, becomes an attractive option.
3. The **tourist** represents the third strategy. Like the vagabond, the tourist moves from place to place. However, their movements are a little more purposeful. They know where they want to go. But they are not like the pilgrim. They do not travel to meet some ultimate goal. They simply go to places to gain new experiences, to see somewhere different or do something they have not done before.

   In postmodern societies people do not devote themselves to creating and cementing a particular identity. Like the tourist seeking new experiences, the equivalent postmodern life strategy involves trying out new identities and always looking for something new to sample.
4. The final strategy is that of the **player**. This involves treating life as a game. Games are played to win, but the result has no lasting consequences. Win or lose, you forget the last game and move on to another one. Similarly, in postmodern societies people can play the game of having particular identities for a time. (For example, they might be a left-wing radical student in their youth but change their politics in middle age.)

   While a person will try to play each identity game well, that will not stop them from changing the game and playing at a new identity once they decide a particular game is over.

Conclusion

Bauman concludes:

> *All four intertwining and interpenetrating postmodern life strategies have in common that they tend to render human relations fragmentary … and discontinuous; they are all up in arms against 'strings-attached' and long-lasting consequences, and militate against the construction of lasting networks of mutual duties and obligations.* Bauman, 1996

There are no solid, lasting identities. The only duty of the postmodern citizen is to 'lead an enjoyable life' by changing identity at will.

Evaluation of Hall and Bauman

Despite the differences between them, Stuart Hall and Zygmunt Bauman both argue that there has been a general movement away from relatively stable identities, based upon social factors such as class, towards more fragmented identities. Bauman in particular stresses the extent to which people can choose identities, while Hall places more emphasis on the increasing importance of ethnicity in shaping identity. These views have been criticized on a number of grounds.

1 Some sociologists deny that class has lost its importance as a source of identity. For example, Marshall *et al.* (1988) argue that in Britain people still see themselves as members of classes and that class continues to influence people's beliefs as well as their life chances (see p. 63).

Similarly, in a discussion of class, politics and identity, Frank McDonough (1997) argues that 'pronouncing the death of class in British society does seem premature'. McDonough accepts that there have been some changes in, for example, working-class life, including a growth in consumerism. However:

> *This cultural revolution has not completely led to the working class no longer feeling working class. When account is taken of what the working class say about class, we find they still do not feel middle class. They still believe that class has a detrimental impact on their life. They still consider class to be an important part of British life.* McDonough, 1997

McDonough also believes that class divisions remain important in British politics.

2 Some feminists argue that gender remains the dominant source of identity. Although difference feminists stress the variety of identities that women have (see pp. 470–1), radical feminists continue to see gender as the principal source of identity, as well as the main source of exploitation in patriarchal societies (see p. 101 and pp. 109–10 for discussions of radical feminism). They therefore contradict Bauman's view that identities are freely chosen rather than related to social factors, and they suggest that gender is a more important source of identity than Hall's work seems to imply.

3 Richard Jenkins (1996) argues against Hall's view that **reflexivity** – reflecting upon your identity – is distinctively modern. According to Jenkins, long before modernity, people were self-conscious about their identity and would seek to change it. Jenkins says:

> *Saint Augustine's Confessions, written more than 1,500 years ago, is a testament to the possibilities for reforging the self, offered as an example for others. Going back nearly another thousand years, one can understand Buddhism as a project for the reformation of selfhood.* Jenkins, 1996

To Jenkins, there is nothing new about being self-conscious about your identity – it is a universal feature of being human.

4 Jenkins also believes that writers such as Bauman greatly exaggerate the degree to which identities are fragmented, short-lived and freely chosen in contemporary societies. He is as sceptical about the claim that there is a distinctive postmodern type of identity as he is about the claim that modernity ushered in a radical change in identity.

Jenkins accepts that there have been some changes in identity – for example, feminism has increased the importance of gender as a source of identity – but he denies that the changes are fundamental. He says:

> *Most commentators on postmodernism are on a historicist mission by any other name, substituting a metanarrative of fragmentation for the old story of progress. In the pursuit of such grand themes, the mundane is likely to be overlooked.* Jenkins, 1996

Jenkins is accusing postmodernists of doing exactly what they object to other theories doing: producing grand theories or metanarratives which are not soundly based.

Unlike postmodernists, Jenkins believes that identity remains rooted in social experience and membership of social groups, and it is not something that can just be changed at will. His ideas will now be examined.

Richard Jenkins – identity as a social product

Individual and collective identity

Richard Jenkins (1996) argues that identities contain elements of the 'individually unique' and the 'collectively shared'. While each individual has an identity which is personal to them, those identities are shaped through membership of social groups. The individual elements of identity emphasize difference, the collective elements similarities, but the two are closely related.

Using the ideas of symbolic interactionists such as George Herbert Mead (see pp. 881–2), Jenkins argues that identity is formed in the process of socialization. Through this process people learn to distinguish the socially significant similarities and differences between themselves and others.

In childhood, certain identities take on primary importance and remain relatively stable throughout people's lives. Jenkins says, 'selfhood, humanness, gender, and, under some circumstances, kinship and ethnicity, are primary identities, more robust and resilient to change in later life than other identities'.

Although all social identities can change, they are much less easy to change than postmodernists such as Bauman suggest. Furthermore, 'social identity is never unilateral' – people's identities are always formed in relationship to other people.

Drawing on the ideas of the interactionist Erving Goffman, Jenkins argues that in everyday life people are concerned to manage impressions of themselves – to give the impression of themselves they want others to see. Identities are formed as people try to get others to see them as they want to be seen. They may or may not be successful. If unsuccessful they may find it difficult to sustain the identity they prefer. (These ideas are based partly on labelling theory – see pp. 334–9.)

Identities are not just concerned with our own impressions of ourselves, but also with our impressions of

others, and others' impressions of us. Identity is both **internal** – what we think our own identity is – and **external** – how others see us. Identities are formed and stabilized in a dialectical relationship between these internal and external factors – they interact to produce an identity.

External factors – how others see us and react to us – may contradict and undermine, or support and strengthen, our view of ourselves. Either way, identity emerges out of this relationship between ourselves and others. Jenkins says:

> *Your external definition of me is an inexorable part of my internal definition of myself – even if only in the process of rejection or resistance – and vice versa. Both processes are among the routine everyday practices of actors. Nor is one more significant than the other.* Jenkins, 1996

Power and identity

To Jenkins, identity formation is not simply related to individual interactions. It is also related to larger social groups. Interaction leads to the construction of boundaries, or dividing lines, between different social groups which carry different identities. For example, the distinction between men and women, and between working class, middle class and underclass, has implications for people's identities.

The ability to claim identities for oneself and to attribute particular identities to others is essentially a question of power. Some groups have more power than other groups to claim identities for themselves and to attribute identities to others. For example, the poor and the unemployed, living in inner-city areas, may have little power to resist being seen as part of an 'underclass'.

Furthermore, identities are closely related to social positions, particularly in organizations. Organizations classify people by job title and rank and people are not free to choose their own position within organizations. A cleaner at the BBC cannot simply choose to become director general in order to change his or her identity.

The existence of identities associated with particular social groups and positions in organizations means that identity is never completely fluid and simply a matter of choice. Jenkins says: 'Social identities exist and are acquired and allocated within power relations. Identity is something over which struggles take place and with which stratagems are advanced.'

The Black Power movement in the USA, and feminist and gay liberation movements, are examples of groups organizing to change the widely held perceptions of particular social identities. They were not simply the struggles of individuals to gain a more positive social identity. They were (and are) the struggles of social groups which sought a more positive social identity for the group as a whole.

Evaluation

While Jenkins's views are different in some ways from those of Hall (for example, over whether reflexivity first developed with modernity), they are particularly antagonistic towards the claims of postmodernists such as Bauman.

Jenkins's work seems to be on strong ground in arguing that humans are not simply free to choose their own identity, that some identities (such as gender) are not easy to change, and that identities are social as well as individual. He puts forward a strong case in arguing that any change in the nature of identity associated with a supposed shift to postmodernity has been exaggerated.

However, some sociologists argue for a position between that of Bauman and that of Jenkins. The work of one such sociologist will now be considered.

Harriet Bradley – *Fractured Identities*

In a review of studies of identity and inequality, Harriet Bradley (1997) argues that neither modern nor postmodern conceptions of identity are adequate on their own. She says: 'A key objective is to pull together classical or modernist approaches to understanding inequalities with the newer perspectives inspired by postmodernism and poststructuralism.'

As a starting point, Bradley identifies a number of differences between these two approaches.

Modernist and postmodern approaches to identity

1 Modernist approaches emphasize the importance of structures (such as class structures or patriarchy) in explaining identity. Postmodern approaches emphasize choice.
2 Modernist approaches tend to suggest that society is **polarizing** (for example, between rich and poor). Postmodern approaches see societies, and the identities of its members, **fragmenting** into many different groups.
3 Modernist approaches tend to see class or gender as key sources of identity. Postmodern approaches often argue that class is disappearing. They deny that women are in any sense a unified group with a single identity. They argue that there are numerous different sources of identity. More stress is placed in postmodern thinking on 'race', ethnicity, nationality, culture and religion, as diverse, but interconnected, sources of identity.
4 Modernist approaches see societies as relatively predictable, with a degree of social order. Postmodern approaches emphasize 'chaos and confusion, the limitless welter of apparently unique events'.
5 Modernist approaches stress material sources of power, particularly control over resources such as money. Postmodern approaches emphasize the importance of the cultural and symbolic. From the postmodern point of view, power stems from the control over discourse – over how people talk and think about issues or social groups. Meanings are seen as central.

The problems of modernist and postmodern approaches

Bradley believes that neither modernist nor postmodern positions on any of these issues are entirely satisfactory. For

example, she says, 'Societies are chaotic, but also orderly; behaviour is infinitely variable, but also regular and predictable; social relations change, but are also stable and persistent.'

Similarly, she argues that **structured social inequalities** remain important; they have not disappeared. However, such inequalities no longer shape identities in as straightforward a way as they used to; there is more fluidity and choice involved in identity. But choice is not absolute: it is constrained by the existence of certain **dynamic** relationships. Bradley prefers the term 'dynamic' to the term 'structure', because she believes the idea of structure exaggerates the degree to which social relationships are solid and fixed. There are, for example, class dynamics which affect people's life chances and identities, but these do not stand still. Class dynamics are in a constant process of change.

Furthermore, power does not just come from meanings and discourse, important though these are. Bradley says: 'It would be nice if the social world were no more than a contestation of meanings, so that, merely by renaming the world, we could change it.' But this is not the case. A number of feminists have contributed to 'rewriting history from female points of view; yet it must be acknowledged to have had as yet rather little effect on the massive exploitation of women by entrepreneurs around the world'. She goes on: 'men are able to dominate women not only by dominating them in discourse, but also by controlling the distribution of social wealth' – for example, by giving them lower-paid jobs.

Nevertheless, exploitation cannot begin to be challenged until oppressed groups are able to attack the discourses that portray the oppression as inevitable or desirable. Women had to challenge the discourse of female inferiority before liberation of women became a possibility; black people had to challenge the discourse of slavery, and so on. Bradley argues: 'both materiality and meaning are aspects of constraining power relations', and it makes no sense to emphasize one to the exclusion of the other.

Four aspects of inequality

In her study, Bradley examines four aspects of inequality: class, gender, 'race' and ethnicity, and age. Although she sees these as the most important types of inequality and sources of identity, she accepts that there are other important social divisions: examples include sexuality and disability.

Although these inequalities and sources of identity can be analysed separately, in practice they interact with each other in a dynamic way. Bradley says:

> *It has become almost a commonplace to say that classes are gendered and that gender relations are class-specific. Similarly, the other dimensions of 'race'/ethnicity and age impinge on individual class and gender experience and in any particular concrete example it is hard to separate out the different elements.* Bradley, 1997

Bradley does not see any one source of inequality as being of primary importance. She sees all as significant. This contrasts with Marxists who see class as central, feminists who see gender as central, and some anti-racists who believe that 'race'/ethnicity is most important.

Inequalities and identities

How do these inequalities relate to identity? Bradley does not believe that there is a straightforward relationship between inequality and identity. The importance of inequalities for identity varies over time and with individual circumstances.

Bradley accepts that postmodernists have a point in arguing that there is a good deal of choice over identity and that identities are to some extent fragmented. However, Bradley still sees identities as rooted in membership of social groups. It will be difficult for a young African Caribbean woman to see herself as white, upper-class, elderly or male.

Furthermore, social factors tend to bring certain identities to prominence, while reducing the significance of others. Although precise predictions about the identities that people will adopt are impossible, it is possible to discern more general trends. Bradley says:

> *For example, it is suggested that changes in work and the break-up of old urban communities are currently acting to weaken class identities. Or again, for Afro-Caribbeans in Britain 'race' is arguably a more potent source of identity than class because it is so visible.* Bradley, 1997

Three levels of identity

Identities tend to be grounded in inequalities, social divisions and differences. However, the importance of particular inequalities, divisions and differences for identity varies from place to place, from time to time, and from individual to individual. Bradley therefore believes it is useful to conceive of identity as working at three different levels:

1. **Passive identities** are 'potential identities'. The potential exists for them to become important, in the way that individuals see themselves and others see them, but the identity is lying largely dormant. Bradley sees class identity in this way. Most British people accept that class inequalities exist, but most of the time they do not see themselves as members of a class. However, events or circumstances can raise consciousness of class and its importance as a source of identity.
2. **Active identities** 'are those which individuals are conscious of and which provide a base for their actions. They are positive elements for an individual's self identification although we do not necessarily think of ourselves continually in terms of any single identity.' For example, a woman who is experiencing sexual harassment from a man is likely to respond to the experience in terms of her gender identity, but at other times another identity might be to the fore.
3. **Politicized identities** exist where identity provides 'a more constant base for action and where individuals constantly think of themselves in terms of an identity'. Such identities are formed through political action, through campaigners highlighting the importance of the identity and using it as a basis for organizing collective action. For example, feminists succeeded in transforming gender into a politicized identity for many women in the 1970s and 1980s; and at times gay rights campaigners have achieved the same kind of politicized identity for many gays and lesbians.

Having outlined her general theory of identity, Bradley then goes on to examine the significance of class, gender, 'race'/ethnicity and age in producing identities in contemporary Britain.

Class and identity

As discussed above, Bradley does not see class as the strongest source of identity in contemporary Britain. She sees it as being mainly a source of passive identity. This is partly because class is less visible and obvious in the everyday world than age, 'race'/ethnicity and gender. However, Bradley does not agree with the argument of postmodernists that class is dying out or disappearing. Rather, there is evidence of class both polarizing and fragmenting.

Bradley quotes a number of studies which show that, far from being reduced, inequalities in countries such as Britain are increasing. Put simply, the rich are getting much richer, while the poor are becoming slightly worse off (see pp. 35–41 and 88–9 for summaries of studies that reach similar findings). This creates the potential for class to be an increasingly important source of identity.

However, Bradley also detects evidence that class is **fragmenting**. She argues that Weber's ideas on class status and party (see pp. 29–31) can be used as a basis for understanding a situation in which there is a plurality of classes which are cross-cut by different status groups (such as ethnic groups), and in which many political organizations and pressure groups are no longer based on class.

The class structure has fragmented, with the development of an 'underclass' (which Bradley sees as a marginal group outside the class structure), and a big increase in self-employment. Furthermore, 'classes are split by region, public or private sector membership, gender or ethnic origins, amongst other things'.

Bradley therefore concludes: 'Neither class, as a set of lived economic relationships, nor class analysis, as a set of social categories, is dead. But there must be recognition of how class relations are shaped by other forms of inequality.'

Gender and identity

In discussing theories of gender, Bradley notes a move away from theories which saw women as a single group, united by their common experience of oppression, towards theories which see women (and indeed men) as being fragmented into different groups. The former type of theory included radical, Marxist and liberal feminism (see pp. 100–3), while the latter type includes black, postmodern and difference feminism (see pp. 103–4, 115–19 and 470–1).

Bradley believes that both types of theory are important and both provide insight into the formation of identity. She notes that some commentators in the popular media believe that inequality between women and men is a thing of the past. Bradley denies that this is so, and believes that the common experience of disadvantage and sexism provides a basis for a common identity for women.

However, not all women experience disadvantage to the same extent or in the same ways. For example, black feminists have suggested that the family is experienced differently by white and black women. White feminists see the family as a source of patriarchal oppression. Black feminists experience the black family (which is quite likely to be headed by a woman) as a source of solidarity and as a bulwark against oppression.

To Bradley, gender – both as a general category, and in terms of differences between groups of women and groups of men – is a very important source of identity in contemporary Britain. Furthermore, gender is an active politicized identity for women as a result of the influence of feminism.

More recently, gender has started to become politicized for men. Men used to take the experience of being male for granted – it was seen as the norm, and being female was seen as a deviation from the norm. However, masculinity has begun to be politicized, with the development of men's movements, and demands for male rights (for example, rights over access to children after divorce), and in a 'backlash' against feminism (see p. 132).

That does not mean that all men and all women experience gender as their main source of identity in all circumstances. Like other sources of identity, it interacts with a variety of other sources. There is a plurality of ways to be a woman or to be a man – as well as class and 'race'/ethnicity, age and sexuality are also important. For example, Bradley argues:

> *For a post-pubescent exploring the pleasures (and problems) of her newly sexualized body in relation to young men, the experience of womanhood is quite different from that of an ageing post-menopausal woman, struggling to adjust to bodily changes in a culture that puts a high value on youth and fertility.* Bradley, 1997

Similarly, gay men and lesbians will have different experiences of masculinity or femininity, and have rather different identities from their heterosexual counterparts. Thus, while gender is a crucial source of identity, its interactions with other sources of identity are very important.

'Race'/ethnicity and identity

Like gender, 'race'/ethnicity has become a more important source of identity in contemporary societies than class, and it is more likely to produce active and politicized identities. Sometimes this is partly due to the visibility of skin colour differences between supposed 'races', but this is not always the case. For example, the violence and 'ethnic cleansing' in the former Yugoslavia occurred between different white ethnic groups.

To a considerable extent the importance of 'race'/ethnicity as a source of identity depends upon how it is used politically to mobilize groups and provide them with a sense of belonging and history. For example, the Black Power movement of the 1960s led to many British and American people from diverse non-white ethnic groups identifying with an oppressed, non-white minority. However, by the 1970s a stronger sense of African identity had developed among black British and American people. By the 1980s:

> *the move towards ethnic particularism might lead people to identify more narrowly, say with a specific Caribbean island or region in the Indian sub-continent. In the 1990s political thinking ... may encourage people to adopt 'hyphenated' identities: Mexican-American, British-Indian and so forth.* Bradley, 1997

This can lead to people having somewhat confused ethnic identities, particularly if they move from a former colony in which they were born to a Western society. Once again, though, political mobilization is important. For example, the identity of a British Muslim has assumed more importance than other identities (such as being Pakistani) among some people of Asian origin in Britain as a result of the revival of Islam as a world religion (see pp. 444–8 for a discussion of Islamic revival).

For dominant ethnic groups, such as white people in Britain or the USA, ethnic identity is a rather less politicized identity. It tends to be taken as the norm and only becomes an active part of identity in certain circumstances. In Britain, Scottish and Welsh ethnic identities are more active and politicized than an English identity, but an English identity can become important in some contexts (such as sporting events or foreign travel).

Age and identity

Bradley describes age as 'the neglected dimension of inequality'. As a source of identity, age is important for individuals. Young people have legal constraints on what they are allowed to do; older people face ageism; and there are, of course, physiological differences between age groups which affect identity.

However, Bradley sees age as 'more problematic' as 'a basis of collective social identity'. Political parties are not usually organized to represent age groups, and only a few pressure groups are concerned with age. Furthermore, 'age as an issue is very low on the political agenda'. Thus, to Bradley, age is primarily part of individual identity and only rarely becomes part of an active or politicized identity. She identifies two main reasons for this:

1. Individuals move through different age groups and are aware that they will not stay young, middle-aged or old for ever. The temporary nature of their membership of an age group militates against the development of a stable, long-lasting identity.
2. Unlike other types of stratification, the most powerful group is in the middle. The most disadvantaged age groups, the young and the old, are likely to have little in common to form a basis for making common cause with one another.

However, there are some examples of age becoming a more active identity. Some aspects of youth culture express a sense of conflict with adults. Bradley quotes the classic song by the Who, 'My Generation':

People try to put us down
Just because we get around.
The things they do look awful cold
Hope I die before I get old.

Nevertheless, the more political aspects of youth culture are more likely to be related to other aspects of stratification than to age, particularly 'race'/ethnicity. (See, for example, the work of Paul Gilroy, pp. 179–81.) Political parties may have specific sections for the young (for example, Young Conservatives), but they are not wholly or mainly concerned with age-related issues.

Despite the limited importance of age as an active or politicized source of identity among the young, Bradley does note two examples of youth-related issues coming to the fore:

1. In 1960s America, Britain and other European countries, the radical student movement was partly based around age-related issues. This included demands for educational reform, sexual liberation and an end to what was seen as the bureaucratic and materialistic culture of the middle-aged.
2. In Britain in the 1990s something of a 'coalition of various youth interests (New Age travellers, ravers, environmental groups and "tribes")' got together to campaign against the Criminal Justice Bill. However, Bradley suggests that the unifying theme of this coalition – the 'right to party' – may not be sufficiently political to form the basis for a more lasting movement.

Among older people there have been some examples of political mobilization. In America, a radical group called the Grey Panthers has campaigned for the rights of the elderly. However, only a very small minority of older people get involved in political activities related to age. Their circumstances vary widely. They may be affluent or very poor, relatively young and vigorous or extremely elderly and very frail. In these circumstances it is hard for them to identify strongly with each other, let alone with the young (the other disadvantaged age group). Bradley suggests that the old may become more political in the future, though, as the generation who were involved in the feminist and student movements of earlier decades reaches retirement age.

Conclusion

Bradley concludes that in contemporary societies stratification systems and identities are becoming both **polarized** and **fragmented**. There is increasing polarization between the rich and the poor and between the young and the (increasingly long-lived) old. There is also some polarization between ethnic groups – with the re-emergence of nationalist and fascist groups determined to advocate racist policies – and between the affluent elderly and the poor elderly.

Inequality has not gone away. Sexism and racism continue to exist alongside ageism, class inequality and other sources of disadvantage. Gender and 'race'/ethnicity are currently in the ascendancy over class as sources of active and politicized identities. Age remains more important in terms of individual identities than collective ones. However, all are still important as sources of identity and there is fragmentation and division in each of them.

As a result, people in contemporary societies tend to have **fractured identities**. They lack a single identity that overarches all others. Nevertheless, people's identities are still essentially social. While there is an element of choice over identity, this is not as great as postmodernists believe. Bradley says, 'Few of us can, as yet, choose to be English, male and middle class if we were born Indian, female and working class.'

To Bradley, the fracturing of identities is not new. There have always been divisions between and within different sources of identity, which have made it possible for individuals to have fractured identities. However, recent

changes in society have led to increased fragmentation, and people have become more aware of the multiple sources of identity open to them.

Bradley concludes that both modernist and postmodern theories are necessary to understand identity and social change. She says:

> *A reworked version of modernist analysis, benefiting from the critical insights of postmodern and poststructuralist thought, offers the best hope for an adequate understanding of the double and contradictory nature of contemporary society, both fragmenting and polarizing. Such an approach must grasp the persisting nature of social hierarchies as well as exploring the interplay of relationships which gives rise to the fractured identities characteristic of post-capitalist societies.* Bradley, 1997

Identity, leisure and consumerism

As discussed above, postmodern theories of identity lay great stress on the choices individuals make to contruct their own identity. If people no longer get their sense of identity from their work, their class background, their gender or their ethnic group, then their leisure choices and the products they consume are seen as increasingly important in contructing identity.

This section examines arguments about whether leisure has changed in character from being modern to postmodern and in the process has become a more important source of identity. After a general discussion about the changes in leisure, the role of one type of leisure, consumption, in the construction of identity will be examined.

Chris Rojek – *Decentring Leisure*

Leisure, modernity and postmodernity

In his book, *Decentring Leisure* (1995), Rojek explores the changing nature of leisure in advanced capitalist societies. He argues that in order to understand leisure better it needs to be **decentred**. By this he means that leisure should not be seen as a clearly demarcated aspect of social life which can be studied in its own right. The experience of leisure cannot be separated out from other experiences.

Rojek is generally supportive of the idea that there has been a shift to postmodernity, although he believes that modernity and postmodernity overlap and advanced societies have not yet become wholly postmodern. Nevertheless, as societies have moved towards postmodernity, the meaning of leisure has become less clear. Modern societies had a relatively clear idea about what leisure was. Leisure was associated with the idea of freedom and tended to be seen as involving escape from more constrained and limited areas of social life such as work or education. As such, leisure was not an important part of an individual's identity, which largely derived from other aspects of life, particularly work. In modern societies leisure was a means of escaping and experiencing some freedom from one's main social roles.

With the advent of postmodernity, the distinction between leisure and other areas of social life, such as work, becomes much more confused. For example, more and more people work in leisure industries, people can experience fun and enjoyment at work, they can even see going to work as a leisure pursuit. Conversely, people can experience 'routine and confinement' when they are engaged in activities that are supposed to be leisure pursuits.

Modern societies tend to contrast authentic with inauthentic experience and to celebrate the authentic as being superior to the inauthentic. For example, going to see an authentic historical building, say the Tower of London, is superior to visiting a model of it or looking at a picture. In modern culture there is also an emphasis on the planning of leisure. Leisure is organized and given a sense of purpose for the participants.

However, in postmodern leisure, people are less likely to seek the authentic experience. Virtual reality machines, models and representations of things, 'simulation and hyperreality', are fully accepted as valid in leisure activities. Furthermore, leisure is less planned and purposeful. People are less likely to pursue leisure activities for particular purposes, but take part in them just for the sake of it. Leisure becomes an end in itself rather than an escape from work or part of planned activities designed to achieve goals such as self-improvement.

Postmodernity, leisure and identity

This change has important consequences for people's sense of self – their sense of identity. Postmodernism 'outflanks the notion of the integrated self which underpins modernist thought'. For example, in modernist thought people pass through different stages in the life cycle. At each stage people have a strong sense of who they are and engage in leisure pursuits appropriate to their age-group identity. Young people will go out socializing, middle-aged people will have more home-centred leisure, older people will spend more times on hobbies, and so on. To Rojek, such assumptions do not apply with postmodernism. For example, older people might continue to go to night clubs and rock concerts, and young people might well engage in more sedate pursuits associated in modern thinking with older age groups.

Postmodernism breaks down a whole series of barriers between areas of social life. Rojek says:

> *The barriers between home and abroad, public and private life, work and leisure, childhood and old age, male roles and female roles, white and ethnic cultures cease to be treated as given 'facts' of life. Instead there is more emphasis on ambivalence, variability, flexibility and individualism.* Rojek, 1995, p. 172

Societies become more pluralistic in the lifestyles and identities of their members, and less rigid in terms of who can adopt particular identities. **Identity politics** becomes more important for people. They can pick and choose who to be and are not even limited by their biological makeup. For example, white people can choose to listen to, and identify with, the music of black people; men can dress as women and vice versa.

Leisure plays a central role in identity politics. In leisure activities people can construct their own identities – they

can choose who to be. In modern societies leisure reflects who you are. The sorts of leisure activities you engage in are shaped by factors such as your job, your sex and your ethnic group. With postmodernism, leisure increasingly creates identity – you become who you are through your leisure.

Evaluation of Rojek

Rojek's work tends to be rather abstract and to make very general statements about the nature of leisure. As such it exaggerates and simplifies the changes in leisure that he claims have taken place. Although Rojek denies that there is a clear-cut distinction between modern and postmodern leisure, he nevertheless ends up characterizing them as being very different. Furthermore, Rojec provides little in the way of systematic evidence that the nature of identity has changed. People's jobs, their class background, their age, their ethnic background and so on may still be much more important as sources of identity than their leisure pursuits.

In some ways a more balanced account of leisure and identity is provided by Sheila Scraton and Peter Bramham, who are more critical of postmodern ideas.

Sheila Scraton and Peter Bramham – leisure, postmodernity and identity

Modernity

According to Sheila Scraton and Peter Bramham (1995), 'Leisure has been seen as a product of modernity, and of industrial capitalism which demarcated time, as defined by the clock, into segments to be bought and sold like any other commodity, at market rates.' Drawing on the work of the historian E.P. Thompson (1967), they argue that, before industrialization and the advent of modernity, there was no clear distinction between work and leisure. Time was governed by the cycles of the seasons and those of night and day. Work activities and leisure activities were intermingled.

However, with the advent of the factory system and the new system of paying workers for their time rather than for what they produced, a strong distinction between work time and non-work time began to be established.

According to Scraton and Bramham, 'Modernity, or industrial society, was essentially a class based or mass society.' Fordist production techniques, which used assembly lines for the mass production of standardized products, became dominant. Systematic, rational planning is also a feature of modernity and these aspects of modernity influenced the development of leisure.

Modernity and leisure

Scraton and Bramham argue that 'Organized leisure was part and parcel of the modern project. It was the time left over from work and paid employment which could be filled with acceptable free-time activities or relaxations supporting existing economic and political arrangements.' The state and the voluntary sector became involved in organizing leisure which was supposed to benefit individuals and/or society.

However, the idea of rational, planned, organized leisure for the masses began to lose some of its influence after the Second World War. Scraton and Bramham suggest that:

> *The influence of American culture through rock and roll, teenage subcultures, the women's movement and the presence of distinctive minority ethnic groups and diverse cultural patterns, all raised questions about the homogeneous and unidirectional nature of rational leisure and highlighted the growing fragmentation and diversity of free time tastes and activities.* Scraton and Bramham, 1995, p. 20

These developments heralded changes which some researchers have come to characterize as the development of postmodern leisure.

Postmodern leisure

Scraton and Bramham identify a number of features of post-war leisure which have come to be seen as postmodern:

1. If modern leisure was based on organizations planning leisure, postmodern leisure is based on individuals buying products and services. Modern leisure was disciplined whereas postmodern leisure is more concerned with self-indulgence. You do what you want to do rather than what others tell you is good for you. Postmodern leisure has been compared to the shopping mall where you are spoilt for choice and are encouraged to indulge yourself as much as possible.
2. Scraton and Bramham draw on the work of Giddens. Although Giddens prefers the concept of high modernity to postmodernity (see pp. 895–9), Scraton and Bramham believe that Giddens's theories are similar to those of postmodernists. To Giddens (1991), **lifestyle** becomes increasingly important in modern societies. Giddens defines lifestyles as involving the creation of a sense of identity, rather than meeting utilitarian needs, such as needs for food, housing, a regular income and so on.

   Leisure becomes an expression of the pursuit of a particular lifestyle, rather than a search for self-improvement or relaxation. It becomes playful, a means to express who you are. Scraton and Bramham say: 'The importance of rational recreation, games and team spirit, fair play and traditional sporting values are undermined by individualism, privatisation and commercialism.' People's identities become more wrapped up in the sort of consumer goods they consume and their choice of pastimes, rather than in their jobs, their families or their community.
3. Postmodern leisure also involves an increased concern with the body. While the rational leisure of modernity was concerned with bodily health and fitness, postmodern leisure associates this with the individual's pursuit of particular lifestyles and identities. Scraton and Bramham argue that 'working out' on multi-gyms, exercise bikes and similar devices is 'all part of the postmodern quest to develop a distinctive lifestyle, desired body shape and social identity. Appearance and image are all.'

An evaluation of postmodern theories of leisure

So far, Scraton and Bramham simply describe the kind of changes in leisure described by postmodernists, and they are happy to acknowledge that many of the changes described by postmodern theories of leisure have taken place. However, they argue that these changes affect some groups more than others. In particular, postmodern leisure is largely the preserve of more affluent members of society.

Many people do not enjoy the choices which postmodern theories suggest are available to everybody. Many do not have the time or the money to engage in playful, postmodern pursuits. For example, Scraton and Bramham deny that shopping can always be seen as providing the opportunity to construct a personal identity through making elaborate lifestyle choices. They say:

> *For many women shopping remains functionally about trying to feed and clothe a family on a restricted income. It takes place in local shops, markets and Oxfam and the transport costs alone constrain any choice there may be to enter the bright lights of the shopping mall.* Scraton and Bramham, 1995, p. 29

The types of leisure activities people engage in are not just restricted by lack of resources. Leisure remains gendered. Scraton and Bramham point out that video games and virtual reality technology are mostly enjoyed by men, and most games involve aggression and violence. Sex tourism to countries like Thailand is almost exclusively male-oriented, although it is young women who are exploited through it.

Racism is another important feature of society that restricts leisure choices. Scraton and Bramham quote research which suggests that racism is endemic in many sports, making it difficult for minority ethnic men and women to fulfil their potential. Scraton and Bramham therefore argue that:

> *By focusing on pleasures, fantasies and pastiche, postmodernism neglects many people's lives which remain influenced by their experiences of poverty, gender and racism. This is political and social reality and if we are to study and understand leisure in times of change we must explore postmodern leisure but without losing sight of persistent social inequalities.* Scraton and Bramham, 1995, p. 34

In more recent work, Scraton and Bramham (2001) emphasize that some people do enjoy the benefits of choice in leisure, but others continue to be restricted throughout their lives and therefore have less opportunity to use leisure to shape their identity. Amongst the over-fifties, for example,

> *There is no doubt that some people … are thoroughly enjoying the benefits of travel, weekend breaks, opportunities of excitement through risk sports and new technology. However, for others, leisure, rather than being a separate sphere of consumption, remains strongly linked to previous and current paid work opportunities.* Scraton and Bramham, 1995, p. 56

Research suggests that those who continue to work in their fifties spend more time on leisure and engage in a greater variety of leisure pursuits than those without work.

Conclusion

Both Rojek and Scraton and Bramham believe that leisure is becoming increasingly important in shaping identity, but Scraton and Bramham in particular emphasize that leisure, lifestyle and therefore identity choices are much more restricted for some than for others.

Consumerism, personal appearance and identity

Some of the most important ways in which individuals can manipulate their identity is through their personal appearance – through changing their bodies, their make-up, the clothes they wear, or their hairstyle – and through their personal possessions. As consumers, people can purchase a wide range of goods or services – such as new clothes, cars, cosmetic surgery, tattoos, or mobile phones – which may influence the way that others perceive their identity, and the way individuals perceive themselves.

This section examines studies which look at the relationship between consumerism and personal identity through case studies of particular types of consumption. It starts with studies of one of the most recent of fashion accessories – the mobile phone – before looking at more traditional aspects of fashion. It includes studies which tend to support a postmodern view that people are free to construct their own identities through consumerism, and studies which suggest that people's choice of consumer products is restricted by existing social identities, social structures or differences in power.

James Katz and Satomi Sugiyama – 'Mobile phones as fashion statements'

Mobiles and decorative display

James Katz and Satomi Sugiyama (2005) see the mobile phone both as 'a physical item and an item of decorative display' (p. 63). Early mobile phones were expensive and few could afford them unless they were rich or it was vital to a person's business. It was therefore a **status symbol** – a mark of your prestige – if you could afford a mobile phone.

However, as the price of ownership has come down, mobile phones have become as much a **fashion statement** as a utilitarian item on which to make phone calls. As a fashion statement, mobiles provide information about their owner and help to establish their identity. Katz and Sugiyama describe the mobile phone as a 'miniature aesthetic statement' (p. 64). Mobiles are particularly important for the young because they allow a young person to control their own communications without parental control. This allows them to develop a sense of independence as an individual and a unique sense of self.

Early mobiles appeared in the late 1980s and tended to emphasize futuristic design. For example, the early Motorola was based on communication devices in the TV and film series *Star Trek*. Advertising campaigns for mobile phones emphasized science and technology; they were used to represent modernity and Western values. The advertisements also tended to link mobile phones to youth and novelty, with claims that they were cutting-edge technology and design.

Companies also tried to associate mobiles with high status and glamour. For example, Nokia distributed phones free to Hollywood stars, and various companies have paid to place their mobiles in Hollywood films. As the technology became more mature and mobile use became more widespread there was an increased emphasis on the relationship between mobile phones and fashion. For example, Siemens has used adverts which compare mobiles to fashion items such as watches and jewellery. Vodafone has used fashion models in their mobile phone adverts to emphasize that the right mobile is essential to establish a fashionable identity.

To see how effective advertising campaigns had been and to find out if mobiles were perceived as fashion items linked to identity, Katz and Sugiyama carried out group interviews at a US university. Although a few students saw mobiles as simply utilitarian objects, the majority did think of them as a fashion item which said something about the identity of the owner. For example, over half the interviewees thought it was important that their mobile 'should look cool'. Katz and Sugiyama also report research from Japan which shows that even heavy users of mobiles place style above battery life in their list of priorities.

Enhancing identity

Some people go to extremes to ensure that their identity is enhanced by their mobile. One company, Vertu, manufactures mobiles with a platinum casing and a sapphire crystal screen (costing $26,000), and gem-encrusted handsets are popular in China. Simply owning a mobile is important in poor societies. Katz and Sugiyama refer to research in Asia which suggests that mobiles are an '**aspirational statement**'.

In countries throughout the world and even for those with low income, mobiles can be used to make a statement about who you are. People increasingly personalize their mobiles – for example, with cases, stickers, and ringtones to make them more individual. Even the way that you carry and display your mobile can be important and can help to enhance self-image. For example, 'digithongs' (body carrier straps) are become more common. Some women may carry mobiles in their cleavage/bra to enhance their own (and the mobile's) sexiness.

Katz and Sugiyama therefore believe that mobiles

like other fashion items are used as a device to project a sense of identity and self into public arenas. It can become an aesthetic object that people adopt and modify according to their sense of self and group affiliations. Katz and Sugiyama, 2005, p. 77

Even though most mobiles are mass-produced, they do not lead to a mass culture. The meaning of objects is modified by consumers.

Rich Ling – fashion, mobile phones and group identity

Rich Ling is a Norwegian sociologist who has conducted interview research on the meaning of mobile phones among teenagers in Norway (Ling, 2000). Like Katz and Sugiyama, he sees mobiles as a fashion item. However, compared to Katz and Sugiyama, he places more emphasis on mobiles as a source of group identity as well as a source of individual identity. From Ling's point of view, mobiles can be used to express group membership as much as individual uniqueness.

Ling conducted interviews in 1997 and 1999–2000 to discover how attitudes to mobile phones as a fashion item had changed. Like Katz and Sugiyama, he argues that mobiles are not just a functional device but can also be understood as a fashion item. (Sometimes they are deliberately used to *breach* rules of fashion.) As mobiles become more and more common, they are increasingly becoming part of the individual's '**personality kit**' – one of the tools they have to express their personality to others. Amongst teenagers, the ownership and display of mobiles is an important part of their lifestyle.

Fashion and identity

Ling argues that fashion generally is a way of communicating personal intention or status to others. Material objects such as mobile phones help the individual to express group identities such as those related to class, gender, ethnic and subcultural differences. **Props** such as clothes or mobiles announce who we are and what groups we belong to.

Following the work of the sociologist George Simmel, Ling argues that fashion involves both the desire for an individual statement and an expression of group membership. Teenagers in particular need to establish a distinct identity in order to separate from parents. However, they also need to collaborate with peers to mark themselves off from other generations and from other types of teenager. In this process, they include others who are seen as part of the same group, and exclude those who are regarded as different. Fashion, including mobile phone fashion, is used to mark the boundaries of distinct subcultures.

However, a problem with fashion is that it is always changing. It is like a **wave** – to be fashionable you need to join when the wave is rising but leave before it reaches a crest. If you leave it too late, or jump on a fashion bandwagon when everybody else has already joined, it is no longer fashionable but has become **popular taste**. When something becomes too popular, it no longer marks you out as fashionable.

To be fashionable, therefore, you need the 'right' mobile at the right time. In addition you increasingly need the 'right' ringtone and accessories and to display your mobile in the right way. Failure in this regard can lead to your exclusion from the most fashionable groups of teenagers.

Not everybody accepts these rules. Some individuals identify instead with **anti-fashion**. They try to show their contempt for fashion by deliberately doing the opposite of what is fashionable. Anti-fashion can be the basis for the formation of distinct groups and subcultures. However, Ling suggests that even this offers no escape from fashion in the formation of identity. This is because adopting anti-

fashion implies an understanding of fashion. Furthermore, like fashionable groups, anti-fashion groups also exclude some teenagers and include others based upon their choice of mobiles, clothes and other fashion items.

Changing fashions in mobile phones

Having discussed the role of fashion items in the formation of identities, Ling goes on to look at changing fashions in relation to mobiles. In Norway in 1997 pagers were still popular and mobiles were only owned by a minority of teenagers. However, even then, people were already starting to distinguish between 'cool' and 'uncool' mobiles. For example, at that time a yellow Nokia which lit up was considered particularly fashionable.

However, owning a mobile, even an expensive or fashionable one, was not necessarily a way to gain acceptance. At that time mobile phones were associated with yuppie culture. Those who were ostentatious or showy in displaying and using mobiles in public places were seen as vulgar. They were too unsubtle in trying to show off their status to others. In Norway the term **harry** is used to denote tackiness and vulgarity. Students who self-importantly used mobiles in public, acting as if they were important business people, could be seen as *harry*. They could also be seen as **soss** – a Norwegian word meaning pompous. Whether somebody was seen as *harry* or *soss*, or not, was an important marker of their status as an insider or an outsider – as part of the group or excluded from it. In the case of some mobile phone users the identity they wished to communicate – an identity where they were important and fashionable – was not the identity conveyed to the observers. Instead they were seen as pretentious, pompous and vulgar.

By 2000 mobiles were owned by most teenagers and simply having or not having one was not a significant source of identity or marker of group membership. Now the age, price, size and style of phones were becoming more important markers. Having a mobile was no longer thought of as snobby; indeed, it was an embarrassment to be seen with an old, outdated or bulky phone (a 'brick'). The colour, facilities, shape and size of the phone marked you out as someone who was *in*, or *out*, among fashionable groups. If you could not afford a fashionable mobile you could try to personalize it to promote a more individualized identity.

Owning a mobile in itself was no longer thought to be *harry* or *soss*, but the way you displayed it could be. One respondent said it was not cool to show off your mobile by having it on a belt. Another said it 'looked dumb' to have a lot of sunflowers or dinosaurs on your phone. Most *harry* of all was talking very loudly into a phone on a bus or in some other public place. Some Norwegian teenagers deliberately followed anti-fashion, choosing to have old or unfashionable phones to show they did not care about the latest trends.

Ling suggests that the use of derogatory terms such as *soss* or *harry* helps to enforce **group identity** in adolescent culture. Often when people step outside group norms we ignore it, to avoid disrupting the interaction, but terms like *harry* and *soss* are used to show that someone has stretched the boundaries beyond what is acceptable. This helps to establish boundaries between acceptable and unacceptable behaviour, and to shape identity in relation to membership of groups.

Ling sees the use of derogatory terms as a form of power. Making judgements about others implies that you have the right to determine what (and who) is cool and what (and who) is not.

Evaluation

Ling's work suggests that postmodern approaches to the use of objects to produce identity may exaggerate the degree to which individuals can choose their identity. Beliefs about what is and is not fashionable can be used to exclude people, or include them, in social groups. Peer groups can exercise considerable power over the acceptance or rejection of the identity or identities which a person wishes to express.

The next study to be considered also stresses the importance of fashion in expressing group identity, but it goes much further than Ling's work in rejecting postmodern views on the extent to which people can choose fashion to create individualized identities.

Jennifer Craik – *The Face of Fashion*

Male dominance

Jennifer Craik (1994) argues that what women wear cannot be seen as simply an individual choice. She believes that fashion is strongly influenced by power structures in society. In particular, she argues that women's fashion is dominated by men and reflects male interests. Furthermore, clothing is a very important part of gender identity, as 'gender, especially femininity, is worn through clothes' (p. 56).

Since the 1920s fashion designers have increasingly acted as arbiters of what is 'in' or 'out'. Designer fashion (or couture) 'markets dreams, lifestyles and fantasies for a tiny elite of women' (p. 59), but these designers in turn influence mass-market fashion chains and, through this, ordinary women. Craik claims that 'many women are influenced by general trends in fashion and follow – albeit at a distance – the activities of the fashion industry' (p. 59). The fashion industry is therefore shaping gender identity and encouraging women to aspire to particular lifestyles.

However, most women will not be able to fully achieve the glamorous lifestyles portrayed by the fashion industry, and high street designs will compromise, toning down extravagant design to provide more practical, wearable clothing. In this process there is a tension between the ideals of femininity portrayed through couture, and the practical reality of female roles. However, because most designers are men, the emphasis tends to be more on ideals of femininity than on practicality. The dominance of male designers leads to women wearing clothes that please men rather than clothes that meet their needs. Increasingly, female clothes 'allude to persons as sexual beings' (p. 56), much more than would have been considered acceptable in previous decades.

Fashion and body shape

As part of this process, women are encouraged to look like the models and style icons who wear fashionable clothes. Alongside the fashion industry, books and magazines provide advice to women about how to improve their 'look'. For example, Craik discusses a book entitled

The Princess of Wales Fashion Handbook (published in 1994), which advised women on how to look as good as Diana:

> *Diana's thin (model-like) body was endorsed as the ideal body shape. Clothes that suited this canonical body shape would not suit other bodies so the outfits were adapted for four 'flawed' body shapes: hourglass; pear-shaped; short-waisted; and top-heavy. The adaptations involved disguising body-flaws.* Craik, 1994, p. 62

'Misshapen' bodies were seen as a problem that needed dealing with. Through fashion – an industry which is largely dominated by men – men were therefore 'managing the feminine body' – telling women how they should look.

Craik argues that the desire for a fashionable identity leads to women regulating their own bodies in ways ultimately shaped by masculine power. It can lead to excessive dieting and various eating disorders such as bulimia nervosa and anorexia nervosa. Since most women are unable to attain the ideal body shape, many women become anxious and, as a result, 'the feminine body is the site of severe conflict and prodigious labour' (p. 69).

Craik concludes that rather than allowing women to express individual identity, fashion tends to reproduce gender inequality. It reinforces male dominance, and the apparent sense of freedom that women experience when shopping for clothes is largely an illusion. Most women are unwilling to risk being seen as unfeminine by ignoring the dictates of fashion.

However, this does not apply to all women. Fashion is also a **site of struggle** where different groups compete to get their ideas accepted. Some women deliberately defy the rules of fashion and rebel against the fashion industry. For example, they might choose to wear dungarees rather than traditionally feminine clothes. Thus, although fashion usually reproduces traditional gender roles and identities, it can also be used to challenge them.

Evaluation

Craik makes out a strong case that the construction of identity is influenced by wider structures of inequality in society. Craik concentrates on gender inequality and identity, but other types of inequality such as class and ethnicity may have an important influence as well.

For example, Angela McRobbie (1994) argues that class has as much influence as gender on the development of fashion. Craik emphasizes the extent to which gender identities are reproduced through fashion, and discusses those who oppose conventional styles. McRobbie believes that clothes are used in an oppositional way, to attack conventional identities, more frequently than Craik suggests. For example, punks, hippies and women dressing in men's clothing styles have all disrupted the conventional relationship between identity and clothing. However, McRobbie suggests that even these attempts at opposition to mainstream fashion often have only temporary success. Fashion designers often start to incorporate oppositional styles into their own designs, thus neutralizing the opposition. Therefore, from McRobbie's point of view, theories such as those put forward by Craik do not fully represent the complexity of the relationship between identity, consumers, fashion and gender.

Summary and conclusions

Although culture, socialization and identity are discussed in separate sections of the chapter, the three topics are closely linked. Culture is reproduced through socialization, and the way an individual is socialized and their position within a culture or cultures are very important in shaping their identity.

Most of the early theorists of culture adopted what some would see as a modernist approach to these topics. These approaches have tended to use a rather monolithic and static model of the relationship between culture, socialization and identity. For example, functionalists and traditional Marxists believe that most people are effectively socialized into accepting the culture of the society or class into which they are born, and their identity stems very much from their social position.

As theories of culture, socialization and identity have developed they have tended to move further away from this sort of model. Postmodernists, for example, take a very different view. They argue that there are many different cultures and subcultures in contemporary societies. They believe that identities are not fixed and that people do not simply accept an identity that stems from the position in society they are born into and the way they are socialized. They argue that in consumer societies we do not just choose the products we buy, we can also largely choose who we are.

However, as work such as Harriet Bradley's discussion of identity and Jennifer Craik's study of fashion suggests, social divisions cannot be ignored in the study of culture, socialization and identity. Factors such as our class, ethnic group, age and gender continue to influence our culture, the way we are brought up, and our, and other people's, sense of who we are. While culture, socialization and identity may be less rigid and more varied than in the past, there are still strong social influences on the form they take, and these exist over and above the decisions of individuals.

CHAPTER 12
Communication and the media

by Paul Trowler
(with revisions by Sarah Burch)

... the social construction of identity today is the knowing construction of identity. Your life is your project – there is no escape. The media provides some of the tools which can be used in this work. Gauntlett, 1998

Introduction: understanding 'the media'

The concept of 'the media' can refer to a variety of things:

- **Technologies** such as television, DVD and ICT (information and communication technologies). These usually involve bundles of technologies used in conjunction: computers, modems and telephony for ICT, for example.
- **Modes of communication**: print (newspapers, books, magazines); visual (television, film); aural (radio).
- **Organizations**, such as the BBC or News International, which are involved in producing and distributing messages of various kinds.
- **People** who work within such organizations: for example, news reporters, producers, editors.
- **Methods of disseminating messages to audiences** (as distinguished from the technologies used in that dissemination): for example, films shown within cinema complexes or in single-screen cinemas, football matches shown on satellite television in crowded pubs or in people's homes.

The term media is used rather too broadly in popular language. Academically, it is useful to distinguish between **mass media**, where a message is conveyed from one point to a very large number of other points; **interactive media**, which provide a limited degree of communication back from individual points to a message's point of origin; **interpersonal media**, where messages are conveyed between single points; and **network media**, which permit messages to be conveyed between single points or small or large numbers of points in any direction.

The term **new media** is used to describe those aspects of the media associated with ICT. Like the term 'media', 'new media' refers to hardware and software, as well as media institutions and the people and practices in them and outside them. Unlike mass media, new media tend to be focused on smaller audiences with specific interests. The term 'narrowcasting' (as opposed to broadcasting) highlights this difference. New media are often interactive, with messages flowing both ways, and frequently involve networks of communication.

Technological developments in ICT, such as the expansion and enhancement of the internet and larger and faster digital storage technologies, have allowed the new media to both diversify and spread. Cable, terrestrial and satellite television channels, plus widespread cheap access to the internet and digital technology, have flowed rapidly from the UK and USA to many other parts of the world.

In 2005/6, 65 per cent of UK households had digital television, a considerable increase from 19 per cent in 1996/7 (National Statistics, 2007a). Amongst children, 65 per cent of 8- to 15-year-olds own a mobile phone, 50 per cent have their own games console (whilst a further third use a console belonging to the household), and 48 per cent use the internet at home (Ofcom, 2006a).

In 2006, an estimated 57 per cent of people in Britain had internet access (National Statistics, 2006), and 60 per cent of people had used the internet in the last three months, a rise of one-quarter since 2001/2 (National Statistics, 2007b). Frequency of internet access is also increasing rapidly, with 59 per cent of all internet users aged 16 and over going online daily or almost daily (National Statistics, 2007b).

With the development of web 2.0 technology, use of the internet is becoming much more dynamic. There has been an upsurge in activities such as blogging and social networking. In 2007, the social networking sites Bebo, MySpace and Facebook reached 34, 32 and 24 per cent respectively of the UK online population (Comscore, 2007).

In his book *Understanding Media* (1964) the Canadian sociologist Marshall McLuhan suggested that developments in communication were the main force for change in human society. For example, when printing was invented and when electronic media were developed, important social changes began to take place. For McLuhan, therefore, the real importance of the media lies not in their content, but in the way they themselves alter our social world.

McLuhan was the prime exponent of a theoretical position called **media determinism**, also referred to as **technological determinism**. Today, we see a dynamic and complex relationship between communications media, and increasingly the new media, and social change.

As the media have changed, so has the study of the media. Early media sociologists tended to concentrate on newspapers and television and paid particular attention to news content. More recent sociology has also studied other media, especially new media, and a broader range of content. It has shown that audience responses to media content can be highly individual. Such responses can include pleasure or anger, changes in behaviour, and increased understanding, as well as other experiences.

Many sociologists now suggest that each of us makes our own interpretations of media messages, in a significant shift away from the determinism of McLuhan's approach. However, they also believe that these interpretations are influenced by our particular social contexts: for example, our ethnicity, our gender and our occupation.

Many postmodernist sociologists regard media messages (or 'texts', as such sociologists call them) as **polysemic**: in other words, each media message or text is capable of being interpreted in a variety of ways. They can also be read **intertextually**; that is, texts will be read in relation to other texts. Many sociologists also stress the influence of the immediate context of viewing on our interpretation of media messages: for example, whether a message is viewed at home or elsewhere, alone or with others, while doing nothing else or engaged in other activities.

The structure and content of the media

Pluralist theories

Pluralism is a label generally applied to theories of the media that were popular in the first seventy years of the twentieth century (see Chapter 9 for a more detailed description of pluralism).

Pluralists argue that society is made up of many interacting but competing sections. These sections of society have more or less equal access to resources and influence, and they are policed by a benevolent and neutral state operating in the public interest. According to pluralists, different parts of the media cater to these various sections of society. The media reflect society: just as there is diversity within society, so there is diversity in media content. Because the media reflect society in this way, they are unlikely to have much effect in changing society.

Pluralism appears in the work of many media commentators, particularly in the ideas of media workers themselves. Indeed, many of the early studies of media content and effects that came to be labelled pluralist were funded by the media industry.

Personal Influence by Elihu Katz and Paul Lazarsfeld is a classic pluralist text. It was published in 1955 and based on data collected in 1945. The basic question underlying this study is how far the media influence opinions and attitudes, particularly political opinions and voting behaviour. Katz and Lazarsfeld note:

> ***Fundamentally all communications research aims at the study of effect [but] there are a variety of possible effects that the mass media may have upon society, and several different dimensions along which effects may be classified.***
> Katz and Lazarsfeld, 1955

They argue that in general the media have a rather limited influence. This is because the mass communication process can be affected in unpredictable ways by five 'variables':

1 Variable exposure, access or attention to media messages. Personal, political, practical or technological factors can shape the nature and extent of an individual's or group's exposure to any particular message or medium.
2 The type of medium used to convey the message has an important impact on the power of the message. For example, television footage of starving children may have a more powerful effect than a newspaper report about the same subject.
3 The nature of the content, and the form, presentation and language of the message, will have important consequences for its effect. An example of this was the national response to the killing of black teenager Stephen Lawrence in 1993 after its reporting in the press and other media, and the

subsequent changes to recruitment and training practices in the police service.

4 Beliefs and attitudes among members of the audience can modify or completely distort the meaning of a given message:

> *For example, a prejudiced person whose attitude towards an out-group is strongly entrenched may actively resist a message of tolerance in such a way that the message may be perceived as a defence of prejudice or as irrelevant to the subject of prejudice entirely.* Katz and Lazarsfeld, 1955

5 Leaders and opinion makers within communities can mediate messages received from the mass media. For example, people tend to vote in the way their spouses, parents, fellow club members or fellow employees vote, not in the way dominant media messages tell them to vote. Thus, pluralists argue that power and status are of little relevance in this context: 'Some individuals of high social status apparently wield little independent influence and some of low status have considerable personal influence' (Katz and Lazarsfeld, 1955).

It is often argued that media pluralism is associated with the liberal democracies of the West, although this can be disputed (Woods, 2007). Support for the principle of media pluralism comes from institutions at national and international levels. The European Broadcasting Union, for example, argues that media pluralism is a broad issue. The central principle is that citizens must have free access to a range of diverse opinion, and this should be supported by the use of regulatory authorities and legislation (Commission of the European Communities, 2007). The World Press Freedom Committee is an organization which campaigns for and monitors press freedom internationally. Its Charter for a Free Press has been endorsed by bodies such as the UN and UNESCO (WPFC, 2007).

However, support for the principle of media pluralism does not necessarily mean that it occurs in practice. Criticisms of the pluralist perspective are discussed below.

Criticisms of pluralism

The next section examines the main criticisms of this kind of pluralist thinking, particularly those made by Marxist and neo-Marxist writers. However, there are two important general criticisms that are often made.

First, it is claimed that pluralist theorists are frequently part of, or funded by, the media industries themselves. Early pluralists, called 'administrative researchers', were funded in this way, which raised questions about their impartiality (Boyd-Barrett, 1995). Greg Philo, Director of the Glasgow Media Group, accused the major pluralist critic of their work, Martin Harrison, of more or less being a spokesperson for Independent Television News (ITN), which provided Harrison with selective access to transcripts of its news coverage and used him in its own interests.

Second, the pluralists' claim that the media are generally diverse and neutral is criticized in terms of what Jay Blumler and Michael Gurevitch (1995) call the 'emergent shared culture' of politicians and press and television journalists.

Blumler and Gurevitch claim that journalists and politicians depend on one another and adapt to one another's requirements. Politicians need journalists to help them persuade people to adopt a certain view (of themselves, their party or what they are trying to achieve). Journalists need politicians for the interviews, news, action and comment they require. Rules and understandings emerge on both sides and a certain degree of trust is built up. Patterns of behaviour develop and become simply 'what is expected'. Interaction between journalists and politicians becomes predictable and taken for granted.

The result, though, is that journalistic diversity narrows, journalistic 'objectivity' is compromised, and media content becomes prey to professional 'spin doctors'. It was for these reasons that *Guardian* newspaper journalists refused for a time to participate in the parliamentary lobby system. This system formed a major part of the shared culture by giving newspapers access to privileged (and heavily 'spun') information as long as the sources of such information were not disclosed.

This difficulty with the pluralist point of view also becomes apparent in situations such as the 2003 coalition attack on Iraq. Around 500 'embedded' journalists were allowed to travel with British and American troops to report from battle scenes. This made it difficult to achieve 'impartial' reporting when the most newsworthy material was accessible only from one side of the conflict and from journalists who quickly formed personal attachments to the troops they were living with and who were protecting them. This was evident from the occasional slip: 'Our task – um, the task of the unit I am travelling with – was to attack Iraqi sniper positions.'

However, as we shall see, the main difficulty with the pluralist model is that it assumes rather than demonstrates that media content as a whole is highly diverse. The two theories examined below challenge this assumption and so reach quite different conclusions about the nature of media effects.

Marxist theories

Marxist theories sharply contradict pluralism (see Chapter 9). In *The German Ideology*, Karl Marx states, 'in every epoch, the ruling ideas are the ideas of the ruling class' (Marx and Engels, 1970, first published 1846). Contemporary Marxists believe the media are the means by which the ideas of the ruling class maintain their dominance as the ruling ideas.

Marxists argue, for example, that ruling ideas are very apparent in advertising: adverts help promote manufactured goods by stimulating aspirations about lifestyles and ways of behaving generally. They attach '**connotative codes**' to material objects: in other words, advertised products become laden with a range of positive attitudes, feelings and desires within an audience, which help the products to sell.

Politically, the ruling ideas set the agenda, excluding some possibilities and normalizing others so that they become 'just common sense'. Ruling ideas control the information we have about the world and even shape our leisure activities. Marxists claim this is largely because the capitalist class has access to the resources which enable its members to present their ideas as 'normal'.

Consequently, there is a striking lack of diversity within media messages. Although media sources and messages appear diverse, in reality there is centralized ownership: a few media corporations own and operate most media. These media corporations are huge and they dominate the industry. The many businesses within these corporations support and promote each other's operations.

For example, the film *Transformers: The Movie* was released in 2007, taking $155.4 million in its first week, a new record for a non-sequel film (McClintock, 2007). The film was produced by Dreamworks in partnership with Paramount and Hasbro, and directed by Michael Bay. However, the film is simply the latest chapter in a long-running franchise which has had many different merchandising strands.

Transformers began as a Japanese toy line, which Hasbro began marketing in the USA in the 1980s (Smith, 2007). Transformers storylines have been developed by Marvel comics and in cartoon series. The toy line has been through several series, being relaunched in different 'generations' in different countries. It has also featured in successful video games, and new games based on the 2007 film and using the voices of the leading actors are under development across a range of gaming platforms (Gaudiosi, 2007).

The film has explicit tie-ins with a number of other large businesses whose products feature within it, such as General Motors, who have supplied the vehicles for a number of films directed by Michael Bay (Schiller, 2007). The film, the toys and the numerous other spin-off products thus achieve saturation coverage on a global basis. They mutually reinforce each other in terms of publicity.

The huge corporations involved in such ventures are able to capitalize on the following advantages to achieve domination of the media market:

1 **Levels of expenditure and economies of scale**: only global corporations have access to levels of investment capital to mount projects like *Transformers: The Movie*. Vast resources are also available to market and promote products. Producing huge volumes of merchandising for sale worldwide means profit levels are higher. There is no market competition in this elite area.
2 **Synergy**: this is the idea that separate entities working together can achieve things that none could individually. As is evident from the example above, a concept such as Transformers can be repackaged as a soundtrack, computer game, TV series, etc. Each feeds and promotes the other, so that the whole is greater than the sum of the parts. Meanwhile, parts of the same media empire will support other parts: this is called **cross-promotion**.
3 **Branding**: media empires use their size and financial muscle to create images associated with their brands and so ensure that their products are more desirable than those of their competitors. The Disney brand, for example, has particular associations in people's minds, which do not appear there accidentally and can be used to sell products.
4 **Globalization**: only the huge media corporations are able to sell on a global scale. For example, the holdings and media interests of Rupert Murdoch's News Corporation now spread around the world, in book publishing, television companies, cable companies, newspapers, film companies and, of course, satellite television. Murdoch himself says the company's satellite and TV channels reach three-quarters of the world's population. Here, there is no serious competition.

Four major trends in media ownership can be identified over recent decades:

1 Concentration of ownership – or monopolization, as Marx called it
2 Growth
3 Integration
4 Globalization

Concentration of ownership

Researchers measure the concentration of total revenue in an industry by means of the concept of **concentration ratio**, or **CR**. Thus, CR4 is the ratio of total revenue going to the top four companies in that industry, and CR8 is the ratio for the top eight companies. If CR8 for an industry is above 75 per cent or CR4 is above 50 per cent, the industry is considered highly concentrated.

Ben Bagdikian has been tracking the concentration ratio of media industries for years in sequential editions of his book *The Media Monopoly*. The ratio is increasing across most sectors, though in some (for example, the film industry) the ratio has been climbing faster than in others (for example, consumer magazines).

In the most recent edition, *The New Media Monopoly* (2004), Bagdikian identifies a startling increase in concentration. In 1985, fifty corporations dominated the mass media. By 2003, this had narrowed to five dominant media corporations, thus giving considerable power to the five men who lead them.

> *Five global-dimension firms, operating with many of the characteristics of a cartel, own most of the newspapers, magazines, book publishers, motion picture studios, and radio and television stations in the United States. Each medium they own, whether magazines or broadcast stations, covers the entire country, and the owners prefer stories and programs that can be used everywhere and anywhere. Their media products reflect this.* Bagdikian, 2004

These five corporations are Time Warner, Walt Disney, News Corporation, Viacom and Bertelsmann. They control the vast majority of the 178,000 media outlets in the USA. Although they are in competition with one another, they also cooperate and share resources. They have 141 joint business ventures, for example, so Bagdikian argues they are in effect business partners. Their combined influence has a massive impact on US society, as well as having considerable global presence.

Growth

Big media corporations have been merging with or buying out other businesses for many years, growing in size as they swallow up competitors, thus reducing competition and the possibilities of competition. For example, Time Warner is the largest media firm in the world. It has become so via a process of accumulations and mergers. Its merger with America Online in 2000 was the largest ever takeover.

A company which has identified itself as operating with an alternative business ethos is Google. Its corporate

philosophy includes such statements as 'You can make money without doing evil' and 'You can be serious without a suit' (Google, 2007a).

Google started out in 1996 as a search engine, set up by two students, Larry Page and Sergei Brin. It was first registered as a private company in 1998 and was floated in 2004 (Google, 2007b), resulting in a market valuation of over $23 billion in spite of some anxieties over the dot.com market and Google's performance (Webb, 2004). Since then, it has expanded massively, with its range of activities now including email, a variety of reference materials such as GoogleScholar and mapping, and features such as document sharing, instant messaging and sale of advertising.

Google has entered into a series of acquisitions, such as the purchase of Blogger, and partnerships with other enterprises such as Yahoo! in order to expand. In 2006, it acquired YouTube, the hugely popular video-sharing website which has been estimated to account for 60 per cent of videos viewed online (Clark, 2006). Larry Page has made it clear that his vision for Google is that it should expand still further to become a massive enterprise (Nuttall and Waters, 2007).

Whatever Google's corporate ethos, it has become a hugely influential player in the new media economic and technological landscape. From a Marxist perspective, this growth in the power of capitalism is both predictable and alarming.

Integration

As well as the increased scale of media businesses, another characteristic that strengthens them and diminishes competition is the variety of businesses within them. Media giants such as Viacom are involved in all aspects of the media: television, publishing, cable, video, the internet.

The integration is both horizontal and vertical. **Horizontal integration** refers to the different types of media – this allows a media giant to market the same products across different media, as noted above in the case of the *Transformers* film. Viacom's ownership of the Star Trek franchise has allowed it to develop and promote products that include books, programmes, films, computer games and a theme park (Croteau and Hoynes, 2001).

Digital media have begun to make this kind of cross-media integration much easier through the process of **convergence**: DVDs and even CDs as storage devices assist companies like Viacom in promoting its products across a variety of media types: video, PC games, video game consoles, etc. Already, filmless digital cinemas are downloading films from the internet and showing them on computerized projection facilities. Eventually it seems probable that most content will be downloaded from the internet via broadband links, at a charge. This has been recognized by Bill Gates, founder of Microsoft:

> *Capitalism, demonstrably the greatest of the constructed economic systems, has in the past decade clearly proved its advantages over the alternative systems. As the internet evolves into its broadband, global interactive network, those advantages will be magnified. Product and service providers will see what buyers want a lot more efficiently than ever before and consumers will buy more efficiently. Adam Smith would be pleased.* Quoted in Patelis, 2000

Vertical integration means owning companies involved in the production, distribution, exhibition and sale of a single type of media product. Thus Viacom owns both film production and distribution companies (for example, Paramount), as well as the venues to exhibit films (UCI cinema chain) and stores to sell video and DVD versions of them (Blockbuster). After the cinema and rental life of a film is over it will be shown on cable channels such as the Movie Channel or Comedy Central, also owned by Viacom.

Referring to the Viacom/CBS merger, Croteau and Hoynes say:

> *By understanding the basic idea of integration, we can understand why many industry observers saw the Viacom/CBS deal as a logical one. First, CBS was the owner of one of the premier exhibition spaces: the CBS network, one of the 'Big Four' television networks. However, it did not have major program production facilities ... Viacom, however, was very strong in production but owned only a 50 per cent stake in a very small broadcast network, UPN. It did not, therefore, have a premier venue for broadcasting. Bringing Viacom and CBS together created a new company with much better vertical integration.* Croteau and Hoynes, 2001

In addition, the same individuals tend to appear on the boards of different corporations, both within the media and in other crucial sectors of the economy. This is partly because large corporations themselves are no longer just media corporations but are also involved in many sectors of the capitalist economy: Sony owns Columbia, Westinghouse owns CBS, General Electric owns NBC, and so forth.

Globalization

As noted above, in the example of the film *Transformers*, the reach of media corporations is now global. New markets are tapped, local competition is crushed and the benefits of economies of scale are reaped.

Viacom, for example, is a truly global player, particularly after its merger with CBS. Its complete holdings are too numerous to list in full here, but they can be viewed on its website: www.viacom.com (see also the subscription site www.cjr.org/owners). They include CBS television and affiliates, multiple cable and satellite television stations (including MTV, Nickelodeon and others), over 160 radio stations, many film and television production and distribution companies (including Paramount, MTV Films and UIP), as well as multiple publishing ventures, theme parks, Blockbuster video stores, UCI cinemas and so on. Blockbuster alone has 6,000 stores in twenty-seven countries. Nickelodeon distributes children's programming in over 100 countries, has cable channels across the globe and has theme parks in Australia and elsewhere.

However, increasingly, Viacom sets up local companies to extend its global reach: MTV India, MTV Southeast Asia (a joint venture with Polygram) and MTV Nordic are examples. Together, Viacom's MTV channels are available in more than 300 million households in eighty-two countries (Croteau and Hoynes, 2001).

It is also notable that the most powerful global players come from the USA and thus particular types of cultural

artefacts are transmitted. The USA is the largest exporter of media products – official US figures for revenue gained from film and television tape rentals showed a rise from $2.5 billion in 1992 to $10.4 billion in 2004 (Thussu, 2005).

The globalized media transform the nature of territory and programmes themselves. In relation to television, Chalaby comments that: 'International TV channels are not simply deterritorializing but deterritorialized cultural artefacts themselves. Many of their features, including coverage, schedule and patterns of production, tear apart the relation between place and television' (2005, p. 8).

However, it is very unlikely that globalization will mean complete homogenization of programme content and advertisements. Local cultures mean that media content often needs to be different for different cultures. Strong evidence for this was found in a very large study of media use by children across Europe, described in more detail below (p. 735): 'Genres and media types evolve in a dialogue between the local, the national and the global, with Anglo-American norms gaining increasing importance as children grow older' (Livingstone and Bovill, 2001).

The logic of capitalism

For most Marxists, it is the **logic of capitalism** which dictates the content and effects of the mass media. The poor and the powerless are not a profitable market for large capitalist corporations and so they are largely ignored. Media products which fail to attract advertisers can be driven out of business.

Bagdikian also shows that capitalism's corporate logic means that the interests of the affluent extend into news coverage too. He argues that:

> *Most business pages consist of corporate propaganda in the form of press releases run without significant changes or printed verbatim. Each day millions of expensive pages of stock market quotations are printed, even though only a small minority of American households actively trade in the stock market.* Bagdikian, 2004, p. 161

This 'logic of capitalism' argument even appeals to researchers who are not Marxists. In 'Television and beyond' (1990), Ellen Wartella and others show that there is very little diversity in children's programming as a result of the same capitalist logic. Wartella *et al.* conducted a survey of all audio-video programming available to children in the Champaign/Urbana area of Illinois in the USA. The survey results showed extremely limited variety (different programmes across different types of media) and extremely limited diversity (different types of programming within one medium). Diversity was only available to those families who could afford cable television:

> *The most striking characteristic of these data is their clear indication that there is no diversity of children's programming on commercial television. All the weekday commercial children's programmes are cartoons; two thirds of these are toy related ... Weekend commercial television provides minimal diversity: only 3 of the 28 commercial children's programmes over the weekend are not cartoons.* Wartella *et al.*, 1990

Those who could afford to subscribe to cable, however, had access to a far wider variety of programmes, including live action, comedy, drama, quiz shows, instructional programmes and so on. The study thus confirms the predictions made by earlier authors, such as Garnham (1986), who foresaw the polarization of society into one section rich in media and information, and another section poor in media and information:

> *A two-tier market divided between the information rich, provided with high-cost specialized information and cultural services, and the information poor, provided with increasingly homogenized entertainment series on a mass scale.* Garnham, 1986

This disparity in access to information is particularly striking in relation to internet access worldwide. As Table 12.1 indicates, there has been considerable global growth in internet usage in the twenty-first century. However, while the most significant growth has occurred in the developing world, there are far higher rates of access within the West. For example, 3.6 per cent of the population in Africa has access, compared to 69.5 per cent in North America (internetworldstats.com, 2007).

Table 12.1 World internet usage and population statistics

World regions	Population (millions) (2007 est.)	Population % of world	Internet usage, latest data (millions)	% Population (penetration)	Usage % of world	Usage growth 2000–2007
Africa	933.4	14.2	33.5	3.6	2.9	643.1
Asia	3,712.5	56.5	436.8	11.8	37.2	282.1
Europe	809.6	12.3	321.9	39.8	27.4	206.2
Middle East	193.5	2.9	19.5	10.1	1.7	494.8
North America	334.5	5.1	232.7	69.5	19.8	115.2
Latin America/Caribbean	556.6	8.5	110.0	19.8	9.4	508.6
Oceania/Australia	34.5	0.5	18.8	54.5	1.6	146.7
WORLD TOTAL	6,574.7	100.0	1,173.1	17.8	100.0	225.0

Source: Internetworldstats.com (2007) 'Internet usage statistics – the big picture': http://www.internetworldstats.com/stats.htm

Media moguls' manipulation

For another strand of Marxist thinking, however, the processes involved are less subtle than those just described. The direct manipulation of media content by corporation chiefs is well documented. For example, newspaper editors working for Rupert Murdoch tell stories about his telephone calls directing the content of the front page. They admit that this influences their decisions and leads to self-censorship (Evans, 1994).

Murdoch's influence can be observed across a range of territories. A successful strategy has been to engage with local culture and concerns, yet impose a distinctive imprint on the news agenda.

Thussu (2007) outlines the 'Murdochization' of news in India. India permits foreign corporations to run news stations, which is unusual amongst Asian countries. Television is a particularly powerful medium, given the comparatively low levels of literacy. Murdoch's Star TV is comprised of a number of channels, including Star News. The proliferation of news channels has led to fierce competition and an increased emphasis on 'infotainment', but Star News has the resources to be a very influential player. Thussu argues that:

> *Star News is leading the way with a news agenda that emphasizes metropolitan concerns, with an obsessive interest in glamour, crime and celebrity culture. At the heart of this agenda is the popularization of news by making it accessible and entertaining, thus expanding the audience base for advertisers as well as promoting synergies among Murdoch's entertainment and news operations in India.* Thussu, 2007, p. 599

In Britain, Murdoch's Sky satellite network appears all-conquering, with competition being crushed as it appears: first Sky took over BSB, with its high-technology satellite broadcasting; then OnDigital failed to compete with Sky television, leaving Sky with little or no serious competition, and viewers with little alternative to Sky's very American populist programming. In 2007, Sky withdrew its most popular channel, Sky One, from its rival Virgin Media, with damaging effects on Virgin Media's customer base.

All of this makes pluralist views like the following seem naive:

> *We are in the midst of a digital maelstrom which is reshaping the traditional computing, telecommunications and consumer electronic industries and promises unprecedented choice for consumers and a new multimedia-rich world of information.* Taylor, 1998

Criticisms of Marxism

Marxist perspectives tend to underestimate the state's regulation of the media, which can set limits to media ownership, and hence control of content – a point pluralists stress. For example, Rupert Murdoch was excluded from bids for the fifth national terrestrial television channel in the UK (Channel 5) because of his extensive media ownership. Similarly, in April 2000 Microsoft was found guilty of violating anti-trust laws, in a case brought by the American Justice Department. The judge found that:

> *Microsoft has demonstrated that it will use its prodigious market power and immense profits to harm any firm that insists on pursuing initiatives that could intensify competition against one of Microsoft's core products. Microsoft's past success in hurting such companies and stifling innovation deters investment in technologies and businesses that exhibit the potential to threaten Microsoft. The ultimate result is that some innovations that would truly benefit consumers never occur for the sole reason that they do not coincide with Microsoft's self-interest.*
> Croteau and Hoynes, 2001

The result of the case was the court-imposed regulation of Microsoft's activities in order to increase competition in the market and reduce Microsoft's monopolistic power, as the Justice Department had wanted.

In Europe, European Union competition law was applied to a proposed joint pay television venture between the Kirch Group, Deutsche Telekom and Bertelsmann. The proposal was ruled incompatible with European competition rules because it would have inhibited the entry of others into the German market: Kirch already had a cable monopoly and the other two firms dominated programming and pay television.

Jeanette Steemers concludes:

> *Broadcasting is far from dead, but its future health with regard to market dominance, and the safeguarding of plurality and diversity, depends on the outcome of regulatory efforts at both a national and EU level.*
> Steemers, 1999

Not all commentators agree that concentration is occurring at the rate described by writers such as Bagdikian. Compaine (2004) states that whilst concentration has increased, it has done so only by a small amount over the last decade or so. The media industry should be seen as fluid and dynamic. Compaine argues that company break-ups and the emergence of new companies receive less attention than mergers and takeovers.

A related point is that Marxist perspectives usually focus on media ownership. If, however, we consider audiences, it soon becomes clear that terrestrial television is the 'most consumed' medium. In general, people spend seven times longer watching television than reading newspapers. Ofcom figures reveal that time spent watching television is increasing. In 2005, weekly viewing hours averaged 25.34, an increase of 11 minutes from 2001 (Ofcom, 2006b).

For pluralists, the dominance of television is reassuring because it is the medium over which national government and regulative bodies, such as the Independent Television Commission and the Broadcasting Standards Commission, have the most control.

According to pluralist theories, the content of the media is largely dictated by market demand rather than by ruling ideas and the interests of the affluent. Thus, control rather than ownership is the important factor in determining the output of the media.

Market share and profitability are of main interest to managers, not social or political influence. For example, although Rupert Murdoch's News Corporation bought Fox Television in the mid-1980s, it became successful by broadcasting anti-establishment programmes like *Married ... with Children* and *The Simpsons*. These series challenged 'traditional' family values, in sharp contrast to bland

programmes on other channels such as *The Cosby Show*. Profits rose and Fox did well, beating the powerful and well established CBS on viewing figures for 18- to 49-year olds in 1993.

Ignoring or manipulating the demands of the market can prove expensive, as News Corporation discovered when it took over *TV Guide* magazine and moved its editorial content downmarket. It lost sales of half a million copies in the first year of ownership. There had been a place in the market for serious journalism in this listings magazine. By removing it the magazine lost its distinctiveness and its market share.

Postmodernists argue that power is not concentrated in a few hands; rather, power circulates in a fluid way. For example, public opinion triumphed over corporate interest, with the assistance of the media, when a campaign organized via Facebook resulted in HSBC bank backing down on the introduction of overdraft fees for students.

In 2007, HSBC announced it would be imposing overdraft fees for new graduates, who had previously been accustomed to free accounts. A 'viral campaign' on Facebook, reported in the *Guardian* newspaper, gathered over 5,000 signatories in a matter of days. Actions including 'flash queuing' were planned, where apparently spontaneous queues of students would block and disrupt branches of HSBC at prearranged times with queries about their accounts. HSBC backed down and entered into talks with the National Union of Students (Levene, 2007).

This example shows that, as such issues arise, some groups become active and mobilize their forces to do battle. The outcomes of these battles are not predetermined and the role of the media varies from one to another.

We will look at postmodernist theories in more detail below (see pp. 726–7).

Neo-Marxist theories: cultural hegemony

Neo-Marxist arguments place less emphasis than Marxist ones on the logic of capitalism to explain the content and effects of the mass media. Rather, they stress the idea that the culture of the dominant class is reproduced in taken-for-granted ways through the mass media. This is part of what is known as **cultural hegemony**: the domination of one set of ideas over others.

This hegemonic model is a more sophisticated version of Marxism. It is associated with the work of the Italian Marxist Antonio Gramsci, as well as with members of the Frankfurt School for Social Research, such as Theodor Adorno, Louis Althusser and Max Horkheimer. Such thinkers view ideology (see below) as more important than the simple pursuit of economic interest. Most people (journalists and others) genuinely act according to their beliefs, which are not necessarily determined by (although they are linked to) their class position. Dominance is instead accomplished at the unconscious level by the 'culture industry'.

Neo-Marxists argue that the media make meanings and organize them into systems or codes which help to make the world comprehensible to viewers and readers: they provide order and help us link together what would otherwise appear to be separate events. However, only a relatively small number of codes – organized into an ideology – are used to interpret reality: these become taken-for-granted sets of ideas. They are so taken for granted that they are 'invisible' to those who use them to interpret the world.

This hegemonic view does not suggest that there is no space available for competing viewpoints: the media-propagated ideology is dominant, but it is not monopolistic. Rather, the social world involves a struggle between competing ideologies and there are challenges to current social organization.

Stuart Hall and cultural hegemony

Stuart Hall (1995, first published 1982) argues that each culture in society has a different way of classifying the world. All of the ways in which a culture communicates, including the communications of the mass media, contain systems of signs which represent aspects of its worldview. Different kinds of meaning can be given to the same set of events. For one dominant meaning to emerge and be produced regularly it has to acquire a kind of taken-for-grantedness, Hall argues. Alternative meanings are downgraded and made to seem incredible, even unthinkable or unsayable.

According to Hall, the media **encode** the meanings of the powerful. They are able to do this because they – or at least the majority of them – operate within a framework of consensus. This consensus is constructed: it is an educated, learnt consent, to which the media are central. This is rarely the result of conscious or deliberate manipulation by the state or by powerful interests. Indeed, if it were recognized as being a conscious effort to construct a consensus the legitimacy of media messages would be undermined. Rather, it is unconscious, taken for granted. For instance:

> *When phrasing a question ... a broadcasting interviewer simply takes it for granted that rising wage demands are the sole cause of inflation, he is both 'freely formulating a question' on behalf of the public and establishing a logic which is compatible with the dominant interests in society ... The ideology has 'worked' in such a case because the discourse has spoken itself through him/her.* Hall, 1995, first published 1982

Cultural hegemony and the social construction of meaning

Hall's approach fits very closely with the direction sociology took during the 1980s. This new direction became known as the **linguistic turn**: the examination of the ways in which patterns of communication in society shape our view of reality. Jonathan Potter and Margaret Wetherell (1987) use a newspaper article as an example of this approach:

Islamic Terrorists Blow Up Plane

In Beirut last night the hijackers of the British Airways 727 finally released the passengers and crew. As the gunmen left they detonated a large quantity of explosive and the plane was quickly gutted by fire. This followed a period of intense negotiation in which the authorities made it clear that they were not going to meet the hijackers' main demands.

Potter and Wetherell make a number of points about this article. First, a newspaper reader would be very familiar with this type of story. It fits into a stereotypical pattern which we categorize as 'hijackings'. Second, some of the terms in the story are loaded with evaluations: 'the gunmen', 'hijackers' and 'terrorists' all have negative associations. Third, the combined effect is to place this story firmly into ways of thinking and understanding the world in much the way that Stuart Hall suggests.

Discourse analysis

Norman Fairclough (1995) shows how discourse analysis can uncover the role of the media in the production of cultural hegemony. (For a discussion of discourse analysis, see pp. 559–60.)

In his study of a 1993 edition of the television programme *Crimewatch UK*, Fairclough describes how a crime is re-enacted for the cameras, how the presenter comments on it and appeals for help, and how at the end a police officer provides further information. Friends, family and sometimes victims themselves are included in the presentation, as are members of the rescue services. Thus, there are three 'voices': police, journalists and 'ordinary people'.

The commentary to the re-enactment provides immediacy by using the historic present tense ('It's six o'clock and Claire is …') and by appealing directly to the viewer ('Were you in the vicinity?'). The personal lives of victims are described in detail and witnesses speak in everyday language ('It suddenly dawned on me …') so that the presentation is made more like a soap opera. Another kind of programme, the biography, is also alluded to ('She was in the Duke of Edinburgh Scheme'), as are police dramas.

In discourse analysis this is referred to as **intertextuality**: the styles, methods and content of different sorts of texts (in this case, television programmes) are drawn upon and used in other contexts. Fairclough demonstrates the complex nature of *Crimewatch*'s discourse in this regard, with its mix of textual styles including drama, narrative, public appeal, police work and biography.

According to Fairclough, programmes like *Crimewatch* work to bring together the state and the people. Politicians and state institutions have lost much of their public credibility, and there is a crisis of legitimacy for the police, who are often portrayed as corrupt and inept, in contrast to a nostalgic vision of 'the bobby on his beat' in the past. *Crimewatch* serves to construct a relationship of trust and cooperation. The programme presents the work of policing as a joint effort between police, journalists and ordinary people.

The key point of this approach is that discourse does not just represent reality – it creates it. A problem with discourse analysis, however, is that it represents only the analyst's reading: in this case, Fairclough's. Messages are **polysemic** (that is, they potentially have multiple meanings) and audience reception studies (discussed below) show how difficult it is to decode media messages.

Fairclough acknowledges this at the end of his account. He explains that *Crimewatch* legitimizes police work and redefines the relationship between the public and the state: 'Or at least appears to do so: it would be fascinating to know what audiences make of this programme.'

This problem is apparent in John Fiske's reading of California District Attorney Gil Garcetti's televised response to the acquittal of O.J. Simpson, the famous black sportsman accused of murdering his wife and her friend:

> *'Apparently', [Garcetti] said, 'the decision was based on emotion that overlapped reason.' On the jury that reached this decision sat eight African American women, and only one white person, and in the word 'emotion' Garcetti was simultaneously blackening and feminizing the verdicts. Loaded into his opposition between 'reason' and 'emotion' were the social differences between the knowledges of a white, rational, educated male … and of a black, emotional, uneducated female.* Fiske, 2000

The reading of a single sentence in this way is highly contestable.

The Glasgow Media Group and cultural hegemony

The Glasgow Media Group has made many studies of television news. (Its website can be found at www.gla.ac.uk/centres/mediagroup.) It concludes that the worldview of journalists serves to predetermine and structure what is to be taken as important or significant and what interpretation is to be placed upon it. This fundamentally affects the character and content of 'the news'. The Group's studies examine the evidence to test and illustrate the cultural hegemony argument.

In *Bad News* (1976), *More Bad News* (1980), *Really Bad News* (1982) and *War and Peace News* (1985) content analyses of television output, and the quantification of types of stories and the way they are presented, are used to demonstrate the partial nature of television news reporting (see Chapter 14 for a discussion of content analysis). The Group concludes:

- The discourse of broadcast news is 'ideologically loaded'. Phrases which evoke attitudes and emotions ('connotative codes'), such as 'trouble', 'radical' and 'pointless strike', all structure listeners' perspectives on stories.
- Visuals are similarly loaded with connotative codes. The camera recording from behind police lines encourages the viewer to identify with the police. The contrast between calm studio shots of managers being interviewed and groups of strikers shouting over each other at the factory gates reinforces dominant messages of dangerous strikers.
- Stories are reported in a way that reproduces the viewpoint of powerful interests because these interests have greater access to the media. Their viewpoints appear 'normal' to journalists.
- Media professionals set the agenda about the most important issues of the day. For example, the effects of strikes are more likely to be reported than their causes. Picket-line violence is emphasized rather than police violence and intimidation. Such dominant themes are likely to recur in the news and serve to reinforce each other.

- Content analysis by the Group suggests that news coverage of party politics is sympathetic towards the political centre ground. What media professionals see as 'extremism' will be treated unsympathetically or remain unreported.

In these ways and others, television news very largely echoes the interests and attitudes of the dominant class in society. The effects of this worldview are twofold. First, it defines what counts as 'news', whose opinions are important enough to be sought, who should be interviewed and so on. Second, it provides journalists with a way of interpreting events and 'explaining' them.

In *War and Peace News* (1985) and *Getting the Message* (1993) the Glasgow Media Group add some elements from traditional Marxist theory to their analysis of media bias. For example, they stress the pressures on broadcasting journalists to present the establishment viewpoint, even if it does not accord with their own view. Sometimes, however, journalists can escape these pressures and present a critical point of view or even one that is anti-establishment. Jonathan Dimbleby is named specifically as a television journalist whose views are out of the ordinary for a journalist, and who has been able to use the media to express them.

In their 1990 publication, *Seeing and Believing*, edited by Greg Philo, the Glasgow Media Group moved from studies of media content to audience studies, usually using group discussions and various group exercises. Here they note, in agreement with Stuart Hall, that audiences do not always accept or believe what they are told. The cultural background of the audience, their experience (of actually being on a picket line, for example) and other characteristics can enable them to 'read' media messages in a variety of ways.

The Glasgow Media Group has moved from a position which simply 'read off' or assumed media effect from an examination of media content. It now theorizes what it calls a **circuit of communication**. This circuit is a system of communication in which production, content and reception of messages are constantly affecting each other, although in unequal ways.

Philo and Miller (2005) define the four key elements of the communication process as:

1. **Social and political institutions**, such as business organizations, government, lobbyists, the PR industry, research and interest groups. These influence the supply of information and adopt planned media strategies as part of their image management approach. This increasingly takes place at supranational as well as national levels.

> *Contemporary corporate and governmental public relations activities are terminally lacking in good faith, they debase the political language and stride forward hand in hand with an increasingly commercialised media – ever ready to take handouts from PR operatives.* Philo and Miller, 2005, p. 100

2. **The media and their content**, including both factual and fictional forms. Within news broadcasting, the media tend to prioritize certain types of issue and to cultivate certain types of relationship. Official sources tend to be accorded most weight, but increasingly commercial forces drive media content. This is reflected in the shift towards lifestyle features, reality TV and live reports, away from detailed or investigative journalism.
3. **The public**, which consists of different social, professional and political groups. The audience will bring varying degrees of prior knowledge to their understanding of reported events, just as they will bring different cultural values and interests.
4. **Decision makers**, in different tiers of government, as well as in other social and political institutions.

The circuits of communication approach involves simultaneous examination of these elements in order to understand how media content is both produced and received. From the Glasgow Media Group perspective, clear agendas drive the news, but some sections of the audience may be critical of the messages conveyed, particularly if they have direct experience of the issues being reported.

In their research into understandings of the Israeli/Palestinian conflict, for example, the Group found that audiences had little knowledge of the background to the conflict. In a sample of 300 young people, 71 per cent did not realize that when a news story contained a reference to 'occupied territories' it was in fact the Israelis who were the occupiers.

The Glasgow Media Group argue that this is because news broadcasts centre on conveying dramatic images of current events rather than explaining the context. However, they also believe that in this case broadcasters shy away from challenging a strong pro-Israeli stance on the part of the US establishment, which is also shared by the UK to some extent.

In other research, an audience sample was initially uninterested in coverage of African conflicts, but their interest increased dramatically when the background and meaning of events were explained.

Criticisms of cultural hegemony

Theories of cultural hegemony are criticized by pluralists, who point out that not all journalists share a dominant ideology. Many journalists attempt to expose the unacceptable side of capitalism. The Watergate scandal, which toppled from power the US president Richard Nixon, is just one example of the sort of work of such reporters.

Similarly, in the late 1990s, press reporting of Tory 'sleaze' was instrumental in triggering the downfall of three Conservative politicians: Neil Hamilton, Jonathan Aitken and Jeffrey Archer.

The model of cultural hegemony assumes a single unified culture among media professionals, but this is highly questionable. Postmodern perspectives argue that organizations have multiple cultures, many of which can be in conflict. An example of such cultural complexity in a media organization is provided by journalist Mike Royko, who describes the purchase of the *Chicago Sun-Times*, a successful quality newspaper, by Rupert Murdoch's News Corporation:

We knew that there had been publications that he basically left alone, like the Village Voice, *and we thought that he might do that here, since this was a very successful quality newspaper. But as soon as his people started coming in, it was clear that this wasn't their intention. They come in like a bunch of pirates. It's unusual for a Chicago newspaper guy to view somebody coming in as a bunch of thugs – I mean, we're generally thought of as pretty hard-nosed newspaper people.* Belfield et al., 1994

Pluralists argue that the media cannot reflect the views of the dominant class in Britain because sections of that class are highly critical of much of the political and other reporting of the broadcast media. Like media professionals, the dominant class is itself extremely varied in character. Those on the political right frequently argue that there is a liberal 'bias' in the BBC and some of the other media. Throughout the 1980s there were numerous instances of the Conservative administration complaining about BBC reportage.

These anxieties have continued to surface. In 2007, an internal BBC report identified a liberal consensus amongst staff (Gibson, 2007). In particular, it highlighted concerns about how to fulfil the BBC's statutory brief of impartiality in the face of intensive single-issue campaigns, such as 'Make Poverty History' and Live 8.

Organizational factors and media content

The internal characteristics of media organizations provide useful information which helps to explain media content and effects. For instance, Jonathan Bignell (1997) points out that 'news' is not a fixed category: how it is interpreted depends on the type of media involved. Quality newspapers have more foreign news, tabloids more personality-based news. It is the professional workers within media organizations who make selections based on the values within their organization.

Galtung and Ruge (1965) describe the conscious and unconscious criteria used by journalists in this process. The more criteria a potential story fulfils, the more likely it is that the story will be printed. Here are some of the criteria that Galtung and Ruge list:

- **Frequency**: short-lived events are preferred to long drawn-out events.
- **Threshold**: the more intense the event, the more preferred it is (for example, a very large annual increase in road deaths as opposed to a small one).
- **Unambiguity**: the more easily interpreted an event is, the better, particularly if it fits into a known category of news stories, such as 'royal stories'.
- **Meaningfulness**: relevance to the assumed reader.
- **Consonance**: the story's closeness to the assumed reader's expectations or desires (for example, the demand for news about a royal marriage).
- **Unexpectedness**: unexpected events are preferred to expected ones.
- **Reference to elite nations**: stories about powerful (rather than powerless) nations are preferred.
- **Reference to elite persons**: stories about powerful or famous people are preferred to stories about powerless or obscure people.
- **Reference to persons**: stories which can be simplified by personifying the issues into one or more people are desirable, especially if there is conflict between these people.
- **Reference to something negative**: bad news is more newsworthy than good news.

Other factors affecting media content

This approach has its limitations. Oliver Boyd-Barrett (1995) points out that media professionals are also influenced by social structures over which they have limited control. He claims that studies such as that of Galtung and Ruge (1965) fail to explore the origin of the sets of values they identify. They stress what is known as **active gatekeeping**: the systematic inclusion or exclusion of certain types of content. They attribute too much to human agency and remain unaware of the structural constraints placed upon it. As Boyd-Barrett puts it, news values have to be 'explained as well as identified'. Cultural hegemony theories are able to do this in terms of the dominant worldview, which shapes the perceptions and choices of media professionals.

There are other sets of structural factors which condition media content. First, there are recurrent practices within organizations, habitual behaviours which have grown up over a long period of time. They are not necessarily obvious to media professionals or to audiences because they are so taken for granted. Here is an example from American television:

In the television industry ... the evening news programme ... will open with a teaser of the top few stories and a brief tape clip [and] will feature a half-dozen hard news stories, all or almost all with tape; none ... longer than 90 seconds. There will be a male and female anchor (the male ... older than the female), a weather person, and a sports anchor. One or two will be members of a minority group ... The news team will send us off with a 'feel good feature'. The form is set and so familiar we rarely notice it, much less stop to ask why. A large part of the answer ... is that there are industrywide constraints – unwritten 'rules' that characterize what TV is ... They maintain themselves because they are familiar, taken for granted ... by both those in the industry and the audience. Grossberg et al., 1998

CBS president Rob Wood said that his freshest ideas came in his early years at the top. After a time 'you learn the rules too well and don't think in new directions' (Turow, 1982).

Second, there are the constraints of production processes, which frequently affect what is possible. The origins of much news coverage, for example, often lie in official sources such as press conferences, parliamentary reports and camera coverage, interviews with government ministers, or reports from journalists 'embedded' with the military. Regular 'diary' events provide a staple diet for news organizations, reappearing each year.

The demand for a constant, predictable supply of news to the newsroom demands that this is so. Technical conditions often influence what is not in the news: the absence of cameras or the costs associated with news-gathering in distant places will mean that some stories never reach the newsroom.

Role and influence of the media: audiences and their responses

This section explores the relationship between media messages and the audience. Sociological thinking about this relationship has developed from simple models of cause and effect to increasingly complex models about the nature of media texts, the audience and 'effects'. It is important to note that this has been an extremely intensive area of research into the media; however:

> *if, after over sixty years of a considerable amount of research, direct effects of media upon behaviour have not been clearly identified, then we should conclude that they are simply not there to be found.* Gauntlett, 1998

Gauntlett may be right, or it may be that the effects, and their causes, are subtle, complex and difficult to pin down. If the latter is the case then perhaps the theories and methods of research used need to be developed further.

The hypodermic model

Store withdraws video game after brutal killing

Source: *Daily Mail*, 29 July 2004

This early model makes an analogy between media messages and a drug injected by a hypodermic syringe. The medium itself (television, newspapers, film, etc.) is the syringe; the medium's message or content is what is injected. The audience is the patient.

The concept of **narcotization** also draws on this model: narcotization refers to the political, physical and mental apathy supposedly induced by the mass media. Herbert Marcuse wrote in *One Dimensional Man* (1964): 'the hypnotic power of the mass media deprives us of the capacity for critical thought which is essential if we are to change the world'.

Shannon and Weaver's (1949) early model of media effect, shown in Figure 12.1, is essentially a hypodermic model, although the authors recognize that external factors ('noise') may introduce differences between the message transmitted and that received.

The hypodermic model is now out of favour, but in early studies of the media it was usually at least implicit. Laboratory studies conducted by psychologists such as

Figure 12.1 Shannon and Weaver's model of communication

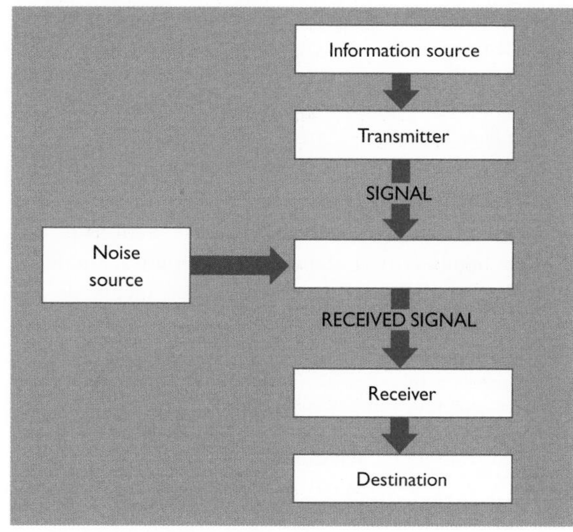

Source: C. Shannon and W. Weaver (1949) *The Mathematical Theory of Communication*, University of Illinois Press, Urbana.

Bandura, Ross and Ross (1963) looked for simple cause-and-effect relationships between a media message and the audience response. They concluded that film images were as effective in teaching aggression as real-life models, particularly in boys, who tended to imitate the postures, actions and words of film aggressors they had seen.

For Bandura and his colleagues, their experiments confirmed the 'imitative' model of media effects. This is a development of the **social learning approach**, which suggests that people learn new behaviours through their observation of the behaviour of others (Miller and Dollard, 1941). This is a very simple hypodermic model, to which Bandura added the idea that learning is more effective if the observed behaviour is reinforced in the daily life of the observer, including via media messages. Seeing attractive film characters behaving in particular ways and being rewarded for their behaviour tends to reinforce imitative behaviour. This is referred to as **the disinhibitory effect**.

There are a number of problems with this kind of approach:

1. It is unable to define what it means by 'violence' or other behaviours that are supposedly imitated:

   > *There appears to be considerable confusion as to what is filmed aggression. For some it is an adult hitting a ... doll, for others a prize fight, and for [others] ... it is Westerns or war shows. Few investigators, if any, seem to be concerned that different types of filmed aggression will have different effects on different types of children.* Noble, 1975

2. As we have already discussed, audiences are highly diverse and have different responses.
3. The imitative or social learning model tends to concentrate on short-term effects only, and ignores the cumulative effects of exposure to many messages in the normal course of daily life.
4. The model largely fails to take into account the different 'uses' audience members make of media content and the different ways there are of interacting

with the media (for example, whether a television programme is watched closely or used as background).

5 The model ignores other media effects. Eysenck and Nias (1978) point out that media messages may enable individuals to express and discharge powerful emotions safely – a process called **catharsis** – and thus prevent behaviours that might otherwise have happened. Media messages may desensitize individuals to the effects of violence (for example, by not showing them), but they may also sensitize individuals to violence when its effects are shown, thus perhaps preventing violence in real life.

However, despite all these problems, this model of media effects is still very popular. The mass media themselves tend to reproduce it when they report crimes that were supposedly 'caused' by the media. Politicians and campaigners against sex and violence in the media also assume this model when they argue for greater censorship or complain about particular programmes.

The normative model and the two-step flow

'Normative' refers to ways of behaving that come to be considered as 'normal' and that regulate social interaction. The **normative model** is a more sophisticated social theory of media influence than the hypodermic model.

Studies in the 1940s and 1950s such as Robert Merton's *Mass Persuasion* (1946) and Katz and Lazarsfeld's *Personal Influence* (1955) (see pp. 712–13) discovered that a **two-step flow** process of media influence was operating. The first step is when a media message actually reaches a member of the audience. The second step is its interpretation and influence, which are affected by social interaction. Such social interaction means that other people, but especially those whose views are respected ('opinion leaders'), shape how an individual responds to the media and any effects that the media have.

Advertising campaigns may choose to utilize the two-step model. Vernette (2004) discusses ways in which women's fashion can target opinion leaders via media plans, especially utilizing magazines. He states that this entails a three-stage approach. First, opinion leaders must be identified. Second, the specific areas in which individuals can act as opinion leaders need to be established. Third, the media affinity of the opinion leaders must be assessed to determine how best they can be reached via media messages.

Vernette's research, based in France, found that the typical profile of a fashion opinion leader was a female employee or student aged between 15 and 35. These individuals tended to display lifestyle values of 'open-mindedness, wanderlust, throwing parties [and] the importance given to friends' (Vernette, 2004, p. 96). The identified opinion leaders were more exposed to advertising than non-leaders, as they read many more magazines, and they discussed advertising more frequently. Vernette was also able to identify specific magazines that appealed to opinion leaders, thus ensuring that advertisements placed within them would reach the target group, who would then go on to discuss these brands with non-leaders within their social networks.

An extension of the two-step flow idea is the multi-step flow model, which recognizes that there are successive stages in the social interpretation of media messages. Such messages are discussed and used in everyday life and become integrated into the cultural world. An example of this process is provided by Dorothy Hobson (1990). Hobson describes her research on 'Jacqui', a telephone sales manager for an internationally known pharmaceutical company. Jacqui describes how women in her office spent some of their working day:

> *Somebody would say something like 'Who saw* Coronation Street *last night?' and Anita would say 'Oh, I saw it!' and you'd sort of have Mary sitting there going 'Oh, my God!' and making comments about* Coronation Street *and doing some stupid impression beneath the desk and you'd say 'Shut up Mary, shut up!' and everybody would go 'Ssh, ssh, Anita, tell us what happened' … Anita … would go into great detail about what had happened and … everybody would sit and listen and if you'd seen it the night before and she missed bits out you'd say 'Er, wait a minute, he wasn't very happy about that', or whatever.*
> Hobson, 1990

The conversation quickly turned to their own lives and interests and to discussions of what they would do if they were in the same circumstances as the characters. Women in the office were enticed to watch these programmes just so that they could join in the discussions.

Hobson's kind of approach is useful because it focuses clearly on media audiences and what they do with messages. However, it pictures people as strongly conditioned by their environment, particularly by opinion leaders and by social norms. In practice people can create and change norms, break them and redefine them. The theory is also unclear about whether the norms are based on consensus or whether they are imposed on people by powerful groups within society.

The uses and gratifications model

The **uses and gratifications model** stresses that different people use the media in different ways in order to obtain different sorts of pleasure or meet different sorts of needs. Individuals are viewed as active interpreters and choice-makers, rather than as passive receivers of media messages. For example, two people watching a party political broadcast might be satisfying very different needs, or obtaining very different gratifications.

Dennis McQuail (1972) suggests there are the following types of uses and gratifications available from the media:

- **Diversion**: an escape from routine.
- **Personal relationships**: (a) surrogate membership of a community, like that in *Hollyoaks* or *Coronation Street*, or (b) enabling us to operate better in a real community, like Jacqui's workmates.
- **Personal identity**: helping us to explore and confirm our identity – for example, the person who sees using the internet as confirming their self-image as up to date and efficient. Media use may also challenge and weaken one's sense of identity.
- **Surveillance**: the feeling of knowing what's going on – for example, information from the news about the chancellor's annual budget.

The European study reported in Livingstone and Bovill (2001) (see p. 716) also found evidence of children in different countries finding uses and deriving gratifications differently for different media. They found that children used television and video for excitement, with electronic games also used for this purpose. TV and video in particular were also used in the avoidance of boredom. Learning was another use – mostly from print and electronic media and the internet.

In his early work, James Lull (1990) also adopted the uses and gratifications model. He made a list of the social uses of television, shown in Table 12.2. It is clear that men and women use the media in different ways and obtain different types of gratifications. Some types of media and media messages may not be gratifying at all for some women. Likewise, older retired people and younger people are likely to derive different gratifications from media content. (These points are discussed in more detail below.)

However, the uses and gratifications approach fails to raise important questions about why people have particular needs or why they choose specific forms of gratification. In particular it suggests that 'needs' are pre-existent. In fact the media can also create needs (for example, advertising can be very effective in creating the 'need' for a particular product). Like the hypodermic model it treats people as asocial and does not recognize that needs are partly socially created (in this it is different from the normative approach). It focuses on individual differences, personality and psychology, and ignores the cultural context and social background which structure audience responses.

The uses and gratifications approach is functionalist (see pp. 7–9) in character, suggesting that the media perform a function but ignoring the dysfunctional nature of the media.

Table 12.2 The social uses of television

Structural
Environmental: background noise; entertainment
Regulative: punctuation of time and activity; talk patterns
Relational
Communication facilitation: experience common ground; conversational entrance; anxiety reduction; agenda for talk; value clarification
Affiliation/avoidance: physical, verbal contract/neglect; family solidarity; family relaxant; conflict reduction; relationship maintenance
Social learning: decision making; behaviour modelling; problem solving; value transmission; legitimization; information dissemination; schooling
Competence/dominance: role enactment; role reinforcement; substitute role portrayal; intellectual validation; authority exercise; gatekeeping; argument facilitation

Source: J. Lull (1990) *Inside Family Viewing: Ethnographic Research on Television's Audiences*, Routledge, London.

The interpretative model

In the **interpretative model**, audiences are believed to 'filter' media messages. Not only do people use the media in different ways; they also attend to and receive media messages in a selective way, ignoring, reacting to, forgetting or reinterpreting messages according to their own viewpoint. In other words they actively interpret the media message. James Halloran (1970) points out that this approach helped researchers to 'get away from the habit of thinking in terms of what media do to people, and to substitute for it the idea of what people do with the media'.

One important way in which people engage with media messages is **intertextually**; that is, they may read one text in relation to others (Fiske, 1988), or they may use one message system (for example, newspaper accounts of the lives of stars) to engage with another (for example, a television programme which includes one of those stars as an actor). Fiske notes that in watching a soap opera a viewer will move between different levels:

- **Engagement**: 'I felt I was really there with the characters.'
- **Detachment**: 'He will die on this journey because I've heard the actor wants to leave the series.'
- **Referential**: 'That man is very much like my own boss.'

According to Fiske, any one text is necessarily read in relationship to others: an audience brings a range of textual knowledge to bear. For Fiske, the audience is powerful: it is people who make popular culture in the way they respond to, consume or reject the offerings of the media. The culture industry is far from the all-powerful meaning-maker that Adorno and others would have it be.

David Buckingham: reading audiences

The ways in which people interpret the media partly depend on their level of media literacy. David Buckingham (1993) suggests that someone with only a low level of television literacy might be able to do the following:

- Distinguish between voices on a soundtrack or between figures and backgrounds.
- Understand the principle of editing and follow a narrative.
- Relate sound and image tracks together.
- Grasp elements of 'television grammar' such as camera angles and movements.

This sort of understanding of television might be typical of a child. However, Buckingham suggests that someone with a higher level of television literacy might be able to read 'behind' the screen images and sounds and do the following:

- Categorize programmes into types and understand their different conventions.
- Describe different ways of producing narrative structure and be aware of the way narrative time is manipulated through editing.
- Infer character traits and construct psychologically coherent characters from a few clues.
- Be aware of how viewers are invited to identify with particular characters.

- Understand the production process and the circulation and distribution of programmes.
- Infer the motivations and intentions of programme producers.

Clearly, these different levels of media literacy will influence the interpretation process.

Although the interpretative model was a useful step forward in understanding media effects, it has a number of problems. Media messages are much stronger than this model often suggests: they carry a dominant and powerful influence. Also, media messages are not isolated. They are repeated frequently and are reinforced in different ways in different media: they have a cumulative impact.

Similarly, the model sees individuals as interpreting messages in a very isolated way. In fact people belong to cultures and subcultures which provide them with particular ways of looking at the media. A person's subculture strongly influences whether they accept, alter or reject the dominant meaning of a media message, as Morley's *Nationwide* study showed (see below).

The structured interpretation model

This model builds on the interpretative model discussed above. It agrees that the audience can interpret media messages in different ways, but suggests there is a **preferred reading** or dominant message, in the way Hall suggests (see p. 718).

So, for example, a news item about the Queen's birthday may be capable of being interpreted in different ways, but one of these is 'easier' than the others because of the way in which the story is presented and because of the general culture in which the item is produced and consumed ('**encoded**' and '**decoded**', to use the jargon). In the UK, the preferred reading might be admiration for a selfless woman who performs public duties in the national interest.

However, complications exist because there are numerous subcultures involved when a single mass media message (or '**text**') is received. To understand a text, researchers cannot just 'read' it themselves but must understand how it is read by different audiences within different subcultures. These subcultures could be associated with age, gender, ethnicity, class, religion, geography, etc.

Some of these audiences are sophisticated and have the ability to read a text in more than one way. For example, a young Muslim audience may react differently to footage of the war in Iraq compared with a young non-Muslim audience. However, reactions cannot simply be inferred on the basis of membership of one group. Muslims watching may also respond as British citizens and as young people, as well as having their responses mediated by factors such as gender or education. The dominant reading is not necessarily the one that all audiences make.

Ien Ang (1991) notes that audiences have traditionally been seen as an undifferentiated mass, in the same way as we think of 'the population' or 'the nation'. Ang argues that we must avoid this sort of model and instead take account of the everyday practices and experiences of audiences themselves. The structured interpretation model attempts to do this.

David Morley and the Nationwide *audience*

David Morley's (1980) study was important because it related 'meaning' to social location. The study focused on audience reception of the daily television magazine programme *Nationwide*, and explored the reactions and readings of a panel of respondents.

Morley played a recording of a single programme item to eighteen groups. The different groups had very different educational, social and economic backgrounds. A second programme item was shown to a further eleven groups, which this time included groups from trade unions and management training centres.

Morley concluded that different socio-economic classes interpret the meaning of a television programme in different ways, although there is no one-to-one relationship between class location and reading.

The media messages in the study were encoded in such a way as to make perfect sense to the bank managers among the respondents. However, the trade unionists saw the *Nationwide* coverage as biased towards management. Younger management trainees saw the coverage as favouring the unions. Meanwhile, middle-class students criticized the programme for its superficiality, and the group of mainly black working-class students saw it as too detailed and boring. Thus, one group approached the programme for information, the other for entertainment. Morley concludes:

> *These examples of the totally contradictory readings of the same programme item ... do provide us with the clearest examples of the way in which the 'meaning' of a programme or a 'message' depends upon the interpretive code which the audience brings to the decoding situation.*
> Morley, 1992

According to Morley, the production of a meaningful message by media professionals in television discourse is always the result of 'work'. It always contains more than one potential 'reading': that is, it is **polysemic**.

Finally, the activity of 'getting meaning' from the message is also complex, however transparent and 'natural' it seems. Morley shows that social location is important in providing a set of cultural 'tools' which we use, usually unconsciously, to decode media messages. These include the language, concepts and assumptions associated with a subculture, other social location or ideological position. Developing Morley's work, Croteau and Hoynes (2001) refer to these as **discursive resources** and point out that different groups of people in society have access to different sets of discursive resources for decoding media messages.

This raises a question about whether the structured interpretation model adopts an over-determined view of individuals, whose attitudes and views are largely conditioned by the social groups to which they belong. Instead of seeing the audience as an undifferentiated mass, as earlier models have done, or even seeing them as divided by class, age, etc. as this one does, postmodernists argue that we need to see them as people interacting with the media in specific social situations. The same person will perceive and react to the same media message in different ways in different contexts. It is therefore difficult or impossible to make generalizations about 'the audience' as such.

Understanding audience reception: the third phase

Pertti Alasuutari (1999) suggests that we can categorize the audience reception approaches examined above under two headings, and that a third approach to understanding the reception of media messages is about to mature.

The first generation of reception research, at its peak during the 1970s, is associated with Hall's notion of encoding and decoding (see p. 718). The new aspect of this compared to many previous studies was its recognition that media texts undergo a process of 'translation', both when they are assembled by specialist groups in the media and when they are read by the audience. Events and messages are encoded or conveyed by means of **signs**. For example, smoking may be used as a 'sign' of a bad as opposed to a good character.

Hall noted that before a message can be put to a use or satisfy a need it must be meaningfully decoded. The emphasis on this process, rather than on simplistic 'effects', marked the start of increasingly sophisticated audience reception studies.

Morley's *Nationwide* research also fits this model and confirms Hall's suggestion that media messages can be decoded differently:

- The **hegemonic code** is the preferred reading encoded by the media professionals.
- The **professional code** interprets messages according to the culture of the professional group to which the viewer belongs.
- The **negotiated code** modifies but does not totally reject the preferred reading.
- The **oppositional code** is one in which the viewer comprehends the message but rejects it.

Crucial to all this is the concept of the **interpretative community**: the culturally coherent group that tends to decode messages in a consistent way.

The second generation of reception studies, from the 1980s, usually relied on ethnographic approaches (see Chapter 14) to study the audience. Such studies often focused on the politics of gender as it related to media messages. So, for example, Lull (1990), Morley (1986) and Silverstone (1991) concentrated on the social uses and the gendered nature of television, particularly within the family. The emphasis of such studies is on the everyday life of a small group of people – not the characteristics of a larger interpretative community – and its implications for the reception of media messages. Some of these studies are discussed below.

Now, a 'third generation' of audience reception studies is developing. Influenced by postmodernist thinking and the linguistic turn in sociology and cultural studies (see p. 718), it adopts what Alasuutari calls 'a constructionist view'. This has begun to question the very notion of 'the audience' itself. Here the identities of the audience are seen as being in flux: people live their lives increasingly in an experimental way, trying new identities and ways of living (Beck, 2002). Gauntlett suggests:

> *Television programmes, pop songs, adverts, movies and the Internet all ... provide numerous kinds of 'guidance' – not necessarily in the obvious form of advice-giving, but in the myriad suggestions of ways of living which they imply. We lap up this material because the social construction of identity today is the knowing construction of identity. Your life is your project – there is no escape. The media provides some of the tools which can be used in this work. Like many other toolkits, however, it contains some good utensils and some useless ones; some that might give beauty to the project and some that might spoil it.*
> Gauntlett, 1998

So the media themselves are now seen as an important part of culture, rather than as a series of separate message generators. As a result, emphasis is placed on the discourses within which 'the public', 'the audience' and 'the world' are understood by audiences and programme makers, and how audiences and programme makers understand themselves. These more recent studies are rooted in a postmodernist approach to understanding the world and the changing nature of the world itself.

Postmodernity, postmodernism and the media

While 'postmodernism' is a philosophical approach to understanding the world, 'postmodernity' is a description of what the world is like, at least as depicted by postmodernists. (For a more detailed discussion of postmodernity, see Chapter 15.)

Postmodernity is a condition which is media-saturated: the media are not just one aspect among many of that condition, but are its intimate, defining aspect. In postmodernity the norm is complexity: there are many meanings and not one deep, profound meaning. Access to the multitude of messages transmitted via the media provides access to these meanings.

For Jean Baudrillard (1988), the communication/media revolution meant that people are engulfed by information to such an extent that the distinction between reality and the word/image which portrays it breaks down into a condition he called **hyperreality**. In this condition – another key characteristic of postmodernity – words, images and the information they convey become open to multiple interpretations, mirroring the breakdown of 'objectivity'. Commenting on this phenomenon, John Fiske (1996) notes:

> *In one hour's television viewing, one of us is likely to experience more images than a member of a non-industrial society would in a lifetime [so] we do not just experience more images ... we live with a completely different relationship between the image and other orders of experience.* Quoted in Lacey, 2002

Media messages are not simply interpreted in one way by a passive audience, but are read in many ways by different portions of the audience or even by the same people at different times. Lash (1999) notes that everyday life becomes pervaded with a reality – in TV, adverts, video, the Walkman, radio-cassette and CD decks in cars, DVD, cable and satellite – which increasingly comprises representations.

Sherry Turkle (1996) echoes Jean Baudrillard when she talks about television as part of the postmodern 'culture of simulation', where we learn to identify with

the simulated world of television more readily than we do with the real world around us. For instance, the bar featured in the television series *Cheers* figured so prominently in the imagination because most people do not have a neighbourhood place where 'everybody knows your name'. Instead, they identified with the place on the screen. Recently, it was given life off the screen as well. Bars designed to look like the one in *Cheers* have sprung up all over the USA, most poignantly in airports, the most anonymous of places. Here, no one will know your name, but you can always buy a drink or a souvenir sweatshirt.

According to Turkle, such simulation has laid the groundwork for the next development in the relationship between reality and simulation. Computers and the virtual worlds they now provide are already adding another dimension to the mediated experience of reality. This can be illustrated by the huge rise in popularity of virtual reality sites such as Second Life, which Jeffries (2006) reports, 'has more than 800,000 registered users, is growing at the extraordinary rate of 20% a month, and is developing an economy larger than those of some real countries'.

In Second Life, users can create their own characters, using avatars. Increasingly, there is crossover between the virtual world and real life, as groups play virtual concerts, property can be leased and companies can advertise.

The global and the local

Postmodernity removes the distinction between the global and the local by linking them with technologies associated with travel and communication, particularly media technologies. Television news in particular plays an increasingly important global role.

The globalization of television news has led to its domination by a mainstream Anglo-American point of view, largely as a result of the limited number of news agencies around the world. Although Oliver Boyd-Barrett (1998) argues that there is an increasing diversity of such news agencies, he concludes that a few major agencies, such as Agence France-Presse, Associated Press, World Television News and Reuters – located primarily in the USA, the UK and France – have dominance in the provision of news.

Baudrillard claimed that one effect of all this is to blur the distinction between image and reality, as we saw in the example of the *Cheers* bar. Another is to undermine traditional concepts and old certainties such as 'duty', 'authority', 'hierarchy' and so on. This is because values are seen as relative, not absolute.

According to theories of postmodernity, we create our own set of values and understandings from the global information around us. In particular the search for a 'true' or authentic self gives way to a 'playfulness' in which personal identity is experimental, expressed and invented through choices of lifestyle. Lifestyles are chosen primarily by selecting those on offer through the media.

Criticisms of postmodernism

Postmodernism has been criticized and attacked from a variety of different points of view (see Chapter 15). For example, Frank Webster (1999) claims there has been no profound change in society as a result of the 'information explosion'. He says that this way of thinking sees technological change as causing social change. This ignores the fact that technologies, like media messages, are interpreted and used in particular ways in particular social contexts, and that technology and society interact with each other.

Webster also argues that postmodernist accounts of the information-rich society fail to ask – much less answer – some important questions: 'What sort of information has increased? Who has generated what kind of information, and for what purposes and with what consequences has it been generated?'

According to Lerner (1994), the failure of postmodernism to answer such questions has had the effect of obscuring poverty, oppression and various forms of inequality around the world, thus foiling attempts to make the world better and more egalitarian.

The media and violence

One area which can be used to illustrate the problematic relationship between the media and audiences is violence. The phrase 'television violence' is often used to express the common fear that violent imagery in programmes breeds aggression in viewers. This links in with the hypodermic model discussed earlier (pp. 722–3).

This fear has also been extended to other forms of media, such as video gaming. Doyle points out that much research on crime simply assumes that the media exert an impact, yet this view has been difficult to substantiate empirically.

> *In something of a parallel to the criminological quest for 'the cause' of crime, some media-effects researchers have continued to search for a reductive lone 'magic bullet' (Cumberbatch and Howitt 1989) – some universal law of how the media directly affects audiences.*
> Doyle, 2006, p. 871

School violence has come to symbolize many of the fears concerning media influence, in particular incidents in the USA such as the Columbine High School shooting in 1999. Two male students, aged 17 and 18, arrived at the school and embarked upon a planned series of killings. During the course of the day, they killed thirteen people and finally took their own lives.

Although by no means the first school shooting in the USA, the killings attracted vast media coverage, much of which focused on youth trends and issues, with blame being variously attached to video games, music and bullying (McCabe and Martin, 2005).

Since Columbine there has been a rising incidence of school shootings, which has led to speculation that the coverage promotes 'copycat' violence. In 2007, shootings took place at Virginia Tech university in the USA, and the gunman left a filmed message, which seemed to portray the Columbine killers as heroes (Deppa, 2007). This message was widely broadcast, which led to concerns that it might in turn fuel further shootings.

Discussing Columbine and studies that employ the idea of copycat violence, McCabe and Martin go on to say:

Add the fact that violence on television is not often immediately punished, that the perpetrators of violence remain relatively unharmed, and that they are also often portrayed as heroic, and it is understandable that copycat violence is appealing. With the continuous coverage of Columbine after the fact, it stands to reason that other incidents should follow. In fact, one incident occurred within a month of Columbine and four within a year of Columbine.

On the subject of school shootings, whether student shooters believe that the media provides them with the ideas and details to carry out such events or whether they perceive that the media has made a celebrity of previous shooters, it certainly is likely that copycat crimes are a very strong possibility. McCabe and Martin, 2005, p. 48

Whilst the idea that student shooters were copying other reported crimes cannot be discounted, it is notable how little empirical evidence is employed in the copycat theory, which rests largely on assumptions and common-sense notions. Indeed, it is unclear from the discussion above which violence is being copied – television violence in general or coverage of school shootings. If the latter, it could hardly be said that the perpetrators remain relatively unharmed or that the violence goes unpunished.

Methodological difficulties in assessing media effects

The above example illustrates some of the difficulties in using empirical evidence to establish the impact of the media on levels of violence. These difficulties are by no means restricted to violent crime, but apply more generally to all forms of crime. Doyle (2006) offers the following cautions regarding research on crime and the media:

- Analysing the texts themselves is not enough; effects on audiences cannot simply be inferred, whichever theoretical approach is used.
- 'Crime in the media' is often treated as if it is a single phenomenon, yet the media, in all its different forms, organizations and contexts, is incredibly diverse.
- Audiences are not homogeneous, as is discussed throughout this chapter. The next section explores in more detail differentiation in relation to social groups.
- Defining and measuring influence within different research traditions has proved difficult. Research has sometimes used quite crude methods – Doyle gives the example of simply counting how much television people watch in order to define them as light or heavy viewers.
- Identifying causality is problematic. For example, fear of crime and viewing of crime programmes seem to be linked, yet it is difficult to establish which comes first. Research which operates under experimental conditions in order to control people's exposure to violent imagery may be difficult to generalize to real-life situations.

Doyle concludes by arguing that it is often easier to demonstrate the impact of the media on politics and policy making than on the audience. This idea is returned to in a more detailed consideration of moral panics later in the chapter (see pp. 730–1).

Role and influence of the media: images and social groups

Popular discussions of the media often focus on their impact on particular social groups. The discussions usually concern whether the media have a negative impact on the social position of women, for example, or minority ethnic groups, different social classes, young or old people, or people with disabilities.

A useful way of looking at this issue is to consider the different phases that media messages pass through: this is known as the **message trajectory**. Four such phases can be readily identified:

1. The media institutions and the message formulation stage
2. The media message content: the nature of the 'text'
3. The audience: behaviour and reception
4. The effects or impact of the message

The following sections discuss these four phases in relation to the various social groups listed above. However, in reality, each of these groups intersects with others: any individual will simultaneously be a member of several social groups – for example, young and disabled. It is important to remember this; otherwise instances of multiple discrimination can remain hidden.

The representation of social groups within media institutions

The representation of social groups within media institutions has an influence on how messages are formulated. Although there have been considerable changes, it is notable that those most commonly in positions of power are older, white, able-bodied men. This picture is not uniformly reflected across all sections and levels of the media, however.

Gender

Creedon (1989) points out that there has been a 'gender switch' in media industries, so that the media are dominated by 'pink collar' workers (that is, women).

However, Croteau and Hoynes (2001) show that in the USA in the mid-1990s women occupied only 6 per cent of top newspaper management positions, wrote only 19 per cent of front-page stories, occupied only 20 per cent of news director posts in television stations, and presented only 20 per cent of television news reports. A 'glass ceiling' is effectively in operation within the media.

Comparable figures apply in other media and the percentages are similar or more pronounced in other nations. Issues which are of particular concern to women are therefore frequently ignored or trivialized. According

to some researchers this is due to conscious manipulation by men; according to others it is the result of patriarchal cultural hegemony.

Ethnicity

Although there is a high proportion of black and Asian television presenters (BSC, 1999), there are very few representatives of minority ethnic groups in more senior management positions. In 2001, Greg Dyke, then Director General of the BBC, famously declared it to be 'hideously white' (Dyke, 2002). Although a number of initiatives were launched to promote ethnic diversity, Hundal (2006) claims that there has been little significant change.

In North America, the media, at least in part, are more open to previously excluded minorities. Yet unequal practices remain. Benson (2005) reports that between 1978 and 2000 the proportion of members of minority ethnic groups in the total population rose from 19 per cent to nearly 30 per cent. Across the same period, the proportion of minority ethnic newspaper journalists rose from 4 per cent to 12 per cent, and amongst television journalists the proportion was higher at 20 per cent. However, under 10 per cent of editorial management roles in both industries are held by minority ethnic journalists.

Studies of influential Sunday morning news programmes show that there is still a strong ethnic and gender bias, as illustrated in Figures 12.2 and 12.3. Guests on the programmes are overwhelmingly male and white.

Class, age and disability

People in senior positions in media organizations are mostly middle-class and usually older than most other media workers.

People with disabilities are rather poorly represented within media institutions. Anne Karpf notes in *Doctoring the Media* (1988): 'Employment is the nub of the problem. As long as media images of disability continue to be shaped by able-bodied people, and intended for an able-bodied audience, the stereotypes will flow.'

Representations of social groups in media texts

Media representations of social groups vary considerably. The treatment of minority ethnic groups is very different, for example, in popular newspapers compared to the treatment in television comedy and film. Changes in social attitudes and awareness over the years have led in some cases to marked differences in the representation of particular social groups in the same media.

The explosion in demand for media 'software' – programming content – means that no matter how old or challenging to contemporary views, many programmes are continuously recycled by cable and satellite companies. This diversity makes generalizing about media representations of social groups both difficult and hazardous.

Representations of gender in the media

The relative numbers of women and men portrayed in the media depend very much on the particular medium and type of programme. On terrestrial and satellite television, for example, males outnumber females in all programme types (BSC, 1999), but a higher percentage of those females are likely to be portrayed in major roles.

However, numbers alone are not the most important criterion. The nature of the representation is important.

Traditionally limited roles for women in early films and television comedies are less likely to be found in modern productions. Thus *Buffy the Vampire Slayer* is quite a different sort of young woman (and potential role model) when compared to the roles played by women in

Figure 12.2 Total guests on Sunday morning TV news programmes in the USA, by gender, 2005–6

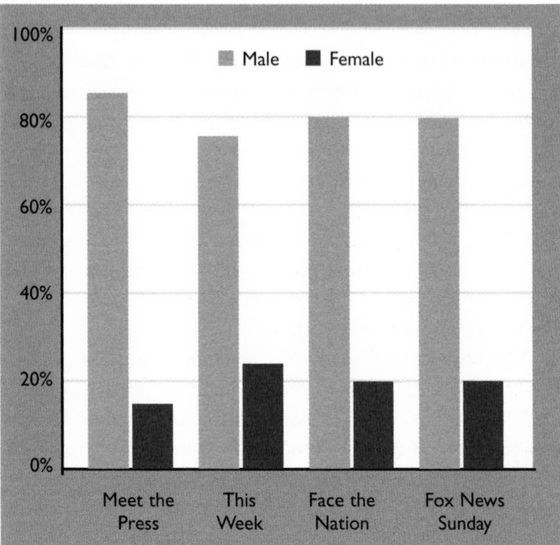

Source: Media Matters (2007) 'Sunday shutout: the lack of gender and ethnic diversity on the Sunday morning talk shows': http://mediamatters.org/SundayShowDiversity

Figure 12.3 Total guests on Sunday morning TV news programmes in the USA, by ethnicity, 2005–6

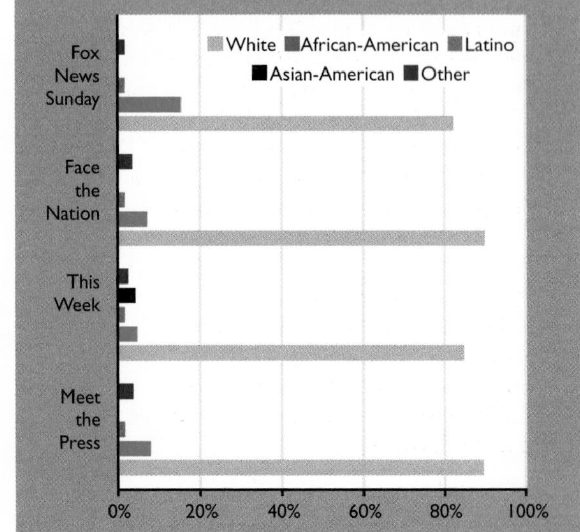

Source: Media Matters (2007) 'Sunday shutout: the lack of gender and ethnic diversity on the Sunday morning talk shows': http://mediamatters.org/SundayShowDiversity

Figure 12.4 Women news presenters make unpalatable facts more human, more watchable and improve ratings

Source: Topfoto

Table 12.3 Level of appearance, by gender (terrestrial television)

Level of appearance	Male N	Male %	Female N	Female %	Total N	Total %
Major role	1,482	16	1,080	23	2,562	18
Minor role	1,474	16	693	15	2,168	16
Incidental/ interviewee	6,217	68	2,922	62	9,139	66
Totals	9,174	100	4,695	100	13,869	100

Source: BSC (1999) *Monitoring Report* 7, Broadcasting Standards Commission, London, p. 100.

film and television of the 1950s and 1960s. Meanwhile, representations of men have softened too, with the Superman of *Smallville* or *The New Adventures of Superman* being quite different from earlier versions – he is more sensitive and 'feminine'.

However, it is important to remember that the earlier forms of gender representation do not simply go away – increasingly, they live on as old programmes are recycled on cable and satellite television, so that audiences are exposed to both old-style and newer images of gender. Furthermore, different aspects of the media represent gender in very different ways. Ivory (2006) argues that representations within video games may be one reason why most gamers are still male. He found that female characters were under-represented and often portrayed in a heavily sexualized way.

Non-fictional television programmes also tend to present a limited range of images of women. While newsreaders are increasingly likely to be women, this trend can be linked to the growing '**intimization**' of television news. This new stress on intimacy and emotion – traditionally regarded as feminine attributes – has provided an employment opportunity for women, whereas the earlier 'rationalistic' approach to the news was more clearly linked to male values.

However, while news and weather presenters are much more likely to be female than in the past, they are usually young and attractive. Such trends are not difficult to associate with the domination of news provision by global corporations discussed above (see pp. 714–15).

These aspects of the feminization of news are reflected in magazines for women. Gauntlett (2002) argues that contemporary women's magazines such as *Cosmopolitan* and *Glamour* present a fairly consistent set of messages about what is important (primarily personal beauty and sex), with advice on how to reach the ideal being offered.

Nowadays men's lifestyle magazines, such as *FHM*, *Maxim* and *Loaded*, offer a kind of mirror to this:

> *Men's lifestyle magazines represent a reassertion of old-fashioned masculine values, or a 'backlash' against feminism. Whilst certain pieces in the magazines might support such an argument, this is not their primary purpose or selling point. Instead ... their existence and popularity shows men rather insecurely trying to find their place in the modern world, seeking help regarding how to behave in relationships, and advice on how to earn the attention, love and respect of women and the friendship of other men.* Gauntlett, 2002

Advertising is also a significant medium of representation. Whilst some gender stereotyping may be less overt, in that women are not exclusively cast as the sole custodians of domestic responsibilities, for example, persistent characterizations live on. Scharrer *et al.* (2006), in a content analysis of US prime-time commercials featuring household tasks, found that men were usually portrayed as amusingly incompetent and inept. Thus women continued to be implicitly portrayed as uniquely competent in the domestic realm.

New media, by contrast, present a particularly difficult area in which to characterize representations of men and women. There is such a variety of representation, and so far such a lack of an obviously 'mainstream' sector of the new media, that simple overviews of representation are impossible. Representations of both men and women range from the one-dimensionally sexual representation of hard and soft pornography, to the very sophisticated, nuanced or non-traditional representations found in e-zines, discussion sites and special interest websites.

Representations of sexuality in the media

Representations of gender intersect with representations of sexuality. Sex and sexuality in the media is an issue that raises concern, even 'moral panic', amongst some sections of the population and the media themselves. The concept of a **moral panic** is one that has been widely used within sociology and particularly within criminology. It stems mainly from Cohen's influential *Folk Devils and Moral Panics: The Creation of the Mods and Rockers* (2002, first published 1972).

This model of studying representations and their consequences has different stages. The media sensationalize a fairly mundane event or issue, often based around a social group, which initiates a process of **deviance amplification**. This entails a series of media commentators, politicians and other authorities, whom Cohen terms 'socially accredited experts', delivering moral condemnation.

Moral panics often occur in periods of dislocating social change. They reflect wider social anxieties and serve to consolidate social norms.

Jewkes explains the operation of the deviancy amplification spiral as describing:

> *what happens when a society outlaws a particular group. As negative social reaction escalates and the 'deviants' become increasingly isolated, they become more and more criminally oriented. The spiral of deviancy may go on for weeks or even months, but it never spirals out of control for a number of reasons. Media interest will eventually wane and move on to other issues and, after a period of time, the 'folk devil' becomes familiar and therefore is perceived as being less of a threat. Ways of coping with the perceived threat are evolved, either as a result of new legislation introduced to minimize or eliminate the problem, or more mundane strategies evolved by the people most affected.* Jewkes, 2004, p. 69

In reporting the coverage of a number of 'moral panics', Chas Critcher (2003) notes the very different ways in which parts of the media reported the issues. With Aids, for example, sections of the press initially depicted the disease as a 'gay plague', blaming a stereotyped 'deviant minority' for the problem. However, there were other representations. Gay and medical groups were able to use a range of media to argue for a more balanced view. Later, the government delivered a leaflet to every house with the slogan 'Don't die of ignorance', and a television advertising campaign was also launched. In the end the anti-gay message of some sections of the press was subsumed under a message of safe sex and harm minimization.

Although this example does not refer to criminal activity, a similar reaction against 'deviancy' can be observed. The example illustrates ways in which the moral panic becomes contained. Gillet (2003) argues that much gay activism became institutionalized and assimilated.

Conversely, the story is a very different one for another 'deviant minority' – paedophiles. Here, according to Critcher, there has been a moral panic about 'stranger danger', which constructed a figure of fear and hate under the blanket category 'paedophile'. Actual threats to children – for example, road traffic accidents and abuse by members of their own family – far greater threats statistically – are obscured rather than clarified by the media's representation of and panic about paedophiles. That scary name, with a hint of medical terminology about it, serves to label a few strangers as psychopaths and to render everyone else as 'just normal'.

Jewkes (2004) identifies a number of problems with the moral panic model. She argues that not all groups can be seen as equally maligned, as some may be more unfairly targeted than others, as in the two examples above. Concepts of deviancy and morality are used rather simplistically, with little concern for the context of social inequalities in which they operate.

McRobbie and Thornton (1995) point out that early versions of the moral panic model tended to conceive of society as one entity which shared a reaction of panic, whilst more recent understandings, influenced by postmodern sensibilities, would take a more differentiated approach.

Representations of ethnicity in the media

Generalizing about representations of ethnicity in the media is also difficult, as some subsections of broadcast, print and film media are oriented to and sensitive towards questions of ethnicity (for example, programmes and satellite channels dedicated to Asian issues, magazines for those with Caribbean roots, etc.) and represent minority ethnic groups in appropriate ways. Even parts of the 'white establishment' media can be sympathetic and campaign for better treatment of minorities in the media (Wilcox, 1992). It is difficult also because different minority ethnic groups are represented in different ways in the media.

Tabloid newspapers often stereotype the cultural values and norms of behaviour of some minority groups. Stories are frequently cast in terms of the threat posed by minority ethnic groups: by their increasing numbers or criminality, or in some other way.

Television, meanwhile, portrays a particularly restricted range of social roles for minority ethnic groups. The Broadcasting Standards Commission (1999) found that in terrestrial and satellite television, members of minority ethnic groups appeared in 42 per cent of programmes, accounting for 7 per cent of all people with a speaking role. They were best represented in children's programmes. The occupation portrayal of members of minority ethnic groups in television programming is strongly skewed.

Sarita Malik summarizes some of the distinctive ways in which racial groups are represented on television:

> *Afro-Caribbeans are mostly seen in social issue discourses, music and light entertainment, sports and comedy … Black people in general are less often seen in one-off dramas, major roles, big-budget landmark productions, British films, and non 'race-related' documentaries and news stories, or in positions of expertise … Asians, on the whole, are more usually marked by their absence. A Broadcasting Standards Commission report … found that 32 per cent of Asian representation on ITV was accounted for by one Asian newsreader (Shulie Ghosh) and one Asian character in Coronation Street (Vikram Desai). Even on BBC 2 … it was found that 97 per cent of speaking parts were White and only 1 per cent was Asian.* Malik, 2002

In the USA there are a considerable number of 'black shows' on network television, but they are predominantly situation comedies, are found mostly on the newest network TV channels and the numbers televised are declining (Gray, 2000).

However, simple content analysis studies of the representation of different minority ethnic groups in the media are limited in what they can tell us. Malik (2002) talks instead about a 'racialized regime of representation', by which she means that the black experience is represented in distinctively patterned ways, different from the ways in which other groups are represented. This regime changes over time and relates not only to the images and other representations of black people in the media, but also to the way their experiences become understood by audiences.

By contrast, 'whiteness' is represented as the norm in the media: it is invisible because it is taken for granted. Malik refers to this as 'social whiteness':

> *Whilst Black people have been racialized in representation, White people have been shown to have no obvious race to represent, rarely being directed to think of themselves as having a racial identity.* Malik, 2002

Other studies have moved further away from looking at the content of media messages and towards the beliefs they appeal to: beliefs that may or may not be widely shared. An example is the highly publicized trial of the black sportsman O.J. Simpson, accused of murdering his wife and her friend. Here, different political factions struggled with each other to use the case to promote their narratives about 'race'. The ways in which the trial of Simpson and Simpson himself were represented on television and in the press were multiple and complex, not singular or simple. Their 'effects' on audiences, therefore, were similarly diverse and hard to pin down or describe in simple terms. Nor were they shaped in accidental ways.

The racist murder of Stephen Lawrence in 1993 illustrates this point. Between 1993 and 1998 the *Guardian* newspaper produced 347 reports on the case. Their focus was predominantly on the actions and failings of the police, courts and ministers in pursuing his racist murderers and bringing them to justice (Cottle, 2000). The agendas pursued throughout the case were political, powerful and explicit.

Cottle (2000) agrees that studies in this area 'provide us with evidence of the general patterns, impoverished representations and sometimes starkly racist portrayal found in both UK and US mainstream media'. However, Cottle notes that simple counts of 'representation-types' are too static and simplistic in the way they conceive of representation in the media. The representations of 'race' and ethnicity on television and in newspapers cannot simply be 'counted', he argues, but rather must be understood as signs which can be read in multiple ways, though there may be a preferred reading which editors, authors and producers attempt to impose.

Thus, for example, Cottle's study of 'raced' media events shows that the preferred readings of representations of 'race' might serve a conservative political agenda (as in the case of 'raced' representations of urban disorder in the USA), or they might serve a liberal multiculturalist agenda (as in the case of television news coverage of carnivals in the UK). However, the preferred reading might not be the one actually made:

> *I observed how ethnic minorities are now often portrayed in deliberate 'multiculturalist' ways through a (superficial) focus on cultural festivities, individual success stories and cultural exotica of ethnic minority cultures ... Despite the best intentions of producers, such 'multiculturalist' representations ... may actually serve to reinforce culturally sedimented views of ethnic minorities as 'Other' and simultaneously appear to give the lie to ideas of structural disadvantage and continuing inequality.* Cottle, 2000

Representations of class in the media

Glennon and Butsch (1982) studied television representations of social-class lifestyles in family contexts between 1941 and 1978. They collected information on 218 family series. All of these were American prime-time programmes, mostly (86 per cent) situation comedies, but there were also family dramas, adventure serials and cartoons. Their uniting feature was that the main characters were members of a family and most of the interactions portrayed were within the family. The study found:

- Working-class families were under-represented and middle-class families over-represented.
- Almost half had professional heads of household (two-thirds were either managers or proprietors; in reality, a quarter of the American workforce in 1970).
- Blue-collar workers were portrayed as heads of household in 4 per cent of the series (36 per cent in reality).
- Glamorous and successful families were portrayed most: many of the families were portrayed as extremely wealthy.
- In the few working-class families represented, some were portrayed as upwardly mobile; others were portrayed with an unintelligent father (Glennon and Butsch argue that these two themes undermine the dignity of working-class family life).
- The effort of moving from a working-class to a middle-class family lifestyle was underestimated.

Glennon and Butsch made some attempt to analyse the way these classes were portrayed. For example:

- In the middle-class families, parents were usually portrayed as coping effectively with problems.
- Many working-class fathers were portrayed in a comic way and laughed at by the rest of the world.

However, it is arguably inappropriate for large content analysis studies like that of Glennon and Butsch to make these kinds of judgements. That is because they often hide assumptions about what messages mean in the first place (for example, 'portrayed as unintelligent' is itself a judgement made by the researcher). Neither do they tell us anything about how these messages are received by the audience.

Studies of representations of social class in non-fiction television were conducted by the Glasgow Media Group (particularly in 1976, 1980 and 1982). Their findings are summarized in detail on pp. 719–20. It is interesting to note that for the Glasgow Media Group the working class is generally portrayed as 'trouble' on television news, in very much the same way as working-class youth (see below). From a neo-Marxist perspective this is no surprise: the media are simply acting against counter-hegemonic groups in an effort to sustain ideological dominance.

Representations of age in the media

Pearson (1983) argues that contemporary images usually categorize youth as a problem. This is often contrasted in the media with a Golden Age (usually twenty years ago) when young people knew their place, there was little crime and people respected the police. Pearson's account of his search through press archives reveals that, no matter what the date, this same story is told: the Golden Age is always around twenty years previously. The media are in a permanent panic about whatever manifestation of 'youth as a problem' is current: the Hooligans of Victorian times, the Teds of the 1950s or the Travellers of today.

It is young people who are most frequently the subject of moral panics (this issue is discussed in more detail on p. 360). Estrada (2001) examined responses to youth violence in Sweden. He argues that crime statistics are at variance with other data sources:

- Victim and self-report surveys amongst 16- to 24-year-olds since 1978 show more or less stable levels of violence.
- Hospital statistics since 1973 show an overall stable level of admissions due to injuries caused by violence amongst 10- to 25-year-olds.
- Cause-of-death statistics do not show a rise in the level of fatal violence.
- However, official crime statistics show a marked increase in violent offending amongst youths, principally from the 1980s onwards, with rates of juvenile assault convictions per 1,000 inhabitants ranging from approximately 1.5 in the early 1980s to almost 6 by the mid-1990s.

Criminological research has long emphasized the need for caution in the interpretation of crime statistics. A rise in the rate of convictions for violent crimes cannot be assumed automatically to correspond to a rise in the actual incidence of violence. Crime rates can be affected by a number of factors, including changes in recording practices, changes in sentencing and redefinitions of criminal offences.

Crime statistics are, as Estrada says, sensitive to changes in our response to violence rather than reflecting violence itself. This alerts us to some of the difficulties inherent in establishing causal relationships between the media and crime.

Nonetheless, Estrada argues that one interpretation of the rising juvenile crime rate is that there is a deviancy amplification spiral (see p. 730). He states that policies towards youth offending have shifted from treatment to just deserts, resulting in an intensified focus on young offenders' actions, particularly violent ones. This has led to more reporting of crimes, thus initiating deviancy amplification.

Estrada identifies a noticeable change in the tone of stories relating to juvenile crime. In the early 1980s, the young offender is represented as 'a problem child with a difficult family background', but by the mid-1980s, the portrayal has changed to that of a cold, ruthless thrill-seeker, with no mention of social circumstances.

Estrada points out some of the problems of identifying exactly what constitutes a 'panic', but draws on aspects of Cohen's model in highlighting the media's role.

What about media images of older people? Susan Sontag (1978) points out that there is a 'double standard of ageing': women are required to match up to a youthful ideal all their lives, but men are not. There are very positive images of ageing for men. This gender distinction needs to be taken into account in any discussion of media representation of the elderly.

Signorelli's (1989) content analysis of over 14,000 American television characters between 1969 and 1981 found that the very old and the very young were under-represented in prime-time dramatic fiction. Older characters were less likely to be presented as 'good', but less likely to be involved in violence than younger characters. Some 70 per cent of older men and 80 per cent of older women were treated discourteously and as low-status persons. However, representation is patchy. For example, Dail (1988) found that older women in soap operas were likely to be portrayed in a positive way.

This patchiness is also found in other media. On Radio 4, for example, there are more older men than older women. In sports broadcasting there is a tradition of the positively portrayed older sportsman, moving on into semi-retirement (with a bit of commentating on the side). One or two examples of women in the same position do exist, but their numbers are far smaller.

As in other aspects of media representations, there is evidence of considerable change over time. In industrialized countries around the world, people aged over 50 have become a larger part of the population, as birth rates decline and life expectancy increases. These same people are increasingly likely to be affluent in retirement as a result of economic and social changes.

Featherstone and Hepworth (1995) show how the magazine *Retirement Choice* presents positive images of ageing, in recognition of the new large market. However, they are still critical of representations of age within its pages. Ageing is represented as 'an extended plateau of active middle age ... a period of youthfulness and active consumer lifestyles'. The message *Retirement Choice* propagates is that the ageing process is a matter of making the right lifestyle (and hence consumer) decisions. Difficult issues such as decline and dependency are avoided.

Representations of disability in the media

Research undertaken by the BBC, the Broadcasting Standards Commission and the Independent Television Commission (Sancho, 2003) shows that representations of disability appear in approximately 11 per cent of television programmes and 1 per cent of speaking roles. The study found that media professionals believed that audiences were not ready for any significant expansion in the presence of disabled people on television. However, viewers were largely happy to see greater representation.

As can be seen from Table 12.4, disabled people tended to feature more in certain kinds of programmes than in others. They are most commonly represented in fiction and factual programming; very few are featured in entertainment or sport. The presence of sporting representations in 2000 is accounted for by coverage of the Paralympics. (Data on children's programming in Table 12.4 may not capture the full representation of disability portrayals as the sample was based on peak-time slots.)

Longmore (1987) listed the following forms of representation of disabled people on television:

- Disability or physical handicap as an emblem of evil
- The disabled as monsters
- Disability as a loss of one's humanity
- Disability as total dependency and lack of self-determination
- The image of the disabled as a maladjusted person
- Disability with compensation or substitute gift (for example, the blind having compensatory powers)
- Disability leading to courageousness or achievement
- Disability and sexuality: as a sexual menace, deviancy, danger stemming from loss of control.

Cumberbatch and Negrine (1992) add the following to Longmore's list:

- Disability as an object of fun or pity
- The disabled as the object of charity.

Table 12.4 Representation of disability in television programmes in Britain between 1997 and 2002

Programme type	1997 N (%)	1998 N (%)	1999 N (%)	2000 N (%)	2001 N (%)	2002 N (%)
News	22 (15)	12 (12)	23 (19)	30 (21)	39 (26)	20 (17)
Factual	36 (24)	29 (29)	39 (32)	39 (27)	40 (27)	30 (25)
Entertainment	8 (5)	5 (5)	9 (7)	7 (5)	8 (5)	6 (5)
Sport				21 (14)		
Religion	4 (3)	3 (3)	2 (2)		1 (1)	
Children's			1 (1)	1 (1)	3 (2)	
Fiction	58 (39)	35 (35)	33 (27)	31 (21)	27 (18)	53 (44)
Film	20 (14)	17 (17)	15 (12)	17 (12)	32 (21)	11 (9)
TOTAL	148	101	122	146	150	120

NB: Percentages may not total 100 per cent due to rounding.

Source: Sancho, J. (2003) 'Disabling prejudice. Attitudes towards disability and its portrayal on television': www.ofcom.org.uk, p. 100.

These authors suggest that what is missing among these stereotyped representations:

> *is the portrayal of people with disabilities as an integral part of life ... When people with disabilities do appear on the screen, their presence and their actions are determined by the nature of the disabilities ... he/she is much less likely to appear as a person, an individual, who happens also to have a disability.* Cumberbatch and Negrine, 1992

The enduring nature of these stereotypes is reflected in Harnett's (2000) examination of images of disability in popular television. Harnett identifies many of these forms of representation, highlighting in particular the 'evil avenger' and the 'supercrip'. The 'evil avenger' continues the tradition of disabled people being associated with malice and wrongdoing. The 'supercrip' is a heroic portrayal of a disabled person overcoming adversity in a spectacular way, often carrying the assumption that the disabled person should aspire to be 'cured'.

When disabled people are directly involved in creating representations, portrayals can be very different. Thoreau (2006) analysed representations within *Ouch!* – a BBC web magazine produced mainly by people with disabilities. Most writers, whilst broadly identifying themselves as disabled, did not specify any particular form of disability, thus resisting the idea of classification. Disability was often discussed with humour and a sense of irony. Articles featured on the website covered a great variety of topics, unlike articles in the mainstream press, which tend to focus on health issues in association with disability.

However, even this site does not convey a fully comprehensive or diverse representation of people with disabilities.

> *Disabled people were presented as multidimensional people with varied interests. Yet despite this variety of topics, the sample was found to represent a rather selective picture of disability. Issues of class, gender, ethnicity, or sexuality were rarely mentioned within the sample.* Thoreau, 2006, p. 459

The audience: behaviour and reception

Our discussion of media images of social groups has highlighted the importance of **reception analysis**: of understanding how the audience interprets and uses media content, in what circumstances and why. This section examines these issues in relation to the five groups examined above.

Gender and audience reception

Radical feminists have tended to adopt a fairly optimistic approach to understanding women's relationship to the media. They regard women as empowered readers of media messages, and stress the processes women use to decode media messages and their ability to resist and even gain pleasure from such messages.

Ang's (1985) study of the female audience of *Dallas* identified the pleasures that women obtained from the programme. More recent studies have also stressed the importance of the television viewing context. For example, Hargrave (1999) shows that adults viewing television with children are more likely to react negatively to sex scenes than when viewing alone or with other adults.

Context is also important in the relationship between a particular audience and a specific medium. For many authors, the technologies of the mass media are themselves highly gendered: in other words, they are clearly associated with a gender identity. Gender identity in this context refers to the beliefs, values and feelings people have about themselves and about media technology and content.

Skirrow (1986) uses the related concept of **gender valence**, which is a measure of the degree to which media technology or content involves male or female gender identities. For example, according to Skirrow, video games 'are particularly unattractive [to women] since they are part of a technology which ... is identified with male power, and they are about mastering a specifically male anxiety in a specifically male way'.

Similarly, Turkle (1988) argues that women 'use their rejection of computers ... to assert something about

themselves as women … It is a way to say that it is not appropriate to have a close relationship with a machine.' The computer is a cultural symbol of what a woman is not. In rejecting computers women are rejecting something they see as gender-coded.

Livingstone and Bovill's (2001) study of children and young people's use of media in Europe found that boys are more technologically oriented than girls. Girls are more likely to have books, while boys are more likely to have computers in their bedrooms.

Distinctions were even sharper when use rather than just availability was examined. There are important gendered differences in preferences for media content. Girls are more likely to listen to music and read, boys to use high-tech media such as games consoles. 'Boys' culture is game dominated. Girls' culture is all about relationships and talk.' However, the differences are small and diminishing, with girls increasingly stepping into the so-called male territories.

Gray (1987) notes that people say that women generally avoid computers and video games because they are too complex. However, women routinely use other complex equipment (which men often claim not to be able to operate), such as sewing machines, microwave ovens and washing machines. For Gray, an important factor in all this is men's domination of domestic leisure, which alienates women from the technology associated with it.

By contrast, the telephone is the key technology that many women would hate to lose because it is a way of 'saving the sanity' of those who have a sense of isolation in their homes. Similarly, Hobson (1980) suggests that radio has a female gender valence and is particularly important for working-class women with young children, as it helps structure their day and links them with the outside world.

This picture of gendered technology use may be changing with the growth of different forms of new media. There has been a phenomenal expansion in interactive media, most notably social networking sites such as Facebook and MySpace. In 2007, London became the biggest network site on Facebook, with 790,615 registered users (Kiss, 2007).

Ofcom (2006) reported that amongst 12- to 15-year-olds, girls are more likely than boys to use the internet on their own (23 per cent compared to 11 per cent) and to spend more on mobile phone use. In 2007, women in the 25–34 and 35–49 age brackets for the first time spent more time online than men (Ofcom, 2007).

Sexuality and audience reception

The age of the audience has been one key concern among researchers into the depiction of sexuality in the media. This is because younger viewers have little or no real-life experience of sex and they are more susceptible to influence – they are blank sheets on which the media can write. Older viewers, however, with real-world experience, are thought to be more media-literate and so receive and interpret messages about sexuality in a more discerning way. Some studies have concluded, for example, that in the absence of other sources of information, 'the sexual lessons young viewers derive from television foster an inaccurate image of sex that can lead to unrealistic expectations, frustration and dissatisfaction' (Gunter and McAleer, 1997).

Gender is a second important variable. Men and women tend to 'read' pornography differently, for example, perhaps because it is largely produced for the male gaze. Studies show that both male and female audiences can be aroused by depictions of consenting sex in which the roles of men and women are equal. But this changes when sex and violence are mixed, as in rape scenes, or where non-consent by the woman is apparent in the representation of sex. In such portrayals women's reactions are generally different.

However, the uses and gratifications theory (pp. 723–4) suggests that different individuals select and use such content for different reasons, have different levels of attention, and interpret the content differently according to the function it fulfils for them, so it will have different effects on attitudes and understandings for different people. It is, in short, extremely difficult to generalize about structural differences in audience reception of depictions of sexuality in the media as a whole.

Ethnicity and audience reception

The interpretative model of media messages highlights the polysemic nature of media texts (see p. 725). This is particularly evident with issues of ethnicity. Let us take as an example *The Cosby Show*, the most popular American television comedy in history.

A successful upper middle-class black family (the Huxtables) is presented extremely favourably in a variety of comedy situations. The lead actor, Bill Cosby, is himself popular, rich and successful and in the show the boundaries between the real Cosby and the fictional Dr Huxtable are blurred (as the title of the show illustrates).

The programme could be interpreted in terms of the Huxtable family (and Bill Cosby) as positive representations of what American black people can become – that is, as depicting positive role models. Alternatively, the programme could be read as depicting an extremely unrepresentative group of black people who are isolated from, and ignore, the problems of racism, deprivation and underachievement that disproportionately affect black people in the USA.

Jhally and Lewis (1992) demonstrate the importance of understanding social differentiation within the audience and the need to distinguish between types of response to media messages. One interesting finding of their study was the degree to which respondents viewed *The Cosby Show* as real. Both black and white respondents had no difficulty in making statements about black people based on their experience of the Huxtables. The authors note:

> *The line between the TV world and the world beyond the screen has, for most people, become exceedingly hazy. We watch at one moment with credulity, at another with disbelief. We mix scepticism with an extraordinary faith in television's capacity to tell the truth. We know that the Huxtables are not real yet we continually think about them as if they were.* Jhally and Lewis, 1992

The overall response to *The Cosby Show* was heavily conditioned by the ethnicity of the person watching it. Black interviewees tended to discuss the show in terms of racial stereotyping. Generally, they contrasted the portrayal of the Huxtables very favourably with other programmes

Figure 12.5 The Fresh Prince: predictable sequences and emotional cues

Source: Rex Features

containing representations of minorities. *The Cosby Show*, however, confronts black viewers with a difficulty. Do they go along with the show's fiction that 'there are black millionaires all over the place', thus ignoring the deep racial divisions in the USA? Or do they consult their own experience for a more realistic view of American blacks, but then leave themselves open to charges of stereotyping and fatalism?

For white viewers, there is no such problem. They come to believe that there is room for minorities to succeed purely by their own efforts. This, for Jhally and Lewis, is simply a more sophisticated form of racism: other blacks have failed to succeed where the Huxtables have not, and their lack of success must, therefore, be their own fault.

Jhally and Lewis conclude that the overall effect of *The Cosby Show* is negative, for it masks persistent divisions of 'race' and class in the USA.

Gray (2000) agrees with this general conclusion. Black situation comedies like *The Cosby Show*, *Fresh Prince of Bel Air* and *Martin* move their characters through predictable sequences, with action and emotional cues heavily laden with studio-audience laughter and laugh tracks. While mildly amusing and giving the feel of being steeped in contemporary urban black culture, such shows have the effect of ghettoizing representations of black people. In fact, Gray argues, the most integrated casts and storylines are found in hour-long dramatic programmes like *ER*, *Homicide* and *NYPD Blue*.

Jhally and Lewis's study is one of the few that examine minority ethnic audiences. Despite the academic attention given these days to audience reception of media texts, rather than the texts themselves, this is perhaps surprising. It is clear that use of minority ethnic actors is a 'double-edged sword', as a 2003 report for the Broadcasting Standards Commission put it, tending to 'polarize the community between those who see the individual representation as positive and those that see it as tokenistic or stereotypical' (Fletcher, 2003).

Recent thinking in this area suggests that reception among particular ethnic groups will itself be complex, mediated by 'hybrid cultures' and 'diasporic consciousness'. Members of minority ethnic groups do not have simple, singular identities, but complex and sometimes contested subject positionings. How these play out will have important consequences for their readings of media texts (Cottle, 2000).

Karen Ross's study of 353 people from a variety of minority ethnic groups in thirty-five ethnically specific focus groups demonstrates this well:

> *For so many people in this study, 'multicultural' has come to mean cultural homogeneity, a proliferation of uni-cultures into which all their disparate and diverse voices, interests, views, identifications and practices dissolve into a formal mass of stereotypical essences; this is what Caribbean people are like, this is what Asian people do ... There is an aching desire for black minority experiences to be created, reported, discussed and interpreted in ways which recognize their humanity, not simply their blackness.*
> Ross, 2000

The next section explores the ideas of hybrid cultures and contested subject positionings in more detail through the work of Marie Gillespie.

Ethnicity, identity construction and the media

Marie Gillespie (1995) shows how television and video are used to recreate the culture of South Asians in London and how these media are also leading to cultural change. Her study is an account of young Punjabis (14- to 18-year-olds) living in Southall, west London, where Punjabis comprise the largest single Asian community outside the Indian subcontinent. Her work took place from 1988 to 1991, during which time the *fatwa* (death sentence) was pronounced against the author Salman Rushdie, the Gulf War was fought, and communism in Eastern Europe collapsed.

Gillespie found that the young people used television and video to redefine their ethnicity. A range of choices is available to young Punjabis – from *Neighbours* to Indian sacred soaps like the *Mahabharata*. This encourages the young people to compare, contrast and criticize cultures, including those of their parents. They dream of an essentially American lifestyle represented in advertisements for Coca-Cola and Levi jeans. However, they are not duped, neither do they live in a fantasy world. They are able to reflect on cultural differences even when they are drawn into a programme and identify with its characters, as tends to happen with *Neighbours*. For example, one young girl uses *Neighbours* as a kind of mirror to reflect on gender roles:

> *You can see that families in* Neighbours *are more flexible, they do things together as a family, they don't expect that girls should stay at home and do housework and cooking, boys and girls are allowed to mix much more freely ... Indian families do go out together to eat ... but most of us can only go out with the family, they can't go out with their mates like the boys do ... Boys live on the outside and girls on the inside.* Gillespie, 1995

News reports of the first Gulf War had the same kind of function, but in relation to religion and national and international loyalties. The young people were torn between identifying with the Iraqi Muslims or with the USA and its allies; between whether or not to adopt their parents' view of the conflict (itself based on their experi-

ence of colonialism); and whether or not to adopt a critical stance towards the reporting of the war. This highlighted their sense of hybrid national and cultural identity, but at the same time gave them the freedom to make choices – a sense of uncertainty, but also of global interconnectedness.

More recently, during the war in Afghanistan and the second Gulf War, the Arab news agency Al-Jazeera has become highly visible. Controversial both within and outside Arab media, it has provided a different voice and perspective on key international events.

Television and video thus enable the young people in Gillespie's study to 'stand outside' their parents' culture and to judge it against a large number of alternatives. They could also go on to change it, to construct new and original versions of ethnicity, and to define what it is to be a young British Asian. These young people are informed and active 'readers' of media texts, not passive receivers. The effect of the media is, on the whole, to empower them.

Social class and audience reception

Ann Gray (1992) shows how class and gender interact in the use of the media. Gender identities influence media use, of course, but so do the social contexts of use and the gendered relationships of power in the household.

Gray shows the importance of class, gender and viewing context for the use of television and video. Her in-depth research into the video use of thirty women of different social classes shows clear differences between social classes I (professional) and II (intermediate) compared to IIIn (skilled non-manual) and IIIm (skilled manual), though Gray was not able to come to firm conclusions about social classes IV (partly skilled) and V (unskilled).

Social classes IIIn and IIIm had a far greater reported use of television and video than social classes I and II. The differences between the viewing habits of men and women were much clearer in IIIn and IIIm than in I and II. The higher the social class, the more concern there was about children using the television and video 'too much' and the more effort was made to control their use. The lower the social class, the more television and video were an accepted (and dominant) part of life and conversation. The higher the social class, the more preference there was for 'classics' and British productions (a perceived sign of quality).

In all classes, however, the context was important and affected how women used video. The context of viewing could be all the family together, children only, male and female together, male only, or female only. In all classes women tended to give control of viewing to men, citing their employment as justification.

Men enjoyed documentaries, current affairs and (especially in classes IIIn and IIIm) sport. Politics, space, science, science fiction, and action adventure were also 'men's domains' in the all-male context. Men tended to archive tapes and organize their viewing more than women. Soap operas, 'weepies', romance and costume drama were enjoyed by the women watching alone in all classes. However, women with higher education were more likely to have similar tastes to their partners. For classes I and II, men and women agreed that the following was a correct representation of taste:

Positive	*Negative*
classics	popular
quality	trash
important	trivial
British	American

In contrast, classes IIIn to V agreed that the following was important:

'Male' genres	*'Female' genres*
hard	soft
tough	soppy
real	fantasy
serious	silly
factual	fictional

However, all the women enjoyed programmes that stressed personal relationships, believable characters and a strong story. So, across the classes, there is this polarity:

Male	*Female*
heroic	romantic
public	domestic
societal	familial
physical	emotional

Age and audience reception

Barry Gunter and Jill McAleer (1997) investigated children's use and reception of television in the home. They note that for 4- to 24-year olds the number of hours spent watching television remained relatively constant between 1982 and 1994, at around 2.8 hours per day – less than all other age groups. This contrasts with the viewing practices of older, retired people, as reported by Gauntlett and Hill (1999), who found that older people tended to 'allow' themselves to watch more television as their social contacts and mobility diminished.

Gunter and McAleer found no strong evidence that television displaces other activities. Instead, they found that the more the children have access to different media in the home, the more they try to do. Sometimes children performed two activities at the same time, such as reading and watching television.

Similarly, older people derived particular benefits from television:

> *It was both comfort and company in times of illness and grief, although its reminder of happier times made it a double-edged, bittersweet pleasure. Older viewers felt that television kept them in touch with the world, and mentally active. Television gave these viewers a 'virtual mobility', its ability to show them other parts of the world was frequently acknowledged.* Gauntlett and Hill, 1999

Older people are now using the internet in greater numbers. Whilst only one in six are internet users, which is a lower proportion than for any other age group, those aged 65 and over now spend the most time a month online (41.6 hours) (Ofcom, 2007).

David Buckingham: children and television

We have seen how the level of media literacy affects the sophistication with which people are able to read media messages. One hypothesis is that children are likely to be

less media literate than adults and so are more vulnerable to a 'hypodermic' effect of media messages. However, David Buckingham's (1993) work on children and advertising tends to contradict this view.

Children are clearly aware of the functions of advertising and sceptical about it. For example, 8-year-old Ben said, 'They're trying to persuade people to buy things or do things'; and Nancy, also 8, said, 'That's why they advertise it, because they can't get anyone to buy it, so they just try and … make it look really good.' While children also gave some more imaginative reasons for advertising (for example, 'to allow the actors to change their clothes' and 'to allow people to go to the toilet'), all the children except one who gave this sort of reason also gave answers like Ben's and Nancy's.

Buckingham came to a number of conclusions. While children said that they pestered their parents to buy things they had seen, this was done with the realization that they probably would not get them (they were 'trying it on'). They did not seriously ask for things they knew they would not get. They substituted these with requests they knew were more realistic.

At Christmas time children consciously used advertisements to help them because they knew they would be asked what they wanted for Christmas and so they needed to generate a list. This finding confirms the uses and gratifications model rather than the hypodermic model of media effects (see pp. 723–4).

According to Buckingham, children saw 'other people' as being influenced by advertisements, but they hardly ever saw themselves as influenced in this way. These 'other people' were usually children younger than themselves. Children were critical, even cynical, about free gifts and the quality of merchandise being advertised generally.

They applied their own interpretations to the content of advertisements. People appearing in adverts were described as 'ugly', 'stupid', 'prattish', 'wallies' and 'boring old has-beens'. (10-year-old Anne complained that adverts showing women doing the washing and ironing were sexist, and Donna, also 10, was unhappy about the fact that boys' sports got most prominence.)

Children applied their well-developed television literacy (see pp. 724–5) to advertisements. They were able to read the intentions of the advertisers (seeing who the advert was aimed at) and discuss technical aspects of its production. They were 'wise consumers'. Some reported that before buying a toy they had seen on television they tested those their friends had bought. Others reported comparing prices of similar goods in different shops. Children often remembered an advert very well, but could not associate it with any particular product.

Although these results suggest that children are very active in interpreting, modifying and even rejecting advertising messages, Buckingham qualifies this conclusion. First, although these sorts of responses to advertisements give children mental defences against the hypodermic injection of the message, there is no guarantee about when, or if, such defences will be used. Children may have defences, but they may not use them.

Second, the methods used in this study made it more likely that these defences would be shown. Buckingham said that the children interviewed seemed to be competing with each other to see who could be the most cynical and clever about adverts.

Third, while the children were generally sceptical about advertising, they displayed a great enthusiasm for watching adverts. Buckingham suggests that children derive a great deal of pleasure from adverts. They enjoy using catchphrases, parodying adverts and singing the songs in adverts – although they often invent new words! Buckingham partly agrees with the conclusion reached by Nava and Nava (1990) that 'young people consume commercials independently of the product which is being marketed'.

Disability and audience reception

Cumberbatch and Negrine (1992) held discussion groups with people who themselves had disabilities, with carers, with families of those with disabilities and with able-bodied people, about their responses to images of disability on television and in films. They also conducted a survey about attitudes towards people with disabilities.

Their findings confirm those of audience reception studies in other areas, such as Hartmann and Husband's (1974) study of responses to media representations of black people. Real-life contact with a minority group represented in media messages, or being a member of such a group, gives a particular perspective on the message and enables members of the audience to 'read' it in alternative ways.

Effects or impact of the message

Gender and media 'effects'

How theorists interpret the effects of media messages largely depends on the model of media content and influence they subscribe to. The impact of media content on gender roles, for example, is quite clear to those who adopt fairly simple hypodermic and social learning models of media influence. For instance, Provenzo argues that sexist representations in video games have important influences on males:

> *[Males] come to assume from the images provided by the games (as well as other sources from the media and the general culture) that women are indeed the 'weaker sex' and constantly in need of aid or assistance. Thus the games not only socialize women to be dependent, but also condition men to assume dominant gender roles.* Provenzo, 1991

Similarly, Frueh and McGhee (discussed in Tuchman *et al.*, 1978) also adopted a simple model of 'effect'. They interviewed American kindergarten children about the amount of time they spent watching television, testing the extent and direction of their sex-typing. Traditional sex-role stereotyping was positively correlated by Frueh and McGhee with heavy viewing. According to this research, women are persuaded to accept and 'go along' with their role: they undergo a process of 'modelling', that is, imitating a role model seen on television.

Beuf's (1974) study argues that some girls aged between 3 and 6 have abandoned their ambitions even by that early age. The implication of this kind of work is that, because of the small number of high-status females in the media available for girls to imitate, the ambitions of real women are limited. The power of the media in this respect is strong, according to Beuf, because the average American

girl will have spent more time in front of the television by the time she is 15 than she will have spent in the classroom.

Beuf also argues that women suffer anxiety and stress because advertising and soap operas create concerns in women about their body image, the need to purchase products to keep them attractive and the competition with other women to get and keep a man. Beuf's views are echoed in recent concerns about the effect of 'size zero' models on women's health and self-image.

According to socialist feminists (see pp. 101–2), media content sustains and perpetuates the capitalist system and the support role of women. Big business effectively controls the editorial content of women's magazines, in particular. That women are portrayed in traditional ways is in the interests of the capitalist class: it justifies using women as a reserve labour force. Kath Davies argues:

> *Since those who control the media are almost all (rich) men, there is every incentive for them to present the capitalist, patriarchal scheme of things as the most attractive system available – and to convince the less privileged that the oppression and limitations of their lives are inevitable.* Davies et *al.*, 1987

However, such straightforward capitalist manipulation of the media is not considered particularly important by many other socialist feminists. Most adopt either a cultural hegemony model of influence or the more sophisticated 'logic of capitalism' version of Marxism in explaining the influence of the media on women (see pp. 716–17).

Angela McRobbie (1991) is in the latter category. She notes how women's magazines have to attract advertising – their articles on make-up surrounded by adverts for eyeliner, hair-mousse and lipstick. Fashion and celebrity, prominent in such magazines, are also tied into the system of consumption. It is part of the 'inner logic' of these magazines that consumption is a natural feature of readers' experience, so that it is seen as extremely unusual not to be interested in 'hairstyles, "cleansing" and all the other intimate rituals that are an intrinsic part of being a woman in contemporary consumer culture'.

Liberal feminists' interest in sex roles usually leads them to concentrate on content analyses of the media, though they tend to take for granted the effects of the stereotyped content they usually find. Gaye Tuchman argues that the media in general, and television advertisements in particular, perform the symbolic annihilation of women: 'The analyses of television commercials support the … hypothesis … [that] commercials neglect or rigidly stereotype women' (Tuchman *et al.*, 1978).

However, media content can be changed by a conscious process of rooting out those elements in society which perpetuate such stereotypes. Tuchman believes this is increasingly the case:

> *The mass media deal in symbols and their symbolic representations may not be up to date. A time lag may be operating … As values change, we would expect the images of society presented in the media to change.*
> Tuchman et *al.*, 1978

Sexuality and media 'effects'

Views of the effects of sexual explicitness in the media are divergent. For some, it is functional, having an educative

Figure 12.6 The influence of magazine advertisements on women in a consumer culture

Source: Roger Scruton.

and entertaining role, and even a cathartic one – that is, releasing energies that might otherwise be destructive.

Studies of both men and women suggest that the uses and gratifications model of media effects applies to the representation of sexuality in the media. Entertainment, passing the time, curiosity satisfaction, education and as a prelude to sex or masturbation are some of the benefits reported by both sexes.

A study by Perse (1994) categorized these benefits into sexual enhancement, diversion, sexual release and substitution. Gender differences in relation to this, where they exist, tend to be small: for example, in Perse's study, men scored higher than women on the use of sexual materials for sexual release and for substitution.

For moralists, on the other hand, sexually explicit material can be desensitizing, leading to more immorality in society and undermining fundamental values. Feminists too tend to argue that sexually explicit material will demean and objectify women and lead men to have undesirable attitudes towards women in real life. Donnerstein (1980), in a series of publications in the 1980s, confirmed this fear, finding that portrayals of aggressive erotica tended to produce distorted beliefs about women in young males.

Similarly, according to 'cultivation theory', long-term exposure to sexually explicit material on television will influence viewers' understandings about the real world. However, cultivation theory assumes a common, consistent message socializing people into a distorted view of reality. This is only sometimes the case: it happened with paedophilia but not with Aids and its relationship to homosexuality (see p. 731). It does not happen in relation to images of sexuality or the depiction of the different sexualities of men and women: representations of sexuality are very different in different media and for different dimensions of sexuality.

Ethnicity and media 'effects'

In terms of ethnicity, too, the model of media effects adopted by a researcher will have important consequences for the way they gather and interpret their data.

Van Dijk (1991) provides an example. He reports the initial results of a study of the effects of press reports on 'race' on people's perceptions of race issues. Based on interviews designed to reveal how people recall and re-tell press stories, the conclusions were as follows:

- People recall stories even from years ago: time is not a major factor.
- Where an event is massively reported, individuals can integrate the story into their understanding of reality and their more general knowledge about, for example, a particular group of immigrants.
- Where the reader has a good understanding of the issues already, stories are more likely to be recalled and integrated into their ideas.

According to van Dijk, virtually no reader challenges the interpretation of immigration issues put forward in the press (and which come from elite groups in society). The possibility that different audiences will interpret the text in different ways (as reception analysis would suggest) is discounted by van Dijk.

The hypodermic model can give rise to fears that the attitudes which are 'injected' into the audience will quickly result in action; that media-inspired racial prejudice, for example, will turn into racial discrimination; or worse, that race hatred will turn into race killings.

However, most studies suggest that direct experience affects the impact of media messages. Hartmann and Husband's (1974) study on children's attitudes towards 'race' is a case in point. Part of the sample they selected for study lived in the West Midlands and Yorkshire (where there is a high density of Asian groups), and another part lived in Teesside and Glasgow (where there is not). Hartmann and Husband found that children in Teesside and Glasgow were more likely to view race relations in terms of 'conflict', 'threat' and 'numbers' because virtually all their information on the issue came from the media rather than actual experience.

Recent studies have emphasized the importance of class and other differences in audiences in conditioning the nature of media effects. If it is the case (as the Glasgow Media Group and others suggest) that the media encode a culturally skewed view of the world, then this will be interpreted differently by different sections of the audience. In terms of social class and gender, for example, Andrea Press concludes:

> *Because the vast majority of television characters are middle class or upper class, my study indicates that television seems to support what I call a 'hegemony of middle-class realism' for working-class women, and as such may operate in part to blind working-class women to the realities of their own situation in society. When their experience is addressed directly ... working-class women are moved to articulate their difference from, and reality apart from, these images ... For middle-class women, however, already living the middle-class material life depicted in the vast majority of television products, television's hegemonic importance rests more in the form of the family, and of women's role within it.* Press, 1995

Age and media 'effects'

We have already seen how Gillespie (1995) describes the importance of the mass media for young Punjabi Londoners. Dick Hebdige (1988, first published 1979), however, argues that any attempt to understand youth subcultures must take into account how the mass media structure the way society is perceived by the young people within them. Their subcultures are based both on the realities of their social situation and on perceptions of it mediated by the mass media – see Figure 12.7.

From a neo-Marxist point of view, Hebdige argues that the media's role is to 'absorb' youth subcultures into mainstream society. Instead of allowing young people to resist capitalist society, the capitalist world attempts to neutralize them through incorporation. The mass media are an extremely important part of this process. The media portray members of youth subcultures as 'just normal kids underneath', the sons and daughters of Mr and Mrs Average, just going through a phase.

Another way of neutralizing youth resistance is what Hebdige calls the **commodity** form of incorporation. Here, youth cultural signs (dress or music, for example) are converted into mass-produced objects and sold on the high street. In this process they lose their threatening and oppositional meanings. The capitalist market effectively takes artefacts away from young people, alienating them from their own subculture. Furthermore, the market 'normalizes' the symbols of resistance by turning them into a 'leisuretime only' style.

Hebdige's is a neo-Marxist perspective. For some postmodernist writers like Gillespie (1995), however, the young are more empowered than Hebdige suggests, and the media are empowering rather than oppressive.

The promotion of a culture of consumerism can be seen in the extensive range of products and fee-paying services associated with social networking sites aimed

Figure 12.7 Youth subcultures

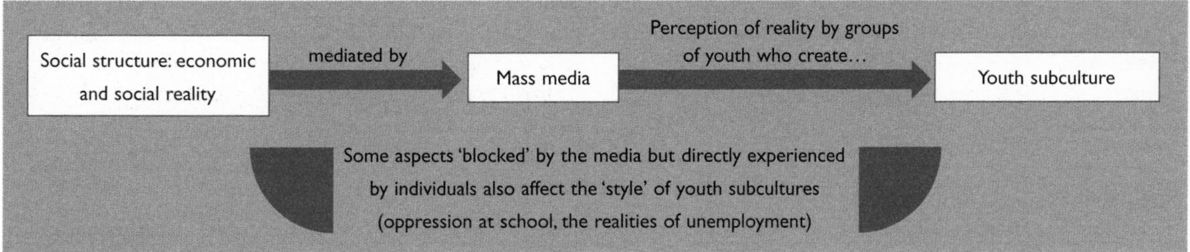

Source: D. Hebdige (1988) *Subculture: The Meaning of Style*, Routledge, London.

exclusively at children. For example, Wall (2007) reports on the Webkinz range of soft toys, which is linked to a website. The toys are aimed at children between 6 and 13 years old. By entering their toy's code, a child is able to create an animated version of it. These virtual pets can then be nurtured and played with online, using the currency of 'Kinzcash'. If the pets are allowed to become ill, the child must purchase virtual medicine for them. Subscriptions last a year, after which time another toy must be purchased.

Wall argues that the brand utilizes a range of strategies to keep children loyal, engaged and spending. This promotes consumerism as fun, without conveying any critical awareness to children. The success of this strategy can be seen in the fact that 2 million toys have been sold since 2005. In May 2007, 4.1 million unique users visited the website (Wall, 2007).

Disability and media 'effects'

Cumberbatch and Negrine (1992) argue that the character of an audience conditions the effects of the stereotyped representations of people with disabilities on television and film. In particular, those with personal experience of living with disability are able to reject or reinterpret dominant readings. For those without this experience, television's treatment of disability tends to mean that it is seen as an 'issue' and as 'a problem'.

> *People with disabilities wish to be seen on television because they are part of life and not alien to it. They do not want to use the box as a soap box but as a 'window on the world' in which they exist ... [But the] achievement of integration is one that more 'positive' imagery alone is unlikely to win single-handedly. Other major social changes would have to take place to accompany the desire to achieve that aim; and such changes would need to include the provision of access to all facets of life, something that will happen only, in the view of many discussants, when people with disabilities are asked about their attitudes, feelings and needs and are not just given what others think they need.* Cumberbatch and Negrine, 1992

Cumberbatch and Negrine highlight an issue at the forefront of much recent thinking about media 'effects': the idea that media messages should not be viewed as isolated from the social context in which they are propagated, but should be considered holistically, that is, in combination with all surrounding circumstances. As Jenny Kitzinger (1999) says, 'Media power does not exist in a vacuum, and audience reception is not an isolated encounter between an individual and a message.' Alasuutari (1999), too, reminds us that media messages are simply part of social life. Studying them out of context is likely to result in misapprehensions about their role and power.

Summary and conclusions

The role and influence of the media can be examined at various levels. Its structure and organization are understood differently depending on theoretical perspectives.

Media determinism is an approach which emphasizes the technological power of the media, seeing it as a key driver of social change, although this has increasingly been seen as simplistic. Pluralists conceive of the media as diverse and balanced by virtue of reflecting many different voices and interests. Hence, the media are seen as reflecting rather than changing society. Marxist and neo-Marxist analyses, in contrast, emphasize the concentrated ownership of the media and the way in which particular dominant agendas are pursued. There is a strong emphasis on the global reach of a limited number of media corporations and their influence on cultural products.

Early studies of the media tended to conceive of both mass media and audiences as monolithic entities. Anxieties about media effects also reflected wider social concerns, while the groups deemed most influenced, such as young people, served as a barometer for the health of society. While such analyses continue to feature heavily in both academic and popular debate, the influence of postmodernism has led to more complex understandings.

Models of the impact of the media have increasingly placed a greater emphasis on differences in the way texts are interpreted. Audiences are now perceived as differentiated, receiving messages selectively according to their own interests and experiences. Factors such as gender, age, class and ethnicity play a major role in shaping responses, although it is important to remember that audience reactions cannot simply be inferred from membership of a particular social group.

Notwithstanding this cultural turn, theoretical perspectives such as cultural hegemony which demonstrate the pervasive power of dominant ideological messages continue to be influential.

However, the area of communication is rapidly evolving. Its landscape is being transformed by the growth in new media, such as social networking, gaming, instant messaging and mobile phone use. These new forms of media are becoming increasingly diverse and interactive, generating different types of engagement.

CHAPTER 13
Age and the life course

The roles and norms that society allocates to age groups create barriers and opportunities. Vincent, 2006

Introduction

This chapter examines a relatively neglected area of study, the sociology of age and the life course. The concept of age is a simple one: it refers to the time elapsed since an individual was born. This is sometimes known as **chronological age**.

Ideas of age and ageing are often seen in biological and psychological terms. Birth, developing to physical maturity, ageing and death are part of universal biological processes which affect all human beings. These processes are linked to the psychological development of individuals. Many psychologists have suggested that there are distinct phases of psychological development which correspond to biological ageing.

Sociologists do not question the idea that age and ageing are linked to biological and psychological development, but they argue that they cannot be fully understood without reference to their social context. Just as 'race' and sex were once seen in purely biological/psychological terms but are now viewed sociologically through concepts such as ethnicity and gender, age can also be seen in sociological terms. From this perspective, age can be seen as, in part, a social construction.

For example, the meanings, roles and identities associated with being a particular age vary from society to society. Historical research suggests that the idea of a prolonged childhood during which it is inappropriate for the young to do paid work is a relatively recent phenomenon. In medieval Europe, 'children' were expected to work and take part in adult social life from a very young age (see pp. 759–60).

Similarly, the meaning of old age varies from society to society. In some traditional societies, the elderly are revered for their wisdom and have high social status and considerable power. As Giddens (2006) points out, this has traditionally been the case in China and Japan. However, Giddens notes that in contemporary Western societies the elderly tend to be seen as 'non-productive, dependent people who are out of step with the times' (2006, p. 183). On the other hand, youth is valued to such an extent that a fortune is spent on attempts by individuals to make themselves appear or feel younger. Cosmetic surgery, Viagra (the anti-impotence drug), skin creams and makeover TV programmes all offer the promise of rejuvenation.

The meaning of age is also linked to the longevity of people in different societies. A particular chronological age has a very different meaning in a society where life expectancy is less than 40 years compared to in a society where life expectancy is over 70.

In 2004 life expectancy at birth in Zimbabwe was 38 for males and 37 for females, but in Britain it was 76 for males and 81 for females. In Switzerland it was even higher, with men living on average until 79 and women until 84 (World Bank, 2007). Stephen Hunt (2005) points

out that in the UK as recently as 1900 life expectancy for women was around 48 years and for men around 50.

These differences in life expectancy have been attributed to a variety of social factors (see pp. 298–306), and in turn they influence what is considered old in different societies at different times.

Because of the variations in the meaning of age in different societies, Giddens argues that sociologists should analyse age in terms of social age rather than chronological or biological age. By **social age** he means 'the norms, values and roles that are culturally associated with a particular chronological age. Ideas about social age differ from one society to another and, at least in modern industrial societies, change over time as well' (Giddens, 2006, p. 183).

Age is not just of sociological importance because its meaning varies from society to society, but also because it is an aspect of stratification. As mentioned above, the status and power of the elderly vary between societies. However, all types of inequality can be shaped by age.

John A. Vincent notes that 'The roles and norms that society allocates to age groups create barriers and opportunities' (2006, p. 197). These barriers and opportunities affect the status, power, wealth and income enjoyed by different age groups in each society. Thus, to use a simple example, in Britain those over 65 have much less opportunity to participate in the labour market than adults under this age. Although there are some very wealthy older people, those old enough to draw their pension have high rates of poverty in Britain.

These introductory points will now be developed further through an examination of some of the key concepts in the sociology of age.

Jane Pilcher – the sociological study of age

The dimensions of age

Jane Pilcher argues that age can be understood as having three significant dimensions:

1. First, age has 'a biological or physiological dimension, so that, over time, the appearance and physical capabilities of our bodies change quite dramatically' (Pilcher, 1995, p. 5).
2. Second, 'as human beings, we live in societies, each with culturally defined expectations of how persons of particular ages are supposed to behave' (p. 5). Therefore, the **social interpretation** of the biological process of ageing varies between and within societies, meaning that different people will experience ageing in different ways.
3. Third, ageing always takes place within a particular historical period. A group born in the same historical period is known as a **cohort**. However, there are no clear dividing lines between one cohort and the next. For example, a group born in the same year might be seen as a cohort, or alternatively a group born in the same decade could be seen as one.

   By virtue of when they were born, a cohort will tend to experience the same historical events, and to some extent the same opportunities and constraints. For example, all those born between 1910 and 1920 in Britain, who survived long enough, experienced the Second World War and its aftermath as adults, which will have affected their lifestyle, career opportunities and outlook.

   The term **generation** is sometimes used to refer to a cohort. For example, somebody might talk of the 'sixties generation' to refer to those who experienced that decade as young adults. However, in kinship studies generation is used to refer more precisely to parent–child–grandchild relationships, so cohort is a more precise and unambiguous term to describe a group who were born around the same time.

Pilcher argues that age is a product of the interaction between these three elements. The stage a person has reached in the physiological process of ageing, the interpretation placed on age within the society in which they live, and the historical period in which they were born and live interact to shape each person's experience of age in society.

Age is therefore a complex phenomenon. Furthermore, because a person's age constantly changes, it is more transient than other social divisions such as those based on gender, ethnicity or even social class. On the other hand, people remain members of the same cohort and each cohort grows up together and lives through the same historical experiences.

Life course and life cycle

In the early sociology of age the term **life cycle** was often used to refer to the varying experiences of those passing through stages of life such as childhood, adolescence and youth, becoming parents, middle age, old age and death. However, Pilcher argues that the idea of a life cycle implies that there are set stages through which people pass. She follows other sociologists of age in arguing that this is a misleading term because it implies that these stages are universal and inevitable.

In reality, there is no universal life cycle since the process of ageing is experienced differently within and between societies. As discussed above, for example, childhood and old age have different meanings and are associated with different roles in different societies. Pilcher therefore prefers the term 'life course' to life cycle. The concept of the **life course** refers to 'a socially defined "timetable" of behaviours deemed as appropriate for particular life stages within any one society' (Pilcher, 1995, p. 4).

Pilcher further argues that the life course does not just vary between societies, but also within societies. Males and females and different ethnic groups, for example, can experience the life course differently because of different meanings given to the processes involved. For example, some ethnic groups may be more deferent to the elderly than others. In Western societies youthfulness may be regarded as more important for women than for men. Actresses and female TV presenters, for example, may find it more difficult to find work as they get older, compared to their male counterparts.

Age structure

The experience of age may also be affected by the age structure of the population. The **age structure** describes 'The relative size of age groups within a population at any

one point in time' (Pilcher, 1995, p. 7). It is affected by the interaction between fertility, mortality and migration.

- For example, if women choose to have fewer babies than in the past, the proportion of children in the population will fall.
- Migration often involves disproportionate numbers of young adults, which will boost this group in the population and change the overall population structure. If migrants include a high proportion of fertile young women, this will also affect the birth rate and consequently the age structure.
- Mortality has a particular impact on the proportion of elderly in the population. If a higher proportion of adults survive into old age the age structure will become more top-heavy.

Figures 13.1 and 13.2 show the age structure of Britain in 1871 and 1991. There is a marked difference between the two caused by the much higher rates of fertility and mortality in 1871 compared with 1991. To put it simply, people had many more children in 1871 but fewer survived into old age.

These changes have led to an ageing of the population, creating potential problems for Britain and similar societies. An increasing proportion of the elderly come to rely upon the work and taxes of a declining proportion of working-age adults, placing strains on the economy. This has been described as the 'demographic time-bomb'. In the process, the shape of the age structure bar chart has gradually changed from that of a pyramid to that of a beehive.

Particular historical events such as large-scale migration or wars can also affect the age structure, increasing or decreasing the proportion of adults or children in the population. For example, despite the deaths of considerable numbers of adults during the Second World War, the years following peace produced a 'baby boom' and consequently a large cohort of so-called 'baby boomers'.

Figure 13.1 Age structure of England and Wales in five-year age groups, 1871

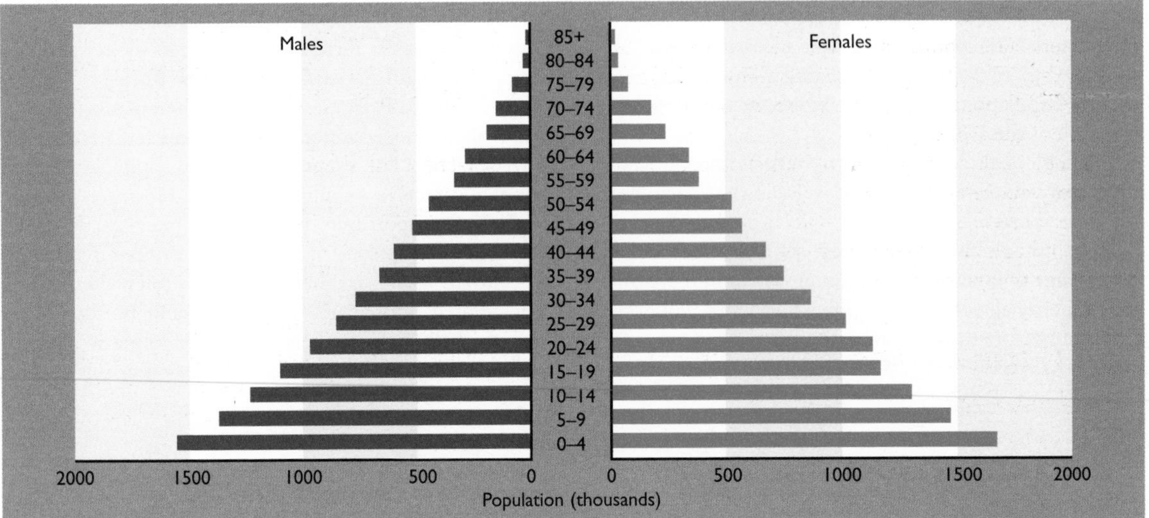

Source: J. Pilcher (1995) *Age and Generation in Britain*, Oxford University Press, Oxford, p. 9.

Figure 13.2 Age distribution of residents: Great Britain, 1991

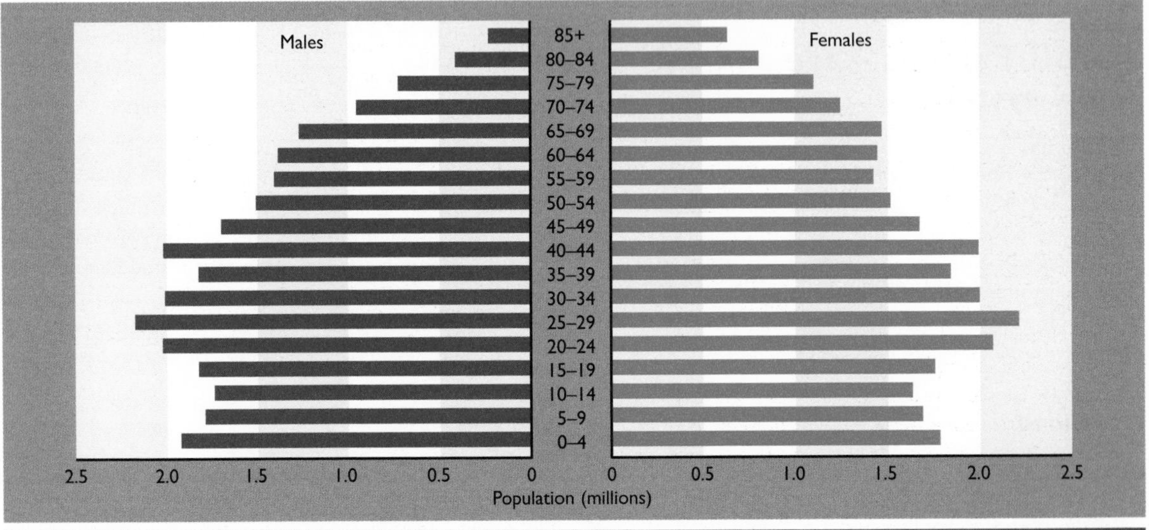

Source: J. Pilcher (1995) *Age and Generation in Britain*, Oxford University Press, Oxford, p. 7.

Figure 13.3 UK population, by gender and age, mid-2006

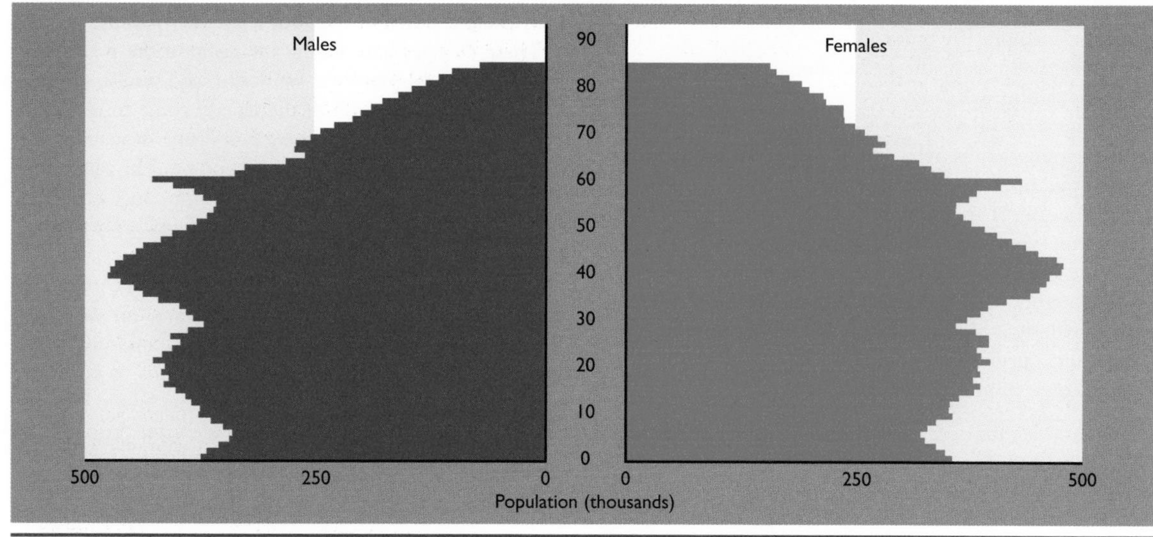

Source: National Statistics, *Population Estimates*: http://www.statistics.gov.uk/cci/nugget.asp?id=6

By mid-2005 the average age in Britain was 38.8, compared to 34.1 in 1971, indicating a continuing ageing of the population. Figure 13.3 shows the population structure of the UK in 2006.

Pilcher concludes that the 'understanding of cultural and historical *context*' is key to developing the sociological analysis of age.

Most sociologists now agree with Pilcher, but the importance of context was not so prevalent in the work of early functionalist theorists of age. Their work will now be examined before looking at competing perspectives in the sociology of age.

Functionalist perspectives on age

Talcott Parsons – age and the social system

An example of a functionalist perspective on age is provided by the work of Talcott Parsons (1954, first published 1942). As in other areas, Parsons related age differences to the overall functioning of the social system. He believed that differences in the social roles associated with age groups were vital for the smooth functioning of society. However, he did accept that in US society there can be tensions between age groups.

Childhood

Parsons believed that in all societies childhood is a period when socialization into society's culture takes place. Children learn the norms and values associated with different social roles, which enables them to contribute to society as adults (see pp. 463–4 for Parsons's views on the family).

According to Parsons, in the USA there is less differentiation in the socialization of males and females than in other societies. For example, both girls and boys attend school and receive a similar education. However, girls get much more opportunity than boys to practise adult roles in childhood. Parsons assumed that women tended to concentrate upon mother/housewife roles while men concentrated upon paid work and being breadwinners. Girls can help their mothers around the home while boys are unlikely to be able to help their fathers at work.

Adolescence

Parsons argued that adolescence is a time when children begin to develop independence from their parents. In industrial societies such as the USA it is essential that the workforce is mobile so that it can move to where workers are needed by manufacturing industry. The nuclear family is functionally well adapted to this type of society since it is self-sufficient and does not rely upon extended kinship networks (see pp. 474–5). For the smooth functioning of society, it is vital that children develop independence from their parents and shift their primary loyalty from their parents to their marriage partner.

Youth culture therefore involves a degree of rebellion against parental discipline, which can cause conflict between the generations. Adolescents put much emphasis on establishing their independence and on personal attractiveness. Although the transition towards adult roles may not always be a smooth one, it does help to create independent individuals within nuclear families who are well adapted to the needs of industrial societies.

Old age

Industrial societies do, however, bring problems for the elderly. Parsons noted that the elderly have less status in US society than in most other types of society. Once

children have grown up and men have retired, the elderly lose their most important social roles. In addition, they may be relatively isolated from their children who tend to focus more on their marriage partners and their own children than they do on their parents. Parsons therefore said that 'By comparison with most other societies the United States assumes an extreme position in the isolation of old age from participation in the most important social structures and interests' (1954, p. 102).

Parsons did acknowledge, however, that the significance of age differences varies within society. For example, farming families tend to have less separation of generations than other families in the USA. Both adolescents and the elderly can make some contribution to running a farm and this can reduce the structural isolation of the elderly. (For a functionalist perspective on youth, see pp. 766–8.)

Evaluation

Parsons's views have been widely criticized.

Jenny Hockey and Allison James note that his theory has been attacked for 'its determinism, its overemphasis on conformity and consensus and neglect of inequalities' (2003, p. 160). Although Parsons acknowledged that adolescents can rebel against their parents, according to his theory they seem to do so simply because the social structure needs them to. However, many studies of youth subcultures stress that youths actively and creatively produce subcultures rather than passively act out roles ascribed to them by society (see pp. 771–82).

Apart from rebellious adolescents, Parsons assumes that different age groups conform to generally agreed roles. However, postmodern theories suggest that age differences are breaking down; feminist theorists criticize Parsons for assuming that women both are and should be socialized into 'feminine' roles as mothers and housewives; while conflict theories stress that Parsons ignores the conflict and exploitation involved in relationships between age groups. Conflict theories will now be examined.

Conflict perspectives on age and generation

The political economy of old age

Conflict perspectives see age as another aspect of stratification along with social class, ethnicity, gender and other social characteristics which lead to inequality. Age differs from social class, ethnicity and gender in that all members of society, or at least all those who survive into old age, pass through the different stages of the life course. However, this has not prevented some conflict theorists from arguing that age is also a very important source of structured social inequality.

John Bond, Roger Briggs and Peter Coleman argue that conflict approaches have had most influence in developing what they call the 'political economy of old age' (1993b, p. 34). The **political economy of old age** explores the relationship between the labour market, government policy and social class.

For example, Peter Townsend (1979) studied the link between old age, poverty and social class. He argues that inadequate state pensions lead to poverty amongst those who are from lower social class backgrounds. During their working lives these people have too little income to save for retirement, and they are less likely than the middle or upper classes to have private pensions; thus they find themselves liable to poverty in old age. Bond *et al.* sum up this line of argument in the following way:

> *Society tends to reward present work; it does not reward past work and therefore it does not reward old age. Elderly people are discriminated against by economic and social policies which benefit the young employed and the well-off. Thus, poverty in old age and the dependent status of elderly people are related to low resources and restricted access to resources through the life-cycle.*
>
> Bond *et al.*, 1993b, p. 34

The political economy of old age approach illustrates how conflict perspectives can be applied to one part of the life course. However it does not provide an overall perspective on age throughout the life course. John A. Vincent has gone further than other sociologists in analysing age as an aspect of social stratification and in doing so developing a conflict perspective on age. His work will now be examined.

John A. Vincent – age, stratification and inequality

Age and differentiation

John A. Vincent (1995, 2006) believes that age is an important way of differentiating people in all societies. As a consequence it is a form of stratification, a source of inequality and potentially a source of exploitation, conflict and discrimination.

Age differentiation can shape life chances and in some societies it is a very significant social division. However, the degree to which it is used to differentiate groups, the criteria that are used for differentiation and the social significance of age all vary from society to society and over time.

The life course of individuals is affected differently by the social divisions of age as age interacts with class, gender and ethnicity to affect the ways in which age is experienced. For example, the social significance of ageing can be different for men and women; elderly family members may be treated differently in different ethnic groups; and social class can affect whether a person becomes poor in old age.

To Vincent, life courses are part of the social structure because 'they have general and observable patterns, shaped by norms and values' (2006, p. 214). However, people experience ageing differently as biography and social structure interact to shape the experience of different cohorts, different classes, genders and ethnic groups.

Variations between societies

Vincent (2006) starts by noting that the significance of age varies between societies. In relatively egalitarian societies, such as that of the Mbuti in Africa, there is relatively little differentiation between age groups and between men and women. Although there are minor differences in the social roles of different age groups, all groups have a say in collective decision making, so that power is not concentrated in the hands of a few.

Vincent (1995) argues that age differentiation is greater in societies where private property is inherited since the inheritance of wealth allows some groups to develop more power than others. For example, some villages in rural India tend to be dominated by adult males who own most of the wealth. They are highly **patriarchal** and Vincent points out that patriarchy 'involves not only the domination by male members of the household over females but also of the older (particularly the senior generation) over the younger' (2006, p. 195). In these circumstances, conflict between generations can occur, with younger males anxious to take control of land owned by older males.

Chronological age is not necessarily very important even in societies which differentiate strongly between age groups. Many non-Western societies mark stages in the life course through rituals, initiation ceremonies or **rites of passage**. The age group someone is seen as belonging to depends not on chronological age, but on whether or not they have undergone the rite of passage.

Historical changes in Western societies

The existence of private property is one factor leading to differentiation between age groups, and Vincent (2006) believes that such differentiation has increased with the development of Western capitalist industrial societies. He argues that in Western Europe between 1600 and 1850 the number of years a person had lived (their chronological age) was of little social significance. Sometimes people did not even remember their age. In rural economies chronological age mattered little. Even quite young children would contribute to work on the land. Few people survived into old age, but if they did there was no normal age of retirement.

In the nineteenth century the development of state education and restrictions on the age at which children could work, and in the twentieth century the establishment of retirement ages and pensions, all made chronological age more important. Age was increasingly associated with legal rights and restrictions, as the law specified, for example, the age at which people could leave school, work, get married, have sex and so on.

In industrial capitalist or 'modern' societies the key life stage has become working age, because it is work that provides people with most status and income.

Social divisions and age

Social divisions between groups of different ages or at different points in the life course vary between societies and can take several forms.

1 **Age strata** or **age classes** are 'groups of people of the same age who, by virtue of this characteristic, have distinct life chances and similar social rights' (Vincent, 2006, p. 197). These groups are similar to social classes because belonging to an age stratum affects life chances and the members can also be seen as having common interests. For example, Stevi Jackson and Sue Scott (2006) see childhood in contemporary Britain and similar societies as a form of subordination. The existence of different rights for different age groups creates contradictions and the possibility of conflict. Universalistic values, which require everybody to be treated equally, are contradicted by the unequal way in which the law treats the rights of children. Children, for example, do not have the right to vote and are not protected from some forms of violence (such as smacking by parents) to the same extent as adults.
2 **Generation** refers to position within the family – for example, the relationship between grandparents, parents and children. Generation can also be a basis for conflict. For example, there can be conflict over the issue of whether children care for elderly parents, or the extent to which parents give their adult children financial help.
3 **Cohort**, as discussed above (see p. 744), refers to 'groupings of people born at the same time' (Vincent, 2006, p. 197). According to Vincent, cohorts can develop a sense of common identity which has some similarities to the sense of identity that might develop amongst members of the same class or ethnic group. Cohorts experience the same historical changes and this can affect both a group's outlook and life chances. For example, cohorts who became adults and entered the labour market in the late 1950s and 1960s experienced the liberalization of social attitudes at that time, such as greater acceptance of extramarital sex. They also had greater opportunities for upward social mobility than later and earlier cohorts because they entered the labour market during a time of economic boom.

Age, generation and cohort can all, then, be the basis for stratification and the development of group identities. They interact (along with other forms of stratification) in complex ways to affect the identities and opportunities of individuals and groups in society as they are shaped by historical changes. By understanding the relationship between these different elements it is possible to make sense of the experience of particular groups. Vincent explains this, saying:

> *for any particular moment in time, those who are old appear to have certain characteristics. However, when viewed critically, these characteristics may not be due to advancing years per se but to cultural conventions that define differences between age strata or cohort experiences of specific historical circumstances.* Vincent, 2006, p. 199

The meanings and opportunities attached to being, for example, in your early sixties were very different thirty years ago compared to now, and will also change considerably in the future.

Inequality and older people

Vincent uses the example of the position of older people to illustrate the extent to which age can be linked to

stratification and inequality. Old age is often characterized by material deprivation – the elderly are more likely to be poor than other groups in the population. This is particularly true of women and those from working-class backgrounds. For these groups, low pay and/or part-time work during their working lives may have restricted their entitlement to pensions. Vincent notes that since 1979 the value of state pensions has declined relative to average wages, making relative poverty more likely for those dependent on the state for an income after retirement.

Women, on average, live longer than men and therefore tend to have more years' dependence upon pensions. The oldest pensioners tend to be worse off than younger pensioners, further adding to the deprivation of elderly women.

Government statistics – see Table 13.1 – show that middle age groups spend significantly more than older or younger people on leisure goods, leisure services and so on. Vincent says: 'These figures document a growing substantial material inequality (and by implication social division) between older people and the general population and a growing differentiation amongst older people themselves' (2006, p. 208).

Vincent believes that this growing division cannot be seen as a product of biological ageing or as an inevitable result of the frailty of older people. In other societies, at other times, people have worked well beyond the age of 65, and Vincent believes that in Western society today many people over this age would be perfectly capable of continuing to work. However, retirement age has been created partly to manage the supply of labour in times when there is a surplus and high unemployment. A relatively early retirement age allows unemployment levels to be minimized. In addition, some financial services companies, such as those selling pensions, have an interest in encouraging retirement at a relatively early age.

Recently, there has been something of a moral panic – an exaggerated outbreak of public fear – about the consequences of an ageing population. It has been claimed that there will be too few people of working age to support and care for a growing group of older people. However, Vincent believes that this problem has been greatly exaggerated and in reality the main problem is one of wealth distribution. If the state redistributed sufficient income from businesses and the wealthy, it could easily afford to pay for the care of the elderly.

Vincent views the concentration on the future costs of an ageing population as an ideological distraction. Other issues which might result in future expense on a greater scale include global warming and the disposal of nuclear waste, but they are not discussed as an economic problem to the same extent as an ageing population.

To Vincent, then, the 'problem' of old age is largely a social creation. This problem is exacerbated by the existence of ageism, which can be every bit as discriminatory as sexism or racism. Indeed there is less legislation banning ageism than there is for these other forms of discrimination. Employers still routinely discriminate against older applicants for jobs in a way that would not be acceptable in the case of female or minority ethnic applicants.

However, just as the working class and minority ethnic groups have fought for increased rights, there is some evidence of efforts by older people to do the same. Vincent asks whether the 'sixties' generation will 'seek liberation from the cultural constraints of ageism' (2006, p. 213). He also points out that old age can lead to liberation from the constraints of middle age such as paying a mortgage and caring for children.

Table 13.1 Average weekly household expenditure in pounds by age of head of household, 2000–1

	Under 30	30–49	50–64	65–74	75 and over	All households
Housing (net)	78.70	84.00	56.80	34.80	30.30	63.90
Fuel and power	9.90	12.30	13.00	11.80	10.00	11.90
Food and non-alcoholic drinks	55.00	73.60	67.10	47.00	34.70	61.90
Alcoholic drink	18.70	17.90	17.40	7.90	4.90	15.00
Tobacco	7.50	6.90	7.20	3.90	1.80	6.10
Clothing and footwear	25.00	29.80	21.10	12.20	5.80	22.00
Household goods	28.20	37.30	37.80	28.90	14.40	32.60
Household services	20.80	26.90	21.70	17.60	11.80	22.00
Personal goods and services	16.30	17.00	15..70	11.20	7.50	14.70
Motoring	52.00	67.30	67.60	32.70	15.40	55.10
Fares and other travel costs	12.00	11.80	10.10	5.40	2.50	9.50
Leisure goods	18.80	25.60	19.60	14.20	7.30	19.70
Leisure services	38.30	61.20	60.80	34.90	22.40	50.60
Miscellaneous	0.60	1.20	0.60	0.20	0.10	0.70
All expenditure groups	381.70	472.80	416.40	262.60	169.10	385.70

Source: J.A. Vincent (2006) 'Age and old age' in G. Payne (ed.) *Social Divisions*, 2nd edn, Palgrave Macmillan, Basingstoke, p. 208.

As with other social divisions and types of stratification, the nature and extent of inequality change over time. Vincent concludes: 'we must consider the life-course as a social process, rather than a static social divide between generation or cohort' (2006, p. 214).

Evaluation

Vincent provides a useful discussion of the relationship between inequality and age and how this relates to social change. He shows an awareness of the variety of ways in which age can be related to social divisions and affect people's life chances. However, his views are not supported by postmodernists who believe that differentiation between age groups is weakening or even breaking down (see pp. 754–6).

From the point of view of feminists Vincent is right to acknowledge that age-based inequalities interact with gender inequalities, but feminist theorists tend to see gender inequalities as the key to understanding other forms of inequality. Their views will now be examined.

Feminist perspectives on age and the life course

Like conflict perspectives, feminist perspectives on age and the life course emphasize the relationship between inequality and age. However, they link this inequality in one way or another to gender inequality.

The first example of a feminist approach examined below discusses the parallels between the oppression of women and the oppression of children, while the second looks at the way ageing affects women differently compared to men.

Ann Oakley – feminism and childhood

The feminist sociologist Ann Oakley (1994) argues that there are many similarities between the position of women and the position of children in society. In the nineteenth century the positions of women and children were very similar. Since then the position of women has improved, but the position of children has not – they are still very disadvantaged compared to other social groups.

Minority groups

Both women and children are members of social **minority groups**. Minority groups are regarded by society as being physically or culturally different from others. On the basis of this difference it is deemed acceptable that they receive unequal treatment. Minority groups often have fewer rights as citizens. Women have fought for and gained most citizenship rights such as the right to vote and own property, but children still lack such rights.

Nevertheless, women are sometimes seen as more childlike than men – for example, they are seen as less logical, more emotional and more in need of protection. Both women and children are often seen as not being capable of knowing what is good for them.

In the past, women were excluded from some forms of paid work because it was thought that such work would harm them. Today, children are still 'protected' by having severe limits placed on their right to work and earn a living. They are given no choice in the matter since society believes that childhood 'should be a time of fun' (Oakley, 1994, p. 16). Partly as a result of this, children are more likely to be in poverty than adults, just as women are more likely to be in poverty than men.

Not only are there many similarities in the oppression of women and the oppression of children, but this oppression is interlinked. Women and children are embedded in each other's lives since women are primarily responsible for childcare and this responsibility helps to restrict their opportunities. Oakley therefore says, 'a comparative sociography of children and women conveys a picture of *mutual dependence* and *interdependence* and *mutual oppression*' (1994, p. 19).

Children's rights

Despite interconnections between the positions of women and children, Oakley is clear that children have much further to go before their lack of rights is seriously addressed. Gender issues are now taken seriously in society and the study of sociology, but childhood issues are still marginalized. Children themselves are not organized and their views are not taken seriously by most adult researchers. Adults still speak for children and children's own voices are rarely heard.

Issues of childhood have not been integrated into sociological theory in the same way that issues of gender have. Children are usually seen in terms of socialization into adult roles, not as social actors in their own right. Sociology, including the sociology of childhood, is still adult-centred, seeing children in terms of what they will become (i.e. adults), rather than studying their experiences as children.

Similarly, society is adult-centred, organizing institutions such as schools in terms of adult needs rather than in terms of what children want. Children are simply required to conform to the demands adults make on them.

Oakley concludes by discussing the radical feminist Shulamith Firestone (1972; see pp. 104–5). Firestone believed that while children and women are locked together in mutual, patriarchal oppression, the rights of adults and children do conflict. If children are to be freed from oppression, then women will have to relinquish some rights over their children.

To Oakley, though, ultimately both women and children will only be freed from oppression through radical social change. She says:

> *the crucial point here is the social and economic fabric within which the rights of different groups are set against one another. In this, and with so much else, the answer lies in the generation of a different sort of society – one whose structures do not have to deprive some people of freedom in order to give it to others.* Oakley, 1994, p. 32

Linda R. Gannon – *Women and Aging*

Ageing for men and women

In *Women and Aging: Transcending the Myths*, Linda Gannon (1999) examines what she sees as myths about differences in the process of ageing for men and women.

Gannon argues that differences in the ageing process between the two sexes are often portrayed as being a consequence of biological differences. However, she claims that in reality ageing sometimes affects women more adversely than men as a result of 'lifestyles, habits, expectations and roles that place women at risk' (1999, p. 1).

The physical and psychological health of women can suffer as they get older because of environmental and social problems rather than biological ageing. Gannon says, 'with age, biology becomes relatively less important as the combined influences of pollution, trauma, sexism, ageism, poverty and access to quality health care accumulate over a lifetime' (1999, p. 1). Women tend to be materially disadvantaged compared to men because they tend to be paid less and have more caring responsibilities.

Science and female ageing

However, 'scientific' views about the ageing of women pay little, if any, attention to such factors and instead claim that biological factors are much more important. According to Gannon, scientific views have three main characteristics.

1. They tend to be **androcentric**. They see men as the norm and women as a deviation from the norm. Gannon says, 'the ideology of androcentrism is the basis for a culture in which men's bodies, feelings, activities, behaviours, interests, desires and occupations are taken as "the point of reference"; women are ignored or characterized as deviant' (1999, p. 3). Normality is what men do and desire. For example, female hormones are seen as a problem during menstruation and women may receive medical treatment to counteract 'premenstrual syndrome'. However, men's hormones are not normally seen as a medical problem worthy of treatment, even if high levels of testosterone are associated with aggression and violence.
2. Scientific approaches see differences in the ageing of men and women as biologically determined. However, Gannon dismisses this belief as a patriarchal ideology. For example, a discourse has developed which portrays women as inferior to men because they are seen as more likely to suffer from the bone disease osteoporosis as they age. In reality, Gannon claims, environmental factors, such as low female rates of participation in sport, explain the higher rate of osteoporosis amongst some groups of women. African American women do not suffer from higher rates of this disease than African American men, demonstrating that gender alone cannot explain the difference.
3. Scientific approaches are also **dualistic**. Dualistic notions divide the world into two opposite categories, such as mind/body, normal/diseased and sick/well. To Gannon dualisms are often artificial and misleading. For example, as the body ages its capacities change and these changes are often misleadingly viewed as diseases. Because of the normal/diseased dualism there is no alternative category to describe the body's changed state as it ages.

The menopause and male power

Gannon illustrates these points by applying them to the way the menopause is viewed. The menopause occurs when a woman's ovaries cease to produce an egg every four weeks, menstruation comes to an end and the levels of oestrogen decline.

In the dualism of normal/diseased, male scientists have labelled the menopause as a disease. It is described as creating 'estrogen deficiency' (estrogen is the US spelling of oestrogen) as the levels of oestrogen are seen as being abnormally low. In reality post-menopausal levels of oestrogen are just as 'normal' as levels before the menopause.

The scientific evidence suggests that lower rates of oestrogen have a mixture of advantages and disadvantages for women's health. Nevertheless, because the menopause is seen as a disease, it is frequently treated with hormone replacement therapy (HRT).

Because they adopt biological deterministic approaches, scientists attribute a whole range of 'problems' – from low sex drive to osteoporosis (see above) – to the menopause, despite a lack of evidence demonstrating that it is the cause. For example, research shows that the sex drive of post-menopausal women varies considerably and in a significant number of cases it increases not decreases.

Gannon concludes that the way the menopause is viewed is androcentric. Men too produce lower levels of androgen hormones as they get older, but this is not viewed as abnormal or seen as a medical problem requiring intervention.

The ideology of this aspect of the process of ageing in women has two main effects:

1. It increases male power. Labelling the menopause as a disease 'advances patriarchal ideology by rendering all women over 50 sick and in need of help – reinforcing their inferior status throughout life' (Gannon, 1999, p. 8).
2. It disguises the real causes of the problems of women as they age, which are the 'economic and political oppression of women – both of which intensify with age' (p. 9).

Evaluation of feminist perspectives

Gannon's work makes an important contribution to the study of age and the life course, showing that the experience and social meaning of ageing may be different for men and women. It suggests that ageism may be experienced acutely by women because of the way it interacts with patriarchy.

Ann Oakley draws attention to the subordinate position of children in society and links this to patriarchal relations. However, sociologists such as Oakley can be criticized when they argue that the subordination of children and the subordination of women can be seen as part of the same patriarchal system. Michael Wyness (2006) argues that the fact that women as well as men exercise power over children makes it difficult to see the subordination of children and of women as part of the same structure. Furthermore, children sometimes suffer abuse at the hands of women. Wyness therefore argues that, 'Ultimately, patriarchy is a system governed by gendered not age-related structures' (2006, p. 39).

Interpretive perspectives on age

Social construction

Both conflict and feminist perspectives on age are critical of the idea that age can be seen solely in biological and chronological terms. Age cannot be understood simply in terms of scientific facts, but instead must be understood in its social context. Indeed all sociological perspectives believe that an understanding of society is crucial to an understanding of age.

Interpretive approaches place particular emphasis upon the meanings attached to age. As Jane Pilcher says, 'Interpretivist perspectives are concerned ... with *understanding* the meaning social phenomena have for individuals and with the *processes* through which individuals interpret and understand the world' (1995, p. 28).

Interpretive perspectives place less emphasis than conflict and feminist perspectives on the way social structures (such as class and patriarchy) shape those meanings. Instead they tend to see the meanings as shaping the social world and affecting the behaviour of members of society. Thus interpretive sociologists are interested in the meanings attached to categories such as childhood, youth or old age, and the effects that those meanings have.

Interpretive perspectives have therefore tended to support the idea that age categories are a **social construct** – they are the product of social definitions, not natural, biological categories. Social constructionism has influenced other sociological approaches examined in this chapter including that of Aries (see pp. 759–60).

The influence of the interpretive perspective

Prout and James (1990, discussed in Pilcher, 1995) see interpretivist sociology as influencing the sociology of age in two main ways:

1 It has led to the questioning of commonsense ideas about age. For example, it has questioned ideas about the inevitability of childhood as a period when children must be highly dependent on parents, and of old age as a time when the quality of people's lives deteriorates.

2 It has encouraged an examination of the social world from the perspective of its participants, including disempowered groups such as children. Thus, for example, it has stimulated studies which take children seriously as social actors in their own right (see p. 765).

The ideas behind interpretive perspectives on age – that age categories are largely social constructs, that commonsense views of age can be questioned, and that age can be studied from the viewpoint of those in all age groups – have been very influential.

There is a good deal of overlap between interpretive and other perspectives in sociology. Many sociologists primarily influenced by other perspectives (including conflict theory, feminism and postmodernism) have accepted at least some aspects of interpretive approaches. For example, Gannon (1999; see above), while primarily seeing age from a feminist perspective, was influenced by interpretivism when studying the different meanings of old age for men and women. Similarly, predominantly interpretive approaches have been influenced by other perspectives in sociology, as the next study to be discussed will show.

Jenny Hockey and Allison James – *Growing Up and Growing Old*

The work of Jenny Hockey and Allison James (1993) draws upon interpretive perspectives in examining the meanings attached to growing up and growing old in contemporary society. Hockey and James argue that the meaning of old age is linked to the meaning of childhood. Through an examination of a range of secondary sources and the use of their own ethnographic studies of old people's homes, they argue that the elderly are often compared to children and treated as if they were children.

Although Hockey and James concentrate primarily on language and the interpretation of meanings in line with interpretive perspectives, they also incorporate elements of conflict perspectives into their study. They examine how the meanings attributed to childhood and old age lead to differences in power between different age groups and can cause conflict.

Childhood and adulthood

Hockey and James argue that in modern Western societies, **personhood** – being accepted as an individual who is a full member of society – depends upon being accepted as an adult. Adults are autonomous individuals with rights but also responsibility for their own actions. Other groups are not given the status of personhood. For example, those with 'mental handicaps' and children are not seen as full persons who should be able to make their own choices and take responsibility for their actions.

Modern ideas of childhood believe that children should be separated and excluded from the public, adult

world and largely live their lives in families, schools, nurseries and other specialist places for children. Children are seen as being close to nature and lacking the rationality of adults. They are seen as innocent and easy to corrupt. They are therefore vulnerable and dependent on adults both for care and for protection from the corrupting world of adults.

Childhood is the 'other' of adulthood, its opposite which helps define adulthood as being about independence and autonomy. Because childhood is seen in this way children are kept in a state of dependency on adults (see pp. 759–64 for a discussion of changing ideas on childhood).

Infantilized old age

Old age is often linked to childhood. In the media and everyday life the elderly and childhood are often linked together. Hockey and James point out that 'very old people may jokingly be described as entering their "second childhood", or as going "ga ga" when their memories fade' (1993, p. 17). The term 'ga ga' refers, of course, to the noise made by babies who cannot yet talk. They are helpless, unable to express their own wishes and totally dependent on adults to care for them.

Stereotypes of elderly women see them as 'little old ladies' – harmless perhaps, but also powerless and passive like an infant. In the media, children and the elderly are often portrayed as having an affinity with one another because they are both dependent. In the film *Cinema Paradiso*, for example, an elderly man and a young boy find a common bond through the cinema; and the elderly and the young are often juxtaposed in adverts.

Everyday talk, stereotypes and the media all serve to make old age appear similar to childhood. In the process old age is **infantilized**. The elderly are made to seem childlike and as a result they lose the status of being adults who have full personhood.

The consequences of this were demonstrated in studies by Jenny Hockey of old people's homes. Hockey found that the clients of old people's homes were often treated like children. They were not allowed to keep their own money, which instead was looked after by the staff who would give them 'pocket money' if they needed it. The privacy of their body was often invaded, as staff members washed, bathed or dressed them. They were expected not to be sexually active and they were given few choices about daily routine such as when they ate or even when they went to the toilet. As Hockey and James say, 'residential homes for the elderly may effectively encourage social dependency by reducing people's opportunities for independence and self determination' (1993, p. 33).

Dependence, independence and resistance

Hockey and James argue that both childhood and old age are social constructs. They are linked by the common theme of dependency yet both children and the elderly could be much more independent than society usually allows them to be.

For example, in the past children did much more work than they do today, and retirement policies deny many older people, who are perfectly capable of working, the opportunity to do so. Hockey and James note that similar characteristics of dependency are often attributed to the disabled who also can be restricted and excluded as a result.

However, Hockey and James do not believe that those who are marginalized, excluded and made dependent always accept their status lying down. In line with conflict theory, Hockey and James argue that they are capable of resisting their status. Resistance can take three forms.

1. They can use alternative sources of power to resist. For example, wealthy elderly people might wield high power because of their wealth, elderly men can still exert some patriarchal power over female carers and so on.
2. A second method of resistance is to deny membership of a subordinate group and to pretend to belong to one of a higher status. Teenagers often pretend to be 18 in order to buy alcoholic drinks. Elderly people may cling on to roles which make them feel or appear younger. Jenny Hockey's research in an old people's home described one resident, Sissy, taking on the role of visitor to cheer up and support more frail residents.
3. Being a member of a disadvantaged social group can in itself be a source of power. It provides opportunities to mock the way you are treated. Hockey recounts how residents of the old people's home would act in deliberately childish ways – sticking their tongue out, for example – in response to being infantilized by care workers. As well as symbolic resistance such as this, some residents were deliberately obstructive. Some refused to hurry to lunch, some demanded to go to the toilet at inconvenient times, others would turn a deaf ear to requests or instructions from care staff. Some residents made frequent and stark comments on their own impending demise, and thereby resisted the taboo in the home against discussing death. This discomfited many care staff but was a way in which some of the residents were able to assert a measure of independence until the end.

Conclusion and evaluation

Hockey and James provide an interesting discussion of the way in which childhood and old age are linked through the process of infantilization. Their work provides a good illustration of how a sociological understanding of age and the life course can be developed through analysing the meaning given to age in particular societies. As such, it is just one example of an interpretive approach to age. Other examples are discussed later in the chapter (see pp. 759–60, 782–4).

Interpretive approaches in sociology are often accused by structural and conflict theorists of ignoring inequality and social structure, but Hockey and James show an awareness of issues related to power, social class, gender and ethnicity. Like a lot of sociological work on age, therefore, it has been influenced by more than one sociological perspective.

'ostmodern perspectives on age

Jane Pilcher – modernity, postmodernity and the life course

The life course and modernity

Jane Pilcher (1995) argues that it is possible to see the stages of the life course in contemporary Western societies as a product of **modernity** in general and **industrialization** in particular. These stages (consisting of an extended childhood, a period of youth, adulthood, and old age, which starts with retirement) have been strongly shaped by the way the labour market has developed. Pilcher says, 'childhood and youth have emerged via a process of their progressive exclusion from the labour market and their increasing containment within the education system' (1995, p. 146). The exclusion of those beyond retirement age from the labour market has 'led old age to be constructed as a period of dependency and relative powerlessness' (p. 147).

Prior to the industrial revolution, both children and the old were usually involved in work if they were able to contribute. Childhood was much shorter, the category of youth was of little importance and being elderly was not so clearly demarcated by chronological age. Pilcher concludes, therefore, that 'The form and characteristics of the modern British life course itself can, then, be argued to be the product of the interrelations of societal institutions as they have developed under conditions of modernity' (1995, p. 147).

Postmodernity and the life course

Having outlined the main features of the life course under modernity, Pilcher goes on to note that it is increasingly argued that the modern form of the life course is breaking down. The different phases of the life course are becoming more disorderly. The boundaries between different stages are becoming increasingly blurred.

As people become more concerned about self-identity they may present themselves or act in ways which contradict the norms associated with different life-course stages. For example, children may dress more like adults and old or middle-aged people may dress in youthful styles – risking being called 'mutton dressed as lamb'. Wide variations in the age of marriage and childbearing, increased longevity, early retirement, advances in medicine, the development of cosmetic surgery and IVF treatment have all undermined the relatively clear-cut stages of the life course associated with modernity.

Pilcher says:

> *Some theorists have argued that, in effect, the life course is becoming deinstitutionalized and destandardized, that age-based transitions and norms, forms and standards of behaviour, which previously were fairly strictly defined, regulated and orderly, are becoming less fixed, less constraining, less orderly.* 1995, p. 149

From this point of view, people have far more choice than in the past about how their age affects their life.

Pilcher herself is not convinced that dramatic changes have taken place. She admits that the effects of age in society are changing so that the life course is becoming less rigid. However, she also says that 'the balance of the evidence … points to the continuing importance of age-based social divisions' (1995, p. 150).

Some theorists, however, believe that the changes are more profound than Pilcher acknowledges and are more supportive of postmodern theories.

Mike Featherstone and Mike Hepworth – 'The mask of ageing'

The deconstruction of the life course

Mike Featherstone and Mike Hepworth argue that there are 'emergent cultural tendencies' (1991, p. 373), particularly in the middle classes, towards postmodern forms of the life course. For some people, the experience of the life course has changed in line with postmodern theory.

Like Pilcher, Featherstone and Hepworth believe that industrialization in modern societies led to the increasing importance of chronological age and the 'institutionalisation of the life course socially structured into orderly sequences' (1991, p. 372). In recent times, though, the life course has begun to be **deconstructed**, or broken down, for some groups, making it less predictable. The central features of this process are:

1. **De-differentiation** – a process in which the differences between stages in the life course become less clear.
2. **Deinstitutionalization** – a process in which the institutions of society become less closely associated with maintaining different phases of the life course.

There are many aspects of these changes:

1. Children and adults are becoming more alike – in terms of gestures, postures, leisure pursuits, ways of dressing and so on they are becoming more similar to one another.
2. Childhood is becoming less separate from other stages of the life course because the segregation of children from adult life is becoming impossible. The media intrude into the formerly private life of the family, bringing adult concerns into the lives of children.
3. Middle-class adults reaching retirement with good pensions can afford to continue to enjoy consumer-culture lifestyles, having a high disposable income to spend on leisure goods and services.
4. Some of this spending goes on 'body maintenance'. They can slow down mental, sexual and physical decline with the help of healthy diets, regular exercise, cosmetics, drugs, surgical intervention and so on.
5. The 'baby boomers' born after the Second World War who grew up in the 1960s are taking with them into old age many of the values and cultural tastes of their

youth. Unlike previous generations they try to maintain youthful lifestyles as they age.

6 Increasingly people reject chronological age – the number of years lived – as an indicator of their real selves. They regard chronological age as a **mask** which hides their more youthful essential, inner self. Featherstone and Hepworth quote research which suggests that many people believe that age should be seen in terms of the age you feel or the age you look, rather than in terms of the number of years you have lived. Based on these criteria, people see themselves as having a **personal age** different from their chronological age, usually seeing themselves as younger than their birth certificate indicates.

7 Ageing has increasingly come to be seen in positive terms rather than as part of an inevitable decline towards infirmity and dependence. Middle age or mid-life is seen as lasting longer than was previously thought, so that only the very elderly are expected to be powerless and dependent. Even after retirement from paid work many middle-class people continue to make a valuable contribution to the community (for example, through voluntary work). They often retain considerable economic, cultural, social or symbolic capital (see pp. 67–9 for a discussion of different types of capital), making them far from powerless.

Conclusion

Featherstone and Hepworth conclude that the baby-boomer generation have done much to break down the stereotypes of old age and increase the range of options and identities open to the middle class as they get older. They acknowledge, however, that these benefits have not been enjoyed to the same extent by lower classes who have fewer resources to take with them into old age. Nor can these changes overcome the loss of status and opportunity for those whose bodies seriously decline. For example, the incontinent or infirm elderly have difficulty maintaining a youthful self-identity, and their social and leisure opportunities are severely restricted.

Featherstone and Hepworth are therefore guarded in accepting postmodern ideas, but they do believe that the societal trend is towards a more flexible life course, in line with the predictions of postmodern theory.

Andrew Blaikie – *Ageing and Popular Culture*

Consumer culture and age

Andrew Blaikie (1999) is a stronger advocate of postmodernism than either Pilcher or Featherstone and Hepworth. He concentrates on the image of retirement, arguing that attitudes to retirement have changed dramatically and stereotypes of old age have broken down. He attributes this partly to the development of **consumer culture**.

With an ageing population, those over retirement age make up an increasingly numerous group. They have become an important market for companies wishing to sell goods and services. While marketing and the media still emphasize youthful vitality much of the time, they also stress the importance of trying to retain that youthfulness into later life. It is stressed that rejuvenation is possible with such products and services as liposuction, anti-wrinkle creams and face-lifts.

In modern societies, where production rather than consumption was dominant, the elderly were not valued because they were considered too old to work. Because knowledge changed rapidly, their experience was not valued. However, in postmodern consumer societies these handicaps no longer apply because the elderly can consume just like younger age groups.

Challenging stereotypes

The stereotypes of ageing have been challenged by media figures who appear to retain their youthfulness much longer than would be expected. Role models of successful ageing include Cliff Richard, Mick Jagger, David Bowie, Raquel Welch, Joan Collins and Paul McCartney, all of whom are perceived as living full lives and looking glamorous.

Some magazines portray positive aspects of life after retirement. For example, the magazine *Choice* emphasizes in its title that the retired have many options open to them and can live full and rewarding lives. In the media there are more and more positive images of older people enjoying life and being active.

This idea has filtered through to the professions which deal with those in later life. Blaikie discusses research which suggests that professionals such as health workers and social workers see it as normal for older people to be self-reliant, sexually active and healthy, at least in the early years of retirement.

Four stages of life

Blaikie supports a view of the life course put forward by the social historian Peter Laslett (1989). Laslett argued that there are now four stages of life:

1 The first age of childhood is characterized by dependence, immaturity and socialization.
2 The second age of adulthood is characterized by maturity, independence and responsibility.
3 The third age follows retirement and is characterized by Laslett as a period of personal fulfilment. Freed from the responsibility of parenthood and employment, people are relatively free to choose their own pursuits and to fulfil ambitions.
4 The fourth age relates to physical decline and is characterized by 'dependence, decrepitude and death'.

The emphasis on choice and opportunity in later life in this analysis reflects the postmodern emphasis on the ability of individuals to choose their own identities.

The end of old age?

People are no longer so restricted by their age. Blaikie says, 'To talk of the "end of old age" is perhaps to overstate the issue' (1999, p. 210), but he goes on to say, 'the appropriate metaphor is no longer one of life as a clearly defined journey but of a bewildering maze' (pp. 210–11). In this maze, people have multiple selves; their identity is much more a matter of choice rather than being determined by age.

speculates that in the future medical advances ncrease longevity and good health amongst the population further. This could break down stereo- about old age even further and bring society closer he 'end of old age'.

However, Blaikie does not completely accept the idea that old age has become a time of fulfilment and choice. He argues that there are still significant problems faced by the elderly.

1. The positive images of old age make those who cannot live active, fulfilled lives after retirement seem like deviants. They may receive more criticism for their failure than sympathy for their plight.
2. The emphasis on active and youthful retirement tends to deny the reality of ultimate physical decline and death. While many people are healthy and active after 65, some are not and their options are much more restricted than positive images of old age would suggest.
3. Class, gender and ethnic divisions continue to shape the experience of old age. White men from higher social classes tend to enjoy more prosperous and fulfilling retirements than other groups.

Realistically, then, 'Most older people stand to be neither particularly affluent, nor desperately infirm: they are relatively poor but also fit and active, with partial, remedial disabilities and dependencies as they grow older' (Blaikie, 1999, pp. 214–15).

Postmodernism and age – conclusion

Postmodern views on age and the life course run the risk of exaggerating the degree to which society has been freed from the influence of age on social life. However, all the approaches examined here accept that the changes they discuss are limited and recognize that biology continues to prevent age differences from disappearing. They identify some important social trends and advance a strong argument that the life course has become less rigid than in the past.

Perhaps the arguments are more convincing when applied to older age groups. It is less apparent that the significance of life-course stages has declined for children (see, for example, the work of Jenks, pp. 761–3). Childhood will now be examined.

Childhood

The dominant framework

Commonsense and childhood

Michael Wyness argues that commonsense thinking sees childhood as 'a natural and inevitable phase that we all go through before we reach adulthood' (2006, p. 7). Childhood therefore tends to be taken for granted as a biological state through which all those who become adults pass. Wyness says:

> *If we are pushed to define childhood, the invocation of 'nature' directs us towards thinking about children's 'natural', biological incapacities. Children are physically smaller and weaker than adults are. Common sense suggests that their size and stature are visible markers of difference.* 2006, p. 7

From this commonsense perspective the nature of childhood is seen as deriving from the biological attributes of children. The experience of childhood follows from the physical and mental immaturity of children. Childhood is seen as something which is inevitably experienced by all humans and which has key features in common across cultures and over time. It is viewed as 'a universal and natural phenomenon largely because, irrespective of context, children are smaller, weaker and less physiologically developed than adults' (Wyness, 2006, p. 117).

Key features of the dominant framework

These assumptions about childhood are part of what Prout and James (1997) referred to as the 'dominant framework' within which children and childhood have been viewed. Drawing on the ideas of Prout and James and others, Wyness identifies the key features of the dominant framework (see Figure 13.4):

1. Childhood and adulthood are seen as **dichotomous** or as opposites. Figure 13.4 illustrates this dichotomous view. Children are seen as being closer to nature than adults. They gradually acquire culture, morality and the ability to take part in social life through a process of development and socialization, but initially they are dominated by biological urges, they have no culture and cannot take an active part in social life.

   Children are seen as simple because they have not yet developed the complex and sophisticated ways of

Figure 13.4 The dominant framework

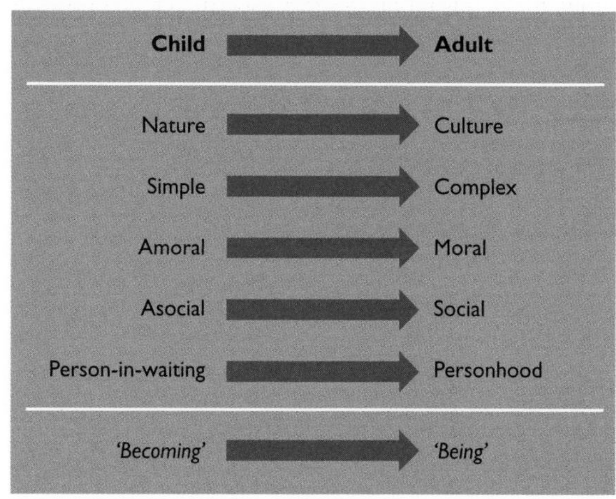

Source: A. Prout and A. James (1997) 'A new paradigm for the sociology of childhood?' in A. James and A. Prout (eds) *Constructing and Reconstructing Childhood*, 2nd edn, Falmer, London.

acting and interacting with one another used by adults. For example, children gradually develop the ability to understand and use complex language.

Childhood is seen as a phase involving a process in which children, as incomplete persons, progress towards adulthood. Adulthood is seen as a state in which personhood has been attained. This approach therefore adopts a **deficit model of childhood** – children are defined in terms of their lack of adult attributes.

2 This links to what Wyness calls children's 'lack of ontology'. Children are not seen as an entity in their own right but 'are conceptualised in terms of what they will become rather than what they are … children are incomplete beings whereas adults are fully constituted social beings'. As a consequence of this approach, 'social scientists have tended to look at children simply in terms of the adults they will become' (Wyness, 2006, p. 120). They have stressed, for example, how problematic childhoods (for example, those involving abuse, neglect or family instability) might create problems (such as criminality) when the children grow up. They have been less concerned with children's experiences during childhood itself.
3 Children are seen as **proto-individuals** – that is, the earliest or most primitive stage of individual. Children are seen as individuals because they are not seen as part of a group with a group culture. There is an 'emphasis on the singular *child* rather than children and their collective practices'. Seeing the child as a primitive or early-stage individual 'further strengthens the idea that children are not of society. Children are seen as unfinished objects who require the continuous involvement of socialising adults before they are complete and can enter society as complete members' (Wyness, 2006, p. 121).

James Prout (2005) argues that the dominant framework, which sees the child as an incomplete individual, is an aspect of **modernity**. Modernity emphasizes the importance of rationality (see pp. 890–1), and becoming rational is an essential part of how the dominant perspective views growing up. According to Prout, the dominant perspective associates childhood with irrationality, incompetence and play, whereas adulthood is associated with rationality, competence and work. Children are not seen as capable of making rational calculations, competently pursuing their aims or using rationality to transform nature through work.

Although childhood might not be associated with rationality or science, the dominant framework has adopted rational scientific methods for studying childhood.

Developmentalism

According to Wyness (2006), the dominant framework has itself been dominated by psychological research using scientific methods. The research has often taken place in the laboratory because it has been looking for universal features of childhood, not features specific to particular societies at particular times.

This approach has tried to measure and assess the 'transition from becoming to being' (Wyness, 2006, p. 122) – the process by which children become adults. It has adopted what Wyness calls an **ages and stages** approach which assumes that children develop through set stages at predictable ages.

Jean Piaget

The most influential ages and stages approach to childhood was put forward by Jean Piaget (1896–1980), a Swiss developmental psychologist. Piaget (1932) believed that children learned as they attempted to adapt to their environment, and as they did so they passed through four main stages of development. These stages were sequential – you had to pass through one stage before you could move on to the next – and occurred at roughly the same ages for children in all societies.

The four stages of child development identified by Piaget were:

1 The **sensorimotor stage**, which lasts from birth until about 18 months. In this stage the infant responds to immediate stimuli and is not able to plan ahead. The child has no internal concept of objects so if he or she cannot see or touch them the child does not believe they exist.
2 The **preoperational stage**, which starts at around 18 months and finishes when the child is about 6 years old. From around 18 months the child develops concepts of objects and believes objects exist even when they cannot be seen or touched (known as **object permanence**). The child starts to use symbols such as words, which stand for something else.
3 The **concrete operational stage**, which takes places roughly between the ages of 6 and 12. By this stage the child begins to learn general rules about how the world can be manipulated or changed. He or she learns that **reversibility** is possible – for example, a ball of clay can be made back into a ball after it has been reshaped.
4 The final stage is the **formal operational stage**, which commences when the child is about 12 and develops further through the teenage years. Formal operations involve children applying abstract rules or principles to solving problems. This allows the child to plan ahead.

Piaget's developmental scheme sees children as moving towards the ability to be rational and apply logic. Describing Piaget's scheme, Wyness says, 'By children's early teens they are capable of much more abstract reasoning; children can theorise and hypothesise about their environments and the worlds of others' (2006, p. 123).

Criticisms of the dominant framework

Although the dominant framework has indeed dominated both commonsense and psychological thinking about childhood for many years, it has increasingly been questioned by sociologists. Those adopting different sociological perspectives have identified a variety of weaknesses with the dominant model.

1 Many sociologists have argued that childhood does not follow a series of fixed, predictable stages in all

places at all times. They have seen the idea of childhood as a social construction which varies from place to place and time to time (see the discussion of Aries's work on pp. 759–60).

2 Stevi Jackson and Sue Scott (2006) point out that the experience of childhood is shaped by other social divisions such as class, gender and disability, which makes universal generalizations about children misleading. Developmental psychology tends to see children as isolated individuals, and many sociologists argue that it is impossible to ignore the role of social groups in how children develop. The socialization of children in different social groups (see pp. 686–92 for a discussion of socialization) will inevitably vary and will affect the way children grow up.

3 Berry Mayall (2004) argues that developmental psychology tends to have a cultural bias towards Western, particularly Anglo-American, ideas about childhood and child rearing. While it claims to state universal truths about how children develop, in reality it simply describes Western views about how children *should* develop. For example, many other societies place much less emphasis on the development of rationality as one of the ultimate goals of child development.

4 All of the above criticisms question the explanations and descriptions of child development put forward within the dominant framework. However, some critics raise more fundamental questions about the whole idea that childhood should be studied from a developmental point of view. Whether children are seen as inevitably passing through certain biologically given stages or are seen as being socialized, the emphasis is on the process of becoming an adult. However, Jackson and Scott (2006) argue that:

> *Contemporary sociological approaches suggest that rather than viewing children as future adults in the making, we should focus on children's own lives and activities. This involves a shift away from the idea of the child as 'becoming' an adult to the child being conceptualised as an active social agent.* 2006, p. 217

In other words, from this point of view, children actively create their own social worlds, which should be studied in their own right. Children should not be regarded as passively passing through stages or being moulded through socialization by adults. Mayall, for example, believes that sociology should concentrate on 'the present tense of childhood – the quality of how it is lived now' and 'point to children's competences in and knowledge about the social worlds they live in' (2004, p. 40).

5 Following on from the above, Mayall argues that the dominant framework emphasizes the needs of children, needs which are met by adults so that children can develop 'normally'. However, seeing children as competent social actors in their own right shifts the emphasis towards children's rights. Children are denied many rights (such as the right to vote or to manage their own financial affairs) which are taken for granted by adults. Some sociologists believe that the lack of children's rights can be oppressive and that a focus on rights can potentially lead to improvements in the lives of children (see pp. 764–6 for more details).

6 According to the dominant framework, childhood is a natural, biological state, and the social division between children and adults is also natural. However, from another point of view, age in general, and childhood in particular, is a form of social stratification. Structural and conflict theories of sociology tend to see childhood very differently from the dominant paradigm which they believe obscures the inequality between different groups of children and between adults and children (see pp. 747–50).

As this section develops, these and other alternative viewpoints will be examined in more detail. First, we will consider the view that childhood is a social construction rather than a natural state.

Childhood as a social construction

Cross-cultural comparisons

The idea that childhood is a social construction has been put forward by many sociologists in various forms. Despite differences between advocates of this view, all agree that the idea of childhood, if it exists at all, varies from place to place and time to time.

Contemporary Western societies have distinctive ideas about childhood and it is often assumed that these ideas are normal and universal. From a social constructionist point of view they are not. A number of examples can illustrate this point.

1 In some societies it is still considered quite normal for children to do substantial amounts of work. Michael Wyness (2006) discusses a study of Mexico (Blasco, 2005) which found that, until the recent introduction of compulsory secondary education, most teenage children spent their teenage years in paid work and domestic employment.

2 According to Amnesty International (2007), there are an estimated 300,000 child soldiers in the world, actively involved in fighting in more than thirty countries including the Democratic Republic of Congo, Sudan, Colombia and Afghanistan. Some of them have been victims of torture and some are beaten to make sure they obey orders. The availability of light and cheap weapons means that children aged 10 or even younger are sometimes used to fight. Children have also been forced to kill members of their own families, and female child soldiers have been raped or used to provide sexual services.

3 Ruth Bennedict (1955, discussed in Pilcher, 1995) found wide cultural variations in the roles of children. In Samoa children were not considered too young to do dangerous or physically demanding tasks. In

Tikopia in the Western Pacific, children's individuality was respected and they were not expected to be obedient. Amongst Australian Aborigines in the 1920s children were not discouraged from playing sexual games. Bennedict concluded that compared to Western societies some other societies differentiated much less between adulthood and childhood.

Social constructionist theories have argued that contemporary Western ideas of childhood have only developed comparatively recently. The next section examines the historical development of ideas about childhood.

The historical development of childhood

Philippe Ariès – *Centuries of Childhood*

Children in medieval times

One of the earliest and most influential theories of childhood as a social construction was advanced by Philippe Ariès (1973, first published 1960). Ariès discussed changes in the nature of childhood in Europe since medieval times. He argued that in medieval times (between roughly the twelfth and sixteenth centuries) a modern conception of childhood did not exist. He said that, 'as soon as the child could live without the constant solicitude of his mother, his nanny or his cradle-rocker, he belonged to adult society' (Ariès, 1973, p. 125).

In early medieval times many people did not even know their chronological age since it had little social significance. At that time many children died before reaching adulthood. Children were not therefore accorded the importance attached to them today. For example, parents did not get painters to do portraits of their children and mourning was kept to a minimum when a child died. Ariès commented that:

> *No one thought of keeping a picture of a child if that child had either lived to grow to manhood or had died in infancy. In the first case childhood was simply an unimportant phase of which there was no need to keep any record; in the second case, that of a dead child, it was thought that the little thing that had disappeared so soon in life was not worthy of remembrance.* Ariès, 1973, p. 36

People did not 'think that every child already contained a man's personality' (p. 37). Instead children were seen as insignificant and incomplete. It was only in the sixteenth century that portraits of children who had died began to appear, indicating that modern ideas of childhood had begun to develop.

According to Ariès, at the start of the medieval period modern conceptions of childhood did not exist. Once children were physically capable of undertaking work, they were expected to help out and to take on what are now seen as adult roles. However, work did not take up as much time as it does now for adults and a lot of time was spent on play and pastimes. There was little difference between children's and adults' games and pastimes; all ages joined in on an equal footing.

There were also few specialist clothes for children and so children were dressed like miniature adults.

Today children are regarded as innocent and in need of protection from adults and adult concerns, particularly in relation to sex. According to Ariès, this was not the case in the past. For example, he put forward evidence from accounts of French and Spanish royalty to suggest that it was not taboo to make sexual references to children or even to touch children's genitals.

In short, childhood was not viewed as a special time of innocence when children had to be sheltered. Children were simply seen as small adults.

The emergence of childhood

However, this gradually began to change towards the end of the medieval era. Children's toys and clothes were introduced, people started keeping paintings of children, children's deaths were mourned more and taboos about children and sexuality developed.

Ariès argued that these changed attitudes stemmed partly from churchmen who began to see children as 'fragile creatures of God who needed to be both safeguarded and reformed' (1973, p. 129). Seventeenth-century moralists were also important. They 'were eager to ensure disciplined and rational manners' among children. Most important of all, though, was the development of modern schools.

In medieval schools all age groups were educated together. In France, in the eighteenth and nineteenth centuries children started to be separated into age groups as age became the organizing principle of education. As more children went to school, they became more segregated from the adult world as children were increasingly regarded as vulnerable and in need of protection.

By this time more children were surviving into adulthood and parents were investing more time and interest in their children's future. At the same time families were becoming more privatized and separated from the world outside. As in schools, children were increasingly kept apart from adults. The idea of childhood as a time of innocence and that children were an investment for the future became increasingly dominant.

Ariès argued that it became accepted that 'the child was not ready for life, and that he had to be subject to a special treatment, a sort of quarantine before he was allowed to join the adults' (1973, p. 396). In caring for children, the family 'assumed a moral and spiritual function, it moulded bodies and souls'. Children were subject to hard discipline in schools and families to ensure that they were moulded into the correct shape, but society had become much more concerned with children, much more **child-centred** than it had ever been in medieval times.

By the twentieth century, specialist sciences such as psychology, psychoanalysis and paediatrics had developed

to give further emphasis to the needs of children. Ariès concluded that now, 'Our world is obsessed by the physical, moral and sexual problems of childhood' (1973, p. 395).

Evaluation

The work of Ariès has generated considerable discussion and debate. Jane Pilcher notes a number of criticisms which have been put forward.

1. His work has been seen as value-laden. Ariès implies in his work that more recent child-centred views of childhood are superior to earlier views which allowed children to be treated in ways which would be considered unacceptable today. Critics have argued that Ariès allows his own values to distort his work, leading him to be over-critical of medieval child rearing.
2. Ariès has also been criticized for arguing that there was no concept of childhood in medieval times. Others have suggested that it would be more accurate to say that ideas on childhood were simply different at that time rather than absent altogether.
3. Ariès has also been criticized for generalizing about childhood on the basis of data largely confined to French aristocratic families. One of these critics, Edward Shorter, has developed his own ideas on the way that childhood has changed.

Edward Shorter – *The Making of the Modern Family*

Edward Shorter (1976) fills in some of the gaps in the research of Philippe Ariès. Shorter examines evidence from a range of European societies and not just France. Furthermore, he looks at research on peasant and working-class families as well as those of higher classes. His focus is on family life in general rather than specifically on childhood, but his research has important implications for the understanding of childhood.

Motherhood

Shorter argues that there is no such thing as maternal instinct. His evidence suggests that in seventeenth- and early eighteenth-century Europe mothers showed little interest in bonding with their children or providing special attention to meet their needs. Mothers did not regard children as anything special; they were seen as no more important than other aspects of their lives.

Mothers could handle children quite roughly and an infant's movements were often restricted by swaddling. Babies were usually left to cry rather than being picked up and comforted. Some mothers left their babies in the care of wet nurses and had relatively little to do with them themselves.

Shorter sees this indifference towards children as tantamount to neglect and argues that it was, at least in part, responsible for high mortality rates. Like Ariès, he argues that modern conceptions of childhood did not exist in the seventeenth and eighteenth centuries.

Changing attitudes to children

Around the middle of the eighteenth century, however, family life and attitudes began to change, at least amongst the more affluent members of society. This was caused by three factors.

1. The idea of romantic love began to develop. People began to marry for love – rather than, for example, to have children or for financial security. As a result, children became seen as more important. As the products of a special relationship – that between husband and wife – the children too were seen as special.
2. Thinkers such as the French philosopher Jean Jacques Rousseau started to popularize the idea that all children were born good and had the potential to develop into reasoning adults if they were brought up sensitively by parents.
3. Developing on the ideas of thinkers such as Rousseau, ideas about the correct or best ways to raise children began to circulate, which in turn influenced mothers.

According to Shorter, by the twentieth century, attitudes towards children and ideas about mothering were very different from those in the seventeenth and early eighteenth centuries. Women were deeply concerned to be 'good mothers'. They were very concerned to care for children properly and to place children at the centre of their lives.

The harshness of early centuries had been replaced by a desire for closeness with children and a desire to nurture and develop them. As a result, mothers developed a **sacrificial** role, Children were so important to mothers that they were now willing to sacrifice their own interests and well-being to help their children develop as well as possible. As families became more child-centred, modern ideas on the importance of childhood also developed.

Evaluation

Shorter's research is based on wider evidence than that of Ariès, but it reaches similar conclusions about the way that childhood has changed. Shorter explains the changes largely in terms of changing ideas; Ariès also emphasizes the importance of ideas along with the development of schooling and the reduction in mortality rates.

However, some sociologists have argued that material factors might be important in explaining the changing nature of childhood.

Other explanations of the development of childhood

Postman (1982) argues that technological change explains the rise of modern ideas about childhood. In particular he argues that the development of the printing press in the late fifteenth century meant that adults increasingly required children to learn to read. Learning to read is a gradual process in which skills are built up slowly, and this encouraged the idea that children were different from adults and needed educating gradually to become like adults.

Eventually the learning of reading was institutionalized through mass schooling. The idea that children needed to pass through age-related stages in their development as they progressed towards adulthood became accepted and modern ideas on childhood were born.

Postman's ideas suggest that both Ariès and Shorter correctly identified the direction of change in the development of childhood, but failed to fully explain why this happened. However, Postman's ideas may attach too much importance to one specific social change, when a variety of factors may explain the emergence of modern childhood.

For example, Jane Pilcher (1995) argues that changes in employment legislation were also important. The Factory Acts of the nineteenth century increasingly excluded children from more and more places of work, and these Acts helped to prepare the ground for the later development of mass schooling.

Whatever the minor differences between these writers, however, all agree that at some point in the last few centuries, a new, child-centred notion of childhood developed in Western societies. Jane Pilcher sums up what many sociologists believe about the changing nature of childhood. She says:

> *The modern conception of childhood as 'institutionalized separateness' has emerged gradually over several centuries in Britain. It has not enveloped all categories of children (female, male, the lower classes, rural and urban children) in exactly the same ways and at exactly the same points in history. Nevertheless, the direction of change has been towards an increasing division in British society between the world of the child and the world of the adult, and a lengthening of the chronological markers attached to childhood.* Pilcher, 1995, p. 39

Modern and postmodern childhood

The writers reviewed in the previous section all concur that a new, modern type of childhood has developed in Western societies. However, some sociologists have begun to argue that childhood has moved beyond the modern stage and is entering a period of postmodernity or late modernity, where once again the idea of childhood is changing. One such writer is Christopher Jenks.

Christopher Jenks – childhood and postmodernity

Jenks (2005) believes that the account of the development of childhood put forward by Ariès is essentially correct. He comments that 'critiques of Ariès rarely succeed in achieving more than a modification of his central ideas' (Jenks, 2005, p. 59). However, Jenks develops a more sophisticated theory of childhood in modernity and then goes on to argue that childhood has begun to change further in postmodern/late modern society.

Childhood and modernity

Jenks characterizes the development of modern childhood in terms of a shift from the Dionysian image of the child to the Apollonian image.

The **Dionysian** image of the child is based upon Dionysus, the 'prince of wine, revelry and nature'. According to this image, children love pleasure and are curious and adventurous. In the pursuit of pleasure children can get themselves into all sorts of trouble and can, potentially, act in evil ways. Children are therefore in need of strict moral guidance and control if they are to grow up to be responsible adults.

There is little sentimentality about children according to this image, and strict discipline can be used to control children. According to Jenks, the Dionysian image was typical of pre-industrial societies, but it survived well into the modern era. In the eighteenth and early nineteenth centuries, for example, children were employed in mines and factories and as chimney sweeps, with little concern for their well-being.

In the twentieth century the Dionysian image survived partly through the influence of psychoanalysis. The founder of psychoanalysis, Sigmund Freud, believed that natural drives from the *id* made children potentially selfish and this needed to be controlled through the development of a conscience or *super ego*. Freud also saw children as sexual and therefore far from innocent.

Despite the survival of the Dionysian image, it was gradually overtaken by an alternative **Apollonian** image of the child (from the Greek god Apollo). Jenks traces the development of the Apollonian image back to *Emile* published by Rousseau in 1762. Rousseau was a leading Enlightenment philosopher and he is therefore associated with the development of modernity (see pp. 890–1 for a discussion of the Enlightenment and modernity).

Rousseau believed that children are born good but are quite different from adults. Because they are different they cannot be treated like adults. They need more careful handling, and the good side of their nature must be coaxed out of them sympathetically. Each child is an individual and therefore special.

From such notions, the modern idea of the child developed. This in turn influenced ideas on child-centred education, the unsuitability of work for children, the avoidance of harsh or physical punishment, and the belief that children needed to be 'enabled', encouraged and facilitated' (Jenks, 2005, p. 65).

Jenks does not believe that this resulted in children being left free to do whatever they wanted. Instead new ways of monitoring and controlling children were introduced. Harsh physical violence against children was no longer common, and instead they were increasingly disciplined through the monitoring and control of space. They were restricted in where they could go at particular times and restricted in what they could do in different settings.

With the extension of schooling, children spent more time sitting behind a desk and were expected to conform

to school rules. In school, children who misbehaved might be sent to a 'reading corner'. Out of school, children were increasingly kept out of most public spaces unless accompanied by an adult, giving them less freedom to go where they wished and fewer opportunities to escape from watchful eyes monitoring their behaviour.

Much of this monitoring and observation was provided by the family. Jenks does not see the family as simply based upon emotional attachment or love. To Jenks, the modern family 'has become the basic unit of social cohesion in advancing capitalism, and though loving and supportive in its self-image it has become the very epitome of the rational enterprise' (2005, p. 105).

Families became rational enterprises organized to develop children so that they became productive and well-adapted adults. The modern idea of progress through growth and development became the main focus and purpose of family life. Childhood was concerned with **futurity** – what the child would become in the future – just as modernity looks to a future, improved society.

Late modern/postmodern childhood

Jenks believes that modernity has now been superseded by a new era. He refers to this new era both as late modernity and as postmodernity, using these terms interchangeably.

Jenks, like many other sociologists, believes that the new era has resulted in a destabilization of people's identities, so that they no longer have a secure, grounded sense of who they are. Class solidarity has broken down, family life is insecure with frequent divorce, and people change jobs more often than in the past.

People develop a **reflexive sense of self** – they constantly monitor, revise, try to change their sense of who they are (see pp. 895–9 for a discussion of similar ideas). This can make people anxious and unsure about their identity since it no longer has firm foundations. Furthermore, Jenks agrees with postmodernists that people have lost their belief in the inevitability of progress and their uncritical optimism about the future.

Having outlined what he sees as the main changes associated with late modern or postmodern societies, Jenks goes on to examine the effects of these changes on childhood. He draws heavily on the work of Ulrich Beck (1992), who argued in his book *Risk Society* (see pp. 86–8) that childhood was changing.

According to Beck, children have become the final source of **primary relationships** – the most fulfilling and unconditional relationships, which last and from which people obtain the most satisfaction. Wives, husbands or partners used to be seen as the most important source of primary relationships, but an increasing proportion of such relationships break down through divorce, or separation. Because of this, parents now attach more importance to relationships with their children. While a marriage might end, you cannot stop being the mother or father of your children.

Although this might sound like simply a more intense version of the child-centredness of modernity, Jenks believes that it involves more fundamental changes in parent–child relationships. In the past, the emphasis was on progressing the child's development, looking to the future. However, in postmodernity the emphasis is on nostalgia for a time when identities and relationships were more permanent.

Parent–child relationships remind adults of the more stable relationships and identities of the past. The relationship with children becomes the one thing on which adults can rely and they cling on to it in the uncertainty and instability of the postmodern world. Jenks says:

> *whereas children used to cling to us, through modernity, for guidance into their/our 'futures', now we, through late modernity, cling to them for 'nostalgic' groundings because (social) change is both intolerable and disorienting for us. They are lover, friend, workmate and, at a different level, symbolic representations of society itself.* Jenks, 2005, p. 112

Jenks believes that children have come to represent 'the sustainable, reliable, trustworthy, not outmoded treasury of social sentiments' (p. 113). With so much uncertainty in the world, children represent the possibility of strong social relationships continuing to exist.

However, there is still some ambiguity about childhood. According to Jenks, we live in a society in which the independence of the individual is seen as a necessity, and it is seen as necessary for children to develop this independence. Yet, as 'the symbolic refuge of trust, dependency and care in human relations' (p. 115), there is a strong sense that children need to be protected so that the last vestiges of the old society do not disappear.

Child abuse

In these circumstances, it is not surprising that there is considerable anxiety about childhood. Childhood is so precious and symbolic that there is great concern if it is seen as under threat. This sense of anxiety is revealed in attitudes towards child abuse.

Child abuse has become increasingly evident in contemporary society, with many more allegations of abuse than in the past and much more publicity given to the issue. Jenks argues that at least some of this increase is probably due to increased reporting as a result of increased awareness and concern. This increased concern has not been caused by a dramatic increase in abuse but by the symbolic importance of childhood.

There is more surveillance of childhood because of what childhood represents. People are therefore more aware of abuse and more fearful for their children. For example, many parents are worried about abduction and reluctant to let children go out without adult supervision. But however much parents want to protect their children from real or imagined threats, they ultimately feel that they cannot guarantee their safety. This is because they feel insecure themselves. The pace of social change means that nothing feels safe. Jenks says:

> *'childhood' sustains the 'meta-narrative' of society itself, and abuse, both real and supposed, expresses our current ambivalence towards and impotence in the face of constantly changing structural conditions. As we see less coherence and sustained meaning in the experience of our own subjectivity and our relationships with others, we witness more symbolic abuse of children.* 2005, p. 115

The disappearance of childhood?

Having discussed the way in which childhood is changing in late modern or postmodern society, Jenks goes on to consider whether childhood is disappearing. The suggestion that childhood was disappearing was raised in 1994 by Neil Postman.

Postman argued that the distinction between childhood and adulthood was being eroded to such an extent that childhood was disappearing as a distinct stage in the life course. The main reason for this was the development of the mass media. According to Postman, media such as television had led to children seeing images (such as images of sex and violence) which had previously been largely inaccessible to them. Because children could now learn about virtually anything from the media, childhood was no longer a time of innocence.

Jenks accepts that there is some truth in this argument, but he does not accept it completely. He agrees that there is anxiety about the loss of innocence in childhood. For example, in 1993 a toddler, James Bulger, was abducted from a shopping centre in Liverpool and violently killed by two older children. In line with Postman's ideas, they were allegedly motivated by having watched a violent, adult video.

The public responded with both horror and confusion. They were horrified and confused because the murderous children totally contradicted the Apollonian image of the innocent child, although the victim fitted this image well. The case fed into anxieties about the lack of stability in society and exacerbated concerns about protecting children. However, it now seemed that children needed to be protected from other children as well as from adults. Society, it seemed, had to both protect children and control them.

This resulted in increased concern about children's anti-social behaviour, and their use of adult-oriented media, and led to demands to hold children responsible for criminal activity. This contradicted previous moves towards giving children greater liberty and say in their own affairs. For example, the Children's Act of 1989 allowed children the right to express a preference for which parent had custody in divorce cases.

Jenks agrees with Postman that there is concern about the death of childhood, or at least a loss of innocence amongst children. However, Jenks does not believe that childhood is disappearing. Society continues to impose rules on many aspects of childhood because of its symbolic importance. Children are still highly regulated and restricted by legal constraints governing their sexuality, education, behaviour in public places, alcohol consumption, political rights (or lack of them) and so on.

Even though people are more aware that children can be violent, society is unwilling to accept that the idea of childhood is a social construction rather than a natural, biological category. Jenks himself suggests that it is now misleading to believe that such a thing as 'childhood' exists in reality. In contemporary society, the experiences and behaviour of children are extremely varied, and any single view of what childhood is will not do justice to the differences that exist between children. Jenks concludes: 'surely we have to eject any monolithic category of "the child" and work instead with the more pluralistic conceptions of "childhoods", "children" and "childlikeness"?' (2005, p. 135).

Evidence in support of Jenks

Jenks puts forward an ambitious, complex, wide-ranging and interesting theory of how childhood is changing. However, it is backed up by very little empirical evidence. That does not necessarily mean that his interpretation is incorrect. There is some evidence to support some aspects of his theory.

1. A study of parenthood by Caroline Gatrell (2005) found support for the idea that some parents saw their relationship with their children as more important than their relationship with their partner. Gatrell carried out in-depth interviews with twenty women who combined motherhood with a career, and eighteen men who were the partners of the women. She found that fathers were increasingly involved with their children. For example, some fathers reduced their working hours to spend more time with their children. Furthermore they then assumed more direct responsibility for routine aspects of childcare rather than acting as the mother's helper. They attached considerable importance to developing an emotional bond with their children, and some saw this as a long-term investment in an intimate relationship which might outlast their marriage or partnership.
2. There is evidence that parents are very concerned to protect their children from what they see as a dangerous world. In a national survey of the attitudes of parents and children in Britain (Madge, 2006), nearly half of the adults thought that parents were over-protective of their children. More than three-quarters of the children believed that their parents worried too much about them being in danger.
3. Madge's survey also found evidence that there was anxiety about childhood being under threat because children were growing up too quickly: 78 per cent of adults questioned agreed that 'Children and teenagers have to grow up too quickly' (Madge, 2006, p. 51). Furthermore, 65 per cent of 'white' children and 56 per cent of children from other ethnic groups thought that children grew up too quickly.

Evidence to contradict Jenks

However, it is also possible to find evidence from such studies which contradicts some of the claims of Jenks. For example, Gatrell's study found a strong career orientation amongst mothers, implying that they were less child-centred than in the past.

Neither of the above studies was designed to explicitly test Jenks's ideas. For example, Gatrell's study used a sample of exclusively middle-class parents, who may not have been representative of the population as a whole. While sociologists have developed sophisticated theories of how childhood is changing, for the most part they have not collected detailed evidence to test the theories.

Conclusion

Theories of childhood have tended to generalize about childhood as a whole. In his conclusion, Jenks suggests that

such generalizations may be misleading because a plurality of childhoods exists. However, Jenks himself is guilty of generalizing about the changing nature of childhood and he fails to examine the variety of different childhoods he acknowledges.

Alan Prout (2005) agrees with Jenks about many other changes in childhood, but develops the idea of diversity further. For example, he notes the vast differences in childhood in the wealthiest countries compared to the poorest. He quotes UNICEF figures which show that children in the poorest 20 per cent of countries are more than twice as likely to die before reaching adulthood, compared to children in the richest 20 per cent of countries.

Prout also suggests that divisions within countries are important. In Britain, children from poorer backgrounds have higher rates of illness, do less well in education and probably suffer more neglect and abuse than children from richer backgrounds. Prout suggests that increasing family diversity (see pp. 482–95) leads to greater variety in the experience of children, and he notes that factors such as class, ethnicity, disability and gender also contribute to the diversity of childhood experiences.

Although Jenks does not discuss the diversity of childhood in detail, he does at least acknowledge it. The same cannot be said for writers such as Ariès, who assume that a single type of childhood is dominant at any one point in history. However, both Ariès and Jenks largely view childhood in terms of changes in the wider society and say little about childhood from the point of view of children. As the next section will show, this is not true of all sociologists of childhood.

Berry Mayall – the sociology of children

Sociology and children

Berry Mayall (2004) is critical of much of the sociology of childhood. She argues that it tends to see childhood in terms of the viewpoint and priorities of adults. It can therefore be accused of being **adultist**. Children are routinely portrayed as the passive recipients of socialization (or, as Mayall puts it, as **socialization projects**), or as simply the occupants of the social role of childhood. As in society, where children's views are rarely solicited or listened to, so it is in sociology. However, Mayall argues that a number of factors have led some sociologists to start to take children more seriously.

1 The women's movement led to the opening up of sociology to one disadvantaged group – women. This paved the way for other groups to be given more attention. One such group is children.

2 A children's rights movement has gained momentum in its own right since the Second World War. For example, the United Nations Convention on the Rights of the Child established the principle that children should be seen as having rights in the same way as adults.

3 Within sociology some writers began to question the way that children were portrayed. For example, Jens Qvortrup (1991) argued that the economic importance of children was seriously underestimated. Writing a report on an international study of childhood, he noted that children did a great deal of hidden work which made a significant contribution to the economy but which was largely ignored by economists.

The present tense of childhood

As a result of such factors, Mayall has begun to emphasize what she calls the **present tense of childhood**. Childhood should not be seen as preparation for adulthood. Instead, the sociology of childhood should concentrate on studying what it is like being a child and it should take children's point of view seriously.

Linked to this is a political stance which supports greater rights for children. Mayall believes that societies such as Britain give children far too few rights. Children are vulnerable up to a point because of their small physical size and biological immaturity. However, most of their vulnerability stems not from their chronological age, but from the way society treats them. Mayall says:

> *there is socially constructed vulnerability, the ideas, policies and practices that adults put in place which confirm children in social inferiority and dependence. Children are vulnerable because adults do not have respect for their rights; they lack political, social and economic power.* Mayall, 2004, p. 43

For example, children have found it difficult to get protection from adult abuse because children's claims are not taken as seriously as those of adults. Children lack the economic power to walk away from an abusive household and, because they cannot vote, they lack the political power to make the issue a priority. Similarly, children have little say in how the education system runs, and they have little freedom to participate in politics or to earn their own living.

Mayall argues that the powerlessness of children is not inevitable. For example, in some countries children have greater rights than in Britain. In Scandinavian countries such as Norway and Sweden, Mayall claims, until relatively recently children made a significant economic contribution to society through work in household businesses.

In these countries, children have more rights than in Britain and are allowed to do more work. For example, children do important work which helps to keep schools running. Although they do not have the same rights as adults, they have more recognition as citizens of these states. Furthermore, children, in Britain and elsewhere, also sometimes take on adult roles very competently when circumstances make this necessary. For example, older children sometimes end up caring for parents and younger siblings if their parents are ill or disabled.

The new sociology of children

Mayall believes that in order to explore and develop the potential for improving the position of children in society it is necessary to develop a new **sociology of children** rather than a sociology of childhood. A sociology of children recognizes the competence of children as social actors and the crucial role children play in shaping their own lives. Mayall says:

> *Children are understood as agents in their learning from their earliest days. Children do things that make a difference to relationships and to their own lives. Children have knowledge about what matters to them. They make assessments of events and of relations. They have clear moral sense, learned from their earliest encounters with dilemmas in daily life.* 2004, p. 43

According to Mayall, research on children has become increasingly popular. For example, the Economic and Social Research Council in the UK funded twenty-two projects of this sort on children aged 5–16 between 1997 and 2000.

Mayall then goes on to illustrate the benefits of the sociology of children with reference to three areas of study.

1. In the study of poverty, research on children has revealed the damaging effects of poverty on the experience of children. It has helped to encourage the Blair/Brown Labour governments to establish targets for reducing child poverty (although the targets have not been met, see p. 258).
2. Physical violence against children has also been studied. According to Mayall, this has served to highlight the fact that children's rights are still denied. The government has failed to ban the smacking of children although there has been pressure to do so and violence of this nature against anyone other than children is illegal. Mayall says:

> *Government views on 'smacking' again reflect government views on childhood as preparation, as socialisation, where the future takes precedence over the present. These views also reflect respect for parental rights over children's rights. And they point to the low social status of childhood, a status which is deemed not to merit respect. 'Smacking' is a symbol of political contempt for children and for childhood.* 2004, p. 50

3. The sociology of children has also helped to develop an understanding of education. From an adult point of view, children in school tend to be portrayed as '*incompetent, immature, morally suspect pupils*'. The school is there to teach them competences, to help them mature and to control their behaviour as it encourages the development of morality. But research suggests that children see themselves and the role of school very differently. They want to learn at school, but they believe that they would learn more effectively if they were given more respect and more say in their learning. Mayall says:

> *they want to learn, to choose what and when to learn, to have teachers who work as partners or enablers who help them learn. Many of them want to see a more open school, where students engage too with the outside world.* 2004, p. 51

From this point of view, 'schools should be reconceptualised as resource-centres for children'.

Conclusion

Mayall concludes that the sociology of children should link with a children's rights movement, just as the sociology of gender linked with the women's rights movement (see Chapter 2). A prerequisite for this is that children are genuinely heard in research. In the past, most research on children involved observation. But Mayall believes that research based on interviews is better because it allows children to voice their own issues and concerns in a way that promotes more equal rights between adults and children.

Evaluation

Mayall is just one of a number of sociologists advocating and developing the sociology of children. She makes important criticisms of sociologies of childhood and demonstrates how listening to children can enhance an understanding of the social world. Her views on increasing the rights of children go much further than most politicians and members of society would accept at present. However, the demands for women's rights were widely thought to be fanciful at the start of the twentieth century, but did gradually gain acceptance. Perhaps the same will happen with children's rights.

Nevertheless an important difference remains between the campaigns for women's rights and those for children's rights. Women campaigned for their own rights and female sociologists analysed their own situation. At the moment it is still largely adults campaigning for children's rights and it is exclusively adults researching the sociology of children. When campaigns for children's rights are led by children and children are studied by child sociologists, then the role of children will truly have changed.

Youth

Introduction – youth as a stage of transition

Jane Pilcher argues that, 'The concept of youth, like that of childhood, is a way of understanding the "growing up" stages in the life course' (1995, p. 58). Pilcher claims that youth are seen both in terms of their past – they are no longer children – and their future – they have not yet become adults. She therefore says that 'youth is best understood as a stage of *transition*' between childhood and adulthood.

In contemporary Western societies this process of transition can involve the start of withdrawal from full-time education and a move towards employment; and a move away from the family of origin and parents' household towards setting up their own household, and

the establishment of a 'family of destination' with a sexual partner (see p. 770). However, the timing of any such transitions varies from individual to individual, and the nature of such transitions varies between societies.

Furthermore, the age at which people leave childhood behind and the age at which they become adult are not clearly defined. As we have already seen (see pp. 758–61), many sociologists see childhood as a social construction which varies between societies, so the chronological age at which it is seen as ending also varies.

In some societies, initiation ceremonies clearly and definitively mark the passage from youth to adulthood. For example, the Nandi people of Kenya mark the passage of boys into adulthood with a circumcision ceremony. For the Bemba people of Zambia, a girl's transition to womanhood takes place when she has her first period. It is marked with the Chisunga ceremony where the girl is washed ceremonially and isolated indoors for a time before she is permitted to return to the community.

Western societies, however, do not attach as much importance to such defining rites of passage.

Youth and puberty

In all societies youth is partly associated with the biological changes of puberty. Puberty is a universal biological phenomenon involving such changes as the development of secondary sex characteristics (such as bodily hair), the development of reproductive organs, rapid skeletal growth, the development of increased strength and endurance, hormonal changes and so on. However, the exact timing of these changes is influenced by environmental factors such as diet and stress, so it varies between and within societies and over time. Puberty does not therefore correspond exactly to particular chronological ages.

Furthermore, Pilcher points out that although puberty in contemporary Britain takes place in the early teenage years, 'young people are not regarded or treated as adults merely because their bodies have matured' (1995, p. 60). Adult rights and responsibilities as defined by the legal system are recognized at different ages. For example, at 16 you are allowed to have sexual intercourse and marry with parental consent, but you cannot vote in elections, buy alcohol or tobacco or marry without parental approval until you are 18. Only when you are 25 do you receive adult levels of income support.

A person's eighteenth birthday is seen as important, but it does not clearly mark a transition to adulthood in the same way as ceremonies or rites of passage do in some other societies. Therefore, just as there are no clear boundaries between childhood and youth in contemporary Britain, there are also no clear boundaries between youth and adulthood.

The development of modern youth

Earlier in this chapter (see pp. 759–61) it was suggested that contemporary ideas of childhood did not develop until the post-industrial era. Some research suggests that conceptions of youth have also changed since pre-industrial times.

Jane Pilcher discusses the work of Gillis (1974), who argued that before the industrial revolution Western societies saw youth as stretching from about the age of 7 until marriage, which might not occur until the mid- or even late twenties. Youth involved a 'gradually more extensive detachment from the family of origin' (Pilcher, 1995, p. 64). Youths were semi-independent but did not achieve complete independence until marriage. In this era, youth was sometimes associated with the apprenticeship system whereby the young apprentice would often be housed by a master for whom they worked as they learnt their trade. Other youths were servants in wealthy households.

However, with the industrialization and urbanization of the industrial revolution the number of servants and the apprentice system declined, and young people were more likely to stay in the parental home until marriage. Modern conceptions of youth began to develop during the nineteenth century, when factory legislation banned child labour, and state education was introduced. As Pilcher puts it, 'the younger age group of youth became increasingly subject to parental and other institutional controls' (1995, p. 64).

At the same time, youth came to be seen as a time of vulnerability during which young people needed protection from corrupting influences. Psychological and social theories about the supposed turmoil of teenage years justified a range of protective legislation and encouraged organizations such as the Scouts to develop in order to exercise a positive influence on youth. It was believed that youth should be a carefree time with few responsibilities, but that care was needed to stop youths from becoming deviant. Gillis believes that this conception of youth developed first in the middle class, but gradually spread to encompass all classes.

Arguably, many of the characteristics of youth and concerns about youth which developed in the nineteenth century remain important today. There are still fears about youths becoming deviant, and there is still a widespread view that teenage years involve turmoil and vulnerability. However, there is also public concern and sociological interest in the way that youth is changing. These issues will be addressed below, after a consideration of functionalist views on youth.

S.N. Eisenstadt – 'Archetypal patterns of youth'

Youth, biology and culture

The functionalist sociologist S.N. Eisenstadt (1963) believed that youth had biological and cultural components. He argued that although 'the basic biological processes of maturation ... are probably more or less similar in all human societies, their cultural definition varies from society to society, at least in details' (Eisenstadt, 1963, p. 24).

Despite accepting that youth varies between societies, Eisenstadt nevertheless believed that a youth stage in life has a very similar role in all societies. Whatever the particular definition, it is always a transitory stage, culminating in a person becoming a full, adult member of society. As such, youth as a stage in the life cycle has vital functions for society.

The functions of youth

The first of these functions is the development of the individual personality so that each person acquires 'the mechanism of self-regulation and self-control' (Eisenstadt, 1963, p. 26). In all societies, youth is organized in order to complete the development of adult personalities. It allows the individual to reach the stage where they no longer need to be directed by an older person, but can largely direct their own behaviour because they have been successfully socialized.

The second function, which follows from the first, is the transmission of the core values of society. Eisenstadt said that youth is 'the purest manifestation and repository of ultimate cultural and societal values' (1963, p. 27). This is because it is the stage where society tries to complete the shaping of future adults into the sort of people that society wants.

The third function of youth is the development of self-identity. If a successful transition takes place during youth, the individual will have a clear sense of who they are and their role in society.

Eisenstadt summarized the archetypal features of youth as:

> *The transition from childhood and adolescence to adulthood, the development of personal identity, psychological autonomy and self-regulation, the attempt to link personal temporal transition to general cultural images ... and to link psychological maturity to the emulation of definite role models.* Eisenstadt, 1963, p. 28

Youth is therefore a time when the individual needs both to develop conformity to societal norms and to develop individuality and self-identity, implying a greater degree of independence than that enjoyed by children. During youth, people may enjoy greater freedom than during adulthood, because they may not yet have all the responsibilities of adult life (for example, looking after or providing for children). But this freedom can be contradicted by the need of society to control and direct the development of young people in line with societal values. This contradiction can be unsettling, making youth a potentially traumatic and troubling phase of life.

Variations between societies

Although Eisenstadt identified some universal aspects of youth, which he therefore saw as present in all societies, he acknowledged that the nature of youth varies between societies to some extent. He saw these variations as the result of three factors:

1. The more complex the division of labour, the less the influence age will have on social roles. In simple societies with little division of labour, age is a very important criterion for allocating roles – for example, the roles of tribal elder or warrior. In more complex, industrial societies, age differences are less clear-cut.
2. The second factor is the values of a society. If a society values characteristics associated with particular age groups, then divisions based on age will be stronger. For example, if physical vigour is valued, this may enhance the status of the young, but if knowledge of societal customs is valued, this may favour older people.
3. A third factor concerns the role of the family. In some societies, full adult status can be obtained within the context of the family. In others, this is not the case and youths have to accomplish the transition by developing independence outside the family. In such societies, peer groups assume great importance as a context in which independence can be developed. Such societies may also have youth organizations, developed by adults, to exercise some influence on how youths mature, perhaps to counteract negative influences of peer groups which may not always support societal values.

Youth and modern industrial societies

Eisenstadt argues that there have always been some societies – for example, the Zulus and the Masai in Africa – in which youths have considerable independence and autonomy. However, modern industrial societies tend to give more freedom to youths than other types of society.

Modern industrial societies have a complex division of labour which tends to make the roles of different age groups less well defined. They operate in terms of **universalistic values**. People are judged according to what they can do rather than who they are, so assumptions about the roles of different age groups are not so clear-cut. Significantly, in industrial societies kinship groups lose a lot of their importance for determining adult roles. Adult roles do not stem directly from an individual's family of birth but must be earned as he or she passes through the education system and enters employment. Such societies also require more individual personalities than pre-industrial societies.

The degree of freedom accorded to youth in modern industrial societies can cause problems. Peer groups assume a very important role, and if they develop deviant subcultures youth can be at odds with society's values. Organizations such as the YMCA and the Scouts were developed to try to control and direct youth, but were only partly successful. Young people can become somewhat isolated and segregated from the adult world; they are often uncertain of their future adult roles and therefore may not have clear role models. Young people can even develop revolutionary movements (such as student protest movements), at odds with society's values, in their search for identity.

Nevertheless, Eisenstadt was optimistic about the developing role of youth in modern industrial societies. He believed that greater freedom gave young people more room to develop the individual personalities needed in modern societies which emphasize individual achievement. This freedom provides opportunities for future adults to develop their own moralities tying in to future roles. This is useful in a society in which there is greater variety in moral values because, with an increased division of labour, individuals need to act differently in specific work roles. (For example, soldiers and nurses need to have somewhat different values to carry out their roles effectively.) Eisenstadt concluded:

> *These new conditions have enhanced the possibility of flexibility in linking cultural values to social reality; they have enhanced the scope of personal and cultural creativity and the development of different personal culture. They have created the possibility of youth's developing ... [a] direct identification with moral values, an awareness of the predicaments of moral choice that exist in any given situation, and individual responsibility for such choices.* Eisenstadt, 1963, p. 41

Thus, although a single, detailed set of values may not be transmitted to all youths, this stage in life still functions to encourage individuals to make choices in line with the basic values of society.

Evaluation

Although Eisenstadt recognized that the nature of youth varied between societies and over time, he said little about variations within societies at a single point in history. Thus Jane Pilcher says, 'Functionalist accounts refer to youth cultures in a uniform, undifferentiated way, probably with American, white, urban, middle-class males as their role model' (1995, p. 69). There is no discussion of the possible restrictions in the freedom of youth that might result from racism, poverty or gender inequality.

Furthermore, Eisenstadt rather assumed that, on the whole, youths would be successfully prepared for adult roles even if adolescence could be a traumatic time. Writing in the 1950s and 1960s, a time of steady economic growth and full employment, Eisenstadt had nothing to say about how transitions to adulthood could be disrupted by social change. Sociologists writing in later decades have sometimes seen youth transitions as more problematic than Eisenstadt.

Youth and the transition to adulthood in Britain

Youth transition research

Writing in 2004, Robert MacDonald, Tracy Shildrick and Mark Cieslik noted that British research on youth was largely divided into two types of study. First, there were studies of subculture which started with the work of the Birmingham Centre for Contemporary Cultural Studies (see pp. 771–4). Second, there were studies which examined the process of transition from youth to adulthood. This section examines work from the second tradition.

Youth transition research attained considerable prominence in the 1980s, largely as a result of the growth of mass youth unemployment during the economic recession of the late 1970s and early 1980s. Writers such as Kenneth Roberts (1984) argued that traditional patterns of transition from youth to adulthood were being undermined by social and economic change.

Roberts argued that in the 1950s and 1960s there were often **abrupt transitions** from school to work. There were very high levels of employment so it was easy for school leavers to find work. Most coped well with going straight into a job, despite the claims of some critics that school leavers were ill-prepared for work by the education system. Roberts claimed that if there were problems, it was often the result of poor work or poor employers rather than any inherent problem with the school leavers.

By the late 1970s the transition between school and work was becoming more **gradual**. Rather than going straight into work, the high levels of unemployment meant that youths often went on to training schemes such as YOP (Youth Opportunities Scheme) or YTS (Youth Training Scheme) in order to be trained for work.

The government argued that such schemes were necessary because young people were leaving school without the appropriate skills or even the right attitude to go into paid jobs. Taking part in the schemes would make them employable. However, Roberts argued that 'There is a huge credibility gap between official accounts and young people's experiences of these schemes' (1984, p. 8).

The schemes were criticized for teaching few useful skills. Where they involved work experience, critics argued that they were simply providing employers with temporary workers at the government's expense and were doing nothing to cut unemployment. (See pp. 620–1 for a discussion of training schemes and vocational education.) Furthermore, some of those who were placed on schemes simply became long-term unemployed, delaying the transition to adult work roles indefinitely.

Structural change and government policies

MacDonald *et al.* (2004) argue that the change in the nature of the transition to work and adulthood had little to do with youths being unemployable. Instead, it was caused by a number of structural changes and government policies. These included:

1. Structural unemployment caused by changes in the economy accompanying a process of **deindustrialization**. With the rapid loss of manufacturing jobs there was also a rapid decline in apprenticeships.
2. Certain regional labour markets (for example, the northeast) were particularly affected and high rates of youth unemployment continued into the 1980s and 1990s.
3. Changes in benefits which reduced the entitlements of young people forced them to join government training schemes if they could not find work.
4. At the same time, opportunities in both further education and higher education were expanded and people who would not previously have continued in post-compulsory education were encouraged to stay on.

Postmodernism and youth transitions

MacDonald *et al.* comment that:

> *A number of adjectives have been used to describe the consequences for young people of these changes. Youth sociologists have conjured with notions of 'long', 'broken', 'extended', 'protracted', 'uneasy' and 'fractured' transitions to describe the way that changes in the world of work, education and training have extended the youth phase. Young people now make lengthier transitions to adulthood, experience longer periods of dependency upon parents and have delayed access to the identities and activities which were previously regarded as signifying adult status (e.g. earning a wage, leaving the parental home, the establishment of long-term partnerships, parenthood).* MacDonald *et al.*, 2004, p. 19

MacDonald *et al.* argue that there is little disagreement that changes have taken place in the nature of the transition between youth and adulthood in Britain, but there are disagreements about how this change should be interpreted. They note that those influenced by postmodernism believe that transitions have become much more a matter of individual choice. Young people can choose, for example, whether to be a student, seek work, pursue a career, have a gap year, travel, work abroad and so on.

From this point of view, social divisions such as class, gender and ethnicity do not shape people's identities or limit their choices in the same way as they did in the past. These ideas are examined in the following study.

Andy Furlong and Fred Cartmel – *Young People and Social Change*

Theories of social change

Andy Furlong and Fred Cartmel (1997, 2006) examine the changing experiences of youth in Britain in the light of recent social changes. In particular they use a wide range of evidence to examine theories of social change as they apply to youth. They focus on three theories:

1. They examine postmodern theories, such as those of Lyotard and Baudrillard (see pp. 891–4). According to Furlong and Cartmel, postmodernists believe that 'structural analysis has lost its validity' and 'patterns of behaviour and individual's life chances have lost their predictability and post-modernism involves a new and much more diverse set of lifestyles' (1997, p. 1). However, Furlong and Cartmel are rather dismissive of postmodernism. While they do not deny that important changes have been taking place, they do not see them as involving a break with modernity. They argue that modernity has always involved a variety of lifestyles and a sense of uncertainty. For example, in the nineteenth century Durkheim used concepts of anomie and egoism to describe the uncertainty produced in modern societies (see pp. 795–8).
2. However, Furlong and Cartmel take theories which suggest that modernity has changed, without being totally transformed, rather more seriously. One such theory is Anthony Giddens's idea that societies have entered a period of **high modernity** (Giddens, 1990, 1991). For Giddens this involves the loss of a firm foundation for individual identity. Instead people have to think constantly about who they are. Creating a sense of identity becomes an individual's project rather than something that flows automatically from their place in society. Giddens uses the term reflexivity to describe the continual reflection involved in creating an identity. (See pp. 692–704 for a discussion of identity.)
3. Another theory which Furlong and Cartmel take seriously is Ulrich Beck's (1992) theory of **risk society** (see pp. 86–8). In the risk society all social groups are exposed to increasing uncertainty, caused by science and technology and changes in society. These risks cut across class boundaries and consequently class becomes much less important as a source of identity. People begin to act less as members of social groups such as social classes, and instead negotiate their way through life as individuals. The **individualization** of social life makes social life less predictable and disrupts previous patterns of behaviour. There is much more choice for individuals, including youths, about the direction they take because they are no longer bound by expectations linked with social divisions such as class, gender and ethnicity.

The transition to adulthood as a journey

Furlong and Cartmel neatly describe how the changes discussed by Giddens, Beck and similar writers could apply to youth. They compare the transitions involved in becoming an adult to a journey. In the 1960s and 1970s the journey was rather like a trip by rail.

> *Within the school young people join trains which are bound for different destinations. The trains they board are determined by factors like social class, gender and educational attainment. Once the train journey has begun, opportunities to switch destinations are limited.* Furlong and Cartmel, 1997, p. 6

Furthermore, because they spend so long with other people on the train, young people tend to develop a sense of camaraderie. If they are not satisfied with what is happening on the train, then they work together to change it.

However, this era of class solidarity and class and gender and ethnic divisions may not fit with the experience of youth today. A more contemporary comparison is with car journeys in an era when many of the railways have closed down. Unlike trains, which must stick to predetermined rails, 'the car driver is able to select his or her route from a vast number of alternatives'. The driver is therefore faced with the need to make decisions – for example, whether to take the motorway or another road, whether to leave the road if they meet a traffic jam, or even whether to change their destination or turn back. In their own car they are relatively isolated from others travelling on the same roads and it seems that their individual decisions are crucial to how the journey goes.

So far this analogy fits the ideas of writers such as Giddens and Beck. It describes an individualized society in which people choose their road or path while constantly making decisions. Whatever choice they make, they risk traffic jams, accidents or slow-moving traffic. However, Furlong and Cartmel argue that this is not the full story. This is because the success of the driver's journey depends partly upon the car they are driving. They say:

> *what many of the drivers fail to realize is that the type of car which they have been allocated at the start of the journey is the most significant predictor of the ultimate outcome. Those with inferior cars can find themselves spending significant periods off the road.* Furlong and Cartmel, 1997, p. 7

By the use of this analogy, Furlong and Cartmel are indicating that although they accept that the transition to adulthood is more varied, and involves more choice, than in the past, social divisions still shape people's life chances.

Key aspects of the transition to adulthood

Furlong and Cartmel then go on to look at evidence of changes in the transition between youth and adulthood in Britain. They do so in the context of the key areas which are involved in this transition. Following the work of Coles (1995), they argue that there are three crucial aspects of the transition between youth and adulthood:

1. The **transition from school to work**. Once individuals have found and taken on full-time employment then one aspect of the transition is complete.
2. The **domestic transition** involves moving away from the family of origin (for example, parents or parents' family) to the family of destination which the individual establishes with a partner.
3. The **housing transition**, which involves getting one's own housing rather than living with parents.

Furlong and Cartmel accept that there have been significant changes in all these areas. They go on to discuss these changes in relation to theories of social change.

The school to work transition

In education, youth transitions have been affected by the expansion of post-compulsory education which, for many young people, delays the move to full-time employment, a crucial part of the transition to adulthood. There is also more differentiation of schools, qualifications and further and higher educational institutions. All this gives the impression of greater individual choice.

Furthermore, the educational achievements of girls have overtaken those of boys, and girls have many more educational opportunities than they once did.

However, from a review of the evidence, Furlong and Cartmel argue that educational achievements are still strongly influenced by class. Children from middle-class backgrounds still do much better than children from working-class backgrounds. All groups gain more qualifications than they did in the past, but with the decline of unskilled work more qualifications are needed to get even working-class jobs. It is still predominantly higher classes who attend elite universities, and it is the middle classes who have taken up most of the extra places in higher education. (See pp. 625–6 for evidence which supports these views.)

Furlong and Cartmel also believe that gender still has some influence. Although females are doing better than males in terms of level of qualifications, subject choice in school and vocational and higher education is still strongly gendered.

Furlong and Cartmel therefore accept that transitions between school and work have become more protracted and more varied, but believe that class and gender still play an important part in determining the destinations at the end of the transition.

Domestic and housing transitions

As with the school to work transition, Furlong and Cartmel believe that the domestic and housing transitions have become more varied and complex, and in some cases more protracted. Many young people remain in a state of semi-independence (or semi-dependency, from another point of view) for several years. Social policies have encouraged this trend as changes in the benefits system mean that young people now have to wait until the age of 25 before they can claim full adult benefits. This tends to delay the domestic and housing transitions.

Nevertheless, on average, people in Britain are leaving parental homes earlier than in the past. However, often this is not to set up a new family of destination in their own housing. Many young people leave to become students. Most students go back to their family of origin during holidays and some return to live there once their course is finished. Some end up living with other students or friends without establishing a new family, in what Furlong and Cartmel describe as **intermediary households**.

Thus, rather than there being a clear transition to adulthood as young people get jobs and start new families in their own homes, the situation is more complex. Class and gender continue to exercise a strong influence on these transitions. For example, women tend to marry or move in with a partner at a younger age than men. Housing transitions tend to be different for different classes. Working-class youth find it more difficult than middle-class youth to afford the cost of buying a house. With a lack of social housing (council or housing association) available, the housing transition may be delayed. Some working-class youths end up homeless.

Furlong and Cartmel therefore say that, 'In some respects, it can be argued that recent changes in domestic and housing transitions reflect an increase in the range of possibilities open to young people' (1997, p. 51). The changes have involved an **extension** and **desequencing** of transitions so that the complete transition to adulthood takes longer than in the past and often does not follow a predictable sequence.

Furlong and Cartmel (2006) note that this has led some to suggest that there is a new phase in the life course, characterized by semi-dependency, which should be called **young adulthood**. However, while there is greater choice and individualization during this stage, in some respects there also tends to be greater reliance upon families of origin for longer than in the past. In addition, the transitions remain highly structured by class and gender.

Conclusion

Furlong and Carmel conclude that there is 'an essential continuity with the past' (2006, p. 109). To them,

modernity and late modernity are similar in many respects. Some individualization has taken place and there is greater choice in the transition from youth to adulthood. However, choice is not equally distributed, with the middle class having more choice than the working class.

While most people feel that class has lost most of its influence on social life. Furlong and Cartmel see this as an **epistemological fallacy**. By this they mean that people's feelings are not a good guide to reality because class continues to have a profound influence on life chances – for example, educational achievement.

This does not mean that class is as important as it used to be in all areas of social life. For example, leisure and youth culture have become less class-based. But this just obscures the fact that the timing of the transition to adulthood and the position that is gained after the transition are both strongly influenced by class and other social factors. Furlong and Cartmel conclude that:

> *some of the problems faced by young people in modern Britain stem from an attempt to negotiate difficulties on an individual level. Blind to the existence of powerful chains of interdependency, young people frequently attempt to resolve collective problems through individual action and hold themselves responsible for their inevitable failure.* 2006, p. 114

Youth subcultures

As discussed earlier, the second major strand in research on youth in Britain, after the study of transitions, involves the study of youth culture and youth subcultures. Research on youth subcultures was pioneered in the 1970s by a group of sociologists in Birmingham who adopted a neo-Marxist approach. Their work saw class as a crucial factor influencing the development of youth culture.

The Birmingham Centre for Contemporary Cultural Studies

In the 1970s and 1980s the Centre for Contemporary Cultural Studies (CCCS) at Birmingham University started to study youth subcultures which had developed in Britain from the 1950s onwards. The work of the CCCS provides the starting point for subsequent research on youth culture. Even quite recent research can be seen as a development of, or reaction against, the views of the CCCS.

Resistance through Rituals

In *Resistance through Rituals* (Hall and Jefferson, 1976), John Clarke, Stuart Hall, Tony Jefferson and Brian Roberts (1976) outline a theoretical approach to the study of youth cultures. They do so within a broadly Marxist framework, arguing that material circumstances impose limits on the sorts of cultures people can develop. These cultures are seen as being closely related to class divisions. However, rather than simply reproducing class-based cultures, subcultures are seen as a creative response by some young people to the class situation they find themselves in.

Cultures and material life

According to Clarke *et al.*:

> *the 'culture' of a group or class is the distinctive 'way of life' of the group or class, the meanings, values and ideas embodied in institutions, in social relations, in systems of beliefs, in mores and customs, in the uses of objects and material life.* Clarke et al., 1976

Individuals are born into particular cultures and these tend to shape the way in which they see the world – their **maps of meaning**, as Clarke *et al.* term it. However, these maps of meaning and their associated cultures change as history unfolds and as members of social groups actively create cultures and innovate. But groups cannot just create new cultures at will. Cultures always relate to experiences and sets of material circumstances and are always partly shaped by pre-existing cultures.

Furthermore, cultures exist in hierarchical relationship to one another. The culture of dominant groups is always likely to be more powerful than the cultures of less powerful groups. But Clarke *et al.* deny that a whole society's culture will ever be dominated by one ruling-class ideology.

Hegemony

Clarke *et al.* draw extensively on the theories of the Italian Marxist, Gramsci (see pp. 539–40). Gramsci argued that in order to achieve political and ideological domination (which he called **hegemony**) powerful classes always had to struggle against competing ideologies and make compromises with other less powerful classes. Dominant ideology can always be opposed and hegemony is never complete. Clarke *et al.* adopt a similar position. They say:

> *Other cultural configurations will not only be subordinate to this dominant order: they will enter into struggle with it, seek to modify, negotiate, resist or even overthrow its reign – its hegemony. The struggle between classes over material and social life thus always assumes a continuous struggle over the distribution of 'cultural power'.* Clarke et al., 1976

It might be an unequal struggle, but it is a struggle nonetheless. Subordinate cultures will generally try to win space, to make room for their own distinctive lifestyles, values and institutions away from the influence of more powerful cultures. An example is the traditional working-class neighbourhood, dating from the 1880s, with its distinctive physical layout – 'the networks of streets, houses, corner shops, pubs and parks' – and social relationships – 'the networks of kin, friendship, work and neighbourly relations'. The working class exercised considerable informal control over these areas.

Youth subcultures

To Clarke *et al.*, youth subcultures often represent creative attempts to try to maintain or win autonomy or space from dominant cultures. They win 'cultural space in the neighbourhood and institutions, real time for leisure and

recreation, actual room on the street-corner'. They are partly shaped by the parent culture of the class from which they originate (for example, working class or middle class), but they are distinct from it.

Youth cultures create their own distinctive style: for example, by choosing a style of dress and listening to a particular type of music. The styles adopted by individual cultures represent an attempt to '"solve", but in an imaginary way, problems which at the concrete material level remain unresolved'. There tends to be a **homology** between the styles chosen and the values and ideas being expressed. That is, objects and styles are chosen by groups which fit the meanings they are expressing. Elements of style might therefore reflect class differences.

Youth subcultures emphasize the importance of **authenticity**. It is seen as paramount that a subculture is genuine and not a media creation. Once the media start to portray a youth subculture, it becomes distorted and influenced by ruling-class ideology.

The example of Teddy boys can be used to illustrate these arguments.

Tony Jefferson – Teddy boys

Tony Jefferson (1976) argues that the youth culture of Teddy boys (or Teds) represented an attempt to recreate the sense of working-class community, which came under threat in the postwar period from urban redevelopment and growing affluence in some sections of the working class.

Unskilled working-class youth felt that their social status was being undermined and their 'territory' was under threat from the urban planners and from a growing minority ethnic presence in their neighbourhood. They responded by forming groups in which members had a strong sense of loyalty to one another and were willing to fight over their territory. Their style of dress incorporated Edwardian-style jackets, bootlace ties and suede shoes.

Jefferson sees aspects of this style as part of an attempt to buy status. For example, Edwardian-style jackets were originally worn by 'upper-class dandies' in Edwardian times, and by wearing them Teds hoped that some of the status of this group would rub off on them. Bootlace ties appeared to come from American Western films, in which they were worn by the 'slick city gambler whose social status was, grudgingly, high because of his ability *to live by his wits* and outside the traditional working-class mores of society'. Like their counterparts in the Westerns, the Teddy boys felt themselves to be outsiders who needed to live by their wits. They were seeking something of the status of the city gambler and so adopted part of their dress.

To Clarke *et al.*, youth cultures do not solve the fundamental problems of working-class youth, but they do offer 'imaginary solutions'. Working-class youth can at least feel they are doing something to protect their territory, gain status and recreate community. They also challenge and resist dominant ideologies without really threatening them. Youth cultures are part of the continuing struggle for cultural hegemony, born out of class cultures, but distinct from them. They are actively created by their members who develop their own styles as a way of expressing their situation and its contradictions, or their aspirations.

Dick Hebdige – *Subculture: The Meaning of Style*

Subculture and style

Dick Hebdige was one of the contributors to *Resistance through Rituals* (Hebdige, 1976). He then went on to develop his own approach to the understanding of subcultures in *Subculture: The Meaning of Style* (1979, 1988). Like the CCCS, Hebdige saw class as key to understanding subcultures, but he also drew extensively on other theoretical approaches. In particular he used **semiotics** (also known as semiology) in order to try to understand the meaning of a number of post-war British youth subcultures.

Semiotics was first developed by Ferdinand de Saussure (1857–1913). It is a method of interpreting the meaning of **signs**: words or objects which have a specific meaning within culture. Semiotics is based upon a distinction between the **signified** (the meaning of a word, object or image) and the **signifier** (the sound of a word, the physical object or the image). Together the signifier and signified are a sign.

The meaning of signs is based on contrasts with other signs: they are defined in terms of their difference compared to other things (see pp. 678–9 for a full description of semiotics/semiology). To Hebdige, it was possible to understand the meaning of the quiff of the Teddy boy, the safety pins of punks or the music of the mods, using semiology.

Each youth subculture developed its own style and each took everyday objects and transformed their meaning. Hebdige says: '"humble" objects can be magically appropriated; "stolen" by subordinate groups and made to carry "secret" meanings: meanings which express, in code, a form of resistance to the order which guarantees their continued subordination'.

Teddy boys transformed the meaning of Edwardian suits and pointed boots. Punks transformed the meaning of safety pins and ripped jeans. They became gestures of defiance against society. They came to signify membership of particular subcultures and the whole complex set of meanings that each subculture expressed. Each subculture defines itself in opposition to **mainstream culture**. It is a self-conscious repudiation of the widely shared lifestyle and taste of the bulk of the population. For example, subcultures reject pop music and conventional clothing. Each subculture is also spectacular: it creates a **spectacle** and is intended to get noticed.

Skinheads and mods

Like Saussure, Hebdige believes that meanings derive from internal systems of differences. Just as a dictionary defines words in terms of their differences and similarities to other words, so the meaning of clothing is defined in terms of differences and similarities to other types of clothing. For example, skinheads wore 'cropped hair, braces, short, wide Levi jeans or functional Sta-prest trousers, plain or striped button-down Ben Sherman shirts and highly polished Doctor Marten boots'. Their appearance was a kind of exaggerated version of the working-class manual labourer and expressed the image of the 'hard' working-class man.

On the other hand, mods adopted a more respectable appearance, which reflected aspirations to be upwardly mobile and join the middle class. However, their dress and style were certainly different from those of most middle-class people. Despite their 'apparently conservative suits in respectable colours', their style expressed an 'emotional affinity with black people' and a love of the world of 'cellar clubs, discotheques, boutiques and record shops', which was outside the 'straight world' of the respectable middle class.

The mods' dress allowed them to move fairly easily between work and leisure, but at the same time they disrupted the conventional meanings of some of the clothes they wore. Hebdige says:

> *Quietly disrupting the orderly sequence which leads from signifier to signified, the mods undermined the conventional meaning of 'collar, suit and tie', pushing neatness to the point of absurdity ... they were a little too smart, somewhat too alert, thanks to amphetamines.* Hebdige, 1979

Black subcultures

Black British people also developed distinctive subcultures based upon differences and similarities to other styles of dress. In the first post-war phases of immigration from the West Indies, the first-generation migrants adopted smart and conventional dress which reflected their aspirations to succeed in Britain. They wore 'rainbow mohair suits and picture ties ... neatly printed frocks and patent leather shoes'. However:

> *all hopes of ever really fitting in were inadvertently belied by every garish jacket sleeve – too loud and jazzy for contemporary British tastes. Both the dreams and the disappointments of an entire generation were thus inscribed in the very cut (ambitious and improbable) of the clothes in which it chose to make its entrance.* Hebdige, 1979

By the 1970s the disappointments that stemmed from racism and high levels of unemployment began to be expressed in the clothes and subcultural style of Rastafarians. British Rastafarians expressed their alienation from British culture by adopting simple clothes with an African feel to them. Army surplus stores provided garments able to express 'sinister guerrilla chic'. The key themes of Rastafarian style were resistance to the dominance of white culture and the expression of black identity.

Punk

Reggae, Rastafarianism and their associated styles influenced white youth culture, but their association with blackness precluded their wholesale adoption by white youth. In the 1970s white youth developed their own subculture – punk – which Hebdige analyses in detail.

To Hebdige, punk almost rewrote the rules of semiology, in certain respects changing the way signs were used to convey meaning. Punk drew some meaning from reggae and Rastafarianism. Some punk groups, such as the Clash, incorporated reggae rhythms into their music, and some punks wore the red, gold and green of Rastafarians.

Punk also adopted an element of the Rastafarian opposition to being seen as British (rather than African). Punks explicitly attacked conventional notions of being British – for example, in the Sex Pistols' songs 'Anarchy in the UK' and 'God Save the Queen'.

But punk also defined itself in opposition to certain types of music. It disliked the empty commercialism of the Glam Rock of artists such as Alvin Stardust and Gary Glitter; but it was also critical of artists who were seen as pretentious (such as David Bowie and Roxy Music). Punk attacked the existing music industry and tried to break down the barrier between performer and audience. It celebrated the amateurish nature of many punk bands and encouraged anybody who could play a couple of chords on a guitar to form their own band.

Behind punk was a claim to 'speak for the neglected constituency of white lumpen youth', and a desire to 'act out alienation'. It was undoubtedly British, but it 'was predicated upon a denial of place. It issued out of nameless housing estates, anonymous dole queues, slums-in-the-abstract. It was blank, expressionless, rootless.' Unlike Rastafarianism, it gave no hope for the future. There was no equivalent to the return to Africa which held the promise of redemption for British Rastafarians. Instead, there was simply, in the Sex Pistols' words, no future.

Punk and chaos

Hebdige comments: 'The punk subculture, then, signified chaos at every level.' Part of this chaos involved radical departures in the way signifiers were used. It was not just that punks took such ordinary objects as safety pins, bin liners and toilet chains and transformed them into fashion accessories. They were also able to detach symbols from their conventional meanings. For example, some punks and punk groups took the swastika as a signifier, but it 'was wilfully detached from the concept (Nazism) it conventionally signified'. Used by punks, the swastika was no longer a symbol of racism – most punks were strongly anti-racist. Instead, it was used simply to signify a lack of meaning. Hebdige says, 'the central value "held and reflected" in the swastika was the communicated absence of any such identifiable values'.

Signifying practices

Hebdige argues that conventional semiotics is unable to deal with the meaning of punk, where signifiers were separated from what they signified. He therefore uses the idea of **signifying practice** to understand the nature of signs in punk subculture.

According to the idea of signifying practice, the traditional relationship between langue (the structure of language) and parole (individual uses of language) is reversed. Langue is no longer seen as more important than parole. Rather than meaning deriving from the overall structure of language, it derives more from the position of the person using it. Thus the meaning of the swastika no longer comes from its relationship to other signifiers (such as 'racism' or 'Nazism'), but from the fact that it was punks who were using the concept. The idea of signifying practices sees language as something that is fluid and capable of changing its meaning. Language is always in the process of being used; its meaning changes, and it is never fixed as it appears to be in dictionaries. Punk is an example of the 'triumph ... of the signifier over the signified'.

Punk and the ruling class

Although Hebdige draws primarily on semiology to develop his ideas on youth subcultures, he also makes use of Marxist ideas. He sees all subcultures 'as a form of resistance ... in which the experienced contradictions and objections to ... ruling ideology are obliquely represented in style'. Although they might pose no major threat to the ruling class, they do produce what Hebdige calls 'noise' – an alternative source of ideas which interferes with ruling-class attempts to create the impression of societal harmony.

Thus, Hebdige's work fits with the approach of the CCCS as it is **neo-Marxist**, combining non-Marxist theory (in this case semiology) with traditional Marxist concepts such as class, ruling-class ideology and alienation.

Evaluation of the CCCS and Hebdige

The work of the CCCS (including Hebdige) was important, not just in trying to develop a neo-Marxist approach to youth subcultures, but also in encouraging sociologists to take youth culture seriously. As we will see, even those who are highly critical of this work often use it as a starting point.

However, the neo-Marxist elements of their approach have fallen out of fashion. Some have seen these theories as exaggerating the importance of class at the expense of other social divisions such as gender and ethnicity. Others, influenced by postmodernism, have questioned whether such social divisions are really important in a consumer society. They have also questioned whether distinctive subcultures still exist. The following are just some of the major criticisms that have been put forward.

1. Neo-Marxist theories such as those developed by the CCCS and Hebdige are not always accepted by conventional Marxists. From the point of view of traditional Marxism they fail to fully acknowledge the importance of the economic base in shaping culture, which is part of the superstructure (see pp. 667–9).
2. Studies such as those of Hebdige are only as good as the interpretations put forward, and subcultures can be interpreted in different ways. There is no evidence in Hebdige's work that the Teddy boys, mods or punks actually saw their own subcultures in the same way as Hebdige saw them. He did not, for example, conduct in-depth interviews with members of subcultures to check that their views corresponded with his own. To other sociologists this could be seen as making his work too subjective and lacking in validity.

Andy Bennett and Keith Kahn-Harris (2004) identify a number of other criticisms of Hebdige and the CCCS.

3. The CCCS failed to carry out studies to establish that the subcultures discussed were almost exclusively working-class. They simply assumed that members were working-class and that subcultures had a class basis. Other sociologists have argued that the growth of consumerism has provided opportunities for identities to develop which are based on taste not class, and cut across class boundaries.
4. The CCCS placed little emphasis on ethnicity and locality as influences on the formation of subcultures, which cut across class boundaries. Researchers in the USA have examined the crucial role of 'race' and ethnicity in the development of subcultures based on hip-hop and other black musical styles. The CCCS also assumed that each subculture took a particular form throughout Britain, but some researchers have emphasized that subcultures can be more regionally or locally based.
5. The CCCS has little to say about youth who are not members or followers of any subculture. Bennett and Kahn-Harris say there is only one 'cursory' mention of such youth in the whole of *Resistance through Rituals*. As they probably make up the majority of youth, it is a serious omission. Furthermore, the CCCS fails to explain why subcultures are attractive to some working-class youth, but not to others who have a similar position in society.
6. Another criticism that has been put forward is that the CCCS greatly exaggerate the extent to which youth subcultures are oppositional to mainstream culture. Not only may it be misleading to assume that there is a single, mainstream culture rather than several, but subcultures might simply be more about having fun than expressing resistance to society.
7. These approaches also neglected girls and concentrated very largely on males within subcultures. As we will see, this problem was discussed in *Resistance through Rituals*, but nevertheless the CCCS can be accused of failing to acknowledge the role of females in subcultures and concentrating on subcultures which were male-dominated (see below).
8. The strongest criticisms are put forward by a variety of postmodern theorists. Some not only deny that class plays an important part in subcultures but even question whether well-defined subcultures ever really existed. Even if they once did, postmodernists tend to argue that the concept of subculture is not useful for describing the nature of youth culture today (see pp. 777–8).

These and other criticisms have given rise to a whole range of alternative ways of theorizing subcultures or youth culture. As such the early work of the CCCS has stimulated much of the later research, even that of postmodernists who are probably the most critical of neo-Marxist theories. However, before examining postmodern views, we will first consider the accusation that early subculture theory neglected females.

Gender and youth subcultures

Angela McRobbie and Jenny Garber – the neglect of gender?

One of the contributions to *Resistance through Rituals* (Hall and Jefferson, 1976) was written by Angela McRobbie and Jenny Garber. McRobbie and Garber noted that there

was a noticeable absence of girls both in the other chapters in the volume and in other studies of youth subcultures. They raised two possible reasons for this: either girls participated a lot less in subcultures, or they did participate in substantial numbers and the way the research was being done rendered them invisible.

When girls were mentioned by subcultural researchers they were often described in terms of their physical attractiveness. Furthermore, McRobbie and Garber note that some researchers seemed to have difficulty eliciting responses from girls during research. They discuss a study by Paul Willis of motorbike subcultures in which he describes the girls as 'giggling' in response to questions and not being very forthcoming. Consequently, most of his data came from the males in the groups.

McRobbie and Garber therefore argue that girls, where they are mentioned at all, are usually portrayed as marginal. However, this marginality may be more apparent than real and could stem from either the reluctance of girls to talk to male researchers, or in some cases sexist assumptions made by the researcher.

Nevertheless McRobbie and Garber believe that girls did play a smaller role in subcultures than boys. Partly, these subcultures were dominated by boys in line with male dominance in society in general. Partly, the limited role of girls was a self-fulfilling prophecy. Both the mass media and academic studies portrayed females as marginal, and therefore youth subcultures had relatively little attraction for girls.

However, McRobbie and Garber believe that the main reason was probably that the position of young women was **structurally different** from that of young men. They speculate that girls might have their own culture, separate from the male-dominated subcultures studied by male researchers.

McRobbie and the culture of femininity

The possibility that girls might have a separate, less visible culture was taken up by McRobbie in later research (1978). She conducted a study of fifty-six working-class girls aged 14–16 who attended a youth club. According to McRobbie these girls faced a restricted future. Given a lack of qualifications and limited job opportunities at the time, they were unlikely to get a job which was sufficiently well paid to support themselves.

Marriage therefore seemed a more or less inevitable future path since by having a better paid husband or two earners in the household they might be able to afford their own home and be able to start a family. Despite their restricted future options, the **culture of femininity** – friendship and a shared culture with other girls – made life bearable.

The culture of femininity involved a tendency to have a 'best friend' – another girl. Although this might seem to exclude boys, in fact best friends were tied up with the desire to attract a man. The girls thought that it would be easier to go out in pairs looking for a man than as individuals.

Furthermore, within the friendship pair there was a strong emphasis on fashion and make-up. This formed part of the **ideology of romance** in which friendship with another girl was seen as a stepping-stone towards romance and marriage. Another important part of the ideology of romance was the idolization of male pop stars or other male media figures. McRobbie saw this as essentially preparation for having real boyfriends.

Despite the ideology of romance, the girls were under no illusions that married life would be perfect. Their own experience of family life – observing their mothers and sisters – taught them that married life could be less than blissful and that romance did not always last. Nevertheless they were still fascinated by marriage as the only way to gain some status in society. Furthermore they were trapped materially and ideologically with no other realistic means of improving their lives.

Bedroom culture

McRobbie argues that the culture of femininity is largely missed by researchers into youth subcultures because it is not as public and not as spectacular as male-dominated youth subcultures. It exists mainly in private space and could be seen as a **bedroom culture**. The bedroom is a space into which girls retreat away from the outside world and away from the risk of being humiliated or harassed by boys. Researchers were unlikely to be allowed into this space.

Furthermore, the culture of femininity was largely missed by researchers because it did not fit the theoretical model of neo-Marxists who were looking for evidence of heroic resistance to dominant ideology by subordinate classes.

Sian Lincoln – bedroom culture in the 1990s

Although McRobbie's research on bedroom culture, the culture of femininity and the ideology of romance is old, some more recent researchers have argued that aspects of this culture still exist.

Research by Sian Lincoln (2004) into a small sample of Mancunian girls found that a bedroom culture still existed in the 1990s. The bedroom was still a space where girls cultivated friendships with other girls. However, girls' bedrooms were no longer as private as they had once been. Televisions and access to the internet were common, and so the outside world was allowed in. Furthermore, girls no longer excluded males from their bedrooms as they were now more likely to allow boyfriends in, though they remained predominantly female territory.

Helen Reddington – the importance of girls in subcultures

Although she was highly critical of male subcultural researchers, McRobbie did find legitimate reasons for the relative absence of girls in subcultural research. McRobbie believed that subcultures, at least in the 1970s, were male-dominated. However, different conclusions were reached by Helen Reddington (2003).

Reddington argues that, 'There is perhaps no better example of male hegemonic control over popular cultural history than the rewrite of punk to exclude the very large and productive presence of young women in the subculture from the very beginning' (2003, p. 239). Punk fashion

was strongly influenced by the female fashion designer Vivienne Westwood. There were also numerous bands which were either all female or had female members. Examples include Siouxsie and the Banshees, X-Ray Spex, The Adverts and the Dollymixtures.

Reddington argues that the high levels of participation by women were partly due to the ethos of punk. Punk was based upon the principle that anybody could have a go at playing music and expressing themselves. It was acceptable for punk musicians to learn to play through performance rather than waiting to become technically accomplished before taking to the stage. Furthermore, there was often a local punk scene and you did not need the approval of (usually) male music business professionals to get involved. Punk bands often lent each other equipment, so the usual financial barriers to joining a band, which particularly held back girls, were not present.

Reddington therefore believes that, in the case of punk at least, the neglect of females had nothing to do with their absence but simply reflected bias from male academics and others who wrote about punk. Reddington believes that women were central in punk bands but their roles have been unfairly reduced 'to the status of sub-subculture or indeed subculturette' (2003, p. 250).

The evidence therefore suggests that the neglect of females in youth subcultures may be partly a result of their lack of participation in some subcultures, but it is also partly due to their neglect by predominantly male researchers. The issue of gender and subculture will also be raised in relation to other studies examined in this section.

Sarah Thornton – *Club Cultures*

One of the most influential studies of youth culture since the CCCS pioneered this area of research is Sarah Thornton's *Club Cultures* (1995). Thornton's study concentrates on a rather different phenomenon to the mods, punks and Teds studied by the CCCS. She carried out an ethnographic study of dance music, clubs and raves in the early 1990s.

Thornton acknowledges that she was influenced by the Birmingham research but points out that her work differs in a number of ways:

1. Thornton does not see club cultures as primarily oppositional to a dominant culture.
2. She does not emphasize the importance of class in shaping club culture.
3. Clubbing is not characterized by close-knit groups who hang around much of the time united by their common culture. Rather, clubbers come together at specific times at specific dance events. Club cultures are therefore more a scene which people take part in on a part-time basis rather than a complete lifestyle.
4. Thornton does not draw upon the theories of Gramsci in developing her ideas but instead gets most of her inspiration from the work of Pierre Bourdieu (see pp. 539–40).

Subcultural capital

Although Bourdieu was himself influenced by Marxist theory, Thornton is not concerned so much with inequality within society as a whole, but more with inequality within club culture itself. Thornton argues that the most important aspect of club culture is the way it is used by the young to differentiate amongst themselves.

Bourdieu argues that there are different forms of capital – economic capital, social capital and cultural capital – which can be used to obtain wealth, status or power in society. Thornton suggests that there is another type of capital, **subcultural capital**, which is also important. Subcultural capital can sometimes be used to gain economic capital – for example, if you become a DJ in club culture – but its main value is in providing status to the clubber.

Thornton sees dance club cultures as **taste cultures** in which the demonstration of good taste, or hipness, gets you social approval and recognition. Thornton says:

> *Subcultural capital conveys status on its owner in the eyes of the relevant beholder ... Just as books and paintings display cultural capital in the home, so subcultural capital is objectified in the form of fashionable haircuts and well-assembled record collections (full of well-chosen, limited edition 'white label' twelve inches and the like). Just as cultural capital is personified in good manners and urbane conversation, so subcultural capital is embodied in the form of being 'in the know', using (but not over-using) current slang and looking as if you were born to perform the latest dance styles.* Thornton, 1995, pp. 11–12

In dance culture you have to keep up with the latest trends to maintain subcultural capital. You need to know where and when you should go clubbing, in order to experience and be seen at the most fashionable clubs. However, you must guard against continuing to enjoy music which is too popular or which has become too mainstream to provide subcultural capital.

By the middle of 1989 media coverage had made acid house culture too popular to be hip. Acid house fans came to be seen as sheep, following media trends. The men were dismissed as 'mindless ravers' or 'Acid Teds'. 'Teds were understood to travel in same-sex mobs, support football teams, wear Kickers boots and be "out of their heads"' (Thornton, 1995, p. 100). They were looked down on just as much as their female equivalents, 'raving Sharons' and 'Techno Tracys' who revealed their lack of hipness by dancing around their handbags.

Class, age, gender and clubbing

These men and women were certainly not hardcore clubbers. Although Teds, Sharons and Tracys were all seen as working-class stereotypes, there was no clear match between class and subcultural capital in club cultures. Although many hardcore clubbers were working-class, some public school-educated youth would put on working-class accents to gain acceptance in club culture. Furthermore, 'Subcultural capitals fuel rebellion against, or rather escape from, parental class' (Thornton, 1995, p. 12). Club culture cuts across all social divisions (class, gender, ethnicity, 'race', sexuality), but not age.

The most avid clubbers are aged 15–19, with the 20–24 age group the next most keen. Going to dance clubs is part of growing up:

> *a rite of passage which marks adolescent independence with the freedom to stay out late with friends beyond the*

neighbourhood in a space which is relatively their own. Clubs allow their patrons to indulge in the 'adult' activities of flirtation, sex, drink and drugs, and explore cultural forms (like music and clothes) which confer autonomous and distinct identities. Thornton, 1995, p. 16

Clubbing starts at around the age of 15 because it is the age at which children start to gain sufficient independence to go out at night. It declines as young people go through their twenties because they move out of the parental home and no longer need to go to clubs to find space away from parents to engage in adult activities.

Apart from age, the most important social division in club culture, according to Thornton, is gender. From the start, girls are more likely to go clubbing than boys, partly because boys engage in a wider range of out-of-home leisure activities than girls, particularly playing sports. However, the feminine is accorded less status in dance culture than the masculine. For example, mainstream pop music is associated with femininity and is looked down on as the lowest of the low. Working-class girls with the least hip musical tastes are regarded with the most contempt.

Thornton therefore argues that dance cultures cannot be seen as a form of rebellion against ruling-class dominance, as CCCS theorists claimed for the subcultures they studied. By looking down on a relatively powerless group, dance cultures were reproducing not challenging existing power relations.

Clubbing and the media

Club culture also fails to challenge dominant power relations in its attitude to the media. Although hardcore clubbers reject the musical styles that get most airplay, subcultural capital is still a product of the media. Local micro-media such as flyers are used to bring clubbers together, and niche media, such as parts of the music press, are key arbiters of hipness.

Without the media there would be no way of communicating the degrees of subcultural capital associated with different clubs, DJs or musical styles. Therefore, despite the apparent rejection of the media by the hardcore, the media are integral to the production of club cultures. The tastes of the hardcore are as much a product of the media as the mainstream tastes of those they look down on.

Evaluation

Thornton's work has been influential. It took the study of youth subculture in a different direction from the work of the CCCS. It examined the importance of a range of social divisions (including gender and age) without concentrating on class, and showed that youth subcultures may have little to do with resisting dominant culture. Thornton also showed that dance cultures were more varied and changed rapidly, so they never assumed a single subcultural style in the same way as Teds, punks or mods.

Thornton's work links the study of subcultures or youth cultures to youth as a period of transition between childhood and adulthood, while retaining the emphasis on cultural style found in the work of the CCCS. However, Thornton does not systematically relate her work to wider changes in society as a whole. She mentions theories such as postmodernity and globalization, but focuses mainly on dance cultures themselves, and her writing draws as much on the work of Bourdieu as it does on postmodern writers. Much of the more recent work on subcultures or youth culture has been more strongly influenced by postmodernism.

Andy Bennett – neo-tribes

In an influential article, Andy Bennett (1999) questioned whether the concept of subculture was useful for describing groups of youths who shared similar tastes in style and music. Bennett described the term 'subculture' as 'little more than a convenient catch-all'.

Like Thornton, Bennett uses dance music as an example to develop his theoretical argument. He develops Thornton's view that youth cultures have become less distinct, more varied and less well defined than they were in the past, saying 'an alternative theoretical framework needs to be developed which allows for the pluralistic and shifting sensibilities of style that have increasingly characterized youth "culture" since the post-Second World War period' (Bennett, 1999, p. 599).

The CCCS

Bennett starts by evaluating the work of the CCCS. He accepts that the CCCS were important in developing the study of 'the new style-orientated post-war youth culture' (p. 601), but thinks that their analysis was seriously flawed.

The CCCS largely ignored mainstream subcultures such as glitter rock (which was based around performers such as Gary Glitter and Slade) and Rollermania (based around the Bay City Rollers). Bennett also argues that the CCCS greatly exaggerated and misinterpreted the influence of class. For example, he claims that punk largely developed amongst middle-class art school students rather than the working class. Furthermore, he suggests that youth were largely using their increased consumer spending power to break away from the constraints of class identities rather than to express class identities.

Bennett does not therefore believe that different 'subcultures' were tied to class in the way that the CCCS believed. He goes on to say that the CCCS have been extensively criticized, but one aspect of their work has remained unchallenged. The term 'subculture' is still seen as appropriate for describing youth groups, and Bennett argues that it is high time this was questioned.

Problems with the concept of subculture

The main reason why the term 'subculture' should be questioned is that:

there is very little evidence that even the most committed groups of youth stylists are in any way as 'coherent' or 'fixed' as the term 'subculture' implies. On the contrary, it seems to me that so-called youth 'subcultures' are prime examples of the unstable and shifting cultural affiliations which characterize late modern consumer societies.
Bennett, 1999, p. 605

Bennett claims that clearly defined subcultures do not exist among contemporary youth. Instead youth assume certain identities in particular settings. For example, at a

rave a person may assume an identity, but the next day in a different setting (for example, at work) the identity of the previous night will not be important.

Furthermore, there is much greater choice of cultural styles – for example, in music – than there was in the past. Dance music, which uses sampling from different genres of music, cuts across distinct tastes or subcultures. Dance music might sample pop songs or heavy metal or reggae. In this way it links the audience to a variety of tastes, each of which will appeal to some consumers more than others and link to a greater or lesser extent to other identities. Thus clubbers who also like heavy metal will identify more with dance music that samples that type of music than other clubbers.

Dance music therefore breaks down the barriers between musical styles and tastes and illustrates the variety and choice available. It allows consumers to pick and mix rather than having to choose one style or taste exclusively. The musical taste, and identity, of the individual have become 'multi-faceted'.

Clubbers can also go to different types of club on different nights, assuming whatever identity is appropriate in that location. Bennett says, '"clubbing" appears to be regarded less as a singularly defined activity and more as a series of fragmented, temporal experiences as they move between different dance floors and engage with different crowds' (1999, p. 611).

Although Bennett concentrates on musical styles predominantly followed by white youth, he also discusses music followed more by minority ethnic youth. He claims that there is little difference between white and minority ethnic groups in that both follow a variety of musical styles and adopt different identities in different settings. Thus British Asian youths enjoy chart music in some contexts, but in others, such as a mela (an Asian cultural or religious fair or festival), they will listen to bhangra, a distinctively Asian type of popular music.

Neo-tribes and lifestyles

Bennett argues that in these circumstances new concepts are needed to describe and understand the tastes of contemporary youth.

First, the concept of subculture should be replaced with the concept of **neo-tribe**. This concept derives from the work of the sociologist Michel Maffesoli (1996) who coined the term **tribus** (or tribes) to describe contemporary youth. Drawing on Maffesoli, Bennett argues that neo-tribes involve loose associations of consumer groups (such as consumers of dance music) who come together in particular settings where they express similar tastes. They do not form coherent groups outside those settings, but when they are together they are influenced by one another and express similar tastes.

According to Maffesoli, neo-tribes are a comparatively new phenomenon and they are a reflection of change in society which involves a move to postmodernism. However, Bennett believes they are part of a longer-developing trend – he argues that there has been a gradual shift from a modern to a late modern society. But, however the change in society is defined, both Maffesoli and Bennett believe that traditional identities based on locality, gender and occupation are breaking down, leading people to move between different neo-tribes expressing different identities.

Second, Bennett believes that the term 'lifestyle' is preferable to 'way of life' (or culture) when describing these groups and the way people live in society today. While 'way of life' implies patterns of behaviour handed down from generation to generation – for example, in social classes – 'lifestyle' implies the choices made by consumers. People might choose a lifestyle that reflects class differences, but that is a choice, not something shaped by the structure of society. For example, Bennett argues that followers of the band Oasis adopt 'an image consisting of training shoes, football shirts and duffel coats, which is designed to illustrate their collective sense of working classness' (1999, p. 607). But even though it is based on class, it is still a self-constructed identity and fans of the band are not all of working-class origin.

Conclusion

Bennett stops just short of adopting a postmodern theory of society and youth. Nevertheless he comes very close to doing so and most postmodernists would agree with the central claims of his argument. His emphasis on consumption, on the decline of traditional identities, and on the 'shifting nature of youth's musical and stylistic preferences and the essential fluidity of youth cultural groups' (1999, p. 614), gives his work a strong affinity with postmodern theories of youth. One such theory will now be examined.

David Muggleton – *The Postmodern Meaning of Style*

Modern and postmodern subcultures

In *Inside Subculture: The Postmodern Meaning of Style* (2000), David Muggleton examines whether youth subcultures can be seen as modern or postmodern. He starts by outlining the ideal types of modern and postmodern subculture. The idea of ideal type was developed by Max Weber to describe the theoretically perfect example of a phenomenon against which actual examples can be compared. Thus if actual subcultures come closer to the ideal type of postmodern subculture than to the ideal type of modern subculture, then that suggests that postmodern theories have some merit. The ideal types are shown in Table 13.2.

According to this analysis, members of a modern subculture would identify strongly with the subculture, have a very similar choice of style (e.g. in clothes or music), see a clear-cut distinction between those who were and were not members of the subculture, and be strongly committed to the subculture which gives them their main identity and a strong set of values and beliefs. Members would tend to stick with a subculture rather than moving between one subculture and another. The subculture would be politically opposed to other groups in society and hostile to the mass media, and it would believe that there was a strong distinction between authentic members and those who had merely jumped on a media-created bandwagon and copied the subculture's style.

In contrast, postmodern subcultures are much less clearly defined, with less clear boundaries between members and non-members, more movement between subcultures, a weaker sense of commitment, greater

Table 13.2 The ideal types of modern and postmodern subculture

Modern	Postmodern
Group identity	Fragmented identity
Stylistic homogeneity	Stylistic heterogeneity
Strong boundary maintenance	Boundary maintenance weak
Subculture provides main identity	Multiple stylistic identities
High degree of commitment	Low degree of commitment
Membership perceived as permanent	Transient attachment expressed
Low rates of subcultural mobility	High rates of subcultural mobility
Stress on beliefs and values	Fascination with style and image
Political gesture of resistance	Apolitical sentiments
Anti-media sentiments	Positive attitude towards media
Self-perception as authentic	Celebration of the inauthentic

Source: D. Muggleton (2000) *Inside Subculture: The Postmodern Meaning of Style*, Berg, Oxford, p. 52.

Figure 13.5 Hybrid culture

Source: Photofusion

variety in the styles adopted within the group, and a greater emphasis on style than on beliefs. A postmodern subculture is not political and enjoys playing around with different styles without worrying about their authenticity. It also celebrates use of the mass media rather than seeing it as a sign of a lack of authenticity.

In addition, Muggleton suggests that modern subcultures are much more strongly influenced by class differences (as the CCCS claimed) than postmodern subcultures.

Having outlined these differences, Muggleton discusses his own empirical research which attempted to test whether there had been a shift to postmodern subcultures. Muggleton conducted interviews with fifty-seven young people (forty-three male and fourteen female). Three of the interviews were conducted in Preston, Lancashire and the remainder in Brighton. All took place between 1993 and 1995. Members of the sample were approached and interviewed in pubs or clubs. Muggleton then analysed whether the respondents corresponded more closely to modern or postmodern characteristics.

Individuality and subcultural affiliation

Muggleton found that few of those he interviewed expressed a strong affiliation to a particular subculture. Most disliked being labelled as belonging to a particular group, although one did say unequivocally that they were a punk and another a goth. Other respondents would qualify subcultural attachment, saying, for example, that they were 'mod-y' rather than a mod or 'punkish' rather than a punk.

Most were much more concerned to assert their individuality rather than group identity. Indeed some, who loosely identified with a subculture, emphasized that belonging to a subculture was all about expressing individuality. Thus a true punk would not look like other punks but would have their own distinctive style.

Some respondents just described themselves as individuals even if they appeared to conform to some extent to a subcultural style. Although you had to fit in with others, you also had to stand out and be different, even within a subculture. The most important rule was that you should not conform to society as a whole.

Some individuals mixed elements from different subcultures. For example, Peter saw himself as part biker, part skateboarder, but overall believed he fitted in with just about everyone. Robin was influenced by both punk and Teddy boy style.

Muggleton therefore saw subcultures as **liminal**. Liminal means on the threshold or in-between clear social identities. The vast majority of respondents were either on the fringe of subcultural membership or had mixed identities. However, there was still some degree of affiliation with particular subcultures. Muggleton therefore claims that 'Subcultures can therefore be understood, somewhat paradoxically, as collective expressions and celebrations of individualism' (2000, p. 79).

Commitment, appearance and the self

In terms of individuality and affiliation, the sample interviewed by Muggleton corresponded much more closely to the postmodern rather than the modern ideal type of subculture. In terms of commitment, appearance and the self, however, there was some evidence that people were rather more involved with subcultures than it first appeared.

Some of those interviewed had long-term affiliations to particular subcultures. However, that did not mean that

they did not change at all. Dressing in exactly the same way for long periods was rather looked down on, but so were frequent, radical changes of style. Instead, slow evolutionary development of a person's style was seen as most desirable. Muggleton says:

> *Stylistic change is regarded positively – an important criterion of authenticity. But change is best understood in transformative terms, as a gradual, partial and evolutionary process, not in sudden shifts in whole identities, as some postmodern theorists would have it.* Muggleton, 2000, p. 103

There was not much evidence that people switched between subcultures frequently. Even those who did change their outward appearance, or dressed more formally in the week and in a subcultural style at weekends, still felt a sense of subcultural identity. People did not playfully change identities or pretend to be something they were not very often; they wanted to be true to themselves. There was a tendency as well to define authentic membership of a subculture in terms of a person's identity rather than superficial aspects of style. Thus a true punk was someone who saw themselves as a punk and thought like a punk, rather than somebody wearing safety pins or bondage clothes.

Divisions between groups

The CCCS, and modern conceptions of subcultures generally, portray subcultures as being highly distinctive and hostile to one another. Thus, traditionally, there has been hostility between mods and rockers (or bikers), punks and hippies and so on. However, Muggleton found little evidence of such outright hostility or indeed such clear divisions between groups.

With more people in a liminal position between different subcultures or on the fringe of subcultures, the edges of subcultures had become blurred. One respondent had, over the years, moved from a primary affiliation to Teds to a punk affiliation; another had moved from seeing himself as a hippy to being a punk. Neither experienced this as being too contradictory because they found within both subcultures some continuity and room for their individuality.

Muggleton argues that all subcultures share hostility to the mainstream and respect for individuality, meaning that 'ideological distinctions that were thought to set particular subcultures in opposition have been over-emphasised' (2000, p. 127). Muggleton says that 'the characteristics of homogeneity, fixity and demarcation, as emphasised in the CCCS approach, appear increasingly irrelevant'. He therefore agrees with Bennett that there is some merit in the concept of neo-tribe, which indicates 'a diffuse grouping with insubstantial boundaries' (p. 128).

The media and politics

Muggleton also rejects the view of the media put forward by the CCCS. They believed that once the media started portraying a subculture and spreading its fashions and style to groups of consumers, then that subculture would lose its authenticity. The subculture became watered down and became little more than a commercialized fashion trend.

However, Muggleton argues that the media are deeply involved – not just in the spread of subcultural styles, but even in the birth of subcultures. For example, the audiences at Sex Pistols concerts did not adopt punk style until the Sex Pistols appeared in a notorious TV interview in December 1976 where they swore repeatedly at the interviewer, Bill Grundy. The subculture's identity only really developed from this point onwards. In this respect, Muggleton's views are close to those of Thornton (see above).

Muggleton, is equally dismissive of the CCCS view that subcultures are political in the sense that they oppose ruling-class, or bourgeois, hegemony. He found no evidence of this in his interviews. The respondents denied any political motive and tended to describe themselves as apolitical or as having little interest in politics. Instead they expressed a 'liberal declaration of freedom of expression' (Muggleton, 2000, p. 149). They had no strong political views as such, and simply wanted to be themselves.

Conclusion

Muggleton concludes that, on the whole, postmodern interpretations of subcultures are much more plausible than modern interpretations. Although individuals felt a considerable degree of commitment to subcultures and they were an important source of individual identity, the actual subcultures themselves were not very distinct and a general commitment to being an individual was common across all subcultures.

Muggleton says, 'Subculturalists are postmodern in that they demonstrate a fragmented, heterogeneous and individualistic stylistic identification' (2000, p. 158). However, Muggleton rejects more extreme versions of postmodernism because he found no evidence that subculturalists had a superficial attitude towards subcultures or frequently changed identity or affiliation. Being an authentic subculturalist was still important to people; they were not simply trying out different styles for fun.

Evaluation

Both Bennett and Muggleton are very critical of the CCCS view of subcultures. They agree that it is no longer appropriate to see subcultures as well-defined, distinctive groups whose members share the same lifestyle. However, in part, these conclusions may be the result of the type of data used in their research. Bennett, like Thornton, studied clubbing, which could be seen more as a weekend leisure pursuit rather than as a whole way of life. Muggleton did not try to identify committed members of subcultures, but instead interviewed a selection of people he found in pubs and clubs.

The final study in this section examined a group much more like a conventional subculture – goths.

Paul Hodkinson – 'The goth scene and (sub)cultural substance'

The goth scene

Paul Hodkinson (2004) carried out a study of goths between 1996 and 2000 using ethnographic methods of research including participant observation and interviews.

According to Hodkinson, the goth scene first emerged in the 1980s out of a combination of punk, glam rock, New

Romantics and other influences. In the late 1980s, bands associated with the goth scene such as The Cure, The Sisters of Mercy and The Mission gained considerable commercial success, but in the 1990s the popularity of these groups declined. Nevertheless, 'a distinct, small-scale and relatively bonded goth scene has survived and developed in and beyond Britain, predominantly outside the realms of mass media and commerce' (Hodkinson, 2004, pp. 135–6). It is characterized by music with 'sinister or sombre sounds and lyrics while the style has been dominated consistently by black hair and clothing, as well as the tendency for both males and females to wear distinct styles of make-up' (p. 138).

Goths and the CCCS

Comparing his findings on goths with the claims of the CCCS, Hodkinson found plenty of differences. There was more fluidity in participation in the goth scene than in the subcultures of the 1970s. Some individuals moved in and out of the scene, and some went to watch non-goth bands. There was variation in the degree of commitment. Some dressed as goths nearly all the time, while others only got 'gothed up' periodically.

Contrary to the CCCS approach, there was no clear relationship between goths and a particular class – they came from a variety of class backgrounds. Although most were middle-class, Hodkinson found no evidence that goth culture was expressing particular middle-class values. Furthermore, goths denied that there was any special meaning in the sombre and dark style of the scene. Instead they saw it as a way to have fun by getting dressed up, listening to music they enjoyed, meeting friends and sometimes getting drunk.

Furthermore, the development of the style was closely linked with its promotion through the mass media and goths did not see this as undermining the authenticity of the goth scene. Hodkinson therefore says:

> *the extent of the links with media and commerce, and the lack of any absolute meaning, function or class identity signified by the style would invalidate use of the structuralist slant placed on the notion of subculture by the Birmingham theorists [the CCCS].* Hodkinson, 2004, p. 139

Subcultural substance

However, that does not mean that Hodkinson accepts the views of writers such as Bennett – that subcultures have been replaced by neo-tribes – or Muggleton – that subcultures have become postmodern. Hodkinson found that despite all the above points, goths had considerable **subcultural substance**. By this he means that they retained crucial features of subcultures, including '*consistent distinctiveness* in group values and tastes, a strong sense of *shared identity*, practical *commitments* among participants, and a significant degree of *autonomy* in the facilitation and operation of the group' (2004, pp. 141–2).

Goths are consistently distinctive because, despite individual variations, they and others can easily distinguish members of the subculture from non-members. Members also had a clear sense of identity as goths. For example, one respondent, Joe, said, 'I dress in black and I'm a goth because that's what I do, I dress in black and I'm a goth – end of story' (Hodkinson, 2004, p. 144).

Figure 13.6 Goths

Source: Rex Features

Respondents also expressed a sense of shared identity with other goths who lived elsewhere and they did not know personally. Goths therefore had a **translocal** sense of identity – that is, a sense of identity that transcended local boundaries. This shared sense of identity was reinforced by a shared dislike of **trendies**, 'a perceived homogeneous mainstream grouping who were not only disliked because of the verbal and physical threat to goths that they were felt to pose, but also as a result of the perceived superficiality of their tastes'. There was therefore a clear sense of insiders and outsiders, which is typical of subcultures.

Although there were variations between individuals, goths also showed their commitment to the group through the frequency of their participation in goth life or style. Most spent much, though not all, of their leisure time socializing with other goths and enjoying goth culture (e.g. fashion or music), and they spent much of their spare money on goth artefacts. Hodkinson therefore argues that, 'while few literally "ate, breathed and slept goth", the levels of group commitment exhibited by most participants would not have been captured by notions such as neo-tribe, which imply a more fickle sensibility' (2004, p. 146).

Similarly, Hodkinson rejects Muggleton's concept of a postmodern subculture. The majority of goths were not fickle and did not, to use Muggleton's concept, have a liminal relationship to the group. Most of those who became seriously involved with a goth lifestyle stuck with it for a long time. Some even went on to earn their living from goth culture, setting up specialist shops or services for goths. The existence of these services gave goths a degree of self-sufficiency or relative autonomy from other parts of society.

As well as those who earned a living full-time from goth culture, there were a lot of part-time entrepreneurs and unpaid volunteers who might, for example, organize gigs or give out flyers to promote them. Furthermore, there were a number of goth websites and forums which allowed goths from different areas to keep in touch.

Conclusion and evaluation

Hodkinson concludes that goths certainly have enough cultural substance to be considered a subculture. However, he does not agree with the CCCS that the subculture can

be explained in neo-Marxist terms as both a product of and expression of class differences.

In part, Hodkinson's conclusions may have been a result of the particular subculture he chose to study, and the way he conducted his research. Goths may be one of the strongest and most distinctive subcultures amongst contemporary youth. Hodkinson's ethnographic research methods, which included participant observation, enabled him to immerse himself in the goth scene, allowing him to understand the commitment of the most involved goths. Muggleton's methods, on the other hand – which involved interviewing a sample of young people in pubs and clubs – were unlikely to uncover those members of subcultures with the strongest commitments.

If Hodkinson is to be believed, then at least some youth subcultures are still alive and well. Thus Hodkinson believes that the CCCS were justified in the use of the term 'subculture'. In other respects, Hodkinson, like most other recent sociologists of youth culture/subculture, rejects the claims of the CCCS, particularly the claim that subcultures can be seen as an expression of class position.

However, unlike the CCCS, recent theories tend to have little to say about why subcultures adopt the styles they do, or why particular individuals follow one style rather than another. In this respect they are rather less ambitious than the CCCS when they first tried to decode the meaning of subcultures in the 1970s.

Later life and old age

The nature of later life and old age

Chronological and non-chronological definitions

Just as there are no clear definitions of childhood (see pp. 758–9), or youth (see pp. 765–6), there are no clear definitions of the age at which adulthood ends and later life begins. The social definition of old age varies from society to society and over time.

Jane Pilcher (1995) argues that in Europe before the industrial revolution there was not a chronological definition of old age. Pilcher quotes Featherstone and Hepworth (1990) who argued that old age began when people became 'helpless and dependent' rather than when they had lived for a particular number of years.

However, modern industrial societies have increasingly seen retirement from employment, and/or eligibility for a state pension, as defining old age. In many jobs, people are still able to retire and take an occupational pension at 60. They may also be able to retire earlier with a reduced pension, but the trend is towards delaying the age at which occupational pensions can be drawn in order to save money.

Using the age of retirement or entitlement to a state pension as the start of old age is rather arbitrary since the age at which this happens depends upon employment conditions or state policies rather than upon any evaluation of the person's ability to work. Currently, the state pension age in Britain is 65 for men and women, though it was formerly 60 for women. The Pensions Act 2007 stipulates that the state pension age will rise from 65 to 68 between 2024 and 2046. This change is largely a response to the rising costs of pensions with an ageing population (see pp. 744–6).

Not only is a definition of old age based upon state pension age arbitrary – it also means that the period defined as old age can last for up to around forty years. As Jane Pilcher comments, 'Grouping all those age 60/65 and above in one category tends to discourage an awareness of the range of experiences within old age' (1995, p. 99). Pilcher notes that some commentators distinguish between the 'young old' or 'young elderly' aged 65–74 and the 'old old' or 'old elderly', aged 75–84, with those who are 85 or older seen as the 'oldest old' or 'very elderly'.

Perhaps a more useful distinction is put forward by Peter Laslett (1989) who distinguishes between the **third age** (when you retire and have fewer responsibilities than you did as an adult) and the **fourth age** (when physical and/or mental decline begins to seriously limit you). This has the advantage of avoiding the use of an arbitrary chronological cut-off point as a definition, though a problem with this approach is that the boundary between the third and fourth ages is not clear-cut because physical or mental decline is a matter of degree.

Variations between societies

Pilcher claims that 'Every known society has been known to define people as "old" on the basis of chronology, physiology or generation' (1995, p. 110). However, the point in life at which old age is seen as beginning, and the social meanings attached to it, vary. 'Old' people may be expected to be active or inactive, relatively dependent or independent, and they may be given high or low status. Pilcher suggests a number of reasons for these differences:

1. The type of social organization is important. Nomadic societies tend not to value the elderly because if they are frail they can be a burden when moving from place to place. The elderly may be abandoned or even encouraged to commit suicide for the good of the social group. However, non-nomadic societies tend to value older people since they may be able to make a greater contribution to social life.
2. The importance to society of the skills and knowledge of the elderly affects their status. In pre-literate societies where the culture and skills are passed down by word of mouth, the old may be valued for their knowledge and wisdom. For example, native American societies such as the Sioux and the Cheyenne tended to value the old highly. The elderly tend to be less highly valued in societies which are literate and change rapidly. In such societies, knowledge can be passed on through written sources and the experience of the elderly can soon become obsolete. For these reasons, the elderly tend to have a lower status in advanced industrial societies than in pre-literate societies.
3. The position of the elderly in society is also affected by control over economic resources. If the young can only gain access to such resources through the elderly, then the elderly tend to be treated with respect. (See Vincent's discussion of old age and inequality, pp. 748–50.)

4 Pilcher says that 'cultural attitudes towards death and the afterlife' (1995, p. 111) are also important. For example, the Sherbro people of Sierra Leone interpret incoherent speech by the elderly as a sign that they can communicate with ancestors, and this enhances their status. Amongst the Venda-speaking people of South Africa, old age is seen as desirable because it is evidence of approaching contact with the spirit world – and people positively welcome signs of ageing such as greying hair. However, in other societies where life before death is seen as more important than the afterlife, signs of ageing are less likely to be welcomed.

Variations within societies

Not only does the meaning of old age vary between societies and over time, but it also varies within each society. The experience of old age is affected by a number of factors.

Gender

The characteristics attributed to older members of society and the opportunities open to them can vary by gender. Pilcher quotes a study by Arber and Ginn (1991) which found that, in Britain, 'older women more commonly than men are characterised as slow, stupid, unhealthy, unattractive and dependent' (Pilcher, 1995, p. 112). Sexism and ageism can combine to make the lives of older women particularly difficult.

Sara Arber (2006) notes a number of differences in the positions of men and women in old age:

1 Women tend to live longer than men. However, the gap in life expectancy is narrowing. In 1981, women in Britain lived on average six years longer than men, but by 2001 this gap was down to 4.6 years. This was partly due to more women suffering from obesity and stress and engaging in risky behaviour such as drinking to excess and smoking.
2 Because women live longer, and their spouse may die before them, they are less likely to be married in old age than men. Consequently, fewer women than men have a partner to care for them if they are ill or disabled. Partly as a result of this, elderly women are more likely to live in residential care homes than elderly men.
3 Older women are also more likely to live in poverty than older men. Because of greater involvement in childcare, and a tendency to have less well-paid jobs, women are less likely to have built up an entitlement to an adequate occupational pension. Arber notes that in 2001, 24 per cent of women over 65 who were not married were receiving income support, compared to 15 per cent of men.

However, Arber believes that older women are becoming more independent in later life than they once were. For example, more are finding new intimate partners, but are living separately from them so that they do not have to care for them. (This is sometimes known as 'living apart together'.)

Nevertheless, Arber is still pessimistic about the prospects for gender inequality disappearing in old age. She says, 'Older married men will continue to be the most advantaged group both in terms of pensions and access to carers should they become sick or disabled' (Arber, 2006, p. 61). She concludes that the next generation of women who reach old age will be little better off than the current generation, because they will still have inferior pension entitlements compared to men. (See also the work of Gannon, pp. 751–2.)

Ethnicity

Ethnicity also has an effect on the experience of old age. James Nazroo (2006) quotes data from the Health Survey for England which shows that all minority ethnic groups have more ill health in old age than the population as a whole. Those of Bangladeshi and Pakistani origin have particularly poor health. For example, in 2001, diabetes rates amongst men of Pakistani ethnic origin aged 55 or over approached 40 per cent, compared to less than 10 per cent amongst men in the general population.

Nazroo suggests that health inequalities between ethnic groups are linked to inequalities of income and wealth. However, he also notes that there is mounting evidence that older members of minority ethnic groups have more contact with family members, stronger social networks and more opportunity to take part in community life than older white people. This might reflect the higher incidence of extended family households among some minority ethnic groups (see pp. 488–92).

On the other hand, Anthony Giddens (2006) points out that members of minority ethnic groups tend to have lower-than-average incomes in old age. He quotes research which suggests that older Asian women are particularly unlikely to have occupational pensions.

Social class

There is a great deal of evidence that ageing is affected by social class. Alan Walker and Liam Foster (2006) see class as a 'critical factor' in how old age is experienced.

Class has a very big impact on pension entitlement. Not only are those in professional and managerial jobs likely to be paid more when working than those in manual jobs, but they are also more likely to be entitled to occupational pensions and less likely to have experienced periods of unemployment.

In 2001/2, 90 per cent of retired men who had worked in professional/managerial jobs were receiving an occupational pension, compared to 62 per cent of men who had worked in a routine/manual job. The corresponding figures for women were 64 per cent for the highest class and just 34 per cent for the lowest class. Walker and Foster also point out that 'there is an enduringly strong relationship between health status and occupational class' (2006, p. 50), and class has a major impact on life expectancy (see pp. 298–303).

Cohort

Cohort can also have an impact. As Pilcher (1995) points out, different cohorts may have different levels of pension provision, which affects living standards in old age. In Britain, the ageing of the population and the volatility of the stock market have led to problems with pension provision for older people – in some cases leading to reductions in pensions and the raising of pension ages.

Conclusion

Although physical change is an inevitable consequence of biological ageing, and all societies make distinctions

between age groups, there is no clear-cut definition of old age. The chronological age you need to reach before being considered old varies, both over time and between societies, as does the social role of elderly people.

While age is an important aspect of inequality, it interacts with other social factors in shaping people's experiences and opportunities. Class, gender and ethnicity all influence how satisfactory, or otherwise, the experience of later life is likely to be.

Not surprisingly, sociological attempts to understand old age tend to prioritize social over biological factors, but some early theories did give prominence to biological aspects of ageing, as the next section will illustrate.

Elaine Cumming and William E. Henry – the functionalist disengagement theory of old age

Disengagement

Elaine Cumming and William E. Henry (1961) were unusual amongst sociological theorists of age in arguing that the marginalization of old people was actually functional for society. They argued that the **disengagement** of people from social roles was necessary and beneficial for society.

Cumming and Henry claim that, as people age, they lose **ego energy** – that is, they lose vitality. Their health usually declines and they become more self-absorbed. These changes make the elderly less well equipped than they were to carry out important social roles. They become less capable of performing work roles, civic roles (such as doing voluntary work or being active in politics) and any other roles for which physical well-being is necessary. If people continue in these roles into old age, it will have a number of negative consequences:

1. The roles will not be carried out particularly well, causing problems for the effective functioning of society.
2. Older people will block opportunities for younger people by continuing to occupy key positions. There is a danger in these circumstances that society will stagnate because it will not benefit from the fresh and innovative ideas of new generations.
3. Attempting to maintain previous roles beyond an age when they can comfortably perform them leads to frustration and fatigue for older people. Old people themselves will benefit from disengagement. Gradual disengagement from society allows them to maintain higher morale.

Ultimately, the disengagement of the individual from society occurs when they die.

Gradual disengagement allows society to adapt as it ceases to be dependent on the contributions of ageing individuals. It also gives the individual time to come to terms with their approaching demise.

According to Cumming and Henry, like death itself disengagement is an inevitable and universal process. But it is also beneficial to society. To support their theory, Cumming and Henry put forward a variety of evidence to show that most people do indeed gradually disengage from society once they have reached retirement age.

Criticisms of disengagement theory

Stephen Hunt (2005) notes a number of criticisms of disengagement theory:

1. It assumes that older people wish to disengage from previous social roles when in reality they may not want to.
2. Some people may not be able to disengage because they have a financial need to continue working, or they have responsibilities – for example, caring for a disabled relative – which they cannot give up because there is no alternative.
3. Disengagement might actually do more harm to society than good. It potentially wastes valuable human resources by encouraging premature withdrawal from social roles.
4. Disengagement theory might underestimate the importance of the social roles that are undertaken by the elderly. For example, there is evidence that grandparents are increasingly important in looking after children while mothers are at work.

Even stronger criticisms of Cumming and Henry are put forward by Chris Phillipson and Jan Baars (2007). They quote Hochschild (1975) who pointed out that a significant proportion of people in Cumming and Henry's own data did not withdraw from previous social roles to any great extent after retirement. Cumming and Henry either dismissed these people as simply bad at adjusting to old age, or praised them as a 'biological or psychological elite'.

However, it may be that people do not have to be members of an 'elite' to continue in important roles after retirement – perhaps most people could do so. The problem is that they are prevented from continuing to make a contribution by obstacles placed in their way by society, such as compulsory retirement or ageism.

Hochschild therefore criticized Cumming and Henry for failing to distinguish social from physical and psychological aspects of ageing, and thereby confusing biological causes of disengagement with social causes. Not surprisingly, most sociologists who have studied old age see social causes as far more important than biological ones.

Alternatives to disengagement theory

Earlier sections of this chapter have examined a number of theories of old age in considerable detail. All of these theories are critical of disengagement theory.

The interpretation of old age

Hockey and James (1993) do not see the social roles of the elderly as a product of a functional disengagement from society. Instead they argue that the role of the elderly results from an interpretation of old age in which the elderly are **infantilized** (see pp. 752–3).

Feminist views

Gannon (1999) argues from a feminist viewpoint that patriarchal ideology shapes the way in which older women are viewed in society. She dismisses scientifically

based claims that women are inferior to men as they age, seeing these as distorted by male power (see pp. 751–2).

Political economy and structured dependency

Both Gannon and Hockey and James see the nature of old age in society as, at least in part, a social construction. They emphasize the importance of ideas in shaping old age, although Gannon also links this to power.

John Vincent (1995) argues that political economy approaches to old age attach much more importance to issues of power and see the disadvantages of the elderly as linked to **structured dependency**. In these respects political economy approaches have much in common with Marxist perspectives. From the viewpoint of political economy, the elderly tend to be dependent, disadvantaged and poor, not as a result of biological decline or an inevitable disengagement that follows from it, but because society is structured in such a way as to make them dependent. Compulsory retirement ages and the provision of state pensions and welfare services for the elderly tend to make them dependent whether they like it or not. Vincent also argues that dependence in old age is linked to other forms of inequality such as ethnicity and class (see pp. 747–50).

Postmodernism

Postmodern perspectives adopt a very different viewpoint. For example, Blaikie (1999) argues that old age need not be a time of dependency and decline, but can be a time of increased choice and opportunity in a consumer culture. Although age eventually catches up with people, at least in the early years of retirement old age is much less of a barrier to living an active life than it once was. Blaikie even speculates that medical advances may eventually make decline and dependency in old age a thing of the past (see pp. 755–6).

Conclusion

Political economy approaches can be accused of having an over-pessimistic view of old age, while postmodern perspectives can equally be accused of having an overly optimistic approach. However, both may be an advance over disengagement theory because they recognize that the nature of old age varies from society to society and that there is nothing inevitable about the social roles of the elderly in any one society at a particular point in history.

Summary and conclusions

Age and the life course is an increasingly important area of study in sociology.

Early assumptions that chronological age and biology are the keys to understanding this area of social life have been progressively challenged. Sociologists no longer see age simply in terms of physical and psychological maturation, leading to a period of adult maturity followed by inevitable decline. By studying historical attitudes to age and by comparing different societies, they have been able to show that the meaning of age and the social roles associated with it are, to a considerable extent, a social construction. They have also shown that whether in childhood, youth or old age a greater variety of roles is possible than are usually found in any particular society at any particular time.

Some sociologists emphasize the extent to which society constrains the behaviour of people in different age groups and creates inequality between these groups. Thus Marxists/political economists and feminists link age to wider structures of inequality and power in society. Other sociologists, particularly postmodernists, suggest that the constraints and social roles associated with age are breaking down as people become able to choose whether or not to conform to traditional notions of appropriate age-related behaviour.

Writers such as Hockey and James (2003) argue that neither of these approaches is adequate on its own, but both have important insights to add to our understanding of the life course. People do have some choice over the social identities they assume, but they are also limited by social structures and power relations.

Furthermore, Hockey and James believe that although social factors are crucial in shaping the life course, biology cannot be ignored, as people's bodies do change and offer different possibilities as they age. Hockey and James see 'ageing as a fundamentally embodied process' (2003, p. 9) as well as a social one.

Nevertheless, within the constraints of bodily ageing and the social definitions related to age, people have some choices about the way ageing affects their identity and their life. These choices are reflected in the variety and creativity of youth subcultures and in the variations in the social roles of older people. The process of ageing for individuals is therefore somewhat unpredictable. Hockey and James argue that you should see 'the passage of a lifetime less as the mechanical turning of a wheel and more as the unpredictable flow of a river' (2003, p. 5).

CHAPTER 14
Methodology

... values are integral to sociology and indeed to all disciplines, but that does not prevent rational debate and the empirical testing of theories. Holborn, 2004

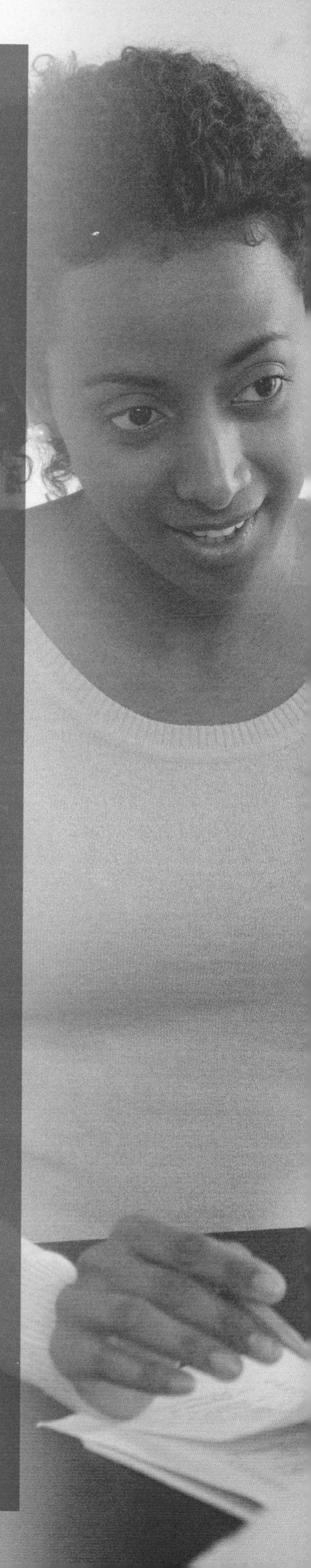

Introduction

Any academic subject requires a **methodology** to reach its conclusions: it must have ways of producing and analysing data so that theories can be tested, accepted or rejected. Without a systematic way of producing knowledge, the findings of a subject can be dismissed as guesswork, or even as common sense made to sound complicated. Methodology is concerned with both the detailed research methods through which data are collected, and the more general philosophies upon which the collection and analysis of data are based.

As we have seen in this book, most areas of sociology are riven with controversy. Methodology is no exception to this general rule. One of the main areas of disagreement concerns – in the most general terms – whether sociology should adopt the same methods as (or similar methods to) those employed in science.

Sociology first developed in Europe in the nineteenth century when industrialization resulted in massive social changes. Accompanying these social changes were intellectual changes, during which science started to enjoy a higher reputation than ever before. Science appeared to be capable of producing objective knowledge that could be used to solve human problems and increase human productive capacity in an unprecedented way. It was not surprising, therefore, that many early sociologists chose to turn to science for a methodology on which to base their subject.

However, not all sociologists have agreed that it is appropriate to adopt the methodology of the natural sciences. For these sociologists, studying human behaviour is fundamentally different from studying the natural world. Unlike the subject matter of, for example, chemistry or physics, people possess consciousness, which means (from the point of view of some sociologists) that sociology requires a different type of methodology from science.

In the above terms, it was possible to identify two broad traditions within sociology:

1. Those who advocated the use of **scientific** and usually **quantitative** methods (numerical statistical methods).
2. Those who supported the use of more **humanistic** and **qualitative** methods.

However, it was never the case that all sociologists fitted neatly into these categories. Furthermore, as will become clear, there are divisions *within* these two broad camps as well as *between* them.

In recent years, some sociologists have questioned the need for such a rigid division between quantitative and qualitative methodology, and have advocated combining the two approaches. Other sociologists have advocated methods associated with critical social science or with postmodernism.

Critical social science tends to favour more qualitative methods, but it is not exclusively associated with such methods. The central feature of critical social science is that it links research with trying to transform society. It therefore rejects the view of many sociologists – including many of the advocates of the two approaches discussed above – that researchers should be impartial. Instead, it sides with those it sees as the disadvantaged and oppressed groups in society. It seeks to develop any methods that will help to liberate these groups from their oppression.

Feminists are among the most influential of critical social scientists, and some feminists have argued that distinctive feminist methodologies should be adopted.

Postmodernists have developed their approaches to methodology relatively recently. They tend to reject the belief that researchers can ever discover some objective truth about the social world. Instead, they believe that all that can be done is to examine the social world from the viewpoint of the different actors within it, and to deconstruct or take apart existing explanations of society. They reject the claims of traditional quantitative, qualitative and critical researchers that it is possible to determine the truth about society. Whatever method is used, researchers will be left with many different accounts of the social world, and no particular account can be singled out as being better than the others.

Critical social science and postmodernism will be examined in detail later in the chapter, but first the contrast between quantitative and qualitative approaches will be discussed in greater depth.

'Scientific' quantitative methodology

As the introduction suggested, some sociologists have tried to adopt the methods of the natural sciences. In doing so they have tended to advocate the use of quantitative methods. The earliest attempt to use such methods in sociology is known as **positivism**.

Positivism, Durkheim and sociology

The French writer Auguste Comte (1798–1857) was the first person to use the word 'sociology', and he also coined the term 'positive philosophy' (Comte, 1986, first published in the 1840s). Comte believed there was a hierarchy of scientific subjects, with sociology at the pinnacle of that hierarchy. Comte was confident that scientific knowledge about society could be accumulated and used to improve human existence so that society could be run rationally without religion or superstition getting in the way of progress.

Emile Durkheim (1858–1917) advocated a similar methodology to that of Comte. He has been widely regarded as a positivist. Durkheim's classic study *Suicide* (1970, first published 1897) is often seen as a model of positivist research and it does indeed follow many of the methodological procedures of positivism. Certain aspects of Durkheim's work will be used to illustrate the positivist approach. However, strictly speaking, Durkheim was not a positivist. As the discussion below will show, he did not follow the positivist rule which states that sociological study should be confined to observable or directly measurable phenomena.

Social facts

First, as a positivist, Comte believed that the scientific study of society should be confined to collecting information about phenomena that can be objectively observed and classified. Comte argued that sociologists should not be concerned with the internal meanings, motives, feelings and emotions of individuals. Since these mental states exist only in the person's consciousness, they cannot be observed and so they cannot be measured in any objective way.

Durkheim agreed that sociologists should confine themselves to studying **social facts**. He argued: 'The first and most fundamental rule is: *Consider social facts as things*' (Durkheim, 1938, first published 1895). This means that the belief systems, customs and institutions of society – the facts of the social world – should be considered as things in the same way as the objects and events of the natural world.

However, Durkheim did not believe that social facts consisted only of those things that could be directly observed or measured. To Durkheim, social facts included such phenomena as the belief systems, customs and institutions of society. Belief systems are not directly measurable or observable, since they exist in the consciousness of humans. Nevertheless, Durkheim saw them as existing over and above individual consciousness. They were not chosen by individuals and they could not be changed at will. Social facts, such as the customs of a particular profession, were external to each individual and constrained their behaviour. That is, each person had their options limited by the existence of customs and practices.

In Durkheim's view, society is not simply a collection of individuals, each acting independently in terms of his or her particular psychology or mental state. Instead, members of society are directed by collective beliefs, values and laws – by social facts which have an existence of their own. Social facts therefore make individuals behave in particular ways. Durkheim's definition and use of the term 'social facts' distinguish him from positivists such as Comte. In many other respects, though, he followed the logic and methods of positivism. (The differences between Durkheim's approach and positivism are further discussed on p. 797.)

Statistical data

The second aspect of positivism concerns its use of **statistical data**. Positivists believed it was possible to classify the social world in an objective way. Using these classifications it was then possible to count sets of observable social facts

and so produce statistics. For example, Durkheim (1970) collected data on social facts such as the suicide rate and membership of different religions.

Correlation

The third stage of positivist methodology entails looking for correlations between different social facts. A **correlation** is a tendency for two or more things to be found together, and it may refer to the strength of the relationship between them. In his study of suicide, Durkheim found an apparent correlation between a particular religion, Protestantism, and a high suicide rate.

Causation

The fourth stage of positivist methodology involves a search for **causal connections**. If there is a strong correlation between two or more types of social phenomena, then a positivist sociologist might suspect that one of these phenomena was causing the other to take place. However, this is not necessarily the case, and it is important to analyse the data carefully before any such conclusion can be reached.

The example of class and criminality can be used to illustrate this point. Many sociologists have noted a correlation between being working-class and a relatively high chance of being convicted of a crime. This has led some (for instance, Robert Merton, 1968) to speculate that being working-class was one factor which might cause people to commit criminal acts. This can be illustrated simply as:

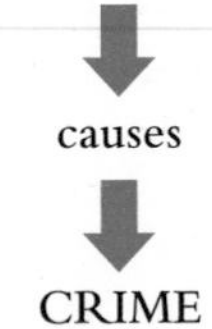

However, there are other possibilities that might explain the correlation. It could be that a similar proportion of criminals come from all social classes but that conviction for crime causes criminals of middle-class origin to be downwardly socially mobile, and to become working-class, since their criminal records might prevent them from obtaining non-manual work. In other words, it is being criminal that causes a person to become working-class, and not the other way round. This is illustrated as:

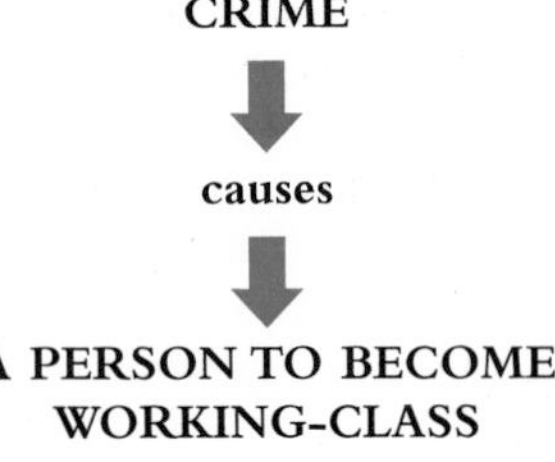

Furthermore, there is the even more serious possibility that an apparent connection between two social phenomena might be a **spurious** or **indirect correlation**. This occurs when two or more phenomena are found together but have no direct connection to each other: one does not therefore cause the other. It may be that some third factor has a causal relationship to both the phenomena or factors being examined. For example, it may be that gender is related both to social class and to the likelihood of committing a crime, and that class and crime are not directly connected at all. Men may be more likely to commit crimes than women and may also be more likely to have manual jobs. Thus the original correlation discovered could be a product of the concentration of men in the working class, as the diagram below illustrates:

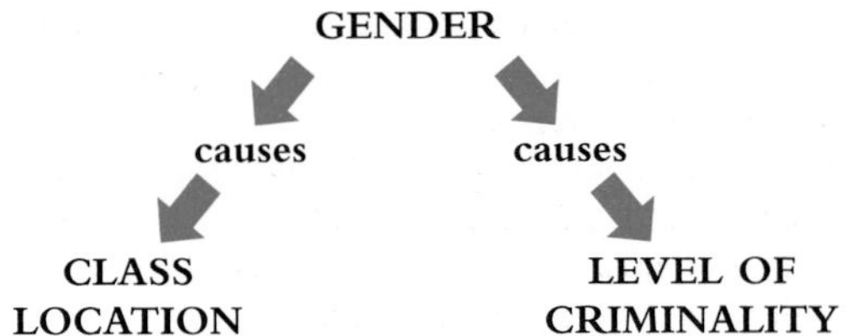

A further possibility is that the police discriminate against the working class and arrest more members of that class than of the middle class, even though the middle class are just as prone to crime.

Multivariate analysis

In order to overcome the problem of spurious correlation, Durkheim devised a technique known as **multivariate analysis**. This involves trying to isolate the effect of a particular independent variable upon the dependent variables. The **dependent variable** is the thing that is caused (in the example used above, crime); the **independent variable(s)** is/are the factor or factors that cause the dependent variable. In the diagram above, gender is an example of an independent variable.

To assess the influence of a particular independent variable – that is, to see if it is more or less important than another independent variable – it may be possible to produce comparisons where one variable is held constant, and the other is changed. For instance, the effect of gender on criminality could be isolated from the effect of class by comparing working-class men and women to see whether their crime rates were similar or different.

With the aid of computers and sophisticated statistical techniques, quantitative researchers can analyse the relative importance of many different variables. Durkheim had to make do with less sophisticated research procedures, but he used the same logic in his study of suicide. For example, he checked whether or not Protestantism was associated with a high suicide rate regardless of nationality by examining suicide rates in a range of countries.

Laws of human behaviour

Positivists believe that multivariate analysis can establish causal connections between two or more variables. If these findings are checked in a variety of contexts (for example, in different societies at different times), then the researchers can be confident that they have attained the ultimate goal of positivism: a **law of human behaviour**.

A scientific law consists of a statement about the relationship between two or more phenomena which is true in all circumstances. Thus Newton's three Laws of Motion were supposed to describe the ways in which matter would always move. Similarly, Comte and Durkheim believed real laws of human behaviour could be discovered.

Durkheim claimed to have discovered laws of human behaviour that governed the suicide rate. According to Durkheim, the suicide rate always rose during a time of economic boom or slump.

Comte believed he had discovered a law that all human societies passed through three stages: the theological, the metaphysical, and the positive. In the first stage humans believed that events were caused by the actions of gods; in the second, events were held to be caused by abstract forces; in the third, scientific rationality triumphed, so that scientific laws formed the basis of explanation.

Positivists and Durkheim, then, believe that laws of human behaviour can be discovered by the collection of objective facts about the social world in a statistical form, by the careful analysis of these facts, and by repeated checking of the findings in a series of contexts. From this point of view, humans have little or no choice about how they behave. What takes place in their consciousness is held to be irrelevant, since external forces govern human behaviour: people react to stimuli in the environment in a predictable and consistent way. They may also have little or no awareness of the factors shaping their actions. These can be uncovered through studying statistical patterns.

The implication is that humans react directly to a stimulus without attaching a meaning to it first. (A simple example would be that of a motorist who sees the stimulus of a red light, and who automatically reacts to it by stopping.) It is this implication of the positivist approach that has attracted the strongest criticism, as will become clear as the chapter develops.

Positivism is based upon an understanding of science that sees science as using a mainly **inductive methodology**. An inductive methodology starts by collecting the data. The data are then analysed, and out of this analysis theories are developed. Once the theory has been developed it can then be tested against other sets of data to see if it is confirmed or not. If it is repeatedly confirmed, then Durkheim and positivists such as Comte assume they have discovered a law of human behaviour.

Karl Popper – falsification and deduction

Despite the undoubted influence of positivist methodology within sociology, the inductive method on which it is usually based has not, by any means, been accepted by all scientists. Indeed, many scientists now advocate and use an alternative, **deductive approach**. Although the logic of the deductive approach is similar in many ways to positivism, the differences have important implications.

This alternative methodology in both natural science and sociology is supported by Karl Popper in his book *The Logic of Scientific Discovery* (1959). The deductive approach reverses the process of induction. It starts with a theory and tests it against the evidence, rather than developing a theory as a result of examining the data.

Popper argues that scientists should start with a 'hypothesis' or a statement that is to be tested. This statement should be very precise, and should state exactly what will happen in particular circumstances. On the basis of the hypothesis it should be possible to deduce predictions about the future. Thus, for example, Newton's Law of Gravity enables hypotheses to be made about the movement of bodies of a given mass, and these hypotheses can then be used to make predictions which can be tested against future events.

According to Popper, it matters little how a scientific theory originates. It does not, as positivists suggest, have to come from prior observation and analysis of data. Scientists can develop theories however they wish – their theories might come to them in dreams or in moments of inspiration. What is important, and what makes them scientific, is their ability to be tested by making precise predictions on the basis of the theory.

Popper differs from positivists in that he denies that it is ever possible to produce laws that will necessarily be found to be true for all time. He argues that, logically, however many times a theory is apparently proved correct because predictions made on the basis of that theory come true, there is always the possibility that at some future date the theory will be proved wrong, or 'falsified'. For example, to Popper, the hypothesis 'all swans are white' is a scientific statement because it makes a precise prediction about the colour of any swan that can be found. But, however many times the statement is confirmed – if five, five hundred or five thousand swans are examined and found to be white – the very next swan examined may prove to be black and the hypothesis will be falsified. Laws, whether of natural science or of human behaviour, do not, from this point of view, necessarily have the permanence attributed to them by positivists.

Popper suggests that scientists have a duty to be objective, and to test their theories as rigorously as possible. Therefore, once they have formulated hypotheses, and made predictions, it is necessary to try constantly to find evidence that disproves or falsifies their theories. In the natural sciences one method that has been developed in order to falsify theories is the laboratory experiment. This method, and its relevance to sociology, will now be examined. Popper's view of science will be evaluated later in the chapter (see pp. 847–51).

The laboratory experiment and sociology

The word 'science' conjures up an image of researchers in white coats carrying out experiments in laboratories. This image is not usually associated, however, with sociology. Indeed, sociologists very rarely carry out laboratory experiments even if they support the use of 'scientific' methods in their research. The reasons for this will be examined later, but, first, why does the laboratory experiment enjoy such popularity in natural science?

The main reason why scientists use the laboratory experiment is because it enables them to test precise predictions in exactly the way that Popper advocates. Laboratories are controlled environments in which the researcher can manipulate the various independent variables however they

wish. They can calculate the effects of a single independent variable while removing the possibility that any other factors are affecting the dependent variable they are studying. This is achieved through the use of a **control** with which to compare the experiment.

For example, if an experimenter wished to determine the importance of the independent variable, light, on the growth of plants, they could set up a laboratory experiment to isolate the effects of light from other independent variables. Thus the experimenter would set up an experiment and a control in which every variable other than the amount of light was held constant. Two sets of matched plants of the same species, age, condition and size would be kept at the same temperature, in an environment of the same humidity, planted in the same type and amount of soil, and given the same amount of water at the same time. The control group of plants would be exposed to a given intensity of light for a given period of time. The experiment group could be exposed to either more or less light than the control group. The results would be observed, measured and quantified. A single variable – light – would have been isolated to find the effects it had, independently of all the other variables.

A laboratory experiment such as this allows the researchers to be far more confident that they have isolated a particular variable than they would have been had they observed plants in the wild, where it would not be possible to regulate the various independent variables so tightly. Furthermore, the laboratory experiment facilitates replication: so long as the precise nature of the experiment is recorded, other scientists can reproduce identical conditions to see if the same results are obtained.

From Popper's point of view, the experimental method is extremely useful because it allows the sort of precision in the making and repeated testing of predictions that he advocates. Laboratory experiments are quite frequently used in some 'social sciences', particularly psychology, but sociologists almost never make use of them. There are four main reasons for this:

1 Laboratories are unnatural situations. Members of society do not, in the normal course of events, spend their time under observation in laboratories. The knowledge that they are being studied, and the artificiality of the situation, might well affect the behaviour of those involved and distort the results so as to make them of little use. Because the results obtained in a laboratory may have little relationship to how people might behave outside the laboratory, the results of experiments lack external validity (see p. 816 for a definition of external validity).
2 If subjects are not informed of the nature of the experiment prior to its commencement, then this raises ethical issues. Payne and Payne (2004) point out that sociological research ethics usually involve prior approval from subjects based on informed consent in which the subjects know the purpose of the research. Psychological research ethics tend only to require the subjects to be given full information after the experiment, which partly explains why psychologists make more use of the laboratory experiment than sociologists.
3 Genuine matching of humans to enable another variable or variables to be altered may be impossible. As Payne and Payne say, 'what does matching really mean when we are dealing with complex entities such as humans beings? Even if we can agree on which factors should be matched – and this could be a long list – there are great practical difficulties in finding people to match into pairs' (2004, p. 86). This can restrict the sample size and therefore the reliability of the results.
4 It is impractical to carry out experiments in laboratories on many of the subjects of interest to sociologists. It is not possible to fit a community – let alone a whole society – into a laboratory. Nor is it possible to carry out a laboratory experiment over a sufficiently long time-span to study social change.

One area of study which has used experiments, which has been discussed both by psychologists and by sociologists, is the media and violence. A famous psychological study by Bandura (1965, discussed in Gross, 1992) examined the effects on children of viewing media images of violence. All the children were shown a film of a man behaving aggressively towards a bobo doll (a doll which returns to a standing position after being knocked down). In the film seen by one group, another adult entered the room and criticized the man for attacking the doll; in a second group an adult praised the man for his behaviour; and in a third group nobody entered the room to pass comment. All the children were then placed individually in a room which included a bobo doll amongst other toys. It was found that the children who had watched the film where the man had been criticized for being aggressive were least likely to be aggressive.

However, sociologists who have studied the media effects of violence are critical of this and similar studies. They argue that an unnatural experiment such as this does not give any indication of whether the short-term effects of watching a film would be repeated over the longer term, and in real social settings where other variables are likely to influence behaviour. Furthermore, the experiment could be seen as unethical for encouraging aggression in children.

A number of sociologists who have studied the media reject approaches that assume that the media have a direct effect on behaviour (sometimes called the hypodermic model, see pp. 722–3). Most recent sociological approaches to the media emphasize the active role played by participants in interpreting and responding to the media, and do not believe that experimental research is a valid way of assessing the effects of the media on audiences (see p. 728).

Field experiments

As a consequence of the above difficulties, when sociologists do carry out experiments they are normally outside a laboratory. Such experiments are known as **field experiments**. They involve intervening in the social world in such a way that hypotheses can be tested by isolating particular variables.

For example, Rosenthal and Jacobson (1968) tested the hypothesis that self-fulfilling prophecies could affect educational attainment by manipulating the independent variables of the pupils' IQ (intelligence quotient) scores known to teachers (see p. 639).

In another experiment, Sissons observed the reactions of members of the public when they were asked for directions by an actor. The location of the experiment was held constant (it took place outside Paddington station), but the appearance of the actor varied. Halfway through the experiment the actor changed from being dressed as a businessman to being dressed as a labourer. Sissons found that the public were more helpful when the actor was dressed as a businessman rather than as a labourer (discussed in McNeill, 1985).

Brown and Gay (1985) conducted field experiments in which they made bogus applications for jobs by letter and telephone, identifying themselves as being from different ethnic groups (white, Asian and African Caribbean). They found that the applications from supposedly non-white candidates were less likely to lead to a job interview than those from supposedly white candidates (see p. 204).

Although field experiments overcome the problem of experiments taking place in an unnatural setting, these experiments do have other problems associated with them. First, it is not possible to control variables as closely as it is in the laboratory. Thus in Sissons's experiment, for example, it was not possible to carry out the two experiments at the same time and the same place, and, since they took place at different times, factors such as the weather and the time of day might have affected the results.

Second, in some field experiments, the fact that an experiment is taking place can affect the results. This is often known as the **Hawthorne effect**, after a famous experiment conducted at the Hawthorne works of the Western Electricity Company in Chicago and analysed by Elton Mayo (1933). The experiment was intended to test various hypotheses about worker productivity. Variables such as room temperature, the strength of the lighting and the length of breaks were varied, but, irrespective of whether working conditions were improved or made worse, productivity usually increased. It appeared that the workers were responding to the knowledge that an experiment was taking place rather than to the variables being manipulated.

To avoid the Hawthorne effect (which can render the results of experiments worthless), it is necessary that the subjects of experimental research are unaware that the experiment is taking place. This, however, raises a further problem: the morality of conducting experiments on people without their consent. Some sociologists strongly object to doing this. Some experiments, such as Sissons's, may not have great moral implications, but others do. In Rosenthal and Jacobson's experiment (described above) the researchers may have held back the educational careers of some children by lying to their teachers.

Although field experiments open up greater possibilities than laboratory experiments, they are still likely to be confined to small-scale studies over short periods of time. Experimentation on society as a whole, or on large groups in society, is only likely to be possible with the consent of governments. Few governments are willing to surrender their authority to social researchers who are keen to test the theories and hypotheses they have developed! In any case the cost would be enormous and funds for research are limited. In these circumstances sociologists normally rely upon studying society as it is, rather than trying to manipulate it so that their theories can be tested directly.

The comparative method

The **comparative method**, as its name suggests, involves the use of comparisons. These may be comparisons of different societies, of groups within one or more societies, and comparisons at the same or different points in time. Victor Jupp points out that a variety of research techniques make use of the comparative method, including 'content analysis (the comparison of documents), historical analysis (comparison of time periods) and analysis of official statistics (comparison of areas, groups or time periods in terms of social indicators' (2006, p. 33). Unlike the experiment, the comparative method is based upon an analysis of what has happened, or is happening in society, rather than upon situations artificially created by a researcher. The data used in the comparative method may come from any of the primary or secondary sources discussed in detail later in this chapter.

The comparative method overcomes some of the problems involved with experimentation in 'social sciences'. Moral problems are not as acute as in experimentation, since the researcher is not intervening directly in shaping the social world. Furthermore, the researcher is less likely to affect artificially the behaviour of those being studied, since the data, at least in theory, come from 'natural' situations.

The comparative method uses a similar 'scientific' logic to that employed by positivists, or to that used in the deductive approach supported by Popper. Systematic comparisons can be used either to establish correlations and ultimately causal connections and supposed 'laws', or to rigorously test hypotheses.

This method can be used to isolate variables to try to uncover the cause or causes of the social phenomenon being studied. It can be a far less convenient approach than laboratory or field experimentation. There is no guarantee that the available data will make it possible to isolate variables precisely when comparing, for example, the development of two different societies. There may be many ways in which they differ, and determining which independent variables caused the differences in the societies may not be straightforward.

The comparative method is superior to the experiment, though, in that it allows sociologists to study the causes of large-scale social change over long periods of time. The historical development of societies can be studied; this is not feasible using experiments.

The comparative method has been widely used in sociology, particularly but by no means exclusively by those advocating a 'scientific' quantitative approach to the subject. The major founders of the discipline – Marx, Durkheim and Weber – all employed the comparative method.

Marx (1974, 1978, first published 1909 and 1867) compared a wide variety of societies in order to develop his theory of social change and to support his claim that societies passed through different stages (see pp. 867–71 for further details).

Durkheim, too, used the comparative method in his study of the division of labour and the change from mechanical to organic solidarity (Durkheim, 1947, first published 1893) (see pp. 858–9 for further details). Durkheim's study of suicide (which is considered later in this chapter) is a classic example of how detailed statistical analysis – involving the comparison of different societies, different groups within society, and different time periods

– can be used to try to isolate the variables that cause a social phenomenon (see pp. 795–8).

In *The Protestant Ethic and the Spirit of Capitalism* (1958, first published 1930), Weber systematically compared early capitalist countries in Western Europe and North America with countries such as China and India to try to show a correlation between early capitalism and Calvinism (see pp. 406–8).

Modern sociologists have followed in the footsteps of Marx, Durkheim and Weber. There are numerous examples of the use of this method throughout this book, including Cicourel's comparison of juvenile justice in two Californian cities (see pp. 339–40), Michael Mann's comparison of networks of power in different territories (see pp. 557–9), and Fiona Devine's comparison of affluent workers in Luton in the 1990s and similar workers in the 1960s (see pp. 59–60).

Interpretive and qualitative methodology

Despite the considerable influence of the 'scientific' approaches to sociological methodology described above, an alternative series of interpretive or qualitative approaches has long existed within sociology. These approaches claim either that 'scientific' approaches are inadequate on their own for collecting, analysing and explaining data, or that they are totally inappropriate in a subject that deals with human behaviour. Thus some sociologists who advocate the use of interpretive and qualitative approaches suggest that they should be used to supplement 'scientific' quantitative methodology; others that they should replace 'scientific' approaches.

Qualitative data

Quantitative data are data in a numerical form: for example, official statistics on crime, suicide and divorce rates. By comparison, **qualitative data** are usually presented in the form of words. An example would be a description of a group of people living in poverty, providing a full and in-depth account of their way of life, or a transcript of an interview in which people describe and explain their attitude towards and experience of religion.

Compared to quantitative data, qualitative data are usually seen as richer, more vital, as having greater depth and as more likely to present a true picture of a way of life, of people's experiences, attitudes and beliefs.

The interpretive approach

Sociologists who take an **interpretive approach** are usually the strongest advocates of qualitative data. They argue that the whole basis of sociology is the interpretation of social action. Social action can only be understood by interpreting the meanings and motives on which it is based. Many interpretive sociologists argue that there is little chance of discovering these meanings and motives from quantitative data. Only from qualitative data – with its greater richness and depth – can the sociologist hope to interpret the meanings that lie behind social action.

Some interpretive sociologists reject the use of natural science methodology for the study of social action. They see the subject matter of the social and natural sciences as fundamentally different. The natural sciences deal with matter. Since matter has no consciousness, its behaviour can be explained simply as a reaction to external stimuli. It is compelled to react in this way because its behaviour is essentially meaningless.

Unlike matter, people have consciousness. They see, interpret and experience the world in terms of meanings; they actively construct their own social reality. Meanings do not have an independent existence, a reality of their own which is somehow separate from social actors. They are not imposed by an external society that constrains members to act in certain ways. Instead, they are constructed and reconstructed by actors in the course of social interaction.

People do not react automatically to external stimuli as positivists claim. Instead, they interpret the meaning of a stimulus before responding to it. Motorists who see a red light will not automatically stop in response to this stimulus. They will attach a meaning to the stimulus before acting. Motorists might conclude that the light is a decoration on a Christmas tree, and not a traffic signal, or alternatively that it indicates that a nearby building is a brothel. Having established the meaning of the stimulus to their own satisfaction, the motorists will then decide how they wish to respond. Motorists being pursued by the police might jump a red light rather than stop. If the stimulus is regarded as a decoration, motorists might stop to admire it, or continue on their way without giving the light a second thought. Clearly, the motorist who concludes that the red light is advertising a brothel might respond in a variety of ways!

Whatever action is taken by an individual, advocates of interpretive sociology would argue that the causal explanation of human behaviour is impossible without some understanding of the subjective states of the individuals concerned. Thus a positivist might be content to discover what external factors led to a certain type of human behaviour, while an advocate of a more qualitative approach would be interested in the meaning attached to the behaviour by those engaging in it.

It is at this point that opponents of positivist and 'scientific' methods begin to diverge. While some, such as Weber, regard the understanding of meaning as necessary to making causal explanations possible, others, such as phenomenologists, regard understanding as the end product of sociological research and they reject the possibility of producing causal explanations at all.

The implications of three qualitative interpretive sociological approaches for methodology will now be briefly examined. They are dealt with in more detail in the next chapter.

Max Weber

Weber defined sociology as the study of social action (Weber, in Gerth and Mills, 1948). Action is social when it takes account of other members of society. Weber believed that an explanation of social action necessitated an understanding of the meanings and motives that underlie human behaviour. The sociologist must interpret the meanings given to actions by the actors themselves. For instance, in order to explain why an individual was chopping wood, the sociologist must discover the person's motives for doing so – whether they were doing it to earn money, to make a fire, to work off anger or for some other motive. According to Weber, understanding motives could be achieved through ***verstehen*** – imagining yourself to be in the position of the person whose behaviour you were seeking to explain.

Weber's emphasis on meanings and motives is obvious throughout his work. For example, in *The Protestant Ethic and the Spirit of Capitalism* (1958) one of his main concerns was to interpret the beliefs and motives of the early Calvinists (see pp. 406–8). However, he was not simply concerned with understanding meanings and motives for their own sake. Weber wanted to explain social action and social change. He was interested in causality.

This can be seen clearly from *The Protestant Ethic and the Spirit of Capitalism*. Using the comparative method, Weber systematically compared the characteristics of early capitalist countries and technologically advanced oriental societies. By doing so he claimed to have isolated 'ascetic' Protestantism as a variable that contributed to the rise of capitalism. He saw the moral and religious beliefs and motives of the early Calvinists as one of the main factors accounting for the emergence of capitalism in the West. (For a fuller account of Weber's methodology, see pp. 874–5.)

Symbolic interactionism

Symbolic interactionists do not reject the attempt to establish causal relationships within sociology; indeed, they see this as an important part of the sociologist's work. However, they tend to believe that statistical data do not provide any great insight into human behaviour. Interactionists see human behaviour as largely governed by the internal processes by which people interpret the world around them and give meaning to their own lives.

In particular, interactionists believe that individuals possess a 'self-concept', or image of themselves, which is built up, reinforced or modified in the process of interaction with other members of society. Thus human beings have an image of what sort of person they are, and they will tend to act in accordance with that image. They might see themselves as caring or tough, honest or dishonest, weak or strong, and their behaviour reflects this sense of their own character.

The responses of others to an individual may make it impossible for him or her to sustain a particular self-concept; the self-concept will change, and in turn the behaviour of the individual will alter accordingly. Thus interactionists have tried to show how the labelling of people as deviant, or as educational successes or failures, can produce self-fulfilling prophecies in which their behaviour comes to live up (or down) to the expectations of others. (For details of these labelling theories, see pp. 334–9 and 638–41.)

The implications of these views for sociological methodology have been developed by the American interactionist Herbert Blumer (1962). Blumer rejects what he regards as the simplistic attempts to establish causal relationships which characterize positivist methodology.

As an example, Blumer refers to the proposition that industrialization causes the replacement of extended families with nuclear families. He objects to the procedure of isolating variables and assuming that one causes the other with little or no reference to the actor's view of the situation. He argues that data on the meanings and interpretations which actors give to the various facets of industrialization and family life are essential before a relationship can be established between the two factors.

Blumer claims that many sociologists conduct their research with only a superficial familiarity with the area of life under investigation. This is often combined with a preoccupation with aping the research procedures of the natural sciences. The net result is the imposition of definitions on the social world with little regard for their relevance to that world. Rather than viewing social reality from the actor's perspective, many sociologists have attempted to force it into predefined categories and concepts. This provides little chance of capturing social reality, but a very good chance of distorting it.

In place of such procedures Blumer argues that sociologists must immerse themselves in the area of life that they seek to investigate. Rather than attempting to fit data into predefined categories, they must attempt to grasp the actor's view of social reality. This involves 'feeling one's way inside the experience of the actor'. Since action is directed by actors' meanings, the sociologist must 'catch the process of interpretation through which they construct their action'. This means that the researcher 'must take the role of the acting unit whose behaviour he is studying'.

Blumer offers no simple solutions as to how this type of research may be conducted. However, the flavour of the research procedures he advocates is captured in the following quotation:

> *It is a tough job requiring a high order of careful and honest probing, creative yet disciplined imagination, resourcefulness and flexibility in study, pondering over what one is finding, and a constant readiness to test and recast one's views and images of the area.* Blumer, 1962

(For a detailed discussion of symbolic interactionism, see pp. 881–4.)

Phenomenology

The nature of social reality

Phenomenology represents the most radical departure from the 'scientific' quantitative methodology examined at the start of the chapter. Angie Titchen and Dawn Hobson say that **phenomenology** 'is the study of lived, human phenomena within everyday social contexts in which the phenomena occur from the perspective of those who experience them. Phenomena comprise any thing that human beings live/experience' (2005, p. 121).

2 **Thanatation** is a type of suicide, or suicide attempt, which occurs when a person is uncertain about themselves. The suicide attempt is a gamble which may or may not be survived, according to fate or chance. If the attempt does not result in death, the person learns that they are capable of facing death. In some cases the person may be exhilarated by the thrill of the risk taking and they may make several suicide attempts. Taylor gives as examples the novelist Graham Greene, who periodically played Russian roulette with a revolver, and the poet Sylvia Plath, who deliberately risked death by driving her car off the road.

The other two types are **symphysic** or **other-directed suicides**:

3 **Sacrifice suicides** occur when a person is certain that others have made their life unbearable. The person who takes their own life often attributes the blame for their death to others so that they will feel guilty or will suffer criticism from other members of society. For example, Taylor refers to a case in which a 22-year-old man killed himself because his wife was in love with his elder brother and she wanted a divorce. The man left letters making it clear that he felt that his wife and brother were responsible for his death.

4 **Appeal suicides** and suicide attempts result from the suicidal person feeling uncertainty over the attitudes of others towards them. The suicide attempts are a form of communication in which the victim tries to show how desperate they are, in order to find out how others will respond. Suicide attempts may involve trying to persuade others to change their behaviour, or they may offer them chances to save the victim. Such attempts 'combine the wish to die and the wish for change in others and improvement in the situation; they are acts both of despair and of hope'.

For example, a woman slashed herself with a bread knife in front of her husband after he had discovered her having sex with a neighbour. Her husband took her to hospital and she survived. She later said she was unsure whether or not she would bleed to death but wanted to show her husband how much she loved him and to appeal for forgiveness through her actions.

In another case a man took an overdose of barbiturates in a car parked in front of his estranged wife's house. He left a note for his wife saying what he had done. However, a dense fog obscured the car and his wife did not see him when she returned to the house and therefore could not save him.

Taylor also refers to Marilyn Monroe's death. She had rung her doctor before taking her fatal overdose, and on previous occasions when she had rung him in an agitated state he had come round to calm her down. His failure to do so on this occasion removed any chance of discovery and rescue.

Evaluation of Taylor

Taylor's theory has some advantages over the other sociological theories examined so far. For example, it helps to explain why some suicide victims leave notes and others do not, why some suicide attempts seem more serious than others, and why some take place in isolation and others in more public places. However, his theory is hard to test. It rests upon the meanings given to suicidal actions by those who take part in them, and these meanings can be interpreted in different ways.

For those whose suicide attempts result in death the meanings can only be inferred from circumstantial evidence, since they are no longer able to explain their motives. Individual suicides may result from a combination of motives, with the result that they do not fit neatly into any one category.

Quantitative and qualitative methodology

The preceding sections of this chapter have outlined and illustrated the differences between these two broad approaches to methodology. Ray Pawson (1989) described the impression that such descriptions tend to give to many students. He says many students 'have their minds firmly fixed upon an image of a methodological brawl in which the beleaguered minority (the phenomenologists) have been for years trying to survive the onslaught of the wicked majority (the positivists)'. He claims that such a view is highly misleading.

Pawson is correct to point out that the distinction between positivism and phenomenology has sometimes been exaggerated, and some of his points will be examined shortly. However, the disputes are real. When Hindess (1973) says 'a manuscript produced by a monkey at a typewriter would be no less valuable' than the work of phenomenologists, he illustrates the strength of feeling of some of the methodological battles that have taken place. Nevertheless, a number of points should be made to put these disputes into perspective:

1 Even those who have strongly advocated and are closely associated with either a quantitative or qualitative approach have not necessarily stuck rigidly to their own supposed methodological principles. Douglas (1967) pointed out how Durkheim in his study of suicide strayed away from basing his analysis entirely on 'social facts', and dealt with the subjective states of individuals. For example, he gave mental sketches of what it felt like to be a Roman Catholic or a Protestant, in order to explain why their suicide rates should be so different.

At the other extreme, even one of the most ardent critics of quantitative methods, Cicourel (1976), made extensive use of statistical data. In his study of juvenile justice in two Californian cities he collected statistics on law enforcement in the two cities, and he

used a systematic comparison of the cities in order to explain their differing crime rates.

Payne and Payne point out that qualitative techniques 'often draw on some of the stock-in-trade of what are normally regarded as quantitative techniques' (2004, p. 179). For example, ethnomethodologists sometimes carry out research into how people talk, which they call conversational analysis. This involves detailed measurement of the time spent saying different things. Grounded theory (see p. 835) is advocated by symbolic interactionists such as Glaser and Strauss (1967), but it involves developing hypotheses in just the same way as experiments.

2 It can be argued that the 'methodological brawl' mentioned above has come to an end. Pawson (1989) says the idea that 'positivists and phenomenologists are always at logger heads is a sixties hangover; nowadays it is much more accurate to describe the relationship between those who do qualitative and those who do quantitative research as one of truce'. Many sociologists get on with actually doing research without worrying too much about the philosophical basis of that research. As the later sections on primary sources will show, practical difficulties have at least as much influence on the choice of research methods as theoretical considerations. Furthermore, many sociologists now advocate methodological pluralism (see pp. 845–7), where a mixture of quantitative and qualitative methods is used.

3 Finally, new philosophies of science and new approaches to methodology have now made the disagreements of positivists and phenomenologists look somewhat outdated. The realist conception of science, which will be discussed in a later section (see pp. 850–1), does not imply that science should be concerned only with that which can be observed directly. In this respect it does not exclude the use of qualitative methods in a 'social science' such as sociology. Critical social science, particularly feminism, and postmodern sociology offer distinctive perspectives on methodology which do not fit neatly into either camp in the disputes between positivist and interpretive sociologists.

Despite the above arguments, a considerable number of sociologists still use the distinction between qualitative and quantitative methods. One example is Alan Bryman (2001). He argues that 'the status of the distinction' between quantitative and qualitative methods 'is ambiguous, because it is almost simultaneously regarded by some writers as a fundamental contrast and by others as no longer useful or even simply as "false"'. Bryman himself chooses to continue using the distinction, arguing that, if anything, it is becoming more widely used by sociologists. Furthermore, he believes 'it represents a useful means of classifying different methods of social research and … it is a helpful umbrella for a range of issues concerned with the practice of social research'.

We will now examine critical social science and postmodern approaches to methodology, before looking at specific research methods.

Critical social science methodology

Lee Harvey – critical social research

The nature of critical social research

Critical social science embraces all those approaches in sociology which aim to be critical of society in order to facilitate social change. Criticism of some sort is present in most social science but, according to its advocates, critical social science goes beyond simply criticizing. According to Lee Harvey (1990), the key characteristic of critical social science is that 'critique is an integral part of the process … A critical research process involves more than appending critique to an accumulation of "fact" or "theory" gathered via some mechanical process, rather it denies the (literally) objective status of knowledge.'

This approach does not believe that you can simply discover the truth by using the appropriate quantitative or qualitative methods. Instead, it believes that 'knowledge is a process' in which you move towards understanding the social world. Knowledge is never completed, it is never finished, because the social world is constantly changing.

Furthermore, knowledge can never be separated from values. As members of the social world, researchers are bound to be influenced by their values and those of society. However, their aim should be to try to get beyond the dominant values of society, to try to see what is going on underneath the surface.

Thus, critical social scientists tend to believe that the way society appears to its members can be misleading. Things that are taken for granted need to be seen in a different light so that the true values underlying them can be revealed. Once this has been done, it may be possible to use the new knowledge to transform society.

Examples of critical social research

Harvey uses the example of feminist studies on housework to illustrate the approach. According to him, feminists have been able to show that housework should be seen as real work, just like paid work. Like paid work it creates things of value and it has a crucial role in the economy. Male-dominated commonsense views of housework have devalued it and seen it as unimportant. By revealing the true nature of housework, feminists have been able to encourage social changes in which women have demanded that the value of their unpaid work is recognized (see pp. 497–9 for a discussion of housework).

Critical social research is particularly concerned with revealing oppressive structures so that such structures

might be changed. Harvey says: 'It is important that the account be located in a wider context which links the specific activities with a broader social structural and historical analysis.' Thus, an analysis of housework can be linked to changes in the role of women in society with the rise of industrial capitalism (see pp. 108–9) and the development of patriarchy (see pp. 111–14).

There are numerous examples of critical social science. Harvey sees the work of Karl Marx (see, for example, pp. 867–72) and Paul Willis's study of working-class lads in the education system (see pp. 605–8) as examples.

Harvey generally divides critical social science studies into three main types, which concentrate on class, gender, and ethnicity and racism. Of course, some of the best critical social research examines all three simultaneously. However, these categories are by no means exhaustive, and critical social scientists also examine issues such as sexuality and disability – indeed, any area where some social groups can be seen as systematically disadvantaged or oppressed.

The main features of critical social research

Harvey sees critical social research as having the following main features.

1 Abstract concepts and ideology

It uses abstract concepts such as housework, but goes beyond simply carrying out empirical studies based on such concepts. Thus, instead of just measuring who does housework tasks, critical research tries to examine how such concepts relate to wider social relationships. Housework is seen as a **work relationship** rather than as simply a set of tasks to be performed. In this way critical research tries to get beneath the surface of social reality. This involves trying to overcome the dominant **ideology** or ideologies.

Distorted ideological beliefs may be related to dominant classes or to patriarchal or racist beliefs. They mask the material reality that lies behind these beliefs. In Marxist theory, for example, the ideology of wage labour as a free and fair exchange between employer and employee disguises the material advantages enjoyed by the employer as the owner of the means of production.

2 Totality, structure and history

Each abstract concept and particular belief cannot be examined in isolation. According to Harvey it is necessary to relate each bit of a society to a **totality**. Harvey says: 'Totality refers to the view that social phenomena are interrelated and form a total whole.' For example, in *The New Criminology* (1973), Taylor *et al.* advocate trying to understand the actions of criminals in the context of society as a whole (see pp. 343–4).

Critical social scientists see societies as possessing **structures**. Structures constrain or limit what people can do, but also make social actions possible. For example, the structures of capitalist societies make it difficult for members of the working class to set up their own businesses to compete with big capitalist companies. On the other hand, they make it possible for some capitalists to make substantial profits.

Structures, though, are not static; they change. Studies of society therefore need to be related to particular **historical contexts**. One needs to examine how particular societies have changed over time in order to understand them at any particular point in time. Thus, studies of the working class need to take account of how the economy and the labour market have changed since the advent of capitalism (see pp. 56–63 for examples).

3 Deconstruction, essence and reconstruction

Critical social researchers proceed through a process of **deconstruction** and **reconstruction**. In the process of deconstruction the different elements of particular areas of social life are taken apart in order to try to discover an **essence**. The essence is the 'fundamental concept that can be used as the key to unlocking the deconstructive process'. Thus, for example, the essence of capitalism, according to Marx, is 'the commodity form', while the essence of housework, according to Christine Delphy, is a set of work relationships in the context of family life.

Reconceptualization – thinking of familiar aspects of social life in unfamiliar ways – is the key to discovering essences through deconstruction. This process is never finished. Harvey says that critical research:

> *involves a constant questioning of the perspective and analysis the researcher is building up. It is a process of gradually, and critically, coming to know through constant reconceptualization. This means that the selection of a core concept for analysis is not a once-and-for-all affair.*
> Harvey, 1990

The process of deconstruction does not follow a pre-set path, as laid down by, for example, positivists. The development and testing of hypotheses and the collection of empirical data can all proceed 'in parallel'. The process involves 'a constant shuttling back and forwards between abstract concept and concrete data; between social totalities and particular phenomena; between current structures and historical development; between surface appearance and essence; between reflection and practice'. Some of the process does involve '"armchair" speculation', but empirical studies can also be carried out by whatever methods are most suitable.

Deconstruction leads to reconstruction. The researcher aims in the end to 'lay bare the essential relationships that are embedded in the structure'. They develop theoretical insights which allow the phenomena under investigation to be seen in a new way. A good example is Paul Willis's study of the transition from school to work among working-class 'lads'. Willis reveals how the lads' rebellion at school serves as a preparation for the alienating shop-floor jobs they end up doing. According to Willis, the lads thereby actively contribute to maintaining their own oppression (see pp. 605–8 for details).

4 Praxis

Critical social research is not just a theoretical activity, it is also a form of **praxis**. Harvey defines praxis as 'practical reflective activity. Praxis does not include "instinctive" or "mindless" activity like sleeping, breathing, walking, and so on, or undertaking repetitive work tasks. Praxis is what changes the world.'

The point of research is to improve the world. Researchers are interested in whether there is any potential for the oppressed groups being studied to come

together to change their situation. If these groups come to understand their situation better, they are more likely to resist or challenge the structures that oppress them. To Harvey, far from being a neutral, uninvolved observer of society, the researcher should be an involved and committed participant in the social world. The involvement should be directed towards developing a radical praxis within oppressed social groups.

Research methods

Critical social science is not tied to any single research method. Critical social scientists have used a full range of methods, including questionnaires, interviews, case studies, ethnography and semiology (see pp. 822–6, 826–31, 820, 831–2 and 843 for discussions of these methods). However, this approach does tend to be sympathetic towards methods which allow the social world to be seen from the viewpoint of those who are oppressed.

Some feminists have advocated the use of interviews (see pp. 809–10); Goldthorpe and Lockwood (whom Harvey describes as critical social researchers) used questionnaires (see pp. 58–9); while critical ethnography is perhaps the most popular of all the methods used by such researchers (see pp. 835–6).

Unlike positivist and interpretive approaches to methodology, the emphasis is not so much upon the preferred technique, but upon the purpose of the research. Any method is permissible so long as it allows the researcher to get beneath the surface of social life and has the potential for helping to change society. Harvey concludes: 'Although not susceptible to simple methodic prescriptions critical social research lies at the very heart of emancipatory sociological enquiry.'

Criticisms of critical social research

Martyn Hammersley (1992) identified a number of problems with critical social research:

1. First, he believes that there are problems in identifying sources of oppression in order to orientate research. Although critical social researchers identify a range of sources of oppression (principally class, gender and ethnicity), there may be others which they have not identified. Furthermore, it is not clear how they can clearly distinguish oppressor from non-oppressor. Hammersley (1992) says, 'many people may be simultaneously oppressor and oppressed'. If critical research is focused on understanding the viewpoint of the oppressed, it becomes difficult to carry out if oppressors might in some ways be oppressed themselves. It becomes hard to know who to interview or who to observe.
2. Hammersley believes there are problems with the whole concept of oppression, and differing ideas of needs and interests. There might be very different viewpoints on what a group needs and what their interests are. There may also be many different views on, and dimensions of, oppression. Hammersley believes that, in the end, needs, interests and what constitutes oppression are subjective judgements. As it is unlikely that all human needs and preferences can be met in society, some judgement has to be made about which needs and interests are legitimate and which are not.
3. Hammersley believes critical researchers tend to argue that 'there is a single set of values that everyone would agree on if it were not for the effects of ideology on our thinking'. If this were the case, it might get around the problem of deciding who was oppressed. However, Hammersley argues that this could never be achieved. Individuals, never mind social groups, can be in two (or more) minds about what is just, fair or in their interests. Furthermore, the interests of different oppressed groups might clash. For example, a religious minority might be oppressed in a society because of their beliefs. However, the religion might be highly patriarchal and oppressive of women. In such a case it becomes unclear whether the critical researcher should focus upon revealing the oppression of the religious minority, or of the women within that minority. If they try to do both they risk the contradictory position of arguing both that the religion should be tolerated and that its oppression of women should not be tolerated.
4. According to Hammersley, critical researchers try to establish the truth of their arguments either by getting oppressed groups to agree with their findings, or by showing that the findings have been successful in combating oppression. There are problems with both of these methods.

   First, oppressed groups may not be able to evaluate the truth of social science theories because they may be suffering from some sort of false consciousness. How do you know that they have cast off false consciousness and can now see the truth?

   Second, you cannot assume that even a correct theory will automatically produce social changes which overcome oppression. Many other factors apart from the production of theories will determine whether oppressed people are emancipated. As Hammersley says:

   > *Theories are not simply applied but used in association with practical knowledge. And, if this is the case, the achievement of emancipation depends on much more than the truth of the theory, and so failure to achieve emancipation does not tell us that the theory is false.*
   > Hammersley, 1992

Because of the above points Hammersley denies that critical social researchers have succeeded in producing an acceptable alternative to conventional methodology for establishing the truth. If this is the case, then critical social research 'becomes simply research directed towards serving the interests of some particular group, whose interests may conflict with others, including those of other oppressed groups'.

Phil Carspecken – a defence of critical social research

Despite the sorts of criticism advanced by writers such as Hammersley, some researchers argue that it is possible to

produce an acceptable critical social science methodology. Writing in 1996, Phil Carspecken argued that critical social researchers had failed to develop a detailed methodology. He attempted to put this right.

Carspecken believes that critical research need not be biased because the researchers engaging in it have value commitments. Critical researchers should not just look for the facts which fit their theories. Like researchers from other traditions, they should be open to finding evidence which contradicts their theories and challenges their values. They should always be open to changing their standpoints in the light of what they find during the course of research. Furthermore, research needs to be systematic and careful. It should go through a number of stages to reach conclusions which can be widely accepted as being close to the truth. Carspecken suggests the following stages.

The process of research

1 **Compiling the primary record.** In the first stage the researcher immerses themselves in the social life of the group or site being studied. They take notes and may use video- or audiotape. The researcher tries to develop a preliminary understanding of the social world from the viewpoint of those being studied.
2 **Preliminary reconstructive analysis.** In this stage the researcher starts to analyse what they found in the first stage. They look particularly for 'interaction patterns, their meanings, power relationships, roles, interactive sequences' and so on.
3 **Dialogical data generation.** In this stage the researcher starts talking to those being studied and discusses the preliminary findings with them. The subjects of research have an opportunity to influence the way the researcher is thinking and help him or her decide how convincing the initial ideas are. Carspecken says this 'democratizes the research process'. Interviews and discussion groups will be used at this stage.
4 **Discovering system relations.** Once stage 3 is well under way the researcher begins to broaden the study to try to link their specific findings to other parts of social life. For example, the relationships found in a school might be linked to the content of the mass media, the local labour market or changing conceptions of masculinity and femininity.
5 **Using system relations to explain findings.** Only in the final stage does the researcher begin to produce causal explanations of what they have found. Links are made to social structures and particular attention may be paid to 'class, race, gender and political structures of society'.

Establishing truth claims

Why, though, should people believe the results of such research? Will it not simply reflect the biases and values that the researcher started with? Carspecken believes not. First, the features of social life uncovered by researchers are the basis on which the theories are developed. They are not simply based on the researcher's abstract ideas. Second, the subjects of the research have a chance to confirm or contradict the initial understandings developed by the researcher. Third, Carspecken develops a sophisticated analysis of how conclusions may be reached about whether the findings of research are true or not.

Like Popper (see p. 790), Carspecken does not believe social scientists can produce statements that will necessarily be regarded as true for all time. Even if everyone agreed that something was true, this view might be rejected in some future society. However, in essence, whether something is regarded as true or not ultimately depends upon whether people can agree that it is true. A truth claim – a claim that something is true – is always an act of communication. It is an attempt by one person or group to assert to other people that something is true. Establishing the truth is therefore a communicative process.

The way to check whether a truth claim stands up to scrutiny is to see whether other people agree with it. The only way to do that is to allow others a chance to accept or refute the truth claim. Traditional science considers truth claims by limiting those who are allowed to express an opinion on them to the scientists. Only experts have their views taken seriously. In critical social research, those who are being studied have a say as well as other social scientists. In studying social life, the participants – the children in a classroom, the workers in an office, the members of families and so on – are the experts. Checking whether they can be convinced by the social researchers' theory is a key part of testing whether it is true.

However, there are some problems involved in checking the findings of research by seeing whether people will agree with them or not. People often agree with things not because they believe them, but because of power relationships. Following the work of Habermas (1984), Carspecken believes that communications can be distorted where some of those communicating have power over others involved. To use a simple example, if someone holds a gun to your head and threatens to kill you, you are likely to agree with whatever they say regardless of whether you believe it.

Critical researchers should therefore be aware of these sources of distortion. They should try to ensure that they eliminate, as far as possible, power relationships between themselves and those being studied. Thus, Carspecken believes that, as a researcher, you should:

> *establish supportive, non-authoritarian relationships with the participants in your study. Actively encourage them to question your own perceptions. Be sure that participants are protected from any harm that your study could produce, and be sure that they know they are protected.*
> Carspecken, 1996

However, researchers should also challenge beliefs that may result from power relationships. Thus, for example, women who believe that their husband or male partner should be able to tell them what to do could have their beliefs challenged by a researcher. The researcher would have to find out whether the women in question could be persuaded that the relationship was patriarchal.

The subjects of the research are not the only ones who need to be persuaded of the researcher's truth claims. Other social scientists and readers of the research need to be persuaded, too. Of course, the research will be

evaluated by people whose views are influenced by the power relationships in which the researcher is involved. The researcher will therefore be unlikely to persuade everybody of the truthfulness of their work. Nevertheless, their aim should be to make the findings as convincing as possible.

While checks on the validity of truth claims do in the end come down to a matter of opinion, Carspecken does not believe that what people believe is just random. To him, what people will accept is affected by what is real. He argues that 'a single, real, world exists independently from any cultural categories used to describe it and act in relation to it'. This real world 'resists' human actions. People find that there are some ways in which it allows them to behave, and some ways in which it limits their behaviour. For example, if people believed that broken glass was not sharp, and acted towards it accordingly, they would soon find themselves cut and bleeding. It would be hard to sustain the belief that broken glass was not sharp, and cultural beliefs would be likely to change.

Beliefs tend to fall into line with reality because of people's experiences. Of course, this does not always happen. People can believe things in spite of experiences which suggest that the beliefs are mistaken. Furthermore, many beliefs are far more complicated than the above example, and cannot easily be tested against experience. Nevertheless, the idea that a real world exists and that it can resist human actions allows Carspecken to claim that ultimately there can be a sound foundation for people trying to agree on what is true and what is not.

Feminist methodology

Approaches to feminist methodology

Perhaps feminist approaches to critical research are the most developed ones. There have been numerous attempts to develop feminist ways of doing or approaching research, but three approaches have been particularly influential:

1. The **attack on 'malestream' research**. This involves a criticism of previous, male-dominated, mainstream research. Often referred to by feminists as 'malestream' research, it is criticized for being based upon sexist or patriarchal principles.
2. The claim that there can be distinctive **feminist research methods**. This approach argues that the more conventional 'scientific' methods used by men are not particularly good at helping the researcher to understand social reality – particularly, though not exclusively, the reality of women.
3. The claim that feminism can reveal a distinctive **epistemology**, or theory of knowledge, which is superior to other epistemologies.

The attack on 'malestream' research

This is perhaps the least controversial of feminist approaches to methodology. Rather than trying to construct a completely new feminist approach, it tries to rectify the mistakes of previous, dominant and male-oriented research methodologies. From this point of view, research has generally been carried out about men, by men and for men.

Pamela Abbott, Claire Wallace and Melissa Tyler (2005) provide a comprehensive list of feminist criticisms of 'malestream' sociology. They say:

> *Feminists from a variety of perspectives have made a number of criticisms of sociology. These are based primarily on the view that*
> 1. *sociology has been mainly concerned with research on men, and by implication with theories and concepts that apply primarily to men's lives;*
> 2. *research findings based on all-male samples are generalized to the whole of the population;*
> 3. *areas and issues of concern to women are frequently overlooked or seen as unimportant;*
> 4. *when they are included in research they are often presented in a distorted and stereotypical way;*
> 5. *when sex and gender are included in research they tend to be just 'added on', ignoring the extent to which the explanatory theories used are ones which have justified the subordination and exploitation of women.*
>
> Abbot et *al.*, 2005

A number of examples included in this book can illustrate these points:

- According to Carol Smart (1976), the sociology of crime and deviance was, until the late 1970s, almost exclusively the sociology of male crime and delinquency (see p. 367). Studies such as those by Merton, Cohen, and Cloward and Ohlin (see pp. 323–6) almost completely ignored women, yet assumed that they applied to criminals in general and not just male criminals.
- As Ann Oakley (1974) points out, housework was seen as too unimportant to be studied by social scientists until her own pioneering work.
- Michelle Stanworth (1984) criticizes John Goldthorpe's class scheme for, generally, allocating wives to classes based upon their husbands' occupations (see p. 77).
- Male social scientists such as Talcott Parsons have been accused of providing sexist, biologically based explanations of female behaviour (see pp. 96–7 and 463–4).

There have also been frequent criticisms of the use of sexist language in social research. For example, Margaret Eichler (1991) points out that terms such as 'men' and 'mankind' have often been used to refer to people in general.

Evaluation

These sorts of criticism of 'malestream' sociology have been very influential and widely accepted. The numbers of

sociological studies of women, studies of issues important to women, and studies which examine female perspectives on social life, have proliferated. It has become much less common for sociologists to try to generalize about people of both sexes on the basis of male samples. The sociological study of women, by women and for women has become much more commonplace.

Sexist language in sociology has also become much less common. For example, the British Sociological Association's 'Ethical Guidelines' state that sexist language is unacceptable, and it is banned from the organization's journal *Sociology* (see the 'Notes for contributors' in any edition of the journal).

Although the problems of 'malestream' sociology have certainly not been eliminated, they have been greatly reduced and the arguments advanced for non-sexist sociology have become relatively uncontentious. Other feminist approaches to research methods, though, are much more controversial.

Feminist research methods

Ann Oakley – approaches to interviewing

The masculine model of interviewing

Perhaps the best-known and most influential argument that there should be distinctive feminist research methods is advanced by Ann Oakley (1981). In particular, she argues that there is a feminist way of conducting interviews which is superior to a more dominant, masculine model of such research.

By studying the instructions of various methodology books which describe the techniques of interviewing, Oakley is able to discover the main features of the masculine approach to interviewing. She says, 'the paradigm of the "proper" interview appeals to such values as objectivity, detachment, hierarchy and "science" as an important cultural activity which takes precedence over people's more individualized concerns'.

Although they can be friendly in order to establish some minimum rapport, interviewers must maintain their distance, to avoid becoming too involved with respondents. Certainly, any emotional involvement between interviewer and respondent must be avoided at all costs.

The interviewees must be manipulated as 'objects of study/sources of data'. They must always have a passive role, and must never become active in shaping the interview. If the interviewee asks the interviewer questions, the interviewer should not answer and should make it clear that he or she is there to ask questions and not to answer them.

Interviewing of this type emphasizes the importance of producing reliable data that can be repeated and checked. Interviewers have to avoid expressing any opinion of their own. To do so will influence the answers of the respondents and lead to bias in the research.

The feminist approach to interviewing

Having outlined the masculine approach to interviewing, Oakley proceeds to suggest a feminist alternative. She draws upon her own experience of interviewing women about becoming mothers. She conducted 178 interviews, with most women being interviewed twice before the birth of their child and twice afterwards. In some cases Oakley was actually present at the birth. On average, each of the women was interviewed for more than nine hours.

Oakley found that the women often wanted to ask her questions. Instead of avoiding answering them, Oakley decided to answer their questions as openly and honestly as she could. Some of the questions were about her and her research, others were requests for information about childbirth or childcare. In some cases the women were anxious about some aspect of childcare or childbirth, and often they had failed to get satisfactory answers from medical staff. In these circumstances Oakley found it impossible to refuse to answer their questions. She was asking a great deal of the interviewees at a difficult time in their lives, and it was only reasonable that she should give something back in return.

Oakley decided to make the research more collaborative. Instead of looking at the women as passive respondents, she wanted them to become her collaborators and friends. Indeed, it was often the interviewees who took the initiative in developing the relationship further. Many expressed an interest in the research and wanted to become more involved. Some rang her up with key pieces of information. Oakley claims, 'the women were reacting to my own evident wish for a relatively intimate and non-hierarchical relationship'.

Oakley tried to make sure that she did not exploit the interviewees. She asked permission to record interviews and use the information. While she was at the mothers' houses she gave them help with childcare or housework if they needed it. She discussed her own experiences of childbirth with the women who were interested, and tried to offer advice on where they could get help with particular problems.

Oakley's objectives in adopting such an approach were not just to give some help to the women and to avoid exploiting them, in return for their participation. She also believed it improved the quality of the research. It allowed her to get closer to the subjective viewpoints of the women being studied. It also played some role in trying to change and improve the experience of becoming a mother for the women involved. Oakley says:

> *Nearly three-quarters of the women said that being interviewed had affected them and the three most common forms this influence took were in leading them to reflect on their experiences more than they would otherwise have done; in reducing the level of their anxiety and/or in reassuring them of their normality; and in giving a valuable outlet for the verbalization of feelings.* Oakley, 1981

Oakley concludes that interviewing that breaks down the barriers between researchers and their subjects is preferable to masculine, 'scientific' interviewing. She says, a feminist methodology:

> *requires, further, that the mythology of 'hygienic' research with its accompanying mystification of the researcher and the researched as objective instruments of data production be replaced by the recognition that personal involvement is more than dangerous bias – it is the condition under which people come to know each other and to admit others into their lives.* Oakley, 1981

Evaluation

Oakley's approach to interviewing has been quite influential among feminists and her ideas are widely quoted in books about methodology. Her approach fits in well with the main aims of feminist research put forward by DeVault (1996, discussed in Burns and Walker, 2005). DeVault believes that feminist research should minimize harm to those being researched and minimize the control exercised by the researcher, and it should produce research of value to women which can be used to improve their lives. DeVault's own research (1991), in which she interviewed women about the burden of preparing food for a family, illustrated how feminist research could benefit from the sort of principles laid down by Oakley.

However, some critics, although generally sympathetic to Oakley's approach, have argued that it is not original or distinctively feminist.

Ray Pawson argues that Oakley simply elaborated on conventional ways of conducting unstructured interviews. He says:

> *This vision of interviewing-as-fieldwork is precisely that urged from the traditional doctrines of interpretive, phenomenological or humanistic sociology. There is a time-honoured tradition of positivism-bashing in general and structured-interviewing bashing in particular, and this feminist approach is essentially a repetition of this literature.* Pawson, 1992

The differences between structured and unstructured interviewing will be discussed later in the chapter (see p. 826). However, it can be argued that there are some features of Oakley's approach which go beyond conventional approaches to unstructured interviewing. For example, even unstructured interviewing is not normally supposed to involve advising and helping the interviewees, since it is thought that such interventions might affect the findings. Oakley's approach to feminist interviewing incorporates elements of critical research which are not typical of other types of interpretive research.

Feminist standpoint epistemology

Perhaps the most influential of feminist epistemologies is what has been called **standpoint epistemology**. From this point of view, the way in which women experience social life gives them unique insights into how society works. Sandra Harding (1986) says: 'The feminist standpoint epistemologies ground a distinctive feminist science in a theory of gendered activity and social experience.' That is, they believe that feminist knowledge can only come from examining the unique experiences of women in societies in which men and women experience social life in different ways.

Standpoint epistemology generally does not deny that it is possible to discover the truth about society. However, instead of believing that the truth can be established through the observation of facts and the discovery of statistical relationships, it seeks to find the truth through understanding women's experiences. Furthermore, it tends to believe that no one version of the truth can explain everything. Although women have certain experiences in common, there are also big differences between groups of women, and their different experiences need to be explored before a full picture of the social world can be produced.

Liz Stanley and Sue Wise are among the advocates of standpoint epistemology. They argue in favour of 'theory derived from experience' which is 'constantly subject to revision in the light of that experience' (Stanley and Wise, 1990). They say feminist research should be 'not only located in, but proceed from, the grounded analysis of women's experiences'. By examining their experiences the feminist researcher can understand the world.

According to Stanley and Wise, 'all knowledge, necessarily, results from the conditions of its production, is contextually located, and irrevocably bears the marks of its origins'. Generally speaking, sociology has usually expressed 'the practices and knowledge of highly particular white, middle-class, heterosexual men'. Feminist standpoint epistemology replaces this with a view of the world developed through the experiences of oppressed women. Oppressed women are in a special position, able through their experiences to see through the ideology of their male oppressors.

However, Stanley and Wise do not believe that all women experience the world in the same way. For example, black, lesbian and working-class women have different experiences from those of their white, heterosexual and middle-class counterparts. Stanley and Wise therefore support the view that feminist epistemology needs to look at different standpoints and should not try to pretend that one set of knowledge can deal with the experiences of very different groups of women. They are in favour of a plurality of feminist theories deriving from the study of different oppressed groups. No one theory should be allowed to be dominant.

Although Stanley and Wise accept the need for a plurality of theories, they do not go as far as some postmodernists who deny that any methodology can deliver a true picture of social life (see pp. 811–12). To Stanley and Wise, the viewpoints of different women need to be examined simply because women do have real, different experiences. Feminist methodology needs to uncover these different and often previously neglected experiences in order to develop a fuller understanding of the social world.

Criticisms of feminist standpoint epistemology

Ray Pawson (1992) argues that such epistemologies run into major problems when those being studied continue to see the world in terms that the researcher finds unconvincing. Thus, for example, feminist researchers are unlikely to give much credence to women's views that it is 'natural' for women to do the housework and for men to be dominant. Sometimes, however much they try to persuade the women being studied to see things differently, the women may stick to beliefs which feminists see as reflecting patriarchal ideology. In such cases researchers may find themselves going against what their respondents believe, or, alternatively, having to accept views which they believe to be untrue.

According to Pawson, a further problem with standpoint epistemology is that it puts all the emphasis upon studying the experiences of the oppressed. This effectively rules out studying the oppressors (in this case men), even though studying oppressors might reveal at least as much about the nature of oppression as studying the oppressed.

Pawson is also unpersuaded by the view that you can simply describe a plurality of different viewpoints. Sometimes the viewpoints of groups of women, grounded in different experiences, may contradict one another. Unless the researcher decides to say that one viewpoint is better than another, they end up having to accept contradictory beliefs. This leads them down the path of **relativism**. They are no longer trying to explain society as it really is; they are reduced to accepting all viewpoints as equally valid. Different feminist views of the world are only true for particular groups of women; none can claim to describe society as it really is for everybody. In these circumstances sociology loses any claim to be able to produce knowledge which is superior to the commonsense knowledge of ordinary members of society.

Pawson's criticisms tend to generalize about feminist methodologies and epistemologies and are not particularly sensitive to variations between them. Not all feminist standpoint epistemologies are relativistic; some do not see the viewpoints of all groups of women as equally valid. Indeed, the accusation of relativism could be more justly directed against postmodern methodology (see p. 837) than feminist methodology. Furthermore, as we have seen above, critical social scientists such as Phil Carspecken have tried to deal with some of the apparent problems with methodologies that take the viewpoint of the oppressed seriously (see pp. 806–8).

Critical and feminist approaches to methodology will be discussed further as the chapter develops.

Postmodern methodology

Varieties of postmodern methodology

There is no single type of methodology accepted by all postmodernists. Some postmodernists, such as David Harvey (1990), see postmodernity largely in terms of changes in society. They do not believe that the nature of knowledge has changed or that radical new methodologies are needed to replace old ones. They therefore tend to use conventional methods and conventional sources of data. Thus, Harvey analyses statistical economic data and tries to interpret cultural trends from a number of secondary sources. From the viewpoint of such writers, existing methodologies, whether quantitative or qualitative, are quite adequate for the analysis of society.

However, most postmodernists are much more critical of conventional research methods. Many make a sharp distinction between modern and postmodern epistemology. **Modern epistemology** (or theory of knowledge) tends to claim that the truth can be discovered by the use of the correct techniques. Those who advocate both deductive and inductive methods (see p. 790), and even critical social scientists (see pp. 804–8), believe that procedures can be used to evaluate what is true and what is not. While Popper and critical sociologists may not believe that the final truth can be established, they do at least believe it is possible to rule out some knowledge as being untrue.

Epistemological postmodernists argue that there is no basis even for ruling out some knowledge as being untrue. Lyotard (1984), for example, dismisses all knowledge based upon modern epistemologies as deriving from 'metanarratives' (see pp. 891–2). Metanarratives are big stories about the world and are essentially opinions rather than objective knowledge.

Lyotard rejects the claims of all 'scientific' subjects and believes that all knowledge is essentially a form of storytelling. He sees all stories as equally valid and offers no way of distinguishing between true and untrue stories. The implication of this view is that postmodern methodology should simply consist of allowing different people to tell their stories. No attempt should be made to try to establish that any particular stories are better than any others.

Some postmodernists have tried to develop postmodern ethnography as a way of allowing the voices of diverse social groups to be heard (see p. 837 for a discussion of postmodern ethnography). Postmodern ethnography allows epistemological postmodernists to collect some of their own data. However, much postmodern sociology is not so concerned with creating new knowledge as with attacking existing knowledge. Many such approaches have drawn on the work of Jacques Derrida as a basis for criticizing other sociologists' work (see Kamuf, 1991, for extracts from Derrida).

Derrida believed that language could never truly represent an external, objective reality. Language is simply a self-contained system in which words are defined in terms of other words. Because of this, scientists, sociologists and indeed anyone else should not be believed if they claim to have established the absolute truth. Therefore the work of such writers should be deconstructed.

Deconstruction involves examining texts (anything containing written language) and taking them apart. In this process Derrida believed that the inherent contradictions built into existing knowledge could be revealed (see pp. 116–17 for further details). The technique of deconstruction is often used by postmodernists to attack and try to undermine texts such as existing sociological theories. This strand of postmodern methodology is therefore based around the critique of secondary sources (see pp. 842–3) rather than the creation of new knowledge.

Criticisms of epistemological postmodernism

Postmodern methodology has been widely accused of adopting a position of complete relativism. That is, it argues that knowledge simply depends upon your point of view, and that one person's view is as good as any other

Alvesson himself admits: 'There is an overwhelming risk that a heavy inspiration from postmodernism might add more destructive confusion than constructive confusion.'

In trying to avoid too much destructive confusion, Alvesson fails to stick to the logic of the postmodern position. He provides no clear way of distinguishing between high-ambiguity and low-ambiguity issues, and even low-ambiguity issues are subject to some doubt. For example, some people have questioned the size of the Nazi Holocaust and whether sexually transmitted HIV leads to AIDS. Alvesson argues that postmodernism should be taken seriously 'but not too seriously', but he is not very clear about when these different degrees of seriousness should be employed.

Postmodern methodology will be discussed further later in the chapter (see p. 837).

The next section will deal with the major issues involved in actually carrying out research. It begins with a consideration of how researchers go about selecting topics for research, and goes on to examine the practical and theoretical issues involved in collecting and analysing data.

The research process

Choosing a topic for research

Before embarking upon research, sociologists have to decide what they are going to study. This choice may be affected by a number of factors.

Values

The values and beliefs of the researcher will obviously play some part. Sociologists are unlikely to devote considerable time and energy to issues that they think are unimportant or trivial. For example, Peter Townsend's values led him to regard poverty as an important problem in contemporary industrial societies (see pp. 217–18), while Paul Heelas believed that the New Age movement and alternative spiritualities were worthy of attention (see pp. 420–1).

Developments in sociology and in society

What a researcher believes is important may be influenced by developments within the discipline of sociology, or developments in the wider society. Sociology is a profession as well as a discipline, and many sociologists wish to advance their careers by criticizing or developing the work of fellow sociologists, or by trying to resolve some key sociological issue. This might explain why so many sociologists have followed Durkheim in studying suicide, while other areas of social life have been comparatively neglected.

Similarly, routine clerical workers have been studied more than some other sections of the stratification system. This group is often seen as a crucial test of Marxist and Weberian theories of stratification. Groups of less theoretical interest to sociologists, such as agricultural labourers, have been studied less often.

In the sociology of religion, apparent examples of religious revival, such as the revival of Islam and the New Christian Right in the USA, have been studied partly in order to evaluate the theory of secularization.

When there are major changes in society, sociologists are likely to study them. Sociology was born in the nineteenth century, largely out of a concern about the changes wrought by the industrial revolution. More recently, sociologists have studied apparent social changes in terms of theories and concepts such as postmodernism (see pp. 891–4) and high modernity (see pp. 895–9).

Specific government policies can also stimulate research. Hence, for example, the concern with markets and competition in the contemporary sociology of education (see pp. 618–20), and the concern with 'social exclusion' in studies of social policy since the British Labour government established a Social Exclusion Unit (see p. 258).

Funding

A very important factor affecting the choice of research topic is the availability or otherwise of grants to finance the research. The people and organizations who hold the purse strings can act as **gatekeepers** – people who decide whether or not researchers are able to carry out research or not. Research funds may come from charitable foundations – such as the Nuffield and Rowntree foundations – from industry, or from government – in Britain, usually via the Economic and Social Research Council (or ESRC). The European Union sometimes provides funds for sociological research.

Some small-scale research requires little funding, but major research projects can be very expensive, and the sort of research that gets done can be very strongly influenced by those who hold the purse strings. Payne *et al.* (1977) suggested that the SSRC (the predecessor of the ESRC) 'had no pretensions to being anything other than a government organization'. As an important source of funding for British sociology it tended to restrict the amount of sociological research that was critical of the government of the day.

Tim May (2001) argues that governments may be actively hostile to research which attacks their policies or which advocates an agenda different from their own. He says: 'there are periodic attacks on the legitimacy of research that runs counter to government expectation'.

Industrial providers of research grants tend to want some practical benefits from the money they spend, so research into organizations and industrial sociology is most likely to receive funding from this source.

Practicalities

Other practical difficulties apart from money can affect the topics chosen by sociologists for their research. The availability of existing data on a topic or the practicality of collecting data will both have an influence. Durkheim chose to study suicide partly because statistics were available

from many European countries (see pp. 795–7). Some important groups in the population – for example, senior politicians and the directors of top companies – rarely form the basis of detailed studies. This is partly due to their unwillingness to reveal their activities to sociological scrutiny. The powerful can sometimes act as gatekeepers determining who, if anybody, is allowed to gain access to data, people or locations in order to conduct research. Other relatively powerless groups, such as delinquent gangs, have been subject to detailed and frequent study.

Ethics

Even when researchers are able to carry out research, they may not do so for ethical reasons. Mark Israel and Iain Hay (2006) argue:

> *ethical behaviour helps protects individuals, communities and environments, and offers the potential to increase the sum of good in the world. As social scientists 'trying to make the world a better place' we should avoid (or at least minimize) doing long-term, systematic harm to those individuals, communities and environments.* Israel and Hay, 2006, p. 2

Furthermore, the behaviour of social scientists is constrained by codes of ethics (such as those of the British Sociological Association and the British Society of Criminology) and sometimes by the ethical guidelines of research committees in universities. Although individual codes of ethics vary, Israel and Hay identify some principles which most codes have in common and which can affect the choice of research methods.

1. Most social scientists follow guidelines which require **informed consent** from participants before research is allowed. Informed consent involves the participants voluntarily agreeing to participate in research, having substantially understood what the research involves. If the need for informed consent is accepted, this can prevent researchers from carrying out covert research or misleading the participants about the nature of the research. This poses particular problems for laboratory or field experiments where the behaviour of participants may alter if they know what the research is aiming to discover (see pp. 790–2). It also makes research difficult when studying interaction between large numbers of people, or when some participants are unlikely to give consent. For example, as Israel and Hay point out, it has created complications for researchers investigating the relationship between drug users and drug dealers, since the latter may be particularly unwilling to consent to taking part in research.

   Israel and Hay note that many codes of ethics require parental consent for children to take part in research. This has greatly restricted research into homeless teenagers in the USA, since parents or guardians are not readily available to give their consent.
2. **Confidentiality** is also a requirement of most ethical codes. Some research may be difficult because governments, police or courts might require researchers to disclose research findings. For example, Fitzgerald and Hamilton (1996, discussed in Israel and Hay, 2006) suspended their research on Australian drug users because they feared that the police would issue a warrant requiring them to disclose confidential information. Such problems can become particularly acute if researchers are studying serious offending such as paedophilia, murder, organized crime or terrorism. In some research it may be very difficult to disguise the identity of participants. For example, Fiona Brookman (1999) argues that it is difficult to keep the identity of murderers who have been interviewed for research purposes confidential if their cases have received a lot of publicity. Even sketchy details of their offences can make it easy to guess their identity.
3. The ultimate purpose of having research ethics is **to avoid harm and do good**. Israel and Hay comment that 'Contemporary researchers are normally expected to minimize risks of harm or discomfort to participants (the principle of non-maleficence). In some circumstances they may also be expected to promote the well-being of participants (the principle of beneficence)' (2006, p. 95). While beneficence is certainly desirable, non-maleficence is seen as essential to most researchers. This may lead them to avoid certain types of research, or at least to be very careful about the way they conduct research. For example, Israel and Hay note that one study of domestic violence in Mexico led to some of the research subjects being re-victimized by their partners because they had spoken to the researcher.

   Feminists and critical social scientists are particularly concerned with doing good through research (see pp. 808–11 and 804–8), and this restricts their choice of research topic to those where they can challenge the exploitation of women or other groups regarded as being oppressed.

Despite widespread agreement on some basic ethical principles, there are also some areas of disagreement. For example, researchers with different values may disagree about the circumstances, if any, in which informed consent is not necessary, and about issues such as what constitutes doing good. The ethics of individuals will vary, and for some it will considerably restrict the range of topics that they are willing to research.

Primary sources

Primary sources of information consist of data collected by researchers themselves during the course of their work. **Secondary sources** consist of data that already exist. Primary sources would include data collected by researchers using questionnaires, conducting interviews or carrying out participant observation. Secondary sources include official statistics, mass media products, diaries, letters, government reports, the content of web pages on the internet, other sociologists' work, and historical and contemporary records. Secondary sources will be discussed later.

Choosing a primary research method

Some of the factors that influence the choice of research topic can also influence the choice of research method used to study that topic. For example, the source of funding for a proposed project might well specify the type of method to be employed. Many funding bodies support the use of more quantitative methods. Janet Finch (1986), for example, describes the 'dominance achieved by quantitative methods, and the (at best) secondary place which qualitative methods were accorded' in the development of British social policy research.

However, the most important factors influencing the choice of research method are the topic to be studied and the theoretical and practical considerations. Some topics lend themselves more readily to the use of quantitative techniques such as questionnaires: for example, research into voting in Great Britain tends to involve large-scale studies using quantitative statistical techniques because of the sheer numbers necessarily involved in the research if the data are to be of any use. Other topics, such as behaviour in classrooms, lend themselves more readily to qualitative methods.

As the earlier sections of this chapter have shown, those who support a particular theoretical approach tend to use either quantitative or qualitative methods. This commitment may well be the major influence on their choice of research method.

Reliability

Many of the debates about the merits of particular research methods focus on questions of reliability and validity. In the natural sciences, data are seen to be 'reliable' if other researchers using the same methods of investigation on the same material produce the same results. By replicating an experiment it is possible to check for errors in observation and measurement. Once reliable data have been obtained, generalizations can then be made about the behaviour observed.

No sociologist would claim that the social sciences can attain the standards of reliability employed in the natural sciences. Many would argue, however, that sociological data can attain a certain standard of reliability.

Generally speaking, quantitative methods are seen to provide greater reliability. They usually produce standardized data in a statistical form. This means that the research can be repeated and the results checked. Questionnaires can be used to test precise hypotheses which the researcher has devised.

Qualitative methods are often criticized for failing to meet the same standards of reliability. Such methods may be seen as unreliable because the procedures used to collect data can be unsystematic, the results are rarely quantified, and there is no way of replicating a qualitative study and checking the reliability of its findings.

Validity

Data are 'valid' if they provide a true picture of what is being studied. A valid statement gives a true measurement, description or explanation of what it claims to measure or describe. It is an accurate reflection of social reality. Data can be reliable without being valid. Studies can be replicated and produce the same results, but those results may not be a valid measure, description or explanation of the social world.

Alan Bryman (2001) outlines four types of validity:

1. **Measurement validity** (also known as **construct validity**) concerns whether a measure being employed really measures what it claims. For example, some sociologists have questioned whether IQ tests really measure innate intelligence (see p. 627), and whether church attendance statistics really measure the strength of religious beliefs (see pp. 433–4).
2. **Internal validity** relates to causality and 'is concerned with whether a conclusion that incorporates a causal relationship between two or more variables holds water'. Throughout this book, causal explanations put forward by some sociologists have been questioned by others. For example, many different causal explanations of criminality (see Chapter 6) and differential educational achievement (see Chapter 10) have had their validity questioned.
3. **External validity** concerns whether the results of a particular study can be generalized to groups or situations other than those of the study itself. For example, Beverley Skeggs's (1997) study of eighty-three working-class women in a single town in northwest England may lack external validity in relation to working-class women elsewhere (see pp. 70–2).
4. **Ecological validity** refers to the problem of whether 'social scientific findings are appropriate to people's everyday natural setting' (Bryman, 2001). The more unnatural a research setting and the more distant it is from everyday life, the more its ecological validity can be questioned. Thus laboratory experiments may lack ecological validity (see pp. 790–1). Some sociologists believe that questionnaires are also too remote from natural or normal social interaction to possess ecological validity (see pp. 824–6).

Supporters of qualitative methods often argue that quantitative methods lack validity. For example, a questionnaire may produce neat, tidy quantitative data. But the process of completing a questionnaire is a long way from people's normal everyday behaviour. As a result, this research method and the data it produces may lack ecological validity.

Quantitative methods are seen to lack the depth to describe accurately the meanings and motives that form the basis of social action. They use categories imposed on the social world by sociologists – categories that may have little meaning or relevance to other members of society. They are therefore lacking in measurement validity.

As a consequence of these problems, some qualitative researchers believe quantitative research is unlikely to have internal validity. It may well reach incorrect conclusions about the causes of social phenomena. To many interpretive sociologists, only qualitative methods can overcome these problems and provide a valid picture of social reality.

Some qualitative researchers (for example, some feminists) advocate the use of **respondent validation** to

overcome problems of validity. This involves respondents checking research findings so that they can correct any misinterpretations or inaccuracies. However, as Rosaline Barbour (2001) points out, this does not guarantee validity. For example, when the interpretations of the researcher and the respondent are different, it is not necessarily the interpretation of the respondent which is superior. The researcher may have more of an overview of the aspect of social life being studied than the respondent and may therefore be in a better position to produce a valid interpretation. Despite the claims of many interpretive researchers that their methods offer greater validity than quantitative methods, the possibility of conflicting interpretations always makes qualitative research open to the accusation of lacking validity as well.

Practicality

Researchers are sometimes attracted to quantitative methods because of their practicality. Quantitative methods are generally less time-consuming and require less personal commitment. It is usually possible to study larger and more representative samples, which can provide an overall picture of society. Qualitative research often has to be confined to the study of small numbers because of practical limitations. It is more suited to providing an in-depth insight into a smaller sample of people.

Ethics

As in the choice of topic, ethics can also affect the choice of method. Researchers will tend not to choose methods where confidentiality and informed consent are not possible, or where they believe harm will come to the subjects. Ethical issues help to explain why sociologists rarely use experimental methods or covert observation, where informed consent may be difficult or impossible. Some feminist researchers, such as Ann Oakley, choose informal interviewing methods because they believe such methods give most opportunity to benefit the subjects of research in various ways (see pp. 809–10).

These points will be developed in the following sections.

Choosing a sample

Once a sociologist has chosen a topic for research and a method to carry out that research, they need to decide upon a 'sample': that is, the actual individuals to be studied. All research involves some sort of **sampling**, some selection of who or what to study. Those researchers who advocate 'scientific' quantitative methods tend to support the use of sophisticated sampling techniques, and often claim to be able to generalize on the basis of their findings. Those who support interpretive qualitative methods tend to study smaller numbers of people, so their studies are less likely to require complex sampling techniques.

A **sample** is a part of a larger population. It is usually selected to be representative of that population: those included in the sample are chosen as a cross-section of the larger group. The use of samples saves the researcher time and money, since it reduces the number of individuals to be studied. If the sample is chosen carefully, it is possible to generalize from it: that is, to make statements about the whole relevant population on the basis of the sample.

The first stage in sampling involves identifying the **target population**. A population in this sense includes all the relevant sampling units. The **sampling unit** is the individual person or social group in that population. In a study of voting in Britain the relevant population would be all those entitled to vote, and the sampling unit would be the individual voter.

Having determined the sampling unit and the population, the researcher might then try to obtain or to produce a **sampling frame**. In a study of voting there is a ready-made sampling frame – the electoral register – since a sampling frame is simply a list of all the relevant sampling units in the population.

It is important that the sampling frame is as comprehensive as possible: if it is not, the sample might be seriously distorted. Researchers have in the past sometimes used telephone directories as a sampling frame for the population of a particular area, but the directory would not have included those who had ex-directory numbers and those without a telephone. Since the latter would probably have been people on low incomes, the results of a study on (for example) voting intentions based upon this sampling frame might be seriously misleading.

Often, even apparently comprehensive sampling frames contain omissions. For example, the electoral register does not include all adults living in Britain. Foreign nationals (except for some citizens of the Republic of Ireland), those who have failed to register as voters, and members of the House of Lords are among those who would be excluded. The introduction of the Poll Tax in the early 1990s led to large numbers of people avoiding enrolment on the electoral register in an attempt to get out of paying the tax.

Studies use imperfect sampling frames. The early British Crime Surveys used the electoral register (see pp. 329–30 for details of these surveys). Pat Mayhew (quoted in McNeill, 1988), the Principal Research Officer responsible for the Surveys, admitted that the most comprehensive sampling frame was not the electoral register, but the Postcode Address File. Mayhew noted that the electoral register did not include many people in institutions (such as mental hospitals and prisons), who may be particularly prone to being the victims of crime.

Later British Crime Surveys did start using the Postcode Address File. However, even that is not perfect. A sample using this as a sampling frame would be likely to under-represent the homeless. Furthermore, researchers usually rely upon the 'Small User File' of the Postcode Address File and this excludes addresses which normally receive twenty-five or more items of mail per day. As Sara Arber (1993) points out, a few households which receive unusually large volumes of mail will not be included in samples using this sampling frame.

One government study, the census, avoids the problems of sampling by studying all, or very nearly all, members of the population. By law every household in Britain has to complete a census form, although some individuals (including many of the homeless) may slip through the net.

Sociologists lack the resources to carry out such comprehensive studies as the census, and so they usually try to select a sample that contains the same proportions of people with relevant characteristics as are present in the

population under consideration. If that population contains 60 per cent women and 40 per cent men, then the sample should contain 60 per cent women and 40 per cent men. Other important characteristics such as age, occupation, ethnic origin and religion are often taken into account by researchers as they select their sample.

Other, more specialized factors may be taken into account, depending upon the nature of the research. Opinion polls on voting intentions usually use a sample from a variety of constituencies chosen according to the share of the vote won by the major parties in those constituencies at the previous election. Thus a number of 'safe' Labour, 'safe' Conservative and more marginal seats would be included. Clearly, the results would be distorted if the sample was chosen entirely from safe Labour seats.

In a study of education the researcher might wish to select the sample so as to ensure that the types of schools attended by those in the sample reflect the proportions in the population as a whole.

If sampling has been carried out satisfactorily, researchers should be able to **generalize** on the basis of the results. This means that they should be able to make statements about the whole population without having conducted research into every member of that population. For example, opinion pollsters often claim to be able to predict the results of an election in Britain to within a couple of percentage points on the basis of a sample of perhaps one or two thousand people.

Different methods of producing a sample will now be examined.

Types of sampling

Random and systematic sampling

This is the simplest way to select a large sample. Using **random sampling** the researcher ensures that each sample unit has an equal chance of being chosen to take part in the research. This is often achieved by assigning numbers to each sample unit and selecting members of the sample by using a random number table. The nearest everyday equivalent to this is picking numbers out of a hat.

A less time-consuming, though slightly less random, method is to select, say, every tenth or twentieth number on a list. Since this method is not truly random it is known as **systematic sampling**.

Random sampling is not ideal. It relies on statistical probability to ensure the representativeness of the sample. In simple terms, it is based upon the so-called 'law of averages', and a relatively large sample is needed for the researcher to be confident that the sample will be genuinely representative. Researchers therefore generally prefer to use the method we will discuss next: stratified random sampling.

Stratified random sampling

Stratified random sampling involves the division of the sampling frame into groups in order to ensure that the sample is representative. The researcher identifies the important variables that need to be controlled and allocates the sampling units to different groups according to these variables.

For example, the researcher might identify gender and class as important variables. In this case the population would be divided into working-class males, working-class females, middle-class males, middle-class females, upper-class males and upper-class females. The sample would then be selected at random from each of these groups, ensuring that the proportions of the sample in each category were the same as the proportions in the population as a whole. If 20 per cent of the population were found to be working-class females, 20 per cent of the sample would be working-class females.

This is an effective method of choosing a representative sample because it allows the researcher to control the variables that are seen as important. It requires a smaller sample size to ensure representativeness than random sampling. However, stratified random sampling is often not practicable. Even if a sampling frame is available, it often does not contain the information necessary to divide the population into groups. Opinion pollsters can use the electoral register as a sampling frame, but it does not provide information such as the occupations of the electorate. For this reason it cannot be used to produce a stratified random sample.

Quota sampling

Quota sampling allows researchers to control variables without having a sampling frame. When quota sampling is used, the interviewers are told how many respondents with particular characteristics to question, so that the overall sample reflects the characteristics of the population as a whole. For example, an interviewer might be required to administer a questionnaire to ten married females and ten married males aged between 20 and 35, five unmarried men and women of the same age group and so on. Once the quota for a particular category has been filled, responses will not be collected from people in that category.

This is a particularly useful method of sampling when the overall proportions of different groups within a population are known. Government population statistics could be used to set the quota for a representative sample of different age groups in the British population. As Sara Arber (1993) points out, it is also generally quicker and cheaper than using random sampling. There is no need to revisit those chosen in your sample if they are not available on the first visit. If someone refuses to cooperate, you can simply find someone else with the same characteristics. When speed is of the essence – for example, if you want to conduct an opinion poll on voting on the day of an election – then quota sampling may be the only practical option.

Despite the simplicity of quota sampling, it does have both theoretical and practical drawbacks in some circumstances.

Quota sampling is not truly random because each person within the population does not have an equal chance of being chosen. For example, a researcher stopping people on a particular street at a particular time can only question people who happen to be in that place at that time. The lack of genuine randomness may distort the results. For example, a researcher for a political opinion poll who questions people at 11 o'clock on Tuesday morning in a city centre would be unlikely to gain much response from those who work in the surrounding rural area.

Stopping people in the street may lead to a low response rate. Many people may refuse to cooperate, and those who do cooperate might be untypical of the population as a whole in a way that was not anticipated when the original quotas were set up. Julia Davidson says:

> *the people who are interviewed are those who are available and on the streets at the time of the fieldwork, and those who agree to form a volunteer sample might be those who have a particular interest in the topic or hold especially strong views about it. They are a self-selected sample and there is no way of knowing if their views are representative.* Davidson, 2006, p. 197

Quota sampling usually requires the researcher to ask a number of personal questions to determine whether the respondent has the characteristics of a quota group on which information is required. Asking such questions at the start of an interview might put some interviewees off, and put others on their guard, so that their responses are not as open and honest as they might otherwise have been.

Furthermore, practical problems can arise in filling quotas. For example, it can be difficult to fill quotas consisting of people from minority groups, such as religious sects or small minority ethnic groups.

Despite these limitations quota sampling continues to be used because there are circumstances when random or stratified random sampling is not possible.

Multi-stage sampling

Multi-stage sampling can save the researcher time and money, although it reduces the extent to which the sample is genuinely random. It simply involves selecting a sample from another sample. It is often used in opinion polls on voting intentions. As Alan Aldridge and Ken Levine (2001) point out, it saves time and money where there is 'a very large, perhaps national, target population'.

In the first stage, a few constituencies, which, on the basis of previous research, appear to represent a cross-section of all constituencies, are selected. Some rural and some urban constituencies would be included and previous election results would be used to check that the constituencies selected are a reasonable mixture in terms of party support. In the second stage, individual respondents are chosen from within these constituencies.

If multi-stage sampling was not used in this sort of research, opinion poll organizations would incur the prohibitive expense of sending researchers to every constituency in the country, to interview a mere three or four people in each to get an overall sample of 2,000. However, in multi-stage sampling the loss of randomness may be accompanied by an increase in sampling error.

Snowballing

Snowballing is a very specialized type of sampling and is usually only used when other methods are not practical. It involves using personal contacts to build up a sample of the group to be studied. Aldridge and Levine (2001) argue that this type of sampling is most appropriate where there is no sampling frame, where examples of the people to be studied are rare or widely spread, and where the people of interest are likely to know each other and they will help the researcher find more contacts. For example, it was used by Laurie Taylor (1984) when he persuaded John McVicar, a former criminal, to obtain introductions to members of the London underworld of professional crime. Taylor then used these contacts to obtain introductions to more criminals.

Clearly, such samples cannot be representative since, to have any chance of being included, those studied must be part of a network of personal contacts. But for groups such as professional criminals it is not easy to use other ways of obtaining a sample.

Non-representative sampling

Sociologists do not always try to obtain representative cross-sections of the population they wish to study. According to Bryman (2001), the use of convenience samples is common in social research. He defines a **convenience sample** as 'one that is simply available to the researcher by virtue of its accessibility'. It is thus chosen entirely for practical reasons and can have no claims to being representative. However, there are sometimes theoretical reasons for choosing a deliberately non-representative sample. A non-representative sample is sometimes referred to as a **purposive sample** – it is chosen for a particular purpose.

In terms of Popper's views of science (see p. 790), researchers should try to disprove or falsify their theories. This means looking for untypical examples of a phenomenon which do not fit a particular theory. For example, in examining the view that differences in the behaviour of men and women are primarily shaped by biological rather than cultural differences, sociologists such as Ann Oakley have tried to find untypical examples of human behaviour (see p. 97). Feminist sociologists claim to have falsified the biological arguments about the behaviour of men and women by finding examples of societies in which women behave in ways more usually associated with men and vice versa. (For examples, see pp. 92–100.)

Goldthorpe *et al.*'s rejection of the embourgeoisement hypothesis (see pp. 58–9) provides an interesting example of the use of a non-representative sample (Goldthorpe *et al.*, 1968a, 1968b, 1969). The embourgeoisement hypothesis stated that large numbers of affluent workers were becoming middle-class as a result of their rising living standards. On the basis of available evidence, Goldthorpe *et al.* doubted this claim.

To test the embourgeoisement hypothesis Goldthorpe *et al.* selected a sample from the most affluent manual workers. If any manual workers were becoming middle-class, it would be members of this 'untypical' group. The research results showed little or no evidence of embourgeoisement. Having chosen the group most likely to confirm the hypothesis, Goldthorpe *et al.* felt confident in rejecting the theory of embourgeoisement.

Fiona Devine (1992, 1994) used a sample of similar workers in a later study of Luton workers which examined how far the working class had changed in the intervening period (see pp. 59–60).

Some sociologists have argued that it is important to study the best-informed members of social groups rather

than a cross-section of a group. Thus, the interactionist Herbert Blumer thought that you should seek and question the most acute observers of a group or aspect of social life, since 'a small number of such individuals, brought together as a discussion group, is more valuable many times over than any representative sample' (Blumer, 1969).

Case studies and life histories

Case studies

In general, case studies make no claims to be representative. A **case study** involves the detailed examination of a single example of something and is therefore bound to lack external validity. Thus a case study could involve the study of a single institution, community or social group, an individual person, a particular historical event, or a single social action.

Howard Becker (1970) has described one aim of case studies as the attempt 'to arrive at a comprehensive understanding of the group under study'. Ken Pryce's (1979) participant observation study of a single West Indian community in the St Paul's area of Bristol attempted, at one level, simply to understand that particular community. Shane Blackman (1997) conducted a detailed ethnographic study of the homeless in Brighton in order to understand how that group experienced and saw the social world; and Naomi Klein (2000) carried out case study research in a free-trade zone to examine how multinational corporations treated the workers manufacturing their products.

However, case studies can be used, as Becker claims, 'to develop more general theoretical statements about regularities in social structure and process'. As mentioned above, a case study of a particular society can be used to falsify a general theory about social life. Thus Gough's (1959) study of Nayar society showed that family structures based upon a marital bond are not universal (see pp. 460–1). Steve Craine's (1997) study of school leavers in Manchester was able to falsify the belief of some theorists that an underclass culture was passed down from generation to generation (see pp. 245–7).

Case studies can also be used to produce **typologies**, or a set of categories defining types of a social phenomenon. Douglas (1967) suggested that case studies could be used to discover the different types of suicide by uncovering the different social meanings of suicide.

Case studies may be useful for generating new hypotheses which can then be tested against other data or in later studies. Paul Willis's (1977) study of a single school produced a number of hypotheses about the relationship between education and capitalist societies, which have proved to be a useful focus for research and the development of theories by other sociologists of education (see pp. 605–8). Dick Hobbs and Colin Dunningham (1998) used their case studies of individuals involved in organized crime to develop hypotheses about changes in the nature of local and global relationships in criminal networks (see pp. 358–9).

Bryman (2001) suggests that sometimes case studies can be seen as 'intensive analysis' where the 'quality of the theoretical reasoning' is more important than the representativeness of the sample.

A useful way of thinking about the benefits of using case studies is provided by Yin's distinction between different sorts of case study (Yin, 1984, discussed in Bryman, 2001). Yin distinguished between:

1. The **critical case**, where a particular example is useful for testing a hypothesis. Bryman quotes an example of a study of a religious cult which examined how members reacted when the world failed to end on the day predicted by their religion (Festinger *et al.*, 1956, discussed in Bryman, 2001).
2. The **unique case**, where there is only one known example of something. For example, Margaret Mead carried out research in Samoa, where she believed that gender relations were unlike those of all other societies.
3. The **revelatory case**, where the researcher can gain access to an aspect of social life which was previously inaccessible. Research by Eliot Liebow (1967) into unemployed black people in the USA (see p. 241) has been seen as revelatory case study research, and Eileen Barker's (1984) research into the religious sect of the 'Moonies' could be seen in the same light (see p. 846).

A major drawback of case study research is that it is not possible to generalize on the basis of its findings. It is impossible to determine how far the findings of a study into one example of a social phenomenon can be applied to other examples.

Alan Bryman (1988) suggests that one way to overcome this problem is to carry out or use a number of case studies of the same type of phenomenon. For example, Shoshana Zuboff (1988) carried out case study research in eight organizations in order to try to make generalizations about the impact of information technology. The Kendal Project (Heelas *et al.*, 2005) incorporated three case studies of different types of alternative spirituality so that some generalizations could be made about the types of practices and beliefs common within the 'holistic milieu' (see pp. 444–5).

However, as Bryman (2001) points out, it may be difficult to make direct comparisons of the results of studies carried out either by different people, or by the same person at different times. The data are likely to be more systematic if a single researcher, or group, collects data on a number of social groups at the same time. However, if this is done, the research ceases to be a case study as such.

Life histories

Life histories are a particular type of case study – the whole study concerns one individual's life. They can be carried out using a variety of methods, but most frequently use extended, unstructured interviews. Some life histories make considerable use of personal documents. The following are some examples: a study of the life of a Polish peasant conducted by Thomas and Znaniecki; Gordon Allport's 'Letters from Jenny', a study of an ageing woman; and Robert Bogdan's study of Jane Fry, a transsexual. (All of these examples are discussed in Plummer, 1982.)

Like case studies, life histories, by their very nature, use an untypical sample. However, Ken Plummer argues that they have a number of uses and can be of considerable value in developing sociological theory.

Plummer suggests that life histories can be used as a 'sensitizing tool'. They can help the researcher develop an understanding of the meaning of concepts used by those she or he is studying. The 'rich detail' of life-history data can help cut through the 'dense jargon' that makes so much theoretical sociology difficult to comprehend. The life history allows the researcher to see the world from the social actor's point of view. This viewpoint is one that may challenge the assumptions and preconceptions of outsiders. For example, Plummer claims that Bogdan's study shows how transsexualism can seem a rational and reasonable choice from the actor's point of view, rather than a sickness, as it appears to be to some psychiatrists.

Like case studies in general, life histories can be used to falsify existing theories or to inspire new ones. A number of life histories can be used together to develop a theory, test it and refine it, and then test it again. Plummer refers to this theoretical approach as 'analytic induction'. The first life history allows the researcher to make preliminary hypotheses. These can be tested in subsequent life-history research. Where the hypotheses are found wanting, they can be modified to fit the extra cases. As research proceeds, the sociologist develops increasingly useful theories and generalizations. (This approach is similar to the 'grounded theory' advocated by Glaser and Strauss, 1967: see p. 835 for further details.)

Some feminist researchers argue that life-history research is useful for helping women to understand their situation, and, once they have understood, helping them to change it. Thus Maria Mies (1993) found that discussing life histories with female victims of violence helped the women to understand 'that their own experience of violence was not just their individual bad luck, or even their fault, but there is an objective social basis for this private violence by men against women and children'.

For critical researchers generally, life-history research can help to raise people's consciousness and awareness of their own exploitation by encouraging them to reflect upon the factors that have shaped their life experiences.

Life histories also have their place in postmodern research. With their emphasis on the fluidity of social life and variations in people's experiences, postmodernists tend to be interested in studying the lives of individuals. A good example is the research of Judith Stacey (1996) into the lives of 'Pam' and 'Dotty' (see pp. 517–19).

Recently, there have been some studies which use the life-history approach but involve the study of several lives rather than just one. For example, C. Squire (2000) used the life histories of thirty-four people who were HIV-positive to study people's experiences of living with HIV.

Pilot studies

Having selected a research method and chosen a method of selecting a sample, some sociologists carry out a pilot study before embarking upon the main research project. A **pilot study** is a small-scale preliminary study conducted before the main research in order to check the feasibility or to improve the design of the research. Pilot studies are not usually appropriate for case studies, but they are frequently carried out before large-scale quantitative research in an attempt to avoid time and money being wasted on an inadequately designed project.

A pilot study is usually carried out on members of the relevant population, but not on those who will form part of the final sample. This is because it might influence the later behaviour of research subjects if they had already been involved in the research.

Pilot studies can be useful for a number of reasons:

1. If interviews or questionnaires are to be used, the questions can be tested to make sure that they make sense to respondents – that is, they produce the sort of information required and are unambiguous. Pilot studies were carried out in the ESRC's *Social Change and Economic Life Initiative* study (which studied social change in six British local labour markets). They were used for 'testing questionnaire items, the placing of the work history schedule, interview length, and the contact procedure' (Gallie, 1994b). The researchers believed that this helped them to improve the reliability and response rate of their research.
2. Pilot studies may help researchers develop ways of getting the full cooperation of those they are studying. In a pilot study for her research into housebound mothers, Hannah Gavron (1966) found it was necessary to establish a rapport with the respondent if she was to get full, open and honest answers. She therefore spent some time chatting to the respondent informally before starting the interview.
3. Pilot studies may be used to develop the research skills of those taking part. When Rex and Tomlinson (1979) studied immigrants in Birmingham they used their pilot study to train the amateur interviewers they were using. Pilot studies can also 'allow the researcher to determine the adequacy of instructions to interviewers' (Bryman, 2001).
4. The pilot study may determine whether or not the research goes ahead. The researchers might discover insurmountable practical problems which lead to them dropping the project. In some cases a pilot study might be used to convince a funding organization of the usefulness of a particular project. If the pilot study is unsuccessful, the full study may be abandoned.

Social surveys

Social surveys can be defined as research projects which collect standardized data about large numbers of people. Aldridge and Levine (2001) argue that the key characteristic of a survey is 'that we collect the same information about all cases in a sample'.

The data are usually in a statistical form, and the most practical way of collecting such data is through the use of questionnaires, which may or may not be administered by an interviewer. Other types of research method, such as unstructured interviewing or observation, would be less suitable for collecting standardized information about large groups because they would be both time-consuming and difficult to translate into a statistical form.

Stephen Ackroyd and John A. Hughes (1981) distinguished three main types of survey:

1 The **factual survey** is used to collect descriptive information. The government census can be seen as a type of factual survey. This survey method has often been used to collect data on poverty and social exclusion – for example, by David Gordon *et al.* (2000) (see pp. 220–2). Paul Heelas and Linda Woodhead supervised a factual survey which identified the number of organizations and people involved in religious and spiritual activities in Kendal (see pp. 444–5).
2 The **attitude survey** is often carried out by opinion poll organizations. Instead of producing descriptive information about the social world, this type of survey attempts to discover the subjective states of individuals. Many polling organizations collect information about attitudes to political policies and personalities. Information on attitudes is often collected by sociologists interested in voting – for example, Evans *et al.* (1999) (see pp. 582–3). Sociologists who study stratification, such as Marshall *et al.* (1988), sometimes collect data on attitudes in order to examine the issue of class consciousness (see p. 60 for further details).
3 The **explanatory survey** is more ambitious than the other types, since it goes beyond description and tries to test theories and hypotheses or to produce new theories. Most sociological surveys contain some explanatory element. Marshall *et al.* (1988), for example, tested the theory that routine white-collar workers had become proletarianized (see p. 52).

Surveys such as that carried out by Townsend into poverty (see pp. 217–18) are designed to be both descriptive and explanatory. Townsend used survey data both to measure the extent of poverty and to develop theories to explain it (Townsend, 1979, 1993; Townsend *et al.*, 1987).

Researchers usually want to be able to generalize from social surveys, and so surveys are based on carefully selected samples. The success of any survey depends ultimately on the quality of the data it produces. Most social surveys use questionnaires as a means of data collection. The advantages and disadvantages of this method and the reliability and validity of the data it produces will now be examined.

Questionnaires

A **questionnaire** consists simply of a list of pre-set questions. In questionnaire research the same questions are usually given to respondents in the same order so that the same information can be collected from every member of the sample.

Administering questionnaires

Questionnaires may be administered in a number of ways. Often they are given to individuals by interviewers, in which case they take the form of structured interviews. This method was used by Gordon Marshall and colleagues in their study of class (Marshall *et al.*, 1988). and in the ESRC's *Social Change and Economic Life Initiative* (Scott, 1994) (see above).

Structured interviews have the advantage of having a trained interviewer on hand to make sure that the questionnaire is completed according to the instructions and to clarify any ambiguous questions. But questionnaires administered by interviewers involve the problem of **interviewer bias**. This means that the responses given are influenced by the presence of the researcher. (See pp. 829–30 for a discussion of interviewer bias.) In addition, this method is expensive compared to the following alternatives.

The **postal questionnaire**, as its name suggests, is mailed to respondents with a stamped addressed envelope for return to the researcher. It provides an inexpensive way of gathering data, especially if respondents are dispersed over a wide geographical area. The return rate, though, does not often exceed 50 per cent of the sample population and is sometimes below 25 per cent. This may seriously bias the results, since there may be systematic differences between those who return questionnaires and those who do not. For example, the main response to a postal questionnaire on marital relationships might come from those experiencing marital problems and wishing to air their grievances. If most non-respondents were happily married, the researcher would be unjustified in making generalizations about married life on the basis of the returned questionnaires.

A second method, and one that obtains a far higher return rate, is to administer the questionnaire to a group, such as a class of students or workers at a union meeting. This method is less expensive than dealing with individual respondents, while maintaining the advantages of the presence of an interviewer. However, the interviewer must ensure that respondents do not discuss questions within the group, since this might affect their answers.

A third way of administering a questionnaire is to ask the questions over the telephone. This is often done by market research firms or marketing departments of companies, but it is not usually regarded as satisfactory by sociologists. As Aldridge and Levine (2001) point out, it is hard to establish rapport in such interviews, disadvantaged groups tend to be under-represented in samples, it is difficult to ask sensitive questions, respondents cannot be expected to remember a wide range of possible answers to fixed-choice questions, and visual aids cannot be used. Furthermore, the response rate may be low because many people associate telephone questionnaires with marketing and this makes them unwilling to cooperate.

A fourth possibility is to administer questionnaires by e-mail. Geoff Payne and Judy Payne (2004) suggest that this may be a useful way of contacting dispersed groups of people, or those who might not wish to be questioned face-to-face. It has been used, for example, in a study of people who commit self-harm. On the other hand, a problem of this method is that genuine anonymity is difficult to assure since it is possible to track the source of an e-mailed response. The biggest problem may be that the sample is restricted to those with access to computers and may therefore be unrepresentative, although the significance of this will diminish as the number of people without e-mail and internet access falls.

Producing questionnaires and analysing the data

Questionnaires tend to be used to produce quantitative data. Sometimes researchers may not have very clear hypotheses and will ask a wide range of questions on a topic. However, they must have some idea of what factors are important or interesting before they can start to construct a questionnaire.

In the process of choosing questions, researchers have to **operationalize** concepts. In other words, abstract concepts have to be translated into concrete questions which make it possible to take measurements relating to those concepts.

Sociologists classify the social world in terms of a variety of concepts. For instance, social class, power, family, religion, alienation and anomie are concepts used to identify and categorize social relationships, beliefs, attitudes and experiences which are seen to have certain characteristics in common. In order to transpose these rather vague concepts into measuring instruments, a number of steps are taken.

First, an **operational definition** is established. This involves breaking the concept down into various **components** or **dimensions** in order to specify exactly what is to be measured. Thus, when Gordon Marshall and colleagues (1988) operationalized the concept of class, they adopted the definitions of class categories used by E.O. Wright and John Goldthorpe.

Once the concept has been operationally defined in terms of a number of components, the second step involves the selection of **indicators** for each component. For example, in measuring class consciousness Marshall *et al.* (1988) collected questionnaire data on aspects of class consciousness such as whether respondents identified themselves as being members of a class, whether they believed class was still important and whether they believed inequality was too great in Britain (see p. 63).

Third, indicators of each dimension are put into the form of a series of questions that will provide quantifiable data for measuring each dimension. Thus indicators of class consciousness became questions such as 'Do you think the distribution of income and wealth is a fair one?' and 'Do you think there are any important issues which cause conflicts between those who run industry and those who work for them?' (Marshall *et al.*, 1988).

Researchers have a number of choices to make during the process of operationalizing concepts in questionnaires. First they have to decide what form of question to ask.

Questions may be open-ended, such as: 'Under what circumstances do you think a person could move from one class to another?' **Open-ended** questions allow the respondents to compose their own answers rather than choosing between a number of given answers. This may be more likely to provide valid data, since respondents can say what they mean in their own words. However, this kind of response might be difficult to classify and quantify. Answers must be interpreted carefully before the researcher is able to say, for example, that a certain percentage of respondents attribute good industrial relations to effective management, an efficient union, high pay, or something else.

A second type of question, sometimes known as a **closed** or **fixed-choice** question, requires a choice between a number of given answers. For example, the following question was asked in a survey of white people in Britain:

If a close relative were to marry an ethnic minority person most white people:

Would not mind
Would mind a little
Would mind very much
Can't say

Modood *et al.*, 1997

Sometimes the respondent is asked to choose between two stated alternatives. For example:

In the past there was a dominant class which largely controlled the economic and political system, and a lower class which had no control over economic or political affairs. Some people say that things are still like this, others say it has now changed. What do you think? Has it changed, or stayed the same? Marshall et *al.*, 1988

A similar type of question requires the respondent to agree or disagree with a particular statement. For example:

A number of ideas have been put forward in order to overcome Britain's economic problems. (For each one indicate whether you agree or disagree.)

a. Leaving it to market forces to revive the economy.
b. Income policies which increase the wages of the low paid rather than the high paid.
c. Increasing income tax in order to increase welfare benefits.
d. Import controls to protect Britain from competition from abroad.
e. Increased taxes on the profits of successful companies in order to maintain jobs in declining industries.
f. Increased government spending to revive the economy.

Marshall et *al.*, 1988

Such questions often employ a **Likert scale** (Aldridge and Levine, 2001), where respondents are given a range of options from 'Strongly agree' to 'Strongly disagree'.

Compared to the open-ended type, fixed-choice questions provide responses that can be more easily classified and quantified. It requires relatively little time, effort and ingenuity to arrive at statements describing the percentages of respondents who gave different answers.

However, fixed-choice questions do not allow the respondent to qualify and develop their answers. It is therefore difficult for researchers to know exactly what they are measuring. For example, when respondents agree that there are issues which divide management and workers, it is not clear what the respondents think those issues are. They might be quite different from the sorts of issues the researchers think might be divisive. Other questions can be added to clarify what respondents mean, but some sociologists would argue that in-depth, unstructured interviews would be better than structured ones for determining the extent and strength of class consciousness.

If open-ended questions are used, and the researcher wants the data to be in a statistical form, it becomes necessary to code the answers. **Coding** involves identifying a number of categories into which answers can be placed. The researcher usually examines the answers given and establishes the principal types of answer that have

been provided. Thus, in the British Crime Survey of 1998, the answers to an open-ended question on the reasons why people had not reported crimes were put into classifications such as: 'Too trivial', 'Police couldn't do anything', 'Dealt with ourselves', 'Dislike/fear of police', 'Inconvenient to report', 'Police would not be interested', 'Fear of reprisal', 'Reported to other authorities' and 'Other answers' (Mirrlees-Black *et al.*, 1998).

Once the data have been collected and classified, it is necessary to analyse them. In an explanatory survey this often involves using multivariate analysis to determine the relationships between the variables. For example, Leon Feinstein (2003) tried to measure the relative importance of parents' jobs, and the amount of interest parents took in their children's education, in determining the children's educational performance (see p. 630).

Questionnaires are often designed to test a particular hypothesis. Marshall *et al.* (1988) used them to test various theories of stratification. In such cases the data are analysed in relation to the hypotheses that are being tested. The analysis of data from descriptive or attitude surveys is often more straightforward. Sometimes it involves little more than statements about the percentages of respondents who gave particular replies.

The advantages of questionnaires

Questionnaire research is certainly a practical way to collect data. Although designing the questionnaire and carrying out pilot studies may take some time, once this has been done questionnaires can be used to collect large quantities of data from considerable numbers of people over a relatively short period of time. Thus Gordon *et al.* (2000), in their study of poverty, used a sample of 1,534 people (see pp. 220–2 for further details), while the British Crime Survey of 2005–6 (see pp. 329–30) used a sample of some 49,000 households (Grant *et al.*, 2006). Such large samples cannot be studied using more in-depth research methods without incurring prohibitive costs.

Even when questionnaires are administered by interviewers this involves relatively little personal involvement, or danger or sacrifice on the part of the researcher, when compared with some participant observation studies. The results of questionnaire research can be relatively easily quantified, and with the assistance of computers the data can be analysed quickly and efficiently. Using computers, the relationships between many different variables can be examined. Many sociological and other social science researchers use the *Statistical Package for Social Sciences* computer programme, which can rapidly produce complex statistical analyses.

To some quantitative researchers, however, the theoretical advantages are more important than the practical ones. Although relatively few sociologists today claim to be positivists, a considerable number support the use of quantitative data on the grounds that it can be analysed more 'scientifically' and objectively than qualitative data. Quantitative data can be considered more reliable than qualitative data. Since each individual respondent answers precisely the same questions in the same order, they are all responding to the same stimuli. Any differences in response should, in theory, reflect real differences between respondents. Furthermore, the figures produced can be checked by other researchers, and their reliability should therefore be high.

Only when the data are quantified by means of reliable measuring instruments can the results of different studies be directly compared. Thus studies of British elections over several decades have produced data that can be used to determine changing patterns of voting and changing social attitudes within the British electorate. Sanders *et al.* (2005), in their study of the 2005 British election, were able to use data from their own and other election studies to reveal changes in voting behaviour (see p. 582).

From a positivist point of view, statistical data from questionnaires can be analysed so that new theories can be produced. More typically, however, such data are used to test existing hypotheses, since the researcher must have a reasonably clear idea of the sort of information that is important before they set the questions. Whether questionnaires are used inductively (as in the former case) or deductively (as in the latter), they can be used to try to establish causal relationships through multivariate analysis. Many sociologists regard questionnaires as a suitable method for testing precise hypotheses in a rigorous manner: for example, Marshall *et al.* (1988) used questionnaire data to back up their claim that they had falsified the proletarianization thesis (see p. 52).

As has already been mentioned, questionnaire research can generally use larger samples than qualitative methods. For this reason, sociologists who have carried out a social survey tend to feel more justified in generalizing about a wider population than those who have carried out an in-depth study of a smaller number of people. This is particularly likely where a questionnaire is used in conjunction with sophisticated sampling techniques so that the researcher can be confident that the sample is representative. Researchers into such areas of social life as poverty, voting, crime and stratification, who have carried out social surveys using questionnaires, have not hesitated to make claims about the British population as a whole, not just those questioned during the research.

Despite the importance of the theoretical points discussed above, questionnaires are not just used by positivists or those who strongly believe in the advantages of quantitative data. In many circumstances they are used when resources are limited and data are needed on large numbers of people. They are particularly useful when straightforward descriptive data are required. However, the validity of the statistical data, particularly when produced for explanatory surveys, has been questioned by some sociologists who advocate a more interpretive, qualitative approach. These criticisms will now be examined.

The disadvantages of questionnaires

Interpretive sociologists vary in their views on survey research and the data it produces. Weber's methodological position implies that such data can be one – but only one – of the types of data required in sociological research. Interactionists often see statistical data as inadequate for producing sociological explanations of human behaviour. Phenomenologists go further, for they see the data produced as an artificial creation of the researcher. Above all, critics argue that, despite the reliability of questionnaire data, it lacks validity. To phenomenologists in particular,

the methodological assumptions on which questionnaires are based are entirely false. They put forward six main objections:

1 It cannot be assumed that different answers to the same question reflect real differences between respondents. However much care is taken with the wording of questions, respondents may interpret them differently. People who choose the same response may not mean the same thing. People who choose different responses may not mean different things. This may result from the wording of questions. For example, the word 'uptight' in low-income black American areas usually refers to a close relationship between friends, but when it entered the vocabulary of mainstream America it changed its meaning to anxious and tense. Even common words and phrases carry different associations for different groups. As Irwin Deutscher (1977) observes: 'Within a society, as well as between societies, the sociologist seeks information from and about people who operate verbally with different vocabularies, different grammars and different kinds of sounds.' Thus a questionnaire, which provides little opportunity to qualify meaning, might not provide comparable data when administered to members of different social groups.

2 In designing the questionnaire researchers assume that they know what is important. Respondents cannot provide information that is not requested, they cannot answer questions that are not asked. For this reason, it is difficult to develop hypotheses during the course of the research and researchers are limited to testing those theories that they have already thought of. This is a form of **researcher imposition** – a situation where researchers impose their own assumptions on research.

3 Questionnaire research involves the operationalization of concepts, and some interpretive sociologists argue that such procedures also involve researcher imposition and consequently produce a distorted picture of the social world. The process of breaking down a concept so that it can be quantified imposes sociological constructs, categories and logic on the social world. Thus, when Blauner sought to measure alienation among workers, he employed a concept which might have had no reality in the social world he sought to understand. Indeed, Blauner (1964) admits: 'It is difficult to interpret a finding that 70 per cent of factory workers report satisfaction with their jobs because we do not know how valid or reliable our measuring instrument is.' The workers were not allowed to reveal their attitudes to their work in their own way. As the phenomenologist Michael Phillipson (1972) observes, 'the instruments of the observer create the very order they are supposedly designed to reveal'.

4 The validity of the data may be reduced by the unwillingness or inability of respondents to give full and accurate replies to questions. Quite simply, respondents may lie. Attempts to check the accuracy of self-report studies on crime (see p. 331) have found that some 20 per cent of respondents do not tell the truth. Even if respondents want to tell the truth they may be unable to do so because of faulty memory or because they lack the relevant information. Thus the British Crime Surveys may have underestimated the amount of unreported crime because victims may have been unaware or may have forgotten that they had been the victims of crime.

Furthermore, even when respondents are honest, and not hampered by ignorance or forgetfulness, there are some types of questions where the validity of the answers can still be queried. This is particularly true of questions about attitudes. It cannot be assumed that stated attitudes will be translated into actual behaviour.

For instance, in the 1930s La Pierre (1934) travelled to 251 establishments – such as restaurants, hotels and campsites – in the USA with two Chinese people. They were refused service or accommodation at only one of these places, yet when the same establishments were sent a questionnaire a few months later, only one said they would accept Chinese customers.

When observation or participant observation is used, the researcher relies less on respondents' accounts and may therefore have more chance of producing valid data.

5 A fifth reason for doubting the validity of questionnaire data is the distance maintained between the researcher and the subject of the research, particularly in the case of postal questionnaires. As Alan Bryman puts it:

> *The quantitative researcher adopts the posture of an outsider looking in on the social world. He or she applies a preordained framework on the subjects being investigated and is involved as little as possible in that world. This posture is the analogue of a detached scientific observer.* Bryman, 1988

To a positivist this approach encourages objectivity, but to an interpretive sociologist it precludes the possibility of understanding the meanings and motives of the subjects of the research. Unlike participant observation, the researcher does not undergo similar experiences to the subjects of the research, and so cannot draw so easily on experience to understand the behaviour of those being studied. Using questionnaires it is not possible to see how people act and react towards each other, nor is it possible to examine the way in which self-concepts change during the course of interaction. Interactionists in particular do not believe that the researcher can gain genuine insights into the subjective states underlying the behaviour of those being studied unless the researcher gets close to those they are studying.

Some feminists and critical social scientists also object to questionnaire research on similar grounds. They believe it is important to involve the subjects of research in the research process. This has a number of advantages. It allows the subjects to contribute to evaluating the research; it allows the researcher to avoid exploiting them; and it enables the consciousness of exploitation to develop.

For example, Victor Jupp and Clive Norris (1993) comment that critical researchers in criminology

have a 'theoretical and political aversion to the highly formal quantitative and positivist approaches of conventional criminology'. They associate such methods with using data to control criminals and deviants, whereas their aims are more directed at liberating people from the controls which restrict them. They see this as better achieved through methods which are 'qualitative, naturalistic and non-positivist and include life-history and other informal interviews, observational methods, especially participant observation, case studies and social history research'.

6 Finally, when open-ended questions are used, and the researcher requires quantitative data, coding of answers will take place. As in the operationalization of concepts, this involves researchers imposing their own order on the data. The differences in the precise answers given to questions are glossed over, as answers which are not identical are placed together in a single category. This process obscures the differences that exist between the answers.

Questionnaire research – conclusions

Despite the strength of these criticisms, most sociologists accept that there is a place for survey research in sociology. After all, there would be little point in carrying out participant observation or in-depth interviewing to discover the percentages of males and females who watched television every evening.

Furthermore, even some feminists believe that quantitative questionnaire research has its uses. For example, Toby Epstein Jayaratne (1993) points out that quantitative research, such as that which uses questionnaires, has been useful in documenting the extent of sexism in certain institutions. The critical social scientist Lee Harvey (1990) sees some questionnaire research (such as that undertaken by Goldthorpe *et al.*) as falling within the tradition of critical research.

It is usually when statistical data from questionnaires are used to try to establish causal relationships that opponents of quantitative research become most concerned about the validity of the data being used. However, such research does often provide useful data on social structures which may shape behaviour without individuals being aware of it. Thus studies of social class and social mobility produce findings about people's life chances which could not be produced using other methods (see pp. 75–82 for examples). When used alongside qualitative methods, questionnaire research can certainly make a crucial contribution towards developing as full a picture as possible of social life.

Interviews

Types of interview

Interviews take a number of forms, depending upon how structured they are. A completely **structured interview** is simply a questionnaire administered by an interviewer who is not allowed to deviate in any way from the questions provided. The interviewer simply reads out the questions to the respondent. At the other extreme, a totally **unstructured interview** takes the form of a conversation where the interviewer has no predetermined questions. Most interviews fall somewhere between these two extremes.

Interviews of a more structured type may allow the interviewer to probe the respondents' answers so that they can, if necessary, be clarified. The interviewer may also be allowed to prompt the interviewee, that is, give them extra guidance to help them answer the question. Goldthorpe *et al.*'s team of researchers were able to prompt interviewees who could not decide how to answer a question about whether they had actively done anything to find a different job, by suggesting that they might have read job adverts in local newspapers (Goldthorpe *et al.*, 1968a).

In more unstructured interviews the conversation develops naturally, unless the respondent fails to cover an area in which the researcher is interested. Eventually the interviewer will direct the conversation back to the areas he or she wishes to cover. Marjorie DeVault, for example, in her study *Feeding the Family* (1991), had some questions which she made sure every interviewee answered, but she also allowed them to talk freely around one general question. She told them that she wanted to talk about 'all the housework that has to do with food: cooking, planning, shopping, cleaning up'.

Some interviewers have a schedule of topics they wish to cover and they make sure that at some point the conversation comes back to these topics.

Some feminist researchers, such as Ann Oakley, are advocates of very unstructured interviews in which the researcher and person being interviewed become collaborators in the research and sometimes friends (see pp. 809–10). Critical social researchers also usually prefer unstructured interviewing.

As highly structured interviews are very similar to questionnaires, the rest of this discussion of interviews will concentrate on interviews of a less structured variety.

Interviewing styles

Having a conversation with somebody is extremely common in human interaction, and it might be thought that interviewing requires no special preparation. However, the sociological researcher needs to overcome the problems of making contact with – and gaining the cooperation of – respondents. Having made contact, and persuaded a person to take part in the interview, the researcher then needs to try to ensure that the respondent gives full, honest and open answers.

Interviewers use a variety of methods to make contact with respondents. They may telephone in advance, write letters or turn up at interviewees' houses. At the initial point of contact it is important that the interviewers establish why they wish to carry out the interview and what the information is to be used for. They may also need to explain how the interviewee was selected and why they are suitable for research.

The most common way of conducting interviews is to be **non-directive**: to refrain from offering opinions, to avoid expressions of approval and disapproval. Often an interviewer will spend some time trying to establish rapport or understanding between themselves and the

interviewee. They may do this simply by talking informally before the interview proper starts. Once the interviewee feels that they are not going to be criticized or judged, that they can talk freely and can rely upon a sympathetic audience, it is hoped that they will talk with honesty and openness. Since the respondent does not have to answer the questions (and since they may be asked about private or personal aspects of their lives which they would not usually discuss with a stranger), it is often argued that non-directive interviewing is the most effective type of interviewing.

In contrast, Howard Becker (1970) suggests that interviewers may be inhibited by adopting this relatively passive approach and a 'bland, polite style of conversation'. He suggests that on certain occasions a more active and aggressive approach can provide much fuller data. This involves the interviewer taking 'positions on some issues' and using 'more aggressive conversational tactics'.

Becker adopted these tactics in his interviews with Chicago school teachers. He claims that American school teachers believe they have a lot to hide from what they regard as a 'prying, misunderstanding, and potentially dangerous public'. They are therefore unlikely to volunteer certain information. By adopting an aggressive stance, being sceptical, and at times even pretending to be stupid, Becker managed to prise out much of this information. In particular, he claimed to have uncovered the ways that teachers categorized and evaluated students in terms of their class and ethnic backgrounds – information they would have preferred to have kept hidden for fear of being accused of prejudice and discrimination. Becker states: 'I coerced many interviewees into being considerably more frank than they had originally intended.'

Becker suggests this approach is particularly useful for one-off interviews. Similar information can be picked up more subtly over a series of interviews without running the risk of antagonizing respondents. The apparent success of Becker's rather unorthodox tactics suggests there is no one best way of interviewing.

Some sociologists who, like Becker, reject non-directive interviewing believe that interviewers should be empathetic towards interviewees rather than aggressive. Thus the feminist researcher Ann Oakley (1981), in her study of childbirth and childcare, became closely involved with the women she was studying. She advised them and sometimes even gave them help, and she encouraged them to become actively involved in the research process (see pp. 809–10 for details).

Individual and group interviews and focus groups

It is normal for a single interviewer to interview a single respondent. This has a number of advantages. It may be easier to establish rapport, confidentiality can be ensured, and the respondent is not distracted or influenced by the presence of other interviewees. In some circumstances, though, sociologists have carried out group interviews.

For example, Paul Willis (1977), in his study of education, interviewed several of the 'lads' together (see pp. 605–8 for further details). It can be argued that this

Figure 14.3 Paul Willis used group interviews – some question their validity

Source: Getty Images

might be more likely to produce valid data than a one-to-one interview. The lads' activities usually took place in a group context, and a group interview would reflect this. In group interviews Willis was able to observe interaction between the lads, and they felt more at ease than when talking alone to an older and middle-class interviewer.

James Holstein and Jaber Gubrium (1995) argue that group interviews are valuable because they 'allow diverse categorizations and sentiments to emerge, showing how participants flesh out, alter, or reconstruct viewpoints in response to challenges'. They believe that having many voices present (which they call **multivocality**) broadens interviews and can make the participants more reflexive. They think more deeply about their answers and reflect critically upon them in their responses to others.

This view of interviewing is rather different from the view that sees interviews as simply uncovering the facts – as untainted by the interview process as possible. Instead, it sees the interview as an active process in which knowledge is created through interaction. This type of group interview tends, therefore, to be favoured by interactionist, interpretive and critical sociologists.

A similar style of interview – the **focus group** – is also used by political parties who want more in-depth data on public opinion than that provided by opinion polls. Alan Bryman defines a focus group as:

> *a form of group interview in which: there are several participants (in addition to the moderator/facilitator); there is an emphasis in the questioning on a particular fairly tightly defined topic; and the accent is on interaction within the group and the joint construction of meaning.* Bryman, 2001

Bryman comments that this method often leads to greater probing of '*why* people feel the way they do' than is achieved by the individual interview. Furthermore, Bryman believes the focus group fits well with aspects of symbolic interactionist theory. This is because it 'offers the researcher the opportunity to study the ways in which individuals collectively make sense of a phenomenon and construct meaning around it'.

David Morgan (2006) suggests that it can be useful to use this research method with groups of individuals who have a shared interest or area of expertise. They can then stimulate each other to continue the conversation, meaning that intervention by the interviewer is minimized and the research becomes genuinely unstructured.

Similarly, Sue Wilkinson (2004) argues that focus groups are more 'naturalistic' – closer to real social life – than one-to-one interviews. They are useful for interviewers who wish to get used to the normal, everyday way of talking of members of groups who may talk very differently from themselves.

According to Wilkinson, some feminists believe that focus groups are more egalitarian than one-to-one interviews. They are less dominated by the interviewer and therefore more in keeping with feminist ethics. Wilkinson concludes that:

> *Focus groups are a method of choice when the objective of the research is primarily to study talk, either conceptualized as a 'window' on participants' lives or their underlying beliefs and opinions, or as constituting a social context in its own right, amenable to direct observation.* 2004, p. 194

However, Wilkinson believes that focus groups are less useful for making systematic comparisons between social groups.

The advantages of interviews

Whatever format is used, interviews are seen as a useful research method by many different types of sociologist. Although they represent something of a compromise between more structured research methods such as questionnaires and the more in-depth methods such as participant observation, they can be adapted to suit both the practical needs and theoretical preferences of different sociologists.

Those who support the use of more quantitative methods tend to prefer interviews to participant observation. Compared to participant observation, interviews can utilize larger samples, so generalizations are more justified. With some coding of responses it is possible to produce statistical data from interviews, and it is easier to replicate the research and check results. Because there is usually some degree of structure in an interview it is easier to make direct comparisons than it is by using data from participant observation.

To sociologists who prefer more qualitative methods, interviews have clear advantages over questionnaires. The concepts and words used by interviewer and interviewee alike can be clarified; the researchers' concepts are less likely to be imposed on the social world; issues can be explored in greater depth; and the researcher does not limit the responses to fixed choices. For these reasons interviews can be useful for generating new hypotheses and theories which the researcher would not otherwise have thought of.

For example, in Simon Winlow's (2001) study of crime in Sunderland, interviews with some of Sunderland's ageing 'hard men' allowed Winlow to develop novel theories about ways in which crime had changed in the city.

The above arguments, though, do not explain why sociologists should sometimes choose to use interviews in preference to all other research methods. They are not as reliable as questionnaires and they are not likely to produce data as valid as that generated by participant observation.

A major reason for the widespread use of interviews is their sheer practicality. There is no other method which allows access to so many different groups of people and different types of information. As Ackroyd and Hughes put it:

> *Using as data what the respondent says about himself or herself potentially offers the social researcher access to vast storehouses of information. The social researcher is not limited to what he or she can immediately perceive or experience, but is able to cover as many dimensions and as many people as resources permit.* Ackroyd and Hughes, 1981

In short, interviews are more flexible than any other research method. They can be used to extract simple factual information from people. They can be used to ask people about their attitudes, their past, present or future behaviour, their motives, feelings and other emotions that cannot be observed directly. Interviewers can explore each question or issue in as much depth or superficiality as they wish. The range of information available from interviews can be demonstrated from the following examples.

Howard Becker (1963) used interviews to study fifty marijuana smokers. Via interviews he was able to explore the whole of the 'deviant career' of the drug users, from the time they first tried the drug to when they became regular users involved with a subculture of marijuana smokers. Interviewing allowed Becker to discuss the motives and circumstances that led to them trying the drug and continuing to use it.

Interviews are often used to carry out research into groups who might not otherwise consent to being the subject of research. Laurie Taylor (1984) could only produce data about professional crime in Britain because he was able to gain the trust of the criminals he interviewed. Clearly, participant observation would have been out of the question, and he would have been unlikely to have obtained a satisfactory response rate using postal questionnaires. Furthermore, because of Taylor's lack of familiarity with professional criminals he might have had difficulty deciding what questions to ask.

Once again, the flexibility and practicality of interviews are evident. Similar comments are applicable to the studies of criminal networks by Dick Hobbs and Colin Dunningham (1998) (see pp. 358–9), which used life-history interviews with professional criminals connected with one particular locality.

Apart from their practicality, there are some theoretical advantages to interviews compared with other methods.

From the viewpoint of some feminist and critical researchers, interviews allow close collaboration between interviewer and interviewee so that they can become partners in the research.

Interviews allow the opportunity for critical reflection by all those involved, so that they can examine and sometimes change the perspectives through which they see the world. This is important for critical researchers, whose objective is to change the social world. Such opportunities may not always be possible in participant observation studies where the flow of social life limits time for reflection. Some sociologists have gone as far as arguing that the interviewing process itself creates new knowledge rather than just revealing data that was previously present in the interviewees' heads (Holstein and Gubrium, 1995).

The disadvantages of interviews

Stephen Ackroyd and John A. Hughes observed:

> *The foundations of interviewing are to be found in the mundane observation that people can report on what they feel, tell others about aspects of their lives, disclose what their hopes and fears are, offer their opinions, state their beliefs, answer questions about who they see regularly, what they did last week, how much they spend on food, and so on, to put it simply they can impart masses of information about themselves.*
>
> Ackroyd and Hughes, 1981

The problem is that these masses of information may be neither valid nor reliable. Interviews have many of the same drawbacks as questionnaires: the responses given may not be accurate and may not reflect real behaviour. Respondents may lie, may forget, or may lack the information required.

To give a simple example, some of the criminals interviewed by Laurie Taylor (1984) later claimed they had made up fanciful stories about their escapades in order to see how gullible Taylor was.

However, even if respondents are not handicapped by forgetfulness or ignorance, and have no wish to deceive, they may still not give valid answers. As critics of questionnaire data have pointed out, interviewees may not act in accordance with their stated beliefs. When reflecting on past events they may alter their interpretation in the light of subsequent experience. Because interviews are artificial, Cicourel has asked whether they 'capture the daily life, conditions, opinions, values, attitudes, and knowledge base of those we study as expressed in their natural habitat' (quoted in Bryman, 1988).

David Matza's (1964) work on delinquents in the USA can illustrate the sort of problem that arises with interview data (see pp. 377–8 for further details). Matza interviewed 100 delinquents in training school and found that a surprisingly large number of them disapproved of most crimes. Matza concluded that delinquents did not, on the whole, strongly reject society's values. Critics, however, have pointed out that, apart from the question of how truthful the delinquents were, Matza failed to take account of the possibility that they had modified their views as a result of their punishment. At the time of their offences they may have regarded the laws they were breaking contemptuously and only later did they change their minds.

Interviewees may also be influenced by the presence of the researcher. The answers given may be influenced by the way the interviewees define the situation.

William Labov (1973), for instance, found that young black American children responded differently when interviewed in different contexts. Interviewed by a white interviewer in a formal setting, the children said little when asked to describe a toy jet plane. This type of evidence had led some psychologists to conclude that these children were linguistically deprived and that this deprivation contributed to their failure in education. However, Labov produced evidence to show that the apparent linguistic deprivation was the result of interviewing techniques and not a genuine reflection of the children's linguistic ability. When the children were interviewed by a black interviewer in a formal setting they were more forthcoming. When the children sat on the floor with the interviewer, and they were able to bring their best friend with them, they opened up and became fluent and articulate.

Labov argued that when the children defined the situation as hostile they were unable to demonstrate their real abilities. When they defined the situation as friendly they were able to give a much better account of themselves. Clearly, such factors as the age, skin colour, sex, clothing and accent of the interviewer may affect the interviewees' definition of the interview, and so affect their behaviour.

A further problem with unstructured interviews is that there is more opportunity for the interviewer (usually without realizing it) to direct the interviewee towards giving certain types of response. Consciously or unconsciously, respondents might give the sort of answers that they believe the interviewer wants to hear, rather than saying what they truly believe. This problem is known as

interviewer bias. It can never be totally eliminated from interview research, simply because interviews are interaction situations.

Interviewer bias was demonstrated in a study conducted by Stuart A. Rice in 1914 (discussed in Deming, 1971). Two thousand destitute men were asked, among other things, to explain their situation. There was a strong tendency for those interviewed by a supporter of Prohibition to blame their decline on alcohol; but those interviewed by a committed socialist were much more likely to explain their plight in terms of the industrial situation. The interviewers apparently had their own views on the reasons for destitution, which they communicated to the respondents.

In order to conduct an interview successfully and interpret the responses correctly the interviewer must also be aware of the social conventions of those being interviewed. For example, certain activities may be regarded as more 'socially desirable' by members of one group than by members of another. As a result there may be differences between social groups in terms of their members' willingness to admit to particular activities.

The importance of this can be seen from a study conducted by Bruce Dohrenwend in New York to investigate the relationship between mental health and ethnicity (discussed in Phillips, 1971). Respondents were asked whether or not they had experienced a list of symptoms associated with mental illness. Compared with Jews, Irish and blacks, Puerto Ricans reported experiencing more of the symptoms and therefore appeared to have a higher rate of mental illness. Yet Dohrenwend found that the symptoms were regarded as less undesirable by Puerto Ricans than by members of the other ethnic groups. As a result, they were more ready to admit to them. Such findings cast serious doubt on the validity of interview data and therefore on the use to which those data are put.

Interviews – conclusion

In all research methods the procedures used by the researcher influence the sort of data produced. Interviews are no exception. Nigel Fielding (1993b) argues that there are three main perspectives on the merits of interview data:

1. Positivists believe that interviews can produce valid and fairly reliable data so long as standardized interviews are used and care is taken to avoid interviewers letting their own views become known to interviewees. The greater the detachment and impartiality of the researcher, the more valid and reliable the data will be.
2. Symbolic interactionists, on the other hand, recognize 'no clearcut distinction between research interviews and other forms of social action … For interactionists, the data are valid when a deep mutual understanding has been achieved between interviewer and respondent.' From this viewpoint, the interactive nature of interviews helps the production of valid knowledge, rather than gets in the way.
3. From the viewpoint of ethnomethodologists, interviews 'do not report on an external reality displayed in respondents' utterances but on the internal reality constructed as both parties contrive to produce the appearance of a recognizable interview'. Interviews then become the objects of study rather than sources of data. Ethnomethodologists can study them to reveal the informal tacit understandings which shape the way interviews are conducted.

A fourth perspective – that of critical researchers and feminists – is not mentioned by Fielding. It can be argued that this perspective comes close to that of interactionists. However, in addition, critical and feminist researchers also see interviews as an opportunity for interviewers and interviewees to see through the ideologies of social life, to reflect together on the social world being studied, and, ultimately, to begin to change that reality so that it becomes less exploitative.

Positivists, symbolic interactionists and critical researchers all see interviews as having some value in producing data that can to some extent describe reality. However, Hammersley and Gomm (2004) review four main arguments which suggest that interviews should no longer be seen as a source of valid data:

1. Some critics of interviews reject the idea that 'what people say somehow represents, or derives from, "what goes on inside their heads"'. According to this view, internal feelings, motives, intentions and so on cannot be adequately expressed through verbal responses in interviews. Hammersley and Gomm call this argument the 'discursive psychology' approach.
2. Another argument questions the view that 'accounts can ever represent reality at all', whether the reality is inside people's heads or external to them. From this point of view, 'Reality is constituted in the telling, rather than having characteristics that are independent of the telling.' This view has similarities with the philosophy of language developed by the poststructuralist Jacques Derrida (see pp. 116–17).
3. A slightly less extreme criticism is advanced by those who propose 'severe methodological caution'. They do not suggest it is impossible to produce valid data through interviewing, but they believe that relying on interviewees' accounts lacks the rigour of scientific research. From this point of view, careful observation by the researcher would be preferable to interviews, since the researcher is likely to be more objective and systematic than an interviewee.
4. Finally, Hammersley and Gomm outline the argument that interviews are unnatural social situations and the context affects the behaviour of interviewees so much that the resulting data cannot be seen as valid. This problem is sometimes referred to as one of ecological validity (see p. 816).

Hammersley and Gomm do not believe that any of these arguments succeed in demonstrating that interviews are useless to researchers.

In response to the first argument, Hammersley and Gomm believe it is 'absurd to deny that individuals have unique personal experiences that they can talk about … that may not be immediately accessible to others'. The descriptions of themselves and their feelings offered by interviewees may not exactly or directly describe what is going on in their head, but it does offer some indication of 'what people think and what they have experienced'. Much of social life rests upon the belief that people can

report on such things. Without this assumption, such social encounters as medical consultations, criminal trials and educational classes would be impossible or pointless.

Hammersley and Gomm are equally dismissive of the second argument. Although ideas have to be expressed through linguistic concepts, which may not exactly match what they are describing, 'concepts do not create something out of nothing but capture the nature of some aspect of reality more or less adequately'. In any case, it is self-defeating to argue that it is impossible to know anything for certain. They say: 'As has been recognized for millennia, we cannot claim that it is impossible to know anything without simultaneously implying that we can know at least one thing, namely that no knowledge is possible.'

Hammersley and Gomm are more sympathetic to the methodological caution expressed in the third criticism. They accept that 'interviewees' accounts are more likely to be affected by error and bias than researchers' own observational reports', but they still think the problem is exaggerated. Researchers may well produce biased reports. The same sort of problem affects all research methods and is a matter of degree. To some extent, you can guard against the problems of validity in interviews by cross-checking results with data from other sources (see pp. 845–7 on triangulation).

Similarly, Hammersley and Gomm believe that the problem of ecological validity is not unique to interviews. Questionnaires, like interviews, are unnatural situations. And behaviour in natural settings may be affected if those being studied are aware that they are being watched (see p. 910). Even if that is not the case, you can argue that it is impossible to generalize from observations in one setting to what might happen in others. Ecological validity is always an issue in research, and Hammersley and Gomm therefore see it as no reason to abandon interviewing. They conclude: 'the fact that interviews are a distinctive type of situation does not necessarily mean that what happens in them carries no reliable implications about people's attitudes, perspectives [and] ... their behaviour in other situations'.

Although Hammersley and Gomm reject these radical critiques of interviewing, they believe they are useful in pointing out some problems with interviews. Although, in their opinion, the use of interviews should not be abandoned, researchers should become 'more circumspect in what inferences [they] draw from interview data' and they should try to avoid relying completely on interviews for their data. Like an increasing number of researchers, Hammersley and Gomm advocate using several methods together in research (see pp. 845–7 for a discussion of methodological pluralism or triangulation).

(For details of postmodernist and feminist views on interviews, see pp. 813–14 and 809–10.)

Observation and participant observation

Observation

All sociological research involves observation of some sort. The use of observation is not confined to researchers advocating any particular methodological approach. Thus positivists believe that the social world can be objectively observed, classified and measured. Observation has also frequently been used by qualitative social researchers: numerous interactionist sociologists have observed interaction in the classroom when studying education. Similarly, in studying suicide, the ethnomethodologist J. Maxwell Atkinson (1978) observed the process of decision making in coroners' courts.

However, there are limits to the situations in which social life can be observed in 'natural' settings without affecting the validity of the data produced. There are a considerable number of social situations in which the presence of an observer is prohibited, or is unlikely to be allowed. Sociologists who study politics are not allowed to observe the deliberations of the British Cabinet, nor can they observe private conversations between members of the government and their senior officials. Sociologists interested in family life are unlikely to be allowed to observe interaction between married couples in the bedroom, nor is it likely that sociologists who study work will be able to observe the board meetings of large companies.

Even when observation is allowed, the researcher's presence might alter the behaviour of those being observed to such an extent that the data are of little use. In small, closely-knit social units such as families, those observed can hardly be expected to act naturally with an observer present.

Despite this, in certain situations sociologists might judge that some useful and valid data can still be produced. For example, in his study of secondary schooling, David Hargreaves (1967) found that some teachers he observed altered their behaviour considerably. Some refused to talk to the class as a whole when he was present. But others appeared to carry on as normal, and Hargreaves believed that some of his data were therefore valid (see p. 641 for further details of Hargreaves's study). In such situations the longer the researcher observes, the more likely those being studied are to forget about his or her presence, and the more likely they are to act naturally.

Given the danger that the researcher will influence those being studied, valid data can most reasonably be expected to be produced when the presence of passive outsiders is quite normal. Thus, in courtrooms, in the Visitors' Gallery of the House of Commons, or on the terraces at a football match, a sociological researcher is able to blend into the background without any great difficulty. In other circumstances it may be necessary for the observer to get involved in the activities of those being studied. To be accepted, she or he will have to become a **participant observer**.

Ethnography and participant observation

Ethnography is described by Geoff Payne and Judy Payne as 'the production of highly detailed accounts of how people in a social setting lead their lives, based upon systematic and long-term observation of, and conversation with, informants (2004, p. 71). It is essentially the study of a way of life. It was first introduced into the social sciences by anthropologists who studied small-scale, pre-industrial societies.

Bronislaw Malinowski's study of the Trobriand Islands (Malinowski, 1954) (pp. 397–8) is an example of an

ethnographic study. Anthropologists increasingly recognized the need to get as close as possible to the societies they were investigating. More recently, the same approach has been applied to the study of groups within modern/postmodern societies.

Ethnography can take various forms and is used by sociologists of different types. It is widely used by symbolic interactionists, and **critical ethnography** is a common type of study among critical social scientists (see pp. 835–6). Ethnography can use different qualitative research methods, but the most common are in-depth interviews, participant observation, and the use of qualitative documents. It may also involve collecting some quantitative data. However, participant observation is often the most important single method used in ethnographic studies.

As a means for gathering data, **participant observation** has a long history in sociology. It has been used by researchers with widely differing theoretical perspectives. As such it is a research technique which has been adapted to meet the requirements of sociologists with various views on the nature of social reality. However, it has been particularly associated with the work of symbolic interactionists such as Herbert Blumer, Howard Becker and Erving Goffman.

Participant observation became widely employed in the USA in the 1960s and since then has been regarded by many sociologists as the most appropriate way of obtaining qualitative data.

Joining the group, collecting and recording the data

One of the most important decisions that participant observers have to make is how to approach the social group they wish to join. Researchers may decide to be an overt participant observer, where they declare their true identity and purpose, or a covert participant observer, where the fact that they are a researcher is not revealed. Sometimes researchers choose to be partially open but do not provide those being studied with the full story.

Some researchers strongly advocate being open from the start, arguing that it is both morally and practically the best way to carry out participant observation. It allows the researcher to meet the ethical requirement of informed consent stipulated in many codes of ethics (see p. 815).

The American sociologist Ned Polsky, in his study of *Hustlers, Beats and Others* (1967), suggests that it is morally correct to be truthful, and that the research can easily be ruined if the covert participant observer is uncovered. Another advantage is that the open researcher may be able to avoid participation in distasteful, immoral or illegal behaviour. For example, Howard Parker (1974), when studying Liverpool delinquents, could refuse to take part in the theft of car radios without damaging his relationship with the people he was studying.

Furthermore, the researcher is free to ask questions without arousing suspicion. In a study of female sexuality and its relationship to masculinity among a group of students at a further education college, Beverley Skeggs (1991) was open about her research and argued that her 'age, clothing, attitude and marginal status as a part-time teacher enabled the students not to see me as part of the establishment'.

Some researchers are selective about who they are open with. For example, Teela Sanders (2004) was open about her research with workers in the sex industry. She spent many hours observing interaction between clients and sex workers in brothels (though not the sexual activity). Although open with the sex workers, she did not tell the clients that she was conducting research, to avoid influencing their behaviour. On occasions she had to make excuses when clients requested sex with her.

Sometimes researchers are less open, without actually lying to those they are studying. William Foote Whyte (1955), in a classic study of an Italian American slum, simply described himself as a writer without elaborating further. Ken Pryce (1979), in his study of the West Indian community in Bristol, found that he could be quite open with some of the groups, but with others (such as those engaged in illegal activities) he had to be more guarded.

The main disadvantage of being open is that it may affect the behaviour of those being studied. 'Doc', one of the key members of the street-corner gang studied by Whyte (1955), said to him, 'You've slowed me up plenty since you've been down here. Now, when I do something, I would have to think that Bill Whyte would want to know about it and how to explain it. Before I used to do things by instinct.' The knowledge that they are being observed can influence people's behaviour as they become more self-conscious and think about their actions.

An obvious advantage of covert participant observation is that the members of the group being studied are not likely to change their behaviour as a result of being studied, since they are kept in ignorance of the fact that they are being observed for research purposes. Some studies may not be possible without participant observation being covert, either because the group would change its behaviour too much, or because the researcher would not be allowed to join in the first place.

For example, Nigel Fielding (1993a) argues that he would not have been able to conduct his study of the National Front (a very right-wing and racist political party in Britain) without conducting covert research, because of the members' hostility to sociology.

Another researcher, who called himself 'James Patrick', had to keep even his name secret as he feared for his personal safety when studying violent Glasgow gangs (Patrick, 1973). Similarly, William Chambliss (1978) needed to maintain secrecy when conducting a study of organized crime in Seattle (see p. 342). Researchers have also had to keep their work secret when studying such groups as the Masons and certain religious sects.

If secrecy is maintained, then the researcher has little choice but to become a full participant in the group. However, if the researcher is open, there is an element of choice in the degree of involvement. Some researchers remain fairly detached. Others become much more involved. Ken Pryce (1979) found himself going to clubs and blues dances, drinking with and talking to local residents well past midnight during his study of West Indian life in Bristol.

Becoming too much of a participant can cause difficulties. In particular the researcher may experience the problem of 'going native'. They may become so much a

part of the group that they are unable to stand back and analyse the situation objectively.

Nigel Fielding argues that, in collecting data, 'One must maintain a certain detachment in order to take that data and interpret it.' On the other hand, those who experience this problem have at least achieved complete acceptance by the group and they may well have a true insider's view.

Perhaps the most complete insider's view can be provided by insiders who become sociological researchers, and use their own experiences as a source of data. Simon Holdaway (1983) was a police officer for a number of years before becoming a sociologist, and could genuinely claim to provide a view from *Inside the British Police.*

The more detached participant observer can perhaps be more objective, but may not understand the behaviour of those being studied quite as well. Fielding comments that there can be a problem in some overt research of '"not getting close enough", of adopting an approach which is too superficial and which merely provides a veneer of plausibility for an analysis to which the researcher is already committed'. In other words the researcher avoids risking challenging their own preconceived ideas by not digging too deeply into the social world of those being studied.

However, very often the researcher cannot predict how involved they will become. It depends to some extent upon how much rapport they build up with the subjects of their research. To be successful, the participant observer must gain the trust of those observed.

In his study of black 'street-corner' men in Washington, DC (see pp. 241–2), Elliot Liebow (1967) had to win over Tally, the leader of the group. Only when Liebow had gained Tally's trust did Tally admit that he had lied to him at the start of their acquaintance.

The close and relatively long-lasting relationships established through participant observation provide greater opportunities for developing trust than are provided by other research techniques. Interviews and questionnaire surveys usually involve one-off, short-lived encounters.

Particularly with groups such as low-income blacks and teenage gangs, a relationship of trust is necessary to secure cooperation. As Lewis Yablonsky (1973) notes from his research on teenage gangs: 'Their characteristic response to questionnaires investigating the gang's organization or personal activities is one of suspicion and distrust. To the gang boy every researcher could be a "cop".' In this type of situation participant observation is more likely to provide valid data than other research techniques.

Once the researcher has entered the group and gained its trust, he or she must then go about collecting the data and recording it. Much of this involves watching and waiting, and taking part where necessary, but some participant observers have supplemented the data gained in this way with some interviewing. This has the advantage of allowing the researcher to request the precise information required, without waiting for it to crop up in normal conversation. It is obviously only possible where the research is overt. Whyte (1955) used interviews with a 'key informant', 'Doc', to gain most of the background information required. Pryce (1979) made extensive use of formal and informal interviews.

Recording the data from interviews can be relatively straightforward: Pryce used a tape recorder. Recording data from participant observation is more difficult. Tape recorders would probably inhibit the natural behaviour of those being studied. Taking notes could have a similar effect, and may in any case be impracticable. Most researchers have to opt for the best means available: committing what has taken place to memory, and writing it down as soon as possible. Ditton (1977) used to retire to the toilet to take notes in private. Pryce had to wait until he got home. He said:

> *I had to rely heavily on memory, my method was to write down these observations as soon as possible after hearing or observing them. The rule of thumb I constantly exercised was to record them while they were still fresh in my mind, generally the same day ... I believe most of the information I recorded in this way was fairly accurate, if not accurate word for word, accurate in tone, flavour and in the emotions expressed.* Pryce, 1979

Not all sociologists, though, would accept Pryce's claim.

The advantages of participant observation

Supporters of participant observation have argued that, compared to other research techniques, it is least likely to lead to sociologists imposing their reality on the social world they seek to understand. It therefore provides the best means of obtaining a valid picture of social reality.

With a structured interview (a predetermined set of questions which the interviewee is requested to answer) or a questionnaire (a set of printed questions to which the respondent is asked to provide written answers) sociologists have already decided what is important. With pre-set questions they impose their framework and priorities on those they wish to study. By assuming that the questions are relevant to the respondents they have already made many assumptions about their social world.

Although participant observers begin the work with some preconceived ideas (for example, they will usually have studied the existing literature on the topic to be investigated), at least they have the opportunity directly to observe the social world.

The value of this opportunity is clear from Whyte's (1955) observations: 'As I sat and listened, I learned the answers to questions I would not have had the sense to ask if I had been getting my information solely on an interviewing basis.' Intensive observation over a period of years provided Whyte with a picture of what was important in the lives of the Italian Americans he studied. Without this exposure to their daily routine he would have remained ignorant of many of their priorities. Had he relied solely on interviews, this ignorance would have prevented him from asking important and relevant questions.

Liebow (1967) was particularly concerned about the danger of distorting the reality he wished to observe. He stated that, from the outset of his research, 'there were by design, no firm presumptions of what was or was not relevant'. He did his best simply to look and listen and to avoid any preconceptions of what was or was not important.

Liebow chose participant observation because he believed the method would provide a 'clear, firsthand picture' of the 'life of ordinary people, on their grounds and on their terms'. By observing what was said and done, where, when and by whom, he hoped to discover how a group of black street-corner men saw and organized their lives. Liebow claims: 'Taking this inside view makes it easier to avoid structuring the material in ways that might be alien to the material itself.'

In participant observation, it is also more difficult for the people being studied to lie or mislead the researcher than it is in other research methods. The researcher is on the spot and witnesses actual behaviour rather than relying upon people's accounts of their lives.

Where the researcher gains data from talking to those being studied, the validity of the data may be greater than in informal interviews. For example, the feminist researcher Beverley Skeggs (1991) argues that she was able to obtain valid data on the sexuality of young women because of the closeness of the relationship she developed with them. She says:

> *Their comments on their own sexual responses came from small soirées in my flat or their bedrooms. The discussions often became so intimate and animated that I think the idea that they were speaking for research purposes became lost in the desire to discuss contentious issues in a safe situation.* Skeggs, 1991

Participant observation is a particularly appropriate method for symbolic interactionists because it allows an understanding of the world from the subjective point of view of the subjects of the research. Because researchers experience many of the same events as those observed, they are better able to put themselves in their position and to understand why they interact with others in particular ways.

Pryce (1979) felt that participant observation allowed him to understand and explain the subjective views of some West Indians in Bristol. He said, 'There is a tendency to either ignore or disregard the subjective feelings of members of the West Indian minority.' One of those subjective feelings was the belief of some that there was no point in trying to earn a living through ordinary employment, which was dismissed as 'slave labour' and 'shit work'.

Interactionists believe that behaviour is largely governed by the self-concept held by an individual. Self-concepts are not fixed and static, but change during the course of interaction. Similarly, the meanings people attach to their own behaviour change as the context in which that behaviour takes place alters. Participant observation studies are often carried out over an extended period of time and it is therefore possible to study the process through which such changes happen.

This can be illustrated by Jock Young's (1971) study of marijuana smokers in Notting Hill. He found that the behaviour, the meaning attached to that behaviour, and the self-concepts of those involved altered in response to police attempts to discourage marijuana smoking. The drug users in the area became more secretive, attached more importance to taking the drug, and in response to what they saw as persecution they saw themselves as being in opposition to some of society's values. (For further details, see pp. 335–6.) Such changes and the way they came about would have been difficult to identify and explain on the basis of interview or questionnaire data.

Many interactionists see observation or participant observation as the best means of studying interaction. Much interaction takes place almost instinctively, and those involved cannot be expected to recall precise details if asked in an interview. Furthermore, it is difficult for complete participants to be detached and objective when discussing their relationships with others. It is easier, for example, for an outsider to comment on group relationships. Howard Parker (1974) was able to describe in detail the relationships between members of delinquent gangs he studied in Liverpool. Simon Winlow (2001) could provide detailed descriptions of the interaction involved around fights in Sunderland which he observed while doing participant observation as a 'bouncer' (see pp. 383–6).

Critics of participant observation argue (as will be discussed later) that the findings of such studies lack objectivity, that they are unreliable and depend too much upon the interpretations of the observer. Defenders of this research method generally believe that these objections can be overcome, and that participant observation can be made sufficiently systematic to be regarded as a reliable as well as valid research method.

Participant observation provides in-depth studies which can serve a number of useful purposes. In particular, participant observation is useful for generating new hypotheses. Rather like unstructured interviews, participant observation can go in unexpected directions and so can provide sociologists with novel insights and ideas. Although less useful for testing hypotheses, because the type of data produced is not entirely under the control of the researcher, it may be useful for falsifying theories. Thus Parker's (1974) study of British delinquents could be used to test how far Albert Cohen's explanation of American delinquency (see p. 325) is applicable to Britain.

Participant observation has the great advantage of a high level of ecological validity (see p. 816). As one of the few methods that collect data in natural social settings, its supporters believe that it is perhaps the most valid of all research methods.

The limitations and disadvantages of participant observation

Participant observation has many practical disadvantages. It is often very time-consuming. Cicourel (1976) spent four years studying juvenile justice in California. Beverley Skeggs (1997) spent a total of twelve years conducting ethnographic research following the lives of women who had been on a 'caring' course at a further education college in England.

The researcher can usually only study a very small group of people and has to be physically present for the research to proceed. In personal terms such research may be highly inconvenient and demanding. The researcher may be required to move house, to live in an area they would not otherwise choose, and to mix with people they would rather avoid. They may find it necessary to engage in activities they dislike in order to fit in with the group, and they may even face personal danger. 'James Patrick' left Glasgow in a hurry when the gang violence began to sicken him and he felt concerned for his own safety (Patrick, 1973).

There are also limits on who can be studied using this method. Higher-class and more powerful groups in society, in particular, may exclude participant observers. Individual researchers may lack the skills, knowledge or personality to be accepted by a particular group.

More serious, though, are the theoretical objections that have been raised.

First, to quantitative researchers, the samples used in participant observation are too small and untypical for generalizations to be made on the basis of the findings. Any conclusions can only apply to the specific group studied. Thus, Winlow (2001) may not have been justified in making claims about crime in cities other than Sunderland.

Second, such studies cannot be replicated, so the results cannot be checked. It is therefore difficult to compare the results with the findings of other studies. The data from participant observation rely upon the particular interpretations of a single individual, and are specific to a particular place and time.

Cicourel (1976) admits that his participant observation study relied heavily upon his own observational and interpretive skills. If the reader has little faith in Cicourel's skills, then they will have little reason to accept his findings. It is quite possible that a different researcher would have reached different conclusions. As Whyte (1955) admitted: 'To some extent my approach must be unique to myself, to the particular situation, and to the state of knowledge existing when I began research.'

Moreover, the account of social life produced by participant observation is the result of a highly selective method of data collection. The participant observer usually records only a small fraction of all possible data that he or she could have used. The observer selects what to record and what to omit and imposes a framework upon the data in the process of interpreting it. Martyn Hammersley (1992) points out that an ethnographer could have produced many different descriptions of the same setting. He says: 'there are multiple, non-contradictory, true descriptions of any phenomenon'. In this situation it may be difficult to accept a particular researcher's description as reflecting anything more than a personal perspective.

A third theoretical objection is that the validity of the data is bound to be affected by the presence of the researcher, since the group being studied will not act naturally. This point is rejected by many participant observers. Whyte, for example, felt that eventually he was able to blend into the background so that social life carried on as normal around him.

To critics – particularly those who support the use of positivist methods – participant observation is simply 'unscientific'. It is not systematic or rigorous; its findings cannot be checked; the research cannot be replicated; it is a subjective rather than objective research method. However, some interactionist sociologists have suggested that this sort of qualitative research need not lack rigour.

Glaser and Strauss (1967) claimed that qualitative research could be used to generate and refine what they called **grounded theory**. The whole process of collecting and analysing qualitative data can be systematic. Theories can be produced which are grounded in the data and in the real social world.

In the early stages the researcher starts to develop categories and then further data are collected to see if they fit with these categories. Hypotheses begin to emerge as the initial hunches of the researcher are backed up or refuted by the data that is being produced. Causal explanations can be produced, and may be tested in follow-up studies.

Becker (1970) showed how this sort of approach could be used when he was studying the behaviour of medical students. From observing the behaviour and listening to the comments of medical students he began to distinguish between 'cynical' and 'idealistic' attitudes to medicine. In the former case, patients tended to be regarded as little more than animated visual teaching aids; in the latter, as human beings whose pain and suffering the students felt a duty to relieve. Having found that these categories seemed to work, Becker went on to observe how often and in what circumstances the students were cynical or idealistic. Noting that students tended to be idealistic when talking to other students, Becker advanced the hypothesis that 'students have "idealist" sentiments' but 'group norms may not sanction their expression'.

Becker said it was perfectly possible to check the hypotheses produced by participant observation, and that this research method need not be unsystematic. He said of participant observation: 'the technique consists of something more than merely immersing oneself in data and having "insights"'.

In a book edited by Anselm Strauss and Juliet Corbin (1997) a range of individual studies apply grounded theory to research on topics as diverse as understanding chronic pain, cancer research, the activities of headhunting companies, abusive relationships, and contemporary Japanese society.

However, writers such as Hammersley still question the ability of ethnographic research to develop theoretical understanding. Hammersley (1992) says: 'Grounded theorizing seeks both to represent concrete situations in their complexity and to produce abstract theory. It thus operates under conflicting requirements.'

Descriptive accounts can concentrate on the unique features of a particular social situation, but developing theory does require making some generalization beyond the setting being studied. According to Hammersley, this is only possible if a number of cases are studied to see whether they conform to a theory. Yet very few ethnographers have even attempted to compare a range of case studies using ethnographic methods, and those who have done so generally rely upon interviews rather than participant observation.

Furthermore, Hammersley believes that the claim of some ethnographers that they are developing theories 'presupposes that there are scientific laws of human social life ... Yet few ethnographers today believe there are such laws.' To Hammersley, then, there is little basis for arguing that ethnography can be used to develop theory. However, this position is totally rejected by advocates of critical ethnography.

Critical ethnography

Critical ethnography is the sort of ethnography advocated by supporters of critical social science (see pp. 804–8).

Unlike Hammersley, critical ethnographers believe that ethnography can be used both to develop and to test theories, including theories that examine the structure of society as a whole.

Paul Willis's (1977) study of the transition from school to work among a group of working-class 'lads' is sometimes seen as the first example of a critical ethnography (see pp. 605–8). Willis relied largely upon data from interviews, but other critical ethnographers have made use of participant observation and other methodologies.

Since Willis's study there have been numerous examples of critical ethnographies. These include Sallie Westwood's (1984) study of female factory workers, Beverley Skeggs's (1997) study of working-class women who had been to a further education college, and Máirtín Mac an Ghaill's (1994) study of the development of masculinity in an English state secondary school.

As discussed earlier in the chapter, critical social scientists believe that research should involve close collaboration between researchers and their subjects; that studying oppressed groups can help to reveal the hidden and oppressive structures of unequal societies; and that research can be instrumental in changing society.

Steven Jordan and David Yeomans (1995) see critical ethnography as providing a way for researchers to understand how oppression is experienced by the oppressed by sharing some of the same experiences. Phil Carspecken (1996) argues that critical ethnographers are 'concerned about social inequalities, and we direct our work towards positive social change'. He goes on: 'We use our research, in fact, to refine social theory rather than merely to describe social life.'

Máirtín Mac an Ghaill's study *The Making of Men* (1994) illustrates the main features of critical ethnography. Mac an Ghaill tries to develop theories of masculinity (particularly those of R.W. Connell, discussed on pp. 138–41) by studying eleven heterosexual young men in a British state secondary school in the Midlands, and a second group of homosexual young men from a range of educational institutions in the same area. He tries to use elements of feminist methodology and argues for an approach to research based on 'collaboration, reciprocity and reflexivity'.

Mac an Ghaill tries to use the research process to challenge the assumption that heterosexuality is preferable to homosexuality, and he also encourages the young men to question dominant ideas on what makes you a true man. For example, he discusses with the homosexual students the way in which conventional ideas of masculinity largely prevent emotional closeness between men. In the course of his research he seems to have some success in encouraging the gay students to value positively their conceptions of masculinity, rather than being defensive in the face of hostility from heterosexuals. The study tries to relate changes in conceptions of masculinity to changes in the British education system and in the wider society.

An evaluation of critical ethnography

As with grounded theory and critical social research in general, Martyn Hammersley (1992) is hostile to critical ethnography. As discussed above, he sees problems in basing research around the concept of oppression and he questions the belief that the validity of theories can be checked by the subjects of research.

However, some critical ethnographers have tried to develop rigorous approaches that overcome the sorts of objections commonly directed at this research method. One such approach was developed by Patti Lather (1986).

Lather accepts that critical ethnography can sometimes be criticized for using circular arguments. The ethnographic description is used both for developing theory and for testing it. Experience comes to be interpreted in terms of the theory, yet the experience is also used to confirm the theory. To break out of the circle, Lather recommends four procedures:

1 **Triangulation** involves the use of different research methods to cross-check the validity of the data. Thus, for example, participant observation can be used to check the validity of data gained from interviews (see pp. 845–7 for a discussion of triangulation).
2 **Construct validity** involves a 'ceaseless confrontation with and respect for the experiences of people in their daily lives to avoid theoretical imposition' (Lather, 1986). From Lather's point of view, this is only possible in ethnographic research; questionnaire-type research tends to be guilty of imposing theoretical constructs on the explanation of behaviour without examining whether they have real relevance in understanding people's lives (see criticisms of questionnaire research, pp. 824–6).
3 **Face validity** is achieved through recycling the findings through at least some of those being studied, while being aware that they may be suffering from false consciousness. Although Hammersley is critical of doing this, Lather believes it is useful as one check on the validity of findings. It helps ensure that the researcher has not fundamentally misunderstood the viewpoint of those being studied and therefore completely failed to grasp the framework within which they choose how to act.
4 **Catalytic validity** refers to 'the degree to which the research process reorients, focuses, and energizes participants towards knowing reality in order to transform it'. Again, this objective is rejected by critics of this type of research, but it does perhaps provide one indication of whether the research has gone beyond the commonsense understandings of the people being studied.

Critical ethnography certainly retains problems despite attempts by some sociologists to develop it and overcome objections. As Irlam Siraj-Blatchford (1995) points out, critical ethnography does tend to assume that you should study the oppressed. It therefore neglects the study of oppressors, who might be able to offer even more insight than the oppressed into the way oppression works.

Furthermore, critical ethnography has by no means overcome all the problems in testing the validity and reliability of data. However, the same is true of other research methods. Critical ethnographers such as Patti Lather and Phil Carspecken use the subjects of research as an additional check on data rather than as an alternative to conventional checks on the data.

Postmodern ethnography

While critical ethnography hopes to penetrate beyond common sense to reveal hidden structures of oppression, postmodern ethnography has no such aims. Some postmodernists do see themselves as opposing oppression, but they do so by undermining all claims to discover the truth, rather than by trying to replace commonsense truths with an analysis of oppressive structures.

Postmodern ethnography rejects any claim to produce objective descriptions of social life, never mind explanations. However, it does follow critical ethnography in emphasizing cooperation with those being studied. Stephen A. Tyler describes postmodern ethnography as:

> *a cooperatively evolved text consisting of fragments of discourse intended to evoke in the minds of both reader and writer an emergent fantasy of a possible work of commonsense reality, and thus to provoke an aesthetic integration that will have a therapeutic effect.* Tyler, 1997, first published 1986

Tyler seems to be arguing that postmodern ethnography should act very much like a work of literature. It is designed to stimulate the imagination, to make people think about the lives of other people, not to describe reality in any objective way. Indeed, he argues it is, 'in a word, poetry – not in its textual form but in its return to the original context and function of poetry … [which] evoked memories of the ethos of community'.

To Tyler, this type of ethnography should acknowledge that there can be many different viewpoints within a social group. It is not the ethnographer's job to decide between these different viewpoints and produce a single account, but to record the variety of perspectives. A postmodern ethnography may take a form in which different versions are published together (as in the different gospels in the Bible), but the precise form it will take cannot be decided in advance. Instead, the researcher and those who are being studied must work together and find a format that will preserve the diversity of views in the social group.

The author is much less important than in traditional sociological studies. The author is not seen as being in a privileged, superior position to those being studied. She or he is not seen as having any special ability to produce an analysis of social reality which can rise above the subjective views of those being studied. Tyler says: 'The whole ideology of representational significance is an ideology of power. To break its spell we would have to attack writing, totalistic representational signification, and authorial authority.' Like Jean-François Lyotard (see pp. 891–3), Tyler seems concerned that any claims to have discovered the truth will be used to produce metanarratives – big stories about truth and fiction, right and wrong. These in turn may be used to dominate and oppress groups of humans.

Tyler admits that postmodern ethnography will not produce a coherent account of social life. It will be 'fragmentary' and will not be 'organized around familiar ethnological categories such as kinship, economy and religion'. However, he does not see this as a particular problem. For Tyler, the fragmentary nature of postmodern ethnography is desirable: 'We confirm in our consciousness the fragmentary nature of the postmodern, for nothing so defines our world as the absence of a synthesizing allegory.' In other words, people experience the social world as fragmented and cannot find any single way of understanding it. An individual's social life is experienced as many different stories which are not closely linked to one another. Tyler concludes: 'Postmodern ethnography captures the mood of the postmodern world, for it, too, does not move toward abstraction, away from life, but back to experience. It aims not to foster the growth of knowledge but to restructure experience.'

Postmodern ethnography – an evaluation

For an approach which advocates a move away from abstraction and back to experience, Tyler's description of postmodern ethnography is highly abstract. He provides no concrete example of postmodern ethnography and no detailed suggestions as to how to conduct it. Furthermore, his approach seems somewhat contradictory. He argues that postmodern ethnography should be more than 'an edited collection of authored papers' written by participants in social life, yet he wishes to give no special privileges to the ethnographer. Indeed, it is unclear why an ethnographer is needed at all, since the opinions of the author are seen to be no better than those of the people being studied.

Furthermore, if ethnography should act like a poem, stimulating the imagination, it is again unclear why it is needed. Fiction can perform the task of stimulating the imagination at least as well as writing that claims to have some basis in real experience.

Tyler's arguments could, therefore, be seen as self-defeating. By arguing that ethnography is really no different from fiction he makes a case for abandoning ethnography altogether.

Postmodern ethnography suffers from the same problem of extreme relativism (in which no view is better than any other) which afflicts a number of other versions of postmodernism (see pp. 894–5 and 811–12).

(See pp. 812–14 for a discussion of Alvesson's more 'pragmatic' postmodern approach to methodology.)

Longitudinal research

In most sociological studies, researchers study a group of people for a relatively short period of time. They analyse their data, produce a report on their research and move on to new endeavours. However, some researchers study a group over an extended period, collecting data on them at intervals. Such studies are known as **longitudinal** or **panel studies**.

Longitudinal studies were first used by researchers in the USA in the 1940s to measure changes in public attitudes. It was seen as more reliable to follow a particular sample over a period of time when measuring changing attitudes, than to select a new sample from time to time. By using a 'panel' the researcher could be sure that changes in the attitudes measured did not result from changes in the composition of the sample.

Longitudinal studies originated as extended attitude surveys. Since then, they have usually been used to collect quantitative data in social surveys, though not necessarily about attitudes. Sometimes a particular age group or cohort is followed over a number of years. The Child

Health and Education Survey has tried to follow the development of every child born in Britain between the 3rd and 9th of March 1958. Although it started as a medical study, it has subsequently been used to investigate education and employment as the subjects have aged (Payne and Payne, 2004).

Another example is provided by D.J. West and D.P. Farrington's *Who Becomes Delinquent?* (1973). This study was concerned with 411 London schoolboys. It followed their development from age 8 to 18 in order to determine what factors were associated with delinquency.

An ongoing longitudinal study is the British Household Panel Survey (discussed in Aldridge and Levine, 2001), which is conducted by the Institute of Social and Economic Research at the University of Essex. This survey is based upon periodic interviews with around 10,000 people from a sample of some 5,500 British households. It provides useful data on various aspects of social change in British families (see, for example, Berthoud and Gershuny, 2000). Heather Laurie and Jonathan Gershuny's (2000) findings on domestic labour and money management (see p. 500) are based upon this study.

Longitudinal studies are usually large-scale quantitative studies, but some qualitative studies also extend over considerable periods of time. Alan Bryman (1988) comments: 'There is an implicit longitudinal element built into much qualitative research, which is both a symptom and a cause of an undertaking to view social life in processual, rather than static terms.' In other words, methods such as participant observation are based upon the assumption that social life should be explained in terms of an unfolding story.

A major advantage of any longitudinal study is its ability to pick up such changes; a study extending over a shorter time-span cannot, and so the results can be misleading. Beverley Skeggs's (1991, 1997) study of a group of young women during and after studying at a further education college followed the women for a total of twelve years.

Supporters of longitudinal studies also see them as more likely to provide valid data than other types of research. As W.D. Wall and H.L. Williams (1970) point out, retrospective studies which ask people to report on past events in their lives rely upon fallible human memories. Wall and Williams also say: 'Human beings naturally seek for causes and may unconsciously fabricate or exaggerate something to account for the present state of affairs.' Longitudinal studies help to overcome this problem because recent events are less likely to have been reinterpreted in the light of subsequent consequences.

Quantitative longitudinal studies often examine a large number of variables because the researchers are unsure what data may prove to be important or required later in the research. For example, West and Farrington (1973) collected information relating to no less than 151 variables in their study of delinquency. Although the researcher still has to decide what variables to study, examination of so many limits the extent to which they impose their own theories upon the research.

Longitudinal studies do, of course, have disadvantages. It may be necessary to select people who are accessible and willing to cooperate over an extended period. Furthermore, the size of the sample is liable to fall as some individuals become unwilling to continue to take part, or prove impossible to trace. The British Household Panel Survey lost around half of its respondents by the tenth year of the research (Payne and Payne, 2004).

More serious criticisms question the overall validity of the data. Quantitative longitudinal studies collect data using such research methods as questionnaires and interviews. As earlier sections have shown, some sociologists question the validity of data collected in this way. A particular problem with longitudinal studies is that the subjects of the research are conscious of the fact that their behaviour is being studied. This may influence them and change their behaviour because they think more carefully about their actions.

Secondary sources

Secondary sources consist of data that have already been produced, often by people other than sociologists. Secondary data produced by the government are often used by sociologists. Organizations such as trade unions, companies and charities are a useful source of data, as are documents such as letters, diaries and autobiographies produced by individuals. The secondary sources used by sociologists may be contemporary or historical, and the data available from them may be primarily qualitative or quantitative. When sociologists refer to existing sociological studies by other writers in their own research, these become secondary sources.

Sociologists often use secondary sources for practical reasons. They can save time and money and they may provide access to historical data that cannot be produced using primary research because the events concerned took place before current members of society were born.

Secondary sources are invaluable to sociologists, but they have to be used with great caution. Their reliability and validity are open to question, and often they do not provide the exact information required by a sociologist.

Specific types of secondary sources will now be examined. At the end of the section there will be a general discussion on how to evaluate all types of secondary sources.

Official statistics

A vast range of statistics are produced by the government. In recent years the Government Statistical Service (which was set up in 1941) has coordinated the production of government statistics, but the production of large-scale statistical data goes back at least to 1801, when the first census was conducted.

Sociologists interested in demography have used statistical data from the census and elsewhere to examine a wide range of topics, which include birth and death rates, marriage and fertility patterns, and divorce. Sociologists who study deviance have used official crime and suicide statistics. The many official economic statistics are of interest to sociologists concerned with work. Figures on inflation,

unemployment and employment, strikes and productivity have also been used. Indeed, almost every area of sociological research has found some use for official statistics.

Some statistics, such as unemployment figures, are published monthly; others, such as crime statistics, annually. Information from the census is produced once every decade. The statistics are readily available through publications such as the annual *Social Trends* and *Annual Abstract of Statistics* and the government's website www.statistics.gov.uk.

Much of the statistical information made available by the government would not exist if it were left to sociologists. They lack the resources and power to carry out the work that goes into producing these data. For example, each household is compelled by law to return a census form, and has a legal duty to provide accurate information; it would be impossible for sociologists to obtain this information independently.

Official statistics are easily accessible and cost sociologists nothing to produce. Sociologists generally acknowledge that such statistics are useful, but they do not necessarily agree about what use can be made of them. Some sociologists do not accept the reliability and validity of official statistical data, while others are prepared to place more trust in them.

In the past, some positivists tended to accept official statistics uncritically. Durkheim (1970, first published 1897) believed suicide statistics were sufficiently reliable and valid to measure the extent and social distribution of suicide (see pp. 795–7). Using official statistics, he tried to establish correlations between suicide and other 'social facts', and ultimately to discover causal relationships and laws of human behaviour.

Similarly, many of the early structural and subcultural theories of crime were based upon the assumption that the official crime statistics accurately identified the working class as the group most prone to criminal activity (see pp. 325–7).

Today, sociologists are more cautious about the use of official statistics in areas of social life such as suicide and crime, but most would accept the reliability and validity of statistics from the census. (Earlier parts of this book have shown how inaccurate some official statistics can be – for instance, many crimes remain unreported and as such cannot be recorded in official data: see pp. 329–30.)

Victimization and self-report studies

However, many researchers believe problems like these can be overcome. For example, **victimization** or **self-report studies** use questionnaires administered to members of the population in order to determine the extent of reported and unreported crime. The British Crime Surveys provide examples of victimization studies (see pp. 329–30 for further details). Graham and Bowling (1995) conducted a large-scale self-report study, *Young People and Crime*, for the British government's Home Office.

It is sometimes argued that on the basis of such studies it is possible to estimate the real amount of crime in society as a whole, and to calculate the extent of criminality in social groups. The figures can be used to determine the accuracy of official figures, and appropriate adjustments can then be made to them. Even so, as Peter Eglin (1987) points out, 'The question remains, however, whether an error estimate calculated for some set of, say, national statistics in some given year will be generalizable to other times or other places.'

An even more serious problem concerns the question of the validity of the answers given by respondents in surveys. Stephen Box (1981) noted that in self-report studies respondents may exaggerate their criminality, or alternatively they might be unwilling to admit to their crimes. In effect, self-report studies measure how many crimes people say they have committed, rather than the actual number.

Furthermore, in measuring the criminality or delinquency of an individual, the researcher has to decide what offences or actions to include in the list of questions. For example, in a study of delinquency by D.J. West and D.P. Farrington (1973), respondents were asked thirty-eight questions. These included questions about stealing school property worth more than 5p, and about annoying, insulting or fighting other people (strangers) in the street. The precise wording and number of questions included in the questionnaire ultimately determine the amount of crime or delinquency uncovered – and in any case, respondents may interpret the questions in different ways.

Whether or not an offence is included in the statistics depends upon the choices made by the researcher. In the British Crime Surveys the researchers discount certain events because they do not believe that they constitute crimes. The statistics produced by such studies are therefore of dubious validity.

However, several sociologists believe that self-report and victimization studies provide some indication of the real extent of crime, and that they help to correct the misleading impression (provided by the official figures) that crime is an overwhelmingly working-class phenomenon.

A phenomenological view

Ethnomethodologists and phenomenologists reject the use of statistics for measuring or determining the causes of the social facts to which they claim to refer. As earlier parts of this book show, sociologists such as Cicourel (1976) and Atkinson (1978) believe that statistics are the product of the meanings and taken-for-granted assumptions of those who construct them. Thus, Cicourel claims that the stereotypes held by the police and juvenile officers lead to youths from lower social classes being more likely to be seen as delinquent. Justice is negotiable and statistics produced by official agencies are socially created (see pp. 339–40). Similarly, Atkinson describes how the commonsense theories held by coroners influence the way they categorize sudden deaths (see pp. 801–2). Both Cicourel and Atkinson regard official statistics as social creations.

This does not mean that official statistics are of no sociological interest. Indeed, phenomenological sociologists believe they are important: they can be studied in order to discover how they are produced. This helps the sociologist to understand the commonsense theories, taken-for-granted assumptions, stereotypes and categorization procedures of officials involved in the production of the statistics. To writers such as Cicourel, this is the only use that can be made of official statistics, including census

statistics, which appear to be based upon far more objective categories. To Cicourel, all statistics involve classifying things as 'this' or 'that', and such decisions are subjective.

Cicourel's views may become less convincing, though, when applied to such data as the age and sex distribution of a population. There may be considerable room for interpretation when considering whether an act is criminal or a sudden death is a suicide. There is less room for interpretation when deciding whether somebody is male or female. As Alan Bryman (2001) says, 'some forms of official statistics are probably very accurate by almost any set of criteria, such as statistics relating to births, marriages and deaths'.

A conflict view

In response to both positivist and phenomenological views, a number of conflict sociologists have developed alternative perspectives on official statistics. They argue that official statistics are neither hard facts, nor subjective meanings. Instead, they consist of information which is systematically distorted by power structures in society. Ian Miles and John Irvine (1979) argue that official statistics are 'developed in support of the system of power and domination that is modern capitalism – a system in which the state plays a particularly important role'.

Miles and Irvine do not believe that statistics produced by the government are complete fabrications, because, as they point out, such a viewpoint would be unable to explain why the state frequently publishes figures that are embarrassing to the government. For instance, figures on inflation, crime and unemployment often seem to suggest that government policies are not working. The statistics are not complete distortions, but they are manipulated through the definitions and collection procedures used so that they tend to favour the interests of the powerful.

Miles and Irvine say that official statistics are produced according to the needs of the various state agencies for information to coordinate their activities and justify their programmes. They are related to a single ideological framework underpinning the concepts and categories employed.

This view appeared to be supported when the Thatcher government appointed Derek Rayner in 1980 to review the British government's statistical services. Rayner proposed considerable cut-backs in the statistics produced and wanted them confined strictly to information directly needed by the government. Most of his recommendations were implemented. In the wake of the changes introduced following the report, 'The government was repeatedly accused of delaying, suppressing, abolishing and manipulating data for its own ends' (Levitas, 1996).

Ruth Levitas mentions a number of examples. The basis for calculating unemployment figures was frequently changed, almost always with the effect of reducing recorded levels of unemployment. Figures on public expenditure were also manipulated. Income from the sale of public assets was artificially used to reduce recorded levels of expenditure, rather than being treated as income. Waiting lists for NHS patients were reduced by removing from the lists those who were unable to keep appointments for operations.

Certain figures which might be damning to the government were not produced or published. For example, census statistics no longer included deaths by social class, which might have revealed a growing gap between the life expectancies of different classes. The government changed the data it produced on poverty, making it difficult to compare poverty rates with previous years (see pp. 223–4).

Levitas comments: 'By the end of the 1980s, public confidence in official statistics was at an all-time low.' Although some attempts were made in the 1990s to make British official statistics less politically biased, critics believe that they still reflect the ideology of the government. In the 1995 edition of the Central Statistical Office's annual publication *Social Trends*, an editorial by Muriel Nissel (the first editor of the publication), which was critical of government manipulation of statistical services, was withdrawn by the Office's director, Bill McLennan.

Conflict sociologists often question the categories used in official statistics. Thus, Theo Nichols (1996) argues from a Marxist point of view that the categories used in the census and other official statistics disguise the true nature of class in capitalism. Most are based on the Registrar General's scale, which uses status as an indicator of social class. To Nichols (as a Marxist), class is based upon the relationship to the means of production. Thus the official statistics give the impression of a status hierarchy and disguise the existence of classes that are in opposition to each other as exploiters and exploited. (New classifications were used for the 2001 census. These were based on a largely Weberian view of class and, like the previous scheme, included no separate category for a ruling class.)

Like phenomenologists, conflict sociologists tend to believe that official statistics are invalid for measuring the things they refer to, but that they do reveal something about those who produce them. However, rather than seeing them as based merely upon subjective meanings, conflict sociologists see them as reflecting the ideological frameworks that are produced by dominant social groups. Official statistics can therefore be analysed to uncover those frameworks and the power structures that produce them.

Official statistics – conclusion

Despite all the above problems, most sociologists do regard official statistics as providing some useful data on phenomena they measure. As suggested above, some statistics, such as those on births, marriages and deaths, can be considered to be both valid and quite reliable.

David Byrne states that all statistics are constructs, 'not crude facts which are given' (2006, p. 200). Nevertheless, he believes that most social scientists do see them as useful. He says:

> *the reasonable position adopted by most social scientists is that they are made out of something, not nothing, and that provided we pay careful attention to the ways in which they are made, and in particular the processes of operationalization, they can be of very considerable value to us.* Byrne, 2006, p. 200

Alan Bryman (2001) suggests that official statistics can be considered useful because they are a relatively

unobtrusive measure of social life. The idea of an unobtrusive measure was first used by Denzin, who defined it as 'any method of observation that directly removes the observer from the set of interactions or events being studied' (Denzin, 1970, quoted in Bryman, 2001).

In much research, those being studied are aware that they are participating in a research project and this may affect their behaviour and undermine the validity of the research. This difficulty is sometimes known as the problem of **reactivity**. Many official statistics are collected as a matter of course as part of the everyday procedures of government agencies and are therefore relatively unobtrusive. Bryman therefore concludes: 'Official statistics represent a form of unobtrusive method and enjoy certain advantages (especially lack of reactivity) because of that.'

Historical sources

Historical documents are of vital importance to sociologists who wish to study social change which takes place over an extended period of time. There are limits to the period over which a sociological study using primary sources can extend, and past events may be important in understanding how contemporary patterns of social life came about.

One area in which historical statistical sources have been of considerable importance is the study of family life. Chapter 8 showed how the development of family life since before the industrial revolution has been a major topic of sociological enquiry.

Peter Laslett (1972, 1977) made extensive use of parish records in order to discover how common nuclear and extended families were in pre-industrial England. Such data have been most useful in correcting the assumption that extended family households were the norm in pre-industrial Britain (see pp. 475–6). However, findings based upon such secondary sources need to be used with caution. Many parish records have not survived, and the documents that Laslett used relate only to particular villages which happened to have complete records. It may therefore be dangerous to accept generalizations based upon such findings.

Michael Anderson's (1971) research on the family (see p. 476) was based upon early census statistics which are more readily available. Nevertheless, Anderson chose to concentrate on one town, Preston, so the patterns of family life described are again not necessarily representative. Anderson also pointed out that census statistics do not provide an in-depth picture of family relationships. He listed the sorts of descriptive, qualitative data that can be used to supplement statistical data in the historical study of the family as:

> *tracts, reports of missionary and charitable societies, descriptions of crimes, newspaper investigations into the condition of the people, parliamentary investigations and the evidence of some witnesses to them, speeches in parliamentary debates and some aspects of novels.*
> Anderson, 1980

Like qualitative data from primary research, qualitative secondary sources may be unreliable and are open to a number of interpretations. Many of the secondary sources mentioned above are highly subjective and are likely to reflect the ideologies of those who produced them. Nevertheless, they do reveal something of the perspectives of their producers.

Whatever the problems of historical research, without using historical documents sociologists would be confined to producing a rather static view of social life. Without such documents, Max Weber (1958) would have been unable to consider the influence of religion on the development of capitalism (see pp. 406–8), and Michael Mann (1986) would not have had the opportunity to discuss the relationship between different sources of social power throughout history (see pp. 557–9).

Life documents

Life documents are created by individuals and record details of that person's experiences and social actions. They are predominantly qualitative and may offer insights into people's subjective states. They can be historical or contemporary and can take a wide variety of forms. Ken Plummer illustrates this diversity when he says:

> *People keep diaries, send letters, take photos, write memos, tell biographies, scrawl graffiti, publish memoirs, write letters to the papers, leave suicide notes, inscribe memorials on tombstones, shoot films, paint pictures, make music and try to record their personal dreams.*
> Plummer, 1982

All of these sources, along with many others, have the potential to be useful to sociologists.

The use of life documents has a long history in sociology. Their use was popularized by W.I. Thomas and F. Znaniecki in their study *The Polish Peasant in Europe and America* (1919). Thomas and Znaniecki made use of 764 letters, a lengthy statement by one Polish peasant about his life, reports from social work agencies, court reports, and articles from Polish newspapers. From such sources they tried to understand and explain the experience of migration for the hundreds of thousands of Polish people who moved to America in the early years of the twentieth century.

The study was widely regarded as a classic at the time but, according to Plummer (1982), it is now rarely mentioned and infrequently read. This is partly because life documents have fallen out of favour as a source for sociologists. Those who favour more quantitative methods tend to regard life documents as an inadequate source of data. Such documents are difficult to obtain and the ones that exist are likely to cover an unrepresentative sample of the population.

Like all data, personal documents are open to interpretation. They may say more about the subjective states of individuals than the events they are describing. It is unlikely that the husband, wife or political opponent of a diary writer would describe events in quite the same way.

Personal documents that are meant to be read by others (such as letters and autobiographies) may be written with an audience in mind. As Ponsonby once commented, 'letters may be said to have two parents, the writer and the recipient' (quoted in Plummer, 1982). Such documents may be designed more to justify actions than as a real attempt to explain the writer's feelings or motives.

Diaries, when they are available, may have greater validity if they are not intended for public consumption. One way of overcoming the scarcity of diaries and the unrepresentative nature of the examples that exist, is for the researcher to prompt those being studied to keep diaries. Young and Willmott (1973) asked the subjects of their research into family life in London to keep diaries, recording how much time they spent on different activities and how they felt about them. Oscar Lewis (1961), studying poverty in Mexico, persuaded a number of families to keep detailed diaries recording the events of a single day. Such diaries may be more systematic than those obtained by chance; however, they may be less valid. The awareness that they will be used for research might influence the details included by their writers.

Despite these limitations, Plummer believes that personal documents should play a crucial role in sociology. Using them as a source avoids a preoccupation with abstract theories 'which can kill off any concern for the joy and suffering of active human beings'. Compared to other secondary sources, personal documents allow much greater insight into the subjective states of individuals, which in turn shape their behaviour.

Plummer supports symbolic interactionist approaches to studying social life. From this point of view, some sort of participant observation may be the ideal method for studying social life. Where this type of research is not possible, life documents are the best alternative, since they offer insights into the 'ordinary ambiguous personal meanings' that shape people's actions in their everyday lives. (More details of Plummer's theoretical standpoint are included in the section on case studies and life histories – see pp. 820–1.)

A relatively new type of life document that has attracted attention from researchers is the e-mail. Alan Bryman (2001) comments that the advent of e-mails may have meant a reduction in the number of letters written, but e-mails offer an alternative documentary source. As an example, Bryman quotes a study by B.F. Sharf (1999), which utilized a managed list of e-mail addresses to conduct research into rhetoric about breast cancer.

The mass media and content analysis

Many parts of the mass media are notoriously inaccurate. Sociologists would, for example, be unlikely to turn solely to a national newspaper for an objective account of social life in Britain. Although some parts of the mass media may provide sociologists with useful data, their main importance is as objects of study. As with official statistics, mass media reports can be used to analyse the ideologies of those who produce them. Some sociologists have been highly critical of parts of the mass media for producing distorted images of society which might mislead the public or adversely affect the socialization of children.

There are a number of different approaches to carrying out **content analysis**, in which researchers analyse the content of documents. These may be largely quantitative, largely qualitative, or combine both approaches. Ray Pawson (1995) identifies four main approaches to carrying out content analysis:

1 **Formal content analysis**. Here the emphasis is upon objectivity and reliability. A systematic sample of texts is collected for study, a classification system is devised to identify different features of this text, and these features are then counted. For example, G. Lobban (1974) conducted a study of the portrayal of gender roles in children's reading schemes. She listed and counted the toys and pets that children had, the activities they engaged in, the skills they learned, and the roles that adults were shown in (see p. 644). The method is reliable because other researchers can repeat the same techniques to check the findings. The same method can also be replicated to carry out comparative studies. For example, Lesley Best (1993) repeated Lobban's research in the 1990s (see pp. 644–5).

   The simplicity and reliability of quantitative content analysis make it appealing. However, it is not without its problems. Simply counting the number of items tells you nothing about their significance, and the meanings of the texts or images being studied can only be implied. As Ray Pawson points out, there is an assumption that the audience are simply passive consumers of the message, and no attempt is made to examine how they actually interpret the messages in the text.

2 **Thematic analysis**. The second approach identified by Pawson is thematic analysis. Pawson says:

   > *The idea is to understand the encoding process, especially the intentions that lie behind the production of mass media documents. The usual strategy is to pick on a specific area of reportage and subject it to a very detailed analysis in the hope of unearthing the underlying purposes and intentions of the authors of the communication.* Pawson, 1995

   Thematic analysis is sometimes aimed at discovering the ideological biases of journalists and others involved in the production of mass media documents. Pawson cites the example of Keith Soothill and Sylvia Walby's (1991) study of newspaper reporting of sex crimes such as rape. Soothill and Walby found that the reporting tended to emphasize the danger of being raped in public places and the pathological nature of individual rapists. It tended to ignore the prevalence of rape by partners and friends of victims, and the wider context of patriarchal power within which sex crimes take place. According to Pawson, the main method involved in such studies is simply the repetition of examples.

   Critics of such studies argue that they rarely use scientific samples, and they therefore tend to use examples selectively to fit the preferred interpretation of the researchers. Like formal content analysis, there is no attempt to check whether consumers of the media interpret the messages in the same way as the researchers.

3 **Textual analysis**. This approach involves examining the 'linguistic devices within the documents in order to show how texts can be influential in encouraging a particular interpretation'. For example, it looks at how different words are linked together so that readers will interpret stories in a particular way. An

example is the Glasgow Media Group's (1976) study of television reporting of strikes. It found that strikers tended to be described using verbs such as 'claim' or 'demand', while management tended to have verbs such as 'offer' or 'propose' applied to them. This meant that readers tended to view strikers as actively causing the strikes and being unreasonable, while managers were viewed as being more reasonable and as the passive victims of the strikers. The linking of visual images and words can also be studied in this way.

Textual analysis often involves the use of **semiology** (or **semiotics**), or the analysis of signs. Semiology involves analysing the meaning of signs with reference to the cultural codes within which they are embedded. Thus, for example, the meaning of a Western would be understood in the context of the meanings of other Westerns.

As with thematic analysis, the main methodological problem with textual analysis is that it relies heavily upon the researcher's interpretation. This may not correspond to the interpretation of members of the audience or of other researchers. As John Scott comments, 'Any reading of a text reflects the standpoint of the reader, and semiotics has provided no clear basis on which the validity of a particular reading can be demonstrated' (2006, p. 298). (For a more detailed discussion of semiology, see pp. 679–80.)

4 **Audience analysis.** This approach overcomes some of the problems of earlier approaches by focusing on the responses of the audience as well as the content of the mass media. This then provides some check on the researcher's interpretation of the message and it recognizes that audiences actively interpret messages rather than just being passive. Sometimes audiences reject the messages apparently being advanced by the media.

Pawson discusses an early example of this approach, provided by a study of *Nationwide* (a British news programme) conducted by Morley (1980). The study found that groups such as shop stewards tended to be more critical and sceptical about *Nationwide*'s coverage of the news than groups such as bank managers.

Critics argued that Morley's study, which involved viewing and talking about *Nationwide* in groups, created a rather artificial research setting. Furthermore, there is no guarantee that people are fully open and honest in discussing their reactions to the mass media with researchers. The messages of the media may have a long-term influence on people's interpretations of the social world around them, and such effects are difficult to pick up in audience research.

More thorough studies may try to combine a range of methods. The work of the Glasgow Media Group (1976) illustrates some of the benefits of combining methods. In their first study they combined formal, thematic and textual analysis. They used quantitative counts to analyse the words used in newscasts and also looked in great detail at particular sentences. Their findings were used to develop a thematic understanding of the coverage of industrial relations. They did not carry out audience research, but there is no reason why such research could not be complemented by studies of the audience as well.

More recently, Greg Philo and David Miller (2002) of the Glasgow Media Group have developed a way of studying the media which involves the use of several methods to collect data on different aspects of the **circuit of communication**. The idea of the circuit of communication describes the way that messages circulate as social and political institutions influence the supply of information – the media present a particular content, the audience interpret the content, and decision makers react to audience interpretations and media content.

Philo and Miller did not just carry out research into the content of the media, but also researched the way audiences interpreted the content, and examined the wider social and political context in which media messages are created and received. In a study of the conflict in Palestine, they used thematic and textual analysis of the content of television coverage as well as interviews and focus groups to study audience understanding of, and reaction to, the broadcast messages.

John Scott – assessing secondary sources

John Scott (1990a, 1990b) has provided some useful guidelines for evaluating secondary sources (or, as he calls them, documents). The criteria can be applied to all secondary sources, including existing sociological research. They offer systematic ways of trying to ensure that researchers use secondary sources with as much care as they employ in producing primary data.

Scott identifies four criteria:

1 **Authenticity** – this refers to the question of how genuine a document is. There are two aspects of authenticity: soundness and authorship. Scott (1990a) says: 'A sound document is one which is complete and reliable. It should have no missing pages or misprints and, if it is a copy of an original, it should be a reliable copy without errors of transcription.' When the document is not sound, the researcher needs to consider carefully how far the omissions detract from its reliability and validity.

The question of authorship concerns who the document was written by. Many documents are not actually produced by those to whom they are attributed. For example, many letters signed by the prime minister may have been written by civil servants and might reveal little about the prime minister's own views. The most extreme problem of authenticity occurs when documents are faked, as in the case of the so-called 'Hitler Diaries', which were originally authenticated as the work of Hitler but which later proved not to be genuine.

2 **Credibility** – this issue relates to the amount of distortion in a document. Any distortion may be related to sincerity or accuracy. In a **sincere document** the author genuinely believes what they write. This is not always the case. The author may hope to gain advantage from deceiving readers. For example, politicians may distort accounts of their actions or motives in their diaries or memoirs to justify what they have done. Inaccuracy might result from unintended distortions, such as when an account

is written some time after the events described and faulty memory makes absolute accuracy impossible.

3 **Representativeness** – Scott points out that 'sampling of documents must be handled as carefully and as systematically as the sampling of respondents in a survey'. A researcher must be aware of how typical or untypical the documents being used are, 'in order to be able to assign limits to any conclusions drawn'.

   Two factors which may limit the possibility of using representative documents are: survival and availability. Many documents do not survive because they are not stored, and others deteriorate with age and become unusable. This is obviously a particular problem when doing historical research in sociology. Other documents are deliberately withheld from researchers and the public gaze, and thus do not become available. For example, many official documents are not made available for thirty years; others which are classified as secret may never be made public. Individuals and private organizations may also be unwilling to make many of their documents available to researchers.

4 **Meaning** – this concerns the ability of a researcher to understand the document. At one level, the researcher may have difficulty with literal understanding. It may be written in a foreign language, in old-fashioned handwriting, or it could use archaic vocabulary which is difficult to comprehend.

   Interpretive understanding is even more difficult to achieve: it involves 'understanding of what the document actually signifies'. For example, there has been a long-standing debate about whether suicide statistics signify more about suicides or about the officials who define certain acts as suicides (see pp. 795–803).

   Some of the problems involved in deciphering meaning are discussed in the section on the mass media (see pp. 710–41). Whether quantitative content analysis or qualitative semiotic analysis is chosen, interpretive understanding is always open to debate.

Scott shows that all secondary sources need to be evaluated and used with great care. Research using such sources needs to be as systematic and rigorous as research which produces primary data. The same care should be employed when reading and using existing sociology books and studies. In particular, as Scott points out, 'readers must always be aware of the interests and commitments of authors', since these may influence the way that secondary and other sources are interpreted and used.

Stuart Stein – the internet as a secondary source

John Scott's criteria for evaluating secondary sources can be applied to any type of secondary source, including the internet. The internet has rapidly established itself as an invaluable source for sociology students, lecturers and researchers. It makes a vast amount of material from a very diverse range of sources readily available to anyone with internet access. However, as Stuart Stein (2002) argues, there is little or no vetting of material on most internet sites. Unlike most written publications:

> *There is no need for submission of proposals to publishers and editorial committees with the attendant refereeing processes. Commercial and scholarly considerations operate to a substantially lesser degree, if at all. Finally, there is no post-publication evaluation system in place that approximates reviews published in scholarly journals, bibliographies and citation indexes.* Stein, 2002

For these reasons, Stein believes internet sources need to be used with particular caution. He suggests that the following criteria need to be considered when using material from the internet.

1 **Authorship**. The user needs to consider whether the authorship of the material on the web page is clearly identified and whether the identity of the compiler of the page (who may be a different person) is also clear. If the authorship is not clear, it is particularly important to seek another source to verify the information.
2 **Authority of the author**. The credibility and authority of the author can be evaluated in terms of criteria such as their qualifications, previous publications and the organization for which they work. Thus authors who work for government departments, universities or reputable research organizations – such as the Rowntree Foundation – have more credibility than those who do not. If they are well qualified with higher degrees and have had work published previously, then their credibility is enhanced.
3 **Authority of the material**. The material has more authority if, like published work, there are references to the sources used by the writer. This allows the user to check whether the material faithfully represents the sources consulted.
4 **Authority of the site/organization**. Stein suggests: 'It is a reasonable assumption that material provided on the website of a major international organization, a research institute, a think-tank, or a college or university is likely to be more authoritative than similar material on a personal web page or site.' However, even if the site or organization appears reputable, some caution needs to be exercised. There may be a disclaimer in which the organization refuses to accept responsibility for the content, or there may be material on a university site which has been produced by a student rather than an academic. Stein also points out that it is sometimes possible to find pages produced by individuals which are 'unrivalled in the depth and breadth of the subject matter they address' compared to other websites.
5 **Currency**. The user of web pages as a secondary source also needs to consider whether the pages are up to date or current. This is not always possible, as not all sites indicate when material is added. Although such sites need to be used cautiously, the material may still be useful despite the lack of dates.
6 **Pressure groups/objectivity**. As in the case of other secondary sources, researchers, lecturers and students need to be aware of the interests of those who have produced the web material. For example, material produced by political parties or pressure groups is likely to reflect particular values. However, the material may still be extremely useful, depending on the goals of the person using the information. Stein suggests that the content of the website of the

white supremacist organization Aryan Nation is unlikely to provide an objective account of social reality, but it may well provide insights into the racist ideology of its supporters.

Stein is careful, therefore, to stress that there are many different ways in which material on the internet can be used by sociologists other than as a source of reliable and valid information. The content of the internet can provide insight into those who produce the pages, as well as the topics about which they are written.

Teela Sanders – the internet and research on sex work

Teela Sanders (2005) discusses some of the advantages and disadvantages of using the internet for research in the context of her own study of sex work (Sanders, 2004). Sanders used some traditional methods in her study: she observed interaction in the foyers of brothels and massage parlours, she carried out fifty-six in-depth interviews with sex workers, and spoke informally to over 200 women. However, she also used the internet, both as a source of information and as a way of recruiting a sample for interviewing.

Sanders argues that internet research can sometimes provide access to information which would not otherwise be available, especially in relation to secretive or illicit activities. She was able to gather ethnographic information about the sex industry using the website *Punternet*. The site provided message boards, 'field reports' from clients of sex workers, and it generally facilitated the exchange of information between sex workers, and between them and their clients. Sanders was able to carry out what she calls **virtual observations** using the site.

Before the advent of the internet, Sanders argues, it would not have been possible to observe the community of sex workers in the same way, because it was the internet which allowed geographically dispersed sex workers and their clients to communicate together as a virtual community in the first place. She says: 'Previously, buyers and sellers of sex communicated only on a private and individual basis, whereas now ... these interactions have entered into the public domain' (Sanders, 2005, p. 70). Furthermore, she says that 'Through the Internet the researcher can now be privy to other aspects of sexual behaviour that have been hidden and largely clandestine' (p. 70).

Conducting such research can raise ethical issues, since it may be impossible to gain consent from those who post messages on websites. However, since the contributors use pseudonyms there is little problem in maintaining anonymity. Where content is available publicly, ethics committees usually consider that informed consent is not necessary.

As well as being a source of information about the world described in the web pages on the internet, the cyber world can be considered a social setting in its own right. The understanding Sanders gained of the sex industry from research in the cyber world complemented the understanding she gained from the study of face-to-face interaction.

Sanders also used the internet to seek sex workers who were willing to be interviewed. She e-mailed twenty sex workers, asking them if they would take part in the research. This was a relatively easy way to contact a population which is generally hard to reach and potentially suspicious of researchers. In the event, only five agreed to face-to-face interviews and two agreed to be interviewed by e-mail.

However, Sanders was able to learn from the experience. For example, one of those contacted posted her request on the *Punternet* notice-board and complained that Sanders had given too little information to prove that she was a genuine researcher. She therefore got feedback on the inadequacy of one aspect of her research method from a non-respondent.

Sanders also suggests that e-mail interviewing can have significant advantages. It reduces the likelihood of interviewer bias, as the interviewer is not physically present. It can also encourage some people to participate who might not be willing to meet face-to-face.

Although Sanders found web-based research useful, she recognizes that it has considerable drawbacks. It was difficult to assess the validity of the data posted on the website. Sanders found that 'the structured e-mail interviews did not produce the detailed, rich data that I acquired through face-to-face questioning' (2005, p. 75). It was also very difficult to clarify concepts using e-mail, leading to misunderstandings with respondents.

The impersonal nature of the process made it difficult to establish any rapport with the respondents, there was no chance to observe non-verbal communications, and the response rate was low.

Sanders comments that 'the advantages of the virtual arena – anonymity, privacy, access, heightened self-disclosure, fluidity of time and space – did not allow some types of data to be observed and understood' (2005, p. 78). She therefore concludes that internet research is most useful when combined with other methods. This view – that it is often best to combine methods – is widely held amongst sociologists.

Combining methods and triangulation

As an earlier section indicated (pp. 803–4), it is difficult to see quantitative and qualitative methods as mutually exclusive. Increasingly, sociologists are combining both approaches in single studies. As Bryman puts it:

> *The rather partisan, either/or tenor of debate about quantitative and qualitative research may appear somewhat bizarre to an outsider, for whom the obvious way forward is likely to be a fusion of the two approaches so that their respective strengths might be reaped.* Bryman, 1988

In reality, the degree to which quantitative and qualitative approaches are different has been exaggerated. Bryman points out: 'Most researchers rely primarily on a method associated with one of the two research traditions, but buttress their findings with a method associated with the other tradition.' The practice of combining quantitative and

qualitative research has a long history, and is evident in the approach advocated by Weber (see pp. 874–5). Combining different methods is sometimes referred to as methodological pluralism and sometimes as triangulation. However, as we shall see, the term 'triangulation' is sometimes reserved for a specific type of methodological pluralism.

Examples of combining methods

Methodological pluralism is an increasingly common feature of social research. The following are a few examples of how methodological pluralism has been used.

In her study of the Unification Church, or Moonies, Eileen Barker (1984) used participant observation, questionnaires and in-depth interviewing. She claimed that this combination of methods allowed her to 'see how the movement as a whole was organized and how it influenced the day-to-day actions and interactions of its members'. She tried to test hypotheses formulated from qualitative data using questionnaires.

Quantitative techniques have been used to analyse data systematically from observation or participant observation. For example, Delamont (1976) used the Flanders Interaction Analysis Categories in her studies of classroom interaction. These allowed her to categorize the different types of interaction and to time them in order to determine differences in the educational experience of boys and girls. She used qualitative data to explain the reasons for the quantitative relationships she found.

Amanda Coffey and Paul Atkinson (1996) note that qualitative data can be analysed in many different ways. One method is the systematic coding of different types of data so that related pieces of data can be easily found and linked together. Furthermore, computer programmes, such as *Ethnograph, QUALPRO and ATLAS/ti*, are now sometimes used to make the analysis of qualitative data easier and more systematic.

Combining different methods is not confined to the use of primary data. Simon Winlow (2001) used participant observation, informal interviewing and secondary sources such as previous studies of working-class life in Sunderland, in his study of bouncers and crime in the city. The secondary sources allowed him to relate his findings on contemporary patterns of crime to historical changes in the working class (see pp. 383–6). As discussed above, Teela Sanders (2004) used the internet as a secondary source as well as carrying out e-mail and face-to-face interviews and observations in her study of sex work.

Reasons for combining methods

Martyn Hammersley (1996, discussed in Bryman, 2001) distinguished three approaches to research which uses several research methods:

1. **Triangulation**. Although this term is often used to refer to any research involving the use of several methods, Hammersley uses it to refer specifically to research where quantitative and qualitative research methods are used to cross-check the findings produced by the other methods. So, for example, the findings produced in a small number of in-depth interviews might be checked by administering questionnaires to a larger sample of people.
2. **Facilitation**. This approach involves using one research method to assist in the use of another method. For example, participant observation or interviews might be used to generate ideas which could be used to produce questions for a questionnaire.
3. **Complementarity**. In this case 'two research strategies are employed in order that different aspects of an investigation can be dovetailed' (Bryman, 2001). For example, questionnaires might be used to produce factual, statistical data, while a more qualitative method is employed to understand the meanings and motives behind the patterns found in the statistics.

Bryman himself elaborates on this classification and identifies ten ways in which multi-strategy research can be used:

1 The logic of triangulation

This follows Hammersley's definition of triangulation described above. As an example, Bryman quotes a study by Webb *et al.* (1996) of young people's attitudes towards different types of alcoholic drinks. Questionnaires were used to check the results of focus group research. According to Bryman, the main advantage of triangulation is that it increases confidence in the research findings.

2 Qualitative research facilitates quantitative research

Qualitative research might be useful for generating hypotheses to be tested in quantitative research. It might also be used to aid measurement. For example, it can help researchers to operationalize complex concepts in questionnaires through an understanding of what the concepts mean to those being studied. The British Household Panel Survey (see p. 838) used discussions and interviews to clarify the concepts included in questionnaires.

3 Quantitative research facilitates qualitative research

A good example of this is when questionnaires are used to identify people suitable for inclusion in a sample to be studied using qualitative methods. This can save researchers a lot of time which would otherwise be wasted in carrying out research on people from whom no useful data is likely to be obtained.

4 Filling in the gaps

Sometimes research might employ one main method but find that this leaves gaps in the data which need to be filled. For example, ethnographers doing participant observation might also carry out interviews to find out about aspects of the social group and its history that they have been unable to observe. For example, William Foot Whyte (1955) interviewed 'Doc', a leader of the street-corner gang he was studying using participant observation.

5 Static and processual features

In some circumstances quantitative methods are used to study the more stable aspects of social life while qualitative methods are employed to study changes. For example, Stephen Ball (1981) in his study of 'Beachside Comprehensive' (see p. 640) used questionnaires to determine friendship networks, and observation to examine how the children progressed through schooling.

6 Researchers' and participants' perspectives
In this case, researchers use qualitative data to 'gain access to the perspectives of the people they are studying; and quantitative data which will allow them to explore specific issues in which they are interested'. Bryman uses the example of a study by Milkman (1997) of a car plant in the USA. Milkman used focus groups and semi-structured interviews to find out how the workers felt about their work, and questionnaires to collect specific data from some workers who had accepted redundancy from the plant.

7 The problem of generality

Qualitative research usually employs a small sample for practical reasons. It may be supplemented by quantitative research using a larger sample to make it possible to generalize from the findings.

8 Qualitative research facilitating the interpretation of the relationship between variables
Quantitative research might identify general patterns, but qualitative research can help to explain why those patterns exist. For example, Gillborn and Youdell (2001) combined the use of school statistics on the achievement of pupils from different class and ethnic backgrounds in two schools, with in-depth interviews and observation (see pp. 656–7). The qualitative methods revealed the reasons why some groups were achieving less than other groups in the schools.

9 Studying different aspects of a phenomenon
Different aspects of a phenomenon might lend themselves to the use of different research methods. An example, discussed by Bryman, is the study of family obligations by Janet Finch (1989). Quantitative methods were used to find out about what people thought family obligations were in theory, while qualitative methods were used to examine how they actually worked in practice.

10 Solving a puzzle
Sometimes research throws up unexpected results which are hard to explain. Researchers might need to use a different method from that used initially to try to understand their findings. Sutton and Rafaeli (1988) conducted a study in the USA of how often shop assistants in convenience stores smiled. They expected to find that they smiled more in shops where sales were booming, but actually found that they smiled more in shops where there was a shortage of customers. To discover why this was, they decided to carry out observation, participant observation and in-depth interviews. They found that the results could be explained in terms of pressure on staff. In busy shops, staff had 'less time and inclination for the pleasantries associated with positive emotions' (Bryman, 2001).

Conclusion

Bryman (1988) believes that both qualitative and quantitative research have their own advantages. Neither can produce totally valid and completely reliable data, but both can provide useful insights into social life.

Generally, quantitative research tends to produce rather static pictures, but it can allow researchers to examine and discover overall patterns and structures in society as a whole. Qualitative research is less useful for discovering overall patterns and structures, but it allows a richer and deeper understanding of the process of change in social life. Bryman says: 'A division of labour is suggested here in that quantitative research may be conceived of as a means of establishing the structural element in social life, qualitative research the processual.'

However, Bryman (2001) does not believe that methodological pluralism is a panacea that can solve all research problems. He says:

> *[It] may provide a better understanding of a phenomenon than if one method had been used. It may also frequently enhance our confidence in our own or others' findings … But the general point remains, that multi-strategy research, while offering great potential in many instances, is subject to similar constraints and considerations as research relying on a single method or research strategy.*
> Bryman, 2001

Sociology and science

Scientific methodology

The early parts of this chapter described how sociologists have adopted varying views on the relationship between sociology and science. Positivists claim that science uses established methods and procedures, and that these methods and procedures can be applied to the social sciences. They believe that social facts can be observed objectively, measured and quantified. Analysis of statistics can reveal correlations, causes and ultimately laws of human behaviour. From this point of view, sociological studies using such methods can be considered to be scientific. Positivists see the use of scientific methods as highly desirable, and they tend to be critical of those sociologists who study subjective and unobservable mental states.

Popper (1959) also saw it as highly desirable that sociology should be scientific, but argued that science is a deductive rather than an inductive methodology. Scientists should make precise predictions on the basis of their theories so that they can strive conscientiously to falsify or disprove them. Popper rejected many sociological theories as being unscientific because they were not sufficiently precise to generate hypotheses that could be falsified. He was particularly critical of Marxism for failing to make precise predictions: for example, for failing to specify exactly when and under what circumstances a proletarian revolution would take place in capitalist societies. Marxism cannot be falsified, since the day of the proletarian revolution and the dawning of the truly communist society is pushed further into the future. Marxism is an article of faith rather than a scientific theory.

Like positivists, then, Popper believed it was possible for 'social sciences' in general, and sociology in particular, to become scientific by following a particular set of

methodological procedures. He parted company with positivists in denying that science can deliver the final, incontrovertible truth, since the possibility of falsification always exists. Instead, he believed that the longer a theory has stood the test of time, and the more often researchers have failed to falsify it, the closer it is likely to be to the truth.

Phenomenologists reject the view that natural science methodology is appropriate to sociology. To phenomenologists, objective observation and measurement of the social world are not possible. The social world is classified by members of society in terms of their own stereotypes and taken-for-granted assumptions. In these circumstances the social world cannot be measured objectively; statistics are simply the product of the categorization procedures used. The best that sociologists can hope to do is to study the way that members of society categorize the world around them. They cannot collect meaningful statistical data and establish correlations, causal connections and laws. Indeed, phenomenologists reject the whole possibility of finding laws of human behaviour.

The social context of science

All of the views discussed so far are based upon the assumption that there are established methods and procedures that characterize science. However, as Kaplan (1964) pointed out, it is necessary to distinguish between 'reconstructed logics' and 'logics in use'.

Reconstructed logics consist of the methods and procedures scientists claim to use. Both positivism and Popper's methodological approach represent reconstructed logics. However, there is no guarantee that scientists actually do follow such procedures. **Logics in use** refer to what scientists actually do during their research, and this may depart considerably from their reconstructed logics.

Michael Lynch (1983) conducted research in a psychobiological laboratory, which illustrated how scientists may be less objective than they claim. The scientists studied brain functioning by examining thin slices of rats' brains under microscopes. Photographs and slides of the brain slices were examined to see how useful they were in developing theories of brain functioning.

Sometimes, unexplained features were found in the photographs. Very often these were put down to some error in the production of the photograph or slide: they were seen as artefacts, rather than being a real feature of the rat's brain. (An **artefact** is something produced by the research process which does not exist in the phenomenon being studied.) Some of these features were held to be an error in staining, others were believed to be the result of scratching of the specimen when it was being sliced.

There was much discussion in the laboratory about whether these features were artefacts or not. In reaching their conclusions, the scientists were influenced by their existing theories, and the types of features they were looking for and expected to find. If the visible marks on the slide or photograph did not fit their theories of how rats' brains functioned, they were much more likely to dismiss the marks as errors. Their interpretations of the data were guided by their theories.

Far from following Popper's methodology and striving to falsify their theories, the researchers tried to use the evidence to confirm them. Many scientists may be reluctant to dismiss perhaps years of intellectual effort and research because a single piece of evidence does not support the theory that they have developed.

The social context of Darwin's theory of evolution

It may also be the case that the sorts of theories that are developed in the first place – and which scientists try to confirm rather than falsify – are influenced by social factors rather than the detached pursuit of objective knowledge. Roger Gomm (1982) used Darwin's theory of evolution as an example to illustrate this.

Darwin claimed that species developed and evolved by a process of natural selection. Most followers of Darwin believed this process took place gradually. Natural selection occurred through adaptation to the environment. Genetic differences between members of a species make some better suited to survival in a particular environment. Those that have a better chance of survival are more likely to produce offspring and so shift the species towards their genetic characteristics. For example, giraffes with longer necks may have been more likely to survive and produce offspring than those with shorter necks because they were able to feed off leaves which other species and certain members of their own species could not reach.

Gomm points out that the ideas of natural selection and gradual evolution are not supported by all of the evidence. According to Gomm, Darwin himself did not believe that evolution was a gradual process, but that it was initiated by sudden genetic changes or mutations. Fossil records do not support the gradualist theory of evolutionary change; instead, there appear to be rapid periods of genetic change and eras of mass extinction.

Gomm claims that the popularity of 'gradualism' was not the result of careful interpretation of the evidence, but the theory was popular 'because it lined up with a preference for gradual social and political change among the dominant social groups of the time'. Darwin's theories were often misused – for example, by the English functionalist sociologist Herbert Spencer – to indicate how societies should be run. Those in power did not want it to appear that revolutionary change was the answer to society's problems, because it could undermine their dominance.

The idea of natural selection suggests, as Herbert Spencer put it, 'survival of the fittest'. The weak – those unsuited to survival in a particular environment – must perish to ensure the healthy genetic development of a species. In this theory, competition is the key to genetic and evolutionary progress.

However, as Gomm points out, 'the idea of natural selection as a red in tooth and claw struggle for survival is only a half truth at best. It leaves out of account the extent to which individuals within a species cooperate with each other.'

In his book *Mutual Aid* (published in 1902), the Russian anarchist Prince Peter Kropotkin amassed a wealth of evidence to show that cooperation rather than conflict allowed animals to survive in flocks, herds or other groups. Many animals are best able to resist predators, or at least ensure that casualties are minimized, in such groupings.

Why then was Darwin's competitive vision of the natural world preferred to Kropotkin's equally carefully

argued cooperative vision? Gomm argues it was because Darwin's views fitted more closely with the ideologies of dominant social groups in Victorian Britain:

1 It justified the free-market capitalist system and did not support socialist ideas which argued for state intervention in the economy.
2 It legitimated harsh social policies which saw the poor as 'unfit' and therefore as not worthy of much assistance. (See p. 238 for details of Herbert Spencer's Darwinist views on poverty.)
3 Since evolution allowed species to be seen as superior or inferior, it allowed groups within the species to be placed on an evolutionary scale. Gomm argues that the idea of evolution as progress 'allowed the Victorians to lay out the peoples of the world on an evolutionary ladder, with Australian Aboriginals at the bottom (least evolved) and Victorian intellectual males at the top'. It therefore justified the colonization of non-Western people on the grounds that the British Empire would civilize them.

A similar use of a scientific theory to legitimate the domination of one group by another (in this case, women by men) is provided by sociobiology (see pp. 94–6).

Thomas Kuhn – paradigms and scientific revolutions

The preceding section argues that the interpretation of evidence is governed by the theories that scientists hold, and that these theories themselves may be influenced by social and ideological factors. This suggests that in practice scientists operate in very different ways from those advocated by Popper or positivists.

Thomas Kuhn (1962) developed an analysis of science which also saw science as being far from the objective pursuit of knowledge. In *The Structure of Scientific Revolutions*, Kuhn argued that science was characterized by a commitment to a scientific paradigm. A **paradigm** consists of a set of beliefs shared by a group of scientists about what the natural world is composed of, what counts as true and valid knowledge, and what sort of questions should be asked and what sort of procedures should be followed to answer those questions.

A paradigm is a complete theory and framework within which scientists operate. It guides what evidence is collected, how that evidence is collected, and how it should be analysed and explained. When scientists work within a paradigm, they tend to look for data that support and refine that paradigm. The way that scientists perceive the world around them is also governed by the paradigm – they see the world in ways that are consistent with the paradigm.

Kuhn did not believe that the same methods and procedures are found throughout scientific history; rather, they are specific to particular sciences at particular times. Nor did Kuhn believe that scientists are entirely objective – paradigms are not accepted or rejected on the basis of evidence alone. Each paradigm has a social base, in that it is grounded in a community of scientists committed to a particular view of the world or some part of it. Older scientists trained to think within the framework provided by an established paradigm find it difficult to see the world in any other way. Furthermore, they have a vested interest in maintaining it, for their academic reputations and careers rest upon the work they have done within that paradigm. Consequently, scientists may ignore evidence that does not fit 'their' paradigm.

Scientific revolutions

Scientific beliefs do change, but, according to Kuhn, rather than changing gradually they are changed by scientific revolutions. In a scientific revolution one scientific paradigm is replaced by another: for instance, when Newton's paradigm in physics was replaced by Einstein's.

Change in science is not a gradual process of accumulating new knowledge, but a sudden move from one paradigm to another. This occurs when an accepted paradigm is confronted by so many 'anomalies', or things it cannot explain, that a new paradigm is developed, which does not suffer from the same anomalies. A community of scientists may resist the change, but, once a new generation of scientists who have been trained within the new paradigm start practising, the new paradigm is accepted. A science then returns to its 'normal' state in which the paradigm is elaborated and developed, but the framework that it lays down is largely unquestioned.

Kuhn's work raises serious questions about other views of science. To Kuhn, a scientific subject is one in which there is, at least most of the time, an agreed paradigm. There is no guarantee, however, that the accepted paradigm is correct: it may well be replaced by a new paradigm in the future. Scientific training has more to do with learning to see the physical world in a particular way than it has to do with a commitment to discovering the truth through objective research.

If Kuhn's view of science is accepted, then it is doubtful if sociology can be seen as a science. The sociological community has not accepted one paradigm, or, in sociological vocabulary, one 'perspective'. Marxists, functionalists, feminists, interactionists, ethnomethodologists and postmodernists all see the social world in different ways: they ask different questions and get different answers. Even within a perspective there is a lack of consensus. There are many variations within Marxism and feminism, and within functionalism Durkheim and Parsons reached different conclusions on many issues, and they did not analyse societies in the same ways.

In this situation, sociology can be regarded as 'pre-paradigmatic' – a single paradigm has not yet been accepted – and, as such, sociology is pre-scientific. It could, of course, become scientific if sociologists were to agree upon a perspective that all practitioners of the subject could accept. Given the present state of the subject, such an outcome seems highly unlikely.

Whether it is desirable for sociology to become a science is questionable. Sociology seems to exist almost in a permanent state of revolution, but the constant conflict may help to push the subject forward at a rapid pace.

Criticisms of Kuhn

Although influential, Kuhn's work has been criticized. It has been seen as having little relevance to social science and as being based upon inadequate evidence. Anderson,

Hughes and Sharrock (1986) argue that Kuhn is doing no more than describing natural science, and his views have little relevance to sociology. Furthermore, they believe he has underestimated the degree to which there is conflict and disagreement in natural science. Most of the time alternative paradigms are debated. Anderson *et al.* claim that a careful examination of the history of science shows that 'the periods of revolution grow in size while those of settled "normality" contract'.

The realist view of science

From the discussion so far, it would appear that it is either impossible or undesirable for sociology to be a science. Despite the claims of positivists and Popper, it seems inappropriate for a subject that deals with human behaviour to confine itself to studying the observable, to ignore the subjective, to try to falsify theories or to make precise predictions. However, partly in response to such problems, the **realist** theory of science – which stresses the similarities between social and natural science – has been developed.

Realists such as Roy Bhaskar (1979), Russell Keat and John Urry (1982) and Andrew Sayer (1984) argue that none of the above points disqualifies sociology from being a science. They believe that positivists, Popper, and indeed Kuhn, are mistaken about the nature of science.

'Closed' and 'open' systems

Sayer (1984) argues that there is a difference between **closed** and **open systems** as objects of scientific study. Within closed systems all the relevant variables can be controlled and measured. In scientific laboratory experiments closed systems may be produced; and certain branches of science such as physics and chemistry have much more scope for the study of closed systems than others.

There are many areas of science in which all the relevant variables cannot be controlled or measured. As a result, it is not possible to make the precise predictions advocated by Popper. For example, doctors cannot predict with certainty who will become ill; seismologists cannot predict exactly when an earthquake will occur; and meteorologists cannot predict the weather with anything like absolute precision. In all of these cases the reasons for the lack of precision are similar – some of the variables cannot be measured, or the processes involved are too complex for accurate predictions to be made.

Sociology has similar problems. Within society as a whole, or within a social group, innumerable variables may influence what happens. Thus sociologists cannot be expected to be able to predict exactly what the divorce rate will be in five years' time, or whether a revolution will occur within a given period of time.

Human consciousness

However, even if it is accepted that a science does not need to make predictions, this still leaves the problem of human consciousness to be dealt with. As outlined earlier, positivists believe that a science should confine itself to the study of the observable, whereas interpretive sociologists believe that reference must be made to internal and unobservable meanings and motives in explaining human behaviour. Realists point out, though, that science itself does not confine itself to studying observable phenomena. As Keat and Urry (1982) say, scientists may 'postulate the existence of entities which have not been observed, and may not be open to any available method of detection'.

Viruses, sub-atomic particles and magnetic fields all form part of scientific theories, despite the impossibility (at present) of directly observing them. Scientists cannot easily observe continental drift, because it takes place too slowly, nor can they see the mechanisms that produce it, because they are below the earth's surface. Darwin could not observe evolution, because it took place too slowly.

Causality

To realists, then, both Popper and positivists have failed to define science accurately, and so the objections raised by interpretive sociologists to seeing sociology as a science become irrelevant. Realists see science as the attempt to explain the causes of events in the natural or social world in terms of underlying and often unobservable structures, mechanisms and processes. Realists produce causal explanations and explain them in terms of such structures, mechanisms and processes. An example of a mechanism or process in science would be Darwin's idea of natural selection. In sociology, examples include ideas on the concentration of capital and the pauperization of the proletariat.

To realists, explaining the mechanisms through which events take place is a vital part of causal explanation. This requires the researcher to specify which factors or variables determine whether these mechanisms operate. For example, in different conditions the concentration of capital might be slowed down, speeded up or halted. Similarly, in Darwin's theory of evolution the actual consequences of the operation of natural selection depend upon the precise and changing environmental conditions in which species evolve.

According to realists, events take place and mechanisms operate within the context of **structures**. Keat and Urry (1982) argue that a structure is a 'system of relationships which underlie and account for the sets of observable social relationships and those of social consciousness'. Similarly, Sayer (1984) defines structures as 'sets of internally related objects or practices'.

Sayer uses the example of the relationship between landlords and tenants to illustrate a structure in society. The existence of a landlord depends upon the existence of tenants, and 'the landlord–tenant relation itself presupposes the existence of private property, rent, the production of an economic surplus and so on; together they form a structure'.

Structures impose limitations or constraints upon what happens, but mechanisms and the variables that affect them determine the actual course of events. For example, the structure of relationships between landlords and tenants does not determine which individual occupies the property being rented, but it does determine that the tenant pays rent and the landlord does not.

Structures are often unobservable, but a natural or social scientist can work out that they are there by

observing their effects. Social classes cannot be seen, nor can the infrastructure and superstructure of society, but to a Marxist they are real.

Science and sociology

According to the realist view of science, much of sociology is scientific. To realist sociologists such as Keat and Urry (1982), Marxist sociology is scientific because it develops models of the underlying structures and processes in society, which are evaluated and modified in the light of empirical evidence. Unlike positivists, realists do not automatically reject interpretive sociology as unscientific, because they believe that studying unobservable meanings and motives is perfectly compatible with a scientific subject.

From this point of view, there is relatively little difference between social and natural sciences. Some branches of natural science which have the luxury of studying 'closed' systems can be more precise than sociology, but others face the same difficulty as sociology in trying to deal with highly complex open systems. Both natural sciences and sociology have common aims: they try to develop models and theories that explain the world as objectively as possible on the basis of the available evidence.

Whether sociology can be completely objective is the subject of the final section.

Methodology, values and objectivity

One of the reasons why sociologists have been so concerned with the question of whether sociology is a science is because of the widespread assumption that science is **objective**, or **value-free**. Robert Bierstedt stated:

> *Objectivity means that the conclusions arrived at as the result of inquiry and investigation are independent of the race, colour, creed, occupation, nationality, religion, moral preference, and political predisposition of the investigator. If his research is truly objective, it is independent of any subjective elements, any personal desires, that he may have.* Bierstedt, 1963

However, even Bierstedt's own definition of objectivity may reveal his values. By assuming that the investigator is male, Bierstedt could be accused of having a patriarchal bias in his work. The quest for objectivity may not be as straightforward as it first appears.

Many of the founders of sociology believed that sociology could and should be value-free. Early positivists such as Comte and Durkheim argued that objectivity was attainable by adopting a 'scientific' methodology. Marx also believed his sociology was objective and 'scientific', although he saw society very differently. Weber did not think complete value-freedom was possible, but he did believe that, once a topic for research had been chosen, the researcher could be objective. He argued that sociologists should not make value judgements, that is, they should not state what aspects of society they found desirable or undesirable.

Despite the claims of these important sociologists, it is doubtful whether their own work met the criteria necessary for complete value-freedom.

Functionalists in general have been accused of holding politically conservative views in assuming that existing social institutions serve a useful purpose. This implies that anything other than slow evolutionary change is harmful to society.

Durkheim accepted the need for certain changes in society, but his personal values are evident in his belief that the inheritance of wealth should be abolished and professional associations should be established (see pp. 858–9).

Few would claim that Marx's sociology was free from his political and moral beliefs. Marx's desire for proletarian revolution influenced most aspects of his work.

Weber's work often appears more value-free than that of functionalists or Marxists, but there is little doubt that his personal values influenced his research. Weber's writings on bureaucracy (see pp. 874–8) were strongly influenced by his fear that bureaucratic organizations would stifle human freedom. In his words: 'What can we oppose to this machinery in order to keep a portion of mankind free from this parcelling-out of the soul, from this supreme mastery of the bureaucratic way of life?' (quoted in Nisbet, 1967).

Even if it is true that such eminent sociologists allowed their values to influence their research, it does not necessarily follow that it is impossible to achieve value-freedom in sociology. To many contemporary sociologists, there is, however, no prospect of a completely value-free sociology. According to this view, total objectivity is impossible because values inevitably enter every stage of the production of sociological knowledge.

Weber recognized that values would influence the choice of topics for study. He argued that the sociologist had to have some way of choosing from the almost infinite number of possible areas of social life that could be studied. Weber believed that 'value relevance' would influence the choice. Researchers would choose to research topics which they thought were important, and, more significantly, which they thought were of central importance to society. Weber himself chose to study the advent of capitalism and the nature of bureaucracy, because he saw these as the most important developments in Western societies.

The values of other sociologists have also been evident in their choice of topics for research. Peter Townsend demonstrated his belief that poverty is a serious problem by devoting years of his life to its study (see pp. 217–18). Marxists have shown the importance they attach to inequality in their studies of wealth, income and stratification. Feminists have revealed their values by deciding that it is important to study such aspects of social life as domestic violence, rape and housework. Simply by selecting an issue to study, sociologists reveal what aspects of society they believe are significant.

Having selected a topic, sociologists then choose what aspects of that topic to study, and what approach they are

going to adopt. According to Alvin Gouldner (1970), this involves making 'domain assumptions'. These are the basic assumptions that sociologists make about the nature of social life and human behaviour. Gouldner said:

> *Domain assumptions about man and society might include, for example, dispositions to believe that men are rational or irrational; that society is precarious or fundamentally stable; that social problems will correct themselves without planned intervention; that human behaviour is unpredictable; that man's true humanity resides in his feelings and sentiments.* Gouldner, 1970

Gouldner believed that in practice all sociologists tend to commit themselves to a particular set of domain assumptions, and these direct the way that research is conducted and conclusions are reached. Without some starting point, research cannot proceed and sociological knowledge cannot be created. Domain assumptions about human behaviour – such as whether it is governed by external or internal stimuli and whether it is rational or irrational – will tend to determine whether quantitative or qualitative methods are adopted.

In designing and carrying out research all researchers have to be selective. When producing a questionnaire or planning an interview, some questions have to be chosen and others excluded. The choice will be influenced by the theories and hypotheses to which a particular researcher attaches credibility. Once the data have been collected, researchers need to interpret the results, and very often the results do not speak for themselves.

For example, in the debate about secularization, the development of sects, cults and the New Age has been variously interpreted both as evidence for and as evidence against the theory of secularization, depending on the standpoint of the researchers (see pp. 439–40).

Interpretive sociologists have tended to be very critical of those using quantitative methods. They have argued that many sociologists simply impose their own views of reality on the social world. As a result, they distort and misrepresent the very reality they seek to understand. Research techniques such as interviews, questionnaires and social surveys are a part of this process of distortion. They come between the sociologist and the social world and so remove any opportunity he or she might have of discovering social reality.

From this point of view, direct observation of everyday activity provides the most likely, if not the only, means of obtaining valid knowledge of the social world. This at least allows researchers to come face-to-face with the reality they seek to understand. Since the social world is seen to be a construction of its members, that world can only be understood in terms of members' categories and constructs. Thus Jack Douglas (1971) argued that sociologists must 'study the phenomena of everyday life on their own terms', they must 'preserve the integrity of that phenomena'.

While phenomenologists might be looking in the right direction, the problem of validity remains unsolved. Though face-to-face with social reality, the observer can only see the social world through their own eyes. No two sociologists will see that world in exactly the same way. A participant observer cannot note and record everything that happens in their presence and, like the sociologist devising a questionnaire, has to be selective. In these circumstances the researcher's values will influence what events they believe to be important.

Critical researchers believe it is important to understand how the social world is seen from the viewpoint of those being studied. However, they do not accept that this alone will produce objective knowledge. To them, it is also important to look beyond the common-sense knowledge of people to uncover the structures of oppression which lie behind everyday life (see pp. 804–8). However, critics believe that the oppressive structures they discover simply reflect their own prejudices: feminists will always find patriarchal oppression, Marxists will find class exploitation, critical gay sociologists will find homophobia, and anti-racists will find racism.

Because of these sorts of considerations, Derek Phillips (1973) argued: 'An investigator's values influence not only the problems he selects for study but also his methods for studying them and the sources of data he uses.' In 'Anti-Minotaur: the myth of a value-free sociology' (1975), Gouldner made a similar point. He argued that, just as the bull and the man in the mythical Minotaur cannot be separated, so facts and values cannot be separated in sociological research.

Weber argued that sociologists' values should be kept out of their research, and that they should not make value judgements – judgements about right or wrong. Gouldner regarded this as dishonest. Since sociologists must have values, they should be open about them so that others can decide for themselves to what degree values have influenced the research. Gouldner said:

> *If sociologists ought not to express their personal values in the academic setting, how then are students to be safeguarded against the unwitting influence of these values which shape the sociologists' selection of problems, his preferences for certain hypotheses or conceptual schemes, and his neglect of others? For these are unavoidable and, in this sense, there is and can be no value-free sociology. The only choice is between an expression of one's values, as open and honest as it can be … and a vain ritual of moral neutrality which, because it invites men to ignore the vulnerability of reason to bias, leaves it at the mercy of irrationality.* Gouldner, 1975

Some postmodernists, such as Lyotard (1984), reject altogether the possibility of producing any objective knowledge. To Lyotard, the creation of knowledge is just a language-game which can only be judged in terms of its saleability. There is no way of distinguishing between true and untrue knowledge, no way of being objective. For many postmodern writers, knowledge simply reflects the viewpoint and the values of different social groups. No one viewpoint and set of values can be seen as superior to any other. As Martyn Hammersley (1995) says, postmodernism involves 'a sustained scepticism and distrust of all claims to knowledge'.

Given these problems, sociology might appear to consist of little more than personal opinions. If this were the case there would seem little point in the subject existing. However, some sociologists believe it is positively desirable for sociologists to be committed to certain values. For example, Phil Carspecken (1996), along with other critical social scientists, believes sociologists should be committed to changing the world.

Nevertheless, this does not prevent sociologists from trying to avoid bias in their research. Although humans might view the world differently, there is an objective world which 'resists' human action. For example, a person cannot walk through a brick wall, whether they think it exists or not. The way that the material world resists our actions provides some basis for reaching agreement about objective statements. Truth claims – claims that you have made an objective statement – are based upon reaching such agreements about what does and does not exist. These agreements in turn can be used to evaluate the claims of different theories. A critical researcher cannot therefore find whatever they want to find.

Empirical investigations, which are more than the subjective interpretations of individuals, mean that sociology can be more than just value-laden opinions. Truth claims, even if accepted now, may be rejected at some point in the future. A consensus about what is and is not true may break down. However, because they are based upon reaching agreements about what is true, they have a more solid foundation than individual interpretations.

Carspecken (1996) even argues that, up to a point, values can be evaluated as well. He uses the example of somebody arguing that poverty is not bad because 'there has always been poverty and always will be; it is natural'. In this case the value claim that poverty is not bad can be critically examined by using examples of societies which have no poverty, and by trying to show that some things which are natural are not necessarily good. Carspecken says: 'We might point to many things in nature that are morally repugnant to human beings and claim that humans must alter nature and establish morality through their own efforts.'

Such arguments can only proceed by finding some sort of common ground – something which all those discussing the issue can agree is good or bad. Such common ground may not always be attainable, but often it is, and some rational evaluation of values becomes possible.

If Carspecken's views are correct, then values are integral to sociology and indeed to all disciplines, but that does not prevent rational debate and the empirical testing of theories. Sociology can make claims about the truth and hope to gain acceptance for them. From this viewpoint, sociologists should also accept and welcome a commitment to using the production of sociological knowledge to try to improve society.

Summary and conclusions

All sociologists who wish to carry out research have to use one method or another, or a combination of several. The type of method that they use is undoubtedly guided by their values and by the theoretical perspective that most influences their work. However, it is probably true that researchers are increasingly using several methods in particular studies, and most sociologists are not very rigid about what they consider to be the best methods to use.

Methodology is guided as much by practicalities as it is by theories, ethics and values. No research method produces knowledge which is perfect and cannot be contested. Inevitably, all research gives a partial view of social reality, and there is always some room to question the validity and/or reliability of any study.

However, by being self-critical, researchers can try to minimize the extent to which their research distorts social reality. By being explicit about their methods, they allow other researchers to evaluate their work and, if they wish, to conduct their own research to check if they get similar results.

Social science research influences, at least to some extent, social policies, and without it policy makers would have little idea about whether their policies were having any positive effect. Whatever the imperfections of social science research, without it social policies would have to be based on little more than guesswork.

CHAPTER 15
Sociological theory

The sociological imagination is more important than ever if we are to control the risks found in contemporary societies, and fulfil the potential for improving people's lives.

Introduction

A theory is a set of ideas that provides an explanation for something. A sociological theory is a set of ideas that provides an explanation for human society. Critics of sociology sometimes object to the emphasis that sociologists place on theory, and suggest it might be better to let 'the facts' speak for themselves. But there are no facts without theory. For example, in Western society, the generally accepted facts that the world is round and that it orbits the sun are inseparable from theories that explain the nature and movement of heavenly bodies. However, in some non-Western societies whose members employ different theories, the view that the world is flat and the solar system revolves around it is accepted as a statement of fact. Clearly, the facts do not speak for themselves.

Like all theory, sociological theory is selective. No amount of theory can hope to explain everything, or account for the infinite amount of data that exist, or encompass the endless ways of viewing reality. Theories are therefore selective in terms of their priorities and perspectives and the data they define as significant. As a result, they provide a particular and partial view of reality.

There are a wide variety of sociological theories, and they can be grouped together according to various criteria. One of the most important of these is the distinction between **structural** perspectives and **social action** perspectives. This distinction will form the framework for the early parts of this chapter. However, there is also an important distinction between **modern** and **postmodern** perspectives in sociology. This distinction will be discussed in detail later in the chapter.

Structural versus social action theories

Structural perspectives and social action perspectives differ in the way they approach the analysis of society. Structural, or macro, perspectives analyse the way society as a whole fits together. Thus, despite their differences, both functionalism and Marxism use a model of how society as a whole works. Many functionalists base their model of society around the assumption of functional prerequisites or basic needs, and go on to explain how different parts of society help to meet those needs. Marxists, on the other hand, see society as resting upon an economic base or infrastructure, with a superstructure rising above it. They see society as divided into social classes which have the potential to be in conflict with each other.

The main differences between functionalist and Marxist perspectives, then, concern the ways in which they characterize the social structure. Functionalists stress the extent to which the different elements of the social structure fit together harmoniously. Marxists stress the lack of fit

between the different parts, particularly social classes, and so emphasize the potential for social conflict.

Marxism is one example of a conflict perspective. There are a variety of interpretations and adaptations of Marx's work, and some neo-Marxists question some of the concepts used by Marx, while accepting his overall approach. Other conflict theorists agree with Marx and neo-Marxists that there is conflict in society, but disagree about the causes and types of conflict. They draw upon the work of Max Weber, who argued that many groups, apart from classes, can be in conflict for the scarce resources in society (see pp. 29–30).

Not all sociological perspectives base their analysis upon an examination of the structure of society as a whole. Rather than seeing human behaviour as being largely determined by society, they see society as being the product of human activity. They stress the meaningfulness of human behaviour, denying that it is primarily determined by the structure of society.

These approaches are variously called social action approaches, interpretive sociology, or micro sociology. Max Weber was the first sociologist to advocate a social action approach (although he also uses elements of a structural approach in parts of his work). In contemporary sociology there are two main varieties of this type of sociology.

Symbolic interactionists try to explain human behaviour and human society by examining the ways in which people interpret the actions of others, develop a self-concept or self-image, and act in terms of meanings. They do not deny the existence of some elements of a social structure: for example, they acknowledge the presence of social roles, and some interactionists also use the concept of social class. However, they believe that the social structure is fluid and constantly changing in response to interaction.

Ethnomethodology moves even further from a structural approach by denying the existence of a social structure as such. To ethnomethodologists, the social world consists of the definitions and categorizations of members of society. These subjective meanings are social reality. The job of the sociologist, in their view, is to interpret, describe and above all to understand this subjective reality.

It is not possible to provide clear dividing lines between sociological perspectives. There are many approaches that do not fit neatly even into such broad categories as structural or social action perspectives. For example, the description of Marx's social theories later in this chapter will show that elements of a social action approach can be found within his work; and Weber's work also uses elements of both types of perspective. Nevertheless, it is reasonable to divide much sociology into these two categories, because the emphasis within perspectives like functionalism and Marxism is so different from that found within interactionism and ethnomethodology.

Some sociologists have made a conscious attempt to bridge the apparent gulf between social action and structural perspectives. Max Weber was arguably the first sociologist to try to combine an analysis of the structures of society with analysis of individual social actions; more recently, the sociologist Pierre Bourdieu combined structural and social action approaches in the study of social stratification; and Anthony Giddens, another sociologist, has also tried to bridge the gap that seems to separate structural and social action approaches.

Some of the most recent approaches within sociology have not been particularly concerned with issues to do with the difference between structural and social action perspectives. Postmodernism, in particular, defies categorization in these terms.

Much of the inspiration for postmodernism comes from the poststructuralist perspectives discussed in Chapter 11 (see pp. 681–2). Poststructuralism takes the analysis of language as its starting point, rather than the analysis of social structures or social action. However, most postmodernists tend to be hostile to structural perspectives that claim to be able to explain how society works. Postmodernists generally reject the claim that any single theory is able to explain the social world.

This brief summary cannot do justice to the subtleties and complexities of sociological theory. Some of these complexities will be examined later in this chapter, but it is important to note that the chapter is far from comprehensive. There are a number of other perspectives that have not been included. Furthermore, sociology is a developing discipline and sociological perspectives are continually being refined and developed in the light of theoretical debate and empirical investigation. Nevertheless, it is possible to outline the central features of the most influential perspectives in the discipline.

Functionalism

Introduction

Functionalist analysis has a long history in sociology. It is prominent in the work of Auguste Comte (1798–1857) and Herbert Spencer (1820–1903), two of the founding fathers of the discipline. It was developed by Emile Durkheim (1858–1917) and refined by Talcott Parsons (1902–79). During the 1940s and 1950s functionalism was the dominant social theory in American sociology. Since that time it has steadily dropped from favour, partly because of damaging criticism, partly because other approaches are seen to answer certain questions more successfully, and partly because it simply went out of fashion.

Society as a system

Functionalism views society as a system: that is, as a set of interconnected parts which together form a whole. The basic unit of analysis is society, and its various parts are understood primarily in terms of their relationship to the whole.

The early functionalists often drew an analogy between society and an organism such as the human body. They argued that an understanding of any organ in the body, such as the heart or lungs, involves an understanding of its relationship to other organs and, in particular, its contribution towards the maintenance of the organism. In the same way, an understanding of any part of society requires an analysis of its relationship to other parts and, most importantly, its contribution to the maintenance of society. Continuing this analogy, functionalists argued that,

just as an organism has certain basic needs that must be satisfied if it is to survive, so society has basic needs that must be met if it is to continue to exist. Thus social institutions such as the family and religion are analysed as a part of the social system rather than as isolated units. In particular, they are understood with reference to the contribution they make to the system as a whole.

Functional prerequisites

These basic needs or necessary conditions of existence are sometimes known as the **functional prerequisites** of society. Various approaches have been used to identify functional prerequisites.

Some sociologists have examined a range of societies in an attempt to discover what factors they have in common. For example, Davis and Moore (1967, first published 1945) claimed that all societies have some form of social stratification, and George Peter Murdock (1949) maintained that the family exists in every known human society. From these observations it is assumed that institutional arrangements, such as social stratification and the family, meet needs that are common to all societies. Thus, from the universal presence of social stratification, it is argued that all societies require some mechanism to ensure that social positions are adequately filled by motivated persons. From the universality of the family, it is assumed that some mechanism for the reproduction and socialization of new members is a functional prerequisite of society.

However, the problem with this approach is its assumption that the presence of the same institution in every society indicates that it meets the same need. The fact that a form of stratification exists in all societies does not necessarily mean that it reflects 'the universal necessity which calls forth stratification in any social system', as Davis and Moore claim. Put another way, it cannot be assumed that stratification systems perform the same function in all societies. (Davis and Moore's theory of stratification is outlined in Chapter 1, pp. 22–3.)

An alternative approach to the identification of functional prerequisites involves an analysis of those factors that would lead to the breakdown or termination of society. Thus Marion J. Levy (1952) argued that a society would cease to exist if its members became extinct, if they became totally apathetic, if they were involved in a war of all against all, or if they were absorbed into another society. Therefore, in order for a society to survive, it must have some means of preventing these events from occurring. These means are the functional prerequisites of society.

For example, to ensure that members of society do not become extinct, a system for reproducing new members and maintaining the health of existing members is essential. This involves role differentiation and role assignment. Individuals must be assigned to produce food and to reproduce and care for new members of society. In order for these essential services to be maintained, individuals must be sufficiently motivated to perform their roles. If they were totally apathetic, the social system would collapse through lack of effort. A system of goals and rewards is necessary to motivate members of society to want to do what they have to do in order to maintain the system.

By specifying the factors that would lead to the termination of society, Levy claimed to have identified the basic requirements that must be met if society is to survive.

The problem with this approach to the specification of functional prerequisites is its reliance on common sense and ingenuity. In the case of a biological organism it is possible to identify basic needs, since it can be shown that if these needs are not met, the organism dies. However, societies change rather than die. As a result, it is not possible to identify unequivocally those aspects of a social system that are indispensable to its existence. Functionalists using Levy's approach have drawn up lists of functional prerequisites that are often similar in content but never quite the same.

A related approach involves the deduction of functional prerequisites from an abstract model of the social system. For example, if society is viewed as a system, certain survival needs can be deduced from an abstract model of the system. Any system is made up of interconnected parts. If a system is to survive, there must be a minimum amount of integration between its parts. There must be some degree of fit, which requires an element of mutual compatibility of the parts. From this type of analysis, the functional prerequisites of society may be inferred. Thus any social system requires a minimum amount of integration between its parts.

From this assumption, functional analysis turns to an examination of the parts of society, to investigate how they contribute to the integration of the social system. In this respect, religion has often been seen as a powerful mechanism for social integration. Religion is seen to reinforce the basic values of society. Social norms, which derive from these values, structure and direct behaviour in the various institutions of society. The parts of the social system are integrated in that they are largely infused with the same basic values. Were the various institutions founded on conflicting values, the system would tend to disintegrate.

Since religion promotes and reinforces social values, it can be seen as an integrating mechanism. But the problem with deducing functional prerequisites such as integration from an abstract model of the social system is that they are inferred rather than unequivocally identified.

The concept of function

The concept of 'function' in functionalist analysis refers to the contribution of the part to the whole. More specifically, the function of any part of society is the contribution it makes to meeting the functional prerequisites of the social system. Parts of society are functional in so far as they maintain the system and contribute to its survival. Thus a function of the family is to ensure the continuity of society by reproducing and socializing new members. A function of religion is to integrate the social system by reinforcing common values.

Some functionalists, particularly Robert Merton (1968), employ the concept of 'dysfunction' to refer to the effects of any social institution which detract from the maintenance of society. However, in practice, they have been primarily concerned with the search for functions, and relatively little use has been made of the concept of dysfunction.

The ideology of functionalism

Functionalist analysis has focused on the question of how social systems are maintained. This focus has tended to

individuals, groups or society as a whole. Thus, poverty may be seen as dysfunctional for the poor, but functional for the non-poor and for society as a whole.

Merton suggested that the postulate of universal functionalism should be replaced by 'the provisional assumption that persisting cultural forms have a net balance of functional consequences either for the society considered as a unit or for subgroups sufficiently powerful to retain these forms intact, by means of direct coercion or indirect persuasion'.

The problem of indispensability

Merton's third criticism was directed towards the 'postulate of indispensability'. This assumption states that certain institutions or social arrangements are indispensable to society. Functionalists have often seen religion in this light. For example, Davis and Moore (1967, first published 1945) claim religion 'plays a unique and indispensable part in society'.

Merton questioned the assumption of indispensability, arguing that the same functional prerequisites may be met by a range of alternative institutions. Thus there is no justification for assuming that institutions such as the family, religion and social stratification are a necessary part of all human societies.

To replace the idea of indispensability, Merton suggested the concept of 'functional equivalents' or 'functional alternatives'. From this point of view, a political ideology such as communism can provide a functional alternative to religion. It can meet the same functional prerequisites as religion. However, Merton was still left with the problem of actually identifying functional prerequisites.

Merton argued that the postulates of the functional unity of society, universal functionalism and indispensability are little more than articles of faith. They are matters for investigation and should not form prior assumptions.

Merton claimed his framework for functionalist analysis removed the charge that functionalism is ideologically based. He argued that the parts of society should be analysed in terms of their 'effects' or 'consequences' on society as a whole and on individuals and groups within society. Since these effects can be functional, dysfunctional or non-functional, Merton claimed that the value judgement present in the assumption that all parts of the system are functional was therefore removed.

Functionalism – a critique

Teleology

Functionalism has been subjected to considerable criticism. Part of this criticism is directed at the logic of functionalist enquiry. In particular, it is argued that the type of explanation employed is **teleological**.

A teleological explanation states that the parts of a system exist because of their beneficial consequences for the system as a whole. The main objection to this type of reasoning is that it treats an effect as a cause. Thus Davis and Moore's theory of stratification outlines the positive effects or functions of social stratification and then proceeds to argue that these effects explain its origin. But an effect cannot explain a cause, since causes must always precede effects. Therefore, the effects of stratification cannot occur until a system of social stratification has already been established.

It may be argued that members of society unconsciously respond to social needs, and so create the institutions necessary for the maintenance of society. However, there is no evidence of the existence of such unconscious motivations.

Assessing effects

Functionalism is on stronger logical ground when it argues that the continued existence of an institution may be explained in terms of its effects. Thus, once an institution has originated, it continues to exist if, on balance, it has beneficial effects on the system. But there are problems with this type of explanation. It is extremely difficult to establish that the net effect of any institution is beneficial to society. A knowledge of all its effects would be required in order to weigh the balance of functions and dysfunctions. As the debate on the functional merits and demerits of stratification indicates, there is little evidence that such knowledge is forthcoming (see Chapter 1, pp. 21–3).

The problems involved in assessing the effects of a social institution may be illustrated in terms of the analogy between society and a physical organism. Biologists are able to show that certain parts of an organism make positive contributions to its maintenance, since, if those parts stopped functioning, life would cease. Since societies change rather than die, sociologists are unable to apply similar criteria. In addition, standards exist in biology for assessing the health of an organism. In terms of these standards, the contribution of the various parts can be judged. There are no comparable standards for assessing the 'health' of a society. For these reasons there are problems with the argument that a social institution continues to exist because, on balance, its effects are beneficial to society.

Value consensus and social order

Functionalists such as Parsons, who see the solution to the problem of social order in terms of value consensus, have been strongly criticized.

First, their critics argue that consensus is assumed rather than shown to exist. Research has failed to reveal unequivocally a widespread commitment to the various sets of values that are seen to characterize Western society.

Second, the stability of society may owe more to the absence, rather than the presence, of value consensus. For example, a lack of commitment to the value of achievement by those at the bottom of stratification systems may serve to stabilize society. Thus Michael Mann argues that, in a society where members compete for unequal rewards, 'cohesion results precisely because there is no common commitment to core values' (quoted in Mennell, 1974). If all members of society were strongly committed to the value of achievement, the failure in terms of this value of those at the base of the stratification system might well produce disorder.

Third, consensus in and of itself will not necessarily result in social order. In fact it may produce the opposite result. As Pierre van den Berghe notes, 'consensus on norms such as extreme competition and individualistic laissez-faire, or suspicion and treachery … or malevolence and

resort to witchcraft is hardly conducive to social solidarity and integration' (quoted in Mennell, 1974). Therefore, the content of values rather than value consensus as such can be seen as the crucial factor with respect to social order.

Determinism

Functionalism has been criticized for what many see as its deterministic view of human action. Its critics have argued that, in terms of functionalist theory, human behaviour is portrayed as determined by the system. In particular, the social system has needs, and the behaviour of its members is shaped to meet these needs. Rather than creating the social world in which they live, people are seen as creations of the system.

Thus David Walsh (1972) argues that Parsons treats human action 'as determined by the characteristics of the system per se'. By means of socialization, humanity is programmed in terms of the norms and values of the social system; it is kept on the straight and narrow by mechanisms of social control that exist to fulfil the requirements of the system; its actions are structured in terms of social roles that are designed to meet the functional prerequisites of society. Humanity is pictured as an automaton, programmed, directed and controlled by the system.

Walsh rejects this view of humanity. Arguing from a phenomenological perspective, he claims humanity actively constructs its own social world rather than being shaped by a social system that is somehow external to its being. Walsh maintains that the concept of a social system represents a 'reification' of the social world. Functionalists have converted social reality into a natural system external to social actors. In doing so, they have translated the social world into something that it is not. They have tended to portray the social system as the active agent, whereas, in reality, only human beings act.

Coercion and conflict

Critics of functionalism have argued that it tends to ignore coercion and conflict. For example, Alvin Gouldner (1970) states: 'While stressing the importance of the ends and values that men pursue, Parsons never asks whose ends and values these are. Are they pursuing their own ends or those imposed upon them by others?'

Few functionalists give serious consideration to the possibility that some groups in society, acting in terms of their own particular interests, dominate others. From this point of view, social order is imposed by the powerful, and value consensus is merely a legitimation of the position of the dominant group.

In his criticism of one of Parsons's major works, *The Social System*, David Lockwood (1970) argues that Parsons's approach is 'highly selective in its focus on the role of the normative order in the stabilization of social systems'. In focusing on the contribution of norms and values to social order, Parsons largely fails to recognize the conflicts of interest that tend to produce instability and disorder. Lockwood argues that, since all social systems involve competition for scarce resources, conflicts of interest are built into society. Conflict is not simply a minor strain in the system which is contained by value consensus. Rather, it is a central and integral part of the system itself.

Functionalism reconsidered

Despite the widespread criticism of functionalism, it should not be rejected out of hand. Durkheim's work, for example, has provided insights that have helped modern sociologists to understand contemporary societies. Jonathon H. Turner and Alexandra Maryanski (1979) argue that, although functionalism has many flaws, it remains useful. Many of its basic assumptions still guide much sociological research: for example, the assumption that society should be seen as an integral whole; that its parts are interdependent; that social institutions exist and they do have effects; and that society is structured and the social structure directs human behaviour.

Social capital

Robert D. Putnam – *Bowling Alone*

Introduction

Although it would be difficult to find any sociologists today who would call themselves functionalists, there are some sociologists who have developed theories which have a good deal in common with functionalism. Robert D. Putnam is a case in point.

Putnam published an influential and widely read book, *Bowling Alone*, in 2000, in which he claimed that since the 1950s and 1960s the USA had experienced a serious decline in what he terms **social capital**. The concept of social capital as used by Putnam emphasizes the importance of the bonds between individuals which bring them together in society.

Like functionalists, Putnam sees the bonds that unite people as part of a society as crucial to the well-being of the society as a whole. His ideas on social capital are somewhat reminiscent of Durkheim's discussion of the need for 'social solidarity' (see pp. 858–9). Indeed at one point in *Bowling Alone* Putnam refers to Durkheim's study of suicide to support his claim that a lack of social capital can have negative effects such as an increase in suicide rates.

Despite these similarities, Putnam could not be called a functionalist and his writings make a distinctive contribution to sociological theory in their own right.

Social capital and generalized reciprocity

Putnam defines social capital as 'connections among individuals – social networks and the norms of reciprocity and trustworthiness that arise from them' (2000, p. 19). Social capital is manifested in such phenomena as taking part in clubs and organizations, socializing with people outside one's immediate family, taking part in politics, doing voluntary work, and playing sports, particularly team sports.

To Putnam, social capital is useful both for individuals and for society. For example, individuals with high levels of social capital tend to be happier than those with lower levels, and social networks can be useful for finding

employment. But even more important are the benefits for society in general. Strong social networks tend to foster mutual obligations between people – people feel obliged to be helpful and to behave in moral ways towards those with whom they are involved in social networks.

People behave well towards others in dense social networks (where many people have links with one another) in the expectation that others will behave well towards them in return. In a dense social network (such as a village) an individual might expect other individuals to reciprocate their kind, generous or considerate behaviour directly at some point in the future. In addition, it is important to maintain one's reputation so that other people will be happy to deal with you because they trust you. In a dense social network reciprocation builds up trust, and, in Putnam's words, 'trustworthiness lubricates social life' (2000, p. 21).

In a large, complex society, local and dense social networks in which most people know one another may not be present. However, in societies where people possess a lot of social capital it is possible to build up a norm of what Putnam calls **generalized reciprocity**. When this occurs people routinely take the interests of others into account when acting. This is not because they expect that particular person to do them a favour later, but because this is the accepted way of behaving in society.

Putnam describes generalized reciprocity in the following way: 'I'll do this for you without expecting anything specific back from you, in the confident expectation that someone else will do something for me down the road' (2000, p. 21). In the end, everybody benefits from this situation:

> *A society characterized by generalized reciprocity is more efficient than a distrustful society, for the same reason that money is more efficient than barter. If we don't have to balance every exchange instantly, we can get a lot more accomplished.* Putnam, 2000, p. 21

Putnam admits that although high levels of social capital usually benefit society, social capital can also be used in a harmful way. He says, 'Social capital ... can be directed towards malevolent, anti-social purposes just like any form of capital' (Putnam, 2000, p. 22). He gives the example of Timothy McVeigh, a ring-wing American terrorist who bombed the Federal building in Oklahoma City in 1995, killing 168 people and injuring over 800. In order to accomplish this, McVeigh needed considerable social capital to gain assistance from the other people involved in the plot. The plot was partly hatched while bowling with co-conspirators.

Similarly, social capital can be used in pursuit of sectarianism or to facilitate corruption. Putnam therefore distinguishes between two types of social capital.

- **Bonding social capital** reinforces the connections within groups and constitutes 'a kind of sociological superglue' (2000, p. 23). However, as suggested above, it can be used in a negative way. It is essential, therefore, that bridging social capital is also widespread.
- **Bridging social capital** reaches out to form connections between diverse social groups and allows information to travel between groups. Bridging social capital acts more like WD-40, lubricating social life.

Many organizations develop both types of social capital. For example, black churches produce bonding within black ethnic groups, but also bridging across class lines as they have both working-class and middle-class members.

The decline of social capital

Having established the importance of the different types of social capital, Putnam goes on to document what he sees as the decline of social capital in the USA. He argues that between the late 1950s and the middle of the 1960s social capital reached a peak, and since then it has declined. He uses a vast range of evidence to back up his case. The following are just some examples.

1. Political participation has declined. Voter turnout has fallen and fewer people are active in political parties.
2. Other forms of civic participation have also declined markedly. People are less likely than they were in the past to serve on local committees, make speeches, sign petitions or attend public meetings on town or school affairs. For example, between 1973–4 and 1993–4 the number of people who held a position as an officer of a club or organization fell by 42 per cent.
3. Between the 1960s and the 1990s there was a slow, but significant, decline in church membership of about 10 per cent.
4. In the mid-1950s, 32.5 per cent of the US workforce were unionized, but by 1998 this was down to 14.1 per cent, and the proportion of professionals who were members of their professional association had also declined.
5. Fewer people are involved in volunteering for charity work. Membership of some organizations, such as environmental groups, has increased, but most people in such groups play little active part and simply pay membership fees or give donations.
6. Participation rates in sport have fallen, especially team sports. Bowling remains popular, but people are much less likely to take part in bowling leagues and instead go bowling with close friends or family, or even go bowling alone.
7. Putnam also believes that informal social connections have declined. Here he distinguishes between ***machers*** (people who make things happen in the community), and ***schmoozers*** who are more involved in informal socializing. The figures discussed above indicate that the number of machers has declined, and other evidence suggests that *schmoozing* is waning as well. Survey research shows that in the mid- to late 1970s Americans entertained friends on average fourteen to fifteen times per year, but this had fallen to eight times by the late 1990s. Over the same period, Americans had become less likely to go to bars and nightclubs, and less likely to play cards with one another, attend parties or socialize with neighbours. People tend to focus more on their immediate family, but even here there is evidence of a decline in *schmoozing* as families are less likely to eat meals together than in the past.

Putnam believes that all this has taken its toll on the norms of reciprocity and the sense of trust which come with dense social networks. In 1952 over 50 per cent of

people thought people were 'as honest and moral as they used to be', but by 1998 this was down to around 28 per cent. Behaviour such as 'violent aggressive driving' has increased, and research shows that people are much less likely to stop at 'stop' signs while driving than they used to be. Furthermore, hitchhiking has virtually disappeared – another indication of the decline of trust.

Putnam accepts that there are some trends which seem to be going against this tide. Encounter groups, reading groups and self-help groups have all grown in popularity, but members are largely dealing with personal issues and such groups seem to have little spin-off in terms of developing wider social contacts.

The telephone has provided opportunities for *schmoozing*, but research suggests that telephone conversations tend to reinforce old friendships rather than produce new ones.

The internet and email have facilitated the development of new groups based on shared interests among geographically dispersed people, including 'BMW fanciers, bird-watchers and white supremacists' (Putnam, 2000, p. 172). However, these forms of communication are quite limited. Non-verbal communication is not possible through email, and this is important for building up trust. It is also likely that people increasingly stick to their own narrow interest groups (a process Putnam calls **cyberbalkanization**), thus reducing the amount of bridging social capital.

Although Putnam admits that it is too early to know exactly what effects new forms of communications will have on social capital, he concludes that there is little evidence that they will compensate for the marked decline of social capital in most areas of social life.

Reasons for the decline of social capital

Putnam goes on to examine the reasons for the decline of most types of social capital and argues that a range of factors have contributed to the change.

1 Increased employment of married women in dual-career families has reduced the time available to many people to participate in civic activities. Putnam estimates that this has contributed about 10 per cent of the decline in social capital.
2 Urban sprawl has led to people spending longer commuting to work and has disrupted communities so that neighbours have less in common with each other and less time to socialize. Putnam thinks that this is responsible for, again, around 10 per cent of the change.
3 Strong circumstantial evidence suggests that the increasing importance of television and other forms of electronic entertainment (such as computer games and DVDs) has also played a part. Putnam says that 'we are watching more TV, watching it more habitually, more pervasively, and more often alone, and watching more programs that were associated specifically with civic disengagement (entertainment, as distinct from news)' (2000, p. 246). This he believes accounts for some 25 per cent of the decline.
4 Putnam believes that by far the most important factor is a generational difference. He distinguishes between the 'baby boom generation' born between 1946 and 1964, and the 'X generation' born between 1965 and 1980. Baby boomers were influenced by events in the 1960s such as the civil rights movement, the assassinations of Martin Luther King and John F. Kennedy, and the trauma of the Vietnam War, all of which stimulated interest and involvement in public affairs. On the other hand, 'generation X'ers'

came of age in an era that celebrated personal goods and private initiative over shared public concern. Unlike boomers, who were once engaged, X'ers have never made the connection to politics so they emphasize the personal and private over the public and collective. Putnam, 2000, p. 259

They have been influenced by the uncertainty caused by economic problems in the 1970s and 1980s, and the insecurity caused by high rates of family breakdown, and they have had no 'collective success stories' such as winning the Second World War or the progress in combating racism. Lacking such sources of inspiration and facing personal uncertainty, they have become more materialistic than the previous generation were when they were young.

All this, Putnam suggests, may be 'part of a larger societal shift towards individual and material values and away from communal values' (2000, p. 272). Putnam thinks that the generational difference could explain about half of the decline in social capital.

Consequences and solutions

Putnam argues that the decline of social capital is of much more than academic interest since inter-personal bonds are crucial to the well-being of society. He quotes evidence which suggests that children flourish in the US states where there are high levels of social capital, but do poorly in education, are less healthy and are more likely to be involved in crime in states where social capital is low. He claims that in high social capital areas, 'public spaces are cleaner, the streets are friendlier and the streets are safer' (Putnam, 2000, p. 307). Economic prosperity is more likely in areas where 'trust and social networks flourish, individuals, firms and neighborhoods and even nations prosper' (p. 319).

In addition, people tend to be healthier and live longer, and, as Durkheim's study claimed, high levels of integration lead to lower suicide rates. A final advantage of high levels of social capital is that people take more interest in politics, participate more and tend to contribute more to their local communities.

Putnam does not deny that dense social networks can have a dark side – for example, they can support racist views. However, the evidence he reviews suggests that those who are engaged in civic life tend to be more tolerant than others. Social networks can also lead to financial advantages for those who have useful contacts. However, Putnam uses data which show that the US states with the highest levels of social capital are also the most egalitarian ones. So long as bonding social capital is balanced by bridging capital, then the dark side of social capital is unlikely to come to the fore.

Putnam admits that reversing the trend which has led to the decline of social capital will not be easy. However, a number of measures can be taken to make progress in that direction. These include improved civic education, encouraging community service amongst school children,

increasing the social connectivity of part-time workers at places of employment, planning cities to reduce urban sprawl and encourage a sense of community, and using the internet to build local social contacts as well as national and international ones.

In *Better Together* (2003), Robert Putnam and Lewis Feldstein examine a range of projects which they believe have increased social capital. For example, in Chicago local library branches are thriving and new branches opening. This has happened because they have started acting as community centres where social networks can develop and prosper. They host adult reading groups and bring in groups of school children who can get help with homework.

Such initiatives might be small-scale and are not a panacea. However, Putnam believes that they show that progress is possible, and that the combined effect of numerous initiatives could make a significant difference to levels of social capital and, in doing so, could do much to improve American society.

Evaluation

Putnam's ideas on social capital have proved influential and have been taken up by influential individuals such as David Halpern (2005), a senior policy adviser in Tony Blair's Prime Minister's Strategy Unit. However, Putnam is not the only theorist of social capital and his ideas are contradicted by the work of Pierre Bourdieu; and his work is criticized directly by some critics.

Pierre Bourdieu (1984) also discusses social capital, but unlike Putnam he sees its primary role as creating or sustaining class inequality. He sees social capital as something that is used by advantaged social classes to maintain or enhance their advantages over other groups (see pp. 87–9).

Bourdieu's work suggests that Putnam might underestimate the possible negative consequences of social capital, a theme taken up by John Field. Field notes that Bourdieu's work shows that 'actors can use their social capital ... as a means of accessing resources of status and privilege that increase their standing at the expense of others' (2003, p. 74). Field also emphasizes much more than Putnam that social capital can be put to perverse uses.

Social capital has been used to sustain networks of paedophiles, drug users, and organized crime. Furthermore, 'group identification can also involve stereotyping of outsiders' (p. 83), which can encourage forms of discrimination such as racism, homophobia or sexism. Field therefore says that Putnam is 'vulnerable to the accusation of functionalism' (p. 40). Like functionalists, he assumes that an aspect of society, in this case social capital, is beneficial to society as a whole, and he is therefore biased towards looking towards the 'bright side'.

Field also documents many other criticisms that have been levelled at Putnam.

1 He has been accused of simply assuming that dense social networks create trust, whereas in reality they can also sometimes produce distrust and hostility.
2 Feminists have criticized him for generalizing about gender differences in a sexist way. For example, at one stage Putnam suggests that women are much more likely than men to be *schmoozers* and he claims that men are much more likely to be *machers*.
3 Putnam tends to see the decline of social networks as a distinct process rather than as part of much wider changes in society as a whole. Field suggests that from the point of view of writers such as Beck (see pp. 86–8) and Giddens (see pp. 895–8), it is simply part of a much wider shift towards individualism or reflexivity in society as a whole. Viewed from this perspective, there is little point in trying to rebuild social capital since these wider social changes are likely to continue whatever attempts are made to counteract them.
4 Although Putnam was writing about America, others have suggested that his ideas are not applicable elsewhere. P. Hall (1999, quoted in Field, 2003) reviewed the evidence from Britain and found nothing to suggest that social capital is declining.

Despite highlighting these criticisms, Field himself is broadly sympathetic to Putnam's work. He claims there is good evidence that levels of social capital can have an influence on social life, and it is therefore an important variable and useful concept in sociology.

Field also believes that the concept of social capital is helpful in examining the relationship between the individual and the social structure. It focuses on an intermediate level of analysis or 'meso-level social structures' which link individuals and society. Such structures include 'family, neighbourhood, voluntary associations and public institutions' (Field, 2003, p. 139). It allows such structures to be examined in a systematic way 'as integrating elements between individuals and the wider social structures' (p. 139).

Field concludes by arguing that the concept of social capital as developed by Putnam emphasizes the importance of relationships, and 'This perhaps implies ... a return to Durkheimian concerns with social solidarity' (p. 140).

While functionalism itself may not be thriving as a perspective, some of the ideas and issues associated with it continue to be addressed in novel ways by contemporary sociologists.

Conflict perspectives

There are many varieties of conflict perspectives within sociology. This section will deal with some of the more influential ones. Despite their differences, all have a model of society as a whole, and all adopt a structural approach. Furthermore, all conflict perspectives use, in one form or another, the notion that there are groups in society that have different interests. In this respect they believe that social arrangements will tend to benefit some groups at the expense of others. Because of the existence of different interests, the potential for, and likelihood of, conflict is always present. Different groups pursuing their separate interests are likely to clash and produce some degree of instability in society.

Conflict theorists tend to agree that the existence of groups with different interests does not mean that they will be in conflict all the time. There may be periods of truce, or it may be that some social groups are persuaded that their interests are not different from those of other groups. Nevertheless, periods of harmony do not last for ever, and eventually conflict will return.

Conflict theories differ from functionalism in stressing the existence of competing groups, while functionalists stress cooperation between social groups. (Most functionalists believe that all members of society share the same interests and that there is a consensus over society's values.)

Conflict theories also differ from each other in important respects. Some theories stress conflict between particular social groups. For example, most forms of feminism see conflict between men and women as the central feature of society. (Feminism was discussed in detail in Chapter 2.) The racism approach to explaining ethnic disadvantage focuses on conflict between ethnic groups (see pp. 168–84).

Many conflict theories take their inspiration from the work of Karl Marx or Max Weber. Marxist and Weberian conflict theories tend to disagree over the precise basis on which society is divided into different groups, and the exact nature of the conflict that results from these divisions.

Marxism

Introduction

This section will focus on certain major themes in the work of Karl Marx (1818–83). Marx's views on various aspects of society have been examined in other chapters of the book. This section will seek to combine them into an overall perspective (see particularly Marx and Engels, 1950a, first published 1848, 1950b; Marx, 1974, first published 1909; Bottomore and Rubel, 1963).

The volume of Marx's writings over a period of about forty years was enormous. Many of his major projects remained unfinished, and part of the material published after his death was drawn from rough notes outlining future projects. Marx's writings contain inconsistencies, ambiguities and changes in emphasis. For these reasons there are many and varied interpretations of his work. This section, therefore, represents a particular interpretation of his ideas.

The historical perspective

Marx regarded people as both the producers and the products of society. They make society and themselves by their own actions. History is therefore the process of human self-creation. Yet people are also a product of society: they are shaped by the social relationships and systems of thought that they create. An understanding of society therefore involves a historical perspective which examines the process whereby humanity both produces, and is produced by, social reality.

A society forms a totality and can only be understood as such. The various parts of society are interconnected and influence each other. Thus, economic, political, legal and religious institutions can only be understood in terms of their mutual effect. Economic factors, however, exert the primary influence and largely shape other aspects of society.

The history of human society is a process of tension and conflict. Social change is not a smooth, orderly progression which gradually unfolds in harmonious evolution. Instead, it proceeds from contradictions built into society, which are a source of tension and ultimately the source of open conflict and radical change.

Dialectical materialism

It is often argued that Marx's view of history is based on the idea of the **dialectic**. Dialectical movement represents a struggle of opposites, a conflict of contradictions. Conflict provides the dynamic principle, the source of change. From this viewpoint, any process of change involves tension between incompatible forces. The struggle between incompatible forces grows in intensity until there is a final collision. The result is a sudden leap forward, which creates a new set of forces on a higher level of development. The dialectical process then begins again, as the contradictions within this new set of forces interact and conflict, and propel change.

The idea of dialectical change was developed by the German philosopher Hegel. Hegel applied it to the history of human society, and in particular to the realm of ideas. He saw historical change as a dialectical movement of human ideas and thoughts. Hegel believed that society is essentially an expression of these thoughts. Thus, in terms of the dialectic, conflict between incompatible ideas produces new concepts which provide the basis for social change.

Marx rejected the priority Hegel gave to thoughts and ideas. He argued that the source of change lies in contradictions – in the economic system in particular, and in society in general. As a result of the priority he gives to economic factors – to 'material life' – Marx's view of history is often referred to as **dialectical materialism**. Since people's ideas are primarily a reflection of the social relationships of economic production, they do not provide the main source of change. It is in contradictions and conflict in the economic system that the major dynamic for social change lies. Since all parts of society are interconnected, however, it is only through a process of interplay between these parts that change occurs.

The material basis of social life

History begins when humans actually produce their means of subsistence, when they begin to control nature. At a minimum, this involves the production of food and shelter. Marx argued: 'The first historical act is, therefore, the production of material life.'

Production is a social enterprise, since it requires cooperation. People must work together to produce the goods and services necessary for life. From the social relationships involved in production develops a 'mode of life' which can be seen as an expression of these relationships. This mode of life shapes human nature. In Marx's words: 'As individuals express their life so they are. What they are, therefore, coincides with their production, with what they produce and how they produce it.' Thus the nature of humanity, and the nature of society as a whole, derive primarily from the production of material life.

The emergence of contradictions

The major contradictions that propel change are found in the economic infrastructure of society. At the dawn of human history, when humans supposedly lived in a state of primitive

communism, those contradictions did not exist. The means of production and the products of labour were communally owned. Since each member of society produced both for themselves and for society as a whole, there were no conflicts of interest between individuals and groups.

However, with the emergence of private property and, in particular, private ownership of the means of production, the fundamental contradiction of human society was created. Through its ownership of the means of production, a minority is able to control, command and enjoy the fruits of the labour of the majority. Since one group gains at the expense of the other, a conflict of interest exists between the minority who own the means of production and the majority who perform productive labour. The tension and conflict generated by this contradiction are the major dynamic of social change.

For long periods of history, people are largely unaware of the contradictions that beset their societies. This is because their consciousness – their view of reality – is largely shaped by the social relationships involved in the process of production. Marx maintained: 'It is not the consciousness of men that determines their being, but, on the contrary, their social being determines their consciousness.'

The primary aspect of an individual's social being is the social relationships they enter into for the production of material life. Since these relationships are largely reproduced in terms of ideas, concepts, laws and religious beliefs, they are seen as normal and natural. Thus, when the law legitimizes the rights of private property, when religious beliefs justify economic arrangements, and the dominant concepts of the age define them as natural and inevitable, members of society will be largely unaware of the contradictions they contain.

In this way the contradictions within the economic infrastructure are compounded by the contradiction between human consciousness and objective reality. This consciousness is false. It presents a distorted picture of reality, since it fails to reveal the basic conflicts of interest that exist in the world that humanity has created.

For long periods of time, humanity is, at most, vaguely aware of these contradictions; yet even a vague awareness produces tension. This tension will ultimately find full expression and be resolved in the process of dialectical change.

Alienation

The course of human history involves a progressive development of the means of production – a steady increase in human control over nature. This is paralleled by a corresponding increase in human alienation, an increase that reaches its height in capitalist society.

Alienation is a situation in which the creations of humanity appear to humans as alien objects. Such creations are seen as independent from their creators and invested with the power to control them. People create their own society, but will remain alienated until they recognize themselves within their own creation. Until that time, humans will assign an independent existence to objects, ideas and institutions and be controlled by them. In the process they lose themselves, become strangers in the world they created: they become alienated.

Religion provides an example of human alienation. In Marx's view, 'Man makes religion, religion does not make man.' However, members of society fail to recognize that religion is of their own making. They assign to the gods an independent power, a power to direct their actions and shape their destiny. The more people invest in religion, the more they lose themselves. In Marx's words, 'The more man puts into God, the less he retains of himself.' In assigning their own powers to supernatural beings, people become alienated from themselves. Religion appears as an external force controlling human destiny, whereas, in reality, it is human-made.

Religion, though, is a reflection of a more fundamental source of alienation. It is essentially a projection of the social relationships involved in the process of production. If people are to find themselves and abolish illusions of religion, they must 'abandon a condition which requires illusions'. Humanity must therefore eradicate the source of alienation in the economic infrastructure. (Marxist views on religion are examined in Chapter 7, pp. 399–401.)

In Marx's view, productive labour is the primary, most vital human activity. In the production of objects, people 'objectify' themselves; they express and externalize their being; then they lose themselves in the object. The act of production then results in human alienation. This occurs when people regard the products of their labour as commodities, as articles for sale in the market-place. The objects of their creation are then seen to control their existence. They are seen to be subject to impersonal forces, such as the law of supply and demand, over which they have little or no control. In Marx's words, 'the object that labour produces, its product, confronts it as an alien being, as a power independent of the producer'. In this way people are estranged from the objects they produce; they become alienated from the most vital human activity – productive labour.

Alienation and capitalism

Alienation reaches its height in capitalist society, where labour is dominated by the requirements of capital, the most important of which is the demand for profit. These requirements determine levels of employment and wages, the nature and quantity of goods produced, and their method of manufacture.

Workers see themselves as prisoners of market forces over which they have no control. They are subject to the impersonal mechanisms of the law of supply and demand. They are at the mercy of the periodic booms and slumps that characterize capitalist economies. The workers therefore lose control over the objects they produce and become alienated from their product and the act of production. Their work becomes a means to an end, a means of obtaining money to buy the goods and services necessary for their existence. Unable to fulfil their being in the products of their labour, the workers become alienated from themselves in the act of production. Therefore, the more the workers produce, the more they lose themselves. In Marx's words, 'the greater this product the less he is himself'.

In Marx's view, the market forces that are seen to control production are not impersonal mechanisms beyond the control of humanity: they are human-made. Alienation is therefore the result of human activity rather than external forces with an existence independent of

humanity. If the products of labour are alien to the worker, they must belong to somebody else. This somebody else is the capitalist who owns and controls the means of production and the products of labour, who appropriates the wealth that labour produces.

Alienation therefore springs not from impersonal market forces but from relationships. Alienation will come to an end when the contradiction between human consciousness and objective reality is resolved. Then people will realize that the situation in which they find themselves is human-made and therefore subject to change by human action.

Communism

Given the priority Marx assigns to economic factors, an end to alienation involves a radical change in the economic infrastructure. In particular, it requires the abolition of private property and its replacement by communal ownership of the means of production – that is, the replacement of capitalism by communism.

Marx saw communism as 'the positive abolition of private property and thus of human self-alienation and therefore the real reappropriation of the human essence by and for man. This is communism as the complete and conscious return of man himself as a social, that is human being.'

In communist society conflicts of interest will disappear and antagonistic groups such as capitalists and workers will be a thing of the past. The products of labour will no longer be appropriated by some at the expense of others. With divisions in society eradicated, humans will be at one with their fellows, truly social beings. As such they will not lose themselves in the products of their labour. They will produce both for themselves and others at one and the same time.

In this situation 'each of us would have doubly affirmed himself and his fellow man'. Since individuals are at one with their fellows, the products of their labour, in which they objectify themselves, will not result in the loss of self. In productive labour each member of society contributes to the well-being of all and so expresses both their individual and social being. The objects that they produce are owned and controlled at once by themselves and their fellow humans.

Class

In Marx's view, humans are essentially social beings. He writes: 'society does not consist of individuals, but expresses the sum of interrelations, the relations within which these individuals stand'. An understanding of human history therefore involves an examination of these relationships, the most important of which are the relations of production.

Apart from communities based on primitive communism at the dawn of history, all societies are divided into social groups known as classes. The relationship between classes is one of antagonism and conflict. Throughout history, opposing classes have stood in 'constant opposition to one another, carried on an uninterrupted, now hidden, now open fight that each time ended either in a revolutionary reconstruction of society at large, or in the common ruin of contending classes'.

Class conflict forms the basis of the dialectic of social change. In Marx's view, expressed in the opening line of the Communist Manifesto, 'The history of all hitherto existing society is the history of the class struggle' (Marx and Engels, 1950a, first published 1848).

The two-class model

Class divisions result from the differing relationships of members of society to the means of production. The structure of all societies may be represented in terms of a simplified two-class model, consisting of a ruling and a subject class. The ruling class owes its dominance and power to its ownership and control of the means of production. The subjection and relative powerlessness of the subject class are due to its lack of ownership and therefore lack of control of the means of production.

The conflict of interest between the two classes stems from the fact that productive labour is performed by the subject class, yet a large part of the wealth so produced is appropriated by the ruling class. Since one class gains at the expense of the other, the interests of their members are incompatible. The classes stand opposed as exploiter and exploited, oppressor and oppressed. The labour of the subject class takes on the character of 'forced labour'. Since its members lack the necessary means to produce for themselves, they are forced to work for others.

Although Marx saw capitalism as characterized by a central struggle between two main classes – the bourgeoisie and the proletariat – he did recognize the existence of other classes. Some classes were left over from previous eras (such as the landowning aristocracy and peasants), and there were intermediate classes (such as the petty bourgeoisie of the self-employed and people with their own small businesses). Marx also recognized that there was a growing middle class of administrative workers in capitalist businesses, although he made little attempt to discuss the implications of this. (See articles such as 'The class struggles in France' and 'The Eighteenth Brumaire of Louis Bonaparte' – both in Marx and Engels, 1950 – for examples of Marx's more complex views on class.)

However, to Marx, these complications merely obscured the central importance of the two-class struggle, which would be at the heart of capitalism as it developed.

Class and consciousness

Members of both the main social classes are largely unaware of the true nature of their situation, of the reality of the relationship between ruling and subject classes. Members of the ruling class assume their particular interests are those of society as a whole; members of the subject class accept this view of reality and regard their situation as part of the natural order of things. This false consciousness is due to the fact that the relationships of dominance and subordination in the economic infrastructure are largely reproduced in the superstructure of society. In Marx's words, the relations of production constitute 'the real foundation on which rise legal and political superstructures and to which correspond definite forms of social consciousness. The mode of production in material life determines the general character of the social, political and spiritual processes of life.'

Ruling-class dominance is confirmed and legitimated in legal statutes, religious proscriptions and political legislation. The consciousness of all members of society is infused with ruling-class ideology, which proclaims the essential rightness, normality and inevitability of the status quo.

While the superstructure may stabilize society and contain its contradictions over long periods of time, this situation cannot be permanent. The fundamental contradictions of class societies will eventually find expression and will finally be resolved by the dialectic of historical change.

A radical change in the structure of society occurs when a class is transformed from a 'class in itself' to a 'class for itself'. A 'class in itself' refers to members of society who share the same objective relationships to the means of production. Thus, as wage labourers, members of the proletariat form a class in itself.

However, a class only becomes a 'class for itself' when its members are fully conscious of the true nature of their situation; when they are fully aware of their common interests and common enemy; when they realize that only by concerted action can they overthrow their oppressors; and when they unite and take positive, practical steps to do so. When a class becomes a class for itself, the contradiction between the consciousness of its members and the reality of their situation is ended.

Social change

The transition from feudalism to capitalism

A class becomes a class for itself when the forces of production have developed to the point where they cannot be contained within the existing relations of production. In Marx's words: 'For an oppressed class to be able to emancipate itself, it is essential that the existing forces of production and the existing social relations should be incapable of standing side by side.' Revolutionary change requires that the forces of production, on which the new order will be based, have developed in the old society. Therefore, the 'new higher relations of production never appear before the material conditions of their existence have matured in the womb of the old society.'

This process may be illustrated by the transition from feudal to capitalist society. Industrial capitalism gradually developed within the framework of feudal society. In order to develop fully, it required 'the free wage labourer who sells his labour-power to capital'. This provides a mobile labour force that can be hired and fired at will, and so efficiently utilized as a commodity in the service of capital. However, the feudal relations of production, which involved 'landed property with serf labour chained to it', tended to prevent the development of wage labourers.

Eventually, though, the forces of production of capitalism gained sufficient strength and impetus to lead to the destruction of the feudal system. At this point the rising class, the bourgeoisie, became a class for itself, and its members united to overthrow the feudal relations of production. When they succeeded, the contradiction between the new forces of production and the old relations of production was resolved.

Once a new economic order is established, the superstructure of the previous era is rapidly transformed. The contradiction between the new infrastructure and the old superstructure is now ended. Thus the political dominance of the feudal aristocracy was replaced by the power of the newly enfranchised bourgeoisie. The dominant concepts of feudalism, such as loyalty and honour, were replaced by the new concepts of freedom and equality. In terms of the new ideology, the wage labourer of capitalist society is free to sell his or her labour power to the highest bidder. The relationship between employer and employee is defined as a relationship between equals: the exchange of labour for wages as an exchange of equivalents.

But the resolution of old contradictions does not necessarily mean an end to contradictions in society. As in previous eras, the transition from feudalism to capitalism merely results in the replacement of an old set of contradictions by a new set.

The transition from capitalism to communism

The predicted rise of the proletariat is not strictly analogous with the rise of the bourgeoisie. The bourgeoisie formed a privileged minority of industrialists, merchants and financiers who forged new forces of production within feudal society. The proletariat forms an unprivileged majority which does not create new forces of production within capitalist society.

Marx believed, however, that the contradictions of capitalism were sufficient to transform the proletariat into a class for itself and bring about the downfall of the bourgeoisie. He saw the magnitude of these contradictions and the intensity of class conflict steadily increasing as capitalism developed. Thus there is a steady polarization of the two major classes as the intermediate strata are submerged into the proletariat. As capital accumulates, it is concentrated more and more into fewer hands – a process accompanied by the relative pauperization of the proletariat.

Production assumes an increasingly social and cooperative character as larger and larger groups of workers are concentrated in factories. At the same time the wealth produced by labour is appropriated by fewer and fewer individuals, as greater competition drives all but the larger companies out of business.

Such processes magnify and illuminate the contradictions of capitalism and increase the intensity of conflict. It is only a matter of time before members of the proletariat recognize that the reality of their situation is the alienation of labour. This awareness will lead the proletariat to 'a revolt to which it is forced by the contradiction between its humanity and its situation, which is an open, clear and absolute negation of its humanity'. (Marxist views on class and class conflict are outlined in Chapter 1, pp. 26–9.)

The communist society, which Marx predicted would arise from the ruins of capitalism, will begin with a transitional phase, 'the dictatorship of the proletariat'. Once the communist system has been fully established, the dictatorship's reason for being (and therefore its existence) will end. Bourgeois society represents 'the closing chapter of the prehistoric stage of human society'. The communist society of the new era is without classes, without contradictions. The dialectical principle now ceases to operate. The contradictions of human history have now been negated in a final harmonious synthesis.

Marxism – a critique

Judging from the constant reinterpretations, impassioned defences and vehement criticisms of Marx's work, his ideas are as alive and relevant today as they ever were. Specific criticisms of Marx's views on society have been examined in previous chapters and will not therefore be covered in detail in this section.

Many of his critics have argued that history has failed to substantiate Marx's views on the direction of social change. Thus they claim that class conflict, far from growing in intensity, has become institutionalized in advanced capitalist society. They see little indication of the proletariat becoming a class for itself. Rather than moving towards a polarization of classes, they argue that the class structure of capitalist society has become increasingly complex and differentiated. In particular, a steadily growing middle class has emerged between the proletariat and bourgeoisie.

Turning to communist society, critics have argued that history has not borne out the promise of communism contained in Marx's writings. Significant social inequalities are present in communist regimes, and there are few, if any, signs of a movement towards equality. The collapse of communism in Eastern Europe and the Soviet Union in the late 1980s and early 1990s suggests that the promise of communism has been replaced by the desire for Western-style democracies.

Particular criticism has been directed towards the priority that Marx assigned to economic factors in his explanation of social structure and social change.

Max Weber's study of ascetic Protestantism argued that religious beliefs provided the ethics, attitudes and motivations for the development of capitalism. Since ascetic Protestantism preceded the advent of capitalism, Weber maintained that, at certain times and places, aspects of the superstructure can play a primary role in directing change (see Chapter 7, pp. 406–8).

However, as previous chapters have indicated, Marxism is sufficiently flexible to counter such criticism, and to provide explanations for historical changes that have occurred since Marx's death.

Economic determinism

This section closes with a brief examination of what many see as the central issue of Marxism – the question of 'economic determinism'. Critics have often rejected Marxism on this basis, although they admit that the charge of economic determinism is more applicable to certain of Marx's followers than to Marx himself.

It is possible to select numerous quotations from Marx's writings that support the views of his critics. In terms of these quotations, history can be presented as a mechanical process directed by economic forces which follow 'iron laws'. Humans are compelled to act in terms of the constraints imposed by the economy, and passively respond to impersonal forces rather than actively construct their own history. Thus the proletariat is 'compelled' by its economic situation to overthrow the bourgeoisie. The contradictions in the capitalist infrastructure will inevitably result in its destruction. The superstructure is 'determined' by the infrastructure, and human consciousness is shaped by economic forces independent of human will and beyond humanity's control. In this way, Marx can be presented as a crude positivist who sees causation solely in terms of economic forces.

A defence of Marx

On closer examination, however, Marx's writings prove more subtle and less dogmatic than many of his critics have suggested. Marx rejected a simplistic, one-directional view of causation. Although he gave priority to economic factors, they form only one aspect of the dialectic of history. From this perspective, the economy is the primary but not the sole determinant of social change. The idea of the dialectic involves an interplay between the various parts of society. It rejects the view of unidirectional causation proceeding solely from economic factors. Instead, it argues that the various parts of society are interrelated in terms of their mutual effect.

Marx described the economic infrastructure as the 'ultimately determinant element in history'. Yet Engels argued:

> *If somebody twists this into saying that the economic element is the only determining one, he transforms that proposition into a meaningless, abstract and senseless phrase. The economic situation is the basis, but the various elements of the superstructure ... also exert their influence upon the course of the historical struggle and in many cases preponderate in determining their form.*
> Marx and Engels, 1950b

Thus the various aspects of the superstructure have a certain degree of autonomy and a part to play in influencing the course of history. They are not automatically and mechanically determined by the infrastructure.

Marx consistently argued that 'man makes his own history'. The history of human society is not the product of impersonal forces; it is the result of people's purposive activity. In Marx's view, 'It is not "history" which uses men as a means of achieving – as if it were an individual person – its own ends. History is nothing but the activity of men in pursuit of their ends' (Marx, quoted in Bottomore and Rubel, 1963). Since people make society, only people can change society.

The idea that Marx was a crude determinist is not therefore supported by a close reading of his work. Economic conditions set the context in which history unfolded, but they did not completely determine what happened.

The collapse of communism in the Soviet Union and Eastern Europe certainly undermined the credibility of communism as a political project, but it also helped to ensure that capitalism became even more dominant in the world. In this context, Marx's analysis of capitalism is potentially very important and some writers have argued that Marx made some accurate predictions about the future development of capitalism.

The US economist John Cassidy published an article in 1997 (which originally appeared in the *New York Times*) which claimed that Marx would be 'The Next Big Thinker'. Writing with Engels in 1848, Marx predicted that capitalism would spread throughout the world as capitalists sought to find new markets to maintain profitability. Cassidy believes that Marx correctly identified the dynamic behind the process of globalization. He also praises Marx for recognizing that even in the highly productive world of advanced capitalism, some workers

would still be very poor. This is certainly true of many workers in the 'third world'.

Cassidy also agrees wholeheartedly with Marx's view that as capitalism developed, more and more power would be concentrated in the hands of capitalists. The growth of giant corporations with a bigger turnover than the Gross Domestic Product of many nation-states seems to support Marx's view that wealth, and with it power, would become increasingly concentrated in the hands of a few.

Cassidy concludes that capitalism may have changed in many ways since the nineteenth century, but Marx's work remains very useful for understanding how capitalism works.

Neo-Marxism

Neo-Marxists are sociologists whose work has been inspired by Marx's theories, but who nevertheless have developed a distinctive approach of their own. In one way or another they have broken with conventional Marxist theory in order, as they see it, to understand society more adequately.

There is no clear dividing line between Marxists and neo-Marxists. As the last section indicated, there are various interpretations of Marx's work, and it is possible for Marxists to disagree without rejecting Marx's overall approach. Nevertheless, some sociological theories that might be described as Marxist are sufficiently different from Marx's own work to merit the description of 'neo-Marxist'.

Antonio Gramsci

Most neo-Marxist perspectives are characterized by the use of some concepts that are different from those that Marx used. Generally, they reject the extent to which Marx concentrated upon economic, material factors in determining the historical development of societies. An example of neo-Marxism, the work of Antonio Gramsci, was examined in Chapter 9 (see pp. 539–40).

Gramsci (1891–1937) suggested that ownership of the means of production was not sufficient to guarantee that a ruling class would monopolize power in a society. In order to maintain its leadership and dominance, or, as he called it, 'hegemony', a ruling class had actively to try to win support from other members of society. Gramsci did not believe the ruling class could ever rely upon false class consciousness to guarantee its position, since all members of the subject classes had some awareness of their exploitation. The ruling class needed to make some real concessions to other groups in society in order to win their support. Thus the state could not always act exclusively in the interests of the owners of the means of production.

Gramsci also differed from Marx in placing greater emphasis on the importance of divisions within classes as well as between classes. Thus, for example, agricultural and industrial workers might to some extent have different interests, and the state might exploit the existence of these divisions in order to maintain ruling-class hegemony.

Like many neo-Marxists, Gramsci attached rather more importance than Marx to the culture of a society, and to the institutions of the superstructure, such as the church, the mass media and the education system. He also placed more stress upon the role of ideas in maintaining political stability.

Marxism and other perspectives

Some neo-Marxists have tried to develop Marxism by drawing upon other sociological perspectives. For example, Paul Willis (1977), in his study of the transition from school to work (see pp. 605–8), combined a Marxist analysis of society with a study of small-scale interaction that owes much to an interactionist perspective.

Similarly, Ian Taylor, Paul Walton and Jock Young in *The New Criminology* (1973) argued that the insights of various sociological perspectives were necessary in order to produce a 'fully social theory' of crime. Taylor *et al.* nevertheless claimed their theory would only make sense if the insights of other perspectives were related to an overall Marxist framework for the analysis of society.

Neo-Marxism – a critique

Much of the appeal of Marx as a sociologist lies with the simplicity of his basic theory. This simplicity is both its principal strength and its main weakness. On the one hand, it provides the basis for a study of society that has a clear starting point. From this starting point it is possible to develop logically connected arguments and to make predictions about the development of societies. On the other hand, it leaves Marx open to the criticism that he has ignored important factors that influence social life.

Neo-Marxism has developed as a response both to the criticisms levelled at Marx, and to developments in societies since his death which seem to undermine his theory. Neo-Marxists have been able to overcome some criticisms of Marx, but in doing so have left themselves open to the claim that they have developed no clear alternative approach to understanding society.

Neo-Marxists attach more importance in their theories to cultural and ideological aspects of society. But they are generally unable to specify when, and in what circumstances, cultural or economic factors are more important in shaping society. Some neo-Marxists move so far away from Marx that their views seem little different from some of the theories that will now be examined.

Conflict theory

Conflict theory has its origins in the work of Max Weber. As Chapter 1 indicated (see pp. 29–32), Weber rejected the view that the division between the owners and non-owners of property was the only significant division between groups in society. He argued that there could be numerous divisions within the two basic classes, depending upon the 'market situation' of individuals (Weber, 1978, first published in the 1920s).

Furthermore, he suggested that people could be divided by their status situation and political interests as well as by their economic position. 'Parties' could be formed on the basis of status groupings or classes, but it was also possible for them to cut across class or status groups.

Weber's views on classes, status groups and parties reflect the main themes of conflict theory. Conflict theorists argue that the social structure is much more complex than Marx's work suggests. It consists of many different groups, not just two classes. Furthermore, although conflict theorists accept that these groups have different interests, these interests are not just economic. For example, a particular group might strive for greater prestige or status rather than greater economic power.

In a neat summary of conflict theory, Ian Craib (1984) describes it in the following way: 'Society is like a more or less confused battle ground. If we watch from on high, we can see a variety of groups fighting each other, constantly forming and reforming, making and breaking alliances.'

Conflict theory strongly influenced the work of John Goldthorpe on stratification (see Chapter 1). However, in order to illustrate and evaluate conflict theory, the work of another sociologist, Ralf Dahrendorf, will now be examined.

Ralf Dahrendorf – authority and conflict

Post-capitalism

Dahrendorf's conflict theory arose out of a critical evaluation of the work of Karl Marx (Dahrendorf, 1959). Dahrendorf accepted that Marx's description of capitalism was generally accurate in the nineteenth century when Marx was writing, but he argued that in the twentieth century it had become outdated as a basis for explaining conflict. Dahrendorf argued that important changes had taken place in countries such as Britain and the USA. They were now 'post-capitalist' societies.

Dahrendorf claimed that, far from the two main classes becoming polarized, as Marx had predicted, the opposite had happened. The proportion of skilled and semi-skilled workers had grown, as had the size of the 'new middle class' of white-collar workers, such as clerks, nurses and teachers. Inequalities in income and wealth had been reduced, partly because of changes in the social structure, and partly because of measures taken by the state. Social mobility had become more common, and, crucially, the link between ownership and control in industry had been broken. Managers, rather than owners, exercised day-to-day control over the means of production.

In these circumstances, Marx's claim that conflict was based upon the ownership or non-ownership of wealth was no longer valid. This was because there was no longer a close association between wealth and power. Shareholders, for example, might own the wealth of a company, but in practice they did not exercise close control over the management.

In view of these changes, Dahrendorf argued that conflicts were no longer based upon the existence of the two classes identified by Marx, nor were they based upon economic divisions. Instead, Dahrendorf saw conflict as being concerned with authority.

Authority

To Dahrendorf, authority is legitimate power attached to the occupation of a particular social role within an organization. Thus, for example, a manager in a company, or a teacher in a classroom, has the right to take certain decisions regardless of the wishes of the workforce or pupils. All organizations – or associations, as Dahrendorf calls them – have positions of domination and subjection. Some are able to take decisions legitimately and issue commands, and others are not. It is this situation which Dahrendorf saw as the basis for conflict in 'post-capitalist' societies.

Authority and quasi-groups

Dahrendorf believed that the existence of dominant and subordinate positions produces a situation in which individuals have different interests. Those occupying dominant positions have an interest in maintaining a social structure that gives them more authority than others, while those in subordinate positions, on the other hand, have an interest in changing it. This conflict of interests is present in a much wider range of social relationships than the economic conflict of interests between the ruling class and the subject class that Marx identified as the basis for conflict in society.

As a consequence, there are many different 'quasi-groups' or potential groups that could be in conflict with each other. Some of these quasi-groups will join together and act to pursue their common interests. Individuals may belong to a whole variety of different groups, and they are not necessarily confined in all areas of social life to subordinate or dominant groups. Thus a person who is a manager and has a position of authority in a company will tend to act to maintain that authority; but if, for example, the same person has a subordinate position in a religious organization, they may try to change the organization to increase their own authority.

Dahrendorf and conflict theory – a critique

Not surprisingly, Marxists do not accept Dahrendorf's view that Marx's theory is no longer applicable to contemporary societies. For example, the British Marxist John Westergaard (1996) believes Britain is still fundamentally divided between two classes, and he denies that inequality between rich and poor has been decreasing in recent decades.

More importantly, though, some sociologists question whether Dahrendorf's approach can actually explain conflict. Ian Craib (1984) points out that Dahrendorf admits that subordinate groups may defer to the authority of dominant groups as well as challenging it. Thus members of a workforce may work conscientiously or they may strike, but Dahrendorf fails to explain adequately why they will follow one course rather than another.

More generally, conflict theory, whether Dahrendorf's or that of other writers, has been accused of being 'almost wholly macroscopic and as a result has little to offer to our understanding of individual thought and action' (Ritzer and Goodman, 2003, p. 258). It also produces a rather confused picture of the social structure. Society is portrayed as consisting of so many different groups, all of which may be in conflict with each other, that it is difficult to get a clear picture of how society works. It is not clear what the end result of the conflict will be: who will win and who

will lose. Nor does conflict theory provide an adequate explanation of why one group will be successful and another will not. Marxism and neo-Marxism give more coherent answers to these types of question. On the other hand, conflict theory is able to encompass conflict between such groups as men and women, which does not fit neatly into a Marxist framework for understanding society.

Conflict theory represented an important break from Marxism and helped to provide the basis for the development of some later theories. In particular, poststructuralists and postmodernists have gone much further in arguing that there are numerous types of social division and sources of inequality. Indeed, poststructuralists and postmodernists think more in terms of difference than division and inequality (see pp. 890–5 for a discussion of postmodernism).

Social action and interpretive perspectives

Sociologists who adopt social action or interpretive perspectives usually reject the view that society has a clear structure that directs individuals to behave in certain ways. Some social action theorists do not deny the existence of a social structure, but see this structure as rising out of the action of individuals. Thus Weber, who to some extent spans the gap between structural and social action perspectives, acknowledges the existence of classes, status groups and parties, but he challenges the view of Durkheim that society exists independently of the individuals who make up society. Symbolic interactionists accept the existence of social roles, but deny that these roles are fixed and inflexible, or determined by the supposed 'needs' of the social system. Phenomenology and ethnomethodology represent a much more radical rejection of structural perspectives. They deny the existence of any sort of social structure.

All of these perspectives argue that sociologists need to understand and interpret human behaviour and discover the meanings that lie behind it. Phenomenology and ethnomethodology claim that sociology can go no further than reaching an understanding of the meanings that individuals attach to the world around them.

These perspectives will now be examined in detail.

Max Weber

The German sociologist Max Weber (1864–1920) is widely regarded as one of the three great founders of sociology, with Marx and Durkheim. Although Weber identified aspects of the social structure such as class, parties, status groups (see pp. 29–30) and bureaucracies, all of these groupings were made up of individuals carrying out social actions. Furthermore, it was social actions which, according to Weber, should be the focus of study in sociology.

Social action

In one of his most important works, *Economy and Society* (1978, first published in the 1920s), Weber said: 'Sociology (in the sense in which this highly ambiguous word is used here) is a science concerning itself with the interpretive understanding of social action and thereby with a causal explanation of its course and consequences.' By making this statement Weber was trying to spell out the precise limits of what could and could not be explained in sociological terms.

To Weber, a social action was an action carried out by an individual to which a person attached a meaning; an action which, in his words, 'takes account of the behaviour of others and is thereby oriented in its course'. Thus an action that a person does not think about cannot be a social action. For example, an accidental collision of bicycles or an involuntary cry of pain are not social actions because they are not the result of any conscious thought process. Furthermore, if an action does not take account of the existence and possible reactions of others, it is not social. If a person prays in private, in secrecy, it cannot be a social action – nobody knows about it and the actor could not be taking account of the possible actions of others.

Social action and Verstehen

Having identified the subject matter of sociology, Weber went on to suggest how social action could be explained. Before the cause of a social action could be found, it was necessary to understand the meaning attached to it by the actor. He distinguished two types of understanding.

First, he referred to *aktuelles Verstehen*, which can roughly be translated as direct observational understanding. For example, it is possible to understand that someone is angry by observing their facial expression. Similarly, it is possible to understand what is happening when a woodcutter hits a piece of wood with an axe – that is, the woodcutter is chopping wood. However, this is not, to Weber, a sufficient level of understanding to begin to explain social action.

The second type of understanding is *erklärendes Verstehen*, or explanatory understanding. In this case the sociologist must try to understand the meaning of an act in terms of the motives that have given rise to it. Thus *erklärendes Verstehen* would require an understanding of why the woodcutter was chopping wood. Was it in order to earn a wage, to make a fire, or to work off anger? To achieve this type of understanding it is necessary to put yourself in the shoes of the person whose behaviour you are explaining. You should imagine yourself in their situation to try to get at the motives behind their actions.

Causal explanations

Even this level of understanding is not sufficient to explain a series of actions or events. For a full causal explanation it is necessary to determine what has given rise to the motives that led to the actions. Here Weber advocated the use of methods closer to a positivist approach. He attempted to discover connections between events and to establish causal relationships. This can be seen from his study, *The Protestant Ethic and the Spirit of Capitalism* (1958, first published 1904) (see pp. 406–8).

Weber tried to show that there was a relationship between ascetic Protestantism and capitalism. He claimed ascetic Protestantism preceded capitalism and was found almost exclusively in those countries that became capitalist. Nevertheless, this was not sufficient to convince Weber that there was a causal connection between the two, because it did not establish how or why ascetic Protestantism contributed to the rise of capitalism. In order to establish this link, Weber tried to understand the motives of ascetic Protestants for adopting capitalist behaviour. He believed their main motive was to convince themselves that they were predestined to go to heaven.

Weber's work on the rise of capitalism illustrates his belief that social actions, particularly those involving large numbers of people behaving in similar ways, could lead to large-scale social changes such as the advent of capitalism. Furthermore, even when Weber sounds rather like a structuralist sociologist, he usually insists he is really describing a type of social action. Thus, while society might contain institutions and social groups, these institutions and social groups are composed of individuals engaged in social action. Weber said:

> *When reference is made in a sociological context to a state, a nation, a corporation, a family or an army corps, or to similar collectivities, what is meant is ... only a certain kind of development of actual or possible social actions of individual persons.* Weber, 1958, first published 1904

Social action and bureaucracy

Weber's general views on the relationship between institutions and social action can be illustrated by his important work on bureaucracies. **Bureaucracies** might be seen as institutions that closely control and direct human behaviour or social actions. Although Weber was aware of, and indeed concerned about, the power of bureaucracies in restricting human freedom, he nevertheless saw them as composed of individuals carrying out social actions. Thus he believed bureaucracies consisted of individuals carrying out **rational social actions** designed to achieve the goals of bureaucracies.

Significantly, Weber saw the whole development of modern societies in terms of a move towards rational social action. Thus, to Weber, modern societies were undergoing a process of **rationalization**, as affective or emotional action and action directed by custom and tradition (traditional action) became less important. Weber's views on bureaucracy will now be examined in detail.

Bureaucracy and rationalization

Weber (1947) believed bureaucratic organizations were the dominant institutions of industrial society. We will examine Weber's definition of bureaucracy in detail shortly but, briefly, he saw it as an organization with a hierarchy of paid, full-time officials who formed a chain of command. A bureaucracy is concerned with the business of administration: with controlling, managing and coordinating a complex series of tasks.

Bureaucratic organizations are increasingly dominating the institutional landscape: departments of state, political parties, business enterprises, the military, education and churches are all organized on bureaucratic lines.

To appreciate the nature of modern society, Weber maintained that an understanding of the process of bureaucratization is essential. Marxists see fundamental differences between capitalist and socialist industrial societies. To Weber, their differences are minimal compared to the essential similarity of bureaucratic organization. This is the defining characteristic of modern industrial society.

Bureaucracy and rational action

Weber's view of bureaucracy must be seen in the context of his general theory of social action. He argued that all human action is directed by meanings. Thus, in order to understand and explain an action, the meanings and motives that lie behind it must be appreciated. Weber identified various types of action that are distinguished by the meanings on which they are based. These include 'affective' or 'emotional action', 'traditional action' and 'rational action'.

1. **Affective or emotional action** stems from an individual's emotional state at a particular time. A loss of temper which results in verbal abuse or physical violence is an example of affective action.
2. **Traditional action** is based on established custom. Individuals act in a certain way because of ingrained habit: because things have always been done that way. They have no real awareness of why they do something; their actions are simply second nature.
3. By comparison, **rational action** involves a clear awareness of a goal: it is the action of a manager who wishes to increase productivity or of a builder contracted to erect a block of flats. In both cases the goal is clearly defined. Rational action also involves a systematic assessment of the various means of attaining a goal and the selection of the most appropriate means to do so. Thus, if a capitalist in the building trade aimed to maximize profit, he or she would carefully evaluate factors such as alternative sites, raw materials, building techniques, labour costs and the potential market, in order to realize his or her goal. This would entail a precise calculation of costs and the careful weighing up of the advantages and disadvantages of the various factors involved. The action is rational since, in Weber's words, rational action is 'the methodical attainment of a definitely given and practical end by means of an increasingly precise calculation of means'.

Weber believed rational action had become the dominant mode of action in modern industrial society. He saw it expressed in a wide variety of areas: in state administration, business, education, science, and even in Western classical music. He referred to the increasing dominance of rational action as the 'process of rationalization'.

Bureaucratization is a prime example of this process. A bureaucratic organization has a clearly defined goal. It involves the precise calculation of the means to attain this goal and systematically eliminating those factors that stand in the way of the achievement of its objectives. Bureaucracy is therefore rational action in an institutional form.

Bureaucracy and control

Bureaucracy is also a system of control. It involves a hierarchical organization in which superiors strictly control and

discipline the activities of subordinates. Weber argued that, in any large-scale task, some people must coordinate and control the activities of others. He stated: 'the imperative coordination of the action of a considerable number of men requires control of a staff of persons'. In order for this control to be effective, it must be regarded as **legitimate**. There must be a 'minimum of voluntary submission' to higher authority.

Legitimacy can be based on various types of meanings. For example, it can result from traditional or rational meanings, and therefore can take the form of traditional authority or rational authority. The form of the organizational structure derives from the type of legitimacy on which it is based. In Weber's words:

> *According to the kind of legitimacy which is claimed, the type of obedience, the kind of administrative staff developed to guarantee it and the mode of exercising authority, will all differ fundamentally.* Weber, 1978

To understand bureaucracy, it is therefore necessary for us to appreciate the type of legitimacy on which bureaucratic control is based.

Weber identified three forms of legitimacy, which derive from the three types of social action discussed above. Affective, traditional and rational actions each provide a particular motive for obedience, a motive based respectively on emotion, custom and rationality. These types of legitimate control are 'charismatic authority', 'traditional authority' and 'rational–legal authority'. Each results in a particular form of organizational structure. Weber constructed models to represent each type of authority.

Charismatic authority and organizational structure

Organizational structures that derive from **charismatic authority** are fluid and ill-defined. Those who occupy positions of authority either share the charisma of the leader or possess a charisma of their own. They are not selected on the basis of family ties to the leader or on the basis of technical qualifications. There is no fixed hierarchy of officials and no legal rules govern the organization of leaders and followers. Jesus's disciples provide an example of leadership positions in a charismatic movement.

There is no systematically organized economic support for the movement; its members typically rely on charity or plunder. Since charismatic authority depends for its control on the person of the leader, it is necessarily short-lived. After the leader's death, the movement must become 'routinized' in terms of either traditional or rational–legal authority, if it is to survive. Thus the organizational control of the Christian church is no longer directly based on the charisma of its founder. Instead, it has been routinized in terms of both traditional and rational–legal authorities.

Traditional authority and organizational structure

The organizational structure that derives from the second type of authority, **traditional authority**, takes two main forms: the first is a household that includes relatives, favourites and servants who are dependent on the head of the household; the second is a system of vassals such as feudal lords who swear an oath of loyalty to the king or queen and hold land on this basis. The duties of both the household retainers and the vassals are defined by custom but may be changed according to the inclination of the particular ruler. This organizational structure is of little importance in contemporary societies.

Rational–legal authority and organizational structure

Like other forms of authority, **rational–legal authority** produces a particular kind of organizational structure. This is **bureaucracy**, which Weber defined as 'a hierarchical organization designed rationally to coordinate the work of many individuals in the pursuit of large-scale administrative tasks and organizational goals'.

Weber constructed an ideal type of the rational–legal bureaucratic organization. He argued that bureaucracies in modern industrial society are steadily moving towards this 'pure' type. The ideal type of bureaucracy contains the following elements:

1. 'The regular activities required for the purposes of the organization are distributed in a fixed way as official duties' (Gerth and Mills, 1948). Each administrative official has a clearly defined area of responsibility. Complex tasks are broken down into manageable parts, with each official specializing in a particular area. For example, state administration is divided into various departments such as education, defence and the environment. Within each department every official has a clearly defined sphere of competence and responsibility.
2. 'The organization of offices follows the principle of hierarchy; that is every lower office is under the control and supervision of a higher one' (Weber, 1978). A chain of command and responsibility is established whereby officials are accountable to their immediate superior both for the conduct of their own official duties and for that of everybody below them.
3. The operations of the bureaucracy are governed by 'a consistent system of abstract rules' and the 'application of these rules to particular cases' (Gerth and Mills, 1948). These rules clearly define the limits of the authority held by various officials in the hierarchy. Obedience to superiors stems from a belief in the correctness of the rules. The rules also lay down fixed procedures for the performance of each task. They impose strict discipline and control, leaving little room for personal initiative or discretion.
4. The 'ideal official' performs his or her duties in 'a spirit of formalistic impersonality … without hatred or passion' (Weber, 1978). The activities of the bureaucrat are governed by the rules, not by personal considerations such as feelings towards colleagues or clients. The actions are therefore rational rather than affective. Business is conducted 'according to calculable rules and "without regard for persons"'.
5. Officials are appointed on the basis of technical knowledge and expertise. Weber stated: 'Bureaucratic administration means fundamentally the exercise of control on the basis of knowledge. This is the feature of it which makes it specifically rational.' Thus officials are selected in terms of the contribution their partic-

ular knowledge and skills can make to the realization of organizational goals. Once appointed, the official is a full-time paid employee and his or her occupation constitutes a career. Promotion is based on seniority or achievement or a combination of both.

6 Bureaucratic administration involves a strict separation of private and official income. Officials do not own any part of the organization for which they work, nor can they use their position for private gain. In Weber's words, 'bureaucracy segregates official activity as something distinct from the sphere of private life'.

The 'technical superiority' of bureaucracy

The ideal type of bureaucracy is never completely achieved in reality. Several of its characteristics are found in the state administrations of Ancient Egypt, China and the later stages of the Roman Empire. The ideal type is most closely approximated in capitalist industrial society, where it has become the major form of organizational control.

The development of bureaucracy is due to its 'technical superiority' compared to organizations based on charismatic and traditional authority. Weber argued: 'The decisive reason for the advance of bureaucratic organization has always been its purely technical superiority over any other form of organization.' This technical superiority stems from the combination of specialist skills subordinated to the goals of the organization. Personal emotions and interests, which might detract from the attainment of those goals, are excluded; while a set of rational rules is designed specifically to further the objectives of the organization. Compared to other forms of organization, tasks in a bureaucracy are performed with greater precision and speed, and with less friction and lower costs.

Bureaucracy and freedom

Although Weber appreciated the technical advantages of bureaucratic organization, he was also aware of its disadvantages. He saw the strict control of officials restricted to very specialized tasks as a limitation of human freedom. The uniform and rational procedures of bureaucratic practice largely prevent spontaneity, creativity and individual initiative. The impersonality of official conduct tends to produce 'specialists without spirit'. Bureaucratic organization produces an iron cage which imprisons and restricts people.

Weber foresaw the possibility of people being trapped in their specialized routines, with little awareness of the relationship between their jobs and the organization as a whole. He wrote: 'It is horrible to think that the world would one day be filled with little cogs, little men clinging to little jobs and striving towards the bigger ones.'

Weber also foresaw the danger of bureaucrats becoming preoccupied with uniformity and order, losing sight of all else and becoming dependent on the security provided by their highly structured niche in the bureaucratic machine. He believed it was as if:

> *we were deliberately to become men who need 'order' and nothing but order, become nervous and cowardly if for one moment this order wavers, and helpless if they are torn away from their total incorporation in it.* Weber, 1978

To Weber, the process of rationalization, of which bureaucracy is the prime expression, is basically irrational. It is ultimately aimless, since it tends to destroy the traditional values that give meaning and purpose to life. For him, the 'great question' is 'what can we oppose to this machinery in order to keep a portion of mankind free from this parcelling-out of the soul, from this supreme mastery of the bureaucratic way of life?' (quoted in Nisbet, 1967).

Despite his forebodings, Weber thought bureaucracy was essential to the operation of large-scale industrial societies. In particular, he believed the state and economic enterprises could not function effectively without bureaucratic control. It therefore made little sense to try to dispense with bureaucracies.

However, Weber was fearful of the ends to which bureaucratic organization could be directed. It represented the most complete and effective institutionalization of power so far created. In Weber's eyes, 'bureaucracy has been and is a power instrument of the first order – for the one who controls the bureaucratic apparatus' (Weber, 1978).

Weber was particularly concerned about the control of state bureaucratic administration. He saw two main dangers if this control was left in the hands of bureaucrats themselves:

1 Particularly in times of crisis, bureaucratic leadership would be ineffective. Bureaucrats are trained to follow orders and conduct routine operations rather than to make policy decisions and take initiatives in response to crises.
2 In capitalist society, top bureaucrats may be swayed by the pressure of capitalist interests and tailor their administrative practices to fit the demands of capital.

Weber argued that these dangers could only be avoided by strong parliamentary control of the state bureaucracy. In particular, professional politicians must hold the top positions in the various departments of state. This would encourage strong and effective leadership, since politicians are trained to take decisions. In addition, it would help to open the bureaucracy to public view and reveal any behind-the-scenes wheeling and dealing between bureaucrats and powerful interests. Politicians are public figures, open to public scrutiny and the criticism of opposition parties. They are therefore accountable for their actions.

Bureaucrats and politicians

Even with politicians at the head of state bureaucracies, problems remain. Weber observed: 'The political master always finds himself vis-à-vis the trained official, in the position of a dilettante facing the expert.'

Professional politicians lack the technical knowledge controlled by the bureaucracy and may have little awareness of its inner workings and procedures. They are largely dependent on the information supplied by bureaucrats and on their advice as to the feasibility of the measures the politician wishes to take. The politician may well end up being directed by the bureaucrat.

Weber believed that only strong parliamentary government could control state bureaucracy. He suggested that state bureaucrats should be made directly and regularly accountable to parliament for their actions. The procedure for doing this was the parliamentary committee, which would systematically cross-examine top civil servants. In

Weber's view, 'this alone guarantees public supervision and a thorough inquiry'.

Weber's view of bureaucracy is ambivalent. He recognized its 'technical superiority' over all other forms of organization. He believed it was essential for the effective operation of large-scale industrial society. While he saw it as a threat to responsible government, he believed this threat could be countered by strong political control. However, he remained pessimistic about the consequences of bureaucracy for human freedom and happiness.

Materialism and idealism

Given the importance Weber attached to social action, it is not surprising that he also attached considerable importance to the role of ideas in shaping social life. Weber was very much opposed to what he saw as the one-sided materialism of Marxism. He denied that human beliefs were entirely shaped by material or economic forces; indeed, his work on Protestantism suggested that religious beliefs could transform an economic system.

However, Weber was equally concerned to reject a one-sided idealism that saw human history as directed by the ideas and beliefs held by people. Instead, Weber maintained that both material factors and beliefs were important. He believed religious beliefs could develop quite independently of material factors – for example, through theological arguments within a church. On the other hand, new beliefs would only be taken up if circumstances made them likely to thrive. Thus, material circumstances might affect whether or not ideas became widely accepted, but they did not determine what ideas were produced in the first place.

Weber adopted a similar type of argument to explain the role of religion in the advent of capitalism. To Weber, before capitalism could fully develop it was necessary to have both the appropriate beliefs and the appropriate material circumstances. In a simple tribal society neither would be present. According to Weber, many oriental societies had the economic conditions that could have led to capitalism, but they lacked a religion that encouraged rational activity. Countries such as Britain and the USA had both the material conditions and the beliefs of ascetic Protestantism, which were necessary preconditions for the development of capitalism.

Weber – a critique

Weber has undoubtedly made a great contribution to the development of modern sociology, although, like the other classical sociologists, his work has been hotly debated.

A central weakness of Weber's sociology can be identified. He has been accused of 'methodological individualism' – a criticism summed up by David Lee and Howard Newby (1983) in the following way: 'Weber was willing to treat all social forces and pressures as if they could be explained (or reduced) to the actions and purposes of seemingly isolated individuals.' The structural approaches examined earlier, particularly those of Durkheim and Marx, were strongly opposed to any such view.

Furthermore, in Weber's own work, his social action approach exists rather uneasily alongside his views on particular types of social institution. Thus it is hard to reconcile his view that bureaucracies could severely restrict human freedom, or that society was divided into social classes, with his claim that society simply consisted of individuals choosing courses of action according to their motives.

Weber's views on bureaucracy and the importance of rationalization to the development of modernity have been the subject of extensive discussion. As we will see below, writers such as Ritzer have largely endorsed and developed Weber's ideas. On the other hand, postmodernists generally argue that bureaucratic organizations are no longer the dominant institutions in contemporary societies. They believe that organizations have become much more flexible, less governed by rules and less hierarchical. For example, Stewart Clegg (1992) argues that post-Fordist flexible firms are far less rigid than traditional bureaucracies. He sees the trend towards this type of work organization as evidence of a shift towards postmodern organizations.

From a different perspective, some interpreters of Weber have argued that there are reasons to suppose that bureaucratic domination is not inevitable even within modern societies. Thus Larry Ray and Michael Reed (1994) believe the 'iron cage' of bureaucracy can be challenged.

Organizations are not always successful in persuading people that what they are doing can be justified simply in terms of its rationality. In modern societies people may question the ends that are being pursued rationally. According to Ray and Reed, such ends would only be regarded as legitimate if people had agreed to them. There were therefore at least two directions in which modern societies could develop: 'the iron cage on the one hand, and the expansion of discursive rational legitimation on the other'. In other words, there could be increasing emphasis on democratic control of organizational ends.

If Ray and Reed are correct, then perhaps pessimistic interpretations of the consequences of bureaucracy may be misplaced or exaggerated.

Whatever the merits of Weber's views on bureaucracy, they have proved enormously influential. His views have shaped much of the debate within the sociology of organizations, and his claims about rationalization have been central to debates about modernity and postmodernity (see pp. 890–9 for a discussion of modernity and postmodernity). Furthermore, they have influenced some contemporary theorists, such as George Ritzer.

George Ritzer – *The McDonaldization of Society*

The importance of McDonald's

George Ritzer (1996) supports the Weberian view that, far from dying out, bureaucratic organization is becoming increasingly important. Like Weber, he argues that the drive towards bureaucratization and rationalization is largely motivated by profit. Companies believe they can cut costs and increase profits through rationalization. Even non-profit-making organizations, such as charities, may adopt this approach to reduce costs so that they can survive and expand.

Ritzer argues that the model of bureaucracy has developed since the time when Weber was writing, so that now, if anything, it is even more rationalized and impersonal. In some cases it is inhumane. The contemporary model of rationalization is exemplified by the fast-food restaurant, which in turn is exemplified by McDonald's. McDonald's has been enormously successful and has outlets in many countries, including Russia, China and in Makkah in Saudi Arabia.

Ritzer believes the principles of rationalization adopted by McDonald's have spread to many types of organization. As well as influencing other important fast-food chains (such as Burger King and Pizza Hut), the principles on which McDonald's operates have been copied by local companies and organizations throughout the world. For example, in Paris there are fast-food croissanteries, and in India you can buy fast-food mutton burgers courtesy of a chain called Nirula's.

McDonaldization has also affected areas such as health care and undertaking. But what exactly are these principles which McDonald's and similar chains have done so much to popularize?

The principles of McDonaldization

Ritzer (1996) argues: 'McDonald's has succeeded because it offers consumers, workers and managers efficiency, calculability, predictability and control.'

Ritzer defines **efficiency** as 'the optimum method for getting from one point to another'. To the customers of McDonald's this means 'the best way of getting from being hungry to being full'. In a world in which many consumers are in a rush, but need to eat, fast food can offer the best solution. Cooking at home and visiting traditional restaurants are inefficient because it can take hours to get fed, whereas in McDonald's it takes minutes.

Ray Kroc, the founder of the McDonald's chain, was obsessed with efficiency. He examined every part of the process of producing a hamburger meal, simplified it and made it quicker. For example, he found that the process was speeded up if the buns supplied to the restaurants were pre-sliced. He even determined the optimum amount of wax to put on the pieces of paper separating individual beefburgers to make them easy to separate. From 1975, efficiency was increased in many outlets by the introduction of the drive-through.

The products supplied in McDonald's are simplified so that generally they do not have to be eaten with utensils. This reduces the cost of supplying utensils and having to wash them. Customers are also 'put to work' to speed up the process and cut costs. Thus customers have to wait in line to be served rather than having a waitress/waiter serve them, and they are expected to clear their own tables when they have finished eating.

The principles of greater efficiency are spreading to other types of organization. In some universities there is increasing use of time-saving multiple-choice exams which can be marked and graded by computer. In the USA patients with minor problems can walk in off the streets to get instant treatment or advice in emergency medical centres. In Moscow eye microsurgery is carried out using a conveyor system, so that each patient can have their eye problems corrected in just three minutes.

In many areas, the principle of putting customers to work has been adopted. For example, bank customers carry out their own transactions using ATM machines, while supermarkets rely upon customers choosing and moving the products they want, loading them onto a conveyor belt and taking them off again.

In McDonald's, 'quantity (especially a large quantity) tends to become a surrogate for quality'. There is an emphasis on producing a high quantity of goods at a rapid speed. The customers get a lot of food quickly, and the managers get a lot of work out of workers. However, the customers may not get 'a quality dining experience' because they are rushed and they have a limited choice.

In McDonald's the emphasis is very much on size (e.g. the 'Big Mac'). However, to some extent it is an 'illusion of quantity'. The large bun surrounding a beefburger makes it seem larger than it really is. The boxes used for fries get bigger towards the top, making them appear as generous overflowing portions whereas they are actually quite small. The quality of the service is measured in terms of speed rather than customer satisfaction.

Quantification has also become increasingly important in education. In US universities courses are often rated by students using a scale from one to five. Academics are increasingly judged by the quantity of publications they produce. In companies, time and motion studies have been used to quantify the work done by employees, while in politics there is increasing emphasis on opinion poll ratings. According to Ritzer, the spread of computer technology has made calculability an increasingly pervasive feature of social life. Ritzer says:

> *Rationalization involves the increasing effort to ensure predictability from one time or place to another. A rationalized society therefore emphasizes such things as discipline, order, systematization, formalization, routine, consistency, and methodical operation.* Ritzer, 1996

McDonald's make their restaurant chain predictable for customers by standardizing the interior of the restaurants, the interaction between employees and customers, employee behaviour and the products themselves. Although the restaurants are not identical, the colours, logos and golden arches are ubiquitous. Thus you can enter a McDonald's anywhere in the world and find the surroundings familiar.

McDonald's staff are given a strict series of steps to follow when serving customers and some of their words are scripted. Even customers tend to become used to the routines. Ritzer describes how his own children told him off for not clearing his table in a McDonald's. Employees are given strict dress codes and uniforms. To ensure that McDonald's managers act predictably, they must attend 'Hamburger University', branches of which are spread around the world. Even the 'professors' are taught to teach from prepared scripts produced centrally.

Predictability is now increasingly creeping into creative products. Thus the film industry uses sequels (for example, *The Godfather*, *Star Wars* and *Back to the Future*) to give customers a familiar and predictable product. Shopping malls, frozen TV dinners, package holidays and suburban housing estates all make consumption much more predictable than it used to be.

Eradicating unpredictability, inefficiency and uncertainty can be achieved through developing greater **control** over workers. One way McDonald's has achieved this is by making tasks such as cooking so simple that they do not need to employ skilled workers who use their own judgement. Technology is used to limit the scope for individual initiative. Workers do not have to judge when a cup is full – an automatic sensor switches off the flow of drink from a dispensing machine. Indeed, the processes have been made so simple that 'one university has built a robot that serves hamburgers at the campus restaurant' (Ritzer, 1996).

Customers are potentially troublesome – they might interrupt the routines – but they too can be controlled to some extent. One useful device is the conveyor-like system of the drive-through, the car acting as the conveyor. However, even in restaurants, customers are encouraged to conform by their socialization into the norms of appropriate behaviour. Other fast-food chains use uncomfortable chairs or security guards to ensure that customers do not linger too long at their tables.

Ritzer believes all kinds of institutions are adopting a range of new techniques to ensure conformity from staff and customers. The 'clock and the lesson plan' are used to control teachers. Computers are used to monitor employee behaviour down to the smallest detail. For example, United Airlines requires its telephone reservations staff to press a 'potty button' on their computer if they are going to the toilet. The world of politics is manipulated so that 'most people never see a politician except on TV, most likely in a firmly controlled format designed to communicate the exact message and image desired by the politicians and their media advisers'.

The irrationality of rationality

Ritzer acknowledges that McDonaldization has some advantages. It can offer 'increased efficiency, predictability, calculability, and control through the substitution of non-human for human technology'. However, its effects can often be quite irrational and counter-productive.

Fast-food restaurants can generate lengthy queues at tills, so that customers wait in line for long periods. They are not efficient for customers, who are required to do their own unpaid work in getting served and clearing the table. Supermarkets can be inefficient for customers because they have to search through so many products for the ones they want.

Many workers in McDonaldized systems have little enthusiasm for their work and end up having low levels of productivity. Companies compensate for this by paying them low wages. The costs for customers are often high. Soft drinks in fast-food outlets usually cost much more than they would from shops.

To Ritzer, McDonaldization also leads to the substitution of illusion for reality. For example, McDonald's itself 'tries to create the illusion that people are having fun, that they are getting lots of french fries, that they are getting a bargain when they purchase their meal'. A McDonaldized society also creates (in a phrase borrowed from Daniel Boorstin) 'pseudo events' – events which are staged but pretend to give people real experiences. Package holidays and international villages in amusement parks are examples.

McDonaldization is irrational because it is dehumanizing and threatens people's health. The presence of 'a lot of fat, cholesterol, salt and sugar' in much fast food can contribute to high blood pressure and cholesterol levels. Furthermore, the fast-food industry produces large amounts of rubbish, particularly styrofoam, which is not biodegradable. It also requires the growing and felling of large areas of forest for its packaging

According to Ritzer, McDonaldization dehumanizes people by getting them to act in standardized ways and preventing them from being creative or imaginative. Fast-food restaurants dehumanize customers. Ritzer says: 'By eating on a sort of assembly line, the diner is reduced to an automaton made to rush through a meal with little gratification derived from the dining experience or from the food itself.'

Contact between humans is routinized and minimized. There is little or no chance of developing rewarding relationships in McDonaldized contexts. Fast-food restaurants undermine the idea of 'family meals' in which there is time for conversation. McDonaldization undermines ethnic and regional diversity in food.

Higher education becomes 'like processing meat' and in the workplace 'you become a mechanical nut'. This can have dangerous consequences. For example, airline pilots become highly dependent on autopilots and may find it harder to use their initiative in an emergency.

Resisting McDonaldization

From Ritzer's point of view, the worst possible future would be one in which McDonaldization creates an 'iron cage' in which people lose control over the supposedly rational systems they have created, and become controlled by them. Ritzer is generally pessimistic about the future. He does not believe the general trend towards McDonaldization can be broken. Nevertheless, he does believe there are things that can be done to slow it down. Indeed, he gives some practical advice to readers on how to subvert the trend. This includes returning junk mail to the post office, avoiding restaurants that use styrofoam packaging, trying to humanize visits to McDonald's by engaging the staff in conversation and dwelling over meals, watching as little TV as possible, avoiding daily routines, using local and independent retailers and service providers rather than national or international chains, and so on.

Conclusion – bureaucracy, McDonaldization and modernity

In many ways Ritzer's views represent an updated version of Weber's arguments about the rationalization of the world. They have been interpreted by writers such as Paul Thompson and David McHugh (1995) as showing that bureaucratic principles are spreading into many areas of social life rather than disappearing. As such, Ritzer's views could be seen as supportive of theories of modernity rather than postmodernity.

Although some of the developments Ritzer notes (such as the creation of illusions) do fit with certain theories of postmodernity, the central arguments about rationalization are more in keeping with claims that societies remain modern. Ritzer (1996) says: 'McDonaldization shows no

sign of disappearing and being replaced by postmodern forms. It is a highly rational modern phenomenon yielding among other things, extremely rigid structures.' Nevertheless, it does exhibit postmodern characteristics at the same time.

Ritzer's arguments are backed up by numerous examples. However, he uses a wide definition of McDonaldization, which allows him to use examples (such as a politician's use of the media) which seem to be far removed from the fast-food restaurant. Advocates of theories of post-Fordism (see p. 127) would argue that there is a move towards non-standardized products and less bureaucratic organizations. They too have examples to back up their arguments. Although Ritzer may have identified a trend in contemporary societies, he ignores trends which contradict his approach.

Symbolic interactionism

Symbolic interactionism (usually referred to as interactionism in earlier chapters) is a distinctly American branch of sociology. It developed from the work of a group of American philosophers who included John Dewey, William I. Thomas and George Herbert Mead. Like Max Weber, symbolic interactionists are concerned with explaining social actions in terms of the meanings that individuals give to them. However, they tend to focus on small-scale interactions rather than large-scale social change.

George Herbert Mead (1863–1931) is generally regarded as the founder of symbolic interactionism. His views will now be examined.

George Herbert Mead

Symbols

In Mead's view, human thought, experience and conduct are essentially social (Mead, 1934). They owe their nature to the fact that human beings interact in terms of symbols, the most important of which are contained in language. A symbol does not simply stand for an object or event: it defines it in a particular way and indicates a response to it. Thus the symbol 'chair' not only represents a class of objects and defines them as similar, it also indicates a line of action: that is, the action of sitting.

Symbols impose particular meanings on objects and events and, in doing so, largely exclude other possible meanings. For example, chairs may be made out of metal, cane or wood, and on this basis be defined as very different objects. However, such differences are rendered insignificant by the fact that they are all categorized in terms of the symbol 'chair'. Similarly, chairs can be stood on, used as a source of fuel or used as a means of assaulting someone; but the range of possible activities that could be associated with chairs is largely excluded by the course of action indicated by the symbol 'chair'.

Symbols provide the means whereby humans can interact meaningfully with their natural and social environment. They are human-made and refer not to the intrinsic nature of objects and events but to the ways in which people perceive them.

Without symbols there would be no human interaction and no human society. Symbolic interaction is necessary since humans have no instincts to direct their behaviour. Humans are not genetically programmed to react automatically to particular stimuli. In order to survive they must therefore construct and live within a world of meaning. For example, they must classify the natural environment into categories of food and non-food in order to meet basic nutritional requirements. In this way humans define both the stimuli and their response to them. Thus, when hunters on the African savannah categorize antelope as a source of food, they define what is significant in the natural environment and their response to it. Via symbols, meaning is imposed on the world of nature, and human interaction with that world is thereby made possible.

Role-taking

Social life can only proceed if the meanings of symbols are largely shared by members of society. If this were not the case, meaningful communication would be impossible. However, common symbols provide only the means by which human interaction can be accomplished. In order for interaction to proceed, each person involved must interpret the meanings and intentions of others. This is made possible by the existence of common symbols, but actually accomplished by means of a process that Mead termed 'role-taking'.

The process of role-taking involves one person taking on the role of another by imaginatively placing themselves in the position of the person with whom they are interacting. For example, if a person observes another smiling, crying, waving a hand or shaking a fist, they will put themselves in that person's position in order to interpret the intention and meaning. On the basis of this interpretation they will make their response to the action of the other.

Thus, if an individual observes someone shaking a fist, they may interpret this gesture as an indication of aggression, but their interpretation will not automatically lead to a particular response. They may ignore the gesture, respond in kind, attempt to defuse the situation with a joke, and so on. The person with whom they are interacting will then take their role, interpret their response and either continue or close the interaction on the basis of this interpretation. In this respect human interaction can be seen as a continuous process of interpretation, with each taking the role of the other.

The self

Mead argued that, through the process of role-taking, individuals develop a concept of 'self'. By placing themselves in the position of others they are able to look back upon themselves. Mead claimed the idea of a self can only develop if the individual can 'get outside himself (experientially) in such a way as to become an object to himself'. To do this they must observe themselves from the standpoint of others. Therefore, the origin and development of a concept of self lie in the ability to take the role of another.

Mead distinguished two aspects of the self. The 'me' is your definition of yourself in a specific social role. For example, you might see yourself as a 'good parent' or a 'loyal friend'. The 'I' is your opinion of yourself as a whole. The 'I', which can also be called your 'self-concept', is built up from the reactions of others to you, and the way you interpret those reactions. It can exercise considerable influence over your behaviour. For example, if you see yourself as cowardly on the basis of the self-concept you have built up, you are unlikely to act bravely in dangerous situations.

The notion of self is not inborn, it is learned during childhood. Mead saw two main stages in its development. The first, known as the **play stage**, involves children playing roles that are not their own. For example, children may play at being a parent, a doctor or a nurse. In doing so they become aware that there is a difference between themselves and the role they are playing. Thus the idea of a self is developed as the child takes the role of a make-believe other.

The second stage in the development of self is known as the **game stage**. In playing a game, children come to see themselves from the perspective of the various participants. In order to play a game such as football or cricket, children must become aware of their relationship to the other players. They must place themselves in the roles of the others in order to appreciate their own particular role in the game. In doing so, they see themselves in terms of the collective viewpoint of the other players. In Mead's terminology, they see themselves from the perspective of 'the generalized other'.

In Mead's view, the development of a consciousness of self is an essential part of the process of becoming a human being. It provides the basis for thought and action, and the foundation for human society. Without an awareness of self, the individual could not direct action or respond to the actions of others. Only by acquiring a concept of self can the individual take the role of self. In this way, thought is possible, since in Mead's view the process of thinking is simply an 'inner conversation'. Thus, unless individuals are aware of the self, they will be unable to converse with themselves and thought will be impossible.

By becoming 'self-conscious', people can direct their own action by thought and deliberation. They can set goals for themselves, plan future action and consider the consequences of alternative courses of action. With an awareness of self, individuals are able to see themselves as others see them. When they take the role of others, they observe themselves from that standpoint and become aware of the views of themselves that others hold.

This provides the basis for cooperative action in society. Individuals will become aware of what is expected of them and will tend to modify their actions accordingly. They will be conscious of the general attitudes of the community, and judge and evaluate themselves in terms of this generalized other. From this perspective, thought becomes 'an inner conversation going on between this generalized other and the individual'. Thus people are constantly asking what other people will think and expect when they reflect upon themselves.

In this way conduct is regulated in terms of the expectations and attitudes of others. Mead argued: 'It is in the form of the generalized other that the social process influences the behaviour of the individuals involved in it … that the community exercises control over the conduct of its individual members.'

Culture, social roles and institutions

Mead accepted that a society has a culture, and that this culture suggests appropriate types of behaviour for particular social roles. For example, a culture might specify that the role of doctor should not involve anything that might harm patients.

People will tend to act in ways that are consistent both with the expected behaviour in a particular role, and with that person's concept of self. From Mead's point of view, social institutions such as the family or the state have an existence in the sense that particular social roles are attached to them. Thus the institution 'the family' consists of the social roles of mother, father, daughter, son, sister, brother and so on.

Although the existence of a culture and social roles does shape human behaviour to some extent, humans still have considerable choice as to how they behave. Mead gave a number of reasons why this is so:

1. Many cultural expectations are not specific. Society may, for example, demand that people wear clothes, but there is usually considerable freedom as to which clothes to wear.
2. Individuals have considerable choice as to which roles they enter: for example, they have an element of choice in what job they do.
3. Some social roles encourage a diversity of behaviour: for example, fashion designers are encouraged to develop novel designs.
4. Society does not have an all-embracing culture. Subcultures exist and people can choose which of them to join.
5. Many cultural meanings indicate possibilities rather than requirements. Thus the symbol 'chair' suggests the possibility that people can sit on the object, but they are not compelled to do so.
6. At times it may be impossible to act in accordance with a social role: for example, parents may find themselves unable to care adequately for their children. In such circumstances new and innovative behaviour is necessary.

Social roles are not therefore fixed or unchanging; in reality they are constantly being modified in the course of interaction.

The individual and society

Mead's view of human interaction sees humans as both actively creating the social environment and being shaped by it. Individuals initiate and direct their own action, while at the same time being influenced by the attitudes and expectations of others in the form of the generalized other. The individual and society are regarded as inseparable, for the individual can only become a human being in a social context. In this context individuals develop a sense of self, which is a prerequisite for thought. They learn to take the roles of others, which is essential both for the development of self and for cooperative action. Without communication in terms of symbols whose meanings are shared, these processes would not be possible. Humanity therefore lives in a world of symbols that give meaning and significance to life and provide the basis for human interaction.

Herbert Blumer

The basic premises of symbolic interactionism

Blumer, a student of George Herbert Mead, systematically developed the ideas of his mentor (Blumer, 1962). In Blumer's view, symbolic interactionism rests on three basic premises:

1 Human beings act on the basis of meanings that they give to objects and events, rather than simply reacting either to external stimuli such as social forces, or to internal stimuli such as organic drives. Symbolic interactionism therefore rejects both societal and biological determinism.
2 Meanings arise from the process of interaction, rather than simply being present at the outset and shaping future action. To some degree, meanings are created, modified, developed and changed within interaction situations rather than being fixed and pre-formed. In the process of interaction actors do not slavishly follow pre-set norms or mechanically act out established roles.
3 Meanings are the result of interpretive procedures employed by actors within interaction contexts. By taking the role of the other, actors interpret the meanings and intentions of others. By means of 'the mechanism of self-interaction', individuals modify or change their definition of the situation, rehearse alternative courses of action and consider their possible consequences. Thus the meanings that guide action arise in the context of interaction via a series of complex interpretive procedures.

Blumer argues that the interactionist perspective contrasts sharply with the view of social action presented by mainstream sociology. He maintains that society must be seen as an ongoing process of interaction, involving actors who are constantly adjusting to one another and continuously interpreting the situation.

By contrast, mainstream sociology, and functionalism in particular, have tended to portray action as a mechanical response to the constraints of social systems. This view fails to see 'the social actions of individuals in human society as being constructed by them through a process of interpretation. Instead, action is treated as a product of factors which play on and through individuals.' Rather than actively creating their own social world, humans are pictured as passively responding to external constraints. Their actions are shaped by the needs of social systems and the values, roles and norms that form a part of those systems. Blumer rejects this view, arguing:

> *the likening of human group life to the operation of a mechanical structure, or to the functioning of a system seeking equilibrium, seems to me to face grave difficulties in view of the formative and explorative character of interaction as the participants judge each other and guide their own acts by that judgement.* Blumer, 1962

Social action and social systems

Although he is critical of those who see action as a predictable and standardized response to external constraints, Blumer accepts that action is to some degree structured and routinized. He states: 'In most situations in which people act towards one another they have in advance a firm understanding of how to act and how other people will act.'

However, such knowledge offers only general guidelines for conduct. It does not provide a precise and detailed recipe for action that is mechanically followed in every situation. Within these guidelines there is considerable room for manoeuvre, negotiation, mutual adjustment and interpretation.

Similarly, Blumer recognizes the existence of social institutions and admits they place limits on human conduct; but even in situations where strict rules prevail, such as in bureaucratic organizations, there is still considerable room for human initiative and creativity. Even when action appears particularly standardized and structured, this should not be taken as an indication that actors are merely responding to external forces. Blumer argues:

> *The common repetitive behaviour of people in such situations should not mislead the student into believing that no process of interpretation is in play; on the contrary, even though fixed, the actions of the participating people are constructed by them through a process of interpretation.* Blumer, 1962

Thus, standardized action is constructed by social actors, not by social systems.

Much of Blumer's work is concerned with developing an appropriate methodology for his view of human interaction. This aspect of his work is discussed in Chapter 14 (see p. 794).

Examples of interactionist sociology can be found on pp. 334–9 and 688–90.

Symbolic interactionism – a critique

Interaction in a vacuum

Interactionists have often been accused of examining human interaction in a vacuum. They have tended to focus on small-scale face-to-face interaction, with little concern for its historical or social setting. They have concentrated on particular situations and encounters, with little reference to the historical events leading up to them or the wider social framework in which they occur. Since these factors influence the particular interaction situation, the scant attention they have received has been regarded as a serious omission. Thus, in a criticism of Mead, Ropers argues: 'The activities that he sees men engaged in are not historically determined relationships of social and historical continuity; they are merely episodes, interactions, encounters, and situations' (quoted in Meltzer *et al.*, 1975).

The origin of norms

While symbolic interactionism provides a corrective to the excesses of societal determinism, many critics have argued it has gone too far in this direction.

Although they claim that action is not determined by structural norms, interactionists do admit the presence of such norms. However, they tend to take them as given

rather than explaining their origin. As William Skidmore (1975) comments, interactionists largely fail to explain 'why people consistently choose to act in given ways in certain situations, instead of in all the other ways they might possibly have acted'.

In stressing the flexibility and freedom of human action, interactionists tend to downplay the constraints on action. In Skidmore's view, this is due to the fact that 'interactionism consistently fails to give an account of social structure'. In other words, it fails to explain adequately how standardized normative behaviour comes about and why members of society are motivated to act in terms of social norms.

The source of meanings

Similar criticisms have been made with reference to what many see as the failure of interactionists to explain the source of the meanings to which they attach such importance. As the chapters on education and crime and deviance have shown, interactionism provides little indication of the origins of the meanings in terms of which individuals are labelled by teachers, police and probation officers (see Chapter 10, pp. 638–41, and Chapter 6, pp. 334–9).

Critics argue that such meanings are not spontaneously created in interaction situations. Instead, they are systematically generated by the social structure. Thus Marxists have argued that the meanings that operate in face-to-face interactions are largely the product of class relationships. From this viewpoint, interactionists have failed to explain the most significant thing about meanings: their origin.

Phenomenology

Phenomenology is a branch of European philosophy which was first developed by Edmund Husserl (1859–1938), and which was developed along more sociological lines by Alfred Schutz (1899–1959). Schutz was a pupil of Husserl's who moved to the USA after the rise of fascism in Europe.

Phenomenology differs from the social action approaches that have been examined so far in that it denies the possibility of explaining social action as such. Its emphasis is upon the internal workings of the human mind and the way that humans classify and make sense of the world around them. It is not concerned with the causal explanation of human behaviour in the same way as other perspectives. Phenomenologists try to understand the meaning of phenomena or things, rather than explaining how they came into existence.

Making sense of sensory experience

According to phenomenologists, individuals only come into contact with the outside world through their senses: touch, smell, hearing, sight and taste. It is not possible to know about the outside world except through these senses. Simply possessing senses, though, is not enough for a person to be able to make any sense out of the world. If humans took their sense experiences at face value, they would be confronted by an unintelligible mass of impressions – of colours, lights, sounds, smells, feelings and tastes – that were meaningless.

In order to overcome this problem, humans begin to organize the world around them into phenomena; they classify their sense experiences into things that appear to have common characteristics. For example, a distinction may be made between animate and inanimate objects. This distinction may be refined by dividing animate objects into mammals and non-mammals. Mammals may be divided into different species and species subdivided into different breeds. Thus humans have a series of shorthand ways of classifying and understanding the world external to their own consciousness. For example, a small white animal making a barking noise may be identified as a poodle.

Husserl (1931) did not believe that this process was in any sense objective; the classification of phenomena was entirely a product of the human mind, and could not be evaluated in terms of whether it was true or false. He did not deny the existence of physical objects beyond and outside the human mind, but he argued that, since people could only come into contact with them through their senses, they could never be sure about their true nature. Thus, in trying to secure knowledge, humans had to 'bracket' reality and commonsense beliefs: that is, put them, as it were, inside brackets and forget about whether they were true or false. Once they had done this, they could turn their attention to a phenomenological understanding of the world.

Husserl argued that, in order to understand social life, phenomenologists should study the way that humans placed the external world into categories by distinguishing particular phenomena. In doing so it would be possible to understand the meaning of a phenomenon by discovering its essence. What Husserl meant by this was that the researcher could find the distinguishing features (the essence) of a group of things (or phenomena) which humans classed together. Thus, for example, it might be found that a distinguishing feature – part of the essence – of a boat was that it could float.

In Chapter 14 the description of Atkinson's work on suicide (pp. 801–2) shows how he tried to understand the nature of the phenomenon suicide by investigating how coroners distinguished it from other types of death.

Alfred Schutz – the phenomenology of the social world

The general approach adopted by phenomenology is a type of philosophy of knowledge, rather than a sociological perspective. Alfred Schutz (1972, first published 1932) was the first to try to explain how phenomenology could be applied to develop insights into the social world.

Schutz's main contribution was to insist that the way that humans classified and attached meaning to the outside world was not a purely individual process. Humans developed what he called **'typifications'** – the concepts attached to classes of things that are experienced. Thus, a 'bank manager', a 'football match', 'dusting' and 'a tree' are

examples of typifications. These typifications are not unique to each person, but are shared by members of a society. They are passed on to children through learning a language, reading books or speaking to other people.

By the use of typifications, people are able to communicate with others on the basis of the assumption that they see the world in the same way. Gradually, a member of society builds up a stock of what Schutz calls 'commonsense knowledge', which is shared with other members of society and allows humans to live and communicate together.

Schutz believes such knowledge is essential to accomplish practical tasks in everyday life. For example, he describes the way in which a simple act such as posting a letter rests upon commonsense knowledge and the existence of shared typifications. The person posting the letter assumes another person (a postal worker whom they may never have met) will be able to recognize the piece of paper with writing on it as a letter, and will deliver it to the address on the envelope. The person also assumes the recipient of the letter – again someone they might not have met – will have commonsense knowledge similar to their own, and will therefore be able to understand the message, and react in an appropriate way.

Although Schutz stresses that knowledge is shared, he does not think it is fixed and unchanging. Indeed, commonsense knowledge is constantly modified in the course of human interaction. Schutz acknowledges that each individual has a unique biography, and interprets and experiences the world in a slightly different way; but the existence of a stock of commonsense knowledge allows humans to understand, at least partly, each other's actions. In doing so, they convince themselves that there are regular and ordered patterns in the world, and in social life. From this point of view, humans create between themselves the illusion that there is stability and order in society, when in reality there is simply a jumble of individual experiences that have no clear shape or form.

Ethnomethodology

Ethnomethodology was first developed in the 1960s. Many of the concerns of ethnomethodology have reflected the type of approach developed by Schutz. Schutz, however, did not carry out detailed research into social life; he merely speculated about the nature of society. Ethnomethodologists have applied phenomenological ideas in carrying out research.

In 1967 Harold Garfinkel first coined the term 'ethnomethodology'. Roughly translated, **ethnomethodology** means a study of the methods used by people. It is concerned with the methods used by people (or 'members', as ethnomethodologists refer to them) to construct, account for and give meaning to their social world.

Social order as a fiction

Ethnomethodologists follow Schutz in believing there is no real social order, as other sociological perspectives assume. Social life appears orderly to members of society only because members actively engage in making sense of social life. Societies have regular and ordered patterns only because members perceive them in this way.

Social order therefore becomes a convenient fiction – an appearance of order constructed by members of society. This appearance allows the social world to be described and explained, and so made knowable, reasonable, understandable and accountable to its members. It is made accountable in the sense that members of society become able to provide descriptions and explanations of their own actions, and of the society around them, which are reasonable and acceptable to themselves and others. Thus, in Atkinson's study of suicide, coroners were able to justify and explain their actions to themselves and to others in terms of the commonsense ways they went about reaching a verdict.

The point of ethnomethodology, according to Zimmerman and Wieder (1971), is to explain 'how members of society go about the task of seeing, describing, and explaining order in the world in which they live'. Ethnomethodologists have therefore conducted investigations into the techniques used by members to achieve the appearance of order. Two studies will now be examined in detail to illustrate the above points.

Harold Garfinkel

The documentary method

Garfinkel (1967) argues that members employ the 'documentary method' to make sense of and account for the social world, and to give it an appearance of order. This method consists of selecting certain aspects of the infinite number of features contained in any situation or context, defining them in a particular way, and seeing them as evidence of an underlying pattern. The process is then reversed and particular instances of the underlying pattern are used as evidence for the existence of the pattern. In Garfinkel's words, the documentary method:

> *consists of treating an actual appearance as 'the document of', as 'pointing to', as 'standing on behalf of' a presupposed underlying pattern. Not only is the underlying pattern derived from its individual documentary evidences, but the individual documentary evidences, in their turn, are interpreted on the basis of 'what is known' about the underlying pattern. Each is used to elaborate the other.*
> Garfinkel, 1967

For example, in the case of Atkinson's study of coroners, those deaths defined as suicide were seen as such by reference to an underlying pattern. This pattern is the coroner's commonsense theory of suicide. However, at the same time, those deaths defined as suicide were seen as evidence for the existence of the underlying pattern. In this way, particular instances of the pattern and the pattern itself are mutually reinforcing and are used to elaborate each other. Thus the documentary method can be seen as 'reflexive'. The particular instance is seen as a reflection of the underlying pattern and vice versa.

Garfinkel argues that social life is 'essentially reflexive'. Members of society constantly look at particular activities and situations in terms of presumed underlying patterns, and in turn confirm the existence of those patterns by

referring to particular expressions of them in activities and situations. In this way, members produce accounts of the social world that not only make sense of and explain, but actually constitute, that world. Thus, in providing accounts of suicide, coroners are actually producing suicide. Their accounts of suicide constitute suicide in the social world.

In this respect, accounts are a part of the things they describe and explain. The social world is therefore constituted by the methods and accounting procedures in terms of which it is identified, described and explained. Thus the social world is constructed by its members by the use of the documentary method. This is what Garfinkel means when he describes social reality as 'essentially reflexive'.

An experiment in counselling

Garfinkel claims to have demonstrated the documentary method and its reflexive nature by an experiment conducted in a university department of psychiatry.

Students were invited to take part in what was described as a new form of psychotherapy. They were asked to summarize a personal problem on which they required advice and then ask a counsellor a series of questions. The counsellor sat in an adjoining room; the student and the counsellor could not see each other and communicated via an intercom. The counsellor was limited to responses of either 'yes' or 'no'. Unknown to the student, the 'counsellor' was not a counsellor and the answers received were evenly divided between 'yes' and 'no', their sequence being predetermined in accordance with a table of random numbers.

In one case a student was worried about his relationship with his girlfriend. He was Jewish and she was a gentile. He was worried about his parents' reaction to the relationship and the problems that might result from marriage and children. His questions related to these concerns. Despite the fact that the answers he received were random and given without reference to the content of questions, and sometimes contradicted previous answers, the student found them helpful, reasonable and sensible. Similar assessments of the counselling sessions were made by the other students in the experiment.

From comments made by students on each of the answers they received, Garfinkel draws the following conclusions. Students made sense of the answers where no sense existed; they imposed an order on the answers where no order was present. When answers appeared contradictory or surprising, the students assumed the counsellor was unaware of the full facts of their case. The students constructed an appearance of order by using the documentary method. From the first answer they perceived an underlying pattern in the counsellor's advice. The sense of each following answer was interpreted in terms of the pattern, and at the same time each answer was seen as evidence for the existence of the pattern.

Thus the students' method of interpretation was reflexive. Not only did they produce an account of the counselling session, but the account also became a part of, and so constituted, the session. In this way the accounting procedure described and explained, and also constructed and constituted, social reality at one and the same time.

Garfinkel claims the counselling experiment highlights and captures the procedures that members are constantly using to construct the social world in their everyday lives.

Indexicality

This experiment can also be used to illustrate the idea of 'indexicality', a central concept employed by Garfinkel and other ethnomethodologists. **Indexicality** means that the sense of any object or activity is derived from its context; it is 'indexed' in a particular situation. As a result, any interpretation, explanation or account made by members in their everyday lives is made with reference to particular circumstances and situations.

Thus the students' sense of the counsellor's answers was derived from the context of the interaction. From the setting – a psychiatry department – and the information they were given, the students believed the counsellor was what he claimed to be and that he was doing his best to give honest and sound advice. His answers were interpreted within the framework of this context. If identical answers had been received from fellow students in a coffee bar, the change of context would probably have resulted in a very different interpretation. Such responses from fellow students might have been seen as evidence that they had temporarily taken leave of their senses, or were having a joke at their friend's expense, or they were drunk and so on.

Garfinkel argues that the sense of any action is achieved by reference to its context. Members' sense of what is happening depends on the way they interpret the context of the activity concerned. In this respect their understanding and accounts are indexical: they make sense in terms of particular settings.

Disrupting the social world

Garfinkel encouraged his students actually to disrupt the social world in order to reveal the way that members made sense of it and reached understandings. For example, he suggested they go into supermarkets and haggle over the price of goods, or go back to their own homes and act as if they were lodgers. In such ways they would demonstrate the fragile nature of social order. The victims of these experiments found it difficult or impossible to index them in the situation in which they took place. Thus parents, faced with a child acting as a lodger in their own home, became perplexed or angry, and desperately tried to make sense of their child's actions by, for example, believing that the child must be ill.

Ethnomethodology and mainstream sociology

Garfinkel (1967) argues that mainstream sociology has typically portrayed people as 'cultural dopes' who simply act out the standardized directives provided by the culture of their society. Garfinkel states: 'By "cultural dope" I refer to the man-in-the-sociologist's-society who produces the stable features of society by acting in compliance with preestablished and legitimate alternatives of action that the common culture provides.'

In place of the 'cultural dope' the ethnomethodologist pictures the skilled member who is constantly attending to the particular, indexical qualities of situations, giving them meaning, making them knowable, communicating this knowledge to others and constructing a sense and appear-

ance of order. From this perspective, members construct and accomplish their own social world rather than being shaped by it.

The nature of social reality

Ethnomethodologists are highly critical of other branches of sociology. They argue that 'conventional' sociologists have misunderstood the nature of social reality. They have treated the social world as if it has an objective reality that is independent of members' accounts and interpretations. Thus they have regarded aspects of the social world such as suicide and crime as facts with an existence of their own. They have then attempted to provide explanations for these 'facts'.

By contrast, ethnomethodologists argue that the social world consists of nothing more than the constructs, interpretations and accounts of its members. The job of the sociologist is therefore to explain the methods and accounting procedures that members employ to construct their social world. According to ethnomethodologists, this is the very job that mainstream sociology has failed to do.

The documentary method and mainstream sociology

Ethnomethodologists see little difference between conventional sociologists and the person in the street. They argue that the methods employed by sociologists in their research are basically similar to those used by members of society in their everyday lives. Members employing the documentary method are constantly theorizing, drawing relationships between activities and making the social world appear orderly and systematic. They then treat the social world as if it had an objectivity separate from themselves.

Ethnomethodologists argue that the procedures of conventional sociologists are essentially similar. They employ the documentary method, theorize and draw relationships, and construct a picture of an orderly and systematic social system. They operate reflexively like any other member of society. Thus, when functionalists see behaviour as an expression of an underlying pattern of shared values, they also use instances of that behaviour as evidence for the existence of the pattern. By means of their accounting procedures, members construct a picture of society. In this sense, the person in the street is their own sociologist. Ethnomethodologists see little to choose between the pictures of society that people create and those provided by conventional sociologists.

Ethnomethodology – a critique

Alvin Gouldner (1970) pours scorn upon ethnomethodology for dealing with trivial aspects of social life, and revealing things that everybody knows already. He gives an example of the type of experiment advocated by Garfinkel. An ethnomethodologist might release chickens in a town centre during the rush hour, and stand back and observe as traffic was held up and crowds gathered to watch and laugh at police officers chasing the chickens. Gouldner goes on to explain that Garfinkel might say that the community has now learned the importance of one hitherto unnoticed rule at the basis of everyday life: chickens must not be dropped in the streets in the midst of the rush hour.

More seriously, critics have argued that the members who populate the kind of society portrayed by ethnomethodologists appear to lack any motives and goals. As Anthony Giddens (1977) remarks, there is little reference to 'the pursuance of practical goals or interests'. What, for example, motivated the students in Garfinkel's counselling experiment?

There is little indication in the writings of ethnomethodologists as to why people want to behave or are made to behave in particular ways. Nor is there much consideration of the nature of power in the social world and the possible effects of differences in power on members' behaviour. As Gouldner notes:

> *The process by which social reality becomes defined and established is not viewed by Garfinkel as entailing a process of struggle among competing groups' definitions of reality, and the outcome, the commonsense conception of the world, is not seen as having been shaped by institutionally protected power differences.* Gouldner, 1970

Critics have argued that ethnomethodologists have failed to give due consideration to the fact that members' accounting procedures are conducted within a system of social relationships involving differences in power.

Many ethnomethodologists appear to dismiss everything that is not recognized and accounted for by members of society. They imply that, if members do not recognize the existence of objects and events, they are unaffected by them. But, as John H. Goldthorpe (1973) pointedly remarks in his criticism of ethnomethodology, 'if for instance, it is bombs and napalm that are zooming down, members do not have to be oriented towards them in any particular way, or at all, in order to be killed by them'. Clearly, members do not have to recognize certain constraints in order for their behaviour to be affected by them. As Goldthorpe notes, with reference to the above example, death 'limits interaction in a fairly decisive way'.

Finally, the ethnomethodologists' criticism of mainstream sociology can be redirected towards themselves. As Giddens remarks, 'any ethnomethodological account must display the same characteristics as it claims to discern in the accounts of lay actors'. Ethnomethodologists' accounting procedures therefore become a topic of study like those of conventional sociologists or any other member of society. In theory, the process of accounting for accounts is never-ending. Carried to its extreme, the ethnomethodological position implies that nothing is ever knowable.

Whatever its shortcomings, however, ethnomethodology asks interesting questions.

Uniting structural and social action approaches

The earlier parts of this chapter have shown how sociology can be divided into two types of approach. Structural

approaches, such as functionalism and some versions of Marxism, emphasize the way in which the structure of society directs human behaviour. Social action or interpretive approaches (such as those advocated by Weber), and symbolic interactionists and ethnomethodologists, argue that humans create society through their own actions. This distinction is not neat and clear-cut: most perspectives in sociology show some concern with both social structure and social action; but most perspectives emphasize one aspect of social life at the expense of another.

However, many sociologists have argued that it would be desirable to produce a sociological theory that combined an understanding of social structure and social action. C. Wright Mills (1959), for example, claimed: 'The sociological imagination enables its possessor to understand the larger historical scene in terms of its meaning for the inner life and external career of a variety of individuals' (see p. 17). It has often seemed as though sociologists could only understand one of these elements at a time. They might try to understand the 'larger historical scene' using a structural perspective; or alternatively they might try to understand the life of individuals using a social action approach. Generally, they do not attempt to understand both simultaneously.

Anthony Giddens – the theory of structuration

The duality of structure

The British sociologist Anthony Giddens (1977, 1979, 1984) has attempted to overcome the division between structure and action. Although the details of his argument are complex, his basic point is simple. Giddens claims structure and action are two sides of the same coin. Neither structure nor action can exist independently; both are intimately related.

Social actions create structures, and it is through social actions that structures are produced and reproduced, so that they survive over time. Indeed, Giddens (1984) uses a single word, 'structuration', to describe the way that structures relate to social actions, so that certain sets of social relationships survive over space and time. Giddens talks about the 'duality of structure', to suggest both that structures make social action possible, and at the same time that social action creates those very structures. He says, 'structure has no existence independent of the knowledge that agents have about what they do in their day-to-day activity'. In other words, it is you, I, and every other individual, who create structures.

The clearest way that Giddens explains this is using the examples of language and speech. The English language is, to Giddens, a structure; it is a set of rules about how to communicate, which seems independent of any individual. The grammar and vocabulary of English cannot simply be changed at will by members of society. Yet, if the language is to be reproduced, if it is to survive, it must be spoken or written by individuals in ways that follow its existing rules. Thus, Giddens says, 'when I utter a grammatical English sentence I contribute to the reproduction of the English language as a whole'.

The structure of the language ultimately depends upon the people who use it. For the most part, competent English speakers will follow the rules of English and reproduction will take place. However, this is not inevitable. Languages change: new words are invented and accepted by being used; some old words are forgotten and fall into disuse. Human agents, by their actions, can therefore transform as well as reproduce structures.

Rules and resources

In social life in general, Giddens identifies two aspects of structure: 'rules' and 'resources'.

Rules are procedures that individuals may follow in their social life. Sometimes interpretations of these rules are written down: for example, in the form of laws or bureaucratic rules. Such written expressions are not the rules themselves. Thus a rule might state that shopping involves paying a shop assistant, while the written interpretation of a rule of this sort might be the law of theft. Such structural rules can either be reproduced by members of society or they can be changed through the development of new patterns of interaction.

The second aspect of structure, resources, also comes into being through human actions and can be changed or maintained by them. Resources take two forms: allocative and authoritative.

Allocative resources include raw materials, land, technology, instruments of production and goods. For Giddens, such resources are never just there, given by nature; they only become resources through human actions. Thus land is not a resource until someone farms it or puts it to some other use.

Authoritative resources are non-material resources that result from some individuals being able to dominate others. In other words, they involve the ability to get others to carry out a person's wishes, and in this way humans become a resource that other individuals may be able to use. As in other parts of his theory, Giddens insists that authoritative resources only exist in so far as they are produced by human interaction. Authority is not something a person has unless they are actually using it.

Social systems

Having discussed what he means by structure, Giddens goes on to explain what he sees as the nature of social systems and institutions. A social system, he argues, is simply a pattern of social relations that exists over a period of time and space. Thus, for example, nineteenth-century Britain is a social system because it was a geographically defined space, over a particular period of time, where there were certain reproduced sets of social relationships and social practices. Of course, Giddens would not believe that Britain was the same 'system' in 1899 as it was in 1801; social relationships and practices would have changed continually as patterns of interaction changed.

Similarly, institutions such as the state or bureaucracies are seen by Giddens as patterns of behaviour that display some continuity over time, but which may also change as time passes.

Agency and reproduction

Giddens's views on structures, systems and institutions are closely tied in with his idea of human action (or 'agency'

as he usually refers to it), since they are all part of the 'duality of structure'. According to Giddens, human agents are constantly intervening in the world by their actions, and in doing so they have the capacity to transform it. He would not, though, accept the view that individuals create society, any more than he would accept that society determines individual behaviour. Structure affects human behaviour because of the knowledge that agents have about their own society. There is a large stock of 'mutual knowledge' of 'how to go on', or how to get things done.

From what they have learnt, agents know how to go about their everyday lives and accomplish objectives. For example, 'competent' members of society know how to go to a bar and order a round of drinks, just as other competent members know how to serve the customer ordering the drinks. Routine, mundane behaviour like this is constantly carried out and much of it requires little thought. This is so because the agents involved are drawing upon their knowledge of the rules of society, which exist in the structure of society. At the same time they are making use of resources that are also part of the structure of society. They make use of material commodities – such as money, drinks and glasses – and authoritative resources, such as the right of the bar staff to demand payment – a right that is recognized by the customers.

Giddens seems to think that humans have a basic desire for some degree of predictability in social life. They have a need for what he calls 'ontological security' or 'confidence and trust that the natural and social worlds are as they appear to be'. He suggests tentatively that this may be connected to the human 'basic security system', essentially a natural concern with the physical survival of the body. Thus it would be unsettling if people did not know whether they were expected to have to give money to, or take money from, bar staff, and even more unsettling if they were to worry that the bar staff were not what they seemed, and were a group of mass murderers intent upon poisoning their customers.

Agency and transformation

According to Giddens, the existence of mutual knowledge, and a need for ontological security, tend to produce regulations in social life. Patterns of behaviour are repeated, and in this way the structure of society, the social system and the institutions are all reproduced.

However, this whole process also involves the ever-present possibility that society can be changed. Agents do not have to behave as others do, nor do they necessarily act in accordance with their habits for ever. Giddens describes 'the reflexive monitoring of actions' in which humans are constantly able to think about what they are doing and consider whether their objectives are being achieved. If they are not being achieved, then agents may start to behave in new ways, patterns of interaction may change, and with them the social structure.

For Giddens, the very concepts of 'agent' and 'agency' involve people having the ability to transform the world around them through their actions, as well as being able to reproduce it. That does not mean that agents necessarily transform society, or for that matter reproduce it in ways that they intend. Human actions may well have consequences that were not anticipated by the agents involved. Giddens gives the example of going home and switching on a light in order to illuminate a room. An unintended consequence of this might be that a burglar is alerted and flees the house, and in doing so is apprehended by the police, and ultimately ends up spending several years in prison.

Such unintended consequences can also result in patterns of social life that were not necessarily intended to be produced by any individual. Thus, for example, decisions by individuals in society about where to live might produce a situation, which nobody had actually intended, in which some inner-city areas start to decay and develop a concentration of social problems.

Determinism and voluntarism

In his theory of the duality of structure, Giddens tries to show how the traditional distinction between social structure and social action does not necessitate seeing society in terms of one or the other: structure and agency are locked together in the processes through which social life is reproduced and transformed.

In a similar fashion, Giddens tries to resolve the dispute between determinists – who believe that human behaviour is entirely determined by outside forces – and voluntarists – who believe that humans possess free will, and can act as they wish. Giddens believes neither theory to be true, but he sees both as having some element of truth. He believes that only in very exceptional circumstances are humans completely constrained.

Complete constraint only occurs where physical force is used – for example, where a person is unwillingly knocked to the ground by someone else. In all other circumstances, even where people claim to 'have no choice', there are options open to them. Thus, if a person holds a gun to someone's head and threatens to shoot them if they do not hand over some money, the option of refusing is still open, even though there is a risk of death by making that choice. In other words, it is nearly always possible to 'do otherwise', to do something different. Constraints, according to Giddens, do not therefore determine actions, but operate 'by placing limits upon the range of options open to an actor'.

In society, humans are constrained by the existence of power relationships. Giddens sees all social action as involving power relationships. He sees power as the ability to make a difference, to change things from what they would otherwise have been, or, as he puts it, 'transformative capacity'. For Giddens, the idea of human agency involves the idea of transformative capacity, and this capacity of power may be used to change things, or the actions of other people. It can therefore be used to exercise power over other people, and so constrain people and reduce their freedom. At the same time, though, power also increases the freedom of action of the agents who possess it. What restricts one person, enables another to do more.

Most of Giddens's work is highly abstract, and he offers few examples of how his theory of structuration could be applied to the study of society. However, he does praise Paul Willis's book *Learning to Labour* (1977). (For details of the study, see pp. 605–7.)

Giddens claims that Willis's work shows how structures can be actively reproduced by the action of agents as an

unintended consequence of their actions. Thus, by their rejection of school and their determination to do manual jobs, 'the lads' in Willis's study reproduce some general features of capitalist–industrial labour.

Furthermore, constraints are not simply experienced as external forces of which they are passive recipients. Instead, the lads are actively involved in making the decisions that come to constrain them. Because they choose not to work hard at school, they end up with very limited options in later life when they are choosing what work to do.

Giddens claims that, if sociology is to progress beyond the division between action and structure, it requires more studies like Willis's, which show how structures are reproduced by purposeful human agents.

Criticisms of Giddens

Margaret S. Archer (1982) criticizes Giddens for locking agency and structure too tightly together. She suggests that the concepts have different implications. The idea of structure tends to stress the limits on human action; the idea of agency stresses the existence of free will; and the two are never reconciled. In her view, Giddens puts too much emphasis on the ability of agents to transform structures simply by changing their behaviour. Giddens's work implies that, if people were to start acting differently tomorrow, then all of society's structures would immediately be changed.

According to Archer, this is not the case. The possibilities for changing social structures, and the extent to which humans have the ability to transform the social world, depend upon the nature of the social structures.

Archer uses the example of Fidel Castro's policy on illiteracy when he took power in Cuba. He wanted to conquer illiteracy by getting each literate person to teach an illiterate person to read. Archer points out that literacy could not be achieved overnight, and, furthermore, how quickly it could be achieved depended upon a structural feature of Cuban society: the percentage of the population who were literate. Thus, if 1 per cent of the population were literate, a much more lengthy period would be involved than if 50 per cent were literate. This demonstrates to Archer that structural features of society cannot just be changed at will, at least not on the time scale that the actors involved might wish for.

Archer similarly takes Giddens to task for suggesting that 'material resources' only enter social life and exercise a constraining influence on social actions when humans choose to make use of them. She points out that a flood or volcanic eruption, or a shortage of land, is not the product of human will, but it exercises a real, material constraint on options, regardless of human actions. To give another example, once all the coal in the ground has been burned, it cannot be burned again.

In short, Archer suggests that people cannot just change or reproduce society as they wish. Some structural features of society are beyond their control and constrain behaviour. She accepts that humans have both some degree of freedom and some limits on how they act, but a theory that does not move beyond this generalization says little.

Giddens notes both the possibility of freedom of action and social change, and the constraints and the reproduction of social institutions. What Giddens does not do, though, is explain which of these will happen in particular circumstances. Archer says: 'The theory of structuration remains incomplete because it provides an insufficient account of the mechanisms of stable replication versus the genesis of new social forms.'

Modernity, postmodernity and postmodernism

Introduction

The distinction between modernity and postmodernity and the theory of postmodernism has become increasingly important in recent times. Theorists such as Durkheim, Weber and Marx have been seen by some as epitomizing modern sociology. Modern theories claimed to be able to provide a comprehensive and definitive theory of society. Postmodern theorists deny this is possible.

Before considering these issues in detail, it is useful to distinguish between modern theories and postmodernism on the one hand, and theories of modernity and postmodernity on the other.

Modern theories and **postmodernism** use different theoretical approaches to studying sociology. For example, modern sociological theory, such as that of Weber, Marx and Durkheim, believes it is possible to find out the objective truth about society, whereas postmodernism does not.

Modernity and **postmodernity** are terms used to describe different eras in the development of human societies. While some people believe Western societies have moved from modernity to postmodernity, others do not agree. Thus the debate about modernity, postmodernity, modernism and postmodernism is a debate both about the extent to which society has changed and about the sort of theoretical approach that should be used in sociology.

This section will first examine what is meant by the idea of modernity before going on to consider theories of postmodernity and postmodernism. It will conclude by considering the arguments of sociologists who believe that modern sociological theories and theories of modernity remain preferable to postmodernism and theories of postmodernity.

Modernity

Premodern and modern

Many of the classic nineteenth-century sociologists, such as Comte, Durkheim, Weber and Marx, shared a common intellectual interest in the social changes associated with industrialization. They all saw these changes as having shaped modernity. Comte and Weber, in particular, saw such changes as involving the progressive triumph of scientific rationality.

Comte believed modern society would be dominated by science. The influence of religion, superstition and philosophy would be replaced by 'positivist' science (see pp. 429–30). Weber fully believed the modern age would be increasingly shaped by rationalization and bureaucracy as affective and traditional actions became less important (see pp. 874–8).

Marx and Durkheim put less emphasis on scientific and rational thinking, but both had strong beliefs that society was developing progressively: in Marx's case, towards a communist utopia (see pp. 867–72); in Durkheim's case, towards a complex society based upon organic solidarity (see pp. 858–9).

All of them believed they had used scientific analysis to uncover the big story (called 'metanarrative' by some postmodernists) of human development. All thought they could outline the future direction of social change.

The belief in progress and the faith placed in science can both be seen as characteristic of modern thinking. Many sociologists would suggest that in premodern societies, such as simple tribal societies, religion, superstition and tradition formed the basis of social life. There was little conception of social change as progressive. Instead, following the seasons, social change was seen as circular (see pp. 5–6 for a description of premodern societies).

The Enlightenment

Modern ways of thinking are usually seen as having their origins in the eighteenth-century Enlightenment. This was a broad European intellectual movement which sought to sweep away the prejudices of previous generations, and replace them with a more rational basis for social life. David Harvey, a commentator on postmodernism, describes the Enlightenment in the following way:

> *The idea was to use the accumulation of knowledge generated by many individuals working freely and creatively for the pursuit of human emancipation and the enrichment of daily life. The scientific domination of nature promised freedom from scarcity, want, and the arbitrariness of natural calamity. The development of rational forms of social organization and rational modes of thought promised liberation from the irrationalities of myth, religion, superstition, release from the arbitrary use of power as well as from the dark side of our own human natures.* Harvey, 1990

The hopes of Enlightenment thinkers were reflected in the French Revolution, and inherited by the nineteenth-century sociologists mentioned above.

Postmodernism and the Enlightenment

Postmodern theorists tend to argue that the Enlightenment 'project' (the aims of Enlightenment thinkers) has been abandoned in contemporary societies. People no longer believe in the inevitability of progress, the power of science to solve all problems, the perfectibility of humanity or the possibility of running societies in a rational way.

People are more pessimistic about the future and much less willing to believe that the truth can be found in grand theories or ideologies such as Marxism. There is now a much wider variety of beliefs and most people are unwilling to accept that one set of ideas gives the absolute truth and all others are false. They see no simple recipe for solving the world's problems. Postmodernists welcome these changes.

Postmodernism and architecture

These changes are reflected in architecture, where the term 'postmodernism' was first adopted. Modern architecture was characterized by the use of new, cheap and efficient materials to mass-produce housing or offices for urban populations. The application of scientific knowledge, using such materials as steel, concrete and glass, would enable problems of accommodating people to be solved.

The Swiss-born modern architect Le Corbusier saw architecture as producing 'machines for modern living'. He advocated the building of the type of functional high-rise tower block that was to become a common feature of towns and cities throughout the world.

However, by the 1970s, tower blocks were beginning to fall out of favour. Charles Jencks (quoted in Harvey, 1990) dates the end of modernism in architecture from the destruction of the Pruitt-Igoe housing development in St Louis in 1972.

According to some theorists, modern architecture has given way to postmodern architecture. This distrusts the scientific and idealistic approach of modern architecture and, instead of looking to a high-tech future, borrows from the past. According to Harvey, examples of postmodern architecture include 'imitation medieval squares and fishing villages, custom-designed or vernacular housing, renovated factories and warehouses, and rehabilitated landscapes of all kinds'. Prince Charles's denunciations of modern architecture for defacing cities such as London can be seen as a typical postmodern attitude.

According to the theory of postmodernism, we have lost faith in all grand plans for the future of humanity, not just in architecture but in all areas of social life. Diversity is the order of the day. We have entered an era in which anything goes, all styles and fashions are permissible so long as none is taken too seriously. If this is true, then it seems to challenge the assumptions on which the foundations of sociology were laid.

The next sections will outline the claims of some postmodern theorists in more detail, starting with those who give strongest support to the concept and its implications. These writers do not just believe that we have entered an era of postmodernity, they also believe that all modern theories of society are unacceptable and outdated.

Jean-François Lyotard – postmodernism and knowledge

Language-games

The French theorist Lyotard (1984) argues that post-industrial society and postmodern culture began to develop at the end of the 1950s, although the rate of development and the stage reached vary between and within countries.

> *Lyotard sees these developments as related to technology, science and some social developments, but, most*

importantly, to changes in language. The key concept he uses is that of language-games. Lyotard seems to see social life as being organized around these language-games. Language-games serve to justify or legitimate people's behaviour in society. They are games in which the participants can try to assert certain things to be true or right. Each statement or utterance is a 'move' that may aid the participant in trying to win the game – to get their version of what is true or right accepted.

Narrative

In simple or pre-industrial societies, such as the South American tribe the Cashinahua, narrative – the telling of stories, myths, legends and tales – is the principal language-game. The narrator establishes their right to speak and the legitimacy of what they are saying according to who they are. They start the story by giving their Cashinahua name to show that they are an authentic member of the tribe who has had the story passed down to them. It is therefore an example of self-legitimation: what they say should be accepted because of who they are. Narratives help to convey the rules on which social order is based; they play a key role in socialization.

Science and metanarratives

With the Enlightenment, narrative language-games were largely replaced by scientific 'denotative' games. The scientist sees narrative as 'belonging to a different mentality: savage, primitive, underdeveloped, backward, alienated, composed of opinions, custom, authority, prejudice, ignorance, ideology'. In denotative language-games it is irrelevant who is speaking; statements are judged as to whether they are true or false. Scientific statements are scrutinized and are 'subject to argumentation or proof' by other participants in the game. Evidence and rational argument are employed to establish whether a statement should be accepted or rejected.

However, probing deeper, Lyotard argues that science is unable to rid itself entirely of narrative knowledge. Science tries to maintain distance between itself and social conventions so that it can remain objective. But this raises the question of the purpose of science. How can the vast expenditure on science be justified if it is kept separate from social life?

In the end, science rests upon metanarratives – narratives that give meaning to other narratives. Metanarratives give a sense of purpose to scientific endeavour and a sense of direction to social life. They suggest that humans can progress, through science, towards defeating ignorance and oppression. Science can help humans to conquer nature and become more self-conscious.

These metanarratives have had a major influence on Western thought, from the French Revolution to twentieth-century Marxism. Knowledge is also justified as being good in itself, enabling human beings to fulfil their potential.

Postmodernism

According to Lyotard, metanarratives of human emancipation, self-fulfilment and social progress are undermined by the advent of postmodernism. An 'incredulity towards metanarratives' develops. People no longer believe that reason can conquer superstition, that humans can be perfected or that communism can produce a perfect society, for example.

The postmodern era has two main characteristics. First, the search for truth is abandoned as denotative language-games fall into disrepute. Knowledge fragments into a multiplicity of different language-games that are specific to particular areas of science or social life. Diversity is the order of the day as people lose faith in the search for one great truth that unites and justifies all knowledge.

Second, denotative language-games are replaced by technical language-games. Here, statements are judged not by whether they are true, but by whether they are useful and efficient or not. Emphasis shifts from the ultimate ends of human activity, towards the technical means through which things can be achieved. In universities, for example, researchers ask what use something is rather than whether it is true. Research becomes geared to producing knowledge that is saleable.

Knowledge and computer technology

Lyotard does not devote much attention to explaining how these changes have come about. However, he seems to attribute most importance to technology. He says postmodernism rests upon the 'miniaturization and commercialization' of machines. Computer technology has become the principal 'force of production'.

Most postmodern scientific developments are concerned with communication, language and information storage. Knowledge that cannot be translated into a form usable by computers tends to get lost or disregarded. Increasingly, economic activity centres around information technology. Social life is monitored and controlled more and more by computerized machines; and control over knowledge becomes the major source of power.

Knowledge is no longer an end in itself, but something to be bought and sold, perhaps even fought over. Lyotard speculates that future wars will not be about territorial disputes, but about disputes over the control of knowledge.

To Lyotard, postmodern society is based on the production and exchange of knowledge that can be sold. Grand theories of truth, justice and progress have fallen out of fashion. Language-games concern whether things are efficient and saleable rather than whether they serve some ultimate human purpose or goal.

Lyotard's analysis sometimes sounds like a Marxist attack on capitalism. In fact, though, he praises the consequences of postmodernism. The search for truth in modern thinking led only to 'as much terror as we can take' (for example, repression under Stalin in the communist USSR). Postmodernism offers the possibility of tolerance and creative diversity, in which humans are not corrupted by some doctrinaire metanarrative.

Lyotard – a critique

Like most advocates of postmodernism, Lyotard indulges in a number of paradoxes. While attacking metanarratives, Lyotard himself makes the most sweeping generalizations about the direction of human development, as well as

making moral judgements about its desirability. While dismissing the possibility of objective knowledge, he claims to have identified and accurately described the development of key features of human societies.

The evidence Lyotard uses to support his claims is sparse, leaving the reader with little reason to prefer Lyotard's language-game to that of other social theorists. While rejoicing in diversity, Lyotard ends up celebrating language-games conducted according to one set of rules – those of the technical language-game. Terry Eagleton, a Marxist critic of Lyotard, sees this as nothing more than a justification for capitalism and the pursuit of profit regardless of the human consequences (quoted in Connor, 1989).

Jean Baudrillard – *Simulations*

Baudrillard does not explicitly discuss the concept of postmodernism in his most influential book, *Simulations* (1983). Nevertheless he is widely seen as a postmodern theorist. Like Lyotard, he sees societies as having entered a new and distinctive phase, and he relates this change to language and knowledge. Unlike Lyotard, he is rather pessimistic about the consequences of this change, seeing it as a kind of trap from which escape is impossible.

Signs and the economy

Baudrillard argues, in contradiction to Marxists, that society has moved away from being based upon production and being shaped by the economic forces involved in exchanging material goods. The central importance of the buying and selling of material goods has now been replaced by the buying and selling of signs and images, which have little if any relationship to material reality. Baudrillard is not explicit about what he means in this context, but examples might include the ways in which cars, cigarettes, pop stars and political parties have become more associated with images than any substance that might lie behind them (engines, nicotine content, music and policies, respectively). The images are everything, the reality nothing.

The development of signs

Baudrillard argues that signs in human culture have passed through four main stages:

1. In the first stage, signs (words, images, etc.) are a 'reflection of a basic reality'.
2. In the next stage, the sign 'masks and perverts some basic reality'. Images become a distortion of the truth, but they have not lost all connection with things that really exist.
3. In the third stage, the sign 'masks the absence of some basic reality'. For example, icons may disguise the fact that God does not exist.
4. Finally, the sign 'bears no relation to any reality whatsoever: it is its own pure simulacrum'. A **simulacrum** is an image of something that does not exist and has never existed. To Baudrillard, modern society is based upon the production and exchange of free-floating images. Signifiers (words and images) have no connection with anything real that is signified (the things that words and images refer to).

Examples of simulacra

Baudrillard provides a number of examples to illustrate this rather sweeping claim. Disneyland is described as 'a perfect model' of a simulacrum. It is a copy of imaginary worlds such as 'Pirates, the Frontier, Future World'.

Simulacra are not confined to theme parks. According to Baudrillard the whole of Los Angeles is a kind of make-believe world founded upon stories and images that have no grounding in reality: it is 'nothing more than an immense script and a perpetual motion picture'.

In contemporary society the predominance of signifiers tends to destroy any basic reality to which they might refer. Baudrillard gives the examples of a Filipino tribe called the Tasaday, the mummy of Rameses II, and a family called the Louds, who were the subject of a fly-on-the-wall television documentary in the USA.

The Tasaday Indians were discovered in a remote area of the Philippines and began to be studied by anthropologists. However, the government believed the traditional culture of the Tasaday was being destroyed by this process, and decided to return them to the jungle and isolate them from contemporary civilization. Thus they were turned into a simulation of a primitive society. They were no longer in their original and natural state, but they had come to represent all primitive peoples to Western scientists.

Science and technology also destroyed the originality of the mummy of the Egyptian Pharaoh Rameses II. Once the mummy was removed from its original site and placed in a museum, it began to deteriorate and scientific techniques were used to try to preserve it. At the same time, though, they altered it and destroyed its authenticity.

The Louds family was similarly destroyed. Chosen as a 'typical' Californian family, 300 hours of film of their life were broadcast. During the process the family fell apart and they went their separate ways. Whether or not this was due to television, the reality of the family was inevitably changed by the fact that they had become the object of a public spectacle.

Attempts to capture reality unavoidably lead to its destruction, so that science and television culture capture nothing but images of things that never existed or have already been destroyed.

Power and politics

Baudrillard is consistently gloomy about the consequences of all this. If it has become impossible to grasp reality, it is also impossible to change it. Society has 'imploded' and become like a black hole in which nothing can escape the exchange of signs with no real meaning. For example, the meaning of a terrorist outrage becomes arbitrary. It can equally easily be interpreted as the work of left-wingers or right-wingers or political moderates who want to discredit extremists of both sides.

In Baudrillard's view, power is no longer unequally distributed, it has just disappeared. Nobody can exercise power to change things. He compares the situation to nuclear deterrence where the two sides cancel each other out and make action impossible. While President Kennedy was assassinated because he might have real power, Johnson, Nixon, Ford and Reagan were merely puppets without any genuine chance of changing America or the outside world.

With the end of the real and its substitution by simulacra, and the end of effective power, we are all trapped in a kind of prison, deprived of our freedom to change things, and condemned to the interminable exchange of meaningless signs.

Television

Baudrillard, then, differs from Lyotard in that he sees humans as trapped into a type of powerless uniformity, and not liberated by plurality and diversity.

If anything, Baudrillard is even more vague than Lyotard in explaining how the postmodern era came about. However, he does seem to attach special importance to the mass media and to television in particular. He talks about 'the dissolution of life into TV' and says: 'TV watches us, TV alienates us, TV manipulates us, TV informs us'. It seems that it is television that is primarily responsible for ushering in a situation where image and reality can no longer be distinguished.

Baudrillard – a critique

Baudrillard's writing is highly abstract and it offers no systematic evidence to justify its case. For example, Baudrillard makes no attempt to show that individuals are immersed in the world of television, that Disneyland is seen as anything more than fantasy by its customers, or that the residents of Los Angeles have lost their grip on reality. His analysis of politics degenerates into totally unsubstantiated assertions. For example, he describes Reagan as a 'puppet' who, in common with other 'postmodern' politicians, has no power.

David Harvey accepts that Reagan's election might have owed a good deal to his television image, but argues that the reality of his policies and their very real effects on the lives of many Americans cannot be denied. He says:

> *A rising tide of social inequality engulfed the United States in the Reagan years, reaching a postwar high in 1986 ... Between 1979 and 1986, the number of poor families with children increased by 35 per cent ... In spite of surging unemployment (cresting at over 10 per cent by official figures in 1982) the percentage of unemployed receiving any federal benefit fell to only 32 per cent, the lowest level in the history of social insurance.* Harvey, 1990

In addition, nearly 40 million people were left with no medical insurance. Perhaps, then, it is Baudrillard who has lost his grasp on reality rather than the 'postmodern' world.

In his later work, Baudrillard (1995) goes as far as claiming that the Gulf War (in which the USA, Britain and other countries attacked Iraq as a response to its invasion of Kuwait) did not take place. From Baudrillard's point of view, the Gulf War was just a series of images produced by the media with no evidence that what they depicted was real. Such views display Baudrillard's lack of grip on reality, since there are innumerable eyewitnesses to the events, not to mention graves containing the corpses of those who died during the war.

(For further descriptions and evaluations of postmodernism in relation to particular topics, see pp. 84–6, 115–19, 198–204, 386–90, 451–6, 512–19, 562–5, 609–12, 682–6, 754–6 and 811–14.)

Greg Philo and David Miller – a critique of postmodernism

Postmodernism, social science and language

Despite the popularity of postmodernism, it has been strongly attacked by some sociologists. Greg Philo and David Miller (2001) see the popularity of postmodernism as part of a wider trend in the social sciences. This trend emphasizes the importance of language and denies that social scientists can explain and understand an objective reality. It is reflected in the popularity of writers such as Derrida and the influence of Foucault's idea of discourse (see pp. 116–17 and 558–62).

Philo and Miller characterize these views in the following way: 'The essence of these arguments is that reality is always constituted for us through language. The meaning of language is negotiated, therefore "reality" is negotiated.' In the work of some postmodernists this view is taken even further 'to the assertion that reality "only" consists for us as what is constituted in language'. Thus Lyotard sees the development of society as involving changes in language-games, while Baudrillard believes the development of simulacra makes it impossible to represent reality through language.

Like those who have criticized particular postmodernists, Philo and Miller see the denial of the possibility of describing or analysing an objective reality as dangerous. It is dangerous because it encourages political apathy. The implication of the postmodernist view is that 'ideologies cannot be challenged because one definition of the real is in principle as good as another'.

From this point of view, it is as valid to deny that the Nazis murdered large numbers of people in concentration camps as it is to argue that the murders really took place. Lyotard himself argued that it was no longer meaningful to use terms such as 'Nazis' and 'death camps' because they 'have become so laden with ethical judgements that there is an irreducible conflict of interpretation' over what they mean.

However, Philo and Miller suggest the emotional and ethical connotations of a word such as 'Auschwitz' are grounded in the 'actual horror which it represents'. To deny the reality of that horror makes it impossible to expose the consequences of fascism or to engage in any rational discussion about whether Nazi ideology should be seen as less desirable than other ideologies.

Sociology and media and cultural studies

Philo and Miller are insistent that sociology needs to remain concerned with real political and social issues and must avoid becoming trapped in endless discussions of the meaning of language. In media and cultural studies, postmodernists tend to be obsessed with minute changes in popular taste and popular culture (see pp. 684–6 for a discussion of postmodernism and popular culture).

Furthermore, in line with Baudrillard's theory of simulacra, postmodernists analyse media images as if they had no connection with reality. From a postmodern point of view, such images can be interpreted in any way the audiences choose. To Baudrillard, the Gulf War was no more than images on a TV screen.

However, Philo and Miller's own research on the media and its audiences shows that none of this is true. Audiences are well aware there is some reality behind TV images. They also know that TV representations of reality are distorted and imperfect.

Nevertheless, the interpretations placed on TV messages are not random; they tend to favour certain viewpoints over others and this influences audiences. For example, in their own research into coverage of the Israeli–Palestinian conflict, Philo and Miller show that many members of the audience were not fully aware of the fact that Israel has been occupying Palestinian territory for decades.

To Philo and Miller, it is perfectly possible to compare media images with reality and to highlight inaccuracies and misrepresentations. They say:

> *a media image is a measurable part of reality in its own right and the processes by which it is manufactured can be analysed and exposed. The exposure of how this part of reality has been constructed can have an impact on beliefs about the validity of the descriptions which are being offered.* Philo and Miller, 2001

In their research Philo and Miller found that members of the audience for TV news were interested in alternative accounts of the Israeli–Palestinian conflict and were able to assess critically the merits of different accounts of the nature and causes of the problem. Philo and Miller say: 'Audience members can and do distinguish between media hype and what are judged to be more authentic accounts.'

Conclusion

Philo and Miller believe, then, that reality exists, that it can be described and analysed by social scientists, that media audiences can distinguish between reality and myth, that distortions of reality by the media can be exposed, and that it is essential to be critical of accounts of reality that are seriously distorting. They reject the postmodern belief that all accounts of the world are equally valid and that political arguments are pointless.

Postmodernists tend to portray the contemporary social world as one in which people are free to consume as they please, and to create and recreate identities as they see fit. Philo and Miller adopt a very different position and support the view of critical social science (see pp. 804–8). To them, people are still constrained by growing inequalities of wealth and income (see pp. 35–41), the growing power of capitalist corporations (see pp. 551–2) and the increasing influence of market forces in social life (see pp. 272–3). Postmodernists, with their obsessive interest in culture and style, miss the point that culture is partly shaped by the capitalist economy and differences in what rich and poor can afford to consume. Philo and Miller therefore conclude:

> *The growth of consumption and fragmentation of styles does not signify a new type of society. Without understanding this there is little that media studies or social science can offer that is critical of the society which we do have. Reducing social critique to ironic commentaries does not remove the social structures which position and limit us as we are – it simply reduces our ability to do anything about them.* Philo and Miller, 2001

Modern theories of society and the sociology of modernity

There are numerous sociologists who believe that the basic principles of modern sociological theories remain valid. They believe it is possible to analyse the social world rationally, to develop coherent theories of that social world, and to intervene to improve it. Such sociologists reject the claims of postmodernists that metanarratives are dangerous, that all knowledge is relative and that the Enlightenment project of improving society has reached the end of the road.

A good example of such a view is provided by the work of Kenan Malik (see pp. 202–4). Malik claims that racism is not a product of modernity, but a consequence of the social relations of capitalism. He believes that Enlightenment thinking provides a foundation for the belief that humans should be treated equally. He points out that the postmodernist's emphasis on plurality and diversity can be used as an excuse to support and justify inequality.

Throughout this book there are numerous examples of sociologists who continue to use a modern approach in analysing society, and who also continue to insist that it is possible to improve society. A few examples are: Gordon Marshall and his colleagues' work on class inequality (see p. 63); Wilkinson's studies of the relationship between inequality and ill-health (see p. 303); Sylvia Walby's theory of patriarchy (see pp. 111–14); and Jock Young's analysis of the 'exclusive society' (see pp. 350–3). Whatever the merits of the work of such sociologists, the types of approach used by them suggest that modern sociological theory and research are far from exhausted.

Anthony Giddens – high modernity and beyond

Anthony Giddens is one of the most influential of those sociologists who reject both the claims of postmodernism and the theory of postmodernity. Like the sociologists mentioned above, Giddens (1990) does not accept that all Enlightenment thinking must be abandoned, that metanarratives no longer have a place or that all knowledge is relative in a new era of postmodernity. Nevertheless, Giddens does believe that significant changes have taken place within modernity and he believes that postmodernity might develop in the future.

The central features of modernity

Giddens starts his analysis by contrasting modern and traditional societies. He argues that, compared to traditional societies, modern societies are characterized by

a more rapid pace of change. Furthermore, the scope of change is much greater than in traditional societies. Changes rapidly encompass virtually the whole of the globe and are not confined to geographically limited areas.

Giddens argues that a number of key features of modernity have led to the rapid pace and widespread scope of change:

1 There is a process of **time–space distanciation**. This involves the separation of time from space. In modernity, what time it is does not depend upon where you are. In pre-industrial societies time was not standardized across the globe, and time therefore depended on where you were. By the twentieth century all parts of the world used a standardized system of recording time. This allowed the development of railway, and later airline, timetables, which made it possible to coordinate the movement of goods and people across space, over time.
2 Time–space distanciation was important as a crucial **disembedding** mechanism. Giddens (1990) describes disembedding as 'the "lifting out" of social relations from local contexts of interaction'. Disembedding allows people to relate to and interact with others who do not live in the local area. It reduces the importance of local contacts and starts to break down geographical constraints. Thus time–space distanciation was a disembedding mechanism partly because it made travel easier.
3 Another important disembedding mechanism was the development of **symbolic tokens**. By far the most important type of symbolic token is money. Money allows the interchange of goods and services between people who have never met each other. It allows these exchanges to take place over long distances without face-to-face bartering. The existence of credit allows the deferment of payments, reducing the obstacles that time limits previously imposed on conducting exchanges.
4 Another important disembedding mechanism is the development of **expert systems**. Giddens defines these as 'systems of technical accomplishment or professional expertise that organize large areas of the material and social environment in which we live today'. Examples of expert systems include engineering and medicine. Expert systems allow people living in modernity to carry out their day-to-day activities and to accomplish things without any knowledge of the technicalities of what they are doing. For example, motorists can drive around without any knowledge of how to build roads; patients can undergo heart surgery without knowing how it is carried out; and airline passengers can cross continents without having any knowledge of aeronautical engineering. Like other disembedding mechanisms, expert systems allow many aspects of social life to proceed without the need for personal relationships between those involved.
5 As a result of the changes discussed above, modernity results in the basis of **trust** changing. In pre-industrial societies you trusted somebody because you knew them, and/or because their local reputation suggested they were trustworthy. With modernity you place your trust in the expert systems that train people and monitor and regulate their behaviour. For example, you do not have to know an airline pilot and the airline's mechanics personally before you will board a plane. You trust that the training of the pilot and the mechanics, the technology used in the plane and the procedures for servicing and flying the aircraft are sufficiently reliable for you to undertake the journey.
6 Along with disembedding mechanisms, a crucial feature of modernity is the development of greater **reflexivity**. Reflexivity refers to the 'reflexive monitoring of action': that is, the way in which humans think about and reflect upon what they are doing in order to consider acting differently in the future.

   Humans have always been reflexive up to a point, but in pre-industrial societies the importance of tradition limited reflexivity. Humans would do some things simply because they were the traditional things to do. With modernity, tradition loses much of its importance and reflexivity becomes the norm. Giddens says: 'The reflexivity of modern social life consists in the fact that social practices are constantly examined and reformed in the light of incoming information about those very practices, thus constitutively altering their character.' This produces constant change and a permanent state of uncertainty.

   Giddens does not agree with postmodernists such as Lyotard that modernity produces metanarratives that are accepted as the absolute truth. Instead, according to Giddens, modernity undermines all certainty. All knowledge is constantly reviewed and is always likely to be revised. This is most obvious in the social sciences, where there is constant theoretical dispute and frequent development of new theories. Indeed, Giddens believes sociology has a central place in the reflexivity of modernity. He describes sociology as 'the most generalized type of reflection upon modern social life' (Giddens, 1991).

   The existence of sociological knowledge reflects back upon society and helps to shape the very social life it describes. According to Giddens, sociological thinking becomes embedded in society, it shapes the way people see the world, and influences their decisions. For example, people considering whether to marry are almost certain to be aware of sociological knowledge about the existence of high divorce rates and arguments about the instability of the family as an institution. Whether or not they decide to marry, awareness of such issues is bound to have some effect on their thinking. If they do get married, this awareness is likely to have some influence on the way they conduct their marriage. This in turn may affect future divorce rates. Giddens (1990) therefore believes 'modernity is itself deeply and intrinsically sociological'.
7 To Giddens, modernity is **globalizing**. Disembedding and reflexivity allow social interaction to stretch across the globe, with the result that social life in particular localities is increasingly shaped by events taking place far away (see Chapter 9, pp. 554–5, for more details of Giddens's views on globalization).

The institutions of modernity

According to Giddens, modernity is based upon four key institutions:

1 **Capitalism**. Giddens (1990) defines capitalism as 'capital accumulation in the context of competitive labour and productive markets'. He sees capitalism as 'intrinsically unstable and restless'. Capitalists are always seeking new markets and trying to develop new products in the pursuit of profit. This makes modernity rather unsettling for the individual and contributes to the process of globalization.
2 **Industrialism**. This involves 'the use of inanimate sources of material power in the production of goods, coupled to the central role of machinery in the production process'. Industrialism produces a massive increase in the productivity of human labour.
3 **Surveillance**. This refers to 'the supervision of subject populations in the political sphere' (Giddens, 1991). In modernity the state devises a range of administrative systems to monitor the behaviour of populations so that people can be controlled (see the work of Foucault, discussed on pp. 558–62).
4 **Military power**. This concerns 'the control of the means of violence in the context of the industrialization of war' (Giddens, 1990). From the First World War onwards, military technology allowed ever-greater destructive power to be used in warfare.

Living in modernity

Modernity does not just consist of a number of institutions; it is also a lived experience for individuals. Giddens considers two sociological theories of the experience of modernity:

1 For Weber, modernity was largely experienced in terms of the '"steel-hard" cage of bureaucratic rationality' (Giddens, 1990). People were trapped in the logic of bureaucratic rationality, and had little freedom to express themselves.

   Giddens rejects this view. He argues: 'Rather than tending inevitably towards rigidity, organizations produce arenas of autonomy and spontaneity – which are often less easy to achieve in smaller groups.'
2 For Marx, modernity was experienced as 'a monster'. It was characterized by the exploitation of the mass of the population, who were alienated from their true humanity by the nature of capitalist work. However, Marx did believe that the monster could be tamed with the advent of a communist society.

   Giddens also rejects this view. He does not see modernity in such a negative light. As well as having some negative effects, it opens up new possibilities in people's lives which were not available in premodern societies.

Giddens develops an alternative image of modernity. He sees it as similar to a 'juggernaut – a runaway engine of enormous power which, collectively as human beings, we can drive to some extent but which also threatens to rush out of our control and which could rend itself asunder'.

It threatens to rush out of control because there are certain **high consequence risks** that characterize the most recent phase of modernity and which threaten to destroy human society. These risks are:

1 The 'growth of totalitarian power': this comes from the existence of systems of surveillance which make the close control of populations feasible.
2 The 'collapse of economic growth mechanisms': this stems from the unpredictability of capitalism with its booms and slumps, and the finite nature of certain resources (such as oil) on which capitalism currently depends.
3 'Nuclear conflict or large-scale warfare' remains a real possibility while a number of nations possess the means of mass destruction. Nobody can be sure that the principle of deterrence among major military powers will continue to work indefinitely.
4 'Ecological decay or disaster' is also a real possibility, with nuclear accidents (like that at Chernobyl), global warming, the depletion of the ozone layer, and other, as yet unforeseen, possibilities threatening human life on earth.

To Giddens, high modernity could end with disaster of one sort or another. The juggernaut might career out of control and come to an abrupt end in a crash. However, he sees this as only one possibility. Attempts to steer the juggernaut of high modernity may be successful and are still worthwhile.

Steering the juggernaut

Giddens rejects the view of postmodernists that planned intervention in society is neither desirable nor effective. He admits there are problems with the Enlightenment view that modernity can be rationally planned, and that society can be perfected through such planning. Giddens argues there is always an element of uncertainty and unpredictability in planning society. This stems from the reflexivity of social life, as discussed earlier. Sociological knowledge and theories can result in changes in the societies that they are trying to describe and analyse.

The nature of society can never be entirely pinned down, since the attempt to understand it can at the same time change it. Furthermore, societies are highly complex. Attempts to intervene to change society can have unintended consequences and end up doing more harm than good.

However, none of this means it is impossible to try to steer the juggernaut of modernity at least roughly in the direction in which you want to go. Knowledge about society may be imperfect, but it is not useless. The effects of intervention in society may be somewhat unpredictable, but lack of intervention is even more likely to end in calamity. With care, there is a good chance that the high consequence risks that threaten modernity will be avoided, and that human society will progress further.

Modernity and 'post-modernity'

Unlike theorists of postmodernity, Giddens believes we still live in an era of modernity or high modernity. He does not entirely reject the idea of 'post-modernity', however, (unlike most theorists, Giddens hyphenates this

term). Instead of seeing postmodernity as something that has already been attained, he uses the term to describe a type of society that may come into existence in the future. According to Giddens, a 'post-modern' society will move beyond each of the four dominant institutional structures of modernity. The main institutions of a 'post-modern' social order are shown in Figure 15.1.

The four transformations that would take place in the shift from modernity to 'post-modernity' are as follows:

1 Capitalism would be transformed into a **post-scarcity system**. Markets would continue to exist, but they would not produce the inequality typical of modernity because there would be an ample supply of goods for everybody. This would be achieved partly through economic growth, but also through people in the richer countries scaling down their aspirations. People will accept a lower standard of living because of 'development fatigue'. According to Giddens, there is evidence that people in richer countries are becoming tired of the negative consequences of unlimited economic growth. They are unhappy with overcrowded roads, pollution and soaring house prices. People are coming to understand that there are ecological limits to how much economic growth the environment can stand. They are therefore becoming willing to accept that lower incomes might actually improve the quality of people's lives. Richer nations would have to accept the need to share some wealth with poorer nations if a post-scarcity system were to be achieved.
2 Societies based on surveillance would be replaced by societies in which there was **multi-layered democratic participation**. The development of techniques of surveillance helps to convince governments that the cooperation and support of populations are essential for the effective exercise of power. People increasingly demand the right to have a say in all aspects of their lives, at local, national and even global level. There are 'pressures towards democratic participation in the workplace, in local associations, in media organizations, and in transnational groupings of various sorts.'
3 In a postmodern society the dominance of military power would give way to **demilitarization**. Globalization and the accompanying increase in interdependence between nations are likely to mean that going to war makes little sense. Long-established borders between nations will increasingly be accepted, and disputes over territory are likely to become infrequent. Furthermore, states will be keen to reduce the enormous costs of building up armed forces or fighting wars.
4 Finally, industrialism would be superseded by the **humanization of technology**. With the development of areas such as genetics and biotechnology, people are becoming increasingly aware of the need to exercise control over technology to prevent it having disastrous consequences. They are likely to become concerned over issues such as human cloning, transplanting animal organs into humans, and genetically modified crops. Such concerns would lead, in a 'post-modern' society, to strict limits being placed on the development and use of technology to prevent it causing environmental disaster or human tragedy.

(For more details of Giddens's theories, see pp. 554–5, 512–13 and 452–3.)

Figure 15.1 The contours of a 'post-modern' order

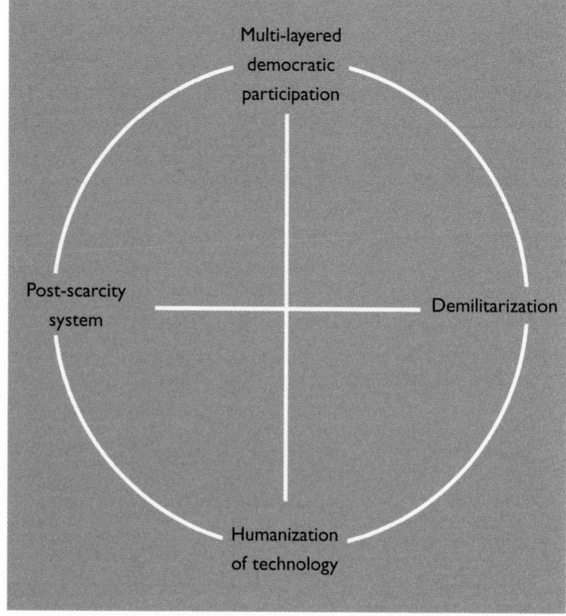

Source: A. Giddens (1990) *The Consequences of Modernity*, Polity Press, Cambridge, p. 164.

Evaluation and conclusions

Giddens's vision of a 'post-modern' society is (as he admits) a rather idealistic one. It is hard, for example, to envisage richer countries readily sharing their wealth with poorer ones, or people in the richer countries accepting that their living standards will not grow in the future.

L.B. Kaspersen (2000) argues that Giddens also underestimates the extent to which material inequalities stemming from class continue to constrain behaviour. Kaspersen believes, for example, that the 'well-educated doctor' has more choices in life than the poor 'single mother with three kids'. Similarly, Kenneth H. Tucker (1998) believes that some of Giddens's more recent work exaggerates the ability of individuals to shape their own lives, and even to transform society.

Another weakness of Giddens's work is that it lacks a theory of culture. Kaspersen (2000) argues that Giddens writes as if everybody living in modern societies experiences modernity in much the same way. In reality, differences in culture between a variety of groups in modern societies (such as ethnic and class groups) significantly affect how people experience social life and how they behave.

Kaspersen says Giddens cannot 'explain … why people act differently, why rules and resources utilized in action are not the same for all, or why the agents have very different practices'. Kaspersen goes on to illustrate this point. He says: 'we may take a seamstress, a lawyer, a retired policeman, and a shopkeeper. Their day-to-day lives are quite varied, their daily activities are differently structured, they have entirely unequal possibilities for action.' To Kaspersen, Giddens

exaggerates individual freedom of action, and neglects concepts such as culture, which address how individuals experience and respond to wider structures.

Despite some problems with Giddens's work, it does provide an alternative perspective to those of postmodernism and theories of postmodernity. It suggests that claims that we have entered postmodernity may, at best, be premature. More importantly, it suggests that sociological analysis remains possible and desirable.

If the arguments of postmodernism were accepted, then all attempts to understand social structures and to shape the future development of society as a whole would be abandoned. Using Giddens's analogy, this would involve taking your hands off the steering wheel of the juggernaut and trusting to fate that it will not crash.

Sociological knowledge may be imperfect, and attempts to shape society may not always succeed, but most sociologists still believe that these endeavours are worthwhile. More than that, it can be argued that the sociological imagination is more important than ever if we are to control the risks found in contemporary societies, and fulfil the potential for improving people's lives.

Summary and conclusions

This chapter has outlined and discussed a wide range of sociological theories. Other chapters have examined yet more theories, such as various types of feminism (see pp. 100–4) and poststructuralism (see pp. 681–2) including the influential theories of Foucault (see pp. 558–62).

There are many differences between perspectives. To simplify, some of the disagreements concern whether society is characterized more by consensus (functionalism) or by conflict (Marxism, conflict theory, feminism); whether you should study social structure (functionalism and Marxism), social action (symbolic interactionism, ethnomethodology), or both (Weber, Giddens); whether the objective study of society is possible (functionalism, Marxism, and, for the most part, Weber), or it is not (ethnomethodology, postmodernism, poststructuralism and some types of feminism); and whether we continue to live in modernity (Marxists, Weberians and some feminists), or we have moved beyond modernity (postmodernists).

Most of the differences of view appear irreconcilable: they directly contradict one another; there is apparently no middle ground. Different sociologists sometimes seem to work within completely different paradigms (see p. 849), making sociology a fragmented and divided discipline.

However, Ritzer and Goodman (2003) believe that the boundaries between different perspectives are breaking down. Many, perhaps most, sociologists draw their inspiration from a variety of sources rather than working simply within one perspective or paradigm. Ritzer and Goodman say, 'Previously, one was limited largely to the ideas internal to the perspective one had opted into. Now the entire range of theoretical perspectives is open to everyone' (2003, p. A-18).

On the whole, Ritzer and Goodman welcome this. They admit that it may seem that sociological theory is in 'turmoil', but they argue that the ability of researchers to draw on such a variety of theories has led to much interesting and insightful sociology. For example, Ritzer and Goodman note that Ritzer's own ideas on McDonaldization (see pp. 878–81) draw heavily on Weber, but are also influenced by ideas from Marxist theory and postmodernism.

Ritzer and Goodman argue that different theories concentrate on different levels of analysis: some on the microscopic (for example, social action theories such as interactionism), and some on the macroscopic (for example, structural theories such as Marxism). Some concentrate on subjective elements in social life, others on the objective. In principle there is no reason why these different elements cannot be brought together into a more integrated sociological paradigm.

While the idea of an integrated sociological perspective remains some way off, Ritzer and Goodman believe that the current situation still provides 'exciting opportunities to create new perspectives' out of the multiplicity of theories available to sociologists today (2003, p. A-22).

Bibliography

Abbas, T. (2005) 'British South Asian Muslims: state and multicultural society' in Abbas (ed.) (2005).
(ed.) (2005) *Muslim Britain: Communities Under Pressure*, Zed Books, London.
Abbott, P. and Payne, G. (1990) 'Women's social mobility: the conventional wisdom reconsidered' in G. Payne and P. Abbott, *The Social Mobility of Women*, Falmer Press, Basingstoke.
Abbott, P. and Wallace, C. (1992) *The Family and the New Right*, Pluto Press, London.
(1997) *An Introduction to Sociology: Feminist Perspectives*, 2nd edn, Routledge, London.
Abbot, P., Wallace, C. and Tyler, M. (2005) *An Introduction to Sociology: Feminist Perspectives*, 3rd edn, Routledge, Abingdon.
Abercrombie, N. and Urry, J. (1983) *Capital Labour and the Middle Classes*, Allen & Unwin, London.
Abercrombie, N., Hill, N. and Turner, B.S. (1980) *The Dominant Ideology Thesis*, Allen & Unwin, London.
Abraham, J. (1995) *Divide and School: Gender and Class Dynamics in Comprehensive Education*, Falmer Press, London.
Acheson, D. (1998) *Independent Inquiry into Inequalities in Health*, HMSO, London.
Ackernecht, E.A. (1982) *A Short History of Medicine*, Johns Hopkins University Press, Baltimore, MD.
Ackers, P., Smith, C. and Smith, P. (1996) 'Against all odds? British trade unions in the new workplace' in P. Ackers *et al.* (eds) *The New Workplace and Trade Unionism: Critical Perspectives on Work and Organization*, Routledge, London.
Ackroyd, S. and Hughes, J.A. (1981) *Data Collection in Context*, Longman, London.
Adam, B., Beck, U. and Van Loon, J. (eds) (2000) *Risk Society and Beyond*, Sage, London.
Adkins, L. (1995) *Gendered Work: Sexuality, Family and the Labour Market*, Open University Press, Milton Keynes.
Adler, F. (1975) *Sisters in Crime*, McGraw Hill, New York.
Adler, Z. (1987) *Rape on Trial*, Routledge & Kegan Paul, London.
Adorno, T.W. *et al.* (1950) *The Authoritarian Personality*, Harper, New York.
Aginsky, B.W. (1940) 'An Indian's soliloquy', *American Journal of Sociology*, vol. 46, pp. 43–4.
(1968) 'A Pomo's soliloquy' in A. Dundes (ed.) *Every Man His Way: Readings in Cultural Anthropology*, Prentice-Hall, Englewood Cliffs, NJ.
Agulnik, P., Burchardt, T. and Evans, M. (2002) 'Response and prevention in the British welfare state' in Hills *et al.* (eds) (2002).
Ahmad, W.I.U. (ed.) (1993) *'Race' and Health in Contemporary Britain*, Open University, Buckingham.
Ahmed, A. and Donnan, H. (eds) (1994) *Islam, Globalization and Postmodernity*, Routledge, London.
Alasuutari, P. (ed.) (1999) *Rethinking the Media Audience*, Sage, London.
Alcock, C., Payne, S. and Sullivan, S. (2004) *Introducing Social Policy*, Prentice-Hall, London.
Alcock, P. (1994) 'Back to the future: Victorian values for the twenty-first century' in C. Murray (1994).
(1997) *Understanding Poverty*, 2nd edn, Macmillan, Basingstoke.
(2003) *Social Policy in Britain*, 2nd edn, Palgrave Macmillan, Basingstoke.
Aldridge, A. (2000) *Religion in the Contemporary World: A Sociological Introduction*, Polity Press, Cambridge.
Aldridge, A. and Levine, K. (2001) *Surveying the Social World: Principles and Practice in Survey Research*, Open University Press, Buckingham.
Alexander, Claire E. (2000) *The Asian Gang: Ethnicity, Identity, Masculinity*, Berg, Oxford.
Allan, G. (1985) *Family Life: Domestic Roles and Social Organization*, Blackwell, London.
Allan, G. and Crow, G. (2001) *Families, Households and Society*, Palgrave, Basingstoke.
Allen, C. (2005) 'From race to religion: the new face of discrimination' in Abbas (ed.) (2005).
Allen, H. (1987) *Justice Unbalanced*, Open University Press, Buckingham.
(1989) 'Fines for women: paradoxes and paradigms' in P. Carlen and D. Cook (eds) *Paying for Crime*, Open University Press, Milton Keynes.
Allen, S. and Watson, A. (1986) 'The effects of unemployment: experience and response' in S. Allen *et al.* (eds) (1986).
Allen, S., Watson, A., Purcell, K. and Wood, S. (eds) (1986) *The Experience of Unemployment*, Macmillan, London.
Almond, B. (2006) *The Fragmenting Family*, Oxford University Press, Oxford.
Almond, G.A., Appleby, R.S. and Sivan, E. (2003) *Strong Religion: The Rise of Fundamentalism Around the World*, University of Chicago Press, Chicago.
Althusser, L. (1969) *For Marx*, Penguin, London.
(1971) *Lenin and Philosophy, and Other Essays*, New Left Books, London.
Alvesson, M. (2002) *Postmodernism and Social Research*, Open University Press, Buckingham.
Amin, A. (ed.) (1994) *Post-Fordism: A Reader*, Blackwell, Oxford.
Ammerman, N. (1990) *Baptist Battles: Social Change and Religious Conflict in the Southern Baptist Convention*, Rutgers University Press, New Brunswick, NJ.
Amnesty International (2007) *Child Soldiers: A Global Issue*. http://web.amnesty.org/pages/childsoldiers-background-eng
Anderson, B. (1983) *Imagined Communities*, Verso, London.
Anderson, E. (1994) 'The code of the streets', *Atlantic Monthly*, vol. 5, pp. 80–94.
(1999) *Code of the Streets: Decency, Violence and Moral Life of the Inner City*, W.W. Norton, New York.
Anderson, M. (1971) 'Family, household and the Industrial Revolution' in M. Anderson (ed.) (1971).
(ed.) (1971) *Sociology of the Family*, Penguin, Harmondsworth.
(1977) 'The historical study of family structure' in M. Bulmer (ed.) *The Historical Study of Family Structure*, Macmillan, London.
(1980) *Approaches to the History of the Western Family 1500–1914*, Macmillan, London.
Anderson, R.J., Hughes, J.A. and Sharrock, W.W. (1986) *Philosophy and the Human Sciences*, Croom Helm, London.
(eds) (1987) *Classic Disputes in Sociology*, Allen & Unwin, London.
Andreski, S. (ed.) (1971) *Herbert Spencer*, Nelson, London.
Ang, I. (1985) *Watching Dallas*, Methuen, London
(1991) *Desperately Seeking the Audience*, Routledge, London.
Annandale, E. (1998) *The Sociology of Health and Medicine*, Polity Press, Cambridge.
Anning, A. (2006) 'Early years education: mixed messages and conflicts' in D. Kassem, E. Mufti and J. Robinson (eds) *Education Studies: Issues and Critical Perspectives*, Open University Press, Maidenhead.
Annual Survey of Hours and Earnings 2005, National Statistics, London (available online).
Ansari, H. (2005) 'Attitudes to jihad, martyrdom and terrorism among British Muslims' in Abbas (ed.) (2005).
Anthias, F. and Yuval-Davis, N. (1992) *Race, Nation, Gender, Colour and Class and the Anti-racist Struggle*, Routledge, London.
Antoun, R. (1994) 'Sojourners abroad: migration for higher education in a post-peasant Muslim society' in Ahmed and Donnan (eds) (1994).
Apple, M.W. (1997) 'What postmodernists forget: cultural capital and official knowledge' in Halsey *et al.* (eds) (1997).
Arber, S. (1993) 'The research process' in N. Gilbert (ed.) *Researching Family Life*, Sage, London.
(2000) *Socio-economic Circumstances, Lone Parents and Children's Utilisation of Health Services*, Department of Health, London.
(2006) 'Gender and later life: change, choice and constraints' in Vincent *et al.* (eds) (2006).
Arber, S. and Ginn, J. (1991) *Gender and Later Life*, Sage, London.
Arber, S., Dale, A. and Gilbert, N. (1986) 'The limitations of existing social class classifications of women' in A. Jacoby (ed.) *The Measurement of Social Class*, Social Research Association, Guildford.
Archer, J. and Lloyd, B. (2002) *Sex and Gender*, 2nd edn, Cambridge University Press, Cambridge.
Archer, L. (2003) *Race, Masculinity and Schooling: Muslim Boys and Education*, Open University Press, Maidenhead.
Archer, L., Hutchings, M. and Ross, A. (2003) *Higher Education and Social Class: Issues of Exclusion and Inclusion*, Routledge, London.
Archer, M.S. (1982) 'Morphogenesis versus structure and action', *British Journal of Sociology*, vol. 33, no. 4.

Arensberg, C.M. and Kimball, S.T. (1968) *Family and Community in Ireland*, 2nd edn, Harvard University Press, Cambridge, MA.

Ariès, P. (1973, first published 1960) *Centuries of Childhood*, Penguin, Harmondsworth.

(1981) *The Hour of Our Death*, Allen Lane, London.

Armstrong, D. (1983) *The Political Anatomy of the Body*, Cambridge University Press, Cambridge.

Armstrong, K. (1993) *The End of Silence: Women and the Priesthood*, Fourth Estate, London.

(2001) 'The war we should fight', *Guardian*, October 13.

Arnold, M. (1960, first published 1869) *Culture and Anarchy*, Cambridge University Press, Cambridge.

Arnot, M. and Weiner, G. (1987) *Gender Under Scrutiny*, Hutchinson, London.

Aron, R. (1967) 'Social class, political class, ruling class' in R. Bendix and S.M. Lipset (eds) (1967).

(1968 and 1970) *Main Currents in Sociological Thought*, vols 1 and 2, Penguin, Harmondsworth.

Atkinson, J. (1978) 'Societal reactions to suicide' in *Discovering Suicide*, Macmillan, London.

(1978) *Discovering Suicide*, Macmillan, London.

(1985) 'The changing corporation' in David Clutterbuck (ed.) *New Patterns of Work*, Gower, Aldershot.

Auletta, K. (1991) *Three Blind Mice: How the TV Networks Lost their Way*, Random House, New York.

Back, L. (1996) *New Ethnicities and Urban Culture*, UCL Press, London.

Badawi, L. (1994) 'Islam' in J. Holm and J. Bowker (eds) (1994).

Bagdikian, B. (1997) *The Media Monopoly*, Beacon Press, Boston, MA.

(2004) *The New Media Monopoly*, Beacon Press, Boston, MA.

Baechler, J. (1979) *Suicides*, Blackwell, Oxford.

Bainbridge, W.S. and Stark, R. (1979) 'Cult formation: three compatible models', *Sociological Analysis*, no. 40.

Bakx, K. (1991) 'The "eclipse" of folk medicine in western society', *Sociology of Health and Illness*, vol. 13, pp. 20–8.

Ball, S.J. (1981) *Beachside Comprehensive. A Case-study of Secondary Schooling*, Cambridge University Press, Cambridge.

(1990) *Politics and Policy Making in Education*, Routledge, London.

Ball, S.J., Bowe, R. and Gewirtz, S. (1994) 'Market forces and parental choice' in S. Tomlinson (ed.) *Educational Reform and its Consequences*, IPPR/Rivers Oram Press, London.

Ballard, R. (1982) 'South Asian families' in R. Rapoport *et al.* (eds) (1982).

(1990) 'Marriage and kinship' in C. Clarke, C. Peach and S. Vertovec (eds) *South Asians Overseas*, Cambridge University Press, Cambridge.

(2002) 'Race, ethnicity and culture' in M. Holborn (ed.) (2002).

Ballard, R. and Ballard, C. (1977) 'The Sikhs' in J.L. Watson (ed.) *Between Two Cultures*, Blackwell, Oxford.

Bandura, A. (1965) 'Influences of model's reinforcement contingency on the acquisition of imitative responses', *Journal of Personality and Social Psychology*, vol. 1, pp. 589–95.

Bandura, A., Ross, D. and Ross, S.A. (1963) 'The imitation of film-mediated aggressive models', *Journal of Abnormal and Social Psychology*, vol. 66, no. 1, pp. 3–11.

Banton, M. (1987) *Racial Theories*, Cambridge University Press, Cambridge.

(1997) *Ethnic and Racial Consciousness*, 2nd edn, Longman, London.

Bara, J. and Budge, I. (2001) 'Party policy and ideology: still New Labour?' in P. Norris (ed.) (2001).

Barak, G. (1994) 'Crime, criminology and human rights: towards an understanding of state criminality' in G. Barak (ed.) (1994).

(ed.) (1994) *Varieties of Criminology: Readings from a Dynamic Discipline*, Praeger, Westport, CN.

Barash, D. (1979) *The Whisperings Within*, Harper & Row, New York.

Barber, B. (1963) 'Some problems in the sociology of professions', *Daedalus*, vol. 92, no. 4.

Barbour, R. (2001) 'Checklists for improving rigour in qualitative research: a case of the tail wagging the dog?' *British Medical Journal*, vol. 322, pp. 1115–17.

Barham, C. (2002) 'Economic activity and the labour market', *Labour Market Trends*, February, National Office for Statistics, London.

Barker, D.L. and Allen, S. (eds) (1976) *Dependence and Exploitation in Work and Marriage*, Longman, London.

Barker, E. (1984) *The Making of a Moonie*, Blackwell, Oxford.

(1985) 'New religious movements: yet another great awakening?' in P.E. Hammond (ed.) *The Sacred in a Secular Age*, University of California Press, Berkeley, CA.

Barker, M. (1989) *Comics: Ideology, Power and the Critics*, Manchester University Press, Manchester.

Barker, M. *et al.* (1994) 'The video violence debate: media researchers respond', press release reacting to the Newson report signed by 23 leading media researchers.

Barlow, A., Duncan, S., James, G. and Park, A. (2001) 'Just a piece of paper? Marriage and cohabitation' in A. Park *et al.* (eds) (2001).

Barlow, A., Duncan, S. and James, G. (2002) 'New Labour, the rationality mistake and family policy in Britain' in A. Carling *et al.* (eds) (2002).

Barnet, R.J. and Cavanagh, J. (1994) *Global Dreams: Imperial Corporations and the New World Order*, Simon & Schuster, New York.

Barrett, M. and McIntosh, M. (1982) *The Anti-social Family*, Verso, London.

Barrett, M. and Phillips, A. (1992) *Destabilising Theory: Contemporary Feminist Debates*, Polity Press, Cambridge.

Barron, R.D. and Norris, G.M. (1976) 'Sexual divisions and the dual labour market' in D.L. Barker and S. Allen (eds) (1976).

Barrow, J. (1982) 'West Indian families: an insider's perspective' in R. Rapoport *et al.* (eds) (1982).

Barry, B. (2002) 'Social exclusion, social isolation and the distribution of income' in Hills *et al.* (eds) (2002).

Bartholomew, J. (2006) *The Welfare State We're In*, Politico's, London.

Bartle, J. and Laycock, S. (2006) 'Elections and voting' in Dunleavy *et al.* (eds) (2006).

Bartlett, W. and Le Grand, J. (1993) 'Quasi markets and educational reform' in Le Grand and Bartlett (eds) (1993).

Basit, T.N. (1997) *Eastern Values; Western Milieu: Identities and Aspirations of Adolescent British Muslim Girls*, Ashgate, Aldershot.

Baudrillard, J. (1983) *Simulations*, Semiotext, New York.

(1985) 'The ecstasy of communication' in H. Foster (ed.) *Postmodern Culture*, Pluto Press. London.

(1988) *The Ecstasy of Communication*, Semiotext, New York.

(1995) *The Gulf War Did Not Take Place*, Power Publications, Sydney.

Bauman, Z. (1989) *Modernity and the Holocaust*, Cornell University Press, New York.

(1992) *Intimations of Postmodernity*, Routledge, London.

(1996) 'From pilgrim to tourist – or a short history of identity' in Hall and du Gay (eds) (1996).

Baxandall, L. and Morawski, S. (eds) (1974) *Karl Marx and Frederick Engels on Literature and Art*, International General, New York.

Baylis, J. and Smith, S. (2005) *The Globalization of World Politics*, 3rd edn, Oxford University Press, Oxford.

Beck, U. (1992) *Risk Society: Towards a New Modernity*, Sage, London.

(2002) ' A life of one's own in a runaway world: Individualization, globalization and politics' in U. Beck and E. Beck-Gernsheim, *Individualization*, Sage, London.

Beck, U. and Beck-Gernsheim, E. (1995) *The Normal Chaos of Love*, Polity Press, Cambridge.

Becker, H.S. (1963) *Outsiders*, Free Press, New York.

(1970) *Sociological Work*, Transaction Books, New Brunswick, NJ.

(1974) 'Labelling theory reconsidered' in P. Rock and M. McIntosh (eds) *Deviance and Social Control*, Tavistock, London.

Becker, M.H., Haefner, D.P., Kasl, S.V. *et al.* (1977) 'Selected Psychological Models and Correlates of Individual Health-related Behaviours', *Medical Care*, vol. 15, no. 5, suppl., pp. 27–46.

Beckford, J.A. (1985) *Cult Controversies*, Tavistock, London.

(1996) 'Postmodernity, high modernity and new modernity: three concepts in search of religion' in K. Flanagan and P. Jupp (eds) *Postmodernity, Sociology and Religion*, Macmillan, Basingstoke.

Beechey, V. (1983) 'The sexual division of labour and the labour process: a critical assessment of Braverman' in S. Wood (ed.) *The Degradation of Work? Skill, Deskilling and the Labour Process*, Hutchinson, London.

(1986) 'Women and employment in contemporary Britain' in V. Beechey and E. Whitelegg (eds) *Women in Britain Today*, Open University Press, Milton Keynes.

Belfield, R., Hird, C. and Kelly, S. (1994) *Murdoch: The Great Escape*, Time Warner.

Bell, C.R. (1968) *Middle Class Families*, Routledge & Kegan Paul, London.

Bell, N.W. and Vogel, E.F. (eds) (1968) *A Modern Introduction to the Family*, rev. edn, Free Press, New York.

Bendix, R. and Lipset, S.M. (eds) (1967) *Class, Status, and Power*, 2nd edn, Routledge & Kegan Paul, London.

Bennedict, R. (1955) 'Continuities and discontinuities in cultural conditioning' in Mead and Wolfenstein (eds) (1955).

Bennett, A. (1999) 'Subcultures or neo-tribes? Rethinking the relationship between youth, style and musical taste' *Sociology*, vol. 33, no. 3.
Bennett, A. and Kahn-Harris, K. (eds) (2004) *After Subculture: Critical Studies in Contemporary Youth Culture*, Palgrave Macmillan, Basingstoke.
Benson, R. (2005) 'American journalism and the politics of diversity', *Media, Culture and Society*, vol. 27, no. 1, pp. 5–20.
Benston, M. (1972) 'The political economy of women's liberation' in N. Glazer-Malbin and H.Y. Waehrer (eds) *Woman in a Man-Made World*, Rand-McNally, Chicago.
Benzeval, M. (1997) 'Health' in Walker and Walker (eds) (1997).
Berger, B. and Berger, P.L. (1983) *The War Over the Family*, Hutchinson, London.
Berger, J. (1972) *Ways of Seeing*, Penguin, Harmondsworth.
Berger, P.L. (1966) *Invitation to Sociology*, Penguin, Harmondsworth.
(1970) *A Rumour of Angels: Modern Society and the Rediscovery of the Supernatural*, Allen Lane, London.
Bernard, J. (1957) *Social Problems at Mid Century*, Holt, Rinehart & Winston, New York.
(1976) *The Future of Marriage*, Penguin, Harmondsworth.
Bernardes, J. (1997) *Family Studies: An Introduction*, Routledge, London.
Bernstein, B. (1961) 'Social class and linguistic development: a theory of social learning' in Halsey *et al.* (eds) (1961).
(1970) 'A socio-linguistic approach to social learning' in P. Worsley (ed.) *Modern Sociology: Introductory Readings*, Penguin, Harmondsworth.
(1971) 'Education cannot compensate for society' in B.R. Cosin *et al.* (eds) *School and Society*, Routledge & Kegan Paul, London.
(1972) 'Language and social context' in P.P. Giglioli (ed.) *Language and Social Context*, Penguin, Harmondsworth.
(1996) *Pedagogy, Symbolic Control and Identity*, Taylor & Francis, London.
Berthoud, R. (2000) 'Introduction: the dynamics of social change' in Berthoud and Gershuny (eds) (2000).
Berthoud, R. and Beishon, S. (1997) 'People, families and households' in Modood *et al.* (eds) (1997).
Berthoud, R. and Gershuny, R. (eds) (2000) *Seven Years in the Lives of British Families*, Policy Press, Bristol.
Best, L. (1993) '"Dragons, dinner ladies and ferrets": sex roles in children's books', *Sociology Review*, February.
Beuf, A. (1974) 'Doctor, lawyer, household drudge', *Journal of Communication*, vol. 24, no. 2, pp. 142–5.
Beveridge, W. (1942) *Social Insurance and Allied Services*, HMSO, London (extracts reprinted in *The Modern History Sourcebook* www.fordham.edu/halsall/mod1942beveridge.htm).
Beyer, P. (1994) *Religion and Globalization*, Sage, London.
Beynon, H. (1992) 'The end of the industrial worker?' in N. Abercrombie and A. Warde (eds) *Social Change in Contemporary Britain*, Polity Press, Cambridge.
Bhaskar, R. (1979) *The Possibility of Naturalism*, Harvester Press, Brighton.
Bhatt, C. (1994) 'New foundations: contingency, indeterminacy and Black translocality' in J. Weeks (ed.) *The Lesser Evil and the Greater Good*, Rivers Oram Press, London.
Bhatti, G. (1999) *Asian Children at Home and at School: An Ethnographic Study*. Routledge, London.
Bierstedt, R. (1963) *The Social Order*, McGraw-Hill, New York.
Biggs, S. (1993) *Understanding Ageism*, Open University Press, Milton Keynes.
Bignell, J. (1997) *Media Semiotics: An Introduction*, Manchester University Press, Manchester.
Birch, A.H. (2001) *The Concepts and Theories of Democracy*, Routledge, London.
Bird, J. (1999) *Investigating Religion*, Collins Educational, London.
Birke, L. (1986) *Women, Feminism and Biology*, Wheatsheaf, Brighton.
Blackburn, R.M. and Mann, M. (1975) 'Ideology in the non-skilled working class' in M. Bulmer (ed.) *Working Class Images of Society*, Routledge & Kegan Paul, London.
Blackburn, R.M. and Stewart, A. (1977) 'Women, work and the class structure', *New Society*, 1 September.
Blackledge, D. and Hunt, B. (1985) *Sociological Interpretations of Education*, Croom Helm, London.
Blackman, S. (1997) '"Destructing a Giro": a critical and ethnographic study of the youth "underclass"' in R. MacDonald (ed.) *Youth, the 'Underclass' and Social Exclusion*, Routledge, London.
Blackstone, T. and Mortimore, J. (1994) 'Cultural factors in child-rearing and attitudes to education' in B. Moon and A.S. Mayes (eds) *Teaching and Learning in the Secondary School*, Routledge, London.
Blaikie, A. (1999) *Ageing and Popular Culture*, Cambridge University Press, Cambridge.
Blair, M. (2001) *Why Pick On Me? School Exclusion and Black Youth*, Trentham Books, Stoke-on-Trent.
Blanden, J., Greg, P. and Machin, S. (2005) *Intergenerational Mobility in Europe and North America*, Centre for Economic Performance, London.
Blane, D., Bartley, M. and Davey-Smith, G. (1997) 'Disease Aetiology and Materialistic Explanations of Socio-economic Mortality Differentials', *European Journal of Public Health*, vol. 7, pp. 385–91.
Blasco, M. (2005) 'Mobilising family solidarity: rights, responsibilities and secondary schooling in urban Mexico' in Goddard *et al.* (eds) (2005).
Blauner, R. (1964) *Alienation and Freedom*, University of Chicago Press, Chicago.
(1972) 'Work satisfaction and industrial trends in modern society' in P. Worsley (ed.) *Problems of Modern Society*, Penguin, Harmondsworth.
Blaxter, M. (1983) 'The Cause of Disease: Women Talking', *Social Science and* Medicine, vol. 17, pp. 59–69.
(1990) *Health and Lifestyles*, Routledge, London.
Blaxter, M. and Peterson, E. (1982) *Mothers and Daughters: A Three Generational Study of Health Attitudes and Behaviour*, Heinemann, London.
Bleier, R. (1984) *Science and Gender*, Pergamon Press, New York.
Blumer, H. (1962) 'Society as symbolic interaction' in A.M. Rose (ed.) *Human Behaviour and Social Processes*, Routledge, London.
(1969) *Symbolic Interactionism*, Prentice-Hall, Englewood Cliffs, NJ.
Blumler, J. and Gurevitch, M. (1995) 'Politicians and the press: an essay on role relationships' in Boyd-Barrett and Newbold (eds) (1995).
Blunkett, D. (1999) *Tackling Social Exclusion: Empowering People and Communities for a Better Future*, DfEE, London.
(2001) *Politics and Progress*, Politico's Publishing, London.
Bodmer, W.F. (1972) 'Race and IQ: the genetic background' in K. Richardson and D. Spears (eds) *Race, Culture and Intelligence*, Penguin, Harmondsworth.
Boh, K. (1989) 'European family life patterns – a reappraisal' in K. Boh *et al.* (eds) *Changing Patterns of European Life*, Routledge, London.
Bond, J., Coleman, P.G. and Peace, S. (eds) (1993a) *Ageing in Society: An Introduction to Social Gerontology*, Sage, London.
Bond, J., Briggs, R. and Coleman, P. (1993b) 'The study of ageing' in Bond *et al.* (eds) (1993a).
Bond, J., Pearce, S., Dittmann-Kohli, F. and Westerhof, G. (eds) (2007) *Ageing in Society*, 3rd edn, Sage, London.
Booth, C. (1902–3) *Life and Labour of the People of London*, Macmillan, London.
Bordua, D. (1962) 'A critique of sociological interpretations of gang delinquency' in M.E. Wolfgang *et al.* (eds) *The Sociology of Crime and Delinquency*, John Wiley & Sons, New York.
Borthwick, G., Ellingworth, D., Bell, C. and MacKenzie, D. (1991) 'The social background of British MPs', *Sociology*, November.
Bottomore, T.B. (1993) *Elites and Society*, 2nd edn, Routledge, London.
Bottomore, T.B. and Rubel, M. (eds) (1963) *Karl Marx: Selected Writings in Sociology and Social Philosophy*, Penguin, Harmondsworth.
Bottoms, A. (2007) 'Environmental criminology' in M. Maguire, R. Morgan and R. Reiner (eds) *Oxford Handbook of Criminology*, 4th edn, Oxford University Press, Oxford.
Boudon, R. (1974) *Education, Opportunity and Social Inequality*, John Wiley & Sons, New York.
Boulton, M.G. (1983) *On Being a Mother*, Tavistock, London.
Bourdieu, P. (1971) 'Intellectual field and creative project' and 'Systems of education and systems of thought' in M. Young (ed.) *Knowledge and Control*, Collier-Macmillan, London.
(1973) 'Cultural reproduction and social reproduction' in R. Brown (ed.) (1973).
(1974) 'The school as a conservative force: scholastic and cultural inequalities' in J. Eggleston (ed.) *Contemporary Research in the Sociology of Education*, Methuen, London.
(1984) *Distinction: A Social Critique of the Judgement of Taste*, Routledge & Kegan Paul, London.
(1993) *Sociology in Question*, Sage, London.
(1994) 'Structures, *habitus* and practices' in Giddens *et al.* (eds) (1994).
Bourdieu, P. and de Saint-Martin, M. (1974) 'Scholastic excellence and the values of the educational system' in J. Eggleston (ed.) *Contemporary Research in the Sociology of Education*, Methuen, London.

Bourdieu, P. and Passeron, J. (1977) *Reproduction in Education, Society and Culture*, Sage, London.

Bowles, S. and Gintis, H. (1976) *Schooling in Capitalist America*, Routledge & Kegan Paul, London.

Bowling, B. and Phillips, C. (2002) *Racism, Crime and Justice*, Longman, Harlow.

Box, S. (1981) *Deviancy, Reality and Society*, Holt, Rinehart & Winston, London.

Box, S. and Hale, C. (1983) 'Liberation and female criminality in England and Wales', *British Journal of Criminology*, vol. 23, no 1.

Boyd-Barrett, O. (1995) 'Early theories in media research' in Boyd-Barrett and Newbold (eds) (1995).
(1995) 'The analysis of media occupations and professionals' in Boyd-Barrett and Newbold (eds) (1995).
(1998) '"Global" news agencies' in Boyd-Barrett and Rantanen (eds) (1998).

Boyd-Barrett, O. and Newbold, C. (eds) (1995) *Approaches to Media: A Reader*, Arnold, London.

Boyd-Barrett, O. and Rantanen, T. (eds) (1998) *The Globalization of News*, Sage, London.

Bradbury, B. and Janti, M. (1999) 'Child poverty across industrialized nations', *Innocenti Occasional Papers*, September.

Bradley, H. (1997) *Fractured Identities: Changing Patterns of Inequality*, Polity Press, Cambridge.
(1997) 'Review of Jan Pakulski and Malcolm Waters, *The Death of Class*', *Sociology*, vol. 31, no. 1, pp. 164–5.

Bradley, H., Erickson, M., Stephenson, C. and Williams, S. (2000) *Myths at Work*, Polity Press, Cambridge.

Bradshaw, J. (2001) 'Child poverty under Labour' in Fimister (ed.) (2001).

Bradshaw, J., Mitchell, D. and Morgan, J. (1987) 'Evaluating adequacy: the potential of budget standards', *Journal of Social Policy*.

Braithwaite, J. and Drahos, P. (2000) *Global Business Regulation*, Cambridge University Press, Cambridge.

Brannen, J. (2003) 'The Age of Beanpole Families', September, *Sociology Review*.

Brannen, J., Moss, P. and Mooney, A. (2000) *Connecting Children: Care and Family Life in Later Childhood*, Routledge, London.

Brantingham, P.J. and Brantingham, P.L. (1991) *Environmental Criminology*, revised edn, Waveland Press, Prospect Heights, IL.

Braverman, H. (1974) *Labor and Monopoly Capitalism*, Monthly Review Press, New York.

Breen, R. (ed.) (2004) *Social Mobility in Europe*, Oxford University Press, Oxford.

Brewer, M., Clark, T. and Goodman, A. (2002) *The Government's Child Poverty Target: How Much Progress Has Been Made?* Institute for Fiscal Studies, London.

Brewer, M., Goodman, A. and Shephard, A. (2002) *How has Child Poverty Changed Under the Labour Government?* Institute for Fiscal Studies, London.
(2003) *How has Child Poverty Changed Under the Labour Government? An Update*, Institute for Fiscal Studies, London.

Brewer, M., Goodman, A., Shaw, J. and Sibieta, L. (2006) *Poverty and Inequality in Britain*, Institute for Fiscal Studies, London.

Brewer, R.M. (1993) 'Theorizing race, class and gender: the new scholarship of Black feminist intellectuals and Black women's labor' in S.M. James and A.P.A. Busia (eds) *Theorizing Black Feminisms*, Routledge, London.

Bridgewood, A. and Savage, D. (1993) *1991 General Household Survey*, HMSO, London.

Brierley, P. (1991) *'Christian' England*, MARC Europe, London.
(ed.) (1998) *UK Christian Handbook*, MARC Europe, London.
(2001) *Religious Trends 3, 2002/2003*, Christian Research, London.
(2005) *UK Christian Handbook: Religious Trends 5*, Christian Research, London.
(2006a) *Pulling Out of the Nose Dive: A Contemporary Picture of Churchgoing*, Christian Research, London.
(2006b) *UK Christian Handbook: Religious Trends 6*, Christian Research, London.

Briggs, A. (2000, first published 1969) 'The welfare state in historical perspective' in Pierson and Castles (eds) (2000).

Bringa, T. (1996) *Being Muslim the Bosnian Way*, Princeton University Press, Princeton, NJ.

British Crime Survey 2002–2003, Home Office, London.

British Crime Survey 2003–2004, Home Office, London.

Brittain, E. (1976) 'Multiracial education. Teacher opinions on aspects of school life', *Educational Research*, vol. 18, no. 2.

Britten, N. and Heath, A. (1983) 'Women, men and social class' in E. Gamarnikow, D. Morgan, J. Purvis and D. Taylorson, *Gender, Class and Work*, Heinemann, London.

Broadcasting Standards Commission (1999) *Monitoring Report 7*, BSC, London.

Brookman, F. (1999) 'Assessing and analysing police murder files' in Brookman *et al.* (eds) (1999).
(2005) *Understanding Homicide*, Sage, London.

Brookman, F., Noaks, L. and Wincup, E. (eds) (1999) *Qualitative Research in Criminology*, Ashgate, Aldershot.

Brooks, A. (1997) *Postfeminisms: Feminisms, Cultural Theory and Cultural Forms*, Routledge, London.

Brown, C. (1984) *Black and White in Britain: The Third PSI Survey*, Heinemann, London.

Brown, C. and Gay, P. (1985) *Racial Discrimination 17 Years after the Act*, Policy Studies Institute, London.

Brown, C.G. (1992) 'A revisionist approach to religious change' in Bruce (ed.) (1992).

Brown, G.W. and Harris, T.O. (1978) *Social Origins of Depression: A Study of Psychiatric Disorder in Women*, Tavistock, London.
(eds) (1989) *Life Events and Illness*, Guildford Press, London.

Brown, M. (1995) 'Demographic trends' in Burghes and Brown (1995).

Brown, M. and Madge, N. (1982) *Despite the Welfare State*, Heinemann, London.

Brown, M.E. (1997) 'Causes and implication of ethnic conflict' in M. Guibernau and J. Rex (eds) *The Ethnicity Reader*, Polity Press, Cambridge.

Brown, P. (1995) 'Naming and Framing: The Social Construction of Diagnosis and Illness', *Journal of Health and Social Behaviour*, extra issue, pp. 34–52.

Brown, P. and Lauder, H. (1997) 'Education, globalization and economic development' in Halsey *et al.* (eds) (1997).

Brown, P., Halsey, A.H., Lauder, H. and Wells, A. (1997) 'The transformation of education and society: an introduction' in Halsey *et al.* (eds) (1997).

Brown, R. (ed.) (1973) *Knowledge, Education and Cultural Change*, Tavistock, London.

Browne, D. (1990) *Black People, Mental Health and the Courts*, NACRO, London.

Brownmiller, S. (1970) 'Sisterhood is powerful', *New York Times Magazine*, 15 March.
(1978) *Against Our Will*, Penguin, Harmondsworth.

Brubaker, R. (1996) *Nationalism Reframed: Nationhood and the National Question in the New Europe*, Cambridge University Press, Cambridge.

Bruce, S. (1985) *No Pope of Rome: Militant Protestantism in Modern Scotland*, Mainstream, Edinburgh.
(1986) *God Save Ulster! The Religion and Politics of Paisleyism*, Oxford University Press, Oxford.
(1988) *Rise and Fall of the New Christian Right in America*, Clarendon Press, Oxford.
(1992) 'Religion in the modern world' in M. Haralambos (ed.) *Developments in Sociology*, vol. 8, Causeway Press, Ormskirk.
(1995) *Religion in Modern Britain*, Oxford University Press, Oxford.
(1996) *Religion in the Modern World: From Cathedrals to Cults*, Oxford University Press, Oxford.
(2000) *Fundamentalism*, Polity, Cambridge.
(2001) 'Religion, the global and the post-modern' in M. Haralambos (ed.) *Developments in Sociology*, vol. 17, Causeway Press, Ormskirk.
(2002) *God is Dead*, Blackwell, Oxford.

Brunsdon, C. (1997) *Screen Tastes: Soap Opera to Satellite Dishes*, Routledge, London.

Bryman, A. (1988) *Quantity and Quality in Social Research*, Unwin Hyman, London.
(2001) *Social Research Methods*, Oxford University Press, Oxford.

Bryson, V. (1992) *Feminist Political Theory. An Introduction*, Macmillan, London.
(1999) *Feminist Debates: Issues of Theory and Political Practice*, Palgrave, Basingstoke.

BSC (1999) *Monitoring Report 7*, Broadcasting Standards Commission, London.

Buchanan, J. and Tullock, G. (1962) *The Calculus of Consent*, University of Michigan Press, MI.

Buckingham, D. (1993) *Children Talking Television*, Taylor & Francis, Lewes.

Buckle, A. and Farrington, D.P. (1984) 'An observational study of shoplifting', *British Journal of Criminology*, vol. 24, no. 1.

Budge, I. (1999) 'Party policy and ideology: reversing the 1950s?' in Evans and Norris (eds) (1999).

Bullock, A. and Trombley, S. (eds) (1999) *The New Fontana Dictionary of Modern Thought*, Fontana, London.

Burchardt, T. Le Grand, J. and Piachaud, D. (2002) 'Introduction' in Hills *et al.* (eds) (2002).

Burawoy, M. (1979) *Manufacturing Consent*, University of Chicago Press, Chicago.

Burchell, B. and Rubery, J. (1994) 'Divided women: labour market segmentation and gender segregation' in Scott (ed.) (1994).

Burgess, R.G. (1994) 'Education: an agenda for change' in Haralambos (ed.) (1994).

Burghes, L. (1996) 'Debates on disruption: what happens to children of lone parents' in E.B. Silva (ed.) *Good Enough Mothering? Feminist Perspectives on Lone Motherhood*, Routledge, London.

Burghes, L. and Brown, M. (1995) *Single Lone Mothers: Problems, Prospects and Policies*, Family Policy Studies Centre, London.

Burgoyne, J. and Clark, D. (1982) 'Reconstituted families' in Rapoport *et al.* (eds) (1982).
(1984) *Making a Go of It: A Study of Stepfamilies in Sheffield*, Routledge & Kegan Paul, London.

Burns, D. and Walker, M. (2005) 'Feminist methodology' in Somekh and Lewin (eds) (2005).

Bury, M. (1982) 'Chronic illness as biographical disruption', *Sociology of Health and Illness*, vol. 4, no. 2, pp. 167–82.
(1991) 'The sociology of chronic illness: a review of research and prospects', *Sociology of Health and Illness*, vol. 23, no. 3, pp. 263–85.
(1997) *Health and Illness in a Changing Society*, Routledge, London.

Butler, D. and Kavanagh, D. (1997) *The British General Election of 1997*, Macmillan, Basingstoke.
(2002) *The British General Election of 2001*, Palgrave, Basingstoke.

Butler, D. and Rose, R. (1960) *The British General Election of 1959*, Frank Cass, London.

Butler, D. and Stokes, D. (1974) *Political Change in Britain*, Macmillan, London.

Butler, J. (1990) *Gender Trouble: Feminism and the Subversion of Identity*, Routledge, London.

Butler, T. and Savage, M. (eds) (1995) *Social Change and the Middle Classes*, UCL Press, London.

Byrne, D. (1999) *Social Exclusion*, Open University Press, Buckingham.
(2006) 'Official statistics' in Jupp (ed.) (2006).

Cabinet Office (2003) *Ethnic Minorities and the Labour Market*, Cabinet Office, London.

Calhoun, C. (1997) 'Family outlaws: rethinking the connections between feminism, lesbianism and the family' in H.L. Nelson (ed.) *Feminism and Families*, Routledge, London.

Callahan, S. (1997) 'Gays, lesbians, and the use of alternative reproductive technologies' in H.L. Nelson (ed.) *Feminism and Families*, Routledge, London.

Callender, C. (2001) 'Changing student finances in higher education: policy contradictions under new labour', *Widening Participation and Lifelong Learning*, vol. 3, no. 2.

Callender, C. and Jackson, J. (2004) *Fear of Debt and Higher Education Participation*, Families & Social Capital ESRC Research Group, London South Bank University, London.

Callinicos, A. (2003) *An Anti-Capitalist Manifesto*, Polity Press, Cambridge.

Calnan, M. (1987) *Health and Illness: The Lay Perspective*, Tavistock, London.

Campbell, A. (1981) *Delinquent Girls*, Blackwell, Oxford.

Campbell, R. and Lovenduski, J. (2005) 'Winning women's votes? The incremental track to equality' in Norris and Wlezien (eds) (2005).

Campion, M.J. (1995) *Who's Fit to be a Parent?* Routledge, London.

Cant, S. and Sharma, U. (1999) *A New Medical Pluralism? Alternative Medicine, Doctors, Patients and the State*, UCL Press, London.

Cantle, T. (2001) *Community Cohesion: A Report of the Independent Review Team*, Home Office, London.

Caplan, L. (ed.) (1987) *Studies in Religious Fundamentalism*, Macmillan, London.

Carlen, P. (1988) *Women, Crime and Poverty*, Open University Press, Milton Keynes.
(1992) 'Criminal women and criminal justice: the limits to, and potential of, feminist and left realist perspectives' in Matthews and Young (eds) (1992).
(1997) 'Women in the criminal justice system' in Haralambos (ed.) (1997).

Carling, A., Duncan, S. and Edwards, R. (eds) (2002) *Analysing Families: Morality and Rationality in Policy and Practice*, Routledge, London.

Carmichael, S. and Hamilton, C.V. (1968) *Black Power: The Political Liberation in America*, Boston, Cape.

Carpenter, M. (1993) 'The subordination of nurses in health care: towards a social divisions approach' in E. Riska and K. Weger (eds) *Gender, Work and Medicine: Women and the Medical Division of Labour*, Sage, London.

Carrabine, E., Iganski, P., Lee, M., Plummer, K. and South, N. (2004) *Criminology: A Sociological Introduction*, Routledge, London.

Carr-Hill, R. (1987) 'The inequalities in health debate: a critical review of the issues', *Journal of Social Policy*.

Carricaburu, D. and Pierret, J. (1995) 'From biographical disruption to biographical reinforcement: the case of HIV-positive men', *Sociology of Health and Illness*, vol. 17, pp. 65–88.

Carr-Saunders, A.M. and Wilson, P.A. (1993) *The Professions*, Oxford University Press, Oxford.

Carspecken, P. (1996) *Critical Ethnography in Educational Research*, Routledge, New York.

Carstairs, V. and Morris, R. (1989) 'Deprivation: explaining differences in mortality between Scotland and England and Wales', *British Medical Journal*, vol. 299, pp. 886–9.

Carter, R.L and Hill, K.Q. (1979) *The Criminal's Image of the City*, Pergamon Press, New York.

Cartwright, A. and Anderson, R. (1981) *General Practice Revisited: a Second Study of Patients and their Doctors*, Tavistock, London.

Casanova, J. (1994) *Public Religions in the Modern World*, University of Chicago Press, Chicago.
(2003) 'Beyond European and American exceptionalisms' in Davie *et al.* (eds) (2003).

Cashmore, E.E. (1985) 'Rewriting the script', *New Society*, December.
(1989) *United Kingdom?* Unwin Hyman, London.
(1996) *Dictionary of Race and Ethnic Relations*, Routledge, London.

Cassidy, J. (1997) 'The next big thinker', *The Independent on Sunday*, 7 December.

Castles, S. (2000, first published 1999) 'Citizenship and the other in the age of migration' in Castles (2000).
(2000) *Ethnicity and Globalisation*, Sage, London.

Castles, F.G. and Dowrick, S. (1990) 'The impact of government spending levels on medium-term economic growth in the OECD, 1960–85', *Journal of Theoretical Politics*, vol. 2, no. 2, pp. 173–204.

Castles, S. and Kosack, G.C. (1973) *Immigrant Workers and Class Structure in Western Europe*, Oxford University Press, Oxford.

Castles, S. and Miller, M.J. (1993) *The Age of Migration*, Macmillan, London.

Centre for Contemporary Cultural Studies (1978) *Women Take Issue*, Hutchinson, London.
(1981) *Unpopular Education*, Hutchinson, London.
(1982) *The Empire Strikes Back*, Hutchinson, London.

Chalaby, J. (2005) 'Towards an understanding of media transnationalism' in J.K. Chalaby (ed.) *Transnational Television Worldwide: Towards a New Media Order*, I.B. Tauris & Co., London, pp. 1–13.

Chamberlain, M. (1999) 'Brothers and sisters, uncles and aunts: a lateral perspective on Caribbean families' in Silva and Smart (eds) (1999).

Chamberlayne, P., Bornat, J. and Wengraf, T. (eds) (2002) *The Turn to Biographical Methods in Social Science: Comparative Issues and Examples*, Routledge, London.

Chambliss, W.J. (1973) 'The Saints and the Roughnecks', *Society*, vol. 11, pp. 224–31.
(1976) 'Functional and conflict theories of crime' and 'The state and criminal law' and 'Vice, corruption, bureaucracy and power' in Chambliss and Mankoff (1976).
(1978) *On the Take: From Petty Crooks to Presidents*, Indiana University Press, Bloomington.
(1989) 'State organised crime' in N. Passas (ed.) *Organised Crime*, Dartmouth, London.

Chambliss, W.J. and Mankoff, M. (1976) *Whose Law? What Order?* John Wiley & Sons, New York.

Chandler. J. (1993) 'Women outside marriage', *Sociology Review*, April.

Charles, N. (1993) *Gender Divisions and Social Change*, Harvester Wheatsheaf, Hemel Hempstead.
(2002) *Gender in Modern Britain*, Oxford University Press, Oxford.

Charlesworth, S.J. (2000) *A Phenomenology of Working Class Experience*, Cambridge University Press, Cambridge.

Charlton, J.I. (1998) *Nothing About Us, Without Us: Disability, Oppression and Empowerment*, University of California Press, Berkeley.

Charmaz, K. (1983) 'Loss of self: a fundamental form of suffering in the chronically ill', *Sociology of Health and Illness*, vol. 5, pp. 168–95.
(1993) *Good Days, Bad Days: The Self in Chronic Illness and Time*, Rutgers University Press, New Brunswick, NJ.
Cheal, D. (1991) *The Family and the State of Theory*, Harvester Wheatsheaf, Hemel Hempstead.
Chesler, P. (1972) *Women and Madness*, Doubleday, New York.
Chesney-Lind, M. (1997) *The Female Offender: Girls, Women and Crime*, Sage, Thousand Oaks, CA.
Chester, R. (1975) 'Divorce' in E. Butterworth and D. Weir (eds) *The Sociology of Modern Britain*, rev. edn, Fontana, Glasgow.
(1985) 'The rise of the neo-conventional family'. *New Society*, 9 May.
Chitty, C. (2002) *Understanding Schools and Schooling*, RoutledgeFalmer, London.
Chomsky, N. (1996) *Powers and Prospects: Reflections on Human Nature and the Social Order*, Pluto Press, London.
(1999) *Profit over People: Neoliberalism and the Global Order*, Seven Stories Press, New York.
(2000) *Rogue States: The Rule of Force in World Affairs*, Pluto Press, London.
(2002) *Media Control: The Spectacular Achievement of Propaganda*, Seven Stories Press, New York.
(2003) *Power and Terror: Post-9/11 Talks and Interviews*, Seven Stories Press, New York.
(2006) *Imperial Ambitions*, Penguin, Harmondsworth.
Chrisman, N.J. (1977) 'The Health Seeking Process: An Approach to the Natural History of Illness', *Culture, Medicine and Psychiatry*, vol. 1, pp. 351–77.
Chryssides, G. (1994) 'Britain's changing faiths: adaptation in a new environment' in G. Parsons (ed.) (1994).
Chubb, J. and Moe, T. (1997) 'Politics, markets and the organization of schools' in Halsey *et al.* (eds) (1997).
Chunn, D., Boyd, S.C. and Menzies, R. (2003) *Toxic Criminology: Environment, Law and the State in Canada*, Fernwood Publishing, Halifax.
Cicourel, A.V. (1976) *The Social Organization of Juvenile Justice*, Heinemann, London.
Cicourel, A.V. and Kitsuse, J.I. (1963) *The Educational Decision-Makers*, Bobbs-Merill, Indianapolis.
(1971) 'The social organization of the high school and deviant adolescent careers' in B.R. Cosin *et al.* (eds) *School and Society*, Routledge & Kegan Paul, London.
Cixous, H. (1981a) 'The laugh of the Medusa' in E. Marks and I. de Courtivron (eds) (1981) *New French Feminisms*, Schoken Books, New York.
(1981b) 'Castration or decapitation?' *Signs*, Autumn.
Clancy, A. *et al.* (2001) *Crime policing and Justice: The Experience of Ethnic Minorities. Findings from the 2000 British Crime Survey*, Home Office Research study 223, Home Office, London.
Clapp, R., Howe, G. and Jacobs Lefevre, M. (2005) *Environmental and Occupational Causes of Cancer: A Review of Recent Scientific Literature*, Lowell Center for Sustainable Production, University of Massachusetts Lowell.
Clark, A. (2006) 'Google nets YouTube in $1.65bn takeover', *Guardian*, 10 October.
(2007) 'Downfall of Citizen Black', *Guardian*, 14 July.
Clarke, H., Sanders, D., Stewart, M. and Whiteley, P. (2004) *Political Choice in Britain*, Oxford University Press, Oxford.
Clarke, J. and Critcher, C. (1985) *The Devil Makes Work: Leisure in Capitalist Britain*, Macmillan, London.
Clarke, J. and Willis, P. (1984) 'Introduction' in I. Bates *et al.* (eds) *Schooling for the Dole?* Macmillan, London.
Clarke, J., Hall, S., Jefferson, T. and Roberts, B. (1976) 'Subcultures, cultures and class' in Hall and Jefferson (eds) (1976).
Clarke, J.N. (1992) Cancer, heart disease and AIDS: what do the media tell us about these diseases?' *Health Communication*, vol. 4, no. 2.
Clegg, S.R. (1992) 'Modern and postmodern organizations', *Sociology Review*, vol. 1, no. 4.
Clement, B. (1997) 'Work injuries not being investigated', *Independent*, 13 November, p. 4.
Clinard, M.B. (1974) *Sociology of Deviant Behavior*, 4th edn, Holt, Rinehart & Winston, New York.
Cloward, R.A. and Ohlin, L.E. (1961) *Delinquency and Opportunity*, Free Press, Glencoe.
Coard, B. (1971) *How the West Indian Child is Made Educationally Subnormal in the British School System*, New Beacon Books, London.
Coates, K. and Silburn, R. (1970) *Poverty: The Forgotten Englishmen*, Penguin, Harmondsworth.
Coffey, A. and Atkinson, P. (1996) *Making Sense of Qualitative Data: Complementary Research Strategies*, Sage, London.
Cohen, A.K. (1955) *Delinquent Boys*, Free Press, Glencoe.
(1966) *Deviance and Control*, Prentice-Hall, Englewood Cliffs, NJ.
Cohen, L.E. and Felson, M. (1979) 'Social change and crime rate trends: a routine activities approach', *American Sociological Review*, vol. 44, pp. 588–608.
Cohen, P. (1984) 'Against the new vocationalism' in I. Bates *et al.* (eds) *Schooling for the Dole?* Macmillan, London.
Cohen, R. (1994) *Frontiers of Identity: The British and the Others*, Longman, Harlow.
Cohen, R. (2006) *Migration and its Enemies: Global Capital, Migrant Labour and the Nation-State*, Ashgate, Aldershot.
Cohen, R. and Rai, S.M. (2000) *Global Social Movements*, Athlone Press, London.
Cohen, S. (2001) *States of Denial: Knowing about Atrocities and Suffering*, Polity Press, Cambridge.
Cohen, S. (2002) *Folk Devils and Moral Panics: The Creation of the Mods and Rockers*, 3rd edn, Routledge, London.
Coles, B. (1995) *Youth and Social Policy*, UCL Press, London.
Colle, R.D. (1973) 'Negro image in the mass media: a case study in social change' in R.F. Hixon (ed.) *Mass Media: A Casebook*, Thomas Y. Crowell, New York.
Colley, A. (1998) 'Gender and subject choice in secondary education' in J. Radford (ed.) *Gender and Choice in Education and Occupation*, Routledge, London.
Collier, R. (1998) *Masculinities, Crime and Criminology*, Sage, London.
Collins, P.H. (1990) *Black Feminist Thought*, Unwin Hyman, London.
Colquhoun, R. (1976) 'Values, socialization and achievement' in J. Beck *et al.* (eds) *Worlds Apart: Readings for a Sociology of Education*, Collier-Macmillan, London.
Commission of the European Communities (2007) 'Media pluralism in the member states of the European Union', Commission Staff Working Document, SEC 32. http://www.ebu.ch/CMSimages/en/BRUDOC_INFO_EN_335_tcm6-49399.pdf?display=EN
Commission for Racial Equality (2002) *It Could Be You: There is a Law Against Racial Discrimination*, CRE, London.
Compaine, B. (2004) 'Domination fantasies: does Rupert Murdoch control the media? Does anyone?', *Reason*, vol. 35, no. 8, pp. 26–9.
Comscore (2007) Press Release. 'Bebo becomes the most visited social networking site in the UK'. http://www.comscore.com/press/release.asp?press=1571
Comte, A. (1986) *The Positive Philosophy*, Bell & Sons, London.
Connell, R.W. (1987) *Gender and Power*, Polity Press, Cambridge.
(1995) *Masculinities*, Polity Press, Cambridge.
(2000) *Gender*, Polity Press, Cambridge.
Connolly, P. (1998) *Racism, Gender Identities and Young Children*, Routledge, London.
Connor, H. (2006) 'It pays to be one of the top 10', *Observer*, 16 April, Business and Media, pp. 4–5.
Connor, H., Tyers, C., Modood, T. and Hillage, J. (2004) *Why the Difference? A Closer Look at Higher Education Minority Ethnic Students and Graduates*, DfES research report RR552. www.dfes.gov.uk/research/data/uploadfiles/RB552.pdf
Connor, S. (1989) *Postmodernist Culture*, Blackwell, Oxford.
Conrad, P. (1994) Wellness as virtue: morality and the pursuit of health. *Culture, Medicine and Psychiatry*, vol. 18, pp. 385–401.
Conrad, P. and Schneider, J. (1980) *Deviance and Medicalization: From Badness to Sickness*, Mosby, St Louis.
Coontz, S. and Henderson, P. (eds) (1986) *Women's Work. Men's Property*, Verso, London.
Cooper, D. (1972) *The Death of the Family*, Penguin, Harmondsworth.
Cooper, H., Arber, S., Fee, L. and Ginn, J. (1999) *The Influence of Social Support and Social Capital on Health: A Review and Analysis of British Data*, Health Education Authority, London.
Cornwell, J. (1984) *Hard Earned Lives: Accounts of Health and Illness from East London*, Tavistock, London.
Corrigan, P. (1981) *Schooling the Smash Street Kids*, Macmillan, London.
Coser, L.A. (1977) *Masters of Sociological Thought*, 2nd edn, Harcourt Brace Jovanovich, New York.
Cottle, S. (ed.) (2000) *Ethnic Minorities and the Media*, Open University Press, Buckingham.
Cotton, J. (2004) 'Homicide' in Povey (ed.) (2004).
Cowley, P. (2001) 'The Commons: Mr Blair's lapdog?' in Norris (ed.) (2001).
Cox, O.C. (1970) *Caste, Class and Race*, Monthly Review Press, New York.

CPAG (2006a) *Media Briefing: The Government's Child Poverty Targets*, Child Poverty Action Group, London.
(2006b) *Poverty: The Facts: Update 2006*, Child Poverty Action Group, London.
Crace, J. (2006) 'Hidden triumphs', *Guardian*, 7 November.
Cracknell, D., Oakshott, I. and Schofield, A. (2007) 'Here comes trouble: Gordon's great talent contest', *The Sunday Times*, 1 July, pp. 13–15.
Craib, I. (1984) *Modern Social Theory*, Wheatsheaf Books, Brighton.
Craik, J. (1994) *The Face of Fashion: Cultural Studies in Fashion*, Routledge, London.
Craine, S. (1997) 'The "Black Magic Roundabout": cyclical social exclusion and alternative careers' in R. MacDonald (ed.) *Youth, the 'Underclass', and Social Exclusion*, Routledge, London.
Creedon, P. (1989) *Women in Mass Communication: Challenging Gender Values*, Sage, London.
Crewe, I. (1983) 'The disturbing truth behind Labour's rout', *Guardian*, 13 June.
(1986) 'On the death and resurrection of class voting: some comments on how Britain votes', *Political Studies*.
(1987a) 'A new class of politics', *Guardian*, 16 June.
(1987b) 'Tories prosper from a paradox', *Guardian*, 15 June.
(1988) 'The grim challenge of the ballot box', *Guardian*, 1 October.
(1992) 'Changing votes and unchanging voters', *Electoral Studies*, December.
(1992) 'Why did Labour lose (yet again)?', *Politics Review*, September.
Crewe, I. and Thompson, K. (1999) 'Party loyalties: dealignment or realignment?' in Evans and Norris (eds) (1999).
Criddle, B. (1988) 'Candidates' in Butler and Kavanagh (eds) (1988).
(2005) 'MPs and candidates' in Kavanagh and Butler (eds) (2005).
Critcher, C. (2003) *Moral Panics and the media*, Open University Press, Buckingham.
Critcher, C., Dicks, B. and Waddington, D. (1992) 'Portrait of despair', *New Statesman and Society*, 23 October.
Croall, H. (1998) *Crime Society in England*, Longman, Harlow.
Crompton, R. (1993) *Class and Stratification: An Introduction to Current Debates*, Blackwell, Oxford.
(1997) *Women and Work in Modern Britain*, Oxford University Press, Oxford.
Crompton, R. and Jones, G. (1984) *White-Collar Proletariat. Deskilling and Gender in Clerical Work*, Macmillan, London.
Crompton, R. and Le Feuvre, N. (1996) 'Paid employment and the changing system of gender relations', *Sociology*, vol. 30, no. 3.
Crompton, R. and Scott, J. (2005) 'Class analysis: beyond the cultural turn' in Devine *et al.* (eds) 2005.
Cromwell, P.F., Olsen, J.N. and Avary D'A.W. (1991) *Breaking and Entering: An Ethnographic Analysis of Burglary*, Sage, Newbury Park, CA.
Crook, S., Pakulski, J. and Waters, M. (1992) *Postmodernization: Changes in Advanced Society*, Sage, London.
Crosland, A. (1981) *Future of Socialism*, Cape, London.
Croteau, D. and Hoynes, W. (2000) *Media Society: Industry, Images and Audiences*, Pine Forge, London.
(2001) *The Business of the Media: Corporate Media and the Public Interest*, Pine Forge Press, Thousand Oaks, CA.
Crouch, C. (2005) *Post-Democracy*, Polity Press, Cambridge.
Cully, M., Woodland, S., O'Reilly, A. and Dix, G. (1999) *Britain at Work: As Depicted in the 1998 Workplace Survey*, Routledge, London.
Cumberbatch, G. and Negrine, R. (1992) *Images of Disability on Television*, Routledge, London.
Cumming, E. and Henry, W.E. (1961) *Growing Old: The Process of Disengagement*, Basic Books, New York.
Curran, J. (ed.) (2000) *Media Organizations in Society*, Arnold, London.
Curran, J. and Gurevitch, M. (eds) (1996) *Mass Media and Society*, Arnold, London.
Currer, C. and Stacey, M. (eds) (1986) *Concepts of Health, Illness and Disease: A Comparative Perspective*, Berg, Leamington Spa.
Curtice, J. and Park, A. (1999) 'Region: New Labour, new geography?' in Evans and Norris (eds) (1999).
Curtin, P.D. (1965) *The Image of Africa*, Macmillan, London.
Curtis, P. (2003) 'Action zones' "limited" effect on school results', *Guardian*, 7 April.
Dahl, R.A. (1961) *Who Governs?* Yale University Press, New Haven.
(1973) 'A critique of the ruling elite model' in Urry and Wakeford (eds) (1973).
(1984) *Modern Political Analysis*, 4th edn, Prentice-Hall, Englewood Cliffs, NJ.
Dahrendorf, R. (1959) *Class and Class Conflict in an Industrial Society*, Routledge & Kegan Paul, London.
Dail, P.W. (1988) 'Prime time portrayals of older adults in the context of family life', *The Gerontologist*, vol. 28, no. 5, pp. 700–6.
Daily Mail (2004) 'Store withdraws video game after brutal killing', *Daily Mail*, 29 July.
Dale, R. (1986) 'Examining the gift-horse's teeth: a tentative analysis of TVEI' in S. Walker and J. Barton, *Youth, Unemployment and Schooling*, Open University Press, Milton Keynes.
Daly, M. (1978) *Gyn/Ecology: The Metaethics of Radical Feminism*, Beacon Press, Boston.
Daly, M. and Lewis, J. (2000) 'The concept of social care and the analysis of contemporary welfare states', *British Journal of Sociology*, vol. 51, no. 2.
Darwin, C. (1968, first published 1859) *On the Origin of Species*, Penguin, Harmondsworth.
Davey-Smith, G. and Gordon, D. (2000) 'Poverty across the lifecourse and health' in Pantazis and Gordon (eds) (2000).
Davey-Smith, G., Neaton, J.D., Wentworth, D., Stamler, R. and Stamler, J. (1996) 'Socio-economic differentials in mortality risk among men screened for the multiple risk factor intervention trial: part 1 – results for 300,685 white men', *American Journal of Public Health*, vol. 86, pp. 497–504.
Davidson, J. (2006) 'Non-probability non-random sampling' in Jupp (ed.) (2006).
Davie, G. (1989) 'Religion' in Haralambos (ed.) (1989).
(1994) *Religion in Britain Since 1945: Believing Without Belonging*, Blackwell, Oxford.
(2002) *Europe: The Exceptional Case*, Darton, Longman & Todd, London.
(2006) 'The future of religion and its implication for social sciences' in Droogers *et al.* (eds) (2006).
Davie, G., Woodhead, L. and Heelas, P. (eds) (2003) *Predicting Religion: Christian Secular and Alternative Futures*, Ashgate, Aldershot.
Davies, J. (1999) 'International comparison of labour market disputes in 1997', *Labour Market Trends*, April, National Office for Statistics, London.
Davies, K. *et al.* (1987) *Out of Focus: Writing on Women and the Media*, Women's Press, London.
Davis, K. and Moore, W.E. (1967, first published 1945) 'Some principles of stratification' in Bendix and Lipset (eds) (1967).
Davis, M. (1990) *City of Quartz: Excavating the Future in Los Angeles*, Verso, London.
Day, D. (1991) *The Eco-Wars*, Paladin, London.
Day, R. and Day, J. (1977) 'A review of the current state of negotiated order theory: An appreciation and a critique', *Sociological Quarterly*, 18, pp. 126–42.
Deakin, N. (1990) 'Mr Murray's Ark' in C. Murray, *The Emerging British Underclass*, Institute of Economic Affairs, London.
Dean, H. (1991) 'In search of the underclass' in P. Brown and R. Scase (eds) *Poor Work: Disadvantage and the Division of Labour*, Open University Press, Milton Keynes.
Dean, H. and Taylor-Gooby, P. (1992) *Dependency Culture: The Explosion of a Myth*, Harvester Wheatsheaf, Hemel Hempstead.
de Beauvoir, S. (1953, first published 1949) *The Second Sex*, Jonathan Cape, London.
Delamont, S. (1976) 'Beyond Flanders' fields: the relationship of subject matter and individuality to classroom style' in M. Stubbs and S. Delamont (eds) *Explorations in Classroom Observation*, Wiley, Chichester.
Delphy, C. (1984) *Close to Home*, Hutchinson, London.
Delphy, C. and Leonard, D. (1992) *Familiar Exploitation*, Polity Press, Cambridge.
Demaine, J. (ed.) (2001) *Sociology of Education Today*, Palgrave, Basingstoke.
Deming, W.E. (1971) 'On errors in surveys' in B.J. Franklin and H. Osborne (eds) *Research Methods*, Wadsworth, Belmont, NJ.
Dench, G., Gavron, K. and Young, M. (2006) *The New East End: Kinship, Race and Conflict*, Profile Books, London.
Dennis, N. (1975) 'Relationships' in E. Butterworth and D. Weir (eds) *The Sociology of Modern Britain*, rev. edn, Fontana, Glasgow.
Dennis, N., Henriques, F. and Slaughter, C. (1956) *Coal is our Life*, Eyre & Spottiswoode, London.
Denver, D. (2002) 'The results: how Britain voted (or didn't)' in Geddes and Tonge (eds) (2002).
Denzin, K. (1970) *The Research Act in Sociology*, Aldine, Chicago.
Department of Health (1996) *Low Income, Food, Nutrition and Health: Strategies for Improvement*, DOH, London.
(1999) *Saving Lives: Our Healthier Nation*, Stationery Office, London.

Department of Work and Pensions (2002) *Opportunity for All: Monitoring Poverty and Social Exclusion*, DWP, London.

Deppa, J. (2007) 'Coping with a killer's "manifesto"', *Chronicle of Higher Education*, 11 May.

Desai, M. (1986) 'Drawing the line: on defining the poverty threshold' in P. Golding (ed.) *Excluding the Poor*, Child Poverty Action Group, London.

Desai, P. (1999) 'Spaces of identity, cultures of conflict: the development of new British Asian identities', Ph.D. thesis, Goldsmiths College London.

Deutscher, I. (1977) 'Asking questions (and listening to answers)' in M. Bulmer (ed.) *The Historical Study of Family Structure*, Macmillan, London.

DeVault, M.L. (1991) *Feeding the Family: The Social Organization of Caring as Gendered Work*, University of Chicago Press, Chicago.
(1996) 'Talking back to sociology: distinctive contributions of feminist methodology', *Annual Review of Sociology*, vol. 22, pp. 29–50.

Devine, F. (1992) *Affluent Workers Revisited*, Edinburgh University Press, Edinburgh.
(1994) '"Affluent workers" revisited', *Sociology Review*, vol. 3, February.

Devine, F., Savage, M., Scott, J. and Crompton, R. (eds) (2005) *Rethinking Class: Culture, Identities and Lifestyle*, Palgrave Macmillan, Basingstoke.

Dewey, J. (1953) *Democracy and Education: An Introduction to the Philosophy of Education*, Macmillan, New York.

Dex, S. and McCulloch, A. (1997) *Flexible Employment: The Future of Britain's Jobs*, Macmillan, Basingstoke.

DfES (2002) *2002 Spending Review: Investment for Reform*, Department for Education and Skills, London.
(2003) *Youth Cohort Study: The Activities and Experiences of 18 Year Olds: England and Wales 2002*, Department for Education and Skills, London.

Dickens, P. (2001) 'Linking the social and natural sciences: Is capital modifying human biology in its own image?' *Sociology*, vol. 35, no. 1, pp. 93–101.

Dickinson, R. Harindrath, R. and Linne, O. (eds) (1998) *Approaches to Audiences*, Arnold, London.

Dixon, B. (1978) *Beyond the Magic Bullet*, George Allen & Unwin, London.

Ditton, J. (1977) *Part-time Crime*, Macmillan, London.

Dobash, R. and Dobash, R. (1979) *Violence Against Wives*, Open Books, London.

Donald, J. (1992) *Sentimental Education*, Verso, London.

Donald, J. and Rattansi, A. (eds) (1992) *'Race' Culture and Difference*, Sage, London.

Donnerstein, E. (1980) 'Aggressive erotica and violence against women', *Journal of Personality and Social Psychology*, vol. 39, pp. 269–77.

Dorais, M. (2004) *Dead Boys Can't Dance: Sexual Orientation, Masculinity and Suicide*, McGill-Queen's University Press, Montreal.

Douglas, J.D. (1967) *The Social Meanings of Suicide*, Princeton University Press, Princeton, NJ.
(ed.) (1971) *Understanding Everyday Life*, Routledge & Kegan Paul, London.

Douglas, J.W.B. (1964) *The Home and the School*, MacGibbon & Kee, London.

Douglas, J.W.B., Ross, J.M. and Simpson, H.R. (1970) *Natural Symbols*, Barrie & Jenkins, London.

Douglas, M. (1973) *Natural Symbols: Explorations in Cosmology*, Penguin, Harmondsworth.

Downes, D. and Rock, P. (1988) *Understanding Deviance*, 2nd edn, Clarendon Press, Oxford.

Dowse, R.E. and Hughes, J.A. (1972) *Political Sociology*, John Wiley & Sons, London.

Doyal, L. (1995) *What Makes Women Sick*, Macmillan, London.

Doyal, L. with Pennell, I. (1979) *The Political Economy of Health*, Pluto Press, London.

Doyle, A. (2006) 'How not to think about crime in the media', *Canadian Journal of Criminology and Criminal Justice*, vol. 48, no. 6, pp. 867–85.

Drane, J. (1999) *What is the New Age Still Saying to the Church?* Marshal Pickering, London.

Driver, G. (1982) 'West Indian families: an anthropological perspective' in Rapoport *et al.* (eds) (1982).

Driver, G. and Ballard, R. (1981) 'Contemporary performance in multiracial schools: South Asian pupils at 16 plus' in A. James and R. Jeffcoate (eds) *The School in the Multicultural Society*, Harper & Row, London.

Droogers, A., Clarke, P.B., Davie, G., Greenfield, S.M. and Versteeg, P. (eds) (2006) *Playful Religion: Challenges for the Study of Religion*, Eburon, Delft.

Duncombe, J. and Marsden, D. (1995) 'Women's "triple shift": paid employment, domestic labour and "emotion work"', *Sociology Review*, vol. 4, no. 4, April.

Dunleavy, P., Heffernan, R., Cowley, P. and Hay, C. (eds) (2006) *Developments in British Politics 8*, Palgrave Macmillan, Basingstoke.

Dunne, G.A. (1999) 'A passion for "sameness"? Sexuality and gender accountability' in Silva and Smart (eds) (1999).

Durcan, J., McCarthy, W.E.J. and Redman, G.P. (1983) *Strikes in Post-War Britain*, Allen & Unwin, London.

Durkheim, E. (1938) *The Rules of Sociological Method*, Free Press, New York.
(1947) *The Division of Labour in Society*, Free Press, New York.
(1957) *Professional Ethics and Civic Morals*, Routledge & Kegan Paul, London.
(1961) *Moral Education*, Free Press, Glencoe.
(1961) *The Elementary Forms of the Religious Life*, Collier Books, New York.
(1970) *Suicide: A Study in Sociology*, Routledge & Kegan Paul, London.

Durkheim, E. and Mauss, M. (1963, first published 1903) *Primitive Classification*, Cohen & West, London.

DWP (2004) *The British Lone Parent Cohort and their Children 1991 to 2001*, DWP, London.
(2006) *Households Below Average Income 2004/05*, DWP, London.
(2006) *Lone Parents Work Focused Interviews/New Deal for Lone Parents: Combined Evaluation and Further Net Impacts*, DWP, London.

Dyke, G. (2002) 'Diversity in public broadcasting: a public service perspective', speech given at the Commonwealth Broadcasting Association Conference in Manchester. http://www.bbc.co.uk/pressoffice/speeches/stories/dyke_cba.shtml

Eatwell, J. (1996) *Global Unemployment: Loss of Jobs in the 1990s*, M.E. Sharpe, New York.

Edgell, S. (1980) *Middle-class Couples*, Allen & Unwin, London.
(1993) *Class*, Routledge, London.

Ednesor, T. (2000) 'A welcome back to the working class', *Sociology*, vol. 34, no. 4.

Edwards, P. (1995) 'Strikes and industrial conflict' in Edwards (ed.) (1995).
(ed.) (1995) *Industrial Relations: Theory and Practice in Britain*, Blackwell, Oxford.

Edwards, P., Hall, M., Hyman, R. *et al.* (1998) 'Great Britain: from partial collectivism to neo-liberalism to where?' in Ferner and Hyman (eds) (1998).

Edwards, P.K. and Scullion, H. (1982) *The Social Organization of Industrial Conflict. Control and Resistance in the Workplace*, Blackwell, Oxford.

Edwards, R. (1979) *Contested Terrain, the Transformation of the Workplace in the Twentieth Century*, Heinemann, London.

Eglin, P. (1987) 'The meaning and use of official statistics' in Anderson *et al.* (eds) (1986).

Ehrenreich, B. and Ehrenreich, J. (1979) 'The professional-managerial class' in P. Walker (ed.) *Between Labour and Capital*, Harvester Press, Sussex.

Ehrenreich, B. and English, D. (1978) 'The "Sick Women of the Upper Classes"' in Ehrenreich (ed.) (1978).

Ehrenreich, J. (ed.) (1978) *The Cultural Crisis of Modern Medicine*, Monthly Review Press, London.

Ehrhardt, D.A. (1969) 'Early androgen stimulation and aggressive behaviour in male and female mice', *Physiology and Behaviour*, no. 4.

Eichler, M. (1991) *Nonsexist Research Methods: A Practical Guide*, Routledge, London.

Eisenberg, D.M., Kessler, R.C., Van Rompay, M.I., Kaptchuk, T.J., Sonja, A., Wilkey, S.A., Appel, S. and Davis, R.B. (2001) 'Perceptions about complementary therapies relative to conventional therapies among adults who use both: results from a national survey', *Annals of Internal Medicine*, vol. 135, no. 5, pp. 344–51.

Eisenberg, L. (1977) 'Disease and illness: distinctions between professional and popular ideas of sickness', *Culture, Medicine and Psychiatry*, vol. 1, pp. 9–23.

Eisenstadt, S.N. (1963) 'Archetypal patterns of youth' in E.H. Erickson (ed.) (1963).

Elias, N. (1978) *The Civilizing Process. Vol. 1 The History of Manners*, Blackwell, Oxford.
(1985) *The Loneliness of Dying*, Blackwell, Oxford.

Elliot, L. (1998) 'A tale of two catastrophes', *Guardian*, 7 November, p. 1.

El Saadawi, N. (1980) *The Hidden Face of Eve: Women in the Arab World*, Zed Books, London.

Engels, F. (1969) 'On the history of early Christianity' in N. Birnbaum and G. Lenzer (eds) *Sociology and Religion: A Book of Readings*, Prentice-Hall, Englewood Cliffs, NJ.
(1972) *The Origin of the Family, Private Property and the State*, Lawrence & Wishart, London.
(1973) *The Condition of the Working Class in England in 1844*, Progress Publishers, Moscow.
(1974, first published 1903) 'German socialism in verse and prose II' in Baxandall and Morawski (eds) (1974).
(1974) *The Condition of the Working Class in England*, Progress Publishers, Moscow.

Epstein, D., Elwood, J., Hey, V. and Maw, J. (1998) 'Schoolboy frictions: feminism and "failing boys"' in D. Epstein *et al.*, *Failing Boys?* Open University Press, Buckingham.

Equal Opportunities Commission (2001) *Women and Men in Britain: Professional Occupations*, Manchester.
(2002a) *Facts about Men and Women in Great Britain*, Manchester.
(2002b) *Women and Men in Britain: Management*, Manchester.
(1997) *Pay*, Manchester.
(2006) *Sex and Power: Who Runs Britain?* Manchester.

Erickson, E.H. (ed.) (1963) *Youth: Change and Challenge*, Basic Books, New York.

Eriksen, T.H. (1993) *Ethnicity and Nationalism*, Pluto Press, London.
(2002) *Ethnicity and Nationalism: Anthropological Perspectives*, 2nd edn, Pluto Books, London.

Ernst, E. and White, A. (2000) 'The BBC survey of the use of complementary therapy in the UK', *Complementary Medicines in Therapy*, vol. 8, no. 1, pp. 32–6.

Estrada, F. (2001) 'Juvenile violence as a social problem. Trends, media attention and social response', *British Journal of Criminology*, vol. 41, pp. 639–55.

Evans, G. and Norris, P. (eds) (1999) *Critical Elections: British Parties and Voters in Long-Term Perspective*, Sage, London.

Evans, G., Heath, A. and Payne, C. (1999) 'Class: Labour as a catch-all party?' in Evans and Norris (eds) (1999).

Evans, H. (1994) *Good Times, Bad Times*, Phoenix.

Evans-Pritchard, E.E. (1951) *Social Anthropology*, Cohen & West, London.

Eysenck, H. (1971) *Race, Intelligence and Education*, Temple Smith, London.

Eysenck, H. and Nias, D.K. (1978) *Sex, Violence and the Media*, Temple Smith, London.

Fagin, L. and Little, M. (1984) *The Forsaken Families*, Penguin, Harmondsworth.

Fairclough, N. (1989) *Language and Power*, Longman, London.
(1995) *Media Discourse*, Arnold, London.

Faludi, S. (1992) *Backlash: The Undeclared War Against Women*, Chatto & Windus, London.

Farrington, D.P. and Morris, A.M. (1983) 'Sex, sentencing and reconviction', *British Journal of Criminology*, vol. 23, no 3.

Fausto-Sterling, A. (2000) *Sexing the Body: Gender Politics and the Construction of Sexuality*, Basic Books, New York.

Featherstone, M. (1990) *Global Culture: Nationalism, Globalization and Modernity*, Sage, London.
(1991) *Consumer Culture and Postmodernism*, Sage, London.
(1991) 'The Body in Consumer Culture' in Featherstone *et al.* (eds) (1991).

Featherstone, M. and Hepworth, M. (1990) 'Images of ageing' in J. Bond and P. Coleman (eds) *Ageing in Society*, Sage, London.
(1991) 'The mask of ageing' in Featherstone *et al.* (eds) (1991).
(1995) 'Images of positive ageing' in M. Featherstone and A. Wernick (eds) *Images of Ageing*, Routledge, London.

Featherstone, M., Hepworth, M. and Turner, B.S. (eds) (1991) *The Body, Social Process and Cultural Theory*, Sage, London.

Feeley, D. (1972) 'The family' in L. Jenness (ed.) *Feminism and Socialism*, Pathfinder Press, New York.

Feinstein, L. (1998) 'Which children succeed and why', *New Economy*, vol. 5, no. 2, June.
(2003) 'Very early evidence: how early can we predict future educational achievement?' *Centrepiece*, vol. 8, no. 2.

Felson, M. (2002) *Crime and Everyday Life*, 3rd edn, Sage, London.

Fenton, S., with Reiner, R. and Hamnett, I. (1994) *Durkheim and Modern Sociology*, Cambridge University Press, Cambridge.
(1999) *Ethnicity: Racism, Class and Culture*, Macmillan, Basingstoke.

Ferguson, M. (1983) *Forever Feminine: Women's Magazines and the Cult of Femininity*, Heinemann, London.

Fernando, S. (2002) *Mental Health, Race and Culture*, Palgrave, Basingstoke.

Ferner, A. and Hyman, R. (eds) (1998) *Changing Industrial Relations in Europe*, Blackwell, Oxford.

Ferrell, J. (2004) 'Scrunge City' in J. Ferrell, K. Hayward, W. Morrison and M. Presdee (eds) *Cultural Criminology Unleashed*, Routledge, London.

Ferri, E. and Smith, K. (1996) *Parenting in the 1990s*, Family Policy Studies Centre, London.

Festinger, J., Riecken, H. and Scachter, S. (1956) *When Prophecy Fails*, Harper & Row, New York.

Field, J. (2003) *Social Capital*, Routledge, London.

Fieldhouse, E. and Cutts, D. (2005) 'The Liberal Democrats: steady progress or failure to seize the moment' in Geddes and Tonge (eds) (2005).

Fielding, N. (1993a) 'Ethnography' in N. Gilbert (ed.) *Researching Social Life*, Sage, London.
(1993b) 'Interviewing' in N. Gilbert (ed.) *Researching Social Life*, Sage, London.

Fielding, T. (1995) 'Migration and middle-class formation in England and Wales' in Butler and Savage (eds) (1995).

Fimister, G. (2001) *An end in Sight? Tackling Child Poverty in the UK*, Child Poverty Action Group, London.

Finch, J. (1989) *Family Obligations and Social Change*, Polity Press, Cambridge.

Fine, G.A. (2006, first published 1981) 'Friends, impression management and preadolescent behaviour' in Handel (ed.) (2006).

Finkelstein, V. (1980) *Attitudes and Disabled People: Issues for Discussion*, World Rehabilitation Fund, New York.

Finn, D. (1987) *Training Without Jobs*, Macmillan, London.

Firestone, S. (1972) *The Dialectics of Sex*, Paladin, London.

Fiske, J. (1988) *Television Culture*, Methuen, London.
(1996) 'Postmodernism and television' in Curran and Gurevitch (eds) (1996).
(2000) 'White watch' in Cottle (ed.) (2000).

Fitzgerald, J. and Hamilton, M. (1996) 'The consequences of knowing: ethical and legal liabilities in illicit drugs research', *Social Science and Medicine*, vol. 43, no. 11.

Flaherty, J., Veit-Wilson, J. and Dornan, P. (2004) *Poverty: The Facts*, 5th edn, Child Poverty Action Group, London.

Fletcher, D. (2003) *Reaching the Ethnic Consumer*, Broadcasting Standards Commission, London.

Fletcher, R. (1966) *The Family and Marriage in Britain*, Penguin, Harmondsworth.
(1988) *The Shaking of the Foundations. Family and Society*, Routledge, London.

Flood-Page, C., Campbell, S., Harrington, V. and Miller, J. (2000) Youth Crime Findings from the 1998/99 Youth Lifestyles Survey, Home Office Research 209, Home Office, London.

Focus on Social Inequalities 2004, National Statistics, London (available online).

Forster, G. and Anderson, B. (1978) *Medical Anthropology*, Wiley, London.

Foucault, M. (1967) *Madness and Civilization*, Tavistock, London.
(1971) *Madness and Civilization*, Tavistock, London.
(1973) *The Birth of the Clinic*, Tavistock, London.
(1988) 'The ethic of care for the self as a practice of freedom' in J. Bernauer and D. Rassmussen (eds) *The Final Foucault*, MIT Press, Boston, MA.
(1991) *Discipline and Punish: The Birth of the Prison*, Penguin, Harmondsworth (first published as *Surveiller et punir*, 1975).

Fox Harding, L. (1996) *Family, State and Social Policy*, Macmillan, Basingstoke.

Francesconi, M. and Gosling, A. (2005) *Career Paths of Part-time Workers*, Equal Opportunities Commission, Manchester.

Francis, B. (1999) 'Lads, lasses and (New) Labour: 14–16-year-old student responses to the "laddish behaviour and boys' underachievement" debate', *British Journal of Sociology of Education*, vol. 20, pp. 357–73.
(2000) *Boys, Girls and Achievement: Addressing the Classroom Issues*, Routledge/Falmer, London.
(2006) 'Heroes or zeroes? The discursive position of "underachieving boys" in English neo-liberal education policy', *Journal of Education Policy*, vol. 21, no. 2, pp. 187–200.

Francis, B. and Skelton, C. (2005) *Reassessing Gender and Achievement: Questioning Contemporary Key Debates*, Routledge, Abingdon.

The Frankfurt Institute for Social Research (1973) *Aspects of Sociology*, Heinemann, London.

Fraser, D. (1984) *The Evolution of the British Welfare State*, Macmillan, Basingstoke.
Fraser, N. (1995) 'Politics, culture and the public sphere: towards a postmodern conception' in L. Nicholson and S. Seidman (eds) *Social Postmodernism: Beyond Identity Politics*, Cambridge University Press, Cambridge.
French, J. and French, P. (1993) 'Gender imbalances in the primary classroom: an interactional account' in P. Woods and M. Hammersley (eds) *Gender and Ethnicity in Schools: Ethnographic Accounts*, Routledge, London.
Freud, S. (1973) *Introductory Lectures on Psychoanalysis*, Penguin, Harmondsworth.
Freund, P.E.S. and McGuire, M.B. (1991) *Health, Illness and the Social Body: A Critical Sociology*, Prentice-Hall, Englewood Cliffs, NJ.
Freund, P., McGuire, M. and Podhurst, L. (2003) *Health, Illness and the Social Body*, 4th edn, Pearson, Upper Saddle River, NJ.
Frieden, J.A. (1991) 'Invested interests: the politics of national economies in a world of global finance', *International Organizations*, vol. 45, Autumn.
Friedman, A. (1977) *Industry and Labour: Class Struggle at Work and Monopoly Capitalism*, Macmillan, London.
Friedman, M. (1962) *Capitalism and Freedom*, Chicago University Press, Chicago.
Friedman, N.L. (1976) 'Cultural deprivation: a commentary on the sociology of knowledge' in J. Beck *et al.* (eds) *Worlds Apart: Readings for a Sociology of Education*, Collier-Macmillan, London.
Friedson, E. (1970) *Profession of Medicine: A Study of Sociology of Applied Knowledge*, Harper Row, New York.
(1994) *Professionalism Reborn: Theory, Prophecy and Policy*, University of Chicago Press, Chicago.
Frosh, S. (1999) 'Identity' in A. Bullock and S. Trombley (eds) *The New Fontana Dictionary of Modern Thought*, HarperCollins, London.
Fryer, D. (1995) 'Labour market disadvantage, deprivation and mental health', *The Psychologist*, vol. 8, no. 6, pp. 256–72.
Fukuyama, F. (1992) *The End of History and the Last Man*, Profile Books, London.
Fuller, M. (1984) 'Black girls in a London. comprehensive school' in M. Hammersley and P. Woods (eds) *Life in School, the Sociology of Pupil Culture*, Open University Press, Milton Keynes.
Furlong, A. and Cartmel, F. (1997) *Young People and Social Change: Individualization and Risk in Late Modernity*, Open University Press, Buckingham.
(2006) *Young People and Social Change: Individualization and Risk in Late Modernity*, 2nd edn, Open University Press, Buckingham.
Furlong, V.J. (1984) 'Interaction sets in the classroom: towards a study of pupil knowledge' in M. Hammersley and P. Woods (eds) *Life in School, the Sociology of Pupil Culture*, Open University Press, Milton Keynes.
Gaine, C. and George, R. (1999) *Gender, 'Race' and Class in Schooling: A New Introduction*, Falmer Press, London.
Galindo-Rueda, F., Marcenaro-Gutierrez, O. and Vignoles, A. (2004) 'The widening socio-economic gap in UK higher education', Centre for the Economics of Education Discussion Paper, London School of Economics and Political Science, London.
Gallie, D. (1978) *In Search of the New Working Class*, Cambridge University Press, Cambridge.
(1988) 'Employment, unemployment and social stratification' in D. Gallie (ed.) *Employment in Britain*, Blackwell, Oxford.
(1994a) 'Are the unemployed an underclass? Some evidence from the social change and economic life initiative', *Sociology*, vol. 28, no. 3, pp. 737–57.
(1994b) 'Methodological appendix' in A.M. Scott (ed.) (1994).
(1994c) 'Patterns of skill change: upskilling, deskilling or polarisation?' in Penn *et al.* (eds) (1994).
Gallie, D. and Rose, M. (1996) 'Employer policies and trade union influence' in Gallie *et al.* (eds) (1996).
Gallie, D. and Vogler, C. (1994) 'Unemployment and attitudes to work' in Gallie *et al.* (eds) (1994).
Gallie, D., Gershuny, J. and Vogler, C. (1994) 'Unemployment, the household and social networks' in Gallie *et al.* (eds) (1994).
Gallie, D., Penn, R. and Rose, M. (1996) 'The British debate on trade unionism: crisis and continuity' in Gallie *et al.* (eds) (1996).
(eds) (1996) *Trade Unionism in Recession*, Oxford University Press, Oxford.
Galtung, J. and Ruge, M. (1965) 'The structure of foreign news', *Journal of Peace Research*, vol. 2, no. 1, pp. 64–91.
Gannon, L.R. (1999) *Women and Aging: Transcending the Myths*, Routledge, London.
Gans, H.J. (1973) *More Equality*, Pantheon, New York.
(1974) *Popular Culture and High Culture*, Basic Books, New York.
Garfinkel, H. (1967) *Studies in Ethnomethodology*, Prentice-Hall, Englewood Cliffs, NJ.
Garnett, M. (2005) 'Groups and democracy', *Politics Review*, November.
(2006) 'Is the Conservative Party Conservative?' *Politics Review*, February.
Garnham, N. (1986) 'The media and the public sphere' in P. Golding *et al.*, *Communicating Politics*, Leicester University Press, Leicester.
Gates, B. (1996) *The Road Ahead*, Penguin, London.
Gaudiosi, J. (2007) 'LeBoeuf, Fox role play for "Transformers"', *Hollywood Reporter*, 17 May. http://www.hollywoodreporter.com/hr/search/article_display.jsp?vnu_content_id=1003586403
Gatrell, C. (2005) *Hard Labour: The Sociology of Parenthood*, Open University Press, Milton Keynes.
Gauntlett, D. (1998) 'Ten things wrong with the "effects model"' in R. Dickinson, R. Harindrath and O. Linne (eds). Also available at http://www.leeds.ac.uk/ics/arts-dg.htm.
(2002) *Media, Gender and Identity: An Introduction*, Sage, London.
Gauntlett, D. and Hill, A. (1999) *TV Living: Television Culture and Everyday Life*, Routledge and BFI, London.
Gavron, H. (1966) *The Captive Wife*, Routledge & Kegan Paul, London.
Geaves, R. (2005) 'Negotiating British citizenship and Muslim identity' in Abbas (ed.) (2005).
Geddes, A. and Tonge, J. (2001) *Labour's Second Landslide: The British General Election 2001*, Manchester University Press, Manchester.
(eds) (2005) *Britain Decides: The UK General Election 2005*, Palgrave Macmillan, Basingstoke.
George, S. (1988) *A Fate Worse than Debt*, Grove Press, New York.
George, V. and Wilding, P. (1994) *Welfare and Ideology*, Harvester Wheatsheaf, London.
Gershuny, J. (1992) 'Changes in the domestic division of labour in the UK 1975–87: dependent labour versus adaptive partnership' in A. Abercrombie and A. Warde (eds) *Social Change in Contemporary Britain*, Polity Press, Cambridge.
(1994) 'The psychological consequences of unemployment: an assessment of the Jahoda thesis' in Gallie *et al.* (eds) (1994).
(1999) 'The work/leisure balance and the new political economy of time', mimeo, Colchester Institute for Social and Economic Research, University of Essex.
Gerth, H.H. and Mills, C.W. (eds) (1948) *From Max Weber, Essays in Sociology*, Routledge & Kegan Paul, London.
(1954) *Character and Social Structure*, Harcourt Brace, New York.
Gewirtz, S. (2001) 'Cloning the Blairs: New Labour's programme for the resocialization of working-class parents', *Journal of Education Policy*, vol. 16, no. 4.
Gewirtz, S., Ball, S.J. and Bowe, R. (1995) *Markets, Choice and Equity in Education*, Open University Press, Buckingham.
Ghaill, M. Mac an (1992) 'Coming of age in 1980s England: reconceptualizing black students' schooling experience' in D. Gill, B. Mayor and M. Blair (eds) *Racism and Education: Structures and Strategies*, Sage, London.
(1994) *The Making of Men: Masculinities, Sexualities and Schooling*, Open University Press, Milton Keynes.
Gibbons, D.C. and Jones, J.F. (1975) *The Study of Deviance*, Prentice-Hall, Englewood Cliffs, NJ.
Gibbs, J. and Martin, W. (1964) *Status Integration and Suicide*, University of Oregon Press, Oregon.
Gibney, M.J. (2004) 'A thousand little Guantanamos: western states and measures to prevent the arrival of refugees' in Tunstall (ed.) (2004).
Gibson, C. (1994) *Dissolving Wedlock*, Routledge, London.
Gibson, O. (2007) 'Internal report attacks BBC's liberal consensus: study criticises "comfort zone" in staff's thinking: Make Poverty History and Vicar of Dibley singled out', *Guardian*, 19 June.
Giddens, A. (1970) '"Power" in the recent writings of Talcott Parsons' in P. Worsley (ed.) *Modern Sociology: Introductory Readings*, Penguin, Harmondsworth.
(1973) *The Class Structure of the Advanced Societies*, Hutchinson, London.
(1977) *Studies in Social and Political Theory*, Hutchinson, London.
(1979) *Central Problems in Social Theory*, Macmillan, London.
(1984) *The Constitution of Society*, Polity Press, Cambridge.
(1990) *The Consequences of Modernity*, Polity Press, Cambridge.
(1991) *Modernity and Self-Identity: Self and Society in the Late Modern Age*, Polity Press, Cambridge.
(1992) *The Transformation of Intimacy: Sexuality, Love and Eroticism in Modern Societies*, Polity Press, Cambridge.

(1994) *Beyond Left and Right: The Future of Radical Politics*, Polity Press, Cambridge.
(1997) *Sociology*, 3rd edn, Polity Press, Cambridge.
(1999) *The Third Way: The Renewal of Social Democracy*, Polity Press, Cambridge.
(2000) *The Third Way and its Critics*, Polity Press, Cambridge.
(2006) *Sociology*, Polity Press, Cambridge.

Giddens, A., Held, D., Hubert, D., Seymour, D. and Thompson, J. (1994) *The Polity Reader in Social Theory*, Polity Press, Cambridge.

Gilchrist, R., Phillips, D. and Ross, A. (2003) 'Participation and potential participation in UK higher education' in Archer *et al.* (eds) (2003).

Giles, C. and Johnson, P. (1994) *Taxes Down, Taxes Up: The Effects of a Decade of Tax Changes*, Institute for Fiscal Studies, London.

Giles, C. and Webb, S. (1993) *Poverty Statistics: A Guide for the Perplexed*, Institute for Fiscal Studies, London.

Gill, C. (1985) *Work, Unemployment and the New Technology*, Polity Press, Cambridge.

Gillborn, D. and Mirza, H.S. (2000) *Educational Inequality: Mapping Race, Gender and Class. A Synthesis of Research*, Ofsted, London.

Gillborn, D. and Youdell, D. (2000) *Rationing Education: Policy, Practice, Reform and Equity*, Open University Press, Buckingham.
(2001) 'The new IQism: intelligence, "ability" and the rationing of education' in Demaine (ed.) (2001).

Gillespie, M. (1995) *Television, Ethnicity and Cultural Change*, Routledge, London.

Gillet, J. (2003) 'Media activism and internet use by people with HIV/AIDS', *Sociology of Health and Illness*, vol. 25, no. 6, pp. 608–24.

Gilligan, J. (2001) *Preventing Violence*, Thames & Hudson, London.

Gillis, J. (1974) *Youth and History*, Academic Press, New York.

Gilmore, D. (1990) *Manhood in the Making: Cultural Concepts of Masculinity*, Yale University Press, New Haven, CT.

Gilroy, P. (1982) 'The myth of black criminality' in *Socialist Register*, Marlin Press, London.
(1983) 'Police and thieves' in Centre for Contemporary Cultural Studies, *The Empire Strikes Back*, Hutchinson, London.
(1987) *There Ain't No Black in the Union Jack*, Hutchinson, London.
(1992) 'The end of antiracism' in J. Donald and A. Rattansi (eds) (1992).

Ginsburg, N. (1979) *Class, Capital and Social Policy*, Macmillan, London.
(1997) 'Housing' in Walker and Walker (eds) (1997).

Giroux, H. (1984) 'Ideology, agency and the process of schooling' in L. Barton and S. Walker (eds) *Social Crisis and Educational Research*, Croom Helm, London.

Gittins, D. (1993) *The Family in Question*, 2nd edn, Macmillan, Basingstoke.

Gladwin, T. (1967) *Poverty USA*, Little Brown, Boston, MA.

Glaser, B. and Strauss, A. (1965) *Awareness of Dying*, Aldine, Chicago.
(1967) *The Discovery of Grounded Theory*, Aldine, Chicago.
(1968) *Time for Dying*, Aldine, Chicago.

Glasgow University Media Group (1976) *Bad News*, Routledge & Kegan Paul, London.
(1980) *More Bad News*, Routledge & Kegan Paul, London.
(1982) *Really Bad News*, Writers & Readers, London.
(1985) *War and Peace News*, Open University Press, Milton Keynes.
(2007) http://www.gla.ac.uk/centres/mediagroup

Glasgow University Media Group and Eldridge, G. (ed.) (1993) *Getting the Message: News, Truth and Power*, Routledge, London

Glasner, P. (1977) *The Sociology of Secularisation*, Routledge & Kegan Paul, London.

Glass, D.V. (ed.) (1954) *Social Mobility in Britain*, Routledge & Kegan Paul, London.

Glass, D.V. and Hall, J.R. (1954) 'Social mobility in Britain: a study of intergenerational changes in status' in Glass (ed.) (1954).

Glatter, R., Woods, A. and Bagley, C. (1997) 'Diversity, differentiation and hierarchy: school choice and parental preferences' in Glatter *et al.* (eds) (1997).
(eds) (1997) *Choice and Diversity in Schooling: Perspectives and Prospects*, Routledge, London.

Glendinning, C. and Millar, J. (1994) *Women and Poverty in Britain: The 1990s*, Harvester Wheatsheaf, Hemel Hempstead.

Glennon, L.M. and Butsch, R. (1982) 'The family as portrayed on television, 1946–1978' in D. Pearl *et al.* (eds) *Television and Behavior*, National Institute of Mental Health, Rockville, MD.

Glock, C.Y. and Stark, R. (1965) *Religion and Society in Tension*, Rand McNally, Chicago.
(1969) 'Dimensions of religious commitment' in Robertson (ed.) (1969).

Goddard, J. *et al.* (eds) (2005) *The Politics of Childhood: International Perspectives*, Palgrave Macmillan, Basingstoke.

Goffman, E. (1959) *The Presentation of Self in Everyday Life*, Doubleday Anchor, New York.
(1968) *Asylums*, Penguin, Harmondsworth.
(1970) *Stigma: Notes on the Management of Spoiled Identity*, Penguin, Harmondsworth.

Gold, M. (1977) 'A crisis of identity: the case of medical sociology', *Journal of Health and Social Behaviour*, vol. 18, pp. 160–8.

Goldberg, D.T. (1993) *Racist Culture: Philosophy and the Politics of Meaning*, Blackwell, Oxford.

Goldmann, L. (1964) *The Hidden God*, Routledge & Kegan Paul, London.

Goldstein, H. (1987) 'Gender bias and test norms in educational selection' in Arnot and Weiner (1987).

Goldthorpe, J.H. (1973) Review article 'A revolution in sociology?' *Sociology*, September.
(1980) *Social Mobility and Class Structure in Modern Britain*, Clarendon Press, Oxford.
(1983) 'Women and class analysis: in defence of the conventional view', *Sociology*, no. 14.
(1995) 'The service class revisited' in Butler and Savage (eds) (1995).

Goldthorpe, J.H. and Payne, C. (1986) 'On the class mobility of women', *Sociology*, vol. 20.
(1986) 'Trends in integenerational mobility in England and Wales 1979–83', *Sociology*, vol. 20.

Goldthorpe, J.H., Lockwood, D., Bechhofer, F. and Platt, J. (1968a) *The Affluent Worker: Industrial Attitudes and Behaviour*, Cambridge University Press, Cambridge.
(1968b) *The Affluent Worker: Political Attitudes and Behaviour*, Cambridge University Press, Cambridge.
(1969) *The Affluent Worker in the Class Structure*, Cambridge University Press, Cambridge.

Goldthorpe, J.H., Llewellyn, C. and Payne, C. (1987) *Social Mobility and Class Structure in Modern Britain*, 2nd edn, Clarendon, Oxford.

Gomm, R. (1982) 'Science and values' in R. Gomm and P. McNeill, *Handbook for Sociology Teachers*, Heinemann, London.
(1996) 'Mental health and inequality' in Heller *et al.* (eds) (1996).

González, N.L. (1970) 'Toward a definition of matrifocality' in N.W. Whitten and J.F. Szwed (eds) *Afro-American Anthropology*, Free Press, New York.

Goode, W.J. (1971) 'A sociological perspective on marital dissolution' in Anderson (ed.) (1971).

Goodhart, D. (2004) 'Discomfort of strangers', *Guardian*, 24 February.

Goodman, A. (2001) 'What happened to income inequality in the 1990s? *Institute for Fiscal Studies Update*, Autumn.

Goodman, A., Johnson, P. and Webb, S. (1997) *Inequality in the UK*, Oxford University Press, Oxford.

Goodman, A., Myck, M. and Shephard, A. (2003) *Sharing in the Nation's Prosperity? Pensioner Poverty in Britain*, Institute for Fiscal Studies, London.

Google (2007a) 'Corporate information: our philosophy'. http://www.google.com/corporate/tenthings.html
(2007b) 'Corporate information: Google milestones'. http://www.google.com/intl/en/corporate/history.html

Gordon, D. *et al.* (2000) *Poverty and Social Exclusion in Britain*, Joseph Rowntree Foundation, York.

Gordon, D.M. (1976) 'Class and the economics of crime' in Chambliss and Mankoff (1976).

Gordon, L. (1984) 'Paul Willis – education, cultural production and social reproduction', *British Journal of Sociology of Education*, vol. 5, no. 2.

Gough, E. (1959) 'Is the family universal? The Nayor case' in N.W. Bell and E.F. Vogel (eds) *A Modern Introduction to the Family*, Collier-Macmillan, London.

Gough, K. (1972) 'An anthropologist looks at Engels' in N. Glazer-Malbin and H.Y. Waehrer (eds) *Woman in a Man-Made World*, Rand McNally, Chicago.

Gouldner, A.W. (1970) *The Coming Crisis of Western Sociology*, Basic Books, New York.
(1975) 'Anti-Minotaur: the myth of a value-free society' in Gouldner (1975).
(1975) *For Sociology*, Penguin, Harmondsworth.

Gove, W. (1982) 'The current status of labelling theory in mental illness', *American Journal of Sociology*, vol. 78, pp. 812–35.

Government Actuary's Department (2005) *New Marital Status Projections for England and Wales*, GAD, London.

Goy, R. and Phoenix, C.H. (1971) 'The effects of testosterone propionate administered before birth on the development of behaviour in genetic female rhesus monkeys' in C.H. Sawyer and R.A. Gorski (eds) *Steroid Hormones and Brain Function*, University of California Press, Berkeley, CA.

Grafton, T., Miller, H., Smith, L., Vegoda, M. and Whitfield, R. (1987) 'Gender and curriculum choice' in Arnot and Weiner (1987).

Graham, H. (1984) *Women, Health and Family*, Harvester Wheatsheaf, Brighton.

(1993) *When Life's a Drag: Women, Smoking and Disadvantage*, HMSO, London.

Graham, H. and Blackburn, C. (1998) 'The socio-economic patterning of health and smoking behaviour among mothers with young children on income support', *Sociology of Health and Illness*, vol. 20, no. 2, pp. 215–40.

Graham, H. and Oakley, A. (1986) 'Competing ideologies of reproduction: medical and maternal perspectives on pregnancy' in Currer and Stacey (eds) (1986).

Graham, J. and Bowling, B. (1995) *Young People and Crime*, HMSO, London.

Gramsci, A. (1971) *Selections from the Prison Notebooks*, Lawrence & Wishart, London.

Grant, C., Bolling, K. and Sexton, M. (2006) *2005–2006 British Crime Survey Technical Report*, Home Office, London.

Grant, W. (1999) 'Pressure groups' in Haralambos (ed.) (1999).

(2003) 'Making economic policy', *Politics Review*, February, pp. 2–5.

Grant, W. and Marsh, D. (1977) *The Confederation of British Industry*, Hodder & Stoughton, London.

Gray, A. (1987) 'Behind closed doors: women and video' in H. Baehr and G. Dyer (eds) *Boxed In*, Routledge, London.

(1992) *Video Playtime*, Routledge, London.

(1999) 'Audience and reception research in retrospect' in Alasuutari (ed.) (1999).

Gray, H. (2000) 'Black representation in the post-network, post-civil rights world of the global media' in Cottle (ed.) (2000).

Gray, J.A. and Buffery, A.W.H. (1971) 'Sex differences in emotional and cognitive behaviour in mammals including man: adaptive and neural bases', *Acta Psychologia*, no. 35.

Greeley, A. (1972) *Unsecular Man: The Persistence of Religion*, Shocken Books, New York.

(1994) 'A religious revival in Russia?' *Journal for the Scientific Study of Religion*, vol. 33, no. 3, pp. 253–72.

Green, A. (1997) *Education, Globalization and the Nation State*, Macmillan, London.

Green, E., Hebron, S. and Woodward, D. (1990) *Women's Leisure, What Leisure?* Macmillan, London.

Greer, G. (1970) *The Female Eunuch*, Paladin, London.

(2000) *The Whole Woman*, Anchor, London.

Grimshaw, D. and Rubery, G. (2001) *The Gender Pay Gap: A Research Review*, Equal Opportunities Commission, Manchester.

Grint, K. (1991) *The Sociology of Work: An Introduction*, Polity Press, Cambridge.

(1992) 'The sociology of work' in M. Haralambos (ed.) *Developments in Sociology*, vol. 8, Causeway Press, Ormskirk.

(1998) *The Sociology of Work*, 2nd edn, Polity Press, Cambridge.

Grint, K. and Woolgar, S. (1992) 'Computers, guns, and roses: what's social about being shot?' *Science, Technology and Human Values*, vol. 17, no. 3.

(1997) *The Machine at Work: Technology, Work and Organization*, Polity Press, Cambridge.

Gross, R. (1992) *Psychology: The Science of Mind and Behaviour*, 2nd edn, Hodder & Stoughton, London.

Gross, R.M. (1994) 'Buddhism' in Holm and Bowker (eds) (1994).

Grossberg, L. (1988) 'Wandering audiences, nomadic critics', *Cultural Studies*, vol. 2, no. 3, pp. 377–92.

(1994, first published 1986) 'The deconstruction of youth' in J. Storey (ed.) *Cultural Theory and Popular Culture: A Reader*, Harvester Wheatsheaf, Hemel Hempstead.

Grossberg, L., Wartella, E. and Whitney, D.C. (1998) *Mediamaking: Mass Media in a Popular Culture*, Sage, London.

Gunter, B. and McAleer, J. (1997) *Children and Television*, 2nd edn, Routledge, London.

Habermas, J. (1984) *The Theory of Communicative Action*, vol. 1, Heinemann, London.

Hacker, H.M. (1972) 'Women as a minority group' in N. Glazer-Malbin and H.Y. Waehrer (eds) *Woman in a Man-Made World*, Rand McNally, Chicago.

Hadaway, C.K., Marler, P.L. and Chaves, M. (1993) 'What the polls don't show: a closer look at US church attendance', *American Sociological Review*, vol. 58.

Haddon, L. (ed.) (1997) *Themes in Mobile Telephony*, COST Home and Work Group, Telia, Stockholm.

Hakim, C. (2004) *Key Issues in Women's Work: Female Diversity and the Polarisation of Women's Employment*, Glasshouse Press, London.

Halbwachs, M. (1930) *Les Causes de Suicide*, Alcan, Paris.

Hall, E.T. (1966) *The Hidden Dimension*, Doubleday, New York.

(1973) *The Silent Language*, Doubleday, New York.

Hall, P., Brockington, I., Levings, J. and Murphy, C. (1993) 'Comparisons of responses to the mentally ill in two communities', *British Journal of Psychiatry*, vol. 162, pp. 99–108.

Hall, S. (1980) 'Encoding/decoding' in S. Hall, D. Hobson, A. Lowe and P. Willis (eds) *Culture, Media and Language*, Hutchinson, London.

(1992) 'Our mongrel selves', *New Statesman and Society*, 19 June.

(1992) 'The question of cultural identity' in Hall *et al.* (eds) (1992).

(1995, first published in 1982) 'The rediscovery of 'ideology': return of the repressed in media studies' in Boyd-Barrett and Newbold (eds) (1995).

(1996) 'New ethnicities' in D. Morley and K.-H. Chen (eds) *Stuart Hall: Critical Dialogues in Cultural Studies*, Routledge, London.

Hall, S. and Jefferson, T. (eds) (1976) *Resistance through Rituals: Youth Subcultures in Post-war Britain*, Hutchinson, London.

Hall, S., Critcher, C., Jefferson, T., Clarke, J. and Roberts, B. (1978 and 1979) *Policing the Crisis*, Macmillan, London.

Hall, S. *et al.* (1982) *The Empire Strikes Back*, Hutchinson, London.

Hall, S., Held, D. and McGrew, T. (eds) (1992) *Modernity and its Futures*, Polity Press, Cambridge.

Halliday, F. (1994) 'The politics of Islamic fundamentalism: Iran, Tunisia and the challenge to the secular state' in A. Ahmed and H. Donnan (eds) *Islam, Globalization and Postmodernity*, Routledge, London.

Halloran, J. (1970) *The Effects of Television*, Panther, St Albans.

Hallsworth, S. (1994) 'Understanding new social movements', *Sociology Review*, vol. 4, no. 1.

Halpern, D. (1999) 'Social capital: the new golden goose', Faculty of Social and Political Sciences, Cambridge University. Unpublished review, cited in *Social Capital: A Review of the Literature*, Social Analysis and Reporting Division, Office for National Statistics, October 2001.

(2005) *Social Capital*, Polity Press, Cambridge.

Halsey, A.H. (1977) 'Towards meritocracy? The case of Britain' in J. Karabel and A.H. Halsey (eds) *Power and Ideology in Education*, Oxford University Press, New York.

(1977) 'Whatever happened to positive discrimination?' *The Times Educational Supplement*, 21 January.

Halsey, A.H., Floud, J. and Anderson, C.A. (1961) *Education, Economy and Society*, Free Press, New York.

Halsey, A.H., Heath, A. and Ridge, J.M. (1980) *Origins and Destinations*, Clarendon Press, Oxford.

Halsey, A.H., Lauder, H., Brown, P. and Wells, A. (eds) (1997) *Education: Culture, Economy, Society*, Oxford University Press, Oxford.

Halsey, M. (2004) 'Against "green" criminology', *British Journal of Criminology*, vol. 44, no. 6, pp. 833–53.

Halsey, M. and White, R. (1998) 'Crime, ecophilosophy and environmental harm', *Theoretical Criminology*, vol. 2, no. 3, pp. 345–71.

Hamilton, M. (1995) *The Sociology of Religion: Theoretical and Comparative Perspectives*, Routledge, London.

(1998) 'Secularisation: now you see it, now you don't', *Sociology Review*, vol. 7, no. 4, April.

Hammersley, M., 'Staffroom racism' (unpublished manuscript).

(1992) *What's Wrong with Ethnography?* Routledge, London.

(ed.) (1993) *Social Research: Philosophy, Politics and Practice*, Sage, London.

(1995) *The Politics of Social Research*, Sage, London.

(1996) 'The relationship between qualitative and quantitative research: paradigm loyalty versus methodological eclecticism' in Richardson (ed.) (1996).

Hammersley, M. and Gomm, R. (2004) 'Recent radical critiques of interviewing' in Holborn (ed.) (2004).

Hamnett, M. and Connell, J. (1981) 'Diagnosis and cure: the resort to traditional and modern medical practitioners in the North Solomons, Papua and New Guinea', *Social Science and Medicine*, vol. 15B, pp. 480–98.

Handel, G. (ed.) (2006) *Childhood Socialization*, 2nd edn, Aldine Transaction, New Brunswick.

Hannerz, U. (1969) *Soulside: Inquiries into Ghetto Culture and Community*, Columbia University Press, New York.

Hannon, L. and Defronzo, J. (1998) 'The truly disadvantaged: public assistance and crime', *Social Problems*, vol. 45.
Hantrais, L. and Letablier, M.T. (1996) *Families and Family Policies in Europe*, Longman, London.
Haralambos, M. (ed.) (1994) *Developments in Sociology*, vol. 10, Causeway Press, Ormskirk
(ed.) (1995) *Developments in Sociology*, vol. 11, Causeway Press, Ormskirk.
(ed.) (1997) *Developments in Sociology*, vol. 13, Causeway Press, Ormskirk.
(ed.) (1999) *Developments in Politics*, vol. 10, Causeway Press, Ormskirk.
(ed.) (1999) *Developments in Sociology*, vol. 15, Causeway Press, Ormskirk.
(ed.) (2001) *Developments in Sociology*, vol. 17, Causeway Press, Ormskirk.
Hardill, I., Green, A., Dudlestone, A. and Owen, D.W. (1997) 'Who decides what? Decision making in dual career households', *Work, Employment and Society*, vol. 11, no. 2.
Harding, S. (1986) *The Science Question in Feminism*, Open University Press, Milton Keynes.
(ed.) (1987) *Feminism and Methodology*, Open University Press, Milton Keynes.
Hargrave, A. (1999) *Sex and Sensibility*, Broadcasting Standards Commission, London.
Hargreaves, A. (1982) 'Resistance and relative autonomy theories: problems of distortion and incoherence in recent Marxist analyses of education', *British Journal of Sociology of Education*, vol. 3, no. 2.
Hargreaves, D.H. (1967) *Social Relations in a Secondary School*, Routledge & Kegan Paul, London.
(1976) 'Reactions to labelling' in M. Hammersley and P. Woods (eds) *The Process of Schooling*, Routledge & Kegan Paul, London.
(1982) *The Challenge for the Comprehensive School*, Routledge & Kegan Paul, London.
Hargreaves, D., Hester, S. and Mellor, F. (1975) *Deviance in Classrooms*, Routledge & Kegan Paul, London.
Harnett, A. (2000) 'Escaping the "Evil Avenger" and the "Supercrip": images of disability in popular television', *Irish Communications Review*, vol. 8, pp. 21–9.
Harrington, M. (1963) *The Other America: Poverty in the United States*, Penguin, Harmondsworth.
Harris, N. (1971) *Beliefs in Society*, Penguin, Harmondsworth.
(1992) *The Urban Environment in Developing Countries*, UNDP, New York.
Harrison, N. (1985) *TV News: Whose Bias?* Policy Journals, Berkshire.
Hart, N. (1976) *When Marriage Ends: A Study in Status Passage*, Tavistock, London.
(1981) 'The unhappy marriage of Marxism and feminism: toward a more progressive union' in Lydia Sargent (ed.) *The Unhappy Marriage of Marxism and Feminism: A Debate on Class and Patriarchy*, Pluto Press, London.
(1982) 'Is capitalism bad for your health?' *British Journal of Sociology*, vol. 33, no. 3, pp. 435–43.
(1985) *The Sociology of Health and Medicine*, Causeway Press, Ormskirk.
Hartmann, H. (1981) 'The unhappy marriage of Marxism and feminism: towards a more progressive union' in Lydia Sargent (ed.) *The Unhappy Marriage of Marxism and Feminism: A Debate on Class and Patriarchy*, Pluto Press, London.
Hartmann, P. and Husband, C. (1974) *Racism and the Mass Media*, Davis-Poynter, London.
Harvey, D. (1990) *The Condition of Postmodernity*, Blackwell, Oxford.
Harvey, L. (1990) *Critical Social Research*, Unwin Hyman, London.
Haste, H. (1993) *The Sexual Metaphor*, Harvester Wheatsheaf, Hemel Hempstead.
Hatcher, R. (2005) 'Business sponsorship of schools: for-profit takeover or agents of neoliberal change?' http://journals.aol.co.uk./rikowskigr/Volumizer/entries/2005/11/07
Haug, M. (1973) 'Deprofessionalization: An alternative hypothesis for the future', *Sociological Review Monograph*, vol. 20, pp. 195–211.
Hawkins, K. (1984) *Unemployment*, 2nd edn, Penguin, Harmondsworth.
Hayek, F.A. (1986, first published 1944) *The Road to Serfdom*, Routledge, London.
Haylett, C. (2001) 'Illegitimate subjects? Abject whites, neoliberal modernisation and middle class multiculturalism', *Environment and Planning D: Society and Space*, vol. 19, pp. 351–70.
Hayward, K. (2004) 'Space: the final frontier' in Ferrell *et al.* (eds) (2004).
Hayward, K. and Young, J. (2004) Cultural criminology: some notes on the script', *Theoretical Criminology*, vol. 8, pp. 259–73.
Heath, A. (1981) *Social Mobility*, Fontana, Glasgow.
(1992) 'The attitudes of the underclass' in D.J. Smith (ed.) *Understanding the Underclass*, Policy Studies Institute, London.
Heath, A. and Britten, N. (1984) 'Women's jobs do make a difference: a reply to Goldthorpe', *Sociology*, vol. 18, no. 4, pp. 475–90.
Heath, A., Jowell, R. and Curtice, J. (1985) *How Britain Votes*, Pergamon, Oxford.
(1987) 'Trendless fluctuation: a reply to Crewe', *Political Studies*.
(1994) 'Can Labour win?' in A. Heath, R. Jowell, J. Curtice with B. Taylor (eds) *Labour's Last Chance?* Dartmouth Publishing, Aldershot.
Health Education Authority (1994) *British Health and Lifestyle Survey*, HEA, London.
Hebdige, D. (1988) *Subculture: The Meaning of Style*, Routledge, London.
Heelas, P. (1996) 'De-traditionalisation of religion and self: the New Age and postmodernity' in K. Flanagan and P. Jupp (eds) *Postmodernity, Sociology and Religion*, Macmillan, Basingstoke.
(1996) *The New Age Movement*, Blackwell, Oxford.
(ed.) (1998) *Religion, Modernity and Postmodernity*, Blackwell, Oxford.
Heelas, P. and Seel, B. (2003) 'An ageing New Age?' in Davie *et al.* (eds) (2003).
Heelas, P. *et al.* (2003) *Bringing the Sacred to Life: The Crisis of Traditional Religion and the Rise of Wellbeing Spirituality*, Blackwell, Oxford.
Heelas, P., Woodhead, L., Seel, B., Tusting, K. and Szerszynski, B. (2005) *The Spiritual Revolution: Why Religion is Giving Way to Spirituality*, Blackwell, Oxford.
Heidensohn, F. (1985) *Women and Crime*, Macmillan, London.
(1987) 'Gender and crime' in Maguire *et al.* (eds) (1997).
(1997) 'Gender and crime' in Maguire *et al.* (eds) (1997).
(2002) 'Gender and crime' in Maguire *et al.* (eds) (2002).
Hekman, S.J. (1990) *Gender and Knowledge: Elements of a Postmodern Feminism*, Polity Press, Cambridge.
Held, D. and McGrew, A. (2002) *Globalization/Anti-Globalization*, Polity Press, Cambridge.
Heller, T., Reynolds, J., Gomm, R., Muston, R. and Pattison, S. (eds) (1996) *Mental Health Matters: A Reader*, Macmillan, Basingstoke.
Helman, C. G. (1986) 'Feed a cold, starve a fever: folk models of infection in an English suburban community' in Currer and Stacey (eds) (1986).
Henwood, F. and Miles, I. (1987) 'Unemployment and the sexual division of labour' in David Fryer and Philip Ullah, *Unemployed People*, Open University Press, Milton Keynes.
Herberg, W. (1960) *Protestant – Catholic – Jew*, rev. edn, Anchor Books, New York.
Hermes, J. (1995) *Reading Women's Magazines*, Polity Press, Cambridge.
Hernstein, R. and Murray, C.A. (1994) *The Bell Curve: Intelligence and Class Structure in American Life*, Free Press, New York.
Hewitt, C.J. (1974) 'Elites and the distribution of power in British society' in P. Stanworth and A. Giddens (eds) *Elites and Power in British Society*, Cambridge University Press, Cambridge.
Hickox, M.S.H. (1982) 'The Marxist sociology of education: a critique', *British Journal of Sociology*, December.
Hill, D. (2006a) 'Neoliberal and neoconservative global and national capital and the class war from above: some implications for social class analysis', *Journal for Critical Education Policy Studies*, vol. 4, no. 1.
(2006b) 'New Labour's education policy' in D. Kassem, E. Mufti and J. Robinson (eds) *Education Studies: Issues and Critical Perspectives*, Open University Press, Maidenhead.
Hill, M. (2003) *Understanding Social Policy*, 7th edn, Blackwell, Oxford.
Hill, M. and Tisdall, K. (1997) *Children and Society*, Prentice Hall, Harlow.
Hills, J. (1995) *Inquiry into Income and Wealth*, Joseph Rowntree Foundation, York.
(2002) 'Does a focus on social exclusion change the policy response?' in Hills *et al.* (eds) (2002).
Hills, J, and Stewart, K. (eds) (2005) *A More Equal Society? New Labour, Poverty, Inequality and Exclusion*, Policy Press, Bristol.
(2005) 'A tide turned but mountains yet to climb' in Hills and Stewart (eds) (2005).
Hills, J., Le Grand, J. and Piachaud, D. (eds) (2002) *Understanding Social Exclusion*, Oxford University Press, Oxford.
Hindess, B. (1973) *The Use of Official Statistics in Sociology: A Critique of Positivism*, Macmillan, London.
(1996) *Discourses of Power: From Hobbes to Foucault*, Blackwell, Oxford.

Hine, C. (ed.) (2005) *Virtual Methods: Issues on Social Research on the Internet*, Berg, Oxford.

Hinnels, J. (1997) *The New Handbook of Living Religions*, Blackwell, London.

Hirschi, T. (1969) *Causes of Delinquency*, University of California Press, Berkeley, CA.

Hirst, P. and Thompson, G. (1996) *Globalization in Question*, Polity Press, Cambridge.

HMSO (published annually) *Social Trends*, HMSO, London.
(2002a) *Living in Britain: Results from the 2000/2001 General Household Survey*, HMSO, London.
(2002b) *UK 2003*, HMSO, London.

Hobbs, D. and Dunninghan, C. (1998) 'Glocal organised crime: context and pretext' in Ruggiero *et al.* (eds) (1998).

Hobsbawm, E.S. (1970) *Industry and Empire*, Penguin, Harmondsworth.

Hobson, D. (1980) 'Housewives and the mass media' in S. Hall *et al.*, *Culture, Media, Language*, Hutchinson, London.
(1990) in M. Brown, *TV and Women's Culture*, Sage, London.

Hochschild, A.R. (1975) 'Disengagement theory: a critique and proposal', *American Sociological Review*, vol. 40, pp. 533–69.
(1983) *The Managed Heart: Commercialisation of Human Feeling*, University of California Press, CA.

Hockey, J. and James, A. (1993) *Growing Up and Growing Old: Ageing and Dependency in the Life Course*, Sage, London.
(2003) *Social Identities across the Life Course*, Palgrave Macmillan, Basingstoke.

Hodkinson, P. (2004) 'The goth scene and (sub)cultural substance' in Bennett and Kahn-Harris (eds) (2004).

Holborn, M. (2001) 'Anthony Giddens and the theory of modernity' in Haralambos (ed.) (2001).
(ed.) (2002) *Developments in Sociology*, vol. 18, Causeway Press, Ormskirk.
(ed.) (2003) *Developments in Sociology*, vol. 19, Causeway Press, Ormskirk.
(ed.) (2004) *Developments in Sociology*, vol. 20, Causeway Press, Ormskirk.
(2005) 'Killing and society: towards a sociology of homicide' in Holborn (ed.) (2005).
(ed.) (2005) *Developments in Sociology*, vol. 21, Causeway Press, Ormskirk.

Holdaway, S. (1983) *Inside the British Police*, Blackwell, Oxford.

Hollingshead, G., Nicholls, P. and Tailby, S. (2003) *Employee Relations*, 2nd edn, Prentice-Hall, Harlow.

Holm, J. (1994) 'Introduction: raising the issues' in Holm and Bowker (eds) (1994).

Holm, J. and Bowker, J. (eds) (1994) *Women in Religion*, Pinter, London.

Holstein, J.A. and Gubrium, J.F. (1995) *The Active Interviewer*, Sage, London.

Holton, R. and Turner, B. (1989) *Max Weber on Economy and Society*, Routledge & Kegan Paul, London.

Home Office (2000a) *Statistics on Race and the Criminal Justice System, 2000*, Home Office, London.
(2000b), *Statistics on Women and the Criminal Justice System*, Home Office, London.
(2005) *Households Below Average Income Survey 2002/03*, Home Office, London.
(2006) *Statistics on Race and the Criminal Justice System, 2005*, Home Office, London.

Hood, R. (1992) *Race and Sentencing*, Clarendon Press, Oxford.

hooks, b. (1981) *Ain't I a Woman: Black Women and Feminism*, South End Press, Boston, MA.
(1982) *Black Looks: Race and Representation*, Macmillan, London.

Hopkins Burke, R. (2001) *An Introduction to Criminological Theory*, Willan Publishing, Cullompton, Devon.

Hoque, K. and Noon, M. (1993) 'Racial discrimination in speculative applications: new optimism six years on?' *Human Resource Management Journal*, vol. 9, no. 3.

Hosking, G. (1988) 'Religion and the atheist state', *The Listener*, 8 December.

Houston, D.M. and Marks, G. (2003) 'The role of planning and workplace support in returning to work after maternity leave', *Journal of Industrial Relations*, vol. 41, no. 2.

Howard, M. (1997) 'Cutting Social Security' in Walker and Walker (eds) (1997).

Howard, M., Garnham, A. Fimister, G. and Veit-Wilson, J. (2001) *Poverty: the Facts*, 4th edn, Child Poverty Action Group, London.

Howlett, B.C., Ahmad, W.I. and Murray, R. (1992) 'An Exploration of White, Asian and Afro-Caribbean Peoples' Concepts of Health and Illness Causation', *New Community*, vol. 18, no. 2, pp. 281–92.

Hudson, K. (1970) *The Place of Women in Society*, Ginn, London.

Hughes, G. (1991) 'Taking crime seriously? A critical analysis of New Left realism', *Sociology Review*, vol. 1, no 2.

Hundal, S. (2006) 'The BBC's still "hideously white"', *Guardian*, 19 June.

Hunt, D. (1999) *O. J. Simpson Fact and Fictions: New Rituals in the Construction of Reality*, Cambridge University Press, Cambridge.

Hunt, S. (2005) *The Life Course: A Sociological Introduction*, Palgrave Macmillan, Basingstoke.

Hunter, J.D. (1987) *Evangelism: The Coming Generation*, University of Chicago Press, Chicago.

Huntington, S.P. (1993) 'The clash of civilizations', *Foreign Affairs*, Summer.

Husserl, E. (1931) *Ideas*, Allen & Unwin, London.

Hutchings, M. (2003) 'Financial barriers to participation' in Archer *et al.* (eds) (2003).

Hutton, W. (2002) 'By the left, quick march', *Observer*, 21 July.

Hyman, H.H. (1967) 'The value systems of different classes' in Bendix and Lipset (eds) (1967).

Hyman, R. (1984) *Strikes*, 3rd edn, Fontana, Aylesbury.

Illich, I. (1973) *Deschooling Society*, Penguin, Harmondsworth.
(1975) *Medical Nemesis*, Calder & Boyars, London.
(1976) *Limits to Medicine*, Marion Boyars, London.

Illsley, R. (1986) 'Occupational class, selection and the production of inequalities in health', *Quarterly Journal of Social Affairs*, vol. 2, pp. 151–65.
(1987) 'The health divide: bad welfare or bad statistics?' *Poverty*, vol. 67, pp. 16–17.

Imray, L. and Middleton, A. (1983) 'Public and private: marking the boundaries' in E. Gamarnikow, D. Morgan *et al.* (eds) *The Public and the Private*, Heinemann, London.

Internetworldstats.com (2007) 'Internet usage statistics – the big picture'. http://www.internetworldstats.com/stats.htm

IPA (1999) *Trends in Television*, IPA, London.

Ireson, J. and Hallam, S. (2001) *Ability Grouping in Education*, Paul Chapman Publishing, London.

Ireson, J., Hallam, S. and Hurley, C. (2001) 'Ability grouping in the secondary school: effects at Key Stage 4', Institute of Education, University of London.

Irvine, J., Miles, I. and Evans, J. (eds) (1979) *Demystifying Social Statistics*, Pluto Press, London.

Israel, M. and Hay, I. (2006) *Research Ethics for Social Scientists*, Sage, London.

Ivory, J.D. (2006) 'Still a man's game: gender representations in online reviews of video games', *Mass Communication and Society*, vol. 9, no. 1, pp. 103–14.

Jackman, R. (1998) 'Unemployment and labour market policy', *Economic Review*, February.

Jackson, C. (2006) *Lads and Ladettes in School: Gender and a Fear of Failure*, Open University Press, Maidenhead.

Jackson, S. and Scott, S. (2006) 'Childhood' in Payne (ed.) (2006).

James, A. and Prout, A. (eds) (1990) *Constructing and Reconstructing Childhood*, Falmer, London.
(eds) (1997a) *Constructing and Reconstructing Childhood*, 2nd edn, Falmer, London.
(1997b) 'Re-presenting childhood: time and transition in the study of childhood' in James and Prout (eds) (1997a).

James, E. (1970) *America Against Poverty*, Routledge & Kegan Paul, London.

James, N. (1989) 'Emotional labour: skill and work in the regulation of feelings', *Sociological Review*, vol. 3.

Jamous, H. and Peloille, B. (1970) 'Changes in French University Hospital System' in J.A. Jackson (ed.) *Professions and Professionalization*, Cambridge University Press, Cambridge.

Jary, D. and Jary, J. (1991) *Collins Dictionary of Sociology*, HarperCollins, London.

Jayaratne, T.E. (1993) 'The value of quantitative methodology for feminist research' in Hammersley (ed.) (1993).

Jefferson, T. (1976) 'Cultural responses of the Teds: the defence of space and status' in Hall and Jefferson (eds) (1976).
(1997) 'Masculinities and crime' in M. Maguire *et al.* (eds) *The Oxford Handbook of Criminology*, Oxford University Press, Oxford.

Jeffries, S. (2006) 'You only live twice: after the success of MySpace, Bebo and YouTube, virtual reality site Second Life is fast becoming the hottest thing on the web', *Guardian*, 7 October.

Jencks, C. (1975) *Inequality: A Reassessment of the Effect of Family and Schooling in America*, Penguin, Harmondsworth.
(1993) *Culture*, Routledge, London.
Jenkins, J. (2002) *Patterns of Pay: Results of the 2001 New Earnings Survey*, Office for National Statistics, London.
Jenkins, R. (1992) *Pierre Bordieu*, Routledge, London.
(1996) *Social Identity*, Routledge, London.
Jenks, C. (2005) *Childhood*, 2nd edn, Routledge, London.
Jensen, A.R. (1973) *Educational Differences*, Methuen, London.
Jessop, B. (1990) *State Theory*, Pennsylvania State University Press, Pennsylvania.
(2002) *The Future of the Capitalist State*, Polity Press, Cambridge.
Jewkes, Y. (2004) *Media and Crime*, Sage, London.
Jewson, N. (1976) 'The disappearance of the sick man from medical cosmology, 1770–1870', *Sociology*, vol. 10, pp. 225–44.
Jhally, S. and Lewis, J. (1992) *Enlightened Racism:* The Cosby Show, *Audiences, and the Myth of the American Dream*, Westview Press, Oxford.
Johnson, D. (1982) 'Families and educational institutions' in Rapoport *et al.* (eds) (1982).
Johnson, J.H. (1996) 'The real issues for reducing poverty' in M.R. Darby (ed.) *Reducing Poverty in America: Views and Approaches*, Sage, Thousand Oaks, CA.
Johnson, R. (1991) 'A new road to serfdom? A critical history of the 1988 Act' in Department of Cultural Studies, University of Birmingham, *Education Limited: Schooling and Training and the New Right since 1979*, Unwin Hyman, London.
Johnson, T.J. (1972) *Professions and Power*, Macmillan, London.
Johnstone, R., Pattie, C. and Rossiter, D. (2005) 'The election results in the UK regions' in Norris and Wlezien (eds) (2005).
Jones, K. (2003) *Education in Britain: 1944 to the Present*, Polity Press, Cambridge.
Jones, N. (1986) *Strikes and the Media: Communication and Conflict*, Blackwell, Oxford.
Jones, S. (1991) 'We are all cousins under the skin', *The Independent*, 12 December.
(1994) *The Language of the Genes*, Flamingo, London.
(1998) *Criminology*, Butterworths, London.
(ed.) (1999) *Doing Internet Research: Critical Issues and Methods for Examining the Net*, Sage, Thousand Oaks, CA.
(2001) *Criminology*, 2nd edn. Butterworths, London.
Jordan, B. (1989) 'Universal welfare provision creates a dependent population. The case against', *Social Studies Review*, November.
Jordan, S. and Yeomans, D. (1995) 'Critical ethnography: problems in contemporary theory and practice', *British Journal of Sociology of Education*, vol. 16, no. 3.
Jorgenson, J. (1991) 'Co-constructing the interviewer/co-constructing the family' in Steier (ed.) (1991).
Joshi, H., Wiggins, R.D., Bartley, M., Mitchell, R., Gleave, S. and Lynch, K. (2000) 'Putting health inequalities on the map: does where you live matter and why?' in H. Graham (ed.) *Understanding Health Inequalities*, Open University Press, Buckingham.
Jowell, R., Witherspoon, S. and Brook, L. (eds) (1989) *British Social Attitudes: Special International Report*, Gower, Aldershot.
Jowell, R., Curtice, J., Park, A., Brook, L., Thompson, K. and Bryson, C. (eds) (1998) *British Social Attitudes: The 15th Report*, Ashgate, Aldershot.
(2000) *British Social Attitudes, The 17th Report, Focussing on Diversity*, National Centre for Social Research, London.
Jupp, V. (2006) 'Comparative method' in Jupp (ed.) (2006).
(ed.) (2006) *The Sage Dictionary of Social Research Methods*, Sage, London.
Jupp, V. and Norris, C. (1993) 'Traditions in documentary analysis' in Hammersley (ed.) (1993).
Kamuf, P. (ed.) (1991) *A Derrida Reader: Between the Blinds*, Harvester Wheatsheaf, Hemel Hempstead.
Kaplan, A. (1964) *The Conduct of Inquiry*, Chandler Publishing, New York.
Karpf, A. (1988) *Doctoring the Media: The Reporting of Health and Medicine*, Routledge, London.
Kaspersen, L.B. (2000) *Anthony Giddens*, Blackwell, Oxford.
Katz, E. and Lazarsfeld, P. (1955) *Personal Influence: The Part Played by People in the Flow of Mass Communication*, Free Press, Glencoe, IL. (Quotations in the text are from the extract in Boyd-Barrett and Newbold (eds) (1995) and from the commentary by J. Curran, M. Gurevitch and J. Woollacott in the same volume.)
Katz, J. (1988) *Seductions of Crime*, Basic Books, New York.
Katz, J.E. and Sugiyama, S. (2005) 'Mobile phones as fashion statements: the co-creation of mobile communication's public meaning' in Ling and Pedersen (eds) (2005).
Kaur-Singh, K. (1994) 'Sikhism' in Holm and Bowker (eds) (1994).
Kautsky, K. (1953) *Foundations of Christianity*, Russell, New York.
Kavanagh, D. and Butler, D. (eds) (2005) *The British General Election of 2005*, Palgrave Macmillan, Basingstoke.
Kay, T. (1989) 'Unemployment' in Haralambos (ed.) (1989).
Keat, R. and Urry, J. (1982) *Social Theory as Science*, 2nd edn, Routledge & Kegan Paul, London.
Keddie, N. (1973) 'Classroom knowledge' in M. Young (ed.) *Tinker, Tailor – The Myth of Cultural Deprivation*, Penguin, Harmondsworth.
Keefe, J. and Hordley, M. (2002) 'Measuring unemployment', *Economics Today*, November.
Kellehear, A. (1990) *Dying of Cancer: The Final Year of Life*, Harwood, London.
Kellner, P. and Wilby, P. (1980) 'The 1: 2: 4 rule of class in Britain', *Sunday Times*, 13 January.
Kelly, A. (1987) *Science for Girls*, Open University Press, Milton Keynes.
Kelvin, P. and Jarrett, J.E. (1985) *Unemployment. Its Social Psychological Effects*, Cambridge University Press, Cambridge.
Kempson, E. (1996) *Life on a Low Income*, Joseph Rowntree Foundation, York.
Kendal Project (2001a) *Newsletter no. 1*, http.www.kendalproject.org.uk/
(2001b) *Newsletter no. 2*, http.www.kendalproject.org.uk/
(2002) *Newsletter no. 3*, http.www.kendalproject.org.uk/
Kepel, G. (1994) *The Revenge of God: The Resurgence of Islam, Christianity and Judaism in the Modern World*, Polity Press, Cambridge.
Kerr, C., Dunlop, J.T., Harbison, F.H. and Mayers, C.A. (1962) *Industrialism and Industrial Man*, Heinemann, London.
Kessler, S.J. and McKenna, W. (1978) *Gender: An Ethnomethodological Approach*, John Wiley & Sons, New York.
Keynes, J.M. (1936) *The General Theory of Employment, Interest and Money*, Macmillan, London.
Kincaid, J.C. (1973) *Poverty and Equality in Britain: A Study of Social Security and Taxation*, Penguin, Harmondsworth.
Kinsey, R., Lea, J. and Young, J. (1986) *Losing the Fight Against Crime*, Blackwell, Oxford.
Kiss, J. (2007) 'London takes Facebook capital crown', *Guardian*, 20 July.
Kitzinger, J. (1999) 'A sociology of media power: key issues in audience reception research' in G. Philo (ed.) *Message Received*, Longman, London.
Klein, N. (2000) *No Logo*, Flamingo, London.
Klineberg, O. (1971) 'Race and IQ', *Courier*, November.
Kling, R. (1991) 'Computerization and social transformations', *Science, Technology and Human Values*, vol. 16, no. 3.
(1992) 'Audiences, narratives and human values in social studies of technology', *Science, Technology and Human Values*, vol. 17, no. 3.
Kluckhohn, C. (1951) 'The concept of culture' in D. Lerner and H.D. Lasswell (eds) *The Policy Sciences*, Stanford University Press, Stanford.
Knutssen, J. (1977) *Labelling Theory: A Critical Examination Scientific Reference Group*, National Swedish Council for Crime Prevention, Stockholm.
Koffman, J., Phulop, N.J., Pashley, D. and Coleman, K. (1997) 'Ethnicity and the Issue of Psychiatric Beds: A One Day Survey in North and South Thames Regions', *British Journal of Psychiatry*, vol. 171, pp. 238–41.
Kuhn, T.S. (1962) *The Structure of Scientific Revolutions*, University of Chicago Press, Chicago and London.
Kumar, K. (1978) *Prophecy and Progress: The Sociology of Industrial and Post-Industrial Society*, Penguin, Harmondsworth.
Labov, W. (1973) 'The logic of nonstandard English' in N. Keddie (1973).
Lacan, J. (1977) *Écrits: A Selection*, Tavistock, London.
Lacey, N. (2002) *Media Institutions and Audiences: Key Concepts in Media Studies*, Palgrave, Basingstoke.
Lader, D., Short, S. and Gershuny, J. (2006) *The Time Use Survey 2005*, Office for National Statistics, London.
Laing, R.D. and Esterson, A. (1964) *Sanity, Madness and the Family*, Penguin, Harmondsworth.
(1970) *Sanity, Madness and the Family*, Penguin, Harmondsworth.
Lambert, J. *et al.* (1984) *The Image of the Elderly on TV*, University of the Third Age, Cambridge.
Lane, D. (1970) *Politics and Society in the USSR*, Weidenfeld & Nicolson, London.

(1976) *The Socialist Industrial State*, Allen & Unwin, London.
Lansley, S. (2006) *Rich Britain: The Rise and Rise of the New Super-Wealthy*, Politico's, London.
La Pierre, R.T. (1934) 'Attitudes versus actions', *Social Forces*, vol. 13.
Laqueur, T. (1990) *Making Sex: Body and Gender from the Greeks to Freud*, Harvard University Press, Cambridge, MA.
Larkin, C. (2004) 'The effects of taxes and benefits on household income 2002–03', *Economic Trends 2004*, no. 607, National Statistics, London.
Lash, S. (1990) *Sociology of Postmodernism*, Routledge, London.
(1999) *Another Modernity, a Different Rationality*, Blackwell, Oxford.
Lash, S. and Urry, J. (1994) *Economies of Signs and Space*, Sage, London.
Laslett, P. (1972) 'Mean household size in England since the sixteenth century' in P. Laslett (ed.) *Household and Family in Past Time*, Cambridge University Press, Cambridge.
(1977) *Family Life and Illicit Love in Earlier Generations*, Cambridge University Press, Cambridge.
(1983) 'Family and household as workgroup and kingroup' in R. Wall, J. Robin and P. Laslett (eds) *Family Forms in Historic Europe*, Cambridge University Press, Cambridge.
(1984) 'The family as a knot of individual interests' in R.M. Netting, R.R. Wilk and E.J. Arnould (eds) *Households*, University of California Press, Berkeley, CA.
(1989) *A Fresh Map of Life: The Emergence of the Third Age*, Weidenfeld & Nicolson, London.
Lather, P. (1986) 'Research as praxis', *Harvard Educational Review*, vol. 56, no. 3.
Lauder, H. (1997) 'Education, democracy and the economy' in Halsey *et al.* (eds) (1997).
Lauder, H., Hughes, D. *et al.* (1999) *Trading in Futures: Why Markets in Education Don't Work*, Open University Press, Buckingham.
Lauder, H., Brown, P., Dillabough, J. and Halsey, A.H. (2006) *Education, Globalization, and Social Change*, Oxford University Press, Oxford.
Laurie, H. and Gershuny, J. (2000) 'Couples, work and money' in Berthoud and Gershuny (eds) (2000).
Law, I. (1997) *Privilege and Silence: 'Race' in the British News during the General Election Campaign 1997*, University of Leeds, Leeds.
Lawler, J. (1991) *Behind the Screens: Nursing, Somology and the Problem of the Body*, Churchill Livingstone, Edinburgh.
Lawler, S. (2005) 'Introduction: class, culture and identity', *Sociology*, vol. 39, no. 5, pp. 797–806.
Lawrence, E. (1982) 'In the abundance of water the fool is thirsty: sociology and black pathology' in Centre for Contemporary Cultural Studies (1982).
(1982) 'Just plain common sense: the "roots" of racism' in Centre for Contemporary Cultural Studies (1982).
Lawrence, S.C. and Bendixen, K. (1992) 'His and hers: male and female anatomy in anatomy texts for US medical students 1890–1989', *Social Science and Medicine*, vol. 35, no. 7, pp. 925–34.
Lawrie, L. and Brown, R. (1992) 'Sex stereotypes, school subject preferences and career aspirations', *British Journal of Educational Psychology*, vol. 62.
Lawson, R. (1995) 'The challenge of "new" poverty: lessons from Europe and North America' in K. Funken and P. Cooper (eds) *Old and New Poverty: The Challenge for Reform*, Rivers Oram Press, London.
Lawton, D. (1989) *Education, Culture and the National Curriculum*, Hodder & Stoughton, London.
Lawton, J. (2000) *The Dying Process: Patients' Experiences of Palliative Care*, Routledge, London.
(2002) 'Contemporary hospice care: the sequestration of the unbounded body and "dirty dying" in England' in S. Nettleton and U. Gustaffson (eds) *The Sociology of Health and Illness*, Polity Press, Cambridge.
Layton-Henry, Z. (1992) *The Politics of Immigration*, Blackwell, Oxford.
Lea, J. (1992) 'The analysis of crime' in Young and Matthews (1992).
(1998) 'Criminology and postmodernity' in Walton and Young (eds) (1998).
Lea, J. and Young, J. (1984) *What is to be Done about Law and Order?* Penguin, Harmondsworth.
Leach, E. (1970) *Lévi-Strauss*, Fontana, London.
Leach, E.R. (1967) *A Runaway World?* BBC Publications, London.
Lee, D. and Newby, H. (1983) *The Problem of Sociology*, Hutchinson, London.
Lee, D.J. and Turner, B.S. (1996) 'Introduction: myths of classlessness and the "death" of class analysis' in Lee and Turner (eds) (1996).
(eds) (1996) *Conflicts about Class*, Longman, Harlow.
The Leeds Revolutionary Feminist Group (1982) 'Political lesbianism: the case against heterosexuality' in M. Evans (ed.) *The Woman Question*, Fontana, London.
Le Grand, J. (1982) *Strategy of Equality: Redistribution and the Social Services*, Allen & Unwin, London.
(1985) *Inequalities in Health: The Human Capital Approach*, Welfare State Programme Pamphlet No. 1, London School of Economics, London.
(1987) 'The middle-class use of the British social services' in R.E. Goodin and J. Le Grand, *Not Only the Poor*, Allen & Unwin, London.
Le Grand, J. and Bartlett, W. (eds) (1993) *Quasi Markets and Social Policy*, Macmillan, London.
Le Grand, J. and Levitas, R. (1998) *The Inclusive Society? Social Exclusion and New Labour*, Palgrave, Basingstoke.
Lehemann, P. and Wirtz, C. (2004) *Household Formation in the EU – Lone Parents*, Eurostat, Brussels.
Lemert, E.M. (1972) *Human Deviance, Social Problems, and Social Control*, 2nd edn, Prentice-Hall, Englewood Cliffs, NJ.
Lenin, V.I. (1969) *Selected Works*, Lawrence & Wishart, London.
Lerner, A. (1994) 'My generation', *Tikkun*, vol. 9, no. 2, pp. 56–8.
L'Esperance, J. (1977) 'Doctors, Women and Nineteenth Century Society: Sexuality and Role' in J. Woodwards and D. Richards (eds) *Health Care and Popular Medicine in Nineteenth Century England*, Croom Helm, London.
Levene, T. (2007) 'HSBC faced down on Facebook', *Guardian*, 1 September.
Levin, H.M. and Belfield, C.R. (2006) 'The marketplace in education' in Lauder *et al.* (eds) (2006).
Lévi-Strauss, C. (1963) *Structural Anthropology*, Penguin, Harmondsworth.
(1986, first published 1963) *The Raw and the Cooked*, Penguin, Harmondsworth.
Levitas, R. (1996) 'The legacy of Rayner' in Levitas and Guy (eds) (1996).
(1998) *The Inclusive Society? Social Exclusion and New Labour*, Macmillan, Basingstoke.
Levitas, R. and Guy, W. (eds) (1996) *Interpreting Official Statistics*, Routledge, London.
Levitas, R., Head, E. and Finch, N. (2006) 'Lone mothers, poverty and social exclusion' in Pantazis *et al.* (eds) (2006).
Levy, M.J. (1952) *The Structure of Society*, Princeton University Press, Princeton, NJ.
Lewis, L. (1990) 'Consumer girl culture' in M. Brown, *TV and Women's Culture*, Sage, London.
Lewis, O. (1959) *Five Families*, Basic Books, New York.
(1961) *The Children of Sanchez*, Random House, New York.
(1966) *La Vida*, Random House, New York.
Licht, B.G. and Dweck, C.S. (1987) 'Some differences in achievement orientations' in Arnot and Weiner (1987).
Liebow, E. (1967) *Tally's Corner*, Little Brown, Boston, MA.
Lincoln, S. (2004) 'Teenage girls' "bedroom culture": codes versus zones' in Bennett and Kahn-Harris (eds) (2004).
Ling, R. (1997) '"One can talk about common manners": the use of mobile telephones in inappropriate situations' in Haddon (ed.) (1997).
(2000) '"'It is in'. it doesn't matter if you need it or not, just that you have it": fashion and the domestication of the mobile'. http://www.telenor.no/fou/prosjecter/Fremitidens-E202000%20in.doc
Ling, R. and Pedersen, P. (eds) (2005) *Mobile Communications: The Re-negotiation of the Social Sphere*, Springer, London.
Linton, R. (1945) 'Present world conditions in cultural perspective' in R. Linton (ed.) *The Science of Man in World Crisis*, Columbia University Press, New York.
Lipset, S.M. (1981, first published 1959) *Political Man*, Johns Hopkins University Press, Baltimore, MD.
Lister, R. (1995) 'Women in poverty' in K. Funken and P. Cooper (eds) *Old and New Poverty: The Challenge for Reform*, Rivers Oram Press, London.
(1996) 'Back to the family: family policies and politics under the Major government' in H. Jones and J. Millar (eds) *The Politics of the Family*, Avebury, Aldershot.
(2001) 'Towards a citizen's welfare state: the 3 + 2 "R"s of welfare reform', *Theory, Culture and Society*, vol. 18, no. 2.
(2004) *Poverty*, Polity, Cambridge.
Littler, C. (1983) 'Deskilling and changing structures of control' in S. Wood (ed.) *The Degradation of Work? Skill, Deskilling and the Labour Process*, Hutchinson, London..

Littler, C.R. and Salaman, G. (1984) *Class at Work*, Batsford, London.
Livingstone, S. and Bovill, M. (eds) (2001) *Children and Their Changing Media Environment: A European Comparative Study*, Lawrence Erlbaum, London.
Lobban, G. (1974) 'Data report on British reading schemes', *Times Educational Supplement*, 1 March.
Lobstein, T. (1995) 'The Increasing Cost of a Healthy Diet', *Food Magazine*, vol. 31, p. 17.
Lockwood, D. (1958) *The Blackcoated Worker*, Allen & Unwin, London.
(1970) 'Some remarks on "The social system"' in P. Worsley (ed.) *Modern Sociology: Introductory Readings*, Penguin, Harmondsworth.
(1982, first published 1966) 'Sources of variation in working class images of society' in A. Giddens and D. Held (eds) *Classes, Power and Conflict*, Macmillan, London.
(1988) 'The weakest link in the chain' in D. Rose (ed.) *Economic Change and Social Stratification*, Hutchinson, London.
Lombroso, C. (1876) *L'Uomo Delinquente*, Hoepli, Milan.
Lombroso, C. and Ferrero, W. (1958) *The Female Offender*, Philosophical Library, New York.
London Chamber of Commerce (2006) *Corporate Leadership*, London Chamber of Commerce, London.
Longmore, F. (1987) 'Screening stereotypes: images of disabled people in TV and motion pictures' in A. Gartner and T. Foe (eds) *Images of the Disabled, Disabling Images*, Praeger, New York.
Lovenduski, J. (2001) 'Women and politics: minority representation of critical mass?' in Norris (ed.) (2001).
Lovering, J. (1994) 'Employers, the sex-typing of jobs, and economic restructuring' in A.M. Scott (ed.) (1994).
Lukes, S. (1974) *Power: A Radical View*, Macmillan, London.
(2006) *Power: A Radical View*, 2nd edn, Palgrave Macmillan, Basingstoke.
Lull, J. (1990) *Inside Family Viewing: Ethnographic Research on Television's Audiences*, Routledge, London.
Lupton, T. and Wilson, C.S. (1973) 'The social background and connections of "top decision makers"' in Urry and Wakeford (eds) (1973).
Lynch, M. (1983) *Art and Artefact in Laboratory Science*, Routledge & Kegan Paul, London.
Lynch, M. and Stretsky, P. (2003) 'The meaning of green: contrasting criminological perspectives', *Theoretical Criminology*, vol. 7, no. 2, pp. 217–38.
Lynch, P. (2006) 'The challenges for Cameron', *Politics Review*, September.
Lyng, S. (1990) 'Edgework: a social-pyschological analysis of voluntary risk taking', *American Journal of Sociology*, vol. 95, no. 4, pp. 887–921.
Lyon, D. (1996) 'Religion and the postmodern, old problems, new prospects' in K. Flanagan and P. Jupp (eds) *Postmodernity, Sociology and Religion*, Macmillan, Basingstoke.
(2000) *Jesus in Disneyland: Religion in Postmodern Times*, Polity Press, Cambridge.
Lyotard, J.F. (1984) *The Postmodern Condition*, Manchester University Press, Manchester.
Mac an Ghaill (see under Ghaill).
McCabe, B.A. and Martin, G.M. (2005) *School Violence, the Media and Criminal Justice Responses*, Peter Lang, New York.
McClintock, P. (2007) '"Transformers" change weekend take', *Variety*, 9 July. http://www.variety.com/article/VR1117968252.html?categoryid=13&cs=1
McCrone, D. (1998) *The Sociology of Nationalism*, Routledge, London.
Macdonald, D. (1957) 'A theory of mass culture' in Rosenberg and White (eds) (1957).
Macdonald, K. (1997) *The Sociology of the Professions*, Sage, London.
MacDonald, R., Shildrick, T. and Cieslik, M. (2004) 'The sociology of youth' in Holborn (ed.) (2004).
McDonough, F. (1997) 'Class and politics' in M. Storry and P. Childs (eds) *British Cultural Identities*, Routledge, London.
McDonough, R. and Harrison, R. (1978) 'Patriarchy relations of production' in A. Kuhn and A.M. Wolpe (eds) *Feminism and Materialism*, Routledge & Kegan Paul, London.
McDowell, L. (1992) 'Gender divisions in a post-Fordist era: new contradictions or the same old story?' in M. McDowell and R. Pringle (eds) *Defining Women: Social Institutions and Gender Divisions*, Polity Press, Cambridge.
McGlone, F., Park, A. and Roberts, C. (1996) 'Relative values: kinship and friendship' in R. Jowell *et al.* (eds) *British Social Attitudes: The 13th Report*, Dartmouth, Aldershot.
McGlone, F., Park, A. and Smith, K. (1998) *Families and Kinship*, Family Policy Studies Centre, London.
McGuire, M.B. (1981) *Religion, the Social Context*, Wadsworth Publishing, California.
Machin, S. and McNally, S. (2006) *Gender and School Achievement in English Schools*, Centre for the Economics of Education, London.
MacInnes, J. (1987) *Thatcherism at Work*, Open University Press, Milton Keynes.
McIntosh, M. (1996) 'Social anxieties about lone motherhood and ideologies of the family: two sides of the same coin' in E.B. Silva (ed.) *Good Enough Mothering: Feminine Perspectives on Lone Motherhood*, Routledge, London.
MacIntyre, S. (1993) 'Gender differences in the perceptions of common cold symptoms', *Social Science and Medicine*, Blackwell, Oxford.
Macionis, J.J. and Plummer, K. (1997) *Sociology: A Global Introduction*, Prentice-Hall, NJ.
Mack, J. and Lansley, S. (1985) *Poor Britain*, Allen & Unwin, London.
(1992) *Breadline Britain 1990s, the Findings of the Television Series*, London Weekend Television, London.
McKay, J. (1982) 'Primordial and mobilisationist approaches to ethnic phenomena', *Ethnic and Racial Studies*.
McKenzie, R.T. (1969) 'Parties, pressure groups and the British political process' in R. Rose (ed.) *Studies in British Politics*, 2nd edn, Macmillan, London.
McKenzie, R.T. and Silver, A. (1968) *Angels in Marble*, Heinemann, London.
(1972) 'The working class Tory in England' in P. Worsley (ed.) *Problems of Modern Society*, Penguin, Harmondsworth.
MacKenzie, W.J.M. (1969) 'Pressure groups in British Government' in Rose (ed.) (1969).
McKeown, T. (1979) *The Role of Medicine*, Blackwell, Oxford.
McKie, L. and Chunningham-Burley, S. (eds) (2005) *Families in Societies: Boundaries and Relationships*, Policy Press, Bristol.
McKinlay, J. (1974) 'The case for refocusing upstream: the political economy of illness' quoted in Ehrenreich (ed.) (1978).
McKinlay, J. and Arches, J. (1985) 'Towards proletarianization of physicians', *International Journal of Health Sciences*, vol. 15, pp. 161–95.
McKnight, A. (2002) 'Low-paid work: drip-feeding the poor' in Hills *et al.* (eds) (2002).
(2005) 'Employment' in Hills and Stewart (eds) (2005).
McKnight, A. Glennerster, H. and Lupton, R. (2005) 'Education, education, education … : an assessment of Labour's success in tackling educational inequalities' in Hills and Stewart (eds) (2005).
McLanahan, S. and Booth, K. (1991) 'Mother-only families' in A. Booth (ed.) *Contemporary Families*, National Council on Family Relations, Minneapolis, MN.
McLaughlin, E. (2001) 'Political violence, terrorism and states of fear' in J. Muncie and E. McLaughlin (eds) *The Problem of Crime*, 2nd edn, Sage, London.
McLennan, G. (1989) *Marxism, Pluralism and Beyond*, Polity Press, Cambridge.
McLuhan, M. (1964) *Understanding Media: The Extensions of Man*, New American Library, New York.
MacNeil, C. (1990) 'The National Curriculum: a Black perspective' in B. Moon (ed.) *New Curriculum – National Curriculum*, Hodder & Stoughton, London.
McNeill, P.A. (1985) Research Methods, Tavistock, London.
(1988) 'Chronicle of crime: an interview with Pat Mayhew', *New Statesman and Society*, 9 December.
Macpherson, Sir W. (1999) *The Stephen Lawrence Inquiry*, Stationery Office, London.
McQuail, D. (1972) *The Sociology of Mass Communications*, Penguin, Harmondsworth.
McRobbie, A. (1978) 'Working class girls and the culture of femininity' in Centre for Contemporary Cultural Studies (1978).
(1991) 'Romantic individualism and the teenage girl', reprinted in A. McRobbie, *Feminism and Youth Culture*, Macmillan, London.
(1994) *Postmodernism and Popular Culture*, Routledge, London.
McRobbie, A. and Garber, J. (1976) 'Girls and subcultures' in Hall and Jefferson (eds) (1976).
McRobbie, A. and Thornton, S. (1995) 'Rethinking "moral panic" for multi-mediated social worlds', *British Journal of Sociology*, vol. 46, pp. 559–74.
Madanipour, A. (1998) 'Social exclusion and space' in Madanipour *et al.* (eds) (1998).
Madanipour, A., Cars, G. and Allen, J. (1998) *Social Exclusion in European Cities*, Jessica Kingsley, London.
Madge, N. (2006) *Children These Days*, Policy Press, Bristol.

Maduro, O. (1982) *Religion and Social Conflicts*, Orbis Books, New York.

Maffesoli, M. (1996) *The Time of the Tribes: The Decline of Individualism in Mass Society*, Sage, London.

Maguire, M. (2002) 'Crime statistics: The 'data explosion' and its implications' in Maguire *et al.* (eds) (2002).

Maguire, M., Morgan, R. and Reiner, R. (eds) (1997) *The Oxford Handbook of Criminology*, 2nd edn, Clarendon Press, Oxford.
(2002) *The Oxford Handbook of Criminology*, 3rd edn, Oxford University Press, Oxford.

Malik, K. (1996) *The Meaning of Race*, Macmillan, Basingstoke.

Malik, S. (2002) *Representing Black Britain*, Sage, London.

Malinowski, B. (1954) *Magic, Science and Religion and Other Essays*, Anchor Books, New York.

Mangin, W. (1968) 'Poverty and politics in cities of Latin America' in W. Bloomberg and H.J. Schmandt, *Urban Poverty: Its Social and Political Dimensions*, Sage, Beverly Hills, CA.

Mankoff, M. (1976) 'Introduction to perspectives on the problem of crime' in W.J. Chambliss and M. Mankoff (1976).

Mann, K. (1992) *The Making of an English Underclass*, Open University Press, Milton Keynes.

Mann, M. (1973) *Consciousness and Action among the Western Working Class*, Macmillan, London.
(1986) *The Sources of Social Power*, vol. 1, Cambridge University Press, Cambridge.
(1993) *The Sources of Social Power*, vol. 2, Cambridge University Press, Cambridge.

Mannheim, H. (1960) *Comparative Criminology*, Routledge & Kegan Paul, London.

Mannheim, K. (1948) *Ideology and Utopia*, Routledge & Kegan Paul, London.

Manning, A. and Swaffield, J. (2005) *The Gender Gap in Early-Career Wage Growth*, London School of Economics Centre for Economic Performance, London.

Marcuse, H. (1964) *One Dimensional Man*, Routledge & Kegan Paul, London.

Marsh, D. (ed.) (1983) *Pressure Politics*, Junction Books, London.

Marsh, D. and Locksley, G. (1983) 'Labour: the dominant force in British politics?' in Marsh (ed.) (1983).

Marshall, G. (1982) *In Search of the Spirit of Capitalism: Max Weber and the Protestant Ethic Thesis*, Hutchinson, London.
(1990) 'John Goldthorpe and class analysis' in J. Clark *et al.* (eds) *John H. Goldthorpe: Consensus and Controversy*, Falmer Press, Basingstoke.
(1997) *Repositioning Class: Social Inequality in Industrial Societies*, Sage, London.

Marshall, G. and Swift, A. (1993) 'Social class and social justice', *British Journal of Sociology*, June.
(1996) 'Merit and mobility: a reply to Peter Saunders', *Sociology*, vol. 30, no. 2, pp. 375–86.

Marshall, G., Newby, H., Rose, D. and Vogler, C. (1988) *Social Class in Modern Britain*, Hutchinson, London.

Marshall, T.H. (1950) *Citizenship and Social Class*, Cambridge University Press, Cambridge.
(2000, first published 1950) 'Citizenship and social class' in Pierson and Castles (eds) (2000).

Marsland, D. (1989) 'Universal welfare provision creates a dependent population. The case for', *Social Studies Review*, November.
(1992) 'The roots and consequences of paternalistic collectivism', *Social Policy and Administration*, vol. 26, no. 2, pp. 144–50.
(1996) *Welfare or Welfare State? Contradictions and Dilemmas in Social Policy*, Macmillan, London.

Martin, C. and McQueen D. (eds) (2000) *Readings for a New Public Health*, Edinburgh University Press, Edinburgh.

Martin, C.J., Platt, S.D. and Hunt, S. (1987) 'Housing Conditions and Health', *British Medical Journal*, vol. 294, pp. 1125–7.

Martin, D. (1967) *A Sociology of English Religion*, Heinemann, London.
(1969) *The Religious and the Secular*, Routledge & Kegan Paul, London.
(1978) *A General Theory of Secularisation*, Blackwell, Oxford.
(1991a) *Tongues of Fire: The Explosion of Protestantism in Latin America*, Blackwell, Oxford.
(1991b) 'The secularisation issue: prospect and retrospect', *British Journal of Sociology*, vol. 42, no. 3.

Marx, K. (1964, first published in the 1840s) *The Economic and Philosophical Manuscripts*, International Publishers, New York.
(1974, first published 1909) *Capital*, vol. 3, Lawrence & Wishart, London.
(1978, first published 1867) *Capital*, vol. 1, Penguin, Harmondsworth.
See also under Bottomore and Rubel, and McLellan.

Marx, K and Engels, F. (1950a, first published 1848) 'Manifesto of the Communist Party' in K. Marx and F. Engels, *Selected Works*, vol. 1, Foreign Languages Publishing House, Moscow.
(1950b) *Selected Works*, vol. 2, Foreign Languages Publishing House, Moscow
(1957) *On Religion*, Progress Publishers, Moscow.
(1970, first published 1846) *The German Ideology*, International Publishers, New York.

Mason, D. (1982) 'After Scarman, a note on the concept of institutional racism', *New Community*, Summer.

Matthews, R. (1992) 'Replacing "broken windows": crime, incivilities and urban change' in Matthews and Young (eds) (1992).
(1993) 'Squaring up to crime', *Sociology Review*, vol. 2, no. 3.

Matthews, R. and Young, J. (1992) 'Reflections on realism' in Young and Matthews (eds) (1992).
(eds) (1992) *Issues in Realist Criminology*, Sage, London.

Matza, D. (1964) *Delinquency and Drift*, John Wiley & Sons, New York.
(1969) *Becoming Deviant*, Prentice Hall, Englewood Cliffs, NJ.

Mawby, R.I. and Batta, I.D. (1980) 'Asians and crime: the Bradford experience', Scope Communication, London.

May, T. (2001) *Social Research: Issues, Methods and Process*, 3rd edn, Open University Press, Buckingham.

Mayall, B. (ed.) (1994) *Children's Childhoods Observed and Experienced*, Falmer, London.
(2004) 'Sociologies of childhood' in Holborn (ed.) (2004).

Mayhew, P. and Aye Maung, N. (1992) *Surveying Crime, Findings from the 1992 British Crime Survey*, Home Office Research and Statistics Department, London.

Mayhew, P., Elliot, D. and Dowds, L. (1989) *The 1988 British Crime Survey*, HMSO, London.

Mayo, E. (1933) *The Human Problems of an Industrial Civilization*, Macmillan, New York.

Mead, G.H. (1934) *Mind, Self and Society*, edited by C. Morris, University of Chicago Press, Chicago.

Mead, M. and Wolfenstein, M. (eds) (1955) *Childhood in Contemporary Cultures*, University of Chicago Press, Chicago.

Mechanic, D. (1968) *Medical Sociology*, Free Press, New York.

Media Matters (2007) 'Sunday shutout: the lack of gender and ethnic diversity on the Sunday morning talk shows'. http://mediamatters.org/SundayShowDiversity

Medved, M. (1992) *Hollywood vs. America*, HarperCollins, London.

Meehan, E.R. and Riordan, E. (eds) (2001) *Sex and Money: Feminism and Political Economy in the Media*, University of Minnesota Press, Minneapolis.

Meldrumm, M. *et al.* (2005) 'The role of occupation in the development of chronic obstructive pulmonary disease (COPD)', *Occupational and Environmental Medicine*, vol. 62, pp. 212–14.

Meltzer, B.N., Petras, J.W. and Reynolds, L.T. (1975) *Symbolic Interactionism*, Routledge & Kegan Paul, London.

Mennell, S. (1974) *Sociological Theory*, Nelson, London.

Merton, R. (1946) *Mass Persuasion*, NYFP.

Merton, R.K. (1968) *Social Theory and Social Structure*, enlarged edn, Free Press, New York.

Messerschmidt, J.M. (1993) *Masculinities and Crime: Critique and Reconceptualization of Theory*, Rowman & Littlefield, Lanham, MD.

Meyer, A.G. (1965) *The Soviet Political System*, Random House, New York.

Mhlanga, B. (1999) *Race and Crown Prosecution Service Decisions*, Stationery Office, London.

Microsoft monopoly court case Findings of Fact: www.usdoj.gov/atr/cases/f3800/msjudgex.htm.

Midwinter, E. (1975) 'The community school' in J. Rushton and J.D. Turner (eds) *Education and Deprivation*, Manchester University Press, Manchester.

Mies, M. (1986) *Patriarchy and Accumulation on a World Scale*, Zed Books, London.
(1993) 'Towards a methodology for feminist research' in Hammersley (ed.) (1993).

Miles, A. (1981) *The Mentally Ill in Contemporary Society*, Martin Robertson, Oxford.

Miles, I. and Irvine, J. (1979) 'The critique of official statistics' in Irvine *et al.* (eds) (1979).

Miles, R. (1989) *Racism*, Routledge, London.
(1993) *Racism after Race Relations*, Routledge, London.

Miliband, R. (1969) *The State in Capitalist Society*, Weidenfeld & Nicolson, London.
(1972) 'Poulantzas and the capitalist state', *New Left Review*, no. 82.

(1974) 'Politics and poverty' in D. Wedderburn (ed.) *Poverty, Inequality and Class Structure*, Cambridge University Press, Cambridge.
(1977) *Marxism and Politics*, Oxford University Press, Oxford.
Milkman, R. (1997) *Farewell to the Factory: Auto Workers in the Late Twentieth Century*, University of California Press, Berkeley.
Mill, J.S. and Taylor, H. (1974, first published 1869) *The Subjection of Women*, Oxford University Press, Oxford.
Millar, J. and Glendinning, C. (1989) 'Gender and Poverty', *Journal of Social Policy*, vol. 18, no. 3, pp. 363–81.
Millar, J. and Glendinning, C. (1992) '"It all really starts in the family": gender divisions and poverty' in C. Glendinning and J. Millar (eds) *Women and Poverty in Britain: the 1990s*, Harvester Wheatsheaf, Hemel Hempstead.
Miller, A.S. and Hoffman, J.P. (1995) 'Risk and religion: an explanation of gender differences in religion', *Journal for the Scientific Study of Religion*, vol. 34, no. 1.
Miller, N.E. and Dollard, J. (1941) *Social Learning Theory and Imitation*, Yale University Press, New Haven, CN.
Miller, S.M. and Roby, P. (1970) 'Poverty: changing social stratification' in Townsend (ed.) (1970).
Miller, W.B. (1962) 'Lower class culture as a generating milieu of gang delinquency' in M.E. Wolfgang *et al.* (eds) *The Sociology of Crime and Delinquency*, John Wiley & Sons, New York.
Millerson, G.L. (1964) *The Qualifying Association*, Routledge, London.
Millett, K. (1970) *Sexual Politics*, Doubleday, New York.
Mills, C. (1995) 'Managerial and professional work-histories' in Butler and Savage (eds) (1995).
Mills, C.W. (1951) *White Collar: The American Middle Classes*, Oxford University Press, New York.
(1956) *The Power Elite*, Oxford University Press, New York.
(1959) *The Sociological Imagination*, Oxford University Press, New York.
Mingione, E. (1996) *Urban Poverty and the Underclass: A Reader*, Blackwell, Oxford.
Mirrlees-Black, C., Budd, T., Partridge, S. and Mayhew, P. (1998) *The 1998 British Crime Survey*, Home Office Information and Publications Group, London.
Mirza, H. (1992) *Young, Female and Black*, Routledge, London.
(1997) 'Introduction: mapping a genealogy of Black British feminism' in Mirza (ed.) (1997).
(ed.) (1997) *Black British Feminism: A Reader*, Routledge, London.
Mitsos, E. and Browne, K. (1998) 'Gender differences in education: the underachievement of boys', *Sociology Review*, vol. 8, no. 1.
Modood, T. (1997) 'Employment' and 'Culture and identity' in Modood *et al.* (1997).
(1997) 'Qualifications and English language' in Modood *et al.* (1997).
(2004) 'Capitals, ethnic identity and educational qualifications', *Cultural Trends*, vol. 13, no. 2, pp. 87–105.
(2006) 'Ethnicity, Muslims and higher education entry in Britain', *Teaching in Higher Education*, vol. 11, no. 2, pp. 247–50.
Modood, T., Beishon, S. and Virdee, S. (1994) *Changing Ethnic Identities*, PSI, London.
Modood, T., Berthoud, R. *et al.* (1997) *Ethnic Minorities in Britain: Diversity and Disadvantage*, PSI, London.
Moir, A. and Jessel, D. (1997) *A Mind to Crime: The Controversial Link between Mind and Criminal Behaviour*, Signet, London.
Mooney, J. (1965) *The Ghost-Dance Religion and the Sioux Outbreak of 1890*, Phoenix Books, Chicago.
(1998) 'Moral panics and the New Right: single mothers and feckless fathers – is this really the key to the crime problem?' in Walton and Young (eds) (1998).
Morawski, S. (1974) 'Introduction' in Baxandall and Morawski (eds) (1974).
Morgan, D. (2006) 'Focus groups' in Jupp (ed.) (2006).
Morgan, D.H.J. (1975) *Social Theory and the Family*, Routledge & Kegan Paul, London.
(1986) 'Gender' in R. Burgess (ed.) *Key Variables in Social Investigation*, Routledge & Kegan Paul, London
(1994) 'The family' in Haralambos (ed.) (1994)
(1996) *Family Connections: An Introduction to Family Studies*, Polity Press, Cambridge.
(1999) 'Risk and family practices: accounting for change and fluidity in family life' in Silva and Smart (eds) (1999).
Morgan, M., Calnan, M. and Manning, N. (1985) *Sociological Approaches to Health and Medicine*, Routledge, London.
Morgan, P. (1995) *Farewell to the Family?* Institute for Economic Affairs, London.
(2003) 'The family today' in Holborn (ed.) (2003).
Morley, D. (1980) *The Nationwide Audience*, British Film Institute, London.
(1986) *Family Television*, Comedia, London.
(1992) *Television Audiences and Cultural Studies*, Routledge, London.
Morris, L. (1994) *Dangerous Classes: The Underclass and Social Citizenship*, Routledge, London.
(2002) *Managing Migration: Civic Stratification and Migrants' Rights*, Routledge, London.
Morris, N. (2003) 'Blunkett accused of manipulating falling figures', *Independent*, 23 May.
Mosca, G. (1939) *The Ruling Class*, McGraw-Hill, New York.
Moynihan, R. and Smith, R. (2002) 'Too much medicine? Almost certainly', *British Medical Journal*, vol. 324, pp. 859–60.
Muggleton, D. (2000) *Inside Subculture: The Postmodern Meaning of Style*, Berg, Oxford.
Muggleton, D. and Weinzierl, R. (eds) (2003) *The Post-Subcultures Reader*, Berg, Oxford.
Murdock, G.P. (1949) *Social Structure*, Macmillan, New York.
Murray, C. (1984) *Losing Ground*, Basic Books, New York.
(1989) 'Underclass', *Sunday Times Magazine*, 26 November.
(1994) *Underclass: The Crisis Deepens*, IEA, London.
(2001) *Underclass + 10*, Institute for the Study of Civil Society, London.
Nash, K. (2000) *Contemporary Political Sociology: Globalization, Politics and Power*, Blackwell, Oxford.
National Statistics (2006) 'Internet access'. http://www.statistics.gov.uk/cci/nugget.asp?id=8
(2007a) 'Use of ICT at home'. http://www.statistics.gov.uk/cci/nugget.asp?id=1710
(2007b) 'Use of the internet'. http://www.statistics.gov.uk/CCI/nugget.asp?ID=1711&Pos=2&ColRank=1&Rank=160
Nava, M. and Nava, O. (1990) 'Discriminating or duped?' *Cultural Studies*, vol. 1, pp. 15–21.
Navarro, V. (1977) *Medicine under Capitalism*, Martin Robertson, London.
(1978) *Class, Struggle, the State and Medicine*, Martin Robertson, London. (1980) 'Work, ideology and science: the case of medicine', *Social Science and Medicine*, vol. 14A, pp. 231–7.
(1986) *Crisis, Health and Medicine*, Tavistock, London.
Nazroo, D.Y. (1997) *The Health of London's Minorities*, Policy Studies Institute, London.
Nazroo, J. (2006) 'Ethnicity and old age' in Vincent *et al.* (eds) (2006).
Nazroo, J., Edwards, A. and Brown, G. (1998) 'Gender differences in the prevalence of depression: artefact, alternative disorders, biology or roles', *Sociology of Health and Illness*, vol. 20, pp. 312–30.
Needham, R. (1963) 'Introduction' in Durkheim and Mauss (1963).
Nelken, D. (2002) 'White-collar crime' in Maguire *et al.* (eds) (2002).
Nelson, G.K. (1986) 'Religion' in M. Haralambos (ed.) *Developments in Sociology*, vol. 2, Causeway Press, Ormskirk.
Nelson, H.L. (ed.) (1997) *Feminism and Families*, Routledge, New York.
Nettleton, S. (1995) *The Sociology of Health and Illness*, Polity Press, Cambridge.
New Earnings Survey 2005, National Statistics, London (available online).
Newburn, T. and Stanko, E. (1994) 'Men, masculinity and crime' in Newburn and Stanko (eds) (1994).
(eds) (1994) *Just Boys Doing Business: Men, Masculinities and Crime*, Routledge, London.
Newson, E. (1994) *Video Violence and the Protection of Children*, Broadcasting Standards Research Monographs, London.
NHS Information Centre (2006) 'Statistics on obesity, physical activity and diet: England, 2006'. http://www.ic.nhs.uk/pubs/obesity/opan06/file
Nicholas, S., Kershaw, C. and Walker, A. (2007) *Crime in England and Wales 2006/7*, Home Office Statistical Bulletin, London.
Nichols, T. (1996) 'Social class: official, sociological and Marxist' in Levitas and Guy (eds) (1996).
Nichols, T. and Beynon, H. (1977) *Living with Capitalism*, Routledge & Kegan Paul, London.
(1979) 'Social class: official, sociological and Marxist' in Irvine *et al.* (eds) (1979).
Nicholson, J. (1993) *Men and Women: How Different Are They?* Oxford University Press, Oxford.
Nicholson, L. (1997) 'The myth of the traditional family' in H.L. Marsh (ed.) *Feminism and Families*, Routledge, New York.

Niebuhr, H.R. (1929) *The Social Sources of Denominationalism*, Shoe String Press, Connecticut.
Nisbet, R.A. (1967) *The Sociological Tradition*, Heinemann, London.
Noble, G. (1975) *Children in Front of the Small Screen*, Constable, London.
Nolan, B. and Whelan, C.T. (1996) *Resources, Deprivation and Poverty*, Clarendon Press, Oxford.
Nord Anglia (2007) www.nordanglia.com
Nordlinger, E.A. (1966) (1981) *On the Autonomy of the Democratic State*, Harvard University Press, Cambridge, MA.
Norman, F., Turner, S., Granados, J., Schwarez, H., Green, H. and Harris, J. (1988) 'Look, Jane, look: anti-sexist initiatives in primary schools' in G. Weiner (ed.) *Just a Bunch of Girls*, Open University Press, Milton Keynes.
Norris, P. (1997) 'Anatomy of a Labour landslide', *Parliamentary Affairs*, vol. 50.
(1999a) 'New politicians? Changes in party competition at Westminster' in Evans and Norris (eds) (1999).
(1999b) 'Gender: a generation gap?' in Evans and Norris (eds) (1999).
(ed.) (2001) *Britain Votes 2001*, Oxford University Press, Oxford.
Norris, P. and Evans, G. (1999a) 'Introduction: understanding electoral change' in Evans and Norris (eds) (1999).
(1999b) 'Conclusion: was 1997 a critical election?' in Evans and Norris (eds) (1999).
Norris, P. and Wlezien, C. (eds) (2005) *Britain Votes 2005*, Oxford University Press, Oxford.
(2005) 'Conclusions' in Norris and Wlezien (eds) (2005).
Nozick, R. (1974) *Anarchy, State and Utopia*, Blackwell, Oxford.
Nuttall, C. and Waters, R. (2007) 'Hirings soar, profits fall … but it's just "Google being Google"', *The Financial Times*, 23 July.
Oakley, A. (1972) *Sex, Gender and Society*, Temple Smith, London.
(1974) *Housewife*, Allen Lane, London.
(1974) *The Sociology of Housework*, Martin Robertson, Oxford.
(1981) 'Interviewing women: a contradiction in terms' in Roberts (ed.) (1981).
(1981) *Subject Women*, Martin Robertson, Oxford.
(1982) 'Conventional families' in Rapoport *et al.* (eds) (1982).
(1994) 'Parallels and differences between children's and women's studies' in Mayall (ed.) (1994).
(2002) *Gender on Planet Earth*, Polity Press, Cambridge.
Oakley, A. and Oakley, R. (1979) 'Sexism in official statistics' in Irvine *et al.* (eds) (1979).
Oakley, R. (1982) 'Cypriot families' in Rapoport *et al.* (eds) (1982).
O'Brien, M. and Jones, D. (1996) 'Revisiting family and kinship', *Sociology Review*, February.
Observer (2001) 'Race in Britain: the 2001 *Observer* poll', *Observer Race in Britain Special Edition*, 25 November.
Ofcom (2006a) Media Literacy Audit: Report on media literacy amongst children. http://www.ofcom.org.uk/advice/media_literacy/medlitpub/medlitpubrss/children/children.pdf
(2006b) The Communications Market 2006 Overview. http://www.ofcom.org.uk/research/cm/cm06/overview06/consumer/
(2007) The Communications Market 2007 Key Points. http://www.ofcom.org.uk/research/cm/cmr07/cm07_print/cm07_1.pdf
Ogden, J. (1992) *Fat Chance: The Myth of Dieting Explained*, Routledge, London.
Ohmae, K. (1994) *The Borderless World*, HarperCollins, London.
Oliver, M. (1990) *The Politics of Disablement*, Macmillan, Basingstoke.
ONS (2001) *The Time Use Survey 2000*, Office for National Statistics, London.
Oppenheim, C. (1997) 'The growth of poverty and inequality' in Walker and Walker (eds) (1997).
Oppenheim, C. and Harker, L. (1996) *Poverty: The Facts*, 3rd edn, CPAG, London.
Ortner, S.B. (1974) 'Is female to male as nature is to culture?' in M.Z. Rosaldo and L. Lamphere (eds) *Woman, Culture and Society*, Stanford University Press, Stanford, CA.
O'Toole, R. (1984) *Religion: Classic Sociological Approaches*, McGraw Hill, Toronto.
Page, R.M. (2002) 'New Labour and the welfare state' in Holborn (ed.) (2003).
(2005) 'Labour governments and the welfare state: past and present' in Holborn (ed.) (2005).
Pahl, R. (1984) *Divisions of Labour*, Blackwell, Oxford.
(1989) *Money and Marriage*, Macmillan, Basingstoke.
(1993) 'Money, marriage and ideology: holding the purse strings', *Sociology Review*, September.
Pakulski, J. and Waters, M. (1996) *The Death of Class*, Sage, London.
Palmer, G., Carr, J. and Kenway, P. (2005) *Monitoring Poverty and Social Exclusion in Britain 2005*, Joseph Rowntree Foundation, York.
Pamuk, E.R. (1985) 'Social Class Inequality in Mortality from 1921 to 1972 in England and Wales', *Population Studies*, vol. 39, pp. 17–31.
Pantazis, C. and Gordon, D. (eds) (2000) *Tackling Inequalities: Where Are We Now and What Can be Done?* Policy Press, Bristol.
Pantazis, C., Gordon, D. and Levitas, R. (eds) (2006) *Poverty and Social Exclusion in Britain*, Policy Press, Bristol.
Parekh, B., *et al.* (2000) *The Future of Multi-Ethnic Britain: Report of the Commission on the Future of Multi-Ethnic Britain, The Parekh Report*, Profile Books, London.
Pareto, V. (1963) *A Treatise on General Sociology*, edited by A. Livingstone, Dover Publications, New York.
Park, A. (ed.) (2001) *British Social Attitudes Survey*, Sage, London.
Park, A., Curtice, J., Thompson, K., Jarvis, L. and Bromley, C. (eds) (2001) *British Social Attitudes: The 18th Report, Public Policy, Social Ties*, Sage, London.
Park, R.E. (1950) *Race and Culture*, Free Press, Glencoe.
Parker, H.J. (1974) *View from the Boys*, David & Charles, Newton Abbot.
Parker, R. (1982) 'Families and social policy: an overview' in Rapoport *et al.* (eds) (1982).
Parker, S. (1976) 'Work and leisure' in E. Butterworth and D. Weir, *The Sociology of Leisure*, Allen & Unwin, London.
Parkin, F. (1968) *Middle-Class Radicalism*, Manchester University Press, Manchester.
(1972) *Class Inequality and Political Order*, Paladin, St Albans.
(1977) Review of 'Class in a capitalist society' by J. Westergaard and H. Resler, *British Journal of Sociology*, March.
Parry, G. (1969) *Political Elites*, Allen & Unwin, London.
Parry, N. and Parry, J. (1976) *The Rise of the Medical Profession*, Croom Helm, London.
(1977) 'Social closure and collective social mobility' in Scase (ed.) (1977).
Parsons, T. (1937) *The Structure of Social Action*, McGraw-Hill, New York.
(1951) *The Social System*, Free Press, New York.
(1954, first published 1942) 'Age and sex in the social structure of the United States' in *Essays in Sociological Theory*, Free Press, New York.
(1955) 'The American family: its relations to personality and social structure' in Parsons and Bales (eds) (1955).
(1959) 'The social structure of the family' in R.N. Anshen (ed.) *The Family: Its Functions and Destiny*, Harper & Row, New York.
(1960) *Structure and Process in Modern Societies*, Free Press, Chicago.
(1961) 'The school class as a social system' in Halsey *et al.* (1961).
(1964) *Essays in Sociological Theory*, Free Press, New York.
(1965a) 'Religious perspectives in sociology and social psychology' in W.A. Lessa and E.Z. Vogt (eds) *Reader in Comparative Religion: an Anthropological Approach*, 2nd edn, Harper & Row, New York.
(1965b) 'The normal American family' in S.M. Farber (ed.) *Man and Civilization: The Family's Search for Survival*, McGraw-Hill, New York.
(1967) *Sociological Theory and Modern Society*, Free Press, New York.
(1969) 'Family and church as "boundary" structures' in N. Birnbaum and G. Lenzer (eds) *Sociology and Religion: A Book of Readings*, Prentice-Hall, Englewood Cliffs, NJ.
(1969) *Politics and Social Structure*, Free Press, New York.
(1975) 'The Sick Role and the Role of the Physician Reconsidered', *Millbank Memorial Fund Quarterly: Health and Society*, vol. 53, pp. 257–78.
(1977) *The Evolution of Societies*, edited by J. Toby, Prentice-Hall, Englewood Cliffs, NJ.
Parsons, T. and Bales, R.F. (eds) (1955) *Family, Socialization and Interaction Process*, Free Press, New York.
Patelis, K. (2000) 'The political economy of the Internet' in J. Curran (ed.). *Media Organizations in Society*, Arnold, London.
Pateman, C. (1988) 'The patriarchal welfare state' in A. Guttman (ed.) *Democracy and the Welfare State*, Princeton University Press, Princeton.
Paterson, K. (1981) 'Theoretical perspectives in epidemiology – a critical appraisal', *Radical Community Medicine*, vol. 2, pp. 23–33.
Patrick, J. (1973) *A Glasgow Gang Observed*, Eyre Methuen, London.
Patterson, S. (1965) *Dark Strangers*, Penguin, Harmondsworth.
Pawson R. (1989) 'Methodology' in Haralambos (ed.) (1989).
(1992) 'Feminist methodology' in M. Haralambos (ed.) *Developments in Sociology*, vol. 8, Causeway Press, Ormskirk.
(1995) 'Methods of content/document/media analysis' in Haralambos (ed.) (1995).

Payne, G. (2006) 'An introduction to social divisions' in Payne (ed.) (2006).

(ed.) (2006) *Social Divisions*, 2nd edn, Palgrave Macmillan, Basingstoke.

Payne, G. and Grew, C. (2005) 'Unpacking "class ambivalence": some conceptual and methodological issues in unpacking class cultures', *Sociology*, vol. 39, no. 5, pp. 893–90.

Payne, G. and Payne, J. (2004) *Key Concepts in Social Research*, Sage, London.

Payne, G., Ford, G. and Robertson, C. (1977) 'A reappraisal of social mobility in Britain', *Sociology*, May.

Peach, C. (2005) 'Muslims in the UK' in Abbas (ed.) (2005).

Pearce, F. (1976) *Crimes of the Powerful*, Pluto Press, London.

Pearce, F. and Tombs, S. (1993) 'US capital versus the Third World: Union Carbide and Bhopal' in Pearce and Woodiwiss (1993).

Pearce, F. and Woodiwiss, M. (1993) *Global Crime Connections*, Macmillan, Basingstoke.

Pearson, G. (1983) *Hooligan: A History of Respectable Fears*, Macmillan, London.

Pearson, M. (1991) 'Ethnic differences in infant health', *Archives of Diseases in Childhood*, vol. 66, pp. 88–90.

Penn, R. (1981) 'The Nuffield class categorization', *Sociology*, vol. 36.

(1983) 'Skilled manual workers in the labour process' in Wood (ed.) (1982).

(1984) *Skilled Workers in the Class Structure*, Cambridge University Press, Cambridge.

Penn, R., Rose, M. and Rubery, J. (eds) (1994) *Skill and Occupational Change*, Oxford University Press, Oxford.

Perse, E. (1994) 'Uses of erotica and acceptance of rape-myths', *Communication Research*, vol. 21, no. 4, pp. 488–515.

Pevalin, D.J. and Rose, D. (2004) *Social Capital for Health*, Health Development Agency, London.

Phelps Brown, Sir Henry and Pierson, J. (1999) 'Labour theory of value' in Bullock and Trombley (eds) (1999).

Phillips, C. and Bowling, B. (2002) 'Racism, ethnicity, crime and criminal justice' in Maguire *et al.* (eds) (2002).

Phillips, C. and Brown, D. (1998) *Entry into the Criminal Justice System: A Survey of Police Arrests and their Outcomes*, Home Office, London.

Phillips, D.L. (1971) *Knowledge From What?* Rand McNally, Chicago.

(1973) *Abandoning Method*, Jossey-Bass, San Francisco.

Phillipson, C. and Baars, J. (2007) 'Social theory and social ageing' in Bond *et al.* (eds) (2007).

Phillipson, M. (1972) 'Theory, methodology and conceptualization' in P. Filmer *et al. New Directions in Sociological Theory*, Collier-Macmillan, London.

Philo, G. (ed.) (1990) *Seeing and Believing: The Influence of Television*, Routledge, London.

(ed.) (1999) *Message Received: Glasgow Media Group Research 1993–1998*, Longman, London.

Philo, G. and Miller, D. (eds) (2001) *Market Killing: What the Free Market Does and What Social Scientists Can Do About It*, Longman, Harlow.

(2002) 'Circuits of communication and power: recent developments in media sociology' in Holborn (ed.) (2002).

(2005) 'Communication and power: production, consumption and reproduction' in Holborn (ed.) (2005).

Philo, G., Secker, J., Platt, S., Henderson, L., McLaughlin, G. and Burnside, J. (1996) 'Media images of mental distress' in Heller *et al.* (eds) (1996).

Phizaklea, A. and Miles, R. (1980) *Labour and Racism*, Routledge & Kegan Paul, London.

Piachaud, D. (1981) 'Peter Townsend and the Holy Grail', *New Society*, 10 September.

(1987) 'Problems in the definition and measurement of poverty', *Journal of Social Policy*.

Piachaud, D. and Sutherland, H. (2001) 'Child poverty: aims, achievements and prospects for the future', *New Economy*, vol. 8, no. 2.

Piaget, J. (1932) *The Moral Judgement of the Child*, Macmillan, New York.

(1977) *The Development of Thought: Equilibrium of Cognitive Structures*, Viking Press, New York.

Pierson, C. (2006) *Beyond the Welfare State: The New Political Economy of Welfare*, 3rd edn, Polity Press, Cambridge.

Pierson, C. and Castles, F.G. (eds) (2000) *The Welfare State Reader*, Polity Press, Cambridge.

Pilcher, J. (1995) *Age and Generation in Modern Britain*, Oxford University Press, Oxford.

Pilgrim, D. and Rogers, A. (1999) *The Sociology of Mental Health and Illness*, Open University Press, Buckingham.

Pilkington, A. (1984) *Race Relations in Britain*, UTP, Slough.

(1993) 'Race and ethnicity' in M. Haralambos (ed.) *Developments in Sociology*, vol. 9, Causeway Press, Ormskirk.

(1997) 'Ethnicity and education' in Haralambos (ed.) (1997).

(1999) 'Racial disadvantage and ethnic diversity' in Haralambos (ed.) (1999).

(2002) 'Cultural representations and changing ethnic identities in a global age' in Holborn (ed.) (2002).

(2003) *Racial Disadvantage and Ethnic Diversity in Britain*, Palgrave Macmillan, Basingstoke.

(2005) 'Social cohesion, racial equality and ethnic diversity' in Holborn (ed.) (2005).

Pill, R. and Stott, N.C.H. (1986) 'Concepts of illness causation and responsibility: some preliminary data from a sample of working-class mothers' in Currer and Stacey (eds) (1986).

Pines, J. (1992) *Black and White in Colour: Black People in British Television since 1936*, BFI, London.

Piore, M. (1986) 'Perspectives on labour market flexibility', *Industrial Relations*, vol. 45, no. 2.

Platt, L. (2002) *Parallel Lives? Poverty among Ethnic Minority Groups in Britain*, Child Poverty Action Group, London.

(2006) 'Poverty' in Payne (ed.) (2006).

Plummer, K. (1979) 'Misunderstanding labelling perspectives' in D. Downes and P. Rock (eds) *Deviant Interpretations*, Martin Robertson, London.

(1982) *Documents of Life: Introductions to the Problems and Literature of a Humanist Method*, Allen & Unwin, London.

Poggi, G. (1978) *Development of the Modern State*, Hutchinson, London.

Pollak, O. (1950) *The Criminality of Women*, University of Philadelphia Press, Philadelphia.

Pollert, A. (1981) *Girls, Wives, Factory Lives*, Macmillan, London.

(1988) 'Dismantling flexibility', *Capital and Class*, no. 34.

(1996) 'Gender and class revisited; or the poverty of "patriarchy"', *Sociology*, vol. 30, no. 4.

Polsky, N. (1967) *Hustlers, Beats and Others*, Aldine, New York.

Popay, J. and Bartley, M. (1989) 'Conditions of Labour and Women's Health' in C. Martin and D. McQueen (eds) *Readings for a New Public Health*, Edinburgh University Press, Edinburgh.

Popper, K.R. (1959) *The Logic of Scientific Discovery*, Hutchinson, London.

Population Trends (2005, 2006) Office for National Statistics, London.

Postman, N. (1982) *The Disappearance of Childhood*, W.H. Allen, London.

Potter, J. and Wetherell, M. (1987) *Discourse and Social Psychology*, Sage, London.

Poulantzas, N. (1969) 'The problem of the capitalist state', *New Left Review*, no. 58.

(1976) 'The capitalist state: a reply to Miliband and Laclau', *New Left Review*, January–February.

Pound, P., Gompertz, P. and Ebrahim, S. (1998) 'Illness in the context of older age: the case of stroke', *Sociology of Health and Illness*, vol. 20, pp. 559–72.

Povey, D. (ed.) (2004) *Crime in England and Wales, Supplementary Volume 1: Homicide and Gun Crime*, National Statistics, London.

The Power Inquiry (2006) *Power to the People: The Report of Power: An Independent Inquiry into Britain's Democracy*, Joseph Rowntree Foundation, York.

Power, S., Edwards, T., Whitty, G. and Wigfall, V. (2003) *Education and the Middle Class*, Open University Press, Buckingham.

Presdee, M. (2004) 'Burning issues: young people and the fascination for fire'. http://www.culturalcriminology.org/papers/presdee-fire.pdf

Press, A. (1995) 'Class and gender in the hegemonic process: class differences in women's perceptions of television realism and the identification with television characters' in Boyd-Barrett and Newbold (eds) (1995).

Pringle, R. (1992) 'What is a secretary?' in M. McDowell and R. Pringle (eds) *Defining Women: Social Institutions and Gender Divisions*, Polity Press, Cambridge.

Prout, A. (2005) *The Future of Childhood*, Routledge Falmer, London.

Prout, A. and James, A. (1990) 'A new paradigm for the sociology of childhood?' in James and Prout (eds) (1990).

Provenzo, E. (1991) *Video Kids: Making Sense of Nintendo*, Harvard University Press, Cambridge, MA.

Pryce, K. (1979) *Endless Pressure*, Penguin, Harmondsworth.

Pulzer, P.G. (1967) *Political Representation and Elections in Britain*, Allen & Unwin, London.
Punch, M. (1996) *Dirty Business: Exploring Corporate Misconduct*, Sage, London.
Purdy, L.M. (1997) 'Babystrike!' in H.L. Marsh (ed.) *Feminism and Families*, Routledge, New York.
Putnam, R. (1983) *Making Democracy Work: Civic Traditions in Modern Italy*, Princeton University Press, Princeton, NJ.
Putnam, R. and Feldstein, L. (2003) *Better Together: Restoring the American Community*, Simon & Schuster, New York.
Putnam, R.D. (1995) 'Tuning in, tuning out: the strange disappearance of social capital in America', *Political Science and Politics*, 28, 664–83.
(2000) *Bowling Alone: The Collapse and Revival of American Community*, Simon & Schuster, New York.
Puwar, M. (1997) 'Gender and political elites: women in the House of Commons', *Sociology Review*, November, pp. 2–6.
Qvortrup, J. (1991) *Childhood as a Social Phenomenon*, Eurosocial Report, Vienna.
Randall, G.J. (1987) 'Gender differences in pupil-teacher interaction in workshops and laboratories' in Weiner and Arnot (eds) (1987).
Ranson, S. (1996) 'Markets or democracy for education' in Ahier *et al.* (eds) (1996).
Rapoport, R. (1989) 'Ideologies about family forms – towards diversity' in K. Boh *et al.* (eds) *Changing Patterns of European Family Life*, Routledge, London.
Rapoport, R. and Rapoport, R.N. (1971) *Dual-Career Families*, Penguin, Harmondsworth.
(1975) *Leisure and the Family Life-Cycle*, Routledge, London.
(1982) 'British families in transition' in Rapoport *et al.* (eds) (1982).
Rapoport, R.N., Fogarty, M.P. and Rapoport, R. (eds) (1982) *Families in Britain*, Routledge & Kegan Paul, London.
Rattansi, A. (1994) '"Western" racisms, ethnicities and identities in a "postmodern" frame' in Rattansi and Westwood (eds) (1994).
Rattansi, A. and Westwood, S. (eds) (1994) *Racism, Modernity and Identity*, Polity Press, Cambridge.
Ray, L. and Read, M. (1994) *Organizing Modernity: New Weberian Perspectives on Work Organizations*, Routledge, London.
Reay, D., David, M.E. and Ball, S. (2005) *Degrees of Choice: Class, Race, Gender and Higher Education*, Trentham Books, Stoke-on-Trent.
Reddington, H. (2003) '"Lady" punks in bands: a subculturette?' in Muggleton and Weinzierl (eds) (2003).
Rees, T. (1992) *Women and the Labour Market*, Routledge, London.
Refugee Council (2005) Briefing, Asylum and Immigration Act 2004: an update, March.
Reich, R. (1997) 'Why the rich are getting richer and the poor poorer' in Halsey *et al.* (eds) (1997).
Reid, I. (1998) *Class in Britain*, Polity Press, Cambridge.
Rein, M. (1970) 'Problems in the definition and measurement of poverty' in Townsend (ed.) (1970).
Reiner, R. (1994) 'Crime, law and deviance: the Durkheim legacy' in Fenton (1994).
Renaud, M. (1975) 'On the structural constraints to state intervention in health', *International Journal of Health Services*, 5, pp. 559–72.
Rex, J. (1970) *Race Relations in Sociological Theory*, Weidenfeld & Nicolson, London.
(1974) 'Capitalism, elites and the ruling class' in P. Stanworth and A. Giddens (eds) *Elites and Power in British Society*, Cambridge University Press, Cambridge.
(1986) *Race and Ethnicity*, Open University Press, Milton Keynes.
Rex, J. and Moore, R. (1967) *Race, Community and Conflict*, Institute of Race Relations/Oxford University Press, London.
Rex, J. and Tomlinson, S. (1979) *Colonial Immigrants in a British City*, Routledge & Kegan Paul, London.
Reynolds, D. (1984) 'Relative autonomy reconstructed' in L. Barton and S. Walker (eds) *Social Crisis and Educational Research*, Croom Helm, London.
Reynolds, T. (2002) 'Re-analysing the Black family' in Carling *et al.* (eds) (2002).
Richardson, B. (ed.) (2005) *Tell It Like It Is: How Our Schools Fail Black Children*, Bookmarks Publications and Trentham Books, Stoke-on-Trent.
Richardson, J. (1987) 'Race' in M. Haralambos (ed.) *Developments in Sociology*, vol. 3, Causeway Press, Ormskirk.
(1990) 'Race' in M. Haralambos (ed.) *Developments in Sociology*, vol. 6, Causeway Press, Ormskirk.
(ed.) (1996) *Handbook of Research Methods for Psychology and Social Sciences*, BPS Books, Leicester.
Richardson, J. and Lambert, J. (1985) *The Sociology of Race*, Causeway Press, Ormskirk.
Richardson, J.J. and Jordan, A.G. (1979) *Governing under Pressure*, Martin Robertson, Oxford.
Rikowski, G. (1997) 'Scorched earth: prelude to rebuilding Marxist educational theory', *British Journal of Sociology of Education*, vol. 18, no. 4.
(2001) *The Battle in Seattle: Its Significance for Education*, Tufnell Press, London.
(2002) 'Globalization and education: a paper prepared for the House of Lords Select Committee on Economic Affairs, Inquiry into the Global Economy'.
www.leeds.ac.uk./educol/documents/00001941.htm
(2005) 'In the dentist's chair: a response to Richard Hatcher's critique of *Habituation of the Nation* – Part One'.
www.flowideas.co.uk/print.php?page=147
Risman, B. J. and Myers, K. (2006) 'As the twig is bent: children reared in feminist households' in Handel (ed.) (2006).
Rist, R. (1970) 'Student social class and teacher expectations: the self-fulfilling prophecy in ghetto education', *Harvard Educational Review*, vol. 40.
Ritzer, G. (1996) *The McDonaldization of Society*, 3rd edn, Pine Forge Press, London.
(1998) *The McDonaldization Thesis*, Sage, London.
(ed.) (2002) *McDonaldization: The Reader*, Pine Forge Press, London.
Ritzer, G. and Goodman, D.J. (2003) *Sociological Theory*, 6th edn, McGraw Hill, New York.
Roach, J.L. and Roach, J.K. (eds) (1972) *Poverty: Selected Readings*, Penguin, Harmondsworth.
Robbins, T. and Robertson, R. (1987) *Church-state Relations: Tensions and Transitions*, Transaction Books, New Brunswick.
Roberts, E. (1984) *A Woman's Place: An Oral History of Working Class Women 1890–1940*, Basil Blackwell, Oxford.
Roberts, K. (1978) *Contemporary Society and the Growth of Leisure*, Longman, New York.
(1984) *School Leavers and Their Prospects*, Open University Press, Milton Keynes.
(1986) 'Leisure' in M. Haralambos (ed.) *Developments in Sociology*, vol. 2, Causeway Press, Ormskirk.
(1997) 'Is there an emerging British "underclass": the evidence from youth research' in R. MacDonald (ed.) *Youth, the 'Underclass' and Social Exclusion*, Routledge, London.
(2001) *Class in Modern Britain*, Palgrave, Basingstoke.
Roberts, K., Cook, F.G., Clark, S.C. and Semeonoff, E. (1977) *The Fragmentary Class Structure*, Heinemann, London.
Roberts, K., Noble, M. and Duggan, J. (1984) 'Youth unemployment: an old problem or a new life-style?' in K. Thompson (ed.) *Work, Employment and Unemployment*, Open University Press, Milton Keynes.
Robertson, R. (ed.) (1969) *Sociology of Religion*, Penguin, Harmondsworth.
(1970) *The Sociological Interpretation of Religion*, Blackwell, Oxford.
(1987) 'Church-state relations and the world system' in Robbins and Robertson (1987).
Rock, P. and Cohen, S. (1970) 'The Teddy boys' in V. Bogdanor and R. Skidelsky, *The Age of Affluence*, Macmillan, London.
Rogers, C. (1982) *The Social Psychology of Schooling*, Routledge & Kegan Paul, London.
Rojek, C. (1995) *Decentring Leisure: Rethinking Leisure Theory*, Sage, London.
Roof, W.C. and McKinney, W. (1987) *American Mainline Religion*, Rutgers University Press, New Brunswick, NJ.
Ropers, R.H. (1991) *Persistent Poverty: The American Dream Turned Nightmare*, Plenum Press, New York.
Rosaldo, M.Z. (1974) 'Women, culture and society: a theoretical overview' in M. Rosaldo and L. Lamphere (eds) *Women, Culture and Society*, Stanford University Press, Stanford, CA.
Rose, A.M. (ed.) (1967) *The Power Structure: Political Process in American Society*, Oxford University Press, New York.
Rose, D. and Marshall, G. (1988) 'Developments' in M. Haralambos (ed.) *Sociology*, vol. 4, Causeway Press, Ormskirk.
Rose, M. (1996) 'Still life in Swindon: case studies in union survival and employer policy in a "sunrise" labour market' in Gallie *et al.* (eds) (1996).
Rose, N. (1989) *Governing the Soul: Shaping the Private Self*, Routledge, London.
Rose, S., Kamin, L.J. and Lewontin, R.C. (1984) *Not in Our Genes. Biology, Ideology and Human Nature*, Penguin, Harmondsworth.

Rosen, H. (1974) *Language and Class*, 3rd edn, Falling Wall Press, Bristol.
Rosenberg, B. (1957) 'Mass culture in America' in Rosenberg and White (eds) (1957).
Rosenberg, B. and White, D.M. (eds) (1957) *Mass Culture: The Popular Arts in America*, Free Press, New York.
Rosenberg, C. (1989) 'Disease in history: frames and framers', *Millbank Quarterly*, 67, suppl., pp. 1–15.
Roseneil, S. (2005) 'Living and loving beyond the boundaries of the heteronorm: personal relationships in the 21st century' in McKie and Chunningham-Burley (eds) (2005).
Rosenhan, D.L. (1973) 'On being sane in insane places', *Science*, vol. 179, pp. 250–8.
Rosenthal, R. and Jacobson, L. (1968) *Pygmalion in the Classroom*, Holt, Rinehart & Winston, New York.
Ross, A. (2003) 'Access to higher education' in Archer *et al.* (eds) (2003).
Ross, K. (2000) 'In whose image? TV criticism and black minority viewers' in Cottle (ed.) (2002).
(2002) 'Selling women (down the river): Gendered relations and the political economy of broadcast news' in Meehan and Riordan (eds) (2002).
Routh, R. (1980) *Occupation and Pay in Great Britain 1906–79*, Macmillan, London.
Rowbotham, S. (1973) *Woman's Consciousness, Man's World*, Penguin, Harmondsworth.
(1982) 'The trouble with patriarchy' in M. Evans (ed.) *The Woman Question*, Fontana, London.
(1998) 'The trouble with "patriarchy"', *New Statesman*, December, pp. 970–1.
Rowntree, S. (1901) *Poverty: A Study of Town Life*, Macmillan, London.
(1941) *Poverty and Progress*, Longman, London.
Rowntree, S. and Lavers, G. (1951) *Poverty and the Welfare State*, Longman, London.
Ruggiero, V. (1992) 'Realist criminology: a critique' in Young and Matthews (eds) (1992).
(1996) *Organised and Corporate Crime in Europe: Offers that Cannot be Refused*, Dartmouth, Aldershot.
Ruggiero, V., South, N. and Taylor, I. (eds) (1998) *The New European Criminology: Crime and Social Order in Europe*, Routledge, London.
Runciman, W.G. (1990) 'How many classes are there in contemporary British society?' *Sociology*, vol. 24, pp. 378–96.
Runnymede Trust (1997) *Islamophobia*, Runnymede Trust, London.
Russell, A. (2002) 'The general election of 2001: Continuity, apathy and disillusion' in Holborn (ed.) (2002).
Rutherford, J. (1988) 'Who's that man?' in R. Chapman and J. Rutherford (eds) *Male Order: Unwrapping Masculinity*, Lawrence & Wishart, London.
Ryan, W. (1971) *Blaming the Victim*, Orbach & Chambers, London.
Sabel, C. (1982) *Work and Politics: The Division of Labour in Industry*, Cambridge University Press, Cambridge.
Safilios-Roschild, C. (1970) *The Sociology and Social Psychology of Disability and Rehabilitation*, Random House, New York.
Saggar, S. and Heath, A. (1999) 'Race: towards a multicultural electorate?' in Evans and Norris (eds) (1999).
Said, E.W. (1978) *Orientalism*, Penguin, Harmondsworth.
(1995) *Orientalism: Western Conceptions of the Orient*, Penguin, Harmondsworth.
(1997) *Covering Islam: How the Media and the Experts Determine How We See the Rest of the World*, Vintage, London.
Saks, M. (1998) 'Medicine and complementary medicine' in G. Scambler, *Modernity, Medicine and Health: Medical Sociology Towards 2000*, Routledge, London.
Sancho, J. (2003) 'Disabling prejudice. Attitudes towards disability and its portrayal on television'. http://www.ofcom.org.uk/static/archive/bsc/pdfs/research/disability.pdf#search=%22disabling%20prejudice%22
Sanders, D., Clarke, H., Stewart, M. and Whiteley, P. (2001) 'The economy and voting' in Norris (ed.) (2001).
(2005) *The 2005 General Election in Great Britain: Report for the Electoral Commission*, University of Essex, Essex.
Sanders, T. (2004) *Sex Work*, Willan, Cullompton, Devon.
(2005) 'Researching the online sex work community' in Hine (ed.) (2005).
Sarlvick, B. and Crewe, I. (1983) *Decade of Dealignment*, Cambridge University Press, Cambridge.
Sarup, M. (1988) *An Introductory Guide to Post-Structuralism and Postmodernism*, Harvester Wheatsheaf, Hemel Hempstead.
Sassi, S. (2005) 'Tackling health inequalities' in Hills and Stewart (eds) (2005).
Saunders, P. (1990) *Social Class and Stratification*, Routledge, London.
(1993) 'Citizenship in a Liberal Society' in B.S. Turner (ed.) *Citizenship and Social Theory*, Sage, London.
(1996) *Unequal but Fair? A Study of Class Barriers in Britain*, IEA, London.
Saussure, F. (1966, first published in English, 1959) *Course in General Linguistics*, McGraw-Hill, New York.
Savage, M. (2005) 'Working-class identities in the 1960s: revisiting the affluent worker studies', *Sociology*, vol. 39, no. 5, pp. 929–48.
Savage, M. and Butler, T. (1995) 'Assets and the middle classes in Britain' in Butler and Savage (eds) (1995).
Savage, M. and Egerton, M. (1997) 'Social mobility, individual ability and the inheritance of class inequality', *Sociology*, vol. 31, no. 4.
Savage, M., Barlow, J., Dickens, P. and Fielding, T. (1992) *Property, Bureaucracy and Culture: Middle Class Formation in Contemporary Britain*, Routledge, London.
Savage, M., Bagnall, G. and Longhurst, B. (2001) 'Ordinary, ambivalent and defensive: class identities in the Northwest of England', *Sociology*, vol. 35, no. 4.
Savelsberg, J.J. (1995) 'Crime, inequality and justice in Eastern Europe' in J. Hagan and R.D. Peterson (eds) (1995) *Crime and Inequality*, Stanford University Press, Stanford, CA.
Sayer, A. (1984) *Method in Social Science*, Hutchinson, London.
(2005) 'Class, moral worth and recognition', *Sociology*, vol. 39, no. 5.
Scambler, G. (2002) *Health and Social Change: A Critical Theory*, Open University Press, Buckingham.
Scambler, G. and Hopkins, A. (1986) 'Being epileptic: coming to terms with stigma', *Sociology of Health and Illness*, vol. 8, pp. 26–43.
Scambler, G., Scambler, A. and Craig, D. (1981) 'Kinship and friendship networks and women's demand for primary care', *Journal of the Royal College of General Practitioners*, vol. 26, pp. 746–50.
Scase, R. (ed.) (1977) *Industrial Society: Class, Cleavage and Control*, Allen & Unwin, London.
Scharrer, E., Kim, D.D., Lin, K. and Liu, Z. (2006) 'Working hard or hardly working? Gender, humor, and the performance of domestic chores in television commercials', *Mass Communication and Society*, vol. 9, no. 2, pp. 215–38.
Scheff, T. (1966) *Being Mentally Ill: A Sociological Theory*, Aldine, Chicago.
Schifferes, S. (2004) 'Election reveals divided nation', *BBC News*, 3 November.
http://news.bbc.co.uk/1/hi/world/americas/3973197.stm
Schiller, G. (2007) 'Firing on all cylinders', *Hollywood Reporter*, 27 June. http://www.hollywoodreporter.com/hr/content_display/news/e3ib489c7d121532c79a336bb2902e48691
Schultz, T.W. (1961) 'Investment in human capital', *American Economic Review*, March.
Schutz, A. (1972, first published 1932) *The Phenomenology of the Social World*, Heinemann, London.
Schwartz, A.J. (1975) 'A further look at the "culture of poverty": ten Caracas barrios', *Sociology and Social Research*, July.
Schwendinger, H. and Schwendinger, J. (1975) 'Guardians of order or defenders of human rights?' in I. Taylor, P. Walton and J. Young (eds) *Critical Criminology*, Routledge & Kegan Paul, London.
Scott, A. (2000) 'Risk society or angst society? Two views of risk, consciousness and community' in Adam *et al.* (eds) (2000).
Scott, A.M. (ed.) (1994) *Gender Segregation and Social Change*, Oxford University Press, Oxford.
Scott, H. (1976) *Women and Socialism*, Allison & Busby, London.
Scott, J. (1982) *The Upper Classes. Property and Privilege in Britain*, Macmillan, London.
(1985) 'The British upper class' in D. Coates, G. Johnston and R. Bush (eds) *A Socialist Anatomy of Britain*, Polity Press, Cambridge.
(1990a) 'Documents in social research', *Social Studies Review*, September.
(1990b) *Matter of Record: Documentary Sources in Social Research*, Polity Press, Cambridge.
(1991) *Who Rules Britain?* Polity Press, Cambridge.
(1997) *Corporate Business and Capitalist Classes*, Oxford University Press, Oxford.
(2005) 'Social mobility: occupational snakes and ladders', *Sociology Review*, November.
(2006) 'Textual analysis' in Jupp (ed.) (2006).
Scraton, S. (1992) 'Leisure' in M. Haralambos (ed.) *Developments in Sociology*, vol. 8, Causeway Press, Ormskirk.
Scraton, S. and Bramham, P. (1995) 'Leisure and postmodernity' in Haralambos (ed.) (1995).

(2001) 'Changing work and leisure relations' in Haralambos (ed.) (2001).
Sefton, T. and Sutherland, H. (2005) 'Inequality and poverty under New Labour' in Hills and Stewart (eds) (2005).
Seidler, V.J. (1989) *Rediscovering Masculinity: Reason, Language and Sexuality*, Routledge, London.
(1994) *Unreasonable Men: Masculinity and Social Theory*, Routledge, London.
Select Committee on Education and Skills (2005) Fifth Report, Summary, www.publications.parliament.uk/pa/cm200405/cmselect/cmeduski/86/8603.htm
Sen, A.K. (1981) *Poverty and Famines: An Essay on Entitlement and Deprivation*, Clarendon Press, Oxford.
(1985) 'Poor relatively speaking', *Oxford Economic Papers*.
(2002) 'Perception versus observation', *British Medical Journal*, vol. 324, pp. 860–1.
Sewell, T. (1997) *Black Masculinities and Schooling*, Trentham Books, Stoke-on-Trent.
Shakespeare, T. (1994) 'Cultural representations of disabled people: dustbins for disavowal', *Disability and Society*, no. 9, vol. 3, pp. 283–301.
Shannon, C. and Weaver, W. (1949) *The Mathematical Theory of Communication*, University of Illinois Press, Urbana, IL.
Share Ownership 2005, National Statistics, London (available online).
Sharf, B. F. (1999) 'Beyond nettiquette: the ethics of doing naturalistic discourse research on the Internet' in S. Jones (ed.) (1999).
Sharma, U. (1992) *Complementary Medicine Today. Practitioners and Patients*, Routledge, London.
Sharp, R. and Green, A. (1975) *Education and Social Control*, Routledge & Kegan Paul, London.
Sharpe, S. (1976) *Just Like a Girl: How Girls Learn to be Women*, Penguin, Harmondsworth.
(1994) *Just Like a Girl*, 2nd edn, Penguin, Harmondsworth.
Shaw, C.R. and McKay, H.D. (1942) *Juvenile Delinquency and Urban Areas*, University of Chicago Press, Chicago.
Shaw, M., Dorling, G. and Davey, G. (1999) *The Widening Gap*, Policy Press, Bristol.
Sheeran, Y. (1993) 'The role of women and family structure', *Sociology Review*, April.
Shephard, A. (2003) *Inequality Under the Labour Government*, Institute for Fiscal Studies, London.
Shepherd, J. (2007) 'League tables', *Guardian*, 11 January.
Shilling, C. (1991) 'Educating the body: physical capital and the production of social inequalities', *Sociology*, vol. 25, pp. 653–72.
(2003) *The Body and Social Theory*, 2nd edn, Sage, London.
Shils, E. (1978) 'Mass society and its culture' in Davison *et al.* (eds) (1978).
Shiner, L. (1971) 'The concept of secularization in empirical research' in K. Thompson and J. Tunstall (eds) *Sociological Perspectives*, Penguin Books, Harmondsworth.
Shorter, E. (1976) *The Making of the Modern Family*, Penguin, Harmondsworth.
Signorelli, N. (1989) 'Television and conceptions about sex roles: maintaining conventionality and the status quo', *Sex Roles*, vol. 21, pp. 341–60.
Siltanen, J. and Stanworth, M. (eds) (1984) *Women and the Public Sphere*, Hutchinson, London.
Silva, E.B. and Smart, C. (1999) 'The "new" practices and policies of family life' in Silva and Smart (eds) (1999).
(eds) (1999) *The New Family?* Sage, London.
Silverman, D. (1970) *The Theory of Organisations*, Heinemann, London.
(1985) *Qualitative Method and Sociology*, Gower, Aldershot.
(ed.) (2004) *Qualitative Research: Theory, Method and Practice*, Sage, London.
Silverstone, R. (1991) 'From audiences to consumers: the household and the consumption of communication and information technologies', *European Journal of Communication*, vol. 6, pp. 135–54.
(1994) *Television and Everyday Life*, Routledge, London.
Simmons, J. *et al.* (2002) *Crime in England and Wales, 2001/2002*, Home Office, London.
Sinclair, S. (2003) 'Poverty and social exclusion' in Holborn (ed.) (2003).
Sinfield, A. (1981) *What Unemployment Means*, Martin Robertson, Oxford.
Siraj-Blatchford, I. (1995) 'Critical social research and the academy: the role of organic intellectuals in educational research', *British Journal of Sociology of Education*, vol. 16, no. 2.
Sissons, M. (1970) *The Psychology of Social Class*, Open University Press, Milton Keynes.
Situ, Y. and Emmons, D. (2000) *Environmental Crime: The Criminal Justice System's Role in Protecting the Environment*, Sage, London.
Skeggs, B. (1991) 'Challenging masculinity and using sexuality', *British Journal of Sociology of Education*, vol. 12, no. 2.
(1997) *Formations of Class and Gender*, Sage, London.
(2005) 'The making of class and gender through visualizing moral subject formation', *Sociology*, vol. 39, no. 5, pp. 965–82.
Skellington, R. and Morris, P. (1992) *'Race' in Britain Today*, Sage, London.
(1996) *'Race' in Britain Today*, 2nd edn, Open University Press, Milton Keynes.
Skidmore, W. (1975) *Theoretical Thinking in Sociology*, Cambridge University Press, Cambridge.
Skirrow, G. (1986) 'Hellivision: an analysis of video games' in C. McCabe (ed.) *High Theory/Low Culture*, Manchester University Press, Manchester.
Sklair, L. (1993) 'Going global: competing models of globalization', *Sociology Review*, November.
(1995) *Sociology of the Global System*, 2nd edn, Prentice-Hall/Harvester Wheatsheaf, Hemel Hempstead.
(2003) 'Globalization, capitalism and power' in Holborn (ed.) (2003).
Skocpol, T. (1979) *States and Social Revolutions*, Cambridge University Press, Cambridge.
(1985) 'Bringing the state back in: strategies of analysis in current research' in P. Evans, D. Rueschemeyer and T. Skocpol (eds) *Bringing the State Back In*, Cambridge University Press, Cambridge.
Slapper, G. and Tombs, S. (1999) *Corporate Crime*, Longman, London.
Slattery, M. (1985) *Urban Sociology*, Causeway Press, Ormskirk.
Sloane, P.J. (1994) 'The gender wage differential and discrimination in six SCELI labour markets' in A.M. Scott (ed.) (1994).
Smart, C. (1976) *Women, Crime and Criminology*, Routledge & Kegan Paul, London.
(1979) 'The new female criminal: reality or myth', *British Journal of Criminology*, vol. 19.
(1989) *Feminism and the Power of Law*, Routledge, London.
(1995) 'Feminist approaches to criminology, or postmodern woman meets atavistic man' in Smart (1995).
(1995) *Law, Crime and Sexuality: Essays in Feminism*, Sage, London.
Smart, C. and Neale, B. (1999) *Family Fragments?* Polity Press, Cambridge.
Smith, A. and Jacobson, B. (1988) *The Nation's Health: A Strategy for the Future*, King's Fund, London.
Smith, D.J. (ed.) (1992) *Understanding the Underclass*, Policy Studies Institute, London.
(1997) 'Ethnic origins, crime and criminal justice' in Maguire *et al.* (eds) (1997).
Smith, G., Smith, T. and Wright, G. (1997) 'Poverty and schooling: choice, diversity or division?' in Walker and Walker (eds) (1997).
Smith, M.J. (2005) 'It's not the economy stupid! The disappearance of the economy from the 2005 campaign' in Geddes and Tonge (eds) (2005).
Smith, M.R. (2007) 'Hasbro banking on "Transformers" change', *Yahoo!* Finance, 18 June. http://biz.yahoo.com/ap/070618/transformers_hasbro.html?.v=5
Smith, P. and Morton, G. (1993) 'Union exclusion and the decollectivization of industrial relations in contemporary Britain', *British Journal of Industrial Relations*, vol. 31, no. 1.
Smith, T. and Noble, M. (1995) *Education Divides: Poverty and Schooling in the 1990s*, CPAG, London.
Snider, L. (1993) 'The politics of corporate crime control' in Pearce and Woodiwiss (1993).
Social Trends 1998, Office for National Statistics, London.
Social Trends 2006, Office for National Statistics, London.
Solomos, J. (1986) 'Varieties of Marxist conceptions of "race", class and the state: a critical analysis' in J. Rex (ed.) *Theories of Race and Ethnic Relations*, Cambridge University Press, Cambridge.
(1993) *Race and Racism in Britain*, 2nd edn, Macmillan, London.
Solomos, J. and Back, L. (1996) *Racism and Society*, Macmillan, London.
Solomos, J., Findlay, B., Jones, S. and Gilroy, P. (1982) 'The organic crisis of British capitalism and race: the experience of the seventies' in Centre for Contemporary Cultural Studies (1982).
Sombart, W. (1907) *Luxury and Capitalism*, University of Michigan Press, Ann Arbor.

Somekh, B. and Lewin, C. (eds) (2005) *Research Methods in Social Science*, Sage, London.

Somerville, J. (2000) *Feminism and the Family: Politics and Society in the UK and USA*, Macmillan, Basingstoke.

Sontag, S. (1978) 'The double standard of ageing' in V. Carver and P. Liddiard (eds) *An Ageing Population*, Hodder & Stoughton, London.
(1988) *Illness as a Metaphor*, Penguin, Harmondsworth.

Soothill, K. and Walby, S. (1991) *Sex Crime in the News*, Routledge, London.

South, N. (1997) 'Drugs: use, crime and control' in M. Maguire *et al.* (eds) *The Oxford Handbook of Criminology*, 2nd edn, Oxford University Press, Oxford.
(1998) 'A green field for Criminology? A proposal for a perspective', *Theoretical Criminology*, vol. 2, no. 2, pp. 211–34.

Spencer, H. (1971) *Structure, Function and Evolution*, Nelson, London.

Spender, D. (1983) *Invisible Women: Schooling Scandal*, Women's Press, London.

Spicker, P. (1993) *Poverty and Social Security*, Routledge, London.

Spiro, M.E. (1965) 'Religion: problems of definition and explanation' in Banton (ed.) (1965).

Squire, C. (2000) 'Situated selves, the coming-out genre and equivalent citizenship in narratives of HIV' in Chamberlayne *et al.* (eds) (2000).

Stacey, J. (1993) 'Untangling feminist theory' in D. Richardson and V. Robinson (eds) *Introducing Women's Studies*, Macmillan, London.
(1996) *In the Name of the Family: Rethinking Family Values in the Postmodern Age*, Beacon Press, Boston, MA.

Stacey, M. (1960) *Tradition and Change: A Study of Banbury*, Oxford University Press, Oxford.

Stanko, E.A. (1988) 'Keeping women in and out of line: sexual harassment and occupational segregation' in S. Walby (ed.) *Gender Segregation at Work*, Open University Press, Milton Keynes.

Stanley, L. and Wise, S. (1990) 'Method, methodology and epistemology in feminist research process' in Wise (ed.) (1990).

Stanworth, M. (1983) *Gender and Schooling*, Hutchinson, London.
(1984) 'Women and class analysis: a reply to John Goldthorpe', *Sociology*, vol. 18, no. 2.

Stark, R. and Glock, C.Y. (1968) *American Piety: The Nature of Religious Commitment*, University of California Press, Berkeley, CA.

Stark, W.S. and Bainbridge, W.A. (1985) *The Future of Religion*, University of California Press, Berkeley, CA.

Steemers, J. (1999) 'Broadcasting is dead. Long live digital choice' in H. Mackay and T. O'Sullivan (eds) *The Media Reader: Continuity and Transformation*, Sage, London.

Steier, F. (1991) *Research and Reflexivity*, Sage, London.

Stein, S. (2002) *Sociology on the Web*, Prentice-Hall, Harlow.

Stevenson, K. and Brearley, N. (1991) 'Left realism in criminology and the return to consensus theory' in R. Reiner and M. Cross *Beyond Law and Order. Criminal Justice Policy and Politics into the 1990s*, Macmillan, Basingstoke.

Stewart, A., Prandy, K. and Blackburn, R.M. (1980) *Social Stratification and Occupations*, Macmillan, London.

Stoker, G. (2006) *Why Politics Matters: Making Democracy Work*, Palgrave Macmillan, Basingstoke.

Stoller, R. (1968) *Sex and Gender: On the Development of Masculinity and Femininity*, Science House, New York.

Stones, R. (1996) *Sociological Reasoning: Towards a Post-modern Sociology*, Macmillan, Basingstoke.

Storey, J. (1997) *An Introductory Guide to Cultural Theory and Popular Culture*, 2nd edn, Harvester Wheatsheaf, Hemel Hempstead.
(2003) *Inventing Popular Culture*, Blackwell, Oxford.

Strathdee, R. (2003) 'Labour market change, vocational education and training, and social class' in Holborn (ed.) (2003).

Strauss, A. and Corbin, J. (eds) (1997) *Grounded Theory in Practice*, Sage, Thousand Oaks, CA.

Streeter, M. (1997) 'Asbestos killed my husband, so I don't mind that I'm dying too', *Independent on Sunday*, 16 November, p. 5.
(1997) 'Shouting "taxi" to hail a cab, and other crimes you commit every day', *The Independent*, 29 November, p. 9.

Strinati, D. (1995) *An Introduction to Theories of Popular Culture*, Routledge, London.

Strong, P.M. (1979) *The Ceremonial Order of the Clinic: Patients, Doctors and Medical Bureaucracies*, Routledge, London.

Sudnow, D. (1967) *Passing On: The Social Organization of Dying*, Prentice-Hall, Englewood Cliffs, NJ.

Sugarman, B. (1970) 'Social class, values and behaviour in schools' in M. Craft (ed.) *Family, Class and Education*, Longman, London.

Sullivan, A. (2001) 'Cultural capital and educational attainment', *Sociology*, vol. 35, no. 4, November.

Sullivan, O. (1996) 'Time co-ordination, the domestic division of labour and affective relations: time use and enjoyment of activities within couples, *Sociology*, vol. 30, no. 1, p. 85.

Sussman, M.B. and Burchinal, L.G. (1971) 'The kin family network in urban-industrial America' in Anderson (ed.) (1971).

Sutherland, E.H. (1960) *White Collar Crime*, Holt, Rinehart & Winston, New York.
(1962) 'Is "white collar crime" crime?' in M.E. Wolfgang *et al.* (eds) *The Sociology of Crime and Delinquency*, John Wiley & Sons, New York.

Sutton Trust (2005a) *The Educational Background of the UK's Top Solicitors, Barristers and Judges*, Sutton Trust, London.
(2005b) *The Educational Background of Members of the House of Commons and the House of Lords*, Sutton Trust, London.
(2006) *The Educational Background of Leading Journalists*, Sutton Trust, London.

Sutton, R. and Rafaeli, A. (1988) 'Untangling the emotions between displayed emotions and organizational sales', *Academy of Management Journal*, no. 31.

Swann, Lord (1985) *Education for All: A Brief Guide*, HMSO, London.
(1985) *Education for All*, Commd. No. 9453, HMSO, London.

Sweeney, K. and McMahon, D. (1998) 'The effect of Jobseeker's Allowance on the claimant count', *Labour Market Trends*, April.

Sykes, G.M. and Matza, D. (1962) 'Techniques of neutralization: a theory of delinquency' in M.E. Wolfgang *et al.* (eds) *The Sociology of Crime and Delinquency*, John Wiley & Sons, New York.

Tailby, S. (2003) 'Flexibility' in Hollingshead *et al.* (2003).

Tambiah, S.J. (1990) *Magic, Science, Religion and the Scope of Rationality*, Cambridge University Press, Cambridge.

Tasker, Y. (1998) *Working Girls: Gender and Sexuality in Popular Culture*, Routledge, London.

Taylor, C. (1991) *The Ethics of Authenticity*, Harvard University Press, London.

Taylor, D. (1987) 'Incipient fundamentalism: religion and politics among Sri Lankan Hindus in Britain' in Caplan (ed.) (1987).

Taylor, F.W. (1947) *Scientific Management*, Harper & Row, New York.

Taylor, I. (1992) 'Left realist criminology and the free market experiment in Britain' in Young and Matthews (eds) (1992).
(1997) 'The political economy of crime' in M. Maguire *et al.* (eds) *The Oxford Handbook of Criminology*, 2nd edn, Oxford University Press, Oxford.
(1998a) 'Crime, market-liberalism and the European idea' in Ruggiero *et al.* (eds) (1998).
(1998b) 'Free markets and the costs of crime: an audit of England and Wales' in Walton and Young (eds) (1998).

Taylor, I., Walton, P. and Young, J. (1973) *The New Criminology*, Routledge & Kegan Paul, London.

Taylor, L. (1971) *Deviance and Society*, Michael Joseph, London.
(1984) *In the Underworld*, Unwin Paperbacks, London.

Taylor, L. and Walton, P. (1971) 'Industrial sabotage: motives and meanings' in S. Cohen (ed.) (1971).

Taylor, M. (2006) 'Guidelines ban covert pupil selection', *Guardian*, 9 September.

Taylor, P. (1998) 'Visions of a multi-media rich millennium', *Financial Times* (IT supplement), 6 May.

Taylor, S. (1982) *Durkheim and the Study of Suicide*, Macmillan, London.
(1989) *Suicide*, Longman, London.
(1990) 'Beyond Durkheim: sociology and suicide', *Social Studies Review*, November.

Tesh, S. (1988) *Hidden Arguments*, Rutgers University Press, New Brunswick, NJ.

Tham, H. (1998) 'Crime and the welfare state: the case of the United Kingdom and Sweden' in Ruggiero *et al.* (eds) (1998).

Thane, P. (1982) *The Foundations of the Welfare State*, Longman, Harlow.

Thomas, E.M. (1969) *The Harmless People*, Penguin, Harmondsworth.

Thomas, M., Walker, A., Willmott, A. and Bennett, N. (1998) *Living in Britain: Results from the 1996 General Household Survey*, Office for National Statistics, London.

Thomas, W.I. and Znaniecki, F. (1919) *The Polish Peasant in Europe and America*, University of Chicago Press, Chicago.

Thompson, E.P. (1967) 'Time, work discipline and industrial capitalism', *Past and Present*, no. 38.

Thompson, P. (1983) *The Nature of Work: An Introduction to Debates on the Labour Process*, Macmillan, London.
(1993) 'The labour process: changing theory changing practice', *Sociology Review*, vol. 3, no. 2.

Thompson, P. and McHugh, D. (1990) *Work Organisations*, Macmillan, London.
(1995) *Work Organizations: A Critical Introduction*, 2nd edn, Macmillan, Basingstoke.
(2002) *Work Organizations*, 3rd edn, Palgrave, Basingstoke.
Thoreau, E. (2006) 'Ouch! An examination of the self-representation of disabled people on the internet', *Journal of Computer-Mediated Communication*, vol. 11, pp. 442–68.
Thorne, B. (1992) *Rethinking the Family: Some Feminist Questions*, Longman, New York.
(1993) *Gender Play: Girls and Boys in School*, Open University Press, Buckingham.
Thornton, S. (1995) *Club Cultures: Music, Media and Subcultural Capital*, Polity Press, Cambridge.
(1997) 'General introduction' in K. Gelder and S. Thornton (eds) *The Subcultures Reader*, Routledge, London.
Thrupp, M. and Hursh, D. (2006) 'The limits of managerialist school reform: the case of target-setting in England and the USA' in H. Lauder *et al.* (eds) *Education, Globalization and Social Change*, Oxford University Press, Oxford.
Thussu, D.K. (2005) 'Mapping global media flow and contra-flow' in D.K. Thussu (ed.) *Media on the Move: Global Flow and Contra-flow*, Routledge, London.
(2007) 'The "Murdochization" of news? The case of Star TV in India', *Media, Culture and Society*, vol. 29, no. 4, pp. 593–611.
Titchen, A. and Hobson, D. (2005) 'Phenomenology' in Somekh and Lewin (eds) (2005).
Titmuss, R. (1968) *Commitment to Welfare*, Allen & Unwin, London.
(2000, first published 1968) 'Universalism versus selection' in Pierson and Castles (eds) (2000).
Tocqueville, A. de (1945, first published 1835) *Democracy in America*, vol. 1, Vintage, New York.
Todd, M.J. and Taylor, G. (eds) (2004) *Democracy and Participation: Popular Protests and New Social Movements*, Merlin Press, London.
Tomka, M. (1995) 'The changing social role of religion in Eastern and Central Europe: religion's revival and its contradiction', *Social Compass*, vol. 42, no. 1.
Tomlinson, S. (2005) *Education in a Post-welfare Society*, 2nd edn, Open University Press, Maidenhead.
Tong, R. (1998) *Feminist Thought: A More Comprehensive Introduction*, Westview Press, Boulder, CO.
Towler, R. (2003) *The public's view 2002*, Broadcasting Standards Commission, London.
Townsend, P. (1970) 'Measures and explanations of poverty in high and low income countries' in Townsend (ed.) (1970).
(ed.) (1970) *The Concept of Poverty*, Heinemann, London.
(1974) 'Poverty as relative deprivation' in D. Wedderburn (ed.) *Poverty, Inequality and Class Structure*, Cambridge University Press, Cambridge.
(1979) *Poverty in the United Kingdom*, Penguin, Harmondsworth.
(1993) *The International Analysis of Poverty*, Harvester Wheatsheaf, Hemel Hempstead.
(1995) 'The need for a new international poverty line' in K. Funken and P. Cooper (eds) *Old and New Poverty: The Challenge for Reform*, Rivers Oram Press, London.
(1997) 'Poverty and policy: what can we do about the poor?' *Sociology Review*, September, pp. 15–19.
Townsend, P. and Davidson, N. (1982) *Inequalities in Health: The Black Report*, Penguin, London.
Townsend, P., Corrigan, P. and Kowarzik, U. (1987) *Poverty and Labour in London*, The Low Pay Unit, London.
Townsend, P., Phillimore, P. and Beattie A. (1988) *Health and Deprivation: Inequality in the North*, Routledge, London.
Troeltsch, E. (1981) *The Social Teachings of the Christian Churches*, vols 1 and 2, University of Chicago Press, Chicago.
Trowler, P. (1995) *Investigating Education and Training*, Collins Educational, London.
(2003) *Education Policy*, 2nd edn, Routledge, London.
Troyna, B. and Carrington, B. (1990) *Education, Racism and Reform*, Routledge, London.
Tuchman, G. *et al.* (eds) (1978) *Hearth and Home: Images of Women in the Mass Media*, Oxford University Press, New York.
Tucker, K.H. (1998) *Anthony Giddens and Modern Social Theory*, Sage, London.
Tumin, M.M. (1967) *Social Stratification: The Forms and Functions of Social Inequality*, Prentice-Hall, Englewood Cliffs, NJ.
(1967) 'Some principles of stratification: a critical analysis' in Bendix and Lipset (eds) (1967).
Tunstall, J. (1962) *The Fishermen*, MacGibbon & Kee, London.
Tunstall, K.E. (ed.) (2004) *Displacement, Asylum, Migration: The Oxford Amnesty* Lectures, Oxford University Press, Oxford.
Turkle, S. (1988) 'Computational reticence' in C. Kramarae (ed.) *Technology and Women's Voices*, Routledge, London.
(1996) *Life on the Screen: Identity in the Age of the Internet*, Weidenfeld & Nicolson, London.
Turner, B.S. (1991) 'Recent developments in the theory of body' in M. Featherstone, M. Hepworth and B.S. Turner (eds) *The Body, Social Process and Cultural Theory*, Sage, London.
(1992) *Regulating Bodies: Essays in Medical Sociology*, Routledge, London.
(1995) *Medical Power and Social Knowledge*, Sage, London.
Turner, J.H. and Maryanski, A. (1979) *Functionalism*, Benjamin/Cummings Publishing, California.
Turow, J. (1982) 'Unconventional programs on television: an organizational perspective' in J.S. Ettema and D.C. Whitney (eds) *Individuals in Mass Media Organizations: Creativity and Constraint*, Sage, Beverly Hills, CA.
Twaddle, A.C. (1982) 'From Sociology to the Sociology of Health: Some changing concerns in the sociological study of health and treatment' in T. Bottomore, M. Sokolowska and S. Nowak (eds) *Sociology: The State of the Art*, Sage, London.
Tyler, S.A. (1997, first published 1986) 'Post-modern ethnography' in K. Gelder and S. Thornton (eds) *The Subcultures Reader*, Routledge, London.
United Nations (1995) *The Copenhagen Declaration and Programme of Action: World Summit for Social Development*, United Nations, New York.
(2005) *Human Development Report 2005*, United Nations, New York.
Universities UK (2005) 'Survey of higher education students' attitudes to debt and term-time working and their impact on attainment', London South Bank University, London.
Unschuld, P. (1986) 'The conceptual determination of individual and collective experiences of illness' in Currer and Stacey (eds) (1986).
Urry, J. (1990) *The Tourist Gaze: Leisure and Travel in Contemporary Societies*, Sage, London.
(1998) 'Contemporary transformations of time and space' in P. Scott (ed.) *The Globalization of Higher Education*, Open University/SRHE, Buckingham.
Urry, J. and Wakeford, J. (eds) (1973) *Power in Britain*, Heinemann, London.
Usher, R. and Edwards, R. (1994) *Postmodernism and Education*, Routledge, London.
Usher, R., Bryant, I. and Johnston, R. (1997) *Adult Education and the Postmodern Challenge*, Routledge, London.
Valentine, C.A. (1968) *Culture and Poverty*, University of Chicago Press, Chicago.
Valentine, C.A. and Valentine, B.L. (1970) 'Making the scene, digging the action, and telling it like it is: anthropologists at work in a dark ghetto' in N.E. Whitten Jr. and J.F. Szwed (eds) *Afro-American Anthropology*, Free Press, New York.
van Dijk, T. (1991) *Racism and the Press*, Routledge, London.
Van Reenen, J. (2004) 'Active labour market policies and the British New Deal for unemployed youth in context' in R. Blundell, D. Card and R. Freeman (eds) *Seeking a Premier League Economy*, University of Chicago Press, Chicago.
Veit-Wilson, J. (1998) *Setting Adequacy Standards*, Policy Press, Bristol.
Vernette, E. (2004) 'Targeting women's clothing fashion opinion leaders in media planning: an application for magazines', *Journal of Advertising Research*, vol. 44, no. 1, pp. 90–107.
Vernon, P.E. (1969) *Intelligence and Cultural Environment*, Methuen, London.
(1971) *Sovereignty at Bay: The Multinational Spread of US Enterprise*, Basic Books, New York.
Vincent, J.A. (1995) *Inequality and Old Age*, UCL Press, London.
(2006) 'Age and old age' in Payne (ed.) (2006).
Vincent, J.A., Phillipson, C.R. and Downs, M. (eds) (2006) *The Futures of Old Age*, Sage, London.
Virdee, S. (1997) 'Racial harassment' in Modood *et al.* (1997).
Voas, D. and Crockett, A. (2005) 'Religion in Britain: neither believing nor belonging', *Sociology*, vol. 39, no. 1.
Vogel, E.F. and Bell, N.W. (1968) 'The emotionally disturbed child as the family scapegoat' in Bell and Vogel (eds) (1968).
Vulliamy, E., McDonald, H., Bhatia, S. and Bright, M. (1998) 'Clinton bombed civilians on purpose', *Observer*, 23 August.

Wadsworth, M.E.J. (1986) 'Serious illness in childhood and its association with later life achievement' in R.G. Wilkinson (ed.) *Class and Health: Research and Longitudinal Data*, Tavistock, London.
Waitzkin, H. (1971) 'Latent functions of the sick role in various institutional settings', *Social Science and Medicine*, vol. 5, pp. 45–75.
Wakefield, A.J., Murch, S.H., Anthony, A. *et al.* (1998) 'Ileal-lymphoid-nodular hyperplasia, non-specific colitis, and pervasive developmental disorder in children', *Lancet*, 351.
Walby, S. (1986) *Patriarchy at Work*, Polity Press, Cambridge.
(1990) *Theorizing Patriarchy*, Blackwell, Oxford.
(1992) 'Post-post-modernism? Theorizing social complexity' in M. Barrett and A. Phillips (eds) *Destabilizing Theory: Contemporary Feminist Debates*, Polity Press, Cambridge.
(1997) *Gender Transformations*, Routledge, London.
Waldron, I. (1983) 'Sex differences in illness incidence prognosis and mortality: issues and evidence', *Social Science and Medicine*, vol. 17, pp. 1107–23.
Walker, A. (1990) 'Blaming the victims' in C. Murray, *The Emerging British Underclass*, Institute of Economic Affairs, London.
(1997) 'Introduction: the strategy of inequality' in Walker and Walker (eds) (1997).
Walker, A. and Foster, L. (2006) 'Ageing and social class: an enduring relationship' in Vincent *et al.* (eds) (2006).
Walker, C. and Walker, A. (1994) 'Poverty and the poor' in Haralambos (ed.) (1995).
(1997) 'Poverty and social exclusion' in Haralambos (ed.) (1997).
(eds) (1997) *Britain Divided: The Growth of Social Exclusion in the 1980s and 1990s*, Child Poverty Action Group, London.
Walker, R. (1987) 'Consensual approaches to the definition of poverty', *Journal of Social Policy*.
Walkerdine, V., Lucey, H. and Meldoy, J. (2001) *Growing Up Girl: Psychosocial Explorations of Gender and Class*, Palgrave, Basingstoke.
Walklate, S. (1995) *Gender and Crime: An Introduction*, Harvester Wheatsheaf, Hemel Hempstead.
(1998) *Understanding Criminology: Current Theoretical Debates*, Open University Press, Buckingham.
Wall, M. (2007) 'Virtual worlds for kids take off', *Guardian*, 9 August.
Wall, W.D. and Williams, H.L. (1970) *Longitudinal Studies and the Social Sciences*, Heinemann, London.
Wallerstein, I. (1991) 'The construction of peoplehood: racism, nationalism, ethnicity' in E. Balibar and I. Wallerstein (eds) *'Race', Nation, Class*, Verso, London.
Wallis, R. (1976) *The Road to Total Freedom: A Sociological Analysis of Scientology*, Heinemann, London.
(1984) *The Elementary Forms of the New Religious Life*, Routledge & Kegan Paul, London.
Wallis, R. and Bruce, S. (1986) *Sociological Theory, Religion and Collective Action*, Queen's University, Belfast.
Walsh, D. (1972) 'Functionalism and systems theory' in P. Filmer *et al.*, *New Directions in Sociological Theory*, Collier-Macmillan, London.
Walsh, V. (1980) 'Contraception: the growth of a technology' in Brighton Women and Science Group (ed.) *Alice through the Microscope: The Power of Science over Women's Lives*, Virago, London.
Walter, N. (1998) *The New Feminism*, Little Brown, London.
Walton, P. (1998) 'Big science: dystopia and utopia – establishment and criminology revisited' in Walton and Young (eds) (1998).
Walton, P. and Young, J. (eds) (1998) *The New Criminology Revisited*, Macmillan, Basingstoke.
Wannamethee, S.G. and Shaper, A.G. (1997) 'Socio-economic status within social class and mortality: a prospective study in middle-aged British men', *International Journal of Epidemiology*, vol. 26.
Ward, H. (1983) 'The anti-nuclear lobby: an unequal struggle' in Marsh (ed.) (1983).
Warr, P., Banks, M. and Ullah, P. (1985) 'The experience of unemployment among black and white urban teenagers', *British Journal of Psychology*, vol. 76.
Wartella, E., Heinz, K., Aidman, A. and Mazzarella, S. (1990) 'Television and beyond: children's video in one community', *Communication Research*, vol. 17, no. 1, pp. 45–64.
Warton, A.S. (2005) *The Sociology of Gender*, Blackwell, Malden, MA.
Warwick, D. and Littlejohn, G. (1992) *Coal, Capital and Culture*, Routledge, London.
Wasoff, F., Jamieson, L. and Smith, A. (2005) 'Solo living, individual and family boundaries: findings from secondary analysis' in McKie and Chunningham-Burley (eds) (2005).
Watson, H. (1994) 'Women and the veil: personal responses to global process' in A. Ahmed and H. Donnan (eds) *Islam, Globalization and Postmodernity*, Routledge, London.
Watts, A.G. (1983) *Education, Unemployment and the Future of Work*, Oxford University Press, Oxford.
Waugh, D. (2000) *Geography: An Integrated Approach*, 3rd edn, Nelson, Walton-on-Thames.
Webb, C.L. (2004) 'Google's IPO: grate expectations', *Washington Post*, 19 August: http://www.washingtonpost.com/wp-dyn/articles/A14939-2004Aug19.html
Webb, E.J. *et al.* (1966) *Unobtrusive Measures: Nonreactive Measures in the Social Sciences*, Rand McNally, Chicago.
Weber, M. (1947) *The Theory of Economic and Social Organizations*, Free Press, New York.
(1958) *The Protestant Ethic and the Spirit of Capitalism*, Charles Scribner's Sons, New York.
(1963) *The Sociology of Religion*, Beacon Press, Boston, MA.
(1978) *Economy and Society*, University of California Press, Berkeley, CA.
See also under Gerth and Mills.
Webster, F. (1999) 'What Information Society?' in H. Mackay and T. O'Sullivan (eds) *The Media Reader: Continuity and Transformation*, Sage, London.
Weedon, C. (1994, first published 1987) 'Feminism and the principles of poststructuralism' in J. Storey (ed.) *Cultural Theory and Popular Culture*, Harvester Wheatsheaf, Hemel Hempstead.
Weeks, J., Donovan, C. and Heaphey, B. (1999) 'Everyday experiments: narratives of non-heterosexual relationships' in Silva and Smart (eds) (1999).
Weiner, G., Arnot, M. and David, M. (1997) 'Is the future female? Female success, male disadvantage, and changing gender patterns in education' in Halsey *et al.* (eds) (1997).
Wellman, D. (1993) *Portraits of White Racism*, 2nd edn, Cambridge University Press, Cambridge.
West, D.J. (1982) *Delinquency: Its Roots, Careers and Prospects*, Heinemann, London.
West, D.J. and Farrington, D.P. (1973) *Who Becomes Delinquent?* Heinemann, London.
Westergaard, J. (1992) 'About and beyond the "underclass": some notes on influences of social climate on British sociology today', *Sociology*, vol. 26, no. 4, pp. 575–87.
(1995) *Who Gets What? The Hardening of Class Inequality in the Late Twentieth Century*, Polity Press, Cambridge.
(1996) 'Class in Britain since 1979: facts, theories and ideologies' in Lee and Turner (eds) (1996).
(1996) 'Class today: fashion at odds with the facts', *Social Science Teacher*, vol. 25, no. 1, pp. 2–6.
Westergaard, J. and Resler, H. (1976) *Class in a Capitalist Society*, Penguin, Harmondsworth.
Westwood, S. (1984) *All Day, Every Day: Factory and Family in the Making of Women's Lives*, Pluto Press, London.
Whelehan, I. (1995) *Modern Feminist Thought: From the Second Wave to 'Post-Feminism'*, Edinburgh University Press, Edinburgh.
(2000) *Overloaded: Popular Culture and the Future of Feminism*, Women's Press, London.
White, M., Hall, S. and Elliott, L. (2003) 'Hain forced to retreat on rich tax', *Guardian*, 21 June.
White, R. (2007) 'Green criminology and the pursuit of social and ecological justice' in P. Bierne and N. South (eds) *Issues in Green Criminology*, Willan, Cullompton.
Whiteley, P. (1983) *The Labour Party in Crisis*, Methuen, London.
Whiteley, P., Clarke, H., Sanders, D. and Stewart, M. (2001) 'Turnout' in Norris (ed.) (2001).
Whiteley, P., Stewart, M., Sanders, D. and Clarke, H. (2005) 'The issue agenda and voting in 2005' in Norris and Wlezien (eds) (2005).
Whitty, G. (1989) 'The New Right and the national curriculum: state control or market forces', *Journal of Education Policy*, vol. 40, no. 4.
(2002) *Making Sense of Education Policy*, Sage, London.
Whitty, G., Rowe, G. and Aggleton, P. (1994) 'Discourse in cross-curricular contexts: limits to empowerment', *International Studies in the Sociology of Education*, vol. 9, no. 2.
Whyte, W.F. (1955) *Street Corner Society*, 2nd edn, University of Chicago Press, Chicago.
Wilcox, D. (1992) (no title) in J. Pines, *Black and White in Colour: Black People in British Television since 1936*, BFI, London.
Wiles, P. and Costello, A. (2000) 'The road to nowhere: the evidence for travelling criminals', Home Office Research Study 207, Home Office, London.
Wilkinson, R. (1996) *Unhealthy Societies: The Afflictions of Inequality*, Routledge, London.

Wilkinson, S. (2004) 'Focus group research' in Silverman (ed.) (2004).
Wilkstrom, P.-O.H. (1991) *Urban Crime, Criminals and Victims: The Swedish Experience in an Anglo-American Comparative Perspective*, Springer-Verlag, New York.
Williams, G. (1984) 'The genesis of chronic illness: narrative reconstruction', *Sociology of Health and Illness*, vol. 6, pp. 175–200.
Williams, H. (2006) *Britain's Power Elites: The Rebirth of a Ruling Class*, Constable, London.
Williams, J. and Watson, G. (1996) 'Mental health services that empower women' in Heller *et al.* (eds) (1996).
Williams, R. (1961) *Culture and Society*, Penguin, Harmondsworth.
(1963) *Culture and Society 1780–1950*, Penguin, Harmondsworth.
(1965) *The Long Revolution*, Penguin, Harmondsworth.
(1976) *Keywords*, Croom Helm, London.
(1978) 'Forms of English fiction in 1848' in F. Barker *et al. 1848: The Sociology of Literature*, proceedings of the Essex conference on the sociology of literature, University of Essex, Colchester.
Willis, P. (1977) *Learning to Labour*, Saxon House, Farnborough.
(1984) 'Youth unemployment, a new social state', *New Society*, 29 March.
Willmott, P. (1963) *The Evolution of a Community: A Study of Dagenham after Forty Years*, Routledge & Kegan Paul, London.
(1988) 'Urban kinship past and present', *Social Studies Review*, November.
Wilson, B. (2003) 'Prediction and prophecy in the future of religion' in Davie *et al.* (eds) (2003).
Wilson, B.R. (1966) *Religion in a Secular Society*, C.A. Watts, London.
(1970) *Religious Sects*, Weidenfeld & Nicolson, London.
(1976) *Contemporary Transformations of Religion*, Oxford University Press, London.
(1982) *Religion in Sociological Perspective*, Oxford University Press, Oxford.
Wilson, E.O. (1975) *Sociobiology: The New Synthesis*, Harvard University Press, Cambridge, MA.
Wilson, J.Q. (1975) *Thinking about Crime*, Basic Books, New York.
Wilson, J.Q. and Hernstein, R. (1985) *Crime and Human Nature*, Simon & Schuster, New York.
Wilson, J.Q. and Kelling, G. (1982) 'Broken windows', *Atlantic Monthly*, March, pp. 29–38.
Wilson, R. (1963) *Difficult Housing Estates*, Tavistock, London.
Wilson, W.J. (1987) *The Truly Disadvantaged*, University of Chicago Press, Chicago.
(1991) 'Studying inner-city dislocations', *American Sociological Review*.
Winlow, S. (2001) *Badfellas: Crime, Violence and New Masculinities*, Berg, Oxford.
Wintour, P. and Cohen, N. (1997) 'Poverty unit to target truants', *Observer*, 7 December, p. 2.
Witz, A. (1992) *Professions and Patriarchy*, Routledge, London.
(1993) 'Women at work' in D. Richardson and V. Robinson (eds) *Introducing Women's Studies*, Macmillan, London.
Witz, A. and Woodward, K. (eds) (2000) *Questioning Identity: Gender, Class, Nation*, Routledge, London.
Wolff, J. (1981) *The Social Production of Art*, Macmillan, London.
Women and Work Commission (2006) *Shaping a Fairer Future*, Women and Work Commission, London.
Wood, S. (1989) 'The transformation of work?' in Wood (ed.) (1989).
(ed.) (1989) *The Transformation of Work?* Unwin Hyman, London.
Woodhead, L. (2001) 'The impact of feminism on the sociology of religion: from gender-blindness to gendered difference' in R.K. Fenn (ed.) *The Blackwell Companion to the Study of Religion*, Blackwell, Oxford, pp. 67–84.
(2004) 'Gendering secularization theory'. Lecture delivered in Copenhagen, October 2004.
(2005) 'Gendering secularization theory', *Kvinder, Køn og Forskning* (*Women, Gender and Research*; Denmark), vol. 1, pp. 24–35.
(2007) 'Gender differences in religious practice and significance' in J. Beckford and N.J. Demerath (eds) *Handbook of the Sociology of Religion*, Sage, London.
Woodiwiss, A. (1996) 'Searching for signs of globalization', *Sociology*, vol. 30, no. 4.
Woodiwiss, M. (1993) 'Crime's global reach' in Pearce and Woodiwiss (1993).
Woods, J. (2007) 'Democracy and the press: a comparative analysis of pluralism in the international print media', *Social Science Journal*, vol. 44, no. 2, pp. 213–30.
Woods, P. (1979) *The Divided School*, Routledge & Kegan Paul, London.
(1983) *Sociology and the School. An Interactionist Viewpoint*, Routledge & Kegan Paul, London.
Woods, P.A., Bagley, C. and Glatter, R. (1998) *School Choice and Competition: Markets in the Public Interest?* Routledge, London.
Woodward, K. (2000) 'Questions of identity' in K. Woodward (ed.) *Questioning Identity: Gender, Class, Nation*, Open University Press, Milton Keynes.
Woolf, A. (2002) *Does Education Matter? Myths about Education and Economic Growth*, Penguin, Harmondsworth.
Woolgar, S. and Grint, K. (1991) 'Computers and the transformation of social analysis', *Science, Technology and Human Values*, vol. 16, no 3.
World Bank (2007) *World Development Report 2007, Development and the Next Generation*, World Bank, New York.
World Health Organization (1974) Alma Ata Declaration, WHO.
World Press Freedom Committee (2007) Fundamentals. http://www.wpfc.org/Fundamentals.html
Wright, A. (1994) 'Judaism' in Holm and Bowker (eds) (1994).
Wright, C. (1992) 'Early education: multiracial primary school classrooms' in D. Gill, B. Mayor and M. Blair (eds) *Racism and Education: Structures and Strategies*, Sage, London.
Wright, E.O. (1978) *Class, Crisis and the State*, New Left Books, London.
Wrigley, N. (1998) 'How British retailers have shaped food choice' in A. Murcott (ed.) *The Nation's Diet: The Social Science of Food Choice*, Longman, London.
Wrong, D.H. (1961) 'The oversocialized conception of man in modern sociology', *American Sociological Review*, vol. 26, pp. 183–93.
Wyness, M. (2006) *Childhood and Society: An Introduction to the Sociology of Childhood*, Palgrave Macmillan, Basingstoke.
Wynne, D. (1998) *Leisure, Lifestyle and the New Middle Class*, Routledge, London.
Yablonsky, L. (1973) *The Violent Gang*, Penguin, Baltimore, MD.
Yin, R.K. (1984) *Case Study Research: Design and Methods*, Sage, Beverly Hills, CA.
Yinger, J.M. (1981) 'Towards a theory of assimilation and dissimilation', *Ethnic and Racial Studies*.
Young, J. (1971) 'The role of the police as amplifiers of deviancy, negotiators of reality and translators of fantasy' in S. Cohen (ed.) *Images of Deviance*, Penguin, Harmondsworth.
(1992) 'Ten points of realism' in Young and Matthews (eds) (1992).
(1993) 'Incessant chatter: recent paradigms in criminology' in M. Maguire *et al.* (eds) *The Oxford Handbook of Criminology*, Oxford University Press, Oxford..
(1997) 'Left realist criminology: radical in its analysis, realist in its policy' in M. Maguire *et al.* (eds) *The Oxford Handbook of Criminology*, 2nd edn, Oxford University Press, Oxford.
(1999) *The Exclusive Society*, Sage, London.
(2002) 'Crime and social exclusion' in Maguire *et al.* (eds) (2002).
Young, J. and Matthews, R. (1992) 'Questioning left realism' in Matthews and Young (eds) (1992).
(eds) (1992) *Rethinking Criminology: the Realist Debate*, Sage, London.
Young, M. and Willmott, P. (1961) *Family and Kinship in East London.*, Penguin, Harmondsworth.
(1973) *The Symmetrical Family*, Penguin, Harmondsworth.
Zaretsky, E. (1976) *Capitalism, the Family and Personal Life*, Pluto Press, London.
Zimbalist, A. (ed.) (1979) *Case Studies on the Labor Process*, Monthly Review Press, London.
Zimmerman, D.H. (1971) 'The practicalities of rule use' in J.D. Douglas (ed.) *Understanding Everyday Life*, Routledge & Kegan Paul, London.
Zimmerman, D.H. and Wieder, D.L. (1971) 'Ethnomethodology and the problem of order' in J.D. Douglas (ed.) *Understanding Everyday Life*, Routledge & Kegan Paul, London.
Zobrowski, M. (1952) 'Cultural components in response to pain', *Journal of Social Issues*, 8, pp. 16–30.
Zola, I.K. (1973) 'Pathways to the doctor: from person to patient', *Social Science and Medicine*, vol. 7, pp. 677–89.
(1981) 'Medicine as an institution of social control' in P. Conrad and R. Kern (eds) *The Sociology of Health and Illness: Critical Perspectives*, St Martin's Press, New York.
Zuboff, S. (1988) *In the Age of the Smart Machine*, Basic Books, New York.

Index

B

C

F

G

H

I

J

M

N

O

P

S

W